Orchid Species Culture

Orchid Species Culture
Dendrobium

by
Margaret L. Baker
and
Charles O. Baker

TIMBER PRESS
Portland, Oregon

Copyright © 1996 by Timber Press, Inc.
All rights reserved.

Printed in Singapore

Timber Press, Inc.
The Haseltine Buildling
133 S.W. Second Avenue, Suite 450
Portland, Oregon 97204, U.S.A.

Library of Congress Cataloging-in-Publication Data

Baker, Margaret L.
    Orchid species culture. Dendrobium / Margaret L. Baker and
Charles O. Baker.
      p.   cm.
    Includes bibliographical references (p.   ).
    ISBN 0-88192-360-5 (hardback)
    ISBN 0-88192-366-4 (paperback)
    1. Orchid culture. 2. Dendrobium. 3. Orchids. 4. Species.
I. Baker, Charles O. II. Title.
SB409.B25   1991 suppl.
635.9'3415—dc20   96-4992
                                                      CIP

This book is dedicated to those orchid lovers who have gone before: the explorers, scientists, writers, and growers. Their contributions to our accumulated knowledge have made this book possible.
—M. L. B. and C. O. B.

Contents

Prologue 9
1. Sample Format and General Cultural Recommendations 13
   General Information 13
   Cultural Recommendations 14
   Plant and Flower Information 20
2. *Dendrobium* 23
   General Information 23
   Species Culture 33
Appendix A: Orchid Growing Problems 783
   I. Preventing Disease 785
   II. Identifying and Treating Plant Problems 787
      Glossary of Terms 787
      Guide to Symptoms 788
      Pathogens 796
      Pests 820
      Nutrients 826
   III. Using Chemicals Safely 833
Appendix B: Unit Conversions and Formulas for Greenhouse Management 836
Bibliography 839
   References 839
   List of Sources 852

Prologue

This is the second in a series of books on the cultivation of individual orchid species. As with the first volume, which covered the genera *Pescatorea, Phaius, Phalaenopsis, Pholidota, Phragmipedium,* and *Pleione,* this book uses climate data as the basis for Cultural Recommendations for *Dendrobium.*

Readers of volume one will find the format nearly identical to the first volume. However, due to the overwhelming size of this work it was necessary to conserve space where possible. Therefore, for those categories for which information is not available for a particular species, the category heading has been deleted entirely instead of including the heading followed by N/A as in the first volume. Readers should know every attempt was made to provide information in each category. If information is missing it is not an error, we were simply unable to locate the information for that particular species. On the other hand, some of the information is more comprehensive. Without a recent review of the genus there is no easily available reference that growers can use for help in identifying a plant. We have attempted to include a little more information without becoming involved in a scientific plant description. Taxonomic descriptions are available from the references listed for each species. We hope this approach will assist growers in confirming that the plant under discussion is in fact the plant they are trying to grow.

Another change is the addition of the describers' name to the species name. In the last volume we were able to work with taxonomic reviews of the genera, and duplicate names were not a problem. However, the situation is very different for *Dendrobium.* There is no recent review of the genus to use as the basis for this volume. A number of the species names have been used more than once, so the describers' name is essential to know what plant is being discussed.

Readers will also recognize the Appendices at the end of the book. They are included for ease of use and for those who do not have volume one available. Appendix A has been revised as needed to reflect changes in the world of approved chemicals for pests and diseases.

For those not familiar with our first volume, our goal is to make information on species culture readily available, easy to use, and as complete as possible. The cultural guidelines were developed from data we originally compiled to help us grow our own, ever-increasing collection of orchid species. The guidelines are based on climate data for each species' native habitat together with cultivation notes and growers' observations, which are included when available. These notes were primarily gleaned from the books listed in the Bibliography, but observations based on personal experience as well as on the expertise of other species growers are also included.

We reluctantly concluded that the only available source for the information we needed to grow our many species was weather data from the species' original habitats. After researching the plants' native habitats, we acquired global tropical and subtropical climate records to use as the basis for developing our own guidelines. Frequently, the temperatures recorded at the nearest weather station were for an elevation different from that of the habitat. Consequently, it required adjusting to reflect the probable temperatures at the elevation where the plants were actually found. Standard atmospheric lapse-rate formulas were used to calculate these probable temperatures.

Although the initial impetus for this undertaking was our desire to grow some of the difficult species, we quickly found the information so helpful that we extended our research to include the more easily grown species in our collection. All plants were healthier when the growing conditions were modified to approximate the environmental conditions indicated by the weather data. Whenever a particular plant languished or failed to bloom, it became an easy process to determine what cultural changes were needed.

In addition, the climate information is especially helpful when acclimating a recently imported plant. By knowing the seasonal climatic conditions in the plant's original habitat, we can provide a gradual transition during the time required for it to adapt to the seasons in the Northern Hemisphere, resulting in a dramatic reduction in the number of plants lost to stress.

The weather records are equally useful whenever we deal with reluctant hybrids. By referring to the growing and habitat conditions required by the parent species, we often discover clues to the hybrid's hereditary cultural requirements and possible bloom initiators.

When a flower illustration intrigues us, we turn to this compiled information to decide whether we should acquire the plant. Can we provide the environment the plant needs to thrive? How long do the flowers last? Are they fragrant? How large are the flowers relative to plant size? Although complete data are not available for all species, the compiled information has proved helpful in a variety of ways.

We believe that as growers we have a responsibility to help reduce whatever pressure our hobby is exerting on populations of wild plants and their natural habitats. Every species grower can contribute to the effort by refusing to purchase wild plants, by growing his or her own species well, and by propagating and making species seedlings available to others as inexpensively as possible.

The world's tropical rainforests are being destroyed at appalling speed, and at the current rate of destruction, many natural habitats will soon be beyond salvage. Orchid species growers have a unique opportunity to help preserve a genetic resource that may become the only source of orchid plant material available to future generations.

We sincerely hope that others will join us in making this series of orchid culture books an ongoing project. With this compilation of information as a starting point, perhaps we all can expand our knowledge of how best to grow our orchid species and benefit from each other's experience. To that end, we would appreciate hearing from anyone with additional habitat details or information concerning propagation, the time required for species seeds to be sufficiently mature to be sown with green-pod techniques, or the growing time required for seedlings to reach blooming size. Accounts of personal growing experience, either successful or disastrous, would also be most helpful.

Included for each species is a list of references that may be consulted for taxonomic information, additional habitat details, or plant illustrations such as botanical drawings or photographs. Since a recent review of the genus was unavailable, we depended upon a variety of publications, listing the species and synonyms as we found them. Throughout, our aim is to provide cultural not taxonomic information.

Prologue

To say that finishing this book brings a sense of relief is certainly an understatement. Only fools or angels would tackle the genus *Dendrobium,* and we most certainly do not qualify as angels. It must have been our naïveté that led us into this project, but it was most certainly stubborness that finished the book. Some might even go so far as to say we were pigheaded, but we prefer to view it as resolve.

We would like to express our most sincere appreciation to the following: Pamela Burns-Balogh of Koeltz Books U. S. A., without whose kind and generous assistance with reference materials we simply could not have assembled the data for this book; Paul Kores of Tulane University, who kindly lent proof sheets of his work in Fiji before the book was available in print and copies of reference materials he had available; Rudolf Jenny from Switzerland, who sent us copies of references from Europe that we had been unable to find in the states; the Missouri Botanical Garden Library staff, who allowed us to spend a week monopolizing their copy machine (a special note of thanks to the library volunteers without whose help the library would not be such a wonderful place in which to work); Dr. Gunnar Seidenfaden of Denmark for sharing taxonomic information not yet in print; Dr. Phillip Cribb of England for reviewing our general discussion in Chaper 2; the Huntington Botanical Library staff, who allowed us access to their reference materials and tolerated our invasion of their very crowded working space; Frannie Farrell and Suzanne Copenhagen for editorial help at Timber Press; the Library staff at the California Academy of Sciences, who let us dominate their time and equipment for several days; the National Climate Centre, Bureau of Meteorology, Australia, and particularly Robin Hicks for help in obtaining some of the climate data for Papua New Guinea; the librarians of numerous herbaria, colleges, and universities, who lent or copied the material needed. Special appreciation is extended to the library at Oregon State University in Corvallis, Oregon and the Multnomah County Library in Portland, Oregon. Their patience and assistance have been invaluable.

The following words are attributed to the 18th-century Swedish botanist Carl Linnaeus. They express sentiments we humbly share:

If you have remarked errors in me, your superior wisdom must pardon them. Who errs not while perambulating the domain of nature? Who can observe everything with accuracy? Correct me as a friend, and I as a friend will requite with kindness.

1
Sample Format and General Cultural Recommendations
General Information

SUBFAMILY: *Botanical name of subfamily.*

TRIBE: *Botanical name of tribe.*

SUBTRIBE: *Botanical name of subtribe.*

GENUS: *Botanical name of genus.*

SPECIES: *Botanical name of species.* The plant name is followed by the name of the original describer. Artificial hybrids are not included, but natural hybrids, which are sometimes sold as species, are listed alphabetically with their parentage indicated. The information provided for parent species may be consulted for cultural information.

AKA *(Also Known As): Other names used over the years and now considered synonymous.* As growers, we generally find name changes more frustrating than illuminating, and from our vantage point they sometimes appear frivolous and unnecessary. However, since beginning this work with individual species, we have come to appreciate some of the problems the taxonomist faces. The more widespread or variable a species is, the greater the number of names given to it. Botanical explorers and early taxonomists did not have the communication systems and computer technology available today and generally described each species as they found it in their area. Even today, taxonomists are plagued with genuine differences of opinion as well as missing or incomplete type specimens. Many of the original specimen collections have been damaged or lost to war, insects, or neglect.

Again, the synonyms here are not included for taxonomic purposes, but to help growers who are using outdated books that may discuss a plant under another name. They may also be helpful when a species is sold under different names.

ORIGIN/HABITAT: *The points of origin, used as the basis for selecting appropriate weather records.* We have included available notes on the species' natural habitat when this information was available. Habitat elevations are usually approximated, and all figures are rounded for ease of use.

CLIMATE: *The climate in each species' native habitat.* All temperatures are as correct as possible for the habitat of the species and may be used as shown; they do not require modification by the grower.

The first paragraph in this category gives the World Meteorological Organization station number, station name, latitude, longitude, elevation, and record temperatures, which are given as recorded at the station. If both station and habitat elevation are given, all temperatures are calculated to the nearest tenth of a degree in both Fahrenheit and Celsius and reflect the probable climate at the orchids' elevation. Growers should take care to avoid record temperatures and calculated extremes, since *plants may not survive exposure to the extremes.* Record temperatures do not take into account the strong influence of local terrain and microclimate within the orchid habitat. Consequently, they can be considered approximations only, and they are included to indicate how precise environmental control should be for each plant, not to serve as norms in plant culture.

Temperatures in the climate tables are rounded to the nearest whole degree Fahrenheit and to the nearest tenth of a degree Celsius. (Note, however, that Celsius temperatures were computed from *unrounded* Fahrenheit figures, an approach that increases the accuracy of the Celsius temperatures, but may result in seeming discrepancies when the rounded Fahrenheit temperatures and Celsius "equivalents" appear side by side.)

If a plant is growing and blooming well in an artificial environment, the conditions are obviously adequate, and altering them might not be beneficial. In such cases, plants which have been propagated and raised in a greenhouse may have adapted in order to survive. However, if a plant is not thriving or blooming satisfactorily, growing conditions should be gradually modified to more closely resemble those in its natural habitat.

Weather records provide seasonal temperature ranges, rainfall patterns, and day/night temperature fluctuations (diurnal range). These components describe a generally appropriate growing environment. The records do not necessarily reflect the exact conditions in the orchids' microclimate and should be used as a guide only. No attempt should be made to duplicate climate exactly since all the information is averaged. Most species will be healthiest if rainfall cycles and seasonal temperature ranges are at least approximated in cultivation. However, species which are difficult to cultivate will be healthiest in a growing environment that recreates the conditions in their native habitat as closely as possible.

A climate table is provided for each species; the month in which the observations were made corresponds to the month given in the table for the hemisphere in which the station is located. These tables are structured so that they may be used by growers world-wide, and we hope readers will find them genuinely easy to use. As many have discovered, some of the excellent cultural information written for growers in the Southern Hemisphere is awkward for those who live north of the equator, where seasons are opposite, or who think in terms of degrees Fahrenheit (°F) and inches (in.). Conversely, it is cumbersome for those who measure temperature in degrees Celcius (°C) and rainfall in millimeters (mm) to adapt cultural information written for growers in the United States.

To use the climate tables, orchid growers north of the equator should start with the line labeled "N/HEMISPHERE," the seasonal guide at the top of the table. All numbers in the columns below apply to the months shown on the top line. Temperature is given in both °F and °C, and rainfall in both inches and millimeters. The months shown on the line labeled "S/HEMISPHERE," the seasonal guide at the bottom of the table, reflect the corresponding seasons south of the equator. Southern growers need only read the chart from bottom to top to find the same information available to top-to-bottom readers in the North. The seasonal guides for both Northern and Southern Hemispheres begin and end in midwinter.

N/HEMISPHERE   JAN FEB MAR APR MAY JUN JUL AUG SEP OCT NOV DEC

Calendar guide for the Northern Hemisphere.

Climate

°F AVG MAX: *Average maximum temperature per month expressed in degrees Fahrenheit.*

°F AVG MIN: *Average minimum temperature per month expressed in degrees Fahrenheit.*

DIURNAL RANGE: *Range between day and night temperatures expressed in degrees Fahrenheit.* Diurnal range is often overlooked when plants are cultivated outside their natural habitat. The diurnal fluctuation can be critical for some species, and this range, rather than absolute low temperatures, is often the factor that induces flowering. Unless night temperatures decline by approximately the number of degrees indicated, the plants are unable to rest, and some chemical functions are inhibited.

Diurnal range is determined by many factors, chief among which is the characteristic of different materials to transfer heat at different speeds. Solid surfaces, like the earth, gain and lose heat more rapidly than the surrounding air. As a result, maximum heating or cooling occurs during clear, calm weather when the process of heat absorption or radiation is undisturbed. (It is this differing rate of heat loss that causes surface frost to form even when air temperatures do not fall to freezing.) Conversely, the difference between day and night temperatures is lowest during windy, overcast weather because both wind and clouds moderate temperatures by altering the amount of radiational heating and cooling that can occur. Wind moderates temperatures by mixing the surface air layer with higher air layers, thereby slowing the rate at which the earth is warmed or cooled. Clouds influence temperatures by allowing the passage of a portion of the incoming energy from the sun (short-wave radiation). The incoming radiation is absorbed, warming the earth's surface. Energy is then reradiated by the earth in the form of long-wave radiation, which is unable to penetrate clouds. This causes the phenomenon known as the "greenhouse effect," since clouds act in the same manner as the skin on a greenhouse by preventing the loss of heat.

RAIN/INCHES: *Average monthly rainfall expressed in inches.* Average rainfall figures are an important indication of suitable watering patterns, showing whether a plant requires high or low moisture levels as well as indicating seasonal increases and decreases in available moisture. Precise rainfall measurements are valid only for the location where the observations were made and cannot accurately be adjusted for elevation, since local terrain is an important determining factor.

HUMIDITY: *Average monthly relative humidity expressed as a percentage.* In the tropics, extremes normally range at least 10% above and below the average. High humidity during a period of low rainfall indicates that some moisture is probably available in the form of dew, fog, mist, or low clouds.

BLOOM SEASON: *Probable bloom times.* An asterisk (*) marks the months when blooming occurs. Multiple asterisks indicate a higher incidence of blooming. Records of blooming in the wild and collection reports were used when available, but our primary source of information was the extensive work done by Robert M. Hamilton and published in 1988 in *When Does It Flower?* In preparing his volume, Hamilton compiled bloom reports for greenhouse-cultivated plants in the Northern Hemisphere.

DAYS CLR @ 7AM, 8AM, 2PM, 4PM, and so on: *Average number of clear (clr) days per month at the hour indicated.* A day qualifies as clear when visibility is 3 miles (4.8 km) or greater and when clouds cover 0.3 or less of the sky. Because the records do not take into account the transparency of the clouds, the sun may seem quite bright even though the weather cannot be classified as clear.

While the information is valid only for the station where the observation was taken, it indicates general patterns of high and low available light. When combined with seasonal light variations, the data provide an indication of the time of day and season when a species is most likely to benefit from increased or decreased light, another factor often critical for blooming. Unfortunately, the information is frequently unavailable, and the time when observations are made varies from one location to another. Some stations report sky cover once a day, while others report several times daily. Whenever possible, records are included for morning and afternoon since orchid habitats frequently have morning fog or afternoon clouds.

RAIN/MM: *Average rainfall per month expressed in millimeters.*

°C AVG MAX: *Average maximum temperature per month expressed in degrees Celsius.*

°C AVG MIN: *Average minimum temperature per month expressed in degrees Celsius.*

DIURNAL RANGE: *Range between day and night temperatures expressed in degrees Celsius.*

S/HEMISPHERE   JUL AUG SEP OCT NOV DEC JAN FEB MAR APR MAY JUN
Calendar guide for the Southern Hemisphere

Cultural Recommendations

The information in this section has been especially tailored to meet growers' needs. Most growers do not work with precision equipment in sophisticated laboratories, hence they are not concerned with fractional degrees of temperature. Accordingly, all temperatures have been rounded to the nearest whole degree. Temperatures are given first in °F, with °C in parentheses.

A healthy, well-grown plant generally escapes most insect and disease damage, while a plant under stress is very susceptible to additional harm from disease and insects. Normally, plant stress is caused by poor cultural and environmental conditions. Some general symptoms of plant stress are included throughout the volume under the heading "Plant and Flower Information." Genus-specific indicators are included in the "General Information" at the beginning of each chapter.

LIGHT: *Approximate light levels, expressed in footcandles (fc).* These light levels may be used as a starting point, but it is important to watch each plant carefully and to modify the light at the first indication of stress (as described under the heading "Leaves" below). Light levels should always be changed gradually.

Plants generally utilize morning light most effectively, since their metabolism is frequently most active in the morning; but as with most rules, there are exceptions. If the habitat climate shows frequent morning overcast, then the plant may benefit from higher light in the afternoon.

Greenhouse plants should be watched carefully during seasonal shifts in light patterns to guard against the possibility of sunburn. Species grown in light which is too low may not bloom, but low light seldom causes the serious damage that can result from excessively high light.

Cultivated species may adapt to different light conditions, but they are unlikely to thrive and may not bloom unless they receive light at the appropriate levels and times. The most widely distributed species are those most likely to be adaptable to various light levels. The following generally accepted cultural divisions describe light levels:

Very high. Over 5000 footcandles—nearly full sun except at midday, when full summer sun in most latitudes may reach 10,000 fc. Full sunlight through clean fiberglass is usually 5000–7000 fc on a clear day.

High. 4000–5000 footcandles—bright light, just under 50% of the full midday sun. Although most plants utilize light most efficiently at 5000 fc, many orchids use light most efficiently at much lower levels.

Intermediate. 1800–4000 footcandles—dappled sunlight.

Low. 1000–1800 footcandles—reduced sunlight, so that if a hand is passed over the leaves it does not produce a shadow.

Very low. Less than 1000 footcandles—deep shade.

Light can be measured with a light meter. If no direct-reading light meter is available, footcandles may be measured with a 35 mm camera that has through-the-lens metering. The procedure is simple. First, set the camera for a film speed of ASA 25 and a shutter speed of $1/60$ second. Center the needle in the viewfinder by adjusting the camera's f/stop while focusing on a clean, white sheet of paper which has been placed where the plant actually grows. Then convert the f/stops to approximate footcandles as follows:

f/2:	f/2.8:	f/4:	f/5.6:	f/8:	f/11:	f/16:
100 fc	200 fc	370 fc	750 fc	1500 fc	2800 fc	5000 fc

When artificial lights are used in the growing area, the f/stop readings may be quite low and yet the light may be adequate. Artificial light is constant, whereas natural light fluctuates during the day as the wind moves leaves and clouds, causing shadows.

Orchids grown in the home normally require supplemental lighting. Fluorescent lights are most frequently used in a one-to-one ratio of cool-white and Gro-Lux bulbs which provide nearly full-spectrum light. Growers also successfully use the newer "full-spectrum" fluorescent and high-intensity lights. Halide lights should be combined with sodium bulbs since alone they are deficient in red portions of the light spectrum, which prevents flowering in some species. Artificial lights are easily controlled by timers to provide seasonal fluctuation, increasing and decreasing light levels each month. Most species do well with 11–14 hours of light, which the following schedule provides:

Jan. (Jul.)	6:30 a.m.–6:00 p.m.	Jul. (Jan.)	5:00 a.m.–7:00 p.m.
Feb. (Aug.)	6:00 a.m.–6:00 p.m.	Aug. (Feb.)	5:30 a.m.–6:30 p.m.
Mar. (Sep.)	5:30 a.m.–6:00 p.m.	Sep. (Mar.)	5:30 a.m.–6:00 p.m.
Apr. (Oct.)	5:30 a.m.–6:30 p.m.	Oct. (Apr.)	6:00 a.m.–6:00 p.m.
May (Nov.)	5:00 a.m.–7:00 p.m.	Nov. (May)	6:30 a.m.–6:00 p.m.
Jun. (Dec.)	5:00 a.m.–7:00 p.m.	Dec. (Jun.)	6:30 a.m.–5:30 p.m.

Seedlings need very low light, starting at 200 fc when they are just out of the flask. During the following years, light should gradually be increased to mature-plant levels as the plants reach blooming size.

Studies indicate that seedlings grow more rapidly if given 14–16 hours of light year-round. However, extending light in the general growing area may adversely affect blooming in mature plants. Consequently, either seedlings should be grown in a separate area, or the light should be blocked from other plants in the same area. See the discussion of bloom initiators under "Flowers" later in this chapter.

TEMPERATURES: *Correct growing temperatures and diurnal range for the species during periods of active growth.* Unless the plant is unusually adaptable, temperatures outside the recommended range will cause plant stress and lead to disease. Changes should be introduced gradually, allowing the plant time to adjust. This is true even for plants being grown at temperatures outside the range found in their natural habitat and not thriving.

Newly imported plants often require months to become acclimated to their changed environment. Once the plant is placed in the location with the best possible conditions, it should not be moved around within the greenhouse. Each position in the greenhouse has its own microclimate to which the plant adapts little by little. Anytime a plant is moved, it must adjust to slightly different conditions, and the acclimating process is slowed.

Plants gain and lose water through their leaves. High humidity provides necessary moisture, while low humidity allows cooling through the evaporative process. When temperatures are high, humidity levels must be optimized in order to maintain the proper balance between the plants' need for moisture to replace the water lost through transpiration and the plants' need for the cooling that evaporation provides. When air movement is adequate, this balance is less critical.

Air circulation is important, as it moves fresh air over the leaves, renewing available carbon dioxide near the leaf surfaces. In fact, air circulation may be the single most important factor in preventing disease. Moving air is critically important in hot or excessively humid environments because it moves the thin layer of moisture-laden air from around the leaf, allowing additional evaporation and the associated cooling to continue. Air movement is sufficient if plants gently wave in the circulating air.

Orchid growers frequently use the terms *warm*, *intermediate*, and *cool* to indicate the temperatures required during a plant's growing season. The following table defines the generally accepted divisions and includes suggested temperature ranges for *very warm* and *very cool* categories.

	Daytime Highs	**Nightime Lows**
Very warm	Above 85°F (29°C)	68–75°F (20–24°C)
Warm	75–85°F (24–29°C)	62–68°F (17–20°C)
Intermediate	65–80°F (18–27°C)	55–62°F (13–17°C)
Cool	60–75°F (16–24°C)	50–55°F (10–13°C)
Very cool	Below 65°F (18°C)	Below 50°F (10°C)

These categories provide a convenient means of indicating an appropriate temperature range, and the classifications work well for some species. To illustrate, temperatures for a low-elevation equatorial plant can accurately be described as *very warm* throughout the year. The categories could describe any species' requirements, but unfortunately, variations in day, night, summer, and winter conditions are seldom specified by means of this shorthand. A plant requiring a wide diurnal range might be classified as needing *warm* days and *cool* nights, or a plant requiring a winter rest might be designated as needing *intermediate* summers and *very cool* winters. The slight expansion of the shorthand reflected in the table above could dramatically reduce the number of plants lost through ignorance and vastly increase orchid growers' enjoyment of species.

Nearly all plants require at least a variation of 10°F (6°C) between day and night temperatures. Note that habitats vary widely in diurnal range, and individual species have distinct requirements.

Seedlings are healthiest when grown at temperatures in the middle of the range recommended for mature plants.

HUMIDITY: *Correct relative humidity levels for the species.* Relative humidity is a ratio between the amount of water vapor present and the amount the air can hold at a given temperature. Warm air is able to hold more water vapor than cold air before becoming saturated (100% relative humidity). Therefore, if water vapor remains constant, relative humidity will decrease as the temperature rises. Conversely, relative humidity will increase as temperatures decline. If air coming in contact with a cold surface causes the temperature to fall to the point where relative humidity becomes 100%, the water vapor condenses (becomes liquid), resulting in nighttime condensation in the greenhouse, morning dew, or the beads of moisture on a glass containing a cold drink. Humidity records do not reflect the influence of a plant's microclimate. Higher relative humidity is generally found near streams, in marshes, or in dense undergrowth.

Even when relative humidity above 75–90% is indicated by the climate table, a midafternoon reading of 50% is usually appropriate, though the ideal level depends to a large extent on the diurnal range in the greenhouse. Optimum relative humidity is generally as high as possible during the day, short of levels that produce condensation as temperatures decline. Each grower will need to devise his or her own optimum midday humidity levels.

If low humidity is a problem, moisture in the greenhouse can be increased by using evaporative coolers, spraying the floor, or misting the air. Humidity can be increased in a small area, or in the home, by using humidity trays. These should be larger in diameter than the plants. Heavy wire mesh may be used to keep the plants above the water, or the trays may be filled with gravel so that the pots never stand in water.

A plant's ability to utilize water vapor directly from the air depends upon the temperature. Absorption is most efficient when temperatures are 43–82°F (6–28°C), with optimum efficiency at 70°F (21°C). Outside this temperature range, the capacity for absorption decreases rapidly.

Recommended relative humidity levels may be designated as follows:

Very high   80% or more   *Intermediate*   50–70%
High   70–80%   *Low*   Below 50%

Seedlings will be healthiest when grown at the highest humidity levels indicated for the species.

WATER: *Water requirements for the species*. These are indicated by the rainfall patterns shown in the climate tables, which should be approximated in cultivation. The cycles need not be exact, and growers should modify them to meet their plants' needs. However, if wet/dry cycles exist in nature, cultivated plants will benefit from a dry period, or at least a drier rest.

Orchids should generally be kept moist during the growing season. Overwatering can be fatal since air around the roots is just as vital as moisture. Both overwatering and deteriorating medium result in insufficient air around the roots, creating a situation conducive to root rot. It is particularly important to avoid excess water when temperatures or light levels are low.

As a general rule, potted orchids should be watered or misted weekly to biweekly in winter unless they require a dry rest, in which case they should be misted only enough to prevent desiccation. Watering should be increased to approximately twice weekly during periods of active growth. Plants mounted on slabs or rafts require daily misting during dry winter weather, while they may need misting several times a day during hot, dry summer weather.

Warmer temperatures, higher light, and lower relative humidity all increase a plant's need for moisture. The opposite is also true: high relative humidity, low light, and low temperatures all reduce the need for water at the roots. Optimal frequency of watering varies with the species, the season, and the environment.

The average relative humidity in the growing area is an excellent indication of the total moisture available to the plants. Since midday readings are normally the lowest and the first to reflect a decline in available moisture, growers use them most often to show when plants need water. For example, if midday readings have averaged 50% but suddenly fall to 35–40%, the grower knows that the plants will benefit from an immediate increase in humidity. This can be achieved by misting the greenhouse walks or running an evaporative cooler. In addition, the grower should plan a thorough watering for the following morning.

The following tips on watering may be helpful to growers:

- Water or mist plants early in the morning. This helps prevent disease by allowing the foliage to dry before evening.
- In winter, water on mornings when the day will be bright and sunny.
- If plants become too dry, water them several times in quick succession until the medium is resaturated.
- Water plants in new medium often. New medium drains rapidly, providing better root aeration, but it requires more frequent watering.
- Decrease water slightly as the medium ages and begins breaking down.
- Do not mist leaves if light levels are high. Water droplets refract and intensify the light, which may cause tissue damage.
- Never use chemically softened water, as the salts used in the softening process accumulate in the pot and may kill the plant.
- Use water that is slightly acid (5.5–5.8 pH), which most orchids prefer.
- Water plants in small pots faithfully, since they dry out more rapidly than those in larger pots, seedling trays, or community pots.
- Water seedlings and young plants carefully. They should never be allowed to dry out.

FERTILIZER: *Recommended strength, plus type and frequency of application*. Excess fertilizer is more harmful to orchids than a slight deficiency, particularly when light levels are low or the plants are dry. Symptoms of nutrient and trace-element deficiencies are discussed in depth in Appendix A.

Essential plant nutrients are classified as either macronutrients or micronutrients. Macronutrients, required in relatively large amounts, include carbon (C), hydrogen (H), and oxygen (O), which are available directly from the atmosphere, together with nitrogen (N), phosphorus (P), and potassium (K), which are usually applied as fertilizer. The last 3 nutrients are listed as percentages in the above order on commercial fertilizer containers. Thus, 30–20–10 contains 30% nitrogen, 20% phosphorus, and 10% potassium, while 10–10–10 contains equal parts of these elements. Other nutrients required in moderately large amounts are calcium (Ca), magnesium (Mg), and sulfur (S).

Micronutrients, or trace minerals, are also necessary for good plant growth, but in much smaller amounts—sometimes in quantities as small as a few parts per billion. These trace minerals include boron (B), chlorine (Cl), cobalt (Co), copper (Cu), iron (Fe), manganese (Mn), molybdenum (Mo), and zinc (Zn). Organic media usually provide sufficient trace elements for orchids, but some growers prefer to make an application of trace minerals in spring and another in midsummer. Growers using non-organic media should either select a fertilizer containing trace elements or periodically apply trace minerals, since they are not otherwise available to the plants. Most commercial fertilizers formulated for indoor plants contain trace minerals even though they may not be listed on the label. (Fertilizer labeling laws in the United States require manufacturers to guarantee the analysis shown on the label. Because the manufacturers are reluctant to guarantee the exact levels of micronutrients, they simply do not list them.)

Plants grown in soft-water areas are more likely to benefit from applications of trace elements than those grown in hard-water areas. Extreme caution should be exercised when applying supplementary trace minerals since an excessive amount can do more damage than a deficiency. Trace elements should never be applied at a higher rate or more frequently than recommended.

Fertilizing dry plants may cause root damage. This can be avoided by always saturating the medium before applying fertilizer, or by using very dilute solutions.

An unhealthy salt buildup is also indicated by discolored root-tips or by white deposits on the leaves or the surface of the pot. A potentially toxic salt accumulation may be prevented by allowing some water (10% of the volume of the pot) to drain through each time the plant is watered, and by flushing or leaching the medium with large quantities or water every few weeks. Plants growing in hard-water areas may be healthier if the pots are flushed more frequently. Species extremely sensitive to salt accumulations may be flushed at every watering.

The pot should be watered at least an hour before it is to be flushed, allowing time for moisture to dissolve the salt crystals. Then an amount of water equal to twice the volume of the pot should be run through the pot. For example, a 6 in. (15 cm) pot holds approximately 2.5 qts. (2.4 liters) of water, so 5 qts. (4.7 liters) should be used to flush the pot. Flushing should be done before fertilizer is applied.

Since orchids are supremely efficient at absorbing nutrients, all fertilizers must be applied in weak solutions. They should be mixed at 10–50% of the strength recommended for garden plants.

Orchid growers in the Northern Hemisphere are sharply divided over the use of organic fertilizers. This will surprise growers from other parts of the world, who use dilute manure tea almost exclusively for both terrestrial and epiphytic orchids. The key to success with any fertilizer is sufficient dilution. Different types of fertilizers have distinct advantages and disadvantages.

Organic fertilizers are particularly beneficial since they contain natural trace minerals, they are less likely to destroy helpful microorganisms, and they reduce the risk of salt buildup. However, growers may find the odor objectionable. Commercial compounds such as fish fertilizer should be mixed at $\frac{1}{4}$–$\frac{1}{2}$ the recommended strength, or $\frac{1}{10}$ the recommended strength if used as a foliar spray. Manure tea is recommended by many growers, but it is difficult to ascertain the strength of the dilution. As a consequence, organic fertilizers are frequently mixed and applied at or near garden-plant strength, causing severe injury to orchids.

Composted manure (the type purchased in bags at gardening stores) may be made into manure tea as follows. These guidelines do not apply when using fresh manure.

- Measure the small amount of composted manure necessary to produce fertilizer of the desired strength.

    1 tsp. per gal. (3.8 liters) is approximately equivalent to commercial fertilizer mixed at $\frac{1}{10}$ tsp. per gal. (3.8 liters).

    2.5 tsp. per gal. (3.8 liters) is approximately equivalent to commercial fertilizer mixed at $\frac{1}{4}$ tsp. per gal. (3.8 liters).

    5 tsp. per gal. (3.8 liters) is approximately equivalent to commercial fertilizer mixed at $\frac{1}{2}$ tsp. per gal. (3.8 liters).

- Mix the manure with 1 cup (236 ml) of water, and allow it to steep overnight or longer.
- Strain the liquid, then add enough water to make 1 gal. (3.8 liters) of fertilizer solution.

The following ratios of nitrogen, phosphate, and potassium are approximate values for manure of different types.

Manure	% Nitrogen	% Phosphate	% Potassium
Chicken	30	14	7
Cow	10	3	8
Hog	13	7	11
Horse	15	5	13

Chemical compounds are readily available, clean, odorless, and easier to dilute to a specified level. However, if used in excess, they destroy microorganisms critical to plant health, and they are more likely to result in excessive salt buildup.

Delayed-release fertilizers should not be used with most orchids.

REST PERIOD: *Recommended conditions during the resting phase of the annual growth cycle.* As always, changes in growing conditions should be introduced gradually, allowing the plants time to adjust. Some species are healthiest if growing conditions are maintained year-round, while for other species a rest period is as vital as light, air, or water. Since rest-period conditions often induce the formation of flowers, information on bloom initiators is also included here.

When an unusually cool or unusually dry rest period is indicated by the climate in the species' native habitat, the plants may be healthier in cultivation if given a rest not quite so long, so dry, or so cold. In fact, the microclimate in the native habitat may prevent exposure to extreme conditions. Plants in the wild normally have extremely long roots which collect and store moisture when it is available, whereas cultivated plants have shorter roots which provide less insurance against drought.

Fertilizer should always be reduced during the rest period. Plants need less food when they are not actively growing or when light levels are low. In addition, they use nitrogen less efficiently when temperatures are cool. Continued applications of fertilizer during the rest period only contribute to salt buildup in the medium and do not benefit the plant.

Whether orchids require a rest period is another subject on which growers are sharply divided. In our view, if a plant is growing and blooming well, the growing conditions should not be changed whatever they happen to be. However, when a plant is not thriving, conditions should be altered in the direction indicated by the climate in the plant's native habitat.

The relationship between temperature and water is critical. If plants which adapt to a variety of conditions are grown in warm temperatures, then watering should be continued but perhaps reduced during winter. *If temperatures are cool, water must be reduced.* As a general rule, the cooler the temperatures, the lower the plant's water requirements.

Growers in tropical and subtropical regions may instinctively take advantage of microclimates in their growing area by placing cool-growing plants near an evaporative cooler, by placing low-light species under a bench, by reducing water in winter when days are cooler, by increasing diurnal range through less intensive heating or cooling, by removing shading in winter, and by tending to select species which do well in their conditions. All these techniques may be applied deliberately when cultivating subtropical to temperate-zone orchids in warm climates.

Growers in cooler regions also use microclimates in their growing areas by placing plants requiring high light near a south (or north in the Southern Hemisphere) wall, by setting cool-growing plants near the floor and warm-growing plants near a heater, by reducing water dramatically when humidity is high, and by choosing to grow plants which do well in their area. Again, these are techniques that growers may apply deliberately.

Many orchids which grow well where nights are warm may also grow well at cooler temperatures. While low-altitude equatorial species are unlikely to survive drying, cold nights, or a wide diurnal range, others, such as high-altitude species of *Pleione,* simply will not survive without a cool, dry rest, and many *Cymbidium* species will not bloom without cooler temperatures or an increase in diurnal range. Reading about attempts by growers in low-elevation, tropical climates to induce flowering in cool-growing *Cymbidium* by icing their plants is enough to bring a smile to a temperate-zone grower, while endless discussions regarding techniques for maintaining warm night temperatures are of little interest to growers closer to the equator.

Greenhouse heating costs are a definite concern for most growers in seasonal, temperate latitudes, just as cooling is a consideration for growers in hot climates. By concentrating on adaptable species or those that require the least heating or cooling, growers can dramatically reduce overhead costs. For example, in the maritime Pacific Northwest region of the United States and Canada, the cost of heating increases 3–5% for each additional 1 °F (0.6°C) of heat maintained in winter, which means that if plants will grow well at 50°F (10°C) but a minimum temperature of 60°F (15.6°C) is being maintained, the cost of heating the greenhouse is 30–50% higher than it needs to be. Growers in other parts of the world or in other climatic regions may have a different cost basis, but the principle is the same and applies to the costs of summer cooling as well.

GROWING MEDIA: *Recommended media and repotting schedules, based on reports from successful growers.* Growers in different areas use various media, their choice frequently reflecting local availability and cost. No one medium is ideal for all plants or for growers in every area. Mixes that work well in dry climates may retain too much water for areas with high relative humidity, while mixes designed to encourage rapid drainage in a moist environment may cause similar plants to become desiccated in areas with low atmospheric moisture.

Growing Media

A medium must drain quickly so that roots are never soggy, but it should retain enough moisture to keep the roots damp between waterings. A rapidly draining medium is preferable in areas with high relative humidity, while a moisture-retaining medium is advantageous in areas with low atmospheric moisture.

A single-ingredient medium is generally easier to manage than a mixture. Also, equally sized particles provide more air circulation than mixtures of fine and coarse materials, since the smaller pieces fill the air spaces between larger chunks.

The acidity or alkalinity of an orchid medium, indicated by its pH, is a variable often overlooked by growers, although it may play a critical role in whether a plant does well in a particular medium.

Under acid conditions, some nutrients, including calcium, phosphorus, and magnesium, undergo chemical changes allowing them to combine with other elements, thereby forming compounds which make them unavailable to the plants. As a result, plants grown in an overly acid environment may be deficient in these nutrients. Other nutrients become more available to plants under acid conditions. Manganese and aluminum, for instance, are so highly soluble in an acid environment that a plant may absorb them in toxic levels. Deficiencies may occur when some nutrients are displaced by excessive quantities of other nutrients, rather than as a result of an actual shortage.

Excessive alkalinity also affects the availability of nutrients. Deficiencies of boron, copper, iron, manganese, phosphorus, and zinc are common in alkaline soils.

The pH scale is the standard means of indicating the relative acidity or alkalinity of any substance. The scale ranges from 0 (acid) to 14 (alkaline), with 7 being neutral. It is logarithmic, like the Richter scale used to indicate the strength of an earthquake. Consequently, a pH of 5 is 10 times more acid than a pH of 6, and 100 times more acid than a pH of 7.

Technically, pH indicates the concentration of hydrogen ions in a given amount of water rather than the acidity of the medium itself. Thus, in the case of plant medium, what is actually measured is the number of hydrogen ions that can move from the medium to the water which clings to the surface of that medium.

The range of pH that is normally of interest to most plant growers is 5–8 (pH 5.5–6.5 for orchid growers). However, some orchid species grow in very acid habitats with readings as low as 3.5.

Very little work has been done relative to the pH requirements of individual orchid species, but descriptions of the natural habitat often give clues to the acidity or alkalinity in the plants' microclimate. Acidic or low pH conditions may be indicated by the presence of certain plants, such as moss, mountain laurel, oak trees, pitcher plants, and rhododendrons. In general, acid habitats tend to be wet: bogs and marshes are usually the most acid. At the other extreme, alkalinity or high pH is common in dry areas. Under extremely alkaline conditions, mineral salt deposits may form a surface crust. In most cases, alkaline soils occur when the base material is high in lime.

Soil pH is normally measured by adding distilled (neutral) water equal to 2.5 times the volume of the soil being tested, then obtaining a value using either a pH meter or litmus paper. This technique is not practical when dealing with orchid potting materials such as chunky bark or cork, but if the material is pulverized, it might be used. An alternate technique is to collect the water that runs out of the pot (since what matters is the pH at the roots) and to measure its pH.

The pH may be adjusted when a plant's pH requirement is known. Water may safely be acidified by adding citric acid at the rate of approximately ¼–⅓ tsp. per gal. of water (250 mg per liter) until the desired pH is reached. Potting medium may be made less acid by sprinkling dolomite lime on the surface of the pot.

The acidity in fir bark or sphagnum is desirable for most orchids, which generally prefer an acidic medium. When using an inert medium, it is best to select a fertilizer that provides the proper acidity. It should be noted that the medium becomes more acid as decomposition takes place. Consequently, plant growth often slows as a medium breaks down. This occurs not only because air is less available to the roots, but also because the medium may become too acid for the plant to utilize nutrients properly.

Commonly used media are listed below, with observations on the advantages and disadvantages of each.

Activated charcoal retains moisture, does not break down, improves aeration, absorbs excess salts and chemical contaminants, and helps produce a healthier plant when added to potting mixes. Some growers feel that charcoal absorbs salts and chemical contaminants so efficiently that in time, water released by the charcoal may be toxic to the plant. They recommend replacing the charcoal every year. *Vanda* and *Oncidium* species are sometimes grown in charcoal alone, but 10–20% charcoal and 80–90% other ingredients is a more usual ratio for most orchids.

Coconut husks and fiber work well in the tropics but for unknown reasons are less satisfactory in temperate-zone greenhouses. This material retains large amounts of moisture and contains high levels of nutrients, so that additional fertilizer is not needed. The fibers tend to become tightly packed, restricting aeration.

Cork slabs and nuggets are often used with orchids that must dry out between waterings. The cork may be mixed with activated charcoal. It breaks down slowly unless attacked by insects such as sow bugs and millipedes, which pulverize it in short order. The best results are reported in temperate zones, because cork often breaks down within a year in warm climates.

Cypress-bark slabs are used for mounting orchids. The material is decay-resistant.

Fir bark, with a pH of 5, is the most frequently used medium in North America because it is readily available and moderately inexpensive. In tropical climates, however, it tends to break down rapidly. Bark is available in graded sizes; as a general rule, the finer a plant's roots or the higher a plant's moisture needs, the smaller the bark should be. Before it is used for potting, bark should be soaked in water at least 3 hours, and preferably 24 hours, to allow it to absorb moisture. Watering dry bark after potting is not sufficient. If bark alone dries out too quickly, then perlite, sphagnum moss, or chopped tree-fern may be added at a ratio of approximately 4 parts bark to 1 part moisture-retentive medium.

Gravel and lava rock permit rapid drying, but plants in these media must be faithfully watered. They also require a complete fertilizer which includes trace minerals. Many epiphytic orchids will grow in almost anything that provides excellent drainage.

Oak or beech leaves are sometimes added to terrestrial mixes. The leaves are collected fresh and should be shredded before they are added to the medium. The addition of fibrous loam or screened, composted manure (not garden soil) is also suggested for these mixes, but these ingredients break down in about 6 months so should be used in a small quantity relative to coarse grit or sand.

Osmunda is acid, with a pH of 4.3. The woody-fibered root of the osmunda fern, it was used almost exclusively for many years, but it has become prohibitively expensive. It provides a good balance of air and water, breaks down slowly, and supplies many nutrients. In fact, when this medium is used, fertilizer should not be applied more than once a month. On the negative side, it is somewhat difficult to repot plants in osmunda without damaging the roots. The medium should be soaked before it is used for potting.

Peat moss, ancient sphagnum from peat beds, is normally acid, with a pH of 3.5–5.0, but is sometimes almost neutral. It is available in milled, coarse, or chunky forms. The moss itself contains few nutrients. Once moist, it can hold 10–20 times its weight in water; but when dry it tends to shed water, making it difficult to remoisten. It is sometimes included in terrestrial mixes but is seldom used with epiphytic orchids except as chunks.

Perlite (sponge rock), with a pH of 7.0–7.5, increases both water retention and aeration. It contains no essential elements and does not hold nutrients. Perlite does not decompose, helps keep the medium open, and holds amazing quantities of water on its surface. This water is released as the surrounding medium dries out and is available when the plant needs moisture. The perlite stays cool in a warm environment, which should be helpful for plants requiring cooler temperatures.

Perlite is available in several sizes, but coarse or chunky forms known as sponge rock are most often used for orchids. Perlite should be purchased with care since fluoride levels range from 1–17%, and high fluoride is toxic, causing severe leaf-tip burn. Perlite is frequently included as an additive to increase water retention. Increasingly, it is being used alone, and growers report excellent root growth in this medium. A complete fertilizer with trace minerals should be used for plants in perlite, as with other non-organic media.

Redwood bark is very acid, with a pH of 3.5, which inhibits fungus growth. It is sometimes used as a medium but is more often a component in mixes. It absorbs moisture rapidly and stays very wet. The pH may be raised by adding a mixture of 50% dolomite lime and 50% powdered oyster shell at the rate of ½ lb. per cubic ft. of medium (8 kg per cubic m).

Rice hulls, with a pH of approximately 5.5, are often included in medium mixes, though they become too tightly packed when used alone. The hulls break down slowly, keep terrestrial mixes open, retain moisture, and provide a long-lasting source of potassium. Rice hulls have proved particularly beneficial in seedling mixes.

Rock wool is sterile, has a pH of 5.5, and does not decompose. It is available in several forms with varying capacities for holding and repelling water. Insects and snails avoid the material, but mice love it. When shredded rock wool is used, it is usually mixed by volume with 30% styrofoam beads, which help keep it from becoming too tightly packed. Covering the surface of the pot with small gravel helps prevent the growth of moss or foul-smelling black algae which may grow on the rock wool.

Plants in this non-organic medium must be fertilized faithfully during periods of active growth, and trace minerals should also be applied 1 or 2 times during the summer. However, determining the appropriate fertilizer can be difficult. Urea-based fertilizers are washed out before breaking down enough to be used by the plant. Reports indicate that during dark winter weather, fertilizer is absorbed, changing the electrical conductivity and doubling the strength of the fertilizer.

Sphagnum moss, with a pH of 3.5, is frequently recommended as a medium, and both live and dried strands are used with orchids. While sphagnum may be used alone for some species, it tends to become tightly packed, so it is usually cut into short pieces and mixed with other ingredients such as perlite or tree fern.

When live sphagnum is included in the potting mix, baskets are highly recommended, but white or translucent plastic pots may also be used. The diffused light transmitted by the light-colored plastic is needed to keep the moss inside the pot alive. In dark pots, only the surface layer of moss continues to live. Both chlorine and concentrated fertilizers kill the moss. Watering with rainwater eliminates the problem, and tap water may be used if it has been held in an open container at least 24 hours, allowing the chlorine to escape from the water.

When the moss is kept alive, it produces natural fertilizers adequate for most orchids, and many growers use no additional fertilizer. If fertilizer is added, the plants should be foliar fed with a dilute solution (0.1 tsp. per gal. or 3.8 liters) of fish fertilizer or an equally dilute solution of manure tea. Chemical fertilizer may be used as a foliar feed, but it is more damaging to the moss than organic fertilizers. Even dilute fertilizers should not be applied directly to the moss.

Orchids appear to benefit from the use of live sphagnum moss, providing that the plant needs the constant moisture necessary to keep the moss alive. Sphagnum works well where low humidity is a problem, particularly if coarse perlite or charcoal is added to increase aeration and drainage. It is an excellent medium for species with high annual rainfall in their natural habitats. Live moss tends to become tightly packed when used alone, so most growers prefer to mix it with other ingredients.

Live sphagnum moss is extremely useful in revitalizing weak or sickly plants or establishing back bulbs or small plant divisions. To treat a weak plant, soak it in Natriphene* for an hour or more, then place it on top of live moss in a clear, covered container or plastic bag with optimum growing temperatures for the species. This treatment is often very successful. It was formerly thought that the acidity of sphagnum helped prevent disease, but there are indications that the live moss may also produce a beneficial natural fungicide.

Tree-fern fiber, from large, tropical tree ferns, is frequently used with good success, either alone or mixed with other media. This material is slow to break down even in warm climates, and though it appears very porous, it holds a surprising amount of water. It should not be used for species that require rapid drying. Like fir bark, it should be soaked before it is used for potting.

Vermiculite is an expanded mica that holds tremendous quantities of water for long periods of time. It has a neutral pH of 6.5–7.2, is light and sterile, and contains a high level of magnesium and potassium. It can be a beneficial addition to terrestrial mixes for plants which live in bogs, experience flooding, or require constant moisture. It stays too wet, however, to be suitable for use with most epiphytic orchids. Fertilizer should be decreased if vermiculite is used, since this medium absorbs large quantities of nutrients whenever fertilizer is applied. Small quantities of vermiculite in seedling mixes could help prevent the media from drying out. Horticultural-grade vermiculite should be used since other grades may be excessively alkaline.

Walnut shells mixed with charcoal and perlite are used successfully by some growers. Nut shells should be avoided in areas with soft water and high humidity, where they rapidly deteriorate and become covered with a fungal growth which prevents air from reaching the roots.

Orchids are usually grown in pots or baskets, but pendent plants and those requiring additional air circulation are healthier if mounted on rafts or hanging plaques if humidity is high or the plant is misted faithfully. Rafts are plaques which are laid horizontally on the bench.

A variety of containers are used for potting, including open baskets, unglazed clay pots, and most commonly, plastic pots. Each type of container has advantages and disadvantages. Baskets allow the greatest air circulation and dry most rapidly. Clay pots provide some evaporative

---

*Throughout this volume, mention of a trademark or proprietary product does not constitute a guarantee or warranty of the product by the publisher or authors and does not imply its approval to the exclusion of other products.

Growing Media

cooling and some air transfer through the porous clay; because of their weight, they are preferable for top-heavy plants. Plastic pots are lightweight and easy to clean and sterilize for reuse. However, when plastic is used, moisture retention may be excessive and air circulation is poor. The pot used to hold a medium is usually not critical, though some species do poorly without ample air to the roots, while others do poorly if allowed to dry out.

Plastic pots should be modified with extra drainage holes to increase air circulation and prevent the medium from becoming stale. The extra holes can easily be punched with a hot soldering iron. Because the fumes are noxious, this should be done outside or in a well-ventilated area. A 4 in. (10 cm) pot should have about 1 sq. in. (2–3 sq. cm) of drainage, or 8–9 holes ⅜ in. (1 cm) in diameter. A 6 in. (15 cm) pot needs drainage increased to about 2 sq. in. (5 sq. cm) or about 20 holes. Increasing root aeration will probably eliminate most problems associated with root rot.

Repotting is best done when the plant resumes active growth in the spring or summer, preferably just as new roots begin to grow, but it is sometimes delayed until immediately after flowering. Exceptions are noted for individual species. Generally, if new leaves are growing, so are the roots. Withholding water for a few days before repotting makes the roots of most species more flexible and less prone to injury. After repotting, plants should be rested without food or water for 7–10 days, which will allow any bruised or broken roots to heal. During this period, the foliage may be misted if necessary to prevent desiccation. When watering is resumed, using a hormone and vitamin B-1 solution such as Superthrive will encourage new growth.

Most orchids respond well to new medium and grow more vigorously if repotted annually. The inevitable exceptions are noted for individual species. Orchids generally outgrow their pots in 18–24 months, which is about how long fir bark lasts before breaking down. Some growers suggest mixing about 20% old medium with 80% new bark to increase the moisture retention of the new mix. However, medium should not be reused unless it has been sterilized or is known to be free from disease and insects.

Seedlings should be potted in a relatively fine medium such as ⅛–¼ in. (3–6 mm) bark, and they will grow most rapidly if repotted annually. Physan should not be used when deflasking as it adversely affects some seedlings.

MISCELLANEOUS NOTES: *Supplementary information.*

Orchid diseases are treated comprehensively in Appendix A.

Sterilizing is the best means of preventing disease, which is frequently transmitted from plant to plant by repotting in contaminated pots. Tools and fingernails may also carry disease pathogens. Through careless cultural practices, growers may carry diseases from one plant to another, often without realizing that a plant being cut or examined is diseased. Fingernails are frequently the culprit.

Everything that comes in contact with a diseased plant should be sterilized before each reuse. Sterilization procedures are discussed in detail in Appendix A under the heading "Preventing Disease."

Mineral or fertilizer salt deposits on pots or humidity trays may be dissolved with oxalic acid, which is available from commercial janitorial suppliers. Once the deposits have been dissolved, the pots and trays should be rinsed and sterilized.

Mycorrhizae play an important but little-understood role in orchid culture. The seeds of virtually all plant genera contain nutrients adequate to sustain the plantlets through the stages of germination and production of their first true leaves, after which time the seedlings can produce adequate food supplies independently. Orchid seeds, however, are tiny and contain none of the nutrients necessary for the seedlings to survive. As a consequence, following germination, the developing protocorms are totally dependent upon fungi to supply their food until they are able to produce their own through photosynthesis.

This unusual characteristic of orchid seed, the essential mycorrhizae, and the symbiotic relation between the two became apparent when growers found that orchid seeds grew only when sown around a mature plant. The seedlings needed to be infected with fungus from the adult plant in order to obtain food for survival. The situation changed when a sterile germinating method was developed. Growers using this technique provide nutrients the protocorm can use directly, thereby eliminating the need for fungi.

More recently, plant scientists have discovered that mycorrhizae are essential to the health and survival of many higher order plants. In fact, as research on this topic is extended, it appears that essentially all higher plants require and develop symbiotic relationships with one or more mycorrhizal species. At present, however, we have little information on the specific requirements of adult orchids.

Plant scientists know that protocorms cannot survive without the fungi, and that the relationship continues throughout the life of the orchid. But research has not yet revealed whether the relationship is necessary for the health or survival of mature orchids, since attempts to confirm this have been inconclusive. Interesting questions have been raised, and avenues of speculation opened; but additional research will be necessary before we know whether plant-mycorrhizal relationships play an important role in orchid culture.

If information bearing on the mycorrhizae associated with particular orchid species becomes available, it will be included in species listings under "Miscellaneous Notes."

Plant and Flower Information

PLANT SIZE AND TYPE: *General information on size and growth habit.* Like the information under "Cultural Recommendations," the information in this section has been especially tailored to the needs of growers. Because growers are not ordinarily concerned with fractional measurements, all figures have been rounded to the nearest whole number. Measurements are given in inches with metric equivalents in parentheses.

Measurements of plant size refer to the vegetative growths and do not include the height of the inflorescence. When a plant's growth habit is such that a height measurement is not an appropriate indicator of size (as for *Phalaenopsis*), the plant is described as "large," "moderate," or "small" in relation to other members of the same genus.

Plants are identified as sympodial (having multiple growths) or monopodial (having a single growth) and as epiphytic (tree-growing), lithophytic (rock-growing), or terrestrial (ground-growing). Because size is influenced by maturity, adaptability, and growing environment, cultivated plants may be various sizes and still be healthy.

Poor overall growth usually indicates a cultural problem. It is frequently the result of root deterioration caused by overwatering, insufficient air to the roots because of deteriorated medium, or salt buildup. Unhealthy plants should be unpotted and examined carefully. Damaged roots should be removed, the plant repotted in new medium, and attention paid to providing the best possible environment for the species. When a plant's root system is inadequate or the environment is too cool, the plant may be unable to utilize available food. Unfortunately, growers often respond to poor growth by increasing water and fertilizer, which not only fails to solve the problem but compounds it by contributing to salt buildup. The following plant and root abnormalities indicate common cultural problems. (See Appendix A for a more complete list of symptoms indicating problems with pathogens, pests, or nutrients.)

Black root-tips are usually caused by salt buildup.

Discolored root-tips indicate damage from salt buildup.

Hard, wrinkled plants result from high light and inadequate moisture.

Poorly developed roots may occur when trace minerals are inadequate.

Root rot is a common and very serious problem caused by overwatering. It often occurs when the medium breaks down and watering is not decreased. Since damaged roots provide an entry point for disease organisms, symptoms of root rot may first be noticed on other plant parts. Anytime a symptom might be related to root deterioration, the plant should be removed from the pot and the roots checked for rot. If the roots are soft or black, all damaged areas should be trimmed back to healthy tissue, and the plant should be soaked in Natriphene at least an hour. After a thorough soaking, the plant should be repotted in fresh medium.

Short roots may indicate excessive water or fertilizer.

Smaller new growths are more likely to result from inappropriate growing conditions than from insufficient fertilizer.

Soft plants may result if light is too low, if humidity is too high, or if too much nitrogen has been given. Such plants seem to be more prone to attack by disease organisms.

PSEUDOBULB: *Length and general description.* This category is omitted from the listings when all members of a genus are monopodial or without pseudobulbs, but it is included if any plants in the genus have pseudobulbs. When a species grows directly from a rhizome or the root ball, without a pseudobulb, "N/A" indicates that the category of information is not applicable.

Wrinkled pseudobulbs indicate water deprivation over a prolonged period. Newer pseudobulbs will become plump when adequate moisture is available to the plant, but older back bulbs may remain wrinkled. With time, back bulbs eventually lose their usefulness to the plant.

LEAVES: *Number, size, and general appearance.* Size measurements refer to length or height rather than width. Leaf information was usually derived from taxonomic descriptions, but information from other sources is also included.

Leaf size and appearance frequently provide the first indication that a plant is stressed. Most successful growers pay very close attention to their plants, examining them frequently in order to observe the first, subtle indications of problems. Every grower would do well to follow this practice, since many problems are easily corrected if detected early.

The following symptoms signal common cultural difficulties. (See Appendix A for a more comprehensive list of symptoms indicating problems with pathogens, pests, or nutrients.)

A brown, discolored patch, usually round, on a curved leaf surface is probably the result of sunburn. The damaged area should be removed, as it offers a point of entry for disease organisms.

Dark green or limp leaves often indicate that the plant is receiving insufficient light or too much nitrogen.

Discolored or damaged leaf surfaces may be caused by ethylene gas but usually result from spider-mite damage.

Heavy leaf loss on orchids that are normally evergreen is a sign of significant stress. But even plants that have lost all their leaves may recover providing their roots are still healthy and they are given the treatment described under "Growing Media" above.

Leaf-tip die-back occurs when insufficient moisture reaches the leaves. The obvious solution is to water more frequently. However, inadequate moisture to the leaves may also occur if the plant has been overwatered to the point of causing root loss. Treatment is suggested above, in the discussion of root rot under "Plant Size and Type."

Leaf-tip die-back also results from hard water, overfertilization, and excessive salt buildup. Excessive salts become concentrated in the tips of the leaves. If the salts have formed white deposits on the leaves, pot, or medium, salt buildup is the most likely cause of the leaf-tip problem.

Pale, yellow-green leaves usually result from high light or insufficient nitrogen. High light is the probable cause if the leaves also appear somewhat dry or wrinkled. Nitrogen deficiency is indicated when the older leaves become yellow. This may result either from an inadequate supply of nitrogen or from a cultural problem which limits the plant's ability to use this nutrient. Possible causes include root damage, cool temperatures, or imbalance of plant nutrients. Rarely, high levels of ethylene gas cause similar symptoms. Ethylene gas is discussed under the heading "Flowers" below, since symptoms of contamination are usually noticed first as sepal wilt in the blossoms.

Red-tinged leaves often indicate that the plant has been exposed to maximum light levels, and additional light could be extremely harmful.

Small leaves on normally large-leaved species may indicate a lack of nitrogen, root loss, or damage from salt buildup.

Spotting on the leaves is usually caused by a fungus (see Appendix A).

Wrinkled or hard leaves result when light levels are excessive or watering is insufficient.

INFLORESCENCE: *Length and appearance of the flower spike.* When a species produces multiple spikes per growth, this information is noted.

The following abnormalities in the flower spike signal cultural problems.

Crooked inflorescences may result if a plant's orientation to the light source is changed while the spike is growing, as the spikes usually grow toward the light.

Excessively long spikes may indicate that light is insufficient.

Unusually short spikes may indicate excessively high light levels.

Seedlings will be healthier if the first flower spike is removed soon after the flowers open, directing the plant's energy towards growth rather than maintaining an early bloom.

FLOWERS: *Approximate number of blooms per inflorescence, size of blossoms, and general appearance.* All information refers to flowers on a healthy, mature plant.

When exact bloom counts are not available, relative number is indicated by a term such as "few" or "many." Unless otherwise noted, diameter measurements are given for flower size.

Descriptions of shape, general form, texture, and color are based on information from a variety of sources. These are not intended to describe any particular flower but merely to indicate what might be expected.

This section also includes information on whether buds open simultaneously or sequentially as well as any available information on how long the blooms generally last.

Reported fragrance is described when possible. Fragrance is frequently dependent on light, temperature, and time of day as well as personal preferences and individual sensitivity to particular scents. A fragrance that is nearly overpowering to one person may be only faintly detectable to another, just as a fragrance that is pleasant for one may be unpleasant for another.

Intense flower color is more likely when light levels at the high end of the appropriate range are combined with temperatures at the low end of the appropriate range. Once flowers are open, a combination of lower light and cooler temperatures helps the blooms stay in good condition. When plants are grown under artificial lights, flower color in some species may be somewhat muddy rather than bright and clear.

Flowers, like other plant parts, may hold clues to the plant's health. The following symptoms indicate culture-related problems which make a plant more susceptible to disease or insect damage.

Black spots or streaks on flower sheaths are caused by a fungus that may also rot the flower buds. Affected sheaths should be removed, and the buds treated with a contact fungicide (see Appendix A). Buds will normally continue to develop unless they have also been infected. Infection may be prevented by increasing air circulation, keeping humidity somewhat low, and avoiding overhead watering when plants are in sheath.

Brown spots on the blossoms may be caused by water droplets as a result of careless watering or condensation resulting from excessively high humidity.

Bud drop may be caused by ethylene gas (see sepal wilt below) but is more likely to result from low light, wide temperature fluctuations, low relative humidity, or temperature shock, which often results from the use of water colder than the environment. The water used for warm-growing species should be at least 62°F (17°C).

Lack of blooms usually results from inappropriate growing conditions. Unfortunately, the precise bloom triggers have not been determined for most orchid species. The individual climate table and the discussion of bloom initiators included in species listings will hopefully assist in determining the most probable critical factor.

Malformed flowers are often caused by exposure to harmful chemicals, but they may also be caused by genetic disorders which cannot be corrected.

Rapid, premature wilting of flowers results when the flowers are pollinated or the pollinia are removed by insects or by accident.

Sepal wilt is nearly always caused by ethylene gas, which is emitted as a result of incomplete combustion of an open flame. A defective heater is normally the source of the problem, but the gas is also produced in abundance by chrysanthemum flowers and ripening fruit, especially apples. In fact, all flowers produce some ethylene as they mature, and this gas causes them to wilt naturally with age. High levels will cause the blooms to age prematurely. Unopened buds are generally not affected unless contamination is severe.

Yellow buds in winter usually indicate inadequate light.

Insufficient winter rest may result in no blooms the following season. Temperature, light, and water cycles are often critical to a species' ability to initiate blooms. Some crop plants are known to require a specific number of hours during which temperatures are below a particular level before the plants produce the hormones necessary to initiate flowering. Other species require a sudden drop in temperatures, while still others depend on an alternating pattern of wet and dry periods.

Many plants respond to increases and decreases in seasonal light levels, which may result from seasonal fluctuations, a distinct pattern of clear days, or high average light levels (for example, some require at least 10 hours of bright light during winter). Because particular light wavelengths may be critical, some plants are difficult to grow under artificial lights. Even plants which need low light levels may require light for a minimum number of hours each day in winter. Light is available 11–13 hours a day throughout the year near the equator, while it may be available only 7 hours a day during midlatitude winters.

Recent research has shown that photoperiodicity may be defined more accurately as the plant's response to hours of darkness rather than its response to hours of light, as was previously thought. Some plants are unable to produce the hormones required to initiate blooms unless they spend the necessary number of hours in darkness. Although experiments have not been conducted with orchids, some species might fail to bloom if the growing area is exposed to nighttime light.

It is interesting to note that growers who supplement the hours of light in temperate latitudes report greater success when light is extended in late afternoon than when it is extended in the early morning.

Insufficient nutrients or trace minerals may result in a plant's being unable to produce flowers. However, fertilizer should not arbitrarily be increased until other environmental conditions have been carefully analyzed. The number of flowers produced by a weak plant normally declines over time.

HYBRIDIZING NOTES: *Chromosome counts and dominant hybridizing characteristics.* The length of time required for seeds to mature refers to the time necessary for the seeds to become sufficiently viable to be used in green-pod culture, which eliminates the need for presterilization. Changes in the appearance of the capsule may indicate that the seeds should be sown immediately; otherwise they will become contaminated and need to be sterilized before being flasked.

Using the climate tables as a guide, growers can select parent plants that will contribute tolerance of warm or cool temperatures to hybrids.

Because seeds may not be viable or pods may fall off prematurely, attempts to propagate plants may fail, particularly attempts to make intergeneric hybrids. Fred Hillerman, author of *An Introduction to the Cultivated* Angraecoid *Orchids of Madagascar* (1986), developed the following technique, which reportedly improves the success rate and has helped him get viable seeds after numerous failed attempts.

- Following the normal procedure, remove the pollen from the pod parent, then load its stigma with pollen from the donor parent.
- Add a small amount of pollen from the receiving plant or its sibling to help prevent rejection.

Unfortunately, when using this technique, growers often cannot be certain that a cross has taken until the plants bloom. However, if the vegetative growth habits of the parents are quite different, the success or failure may be apparent when the seedlings develop leaves.

REFERENCES: *Numbers corresponding to entries in the Bibliography.* Readers seeking additional information may consult the selected sources listed at the close of this volume.

PHOTOS/DRAWINGS: *Numbers corresponding to entries in the Bibliography.* Here readers will find references to species illustrations. Italic type indicates that the photograph or drawing is reproduced in color. Standard type indicates a black-and-white photo or a botanical drawing. This category is not included in synonym listings or for species not recently collected.

Throughout this volume, "N/A" indicates that the information was not available or that the category of information was not applicable.

Synonyms and natural hybrids are listed separately in alphabetical order. Synonyms are followed by a cross-reference to the species or genus name that is now considered valid. Natural hybrid names are followed by a listing of the hybrid's parents.

2
Dendrobium
General Information

SUBFAMILY: Epidendroideae.

TRIBE: *Epidendreae*.

SUBTRIBE: *Dendrobiinae*.

GENUS: *Dendrobium* Swartz.

AKA: In 1859, Professor Lindley wrote, "In fact that whole genus *(Dendrobium)*, if it be one, is in extricable confusion." Many changes have been made during the intervening years. New species have been discovered, species have been renamed because the same name had been used for completely different plants, some species have been lumped, other large variable ones have been split into several new and different species, groups of plants have been moved into other genera, and some have then been returned to *Dendrobium*. After all of this effort, however, Lindley's sentiments are still reiterated by today's botanists as they attempt to resolve the confusion surrounding this genus.

Growers need to be aware that the names listed as AKA (also known as) are as we found them in the literature. Because many of the plant names have been used more than once, they must be further identified by the describer's name. Plants identified as *D. xyz* Rchb.f. are not the same as *D. xyz* Lindley. Both Lindley and Reichenbach f. (The son of H. G. Reichenbach, Sr.) used the same name for different plants. The first use of a name has priority, and the plant given the same name at a later date must be renamed. Without the describers name, and sometimes the date, it is impossible to determine which plant is being discussed.

We have little doubt that many of the plants included here may someday be transferred to other genera or combined under a single plant name. However, our sole purpose is to provide cultural information for all current *Dendrobium* species.

The synonyms included in this category are as we found them in the works listed in each Reference category and the Bibliography.

Over the years, species now assigned to the genus *Dendrobium* have been called *Aclinia, Aporum, Bolbidium, Cadetia, Calcatrippa, Callista, Ceraia, Coelandria, Desmotrichum, Dichopus, Ditulima, Endeisa, Ephemerantha, Froscula, Grastidium, Keranthus, Latouria, Macrostomium, Onychium, Ormostema, Oxystophyllum, Pedilonum, Pierardia, Sarcopodium, Sarcostoma, Scandederis, Schismoceras, Stachyobium, Thelychiton, Thicuania, Tropilis,* and probably others.

Some groups of species originally assigned to *Dendrobium* have been placed in independent genera, though some disagreement exists regarding the status of these genera. In his work *Orchids of Thailand*, Dr. G. Seidenfaden includes species in the genera *Diplocaulobium, Epigeneium, Flickingeria,* and *Goniobulbon*. Dr. P. Cribb also places species formerly described as *Dendrobium* in the genera *Glossorhyncha* and *Cadetia*. T. M. Reeve (ref. 24) in his work with New Guinea *Dendrobium* continues to use the sections developed by Schlechter and J. J. Smith including *Desmotrichuim (Flickingeria)* and *Diplocaulobium*. He does not include in the genus *Dendrobium* those species originally placed in the section (or genus, depending on the botanist) *Cadetia*, which is now generally accepted as an independent genus.

Growers owe a debt of gratitude to botanists working in particular geographical areas or with particular groups of *Dendrobium* species. Their careful studies have helped clarify our understanding of the plants reviewed and serve as the basis for cultural research. Attempts to review the genus as a whole have been unsuccessful. The sheer size of the genus as well as the wide-ranging habitat make it essentially impossible for a single botanist to know all the plants involved. Comparing type specimens is difficult if not impossible, since many of the specimens are in extremely poor condition while others have deteriorated or been destroyed. Even when duplicate specimens exist, they are frequently located in herbaria scattered around the world, making comparative study difficult.

The huge number of superfluous names also complicates *Dendrobium* study. We have included generally accepted synonyms as well as synonyms listed by botanists working with specific groups of plants or in particular geographical areas. When we encountered different synonyms listed by individual botanists, we used the species name from the most recent work unless there appeared to be a genuine difference of opinion. In that case, we included as much information as possible. Mark Clements (ref. 67) proposed numerous new names for Australian *Dendrobium* species. Taxonomists' opinions differ regarding the validity of these names. Whether these new names survive the test of time or become additional superfluous names remains to be seen. Cross-references are included for these names as they are sometimes used by growers and sellers of orchid plants.

Cribb (ref. 82) describes the difficulties he encountered while reviewing sections of the genus *Dendrobium*. In his work on *Dendrobium* in Thailand, Seidenfaden (ref. 453) eloquently expresses his frustration and describes the difficulty of resolving questions as to which name belongs with which plant. Even after exhaustive research, he was sometimes unable to reconcile the problems he encountered in identifying Thailand's 150 *Dendrobium* species.

Although the efforts have been monumental, broad-based attempts to revise the entire genus have only compounded the confusion of names. Fr. Kränzlin, in Engler's *Das Pflanzenreich* (ref. 254), attempted the first wholesale revision of the genus. His reorganization was sufficiently flawed that it has never been considered usable by other botanists, but the names he created are still causing confusion. In fact, Schlechter was so frustrated by Kränzlin's "monograph" that he stated: "The species often are quite incorrectly interpreted and those species which have been clarified by knowledgeable persons, such as J. J. Smith for example, have been shuffled up again. As was recently stated in England, one result of this 'monograph' is that a reappraisal of the genus *Dendrobium* has now become more important than ever."

Even with this stated need, however, little was done with the genus as a whole until 1981 when F. G. Brieger published over 800 new names and combinations that have not been generally accepted by other taxonomists. Then in 1983, S. Rauschert published still more new names, attempting to complete the transfers started by Brieger. Transfers that are not generally accepted by other taxonomists are not included here since our purpose is to provide cultural information and a cross reference of names for growers. It is not intended in any way to be a taxonomic study. Therefore, all references to genus names that are not generally considered valid by other authorities in the field are omitted unless the name applies to the original description.

Additional information regarding the species and names used here may be found in the references cited for each species.

D. moniliforme (Linn.) Swartz is designated as the type species for the genus *Dendrobium* Sw. as recommended by R. E. Holttum, F. G. Brieger, and P. J. Cribb (ref. 201).

Because of the difficult task of revising or changing hybridization records, the International Orchid Comission sometimes continues to register hybrids under names that are no longer considered botanically correct. Whenever possible, we have indicated the name presently used to register hybrids when it differs from the currently accepted botanical name.

SPECIES: *Dendrobium* flowers have 4 pollinia in 2 pairs and the base of the lateral sepals and the column-foot, which is joined to the base of the lip, form a spur-like mentum or hood.

Dendrobium is the second largest genus in the orchid family. Only *Bulbophyllum* has more species. Without a generally accepted review of the genus, the number of valid species is uncertain, but estimates range from 900–2000. For this work, we found 2425 *Dendrobium* names of which 1230 appear to be currently valid. (The preceding statement was written on January 13, 1994 at 9:30 a. m. It was valid until we received a letter from Dr. Gunnar Seidenfaden at 11:30 a. m. in which he shared a number of taxonomic changes that would be published in the near future.) The number of valid species also varies depending on which taxonomist is being followed, and some of the species included here may prove to be invalid; but *it is not the function of this work to determine the validity of any name.* The plant names and synonyms are included as found in the literature available to us.

Botanists divide the genus into closely related groups using the sections or subdivisions devised by Schlechter, sometimes with variations for convenience. However, they frequently disagree regarding which plants belong to which section because some species fall somewhere between sections. These intergrades have frequently forestalled attempts to divide *Dendrobium* into more manageable divisions. Schlechter originally listed 41 sections, but some are now considered separate genera while others have been combined.

Orchid growers frequently refer to sections or groups of closely related plants as a means of trying to generalize cultural instructions. Some common section names that may be encountered in other literature include *Calyptrochilus, Dendrobium, Dendrochoryne, Desmotrichum, Latouria* (*Latourea* in Schlechter), *Formosae* (formerly *Nigrohirsutae*), *Oxyglossum, Pedilonum, Phalaenanthe,* and *Spatulata. Dendrobium* growers may also refer to groups of plants by the name of the most commonly cultivated species such as the "anosmum" or "nobile" group, or by a flower feature such as the "antelope" group, or a growth characteristic such as evergreen, deciduous, soft cane, or hard cane. This approach is frequently very misleading, however, so all sectional designations and horticultural groupings are omitted from this work.

At no time since the work done by early botanists have more *Dendrobium* species been reviewed than in the last 10 years. These reviews have produced a staggering number of name changes. Perplexed growers should remember that taxonomy is an evolving science, and species' names are in a continuous state of flux as new information becomes available. We can only hope that botanists will resist the urge to name or rename a plant until evidence indicating a need for change is irrefutable. We also hope that this listing of species and synonyms will help frustrated growers make the transition to the new names.

In *A Revision of* Dendrobium *Section* Oxyglossum, Reeve and Wood (ref. 385) explain some of the reasons for the recent name changes. They include (1) previous misunderstanding regarding the extent of variability within a species, including the number of color varieties and the variability of veins and keels on flowers on the same plant, (2) the loss of many original specimens during World War II, and (3) the frequent, nearly simultaneous describing of the same plant by British, Dutch, and German explorers working in neighboring countries.

Of particular interest to growers, and in many instances unknown until recently, is how some species respond to a common environment. For example, several of the high-altitude New Guinea species were combined after individual plants, thought to be different species, were placed in the Highland Orchid Collection at Laiagam, Papua New Guinea and grown under uniform conditions. The results surprised both growers and botanists. Many apparent differences, which had originally justified separating plants into different species, simply disappeared when plants were grown under uniform conditions. When available, we have included information regarding how species respond to different conditions in cultivation.

The following references were our primary sources for species names. Included are all *Dendrobium* names listed in *Index Kewensis* (ref. 216–235), including the 5-year supplements through 1990. Several sections of the genus have been reviewed recently, and the synonyms provided in those reviews are given priority in species listings.

Comber, J. B. 1983. The section *Calcarifera* of the genus *Dendrobium* in Java. *Orchid Digest* 47(5):191.

Cribb, P. J. 1983. A revision of *Dendrobium* sect. *Latouria* (Orchidaceae). Reprint *Kew Bulletin* 38(2):229–306.

Cribb, P. J. 1983. *Dendrobium* sect. *Ceratobium (Orchidaceae)* in the Pacific Islands. *Kew Bulletin* 37(4):577–591.

Cribb, P. J. 1986. The 'antelope' dendrobiums. Originally printed as— A Revision of *Dendrobium* Sect. *Spatulata* (Orchidaceae). *Kew Bulletin* 41(3):615–692.

Pradhan, G. M. 1974. Indian species of the *Nigrohirsutae* section of *Dendrobium.* Part I, *Orchid Digest* 38(4):124; Part II, *Orchid Digest* 41(1):4.

Reeve, T. 1983. A revision of *Dendrobium* section *Microphytanthe* (Orchidaceae). *The Orcadian* 7(9):203–206.

Reeve, T., and P. Woods. 1989. A revision of *Dendrobium* section *Oxyglossum* (Orchidaceae). *Notes from the Royal Botanic Garden, Edinburgh* 46(2):161–305. Edinburgh, Scotland.

Schelpe, E. A. 1981. A review of the genus *Dendrobium* section *Callista. Orchid Digest* 45(6):204–210.

Schelpe, E. A. 1985. The section *Formosae* of the genus *Dendrobium.* In K. W. Tan (Ed.), *Proceedings of the 11th World Orchid Conference March 1984, Miami,* pp. 308–310.

Also included in the alphabetical species listing are names given in the geographical floras, unless more recent work disagrees with the validity of the name or synonymy. The floras are frequently dated, but they often provide the only information available and constitute an important source of habitat information.

Australia

Clements, M. A. 1989. Catalogue of Australian orchidaceae. *Australian orchid research,* Vol. 1, ed. by D. L. Jones. Australian Orchid Foundation, 107 Roberts St., Essendon 3040, Victoria, Australia.

Dockrill, A. W. 1969. *Australian indigenous orchids.* Society for Growing Australian Plants, Halstead Press, Sydney, Australia.

Nicholls, W. H. 1969. *Orchids of Australia*. Edited by D. L. Jones and T. B. Muir. Nelson Publishing, Melbourne, Australia.

Upton, Walter T. 1989. Dendrobium *orchids of Australia*. Timber Press, Portland, Oregon, USA.

Burma and the Andaman Islands

Grant, B. [1895] 1966. *Orchids of Burma and the Andaman Islands*. Hanthawaddy Press, Rangoon, Burma. Reprinted by Twin Oaks Books, Greenfield, Wisc.

Ceylon

Dassanayake, M. D., and E. R. Fosberg. 1981. *Flora of Ceylon: a revised handbook*. Oxford and IBH Publishing Co., New Delhi, India.

China

Chen, Sing-Chi, and T. Tang. 1982. A general review of the orchid flora of China. *Orchid biology: reviews and perspectives*. Vol. II. Edited by J. Arditti. Comstock Publishing, Cornell University Press, Ithaca, NY.

Hu, Shiu Ying. 1973. The Orchidaceae of China 5. *Quarterly Journal-Taiwan Museum*, 26, 1–2:150–165.

Lin, Tsian-Piao. 1975. *Native orchids of Taiwan*. Vol. 1. Southern Materials Center, P.O. Box 13–342, Taipei, Taiwan, Republic of China.

Su, Horng-Jye. 1975. *Taiwan orchids,* 2nd ed. Horng-Jye Su, Department of Forestry, National Taiwan University, Taipei, Republic of China.

Fiji Islands

Parham, J. W. 1972. *Plants of the Fiji Islands: Orchidaceae*. Rev. ed. The Government Printer, Suva, Fiji.

Kores, P. 1989. A precursory study to orchids of Figi. *Allertonia* Vol. V. National Tropical Botanic Gardens, Hawaii.

Smith, A. C. 1991. *Flora Vitiensis Nova*. Vol. 5. *Orchidaceae* by P. Kores. National Tropical Botanical Garden, Lawai, Kauai, Hawaii.

India

Banerji, M. L., and P. Pradhan. 1984. *The orchids of Nepal Himalaya*. J. Cramer, Vaduz, India.

Bhattacharjee, S. K. 1977. Distribution of orchid genera in India. *Orchid Digest* 41(1):7.

Bose, T. K., and S. K. Bhattacharjee. 1980. *Orchids of India*. Naya Prokash, Calcutta, India.

Deva, S., and H. B. Naithani. 1986. *Orchid flora of North West Himalaya*. Print & Media Assoc., New Delhi, India.

Santapau, H., and Z. Kapadia. 1964. *The orchids of Bombay*. Government of India Press, Calcutta, India.

Indochina

Seidenfaden, G. 1992. The orchids of Indochina. *Opera Botanica* 114, Copenhagen, Denmark

Java

Backer, C. A., and R. C. Bakhuizen Van Den Brink. 1968. *Flora of Java*, vol. III. Wolters-Noordhoff N. V., Groningen, The Netherlands.

Comber, J. B. 1990. *Orchids of Java*. Bentham-Moxon Trust, Royal Botanic Gardens, Kew, England.

Smith, J. J. [1905] 1984. *Die orchideen von Java*. J. Brill, Leiden, The Netherlands. Reprint, Bishen Singh Mahendra Pal Singh, Dehra Dun, India.

Malaya

Holttum, R. E. 1964. *A revised flora of Malaya*. Vol. 1, *Orchids*. Government Printing Office, Singapore.

New Caledonia

Hallé, N. 1977. *Flore de la Nouvelle Caledonie et Dépendencies*. Vol. 8, *Orchidacées*. Musée national d'histoire naturelle, Paris.

New Guinea

Schlechter, R. R. [1911–1914] 1982. *The Orchidaceae of German New Guinea*. Translated by D. F. Blaxell, H. J. Katz, and J. T. Simmons. Australian Orchid Foundation, Melbourne, Australia.

Van Royen, P. 1980. *The orchids of the high mountains of New Guinea*. J. Cramer, Vaduz.

Philippine Islands

Valmayor, H. 1984. *Orchidiana Philippiniana*. Vols. 1–2. Eugenio Lopez Foundation, Manilla, Philippines.

Ryukyu Islands

Garay, L. A., and H. Sweet. 1974. *Orchids of the southern Ryukyu Islands*. Botanical Museum, Harvard University, Cambridge, Mass.

Solomon Islands and Bougainville

Lewis, B., and P. Cribb. 1991. *Orchids of the Solomon Islands and Bougainville*. Royal Botanic Gardens, Kew, England.

Taiwan

Su, Horng-Jye. 1975. *Taiwan orchids,* 2nd ed. Horng-Jye Su, Department of Forestry, National Taiwan University, Taipei, Republic of China.

Thailand

Seidenfaden, G. 1986. Orchid genera in Thailand, XII. *Dendrobium* Sw. *Opera Botanica* 83, Copenhagen, Denmark.

Vanuatu

Lewis, B., and P. Cribb. 1989. *Orchids of Vanuatu*. Royal Botanic Gardens, Kew, England.

Vietnam

Gagnepain, F. 1932. *Flore Générale de L'Indo-Chine,* Vol. sixieme. Edited by Lecomte, H. and H. Humbert. Masson et Cie, Paris.

Recent work is not available for critical habitats in New Guinea, Borneo, Burma, much of Indonesia, and Indochina. Taxonomic work is underway for Borneo so up-to-date *Dendrobium* information should be available within a few years. Fortunately, the work done by Seidenfaden in Thailand helps with the lack of current information for Burma, Cambodia, Laos, and Vietnam.

A complete bibliography appears at the end of this work.

ORIGIN/HABITAT: New Guinea, with an estimated 350 species, is considered the center of distribution for *Dendrobium*. The natural habitat includes most of the South Pacific islands and extends west to India, south to Australia and southern New Zealand, east to Samoa, and north to Japan and Korea.

There are some plants for which so little information is available that we are unable to select appropriate climate data. We have included the information that is available for these plants, usually only a very generalized or questionable source location and a brief or partial description of the plant and flower. These plants may eventually prove to be valid species waiting to be rediscovered, they may prove to be invalid species, or they may be determined to be the same as a species with a better known name and be reduced to synonymy. Regardless of their eventual status, these plants are unlikely to be available for cultivation.

When habitat location is known but the elevation is unavailable, which occurs frequently with *Dendrobium*, data from the nearest weather station are included. However, adjustments cannot be made to the temperature averages to reflect differences between the station and habitat elevations. The climate data may be used as an indication of seasonal patterns, but growers should use the temperatures and rainfall amounts with extreme caution.

Habitat elevations are rounded to the nearest 50 ft. (10 m), but actual elevation is given for each weather station.

CLIMATE: *Dendrobium* grow primarily in tropical to subtropical climates, but some species grow in temperate midlatitudes or at high elevations in tropical areas. Unless habitat location and elevation are reasonably precise, cultural recommendations cannot be developed using climate records.

Numerous species have been moved to other genera, but many are still sold, grown, shown, and their hybrids registered under the *Dendrobium* name. Although taxonomically these plants are no longer *Dendrobium*, we have included some the more popularly grown ones and indicated their current names in the AKA section. We hope that this will help growers avoid some frustration with the name changes.

Cultural Recommendations

LIGHT: 1000–4000 fc. Light requirements are highly variable depending on the species, but most respond well to high morning or afternoon light. Bright, filtered sunlight is usually appropriate, but full midday sun should generally be avoided, even for those species which grow best in high light. For most species, light should be as high as possible, short of damaging the foliage. In temperate latitudes, most species do well with 50–60% shade cloth in summer. The plants may need no shade at all in late autumn and winter because these are often the brightest seasons in the habitat and bright light may be critically important when growths are maturing. Because *Dendrobium* often require higher light than many other orchids, most species do poorly when grown under artificial lights. Many will grow very well under these conditions but will not bloom, and some will both grow and bloom well. Therefore, growers are cautioned to carefully check the light requirements of any species being considered for light culture. Growers have noted that when a plant has a white flowered variety and a purple flowered variety, the purple form seems to require higher light to bloom satisfactorily.

TEMPERATURES: See individual species listings.

Unfortunately, generalizations cannot be made for temperature requirements for *Dendrobium* species. The determining factor is habitat location and elevation for each species. Plants with a large area of distribution or a wide range in habitat elevation are more likely to be adaptable and relatively easy to cultivate.

Most Australian *Dendrobium* do well when summer days average about 80°F (27°C).

Many cool-growing species may adapt to or survive periods when the daily maximum temperatures exceed those shown in the climate table. This is especially true if night temperatures are cool, air circulation is excellent, and humidity is high.

Some warm-growing species survive winter conditions cooler than indicated, especially if they are kept somewhat dry and if light is low. However, plants may not be as quite as healthy or grow as fast as they would under warmer conditions.

HUMIDITY: See individual species listings. Summer values of 80% or more are common, but winter humidity in some regions may drop to near 40%. Species requiring high humidity should be misted as needed to maintain moisture levels. Air circulation over the leaves and around the roots should be excellent. Most skilled growers consider air circulation one of the most important cultural elements.

Seedlings out of flask require uniformly high humidity and constant air circulation.

WATER: Most species are healthiest if they are watered just as the medium begins to dry. Dull leaves or shriveled pseudobulbs are usually symptoms of inadequate moisture. However, species from regions with prolonged winter dry periods will often need to become shriveled to one extent or another before they will bloom. All *Dendrobium* species require more water when they are actively growing, but esentially none can tolerate a soggy medium. Successful growers report that correct watering may be the single most important element when growing *Dendrobium*.

Cold water may stress plants requiring uniformly warm temperatures.

Midlatitude growers should remember that when winter light is low, days are short, or temperatures are cool, water and humidity must be reduced regardless of the indications in the climate table. Plants simply cannot use as much water under these conditions, and disease results when moisture is excessive.

Evergreen species usually need to be kept moist while actively growing, but even they cannot tolerate soggy conditions and should be allowed to dry slightly before additional moisture is given. They are less likely to require a dry or cold rest period.

Deciduous and hard-cane species are more likely to need a dry or cool period during the winter.

High altitude species usually require year-round moisture. Schlechter (ref. 437) described the high elevation climate in New Guinea as follows: "I formed the opinion that more than double the quantity of rain falls (in the mountains) than on the coast. At an altitude of 3300 ft. (1000 m) it rained nearly every day and one felt this, particularly when it was followed by a few dry days. The clearer part of the day was usually the morning or forenoon with the temperature rising until 10 or 11 a.m. The mist then gathered and in the afternoon the rain set in with short heavy showers. Often it cleared up towards evening before sunset, but only to be followed by fresh mists. The trees and shrubs soon began to drip moisture, leading one to believe that the rain had only then ceased." He further stated, "The fall of dew in the mountains and hill country is very striking, since after a short distance on the march in the early morning, one is as wet as though just coming out of water." Although Schlechter's description applies specifically to New Guinea, the conditions are typical throughout tropical mistforests.

FERTILIZER: *Dendrobium* generally require moderate to heavy applications of fertilizer during periods of active growth. The exceptions to this general rule are the high altitude species from New Guinea which often need very little fertilizer.

Tropical evergreen species should receive nutrients throughout the year. However, fertilizer should be reduced along with water if days are short, light is low, or cultivation temperatures are cool. Their growths need not harden before winter.

Deciduous species require regular applications of nutrients during the growing season, which is sometimes quite short. These plants use relatively large amounts of nutrients to support their rapid growth to maturity. As a general rule, nutrient levels should be high enough so that the canes become as large and healthy as possible. This normally increases the number of blooms the following year. Growers commonly use a high nitrogen fertilizer, such as 30–10–10, during periods of active vegetative growth, changing to a high phosphate fertilizer, such as 10–20–10, near the middle of the growing season. This practice not only promotes blooming but also allows new growths to mature and harden before winter.

Many growers use 30–10–10 fertilizer with the belief that most of the nitrogen is used by the bark medium as it breaks down. A word of caution: recent research with food crops indicates that excess nitrogen may lead to mosaic viral diseases. In addition, excessive nitrogen is known to cause root and pseudobulb rot in *Cattleya*.

Growers have found that *Phalaenopsis* potted in bark do not show reduced growth and flowering when 10–10–10 fertilizer is used most of the time with only occasional applications of 30–10–10. The lower nitrogen levels reportedly slow the breakdown of the bark without retarding plant growth.

This suggests that while nutrient levels should be higher for *Dendrobium* than for many orchids, excessively high nitrogen levels should be avoided. We strongly encourage growers to use a more balanced fertilizer, or to at least alternate applications of the high nitrogen fertilizer with applications of one lower in nitrogen. Excess nitrogen causes soft, rapid vegetative growth that is much more susceptible to disease. Fertilizer applications should always be reduced or eliminated during a rest period, if days are short or light is low, if temperatures are cooler than normal, or if water is reduced.

The micronutrients available from an organic medium may help promote plant growth via the action of unidentified mycorrhizal fungi.

Seedlings should be fertilized with a balanced fertilizer mixed at ¼ recommended strengh.

REST PERIOD: Most *Dendrobium* are usually healthiest when they are given seasonal variations similar to those found in their natural habitats. However, growers report that some species adapt to warmer conditions than are found in their native habitat while others will continue to grow and bloom with conditions much colder than experienced in nature.

Growing conditions often need to be maintained year-round for *Dendrobium* with evergreen leaves. There are numerous exceptions to this general rule, however, and even those plants that require no rest are often healthiest if water and fertilizer are reduced in winter. This is particularly true when the plants are grown in temperate latitudes where winter days are short and light is low. These plants should never be allowed to dry out completely, however, and their leaves and pseudobulbs should not become desiccated or withered.

Winter temperatures in different habitats vary greatly. In cultivation, many species are healthy with winter temperatures of 45°F (7°C), but they may not require sustained periods of temperatures this low. Most subtropical species do well with a 53°F (12°C) winter minimum. In general, they resume growth when night temperatures average about 65°F (18°C). The warmest growing species are healthiest if winter temperatures are about 60°F (16°C), but some lowland equatorial species may prefer even warmer conditions.

Evergreen plants usually retain their leaves for several seasons. However, if temperatures drop below 50°F (10°C), for even a few hours, the leaves may drop.

Deciduous species are most likely to require a cool or dry rest period, although some species that are deciduous in their native habitat are also healthy when allowed to actively grow year-round. Plants tend to drop their leaves when conditions in the habitat are not conducive to growth. The adverse conditions are usually water or temperature related. Growing many *Dendrobium* species, especially the deciduous ones, in tropical areas is challenging and sometimes impossible. The lack of seasonal weather changes often results in new growths beginning before the older ones mature, making it extremely difficult to provide these *Dendrobium* with the needed rest period. Such plants may fail to bloom but often grow luxuriously until they die from exhaustion.

Water and fertilizer should always be reduced when plants are not actively growing, when temperatures are cool, or when light is low. Water temperature should be near the ambient growing temperature. Extremely cold water can cause bud blast and cell collapse.

GROWING MEDIA: The primary requirement for all *Dendrobium* is excellent drainage and constant air movement. Many *Dendrobium* are healthiest when mounted on a slab of cork, tree-fern, or rough-barked hardwood. If plants are potted, a container that is small relative to the plant size may be filled with any medium that provides good air circulation, rapid drainage, and moderate moisture retention. Many growers prefer clay pots for the stability that the additional weight provides and freqently recommend short pots over full height pots. Plants should never be placed in overly large containers. This practice does not increase the time between repottings, but it often results in rot so that the plant dies and never needs to be repotted again. Containers may be filled with fir bark or chopped tree-fern with charcoal added. The rainfall pattern and natural habitat information often provides a clue to the amount of moisture retention needed. When selecting a medium, a plant's requirement for moisture should be balanced with the prevailing conditions in the growing area or greenhouse.

As a general rule, plants with fine, wiry roots will do best in a smaller medium such as shredded tree-fern or small to medium bark, while those with large moisture-retaining roots often need to dry between waterings and a medium such as large cork nuggets or coarse fir bark reduces the risk of excessive moisture retention.

Growers in hard-water areas successfully grow *Dendrobium* in a mixture of charcoal and perlite with about 10% seedling fir bark and coarse sphagnum moss. The bark and moss eventually rot away after the plant is established, leaving just the charcoal and perlite. The charcoal neutralizes the damaging effects of hard water and salt accumulation while the perlite retains some moisture. With this inert mix, plants need not be repotted as often as plants potted in an organic mix.

Dendrobium cannot tolerate stale medium or poor air circulation around the roots, but they have a reputation for blooming best when they are somewhat crowded and root-bound. Plants should be potted in relatively small containers. Most *Dendrobium* prefer a pH of 5–6. Plants are generally healthiest if repotted at least once every 2 years. The medium should always be premoistened before the plants are potted.

Erect species are often top heavy, and growers find that clay or weighted pots help keep the plant from tipping over on the growing bench. These plants also grow well and are relatively easy to manage in hanging pots or baskets.

Tall species may be staked, but the bases of the pseudobulbs must never be buried in the medium.

Pendent species are best grown in hanging pots or baskets or mounted on a cork or tree-fern slab.

Creeping species and very small plants are best mounted on slabs of wood, tree-fern, or coconut husk. Mounts may be covered with sphagnum or birds-nest-fern root to increase moisture retention, but these materials should not be allowed to smother the roots. Live sphagnum moss can be very beneficial, but it sometimes grows taller than the smallest species. Some growers place live moss on the mount and allow it to become established before attaching the plant. This is particularly beneficial for mistzone or cloudforest species. If conditions are correct for the moss to become established, they are also correct for high-altitude orchids.

Lithophytic species are healthiest if slabbed on cork or tied to a rock or an inverted clay pot, providing adequate moisture levels can be maintained. They must be tied firmly for the roots to attach to the mount. Plants attach more readily if the old roots are removed so that the base of the pseudobulbs are close to the slab. When potting is advisable, wire baskets or clay pots with more than just a single drainage hole are preferable to plastic pots. Lithophytic *Dendrobium* generally need better air circulation than is available in plastic pots. Containers should be filled with a moderately large medium. Exact size depends on plant size and available moisture.

Many species do well grown outdoors when the local climate approximates the prevailing conditions in their natural habitat. Plants should be placed where they receive high light during the early part of the day. Full sun at midday should usually be avoided. They may be mounted on a tree with a pad of moss which helps maintain moisture until the plants become established. In appropriate climates, *Dendrobium* species reportedly grow well on Tamarind trees.

Some species do well planted in specially prepared raised beds. The beds should be filled with a rich, perfectly-drained compost, which may include a mix of any of the following ingredients: osmunda, tree fern, sphagnum moss, coarse sand, charcoal, and manure or other fertilizing materials. *Dendrobium* should be potted firmly, and since the plants are sometimes top heavy, they may require staking. The base of the pseudobulbs should never be buried in the compost. The crown of the plant must be above the medium or the pseudobulbs may develop rot. If this occurs, a new growing bud may emerge from the upper portion of the stem, which sometimes indicates a problem at the roots.

Dendrobium must be repotted when the medium begins to break down, which usually occurs after about 2 years. Repotting is normally done in the spring when new roots begin to grow. If any roots are not healthy looking, they should be removed, and the plants should be soaked in in systemic fungicide or one of the general disinfectants discussed in Appendix A.

Newly repotted plants should be shaded and given a short dry period to allow any damaged roots to heal. If new growth has not started, the plants should be kept slightly damp until new roots begin to grow. If the repotted plant has new vegetative growth, it must be given enough water to sustain that growth until the plant becomes established.

Seedlings require a medium that retains moisture, and growers often mix sphagnum moss, coconut fiber, or rockwool with fine fir bark or chopped tree-fern fiber. They indicate that rockwool alone is unsatisfactory. We have successfully used live sphagnum moss over chopped tree-fern or small bark for the first compotting out of flask. Live sphagnum has nearly eliminated the problem of young plants damping off due to infection. Growers indicate that live sphagnum should not be used in pots larger than 4 in. (10 cm), and we prefer to use live moss only in very small pots. Growers recommend potting plants in spring when the transition from flask to the outside world may be less traumatic.

MISCELLANEOUS NOTES: Air circulation is critically important in *Dendrobium* cultivation. Fans should keep the air moving throughout the year.

The bloom season shown in the climate table may be based on cultivation records, plant collection times, or reports from the habitat.

Blooming is initiated by a variety of environmental and physiological factors, but flowering is frequently triggered by changes in light, day length, heat, or moisture. Little specific information is available on a species by species basis. Most research into blooming is oriented toward producing hybrid flowers for the cut flower market, but bloom triggers are included for each species when available. If plants fail to bloom, growers may find the following discussion of known flower inducers helpful when specific information is unavailable.

Growers in areas with a high incidence of cloud cover and consequently low natural light have noticed that white flowered hybrids bloom more dependably than red or purple hybrids. It is thought that this occurs because the red flowered plants require more light, but no studies have been conducted to confirm this observation.

Many *Dendrobium* do not produce flowers until they are exposed to the necessary change in their environment. A byproduct of this characteristic is that flowering may be hurried or delayed by the grower. This is particularly true for many spring flowering species. Depending on what initiates flowering, which is specific to each species, it is often possible to delay blooming by altering the temperature, moisture, or the timing of increased light. Plants rested in cool temperatures frequently bloom about 60 days after being moved to a warm environment. Growers wishing a maximum floral display can try eliminating the rest period for one or more seasons. Many *Dendrobium* whose flowers are triggered by the rest period conditions will treat this as an exceptionally long growing season and produce multitudes of blossoms after the rest period is finally provided.

Inadequate or excessive light during the growing season may prevent the differentiation of cells necessary to produce flower buds.

Photoperiodism is critical for some Dendrobiums, which bloomed as much as 60 days earlier when given 16 hours of dark each day.

Orchids which are forced to bloom by manipulation of light or low temperatures often produce fewer flowers than plants allowed to bloom naturally. Experimental work done with the growth regulator BAP, applied at the rate of 4000 ppm, counteracted this tendency for fewer flowers on forced plants and increased the number of blossoms on unforced plants when the compound was sprayed on mature pseudobulbs.

A number of species with short-lived flowers produce buds which form to a certain stage and then hold on the plant without developing further. The buds usually open 8–12 days after a sudden 10°F (5°C) drop in daytime temperatures. Having all blossoms open simultaneously results in all plants being pollinated on the same day. Plants which are out of step and fail to bloom on that day are ignored by pollinators when their buds do open.

Some *Dendrobium* species will not produce flowers until the newest pseudobulb has fully matured. If plants are kept too warm or too moist, new growths may not be able to harden. Although we know of no specific research, it is possible that a growth hormone produced in the growing tip suppresses the production of the hormones needed for flowering. This phenomenon is better understood in crop plants.

As with other plants, orchid flowers can sometimes be induced by interupting the flow of hormones from the growing tip either by removing it or by cutting the outer layer of the pseudobulb.

Propagating *Dendrobium* may be done by seed, division, and keikis (aerial growths that emerge from nodes on mature pseudobulbs).

When dividing plants, 3–4 mature growths in each division are adequate to continue blooming. When dividing evergreen types, several older growths should be included with the new growths, since blooming often occurs on prior year's growths.

If suitably treated, many species may be propagated from old, leafless canes. The old canes should be wedged upright in a pot and kept barely moist until new buds break from the lateral nodes.

Plants can often be forced to produce Keikis along the stem by removing the upper part of a stem or inflorescence.

New plants may also be started from old inflorescences. After the flowers fade, the spike should be removed and laid in a tray which has been lined with a layer of live sphagnum moss. The propagating tray should then be kept at moderately warm temperatures. If humidity is low, the trays should be covered with clear plastic to maintain moisture levels, as the stems must be kept moist until new plants develop at the nodes. Growers suggest that the old flower spikes be sprayed with Di-hydrogen Orthophosphate 2–3 times at 2-week intervals.

Plantlets propogated from old canes or inflorescences may be removed when their roots are 1 in. (2.5 cm) long. They should then be potted or mounted and treated like a seedling until well established.

Hybrids frequently need a winter rest intermediate between the conditions required by each of the parents. However, hybrids which are difficult to bloom in cultivation may require a rest period corresponding to the one needed by 1 of the parents.

Plant and Flower Information

PLANT SIZE AND TYPE: *Dendrobium* vary in size from very tiny to the largest pseudobulbous plant known. Usually epiphytic or lithophytic, they are always sympodial but have such diverse growth habits that it is sometimes difficult to quickly recognize them as related members of the same genus.

Plant and Flower Information is not always complete because often the only information available is a brief original Latin description which may not have included all the elements desired by growers. The material available to the describing taxonomist was often limited or incomplete.

Plant measurements given here are usually a general description of the range of plant and flower sizes, but they may be based on a single specimen when the original plant description is the only information available. Although the plant and flower information may assist growers in confirming that the plant they have is as labelled, the descriptions are not intended for plant identification.

Growth habit usually conforms to one of the following categories:

Growths may be rhizomelike without pseudobulbs.

Growths may develop regular stems or pseudobulbs that may be clustered or widely spaced.

Growths may have canelike stems with one or many nodes, all or some of which may be swollen. They may be erect or pendent and sometimes arise from a many-noded rhizome.

New growths may arise directly from a node on the old pseudobulb without an interconnecting rhizome.

PSEUDOBULBS: Also called stems or canes, pseudobulbs vary in size from 0.3–192 in (1–488 cm). They are usually jointed, may be woody or fleshy, and often appear knobby. This is caused by nodal or internodal swelling rather than an abnormality. The slowly creeping rhizomes are usually woody and produce numerous hairlike roots which attach tenaciously to the substrata.

The following terms are frequently used to describe the shape of the pseudobulb:

Club-shaped. The pseudobulbs are swollen near the apex and taper toward the base.

Cylindrical. The pseudobulb is stemlike without any prominent swelling, except possibly at the nodes.

Pseudobulbous. The storage organs are swollen at the base.

Spindle-shaped. The pseudobulb is enlarged in the middle and tapers at each end.

LEAVES: One to many. The leaves are usually ovate to oblong or variations of those shapes. They may be flat or terete, grooved, or folded, and appear triangular. The leaves may be deciduous and last a single season or be evergreen and last for several years. When they arise at the apex of the pseudobulb, they usually last for several years. Some species have distichous leaves which grow along the entire length of the stem.

INFLORESCENCE: Flower spikes may be long or short, and some are erect while others are horizontal or pendent. The inflorescences usually emerge from the side of the pseudobulb but some species produce flowers on a leafless independent growth. They often break through the sheath opposite the leaves, but in some instances they appear to emerge from the apex of the pseudobulb. However, these are usually pseudoterminal and actually arise from nodes very near the apex.

Deciduous species tend to produce flower spikes from numerous nodes along the stem, usually opposite the leaf or where the leaf had been. These may be produced singly or in small clusters of 2–4.

Evergreen species tend to produce racemes which emerge from below the leaves. Each stem may produce blossoms from different nodes for several years.

FLOWERS: One to many. The blossoms vary from large to small, but even small flowers may be showy. Some species, many of which are now called *Flickingeria,* have flowers which last a few hours or a single day. Other species produce blossoms which last for months. Most *Dendrobium* species have flowers which last at least 2–3 weeks.

The lip, which often forms a closed spur with the lateral sepals, may be 3-lobed or it may be entire (not divided into lobes). The shape of the lip is highly variable.

Flower color and size are also highly variable and may be influenced by environmental conditions such as light, temperature, and nutrients.

HYBRIDIZING NOTES: Chromosome counts and primary hybridizing characteristics are included for each species when they are available. Most listings of chromosome counts do not include describers' names after the species name. References are included for each count, but multiple references may only indicate that the number was included in a number of compilations of chromosome counts, not that that many researchers actually performed chromosome counts on different plants. When the chromosome count is shown as n = or s =, it indicates that the count is one half the chromosomes needed for a complete plant; while 2n = or g = indicates that the count was made after the male sperm and female ova united and is the number needed for a complete plant.

The most common chromosome counts for *Dendrobium* is $2n = 38$ or $2n = 40$. Hashimoto (ref. 187) indicates that some are both $2n = 38$ and $2n = 40$, while others may vary from $2n = 30$ to $2n = 114$. Polyploidy is indicated when the 2n count is a multiple of the normal n count.

Preliminary studies indicate that species with chromosome counts of $2n = 36$ and $2n = 38$ will hybridize, while species with counts of $2n = 36$ and $2n = 40$ cannot be cross-pollinated. However, since chromosome counts are often variable, a particular plant may pollinate while another may not.

When chromosome counts differ, the disparity may result from various causes. The foremost reason for different counts is that a species may have an unstable genetic makeup resulting in individual plants with different chromosome counts. Other possibilities include misidentification of one of the samples or grouping separate species under a single name.

Johansen (ref. 239) conducted a study of self-compatability in *Dendrobium.* The data collected and the implications of his findings are extremely important for hybridizers. The plants studied were primarily those collected by Seidenfaden in Thailand. In the study, plants were considered self-sterile if the blossom dropped prematurely. Johansen found that 72% of the self-pollinated species were self-sterile. When cross-pollinated, 78% of the attempts produced capsules. Johansen found that compatibility between species was uncommon and only 46 of 254 attempts produced fruit, and these often produced seed in only one direction. Of his crosses, only 6 produced seed in both directions and these were always members of the same section. Although some information from his study has been included, it contains too much to include it all. A careful examination of his work should be considered essential for anyone interested in *Dendrobium* seed propogation.

Despite the findings regarding compatibility, we encourage growers to try it anyway. Growing conditions often make a tremendous difference, even for clones that do not normally produce seed. Regardless of whether the critical factor is temperature, humidity, the age of the flowers, the phase of the moon, or the serenity of the pollinator, just keep trying! Johansen indicates that some clones of *D. crystallinum* were self-compatabile while others were self-sterile and that individual plants may be self-sterile sometimes and self-fertile at other times. Species may have some clones that are self-sterile and others that are self-fertile. Adams (ref. 4) found that self-pollinations of *D. speciosum* were possible if post-pollination conditions are warm, so environmental conditions are sometimes critically important.

From a hybridizer's view point, the most significant conclusion Johansen reached was proof that the simultaneous application of both compatible and incompatible pollen leads to capsule formation providing more compatible pollen is used than incompatible pollen. Growers have often tried this technique. The disadvantage of course is that unless growth patterns are very different when plants are very young it takes a long time to know which pollen resulted in germination.

We have found that plants which normally do not produce seed when self-pollinated are sometimes tricked into producing seed with their own pollen if stigmatic fluid from a compatible plant is placed on the stigmatic surface along with the pollinia. As with most things in nature, the technique does not always work, but by using it, we have obtained capsules on numerous plants that are supposedly self-sterile. The advantage of trying this technique, as opposed to mixing compatible and incompatible pollen, is that the resulting seed produces only the plants desired.

Wilfret and Kamemoto (ref. 568) did extensive studies regarding the crossability of plants belonging to different sections of the genus *Dendrobium*. In their study, pollen that had been stored for up to 6 months at 45°F (7°C) produced viable seed. Pollen was stored in gelatin capsules in an airtight plastic container with packets of calcium chloride (commonly called silica gel) to reduce humidity.

The greatest potential source of new plants is ourselves, the hobby and small commercial growers. We strongly encourage all growers to pollinate their orchid species. One of the difficulties is knowing how long it takes for seed to ripen and when it is viable for use in green-pod culture. The general rule of 2–7 months for green pod is less specific that most growers would like. Johansen (ref. 239) found that the time needed for dry seed to develop varied from 43 days for *D. salaccense (D. philippinense)* to 441 days for *D. heterocarpum*. When known, we have included in Hybridizing Notes for each species the time needed for seed capsules to open. Seeds are usually viable for green pod culture in about 60–80% of the time needed for dry seed. The longer the seeds hold on the mother plant the greater the number of viable seeds and the higher the germination rate.

Growers are encouraged to copy the following form to record pollination information for species in their collection. Anyone willing to share this information is urged to send a us copy so that it can be included in future publications.

The Bakers
3526 S. E. Johnson Creek Boulevard
Portland, Oregon 97222
U. S. A

REFERENCES: 239, 273, 352, 533, 541, 568.

PHOTOS/DRAWINGS: See species listings.

Dendrobium General Information

Pollination Record

Date Pollinated	Pollen Used			Species Name	Pod Development			Days to Viable Seed			Seed Produced?		Notes and Comments
	Self	Sib.	Other		None	Aborted	Matured	Green Pod	Dry Seed		Poor	Good	

The Notes and Comments section may be helpful in recording the type of germinating media and other conditions used for seed germination.

Dendrobium abbreviatum Schlechter. Now considered a synonym of *Diplocaulobium abbreviatum* (Schlechter) A. Hawkes. REFERENCES: 24, 92, 221, 229, 437, 445.

Dendrobium aberrans Schlechter

ORIGIN/HABITAT: Papua New Guinea. Plants grow on tree fern and shady tree trunks in the mossy forests of the Bowutu (Maboro) Mountains south of Lae at 1000–6250 ft. (300–1900 m).

CLIMATE: Station #200192, Garaina, Papua New Guinea, Lat. 7.9°S, Long. 147.1°E, at 2350 ft. (716 m). Temperatures are calculated for an elevation of 3300 ft. (1000 m), resulting in probable extremes of 91°F (33°C) and 43°F (6°C).

N/HEMISPHERE	JAN	FEB	MAR	APR	MAY	JUN	JUL	AUG	SEP	OCT	NOV	DEC
°F AVG MAX	77	79	80	81	82	82	82	82	81	81	80	78
°F AVG MIN	60	60	60	61	60	61	62	62	62	61	61	60
DIURNAL RANGE	17	19	20	20	22	21	20	20	19	20	19	18
RAIN/INCHES	5.8	6.5	8.7	11.1	11.8	11.9	8.9	11.7	11.5	9.9	7.7	5.2
HUMIDITY/%	84	82	82	81	80	80	81	81	82	83	84	84
BLOOM SEASON	*	**		*		*						*
DAYS CLR	N/A											
RAIN/MM	147	165	221	282	300	302	226	297	292	251	196	132
°C AVG MAX	25.0	26.1	26.6	27.2	27.7	27.7	27.7	27.7	27.2	27.2	26.6	25.5
°C AVG MIN	15.5	15.5	15.5	16.1	15.5	16.1	16.6	16.6	16.6	16.1	16.1	15.5
DIURNAL RANGE	9.5	10.6	11.1	11.1	12.2	11.6	11.1	11.1	10.6	11.1	10.5	10.0
S/HEMISPHERE	JUL	AUG	SEP	OCT	NOV	DEC	JAN	FEB	MAR	APR	MAY	JUN

Cultural Recommendations

LIGHT: 2000–3000 fc.

TEMPERATURES: Throughout the year, days average 77–82°F (25–28°C), and nights average 60–62°F (16–17°C), with a diurnal range of 17–22°F (10–12°C).

HUMIDITY: 80–85% year-round.

WATER: Rainfall is heavy year-round with slightly drier conditions in winter. Cultivated plants should never be allowed to dry out completely.

FERTILIZER: ½ recommended strength. A balanced fertilizer should be applied weekly to biweekly throughout the year.

REST PERIOD: Growing conditions vary only slightly during the year. In the habitat, rainfall is slightly lower in winter. Water should be reduced for cultivated plants, especially those grown in the dark, short-day conditions common in temperate latitudes. Fertilizer should be reduced or eliminated anytime water is reduced.

GROWING MEDIA: Plants may be mounted on a tree-fern slab if humidity is high and plants are watered at least once daily in summer. When plants are potted, any open, fast-draining medium may be used. Repotting may be done anytime new roots are growing.

MISCELLANEOUS NOTES: The bloom season shown in the climate table is based on cultivation records. Growers indicate that plants grow easily and rapidly and often produce flowers only 2 years out of flask

Plant and Flower Information

PLANT SIZE AND TYPE: A 2–8 in. (5–20 cm) sympodial epiphyte. Plants always grow in colonies.

PSEUDOBULB: 0.8–1.2 in. (2–3 cm) long. The clustered pseudobulbs are spherical to spindle shaped with 3–4 nodes below the leaves. The stems may be purple, olive-yellow, or glossy green.

LEAVES: 2, rarely 3, at the apex of each growth. The leaves are commonly 2–4 in. (5–10 cm) long, but may reach a length of 7 in. (18 cm). They are oval, leathery, and spreading.

INFLORESCENCE: 2–3 in. (5–8 cm) long. The short inflorescences, which may appear twice each year, are wiry, erect or pendent, and arise near the apex of both old and new growths. The old pseudobulbs produce inflorescences for many years. Flowers are arranged in dense sprays.

FLOWERS: 2–6 per inflorescence. The blossoms are 0.4–0.6 in. (1.0–1.5 cm) across. They are creamy white with pink to purple markings on the outside of the sepals and petals. The deeply incised lip is pure white. The flowers appear round and open fully. The column is often marked with pink.

REFERENCES: 83, 92, 95, 179, 221, 330, 437, 445, 526, 550, 554.

PHOTOS/DRAWINGS: *83*, 437.

Dendrobium abietinum Ridley. See *D. pachyglossum* Parish and Rchb. f. REFERENCES: 254, 395, 454.

Dendrobium acaciifolium J. J. Smith

ORIGIN/HABITAT: The Sula (Soela) Islands on Pulau Seho. Habitat elevation was not included with the original plant description, but the highest elevation on the island is 1500 ft. (460 m). The following climate table should be used with caution as temperatures in the habitat may be a few degrees cooler than indicated. Plants were cultivated in the botanical garden in Bogor, Java.

CLIMATE: Station #97600, Sanana, Pulau Sulawesi, Indonesia, Lat. 2.1°S, Long. 126.0°E, at 7 ft. (2 m). Record extreme temperatures are not available for this location.

N/HEMISPHERE	JAN	FEB	MAR	APR	MAY	JUN	JUL	AUG	SEP	OCT	NOV	DEC
°F AVG MAX	86	85	87	88	88	88	88	87	88	87	87	86
°F AVG MIN	76	76	75	77	77	78	78	76	76	76	78	76
DIURNAL RANGE	10	9	12	11	11	10	10	11	12	11	9	10
RAIN/INCHES	2.8	2.7	1.2	1.8	4.8	5.4	4.1	4.1	5.7	6.6	6.5	7.3
HUMIDITY/%	N/A											
BLOOM SEASON	N/A											
DAYS CLR	N/A											
RAIN/MM	72	69	31	47	122	137	105	104	146	168	165	185
°C AVG MAX	29.9	29.6	30.3	31.0	31.3	31.0	31.0	30.8	30.9	30.3	30.4	29.8
°C AVG MIN	24.4	24.3	24.0	25.2	25.1	25.4	25.3	24.5	24.4	24.6	25.3	24.2
DIURNAL RANGE	5.5	5.3	6.3	5.8	6.2	5.6	5.7	6.3	6.5	5.7	5.1	5.6
S/HEMISPHERE	JUL	AUG	SEP	OCT	NOV	DEC	JAN	FEB	MAR	APR	MAY	JUN

Cultural Recommendations

LIGHT: 2000–3000 fc.

TEMPERATURES: Throughout the year, days average 85–88°F (30–31°C), and nights average 75–78°F (24–25°C), with a diurnal range of 9–12°F (5–6°C).

HUMIDITY: Averages are not available for this location. However, records from other stations in the region indicate that humidity probably exceeds 80% year-round.

WATER: Rainfall is moderate most of the year with a semidry period in winter and early spring. Cultivated plants should be kept moist while actively growing.

FERTILIZER: ¼–½ recommended strength. A balanced fertilizer should be applied weekly to biweekly throughout the year.

REST PERIOD: Growing conditions should be maintained year-round. In cultivation, water should be reduced in winter and plants allowed to dry slightly between waterings. They should not remain dry for long periods, however. Fertilizer should be reduced anytime water is reduced.

GROWING MEDIA: Plants may be mounted on tree-fern or cork slabs or potted in small pots filled with any open, fast-draining medium. Repotting may be done anytime new roots are actively growing.

MISCELLANEOUS NOTES: The plant was described in 1917 in *Bull. Jard. Bot. Buit.* 2nd sér. 25:34.

Dendrobium acanthophippiiflorum

Plant and Flower Information

PLANT SIZE AND TYPE: A 36 in. (91 cm) sympodial epiphyte.

PSEUDOBULB: 36 in. (91 cm) long. The stems, which do not branch, are close together, constricted between nodes, and somewhat flattened. They may be blackish or dirty green.

LEAVES: 6–7 per growth. The leaves, which are 2.4–5.0 in. (6–13 cm) long, are rigid, dirty violet, and laterally flattened.

INFLORESCENCE: Length unavailable. Blossoms are carried on the upper part of the stem.

FLOWERS: 1 per inflorescence. The small flowers are 0.6 in. (1.5 cm) long. Sepals are pale yellow with faint purple stripes. The somewhat lanceolate petals are erect and slightly twisted. The pale yellow lip, which is marked with dark purple veins, is recurved.

REFERENCES: 222.

Dendrobium acanthophippiiflorum J. J. Smith

ORIGIN/HABITAT: Irian Jaya (western New Guinea). Plants grow epiphytically in forests of the Jabi Range near Kwatisore (Wape) on the southwest coast of Teluk Cenderawasih (Geelvink Bay).

CLIMATE: Station #97682, Nabire, Irian Jaya, Lat. 3.3°S, Long. 135.5°E, at 10 ft. (3 m). Record extreme temperatures are not available for this location.

N/HEMISPHERE	JAN	FEB	MAR	APR	MAY	JUN	JUL	AUG	SEP	OCT	NOV	DEC
°F AVG MAX	86	86	86	86	87	87	86	86	87	87	87	87
°F AVG MIN	75	75	76	77	77	76	77	75	75	76	76	76
DIURNAL RANGE	11	11	10	9	10	11	9	11	12	11	11	11
RAIN/INCHES	7.4	11.1	8.5	8.5	7.5	9.0	9.2	10.6	12.1	11.3	10.2	9.8
HUMIDITY/%	N/A											
BLOOM SEASON												*
DAYS CLR	N/A											
RAIN/MM	190	283	217	217	192	228	233	270	308	286	259	248
°C AVG MAX	30.1	29.9	30.1	30.3	30.5	30.6	30.0	30.0	30.5	30.5	30.3	30.3
°C AVG MIN	24.0	24.0	24.3	24.7	24.9	24.5	24.8	24.0	23.8	24.6	24.3	24.2
DIURNAL RANGE	6.1	5.9	5.8	5.6	5.6	6.1	5.2	6.0	6.7	5.9	6.0	6.1
S/HEMISPHERE	JUL	AUG	SEP	OCT	NOV	DEC	JAN	FEB	MAR	APR	MAY	JUN

Cultural Recommendations

LIGHT: 2000–3000 fc.

TEMPERATURES: Throughout the year, days average 86–87°F (30–31°C), and nights average 75–77°F (24–25°C), with a diurnal range of 9–12°F (6–7°C).

HUMIDITY: Averages are not available for this location. However, records from other stations in the region indicate that values are probably 80–85% year-round.

WATER: Rainfall is heavy all year. Cultivated plants should be kept evenly moist. They should never be allowed to dry out completely.

FERTILIZER: ¼–½ recommended strength. A balanced fertilizer should be applied weekly to biweekly throughout the year.

REST PERIOD: Growing conditions should be maintained year-round. Water and fertilizer may be reduced slightly in winter, especially for plants grown in the dark, short-day conditions common in temperate latitudes, but plants should never be allowed to dry out completely.

GROWING MEDIA: Plants may be mounted on tree-fern or cork slabs or potted in any open, fast-draining medium. Repotting may be done anytime new roots are actively growing.

Plant and Flower Information

PLANT SIZE AND TYPE: A 16 in. (40 cm) sympodial epiphyte.

PSEUDOBULB: 16 in. (40 cm) long. The elongated stems are unbranched. The upper part is dilated and flattened.

LEAVES: Many. The lanceolate leaves are 3–5 in. (8–13 cm) long. They are 2-toothed at the apex and irregularly toothed along the recurved margin.

INFLORESCENCE: Short. Inflorescences emerge through the leaf bases.

FLOWERS: 2 per inflorescence. The flowers are 1.2 in. (3 cm) long. Floral segments are white with a red picoteed margin on the lip. The dorsal sepal is oblong-triangular. Lateral sepals are obliquely triangular, sickle-shaped, and recurved. The petals are elliptic- to tongue-shaped. The 3-lobed lip is erect and recurved and decorated with irregular protrusions. The margins of short sidelobes are uneven.

REFERENCES: 220, 470, 478.

Dendrobium acerosum Lindley

AKA: *D. subteres* (Griffith) Lindley.

ORIGIN/HABITAT: Borneo, Indonesia, Malaya, Thailand, and Burma. *D. acerosum* is a very common lowland species in Southeast Asia. It grows on trees and rock faces, always in moderately open places, and frequently in full sun. Millar (ref. 302) reports that *D. acerosum* is also found in the Western District of Papua New Guinea.

CLIMATE: Station #48551, Surat (Ban Don), Thailand, Lat. 9.1°N, Long. 99.3°E, at 10 ft. (3 m). Record extreme temperatures are 105°F (41°C) and 47°F (8°C).

N/HEMISPHERE	JAN	FEB	MAR	APR	MAY	JUN	JUL	AUG	SEP	OCT	NOV	DEC
°F AVG MAX	88	92	95	95	93	91	90	91	90	89	87	86
°F AVG MIN	69	69	70	73	74	74	74	74	73	73	72	71
DIURNAL RANGE	19	23	25	22	19	17	16	17	17	16	15	15
RAIN/INCHES	1.0	0.3	0.4	2.5	6.6	4.5	6.9	5.8	7.1	8.1	12.1	4.0
HUMIDITY/%	82	78	75	79	83	82	82	82	84	87	87	86
BLOOM SEASON			*		*		*				*	*
DAYS CLR @ 7AM	4	3	2	2	1	1	1	1	1	1	1	2
DAYS CLR @ 1PM	2	2	2	1	1	0	0	0	0	0	1	1
RAIN/MM	25	8	10	64	168	114	175	147	180	206	307	102
°C AVG MAX	31.1	33.3	35.0	35.0	33.9	32.8	32.2	32.8	32.2	31.7	30.6	30.0
°C AVG MIN	20.6	20.6	21.1	22.8	23.3	23.3	23.3	23.3	22.8	22.8	22.2	21.7
DIURNAL RANGE	10.5	12.7	13.9	12.2	10.6	9.5	8.9	9.5	9.4	8.9	8.4	8.3
S/HEMISPHERE	JUL	AUG	SEP	OCT	NOV	DEC	JAN	FEB	MAR	APR	MAY	JUN

Cultural Recommendations

LIGHT: 3500–4500 fc.

TEMPERATURES: Summer days average 90–91°F (32–33°C), and nights average 74°F (23°C), with a diurnal range of 16–17°F (9–10°C). Early spring is the warmest season. Highs average 93–95°F (34–35°C), and lows average 70–74°F (21–23°C), with a diurnal range of 19–25°F (11–14°C).

HUMIDITY: 80–85% year-round.

WATER: Rainfall is moderate to heavy from late spring through autumn with a wet/dry seasonal pattern. Cultivated plants should be kept evenly moist while actively growing.

FERTILIZER: ¼–½ recommended strength, applied weekly. A high-nitrogen fertilizer is beneficial from spring to midsummer, but a fertilizer high in phosphates should be used in late summer and autumn.

REST PERIOD: Winter days average 86–92°F (30–33°C), and nights average 69–71°F (21–22°C), with a diurnal range of 15–23°F (8–13°C). In the habitat, winter rainfall is low, but the high average humidity indicates that some moisture is available in the form of dew or morning mist. Cultivated plants should be allowed to dry out between waterings but should not remain dry for extended periods. Occasional early morning mistings between waterings may help prevent plants from becoming too dry.

GROWING MEDIA: Mounting plants on tree-fern or cork slabs accommodates their pendulous growth habit. If plants cannot be mounted because humidity is low or they cannot be watered daily, they may be placed in small pots or hanging baskets filled with any open, fast-draining medium. Repotting is best done in early spring when new roots begin to grow.

MISCELLANEOUS NOTES: The bloom season shown in the climate table is based on cultivation records.

Plant and Flower Information

PLANT SIZE AND TYPE: A 6–10 in. (15–25 cm) sympodial epiphyte or lithophyte.

PSEUDOBULB: 6–10 in. (15–25 cm) long. The stemlike pseudobulbs are slender, flexuous, branching, and usually pendulous.

LEAVES: 7–10 per growth. The persistent leaves, which occur on the basal 60% of the stem, are 1–2 in. (2.5–5.0 cm) long. They are flat, spreading, recurved, sharply pointed, and loosely distichous. Leaves are fleshy and unusually grooved on each side.

INFLORESCENCE: 2–6 in. (5–15 cm) long. Flowers are produced on the apical, leafless portion of the stem.

FLOWERS: 1–3, rarely more, per inflorescence. The small flowers are normally 0.2–0.6 in. (0.5–1.5 cm) long, but plants from Borneo may produce somewhat larger blossoms. Sepals and petals may be white, cream, pale greenish yellow, or pale rose. The sepals, petals, and column foot are usually marked with strong red-purple veins, although some specimens have pale veins. The white lip is narrow, ruffled along the margin, notched at the apex, and curved forward at the tip. It has no sidelobes. It is accented with a yellow or orange spot along the thickened centerline.

HYBRIDIZING NOTES: Chromosome count is 2n = 38 (ref. 151, 153, 187, 273).

REFERENCES: 151, 153, 157, 179, 187, 200, 202, 216, 254, 273, 278, 286, 295, 297, 302, 304, 310, 317, 394, 395, 402, 454, 455.

PHOTOS/DRAWINGS: 200, *304*, *454*, 455.

Dendrobium achillis Rchb. f. See *D. calcaratum* A. Richard.

This synonymy is used in *Index Kewensis* (ref. 216) and Kränzlin (ref. 254), but Lewis and Cribb (ref. 270, 271) do not include *D. achillis* as a synonym of *D. calcaratum*. We did not find any origin and habitat information or any other reference to *D. achillis* as a valid species; the cross reference to *D. calcaratum* is listed as the best information available.

REFERENCES: 216, 254, 270, 271.

Dendrobium acianthum Schlechter

ORIGIN/HABITAT: Northern Papua New Guinea. Plants grow epiphytically in primary forests of the Minjem Valley below 1650 ft. (500 m) and along the Waria River near Jaduna at about 650 ft. (200 m).

CLIMATE: Station #94014, Madang, Papua New Guinea, Lat. 5.2°S, Long. 145.8°E, at 13 ft. (4 m). Temperatures are calculated for a habitat elevation of 1150 ft. (350 m), resulting in probable extremes of 94°F (35°C) and 58°F (15°C).

N/HEMISPHERE	JAN	FEB	MAR	APR	MAY	JUN	JUL	AUG	SEP	OCT	NOV	DEC
°F AVG MAX	79	79	81	81	81	81	81	81	81	83	83	80
°F AVG MIN	73	74	74	74	73	73	73	73	73	72	73	74
DIURNAL RANGE	6	5	7	7	8	8	8	8	8	11	10	6
RAIN/INCHES	4.0	3.4	3.2	8.5	11.2	11.1	10.1	11.3	9.4	11.3	10.5	6.7
HUMIDITY/%	88	87	86	86	86	86	86	85	85	87	88	89
BLOOM SEASON	*								*			
DAYS CLR	N/A											
RAIN/MM	102	86	81	216	284	282	257	287	239	287	267	170
°C AVG MAX	26.2	26.2	27.4	27.4	27.4	27.4	27.4	27.4	27.4	28.5	28.5	26.8
°C AVG MIN	22.9	23.5	23.5	23.5	22.9	22.9	22.9	22.9	22.9	22.4	22.9	23.5
DIURNAL RANGE	3.3	2.7	3.9	3.9	4.5	4.5	4.5	4.5	4.5	6.1	5.6	3.3
S/HEMISPHERE	JUL	AUG	SEP	OCT	NOV	DEC	JAN	FEB	MAR	APR	MAY	JUN

Cultural Recommendations

LIGHT: 2000–3000 fc.

TEMPERATURES: Throughout the year, days average 79–83°F (26–29°C), and nights average 72–74°F (22–24°C), with a diurnal range of 5–11°F (3–6°C). The warmest highs, the coolest lows, and the greatest diurnal range occur in autumn.

HUMIDITY: 85–90% year-round.

WATER: Rainfall is moderate to heavy all year. Cultivated plants should be kept moist but not soggy.

FERTILIZER: ¼–½ recommended strength. A balanced fertilizer should be applied weekly to biweekly throughout the year.

REST PERIOD: Growing conditions should be maintained all year. In the habitat, rainfall decreases somewhat for 3–4 months in winter. Cultivated plants should be allowed to dry slightly between waterings, but they should never dry out completely. In the habitat, light is slightly higher in winter.

GROWING MEDIA: Mounting plants on tree-fern or cork slabs accommodates their pendulous growth habit, but mounted plants must be watered at least once a day in summer. If plants must be potted, an undersized pot may be filled with any open, fast-draining medium. Repotting may be done anytime new roots are actively growing.

MISCELLANEOUS NOTES: The bloom season shown in the climate table is based on collection records.

Plant and Flower Information

PLANT SIZE AND TYPE: An 18–20 in. (45–50 cm) sympodial epiphyte. Plants form clumps which may reach a diameter of 79 in. (200 cm).

PSEUDOBULB: 18–20 in. (45–50 cm) long. The branching stems are reclining or pendent.

LEAVES: Many. Growths are densely covered with leaves that overlap at their bases. The obliquely lanceolate leaves are 0.4–0.8 in. (1–2 cm) long.

INFLORESCENCE: Short. Each growth produces many one-flowered inflorescences from the leaf axils.

FLOWERS: 1 per inflorescence. The small, tulip-shaped flowers are 0.3 in. (0.8 cm) long. Sepals and petals are thick, fleshy, and yellow-green. The lip and anther are dark red-brown.

REFERENCES: 221, 437, 445.

PHOTOS/DRAWINGS: 437.

Dendrobium aciculare Lindley

AKA: *D. setifolium* Ridley and *D. philippinense* Ames are sometimes listed as synonyms, but Seidenfaden (ref. 454) specifically excludes this synonymy. *D. koeteianum* Schlechter is sometimes listed as a synonym, but Seidenfaden (ref. 450) expressed strong reservations regarding this synonymy.

ORIGIN/HABITAT: Southeastern and peninsular Thailand and Borneo. Habitat elevation is unreported, so the following temperatures should be used with caution. Regardless of elevation, seasonal patterns are similar.

CLIMATE: Station #48551, Surat (Ban Don), Thailand, Lat. 9.1°N, Long. 99.3°E, at 10 ft. (3 m). Record extreme temperatures are 105°F (41°C) and 47°F (8°C).

N/HEMISPHERE	JAN	FEB	MAR	APR	MAY	JUN	JUL	AUG	SEP	OCT	NOV	DEC
°F AVG MAX	88	92	95	95	93	91	90	91	90	89	87	86
°F AVG MIN	69	69	70	73	74	74	74	74	73	73	72	71
DIURNAL RANGE	19	23	25	22	19	17	16	17	17	16	15	15
RAIN/INCHES	1.0	0.3	0.4	2.5	6.6	4.5	6.9	5.8	7.1	8.1	12.1	4.0
HUMIDITY/%	82	78	75	79	83	82	82	82	84	87	87	86
BLOOM SEASON	N/A											
DAYS CLR @ 7AM	4	3	3	1	1	1	1	1	1	1	1	2
DAYS CLR @ 1PM	2	2	2	1	1	0	0	0	0	0	1	1
RAIN/MM	25	8	10	64	168	114	175	147	180	206	307	102
°C AVG MAX	31.1	33.3	35.0	35.0	33.9	32.8	32.2	32.8	32.2	31.7	30.6	30.0
°C AVG MIN	20.6	20.6	21.1	22.8	23.3	23.3	23.3	23.3	22.8	22.8	22.2	21.7
DIURNAL RANGE	10.5	12.7	13.9	12.2	10.6	9.5	8.9	9.5	9.4	8.9	8.4	8.3
S/HEMISPHERE	JUL	AUG	SEP	OCT	NOV	DEC	JAN	FEB	MAR	APR	MAY	JUN

Dendrobium acinaciforme

Cultural Recommendations

LIGHT: 3000–4000 fc.

TEMPERATURES: Summer days average 90–91°F (32–33°C), and nights average 74°F (23°C), with a diurnal range of 16–17°F (9–10°C). Early spring is the warmest season. Days average 93–95°F (34–35°C), and nights average 70–74°F (21–23°C), with a diurnal range of 19–25°F (11–14°C).

HUMIDITY: 80–85% year-round.

WATER: Rainfall is moderate to heavy from late spring to autumn, with a 2–3 month dry season in late winter. Cultivated plants should be allowed to dry slightly between waterings.

FERTILIZER: ¼–½ recommended strength. A balanced fertilizer should be applied weekly to biweekly throughout the year.

REST PERIOD: Winter days average 86–92°F (30–33°C), and nights average 69–71°F (21–22°C), with a diurnal range of 15–23°F (8–13°C). In the habitat, winter rainfall is low, but the high average humidity indicates that some moisture is available in the form of dew or morning mist. Cultivated plants should be allowed to dry out between waterings but should not remain dry for extended periods. Occasional early morning mistings between waterings may help prevent plants from becoming too dry.

GROWING MEDIA: Plants may be mounted on tree-fern or cork slabs if humidity is high and plants are watered daily in summer. When plants are potted, any open, fast-draining medium may be used. Repotting may be done anytime new roots are growing.

MISCELLANEOUS NOTES: Plants that produce flowers which last a single day commonly bloom several times during the year. Flowering usually occurs 7–14 days after a sudden 10°F (5°C) drop in daytime temperatures.

Plant and Flower Information

PLANT SIZE AND TYPE: An 8–12 in. (20–30 cm) sympodial epiphyte.

PSEUDOBULB: 8–12 in. (20–30 cm) long. The erect stems are swollen for a few nodes at the base, becoming very slender above. They sometimes branch.

LEAVES: 5–7 per stem. The widely spaced, linear to terete leaves are 1.2–2.0 in. (3–5 cm) long. They are held at a 45° angle to the stem. They are not grooved.

INFLORESCENCE: Short. Inflorescences emerge from nodes near the apex of the stem.

FLOWERS: 1 per inflorescence. The flowers are 0.5 in. (1.3 cm) long. Sepals and petals are yellow with a strong purple tint that becomes most pronounced on the spur. The lip is white with bright purple branching lines on the sidelobes. The uneven front margin is ruffled. The rounded, light yellow keels on the lip have a few orange hairs with red dots at the front. Blossoms last 2 days.

HYBRIDIZING NOTES: Johansen (ref.239) indicates that plants are self-sterile and that flowers dropped 3–4 days after self-pollination. No attempts to cross-pollinate produced capsules, but capsules were produced when *D. aciculare* was used as the female parent and crossed with *D. acinaciforme* Roxburgh. *D. aciculare* did not produce seed when used as a female parent and crossed with *D. setifolium* Ridley.

REFERENCES: 12, 202, 216, 239, 254, 286, 295, 296, 317, 395, 450, 454, 455, 536.

PHOTOS/DRAWINGS: 450, *454, 455*.

Dendrobium acinaciforme Roxburgh

AKA: *D. spatella* Rchb. f. *D. scalpelliforme* Teijsm. and Binn. is sometimes listed as a synonym, but Seidenfaden (ref. 454) expressed reservations regarding this synonymy. In 1992 *Opera Botanica* 114, he includes *D. banaense* Gagnepain as a synonym.

ORIGIN/HABITAT: Widespread across Southeast Asia. The habitat includes India, Burma, Thailand, Laos, Cambodia, Vietnam, China, and Hong Kong. Plants grow in the Khasi (Khasia) Hills of northeastern India at about 3300 ft. (1000 m). In Thailand, they grow near Chiang Mai at 2900–6700 ft. (880–2100 m).

CLIMATE: Station #48327, Chiang Mai, Thailand, Lat. 18.8°N, Long. 99.0°E, at 1100 ft. (335 m). Temperatures are calculated for an elevation of 5000 ft. (1520 m), resulting in probable extremes of 96°F (36°C) and 25°F (−4°C).

N/HEMISPHERE	JAN	FEB	MAR	APR	MAY	JUN	JUL	AUG	SEP	OCT	NOV	DEC
°F AVG MAX	72	77	82	83	81	77	76	74	75	76	73	71
°F AVG MIN	43	44	49	57	61	61	61	62	60	58	53	44
DIURNAL RANGE	29	33	33	26	20	16	15	12	15	18	20	27
RAIN/INCHES	0.3	0.4	0.6	2.0	5.5	6.1	7.4	8.7	11.5	4.9	1.5	0.4
HUMIDITY/%	73	65	58	62	73	78	80	83	83	81	79	76
BLOOM SEASON			*	*	*				*			
DAYS CLR @ 7AM	5	5	2	2	1	0	0	0	0	1	3	3
DAYS CLR @ 1PM	9	8	4	2	0	0	0	0	0	1	3	
RAIN/MM	8	10	15	51	140	155	188	221	292	124	38	10
°C AVG MAX	22.3	25.1	27.9	28.4	27.3	25.1	24.5	23.4	24.0	24.5	22.9	21.7
°C AVG MIN	6.2	6.7	9.5	14.0	16.2	16.2	16.2	16.7	15.6	14.5	11.7	6.7
DIURNAL RANGE	16.1	18.4	18.4	14.4	11.1	8.9	8.3	6.7	8.4	10.0	11.2	15.0
S/HEMISPHERE	JUL	AUG	SEP	OCT	NOV	DEC	JAN	FEB	MAR	APR	MAY	JUN

Cultural Recommendations

LIGHT: 1800–2400 fc. Diffused light is suggested.

TEMPERATURES: Summer days average 74–77°F (23–25°C), and nights average 61–62°F (16–17°C), with a diurnal range of 12–16°F (7–9°C). The warmest temperatures occur in spring. Days average 81–83°F (27–28°C), and nights average 49–61°F (10–16°C), with a diurnal range of 20–33°F (11–18°C).

HUMIDITY: 75–85% from late spring through autumn, dropping to near 60% in late winter and early spring.

WATER: Rainfall is moderate to heavy from late spring through early autumn, but conditions are very dry in winter. Cultivated plants should be kept moist while actively growing, but water should be gradually reduced after new growths mature in autumn.

FERTILIZER: ¼–½ recommended strength, applied weekly. A high-nitrogen fertilizer is beneficial from spring to midsummer, but a fertilizer high in phosphates should be used in late summer and autumn.

REST PERIOD: Winter days average 71–77°F (22–25°C), and nights average 43–44°F (6–7°C), with a diurnal range of 27–33°F (15–18°C). The average low temperatures are below 50°F (10°C) for 3 months and then warm rapidly in spring. Plants should be able to tolerate temperatures a few degrees below freezing, but extremes should be avoided in cultivation. During very cold weather, a plant's chance of surviving with minimal damage is better if it is dry. In the habitat, rainfall averages are very low for 4–5 months in winter, but during the early part of the season the high relative humidity indicates that additional moisture is available from frequent fog, mist, and heavy deposits of dew. Growers sometimes recommend eliminating water in winter, but plants are healthiest if for most of the winter they are allowed to become somewhat dry between waterings but do not remain dry for extended periods. For 1–2 months in late winter, however, conditions are clear, warm, and dry with humidity so low that even the moisture from morning dew is uncommon. Plants should be allowed to dry out completely between waterings and remain dry longer during this time. Occasional early morning mistings between waterings may help keep the plants from becoming too dry. Fertilizer should be greatly reduced or eliminated until water is increased in spring. A cool, dry rest is essential for cultivated plants and should be continued until new growth starts in spring. In the habitat, light is highest in winter, but increased light may not be critical in cultivation.

GROWING MEDIA: Plants may be mounted on tree-fern or cork slabs if

humidity is high and if they are watered at least once a day in summer. If plants are potted, shallow, undersized pots may be filled with any open, fast-draining medium. Repotting is best done in early spring immediately after flowering.

MISCELLANEOUS NOTES: The bloom season shown in the climate table is based on cultivation records. The purple-flowered *D. banaënse* Gagnepain from Vietnam is very similar, and plants with each flower color have been found growing together.

Plant and Flower Information

PLANT SIZE AND TYPE: A 7–13 in. (18–33 cm) sympodial epiphyte.

PSEUDOBULB: 6–12 in. (15–30 cm) long. The slender, slightly zigzag stems are tightly clustered.

LEAVES: 8–12 per growth. The narrow, pointed leaves, which are distichous, succulent, and folded to appear triangular, are 1.5–2.0 in. (3.8–5.0 cm) long. They are curved, held at about a 45° angle to the stem, and moderately widely spaced.

INFLORESCENCE: 3–6 in. (8–15 cm) long. Flowers emerge from nodes on the upper, leafless portion of the stem.

FLOWERS: 1 per inflorescence. The tiny flowers are 0.3 in. (0.8 cm) across. The blossoms have white to greenish yellow sepals and petals. Blossoms are variable in size and lip details. They may have extensive purple in the flower and a distinct cleft at the apex of the lip, or they may have little purple and much yellow on the less-cleft lip. Various color forms have been found growing together. The lip is wavy and notched at the apex. The disk has 3 elevated yellow lines.

HYBRIDIZING NOTES: Chromosome counts are n = 19 (ref. 150, 504, 542) and 2n = 38 (ref. 152, 153, 154, 188, 243). Johansen (ref. 239) indicates that plants are self-sterile and that flowers dropped 5–7 days after self-pollination. *D. acinaciforme* produced seed when crossed with *D. aciculare* but not when crossed with *D. setifolium*.

REFERENCES: 38, 46, 150, 152, 153, 154, 179, 188, 202, 208, 209, 216, 239, 243, 254, 266, 369, 376, 447, 448, 454, 455, 504, 528, 542.

PHOTOS/DRAWINGS: *454*, 455.

Dendrobium aclinia Lindley not Rchb. f. See *D. incurvum* Lindley. REFERENCES: 157, 216, 254, 278, 452, 454.

Dendrobium aclinia Rchb. f. not Lindley

AKA: *D. pseudaclinia* Lindley.

ORIGIN/HABITAT: Widespread on Luzon Island in the Philippines. Plants grow in Zambales Province in the west, Isabela Province in the northeast, Rizal Province in central Luzon, and Quezon Province in the east. They are usually found below 1100 ft. (330 m).

CLIMATE: Station #98327, Clark Air Base, Philippines, Lat. 15.2°N, Long. 120.6°E, at 478 ft. (146 m). Record extreme temperatures are 99°F (37°C) and 61°F (16°C).

N/HEMISPHERE	JAN	FEB	MAR	APR	MAY	JUN	JUL	AUG	SEP	OCT	NOV	DEC
°F AVG MAX	85	87	90	92	92	89	87	86	86	87	86	85
°F AVG MIN	70	70	73	75	76	75	74	74	74	74	73	71
DIURNAL RANGE	15	17	17	17	16	14	13	12	12	13	13	14
RAIN/INCHES	0.8	0.7	0.9	1.5	3.9	10.8	12.6	16.1	13.1	4.9	2.0	0.9
HUMIDITY/%	67	65	64	63	68	79	81	83	84	76	72	70
BLOOM SEASON					*	*	*	*	*	*		
DAYS CLR @ 8AM	5	5	7	9	6	1	0	0	0	3	3	4
DAYS CLR @ 2PM	2	1	2	2	1	0	0	0	0	1	1	1
RAIN/MM	20	18	23	38	99	274	320	409	333	124	51	23
°C AVG MAX	29.4	30.6	32.2	33.3	33.3	31.7	30.6	30.0	30.0	30.6	30.0	29.4
°C AVG MIN	21.1	21.1	22.8	23.9	24.4	23.9	23.3	23.3	23.3	23.3	22.8	21.7
DIURNAL RANGE	8.3	9.5	9.4	9.4	8.9	7.8	7.3	6.7	6.7	7.3	7.2	7.7
S/HEMISPHERE	JUL	AUG	SEP	OCT	NOV	DEC	JAN	FEB	MAR	APR	MAY	JUN

Cultural Recommendations

LIGHT: 2500–3500 fc. In the habitat, clear weather occurs most often in winter and spring. Light is highest in the morning.

TEMPERATURES: Throughout the year, days average 85–92°F (29–33°C), and nights average 70–76°F (21–24°C), with a diurnal range of 12–17°F (7–9°C). The warmest temperatures occur in spring, before the rainy season starts.

HUMIDITY: 80–85% in summer. Humidity decreases to 70–75% in autumn and to near 65% in winter and spring.

WATER: Rainfall is heavy for 4 months in summer, but conditions are dry in winter. Cultivated plants should be kept moist from late spring to early autumn, but water should be gradually reduced after new growths mature.

FERTILIZER: ¼–½ recommended strength, applied weekly. A high-nitrogen fertilizer is beneficial from spring to midsummer, but a fertilizer high in phosphates should be used in late summer and autumn.

REST PERIOD: Growing temperatures should be maintained all year. For 4 months in winter, rainfall averages are low, and even moisture from dew is uncommon. Cultivated plants should be allowed to dry out between waterings in winter, but they should not remain dry for extended periods. Fertilizer should be reduced or eliminated until water is increased in spring. In the habitat, light is highest in winter.

GROWING MEDIA: Plants may be mounted on cork or tree-fern slabs. However, water must be applied at least daily in summer and humidity levels should be high. When plants are potted, any rapidly draining medium may be used. Repotting is best done when new roots are beginning to grow.

MISCELLANEOUS NOTES: The bloom season shown in the climate table is based on collection reports.

Plant and Flower Information

PLANT SIZE AND TYPE: A sympodial epiphyte of unreported size.

PSEUDOBULB: The stems are slender, canelike, and somewhat zigzag.

LEAVES: Many. The deciduous leaves are 2.4 in. (6 cm) long and arranged in 2 rows. They are oblong, tapering at each end, and somewhat leathery.

INFLORESCENCE: Very short. Inflorescences arise from leafless stems.

FLOWERS: 2–3 per inflorescence. Flowers are about 1 in. (2.5 cm) across. The yellow to straw-colored sepals and petals are wider than they are long and may not open fully. The lip is similar to the sepals and petals. All floral segments are similar.

REFERENCES: 12, 216, 296, 536.

Dendrobium acrobaticum Rchb. f. See *D. capillipes* Rchb. f. REFERENCES: 157, 216, 254, 454.

Dendrobium actinomorphum Blatter and Hallberg. See *D. crepidatum* Lindley. REFERENCES: 102, 223, 445, 454.

Dendrobium acuminatissimum (Blume) Lindley

AKA: *Grastidium acuminatissimum* Blume, *D. caudatum* var. *javanica* Teijsm. and Binn. *D. acuminatissimum* (Blume) Lindley var. *latifolium* J. J. Smith is now considered a synonym of *D. quinquecaudatum* J. J. Smith. J. J. Smith (ref. 470) suggested that the description for *D. schwartzkopffianum* Kränzlin sounded very like *D. acuminatissimum* (Blume) Lindley. *D. acuminatissimum* Lindley var. *mamberamense* J. J. Smith is now considered a synonym of *D. angustispathum* J. J. Smith.

ORIGIN/HABITAT: Widespread. Plants are found in Borneo, the Philippines, Papua New Guinea, and numerous Indonesian islands, including Ambon,

Dendrobium acuminatum

Java, and Sumatra. In Sumatra, plants were collected near Padang-Pandjang at about 2800 ft. (850 m), but they usually grow much lower at 100–200 ft. (30–60 m). On Borneo, plants are found in Sabah at 2950–4900 ft. (900–1500 m). In the Philippines, plants are found on Luzon in Benguet Province and near Mt. Maquiling (Makiling) in Dipterocarp forests of Laguna Province. They also grow near Dagami on Leyte, which is located on the east slopes of the mountains south-southwest of Tacloban.

CLIMATE: Station #49613, Tambunan, Sabah (North Borneo), Lat. 5.7°N, Long. 116.4°E, at 1200 ft. (366 m). Temperatures are calculated for an elevation of 4000 ft. (1220 m), resulting in probable extremes of 89°F (32°C) and 45°F (7°C).

N/HEMISPHERE	JAN	FEB	MAR	APR	MAY	JUN	JUL	AUG	SEP	OCT	NOV	DEC
°F AVG MAX	77	78	80	81	81	80	80	80	80	79	78	77
°F AVG MIN	58	56	57	58	59	58	57	57	58	58	58	59
DIURNAL RANGE	19	22	23	23	22	22	23	23	22	21	20	18
RAIN/INCHES	5.8	3.7	5.8	7.5	8.2	7.3	5.1	4.9	6.4	7.0	6.8	6.0
HUMIDITY/%	N/A											
BLOOM SEASON			*		*			*			*	
DAYS CLR	N/A											
RAIN/MM	147	94	147	190	208	185	130	124	163	178	173	152
°C AVG MAX	24.9	25.4	26.5	27.1	27.1	26.5	26.5	26.5	26.5	26.0	25.4	24.9
°C AVG MIN	14.3	13.2	13.8	14.3	14.9	14.3	13.8	13.8	14.3	14.3	14.3	14.9
DIURNAL RANGE	10.6	12.2	12.7	12.8	12.2	12.2	12.7	12.7	12.2	11.7	11.1	10.0
S/HEMISPHERE	JUL	AUG	SEP	OCT	NOV	DEC	JAN	FEB	MAR	APR	MAY	JUN

Cultural Recommendations

LIGHT: 2500–3500 fc.

TEMPERATURES: Throughout the year, days average 77–81°F (25–27°C), and nights average 56–59°F (13–15°C), with a diurnal range of 18–23°F (10–13°C). These temperatures represent conditions in the higher, cooler portions of the habitat. Because plants grow over a wide range of elevations, they should adapt to conditions about 10°F (6°C) warmer than indicated above.

HUMIDITY: Near 80% year-round.

WATER: Rainfall is heavy most of the year, but conditions are slightly drier for 2–3 months in winter. Cultivated plants should be kept moist but not soggy.

FERTILIZER: ¼–½ recommended strength. A balanced fertilizer should be applied weekly to biweekly throughout the year.

REST PERIOD: Growing conditions should be maintained all year. Water and fertilizer should be reduced somewhat in winter, especially for plants grown in the darker, short-day conditions common in temperate-latitude winters. Plants should be allowed to dry slightly between waterings, but they should never dry out completely or remain dry for long periods.

GROWING MEDIA: Mounting plants on cork or tree-fern slabs accommodates their pendent growth habit, but water must be applied at least once daily in summer and humidity must be high. When plants are potted, a hanging basket or shallow, undersized pot may be filled with any open, rapidly draining medium. Repotting is best done in late winter or early spring or immediately after flowering if new roots are growing.

MISCELLANEOUS NOTES: The bloom times in the climate table are based on collection reports, but blooming may occur at any time. *D. acuminatissimum* produces buds which form to a certain stage and then hold on the plant without developing further. The buds open 8 days after a sudden temperature drop. Most plants bloom on the same day when cross-pollination occurs. Plants which for some reason fail to bloom with the others are ignored by pollinators when they do bloom.

Plant and Flower Information

PLANT SIZE AND TYPE: A pendulous, 39 in. (100 cm) sympodial epiphyte. Plants occasionally reach a length of 79 in. (200 cm).

PSEUDOBULB: 39–79 in. (100–200 cm) long. The stems are shiny, yellow-green, slender, clustered, and pendent.

LEAVES: Many per growth. The leaves are about 5 in. (13 cm) long, linear, and grasslike. They grow only on the apical part of the cane.

INFLORESCENCE: Short. The inflorescences emerge from rigid scalelike bracts below the leaves.

FLOWERS: 2 per inflorescence. The flowers are small, but each plant produces many blossoms. The slender sepals, which are 1.3 in. (3.3 cm) long, taper to mere threads at the tips. Blossoms may be pure white, green, or pale yellow marked with red-brown spots. The pointed lip is hairy along the midline. Blossoms are short-lived.

HYBRIDIZING NOTES: Chromosome count is 2n = 40 (ref. 280, 504, 580).

REFERENCES: 12, 25, 75, 111, 216, 254, 277, 280, 296, 310, 373, 435, 445, 469, 470, 479, 504, 516, 536, 580, 592.

PHOTOS/DRAWINGS: 469.

Dendrobium acuminatum H. B. and K. not Lyon or Rolfe ex Ames.

Now considered a synonym of *Pleurothallis acuminata* Lindley. REFERENCES: 45, 216, 254.

Dendrobium acuminatum Lyon not Rolfe ex Ames or H. B. and K.

See *D. lyonii* Ames. REFERENCES: 98, 296, 504, 536, 580.

Dendrobium acuminatum Rolfe ex Ames not H. B. and K. or Lyon.

Now considered a synonym of *Epigeneium acuminatum* (Rolfe) Summerhayes. REFERENCES: 12, 188, 190, 219, 229, 254, 296, 445, 499, 504, 536.

Dendrobium acutifolium Ridley

ORIGIN/HABITAT: Sumatra. Plants were collected near Barong Bharu on the west side of the Barisan Range at 4000 ft. (1220 m).

CLIMATE: Station #96163, Padang, Sumatra, Indonesia, Lat. 0.9°S, Long. 100.4°E, at 19 ft. (6 m). Temperatures are calculated for an elevation of 3950 ft. (1200 m), resulting in probable extremes of 81°F (27°C) and 55°F (13°C).

N/HEMISPHERE	JAN	FEB	MAR	APR	MAY	JUN	JUL	AUG	SEP	OCT	NOV	DEC
°F AVG MAX	74	74	73	73	73	73	74	74	74	74	75	74
°F AVG MIN	61	61	61	61	61	61	61	61	61	62	62	61
DIURNAL RANGE	13	13	12	12	12	12	13	13	13	12	13	13
RAIN/INCHES	10.9	13.7	6.0	19.5	20.4	18.9	13.8	10.2	12.1	14.3	12.4	12.1
HUMIDITY/%	81	82	82	84	85	84	81	81	82	83	81	81
BLOOM SEASON	N/A											
DAYS CLR @ 7AM	5	1	1	0	0	2	2	1	2	2	2	5
DAYS CLR @ 1PM	5	2	2	1	1	3	3	4	3	3	6	5
RAIN/MM	277	348	152	495	518	480	351	259	307	363	315	307
°C AVG MAX	23.3	23.3	22.8	22.8	22.8	22.8	23.3	23.3	23.3	23.3	23.9	23.3
°C AVG MIN	16.1	16.1	16.1	16.1	16.1	16.1	16.1	16.1	16.1	16.7	16.7	16.1
DIURNAL RANGE	7.2	7.2	6.7	6.7	6.7	6.7	7.2	7.2	7.2	6.6	7.2	7.2
S/HEMISPHERE	JUL	AUG	SEP	OCT	NOV	DEC	JAN	FEB	MAR	APR	MAY	JUN

Cultural Recommendations

LIGHT: 2000–3000 fc. Clear summer days are rare, so light is naturally diffused.

TEMPERATURES: Throughout the year, days average 73–75°F (23–24°C), and nights average 61–62°F (16–17°C), with a diurnal range of 12–13°F (7°C). Probable extremes vary only a few degrees from the averages, indicating that plants from this habitat may not tolerate wide temperature fluctuations.

HUMIDITY: 80–85% year-round.

WATER: Rainfall is heavy all year. Cultivated plants should be constantly moist.

FERTILIZER: ¼–½ recommended strength. A balanced fertilizer should be applied weekly to biweekly throughout the year.

REST PERIOD: Growing conditions should be maintained year-round. Water may be reduced somewhat for cultivated plants in winter, especially those grown in the dark, short-day conditions common in temperate latitudes. Plants should never be allowed to dry out completely, however. In the habitat, light is higher for 2–3 months in winter.

GROWING MEDIA: Plants may be mounted on tree-fern or cork slabs if humidity is high and plants are watered at least once daily in summer. When plants are potted, any open, fast-draining medium may be used. They may be repotted anytime new roots are growing.

Plant and Flower Information

PLANT SIZE AND TYPE: A 14–17 in. (35–43 cm) sympodial epiphyte.

PSEUDOBULB: 14–17 in. (35–43 cm) long. The pseudobulbs are slender and stemlike.

LEAVES: The lanceolate leaves are 2.8 in. (7 cm) long and taper to a point. They are deciduous.

INFLORESCENCE: 0.8 in. (2 cm) long. Inflorescences emerge from leafless stems.

FLOWERS: The white blossoms are 0.8 in. (2 cm) long. Sepals and petals are lanceolate. The white lip, which has elevated orange markings at the base, is oblong-lanceolate, rounded, and lightly ruffled.

REFERENCES: 222, 401.

Dendrobium acutilobum Schlechter

ORIGIN/HABITAT: Northern Papua New Guinea. Plants grow at about 1000 ft. (300 m) on forest trees in the Minjem Valley.

CLIMATE: Station #94014, Madang, Papua New Guinea, Lat. 5.2°S, Long. 145.8°E, at 13 ft. (4 m). Temperatures are calculated for an elevation of 1000 ft. (300 m), resulting in probable extremes of 95°F (35°C) and 59°F (15°C).

N/HEMISPHERE	JAN	FEB	MAR	APR	MAY	JUN	JUL	AUG	SEP	OCT	NOV	DEC
°F AVG MAX	80	80	82	82	82	82	82	82	82	84	84	81
°F AVG MIN	74	75	75	75	74	74	74	74	74	73	74	75
DIURNAL RANGE	6	5	7	7	8	8	8	8	8	11	10	6
RAIN/INCHES	4.0	3.4	3.2	8.5	11.2	11.1	10.1	11.3	9.4	11.3	10.5	6.7
HUMIDITY/%	88	87	86	86	86	86	86	85	85	87	88	89
BLOOM SEASON					*							
DAYS CLR	N/A											
RAIN/MM	102	86	81	216	284	282	257	287	239	287	267	170
°C AVG MAX	26.6	26.6	27.7	27.7	27.7	27.7	27.7	27.7	27.7	28.8	28.8	27.1
°C AVG MIN	23.2	23.8	23.8	23.8	23.2	23.2	23.2	23.2	23.2	22.7	23.2	23.8
DIURNAL RANGE	3.4	2.8	3.9	3.9	4.5	4.5	4.5	4.5	4.5	6.1	5.6	3.3
S/HEMISPHERE	JUL	AUG	SEP	OCT	NOV	DEC	JAN	FEB	MAR	APR	MAY	JUN

Cultural Recommendations

LIGHT: 2500–3000 fc.

TEMPERATURES: Throughout the year, days average 80–84°F (27–29°C), and nights average 73–75°F (23–24°C), with a diurnal range of 5–11°F (3–6°C). The warmest highs, the coolest lows, and the greatest diurnal range occur in autumn.

HUMIDITY: 85–90% year-round.

WATER: Rainfall is moderate to heavy all year. The driest conditions occur in late winter. Cultivated plants should be kept moist but not soggy.

FERTILIZER: ¼–½ recommended strength. A balanced fertilizer should be applied weekly to biweekly throughout the year.

REST PERIOD: Growing temperatures should be maintained all year. In the habitat, rainfall decreases for 4 months in winter. Water should be reduced for cultivated plants, but they should not be allowed to dry out completely. Fertilizer should be reduced or eliminated while water is reduced. In the habitat, light is slightly higher in late winter.

GROWING MEDIA: Plants may be mounted on tree-fern or cork slabs if humidity is high and plants are watered at least once daily in summer. When plants are potted, they may be placed in small, shallow pots filled with any open, fast-draining medium. Repotting may be done anytime new roots are growing.

MISCELLANEOUS NOTES: The bloom time given in the climate table is based on a single collection report. It is probable that blooming occurs several times during the year. Flowers last a single day, and their initiation may result from a sudden drop in daytime temperatures.

Plant and Flower Information

PLANT SIZE AND TYPE: A 20–24 in. (50–60 cm) sympodial epiphyte.

PSEUDOBULB: 17–21 in. (43–53 cm) long. The erect stems do not branch.

LEAVES: Several to many. The leaves are 2–3 in. (5–8 cm) long, oval, and erect to spreading.

INFLORESCENCE: Short. Inflorescences arise from flat sheaths at the side of the pseudobulb.

FLOWERS: 2 per inflorescence. The flowers are 0.6 in. (1.6 cm) long and often remain rather closed. Blossoms are rose-red with an orange-yellow keel on the ruffled lip. The sepals, petals, and lip all project forward.

REFERENCES: 92, 221, 437, 445.

PHOTOS/DRAWINGS: 437.

Dendrobium acutimentum J. J. Smith

ORIGIN/HABITAT: Western Sumatra near Bengkulu at about 3950 ft. (1200 m).

CLIMATE: Station #96253, Bengkulu, Sumatra, Indonesia, Lat. 3.9°S, Long. 102.3°E, at 49 ft. (15 m). Temperatures are calculated for an elevation of 3950 ft. (1200 m). Record extreme temperatures are not available for this location.

N/HEMISPHERE	JAN	FEB	MAR	APR	MAY	JUN	JUL	AUG	SEP	OCT	NOV	DEC
°F AVG MAX	75	74	74	74	74	74	75	75	75	75	76	75
°F AVG MIN	59	59	59	60	60	60	60	59	60	61	60	60
DIURNAL RANGE	16	15	15	14	14	14	15	16	15	14	16	15
RAIN/INCHES	6.9	6.8	9.1	13.9	16.0	12.7	16.0	11.5	12.0	8.3	8.4	8.4
HUMIDITY/%	77	78	77	77	79	80	78	76	77	79	77	78
BLOOM SEASON	N/A											
DAYS CLR @ 7AM	5	1	1	1	0	0	2	1	1	1	2	3
DAYS CLR @ 1PM	5	4	3	1	2	3	2	2	3	7	5
RAIN/MM	175	173	231	353	406	323	406	292	305	211	213	213
°C AVG MAX	24.0	23.4	23.4	23.4	23.4	23.4	24.0	24.0	24.0	24.0	24.5	24.0
°C AVG MIN	15.1	15.1	15.1	15.6	15.6	15.6	15.6	15.1	15.6	16.2	15.6	15.6
DIURNAL RANGE	8.9	8.3	8.3	7.8	7.8	7.8	8.4	8.9	8.4	7.8	8.9	8.4
S/HEMISPHERE	JUL	AUG	SEP	OCT	NOV	DEC	JAN	FEB	MAR	APR	MAY	JUN

Cultural Recommendations

LIGHT: 2000–3000 fc.

TEMPERATURES: Throughout the year, days average 74–76°F (23–25°C), and nights average 59–61°F (15–16°C), with a diurnal range of 14–16°F (8–9°C).

HUMIDITY: 75–80% year-round.

WATER: Rainfall is heavy throughout the year, but conditions are slightly drier in winter. Cultivated plants should be kept moist and never be allowed to dry out completely.

FERTILIZER: ¼–½ recommended strength. A balanced fertilizer should be applied weekly to biweekly throughout the year.

REST PERIOD: Growing conditions should be maintained year-round. Water may be reduced somewhat for plants that are grown in the dark, short-day conditions common in temperate-latitude winters, but they should never be allowed to dry completely between waterings.

GROWING MEDIA: Plants may be mounted on tree-fern or cork slabs or potted in small pots filled with any open, fast-draining medium. Repotting may be done anytime new roots are actively growing.

MISCELLANEOUS NOTES: The plant was described in 1917 in *Bul. Jard. Bot. Buit.* 2nd sér. 25:53.

Plant and Flower Information

PLANT SIZE AND TYPE: A 12–14 in. (30–35 cm) sympodial epiphyte.

PSEUDOBULB: 12–14 in. (30–35 cm) long. The pale green stems are clustered.

LEAVES: The dark green leaves are 2.0–3.5 in. (5–9 cm) long. They are twisted at the base. The leaf sheaths are marked with dark spots.

INFLORESCENCE: Short. Inflorescences emerge from nodes on leafless stems.

FLOWERS: 1 per inflorescence. The pale yellow-green flowers are 0.6 in. (1.6 cm) across. The lip, which has no sidelobes, is wavy and recurved.

REFERENCES: 222.

Dendrobium acutisepalum J. J. Smith

ORIGIN/HABITAT: Irian Jaya (western New Guinea). Plants grow on the ground in layers of sphagnum moss in mountain forests and marshes. On Mt. Goliath, plants are found at 5750–10,600 ft. (1750–3230 m). They also grow at 9850–11,300 ft. (3000–3450 m) on ridges in the Kajan Mountains, near the summit of Mt. Wichmann close to Lake Habbema and in the Wissel Lakes area.

CLIMATE: Station #97686, Wamena, Irian Jaya, Lat. 4.1°S, Long. 139.0°E, at 5446 ft. (1660 m). Temperatures are calculated for an elevation of 10,000 ft. (3050 m). Record extreme temperatures are not available for this location.

N/HEMISPHERE	JAN	FEB	MAR	APR	MAY	JUN	JUL	AUG	SEP	OCT	NOV	DEC
°F AVG MAX	60	61	62	61	62	61	62	61	61	64	63	59
°F AVG MIN	45	45	47	47	48	49	48	47	48	50	50	46
DIURNAL RANGE	15	16	15	14	14	12	14	14	13	14	13	13
RAIN/INCHES	3.0	1.9	2.2	4.0	4.6	3.3	2.8	4.2	6.9	3.9	5.4	4.9
HUMIDITY/%	N/A											
BLOOM SEASON			*	*				*				
DAYS CLR	N/A											
RAIN/MM	76	48	56	102	117	84	71	107	175	99	137	124
°C AVG MAX	15.5	16.1	16.7	16.1	16.7	16.1	16.7	16.1	16.1	17.8	17.2	15.0
°C AVG MIN	7.2	7.2	8.3	8.3	8.9	9.4	8.9	8.3	8.9	10.0	10.0	7.8
DIURNAL RANGE	8.3	8.9	8.4	7.8	7.8	6.7	7.8	7.8	7.2	7.8	7.2	7.2
S/HEMISPHERE	JUL	AUG	SEP	OCT	NOV	DEC	JAN	FEB	MAR	APR	MAY	JUN

Cultural Recommendations

LIGHT: 1500–2500 fc.

TEMPERATURES: Throughout the year, days average 59–64°F (15–18°C), and nights average 45–50°F (7–10°C), with a diurnal range of 12–16°F (7–9°C). The warmest temperatures occur in autumn. In the habitat, the warmest temperatures of the day occur in late morning when skies are clear. Clouds and mist develop near noon and continue through the afternoon, thus preventing additional warming. Because of microclimate effects, actual maximum temperatures may be somewhat warmer than indicated by the calculated values above. Reports from the habitat indicate a sharp contrast between day and night temperatures.

HUMIDITY: Information is not available for this location. However, records from nearby stations indicate that humidity probably averages near 80% year-round. High humidity and excellent air circulation are particularly important if temperatures are warm. Placing the plants in front of an evaporative cooler or near a fine mist is very beneficial.

WATER: Rainfall is moderate to heavy through most of the year. In the higher-elevation habitat, rainfall amounts may be greater than indicated in the climate table. In addition, large amounts of water are available from mist and heavy dew, even during periods of reduced rainfall. Cultivated plants should be misted several times daily on the hottest days, but the foliage should always be dry before evening.

FERTILIZER: ¼–½ recommended strength, applied weekly when plants are actively growing. The Royal Botanic Garden in Edinburgh uses a seaweed-based fertilizer for plants from high-elevation New Guinea.

REST PERIOD: Growing conditions should be maintained all year. Rainfall averages are somewhat lower for a month or so in winter with a secondary dry period in midsummer. In cultivation, water may be decreased, but plants should never be allowed to dry out completely. In the habitat, light is slightly higher in winter. Cultivated plants often grow year-round.

GROWING MEDIA: *D. acutisepalum* grows in mossy, mountain forests and in sphagnum moss in marshy areas, indicating that it should be grown in a medium that retains moisture, but is not soggy. A potting mixture of fir bark or chopped tree-fern fiber with moisture-retaining additives is recommended. A surface layer of sphagnum moss might be beneficial. Repotting may be done anytime new roots are growing.

MISCELLANEOUS NOTES: The bloom season shown in the climate table is based on collection reports. *D. acutisepalum* may be difficult to cultivate outside its natural habitat. Botanists working with the New Guinea Highland Orchid Collection near Laiagam at 7216 ft. (2200 m) found that species collected above 10,500 ft. (3200 m) were very difficult to cultivate at lower elevations.

Plant and Flower Information

PLANT SIZE AND TYPE: A 24–31 in. (60–80 cm) sympodial terrestrial.

PSEUDOBULB: 24–31 in. (60–80 cm) long. The stems are erect and clustered. Young stems are covered with sheaths.

LEAVES: 3–10 per growth. The ovate to elliptical leaves are usually erect, 3 in. (8 cm) long, and occur on the apical portion of the stem.

INFLORESCENCE: 10–13 in. (25–32 cm) long. The spikes arise near the apex of the stem from below the leaf bracts.

FLOWERS: 4–11 per inflorescence. The flowers are 1.2–1.6 in. (3–4 cm) across. Flower color is highly variable. Sepals and petals may be crimson or white, and in some specimens, they are green with purple at the base. The lip has a pale yellow midlobe with purple or red veins, and the sidelobes are marked with brown.

REFERENCES: 83, 221, 445, 470, 538.

PHOTOS/DRAWINGS: 83, 538.

Dendrobium adae F. M. Bailey

AKA: *D. ancorarium* Rupp, *D. palmerstoniae* Schlechter.

ORIGIN/HABITAT: Endemic to northeastern Australia. Plants are common on the Cape York Peninsula between the Burdekin and Annan Rivers. They usually grow above 2600 ft. (800 m) in exposed, north- to west-facing locations on cloudforest trees or in protected spots in open forest.

CLIMATE: Station #94295, Ingham, Australia, Lat. 18.7°S, Long. 146.2°E, at 45 ft. (14 m). Temperatures are calculated for an elevation of 3000 ft. (910 m), resulting in probable extremes of 100°F (38°C) and 29°F (–2°C).

N/HEMISPHERE	JAN	FEB	MAR	APR	MAY	JUN	JUL	AUG	SEP	OCT	NOV	DEC
°F AVG MAX	65	67	70	73	75	77	77	77	76	74	71	67
°F AVG MIN	49	51	56	61	64	66	66	65	63	60	55	51
DIURNAL RANGE	16	16	14	12	11	11	11	12	13	14	16	16
RAIN/INCHES	0.6	0.5	0.7	1.3	1.9	5.4	10.9	11.2	7.2	3.3	1.3	1.4
HUMIDITY/%	61	61	62	64	66	70	72	71	70	64	63	63
BLOOM SEASON	*	*	*	*								
DAYS CLR @ 10AM	16	18	15	10	7	7	5	5	9	13	14	15
DAYS CLR @ 4PM	16	18	20	20	17	15	8	5	7	11	14	15
RAIN/MM	15	13	18	33	48	137	277	284	183	84	33	36
°C AVG MAX	18.5	19.6	21.2	22.9	24.0	25.1	25.1	25.1	24.6	23.5	21.8	19.6
°C AVG MIN	9.6	10.7	13.5	16.2	17.9	19.0	19.0	18.5	17.4	15.7	12.9	10.7
DIURNAL RANGE	8.9	8.9	7.7	6.7	6.1	6.1	6.1	6.6	7.2	7.8	8.9	8.9
S/HEMISPHERE	JUL	AUG	SEP	OCT	NOV	DEC	JAN	FEB	MAR	APR	MAY	JUN

Cultural Recommendations

LIGHT: 3500–4500 fc. Strong air movement should be provided year-round.

TEMPERATURES: Summer days average 76–77°F (25°C), and nights average 63–66°F (17–19°C), with a diurnal range of 11–13°F (6–7°C).

HUMIDITY: 70–80% year-round. In the cloudforest habitat, humidity is probably greater than indicated by the climate data. Growers report that plants will tolerate lower humidity levels, however.

WATER: Rainfall is moderate to heavy in summer and early autumn, but conditions are much drier from late autumn to spring. Plants require ample moisture while actively growing, but pot-grown plants should be allowed to dry out between waterings. Water should be gradually reduced in autumn with only light to moderate moisture from autumn through spring.

FERTILIZER: ¼–½ recommended strength, applied weekly. A high-nitrogen fertilizer is beneficial from spring to midsummer, but a fertilizer high in phosphates should be used in late summer and autumn.

REST PERIOD: Winter days average 65–67°F (19–20°C), and nights average 49–51°F (10–11°C), with a diurnal range of 14–16°F (8–9°C). Growers report that D. adae survives 32°F (0°C) for short periods. Although rainfall is lower in winter, some water is available in the cloudforest habitat throughout the year from heavy dew and mist. Cultivated plants should be watered whenever the medium becomes dry. Occasional early morning mistings between waterings may be beneficial. Fertilizer should be reduced or eliminated unless plants are actively growing.

GROWING MEDIA: Plants may be mounted on tree-fern or cork slabs if humidity is high and plants are watered at least once daily in summer. If plants are potted, small, shallow pots should be used with a very open, fast-draining medium. Repotting is best done immediately after flowering.

MISCELLANEOUS NOTES: The bloom season shown in the climate table is based on cultivation records. The plant is considered easy to grow if it has a cool, humid environment with strong air movement. These conditions are critically important. When not in flower, the plants are indistinguishable from D. fleckeri Rupp and C. T. White. Therefore, if a plant is growing poorly using the preceding cultural regime, conditions may be gradually changed to more closely match the Cultural Recommendations given for D. fleckeri.

Plant and Flower Information

PLANT SIZE AND TYPE: A 12–24 in. (30–60 cm) sympodial epiphyte or lithophyte. Plants normally form small- to medium-sized clumps, but some large specimens consist of clusters of 100 pseudobulbs.

PSEUDOBULB: 11–15 in. (28–38 cm) long. The erect to semipendent canes are thin and wiry with a pseudobulbous swelling at the base. The stems become yellow-brown and furrowed with age. Plants found at low elevations are smaller than those from higher locations.

LEAVES: 2–4 at the apex of each growth. The leaves are 2.4–3.0 in. (6.0–7.6 cm) long, narrowly or broadly lanceolate, with a moderately thin texture.

INFLORESCENCE: 3 in. (8 cm) long. Racemes emerge from between the leaves at the apex of the stem.

FLOWERS: 2–6, rarely 9 per inflorescence. The flowers are 0.8–1.6 in. (2–4 cm) across and remain somewhat closed in cloudy weather. The variably colored sepals and petals may be white, light yellow, or greenish, but they turn creamy yellow then apricot before withering. The white to green lip is covered with hairs, which distinguishes it from D. fleckeri. The lip is marked with pale mauve stripes. The column is commonly blotched or speckled with orange-red dots. The spur is short and curved. D. adae occasionally produces flowers of different sexes. Plants are free-flowering, and individual blossoms last 2–3 weeks. Blossoms are highly perfumed, particularly in strong sunlight, with a fragrance resembling orange blossoms.

HYBRIDIZING NOTES: Chromosome count is 2n = 38 (ref. 153, 273). When used as a parent, D. adae generally contributes an erect growth habit, upright raceme, clear colors, and fragrance. Unfortunately, it also tends to reduce the number of flowers.

REFERENCES: 23, 24, 67, 105, 153, 179, 216, 240, 254, 262, 273, 325, 390, 421, 495, 533, 562.

PHOTOS/DRAWINGS: *105*, 240, 325, *390, 533, 562*.

Dendrobium adamsii A. Hawkes

ORIGIN/HABITAT: Widespread on the islands of Kusaie (Kosrae), Truk, and Ponape (Pohnpei) in the Caroline Islands. Plants grow on mossy tree trunks on Mt. Kubersoh, Ponape at about 2100 ft. (640 m).

CLIMATE: Station #91348, Ponape, Caroline Islands, Lat. 7.0°N, Long. 158.2°E, at 121 ft. (37 m). Temperatures are calculated for an elevation of 2100 ft. (640 m). Record extreme temperatures are not available for this location.

N/HEMISPHERE	JAN	FEB	MAR	APR	MAY	JUN	JUL	AUG	SEP	OCT	NOV	DEC
°F AVG MAX	81	82	82	82	82	82	83	82	82	82	82	81
°F AVG MIN	66	65	65	64	64	64	63	62	63	64	64	65
DIURNAL RANGE	15	17	17	18	18	18	20	20	19	18	18	16
RAIN/INCHES	11.1	9.7	14.6	20.0	20.3	16.7	16.2	16.3	15.8	16.0	16.9	18.3
HUMIDITY/%	N/A											
BLOOM SEASON							*					
DAYS CLR	N/A											
RAIN/MM	282	246	371	508	516	424	411	414	401	406	429	465
°C AVG MAX	27.5	28.0	28.0	28.0	28.0	28.0	28.6	28.0	28.0	28.0	28.0	27.5
°C AVG MIN	19.1	18.6	18.6	18.0	18.0	18.0	17.5	16.9	17.5	18.0	18.0	18.6
DIURNAL RANGE	8.4	9.4	9.4	10.0	10.0	10.0	11.1	11.1	10.5	10.0	10.0	8.9
S/HEMISPHERE	JUL	AUG	SEP	OCT	NOV	DEC	JAN	FEB	MAR	APR	MAY	JUN

Cultural Recommendations

LIGHT: 2000–3000 fc. Although cloud cover records are not available for this location, other stations throughout the Caroline Islands report less than 3 days with clear skies each year. Heavy rainfall in all months is an additional indication of relatively low light.

TEMPERATURES: Throughout the year, days average 81–83°F (28–29°C), and nights average 62–66°F (17–19°C), with a diurnal range of 15–20°F (8–11°C).

HUMIDITY: Information is not available for this location, but other stations in the island group report year-round averages of 80–85%.

WATER: Rainfall is very heavy all year. Conditions are slightly drier for 2–3 months in winter, but cultivated plants should never be allowed to dry out completely.

FERTILIZER: ¼–½ recommended strength. A balanced fertilizer should be applied weekly to biweekly throughout the year.

REST PERIOD: Growing conditions should be maintained year-round. Water and fertilizer should be reduced for cultivated plants grown in the dark, short-day conditions common in temperate-latitude winters, but they should not be allowed to dry out completely.

GROWING MEDIA: Plants may be mounted on tree-fern or cork slabs if humidity is high and plants are watered at least once a day in summer. If plants are potted, small, shallow pots may be filled with any open, fast-draining medium. Repotting may be done anytime new roots are growing.

MISCELLANEOUS NOTES: The bloom season shown in the climate table is based on reports from the habitat. Plants that produce flowers which last a single day commonly bloom several times during the year. Flowering usually occurs 7–14 days after a sudden 10°F (5°C) drop in daytime temperatures.

Plant and Flower Information

PLANT SIZE AND TYPE: A 5 in. (13 cm) sympodial epiphyte.

Dendrobium adenanthum

PSEUDOBULB: 5 in. (13 cm) long. The describer indicated that length was based on an incomplete specimen. The stems are yellowish, curved, slightly zigzag, and covered by sheaths.

LEAVES: Many per growth. The slender leaves are leathery, oblong-lanceolate, and usually 2 in. (5 cm) long.

INFLORESCENCE: Short.

FLOWERS: 1–2 per inflorescence. The greenish flowers, which are 1 in. (2.5 cm) across, may have a pinkish tinge on the inside of the petals. The recurved lip is densely covered with hairs and marked with purplish red in the center. The very fragrant blossoms last about 6 hours.

REFERENCES: 189, 228.

Dendrobium adenanthum (Schlechter) J. J. Smith. Now considered a synonym of *Cadetia hispida* (A. Richard) Schlechter. REFERENCES: 46, 221, 271, 472.

Dendrobium adolphi Schlechter. See *D. puniceum* Ridley. REFERENCES: 223, 385.

Dendrobium adpressifolium J. J. Smith. See *D. flexile* Ridley. REFERENCES: 222, 454.

Dendrobium aduncilobum J. J. Smith. Now considered a synonym of *Diplocaulobium aduncilobum* (J. J. Smith) Hunt and Summerhayes. REFERENCES: 213, 224, 230.

Dendrobium aduncum Wallich ex Lindley

AKA: Seidenfaden (ref. 454) includes *D. scoriarum* W. W. Smith as a synonym. He expresses reservations regarding other synonyms, as the records for *D. aduncum*, *D. hercoglossum* Rchb. f., and *D. linguella* Rchb. f. are all mixed up. *D. aduncum* var. *faulhaberianum* (Schlechter) Tang and Wang is a synonym of *D. faulhaberianum* Schlechter.

ORIGIN/HABITAT: Widespread in Southeast Asia. In India, plants grow near Gangtok, Kalimpong, and Darjeeling in the light shade of open forests in tropical valleys below 2600 ft. (800 m). In the Khasi (Khasia) Hills of Meghalaya, plants grow below 2300 ft. (700 m). The habitat extends to Nepal, Bhutan, Burma, and northern Thailand. In Vietnam, plants grow in the Prenn Valley near Dalat at 3950–4250 ft. (1200–1300 m). In China, plants are found on Hainan Island and in the Lo-fan-shan (Lofaushan) Mountains opposite Hong Kong.

CLIMATE: Station #42398, Baghdogra, India, Lat. 26.7°N, Long. 88.3°E, at 412 ft. (126 m). Temperatures are calculated for an elevation of 2000 ft. (610 m), resulting in probable extremes of 99°F (37°C) and 31°F (–1°C).

N/HEMISPHERE	JAN	FEB	MAR	APR	MAY	JUN	JUL	AUG	SEP	OCT	NOV	DEC
°F AVG MAX	69	72	80	85	85	84	84	84	83	82	77	72
°F AVG MIN	45	49	55	63	68	71	72	72	71	65	55	48
DIURNAL RANGE	24	23	25	22	17	13	12	12	12	17	22	24
RAIN/INCHES	0.3	0.7	1.3	3.7	11.8	25.9	32.2	25.3	21.2	5.6	0.5	0.2
HUMIDITY/%	73	68	57	58	74	84	86	85	85	79	75	76
BLOOM SEASON				*	**	**	*		*	*		*
DAYS CLR @ 6AM	21	18	15	11	5	0	1	4	13	23	19	
DAYS CLR @ 12PM	23	16	16	11	2	2	0	2	10	21	18	
RAIN/MM	8	18	33	94	300	658	818	643	538	142	13	5
°C AVG MAX	20.4	22.1	26.5	29.3	29.3	28.8	28.8	28.8	28.2	27.6	24.9	22.1
°C AVG MIN	7.1	9.3	12.6	17.1	19.9	21.5	22.1	22.1	21.5	18.2	12.6	8.8
DIURNAL RANGE	13.3	12.8	13.9	12.2	9.4	7.3	6.7	6.7	6.7	9.4	12.3	13.3
S/HEMISPHERE	JUL	AUG	SEP	OCT	NOV	DEC	JAN	FEB	MAR	APR	MAY	JUN

Cultural Recommendations

LIGHT: 2500–3500 fc. Light levels are lowest in summer when clear days are rare.

TEMPERATURES: Summer days average 84°F (29°C), and nights average 71–72°F (22°C), with a diurnal range of 12–13°F (7°C).

HUMIDITY: Near 85% in summer. Humidity decreases to 75–80% in autumn, and to near 60% in late winter and early spring.

WATER: Conditions are very wet for 5 months in late spring and summer, very dry for 4–5 months in late autumn and winter, with short transition periods in autumn and spring. Cultivated plants should be kept evenly moist from late spring to early autumn, but water should be gradually reduced in autumn after new growths mature.

FERTILIZER: ¼–½ recommended strength, applied weekly. A high-nitrogen fertilizer is beneficial from spring to midsummer, but a fertilizer high in phosphates should be used in late summer and autumn. Summer growth should be rapid to improve flowering the following year.

REST PERIOD: Winter days average 69–72°F (20–22°C), and nights average 45–49°F (7–9°C), with a diurnal range of 23–25°F (13–14°C). Cultivated plants need at least a short, cool, dry rest with reduced fertilizer after the deciduous leaves drop. In the habitat, the dry period is 4–5 months long; but for 3 months, the high humidity indicates that some additional moisture is available from heavy dew. Therefore, conditions are extremely dry for only 1–2 months. Cultivated plants should be allowed to dry out between waterings in winter, but they should not remain dry for extended periods. Occasional early morning mistings between waterings, especially on warm, sunny days, may help prevent the plants from becoming too dry. Fertilizer should be eliminated until water is increased in spring. In the habitat, light is much higher in winter.

GROWING MEDIA: Plants are best mounted on tree-fern slabs to accommodate their semipendent growth habit, but large amounts of water must be provided and high humidity maintained in summer. *D. aduncum* has fine roots and is healthiest in a rapidly draining medium such as osmunda, shredded tree-fern fiber, or fine to medium fir bark. Hanging the plant from the rafters in a greenhouse allows it to droop naturally, showing the flowers to best advantage. Repotting is best done when new roots begin to grow.

MISCELLANEOUS NOTES: The bloom season shown in the climate table is based on cultivation records. Collected plants are dried and used in Chinese medicine. Plants grow over a wide range of habitat and adapt to a variety of conditions.

Plant and Flower Information

PLANT SIZE AND TYPE: A 12–24 in. (30–60 cm) sympodial epiphyte.

PSEUDOBULB: 12–24 in. (30–60 cm) long. The slender canes are uniform in diameter along their entire length. They are pendulous, zigzag, and appear to branch as new growths emerge from nodes on mature stems. This growth habit often results in a somewhat straggly looking plant.

LEAVES: 4–6 per growth. The stems are leafy near the apex. The deciduous leaves are elliptic-lanceolate, 2.0–3.5 in. (5–9 cm) long, with a thin texture.

INFLORESCENCE: 2.8 in. (7 cm) long. Plants normally produce many, short, zigzag racemes from the upper nodes of mature, leafless stems. The flowers on a single pseudobulb may be in full flower, while the buds on another cane are just developing. As a result, the plants are often in bloom for about 3 months.

FLOWERS: 3–5 per inflorescence. The long-lived, fragrant blossoms are 1.0–1.4 in. (2.5–3.5 cm) across and open fully. The semitransparent sepals and petals, which are broad and overlap at the base, are usually white or pink, often tipped with darker pink. Plants from India may bear smaller, pale purple flowers whose color deepens with age. All segments are pointed at the tips. The elliptic lip is broad but appears smaller because it is cupped. The hooked, sharply pointed tip is often a paler color. The lip is pubescent at the apex and along the center line, with a large, glossy callus near the base. The anther cap is dark purple. The blossoms are similar to *D. hercoglossum* Rchb. f. which differs in having the disk completely covered with hairs.

HYBRIDIZING NOTES: Chromosome counts are 2n = 38 (ref. 152, 154, 188) and 2n = 40 (ref. 153, 154, 542).

REFERENCES: 12, 36, 38, 46, 152, 153, 154, 163, 167, 179, 188, 190, 196, 202, 208, 210, 216, 254, 266, 317, 362, 369, 376, 414, 430, 445, 448, 454, 455, 505, 524, 528, 541, 542, 570.

PHOTOS/DRAWINGS: 38, 210, 362, *430, 454.*

Dendrobium aegle Ridley. See *D. erosum* (Blume) Lindley.
REFERENCES: 75, 200, 254, 270, 271, 395, 402, 454, 455. PHOTOS/DRAWINGS: *75, 270.*

Dendrobium aemulans Schlechter. See *D. erosum* (Blume) Lindley.
REFERENCES: 92, 219, 254, 270, 271, 304, 437, 444, 445, 486, 516.

Dendrobium aemulum R. Brown

ORIGIN/HABITAT: Endemic to Australia. *D. aemulum* grows from southeastern New South Wales to northeastern Queensland. Plants occur in the lowlands and mountains to 3950 ft. (1200 m), but they are uncommon on the coastal plain. Plants usually grow on trees in humid areas along streams in open forests, but they are also found in rainforests.

CLIMATE: Station #94576, Brisbane, Australia, Lat. 27.4°S, Long. 153.1°E, at 17 ft. (5 m). Temperatures are calculated for an elevation of 2000 ft. (610 m), resulting in probable extremes of 103°F (40°C) and 28°F (−2°C).

N/HEMISPHERE	JAN	FEB	MAR	APR	MAY	JUN	JUL	AUG	SEP	OCT	NOV	DEC
°F AVG MAX	61	64	69	73	75	78	78	78	75	72	67	62
°F AVG MIN	42	43	48	53	57	60	62	61	59	54	49	44
DIURNAL RANGE	19	21	21	20	18	18	16	17	16	18	18	18
RAIN/INCHES	2.2	1.9	1.9	2.5	3.7	5.0	6.4	6.3	5.7	3.7	2.8	2.6
HUMIDITY/%	62	59	58	57	59	59	63	65	66	64	64	64
BLOOM SEASON	**	***	**	*								
DAYS CLR @ 10AM	17	20	18	11	12	9	5	4	9	14	18	16
DAYS CLR @ 4PM	15	16	15	12	14	12	8	5	8	10	14	14
RAIN/MM	56	48	48	64	94	127	163	160	145	94	71	66
°C AVG MAX	16.4	18.0	20.8	23.0	24.1	25.8	25.8	25.8	24.1	22.5	19.7	16.9
°C AVG MIN	5.8	6.4	9.1	11.9	14.1	15.8	16.9	16.4	15.3	12.5	9.7	6.9
DIURNAL RANGE	10.6	11.6	11.7	11.1	10.0	10.0	8.9	9.4	8.8	10.0	10.0	10.0
S/HEMISPHERE	JUL	AUG	SEP	OCT	NOV	DEC	JAN	FEB	MAR	APR	MAY	JUN

Cultural Recommendations

LIGHT: 3500–4500 fc. Light should be as high as possible, short of burning the leaves. In the habitat, more than half the days are clear each month except during the summer rainy season when skies are clear about 30% of the time. The smallest forms of *D. aemulum* grow in open forests exposed to high light, but the more robust forms tend to grow in shadier habitats.

TEMPERATURES: Summer days average near 78°F (26°C), and nights average 60–62°F (16–17°C), with a diurnal range of 16–18°F (9–10°C). *D. aemulum* also grows in the lowlands, where temperatures may be 5–7°F (3–4°C) warmer than indicated in the climate table.

HUMIDITY: Near 65% most of the year, dropping to 55–60% in winter and spring. However, values are probably greater in the moist, shady habitat. Growers recommend strong air circulation.

WATER: Rainfall is moderate in summer and autumn but is somewhat lower in winter and early spring. However, more water is probably available in the habitat than is indicated by the climate from the low elevation weather station. Cultivated plants need to dry only slightly between waterings from late spring into early autumn. Water should be gradually reduced in late autumn.

FERTILIZER: ¼–½ recommended strength, applied weekly. A high-nitrogen fertilizer is beneficial from spring to midsummer, but a fertilizer high in phosphates should be used in late summer and autumn.

REST PERIOD: Winter days average 61–69°F (16–21°C), and nights average 42–48°F (6–9°C), with a diurnal range of 19–21°F (11–12°C). In cultivation, water should be reduced so that the plants are kept only barely moist until growth resumes in spring. Fertilizer should be reduced or eliminated. Growers indicate that distinct seasonal variation is essential for plant health.

GROWING MEDIA: Plants are best mounted on cork slabs or rough-barked hardwood. If mounted, the plants need daily watering and high humidity in summer. Plants are sometimes grown in clay pots filled with a rapidly draining medium, but most growers report that plants decline when potted. Remounting is best done in early spring, immediately after flowering.

MISCELLANEOUS NOTES: The bloom season shown in the climate table is based on cultivation records. Several plant forms are recognized, and variations are identified by the habitat in which they originate. Thus, they may be identified as the ironbark form, which has cream or white flowers and short, chunky, crowded yellowish stems that may become purplish brown. The brush box form tends to be pendent and grows in heavy shade on *Tristania* species. It has tall slender stems which radiate in a circle. The rainforest form has stout stems. The Casuarina form has short, stout, prominently ribbed, dark stems. The Callitris form has slender pseudobulbs and small, greenish cream blossoms.

Plant and Flower Information

PLANT SIZE AND TYPE: A highly variable, 3–12 in. (8–30 cm) sympodial epiphyte, which occasionally grows lithophytically.

PSEUDOBULB: 2–12 in. (5–30 cm) long. The stems, which vary from short and stout to long and thin, may be green, yellowish, or dark reddish brown when grown in high light. The canes become hard and ridged during the dry season. Small plants are most often erect, but plants with long stems often hang in a tangled disarray. The pseudobulbs, which have 6 nodes, are narrowest near the roots before beginning to swell just above the base. The plant slowly forms a clump.

LEAVES: 2–4 at the apex of each growth. Leaves are frequently about 2 in. (5 cm) long, but they vary with plant size. The leaves are normally ovate to lanceolate, rigid, leathery, and glossy. They are commonly dark green, but if the plants grow in high light, the leaves may be pale dull green.

INFLORESCENCE: 2–4 in. (5–10 cm) long. Each season, old and new stems produce 1 or more racemes which emerge from nodes near the apex. Each pseudobulb may produce a total of about 4 spikes over a period of time.

FLOWERS: 5–7 per inflorescence is common, but spikes may produce 1–20 blooms. The crystalline, spidery flowers are 1.0–1.6 in. (2.5–4.0 cm) across. They have a sweet but delicate fragrance. Sepals are somewhat wider than the petals but both are slender. The segments are normally white or cream, but some clones have blossoms that are suffused with rose or stained with yellow near the apex. Sepals and petals often turn pink before withering. The lip, which is broader and shorter than other segments, is accented with purple markings on the sidelobes and 3 wavy yellow ridges on the midlobe. Individual flowers last about 2 weeks. Flower size and form are highly variable.

HYBRIDIZING NOTES: Chromosome count is 2n = 38 (ref. 151, 154, 187, 188). When used in hybridizing, the narrow sepals and petals tend to be dominant.

REFERENCES: 23, 36, 67, 105, 151, 154, 179, 187, 188, 190, 210, 216, 240, 254, 262, 277, 291, 312, 317, 325, 390, 421, 430, 445, 495, 527, 533, 541, 544.

PHOTOS/DRAWINGS: 105, 210, *240, 291, 312,* 325, *390, 430, 533, 544.*

Dendrobium aeries Hort. See *D. aries* J. J. Smith. REFERENCES: 190.

Dendrobium affine (Decaisne) Steudel

AKA: *Onychium affine* Decaisne, *Dendrobium bigibbum* F. Mueller not Lindley, *D. dicuphum* F. Mueller, *D. dicuphum* F. Mueller var. *album* Hort. ex E. C. Cooper, and *D. dicuphum* F. Mueller var. *grandiflorum* Rupp and Hunt, *D. leucolophotum* Rchb. f., *D. urvillei* Finet. The name *D. dicuphum* has been used to register some hybrids.

ORIGIN/HABITAT: Northern Australia, New Guinea, and the islands of Timor, Seram, and Tanimbar. Plants grow on paperbark trees at low elevations, usually exposed to high light. They are often seen in moist areas such as swamps, small pockets of rainforest, or in trees overhanging streams or lagoons. They also grow at the edges of desert or harsh country, but they do not survive droughts in this habitat.

CLIMATE: Station #94120, Darwin, Australia, Lat. 12.4°S, Long. 130.9°E, at 104 ft. (32 m). Record extreme temperatures are 105°F (41°C) and 55°F (13°C).

N/HEMISPHERE	JAN	FEB	MAR	APR	MAY	JUN	JUL	AUG	SEP	OCT	NOV	DEC
°F AVG MAX	87	89	91	93	94	92	90	90	91	92	91	88
°F AVG MIN	67	70	74	77	78	78	77	77	77	76	73	69
DIURNAL RANGE	20	19	17	16	16	14	13	13	14	16	18	19
RAIN/INCHES	0.0	0.1	0.5	2.0	4.7	9.4	15.2	12.3	10.0	3.8	0.0	0.1
HUMIDITY/%	52	54	57	59	63	69	75	76	73	62	55	54
BLOOM SEASON	*	*	*	*	*	*	*	*	*	*	*	*
DAYS CLR @ 9AM	20	19	17	9	5	3	4	1	6	7	17	17
DAYS CLR @ 3PM	17	19	18	14	6	3	2	1	3	3	13	15
RAIN/MM	0	3	13	51	119	239	386	312	254	97	0	3
°C AVG MAX	30.6	31.7	32.8	33.9	34.4	33.3	32.2	32.2	32.8	33.3	32.8	31.1
°C AVG MIN	19.4	21.1	23.3	25.0	25.6	25.6	25.0	25.0	25.0	24.4	22.8	20.6
DIURNAL RANGE	11.2	10.6	9.5	8.9	8.8	7.7	7.2	7.2	7.8	8.9	10.0	10.5
S/HEMISPHERE	JUL	AUG	SEP	OCT	NOV	DEC	JAN	FEB	MAR	APR	MAY	JUN

Cultural Recommendations

LIGHT: 3500–4500 fc. Light should be as high as possible, short of burning the leaves. Growers recommend placing plants high in the greenhouse for maximum light.

TEMPERATURES: Summer days average 90–92°F (32–33°C), and nights average 77–78°F (25–26°C), with a diurnal range of 13–14°F (7–8°C). The diurnal temperature range and seasonal fluctuations are important for *D. affine*. It is reportedly very difficult to grow in Singapore's uniform climate.

HUMIDITY: 70–75% in summer, falling to 55–60% from autumn to spring at the weather station. However, the plants grow in swampy or other moist habitats where humidity is higher. Growers indicate that excellent air movement is critically important for cultivated plants.

WATER: Rainfall is heavy during the growing season. The rainfall pattern is wet/dry, with an extended dry season. Cultivated plants should be kept evenly moist while actively growing with only a slight drying between waterings. Water should be gradually reduced after new growths mature in autumn, however.

FERTILIZER: ¼–½ recommended strength. A balanced fertilizer should be applied weekly to biweekly.

REST PERIOD: Winter days average 87–91°F (31–33°C), and nights average 67–74°F (19–23°C), with a diurnal range of 17–20°F (9–11°C). Growers report that winter temperatures should not fall below 60°F (16°C). Rainfall is very low from midautumn to early spring. Cultivated plants decline unless given a long dry season, and some growers withhold water completely during the winter rest. Fertilizer should be eliminated until watering is increased in spring. Light should be as high as possible short of burning the foliage.

GROWING MEDIA: Plants are healthiest mounted on cork slabs; but water must be applied at least once a day in summer, and humidity must be high. If plants are potted, the smallest possible pot should be used. Clay pots are preferable to plastic ones, and a rapidly draining medium should be used. Repotting is best done in early spring when new roots begin to grow.

MISCELLANEOUS NOTES: Cultivated plants bloom from late spring through winter, but in the habitat, flowering occurs in autumn and winter at the end of the wet season.

Plant and Flower Information

PLANT SIZE AND TYPE: A 12–24 in. (30–60 cm) erect sympodial epiphyte or lithophyte.

PSEUDOBULB: 10–24 in. (25–60 cm) long, rarely as small as 3 in. (8 cm). The tapered pseudobulbs are most often erect, pale brown, and strongly ribbed and furrowed. They are usually stout and nearly conical, though they are sometimes spindly. They are covered with dry sheaths.

LEAVES: 2–10 per growth. The rigid, leathery leaves are held near the apex of the stem. They are 1–7 in. (3–18 cm) long, ovate-lanceolate to oblong, and often decurved. Leaves may be red along the margin. They may persist for several years or be completely deciduous depending on the environmental conditions.

INFLORESCENCE: 4–20 in. (10–50 cm) long. Inflorescences arise from the apical nodes of both leafy and leafless stems. The racemes are slender and nodding with all flowers facing one direction. Blossoms may be crowded or widely spaced.

FLOWERS: 10–20 per inflorescence. The waxy, long-lived flowers are 1.2–1.6 in. (3–4 cm) across. They open in succession over a month or more. The overlapping sepals and petals are clear, dead white (rarely pink), with green on the outside and at the base of the lip. The sidelobes are marked with 3 maroon or magenta lines. The callus consists of 5 fringed or raised ridges. The column is pale green. Blossoms normally open fully, but some clones may have self-pollinating flowers which do not open properly.

HYBRIDIZING NOTES: Chromosome counts as *D. dicuphum* are 2n = 38 (ref. 504, 580) and 2n = 39 (ref. 151, 154, 187, 188). When used in hybridizing, *D. affine* tends to decrease cane size, increase the number of flowers, lengthen flower life, and improve flower substance, even giving a waxy feel. It often widens sepals and petals, thereby improving flower form. The markings on the lip are frequently passed on to the progeny. *D. affine* is known to hybridize naturally with *D. canaliculatum* R. Brown, but hybrids are uncommon.

REFERENCES: 25, 44, 67, 105, 118, 151, 154, 179, 187, 188, 190, 200, 216, 240, 254, 262, 310, 317, 325, 345, 351, 421, 470, 504, 526, 533, 580.

PHOTOS/DRAWINGS: 240, *262*, 325, *345, 350, 351, 430, 533*.

Dendrobium agamensis J. J. Smith. Sometimes spelled *D. agamense*, it was transferred to *Ephemerantha* by Hunt and Summerhayes, which is now considered synonymous with *Flickingeria*. REFERENCES: 213, 224, 230, 449.

Dendrobium agathodaemonis J. J. Smith. See *D. cuthbertsonii* F. Mueller. REFERENCES: 144, 220, 254, 385, 430, 437, 445, 470, 538. PHOTOS/DRAWINGS: 538.

Dendrobium aggregatum H. B. and K not Roxburgh. Now considered a synonym of *Ornithidium aggregatum* (Kunth) Rchb. f. REFERENCES: 45, 214, 216, 254, 447.

Dendrobium aggregatum Roxburgh not H. B. and K. See *D. lindleyi* Steudel. The International Orchid Commission (ref. 236) registers hybrids under the name *D. aggregatum* and plants are commonly

cultivated under this name. *D. aggregatum* var. *jenkinsii* (Wallich ex Lindley) King and Pantling is now considered a synonym of *D. jenkinsii* Wallich ex Lindley. Massive confusion surrounds the use of the name *D. aggregatum*. For a discussion of the nomenclature problems, see Seidenfaden (ref. 454). REFERENCES: 6, 36, 38, 46, 151, 154, 157, 179, 188, 190, 196, 200, 202, 216, 236, 245, 254, 266, 273, 317, 326, 330, 369, 389, 395, 402, 414, 430, 445, 448, 452, 454, 458, 461, 504, 541, 557, 568, 570, 580. PHOTOS/DRAWINGS: 46, 245, *356, 389, 446, 458, 568.*

Dendrobium agrostophylloides Schlechter

ORIGIN/HABITAT: Northern Papua New Guinea. Plants grow south of Madang on forest trees in the Kani Range at about 3300 ft. (1000 m).

CLIMATE: Station #94010, Goroka, Papua New Guinea, Lat. 6.1°S, Long. 145.4°E, at 5141 ft. (1567 m). Temperatures are calculated for an elevation of 3300 ft. (1000 m), resulting in probable extremes of 93°F (34°C) and 49°F (10°C).

N/HEMISPHERE	JAN	FEB	MAR	APR	MAY	JUN	JUL	AUG	SEP	OCT	NOV	DEC
°F AVG MAX	82	83	84	85	85	84	85	84	84	84	85	83
°F AVG MIN	62	63	63	63	64	65	65	65	66	65	65	63
DIURNAL RANGE	20	20	21	22	21	19	20	19	18	19	20	20
RAIN/INCHES	2.1	2.8	4.6	5.9	6.6	9.3	9.1	10.1	10.7	8.3	4.6	2.0
HUMIDITY/%	70	67	67	67	67	71	72	73	74	71	70	70
BLOOM SEASON					*							
DAYS CLR	N/A											
RAIN/MM	53	71	117	150	168	236	231	257	272	211	117	51
°C AVG MAX	27.9	28.4	29.0	29.5	29.5	29.0	29.5	29.0	29.0	29.0	29.5	28.4
°C AVG MIN	16.7	17.3	17.3	17.3	17.9	18.4	18.4	18.4	19.0	18.4	18.4	17.3
DIURNAL RANGE	11.2	11.1	11.7	12.2	11.6	10.6	11.1	10.6	10.0	10.6	11.1	11.1
S/HEMISPHERE	JUL	AUG	SEP	OCT	NOV	DEC	JAN	FEB	MAR	APR	MAY	JUN

Cultural Recommendations

LIGHT: 2000–3000 fc.

TEMPERATURES: Throughout the year, days average 82–85°F (28–30°C), and nights average 62–65°F (17–18°C), with a diurnal range of 18–22°F (10–12°C). Average highs and lows vary only slightly during the year, indicating that plants may not tolerate wide seasonal fluctuations.

HUMIDITY: 70–75% in summer and autumn, dropping to 65–70% in winter and spring.

WATER: Rainfall is moderate to heavy most of the year but is relatively low for 2–3 months in winter. However, additional moisture is available from dew, fog, and mist, even during periods when rainfall is low. Cultivated plants should be kept moist but not soggy. Additional early morning mistings between waterings are often beneficial, especially on warm, bright, sunny days.

FERTILIZER: ¼–½ recommended strength. A balanced fertilizer should be applied weekly to biweekly throughout the year.

REST PERIOD: Growing temperatures should be maintained all year. Water should be reduced in winter. Plants should dry slightly between waterings, but they should never be allowed to dry out completely. Fertilizer should be reduced or eliminated until water is increased in spring. In the habitat, winter light may be slightly higher.

GROWING MEDIA: Plants may be potted in any open, rapidly draining medium. A small, shallow pot is recommended. Repotting should be done as soon as new roots begin to grow.

MISCELLANEOUS NOTES: The bloom season shown in the climate table is based on collection records.

Plant and Flower Information

PLANT SIZE AND TYPE: A robust, 20–28 in. (50–70 cm) sympodial epiphyte.

PSEUDOBULB: 17–24 in. (43–60 cm) long. The simple, flattened growths arise from a very short rhizome. The stems are densely leafy.

LEAVES: Many. The linear leaves, which may be erect or suberect, are 3–4 in. (8–10 cm) long. The are unequally bilobed.

FLOWERS: 1 per inflorescence. The inverted flowers are 0.5 in. (1.3 cm) across. The oblong sepals and petals are glistening brownish or dark cherry-red. They are recurved at the tips. The 3-lobed lip is roundly oblong with small sidelobes.

REFERENCES: 221, 437, 445.

PHOTOS/DRAWINGS: 437.

Dendrobium agrostophyllum F. Mueller

AKA: *D. muellerianum* Schlechter.

ORIGIN/HABITAT: Australia. Endemic to northeastern Queensland between the Burdekin and Annan Rivers where plants are common. They usually grow on upper tree limbs in cool cloudforests at 2950–4250 ft. (900–1300 m). Plants are occasionally found at lower elevations in gorges or gullies where moist conditions are similar to cloudforests. However, in some locations, plants grow near the ground on small trees and rocks in somewhat exposed positions.

CLIMATE: Station #94295, Ingham, Australia, Lat. 18.7°S, Long. 146.2°E, at 45 ft. (14 m). Temperatures are calculated for an elevation of 3300 ft. (1000 m), resulting in probable extremes of 99°F (37°C) and 28°F (−2°C).

N/HEMISPHERE	JAN	FEB	MAR	APR	MAY	JUN	JUL	AUG	SEP	OCT	NOV	DEC
°F AVG MAX	64	66	69	72	74	76	76	76	75	73	70	66
°F AVG MIN	48	50	55	60	63	65	65	64	62	59	54	50
DIURNAL RANGE	16	16	14	12	11	11	11	12	13	14	16	16
RAIN/INCHES	0.6	0.5	0.7	1.3	1.9	5.4	10.9	11.2	7.2	3.3	1.3	1.4
HUMIDITY/%	61	61	62	64	66	70	72	71	70	64	63	63
BLOOM SEASON	*	*	*							*	*	
DAYS CLR @ 10AM	16	18	15	10	7	5	5	9	13	14	15	
DAYS CLR @ 4PM	16	18	20	20	17	15	8	5	7	11	14	15
RAIN/MM	15	13	18	33	48	137	277	284	183	84	33	36
°C AVG MAX	18.0	19.1	20.7	22.4	23.5	24.6	24.6	24.6	24.1	23.0	21.3	19.1
°C AVG MIN	9.1	10.2	13.0	15.7	17.4	18.5	18.5	18.0	16.8	15.2	12.4	10.2
DIURNAL RANGE	8.9	8.9	7.7	6.7	6.1	6.1	6.1	6.6	7.3	7.8	8.9	8.9
S/HEMISPHERE	JUL	AUG	SEP	OCT	NOV	DEC	JAN	FEB	MAR	APR	MAY	JUN

Cultural Recommendations

LIGHT: 2500–3500 fc.

TEMPERATURES: Summer days average 76°F (25°C), and nights average 64–65°F (18–19°C), with a diurnal range of 11–12°F (6–7°C).

HUMIDITY: 70–80% year-round. In the cloudforest habitat, humidity averages are probably greater than indicated in the climate table.

WATER: Rainfall is heavy for 4–5 months in summer and early autumn but is much lower in winter. In the orchid habitat, however, additional moisture is usually available from mist and heavy dews, even when rainfall is reduced. Plants should be kept moist with only slight drying allowed between waterings from late spring to early autumn, but water should be gradually reduced in late autumn. *D. agrostophyllum* grows in very wet habitats and requires more moisture than most Australian species.

FERTILIZER: ¼–½ recommended strength, applied weekly. A high-nitrogen fertilizer is beneficial from spring to midsummer, but a fertilizer high in phosphates should be used in late summer and autumn.

REST PERIOD: Winter days average 64–66°F (18–19°C), and nights average 48–50°F (9–10°C), with a diurnal range of 16°F (9°C). In the orchids' microclimate, more moisture is available during the dry season than is indicated in the climate table. For cultivated plants, water should be reduced for 3–4 months in winter. However, plants should not be allowed to dry out completely or to remain dry for long periods. Fertilizer should be reduced or eliminated until plants begin actively growing. Winter light should be as high as possible, short of burning the leaves.

GROWING MEDIA: Plants should be mounted on slabs of tree-fern fiber because the growth habit is somewhat rambling. Water must be provided daily in summer, and high humidity should be maintained all year.

Australian growers report that this species requires more water than most Australian *Dendrobium* and cork slabs do not make good mounts as they dry out too rapidly in summer. *D. agrostophyllum* is not particularly well suited for pot culture because of its rambling growth habit, but hanging pots or baskets may be used. If plants are potted, an open, rapidly draining medium should be used. Repotting is best done immediately after flowering or when new roots are growing.

MISCELLANEOUS NOTES: Moderate temperatures, strong air movement, and high humidity levels are very important for this species. The bloom season shown in the climate table is based on reports from the habitat. Growers indicate that plants may bloom in spring and fall in cultivation. This slow-growing, very hardy plant has tough, wiry roots. Collectors note that above 2950 ft. (900 m), plants are almost always lithophytic. Those from higher elevations tend to be more robust, flower later in the season, and produce larger flowers.

Plant and Flower Information

PLANT SIZE AND TYPE: A variable, 6–24 in. (15–60 cm) sympodial epiphyte or lithophyte.

PSEUDOBULB: 6–24 in. (15–60 cm) long, rarely to 35 in. (90 cm). The stem-like pseudobulbs, which arise from a creeping rhizome, are spaced 0.4–2.4 in. (1–6 cm) apart. The rhizome normally grows in a straight line and only rarely branches, thus forming a slender, creeping row of stems. New growths require 2–3 years to mature.

LEAVES: 20 per growth. The upper half of the pseudobulb has thin, grasslike leaves that are 1–4 in. (2.5–10.0 cm) long.

INFLORESCENCE: 2 in. (5 cm). A short raceme arises near the apex of the stem. Older growths may bloom for several seasons, but during a season, only a single node of each stem produces an inflorescence.

FLOWERS: 2–6, rarely 10, per inflorescence. The fragrant, waxy blossoms are 0.6–1.0 in. (1.5–2.5 cm) across and do not open fully. Sepals and petals are buttercup to canary yellow and may be pale or bright. The yellow lip is marked with purplish brown. The flowers last about 3 weeks.

HYBRIDIZING NOTES: Chromosome count is 2n = 38 (ref. 151, 154, 187, 188). When used as a parent, the lip shape, growth habit, and tolerance for cool temperatures tend to be dominant characteristics.

REFERENCES: 23, 24, 67, 105, 151, 154, 179, 187, 188, 216, 240, 254, 262, 263, 264, 389, 390, 421, 445, 533.

PHOTOS/DRAWINGS: 105, 240, *262, 389, 390, 533.*

Dendrobium agusanense Ames

ORIGIN/HABITAT: The Philippines. Plants are found in Agusan and Surigao Provinces in northeastern Mindanao Island. They grow at about 1000 ft. (300 m) in very humid, densely shaded places, often on moss-covered limbs overhanging streams.

CLIMATE: Station #98752, Butuan, Mindanao Island, Philippines, Lat. 8.9°N, Long. 125.5°E, at 148 ft. (45 m). Temperatures are calculated for an elevation of 1000 ft. (300 m). Record extreme temperatures are not available for this location.

N/HEMISPHERE	JAN	FEB	MAR	APR	MAY	JUN	JUL	AUG	SEP	OCT	NOV	DEC
°F AVG MAX	84	84	86	87	89	87	86	87	87	86	85	83
°F AVG MIN	69	69	70	71	72	72	71	71	71	71	71	70
DIURNAL RANGE	15	15	16	16	17	15	15	16	16	15	14	13
RAIN/INCHES	2.0	4.4	2.4	2.1	2.5	4.4	6.3	1.8	3.4	6.5	5.1	4.6
HUMIDITY/%	N/A											
BLOOM SEASON												
DAYS CLR	N/A											
RAIN/MM	51	112	61	53	64	112	160	46	86	165	130	117
°C AVG MAX	29.0	29.0	30.1	30.7	31.8	30.7	30.1	30.7	30.7	30.1	29.5	28.4
°C AVG MIN	20.7	20.7	21.2	21.8	22.3	22.3	21.8	21.8	21.8	21.8	21.8	21.2
DIURNAL RANGE	8.3	8.3	8.9	8.9	9.5	8.4	8.3	8.9	8.9	8.3	7.7	7.2
S/HEMISPHERE	JUL	AUG	SEP	OCT	NOV	DEC	JAN	FEB	MAR	APR	MAY	JUN

Cultural Recommendations

LIGHT: 1200–2500 fc.

TEMPERATURES: Throughout the year, days average 83–89°F (28–32°C), and nights average 69–72°F (21–22°C), with a diurnal range of 13–17°F (7–10°C). The warmest weather occurs in spring.

HUMIDITY: Information is not available for this location. However, reports from nearby stations indicate that averages of 75–85% are common throughout the region.

WATER: Rainfall is moderate most of the year. The driest period occurs in winter and early spring, with a short, secondary dry period in late summer. Cultivated plants should be kept moist with only slight drying allowed between waterings from late spring to autumn.

FERTILIZER: ¼–½ recommended strength. A balanced fertilizer should be applied weekly to biweekly throughout the year.

REST PERIOD: Growing temperatures should be maintained year-round. Water should be reduced in winter and early spring. Plants should be allowed to become somewhat dry between waterings, but they should never dry out completely or remain dry for long periods. Fertilizer should be reduced or eliminated until plants begin actively growing in spring.

GROWING MEDIA: Mounting plants on tree-fern or cork slabs accommodates their pendulous growth habit. However, humidity must be high and plants must be watered at least once a day in summer. If plants cannot be mounted, hanging pots or baskets may be filled with an open, fast-draining medium. Repotting may be done anytime new roots are actively growing.

MISCELLANEOUS NOTES: The bloom season shown in the climate table is based on collection reports.

Plant and Flower Information

PLANT SIZE AND TYPE: A very large, 39–157 in. (100–400 cm) sympodial epiphyte that may reach a length of 197 in. (500 cm).

PSEUDOBULB: 39–157 in. (100–400 cm) long. The stems are pendent.

LEAVES: Many. The distichous, lanceolate leaves are about 4 in. (10 cm) long.

INFLORESCENCE: Very short. Inflorescences emerge through the leaf sheaths opposite the leaves.

FLOWERS: 2 per inflorescence. Blossoms are 0.8–1.2 in. (2–3 cm) across, which is extremely small for the plant size. The fleshy, incurved sepals and petals are green with purple spots. The heaviest spotting occurs on the lip.

REFERENCES: 15, 223, 296, 536.

Dendrobium ajoebii J. J. Smith. Now considered a synonym of *Diplocaulobium ajoebii* (J. J. Smith) Hunt and Summerhayes. REFERENCES: 213, 221, 230, 470, 475.

Dendrobium alabense J. J. Wood

ORIGIN/HABITAT: Sabah (North Borneo). Plants grow on Mt. Kinabalu and other peaks in the Crocker Range at 5400–7550 ft. (1650–2300 m). They are usually found in open areas near ridge summits growing in both scrub and mossy forests.

CLIMATE: Station #49613, Tambunan, Sabah, Lat. 5.7°N, Long. 116.4°E, at 1200 ft. (366 m). Temperatures are calculated for an elevation of 6500 ft. (1980 m), resulting in probable extremes of 81°F (27°C) and 37°F (3°C).

N/HEMISPHERE	JAN	FEB	MAR	APR	MAY	JUN	JUL	AUG	SEP	OCT	NOV	DEC
°F AVG MAX	69	70	72	73	73	72	72	72	72	71	70	69
°F AVG MIN	50	48	49	50	51	50	49	49	50	50	50	51
DIURNAL RANGE	19	22	23	23	22	22	23	23	22	21	20	18
RAIN/INCHES	5.8	3.7	5.8	7.5	8.2	7.3	5.1	4.9	6.4	7.0	6.8	6.0
HUMIDITY/%	N/A											
BLOOM SEASON					*	*						
DAYS CLR	N/A											
RAIN/MM	147	94	147	190	208	185	130	124	163	178	173	152
°C AVG MAX	20.3	20.8	21.9	22.5	22.5	21.9	21.9	21.9	21.9	21.4	20.8	20.3
°C AVG MIN	9.7	8.6	9.2	9.7	10.3	9.7	9.2	9.2	9.7	9.7	9.7	10.3
DIURNAL RANGE	10.6	12.2	12.7	12.8	12.2	12.2	12.7	12.7	12.2	11.7	11.1	10.0
S/HEMISPHERE	JUL	AUG	SEP	OCT	NOV	DEC	JAN	FEB	MAR	APR	MAY	JUN

Cultural Recommendations

LIGHT: 2500–3500 fc.

TEMPERATURES: Throughout the year, days average 69–73°F (20–23°C), and nights average 48–51°F (9–10°C), with a diurnal range of 18–23°F (10–13°C). Average high temperatures fluctuate only 5°F (3°C), and average lows vary only 4°F (2°C) all year. The daily temperature range is much greater than seasonal temperature fluctuations.

HUMIDITY: Averages not available for this location. However, records from nearby stations indicate that values are probably 80–85% year-round. Excellent air circulation should be provided.

WATER: Rainfall is moderate to heavy all year, with a short drier period in winter. Cultivated plants should be kept moist with only slight drying allowed between waterings.

FERTILIZER: $\frac{1}{4}$–$\frac{1}{2}$ recommended strength. A balanced fertilizer should be applied weekly to biweekly throughout the year.

REST PERIOD: Growing conditions vary only slightly through the year. The diurnal range is slightly lower in winter, due to somewhat cooler days. In cultivation, water should be reduced somewhat in winter, especially for plants grown in the dark, short-day conditions common in temperate latitudes. Plants should never be allowed to dry out completely, however. Fertilizer should be decreased when water is reduced or if plants are not actively growing.

GROWING MEDIA: Plants may be mounted on cork or tree-fern slabs if high humidity is maintained and water is applied daily in summer. If plants are potted, any open, rapidly draining medium may be used. Repotting may be done anytime new roots are growing.

MISCELLANEOUS NOTES: The bloom season shown in the climate table is based on collection reports. Plants that produce flowers which last a single day commonly bloom several times during the year. Flowering usually occurs 7–14 days after a sudden 10°F (5°C) drop in daytime temperatures.

Plant and Flower Information

PLANT SIZE AND TYPE: A variable, 3–12 in. (8–30 cm) sympodial epiphyte. Each plant forms a dense clump. When grown in high light, plants are often less than 2 in. (5 cm) tall and become dark purple.

PSEUDOBULB: 0.6–1.2 in. (1.6–3.0 cm) long, occasionally smaller. Growths are pseudobulbous at the base. The upper portion of the stem is slender, flattened, branching, and covered by leaf sheaths. Growths are commonly purplish when young, becoming shiny and straw-yellow when mature.

LEAVES: 4–8 per growth. The linear leaves are 0.7–1.2 in. (1.8–3.0 cm) long.

INFLORESCENCE: Short. Inflorescences emerge from the uppermost nodes of leafless stems.

FLOWERS: 1 per inflorescence. The tiny flowers remain rather closed. Buds emerge from a tuft of bracts and open in succession, each lasting a single day. Sepals and petals are creamy white and lightly spotted with purple. The cream-colored lip is marked with a purple disk and stained with yellow at the base of the midlobe.

REFERENCES: 235, 590, 592.

PHOTOS/DRAWINGS: 590, *592*.

Dendrobium alagense Ames. Sometimes spelled *D. alagensis*, see *D. luzonense* Lindley. REFERENCES: 12, 220, 254, 296, 536.

Dendrobium alaticaulinum P. van Royen

ORIGIN/HABITAT: Northern Papua New Guinea. Plants are found near Keglsugl, about 65 miles (105 km) southwest of Madang, where they normally grow on forest trees at 9000–10,400 ft. (2750–3170 m).

CLIMATE: Botanical garden records, Laiagam, Papua New Guinea, Lat. 5.5°S, Long. 143.5°E, at 7218 ft. (2200 m). Temperatures are calculated for an elevation of 9500 ft. (2900 m), resulting in probable extremes of 83°F (29°C) and 24°F (–4°C).

N/HEMISPHERE	JAN	FEB	MAR	APR	MAY	JUN	JUL	AUG	SEP	OCT	NOV	DEC
°F AVG MAX	68	69	70	68	70	70	74	69	68	70	70	68
°F AVG MIN	47	46	47	47	48	48	47	48	50	49	48	48
DIURNAL RANGE	21	23	23	21	22	22	27	21	18	21	22	20
RAIN/INCHES	4.0	4.8	6.1	7.8	8.5	9.1	8.4	9.6	9.5	8.9	6.3	4.0
HUMIDITY/%	N/A											
BLOOM SEASON					*			*				
DAYS CLR	N/A											
RAIN/MM	102	122	155	198	216	231	213	244	241	226	160	102
°C AVG MAX	20.2	20.8	21.4	20.2	21.4	21.4	23.6	20.8	20.2	21.4	21.4	20.2
°C AVG MIN	8.6	8.0	8.6	8.6	9.1	9.1	8.6	9.1	10.2	9.7	9.1	9.1
DIURNAL RANGE	11.6	12.8	12.8	11.6	12.3	12.3	15.0	11.7	10.0	11.7	12.3	11.1
S/HEMISPHERE	JUL	AUG	SEP	OCT	NOV	DEC	JAN	FEB	MAR	APR	MAY	JUN

Cultural Recommendations

LIGHT: 1800–2500 fc.

TEMPERATURES: Throughout the year, days average 68–74°F (20–24°C), and nights average 46–50°F (8–10°C), with a diurnal range of 18–27°F (10–15°C).

HUMIDITY: Information is not available for this location. However, records from other stations in the region indicate that values are probably 70–80% year-round.

WATER: Rainfall is heavy throughout the year, but conditions are slightly drier for 3–4 months in winter. Cultivated plants should be kept moist.

FERTILIZER: $\frac{1}{4}$–$\frac{1}{2}$ recommended strength. A balanced fertilizer should be applied weekly to biweekly throughout the year.

REST PERIOD: Growing conditions should be maintained all year. Water and fertilizer should be reduced somewhat in winter, especially when plants are grown in the dark, short-day conditions common in temperate latitudes. Plants should dry slightly between waterings, but they should never be allowed to dry out completely. Water and fertilizer should be gradually increased when plants begin growing in spring.

GROWING MEDIA: Mounting plants on tree-fern slabs accommodates the pendent growth habit, but water must be applied at least once daily in summer and humidity must be high. When plants are potted, a mixture of fir bark, osmunda, or chopped tree-fern with moisture-retaining additives is recommended. The medium should be kept moist, but not soggy. A surface layer of sphagnum moss might be beneficial. Repotting may be done anytime new roots are growing.

MISCELLANEOUS NOTES: *D. alaticaulinum* is less demanding than many high-elevation species. Some growers consider it easy to grow, and seedlings have been known to bloom only 2 years out of flask. The bloom season shown in the climate table is based on 2 reports from cultivated plants.

Dendrobium alatum

Plant and Flower Information

PLANT SIZE AND TYPE: A 5–6 in. (13–15 cm) sympodial epiphyte.

PSEUDOBULB: 5 in. (13 cm) long. The slender, pendent stems are somewhat zigzag and sometimes branched. They are pale yellowish brown.

LEAVES: Many. Each growth is leafy along its entire length. The small, deciduous leaves are 0.5–0.7 in. (1.3–1.8 cm) long. They are ovate-lanceolate, dull dark green, thin, and spreading. The distichous leaves are twisted at the base.

INFLORESCENCE: 0.6 in. (1.5 cm) long. The tassel-like inflorescences emerge from nodes on leafless stems.

FLOWERS: 3–8 per inflorescence. The tiny flowers are 0.2 in. (0.4–0.5 cm) across. Sepals and petals may be more or less orange or pink at the base fading to off-white at the tips. The lip is scarlet. The spur is burnt-orange.

HYBRIDIZING NOTES: Chromosome count is $2n = 38$ (ref. 152, 153, 243, 273). *D. alaticaulinum* is known to hybridize naturally with *D. leucocyanum* T. M. Reeve to produce *D.* × *yengiliense* T. M. Reeve.

REFERENCES: 79, 95, 152, 153, 179, 233, 243, 273, 538, 552.

PHOTOS/DRAWINGS: 538, 552.

Dendrobium alatum Persoon. Now considered a synonym of *Maxillaria alata* Ruiz and Pavón. REFERENCES: 216, 254.

Dendrobium albayense Ames

ORIGIN/HABITAT: Widespread throughout the Philippine Islands. Collections are reported from Palawan, Samar, Mindanao, Negros, Luzon, and Leyte Islands. Plants usually grow in trees near swamps and in forests between sea level and 2950 ft. (0–900 m). In Albay Province, plants were collected on the northeastern side of Mt. Mayon. Gagnepain (ref. 266) indicated the plant is also found in southern Vietnam, but this distribution has not been included in recent literature.

CLIMATE: Station #98639, Bacolod, Negros Island, Philippines, Lat. 10.6°N, Long. 122.9°E, at 20 ft. (6 m). Temperatures are calculated for an elevation of 1500 ft. (460 m), resulting in probable extremes of 91°F (33°C) and 62°F (17°C).

N/HEMISPHERE	JAN	FEB	MAR	APR	MAY	JUN	JUL	AUG	SEP	OCT	NOV	DEC
°F AVG MAX	78	79	81	83	84	82	81	81	81	81	80	79
°F AVG MIN	68	68	69	70	72	72	71	71	71	71	70	69
DIURNAL RANGE	10	11	12	13	12	10	10	10	10	10	10	10
RAIN/INCHES	3.9	2.3	1.6	1.5	7.0	8.9	14.8	12.0	11.3	10.3	9.3	6.8
HUMIDITY/%	83	80	79	75	77	82	84	85	85	84	84	84
BLOOM SEASON	*	*	*	*	*				*	*	*	
DAYS CLR @ 8AM	5	5	8	10	4	2	2	1	1	4	5	4
DAYS CLR @ 2PM	3	4	8	11	4	1	1	0	1	2	4	4
RAIN/MM	99	58	41	38	178	226	376	305	287	262	236	173
°C AVG MAX	25.6	26.2	27.3	28.4	29.0	27.8	27.3	27.3	27.3	27.3	26.7	26.2
°C AVG MIN	20.1	20.1	20.6	21.2	22.3	22.3	21.7	21.7	21.7	21.7	21.2	20.6
DIURNAL RANGE	5.5	6.1	6.7	7.2	6.7	5.5	5.6	5.6	5.6	5.6	5.5	5.6
S/HEMISPHERE	JUL	AUG	SEP	OCT	NOV	DEC	JAN	FEB	MAR	APR	MAY	JUN

Cultural Recommendations

LIGHT: 2500–3500 fc.

TEMPERATURES: Throughout the year, days average 78–84°F (26–29°C), and nights average 68–72°F (20–22°C), with a diurnal range of 10–13°F (6–7°C).

HUMIDITY: 80–85% most of the year, but averages decrease to near 75% for 2–3 months in late winter and early spring.

WATER: Rainfall is moderate to heavy most of the year with a 2–3 month semidry period in late winter and early spring. Cultivated plants should never be allowed to dry out completely.

FERTILIZER: ¼–½ recommended strength. A balanced fertilizer should be applied weekly to biweekly throughout the year.

REST PERIOD: Growing temperatures should be maintained all year. Water should be reduced somewhat for cultivated plants for 2–3 months in late winter. They should be allowed to become slightly dry between waterings but should not remain dry for long. Fertilizer should be reduced until plants begin actively growing in spring. In the habitat, light is highest in winter and spring.

GROWING MEDIA: Plants may be mounted on cork or tree-fern slabs if humidity is high and water is applied at least once a day in summer. If plants are potted, any open, fast-draining medium may be used. Repotting is best done when new roots begin to grow or immediately after flowering.

MISCELLANEOUS NOTES: The bloom season shown in the climate table is based on collection reports.

Plant and Flower Information

PLANT SIZE AND TYPE: A 12 in. (30 cm) sympodial epiphyte.

PSEUDOBULB: 12 in. (30 cm) long.

LEAVES: The leaves are 0.6–1.2 in. (1.5–3.0 cm) long.

INFLORESCENCE: Short. Inflorescences emerge from a cushion of fibrous scales that cover the apical nodes opposite rudimentary leaves.

FLOWERS: The small, odorless flowers are white with purple and yellow stripes.

HYBRIDIZING NOTES: Chromosome count is $2n = 40$ (ref. 280, 504, 580).

REFERENCES: 12, 221, 266, 280, 296, 373, 448, 504, 536, 580.

Dendrobium albicolor Ridley. See *D. kentrophyllum* Hooker f. REFERENCES: 190, 254, 395, 454.

Dendrobium albidulum Thwaites ex Trimen. See *D. diodon* Rchb. f. REFERENCES: 216, 254.

Dendrobium albiflorum Ridley. Now considered a synonym of *Cadetia albiflora* (Ridley) Schlechter. REFERENCES: 218, 221, 254, 393, 437.

Dendrobium albiviride P. van Royen. See *D. vexillarius* J. J. Smith. REFERENCES: 233, 385, 538. PHOTOS/DRAWINGS: 538

Dendrobium albosanguineum Lindley

AKA: Sometimes spelled *D. albo-sanguineum*. The name *D. atrosanguineum* E. Morren and DeVos is considered a synonym.

ORIGIN/HABITAT: Burma and Thailand. In Burma, plants grow in the eastern mountain region from Inle Lake in the north to the Tenasserim district near the southern end of the panhandle bordering peninsular Thailand. They are also found in the mountains of northwestern Thailand along the Burma border. They usually grow in the tops of the tallest trees. *D. albosanguineum* is rare and may be well on the way to extinction due to deforestation and overcollecting. Collection reports do not include habitat elevation, which is estimated at 2000 ft. (610 m) in peninsular Burma and 1000 ft. (300 m) in Thailand. Therefore, the following climate data should be used with caution.

CLIMATE: Station #48103, Moulmein, Burma, Lat. 16.4°N, Long. 97.7°E, at 150 ft. (46 m). Temperatures are calculated for an estimated elevation of 2000 ft. (610 m), resulting in probable extremes of 96°F (36°C) and 45°F (7°C).

N/HEMISPHERE	JAN	FEB	MAR	APR	MAY	JUN	JUL	AUG	SEP	OCT	NOV	DEC
°F AVG MAX	83	86	88	89	83	79	77	77	79	82	83	81
°F AVG MIN	60	62	67	70	70	69	69	69	69	69	67	62
DIURNAL RANGE	23	24	21	19	13	10	8	8	10	13	16	19
RAIN/INCHES	0.3	0.2	0.4	3.0	20.3	35.6	46.3	43.4	28.1	8.5	2.1	0.1
HUMIDITY/%	66	68	68	70	81	91	92	93	91	81	75	64
BLOOM SEASON			*	**	*							
DAYS CLR @ 7AM	12	7	5	6	1	0	0	0	0	3	7	12
DAYS CLR @ 1PM	20	13	10	8	3	0	0	0	0	4	12	17
RAIN/MM	8	5	10	76	516	904	1176	1102	714	216	53	3
°C AVG MAX	28.3	29.9	31.1	31.6	28.3	26.1	24.9	24.9	26.1	27.7	28.3	27.2
°C AVG MIN	15.5	16.6	19.4	21.1	21.1	20.5	20.5	20.5	20.5	20.5	19.4	16.6
DIURNAL RANGE	12.8	13.3	11.7	10.5	7.2	5.6	4.4	4.4	5.6	7.2	8.9	10.6
S/HEMISPHERE	JUL	AUG	SEP	OCT	NOV	DEC	JAN	FEB	MAR	APR	MAY	JUN

Cultural Recommendations

LIGHT: 2500–3500 fc.

TEMPERATURES: Summer days average 77–79°F (25–26°C), and nights average 69°F (21°C), with a diurnal range of 8–10°F (4–6°C). Weather is warmest in spring. Days average 88–89°F (31–32°C), and nights average 67–70°F (19–21°C), with a diurnal range of 19–21°F (11–12°C). Because habitat elevation is estimated, temperatures should be used with caution, but seasonal patterns are similar regardless of elevation.

HUMIDITY: 80–90% from late spring to midautumn. Humidity decreases to near 65% in winter.

WATER: Rainfall is very heavy from late spring to autumn, but amounts are greatly reduced in winter. Cultivated plants require frequent and heavy watering while actively growing, but they must be able to dry rapidly after watering. Water should be gradually reduced after new growths mature in autumn.

FERTILIZER: ¼–½ recommended strength. A balanced fertilizer should be applied weekly to biweekly throughout the year.

REST PERIOD: Winter days average 81–86°F (27–30°C), and nights average 60–62°F (16–17°C), with a diurnal range of 23–24°F (13°C). The wide diurnal range results from both warmer days and cooler nights. For 4 months, rainfall averages are very low, but additional moisture is usually available from frequent heavy deposits of dew. Water should be reduced for cultivated plants. They should be allowed to dry somewhat between waterings but should never remain dry for long periods. Occasional early morning mistings between waterings, especially on bright, sunny days, may help prevent plants from becoming too dry. Fertilizer should be reduced or eliminated during the dry period. In the habitat, light is highest in winter and spring.

GROWING MEDIA: Plants are healthiest if mounted on tree-fern or cork slabs as they need to dry rapidly after watering. However, humidity must be high and plants must be watered at least once a day in summer. If plants cannot be mounted, they may be grown in baskets or small pots filled with a very open, fast-draining medium. Repotting may be done anytime new roots are actively growing.

MISCELLANEOUS NOTES: Climate data for the habitat in Thailand indicates that *D. albosanguineum* probably tolerates average low temperatures near 55°F (13°C) for 2–3 months in winter.

Plant and Flower Information

PLANT SIZE AND TYPE: A compact, 6–15 in. (15–38 cm) sympodial epiphyte.

PSEUDOBULB: 5–11 in. (12–28 cm) long. The club-shaped stems are erect and pseudobulbous with swollen internodes.

LEAVES: 5–7 per growth. The lanceolate leaves, which are 3–6 in. (8–15 cm) long, are light green, almost translucent, and deciduous. They overlap at the base, nearly hiding the pseudobulb.

INFLORESCENCE: 2–3 in. (5.0–7.5 cm) long. Paired inflorescences arise from upper nodes on 1- and 2-year-old stems, which may be leafy or leafless.

FLOWERS: 2–7 are common, occasionally up to 10. The distinctive blossoms are fleshy, 2–3 in. (5–8 cm) across, fragrant, and long-lasting. Sepals and petals may be cream-white to pale yellow, sometimes with a purple tinge. The cream-colored lip is notched at the apex and marked with raised, blood-red or maroon blotches on each sidelobe. The anther may be red or maroon.

HYBRIDIZING NOTES: Chromosome count is 2n = 40 (ref. 153, 154, 188, 273). Johansen (ref. 239) indicates that no viable seed was produced when plants were self-pollinated.

REFERENCES: 36, 153, 154, 157, 179, 188, 190, 202, 210, 216, 239, 254, 273, 317, 430, 445, 450, 454, 541, 557, 570.

PHOTOS/DRAWINGS: 210, 430, 454.

Dendrobium alboviride Hayata not Parish or Roxburgh. See *D. linawianum* Rchb. f. REFERENCES: 61, 222, 279, 445, 504.

Dendrobium alboviride Parish not Hayata or Roxburgh. See *D. scabrilingue* Lindley. REFERENCES: 190.

Dendrobium alboviride Roxburgh not Hayata or Parish. S. Y. Hu (ref. 208) lists *D. alboviride* Roxburgh var. *majus* Rolfe as a synonym of *D. lindleyi* var. *majus* (Rolfe) S. Y. Hu. No other references to *D. alboviride* Roxburgh were found. REFERENCES: 208.

Dendrobium album Boxall not Hooker or Wight. Merrill (ref. 296) indicates that the correct name should probably be *D. album* Wight. REFERENCES: 296.

Dendrobium album Hooker not Boxall or Wight. Now considered a synonym of *Maxillaria alba* Lindley. REFERENCES: 190, 216, 254.

Dendrobium album Wight not Boxall or Hooker. See *D. aqueum* Lindley. REFERENCES: 216, 254, 278, 369, 424, 445, 448, 570.

Dendrobium album Williams. See *D. wardianum* Warner. Hawkes (ref. 190) listed this name, but we found no other use of it. REFERENCES: 190.

Dendrobium alderwereltianum J. J. Smith

ORIGIN/HABITAT: Endemic to Sulawesi (Celebes). Plants were collected in the south, on or near Mt. Katong Moan (Katongkoan) and Mt. Sinadji. Habitat elevation is not available, so the following climate data should be used with caution.

CLIMATE: Station #97180, Makassar, Sulawesi, Indonesia, Lat. 5.1°S, Long. 119.6°E, at 46 ft. (14 m). Temperatures are calculated for an elevation of 3300 ft. (1000 m), resulting in probable extremes of 84°F (29°C) and 47°F (9°C).

N/HEMISPHERE	JAN	FEB	MAR	APR	MAY	JUN	JUL	AUG	SEP	OCT	NOV	DEC
°F AVG MAX	75	76	76	76	75	73	73	73	74	75	76	75
°F AVG MIN	59	58	59	61	63	63	63	64	63	63	63	61
DIURNAL RANGE	16	18	17	15	12	10	10	9	11	12	13	14
RAIN/INCHES	1.3	0.4	0.5	1.6	6.7	23.2	28.3	20.9	16.7	6.5	3.6	2.7
HUMIDITY/%	72	67	64	70	77	84	84	85	84	80	79	76
BLOOM SEASON					*	*	*					
DAYS CLR @ 8AM	14	17	15	14	8	4	4	1	4	8	8	11
DAYS CLR @ 2PM	7	7	11	13	9	3	1	1	1	2	6	7
RAIN/MM	33	10	13	41	170	589	719	531	424	165	91	69
°C AVG MAX	24.0	24.6	24.6	24.6	24.0	22.9	22.9	22.9	23.5	24.0	24.6	24.0
°C AVG MIN	15.1	14.6	15.1	16.3	17.4	17.4	17.4	17.9	17.4	17.4	17.4	16.3
DIURNAL RANGE	8.9	10.0	9.5	8.3	6.6	5.5	5.5	5.0	6.1	6.6	7.2	7.7
S/HEMISPHERE	JUL	AUG	SEP	OCT	NOV	DEC	JAN	FEB	MAR	APR	MAY	JUN

Dendrobium alexandrae

Cultural Recommendations

LIGHT: 2500–3500 fc. In the habitat, clear summer days are rare due to the cloud cover associated with the summer rainy season.

TEMPERATURES: Summer days average 73°F (23°C), and nights average 63–64°F (17–18°C), with a diurnal range of 9–10°F (5–6°C). Regardless of habitat elevation, seasonal patterns are similar.

HUMIDITY: Near 85% in summer and early autumn, dropping to 65–70% in winter and early spring.

WATER: Rainfall is heavy from late spring to autumn. For 2–3 months in winter, conditions are much drier. Cultivated plants should be kept moist from late spring to early autumn, but water should be gradually reduced in late autumn.

FERTILIZER: ¼–½ recommended strength, applied weekly. A high-nitrogen fertilizer is beneficial from spring to midsummer, but a fertilizer high in phosphates should be used in late summer and autumn.

REST PERIOD: Winter days average 75–76°F (24–25°C), and nights average 58–61°F (15–16°C), with a diurnal range of 14–18°F (8–10°C). The increased diurnal range results from both warmer days and cooler nights. Rainfall is much lower for about 4 months in winter; and for 2 of these months, conditions are so dry that even dew is uncommon. Water and fertilizer should be reduced for cultivated plants. In early winter, they should be kept barely moist; but for 1–2 months in late winter, plants should be allowed to dry out between waterings. They should not remain dry for extended periods, however. In the habitat, light is highest in winter.

GROWING MEDIA: Plants may be mounted on tree-fern or cork slabs if humidity is high and plants are watered at least once daily in summer. When plants are potted, any open, fast-draining medium may be used. Repotting is best done in early spring when new roots are growing.

MISCELLANEOUS NOTES: The bloom season shown in the climate table is based on reports from the habitat. The plant was described in 1917 in *Bul. Jard. Bot. Buit.* 2nd sér. 25:58.

Plant and Flower Information

PLANT SIZE AND TYPE: A 7 in. (18 cm) sympodial epiphyte.

PSEUDOBULB: 7 in. (18 cm) long.

LEAVES: The spreading, oblong leaves, which are about 2 in. (5 cm) long, are minutely toothed at the apex.

INFLORESCENCE: Short. Inflorescences arise from the axils of the upper leaves.

FLOWERS: 2 per inflorescence. The red flowers are 1.6 in. (4 cm) across. Blossoms have an ovate-oblong dorsal sepal that is recurved at the apex and oblong-triangular lateral sepals. Petals have uneven edges. The erect lip is not thickened.

REFERENCES: 222, 436.

Dendrobium alexandrae Schlechter

AKA: A very rare plant that Cribb (ref. 85) suspects may be a hybrid, with *D. spectabile* (Blume) Miquel as one of its parents.

ORIGIN/HABITAT: Northeastern Papua New Guinea, in the Morobe District. The type specimen was found in the Waria Valley near Gobi (Gobe) at 2950–3600 ft. (900–1100 m). It grew in cool, shady conditions on moss-covered trees in the mistforest.

CLIMATE: Station #200192, Garaina, Papua New Guinea, Lat. 7.9°S, Long. 147.1°E, at 2350 ft. (716 m). Temperatures are calculated for an elevation of 3300 ft. (1000 m), resulting in probable extremes of 91°F (33°C) and 43°F (6°C).

N/HEMISPHERE	JAN	FEB	MAR	APR	MAY	JUN	JUL	AUG	SEP	OCT	NOV	DEC
°F AVG MAX	77	79	80	81	82	82	82	82	81	81	80	78
°F AVG MIN	60	60	60	61	60	61	62	62	62	61	61	60
DIURNAL RANGE	17	19	20	20	22	21	20	20	19	20	19	18
RAIN/INCHES	5.8	6.5	8.7	11.1	11.8	11.9	8.9	11.7	11.5	9.9	7.7	5.2
HUMIDITY/%	84	82	82	81	80	80	81	81	82	83	84	84
BLOOM SEASON											*	*
DAYS CLR	N/A											
RAIN/MM	147	165	221	282	300	302	226	297	292	251	196	132
°C AVG MAX	25.0	26.1	26.6	27.2	27.7	27.7	27.7	27.7	27.2	27.2	26.6	25.5
°C AVG MIN	15.5	15.5	15.5	16.1	15.5	16.1	16.6	16.6	16.6	16.1	16.1	15.5
DIURNAL RANGE	9.5	10.6	11.1	11.1	12.2	11.6	11.1	11.1	10.6	11.1	10.5	10.0
S/HEMISPHERE	JUL	AUG	SEP	OCT	NOV	DEC	JAN	FEB	MAR	APR	MAY	JUN

Cultural Recommendations

LIGHT: 2000–3000 fc. At Kew, the greenhouse is lightly shaded from spring to autumn.

TEMPERATURES: Throughout the year, days average 77–82°F (25–28°C), and nights average 60–62°F (16–17°C), with a diurnal range of 17–22°F (10–12°C). At Kew, the minimum night temperature for *D. alexandrae* is 64°F (18°C), and summer daytime temperatures average 77°F (25°C), but may rise to 90°F (32°C) for short periods.

HUMIDITY: 80–85% year-round. At Kew, humidity is near 100% at night, but it drops to 70% in the afternoon.

WATER: Rainfall is heavy all year, but conditions are slightly drier in winter. Cultivated plants should be kept moist but not soggy.

FERTILIZER: ¼–½ recommended strength. A balanced fertilizer should be applied weekly to biweekly throughout the year. The Royal Botanic Garden in Edinburgh uses a seaweed-based fertilizer for high-elevation plants from New Guinea.

REST PERIOD: Growing conditions vary only slightly during the year. In the habitat, rainfall is slightly lower in winter. Water and fertilizer should be reduced somewhat for cultivated plants, especially those grown in the dark, short-day conditions common in temperate-latitude winters; but they should never be allowed to dry out completely. In the habitat, light is slightly higher in winter.

GROWING MEDIA: Plants may be mounted on slabs of tree-fern fiber if humidity is high and water can be applied at least once daily in summer. If plants are potted, medium-grade fir bark may be used, providing humidity is high. The medium should be kept moist, but not soggy. Drainage and air movement are extremely important. Repotting may be done when new roots are beginning to grow.

MISCELLANEOUS NOTES: The bloom season shown in the climate table is based on cultivation records, and plants bloom at about the same time in nature. Seedlings may not bloom for 7 years.

Plant and Flower Information

PLANT SIZE AND TYPE: A robust, 20–28 in. (50–70 cm) sympodial epiphyte.

PSEUDOBULB: 22 in. (55 cm) long, sometimes smaller. Growths arise from a short rhizome.

LEAVES: 3–4 at the apex of each growth. The elliptic, bluish-green leaves are 4–6 in. (10–15 cm) long. They may be erect or spreading.

INFLORESCENCE: 10 in. (25 cm) long. The laxly flowered inflorescences arise from nodes near the apex of the pseudobulb.

FLOWERS: 3–7 per inflorescence. The large flowers are 2–3, rarely 4 in. (5–8, rarely 10 cm) across. The lanceolate sepals and petals are pale yellow. The margins of the petals are ruffled. The tips of the sepals are somewhat incurved. The white lip has 3 lobes, a callus with short fleshy ridges, and a sharply pointed midlobe. Blossoms are marked with dull purple spots rather than bold reddish lines as found on *D. spectabile*. Schlechter (ref. 437) described the flowers as "magnificent," which was a superlative he rarely used.

REFERENCES: 22, 83, 85, 179, 221, 370, 437.

PHOTOS/DRAWINGS: 22, 370, 437.

Dendrobium alexisense (Schlechter) J. J. Smith

AKA: *Cadetia bigibba* Schlechter. *Cadetia* is again considered a valid genus, so this plant may again be a *Cadetia*.

ORIGIN/HABITAT: Northeastern Papua New Guinea. Plants grow on forest trees at about 150 ft. (50 m) near Alexishafen, just north of Madang.

CLIMATE: Station #94014, Madang, Papua New Guinea, Lat. 5.2°S, Long. 145.8°E, at 13 ft. (4 m). Temperatures are calculated for a habitat elevation of 1000 ft. (300 m), resulting in probable extremes of 95°F (35°C) and 59°F (15°C).

N/HEMISPHERE	JAN	FEB	MAR	APR	MAY	JUN	JUL	AUG	SEP	OCT	NOV	DEC
°F AVG MAX	80	80	82	82	82	82	82	82	82	84	84	81
°F AVG MIN	74	75	75	75	74	74	74	74	74	73	74	75
DIURNAL RANGE	6	5	7	7	8	8	8	8	8	11	10	6
RAIN/INCHES	4.0	3.4	3.2	8.5	11.2	11.1	10.1	11.3	9.4	11.3	10.5	6.7
HUMIDITY/%	88	87	86	86	86	86	86	85	85	87	88	89
BLOOM SEASON									*			
DAYS CLR	N/A											
RAIN/MM	102	86	81	216	284	282	257	287	239	287	267	170
°C AVG MAX	26.6	26.6	27.7	27.7	27.7	27.7	27.7	27.7	27.7	28.8	28.8	27.1
°C AVG MIN	23.2	23.8	23.8	23.8	23.2	23.2	23.2	23.2	23.2	22.7	23.2	23.8
DIURNAL RANGE	3.4	2.8	3.9	3.9	4.5	4.5	4.5	4.5	4.5	6.1	5.6	3.3
S/HEMISPHERE	JUL	AUG	SEP	OCT	NOV	DEC	JAN	FEB	MAR	APR	MAY	JUN

Cultural Recommendations

LIGHT: 2500–3000 fc.

TEMPERATURES: Throughout the year, days average 80–84°F (27–29°C), and nights average 73–75°F (23–24°C), with a diurnal range of 5–11°F (3–6°C). The warmest highs, the coolest lows, and the greatest diurnal range occur in autumn.

HUMIDITY: 85–90% all year.

WATER: Rainfall is heavy from spring through autumn, but conditions are somewhat drier in winter. Cultivated plants should be kept moist but not soggy while actively growing.

FERTILIZER: ¼–½ recommended strength. A balanced fertilizer should be applied weekly to biweekly throughout the year.

REST PERIOD: Growing temperatures should be maintained all year. In the habitat, rainfall decreases somewhat for 3–4 months in winter. In cultivation, water should be reduced and the plants allowed to dry slightly between waterings. Fertilizer should be reduced until water is increased in spring. In the habitat, light is highest in winter.

GROWING MEDIA: Plants may be mounted on tree-fern or cork slabs if humidity is high and plants are watered at least once daily in summer. When plants are potted, any open, fast-draining medium may be used. Repotting is best done in early spring.

MISCELLANEOUS NOTES: The bloom season shown in the climate table is based on collection records.

Plant and Flower Information

PLANT SIZE AND TYPE: A 3–5 in. (8–12 cm) sympodial epiphyte.

PSEUDOBULB: 2–3 in. (5–7 cm) long. The flattened pseudobulbs arise from a very short rhizome.

LEAVES: 1 per growth. The sickle-shaped leaves are 1–2 in. (3–5 cm) long and somewhat leathery.

INFLORESCENCE: The inflorescences are erect to suberect.

FLOWERS: All segments are about 0.2 in. (0.5 cm) long. The linear petals and oval sepals are white. The lip is golden yellow on the midlobe. It is covered by 5 thick pads except at the margin.

REFERENCES: 221, 437, 472.

PHOTOS/DRAWINGS: 437.

Dendrobium algosum Reinwardt. Now considered a *Taeniophyllum* species. REFERENCES: 216, 254.

Dendrobium aliciae Ames and Quisumbing

ORIGIN/HABITAT: Endemic to Luzon Island in the Philippines. Plants grow on Mt. Santo Tomas near Baguio in Benguet Province. They are also reported in Batangas Province.

CLIMATE: Station #98328, Baguio, Philippines, Lat. 16.4°N, Long. 120.6°E, at 4962 ft. (1512 m). Record extreme temperatures are 84°F (29°C) and 46°F (8°C).

N/HEMISPHERE	JAN	FEB	MAR	APR	MAY	JUN	JUL	AUG	SEP	OCT	NOV	DEC
°F AVG MAX	72	73	76	77	76	75	71	71	71	73	74	74
°F AVG MIN	55	56	58	60	61	61	60	60	60	60	59	57
DIURNAL RANGE	17	17	18	17	15	14	11	11	11	13	15	17
RAIN/INCHES	0.9	0.9	1.7	4.3	15.8	17.2	42.3	45.7	28.1	15.0	4.9	2.0
HUMIDITY/%	83	83	83	85	89	90	93	93	92	89	86	84
BLOOM SEASON							*					
DAYS CLR	N/A											
RAIN/MM	23	23	43	109	401	437	1074	1161	714	381	124	51
°C AVG MAX	22.2	22.8	24.4	25.0	24.4	23.9	21.7	21.7	21.7	22.8	23.3	23.3
°C AVG MIN	12.8	13.3	14.4	15.6	16.1	16.1	15.6	15.6	15.6	15.6	15.0	13.9
DIURNAL RANGE	9.4	9.5	10.0	9.4	8.3	7.8	6.1	6.1	6.1	7.2	8.3	9.4
S/HEMISPHERE	JUL	AUG	SEP	OCT	NOV	DEC	JAN	FEB	MAR	APR	MAY	JUN

Cultural Recommendations

LIGHT: 1500–2500 fc. Diffused or dappled light is recommended. Sky-cover records are unavailable, but high elevations are typically cloudy in this region.

TEMPERATURES: Summer days average 71–75°F (22–24°C), and nights average 60–61°F (16°C), with a diurnal range of 11–14°F (6–8°C).

HUMIDITY: 83–93% year-round.

WATER: Rainfall is very heavy from spring to autumn but is greatly reduced in winter. Cultivated plants should be kept moist but not soggy from spring to autumn, but water should be gradually reduced in late autumn.

FERTILIZER: ¼–½ recommended strength, applied weekly. A high-nitrogen fertilizer is beneficial from spring to midsummer, but a fertilizer high in phosphates should be used in late summer and autumn.

REST PERIOD: Winter days average 72–76°F (22–24°C), and nights average 55–58°F (13–14°C), with a diurnal range of 17–18°F (9–10°C). Rainfall is low in the habitat for 2–4 months in winter, but the high humidity and large temperature range indicate that additional moisture is frequently available from dew or fog and mist. Cultivated plants should be kept barely moist in winter, but they should never be allowed to dry out completely. Fertilizer should be reduced or eliminated anytime water is reduced or plants are not actively growing. In the habitat, light may be highest in winter.

GROWING MEDIA: Mounting plants on tree-fern or cork slabs accommodates their pendent growth habit. When plants are mounted, humidity must be high and the plants must be watered at least once a day in summer. If plants are potted, the pots may be filled with any open, fast-draining medium. Repotting is best done in early spring or when new roots are beginning to grow.

MISCELLANEOUS NOTES: The bloom season shown in the climate table is based on collection reports.

Plant and Flower Information

PLANT SIZE AND TYPE: A 39 in. (100 cm) sympodial epiphyte.

Dendrobium alleizettei

PSEUDOBULB: 33–39 in. (85–100 cm) long. The pendulous pseudobulbs, which are slender, clustered, and smooth, do not branch.

LEAVES: Many. Stems are leafy along their entire length. The linear leaves are 3.5–4.5 in. (9–11 cm) long and become smaller toward the apex.

INFLORESCENCE: Very short.

FLOWERS: 2 per inflorescence. The star-shaped flowers are 2.4–4.7 in. (6–12 cm) across, with very long, linear sepals and petals. They are straw-yellow with carmine-red spots. The margin of the large, yellow midlobe is marked with red spots, but the sidelobes are white. The lip is covered with short white hairs.

REFERENCES: 98, 225, 373, 536.

PHOTOS/DRAWINGS: *373, 536.*

Dendrobium alleizettei Gagnepain. See *D. sociale* J. J. Smith.
REFERENCES: 454, Seidenfaden 1992 *Opera Botanica* #114.

Dendrobium allioides J. J. Smith. See *D. violaceum* Kränzlin. REFERENCES: 225, 385, 470.

Dendrobium aloideum Llave and Lexarza. An invalid name used for an unidentified plant from Mexico. REFERENCES: 216, 254.

Dendrobium aloifolium (Blume) Rchb. f.

AKA: Sometimes spelled *D. aloiaefollium* or *D. aloefolium*. Synonyms include *Aporum serra* Lindley, *Aporum micranthum* Griffith, *Macrostomium aloefolium* Blume, *Oxystophyllum macrostoma* Hasskarl, *Dendrobium micranthum* (Griffith) Lindley, and *D. serra* (Lindley) Lindley. Seidenfaden in 1992 *Opera Botanica* #114 includes *D. cochinchinense* Ridley. He indicates that plants from Indochina which have been incorrectly identified as *D. anceps*, *D. albayense*, and *D. acinaciforme* are actually *D. aloifolium*. Seidenfaden (ref. 454) indicates that *D. lobbii* Lindley may be synonymous, but he specifically excludes *D. ramificans* J. J. Smith, which is sometimes listed as a synonym. Merrill (ref. 296) and Valmayor (ref. 536) indicate that *D. aloifolium* Rchb. f. as used by Kränzlin is actually *D. merrillii* Ames.

ORIGIN/HABITAT: Widespread and common in the lowlands of a large region including Borneo, Indonesia, Java, Malaya, Thailand, Cambodia, Laos, and Vietnam. In Thailand, plants grow at about 1000 ft. (300 m) near Chiang Mai. In East and West Java, plants grow in wet areas from sea level to 1650 ft. (0–500 m), and in Borneo they are found in hill forests at 1650–1950 ft. (500–600 m).

CLIMATE: Station #48327, Chiang Mai, Thailand, Lat. 18.8°N, Long. 99.0°E, at 1100 ft. (335 m). Record extreme temperatures are 109°F (43°C) and 38°F (3°C).

N/HEMISPHERE	JAN	FEB	MAR	APR	MAY	JUN	JUL	AUG	SEP	OCT	NOV	DEC
°F AVG MAX	85	90	95	96	94	90	89	87	88	89	86	84
°F AVG MIN	56	57	62	70	74	74	74	75	73	71	66	57
DIURNAL RANGE	29	33	33	26	20	16	15	12	15	18	20	27
RAIN/INCHES	0.3	0.4	0.6	2.0	5.5	6.1	7.4	8.7	11.5	4.9	1.5	0.4
HUMIDITY/%	73	65	58	62	73	78	80	83	83	81	79	76
BLOOM SEASON		*							*	*	*	*
DAYS CLR @ 7AM	5	5	2	2	1	0	0	0	0	1	3	3
DAYS CLR @ 1PM	9	8	4	2	0	0	0	0	0	0	1	3
RAIN/MM	8	10	15	51	140	155	188	221	292	124	38	10
°C AVG MAX	29.4	32.2	35.0	35.6	34.4	32.2	31.7	30.6	31.1	31.7	30.0	28.9
°C AVG MIN	13.3	13.9	16.7	21.1	23.3	23.3	23.3	23.9	22.8	21.7	18.9	13.9
DIURNAL RANGE	16.1	18.3	18.3	14.5	11.1	8.9	8.4	6.7	8.3	10.0	11.1	15.0
S/HEMISPHERE	JUL	AUG	SEP	OCT	NOV	DEC	JAN	FEB	MAR	APR	MAY	JUN

Cultural Recommendations

LIGHT: 3000–4000 fc. Bright light should be provided, along with strong air movement. In the habitat, the heavy cloud cover during the summer rainy season reduces light considerably. Therefore, cultivated plants should be given some shading from spring into autumn.

TEMPERATURES: Summer days average 87–90°F (31–32°C), and nights average 74–75°F (23–24°C), with a diurnal range of 12–16°F (7–9°C). Spring is the warmest time of the year. Days average 94–96°F (35–36°C), and nights average 62–74°F (17–23°C), with a diurnal range of 20–33°F (11–18°C). Temperatures are moderate after the summer wet season starts. While *D. aloifolium* frequently grows in the hills, it also occurs in the warm uniform climate of lowland equatorial regions. The temperatures above may, therefore, represent the coolest conditions this species can tolerate.

HUMIDITY: 80–85% in summer and early autumn, dropping to about 60–65% in late winter and early spring.

WATER: Rainfall is moderate to heavy from late spring through early autumn, but conditions are much drier in winter. Cultivated plants should be kept moist while actively growing, but water should be gradually reduced after new growths mature in autumn.

FERTILIZER: ½ recommended strength, applied weekly. A high-nitrogen fertilizer is beneficial from spring to midsummer, but a fertilizer high in phosphates should be used in late summer and autumn.

REST PERIOD: Winter days average 84–90°F (29–32°C), and nights average 56–57°F (13–14°C), with a diurnal range of 27–33°F (15–18°C). In the habitat, rainfall averages are very low for 4 months in winter, but during the early part of the season the high relative humidity indicates that additional moisture is available from frequent fog, mist, and heavy deposits of dew. Growers sometimes recommend eliminating water in winter, but plants are healthiest if for most of the winter they are allowed to become dry between waterings but do not remain dry for extended periods. However, for 1–2 months in early spring, conditions in the habitat are clear, warm, and dry; and humidity is so low that even the moisture from morning dew is uncommon. During a corresponding time for cultivated plants, water should be limited to an occasional early morning misting if the plant starts to shrivel, or if an extended period of bright, sunny weather is expected. Fertilizer should be eliminated in winter, and resumed only when water is increased in spring. In the habitat, light is highest in winter. In other, warmer habitats, *D. aloifolium* is found in areas with heavy year-round rainfall or much shorter and less severe winter dry seasons. This suggests that if winter growing conditions are warm, plants may need to be watered all year and should be watched carefully for stress if water has been reduced.

GROWING MEDIA: Mounting plants on slabs of cork or tree-fern fiber accommodates their pendulous growth habit, but mounted plants must be watered at least once a day in summer. Additional waterings or mistings may be beneficial on hot, sunny days. Plants may be potted in any open, fast-draining medium. In cultivation, potted plants should be watered once every 2–3 days during bright, hot, summer weather. Repotting is best done in early spring when new roots begin to grow.

MISCELLANEOUS NOTES: The bloom season shown in the climate table is based on collection reports. Plants known as *D. cochinchinense* Ridley often have broader, larger stems and larger flowers than plants cultivated as *D. aloifolium*.

Plant and Flower Information

PLANT SIZE AND TYPE: An 18–35 in. (45–90 cm) sympodial epiphyte.

PSEUDOBULB: 18–35 in. (45–90 cm) long. The pseudobulbs are thin, flattened, clustered, and rarely branched. Initially erect, the stems become pendulous as they mature. Plants often have a reddish tinge, and those that grow in hot and wet areas may become bright red.

LEAVES: Many. The lower leaves are about 1.2 in. (3 cm) long, becoming smaller at the apex. They are ovate and pointed at the tip. The stems are densely leafy on the lower half, which appears almost braided, but the upper half has only leaf bracts. The thick fleshy leaves, which are laterally flattened, alternate along the stem in 2 rows.

INFLORESCENCE: Very short. Inflorescences arise from tufts of dry scales on the 6 in. (15 cm) long, leafless, apical extensions of the stem.

FLOWERS: 1–2 per inflorescence. Extremely small for the plant size, the flowers are usually less that 0.3 in. (0.8 cm) across. They open in succession and each lasts only a few days. Sepals and petals become recurved 1–2 days after opening. They are creamy white to greenish white, sometimes with pale rose spotting on the inside. The straight lip has a deeply notched midlobe and projects forward. The sidelobes are erect. The anther cap is green.

HYBRIDIZING NOTES: Johansen (ref. 239) indicates that plants are self-sterile and that flowers dropped 6 days after self-pollination.

REFERENCES: 25, 36, 75, 190, 200, 202, 216, 239, 254, 266, 278, 286, 295, 296, 310, 317, 394, 395, 402, 445, 447, 448, 454, 455, 469, 474, 482, 536, 592.

PHOTOS/DRAWINGS: 75, 200, *454*, *455*, 469.

Dendrobium aloifolium Swartz.
Schlechter (ref. 437) included this name in a discussion of the section *Aporum*. We found no other reference to it. REFERENCES: 437.

Dendrobium alpestre Royle.
See *D. monticola* Hunt and Summerhayes. REFERENCES: 32, 102, 150, 153, 179, 202, 211, 216, 254, 317, 369, 445, 454, 504.

Dendrobium alpestre Swartz.
Now considered a synonym of *Pleurothallis alpestris* Lindley. REFERENCES: 216, 254.

Dendrobium alpinum P. van Royen.
See *D. rigidifolium* Rolfe. REFERENCES: 83, 233, 538. PHOTOS/DRAWINGS: 538.

Dendrobium alterum Seidenfaden.
See *D. dantaniense* Guilaumin. REFERENCES: 234, 239, 454.

Dendrobium alticola Schlechter
ORIGIN/HABITAT: Northeastern New Guinea. Plants grow in the Bismarck Mountains on forest trees at about 7850 ft. (2400 m).

CLIMATE: Station #94010, Goroka, Papua New Guinea, Lat. 6.1°S, Long. 145.4°E, at 5141 ft. (1567 m). Temperatures are calculated for an elevation of 8000 ft. (2440 m), resulting in probable extremes of 78°F (25°C) and 34°F (1°C).

N/HEMISPHERE	JAN	FEB	MAR	APR	MAY	JUN	JUL	AUG	SEP	OCT	NOV	DEC
°F AVG MAX	67	68	69	70	70	69	70	69	69	69	70	68
°F AVG MIN	47	48	48	48	49	50	50	50	51	50	50	48
DIURNAL RANGE	20	20	21	22	21	19	20	19	18	19	20	20
RAIN/INCHES	2.1	2.8	4.6	5.9	6.6	9.3	9.1	10.1	10.7	8.3	4.6	2.0
HUMIDITY/%	70	67	67	67	67	71	72	73	74	71	70	70
BLOOM SEASON					*							
DAYS CLR	N/A											
RAIN/MM	53	71	117	150	168	236	231	257	272	211	117	51
°C AVG MAX	19.2	19.8	20.3	20.9	20.9	20.3	20.9	20.3	20.3	20.3	20.9	19.8
°C AVG MIN	8.1	8.6	8.6	8.6	9.2	9.8	9.8	9.8	10.3	9.8	9.8	8.6
DIURNAL RANGE	11.1	11.2	11.7	12.3	11.7	10.5	11.1	10.5	10.0	10.5	11.1	11.2
S/HEMISPHERE	JUL	AUG	SEP	OCT	NOV	DEC	JAN	FEB	MAR	APR	MAY	JUN

Cultural Recommendations

LIGHT: 1500–2500 fc. Plants may tolerate higher light, especially in the morning.

TEMPERATURES: Throughout the year, days average 67–70°F (19–21°C), and nights average 47–51°F (8–10°C), with a diurnal range of 18–22°F (10–12°C). In the habitat, the warmest temperatures of the day occur during late morning when skies are clear. Clouds and mist develop near noon and continue through the afternoon preventing additional warming.

HUMIDITY: 70–75% from summer into autumn. Humidity decreases to 65–70% in winter and spring.

WATER: Rainfall is moderate to heavy most of the year, but conditions are slightly drier for 3 months in winter. Cultivated plants should be kept moist. In summer, daily water may be necessary during hot, dry weather. In addition, early morning mistings may be beneficial, especially on bright, sunny days.

FERTILIZER: ¼–½ recommended strength. A balanced fertilizer should be applied weekly to biweekly throughout the year.

REST PERIOD: Growing conditions should be maintained all year. In the habitat, rainfall is lowest in winter, but additional moisture is usually available from dew, fog, and mist. Water should be reduced for cultivated plants, especially those grown in the dark, short-day conditions common during temperate-latitude winters. Cultivated plants should never be allowed to dry out completely, however. Fertilizer should be reduced or eliminated until water is increased in spring. In the habitat, seasonal light variation is minor.

GROWING MEDIA: Plants may be mounted on slabs of tree-fern fiber if water can be applied at least once daily in summer and if humidity is high. If plants are potted, a mixture of fir bark or tree-fern fiber with moisture-retaining additives should be used. A surface layer of live sphagnum moss may be beneficial. The medium should be kept moist, but not soggy. It should never be allowed to dry out completely. Repotting may be done anytime new roots are growing.

MISCELLANEOUS NOTES: The bloom season shown in the climate table is based on reports from the habitat.

Plant and Flower Information

PLANT SIZE AND TYPE: A 16–20 in. (40–50 cm) sympodial epiphyte.

PSEUDOBULB: 14–18 in. (35–45 cm) long. The stems are rigid and non-branching.

LEAVES: The elliptic leaves are 1.2–2.0 in. (3–5 cm) long, smooth, rigid, and erect to spreading.

INFLORESCENCE: Very short. Inflorescences arise from nodes on the side of the pseudobulb.

FLOWERS: 2 per inflorescence. The flowers, which are 0.8 in. (2 cm) across, are spreading, but they do not open fully. Sepals and petals are yellowish with red dots. The column foot has red markings.

REFERENCES: 221, 437, 445.

PHOTOS/DRAWINGS: 437.

Dendrobium altomontanum A. Gilli
ORIGIN/HABITAT: Papua New Guinea. Plants grow near Kasap at about 8850 ft. (2700 m).

CLIMATE: Botanical garden records, Laiagam, Papua New Guinea, Lat. 5.5°S, Long. 143.5°E, at 7218 ft. (2200 m). Temperatures are calculated for an elevation of 8500 ft. (2600 m), resulting in probable extremes of 87°F (30°C) and 28°F (–2°C).

Dendrobium amabile

N/HEMISPHERE	JAN	FEB	MAR	APR	MAY	JUN	JUL	AUG	SEP	OCT	NOV	DEC
°F AVG MAX	72	73	74	72	74	74	78	73	72	74	74	72
°F AVG MIN	51	50	51	51	52	52	51	52	54	53	52	52
DIURNAL RANGE	21	23	23	21	22	22	27	21	18	21	22	20
RAIN/INCHES	4.0	4.8	6.1	7.8	8.5	9.1	8.4	9.6	9.5	8.9	6.3	4.0
HUMIDITY/%	N/A											
BLOOM SEASON	N/A											
DAYS CLR	N/A											
RAIN/MM	102	122	155	198	216	231	213	244	241	226	160	102
°C AVG MAX	22.1	22.6	23.2	22.1	23.2	23.2	25.4	22.6	22.1	23.2	23.2	22.1
°C AVG MIN	10.4	9.9	10.4	10.4	11.0	11.0	10.4	11.0	12.1	11.5	11.0	11.0
DIURNAL RANGE	11.7	12.7	12.8	11.7	12.2	12.2	15.0	11.6	10.0	11.7	12.2	11.1
S/HEMISPHERE	JUL	AUG	SEP	OCT	NOV	DEC	JAN	FEB	MAR	APR	MAY	JUN

Cultural Recommendations

LIGHT: 2000–3000 fc.

TEMPERATURES: Throughout the year, days average 72–78°F (22–25°C), and nights average 50–54°F (10–12°C), with a diurnal range of 18–27°F (10–15°C).

HUMIDITY: Information is not available for this location. However, records from nearby stations indicate that averages are probably near 80% year-round.

WATER: Rainfall is heavy throughout the year, but for 3–4 months in winter, conditions are slightly drier. Cultivated plants should be kept moist with little if any drying allowed between waterings.

FERTILIZER: ¼–½ recommended strength. A balanced fertilizer should be applied weekly to biweekly throughout the year.

REST PERIOD: Growing conditions should be maintained year-round. Water and fertilizer may be reduced somewhat in winter, especially for plants grown in the dark, short-day conditions common in temperate latitudes, but they should never be allowed to dry out completely. Occasional early morning mistings between waterings may be beneficial, particularly on bright, sunny days. In the habitat, light may be slightly higher in winter.

GROWING MEDIA: Plants may be mounted on tree-fern or cork slabs or potted in small pots filled with any open, fast-draining medium. Repotting may be done anytime new roots are growing.

Plant and Flower Information

PLANT SIZE AND TYPE: A 39 in. (100 cm) sympodial epiphyte.

PSEUDOBULB: 39 in. (100 cm) long. The stems are grooved.

LEAVES: The leaves are 0.8–2.0 in. (2–5 cm) long, leathery, and linear-lanceolate.

INFLORESCENCE: The blossoms are densely clustered on the raceme.

FLOWERS: 5–10 per inflorescence. The flowers are 0.5 in. (1.3 cm) long. Sepals and petals are lilac with white at the tips. The lilac lip has an orange margin.

REFERENCES: 146, 234.

PHOTOS/DRAWINGS: 146.

Dendrobium amabile (Loureiro) O'Brien

AKA: *Callista amabilis* Loureiro, *D. bronckartii* Wildeman. Seidenfaden (ref. 454) includes *D. bronckartii* as a synonym, but he suggested that the basis for combining it with *D. amabile* be reviewed. Hawkes (ref. 190) included *D. amabile* as a synonym of *D. thyrsiflorum* Rchb. f. but later works consider them separate species.

ORIGIN/HABITAT: Hainan, China, and near Quang Tri, Vietnam. Habitat elevation was not reported, but closely related species are generally cool growing, so we have estimated habitat elevation at about 4000 ft. (1220 m). Because habitat elevation is estimated, the following climate data should be used with caution.

CLIMATE: Station #48851, Quang Tri, Vietnam, Lat. 16.8°N, Long. 107.2°E, at 36 ft. (11 m). Temperatures are calculated for an estimated habitat elevation of 4000 ft. (1220 m), resulting in probable extremes of 92°F (33°C) and 36°F (2°C).

N/HEMISPHERE	JAN	FEB	MAR	APR	MAY	JUN	JUL	AUG	SEP	OCT	NOV	DEC
°F AVG MAX	60	62	66	74	79	80	79	80	75	70	65	61
°F AVG MIN	50	51	54	59	62	64	65	64	61	59	56	52
DIURNAL RANGE	10	11	12	15	17	16	14	16	14	11	9	9
RAIN/INCHES	6.2	2.6	2.6	2.3	4.0	3.2	3.2	4.4	16.4	22.9	21.0	11.4
HUMIDITY/%	90	92	90	86	82	75	73	76	84	89	89	90
BLOOM SEASON			**	***	***	*	*	**				
DAYS CLR @ 7AM	1	0	1	4	4	3	6	3	3	4	4	2
DAYS CLR @ 1PM	3	3	5	5	3	2	5	2	2	2	1	2
RAIN/MM	157	66	66	58	102	81	81	112	417	582	533	290
°C AVG MAX	15.5	16.6	18.8	23.3	26.1	26.6	26.1	26.6	23.8	21.1	18.3	16.1
°C AVG MIN	10.0	10.5	12.2	15.0	16.6	17.7	18.3	17.7	16.1	15.0	13.3	11.1
DIURNAL RANGE	5.5	6.1	6.6	8.3	9.5	8.9	7.8	8.9	7.7	6.1	5.0	5.0
S/HEMISPHERE	JUL	AUG	SEP	OCT	NOV	DEC	JAN	FEB	MAR	APR	MAY	JUN

Cultural Recommendations

LIGHT: 2500–3500 fc.

TEMPERATURES: Summer days average 79–80°F (26–27°C), and nights average 64–65°F (18°C), with a diurnal range of 14–16°F (8–9°C).

HUMIDITY: 80–90% most of the year, but averages drop to near 75% in summer.

WATER: Rainfall is light to moderate in summer. Heavy rains start in early autumn and continue into early winter. Cultivated plants should be allowed to dry somewhat between waterings but never remain dry for long periods.

FERTILIZER: ¼–½ recommended strength, applied weekly. A high-nitrogen fertilizer is beneficial from spring to midsummer, but a fertilizer high in phosphates should be used in late summer and autumn.

REST PERIOD: Winter days average 60–62°F (16–17°C), and nights average 50–52°F (10–11°C), with a diurnal range of 9–11°F (5–6°C). Although rainfall is lower for about 3 months in late winter and early spring, considerable additional water is available from heavy dew and mist. Cultivated plants should dry slightly between waterings, but they should never dry out completely. Fertilizer should be reduced or eliminated anytime water is reduced. Light should be as high as possible, short of burning the foliage.

GROWING MEDIA: Plants may be mounted on tree-fern or cork slabs if humidity is high and water is applied at least once daily in summer. Any open, fast-draining medium may be used for potting. Repotting is best done immediately after flowering when new roots are growing.

MISCELLANEOUS NOTES: The bloom time shown in the climate table is based on cultivation records for *D. bronckartii*.

Plant and Flower Information

PLANT SIZE AND TYPE: A 35–39 in. (90–100 cm) sympodial epiphyte. Plant information is based on descriptions for *D. bronckartii*.

PSEUDOBULB: 35 in. (90 cm) long. The many ridged and jointed stems are swollen in the middle and taper at each end.

LEAVES: 2–5 per growth. The oblong-lanceolate leaves are leathery, persistent, and 5 in. (13 cm) long. They are held near the apex of the stem.

INFLORESCENCE: 12 in. (30 cm) long. The spikes are long, pendulous, and laxly flowered.

FLOWERS: Several per inflorescence. The flowers are 2.2 in. (5.6 cm) across. Sepals and petals are usually pale rose, but they may be white. Also rose or white, the large circular lip is minutely toothed along the margin. The large, centered patch of orange hairs does not extend all the way to the margin. Long, lateral hairs at the base of the lip differentiate *D. amabile* from other closely related species.

HYBRIDIZING NOTES: Chromosome count is 2n = 40 as *D. bronckartii* (ref. 504, 580).
REFERENCES: 179, 190, 208, 210, 220, 254, 266, 428, 454, 504, 580.
PHOTOS/DRAWINGS: 210, *290*, *428*, 454.

Dendrobium amabile Schlechter. See *D. furcatum* Reinwardt ex Lindley. REFERENCES: 220, 436.

Dendrobium amblyogenium Schlechter

AKA: *D. erosum* Kränzlin not Lindley.
ORIGIN/HABITAT: Endemic to Sulawesi (Celebes) at about 3300 ft. (1000 m). Plants often grow in trees on the forested slopes of Mt. Klabat, a volcano east of Manado at the extreme northeastern tip of the island.
CLIMATE: Station #97014, Manado, Sulawesi, Lat. 1.5°N, Long. 124.9°E, at 264 ft. (80 m). Temperatures are calculated for an elevation of 3000 ft. (910 m), resulting in probable extremes of 88°F (31°C) and 56°F (13°C).

N/HEMISPHERE	JAN	FEB	MAR	APR	MAY	JUN	JUL	AUG	SEP	OCT	NOV	DEC
°F AVG MAX	76	76	76	77	78	78	78	80	80	80	78	77
°F AVG MIN	64	64	64	64	65	64	64	64	64	63	64	65
DIURNAL RANGE	12	12	12	13	13	14	14	16	16	17	14	12
RAIN/INCHES	18.6	13.8	12.2	8.0	6.4	6.5	4.8	4.0	3.4	4.9	8.9	14.7
HUMIDITY/%	84	83	83	83	81	80	75	72	75	77	82	83
BLOOM SEASON			*					*				*
DAYS CLR @ 8AM	4	3	6	11	11	12	12	14	17	12	8	
DAYS CLR @ 2PM	1	1	1	2	1	3	3	4	4	4	1	1
RAIN/MM	472	351	310	203	163	165	122	102	86	124	226	373
°C AVG MAX	24.4	24.4	24.4	25.0	25.5	25.5	25.5	26.7	26.7	26.7	25.5	25.0
°C AVG MIN	17.8	17.8	17.8	17.8	18.3	17.8	17.8	17.8	17.8	17.2	17.8	18.3
DIURNAL RANGE	6.6	6.6	6.6	7.2	7.2	7.7	7.7	8.9	8.9	9.5	7.7	6.7
S/HEMISPHERE	JUL	AUG	SEP	OCT	NOV	DEC	JAN	FEB	MAR	APR	MAY	JUN

Cultural Recommendations

LIGHT: 1200–2400 fc. In the habitat, morning light is highest as skies are usually overcast by afternoon.
TEMPERATURES: Throughout the year, days average 76–80°F (24–27°C), and nights average 63–65°F (17–18°C), with a diurnal range of 12–17°F (7–10°C). Record extreme temperatures are only a few degrees above and below the average temperatures. Plants may be intolerant of wide temperature fluctuations.
HUMIDITY: 80–85% most of the year, dropping to 70–75% in late summer and autumn.
WATER: Rainfall is moderate to heavy all year. The driest weather occurs in late summer when temperatures are warm. Cultivated plants should be kept moist but not soggy. Warm water might be beneficial.
FERTILIZER: ¼–½ recommended strength. A balanced fertilizer should be applied weekly to biweekly throughout the year.
REST PERIOD: Growing temperatures should be maintained all year. The plants may rest during the 1–2 month drier period which occurs in late summer and coincides with the period of greatest diurnal range. Cultivated plants should dry out slightly during this period, but they should never remain dry for long. The heaviest rainfall in the habitat occurs in winter, but water should not be increased for cultivated plants. In fact, water should be reduced somewhat for plants grown in the dark, short-day conditions common in temperate latitudes, but they should not be allowed to dry out completely.
GROWING MEDIA: Plants may be potted in a mixture of fir bark or shredded tree-fern with moisture-retaining additives. A surface layer of sphagnum moss may be beneficial. The medium should be moist, but not soggy. It should never be allowed to dry out completely. Repotting may be done anytime new roots are growing.
MISCELLANEOUS NOTES: The bloom season shown in the climate table is based on collection reports. In the habitat, plants were flowering and carrying fruit in early spring.

Plant and Flower Information

PLANT SIZE AND TYPE: A 26–30 in. (65–75 cm) sympodial epiphyte.
PSEUDOBULB: 28 in. (70 cm) long. The clustered stems arise from a short rhizome.
LEAVES: Many. The linear-lanceolate leaves, which are 1.8–2.8 in. (4.5–7.0 cm) long, are spaced 1.0–1.2 in. (2.5–3.0 cm) apart. They are spreading, smooth, and unequally bilobed at the apex.
INFLORESCENCE: 0.8–1.2 in. (2–3 cm) long. The short racemes are very densely flowered.
FLOWERS: 10–15 per inflorescence. The small flowers are 0.4 in. (1 cm) across. Sepals are oblong. Petals are elliptic with a minute fringe along the margin. Blossoms are pink with whitish tips.
REFERENCES: 221, 436.

Dendrobium amblyornidis Rchb. f.

ORIGIN/HABITAT: Irian Jaya (western New Guinea). Plants grow in the Arfak Mountains at 4800–5000 ft. (1460–1520 m).
CLIMATE: Station #97530, Manokwari, Irian Jaya, Lat. 0.9°S, Long. 134.1°E, at 10 ft. (3 m). Temperatures are calculated for an elevation of 5000 ft. (1520 m), resulting in probable extremes of 77°F (25°C) and 52°F (11°C).

N/HEMISPHERE	JAN	FEB	MAR	APR	MAY	JUN	JUL	AUG	SEP	OCT	NOV	DEC
°F AVG MAX	70	69	71	71	72	70	70	70	70	70	70	69
°F AVG MIN	58	59	58	58	58	59	57	57	58	58	58	58
DIURNAL RANGE	12	10	13	13	14	11	13	13	12	12	12	11
RAIN/INCHES	5.4	5.6	5.0	4.7	4.5	10.3	12.0	9.4	13.2	11.1	7.8	7.3
HUMIDITY/%	87	87	86	84	85	86	86	85	86	86	86	85
BLOOM SEASON	N/A											
DAYS CLR @ 9AM	4	3	3	3	3	3	1	1	2	2	3	7
DAYS CLR @ 3PM	2	2	2	3	1	1	1	1	0	1	0	2
RAIN/MM	137	142	127	119	114	262	305	239	335	282	198	185
°C AVG MAX	20.9	20.3	21.4	21.4	22.0	20.9	20.9	20.9	20.9	20.9	20.9	20.3
°C AVG MIN	14.2	14.7	14.2	14.2	14.2	14.7	13.6	13.6	14.2	14.2	14.2	14.2
DIURNAL RANGE	6.7	5.6	7.2	7.2	7.8	6.2	7.3	7.3	6.7	6.7	6.7	6.1
S/HEMISPHERE	JUL	AUG	SEP	OCT	NOV	DEC	JAN	FEB	MAR	APR	MAY	JUN

Cultural Recommendations

LIGHT: 2000–3000 fc.
TEMPERATURES: Throughout the year, days average 69–72°F (20–22°C), and nights average 57–59°F (14–15°C), with a diurnal range of 10–14°F (6–8°C). Because of microclimate effects, actual maximum temperatures may be as much as 10°F (6°C) warmer than the calculated values in the climate table.
HUMIDITY: Near 85% year-round.
WATER: Rainfall is moderate to very heavy all year. Cultivated plants should be kept moist with only slight drying allowed between waterings.
FERTILIZER: ¼–½ recommended strength. A balanced fertilizer should be applied weekly to biweekly throughout the year.
REST PERIOD: Growing conditions should be maintained year-round. Water and fertilizer may be reduced somewhat in winter, especially for plants grown in the dark, short-day conditions common in temperate latitudes. Plants should never be allowed to dry out completely, however.
GROWING MEDIA: Plants may be mounted on tree-fern or cork slabs if humidity is high and plants watered daily in summer. When plants are potted, any open, fast-draining medium may be used. Repotting may be done anytime new roots are growing.
MISCELLANEOUS NOTES: The stems of *D. amblyornidis* are used by the *Amblyornis inornata* (a plain-Jane bird of paradise) to build elaborate,

hutlike nests in the dense forests where, according to one explorer, "Scarcely a ray of sunshine penetrated the branches. The ground was almost destitute of vegetation."

Plant and Flower Information

PLANT SIZE AND TYPE: A bushy, 24 in. (60 cm) sympodial epiphyte.

PSEUDOBULB: 24 in. (60 cm) long. The stems are strong and thin.

LEAVES: 2 per growth. The pointed, lanceolate leaves are 3.6 in. (9 cm) long.

INFLORESCENCE: Short.

FLOWERS: 1–2 per inflorescence. Blossoms have a wedge-shaped dorsal sepal, with reflexed, sickle-shaped lateral sepals, and linear-lanceolate petals. Sepals and petals are pointed. The oblong lip is wavy with 2 keels on the disk. Flower color was not included in the description.

REFERENCES: 216, 254, 470.

Dendrobium amboinense Hooker f.

AKA: *Callista amboinensis* O. Kuntze.

ORIGIN/HABITAT: Ambon Island in the Moluccas. Habitat elevation is not available, so the following temperatures should be used with caution.

CLIMATE: Station #97724, Ambon/Pattimura, Indonesia, Lat. 3.7°S, Long. 128.1°E, at 33 ft. (10 m). Record extreme temperatures are 96°F (36°C) and 66°F (19°C).

N/HEMISPHERE	JAN	FEB	MAR	APR	MAY	JUN	JUL	AUG	SEP	OCT	NOV	DEC
°F AVG MAX	81	81	83	85	88	88	88	88	88	86	84	82
°F AVG MIN	74	74	74	74	75	76	76	76	76	76	75	74
DIURNAL RANGE	7	7	9	11	13	12	12	12	12	10	9	8
RAIN/INCHES	23.7	15.8	9.5	6.1	4.5	5.2	5.0	4.7	5.3	11.0	20.3	25.1
HUMIDITY/%	83	82	81	80	79	78	78	77	79	82	83	84
BLOOM SEASON				*								
DAYS CLR @ 9AM	1	1	1	6	7	4	3	3	5	5	3	3
DAYS CLR @ 3PM	1	1	2	5	6	1	1	1	2	3	1	3
RAIN/MM	602	401	241	155	114	132	127	119	135	279	516	638
°C AVG MAX	27.2	27.2	28.3	29.4	31.1	31.1	31.1	31.1	31.1	30.0	28.9	27.8
°C AVG MIN	23.3	23.3	23.3	23.3	23.9	24.4	24.4	24.4	24.4	24.4	23.9	23.3
DIURNAL RANGE	3.9	3.9	5.0	6.1	7.2	6.7	6.7	6.7	6.7	5.6	5.0	4.5
S/HEMISPHERE	JUL	AUG	SEP	OCT	NOV	DEC	JAN	FEB	MAR	APR	MAY	JUN

Cultural Recommendations

LIGHT: 2500–3500 fc.

TEMPERATURES: Summer days average 88°F (31°C), and nights average 76°F (24°C), with a diurnal range of 12°F (7°C).

HUMIDITY: 80–85% year-round.

WATER: Rainfall is moderate to heavy all year. Conditions are slightly drier from late spring through summer. Cultivated plants should be kept evenly moist all year with only slight drying allowed between waterings.

FERTILIZER: ¼–½ recommended strength. A balanced fertilizer should be applied weekly to biweekly throughout the year.

REST PERIOD: Growing conditions should be maintained all year. Temperatures are slightly cooler. Winter days average 81–82°F (27–28°C), and nights average 74°F (23°C), with a diurnal range of 7–8°F (4–5°C). A brief semidry period in late spring may be beneficial. Less water is needed for plants grown in the dark, short-day conditions common in temperate latitudes. These plants should never be allowed to dry out completely, however.

GROWING MEDIA: Plants may be potted in any open, moisture-retaining medium. If plants are mounted, high humidity and daily watering are critical, especially during hot, dry weather. Repotting may be done anytime new roots are growing.

MISCELLANEOUS NOTES: The bloom season shown in the climate table is based on a single cultivation record. Plants that produce flowers which last a single day commonly bloom several times during the year. Flowering usually occurs 7–14 days after a sudden 10°F (5°C) drop in daytime temperatures.

Plant and Flower Information

PLANT SIZE AND TYPE: A 14 in. (35 cm) sympodial plant.

PSEUDOBULB: 8 in. (20 cm) long. Stems are jointed, club-shaped, and swollen at the base. The upper portion has 4–6 angles.

LEAVES: 2–3 at the apex of each growth. The leathery leaves, which are about 6 in. (15 cm) long, are oblong-lanceolate and pointed at the tip.

INFLORESCENCE: Short. Inflorescences arise along the apical portion of the stem.

FLOWERS: 2–4 per inflorescence. The spreading flowers are normally about 3 in. (7.6 cm) across, but they may reach a diameter of 7 in. (18 cm). Sepals and petals may be white or cream with red and orange-red veins and red margins. The yellowish lip is also outlined with red or dark purple, and the disk is marked with dark orange spots. Blossoms are short-lived, lasting a single day.

REFERENCES: 25, 179, 190, 210, 216, 254, 310, 437, 445, 468, 541.

PHOTOS/DRAWINGS: 210, 437.

Dendrobium ambotiense J. J. Smith

ORIGIN/HABITAT: Pulau Buru in the Molucca Islands. Elevation and habitat information are unavailable, so the following climate data should be used with caution.

CLIMATE: Station #97700, Namlea, Pulau Buru, Indonesia, Lat. 3.3°S, Long. 127.0°E, at 66 ft. (20 m). Record extreme temperatures are not available for this location.

N/HEMISPHERE	JAN	FEB	MAR	APR	MAY	JUN	JUL	AUG	SEP	OCT	NOV	DEC
°F AVG MAX	84	84	86	87	87	86	85	84	85	86	86	84
°F AVG MIN	75	77	77	78	80	78	77	77	77	77	77	76
DIURNAL RANGE	9	7	9	9	7	8	8	7	8	9	9	8
RAIN/INCHES	3.1	4.4	1.3	1.6	4.0	5.8	6.1	5.3	6.9	2.8	2.0	5.5
HUMIDITY/%	N/A											
BLOOM SEASON									*			
DAYS CLR	N/A											
RAIN/MM	79	111	33	42	101	146	156	136	176	71	50	139
°C AVG MAX	29.0	29.0	29.8	30.4	30.8	30.1	29.5	29.0	29.5	30.3	30.2	29.1
°C AVG MIN	23.9	24.8	25.2	25.8	26.5	25.7	25.3	25.1	25.1	25.2	25.0	24.3
DIURNAL RANGE	5.1	4.2	4.6	4.6	4.3	4.4	4.2	3.9	4.4	5.1	5.2	4.8
S/HEMISPHERE	JUL	AUG	SEP	OCT	NOV	DEC	JAN	FEB	MAR	APR	MAY	JUN

Cultural Recommendations

LIGHT: 2000–3000 fc.

TEMPERATURES: Throughout the year, days average 84–87°F (29–31°C), and nights average 75–80°F (24–27°C), with a diurnal range of 7–9°F (4–5°C).

HUMIDITY: Averages are not available for this location. However, records from nearby stations in the region indicate probable values of 80–85% year-round.

WATER: Rainfall is moderate most of the year, with a 2-month, semidry period in early spring and again in autumn. Cultivated plants should be allowed to dry slightly between waterings.

FERTILIZER: ¼–½ recommended strength. A balanced fertilizer should be applied weekly to biweekly throughout the year.

REST PERIOD: Growing temperatures should be maintained year-round. Water should be reduced somewhat for cultivated plants for 1–2 months in autumn and again in spring. Additional drying should be allowed between waterings, but plants should not remain dry for long periods. Fertilizer should be reduced whenever water is reduced.

GROWING MEDIA: Plants may be mounted on tree-fern or cork slabs or potted in small pots filled with any open, fast-draining medium. Repotting may be done anytime new roots are growing.

MISCELLANEOUS NOTES: The bloom season shown in the climate table is based on reports from the habitat. The plant was described in 1928 in *Bul. Jard. Bot. Buit.* 3rd sér. 9:466.

Plant and Flower Information

PLANT SIZE AND TYPE: A 2.4 in. (6 cm) sympodial epiphyte.

PSEUDOBULB: 1.6 in. (4 cm) long. The widely spaced growths arise from a branching rhizome.

LEAVES: 12 per growth. The linear-lanceolate leaves are about 1.6 in. (4 cm) long, fleshy, laterally compressed, and terminate in a sharp point. They may be erect or recurved.

INFLORESCENCE: Short. The branching inflorescences may arise along the side or at the apex of the stem.

FLOWERS: 1 per branch. The flowers are 0.2 in. (0.6 cm) long. Flower color was not included with the original plant description.

REFERENCES: 224.

Dendrobium amesianum Schlechter. Transferred to *Ephemerantha* by Hunt and Summerhayes, which is now considered a synonym of *Flickingeria*. REFERENCES: 211, 213, 214, 223, 230, 271, 441.

Dendrobium amethystoglossum Rchb. f.

AKA: Sometimes spelled *D. amethystoglossa*.

ORIGIN/HABITAT: Northwestern Luzon in the Philippines. Plants often grow on mossy, limestone cliffs at about 4600 ft. (1400 m) in Benguet Province.

CLIMATE: Station #98328, Baguio, Philippines, Lat. 16.4°N, Long. 120.6°E, at 4962 ft. (1512 m). Record extreme temperatures are 84°F (29°C) and 46°F (8°C).

N/HEMISPHERE	JAN	FEB	MAR	APR	MAY	JUN	JUL	AUG	SEP	OCT	NOV	DEC
°F AVG MAX	72	73	76	77	76	75	71	71	71	73	74	74
°F AVG MIN	55	56	58	60	61	61	60	60	60	60	59	57
DIURNAL RANGE	17	17	18	17	15	14	11	11	11	13	15	17
RAIN/INCHES	0.9	0.9	1.7	4.3	15.8	17.2	42.3	45.7	28.1	15.0	4.9	2.0
HUMIDITY/%	83	83	83	85	89	90	93	93	92	89	86	84
BLOOM SEASON	*	**	**	*	*							
DAYS CLR	N/A											
RAIN/MM	23	23	43	109	401	437	1074	1161	714	381	124	51
°C AVG MAX	22.2	22.8	24.4	25.0	24.4	23.9	21.7	21.7	21.7	22.8	23.3	23.3
°C AVG MIN	12.8	13.3	14.4	15.6	16.1	16.1	15.6	15.6	15.6	15.6	15.0	13.9
DIURNAL RANGE	9.4	9.5	10.0	9.4	8.3	7.8	6.1	6.1	6.1	7.2	8.3	9.4
S/HEMISPHERE	JUL	AUG	SEP	OCT	NOV	DEC	JAN	FEB	MAR	APR	MAY	JUN

Cultural Recommendations

LIGHT: 1500–2400 fc. Diffused or dappled light is recommended. Cloud-cover records are unavailable, but high elevations are typically cloudy in this region.

TEMPERATURES: Summer days average 71–75°F (22–24°C), and nights average 60–61°F (16°C), with a summer diurnal range of 11–14°F (6–8°C). Plants from this habitat are not heat tolerant. If cultivated at warmer temperatures, *D. amethystoglossum* may be considered difficult to grow and buds may drop. Growers report, however, that plants are easy to grow at intermediate to cool temperatures.

HUMIDITY: 85–90% year round.

WATER: Rainfall is very heavy from late spring into autumn, but conditions are much drier in winter. Cultivated plants should be kept moist but not soggy during the growing season, but water should be gradually reduced after new growths mature in autumn. Growers indicate that this water pattern is critically important.

FERTILIZER: ¼–½ recommended strength, applied weekly. A high-nitrogen fertilizer is beneficial from spring to midsummer, but a fertilizer high in phosphates should be used in late summer and autumn.

REST PERIOD: Winter days average 72–76°F (22–24°C), and nights average 55–58°F (13–14°C), with a winter diurnal range of 17–18°F (9–10°C). Growers report that plants readily adapt to winter lows near 50°F (10°C), with a minimum winter temperature of 43°F (6°C). Plants need a cool, dry rest for a minimum of 2 months, but the rest period may last 4 months. Rainfall is low for 2–4 months, but the continuing high humidity indicates that additional moisture is frequently available from fog, dew, or mist. Cultivated plants should be allowed to dry somewhat between waterings, but should never remain dry for long periods. In the habitat, light may be higher in winter.

GROWING MEDIA: Plants may be mounted on tree-fern slabs or potted in any open medium that retains moisture. Repotting is best done after flowering, at the end of the dry season.

MISCELLANEOUS NOTES: The bloom season shown in the climate table is based on cultivation records. In the habitat, plants bloom from late autumn through midwinter. Growers indicate that plants do not survive cultivation in Manila, but they grow well in Honolulu, which is about 5–10°F (3–6°C) cooler. Growers often consider this a problem plant, so careful attention should be paid to cultural requirements.

Plant and Flower Information

PLANT SIZE AND TYPE: An 18–39 in. (45–100 cm) sympodial plant.

PSEUDOBULB: 24–35 in. (60–90 cm) long. The erect or arching stems are about 1 in. (2.5 cm) in diameter. They are canelike, frequently zigzag, with ridges even on young stems. *D. amethystoglossum* is often very large and robust, and in nature, it may form clumps of 15–20 canes.

LEAVES: Several. The oval, pale green leaves are about 3–4 in. (8–10 cm) long and stalkless. They are normally deciduous before flowering, but leaves sometimes last more than a single growing season. Under ideal conditions they are soft and shiny, but they may become leathery anytime water or humidity is inadequate.

INFLORESCENCE: 3–6 in. (8–15 cm) long. Plants produce numerous short, drooping clusters that emerge from nodes near the apex of the stem. Inflorescences are normally borne on leafless pseudobulbs, but they may also emerge from mature, leafy stems.

FLOWERS: 15–20 per inflorescence. The waxy blossoms are about 1.2–1.5 in. (3.0–3.8 cm) across. The white sepals and petals open fully and may have amethyst at the tips. The lip is tubular with a large, vivid purple stain in the center. All floral segments are pointed. Flowers are fragrant and last 3–4 weeks.

HYBRIDIZING NOTES: Chromosome counts are n = 20 (ref. 151, 187) and 2n = 40 (ref. 151, 153, 154, 187, 188, 273).

REFERENCES: 6, 12, 98, 151, 153, 154, 179, 187, 188, 190, 196, 210, 216, 254, 273, 293, 296, 371, 373, 430, 445, 536, 541.

PHOTOS/DRAWINGS: 98, 210, *350, 371, 430*.

Dendrobium amoenum Wallich ex Lindley

AKA: *D. egertoniae* Lindley, *D. mesochlorum* Lindley. Hawkes (ref. 190) also lists *D. aphyllum* (Roxburgh) C. Fischer, but later authors do not include it as a synonym.

ORIGIN/HABITAT: The Himalaya region. The habitat extends from Dehra Dun and Garhwal eastward through central Nepal, Sikkim, Bangladesh, the Khasi (Khasia) Hills in Meghalaya, and Burma. Plants grow at 3300–6550 ft. (1000–2000 m). They are found at the base of trees where they receive ample moisture and protection from extreme temperature fluctuations.

Dendrobium amphigenyum

CLIMATE: Station #42398, Baghdogra, India, Lat. 26.7°N, Long. 88.3°E, at 412 ft. (126 m). Temperatures are calculated for an elevation of 5000 ft. (1520 m), resulting in probable extremes of 89°F (32°C) and 21°F (−6°C).

N/HEMISPHERE	JAN	FEB	MAR	APR	MAY	JUN	JUL	AUG	SEP	OCT	NOV	DEC
°F AVG MAX	59	62	70	75	75	74	74	74	73	72	67	62
°F AVG MIN	35	39	45	53	58	61	62	62	61	55	45	38
DIURNAL RANGE	24	23	25	22	17	13	12	12	12	17	22	24
RAIN/INCHES	0.3	0.7	1.3	3.7	11.8	25.9	32.2	25.3	21.2	5.6	0.5	0.2
HUMIDITY/%	73	68	57	58	74	84	86	85	85	79	75	76
BLOOM SEASON					*	*						
DAYS CLR @ 6AM	21	18	15	11	5	0	1	1	4	13	23	19
DAYS CLR @ 12PM	23	16	16	11	2	2	0	1	2	10	21	18
RAIN/MM	8	18	33	94	300	658	818	643	538	142	13	5
°C AVG MAX	14.9	16.6	21.0	23.8	23.8	23.3	23.3	23.3	22.7	22.1	19.4	16.6
°C AVG MIN	1.6	3.8	7.1	11.6	14.4	16.0	16.6	16.6	16.0	12.7	7.1	3.3
DIURNAL RANGE	13.3	12.8	13.9	12.2	9.4	7.3	6.7	6.7	6.7	9.4	12.3	13.3
S/HEMISPHERE	JUL	AUG	SEP	OCT	NOV	DEC	JAN	FEB	MAR	APR	MAY	JUN

Cultural Recommendations

LIGHT: 2000–3000 fc. Diffused light is suggested in summer.

TEMPERATURES: Summer days average 74°F (23°C), and nights average 61–62°F (16–17°C), with a diurnal range of 12–13°F (7°C). Because of the effects of microclimate, actual summer maximum and winter minimum temperatures in the habitat may be 6–8°F (3–4°C) warmer than indicated in the climate table.

HUMIDITY: 75–85% most of the year, dropping below 60% for 2 months in late winter or early spring.

WATER: Rainfall is extremely heavy in summer, but conditions are much drier in winter. More moisture is available at higher elevations than is recorded at the weather station. Cultivated plants should be kept wet but not soggy from spring to early autumn. Water should be gradually reduced after new growths mature in late autumn.

FERTILIZER: 1/4–1/2 recommended strength, applied weekly. A high-nitrogen fertilizer is beneficial from spring to midsummer, but a fertilizer high in phosphates should be used in late summer and autumn.

REST PERIOD: For 2–4 months in winter, days average 59–70°F (15–21°C), and nights average 35–45°F (2–7°C), with a diurnal range of 23–25°F (13–14°C). Growers are cautioned that actual minimum temperatures may be somewhat warmer than indicated. Plants should tolerate freezing temperatures, at least for short periods, if they are dry at the time; but extremes should be avoided in cultivation. In the habitat, the dry period is 4–5 months long; but for the 3 driest months, the high humidity indicates that some additional moisture is available from heavy dew or mist. Cultivated plants should be allowed to dry out between waterings in winter, but they should not remain dry for extended periods. Occasional early morning mistings between waterings, especially on warm, sunny days, may help prevent the plants from becoming too dry. Fertilizer should be eliminated until water is increased in spring. In the habitat, light is much higher in winter.

GROWING MEDIA: Mounting plants on tree-fern or cork slabs accommodates their pendent growth habit, but humidity must be high and plants need watering at least once daily in summer. Plants may be suspended high in the greenhouse in hanging pots or baskets filled with any open, rapidly draining medium. Repotting is best done immediately after flowering.

MISCELLANEOUS NOTES: The bloom season shown in the climate table is based on reports from the habitat. The cool, dry rest is essential to initiate blooms.

Plant and Flower Information

PLANT SIZE AND TYPE: A 12–30 in. (30–75 cm) sympodial plant.

PSEUDOBULB: 12–20 in. (30–50 cm) long. The pseudobulbous stems are slender and pendulous. The thickened nodes occur at about 2 in. (5 cm) intervals.

LEAVES: Many. The pale green leaves are linear to oblong-lanceolate, 2–4 in. (5–10 cm) long, narrow, wavy, and pointed at the apex. They are quickly deciduous.

INFLORESCENCE: Short. An inflorescence emerges from each upper node on leafless canes, but flowers are held well away from the stem.

FLOWERS: 1–3 per inflorescence, with many on each growth. The blossoms are 1.6–2.0 in. (4–5 cm) across, and may be either wide-opening or rather closed. The broad sepals and petals are white, often becoming amethyst at the tip. The white lip is marked with a purple spot near the tip and a large greenish yellow stain toward the center. It is ovate to nearly round when spread, wavy along the margin, with a small notch at the apex. The spur is swollen at the base. Blossoms have a fragrance reminiscent of violets.

HYBRIDIZING NOTES: Chromosome counts are n = 19 (ref. 154), n = 20 (ref. 150, 154, 504, 542, 580), 2n = 38 (ref. 504, 580), 2n = 40 (ref. 154, 542), and 2n = 80 (ref. 154, 542).

REFERENCES: 32, 38, 46, 102, 150, 154, 157, 190, 202, 210, 216, 254, 277, 278, 294, 317, 358, 369, 374, 376, 430, 445, 504, 541, 542, 557, 570, 577, 580.

PHOTOS/DRAWINGS: 32, 38, 46, 102, 210, 294, *369*, *430*, 570.

Dendrobium amphigenyum Ridley

AKA: *D. fantasticum* L. O. Williams.

ORIGIN/HABITAT: New Guinea. In the Morobe district of Papua New Guinea, plants grow in mossy forests at 5500–7550 ft. (1680–2300 m). In Irian Jaya (western New Guinea), they were collected at 3100 ft. (950 m).

CLIMATE: Station #200192, Garaina, Papua New Guinea, Lat. 7.9°S, Long. 147.1°E, at 2350 ft. (716 m). Temperatures are calculated for an elevation of 6000 ft. (1830 m), resulting in probable extremes of 82°F (28°C) and 34°F (1°C).

N/HEMISPHERE	JAN	FEB	MAR	APR	MAY	JUN	JUL	AUG	SEP	OCT	NOV	DEC
°F AVG MAX	68	70	71	72	73	73	73	73	72	72	71	69
°F AVG MIN	51	51	51	52	51	52	53	53	53	52	52	51
DIURNAL RANGE	17	19	20	20	22	21	20	20	19	20	19	18
RAIN/INCHES	5.8	6.5	8.7	11.1	11.8	11.9	8.9	11.7	11.5	9.9	7.7	5.2
HUMIDITY/%	84	82	82	81	80	80	81	81	82	83	84	84
BLOOM SEASON		*			*			*				
DAYS CLR	N/A											
RAIN/MM	147	165	221	282	300	302	226	297	292	251	196	132
°C AVG MAX	20.0	21.1	21.6	22.2	22.8	22.8	22.8	22.8	22.2	22.2	21.6	20.5
°C AVG MIN	10.5	10.5	10.5	11.1	10.5	11.1	11.6	11.6	11.6	11.1	11.1	10.5
DIURNAL RANGE	9.5	10.6	11.1	11.1	12.3	11.7	11.2	11.2	10.6	11.1	10.5	10.0
S/HEMISPHERE	JUL	AUG	SEP	OCT	NOV	DEC	JAN	FEB	MAR	APR	MAY	JUN

Cultural Recommendations

LIGHT: 2000–3000 fc.

TEMPERATURES: Throughout the year, days average 68–73°F (20–23°C), and nights average 51–53°F (11–12°C), with a diurnal range of 17–22°F (10–12°C).

HUMIDITY: 80–85% year-round.

WATER: Rainfall is heavy most of the year. Conditions are slightly drier in winter. Cultivated plants should be kept moist but not soggy.

FERTILIZER: 1/4–1/2 recommended strength. A balanced fertilizer should be applied weekly to biweekly throughout the year. The Royal Botanic Garden in Edinburgh uses a seaweed-based fertilizer for plants from high-elevation habitats in New Guinea.

REST PERIOD: Growing conditions should be maintained all year. In the habitat, rainfall is slightly lower in winter. Water and fertilizer may be reduced somewhat in winter, especially for plants grown in the dark, short-day conditions common in temperate latitudes. Plants should never be allowed to dry out completely, however. In the habitat, light is probably higher in winter.

GROWING MEDIA: Plants may be mounted on slabs of tree-fern fiber if humidity is high and water is applied at least once daily in summer. If plants are potted, a mixture of fir bark or chopped tree-fern fiber with moisture-retaining additives is suggested. A surface layer of sphagnum moss might be beneficial, especially in dry regions. The medium should be kept moist, but not soggy. It should never be allowed to dry out completely. Repotting may be done anytime new roots are growing.

MISCELLANEOUS NOTES: The bloom season shown in the climate table is based on cultivation and collection records. Botanists indicate that *D. amphigenyum* is often confused with *D. dendrocolloides* J. J. Smith and *D. woodsii* Cribb. Cribb (ref. 83) indicates that *D. dendrocolloides* has a deeply emarginate, 3–lobed lip with the midlobe equal in length to the sidelobes, whereas *D. woodsii* has a midlobe that is shorter and lobules that are tapering and acute.

Plant and Flower Information

PLANT SIZE AND TYPE: A variable, 3–16 in. (8–40 cm) sympodial epiphyte or lithophyte.

PSEUDOBULB: 3–16 in. (8–40 cm) long. The erect pseudobulbs are cylindrical or slightly swollen near the apex. They turn orange-yellow when dry.

LEAVES: 2–3 per growth. The pointed, lanceolate leaves are 2–5 in. (5–12 cm) long, suberect, and leathery.

INFLORESCENCE: 2–3 in. (6–8 cm) long. The suberect inflorescences emerge from nodes at or near the apex of the pseudobulb.

FLOWERS: Few per inflorescence. The small, fleshy flowers are 0.4 in. (1 cm) across. Sepals and petals are cream to green with purple mottling. The purplish lip is clawed and strongly recurved at the base. The midlobe is smaller than the sidelobes.

HYBRIDIZING NOTES: Chromosome count is 2n = 36+2f (ref. 153, 273).

REFERENCES: 83, 153, 179, 222, 273, 400, 554, 574.

Dendrobium amplum Lindley.

Now considered a synonym of *Epigeneium amplum* (Lindley) Summerhayes. REFERENCES: 32, 38, 46, 190, 202, 216, 229, 254, 277, 369, 445, 449, 499, 504, 580. PHOTOS/DRAWINGS: 46.

Dendrobium anamalayanum M. Chandrabose, V. Chandrasekaran, and N. C. Nair

ORIGIN/HABITAT: Endemic to southwest India. Plants were collected in Kavarakal and Donalar, Anamalai, Coimbatore District, Tamil Nadu (Madras). They grow in evergreen forests at 4750–6500 ft. (1450–1980 m).

CLIMATE: Station #43319, Coimbatore, India, Lat. 11.0°N, Long. 77.1°E, at 1298 ft. (396 m). Temperatures are calculated for an elevation of 5600 ft. (1710 m), resulting in probable extremes of 90°F (32°C) and 39°F (4°C).

N/HEMISPHERE	JAN	FEB	MAR	APR	MAY	JUN	JUL	AUG	SEP	OCT	NOV	DEC
°F AVG MAX	72	77	81	83	80	75	73	73	75	74	71	70
°F AVG MIN	51	53	56	60	60	58	57	57	57	57	55	52
DIURNAL RANGE	21	24	25	23	20	17	16	16	18	17	16	18
RAIN/INCHES	0.6	0.4	0.5	1.6	2.5	1.5	1.7	1.2	1.6	6.3	4.0	1.4
HUMIDITY/%	61	56	52	61	68	72	74	73	74	73	73	66
BLOOM SEASON						*			*			
DAYS CLR @ 5PM	16	15	19	11	10	1	1	3	5	9	10	
RAIN/MM	15	10	13	41	64	38	43	30	41	160	102	36
°C AVG MAX	22.1	24.9	27.1	28.2	26.6	23.8	22.7	22.7	23.8	23.2	21.6	21.0
°C AVG MIN	10.4	11.6	13.2	15.4	15.4	14.3	13.8	13.8	13.8	13.8	12.7	11.0
DIURNAL RANGE	11.7	13.3	13.9	12.8	11.2	9.5	8.9	8.9	10.0	9.4	8.9	10.0
S/HEMISPHERE	JUL	AUG	SEP	OCT	NOV	DEC	JAN	FEB	MAR	APR	MAY	JUN

Cultural Recommendations

LIGHT: 3000–4000 fc.

TEMPERATURES: Summer days average 73–75°F (23–24°C), and nights average 57–58°F (14°C), with a diurnal range of 16–17°F (9–10°C). Spring is the warmest season. Days average 80–83°F (27–28°C), and nights average 56–60°F (13–15°C), with a diurnal range of 20–25°F (11–14°C).

HUMIDITY: 70–75% in summer and autumn, dropping to near 50% in late winter.

WATER: Rainfall is low to moderate all year, with autumn being the wet season. However, more moisture is probably available from greater rainfall, mist, and fog in the high elevation habitat than is indicated by the climate data from the low elevation station. Cultivated plants should be kept moist from spring to autumn, but they should be allowed to dry slightly between waterings. Water should be gradually reduced in late autumn after new growths mature.

FERTILIZER: ¼–½ recommended strength, applied weekly. A high nitrogen fertilizer is beneficial from spring to midsummer, but a fertilizer high in phosphates should be used in late summer and autumn.

REST PERIOD: Winter days average 70–77°F (21–25°C), and nights average 51–53°F (10–12°C), with a diurnal range of 18–24°F (10–13°C). Rainfall is very low for 3 months in winter. In addition, conditions are so dry that even dew is uncommon. Cultivated plants should be allowed to dry out between waterings, but they should not remain dry for extended periods. Occasional early morning mistings between waterings may help prevent plants from becoming too dry. Reduce or eliminate fertilizer while water is reduced. Light should be as high as the plant can tolerate, short of burning the foliage.

GROWING MEDIA: Plants may be mounted on tree-fern or cork slabs if humidity is high and plants are watered at least once daily in summer. When plants are potted, any open, fast-draining medium may be used. They may be repotted anytime new roots are growing.

MISCELLANEOUS NOTES: The bloom season shown in the climate table is based on collection reports. All plants bloom at the same time.

Plant and Flower Information

PLANT SIZE AND TYPE: A 1.6–4.0 in. (4–10 cm) sympodial epiphyte.

PSEUDOBULB: 0.8–1.2 in. (2–3 cm) long. The stems are ovoid, greenish pink, and sheathed at the base.

LEAVES: 2 at the apex of each growth. The elliptic leaves are 0.8–2.8 in. (2–7 cm) long.

INFLORESCENCE: 5 in. (13 cm) long. A single inflorescence arises from between the leaves at the apex of the pseudobulb.

FLOWERS: 5–many per inflorescence. The flowers are 0.6 in. (1.6 cm) across. Blossoms are white with a pink tinge. The clawed, 3-lobed lip is broadly obovate with toothlike sidelobes and a serrated front margin.

REFERENCES: 60, 234, 255.

PHOTOS/DRAWINGS: 60.

Dendrobium anceps Swartz

ORIGIN/HABITAT: The Himalaya region from Nepal eastwards to the Tenasserim mountains in Burma. In Nepal, the plants grow at 1000–3300 ft. (300–1000 m). Historically, the plants were thought to have a wider range, but in 1992 *Opera Botanica* #114, Seidenfaden reported that the true *D. anceps* has a more limited distribution.

CLIMATE: Station #42398, Baghdogra, India, Lat. 26.7°N, Long. 88.3°E, at 412 ft. (126 m). Temperatures are calculated for an elevation of 2000 ft. (610 m), resulting in probable extremes of 99°F (37°C) and 31°F (–1°C).

Dendrobium ancorarium

N/HEMISPHERE	JAN	FEB	MAR	APR	MAY	JUN	JUL	AUG	SEP	OCT	NOV	DEC
°F AVG MAX	69	72	80	85	85	84	84	84	83	82	77	72
°F AVG MIN	45	49	55	63	68	71	72	72	71	65	55	48
DIURNAL RANGE	24	23	25	22	17	13	12	12	12	17	22	24
RAIN/INCHES	0.3	0.7	1.3	3.7	11.8	25.9	32.2	25.3	21.2	5.6	0.5	0.2
HUMIDITY/%	73	68	57	58	74	84	86	85	85	79	75	76
BLOOM SEASON	**	*	*	**	**	**				*	*	*
DAYS CLR @ 6AM	21	18	15	11	5	0	1	1	4	13	23	19
DAYS CLR @ 12PM	23	16	16	11	2	2	0	1	2	10	21	18
RAIN/MM	8	18	33	94	300	658	818	643	538	142	13	5
°C AVG MAX	20.4	22.1	26.5	29.3	29.3	28.8	28.8	28.8	28.2	27.6	24.9	22.1
°C AVG MIN	7.1	9.3	12.6	17.1	19.9	21.5	22.1	22.1	21.5	18.2	12.6	8.8
DIURNAL RANGE	13.3	12.8	13.9	12.2	9.4	7.3	6.7	6.7	6.7	9.4	12.3	13.3
S/HEMISPHERE	JUL	AUG	SEP	OCT	NOV	DEC	JAN	FEB	MAR	APR	MAY	JUN

Cultural Recommendations

LIGHT: 2500–3500 fc. Summer light is low due to the heavy cloud cover.

TEMPERATURES: Summer days average 84°F (29°C), and nights average 71–72°F (22°C), with a diurnal range of 12–13°F (7°C).

HUMIDITY: Near 85% in summer. Averages drop to 70–80% in autumn and early winter then decrease further to 55–60% for 2–3 months in late winter and early spring.

WATER: Conditions are very wet for 5 months in summer, very dry for 5 months in winter, with short transition periods in autumn and spring. Cultivated plants should be kept evenly moist from spring to early autumn, but water should be gradually reduced after new growths mature in late autumn.

FERTILIZER: ¼–½ recommended strength, applied weekly. A high-nitrogen fertilizer is beneficial from spring to midsummer, but a fertilizer high in phosphates should be used in late summer and autumn.

REST PERIOD: Winter days average 69–72°F (20–22°C), and nights average 45–49°F (7–9°C), with a diurnal range of 23–25°F (13–14°C). Some growers recommend winter minimums near 59°F (15°C). In the habitat, winter rainfall is low, but additional moisture is often available from heavy deposits of dew. For about a month in late winter or early spring, however, humidity is so low that even the moisture from dew is uncommon. Cultivated plants should be allowed to dry out between waterings in winter, but they should not remain dry for extended periods. Occasional early morning mistings between waterings, especially on warm, sunny days, may help prevent the plants from becoming too dry. Fertilizer should be eliminated until water is increased in spring. In the habitat, light is highest in winter. The cool, dry rest with increased light may be necessary to initiate blooming.

GROWING MEDIA: Plants may be mounted on tree-fern slabs, if humidity is high and plants are watered at least once daily in summer. When plants are potted, any open, fast-draining medium may be used. Repotting is best done immediately after flowering in spring just as new roots begin to grow.

MISCELLANEOUS NOTES: The bloom season shown in the climate table is based on cultivation records. Reports from the habitat indicate that plants bloom in spring following the dry rest period.

Plant and Flower Information

PLANT SIZE AND TYPE: A 6–35 in. (15–90 cm) sympodial epiphyte.

PSEUDOBULB: 6–16 in. (15–40 cm) long. Stems sometimes reach a length of 30 in. (75 cm). The entire growth, including occasional branches, is flattened lengthwise. Stems are hidden by the leaf bases.

LEAVES: Many. Each growth is densely leafy. The fleshy, deciduous leaves are 1–2 in. (2.5–5.0 cm) long. They are distichous on a single plane, ovate-lanceolate, sharply pointed, and tightly folded so as to look flattened.

INFLORESCENCE: Very short. Blossoms appear to rest on the center line of leafy, mature stems and emerge from nodes below each leaf. The flowers are borne on upper surface of the stem. Blossoms are produced from many leaf axils, especially near the apex of the stem.

FLOWERS: 1 per inflorescence. The flowers are 0.6–0.8 in. (1.5–2.0 cm) across, fleshy, and greenish yellow. They have an erect dorsal sepal, large lateral sepals, and smaller petals that project forward parallel to the lateral sepals. The 3-lobed lip is marked with purple along the ruffled margin. Blossoms are faintly fragrant.

HYBRIDIZING NOTES: Chromosome counts are $n = 19 + 0 - 2B$ (ref. 504, 542, 580), $n = 19 + 0 - 6B$ (ref. 154, 542), and $2n = 38$ (ref. 153, 154, 273, 542).

REFERENCES: 32, 38, 46, 153, 154, 157, 179, 190, 196, 202, 210, 216, 254, 266, 273, 294, 369, 371, 376, 445, 447, 448, 454, 504, 542, 580.

PHOTOS/DRAWINGS: 32, 46, 210, *371, 454*.

Dendrobium ancorarium Rupp. See *D. adae* F. M. Bailey.
REFERENCES: 67, 105, 227, 533.

Dendrobium andersonianum F. M. Bailey.
Cribb (ref. 84) suggests that this plant may be a natural hybrid between *D. antennatum* Lindley and *D. lineale* Rolfe. He further indicates that if this parentage is accurate, the name *D.* × *andersonianum* F. M. Bailey will take precedence over the name *D.* × *schumannianum* Schlechter. REFERENCES: 84, 219, 254.

Dendrobium andersonii J. Scott. See *D. draconis* Rchb. f.
REFERENCES: 157, 190, 202, 216, 254, 454.

Dendrobium andreemillarae T. M. Reeve

AKA: Sometimes spelled *D. andreemillariae*.

ORIGIN/HABITAT: Papua New Guinea, in the Marobe and Enga Provinces. Extremely rare, the plants grow at 7750–9850 ft. (2360–3000 m) near Wau on Mt. Kaindi and near Porgera on Mt. Kumbivera.

CLIMATE: Botanical garden records, Laiagam, Papua New Guinea, Lat. 5.5°S, Long. 143.5°E, at 7218 ft. (2200 m). Temperatures are calculated for an elevation of 9500 ft. (2900 m), resulting in probable extremes of 83°F (29°C) and 24°F (−4°C).

N/HEMISPHERE	JAN	FEB	MAR	APR	MAY	JUN	JUL	AUG	SEP	OCT	NOV	DEC
°F AVG MAX	68	69	70	68	70	70	74	69	68	70	70	68
°F AVG MIN	47	46	47	47	48	48	47	48	50	49	48	48
DIURNAL RANGE	21	23	23	21	22	22	27	21	18	21	22	20
RAIN/INCHES	4.0	4.8	6.1	7.8	8.5	9.1	8.4	9.6	9.5	8.9	6.3	4.0
HUMIDITY/%	N/A											
BLOOM SEASON	*	*										
DAYS CLR	N/A											
RAIN/MM	102	122	155	198	216	231	213	244	241	226	160	102
°C AVG MAX	20.2	20.8	21.4	20.2	21.4	21.4	23.6	20.8	20.2	21.4	21.4	20.2
°C AVG MIN	8.6	8.0	8.6	8.6	9.1	9.1	8.6	9.1	10.2	9.7	9.1	9.1
DIURNAL RANGE	11.6	12.8	12.8	11.6	12.3	12.3	15.0	11.7	10.0	11.7	12.3	11.1
S/HEMISPHERE	JUL	AUG	SEP	OCT	NOV	DEC	JAN	FEB	MAR	APR	MAY	JUN

Cultural Recommendations

LIGHT: 2000–3000 fc.

TEMPERATURES: Throughout the year, days average 68–74°F (20–24°C), and nights average 46–50°F (8–10°C), with a diurnal range of 18–27°F (10–15°C).

HUMIDITY: Averages are not available for this location. However, records from other stations in the region indicate that values are probably 70–80% year-round.

WATER: Rainfall is heavy throughout the year, but conditions are slightly drier for 3–4 months in winter. Cultivated plants should be kept moist.

FERTILIZER: ¼–½ recommended strength. A balanced fertilizer should be applied weekly to biweekly throughout the year.

REST PERIOD: Growing conditions should be maintained all year. Water and fertilizer should be reduced somewhat in winter, especially when plants are grown in the dark, short-day conditions common in temperate latitudes. Plants should dry slightly between waterings, but they should never be allowed to dry out completely. Water and fertilizer should be gradually increased when plants begin growing in spring.

GROWING MEDIA: Mounting plants on tree-fern or cork slabs accommodates their drooping, somewhat pendulous growth habit. However, humidity must be high and plants must be watered at least once a day in summer. If plants cannot be mounted, small pots or hanging baskets may be filled with an open, fast-draining medium. Repotting may be done anytime new roots are actively growing.

MISCELLANEOUS NOTES: Plants brought to lower elevations did not survive, indicating that growing requirements must be provided.

Plant and Flower Information

PLANT SIZE AND TYPE: A 6–8 in. (15–20 cm) sympodial epiphyte.

PSEUDOBULB: 1.2–5.1 in. (3–13 cm) long. The slender, cylindrical stems are green to greenish yellow, with blackish nodes. Plants branch and root freely from the nodes of older stems. Root tips are orange.

LEAVES: 2–4 per growth. The spreading leaves are 8–20 in. (20–51 cm) long. They may be narrowly elliptical to broadly ovate.

INFLORESCENCE: Short. Inflorescences are borne on both leafy and leafless stems.

FLOWERS: 1–4 per inflorescence. The large, waxy flowers, which open fully, are 1.0–1.2 in. (2.5–3.0 cm) long. Blossoms are bright purple fading to white on part of the mentum. The lip is orange to red-orange with white along the margin and a purplish tinge at the tip. It resembles a flat-bottomed boat.

REFERENCES: 95, 234, 381.

PHOTOS/DRAWINGS: *95*, 381.

Dendrobium angiense J. J. Smith. Sometimes spelled *D. argiense*, see *D. subclausum* Rolfe. REFERENCES: 144, 221, 470, 486, 588.

Dendrobium angraecifolium Finet. Schlechter (ref. 437) used this name when defining his section *Macrocladium*, but we found no other reference to it. REFERENCES: 437.

Dendrobium angraecifolium Schlechter

AKA: *D. branderhorstii* J. J. Smith.

ORIGIN/HABITAT: New Guinea. In Northern New Guinea, plants grow from sea level to 1300 ft. (0–400 m) along the Waria and Minjem Rivers. In Irian Jaya (western New Guinea), plants known as *D. branderhorstii* were common on Jotéfa Bay, near sea level along the Lorentz River, on the upper Digul River, and at about 800 ft. (240 m) near the border with Papua New Guinea. Plants grow on tall trees in primary forests and on cliffs along the shoreline.

CLIMATE: Station #94014, Madang, Papua New Guinea, Lat. 5.2°S, Long. 145.8°E, at 13 ft. (4 m). Temperatures are calculated for a habitat elevation of 1000 ft. (300 m), resulting in probable extremes of 95°F (35°C) and 59°F (15°C).

N/HEMISPHERE	JAN	FEB	MAR	APR	MAY	JUN	JUL	AUG	SEP	OCT	NOV	DEC
°F AVG MAX	80	80	82	82	82	82	82	82	82	84	84	81
°F AVG MIN	74	75	75	75	74	74	74	74	74	73	74	75
DIURNAL RANGE	6	5	7	7	8	8	8	8	8	11	10	6
RAIN/INCHES	4.0	3.4	3.2	8.5	11.2	11.1	10.1	11.3	9.4	11.3	10.5	6.7
HUMIDITY/%	88	87	86	86	86	86	86	85	85	87	88	89
BLOOM SEASON	*			*			*	*	*		*	
DAYS CLR	N/A											
RAIN/MM	102	86	81	216	284	282	257	287	239	287	267	170
°C AVG MAX	26.6	26.6	27.7	27.7	27.7	27.7	27.7	27.7	27.7	28.8	28.8	27.1
°C AVG MIN	23.2	23.8	23.8	23.8	23.2	23.2	23.2	23.2	23.2	22.7	23.2	23.8
DIURNAL RANGE	3.4	2.8	3.9	3.9	4.5	4.5	4.5	4.5	4.5	6.1	5.6	3.3
S/HEMISPHERE	JUL	AUG	SEP	OCT	NOV	DEC	JAN	FEB	MAR	APR	MAY	JUN

Cultural Recommendations

LIGHT: 2500–3000 fc.

TEMPERATURES: Throughout the year, days average 80–84°F (27–29°C), and nights average 73–75°F (23–24°C), with a diurnal range of 5–11°F (3–6°C). The warmest highs, the coolest lows, and the greatest diurnal range occur in autumn.

HUMIDITY: 85–90% year-round.

WATER: Rainfall is heavy from spring through autumn, but conditions are somewhat drier in winter. Cultivated plants should be kept moist but not soggy while actively growing.

FERTILIZER: ¼–½ recommended strength. A balanced fertilizer should be applied weekly to biweekly throughout the year.

REST PERIOD: Growing temperatures should be maintained all year. In the habitat, rainfall decreases somewhat for 3–4 months in winter. In cultivation, water should be reduced and the plants allowed to dry slightly between waterings, but they should never dry completely. Fertilizer should be reduced until water is increased in spring. In the habitat, light is highest in winter.

GROWING MEDIA: Mounting plants on tree-fern or cork slabs accommodates their pendulous growth habit. However, humidity must be high and plants must be watered at least once a day in summer. If plants cannot be mounted, hanging pots or baskets may be filled with an open, fast-draining medium. Repotting may be done anytime new roots are actively growing.

MISCELLANEOUS NOTES: The bloom season included in the climate table is based on reports from the habitat. Plants that produce flowers which last a single day commonly bloom several times during the year. Flowering usually occurs 7–14 days after a sudden 10°F (5°C) drop in daytime temperatures.

Plant and Flower Information

PLANT SIZE AND TYPE: A 49 in. (125 cm) sympodial epiphyte.

PSEUDOBULB: 39 in. (100 cm) long. The flattened stems are pendulous, branching, and leafy.

LEAVES: Many. The linear-lanceolate leaves are about 10 in. (25 cm) long.

INFLORESCENCE: Very short.

FLOWERS: 2 per inflorescence. The small blossoms, which are thick and fleshy, are pale yellow with an orange-yellow callus. They remain nearly closed and last a single day.

REFERENCES: 219, 254, 437, 444, 445, 470.

PHOTOS/DRAWINGS: 437.

Dendrobium angulatum (Blume) Lindley 1830 not Lindley 1828. Now considered a synonym of *Flickingeria angulata* (Blume) A. Hawkes. REFERENCES: 25, 75, 213, 216, 230, 231, 277, 310, 395, 469.

PHOTOS/DRAWINGS: 469.

Dendrobium angulatum Lindley 1828 not Lindley 1830. See *D. podagraria* Hooker f. REFERENCES: 216, 254, 454.

Dendrobium angustiflorum J. J. Smith

ORIGIN/HABITAT: Irian Jaya (western New Guinea). Plants grow on forest trees on the north-facing slopes of the Gautier Range at about 1300 ft. (400 m). They are also found along the upper Tor River between Berkombor and Gwisterna at about 150 ft. (50 m).

CLIMATE: Station #97690, Sentani/Jayapura, Irian Jaya, Lat. 2.7°S, Long. 140.5°E, at 289 ft. (88 m). Temperatures are calculated for an elevation of 1000 ft. (300 m), resulting in probable extremes of 95°F (35°C) and 66°F (19°C).

N/HEMISPHERE	JAN	FEB	MAR	APR	MAY	JUN	JUL	AUG	SEP	OCT	NOV	DEC
°F AVG MAX	85	87	87	88	88	87	87	86	87	88	88	87
°F AVG MIN	70	70	70	71	71	71	71	71	71	72	71	71
DIURNAL RANGE	15	17	17	17	17	16	16	15	16	16	17	16
RAIN/INCHES	4.1	3.9	5.3	2.9	6.7	7.0	8.3	8.3	8.5	4.6	2.4	5.2
HUMIDITY/%	81	80	80	79	81	81	79	80	80	80	81	80
BLOOM SEASON			*		*							
DAYS CLR @ 9AM	5	3	4	3	2	1	1	0	1	2	2	5
DAYS CLR @ 3PM	4	3	3	3	2	1	3	0	1	2	2	3
RAIN/MM	104	99	135	74	170	178	211	211	216	117	61	132
°C AVG MAX	29.3	30.4	30.4	31.0	31.0	30.4	30.4	29.8	30.4	31.0	31.0	30.4
°C AVG MIN	21.0	21.0	21.0	21.5	21.5	21.5	21.5	21.5	21.5	22.1	21.5	21.5
DIURNAL RANGE	8.3	9.4	9.4	9.5	9.5	8.9	8.9	8.3	8.9	8.9	9.5	8.9
S/HEMISPHERE	JUL	AUG	SEP	OCT	NOV	DEC	JAN	FEB	MAR	APR	MAY	JUN

Cultural Recommendations

LIGHT: 2000–3000 fc.

TEMPERATURES: Throughout the year, days average 85–88°F (29–31°C), and nights average 70–72°F (21–22°C), with a diurnal range of 15–17°F (8–10°C).

HUMIDITY: Near 80% year-round.

WATER: Rainfall is heavy all year with brief semidry periods in spring and autumn. Cultivated plants should be kept evenly moist with only slight drying allowed between waterings.

FERTILIZER: ¼–½ recommended strength. A balanced fertilizer should be applied weekly to biweekly throughout the year.

REST PERIOD: Growing conditions should be maintained year-round. Water may be reduced somewhat for cultivated plants in winter, especially those grown in the dark, short-day conditions common in temperate latitudes. They should never be allowed to dry out completely, however. In the habitat, light is slightly higher in winter.

GROWING MEDIA: Plants may be mounted on tree-fern or cork slabs, if humidity is high and plants are watered at least once daily in summer. When plants are potted, any open, fast-draining medium may be used. Repotting may be done anytime new roots are growing.

MISCELLANEOUS NOTES: The bloom season shown in the climate table is based on reports from the habitat.

Plant and Flower Information

PLANT SIZE AND TYPE: A 7–11 in. (18–28 cm) sympodial epiphyte.

PSEUDOBULB: 3.5 in. (9 cm) long. The pseudobulbs are gray-green.

LEAVES: 2 per growth. The dark green leaves are 3–7 in. (8–18 cm) long.

INFLORESCENCE: 2 in. (5 cm) long. The pubescent racemes are densely flowered.

FLOWERS: Many per inflorescence. The large flowers are 1.2 in. (3 cm) long. The large, linear sepals and much shorter, linear petals open fully. The petals have an uneven margin. Blossoms are yellowish white with a slight greenish cast. The base of the lip is pale green. The ovary and back of the flower are covered with short, soft hairs.

REFERENCES: 221, 470.

Dendrobium angustifolium Ames not (Blume) Lindley.

Now considered a synonym of *Flickingeria chrysographota* (Ames) A. Hawkes. REFERENCES: 213, 296, 536.

Dendrobium angustifolium (Blume) Lindley not Ames.

Frequently listed as a synonym of *D. rumphiae* Rchb. f., it is often now considered a synonym of *Flickingeria angustifolia* (Blume) A. Hawkes. See note at *D. rumphiae* Rchb. f. REFERENCES: 25, 75, 216, 230, 254, 310, 395, 445, 449, 469. PHOTOS/DRAWINGS: 469.

Dendrobium angustipetalum J. J. Smith

ORIGIN/HABITAT: Ambon and Ternate Islands in the Moluccas. Habitat elevation is unreported, so the following climate date should be used with caution.

CLIMATE: Station #97724, Ambon/Pattimura, Indonesia, Lat. 3.7°S, Long. 128.1°E, at 33 ft. (10 m). Record extreme temperatures are 96°F (36°C) and 66°F (19°C).

N/HEMISPHERE	JAN	FEB	MAR	APR	MAY	JUN	JUL	AUG	SEP	OCT	NOV	DEC
°F AVG MAX	81	81	83	85	88	88	88	88	88	86	84	82
°F AVG MIN	74	74	74	74	75	76	76	76	76	76	75	74
DIURNAL RANGE	7	7	9	11	13	12	12	12	12	10	9	8
RAIN/INCHES	23.7	15.8	9.5	6.1	4.5	5.2	5.0	4.7	5.3	11.0	20.3	25.1
HUMIDITY/%	83	82	81	80	79	78	78	77	79	82	83	84
BLOOM SEASON	N/A											
DAYS CLR @ 9AM	1	1	1	6	7	4	3	3	5	5	3	3
DAYS CLR @ 3PM	1	1	2	5	6	1	1	1	2	3	1	3
RAIN/MM	602	401	241	155	114	132	127	119	135	279	516	638
°C AVG MAX	27.2	27.2	28.3	29.4	31.1	31.1	31.1	31.1	31.1	30.0	28.9	27.8
°C AVG MIN	23.3	23.3	23.3	23.3	23.9	24.4	24.4	24.4	24.4	24.4	23.9	23.3
DIURNAL RANGE	3.9	3.9	5.0	6.1	7.2	6.7	6.7	6.7	6.7	5.6	5.0	4.5
S/HEMISPHERE	JUL	AUG	SEP	OCT	NOV	DEC	JAN	FEB	MAR	APR	MAY	JUN

Cultural Recommendations

LIGHT: 2500–3500 fc.

TEMPERATURES: Throughout the year, days average 81–88°F (27–31°C), and nights average 74–76°F (23–24°C), with a diurnal range of 7–13°F (4–7°C).

HUMIDITY: 80–85% year-round.

WATER: Rainfall is moderate to heavy all year, but conditions are slightly drier in late spring and summer. Cultivated plants should be kept evenly moist with only slight drying allowed between waterings.

FERTILIZER: ¼–½ recommended strength. A balanced fertilizer should be applied weekly to biweekly throughout the year.

REST PERIOD: Growing conditions should be maintained all year. In the habitat, rainfall is heaviest in winter, but water and fertilizer should be reduced for cultivated plants, especially those grown in the dark, short-day conditions common in temperate latitudes. However, plants should never be allowed to dry completely. In the habitat, light is highest in spring.

GROWING MEDIA: Plants may be mounted on tree-fern slabs, if humidity is high and plants are watered at least once daily in summer. Mounting accommodates the pendent growth habit. When plants are potted, any open, fast-draining medium may be used. Plants should never be allowed to dry out completely. Repotting may be done anytime new roots are growing.

Plant and Flower Information

PLANT SIZE AND TYPE: A 39 in. (100 cm) sympodial plant.

PSEUDOBULB: 35 in. (90 cm) long. The somewhat flattened stems are pendulous with internodes at 1 in. (2.5 cm) intervals.

LEAVES: Many. The pointed, lanceolate leaves are 4 in. (10 cm) long and unequally bilobed at the apex.

INFLORESCENCE: Short. Inflorescences are numerous and somewhat zigzag.

FLOWERS: 6–8 per inflorescence. The small, green and white flowers are 0.5 in. (1.3 cm) across, but may not open fully. They have lanceolate petals and ovate sepals. The lip is toothed at the apex and accented with slightly elevated lines and violet dots on the sidelobes.

REFERENCES: 219, 254, 437, 468.

Dendrobium angustispathum J. J. Smith

AKA: *D. acuminatissimum* Lindley var. *mamberamense* J. J. Smith.

ORIGIN/HABITAT: Irian Jaya (western New Guinea). Plants are found near the Mamberamo River at about 350 ft. (100 m). They grow terrestrially on rocky ground in the dappled light in a forest of small trees.

CLIMATE: Station #97690, Sentani/Jayapura, Indonesian New Guinea, Lat. 2.7°S, Long. 140.5°E, at 289 ft. (88 m). Record extreme temperatures are 97°F (36°C) and 68°F (20°C).

N/HEMISPHERE	JAN	FEB	MAR	APR	MAY	JUN	JUL	AUG	SEP	OCT	NOV	DEC
°F AVG MAX	87	89	89	90	90	89	89	88	89	90	90	89
°F AVG MIN	72	72	72	73	73	73	73	73	73	74	73	73
DIURNAL RANGE	15	17	17	17	17	16	16	15	16	16	17	16
RAIN/INCHES	4.1	3.9	5.3	2.9	6.7	7.0	8.3	8.3	8.5	4.6	2.4	5.2
HUMIDITY/%	81	80	80	79	81	81	79	80	80	80	81	80
BLOOM SEASON	*											
DAYS CLR @ 9AM	5	3	4	3	2	1	1	0	1	2	2	5
DAYS CLR @ 3PM	4	3	3	3	2	1	3	0	1	2	2	3
RAIN/MM	104	99	135	74	170	178	211	211	216	117	61	132
°C AVG MAX	30.6	31.7	31.7	32.2	32.2	31.7	31.7	31.1	31.7	32.2	32.2	31.7
°C AVG MIN	22.2	22.2	22.2	22.8	22.8	22.8	22.8	22.8	22.8	23.3	22.8	22.8
DIURNAL RANGE	8.3	9.4	9.4	9.4	9.4	8.9	8.9	8.3	8.9	8.9	9.4	8.9
S/HEMISPHERE	JUL	AUG	SEP	OCT	NOV	DEC	JAN	FEB	MAR	APR	MAY	JUN

Cultural Recommendations

LIGHT: 2000–3000 fc.

TEMPERATURES: Throughout the year, days average 87–89°F (31–32°C), and nights average 72–74°F (22–23°C), with a diurnal range of 15–17°F (8–9°C).

HUMIDITY: Near 80% year-round.

WATER: Rainfall is heavy all year with brief semidry periods in spring and autumn. Cultivated plants should be kept evenly moist with only slight drying allowed between waterings.

FERTILIZER: ¼–½ recommended strength. A balanced fertilizer should be applied weekly to biweekly throughout the year.

REST PERIOD: Growing conditions should be maintained year-round. Water may be reduced somewhat for cultivated plants in winter, especially those grown in the dark, short-day conditions common in temperate latitudes. They should never be allowed to dry out completely, however. In the habitat, light is slightly higher in winter.

GROWING MEDIA: Plants may be mounted on tree-fern or cork slabs if humidity is high and plants are watered at least once daily in summer. When plants are potted, any open, fast-draining medium may be used. Repotting may be done anytime new roots are growing.

MISCELLANEOUS NOTES: The bloom season shown in the climate table is based on reports from the habitat.

Plant and Flower Information

PLANT SIZE AND TYPE: An 18–24 in. (45–60 cm) sympodial terrestrial that may be as small as 4 in. (10 cm).

PSEUDOBULB: 4–24 in. (10–60 cm) long. The clustered stems are borne on a short, branching rhizome. They are rigid and shiny.

LEAVES: Many. The linear leaves are 3.6–4.3 in. (9–11 cm) long, light green, and folded.

INFLORESCENCE: Short. Numerous inflorescences emerge through the leaf sheaths between the nodes.

FLOWERS: 2–3, rarely 1 per inflorescence. The flowers are 2 in. (5 cm) long. The white blossoms have violet markings on the lip and orange on the underside. The column is red and white.

REFERENCES: 225, 470.

Dendrobium annae J. J. Smith

ORIGIN/HABITAT: Southwestern Malaya and Lampong Province in southern Sumatra. Plants were cultivated in the botanical garden at Bogor, Java. Habitat elevation is unreported, so the following climate data should be used with caution.

CLIMATE: Station #96755, Bogor, Java, Indonesia, Lat. 6.5°S, Long. 106.8°E, at 550 ft. (170 m). Record extreme temperatures are 96°F (36°C) and 66°F (19°C).

N/HEMISPHERE	JAN	FEB	MAR	APR	MAY	JUN	JUL	AUG	SEP	OCT	NOV	DEC
°F AVG MAX	86	87	88	88	87	85	84	84	85	86	87	86
°F AVG MIN	73	73	73	74	74	74	74	74	74	75	75	74
DIURNAL RANGE	13	14	15	14	13	11	10	10	11	11	12	12
RAIN/INCHES	2.1	1.0	0.5	5.0	8.1	18.8	23.7	20.2	14.4	12.0	11.9	3.4
HUMIDITY/%	72	68	65	66	74	79	84	84	81	79	77	75
BLOOM SEASON											**	**
DAYS CLR @ 7AM	14	14	14	11	5	3	1	2	4	6	10	12
DAYS CLR @ 1PM	9	10	8	5	1	1	0	0	1	1	3	7
RAIN/MM	53	25	13	127	206	478	602	513	366	305	302	86
°C AVG MAX	30.0	30.6	31.1	31.1	30.6	29.4	28.9	28.9	29.4	30.0	30.6	30.0
°C AVG MIN	22.8	22.8	22.8	23.3	23.3	23.3	23.3	23.3	23.3	23.9	23.9	23.3
DIURNAL RANGE	7.2	7.8	8.3	7.8	7.3	6.1	5.6	5.6	6.1	6.1	6.7	6.7
S/HEMISPHERE	JUL	AUG	SEP	OCT	NOV	DEC	JAN	FEB	MAR	APR	MAY	JUN

Cultural Recommendations

LIGHT: 1800–3000 fc.

TEMPERATURES: Throughout the year, days average 84–88°F (29–31°C), and nights average 73–75°F (23–24°C), with a diurnal range of 10–15°F (6–8°C). Cultivated plants may not tolerate wide seasonal temperature fluctuations.

HUMIDITY: 75–85% most of the year, dropping to about 65% for 2–3 months in winter.

WATER: Rainfall is very heavy from spring to autumn, but conditions are very dry for 2 months in winter. During the growing season, plants should never be allowed to dry out completely, but water should be gradually reduced in late autumn.

FERTILIZER: ¼–½ recommended strength, applied weekly. A high-nitrogen fertilizer is beneficial from spring to midsummer, but a fertilizer high in phosphates should be used in late summer and autumn.

REST PERIOD: Growing conditions should be maintained all year, but rainfall is very low for 2–3 months. In cultivation, water should be reduced and the plants allowed to become somewhat dry between waterings. They should not remain dry for prolonged periods, however. Fertilizer may be reduced or eliminated anytime the plant is not actively growing. In the habitat, light is highest in winter.

GROWING MEDIA: Plants may be mounted on tree-fern or cork slabs if humidity is high and plants are watered at least once daily in summer. When plants are potted, any open, fast-draining medium may be used. Repotting may be done anytime new roots are growing.

MISCELLANEOUS NOTES: The bloom season shown in the climate table is based on collection reports.

Dendrobium annamense

Plant and Flower Information

PLANT SIZE AND TYPE: A 39 in. (100 cm) sympodial plant.

PSEUDOBULB: 39 in. (100 cm) long. The stems are clustered, gray-green, and have internodes spaced about 2 in. (5 cm) apart.

LEAVES: The lanceolate leaves are bilobed at the apex.

INFLORESCENCE: Inflorescences emerge above the leaf axils.

FLOWERS: The white flowers are 2 in. (5 cm) across. Blossoms are described as having a beautiful, full form. The petals are broad and ruffled, with dark violet at the tips of the segments. Sepals are narrower than the petals. The lip, which is ruffled at the margin and blotched with dark violet at the tip, is also marked with a dark blotch in the center.

REFERENCES: 25, 219, 254, 445, 469.

PHOTOS/DRAWINGS: 469.

Dendrobium annamense Rolfe.

Plants originated in Vietnam (Annam). Without additional habitat information, climate data cannot be selected. *D. annamense* is a pendulous sympodial epiphyte 16–20 in. (41–51 cm) long with somewhat flattened canes that are swollen at the base. The leaves are oblong, leathery, and 2–3 in. (5–8 cm) long. Inflorescences emerge laterally from nodes on leafless stems. Each Inflorescence bears 3 flowers. The buff-yellow blossoms are 0.9 in. (2.3 cm) long. The dorsal sepal is ovate-triangular, and lateral sepals are triangular, with lanceolate to oblong petals. The broadly oblong lip is ruffled along the edge. REFERENCES: 220, 254, 266, 415, 448.

Dendrobium annuligerum Rchb. f.

Plant origin was given as Marisa. Without habitat location and elevation, climate data cannot be selected. This sympodial orchid has many angled, shiny stems. The edges of the internodes are marked by faint bars. Leaves were not described. Blossoms emerge singly from nodes along the stem. The greenish yellow flowers have an oblong dorsal sepal, somewhat triangular lateral sepals, and ovate petals. Sepals and petals are pointed at the tips. The white lip has greenish yellow markings and purplish bars on the sidelobes. The callus is orange. REFERENCES: 216, 254.

Dendrobium anosmum Lindley

AKA: Seidenfaden (ref. 454) includes *D. leucorhodum* Schlechter, *D. maranthum* Hooker f. not A. Richard, *D. macranthum* Miquel, *D. macrophyllum* Lindley, *D. scortechinii* Hooker f., *D. superbum* Rchb. f. In addition, Valmayor (ref. 536) includes *D. retusum* Llanos as a possible synonym. Seidenfaden and Wood (ref. 455) list only *D. superbum* Rchb. f., while Hawkes (ref. 190) also includes *D. superbum* Rchb. f. var. *anosmum* Rchb. f., and Merrill (ref. 295) includes *D. superbum* Rchb. f. var. *burkei* Rchb. f. The International Orchid Commission (ref. 236) registers *D. anosmum* hybrids under the name *D. superbum*.

ORIGIN/HABITAT: Widespread. Plants are found from the Philippines to New Guinea, including Borneo and many islands in Indonesia. They are also found in Malaya, peninsular Thailand, Laos, Vietnam, and Sri Lanka. On Luzon Island and in Davao Province on Mindanao Island in the Philippines, plants grow in mountain forests usually below 2450 ft. (750 m). *D. anosmum* often grows in association with *Aerides quinquevulnerum* and *Anota violacea*. In Papua New Guinea, plants are common in the Bulolo and Wau areas, where they grow on rough-barked trees from sea level to 4250 ft. (0–1300 m).

CLIMATE: Station #98427, Manila, Luzon, Philippines, Lat. 14.5°N, Long. 121.0°E, at 74 ft. (23 m). Temperatures are calculated for an elevation of 2450 ft. (750 m), resulting in probable extremes of 93°F (34°C) and 50°F (10°C).

N/HEMISPHERE	JAN	FEB	MAR	APR	MAY	JUN	JUL	AUG	SEP	OCT	NOV	DEC
°F AVG MAX	78	80	83	85	85	83	80	79	80	80	79	78
°F AVG MIN	61	61	63	65	67	67	67	67	67	66	64	62
DIURNAL RANGE	17	19	20	20	18	16	13	12	13	14	15	16
RAIN/INCHES	0.9	0.5	0.7	1.3	5.1	10.0	17.0	16.6	14.0	7.6	5.7	2.6
HUMIDITY/%	77	73	70	68	71	81	84	86	87	84	82	79
BLOOM SEASON	**	***	***	***	**	*	*	*	*	*	*	*
DAYS CLR @ 8AM	6	9	14	14	10	3	2	1	1	6	7	6
DAYS CLR @ 2PM	3	6	10	10	8	2	1	1	0	2	2	3
RAIN/MM	23	13	18	33	130	254	432	422	356	193	145	66
°C AVG MAX	25.6	26.7	28.4	29.5	29.5	28.4	26.7	26.2	26.7	26.7	26.2	25.6
°C AVG MIN	16.2	16.2	17.3	18.4	19.5	19.5	19.5	19.5	19.5	19.0	17.8	16.7
DIURNAL RANGE	9.4	10.5	11.1	11.1	10.0	8.9	7.2	6.7	7.2	7.7	8.4	8.9
S/HEMISPHERE	JUL	AUG	SEP	OCT	NOV	DEC	JAN	FEB	MAR	APR	MAY	JUN

Cultural Recommendations

LIGHT: 2000–3000 fc in summer. Bright diffused light is suggested. Morning light is preferred, and plants should be shaded at midday.

TEMPERATURES: Throughout the year, days average 78–85°F (26–30°C), and nights average 61–67°F (16–20°C), with a diurnal range of 12–20°F (7–11°C). The coolest temperatures occur in winter. This climate data represents the coolest portion of the natural habitat.

HUMIDITY: 80–90% in summer and autumn, dropping to near 70% in late winter and spring.

WATER: Rainfall is heavy in summer, moderate in autumn, and light in winter and spring. Cultivated plants should be kept moist during the growing season, but water should be gradually reduced in autumn.

FERTILIZER: ½ recommended strength, applied weekly. A high-nitrogen fertilizer is beneficial from spring to midsummer, while a fertilizer high in phosphates should be used in late summer and autumn. *D. anosmum* grows rapidly in spring and summer, and benefits from higher than normal levels of nutrients.

REST PERIOD: Growing temperatures should be maintained all year. Rainfall is low for 3–4 months in winter, but additional moisture is available from frequent heavy dew. In cultivation, water should be reduced and the plants allowed to dry out between waterings. They should not remain dry for extended periods, however. Fertilizer should also be reduced or eliminated anytime water is reduced. In the habitat, light is highest in winter. Growers indicate that water should be gradually increased in late winter after the flower buds develop.

GROWING MEDIA: Plants are best mounted on tree-fern slabs or placed in hanging baskets to accommodate their pendulous growth habit. Baskets may be filled with any open medium. Humidity should be high and plants should be watered at least once daily in summer. If plants must be potted, the smallest possible pot should be filled with an open, fast-draining medium. Growers in tropical climates indicate that plants are healthiest when grown outdoors on living trees. Repotting is best done in early spring immediately after flowering when new roots are growing.

MISCELLANEOUS NOTES: The bloom season shown in the climate table is based on cultivation records. Flowering may be controlled on cultivated plants by maintaining cool, dry conditions. In the habitat, blooming occurs after the cool, dry season ends. Growers often consider this a problem plant, so careful attention should be paid to cultural needs.

Large-flowered plants generally originate in the Philippines and may be called *D. superbum*. Smaller flowered forms are more likely to originate in Malaya.

Keikis, small aerial plants, may be produced at nodes, especially if the growing eyes are damaged.

Plant and Flower Information

PLANT SIZE AND TYPE: A very large, 39–118 in. (100–300 cm) sympodial epiphyte. Plants occasionally reach a length of 144 in. (370 cm).

PSEUDOBULB: 39–118 in. (100–300 cm) long. However, plants tend to be smaller in cultivation. The cylindrical stems, which may be arching or pendulous, consist of nodes spaced a few inches apart. They become yellow, then silvery gray with age.

LEAVES: Many. The large leaves are oblong-lanceolate, 5–7 in. (12–18 cm) long, pointed at the apex, fleshy, and glossy green. They are carried in 2 rows. The leaves normally last a single season and fall just as the flower buds appear, although they may persist until after blooming if growing conditions are moderate. Leaves should not be removed as they start to dry, as it is very easy to damage the buds forming at the leaf axils.

INFLORESCENCE: Short. Inflorescences arise from nearly every node on mature, leafless stems.

FLOWERS: 1–2 per inflorescence. The flowers are normally 2.8–4.0 in. (7–10 cm) across, but some forms may be smaller and some may not open fully. Flowers vary from dark rose-red to deep lavender, including intermediate shades. The translucent segments are darkest at the base with paler tips. The broad petals and narrower sepals are normally the same color accented with darker veins. Some alba and semialba forms have white sepals and petals with yellow on the lip; but in rare instances, the sepals and petals are white, and the lip is pink. Dourado (ref. 110) stated that the albino form is probably indigenous to the Philippines. The lip is hairy on the inside and usually marked with deep purple stripes in the throat. The stripes may nearly merge, making the lip appear predominantly purple with a white margin. The lip is longer than the dorsal sepal and commonly heart-shaped, but the shape is highly variable. Although not always fragrant, flowers sometimes have a strong, pleasant scent which reminds some of raspberries, but others associate the fragrance with rhubarb or mustard. Blossoms last about 3 weeks, but they may last longer if conditions are cool. Numerous varieties have been described.

HYBRIDIZING NOTES: Chromosome counts are n = 19 (ref. 187, 504, 580), 2n = 38 (ref. 153, 273, 504, 580). As *D. superbum*, counts are n = 19 (ref. 187, 580), 2n = 38 (ref. 151, 187), and 2n = 40 (ref. 187, 504, 580). Counts are 2n = 38 (ref. 504, 580) as *D. leucorhodum* and 2n = 38 (ref. 154, 188) as *D. superbum* var. *album* Hort. Seeds are sufficiently mature for green-pod culture in 160–250 (186) days.

REFERENCES: 6, 12, 25, 36, 92, 98, 108, 110, 151, 153, 154, 179, 187, 188, 190, 196, 200, 202, 207, 210, 216, 236, 254, 266, 273, 281, 286, 293, 296, 298, 302, 304, 317, 326, 371, 373, 389, 395, 402, 425, 430, 436, 437, 445, 448, 454, 455, 458, 468, 470, 474, 482, 483, 504, 524, 536, 537, 569, 570, 580, 586, 592.

PHOTOS/DRAWINGS: 36, 98, *108, 109, 110*, 200, 207, 210, *281, 304, 371, 373, 389, 430*, 437, *454, 455*, 458, *536, 569*.

Dendrobium ansusanum Schlechter. See *D. zippelii* J. J. Smith. REFERENCES: 221, 470, 583.

Dendrobium antelope Rchb. f. See *D. bicaudatum* Reinwardt ex Lindley. REFERENCES: 25, 84, 216, 254.

Dendrobium antennatum Lindley

AKA: *D. d'albertisii* Rchb. f. The International Orchid Commission (ref. 236) registers hybrids under both *D. antennatum* and *D. d'albertisii*.

ORIGIN/HABITAT: New Guinea and adjacent islands. Plants are common in lowland swamps and coastal gallery forests through the entire north and west coasts of New Guinea. Plants may be found between sea level and 3900 ft. (0–1200 m), but they most often grow near 500 ft. (150 m). Plants also grow in the Solomon Islands and Australia, where they are found at about 1050 ft. (320 m) in the McIlwraith Range on the northern Cape York Peninsula. Plants occur in bright locations with high humidity. They are often found along creeks near waterfalls and rapids where the rocky terrain causes breaks in the forest canopy.

CLIMATE: Station #200004, Ambunti, Papua New Guinea, Lat. 4.2°S, Long. 142.8°E, at 164 ft. (50 m). Temperatures are calculated for an elevation of 1000 ft. (300 m), resulting in probable extremes of 96°F (36°C) and 49°F (10°C).

N/HEMISPHERE	JAN	FEB	MAR	APR	MAY	JUN	JUL	AUG	SEP	OCT	NOV	DEC
°F AVG MAX	85	87	87	87	88	87	87	87	87	87	87	86
°F AVG MIN	69	70	71	70	70	70	69	70	70	70	70	71
DIURNAL RANGE	16	17	16	17	18	17	18	17	17	17	17	15
RAIN/INCHES	6.4	7.4	7.7	8.5	9.2	9.4	10.9	10.2	12.2	10.4	8.3	5.2
HUMIDITY/%	N/A											
BLOOM SEASON	*	*	*	*	*	*	*					
DAYS CLR	N/A											
RAIN/MM	163	188	196	216	234	239	277	259	310	264	211	132
°C AVG MAX	29.6	30.7	30.7	30.7	31.2	30.7	30.7	30.7	30.7	30.7	30.7	30.1
°C AVG MIN	20.7	21.2	21.8	21.2	21.2	21.2	20.7	21.2	21.2	21.2	21.2	21.8
DIURNAL RANGE	8.9	9.5	8.9	9.5	10.0	9.5	10.0	9.5	9.5	9.5	9.5	8.3
S/HEMISPHERE	JUL	AUG	SEP	OCT	NOV	DEC	JAN	FEB	MAR	APR	MAY	JUN

Cultural Recommendations

LIGHT: 2000–3000 fc.

TEMPERATURES: Throughout the year, days average 85–88°F (30–31°C), and nights average 69–71°F (21–22°C), with a diurnal range of 15–18°F (8–10°C). Because plants are found over a large area and a fairly wide range of habitat elevations, growers report that they are tolerant of a relatively wide range of cultural conditions.

HUMIDITY: Information is not available for this location. However, records from nearby stations indicate that humidity probably averages near 80% year-round.

WATER: Rainfall is heavy all year, with the greatest amounts falling in summer and early autumn. Cultivated plants should be kept moist but not soggy.

FERTILIZER: ¼–½ recommended strength. A balanced fertilizer should be applied weekly to biweekly throughout the year.

REST PERIOD: Growing conditions should be maintained all year. Growers report that plants do poorly if subjected to temperatures below 55°F (13°C), but others indicate that plants require winter minimum temperatures of 60°F (15°C). In the Australian habitat, winter minimums average 63–65°F (17–18°C). Water and fertilizer should be reduced slightly in winter, especially for plants cultivated in the dark, short-day conditions common in temperate latitudes. However, plants should never be allowed to dry between waterings. In the habitat, light is probably highest in winter.

GROWING MEDIA: Plants may be mounted on tree-fern or cork slabs if humidity is high and plants are watered at least once daily in summer. However, most growers prefer to place plants in a pot filled with an open, fast-draining medium. Repotting should be done annually or at least every second year.

MISCELLANEOUS NOTES: The bloom season shown in the climate table is based on cultivation records. Plants begin blooming when 6–8 in. (15–20 cm) tall. Large cultivated plants usually flower most of the year. In the habitat, blooming lasts from autumn through spring. Plants known as *D. d'albertisii* are generally smaller than plants cultivated as *D. antennatum*. Some growers consider it tricky to grow in cool climates. Growers indicate that increased levels of magnesium in the fertilizer deepens the green color of the petals.

Plant and Flower Information

PLANT SIZE AND TYPE: A variably sized, 8–51 in. (20–130 cm) sympodial epiphyte.

PSEUDOBULB: 8–51 in. (20–130 cm) long. The hard, cylindrical stem is swollen near the base and tapers toward the apex. Plants form slender clumps.

Dendrobium anthrene

LEAVES: 10–14 per growth, on the upper portion of the stem. The leaves are narrow, leathery to succulent, lanceolate, and become smaller near the apex of the stem.

INFLORESCENCE: 8–12 in. (20–30 cm) long. Each growth produces up to 3 long, erect to arching racemes. The inflorescences emerge from the upper leaf axils a few millimeters above the axils of the sheathing bracts.

FLOWERS: 8–15 per inflorescence. Flowers are 1.6–2.0 in. (4–5 cm) across, fragrant, and last up to 6 months. The pale green petals are linear, stiffly erect, 2–3 in. (5–8 cm) long, and mildly twisted. Sepals are usually white or a pale shade of greenish white. They are sometimes suffused with yellow near the apex. The large, white lip is pointed at the tip, somewhat wavy, and marked with purple or violet veins on the sidelobes.

HYBRIDIZING NOTES: Chromosome counts are n = 19 (ref. 504, 580) and 2n = 38 (ref. 152, 243, 504, 580) as both *D. antennatum* and *D. d'albertisii*. After fertilization, the flowers turn yellowish green and persist on the developing capsule without withering. Plants appear to be self-fertile, and in the Solomon Islands, they may be self-pollinating. Seed pods become very large before reaching maturity. When used as a parent, *D. antennatum* transmits its densely clustered growths, long-lasting flowers, the tendency to bloom frequently, and its long, erect to arching racemes. The tendency toward stiffly erect petals persists for several generations. Progeny tend to produce flowers that are intermediate between the 2 parents. *D. antennatum* is thought to hybridize naturally with *D. lineale* Rolfe.

REFERENCES: 25, 67, 82, 84, 86, 105, 116, 152, 179, 190, 196, 200, 216, 236, 240, 243, 254, 262, 263, 271, 302, 304, 310, 317, 342, 343, 351, 371, 390, 421, 430, 437, 444, 445, 458, 470, 504, 510, 516, 526, 533, 537, 551, 554, 568, 570, 580.

PHOTOS/DRAWINGS: *84, 86,* 105, *116,* 200, *240, 262, 304, 342, 343, 351, 371, 390, 430,* 437, 458, *510, 533, 551, 554.*

Dendrobium anthrene Ridley

AKA: Sometimes spelled *D. antherene*.

ORIGIN/HABITAT: Sarawak, Borneo and Sumatra. In Sumatra, plants were collected at 4500 ft. (1370 m) near Sungei Kumbang on an expedition to Kerinci (Korinchi) Peak.

CLIMATE: Station #96163, Padang, Sumatra, Indonesia, Lat. 0.9°S, Long. 100.4°E, at 19 ft. (6 m). Temperatures are calculated for an elevation of 4300 ft. (1310 m), resulting in probable extremes of 80°F (27°C) and 54°F (12°C).

N/HEMISPHERE	JAN	FEB	MAR	APR	MAY	JUN	JUL	AUG	SEP	OCT	NOV	DEC
°F AVG MAX	73	73	72	72	72	72	73	73	73	73	74	73
°F AVG MIN	60	60	60	60	60	60	60	60	60	61	61	60
DIURNAL RANGE	13	13	12	12	12	12	13	13	13	12	13	13
RAIN/INCHES	10.9	13.7	6.0	19.5	20.4	18.9	13.8	10.2	12.1	14.3	12.4	12.1
HUMIDITY/%	81	82	82	84	85	84	81	81	82	83	81	81
BLOOM SEASON	N/A											
DAYS CLR @ 7AM	5	1	1	0	0	2	2	1	2	2	3	5
DAYS CLR @ 1PM	5	2	2	1	1	3	3	4	3	3	6	5
RAIN/MM	277	348	152	495	518	480	351	259	307	363	315	307
°C AVG MAX	22.7	22.7	22.2	22.2	22.2	22.2	22.7	22.7	22.7	22.7	23.3	22.7
°C AVG MIN	15.5	15.5	15.5	15.5	15.5	15.5	15.5	15.5	15.5	16.0	16.0	15.5
DIURNAL RANGE	7.2	7.2	6.7	6.7	6.7	6.7	7.2	7.2	7.2	6.7	7.3	7.2
S/HEMISPHERE	JUL	AUG	SEP	OCT	NOV	DEC	JAN	FEB	MAR	APR	MAY	JUN

Cultural Recommendations

LIGHT: 2000–3000 fc. Diffused light is preferred.

TEMPERATURES: Throughout the year, days average 72–74°F (22–23°C), and nights average 60–61°F (16°C), with a diurnal range of 12–13°F (7°C). Probable extremes vary only a few degrees from the averages, indicating that plants may not tolerate wide temperature fluctuations.

HUMIDITY: 80–85% year-round.

WATER: Rainfall is heavy all year. Cultivated plants should be kept moist but not soggy.

FERTILIZER: ¼–½ recommended strength. A balanced fertilizer should be applied weekly to biweekly throughout the year.

REST PERIOD: Growing conditions should be maintained year-round. Water may be reduced somewhat for cultivated plants in winter, especially those grown in the dark, short-day conditions common in temperate latitudes. They should never be allowed to dry out completely, however.

GROWING MEDIA: Plants may be mounted on tree-fern or cork slabs or placed in small pots filled with any open, fast-draining medium. Repotting may be done anytime new roots are actively growing.

Plant and Flower Information

PLANT SIZE AND TYPE: An 18 in. (45 cm) sympodial epiphyte.

PSEUDOBULB: 18 in. (45 cm) long. The grooved stems consist of segments 0.8 in. (2 cm) long.

LEAVES: 5 in. (13 cm) long. The lanceolate leaves are pointed at the tip. They are deciduous.

INFLORESCENCE: 0.8 in. (2 cm). Racemes are borne near the apex of leafless stems.

FLOWERS: 1–2 per inflorescence. The flowers, which are 1.2–1.6 in. (3–4 cm) long, are described as resembling a large insect. The triangular sepals and elliptical petals are white with a pale yellow or pale rose tinge. They have a yellowish mark near the base. The rounded lip, which is bilobed at the apex, is pale yellow marked with red stripes. The bow-shaped spur is 1.5 in. (3.8 cm) long.

REFERENCES: 254, 286, 394, 401.

Dendrobium apertum Schlechter

ORIGIN/HABITAT: Northern Papua New Guinea. Plants grow on mistforest trees at 4250–4600 ft. (1300–1400 m) in the Bismarck Range and the Waria District of the Dischore Range.

CLIMATE: Station #200192, Garaina, Papua New Guinea, Lat. 7.9°S, Long. 147.1°E, at 2350 ft. (716 m). Temperatures are calculated for an elevation of 4250 ft. (1300 m), resulting in probable extremes of 88°F (31°C) and 40°F (4°C).

N/HEMISPHERE	JAN	FEB	MAR	APR	MAY	JUN	JUL	AUG	SEP	OCT	NOV	DEC
°F AVG MAX	74	76	77	78	79	79	79	79	78	78	77	75
°F AVG MIN	57	57	57	58	57	58	59	59	59	58	58	57
DIURNAL RANGE	17	19	20	20	22	21	20	20	19	20	19	18
RAIN/INCHES	5.8	6.5	8.7	11.1	11.8	11.9	8.9	11.7	11.5	9.9	7.7	5.2
HUMIDITY/%	84	82	82	81	80	80	81	81	82	83	84	84
BLOOM SEASON								*			*	
DAYS CLR	N/A											
RAIN/MM	147	165	221	282	300	302	226	297	292	251	196	132
°C AVG MAX	23.1	24.3	24.8	25.4	25.9	25.9	25.9	25.9	25.4	25.4	24.8	23.7
°C AVG MIN	13.7	13.7	13.7	14.3	13.7	14.3	14.8	14.8	14.8	14.3	14.3	13.7
DIURNAL RANGE	9.4	10.6	11.1	11.1	12.2	11.6	11.1	11.1	10.6	11.1	10.5	10.0
S/HEMISPHERE	JUL	AUG	SEP	OCT	NOV	DEC	JAN	FEB	MAR	APR	MAY	JUN

Cultural Recommendations

LIGHT: 2000–3000 fc.

TEMPERATURES: Throughout the year, days average 74–79°F (23–26°C), and nights average 57–59°F (14–15°C), with a diurnal range of 17–22°F (10–12°C).

HUMIDITY: 80–85% year-round.

WATER: Rainfall is heavy all year. Conditions are slightly drier in winter. Cultivated plants should be kept moist but not soggy.

FERTILIZER: ¼–½ recommended strength. A balanced fertilizer should be applied weekly to biweekly throughout the year.

REST PERIOD: Growing conditions should be maintained all year. In the habitat, rainfall is slightly lower in winter. Water and fertilizer should be reduced somewhat for cultivated plants, especially those grown in the dark, short-day conditions common during temperate-latitude winters. They should never be allowed to dry out completely, however. In the habitat, seasonal light variation is minor.

GROWING MEDIA: To accommodate the somewhat pendulous growth habit, plants may be mounted on tree-fern or cork slabs or potted in small hanging pots or baskets filled with any open, fast-draining medium. Repotting may be done anytime new roots are growing.

MISCELLANEOUS NOTES: The bloom season shown in the climate table is based on cultivation records.

Plant and Flower Information

PLANT SIZE AND TYPE: A 20 in. (50 cm) sympodial epiphyte.

PSEUDOBULB: 18–19 in. (45–48 cm) long. Stems are very slender.

LEAVES: Many. The leaves, which lie on a single plane, are 0.6–1.2 in. (1.5–3.0 cm) long.

INFLORESCENCE: Very short.

FLOWERS: Few. The rose-purple flowers, which are 0.6 in. (1.5 cm) across, open fully.

REFERENCES: 92, 95, 179, 221, 437, 445, 549, 553.

PHOTOS/DRAWINGS: 437, *553*.

Dendrobium aphanochilum Kränzlin

ORIGIN/HABITAT: The Molucca Islands, including Ambon and Seram. On Seram, plants grow in the source mountains of the Makino River at 3300–3600 ft. (1000–1100 m) and in Hatoemeten Pass, south of Manoesela, at 4900–5600 ft. (1500–1700 m). On Ambon, plants are common on Mt. Salhoetoe at about 2600 ft. (800 m).

CLIMATE: Station #49620, Amahai, Seram, Indonesia, Lat. 3.3°S, Long. 128.9°E, at 10 ft. (3 m). Temperatures are calculated for an elevation of 4000 ft. (1220 m), resulting in probable extremes of 83°F (28°C) and 53°F (12°C).

N/HEMISPHERE	JAN	FEB	MAR	APR	MAY	JUN	JUL	AUG	SEP	OCT	NOV	DEC
°F AVG MAX	68	68	70	72	75	75	75	75	75	73	71	69
°F AVG MIN	61	61	61	61	62	63	63	63	63	63	62	61
DIURNAL RANGE	7	7	9	11	13	12	12	12	12	10	9	8
RAIN/INCHES	23.7	15.8	9.5	6.1	4.5	5.2	5.0	4.7	5.3	11.0	20.3	25.1
HUMIDITY/%	83	82	81	80	79	78	78	77	79	82	83	84
BLOOM SEASON					*						*	
DAYS CLR @ 9AM	1	1	1	6	7	4	3	3	5	5	3	3
DAYS CLR @ 3PM	1	1	2	5	6	1	1	1	2	3	1	3
RAIN/MM	602	401	241	155	114	132	127	119	135	279	516	638
°C AVG MAX	19.9	19.9	21.0	22.1	23.8	23.8	23.8	23.8	23.8	22.7	21.6	20.5
°C AVG MIN	16.0	16.0	16.0	16.0	16.6	17.1	17.1	17.1	17.1	17.1	16.6	16.0
DIURNAL RANGE	3.9	3.9	5.0	6.1	7.2	6.7	6.7	6.7	6.7	5.6	5.0	4.5
S/HEMISPHERE	JUL	AUG	SEP	OCT	NOV	DEC	JAN	FEB	MAR	APR	MAY	JUN

Cultural Recommendations

LIGHT: 2000–3000 fc. In the habitat clear days are rare.

TEMPERATURES: Summer days average 75°F (24°C), and nights average 63°F (17°C), with a diurnal range of 12°F (7°C).

HUMIDITY: 75–80% most of the year. Humidity increases to near 85% in winter.

WATER: Rainfall is moderate to heavy throughout the year, but conditions are slightly drier in spring and summer. Plants should be allowed to dry slightly between waterings but should never dry out completely.

FERTILIZER: ¼–½ recommended strength. A balanced fertilizer should be applied weekly to biweekly throughout the year.

REST PERIOD: Winter days average 68–71°F (20–22°C), and nights average 61°F (16°C), with a diurnal range of 7–9°F (4–5°C). In the habitat, winter is the wettest season, but water should not be increased for cultivated plants. In fact, water may be reduced somewhat for plants cultivated in the dark, short-day conditions common in temperate latitudes. However, plants should never be allowed to dry completely between waterings. Fertilizer should be reduced or eliminated anytime water is reduced.

GROWING MEDIA: Mounting plants on tree-fern or cork slabs accommodates their growth habit. However, humidity must be high and plants must be watered at least once a day in summer. If plants cannot be mounted, hanging pots or baskets may be filled with an open, fast-draining medium. Repotting may be done anytime new roots are actively growing.

MISCELLANEOUS NOTES: The bloom season shown in the climate table is based on reports from the habitat. The plant was described in 1928 in *Bul. Jard. Bot. Buit.* 3rd sér. 10:153.

Plant and Flower Information

PLANT SIZE AND TYPE: A 12 in. (30 cm) sympodial epiphyte.

PSEUDOBULB: 12 in. (30 cm) long. The slender stems are lax and curved.

LEAVES: The ovate-lanceolate leaves are 2.4–3.2 in. (6–8 cm) long. They are unequally 2-toothed at the apex.

INFLORESCENCE: Short. Inflorescences emerge from nodes on leafless stems.

FLOWERS: 5–6 per inflorescence. The lovely white flowers are 1.6 in. (4 cm) across. The very wide dorsal sepal is slightly uneven at the apex. Lateral sepals are broadly ovate. The oblong petals are variably uneven to bearded at the tips. About 60% of the lip is decorated with lines.

REFERENCES: 220, 254.

Dendrobium aphrodite Rchb. f.

AKA: *D. nodatum* Lindley.

ORIGIN/HABITAT: The Tenasserim Range near Moulmein, Burma. Plants often grow with *D. albosanguineum* Lindley in the tops of the tallest trees. Habitat elevation was not reported, so the following climate data should be used with caution.

CLIMATE: Station #48103, Moulmein, Burma, Lat. 16.4°N, Long. 97.7°E, at 150 ft. (46 m). Temperatures are calculated for an estimated habitat elevation of 2000 ft. (610 m), resulting in probable extremes of 96°F (36°C) and 45°F (7°C).

N/HEMISPHERE	JAN	FEB	MAR	APR	MAY	JUN	JUL	AUG	SEP	OCT	NOV	DEC
°F AVG MAX	83	86	88	89	83	79	77	77	79	82	83	81
°F AVG MIN	60	62	67	70	70	69	69	69	69	69	67	62
DIURNAL RANGE	23	24	21	19	13	10	8	8	10	13	16	19
RAIN/INCHES	0.3	0.2	0.4	3.0	20.3	35.6	46.3	43.4	28.1	8.5	2.1	0.1
HUMIDITY/%	66	68	68	70	81	91	92	93	91	81	75	64
BLOOM SEASON			*	*	*							
DAYS CLR @ 7AM	12	7	5	6	1	0	0	0	0	3	7	12
DAYS CLR @ 1PM	20	13	10	8	3	0	0	0	0	4	12	17
RAIN/MM	8	5	10	76	516	904	1176	1102	714	216	53	3
°C AVG MAX	28.3	29.9	31.1	31.6	28.3	26.1	24.9	24.9	26.1	27.7	28.3	27.2
°C AVG MIN	15.5	16.6	19.4	21.1	21.1	20.5	20.5	20.5	20.5	20.5	19.4	16.6
DIURNAL RANGE	12.8	13.3	11.7	10.5	7.2	5.6	4.4	4.4	5.6	7.2	8.9	10.6
S/HEMISPHERE	JUL	AUG	SEP	OCT	NOV	DEC	JAN	FEB	MAR	APR	MAY	JUN

Cultural Recommendations

LIGHT: 2500–3500 fc. Plants normally grow in the tops of the tallest trees where light is high. During summer, however, clear days are rare and cloud cover is extremely heavy.

TEMPERATURES: Summer days average 77–79°F (25–26°C), and nights

average 69°F (21°C), with a diurnal range of 8–10°F (4–6°C). Weather is warmest in spring. Days average 88–89°F (31–32°C), and nights average 67–70°F (19–21°C), with a diurnal range of 19–21°F (11–12°C). Habitat elevation is estimated, so temperatures should be used with caution, but seasonal patterns are similar regardless of elevation.

HUMIDITY: 80–90% from late spring to midautumn. Humidity decreases to near 65% in winter.

WATER: Rainfall is very heavy from late spring to autumn, but amounts are greatly reduced in winter. Cultivated plants require frequent and heavy watering while actively growing, but they must be able to dry rapidly after watering. Water should be gradually reduced after new growths mature in autumn.

FERTILIZER: ¼–½ recommended strength. A balanced fertilizer should be applied weekly to biweekly throughout the year.

REST PERIOD: Winter days average 81–86°F (27–30°C), and nights average 60–62°F (16–17°C), with a diurnal range of 23–24°F (13°C). The wide diurnal range results from both warmer days and cooler nights. For 4 months, rainfall averages are very low, but additional moisture is usually available from frequent heavy deposits of dew. Water should be reduced for cultivated plants. They should be allowed to dry somewhat between waterings but should never remain dry for long periods. Occasional early morning mistings between waterings, especially on bright, sunny days, may help prevent plants from becoming too dry. Fertilizer should be reduced or eliminated during the dry period. In the habitat, light is highest in winter and spring.

GROWING MEDIA: Plants may be mounted on cork or tree-fern slabs with a pad of sphagnum. If plants are mounted, high humidity should be maintained and water should be applied at least once a day in summer. If plants are potted, any open, rapidly draining medium may be used. Repotting is best done in spring, immediately after flowering.

MISCELLANEOUS NOTES: The bloom season shown in the climate table is based on cultivation records. *D. aphrodite* has the reputation of being a reluctant bloomer, and growers indicate that the cool, dry rest should be continued until flower buds form. The very rapid vegetative growth occurs during the rainy season.

Plant and Flower Information

PLANT SIZE AND TYPE: A 6–24 in. (15–60 cm) sympodial epiphyte.

PSEUDOBULB: 10–15 in. (25–38 cm) long. However, plant size is variable. The stems are slender, branching, suberect, and very swollen at the nodes.

LEAVES: Few per growth. The oblong-obtuse leaves are 2–3 in. (5–8 cm) long. They are deciduous during the cool, dry season.

INFLORESCENCE: 3 in. (8 cm) long. Inflorescences arise from the uppermost nodes of mature, leafless pseudobulbs. Older stems continue to produce flowers for several bloom seasons.

FLOWERS: 1–2 per inflorescence. The flowers are 2–3 in. (5–8 cm) across and delicately fragrant. They are white to yellowish cream and do not open fully. The lip midlobe is sulfur colored with white along the margin and 2 blood-red or maroon blotches at the base. The anther cap is bright purple and very conspicuous.

HYBRIDIZING NOTES: Chromosome counts are n = 19 (ref. 151) and 2n = 40 (ref. 151, 187).

REFERENCES: 151, 157, 179, 187, 190, 196, 202, 210, 216, 254, 445, 541, 570.

PHOTOS/DRAWINGS: 210.

Dendrobium aphyllum (Roxburgh) C. Fischer

AKA: Hunt (ref. 211) includes the synonyms *Limodorum aphyllum* Roxburgh, *Cymbidium aphyllum* (Roxburgh) Swartz, *Dendrobium cucullatum* R. Brown, *D. madrasense* A. Hawkes, and *D. pierardii* Roxburgh. Seidenfaden and Wood (ref. 455) include only *D. pierardii* as a synonym. In 1992 in *Opera Botanica* #114, Seidenfaden includes *D. pierardii*, *D. evaginatum* Gagnepaign, and *D. oxyphyllum* Gagnepaign. Hawkes (ref. 190) and *Index Kewensis* (ref. 216) include *D. aphyllum* Roxburgh as a synonym of *D. amoenum* Wallich ex. Lindley. The International Orchid Commission (ref. 236) registers hybrids under the name *D. pierardii*.

ORIGIN/HABITAT: Widespread in Southeast Asia. Plants grow in southern and eastern India and the tropical valleys of Sikkim and Nepal where they are found at about 3300 ft. (1000 m). Distribution extends into Burma, southwest China, Thailand, Laos, Vietnam, Malaya, and South Andaman Island. In Burma, plants grow near Moulmein in the Tenasserim Range at 500–4250 ft. (150–1300 m). In China, they are found at 3300–5900 ft. (1000–1800 m). Plants known as *D. pierardii* are usually found in mangrove swamps. They are normally epiphytic, but in deforested areas, they may grow lithophytically.

CLIMATE: Station #42398, Baghdogra, India, Lat. 26.7°N, Long. 88.3°E, at 412 ft. (126 m). Temperatures are calculated for an elevation of 2000 ft. (610 m), resulting in probable extremes of 99°F (37°C) and 31°F (–1°C).

N/HEMISPHERE	JAN	FEB	MAR	APR	MAY	JUN	JUL	AUG	SEP	OCT	NOV	DEC
°F AVG MAX	69	72	80	85	85	84	84	84	83	82	77	72
°F AVG MIN	45	49	55	63	68	71	72	72	71	65	55	48
DIURNAL RANGE	24	23	25	22	17	13	12	12	12	17	22	24
RAIN/INCHES	0.3	0.7	1.3	3.7	11.8	25.9	32.2	25.3	21.2	5.6	0.5	0.2
HUMIDITY/%	73	68	57	58	74	84	86	85	85	79	75	76
BLOOM SEASON	*	***	***	***	**	**	**	*	*	*		*
DAYS CLR @ 6AM	21	18	15	11	5	0	1	1	4	13	23	19
DAYS CLR @ 12PM	23	16	16	11	2	0	1	2	10	21	18
RAIN/MM	8	18	33	94	300	658	818	643	538	142	13	5
°C AVG MAX	20.4	22.1	26.5	29.3	29.3	28.8	28.8	28.8	28.2	27.6	24.9	22.1
°C AVG MIN	7.1	9.3	12.6	17.1	19.9	21.5	22.1	22.1	21.5	18.2	12.6	8.8
DIURNAL RANGE	13.3	12.8	13.9	12.2	9.4	7.3	6.7	6.7	6.7	9.4	12.3	13.3
S/HEMISPHERE	JUL	AUG	SEP	OCT	NOV	DEC	JAN	FEB	MAR	APR	MAY	JUN

Cultural Recommendations

LIGHT: 2500–3500 fc.

TEMPERATURES: Summer days average 84°F (29°C), and nights average 71–72°F (22°C), with a diurnal range of 12–13°F (7°C).

HUMIDITY: Near 85% in summer. Humidity decreases to 75–80% in autumn, and to near 60% in late winter and early spring.

WATER: Conditions are very wet for 5 months in summer, very dry for 5 months in winter, with short transition periods in autumn and spring. Cultivated plants should be kept evenly moist from spring to early autumn, but water should be gradually reduced in late autumn after new growths mature.

FERTILIZER: ¼–½ recommended strength, applied weekly. A high-nitrogen fertilizer is beneficial from spring to midsummer, while a fertilizer high in phosphates should be used in late summer and autumn. Summer growth should be rapid to improve flowering the following year.

REST PERIOD: Winter days average 69–72°F (20–22°C), and nights average 45–49°F (7–9°C), with a diurnal range of 23–24°F (13°C). In the habitat, winter rainfall is low, but additional moisture is often available from heavy deposits of dew. For about a month in late winter or early spring, however, humidity is so low that even the moisture from dew is uncommon. Cultivated plants should be allowed to dry out between waterings in winter, but they should not remain completely dry for extended periods. Fertilizer should be eliminated until water is increased in spring. In the habitat, light is highest in winter. The cool, dry rest with increased light may be necessary to initiate blooming, and some growers recommend that plants be kept completely dry in winter.

GROWING MEDIA: Mounting plants on cork or tree-fern slabs accommodates the pendent growth habit. Growers often place a pad of sphagnum moss between the mount and the plant. If plants are mounted, humidity must be high and plants watered at least once a day in summer. If plants cannot be mounted, hanging pots or baskets may be filled with any open, rapidly draining medium. Containers should be small relative to the plant size. Mounts or baskets reduce the risk of the slender new canes becoming kinked under their own weight. Repotting is best done in spring, immediately after flowering.

MISCELLANEOUS NOTES: The bloom season shown in the climate table is based on cultivation records. In the habitat, blooming occurs in spring. *D. aphyllum* grows over a wide region, so plants may adapt to temperatures 10–12°F (6–7°C) warmer than indicated. Plants are commonly and easily cultivated by many growers, but it can be a difficult species to grow and bloom in warm, tropical climates. Seasonal fluctuations in temperature and rainfall are necessary to induce flowering, and a dry season is particularly important. *D. aphyllum* frequently produces keikis.

Plant and Flower Information

PLANT SIZE AND TYPE: A 24–35 in. (60–90 cm) sympodial epiphyte. Plants known as *D. pierardii* may reach a length of 72 in. (183 cm).

PSEUDOBULB: 24–72 in. (60–183 cm) long. The slender, graceful stems are pendent to semierect and only slightly swollen at the nodes. New growths appear about flowering time.

LEAVES: Many. The leaves, which are usually 4–5 in. (10–13 cm) long, are often smaller near the apex of the cane. They may be linear to ovate, and they are often wavy along the margin. The foliage has a soft texture and is typically deciduous after a single season, though under some conditions leaves may last more than a single year.

INFLORESCENCE: Short. The inflorescences emerge from nodes along the apical 60% of the prior year's leafless stems. The inflorescences are so numerous that the canes appear covered with blossoms.

FLOWERS: 1–3 per inflorescence. Blossoms are 1–2 in. (3–5 cm) across and last about 3 weeks. They have a strong violet fragrance. Sepals and petals may be nearly white or have a pale, rosy-mauve tint with magenta at the tips. The narrowly oblong sepals and broadly oblong petals are fragile and nearly transparent. The lip is cream to bright primrose yellow with purple veins or markings at the base and a greenish yellow disk. The lip is densely hairy on both surfaces. It appears funnel-shaped, but it is nearly round when spread. The lip is highly variable in color, size, and shape.

HYBRIDIZING NOTES: Chromosome counts are n = 19 (ref. 151, 153, 504, 542), 2n = 38 (ref. 152, 153, 188, 243, 504, 542), and 2n = 40 (ref. 150, 153, 542). As *D. pierardii*, counts are n = 19 (ref. 151, 152, 154, 187, 504, 580), n = 19–20 (ref. 187, 504, 580), 2n = 38 (ref. 150, 151, 152, 154, 187, 504, 580), 2n = 40 (ref. 187), and 2n = 57 (ref. 187, 504).

Johansen (ref. 239) indicates that *D. aphyllum* is self-sterile and flowers dropped 5–8 days after self-pollination. When cross-pollinated, capsules opened in 347 days. 95% of the seed contained visible embryos, and 73% germinated. When crossed with *D. lindleyi* Steudel, capsules formed but no seed was produced.

REFERENCES: 6, 32, 36, 38, 46, 71, 102, 119, 150, 151, 152, 153, 154, 165, 179, 187, 188, 190, 196, 202, 208, 210, 211, 216, 224, 236, 238, 239, 243, 247, 254, 266, 278, 317, 326, 369, 371, 376, 402, 430, 447, 448, 452, 454, 455, 458, 504, 510, 523, 528, 541, 542, 569, 570, 577, 580.

PHOTOS/DRAWINGS: 6, 32, *36, 71, 72,* 102, 210, 238, *247, 371, 430, 454, 455, 458, 569.*

Dendrobium apiculiferum J. J. Smith. Although not correctly transferred, Schlechter (ref. 443) considered this plant to be a synonym of *Cadetia apiculifera* (J. J. Smith) Schlechter. REFERENCES: 221, 223, 443, 445, 470, 477.

Dendrobium aporoides (Lindley) Merrill. Now considered a synonym of *Eria aporoides* Lindley. REFERENCES: 222, 280, 296, 373, 504, 536, 580.

Dendrobium appendicula Schlechter

ORIGIN/HABITAT: Northern Papua New Guinea. Plants grow on moss-covered trees in the mistforests of the Finisterre Mountains at about 3000 ft. (910 m).

CLIMATE: Station #200187, Erap, Papua New Guinea, Lat. 6.6°S, Long. 146.7°E, at 850 ft. (260 m). Temperatures are calculated for an elevation of 3300 ft. (1000 m), resulting in probable extremes of 94°F (34°C) and 45°F (7°C).

N/HEMISPHERE	JAN	FEB	MAR	APR	MAY	JUN	JUL	AUG	SEP	OCT	NOV	DEC
°F AVG MAX	80	80	81	82	85	85	85	85	85	84	82	82
°F AVG MIN	61	61	61	62	64	65	64	64	65	63	66	62
DIURNAL RANGE	19	19	20	20	21	20	21	21	20	21	16	20
RAIN/INCHES	3.9	3.9	2.7	3.0	3.0	5.3	5.9	5.9	7.0	3.4	2.4	3.1
HUMIDITY/%	82	81	81	79	75	74	74	74	77	76	80	80
BLOOM SEASON				*								
DAYS CLR	N/A											
RAIN/MM	99	99	69	76	76	135	150	150	178	86	61	79
°C AVG MAX	26.7	26.7	27.2	27.8	29.4	29.4	29.4	29.4	29.4	28.9	27.8	27.8
°C AVG MIN	16.1	16.1	16.1	16.7	17.8	18.3	17.8	17.8	18.3	17.2	18.9	16.7
DIURNAL RANGE	10.6	10.6	11.1	11.1	11.6	11.1	11.6	11.6	11.1	11.7	8.9	11.1
S/HEMISPHERE	JUL	AUG	SEP	OCT	NOV	DEC	JAN	FEB	MAR	APR	MAY	JUN

Cultural Recommendations

LIGHT: 2500–3500 fc.

TEMPERATURES: Throughout the year, days average 80–85°F (27–29°C), and nights average 61–66°F (16–19°C), with a diurnal range of 16–21°F (9–12°C).

HUMIDITY: 75–80% year-round. Despite high average humidity, the habitat may be quite dry during hot afternoons.

WATER: Rainfall is moderate most of the year, but for 4–5 months in summer and early autumn, conditions are somewhat wetter. Cultivated plants should be thoroughly saturated then allowed to dry slightly between waterings in summer and early autumn. Water should be gradually reduced in autumn.

FERTILIZER: ¼–½ recommended strength. A balanced fertilizer should be applied weekly to biweekly throughout the year.

REST PERIOD: Growing temperatures should be maintained all year. In the habitat, rainfall is lowest in winter, but the high humidity indicates that additional moisture is frequently available from heavy dew. Cultivated plants should be allowed to dry somewhat longer between waterings, but they should not remain dry for extended periods. Fertilizer should be reduced until water is increased in spring. In the habitat, seasonal light variation is minor.

GROWING MEDIA: Plants may be mounted on cork slabs or a rough-barked hardwood. If plants are mounted, they need high humidity and watering at least once daily in summer. If plants are potted, the smallest possible pot should be used. Growers report that clay pots are preferable to plastic ones. A rapidly draining medium is recommended. Repotting is best done in early spring immediately after blooming.

MISCELLANEOUS NOTES: The bloom season shown in the climate table is based on collection reports. When describing this plant, Schlechter (ref. 437) commented that it bore an "astonishing resemblance to *Appendicula carnosa* Blume."

Plant and Flower Information

PLANT SIZE AND TYPE: A 4–10 in. (10–25 cm) sympodial epiphyte.

PSEUDOBULB: 4–10 in. (10–25 cm) long. The growth habit is erect to ascending.

Dendrobium appendiculatum

LEAVES: Many. The stems are densely leafy. The linear, spreading leaves are 0.4–0.8 in. (1–2 cm) long.

INFLORESCENCE: Inflorescences emerge from the side of the pseudobulb.

FLOWERS: 1 per inflorescence. The tiny white flowers are 0.2 in. (0.5 cm) across and last only a few days. The lip is uppermost and marked with red. The lateral sepals are joined forming a hood over the lip.

REFERENCES: 92, 221, 437, 445.

PHOTOS/DRAWINGS: 437.

Dendrobium appendiculatum (Blume) Lindley. Now considered a synonym of *Flickingeria appendiculata* (Blume) A. Hawkes. REFERENCES: 75, 213, 216, 230, 231, 254, 277, 310, 395, 449.

Dendrobium appendiculiforme Kränzlin. See *D. distachyum* Lindley. REFERENCES: 218, 253, 254.

Dendrobium appendiculoides Ames. See *D. bunuanense* Ames. REFERENCES: 15, 223, 296, 536.

Dendrobium appendiculoides J. J. Smith

ORIGIN/HABITAT: Irian Jaya (western New Guinea). Plants grow epiphytically in forests on serpentine hills and on spurs of the Cyclops Mountains at about 650 ft. (200 m). They were cultivated in the botanical garden at Bogor, Java.

CLIMATE: Station #97690, Sentani/Jayapura, Irian Jaya, Lat. 2.7°S, Long. 140.5°E, at 289 ft. (88 m). Record extreme temperatures are 97°F (36°C) and 68°F (20°C).

N/HEMISPHERE	JAN	FEB	MAR	APR	MAY	JUN	JUL	AUG	SEP	OCT	NOV	DEC
°F AVG MAX	87	89	89	90	90	89	89	88	89	90	90	89
°F AVG MIN	72	72	72	73	73	73	73	73	73	74	73	73
DIURNAL RANGE	15	17	17	17	17	16	16	15	16	16	17	16
RAIN/INCHES	4.1	3.9	5.3	2.9	6.7	7.0	8.3	8.3	8.5	4.6	2.4	5.2
HUMIDITY/%	81	80	80	79	81	81	79	80	80	80	81	80
BLOOM SEASON							*					
DAYS CLR @ 9AM	5	3	4	3	2	1	1	0	1	2	2	5
DAYS CLR @ 3PM	4	3	3	3	2	1	3	0	1	2	2	3
RAIN/MM	104	99	135	74	170	178	211	211	216	117	61	132
°C AVG MAX	30.6	31.7	31.7	32.2	32.2	31.7	31.7	31.1	31.7	32.2	32.2	31.7
°C AVG MIN	22.2	22.2	22.2	22.8	22.8	22.8	22.8	22.8	22.8	23.3	22.8	22.8
DIURNAL RANGE	8.3	9.4	9.4	9.4	9.4	8.9	8.9	8.3	8.9	8.9	9.4	8.9
S/HEMISPHERE	JUL	AUG	SEP	OCT	NOV	DEC	JAN	FEB	MAR	APR	MAY	JUN

Cultural Recommendations

LIGHT: 2000–3000 fc.

TEMPERATURES: Throughout the year, days average 87–90°F (31–32°C), and nights average 72–74°F (22–23°C), with a diurnal range of 15–17°F (8–9°C).

HUMIDITY: Near 80% year-round.

WATER: Rainfall is moderate to heavy most of the year, with brief, semidry periods in spring and autumn. Cultivated plants should be kept moist with only slight drying allowed between waterings.

FERTILIZER: ¼–½ recommended strength. A balanced fertilizer should be applied weekly to biweekly throughout the year.

REST PERIOD: Growing conditions should be maintained year-round. Water and fertilizer should be reduced somewhat in winter for plants grown in the dark, short-day conditions common in temperate latitudes, but they should never be allowed to dry out completely. In the habitat, light is highest in winter.

GROWING MEDIA: Plants may be mounted on tree-fern or cork slabs or potted in any open, fast-draining medium. Repotting is best done in early spring when new roots are growing.

MISCELLANEOUS NOTES: The roots are naturally very rough.

Plant and Flower Information

PLANT SIZE AND TYPE: A 16 in. (40 cm) sympodial epiphyte.

PSEUDOBULB: 16 in. (40 cm) long. The stems are angled.

LEAVES: Many. The spreading, lanceolate leaves are 2.0–3.5 in. (5–9 cm) long. They are unequally 3-lobed at the apex.

INFLORESCENCE: 1.6–4.3 in. (4–11 cm) long.

FLOWERS: 4–14 per inflorescence. The flowers are 0.7 in. (1.7 cm) long. Blossoms have a somewhat elliptical dorsal sepal, triangular lateral sepals, and petals that are shaped like a parallelogram. The concave, fleshy lip has 3 identical longitudinal ribs which start at the base. The midlobe is cut or notched twice.

REFERENCES: 221, 470, 476.

Dendrobium aprinoides J. J. Smith. Now considered a synonym of *Cadetia aprinoides* (J. J. Smith) A. Hawkes. REFERENCES: 224, 230, 445.

Dendrobium aprinum J. J. Smith. Now considered a synonym of *Cadetia aprina* (J. J. Smith) Schlechter. REFERENCES: 221, 445, 470, 538. PHOTOS/DRAWINGS: 538.

Dendrobium aqueum Lindley

AKA: *D. album* Wight.

ORIGIN/HABITAT: India. Plants grow in the mountains along the east and west sides of the peninsula. They are often found near the top of coffee bushes on abandoned plantations at 3000–7000 ft. (910–2130 m).

CLIMATE: Station #43314, Calicut, India, Lat. 11.3°N, Long. 75.8°E, at 17 ft. (5 m). Temperatures are calculated for an elevation of 5000 ft. (1520 m), resulting in probable extremes of 83°F (28°C) and 41°F (5°C).

N/HEMISPHERE	JAN	FEB	MAR	APR	MAY	JUN	JUL	AUG	SEP	OCT	NOV	DEC
°F AVG MAX	72	73	74	75	74	69	66	67	68	70	71	72
°F AVG MIN	55	57	60	62	62	59	58	58	59	59	58	55
DIURNAL RANGE	17	16	14	13	12	10	8	9	9	11	13	17
RAIN/INCHES	0.4	0.2	0.7	3.6	9.3	33.1	32.5	17.2	7.9	10.3	5.5	1.0
HUMIDITY/%	71	73	73	74	82	87	91	91	87	85	77	74
BLOOM SEASON	*	*						*	*	*	*	
DAYS CLR @ 5AM	19	18	21	12	5	4	2	2	4	4	19	20
DAYS CLR @ 11AM	16	18	23	15	5	3	0	1	6	5	12	14
RAIN/MM	10	5	18	91	236	841	826	437	201	262	140	25
°C AVG MAX	22.0	22.5	23.1	23.6	23.1	20.3	18.6	19.2	19.8	20.9	21.4	22.0
°C AVG MIN	12.5	13.6	15.3	16.4	16.4	14.8	14.2	14.2	14.8	14.8	14.2	12.5
DIURNAL RANGE	9.5	8.9	7.8	7.2	6.7	5.5	4.4	5.0	5.0	6.1	7.2	9.5
S/HEMISPHERE	JUL	AUG	SEP	OCT	NOV	DEC	JAN	FEB	MAR	APR	MAY	JUN

Cultural Recommendations

LIGHT: 3000–4000 fc. The heavy summer cloud cover indicates that some shading is needed from spring through autumn, but light should be as high as the plant can tolerate, short of burning the leaves.

TEMPERATURES: Summer days average 66–69°F (19–20°C), and nights average 58–59°F (14–15°C), with a diurnal range of 8–10°F (5–6°C). Spring is the warmest season. Days average 74–75°F (23–24°C), and nights average 60–62°F (15–16°C), with a diurnal range of 12–14°F (7–8°C).

HUMIDITY: 85–90% in summer, decreasing to 70–75% in winter and spring.

WATER: Rainfall is heavy to extremely heavy most of the year, but conditions are very dry for 3–4 months in winter. Cultivated plants should be watered liberally in summer, as often several times a week during bright, hot weather. Water should be gradually reduced through autumn, greatly reduced in winter, then gradually increased in spring when new growth starts.

FERTILIZER: ¼–½ recommended strength, applied weekly. A high-nitrogen fertilizer is beneficial from spring to midsummer, but a fertilizer high in phosphates should be used in late summer and autumn.

REST PERIOD: Winter days average 72–73°F (22–23°C), and nights average 55–57°F (13–14°C), with a diurnal range of 16–17°F (9–10°C). For cultivated plants, water should be greatly reduced for 3–4 months. Plants should be allowed to dry out between waterings, but they should not remain completely dry for extended periods. Occasional, early morning mistings between waterings may be beneficial, especially on warm, sunny days. Fertilizer should be greatly reduced or eliminated until water is increased in spring. In the habitat, light is highest in winter.

GROWING MEDIA: Mounting plants on tree-fern slabs accommodates their pendulous growth habit, but humidity must be high and plants should be watered at least once daily in summer. If plants are potted, any open, fast-draining medium may be used. Repotting should be done in late spring when new roots begin to grow.

MISCELLANEOUS NOTES: The bloom season shown in the climate table is based on cultivation records.

Plant and Flower Information

PLANT SIZE AND TYPE: A 10–20 in. (25–50 cm) sympodial epiphyte.

PSEUDOBULB: 10–20 in. (25–50 cm) long. The jointed stems are stout, decurved or pendulous, and yellow-green when young. They are largest at the apex.

LEAVES: Many along the entire stem. The dark leaves are 2–7 in. (5–18 cm) long, ovate-oblong, pointed, and sometimes wavy. They are smallest near the apex.

INFLORESCENCE: Short. The inflorescences emerge in succession from leaf axils along the upper half of the current season's growth.

FLOWERS: 1–3 per inflorescence. The attractive blossoms are 1.0–1.5 in. (2.5–3.8 cm) long. Sepals and petals may be white or greenish white. The 3-lobed lip is suffused with pale yellow and decorated with a pale yellow disk. The midlobe is reflexed, downy on the upper surface, and toothed or fringed along the margin.

HYBRIDIZING NOTES: Chromosome count is 2n = 38 (ref. 151, 504, 542, 580).

REFERENCES: 38, 46, 119, 151, 179, 202, 210, 216, 254, 255, 278, 317, 369, 424, 445, 504, 541, 542, 570, 580.

PHOTOS/DRAWINGS: 210.

Dendrobium arachnanthe Kränzlin. See *D. discolor* Lindley. REFERENCES: 67, 84, 220, 254.

Dendrobium arachnites Rchb. f. not Thouars. See *D. dickasonii* L. O. Williams. REFERENCES: 36, 157, 179, 190, 196, 202, 216, 233, 254, 280, 369, 452, 454, 504, 541, 568, 570, 580. PHOTOS/DRAWINGS: 369.

Dendrobium arachnitis Thouars not Rchb. f. Now considered a synonym of *Aëranthes arachnitis* Lindley. REFERENCES: 100, 190, 216, 254, 445.

Dendrobium arachnoideum Schlechter. Now considered a synonym of *Diplocaulobium arachnoideum* (Schlechter) Carr. REFERENCES: 221, 225, 437, 445.

Dendrobium arachnoglossum Rchb. f. Schlechter (ref. 437) includes this name, but refers to the original reference for *D. arachnostachyum* Rchb. f. REFERENCES: 437.

Dendrobium arachnostachyum Rchb. f. See *D. macranthum* A. Richard. REFERENCES: 84, 216, 254, 270.

Dendrobium araneola Schlechter. Now considered a synonym of *Diplocaulobium araneola* (Schlechter) Carr. REFERENCES: 221, 225, 437, 445.

Dendrobium araneum J. J. Smith

ORIGIN/HABITAT: Irian Jaya (western New Guinea). Plants grow on forest trees along the Giriwo River.

CLIMATE: Station #97682, Nabire, Irian Jaya, Lat. 3.3°S, Long. 135.5°E, at 10 ft. (3 m). Record extreme temperatures are not available for this location.

N/HEMISPHERE	JAN	FEB	MAR	APR	MAY	JUN	JUL	AUG	SEP	OCT	NOV	DEC
°F AVG MAX	86	86	86	86	87	87	86	86	87	87	87	87
°F AVG MIN	75	75	76	77	77	76	77	75	75	76	76	76
DIURNAL RANGE	11	11	10	9	10	11	9	11	12	11	11	11
RAIN/INCHES	7.4	11.1	8.5	8.5	7.5	9.0	9.2	10.6	12.1	11.3	10.2	9.8
HUMIDITY/%	N/A											
BLOOM SEASON	*											
DAYS CLR	N/A											
RAIN/MM	190	283	217	217	192	228	233	270	308	286	259	248
°C AVG MAX	30.1	29.9	30.1	30.3	30.5	30.6	30.0	30.0	30.5	30.5	30.3	30.3
°C AVG MIN	24.0	24.0	24.3	24.7	24.9	24.5	24.8	24.0	23.8	24.6	24.3	24.2
DIURNAL RANGE	6.1	5.9	5.8	5.6	5.6	6.1	5.2	6.0	6.7	5.9	6.0	6.1
S/HEMISPHERE	JUL	AUG	SEP	OCT	NOV	DEC	JAN	FEB	MAR	APR	MAY	JUN

Cultural Recommendations

LIGHT: 2000–3000 fc.

TEMPERATURES: Throughout the year, days average 86–87°F (30–31°C), and nights average 75–77°F (24–25°C), with a diurnal range of 9–12°F (6–7°C).

HUMIDITY: Information is not available for this location. However, data from nearby stations indicate that averages are probably near 85% year-round.

WATER: Rainfall is heavy year-round. Cultivated plants should be kept evenly moist.

FERTILIZER: ¼–½ recommended strength. A balanced fertilizer should be applied weekly to biweekly throughout the year.

REST PERIOD: Growing conditions should be maintained year-round. Water and fertilizer may be reduced slightly in winter for plants cultivated in the dark, short-day conditions common in temperate latitudes, but cultivated plants should never be allowed to dry completely.

GROWING MEDIA: Mounting plants on tree-fern or cork slabs accommodates their pendulous growth habit. However, humidity must be high and plants must be watered at least once a day in summer. If plants cannot be mounted, hanging pots or baskets may be filled with an open, fast-draining medium. Repotting may be done anytime new roots are actively growing.

MISCELLANEOUS NOTES: The bloom season shown in the climate table is based on reports from the habitat.

Plant and Flower Information

PLANT SIZE AND TYPE: A 16 in. (40 cm) sympodial epiphyte.

PSEUDOBULB: 16 in. (40 cm) long. The pendulous stems are very branching.

LEAVES: Many. The linear-lanceolate leaves are 1.7 in. (4.4 cm) long. They are erect to spreading, laterally compressed, and pointed.

INFLORESCENCE: Short. The branching inflorescences emerge from nodes along the stem.

FLOWERS: 1 per inflorescence. The flowers are 0.3 in. (0.8 cm) across. They are thick and fleshy with white sepals and petals and a green lip. Blossoms have an ovate-triangular dorsal sepal, obliquely triangular lateral sepals, and oblong petals. All segments are pointed. The curved lip has numerous projections that may resemble small bumps or hairs.

REFERENCES: 221, 470, 477.

Dendrobium aratriferum J. J. Smith. Now considered a synonym of *Diplocaulobium aratriferum* (J. J. Smith) Hunt and Summerhayes. REFERENCES: 111, 213, 220, 230, 254, 445, 470.

Dendrobium araucaricola. Cruttwell (ref. 95) includes this species name (without describers' name) as growing very high in hoop pines in the Mt. Gahavisuka Botanical Sanctuary in Papua New Guinea. REFERENCES: 95.

Dendrobium arcuatum J. J. Smith

ORIGIN/HABITAT: Java, where it may be endemic. Plants grow in the forests on hills facing the south coast of eastern Java. They are found from sea level to 2600 ft. (0–800 m).

CLIMATE: Station #96853, Jogjakarta, Java, Indonesia, Lat. 7.8°S, Long. 110.4°E, at 350 ft. (107 m). Temperatures are calculated for an elevation of 1300 ft. (400 m), resulting in probable extremes of 92°F (33°C) and 59°F (15°C).

N/HEMISPHERE	JAN	FEB	MAR	APR	MAY	JUN	JUL	AUG	SEP	OCT	NOV	DEC
°F AVG MAX	82	83	84	85	83	82	81	81	82	84	83	83
°F AVG MIN	66	66	68	69	69	69	69	69	69	69	69	67
DIURNAL RANGE	16	17	16	16	14	13	12	12	13	15	14	16
RAIN/INCHES	1.6	1.0	1.2	3.7	9.0	13.4	13.9	13.2	12.2	8.3	5.0	3.5
HUMIDITY/%	74	71	69	73	78	82	82	82	81	78	77	74
BLOOM SEASON		*					*	*				
DAYS CLR @ 7AM	9	8	7	8	4	2	2	3	5	7	8	12
DAYS CLR @ 1PM	6	6	3	3	2	0	1	1	1	2	3	5
RAIN/MM	41	25	30	94	229	340	353	335	310	211	127	89
°C AVG MAX	27.7	28.3	28.8	29.4	28.3	27.7	27.1	27.1	27.7	28.8	28.3	28.3
°C AVG MIN	18.8	18.8	19.9	20.5	20.5	20.5	20.5	20.5	20.5	20.5	20.5	19.4
DIURNAL RANGE	8.9	9.5	8.9	8.9	7.8	7.2	6.6	6.6	7.2	8.3	7.8	8.9
S/HEMISPHERE	JUL	AUG	SEP	OCT	NOV	DEC	JAN	FEB	MAR	APR	MAY	JUN

Cultural Recommendations

LIGHT: 3000–4000 fc. Cultivated plants should receive as much light as possible, but some shading is required in summer to prevent leaf-burn.

TEMPERATURES: Throughout the year, days average 81–85°F (27–29°C), and nights average 66–69°F (19–21°C), with a diurnal range of 12–17°F (7–10°C). The warmest temperatures occur in spring.

HUMIDITY: Near 80% in summer and early autumn, dropping to 70% in winter.

WATER: Rainfall is very heavy for 6 months from spring into autumn, but conditions are relatively dry for 3 months in winter. Cultivated plants should be kept moist from spring to early autumn, but water should be gradually reduced through autumn, greatly reduced in winter, then gradually increased in spring when new growth starts.

FERTILIZER: ¼–½ recommended strength. A balanced fertilizer should be applied weekly to biweekly throughout the year.

REST PERIOD: Growing temperatures should be maintained all year. A dry, winter rest is important to plant health, and water should be greatly reduced for 3 months. Plants should be allowed to dry out between waterings, but they should not remain dry for extended periods. Fertilizer should be greatly reduced or eliminated until plants begin actively growing in spring. In the habitat, light is highest in winter.

GROWING MEDIA: Mounting on tree-fern or cork slabs accommodates their horizontal growth habit, but humidity must be high and plants need watering at least once daily in summer. Repotting is best done between flowerings as soon as possible after new roots begin growing.

MISCELLANEOUS NOTES: The bloom season shown in the climate table is based on 2 records for cultivated plants. In its habitat, *D. arcuatum* is very free-flowering and may bloom 5–6 times a year.

Plant and Flower Information

PLANT SIZE AND TYPE: A 7 in. (18 cm) sympodial epiphyte.

PSEUDOBULB: 3 in. (8 cm) long. The stems, which grow horizontally, consist of numerous leafy internodes.

LEAVES: Many. The ovate-lanceolate leaves are 4 in. (10 cm) long. Photos suggest that the leaves, which are arranged in 2 rows, are slightly twisted at the base so that they all face one direction.

INFLORESCENCE: 1.2–1.6 in. (3–4 cm). Several inflorescences emerge from nodes along the apical 65% of leafy and leafless stems. Leafless stems are usually more floriferous.

FLOWERS: 3–6 per inflorescence. The white or yellowish flowers are 2 in. (5 cm) long with a greenish spur that is at least twice as long as the dorsal sepal. The long narrow lip is keeled, prominently nerved, and wavy along the apical margin. It is marked with a few crimson spots.

REFERENCES: 25, 74, 75, 179, 219, 254, 445, 469.

PHOTOS/DRAWINGS: 74, 75, 469.

Dendrobium ardenii Ridley. Sometimes spelled *D. ardeni*, it is now considered a synonym of *Flickingeria angustifolia* (Blume) A. Hawkes. REFERENCES: 213, 220, 223, 398, 449.

Dendrobium arfakense J. J. Smith. Although not correctly transferred, Schlechter (ref. 443) considered this plant to be a synonym of *Cadetia arfakensis* (J. J. Smith) Schlechter. REFERENCES: 221, 223, 443, 445, 470, 475.

Dendrobium argiense J. J. Smith. See *D. subclausum* Rolfe. REFERENCES: 144, 221, 470, 476.

Dendrobium aridum J. J. Smith

ORIGIN/HABITAT: Irian Jaya (western New Guinea). Plants grow in the primary forests of the Nassau mountains at about 3950 ft. (1200 m).

CLIMATE: Station #97686, Wamena, Irian Jaya, Lat. 4.1°S, Long. 139.0°E, at 5446 ft. (1660 m). Temperatures are calculated for an elevation of 3950 ft. (1200 m). Record extreme temperatures are not available for this location.

N/HEMISPHERE	JAN	FEB	MAR	APR	MAY	JUN	JUL	AUG	SEP	OCT	NOV	DEC
°F AVG MAX	80	81	82	81	82	81	82	81	81	84	83	79
°F AVG MIN	65	65	67	67	68	69	68	67	68	70	70	66
DIURNAL RANGE	15	16	15	14	14	12	14	14	13	14	13	13
RAIN/INCHES	3.0	1.9	2.2	4.0	4.6	3.3	2.8	4.2	6.9	3.9	5.4	4.9
HUMIDITY/%	N/A											
BLOOM SEASON					*							
DAYS CLR	N/A											
RAIN/MM	76	48	56	102	117	84	71	107	175	99	137	124
°C AVG MAX	26.6	27.2	27.7	27.2	27.7	27.2	27.7	27.2	27.2	28.9	28.3	26.1
°C AVG MIN	18.3	18.3	19.4	19.4	20.0	20.5	20.0	19.4	20.0	21.1	21.1	18.9
DIURNAL RANGE	8.3	8.9	8.3	7.8	7.7	6.7	7.7	7.8	7.2	7.8	7.2	7.2
S/HEMISPHERE	JUL	AUG	SEP	OCT	NOV	DEC	JAN	FEB	MAR	APR	MAY	JUN

Cultural Recommendations

LIGHT: 2000–3000 fc.

TEMPERATURES: Throughout the year, days average 80–84°F (27–29°C), and nights average 65–70°F (18–21°C), with a diurnal range of 12–16°F (7–9°C). In the habitat, the warmest temperatures of the day occur during late morning, when skies are usually clear. Clouds and mist develop near noon and continue through the afternoon, thus preventing additional warming.

HUMIDITY: Information is not available for this location. However, records from nearby stations indicate that humidity probably averages near 80%

year-round. High humidity is particularly important if temperatures are warm. Placing the plants in front of an evaporative cooler or near a fine mist may be very beneficial on especially warm days.

WATER: Rainfall is light to moderate through most of the year, but large amounts of water are usually available from mist and heavy dew, even during periods of lower rainfall. Cultivated plants should be kept moist with only slight drying allowed between waterings. Good air movement is critically important and should be maintained at all times.

FERTILIZER: ¼–½ recommended strength. A balanced fertilizer should be applied weekly to biweekly throughout the year.

REST PERIOD: Growing conditions should be maintained all year. Conditions are slightly drier for 1–2 months in winter. In cultivation, water may be decreased somewhat, but plants should never be allowed to dry out completely or remain dry for long periods. In the habitat, light is slightly higher in winter.

GROWING MEDIA: Plants may be mounted on tree-fern or cork slabs if humidity is high and plants are watered daily in summer. When plants are potted, any open, fast-draining medium may be used. Repotting is best done in early spring when new roots are growing.

MISCELLANEOUS NOTES: The bloom season shown in the climate table is based on reports from the habitat.

Plant and Flower Information

PLANT SIZE AND TYPE: A 12 in. (30 cm) sympodial epiphyte.

PSEUDOBULB: 12 in. (30 cm) long. The clustered pseudobulbs are erect, unbranched, and somewhat flattened. Numerous stems arise from a short, very branching rhizome.

LEAVES: Many. The erect, linear leaves are 2 in. (5 cm) long.

INFLORESCENCE: Short. Inflorescences emerge along the stem through the leaf sheaths.

FLOWERS: 1 per inflorescence. The tiny flowers are 0.3 in. (0.8 cm) across. The light yellow blossoms have a red lip.

REFERENCES: 225, 470.

Dendrobium aries J. J. Smith

AKA: Sometimes spelled *D. aeries*.

ORIGIN/HABITAT: Irian Jaya (western New Guinea). Plants grow on trees near sea level at the western tip of the island, on Waigeo Island, near Sorong, and in the lowlands of Teminaboean on the southwest coast of the Vogelkop Peninsula. They were cultivated in the botanical garden at Bogor, Java.

CLIMATE: Station #97502, Jefman, Irian Jaya, Lat. 0.9°S, Long. 131.1°E, at 10 ft. (3 m). Record extreme temperatures are 93°F (34°C) and 72°F (22°C).

N/HEMISPHERE	JAN	FEB	MAR	APR	MAY	JUN	JUL	AUG	SEP	OCT	NOV	DEC
°F AVG MAX	85	87	89	89	88	88	88	88	89	90	89	87
°F AVG MIN	77	77	77	78	78	78	79	79	79	79	78	78
DIURNAL RANGE	8	10	12	11	10	10	9	9	10	11	11	9
RAIN/INCHES	13.1	9.7	10.3	8.1	6.9	7.0	7.2	6.6	8.0	9.6	12.4	13.4
HUMIDITY/%	85	86	85	82	82	83	81	81	82	82	85	84
BLOOM SEASON									*	*		
DAYS CLR @ 9AM	2	2	2	5	6	1	6	1	4	5	5	6
DAYS CLR @ 3PM	3	2	3	4	1	1	5	1	2	4	3	5
RAIN/MM	333	246	262	206	175	178	183	168	203	244	315	340
°C AVG MAX	29.4	30.6	31.7	31.7	31.1	31.1	31.1	31.1	31.7	32.2	31.7	30.6
°C AVG MIN	25.0	25.0	25.0	25.6	25.6	25.6	26.1	26.1	26.1	26.1	25.6	25.6
DIURNAL RANGE	4.4	5.6	6.7	6.1	5.5	5.5	5.0	5.0	5.6	6.1	6.1	5.0
S/HEMISPHERE	JUL	AUG	SEP	OCT	NOV	DEC	JAN	FEB	MAR	APR	MAY	JUN

Cultural Recommendations

LIGHT: 3000–4000 fc. Shading is required from spring into early autumn, but throughout the year, plants should receive as much light as possible without burning the foliage.

TEMPERATURES: Throughout the year, days average 85–90°F (29–32°C), and nights average 77–79°F (25–26°C), with a diurnal range of 8–12°F (4–7°C). More temperature variation occurs each day than occurs seasonally.

HUMIDITY: 80–85% year-round.

WATER: Rainfall is moderate to heavy all year, but conditions are a little drier in summer. Cultivated plants should be kept moist with only slight drying allowed between waterings.

FERTILIZER: ¼–½ recommended strength. A balanced fertilizer should be applied weekly to biweekly throughout the year.

REST PERIOD: Growing temperatures should be maintained year-round. Water should be reduced in winter for plants grown in the dark, short-day conditions common in temperate latitudes, but they should never be allowed to dry out completely.

GROWING MEDIA: Plants may be mounted on tree-fern or cork slabs if humidity is high and plants are watered at least once daily in summer. If plants are potted, any open, fast-draining medium may be used. Repotting may be done anytime new roots are growing. Growers report that the roots are sensitive to excess moisture.

MISCELLANEOUS NOTES: The bloom season shown in the climate table is based on cultivation records. *D. aries* is attractive, but seldom cultivated. When not in flower, plants are very similar to *D. discolor* Lindley.

Plant and Flower Information

PLANT SIZE AND TYPE: A 47 in. (120 cm) sympodial epiphyte. Plants occasionally reach a length of 118 in. (300 cm).

PSEUDOBULB: 47 in. (120 cm) long. The stems are canelike.

LEAVES: The oblong leaves are 5–7 in. (12–18 cm) long and unequally bilobed at the tip.

INFLORESCENCE: 6–16 in. (15–41 cm) long. Inflorescences are densely flowered.

FLOWERS: 25–40 per inflorescence. The flowers are 1.4–2.0 in. (3.5–5.1 cm) across. The blossoms have tightly spiraled, erect petals and sharply recurved sepals. The shiny flowers have yellowish brown sepals with yellow margins and pale chestnut brown petals. The yellow lip is marked with 3 violet keels. The rounded midlobe is light brown at the base and yellow-green at the apex. The long lasting blossoms, which are all open at once, have a heavy texture.

REFERENCES: 25, 84, 190, 200, 221, 445, 470, 537.

PHOTOS/DRAWINGS: 84.

Dendrobium aristiferum J. J. Smith

ORIGIN/HABITAT: Rare in Irian Jaya (western New Guinea). Plants grow on Mt. Goliath at about 2950 ft. (900 m). They are found on trees in the shade.

CLIMATE: Station #97876, Tanahmerah, Irian Jaya, Lat. 6.1°S, Long. 140.3°E, at 75 ft. (23 m). Temperatures are calculated for an elevation of 2950 ft. (900 m), resulting in probable extremes of 89°F (31°C) and 55°F (13°C).

N/HEMISPHERE	JAN	FEB	MAR	APR	MAY	JUN	JUL	AUG	SEP	OCT	NOV	DEC
°F AVG MAX	75	76	78	81	82	81	81	80	81	80	78	76
°F AVG MIN	63	62	62	63	64	65	64	64	64	64	65	64
DIURNAL RANGE	12	14	16	18	18	16	17	16	17	16	13	12
RAIN/INCHES	11.5	12.1	14.7	13.2	14.4	15.9	14.5	15.8	17.4	17.3	15.5	11.9
HUMIDITY/%	N/A											
BLOOM SEASON									*			
DAYS CLR	N/A											
RAIN/MM	292	307	373	335	366	404	368	401	442	439	394	302
°C AVG MAX	23.9	24.4	25.6	27.2	27.8	27.4	27.3	26.7	27.2	26.7	25.6	24.4
°C AVG MIN	17.2	16.4	16.6	17.0	17.5	18.1	17.5	17.5	17.5	17.5	18.1	17.5
DIURNAL RANGE	6.7	8.0	9.2	10.2	10.3	9.3	9.8	9.2	9.7	9.2	7.5	6.9
S/HEMISPHERE	JUL	AUG	SEP	OCT	NOV	DEC	JAN	FEB	MAR	APR	MAY	JUN

Dendrobium armeniacum

Cultural Recommendations

LIGHT: 1800–2500 fc.

TEMPERATURES: Throughout the year, days average 75–82°F (24–28°C), and nights average 62–65°F (16–18°C), with a diurnal range of 12–18°F (7–10°C).

HUMIDITY: Information is not available for this location. However, records from nearby stations indicate that humidity probably averages near 85% year-round.

WATER: Rainfall is very heavy all year. Cultivated plants should be kept evenly moist with only slight drying allowed between waterings.

FERTILIZER: ¼–½ recommended strength. A balanced fertilizer should be applied weekly to biweekly throughout the year.

REST PERIOD: Growing conditions should be maintained year-round. Water and fertilizer might be reduced slightly in winter, especially for plants cultivated in the dark, short-day conditions common in temperate latitudes; but they should never be allowed dry out completely. In the habitat, seasonal light variation is minor.

GROWING MEDIA: Plants may be mounted on tree-fern or cork slabs if humidity is high and plants are watered at least once daily in summer. When plants are potted, any open, fast-draining medium may be used. Repotting is best done in early spring when new roots begin to grow.

MISCELLANEOUS NOTES: The bloom season shown in the climate table is based on reports from the habitat. The plant was described in 1911 in *Bul. Jard. Bot. Buit.* 2nd sér. 2:12.

Plant and Flower Information

PLANT SIZE AND TYPE: A sympodial epiphyte of unreported size.

PSEUDOBULB: The stems are square in cross section.

LEAVES: Many. The leaves are 0.5–0.7 in. (1.4–1.7 cm) long. The short, ovate leaves have small teeth and a long bristle at the tip. The sheaths are covered with warts.

FLOWERS: 2–3 per inflorescence. The poppy-red flowers are 0.6 in. (1.6 cm) long. Blossoms have warty, ovate sepals, oblong petals, and a tongue-shaped lip. The lip, which has a horseshoe-shaped callus, is fringed along the incurved apex.

REFERENCES: 221, 445, 470.

Dendrobium armeniacum Cribb

ORIGIN/HABITAT: Endemic to north-central Papua New Guinea. Plants grow in the forests of the Bismarck Mountains at 4900–7900 ft. (1500–2400 m).

CLIMATE: Station #94010, Goroka, Papua New Guinea, Lat. 6.1°S, Long. 145.4°E, at 5141 ft. (1567 m). Temperatures are calculated for an elevation of 6550 ft. (2000 m), resulting in probable extremes of 82°F (28°C) and 38°F (4°C).

N/HEMISPHERE	JAN	FEB	MAR	APR	MAY	JUN	JUL	AUG	SEP	OCT	NOV	DEC
°F AVG MAX	71	72	73	74	74	73	74	73	73	73	74	72
°F AVG MIN	51	52	52	52	53	54	54	54	55	54	54	52
DIURNAL RANGE	20	20	21	22	21	19	20	19	18	19	20	20
RAIN/INCHES	2.1	2.8	4.6	5.9	6.6	9.3	9.1	10.1	10.7	8.3	4.6	2.0
HUMIDITY/%	70	67	67	67	67	71	72	73	74	71	70	70
BLOOM SEASON			*									
DAYS CLR	N/A											
RAIN/MM	53	71	117	150	168	236	231	257	272	211	117	51
°C AVG MAX	21.8	22.4	23.0	23.5	23.5	23.0	23.5	23.0	23.0	23.0	23.5	22.4
°C AVG MIN	10.7	11.3	11.3	11.3	11.8	12.4	12.4	12.4	13.0	12.4	12.4	11.3
DIURNAL RANGE	11.1	11.1	11.7	12.2	11.7	10.6	11.1	10.6	10.0	10.6	11.1	11.1
S/HEMISPHERE	JUL	AUG	SEP	OCT	NOV	DEC	JAN	FEB	MAR	APR	MAY	JUN

Cultural Recommendations

LIGHT: 2500–3500 fc.

TEMPERATURES: Throughout the year, days average 71–74°F (22–24°C), and nights average 51–55°F (11–13°C), with a diurnal range of 18–22°F (10–12°C).

HUMIDITY: 70–75% in summer and autumn, decreasing to 65–70% in winter and spring.

WATER: Rainfall is moderate to heavy most of the year, but conditions are slightly drier for 3 months in winter. Cultivated plants should be kept moist. In summer, daily water may be necessary during hot, dry weather. In addition, early morning mistings may be beneficial, especially on bright, sunny days.

FERTILIZER: ¼ recommended strength. A balanced fertilizer should be applied weekly to biweekly throughout the year. Plants require little or no fertilizer if grown in live sphagnum. In any medium, fertilizer should be very weak. The Royal Botanic Garden in Edinburgh uses a weak, seaweed-based fertilizer for plants from this habitat.

REST PERIOD: Growing conditions must be cool year-round. In the habitat, rainfall is lowest in winter, but dew, fog, and low clouds are common. Water should be reduced somewhat, especially for plants cultivated in the dark, short-day conditions common during temperate-latitude winters. However, cultivated plants should never be allowed to dry out completely. Fertilizer should be reduced or eliminated until water is increased in spring. In the habitat, seasonal light variation is minor.

GROWING MEDIA: Plants are best mounted on tree-fern slabs to accommodate their pendent growth habit, but humidity must be high and plants must be watered at least once a day in summer. If plants are potted, a mixture of fir bark or chopped tree-fern fiber with moisture-retaining additives is recommended. A surface layer of sphagnum moss might be beneficial, especially in drier regions. The medium should be kept moist, but not soggy. Repotting is best done immediately after flowering when new roots are growing.

MISCELLANEOUS NOTES: The bloom season shown in the climate table is based on cultivation records.

Plant and Flower Information

PLANT SIZE AND TYPE: A pendulous, 10 in. (25 cm) sympodial epiphyte.

PSEUDOBULB: 6 in. (15 cm) long. The stems, which yellow with age, usually consist of about 3 nodes. They taper slightly toward the base.

LEAVES: 1–2 at the apex of each growth. The large, apical leaves are 4.3 in. (11 cm) long and thin-textured. They twist at the base so that all lie on a single plane. The leaves are frequently orange.

INFLORESCENCE: 2–3 in. (6–8 cm) long. Inflorescences emerge near the apex of the pseudobulb.

FLOWERS: 3–10 per inflorescence. The small, fleshy blossoms are 0.4–0.8 in. (1–2 cm) across and remain somewhat closed. Flowers may be white or pale greenish ochre. The bright orange lip is marked with red lines and a green callus which bears 3 ridges.

REFERENCES: 83, 95, 179, 234.

PHOTOS/DRAWINGS: 83.

Dendrobium armitiae F. M. Bailey. See *D. baileyi* F. Mueller.

REFERENCES: 254.

Dendrobium aromaticum J. J. Smith

ORIGIN/HABITAT: Irian Jaya (western New Guinea). Plants grow near Humboldt Bay in coastal, hillside forests at about 350 ft. (100 m).

CLIMATE: Station #97690, Sentani/Jayapura, Irian Jaya, Lat. 2.7°S, Long.

140.5°E, at 289 ft. (88 m). Record extreme temperatures are 97°F (36°C) and 68°F (20°C).

N/HEMISPHERE	JAN	FEB	MAR	APR	MAY	JUN	JUL	AUG	SEP	OCT	NOV	DEC
°F AVG MAX	87	89	89	90	90	89	89	88	89	90	90	89
°F AVG MIN	72	72	72	73	73	73	73	73	73	74	73	73
DIURNAL RANGE	15	17	17	17	17	16	16	15	16	16	17	16
RAIN/INCHES	4.1	3.9	5.3	2.9	6.7	7.0	8.3	8.3	8.5	4.6	2.4	5.2
HUMIDITY/%	81	80	80	79	81	81	79	80	80	80	81	80
BLOOM SEASON						*						
DAYS CLR @ 9AM	5	3	4	3	2	1	1	0	1	2	2	5
DAYS CLR @ 3PM	4	3	3	3	2	1	3	0	1	2	2	3
RAIN/MM	104	99	135	74	170	178	211	211	216	117	61	132
°C AVG MAX	30.6	31.7	31.7	32.2	32.2	31.7	31.7	31.1	31.7	32.2	32.2	31.7
°C AVG MIN	22.2	22.2	22.2	22.8	22.8	22.8	22.8	22.8	22.8	23.3	22.8	22.8
DIURNAL RANGE	8.4	9.5	9.5	9.4	9.4	8.9	8.9	8.3	8.9	8.9	9.4	8.9
S/HEMISPHERE	JUL	AUG	SEP	OCT	NOV	DEC	JAN	FEB	MAR	APR	MAY	JUN

Cultural Recommendations

LIGHT: 2500–3500 fc.

TEMPERATURES: Throughout the year, days average 87–90°F (31–32°C), and nights average 72–74°F (22–23°C), with a diurnal range of 15–17°F (8–9°C).

HUMIDITY: Near 80% year-round.

WATER: Rainfall is moderate to heavy most of the year with brief, semidry periods in spring and autumn. Cultivated plants should be kept moist with only slight drying allowed between waterings.

FERTILIZER: 1/4–1/2 recommended strength. A balanced fertilizer should be applied weekly to biweekly throughout the year.

REST PERIOD: Growing conditions should be maintained year-round. Water and fertilizer should be reduced somewhat in winter for plants grown in the dark, short-day conditions common in temperate latitudes, but they should never be allowed to dry out completely. In the habitat, light is highest in winter.

GROWING MEDIA: Plants may be mounted on tree-fern or cork slabs if humidity is high and plants are watered at least once daily in summer. When plants are potted, any open, fast-draining medium may be used. Repotting may be done anytime new roots are growing.

MISCELLANEOUS NOTES: The bloom season shown in the climate table is based on reports from the habitat.

Plant and Flower Information

PLANT SIZE AND TYPE: A 39 in. (100 cm) sympodial epiphyte.

PSEUDOBULB: 39 in. (100 cm) long. The elongated stems are elliptical in cross section.

LEAVES: Many. The pale, matte-green leaves are 5–7 in. (13–17 cm) long. They are lanceolate, spreading, and somewhat twisted at the base.

INFLORESCENCE: Short. Inflorescences emerge through 2 leaf sheaths along the side of the stem.

FLOWERS: 2 per inflorescence. The flowers are 0.6 in. (1.6 cm) across. The faintly fragrant blossoms are creamy yellow with delicate brown dots. Sepals are warty on the backside. The petals are very incurved. The small, 3-lobed lip is curved with longitudinal veins.

REFERENCES: 200, 221, 470, 478.

Dendrobium arthrobulbum Kränzlin.
Described as originating in New Caledonia, but N. Hallé (ref. 173) indicates that it has not been found there. Habitat location and elevation are not available, so climate data cannot be selected. REFERENCES: 173, 221.

Dendrobium articulatum Teijsm. and Binn.
Listed as an invalid name by Kränzlin. REFERENCES: 216, 254.

Dendrobium aruanum Kränzlin.
See *D. mirbelianum* Gaudich. REFERENCES: 67, 84, 220, 254, 437.

Dendrobium ashworthiae O'Brien.
See *D. forbesii* Ridley. REFERENCES: 83, 179, 190, 254, 437, 445.

Dendrobium asperatum Schlechter

ORIGIN/HABITAT: Northern Papua New Guinea. In the Waria District, plants grow on trees in the mountain forests along Waube Creek at about 2300 ft. (700 m).

CLIMATE: Station #200192, Garaina, Papua New Guinea, Lat. 7.9°S, Long. 147.1°E, at 2350 ft. (716 m). Record extreme temperatures are 94°F (34°C) and 46°F (8°C).

N/HEMISPHERE	JAN	FEB	MAR	APR	MAY	JUN	JUL	AUG	SEP	OCT	NOV	DEC
°F AVG MAX	80	82	83	84	85	85	85	85	84	84	83	81
°F AVG MIN	63	63	63	64	63	64	65	65	65	64	64	63
DIURNAL RANGE	17	19	20	20	22	21	20	20	19	20	19	18
RAIN/INCHES	5.8	6.5	8.7	11.1	11.8	11.9	8.9	11.7	11.5	9.9	7.7	5.2
HUMIDITY/%	84	82	82	81	80	81	81	81	82	83	84	84
BLOOM SEASON					*							
DAYS CLR	N/A											
RAIN/MM	148	166	220	282	300	303	227	296	291	251	195	131
°C AVG MAX	26.8	27.5	28.2	28.6	29.3	29.3	29.4	29.4	29.1	28.7	28.2	27.2
°C AVG MIN	16.9	16.9	17.4	17.6	17.4	18.0	18.1	18.2	18.4	17.7	17.7	17.1
DIURNAL RANGE	9.9	10.6	10.8	11.0	11.9	11.3	11.3	11.2	10.7	11.0	10.5	10.1
S/HEMISPHERE	JUL	AUG	SEP	OCT	NOV	DEC	JAN	FEB	MAR	APR	MAY	JUN

Cultural Recommendations

LIGHT: 2500–3500 fc.

TEMPERATURES: Throughout the year, days average 80–85°F (27–29°C), and nights average 63–65°F (17–18°C), with a diurnal range of 17–22°F (10–12°C).

HUMIDITY: Near 80–85% year-round.

WATER: Rainfall is heavy year-round, with a slightly drier period in winter. Cultivated plants should be kept moist with only slight drying allowed between waterings.

FERTILIZER: 1/4–1/2 recommended strength. A balanced fertilizer should be applied weekly to biweekly throughout the year.

REST PERIOD: Growing conditions should be maintained all year. In the habitat, rainfall is slightly lower in winter. Water and fertilizer should be reduced somewhat for cultivated plants, especially those grown in the dark, short-day conditions common in temperate latitudes. Plants should never be allowed to dry out completely, however. In the habitat, seasonal light variation is minor.

GROWING MEDIA: Plants may be mounted on tree-fern or cork slabs if humidity is high and plants are watered at least once daily in summer. When plants are potted, any open, fast-draining medium may be used. They may be repotted anytime new roots are growing.

MISCELLANEOUS NOTES: The bloom season shown in the climate table is based on reports from the habitat. Plants that produce flowers which last a single day commonly bloom several times during the year. Flowering usually occurs 7–14 days after a sudden 10°F (5°C) drop in daytime temperatures.

Plant and Flower Information

PLANT SIZE AND TYPE: A robust, 39 in. (100 cm) sympodial epiphyte.

PSEUDOBULB: 31–33 in. (80–85 cm) long.

LEAVES: The erect to spreading leaves are 5–7 in. (13–17 cm) long.

INFLORESCENCE: Very short. The inflorescences emerge from nodes along the stem.

Dendrobium asperifolium

FLOWERS: 2 per inflorescence. The creamy white blossoms are 1 in. (2.5 cm) across and last a single day. Sepals and petals, which are pointed and narrow, thrust forward. The recurved lip, which has spiny projections on the midlobe, is decorated with orange keels. The column foot is marked with orange-red. Flower sheaths are covered with warts.

REFERENCES: 221, 437, 445.

PHOTOS/DRAWINGS: 437.

Dendrobium asperifolium J. J. Smith. See *D. cuthbertsonii* F. Mueller. REFERENCES: 179, 221, 385, 437, 445, 470.

Dendrobium asphale Rchb. f. Not mentioned in current literature, this species was described without habitat information or country of origin. It is unlikely to be available for cultivation. REFERENCES: 216, 254.

Dendrobium assamicum S. Chowdhury

ORIGIN/HABITAT: Northeastern India in the Assam region. The plant was found about 45 mi. (72 km) east of Gauhati on the road to Nowgong near the village of Nellie. It was growing epiphytically about 20 ft. (6 m) above the ground on *Lagerstroemia speciosa*. Habitat elevation was not reported but is estimated at 500 ft. (150 m), so the following climate data should be used with caution.

CLIMATE: Station #42410, Gauhati, India, Lat. 26.1°N, Long. 91.6°E, at 158 ft. (48 m). Temperatures are calculated for an elevation of 500 ft. (150 m), resulting in probable extremes of 102°F (39°C) and 40°F (4°C).

N/HEMISPHERE	JAN	FEB	MAR	APR	MAY	JUN	JUL	AUG	SEP	OCT	NOV	DEC
°F AVG MAX	75	77	85	87	87	88	89	89	88	86	80	75
°F AVG MIN	50	53	59	67	71	76	77	77	75	70	60	52
DIURNAL RANGE	25	24	26	20	16	12	12	12	13	16	20	23
RAIN/INCHES	0.4	1.2	2.0	5.7	9.3	12.3	12.3	10.3	6.6	2.8	0.6	0.2
HUMIDITY/%	79	72	64	71	82	85	85	86	84	84	83	82
BLOOM SEASON			*	*								
DAYS CLR @ 6AM	6	12	16	11	3	0	0	1	3	7	6	3
DAYS CLR @ 12PM	17	16	18	15	6	1	0	0	2	11	17	19
RAIN/MM	10	30	51	145	236	312	312	262	168	71	15	5
°C AVG MAX	23.8	24.9	29.4	30.5	30.5	31.0	31.6	31.6	31.0	29.9	26.6	23.8
°C AVG MIN	9.9	11.6	14.9	19.4	21.6	24.4	24.9	24.9	23.8	21.0	15.5	11.0
DIURNAL RANGE	13.9	13.3	14.5	11.1	8.9	6.6	6.7	6.7	7.2	8.9	11.1	12.8
S/HEMISPHERE	JUL	AUG	SEP	OCT	NOV	DEC	JAN	FEB	MAR	APR	MAY	JUN

Cultural Recommendations

LIGHT: 2500–3500 fc.

TEMPERATURES: Summer days average 88–89°F (31–32°C), and nights average 76–77°F (24–25°C), with a diurnal range of 12–13°F (7°C).

HUMIDITY: 80–85% most of the year, dropping to 65–70% for 3 months in late winter and early spring.

WATER: Rainfall is heavy during the growing season from spring to early autumn, but conditions are dry for 2–3 months in winter. Cultivated plants should be kept moist but not soggy in spring and summer, but water should be gradually reduced after new growths mature in autumn.

FERTILIZER: ¼–½ recommended strength, applied weekly. A high-nitrogen fertilizer is beneficial from spring to midsummer, but a fertilizer high in phosphates should be used in late summer and autumn.

REST PERIOD: Winter days average 75–55°F (24–25°C), and nights average 50–53°F (10–12°C), with a diurnal range of 23–25°F (13–14°C). Although rainfall is low in winter, additional moisture is available from heavy dew or mist. For cultivated plants, water should be reduced for 2–3 months in winter. They should be allowed to dry out between waterings, but should not remain dry for extended periods. Fertilizer should be reduced or eliminated until water is increased in spring. In the habitat, winter days are frequently clear. The cool, dry rest is usually necessary to induce flowering. Other species from this region may grow in the warm, uniform Singapore climate, but they seldom bloom.

GROWING MEDIA: Mounting plants on tree-fern or cork slabs accommodates their pendent growth habit, but humidity must be high and plants watered at least once daily in summer. When plants are potted, any open, fast-draining medium may be used. Repotting is best done in early spring when new roots are growing.

MISCELLANEOUS NOTES: The bloom season shown in the climate table is based on reports from the habitat.

Plant and Flower Information

PLANT SIZE AND TYPE: A 28 in. (70 cm) sympodial epiphyte.

PSEUDOBULB: 28 in. (70 cm) long. The flattened, pendent stems are swollen at the base with slight swellings at the nodes. After leaf drop, the stems are covered by broken, greyish sheaths.

LEAVES: Many. The alternating leaves, which are 0.2–2.8 in. (0.5–7.0 cm) long, may be ovate or lanceolate. They are deciduous by midwinter.

INFLORESCENCE: Short. The purplish green racemes emerge from nodes through the sheaths covering the leafless stems.

FLOWERS: 1–3 per inflorescence. The showy flowers are 1.0–1.3 in. (2.5–3.2 cm) across. Sepals and petals are incurved at the tips. All segments are light pink with a white tinge. The short lip, which is marked with 2 distinct nerves, is yellow at the tip.

REFERENCES: 64, 235.

Dendrobium asumburu P. van Royen

ORIGIN/HABITAT: Papua New Guinea. Plants grow at 8500–10,000 ft. (2600–3050 m) on the western slopes of Mt. Giluwe. They are found in mountain forests or on subalpine shrubbery.

CLIMATE: Botanical garden records, Laiagam, Papua New Guinea, Lat. 5.5°S, Long. 143.5°E, at 7218 ft. (2200 m). Temperatures are calculated for an elevation of 8500 ft. (2600 m), resulting in probable extremes of 87°F (30°C) and 28°F (−2°C).

N/HEMISPHERE	JAN	FEB	MAR	APR	MAY	JUN	JUL	AUG	SEP	OCT	NOV	DEC
°F AVG MAX	72	73	74	72	74	74	78	73	72	74	74	72
°F AVG MIN	51	50	51	51	52	52	51	52	54	53	52	52
DIURNAL RANGE	21	23	23	21	22	22	27	21	18	21	22	20
RAIN/INCHES	4.0	4.8	6.1	7.8	8.5	9.1	8.4	9.6	9.5	8.9	6.3	4.0
HUMIDITY/%	N/A											
BLOOM SEASON							*		*			
DAYS CLR	N/A											
RAIN/MM	102	122	155	198	216	231	213	244	241	226	160	102
°C AVG MAX	22.1	22.6	23.2	22.1	23.2	23.2	25.4	22.6	22.1	23.2	23.2	22.1
°C AVG MIN	10.4	9.9	10.4	10.4	11.0	11.0	10.4	11.0	12.1	11.5	11.0	11.0
DIURNAL RANGE	11.7	12.7	12.8	11.7	12.2	12.2	15.0	11.6	10.0	11.7	12.2	11.1
S/HEMISPHERE	JUL	AUG	SEP	OCT	NOV	DEC	JAN	FEB	MAR	APR	MAY	JUN

Cultural Recommendations

LIGHT: 2000–3000 fc.

TEMPERATURES: Throughout the year, days average 72–78°F (22–25°C), and nights average 50–54°F (10–12°C), with a diurnal range of 18–27°F (10–15°C). The preceding climate table represents the lower, therefore warmer, portion of the habitat, so plants should easily adapt to conditions that are 5–7°F (3–4°C) cooler than indicated.

HUMIDITY: Information is not available for this location. However, records from nearby stations indicate that averages are probably near 80% year-round.

WATER: Rainfall is heavy all year, but conditions are slightly drier for 3–4 months in winter. Rain falls as heavy showers most afternoons. Skies clear by early evening, then low clouds and mist develop again during the evening and continue until midmorning the next day. The mist is so heavy that trees and shrubs drip moisture soon after the mist forms. Cultivated plants should be kept moist with little if any drying allowed between waterings.

FERTILIZER: ¼–½ recommended strength. A balanced fertilizer should be applied weekly to biweekly throughout the year. The Royal Botanic Garden in Edinburgh uses a seaweed-based fertilizer for high elevation plants from New Guinea.

REST PERIOD: Growing conditions should be maintained year-round. Water and fertilizer may be reduced somewhat in winter, especially for plants grown in the dark, short-day conditions common in temperate latitudes, but they should never be allowed to dry out completely. Occasional early morning mistings between waterings may be beneficial, particularly on bright, sunny days. In the habitat, light may be slightly higher in winter.

GROWING MEDIA: Plants may be mounted on slabs of tree-fern fiber if humidity is high and water is applied at least once daily in summer. If plants are potted, a mixture of fir bark or tree-fern fiber with moisture-retaining additives is recommended. The medium should be kept moist, but not soggy. A surface layer of sphagnum moss might be beneficial in drier regions. Repotting may be done anytime new roots are growing.

MISCELLANEOUS NOTES: The bloom season shown in the climate table is based on collection reports.

Plant and Flower Information

PLANT SIZE AND TYPE: An erect, 31 in. (80 cm) sympodial epiphyte.

PSEUDOBULB: 31 in. (80 cm) long. Stems occasionally branch.

LEAVES: 6–8 on the upper portion of the stem. The leaves, which are 2–4 in. (5–10 cm) long, twist at the base to lie on a single plane. The leaf-sheaths are warty.

INFLORESCENCE: Very short. Inflorescences emerge from nodes on mature stems.

FLOWERS: 3–9 per inflorescence. The flowers are orange with yellow at the tips.

REFERENCES: 233, 538.

PHOTOS/DRAWINGS: 538.

Dendrobium atavus J. J. Smith

ORIGIN/HABITAT: Java. An uncommon plant that was first found near Wlingi. Comber (ref. 75) reported finding plants at about 2600 ft. (790 m) in East Java.

CLIMATE: Station #96881, Madiun, Java, Indonesia, Lat. 7.6°S, Long. 111.4°E, at 361 ft. (110 m). Temperatures are calculated for an elevation of 2600 ft. (790 m), resulting in probable extremes of 88°F (31°C) and 55°F (13°C).

N/HEMISPHERE	JAN	FEB	MAR	APR	MAY	JUN	JUL	AUG	SEP	OCT	NOV	DEC
°F AVG MAX	78	79	80	81	79	78	77	77	78	80	79	79
°F AVG MIN	62	62	64	65	65	65	65	65	65	65	65	63
DIURNAL RANGE	16	17	16	16	14	13	12	12	13	15	14	16
RAIN/INCHES	1.3	0.8	1.2	2.9	7.6	10.2	11.9	10.9	10.4	8.8	5.1	3.2
HUMIDITY/%	60	54	52	52	64	72	77	78	78	74	70	64
BLOOM SEASON			*	*								
DAYS CLR @ 7AM	18	22	21	16	8	4	2	2	3	6	9	16
DAYS CLR @ 1PM	15	17	14	9	4	2	1	1	3	6	11
RAIN/MM	33	20	30	74	193	259	302	277	264	224	130	81
°C AVG MAX	25.3	25.9	26.5	27.0	25.9	25.3	24.8	24.8	25.3	26.5	25.9	25.9
°C AVG MIN	16.5	16.5	17.6	18.1	18.1	18.1	18.1	18.1	18.1	18.1	18.1	17.0
DIURNAL RANGE	8.8	9.4	8.9	8.9	7.8	7.2	6.7	6.7	7.2	8.4	7.8	8.9
S/HEMISPHERE	JUL	AUG	SEP	OCT	NOV	DEC	JAN	FEB	MAR	APR	MAY	JUN

Cultural Recommendations

LIGHT: 2500–3500 fc.

TEMPERATURES: Throughout the year, days average 77–81°F (25–27°C), and nights average 62–65°F (17–18°C), with a diurnal range of 12–17°F (7–9°C).

HUMIDITY: 70–80% most of the year, dropping to 50–55% in late winter and early spring.

WATER: At the weather station, rainfall is heavy from spring through autumn. The wet season is followed by a 2–3 month winter dry season when humidity is so low that even moisture from dew is uncommon. Cultivated plants should be watered frequently during the growing season from late spring to early autumn, but water should be gradually reduced in late autumn.

FERTILIZER: ¼–½ recommended strength. A balanced fertilizer should be applied weekly to biweekly throughout the year.

REST PERIOD: Growing conditions should be maintained year-round. Water and fertilizer should be reduced in winter and the plants allowed to dry out somewhat between waterings. They should not remain dry for long periods, however. In the habitat, light may be higher in winter.

GROWING MEDIA: Plants may be potted in any open, fast-draining medium. Repotting may be done anytime new roots are growing.

MISCELLANEOUS NOTES: The bloom season shown in the climate table is based on reports from the habitat. Plants bloom near the end of the dry season.

When describing *D. atavus*, J. J. Smith considered the possibility that it may have been a peloric flower. Comber (ref. 75) further suggests that it may be a peloric and extremely southern form of *D. fimbriatum* Hooker f.

Plant and Flower Information

PLANT SIZE AND TYPE: A 35 in. (90 cm) sympodial epiphyte.

PSEUDOBULB: 30 in. (75 cm) long. The yellowish purple stems are shiny, zigzag, clustered, and somewhat flattened.

LEAVES: Many. The lanceolate to linear leaves are 6 in. (15 cm) long, unequally bilobed at the apex, and quickly deciduous when the wet season ends.

INFLORESCENCE: 2 in. (5 cm) long. The laxly flowered inflorescences are shorter than the leaves.

FLOWERS: 10 per inflorescence. Blossoms are 1.2 in. (3 cm) across with a lovely, open form. All segments are pure golden yellow and overlap at the base. The sepals are pointed at the tip, but the petals and lip are rounded. The lip margin is curled inward at the tip.

REFERENCES: 25, 75, 219, 254, 445, 469.

PHOTOS/DRAWINGS: 75, 469.

Dendrobium atjehense J. J. Smith

ORIGIN/HABITAT: Northern Sumatra. Plants were found in the Aceh (Atjeh) region. Specific habitat location and elevation are unavailable, so the following climate should be used with caution.

CLIMATE: Station #96009, Lhou, Sumatra, Indonesia, Lat. 5.1°N, Long. 97.2°E, at 7 ft. (2 m). Record extreme temperatures are not available for this location.

N/HEMISPHERE	JAN	FEB	MAR	APR	MAY	JUN	JUL	AUG	SEP	OCT	NOV	DEC
°F AVG MAX	84	86	87	88	88	89	88	88	86	86	85	84
°F AVG MIN	72	72	73	74	75	74	73	73	73	73	73	73
DIURNAL RANGE	12	14	14	14	13	15	15	15	13	13	12	11
RAIN/INCHES	4.8	1.9	3.3	3.2	6.6	2.2	4.8	2.8	5.0	4.6	9.2	7.6
HUMIDITY/%	N/A											
BLOOM SEASON				*								
DAYS CLR	N/A											
RAIN/MM	121	49	85	82	167	57	121	70	128	117	233	192
°C AVG MAX	29.2	30.0	30.7	31.3	31.2	31.5	31.2	31.1	30.1	29.9	29.5	28.9
°C AVG MIN	22.4	22.1	22.5	23.4	23.7	23.5	23.0	22.7	22.9	22.8	22.8	22.7
DIURNAL RANGE	6.8	7.9	8.2	7.9	7.5	8.0	8.2	8.4	7.2	7.1	6.7	6.2
S/HEMISPHERE	JUL	AUG	SEP	OCT	NOV	DEC	JAN	FEB	MAR	APR	MAY	JUN

Dendrobium atractodes

Cultural Recommendations

LIGHT: 2000–3000 fc.

TEMPERATURES: Throughout the year, days average 84–89°F (29–32°C), and nights average 72–75°F (22–24°C), with a diurnal range of 12–15°F (7–8°C).

HUMIDITY: Information is not available for this location. However, records from other stations in the region indicate that humidity is probably 80–85% year-round.

WATER: Rainfall is moderate most of the year with brief semidry periods in midwinter and early summer. Cultivated plants should be kept evenly moist most of the year, with only slight drying allowed between waterings. For a month or so in winter and again in early summer, plants should be allowed to dry somewhat between waterings, but they should not remain dry for long periods.

FERTILIZER: ¼–½ recommended strength. A balanced fertilizer should be applied weekly to biweekly throughout the year.

REST PERIOD: Growing conditions should be maintained year-round. The wettest season is late autumn–early winter, but water should not be increased for cultivated plants during this season, especially those grown in the dark, short-day conditions common in temperate latitudes. In fact, water and fertilizer may be reduced somewhat until light increases in spring, but the plants should not be allowed to dry out completely.

GROWING MEDIA: Plants may be mounted on tree-fern or cork slabs or potted in small pots filled with any open, fast-draining medium. Repotting may be done anytime new roots are actively growing.

MISCELLANEOUS NOTES: The bloom season shown in the climate table is based on collection records. The plant was described in 1932 in *Bul. Jard. Bot. Buit.* 3rd sér. 12:137.

Plant and Flower Information

PLANT SIZE AND TYPE: A sympodial epiphyte of unreported size.

PSEUDOBULB: Longer than 14–19 in. (35–48 cm). The original description was based on an incomplete specimen.

LEAVES: Many. The linear-lanceolate leaves are about 5.5 in. (14 cm) long, but they become somewhat smaller near the apex.

FLOWERS: The flowers are 1.2 in. (3 cm) long. Sepals and petals are snow white. The lip is marked with rows of yellow dots.

REFERENCES: 225.

Dendrobium atractodes Ridley. See *D. heterocarpum* Lindley. REFERENCES: 75, 190, 216, 254, 296, 454.

Dendrobium atromarginatum J. J. Smith. See *D. cuthbertsonii* F. Mueller. REFERENCES: 224, 385, 445.

Dendrobium atropurpureum Ames. See *D. cultratum* Schlechter. REFERENCES: 296, 536.

Dendrobium atropurpureum (Blume) Miquel

AKA: *Oxystophyllum atropurpureum* Blume. Seidenfaden (ref. 454) discusses the confusion surrounding the name *D. atropurpureum*. In his opinion, the misidentification of some specimens has resulted in the following plant names being erroneously listed as synonyms: *Oxystophyllum carnosum* Blume, *D. carnosum* (Blume) Rchb. f., *D. concinnum* Miquel, and *D. excavatum* (Blume) Miquel.

ORIGIN/HABITAT: New Guinea. Ridley (ref. 400) indicated that the plant was collected at sea level in Irian Jaya (western New Guinea). Seidenfaden (ref. 454) states that it is now generally accepted that *D. atropurpureum* is endemic to New Guinea. Schlechter (ref. 437) indicates that it is endemic to Papua New Guinea.

CLIMATE: Station #97690, Sentani/Jayapura, Irian Jaya, Lat. 2.7°S, Long. 140.5°E, at 289 ft. (88 m). Record extreme temperatures are 97°F (36°C) and 68°F (20°C).

N/HEMISPHERE	JAN	FEB	MAR	APR	MAY	JUN	JUL	AUG	SEP	OCT	NOV	DEC
°F AVG MAX	87	89	89	90	90	89	89	88	89	90	90	89
°F AVG MIN	72	72	72	73	73	73	73	73	73	74	73	73
DIURNAL RANGE	15	17	17	17	17	16	16	15	16	16	17	16
RAIN/INCHES	4.1	3.9	5.3	2.9	6.7	7.0	8.3	8.3	8.5	4.6	2.4	5.2
HUMIDITY/%	81	80	80	79	81	81	79	80	80	80	81	80
BLOOM SEASON	N/A											
DAYS CLR @ 9AM	5	3	4	3	2	1	1	0	1	2	2	5
DAYS CLR @ 3PM	4	3	3	3	2	1	3	0	1	2	2	3
RAIN/MM	104	99	135	74	170	178	211	211	216	117	61	132
°C AVG MAX	30.6	31.7	31.7	32.2	32.2	31.7	31.7	31.1	31.7	32.2	32.2	31.7
°C AVG MIN	22.2	22.2	22.2	22.8	22.8	22.8	22.8	22.8	22.8	23.3	22.8	22.8
DIURNAL RANGE	8.3	9.4	9.4	9.4	9.4	8.9	8.9	8.3	8.9	8.9	9.4	8.9
S/HEMISPHERE	JUL	AUG	SEP	OCT	NOV	DEC	JAN	FEB	MAR	APR	MAY	JUN

Cultural Recommendations

LIGHT: 2000–3000 fc.

TEMPERATURES: Throughout the year, days average 87–90°F (31–32°C), and nights average 72–74°F (22–23°C), with a diurnal range of 15–17°F (8–9°C).

HUMIDITY: Near 80% year-round.

WATER: Rainfall is moderate to heavy most of the year with brief, semidry periods in spring and autumn. Cultivated plants should be kept moist with only slight drying allowed between waterings.

FERTILIZER: ¼–½ recommended strength. A balanced fertilizer should be applied weekly to biweekly throughout the year.

REST PERIOD: Growing conditions should be maintained year-round. Water and fertilizer should be reduced somewhat in winter for plants grown in the dark, short-day conditions common in temperate latitudes, but they should never be allowed to dry out completely. In the habitat, light is highest in winter.

GROWING MEDIA: Plants may be mounted on tree-fern or cork slabs, if humidity is high and plants are watered daily in summer. When plants are potted, any open, fast-draining medium may be used. Repotting may be done anytime new roots are growing.

Plant and Flower Information

PLANT SIZE AND TYPE: A sympodial epiphyte of unreported size.

LEAVES: Many. The leaves are 1 in. (2.5 cm) long. They are fleshy, overlapping, and slightly curved.

INFLORESCENCE: Short. The blossoms are held on short peduncles which are covered by several bracts.

FLOWERS: 1 per inflorescence. The thick, fleshy blossoms are dark claret or maroon. The pointed lip has an uneven margin. Flowers are somewhat short-lived.

REFERENCES: 12, 202, 216, 208, 254, 286, 295, 298, 310, 317, 400, 402, 414, 437, 454, 468, 470.

Dendrobium atropurpureum Kränzlin. See *D. lockhartioides* Schlechter. REFERENCES: 436.

Dendrobium atropurpureum J. J. Smith. See *D. moluccense* J. J. Smith. REFERENCES: 479.

Dendrobium atrorubens Ridley not Schlechter

AKA: Sometimes spelled *D. atro-rubens*. Holttum (ref. 200) indicates that *D. atrorubens* is very closely related to *D. sinuatum* (Lindley) Lindley ex Rchb. f., differing primarily in flower color.

ORIGIN/HABITAT: Endemic to Malaya. Plants grow in the mountains at 3000–5000 ft. (910–1520 m), and have been collected from Mt. Jerai (Kedah Peak), Thaiping Hills in Perak, and Dluang Terbank in Pahang. They are usually found on tree stumps and small trees.

CLIMATE: Station #48625, Ipoh, Malaya, Lat. 4.6°N, Long. 101.1°E, at 123 ft. (37 m). Temperatures are calculated for an elevation of 3500 ft. (1070 m), resulting in probable extremes of 88°F (31°C) and 53°F (12°C).

N/HEMISPHERE	JAN	FEB	MAR	APR	MAY	JUN	JUL	AUG	SEP	OCT	NOV	DEC
°F AVG MAX	79	81	82	81	81	81	80	80	79	78	78	78
°F AVG MIN	61	61	62	62	63	62	61	61	62	61	61	61
DIURNAL RANGE	18	20	20	19	18	19	19	19	17	17	17	17
RAIN/INCHES	7.9	3.1	7.6	8.4	6.2	3.6	7.2	6.9	8.8	11.0	13.0	8.9
HUMIDITY/%	76	74	76	78	78	75	76	77	79	82	82	81
BLOOM SEASON	N/A											
DAYS CLR @ 7AM	3	3	3	1	1	2	1	1	0	0	1	2
DAYS CLR @ 1PM	2	2	2	1	1	1	1	0	0	0	0	2
RAIN/MM	201	79	193	213	157	91	183	175	224	279	330	226
°C AVG MAX	26.0	27.1	27.7	27.1	27.1	27.1	26.6	26.6	26.0	25.5	25.5	25.5
°C AVG MIN	16.0	16.0	16.6	16.6	17.1	16.6	16.0	16.0	16.6	16.0	16.0	16.0
DIURNAL RANGE	10.0	11.1	11.1	10.5	10.0	10.5	10.6	10.6	9.4	9.5	9.5	9.5
S/HEMISPHERE	JUL	AUG	SEP	OCT	NOV	DEC	JAN	FEB	MAR	APR	MAY	JUN

Cultural Recommendations

LIGHT: 2500–3500 fc. The plant is usually found on tree stumps and small trees, which suggests open areas with moderately high light.

TEMPERATURES: Throughout the year, days average 78–82°F (26–28°C), and nights average 61–63°F (16–17°C), with a diurnal range of 17–20°F (9–11°C).

HUMIDITY: 75–80% year-round.

WATER: Rainfall is heavy most of the year. The heaviest rainfall occurs in autumn, with a secondary maximum in spring. Brief semidry periods occur in midwinter and midsummer. Cultivated plants should be kept evenly moist with only slight drying allowed between waterings.

FERTILIZER: ¼–½ recommended strength. A balanced fertilizer should be applied weekly to biweekly throughout the year.

REST PERIOD: Growing conditions should be maintained year-round. Water should be reduced somewhat in winter for plants cultivated in the dark, short-day conditions common in temperate latitudes. They should never be allowed to dry out completely, however. Fertilizer may be reduced when the plant is not actively growing or when water is reduced. In the habitat, light is slightly higher in winter.

GROWING MEDIA: Plants may be mounted on cork slabs or a rough-barked hardwood if humidity is high and plants are watered at least once daily in summer. If plants are potted, the smallest possible pot should be used. Growers report that clay pots are preferable to plastic ones. Pots may be filled with any open, rapidly draining medium. Repotting may be done anytime new roots are growing.

Plant and Flower Information

PLANT SIZE AND TYPE: A 6–10 in. (15–25 cm) sympodial epiphyte that may reach an overall length of 24 in. (60 cm).

PSEUDOBULB: 6–10 in. (15–25 cm) long. The pseudobulb sometimes branch, and the branches may root.

LEAVES: Many. The leaves are carried all along the stem. They are lanceolate, red-brown when dry, pointed at the apex, and about 1 in. (2.5 cm) long. The leaves are broader than those of *D. sinuatum*.

INFLORESCENCE: Racemes emerge from lateral nodes below the tip of the stem.

FLOWERS: The small flowers are 0.4–0.8 in. (1–2 cm) across and entirely dark red to reddish purple. The linear lip is 0.1 in. (0.3 cm) wide and bent in the middle. It has a thickened, fleshy toothlike point at the tip.

REFERENCES: 200, 395, 402, 454, 455.

PHOTOS/DRAWINGS: 455.

Dendrobium atrorubens Schlechter not Ridley. See *D. torricellianum* Kränzlin. REFERENCES: 219, 220, 254, 437, 444, 486.

Dendrobium atrosanguineum E. Morren and De Vos.
See *D. albosanguineum* Lindley. REFERENCES: 190, 216, 254.

Dendrobium atrosanguineum Schlechter. This name was included in a list of the duplicate specimens at the Herbarium Bogoriense, in Bogor, Java. We were unable to locate a description or any additional information. REFERENCES: 92.

Dendrobium atroviolaceum Rolfe

ORIGIN/HABITAT: New Guinea. Plants are found in eastern Papua New Guinea and on Rossel Island as well as other islands off the eastern tip of New Guinea. In the Milne Bay District, plants grow on large, rainforest tree-trunks at 1000–2450 ft. (300–750 m). In Irian Jaya (western New Guinea), plants have been reported from the Cyclops Mountains near Jayapura, but habitat elevation was not given.

CLIMATE: Station #94075, Samarai, Sideia Island, Papua New Guinea, Lat. 10.6°S, Long. 150.7°E, at 20 ft. (6 m). Temperatures are calculated for an elevation of 1700 ft. (520 m), resulting in probable extremes of 98°F (37°C) and 58°F (15°C).

N/HEMISPHERE	JAN	FEB	MAR	APR	MAY	JUN	JUL	AUG	SEP	OCT	NOV	DEC
°F AVG MAX	75	75	76	77	79	81	81	82	81	80	78	76
°F AVG MIN	68	67	68	68	69	70	71	71	70	69	69	68
DIURNAL RANGE	7	8	8	9	10	11	10	11	11	11	9	8
RAIN/INCHES	8.1	8.6	10.1	8.7	8.4	6.1	7.0	7.8	10.0	9.8	12.0	11.3
HUMIDITY/%	N/A											
BLOOM SEASON	*	**	***	**	***	*						
DAYS CLR	N/A											
RAIN/MM	206	218	257	221	213	155	178	198	254	249	305	287
°C AVG MAX	24.1	24.1	24.7	25.3	26.4	27.5	27.5	28.0	27.5	26.9	25.8	24.7
°C AVG MIN	20.3	19.7	20.3	20.3	20.8	21.4	21.9	21.9	21.4	20.8	20.8	20.3
DIURNAL RANGE	3.8	4.4	4.4	5.0	5.6	6.1	5.6	6.1	6.1	6.1	5.0	4.4
S/HEMISPHERE	JUL	AUG	SEP	OCT	NOV	DEC	JAN	FEB	MAR	APR	MAY	JUN

Cultural Recommendations

LIGHT: 2000–3000 fc. Growers report that plants flower when grown under broad spectrum fluorescent lighting.

TEMPERATURES: Throughout the year, days average 75–82°F (24–28°C), and nights average 67–71°F (20–22°C), with a diurnal range of 7–11°F (4–6°C).

HUMIDITY: Information is not available for this location. However, records from nearby stations indicate that humidity is probably 70–80% year-round.

WATER: Rainfall is very heavy year-round. Cultivated plants should be kept moist but not soggy.

FERTILIZER: ¼–½ recommended strength. A balanced fertilizer should be applied weekly to biweekly throughout the year.

REST PERIOD: Growing temperatures should be maintained year-round. However, growers indicate that *D. atroviolaceum* grows with winter temperatures of 55°F (13°C) and tolerates 50°F (10°C). In the habitat, winter rainfall is high; but water and fertilizer should be reduced for cultivated plants, especially those grown in the dark, short-day conditions in temperate-latitude winters. Plants should never be allowed to dry out completely, however. In the habitat, seasonal light variation is minor.

GROWING MEDIA: Plants may be mounted on cork slabs, tree-fern, or rough-barked hardwood slabs. If plants are mounted, summer humidity must be high and plants should be watered at least once a day. If plants are potted, the smallest possible pot should be used, and growers report that clay pots are preferable to plastic ones. A rapidly draining medium should be used. Repotting may be done anytime new roots are actively growing.

MISCELLANEOUS NOTES: The bloom season shown in the climate table is based on cultivation records. *D. atroviolaceum* is considered a problem plant by some growers, while others consider it free-flowering and easy to grow.

Plant and Flower Information

PLANT SIZE AND TYPE: An 8–17 in. (20–42 cm) sympodial epiphyte.

PSEUDOBULB: 5–12 in. (12–30 cm) long. The stems, which have 3–6 nodes below the leaves, are spindle-shaped, clustered, and erect. Greenish when young, the pseudobulbs become yellow-brown and furrowed with age.

LEAVES: 2–4 at the apex of each growth. The elliptic leaves are 3–5 in. (8–12 cm) long, tough, and very stiff. They are dark green above and pale yellow-green on the underside.

INFLORESCENCE: 8 in. (20 cm) long. The inflorescences are erect and densely flowered. They emerge at or below the apex of both old and new growths. Each growth continues to produce blooms for many years. The flowers hang on the inflorescence.

FLOWERS: 10–20 per inflorescence. Blossoms are 1.6–3.0 in. (4.0–7.5 cm) across. They are fragrant and extremely long-lasting with a heavy, almost leathery texture. Sepals and petals may be cream, primrose yellow, or greenish white, with purplish spotting near the base. The lip is green on the outside and heavily striped with purple on the inside. The blooms are somewhat nodding. Plants are free flowering.

HYBRIDIZING NOTES: Chromosome count is 2n = 38 (ref. 153, 273, 504, 580). When used as a parent, the offspring often bloom continuously.

REFERENCES: 25, 36, 83, 153, 179, 196, 210, 218, 254, 262, 273, 304, 305, 330, 359, 371, 390, 421, 430, 445, 504, 510, 525, 537, 548, 550, 554, 570, 580.

PHOTOS/DRAWINGS: *36, 83,* 121, 210, *304, 305, 371, 390, 430, 525, 548, 550.*

Dendrobium attenuatum Lindley.

Seidenfaden (ref. 454) discusses the confusion surrounding this plant name. Plants were found in Borneo; but habitat location and elevation are not available, so climate data cannot be selected. Hamilton (ref. 179) reports a single bloom record each month Jul.–Nov. (Jan.–May), but considering the confusion regarding this plant name, these cultivation records may actually apply to other species. A sympodial epiphyte with slender, ascending stems 6–8 in. (15–20 cm) long. Young stems are covered with short black hairs. The long, linear leaves are grasslike. A single blossom is produced on each inflorescence. The small flowers are white. Sepals and petals are rounded at the tips. The lip has an elongated, rounded, spatula-shaped midlobe with a fleshy margin and wartlike like projections in the center. The sidelobes are toothlike. REFERENCES: 17, 179, 216, 254, 278, 286, 295, 310, 454.

Dendrobium augustae-victoriae Kränzlin. See *D. lineale* Rolfe. REFERENCES: 84, 190, 211, 217, 218, 254, 437, 470.

Dendrobium aurantiaco-purpureum Nicholls. See *D. prenticei* (F. Mueller) Nicholls. REFERENCES: 67, 105, 179, 227, 228, 421, 533.

Dendrobium aurantiacum F. Mueller not Rchb. f. Now considered a synonym of *Bulbophyllum schillerianum*. REFERENCES: 67, 105, 216, 254, 445.

Dendrobium aurantiacum Rchb. f. not F. Mueller. See *D. chryseum* Rolfe. REFERENCES: 61, 102, 152, 190, 202, 203, 208, 218, 243, 254, 279, 369, 414, 430, 454. PHOTOS/DRAWINGS: 203.

Dendrobium aurantiflavum P. van Royen. See *D. subclausum* Rolfe. REFERENCES: 233, 538, 588. PHOTOS/DRAWINGS: 538.

Dendrobium aurantiroseum P. van Royen ex T. M. Reeve

ORIGIN/HABITAT: Widespread throughout the mountains of New Guinea. Plants grow epiphytically in loose moss in shady, mountain habitats. Although found at 6900–11,000 ft. (2100–3350 m), they most often grow in the narrow range of 8000–8400 ft. (2440–2560 m).

CLIMATE: Botanical garden records, Laiagam, Papua New Guinea, Lat. 5.5°S, Long. 143.5°E, at 7218 ft. (2200 m). Temperatures are calculated for an elevation of 8500 ft. (2600 m), resulting in probable extremes of 87°F (30°C) and 28°F (–2°C).

N/HEMISPHERE	JAN	FEB	MAR	APR	MAY	JUN	JUL	AUG	SEP	OCT	NOV	DEC
°F AVG MAX	72	73	74	72	74	74	78	73	72	74	74	72
°F AVG MIN	51	50	51	51	52	52	51	52	54	53	52	52
DIURNAL RANGE	21	23	23	21	22	22	27	21	18	21	22	20
RAIN/INCHES	4.0	4.8	6.1	7.8	8.5	9.1	8.4	9.6	9.5	8.9	6.3	4.0
HUMIDITY/%	N/A											
BLOOM SEASON	*	*	*	*		*			*			
DAYS CLR	N/A											
RAIN/MM	102	122	155	198	216	231	213	244	241	226	160	102
°C AVG MAX	22.1	22.6	23.2	22.1	23.2	23.2	25.4	22.6	22.1	23.2	23.2	22.1
°C AVG MIN	10.4	9.9	10.4	10.4	11.0	11.0	10.4	11.0	12.1	11.5	11.0	11.0
DIURNAL RANGE	11.7	12.7	12.8	11.7	12.2	12.2	15.0	11.6	10.0	11.7	12.2	11.1
S/HEMISPHERE	JUL	AUG	SEP	OCT	NOV	DEC	JAN	FEB	MAR	APR	MAY	JUN

Cultural Recommendations

LIGHT: 1500–2500 fc.

TEMPERATURES: Throughout the year, days average 72–78°F (22–25°C), and nights average 50–54°F (10–12°C), with a diurnal range of 18–27°F (10–15°C). The preceding climate table represents the lower, therefore warmer, portion of the habitat, so plants should easily adapt to conditions that are 5–7°F (3–4°C) cooler than indicated.

HUMIDITY: Information is not available for this location. However, records from nearby stations indicate that averages are probably near 80% year-round.

WATER: Rainfall is heavy all year, but conditions are slightly drier for 3–4 months in winter. Rain falls as heavy showers most afternoons. Skies clear by early evening, then low clouds and mist develop again during the evening and continue until midmorning the next day. The mist is so heavy that trees and shrubs drip moisture soon after the mist forms. Cultivated plants should be kept moist, with little if any drying allowed between waterings.

FERTILIZER: ¼–½ recommended strength. A balanced fertilizer should be applied weekly to biweekly throughout the year. The Royal Botanic Garden in Edinburgh uses a seaweed based fertilizer for high elevation plants from New Guinea.

REST PERIOD: Growing conditions should be maintained year-round. Water and fertilizer may be reduced somewhat in winter, especially for plants grown in the dark, short-day conditions common in temperate latitudes, but they should never be allowed to dry out completely. Occasional early morning mistings between waterings may be beneficial, particularly on bright, sunny days. In the habitat, light may be slightly higher in winter.

GROWING MEDIA: Plants grow well on tree-fern slabs or posts in 50% shade but humidity must be high and water applied at least once daily in summer. If plants are potted, a mixture of fir bark or chopped tree-fern with moisture-retaining additives are recommended. A surface layer of sphagnum moss might be beneficial. The medium should be kept moist, but not soggy, and roots should never be allowed to dry out. Repotting may be done anytime new roots are growing.

MISCELLANEOUS NOTES: The bloom season shown in the climate table is based on cultivation records. *D. aurantiroseum* is reportedly very slow growing and difficult to cultivate. Careful attention should be paid to its cultural requirements. Plants grown at Laiagam are reluctant bloomers.

Plant and Flower Information

PLANT SIZE AND TYPE: A 2–4 in. (5–10 cm) sympodial epiphyte.

PSEUDOBULB: 0.8 in. (2 cm) long. The ovoid to spindle-shaped pseudobulbs are borne on a creeping rhizome. They may be green or brown. The stem is rounded at the base and tapers toward the apex. When plants are stressed, the stem becomes wrinkled and spindly.

LEAVES: 1–2 at the apex of new growths. The elliptic-lanceolate leaves are 1.6–3.1 in. (4–8 cm) long. The deciduous leaves are green with purple on the underside.

INFLORESCENCE: 0.8 in. (2 cm) long. Racemes emerge from many nodes on leafless pseudobulbs. Inflorescences are densely many-flowered.

FLOWERS: Many. The smooth, fleshy blossoms are 0.7–1.1 in. (1.8–2.8 cm) long and do not open fully. Flowers last 2–3 months. The rounded sepals and petals are erect and resemble a fan. Sepals and petals are pink to mauve with white at the tips. The lip, which has no sidelobes, is incurved along the side margin. It has a prominent orange to red-orange band with pink or white at the tip of the midlobe.

HYBRIDIZING NOTES: Chromosome count is 2n = 76 (ref. 153, 273).

REFERENCES: 79, 95, 153, 179, 234, 273, 318, 330, 381, 552, 554.

PHOTOS/DRAWINGS: *318, 330,* 381, *552.*

Dendrobium aurantivinosum P. van Royen. See *D. brevicaule* Rolfe. REFERENCES: 233, 385, 538. PHOTOS/DRAWINGS: 538.

Dendrobium aureicolor J. J. Smith. See *D. auricolor* J. J. Smith. REFERENCES: 221.

Dendrobium aureilobum J. J. Smith. Now considered a synonym of *Flickingeria aureiloba* (J. J. Smith) J. J. Wood. REFERENCES: 25, 75, 213, 223, 230, 234, 445, 449.

Dendrobium aureum Lindley. See *D. heterocarpum* Wallich ex Lindley. The International Orchid Commission (ref. 236) registers *D. heterocarpum* hybrids under the name *D. aureum.* REFERENCES: 6, 12, 25, 32, 75, 102, 190, 200, 216, 236, 245, 254, 277, 296, 317, 369, 402, 436, 445, 454, 455, 458, 469, 541, 542, 569, 570.

Dendrobium auricolor J. J. Smith. J. J. Smith originally spelled the name *D. auricolor* and reprinted it as *D. auricolor* (ref. 470), but Hawkes (ref. 191) transferred the plant as *D. aureicolor* to *Diplocaulobium aureicolor* (J. J. Smith) A. Hawkes. The International Orchid Commission (ref. 236) lists *Dendrobium aureicolor* as a synonym of *Diplocaulobium aureicolor,* but they register hybrids under the name *Dendrobium aureicolor.* Blossoms last a single day. REFERENCES: 213, 221, 229, 236, 437, 445, 470.

Dendrobium auriculatum Ames and Quisumbing

ORIGIN/HABITAT: The Philippines. Plants are found in Bulacan Province on Luzon Island and in Davao Province on Mindanao Island. They usually grow on rocks and trees at 2950–3300 ft. (900–1000 m).

CLIMATE: Station #98427, Manila, Luzon, Philippines, Lat. 14.5°N, Long. 121.0°E, at 74 ft. (23 m). Temperatures are calculated for an elevation of 3300 ft. (1000 m), resulting in probable extremes of 90°F (33°C) and 47°F (9°C).

N/HEMISPHERE	JAN	FEB	MAR	APR	MAY	JUN	JUL	AUG	SEP	OCT	NOV	DEC
°F AVG MAX	75	77	80	82	82	80	77	76	77	77	76	75
°F AVG MIN	58	58	60	62	64	64	64	64	64	63	61	59
DIURNAL RANGE	17	19	20	20	18	16	13	12	13	14	15	16
RAIN/INCHES	0.9	0.5	0.7	1.3	5.1	10.0	17.0	16.6	14.0	7.6	5.7	2.6
HUMIDITY/%	77	73	70	68	71	81	84	86	87	84	82	79
BLOOM SEASON	*						*					
DAYS CLR @ 8AM	6	9	14	14	10	3	2	1	1	6	7	6
DAYS CLR @ 2PM	3	6	10	10	8	2	1	1	0	2	2	3
RAIN/MM	23	13	18	33	130	254	432	422	356	193	145	66
°C AVG MAX	24.1	25.2	26.9	28.0	28.0	26.9	25.2	24.7	25.2	25.2	24.7	24.1
°C AVG MIN	14.7	14.7	15.8	16.9	18.0	18.0	18.0	18.0	18.0	17.5	16.3	15.2
DIURNAL RANGE	9.4	10.5	11.1	11.1	10.0	8.9	7.2	6.7	7.2	7.7	8.4	8.9
S/HEMISPHERE	JUL	AUG	SEP	OCT	NOV	DEC	JAN	FEB	MAR	APR	MAY	JUN

Cultural Recommendations

LIGHT: 1800–2400 fc. Diffused or barely dappled light is indicated.

TEMPERATURES: Throughout the year, days average 75–82°F (24–28°C), and nights average 58–64°F (15–18°C), with a diurnal range of 12–20°F (7–11°C).

HUMIDITY: 80–85% in summer and autumn, falling to 70–75% in winter and spring.

WATER: Rainfall is heavy from late spring through autumn, but conditions are dry for 3–4 months in winter. Cultivated plants should be kept moist while actively growing, but water should be gradually reduced in late autumn.

FERTILIZER: ¼–½ recommended strength, applied weekly. A high-nitrogen fertilizer is beneficial from spring to midsummer, but a fertilizer high in phosphates should be used in late summer and autumn.

REST PERIOD: Growing temperatures should be maintained all year. Rainfall is low for 3–4 months in winter, but additional moisture is available from frequent heavy dew. In cultivation, water should be reduced and the plants allowed to dry out between waterings. They should not remain dry for extended periods, however. Fertilizer should also be reduced or eliminated anytime water is reduced. In the habitat, light is highest in winter.

GROWING MEDIA: Plants may be potted in any open, fast-draining medium. The medium should be moist but not soggy. Repotting is best done in early spring when new roots are growing.

MISCELLANEOUS NOTES: The bloom times shown in the climate table are based on collection reports. The preceding climate data represents the coolest, driest portion of the habitat range. In the Mindanao Island habitat, winter low temperatures are 4–6°F (2–3°C) degrees warmer, and the rainfall pattern does not show a winter dry period.

Plant and Flower Information

PLANT SIZE AND TYPE: A 12–31 in. (30–80 cm) sympodial epiphyte or lithophyte.

PSEUDOBULB: 12–31 in. (30–80 cm) long. The smooth stem is greenish yellow.

Dendrobium auriferum

LEAVES: Many. The linear-lanceolate leaves are borne on the lower portion of each growth.

INFLORESCENCE: Blossoms are normally carried on the terminal, leafless portion of the stem.

FLOWERS: 1 per inflorescence. The showy flowers, which are not fragrant, are 2.4 in. (6 cm) across. The blossoms have white petals and a white lip with purple at the base. The spur and lateral sepals are greenish white.

REFERENCES: 225, 373, 536.

PHOTOS/DRAWINGS: *373.*

Dendrobium auriferum Lindley.
Now considered a synonym of *Thrixspermum auriferum* (Lindley) Schlechter. REFERENCES: 208, 216, 254, 277.

Dendrobium auroroseo Lindley.
This name is included by Kränzlin (ref. 254) in his discussion of *D. pictum* Lindley; but in Kränzlin's index, it is spelled *D. auroroseum* Lindley. No additional information was found. REFERENCES: 254.

Dendrobium auroroseum Rchb. f.
Sometimes spelled *D. aureoroseum,* see *D. nudum* Lindley. REFERENCES: 12, 75, 125, 216, 254, 278, 296, 310, 469.

Dendrobium austrocaledonicum Schlechter

AKA: Sometimes spelled *D. austro-caledonicum.* Hunt (ref. 211) includes the synonyms *D. cerinum* Schlechter not Rchb. f., *D. critae-rubrae (critaerubrae)* Guillaumin, *D. garayanum* A. Hawkes and A. H. Heller, *D. inaequale* Finet not Rolfe, and *D. mendoncanum* A. Hawkes.

ORIGIN/HABITAT: Pacific islands, including New Caledonia, Anatom, Erromango, Bougainville, and the Solomon Islands. Plants grow in rainforests at 800–2950 ft. (240–900 m).

CLIMATE: Station #91592, Noumea, New Caledonia, Lat. 22.3°S, Long. 166.5°E, at 246 ft. (75 m). Temperatures are calculated for an elevation of 1000 ft. (300 m), resulting in probable extremes of 97°F (36°C) and 50°F (10°C).

N/HEMISPHERE	JAN	FEB	MAR	APR	MAY	JUN	JUL	AUG	SEP	OCT	NOV	DEC
°F AVG MAX	74	74	76	78	81	84	84	83	83	81	77	75
°F AVG MIN	60	59	61	63	66	68	70	71	70	68	64	62
DIURNAL RANGE	14	15	15	15	15	16	14	12	13	13	13	13
RAIN/INCHES	3.6	2.6	2.5	2.0	2.4	2.6	3.7	5.1	5.7	5.2	4.4	3.7
HUMIDITY/%	73	70	69	67	68	69	71	74	75	76	73	73
BLOOM SEASON			*	*	**		*	*	*			
DAYS CLR @ 11AM	7	9	9	15	12	10	7	6	7	7	7	7
DAYS CLR @ 5PM	7	11	6	11	7	6	5	4	4	5	3	7
RAIN/MM	91	66	64	51	61	66	94	130	145	132	112	94
°C AVG MAX	23.1	23.1	24.2	25.3	27.0	28.6	28.6	28.1	28.1	27.0	24.7	23.6
°C AVG MIN	15.3	14.7	15.8	17.0	18.6	19.7	20.8	21.4	20.8	19.7	17.5	16.4
DIURNAL RANGE	7.8	8.4	8.4	8.3	8.4	8.9	7.8	6.7	7.3	7.3	7.2	7.2
S/HEMISPHERE	JUL	AUG	SEP	OCT	NOV	DEC	JAN	FEB	MAR	APR	MAY	JUN

Cultural Recommendations

LIGHT: 1500–2500 fc.

TEMPERATURES: Summer days average 83–84°F (28–29°C), and nights average 68–71°F (20–21°C), with a diurnal range of 12–16°F (7–9°C).

HUMIDITY: 70–75% most of the year, dropping to near 65% for 1–2 months in spring. Humidity averages may be higher in the rainforest habitat.

WATER: Rainfall is light to moderate all year. Late summer and early autumn are the wettest seasons. In cultivation, moisture should be provided year-round with slight drying allowed between waterings.

FERTILIZER: ¼–½ recommended strength, applied weekly. A high-nitrogen fertilizer is beneficial from spring to midsummer, but a fertilizer high in phosphates should be used in late summer and autumn.

REST PERIOD: Winter days average 74–76°F (23–24°C), and nights average 59–62°F (15–16°C), with a diurnal range of 13–15°F (7–8°C). Rainfall is slightly lower in winter and spring. Cultivated plants should be allowed to become somewhat dry between waterings but should not remain dry for long periods. In the habitat, light is highest in early spring.

GROWING MEDIA: Mounting plants on tree-fern or cork slabs accommodates their pendulous growth habit. However, humidity must be high and plants must be watered at least once a day in summer. If plants cannot be mounted, hanging pots or baskets may be filled with an open, fast-draining medium. Repotting may be done anytime new roots are actively growing.

MISCELLANEOUS NOTES: The bloom season shown in the climate table is based on reports from the habitat. The climate given represents the coolest, driest extremes of the habitat. The weather patterns are the same throughout the range, but locations nearer the equator experience temperatures that are 8–10°F (4–6°C) warmer, and rainfall amounts that are 3–4 times greater.

Plant and Flower Information

PLANT SIZE AND TYPE: A 10–24 in. (25–60 cm) sympodial epiphyte.

PSEUDOBULB: 9–14 in. (23–35 cm) long. The pendent stems are clustered, ribbed, and slightly swollen at the base.

LEAVES: Many. The distichous leaves are oblong, light yellow-green, 0.8–1.6 in. (2–4 cm) long, and unequally bilobed at the apex. They are carried on the upper half of the stem.

INFLORESCENCE: 7 in. (17 cm) long. Inflorescences emerge laterally on the stem.

FLOWERS: 1 per inflorescence. The tiny, waxy flowers, which are 0.8 in. (2 cm) across, may be self-pollinating. The blossoms are initially white, but they turn yellowish or pale orange with age. They are sometimes streaked with darker orange.

REFERENCES: 118, 173, 211, 220, 254, 270, 271, 432, 454, 516.

PHOTOS/DRAWINGS: 173, 270, 271.

Dendrobium axillare Schlechter

ORIGIN/HABITAT: Northern Papua New Guinea. Plants grow on forest trees in the Kani Mountains at about 3300 ft. (1000 m).

CLIMATE: Station #200187, Erap, Papua New Guinea, Lat. 6.6°S, Long. 146.7°E, at 850 ft. (260 m). Temperatures are calculated for an elevation of 3300 ft. (1000 m), resulting in probable extremes of 94°F (34°C) and 45°F (7°C).

N/HEMISPHERE	JAN	FEB	MAR	APR	MAY	JUN	JUL	AUG	SEP	OCT	NOV	DEC
°F AVG MAX	80	80	81	82	85	85	85	85	85	84	82	82
°F AVG MIN	61	61	61	62	64	65	64	64	65	63	66	62
DIURNAL RANGE	19	19	20	20	21	20	21	21	20	21	16	20
RAIN/INCHES	3.9	3.9	2.7	3.0	3.0	5.3	5.9	5.9	7.0	3.4	2.4	3.1
HUMIDITY/%	82	81	81	79	75	74	74	74	77	76	80	80
BLOOM SEASON												*
DAYS CLR	N/A											
RAIN/MM	99	99	69	76	76	135	150	150	178	86	61	79
°C AVG MAX	26.7	26.7	27.2	27.8	29.4	29.4	29.4	29.4	29.4	28.9	27.8	27.8
°C AVG MIN	16.1	16.1	16.1	16.7	17.8	18.3	17.8	17.8	18.3	17.2	18.9	16.7
DIURNAL RANGE	10.6	10.6	11.1	11.1	11.6	11.1	11.6	11.6	11.1	11.7	8.9	11.1
S/HEMISPHERE	JUL	AUG	SEP	OCT	NOV	DEC	JAN	FEB	MAR	APR	MAY	JUN

Cultural Recommendations

LIGHT: 3000–4000 fc.

TEMPERATURES: Throughout the year, days average 80–85°F (27–29°C), and nights average 61–66°F (16–19°C), with a diurnal range of 16–21°F (9–12°C).

HUMIDITY: 75–80% year-round. Despite high average humidity, the habitat may be quite dry during hot afternoons.

WATER: Rainfall is moderate most of the year, but for 4–5 months in summer and early autumn, conditions are somewhat wetter. Cultivated plants should be thoroughly saturated then allowed to dry slightly between waterings in summer and early autumn. Water should be gradually reduced in autumn.

FERTILIZER: ¼–½ recommended strength. A balanced fertilizer should be applied weekly to biweekly throughout the year.

REST PERIOD: Growing temperatures should be maintained all year. In the habitat, rainfall is lowest in winter, but the high humidity indicates that additional moisture is frequently available from heavy dew. Cultivated plants should be allowed to dry somewhat longer between waterings, but they should not remain dry for extended periods. Fertilizer should be reduced until water is increased in spring. In the habitat, seasonal light variation is minor.

GROWING MEDIA: Plants may be mounted on rough-barked hardwood or cork slabs if humidity is high and plants are watered at least once daily in summer. When plants are potted, any open, fast-draining medium may be used. They may be repotted anytime new roots are growing.

MISCELLANEOUS NOTES: The bloom season shown in the climate table is based on a single collection report. Schlechter (ref. 437) indicated that the species is "by no means rare and is found often during the rainy season (in the European winter months)." Plants that produce flowers which last a single day commonly bloom several times during the year. Flowering usually occurs 7–14 days after a sudden 10°F (5°C) drop in daytime temperatures.

Plant and Flower Information

PLANT SIZE AND TYPE: A 31 in. (80 cm) sympodial epiphyte.

PSEUDOBULB: 24–26 in. (60–65 cm) long. The slightly flattened stems are erect to spreading.

LEAVES: Many. The growths are densely leafy. The leaves are 5–6 in. (12–15 cm) long.

INFLORESCENCE: Short. The flattened inflorescences emerge from the leaf axils.

FLOWERS: 2 per inflorescence. The orange-yellow flowers are 1 in. (2.5 cm) long, do not open fully, and last a single day, but Schlechter (ref. 437) described them as beautiful. The sepals and 3-lobed lip have central keels. The lip margins are smooth and rounded.

REFERENCES: 92, 221, 437, 445.

PHOTOS/DRAWINGS: 437.

Dendrobium babiense J. J. Smith

ORIGIN/HABITAT: Kalimantan, Borneo. Plants were collected near Batu Babi and on a ridge near Mt. Dulit at about 3100 ft. (950 m).

CLIMATE: Station #96633, Balikpapan, Borneo, Lat. 1.3°S, Long. 116.9°E, at 10 ft. (3 m). Temperatures are calculated for an estimated elevation of 3000 ft. (910 m), resulting in probable extremes of 82°F (28°C) and 50°F (10°C).

N/HEMISPHERE	JAN	FEB	MAR	APR	MAY	JUN	JUL	AUG	SEP	OCT	NOV	DEC
°F AVG MAX	73	74	74	75	75	75	75	76	76	75	75	74
°F AVG MIN	63	64	64	64	63	63	63	63	63	63	64	64
DIURNAL RANGE	10	10	10	11	12	12	12	13	13	12	11	10
RAIN/INCHES	7.1	6.4	5.5	5.2	6.6	8.1	7.9	8.9	9.1	8.2	9.1	7.6
HUMIDITY/%	82	80	77	78	80	79	82	81	81	82	83	82
BLOOM SEASON									*			
DAYS CLR @ 8AM	4	2	3	3	3	3	2	3	4	4	2	5
DAYS CLR @ 2PM	6	4	5	3	3	1	2	1	2	3	4	5
RAIN/MM	180	163	140	132	168	206	201	226	231	208	231	193
°C AVG MAX	22.9	23.4	23.4	24.0	24.0	24.0	24.0	24.5	24.5	24.0	24.0	23.4
°C AVG MIN	17.3	17.9	17.9	17.9	17.3	17.3	17.3	17.3	17.3	17.3	17.9	17.9
DIURNAL RANGE	5.6	5.5	5.5	6.1	6.7	6.7	6.7	7.2	7.2	6.7	6.1	5.5
S/HEMISPHERE	JUL	AUG	SEP	OCT	NOV	DEC	JAN	FEB	MAR	APR	MAY	JUN

Cultural Recommendations

LIGHT: 2500–3500 fc.

TEMPERATURES: Throughout the year, days average 73–76°F (23–25°C), and nights average 63–64°F (17–18°C), with a diurnal range of 10–13°F (6–7°C).

HUMIDITY: Near 80% year-round.

WATER: Rainfall is heavy all year. Cultivated plants should be kept moist but not soggy.

FERTILIZER: 1/4–1/2 recommended strength. A balanced fertilizer should be applied weekly to biweekly throughout the year.

REST PERIOD: Growing conditions should be maintained all year. Water should be reduced in winter for plants cultivated in the dark, short-day conditions common in temperate latitudes, but they should never be allowed to dry out completely.

GROWING MEDIA: Plants may be mounted or potted. Pots may be filled with any open, fast-draining medium. Repotting may be done anytime new roots are growing.

MISCELLANEOUS NOTES: The bloom season shown in the climate table is based on records from the habitat.

Plant and Flower Information

PLANT SIZE AND TYPE: A 17 in. (43 cm) sympodial epiphyte.

PSEUDOBULB: 17 in. (43 cm) long. Stems are snaky and rigid. The lower 10 in. (25 cm) of the stem is leafy, but the upper part has only rudimentary leaves. The nodes are swollen and flattened above the base.

LEAVES: Many. The oblong-triangular leaves are 1.2 in. (3 cm) long, laterally flattened, fleshy, and pointed.

INFLORESCENCE: Short. Inflorescences emerge from the upper, leafless portion of the stem.

FLOWERS: The tiny, non-fragrant flowers are less than 0.2 in. (0.6 cm) long. Sepals and petals are yellowish. The lip is a deeper yellow with brown markings.

REFERENCES: 59, 221, 286, 295, 474.

Dendrobium baeuerlenii F. Mueller and Kränzlin

AKA: Also spelled *D. bauerlenii* by J. J. Smith and *D. bäuerlerni* by Schlechter.

ORIGIN/HABITAT: New Guinea. In southwestern Papua, plants grow near the Fly River. In Iran Jaya (western New Guinea), plants were collected on the upper Eilanden River, the middle Legarei River at 260 ft. (80 m), and Noordwest River. Plants were cultivated in the botanical garden at Bogor, Java.

CLIMATE: Station #94003, Daru, Papua New Guinea, Lat. 9.1°S, Long. 143.2°E, at 20 ft. (6 m). Record extreme temperatures are 98°F (37°C) and 63°F (17°C).

N/HEMISPHERE	JAN	FEB	MAR	APR	MAY	JUN	JUL	AUG	SEP	OCT	NOV	DEC
°F AVG MAX	81	82	83	85	88	88	88	87	87	86	84	82
°F AVG MIN	74	74	74	76	76	76	76	76	76	76	77	75
DIURNAL RANGE	7	8	9	9	12	12	12	11	11	10	7	7
RAIN/INCHES	3.0	2.2	1.8	2.3	4.6	8.1	11.9	10.4	12.5	12.6	9.4	3.8
HUMIDITY/%	94	93	91	88	85	88	85	87	84	88	91	94
BLOOM SEASON									*			
DAYS CLR	N/A											
RAIN/MM	76	56	46	58	117	206	302	264	318	320	239	97
°C AVG MAX	27.2	27.8	28.3	29.4	31.1	31.1	31.1	30.6	30.6	30.0	28.9	27.8
°C AVG MIN	23.3	23.3	23.3	24.4	24.4	24.4	24.4	24.4	24.4	24.4	25.0	23.9
DIURNAL RANGE	3.9	4.5	5.0	5.0	6.7	6.7	6.7	6.2	6.2	5.6	3.9	3.9
S/HEMISPHERE	JUL	AUG	SEP	OCT	NOV	DEC	JAN	FEB	MAR	APR	MAY	JUN

Cultural Recommendations

LIGHT: 2500–3500 fc.

TEMPERATURES: Throughout the year, days average 81–88°F (27–31°C), and nights average 74–77°F (23–25°C), with a diurnal range of 7–12°F (4–7°C).

HUMIDITY: 85–90% from spring to autumn, increasing to 90–95% in winter.

WATER: Rainfall is heavy from late spring through autumn with a 2–3 month drier season in late winter and early spring. Cultivated plants should be kept wet but not soggy from late spring through early autumn. Water should be gradually reduced in late autumn.

FERTILIZER: 1/4–1/2 recommended strength. A balanced fertilizer should be applied weekly to biweekly throughout the year.

REST PERIOD: Growing temperatures should be maintained all year. Rainfall is low for about 5 months, but the driest part of the season lasts only 2–3 months. However, large quantities of water are available from nightly dew. Cultivated plants should be allowed to dry out between waterings, but they should not remain dry for long periods. Growers indicate that these plants require the same conditions as *D. bigibbum* Lindley with a prolonged dry rest after flowering. Fertilizer should be reduced or eliminated until water is increased in spring. In the habitat, light is probably greater in winter.

GROWING MEDIA: Plants may be mounted on tree-fern or cork slabs if humidity is high and plants are watered at least once daily in summer. When plants are potted, any open, fast-draining medium may be used. Repotting may be done anytime new roots are growing.

MISCELLANEOUS NOTES: The bloom season shown in the climate table is based on collection reports.

Plant and Flower Information

PLANT SIZE AND TYPE: A 24 in. (60 cm) sympodial epiphyte.

PSEUDOBULB: 20 in. (50 cm) long. The pseudobulbs are clustered.

LEAVES: Many. The linear, pointed leaves are 4–5 in. (10–12 cm) long.

INFLORESCENCE: Short. Inflorescences emerge from nodes near the apex of the pseudobulb.

FLOWERS: Few per inflorescence. The pale rose flowers are 0.6 in. (1.5 cm) across. The dorsal sepal is oblong to nearly round and minutely serrated in front. The short lateral sepals are rounded at the apex. For 65% of its length, the lip is completely round, incurved, and minutely toothed. The sidelobes are indistinct.

REFERENCES: 25, 216, 253, 254, 445, 470.

Dendrobium baileyi F. Mueller

AKA: *D. keffordii* F. M. Bailey. Kränzlin (ref. 254) includes *D. armitiae* F. M. Bailey as a synonym of *D. keffordii* F. M. Bailey, which is now considered a synonym of *D. baileyi* F. Mueller. Lewis and Cribb (ref. 271) discuss a species from Choiseul, the Florida Islands, and Malaita that grows below 1150 ft. (350 m). They indicate that it is different but closely related to *D. baileyi*.

ORIGIN/HABITAT: Australia. Plants are found in northeastern Queensland from the McIlwraith Range to Townsville. They grow in lowland rainforests, coastal swamps, or near streams in humid, sheltered locations.

CLIMATE: Station #94283, Cooktown, Australia, Lat. 15.5°S, Long. 145.2°E, at 24 ft. (7 m). Temperatures are calculated for an elevation of 1000 ft. (300 m), resulting in probable extremes of 101°F (39°C) and 43°F (6°C).

N/HEMISPHERE	JAN	FEB	MAR	APR	MAY	JUN	JUL	AUG	SEP	OCT	NOV	DEC
°F AVG MAX	76	77	79	82	85	86	86	85	83	82	79	77
°F AVG MIN	63	64	67	70	72	72	72	72	72	70	67	65
DIURNAL RANGE	13	13	12	12	13	14	14	13	11	12	12	12
RAIN/INCHES	0.9	1.2	0.6	1.0	2.5	6.6	14.4	13.7	15.3	8.8	2.8	2.0
HUMIDITY/%	73	69	68	67	68	71	75	76	77	75	74	75
BLOOM SEASON						*	*					
DAYS CLR	N/A											
RAIN/MM	23	30	15	25	64	168	366	348	389	224	71	51
°C AVG MAX	24.3	24.9	26.0	27.7	29.3	29.9	29.9	29.3	28.2	27.7	26.0	24.9
°C AVG MIN	17.1	17.7	19.3	21.0	22.1	22.1	22.1	22.1	22.1	21.0	19.3	18.2
DIURNAL RANGE	7.2	7.2	6.7	6.7	7.2	7.8	7.8	7.2	6.1	6.7	6.7	6.7
S/HEMISPHERE	JUL	AUG	SEP	OCT	NOV	DEC	JAN	FEB	MAR	APR	MAY	JUN

Cultural Recommendations

LIGHT: 2400–3000 fc. Diffused or barely dappled light is preferred. Direct sunlight should be avoided.

TEMPERATURES: Summer days average 85–86°F (29–30°C), and nights average 72°F (22°C), with a diurnal range of 13–14°F (7–8°C). The diurnal range varies only 3°F (2°C) all year.

HUMIDITY: 70–75% year-round, but humidity is probably greater than indicated in the habitat. Growers recommend a very humid atmosphere.

WATER: Rainfall is moderate to heavy in summer and early autumn, but conditions are drier in winter. Cultivated plants should be kept moist but not soggy while actively growing, but water should be reduced after new growths mature in autumn.

FERTILIZER: ¼–½ recommended strength, applied weekly. A high-nitrogen fertilizer is beneficial from spring to midsummer, but a fertilizer high in phosphates should be used in late summer and autumn. Fertilizer should be eliminated during the dry season. Some growers believe that *D. baileyi* is healthiest if fertilizer is applied at a slightly higher than normal rate, while others report that plants fed regularly with inorganic fertilizers tend to become lush and soft and therefore more prone to insect infestations or disease.

REST PERIOD: Winter days average 76–79°F (24–26°C), and nights average 63–67°F (17–19°C), with a diurnal range of 12–13°F (7°C). Temperatures should never be allowed to drop below 50–55°F (10–13°C) as the plants are very sensitive to cold. Growers indicate that plants quickly drop all leaves, collapse, and die when exposed to temperatures below 54°F (12°C). Rainfall is lower in the habitat in winter, but ample moisture is normally available year-round from heavy dew and mist. Growers indicate that this species requires more water than most dendrobiums, even in winter. While water should be reduced somewhat for cultivated plants in winter, they should never be allowed to dry out completely.

GROWING MEDIA: Plants may be mounted on tree-fern or cork slabs if humidity is high and plants are watered at least once daily in summer. When plants are potted, a very open, fast-draining medium should be used. They may be repotted anytime new roots are growing.

MISCELLANEOUS NOTES: The primary bloom season shown in the climate table is based on reports from the habitat. However, plants may bloom sporadically throughout year. Plants begin blooming while very young. Some growers consider *D. baileyi* difficult to maintain in cultivation, and careful attention should be paid to its cultural requirements.

Plant and Flower Information

PLANT SIZE AND TYPE: An 8–47 in. (20–120 cm) sympodial epiphyte or lithophyte. Plant size is extremely variable.

PSEUDOBULB: Usually 16–24 in. (40–60 cm) long. Stems may be as short as 6 in. (15 cm) or as long as 43 in. (110 cm). The pseudobulbs, which are numerous and stemlike, are normally long and wiry. New growths often require more than a single year to mature. Cultivated plants are normally rather small, but they may grow into a large mass if left undisturbed. Most of the stem is leafy.

LEAVES: Many. The grasslike leaves are dark green, sickle-shaped, and 2–3 in. (5–8 cm) long.

INFLORESCENCE: Very short. The inflorescences emerge from lateral nodes along the upper half of the pseudobulb.

FLOWERS: 1–3 per inflorescence. The fragrant flowers are 2 in. (5 cm) across. They are yellowish on the outside and densely spotted with red or purple on the inside. Sepals and petals, which are very slender and taper to threads at the tips, curl and become tangled as the flower ages. Blossoms last less than a day and remain fully open for only a few hours.

HYBRIDIZING NOTES: Chromosome count is 2n = 38 (ref. 152). *D. baileyi* is seldom used for hybridizing due to the large plant size and short flower life.

REFERENCES: 67, 105, 145, 152, 216, 240, 254, 262, 271, 325, 421, 533.

PHOTOS/DRAWINGS: 105, *145,* 240, 325, *533.*

Dendrobium bairdianum F. M. Bailey. See *D. fellowsii* F. Mueller. REFERENCES: 67, 105, 153, 179, 216, 240, 254, 262, 273, 291, 325, 421, 533.

Dendrobium bambusifolium Parish and Rchb. f. Sometimes spelled *D. bambusaefolium,* see *D. salaccense* (Blume) Lindley. REFERENCES: 97, 152, 154, 157, 188, 202, 216, 254, 454. PHOTOS/DRAWINGS: 97.

Dendrobium bambusinum Ridley

ORIGIN/HABITAT: Irian Jaya (western New Guinea). Plants were collected on the south side of Mt. Jaya (Mt. Carstensz) at 2500–5500 ft. (760–1680 m).

CLIMATE: Station #97796, Kokenau (Kokonau), Irian Jaya, Lat. 4.7°S, Long. 135.4°E, at 10 ft. (3 m). Temperatures are calculated for an elevation of 4000 ft. (1220 m). Record extreme temperatures are not available for this location.

N/HEMISPHERE	JAN	FEB	MAR	APR	MAY	JUN	JUL	AUG	SEP	OCT	NOV	DEC
°F AVG MAX	70	70	73	75	77	76	76	76	77	75	74	71
°F AVG MIN	60	60	61	61	61	62	61	61	61	61	61	60
DIURNAL RANGE	10	10	12	14	16	14	15	15	16	14	13	11
RAIN/INCHES	18.4	15.8	18.9	11.6	9.7	10.6	11.5	15.7	11.6	11.6	16.0	19.9
HUMIDITY/%	N/A											
BLOOM SEASON	N/A											
DAYS CLR	N/A											
RAIN/MM	467	401	480	295	246	269	292	399	295	295	406	505
°C AVG MAX	21.0	21.0	22.7	23.8	24.9	24.4	24.4	24.4	24.9	23.8	23.2	21.6
°C AVG MIN	15.5	15.5	16.0	16.0	16.0	16.6	16.0	16.0	16.0	16.0	16.0	15.5
DIURNAL RANGE	5.5	5.5	6.7	7.8	8.9	7.8	8.4	8.4	8.9	7.8	7.2	6.1
S/HEMISPHERE	JUL	AUG	SEP	OCT	NOV	DEC	JAN	FEB	MAR	APR	MAY	JUN

Cultural Recommendations

LIGHT: 2500–3500 fc.

TEMPERATURES: Throughout the year, days average 70–77°F (21–25°C),

Dendrobium banaense

and nights average 60–62°F (16–17°C), with a diurnal range of 10–16°F (6–9°C).

HUMIDITY: Information is not available for this location. However, averages from nearby stations indicate that values are probably near 85% year-round.

WATER: Rainfall is very heavy all year. Cultivated plants should be kept evenly moist.

FERTILIZER: ¼–½ recommended strength. A balanced fertilizer should be applied weekly to biweekly throughout the year.

REST PERIOD: Growing conditions should be maintained year-round. Water and fertilizer might be reduced slightly in winter for plants cultivated in the dark, short-day conditions common in temperate latitudes. However, plants should never be allowed to dry out completely.

GROWING MEDIA: Plants may be mounted on tree-fern or cork slabs if humidity is high and plants are watered at least once daily in summer. When plants are potted, any open, fast-draining medium may be used. They may be repotted anytime new roots are growing.

Plant and Flower Information

PLANT SIZE AND TYPE: A 12 in. (30 cm) sympodial epiphyte.

PSEUDOBULB: 12 in. (30 cm) long. The slender stems are somewhat flattened.

LEAVES: Many. The leaves are 1.6 in. (4 cm) long, lanceolate, and taper toward the apex. The leaf-tip is unequally bilobed.

INFLORESCENCE: Short. Racemes emerge from nodes along the side of the stem.

FLOWERS: 2 per inflorescence. The thin-textured, greenish flowers are 0.4 in. (1 cm) across. The lip has a very wide, deep indentation between the 2 pointed sections of the midlobe making the 3-lobed lip appear 4-lobed. The flower was described from a dried specimen, and the lip appeared to have darker, possibly orange stripes.

REFERENCES: 222, 400.

Dendrobium banaense Gagnepain. See *D. acinaciforme* Roxburgh. REFERENCES: 136, 224, 266, 448, 454.

Dendrobium bancanum J. J. Smith. Now considered a synonym of *Flickingeria bancana* (J. J. Smith) A. Hawkes. REFERENCES: 213, 220, 231, 254, 449.

Dendrobium bandaense Schlechter

AKA: Cribb (ref. 84) suggests the possibility that *D. bandaense* may be conspecific with *D. mirbelianum* Gaudich.

ORIGIN/HABITAT: The Banda Archipelago, a group of small islands south of Seram. Plants grow between lava pebbles at low elevations near Mt. Api.

CLIMATE: Station #97724, Ambon/Pattimura, Indonesia, Lat. 3.7°S, Long. 128.1°E, at 33 ft. (10 m). Record extreme temperatures are 96°F (36°C) and 66°F (19°C).

N/HEMISPHERE	JAN	FEB	MAR	APR	MAY	JUN	JUL	AUG	SEP	OCT	NOV	DEC
°F AVG MAX	81	81	83	85	88	88	88	88	88	86	84	82
°F AVG MIN	74	74	74	74	75	76	76	76	76	76	75	74
DIURNAL RANGE	7	7	9	11	13	12	12	12	12	10	9	8
RAIN/INCHES	23.7	15.8	9.5	6.1	4.5	5.2	5.0	4.7	5.3	11.0	20.3	25.1
HUMIDITY/%	83	82	81	80	79	78	78	77	79	82	83	84
BLOOM SEASON				*								
DAYS CLR @ 9AM	1	1	1	6	7	4	3	5	5	5	3	3
DAYS CLR @ 3PM	1	1	2	5	6	1	1	1	2	3	1	3
RAIN/MM	602	401	241	155	114	132	127	119	135	279	516	638
°C AVG MAX	27.2	27.2	28.3	29.4	31.1	31.1	31.1	31.1	31.1	30.0	28.9	27.8
°C AVG MIN	23.3	23.3	23.3	23.3	23.9	24.4	24.4	24.4	24.4	24.4	23.9	23.3
DIURNAL RANGE	3.9	3.9	5.0	6.1	7.2	6.7	6.7	6.7	6.7	5.6	5.0	4.5
S/HEMISPHERE	JUL	AUG	SEP	OCT	NOV	DEC	JAN	FEB	MAR	APR	MAY	JUN

Cultural Recommendations

LIGHT: 2500–4000 fc.

TEMPERATURES: Throughout the year, days average 81–88°F (27–31°C), and nights average 74–76°F (23–24°C), with a diurnal range of 7–13°F (4–7°C).

HUMIDITY: 80–85% year-round.

WATER: Rainfall is moderate to heavy all year. Conditions are slightly drier from late spring through summer. Cultivated plants should be kept evenly moist with only slight drying allowed between waterings.

FERTILIZER: ¼–½ recommended strength. A balanced fertilizer should be applied weekly to biweekly throughout the year.

REST PERIOD: Growing conditions should be maintained all year. In the habitat, rainfall is heaviest in winter, but water and fertilizer should be reduced for cultivated plants, especially those grown in the dark, short-day conditions common in temperate latitudes. However, plants should never be allowed to dry completely. In the habitat, light is highest in spring.

GROWING MEDIA: Plants may be mounted on tree-fern or cork slabs if humidity is high and plants are watered at least once daily in summer. When plants are potted, any open, fast-draining medium may be used. Repotting may be done anytime new roots are growing.

MISCELLANEOUS NOTES: The bloom season shown in the climate table is based on reports from the habitat.

Plant and Flower Information

PLANT SIZE AND TYPE: A 14–20 in. (35–50 cm) sympodial terrestrial.

PSEUDOBULB: 14–20 in. (35–50 cm) long. The erect stems are cylindrical.

LEAVES: Many. The oblong-elliptic leaves are 2.8–4.3 in. (7–11 cm) long, leathery, and unequally bilobed at the tip. The leaves are smaller near the apex of the stem.

INFLORESCENCE: Racemes are much longer than the leaves.

FLOWERS: 10–20 per inflorescence. Blossoms are 1.6 in. (4 cm) across. The lanceolate sepals and tongue-shaped petals are greenish yellow. The white, 3-lobed lip has brown veins and yellow callus ridges. The midlobe is ovate and wavy along the margin.

REFERENCES: 25, 84, 220, 254, 433.

Dendrobium banghamii Ames and Schweinfurth. Now considered a synonym of *Epigeneium cymbidioides* (Blume) Summerhayes. REFERENCES: 225, 298.

Dendrobium barbatochlorops Rolfe. Sometimes spelled *D. barbatulo-chlorops*, it was originally spelled *D. barbato-chlorops*. The plant was described as an apparent natural hybrid between *D. barbatulum* Lindley and *D. chlorops* Lindley. REFERENCES: 254, 570.

Dendrobium barbatulum Bateman not Lindley or Wight. See *D. fytchianum* Bateman. REFERENCES: 216, 254.

Dendrobium barbatulum Lindley not Bateman or Wight

ORIGIN/HABITAT: Southern and western India. Plants grow in the mountain forests of the Western Ghats region from Mysore to Travancore. They are usually found on bushes and small trees at about 5000 ft. (1520 m), where they may be exposed to full sun during the dry season.

CLIMATE: Station #43314, Calicut, India, Lat. 11.3°N, Long. 75.8°E, at 17 ft. (5 m). Temperatures are calculated for an elevation of 5000 ft. (1520 m), resulting in probable extremes of 83°F (28°C) and 41°F (5°C).

N/HEMISPHERE	JAN	FEB	MAR	APR	MAY	JUN	JUL	AUG	SEP	OCT	NOV	DEC
°F AVG MAX	72	73	74	75	74	69	66	67	68	70	71	72
°F AVG MIN	55	57	60	62	62	59	58	58	59	59	58	55
DIURNAL RANGE	17	16	14	13	12	10	8	9	9	11	13	17
RAIN/INCHES	0.4	0.2	0.7	3.6	9.3	33.1	32.5	17.2	7.9	10.3	5.5	1.0
HUMIDITY/%	71	73	73	74	82	87	91	91	87	85	77	74
BLOOM SEASON	*	**	**	*	*	*						
DAYS CLR @ 5AM	19	18	21	12	5	4	2	2	4	4	19	20
DAYS CLR @ 11AM	16	18	23	15	5	3	0	1	6	5	12	14
RAIN/MM	10	5	18	91	236	841	826	437	201	262	140	25
°C AVG MAX	22.0	22.5	23.1	23.6	23.1	20.3	18.6	19.2	19.8	20.9	21.4	22.0
°C AVG MIN	12.5	13.6	15.3	16.4	16.4	14.8	14.2	14.2	14.8	14.8	14.2	12.5
DIURNAL RANGE	9.5	8.9	7.8	7.2	6.7	5.5	4.4	5.0	5.0	6.1	7.2	9.5
S/HEMISPHERE	JUL	AUG	SEP	OCT	NOV	DEC	JAN	FEB	MAR	APR	MAY	JUN

Cultural Recommendations

LIGHT: 3500–4500 fc. Cultivated plants need to be shaded during the brightest part of the year, but as much light as possible should be provided from autumn into spring.

TEMPERATURES: Summer days average 66–69°F (19–20°C), and nights average 58–59°F (14–15°C), with a diurnal range of 8–10°F (4–6°C). Spring is the warmest season. Days average 74–75°F (23–24°C), and nights average 60–62°F (15–16°C), with a diurnal range of 12–14°F (7–8°C).

HUMIDITY: 85–90% in summer, decreasing to 70–75% in winter and spring.

WATER: Rainfall is heavy to extremely heavy most of the year, but conditions are very dry for 3–4 months in winter. Cultivated plants should be kept moist from spring to autumn. Water should be gradually reduced in late autumn after new growths mature.

FERTILIZER: ¼–½ recommended strength, applied weekly. A high-nitrogen fertilizer is beneficial from spring to midsummer, but a fertilizer high in phosphates should be used in late summer and autumn.

REST PERIOD: Winter days average 72–73°F (22–23°C), and nights average 55–57°F (13–14°C), with a diurnal range of 14–17°F (8–10°C). Rainfall is very low for 3–4 months in winter, so water should be reduced for cultivated plants. Plants should be allowed to dry out between waterings, but they should not remain completely dry for extended periods. Occasional early morning mistings between waterings may be beneficial, especially on warm, sunny days. Fertilizer should be greatly reduced or eliminated until water is increased in spring. In the habitat, light is highest in winter.

GROWING MEDIA: Plants are best mounted on rafts or slabs if humidity is high and water is applied at least daily in summer. If these conditions cannot be met, plants may be placed in a pot that is small for the plant size. Pots should be filled with a very open, fast-draining medium such as fir bark or cork nuggets. Repotting should be done as soon after flowering as possible.

MISCELLANEOUS NOTES: The bloom season shown in the climate table is based on cultivation records. New growths and flowers appear at about the same time.

Plant and Flower Information

PLANT SIZE AND TYPE: A 6–18 in. (15–45 cm) sympodial epiphyte. *D. barbatulum* is not robust.

PSEUDOBULB: 6–15 in. (15–38 cm) long. The purplish brown pseudobulb is tapered, curved, and swollen at the base. It is more often erect than pendent.

LEAVES: The leaves are 2.4–5.0 in. (6–13 cm) long, narrowly lanceolate, and deciduous.

INFLORESCENCE: The stout inflorescence emerges at or near the apex of the pseudobulb. The blossoms are crowded on the raceme.

FLOWERS: 8–15 per inflorescence. The flowers are 1.0–1.6 in. (2.5–4.0 cm) across. Sepals and petals are commonly pure white, but some clones may be lightly tinged with pink or suffused with a deeper rose-pink. The white lip is flat, ovate, and pointed. The greenish spur is conical. The disk has yellow hairs at the apex and base. The flowers are described as beautiful. Growers indicate that they are good cut flowers.

HYBRIDIZING NOTES: Chromosome counts are n = 20 (ref. 542) and 2n = 38 (ref. 151, 154).

REFERENCES: 38, 46, 119, 151, 154, 179, 190, 202, 210, 216, 228, 244, 254, 255, 278, 317, 369, 424, 430, 445, 459, 541, 542, 570.

PHOTOS/DRAWINGS: 210, 244, 459.

Dendrobium barbatulum Wight not Bateman or Lindley.

See *D. ovatum* (Willdenow) Kränzlin. REFERENCES: 216, 254, 424.

Dendrobium barbatum Cogniaux.

Originally described as originating in Burma. Insufficient habitat information is available to select climate data. The yellow-green plants were described as having slender, club-shaped pseudobulbs 4 in. (10 cm) long. The apex of the stem was covered with numerous distichous leaves 2 in. (5 cm) long. Inflorescences were shorter than the leaves and emerged along the upper part of the stem. The white blossoms were 0.4 in. (1 cm) long with a rosy tint at the apex of the segments. The lanceolate petals were erect. The margin of the 3-lobed lip was covered with elongated hairs and the inner surface of the midlobe had a downy surface. The plant imported to Europe bloomed in midsummer. REFERENCES: 254.

Dendrobium bariense J. J. Smith

AKA: *Cadetia sepikana* Schlechter. *Cadetia* is now considered a valid genus by some botanists, so this plant may again be considered a *Cadetia*.

ORIGIN/HABITAT: Northwestern Papua New Guinea. Plants grow along the Sepik River near Malu at 150–1850 ft. (40–560 m).

CLIMATE: Station #200004, Ambunti, Papua New Guinea, Lat. 4.2°S, Long. 142.8°E, at 164 ft. (50 m). Temperatures are calculated for an elevation of 1000 ft. (300 m), resulting in probable extremes of 96°F (36°C) and 49°F (10°C).

N/HEMISPHERE	JAN	FEB	MAR	APR	MAY	JUN	JUL	AUG	SEP	OCT	NOV	DEC
°F AVG MAX	85	87	87	87	88	87	87	87	87	87	87	86
°F AVG MIN	69	70	71	70	70	70	69	70	70	70	70	71
DIURNAL RANGE	16	17	16	17	18	17	18	17	17	17	17	15
RAIN/INCHES	6.4	7.4	7.7	8.5	9.2	9.4	10.9	10.2	12.2	10.4	8.3	5.2
HUMIDITY/%	N/A											
BLOOM SEASON		*								*		
DAYS CLR	N/A											
RAIN/MM	163	188	196	216	234	239	277	259	310	264	211	132
°C AVG MAX	29.6	30.7	30.7	30.7	31.2	30.7	30.7	30.7	30.7	30.7	30.7	30.1
°C AVG MIN	20.7	21.2	21.8	21.2	21.2	21.2	20.7	21.2	21.2	21.2	21.2	21.8
DIURNAL RANGE	8.9	9.5	8.9	9.5	10.0	9.5	10.0	9.5	9.5	9.5	9.5	8.3
S/HEMISPHERE	JUL	AUG	SEP	OCT	NOV	DEC	JAN	FEB	MAR	APR	MAY	JUN

Cultural Recommendations

LIGHT: 2000–3000 fc.

TEMPERATURES: Throughout the year, days average 85–88°F (30–31°C), and nights average 69–71°F (21–22°C), with a diurnal range of 15–18°F (8–10°C).

HUMIDITY: Information is not available for this location. However, records from other stations indicate that averages are probably near 80% year-round.

WATER: Rainfall is heavy all year, with the greatest amounts falling in summer and early autumn. Cultivated plants should be kept moist with only slight drying allowed between waterings.

FERTILIZER: ¼–½ recommended strength. A balanced fertilizer should be applied weekly to biweekly throughout the year.

REST PERIOD: Growing conditions should be maintained all year. Water and fertilizer should be reduced in winter, especially for plants cultivated in the dark, short-day conditions common in temperate latitudes, but they should never be allowed to dry completely between waterings.

GROWING MEDIA: Plants may be mounted on cork or tree-fern slabs if humidity is high and plants are watered at least once daily in summer. If plants are potted, most growers prefer fir bark, but any open, fast-draining medium may be used. Repotting may be done anytime new roots are growing.

MISCELLANEOUS NOTES: The bloom season shown in the climate table is based on reports from the habitat.

Plant and Flower Information

PLANT SIZE AND TYPE: A 4–7 in. (11–18 cm) sympodial epiphyte.

PSEUDOBULB: 1.4–4.7 in. (3.5–12.0 cm) long. The tiny, square stems are clustered on a very short rhizome.

LEAVES: 1 per growth. The leaf is 2.0–2.8 in. (5–7 cm) long.

INFLORESCENCE: Short.

FLOWERS: Blossoms are 0.2 in. (0.6 cm) long. Flowers are white with a purple margin on the lip.

REFERENCES: 223, 225, 443, 486.

Dendrobium barisanum J. J. Smith

ORIGIN/HABITAT: Western Sumatra. Plants grow at several locations near Bengkulu at about 3300 ft. (1000 m).

CLIMATE: Station #96253, Bengkulu, Sumatra, Indonesia, Lat. 3.9°S, Long. 102.3°E, at 49 ft. (15 m). Temperatures are calculated for an elevation of 3300 ft. (1000 m). Record extreme temperatures are not available for this location.

N/HEMISPHERE	JAN	FEB	MAR	APR	MAY	JUN	JUL	AUG	SEP	OCT	NOV	DEC
°F AVG MAX	77	76	76	76	76	76	77	77	77	77	78	77
°F AVG MIN	61	61	61	62	62	62	62	61	62	63	62	62
DIURNAL RANGE	16	15	15	14	14	14	15	16	15	14	16	15
RAIN/INCHES	6.9	6.8	9.1	13.9	16.0	12.7	16.0	11.5	12.0	8.3	8.4	8.4
HUMIDITY/%	77	78	77	77	79	80	78	76	77	79	77	78
BLOOM SEASON	N/A											
DAYS CLR @ 7AM	5	1	1	1	0	0	2	1	1	1	2	3
DAYS CLR @ 1PM	5	4	3	1	2	3	2	2	2	3	7	5
RAIN/MM	175	173	231	353	406	323	406	292	305	211	213	213
°C AVG MAX	25.2	24.6	24.6	24.6	24.6	24.6	25.2	25.2	25.2	25.2	25.7	25.2
°C AVG MIN	16.3	16.3	16.3	16.8	16.8	16.8	16.8	16.3	16.8	17.4	16.8	16.8
DIURNAL RANGE	8.9	8.3	8.3	7.8	7.8	7.8	8.4	8.9	8.4	7.8	8.9	8.4
S/HEMISPHERE	JUL	AUG	SEP	OCT	NOV	DEC	JAN	FEB	MAR	APR	MAY	JUN

Cultural Recommendations

LIGHT: 2000–3000 fc.

TEMPERATURES: Throughout the year, days average 76–78°F (25–26°C), and nights average 61–63°F (16–17°C), with a diurnal range of 14–16°F (8–9°C).

HUMIDITY: 75–80% year-round.

WATER: Rainfall is heavy all year, but winter is only slightly drier than summer. Cultivated plants should be kept moist and never be allowed to dry completely.

FERTILIZER: ¼–½ recommended strength. A balanced fertilizer should be applied weekly to biweekly throughout the year.

REST PERIOD: Growing conditions should be maintained year-round. Water and fertilizer may be reduced somewhat in winter, especially for plants grown in the dark, short-day conditions common in temperate latitudes. However, cultivated plants should never be allowed to dry completely between waterings. In the habitat, light is highest in winter.

GROWING MEDIA: Plants may be mounted on tree-fern or cork slabs or potted in small pots filled with any open, fast-draining medium. Repotting may be done anytime new roots are growing.

MISCELLANEOUS NOTES: The plant was described in 1917 in *Bul. Jard. Bot. Buit.* 2nd sér. 25:45.

Plant and Flower Information

PLANT SIZE AND TYPE: A sympodial epiphyte of unreported size.

PSEUDOBULB: The unbranched stems are pale yellow-green.

LEAVES: Few. The distichous leaves are 0.5–0.8 in. (1.2–2.0 cm) long. They are oblong to oval, darker on the upper surface, and slightly twisted at the base.

INFLORESCENCE: Short. Inflorescences, which emerge through the leaf bases, hold blossoms close to the stem.

FLOWERS: 1 per inflorescence. The flowers are 0.5 in. (1.2 cm) across. Blossoms may be pale yellow or greenish-white. The lip is distinctly 3-lobed with a wavy midlobe.

REFERENCES: 222.

Dendrobium barringtoniae Swartz.

Now considered a synonym of *Lycaste barringtoniae* Lindley. REFERENCES: 190, 216, 254, 445.

Dendrobium baseyanum St. Cloud

AKA: *D. baseyanum* is often considered as a synonym of *D. teretifolium* var. *fasciculatum* Rupp (*D. calamiforme* Loddiges), but Jones (ref. 240) and Clements (ref. 67) consider it a separate species.

ORIGIN/HABITAT: Australia. Plants are found in northeastern Queensland between Cooktown and Cairns. They grow on trees at low elevations.

CLIMATE: Station #94287, Cairns, Australia, Lat. 16.9°S, Long. 145.8°E, at 7 ft. (2 m). Temperatures are calculated for an elevation of 2000 ft. (610 m), resulting in probable extremes of 103°F (40°C) and 36°F (3°C).

N/HEMISPHERE	JAN	FEB	MAR	APR	MAY	JUN	JUL	AUG	SEP	OCT	NOV	DEC
°F AVG MAX	71	73	76	79	81	83	83	82	80	78	74	72
°F AVG MIN	54	55	57	61	63	66	67	67	66	63	59	57
DIURNAL RANGE	17	18	19	18	18	17	16	15	14	15	15	15
RAIN/INCHES	1.6	1.7	1.7	2.1	3.9	8.7	16.6	15.7	18.1	11.3	4.4	2.9
HUMIDITY/%	69	67	65	65	65	68	72	72	74	73	73	72
BLOOM SEASON				*	*	*						
DAYS CLR @ 10AM	9	11	13	11	6	6	4	5	6	7	11	10
DAYS CLR @ 4PM	8	10	12	16	10	7	4	3	4	6	9	10
RAIN/MM	41	43	43	53	99	221	422	399	460	287	112	74
°C AVG MAX	21.9	23.0	24.7	26.3	27.5	28.6	28.6	28.0	26.9	25.8	23.6	22.5
°C AVG MIN	12.5	13.0	14.1	16.3	17.5	19.1	19.7	19.7	19.1	17.5	15.2	14.1
DIURNAL RANGE	9.4	10.0	10.6	10.0	10.0	9.5	8.9	8.3	7.8	8.3	8.4	8.4
S/HEMISPHERE	JUL	AUG	SEP	OCT	NOV	DEC	JAN	FEB	MAR	APR	MAY	JUN

Cultural Recommendations

LIGHT: 2500–3000 fc.

TEMPERATURES: Summer days average 82–83°F (28–29°C), and nights average 66–67°F (19–20°C), with a diurnal range of 15–17°F (8–10°C).

HUMIDITY: Near 75% summer through autumn, dropping to about 65% in winter and spring.

WATER: Rainfall is heavy from late spring into autumn. Cultivated plants should be watered heavily from late spring to early autumn. Water should then be gradually reduced in late autumn after new growths mature.

FERTILIZER: ¼–½ recommended strength, applied weekly. A high-nitrogen fertilizer is beneficial from spring to midsummer, but a fertilizer high in phosphates should be used in late summer and autumn.

REST PERIOD: Winter days average 71–73°F (22–23°C), and nights average 54–57°F (13–14°C), with a diurnal range of 15–19°F (8–11°C). Water should be reduced for 4–5 months from late autumn into early spring.

Cultivated plants should be kept barely moist, but they should not be allowed to dry out completely. Fertilizer should be reduced or eliminated until water is increased in spring. In the habitat, light is highest in winter.

GROWING MEDIA: Mounting plants on slabs or rafts accommodates their pendent growth habit. However, humidity must be high and the plants must be watered at least once daily in summer. Several waterings a day may be necessary on the hottest days. If plants are potted, a very open and fast-draining medium is recommended. Undersized pots, barely large enough to hold the roots, should be used. Repotting is best done in early spring immediately after flowering when new roots are growing.

MISCELLANEOUS NOTES: The bloom season shown in the climate table is based on reports from the habitat.

Plant and Flower Information

PLANT SIZE AND TYPE: A 20 in. (50 cm) sympodial epiphyte. *D. baseyanum* is the smallest terete-leafed *Dendrobium* in Australia.

PSEUDOBULB: 10 in. (25 cm) long. The slender, branching stems, which may be dark green to yellowish, root only at the base.

LEAVES: 1 per branch. The pendulous, dull green leaves are 10 in. (25 cm) long. They are terete, but not grooved.

INFLORESCENCE: 2.4 in. (6 cm) long. Two stiffly spreading inflorescences emerge near the base of each leaf.

FLOWERS: 4–8 per inflorescence. The flowers are 0.4 in. (1 cm) across. The creamy white blossoms have purplish markings at the base of each segment.

REFERENCES: 67, 105, 228, 240, 533.

Dendrobium basilanense Ames

ORIGIN/HABITAT: The southern Philippines. Plants grow on trees in swamps from sea level to 1300 ft. (0–400 m).

CLIMATE: Station #98836, Zamboanga, Mindanao, Philippines, Lat. 6.9°N, Long. 122.1°E, at 17 ft. (5 m). Temperatures are calculated for an elevation of 650 ft. (200 m), resulting in probable extremes of 94°F (34°C) and 58°F (14°C).

N/HEMISPHERE	JAN	FEB	MAR	APR	MAY	JUN	JUL	AUG	SEP	OCT	NOV	DEC
°F AVG MAX	87	87	88	88	87	86	86	86	86	86	87	86
°F AVG MIN	69	69	70	71	72	72	71	71	71	71	70	69
DIURNAL RANGE	18	18	18	17	15	14	15	15	15	15	17	17
RAIN/INCHES	2.1	2.2	1.5	2.0	3.5	4.2	4.9	4.0	4.7	5.6	4.2	3.4
HUMIDITY/%	78	76	76	77	79	80	80	80	80	81	80	79
BLOOM SEASON	*			*							*	*
DAYS CLR @ 8AM	6	6	8	7	3	1	3	2	4	7	6	5
DAYS CLR @ 2PM	4	3	5	3	1	1	1	2	2	2	2	3
RAIN/MM	53	56	38	51	89	107	124	102	119	142	107	86
°C AVG MAX	30.5	30.5	31.1	31.1	30.5	29.9	29.9	29.9	29.9	29.9	30.5	29.9
°C AVG MIN	20.5	20.5	21.1	21.6	22.2	22.2	21.6	21.6	21.6	21.6	21.1	20.5
DIURNAL RANGE	10.0	10.0	10.0	9.5	8.3	7.7	8.3	8.3	8.3	8.3	9.4	9.4
S/HEMISPHERE	JUL	AUG	SEP	OCT	NOV	DEC	JAN	FEB	MAR	APR	MAY	JUN

Cultural Recommendations

LIGHT: 2500–3500 fc.

TEMPERATURES: Throughout the year, days average 86–88°F (30–31°C), and nights average 69–72°F (21–22°C), with a diurnal range of 14–18°F (8–10°C).

HUMIDITY: Near 80% most of the year, dropping to near 75% in late winter and early spring.

WATER: Rainfall is moderate to heavy from late spring through autumn. Conditions are slightly drier for 4 months in winter and early spring. Cultivated plants should be allowed to dry slightly between waterings but should never dry out completely.

FERTILIZER: ¼–½ recommended strength. A balanced fertilizer should be applied weekly to biweekly throughout the year.

REST PERIOD: Warm temperatures should be maintained year-round. Water and fertilizer should be gradually reduced in late autumn and early winter. In winter, plants should become even drier between waterings than in summer. However, they should not be allowed to remain dry for long periods.

GROWING MEDIA: Plants may be mounted on tree-fern or cork slabs if humidity is high and plants are watered at least once daily in summer. When plants are potted, any open, fast-draining medium may be used. Repotting may be done anytime new roots are growing.

MISCELLANEOUS NOTES: The bloom season shown in the climate table is based on collection reports.

Plant and Flower Information

PLANT SIZE AND TYPE: A 4–16 in. (10–40 cm) sympodial epiphyte.

PSEUDOBULB: 4–16 in. (10–40 cm) long. The stems may be simple or branching.

LEAVES: Many. The leaves are lanceolate, pointed at the tip, and usually 0.4 in. (1 cm) long. They are arranged in 2 rows and cover the stem from base to tip.

INFLORESCENCE: 0.8 in. (2 cm) long. Blossoms are carried in short racemes that emerge from a cushion of fibrous scales opposite rudimentary leaves at the apex of the stem.

FLOWERS: 1. Blossoms open in succession. The small white flowers are 0.2 in. (0.5 cm) across.

REFERENCES: 12, 221, 296, 373, 536.

Dendrobium batakense J. J. Smith. See *D. sociale* J. J. Smith.

REFERENCES: 223, 454.

Dendrobium batanense Ames and Quisumbing. See *D. equitans* Kränzlin. REFERENCES: 151, 152, 179, 187, 225, 243, 373, 536.

PHOTOS/DRAWINGS: 373.

Dendrobium beamanianum J. J. Wood and A. Lamb

ORIGIN/HABITAT: Borneo. Plants grow on the Pinosuk Plateau in Sabah. They are found in the lower mountain forests of Mt. Kinabalu at 3950–5600 ft. (1200–1700 m).

CLIMATE: Station #49613, Tambunan, Sabah, Borneo, Lat. 5.7°N, Long. 116.4°E, at 1200 ft. (366 m). Temperatures are calculated for an elevation of 4800 ft. (1460 m), resulting in probable extremes of 86°F (30°C) and 42°F (6°C).

N/HEMISPHERE	JAN	FEB	MAR	APR	MAY	JUN	JUL	AUG	SEP	OCT	NOV	DEC
°F AVG MAX	74	75	77	78	78	77	77	77	77	77	76	75
°F AVG MIN	55	53	54	55	56	55	54	54	55	55	55	56
DIURNAL RANGE	19	22	23	23	22	22	23	23	22	22	21	19
RAIN/INCHES	5.8	3.7	5.8	7.5	8.2	7.3	5.1	4.9	6.4	7.0	6.8	6.0
HUMIDITY/%	N/A											
BLOOM SEASON											*	
DAYS CLR	N/A											
RAIN/MM	147	94	147	190	208	185	130	124	163	178	173	152
°C AVG MAX	23.4	24.0	25.1	25.6	25.6	25.1	25.1	25.1	25.1	25.1	24.5	24.0	23.4
°C AVG MIN	12.8	11.7	12.3	12.8	13.4	12.8	12.3	12.3	12.8	12.8	12.8	13.4
DIURNAL RANGE	10.6	12.3	12.8	12.8	12.2	12.3	12.8	12.8	12.3	11.7	11.2	10.0
S/HEMISPHERE	JUL	AUG	SEP	OCT	NOV	DEC	JAN	FEB	MAR	APR	MAY	JUN

Cultural Recommendations

LIGHT: 2000–3000 fc.

TEMPERATURES: Throughout the year, days average 74–78°F (23–26°C), and nights average 53–56°F (12–13°C), with a diurnal range of 18–23°F (10–13°C).

HUMIDITY: Information is not available for this location. However, records from nearby locations indicate that humidity probably averages 80–85% year-round.

WATER: Rainfall is moderate to heavy all year with a brief, slightly drier period in winter. Cultivated plants should be kept moist with only slight drying allowed between waterings.

FERTILIZER: ¼–½ recommended strength. A balanced fertilizer should be applied weekly to biweekly throughout the year.

REST PERIOD: Growing temperatures should be maintained all year. Water should be reduced for cultivated plants, especially those grown in the dark, short-day conditions common in temperate-latitude winters, but they should never be allowed to dry out completely. Fertilizer should be reduced or eliminated until water is increased in spring.

GROWING MEDIA: Plants may be mounted on tree-fern or cork slabs if humidity is high and plants are watered at least once daily in summer. When plants are potted, any open, fast-draining medium may be used. Repotting is best done in early spring when new roots begin to grow.

Plant and Flower Information

PLANT SIZE AND TYPE: A 12–24 in. (30–60 cm) sympodial epiphyte.

PSEUDOBULB: 12–24 in. (30–60 cm) long.

LEAVES: 1.2–3.2 in. (3–8 cm) long. The slender leaves are unequally bilobed at the tip. The leaf sheaths are densely covered with black hairs when young, but they become smooth with age.

INFLORESCENCE: 0.4–0.6 in. (1.0–1.5 cm) long. Inflorescences emerge opposite numerous upper leaves.

FLOWERS: 1–3 per inflorescence. A single flower is open at any one time on each inflorescence. The flowers are 1 in. (2.5 cm) across. The stiff, pointed sepals and petals are pale brown to pale creamy-yellow with pale orange or orange-brown veins. The blossoms have an oblong-elliptic dorsal sepal, narrowly elliptic lateral sepals, and linear petals. The fleshy, 3-lobed lip is uppermost. It is pale yellow or pale brown with white keels and brownish yellow at the base. It is more or less covered with a white, mealy powder. The sidelobes are erect. The oval midlobe is very fleshy and roughened.

REFERENCES: 592.

PHOTOS/DRAWINGS: 592.

Dendrobium beccarianum (Kränzlin) Masamune

AKA: *Sarcopodium beccarianum* Kränzlin.

ORIGIN/HABITAT: Sarawak, Borneo. Habitat location and elevation were not included with the original description, so the following climate data should be used with caution.

CLIMATE: Station #96413, Kuching, Sarawak, Lat. 1.5°N, Long. 110.3°E, at 85 ft. (26 m). Record extreme temperatures are 97°F (36°C) and 64°F (18°C).

N/HEMISPHERE	JAN	FEB	MAR	APR	MAY	JUN	JUL	AUG	SEP	OCT	NOV	DEC
°F AVG MAX	88	88	89	90	91	91	91	92	90	90	90	88
°F AVG MIN	72	72	72	72	72	73	72	72	72	72	72	72
DIURNAL RANGE	16	16	17	18	19	18	19	20	18	18	18	16
RAIN/INCHES	27.1	19.7	14.2	9.7	9.0	8.5	6.9	8.8	9.5	12.6	13.1	20.1
HUMIDITY/%	89	88	86	85	85	83	82	83	84	85	87	88
BLOOM SEASON	N/A											
DAYS CLR @ 7AM	1	0	1	2	3	2	4	1	2	1	1	1
DAYS CLR @ 1PM	0	0	0	0	0	1	1	1	0	0	0	0
RAIN/MM	688	500	361	246	229	216	175	224	241	320	333	511
°C AVG MAX	31.1	31.1	31.7	32.2	32.8	32.8	32.8	33.3	32.2	32.2	32.2	31.1
°C AVG MIN	22.2	22.2	22.2	22.2	22.2	22.8	22.2	22.2	22.2	22.2	22.2	22.2
DIURNAL RANGE	8.9	8.9	9.5	10.0	10.6	10.0	10.6	11.1	10.0	10.0	10.0	8.9
S/HEMISPHERE	JUL	AUG	SEP	OCT	NOV	DEC	JAN	FEB	MAR	APR	MAY	JUN

Cultural Recommendations

LIGHT: 2000–3000 fc.

TEMPERATURES: Throughout the year, days average 88–92°F (31–33°C), and nights average 72–73°F (22–23°C), with a diurnal range of 16–20°F (9–11°C). The diurnal range is unusually large for a habitat with so little seasonal variation.

HUMIDITY: 80–90% year-round. High humidity and excellent air circulation are important.

WATER: Rainfall is very heavy all year. Plants should be kept moist but not soggy. Warm water may be beneficial.

FERTILIZER: ¼–½ recommended strength. A balanced fertilizer should be applied weekly to biweekly throughout the year.

REST PERIOD: Growing conditions should be maintained all year. The record low is only 10°F (6°C) below the average lows. Although rainfall remains heavy in winter, water may be reduced somewhat for cultivated plants, especially those grown in the dark, short-day conditions common in temperate latitudes. They should never be allowed to dry out completely, however. In the habitat, light is highest in winter.

GROWING MEDIA: Plants may be mounted on tree-fern or cork slabs if humidity is high and plants are watered at least once daily in summer. When plants are potted, any open, fast-draining medium may be used. They may be repotted anytime new roots are growing.

Plant and Flower Information

PLANT SIZE AND TYPE: A 10–15 in. (25–38 cm) sympodial epiphyte.

PSEUDOBULB: 4–5 in. (10–13 cm) long. The stems are erect, cylindrical, and woody. They are widely spaced and appear to be extensions of the creeping rhizome. The rhizome branches and roots along its entire length.

LEAVES: 3 per growth. The broad, oblong leaves are 6–7 in. (15–17 cm) long. They are sharply pointed with many veins.

INFLORESCENCE: Short. Inflorescences emerge near the apex of the stem.

FLOWERS: 1–3 per inflorescence. The flowers, which remain rather closed, are 0.5 in. (1.3 cm) long. Flower color was not reported.

REFERENCES: 229, 254, 286.

Dendrobium beckleri F. Mueller. See *D. schoeninum* Lindley. *D. beckleri* F. Mueller var. *racemosum* Nicholls is considered a synonym of *D. racemosum* (Nicholls) Clemesha and Dockrill. REFERENCES: 23, 36, 67, 105, 152, 154, 188, 216, 240, 243, 254, 262, 325, 330, 390, 421, 495, 533. PHOTOS/DRAWINGS: *36*, 105, *390*.

Dendrobium begoniicarpum J. J. Smith. See *D. subacaule* Reinwardt ex Lindley. REFERENCES: 221, 385, 445, 470.

Dendrobium bellatulum Rolfe

ORIGIN/HABITAT: Widespread across southeast Asia. Plants are found in northeastern India, including Sikkim and the Khasi (Khasia) Hills. They also grow on the southern Shan Plateau of eastern Burma, in northern Thailand, in the Sedone region of Laos, near Dalat in Vietnam, and in Yunnan and Mengtze Provinces of southwestern China. Plants are normally found in open, deciduous forests at 2950–5600 ft. (900–1700 m), but are reported from as high as 6900 ft. (2100 m).

CLIMATE: Station #48327, Chiang Mai, Thailand, Lat. 18.8°N, Long. 99.0°E, at 1100 ft. (335 m). Temperatures are calculated for an elevation of 4000 ft. (1200 m), resulting in probable extremes of 99°F (37°C) and 28°F (–2°C).

Dendrobium bensoniae

N/HEMISPHERE	JAN	FEB	MAR	APR	MAY	JUN	JUL	AUG	SEP	OCT	NOV	DEC
°F AVG MAX	75	80	85	86	84	80	79	77	78	79	76	74
°F AVG MIN	46	47	52	60	64	64	64	65	63	61	56	47
DIURNAL RANGE	29	33	33	26	20	16	15	12	15	18	20	27
RAIN/INCHES	0.3	0.4	0.6	2.0	5.5	6.1	7.4	8.7	11.5	4.9	1.5	0.4
HUMIDITY/%	73	65	58	62	73	78	80	83	83	81	79	76
BLOOM SEASON	*	*	***	**	*	*	*	*	*	*	*	*
DAYS CLR @ 7AM	5	5	2	2	1	0	0	0	0	1	3	3
DAYS CLR @ 1PM	9	8	4	2	0	0	0	0	0	0	1	3
RAIN/MM	8	10	15	51	140	155	188	221	292	124	38	10
°C AVG MAX	24.1	26.9	29.7	30.2	29.1	26.9	26.4	25.2	25.8	26.4	24.7	23.6
°C AVG MIN	8.0	8.6	11.3	15.8	18.0	18.0	18.0	18.6	17.5	16.4	13.6	8.6
DIURNAL RANGE	16.1	18.3	18.4	14.4	11.1	8.9	8.4	6.6	8.3	10.0	11.1	15.0
S/HEMISPHERE	JUL	AUG	SEP	OCT	NOV	DEC	JAN	FEB	MAR	APR	MAY	JUN

Cultural Recommendations

LIGHT: 3500–4000 fc. In cultivation, *D. bellatulum* is healthiest in a bright, sunny location with only light shade.

TEMPERATURES: Summer days average 77–80°F (25–27°C), and nights average 64–65°F (18–19°C), with a diurnal range of 12–16°F (7–9°C). The warmest weather occurs in spring. Days average 84–86°F (29–30°C), and nights average 52–64°F (11–18°C), with a diurnal range of 20–33°F (11–18°C).

HUMIDITY: 75–85% during most of the year, dropping to near 60% for 2 months in late winter and early spring.

WATER: Rainfall is heavy while plants are actively growing from spring to early autumn. During this season, cultivated plants should be kept moist with little if any drying allowed between waterings. However, water should be gradually reduced after new growths mature in autumn.

FERTILIZER: ¼–½ recommended strength, applied weekly. A high-nitrogen fertilizer is beneficial from spring to midsummer, but a fertilizer high in phosphates should be used in late summer and autumn. Some growers report good success alternating applications of fish emulsion with their regular fertilizer.

REST PERIOD: Winter days average 74–80°F (24–27°C), and nights average 46–47°F (8–9°C), with a diurnal range of 27–33°F (15–18°C). Overnight lows are below 50°F (10°C) for 3 months. Plants should be able to tolerate temperatures a few degrees below freezing for short periods, but extremes should be avoided in cultivation. During very cold weather, a plant's chance of surviving with minimal damage is better if it is dry when temperatures are low. In the habitat, winter rainfall is low for 4–5 months, and humidity falls to 58–65%, indicating distinctly reduced moisture. During the early part of the dry season, however, additional moisture is available from dew and as mist from fog and low clouds. Cultivated plants should be allowed to dry out between waterings, but they should not remain dry for extended periods. Fertilizer should be greatly reduced or eliminated anytime water is reduced. In the habitat, light is slightly higher in winter, but increased light may not be critical in cultivation. Low night temperatures or wide diurnal range may be necessary to initiate blooming.

GROWING MEDIA: Plants are best mounted on tree-fern slabs. When plants must be potted, chopped tree-fern in small clay pots is commonly recommended, but any open, fast-draining medium may be used providing it accommodates the very fine roots. *D. bellatulum* should be potted in the smallest possible clay pot so that roots dry between waterings. Because of this, slab culture is often preferred; but plants must be watered at least once daily in summer. The growths are tightly clustered, so repotting is seldom necessary until the medium breaks down. Growers report that plants may be set back severely by repotting and often require an extended period to recover their normal vigor. Repotting is best done in early spring when new roots are growing.

MISCELLANEOUS NOTES: The bloom season shown in the climate table is based on cultivation records. Although plants bloom most heavily in late spring, *D. bellatulum* is reported in bloom nearly every month of the year except Dec. (Jun.). It is closely related to, and shares the same habitat with, *D. christyanum* which is a slightly larger plant with larger flowers that blooms summer through autumn. Growers often consider *D. bellatulum* a problem plant, so careful attention should be paid to its cultural needs. Plants grow with *D. draconis* Rchb. f. and *D. cariniferum* Rchb. f.

Collected plants are dried and used in Chinese medicine.

Plant and Flower Information

PLANT SIZE AND TYPE: A miniature, 2–4 in. (5–10 cm) sympodial epiphyte.

PSEUDOBULB: 1–3 in. (2.5–8.0 cm) long. The plump, chunky pseudobulbs are ovoid to elliptical, tightly clustered, and ridged lengthwise. They are covered with black hairs that persist for years.

LEAVES: 2–4 per growth. The leathery leaves are 1.2–2.4 in. (3–6 cm) long, dull gray-green, and eventually deciduous. They are bilobed at the apex. The upper surface is textured, and the back of each leaf is covered with black hairs.

INFLORESCENCE: Very short. The blossoms are held very close to the stem. The stems continue to produce flowers for many years even after leaves fall.

FLOWERS: 1, rarely 2 or 3 per inflorescence. The long-lasting blossoms are 1.5–1.8 in. (3.8–4.6 cm) across, which is exceptionally large relative to the plant size. Sepals and petals are creamy white with green veins and sparkle in the light. The lip is brilliantly colored with yellow at the base, a pink or very deep purple patch near the apex, vermilion on the sidelobes, and a bright orange-red tip. The lip has 5 warty keels. The colors deepen as the flower ages. The midlobe turns down sharply at the end. The flowers are faintly fragrant, especially in the evening.

HYBRIDIZING NOTES: Chromosome count is 2n = 38 (ref. 152).

REFERENCES: 36, 38, 46, 152, 165, 179, 190, 196, 208, 210, 219, 233, 245, 254, 266, 291, 330, 332, 333, 349, 366, 369, 371, 414, 429, 430, 445, 447, 448, 454, 524, 528, 568.

PHOTOS/DRAWINGS: *50, 124,* 210, *245, 291, 332, 349, 366, 371, 430, 454.*

Dendrobium bellum J. J. Smith. See *D. eximium* Schlechter.

REFERENCES: 83, 220, 254, 437.

Dendrobium bensoniae Rchb. f.

AKA: Sometimes spelled *D. bensonae*. The International Orchid Commission (ref. 236) lists *D. signatum* as a synonym of *D. bensoniae* Rchb. f. but registers hybrids under the name *D. signatum* Rchb. f. However, Seidenfaden (ref. 454) maintains them as separate species.

ORIGIN/HABITAT: Northeastern India, Burma, and possibly Thailand. Plants grow at about 5000 ft. (1520 m) in the Indian states of Manipur and Mizoram. They are found in the hills of eastern and western Burma from the latitude of Bhamo in the north to the latitude of Moulmein in the south. The original discovery in Burma was reported west of Prome at about 1500 ft. (457 m). Other reports indicate that plants grow at moderate elevations. Although plants are sometimes reported to occur in Thailand, Seidenfaden (ref. 454) indicates that he has been unable to locate records or plants that would confirm these reports.

CLIMATE: Station #48035, Lashio, Burma, Lat. 23.0°N, Long. 97.8°E, at 2450 ft. (747 m). Temperatures are calculated for an elevation of 3300 ft. (1000 m), resulting in probable extremes of 101°F (39°C) and 28°F (−2°C).

Dendrobium bialatum

N/HEMISPHERE	JAN	FEB	MAR	APR	MAY	JUN	JUL	AUG	SEP	OCT	NOV	DEC
°F AVG MAX	71	75	82	86	84	81	80	79	80	79	74	70
°F AVG MIN	43	46	53	59	64	67	67	67	66	61	54	46
DIURNAL RANGE	28	29	29	27	20	14	13	12	14	18	20	24
RAIN/INCHES	0.2	0.4	0.5	2.2	6.7	10.1	11.7	12.8	7.9	5.6	2.9	0.9
HUMIDITY/%	75	66	59	60	71	78	83	85	81	83	80	78
BLOOM SEASON					*	*						
DAYS CLR @ 7AM	1	12	15	13	7	2	0	0	0	0	0	2
DAYS CLR @ 1PM	20	21	22	12	4	0	0	0	2	4	12	18
RAIN/MM	5	10	13	56	170	257	297	325	201	142	74	23
°C AVG MAX	21.8	24.0	27.9	30.1	29.0	27.4	26.8	26.3	26.8	26.3	23.5	21.3
°C AVG MIN	6.3	7.9	11.8	15.1	17.9	19.6	19.6	19.6	19.0	16.3	12.4	7.9
DIURNAL RANGE	15.5	16.1	16.1	15.0	11.1	7.8	7.2	6.7	7.8	10.0	11.1	13.4
S/HEMISPHERE	JUL	AUG	SEP	OCT	NOV	DEC	JAN	FEB	MAR	APR	MAY	JUN

Cultural Recommendations

LIGHT: 2500–3500 fc.

TEMPERATURES: Summer days average 79–81°F (26–27°C), and nights average 67°F (20°C), with a diurnal range of 12–14°F (7–8°C). The warmest weather occurs in spring. Days average 82–86°F (28–30°C), and nights average 53–64°F (12–18°C), with a diurnal range of 20–29°F (11–16°C).

HUMIDITY: 80–85% during the growing season, dropping to near 75% in early winter. Humidity is lowest during clear, dry weather in early spring when it averages 60% for about 2 months.

WATER: Rainfall is heavy while plants are actively growing from late spring to early autumn. During this season, cultivated plants should be kept moist with little if any drying allowed between waterings. However, water should be gradually reduced after new growths mature in autumn.

FERTILIZER: ¼–½ recommended strength, applied weekly. A high-nitrogen fertilizer is beneficial from spring to midsummer, but a fertilizer high in phosphates should be used in late summer and autumn.

REST PERIOD: Winter days average 70–75°F (21–24°C), and nights average 43–46°F (6–8°C), with a diurnal range of 24–29°F (13–16°C). Overnight lows are below 50°F (10°C) for 3 months. Plants should be able to tolerate temperatures a few degrees below freezing for short periods, but extremes should be avoided in cultivation. During very cold weather, a plant's chance of surviving with minimal damage is better if it is dry when temperatures are low. In the habitat, winter rainfall is low for 4–5 months, and humidity falls to near 60% in late winter and early spring, indicating distinctly reduced moisture. During the early part of the dry season, additional moisture is available from dew and as mist from fog and low clouds. For most of the winter, cultivated plants should be allowed to dry out between waterings, but they should not remain dry for extended periods. For 1–2 months in spring, however, weather in the habitat is clear, warm, and dry. Humidity is so low that even moisture from morning dew is uncommon. In cultivation, water should be further reduced to only an occasional early morning misting for 1–2 months. In the habitat, light is slightly higher in winter, but in cultivation increased light may not be critical. Low night temperatures or wide diurnal range may be necessary to initiate blooming. Growers indicate that the plant's health begins to decline in about 2 years unless it rests over winter.

GROWING MEDIA: Mounting accommodates the sometimes pendulous growth habit. Plants may be mounted on tree-fern or cork slabs if humidity is high and plants are watered at least once daily in summer. When plants are potted, any open, fast-draining medium may be used. Repotting is best done in early spring when new roots are growing.

MISCELLANEOUS NOTES: The bloom season shown in the climate table is based on reports from the habitat. *D. bensoniae* usually does not adapt to a warm, uniform climate, and reportedly grows and flowers poorly in Singapore.

Plant and Flower Information

PLANT SIZE AND TYPE: A 12–30 in. (30–75 cm) sympodial epiphyte.

PSEUDOBULB: 10–28 in. (25–70 cm) long. The yellow pseudobulbs, which are fleshy and stemlike, may be erect or pendulous. They are cylindrical without swollen nodes.

LEAVES: More than 1 per growth. Eventually deciduous, the leathery leaves may be linear, lanceolate, or oval and 2–3 in. (5–8 cm) long.

INFLORESCENCE: 2 in. (5 cm) long. Inflorescences, which appear 1 or 2 at a node, emerge from upper nodes of leafless pseudobulbs.

FLOWERS: 1–3 per inflorescence. The sparkling flowers are 2.0–2.5 in. (5–6 cm) across. Sometimes twisted, the sepals and petals may be lavender, greenish, or pure milk-white. The yellow to orange lip is edged with white and marked with a yellow disk in the center. Most clones are decorated with 2 maroon spots in the throat, but in rare instances, the spots are absent, and even more rarely the flowers are pure white without any markings. The lip is downy, concave, toothed along the margin, with a cluster of long, fine hairs on the narrow neck of the lip. The fragrant flowers last longer than 2 months.

HYBRIDIZING NOTES: Chromosome counts are 2n = 38 (ref. 153, 154, 542).

REFERENCES: 6, 153, 154, 157, 190, 200, 202, 210, 216, 236, 254, 266, 369, 430, 445, 448, 454, 541, 542, 557, 570.

PHOTOS/DRAWINGS: 210, *369, 430*, 454, 541.

Dendrobium bialatum J. J. Smith

AKA: *Cadetia parvula* Schlechter. *Cadetia* is now considered a valid genus by some botanists, so this plant may again be considered a *Cadetia*.

ORIGIN/HABITAT: Papua New Guinea. Plants grow at 1500–1950 ft. (450–600 m) in the forests on Mt. Gomadjidji and along Govidjoa Creek in the Waria District.

CLIMATE: Station #200192, Garaina, Papua New Guinea, Lat. 7.9°S, Long. 147.1°E, at 2350 ft. (716 m). Temperatures are calculated for an elevation of 1500 ft. (460 m), resulting in probable extremes of 97°F (36°C) and 49°F (9°C).

N/HEMISPHERE	JAN	FEB	MAR	APR	MAY	JUN	JUL	AUG	SEP	OCT	NOV	DEC
°F AVG MAX	83	85	86	87	88	88	88	88	87	87	86	84
°F AVG MIN	66	66	66	67	66	67	68	68	68	67	67	66
DIURNAL RANGE	17	19	20	20	22	21	20	20	19	20	19	18
RAIN/INCHES	5.8	6.5	8.7	11.1	11.8	11.9	8.9	11.7	11.5	9.9	7.7	5.2
HUMIDITY/%	84	82	82	81	80	80	81	81	82	83	84	84
BLOOM SEASON										*		
DAYS CLR	N/A											
RAIN/MM	147	165	221	282	300	302	226	297	292	251	196	132
°C AVG MAX	28.2	29.3	29.9	30.4	31.0	31.0	31.0	31.0	30.4	30.4	29.9	28.8
°C AVG MIN	18.8	18.8	18.8	19.3	18.8	19.3	19.9	19.9	19.9	19.3	19.3	18.8
DIURNAL RANGE	9.4	10.5	11.1	11.1	12.2	11.7	11.1	11.1	10.5	11.1	10.6	10.0
S/HEMISPHERE	JUL	AUG	SEP	OCT	NOV	DEC	JAN	FEB	MAR	APR	MAY	JUN

Cultural Recommendations

LIGHT: 2500–3500 fc.

TEMPERATURES: Throughout the year, days average 83–88°F (28–31°C), and nights average 66–68°F (19–20°C), with a diurnal range of 20–21°F (11–12°C).

HUMIDITY: 80–85% year-round.

WATER: Rainfall is heavy year-round, with a slightly drier period in winter. Cultivated plants should be kept moist and never be allowed to dry out completely.

FERTILIZER: ¼–½ recommended strength. A balanced fertilizer should be applied weekly to biweekly throughout the year.

REST PERIOD: Growing conditions vary only slightly during the year. In the habitat, rainfall is slightly lower in winter. Water should be reduced for cultivated plants, especially those grown in the dark, short-day conditions common in temperate-latitude winters. Plants should never be allowed to dry out completely, however. Fertilizer should be reduced or eliminated anytime water is reduced.

GROWING MEDIA: Plants may be mounted on tree-fern or cork slabs if humidity is high and the plants are watered at least once daily in summer. When plants are potted, any open, fast-draining medium may be used. Repotting is best done in early spring when new roots are growing.

MISCELLANEOUS NOTES: The bloom season shown in the climate table is based on reports from the habitat.

Plant and Flower Information

PLANT SIZE AND TYPE: A 0.4 in. (1 cm) sympodial epiphyte. *D. bialatum* may be the smallest in the genus.

PSEUDOBULB: 0.1–0.2 in. (0.3–0.5 cm) long. The stems are cylindrical, erect to ascending, and tightly clustered on a rooting rhizome.

LEAVES: 1 per growth. The oblong to oval leaves are 0.2–0.3 in. (0.5–0.8 cm) long.

INFLORESCENCE: Very short. Inflorescences are borne at the base of the leaf near the apex of the stem.

FLOWERS: 1 per inflorescence. Flowers are less than 0.1 in. (0.3 cm) across. Sepals and petals are white. The lip is pale yellow in front. The anther is green.

REFERENCES: 221, 437, 472.

Dendrobium bicallosum Ridley

ORIGIN/HABITAT: Sumatra. Plants grow on Kerinci (Korinchi) Peak at 7300 ft. (2220 m).

CLIMATE: Station #96163, Padang, Sumatra, Indonesia, Lat. 0.9°S, Long. 100.4°E, at 19 ft. (6 m). Temperatures are calculated for an elevation of 7200 ft. (2200 m), resulting in probable extremes of 70°F (21°C) and 44°F (7°C).

N/HEMISPHERE	JAN	FEB	MAR	APR	MAY	JUN	JUL	AUG	SEP	OCT	NOV	DEC
°F AVG MAX	63	63	62	62	62	62	63	63	63	63	64	63
°F AVG MIN	50	50	50	50	50	50	50	50	50	51	51	50
DIURNAL RANGE	13	13	12	12	12	12	13	13	13	12	13	13
RAIN/INCHES	10.9	13.7	6.0	19.5	20.4	18.9	13.8	10.2	12.1	14.3	12.4	12.1
HUMIDITY/%	81	82	82	84	85	84	81	81	82	83	81	81
BLOOM SEASON	N/A											
DAYS CLR @ 7AM	5	1	1	0	0	2	2	1	2	2	3	5
DAYS CLR @ 1PM	5	2	2	1	1	3	3	4	3	3	6	5
RAIN/MM	277	348	152	495	518	480	351	259	307	363	315	307
°C AVG MAX	17.4	17.4	16.8	16.8	16.8	16.8	17.4	17.4	17.4	17.4	17.9	17.4
°C AVG MIN	10.2	10.2	10.2	10.2	10.2	10.2	10.2	10.2	10.2	10.7	10.7	10.2
DIURNAL RANGE	7.2	7.2	6.6	6.6	6.6	6.6	7.2	7.2	7.2	6.7	7.2	7.2
S/HEMISPHERE	JUL	AUG	SEP	OCT	NOV	DEC	JAN	FEB	MAR	APR	MAY	JUN

Cultural Recommendations

LIGHT: 2000–3000 fc.

TEMPERATURES: Throughout the year, days average 62–64°F (17–18°C), and nights average 50–51°F (10–11°C), with a diurnal range of 12–13°F (7°C). Probable extremes vary only a few degrees from the averages, indicating that plants may not tolerate wide temperature fluctuations.

HUMIDITY: 80–85% year-round.

WATER: Rainfall is very heavy all year. Cultivated plants should be constantly moist but not soggy.

FERTILIZER: ¼–½ recommended strength. A balanced fertilizer should be applied weekly to biweekly throughout the year.

REST PERIOD: Growing conditions should be maintained year-round. Water may be reduced somewhat for cultivated plants in winter, especially those grown in the dark, short-day conditions common in temperate latitudes. They should never be allowed to dry out completely, however.

GROWING MEDIA: Mounting plants on tree-fern or cork slabs accommodates their pendulous growth habit. However, humidity must be high and plants must be watered at least once a day in summer. If plants cannot be mounted, small pots or hanging baskets may be filled with an open, fast-draining medium. Repotting may be done anytime new roots are actively growing.

Plant and Flower Information

PLANT SIZE AND TYPE: An 18 in. (45 cm) sympodial epiphyte.

PSEUDOBULB: 18 in. (45 cm) long. The stems are very slender.

LEAVES: The pointed, lanceolate leaves, which are 4 in. (10 cm) long, are somewhat leathery.

INFLORESCENCE: Short. Racemes emerge from upper leaf axils.

FLOWERS: 3–4 per inflorescence. The flowers are 0.6 in. (1.5 cm) across. All segments are white with yellow at the base of the lip. The stalk is pale pink.

REFERENCES: 222, 401.

Dendrobium bicameratum Wallich ex Lindley

AKA: *D. bolboflorum* Falconer ex Hooker f., *D. breviflorum* Lindley.

ORIGIN/HABITAT: India and Southeast Asia. Plants grow at 3900–8000 ft. (1200–2440 m) from the Dehra Dun and Garhwal regions of northern India, across central Nepal, Sikkim, Bhutan, and the Khasi (Khasia) Hills in northeastern India. Distribution continues eastward across Burma, and northern Thailand. Plants commonly grow at the base of trees, where they receive ample moisture and protection from extreme temperature fluctuations.

CLIMATE: Station #42398, Baghdogra, India, Lat. 26.7°N, Long. 88.3°E, at 412 ft. (126 m). Temperatures are calculated for an elevation of 5000 ft. (1520 m), resulting in probable extremes of 89°F (32°C) and 21°F (–6°C).

N/HEMISPHERE	JAN	FEB	MAR	APR	MAY	JUN	JUL	AUG	SEP	OCT	NOV	DEC
°F AVG MAX	59	62	70	75	75	74	74	74	73	72	67	62
°F AVG MIN	35	39	45	53	58	61	62	62	61	55	45	38
DIURNAL RANGE	24	23	25	22	17	13	12	12	12	17	22	24
RAIN/INCHES	0.3	0.7	1.3	3.7	11.8	25.9	32.2	25.3	21.2	5.6	0.5	0.2
HUMIDITY/%	73	68	57	58	74	84	86	85	85	79	75	76
BLOOM SEASON						*	**	**	*			
DAYS CLR @6AM	21	18	15	11	5	0	1	1	4	13	23	19
DAYS CLR @ 12PM	23	16	16	11	2	2	0	1	2	10	21	18
DAYS CLR @ 6PM	15	14	13	10	7	3	1	1	2	14	17	14
RAIN/MM	8	18	33	94	300	658	818	643	538	142	13	5
°C AVG MAX	14.9	16.6	21.0	23.8	23.8	23.3	23.3	23.3	22.7	22.1	19.4	16.6
°C AVG MIN	1.6	3.8	7.1	11.6	14.4	16.0	16.6	16.6	16.0	12.7	7.1	3.3
DIURNAL RANGE	13.3	12.8	13.9	12.2	9.4	7.3	6.7	6.7	6.7	9.4	12.3	13.3
S/HEMISPHERE	JUL	AUG	SEP	OCT	NOV	DEC	JAN	FEB	MAR	APR	MAY	JUN

Cultural Recommendations

LIGHT: 2000–3000 fc. Diffused light is suggested.

TEMPERATURES: Summer days average 74°F (23°C), and nights average 61–62°F (16–17°C), with a diurnal range of 12–13°F (7°C). Due to the effects of the microclimate, actual temperatures in the habitat may be 6–8°F (3–4°C) warmer than indicated.

HUMIDITY: 75–85% year-round. Humidity drops to near 60% in early spring.

WATER: Conditions are very wet for 5 months in summer, very dry for 5 months in winter, with short transition periods in autumn and spring. Cultivated plants should be kept evenly moist from spring to early autumn, but water should be gradually reduced after new growths mature in late autumn.

FERTILIZER: ¼–½ recommended strength, applied weekly. A high-nitrogen fertilizer is beneficial from spring to midsummer, but a fertilizer high in phosphates should be used in late summer and autumn.

Dendrobium bicarinatum

REST PERIOD: For 2–4 months in winter, days average 59–70°F (15–21°C), and nights average 35–45°F (2–7°C), with a diurnal range of 23–25°F (13–14°C). Reports from the habitat indicate than frost is not uncommon. Plants should survive brief exposure to freezing conditions, particularly if they are dry. However, extreme conditions should be avoided in cultivation. In the habitat, winter rainfall is low, but additional moisture is often available from heavy deposits of dew. For about a month in late winter or early spring, however, humidity is so low that even the moisture from dew is uncommon. Cultivated plants should be allowed to dry out between waterings in winter, but they should not remain dry for extended periods. Occasional early morning mistings between waterings, especially on warm, sunny days, may help prevent the plants from becoming too dry. Fertilizer should be eliminated until water is increased in spring. In the habitat, light is highest in winter. The cool, dry rest with increased light may be necessary to initiate blooming.

GROWING MEDIA: Plants may be mounted on tree-fern or cork slabs if humidity is high and plants are watered at least once daily in summer. When plants are potted, any open, fast-draining medium may be used. Repotting is best done in early spring when new roots begin to grow. Repotting after flowering is too late for the plants to become reestablished before winter.

MISCELLANEOUS NOTES: The bloom season shown in the climate table is the same for wild and cultivated plants.

Plant and Flower Information

PLANT SIZE AND TYPE: A 12–18 in. (30–45 cm) sympodial epiphyte. Plants may be as small as 4 in. (10 cm).

PSEUDOBULB: 10–18 in. (25–45 cm) long. The clustered pseudobulbs are erect and taper at the base.

LEAVES: 3–4 per growth. The papery leaves are deciduous, oblong to linear-lanceolate, and 2–4 in. (5–10 cm) long.

INFLORESCENCE: Numerous inflorescences emerge from nodes near the apex of leafy and leafless pseudobulbs. The densely crowded flowers form circular clusters at the apex of the pseudobulb at the level of the leaf bases.

FLOWERS: 2 per inflorescence. The fleshy flowers, which are 0.4 in. (1.0 cm) across, are small for the plant size. The petals and reflexed sepals, which may be greenish or dirty yellow, are marked with rows of dull red or purple speckles. The golden yellow lip is small and fleshy with pink to dark red sidelobes and an hourglass-shaped callus. Flower color is highly variable.

HYBRIDIZING NOTES: Chromosome counts are n = 19 (ref. 150, 154, 542), n = 19 + 0 – 4B (ref. 153), 2n = 38 (ref. 150, 152, 153, 504, 542, 580), and 2n = 40 (ref. 154, 504, 542, 580). Johansen (ref. 239) indicates that plants are self-sterile and that flowers dropped 7–9 days after self-pollination.

REFERENCES: 32, 38, 46, 102, 119, 150, 152, 153, 154, 157, 179, 202, 216, 218, 239, 254, 278, 294, 310, 317, 369, 374, 376, 427, 445, 454, 504, 542, 577, 580.

PHOTOS/DRAWINGS: 32, 46, 102, 427, *454*.

Dendrobium bicarinatum Ames and Schweinfurth.
Now considered a synonym of *Flickingeria bicarinata* (Ames and Schweinfurth) A. Hawkes. REFERENCES: 12, 213, 222, 229, 231, 286.

Dendrobium bicaudatum Kränzlin.
See *D. bicaudatum* Reinwardt ex Lindley. REFERENCES: 436.

Dendrobium bicaudatum Reinwardt ex Lindley

AKA: *D. antelope* Rchb. f., *D. burbidgei* Rchb. f., *D. demmenii* J. J. Smith, *D. minax* Rchb. f., *D. rumphianum* Teijsm. and Binn. The International Orchid Commission (ref. 236) lists hybrids under both *D. minax* and *D. rumphianum*.

ORIGIN/HABITAT: Northern Sulawesi (Celebes), the Sulu Archipelago, and the islands of Ambon and Seram in the Moluccas. On Sulawesi, plants grow from among rocks at sea level to the lower boundary of the mist-forest at about 3300 ft. (0–1000 m).

CLIMATE: Station #97014, Manado, Sulawesi, Lat. 1.5°N, Long. 124.9°E, at 264 ft. (80 m). Temperatures are calculated for an elevation of 3000 ft. (910 m), resulting in probable extremes of 88°F (31°C) and 56°F (13°C).

N/HEMISPHERE	JAN	FEB	MAR	APR	MAY	JUN	JUL	AUG	SEP	OCT	NOV	DEC
°F AVG MAX	76	76	76	77	78	78	78	80	80	80	78	77
°F AVG MIN	64	64	64	64	65	64	64	64	64	63	64	65
DIURNAL RANGE	12	12	12	13	13	14	14	16	16	17	14	12
RAIN/INCHES	18.6	13.8	12.2	8.0	6.4	6.5	4.8	4.0	3.4	4.9	8.9	14.7
HUMIDITY/%	84	83	83	83	81	80	75	72	75	77	82	83
BLOOM SEASON	*			*			*		*	*	*	*
DAYS CLR @ 8AM	4	3	6	11	11	12	12	12	14	17	12	8
DAYS CLR @ 2PM	1	1	1	2	1	3	3	4	4	4	1	1
RAIN/MM	472	351	310	203	163	165	122	102	86	124	226	373
°C AVG MAX	24.4	24.4	24.4	25.0	25.5	25.5	25.5	26.7	26.7	26.7	25.5	25.0
°C AVG MIN	17.8	17.8	17.8	17.8	18.3	17.8	17.8	17.8	17.8	17.2	17.8	18.3
DIURNAL RANGE	6.6	6.6	6.6	7.2	7.2	7.7	7.7	8.9	8.9	9.5	7.7	6.7
S/HEMISPHERE	JUL	AUG	SEP	OCT	NOV	DEC	JAN	FEB	MAR	APR	MAY	JUN

Cultural Recommendations

LIGHT: 1800–2500 fc. The habitat is usually overcast in the afternoon.

TEMPERATURES: Throughout the year, days average 76–80°F (24–27°C), and nights average 64–65°F (18°C), with a diurnal range of 12–17°F (7–9°C). Hot dry conditions or wide temperature fluctuations should be avoided as weather in this habitat is moderate year-round. Record extreme temperatures are only a few degrees above or below the averages. Plants may not tolerant wide temperature fluctuations.

HUMIDITY: 80–85% most of the year, dropping to 70–75% in late summer and autumn.

WATER: Rainfall is moderate to heavy through the year. The driest period occurs in late summer and early autumn. Plants should be kept moist year-round with only slight drying allowed between waterings.

FERTILIZER: ¼–½ recommended strength. A balanced fertilizer should be applied weekly to biweekly throughout the year.

REST PERIOD: Growing temperatures should be maintained all year. The plants may rest during the 1–2 month drier period which occurs in late summer and coincides with the period of greatest diurnal range. Cultivated plants should dry out slightly during this period, but they should never remain dry for long. The heaviest rainfall in the habitat occurs in winter, but water should not be increased for cultivated plants. In fact, water should be reduced somewhat for plants grown in the dark, short-day conditions common in temperate latitudes, but they should not be allowed to dry out completely.

GROWING MEDIA: Mounting accommodates the pendulous growth habit. Plants may be mounted on tree-fern or cork slabs, but in summer they must be watered at least once daily, and more frequently on the hottest days. When plants must be potted, any open, fast-draining medium may be used. Repotting is best done when new roots are growing.

MISCELLANEOUS NOTES: The bloom season shown in the climate table is based on reports from the habitat. Cultivated plants known as *D. minax* bloom throughout the year. Other reports indicate that blooming occurs during the rainy season. *D. bicaudatum* is frequently cultivated in Java.

Plant and Flower Information

PLANT SIZE AND TYPE: A pendulous, 12–20 in. (30–50 cm) sympodial epiphyte.

PSEUDOBULB: 12–20 in. (30–50 cm) long. The clustered, canelike pseudobulbs are swollen near the middle. Stems consist of up to 20 nodes.

LEAVES: Many. The leaves are lanceolate, most often suberect, and 0.5–1.0 in. (1.3–2.5 cm) long, although leaves on plants known as *D. minax* may reach a length of 3.6 in. (9 cm).

INFLORESCENCE: 3–6 in. (8–15 cm) long. Inflorescences emerge from nodes near the apex of the pseudobulbs. Often 2 or more inflorescences are produced at a time, each with 1–3 flowers. They usually do not branch.

FLOWERS: 1–3, rarely 5 per inflorescence. The flowers are 1.4–2.0 in. (3.5–5.0 cm) across. Sepals and petals are linear-lanceolate. The dorsal sepal is recurved. Flower color is variable, but sepals and petals are commonly white, yellow-green, or green, with or without a brown, purple, or red suffusion. The lip, which is pointed at the tip, is white or greenish white marked with purple veins and red keels. The form originally known as *D. minax* is rose-purple with carmine lines on the lip.

HYBRIDIZING NOTES: As a parent, *D. bicaudatum* tends to contribute long-lasting flowers and frequent bloom periods so that plants may be in bloom most of the year. It also contributes short plant stature and the antelope flower shape with stiffly erect petals. The flower form persists for several generations.

REFERENCES: 25, 84, 179, 196, 216, 236, 254, 278, 286, 310, 343, 344, 436, 469, 483.

PHOTOS/DRAWINGS: *84, 343, 344*.

Dendrobium bicolor Lindley. Now considered a synonym of *Eria lindleyi* Thwaites. REFERENCES: 216, 254, 277.

Dendrobium bicolor Persoon. Now considered a synonym of *Maxillaria bicolor* Ruiz and Pavón. REFERENCES: 216, 254.

Dendrobium bicornutum Schlechter

AKA: Kränzlin (ref. 254) and J. J. Smith (ref. 486) considered *D. bicornutum* Schlechter a synonym of *D. lobatum* (Blume) Miquel, but present day taxonomists do not include this synonymy.

ORIGIN/HABITAT: Endemic to Borneo. Plants were reportedly found near Kwaru growing in mangroves as well as high in trees near Moeara Kelindjau. Because we have been unable to find either of these locations, the following climate data should be used with caution.

CLIMATE: Station #96583, Pontianak, Borneo, Lat. 0.0°N, Long. 109.3°E, at 13 ft. (4 m). Temperatures are calculated for an elevation of 1000 ft. (328 m), resulting in probable extremes of 93°F (34°C) and 65°F (18°C).

N/HEMISPHERE	JAN	FEB	MAR	APR	MAY	JUN	JUL	AUG	SEP	OCT	NOV	DEC
°F AVG MAX	84	86	86	86	87	87	86	87	87	86	85	84
°F AVG MIN	71	73	72	72	72	72	71	72	72	72	72	71
DIURNAL RANGE	13	13	14	14	15	15	15	15	16	15	14	13	13
RAIN/INCHES	10.8	8.2	9.5	10.9	11.1	8.7	6.5	8.0	9.0	14.4	15.3	12.7
HUMIDITY/%	85	85	84	84	82	81	79	82	83	87	86	87
BLOOM SEASON						*	*					
DAYS CLR @ 7AM	1	1	1	3	2	4	5	1	2	1	1	2
DAYS CLR @ 1PM	0	0	1	0	0	0	1	1	1	0	1	0
RAIN/MM	274	208	241	277	282	221	165	203	229	366	389	323
°C AVG MAX	28.7	29.9	29.9	29.9	30.4	30.4	29.9	30.4	30.4	29.9	29.3	28.7
°C AVG MIN	21.5	22.6	22.1	22.1	22.1	22.1	21.5	21.5	22.1	22.1	22.1	21.5
DIURNAL RANGE	7.2	7.3	7.8	7.8	8.3	8.3	8.4	8.9	8.3	7.8	7.2	7.2
S/HEMISPHERE	JUL	AUG	SEP	OCT	NOV	DEC	JAN	FEB	MAR	APR	MAY	JUN

Cultural Recommendations

LIGHT: 2000–3000 fc.

TEMPERATURES: Throughout the year, days average 84–87°F (29–30°C), and nights average 71–73°F (22–23°C), with a diurnal range of 13–16°F (7–9°C). The probable extreme temperatures are near the averages, indicating that plants probably cannot tolerate wide temperature fluctuations.

HUMIDITY: 80–85% year-round. Air circulation should be excellent.

WATER: Rainfall is heavy all year. Cultivated plants should receive year-round moisture and never be allowed to dry out completely. Constant air movement is highly recommended. Plants from this habitat are often very sensitive to cold water, which may cause bud blast and cellular damage.

FERTILIZER: ¼–½ recommended strength. A balanced fertilizer should be applied weekly to biweekly throughout the year.

REST PERIOD: Growing conditions should be maintained all year. In the habitat, the heaviest rainfall occurs in winter; but water may be reduced somewhat for cultivated plants, especially those grown in the dark, short-day conditions common in temperate latitudes. Fertilizer should be reduced if water is reduced.

GROWING MEDIA: Plants may be mounted on tree-fern or cork slabs if humidity is high and plants are watered at least once daily in summer. When plants are potted, any open, fast-draining medium may be used. They may be repotted anytime new roots are growing.

MISCELLANEOUS NOTES: The bloom season shown in the climate table is based on reports from the habitat.

Plant and Flower Information

PLANT SIZE AND TYPE: A 48 in. (122 cm) sympodial epiphyte.

PSEUDOBULB: 48 in. (122 cm) long. Stems emerge from a very short rhizome. They are covered by persistent leaf sheaths. The stems occasionally branch.

LEAVES: Many. The lanceolate, pointed leaves are 1.0–1.6 in. (2.5–4.0 cm) long.

INFLORESCENCE: Short. Inflorescences emerge from the side of the stem.

FLOWERS: Few per inflorescence. The flowers, which are very small for the plant size, are 0.4 in. (1 cm) across. The dorsal sepal is ovate-oblong, and the lateral sepals are similar with a very expanded base. The petals are tongue-shaped. The 3-lobed lip is totally smooth.

REFERENCES: 220, 254, 286, 433, 474.

Dendrobium bicornutum (Schlechter) J. J. Smith

AKA: *Cadetia bicornuta* Schlechter. *Cadetia* is again considered a valid genus by some botanists, so this plant may again be a *Cadetia*.

ORIGIN/HABITAT: New Guinea. Plants grow in the Waria District of Papua New Guinea, and along the border between Irian Jaya (western New Guinea) and Papua New Guinea. Habitat elevation was not included with the plant description, so the following climate data should be used with caution.

CLIMATE: Station #200192, Garaina, Papua New Guinea, Lat. 7.9°S, Long. 147.1°E, at 2350 ft. (716 m). Record extreme temperatures are 94°F (34°C) and 46°F (8°C).

N/HEMISPHERE	JAN	FEB	MAR	APR	MAY	JUN	JUL	AUG	SEP	OCT	NOV	DEC
°F AVG MAX	80	82	83	84	85	85	85	85	84	84	83	81
°F AVG MIN	63	63	63	64	63	64	65	65	65	64	64	63
DIURNAL RANGE	17	19	20	20	22	21	20	20	19	20	19	18
RAIN/INCHES	5.8	6.5	8.7	11.1	11.8	11.9	8.9	11.7	11.5	9.9	7.7	5.2
HUMIDITY/%	84	82	82	81	80	80	81	81	82	83	84	84
BLOOM SEASON	*											
DAYS CLR	N/A											
RAIN/MM	148	166	220	282	300	303	227	296	291	251	195	131
°C AVG MAX	26.8	27.5	28.2	28.6	29.3	29.3	29.4	29.4	29.1	28.7	28.2	27.2
°C AVG MIN	16.9	16.9	17.4	17.6	17.4	18.0	18.1	18.2	18.4	17.7	17.7	17.1
DIURNAL RANGE	9.9	10.6	10.8	11.0	11.9	11.3	11.3	11.2	10.7	11.0	10.5	10.1
S/HEMISPHERE	JUL	AUG	SEP	OCT	NOV	DEC	JAN	FEB	MAR	APR	MAY	JUN

Dendrobium bicostatum

Cultural Recommendations

LIGHT: 2000–3000 fc.

TEMPERATURES: Throughout the year, days average 80–85°F (27–29°C), and nights average 63–65°F (17–18°C), with a diurnal range of 17–22°F (10–12°C).

HUMIDITY: 80–85% year-round.

WATER: Rainfall is heavy all year, but conditions are slightly drier in winter. Cultivated plants should be kept moist but not soggy.

FERTILIZER: ¼–½ recommended strength. A balanced fertilizer should be applied weekly to biweekly throughout the year.

REST PERIOD: Growing conditions should be maintained all year. In the habitat, rainfall is slightly lower in winter. Water and fertilizer may be reduced somewhat in winter, especially for plants grown in the dark, short-day conditions common in temperate latitudes. Plants should never be allowed to dry out completely, however. In the habitat, light is probably higher in winter.

GROWING MEDIA: Plants may be mounted on tree-fern or cork slabs if humidity is high and plants are watered at least once daily in summer. When plants are potted, any open, fast-draining medium may be used. Repotting is best done in early spring when new roots begin to grow.

MISCELLANEOUS NOTES: The bloom season shown in the climate table is based on records from the habitat.

Plant and Flower Information

PLANT SIZE AND TYPE: A 5–6 in. (13–16 cm) sympodial epiphyte.

PSEUDOBULB: 1.6–4.0 in. (4–10 cm) long. The erect growths emerge from a very short rhizome.

LEAVES: 1 per growth. The tongue-shaped leaves are 1.8–2.4 in. (4.5–6.0 cm) long, erect, fleshy, and rigid.

INFLORESCENCE: Short. A single inflorescence arises at the apex of the stem.

FLOWERS: 1 per inflorescence. The flowers are 0.5 in. (1.2 cm) across. Sepals and petals are linear. The wavy, tongue-shaped lip has a deeply cut, kidney-shaped midlobe, and triangular sidelobes.

REFERENCES: 225, 474, 486.

Dendrobium bicostatum J. J. Smith. Now considered a synonym of *Flickingeria bicostata* (J. J. Smith) A. Hawkes. REFERENCES: 111, 213, 220, 230, 231, 254, 286, 295, 445.

Dendrobium bidentiferum J. J. Smith. Now considered a synonym of *Diplocaulobium bidentiferum* (J. J. Smith) Kränzlin. REFERENCES: 220, 254, 445, 470.

Dendrobium bidupense Gagnepain. Now considered a synonym of *Eria bidupensis* (Gagnepain) Seidenfaden ex Averyanov. REFERENCES: 137, 227, 448, Seidenfaden 1992 *Opera Botanica* #114.

Dendrobium bifalce Lindley

AKA: *Bulbophyllum oncidiochilum* Kränzlin, *Dendrobium breviracemosum* F. M. Bailey, *D. chloropterum* Rchb. f. and Moore, *D. chloropterum* var. *striatum* J. J. Smith, and *Doritis bifalcis* Rchb. f.

ORIGIN/HABITAT: Timor Island, New Britain, Sabai and Tanimbar Islands, the Solomon Islands, Australia, and New Guinea. In Australia, plants are found primarily on Cape York Peninsula, but they are reported as far south as the Daintree River. In lowland New Guinea and adjacent islands, where plants are common, they usually grow high in trees from sea level to 3300 ft. (0–1000 m). They are also found in humid situations in open savannas, open rainforests, and coastal areas where light is high.

CLIMATE: Station #94035, Port Moresby, Papua New Guinea, Lat. 9.5°S, Long. 147.2°E, at 126 ft. (38 m). Temperatures are calculated for an elevation of 1300 ft. (400 m), resulting in probable extremes of 94°F (35°C) and 60°F (16°C).

N/HEMISPHERE	JAN	FEB	MAR	APR	MAY	JUN	JUL	AUG	SEP	OCT	NOV	DEC
°F AVG MAX	79	78	80	82	84	86	85	83	84	83	82	80
°F AVG MIN	69	69	70	71	72	72	72	72	72	71	71	70
DIURNAL RANGE	10	9	10	11	12	14	13	11	12	12	11	10
RAIN/INCHES	1.1	0.7	1.0	1.4	1.9	4.4	7.0	7.6	6.7	4.2	2.5	1.3
HUMIDITY/%	78	77	78	76	73	71	71	73	74	75	77	78
BLOOM SEASON										*		
DAYS CLR	N/A											
RAIN/MM	28	18	25	36	48	112	178	193	170	107	64	33
°C AVG MAX	26.2	25.6	26.7	27.8	29.0	30.1	29.5	28.4	29.0	28.4	27.8	26.7
°C AVG MIN	20.6	20.6	21.2	21.7	22.3	22.3	22.3	22.3	22.3	21.7	21.7	21.2
DIURNAL RANGE	5.6	5.0	5.5	6.1	6.7	7.8	7.2	6.1	6.7	6.7	6.1	5.5
S/HEMISPHERE	JUL	AUG	SEP	OCT	NOV	DEC	JAN	FEB	MAR	APR	MAY	JUN

Cultural Recommendations

LIGHT: 3500–4000 fc. Plants are usually found high in trees or in other high light situations. Growers report that while plants can grow in full sun, they grow best in light shade.

TEMPERATURES: Summer days average 83–86°F (28–30°C), and nights average 72°F (22°C), with a diurnal range of 11–14°F (6–8°C).

HUMIDITY: 70–80% year-round.

WATER: Rainfall is moderate from late spring through late autumn, followed by a 5–6 month dry season. Cultivated plants should dry slightly between waterings. Plants grown on slabs or rafts should be watered at least daily in summer, and probably more often on the warmest days.

FERTILIZER: ¼–½ recommended strength. A balanced fertilizer should be applied weekly to biweekly throughout the year. Growers indicate that many closely related *Dendrobium* are heavy feeders.

REST PERIOD: Winter days average 78–80°F (26–27°C), and nights average 69–70°F (21°C), with a diurnal range of 9–10°F (5–6°C). Growers indicate that winter lows should be kept above 59°F (15°C). Warm growing temperatures should be maintained all year, but after flowering, a dry rest lasting up to 5 months is required. Not only is rainfall low in winter, but even the moisture from morning dew is seldom available. Cultivated plants should be allowed to dry out between waterings, but they should not remain completely dry for extended periods. Water should be eliminated for a month or so when new growths first appear, as new growths are subject to disease if allowed to stay wet. High light levels should be maintained. Fertilizer should be reduced or eliminated during the dry period.

GROWING MEDIA: Plants are equally healthy in pots or on rafts or slabs, providing they are kept moist after new growths start in spring. Plants are healthiest if watered frequently on a substrate that drains rapidly. Mixes based on medium sized fir bark are successfully used by many growers. New growths are susceptible to damping off, so the potting medium should not be stale or waterlogged. Repotting is best done in early spring when new roots are growing.

MISCELLANEOUS NOTES: The bloom season shown in the climate table is based on cultivation records. Plants grow and flower well in Singapore. Cultivated plants are generally considered easy to grow but difficult to flower. Year-round high light and high humidity are essential.

Plant and Flower Information

PLANT SIZE AND TYPE: A 12–18 in. (30–45 cm) sympodial plant that forms large clumps. It may be epiphytic or lithophytic.

PSEUDOBULB: 5–12 in. (13–30 cm) long. Pseudobulbs are thickest in the middle and taper at the base. The bright yellow stems are ridged and clustered with 5–7 nodes below the leaves.

LEAVES: 2–4 per growth. Leaves are commonly 6 in. (15 cm) long, but they are variable. Leaves are medium green, leathery, oblong, suberect, and somewhat channeled.

INFLORESCENCE: 10–16 in. (25–40 cm) long. Several erect racemes may be produced by each growth. Inflorescences emerge from nodes below the leaf bases. Flowers are clustered at the apex of the long, stiff flower stem. They are held well above the leaves.

FLOWERS: 6–12 per inflorescence. The waxy blossoms are 0.6–1.0 in. (1.5–2.5 cm) across and open fully. They are variable in size and color. Sepals and petals, which may be yellowish or greenish, are marked with dark purple, brown, or maroon spots. The lip may be white, fawn colored, or yellow-green with brownish purple markings on the midlobe. Flowers are long-lasting.

HYBRIDIZING NOTES: Chromosome count is 2n = 38 (ref. 152).

REFERENCES: 25, 67, 83, 105, 152, 179, 190, 200, 216, 240, 243, 254, 262, 263, 271, 302, 304, 310, 371, 421, 437., 444, 445, 470, 510, 533, 537.

PHOTOS/DRAWINGS: 83, *105*, 240, *304*, 437, *533*.

Dendrobium bifarium Lindley

AKA: *D. excisum* Lindley. Seidenfaden (ref. 454) indicates that the taxonomy is very confused and that future name changes may occur when taxonomists reach a consensus.

ORIGIN/HABITAT: Widespread in Southeast Asia. Plants are common on trees in the lowland forests of Malaya from Singapore to Penang. They are also reported in southern Thailand at about 3950 ft. (1200 m), from several locations in Borneo at 3300–5900 ft. (1000–1800 m), and on Ambon Island.

CLIMATE: Station #49613, Tambunan, Sabah, Borneo, Lat. 5.7°N, Long. 116.4°E, at 1200 ft. (366 m). Temperatures are calculated for an elevation of 4800 ft. (1460 m), resulting in probable extremes of 86°F (30°C) and 42°F (6°C).

N/HEMISPHERE	JAN	FEB	MAR	APR	MAY	JUN	JUL	AUG	SEP	OCT	NOV	DEC
°F AVG MAX	74	75	77	78	78	77	77	77	77	76	75	74
°F AVG MIN	55	53	54	55	56	55	54	54	55	55	55	56
DIURNAL RANGE	19	22	23	23	22	22	23	23	22	21	20	18
RAIN/INCHES	5.8	3.7	5.8	7.5	8.2	7.3	5.1	4.9	6.4	7.0	6.8	6.0
HUMIDITY/%	N/A											
BLOOM SEASON		*	*	*	*	*	*	*				
DAYS CLR	N/A											
RAIN/MM	147	94	147	190	208	185	130	124	163	178	173	152
°C AVG MAX	23.4	24.0	25.1	25.6	25.6	25.1	25.1	25.1	25.1	24.5	24.0	23.4
°C AVG MIN	12.8	11.7	12.3	12.8	13.4	12.8	12.3	12.3	12.8	12.8	12.8	13.4
DIURNAL RANGE	10.6	12.3	12.8	12.8	12.2	12.3	12.8	12.8	12.3	11.7	11.2	10.0
S/HEMISPHERE	JUL	AUG	SEP	OCT	NOV	DEC	JAN	FEB	MAR	APR	MAY	JUN

Cultural Recommendations

LIGHT: 2500–3500 fc.

TEMPERATURES: Throughout the year, days average 74–78°F (23–26°C), and nights average 53–56°F (12–13°C), with a diurnal range of 18–23°F (10–13°C).

HUMIDITY: Information is not available for this location. However, records from nearby locations indicate that humidity probably averages 80–85% year-round.

WATER: Rainfall is moderate to heavy all year with a brief, slightly drier period in winter. Cultivated plants should be kept moist with only slight drying allowed between waterings.

FERTILIZER: ¼–½ recommended strength. A balanced fertilizer should be applied weekly to biweekly throughout the year.

REST PERIOD: Growing temperatures should be maintained all year. Water should be reduced for cultivated plants, especially those grown in the dark, short-day conditions common in temperate-latitude winters, but they should never be allowed to dry out completely. Fertilizer should be reduced or eliminated until water is increased in spring.

GROWING MEDIA: Plants may be mounted on tree-fern or cork slabs if humidity is high and plants are watered at least once daily in summer. When plants are potted, any open, fast-draining medium may be used. Repotting may be done after flowering or anytime new roots are growing.

MISCELLANEOUS NOTES: The bloom season shown in the climate table is based on cultivation records.

Plant and Flower Information

PLANT SIZE AND TYPE: A 6–24 in. (15–60 cm) sympodial epiphyte.

PSEUDOBULB: 6–24 in. (15–60 cm) long. The stems have numerous internodes, which at the apex, are about 0.4 in. (1 cm) apart.

LEAVES: Many. The elliptic-oblong leaves, which are 1–2 in. (3–5 cm) long, are twisted at the base so that leaves all face one direction. They are distichous with overlapping leaf bases. The entire stem is leafy.

INFLORESCENCE: Very short. Inflorescences emerge from nodes along the stem, and blossoms appear to rest on the stem.

FLOWERS: 1 per inflorescence. The small flowers, which open fully, are 0.6 in. (1.5 cm) across. Sepals and lanceolate petals are white, but they may have a greenish tinge. The white lip, which is flat and without sidelobes, has several warty ridges. The midlobe is marked with a yellow spot in the center.

REFERENCES: 59, 179, 200, 202, 216, 229, 254, 286, 295, 310, 317, 394, 395, 402, 454, 455, 468, 592.

PHOTOS/DRAWINGS: *454*, 455, *592*.

Dendrobium bifidum Ridley. Now considered a synonym of *Flickingeria appendiculata* (Blume) A. Hawkes.

REFERENCES: 200, 213, 219, 230, 231, 254, 449, 455.

Dendrobium biflorum Kränzlin. See *D. dactylodes* Rchb. f.

REFERENCES: 434.

Dendrobium biflorum A. Richard. See *D. cunninghamii* Lindley.

REFERENCES: 190, 216, 254.

Dendrobium biflorum (Forster) Swartz

AKA: *Epidendrum biflorum* Forster.

ORIGIN/HABITAT: South Pacific Islands. Plants are found on Vitu Levu and Ovalau in Fiji, in Tahiti, Vanuatu, and the Society Islands, as well as east of Fiji on Niue Island. In western Samoa, plants grow near Matautu village on Savaii Island in dense shade and bright conditions on isolated trees or in open forest from sea level to 2950 ft. (0–900 m). In Tahiti, plants have been found at 650–3600 ft. (200–1100 m).

CLIMATE: Station #91762, Apia, Western Samoa, Lat. 13.8°S, Long. 171.8°W, at 7 ft. (2 m). Temperatures are calculated for an elevation of 2000 ft. (610 m), resulting in probable extremes of 86°F (30°C) and 56°F (14°C).

N/HEMISPHERE	JAN	FEB	MAR	APR	MAY	JUN	JUL	AUG	SEP	OCT	NOV	DEC
°F AVG MAX	78	77	77	78	79	78	79	78	79	79	78	78
°F AVG MIN	67	68	67	68	67	67	68	69	67	68	67	67
DIURNAL RANGE	11	9	10	10	12	11	11	9	12	11	11	11
RAIN/INCHES	3.2	3.5	5.2	6.7	10.5	14.6	17.9	15.2	14.1	10.0	6.3	5.1
HUMIDITY/%	76	75	75	77	77	78	81	80	80	78	77	75
BLOOM SEASON	*											*
DAYS CLR @ 1PM	9	10	9	6	3	2	4	2	5	9	5	10
DAYS CLR @ 7PM	12	10	11	7	4	3	2	2	2	5	11	8
RAIN/MM	81	89	132	170	267	371	455	386	358	254	160	130
°C AVG MAX	25.8	25.2	25.2	25.8	26.3	25.8	26.3	25.8	26.3	26.3	25.8	25.8
°C AVG MIN	19.7	20.2	19.7	20.2	19.7	19.7	20.2	20.8	19.7	20.2	19.7	19.7
DIURNAL RANGE	6.1	5.0	5.5	5.6	6.6	6.1	6.1	5.0	6.6	6.1	6.1	6.1
S/HEMISPHERE	JUL	AUG	SEP	OCT	NOV	DEC	JAN	FEB	MAR	APR	MAY	JUN

Dendrobium bigibbum

Cultural Recommendations

LIGHT: 2000–3500 fc.

TEMPERATURES: Throughout the year, days average 77–79°F (25–26°C), and nights average 67–69°F (20–21°C), with a diurnal range of 9–12°F (5–7°C).

HUMIDITY: 75–80% year-round.

WATER: Rainfall is moderate to heavy all year. Conditions are slightly drier for 2–3 months in winter. Cultivated plants should never be allowed to dry out completely.

FERTILIZER: ¼–½ recommended strength. A balanced fertilizer should be applied weekly to biweekly throughout the year.

REST PERIOD: Growing temperatures should be maintained all year. Water should be reduced somewhat for cultivated plants, especially those grown in the dark, short-day conditions common during temperate-latitude winters; but they should dry only slightly between waterings. Fertilizer should be reduced or eliminated anytime water is reduced. In the habitat, light is highest in winter.

GROWING MEDIA: Plants may be mounted on tree-fern or cork slabs if humidity is high and plants are watered at least once daily in summer. When plants are potted, any open, fast-draining medium may be used. Repotting may be done anytime new roots are growing.

MISCELLANEOUS NOTES: The bloom season shown in the climate table is based on reports from the habitat.

Plant and Flower Information

PLANT SIZE AND TYPE: A 16–67 in. (40–170 cm) sympodial epiphyte.

PSEUDOBULB: 16–67 in. (40–170 cm) long. The slender, reedlike stems are closely spaced and arise from a very short rhizome. They are hard, smooth, and shiny with many internodes 0.4–0.6 in (1.0–1.5) cm long. The stems turn yellow when dry.

LEAVES: Many near the apex of each growth. The distichous leaves are 3–6 in. (8–15 cm) long, linear to linear-lanceolate, and somewhat erect.

INFLORESCENCE: Short. Inflorescences emerge from nodes all along the upper part of the stem.

FLOWERS: 2 per inflorescence. Blossoms are pale yellow to creamy-white and pink. They are 1.2 in. (3 cm) long and remain somewhat closed. Sepals and petals are linear-lanceolate tapering to a mere thread at the tip. The lip is deeply and irregularly fringed with 3 raised keels. They are ephemeral, lasting a few hours to a few days.

HYBRIDIZING NOTES: Chromosome count is 2n = 38 (ref. 152, 243).

REFERENCES: 52, 86, 152, 216, 224, 243, 252, 254, 270, 277, 317, 353, 434, 445, 466.

PHOTOS/DRAWINGS: 254, *466.*

Dendrobium bigibbum F. Mueller not Lindley. See *D. affine* (Decaisne) Steudel. REFERENCES: 533.

Dendrobium bigibbum Lindley

AKA: Sometimes spelled *D. biggibum.* Clements (ref. 67) includes the following synonyms. *Callista bigibba* (Lindley) Kuntze (revised), *Callista sumneri* (F. Mueller) Kuntze (revised), *D. bigibbum* var. *album* F. M. Bailey, *D. bigibbum* var. *candidum* Rchb. f., *D. bigibbum* subvar. *candidum* (Rchb. f.) Veitch, *D. bigibbum* Lindley var. *sumneri* (F. Mueller) F. M. Bailey, and *D. phalaenopsis* Fitzgerald var. *statterianum* Hort. ex Sander, *D. sumneri* F. Mueller, *D. bigibbum* Lindley subsp. *phalaenopsis* (Fitzgerald) M. Clements and Cribb. Also see *D. lithocola* D. Jones and M. Clements, *D. phalaenopsis* Fitzgerald, and *D. striaenopsis* M. Clements and D. Jones, the other members of this confused, closely related group of plants.

D. bigibbum and related plants are commonly cultivated, and numerous varieties have been described. Some taxonomists currently recognize 2 subspecies (subsp. *phalaenopsis* Fitzgerald and subsp. *compactum* C. White) and several varieties, but others prefer to simply view the plants as a variable complex.

D. bigibbum subsp. *laratensis* Clemesha from the Tanimbar Islands is frequently confused with the Australian *D. bigibbum.* Clements (ref. 67) indicates that this subspecies was formally described as *D. striaenopsis* M. Clements and D. Jones. Clements (ref. 67) include the following names as synonyms: *D. bigibbum* Lindley var. *albomarginatum* Linden Aug. 1891 not F. M. Bailey Mar. 1891, *D. bigibbum* Lindley subsp. *laratensis* Clemesha, *D. phalaenopsis* Fitzgerald var. *schroderianum* Hort. ex Masters, *D. schroderianum* Hort. ex L. Gentil, which Clements indicates is an illegal name. Clements indicates that Blake (ref. 44) includes additional synonyms.

Clements (ref. 67) reinstated some species names and described new species from the following names that are commonly considered synonyms of *D. bigibbum.* The names are frequently confused and are likely to continue so for some time.

D. bigibbum var. *albomarginatum* F. M. Bailey not Linden. See *D.* × *superbiens* Rchb. f.

D. bigibbum var. *albomarginatum* Linden not F. M. Bailey. See *D. striaenopsis* M. Clements and D. Jones

D. bigibbum var. *albopurpuratum* Hort. See *D. striaenopsis* M. Clements and D. Jones.

D. bigibbum var. *compactum* C. White. See *D. lithocola* D. Jones and M. Clements.

D. bigibbum forma *compactum* (C. White) St. Cloud. See *D. lithocola* D. Jones and M. Clements.

D. bigibbum subvar. *compactum* (C. White) St. Cloud. See *D. lithocola* D. Jones and M. Clements.

D. bigibbum var. *georgei* C. White. See *D.* × *lavarackianum* M. Clements.

D. bigibbum var. *macranthum* F. M. Bailey. See *D. phalaenopsis* Fitzgerald.

D. bigibbum var. *phalaenopsis* (Fitzgerald) F. M. Bailey. See *D. phalaenopsis* Fitzgerald.

D. bigibbum var. *phalaenopsis* (Fitzgerald) F. M. Bailey forma *compactum* (C. White) St. Cloud. See *D. lithocola* D. Jones and M. Clements.

D. bigibbum var. *superbum* Hort. ex Rchb. f. See *D. phalaenopsis* Fitzgerald.

D. bigibbum var. *superbum* subvar. *compactum* (C. White) Dockrill. See *D. lithocola* D. Jones and M. Clements.

D. bigibbum var. *superbiens* (Rchb. f.) F. M. Bailey. See *D.* × *superbiens* Rchb. f.

D. bigibbum var. *venosum* F. M. Bailey. See *D.* × *lavarackianum* M. Clements.

D. bigibbum forma *venosum* (F. M. Bailey) F. M. Bailey. See *D.* × *lavarackianum* M. Clements.

ORIGIN/HABITAT: Australia. Plants grow on the northern tip of the Cape York Peninsula. They are generally found west of the dividing range and north of the Iron Range. The habitat extends northward through the islands of the Torres Strait into southern Papua New Guinea. Plants are found in semiarid regions, usually at low elevations, where they grow on small trees and rocks in bright light.

CLIMATE: Station #94175, Thursday Island, Australia, Lat. 10.6°S, Long. 142.2°E, at 200 ft. (61 m). Record extreme temperatures are 98°F (37°C) and 64°F (18°C).

Dendrobium bigibbum

N/HEMISPHERE	JAN	FEB	MAR	APR	MAY	JUN	JUL	AUG	SEP	OCT	NOV	DEC
°F AVG MAX	82	82	84	86	88	89	87	87	87	86	85	84
°F AVG MIN	73	73	74	76	77	78	77	77	77	77	76	74
DIURNAL RANGE	9	9	10	10	11	11	10	10	10	9	9	10
RAIN/INCHES	0.4	0.2	0.1	0.3	1.5	7.0	18.2	15.8	13.9	8.0	1.6	0.5
HUMIDITY/%	75	72	71	70	69	72	79	80	79	77	75	75
BLOOM SEASON	**	*	*	*			*	*	**	**	**	**
DAYS CLR @ 9AM	3	4	3	2	3	1	0	0	1	4	9	5
DAYS CLR @ 3PM	4	5	6	8	7	2	0	1	1	4	8	6
RAIN/MM	10	5	3	8	38	178	462	401	353	203	41	13
°C AVG MAX	27.8	27.8	28.9	30.0	31.1	31.7	30.6	30.6	30.6	30.0	29.4	28.9
°C AVG MIN	22.8	22.8	23.3	24.4	25.0	25.6	25.0	25.0	25.0	25.0	24.4	23.3
DIURNAL RANGE	5.0	5.0	5.6	5.6	6.1	6.1	5.6	5.6	5.6	5.0	5.0	5.6
S/HEMISPHERE	JUL	AUG	SEP	OCT	NOV	DEC	JAN	FEB	MAR	APR	MAY	JUN

Cultural Recommendations

LIGHT: 3000–4000 fc. The heavy summer cloud cover indicates that some shading is needed from spring through autumn, but light should be as high as the plant can tolerate, short of burning the leaves. Strong air movement should be provided year-round.

TEMPERATURES: Throughout the year, days average 82–89°F (28–32°C), and nights average 73–78°F (23–26°C), with a diurnal range of 9–11°F (5–6°C).

HUMIDITY: 70–80% year-round.

WATER: Rainfall is moderate to heavy during summer and early autumn, but conditions are much drier in winter. Cultivated plants should be kept moist while actively growing, but water should be gradually reduced in autumn. Australian growers recommend a daily morning misting in summer, even for pot-grown plants, with evening mistings when temperatures are above 91°F (33°C).

FERTILIZER: ¼–½ recommended strength, applied weekly. A high-nitrogen fertilizer is beneficial from spring to midsummer, but a fertilizer high in phosphates should be used in late summer and autumn.

REST PERIOD: Growing temperatures should be maintained year-round. Some growers report success with winter minimums near 54°F (12°C). It should be noted, however, that this is colder than the record lows in the habitat. In cultivation, these extremes should probably be avoided; but seed-grown plants are somewhat adaptable and may adjust to these conditions, especially if they are kept very dry. A long dry rest is required in winter. Many growers recommend hanging plants high in the greenhouse and forgetting them for 2–3 months in winter. However, a little rain does fall each month, so an occasional early morning misting should help keep plants from becoming too dry. Growers should maintain high light levels, provide strong air movement, and eliminate fertilizer until watering is resumed in spring. After growth starts, Australian growers strongly recommend using care to keep water from the new growths until they are 2–3 in. (5–8 cm) tall.

GROWING MEDIA: Plants may be mounted or potted. If plants are potted, the pots should be as small as possible and the medium should be very open and fast draining. Excellent drainage is essential. Repotting is best done when the new growth is 2–3 in. (5–7 cm) high and new root growth is evident.

MISCELLANEOUS NOTES: The bloom season shown in the climate table is based on collection reports. Growers indicate that *D. bigibbum* does poorly in Singapore, as it requires a more seasonal climate.

One source indicates that plants are free blooming, with peak blooming Aug.–Nov. (Feb.–Mar.), and that both slightly cooler average temperatures and shorter days (long periods of dark) are required to initiate blooms. It should be remembered, however, that the record low temperature in the habitat is 64°F (18°C) and conditions colder than this should probably be avoided.

Sudden temperature declines may cause flower buds to drop, and cold water should be avoided when plants are in bud. Other growers suggest that bud drop may be caused if plants are allowed to dry out, if humidity is too low, if ethylene gas contaminates the growing area, or if salts are allowed to accumulate.

Australian growers recommend repotting *D. bigibbum* every other year in the smallest possible pots. They also suggest removing all but the newest 4–5 stems. The base of the plants should be kept clean and healthy. Plants seldom develop into specimen plants as they are very prone to dieback.

Plant and Flower Information

PLANT SIZE AND TYPE: A slender, 16–48 in. (40–122 cm) sympodial epiphyte or lithophyte.

PSEUDOBULB: 16–48 in. (40–122 cm) long. The stems are cylindrical with a slight swelling at the base.

LEAVES: 3–12 per growth. The oblong-lanceolate leaves are 3–6 in. (8–15 cm) long. They are flushed with red or purple, and are leathery, rigid, and evergreen for 2 years. The apical 30% of the stems are leafy.

INFLORESCENCE: 8–16 in. (20–41 cm) long. Over a period of several years, each growth produces 1–4 inflorescences from nodes near the apex of the pseudobulb, even after the canes are leafless. The inflorescences are usually arching or horizontal, but they may be pendent. Flowers are nicely spaced along the upper half of the raceme.

FLOWERS: 8–20 per inflorescence, occasionally less. The flowers are 1.2–2.0 in. (3–5 cm) across. Sepals and petals usually curve backward. The showy flowers have a heavy texture, broad overlapping sepals, and narrower petals. Flowers are normally violet, but colors include white, pale to deep lilac, magenta, and purple. All colors are bright and rich. The pubescent lip, which is normally rounded or notched in the center of the blunt midlobe, is often a darker shade than the sepals and petals. Blossoms are highly variable in size and color. Flowers last for months in perfect condition, providing they do not become water spotted, so the plants seem to be in nearly continuous bloom.

HYBRIDIZING NOTES: Chromosome count is 2n = 38 as *D. bigibbum* (ref. 187, 504, 580) and *D. bigibbum* var. *bigibbum* (ref. 504). As *D. bigibbum* var. *compactum* the count is 2n = 38 (ref. 154, 188, 504, 580) and 2n = about 57 (ref. 504, 580). As *D. bigibbum* var. *superbum* the count is n = 19 (ref. 151) and 2n = 38 (ref. 151).

Johansen (ref. 239) indicates that the seeds produced when *D. phalaenopsis* was self-pollinated contained no visible embryos and no seeds germinated. Capsules opened 197 days after pollination. Seeds are sufficiently mature for green-pod sowing in 120–140 (131) days.

Wilfret and Hashimoto (ref. 568) did not get seed when they tried to cross *D. bigibbum* with *D. leonis* (Lindley) Rchb. f. or *D. crumenatum* Swartz. When *D. bigibbum* was crossed with *D. delacourii* Guillaumin, seed was occasionally produced but none was viable. *D. bigibbum* regularly produces a high percentage of viable seed when different clones are cross-pollinated.

As a parent, *D. bigibbum* contributes long-lasting flowers, full flower shape, and long inflorescences, thereby improving a hybrid's potential value for cut flowers. It does not breed true for color.

D. bigibbum hybridizes naturally with *D. discolor* Lindley, producing *D.* × *superbiens* Rchb. f.

REFERENCES: 23, 24, 25, 36, 44, 67, 69, 105, 116, 151, 154, 187, 188, 190, 196, 200, 210, 216, 233, 239, 240, 254, 260, 262, 263, 264, 304, 317, 325, 326, 351, 353, 371, 389, 390, 421, 430, 445, 458, 461, 504, 510, 526, 533, 541, 557, 558, 568, 570, 580.

PHOTOS/DRAWINGS: *36, 69, 105, 116,* 210, 240, *262,* 304, 325, *351, 371, 389, 390, 430, 456,* 458, 461, *526, 533, 541, 558, 568.*

Dendrobium bihamulatum J. J. Smith

ORIGIN/HABITAT: Western Sumatra. Plants grow near Bengkulu at about 3300 ft. (1000 m).

CLIMATE: Station #96253, Bengkulu, Sumatra, Indonesia, Lat. 3.9°S, Long. 102.3°E, at 49 ft. (15 m). Temperatures are calculated for an elevation of 3300 ft. (1000 m). Record extreme temperatures are not available for this location.

N/HEMISPHERE	JAN	FEB	MAR	APR	MAY	JUN	JUL	AUG	SEP	OCT	NOV	DEC
°F AVG MAX	77	76	76	76	76	76	77	77	77	77	78	77
°F AVG MIN	61	61	61	62	62	62	62	61	62	63	62	62
DIURNAL RANGE	16	15	15	14	14	14	15	16	15	14	16	15
RAIN/INCHES	6.9	6.8	9.1	13.9	16.0	12.7	16.0	11.5	12.0	8.3	8.4	8.4
HUMIDITY/%	77	78	77	77	79	80	78	76	77	79	77	78
BLOOM SEASON	N/A											
DAYS CLR @ 7AM	5	1	1	1	0	0	2	1	1	1	2	3
DAYS CLR @ 1PM	5	4	3	1	2	3	2	2	2	3	7	5
RAIN/MM	175	173	231	353	406	323	406	292	305	211	213	213
°C AVG MAX	25.2	24.6	24.6	24.6	24.6	24.6	25.2	25.2	25.2	25.2	25.7	25.2
°C AVG MIN	16.3	16.3	16.3	16.8	16.8	16.8	16.8	16.3	16.8	17.4	16.8	16.8
DIURNAL RANGE	8.9	8.3	8.3	7.8	7.8	7.8	8.4	8.9	8.4	7.8	8.9	8.4
S/HEMISPHERE	JUL	AUG	SEP	OCT	NOV	DEC	JAN	FEB	MAR	APR	MAY	JUN

Cultural Recommendations

LIGHT: 2000–3000 fc.

TEMPERATURES: Throughout the year, days average 76–78°F (25–26°C), and nights average 61–63°F (16–17°C), with a diurnal range of 14–16°F (8–9°C).

HUMIDITY: 75–80% year-round.

WATER: Rainfall is heavy all year, but winter is slightly drier than summer. Cultivated plants should be kept moist but not soggy.

FERTILIZER: ¼–½ recommended strength. A balanced fertilizer should be applied weekly to biweekly throughout the year.

REST PERIOD: Growing conditions should be maintained year-round. Water and fertilizer may be reduced somewhat in winter, especially for plants grown in the dark, short-day conditions common in temperate latitudes. However, cultivated plants should never be allowed to dry completely between waterings. In the habitat, light is highest in winter.

GROWING MEDIA: Plants may be mounted on tree-fern or cork slabs or potted in a small pot filled with any open, fast-draining medium. Repotting may be done anytime new roots are growing.

Plant and Flower Information

PLANT SIZE AND TYPE: An 18 in. (45 cm) sympodial epiphyte.

PSEUDOBULB: 18 in. (45 cm) long. The stems are dark yellow-green, nonbranching, and close together.

LEAVES: Few. The leaves are pale green with a dark suffusion. They are oblong, unequally bilobed at the tip, and somewhat twisted at the base. The leaves often drop from the lower part of the stem.

INFLORESCENCE: Short. Inflorescences emerge through the leaf bases.

FLOWERS: 1 per inflorescence. The flowers are very small. Sepals and petals are white with pale orange markings on the wavy lip.

REFERENCES: 222, 480.

Dendrobium bilamellatum R. S. Rogers. See *D. vexillarius* J. J. Smith. REFERENCES: 223, 385, 406.

Dendrobium bilobulatum Seidenfaden

ORIGIN/HABITAT: Southern peninsular Thailand and the Dalat area of Vietnam. The habitat elevation is estimated, so the following climate data should be used with caution.

CLIMATE: Station #48551, Surat (Ban Don), Thailand, Lat. 9.1°N, Long. 99.3°E, at 10 ft. (3 m). Temperatures are calculated for an elevation of 3000 ft. (910 m), resulting in probable extremes of 95°F (35°C) and 37°F (3°C).

N/HEMISPHERE	JAN	FEB	MAR	APR	MAY	JUN	JUL	AUG	SEP	OCT	NOV	DEC
°F AVG MAX	78	82	85	85	83	81	80	81	80	79	77	76
°F AVG MIN	59	59	60	63	64	64	64	64	63	63	62	61
DIURNAL RANGE	19	23	25	22	19	17	16	17	17	16	15	15
RAIN/INCHES	1.0	0.3	0.4	2.5	6.6	4.5	6.9	5.8	7.1	8.1	12.1	4.0
HUMIDITY/%	82	78	75	79	83	82	82	82	84	87	87	86
BLOOM SEASON	N/A											
DAYS CLR @ 7AM	4	3	3	2	1	1	1	1	1	1	1	2
DAYS CLR @ 1PM	2	2	2	1	1	0	0	0	0	0	1	1
RAIN/MM	25	8	10	64	168	114	175	147	180	206	307	102
°C AVG MAX	25.6	27.9	29.5	29.5	28.4	27.3	26.7	27.3	26.7	26.2	25.1	24.5
°C AVG MIN	15.1	15.1	15.6	17.3	17.9	17.9	17.9	17.9	17.3	17.3	16.7	16.2
DIURNAL RANGE	10.5	12.8	13.9	12.2	10.5	9.4	8.8	9.4	9.4	8.9	8.4	8.3
S/HEMISPHERE	JUL	AUG	SEP	OCT	NOV	DEC	JAN	FEB	MAR	APR	MAY	JUN

Cultural Recommendations

LIGHT: 3500–4000 fc.

TEMPERATURES: Summer days average 80–81°F (27°C), and nights average 64°F (18°C), with a diurnal range of 16–17°F (9°C). Early spring is the warmest season. Days average 83–85°F (28–30°C), and nights average 60–64°F (16–18°C), with a diurnal range of 19–25°F (11–14°C).

HUMIDITY: 80–85% most of the year, dropping to 75–80% in winter and early spring.

WATER: Rainfall is moderate to heavy from late spring through autumn. Conditions are drier in winter. Cultivated plants should be kept moist from late spring into autumn with only slight drying allowed between waterings. Water should be gradually reduced in late autumn.

FERTILIZER: ¼–½ recommended strength. A balanced fertilizer should be applied weekly to biweekly throughout the year.

REST PERIOD: Winter days average 76–82°F (25–28°C), and nights average 59–61°F (15–16°C), with a diurnal range of 15–23°F (8–13°C). Winter rainfall is low for 2–3 months, but additional moisture is available from frequent heavy dew. Water and fertilizer should be reduced and the plants allowed to dry somewhat between waterings. They should not remain dry for long periods, however. In the habitat, light is slightly higher in winter.

GROWING MEDIA: Plants may be mounted on tree-fern or cork slabs if humidity is high and plants are watered at least once daily in summer. When plants are potted, any open, fast-draining medium may be used. Repotting is best done in early spring when new roots are growing.

Plant and Flower Information

PLANT SIZE AND TYPE: An 18–20 in. (45–50 cm) sympodial epiphyte.

PSEUDOBULB: 18–20 in. (45–50 cm) long. The stems, which often branch, curve downward, but they are not pendent.

LEAVES: Many per growth. The triangular, distichous leaves, which have a textured surface, are 0.8 in. (2 cm) long. They are held at a 40° angle to the stem and lie flat along a single plane.

INFLORESCENCE: Very short. Inflorescences arise from the apex of young stems and from the side of leafless stems.

FLOWERS: 1 per inflorescence. The flowers are 0.4 in. (1 cm) across. The sepals and narrow petals are white with fine purple lines. The fan-shaped lip is wavy-margined, deeply split at the apex, and marked with 3 faint purple lines below the bright yellow spot in the center. They are superficially similar to *D. anceps* Swartz.

HYBRIDIZING NOTES: Seed capsules opened in 152 days and only 1% of the seeds germinated. Johansen (ref. 239) indicates that some clones of *D. bilobulatum* could be self-pollinated while others were self-sterile.

REFERENCES: 234, 239, 454.

PHOTOS/DRAWINGS: 454.

Dendrobium bilobum Lindley

AKA: Although not mentioned by recent taxonomists, J. J. Smith (ref. 470) suggests the possibility that *D. isochiloides* Kränzlin and *D. koordersii* J. J. Smith might be synonyms. Kränzlin (ref. 254) suggested that *D. macrum* Schlechter might be a synonym of *D. isochiloides* Kränzlin. When describing their plants, both Lindley and Kränzlin referred to the amazing resemblance to *Isochilus linearis* R. Brown.

ORIGIN/HABITAT: New Guinea, Solomon Islands, Vanuatu, New Caledonia, and Fiji. Plants usually grow in mountain forests at about 2950 ft. (900 m). *D. isochiloides* Kränzlin var. *pumilum* J. J. Smith was found at the base of Nepenthes hill along the Noord River in Irian Jaya (western New Guinea). The plants grew on trees in primary forest. In Papua New Guinea, *D. bilobum* was collected in the Torricelli Mountains at about 1950 ft. (600 m), and *D. isochiloides* was collected near Port Praslin and Port Carteret on New Ireland.

CLIMATE: Station #94004, Wewak, Papua New Guinea, Lat. 3.6°S, Long. 143.7°E, at 16 ft. (5 m). Temperatures are calculated for an elevation of 2000 ft. (610 m), resulting in probable extremes of 91°F (33°C) and 55°F (13°C).

N/HEMISPHERE	JAN	FEB	MAR	APR	MAY	JUN	JUL	AUG	SEP	OCT	NOV	DEC
°F AVG MAX	81	81	81	81	81	81	80	79	80	81	81	81
°F AVG MIN	67	67	67	68	68	68	68	68	67	67	68	67
DIURNAL RANGE	14	14	14	13	13	13	12	11	13	14	13	14
RAIN/INCHES	7.6	4.8	5.3	10.0	13.3	14.5	12.1	11.9	14.9	16.9	15.1	10.8
HUMIDITY/%	80	79	79	78	79	81	82	82	81	82	81	80
BLOOM SEASON	*	*	**	*	*	*	*	*	*	*	*	*
DAYS CLR	N/A											
RAIN/MM	193	122	135	254	338	368	307	302	378	429	384	274
°C AVG MAX	27.5	27.5	27.5	27.5	27.5	27.5	26.9	26.4	26.9	27.5	27.5	27.5
°C AVG MIN	19.7	19.7	19.7	20.3	20.3	20.3	20.3	20.3	19.7	19.7	20.3	19.7
DIURNAL RANGE	7.8	7.8	7.8	7.2	7.2	7.2	6.6	6.1	7.2	7.8	7.2	7.8
S/HEMISPHERE	JUL	AUG	SEP	OCT	NOV	DEC	JAN	FEB	MAR	APR	MAY	JUN

Cultural Recommendations

LIGHT: 2000–3000 fc.

TEMPERATURES: Throughout the year, days average 79–81°F (26–28°C), and nights average 67–68°F (20°C), with a diurnal range of 11–14°F (6–8°C).

HUMIDITY: Near 80% year-round.

WATER: Rainfall is heavy all year, but conditions are slightly drier for 1–2 months in late winter. Cultivated plants should be kept moist and never be allowed to dry out completely.

FERTILIZER: ¼–½ recommended strength. A balanced fertilizer should be applied weekly to biweekly throughout the year.

REST PERIOD: Growing conditions should be maintained year-round. Water should be reduced for plants cultivated in the dark, short-day conditions common during temperate-latitude winters, but they should still not be allowed to dry out completely. Fertilizer should also be reduced if water is reduced. In the habitat, light may be slightly higher in winter.

GROWING MEDIA: A very open and fast-draining medium may be used with either baskets or small pots. Repotting may be done anytime new roots are growing.

MISCELLANEOUS NOTES: The bloom season shown in the climate table is based on cultivation records.

Plant and Flower Information

PLANT SIZE AND TYPE: A 16–20 in. (40–50 cm) sympodial epiphyte.

PSEUDOBULB: 16–20 in. (40–50 cm) long.

LEAVES: Many. The linear leaves are 1.2–1.6 in. (3–4 cm) long and bilobed at the apex. The leaf sheaths have purple speckles. The stems are densely leafy for part of each stem. Collectors indicate that plants collected above 1050 ft. (320 m) have smaller, more numerous leaves than plants collected at lower elevations.

INFLORESCENCE: Short.

FLOWERS: 1 per inflorescence. The very tiny flowers are 0.2 in. (0.5 cm) long. Sepals and petals are greenish yellow. The lip may be purple or red-brown with a greenish apex.

HYBRIDIZING NOTES: Chromosome count is 2n = 38 (ref. 152).

REFERENCES: 152, 179, 216, 243, 254, 270, 271, 310, 317, 470, 516.

PHOTOS/DRAWINGS: 271

Dendrobium biloculare J. J. Smith.

ORIGIN/HABITAT: Irian Jaya (western New Guinea). Plants were collected in the vicinity of Etna Bay. Habitat elevation is unavailable, so the following climate data should be used with caution.

CLIMATE: Station #97682, Nabire, Irian Jaya, Lat. 3.3°S, Long. 135.5°E, at 10 ft. (3 m). Record extreme temperatures are not available for this location.

N/HEMISPHERE	JAN	FEB	MAR	APR	MAY	JUN	JUL	AUG	SEP	OCT	NOV	DEC
°F AVG MAX	86	86	86	86	87	87	86	87	86	87	87	87
°F AVG MIN	75	75	76	77	77	76	77	75	75	75	76	76
DIURNAL RANGE	11	11	10	9	10	11	9	11	12	11	11	11
RAIN/INCHES	7.4	11.1	8.5	8.5	7.5	9.0	9.2	10.6	12.1	11.3	10.2	9.8
HUMIDITY/%	N/A											
BLOOM SEASON	N/A											
DAYS CLR	N/A											
RAIN/MM	190	283	217	217	192	228	233	270	308	286	259	248
°C AVG MAX	30.1	29.9	30.1	30.3	30.5	30.6	30.0	30.0	30.5	30.5	30.3	30.3
°C AVG MIN	24.0	24.0	24.3	24.7	24.9	24.5	24.8	24.0	23.8	24.6	24.3	24.2
DIURNAL RANGE	6.1	5.9	5.8	5.6	5.6	6.1	5.2	6.0	6.7	5.9	6.0	6.1
S/HEMISPHERE	JUL	AUG	SEP	OCT	NOV	DEC	JAN	FEB	MAR	APR	MAY	JUN

Cultural Recommendations

LIGHT: 2000–3000 fc.

TEMPERATURES: Throughout the year, days average 86–87°F (30–31°C), and nights average 75–77°F (24–25°C), with a diurnal range of 9–12°F (6–7°C). Temperature data should be used with caution, however.

HUMIDITY: Information is not available for this location. However, records from nearby stations indicate that humidity is probably about 85% year-round.

WATER: Rainfall is heavy year-round. Cultivated plants should be kept evenly moist. Warm water should be beneficial.

FERTILIZER: ¼–½ recommended strength. A balanced fertilizer should be applied weekly to biweekly throughout the year.

REST PERIOD: Growing conditions should be maintained year-round. Water and fertilizer might be reduced slightly in winter for plants cultivated in the dark, short-day conditions common in the temperate latitudes. However, plants from this area should never be allowed to dry out completely. In the habitat, seasonal light variation is minor.

GROWING MEDIA: Mounting plants on tree-fern or cork slabs accommodates their pendulous growth habit. However, humidity must be high and plants must be watered at least once a day in summer. If plants cannot be mounted, small pots or hanging baskets may be filled with an open, fast-draining medium. Repotting may be done anytime new roots are actively growing.

MISCELLANEOUS NOTES: Bloom season is unavailable. Cribb (ref. 83) indicates that the type specimen is the only known collection.

Dendrobium bimorphum

Plant and Flower Information

PLANT SIZE AND TYPE: A pendulous, sympodial epiphyte of unreported size.

PSEUDOBULB: 3–10 in. (8–26 cm) long. The club-shaped pseudobulbs are grooved and dull yellow when dry.

LEAVES: 2 at the apex of each growth. The leaves are about 5.5 in. (14 cm) long, pointed, and elliptic.

INFLORESCENCE: 6 in. (15 cm) long. The inflorescence emerges from between the leaves at the apex of the pseudobulb.

FLOWERS: 3–5. The flowers are 0.5 in. (1.2 cm) across. The pointed sepals and petals are greenish with violet markings. The lip is marked with violet stripes. The erect sidelobes are nearly as large as the midlobe.

REFERENCES: 83, 219, 254, 445, 470.

PHOTOS/DRAWINGS: 83.

Dendrobium bimorphum J. J. Smith. Now considered a synonym of *Flickingeria*. REFERENCES: 449.

Dendrobium binnendijkii Rchb. f. Now considered a synonym of *Flickingeria fimbriata* (Blume) A. Hawkes. REFERENCES: 213, 216, 220, 231, 254, 436, 445, 449, 469, 536.

Dendrobium binoculare Rchb. f.

ORIGIN/HABITAT: Burma, Laos, Cambodia, and Vietnam. In the hills east of Prome, Burma, plants grow in shady places at about 1000 ft. (300 m).

CLIMATE: Station #48078, Toungoo, Burma, Lat. 18.9°N, Long. 96.5°E, at 162 ft. (49 m). Temperatures are calculated for an elevation of 1000 ft. (300 m), resulting in probable extremes of 106°F (41°C) and 44°F (7°C).

N/HEMISPHERE	JAN	FEB	MAR	APR	MAY	JUN	JUL	AUG	SEP	OCT	NOV	DEC
°F AVG MAX	82	88	94	97	92	86	83	83	86	87	84	80
°F AVG MIN	56	58	66	73	74	72	72	72	72	71	67	59
DIURNAL RANGE	26	30	28	24	18	14	11	11	14	16	17	21
RAIN/INCHES	0.2	0.2	0.3	2.1	8.0	14.4	17.9	18.9	11.7	7.2	1.9	0.4
HUMIDITY/%	67	60	56	57	72	87	88	89	86	82	77	72
BLOOM SEASON	N/A											
DAYS CLR @ 6AM	7	5	6	4	2	0	0	0	1	1	4	5
DAYS CLR @ 12PM	14	13	14	10	2	0	0	0	2	9	14	
RAIN/MM	5	5	8	53	203	366	455	480	297	183	48	10
°C AVG MAX	27.9	31.2	34.6	36.2	33.5	30.1	28.5	28.5	30.1	30.7	29.0	26.8
°C AVG MIN	13.5	14.6	19.0	22.9	23.5	22.4	22.4	22.4	22.4	21.8	19.6	15.1
DIURNAL RANGE	14.4	16.6	15.6	13.3	10.0	7.7	6.1	6.1	7.7	8.9	9.4	11.7
S/HEMISPHERE	JUL	AUG	SEP	OCT	NOV	DEC	JAN	FEB	MAR	APR	MAY	JUN

Cultural Recommendations

LIGHT: 2000–2500 fc. The shady habitat along with the heavy, persistent cloud cover associated with the summer monsoon indicates moderately low light. In cultivation, shading must be provided during the brightest time of the year, but it should be removed before winter.

TEMPERATURES: Summer days average 83–86°F (29–30°C), and nights average 72°F (22°C), with a diurnal range of 11–14°F (6–8°C). Weather is warmest during the bright clear days of spring. Days average 92–97°F (34–36°C), and nights average 66–74°F (19–24°C), with a diurnal range of 18–28°F (10–16°C).

HUMIDITY: Above 80% for 5–6 months from late spring to early autumn. Humidity remains moderately high in early winter, but decreases to 60% or less for about 3 months in late winter and early spring.

WATER: Rainfall is very heavy for 6 months from late spring into autumn, followed by 4–5 very dry months in winter and early spring. Cultivated plants should be kept moist during the growing season, but water should be gradually reduced after new growths mature in late autumn.

FERTILIZER: ¼–½ recommended strength, applied weekly. A high-nitrogen fertilizer is beneficial from spring to midsummer, but a fertilizer high in phosphates should be used in late summer and autumn.

REST PERIOD: Winter days average 80–88°F (27–31°C), and nights average 56–59°F (14–15°C), with a diurnal range of 21–30°F (12–17°C). Rainfall decreases rapidly in autumn, and the habitat is very dry for 4–5 months. Some moisture is still available at the beginning of the rest period because the humidity is high in early winter, resulting in frequent heavy deposits of dew. By late winter, however, the habitat becomes so dry and the humidity falls so low that even the moisture from morning dew is seldom available. In cultivation, water should be reduced and the plants allowed to dry out between waterings. They should not remain completely dry for extended periods, however. Occasional early morning misting on bright winter days may help keep plants from becoming too dry. Fertilizer should be eliminated until water is increased in spring. Light should be as bright as possible, short of burning the foliage.

GROWING MEDIA: Plants may be mounted on tree-fern or cork slabs if humidity is high and plants are watered at least once daily in summer. When plants are potted, any open, fast-draining medium may be used. Repotting may be done anytime new roots are growing.

Plant and Flower Information

PLANT SIZE AND TYPE: A 24 in. (60 cm) sympodial epiphyte, terrestrial, or lithophyte.

PSEUDOBULB: 24 in. (60 cm) long. The stems are slender, rodlike, and vary in length.

LEAVES: Many. The lanceolate leaves are 3–4 in. (8–10 cm) long and pointed at the apex.

INFLORESCENCE: The racemes are ascending to erect.

FLOWERS: 5–9 per inflorescence. The flowers are 2 in. (5 cm) across. The oblong sepals and slightly broader petals are reddish, intensely yellow, or coppery orange. The lip has yellow at the apex and 2 maroon spots at the base. It is pubescent with a toothed margin.

REFERENCES: 157, 202, 216, 254, 447, 448, 454, 541.

Dendrobium bipulvinatum J. J. Smith

ORIGIN/HABITAT: Irian Jaya (western New Guinea). Plants grow on trees near Humboldt Bay at about 150 ft. (50 m). They were found at the forest edge on an *Imperata*-covered hill.

CLIMATE: Station #97690, Sentani/Jayapura, Irian Jaya, Lat. 2.7°S, Long. 140.5°E, at 289 ft. (88 m). Record extreme temperatures are 97°F (36°C) and 68°F (20°C).

N/HEMISPHERE	JAN	FEB	MAR	APR	MAY	JUN	JUL	AUG	SEP	OCT	NOV	DEC
°F AVG MAX	87	89	89	90	90	89	89	88	89	90	90	89
°F AVG MIN	72	72	72	73	73	73	73	73	73	74	73	73
DIURNAL RANGE	15	17	17	17	17	16	16	15	16	16	17	16
RAIN/INCHES	4.1	3.9	5.3	2.9	6.7	7.0	8.3	8.3	8.5	4.6	2.4	5.2
HUMIDITY/%	81	80	80	79	81	81	79	80	80	80	81	80
BLOOM SEASON						*						
DAYS CLR @ 9AM	5	3	3	2	1	1	0	1	2	2	5	
DAYS CLR @ 3PM	4	3	3	3	2	1	3	0	1	2	2	3
RAIN/MM	104	99	135	74	170	178	211	211	216	117	61	132
°C AVG MAX	30.6	31.7	31.7	32.2	32.2	31.7	31.7	31.1	31.7	32.2	32.2	31.7
°C AVG MIN	22.2	22.2	22.2	22.8	22.8	22.8	22.8	22.8	22.8	23.3	22.8	22.8
DIURNAL RANGE	8.4	9.5	9.5	9.4	9.4	8.9	8.9	8.3	8.9	8.9	9.4	8.9
S/HEMISPHERE	JUL	AUG	SEP	OCT	NOV	DEC	JAN	FEB	MAR	APR	MAY	JUN

Cultural Recommendations

LIGHT: 2000–3000 fc.

TEMPERATURES: Throughout the year, days average 87–90°F (31–32°C), and nights average 72–74°F (22–23°C), with a diurnal range of 15–17°F (8–10°C).

HUMIDITY: Near 80% year-round.

WATER: Rainfall is heavy all year with brief semidry periods in spring and autumn. Cultivated plants should be kept evenly moist with only slight drying allowed between waterings.

FERTILIZER: ¼–½ recommended strength. A balanced fertilizer should be applied weekly to biweekly throughout the year.

REST PERIOD: Growing conditions should be maintained year-round. Water may be reduced somewhat for cultivated plants in winter, especially those grown in the dark, short-day conditions common in temperate latitudes. They should never be allowed to dry out completely, however. In the habitat, light is slightly higher in winter.

GROWING MEDIA: Plants may be mounted on tree-fern or cork slabs if humidity is high and plants are watered at least once daily in summer. When plants are potted, any open, fast-draining medium may be used. Repotting may be done anytime new roots are growing.

MISCELLANEOUS NOTES: The bloom season shown in the climate table is based on reports from the habitat.

Plant and Flower Information

PLANT SIZE AND TYPE: A 30 in. (75 cm) sympodial epiphyte.

PSEUDOBULB: 30 in. (75 cm) long. The flattened stems are elongated, spreading, and branching.

LEAVES: Many. The linear-triangular leaves are 1.1 in. (2.8 cm) long along the longest edge. They are overlapping, arranged in 2 rows, and terminate in a sharp point.

INFLORESCENCE: Short. Inflorescences emerge along the side of the stem.

FLOWERS: 1 per inflorescence. The yellow-green blossoms are 0.4 in. (1 cm) long, thick, and fleshy. They have an ovate-oblong dorsal sepal, obliquely triangular lateral sepals, and oblong petals. All segments are pointed. The curved lip is deep brownish red with metallic green in the center. The margin of the lip and callus are hairy. The sidelobes are brownish-red on the outside. The column is a paler shade of brownish red.

REFERENCES: 221, 470, 477.

Dendrobium bismarckiense Schlechter

ORIGIN/HABITAT: Northern Papua New Guinea. Plants are found in the mountains at 4600–6050 ft. (1400–1850 m), where they grow low on the trunks of mistforest trees.

CLIMATE: Station #94010, Goroka, Papua New Guinea, Lat. 6.1°S, Long. 145.4°E, at 5141 ft. (1567 m). Record extreme temperatures are 87°F (31°C) and 43°F (6°C).

N/HEMISPHERE	JAN	FEB	MAR	APR	MAY	JUN	JUL	AUG	SEP	OCT	NOV	DEC
°F AVG MAX	76	77	78	79	79	78	79	78	78	78	79	77
°F AVG MIN	56	57	57	57	58	59	59	59	60	59	59	57
DIURNAL RANGE	20	20	21	22	21	19	20	19	18	19	20	20
RAIN/INCHES	2.1	2.8	4.6	5.9	6.6	9.3	9.1	10.1	10.7	8.3	4.6	2.0
HUMIDITY/%	70	67	67	67	67	71	72	73	74	71	70	70
BLOOM SEASON		*		*		*			*			
DAYS CLR	N/A											
RAIN/MM	54	70	118	151	167	236	230	256	271	211	116	52
°C AVG MAX	24.7	25.1	25.6	26.3	26.2	25.7	25.8	25.6	25.5	25.6	25.9	25.1
°C AVG MIN	13.5	13.8	14.0	14.0	14.2	14.8	15.0	15.2	15.3	15.1	14.7	13.7
DIURNAL RANGE	11.2	11.3	11.6	12.3	12.0	10.9	10.8	10.4	10.2	10.5	11.2	11.4
S/HEMISPHERE	JUL	AUG	SEP	OCT	NOV	DEC	JAN	FEB	MAR	APR	MAY	JUN

Cultural Recommendations

LIGHT: 2000–2500 fc.

TEMPERATURES: Throughout the year, days average 76–79°F (25–26°C), and nights average 56–60°F (14–15°C), with a diurnal range of 18–22°F (10–12°C).

HUMIDITY: 70–75% in summer and autumn, decreasing to 65–70% in winter and spring.

WATER: Rainfall is moderate to heavy most of the year, but conditions are slightly drier for 3 months in winter. Cultivated plants should be kept moist. In summer, daily water may be necessary during hot, dry weather. In addition, early morning mistings may be beneficial, especially on bright, sunny days.

FERTILIZER: ¼–½ recommended strength. A balanced fertilizer should be applied weekly to biweekly throughout the year.

REST PERIOD: Growing conditions must be cool year-round. In the habitat, rainfall is lowest in winter, but dew, fog, and low clouds are common. Water should be reduced somewhat in winter, especially for plants grown in the dark, short-day conditions common in temperate latitudes. Plants should never be allowed to dry out completely, however. Fertilizer should be reduced or eliminated until water is increased in spring. In the habitat, seasonal light variation is minor.

GROWING MEDIA: Plants may be mounted on tree-fern or cork slabs or potted in a small pot filled with any open, fast-draining medium. Repotting may be done anytime new roots are actively growing.

MISCELLANEOUS NOTES: The bloom season shown in the climate table is based on collection and cultivation records.

Plant and Flower Information

PLANT SIZE AND TYPE: An 18 in. (45 cm) epiphyte.

PSEUDOBULB: 12 in. (30 cm) long. The pseudobulbs are clustered on a very short rhizome.

LEAVES: Many. The papery leaves are 5–6 in. (13–15 cm) long, lanceolate, and pointed at the apex.

INFLORESCENCE: The racemes, which are minutely covered with black hairs, emerge from nodes below the apex of the pseudobulb.

FLOWERS: Few per inflorescence. The blossoms are yellowish on the outside and white on the inside. The backs of the sepals are covered with short, black hairs. The smooth lip is white with a golden yellow spot in the center. It has a sharp point at the apex and a distinctly scalloped edge around the nearly round midlobe.

REFERENCES: 179, 219, 254, 437, 444, 445.

PHOTOS/DRAWINGS: 437.

Dendrobium blanche-amesii A. Hawkes and A. H. Heller

AKA: *D. verruculosum* Ames. Valmayor (ref. 536) includes *D. verruculosum* and does not include *D. blanche-amesii* as a synonym.

ORIGIN/HABITAT: The Philippines. Plants grow throughout Luzon Island from Ilocos Norte province on the northwest coast to Sorsogon province at the south end of the island. They are also reported on Leyte Island. Plants are normally found growing on trees in Mangrove swamps.

CLIMATE: Station #98223, Laoag, Philippines, Lat. 18.2°N, Long. 120.5°E, at 13 ft. (4 m). Record extreme temperatures are 100°F (38°C) and 53°F (12°C).

N/HEMISPHERE	JAN	FEB	MAR	APR	MAY	JUN	JUL	AUG	SEP	OCT	NOV	DEC
°F AVG MAX	86	87	89	91	92	90	88	88	88	89	88	87
°F AVG MIN	66	67	70	74	76	76	75	75	75	73	71	69
DIURNAL RANGE	20	20	19	17	16	14	13	13	13	16	17	18
RAIN/INCHES	0.2	0.1	0.1	0.4	4.0	16.8	18.1	22.0	13.0	3.0	1.7	0.3
HUMIDITY/%	71	70	71	71	74	80	83	84	84	76	73	71
BLOOM SEASON					*	*	*	*	*			
DAYS CLR @ 8AM	16	17	23	22	17	7	7	3	6	14	15	16
DAYS CLR @ 2PM	19	19	22	21	12	5	3	4	11	15	15
RAIN/MM	5	3	3	10	102	427	460	559	330	76	43	8
°C AVG MAX	30.0	30.6	31.7	32.8	33.3	32.2	31.1	31.1	31.1	31.7	31.1	30.6
°C AVG MIN	18.9	19.4	21.1	23.3	24.4	24.4	23.9	23.9	23.9	22.8	21.7	20.6
DIURNAL RANGE	11.1	11.2	10.6	9.5	8.9	7.8	7.2	7.2	7.2	8.9	9.4	10.0
S/HEMISPHERE	JUL	AUG	SEP	OCT	NOV	DEC	JAN	FEB	MAR	APR	MAY	JUN

Dendrobium blumei

Cultural Recommendations

LIGHT: 3000–4000 fc. Light is very high from late autumn into spring when skies are clear for more than half the days each month. Cultivated plants need some summer shading. But during the rest of the year, light should be as high as possible, short of burning the foliage.

TEMPERATURES: Summer days average 88–90°F (31–32°C), and nights average 75–76°F (24°C), with a diurnal range of 13–14°F (7–8°C). The warmest weather occurs in spring when days average 2–3°F (1–2°C) warmer than in summer.

HUMIDITY: 80–85% for about 4 months in summer, dropping to 70–75% during the remainder of the year.

WATER: Rainfall is very heavy from late spring into early autumn. This wet season is followed by 5, very dry months from late autumn into spring. Cultivated plants should be kept moist with only slight drying allowed between waterings in the summer growing season. Water should be gradually reduced after new growth matures in autumn.

FERTILIZER: ¼–½ recommended strength, applied weekly. A high nitrogen fertilizer is beneficial from spring to midsummer, but a fertilizer high in phosphates should be used in late summer and autumn.

REST PERIOD: Winter days average 86–87°F (30–31°C), and nights average 66–69°F (19–21°C), with a diurnal range of 18–20°F (10–11°C). Rainfall is very low for about 5 months in winter. However, the mangrove-swamp habitat provides high humidity, and the nightly cooling causes heavy deposits of dew. Cultivated plants should be allowed to dry out between waterings, but they should never remain dry for extended periods. Occasional early morning mistings between waterings may help keep plants from becoming too dry. Fertilizer should be reduced or eliminated until water is increased in spring. In the habitat, light is highest in winter.

GROWING MEDIA: Plants may be mounted on tree-fern or cork slabs if humidity is high and plants are watered at least once daily in summer. When plants are potted, any open, fast-draining medium may be used. Repotting may be done anytime new roots are growing.

MISCELLANEOUS NOTES: The bloom season shown in the climate table is based on collection reports.

Plant and Flower Information

PLANT SIZE AND TYPE: An 18–20 in. (45–50 cm) sympodial epiphyte.

PSEUDOBULB: 15–20 in. (39–50 cm) long. The branched stems are elongated and very slender.

LEAVES: Many. The linear-lanceolate leaves are 2.8–3.6 in. (7–9 cm) long. They taper from a rounded base to a pointed tip. The leaves are grasslike, spreading, and toothed along the edges.

INFLORESCENCE: Inflorescences emerge from nodes on the stem.

FLOWERS: 2 per inflorescence. The odorless flowers are 0.8 in. (2 cm) across. They are bright yellow to greenish yellow. The blossoms are similar to those of *D. ornithoflorum* Ames.

REFERENCES: 12, 13, 191, 221, 229, 536.

PHOTOS/DRAWINGS: 13.

Dendrobium blumei Lindley

AKA: Sometimes spelled *D. blumii*. Seidenfaden (ref. 454) includes *D. boothii* Teijsm. and Binn. and *D. tuberiferum* Hooker f. as synonyms, but these names are not included by Seidenfaden and Wood (ref. 455).

Confusion exists regarding the status of the plants known as *D. blumei* Lindley and *D. planibulbe* Lindley. Valmayor (ref. 536) follows Merrill (ref. 296) in listing *D. blumei* as a synonym of *D. planibulbe*, but J. J. Smith (ref. 469) lists *D. planibulbe* as a synonym of *D. blumei*. Seidenfaden (ref. 454) maintains them as independent species and indicates that the Philippine plant Valmayor refers to as *D. planibulbe* should in fact be *D. blumei*.

ORIGIN/HABITAT: Peninsular Thailand, Malaya, western Java, Borneo, and the Philippines. In Java, plants are found at 1650–1950 ft. (500–600 m). In Malaya, plants grow in shady places. In the Philippines, plants grow in low-elevation swamps on Mindanao, Basilan, and Samar.

CLIMATE: Station #96755, Bogor, Java, Indonesia, Lat. 6.5°S, Long. 106.8°E, at 558 ft. (170 m). Temperatures are calculated for an elevation of 1800 ft. (550 m), resulting in probable extremes of 92°F (33°C) and 62°F (17°C).

N/HEMISPHERE	JAN	FEB	MAR	APR	MAY	JUN	JUL	AUG	SEP	OCT	NOV	DEC
°F AVG MAX	82	83	84	84	83	81	80	80	81	82	83	82
°F AVG MIN	69	69	69	70	70	70	70	70	70	71	71	70
DIURNAL RANGE	13	14	15	14	13	11	10	10	11	11	12	12
RAIN/INCHES	2.1	1.0	0.5	5.0	8.1	18.8	23.7	20.2	14.4	12.0	11.9	3.4
HUMIDITY/%	72	68	65	66	74	79	84	84	81	79	77	75
BLOOM SEASON	*	*				*		*		*		
DAYS CLR @ 7AM	14	14	14	11	5	3	1	2	4	6	10	12
DAYS CLR @ 1PM	9	10	8	5	1	1	0	0	1	1	3	7
RAIN/MM	53	25	13	127	206	478	602	513	366	305	302	86
°C AVG MAX	27.7	28.3	28.8	28.8	28.3	27.2	26.6	26.6	27.2	27.7	28.3	27.7
°C AVG MIN	20.5	20.5	20.5	21.1	21.1	21.1	21.1	21.1	21.1	21.6	21.6	21.1
DIURNAL RANGE	7.2	7.8	8.3	7.7	7.2	6.1	5.5	5.5	6.1	6.1	6.7	6.6
S/HEMISPHERE	JUL	AUG	SEP	OCT	NOV	DEC	JAN	FEB	MAR	APR	MAY	JUN

Cultural Recommendations

LIGHT: 1200–2400 fc. Diffused or barely dappled light is preferred, and direct sunlight should be avoided.

TEMPERATURES: Throughout the year, days average 80–84°F (27–29°C), and nights average 69–71°F (21–22°C), with a diurnal range of 10–15°F (6–8°C). Temperatures at higher elevations are a few degrees cooler with a similar diurnal range and limited seasonal fluctuation. In Malaya and Thailand, day temperatures are about 10°F (6°C) warmer and nights are 2–4°F (1–2°C) warmer than temperatures in Java.

HUMIDITY: 75–85% most of the year, dropping to about 65% for 2–3 months in winter.

WATER: Rainfall is very heavy from spring to autumn, but conditions are very dry in winter. During the growing season, plants should never be allowed to dry out completely, but water should be gradually reduced in late autumn.

FERTILIZER: ¼–½ recommended strength, applied weekly. A high-nitrogen fertilizer is beneficial from spring to midsummer, but a fertilizer high in phosphates should be used in late summer and autumn.

REST PERIOD: Growing conditions should be maintained all year, but rainfall is very low for 2–3 months in winter. In cultivation, water should be reduced and the plants allowed to become somewhat dry between waterings. They should not remain dry for prolonged periods, however. Fertilizer may be reduced or eliminated anytime the plant is not actively growing. In the habitat, light is highest in winter.

GROWING MEDIA: Plants may be mounted on tree-fern or cork slabs if humidity is high and plants are watered at least once daily in summer. When plants are potted, any open, fast-draining medium may be used. Repotting may be done anytime new roots are growing.

MISCELLANEOUS NOTES: The bloom season shown in the climate table is based on collection reports from the Philippines. Plants that produce flowers which last a single day commonly bloom several times during the year. Flowering usually occurs 7–14 days after a sudden 10°F (5°C) drop in daytime temperatures.

Plant and Flower Information

PLANT SIZE AND TYPE: A 5–16 in. (13–40 cm) sympodial epiphyte.

PSEUDOBULB: 4–7 in. (10–18 cm) long. The yellowish growths may reach a length of 16 in. (40 cm). The base is slender, several thickened nodes are angular, but the upper nodes are spindle-shaped and often somewhat flattened. The swollen portion of the stem is 1.2–2.4 in. (3–6 cm) long.

LEAVES: 5–9 per growth. The thick, lanceolate leaves are 1.2–1.6 in. (3–4 cm) long and alternate along the upper part of the stem.

INFLORESCENCE: Inflorescences emerge on the upper, leafless portion of the cane.

FLOWERS: 1 per inflorescence. The short-lived blossoms are 0.4–0.6 in. (1.0–1.5 cm) across, which is small for the plant size. They are lemon scented. Sepals and petals are white to cream with reddish lavender on the outer petals and often with a red spot at the tip of each segment. The outer margins of the petals are uneven. The margin of the yellow lip midlobe appears chopped off and is deeply fringed.

HYBRIDIZING NOTES: Johansen (ref. 239) indicates that plants are self-sterile and that flowers dropped 6–7 days after self-pollination.

REFERENCES: 25, 75, 216, 239, 254, 278, 286, 295, 296, 310, 445, 454, 455, 469, 536.

PHOTOS/DRAWINGS: *454, 455, 469.*

Dendrobium blumii Lindley. See *D. blumei* Lindley. REFERENCES: 25, 216.

Dendrobium bolboflorum Falconer ex Hooker f. See *D. bicameratum* Wall ex Lindley. REFERENCES: 46, 202, 218, 254, 445, 454.

Dendrobium bolbophylli Griffith. Now considered a synonym of *Bulbophyllum griffithii* Rchb. f. REFERENCES: 216, 224, 254.

Dendrobium bonianum Gagnepain. Now considered a synonym of *Eria boniana* (Gagnepain) Tang and Wang. REFERENCES: 136, 139, 224, 266, 448, 505, Seidenfaden 1992 *Opera Botanica* #114.

Dendrobium boothii Teijsm. and Binn. See *D. blumei* Lindley. REFERENCES: 75, 216, 254, 445, 454, 469.

Dendrobium borneense Finet. See *D. pachyphyllum* (Kuntze) Bakhuizen f. REFERENCES: 25, 118, 213, 219, 254, 286, 295, 445, 454.

Dendrobium bostrychodes Rchb. f. Sometimes spelled as *D. bostrichodes.* Thought to have originated on Borneo or nearby offshore islands, but Schelpe (ref. 429) indicates that this species has not been collected recently. It is not known to be in cultivation. Habitat location and elevation are not available, so climate data cannot be provided. The flowers are described as large. Sepals and ruffled petals are white. The wavy, ruffled lip, which is somewhat fiddle-shaped, has numerous warts. It is decorated with red markings. REFERENCES: 216, 254, 286, 295, 429, 454.

Dendrobium boumaniae J. J. Smith

ORIGIN/HABITAT: Western Sumatra. Plants were originally collected near Wai Tenoeng in the Bengkulu district at about 3300 ft. (1000 m). Plants were cultivated in the botanical garden at Bogor, Java.

CLIMATE: Station #96253, Bengkulu, Sumatra, Indonesia, Lat. 3.9°S, Long. 102.3°E, at 49 ft. (15 m). Temperatures are calculated for an elevation of 3300 ft. (1000 m). Record extreme temperatures are not available for this location.

N/HEMISPHERE	JAN	FEB	MAR	APR	MAY	JUN	JUL	AUG	SEP	OCT	NOV	DEC
°F AVG MAX	77	76	76	76	76	76	77	77	77	77	78	77
°F AVG MIN	61	61	61	62	62	62	62	61	62	63	62	62
DIURNAL RANGE	16	15	15	14	14	14	15	16	15	14	16	15
RAIN/INCHES	6.9	6.8	9.1	13.9	16.0	12.7	16.0	11.5	12.0	8.3	8.4	8.4
HUMIDITY/%	77	78	77	77	79	80	78	76	77	79	77	78
BLOOM SEASON	N/A											
DAYS CLR @ 7AM	5	1	1	0	0	2	1	1	1	2	1	3
DAYS CLR @ 1PM	5	4	3	1	2	3	2	2	2	3	7	5
RAIN/MM	175	173	231	353	406	323	406	292	305	211	213	213
°C AVG MAX	25.2	24.6	24.6	24.6	24.6	24.6	25.2	25.2	25.2	25.2	25.7	25.2
°C AVG MIN	16.3	16.3	16.3	16.8	16.8	16.8	16.8	16.3	16.8	17.4	16.8	16.8
DIURNAL RANGE	8.9	8.3	8.3	7.8	7.8	7.8	8.4	8.9	8.4	7.8	8.9	8.4
S/HEMISPHERE	JUL	AUG	SEP	OCT	NOV	DEC	JAN	FEB	MAR	APR	MAY	JUN

Cultural Recommendations

LIGHT: 2000–3000 fc.

TEMPERATURES: Throughout the year, days average 76–78°F (25–26°C), and nights average 61–63°F (16–17°C), with a diurnal range of 14–16°F (8–9°C).

HUMIDITY: 75–80% year-round.

WATER: Rainfall is heavy throughout the year, but conditions are slightly drier in winter. Cultivated plants should be kept moist but not soggy. Only slight drying should be allowed between waterings.

FERTILIZER: ¼–½ recommended strength. A balanced fertilizer should be applied weekly to biweekly throughout the year.

REST PERIOD: Growing conditions should be maintained year-round. Water may be reduced somewhat in winter for plants that are grown in the dark, short-day conditions common in temperate latitudes, but they should never be allowed to dry completely.

GROWING MEDIA: Plants may be mounted on tree-fern or cork slabs or potted in small pots filled with any open, fast-draining medium. Repotting may be done anytime new roots are growing.

MISCELLANEOUS NOTES: The plant was described in 1926 in *Bul. Jard. Bot. Buit.* 3rd sér. 8:55.

Plant and Flower Information

PLANT SIZE AND TYPE: A 10 in. (25 cm) sympodial epiphyte.

PSEUDOBULB: 10 in. (25 cm) long. The clustered stems are elliptical in cross section. They become grooved with age.

LEAVES: The lanceolate leaves are 2.8 in. (7 cm) long. They are shiny and dark green with a violet flush.

INFLORESCENCE: Short. Inflorescences emerge from nodes on leafless stems. The leaf sheaths are pale green with purple dots.

FLOWERS: 1 per inflorescence. The flowers are 1 in. (2.5 cm) across. The sepals and paler petals are yellowish brown with a purple suffusion. The white lip is marked with purple at the apex.

REFERENCES: 224.

Dendrobium bowmanii Bentham

AKA: Sometimes spelled *D. bowmannii.* Synonyms include *D. chalandei* (A. Finet) Kränzlin, *D. mortii* as used by Dockrill, *D. striolatum* Rchb. f. var. *chalandei* Finet. *D. tenuissimum* Rupp is frequently included as a synonym, but Kränzlin (ref. 254) and Clements (ref. 67) consider it a synonym of *D. mortii* F. Mueller.

ORIGIN/HABITAT: New Caledonia and Australia. In Australia, the habitat extends along the east coast, ranging southward from the Herbert River in northeastern Queensland to near Coffs Harbour in northeastern New South Wales. In southern Queensland and northern New South Wales, plants normally grow in dry open areas and on the coastal plains. In drier central Queensland, plants are most often found near mangrove swamps;

Dendrobium boxallii

but further north, they grow in dry country, sometimes well away from the coast, often on trees overhanging creeks. Plants do not grow in moist, high altitude mountains, but they are sometimes found in the drier edges of rainforests, and distribution extends to the western slopes of the dividing range.

CLIMATE: Station #94576, Brisbane, Australia, Lat. 27.4°S, Long. 153.1°E, at 17 ft. (5 m). Record extreme temperatures are 110°F (43°C) and 35°F (2°C).

N/HEMISPHERE	JAN	FEB	MAR	APR	MAY	JUN	JUL	AUG	SEP	OCT	NOV	DEC
°F AVG MAX	68	71	76	80	82	85	85	85	82	79	74	69
°F AVG MIN	49	50	55	60	64	67	69	68	66	61	56	51
DIURNAL RANGE	19	21	21	20	18	18	16	17	16	18	18	18
RAIN/INCHES	2.2	1.9	1.9	2.5	3.7	5.0	6.4	6.3	5.7	3.7	2.8	2.6
HUMIDITY/%	62	59	58	57	59	59	63	65	66	64	64	64
BLOOM SEASON								*	*	*	*	*
DAYS CLR @ 10AM	17	20	18	11	12	9	5	4	9	14	18	16
DAYS CLR @ 4PM	15	16	15	12	14	12	8	5	8	10	14	14
RAIN/MM	56	48	48	64	94	127	163	160	145	94	71	66
°C AVG MAX	20.0	21.7	24.4	26.7	27.8	29.4	29.4	29.4	27.8	26.1	23.3	20.6
°C AVG MIN	9.4	10.0	12.8	15.6	17.8	19.4	20.6	20.0	18.9	16.1	13.3	10.6
DIURNAL RANGE	10.6	11.7	11.6	11.1	10.0	10.0	8.8	9.4	8.9	10.0	10.0	10.0
S/HEMISPHERE	JUL	AUG	SEP	OCT	NOV	DEC	JAN	FEB	MAR	APR	MAY	JUN

Cultural Recommendations

LIGHT: 3500–4500 fc. Light should be as high as possible short of burning the leaves. High light is required to initiate blooms. In the habitat, more than half the days are clear each month except during the summer rainy season when skies are clear approximately 30% of the time. Growers recommend using 40–50% shade cloth.

TEMPERATURES: Summer days average 85°F (29°C), and nights average 67–69°F (19–21°C), with a diurnal range of 16–18°F (9–10°C).

HUMIDITY: 60–65% year-round. Growers recommend brisk air movement.

WATER: Rainfall is moderate in summer and autumn, but conditions are drier in winter. Cultivated plants should be kept moist during the growing season with only slight drying allowed between waterings. Water should be gradually reduced in autumn.

FERTILIZER: ¼–½ recommended strength, applied weekly. A high-nitrogen fertilizer is beneficial from spring to midsummer, but a fertilizer high in phosphates should be used in late summer and autumn.

REST PERIOD: Winter days average 68–76°F (20–24°C), and nights average 49–55°F (9–13°C), with a diurnal range of 18–21°F (10–12°C). Growers recommend that winter lows be kept above 35°F (2°C). Rainfall is relatively low in winter. Cultivated plants should be allowed to become somewhat dry between waterings but should never dry out completely. Growers indicate that plants should be kept just barely moist in winter. Fertilizer should be reduced or eliminated until water is increased in spring. Plants from this habitat require distinct seasonal variation to be healthy. In the habitat, light is highest in winter.

GROWING MEDIA: Mounting plants on slabs of cork, tree-fern, or a rough-barked hardwood accommodates their growth habit. Mounted plants need high humidity and watering at least once daily in summer. If plants are potted, the smallest possible pot should be filled with fir bark, cork nuggets, or other rapidly draining media. Growers report that clay pots are preferable to plastic ones. Repotting is best done immediately after flowering.

MISCELLANEOUS NOTES: The bloom season shown in the climate table is based on reports from the habitat. Plants bloom irregularly in summer-autumn—up to 6 times in succession. All plants in a particular area bloom at the same time. Branches may be removed if the plant becomes too untidy.

Plant and Flower Information

PLANT SIZE AND TYPE: A 16–24 in. (40–60 cm) sympodial epiphyte or lithophyte.

PSEUDOBULB: Variable. New branches emerge from upper nodes of the preceding branch. The straggly, semipendulous plants increase in overall size each growing season.

LEAVES: 2–4 per branch. The terete leaves are 1–5 in. (3–13 cm) long, cylindrical to tapering, with several longitudinal grooves.

INFLORESCENCE: 1–3 in. (2.5–7.6 cm) long. Inflorescences emerge from the base of new leaves near the branch tip.

FLOWERS: 2 (1–4) per inflorescence. The flowers are 1 in. (2.5 cm) across. The narrow sepals and petals remain rather closed. They may be yellow, pale yellowish green, or a pale shade of green or brown. They often have 3–5 red or purple-brown stripes on the rear of the segments. The white lip has a narrow, oval midlobe with a short, sharp tip. Blossoms are lemon-scented and last about 2 weeks. However, buds form rapidly, and plants may bloom 3–4 times in quick succession.

REFERENCES: 67, 105, 118, 173, 216, 240, 254, 263, 533.

PHOTOS/DRAWINGS: 173, 240, *263*, *533*.

Dendrobium boxallii Rchb. f. See *D. gratiosissimum* Rchb. f.
REFERENCES: 216, 254, 430, 445, 454, 541, 570.

Dendrobium braccatum Lindley. Now considered a synonym of *Eria braccata* Lindley. REFERENCES: 216, 254, 277.

Dendrobium brachyacron Schlechter. See *D. violaceum* Kränzlin. REFERENCES: 222, 385, 443.

Dendrobium brachyanthum Schlechter

ORIGIN/HABITAT: Palau Island, Micronesia. Plants grow in dense intermediate forests at 350–1000 ft. (100–300 m).

CLIMATE: Station #91408, Koror Island, Caroline Island group, Lat. 7.3°N, Long. 134.5°E, at 108 ft. (33 m). Temperatures are calculated for an elevation of 650 ft. (200 m), resulting in probable extremes of 91°F (33°C) and 67°F (20°C).

N/HEMISPHERE	JAN	FEB	MAR	APR	MAY	JUN	JUL	AUG	SEP	OCT	NOV	DEC
°F AVG MAX	84	85	85	86	86	86	85	85	85	86	86	85
°F AVG MIN	73	73	73	74	74	73	73	73	73	74	74	73
DIURNAL RANGE	11	12	12	12	12	13	12	12	12	12	12	12
RAIN/INCHES	12.6	6.8	7.7	9.7	16.3	14.6	16.8	16.8	15.4	13.4	10.8	12.7
HUMIDITY/%	86	85	84	85	87	87	87	87	86	86	85	86
BLOOM SEASON		*	*									
DAYS CLR @ 9AM	0	0	0	0	0	0	0	0	0	1	0	0
DAYC CLR @ 3PM	0	0	0	0	0	0	0	0	0	0	0	0
RAIN/MM	320	173	196	246	414	371	427	427	391	340	274	323
°C AVG MAX	29.0	29.4	29.6	30.1	30.1	30.1	29.6	29.6	29.6	30.1	30.1	29.6
°C AVG MIN	22.9	22.9	22.9	23.5	23.5	22.9	22.9	22.9	22.9	23.5	23.5	22.9
DIURNAL RANGE	6.1	6.7	6.7	6.6	6.6	7.2	6.7	6.7	6.7	6.6	6.6	6.7
S/HEMISPHERE	JUL	AUG	SEP	OCT	NOV	DEC	JAN	FEB	MAR	APR	MAY	JUN

Cultural Recommendations

LIGHT: 1800–2500 fc. Clear days are rare in the region, and the plants grow in shady situations in deep forest

TEMPERATURES: Throughout the year, days average 84–86°F (29–30°C), and nights average 73–74°F (23–24°C), with a diurnal range of 11–13°F (6–7°C).

HUMIDITY: Near 85% year-round.

WATER: Rainfall is heavy all year. Cultivated plants should never be allowed to dry out completely.

FERTILIZER: ¼–½ recommended strength. A balanced fertilizer should be applied weekly to biweekly throughout the year.

REST PERIOD: Growing conditions vary only slightly. Water may be reduced somewhat in winter, especially for plants grown in the dark, short-day conditions common in temperate latitudes; but plants should not dry out completely. Fertilizer should be reduced or eliminated anytime watering is reduced.

GROWING MEDIA: Mounting plants on tree-fern or cork slabs accommodates their pendent growth habit. However, humidity must be high and plants must be at least once daily in summer. When plants are potted, any open, fast-draining medium may be used. Repotting may be done anytime new roots are growing.

MISCELLANEOUS NOTES: The bloom season shown in the climate table is based on the collection reports.

Plant and Flower Information

PLANT SIZE AND TYPE: A 14–20 in. (35–50 cm) sympodial epiphyte.

PSEUDOBULB: 5–10 in. (13–25 cm) long. The pendent pseudobulbs, which arise from a very short rhizome, consist of several internodes.

LEAVES: 1 per growth. The leaves, which are roughly equal to the length of the stems, are 6–10 in. (16–25 cm) long.

INFLORESCENCE: 2 in. (5.5 cm) long. The short inflorescences are borne at nodes on the pseudobulbs.

FLOWERS: 2–5 per inflorescence. The white flowers are about 0.7 in. (1.8 cm) across. All segments are smooth, thick, and fleshy.

REFERENCES: 223, 441.

Dendrobium brachycalyptra Schlechter

ORIGIN/HABITAT: Papua New Guinea. Plants grow in the Sepik River region at about 4600 ft. (1400 m).

CLIMATE: Station #200004, Ambunti, Papua New Guinea, Lat. 4.2°S, Long. 142.8°E, at 164 ft. (50 m). Temperatures are calculated for an elevation of 4600 ft. (1400 m), resulting in probable extremes of 84°F (29°C) and 37°F (3°C).

N/HEMISPHERE	JAN	FEB	MAR	APR	MAY	JUN	JUL	AUG	SEP	OCT	NOV	DEC
°F AVG MAX	73	75	75	75	76	75	75	75	75	75	75	74
°F AVG MIN	57	58	59	58	58	58	57	58	58	58	58	59
DIURNAL RANGE	16	17	16	17	18	17	18	17	17	17	17	15
RAIN/INCHES	6.4	7.4	7.7	8.5	9.2	9.4	10.9	10.2	12.2	10.4	8.3	5.2
HUMIDITY/%	N/A											
BLOOM SEASON			*									
DAYS CLR	N/A											
RAIN/MM	163	188	196	216	234	239	277	259	310	264	211	132
°C AVG MAX	23.0	24.1	24.1	24.1	24.6	24.1	24.1	24.1	24.1	24.1	24.1	23.5
°C AVG MIN	14.1	14.6	15.2	14.6	14.6	14.6	14.1	14.6	14.6	14.6	14.6	15.2
DIURNAL RANGE	8.9	9.5	8.9	9.5	10.0	9.5	10.0	9.5	9.5	9.5	9.5	8.3
S/HEMISPHERE	JUL	AUG	SEP	OCT	NOV	DEC	JAN	FEB	MAR	APR	MAY	JUN

Cultural Recommendations

LIGHT: 2000–3000 fc.

TEMPERATURES: Throughout the year, days average 73–76°F (23–25°C), and nights average 57–59°F (14–15°C), with a diurnal range of 15–18°F (8–10°C).

HUMIDITY: Information is not available for this location. However, records from nearby stations indicate that humidity is probably near 80% year-round.

WATER: Rainfall is heavy year-round, with the greatest amounts falling in summer and early autumn. Cultivated plants should be kept moist but not soggy.

FERTILIZER: ¼–½ recommended strength. A balanced fertilizer should be applied weekly to biweekly throughout the year.

REST PERIOD: Growing temperatures should be maintained all year. Water and fertilizer should be reduced somewhat in winter, especially for plants cultivated in the dark, short-day conditions common in temperate latitudes; but plants should never be allowed to dry out completely. In the habitat, seasonal light variation is minor.

GROWING MEDIA: Plants may be mounted on cork or tree-fern slabs if humidity is high and plants are watered at least once daily in summer. When plants are potted, any open, fast-draining medium may be used. Repotting may be done anytime new roots are growing.

MISCELLANEOUS NOTES: The bloom season shown in the climate table is based on collection reports.

Plant and Flower Information

PLANT SIZE AND TYPE: An 8–20 in. (20–50 cm) sympodial epiphyte.

PSEUDOBULB: 8–20 in. (20–50 cm) long. Numerous stems arise from a very short rhizome. They are slender and cylindrical.

LEAVES: Many. The narrow, lanceolate leaves are 1.6–3.2 in. (4–8 cm) long with a sharp point at the tip.

INFLORESCENCE: Very short. The blossoms appear to rest on the stem.

FLOWERS: The flowers are 0.9 in. (2.2 cm) long. Blossoms have very small sepals and petals, about 0.2 in. (0.5cm) long, but the lip is relatively large. The bright orange segments are paler near the tips.

REFERENCES: 223, 443.

Dendrobium brachycarpum A. Richard. Now considered a synonym of *Angraecum brachycarpum* Rchb. f. REFERENCES: 216, 254.

Dendrobium brachycentrum Ridley

ORIGIN/HABITAT: Irian Jaya (western New Guinea). Plants were collected on the south side of Mt. Jaya (Mt. Carstensz) at 500–2500 ft. (150–760 m).

CLIMATE: Station #97796, Kokenau (Kokonau), Irian Jaya, Lat. 4.7°S, Long. 135.4°E, at 10 ft. (3 m). Temperatures are calculated for an elevation of 1500 ft. (460 m). Record extreme temperatures are not available for this location.

N/HEMISPHERE	JAN	FEB	MAR	APR	MAY	JUN	JUL	AUG	SEP	OCT	NOV	DEC
°F AVG MAX	78	78	81	83	85	84	84	84	85	83	82	79
°F AVG MIN	68	68	69	69	69	70	69	69	69	69	69	68
DIURNAL RANGE	10	10	12	14	16	14	15	15	16	14	13	11
RAIN/INCHES	18.4	15.8	18.9	11.6	9.7	10.6	11.5	15.7	11.6	11.6	16.0	19.9
HUMIDITY/%	N/A											
BLOOM SEASON	N/A											
DAYS CLR	N/A											
RAIN/MM	467	401	480	295	246	269	292	399	295	295	406	505
°C AVG MAX	25.6	25.6	27.3	28.4	29.5	28.9	28.9	28.9	29.5	28.4	27.8	26.2
°C AVG MIN	20.0	20.0	20.6	20.6	20.6	21.2	20.6	20.6	20.6	20.6	20.6	20.0
DIURNAL RANGE	5.6	5.6	6.7	7.8	8.9	7.7	8.3	8.3	8.9	7.8	7.2	6.2
S/HEMISPHERE	JUL	AUG	SEP	OCT	NOV	DEC	JAN	FEB	MAR	APR	MAY	JUN

Cultural Recommendations

LIGHT: 2500–3500 fc.

TEMPERATURES: Throughout the year, days average 78–85°F (26–30°C), and nights average 68–70°F (20–21°C), with a diurnal range of 10–16°F (6–9°C).

HUMIDITY: Information is not available for this location. However, averages from nearby stations indicate that values are probably near 85% year-round.

WATER: Rainfall is very heavy all year. Cultivated plants should be kept evenly moist with only slight drying allowed between waterings.

FERTILIZER: ¼–½ recommended strength. A balanced fertilizer should be applied weekly throughout the year.

REST PERIOD: Growing conditions should be maintained year-round. Water and fertilizer may be reduced somewhat for cultivated plants in winter, especially those grown in the dark, short-day conditions common in temperate latitudes. Plants should never be allowed to dry completely, however. In the habitat, seasonal light variation is minor.

GROWING MEDIA: Plants should be kept moist. They are best potted in an open medium and watered often, however, if frequent watering is a problem, plants may be potted in a medium that retains more moisture. Repotting may be done anytime new roots are growing.

Plant and Flower Information

PLANT SIZE AND TYPE: A 9 in. (23 cm) sympodial epiphyte.

PSEUDOBULB: 9 in. (23 cm) long. The quadrangular stems are very slender.

LEAVES: The leaves, which may have been immature when the plant was collected, were 0.8 in. (2 cm) long. They were toothed at the apex and margin.

INFLORESCENCE: Short. Racemes emerge from the apical, leafless portion of the stem.

FLOWERS: 12 per inflorescence. The orange-red flowers are 0.5 in. (1.2 cm) across, with linear petals, and elliptical or oblong sepals. The rounded lip, which is 0.4 in. (1 cm) long, is toothed at the apex.

REFERENCES: 222, 400.

Dendrobium brachypetalum Lindley. Now considered a synonym of *Bulbophyllum mutabile* (Blume) Lindley. REFERENCES: 216, 254, 278, 310, 469.

Dendrobium brachyphyta Schlechter. See *D. vexillarius* J. J. Smith. REFERENCES: 223, 385, 443.

Dendrobium brachypus Rchb. f.

AKA: Commonly considered part of the *D. macropus* alliance of plants, Clements (ref. 67) reinstated species status pending conclusion of research currently being conducted in Australia. See discussion at *D. macropus* (Endl.) Rchb. f. ex Lindley.

ORIGIN/HABITAT: Endemic to Norfolk Island. Plants generally grow on trees, but they are occasionally found on rocks in heavily wooded areas. They are common in the forests of the Mt. Pitt Reserve but less common in other areas around the island.

CLIMATE: Station #94996, Norfolk Island, Australia, Lat. 29.1°S, Long. 167.9°E, at 370 ft. (113 m). Temperatures are calculated for an elevation of 500 ft. (150 m), resulting in probable extremes of 89°F (31°C) and 43°F (6°C).

N/HEMISPHERE	JAN	FEB	MAR	APR	MAY	JUN	JUL	AUG	SEP	OCT	NOV	DEC
°F AVG MAX	65	65	67	69	72	75	78	77	76	73	69	67
°F AVG MIN	57	56	57	60	62	65	67	68	67	65	61	60
DIURNAL RANGE	8	9	10	9	10	10	11	9	9	8	8	7
RAIN/INCHES	6.1	5.4	3.7	3.7	2.6	3.4	3.3	4.3	3.7	5.0	5.7	5.5
HUMIDITY/%	80	83	82	82	82	82	82	85	82	82	83	82
BLOOM SEASON		*	*									
DAYS CLR @ 5AM	5	6	7	5	5	3	4	3	4	5	5	6
DAYS CLR @ 11AM	4	5	5	5	5	4	4	2	3	3	3	3
RAIN/MM	155	137	94	94	66	86	84	109	94	127	145	140
°C AVG MAX	18.1	18.1	19.2	20.3	22.0	23.7	25.3	24.8	24.2	22.5	20.3	19.2
°C AVG MIN	13.7	13.1	13.7	15.3	16.4	18.1	19.2	19.8	19.2	18.1	15.9	15.3
DIURNAL RANGE	4.4	5.0	5.5	5.0	5.6	5.6	6.1	5.0	5.0	4.4	4.4	3.9
S/HEMISPHERE	JUL	AUG	SEP	OCT	NOV	DEC	JAN	FEB	MAR	APR	MAY	JUN

Cultural Recommendations

LIGHT: 2500–3500 fc. Plants require good light and strong air movement.

TEMPERATURES: Summer days average 75–78°F (24–25°C), and nights average 65–68°F (18–20°C), with a diurnal range of 9–11°F (5–6°C).

HUMIDITY: 80–85% year-round.

WATER: Rainfall is moderate throughout the year, with a short, slightly drier period in late spring. Plants are healthiest if allowed to dry between waterings.

FERTILIZER: ¼–½ recommended strength, applied weekly. A high-nitrogen fertilizer is beneficial from spring to midsummer, but a fertilizer high in phosphates should be used in late summer and autumn.

REST PERIOD: Winter days average 65–67°F (18–19°C), and nights average 56–60°F (13–15°C), with a diurnal range of 7–9°F (4–5°C). Water and fertilizer should be reduced somewhat in winter, especially for plants grown in the dark, short-day conditions common in temperate latitudes. They should not remain dry for long periods, however.

GROWING MEDIA: Plants may be mounted on a tree-fern slab or potted in small pots filled with chopped tree-fern. Growers indicate that drainage must be excellent as roots are prone to rot, especially in winter. The fine roots deteriorate quickly if plants are overwatered or if the medium becomes stale. Repotting may be done anytime new roots are actively growing.

MISCELLANEOUS NOTES: The bloom season shown in the climate table is based on cultivation records.

Plant and Flower Information

PLANT SIZE AND TYPE: A 5–22 in. (13–55 cm) sympodial epiphyte or lithophyte.

PSEUDOBULB: 5–22 in. (13–55 cm) long. The swollen, clustered stems taper toward the apex.

LEAVES: 3–4 per growth. The apical leaf is half the size of the lowest leaf.

INFLORESCENCE: 1.6–2.0 in. (4–5 cm) long.

FLOWERS: 3–4 per inflorescence. The flowers are 0.5 in. (1.3 cm) across. The blossoms are peloric and all segments are the same. They are frequently self-pollinating.

HYBRIDIZING NOTES: When used in hybridizing, the plant form, flower color, shape, and size all tend to be dominant. However, when *D. brachypus* is crossed with *D. kingianum* Bidwill ex Lindley, the flower color of *D. kingianum* is dominant.

REFERENCES: 67, 216, 237, 254, 533.

PHOTOS/DRAWINGS: 237, *533*.

Dendrobium brachystachyum Rchb. f. Kränzlin (ref. 254) indicates that this plant should be considered a variety of *D. hookerianum* Lindley. REFERENCES: 254.

Dendrobium brachythecum F. Mueller and Kränzlin. See *D. macrophyllum* A. Richard. REFERENCES: 83, 218, 253, 254, 270, 271, 437, 445.

Dendrobium bracteatum Llave and Lexarza. A plant from Mexico that does not belong in the genus *Dendrobium*. REFERENCES: 216, 254.

Dendrobium bracteosum Rchb. f.

AKA: *D. chrysolabium* Rolfe, *D. dixsonii* F. M. Bailey (also spelled *D. dixsoni*), *D. eitapense* Schlechter, *D. leucochysum* Schlechter, *D. novaehiberniae* Kränzlin, *D. trisaccatum* Kränzlin.

ORIGIN/HABITAT: New Guinea. In Papua, plants were found near Port Praslin and Punam on New Ireland (New Mecklenburg) Island at about 1650 ft. (500 m), on Rossel Island, in the Sepik River region near Aitape (Eitape) at 50–1300 ft. (20–400 m), and along the coast of northwestern Papua New Guinea at about 50 ft. (20 m). In Irian Jaya (western New

Guinea), the plants grow in swamps along the Noord River. They usually grow on forest trees or close to the ground on mangroves in lowland rainforests from sea level to 2300 ft. (0–700 m), but they have been reported as high as 3950 ft. (1200 m).

CLIMATE: Station #94085, Rabaul, New Britain Island, Papua New Guinea, Lat. 4.2°S, Long. 152.2°E, at 28 ft. (9 m). Temperatures are calculated for an elevation of 1150 ft. (350 m), resulting in probable extremes of 96°F (36°C) and 61°F (16°C).

N/HEMISPHERE	JAN	FEB	MAR	APR	MAY	JUN	JUL	AUG	SEP	OCT	NOV	DEC
°F AVG MAX	85	85	87	88	87	86	86	86	86	86	86	86
°F AVG MIN	69	68	69	69	69	69	69	69	69	69	69	69
DIURNAL RANGE	16	17	18	19	18	17	17	17	17	17	17	17
RAIN/INCHES	5.4	3.7	3.5	5.1	7.1	10.1	14.8	10.4	10.2	10.0	5.2	3.3
HUMIDITY/%	74	73	69	70	73	76	77	76	77	77	75	74
BLOOM SEASON				*	*	**	**	**	*	*	*	
DAYS CLR	N/A											
RAIN/MM	137	94	89	130	180	257	376	264	259	254	132	84
°C AVG MAX	29.6	29.6	30.7	31.3	30.7	30.2	30.2	30.2	30.2	30.2	30.2	30.2
°C AVG MIN	20.7	20.2	20.7	20.7	20.7	20.7	20.7	20.7	20.7	20.7	20.7	20.7
DIURNAL RANGE	8.9	9.4	10.0	10.6	10.0	9.5	9.5	9.5	9.5	9.5	9.5	9.5
S/HEMISPHERE	JUL	AUG	SEP	OCT	NOV	DEC	JAN	FEB	MAR	APR	MAY	JUN

Cultural Recommendations

LIGHT: 1000–2000 fc. Some growers recommend *Phalaenopsis* light levels.

TEMPERATURES: Throughout the year, days average 85–88°F (30–31°C), and nights average 68–69°F (20–21°C), with a diurnal range of 16–19°F (9–11°C).

HUMIDITY: Near 75% most of the year. However, humidity is generally 90–100% at night, but during the dry season, averages may drop as low as 35% during the day.

WATER: Rainfall is heavy most of the year, but conditions are slightly drier for 2 months in late winter. Cultivated plants should be kept somewhat moist but not soggy. Growers indicate that although plants are found in wet areas, care should be taken to ensure that the roots are not kept continuously damp.

FERTILIZER: ½ recommended strength. A balanced fertilizer should be applied weekly to biweekly throughout the year. Growers indicate that plants are fast-growing and utilize more fertilizer than many *Dendrobium*.

REST PERIOD: Growing conditions should be maintained all year. Growers indicate that plants tolerate winter lows of 59°F (15°C). Water and fertilizer should be reduced somewhat in winter. Plants should dry slightly between waterings, but they should never be allowed to dry completely. In the habitat, light may be slightly higher in winter.

GROWING MEDIA: Plants may be mounted on tree-fern or cork slabs if humidity is high and plants are watered at least once daily in summer, or they may be placed in shallow pots filled with any open, fast-draining medium. Repotting may be done anytime new roots are growing. When repotting, old canes should not be removed, as they continue flowering for several years. Collectors report that because plants are usually found in areas of high rainfall, the fibrous roots are often covered with moss. They indicate that plants may be difficult to transplant unless they are taken with a piece of the branch on which they are growing.

MISCELLANEOUS NOTES: The bloom season shown in the climate table is based on cultivation records. In the habitat, blooming is heaviest in autumn.

Plants bloom while quite small, but they form large specimen clumps.

Plant and Flower Information

PLANT SIZE AND TYPE: A 10–20 in. (25–50 cm) sympodial epiphyte.

PSEUDOBULB: 8–16 in. (20–40 cm) long. The stemlike pseudobulbs, which consist of many nodes, are yellowish with brown rings. They become furrowed with age. The erect or pendulous stems arise from a very short rhizome.

LEAVES: 6–8 per growth. The narrow, pointed leaves are 1.6–3.2 in. (4–8 cm) long, thin but tough, rich glossy green, and deciduous.

INFLORESCENCE: Short. The densely clustered flowers emerge from the nodes along the stem. The large floral bracts are an easily distinguished characteristic.

FLOWERS: 3–10 per inflorescence. The blossoms, which are 0.5–1.0 in. (1.3–2.5 cm) long, do not open fully. They are fragrant, extremely long-lasting, and stay in perfect condition for 5–6 months. Sepals and petals may be white, greenish, yellow, rose, pink, purple, or dark red. Regardless of sepal and petal color, the pointed lip is always red- to yellow-orange, though it may be flushed with pale violet. Flower size and color are variable.

HYBRIDIZING NOTES: Chromosome count is $2n = 38$ (ref. 152).

REFERENCES: 36, 79, 152, 179, 190, 218, 243, 254, 304, 305, 352, 371, 389, 430, 437, 444, 445, 470, 510, 526, 537, 549, 552, 570.

PHOTOS/DRAWINGS: *36, 79, 304, 305, 350, 371, 389, 430, 437, 510, 549, 552.*

Dendrobium braianense Gagnepain. See *D. capillipes* Rchb. f. REFERENCES: 167, 226, 447, 448, 454.

Dendrobium branderhorstii J. J. Smith. See *D. angraecifolium* Schlechter. REFERENCES: 220, 254, 437, 445, 470.

Dendrobium brandtiae Kränzlin. See *D.* × *superbiens* Rchb. f. REFERENCES: 67, 220, 254, 262, 437.

Dendrobium brassii T. M. Reeve and P. J. B. Woods

ORIGIN/HABITAT: Papua New Guinea. Plants are found in the Port Moresby District of the Central Province, in the Northern Province, and Milne Bay Province but have never been seen in great numbers. They grow epiphytically in exposed *Nothofagus* and *Castanopsis* forests at 4900–7200 ft. (1500–2200 m).

CLIMATE: Station #94035, Port Moresby, Papua New Guinea, Lat. 9.5°S, Long. 147.2°E, at 126 ft. (38 m). Temperatures are calculated for an elevation of 5600 ft. (1700 m), resulting in probable extremes of 80°F (27°C) and 46°F (8°C).

N/HEMISPHERE	JAN	FEB	MAR	APR	MAY	JUN	JUL	AUG	SEP	OCT	NOV	DEC
°F AVG MAX	65	64	66	68	70	72	71	69	70	69	68	66
°F AVG MIN	55	55	56	57	58	58	58	58	58	57	57	56
DIURNAL RANGE	10	9	10	11	12	14	13	11	12	12	11	10
RAIN/INCHES	1.1	0.7	1.0	1.4	1.9	4.4	7.0	7.6	6.7	4.2	2.5	1.3
HUMIDITY/%	78	77	78	76	73	71	71	74	74	75	77	78
BLOOM SEASON	*	*	*				*					
DAYS CLR	N/A											
RAIN/MM	28	18	25	36	48	112	178	193	170	107	64	33
°C AVG MAX	18.3	17.8	18.9	20.0	21.1	22.2	21.7	20.6	21.1	20.6	20.0	18.9
°C AVG MIN	12.8	12.8	13.3	13.9	14.4	14.4	14.4	14.4	14.4	13.9	13.9	13.3
DIURNAL RANGE	5.5	5.0	5.6	6.1	6.7	7.8	7.3	6.2	6.7	6.7	6.1	5.6
S/HEMISPHERE	JUL	AUG	SEP	OCT	NOV	DEC	JAN	FEB	MAR	APR	MAY	JUN

Cultural Recommendations

LIGHT: 2500–3000 fc. Plants require moderately high light with strong air movement year-round. About 50% shading should be provided in summer. Light should be as high as the plants can tolerate, short of burning the foliage.

TEMPERATURES: Throughout the year, days average 64–72°F (18–22°C), and nights average 55–58°F (13–14°C), with a diurnal range of 9–14°F (5–8°C).

Dendrobium brevibulbum

HUMIDITY: 70–75% most of the year, increasing to near 80% in winter. Humidity is probably somewhat greater in the higher elevation forest habitat, however.

WATER: Rainfall is moderate for 5 months in summer, but conditions are drier in winter. Cultivated plants should dry slightly between waterings.

FERTILIZER: ¼–½ recommended strength, applied weekly. A high-nitrogen fertilizer is beneficial from spring to midsummer, but a fertilizer high in phosphates should be used in late summer and autumn.

REST PERIOD: Growing conditions should be maintained all year. In the habitat, rainfall is low for 6–7 months in winter, but additional water is available from dew and mist in the high-elevation habitat. Cultivated plants need less water in winter, especially those grown in the dark, short-day conditions common in temperate latitudes. Plants should be kept moist and never be allowed to dry out completely. In addition to regular waterings, occasional light mistings on clear, sunny mornings may be beneficial. Fertilizer should be reduced anytime water is reduced. In the habitat, winter light is highest.

GROWING MEDIA: Plants may be mounted on tree-fern or cork slabs if humidity is high and plants are watered at least once daily in summer. Any open, fast-draining medium may be used for potting. Repotting may be done anytime new roots are growing.

MISCELLANEOUS NOTES: The bloom season indicated in the climate table is based on cultivation records.

Plant and Flower Information

PLANT SIZE AND TYPE: A 3–9 in. (8–22 cm) sympodial epiphyte.

PSEUDOBULB: 0.2–1.0 in. (0.5–2.5 cm) long. The erect to pendent stems are nearly ovoid and contracted at the middle. Growths are normally tightly clustered, but some plants growing in moss have elongated rhizomes.

LEAVES: 1 per growth. The pointed leaves are 2–6 in. (5–16 cm) long. The leaf blade and stem are green, sometimes suffused with purple.

INFLORESCENCE: Short. Inflorescences emerge at the apex of leafless pseudobulbs.

FLOWERS: 2 per inflorescence. The flowers are 0.9–1.3 in. (2.2–3.2 cm) long. They have purplish-pink to violet sepals and petals with orange at the tip of the lip. Blossoms have an is ovate-elliptic dorsal sepal, triangular lateral sepals, oblong-obovate petals, and a simple to slightly 3-lobed lip. They last about 6 months.

REFERENCES: 179, 235, 385.

PHOTOS/DRAWINGS: *385*.

Dendrobium brevibulbum J. J. Smith. Now considered a synonym of *Epigeneium pulchellum* (Ridley) Summerhayes. REFERENCES: 224, 499.

Dendrobium brevicaule as used by Kränzlin. See *D. pentapterum* Schlechter. REFERENCES: 437, 538.

Dendrobium brevicaule Ridley. P. van Royen (ref. 538) includes this name as a synonym of *D. rupestre* J. J. Smith, but Reeve and Woods (ref. 385) include *D. brevicaule* Ridley as a synonym of *D. vexillarius* J. J. Smith. REFERENCES: 385, 538.

Dendrobium brevicaule Rolfe

AKA: Reeve and Woods (ref. 385) presently recognize 3 subspecies of *D. brevicaule* and synonyms are listed by subspecies.

D. brevicaule subsp. *brevicaule* has also been known as *D. cyatheicola* P. van Royen.

D. brevicaule subsp. *calcarium* (J. J. Smith) T. M. Reeve and P. Woods was originally known as *D. calcarium* J. J. Smith. Other synonyms include *D. aurantivinosum* P. van Royen, *D. montistellare* P. van Royen forma *albescens* P. van Royen, *D. montistellare* P. van Royen forma *montistellare* P. van Royen, and *D. quinquecristatus* P. van Royen.

D. brevicaule subsp. *pentagonum* (Kränzlin) T. M. Reeve and P. Woods was described as *D. pentagonum* Kränzlin. Other synonyms include *D. teligerum* P. van Royen and *D. zaranense* P. van Royen. Reeve and Woods consider *D. saruwagedicum* Schlechter a possible synonym.

ORIGIN/HABITAT: New Guinea. Plants grow epiphytically on subalpine shrubs at 9500–13,100 ft. (2900–4000 m).

CLIMATE: Botanical garden records, Laiagam, Papua New Guinea, Lat. 5.5°S, Long. 143.5°E, at 7218 ft. (2200 m). Temperatures are calculated for an elevation of 10,500 ft. (3200 m), resulting in probable extremes of 80°F (27°C) and 21°F (–6°C).

N/HEMISPHERE	JAN	FEB	MAR	APR	MAY	JUN	JUL	AUG	SEP	OCT	NOV	DEC
°F AVG MAX	65	66	67	65	67	67	71	66	65	67	67	65
°F AVG MIN	44	43	44	44	45	45	44	45	47	46	45	45
DIURNAL RANGE	21	23	23	21	22	22	27	21	18	21	22	20
RAIN/INCHES	4.0	4.8	6.1	7.8	8.5	9.1	8.4	9.6	9.5	8.9	6.3	4.0
HUMIDITY/%	N/A											
BLOOM SEASON		*	*	*								
DAYS CLR	N/A											
RAIN/MM	102	122	155	198	216	231	213	244	241	226	160	102
°C AVG MAX	18.4	19.0	19.5	18.4	19.5	19.5	21.8	19.0	18.4	19.5	19.5	18.4
°C AVG MIN	6.8	6.2	6.8	6.8	7.3	7.3	6.8	7.3	8.4	7.9	7.3	7.3
DIURNAL RANGE	11.6	12.8	12.7	11.6	12.2	12.2	15.0	11.7	10.0	11.6	12.2	11.1
S/HEMISPHERE	JUL	AUG	SEP	OCT	NOV	DEC	JAN	FEB	MAR	APR	MAY	JUN

Cultural Recommendations

LIGHT: 2000–3000 fc.

TEMPERATURES: Throughout the year, days average 65–71°F (18–22°C), and nights average 43–47°F (6–8°C), with a diurnal range of 18–27°F (10–15°C). Plants should easily adapt to conditions that are 5–7°F (3–4°C) cooler than indicated.

HUMIDITY: Information is not available for this location. However, records from other stations in the region indicate that averages are probably 80–85% year-round.

WATER: Rainfall is heavy throughout the year, but conditions are slightly drier for 3–4 months in winter. Cultivated plants should be kept moist.

FERTILIZER: ¼ recommended strength, applied weekly throughout the year. The Royal Botanic Garden in Edinburgh uses a seaweed-based fertilizer for plants from this habitat.

REST PERIOD: Growing conditions should be maintained all year. Water and fertilizer should be reduced somewhat in winter, especially when plants are grown in the dark, short-day conditions common in temperate latitudes. Plants should dry slightly between waterings, but they should never be allowed to dry out completely. Water and fertilizer should be gradually increased when plants begin growing in spring.

GROWING MEDIA: Plants may be potted in live sphagnum moss over a layer of chopped tree-fern or small bark. High humidity is critically important. The potting medium should allow air to the roots but keep them moist. Clay pots with enlarged drainage holes, which are loosely filled with green sphagnum moss and exposed to very fine mist, have been used successfully for closely related species from similar habitats. Repotting may be done anytime new roots are growing.

MISCELLANEOUS NOTES: The bloom season shown in the climate table reflects the peak bloom season in the habitat. Cultivated plants bloom all seasons of the year. Plant size varies and appears to bear a direct relationship to the amount of available light, with higher light producing smaller plants. *D. brevicaule* may be very difficult to cultivate unless cool, moist conditions can be provided.

D. brevicaule subsp. *brevicaule*, which is normally epiphytic on tree fern in alpine grasslands, grows at very high altitudes of 10,988–12,464 ft. (3350–3800 m). It has brilliant orange flowers, and is described as spectacular when in full bloom.

D. brevicaule subsp. *calcarium*, which is highly variable and is the most widespread of the 3 subspecies, grows epiphytically on alpine shrubs at 9500–12,000 ft. (2900–3650 m). It is rarely a terrestrial. The flowers are brilliant orange or orange-red, and the lip is sometimes red. The backs of the sepals are not conspicuously keeled.

D. brevicaule subsp. *pentagonum* grows as an epiphyte at 9840–11,808 ft. (3000–3600 m). The flowers are orange with the typical purple-black anther cap. This subspecies is usually the most branching and has a lax growth habit. Flowers are distinguished by the very large keels on the outside of the lateral sepals.

Plant and Flower Information

PLANT SIZE AND TYPE: An erect, 2–4 in. (5–10 cm) sympodial epiphyte. Plants described as *D. teligerum* were 10 in. (25 cm) tall.

PSEUDOBULB: 0.4–1.2 in. (1–3 cm) long. The pseudobulbs are cylindrical to ellipsoid. They normally have 2 or 3 nodes, but plants described as *D. teligerum* had 5 to many nodes and occasionally branched.

LEAVES: 1–3 per growth. The linear to elliptic leaves are 0.6–1.0 in. (1.5–2.5 cm) long.

INFLORESCENCE: 0.8–1.2 in. (2–3 cm) long. Inflorescences emerge from between the leaves at the apex of the newest growths.

FLOWERS: 1–2 per inflorescence. The flowers are 1.0 in. (2.5 cm) across, which is large for the plant size. Sepals and petals are orange to orange-red. The lip may be the same color as the sepals and petals, or it may be wine-red. The anther cap is grey or purplish black.

REFERENCES: 235, 254, 385, 400, 412, 538.

PHOTOS/DRAWINGS: *385*, 538.

Dendrobium brevicolle J. J. Smith. Now considered a synonym of *Diplocaulobium brevicolle* (J. J. Smith) Kränzlin. REFERENCES: 219, 254, 445.

Dendrobium breviflorum Lindley. See *D. bicameratum* Wall ex Lindley. REFERENCES: 102, 216, 254, 310, 454.

Dendrobium brevifolium Hort. ex Lindley. See *D. devonianum* Paxton. REFERENCES: 216, 254.

Dendrobium brevilabium Schlechter

ORIGIN/HABITAT: Northern Papua New Guinea, in the Waria District. Plants grow on trees in the mistforests of the Dischore Range at about 3950 ft. (1200 m).

CLIMATE: Station #200192, Garaina, Papua New Guinea, Lat. 7.9°S, Long. 147.1°E, at 2350 ft. (716 m). Temperatures are calculated for an elevation of 3950 ft. (1200 m), resulting in probable extremes of 89°F (32°C) and 41°F (5°C).

N/HEMISPHERE	JAN	FEB	MAR	APR	MAY	JUN	JUL	AUG	SEP	OCT	NOV	DEC
°F AVG MAX	75	77	78	79	80	80	80	80	79	79	78	76
°F AVG MIN	58	58	58	59	58	59	60	60	60	59	59	58
DIURNAL RANGE	17	19	20	20	22	21	20	20	19	20	19	18
RAIN/INCHES	5.8	6.5	8.7	11.1	11.8	11.9	8.9	11.7	11.5	9.9	7.7	5.2
HUMIDITY/%	84	82	82	81	80	80	81	81	82	83	84	84
BLOOM SEASON	N/A											
DAYS CLR	N/A											
RAIN/MM	147	165	221	282	300	302	226	297	292	251	196	132
°C AVG MAX	23.8	24.9	25.4	26.0	26.5	26.5	26.5	26.5	26.0	26.0	25.4	24.3
°C AVG MIN	14.3	14.3	14.3	14.9	14.3	14.9	15.4	15.4	15.4	14.9	14.9	14.3
DIURNAL RANGE	9.5	10.6	11.1	11.1	12.2	11.6	11.1	11.1	10.6	11.1	10.5	10.0
S/HEMISPHERE	JUL	AUG	SEP	OCT	NOV	DEC	JAN	FEB	MAR	APR	MAY	JUN

Cultural Recommendations

LIGHT: 2000–3000 fc.

TEMPERATURES: Throughout the year, days average 75–80°F (24–27°C), and nights average 58–60°F (14–15°C), with a diurnal range of 17–22°F (10–12°C).

HUMIDITY: 80–85% year-round.

WATER: Rainfall is heavy all year. Conditions are slightly drier in winter. Cultivated plants should be kept moist but not soggy.

FERTILIZER: ¼–½ recommended strength. A balanced fertilizer should be applied weekly to biweekly throughout the year.

REST PERIOD: Growing conditions should be maintained all year. In the habitat, rainfall is slightly lower in winter. Water and fertilizer should be reduced somewhat for cultivated plants, especially those grown in the dark, short-day conditions common during temperate-latitude winters. They should never be allowed to dry out completely, however. In the habitat, seasonal light variation is minor.

GROWING MEDIA: Plants may be mounted on tree-fern or cork slabs if humidity is high and plants are watered at least once daily in summer. When plants are potted, any open, fast-draining medium may be used. Repotting may be done anytime new roots are growing.

Plant and Flower Information

PLANT SIZE AND TYPE: A 22 in. (55 cm) sympodial epiphyte.

PSEUDOBULB: 20 in. (50 cm) long.

LEAVES: The linear leaves are 2.4–3.5 in. (6–9 cm) long, erect, and spreading.

INFLORESCENCE: Very short. The inflorescences hold the clustered flowers close to the leaves.

FLOWERS: 4–7 per inflorescence. The flowers are 0.5 in. (1.2 cm) long. Shaped like an open cone, sepals and petals are pale rose-red, deepening to scarlet-red at the base of the cone. The lip is cinnabar-red at the tip. The ovary is violet.

REFERENCES: 92, 221, 437, 445.

PHOTOS/DRAWINGS: 437.

Dendrobium brevimentum Cribb (1986).

AKA: This name had already been used by Seidenfaden (ref. 454) to describe a different species.

ORIGIN/HABITAT: Ternate Island in the Moluccas. Plants grow in mountain forests at about 4900 ft. (1500 m).

CLIMATE: Station #97430, Ternate Island, Indonesia, Lat. 0.8°N, Long. 127.4°E, at 75 ft. (23 m). Temperatures are calculated for an elevation of 4900 ft. (1500 m). Record extreme temperatures are not available for this location.

N/HEMISPHERE	JAN	FEB	MAR	APR	MAY	JUN	JUL	AUG	SEP	OCT	NOV	DEC
°F AVG MAX	69	69	70	70	71	70	71	70	70	71	71	70
°F AVG MIN	61	60	61	61	61	60	59	59	60	61	61	61
DIURNAL RANGE	8	9	9	9	10	10	12	11	10	10	10	9
RAIN/INCHES	5.0	6.1	6.7	6.6	9.4	8.4	4.6	2.1	3.1	3.2	7.2	8.2
HUMIDITY/%	N/A											
BLOOM SEASON	N/A											
DAYS CLR	N/A											
RAIN/MM	127	155	170	168	239	213	117	53	79	81	183	208
°C AVG MAX	20.6	20.6	21.1	21.1	21.7	21.1	21.7	21.1	21.1	21.7	21.7	21.1
°C AVG MIN	16.1	15.6	16.1	16.1	16.1	15.6	15.0	15.0	15.6	16.1	16.1	16.1
DIURNAL RANGE	4.5	5.0	5.0	5.0	5.6	5.5	6.7	6.1	5.5	5.6	5.6	5.0
S/HEMISPHERE	JUL	AUG	SEP	OCT	NOV	DEC	JAN	FEB	MAR	APR	MAY	JUN

Cultural Recommendations

LIGHT: 3000 fc.

Dendrobium brevimentum

TEMPERATURES: Throughout the year, days average 69–71°F (21–22°C), and nights average 59–61°F (15–16°C), with a diurnal range of 8–12°F (5–7°C).

HUMIDITY: Information is not available for this location. However, records from nearby stations indicate that humidity is probably near 85% year-round.

WATER: Rainfall is moderate to heavy most of the year. For 2–3 months in late summer and autumn, conditions are somewhat drier. Cultivated plants should be kept moist, with only slight drying allowed between waterings through most of the year. For 1–3 months in late summer and early autumn, however, plants should become moderately dry between waterings, but they should not remain dry for long periods.

FERTILIZER: ¼–½ recommended strength. A balanced fertilizer should be applied weekly to biweekly throughout the year.

REST PERIOD: Growing temperatures should be maintained all year. Water may be reduced somewhat in winter, especially for plants grown in the dark, short-day conditions in temperate latitudes. They should never dry out completely, however. In the habitat, seasonal light variation is minor.

GROWING MEDIA: Plants may be mounted on slabs or potted in any open, fast-draining medium. Repotting may be done anytime roots are actively growing.

MISCELLANEOUS NOTES: Plants are unlikely to be in cultivation, as only a single collection is recorded.

Plant and Flower Information

PLANT SIZE AND TYPE: A 39 in. (100 cm) sympodial epiphyte.

PSEUDOBULB: 39 in. (100 cm) long. The slender, canelike pseudobulbs arise at 0.4–0.8 in. (1–2 cm) intervals from a creeping rhizome.

LEAVES: Numerous. The lanceolate leaves are 1.2–2.0 in. (3–5 cm) long.

INFLORESCENCE: Inflorescences emerge opposite the leaves. Blossoms are produced from nodes above the midpoint of the cane.

FLOWERS: Several per inflorescence. The white flowers are 1.2 in. (3 cm) across, which is small for the plant size.

REFERENCES: 84, 235.

PHOTOS/DRAWINGS: 84.

Dendrobium brevimentum Seidenfaden

ORIGIN/HABITAT: Endemic to Thailand. Plants were originally collected at the Khun Yuan airstrip at about 2050 ft. (620 m) in the northwestern foothills.

CLIMATE: Station #48325, Mae Sariang, Thailand, Lat. 18.2°N, Long. 97.8°E, at 1030 ft. (314 m). Temperatures are calculated for an elevation of 2050 ft. (620 m), resulting in probable extremes of 108°F (42°C) and 38°F (3°C).

N/HEMISPHERE	JAN	FEB	MAR	APR	MAY	JUN	JUL	AUG	SEP	OCT	NOV	DEC
°F AVG MAX	85	89	93	96	91	86	84	84	86	87	86	83
°F AVG MIN	55	54	61	70	73	72	71	71	71	69	65	57
DIURNAL RANGE	30	35	32	26	18	14	13	13	15	18	21	26
RAIN/INCHES	0.3	0.2	0.3	1.9	5.7	9.0	8.4	10.8	8.7	3.7	1.1	0.6
HUMIDITY/%	72	67	57	55	68	83	83	84	83	81	77	75
BLOOM SEASON	N/A											
DAYS CLR @ 7AM	1	16	0	3	4	0	0	0	0	0	0	1
DAYS CLR @ 1PM	24	18	9	5	2	0	0	1	1	6	13	20
RAIN/MM	8	5	8	48	145	229	213	274	221	94	28	15
°C AVG MAX	29.3	31.5	33.7	35.4	32.6	29.8	28.7	28.7	29.8	30.4	29.8	28.2
°C AVG MIN	12.6	12.1	15.9	20.9	22.6	22.1	21.5	21.5	21.5	20.4	18.2	13.7
DIURNAL RANGE	16.7	19.4	17.8	14.5	10.0	7.7	7.2	7.2	8.3	10.0	11.6	14.5
S/HEMISPHERE	JUL	AUG	SEP	OCT	NOV	DEC	JAN	FEB	MAR	APR	MAY	JUN

Cultural Recommendations

LIGHT: 2500–3500 fc.

TEMPERATURES: Summer days average 84–86°F (29–30°C), and nights average 71–72°F (22°C), with a diurnal range of 13–14°F (7–8°C). Spring is the warmest season. Days average 91–96°F (33–35°C), and nights average 61–73°F (16–23°C), with a diurnal range of 18–32°F (10–18°C).

HUMIDITY: 80–85% in summer through early autumn, dropping to near 55% for 2 months in winter.

WATER: Rainfall is heavy for 6 months from spring into early autumn but is very light for 4–5 months in winter and early spring. Cultivated plants should be kept moist while actively growing, but water should be gradually reduced in autumn after new growths mature.

FERTILIZER: ¼–½ recommended strength. A balanced fertilizer should be applied weekly to biweekly throughout the growing season.

REST PERIOD: Winter days average 83–89°F (28–32°C), and nights average 54–57°F (12–14°C), with a diurnal range of 26–35°F (15–19°C). Rainfall is light for 5–6 months from autumn into spring; but during the early part of the dry period, considerable moisture is available from heavy dew and as mist from low clouds and fog. However, for 2 months in spring the weather is clear and dry with humidity so low that even the moisture from dew is uncommon. During most of the winter dry season, cultivated plants should be allowed to dry slightly between waterings, but they should not remain dry for long periods. For 1–2 months in late winter, however, water should be further decreased and the plants allowed to dry completely. An occasional early morning misting during this time may help keep plants from becoming too dry. Fertilizer should be eliminated. In the habitat, light is highest in winter.

GROWING MEDIA: Plants may be mounted on tree-fern or cork slabs or potted in any open, fast-draining medium. Repotting may be done anytime new roots are growing.

Plant and Flower Information

PLANT SIZE AND TYPE: A 10 in. (26 cm) sympodial epiphyte.

PSEUDOBULB: 10 in. (26 cm) long.

LEAVES: Many. The deciduous leaves are 1 in. (2.5 cm) long. They are distichous, flattened, and held at a wide angle to the stem. Young stems are leafy.

INFLORESCENCE: Several per growth. The short inflorescences appear at the apex of young shoots as well as laterally from older, leafless stems.

FLOWERS: 1 per inflorescence. The very small flowers are 0.3 in. (0.7 cm) across. The sepals and petals are dull brownish yellow with 3 purplish veins on the petals. The broadly fan-shaped lip has no sidelobes. It is lighter yellow than the other segments with a brownish yellow spot.

HYBRIDIZING NOTES: Johansen (ref. 239) indicates that plants are self-sterile and that flowers dropped 5–8 days after self-pollination. Attempts to cross *D. brevimentum* with *D. setifolium* Ridley did not produce seed.

REFERENCES: 234, 239, 454.

PHOTOS/DRAWINGS: *454*.

Dendrobium breviracemosum F. M. Bailey. See *D. bifalce* Lindley. REFERENCES: 67, 83, 105, 190, 254, 270, 437, 470.

Dendrobium brinchangense Holttum

AKA: Sometimes spelled *D. brinchangensis*.

ORIGIN/HABITAT: Northern Malaya. Plants have been found only on Mt. Brinchang in the Cameron Highlands at 5500–6000 ft. (1680–1830 m).

CLIMATE: Station #48625, Ipoh, Malaya, Lat. 4.6°N, Long. 101.1°E, at 123 ft. (37 m). Temperatures are calculated for an elevation of 5750 ft. (1750 m), resulting in probable extremes of 80°F (27°C) and 45°F (7°C).

N/HEMISPHERE	JAN	FEB	MAR	APR	MAY	JUN	JUL	AUG	SEP	OCT	NOV	DEC
°F AVG MAX	71	73	74	73	73	73	72	72	71	70	70	70
°F AVG MIN	53	53	54	54	55	54	53	53	54	53	53	53
DIURNAL RANGE	18	20	20	19	18	19	19	19	17	17	17	17
RAIN/INCHES	7.9	3.1	7.6	8.4	6.2	3.6	7.2	6.9	8.8	11.0	13.0	8.9
HUMIDITY/%	76	74	76	78	78	75	76	77	79	82	82	81
BLOOM SEASON				*				*			*	
DAYS CLR @ 7AM	3	3	3	1	1	2	1	1	0	0	1	2
DAYS CLR @ 1PM	2	2	2	1	1	1	1	1	0	0	0	2
RAIN/MM	201	79	193	213	157	91	183	175	224	279	330	226
°C AVG MAX	21.9	23.0	23.6	23.0	23.0	23.0	22.5	22.5	21.9	21.4	21.4	21.4
°C AVG MIN	11.9	11.9	12.5	12.5	13.0	12.5	11.9	11.9	12.5	11.9	11.9	11.9
DIURNAL RANGE	10.0	11.1	11.1	10.5	10.0	10.5	10.6	10.6	9.4	9.5	9.5	9.5
S/HEMISPHERE	JUL	AUG	SEP	OCT	NOV	DEC	JAN	FEB	MAR	APR	MAY	JUN

Cultural Recommendations

LIGHT: 1500–2400 fc. Light should be diffused or dappled, and direct sunlight should be avoided. In the habitat, clear days are quite rare.

TEMPERATURES: Throughout the year, days average 70–74°F (21–24°C), and nights average 53–55°F (12–13°C), with a diurnal range of 17–20°F (9–11°C). The record high does not exceed the warmest average by more than 6°F (3°C), indicating a probable sensitivity to hot temperatures and wide temperature fluctuations.

HUMIDITY: 75–80% year-round.

WATER: Rainfall is heavy most of the year. The heaviest rainfall occurs in autumn with a secondary maximum in spring. Brief semidry periods occur in midwinter and midsummer. Cultivated plants should be kept evenly moist with only slight drying allowed between waterings.

FERTILIZER: ¼–½ recommended strength. A balanced fertilizer should be applied weekly to biweekly throughout the year.

REST PERIOD: Growing conditions should be maintained year-round. Water should be reduced somewhat in winter for plants cultivated in the dark, short-day conditions common in temperate latitudes. They should never be allowed to dry out completely, however. Fertilizer may be reduced when the plant is not actively growing or when water is reduced. In the habitat, light is slightly higher in winter.

GROWING MEDIA: Plants may be mounted on tree-fern or cork slabs if humidity is high and plants are watered at least once daily in summer. When plants are potted, any open, fast-draining medium may be used. Repotting may be done anytime new roots are growing.

MISCELLANEOUS NOTES: The bloom season shown in the climate table is based on reports from the habitat.

Plant and Flower Information

PLANT SIZE AND TYPE: A 28 in. (70 cm) sympodial epiphyte.

PSEUDOBULB: 28 in. (70 cm) long.

LEAVES: The very narrow leaves are 5 in. (13 cm) long. They are widest at the base and narrow evenly to the apex. The leaf sheaths are flushed with purple.

INFLORESCENCE: Very short. Inflorescences emerge from internodes along leafless stems.

FLOWERS: 1–3 per inflorescence. Blossoms are 1 in. (2.5 cm) across. The sepals and petals are white with a lilac tinge. The lip is marked with a yellow patch in the middle.

REFERENCES: 200, 227, 455.

PHOTOS/DRAWINGS: 200, 455.

Dendrobium brisbanense Rchb. f. Sometimes spelled *D. brisbranense*, see *D. gracilicaule* F. Mueller not Kränzlin and discussion at *D. macropus* (Endl.) Rchb. f. ex Lindley. REFERENCES: 67, 105, 216, 254, 270, 317, 533.

Dendrobium bronckartii Wildeman. See *D. amabile* (Loureiro) O'Brien. REFERENCES: 179, 220, 254, 266, 428, 445, 448, 454, 504, 580. PHOTOS/DRAWINGS: *428*.

Dendrobium brongniartii Kränzlin. Now considered a synonym of *Eria aporoides* Lindley. REFERENCES: 12, 220, 254, 296, 536.

Dendrobium broomfieldii (Fitzgerald) Fitzgerald. See *D. discolor* Lindley. REFERENCES: 67, 218, 430.

Dendrobium brunnescens Schlechter

ORIGIN/HABITAT: Northern Papua New Guinea. Plants were collected in the Maboro Mountains of the Waria District. These rare plants were found on forest trees at about 3600 ft. (1100 m).

CLIMATE: Station #200192, Garaina, Papua New Guinea, Lat. 7.9°S, Long. 147.1°E, at 2350 ft. (716 m). Temperatures are calculated for an elevation of 3300 ft. (1000 m), resulting in probable extremes of 91°F (33°C) and 43°F (6°C).

N/HEMISPHERE	JAN	FEB	MAR	APR	MAY	JUN	JUL	AUG	SEP	OCT	NOV	DEC
°F AVG MAX	77	79	80	81	82	82	82	82	81	81	80	78
°F AVG MIN	60	60	60	61	60	61	62	62	62	61	61	60
DIURNAL RANGE	17	19	20	20	22	21	20	20	19	20	19	18
RAIN/INCHES	5.8	6.5	8.7	11.1	11.8	11.9	8.9	11.7	11.5	9.9	7.7	5.2
HUMIDITY/%	84	82	82	81	80	80	81	81	82	83	84	84
BLOOM SEASON												*
DAYS CLR	N/A											
RAIN/MM	147	165	221	282	300	302	226	297	292	251	196	132
°C AVG MAX	25.0	26.1	26.6	27.2	27.7	27.7	27.7	27.7	27.2	27.2	26.6	25.5
°C AVG MIN	15.5	15.5	15.5	16.1	15.5	16.1	16.6	16.6	16.6	16.1	16.1	15.5
DIURNAL RANGE	9.5	10.6	11.1	11.1	12.2	11.6	11.1	11.1	10.6	11.1	10.5	10.0
S/HEMISPHERE	JUL	AUG	SEP	OCT	NOV	DEC	JAN	FEB	MAR	APR	MAY	JUN

Cultural Recommendations

LIGHT: 2000–3000 fc.

TEMPERATURES: Throughout the year, days average 77–82°F (25–28°C), and nights average 60–62°F (16–17°C), with a diurnal range of 17–22°F (10–12°C).

HUMIDITY: 80–85% year-round.

WATER: Rainfall is heavy all year. Conditions are slightly drier in winter. Cultivated plants should be kept moist but not soggy.

FERTILIZER: ¼–½ recommended strength. A balanced fertilizer should be applied weekly to biweekly throughout the year.

REST PERIOD: Growing conditions should be maintained all year. In the habitat, rainfall is slightly lower in winter. Water and fertilizer should be reduced somewhat for cultivated plants, especially those grown in the dark, short-day conditions common during temperate-latitude winters. They should never be allowed to dry out completely, however. In the habitat, seasonal light variation is minor.

GROWING MEDIA: Plants may be mounted on tree-fern or cork slabs if humidity is high and plants are watered at least once daily in summer. When plants are potted, any open, fast-draining medium may be used. Repotting may be done anytime new roots are growing.

MISCELLANEOUS NOTES: The bloom season shown in the climate table is based on collection reports. Plants that produce flowers which last a single day commonly bloom several times during the year. Flowering usually occurs 7–14 days after a sudden 10°F (5°C) drop in daytime temperatures.

Dendrobium brymerianum

Plant and Flower Information

PLANT SIZE AND TYPE: A 14–16 in. (35–40 cm) sympodial epiphyte.

PSEUDOBULB: 14–16 in. (35–40 cm) long. The stems do not branch.

LEAVES: Many. Leaves are about 1.6 in. (4 cm) long, erect to spreading, and elliptic to lanceolate. The growths are densely leafy.

INFLORESCENCE: Short. The inflorescences emerge laterally from the side of the pseudobulb. Flowers are held nearly opposite each other.

FLOWERS: 2 per inflorescence. The short-lived flowers, which last a single day, are 1 in. (2.5 cm) across. The brownish sepals and petals project forward. The fringed, pointed lip is brownish with red-brown markings on the sidelobes. The column is white with orange-yellow markings.

REFERENCES: 221, 437, 445.

PHOTOS/DRAWINGS: 437.

Dendrobium brymerianum Rchb. f.

AKA: *D. histrionicum* Schlechter is a synonym of *D. brymerianum* Rchb. f. var. *histrionicum* Rchb. f.

ORIGIN/HABITAT: Assam in Northeast India, Burma, northern Thailand, the Xieng Khouang region of northern Laos, and southwest China. In Thailand, plants grow at 5000–5200 ft. (1520–1590 m) near Chiang Mai and at 4750 ft. (1450 m) northwest of Pai.

CLIMATE: Station #48327, Chiang Mai, Thailand, Lat. 18.8°N, Long. 99.0°E, at 1100 ft. (335 m) elevation. Temperatures are calculated for an elevation of 5000 ft. (1520 m), resulting in probable extremes of 96°F (36°C) and 25°F (–4°C).

N/HEMISPHERE	JAN	FEB	MAR	APR	MAY	JUN	JUL	AUG	SEP	OCT	NOV	DEC
°F AVG MAX	72	77	82	83	81	77	76	74	75	76	73	71
°F AVG MIN	43	44	49	57	61	61	61	62	60	58	53	44
DIURNAL RANGE	29	33	33	26	20	16	15	12	15	18	20	27
RAIN/INCHES	0.3	0.4	0.6	2.0	5.5	6.1	7.4	8.7	11.5	4.9	1.5	0.4
HUMIDITY/%	73	65	58	62	73	78	80	83	83	81	79	76
BLOOM SEASON		*	**	**	**	*	*		*	*	*	
DAYS CLR @ 7AM	5	5	2	2	1	0	0	0	0	1	3	3
DAYS CLR @ 1PM	9	8	4	2	0	0	0	0	0	0	1	3
RAIN/MM	8	10	15	51	140	155	188	221	292	124	38	10
°C AVG MAX	22.3	25.1	27.9	28.4	27.3	25.1	24.5	23.4	24.0	24.5	22.9	21.7
°C AVG MIN	6.2	6.7	9.5	14.0	16.2	16.2	16.2	16.7	15.6	14.5	11.7	6.7
DIURNAL RANGE	16.1	18.4	18.4	14.4	11.1	8.9	8.3	6.7	8.4	10.0	11.2	15.0
S/HEMISPHERE	JUL	AUG	SEP	OCT	NOV	DEC	JAN	FEB	MAR	APR	MAY	JUN

Cultural Recommendations

LIGHT: 2500–3500 fc.

TEMPERATURES: Summer days average 74–77°F (23–25°C), and nights average 61–62°F (16–17°C), with a diurnal range of 12–16°F (7–9°C). The warmest temperatures occur in spring. Days average 81–83°F (27–28°C), and nights average 49–61°F (10–16°C), with a diurnal range of 20–33°F (11–18°C).

HUMIDITY: 75–85% from late spring through autumn, dropping to near 60% in late winter and early spring.

WATER: Rainfall is moderate to heavy from late spring through early autumn, but conditions are very dry in winter. Cultivated plants should be kept moist while actively growing, but water should be gradually reduced after new growths mature in autumn.

FERTILIZER: ¼–½ recommended strength, applied weekly. A high-nitrogen fertilizer is beneficial from spring to midsummer, but a fertilizer high in phosphates should be used in late summer and autumn.

REST PERIOD: Winter days average 71–82°F (22–28°C), and nights average 43–49°F (6–10°C), with a diurnal range of 27–33°F (15–18°C). The average low temperatures are below 50°F (10°C) for 3 months and then warm rapidly in spring. Plants should be able to tolerate temperatures a few degrees below freezing, but extremes should be avoided in cultivation. During very cold weather, a plant's chance of surviving with minimal damage is better if it is dry. Growers indicate that maintaining cool, dry conditions from the time new growths mature to blooming is important for cultivated plants but that they tolerate night temperatures of 55–60°F (13–16°C). In the habitat, rainfall averages are very low for 4–5 months in winter; but during the early part of the season, the high relative humidity indicates that additional moisture is available from frequent fog, mist, and heavy deposits of dew. Growers sometimes recommend eliminating water in winter, but plants are healthiest if for most of the winter they are allowed to become somewhat dry between waterings but do not remain dry for extended periods. For 1–2 months in late winter, however, conditions are clear, warm, and dry, with humidity so low that even the moisture from morning dew is uncommon. Plants should be allowed to dry out completely between waterings and remain dry longer during this time. Occasional early morning mistings between waterings may help keep the plants from becoming too dry. Fertilizer should be greatly reduced or eliminated until water is increased in spring. A cool, dry rest is essential for cultivated plants and should be continued until new growth starts in spring. In the habitat, light is highest in winter.

GROWING MEDIA: Plants may be mounted on tree-fern or cork slabs if humidity is high and plants are watered at least once daily in summer. When plants are potted, any open, fast-draining medium may be used. Repotting is best done in spring when new roots are beginning to grow.

MISCELLANEOUS NOTES: The bloom season shown in the climate table is based on cultivation records. *D. brymerianum* is considered a problem plant by many growers. Careful attention should be paid to cultural needs, especially the cool, dry winter rest. Growers indicate that blossoms sometimes fail to open, and believe them to be self-pollinating. However, these growers often recommend intermediate to warm temperatures, a recommendation that may be part of the problem.

The fall bloom records are probably for *D. brymerianum* var. *histrionicum*. Growers indicate that plants known as *D. brymerianum* var. *histrionicum* bloom in fall rather than spring and that flowers are sometimes self-pollinating. It is said to be a shorter plant with smaller, duller flowers that may have little or no fringe on the lip.

Plant and Flower Information

PLANT SIZE AND TYPE: An 8–20 in. (20–50 cm) sympodial epiphyte.

PSEUDOBULB: 8–20 in. (20–50 cm) long. The yellowish stems are erect with 2 swollen internodes in the middle.

LEAVES: 6 per growth. The apical leaves are 4–6 in. (10–15 cm) long. They are oblong-lanceolate, thin-textured, and leathery. The shiny, rich green leaves persist for several seasons, but they are eventually deciduous.

INFLORESCENCE: 4 in. (10 cm) long. The inflorescences, which are lateral or subterminal, emerge from nodes near the apex of the stem.

FLOWERS: 1–5 per inflorescence. The extremely fragrant flowers are 2–3 in. (5.0–7.5 cm) across. The bright, golden yellow sepals and petals are spreading, equally sized, and glossy. The lip is sometimes golden yellow and sometimes deep orange. The lip may have a yellow-green midlobe. The margin of the lip is fringed with extended, branching, and rebranching nerves which form an immense beard-like fringe on the lip. The sidelobes are also fringed. Unfortunately, the blossoms are somewhat short-lived.

HYBRIDIZING NOTES: Chromosome counts are $2n = 38$ (ref. 154, 188, 504, 580) and $2n = 40$ (ref. 153, 273, 504, 580). Johansen (ref. 239) indicates that "the number of days to capsule maturity could not be determined exactly because of spontaneous self-pollination."

REFERENCES: 6, 36, 38, 46, 153, 154, 157, 179, 188, 190, 196, 202, 210, 216, 239, 254, 266, 273, 371, 430, 445, 447, 448, 454, 504, 513, 528, 541, 557, 570, 580.

PHOTOS/DRAWINGS: 6, *36,* 210, *292,* 314, *371, 430, 454,* 513, 541, 557.

Dendrobium buffumii A. Hawkes

AKA: *D. roseoflavidum* Schlechter 1923 not 1912.

ORIGIN/HABITAT: Papua New Guinea. Plants grow along the Sepik River.

CLIMATE: Station #200004, Ambunti, Papua New Guinea, Lat. 4.2°S, Long. 142.8°E, at 164 ft. (50 m). Record extreme temperatures are 99°F (37°C) and 52°F (11°C).

N/HEMISPHERE	JAN	FEB	MAR	APR	MAY	JUN	JUL	AUG	SEP	OCT	NOV	DEC
°F AVG MAX	88	90	90	90	91	90	90	90	90	90	90	89
°F AVG MIN	72	73	74	73	73	73	72	73	73	73	73	74
DIURNAL RANGE	16	17	16	17	18	17	18	17	17	17	17	15
RAIN/INCHES	6.4	7.4	7.7	8.5	9.2	9.4	10.9	10.2	12.2	10.4	8.3	5.2
HUMIDITY/%	N/A											
BLOOM SEASON					*							
DAYS CLR	N/A											
RAIN/MM	163	187	196	217	233	240	277	260	311	265	211	132
°C AVG MAX	31.2	32.2	32.4	32.1	32.6	32.2	32.3	31.9	32.1	31.9	31.9	31.7
°C AVG MIN	22.4	22.8	23.2	22.1	23.0	22.8	22.4	22.5	22.7	22.8	22.9	23.1
DIURNAL RANGE	8.8	9.4	9.2	9.3	9.6	9.4	9.9	9.4	9.4	9.1	9.0	8.6
S/HEMISPHERE	JUL	AUG	SEP	OCT	NOV	DEC	JAN	FEB	MAR	APR	MAY	JUN

Cultural Recommendations

LIGHT: 2000–3000 fc.

TEMPERATURES: Throughout the year, days average 88–91°F (31–33°C), and nights average 72–74°F (22–23°C), with a diurnal range of 15–18°F (9–10°C).

HUMIDITY: Information is not available for this location. The habitat is always described as being near water, so humidity probably averages 80–85% year-round. High humidity and strong air movement must be maintained for cultivated plants.

WATER: Rainfall is heavy year-round with the greatest amounts falling in summer and early autumn. Cultivated plants should be moist but not soggy.

FERTILIZER: ¼–½ recommended strength. A balanced fertilizer should be applied weekly to biweekly throughout the year.

REST PERIOD: Growing conditions should be maintained all year. Water and fertilizer should be reduced for plants cultivated in the dark, short-day conditions common in temperate-latitude winters, but plants should never be allowed to dry completely between waterings. In the habitat, seasonal light variation is minor.

GROWING MEDIA: Plants may be mounted on tree-fern or cork slabs if humidity is high and plants are watered daily in summer. When plants are potted, any open, fast-draining medium may be used. Repotting may be done anytime new roots are growing.

MISCELLANEOUS NOTES: The bloom season shown in the climate table is based on the collection report.

Plant and Flower Information

PLANT SIZE AND TYPE: A 14–20 in. (35–50 cm) sympodial epiphyte.

PSEUDOBULB: 14–20 in. (35–50 cm) long. Stems are slender and non-branching.

LEAVES: Many. The pointed, linear leaves are 3.5–4.7 in. (9–12 cm) long.

INFLORESCENCE: Short.

FLOWERS: Few per inflorescence. The flowers are 0.6 in. (1.5 cm) long. Sepals and petals are yellowish violet with yellow at the tips. Sepals are ovate. The margins of the oblong-elliptic petals are minutely fringed. The margin of the lip is serrated.

REFERENCES: 191, 229, 443.

Dendrobium bukidnonense Ames and Quisumbing

ORIGIN/HABITAT: The Philippines. Plants grow in Bukidnon Province on northern Mindanao Island. Habitat elevation was not given; but Bukidnon is located on a mountainous plateau, and elevation is estimated at 3300 ft. (1000 m) based on verbal descriptions and topographical maps. Because elevation has been estimated, the following climate data should be used with caution.

CLIMATE: Station #98751, Malaybalay, Mindanao, Philippines, Lat. 8.2°N, Long. 125.1°E, at 2106 ft. (642 m). Temperatures are calculated for an elevation of 3300 ft. (1000 m), resulting in probable extremes of 89°F (32°C) and 49°F (10°C).

N/HEMISPHERE	JAN	FEB	MAR	APR	MAY	JUN	JUL	AUG	SEP	OCT	NOV	DEC
°F AVG MAX	78	79	81	83	82	79	79	78	79	80	80	79
°F AVG MIN	60	60	60	61	62	62	62	62	62	62	62	61
DIURNAL RANGE	18	19	21	22	20	17	17	16	17	18	18	18
RAIN/INCHES	4.6	3.7	4.0	3.7	10.0	13.0	14.1	13.8	14.2	12.6	7.3	7.0
HUMIDITY/%	85	85	82	79	85	87	87	88	87	86	83	83
BLOOM SEASON												*
DAYS CLR @ 8AM	5	5	11	17	10	7	7	4	5	9	8	10
DAYS CLR @ 2PM	2	1	3	3	1	1	1	1	1	2	1	1
RAIN/MM	117	94	102	94	254	330	358	351	361	320	185	178
°C AVG MAX	25.6	26.2	27.3	28.4	27.8	26.2	26.2	25.6	26.2	26.7	26.7	26.2
°C AVG MIN	15.6	15.6	15.6	16.2	16.7	16.7	16.7	16.7	16.7	16.7	16.7	16.2
DIURNAL RANGE	10.0	10.6	11.7	12.2	11.1	9.5	9.5	8.9	9.5	10.0	10.0	10.0
S/HEMISPHERE	JUL	AUG	SEP	OCT	NOV	DEC	JAN	FEB	MAR	APR	MAY	JUN

Cultural Recommendations

LIGHT: 1800–2500 fc.

TEMPERATURES: Throughout the year, days average 78–83°F (26–28°C), and nights are 60–62°F (16–17°C), with a diurnal range of 16–22°F (9–12°C).

HUMIDITY: 85–90% most of the year, dropping to near 80% in late winter and early spring.

WATER: Rainfall is heavy most of the year, but conditions are slightly drier in winter and early spring. Cultivated plants should be kept moist but not soggy, with only slight drying allowed between waterings.

FERTILIZER: ¼–½ recommended strength. A balanced fertilizer should be applied weekly to biweekly throughout the year.

REST PERIOD: Growing temperatures should be maintained all year. A brief rest probably occurs during the relatively dry winter months. In cultivation, water and fertilizer should be reduced for 2–3 months, especially for plants grown in the dark, short-day conditions common in temperate latitudes. Plants should dry slightly between waterings, but they should never be allowed to dry out completely.

GROWING MEDIA: Plants may be mounted on tree-fern or cork slabs if humidity is high and plants are watered at least once daily in summer. When plants are potted, any open, fast-draining medium may be used. They may be repotted anytime new roots are growing.

MISCELLANEOUS NOTES: The bloom season shown in the climate table is based on collection reports.

Plant and Flower Information

PLANT SIZE AND TYPE: An 8–20 in. (20–50 cm) sympodial epiphyte.

PSEUDOBULB: 6–17 in. (16–43 cm) long. The many-ridged stems have a 1.0–1.6 in. (2.5–4.0 cm) long thickening at the base.

LEAVES: Many. The linear leaves, which are arranged in 2 rows, are 1.6–2.8 in. (4–7 cm) long.

INFLORESCENCE: Short.

FLOWERS: 1 per inflorescence. The flower is 0.6 in. (1.5 cm) across. Blossoms have yellow sepals and white petals with yellow at the tips.

Dendrobium bulbophylloides

REFERENCES: 226, 373, 536.

PHOTOS/DRAWINGS: 373.

Dendrobium bulbophylloides Schlechter not J. J. Smith

ORIGIN/HABITAT: Northern Papua New Guinea. Plants grow in the Kani and Finisterre Ranges at 3300–3950 ft. (1000–1200 m). Plants were recently collected in the Lufa District of the Eastern Highlands Province at about 6900 ft. (2100 m). *D. bulbophylloides* often forms large mats on the trunks of tall, mistforest trees.

CLIMATE: Station #94010, Goroka, Papua New Guinea, Lat. 6.1°S, Long. 145.4°E, at 5141 ft. (1567 m). Record extreme temperatures are 87°F (31°C) and 43°F (6°C).

N/HEMISPHERE	JAN	FEB	MAR	APR	MAY	JUN	JUL	AUG	SEP	OCT	NOV	DEC
°F AVG MAX	76	77	78	79	79	78	79	78	78	78	79	77
°F AVG MIN	56	57	57	57	58	59	59	59	60	59	59	57
DIURNAL RANGE	20	20	21	22	21	19	20	19	18	19	20	20
RAIN/INCHES	2.1	2.8	4.6	5.9	6.6	9.3	9.1	10.1	10.7	8.3	4.6	2.0
HUMIDITY/%	70	67	67	67	67	71	72	73	74	71	70	70
BLOOM SEASON						*	*	*				
DAYS CLR	N/A											
RAIN/MM	54	70	118	151	167	236	230	256	271	211	116	52
°C AVG MAX	24.7	25.1	25.6	26.3	26.2	25.7	25.8	25.6	25.5	25.6	25.9	25.1
°C AVG MIN	13.5	13.8	14.0	14.0	14.2	14.8	15.0	15.2	15.3	15.1	14.7	13.7
DIURNAL RANGE	11.2	11.3	11.6	12.3	12.0	10.9	10.8	10.4	10.2	10.5	11.2	11.4
S/HEMISPHERE	JUL	AUG	SEP	OCT	NOV	DEC	JAN	FEB	MAR	APR	MAY	JUN

Cultural Recommendations

LIGHT: 1800–2500 fc.

TEMPERATURES: Throughout the year, days average 76–79°F (25–26°C), and nights average 56–60°F (14–15°C), with a diurnal range of 18–22°F (10–12°C).

HUMIDITY: 70–75% most of the year, dropping to near 65% in late winter and spring.

WATER: Rainfall is moderate to heavy most of the year, but conditions are slightly drier for 3 months in winter. The high relative humidity and wide temperature range causes frequent heavy deposits of dew. Additional moisture is available as mist from fog and low clouds. Cultivated plants should be kept moist and never be allowed to dry completely. In summer, daily watering may be necessary during hot, dry weather. Additional early morning mistings may be beneficial, especially on bright, sunny days.

FERTILIZER: 1/4–1/2 recommended strength. A balanced fertilizer should be applied weekly to biweekly throughout the year.

REST PERIOD: Growing temperatures should be maintained all year. Water should be reduced in winter, especially for plants grown in the dark, short-day conditions common in temperate latitudes; but plants should never be allowed to dry completely. Fertilizer should be reduced or eliminated until spring. In the habitat, light is probably highest in winter.

GROWING MEDIA: Plants are best mounted on a tree-fern slab to accommodate their mat-forming growth habit. Humidity must be high, however, and the plants watered at least once daily in summer. If plants must be potted, small pots or baskets may be filled with any open, moisture-retaining medium. Repotting may be done anytime new roots are growing.

MISCELLANEOUS NOTES: The bloom season shown in the climate table is based on the primary bloom season in the habitat.

Plant and Flower Information

PLANT SIZE AND TYPE: A small, 1.2 in. (3 cm) sympodial epiphyte.

PSEUDOBULB: 0.2–0.4 in. (0.4–1.0 cm) long. The pseudobulbs, which vary from oblong to cylindrical, may be brown, reddish-brown, or green. New growths may be spaced 0.2–1.1 in. (5–28 cm) apart. They emerge from a branching, mat-forming rhizome. Roots are white with pink tips.

LEAVES: 1 per growth. The ovate to oblong leaves are 0.2–0.8 in. (0.6–2.0 cm) long, thick, fleshy, and nearly erect.

INFLORESCENCE: 0.2 in. (0.5 cm) long. A single inflorescence arises at the apex of newer pseudobulbs. It emerges at the back of the leaf petiole.

FLOWERS: 1 per inflorescence. The fleshy flowers are 0.4 in. (1 cm) across, which is large for the plant size. They may not open fully. Sepals and petals are dull orange to maroon, with some described as brick-red. The lip is darker maroon. Blossoms last 12–24 days.

HYBRIDIZING NOTES: Chromosome count is 2n = 38 (ref. 153, 273).

REFERENCES: 95, 153, 221, 253, 273, 382, 437, 445.

PHOTOS/DRAWINGS: 382, 437.

Dendrobium bulbophylloides J. J. Smith not Schlechter.

Now considered a synonym of *Diplocaulobium kirchianum* (A. Hawkes and A. H. Heller) P. F. Hunt and Summerhayes. REFERENCES: 213, 221, 230, 470, 475.

Dendrobium bulbosum Rojas 1897. An Argentinean orchid.

REFERENCES: 231.

Dendrobium bullenianum Rchb. f.

AKA: Valmayor (ref. 536) includes *D. erythroxanthum* Rchb. f. and *D. topaziacum* Ames as synonyms. Kränzlin (ref. 254) also lists *D. salaccense* Hort. ex Rchb. f. not (Blume) Lindley. Ossian (ref. 350) includes a photograph labeled *D. topaziacum*.

ORIGIN/HABITAT: Western Samoa and the Philippines. In the Philippines, plants grow near Dagami on Leyte, in the provinces of Camarines Sur, Isabela, and Quezon on Luzon, and on Bucas Grande Island, which is located off the northeastern coast of Mindanao. Plants are usually found in forests below 200 ft. (60 m).

CLIMATE: Station #98439, Daet, Philippines, Lat. 14.1°N, Long. 122.9°E, at 36 ft. (11 m). Temperatures are calculated for an elevation of 200 ft. (60 m), resulting in probable extremes of 100°F (38°C) and 59°F (15°C).

N/HEMISPHERE	JAN	FEB	MAR	APR	MAY	JUN	JUL	AUG	SEP	OCT	NOV	DEC
°F AVG MAX	82	83	85	88	90	91	89	89	89	87	85	83
°F AVG MIN	71	71	72	73	74	74	74	74	73	73	73	72
DIURNAL RANGE	11	12	13	15	16	17	15	15	16	14	12	11
RAIN/INCHES	16.2	7.8	7.0	4.9	5.7	5.9	7.9	9.4	10.5	19.3	22.8	21.7
HUMIDITY/%	82	81	81	81	81	80	83	83	84	84	84	84
BLOOM SEASON	*	*		*	*	*	**	*		*	*	*
DAYS CLR @ 8AM	3	4	7	10	8	8	4	4	4	4	3	3
DAYS CLR @ 2PM	3	5	9	10	9	3	1	1	1	3	3	2
RAIN/MM	411	198	178	124	145	150	201	239	267	490	579	551
°C AVG MAX	28.0	28.6	29.7	31.4	32.5	33.0	31.9	31.9	31.9	30.8	29.7	28.6
°C AVG MIN	21.9	21.5	22.5	23.0	23.6	23.6	23.6	23.6	23.0	23.0	23.0	22.5
DIURNAL RANGE	6.1	6.7	7.2	8.4	8.9	9.4	8.3	8.3	8.9	7.8	6.7	6.1
S/HEMISPHERE	JUL	AUG	SEP	OCT	NOV	DEC	JAN	FEB	MAR	APR	MAY	JUN

Cultural Recommendations

LIGHT: 2500–3500 fc.

TEMPERATURES: Summer days average 89–91°F (32–33°C), and nights average 74°F (24°C), with a diurnal range of 15–17°F (8–9°C).

HUMIDITY: 80–85% year-round.

WATER: Rainfall is moderate to heavy all year, but the driest period occurs in spring and summer. Cultivated plants should be kept evenly moist with only slight drying allowed between waterings.

FERTILIZER: ¼–½ recommended strength. A balanced fertilizer should be applied weekly to biweekly throughout the year.

REST PERIOD: Winter days average 82–85°F (28–30°C), and nights average 71–72°F (22–23°C), with a diurnal range of 11–13°F (6–7°C). In the habitat, winter lows are only slightly cooler than summer nights. Growers indicate that plants tolerate winter lows near 54°F (12°C), but it should be noted that this is colder than the record lows in the habitat. Although rainfall is greatest in winter, water should not be increased for cultivated plants, especially those grown in the dark, short-day conditions common in temperate-latitude winters. Fertilizer may be reduced anytime plants are not actively growing.

GROWING MEDIA: Plants may be mounted on tree-fern or cork slabs if humidity is high and plants are watered at least once daily in summer. When plants are potted, any open, fast-draining medium may be used. Repotting may be done anytime new roots are growing.

MISCELLANEOUS NOTES: The bloom season shown in the climate table is based on cultivation records.

Plant and Flower Information

PLANT SIZE AND TYPE: A 10–24 in. (25–60 cm) sympodial epiphyte.

PSEUDOBULB: 10–24 in. (25–60 cm) long. The canelike stems are erect, angular, fleshy, and become furrowed with age. Growth habit resembles *D. secundum* (Blume) Lindley.

LEAVES: The oblong leaves are 2.4–5.5 in. (6–14 cm) long, leathery, and deciduous.

INFLORESCENCE: 2.4 in. (6 cm) long. The densely flowered racemes emerge from the nodes of leafless stems.

FLOWERS: 24–36 per inflorescence. The waxy flowers are about 0.8 in. (2 cm) across. They are bright yellow to amber with red to purple stripes. The stripes are often strongest on the petals and lip.

HYBRIDIZING NOTES: Chromosome count is 2n = 38 as *D. bullenianum* (ref. 154, 188, 504, 580). As *D. topaziacum*, n = 19 (ref. 187) and 2n = 38 (ref. 151, 187, 280, 504, 580). Wilfret and Hashimoto (ref. 568) did not get seed when they crossed *D. bullenianum* with *D. bigibbum* Lindley, *D. crumenatum* Swartz, or *D. delacourii* Guillaumin.

REFERENCES: 12, 36, 101, 151, 154, 179, 187, 188, 190, 216, 254, 280, 296, 371, 430, 504, 536, 568, 580.

PHOTOS/DRAWINGS: *36, 101, 371, 430, 568.*

Dendrobium bullerianum Bateman. See *D. gratiosissimum* Rchb. f. REFERENCES: 190, 216, 254, 430, 445, 454.

Dendrobium bulleyi Rolfe. See *D. longicornu* Lindley. REFERENCES: 208, 221.

Dendrobium buluense Schlechter. See *D. mirbelianum* Gaudich. REFERENCES: 67, 84, 221, 236, 437, 445.

Dendrobium bunuanense Ames

AKA: *D. appendiculoides* Ames.

ORIGIN/HABITAT: The Philippines. On northern Mindanao Island, *D. bunuanense* grows in Bukidnon Province on forest trees at about 5400 ft. (1650 m) on Mt. Candoon.

CLIMATE: Station #98751, Malaybalay, Philippines, Lat. 8.2°N, Long. 125.1°E, at 2106 ft. (642 m). Temperatures are calculated for an elevation of 5400 ft. (1650 m), resulting in probable extremes of 82°F (28°C) and 42°F (6°C).

N/HEMISPHERE	JAN	FEB	MAR	APR	MAY	JUN	JUL	AUG	SEP	OCT	NOV	DEC
°F AVG MAX	71	72	74	76	75	72	72	71	72	73	73	72
°F AVG MIN	53	53	53	54	55	55	55	55	55	55	55	54
DIURNAL RANGE	18	19	21	22	20	17	17	16	17	18	18	18
RAIN/INCHES	4.6	3.7	4.0	3.7	10.0	13.0	14.1	13.8	14.2	12.6	7.3	7.0
HUMIDITY/%	85	85	82	79	85	87	87	88	87	86	83	83
BLOOM SEASON						*	*					
DAYS CLR @ 8AM	5	5	11	17	10	7	7	4	5	9	8	10
DAYS CLR @ 2PM	2	1	3	3	1	1	1	1	1	2	1	1
RAIN/MM	117	94	102	94	254	330	358	351	361	320	185	178
°C AVG MAX	21.7	22.3	23.4	24.5	24.0	22.3	22.3	21.7	22.3	22.8	22.8	22.3
°C AVG MIN	11.7	11.7	11.7	12.3	12.8	12.8	12.8	12.8	12.8	12.8	12.8	12.3
DIURNAL RANGE	10.0	10.6	11.7	12.2	11.2	9.5	9.5	8.9	9.5	10.0	10.0	10.0
S/HEMISPHERE	JUL	AUG	SEP	OCT	NOV	DEC	JAN	FEB	MAR	APR	MAY	JUN

Cultural Recommendations

LIGHT: 2000–3000 fc.

TEMPERATURES: Throughout the year, days average 71–76°F (22–25°C), and nights are 53–55°F (12–13°C), with a diurnal range of 16–22°F (9–12°C).

HUMIDITY: 85–90% most of the year, dropping to near 80% in late winter and early spring.

WATER: Rainfall is heavy most of the year, but conditions are slightly drier in winter and early spring. Cultivated plants should be kept moist but not soggy, with only slight drying allowed between waterings.

FERTILIZER: ¼–½ recommended strength. A balanced fertilizer should be applied weekly to biweekly throughout the year.

REST PERIOD: Growing temperatures should be maintained all year. A brief rest probably occurs during the relatively dry winter months. In cultivation, water and fertilizer should be reduced for 2–3 months, especially for plants grown in the dark, short-day conditions common in temperate latitudes. Plants should dry slightly between waterings, but they should never be allowed to dry out completely.

GROWING MEDIA: Plants may be mounted on a tree-fern or cork slab or potted in small pots filled with any open, fast-draining medium. Repotting may be done anytime new roots are growing.

MISCELLANEOUS NOTES: The bloom season shown in the climate table is based on collection records.

Plant and Flower Information

PLANT SIZE AND TYPE: A 10 in. (25 cm) sympodial epiphyte.

PSEUDOBULB: 10 in. (25 cm) long. The yellow pseudobulbs are jointed and slender. They grow compactly.

LEAVES: The leaves, which are 2-ranked along the stem, are 1.5 in. (3.8 cm) long.

FLOWERS: Few per inflorescence. The white flowers, which are 0.5 in. (1.3 cm) across, are tinged with pink or rose.

REFERENCES: 12, 15, 223, 296, 536.

Dendrobium burbidgei Rchb. f. See *D. bicaudatum* Reinwardt ex Lindley. REFERENCES: 84, 216, 254, 286, 295.

Dendrobium bursigerum Lindley. See *D. secundum* (Blume) Lindley. REFERENCES: 12, 190, 216, 254, 278, 286, 295, 296, 310, 445, 454.

Dendrobium busuangense Ames

AKA: Cribb (ref. 84) states that on further study this species may prove to be only a variant of *D. taurinum* Lindley.

ORIGIN/HABITAT: The Philippine Islands. Plants were collected on Busuanga in the Calamian Islands between Mindoro and Palawan. Habitat

Dendrobium busuangense

description and elevation were not reported. However, topographical maps indicate that the island is generally low lying, with the highest point being about 2150 ft. (655 m) above sea level.

CLIMATE: Station #98526, Coron, Busuanga Island, Philippines, Lat. 12.0°N, Long. 120.2°E, at 48 ft. (15 m). Record extreme temperatures are 99°F (37°C) and 61°F (16°C).

N/HEMISPHERE	JAN	FEB	MAR	APR	MAY	JUN	JUL	AUG	SEP	OCT	NOV	DEC
°F AVG MAX	89	89	90	92	91	88	87	86	87	88	89	88
°F AVG MIN	73	73	74	76	77	75	73	74	74	74	74	73
DIURNAL RANGE	16	16	16	16	14	13	14	12	13	14	15	15
RAIN/INCHES	1.3	0.2	0.2	1.0	6.9	16.4	18.6	20.4	18.9	11.4	5.5	4.9
HUMIDITY/%	81	77	75	74	74	84	88	87	86	84	80	80
BLOOM SEASON									*			
DAYS CLR @ 8AM	12	11	14	11	7	3	2	2	3	7	9	8
DAYS CLR @ 2PM	8	7	14	11	6	2	1	1	3	3	6	6
RAIN/MM	33	5	5	25	175	417	472	518	480	290	140	124
°C AVG MAX	31.7	31.7	32.2	33.3	32.8	31.1	30.6	30.0	30.6	31.1	31.7	31.1
°C AVG MIN	22.8	22.8	23.3	24.4	25.0	23.9	22.8	23.3	23.3	23.3	23.3	22.8
DIURNAL RANGE	8.9	8.9	8.9	8.9	7.8	7.2	7.8	6.7	7.3	7.8	8.4	8.3
S/HEMISPHERE	JUL	AUG	SEP	OCT	NOV	DEC	JAN	FEB	MAR	APR	MAY	JUN

Cultural Recommendations

LIGHT: 2000–3000 fc. The few clear days in summer indicates that shading is required for cultivated plants from spring into autumn. On the other hand, the large number of clear days in winter and early spring indicates that these are the brightest seasons and that light should be increased for cultivated plants, if possible.

TEMPERATURES: Throughout the year, days average 86–92°F (30–33°C), and nights average 73–77°F (23–25°C), with a diurnal range of 12–16°F (7–9°C). Temperatures are warmest in spring.

HUMIDITY: 80–90% most of the year, dropping to near 75% in late winter and spring.

WATER: Rainfall is very heavy from late spring through autumn, but conditions are much drier in winter and early spring. Cultivated plants should be kept moist with only slight drying allowed between waterings during the growing season, but water should be gradually reduced in late autumn.

FERTILIZER: ¼–½ recommended strength, applied weekly. A high nitrogen fertilizer is beneficial from spring to midsummer, but a fertilizer high in phosphates should be used in late summer and autumn.

REST PERIOD: Very warm growing temperatures should be maintained year-round. Rainfall is low for 3–4 months in winter and spring, and 2 of those months are very dry. Not only is rainfall low, but the low humidity and diurnal range indicate that even moisture from dew is uncommon. For most of the winter, cultivated plants should be allowed to dry out between waterings, but they should not remain dry for extended periods. For 1–2 months in late winter, however, water should be reduced even further and the plants allowed to remain dry for longer. Fertilizer should be reduced or eliminated anytime water is reduced. Winter light is highest in the habitat.

GROWING MEDIA: Plants may be mounted if humidity is high and plants are watered at least once daily in summer. When plants are potted, any open, fast-draining medium may be used. Repotting is best done in early spring when new roots are growing.

MISCELLANEOUS NOTES: The bloom season shown in the climate table is based on collection reports. Plants are cultivated in Manila.

Plant and Flower Information

PLANT SIZE AND TYPE: A 79 in. (200 cm) sympodial epiphyte.

PSEUDOBULB: 79 in. (200 cm) long. The yellow stems are canelike.

LEAVES: Many per growth. The leathery, elliptical leaves are approximately 3 in. (7.6 cm) long.

INFLORESCENCE: 20–28 in. (50–70 cm) long. The racemes are laxly flowered.

FLOWERS: 50 or more per inflorescence. The flowers are 2.5–3.0 in. (6.4–7.6 cm) across. The sepals and mentum are pale lavender to purple. The petals and lip are greenish with a lavender-purple tinge. The petals are erect and twisted. The lip is fringed along the wavy margin. Blossoms last about 8 weeks.

REFERENCES: 12, 84, 222, 296, 445, 536.

PHOTOS/DRAWINGS: *536*.

Dendrobium cabadbarense Ames

AKA: Sometimes spelled *D. cabadharense*.

ORIGIN/HABITAT: The Philippines. Plants grow on trees in swampy areas from sea level to 350 ft. (0–100 m) in Agusan Province near Cabadbaran on Mindanao and in Rizal Province of central Luzon.

CLIMATE: Station #98752, Butuan, Mindanao, Philippines, Lat. 8.9°N, Long. 125.5°E, at 148 ft. (45 m). Record extreme temperatures are not available for this location.

N/HEMISPHERE	JAN	FEB	MAR	APR	MAY	JUN	JUL	AUG	SEP	OCT	NOV	DEC
°F AVG MAX	87	87	89	90	92	90	89	90	90	89	88	86
°F AVG MIN	72	72	73	74	75	75	74	74	74	74	74	73
DIURNAL RANGE	15	15	16	16	17	15	15	16	16	15	14	13
RAIN/INCHES	2.0	4.4	2.4	2.1	2.5	4.4	6.3	1.8	3.4	6.5	5.1	4.6
HUMIDITY/%	N/A											
BLOOM SEASON				*		*	*		*			
DAYS CLR	N/A											
RAIN/MM	51	112	61	53	64	112	160	46	86	165	130	117
°C AVG MAX	30.6	30.6	31.7	32.2	33.3	32.2	31.7	32.2	32.2	31.7	31.1	30.0
°C AVG MIN	22.2	22.2	22.8	23.3	23.9	23.9	23.3	23.3	23.3	23.3	23.3	22.8
DIURNAL RANGE	8.4	8.4	8.9	8.9	9.4	8.3	8.4	8.9	8.9	8.4	7.8	7.2
S/HEMISPHERE	JUL	AUG	SEP	OCT	NOV	DEC	JAN	FEB	MAR	APR	MAY	JUN

Cultural Recommendations

LIGHT: 1500–3000 fc.

TEMPERATURES: Throughout the year, days average 87–92°F (31–33°C), and nights average 72–75°F (22–24°C), with a diurnal range of 13–17°F (7–9°C).

HUMIDITY: Information is not available for this location. However, records from nearby stations indicate that averages are probably 75–85%.

WATER: Rainfall is moderate most of the year. The driest period occurs in winter and early spring, with a short, secondary dry period in late summer. Cultivated plants should be kept moist with only slight drying allowed between waterings from late spring to autumn.

FERTILIZER: ¼–½ recommended strength. A balanced fertilizer should be applied weekly to biweekly.

REST PERIOD: Growing temperatures should be maintained year-round. Water should be reduced in winter and early spring. Plants should be allowed to become somewhat dry between waterings, but they should never dry out completely or remain dry for long periods. Fertilizer should be reduced or eliminated until plants begin actively growing in spring.

GROWING MEDIA: Plants may be mounted on cork or tree-fern slabs if humidity is high and water is applied at least once daily in summer. Plants should never become completely dry, even in winter. If plants are potted, any open, fast-draining media may be used. Repotting may be done anytime new roots are growing.

MISCELLANEOUS NOTES: The bloom season shown in the climate table is based on collection reports. Plants that produce flowers which last a single day commonly bloom several times during the year. Flowering usually occurs 7–14 days after a sudden 10°F (5°C) drop in daytime temperatures.

Plant and Flower Information

PLANT SIZE AND TYPE: A 3.5 in. (9 cm) sympodial epiphyte.

PSEUDOBULB: 2.5–3.0 in. (6.4–7.6 cm) long. The pseudobulbs, which are sometimes as small as 1 in. (2.5 cm), are yellow, compact, and 4-angled. They are rigid and unbranched. They are attached to the rhizome by a slender stem.

LEAVES: 2 at the apex of each growth. The oblong leaves are approximately 1.0–1.2 in. (2.5–3.0 cm) long.

INFLORESCENCE: 0.4 in. (1 cm) long. The inflorescence emerges at the apex of the pseudobulb.

FLOWERS: The greenish yellow blossoms are 0.3 in. (0.8 cm) across and thin-textured. The lip is toothed and ruffled. Blossoms are short-lived.

REFERENCES: 12, 222, 296, 536.

Dendrobium cacatua M. Clements and D. Jones

AKA: Clements (ref. 67) includes *D. tetragonum* A. Cunningham var. *giganteum* Leaney, *D. tetragonum* A. Cunningham var *giganteum* Gilbert (in part), *D. tetragonum* A. Cunningham var *hayesianum* as used by Dockrill not P. A. Gilbert. See also *D. tetragonum* A. Cunningham and *D. capitisyork* M. Clements and D. Jones.

ORIGIN/HABITAT: Australia. *D. cacatua* is found from near the Fitzroy River (23.5°S) northward to at least the Iron Range on the northeastern part of Cape York Peninsula (12.8°S). It grows in both high and lowland rainforests from sea level to 5250 ft. (0–1600 m) but is usually found above 2950 ft. (900 m). Although the plant usually grows low on trees in well-shaded situations, it is occasionally found on rocks.

CLIMATE: Station #94294, Townsville, Australia, Lat. 19.3°S, Long. 146.8°E, at 18 ft. (5 m). Temperatures are calculated for an elevation of 3500 ft. (1070 m), resulting in probable extremes of 99°F (37°C) and 28°F (−2°C).

N/HEMISPHERE	JAN	FEB	MAR	APR	MAY	JUN	JUL	AUG	SEP	OCT	NOV	DEC
°F AVG MAX	64	66	69	72	74	76	76	76	75	73	70	66
°F AVG MIN	48	50	55	60	63	65	65	64	62	59	54	50
DIURNAL RANGE	16	16	14	12	11	11	11	12	13	14	16	16
RAIN/INCHES	0.6	0.5	0.7	1.3	1.9	5.4	10.9	11.2	7.2	3.3	1.3	1.4
HUMIDITY/%	61	61	62	64	66	70	72	71	70	64	63	63
BLOOM SEASON	**	**	**							*	*	*
DAYS CLR @ 10AM	16	18	15	10	7	5	5	9	13	14	15	
DAYS CLR @ 4PM	16	18	20	20	17	15	8	5	7	11	14	15
RAIN/MM	15	13	18	33	48	137	277	284	183	84	33	36
°C AVG MAX	17.8	18.9	20.6	22.2	23.3	24.6	24.5	24.4	23.9	22.8	21.1	18.9
°C AVG MIN	8.9	9.7	12.5	15.3	16.9	18.1	18.1	17.5	16.4	14.7	11.9	9.7
DIURNAL RANGE	8.9	9.2	8.1	6.9	6.4	6.5	6.4	6.9	7.5	8.1	9.2	9.2
S/HEMISPHERE	JUL	AUG	SEP	OCT	NOV	DEC	JAN	FEB	MAR	APR	MAY	JUN

Cultural Recommendations

LIGHT: 1800–3000 fc. About 60% shading is required in summer, but the large number of clear winter days in the habitat indicates that light should be increased for cultivated plants from autumn until spring. Strong air movement should be provided at all times.

TEMPERATURES: Summer days average 76°F (24–25°C), and nights average 64–65°F (18°C), with a diurnal range of 11–12°F (6–7°C).

HUMIDITY: Near 70% in summer, dropping to 60–65% during the rest of the year. However, in the rainforest habitat, values are probably 10–15% greater than indicated by the climate data. Humidity for cultivated plants should be 75–85% year-round.

WATER: At lower elevations, rainfall is moderate to heavy during a 5-month summer wet season, followed by a 6–7 month dry season. More water is available in the rainforest habitat from heavy dew and mist than is indicated in the climate data, however. Cultivated plants should be kept moist, with only slight drying allowed between waterings in summer and early autumn. Water should be gradually reduced in autumn after new growths mature. Successful growers report that this species requires "lots of water," and that plants must never be allowed to dry out completely for any length of time.

FERTILIZER: ¼–½ recommended strength, applied weekly. A high-nitrogen fertilizer is beneficial from spring to midsummer, but a fertilizer high in phosphates should be used in late summer and autumn.

REST PERIOD: Winter days average 64–66°F (18–19°C), and nights average 48–50°F (9–10°C), with a diurnal range of 16°F (9°C). Water and humidity may be reduced somewhat, especially for plants grown in the dark, short-day conditions common in temperate-latitude winters. However, plants should never be allowed to dry out completely. Occasional morning mistings between waterings are often beneficial on bright, sunny days. Fertilizer should be reduced or eliminated until plants begin actively growing in spring.

GROWING MEDIA: Mounting plants on cork or tree-fern slabs accommodates their pendulous growth habit. When plants are potted, any open, fast-draining medium may be used. Repotting is best done in early spring when new roots are growing.

MISCELLANEOUS NOTES: The bloom season shown in the climate table is based on reports from the habitat. Plants frequently bloom more than once during the bloom season.

Plant and Flower Information

PLANT SIZE AND TYPE: A 14 in. (35 cm) sympodial epiphyte.

PSEUDOBULB: 14 in. (35 cm) long. The greenish brown stem is wiry on the basal part then expands and becomes 4-angled. Plants are pendulous.

LEAVES: 2–4 per growth. The dark green ovate leaves are 3.5 in. (9 cm) long. They are thin but tough.

INFLORESCENCE: 8 in. (20 cm) long. Inflorescences are extremely slender.

FLOWERS: 2–5 per inflorescence. The fragrant flowers are about 2.8 in. (7 cm) long. The very slender sepals and petals may be a white, pale green, or yellow. The sepals and petals are variably covered with reddish brown spots. A pale green form with a white lip occasionally occurs. The hairy lip is usually marked with red. The sidelobes are broader than the midlobe.

HYBRIDIZING NOTES: When used as a parent, it contributes the tendency to bloom twice a year.

REFERENCES: 67, 68, 235, 240, 533, 564.

PHOTOS/DRAWINGS: 68, *533*, 564.

Dendrobium cacuminis Gagnepain. Now considered a synonym of *Epigeneium cacuminis* (Gagnepain) Summerhayes. REFERENCES: 136, 224, 229, 266, 448, 449, 505.

Dendrobium cadetia (Blume) J. J. Smith. Originally described as *Cadetia biloba* Blume from Irian Jaya (western New Guinea) without precise locality. J. J. Smith indicated that the original description was too incomplete to be able to recognize the plant. *Cadetia* is now considered a valid genus by some botanists. REFERENCES: 220, 470.

Dendrobium cadetiiflorum J. J. Smith

ORIGIN/HABITAT: Irian Jaya (western New Guinea). Plants grow on the ground in thin forests near the Rouffaer River at about 500 ft. (150 m).

CLIMATE: Station #200004, Ambunti, Papua New Guinea, Lat. 4.2°S, Long. 142.8°E, at 164 ft. (50 m). Temperatures are calculated for an elevation of 500 ft. (150 m), resulting in probable extremes of 98°F (37°C) and 51°F (11°C).

N/HEMISPHERE	JAN	FEB	MAR	APR	MAY	JUN	JUL	AUG	SEP	OCT	NOV	DEC
°F AVG MAX	87	89	89	89	90	89	89	89	89	89	89	88
°F AVG MIN	71	72	73	72	72	72	71	72	72	72	72	73
DIURNAL RANGE	16	17	16	17	18	17	18	17	17	17	17	15
RAIN/INCHES	6.4	7.4	7.7	8.5	9.2	9.4	10.9	10.2	12.2	10.4	8.3	5.2
HUMIDITY/%	N/A											
BLOOM SEASON				•								
DAYS CLR	N/A											
RAIN/MM	163	188	196	216	234	239	277	259	310	264	211	132
°C AVG MAX	30.5	31.6	31.6	31.6	32.2	31.6	31.6	31.6	31.6	31.6	31.6	31.1
°C AVG MIN	21.6	22.2	22.7	22.2	22.2	22.2	21.6	22.2	22.2	22.2	22.2	22.7
DIURNAL RANGE	8.9	9.4	8.9	9.4	10.0	9.4	10.0	9.4	9.4	9.4	9.4	8.4
S/HEMISPHERE	JUL	AUG	SEP	OCT	NOV	DEC	JAN	FEB	MAR	APR	MAY	JUN

Cultural Recommendations

LIGHT: 2000–3000 fc.

TEMPERATURES: Throughout the year, days average 87–90°F (31–32°C), and nights average 71–73°F (22–23°C), with a diurnal range of 15–18°F (8–10°C).

HUMIDITY: Information is not available at this location. However, reports from other stations in the region indicate that averages are probably near 80% year-round.

WATER: Rainfall is heavy year-round, with the greatest amounts falling in summer and early autumn. Cultivated plants should be moist but not soggy.

FERTILIZER: ¼–½ recommended strength. A balanced fertilizer should be applied weekly to biweekly throughout the year.

REST PERIOD: Growing conditions should be maintained all year. Water and fertilizer should be reduced for plants cultivated in the dark, short-day conditions common in temperate-latitude winters, but plants should never be allowed to dry completely between waterings. In the habitat, seasonal light variation is minor.

GROWING MEDIA: Plants may be mounted on cork or tree-fern slabs if humidity is high and plants are watered at least once daily in summer. When plants are potted, any open, fast-draining medium may be used. However, fir bark is preferred by most growers. Repotting may be done anytime new roots are growing.

MISCELLANEOUS NOTES: The bloom season shown in the climate table is based on collection records. Collectors indicated that although the plants were numerous in that locality, few were in bloom.

Plant and Flower Information

PLANT SIZE AND TYPE: A 30 in. (75 cm) sympodial terrestrial.

PSEUDOBULB: 30 in. (75 cm) long. Stems are slender and flexible.

LEAVES: Many. The linear leaves are 1.4–2.2 in. (3.5–5.5 cm) long. New leaves are covered with dark hairs, but older leaves are nearly smooth. The underside is densely covered with dots. The leaf sheaths are covered with dark hairs.

INFLORESCENCE: Short. Inflorescences emerge from nodes along the stem.

FLOWERS: 1 per inflorescence. The very light yellow flowers are 0.5 in. (1.2 cm) across. The sepals and petals are arranged in a semicircle. The oblong sepals are recurved. The pointed petals are nearly linear. The 3-lobed lip is concave, fleshy, and longitudinally grooved with small erect sidelobes and a broad midlobe.

REFERENCES: 225, 470.

Dendrobium cadetioides Schlechter. Now considered a synonym of *Diplocaulobium cadetioides* (Schlechter) A. Hawkes. REFERENCES: 92, 221, 229, 437, 445.

Dendrobium caenosicallainum P. van Royen. See *D. vexillarius* J. J. Smith. REFERENCES: 233, 385, 538. PHOTOS/DRAWINGS: 538

Dendrobium caespitificum Ridley. See *D. masarangense* Schlechter. REFERENCES: 222, 385, 400.

Dendrobium caespitosum King and Pantling. See *D. porphyrochilum* Lindley. REFERENCES: 218, 254, 454.

Dendrobium calamiforme Loddiges not Rolfe

AKA: Generally accepted synonyms include *D. baseyanum* St. Cloud and *D. teretifolium* R. Brown var. *album* C. T. White. Clements (ref. 67) includes only *D. teretifolium* R. Brown var. *fasciculatum* Rupp. He retains *D. baseyanum* St. Cloud as a separate entity and refers *D. teretifolium* R. Brown var. *album* C. T. White to a new species *D. dolchophyllum* D. Jones and M. Clements.

ORIGIN/HABITAT: Endemic to eastern Australia. Plants grow in northern Queensland from near the Burdekin River in the south to the Iron Range and Portland Roads in the north. They are found in a variety of habitats from open forests to rainforests to swamps from sea level to 3950 ft. (0–1200 m). They grow in a variety of habitats ranging from deep shade in dense rainforests to full sun in dry grassland. Plants are usually epiphytic, but they also grow on rocks, especially at higher elevations.

CLIMATE: Station #94287, Cairns, Australia, Lat. 16.9°S, Long. 145.8°E, at 7 ft. (2 m). Temperatures are calculated for an elevation of 2000 ft. (610 m), resulting in probable extremes of 103°F (40°C) and 36°F (3°C).

N/HEMISPHERE	JAN	FEB	MAR	APR	MAY	JUN	JUL	AUG	SEP	OCT	NOV	DEC
°F AVG MAX	71	73	76	79	81	83	83	82	80	78	74	72
°F AVG MIN	54	55	57	61	63	66	67	67	66	63	59	57
DIURNAL RANGE	17	18	19	18	18	17	16	15	14	15	15	15
RAIN/INCHES	1.6	1.7	1.7	2.1	3.9	8.7	16.6	15.7	18.1	11.3	4.4	2.9
HUMIDITY/%	69	67	65	65	65	68	72	72	74	73	73	72
BLOOM SEASON			*	*	*	*						
DAYS CLR @ 10AM	9	11	13	11	6	6	4	5	6	7	11	10
DAYS CLR @ 4PM	8	10	12	16	10	7	4	3	4	6	9	10
RAIN/MM	41	43	43	53	99	221	422	399	460	287	112	74
°C AVG MAX	21.9	23.0	24.7	26.3	27.5	28.6	28.6	28.0	26.9	25.8	23.6	22.5
°C AVG MIN	12.5	13.0	14.1	16.3	17.5	19.1	19.7	19.7	19.1	17.5	15.2	14.1
DIURNAL RANGE	9.4	10.0	10.6	10.0	10.0	9.5	8.9	8.3	7.8	8.3	8.4	8.4
S/HEMISPHERE	JUL	AUG	SEP	OCT	NOV	DEC	JAN	FEB	MAR	APR	MAY	JUN

Cultural Recommendations

LIGHT: 2000–3500 fc.

TEMPERATURES: Summer days average 82–83°F (28–29°C), and nights average 66–67°F (19–20°C), with a diurnal range of 15–17°F (8–10°C).

HUMIDITY: 65–75% year-round. In cloudforest habitats, humidity probably averages 10% higher than indicated in the climate table. Cultivated plants are healthiest with high humidity and strong air movement all year.

WATER: Rainfall is heavy from late spring into autumn, with much drier conditions in winter. Cultivated plants should be kept moist from late spring into autumn, but water should be gradually reduced in late autumn. Growers indicate that mounted plants should be misted frequently and never be allowed to dry out completely for any length of time.

FERTILIZER: ¼–½ recommended strength, applied weekly. A high-nitrogen fertilizer is beneficial from spring to midsummer, but a fertilizer high in phosphates should be used in late summer and autumn.

REST PERIOD: Winter days average 71–73°F (22–23°C), and nights average 54–57°F (13–14°C), with a diurnal range of 15–18°F (8–10°C). Australian growers report that plants require a winter minimum temperature of 46°F (8°C). In cultivation, water should be reduced for 4–5 months from late autumn into early spring. The medium should be kept just barely moist. Light, humidity, and air movement should be maintained in winter. Fertilizer should be reduced until water is increased in spring.

GROWING MEDIA: Mounting plants on slabs or rafts accommodates their pendent growth habit. However, high humidity must be maintained and the plants must be watered at least once daily in summer. Several waterings a day may be necessary on the hottest days. If plants are potted, a very open and fast-draining medium is recommended. Undersized pots, barely large enough to hold the roots, should be used. Repotting is best done in spring after flowering when new roots are growing.

MISCELLANEOUS NOTES: The bloom season shown in the climate table is based on reports from the habitat. *D. calamiforme* requires high light and a cool rest to initiate blooming.

Plant and Flower Information

PLANT SIZE AND TYPE: A pendent, 6–30 in. (15–75 cm) sympodial epiphyte or lithophyte. Plants known as *D. baseyanum* are the smallest tereteleafed *Dendrobium* in Australia.

PSEUDOBULB: 2–6 in. (5–15 cm) long.

LEAVES: 1 at the apex of each wiry branch. The terete leaves may be 4–24 in. (10–61 cm) long.

INFLORESCENCE: 1.6–4.0 in. (4–10 cm) long. Racemes are produced 1–2 at a time near the tip of each stem. They are very numerous on a mature plant.

FLOWERS: 4–15 per inflorescence. The spidery sepals and petals are 1.6–3.1 in. (4–8 cm) long and open widely. Size is highly variable. Blossoms are white, cream, or pale yellow. Blossoms have red or purple markings at the base of the sepals and petals and on the lip sidelobes.

HYBRIDIZING NOTES: Chromosome count is 2n = 40 as *D. teretifolium* R. Brown var. *fasciculatum* Rupp (ref. 187). It is known to hybridize naturally with *D. linguiforme* Swartz producing *D.* × *grimesii* C. T. White and Summerhayes and with *D. rigidum* R. Brown forming *D.* × *foederatum* St. Cloud.

REFERENCES: 67, 105, 151, 187, 190, 216, 240, 254, 263, 264, 533.

PHOTOS/DRAWINGS: 240, *533*.

Dendrobium calamiforme Rolfe not Loddiges. See *D. vagans* Schlechter 1911 not 1923. REFERENCES: 55, 223, 252, 417, 466.

Dendrobium calcaratum Lindley not A. Richard. See *D. lobbii* Teijsm. and Binn. REFERENCES: 67, 105, 216, 254, 402, 454, 455.

Dendrobium calcaratum A. Richard not Lindley

AKA: *D. achillis* Rchb. f., *D. separatum* Ames, *D. triviale* Kränzlin. Lewis and Cribb (ref. 270, 271) include only *D. separatum* and *D. triviale* as synonyms.

ORIGIN/HABITAT: New Britain, Samoa, Vanuatu, and the Santa Cruz and Solomon Island groups. In Samoa, plants grow in the crowns of tall rainforest trees at 1000–1850 ft. (300–560 m).

CLIMATE: Station #94085, Rabaul, New Britain, Lat. 4.2°S, Long. 152.2°E, at 28 ft. (9 m). Temperatures are calculated for an elevation of 1150 ft. (350 m), resulting in probable extremes of 96°F (36°C) and 61°F (16°C).

N/HEMISPHERE	JAN	FEB	MAR	APR	MAY	JUN	JUL	AUG	SEP	OCT	NOV	DEC
°F AVG MAX	85	85	87	88	87	86	86	86	86	86	86	86
°F AVG MIN	69	68	69	69	69	69	69	69	69	69	69	69
DIURNAL RANGE	16	17	18	19	18	17	17	17	17	17	17	17
RAIN/INCHES	5.4	3.7	3.5	5.1	7.1	10.1	14.8	10.4	10.2	10.0	5.2	3.3
HUMIDITY/%	74	73	69	70	73	76	77	76	77	77	75	74
BLOOM SEASON		*	*	*	*	*						
DAYS CLR	N/A											
RAIN/MM	137	94	89	130	180	257	376	264	259	254	132	84
°C AVG MAX	29.6	29.6	30.7	31.3	30.7	30.2	30.2	30.2	30.2	30.2	30.2	30.2
°C AVG MIN	20.7	20.2	20.7	20.7	20.7	20.7	20.7	20.7	20.7	20.7	20.7	20.7
DIURNAL RANGE	8.9	9.4	10.0	10.6	10.0	9.5	9.5	9.5	9.5	9.5	9.5	9.5
S/HEMISPHERE	JUL	AUG	SEP	OCT	NOV	DEC	JAN	FEB	MAR	APR	MAY	JUN

Cultural Recommendations

LIGHT: 2500–3000 fc.

TEMPERATURES: Throughout the year, days average 85–88°F (30–31°C), and nights average 68–69°F (20–21°C), with a diurnal range of 16–19°F (9–11°C).

Dendrobium calcariferum

HUMIDITY: 70–80% most of the year. Humidity increases to 90–100% at night but may drop as low as 35% during hot afternoons.

WATER: Rainfall is heavy most of the year, but conditions are slightly drier for 2 months in late winter. Cultivated plants should be kept moist but not soggy.

FERTILIZER: ¼–½ recommended strength. A balanced fertilizer should be applied weekly to biweekly throughout the year.

REST PERIOD: Growing conditions should be maintained all year. Water and fertilizer should be reduced somewhat in winter. Plants should dry slightly between waterings, but they should never be allowed to dry completely. In the habitat, light may be slightly higher in winter.

GROWING MEDIA: Mounting plants on tree-fern or cork slabs accommodates their pendulous growth habit. However, humidity must be high and plants must be watered at least once daily in summer. If plants must be potted to maintain moisture, any open, fast-draining medium may be used. Repotting may be done anytime new roots are growing.

MISCELLANEOUS NOTES: The bloom season shown in the climate table is based on reports from the habitat.

Plant and Flower Information

PLANT SIZE AND TYPE: A 59 in. (150 cm) sympodial epiphyte.

PSEUDOBULB: 59 in. (150 cm) long. The ribbed pseudobulbs, which are swollen at the base, are yellow-green when young becoming maroon with age. They are branched, clustered, and pendent.

LEAVES: Several per growth. Usually 3.5–6.3 in. (9–16 cm) long, the oblong-lanceolate leaves alternate on the upper portion of the stem.

INFLORESCENCE: 0.8 in. (2 cm) long. The mauve inflorescences emerge from nodes near the apex of leafless stems.

FLOWERS: 10–18 per inflorescence. The fleshy, bright orange flowers, which are 0.6 in. (1.5 cm) long, are held in a cluster that hangs from the stem. The dorsal sepal and petals are much shorter than the lateral sepals. Blossoms at the base of the inflorescence develop first.

HYBRIDIZING NOTES: Chromosome count is 2n = 38 (ref. 152).

REFERENCES: 16, 17, 152, 216, 243, 254, 270, 271, 317, 434, 445, 516.

PHOTOS/DRAWINGS: *270*, 271.

Dendrobium calcariferum Carr

ORIGIN/HABITAT: Borneo. Plants grow in Sarawak near Mt. Api at about 3950 ft. (1200 m). Collections have also been made on Mt. Balapan at 1950–2950 ft. (600–900 m).

CLIMATE: Station #96449, Miri, Sarawak, Lat. 4.4°N, Long. 114.0°E, at 13 ft. (4 m). Temperatures are calculated for an elevation of 3500 ft. (1070 m), resulting in probable extremes of 83°F (29°C) and 55°F (13°C).

N/HEMISPHERE	JAN	FEB	MAR	APR	MAY	JUN	JUL	AUG	SEP	OCT	NOV	DEC
°F AVG MAX	74	74	75	76	76	76	76	76	75	75	75	75
°F AVG MIN	62	62	62	63	63	63	62	62	62	62	62	62
DIURNAL RANGE	12	12	13	13	13	13	14	14	13	13	13	13
RAIN/INCHES	16.8	6.5	5.5	4.4	8.2	12.0	8.5	8.4	11.8	11.7	14.5	11.3
HUMIDITY/%	86	86	85	83	83	82	81	81	82	83	84	85
BLOOM SEASON												
DAYS CLR @ 8AM	1	2	4	4	3	2	3	2	2	1	2	2
DAYS CLR @ 2PM	1	1	3	4	2	5	3	2	3	2	1	1
RAIN/MM	427	165	140	112	208	305	216	213	300	297	368	287
°C AVG MAX	23.6	23.6	24.2	24.7	24.7	24.7	24.7	24.7	24.2	24.2	24.2	24.2
°C AVG MIN	16.9	16.9	16.9	17.5	17.5	17.5	16.9	16.9	16.9	16.9	16.9	16.9
DIURNAL RANGE	6.7	6.7	7.3	7.2	7.2	7.2	7.8	7.8	7.3	7.3	7.3	7.3
S/HEMISPHERE	JUL	AUG	SEP	OCT	NOV	DEC	JAN	FEB	MAR	APR	MAY	JUN

Cultural Recommendations

LIGHT: 2000–3000 fc.

TEMPERATURES: Throughout the year, days average 74–76°F (24–25°C), and nights average 62–63°F (17–18°C), with a diurnal range of 12–14°F (7–8°C).

HUMIDITY: 80–85% year-round.

WATER: Rainfall is heavy to very heavy all year, but conditions are slightly drier in winter. Cultivated plants should be kept moist but not soggy.

FERTILIZER: ¼–½ recommended strength. A balanced fertilizer should be applied weekly to biweekly throughout the year.

REST PERIOD: Growing conditions should be maintained all year. In cultivation, water and fertilizer should be reduced in winter, especially for plants grown in the dark, short-day conditions common in temperate latitudes. They should never be allowed to dry out completely, however. In the habitat, seasonal light variation is minor.

GROWING MEDIA: Plants may be mounted on tree-fern or cork slabs if humidity is high and plants are watered at least once daily in summer. When plants are potted, any open, fast-draining medium may be used. They may be repotted anytime new roots are growing.

MISCELLANEOUS NOTES: The bloom season shown in the climate table is based on records from the habitat.

Plant and Flower Information

PLANT SIZE AND TYPE: A 17 in. (43 cm) sympodial epiphyte.

PSEUDOBULB: 17 in. (43 cm) long. The clustered stems are slender and wrinkled.

LEAVES: Many. The linear-lanceolate leaves are less than 4 in. (10 cm) long.

INFLORESCENCE: 1.2–2.0 in. (3–5 cm) long. Inflorescences first appear from the upper nodes of leafy stems. Later inflorescences emerge from lower nodes after the leaves have fallen.

FLOWERS: 6 per inflorescence. The flowers are 0.8–1.2 in. (2–3 cm) across. Blossoms are white with faint magenta stripes and an orange-red tinge. Flowers have an ovate-lanceolate dorsal sepal and oblong-ovate lateral sepals. Petals are contracted at the base and become broadly lanceolate-oblong and truncate. The bilobed lip has an inverted V-shaped keel on the claw and rounded keels on the blade. The margins at the base of the blade have warty cushions, and the balance of the margin is uneven or minutely toothed.

REFERENCES: 59, 225, 286, 586.

Dendrobium calcarium J. J. Smith. See *D. brevicaule* Rolfe.
REFERENCES: 221, 385, 437, 445, 470, 538. PHOTOS/DRAWINGS: 538.

Dendrobium calceolaria Carey ex Hooker. Sometimes spelled *D. calceolarie* or *D. calceolare*, see *D. moschatum* (Buch.-Ham.) Swartz. REFERENCES: 32, 102, 157, 202, 216, 254, 277, 369, 430, 454, 570.

Dendrobium calceolum Roxburgh. Sometimes spelled *D. calceolus*, see *D. roxburghii* Lindley. REFERENCES: 216, 310, 445, 468, 470.

Dendrobium calceolum Wallich. Schlechter (ref. 437) mentions this name and indicates that the plant does not originate in New Guinea. No other reference to this plant name with this describer was found. REFERENCES: 437.

Dendrobium caleyi A. Cunningham not Lindley. Now considered a synonym of *Bulbophyllum exiguum* (F. Mueller) F. Mueller. REFERENCES: 67, 216.

Dendrobium caleyi Lindley not A. Cunningham. See *D. pygmaeum* A. Cunningham. not Lindley. REFERENCES: 254.

Dendrobium calicopis Ridley

ORIGIN/HABITAT: Eastern, southern, and peninsular Thailand, the Langkawi Islands, and Malaya. Plants usually grow at low elevations.

CLIMATE: Station #48430, Prachin Buri, Thailand, Lat. 14.1°N, Long. 101.4°E, at 16 ft. (5 m). Record extreme temperatures are not available for this location.

N/HEMISPHERE	JAN	FEB	MAR	APR	MAY	JUN	JUL	AUG	SEP	OCT	NOV	DEC
°F AVG MAX	91	94	97	97	95	91	90	90	90	89	90	89
°F AVG MIN	69	74	76	78	78	78	77	77	77	76	74	68
DIURNAL RANGE	22	20	21	19	17	13	13	13	13	13	16	21
RAIN/INCHES	1.0	1.0	1.2	4.0	8.3	10.3	11.5	13.9	11.8	6.9	1.6	0.3
HUMIDITY/%	N/A											
BLOOM SEASON	N/A											
DAYS CLR	N/A											
RAIN/MM	25	25	30	102	211	262	292	353	300	175	41	8
°C AVG MAX	32.8	34.4	36.1	36.1	35.0	32.8	32.2	32.2	32.2	31.7	32.2	31.7
°C AVG MIN	20.6	23.3	24.4	25.6	25.6	25.6	25.0	25.0	25.0	24.4	23.3	20.0
DIURNAL RANGE	12.2	11.1	11.7	10.5	9.4	7.2	7.2	7.2	7.2	7.3	8.9	11.7
S/HEMISPHERE	JUL	AUG	SEP	OCT	NOV	DEC	JAN	FEB	MAR	APR	MAY	JUN

Cultural Recommendations

LIGHT: 2000–3000 fc. Heavy, persistent cloud cover greatly reduces light levels in summer. Cultivated plants should be shaded from spring through autumn.

TEMPERATURES: Summer days average 90–91°F (32–33°C), and nights average 77–78°F (25–26°C), with a diurnal range of 13°F (7°C). The warmest weather occurs in spring. Days average 95–97°F (35–36°C), and nights average 76–78°F (24–26°C), with a diurnal range of 17–21°F (9–12°C).

HUMIDITY: Information is not available for this location. However, records from nearby locations indicate that humidity probably averages 80–85% year-round.

WATER: Rainfall is heavy from spring through early autumn. Cultivated plants should be kept moist while actively growing, but water should be gradually reduced in autumn. Cultivated plants may need to be watered several times a week during the warmest and brightest part of the year.

FERTILIZER: ¼–½ recommended strength. A balanced fertilizer should be applied weekly to biweekly throughout the year.

REST PERIOD: Winter days average 89–94°F (32–34°C), and nights average 68–74°F (20–23°C), with a diurnal range of 20–22°F (11–12°C). In the habitat, rainfall is low for 4–5 months from late autumn into early spring, but the nightly cooling and high humidity results in frequent, heavy deposits of dew. Water should be reduced for cultivated plants. They should be allowed to dry slightly between waterings but should not remain dry for extended periods. Fertilizer should also be reduced when less water is used. In the habitat, light is highest in winter.

GROWING MEDIA: Plants may be mounted on tree-fern or cork slabs if humidity is high and plants are watered at least once daily in summer. When plants are potted, any open, fast-draining medium may be used. Repotting is best done at the end of the dry season when new roots are growing.

Plant and Flower Information

PLANT SIZE AND TYPE: A 12–16 in. (30–40 cm) sympodial plant.

PSEUDOBULB: 12–16 in. (30–40 cm) long. The slender stems consist of internodes spaced 0.5–1.0 in. (1.3–2.5 cm) apart.

LEAVES: Many. The leaves are 3.5 in. (9 cm) long. They are spaced approximately 1 in. (2.5 cm) apart along the entire length of the stem.

INFLORESCENCE: 1 in. (2.5 cm). Inflorescences arise from the bare stem.

FLOWERS: 2–6 per inflorescence. The flowers are 1.0–1.2 in. (2.5–3.0 cm) across. White sepals and petals have a rosy tinge. The lip is marked with pink and orange in the throat. It is sometimes decorated with darker, rose-colored freckles. The midlobe has 4 raised veins in the center. The anther is pink.

REFERENCES: 200, 219, 254, 402, 454, 455.

PHOTOS/DRAWINGS: *454, 455.*

Dendrobium caliculimentum R. S. Rogers

AKA: Sometimes spelled *D. caliculi-mentum* or *D. calyculimentum.*

ORIGIN/HABITAT: New Guinea. Plants were found near Sattelberg at 2600–4900 ft. (800–1500 m) and at other locations up to 8500 ft. (2890 m). *D. caliculimentum* is also found on Guadalcanal in the Solomon Islands growing in mossy cloudforests at 6250 ft. (1900 m).

CLIMATE: Station #94048, Finschhafen, Papua New Guinea, Lat. 6.6°S, Long. 147.9°E, at 25 ft. (8 m). Temperatures are calculated for an elevation of 4000 ft. (1220 m), resulting in probable extremes of 80°F (27°C) and 55°F (13°C).

N/HEMISPHERE	JAN	FEB	MAR	APR	MAY	JUN	JUL	AUG	SEP	OCT	NOV	DEC
°F AVG MAX	71	70	70	71	73	75	76	76	74	73	71	71
°F AVG MIN	60	59	59	58	58	59	61	61	61	61	60	60
DIURNAL RANGE	11	11	11	13	15	16	15	15	13	12	11	11
RAIN/INCHES	25.8	22.4	20.9	15.8	11.7	8.9	5.5	3.7	5.3	11.9	18.3	23.2
HUMIDITY/%	88	87	86	86	84	85	84	85	86	88	88	88
BLOOM SEASON		*										
DAYS CLR	N/A											
RAIN/MM	655	569	531	401	297	226	140	94	135	302	465	589
°C AVG MAX	21.6	21.0	21.0	21.6	22.7	23.8	24.4	24.4	23.3	22.7	21.6	21.6
°C AVG MIN	15.5	14.9	14.9	14.4	14.4	14.9	16.0	16.0	16.0	16.0	15.5	15.5
DIURNAL RANGE	6.1	6.1	6.1	7.2	8.3	8.9	8.4	8.4	7.3	6.7	6.1	6.1
S/HEMISPHERE	JUL	AUG	SEP	OCT	NOV	DEC	JAN	FEB	MAR	APR	MAY	JUN

Cultural Recommendations

LIGHT: 1500–2000 fc.

TEMPERATURES: Throughout the year, days average 70–76°F (21–24°C), and nights average 58–61°F (14–16°C), with a diurnal range of 11–16°F (6–9°C). Weather from Guadalcanal and higher elevation New Guinea stations indicates that plants should tolerate nighttime lows near 50°F (10°C).

HUMIDITY: 85–90% year-round.

WATER: Rainfall is very heavy most of the year, but conditions are somewhat drier for 3–4 months in summer. Cultivated plants should be kept moist and never be allowed to dry out completely. During hot weather, plants may need to be watered at least once daily.

FERTILIZER: ¼–½ recommended strength. A balanced fertilizer should be applied weekly to biweekly throughout the year.

REST PERIOD: Growing conditions should be maintained year-round. In the habitat, rainfall is heaviest in winter. However, water and fertilizer should be reduced somewhat for cultivated plants, especially those grown in the dark, short-day conditions common in temperate latitudes. The medium should never be allowed to dry out completely, but leaf surfaces should always be dry before nightfall.

GROWING MEDIA: Mounting plants on tree-fern or cork slabs accommodates their pendulous growth habit. However, humidity must be high and plants must be watered at least once a day in summer. If plants cannot be mounted, small pots or hanging baskets may be filled with an open, fast-draining medium. Repotting may be done anytime new roots are actively growing.

MISCELLANEOUS NOTES: The bloom season shown in the climate table is based on reports from the habitat. Growers indicate that *D. caliculimentum* is more adaptable to cultivation than many high altitude species.

Dendrobium calithyrsos

Plant and Flower Information

PLANT SIZE AND TYPE: A 36–48 in. (91–122 cm) sympodial epiphyte that may be as short as 6–12 in. (15–30 cm) in cultivation.

PSEUDOBULB: 12–48 in. (30–122 cm) long. The pendulous canes, which are thin and ropelike with a slight swelling at the base, are covered by leaf-sheaths. They form straggling clumps.

LEAVES: Many. The lanceolate leaves are up to 1.6 in. (4 cm) long, rigid, and very pointed.

INFLORESCENCE: Very short. Inflorescences arise from nodes at or below the apex of the canes.

FLOWERS: 4–6 per cluster of blossoms. The cone-shaped flowers are 0.6 in. (1.5 cm) long. They are rose to light pink with bright red anther caps. The lip is erect.

REFERENCES: 79, 95, 223, 271, 406, 486, 516, 526, 552.

PHOTOS/DRAWINGS: 95, 552.

Dendrobium calithyrsos. See *D. calothyrsos* Schlechter.
REFERENCES: 454.

Dendrobium callibotrys Ridley. See *D. microglaphys* Rchb. f.
REFERENCES: 200, 254, 286, 395, 402, 455, 495. PHOTOS/DRAWINGS: 200.

Dendrobium callitrophilum B. Gray and D. L. Jones

ORIGIN/HABITAT: Northeastern Queensland, Australia. This species grows on the upper trunk and branches of rough-barked trees, particularly *Callitris macleayana*, at 2300–4050 ft. (700–1240 m), in or along the edge of rain forests.

CLIMATE: Station #94287, Cairns, Australia, Lat. 16.0°S, Long. 145.8°E, at 7 ft. (2m). Temperatures are calculated for an elevation of 3000 ft. (910 m), resulting in probable extremes of 100°F (38°C) and 33°F (1°C).

N/HEMISPHERE	JAN	FEB	MAR	APR	MAY	JUN	JUL	AUG	SEP	OCT	NOV	DEC
°F AVG MAX	68	70	73	76	78	80	80	79	77	75	71	69
°F AVG MIN	51	52	54	58	60	63	64	64	63	60	56	54
DIURNAL RANGE	17	18	19	18	18	17	16	15	14	15	15	15
RAIN/INCHES	1.6	1.7	1.7	2.1	3.9	8.7	16.6	15.7	18.1	11.3	4.4	2.9
HUMIDITY/%	69	67	65	65	65	68	72	72	74	73	73	72
BLOOM SEASON		*	*									
DAYS CLR @ 8AM	9	11	13	11	6	6	4	5	6	7	11	10
DAYS CLR @ 2PM	9	10	12	16	10	7	4	3	4	6	9	10
RAIN/MM	41	43	43	53	99	221	422	399	460	287	112	74
°C AVG MAX	20.1	21.2	22.8	24.5	25.6	26.7	26.7	26.2	25.1	24.0	21.7	20.6
°C AVG MIN	10.6	11.2	12.3	14.5	15.6	17.3	17.8	17.8	17.3	15.6	13.4	12.3
DIURNAL RANGE	9.5	10.0	10.5	10.0	10.0	9.4	8.9	8.4	7.8	8.4	8.3	8.3
S/HEMISPHERE	JUL	AUG	SEP	OCT	NOV	DEC	JAN	FEB	MAR	APR	MAY	JUN

Cultural Recommendations

LIGHT: 3000–4000 fc.

TEMPERATURES: Summer days average 78–80°F (26–27°C), and nights average 63–64°F (17–18°C), with a diurnal range of 15–17°F (8–9°C).

HUMIDITY: Near 75% summer through autumn, dropping to about 65% in winter and spring.

WATER: Rainfall is heavy from late spring into autumn. Cultivated plants should be watered heavily during the growing season. Water should then be gradually reduced in late autumn after new growths mature.

FERTILIZER: ¼–½ recommended strength, applied weekly. A high-nitrogen fertilizer is beneficial from spring to midsummer, while a fertilizer high in phosphates should be used in late summer and autumn.

REST PERIOD: Winter days average 68–73°F (20–23°C), and nights average 51–54°F (11–12°C), with a diurnal range of 17–19°F (9–11°C). Water should be reduced for 4–5 months from late autumn into early spring, but the plants should not be allowed to dry out completely because conditions are wetter in the rain forest habitat than is indicated by the climate data. Fertilizer should be reduced or eliminated until water is increased in spring. In the habitat, winter skies are frequently clear.

GROWING MEDIA: Plants are best mounted on cork slabs or rough-barked hardwood. If mounted, the plants need daily watering and high humidity in summer. Remounting is best done in early spring immediately after flowering.

MISCELLANEOUS NOTES: The bloom season shown in the climate table is based on records from the habitat. David Jones reports that the plant is difficult to maintain in cultivation.

Plant and Flower Information

PLANT SIZE AND TYPE: An 2–12 in. (5–30 cm) sympodial epiphyte.

PSEUDOBULB: 2–12 in. (5–30 cm) long. The slender pseudobulbs are grooved, dark purple, and swollen at the base. They grow in small clumps and root only at the base.

LEAVES: 2 at the apex of each growth. The ovate leaves are 0.8–2.5 in. (2.0–6.5 cm) long. They are thinly leathery.

INFLORESCENCE: 0.3–1.0 in. (0.8–2.5 cm) long. Growths produce 1 or 2 erect to curving inflorescences at the apex or from the lower nodes on older stems.

FLOWERS: 2–4, occasionally up to 6 per inflorescence. The flowers are 0.4–0.6 in. (1.0–1.5 cm) across. The blossoms, which open fully, are initially green to greenish yellow with a creamy center, but they quickly age to apricot. The sepals and petals are suffused with pink at the base except the dorsal sepal which is marked with purplish lines at the base. The sepals, which are much broader than the nearly linear, incurved petals, are pointed near the apex. The 3-lobed lip, which has a scaly surface, is pointed at the tip. The curved, pointed sidelobes are marked with irregular purplish bars. The lip callus consists of 3 yellow keels. The center keel is snaky and extends nearly to the apex.

REFERENCES: Gray, B., and D. L. Jones. 1989. A new species of *Dendrobium* Section Dendrocoryne (Orchidaceae) from North-eastern Queensland. *Proceedings Royal Society of Queensland* 100:105–107.

PHOTOS/DRAWINGS: *Proceedings Royal Society of Queensland* 100:105–107.

Dendrobium calopogon Rchb. f. Sometimes spelled *D. caelopogon*, it is now considered a synonym of *Flickingeria calopogon* (Rchb. f.) A. Hawkes. REFERENCES: 213, 216, 220, 230, 231, 254, 395, 445, 449, 469.

Dendrobium calothyrsos Schlechter. Sometimes spelled *D. calythyrsos* or *D. calythyrsos*. Seidenfaden (ref. 454) indicates that the description of this plant from upper Burma closely resembles *D. chrysotoxum* Lindley, but that he was unable to locate study material necessary to confirm the synonym. No additional habitat information is available.
REFERENCES: 223, 454.

Dendrobium calyptratum J. J. Smith. See *D. subclausum* Rolfe. REFERENCES: 221, 437, 445, 470, 486, 588.

Dendrobium camaridiorum Rchb. f.

ORIGIN/HABITAT: Endemic to New Caledonia. Plants grow in dense, humid forest galleries at 350–1000 ft. (100–300 m).

CLIMATE: Station #91592, Noumea, New Caledonia, Lat. 22.3°S, Long.

166.5°E, at 246 ft. (75 m). Temperatures are calculated for an elevation of 650 ft. (200 m), resulting in probable extremes of 98°F (36°C) and 51°F (10°C).

N/HEMISPHERE	JAN	FEB	MAR	APR	MAY	JUN	JUL	AUG	SEP	OCT	NOV	DEC
°F AVG MAX	75	75	77	79	82	85	85	84	84	82	78	76
°F AVG MIN	61	60	62	64	67	69	71	72	71	69	65	63
DIURNAL RANGE	14	15	15	15	15	16	14	12	13	13	13	13
RAIN/INCHES	3.6	2.6	2.5	2.0	2.4	2.6	3.7	5.1	5.7	5.2	4.4	3.7
HUMIDITY/%	73	70	69	67	68	69	71	74	75	76	73	73
BLOOM SEASON					*	*	*	*	*			
DAYS CLR @ 11AM	7	9	9	15	12	10	7	6	7	7	7	7
DAYS CLR @ 5PM	7	11	6	11	7	6	5	4	4	5	3	7
RAIN/MM	91	66	64	51	61	66	94	130	145	132	112	94
°C AVG MAX	23.7	23.7	24.8	25.9	27.6	29.2	29.2	28.7	28.7	27.6	25.3	24.2
°C AVG MIN	15.9	15.3	16.4	17.6	19.2	20.3	21.4	22.0	21.4	20.3	18.1	17.0
DIURNAL RANGE	7.8	8.4	8.4	8.3	8.4	8.9	7.8	6.7	7.3	7.4	7.2	7.2
S/HEMISPHERE	JUL	AUG	SEP	OCT	NOV	DEC	JAN	FEB	MAR	APR	MAY	JUN

Cultural Recommendations

LIGHT: 1200–2000 fc.

TEMPERATURES: Summer days average 84–85°F (29°C), and nights average 69–72°F (20–22°C), with a diurnal range of 12–16°F (7–9°C).

HUMIDITY: 70–75% most of the year, dropping to near 65% for 1–2 months in spring. Humidity averages may be greater in the forest habitat.

WATER: Rainfall is light to moderate all year. Late summer and early autumn are the wettest seasons. In cultivation, moisture should be provided year-round with only slight drying allowed between waterings.

FERTILIZER: ¼–½ recommended strength, applied weekly. A high-nitrogen fertilizer is beneficial from spring to midsummer, but a fertilizer high in phosphates should be used in late summer and autumn.

REST PERIOD: Winter days average 75–77°F (24–25°C), and nights average 60–63°F (15–17°C), with a diurnal range of 13–15°F (7–8°C). High and low temperatures decline simultaneously, resulting in little change in the diurnal range. Plants cannot tolerate drying out, but in cultivation, water should be reduced if plants are grown in the dark, short-day conditions common in temperate-latitude winters.

GROWING MEDIA: Plants may be mounted on tree-fern or cork slabs if humidity is high and plants are watered at least once daily in summer. When plants are potted, any open, fast-draining medium may be used. Repotting is best done in early spring when new roots are growing.

MISCELLANEOUS NOTES: The bloom season shown in the climate table is based on reports from the habitat.

Plant and Flower Information

PLANT SIZE AND TYPE: An 8–28 in. (20–70 cm) sympodial epiphyte.

PSEUDOBULB: 8–28 in. (20–70 cm) long. Plants consist of numerous rooting branches.

LEAVES: 6–8 per branch. The unequally bilobed leaves are usually 2–4 in. (5–10 cm) long.

INFLORESCENCE: Very short. The blossoms are held near the base of the leaves. The inflorescences, which arise from small appendages along the cane, appear between the leaf nodes near the top of the newest growths.

FLOWERS: 2 per inflorescence. The blossoms are 2 in. (5 cm) long. They are very fragile. The white sepals and petals are extremely long and taper to a slender tip. The pointed lip, which is marked with orange along the center callus, is covered with hairs along each side.

HYBRIDIZING NOTES: Chromosome count is 2n = 38 (ref. 152, 243).

REFERENCES: 152, 173, 216, 243, 254, 432.

PHOTOS/DRAWINGS: 173.

Dendrobium cambridgeanum Paxton.
Sometimes spelled *D. cambridgeum*, see *D. ochreatum* Lindley. REFERENCES: 190, 216, 254, 369, 430, 445, 454, 570.

Dendrobium campbellii Cribb and B. Lewis

ORIGIN/HABITAT: The Solomon Islands. Plants were originally found on Rendova and San Cristobal (Makira) in rainforests below 150 ft. (50 m).

CLIMATE: Station #91520, Honiara, Guadalcanal, Solomon Islands, Lat. 9.4°S, Long. 160.6°E, at 10 ft. (3 m). Record extreme temperatures are 95°F (35°C) and 65°F (18°C).

N/HEMISPHERE	JAN	FEB	MAR	APR	MAY	JUN	JUL	AUG	SEP	OCT	NOV	DEC
°F AVG MAX	86	87	88	88	88	88	88	88	87	88	88	87
°F AVG MIN	72	72	72	72	73	73	74	74	73	73	73	72
DIURNAL RANGE	14	15	16	16	15	15	14	14	14	15	15	15
RAIN/INCHES	6.0	4.4	4.6	7.7	7.7	9.5	14.1	13.3	16.7	10.6	8.1	6.7
HUMIDITY/%	84	82	81	80	81	82	83	83	87	85	85	85
BLOOM SEASON	N/A											
DAYS CLR @ 5AM	6	7	7	5	6	4	3	3	4	4	8	7
DAYS CLR @ 11AM	3	2	2	1	1	1	0	2	2	4	4
RAIN/MM	152	112	117	196	196	241	358	338	424	269	206	170
°C AVG MAX	30.0	30.6	31.1	31.1	31.1	31.1	31.1	31.1	30.6	31.1	31.1	30.6
°C AVG MIN	22.2	22.2	22.2	22.2	22.8	22.8	23.3	23.3	22.8	22.8	22.8	22.2
DIURNAL RANGE	7.8	8.4	8.9	8.9	8.3	8.3	7.8	7.8	7.8	8.3	8.3	8.4
S/HEMISPHERE	JUL	AUG	SEP	OCT	NOV	DEC	JAN	FEB	MAR	APR	MAY	JUN

Cultural Recommendations

LIGHT: 3000–4000 fc.

TEMPERATURES: Throughout the year, days average 86–88°F (30–31°C), and nights average 72–74°F (22–23°C), with a diurnal range of 14–16°F (8–9°C).

HUMIDITY: 80–85% year-round.

WATER: Habitat rainfall is heavy all year, but conditions are slightly drier for 2–3 months in winter. Cultivated plants should be kept moist with only slight drying allowed between waterings.

FERTILIZER: ¼–½ recommended strength. A balanced fertilizer should be applied weekly to biweekly throughout the year.

REST PERIOD: Growing conditions should be maintained year-round. Water and fertilizer may be reduced somewhat for cultivated plants in winter, especially those grown in the dark, short-day conditions common in temperate latitudes. Plants should never be allowed to dry out completely, however.

GROWING MEDIA: Mounting plants on tree-fern or cork slabs accommodates their pendulous growth habit. However, humidity must be high and plants must be watered at least once a day in summer. If plants cannot be mounted, small pots or hanging baskets may be filled with an open, fast-draining medium. Repotting may be done anytime new roots are actively growing.

Plant and Flower Information

PLANT SIZE AND TYPE: A 79 in. (200 cm) sympodial epiphyte.

PSEUDOBULB: 79 in. (200 cm) long. The stems are pendent.

LEAVES: Many. The distichous leaves are elliptic and 4.5 in. (11 cm) long.

INFLORESCENCE: Short. Inflorescences emerge laterally from swellings below the leaf blades.

FLOWERS: 2 per inflorescence. The flowers, which remain rather closed, are about 0.4 in. (1 cm) long. The blossoms are yellow-green with a white spur. The flowers are similar to those of *D. triste* Schlechter from New Guinea, but flower color is different and the back of the sepals are smooth.

REFERENCES: 271.

PHOTOS/DRAWINGS: 271.

Dendrobium camptocentrum Schlechter. See *D. platygastrium* Rchb. f. REFERENCES: 173, 220, 254, 270, 432. PHOTOS/DRAWINGS: 173.

Dendrobium canaliculatum R. Brown

AKA: Most botanists currently recognize several varieties of *D. canaliculatum* including var. *canaliculatum* Prod., for which *D. tattonianum* Bateman is considered a synonym; var. *foelschei* F. Mueller, for which *D. foelschei* F. Mueller is considered a synonym; var. *nigrescens* Nicholls; and var. *pallidum* Dockrill.

Clements (ref. 67), however, includes var. *nigrescens* as a synonym of *D. canaliculatum* var. *canaliculatum*. He reinstated *D. foelschei* F. Mueller with *D. canaliculatum* var. *foelschei* F. Mueller as a synonym and *D. tattonianum* Bateman with *D. canaliculatum* var. *tattonianum* (Bateman) Rchb. f. as a synonym.

Taxonomists obviously differ in their approach to this group of plants. Consequently, the tug-of-war over which plant should be called by what name is apt to continue for some time. Because Clements' work (ref. 67) is the most recent, we have followed his taxonomy. Therefore, for plants previously known as *D. canaliculatum* var. *foelschei*, see *D. foelschei* F. Mueller; for *D. canaliculatum* var. *tattonianum*, see *D. tattonianum* Bateman; and for *D. canaliculatum* var. *nigrescens* and var. *pallidum*, see the following.

ORIGIN/HABITAT: Australia and New Guinea. Plants are found from Cairns in northeastern Australia northward along the Cape York Peninsula into southern Papua New Guinea. They grow almost exclusively on the trunks of paper-barked Melaleuca trees. The orchids are found in a variety of habitats, from swampy areas to semiarid regions and open forest grasslands, between sea level and 2500 ft. (0–760 m). However, they are usually found in humid habitats along streams and on stunted trees in low lying areas that are inundated during the wet season.

CLIMATE: Station #94283, Cooktown, Australia, Lat. 15.5°S, Long. 145.2°E, at 24 ft. (7 m). Temperatures are calculated for an elevation of 1000 ft. (300 m), resulting in probable extremes of 101°F (39°C) and 43°F (6°C).

N/HEMISPHERE	JAN	FEB	MAR	APR	MAY	JUN	JUL	AUG	SEP	OCT	NOV	DEC
°F AVG MAX	76	77	79	82	85	86	86	85	83	82	79	77
°F AVG MIN	63	64	67	70	72	72	72	72	72	70	67	65
DIURNAL RANGE	13	13	12	12	13	14	14	13	11	12	12	12
RAIN/INCHES	0.9	1.2	0.6	1.0	2.5	6.6	14.4	13.7	15.3	8.8	2.8	2.0
HUMIDITY/%	73	69	68	67	68	71	75	76	77	75	74	75
BLOOM SEASON	*	*	*	*	*			*	*	*	*	*
DAYS CLR	N/A											
RAIN/MM	23	30	15	25	64	168	366	348	389	224	71	51
°C AVG MAX	24.3	24.9	26.0	27.7	29.3	29.9	29.9	29.3	28.2	27.7	26.0	24.9
°C AVG MIN	17.1	17.7	19.3	21.0	22.1	22.1	22.1	22.1	22.1	21.0	19.3	18.2
DIURNAL RANGE	7.2	7.2	6.7	6.7	7.2	7.8	7.8	7.2	6.1	6.7	6.7	6.7
S/HEMISPHERE	JUL	AUG	SEP	OCT	NOV	DEC	JAN	FEB	MAR	APR	MAY	JUN

Cultural Recommendations

LIGHT: 3000–4000 fc. In the tropics, plants tolerate nearly full sun. Growers indicate that plants are the most floriferous when light is very bright.

TEMPERATURES: Summer days average 85–86°F (29–30°C), and nights average 72°F (22°C), with a diurnal range of 13–14°F (7–8°C) which varies only 3°F (2°C) through the year.

HUMIDITY: 70–75% most of the year. Humidity drops to about 70% during the winter bloom season. *D. canaliculatum* does not grow well with excessive humidity, but buds may drop if humidity is below 50%.

WATER: Rainfall is very heavy in summer and early autumn, but conditions are much drier in winter. Cultivated plants should be kept moist during the growing season, but water should be reduced in late autumn. Growers indicate that plants are healthiest if given frequent waterings in summer, particularly when temperatures are warm.

FERTILIZER: 1/4–1/2 recommended strength, applied weekly. A high-nitrogen fertilizer is beneficial from spring to midsummer, but a fertilizer high in phosphates should be used in late summer and autumn.

REST PERIOD: Winter days average 76–79°F (24–26°C), and nights average 63–67°F (17–19°C), with little change in the diurnal range. Some growers recommend keeping winter lows above 59°F (15°C); and others report that temperatures of 50°F (10°C), even for a few hours, result in leaf drop. Water should be reduced gradually in autumn. For 3–4 months in winter, plants should be very dry, drier than most *Dendrobium*. In the habitat, plants survive extraordinary droughts. As inflorescences start to grow, water should be increased so that plants are slightly moist. However, the plants should be kept quite dry until new growths are about 2 in. (5 cm) tall because young growths are very susceptible to infection. Fertilizer should be eliminated during the winter dry season. In the habitat, light is highest during the rest period.

GROWING MEDIA: Plants are best mounted on a cork slab, as they are healthiest when the roots are exposed to air. Plants are less vigorous when potted. Remounting is best done in early spring when new roots are actively growing. Some Australian growers have reported good results by growing in pots with wine corks as a medium.

MISCELLANEOUS NOTES: The bloom season shown in the climate table is based on cultivation records. Some growers consider *D. canaliculatum* easy to cultivate, but growers in Melbourne, Australia indicate that plants tend to slowly decline in vigor, suggesting that the plant is not particularly adaptable. High light is essential to initiate blooming.

Plant and Flower Information

PLANT SIZE AND TYPE: A 3–10 in. (8–25 cm) sympodial epiphyte.

PSEUDOBULB: 1–2 in. (2.5–5.0 cm) long, rarely to 6 in. (15 cm). The pear-shaped pseudobulbs resemble clumps of 4–7 onions. Growths are densely clustered and form small to medium mats or clumps.

LEAVES: 3–6 per growth. The fleshy, nearly terete leaves are variable. They are usually 2–4 in. (5–10 cm) long, but may reach a length of 8 in. (20 cm). Environmental conditions, particularly the amount of light, strongly influences leaf size, thickness, and shape which varies from terete to straplike to linear.

INFLORESCENCE: 4–16 in. (10–41 cm) long. Inflorescence length varies with plant size. The slender, rigidly erect inflorescences emerge from nodes near the apex of each growth. Each growth produces 1 to several flower spikes every year and continues to bloom for several years, resulting in well-grown plants being covered with blossoms.

FLOWERS: 12–25, sometimes 60 per inflorescence. The extremely fragrant flowers are 1 in. (2.5 cm) across. They are attractive and curious rather than showy. The slender sepals and petals are normally white to pale yellow-green at the base with varying shades of yellow (var. *canaliculatum*) on the apical half, but color may range from white with pale-yellowish to green tips on the sepals and petals (var. *pallidum*) to deep reddish brown or nearly black which usually shades into lighter colors at the base of the floral segments (var. *nigrescens*). The petals are longer than the sepals and all are twisted less than once. The lip is white with 3 raised keels and red and yellow markings on the sidelobes and disk. The long-lived blossoms last about 5 weeks.

HYBRIDIZING NOTES: Chromosome counts are n = 19 (ref. 151), 2n = 38 (ref. 151, 154, 188, 504, 580), and 2x (ref. 187, 504, 580). When used as a parent, all varieties tend to reduce plant size and most contribute erect racemes, produce long lasting flowers, and increase the number of flowers.

REFERENCES: 23, 25, 36, 67, 84, 105, 151, 154, 179, 187, 188, 196, 210, 216, 240, 254, 260, 262, 263, 277, 291, 302, 304, 309, 317, 325, 342, 344, 351, 352, 371, 390, 421, 430, 445, 504, 526, 533, 541, 551, 568, 570, 580.

PHOTOS/DRAWINGS: *36, 84*, 105, 210, *240, 262, 291, 304, 308,* 325, *342, 344, 351, 371, 390, 430,* 465, *533,* 561, *568.*

Dendrobium cancroides T. E. Hunt

ORIGIN/HABITAT: Northeastern Australia. The habitat extends from the Johnstone River northward to the McIlwraith Range. Plants usually grow at lower elevations in humid, shady situations in the rainforests of mountain gorges, but they are also found in open forests, generally on trees overhanging streams.

CLIMATE: Station #94287, Cairns, Australia, Lat. 16.9°S, Long. 145.8°E, at 7 ft. (2 m). Temperatures are calculated for an elevation of 2000 ft. (610 m), resulting in probable extremes of 103°F (40°C) and 36°F (3°C).

N/HEMISPHERE	JAN	FEB	MAR	APR	MAY	JUN	JUL	AUG	SEP	OCT	NOV	DEC
°F AVG MAX	71	73	76	79	81	83	83	82	80	78	74	72
°F AVG MIN	54	55	57	61	63	66	67	67	66	63	59	57
DIURNAL RANGE	17	18	19	18	18	17	16	15	14	15	15	15
RAIN/INCHES	1.6	1.7	1.7	2.1	3.9	8.7	16.6	15.7	18.1	11.3	4.4	2.9
HUMIDITY/%	69	67	65	65	65	68	72	72	74	73	73	72
BLOOM SEASON					*	*	*					
DAYS CLR @ 10AM	9	11	13	11	6	6	4	5	6	7	11	10
DAYS CLR @ 4PM	8	10	12	16	10	7	4	3	4	6	9	10
RAIN/MM	41	43	43	53	99	221	422	399	460	287	112	74
°C AVG MAX	21.9	23.0	24.7	26.3	27.5	28.6	28.6	28.0	26.9	25.8	23.6	22.5
°C AVG MIN	12.5	13.0	14.1	16.3	17.5	19.1	19.7	19.7	19.1	17.5	15.2	14.1
DIURNAL RANGE	9.4	10.0	10.6	10.0	10.0	9.5	8.9	8.3	7.8	8.3	8.4	8.4
S/HEMISPHERE	JUL	AUG	SEP	OCT	NOV	DEC	JAN	FEB	MAR	APR	MAY	JUN

Cultural Recommendations

LIGHT: 1500–2500 fc. Australian growers recommend about 70% shade and state that strong air movement and high humidity at all times are very important.

TEMPERATURES: Summer days average 82–83°F (28–29°C), and nights average 66–67°F (19–20°C), with a diurnal range of 15–17°F (8–10°C).

HUMIDITY: 70–75% most of the year, dropping to 65% in late winter and spring. In the rainforest habitat, relative humidity may average 10% more than indicated in the climate table. Cultivated plants are healthiest when high humidity and strong air movement are provided year-round.

WATER: Rainfall is heavy from late spring into autumn, but conditions are much drier in winter. Growers indicate that mounted plants should be misted frequently and never be allowed to dry out completely for any length of time.

FERTILIZER: ¼–½ recommended strength, applied weekly. A high-nitrogen fertilizer is beneficial from spring to midsummer, but a fertilizer high in phosphates should be used in late summer and autumn.

REST PERIOD: Winter days average 71–73°F (22–23°C), and nights average 54–57°F (13–14°C), with a diurnal range of 17–19°F (9–11°C). Water should be reduced for 4–5 months from late autumn into early spring so that plants are kept on the dry side, but they should never be allowed to dry out completely. Light, humidity, and air movement should be maintained all year, but fertilizer should be reduced or eliminated until water is increased in spring.

GROWING MEDIA: Mounting plants on tree-fern slabs accommodates their pendent growth habit and produces excellent results if humidity is high and plants are watered at least once daily in summer. Several waterings a day may be necessary during hot weather. If plants must be potted, a very open and fast-draining medium is recommended. Undersized pots, barely large enough to hold the roots, should be used. Repotting is best done in early spring when new roots are growing.

MISCELLANEOUS NOTES: The bloom season shown in the climate table is based on reports from the habitat. Flowering is erratic, however, suggesting that it may be initiated by a sudden drop in daytime temperatures. Plants that produce very short-lived flowers commonly bloom several times during the year. Flowering usually occurs 7–14 days after a sudden 10°F (5°C) drop in daytime temperatures. Plants begin blooming while very young.

Plant and Flower Information

PLANT SIZE AND TYPE: An 8–35 in. (20–90 cm) sympodial epiphyte.

PSEUDOBULB: 8–35 in. (20–90 cm) long. The woody stems are slender, pendulous, slightly flattened, and leafy on the apical half. New growths require more than 1 year to mature. Cultivated plants tend to remain small. Plants seldom consist of more than 15–20 stems, as after reaching that size, one dies for each new stem produced.

LEAVES: 10–20 per growth. The shiny, oval leaves are thin textured, often wavy, and usually dark green. They alternate along the stem but drop quickly from the basal half of the stem. The dark brown leaf sheaths are rough and feel like sandpaper.

INFLORESCENCE: Extremely short. The paired blossoms face each other and are held very close to the stem. Inflorescences emerge opposite the leaf-bases from any node along the stem.

FLOWERS: 2 per inflorescence. Blossoms are about 0.8 in. (2 cm) long and remain rather closed. The fragrant flowers are short-lived, lasting a few hours to 2 days. The blossoms have a thick texture. The pointed sepals and petals are reddish brown with a whitish or yellowish base. They appear warty. Blossoms are normally at least partly hidden by the leaves.

REFERENCES: 67, 105, 145, 227, 240, 262, 304, 421, 533.

PHOTOS/DRAWINGS: 105, *145, 304, 533.*

Dendrobium candidum King and Pantling not Wallich ex Lindley. See *D. spathaceum* Lindley. REFERENCES: 254.

Dendrobium candidum Wallich ex Lindley not King and Pantling

AKA: *D. officinale* Kimura and Migo. H. Wood (ref. 582) expresses doubt regarding this synonymy and indicates that *D. officinale* may be closely related to *D. stricklandianum* Rchb. f.

ORIGIN/HABITAT: Widespread including northern India, China, and Burma. In northeastern India, plants frequently grow on azalea and rhododendron bushes at 6550–7550 ft. (2000–2300 m), but they are most often found on *Quercus lamellosa* growing on ridge tops. Plants also grow on rocks, sand, and decayed trees. The orchids occasionally occur as low as 3300 ft. (1000 m) and as high as 9850 ft. (3000 m). Distribution extends from Manipur on the Burma border, through the Khasi (Khasia) Hills, Sikkim, central Nepal, and the Garhwal district of northern India. *D. candidum* also grows on dry granite rocks at 4000–7000 ft. (1220–2130 m) in northwestern Yunnan Province in southwestern China.

CLIMATE: Station #42147, Mukteswar, India, Lat. 29.5°N, Long. 79.7°E, at 7592 ft. (2314 m). Record extreme temperatures are 91°F (33°C) and 21°F (–6°C).

N/HEMISPHERE	JAN	FEB	MAR	APR	MAY	JUN	JUL	AUG	SEP	OCT	NOV	DEC
°F AVG MAX	51	54	61	69	75	75	69	69	68	65	61	55
°F AVG MIN	36	38	44	52	57	59	59	58	56	50	44	39
DIURNAL RANGE	15	16	17	17	18	16	10	11	12	15	17	16
RAIN/INCHES	1.0	2.1	1.7	1.0	0.3	4.6	11.4	12.8	4.6	3.5	0.3	0.2
HUMIDITY/%	61	55	50	39	44	67	91	93	83	66	55	56
BLOOM SEASON				*	**	***	**	*	*			
DAYS CLR @ 5PM	17	17	15	18	18	12	1	1	6	25	26	21
RAIN/MM	25	53	43	25	8	117	290	325	117	89	8	5
°C AVG MAX	10.6	12.2	16.1	20.6	23.9	23.9	20.6	20.6	20.0	18.3	16.1	12.8
°C AVG MIN	2.2	3.3	6.7	11.1	13.9	15.0	15.0	14.4	13.3	10.0	6.7	3.9
DIURNAL RANGE	8.4	8.9	9.4	9.5	10.0	8.9	5.6	6.2	6.7	8.3	9.4	8.9
S/HEMISPHERE	JUL	AUG	SEP	OCT	NOV	DEC	JAN	FEB	MAR	APR	MAY	JUN

Cultural Recommendations

LIGHT: 2500–3500 fc.

TEMPERATURES: Summer days average 69–75°F (21–24°C), and nights average 58–59°F (14–15°C), with a diurnal range of 10–16°F (6–9°C). Because plants are found over such a wide range of elevations, they should adapt to temperatures 5–7°F (3–4°C) warmer than indicated in the table.

HUMIDITY: Near 90% in summer, dropping to 55–60% in winter. The driest season occurs in spring when humidity drops to near 40% for 2 months.

WATER: Rainfall is moderate to heavy for 5 months in summer. The wet season is followed immediately by 7 very dry months from autumn through spring. Several months are so dry that even morning dew is uncommon. Cultivated plants should be kept moist while actively growing, but water should be gradually reduced after new growths mature in autumn.

FERTILIZER: ¼–½ recommended strength, applied weekly. A high-nitrogen fertilizer is beneficial from spring to midsummer, but a fertilizer high in phosphates should be used in late summer and autumn.

REST PERIOD: Winter days average 51–61°F (11–16°C), and nights average 36–44°F (2–7°C), with a diurnal range of 15–17°F (8–9°C). Water should be reduced for cultivated plants in winter. They should be allowed to dry out between waterings but should not remain dry for extended periods. Occasional early morning mistings between waterings may be beneficial in keeping plants from becoming too dry. In the habitat, light is highest during clear winter weather.

GROWING MEDIA: Plants may be mounted on a tree-fern or cork slabs or potted in small clay pots filled with any open, fast-draining medium. However, a smaller grade medium should be selected to accommodate the plant's very fine roots. Repotting is best done in early spring when new roots are growing.

MISCELLANEOUS NOTES: Blooming occurs from late spring through early summer in the habitat. Unlike most *Dendrobium,* the roots are very fine. Plants are collected, dried, and used in Chinese medicine. They are often cultivated in Chinese medicinal shops as *D. officinale.*

Plant and Flower Information

PLANT SIZE AND TYPE: A 6–12 in. (15–30 cm) sympodial epiphyte or lithophyte. Plants occasionally reach a height of 24 in. (60 cm).

PSEUDOBULB: 6–24 in. (15–60 cm) long. The erect, very slender pseudobulbs are straggling.

LEAVES: Several. Leaves are clustered near the apex of each new growth. They are usually 2–3 in. (5.0–7.5 cm) long, narrowly lanceolate, thin-textured, and deciduous.

INFLORESCENCE: Very short. The inflorescences emerge from leaf nodes after most of the leaves have dropped.

FLOWERS: 1–3 per inflorescence. The flowers are 1.0–1.4 in. (2.5–3.5 cm) across. All segments are white, sometimes with olive-green markings and often with a pink flush on the backside. The oblong-lanceolate lip is white and more or less marked with a yellow spot near the base. The delightful fragrance may be faint or strong. Blossoms last about 2 weeks.

HYBRIDIZING NOTES: Chromosome counts are n = 19 (ref. 504), 2n = 38 (ref. 151, 153, 154, 187, 188, 504, 547, 580), and 2n = 57 (ref. 153).

REFERENCES: 32, 38, 46, 61, 102, 150, 151, 153, 154, 179, 187, 188, 190, 202, 203, 208, 216, 254, 317, 363, 369, 376, 445, 489, 504, 528, 547, 580.

PHOTOS/DRAWINGS: 32, 102, 203, 363.

Dendrobium candoonense Ames. Now considered a synonym of *Flickingeria candoonense* (Ames) Seidenfaden. REFERENCES: 12, 223, 296, 449, 536.

Dendrobium caninum Merrill. Sometimes spelled *D. canicum,* see *D. crumenatum* Swartz. REFERENCES: 67, 190, 223, 296, 454.

Dendrobium capillipes Rchb. f.

AKA: *D. acrobaticum* Rchb. f., *D. braianense* Gagnepain.

ORIGIN/HABITAT: Widespread in Southeast Asia. Distribution extends from Manipur in eastern India through the Moulmein region of Burma into the mountains of northern Thailand. The orchids are also found in the Xieng Kouang region of Laos and in southwest China. Plants usually grow in exposed areas of dry, deciduous forests at 2600–3950 ft. (800–1200 m).

CLIMATE: Station #48325, Mae Sariang, Thailand, Lat. 18.2°N, Long. 97.8°E, at 1030 ft. (314 m). Temperatures are calculated for an elevation of 3000 ft. (910 m), resulting in probable extremes of 104°F (40°C) and 34°F (1°C).

N/HEMISPHERE	JAN	FEB	MAR	APR	MAY	JUN	JUL	AUG	SEP	OCT	NOV	DEC
°F AVG MAX	81	85	89	92	87	82	80	80	82	83	82	79
°F AVG MIN	51	50	57	66	69	68	67	67	67	65	61	53
DIURNAL RANGE	30	35	32	26	18	14	13	13	15	18	21	26
RAIN/INCHES	0.3	0.2	0.3	1.9	5.7	9.0	8.4	10.8	8.7	3.7	1.1	0.6
HUMIDITY/%	72	67	57	55	68	83	83	84	83	81	77	75
BLOOM SEASON		*	**	***	*	*			*			
DAYS CLR @ 7AM	1	16	0	3	4	0	0	0	0	0	0	1
DAYS CLR @ 1PM	24	18	9	5	2	0	0	1	1	6	13	20
RAIN/MM	8	5	8	48	145	229	213	274	221	94	28	15
°C AVG MAX	27.5	29.7	31.9	33.6	30.8	28.1	26.9	26.9	28.1	28.6	28.1	26.4
°C AVG MIN	10.8	10.3	14.2	19.2	20.8	20.3	19.7	19.7	19.7	18.6	16.4	11.9
DIURNAL RANGE	16.7	19.4	17.7	14.4	10.0	7.8	7.2	7.2	8.4	10.0	11.7	14.5
S/HEMISPHERE	JUL	AUG	SEP	OCT	NOV	DEC	JAN	FEB	MAR	APR	MAY	JUN

Cultural Recommendations

LIGHT: 3000–4000 fc. Cultivated plants should be shaded from late spring into autumn, but shading should be reduced or removed in winter. Strong air movement in the growing area is very important.

TEMPERATURES: Summer days average 80–82°F (27–28°C), and nights average 67–68°F (20°C), with a diurnal range of 13–14°F (7–8°C). The warmest season is spring. Days average 87–92°F (31–34°C), and nights average 57–69°F (14–21°C), with a diurnal range of 18–32°F (10–19°C).

HUMIDITY: 80–85% in summer through early autumn, dropping to near 55% for 2 months in winter.

WATER: Rainfall is heavy for 6 months from spring into early autumn but is very light for 4–5 months in winter and early spring. Cultivated plants should be kept moist while actively growing, but water should be gradually reduced in autumn after new growths mature.

FERTILIZER: ¼–½ recommended strength, applied weekly. A high-nitrogen fertilizer is beneficial from spring to midsummer, but a fertilizer high in phosphates should be used in late summer and autumn.

REST PERIOD: Winter days average 79–85°F (26–30°C), and nights average 50–53°F (10–12°C), with a diurnal range of 26–35°F (15–19°C). Rainfall is light for 5–6 months from autumn into spring; but during the early part of the dry period, considerable moisture is available from heavy dew and as mist from low clouds and fog. However, for 2 months in spring the weather is clear and dry with humidity so low that even the moisture from dew is uncommon. During most of the winter dry season, cultivated plants should be allowed to dry slightly between waterings, but they should not remain dry for long periods. For 1–2 months in late winter, however, water should be further decreased and the plants allowed to dry completely. Fertilizer should be eliminated. In the habitat, light is highest in winter.

GROWING MEDIA: Mounting plants on tree-fern or cork slabs accommodates their pendulous growth habit. However, humidity must be high and plants must be watered at least once a day in summer. If plants can-

not be mounted, small pots or hanging baskets may be filled with an open, fast-draining medium. Repotting may be done anytime new roots are actively growing.

MISCELLANEOUS NOTES: The bloom season shown in the climate table is based on cultivation records. Smaller plants are usually found in exposed places in dry, deciduous forests. *D. capillipes* is considered a problem plant by many growers and careful attention should be paid to cultural needs. It is very susceptible to spider mites, particularly if it is stressed by excessively warm, winter temperatures.

Plant and Flower Information

PLANT SIZE AND TYPE: A pendulous, 5–12 in. (13–30 cm) sympodial epiphyte. Plants may be as small as 2–3 in. (5.0–7.5 cm). It is one of the smallest of the yellow-flowered dendrobiums.

PSEUDOBULB: 2–6 in. (5–15 cm) long. The clustered pseudobulbs are 6-noded, fleshy, and somewhat spindle-shaped. They are pale green when young developing yellow stripes as they age.

LEAVES: 3–5 per growth. The deciduous leaves are usually 3–6 in. (8–15 cm) long. They are lanceolate, pointed at the tip, thin, and laxly arranged.

INFLORESCENCE: 3–6 in. (8–15 cm) long. Erect inflorescences are short and threadlike and emerge from many upper nodes on leafless pseudobulbs.

FLOWERS: 1–4 per inflorescence. The flowers are 1.0–1.6 in. (2.5–4.0 cm) across. They are not fragrant. The narrow sepals and round petals are bright golden- to orange-yellow. The broad, rounded petals hide the lateral sepals. The large, round lip, which is a deeper color than the sepals and petals, is slightly wavy along the edges. It has a large golden-yellow disc and reddish stripes in the throat. Although each flower only lasts a few days, the flowers open successively so that a plant may be in bloom for several weeks. The blossoms of this species are a very consistent quality.

HYBRIDIZING NOTES: Chromosome count is 2n = 38 (ref. 504, 580).

REFERENCES: 36, 157, 167, 179, 196, 198, 202, 208, 210, 216, 245, 254, 266, 291, 330, 369, 430, 445, 447, 448, 454, 490, 504, 528, 541, 570, 580.

PHOTOS/DRAWINGS: *36*, *198*, 210, *245*, *291*, 369, *430*, *454*, *490*.

Dendrobium capitellatoides J. J. Smith

ORIGIN/HABITAT: Bangka Island, off the southeast coast of Sumatra. Plants were originally found near the village of Muntok (Mentok). Additional habitat and elevation information is unavailable, so the climate data should be used with caution. *D. capitellatoides* was cultivated at the botanical garden in Bogor, Java.

CLIMATE: Station #96237, Pangkalpinang, Bangka Island, Indonesia, Lat. 2.2°S, Long. 106.1°E, at 109 ft. (33 m). Record extreme temperatures are 94°F (34°C) and 68°F (20°C).

N/HEMISPHERE	JAN	FEB	MAR	APR	MAY	JUN	JUL	AUG	SEP	OCT	NOV	DEC
°F AVG MAX	86	86	86	87	86	85	84	85	86	87	87	86
°F AVG MIN	78	78	77	76	74	74	74	74	74	75	76	77
DIURNAL RANGE	8	8	9	11	12	11	10	11	12	12	11	9
RAIN/INCHES	8.6	6.0	5.9	6.3	11.6	16.3	15.1	12.4	9.9	11.8	9.7	7.5
HUMIDITY/%	76	72	71	75	80	86	84	85	84	82	81	79
BLOOM SEASON	N/A											
DAYS CLR @ 7AM	6	6	6	3	1	0	2	2	2	3	4	3
DAYS CLR @ 1PM	1	2	5	2	0	0	0	0	0	0	0	0
RAIN/MM	218	152	150	160	295	414	384	315	251	300	246	190
°C AVG MAX	30.0	30.0	30.0	30.6	30.0	29.4	28.9	29.4	30.0	30.6	30.6	30.0
°C AVG MIN	25.6	25.6	25.0	24.4	23.3	23.3	23.3	23.3	23.3	23.9	24.4	25.0
DIURNAL RANGE	4.4	4.4	5.0	6.2	6.7	6.1	5.6	6.1	6.7	6.7	6.2	5.0
S/HEMISPHERE	JUL	AUG	SEP	OCT	NOV	DEC	JAN	FEB	MAR	APR	MAY	JUN

Cultural Recommendations

LIGHT: 2000–3000 fc.

TEMPERATURES: Throughout the year, days average 84–87°F (29–31°C), and nights average 74–78°F (23–26°C), with a diurnal range of 8–12°F (4–7°C).

HUMIDITY: 80–85% from late spring through autumn, dropping to 70–75% in winter and early spring.

WATER: Rainfall is heavy year-round, but conditions are driest in winter. Cultivated plants should never be allowed to dry out completely.

FERTILIZER: ¼–½ recommended strength. A balanced fertilizer should be applied weekly to biweekly throughout the year.

REST PERIOD: Growing conditions should be maintained year-round. Water may be reduced somewhat for plants cultivated in the dark, short-day conditions common in temperate-latitude winters, but these plants should still never be allowed to dry out completely.

GROWING MEDIA: Plants may be mounted on tree-fern or cork slabs or potted in small pots filled with any open, fast-draining medium. Repotting may be done anytime new roots are growing.

MISCELLANEOUS NOTES: The plant was described in 1917 in *Bul. Jard. Bot. Buit.* 2nd sér. 25:36.

Plant and Flower Information

PLANT SIZE AND TYPE: A 6 in. (15 cm) sympodial epiphyte.

PSEUDOBULB: 6 in. (15 cm) long. The stems are dark yellow-green, flattened, and somewhat swollen at the base. They occasionally develop short branches.

LEAVES: The flattened leaves are 0.5–1.0 in. (1.3–2.5 cm) long. They are rigid and fleshy.

INFLORESCENCE: Inflorescences emerge from nodes on the upper part of the stem.

FLOWERS: 1–2 per inflorescence. The flowers are 0.7 in. (1.8 cm) long. Sepals and petals are yellowish-white with pale purple stripes. The blossoms have an ovate-triangular dorsal sepal, somewhat triangular lateral sepals, and lanceolate petals.

REFERENCES: 222.

Dendrobium capitellatum Kränzlin. See *D. hypodon*

Schlechter. REFERENCES: 220, 254, 436.

Dendrobium capitellatum J. J. Smith. See *D. kentrophyllum*

Hooker f. REFERENCES: 190, 200, 220, 254, 298, 435, 436, 445, 454.

Dendrobium capitisyork M. Clements and D. Jones

AKA: Clements (ref. 67) includes *D. tetragonum* A. Cunningham var. *giganteum* P. A. Gilbert (in part), *D. tetragonum* A. Cunningham var. *tomentosum* Nicholls. See also *D. tetragonum* A. Cunningham and *D. cacatua* M. Clements and D. Jones.

ORIGIN/HABITAT: Northeastern Queensland, Australia. The habitat extends from the Iron Range to the Fitzroy River. Plants grow in rainforests at moderate to low elevations, usually below 2600 ft. (800 m), but may be found as high as 4100 ft. (1250 m).

CLIMATE: Station #94287, Cairns, Australia, Lat. 16.9°S, Long. 145.8°E, at 7 ft. (2 m). Temperatures are calculated for an elevation of 2000 ft. (610 m), resulting in probable extremes of 103°F (40°C) and 36°F (3°C).

Dendrobium capituliflorum

N/HEMISPHERE	JAN	FEB	MAR	APR	MAY	JUN	JUL	AUG	SEP	OCT	NOV	DEC
°F AVG MAX	71	73	76	79	81	83	83	82	80	78	74	72
°F AVG MIN	54	55	57	61	63	66	67	67	66	63	59	57
DIURNAL RANGE	17	18	19	18	18	17	16	15	14	15	15	15
RAIN/INCHES	1.6	1.7	1.7	2.1	3.9	8.7	16.6	15.7	18.1	11.3	4.4	2.9
HUMIDITY/%	69	67	65	65	65	68	72	72	74	73	73	72
BLOOM SEASON	*	*	*	*						*	*	*
DAYS CLR @ 10AM	9	11	13	11	6	6	4	5	6	7	11	10
DAYS CLR @ 4PM	8	10	12	16	10	7	4	3	4	6	9	10
RAIN/MM	41	43	43	53	99	221	422	399	460	287	112	74
°C AVG MAX	21.9	23.0	24.7	26.3	27.5	28.6	28.6	28.0	26.9	25.8	23.6	22.5
°C AVG MIN	12.5	13.0	14.1	16.3	17.5	19.1	19.7	19.7	19.1	17.5	15.2	14.1
DIURNAL RANGE	9.4	10.0	10.6	10.0	10.0	9.5	8.9	8.3	7.8	8.3	8.4	8.4
S/HEMISPHERE	JUL	AUG	SEP	OCT	NOV	DEC	JAN	FEB	MAR	APR	MAY	JUN

Cultural Recommendations

LIGHT: 1800–2500 fc.

TEMPERATURES: Summer days average 82–83°F (28–29°C), and nights average 66–67°F (19–20°C), with a diurnal range of 15–17°F (8–9°C).

HUMIDITY: 65–75% year-round. In cloudforest habitats, however, humidity probably averages 10% higher than indicated in the climate table. Growers indicate that cultivated plants are healthier if high humidity and strong air movement are provided throughout the year.

WATER: Rainfall is heavy from late spring into autumn, with much drier conditions in winter. Cultivated plants should be kept moist from late spring into autumn, but water should be gradually reduced in late autumn. Mounted plants should be misted frequently and never be allowed to dry out completely for any length of time.

FERTILIZER: ¼–½ recommended strength, applied weekly. A high-nitrogen fertilizer is beneficial from spring to midsummer, but a fertilizer high in phosphates should be used in late summer and autumn.

REST PERIOD: Winter days average 71–73°F (22–23°C), and nights average 54–57°F (13–14°C), with a diurnal range of 17–19°F (9–11°C). Water should be reduced for 4–5 months from late autumn into early spring. Plants should be kept on the dry side, but they should never be allowed to dry out completely. Light, humidity, and air movement should be maintained all winter. Fertilizer should be reduced or eliminated until water is increased in spring.

GROWING MEDIA: Mounting plants on tree-fern or cork slabs accommodates their pendulous growth habit. However, humidity must be high and plants must be watered at least once a day in summer. If plants cannot be mounted, small pots or hanging baskets may be filled with an open, fast-draining medium. Repotting may be done anytime new roots are actively growing.

MISCELLANEOUS NOTES: The bloom season shown in the climate table is based on reports from the habitat. The plants flower sporadically during the bloom season. *D. capitisyork* is considered easy to grow if the environment is warm, humid, and shady.

Plant and Flower Information

PLANT SIZE AND TYPE: A 16 in. (40 cm) sympodial epiphyte or lithophyte.

PSEUDOBULB: 16 in. (40 cm) long. The frequently pendulous plant forms small- to medium-sized clumps. Individual stems are slender and wiry at the base, becoming larger and distinctly 4-angled near the tip. The pseudobulbs are greenish-brown.

LEAVES: 2–4 per growth. The thin, tough leaves are 3 in. (8 cm) long.

INFLORESCENCE: 8 in. (20 cm) long. Inflorescences are extremely slender and wiry.

FLOWERS: 2–5 per inflorescence. The flowers are 2.5 in. (6.5 cm) long. All segments are narrow and taper to an extremely sharp point. The greenish yellow blossoms are larger and more heavily spotted than *D. tetragonum*. The white lip is marked with strong red lines on the sidelobes. Lateral sepals may be straight or twisted and spreading or crossed. The lip has 3, rarely 5, parallel ridges that extend to the base of the midlobe. The sidelobes are much larger than the midlobe.

REFERENCES: 67, 68, 235, 240, 533, 564.

PHOTOS/DRAWINGS: 68, *564*.

Dendrobium capituliflorum Rolfe

AKA: In 1993, Dauncey and Cribb in *Kew Bulletin* 48(3) included *D. capituliflorum* var. *viride* J. J. Smith and *D. confusum* J. J. Smith as synonyms.

ORIGIN/HABITAT: Widely distributed on the Pacific islands. Plants grow at 15–2850 ft. (5–870 m). In New Guinea, they grow in coastal areas, but in the Solomon Islands they occur on ridge-tops. In other areas they have been reported in river ravines, rainforests, open secondary forests, and on rocky outcroppings.

CLIMATE: Station #200187, Erap, Papua New Guinea, Lat. 6.6°S, Long. 146.7°E, at 850 ft. (260 m). Record extreme temperatures are 102°F (39°C) and 53°F (12°C).

N/HEMISPHERE	JAN	FEB	MAR	APR	MAY	JUN	JUL	AUG	SEP	OCT	NOV	DEC
°F AVG MAX	88	88	89	90	93	93	93	93	93	92	90	90
°F AVG MIN	69	69	69	70	72	73	72	72	73	71	74	70
DIURNAL RANGE	19	19	20	20	21	20	21	21	20	21	16	20
RAIN/INCHES	3.9	3.9	2.7	3.0	3.0	5.3	5.9	5.9	7.0	3.4	2.4	3.1
HUMIDITY/%	82	81	81	79	75	74	74	74	77	76	80	80
BLOOM SEASON	*	**	**	*	*						*	*
DAYS CLR	N/A											
RAIN/MM	98	99	68	77	76	135	149	149	179	87	60	78
°C AVG MAX	30.9	30.9	31.7	32.3	34.0	33.9	33.8	33.9	34.0	33.6	32.3	32.0
°C AVG MIN	20.4	20.5	20.7	21.1	22.0	22.5	22.1	22.4	22.5	21.7	23.3	20.9
DIURNAL RANGE	10.5	10.4	11.0	11.2	12.0	11.4	11.7	11.5	11.5	11.9	9.0	11.1
S/HEMISPHERE	JUL	AUG	SEP	OCT	NOV	DEC	JAN	FEB	MAR	APR	MAY	JUN

Cultural Recommendations

LIGHT: 1200–2000 fc. Growers recommend *Phalaenopsis* light levels.

TEMPERATURES: Throughout the year, days average 88–93°F (31–34°C), and nights average 69–74°F (20–23°C), with a diurnal range of 16–21°F (9–12°C).

HUMIDITY: 75–80% year-round.

WATER: Rainfall is moderate most of the year, but conditions are somewhat wetter for 4–5 months in summer and early autumn. Cultivated plants should be thoroughly saturated, then allowed to dry slightly between waterings in summer and early autumn. Water should be gradually reduced in autumn.

FERTILIZER: ¼–½ recommended strength. A balanced fertilizer should be applied weekly to biweekly throughout the year.

REST PERIOD: Growing temperatures should be maintained all year. In the habitat, rainfall is lowest in winter, but the high humidity indicates that additional moisture is frequently available from heavy dew. Cultivated plants should be allowed to dry for somewhat longer between waterings, but should not remain dry for extended periods. Fertilizer should be reduced until water is increased in spring. In the habitat, seasonal light variation is minor.

GROWING MEDIA: Plants may be mounted on tree-fern or cork slabs if humidity is high and plants are watered at least once a day in summer. When plants are potted, shallow pots may be filled with any open, fast-draining medium. Repotting is best done when new roots are growing.

MISCELLANEOUS NOTES: The bloom season shown in the climate table is based on cultivation records. In the habitat, plants bloom from autumn to early winter. Dauncy and Cribb report that in cultivation some long stemmed plants from the Solomon Islands bloom at a different time than plants from other areas.

Plant and Flower Information

PLANT SIZE AND TYPE: A 4–10 in. (10–25 cm) sympodial epiphyte or lithophyte.

PSEUDOBULB: 4–10 in. (10–25 cm) long. The pseudobulbs consist of several nodes that are constricted at the base. The shape varies from spindle-shaped to cylindrical. The green stems become yellow and grooved with age.

LEAVES: Many. The deciduous leaves, which may be dark- to gray-green on the upper surface, are velvety purple or with a violet tint on the underside. They are thinly leathery and unequally bilobed at the tip. The leaf shape is narrowly lanceolate on tall plants and elliptical on shorter plants.

INFLORESCENCE: 2.4 in. (6 cm) long. Dense, ovoid clusters of inflorescences emerge laterally from nodes near the apex of the stem. They arise from both older, leafless pseudobulbs and newer leafy stems.

FLOWERS: 50–60 per inflorescence. The flowers are 0.5 in. (1.3 cm) across and do not open fully. They are green-white with green at the tips of the sepals, the lip plate, and the anther-cap. The blossoms may be smooth or hairy to bumpy. They have an ovate upper sepal and smaller lateral sepals. The oblong-lanceolate petals are pointed at the tips. The mentum is about the same length as the free parts of the lateral sepals. All segments are white to cream with a green tinge. The greenish lip is ovate-lanceolate, pointed, and concave. The anther is also greenish.

HYBRIDIZING NOTES: Chromosome count is 2n = 38 (ref. 152, 154, 188, 504, 580).

REFERENCES: 25, 67, 86, 92, 152, 154, 179, 188, 212, 219, 243, 254, 271, 304, 352, 413, 430, 437, 445, 470, 504, 516, 526, 537, 580.

PHOTOS/DRAWINGS: *271, 304, 430,* 437

Dendrobium capra J. J. Smith

ORIGIN/HABITAT: The Lesser Sunda Islands and eastern Java. Plants grow on trees at low elevations. They are often found in planted teak forests near the base of Mt. Penanggungan north of Mt. Arjuno.

CLIMATE: Station #96933, Surabaja, Java, Indonesia, Lat. 7.2°S, Long. 112.7°E, at 10 ft. (3 m). Record extreme temperatures are 96°F (36°C) and 58°F (14°C).

N/HEMISPHERE	JAN	FEB	MAR	APR	MAY	JUN	JUL	AUG	SEP	OCT	NOV	DEC
°F AVG MAX	87	87	89	90	90	88	88	88	88	88	88	87
°F AVG MIN	70	70	71	73	75	74	74	74	74	74	73	71
DIURNAL RANGE	17	17	18	17	15	14	14	14	14	14	15	16
RAIN/INCHES	0.9	0.2	0.2	0.6	2.3	6.7	10.2	10.7	8.7	5.2	3.5	2.4
HUMIDITY/%	76	71	66	67	72	80	82	83	83	80	80	75
BLOOM SEASON									*	*		
DAYS CLR @ 8AM	13	17	20	17	8	3	3	3	6	8	9	14
DAYS CLR @ 2PM	17	20	21	16	6	2	2	1	2	6	9	17
RAIN/MM	23	5	5	15	58	170	259	272	221	132	89	61
°C AVG MAX	30.6	30.6	31.7	32.2	32.2	31.1	31.1	31.1	31.1	31.1	31.1	30.6
°C AVG MIN	21.1	21.1	21.7	22.8	23.9	23.3	23.3	23.3	23.3	23.3	22.8	21.7
DIURNAL RANGE	9.5	9.5	10.0	9.4	8.3	7.8	7.8	7.8	7.8	7.8	8.3	8.9
S/HEMISPHERE	JUL	AUG	SEP	OCT	NOV	DEC	JAN	FEB	MAR	APR	MAY	JUN

Cultural Recommendations

LIGHT: 3000–4000 fc. Most days are cloudy during the summer rainy season, but more than half the days are clear in winter and early spring. Cultivated plants should be shaded in summer. As much light as possible, short of burning the foliage, should be provided during the remainder of the year. Strong air movement is very important, especially when light is high.

TEMPERATURES: Throughout the year, days average 87–90°F (31–32°C), and nights average 70–75°F (21–24°C), with a diurnal range of 14–18°F (8–10°C).

HUMIDITY: 80–85% in summer and autumn, dropping to near 75% in winter, then decreasing to 65–70% in spring.

WATER: Rainfall is heavy in summer and early autumn, but conditions are very dry in winter and early spring. Cultivated plants should be kept moist, with only slight drying allowed between waterings while actively growing. Water should be gradually reduced in autumn.

FERTILIZER: ¼–½ recommended strength. A balanced fertilizer should be applied weekly to biweekly throughout the growing season.

REST PERIOD: Growing temperatures should be maintained all year. Conditions are dry for 4–5 months in winter and early spring. For 2–3 months at the end of the dry season, humidity declines to near 65%, which is sufficiently low that even moisture from dew is uncommon. Cultivated plants should be watered lightly most of the winter. They should be allowed to dry out between waterings but should not remain completely dry for extended periods. For 1–2 months in late winter, however, water should be restricted to only an occasional misting. Fertilizer should be eliminated until water is increased in spring.

GROWING MEDIA: Plants may be mounted on tree-fern or cork slabs if humidity is high and plants are watered at least once daily in summer. When plants are potted, any open, fast-draining medium may be used. Repotting may be done anytime new roots are growing.

MISCELLANEOUS NOTES: The bloom season shown in the climate table is based on reports from the habitat.

Plant and Flower Information

PLANT SIZE AND TYPE: A 4–17 in. (10–43 cm) sympodial epiphyte.

PSEUDOBULB: 4–17 in. (10–43 cm) long. The erect, somewhat zigzag stems are dull green, canelike, and swollen in the middle.

LEAVES: 4–7 on the upper portion of each growth. The leaves are 3–5 in. (8–13 cm) long, linear-lanceolate, and sharply pointed. They are shiny green sometimes with black spots when young.

INFLORESCENCE: 4–12 in. (10–31 cm) long. The laxly flowered inflorescences emerge horizontally from the leaf bases on leafy stems.

FLOWERS: 5–10 per inflorescence, normally, but occasionally as many as 20. Blossoms are 1.2 in. (3 cm) across. Sepals are slender, but the petals are even narrower. The sepals and petals, which are not twisted, may be lime-green to greenish yellow with a grey strip down the center. The paler lip is nearly yellow with dark brownish-purple markings on the sidelobes and keels.

HYBRIDIZING NOTES: Chromosome count is n = 19 (ref. 151) and 2n = 38 (ref. 187). When used as a parent, *D. capra* tends to contribute an increased number of many-flowered spikes and long-lasting flowers. It usually increases the number of flowers; helps round-out flower shape; and adds yellows, greens, and blue tones to hybrids made with species in the *Phalaenopsis* subsection. Hybrids generally produce good cut flowers.

REFERENCES: 25, 75, 84, 151, 187, 200, 220, 346, 445.

PHOTOS/DRAWINGS: *75, 84, 346.*

Dendrobium carinatum (Linn.) Willdenow

AKA: *Epidendrum carinatum* Linn., *D. robinsonii* Ames.

ORIGIN/HABITAT: The Philippines, Mindoro and Luzon Islands. Plants grow on trees in open, sandy areas in Mountain Province and Rizal and Zambales provinces.

CLIMATE: Station #98328, Baguio, Philippines, Lat. 16.4°N, Long. 120.6°E, at 4962 ft. (1512 m). Record extreme temperatures are 84°F (29°C) and 46°F (8°C).

Dendrobium cariniferum

N/HEMISPHERE	JAN	FEB	MAR	APR	MAY	JUN	JUL	AUG	SEP	OCT	NOV	DEC
°F AVG MAX	72	73	76	77	76	75	71	71	71	73	74	74
°F AVG MIN	55	56	58	60	61	61	60	60	60	60	59	57
DIURNAL RANGE	17	17	18	17	15	14	11	11	11	13	15	17
RAIN/INCHES	0.9	0.9	1.7	4.3	15.8	17.2	42.3	45.7	28.1	15.0	4.9	2.0
HUMIDITY/%	83	83	83	85	89	90	93	93	92	89	86	84
BLOOM SEASON				*	*							
DAYS CLR	N/A											
RAIN/MM	23	23	43	109	401	437	1074	1161	714	381	124	51
°C AVG MAX	22.2	22.8	24.4	25.0	24.4	23.9	21.7	21.7	21.7	22.8	23.3	23.3
°C AVG MIN	12.8	13.3	14.4	15.6	16.1	16.1	15.6	15.6	15.6	15.6	15.0	13.9
DIURNAL RANGE	9.4	9.5	10.0	9.4	8.3	7.8	6.1	6.1	6.1	7.2	8.3	9.4
S/HEMISPHERE	JUL	AUG	SEP	OCT	NOV	DEC	JAN	FEB	MAR	APR	MAY	JUN

Cultural Recommendations

LIGHT: 1200–2400 fc. Diffused or dappled light is recommended. Sky-cover records are unavailable, but high elevations are typically cloudy in this region.

TEMPERATURES: Throughout the year, days average 71–77°F (22–25°C), and nights average 55–61°F (13–16°C), with a diurnal range of 11–18°F (6–10°C). Plants from this habitat are not heat tolerant. Buds may drop if plants are cultivated at temperatures that are too warm; hence, they are sometimes considered difficult to grow.

HUMIDITY: 80–90% year-round.

WATER: Rainfall is very heavy from spring to autumn but is greatly reduced in winter. Cultivated plants should be kept moist but not soggy from spring to autumn. Water should be gradually reduced in late autumn.

FERTILIZER: ½ recommended strength, applied weekly. A high-nitrogen fertilizer is beneficial from spring to midsummer, but a fertilizer high in phosphates should be used in late summer and autumn.

REST PERIOD: Growing temperatures should be maintained all year. Rainfall is low for 2–4 months in winter, but the continuing high humidity indicates that additional moisture is frequently available from fog, dew, or mist. Cultivated plants should be allowed to dry somewhat between waterings, but should never remain dry for long periods. In the habitat, light may be highest in winter.

GROWING MEDIA: Plants may be potted in any open, fast-draining medium. Repotting is best done in early spring when new roots are growing.

MISCELLANEOUS NOTES: The bloom season shown in the climate table is based on cultivation records. Collection reports suggest that in the habitat, plants bloom during the winter dry season.

Plant and Flower Information

PLANT SIZE AND TYPE: A 16 in. (40 cm) sympodial epiphyte.

PSEUDOBULB: 4.3 in. (11 cm) long. Each growth normally consists of several branches. The stems are swollen at the base.

LEAVES: The terete leaves are 2–3 in. (5.0–7.5 cm) long. They are fleshy, rigid, slender, and thickened at the base.

INFLORESCENCE: Inflorescences arise from the leafless apical portion of the stem.

FLOWERS: 1 per inflorescence. The sweetly fragrant flowers are 0.8 in. (2 cm) across. Sepals and petals are greenish yellow with brownish markings. The lip is blotched a dark purple at the base.

REFERENCES: 12, 13, 179, 216, 254, 277, 296, 536.

PHOTOS/DRAWINGS: 13.

Dendrobium cariniferum Rchb. f.

AKA: Seidenfaden (ref. 454) discusses the confusion regarding the species *D. cariniferum*, *D. wattii* (Hooker f.) Rchb. f., and *D. williamsonii* Day and Rchb. f. *D. cariniferum* is sometimes listed as a synonym of *D. williamsonii*. *D. cariniferum* Rchb. f. var. *wattii* Hooker f. is considered a synonym of *D. wattii* (Hooker f.) Rchb. f. In 1992 *Opera Botanica* #114, Seidenfaden differentiates the plants with characteristics included in the following Plant and Flower Information.

ORIGIN/HABITAT: Widespread in Southeast Asia. The habitat extends from the mountains of northeastern India where plants grow at about 5900 ft. (1800 m), through Burma, Indochina, and southwest China. In northwestern Thailand, plants are found at 3600–5000 ft. (1100–1530 m).

CLIMATE: Station #48327, Chiang Mai, Thailand, Lat. 18.8°N, Long. 99.0°E, at 1100 ft. (335 m). Temperatures are calculated for an elevation of 4000 ft. (1219 m), resulting in probable extremes of 99°F (38°C) and 28°F (–2°C).

N/HEMISPHERE	JAN	FEB	MAR	APR	MAY	JUN	JUL	AUG	SEP	OCT	NOV	DEC
°F AVG MAX	75	80	85	86	84	80	79	77	78	79	76	74
°F AVG MIN	46	47	52	60	64	64	64	65	63	65	56	47
DIURNAL RANGE	29	33	33	26	20	16	15	12	15	18	20	27
RAIN/INCHES	0.3	0.4	0.6	2.0	5.5	6.1	7.4	8.7	11.5	4.9	1.5	0.4
HUMIDITY/%	73	65	58	62	73	78	80	83	83	81	79	76
BLOOM SEASON	*	**	*	*								*
DAYS CLR @ 7AM	5	5	2	2	1	0	0	0	0	1	3	3
DAYS CLR @ 1PM	9	8	4	2	0	0	0	0	0	0	1	3
RAIN/MM	8	10	15	51	140	155	188	221	292	124	38	10
°C AVG MAX	24.1	26.9	29.7	30.2	29.1	26.9	26.4	25.2	25.8	26.4	24.7	23.6
°C AVG MIN	8.0	8.6	11.3	15.8	18.0	18.0	18.0	18.6	17.5	16.4	13.6	8.6
DIURNAL RANGE	16.1	18.3	18.4	14.4	11.1	8.9	8.4	6.6	8.3	10.0	11.1	15.0
S/HEMISPHERE	JUL	AUG	SEP	OCT	NOV	DEC	JAN	FEB	MAR	APR	MAY	JUN

Cultural Recommendations

LIGHT: 2500–3500 fc. Growers indicate that plants are healthiest in bright, diffused light.

TEMPERATURES: Summer days average 77–80°F (25–27°C), and nights average 64–65°F (18–19°C), with a diurnal range of 12–16°F (7–9°C). Spring is the warmest season. Days average 84–86°F (29–30°C), and nights average 52–64°F (11–18°C), with a diurnal range of 20–33°F (11–18°C). Both highs and lows are more moderate after the start of the summer wet season.

HUMIDITY: 75–85% most of the year, dropping to near 60% in late winter and early spring.

WATER: Rainfall is heavy from late spring to early autumn, but conditions are much drier in winter and early spring. While actively growing, cultivated plants should be kept moist with little if any drying allowed between waterings. Water should be gradually reduced after new growths mature in autumn, however.

FERTILIZER: ½ recommended strength, applied weekly. A high-nitrogen fertilizer is beneficial from spring to midsummer, but a fertilizer high in phosphates should be used in late summer and autumn.

REST PERIOD: Winter days average 74–80°F (24–27°C), and nights average 46–47°F (8–9°C), with a diurnal range of 27–33°F (15–18°C). Low night temperatures or wide diurnal range may be necessary to initiate blooming. Plants should be able to tolerate temperatures a few degrees below freezing, but extremes should be avoided in cultivation. During very cold weather, a plant's chance of surviving with minimal damage is better if it is dry when temperatures are low. In the habitat, rainfall averages are very low for 4–5 months in winter; but during the early part of the season, the high relative humidity indicates that additional moisture is available from frequent fog, mist, and heavy deposits of dew. Growers sometimes recommend eliminating water in winter, but plants are healthiest if for most of the winter they are allowed to become somewhat dry between waterings but do not remain dry for extended periods. For 1–2 months in late winter, however, conditions are clear, warm, and dry with humidity so low that even the moisture from morning dew is uncommon. Plants should be allowed to dry out completely between waterings and remain dry longer during this time. Occasional early morning mistings between waterings may help keep the plants from becoming too dry. Fertilizer should be greatly reduced or eliminated until water is increased in spring. A cool, dry rest is essential for cultivated plants and should be continued until new growth starts in spring. In the habitat, light is highest in winter.

GROWING MEDIA: Plants may be mounted on tree-fern or cork slabs if humidity is high and plants are watered at least once daily in summer. When plants are potted, any open, fast-draining medium may be used. Repotting is best done immediately after flowering in early spring when new roots are growing.

MISCELLANEOUS NOTES: The bloom season shown in the climate table is based on cultivation records for plants cultivated as *D. williamsonii*. In the habitat, blooming occurs in spring and early summer. *D. cariniferum* is considered a problem plant by many growers and careful attention should be paid to cultural needs. Low night temperatures, wide diurnal range, or the dry winter may be necessary to initiate blooming.

Plant and Flower Information

PLANT SIZE AND TYPE: A 10 in. (25 cm) sympodial epiphyte.
PSEUDOBULB: 8 in. (20 cm) long. The relatively thick stems are covered with hairs.
LEAVES: 4–6 per growth. The relatively broad leaves, which are 2–3 in. (5–8 cm) long, are hairy on the backside.
INFLORESCENCE: Very short. The inflorescence emerges near the apex of the pseudobulb.
FLOWERS: 1 per inflorescence. The flowers are 1.5 in. (3.8 cm) across with distinct keels on the back of the sepals. The keels extend as sharp keels on the ovary. The width of the petals is nearly equal the width of the dorsal sepal. Blossoms may be pale buff marked with golden yellow streaks on the disk, or the sepals and petals may be white with brick-red markings on the lip. Hairs protrude along the nerves. The center callus divides near the tip forming 3 sharp points at the tip.
HYBRIDIZING NOTES: Chromosome count is $2n = 38$ (ref. 504, 580). Johansen (ref. 239) indicates that plants are self-sterile and that flowers dropped 11 days after self-pollination. *D. draconis* Rchb. f. hybridizes with *D. cariniferum*. Either plant may be used as the female parent.
REFERENCES: 25, 38, 46, 157, 202, 210, 216, 239, 245, 254, 369, 429, 430, 437, 445, 454, 504, 528, 541, 568, 580.
PHOTOS/DRAWINGS: 210, *245, 350, 430, 454.*

Dendrobium carinulatidiscum J. J. Smith. Now considered a synonym of *Diplocaulobium carinulatidiscum* (J. J. Smith) A. Hawkes. REFERENCES: 223, 229, 445, 470.

Dendrobium carnicarinum Kores

ORIGIN/HABITAT: Endemic to Viti Levu, Fiji. South of Nandarivatu in Mba Province, plants grow on tree trunks 20–30 ft. (6–9 m) above the ground in the rainforests at 2450–2950 ft. (750–900 m).
CLIMATE: Station #91683, Nausori, Vitu Levu, Fiji, Is., Lat. 18.1°S, Long. 178.6°E, at 19 ft. (6 m). Temperatures are calculated for an elevation of 2700 ft. (820 m), resulting in probable extremes of 89°F (32°C) and 46°F (8°C).

N/HEMISPHERE	JAN	FEB	MAR	APR	MAY	JUN	JUL	AUG	SEP	OCT	NOV	DEC
°F AVG MAX	70	70	71	72	74	76	77	77	77	75	73	71
°F AVG MIN	59	59	60	61	62	64	65	65	65	64	62	60
DIURNAL RANGE	11	11	11	11	12	12	12	12	12	11	11	11
RAIN/INCHES	4.9	8.3	7.7	8.3	9.8	12.5	11.4	10.7	14.5	12.2	10.1	6.7
HUMIDITY/%	77	77	76	75	75	76	76	78	79	79	81	78
BLOOM SEASON	N/A											
DAYS CLR @ 12PM	3	1	0	0	1	1	2	0	0	0	1	0
RAIN/MM	124	211	196	211	249	318	290	272	368	310	257	170
°C AVG MAX	21.2	21.2	21.8	22.3	23.4	24.5	25.1	25.1	25.1	24.0	22.9	21.8
°C AVG MIN	15.1	15.1	15.6	16.2	16.8	17.9	18.4	18.4	18.4	17.9	16.8	15.6
DIURNAL RANGE	6.1	6.1	6.2	6.1	6.6	6.6	6.7	6.7	6.7	6.1	6.1	6.2
S/HEMISPHERE	JUL	AUG	SEP	OCT	NOV	DEC	JAN	FEB	MAR	APR	MAY	JUN

Cultural Recommendations

LIGHT: 2000–3000 fc.
TEMPERATURES: Summer days average 76–77°F (25°C), and nights average 64–65°F (18°C), with a diurnal range of 12°F (7°C).
HUMIDITY: 75–80% year-round.
WATER: Rainfall is moderate to heavy all year. Cultivated plants should be kept moist and never be allowed to dry completely.
FERTILIZER: ¼–½ recommended strength. A balanced fertilizer should be applied weekly to biweekly throughout the year.
REST PERIOD: Winter days average 70–71°F (21–22°C), and nights average 59–60°F (15–16°C), with a diurnal range of 11°F (6°C). Seasonal temperature variation is minor. Winter rainfall is high, but water should be reduced somewhat for cultivated plants, especially those grown in the dark, short-day conditions common in temperate-latitude winters. Plants should never be allowed to dry completely, however. Fertilizer should be reduced or eliminated anytime water is reduced.
GROWING MEDIA: Plants may be mounted on tree-fern or cork slabs if humidity is high and plants are watered at least once daily in summer. When plants are potted, any open, fast-draining medium may be used. Repotting is best done in early spring when new roots are growing.
MISCELLANEOUS NOTES: The plant is known only from the type collection.

Plant and Flower Information

PLANT SIZE AND TYPE: A small sympodial epiphyte of unreported size.
PSEUDOBULB: New growths arise from a very short rhizome.
LEAVES: Several per growth. The linear to linear-lanceolate leaves are 1.0–1.6 in. (2.5–4.0 cm) long and very leathery.
INFLORESCENCE: Very short.
FLOWERS: 1–2 per inflorescence. The yellow to white flowers are 0.6 in. (1 cm) long and remain rather closed. The lip is nearly kidney-shaped.
REFERENCES: 235, 252, 466.
PHOTOS/DRAWINGS: 466.

Dendrobium carnosum Presl. Now considered a synonym of *Maxillaria scabrilinguis*. REFERENCES: 216, 254, 445.

Dendrobium carnosum (Blume) Rchb. f. See *D. concinnum* Miquel. REFERENCES: 25, 59, 75, 200, 208, 216, 254, 286, 298, 317, 435, 454, 455, 469. PHOTOS/DRAWINGS: 200, 469.

Dendrobium carnosum Teijsm. and Binn. See *D. pachyphyllum* (Kuntze) Bakhuizen f. REFERENCES: 213, 216, 254, 310, 317, 454, 469.

Dendrobium carolinense Schlechter

ORIGIN/HABITAT: Patapat, Ponape, Kusaie, and Truk in the Caroline Islands. *D. carolinense* is common at 1000–1950 ft. (300–600 m) in mixed or scrub forest habitats. Plants grow on dead trees with bird's nest fern.
CLIMATE: Station #91348, Ponape, Caroline Islands, Lat. 7.0°N, Long. 158.2°E, at 121 ft. (37 m). Temperatures are calculated for an elevation of 1480 ft. (450 m). Record extreme temperatures are not available for this location.

N/HEMISPHERE	JAN	FEB	MAR	APR	MAY	JUN	JUL	AUG	SEP	OCT	NOV	DEC
°F AVG MAX	82	82	83	84	84	83	83	84	84	84	84	83
°F AVG MIN	73	73	73	73	72	72	71	70	71	71	71	72
DIURNAL RANGE	9	9	10	11	12	11	12	14	13	13	13	11
RAIN/INCHES	13.7	9.4	11.2	12.6	15.2	23.8	22.9	17.1	17.4	15.7	17.0	16.7
HUMIDITY/%	N/A											
BLOOM SEASON									*		*	*
DAYS CLR	N/A											
RAIN/MM	348	239	284	320	386	605	582	434	442	399	432	424
°C AVG MAX	27.5	27.5	28.1	28.6	28.6	28.1	28.1	28.6	28.6	28.6	28.6	28.1
°C AVG MIN	22.5	22.5	22.5	22.5	22.0	22.0	21.4	20.8	21.4	21.4	21.4	22.0
DIURNAL RANGE	5.0	5.0	5.6	6.1	6.6	6.1	6.7	7.8	7.2	7.2	7.2	6.1
S/HEMISPHERE	JUL	AUG	SEP	OCT	NOV	DEC	JAN	FEB	MAR	APR	MAY	JUN

Dendrobium carrii

Cultural Recommendations

LIGHT: 2000–3000 fc.

TEMPERATURES: Throughout the year, days average 82–84°F (28–29°C), and nights average 70–73°F (21–23°C), with a diurnal range of 9–14°F (5–8°C).

HUMIDITY: Information is not available for this location. However, records from nearby stations indicate that humidity is probably near 80% year-round.

WATER: Rainfall is heavy to very heavy all year. Cultivated plants should be kept wet but not soggy.

FERTILIZER: ¼–½ recommended strength. A balanced fertilizer should be applied weekly to biweekly throughout the year.

REST PERIOD: Growing temperatures should be maintained all year. Water and fertilizer should be reduced in winter, especially for plants grown in the dark, short-day conditions common in temperate latitudes. Plants should never be allowed to dry out completely, however. In the habitat, seasonal light variation is minor.

GROWING MEDIA: Plants may be mounted on tree-fern or cork slabs if humidity is high and plants are watered at least once daily in summer. When plants are potted, any open, fast-draining medium may be used. Repotting may be done anytime new roots are growing.

MISCELLANEOUS NOTES: The bloom season shown in the climate table is based on reports from the habitat.

Plant and Flower Information

PLANT SIZE AND TYPE: A 20–28 in. (50–70 cm) sympodial epiphyte.

PSEUDOBULB: 20–28 in. (50–70 cm) long. Stems are wiry, rigid, and do not branch. They are smooth when dry.

LEAVES: Many. The lanceolate leaves are usually 2.4–3.2 in. (6–8 cm) long. The stems are densely leafy.

INFLORESCENCE: Short. Inflorescences emerge from nodes along the sides of the pseudobulbs.

FLOWERS: 2 per inflorescence. The flowers are 2 in. (5 cm) across. Sepals and petals are whitish to reddish white. The nearly circular lip is wine-red to dark red.

REFERENCES: 189, 223, 441.

Dendrobium carrii Rupp and C. T. White

ORIGIN/HABITAT: Australia. Plants grow in cloudforests of the highlands in northern Queensland between the Tully and Annan Rivers. *D. carrii* is found at 3000–4000 ft. (900–1220 m), usually in high light on the outer branchlets in tree tops, and often in exposed and windy conditions. Humidity is normally very high and heavy dew and early morning mists are common.

CLIMATE: Station #94287, Cairns, Australia, Lat. 16.9°S, Long. 145.8°E, at 7 ft. (2 m). Temperatures are calculated for an elevation of 3500 ft. (1070 m), resulting in probable extremes of 98°F (37°C) and 31°F (0°C).

N/HEMISPHERE	JAN	FEB	MAR	APR	MAY	JUN	JUL	AUG	SEP	OCT	NOV	DEC
°F AVG MAX	66	68	71	74	76	78	78	77	75	73	69	67
°F AVG MIN	49	50	52	56	58	61	62	62	61	58	54	52
DIURNAL RANGE	17	18	19	18	18	17	16	15	14	15	15	15
RAIN/INCHES	1.6	1.7	1.7	2.1	3.9	8.7	16.6	15.7	18.1	11.3	4.4	2.9
HUMIDITY/%	69	67	65	65	65	68	72	72	74	73	73	72
BLOOM SEASON			*	*	*							
DAYS CLR @ 10AM	9	11	13	11	6	6	4	5	6	7	11	10
DAYS CLR @ 4PM	8	10	12	16	10	7	4	3	4	6	9	10
RAIN/MM	41	43	43	53	99	221	422	399	460	287	112	74
°C AVG MAX	19.2	20.3	21.9	23.6	24.7	25.8	25.8	25.3	24.2	23.0	20.8	19.7
°C AVG MIN	9.7	10.3	11.4	13.6	14.7	16.4	16.9	16.9	16.4	14.7	12.5	11.4
DIURNAL RANGE	9.5	10.0	10.5	10.0	10.0	9.4	8.9	8.4	7.8	8.3	8.3	8.3
S/HEMISPHERE	JUL	AUG	SEP	OCT	NOV	DEC	JAN	FEB	MAR	APR	MAY	JUN

Cultural Recommendations

LIGHT: 3000–4000 fc.

TEMPERATURES: Summer days average 77–78°F (25–26°C), and nights average 61–62°F (16–17°C), with a diurnal range of 15–17°F (8–9°C).

HUMIDITY: 70–75% most of the year, dropping to 65% in late winter and spring. In the rainforest habitat, however, relative humidity may average at least 10% more than indicated in the climate table. Cultivated plants are healthiest if high humidity and strong air movement are provided all year.

WATER: Rainfall is heavy from late spring into autumn with much drier conditions in winter. Plants should be kept moist from late spring into autumn, but water should be gradually reduced in late autumn. Growers indicate that mounted plants should be misted frequently and never be allowed to dry out completely for any length of time.

FERTILIZER: ¼–½ recommended strength, applied weekly. A high-nitrogen fertilizer is beneficial from spring to midsummer, but a fertilizer high in phosphates should be used in late summer and autumn.

REST PERIOD: Winter days average 66–71°F (19–22°C), and nights average 49–52°F (10–11°C), with a diurnal range of 15–19°F (8–11°C). Australian growers recommend that winter lows not fall below 43°F (6°C). Water should be reduced for 4–5 months from late autumn to early spring. Plants should be allowed to dry slightly between waterings, but they should not remain dry for long periods. Fertilizer may be reduced when temperatures are cool or light is low. In the habitat, winter skies are frequently clear.

GROWING MEDIA: Mounting plants on slabs or rafts produces excellent results if humidity is high and the plants are watered at least once daily in summer. Several waterings a day may be necessary on the hottest days. If plants are potted, a very open and fast-draining medium may be used. Undersized pots, barely large enough to hold the roots, are recommended. Repotting is best done in early spring immediately after blooming when new roots begin to grow.

MISCELLANEOUS NOTES: The bloom season shown in the climate table is based on reports from the habitat.

Plant and Flower Information

PLANT SIZE AND TYPE: A 3–6 in. (8–15 cm) sympodial epiphyte.

PSEUDOBULB: 1–2 in. (2.5–5.0 cm) long. The pseudobulbs arise from a creeping, branching, and very woody rhizome. The plant straggles across the surface rather than forming a mat.

LEAVES: 1–3 per growth. The lanceolate leaves are 2–4 in. (5–10 cm) long, thin, and often twisted.

INFLORESCENCE: 1–3 per growth. The erect inflorescences, which are shorter than the leaves, arise from the apex of the pseudobulb.

FLOWERS: 5–10 per inflorescence. The flowers are 0.4 in. (1 cm) across and remain rather closed. Sepals and petals are dull white to cream. The lip is yellow or orange splashed with light red markings which are heaviest on the midlobe.

REFERENCES: 67, 105, 226, 227, 240, 262, 263, 421, 533.

PHOTOS/DRAWINGS: 105, 240, *533*.

Dendrobium carronii Lavarack and Cribb

AKA: Normally listed as part of the *D. canaliculatum* R. Brown alliance, Clements (ref. 67) considers *D. carronii* an independent species.

ORIGIN/HABITAT: Australia and Papua New Guinea. In Australia, the plants are found from near Coen on the Cape York Peninsula northward to the Jardine River. Distribution then extends across the Torres Straits into Papua New Guinea. Plants usually grow 7–13 ft. (2–4 m) above the ground on *Melaleuca* trees in swamps or open forests, but they are always found in areas with high humidity. They are found from sea level to 1650 ft. (0–500 m).

CLIMATE: Station #94283, Cooktown, Australia, Lat. 15.5°S, Long. 145.2°E, at 24 ft. (7 m). Temperatures are calculated for an elevation of 1000 ft. (300 m), resulting in probable extremes of 101°F (39°C) and 43°F (6°C).

N/HEMISPHERE	JAN	FEB	MAR	APR	MAY	JUN	JUL	AUG	SEP	OCT	NOV	DEC
°F AVG MAX	76	77	79	82	85	86	86	85	83	82	79	77
°F AVG MIN	63	64	67	70	72	72	72	72	72	70	67	65
DIURNAL RANGE	13	13	12	12	13	14	14	13	11	12	12	12
RAIN/INCHES	0.9	1.2	0.6	1.0	2.5	6.6	14.4	13.7	15.3	8.8	2.8	2.0
HUMIDITY/%	73	69	68	67	68	71	75	76	77	75	74	75
BLOOM SEASON	*	**	**	**							*	*
DAYS CLR	N/A											
RAIN/MM	23	30	15	25	64	168	366	348	389	224	71	51
°C AVG MAX	24.3	24.9	26.0	27.7	29.3	29.9	29.9	29.3	28.2	27.7	26.0	24.9
°C AVG MIN	17.1	17.7	19.3	21.0	22.1	22.1	22.1	22.1	22.1	21.0	19.3	18.2
DIURNAL RANGE	7.2	7.2	6.7	6.7	7.2	7.8	7.8	7.2	6.1	6.7	6.7	6.7
S/HEMISPHERE	JUL	AUG	SEP	OCT	NOV	DEC	JAN	FEB	MAR	APR	MAY	JUN

Cultural Recommendations

LIGHT: 1800–2400 fc. Diffused or dappled light is preferred. Direct sunlight should be avoided.

TEMPERATURES: Summer days average 85–86°F (29–30°C), and nights average 72°F (22°C), with a diurnal range of 13–14°F (7–8°C) which varies only 3°F (2°C) through the year.

HUMIDITY: 70–75% most of the year, dropping to 65–70% in winter and spring.

WATER: Rainfall is very heavy in summer and early autumn, but conditions are much drier in winter. Cultivated plants should be kept moist during the growing season, but water should be reduced in late autumn. Growers indicate that plants are healthiest if given frequent waterings in summer, particularly when temperatures are warm.

FERTILIZER: ¼–½ recommended strength, applied weekly. A high-nitrogen fertilizer is beneficial from spring to midsummer, but a fertilizer high in phosphates should be used in late summer and autumn.

REST PERIOD: Winter days average 76–79°F (24–26°C), and nights average 63–67°F (17–19°C), with little change in the diurnal range of 12–13°F (7°C). For 3–4 months in winter, *D. carronii* prefers to be drier than most *Dendrobium*. In the habitat, plants survive extraordinary droughts. As inflorescences start to grow, water should be increased so that plants are very slightly moist, but they must be kept quite dry until new growths are about 2 in. (5 cm) tall. Young growths are very susceptible to infection. Fertilizer should be eliminated during the winter dry season. In the habitat, light is highest during the rest period.

GROWING MEDIA: Plants should be mounted on cork slabs if humidity is high and plants are watered at least once daily in summer. Potted plants are very difficult to maintain in cultivation, but if pots must be used, a very open, fast-draining medium is recommended. Repotting is best done in early spring immediately after flowering when new roots are growing. Repotting at this time allows the plant to reestablish as rapidly as possible.

MISCELLANEOUS NOTES: The bloom season shown in the climate table is based on reports from the habitat.

Plant and Flower Information

PLANT SIZE AND TYPE: A 6 in. (16 cm) sympodial epiphyte.

PSEUDOBULB: 2 in. (5 cm) long. The short, swollen pseudobulbs taper at both ends. When not in flower, *D. carronii* is difficult to differentiate from *D. canaliculatum* R. Brown.

LEAVES: 2–4 per growth. The often purplish leaves are 3–4 in. (8–12 cm) long, thick, and semicylindrical.

INFLORESCENCE: 8 in. (20 cm) long. Inflorescences emerge near the apex of the pseudobulb. Each growth produces 1–3 flower spikes.

FLOWERS: 2–12 per inflorescence. The flowers are 0.8 in. (2 cm) long. Sepals may be white to greenish often suffused with pink or purple. The petals, which are dark brown to purple with white at the base, are occasionally twisted. The yellow to greenish lip is 3-lobed with 3 raised keels and a pointed midlobe. The column is purple. The fragrant blossoms last about 3 weeks.

HYBRIDIZING NOTES: When used as a parent, the plant size of *D. carronii* is usually dominant.

REFERENCES: 67, 84, 234, 240, 261, 262, 526, 533.

PHOTOS/DRAWINGS: *84*, 240, 261, *262, 533*.

Dendrobium carstensziense J. J. Smith. Sometimes spelled *D. carstenziense*, see *D. cuthbertsonii* F. Mueller. REFERENCES: 224, 385.

Dendrobium carunculosum Gagnepain. Now considered a synonym of *Eria carunculoa* (Gagnepain) Seidenfaden ex Averyanov. REFERENCES: 137, 227, 448, Seidenfaden 1992 *Opera Botanica* #114.

Dendrobium caryaecolum Guillaumin

AKA: Sometimes spelled *D. caryicola* or *D. caryaecolon*.

ORIGIN/HABITAT: Vietnam. Plants were originally collected near Dalat from *Carya arborea* trees along the road between Ho Chi Minh City (formerly Saigon) and Dalat. Plants were found 87 miles (140 km) from Ho Chi Minh City. Based on topographical maps of the region, we have estimated the habitat elevation at 1500 ft. (460 m), but the following temperatures should be used with caution.

CLIMATE: Station #48881, Dalat, Vietnam, Lat. 11.1°N, Long. 108.1°E, at 3156 ft. (962 m). Temperatures are calculated for an elevation of 1500 ft. (460 m), resulting in probable extremes of 98°F (37°C) and 48°F (9°C).

N/HEMISPHERE	JAN	FEB	MAR	APR	MAY	JUN	JUL	AUG	SEP	OCT	NOV	DEC
°F AVG MAX	85	87	89	90	89	86	86	85	85	85	84	84
°F AVG MIN	61	62	64	67	70	70	70	70	70	68	65	63
DIURNAL RANGE	24	25	25	23	19	16	16	15	15	17	19	21
RAIN/INCHES	0.2	0.9	1.6	4.6	9.1	6.1	7.7	8.2	10.1	9.7	2.7	1.3
HUMIDITY/%	68	64	65	71	78	81	82	83	84	82	76	73
BLOOM SEASON	N/A											
DAYS CLR @ 7AM	13	13	13	9	5	3	2	2	2	5	7	10
DAYS CLR @ 1PM	8	8	8	2	0	0	0	0	0	1	3	4
RAIN/MM	5	23	41	117	231	155	196	208	257	246	69	33
°C AVG MAX	29.7	30.8	31.9	32.5	31.9	30.3	30.3	29.7	29.7	29.7	29.1	29.1
°C AVG MIN	16.4	16.9	18.0	19.7	21.4	21.4	21.4	21.4	21.4	20.3	18.6	17.5
DIURNAL RANGE	13.3	13.9	13.9	12.8	10.5	8.9	8.9	8.3	8.3	9.4	10.5	11.6
S/HEMISPHERE	JUL	AUG	SEP	OCT	NOV	DEC	JAN	FEB	MAR	APR	MAY	JUN

Cultural Recommendations

LIGHT: 2000–3000 fc. The deciduous forest and semishade habitats indicate that summer light should be low, but optimal cultivation levels are unknown.

TEMPERATURES: Summer days average 85–86°F (30°C), and nights average 70°F (21°C), with a diurnal range of 15–16°F (8–9°C). The warmest temperatures occur in late winter and spring. Days average 89–90°F (32–33°C), nights average 64–70°F (18–21°C), with a diurnal range of 19–25°F (11–14°C).

HUMIDITY: 80–85% in summer, dropping to near 65% in late winter.

WATER: Rainfall is moderate to heavy in summer but is very light for 2 months in winter. Cultivated plants should be kept moist while growing, but water should be gradually reduced after new growths mature in autumn.

FERTILIZER: ¼–½ recommended strength, applied weekly. A high-nitrogen fertilizer is beneficial from spring to midsummer, but a fertilizer high in phosphates should be used in late summer and autumn.

REST PERIOD: Winter days average 84–87°F (29–31°C), and nights average 61–63°F (16–18°C), with a diurnal range of 21–25°F (12–14°C). The increased diurnal range results from warmer days and cooler nights. Rainfall is low for 3–4 months in winter; and for 1–2 months, conditions are so dry that even moisture from dew is uncommon. For cultivated plants, water and fertilizer should be reduced for 2–3 months. Plants should be allowed to dry out between waterings, but they should not remain dry for extended periods. In the habitat, light is highest in winter.

GROWING MEDIA: Plants may be mounted on tree-fern or cork slabs or potted in small pots filled with any open, fast-draining medium. Repotting is best done in early spring when new roots are growing.

Plant and Flower Information

PLANT SIZE AND TYPE: A 12 in. (30 cm) sympodial epiphyte.

PSEUDOBULB: 12 in. (30 cm) long. The erect stems are somewhat zigzag and very slender.

LEAVES: The lanceolate leaves are 2.8 in. (7 cm) long.

INFLORESCENCE: Inflorescences are borne on leafless stems.

FLOWERS: 1–2 per inflorescence. The flowers are 0.8 in. (2 cm) across. The lanceolate sepals and petals are white and pointed at the tip. The ovate lip, which is pale yellow with rose markings, is usually inflexed along the margin.

REFERENCES: 163, 228, 448.

Dendrobium cassythoides A. Cunningham. Now considered a synonym of *Erythrorchis cassythoides*. REFERENCES: 67, 190, 216, 254.

Dendrobium castum Bateman. See *D. moniliforme* (Linn.) Swartz. REFERENCES: 139, 216, 254.

Dendrobium casuarinae Schlechter. See *D. sylvanum* Rchb. f. REFERENCES: 173, 222.

Dendrobium catenatum Lindley. See *D. moniliforme* (Linn.) Swartz. REFERENCES: 139, 190, 208, 216, 254.

Dendrobium cathcartii Hooker f.

ORIGIN/HABITAT: Endemic to northeastern India. Plants grow in Orissa and tropical valleys of the Sikkim region, usually at 2000–2600 ft. (610–790 m).

CLIMATE: Station #42398, Baghdogra, India, Lat. 26.7°N, Long. 88.3°E, at 412 ft. (126 m). Temperatures have been calculated for a habitat elevation of 2000 ft. (610 m), resulting in probable extremes of 99°F (37°C) and 31°F (−1°C).

N/HEMISPHERE	JAN	FEB	MAR	APR	MAY	JUN	JUL	AUG	SEP	OCT	NOV	DEC
°F AVG MAX	69	72	80	85	85	84	84	84	83	82	77	72
°F AVG MIN	45	49	55	63	68	71	72	72	71	65	55	48
DIURNAL RANGE	24	23	25	22	17	13	12	12	12	17	22	24
RAIN/INCHES	0.3	0.7	1.3	3.7	11.8	25.9	32.2	25.3	21.2	5.6	0.5	0.2
HUMIDITY/%	73	68	57	58	74	84	86	85	85	79	75	76
BLOOM SEASON				*	**	**	*	*	*	*	*	*
DAYS CLR @ 6AM	21	18	15	11	5	0	1	1	4	13	23	19
DAYS CLR @ 12PM	23	16	16	11	2	2	0	1	2	10	21	18
RAIN/MM	8	18	33	94	300	658	818	643	538	142	13	5
°C AVG MAX	20.4	22.1	26.5	29.3	29.3	28.8	28.8	28.8	28.2	27.6	24.9	22.1
°C AVG MIN	7.1	9.3	12.6	17.1	19.9	21.5	22.1	22.1	21.5	18.2	12.6	8.8
DIURNAL RANGE	13.3	12.8	13.9	12.2	9.4	7.3	6.7	6.7	6.7	9.4	12.3	13.3
S/HEMISPHERE	JUL	AUG	SEP	OCT	NOV	DEC	JAN	FEB	MAR	APR	MAY	JUN

Cultural Recommendations

LIGHT: 2500–3500 fc. Light levels are lower in summer because of heavy cloud cover.

TEMPERATURES: Summer days average 84°F (29°C), and nights average 71–72°F (22°C), with a diurnal range of 12–13°F (7°C).

HUMIDITY: Near 85% in summer. Averages decrease to 75–80% in autumn, then drop to near 60% in late winter and early spring.

WATER: Conditions are very wet for 5 months in summer and very dry for 5 months in winter, with short transition periods in autumn and spring. Cultivated plants should be kept evenly moist from spring to early autumn, but water should be gradually reduced after new growths mature in late autumn.

FERTILIZER: ¼–½ recommended strength, applied weekly. A high-nitrogen fertilizer is beneficial from spring to midsummer, but a fertilizer high in phosphates should be used in late summer and autumn. Summer growth should be rapid to improve flowering the following year.

REST PERIOD: Winter days average 69–72°F (20–22°C), and nights average 45–49°F (7–9°C), with a diurnal range of 23–25°F (13–14°C). Cultivated plants need at least a short, cool, dry rest with reduced fertilizer. In the habitat, winter rainfall is low but additional moisture is often available from heavy deposits of dew. For about a month in late winter or early spring, however, humidity is so low that even the moisture from dew is uncommon. Cultivated plants should be allowed to dry out between waterings in winter, but they should not remain dry for extended periods. Occasional early morning mistings between waterings, especially on warm, sunny days, may help prevent the plants from becoming too dry. Fertilizer should be eliminated until water is increased in spring. In the habitat, light is highest in winter. The cool, dry rest with increased light may be necessary to initiate blooming.

GROWING MEDIA: Plants may be mounted on tree-fern or cork slabs if humidity is high and plants are watered at least once daily in summer. When plants are potted, any open, fast-draining medium may be used. Repotting is best done in early spring when new roots are growing.

MISCELLANEOUS NOTES: The bloom season shown in the climate table is based on cultivation records.

Plant and Flower Information

PLANT SIZE AND TYPE: A 12–30 in. (30–75 cm) sympodial epiphyte.

PSEUDOBULB: 12–24 in. (30–60 cm) long. Stems are swollen at each internode.

LEAVES: Many, particularly near the apex. The linear-lanceolate leaves are usually 4–6 in. (10–15 cm) long.

INFLORESCENCE: Short. Inflorescences emerge from the middle of the internodes opposite the leaves along the leafy portion of the stem.

FLOWERS: 2 per inflorescence. The flowers are 1 in. (2.5 cm) long. The ovate-lanceolate sepals and narrower petals are golden yellow. The elliptic-oblong, decurved lip has purple markings. All segments are pointed.

HYBRIDIZING NOTES: Chromosome count is n = 19 (ref. 504, 542, 580).

REFERENCES: 38, 46, 179, 202, 218, 254, 369, 376, 445, 448, 454, 504, 542, 580.

PHOTOS/DRAWINGS: 46, *369*.

Dendrobium catillare Rchb. f.

AKA: In 1993 Dauncey and Cribb in *Kew Bulletin* 48(3) included *D. glossotis* Rchb. f. and *D. sertatum* Rolfe as synonyms.

ORIGIN/HABITAT: Endemic to dense forests in the Fiji Islands, including Viti Levu, Kandavu, Vanua Levu, Taveuni, and Yathata. Although *D.*

catillare is found from 100–4900 ft. (35–1500 m), it usually grows at the higher elevations, frequently close to lakes or swamps.

CLIMATE: Station #91683, Nausori, Vitu Levu, Fiji, Is., Lat. 18.1°S, Long. 178.6°E at 19 ft. (6 m). Temperatures are calculated for an elevation of 2700 ft. (820 m), resulting in probable extremes of 89°F (32°C) and 46°F (8°C).

N/HEMISPHERE	JAN	FEB	MAR	APR	MAY	JUN	JUL	AUG	SEP	OCT	NOV	DEC
°F AVG MAX	70	70	71	72	74	76	77	77	77	75	73	71
°F AVG MIN	59	59	60	61	62	64	65	65	65	64	62	60
DIURNAL RANGE	11	11	11	11	12	12	12	12	12	11	11	11
RAIN/INCHES	4.9	8.3	7.7	8.3	9.8	12.5	11.4	10.7	14.5	12.2	10.1	6.7
HUMIDITY/%	77	77	76	75	75	76	76	78	79	79	81	78
BLOOM SEASON	*		*			*		*		*		*
DAYS CLR @ 12PM	3	1	0	0	1	1	2	0	0	0	1	0
RAIN/MM	124	211	196	211	249	318	290	272	368	310	257	170
°C AVG MAX	21.2	21.2	21.8	22.3	23.4	24.5	25.1	25.1	25.1	24.0	22.9	21.8
°C AVG MIN	15.1	15.1	15.6	16.2	16.8	17.9	18.4	18.4	18.4	17.9	16.8	15.6
DIURNAL RANGE	6.1	6.1	6.2	6.1	6.6	6.6	6.7	6.7	6.7	6.1	6.1	6.2
S/HEMISPHERE	JUL	AUG	SEP	OCT	NOV	DEC	JAN	FEB	MAR	APR	MAY	JUN

Cultural Recommendations

LIGHT: 2000–3000 fc.

TEMPERATURES: Summer days average 76–77°F (25°C), and nights average 64–65°F (18°C), with a diurnal range of 12°F (7°C).

HUMIDITY: 75–80% year-round.

WATER: Rainfall is moderate to heavy all year. Cultivated plants should be kept moist and never be allowed to dry completely.

FERTILIZER: ¼–½ recommended strength. A balanced fertilizer should be applied weekly to biweekly throughout the year.

REST PERIOD: Winter days average 70–71°F (21–22°C), and nights average 59–60°F (15–16°C), with a diurnal range of 11°F (6°C). Seasonal temperature variation is minor. Winter rainfall is high, but water should be reduced somewhat for cultivated plants, especially those grown in the dark, short-day conditions common in temperate-latitude winters. Plants should never be allowed to dry completely, however. Fertilizer should be reduced or eliminated anytime water is reduced.

GROWING MEDIA: Plants may be mounted on tree-fern or cork slabs if humidity is high and plants are watered at least once daily in summer. When plants are potted, any open, fast-draining medium may be used. Repotting is best done in early spring when new roots are growing.

MISCELLANEOUS NOTES: The bloom season shown in the climate table is based on reports from the habitat. Blooming occurs intermittently any time of year, but fruits are always present in late spring–early summer.

Plant and Flower Information

PLANT SIZE AND TYPE: An 8–39 in. (20–100 cm) sympodial epiphyte.

PSEUDOBULB: 4–18 in. (10–45 cm) long. The slender, yellow pseudobulbs, which are closely spaced, arise from a very short rhizome. They are cylindrical, pendulous, curving, and somewhat swollen at the base.

LEAVES: Several, near the apex of each growth. The lanceolate leaves are 2.5–6.3 in. (6.5–16.0 cm) long, erect-spreading, and somewhat leathery.

INFLORESCENCE: 0.6 in. (1.5 cm) long. Inflorescences normally emerge from axils near the apex of older, leafless stems, but they occasionally develop on leafy stems. The bracts on the inflorescence are narrowly triangular and obscurely spotted.

FLOWERS: 10–25 per inflorescence. Blossoms are white often with a pink tinge on the mentum. They are occasionally bright pink with white at the tips of the segments. The flowers are 1 in. (2.5 cm) across when spread, but individual blossoms normally remain rather closed. The dorsal sepal and petals tend to be somewhat recurved. The margin of the petals are slightly uneven. The transverse callus points to the claw. The lip is contracted below the midpoint. The inconspicuous sidelobes are often toothed along the margin, but this is an inconsistent characteristic. The curved ovary has wings formed by the valvae.

REFERENCES: 216, 226, 252, 254, 353, 466.

PHOTOS/DRAWINGS: 42, 466.

Dendrobium caudatum Teijsm. and Binn.

D. caudatum var. *javanica* Teijsm. and Binn. is now considered a synonym of *D. acuminatissimum* (Blume) Lindley. *D. caudatum* originated in Sumatra. Additional plant and habitat information was unavailable. REFERENCES: 216, 254, 469.

Dendrobium cavipes J. J. Smith

ORIGIN/HABITAT: Irian Jaya (western New Guinea). A collection was reported near Wespen Creek at about Lat. 4.5°S and Long. 138.5°E. Plants grow on trees in primary forests. Habitat elevation was not reported. Topographical maps for this vicinity indicate that elevation is about 2000 ft. (610 m), but the following climate data should be used with caution.

CLIMATE: Station #97796, Kokenau (Kokonau), Irian Jaya, Lat. 4.7°S, Long. 136.4°E, at 10 ft. (3 m). Temperatures are calculated for an elevation of 2000 ft. (610 m). Record extreme temperatures are not available for this location.

N/HEMISPHERE	JAN	FEB	MAR	APR	MAY	JUN	JUL	AUG	SEP	OCT	NOV	DEC
°F AVG MAX	76	76	79	81	83	82	82	82	83	81	80	77
°F AVG MIN	66	66	67	67	67	68	67	67	67	67	67	66
DIURNAL RANGE	10	10	12	14	16	14	15	15	16	14	13	11
RAIN/INCHES	18.4	15.8	18.9	11.6	9.7	10.6	11.5	15.7	11.6	11.6	16.0	19.9
HUMIDITY/%	N/A											
BLOOM SEASON	*											
DAYS CLR	N/A											
RAIN/MM	467	401	480	295	246	269	292	399	295	295	406	505
°C AVG MAX	24.7	24.7	26.4	27.5	28.6	28.0	28.0	28.0	28.6	27.5	26.9	25.2
°C AVG MIN	19.1	19.1	19.7	19.7	19.7	20.2	19.7	19.7	19.7	19.7	19.7	19.1
DIURNAL RANGE	5.6	5.6	6.7	7.8	8.9	7.8	8.3	8.3	8.9	7.8	7.2	6.1
S/HEMISPHERE	JUL	AUG	SEP	OCT	NOV	DEC	JAN	FEB	MAR	APR	MAY	JUN

Cultural Recommendations

LIGHT: 2500–3500 fc.

TEMPERATURES: Throughout the year, days average 76–83°F (25–29°C), with the coolest days in winter. Nights average 66–68°F (19–20°C), with a diurnal range of 10–16°F (6–9°C).

HUMIDITY: Information is not available for this station. However, records from nearby locations indicate that humidity probably averages near 85% year-round.

WATER: Rainfall is very heavy year-round. Cultivated plants should be kept evenly moist but not soggy.

FERTILIZER: ¼–½ recommended strength. A balanced fertilizer should be applied weekly to biweekly throughout the year.

REST PERIOD: Growing conditions should be maintained year-round. Water and fertilizer might be reduced slightly in winter, especially for plants cultivated in the dark, short-day conditions common in temperate latitudes; but plants should never be allowed to dry out completely. In the habitat, seasonal light variation is minor.

GROWING MEDIA: Because plants must be kept moist, they are easier to manage when potted. Fir bark or any open, fast-draining medium may be used. Repotting may be done anytime new roots are growing.

MISCELLANEOUS NOTES: The bloom season shown in the climate table is based on reports from the habitat. The plant was described in 1908 in *Bul. Dép. Agric. Indes Néerl.* 9:18.

Dendrobium cedricola

Plant and Flower Information

PLANT SIZE AND TYPE: A 14 in. (35 cm) sympodial epiphyte.

PSEUDOBULB: 12 in. (30 cm) long. The pseudobulbs, which are very close together, have nodes every 0.5 in. (1.3 cm).

LEAVES: Many. The lanceolate leaves are 2.8–3.2 in. (7–8 cm) long. The stems are leafy.

INFLORESCENCE: Short.

FLOWERS: 2–4 per inflorescence. The fleshy flowers are 0.6 in. (1.6 cm) across. The sepals and petals are white. The lip, which is rose with yellow hairs, is somewhat scaly or grainy on the backside.

REFERENCES: 220, 254, 437, 445, 470.

Dendrobium cedricola P. van Royen. See *D. dekockii* J. J. Smith. REFERENCES: 233, 385, 538. PHOTOS/DRAWINGS: 538.

Dendrobium celebense J. J. Smith. Transferred to *Ephemerantha celebensis* (J. J. Smith) P. F. Hunt and Summerhayes, which is now considered a synonym of the genus *Flickingeria*. REFERENCES: 213, 220, 230, 436.

Dendrobium celebicum A. Hawkes. Considered a synonym of *D. amabile* Schlechter, which is now considered a synonym of *D. furcatum* Reinwardt ex Lindley. REFERENCES: 230.

Dendrobium cellulosum J. J. Smith. See *D. sulphureum* Schlechter. REFERENCES: 224, 385, 445.

Dendrobium centrale J. J. Smith. Now considered a synonym of *Diplocaulobium centrale* (J. J. Smith) P. F. Hunt and Summerhayes. REFERENCES: 213, 221, 224, 230, 445, 470, 486.

Dendrobium ceraceum Schlechter

ORIGIN/HABITAT: Papua New Guinea. Plants grow in the Sepik River region at 650–1000 ft. (200–300 m).

CLIMATE: Station #200004, Ambunti, Papua New Guinea, Lat. 4.2°S, Long. 142.8°E, at 164 ft. (50 m). Temperatures are calculated for an elevation of 1000 ft. (300 m), resulting in probable extremes of 96°F (36°C) and 49°F (10°C).

N/HEMISPHERE	JAN	FEB	MAR	APR	MAY	JUN	JUL	AUG	SEP	OCT	NOV	DEC
°F AVG MAX	85	87	87	87	88	87	87	87	87	87	87	86
°F AVG MIN	69	70	71	70	70	70	69	70	70	70	70	71
DIURNAL RANGE	16	17	16	17	18	17	18	17	17	17	17	15
RAIN/INCHES	6.4	7.4	7.7	8.5	9.2	9.4	10.9	10.2	12.2	10.4	8.3	5.2
HUMIDITY/%	N/A											
BLOOM SEASON			*									
DAYS CLR	N/A											
RAIN/MM	163	188	196	216	234	239	277	259	310	264	211	132
°C AVG MAX	29.6	30.7	30.7	30.7	31.2	30.7	30.7	30.7	30.7	30.7	30.7	30.1
°C AVG MIN	20.7	21.2	21.8	21.2	21.2	21.2	20.7	21.2	21.2	21.2	21.2	21.8
DIURNAL RANGE	8.9	9.5	8.9	9.5	10.0	9.5	10.0	9.5	9.5	9.5	9.5	8.3
S/HEMISPHERE	JUL	AUG	SEP	OCT	NOV	DEC	JAN	FEB	MAR	APR	MAY	JUN

Cultural Recommendations

LIGHT: 2000–3000 fc.

TEMPERATURES: Throughout the year, days average 85–88°F (30–31°C), and nights average 69–71°F (21–22°C), with a diurnal range of 15–18°F (8–10°C).

HUMIDITY: Information is not available at this location. However, records from other stations in the region indicate that averages are probably near 80% year-round.

WATER: Rainfall is heavy all year, with the greatest amounts falling in summer and early autumn. Cultivated plants should be kept moist but not soggy.

FERTILIZER: ¼–½ recommended strength. A balanced fertilizer should be applied weekly to biweekly throughout the year.

REST PERIOD: Growing conditions should be maintained all year. Water and fertilizer should be reduced for plants cultivated in the dark, short-day conditions common in temperate-latitude winters, but plants should never be allowed to dry completely between waterings. In the habitat, seasonal light variation is minor.

GROWING MEDIA: Plants may be mounted on cork or tree-fern slabs if humidity is high and plants are watered at least once daily in summer. When plants are potted, any open, fast-draining medium may be used, but fir bark is preferred by most growers. Repotting may be done anytime new roots are growing.

MISCELLANEOUS NOTES: The bloom season shown in the climate table is based on collection reports.

Plant and Flower Information

PLANT SIZE AND TYPE: An 18–24 in. (45–60 cm) sympodial epiphyte.

PSEUDOBULB: 18–24 in. (45–60 cm) long. The numerous spreading stems emerge from a very short rhizome.

LEAVES: Many. The lanceolate leaves are 2.4–3.6 in. (6–9 cm) long, pointed at the base, and rounded at the apex.

INFLORESCENCE: Short.

FLOWERS: 4–6 per inflorescence. The waxy flowers are white with brown scales on the backside. The sepals are 0.5 in. (1.3 cm) long. The rounded lip is oblong to ovate with a toothed or lacerated margin and small sidelobes.

REFERENCES: 223, 443.

Dendrobium ceraia Lindley. See *D. crumenatum* Swartz. REFERENCES: 67, 208, 216, 414, 454.

Dendrobium cerasinum Ridley. See *D. puniceum* Ridley. REFERENCES: 218, 254, 385, 393.

Dendrobium ceratostyloides J. J. Smith. Now considered a synonym of *Cadetia ceratostyloides* (J. J. Smith) Schlechter. REFERENCES: 220, 254, 437, 445, 470, 516.

Dendrobium ceraula Rchb. f.

ORIGIN/HABITAT: Luzon Island in the Philippines. Habitat location and elevation are unavailable, so the following climate data should be used with extreme caution.

CLIMATE: Station #98427, Manila, Philippines, Lat. 14.5°N, Long. 121.0°E, at 74 ft. (23 m). Record extreme temperatures are 101°F (38°C) and 58°F (14°C).

N/HEMISPHERE	JAN	FEB	MAR	APR	MAY	JUN	JUL	AUG	SEP	OCT	NOV	DEC
°F AVG MAX	86	88	91	93	93	91	88	87	88	88	87	86
°F AVG MIN	69	69	71	73	75	75	75	75	75	74	72	70
DIURNAL RANGE	17	19	20	20	18	16	13	12	13	14	15	16
RAIN/INCHES	0.9	0.5	0.7	1.3	5.1	10.0	17.0	16.6	14.0	7.6	5.7	2.6
HUMIDITY/%	77	73	70	68	71	81	84	86	87	84	82	89
BLOOM SEASON	N/A											
DAYS CLR @ 8AM	6	9	14	14	10	3	2	1	1	6	7	6
DAYS CLR @ 2PM	3	6	10	10	8	2	1	1	0	2	2	3
RAIN/MM	23	13	18	33	130	254	432	422	356	193	145	66
°C AVG MAX	30.0	31.1	32.8	33.9	33.9	32.8	31.1	30.6	31.1	31.1	30.6	30.0
°C AVG MIN	20.6	20.6	21.7	22.8	23.9	23.9	23.9	23.9	23.9	23.3	22.2	21.1
DIURNAL RANGE	9.4	10.5	11.1	11.1	10.0	8.9	7.2	6.7	7.2	7.8	8.4	8.9
S/HEMISPHERE	JUL	AUG	SEP	OCT	NOV	DEC	JAN	FEB	MAR	APR	MAY	JUN

Cultural Recommendations

LIGHT: 2000–3000 fc.

TEMPERATURES: Throughout the year, days average 86–93°F (30–34°C), and nights average 69–75°F (21–24°C), with a diurnal range of 12–20°F (7–11°C).

HUMIDITY: 80–85% in summer and autumn, dropping to 70–75% in winter and spring.

WATER: Rainfall is heavy from late spring through autumn, but conditions are dry for 3–4 months in winter. Cultivated plants should be kept moist while actively growing, but water should be gradually reduced in late autumn.

FERTILIZER: ¼–½ recommended strength. A balanced fertilizer should be applied weekly to biweekly throughout the year.

REST PERIOD: Growing temperatures should be maintained all year. Rainfall is low for 3–4 months in winter, but additional moisture is available from frequent heavy dew. In cultivation, water should be reduced and the plants allowed to dry out between waterings, but they should not remain dry for extended periods. Fertilizer should also be reduced or eliminated anytime water is reduced. In the habitat, light is highest in winter.

GROWING MEDIA: Mounting plants on tree-fern or cork slabs accommodates their pendent growth habit, but humidity must be high and the plants watered at least once daily in summer. Plants may be placed in hanging pots or baskets filled with any open, fast-draining medium. Repotting may be done anytime new roots are growing.

Plant and Flower Information

PLANT SIZE AND TYPE: An 11 in. (28 cm) long sympodial epiphyte.

PSEUDOBULB: 8 in. (20 cm) long. The densely leafy stems are slender and pendent.

LEAVES: Many. The lanceolate leaves, which have 3 fine teeth at the apex, are usually 3 in. (8 cm) long.

INFLORESCENCE: Short.

FLOWERS: 2 per inflorescence. The white flowers are 2 in. (5 cm) across. Lateral sepals are shorter than the dorsal sepal or petals. Segments are lanceolate, pointed, and curved. The lip is oblong to lanceolate with a small horned callus on both sides of the base.

REFERENCES: 12, 216, 254, 296, 536.

Dendrobium cerinum Rchb. f. not Schlechter. See *D. sanguinolentum* Lindley. REFERENCES: 12, 75, 200, 216, 254, 373, 454, 536. PHOTOS/DRAWINGS: *373.*

Dendrobium cerinum Schlechter not Rchb. f. See *D. austrocaledonicum* Schlechter. REFERENCES: 173, 211, 220, 254, 270, 271, 432.

Dendrobium cervicaliferum J. J. Smith. Now considered a synonym of *Diplocaulobium cervicaliferum* (J. J. Smith) Hunt and Summerhayes. REFERENCES: 213, 221, 230, 470, 475.

Dendrobium chalandei (A. Finet) Kränzlin. See *D. bowmanii* Bentham. REFERENCES: 67, 173, 220, 254. PHOTOS/DRAWINGS: *173.*

Dendrobium chalmersii F. Mueller. See *D. cincinnatum* F. Mueller. REFERENCES: 216, 254, 348, 437.

Dendrobium chamaephytum Schlechter. Now considered a synonym of *Cadetia chamaephyta* Schlechter. REFERENCES: 92, 219, 221, 254, 400, 437, 444, 445, 470, 486, 538. PHOTOS/DRAWINGS: *538.*

Dendrobium chameleon Ames

AKA: *D. longicalcaratum* Hayata, *D. randaiense* Hayata.

ORIGIN/HABITAT: The Philippines and Taiwan. In the Philippines, plants grow on Luzon Island. They are found near Baguio in Benguet Province, near Floridablanca in Pampanga Province, and in Laguna and Sorsogon Provinces. Plants grow on rocks, tree ferns, and tree trunks, or hang from tree branches in moist, shady areas of broadleaf forests at 1950–3300 ft. (600–1000 m). On Taiwan, plants are found in the northern mountains.

CLIMATE: Station #98327, Clark Air Base, Philippines, Lat. 15.2°N, Long. 120.6°E, at 478 ft. (146 m). Temperatures are calculated for an elevation of 3000 ft. (910 m), resulting in probable extremes of 91°F (33°C) and 53°F (12°C).

N/HEMISPHERE	JAN	FEB	MAR	APR	MAY	JUN	JUL	AUG	SEP	OCT	NOV	DEC
°F AVG MAX	77	79	82	84	84	81	79	78	78	79	78	77
°F AVG MIN	62	62	65	67	68	67	66	66	66	66	65	63
DIURNAL RANGE	15	17	17	17	16	14	13	12	12	13	13	14
RAIN/INCHES	0.8	0.7	0.9	1.5	3.9	10.8	12.6	16.1	13.1	4.9	2.0	0.9
HUMIDITY/%	67	65	64	63	68	79	81	83	84	76	72	70
BLOOM SEASON							*	*	*	*		
DAYS CLR @ 8AM	5	5	7	9	6	1	0	0	0	3	3	4
DAYS CLR @ 2PM	2	1	2	2	1	0	0	0	0	1	1	1
RAIN/MM	20	18	23	38	99	274	320	409	333	124	51	23
°C AVG MAX	24.8	25.9	27.6	28.7	28.7	27.0	25.9	25.4	25.4	25.9	25.4	24.8
°C AVG MIN	16.5	16.5	18.2	19.3	19.8	19.3	18.7	18.7	18.7	18.7	18.2	17.0
DIURNAL RANGE	8.3	9.4	9.4	9.4	8.9	7.7	7.2	6.7	6.7	7.2	7.2	7.8
S/HEMISPHERE	JUL	AUG	SEP	OCT	NOV	DEC	JAN	FEB	MAR	APR	MAY	JUN

Cultural Recommendations

LIGHT: 1800–2500 fc.

TEMPERATURES: Throughout the year, days average 77–84°F (25–29°C), and nights average 62–68°F (17–20°C), with a diurnal range of 12–17°F (7–9°C). The warmest temperatures occur in spring, before the rainy season starts.

HUMIDITY: 80–85% in summer. Humidity decreases to 70–75% in autumn and to near 65% in winter and spring.

WATER: Rainfall is heavy for 4 months in summer, but conditions are dry in winter. Cultivated plants should be kept moist from late spring to early autumn, but water should be gradually reduced after new growths mature.

FERTILIZER: ¼–½ recommended strength, applied weekly. A high-nitrogen fertilizer is beneficial from spring to midsummer, but a fertilizer high in phosphates should be used in late summer and autumn.

REST PERIOD: Growing temperatures should be maintained all year. For 4 months in winter, rainfall averages are low, and even moisture from dew is uncommon. Cultivated plants should be allowed to dry out between waterings in winter, but they should not remain dry for extended periods. Fertilizer should be reduced or eliminated until water is increased in spring. In the habitat, light is highest in winter.

GROWING MEDIA: Mounting plants on cork or tree-fern slabs accommodates their pendent growth habit. Humidity should be high and water should be applied daily in summer. If plants are potted, a hanging basket filled with a rapidly draining medium is recommended. Repotting is best done in early spring when new roots begin growing.

MISCELLANEOUS NOTES: The bloom season shown in the climate table is based on cultivation records. In the habitat, flowering is heaviest in autumn and winter.

Plant and Flower Information

PLANT SIZE AND TYPE: A 16–25 in. (40–64 cm) sympodial epiphyte or lithophyte. Plants may reach a length of 72 in. (183 cm).

PSEUDOBULB: 16–25 in. (40–64 cm) long. Stems are somewhat canelike, branching, and thickened at the apex. They are commonly pendent or cascading.

Dendrobium changjiangense

LEAVES: Many. The ovate leaves, which are 1.2–2.4 in. (3–6 cm) long, are arranged in two rows. The leaves remain evergreen through blooming.

INFLORESCENCE: Each plant produces many inflorescences. The racemes emerge from opposite the leaf bracts on the upper nodes of the stem. At the base of the inflorescence is a branch which bears a leafy stem.

FLOWERS: 1–4 per inflorescence. The flowers are 1.2–1.6 in. (3–4 cm) across. The pointed sepals, incurved petals, and spoonlike lip are white, sometimes with a slight lavender tinge, purplish veins, or pink stripes. The blossoms quickly turn yellow.

HYBRIDIZING NOTES: Chromosome count is 2n = 38 (ref. 152, 280, 504, 580) as *D. chameleon* and as *D. longicalcaratum*.

REFERENCES: 12, 18, 62, 98, 152, 193, 208, 220, 254, 279, 280, 296, 373, 445, 497, 504, 528, 536, 580.

PHOTOS/DRAWINGS: 12, 279, *373*, 497, *536*.

Dendrobium changjiangense S. J. Cheng and C. Z. Tang

AKA: Seidenfaden (ref. 454) indicates that this species was previously included with *D. concinnum* Miquel.

ORIGIN/HABITAT: Endemic to Hainan Island, China. Plants are found at about 3300 ft. (1000 m).

CLIMATE: Station #59849, Yinggen, Hainan Island, China, Lat. 19.1°N, Long. 109.9°E, at 797 ft. (243 m). Average temperatures are calculated for an elevation of 2600 ft. (800 m). Record extreme temperatures are not available for this location.

N/HEMISPHERE	JAN	FEB	MAR	APR	MAY	JUN	JUL	AUG	SEP	OCT	NOV	DEC
°F AVG MAX	64	68	74	78	81	82	83	81	78	75	69	64
°F AVG MIN	50	54	57	62	65	67	67	67	65	62	57	50
DIURNAL RANGE	14	14	17	16	16	15	16	14	13	13	12	14
RAIN/INCHES	1.9	1.4	1.7	5.1	7.6	7.0	6.8	9.7	15.1	19.1	7.1	1.9
HUMIDITY/%	N/A											
BLOOM SEASON	N/A											
DAYS CLR	N/A											
RAIN/MM	48	36	43	130	193	178	173	246	384	485	180	48
°C AVG MAX	17.8	20.0	23.4	25.6	27.3	27.8	28.4	27.3	25.6	23.9	20.6	17.8
°C AVG MIN	10.0	12.3	13.9	16.7	18.4	19.5	19.5	19.5	18.4	16.7	13.9	10.0
DIURNAL RANGE	7.8	7.7	9.5	8.9	8.9	8.3	8.9	7.8	7.2	7.2	6.7	7.8
S/HEMISPHERE	JUL	AUG	SEP	OCT	NOV	DEC	JAN	FEB	MAR	APR	MAY	JUN

Cultural Recommendations

LIGHT: 2000–3000 fc.

TEMPERATURES: Summer days average 81–83°F (27–28°C), and nights average 67°F (20°C), with a diurnal range of 14–16°F (8–9°C).

HUMIDITY: Information is not available for this location. However, records from nearby stations indicate that humidity probably averages 80–85% from late spring into autumn, dropping to 70–75% from late autumn into spring.

WATER: Rainfall is heavy from spring through autumn, but conditions are dry for 4 months in winter. Cultivated plants should be kept moist from spring into autumn, but water should be reduced in late autumn.

FERTILIZER: ¼–½ recommended strength, applied weekly. A high nitrogen fertilizer is beneficial from spring to midsummer, but a fertilizer high in phosphates should be used in late summer and autumn.

REST PERIOD: Winter days average 64–68°F (18–20°C), and nights average 50–54°F (10–12°C), with a diurnal range of 14–17°F (8–10°C). While rainfall is lower in winter, additional water is available from heavy dew and overnight mist which are common during the season. Cultivated plants should be watered less frequently in winter. They should be allowed to dry slightly between waterings but should not dry out completely or remain dry for long periods.

GROWING MEDIA: Plants may be mounted on tree-fern or cork slabs if humidity is high and plants are watered at least once daily in summer. When plants are potted, any open, fast-draining medium may be used. Repotting is best done in early spring when new roots begin to grow.

Plant and Flower Information

PLANT SIZE AND TYPE: We have been unable to locate plant and flower descriptions in any language except Chinese, which we are unable to translate. The plant was considered for some time to be synonymous with *D. concinnum*, so information for that species should provide approximate information for *D. changjiangense*.

REFERENCES: 233, 454, 528.

Dendrobium cheesmanae Guillaumin. See *D. dactylodes* Rchb. f. and *D. involutum* Lindley. REFERENCES: 229, 270, 466.

Dendrobium chionanthum Schlechter. Now considered a synonym of *Cadetia chionantha* (Schlechter) Schlechter. REFERENCES: 92, 157, 219, 221, 254, 400, 437, 444.

Dendrobium chlorinum Ridley. See *D. masarangense* Schlechter. REFERENCES: 222, 385, 400.

Dendrobium chloroleucum Ridley. See *D. subflavidum* Ridley. REFERENCES: 200, 221, 402, 455.

Dendrobium chloroleucum Schlechter. See *D. otaguro-anum* A. Hawkes. REFERENCES: 83, 92, 221, 304, 437, 445.

Dendrobium chlorops Lindley. See *D. ovatum* (Linn.) Kränzlin. REFERENCES: 202, 216, 236, 254, 278, 317, 424, 445, 541, 570.

Dendrobium chloropterum Rchb. f. and S. Moore. See *D. bifalce* Lindley. REFERENCES: 67, 83, 105, 179, 190, 216, 254, 271, 437, 444, 445, 470, 516.

Dendrobium chlorostylum Gagnepain

AKA: In 1992 *Opera Botanica* 114, Seidenfaden suggests that this may have been a very desirable clone of *D. nobile* Lindley.

ORIGIN/HABITAT: Vietnam. Plants were originally found in northern Vietnam (Tonkin) in the vicinity of Cha Pa near the Chinese border. Habitat elevation is not available, so the following temperatures should be used with caution.

CLIMATE: Station #48802, Cha Pa, Vietnam, Lat. 22.3°N, Long. 103.8°E, at 5381 ft. (1640 m). Record extreme temperatures are 91°F (33°C) and 28°F (−2°C).

N/HEMISPHERE	JAN	FEB	MAR	APR	MAY	JUN	JUL	AUG	SEP	OCT	NOV	DEC
°F AVG MAX	52	54	65	70	73	73	74	73	72	66	63	57
°F AVG MIN	41	44	52	56	61	63	64	63	61	56	51	46
DIURNAL RANGE	11	10	13	14	12	10	10	10	11	10	12	11
RAIN/INCHES	1.6	2.8	4.7	7.0	14.6	14.0	18.9	18.9	12.6	7.5	4.7	1.6
HUMIDITY/%	86	92	86	82	85	88	88	89	87	93	90	88
BLOOM SEASON	N/A											
DAYS CLR @ 7AM	7	4	6	5	1	2	1	3	5	5	9	7
DAYS CLR @ 1PM	8	3	6	7	2	1	0	0	1	1	3	7
RAIN/MM	41	71	119	178	371	356	480	480	320	190	119	41
°C AVG MAX	11.1	12.2	18.3	21.1	22.8	22.8	23.3	22.8	22.2	18.9	17.2	13.9
°C AVG MIN	5.0	6.7	11.1	13.3	16.1	17.2	17.8	17.2	16.1	13.3	10.6	7.8
DIURNAL RANGE	6.1	5.5	7.2	7.8	6.7	5.6	5.5	5.6	6.1	5.6	6.6	6.1
S/HEMISPHERE	JUL	AUG	SEP	OCT	NOV	DEC	JAN	FEB	MAR	APR	MAY	JUN

Cultural Recommendations

LIGHT: 2400–3000 fc. Diffused light is suggested.

TEMPERATURES: Summer days average 73–74°F (23°C), and nights average 61–64°F (16–18°C), with a diurnal range of 10°F (6°C).

HUMIDITY: 85–90% year-round.

WATER: Rainfall is heavy from spring through autumn, followed by a 2–3 month relatively dry winter season. Cultivated plants should be constantly moist while actively growing, but water should be gradually reduced in autumn.

FERTILIZER: ¼–½ recommended strength, applied weekly. A high-nitrogen fertilizer is beneficial from spring to midsummer, but a fertilizer high in phosphates should be used in late summer and autumn.

REST PERIOD: For 2–3 months in winter, days average 52–57°F (11–14°C), and nights average 41–46°F (5–8°C), with a diurnal range of 10–11°F (6°C). Little change occurs in the diurnal range, as high and low temperatures decline simultaneously. In the habitat, light may be somewhat higher in winter. Although rainfall is low in winter, the unusually high winter humidity indicates additional moisture is available from frequent early morning dew, fog, and mist. In cultivation, water should be reduced and the plants allowed to dry somewhat between waterings, but they should never be allowed to dry out completely. Fertilizer should be reduced or eliminated when the plants are not actively growing.

GROWING MEDIA: Plants may be mounted on tree-fern or cork slabs if humidity is high and plants are watered at least once daily in summer. When plants are potted, any open, fast-draining medium may be used. Repotting is best done in early spring when new roots are growing.

Plant and Flower Information

PLANT SIZE AND TYPE: An 8–12 in. (20–30 cm) sympodial epiphyte.

PSEUDOBULB: 8–12 in. (20–30 cm) long. The club-shaped stems are slender at the base and thickened toward the apex.

LEAVES: The elongated leaves are 4.0–5.5 in. (10–14 cm) long. The base of the leaf attaches directly to the stem without a stalk.

INFLORESCENCE: 1.6–2.8 in. (4–7 cm) long. Inflorescences are borne laterally from nodes along leafy and leafless stems.

FLOWERS: 2–3 per inflorescence. The flowers are 2.8 in. (7 cm) across. Sepals and petals are white in the center with violet-purple at the tips. The intensely purple lip, which is marked with darker purple spots on the upper part of the throat, is 3-lobed with tiny white sidelobes and a large convoluted midlobe.

REFERENCES: 137, 227, 448.

Dendrobium chordiforme Kränzlin

ORIGIN/HABITAT: Papua New Guinea. Plants grow on trees in primary forests near Sattelberg. The habitat elevation is estimated at 4600 ft. (1400 m), so the following temperatures should be used with caution.

CLIMATE: Station #94014, Madang, Papua New Guinea, Lat. 5.2°S, Long. 145.8°E, at 13 ft. (4 m). Temperatures are calculated for an elevation of 4600 ft. (1400 m), resulting in probable extremes of 83°F (28°C) and 47°F (8°C).

N/HEMISPHERE	JAN	FEB	MAR	APR	MAY	JUN	JUL	AUG	SEP	OCT	NOV	DEC
°F AVG MAX	68	68	70	70	70	70	70	70	70	72	72	69
°F AVG MIN	62	63	63	63	62	62	62	62	62	61	62	63
DIURNAL RANGE	6	5	7	7	8	8	8	8	8	11	10	6
RAIN/INCHES	4.0	3.4	3.2	8.5	11.2	11.1	10.1	11.3	9.4	11.3	10.5	6.7
HUMIDITY/%	88	87	86	86	86	86	86	85	85	87	88	89
BLOOM SEASON	**											
DAYS CLR	N/A											
RAIN/MM	102	86	81	216	284	282	257	287	239	287	267	170
°C AVG MAX	19.9	19.9	21.0	21.0	21.0	21.0	21.0	21.0	21.0	22.1	22.1	20.5
°C AVG MIN	16.6	17.1	17.1	17.1	16.6	16.6	16.6	16.6	16.6	16.0	16.6	17.1
DIURNAL RANGE	3.3	2.8	3.9	3.9	4.4	4.4	4.4	4.4	4.4	6.1	5.5	3.4
S/HEMISPHERE	JUL	AUG	SEP	OCT	NOV	DEC	JAN	FEB	MAR	APR	MAY	JUN

Cultural Recommendations

LIGHT: 2500–3000 fc.

TEMPERATURES: Throughout the year, days average 68–72°F (20–22°C), and nights average 61–63°F (20–22°C), with a diurnal range of 5–11°F (3–6°C). The warmest highs, the coolest lows, and the greatest diurnal range occur in autumn. Growers indicate that plants are healthy with intermediate temperatures.

HUMIDITY: Near 85–90% year-round.

WATER: Rainfall is moderate to heavy all year. The driest conditions occur in late winter. Cultivated plants should be kept moist but not soggy.

FERTILIZER: ¼–½ recommended strength. A balanced fertilizer should be applied weekly to biweekly throughout the year.

REST PERIOD: Growing temperatures should be maintained all year. In the habitat, rainfall decreases for 4 months in winter. Water should be reduced for cultivated plants, but they should not be allowed to dry out completely. Fertilizer should be reduced or eliminated while water is reduced. In the habitat, light is slightly higher in late winter.

GROWING MEDIA: Plants may be mounted on tree-fern or cork slabs if humidity is high and plants are watered at least once daily in summer. When plants are potted, any open, fast-draining medium may be used. Repotting is best done in early spring when new roots are growing.

MISCELLANEOUS NOTES: The bloom season shown in the climate table is based on reports from the habitat.

Plant and Flower Information

PLANT SIZE AND TYPE: A sympodial epiphyte of unreported size.

PSEUDOBULB: Probably long. The stems are slender and elongated.

LEAVES: The terete leaves are usually about 12 in. (30 cm) long, but they are sometimes longer.

INFLORESCENCE: Blossoms are widely spaced on the inflorescence.

FLOWERS: Few per inflorescence. The widely spaced white flowers are 0.8 in. (2 cm) across. The dorsal sepal and petals are narrow, but the somewhat triangular lateral sepals are dilated at the base to form the mentum. The heart-shaped lip is decorated with wavy, elevated keels along the centerline.

REFERENCES: 95, 254, 437.

Dendrobium christianae A. H. Heller. See *D. hypodon* Schlechter. REFERENCES: 191, 229, 454.

Dendrobium christyanum Rchb. f.

AKA: *D. margaritaceum* Finet. Many cultivated plants are grown under the name *D. margaritaceum*. Seidenfaden (ref. 454) expresses the opinion that *D. fuerstenbergianum* Schlechter may be a tall form of *D. christyanum*.

ORIGIN/HABITAT: Northern Thailand, Vietnam, and southwest China. Plants grow in cool forests at about 4000 ft. (1220 m).

CLIMATE: Station #48327, Chiang Mai, Thailand, Lat. 18.8°N, Long. 99.0°E, at 1100 ft. (335 m). Temperatures are calculated for a habitat elevation of 4000 ft. (1220 m), resulting in probable extremes of 99°F (38°C) and 28°F (−2°C).

N/HEMISPHERE	JAN	FEB	MAR	APR	MAY	JUN	JUL	AUG	SEP	OCT	NOV	DEC
°F AVG MAX	75	80	85	86	84	80	79	77	78	79	76	74
°F AVG MIN	46	47	52	60	64	64	64	65	63	61	56	47
DIURNAL RANGE	29	33	33	26	20	16	15	12	15	18	20	27
RAIN/INCHES	0.3	0.4	0.6	2.0	5.5	6.1	7.4	8.7	11.5	4.9	1.5	0.4
HUMIDITY/%	73	65	58	62	73	78	80	83	83	81	79	76
BLOOM SEASON						*	**	**	*	*		
DAYS CLR @ 7AM	5	5	2	2	1	0	0	0	0	1	3	3
DAYS CLR @ 1PM	9	8	4	2	0	0	0	0	0	1	3	3
RAIN/MM	8	10	15	51	140	155	188	221	292	124	38	10
°C AVG MAX	24.1	26.9	29.7	30.2	29.1	26.9	26.4	25.2	25.8	26.4	24.7	23.6
°C AVG MIN	8.0	8.6	11.3	15.8	18.0	18.0	18.0	18.6	17.5	16.4	13.6	8.6
DIURNAL RANGE	16.1	18.3	18.4	14.4	11.1	8.9	8.4	6.6	8.3	10.0	11.1	15.0
S/HEMISPHERE	JUL	AUG	SEP	OCT	NOV	DEC	JAN	FEB	MAR	APR	MAY	JUN

Dendrobium chrysanthum

Cultural Recommendations

LIGHT: 2500–4000 fc. Diffused light is appropriate as clear summer days are exceedingly rare. Light should be bright, but direct sunlight should be avoided. Air movement should be excellent.

TEMPERATURES: Summer days average 77–80°F (25–27°C), and nights average 64–65°F (18–19°C), with a diurnal range of 12–16°F (7–9°C). The warmest weather occurs in spring. Days average 84–86°F (29–30°C), and nights average 52–64°F (11°C to 18°C), with a diurnal range of 20–33°F (11–18°C). Both highs and lows are more moderate after the start of the summer wet season.

HUMIDITY: Near 80% in summer and early autumn, decreasing to 65–75% in winter, and dropping to near 60% for 2 months in early spring.

WATER: Rainfall is heavy while plants are actively growing from spring to early autumn. During this season, cultivated plants should be kept moist with little if any drying allowed between waterings. However, water should be gradually reduced after new growths mature in autumn.

FERTILIZER: ¼–½ recommended strength, applied weekly. A high-nitrogen fertilizer is beneficial from spring to midsummer, but a fertilizer high in phosphates should be used in late summer and autumn. Some growers report good success alternating applications of fish emulsion with their regular fertilizer.

REST PERIOD: Winter days average 74–80°F (24–27°C), and nights average 46–47°F (8–9°C), with a diurnal range of 27–33°F (15–18°C). Overnight lows are below 50°F (10°C) for 3 months. Plants should be able to tolerate temperatures a few degrees below freezing for short periods, but extremes should be avoided in cultivation. During very cold weather, a plant's chance of surviving with minimal damage is better if it is dry when temperatures are low. In the habitat, rainfall averages are very low for 4–5 months in winter; but during the early part of the season, the high relative humidity indicates that additional moisture is available from frequent fog, mist and heavy deposits of dew. Growers sometimes recommend eliminating water in winter, but plants are healthiest if for most of the winter they are allowed to become somewhat dry between waterings but do not remain dry for extended periods. For 1–2 months in late winter, however, conditions are clear, warm, and dry with humidity so low that even the moisture from morning dew is uncommon. Plants should be allowed to dry out completely between waterings and remain dry longer during this time. Occasional early morning mistings between waterings may help keep the plants from becoming too dry. Fertilizer should be greatly reduced or eliminated until water is increased in spring. A cool, dry rest is essential for cultivated plants and should be continued until new growth starts in spring. In the habitat, light is highest in winter.

GROWING MEDIA: Plants may be mounted on tree-fern or cork slabs if humidity is high and plants are watered at least once daily in summer. When plants are potted, any open, fast-draining medium may be used. They may be repotted anytime new roots are growing.

MISCELLANEOUS NOTES: The bloom season shown in the climate table is based on cultivation records. The dry winter rest, low night temperatures, or wide diurnal range may be necessary to initiate blooming.

D. christyanum is closely related to and shares the same habitat with *D. bellatulum* Rolfe. *D. bellatulum* differs in being a slightly smaller plant with smaller flowers that blooms in winter.

Plant and Flower Information

PLANT SIZE AND TYPE: A small, 3–6 in. (8–14 cm) sympodial epiphyte.

PSEUDOBULB: 2–3 in. (5–8 cm) tall. The grooved stems consist of 2–4 internodes. They are covered with fine black hairs.

LEAVES: 2–4 per pseudobulb. The leaves are 1.2–2.4 in. (3–6 cm) long, dark green, and covered on the backside with small black hairs.

INFLORESCENCE: Very short. The inflorescences arise from internodes near the apex or on the sides of both old and new pseudobulbs. Each inflorescence produces a single flower, but they may be clustered in groups of 2 or 3.

FLOWERS: 1 per inflorescence. The somewhat elongated flowers are 2 in. (5 cm) across which is very large for the plant size. They are cream to white. The broad, fiddle-shaped lip is marked with a bright orange to yellow patch in the center. The lip does not turn down at the end. The blossoms are long-lasting with a slight but pleasant fragrance.

REFERENCES: 36, 50, 118, 179, 196, 198, 216, 245, 254, 266, 291, 332, 333, 429, 430, 448, 454.

PHOTOS/DRAWINGS: 50, 198, 291, 430, 454.

Dendrobium chrysanthum Wallich ex Lindley

AKA: *D. paxtonii* Lindley.

ORIGIN/HABITAT: Widespread in valleys of the Himalayan foothills from India through Southeast Asia. Plants grow in northeastern India, Burma, northern Thailand, Laos, Vietnam, and Yunan Province of southwest China. They are usually found at 3300–6550 ft. (1000–2000 m).

CLIMATE: Station #48327, Chiang Mai, Thailand, Lat. 18.8°N, Long. 99.0°E, at 1100 ft. (335 m) elevation. Temperatures are calculated for an elevation of 5000 ft. (1520 m), resulting in probable extremes of 96°F (36°C) and 25°F (–4°C).

N/HEMISPHERE	JAN	FEB	MAR	APR	MAY	JUN	JUL	AUG	SEP	OCT	NOV	DEC
°F AVG MAX	72	77	82	83	81	77	76	74	75	76	73	71
°F AVG MIN	43	44	49	57	61	61	61	62	60	58	53	44
DIURNAL RANGE	29	33	33	26	20	16	15	12	15	18	20	27
RAIN/INCHES	0.3	0.4	0.6	2.0	5.5	6.1	7.4	8.7	11.5	4.9	1.5	0.4
HUMIDITY/%	73	65	58	62	73	78	80	83	83	81	79	76
BLOOM SEASON				*	*	*	**	**	**	**	**	*
DAYS CLR @ 7AM	5	5	2	2	1	0	0	0	0	1	3	3
DAYS CLR @ 1PM	9	8	4	2	0	0	0	0	0	0	1	3
RAIN/MM	8	10	15	51	140	155	188	221	292	124	38	10
°C AVG MAX	22.3	25.1	27.9	28.4	27.3	25.1	24.5	23.4	24.0	24.5	22.9	21.7
°C AVG MIN	6.2	6.7	9.5	14.0	16.2	16.2	16.2	16.7	15.6	14.5	11.7	6.7
DIURNAL RANGE	16.1	18.4	18.4	14.4	11.1	8.9	8.4	6.7	8.4	10.0	11.2	15.0
S/HEMISPHERE	JUL	AUG	SEP	OCT	NOV	DEC	JAN	FEB	MAR	APR	MAY	JUN

Cultural Recommendations

LIGHT: 3000–4500 fc. Growers recommend hanging the plant high in the greenhouse for maximum light.

TEMPERATURES: Summer days average 74–77°F (23–25°C), and nights average 61–62°F (16–17°C), with a diurnal range of 12–16°F (7–9°C). The warmest temperatures occur in spring. Days average 81–83°F (27–28°C), and nights average 49–61°F (10–16°C), with a diurnal range of 20–33°F (11–18°C).

HUMIDITY: Near 80% in summer and early autumn, decreasing to 65–75% in winter, and dropping to near 60% for 2 months in early spring. Growers indicate that plants are healthiest when humidity is high.

WATER: Rainfall is heavy while plants are actively growing from spring to early autumn. During this season, cultivated plants should be kept moist with little if any drying allowed between waterings. However, water should be gradually reduced after new growths mature in autumn.

FERTILIZER: ¼–½ recommended strength, applied weekly. A high-nitrogen fertilizer is beneficial from spring to midsummer, but a fertilizer high in phosphates should be used in late summer and autumn.

REST PERIOD: Winter days average 71–77°F (22–25°C), and nights average 43–44°F (6–7°C), with a diurnal range of 27–33°F (15–18°C). In the habitat, overnight low temperatures are below 50°F (10°C) for 3 months and then increase relatively quickly in spring. However, growers indicate that plants grow well with winter nights of 60°F (16°C). Plants should be able to tolerate temperatures a few degrees below freezing, but extremes should be avoided in cultivation. During very cold weather, a plant's chance of surviving with minimal damage is better if it is dry when temperatures are low. In the habitat, rainfall averages are very low for 4–5 months in winter; but during the early part of the season, the high relative humidity indicates that additional moisture is available from frequent fog, mist, and heavy deposits of dew. Plants are healthiest if for most of the winter they are allowed to become somewhat dry between waterings but do not remain dry for extended periods. For 1–2 months in late winter, however, conditions are clear, warm, and dry with humidity so low that even the moisture from morning dew is uncommon. Plants should be allowed to dry out completely between waterings and remain dry longer during this time. Occasional early morning mistings between waterings may help keep the plants from becoming too dry. Fertilizer should be greatly reduced or eliminated until water is increased in spring. A cool, dry rest is essential for cultivated plants and should be continued until new growth starts in spring. In the habitat, light is highest in winter.

GROWING MEDIA: Plants are best placed in hanging baskets filled with an open, fast-draining medium or mounted on tree-fern or cork slabs to accommodate their pendent growth habit. If mounted, humidity should be high and plants should be watered at least once daily in summer. Several waterings a day may be required during hot, dry weather. Repotting is best done in early spring when new roots are growing.

MISCELLANEOUS NOTES: The bloom season shown in the climate table is based on cultivation records. In the habitat, the primary flowering occurs summer through autumn, but plants may bloom sporadically throughout the year. *D. chrysanthum* grows easily in Singapore, but the plants are small and few flowered in that very warm, uniform climate. Growers indicate that it can be difficult in cultivation and careful attention should be given to its cultural requirements. New growth begins after flowering and continues all winter. Collected plants are dried and used in Chinese medicine.

Plant and Flower Information

PLANT SIZE AND TYPE: A 35–118 in. (90–300 cm) sympodial epiphyte.

PSEUDOBULB: 35–118 in. (90–300 cm) long. The stemlike pseudobulbs are slender, ribbed, somewhat swollen in the middle, and naturally curved or pendulous. The plant is very close to and often confused with *D. ochreatum*.

LEAVES: Many. The deciduous leaves are 4–7 in. (10–18 cm) long, ovate, and somewhat twisted at the base. They are bright, shiny green with a rather thin texture. They resemble those of *D. normale* Falconer.

INFLORESCENCE: Very short. Inflorescences emerge opposite the leaves on the upper portion of the stem. Plants bloom on immature, leafy stems. A single specimen plant carried 50 inflorescences.

FLOWERS: 1–3, up to 6 per inflorescence. The waxy flowers are 1.6–2.0 in. (4–5 cm) across and open fully. The rounded sepals and broader petals are bright, deep yellow, golden yellow, or orange. They are held forward and incurved at the tips. The petals are serrated along the margin. The wavy lip is marked with 2 oval spots that may merge to appear as a single blotch, which may be blood-red to brownish purple. The nearly circular, slightly concave lip is pubescent on both surfaces, with long, thin hairs on the upper surface. Blossoms are very fragrant and last 1–2 weeks. Although individual flowers are relatively short-lived, blossoms are produced throughout the summer.

HYBRIDIZING NOTES: Chromosome counts are n = 19 (ref. 154, 504, 542, 580), n = 20 (ref. 150, 152, 542), 2n = 38 (ref. 150, 152, 154, 504, 542, 580), 2n = 40 (ref. 150, 152, 153, 504, 542), 2n = 76 (ref. 153).

REFERENCES: 6, 19, 25, 32, 36, 38, 46, 102, 150, 152, 153, 154, 157, 179, 190, 196, 200, 202, 208, 216, 245, 247, 254, 266, 278, 317, 326, 369, 376, 414, 430, 445, 447, 448, 454, 504, 524, 528, 541, 542, 557, 570, 580.

PHOTOS/DRAWINGS: 32, *36*, 46, 102, 200, *245, 247, 430, 454*.

Dendrobium chryseum Rolfe

AKA: Seidenfaden (ref. 454) includes *D. aurantiacum* Rchb. f. not F. Mueller, *D. clavatum* Lindley not Roxburgh, *D. clavatum* Lindley var. *aurantiacum* (Rchb. f.) Tang and Wang, *D. denneanum* Kerr, *D. flaviflorum* Hayata, *D. rivesii* Gagnepain, *D. rolfei* A. Hawkes and A. H. Heller, *D. tibeticum* Schlechter. For an extensive discussion regarding this synonymy, see Seidenfaden (ref. 454). The International Orchid Commission (ref. 236) registers hybrids under the name *D. clavatum* Lindley.

ORIGIN/HABITAT: Widespread throughout Southeast Asia. Distribution extends from the Garhwal region of northern India eastward through Sikkim, Bhutan, and the Himalayan region of northeast India. The range continues through Burma, northern Thailand, Laos, Vietnam, and southwest China to as far north as Taiwan. *D. chryseum* grows at 4900–6550 ft. (1490–2000 m) over most of the habitat, but plants are found as low as 3300 ft. (1000 m) in northeast India. In Yunnan, China, plants grow on south-facing rocks in sandy gulches at 6000–7000 ft. (1850–2150 m).

CLIMATE: Station #48802, Cha Pa, Vietnam, Lat. 22.3°N, Long. 103.8°E, at 5381 ft. (1640 m). Temperatures are calculated for an elevation of 6000 ft. (1830 m), resulting in probable extremes of 89°F (32°C) and 26°F (−3°C).

N/HEMISPHERE	JAN	FEB	MAR	APR	MAY	JUN	JUL	AUG	SEP	OCT	NOV	DEC
°F AVG MAX	50	52	63	68	71	71	72	71	70	64	61	55
°F AVG MIN	39	42	50	54	59	61	62	61	59	54	49	44
DIURNAL RANGE	11	10	13	14	12	10	10	10	11	10	12	11
RAIN/INCHES	1.6	2.8	4.7	7.0	14.6	14.0	18.9	18.9	12.6	7.5	4.7	1.6
HUMIDITY/%	86	92	86	82	85	88	88	89	87	93	90	88
BLOOM SEASON			*	**	*							
DAYS CLR @ 7AM	7	4	6	5	1	2	1	3	5	5	9	7
DAYS CLR @ 1PM	8	3	9	7	2	1	0	0	1	1	3	7
RAIN/MM	41	71	119	178	371	356	480	480	320	190	119	41
°C AVG MAX	10.0	11.1	17.2	20.0	21.6	21.6	22.2	21.6	21.1	17.8	16.1	12.8
°C AVG MIN	3.9	5.5	10.0	12.2	15.0	16.1	16.6	16.1	15.0	12.2	9.4	6.6
DIURNAL RANGE	6.1	5.6	7.2	7.8	6.6	5.5	5.6	5.5	6.1	5.6	6.7	6.2
S/HEMISPHERE	JUL	AUG	SEP	OCT	NOV	DEC	JAN	FEB	MAR	APR	MAY	JUN

Cultural Recommendations

LIGHT: 2000–2500 fc. Diffused light is suggested.

TEMPERATURES: Summer days average 71–72°F (22°C), and nights average 61–62°F (16–17°C), with a diurnal range of 10°F (6°C). *D. chryseum* also grows at lower elevations and may tolerate temperatures that are as much as 10°F (6°C) warmer than indicated in the climate table.

HUMIDITY: 85–90% year-round.

WATER: Rainfall is heavy from spring into autumn with a 2–3 month winter dry period. Cultivated plants should be constantly moist while actively growing, but water should be gradually reduced in autumn.

FERTILIZER: ¼–½ recommended strength, applied weekly. A high-nitrogen fertilizer is beneficial from spring to midsummer, but a fertilizer high in phosphates should be used in late summer and autumn.

REST PERIOD: Winter days average 50–55°F (10–13°C), and nights average 39–44°F (4–7°C), with a diurnal range of 10–11°F (6°C). In the habitat, light may be somewhat higher in winter. Although rainfall is low in winter, the unusually high winter humidity indicates additional moisture is available from frequent early morning dew, fog, and mist. In cultivation, water should be reduced and the plants allowed to dry somewhat between waterings, but they should never be allowed to dry out completely. Fertilizer should be reduced or eliminated when the plants are not actively growing.

GROWING MEDIA: Plants may be mounted on tree-fern or cork slabs if humidity is high and plants are watered at least once daily in summer. When plants are potted, any open, fast-draining medium may be used. Repotting is best done in early spring when new roots are growing.

Dendrobium chrysobulbon

MISCELLANEOUS NOTES: The bloom season shown in the climate table is based on cultivation records. In the habitat, plants flower in spring or early summer.

Plant and Flower Information

PLANT SIZE AND TYPE: A 16–30 in. (40–75 cm) sympodial epiphyte or lithophyte.

PSEUDOBULB: 16–30 in. (40–75 cm) long. The thin, erect pseudobulbs are pencil-thick along most of their length, but they may be somewhat swollen at the base. Smooth young stems become vertically ridged with age.

LEAVES: Several per growth. The oblong to lanceolate leaves are 4 in. (10 cm) long and notched at the apex.

INFLORESCENCE: 3 in. (8 cm) long. The sharply decurved inflorescences arise from nodes near the apex of prior year's stems.

FLOWERS: 4–6 per inflorescence. Described as beautiful and deliciously fragrant, the glossy, rather short lived flowers are 2–3 in. (5–8 cm) across. The golden yellow sepals and broader petals are normally narrow and pointed, but rounder forms are known. The convolute lip is bright yellow with a dark maroon-purple blotch near the center. It is fuzzy on the upper surface and fringed and ruffled along the margin. Seidenfaden (ref. 454) indicates that plants known as *D. clavatum* have flowers with the deep red blotch on the lip, but plants known as *D. aurantiacum* do not. Rolfe (ref. 414) indicated that *D. clavatum,* which was not fragrant, had deep orange blossoms. Growers indicate that plants known as *D. flaviflorum* from Taiwan are unspotted and usually have 2 blossoms per inflorescence.

HYBRIDIZING NOTES: Chromosome counts as *D. clavatum* are n = 19 (ref. 150, 504, 580) and 2n = 38 (ref. 152, 243). Also, n = 19 and 2n = 38 as *D. aurantiacum* (ref. 152, 243, 504), as *D. denneanum* (ref. 153, 164, 542), and as *D. flaviflorum* (ref. 504).

REFERENCES: 32, 38, 46, 61, 64, 102, 136, 150, 152, 153, 154, 179, 190, 202, 208, 218, 236, 243, 254, 266, 279, 317, 367, 369, 414, 430, 447, 454, 497, 504, 505, 528, 541, 547, 580.

PHOTOS/DRAWINGS: 32, 102, 279, *430,* 454, 497.

Dendrobium chrysobulbon Schlechter. Now considered a *Flickingeria*. REFERENCES: 223, 449.

Dendrobium chrysocephalum Kränzlin. See *D. purpureum* Roxburgh. REFERENCES: 218, 219, 254.

Dendrobium chrysocrepis Parish and Rchb. f.

AKA: H. Wood (ref. 582) indicates that this species should be transferred to the genus *Diplocaulobium.*

ORIGIN/HABITAT: Burma near Moulmein. Habitat elevation is estimated at 4500 ft. (1370 m), so the following temperatures should be used with caution.

CLIMATE: Station #48103, Moulmein, Burma, Lat. 16.4°N, Long. 97.7°E, at 150 ft. (46 m). Temperatures are calculated for an elevation of 4500 ft. (1370 m), resulting in probable extremes of 89°F (32°C) and 38°F (3°C).

N/HEMISPHERE	JAN	FEB	MAR	APR	MAY	JUN	JUL	AUG	SEP	OCT	NOV	DEC
°F AVG MAX	75	78	80	81	75	71	69	69	71	74	75	73
°F AVG MIN	52	54	59	62	62	61	61	61	61	61	59	54
DIURNAL RANGE	23	24	21	19	13	10	8	8	10	13	16	19
RAIN/INCHES	0.3	0.2	0.4	3.0	20.3	35.6	46.3	43.4	28.1	8.5	2.1	0.1
HUMIDITY/%	66	68	68	70	81	91	92	93	91	81	75	64
BLOOM SEASON					*	*	*					
DAYS CLR @ 7AM	12	7	5	6	1	0	0	0	0	3	7	12
DAYS CLR @ 1PM	20	13	10	8	3	0	0	0	0	4	12	17
RAIN/MM	8	5	10	76	516	904	1176	1102	714	216	53	3
°C AVG MAX	23.7	25.4	26.5	27.0	23.7	21.5	20.4	20.4	21.5	23.1	23.7	22.6
°C AVG MIN	10.9	12.0	14.8	16.5	16.5	15.9	15.9	15.9	15.9	15.9	14.8	12.0
DIURNAL RANGE	12.8	13.4	11.7	10.5	7.2	5.6	4.5	4.5	5.6	7.2	8.9	10.6
S/HEMISPHERE	JUL	AUG	SEP	OCT	NOV	DEC	JAN	FEB	MAR	APR	MAY	JUN

Cultural Recommendations

LIGHT: 2000–3000 fc. In the habitat during summer, clear days are rare and the cloud cover is extremely heavy.

TEMPERATURES: Summer days average 69–71°F (20–22°C), and nights average 61°F (16°C), with a diurnal range of 8–10°F (5–6°C). Weather is warmest in spring. Days average 75–81°F (24–27°C), and nights average 59–62°F (15–17°C), with a diurnal range of 13–21°F (7–12°C).

HUMIDITY: 80–90% from late spring to midautumn, dropping to 65–70% in winter.

WATER: Rainfall is very heavy from late spring into autumn, with a 4-month winter dry season. Cultivated plants should be kept evenly moist while actively growing, but water should be gradually reduced in autumn after new growths mature.

FERTILIZER: ¼–½ recommended strength, applied weekly. A high-nitrogen fertilizer is beneficial from spring to midsummer, but a fertilizer high in phosphates should be used in late summer and autumn.

REST PERIOD: Winter weather is moderately cool and dry. Days average 73–78°F (23–25°C), and nights average 52–54°F (11–12°C), with a diurnal range of 23–24°F (13°C). In the habitat, rainfall is low for 4 months, but additional moisture is available from frequent, heavy deposits of dew. Cultivated plants should be allowed to dry out between waterings, but they should never remain dry for long periods. Occasional early morning mistings between waterings may help prevent plants from becoming too dry. Fertilizer should be reduced or eliminated. In the habitat, light is highest in winter.

GROWING MEDIA: Plants may be mounted on slabs of cork or tree-fern fiber with a pad of sphagnum. Mounted plants need high humidity and watering at least daily in summer. If plants are potted, a rapidly draining medium should be used. Repotting is best done in early spring when new roots are growing.

MISCELLANEOUS NOTES: The bloom season shown in the climate table is based on cultivation records. Growers report that this species grows without difficulty as a mounted specimen in a cool greenhouse if it is kept on the dry side during the cooler winter months. Plants that produce very short-lived flowers commonly bloom several times during the year. Flowering usually occurs 7–14 days after a sudden 10°F (5°C) drop in daytime temperatures. Plants begin blooming while very young.

Plant and Flower Information

PLANT SIZE AND TYPE: A 6–10 in. (15–25 cm) sympodial epiphyte.

PSEUDOBULB: 6–10 in. (15–25 cm) long. Pseudobulbs are somewhat swollen above the base, forming a flattened, leafy growth.

LEAVES: 3 or more per growth. The elliptic–lanceolate leaves are 2–3 in. (5.1–7.6 cm) long and pointed at the tip.

INFLORESCENCE: Short. The slender inflorescences arise from old leafless stems.

FLOWERS: 1 per inflorescence. The flowers are 1.0–1.5 in. (2.5–3.8 cm) across. Sepals and petals are golden yellow. The slipper or pear-shaped lip is a deeper yellow or orange color with a dense covering of reddish hairs on the inner surface. Blossoms are short lived.

HYBRIDIZING NOTES: Chromosome count is 2n = about 76 (ref. 504, 580).

REFERENCES: 157, 179, 202, 210, 216, 254, 430, 437, 445, 454, 504, 541, 580, 582.

PHOTOS/DRAWINGS: 210, 254, *430.*

Dendrobium chrysoglossum Schlechter

AKA: The International Orchid Commission (ref. 236) lists *D. chrysoglossum* as a synonym of *D. concavissimum* J. J. Smith and registers hybrids under the latter name.

ORIGIN/HABITAT: Northern Papua New Guinea. Plants grow in the mountains along the Ramu River, in the Finisterre Range, and in various other locations. Plants are often found on *Casuarina* trees in mistforests at 4250–4900 ft. (1300–1500 m). Collections are reported from Bougainville Island.

CLIMATE: Station #94010, Goroka, Papua New Guinea, Lat. 6.1°S, Long. 145.4°E, at 5141 ft. (1567 m). Temperatures are calculated for an elevation of 4600 ft. (1400 m), resulting in probable extremes of 89°F (32°C) and 45°F (7°C).

N/HEMISPHERE	JAN	FEB	MAR	APR	MAY	JUN	JUL	AUG	SEP	OCT	NOV	DEC
°F AVG MAX	78	79	80	81	81	80	81	80	80	80	81	79
°F AVG MIN	58	59	59	59	60	61	61	61	62	61	61	59
DIURNAL RANGE	20	20	21	22	21	19	20	19	18	19	20	20
RAIN/INCHES	2.1	2.8	4.6	5.9	6.6	9.3	9.1	10.1	10.7	8.3	4.6	2.0
HUMIDITY/%	70	67	67	67	67	71	72	73	74	71	70	70
BLOOM SEASON			*			*			*		*	
DAYS CLR	N/A											
RAIN/MM	53	71	117	150	168	236	231	257	272	211	117	51
°C AVG MAX	25.4	26.0	26.5	27.1	27.1	26.5	27.1	26.5	26.5	26.5	27.1	26.0
°C AVG MIN	14.3	14.9	14.9	14.9	15.4	16.0	16.0	16.0	16.5	16.0	16.0	14.9
DIURNAL RANGE	11.1	11.1	11.6	12.2	11.7	10.5	11.1	10.5	10.0	10.5	11.1	11.1
S/HEMISPHERE	JUL	AUG	SEP	OCT	NOV	DEC	JAN	FEB	MAR	APR	MAY	JUN

Cultural Recommendations

LIGHT: 2500–3000 fc.

TEMPERATURES: Throughout the year, days average 78–81°F (25–27°C), and nights average 58–62°F (14–17°C), with a diurnal range of 18–22°F (10–12°C).

HUMIDITY: 70–75% most of the year, dropping to near 65% in late winter and spring.

WATER: Rainfall is moderate to heavy most of the year, but conditions are slightly drier for 3 months in winter. The high relative humidity and wide temperature range cause frequent heavy deposits of dew. Additional moisture is available as mist from fog and low clouds. Cultivated plants should be kept moist and never be allowed to dry completely. In summer, daily watering may be necessary during hot, dry weather. Additional early morning mistings may be beneficial, especially on bright, sunny days.

FERTILIZER: ¼–½ recommended strength. A balanced fertilizer should be applied weekly to biweekly.

REST PERIOD: Growing temperatures should be maintained all year. Water should be reduced in winter, especially for plants grown in the dark, short-day conditions common in temperate latitudes; but plants should never be allowed to dry completely. Fertilizer should be reduced or eliminated until water is increased in spring. In the habitat, light is probably highest in winter.

GROWING MEDIA: Plants may be mounted on tree-fern or cork slabs if humidity is high and plants are watered at least once daily in summer. When plants are potted, any open, fast-draining medium may be used. Repotting is best done in early spring when new roots are growing.

MISCELLANEOUS NOTES: The bloom season shown in the climate table is based on cultivation records. Plants are free-flowering, and the bloom season is variable. The roots are tough and stringy.

Plant and Flower Information

PLANT SIZE AND TYPE: An 8–12 in. (20–30 cm) sympodial epiphyte. Plants occasionally grow to 28 in. (71 cm).

PSEUDOBULB: 8–12 in. (20–30 cm) long. Stems are leafy.

LEAVES: Many. The leaves are usually 2–3 in. (5–8 cm) long.

INFLORESCENCE: Densely flowered inflorescences emerge from leafless stems. Several clusters of flowers are commonly produced on each stem.

FLOWERS: 10–20 per inflorescence. The fan-shaped flowers are 0.5 in. (1.3 cm) across. Sepals and petals are pale pink. The lip is golden yellow to orange. The column is red.

REFERENCES: 179, 221, 304, 430, 437, 445, 516.

PHOTOS/DRAWINGS: *304*, *430*, 437.

Dendrobium chrysographatum Ames. Sometimes

spelled *D. chrysographotum,* it is now considered a synonym of *Flickingeria chrysographata* (Ames) A. Hawkes. REFERENCES: 12, 213, 222, 230, 231, 296, 536.

Dendrobium chrysolabium Rolfe. Also spelled *D. chryso-*

labum, see *D. bracteosum* Rchb. f. REFERENCES: 190, 216, 218, 254, 437, 470.

Dendrobium chrysornis Ridley. See *D. dekockii* J. J. Smith.

REFERENCES: 222, 385, 400.

Dendrobium chrysosema Schlechter

ORIGIN/HABITAT: Papua New Guinea. Plants grow in the Sepik River region at 4450–4900 ft. (1350–1500 m).

CLIMATE: Station #200004, Ambunti, Papua New Guinea, Lat. 4.2°S, Long. 142.8°E, at 164 ft. (50 m). Temperatures are calculated for an elevation of 4600 ft. (1400 m), resulting in probable extremes of 84°F (29°C) and 37°F (3°C).

N/HEMISPHERE	JAN	FEB	MAR	APR	MAY	JUN	JUL	AUG	SEP	OCT	NOV	DEC
°F AVG MAX	73	75	75	75	76	75	75	75	75	75	75	74
°F AVG MIN	57	58	59	58	58	58	57	58	58	58	58	59
DIURNAL RANGE	16	17	16	17	18	17	18	17	17	17	17	15
RAIN/INCHES	6.4	7.4	7.7	8.5	9.2	9.4	10.9	10.2	12.2	10.4	8.3	5.2
HUMIDITY/%	N/A											
BLOOM SEASON									*		*	
DAYS CLR	N/A											
RAIN/MM	163	188	196	216	234	239	277	259	310	264	211	132
°C AVG MAX	23.0	24.1	24.1	24.1	24.6	24.1	24.1	24.1	24.1	24.1	24.1	23.5
°C AVG MIN	14.1	14.6	15.2	14.6	14.6	14.6	14.1	14.6	14.6	14.6	14.6	15.2
DIURNAL RANGE	8.9	9.5	8.9	9.5	10.0	9.5	10.0	9.5	9.5	9.5	9.5	8.3
S/HEMISPHERE	JUL	AUG	SEP	OCT	NOV	DEC	JAN	FEB	MAR	APR	MAY	JUN

Cultural Recommendations

LIGHT: 2000–3000 fc.

TEMPERATURES: Throughout the year, days average 73–76°F (23–25°C), and nights average 57–59°F (14–15°C), with a diurnal range of 15–18°F (8–10°C).

HUMIDITY: Information is not available for this location. However, average humidity in this region normally exceeds 80% year-round.

WATER: Rainfall is heavy year-round, with the greatest amounts falling in summer and early autumn. Cultivated plants should be kept moist but not soggy.

FERTILIZER: ¼–½ recommended strength. A balanced fertilizer should be applied weekly to biweekly throughout the year.

REST PERIOD: Growing temperatures should be maintained all year. Water and fertilizer should be reduced somewhat in winter, especially for plants cultivated in the dark, short-day conditions common in temperate latitudes; but plants should never be allowed to dry out completely. In the habitat, seasonal light variation is minor.

GROWING MEDIA: Plants may be mounted on cork or tree-fern slabs if humidity is high and plants are watered at least once daily in summer. When plants are potted, any open, fast-draining medium may be used. Repotting may be done anytime new roots are growing.

Dendrobium chrysotainium

MISCELLANEOUS NOTES: The bloom season shown in the climate table is based on reports from the habitat.

Plant and Flower Information

PLANT SIZE AND TYPE: A 14–20 in. (35–50 cm) sympodial epiphyte.

PSEUDOBULB: 14–20 in. (35–50 cm) long. Numerous fleshy stems emerge from a very short rhizome.

LEAVES: Many. The lanceolate-elliptic leaves are 4–7 in. (10–18 cm) long.

INFLORESCENCE: Short. Inflorescences are densely flowered.

FLOWERS: Many. The waxy flowers are about 0.8 in. (2 cm) long. The sepals and petals are white on the front and brownish on the back. The back of the sepals have a scalelike covering. The fiddle-shaped lip, which is decorated with large, pale gold spots, is toothed at the apex.

REFERENCES: 223, 443.

Dendrobium chrysotainium Schlechter

AKA: Sometimes spelled *D. chrysotaenium*.

ORIGIN/HABITAT: Endemic to Sulawesi (Celebes). Plants were originally collected at 2600–2950 ft. (800–900 m) along a road near Kakaskassen at the eastern end of the Minahassa Peninsula.

CLIMATE: Station #97014, Manado, Sulawesi, Lat. 1.5°N, Long. 124.9°E, at 264 ft. (80 m). Temperatures are calculated for an elevation of 3000 ft. (914 m), resulting in probable extremes of 88°F (31°C) and 56°F (13°C).

N/HEMISPHERE	JAN	FEB	MAR	APR	MAY	JUN	JUL	AUG	SEP	OCT	NOV	DEC
°F AVG MAX	76	76	76	77	78	78	78	80	80	80	78	77
°F AVG MIN	64	64	64	64	65	64	64	64	64	63	64	65
DIURNAL RANGE	12	12	12	13	13	14	14	16	16	17	14	12
RAIN/INCHES	18.6	13.8	12.2	8.0	6.4	6.5	4.8	4.0	3.4	4.9	8.9	14.7
HUMIDITY/%	84	83	83	83	81	80	75	72	75	77	82	83
BLOOM SEASON									*			
DAYS CLR @ 8AM	4	3	6	11	11	12	12	12	14	17	12	8
DAYS CLR @ 2PM	1	1	1	2	1	3	3	4	4	4	1	1
RAIN/MM	472	351	310	203	163	165	122	102	86	124	226	373
°C AVG MAX	24.4	24.4	24.4	25.0	25.5	25.5	25.5	26.7	26.7	26.7	25.5	25.0
°C AVG MIN	17.8	17.8	17.8	17.8	18.3	17.8	17.8	17.8	17.8	17.2	17.8	18.3
DIURNAL RANGE	6.6	6.6	6.6	7.2	7.2	7.7	7.7	8.9	8.9	9.5	7.7	6.7
S/HEMISPHERE	JUL	AUG	SEP	OCT	NOV	DEC	JAN	FEB	MAR	APR	MAY	JUN

Cultural Recommendations

LIGHT: 2000–3000 fc. In the habitat, morning light is highest as skies are usually overcast by afternoon.

TEMPERATURES: Throughout the year, days average 76–80°F (24–27°C), and nights average 63–65°F (17–18°C), with a diurnal range of 12–17°F (7–10°C). Plants from this habitat may not be heat tolerant and could be difficult to cultivate in hot climates. Record extreme temperatures are only a few degrees above and below the average temperatures. Plants may not tolerate wide temperature fluctuations.

HUMIDITY: 80–85% most of the year, dropping to 70–75% in late summer and autumn.

WATER: Rainfall is moderate to heavy through the year. The driest period occurs in late summer and early autumn. Plants should be kept moist year-round with only slight drying allowed between waterings.

FERTILIZER: ¼–½ recommended strength. A balanced fertilizer should be applied weekly to biweekly throughout the year.

REST PERIOD: Growing temperatures should be maintained all year. The plants may rest during the 1–2 month drier period which occurs in late summer and coincides with the period of greatest diurnal range. Cultivated plants should dry out slightly during this period, but they should never remain dry for long. The heaviest rainfall in the habitat occurs in winter, but water should not be increased for cultivated plants. In fact, water should be reduced somewhat for plants grown in the dark, short-day conditions common in temperate latitudes, but they should not be allowed to dry out completely.

GROWING MEDIA: Plants may be mounted on tree-fern or cork slabs if humidity is high and plants are watered at least once daily in summer. When plants are potted, any open, fast-draining medium may be used. Repotting may be done anytime new roots are growing.

MISCELLANEOUS NOTES: The bloom season shown in the climate table is based on collection reports. When describing this plant, Schlechter (ref. 436) indicated that although the flowers are very similar to *D. confusum* Schlechter, the plants have entirely different growth habits.

Plant and Flower Information

PLANT SIZE AND TYPE: A 16 in. (40 cm) sympodial epiphyte.

PSEUDOBULB: 16 in. (40 cm) long. Stems are swollen in the middle with a slender base and top. The erect stems emerge from a very short, branching rhizome.

LEAVES: Many. The stems are leafy on the upper, slender part except at the apex. The lanceolate leaves are somewhat sickle-shaped.

INFLORESCENCE: Short. Clusters of flowers emerge from nodes near the apex of the stem.

FLOWERS: Several per inflorescence. The fragrant flowers are about 1 in. (2.5 cm) long. Sepals and petals are snow white. The lip is decorated with a yellow central band which is golden yellow in the front.

REFERENCES: 220, 436.

Dendrobium chrysotis Rchb. f. See *D. hookerianum* Lindley.

REFERENCES: 190, 216, 254, 369, 445, 454, 570.

Dendrobium chrysotoxum Lindley

AKA: *D. chrysotoxum* Lindley var. *delacourii* Gagnepain, *D. chrysotoxum* Lindley var. *suavissima* (Rchb. f.) Veitch, and *D. suavissimum* Rchb. f. Seidenfaden (ref. 454) indicates that the description of *D. calythyrsos* Schlechter from upper Burma closely resembles *D. chrysotoxum* Lindley.

ORIGIN/HABITAT: Widespread throughout southeast Asia. The habitat extends from the Sikkim region of India, through Assam and Burma, across Thailand and Laos, and into Yunnan Province of southwest China. *D. chrysotoxum* is reported at 1300–5300 ft. (400–1620 m) throughout this range. In Thailand, plants grow near Chiang Mai in deciduous forests above 2000 ft. (610 m).

CLIMATE: Station #48327, Chiang Mai, Thailand, Lat. 18.8°N, Long. 99.0°E, at 1100 ft. (335 m). Temperatures are calculated for an elevation of 3000 ft. (910 m), resulting in probable extremes of 102°F (39°C) and 32°F (0°C).

N/HEMISPHERE	JAN	FEB	MAR	APR	MAY	JUN	JUL	AUG	SEP	OCT	NOV	DEC
°F AVG MAX	79	84	89	90	88	84	83	81	82	83	80	78
°F AVG MIN	50	51	56	64	68	68	68	69	67	65	60	51
DIURNAL RANGE	29	33	33	26	20	16	15	12	15	18	20	27
RAIN/INCHES	0.3	0.4	0.6	2.0	5.5	6.1	7.4	8.7	11.5	4.9	1.5	0.4
HUMIDITY/%	73	65	58	62	73	78	80	83	83	81	79	76
BLOOM SEASON		*	**	***	***	***	**	*	*			
DAYS CLR @ 7AM	5	5	2	2	1	0	0	0	0	1	3	3
DAYS CLR @ 1PM	9	8	4	2	0	0	0	0	0	1	3	3
RAIN/MM	8	10	15	51	140	155	188	221	292	124	38	10
°C AVG MAX	26.0	28.7	31.5	32.1	31.0	28.7	28.2	27.1	27.6	28.2	26.5	25.4
°C AVG MIN	9.8	10.4	13.2	17.6	19.9	19.9	19.9	20.4	19.3	18.2	15.4	10.4
DIURNAL RANGE	16.2	18.3	18.3	14.5	11.1	8.8	8.3	6.7	8.3	10.0	11.1	15.0
S/HEMISPHERE	JUL	AUG	SEP	OCT	NOV	DEC	JAN	FEB	MAR	APR	MAY	JUN

Cultural Recommendations

LIGHT: 2500–3500 fc. In the habitat, clear days are rare. The plants are adaptable. Growers indicate plants tolerate high light, particularly in the morning.

TEMPERATURES: Summer days average 81–84°F (27–29°C), and nights average 68–69°F (20°C), with a diurnal range of 12–16°F (7–9°C). The warmest weather occurs in spring. Days average 88–90°F (31–32°C), and nights average 56–68°F (13–20°C), with a diurnal range of 20–33°F (11–18°C). Both highs and lows are more moderate after the start of the summer wet season.

HUMIDITY: 80–85% in summer and autumn, dropping to near 60% for 2–3 months in winter and early spring.

WATER: Rainfall is heavy while plants are actively growing from spring to early autumn. During this season, cultivated plants should be kept moist with little if any drying allowed between waterings. However, water should be gradually reduced after new growths mature in autumn. Growers indicate that *D. chrysotoxum* is less demanding of aeration around the roots than many species.

FERTILIZER: ½ recommended strength, applied weekly. A high-nitrogen fertilizer is beneficial from spring to midsummer, but a fertilizer high in phosphates should be used in late summer and autumn. Growers indicate that plants respond to generous fertilizer, but that salt buildup from excess fertilizer or alkaline water may cause shriveling and kill the plant. Short, stubby roots are an indication of excessive salts.

REST PERIOD: Winter days average 78–84°F (25–29°C), and nights average 50–51°F (10°C), with a diurnal range of 27–33°F (15–18°C). The increased diurnal range is due primarily to cooler nights, which occasionally drop to near freezing when the weather is clear and dry. In the habitat, rainfall averages are very low for 4–5 months in winter; but during the early part of the season, the high relative humidity indicates that additional moisture is available from frequent fog, mist, and heavy deposits of dew. Plants are healthiest if for most of the winter they are allowed to become somewhat dry between waterings but do not remain dry for extended periods. For 1–2 months in late winter, however, conditions are clear, warm, and dry with humidity so low that even the moisture from morning dew is uncommon. Plants should be allowed to dry out completely between waterings and remain dry longer during this time. Occasional early morning mistings between waterings may help keep the plants from becoming too dry. Fertilizer should be greatly reduced or eliminated until water is increased in spring. A cool, dry rest is essential for cultivated plants and should be continued until new growth starts in spring. In the habitat, light is highest in winter. Growers indicate that high winter light is needed to encourage flowering.

GROWING MEDIA: Growers recommend potting to help maintain moisture in summer. Any open, fast-draining medium appropriate for the plant size may be used. Plants may be mounted on tree-fern or cork slabs if humidity is high and plants are watered at least once daily in summer. Repotting is best done in early spring immediately after flowering when new roots are growing.

MISCELLANEOUS NOTES: The bloom season shown in the climate table is based on cultivation records. Many growers consider *D. chrysotoxum* a problem plant and careful attention should be given to its cultural requirements. Plants grow well in the warm, uniform climate of Singapore, but they rarely bloom. Low night temperatures or wide diurnal range may be necessary to initiate blooming.

Plant and Flower Information

PLANT SIZE AND TYPE: A 4–12 in. (10–30 cm) sympodial epiphyte. Plants form a large, tightly clustered clump.

PSEUDOBULB: 4–12 in. (10–30 cm) long. The erect pseudobulbs are spindle- or club-shaped and somewhat flattened. The stems, which are variable in size and shape, are usually dark green when young then become grooved, shiny, and yellow with age.

LEAVES: 2–8 near the apex. The number of leaves depends on plant size. The glossy, dark green leaves are usually 4–7 in. (10–18 cm) long. Eventually deciduous, the leathery leaves are long-lasting.

INFLORESCENCE: 6–18 in. (15–46 cm) long. Inflorescences are sometimes erect, but they are more often arching or laxly pendent. They emerge from upper nodes on the most recently matured pseudobulbs. Flowers are attractively spaced on the inflorescence.

FLOWERS: 10–21 per inflorescence. Blossoms are 2 in. (5 cm) across, large compared to plant size. The waxy flowers are gold- to orange-yellow with spreading sepals and large rounded petals. Petals are minutely toothed along the margin. The nearly round lip is fringed, velvety, and ruffled. It is marked with a curved orange or brown band and red streaks in the throat. Flowers are variable in size and color depth, and several varieties have been named. Blossoms are very fragrant and last 2–3 weeks. A single specimen plant grown in a wooden tub in its native area reached 36 in. (91 cm) in diameter and produced 75 inflorescences each with 15–20 blossoms.

HYBRIDIZING NOTES: Chromosome counts are n = 19 (ref. 154, 542), n = 20 (ref. 504, 580), n = 20 + 5f. (ref. 580), 2n = 38 (ref. 151, 153, 154, 187, 188, 504, 542, 580), 2n = 40 (ref. 504, 580), 2n = 38 as *D. chrysotoxum* var. *chrysotoxum* (ref. 504), and 2n = 38 as *D. chrysotoxum* var. *suavissimum* (ref. 504, 580). Johansen (ref. 239) indicates that plants are self-sterile and that flowers dropped 10–11 days after self-pollination. When cross-pollinated, 100% produced capsules which opened 374–393 days after pollination. 87–89% of the seed produced contained visible embryos, and 67–87% germinated.

REFERENCES: 25, 36, 38, 46, 151, 153, 154, 157, 179, 187, 188, 190, 196, 200, 202, 208, 210, 216, 236, 239, 245, 247, 254, 266, 317, 326, 359, 369, 371, 376, 389, 428, 430, 445, 447, 448, 454, 458, 504, 523, 528, 541, 542, 557, 568, 569, 570, 580.

PHOTOS/DRAWINGS: 36, 46, 210, *245, 247, 359, 369, 371, 389, 428, 430, 454, 458, 569.*

Dendrobium chrysotropis Schlechter.

Now considered a synonym of *Diplocaulobium chrysotropis* (Schlechter) A. Hawkes. REFERENCES: 92, 179, 219, 229, 254, 437, 444, 445, 504, 580.

Dendrobium ciliatilabellum Seidenfaden

ORIGIN/HABITAT: Endemic to eastern Thailand. Plants grow near Khao Yai and Khao Khieo at 3600 ft. (1100 m).

CLIMATE: Station #49000, Ban Ta Khli, Thailand, Lat. 15.3°N, Long. 100.3°E, at 100 ft. (30 m). Temperatures are calculated for an elevation of 3600 ft. (1100 m), resulting in probable extremes of 101°F (39°C) and 31°F (−1°C).

N/HEMISPHERE	JAN	FEB	MAR	APR	MAY	JUN	JUL	AUG	SEP	OCT	NOV	DEC
°F AVG MAX	77	82	87	88	85	82	80	79	77	77	77	76
°F AVG MIN	51	58	62	65	65	64	64	63	63	62	58	52
DIURNAL RANGE	26	24	25	23	20	18	16	16	14	15	19	24
RAIN/INCHES	0.1	0.7	1.4	3.4	5.1	5.4	5.5	6.3	11.2	6.2	1.4	0.1
HUMIDITY/%	60	61	60	72	64	75	80	83	85	83	78	68
BLOOM SEASON									*			
DAYS CLR @ 7AM	5	2	4	4	3	0	0	0	0	2	4	5
DAYS CLR @ 1PM	12	7	7	4	1	0	0	0	0	1	3	7
RAIN/MM	3	18	36	86	130	137	140	160	284	157	36	3
°C AVG MAX	25.2	28.0	30.8	31.3	29.7	28.0	26.9	26.3	25.2	25.2	25.2	24.7
°C AVG MIN	10.8	14.7	16.9	18.6	18.6	18.0	18.0	17.5	17.5	16.9	14.7	11.3
DIURNAL RANGE	14.4	13.3	13.9	12.7	11.1	10.0	8.9	8.8	7.7	8.3	10.5	13.4
S/HEMISPHERE	JUL	AUG	SEP	OCT	NOV	DEC	JAN	FEB	MAR	APR	MAY	JUN

Cultural Recommendations

LIGHT: 3000–3500 fc.

TEMPERATURES: Summer days average 79–82°F (26–28°C), and nights average 63–64°F (18°C), with a diurnal range of 16–18°F (9–10°C). The warmest weather occurs in spring. Days average 85–88°F (30–31°C), and nights average 62–65°F (17–19°C), with a diurnal range of 20–25°F (11–14°C).

Dendrobium ciliatum

HUMIDITY: 75–85% from summer into late autumn, decreasing to about 60% in winter.

WATER: Rainfall is moderate to heavy for 7 months from late spring into autumn. The wet season changes rapidly into a 4–5 month dry period that extends from late autumn into spring. Cultivated plants should be kept moist while growing, but water should be reduced after new growths mature in autumn.

FERTILIZER: ¼–½ recommended strength, applied weekly. A high-nitrogen fertilizer is beneficial from spring to midsummer, but a fertilizer high in phosphates should be used in late summer and autumn.

REST PERIOD: Winter days average 76–82°F (25–28°C), and nights average 51–58°F (11–15°C), with a diurnal range of 24–26°F (13–14°C). In the habitat, rainfall is low in winter, and humidity is so low that even morning dew is uncommon. In cultivation, water should be reduced to an occasional light misting for 2–3 months. Fertilizer should be eliminated until water is increased in spring.

GROWING MEDIA: Plants may be mounted on tree-fern or cork slabs if humidity is high and plants are watered at least once daily in summer. When plants are potted, any open, fast-draining medium may be used. Repotting is best done in early spring when new roots are growing.

MISCELLANEOUS NOTES: The bloom season shown in the climate table is based on reports from the habitat.

Plant and Flower Information

PLANT SIZE AND TYPE: An 8–10 in. (20–25 cm) sympodial epiphyte.

PSEUDOBULB: 8–10 in. (20–25 cm) long. The stems are slender with nodes each 1.2–1.4 in. (3.0–3.5 cm). Rooting branches often develop at the nodes.

LEAVES: 2 per growth. The lanceolate, pointed leaves are 2.4 in. (6 cm) long.

INFLORESCENCE: Very short. Inflorescences emerge from nodes along the side of the stem just below the leaves.

FLOWERS: 1 per inflorescence. The cream-yellow flowers are 0.4 in. (1 cm) long and remain rather closed. The lip is marked with purple streaks.

REFERENCES: 234, 454.

PHOTOS/DRAWINGS: 454.

Dendrobium ciliatum Parish ex Hooker f. not (Ruiz and Pavón) Persoon. See *D. venustum* Teijsm. and Binn. REFERENCES: 25, 154, 157, 167, 188, 190, 202, 211, 216, 254, 266, 454, 541, 570, 580.

Dendrobium ciliatum (Ruiz and Pavón) Persoon not Parish ex Hooker f. Now considered a synonym of *Lycaste barringtoniae* (Smith) Lindley. REFERENCES: 190, 216, 254.

Dendrobium ciliferum Bakhuizen. See *D. venustum* Teijsm. and Binn. REFERENCES: 25, 211, 230, 454.

Dendrobium cincinnatum F. Mueller 1884

AKA: Schlechter (ref. 437) indicated that *D. chalmersii* F. Mueller 1882 was certainly identical with *D. cincinnatum* F. Mueller 1884, and that both species belonged to the section *Trachyrhizum*, which would make *D. chalmersii* the correct name. However, Schlechter further indicated that he had never found a member of this section below the cloudforest, thus disagreeing with Millar (ref. 304), who found *D. cincinnatum* at low elevations. Kränzlin (ref. 254) included *D. chalmersii* from southeastern New Guinea in his list of doubtful species, indicating that it was poorly described with no illustration. Ossian (ref. 348) included *D. chalmersii* in the section *Ceratobium*. Cribb (ref. 82) reviewed the section *Ceratobium* in the Pacific Islands, but his work did not extend to New Guinea.

ORIGIN/HABITAT: Papua New Guinea. Plants grow in the Milne Bay region near Wakaiuna on Normandy Island, which is located just northeast of the eastern tip of New Guinea. Millar (ref. 304) reports that even after collecting extensively in Papua, she has never found the plants anywhere else. They usually grow on beech trees, especially *Calophyllum inophyllum*.

CLIMATE: Station #94075, Samarai, Sideia Island, Papua New Guinea, Lat. 10.6°S, Long. 150.7°E, at 20 ft. (6 m). Record extreme temperatures are 104°F (40°C) and 64°F (18°C).

N/HEMISPHERE	JAN	FEB	MAR	APR	MAY	JUN	JUL	AUG	SEP	OCT	NOV	DEC
°F AVG MAX	81	81	82	83	85	87	87	88	87	86	84	82
°F AVG MIN	74	73	74	74	75	76	77	77	76	75	75	74
DIURNAL RANGE	7	8	8	9	10	11	10	11	11	11	9	8
RAIN/INCHES	8.1	8.6	10.1	8.7	8.4	6.1	7.0	7.8	10.0	9.8	12.0	11.3
HUMIDITY/%	N/A											
BLOOM SEASON	N/A											
DAYS CLR	N/A											
RAIN/MM	206	218	257	221	213	155	178	198	254	249	305	287
°C AVG MAX	27.2	27.2	27.8	28.3	29.4	30.6	30.6	31.1	30.6	30.0	28.9	27.8
°C AVG MIN	23.3	22.8	23.3	23.3	23.9	24.4	25.0	25.0	24.4	23.9	23.9	23.3
DIURNAL RANGE	3.9	4.4	4.5	5.0	5.5	6.2	5.6	6.1	6.2	6.1	5.0	4.5
S/HEMISPHERE	JUL	AUG	SEP	OCT	NOV	DEC	JAN	FEB	MAR	APR	MAY	JUN

Cultural Recommendations

LIGHT: 2500–3000 fc.

TEMPERATURES: Throughout the year, days average 81–88°F (27–31°C), and nights average 73–77°F (23–25°C), with a diurnal range of 7–11°F (4–6°C).

HUMIDITY: Information is not available for this location. However, records from nearby stations indicate that humidity is probably 70–80% year-round.

WATER: Rainfall is very heavy year-round. Cultivated plants should be kept moist but not soggy.

FERTILIZER: ¼–½ recommended strength. A balanced fertilizer should be applied weekly to biweekly throughout the year.

REST PERIOD: Growing temperatures should be maintained year-round, but growers indicate that plants are healthy and continue to bloom regularly with winter lows as cold as 55–60°F (13–16°C). In the habitat, winter rainfall is high; but water and fertilizer should be reduced for cultivated plants, especially those grown in the dark, short-day conditions in temperate-latitude winters. Plants should never be allowed to dry out completely, however. In the habitat, seasonal light variation is minor.

GROWING MEDIA: Plants may be mounted on tree-fern or cork slabs if humidity is high and plants are watered at least once daily in summer. When plants are potted, any open, fast-draining medium may be used. Repotting may be done anytime roots are actively growing.

MISCELLANEOUS NOTES: The roots are strong and wiry.

Plant and Flower Information

PLANT SIZE AND TYPE: A 16–31 in. (40–80 cm) sympodial epiphyte. Plants form clumps of 20 or more canes.

PSEUDOBULB: 16–31 in. (40–80 cm) long. The yellow pseudobulbs are slender. Stems are leafy.

LEAVES: Many. The lanceolate leaves are olive green and parchment thin.

INFLORESCENCE: 6 in. (15 cm) long. Inflorescences emerge from nodes along the stem.

FLOWERS: 8–12 per inflorescence. The flowers are long-lasting, faintly fragrant, and measure about 1.2 in. (3 cm) across. The strongly recurved sepals and petals are milky white with pale yellow areas and purple veins. The sepals, which are wider than the petals, are ovate with elongated tips. Petals are serrated along the margin and narrowly pointed. The lip is frilly along the margin.

REFERENCES: 216, 253, 254, 304, 348, 437.

PHOTOS/DRAWINGS: *304*, 348.

Dendrobium cinereum J. J. Smith

ORIGIN/HABITAT: Western Borneo. Plants are found in Kalimantan and near Poring in Sabah. Specific habitat information is unavailable, but habitat elevation is estimated as 2500 ft. (760 m). The following climate data should, therefore, be used with caution.

CLIMATE: Station #49613, Tambunan, Sabah, Borneo, Lat. 5.7°N, Long. 116.4°E, at 1200 ft. (366 m). Temperatures are calculated for an elevation of 2500 ft. (760 m), resulting in probable extremes of 94°F (34°C) and 50°F (10°C).

N/HEMISPHERE	JAN	FEB	MAR	APR	MAY	JUN	JUL	AUG	SEP	OCT	NOV	DEC
°F AVG MAX	82	83	85	86	86	85	85	85	85	84	83	82
°F AVG MIN	63	61	62	63	64	63	62	62	63	63	63	64
DIURNAL RANGE	19	22	23	23	22	22	23	23	22	21	20	18
RAIN/INCHES	5.8	3.7	5.8	7.5	8.2	7.3	5.1	4.9	6.4	7.0	6.8	6.0
HUMIDITY/%	N/A											
BLOOM SEASON	N/A											
DAYS CLR	N/A											
RAIN/MM	147	94	147	191	208	185	130	124	163	178	173	152
°C AVG MAX	27.8	28.3	29.4	30.0	30.0	29.6	29.5	29.4	29.4	28.9	28.3	27.8
°C AVG MIN	17.2	16.0	16.5	17.1	17.6	17.1	16.5	16.5	17.1	17.1	17.1	17.6
DIURNAL RANGE	10.6	12.3	12.9	12.9	12.4	12.5	13.0	12.9	12.3	11.8	11.2	10.2
S/HEMISPHERE	JUL	AUG	SEP	OCT	NOV	DEC	JAN	FEB	MAR	APR	MAY	JUN

Cultural Recommendations

LIGHT: 2000–2500 fc.

TEMPERATURES: Throughout the year, days average 82–86°F (28–30°C), and nights average 61–64°F (16–18°C), with a diurnal range of 18–23°F (10–13°C).

HUMIDITY: Information is not available for this location. However, records from nearby locations indicate that humidity probably averages 80–85% year-round.

WATER: Rainfall is moderate to heavy all year with a brief, slightly drier period in winter. Cultivated plants should be allowed to dry only slightly between waterings.

FERTILIZER: 1/4–1/2 recommended strength. A balanced fertilizer should be applied weekly to biweekly throughout the year.

REST PERIOD: Growing conditions should be maintained all year. Water should be reduced slightly in winter, but the plants should never be allowed to dry out completely. Fertilizer should be reduced anytime plants are not actively growing.

GROWING MEDIA: Plants may be mounted on tree-fern or cork slabs or potted in small pots filled with any open, fast-draining medium. Repotting may be done anytime new roots are growing.

MISCELLANEOUS NOTES: The plant was described in 1920 in *Bul. Jard. Bot. Buit.* 3rd sér. 2:78.

Plant and Flower Information

PLANT SIZE AND TYPE: A 31 in. (80 cm) sympodial epiphyte.

PSEUDOBULB: 31 in. (80 cm) long. The clustered stems are slender, dirty green, shiny, and longitudinally grooved.

LEAVES: Many. The oblong leaves are 3.2–4.0 in. (8–10 cm) long. They are shiny, pearl-grey on the upper surface and dark violet underneath. The leaf sheaths are pale green with a violet suffusion. The nerves are violet.

INFLORESCENCE: Short. Inflorescences are borne at nodes on leafless stems.

FLOWERS: The flowers, which open fully, are about 1 in. (2.5 cm) across with a fragrance that is reminiscent of *Dianthum caryophyllum*. Blossoms are ivory white, often with a purplish suffusion. The blossoms have an erect dorsal sepal, elongated lateral sepals, and recurved petals. The lip is spatula shaped.

REFERENCES: 222, 592.

PHOTOS/DRAWINGS: *592*.

Dendrobium cinnabarinum Rchb. f.

AKA: Hunt (ref. 211) includes the synonyms *D. sanguineum* Rolfe not Swartz and *D. holttumianum* A. Hawkes and A. H. Heller.

ORIGIN/HABITAT: Borneo. Originally reported from Labuan, Sabah (North Borneo), plants have since been found in mountain forests of Sarawak near the limestone pinnacles north of Mt. Api at 3950 ft. (1200 m), in the lower moss forests on Mt. Dulit at 6250 ft. (1900 m), and on Mt. Buda on limestone at 2950–3300 ft. (900–1000 m).

CLIMATE: Station #96449, Miri, Sarawak, Lat. 4.4°N, Long. 114.0°E, at 13 ft. (4 m). Temperatures are calculated for an elevation of 4000 ft. (1220 m), resulting in probable extremes of 82°F (28°C) and 54°F (12°C).

N/HEMISPHERE	JAN	FEB	MAR	APR	MAY	JUN	JUL	AUG	SEP	OCT	NOV	DEC
°F AVG MAX	73	73	74	75	75	75	75	75	74	74	74	74
°F AVG MIN	61	61	61	62	62	62	61	61	61	61	61	61
DIURNAL RANGE	12	12	13	13	13	13	14	14	13	13	13	13
RAIN/INCHES	16.8	6.5	5.5	4.4	8.2	12.0	8.5	8.4	11.8	11.7	14.5	11.3
HUMIDITY/%	86	86	85	83	83	82	81	81	82	83	84	85
BLOOM SEASON									•			
DAYS CLR @ 8AM	1	2	4	4	3	2	3	2	2	1	2	2
DAYS CLR @ 2PM	1	1	3	4	2	5	3	2	3	2	1	1
RAIN/MM	427	165	140	112	208	305	216	213	300	297	368	287
°C AVG MAX	22.7	22.7	23.2	23.8	23.8	23.8	23.8	23.8	23.2	23.2	23.2	23.2
°C AVG MIN	16.0	16.0	16.0	16.6	16.6	16.6	16.0	16.0	16.0	16.0	16.0	16.0
DIURNAL RANGE	6.7	6.7	7.2	7.2	7.2	7.2	7.8	7.8	7.2	7.2	7.2	7.2
S/HEMISPHERE	JUL	AUG	SEP	OCT	NOV	DEC	JAN	FEB	MAR	APR	MAY	JUN

Cultural Recommendations

LIGHT: 2000–3000 fc.

TEMPERATURES: Throughout the year, days average 73–75°F (23–24°C), and nights average 61–62°F (16–17°C), with a diurnal range of 12–14°F (7–8°C).

HUMIDITY: Near 80–85% year-round.

WATER: Rainfall is heavy to very heavy all year, but conditions are slightly drier in winter. Cultivated plants should be kept moist but not soggy.

FERTILIZER: 1/4–1/2 recommended strength. A balanced fertilizer should be applied weekly to biweekly throughout the year.

REST PERIOD: Growing conditions should be maintained all year. In cultivation, water and fertilizer should be reduced in winter, especially for plants grown in the dark, short-day conditions common in temperate latitudes. They should never be allowed to dry out completely, however. In the habitat, seasonal light variation is minor.

GROWING MEDIA: Plants may be mounted on tree-fern or cork slabs if humidity is high and plants are watered at least once daily in summer. When plants are potted, any open, fast-draining medium may be used. Repotting may be done anytime new roots are growing.

MISCELLANEOUS NOTES: The bloom season shown in the climate table is based on records from the habitat.

Plant and Flower Information

PLANT SIZE AND TYPE: A 35 in. (90 cm) sympodial epiphyte.

PSEUDOBULB: 35 in. (90 cm) long. The shiny stem is thin with 8 ridges at the base. Above the base, it is thickened for 3–4 in. (8–10 cm), then becomes very slender again near the tip.

LEAVES: Young leaves are linear-oblong.

INFLORESCENCE: 2 in. (5 cm) long. Inflorescences emerge near the apex of leafless stems.

Dendrobium citrinocastaneum

FLOWERS: 1–3 per inflorescence. The flowers, which Reichenbach described as "resembling scarlet and purple moths sitting on the straw-colored twigs," are 2.0–3.2 in. (5–8 cm) across and somewhat short-lived. They are not fragrant. The lanceolate-oblong sepals and broader, obovate petals are crimson or vermilion with white or light ochre near the base. The small lip, which may be whitish or pale orange, is deep crimson at the frilled tip. The lip is marked with spots, 3–5 purple lines, and a yellow callus. It is very wavy along the front margin. Blossoms are highly variable in size, shape, and coloring.

REFERENCES: 59, 211, 216, 254, 286, 295, 430, 586.

PHOTOS/DRAWINGS: *430.*

Dendrobium citrinocastaneum Burkill. Now considered a synonym of *Epigeneium zebrinum* (J. J. Smith) Summerhayes. REFERENCES: 223, 449, 455, 499.

Dendrobium citrinum Ridley

ORIGIN/HABITAT: Irian Jaya (western New Guinea). Plants were collected on the south side of Mt. Jaya (Mt. Carstensz) at about 5500 ft. (1680 m).

CLIMATE: Station #97796, Kokenau (Kokonau), Irian Jaya, Lat. 4.7°S, Long. 135.4°E, at 10 ft. (3 m). Temperatures are calculated for an elevation of 5500 ft. (1680 m). Record extreme temperatures are not available for this location.

N/HEMISPHERE	JAN	FEB	MAR	APR	MAY	JUN	JUL	AUG	SEP	OCT	NOV	DEC
°F AVG MAX	65	65	68	70	72	71	71	71	72	70	69	66
°F AVG MIN	55	55	56	56	56	57	56	56	56	56	56	55
DIURNAL RANGE	10	10	12	14	16	14	15	15	16	14	13	11
RAIN/INCHES	18.4	15.8	18.9	11.6	9.7	10.6	11.5	15.7	11.6	11.6	16.0	19.9
HUMIDITY/%	N/A											
BLOOM SEASON			*									
DAYS CLR	N/A											
RAIN/MM	467	401	480	295	246	269	292	399	295	295	406	505
°C AVG MAX	18.3	18.3	19.9	21.0	22.2	21.6	21.6	21.6	22.2	21.0	20.5	18.8
°C AVG MIN	12.7	12.7	13.3	13.3	13.3	13.8	13.3	13.3	13.3	13.3	13.3	12.7
DIURNAL RANGE	5.6	5.6	6.6	7.7	8.9	7.8	8.3	8.3	8.9	7.7	7.2	6.1
S/HEMISPHERE	JUL	AUG	SEP	OCT	NOV	DEC	JAN	FEB	MAR	APR	MAY	JUN

Cultural Recommendations

LIGHT: 2500–3500 fc.

TEMPERATURES: Throughout the year, days average 65–72°F (18–22°C), and nights average 55–57°F (13–14°C), with a diurnal range of 10–16°F (6–9°C).

HUMIDITY: Information is not available for this location. However, records from nearby stations indicate that humidity is probably near 85% year-round.

WATER: Rainfall is very heavy year-round. Cultivated plants should be kept evenly moist but not soggy.

FERTILIZER: ¼–½ recommended strength. A balanced fertilizer should be applied weekly to biweekly throughout the year.

REST PERIOD: Growing conditions should be maintained year-round. Water and fertilizer might be reduced slightly in winter, especially for plants cultivated in the dark, short-day conditions common in temperate latitudes; but plants should never be allowed to dry out completely. In the habitat, seasonal light variation is minor.

GROWING MEDIA: Plants may be mounted on tree-fern or cork slabs or potted in small pots filled with any open, fast-draining medium. Repotting may be done anytime new roots are growing.

MISCELLANEOUS NOTES: The bloom season shown in the climate table is based on reports from the habitat.

Plant and Flower Information

PLANT SIZE AND TYPE: A tufted, 1.2–2.0 in. (3–5 cm) sympodial epiphyte.

PSEUDOBULB: 0.4 in. (1 cm) long. The tiny pseudobulbs are wrinkled.

LEAVES: 1 per growth. The leaves are 0.8–1.2 in. (2–3 cm) long.

INFLORESCENCE: 1 in. (2.5 cm) long. The inflorescence is white.

FLOWERS: 1 per inflorescence. The flowers are 0.8 in. (2 cm) long. They are yellowish white with an orange keel. The petals and lip are smaller than the sepals.

REFERENCES: 222, 400.

Dendrobium clarissimum Ridley. See *D. roseatum* Ridley.
REFERENCES: 200, 221, 402, 455.

Dendrobium clausum Schlechter

ORIGIN/HABITAT: Northern Papua New Guinea. Plants grow on forest trees in the Finisterre Range at about 3950 ft. (1200 m).

CLIMATE: Station #200187, Erap, Papua New Guinea, Lat. 6.6°S, Long. 146.7°E, at 850 ft. (260m). Temperatures are calculated for an elevation of 3950 ft. (1200 m), resulting in probable extremes of 92 °F (33°C) and 43°F (6°C).

N/HEMISPHERE	JAN	FEB	MAR	APR	MAY	JUN	JUL	AUG	SEP	OCT	NOV	DEC
°F AVG MAX	78	78	79	80	83	83	83	83	83	82	80	80
°F AVG MIN	59	59	59	60	62	63	62	62	63	61	64	60
DIURNAL RANGE	19	19	20	20	21	20	21	21	20	21	16	20
RAIN/INCHES	3.9	3.9	2.7	3.0	3.0	5.3	5.9	5.9	7.0	3.4	2.4	3.1
HUMIDITY/%	82	81	81	79	75	74	74	74	77	76	80	80
BLOOM SEASON									*			
DAYS CLR	N/A											
RAIN/MM	99	99	69	76	76	135	150	150	178	86	61	79
°C AVG MAX	25.6	25.6	26.1	26.7	28.3	28.5	28.4	28.3	28.3	27.8	26.7	26.7
°C AVG MIN	15.0	14.9	14.9	15.4	16.5	17.1	16.5	16.5	17.1	16.0	17.7	15.4
DIURNAL RANGE	10.6	10.7	11.2	11.3	11.8	11.4	11.9	11.8	11.2	11.8	9.1	11.3
S/HEMISPHERE	JUL	AUG	SEP	OCT	NOV	DEC	JAN	FEB	MAR	APR	MAY	JUN

Cultural Recommendations

LIGHT: 2500–3000 fc.

TEMPERATURES: Throughout the year, days average 78–83°F (26–29°C), and nights average 59–64°F (15–18°C), with a diurnal range of 16–21°F (9–12°C).

HUMIDITY: 75–80% year-round. Despite high average humidity, the habitat may be quite dry during hot afternoons.

WATER: Rainfall is moderate most of the year, but for 4–5 months in summer and early autumn, conditions are wetter. Cultivated plants should be thoroughly saturated then allowed to dry slightly between waterings.

FERTILIZER: ¼–½ recommended strength. A balanced fertilizer should be applied weekly to biweekly throughout the year.

REST PERIOD: Growing temperatures should be maintained all year. In the habitat, rainfall is lowest in winter, but the high humidity indicates that additional moisture is frequently available from heavy dew. Cultivated plants should be allowed to dry for somewhat longer between waterings, but they should not remain dry for extended periods. Fertilizer should be reduced until water is increased in spring. In the habitat, seasonal light variation is minor.

GROWING MEDIA: Plants may be mounted on tree-fern or cork slabs if humidity is high and plants are watered at least once daily in summer. When plants are potted, any open, fast-draining medium may be used. Repotting may be done anytime new roots are growing.

MISCELLANEOUS NOTES: The bloom season shown in the climate table is based on collection reports. Plants that produce flowers which last a single day commonly bloom several times during the year. Flowering usually occurs 7–14 days after a sudden 10°F (5°C) drop in daytime temperatures.

Plant and Flower Information

PLANT SIZE AND TYPE: A 12–16 in. (30–40 cm) sympodial epiphyte.

PSEUDOBULB: 12–16 in. (30–40 cm) long. The pseudobulbs are slightly flattened and erect to spreading. They do not branch.

LEAVES: Many. Growths are densely leafy. The spreading, elliptic leaves are usually 1.8–2.8 in. (4.6–7.1 cm) long.

INFLORESCENCE: Very short. Inflorescences emerge from the leaf axils.

FLOWERS: 2 per inflorescence. The flowers are 0.4 in. (1 cm) across. The blossoms are rather closed. Sepals and petals are pale yellow. The lip is white near the apex and the column foot is marked with an orange-yellow spot. Blossoms normally last a single day, but they may self-pollinate before the flowers open.

REFERENCES: 92, 221, 437, 445.

PHOTOS/DRAWINGS: 437.

Dendrobium clavator Ridley

AKA: *D. mellitum* Ridley.

ORIGIN/HABITAT: The southern part of peninsular Thailand and Malaya. In Malaya, plants grow near Taiping in Perak state and in the states of Johore and Negeri Sembilan.

CLIMATE: Station #48625, Ipoh, Malaya, Lat. 4.6°N, Long. 101.1°E, at 123 ft. (37 m). Record extreme temperatures are 99°F (37°C) and 64°F (18°C).

N/HEMISPHERE	JAN	FEB	MAR	APR	MAY	JUN	JUL	AUG	SEP	OCT	NOV	DEC
°F AVG MAX	90	92	93	92	92	92	91	91	90	89	89	89
°F AVG MIN	72	72	73	73	74	73	72	72	73	72	72	72
DIURNAL RANGE	18	20	20	19	18	19	19	19	17	17	17	17
RAIN/INCHES	7.9	3.1	7.6	8.4	6.2	3.6	7.2	6.9	8.8	11.0	13.0	8.9
HUMIDITY/%	76	74	76	78	78	75	76	77	79	82	82	81
BLOOM SEASON	N/A											
DAYS CLR @ 7AM	3	3	3	1	1	2	1	1	0	0	1	2
DAYS CLR @ 1PM	2	2	2	1	1	1	1	1	0	0	0	2
RAIN/MM	201	79	193	213	157	91	183	175	224	279	330	226
°C AVG MAX	32.2	33.3	33.9	33.3	33.3	33.3	32.8	32.8	32.2	31.7	31.7	31.7
°C AVG MIN	22.2	22.2	22.8	22.8	23.3	22.8	22.2	22.2	22.8	22.2	22.2	22.2
DIURNAL RANGE	10.0	11.1	11.1	10.5	10.0	10.5	10.6	10.6	9.4	9.5	9.5	9.5
S/HEMISPHERE	JUL	AUG	SEP	OCT	NOV	DEC	JAN	FEB	MAR	APR	MAY	JUN

Cultural Recommendations

LIGHT: 2000–3000 fc.

TEMPERATURES: Throughout the year, days average 89–93°F (32–34°C), and nights average 72–74°F (22–23°C), with a diurnal range of 17–20°F (9–11°C). Average highs fluctuate only 4°F (2°C) all year, and average lows vary only 2°F (1°C).

HUMIDITY: 75–80% year-round.

WATER: Rainfall is heavy most of the year. The heaviest rainfall occurs in autumn with a secondary maximum in spring. Brief semidry periods occur in midwinter and midsummer. Cultivated plants should be kept evenly moist with only slight drying allowed between waterings.

FERTILIZER: ¼–½ recommended strength. A balanced fertilizer should be applied weekly to biweekly throughout the year.

REST PERIOD: Growing conditions should be maintained year-round. Water should be reduced somewhat in winter for plants cultivated in the dark, short-day conditions common in temperate latitudes. They should never be allowed to dry out completely, however. Fertilizer may be reduced when the plant is not actively growing or when water is reduced. In the habitat, light is slightly higher in winter.

GROWING MEDIA: Plants may be mounted on tree-fern or cork slabs if humidity is high and plants are watered at least once daily in summer. When plants are potted, any open, fast-draining medium may be used. Repotting may be done anytime new roots are growing.

MISCELLANEOUS NOTES: Plants that produce flowers which last a single day commonly bloom several times during the year. Flowering usually occurs 7–14 days after a sudden 10°F (5°C) drop in daytime temperatures.

Plant and Flower Information

PLANT SIZE AND TYPE: An 8–12 in. (20–31 cm) sympodial epiphyte.

PSEUDOBULB: 8–12 in. (20–31 cm) long. The stems have a short, swollen portion 1–2 internodes long. The slender pseudobulbs are 8–10 angled. *D. clavator* is vegetatively very similar to *D. setifolium* Ridley.

LEAVES: 2–4 per growth. The terete leaves are usually 1.2–3.2 in. (3–8 cm) long, widely spaced, and deciduous.

INFLORESCENCE: Very short. Inflorescences emerge opposite the leaves near the apex of the stem.

FLOWERS: 1 per inflorescence. The nearly upside down flowers are small for the plant size and remain rather closed. Sepals and petals are lanceolate. Blossoms may be yellowish, greenish yellow, or dirty orange, but the petals may be flushed with red. The midlobe of the lip, which is yellowish with purple markings, is toothed or uneven along the front margin. The erect sidelobes have pale red nerves. Flowers last 2 days.

HYBRIDIZING NOTES: Chromosome count is 2n = 38 (ref. 154, 188).

REFERENCES: 154, 188, 200, 254, 395, 402, 450, 454, 455.

PHOTOS/DRAWINGS: 200, 450, 454, 455.

Dendrobium clavatum Lindley not Roxburgh. The describer is sometimes listed as Wallich, see *D. chryseum* Rolfe. REFERENCES: 38, 46, 102, 152, 153, 179, 202, 208, 216, 243, 254, 266, 274, 317, 367, 369, 414, 430, 445, 447, 454, 497, 505, 541, 570, 580. PHOTOS/DRAWINGS: *274, 497.*

Dendrobium clavatum Roxburgh not Lindley. See *D. densiflorum* Lindley. REFERENCES: 216, 254, 454.

Dendrobium clavipes Hooker f. See *D. truncatum* Lindley. REFERENCES: 25, 75, 202, 218, 254, 395, 445, 454, 469. PHOTOS/DRAWINGS: 469.

Dendrobium clavuligerum J. J. Smith. Plants originated from Irian Jaya (western New Guinea). Habitat location and elevation were not reported, so climate data cannot be selected. In the habitat, blooming occurs in winter. A sympodial epiphyte of unreported size. The partial stem available at the time the plant was described was 10 in. (25 cm) long. The numerous, papery leaves are 3 in. (7.5 cm) long, spreading, and somewhat twisted at the base. The short inflorescences bear 2 blossoms. The conspicuous flowers are 1.6 in. (4 cm) long. Sepals and petals are slender. The upper part of the lip is recurved. The midlobe is densely covered with long hairs. The plant was described from a dried specimen and flower color was not available. REFERENCES: 225, 486.

Dendrobium cleistogamum Schlechter

ORIGIN/HABITAT: New Caledonia. *D. cleistogamum* is endemic and rare. It grows on tree trunks near the Ngoye River and in humid mountain forests at 2950–4100 ft. (900–1250 m).

CLIMATE: Station #91592, Noumea, New Caledonia, Lat. 22.3°S, Long. 166.5°E, at 246 ft. (75 m). Temperatures are calculated for an elevation of 3000 ft. (914 m), resulting in probable extremes of 90°F (32°C) and 43°F (6°C).

Dendrobium clemensiae

N/HEMISPHERE	JAN	FEB	MAR	APR	MAY	JUN	JUL	AUG	SEP	OCT	NOV	DEC
°F AVG MAX	67	67	69	71	74	77	77	76	76	74	70	68
°F AVG MIN	53	52	54	56	59	61	63	64	63	61	57	55
DIURNAL RANGE	14	15	15	15	15	16	14	12	13	13	13	13
RAIN/INCHES	3.6	2.6	2.5	2.0	2.4	2.6	3.7	5.1	5.7	5.2	4.4	3.7
HUMIDITY/%	73	70	69	67	68	69	71	74	75	76	73	73
BLOOM SEASON			*			*						
DAYS CLR @ 11AM	7	9	9	15	12	10	7	6	7	7	7	7
DAYS CLR @ 5PM	7	11	6	11	7	6	5	4	4	5	3	7
RAIN/MM	91	66	64	51	61	66	94	130	145	132	112	94
°C AVG MAX	19.4	19.4	20.5	21.6	23.3	25.0	25.0	24.4	24.4	23.3	21.1	20.0
°C AVG MIN	11.6	11.1	12.2	13.3	15.0	16.1	17.2	17.7	17.2	16.1	13.8	12.7
DIURNAL RANGE	7.8	8.3	8.3	8.3	8.3	8.9	7.8	6.7	7.2	7.2	7.3	7.3
S/HEMISPHERE	JUL	AUG	SEP	OCT	NOV	DEC	JAN	FEB	MAR	APR	MAY	JUN

Cultural Recommendations

LIGHT: 1800–2500 fc. Days are frequently clear, indicating relatively high light. However, the humid forest microclimate suggests lower light.

TEMPERATURES: Summer days average 76–77°F (24–25°C), and nights average 61–64°F (16–18°C), with a diurnal range of 12–16°F (7–9°C) which fluctuates only 4°F (2°C) throughout the year.

HUMIDITY: 70–75% year-round with the lower values occurring from late winter to early summer.

WATER: Rainfall is relatively low and consistent all year. The heaviest rain falls in late summer and early autumn. In this region, rain normally falls as heavy showers, so plants might be healthiest if they are allowed to become somewhat dry before being watered thoroughly.

FERTILIZER: ¼–½ recommended strength, applied weekly. A high-nitrogen fertilizer is beneficial from spring to midsummer, but a fertilizer high in phosphates should be used in late summer and autumn.

REST PERIOD: Winter days average 67–69°F (19–21°C), and nights average 52–54°F (11–12°C), with a diurnal range of 13–15°F (7–8°C). In cultivation, water and fertilizer should be reduced somewhat in winter and spring, but plants should not be allowed to remain completely dry for long periods. In the habitat, light is highest in winter.

GROWING MEDIA: Plants may be mounted on tree-fern or cork slabs if humidity is high and plants are watered at least once daily in summer. When plants are potted, any open, fast-draining medium may be used. Repotting is best done in early spring when new roots are growing.

MISCELLANEOUS NOTES: The bloom season shown in the climate table is based on reports from the habitat.

Plant and Flower Information

PLANT SIZE AND TYPE: An 18 in. (45 cm) sympodial epiphyte.

PSEUDOBULB: 18 in. (45 cm) long. The pseudobulbs are quadrangular, slightly zigzag, and clustered. They arise from a very short rhizome.

LEAVES: 9–11 per growth. The distichous leaves are 1.0–1.6 in. (2.5–4.0 cm) long. They are linear, spreading to erect, unequally bilobed, and leathery.

INFLORESCENCE: 1.2 in. (3 cm) long. Inflorescences are held in 2 rows and emerge opposite the base of most leaves.

FLOWERS: 1–3 per inflorescence. The flowers, which are 0.2 in. (0.5 cm) long, are pollinated without opening.

REFERENCES: 173, 220, 254, 432.

PHOTOS/DRAWINGS: 173.

Dendrobium clemensiae Ames. Now considered a synonym of *Diplocaulobium clemensiae* (Ames) A. Hawkes. REFERENCES: 12, 221, 229, 296, 536.

Dendrobium closterium Rchb. f.

AKA: Hallé (ref. 173) includes *D. eleutheroglossum* Schlechter, *D. jocosum* Rchb. f., and *D. myrticola* Kränzlin as synonyms for *D. closterium* var. *jocosum* (Rchb. f.) Hallé.

ORIGIN/HABITAT: Widely distributed on New Caledonia. Plants grow from sea level to 3300 ft. (0–1000 m), but most are found below 1650 ft. (500 m). In the Southern District near Yaouhé, plants grow on the trunks of *Melaleuca viridiflora* Forster at low elevations. In the Northern District, they are found on *Casuarina* trees near Ou Hinna.

CLIMATE: Station #91592, Noumea, New Caledonia, Lat. 22.3°S, Long. 166.5°E, at 246 ft. (75 m). Temperatures are calculated for an elevation of 650 ft. (200 m), resulting in probable extremes of 98°F (36°C) and 51°F (10°C).

N/HEMISPHERE	JAN	FEB	MAR	APR	MAY	JUN	JUL	AUG	SEP	OCT	NOV	DEC
°F AVG MAX	75	75	77	79	82	85	85	84	84	82	78	76
°F AVG MIN	61	60	62	64	67	69	71	72	71	69	65	63
DIURNAL RANGE	14	15	15	15	15	16	14	12	13	13	13	13
RAIN/INCHES	3.6	2.6	2.5	2.0	2.4	2.6	3.7	5.1	5.7	5.2	4.4	3.7
HUMIDITY/%	73	70	69	67	68	69	71	74	75	76	73	73
BLOOM SEASON			*		**	**	**		*			
DAYS CLR @ 11AM	7	9	9	15	12	10	7	6	7	7	7	7
DAYS CLR @ 5PM	7	11	6	11	7	6	5	4	4	5	3	7
RAIN/MM	91	66	64	51	61	66	94	130	145	132	112	94
°C AVG MAX	23.7	23.7	24.8	25.9	27.6	29.2	29.2	28.7	28.7	27.6	25.3	24.2
°C AVG MIN	15.9	15.3	16.4	17.6	19.2	20.3	21.4	22.0	21.4	20.3	18.1	17.0
DIURNAL RANGE	7.8	8.4	8.4	8.3	8.4	8.9	7.8	6.7	7.3	7.3	7.2	7.2
S/HEMISPHERE	JUL	AUG	SEP	OCT	NOV	DEC	JAN	FEB	MAR	APR	MAY	JUN

Cultural Recommendations

LIGHT: 1800–2500 fc.

TEMPERATURES: Summer days average 84–85°F (29°C), and nights average 69–72°F (20–22°C), with a diurnal range of 12–16°F (7–9°C).

HUMIDITY: 70–75% year-round.

WATER: Rainfall is low to moderate throughout the year, but is probably greater in the mountain habitat than the climate data indicates. Cultivated plants should be kept relatively moist, but should be allowed to dry slightly between waterings.

FERTILIZER: ¼–½ recommended strength, applied weekly. A high-nitrogen fertilizer is beneficial from spring to midsummer, but a fertilizer high in phosphates should be used in late summer and autumn.

REST PERIOD: Winter days average 75–77°F (24–25°C), and nights average 60–63°F (15–17°C), with a diurnal range of 13–15°F (7–8°C). High and low temperatures decline simultaneously, resulting in little change in the diurnal range. For cultivated plants, water should be reduced somewhat in winter, particularly for plants grown in the dark, short-day conditions common in temperate latitudes. Plants should not be allowed to dry out completely, however. In the habitat, light is highest in winter.

GROWING MEDIA: Plants may be mounted on tree-fern or cork slabs if humidity is high and plants are watered at least once daily in summer. When plants are potted, any open, fast-draining medium may be used. Repotting is best done in early spring when new roots are growing.

MISCELLANEOUS NOTES: The bloom season shown in the climate table is based on reports from the habitat.

Plant and Flower Information

PLANT SIZE AND TYPE: A 2.4–8.0 in. (6–20 cm) sympodial epiphyte.

PSEUDOBULB: 0.6–1.4 in. (1.5–3.5 cm) long. The swollen stems are carried on a very short rhizome.

LEAVES: 2 per growth. The elliptic leaves, which are unequally bilobed, are 1.4–3.4 in. (3.5–8.5 cm) long. They are erect to spreading with a leathery texture.

INFLORESCENCE: Short. The inflorescence emerges at the apex or from nodes so near the tip that it appears to be apical.

FLOWERS: 2–7 per inflorescence. The yellow flowers are 0.8–1.2 in. (2–3 cm) across. They have protruding sepals. The lip has white crests, red speckles, and a large notch in the midlobe.

REFERENCES: 173, 216, 233, 254, 432.

PHOTOS/DRAWINGS: 173.

Dendrobium cobbianum Rchb. f.
Status unknown. Kränzlin (ref. 254) included *Dendrobium cobbianum* as an uncertain species, and Merrill (ref. 296) specifically excludes it as a Philippine plant. The name is included in several lists of chromosome counts but we suspect that they should refer to *Dendrochilum cobbianum*. REFERENCES: 216, 254, 280, 296, 386, 504, 580.

Dendrobium coccinellum Ridley.
See *D. cuthbertsonii* F. Mueller. REFERENCES: 222, 385, 400.

Dendrobium coccineum Kränzlin

ORIGIN/HABITAT: Ambon Island in the Moluccas. Plants grow on Mt. Saltutu at about 3300 ft. (1000 m).

CLIMATE: Station #97724, Ambon Island, Indonesia. Lat. 3.7°S, Long. 128.1°E, at 33 ft. (10 m). Temperatures are calculated for an elevation of 3300 ft. (1000 m), resulting in probable extremes of 85°F (30°C) and 55°F (13°C).

N/HEMISPHERE	JAN	FEB	MAR	APR	MAY	JUN	JUL	AUG	SEP	OCT	NOV	DEC
°F AVG MAX	70	70	72	74	77	77	77	77	77	75	73	71
°F AVG MIN	63	63	63	63	64	65	65	65	65	65	64	63
DIURNAL RANGE	7	7	9	11	13	12	12	12	12	10	9	8
RAIN/INCHES	23.7	15.8	9.5	6.1	4.5	5.2	5.0	4.7	5.3	11.0	20.3	25.1
HUMIDITY/%	83	82	81	80	79	78	78	77	79	82	83	84
BLOOM SEASON						*						
DAYS CLR @ 9AM	1	1	1	6	7	4	3	3	5	5	3	3
DAYS CLR @ 3PM	1	1	2	5	6	1	1	1	2	3	1	3
RAIN/MM	602	401	241	155	114	132	127	119	135	279	516	638
°C AVG MAX	21.2	21.2	22.3	23.5	25.1	25.1	25.1	25.1	25.1	24.0	22.9	21.8
°C AVG MIN	17.3	17.3	17.3	17.3	17.9	18.5	18.5	18.5	18.5	18.5	17.9	17.3
DIURNAL RANGE	3.9	3.9	5.0	6.2	7.2	6.6	6.6	6.6	6.6	5.5	5.0	4.5
S/HEMISPHERE	JUL	AUG	SEP	OCT	NOV	DEC	JAN	FEB	MAR	APR	MAY	JUN

Cultural Recommendations

LIGHT: 2500–3500 fc.

TEMPERATURES: Throughout the year, days average 70–77°F (21–25°C), and nights average 63–65°F (17–19°C), with a diurnal range of 7–13°F (4–7°C).

HUMIDITY: 80–85% year-round.

WATER: Rainfall is moderate to heavy all year, but conditions are slightly drier from late spring through summer. Cultivated plants should be kept evenly moist with only slight drying allowed between waterings.

FERTILIZER: ¼–½ recommended strength. A balanced fertilizer should be applied weekly to biweekly throughout the year.

REST PERIOD: Growing conditions should be maintained all year. In the habitat, light may be slightly higher in winter. Even though rainfall is heavy in the habitat in winter, water should be reduced for plants grown in the dark, short-day conditions common in temperate latitudes. They should not be allowed to dry out completely, however.

GROWING MEDIA: Plants may be mounted on tree-fern or cork slabs if humidity is high and plants are watered at least once a day in summer. When plants are potted, any open, fast-draining medium may be used. Repotting may be done anytime new roots are growing.

MISCELLANEOUS NOTES: The bloom season shown in the climate table is based on reports from the habitat.

Plant and Flower Information

PLANT SIZE AND TYPE: A 16 in. (40 cm) sympodial epiphyte.

PSEUDOBULB: 16 in. (40 cm) long. The stems are slender and branching with numerous, branching roots.

LEAVES: The linear leaves are 1.2–1.8 in. (3.0–4.5 cm) long and unequally bilobed at the apex. The leaf sheaths are densely covered with pearl-like protrusions.

FLOWERS: The orange flowers are 1.2 in. (3 cm) across. Blossoms have spoon shaped sepals, small oblong petals, and a very small, simple lip. All segments are pointed.

REFERENCES: 220, 254.

Dendrobium cochinchinense Ridley.
See *D. aloifolium* (Blume) Rchb. f. REFERENCES: 254, 266, 395, 448, 454.

Dendrobium cochleatum J. J. Smith

ORIGIN/HABITAT: Irian Jaya (western New Guinea). Plants grow along the Noord River and south of Geluks Hill. They are found on trees in primary forests and on trees rooted in gravel banks.

CLIMATE: Station #97796, Kokenau (Kokonau), Irian Jaya, Lat. 4.7°S, Long. 136.4°E, at 10 ft. (3 m). Record extreme temperatures are not available for this location.

N/HEMISPHERE	JAN	FEB	MAR	APR	MAY	JUN	JUL	AUG	SEP	OCT	NOV	DEC
°F AVG MAX	83	83	86	88	90	89	89	89	90	88	87	84
°F AVG MIN	73	73	74	74	74	75	74	74	74	74	74	73
DIURNAL RANGE	10	10	12	14	16	14	15	15	16	14	13	11
RAIN/INCHES	18.4	15.8	18.9	11.6	9.7	10.6	11.5	15.7	11.6	11.6	16.0	19.9
HUMIDITY/%	N/A											
BLOOM SEASON	*											
DAYS CLR	N/A											
RAIN/MM	467	401	479	295	245	269	293	400	294	296	407	506
°C AVG MAX	28.6	28.4	30.2	31.1	32.1	31.9	31.9	31.7	32.0	31.4	30.7	28.7
°C AVG MIN	22.7	22.6	23.3	23.4	23.5	23.7	23.6	23.5	23.4	23.4	23.5	23.0
DIURNAL RANGE	5.9	5.8	6.9	7.7	8.6	8.2	8.3	8.2	8.6	8.0	7.2	5.7
S/HEMISPHERE	JUL	AUG	SEP	OCT	NOV	DEC	JAN	FEB	MAR	APR	MAY	JUN

Cultural Recommendations

LIGHT: 2500–3500 fc.

TEMPERATURES: Throughout the year, days average 83–90°F (29–32°C), and nights average 73–75°F (23–24°C), with a diurnal range of 10–16°F (6–9°C).

HUMIDITY: Information is not available for this location. However, average humidity in mistforest habitats normally exceeds 80–85% year-round.

WATER: Rainfall is very heavy all year. Cultivated plants should be kept evenly moist but not soggy.

FERTILIZER: ¼–½ recommended strength. A balanced fertilizer should be applied weekly to biweekly throughout the year.

REST PERIOD: Growing conditions should be maintained year-round. Water and fertilizer should be reduced for plants grown in the dark, short-day conditions common in temperate-latitude winters, but they should never be allowed to dry out completely.

GROWING MEDIA: Plants may be potted in any well-drained, moisture-retaining medium. Plants should never be allowed to dry out completely. Repotting may be done anytime new roots are growing.

MISCELLANEOUS NOTES: The bloom season shown in the climate table is based on reports from the habitat. The plant was described in 1908 in *Bul. Dep. Agric. Indes Neerl.* 9:15.

Plant and Flower Information

PLANT SIZE AND TYPE: A 31 in. (80 cm) sympodial epiphyte.

PSEUDOBULB: 31 in. (80 cm) long. The clustered stems are zigzag and flexuous rather than rigid at the apex.

LEAVES: The ovate-lanceolate leaves are 1.4–2.4 in. (3.5–6.0 cm) long. They are sharply pointed with minute serrations at the apex.

INFLORESCENCE: Short.

FLOWERS: 3–8 per inflorescence. The small flowers are 0.7 in. (1.8 cm) long and covered with fine bumps or warts on the outside. Blossoms may be rose-red or orange-red with pale margins. Blossoms have ovate dorsal sepals, lateral sepals that form a long cone, and very small petals. The pale orange lip is paler at the apex. The anther is pale green and the pollinia are olive-green. The ovary is orange. The flowers change color as they age.

REFERENCES: 220, 254, 470.

Dendrobium cochliodes Schlechter

AKA: *D. ruidilobum* J. J. Smith.

ORIGIN/HABITAT: Northern Papua New Guinea and Irian Jaya. Plants grow in the mistforest zone at 1300–5250 ft. (400–1600 m). They are often found on high branches of exposed trees that grow near water.

CLIMATE: Station #94010, Goroka, Papua New Guinea, Lat. 6.1°S, Long. 145.4°E, at 5141 ft. (1567 m). Temperatures are calculated for an elevation of 4000 ft. (1220 m), resulting in probable extremes of 90°F (32°C) and 46°F (8°C).

N/HEMISPHERE	JAN	FEB	MAR	APR	MAY	JUN	JUL	AUG	SEP	OCT	NOV	DEC
°F AVG MAX	80	81	82	83	83	82	83	82	82	82	83	81
°F AVG MIN	60	61	61	61	62	63	63	63	64	63	63	61
DIURNAL RANGE	20	20	21	22	21	19	20	19	18	19	20	20
RAIN/INCHES	2.1	2.8	4.6	5.9	6.6	9.3	9.1	10.1	10.7	8.3	4.6	2.0
HUMIDITY/%	70	67	67	67	67	71	72	73	74	71	70	70
BLOOM SEASON			*		*			*				
DAYS CLR	N/A											
RAIN/MM	53	71	117	150	168	236	231	257	272	211	117	51
°C AVG MAX	26.5	27.1	27.6	28.2	28.2	27.6	28.2	27.6	27.6	27.6	28.2	27.1
°C AVG MIN	15.4	16.0	16.0	16.0	16.5	17.1	17.1	17.1	17.6	17.1	17.1	16.0
DIURNAL RANGE	11.1	11.1	11.6	12.2	11.7	10.5	11.1	10.5	10.0	10.5	11.1	11.1
S/HEMISPHERE	JUL	AUG	SEP	OCT	NOV	DEC	JAN	FEB	MAR	APR	MAY	JUN

Cultural Recommendations

LIGHT: 2500–3500 fc.

TEMPERATURES: Throughout the year, days average 80–83°F (27–28°C), and nights average 60–64°F (15–18°C), with a diurnal range of 18–22°F (10–12°C). The diurnal range is unusually large for a habitat with such constant temperatures.

HUMIDITY: 70–75% from summer into autumn, dropping to 65–70% in winter and spring. Plants require excellent air movement.

WATER: Rainfall is moderate to heavy most of the year, with slightly drier conditions for 3 months in winter. Cultivated plants should be kept moist but not soggy. Occasional early morning mistings may be beneficial, especially on bright, sunny days.

FERTILIZER: ¼–½ recommended strength. A balanced fertilizer should be applied weekly to biweekly throughout the year.

REST PERIOD: Growing temperatures should be maintained all year. In the habitat, rainfall is lowest in winter, but dew and mist from fog and low clouds are common. Water and fertilizer should be reduced somewhat for cultivated plants, especially those grown in the darker, short-day conditions common during temperate latitude winters. Plants should be kept on the dry side, but they should never be allowed to dry out completely. In the habitat, light is higher in winter.

GROWING MEDIA: Plants may be mounted on tree-fern or cork slabs if humidity is high and plants are watered at least once daily in summer. When plants are potted, any open, fast-draining medium may be used. Repotting may be done anytime new roots are growing.

MISCELLANEOUS NOTES: The bloom season shown in the climate table is based on collection reports. Plants may be in bloom most of the year.

Plant and Flower Information

PLANT SIZE AND TYPE: A 24–48 in. (60–122 cm) sympodial epiphyte.

PSEUDOBULB: 24–48 in. (60–122 cm) long. The canelike pseudobulbs are sturdy, robust, and erect. Although tall, the pseudobulbs are small when compared to other closely related plants.

LEAVES: 4–6 per growth. The oblong to elliptic leaves are 2–3 in. (5.0–7.6 cm) long. They become dark green before dropping.

INFLORESCENCE: 8–14 in. (20–35 cm) long. Inflorescences emerge from nodes at the base of the uppermost leaves. Leaves and flowers are crowded at the tip of the stem.

FLOWERS: 6–30 per inflorescence. The flowers may be 1.5–2.0 in. (4–5 cm) long, but size is highly variable. Blossoms are yellow-green with varying amounts of dark bronze-brown flushing. The petals are erect and tightly twisted 3 times. The lip, which is white to greenish yellow with purple or brown veins and keels, curls under 360°. The callus is white with purple along the edge. The anther is golden yellow.

REFERENCES: 25, 84, 221, 304, 344, 437, 445, 485, 486.

PHOTOS/DRAWINGS: *84, 304, 344*, 437.

Dendrobium codonosepalum J. J. Smith

ORIGIN/HABITAT: Irian Jaya (western New Guinea). Plants were collected along the Rouffaer River in primeval forests at about 1000 ft. (300 m).

CLIMATE: Station #200004, Ambunti, Papua New Guinea, Lat. 4.2°S, Long. 142.8°E, at 164 ft. (50 m). Temperatures are calculated for an elevation of 1000 ft. (300 m), resulting in probable extremes of 96°F (36°C) and 49°F (10°C).

N/HEMISPHERE	JAN	FEB	MAR	APR	MAY	JUN	JUL	AUG	SEP	OCT	NOV	DEC
°F AVG MAX	85	87	87	87	88	87	87	87	87	87	87	86
°F AVG MIN	69	70	71	70	70	70	69	70	70	70	70	71
DIURNAL RANGE	16	17	16	17	18	17	18	17	17	17	17	15
RAIN/INCHES	6.4	7.4	7.7	8.5	9.2	9.4	10.9	10.2	12.2	10.4	8.3	5.2
HUMIDITY/%	N/A											
BLOOM SEASON			*									
DAYS CLR	N/A											
RAIN/MM	163	188	196	216	234	239	277	259	310	264	211	132
°C AVG MAX	29.6	30.7	30.7	30.7	31.2	30.7	30.7	30.7	30.7	30.7	30.7	30.1
°C AVG MIN	20.7	21.2	21.8	21.2	21.2	21.2	20.7	21.2	21.2	21.2	21.2	21.8
DIURNAL RANGE	8.9	9.5	8.9	9.5	10.0	9.5	10.0	9.5	9.5	9.5	9.5	8.3
S/HEMISPHERE	JUL	AUG	SEP	OCT	NOV	DEC	JAN	FEB	MAR	APR	MAY	JUN

Cultural Recommendations

LIGHT: 2000–3000 fc.

TEMPERATURES: Throughout the year, days average 85–88°F (30–31°C), and nights average 69–71°F (21–22°C), with a diurnal range of 15–18°F (8–10°C).

HUMIDITY: Information is not available for this location. However, records from other stations in the region indicate that averages are probably near 80% year-round.

WATER: Rainfall is heavy all year, with the greatest amounts falling in summer and early autumn. Cultivated plants should be kept moist but not soggy.

FERTILIZER: ¼–½ recommended strength. A balanced fertilizer should be applied weekly to biweekly throughout the year.

REST PERIOD: Growing conditions should be maintained all year. Water should be reduced for plants cultivated in the dark, short-day conditions common in temperate-latitude winters, but they should never be allowed to dry out completely. Fertilizer should be reduced anytime water is reduced. In the habitat, light is probably highest in winter.

GROWING MEDIA: Plants may be mounted on cork or tree-fern slabs if humidity is high and plants are watered at least once daily in summer. When plants are potted, any open, fast-draining medium may be used, but fir bark is preferred by most growers. Repotting may be done anytime new roots are growing.

MISCELLANEOUS NOTES: The bloom season shown in the climate table is based on reports from the habitat.

Plant and Flower Information

PLANT SIZE AND TYPE: A 16 in. (40 cm) sympodial epiphyte.

PSEUDOBULB: 16 in. (40 cm) long. The quadrangular stems are clustered on a short, branching rhizome.

LEAVES: Several. The obovate to oblong leaves are about 1.4 in. (3.5 cm) long with a sharp point at the tip. They are wavy along the margin.

INFLORESCENCE: Short. The inflorescences, which emerge through the leaf sheaths, are usually borne on leafless stems.

FLOWERS: Few per inflorescence. The flowers are 1.4 in. (3.5 cm) long. New blossoms are red with a violet hue, but with age, they become brick red. The lip has a long fringe.

REFERENCES: 225, 470.

Dendrobium coelandria Kränzlin

ORIGIN/HABITAT: Papua New Guinea and off-shore islands. *D. coelandria* grows near Jimari at about 3300 ft. (1000 m).

CLIMATE: Station #94075, Samarai, Sideia Island, Papua New Guinea, Lat. 10.6°S, Long. 150.7°E, at 20 ft. (6 m). Temperatures are calculated for an elevation of 3300 ft. (1000 m), resulting in probable extremes of 93°F (34°C) and 53°F (12°C).

N/HEMISPHERE	JAN	FEB	MAR	APR	MAY	JUN	JUL	AUG	SEP	OCT	NOV	DEC
°F AVG MAX	70	70	71	72	74	76	76	77	76	75	73	71
°F AVG MIN	63	62	63	63	64	65	66	66	65	64	64	63
DIURNAL RANGE	7	8	8	9	10	11	10	11	11	11	9	8
RAIN/INCHES	8.1	8.6	10.1	8.7	8.4	6.1	7.0	7.8	10.0	9.8	12.0	11.3
HUMIDITY/%	N/A											
BLOOM SEASON					*							
DAYS CLR	N/A											
RAIN/MM	206	218	257	221	213	155	178	198	254	249	305	287
°C AVG MAX	21.2	21.2	21.8	22.3	23.4	24.5	24.5	25.1	24.5	24.0	22.9	21.8
°C AVG MIN	17.3	16.8	17.3	17.3	17.9	18.4	19.0	19.0	18.4	17.9	17.9	17.3
DIURNAL RANGE	3.9	4.4	4.5	5.0	5.5	6.1	5.5	6.1	6.1	6.1	5.0	4.5
S/HEMISPHERE	JUL	AUG	SEP	OCT	NOV	DEC	JAN	FEB	MAR	APR	MAY	JUN

Cultural Recommendations

LIGHT: 2500–3000 fc.

TEMPERATURES: Throughout the year, days average 70–77°F (21–25°C), and nights average 62–66°F (17–19°C), with a diurnal range of 7–11°F (4–6°C).

HUMIDITY: Information is not available for this location. However, records at other locations in the region indicate that averages are probably 70–80% year-round.

WATER: Rainfall is very heavy all year. Cultivated plants should be kept moist but not soggy.

FERTILIZER: ¼–½ recommended strength. A balanced fertilizer should be applied weekly to biweekly throughout the year.

REST PERIOD: Growing conditions should be maintained year-round. While rainfall remains high in the habitat in winter, water should be reduced somewhat for cultivated plants, especially those grown in the darker, short-day conditions common in temperate latitudes. Plants should never be allowed to dry out completely, however. Fertilizer should be reduced until plants begin to actively grow and water is increased in spring.

GROWING MEDIA: Plants may be mounted on tree-fern or cork slabs if humidity is high and plants are watered at least once daily in summer. When plants are potted, any open, fast-draining medium may be used. Repotting may be done anytime new roots are growing.

MISCELLANEOUS NOTES: The bloom season shown in the climate table is based on reports from the habitat.

Plant and Flower Information

PLANT SIZE AND TYPE: A 12–16 in. (30–40 cm) sympodial epiphyte.

PSEUDOBULB: 12–16 in. (30–40 cm) long. The somewhat zigzag stems taper toward the apex.

LEAVES: Many. The grooved, grey-green leaves are 1.6–2.2 in. (4.0–5.5 cm) long. The leaf blade is ovate.

INFLORESCENCE: Very short. The densely flowered inflorescences emerge laterally from leaf axils.

FLOWERS: Few per inflorescence. The scarlet flowers are 0.6 in. (1.6 cm) long. The blossoms have an oblong or ovate dorsal sepal, somewhat triangular lateral sepals, and small, oblong petals. The spoon-shaped lip is minutely toothed along the margin and decorated with raised keels.

REFERENCES: 220, 254.

Dendrobium coeleste Loher. See *D. victoria-reginae* Loher.
REFERENCES: 12, 190, 254, 296, 536.

Dendrobium coeloglossum Schlechter

ORIGIN/HABITAT: Northern Papua New Guinea. Plants usually grow at 1300–2600 ft. (400–800 m), just below the mistforest zone, on the trunks and branches of large, moss-covered, smooth-barked trees. In Irian Jaya (western New Guinea), plants grow near Humboldt Bay at 30 ft. (10 m) and have been collected from a tree on a bare mountain peak at 650 ft. (200 m). Plants were cultivated in the botanical garden at Bogor, Java.

CLIMATE: Station #200192, Garaina, Papua New Guinea, Lat. 7.9°S, Long. 147.1°E, at 2350 ft. (716 m). Record extreme temperatures are 94°F (34°C) and 46°F (8°C).

N/HEMISPHERE	JAN	FEB	MAR	APR	MAY	JUN	JUL	AUG	SEP	OCT	NOV	DEC
°F AVG MAX	80	82	83	84	85	85	85	85	84	84	83	81
°F AVG MIN	63	63	63	64	63	64	65	65	65	64	64	63
DIURNAL RANGE	17	19	20	20	22	21	20	20	19	20	19	18
RAIN/INCHES	5.8	6.5	8.7	11.1	11.8	11.9	8.9	11.7	11.5	9.9	7.7	5.2
HUMIDITY/%	84	82	82	81	80	80	81	81	82	83	84	84
BLOOM SEASON	*	*	*									
DAYS CLR	N/A											
RAIN/MM	148	166	220	282	300	303	227	296	291	251	195	131
°C AVG MAX	26.8	27.5	28.2	28.6	29.3	29.3	29.4	29.4	29.1	28.7	28.2	27.2
°C AVG MIN	16.9	16.9	17.4	17.6	17.4	18.0	18.1	18.2	18.4	17.7	17.7	17.1
DIURNAL RANGE	9.9	10.6	10.8	11.0	11.9	11.3	11.3	11.2	10.7	11.0	10.5	10.1
S/HEMISPHERE	JUL	AUG	SEP	OCT	NOV	DEC	JAN	FEB	MAR	APR	MAY	JUN

Cultural Recommendations

LIGHT: 2500–3500 fc.

TEMPERATURES: Throughout the year, days average 80–85°F (27–29°C), and nights average 63–65°F (17–18°C), with a diurnal range of 17–22°F (10–12°C).

HUMIDITY: 80–85% year-round, dropping to 65–70% for a few hours each afternoon.

Dendrobium coelogyne

WATER: Rainfall is heavy all year with a slightly drier period in winter. Cultivated plants should be kept moist but not soggy.

FERTILIZER: ¼–½ recommended strength. A balanced fertilizer should be applied weekly to biweekly throughout the year.

REST PERIOD: Growing conditions should be maintained all year. In the habitat, rainfall is slightly lower in winter. Water and fertilizer should be reduced somewhat for cultivated plants, especially those grown in the dark, short-day conditions common during temperate-latitude winters. They should never be allowed to dry out completely, however. In the habitat, seasonal light variation is minor.

GROWING MEDIA: Mounting plants on tree-fern or cork slabs accommodates their pendent growth habit, but humidity must be high and plants need to be watered at least once daily in summer. If plants must be potted, a hanging basket filled with any open, fast-draining medium is the easiest to manage. Repotting is best done in early spring when new roots are growing.

MISCELLANEOUS NOTES: The bloom season shown in the climate table is based on reports from the habitat. Plants that produce flowers which last a single day commonly bloom several times during the year. Flowering usually occurs 7–14 days after a sudden 10°F (5°C) drop in daytime temperatures.

Plant and Flower Information

PLANT SIZE AND TYPE: An 8 in. (20 cm) sympodial epiphyte. Plants normally consist of 4–6 stems.

PSEUDOBULB: 8 in. (20 cm) long. Pseudobulbs tend to hang down or lean to one side. They are pale green when immature and become yellow with age. Each stem has several angles, and is slender for half its length before becoming wider. New shoots arise from bracts.

LEAVES: 1–2 per growth. The leaves are 2.5–4.5 in. (6.4–11.4 cm) long.

INFLORESCENCE: Many inflorescences emerge from nodes near the apex of the pseudobulb.

FLOWERS: 2–4 per inflorescence. The flowers are 0.8–1.2 in. (2–3 cm) across. They are creamy white and sulfur yellow with a brown keel on the lip. The thick, fleshy flowers do not open fully and last a single day.

REFERENCES: 221, 304, 437, 445, 470.

PHOTOS/DRAWINGS: *304*, 437.

Dendrobium coelogyne Rchb. f.
Now considered a synonym of *Epigeneium amplum* (Rchb. f.) Summerhayes. REFERENCES: 152, 154, 157, 188, 190, 202, 216, 229, 254, 369, 445, 449, 499, 542.

Dendrobium coerulescens Wallich.
Sometimes spelled *D. caerulescens*, see *D. nobile* Lindley. REFERENCES: 216, 254, 369, 445, 454.

Dendrobium coerulescens Schlechter.
See *D. putnamii* A. Hawkes and A. H. Heller. REFERENCES: 221, 229, 385, 437.

Dendrobium cogniauxianum Kränzlin.
See *D. sylvanum* Rchb. f. and *D. lineale* Rolfe. Hunt (ref. 211) lists *D. cogniauxianum* as a synonym of *D. gouldii*, but Cribb (ref. 84) concurred with Schlechter (ref. 437) in applying parts of the original description of *D. cogniauxianum* to different species. REFERENCES: 84, 190, 211, 217, 218, 254, 437.

Dendrobium collinum (Schlechter) J. J. Smith

AKA: *Cadetia collina* Schlechter. *Cadetia* is again considered a valid genus by some botanists, so this plant may belong to the genus *Cadetia*.

ORIGIN/HABITAT: Widely distributed in northern Papua New Guinea. *D. collinum* grows on trees in primary, hillside forests at 1000–2300 ft. (300–700 m).

CLIMATE: Station #200192, Garaina, Papua New Guinea, Lat. 7.9°S, Long. 147.1°E, at 2350 ft. (716 m). Record extreme temperatures are 94°F (34°C) and 46°F (8°C).

N/HEMISPHERE	JAN	FEB	MAR	APR	MAY	JUN	JUL	AUG	SEP	OCT	NOV	DEC
°F AVG MAX	80	82	83	84	85	85	85	85	84	84	83	81
°F AVG MIN	63	63	63	64	63	64	65	65	65	64	64	63
DIURNAL RANGE	17	19	20	20	22	21	20	20	19	20	19	18
RAIN/INCHES	5.8	6.5	8.7	11.1	11.8	11.9	8.9	11.7	11.5	9.9	7.7	5.2
HUMIDITY/%	84	82	82	81	80	80	81	81	82	83	84	84
BLOOM SEASON	*					*		*	*	*		
DAYS CLR	N/A											
RAIN/MM	148	166	220	282	300	303	227	296	291	251	195	131
°C AVG MAX	26.8	27.5	28.2	28.6	29.3	29.3	29.4	29.4	29.1	28.7	28.2	27.2
°C AVG MIN	16.9	16.9	17.4	17.6	17.4	18.0	18.1	18.2	18.4	17.7	17.7	17.1
DIURNAL RANGE	9.9	10.6	10.8	11.0	11.9	11.3	11.3	11.2	10.7	11.0	10.5	10.1
S/HEMISPHERE	JUL	AUG	SEP	OCT	NOV	DEC	JAN	FEB	MAR	APR	MAY	JUN

Cultural Recommendations

LIGHT: 2500–3000 fc.

TEMPERATURES: Throughout the year, days average 80–85°F (27–29°C), and nights average 63–65°F (17–18°C), with a diurnal range of 17–22°F (10–12°C).

HUMIDITY: Near 80–85% year-round, dropping to 65–70% for a few hours each afternoon.

WATER: Rainfall is heavy all year with a slightly drier period in winter. Cultivated plants should be kept moist but not soggy.

FERTILIZER: ¼–½ recommended strength. A balanced fertilizer should be applied weekly to biweekly throughout the year.

REST PERIOD: Growing conditions should be maintained all year. In the habitat, rainfall is slightly lower in winter. Water and fertilizer should be reduced somewhat for cultivated plants, especially those grown in the dark, short-day conditions common during temperate-latitude winters. They should never be allowed to dry out completely, however. In the habitat, seasonal light variation is minor.

GROWING MEDIA: Plants may be mounted on tree-fern or cork slabs if humidity is high and plants are watered at least once daily in summer. When plants are potted, any open, fast-draining medium may be used. Repotting is best done in early spring when new roots are growing.

MISCELLANEOUS NOTES: The bloom season shown in the climate table is based on collection reports. Plants that produce flowers which last a single day commonly bloom several times during the year. Flowering usually occurs 7–14 days after a sudden 10°F (5°C) drop in daytime temperatures.

Plant and Flower Information

PLANT SIZE AND TYPE: A 6–7 in. (16–18 cm) sympodial epiphyte.

PSEUDOBULB: 2.8–3.6 in. (7–9 cm) long. The slender, acutely 4-angled stems arise from a very short rhizome.

LEAVES: 1 per growth. The broad, oblong leaves are usually 2.4–3.2 in. (6–8 cm) long.

INFLORESCENCE: Short. Inflorescences emerge at the apex of the stem.

FLOWERS: 1 per inflorescence. Blossoms are 0.3 in. (0.7 cm) long. The flowers are pale yellow with red dots on the front of the lip. The dorsal sepal is erect, but all other parts thrust forward. The lip is scalloped and ruffled with pink along the margin and the sidelobes. Flowers last a single day.

REFERENCES: 92, 221, 437, 445, 472.

PHOTOS/DRAWINGS: 437.

Dendrobium collinum J. J. Smith

AKA: *D. planum* J. J. Smith var. *collinum* J. J. Smith.

ORIGIN/HABITAT: Irian Jaya (western New Guinea). Plants grow near sea level on the plain by the Noord River.

CLIMATE: Station #97796, Kokenau (Kokonau), Irian Jaya, Lat. 4.7°S, Long. 136.4°E, at 10 ft. (3 m). Record extreme temperatures are not available for this location.

N/HEMISPHERE	JAN	FEB	MAR	APR	MAY	JUN	JUL	AUG	SEP	OCT	NOV	DEC
°F AVG MAX	83	83	86	88	90	89	89	89	90	88	87	84
°F AVG MIN	73	73	74	74	74	75	74	74	74	74	74	73
DIURNAL RANGE	10	10	12	14	16	14	15	15	16	14	13	11
RAIN/INCHES	18.4	15.8	18.9	11.6	9.7	10.6	11.5	15.7	11.6	11.6	16.0	19.9
HUMIDITY/%	N/A											
BLOOM SEASON												
DAYS CLR	N/A											
RAIN/MM	467	401	479	295	245	269	293	400	294	296	407	506
°C AVG MAX	28.6	28.4	30.2	31.1	32.1	31.9	31.9	31.7	32.0	31.4	30.7	28.7
°C AVG MIN	22.7	22.6	23.3	23.4	23.5	23.7	23.6	23.5	23.4	23.4	23.5	23.0
DIURNAL RANGE	5.9	5.8	6.9	7.7	8.6	8.2	8.3	8.2	8.6	8.0	7.2	5.7
S/HEMISPHERE	JUL	AUG	SEP	OCT	NOV	DEC	JAN	FEB	MAR	APR	MAY	JUN

Cultural Recommendations

LIGHT: 2500–3500 fc.

TEMPERATURES: Throughout the year, days average 83–90°F (28–32°C), and nights average 73–75°F (23–24°C), with a diurnal range of 10–16°F (6–9°C).

HUMIDITY: Information is not available for this location. However, records from nearby locations indicate that humidity probably averages near 85% year-round.

WATER: Rainfall is very heavy all year. Cultivated plants should be kept evenly moist with only slight drying allowed between waterings.

FERTILIZER: 1/4–1/2 recommended strength. A balanced fertilizer should be applied weekly to biweekly throughout the year.

REST PERIOD: Growing conditions should be maintained year-round. Water and fertilizer may be reduced slightly in winter, especially for plants cultivated in the dark, short-day conditions common in the temperate latitudes, but they should never be allowed to dry out completely.

GROWING MEDIA: Plants may be mounted on tree-fern or cork slabs if humidity is high and plants are watered at least once daily in summer. When plants are potted, any open, fast-draining medium may be used. Repotting is best done in early spring when new roots begin to grow.

MISCELLANEOUS NOTES: The bloom season shown in the climate table is based on reports from the habitat.

Plant and Flower Information

PLANT SIZE AND TYPE: A sympodial epiphyte of unreported size.

PSEUDOBULB: The elongated stems are very flattened.

LEAVES: 1.5–2.2 in. (3.7–5.6 cm) long. The lanceolate leaves are semi-twisted at the base and bilobed at the apex.

INFLORESCENCE: Short. Inflorescences emerge through the leaf-sheaths along the side of the stem.

FLOWERS: 2 per inflorescence. The flowers are 0.6 in. (1.6 cm) across. They are yellow-green with red stripes and a red margin on the midlobe and red markings on the sidelobes. Sepals and petals are shiny on the backside. The erect dorsal sepal is lanceolate-triangular, pointed, recurved, and convex. Lateral sepals are obliquely triangular, pointed, and somewhat sickle-shaped. Petals are linear. The erect, recurved lip is 3-lobed. The ovate midlobe is incurved along the ruffled, wavy margin. The ovate-triangular sidelobes are erect.

REFERENCES: 220, 254, 470.

Dendrobium coloratum J. J. Smith

ORIGIN/HABITAT: Irian Jaya (western New Guinea). These rare plants, which were collected on the lower slopes of Mt. Goliath at about 500 ft. (150 m), grow on smooth tree trunks.

CLIMATE: Station #97876, Tanahmerah, Irian Jaya, Lat. 6.1°S, Long. 140.3°E, at 75 ft. (23 m). Temperatures are calculated for an elevation of 500 ft. (150 m), resulting in probable extremes of 97°F (36°C) and 63°F (17°C).

N/HEMISPHERE	JAN	FEB	MAR	APR	MAY	JUN	JUL	AUG	SEP	OCT	NOV	DEC
°F AVG MAX	83	84	86	89	90	89	89	88	89	88	86	84
°F AVG MIN	71	70	70	71	72	73	72	72	72	72	73	72
DIURNAL RANGE	12	14	16	18	18	16	17	16	17	16	13	12
RAIN/INCHES	11.5	12.1	14.7	13.2	14.4	15.9	14.5	15.8	17.4	17.3	15.5	11.9
HUMIDITY/%	N/A											
BLOOM SEASON												
DAYS CLR	N/A											
RAIN/MM	292	307	373	335	366	404	368	401	442	439	394	302
°C AVG MAX	28.1	28.7	29.8	31.4	32.0	31.4	31.4	30.9	31.4	30.9	29.8	28.7
°C AVG MIN	21.4	20.9	20.9	21.4	22.0	22.6	22.0	22.0	22.0	22.0	22.6	22.0
DIURNAL RANGE	6.7	7.8	8.9	10.0	10.0	8.8	9.4	8.9	9.4	8.9	7.2	6.7
S/HEMISPHERE	JUL	AUG	SEP	OCT	NOV	DEC	JAN	FEB	MAR	APR	MAY	JUN

Cultural Recommendations

LIGHT: 2000–3000 fc.

TEMPERATURES: Throughout the year, days average 83–90°F (28–32°C), and nights average 70–73°F (21–23°C), with a diurnal range of 12–18°F (7–10°C).

HUMIDITY: Information is not available for this location. However, records from nearby stations indicate that values are probably near 85% year-round.

WATER: Rainfall is very heavy all year. Cultivated plants should be kept evenly moist but not soggy.

FERTILIZER: 1/4–1/2 recommended strength. A balanced fertilizer should be applied weekly to biweekly throughout the year.

REST PERIOD: Growing conditions should be maintained year-round. Water and fertilizer may be reduced slightly in winter for plants cultivated in the dark, short-day conditions common in temperate latitudes, but they should never be allowed dry completely between waterings.

GROWING MEDIA: Because plants must be kept moist, they are most easily managed when potted. Fir bark or any open, fast-draining medium may be used. Repotting may be done anytime new roots are growing.

MISCELLANEOUS NOTES: The bloom season shown in the climate table is based on reports from the habitat.

Plant and Flower Information

PLANT SIZE AND TYPE: A 12 in. (30 cm) sympodial epiphyte.

PSEUDOBULB: 12 in. (30 cm) long. The flexuous stems are flattened.

LEAVES: The lanceolate leaves are 2.7–3.2 in. (6.8–8.0 cm) long. They are shaped as though they should end in a long tapering point, but instead the apex ends abruptly in 2, obtuse and unequal lobes. They are erect-spreading.

INFLORESCENCE: Inflorescences emerge laterally from flat sheaths.

FLOWERS: 2 per inflorescence. The crimson-red flowers are 0.5 in. (1.3 cm) long. The warty dorsal sepal is concave with a thickened, recurved tip. It curves in between the petals. The lateral sepals are oblong-triangular. The petals are sickle-shaped.

REFERENCES: 221, 470, 476.

Dendrobium comatum (Blume) Lindley. Now considered a synonym of *Flickingeria comata* (Blume) A. Hawkes. REFERENCES: 25,

67, 75, 105, 111, 173, 200, 211, 213, 216, 230, 231, 254, 270, 271, 277, 310, 395, 449, 455, 469, 470, 497, 510, 537. PHOTOS/DRAWINGS: 200, 469, *497, 510*.

Dendrobium compactum Rolfe ex W. Hackett

AKA: Plants from Australia are sometimes labeled *D. compactum,* but they are actually *D. bigibbum* Lindley subsp. *compactum* C. White.

ORIGIN/HABITAT: Burma, Yunnan Province of southwestern China, and northern Thailand. Collections are recorded at 2600–5400 ft. (800–1650 m), but most are from about 4900 ft. (1500 m).

CLIMATE: Station #48327, Chiang Mai, Thailand, Lat. 18.8°N, Long. 99.0°E, at 1100 ft. (335 m). Temperatures are calculated for an elevation of 5000 ft. (1520 m), resulting in probable extremes of 96°F (36°C) and 25°F (–4°C).

N/HEMISPHERE	JAN	FEB	MAR	APR	MAY	JUN	JUL	AUG	SEP	OCT	NOV	DEC
°F AVG MAX	72	77	82	83	81	77	76	74	75	76	73	71
°F AVG MIN	43	44	49	57	61	61	61	62	60	58	53	44
DIURNAL RANGE	29	33	33	26	20	16	15	12	15	18	20	27
RAIN/INCHES	0.3	0.4	0.6	2.0	5.5	6.1	7.4	8.7	11.5	4.9	1.5	0.4
HUMIDITY/%	73	65	58	62	73	78	80	83	83	81	79	76
BLOOM SEASON			*					*	*	*		
DAYS CLR @ 7AM	5	5	2	2	1	0	0	0	0	1	3	3
DAYS CLR @ 1PM	9	8	4	2	0	0	0	0	0	0	1	3
RAIN/MM	8	10	15	51	140	155	188	221	292	124	38	10
°C AVG MAX	22.3	25.1	27.9	28.4	27.3	25.1	24.5	23.4	24.0	24.5	22.9	21.7
°C AVG MIN	6.2	6.7	9.5	14.0	16.2	16.2	16.2	16.7	15.6	14.5	11.7	6.7
DIURNAL RANGE	16.1	18.4	18.4	14.4	11.1	8.9	8.3	6.7	8.4	10.0	11.2	15.0
S/HEMISPHERE	JUL	AUG	SEP	OCT	NOV	DEC	JAN	FEB	MAR	APR	MAY	JUN

Cultural Recommendations

LIGHT: 2500–3500 fc. Bright diffused light is suggested.

TEMPERATURES: Summer days average 74–77°F (23–25°C), and nights average 61–62°F (16–17°C), with a diurnal range of 12–16°F (7–9°C). The warmest temperatures occur in spring. Days average 81–83°F (27–28°C), and nights average 49–61°F (10–16°C), with a diurnal range of 20–33°F (11–18°C).

HUMIDITY: 75–85% from late spring through autumn, dropping to near 60% in late winter and early spring.

WATER: Rainfall is moderate to heavy from late spring through early autumn, but conditions are very dry in winter. Cultivated plants should be kept moist while actively growing, but water should be gradually reduced after new growths mature in autumn.

FERTILIZER: ¼–½ recommended strength, applied weekly. A high-nitrogen fertilizer is beneficial from spring to midsummer, but a fertilizer high in phosphates should be used in late summer and autumn.

REST PERIOD: Winter days average 71–77°F (22–25°C), and nights average 43–44°F (6–7°C), with a diurnal range of 27–33°F (15–18°C). The average low temperatures are below 50°F (10°C) for 3 months and then warm rapidly in spring. Plants should be able to tolerate temperatures a few degrees below freezing, but extremes should be avoided in cultivation. During very cold weather, a plant's chance of surviving with minimal damage is better if it is dry. In the habitat, rainfall averages are very low for 4–5 months in winter, but during the early part of the season the high relative humidity indicates that additional moisture is available from frequent fog, mist, and heavy deposits of dew. Growers sometimes recommend eliminating water in winter, but plants are healthiest if for most of the winter they are allowed to become somewhat dry between waterings but do not remain dry for extended periods. For 1–2 months in late winter, however, conditions are clear, warm, and dry with humidity so low that even the moisture from morning dew is uncommon. Plants should be allowed to dry out completely between waterings and remain dry longer during this time. Occasional early morning mistings between waterings may help keep the plants from becoming too dry. Fertilizer should be greatly reduced or eliminated until water is increased in spring. A cool, dry rest is essential for cultivated plants and should be continued until new growth starts in spring. In the habitat, light is highest in winter.

GROWING MEDIA: Plants are best mounted on a tree-fern slab if humidity is high and plants are watered at least once daily in summer. When plants must be potted, any open, fibrous medium may be used. Repotting is best done in early spring when new roots are growing.

MISCELLANEOUS NOTES: The bloom season shown in the climate table is based on cultivation records. *D. compactum* differs from *D. wilmsianum* Schlechter only in the shape of the lip callus.

Plant and Flower Information

PLANT SIZE AND TYPE: A 3.5 in. (9 cm) sympodial plant.

PSEUDOBULB: 1.2–3.2 in. (3–8 cm) long.

LEAVES: 6 per growth. The deciduous leaves, which are 1.6–3.2 in. (4–8 cm) long, alternate along the stem.

INFLORESCENCE: 1.0–1.6 in. (2.5–4.0 cm) long. Often several on each growth, the inflorescences emerge opposite the leaves on leafy pseudobulbs. Blossoms are densely clustered on the inflorescence.

FLOWERS: 6–10 per inflorescence. The flowers are 0.4 in. (1 cm) across. The white sepals and petals are pointed and erect. The lateral sepals are broadly triangular. The ruffled lip is greenish with white at the base.

HYBRIDIZING NOTES: Chromosome counts are n = 20 (ref. 151) and 2n = 40 (ref. 151, 154, 188).

REFERENCES: 151, 154, 179, 188, 208, 220, 254, 266, 291, 415, 454, 528.

PHOTOS/DRAWINGS: *291, 454*.

Dendrobium complanatum A. Cunningham. Now considered a synonym of *Oberonia complanata*. REFERENCES: 67, 216, 254, 317.

Dendrobium compressicolle J. J. Smith 1912 not 1928.
Now considered a synonym of *Diplocaulobium compressicolle* (J. J. Smith) Hunt and Summerhayes. REFERENCES: 111, 213, 221, 230, 445, 470, 537.

Dendrobium compressicaule J. J. Smith 1928 not 1912

ORIGIN/HABITAT: Western Sumatra and New Guinea. In Sumatra, plants grow on the south slope of Mt. Kerintji at about 4900 ft. (1500 m).

CLIMATE: Station #96163, Padang, Sumatra, Indonesia, Lat. 0.9°S, Long. 100.4°E, at 19 ft. (6 m). Temperatures are calculated for an elevation of 4900 ft. (1500 m), resulting in probable extremes of 78°F (26°C) and 52°F (11°C).

N/HEMISPHERE	JAN	FEB	MAR	APR	MAY	JUN	JUL	AUG	SEP	OCT	NOV	DEC
°F AVG MAX	71	71	70	70	70	70	71	71	71	71	72	71
°F AVG MIN	58	58	58	58	58	58	58	58	58	59	59	58
DIURNAL RANGE	13	13	12	12	12	12	13	13	13	12	13	13
RAIN/INCHES	10.9	13.7	6.0	19.5	20.4	18.9	13.8	10.2	12.1	14.3	12.4	12.1
HUMIDITY/%	81	82	82	84	85	84	81	81	82	83	81	81
BLOOM SEASON									*			
DAYS CLR @ 7AM	5	1	1	0	0	2	1	2	2	2	3	5
DAYS CLR @ 1PM	5	2	2	1	1	3	4	3	3	4	6	5
RAIN/MM	277	348	152	495	518	480	351	259	307	363	315	307
°C AVG MAX	21.6	21.6	21.1	21.1	21.1	21.1	21.6	21.6	21.6	21.6	22.2	21.6
°C AVG MIN	14.4	14.4	14.4	14.4	14.4	14.4	14.4	14.4	14.4	14.9	14.9	14.4
DIURNAL RANGE	7.2	7.2	6.7	6.7	6.7	6.7	7.2	7.2	7.2	6.7	7.3	7.2
S/HEMISPHERE	JUL	AUG	SEP	OCT	NOV	DEC	JAN	FEB	MAR	APR	MAY	JUN

Cultural Recommendations

LIGHT: 2000–3000 fc.

TEMPERATURES: Throughout the year, days average 70–72°F (21–22°C),

and nights average 58–59°F (14–15°C), with a diurnal range of 12–13°F (7°C). Probable extremes vary only a few degrees from the averages, indicating that plants may not tolerate wide temperature fluctuations.

HUMIDITY: 80–85% year-round.

WATER: Rainfall is heavy all year. Cultivated plants should be kept moist but not soggy.

FERTILIZER: ¼–½ recommended strength. A balanced fertilizer should be applied weekly to biweekly throughout the year.

REST PERIOD: Growing conditions should be maintained year-round. Water may be reduced somewhat for cultivated plants in winter, especially those grown in the dark, short-day conditions common in temperate latitudes. They should never be allowed to dry out completely, however.

GROWING MEDIA: Plants may be mounted on tree-fern or cork slabs or potted in small pots filled with any open, fast-draining medium. Repotting may be done anytime new roots are actively growing.

MISCELLANEOUS NOTES: The bloom season shown in the climate table is based on reports from the habitat. Plants that produce flowers which last a single day commonly bloom several times during the year. Flowering usually occurs 7–14 days after a sudden 10°F (5°C) drop in daytime temperatures. The plant was described in 1928 in *Bul. Jard. Bot. Buit.* 3rd sér. 10:57.

Plant and Flower Information

PLANT SIZE AND TYPE: An 8–21 in. (20–53 cm) sympodial epiphyte.

PSEUDOBULB: 6–19 in. (15–48 cm) long.

LEAVES: Many. The flattened, linear-lanceolate leaves are 1.6–2.0 in. (4–5 cm) long and somewhat twisted at the base. The upper part of the stem is leafy.

INFLORESCENCE: Short. Inflorescences emerge from nodes along the stem after the leaves have fallen.

FLOWERS: The blossoms are 0.5 in. (1.3 cm) across. They are white with light violet on the inside. The spur is violet.

REFERENCES: 224.

Dendrobium compressimentum J. J. Smith

ORIGIN/HABITAT: Western Sumatra. Plants grow on Mt. Malintang in the Padang region at about 4700 ft. (1430 m). They are also found on Mt. Gomgak at 4750 ft. (1450 m) and on Mt. Niroe at 5900 ft. (1800 m).

CLIMATE: Station #96163, Padang, Sumatra, Indonesia, Lat. 0.9°S, Long. 100.4°E, at 19 ft. (6 m). Temperatures are calculated for an elevation of 4900 ft. (1500 m), resulting in probable extremes of 78°F (26°C) and 52°F (11°C).

N/HEMISPHERE	JAN	FEB	MAR	APR	MAY	JUN	JUL	AUG	SEP	OCT	NOV	DEC
°F AVG MAX	71	71	70	70	70	70	71	71	71	71	72	71
°F AVG MIN	58	58	58	58	58	58	58	58	58	59	59	58
DIURNAL RANGE	13	13	12	12	12	12	13	13	13	12	13	13
RAIN/INCHES	10.9	13.7	6.0	19.5	20.4	18.9	13.8	10.2	12.1	14.3	12.4	12.1
HUMIDITY/%	81	82	82	84	85	84	81	81	82	83	81	81
BLOOM SEASON		*		*								
DAYS CLR @ 7AM	5	1	1	0	0	2	5	1	2	2	3	5
DAYS CLR @ 1PM	5	2	2	1	1	3	3	4	3	3	6	5
RAIN/MM	277	348	152	495	518	480	351	259	307	363	315	307
°C AVG MAX	21.6	21.6	21.1	21.1	21.1	21.1	21.6	21.6	21.6	21.6	22.2	21.6
°C AVG MIN	14.4	14.4	14.4	14.4	14.4	14.4	14.4	14.4	14.9	14.9	14.4	
DIURNAL RANGE	7.2	7.2	6.7	6.7	6.7	6.7	7.2	7.2	7.2	6.7	7.3	7.2
S/HEMISPHERE	JUL	AUG	SEP	OCT	NOV	DEC	JAN	FEB	MAR	APR	MAY	JUN

Cultural Recommendations

LIGHT: 2000–3000 fc. Diffused light is preferred.

TEMPERATURES: Throughout the year, days average 70–72°F (21–22°C), and nights average 58–59°F (14–15°C), with a diurnal range of 12–13°F (7°C). Probable extremes vary only a few degrees from the averages, indicating that plants may not tolerate wide temperature fluctuations.

HUMIDITY: 80–85% year-round.

WATER: Rainfall is heavy all year. Cultivated plants should be kept moist but not soggy.

FERTILIZER: ¼–½ recommended strength. A balanced fertilizer should be applied weekly to biweekly throughout the year.

REST PERIOD: Growing conditions should be maintained year-round. Water may be reduced somewhat for cultivated plants in winter, especially those grown in the dark, short-day conditions common in temperate latitudes. They should never be allowed to dry out completely, however.

GROWING MEDIA: Plants may be mounted on tree-fern or cork slabs or potted in small pots filled with any open, fast-draining medium. Repotting may be done anytime new roots are growing.

MISCELLANEOUS NOTES: The bloom season shown in the climate table is based on collection reports. The plant was described in 1928 in *Bul. Jard. Bot. Buit.* 3rd sér. 10:63

Plant and Flower Information

PLANT SIZE AND TYPE: A 26–33 in. (67–84 cm) sympodial epiphyte.

PSEUDOBULB: 26–33 in. (67–84 cm) long. The unbranched stems are slightly zigzag at the narrower tip.

LEAVES: Many. The lanceolate to ovate-lanceolate leaves are 3.5–5.0 in. (9–13 cm) long. They are somewhat twisted at the base. When dry, the leaves are rigidly papery.

INFLORESCENCE: Short. Inflorescences emerge from nodes near the apex of the leafless stems.

FLOWERS: 1 per inflorescence. The flowers are 1.4 in. (3.5 cm) long. They are light yellow to greenish yellow often with 2 red streaks near the column.

REFERENCES: 224.

Dendrobium compressistylum J. J. Smith

ORIGIN/HABITAT: Indonesia. Plants are found in Sumatra near Deli and in the Riau Archipelago, just off the southern tip of the Malay Peninsula. They were cultivated in the botanical garden at Bogor, Java. Habitat elevation is not available, so the following temperatures should be used with caution.

CLIMATE: Station #96091, Tandjungpinang, Pulau Bintan, Indonesia, Lat. 0.9°N, Long. 104.5°E, at 54 ft. (16 m). Record extreme temperatures are not available for this location.

N/HEMISPHERE	JAN	FEB	MAR	APR	MAY	JUN	JUL	AUG	SEP	OCT	NOV	DEC
°F AVG MAX	84	87	87	88	87	88	87	87	87	87	85	85
°F AVG MIN	73	72	73	74	74	74	73	73	73	74	74	74
DIURNAL RANGE	11	15	14	14	13	14	14	14	14	13	11	11
RAIN/INCHES	9.2	3.2	7.9	9.5	13.7	6.0	9.6	6.6	8.0	9.0	11.2	12.8
HUMIDITY/%	N/A											
BLOOM SEASON									*			
DAYS/CLR	N/A											
RAIN/MM	234	82	201	240	347	153	244	167	204	228	285	326
°C AVG MAX	29.0	30.4	30.6	31.4	30.5	30.9	30.5	30.6	30.3	30.4	29.7	29.2
°C AVG MIN	22.8	22.4	22.6	23.3	23.4	23.5	22.9	22.9	22.8	23.1	23.1	23.2
DIURNAL RANGE	6.2	8.0	8.0	8.1	7.3	7.4	7.6	7.7	7.5	7.3	6.6	6.0
S/HEMISPHERE	JUL	AUG	SEP	OCT	NOV	DEC	JAN	FEB	MAR	APR	MAY	JUN

Cultural Recommendations

LIGHT: 2000–3000 fc.

TEMPERATURES: Throughout the year, days average 84–88°F (29–31°C), and nights average 72–74°F (22–24°C), with a diurnal range of 11–15°F (6–8°C).

HUMIDITY: Information is not available for this location. However, records from other stations in the region indicate that averages are probably 80–85% year-round.

WATER: Rainfall is very heavy most of the year, with a brief, semidry period in winter. Cultivated plants should be kept moist and never be allowed to dry out completely.

FERTILIZER: ¼–½ recommended strength. A balanced fertilizer should be applied weekly to biweekly throughout the year.

REST PERIOD: Growing conditions should be maintained all year. Water may be reduced somewhat in winter, especially for plants grown in the dark, short-day conditions common in temperate latitudes. Fertilizer should be reduced until water is increased in spring.

GROWING MEDIA: Plants may be mounted on tree-fern or cork slabs or potted in small pots filled with any open, fast-draining medium. Repotting may be done anytime new roots are growing.

MISCELLANEOUS NOTES: The bloom season shown in the climate table is based on collection reports. The plant was described in 1926 in *Bul. Jard. Bot. Buit.* 3rd sér. 8:52.

Plant and Flower Information

PLANT SIZE AND TYPE: A 5 in. (13 cm) sympodial epiphyte.

PSEUDOBULB: 5 in. (13 cm) long. The pale green stems are very flattened. They are clustered and arise from a very short rhizome.

LEAVES: Many. The oblong-triangular leaves are 1.2–1.6 in. (3–4 cm) long. They are distichous, laterally compressed, and pale green.

INFLORESCENCE: Short. Inflorescences emerge near the apex of the stem.

FLOWERS: 1 per inflorescence. The flowers are 0.5 in. (1.3 cm) across. Sepals and petals are pale yellow with purple dots at the base. The 3-lobed lip is pale yellowish brown and yellowish white, recurved, and very wavy.

REFERENCES: 224.

Dendrobium compressum Lindley. See *D. lamellatum* (Blume) Lindley. REFERENCES: 75, 190, 216, 254, 317, 454, 469.

Dendrobium comptonii Rendle

AKA: Lewis and Cribb (ref. 270), Hallé (ref. 173), and Kores (ref. 466) consider plants known as *D. comptonii* from Vanuatu, New Caledonia, and the Fiji Islands to be synonymous with *D. macropus* (Endl.) Rchb. f. ex Lindley. However, Clements (ref. 67) recommends that at least the Australian form be maintained as an independent species. He includes *D. drake-castilloi* Kränzlin, *D. gracilicaule* F. Mueller var. *howeanum* Maiden, and *D. macropus* (Endl.) Rchb. f. ex Lindley subsp. *howeanum* (Maiden) P. Green as synonyms. Also see discussion at *D. macropus* (Endl.) Rchb. f. ex Lindley.

ORIGIN/HABITAT: Widespread on Lord Howe Island, Australia. Plants commonly grow on trees, but when pieces break off, they continue to grow happily on the rocky ground.

CLIMATE: Station #94995, Lord Howe Island, Australia, Lat. 31.5°S, Long. 159.1°E, at 35 ft. (11 m). Record extreme temperatures are 89°F (32°C) and 43°F (6°C).

N/HEMISPHERE	JAN	FEB	MAR	APR	MAY	JUN	JUL	AUG	SEP	OCT	NOV	DEC
°F AVG MAX	65	65	68	70	73	76	78	78	77	74	70	67
°F AVG MIN	55	55	56	59	61	64	67	67	66	63	60	57
DIURNAL RANGE	10	10	12	11	12	12	11	11	11	11	10	10
RAIN/INCHES	7.7	5.3	5.3	5.2	4.5	4.9	4.9	4.2	5.0	6.7	6.2	7.7
HUMIDITY/%	72	70	70	71	72	72	71	69	69	71	71	70
BLOOM SEASON			**	**								
DAYS CLR @ 5AM	5	8	6	7	5	5	6	5	9	7	7	5
DAYS CLR @ 11AM	4	4	5	5	7	6	5	3	5	6	4	3
RAIN/MM	196	135	135	132	114	124	124	107	127	170	157	196
°C AVG MAX	18.3	18.3	20.0	21.1	22.8	24.4	25.6	25.6	25.0	23.3	21.1	19.4
°C AVG MIN	12.8	12.8	13.3	15.0	16.1	17.8	19.4	19.4	18.9	17.2	15.6	13.9
DIURNAL RANGE	5.5	5.5	6.7	6.1	6.7	6.6	6.2	6.2	6.1	6.1	5.5	5.5
S/HEMISPHERE	JUL	AUG	SEP	OCT	NOV	DEC	JAN	FEB	MAR	APR	MAY	JUN

Cultural Recommendations

LIGHT: 2500–3500 fc. Plants require good light and strong air movement.

TEMPERATURES: Summer days average 76–78°F (24–26°C), and nights average 64–67°F (18–19°C), with a diurnal range of 11–12°F (6–7°C).

HUMIDITY: Near 70% year-round.

WATER: Rainfall is moderate all year, with a short, slightly drier period in late spring. Cultivated plants require a delicate balance between too much and too little water. They are healthiest if allowed to dry out between waterings, as the fine roots deteriorate quickly if plants are overwatered or if the medium is allowed to become stale. However, the plants should never be allowed to remain dry for long periods.

FERTILIZER: ¼–½ recommended strength, applied weekly. A high-nitrogen fertilizer is beneficial from spring to midsummer, but a fertilizer high in phosphates should be used in late summer and autumn.

REST PERIOD: Winter days average 65–68°F (18–20°C), and nights average 55–57°F (13–14°C), with a diurnal range of 10–12°F (6–7°C). Water and fertilizer should be reduced somewhat in winter, especially for plants grown in the dark, short-day conditions common in temperate latitudes; but plants should still not remain dry for very long.

GROWING MEDIA: Plants grow well with either pot or slab culture. They may be mounted on tree-fern or cork slabs if humidity is high and plants are watered at least once daily in summer. When plants are potted, any open, fast-draining medium may be used. Repotting is best done in early spring when new roots are growing.

MISCELLANEOUS NOTES: The bloom season shown in the climate table is based on cultivation records.

Plant and Flower Information

PLANT SIZE AND TYPE: A 16 in. (40 cm) sympodial epiphyte or lithophyte.

PSEUDOBULB: 16 in. (40 cm) long. The erect canes are thicker than the stems of plants called *D. macropus*.

LEAVES: 4–6 per growth. The leaves are usually slightly larger and longer than *D. macropus*.

INFLORESCENCE: Shorter than *D. macropus*. The blossoms are clustered at the apex of the inflorescence.

FLOWERS: Many per inflorescence. The flowers are 0.6–0.8 in. (1.5–2.0 cm) across, usually slightly larger than flowers called *D. macropus*. The normally lemon-yellow sepals and petals may be golden yellow, pale yellow, or cream, but they are sometimes green. Some clones have brown blotches on the outside of the sepals and petals. The cream-colored lip is marked with red-pink. The flower fragrance is different than *D. macropus*.

HYBRIDIZING NOTES: Chromosome count is 2n = 38 as *D. gracilicaule* var. *howeanum* (ref. 580).

REFERENCES: 67, 173, 223, 270, 445, 466, 533, 562, 580.

PHOTOS/DRAWINGS: 562.

Dendrobium conanthum Schlechter

AKA: *D. kajewskii* Ames.

ORIGIN/HABITAT: New Guinea and islands of the South Pacific. In New Guinea, plants are found across much of Irian Jaya and Papua. They usually grow near sea level or in swamps, but they are occasionally found as high as 2600 ft. (800 m). In the Santa Cruz Islands, *D. conanthum* is common in rainforests and on mangroves. Distribution also includes the island of Espiritu Santo in Vanuatu and the Admiralty and Solomon Islands.

CLIMATE: Station #200004, Ambunti, Papua New Guinea, Lat. 4.2°S, Long. 142.8°E, at 164 ft. (50 m). Record extreme temperatures are 99°F (37°C) and 52°F (11°C).

N/HEMISPHERE	JAN	FEB	MAR	APR	MAY	JUN	JUL	AUG	SEP	OCT	NOV	DEC
°F AVG MAX	88	90	90	90	91	90	90	90	90	90	90	89
°F AVG MIN	72	73	74	73	73	73	72	73	73	73	73	74
DIURNAL RANGE	16	17	16	17	18	17	18	17	17	17	17	15
RAIN/INCHES	6.4	7.4	7.7	8.5	9.2	9.4	10.9	10.2	12.2	10.4	8.3	5.2
HUMIDITY/%	N/A											
BLOOM SEASON					*			*				
DAYS CLR	N/A											
RAIN/MM	163	187	196	217	233	240	277	260	311	265	211	132
°C AVG MAX	31.2	32.2	32.4	32.1	32.6	32.2	32.3	31.9	32.1	31.9	31.9	31.7
°C AVG MIN	22.4	22.8	23.2	22.8	23.0	22.8	22.4	22.5	22.7	22.8	22.9	23.1
DIURNAL RANGE	8.8	9.4	9.2	9.3	9.6	9.4	9.9	9.4	9.4	9.1	9.0	8.6
S/HEMISPHERE	JUL	AUG	SEP	OCT	NOV	DEC	JAN	FEB	MAR	APR	MAY	JUN

Cultural Recommendations

LIGHT: 2500–3500 fc.

TEMPERATURES: Throughout the year, days average 88–91°F (31–33°C), and nights average 72–74°F (22–23°C), with a diurnal range of 15–18°F (9–10°C).

HUMIDITY: Information is not available for this location. The habitat is always described as being near water, so humidity probably averages 80–85% year-round. Growers recommend that high humidity and strong air movement be provided at all times.

WATER: Rainfall is heavy all year with the greatest amounts falling in summer and early autumn. Cultivated plants should be kept moist but not soggy.

FERTILIZER: ¼–½ recommended strength. A balanced fertilizer should be applied weekly to biweekly throughout the year.

REST PERIOD: Growing conditions should be maintained all year. Water and fertilizer should be reduced for plants cultivated in the dark, short-day conditions common in temperate-latitude winters, but plants should never be allowed to dry completely between waterings. In the habitat, seasonal light variation is minor.

GROWING MEDIA: Plants are best mounted on tree-fern or cork slabs if humidity is high and plants are watered at least once daily. If plants must be potted, hanging baskets may be filled with any open, fast-draining medium. Repotting may be done anytime new roots are growing.

MISCELLANEOUS NOTES: The bloom season shown in the climate table is based on cultivation records. Plants from this habitat are reportedly difficult to maintain in Singapore, but no specific horticultural problem was indicated. Overall climatic conditions are similar at both locations, but average night temperatures in Singapore are about 5°F (3°C) warmer, and the diurnal range averages about 6°F (3°C) less.

Plant and Flower Information

PLANT SIZE AND TYPE: A 24–120 in. (60–305 cm) sympodial epiphyte.

PSEUDOBULB: 24–120 in. (60–305 cm) long. The canelike stems produce side branches from the nodes.

LEAVES: Many. The dark green leaves, which are 1.6–6.0 in. (4–15 cm) long, may be oblong or ovate.

INFLORESCENCE: 12–24 in. (30–60 cm) long. The inflorescences may be erect or suberect. They emerge from both old and new canes.

FLOWERS: 6–30 per inflorescence. Inflorescences commonly produce 15–20 blossoms. The flowers are 1.2 in. (3 cm) across. The undulate, recurved sepals are a unique characteristic of this species. Sepals and petals may be gold or yellow-green with a red-brown flush. They are twisted and curl at the tips. The pointed, yellow lip is marked with dark purple lines. Flower color is highly variable.

HYBRIDIZING NOTES: Chromosome count is 2n = 38 (ref. 152, 153, 243, 273). In the Solomon Islands, *D. macranthum* A. Richard and *D. sancristobalense* Cribb are known to hybridize naturally with *D. conanthum* Schlechter. When used as a parent, *D. conanthum* contributes the tendency to produce plants with numerous flowers. It also improves flower substance in the progeny.

REFERENCES: 25, 82, 84, 152, 153, 221, 243, 269, 270, 271, 273, 304, 306, 345, 437, 445, 470, 516, 537.

PHOTOS/DRAWINGS: *41,* 84, *269,* 270, *271, 304, 306, 345,* 437, *540.*

Dendrobium concavissimum J. J. Smith

AKA: *D. fornicatum* Schlechter. The International Orchid Commission (ref. 236) considers *D. chrysoglossum* Schlechter a synonym of *D. concavissimum* and registers hybrids under the latter name.

ORIGIN/HABITAT: Rare in Iran Jaya (western New Guinea) on Mt Goliath at about 5250 ft. (1600 m) and in the Arfak Range at about 3950 ft. (1200 m). In northeastern Papua New Guinea, plants collected as *D. fornicatum* grew on forest trees of the Maboro and Dischore Ranges at about 4250 ft. (1300 m). Plants also grow on Bougainville in mountain and cloud forests at 4450–6050 ft. (1350–1850 m) and on Sulawesi (Celebes) where they are found near Tondano (Tomohon) on the Minahassa Peninsula at about 2950 ft. (900 m). *D. concavissimum* grows on mossy trees in shady places.

CLIMATE: Station #200192, Garaina, Papua New Guinea, Lat. 7.9°S, Long. 147.1°E, at 2350 ft. (716 m). Temperatures are calculated for an elevation of 4250 ft. (1300 m), resulting in probable extremes of 88°F (31°C) and 40°F (4°C).

N/HEMISPHERE	JAN	FEB	MAR	APR	MAY	JUN	JUL	AUG	SEP	OCT	NOV	DEC
°F AVG MAX	74	76	77	78	79	79	79	79	78	78	77	75
°F AVG MIN	57	57	57	58	57	58	59	59	59	58	58	57
DIURNAL RANGE	17	19	20	20	22	21	20	20	19	20	19	18
RAIN/INCHES	5.8	6.5	8.7	11.1	11.8	11.9	8.9	11.7	11.5	9.9	7.7	5.2
HUMIDITY/%	84	82	82	81	80	80	81	81	82	83	84	84
BLOOM SEASON				*							*	*
DAYS CLR	N/A											
RAIN/MM	147	165	221	282	300	302	226	297	292	251	196	132
°C AVG MAX	23.1	24.3	24.8	25.4	25.9	25.9	25.9	25.9	25.4	25.4	24.8	23.7
°C AVG MIN	13.7	13.7	13.7	14.3	13.7	14.3	14.8	14.8	14.8	14.3	14.3	13.7
DIURNAL RANGE	9.4	10.6	11.1	11.1	12.2	11.6	11.1	11.1	10.6	11.1	10.5	10.0
S/HEMISPHERE	JUL	AUG	SEP	OCT	NOV	DEC	JAN	FEB	MAR	APR	MAY	JUN

Cultural Recommendations

LIGHT: 1500–2500 fc. Plants may tolerate higher light levels, especially in the morning.

TEMPERATURES: Throughout the year, days average 74–79°F (23–26°C), and nights average 57–59°F (14–15°C), with a diurnal range of 17–22°F (9–12°C).

HUMIDITY: 80–85% year-round.

WATER: Rainfall is heavy all year. Conditions are slightly drier in winter. Cultivated plants should be kept moist but not soggy.

FERTILIZER: ¼–½ recommended strength. A balanced fertilizer should be applied weekly to biweekly throughout the year.

REST PERIOD: Growing conditions should be maintained all year. Water and fertilizer should be reduced somewhat for cultivated plants, especially those grown in the dark, short-day conditions common during temperate-latitude winters. They should never be allowed to dry out completely, however. In the habitat, seasonal light variation is minor.

GROWING MEDIA: Plants may be mounted on tree-fern or cork slabs if humidity is high and plants are watered at least once daily in summer. When plants are potted, any open, fast-draining medium may be used. Repotting may be done anytime new roots are growing.

MISCELLANEOUS NOTES: The bloom season shown in the climate table is based on reports from the habitat. The spring bloom season is reported for plants collected on Sulawesi, and the autumn bloom record is for plants from New Guinea.

Plant and Flower Information[c]

PLANT SIZE AND TYPE: A sympodial epiphyte of unreported size.

PSEUDOBULB: The stems are long and branching.

LEAVES: The lanceolate leaves are 1.2–1.6 in. (3–4 cm) long.

INFLORESCENCE: Short.

FLOWERS: 5–7 per inflorescence. The flowers are 0.6 in. (1.5 cm) across with oval sepals and obovate petals. Blossoms have violet sepals and petals and an orange lip. The lip is hood-shaped with a short tooth on each side of the margin.

REFERENCES: 92, 221, 271, 445, 470, 486, 516.

Dendrobium concavum J. J. Smith

AKA: Kränzlin (ref. 254) listed *D. teloense* J. J. Smith as a synonym of *D. concavum*, but Schlechter (ref. 436) strongly disagreed, indicating that *D. concavum* J. J. Smith var. *celebense* J. J. Smith might be synonymous with *D. smithianum* Schlechter. J. J. Smith (ref. 483) expressed reservations regarding Schlechter's conclusions, however.

ORIGIN/HABITAT: Sulawesi (Celebes) near Tondano (Tomohon). Plants grow on trees on the Minahassa Peninsula at about 2950 ft. (900 m).

CLIMATE: Station #97014, Manado, Sulawesi, Lat. 1.5°N, Long. 124.9°E, at 264 ft. (80 m). Temperatures are calculated for an elevation of 3000 ft. (910 m), resulting in probable extremes of 88°F (31°C) and 56°F (13°C).

N/HEMISPHERE	JAN	FEB	MAR	APR	MAY	JUN	JUL	AUG	SEP	OCT	NOV	DEC
°F AVG MAX	76	76	76	77	78	78	78	80	80	80	78	77
°F AVG MIN	64	64	64	64	65	64	64	64	64	63	64	65
DIURNAL RANGE	12	12	12	13	13	14	14	16	16	17	14	12
RAIN/INCHES	18.6	13.8	12.2	8.0	6.4	6.5	4.8	4.0	3.4	4.9	8.9	14.7
HUMIDITY/%	84	83	83	83	81	80	75	72	75	77	82	83
BLOOM SEASON											*	**
DAYS CLR @ 8AM	4	3	6	11	11	12	12	12	14	17	12	8
DAYS CLR @ 2PM	1	1	1	2	1	3	3	4	4	4	1	1
RAIN/MM	472	351	310	203	163	165	122	102	86	124	226	373
°C AVG MAX	24.4	24.4	24.4	25.0	25.5	25.5	25.5	26.7	26.7	26.7	25.5	25.0
°C AVG MIN	17.8	17.8	17.8	17.8	18.3	17.8	17.8	17.8	17.8	17.2	17.8	18.3
DIURNAL RANGE	6.6	6.6	6.6	7.2	7.2	7.7	7.7	8.9	8.9	9.5	7.7	6.7
S/HEMISPHERE	JUL	AUG	SEP	OCT	NOV	DEC	JAN	FEB	MAR	APR	MAY	JUN

Cultural Recommendations

LIGHT: 2000–2500 fc. The habitat is usually overcast in the afternoon.

TEMPERATURES: Throughout the year, days average 76–80°F (24–27°C), and nights average 63–65°F (17–18°C), with a diurnal range of 12–17°F (7–10°C). The average highs vary only 4°F (2°C), and average lows fluctuate only 2°F (1°C), indicating that plants may not tolerate wide temperature fluctuations.

HUMIDITY: 80–85% most of the year, dropping to 70–75% in summer.

WATER: Rainfall is moderate to heavy all year. The driest weather occurs in late summer when temperatures are warm. Cultivated plants should be kept moist but not soggy. Warm water might be beneficial.

FERTILIZER: ¼–½ recommended strength. A balanced fertilizer should be applied weekly to biweekly throughout the year.

REST PERIOD: Growing temperatures should be maintained all year. The plants may rest during the 1–2 month drier period which occurs in late summer and coincides with the period of greatest diurnal range. Cultivated plants should dry out slightly during this period, but they should never remain dry for long. The heaviest rainfall in the habitat occurs in winter, but water should not be increased for cultivated plants. In fact, water should be reduced somewhat for plants grown in the dark, short-day conditions common in temperate latitudes, but they should not be allowed to dry out completely.

GROWING MEDIA: Plants may be mounted on tree-fern or cork slabs or potted in any open, fast-draining medium. Repotting may be done anytime roots are growing.

MISCELLANEOUS NOTES: The bloom season shown in the climate table is based on reports from the habitat.

Plant and Flower Information

PLANT SIZE AND TYPE: A 12–14 in. (31–36 cm) sympodial epiphyte.

PSEUDOBULB: 12–14 in. (31–36 cm) long. The elongated stems are flattened.

LEAVES: 6–8 per growth. The lanceolate leaves are about 1.2 in. (3 cm) long, laterally flattened, and pointed.

INFLORESCENCE: Short. Inflorescences are borne on the upper part of the stem.

FLOWERS: The white flowers are 0.3 in. (0.9 cm) across. Blossoms have ovate sepals, lanceolate petals, and a large conical mentum. The 3-lobed lip has slender, sickle-shaped sidelobes and a concave midlobe which is marked with 3 ridges.

REFERENCES: 219, 254, 436, 468, 483.

Dendrobium concinnum Miquel

AKA: *Oxystophyllum carnosum* Blume, *Oxystophyllum rigidum* Blume, *Dendrobium carnosum* (Blume) Rchb. f. not Presl or Teijsm. and Binn., *D. rigens* Rchb. f., *D. rigidum* (Blume) Miquel not R. Brown or Lindley. Seidenfaden (ref. 454) indicates that the name *D. atropurpureum* has been erroneously used when referring to plants that should have been identified as *D. concinnum*, which is apparently the case of Holttum (ref. 200) and Ridley (ref. 402) who included *D. atropurpureum* Miquel as a synonym of *D. concinnum* or *D. carnosum*.

ORIGIN/HABITAT: Vietnam, Cambodia, Thailand, Malaya, Borneo, and Indonesia. In southern Thailand, plants grow at about 800 ft. (250 m), and in Malaya, it is a lowland species. Common in West Java, the orchids grow on trees in rubber plantations and in the foothills at 1300–3300 ft. (400–1000 m). Plants from Sumatra were collected in first growth jungle at about 3600 ft. (1070 m) near Takengön. In Borneo, plants are found in Sabah and Sarawak. One collection was reported from a small tree on the summit of a limestone crag at about 1000 ft. (300 m) where it was exposed to relatively high light.

CLIMATE: Station #48551, Surat (Ban Don), Thailand, Lat. 9.1°N, Long. 99.3°E, at 10 ft. (3 m). Temperatures are calculated for an elevation of 800 ft. (250 m), resulting in probable extremes of 102°F (39°C) and 44°F (7°C).

N/HEMISPHERE	JAN	FEB	MAR	APR	MAY	JUN	JUL	AUG	SEP	OCT	NOV	DEC
°F AVG MAX	85	89	92	92	90	88	87	88	87	86	84	83
°F AVG MIN	66	66	67	70	71	71	71	71	70	70	69	68
DIURNAL RANGE	19	23	25	22	19	17	16	17	17	16	15	15
RAIN/INCHES	1.0	0.3	0.4	2.5	6.6	4.5	6.9	5.8	7.1	8.1	12.1	4.0
HUMIDITY/%	82	78	75	79	83	82	82	82	84	87	87	86
BLOOM SEASON									*			
DAYS CLR @ 7AM	4	3	3	2	1	1	1	1	1	1	1	2
DAYS CLR @ 1PM	2	2	2	1	1	0	0	0	0	0	1	1
RAIN/MM	25	8	10	64	168	114	175	147	180	206	307	102
°C AVG MAX	29.6	31.8	33.5	33.5	32.4	31.3	30.7	31.3	30.7	30.2	29.1	28.5
°C AVG MIN	19.1	19.1	19.6	21.3	21.8	21.8	21.8	21.8	21.3	21.3	20.7	20.2
DIURNAL RANGE	10.5	12.7	13.9	12.2	10.6	9.5	8.9	9.5	9.4	8.9	8.4	8.3
S/HEMISPHERE	JUL	AUG	SEP	OCT	NOV	DEC	JAN	FEB	MAR	APR	MAY	JUN

Cultural Recommendations

LIGHT: 3500–4000 fc.

TEMPERATURES: Through the year, days average 85–92°F (30–34°C), and nights average 66–71°F (19–22°C), with a diurnal range of 15–25°F (8–14°C). The warmest season is early spring.

HUMIDITY: 80–85% most of the year, dropping to 75–80% for 3 months in winter.

WATER: Rainfall is moderate to heavy from late spring through autumn. Conditions are drier in winter. Cultivated plants should be kept moist from late spring into autumn with only slight drying allowed between waterings. Water should be gradually reduced in late autumn.

FERTILIZER: 1/4–1/2 recommended strength. A balanced fertilizer should be applied weekly to biweekly throughout the year.

REST PERIOD: Growing temperatures should be maintained year-round. Winter rainfall is low for 2–3 months, but additional moisture is available from frequent heavy dew. Water and fertilizer should be reduced and the plants allowed to dry somewhat between waterings. They should not remain dry for long periods, however. In the habitat, light is slightly higher in winter.

GROWING MEDIA: Plants may be potted in any open, fast-draining medium. Repotting is best done in early spring when new roots are growing.

MISCELLANEOUS NOTES: The bloom season shown in the climate table is based on the collection report. Plants may bloom several times a year. Flowering occurs 11 days after a sudden 10°F (5°C) drop in daytime temperatures.

Plant and Flower Information

PLANT SIZE AND TYPE: A 4–8 in. (10–20 cm) sympodial epiphyte.

PSEUDOBULB: 4–8 in. (10–20 cm) long. The tightly clustered stems arise from a very short rhizome. The internodes are 0.4 in. (1 cm) long.

LEAVES: 10–14 per growth. The fleshy leaves, which alternate along the stem, are about 1.6 in. (4 cm) long, but leaf length and shape are variable. They are jointed at the base and often curve toward the stem. They are flattened to lie on a single plane and overlap each other for a considerable distance. In some habitats, the leaves may be deciduous.

INFLORESCENCE: Short. The blossoms rest on the leaves. Inflorescences emerge from leaf bracts of leafy and leafless stems. Although they may arise anywhere on the stem, they are usually near the apex.

FLOWERS: 1–2 per inflorescence. The fleshy flowers are 0.25 in. (0.6 cm) across. Usually pale to bright yellow sometimes with purple spotting, the nearly transparent blossoms may occasionally be entirely red to dark purple. The lip is marked with tiny red spots in the center and a hairy, swollen, kidney-shaped cushion near the apex. The Sumatra collection had yellow flowers with red-brown markings on the sepals.

REFERENCES: 25, 59, 75, 111, 213, 216, 254, 266, 286, 298, 310, 317, 435, 454, 455, 469, 592.

PHOTOS/DRAWINGS: 75, 454, *455*.

Dendrobium confinale Kerr

ORIGIN/HABITAT: Endemic to Thailand. Plants grow on Mt. Chiengdao at about 6050 ft. (1850 m).

CLIMATE: Station #48327, Chiang Mai, Thailand, Lat. 18.8°N, Long. 99.0°E, at 1100 ft. (335 m). Temperatures are calculated for an elevation of 6000 ft. (1830 m), resulting in probable extremes of 93°F (34°C) and 22°F (–6°C).

N/HEMISPHERE	JAN	FEB	MAR	APR	MAY	JUN	JUL	AUG	SEP	OCT	NOV	DEC
°F AVG MAX	69	74	79	80	78	74	73	71	72	73	70	68
°F AVG MIN	40	41	46	54	58	58	58	59	57	55	50	41
DIURNAL RANGE	29	33	33	26	20	16	15	12	15	18	20	27
RAIN/INCHES	0.3	0.4	0.6	2.0	5.5	6.1	7.4	8.7	11.5	4.9	1.5	0.4
HUMIDITY/%	73	65	58	62	73	78	80	83	83	81	79	76
BLOOM SEASON	N/A											
DAYS CLR @ 7AM	5	5	2	2	1	0	0	0	0	1	3	3
DAYS CLR @ 1PM	9	8	4	2	0	0	0	0	0	0	1	3
RAIN/MM	8	10	15	51	140	155	188	221	292	124	38	10
°C AVG MAX	20.5	23.2	26.0	26.6	25.5	23.2	22.7	21.6	22.1	22.7	21.0	19.7
°C AVG MIN	4.4	4.9	7.7	12.1	14.3	14.3	14.3	14.9	13.8	12.7	9.9	4.9
DIURNAL RANGE	16.1	18.3	18.3	14.5	11.2	8.9	8.4	6.7	8.3	10.0	11.1	15.0
S/HEMISPHERE	JUL	AUG	SEP	OCT	NOV	DEC	JAN	FEB	MAR	APR	MAY	JUN

Cultural Recommendations

LIGHT: 1800–2400 fc.

TEMPERATURES: Summer days average 71–74°F (22–23°C), and nights average 58–59°F (15°C), with a diurnal range of 12–16°F (7–9°C). Spring is the warmest season. Days average 78–80°F (26–27°C), and nights average 46–58°F (8–15°C), with a diurnal range of 20–33°F (11–18°C). The warm weather occurs with, or immediately follows, the period of widest diurnal range.

HUMIDITY: 75–80% most of the year, dropping to near 60% in late winter and early spring.

WATER: Rainfall is heavy in summer and autumn, but conditions are dry in winter and early spring. Cultivated plants should be kept moist while actively growing, but water should be gradually reduced in autumn after new growths mature.

FERTILIZER: 1/4–1/2 recommended strength, applied weekly. A high-nitrogen fertilizer is beneficial from spring to midsummer, but a fertilizer high in phosphates should be used in late summer and autumn.

REST PERIOD: Winter days average 68–74°F (20–23°C), and nights average 40–41°F (5°C), with a diurnal range of 27–33°F (15–18°C). The average low temperatures are below 50°F (10°C) for 4 months and then warm rapidly in spring. Plants should be able to tolerate temperatures a few degrees below freezing, but extremes should be avoided in cultivation. During very cold weather, a plant's chance of surviving with minimal damage is better if it is dry. In the habitat, rainfall averages are very low for 4–5 months in winter, but during the early part of the season the high relative humidity indicates that additional moisture is available from frequent fog, mist, and heavy deposits of dew. Growers sometimes recommend eliminating water in winter, but plants are healthiest if for most of the winter they are allowed to become somewhat dry between waterings. They should not remain dry for extended periods, however. For 1–2 months in late winter, conditions are clear, warm, and dry, with humidity so low that even the moisture from morning dew is uncommon. Plants should be allowed to dry out completely between waterings and remain dry longer during this time. Occasional early morning mistings between waterings may help keep the plants from becoming too dry. Fertilizer should be greatly reduced or eliminated until water is increased in spring. A cool, dry rest is essential for cultivated plants and should be continued until new growth starts in spring. In the habitat, light is highest in winter.

GROWING MEDIA: Plants may be mounted on tree-fern or cork slabs if humidity is high and plants are watered at least once daily in summer. When plants are potted, any open, fast-draining medium may be used. Repotting is best done in early spring when new roots are growing.

Plant and Flower Information

PLANT SIZE AND TYPE: A small sympodial epiphyte.

PSEUDOBULB: 1.2–2.0 in. (3–5 cm) long.

INFLORESCENCE: 1.2 in. (3 cm) long. Several inflorescences usually appear from the terminal and subapical nodes of leafless stems.

FLOWERS: 5 per inflorescence. The flowers are 0.4 in. (1 cm) across and remain nearly closed. The white flowers are marked with dense purple veins on the lip.

REFERENCES: 224, 249, 266, 454.

PHOTOS/DRAWINGS: 454.

Dendrobium confluens J. J. Smith

ORIGIN/HABITAT: Buru Island in the Moluccas. Plants grow on trees rooting on peat moors near Likoe Ewali (Koentoeroen) at about 3950 ft. (1200 m).

Dendrobium confundens

CLIMATE: Station #97700, Namlea, Pulau Buru, Indonesia, Lat. 3.3°S, Long. 127.0°E, at 66 ft. (20 m). Temperatures are calculated for an elevation of 3950 ft. (1200 m). Record extreme temperatures are not available for this location.

N/HEMISPHERE	JAN	FEB	MAR	APR	MAY	JUN	JUL	AUG	SEP	OCT	NOV	DEC
°F AVG MAX	71	71	73	74	74	73	72	71	72	73	73	71
°F AVG MIN	62	64	64	65	67	65	64	64	64	64	64	63
DIURNAL RANGE	9	7	9	9	7	8	8	7	8	9	9	8
RAIN/INCHES	3.1	4.4	1.3	1.6	4.0	5.8	6.1	5.3	6.9	2.8	2.0	5.5
HUMIDITY/%	N/A											
BLOOM SEASON	*											
DAYS CLR	N/A											
RAIN/MM	79	112	33	41	102	147	155	135	175	71	51	140
°C AVG MAX	21.8	21.8	22.9	23.4	23.4	22.9	22.3	21.8	22.3	22.9	22.9	21.8
°C AVG MIN	16.8	17.9	17.9	18.4	19.5	18.4	17.9	17.9	17.9	17.9	17.9	17.3
DIURNAL RANGE	5.0	3.8	5.0	5.0	3.9	4.5	4.4	3.9	4.4	5.0	5.0	4.5
S/HEMISPHERE	JUL	AUG	SEP	OCT	NOV	DEC	JAN	FEB	MAR	APR	MAY	JUN

Cultural Recommendations

LIGHT: 2000–3000 fc.

TEMPERATURES: Throughout the year, days average 71–74°F (22–23°C), and nights average 62–67°F (17–20°C), with a diurnal range of 7–9°F (4–5°C).

HUMIDITY: Information is not available for this location. However, average humidity at other stations in the region is near 80% year-round.

WATER: Rainfall is moderate most of the year, with a 2-month, semidry period in early spring and again in autumn. Cultivated plants should be allowed to dry slightly between waterings.

FERTILIZER: ¼–½ recommended strength. A balanced fertilizer should be applied weekly to biweekly throughout the year.

REST PERIOD: Growing temperatures should be maintained year-round. Water should be reduced for cultivated plants in late autumn and again in early spring. Additional drying should be allowed between waterings, but plants should not remain completely dry for long periods. Water may be reduced in winter for plants cultivated in the dark, short-day conditions common in temperate latitudes, but they should not be allowed to dry out completely. Reduce fertilizer anytime water is reduced.

GROWING MEDIA: Plants may be mounted on tree-fern or cork slabs or placed in small pots filled with any open, fast-draining medium. Repotting may be done anytime new roots are growing.

MISCELLANEOUS NOTES: The bloom season shown in the climate table is based on a collection report. The plant was described in 1928 in *Bul. Jard. Bot. Buit.* 3rd sér. 9:466.

Plant and Flower Information

PLANT SIZE AND TYPE: A 3–7 in. (8–18 cm) sympodial epiphyte.

PSEUDOBULB: 1.2–4.7 in. (3–12 cm) long. New growths arise from a short branching rhizome. The pseudobulbs are oblong-ovate when young becoming slender and nearly linear with age.

LEAVES: 1 per growth. The linear-lanceolate leaves are 2.0–2.5 in. (5.0–6.5 cm) long, fleshy, and leathery.

INFLORESCENCE: 1 in. (2.5 cm) long.

FLOWERS: 1 per inflorescence. The long-lasting flowers are 1.7 in. (4.4 cm) long. Blossoms are rose to purple. Sepals and petals taper to a slender point. The lip is erect with a wavy, very recurved midlobe.

REFERENCES: 224.

Dendrobium confundens Kränzlin

ORIGIN/HABITAT: The Aru Islands located in the Arafura Sea between northern Australia and Irian Jaya (western New Guinea). No habitat or elevation information is available, so the following climate data should be used with caution. Schlechter (ref. 437) notes that all closely related orchids grow on isolated trees near the shore, along rivers, or along the forest border so that the orchids receive some direct sun.

CLIMATE: Station #97796, Kokenau (Kokonau), Irian Jaya, Lat. 4.7°S, Long. 136.4°E, at 10 ft. (3 m). Record extreme temperatures are not available for this location.

N/HEMISPHERE	JAN	FEB	MAR	APR	MAY	JUN	JUL	AUG	SEP	OCT	NOV	DEC
°F AVG MAX	83	83	86	88	90	89	89	89	90	88	87	84
°F AVG MIN	73	73	74	74	74	75	74	74	74	74	74	73
DIURNAL RANGE	10	10	12	14	16	14	15	15	16	14	13	11
RAIN/INCHES	18.4	15.8	18.9	11.6	9.7	10.6	11.5	15.7	11.6	11.6	16.0	19.9
HUMIDITY/%	N/A											
BLOOM SEASON						*						
DAYS CLR	N/A											
RAIN/MM	467	401	479	295	245	269	293	400	294	296	407	506
°C AVG MAX	28.6	28.4	30.2	31.1	32.1	31.9	31.9	31.7	32.0	31.4	30.7	28.7
°C AVG MIN	22.7	22.6	23.3	23.4	23.5	23.7	23.6	23.5	23.4	23.4	23.5	23.0
DIURNAL RANGE	5.9	5.8	6.9	7.7	8.6	8.2	8.3	8.2	8.6	8.0	7.2	5.7
S/HEMISPHERE	JUL	AUG	SEP	OCT	NOV	DEC	JAN	FEB	MAR	APR	MAY	JUN

Cultural Recommendations

LIGHT: 2500–3500 fc.

TEMPERATURES: Throughout the year, days average 83–90°F (29–32°C), and nights average 73–75°F (23–24°C), with a diurnal range of 10–16°F (6–9°C).

HUMIDITY: Information is not available for this location. However, records from nearby locations indicate that humidity probably averages near 85% year-round.

WATER: Rainfall is very heavy all year. Cultivated plants should be kept evenly moist but not soggy. Warm water might be beneficial.

FERTILIZER: ¼–½ recommended strength. A balanced fertilizer should be applied weekly to biweekly throughout the year.

REST PERIOD: Growing temperatures should be maintained year-round. The smallest diurnal range occurs in winter. Water and fertilizer might be reduced slightly in winter, especially for plants cultivated in the dark, short-day conditions common in the temperate latitudes. However, plants should never be allowed to dry out completely. In the habitat, seasonal light variation is minor.

GROWING MEDIA: Mounting plants on tree-fern or cork slabs accommodates their pendent growth habit, but humidity must be high and the plants watered at least once daily in summer. Plants may be potted in hanging pots or baskets filled a rapidly draining medium that retains some moisture. The medium should be moist, but not soggy. Repotting may be done anytime new roots are growing.

MISCELLANEOUS NOTES: The bloom season shown in the climate table is based on collection records. Plants that produce very short-lived flowers commonly bloom several times during the year. Flowering usually occurs 7–14 days after a sudden 10°F (5°C) drop in daytime temperatures. Plants begin blooming while very young.

Plant and Flower Information

PLANT SIZE AND TYPE: A pendent, 28 in. (70 cm) sympodial epiphyte.

PSEUDOBULB: 28 in. (70 cm) long. The flattened, basal part of the stem is 4 in. (10 cm) long.

LEAVES: Many. The linear leaves are distichous, 1.6–2.4 in. (4–6 cm) long, and sharply pointed.

INFLORESCENCE: Flowers are borne on the upper, leafless part of the stem.

FLOWERS: The inconspicuous flowers are 0.3 in. (0.8 cm) long. The ovate dorsal sepal is pointed. Lateral sepals are ovate and rounded at the apex. The petals are oblong. The obovate lip has indistinct, rounded sidelobes. Blossoms last a single day.

REFERENCES: 220, 254, 437.

Dendrobium confusum Schlechter not J. J. Smith. See *D. shipmani* A. Hawkes. REFERENCES: 153, 221, 229, 273, 304, 436, 454, 470, 537.

Dendrobium confusum J. J. Smith not Schlechter. See *D. capituliflorum* Rolfe. REFERENCES: 25, 212, 221, 437, 445, 470.

Dendrobium conicum J. J. Smith

ORIGIN/HABITAT: Irian Jaya (western New Guinea). Plants grow on moss-covered trees in the forests of the eastern slopes of the Cyclops Range. Schlechter (ref. 437) indicates that all closely related species grow in the mistforest zone.

CLIMATE: Station #97690, Sentani/Jayapura, Irian Jaya, Lat. 2.7°S, Long. 140.5°E, at 289 ft. (88 m). Temperatures are calculated for an estimated elevation of 2000 ft. (610 m), resulting in probable extremes of 91°F (33°C) and 62°F (17°C).

N/HEMISPHERE	JAN	FEB	MAR	APR	MAY	JUN	JUL	AUG	SEP	OCT	NOV	DEC
°F AVG MAX	81	83	83	84	84	83	83	82	83	84	84	83
°F AVG MIN	66	66	66	67	67	67	67	67	67	68	67	67
DIURNAL RANGE	15	17	17	17	17	16	16	15	16	16	17	16
RAIN/INCHES	4.1	3.9	5.3	2.9	6.7	7.0	8.3	8.3	8.5	4.6	2.4	5.2
HUMIDITY/%	81	80	80	79	81	81	79	80	80	80	81	80
BLOOM SEASON												*
DAYS CLR @ 9AM	5	3	4	3	2	1	1	0	1	2	2	5
DAYS CLR @ 3PM	4	3	3	3	2	1	3	0	1	2	2	3
RAIN/MM	104	99	135	74	170	178	211	211	216	117	61	132
°C AVG MAX	27.4	28.5	28.5	29.1	29.1	28.5	28.5	28.0	28.5	29.1	29.1	28.5
°C AVG MIN	19.1	19.1	19.1	19.6	19.6	19.6	19.6	19.6	19.6	20.2	19.6	19.6
DIURNAL RANGE	8.3	9.4	9.4	9.5	9.5	8.9	8.9	8.4	8.9	8.9	9.5	8.9
S/HEMISPHERE	JUL	AUG	SEP	OCT	NOV	DEC	JAN	FEB	MAR	APR	MAY	JUN

Cultural Recommendations

LIGHT: 2000–3000 fc.

TEMPERATURES: Throughout the year, days average 81–84°F (27–29°C), and nights average 66–68°F (19–20°C), with a diurnal range of 15–17°F (8–9°C).

HUMIDITY: Near 80% year-round.

WATER: Rainfall is heavy all year, with brief semidry periods in spring and autumn. Cultivated plants should be kept moist most of the year, but they should be allowed to become somewhat dry for a few weeks in spring and again in autumn.

FERTILIZER: ¼–½ recommended strength. A balanced fertilizer should be applied weekly to biweekly throughout the year.

REST PERIOD: Growing conditions should be maintained year-round. Water and fertilizer might be reduced slightly in winter, especially for plants grown in the dark, short-day conditions common in temperate latitudes. They should never be allowed to dry completely, however. In the habitat, light is slightly higher in winter.

GROWING MEDIA: Plants may be mounted on tree-fern or cork slabs if humidity is high and plants are watered at least once daily in summer. When plants are potted, any open, fast-draining medium may be used. Repotting is best done in early spring when new roots are growing.

MISCELLANEOUS NOTES: The bloom season shown in the climate table is based on reports from the habitat. The plant was described in 1912 in *Bul. Jard. Bot. Buit.* 2nd sér. 3:72.

Plant and Flower Information

PLANT SIZE AND TYPE: A sympodial epiphyte of unreported size.

PSEUDOBULB: Stems are long and leafy.

LEAVES: The pointed, lanceolate leaves are 2.4–3.5 in. (6–9 cm) long.

INFLORESCENCE: Short. Inflorescences emerge from nodes on leafless stems.

FLOWERS: 10 per inflorescence. The green to yellowish white flowers are 1.2 in. (3 cm) long. Blossoms have an oval dorsal sepal, somewhat triangular lateral sepals, and a fringed, spatula-shaped lip that is incurved at the apex.

REFERENCES: 221, 437, 445, 470.

Dendrobium connatum (Blume) Lindley

AKA: *Onychium connatum* Blume, *Dendrobium subarticulatum* Teijsm. and Binn.

ORIGIN/HABITAT: East and West Java, Sumatra, and Borneo. Plants grow on the lower slopes of Mt. Kinabalu in Sabah (North Borneo) and in Java at 1300–3300 ft. (400–1000 m). In Sumatra, they occur on trees near Padang-Pandjang at about 2800 ft. (850 m). They usually grow low on tree trunks in moderately open areas.

CLIMATE: Station #49613, Tambuan, Sabah (North Borneo), Lat. 5.7°N, Long. 116.4°E, at 1200 ft. (366 m). Temperatures are calculated for an elevation of 3000 ft. (910 m), resulting in probable extremes of 92°F (33°C) and 48°F (9°C).

N/HEMISPHERE	JAN	FEB	MAR	APR	MAY	JUN	JUL	AUG	SEP	OCT	NOV	DEC
°F AVG MAX	80	81	83	84	84	83	83	83	83	82	81	80
°F AVG MIN	61	59	60	61	62	61	60	60	61	61	61	62
DIURNAL RANGE	19	22	23	23	22	22	23	23	22	21	20	18
RAIN/INCHES	5.8	3.7	5.8	7.5	8.2	7.3	5.1	4.9	6.4	7.0	6.8	6.0
HUMIDITY/%	N/A											
BLOOM SEASON							*					
DAYS CLR	N/A											
RAIN/MM	147	94	147	190	208	185	130	124	163	178	173	152
°C AVG MAX	26.7	27.3	28.4	28.9	28.9	28.4	28.4	28.4	28.4	27.8	27.3	26.7
°C AVG MIN	16.1	15.0	15.6	16.1	16.7	16.1	15.6	15.6	16.1	16.1	16.1	16.7
DIURNAL RANGE	10.6	12.3	12.8	12.8	12.2	12.3	12.8	12.8	12.3	11.7	11.2	10.0
S/HEMISPHERE	JUL	AUG	SEP	OCT	NOV	DEC	JAN	FEB	MAR	APR	MAY	JUN

Cultural Recommendations

LIGHT: 2000–3000 fc.

TEMPERATURES: Throughout the year, days average 80–84°F (27–29°C), and nights average 59–62°F (15–17°C), with a diurnal range of 18–23°F (10–13°C).

HUMIDITY: Information is not available for this location. However, records from nearby stations indicate that averages are probably 80–85% year-round.

WATER: Rainfall is moderate to heavy all year with a brief slightly drier period in winter. Cultivated plants should be allowed to dry only slightly between waterings.

FERTILIZER: ¼–½ recommended strength. A balanced fertilizer should be applied weekly to biweekly throughout the growing season.

REST PERIOD: Growing conditions should be maintained all year. Water should be reduced slightly in winter, but the plants should never be allowed to dry out completely. Fertilizer should be reduced anytime plants are not actively growing.

GROWING MEDIA: Plants may be potted in any open, well drained medium. The medium should be moist, but not soggy. Repotting may be done anytime new roots are growing.

MISCELLANEOUS NOTES: The bloom season shown in the climate table is based on collection reports.

Plant and Flower Information

PLANT SIZE AND TYPE: A 20 in. (50 cm) sympodial epiphyte. The plants may become quite large and resemble a small, dense bush.

Dendrobium connexicostatum

PSEUDOBULB: 20 in. (50 cm) long. The stems are close together.

LEAVES: Many. The distichous leaves are about 0.8 in. (2 cm) long. The entire stem is covered with overlapping leaf bases.

INFLORESCENCE: Short. Blossoms emerge laterally from between the leaves. Although inflorescences are produced at numerous nodes, only a few flowers are open at a time.

FLOWERS: 1 per inflorescence. The pale yellowish white flowers are 0.5 in. (1.3 cm) across and open fully. The broadly lanceolate sepals and much smaller petals have green veins. They are sharply pointed at the apex. The spatula-shaped lip has a midlobe covered with green warts and small rounded sidelobes.

REFERENCES: 12, 25, 75, 216, 254, 286, 295, 310, 435, 469, 592.

PHOTOS/DRAWINGS: 75, 469.

Dendrobium connexicostatum J. J. Smith. Now considered a synonym of *Diplocaulobium connexicostatum* (J. J. Smith) Hunt and Summerhayes. REFERENCES: 213, 225, 230, 470.

Dendrobium conostalix Rchb. f. not Kränzlin. See *D. lobbii* Teijsm. and Binn. REFERENCES: 12, 67, 105, 202, 216, 254, 266, 286, 295, 298, 317, 395, 437, 448, 454.

Dendrobium conostalix Kränzlin not Rchb. f. See *D. lacustre* Schlechter. REFERENCES: 436.

Dendrobium consanguineum J. J. Smith

ORIGIN/HABITAT: Molucca Islands. Plants were originally collected near sea level on Ambon Island.

CLIMATE: Station #97724, Ambon/Pattimura, Indonesia, Lat. 3.7°S, Long. 128.1°E, at 33 ft. (10 m). Record extreme temperatures are 96°F (36°C) and 66°F (19°C).

N/HEMISPHERE	JAN	FEB	MAR	APR	MAY	JUN	JUL	AUG	SEP	OCT	NOV	DEC
°F AVG MAX	81	81	83	85	88	88	88	88	88	86	84	82
°F AVG MIN	74	74	74	74	75	76	76	76	76	76	75	74
DIURNAL RANGE	7	7	9	11	13	12	12	12	12	10	9	8
RAIN/INCHES	23.7	15.8	9.5	6.1	4.5	5.2	5.0	4.7	5.3	11.0	20.3	25.1
HUMIDITY/%	83	82	81	80	79	78	78	77	79	82	83	84
BLOOM SEASON					*							
DAYS CLR @ 9AM	1	1	1	6	7	4	3	3	5	5	3	3
DAYS CLR @ 3PM	1	1	2	5	6	1	1	1	2	3	1	3
RAIN/MM	602	401	241	155	114	132	127	119	135	279	516	638
°C AVG MAX	27.2	27.2	28.3	29.4	31.1	31.1	31.1	31.1	31.1	30.0	28.9	27.8
°C AVG MIN	23.3	23.3	23.3	23.3	23.9	24.4	24.4	24.4	24.4	24.4	23.9	23.3
DIURNAL RANGE	3.9	3.9	5.0	6.1	7.2	6.7	6.7	6.7	6.7	5.6	5.0	4.5
S/HEMISPHERE	JUL	AUG	SEP	OCT	NOV	DEC	JAN	FEB	MAR	APR	MAY	JUN

Cultural Recommendations

LIGHT: 2500–3500 fc.

TEMPERATURES: Through the year, days average 81–88°F (27–31°C), and nights average 74–76°F (23–24°C), with a diurnal range of 7–13°F (4–7°C).

HUMIDITY: 80–85% year-round.

WATER: Rainfall is moderate to heavy all year, but conditions are slightly drier in late spring and summer. Cultivated plants should be kept evenly moist with only slight drying allowed between waterings.

FERTILIZER: ¼–½ recommended strength. A balanced fertilizer should be applied weekly to biweekly throughout the year.

REST PERIOD: Growing conditions should be maintained all year. In the habitat, rainfall is heaviest in winter, but water and fertilizer should be reduced somewhat for cultivated plants, especially those grown in the dark, short-day conditions common in temperate latitudes. They should never be allowed to dry completely, however. In the habitat, light is highest in spring.

GROWING MEDIA: Plants may be mounted on tree-fern or cork slabs if humidity is high and plants are watered at least once daily in summer. When plants are potted, medium or coarse fir bark or any open, fast-draining medium may be used.

MISCELLANEOUS NOTES: The bloom season shown in the climate table is based on collection reports.

Plant and Flower Information

PLANT SIZE AND TYPE: A 20 in. (50 cm) sympodial epiphyte.

PSEUDOBULB: 20 in. (50 cm) long. Growths emerge from a short rhizome.

LEAVES: Many. The oblong-ovate leaves are 1.9 in. (4.8 cm) long.

INFLORESCENCE: Inflorescences emerge through the leaf sheaths.

FLOWERS: 2 per inflorescence. The flowers are 0.8 in. (2 cm) across. Blossoms have somewhat triangular sepals and lanceolate petals. They are yellow with lines of lilac spots. The erect lip, which has no sidelobes, is pure white. It is covered with warts. The column is whitish-lilac along the margin and near the apex.

REFERENCES: 222, 479.

Dendrobium conspicuum Bakhuizen f. Now considered a synonym of *Flickingeria grandiflora* (Blume) A. Hawkes. REFERENCES: 25, 75, 230, 449.

Dendrobium constrictum J. J. Smith

AKA: In 1993, Dauncey and Cribb in *Kew Bulletin* 48(3) consider *D. mimiense* Schlecter a possible synonym.

ORIGIN/HABITAT: New Guinea and New Britain Islands. Plants grow on forest trees and on large rocks along streams at 1500–4600 ft. (450–1400 m). Plants were originally collected along the Noord River south of Geluks Hill in the Waria Mountains.

CLIMATE: Station #97796, Kokenau (Kokonau), Irian Jaya, Lat. 4.7°S, Long. 135.4°E, at 10 ft. (3 m). Temperatures are calculated for an elevation of 3000 ft. (910 m). Record extreme temperatures are not available for this location.

N/HEMISPHERE	JAN	FEB	MAR	APR	MAY	JUN	JUL	AUG	SEP	OCT	NOV	DEC
°F AVG MAX	73	73	76	78	80	79	79	79	80	78	77	74
°F AVG MIN	63	63	64	64	64	65	64	64	64	64	64	63
DIURNAL RANGE	10	10	12	14	16	14	15	15	16	14	13	11
RAIN/INCHES	18.4	15.8	18.9	11.6	9.7	10.6	11.5	15.7	11.6	11.6	16.0	19.9
HUMIDITY/%	N/A											
BLOOM SEASON											*	
DAYS CLR	N/A											
RAIN/MM	467	401	480	295	246	269	292	399	295	295	406	505
°C AVG MAX	22.9	22.9	24.5	25.6	26.7	26.2	26.2	26.2	26.7	25.6	25.1	23.4
°C AVG MIN	17.3	17.3	17.9	17.9	17.9	18.4	17.9	17.9	17.9	17.9	17.9	17.3
DIURNAL RANGE	4.6	5.6	6.6	7.7	8.8	7.9	8.3	9.3	8.8	7.7	7.2	6.1
S/HEMISPHERE	JUL	AUG	SEP	OCT	NOV	DEC	JAN	FEB	MAR	APR	MAY	JUN

Cultural Recommendations

LIGHT: 2500–3500 fc.

TEMPERATURES: Throughout the year, days average 73–80°F (23–27°C), and nights average 63–65°F (17–18°C), with a diurnal range of 10–16°F (6–9°C).

HUMIDITY: Information is not available for this location. However, average humidity at other stations in the region indicates probable values near 80% year-round.

WATER: Rainfall is very heavy year-round. Cultivated plants should be kept evenly moist but not soggy.

FERTILIZER: ¼–½ recommended strength. A balanced fertilizer should be applied weekly to biweekly throughout the year.

REST PERIOD: Growing conditions should be maintained year-round. Water and fertilizer might be reduced slightly in winter, especially for plants cultivated in the dark, short-day conditions common in temperate latitudes. Plants should never be allowed to dry out completely, however.

GROWING MEDIA: Plants may be mounted on tree-fern or cork slabs if humidity is high and plants are watered at least once daily in summer. When plants are potted, any open, fast-draining medium may be used. Repotting may be done in early spring when new roots begin to grow.

MISCELLANEOUS NOTES: The bloom season shown in the climate table is based on collection records.

Plant and Flower Information

PLANT SIZE AND TYPE: A small sympodial epiphyte or lithophyte.

PSEUDOBULB: The cylindrical to spindle-shaped growths may be clustered, but they tend to emerge from alternate side of a creeping rhizome. The stems are covered with pale, spotted, tubular leaf-sheaths.

LEAVES: 1–4 in. (2.5–10.0 cm) long. Each growth produces 2–3 dusty green leaves, which may be lanceolate or elliptic. They are recurved, grooved along the midvein, and narrower near the short, unequally bilobed tips.

INFLORESCENCE: 0.6–0.8 in. (1.5–2.0 cm) long. Inflorescences emerge from mature, leafless stems. The bracts are hairy.

FLOWERS: 25–40. The smooth flowers are 0.4 in. (1 cm) long and remain nearly closed. The sepals and petals, which are variable in shape, are white to greenish white. The concave petals and lip nearly enclose the column. The oval lip, which is uneven along the front margin, is narrowed and thickened in the middle. The length of the mentum equals the free portion of the sepals and petals.

REFERENCES: 212, 220, 254, 437, 445, 470, Dauncey and Cribb 1993 *Kew Bulletin* 48(3):545–576.

PHOTOS/DRAWINGS: Dauncey and Cribb 1993 *Kew Bulletin* 48(3):545–576.

Dendrobium convexipes J. J. Smith

ORIGIN/HABITAT: Northern Irian Jaya (western New Guinea). Plants grow on a ridge to Mt. Doorman at 4600–4650 ft. (1400–1420 m), where they are found on trees in a moss-covered *Vaccinium* forest.

CLIMATE: Station #97686, Wamena, New Guinea, Lat. 4.1°S, Long. 139.0°E, at 5446 ft. (1660 m). Temperatures are calculated for an elevation of 4400 ft. (1340 m). Record extreme temperatures are not available for this location.

N/HEMISPHERE	JAN	FEB	MAR	APR	MAY	JUN	JUL	AUG	SEP	OCT	NOV	DEC
°F AVG MAX	78	79	80	79	80	79	80	79	79	82	81	77
°F AVG MIN	63	63	65	65	66	67	66	65	66	68	68	64
DIURNAL RANGE	15	16	15	14	14	12	14	14	13	14	13	13
RAIN/INCHES	3.0	1.9	2.2	4.0	4.6	3.3	2.8	4.2	6.9	3.9	5.4	4.9
HUMIDITY/%	N/A											
BLOOM SEASON				•								
DAYS CLR	N/A											
RAIN/MM	76	48	56	102	117	84	71	107	175	99	137	124
°C AVG MAX	25.8	26.4	26.9	26.4	26.9	26.4	26.9	26.4	26.4	28.0	27.5	25.3
°C AVG MIN	17.5	17.5	18.6	18.6	19.1	19.7	19.1	18.6	19.1	20.3	20.3	18.0
DIURNAL RANGE	8.3	8.9	8.3	7.8	7.8	6.7	7.8	7.8	7.3	7.7	7.2	7.3
S/HEMISPHERE	JUL	AUG	SEP	OCT	NOV	DEC	JAN	FEB	MAR	APR	MAY	JUN

Cultural Recommendations

LIGHT: 1500–2300 fc. Plants may tolerate higher light levels, especially in the morning.

TEMPERATURES: Throughout the year, days average 78–82°F (26–28°C), and nights average 63–68°F (18–20°C), with a diurnal range of 12–16°F (7–9°C). In the habitat, the warmest temperatures of the day occur during late morning when skies are usually clear. Clouds and mist develop near noon, thus preventing additional warming.

HUMIDITY: Information is not available for this location. However, records from nearby stations indicate that humidity probably averages near 80% year-round. High humidity and excellent air circulation are particularly important if temperatures are warm. Placing the plants in front of an evaporative cooler or near a fine mist may be very beneficial on especially warm days.

WATER: Rainfall is light to moderate through most of the year; but large amounts of water are usually available from mist and heavy dew, even during periods of lower rainfall. Cultivated plants should be kept moist with only slight drying allowed between waterings. Good air movement is critically important and should be maintained at all times.

FERTILIZER: ¼–½ recommended strength. A balanced fertilizer should be applied weekly to biweekly throughout the year.

REST PERIOD: Growing conditions should be maintained all year. Conditions are slightly drier for 1–2 months in winter. In cultivation, water may be decreased somewhat, but plants should never be allowed to dry out completely or remain dry for long periods. In the habitat, light is slightly higher in winter.

GROWING MEDIA: Plants may be mounted on tree-fern or cork slabs if humidity is high and plants are watered at least once daily in summer. When plants are potted, any open, fast-draining medium may be used. Repotting may be done anytime new roots are growing.

MISCELLANEOUS NOTES: The bloom season shown in the climate table is based on reports from the habitat.

Plant and Flower Information

PLANT SIZE AND TYPE: A 19 in. (48 cm) sympodial epiphyte.

PSEUDOBULB: 19 in. (48 cm) long. The stems are angled and grooved when dry.

LEAVES: Many. The leaves, which are about 2.2 in. (5.6 cm) long, may be ovate to lanceolate. They are twisted at the base. The shiny leaves and sheaths are dark greenish-violet on the upper surface, but the underside is dull and less violet.

INFLORESCENCE: Short. Inflorescences are borne on leafy and leafless stems.

FLOWERS: 3–5 per inflorescence. The flowers are 0.9 in. (2.3 cm) long. The lanceolate petals are ciliate. Lateral sepals are oblong-triangular and slashed along the margin. The dorsal sepal is ovate. The erect lip is toothed and uneven along the margin. All floral segments are lilac, but the lip is paler at the apex. The tip of the column is tinged with whitish-violet.

REFERENCES: 224, 445, 470.

Dendrobium convexum (Blume) Lindley.

Now considered a synonym of *Flickingeria convexa* (Blume) A. Hawkes. REFERENCES: 25, 67, 75, 105, 200, 213, 216, 230, 231, 254, 277, 310, 395, 435, 445, 449, 455, 469. PHOTOS/DRAWINGS: 469.

Dendrobium convolutum Rolfe

ORIGIN/HABITAT: Northern Papua New Guinea. Collections have been made at low elevations near Finschhafen in Morobe Province, and on the offshore islands in Madang Province.

CLIMATE: Station #94048, Finschhafen, Papua New Guinea, Lat. 6.6°S, Long. 147.9°E, at 25 ft. (8 m). Record extreme temperatures are 93°F (34°C) and 68°F (20°C).

Dendrobium copelandianum

N/HEMISPHERE	JAN	FEB	MAR	APR	MAY	JUN	JUL	AUG	SEP	OCT	NOV	DEC
°F AVG MAX	84	83	83	84	86	88	89	89	87	86	84	84
°F AVG MIN	73	72	72	71	71	72	74	74	74	74	73	73
DIURNAL RANGE	11	11	11	13	15	16	15	15	13	12	11	11
RAIN/INCHES	25.8	22.4	20.9	15.8	11.7	8.9	5.5	3.7	5.3	11.9	18.3	23.2
HUMIDITY/%	88	87	86	86	84	85	84	85	86	88	88	88
BLOOM SEASON	N/A											
DAYS CLR	N/A											
RAIN/MM	655	568	531	402	297	227	140	95	135	301	464	589
°C AVG MAX	28.9	28.3	28.3	28.9	30.0	31.1	31.7	31.7	30.6	30.0	28.9	28.9
°C AVG MIN	22.8	22.2	22.2	21.7	21.7	22.2	23.3	23.3	23.3	23.3	22.8	22.8
DIURNAL RANGE	6.1	6.1	6.1	7.2	8.3	8.9	8.4	8.4	7.3	6.7	6.1	6.1
S/HEMISPHERE	JUL	AUG	SEP	OCT	NOV	DEC	JAN	FEB	MAR	APR	MAY	JUN

N/HEMISPHERE	JAN	FEB	MAR	APR	MAY	JUN	JUL	AUG	SEP	OCT	NOV	DEC
°F AVG MAX	81	81	82	83	85	87	87	88	87	86	84	82
°F AVG MIN	74	73	74	74	75	76	77	77	76	75	75	74
DIURNAL RANGE	7	8	8	9	10	11	10	11	11	11	9	8
RAIN/INCHES	8.1	8.6	10.1	8.7	8.4	6.1	7.0	7.8	10.0	9.8	12.0	11.3
HUMIDITY/%	N/A											
BLOOM SEASON	N/A											
DAYS CLR	N/A											
RAIN/MM	206	218	257	221	213	155	178	198	254	249	305	287
°C AVG MAX	27.2	27.2	27.8	28.3	29.4	30.6	30.6	31.1	30.6	30.0	28.9	27.8
°C AVG MIN	23.3	22.8	23.3	23.3	23.9	24.4	25.0	25.0	24.4	23.9	23.9	23.3
DIURNAL RANGE	3.9	4.4	4.5	5.0	5.5	6.2	5.6	6.1	6.2	6.1	5.0	4.5
S/HEMISPHERE	JUL	AUG	SEP	OCT	NOV	DEC	JAN	FEB	MAR	APR	MAY	JUN

Cultural Recommendations

LIGHT: 2500–3000 fc.

TEMPERATURES: Throughout the year, days average 83–89°F (28–32°C), and nights average 71–74°F (22–23°C), with a diurnal range of 11–16°F (6–9°C).

HUMIDITY: 84–88% year-round.

WATER: Rainfall is very heavy most of the year, but conditions are slightly drier for 3–4 months in summer. Cultivated plants should be kept evenly moist with only slight drying allowed between waterings.

FERTILIZER: ¼–½ recommended strength. A balanced fertilizer should be applied weekly to biweekly throughout the year.

REST PERIOD: Growing conditions should be maintained year-round. In the habitat, rainfall is heaviest in winter. In cultivation, water and fertilizer may be reduced somewhat, especially for plants grown in the dark, short-day conditions common in temperate latitudes. Plants should never be allowed to dry completely, however. In the habitat, seasonal light variation is minor.

GROWING MEDIA: Plants may be potted in any open, fast-draining medium that stays moist, but not soggy. Repotting may be done anytime new roots are growing.

MISCELLANEOUS NOTES: Pictured and discussed as an unnamed species by Millar (ref. 304).

Plant and Flower Information

PLANT SIZE AND TYPE: A 12 in. (30 cm) sympodial epiphyte.

PSEUDOBULB: 12 in. (30 cm) long. The yellow stems have 4–5 nodes below the leaves.

LEAVES: 3 at the apex of each growth. The elliptic-lanceolate leaves are usually 5 in. (13 cm) long.

INFLORESCENCE: 4–5 in. (10–13 cm) long. Inflorescences are suberect.

FLOWERS: Few per inflorescence. The flowers are 1.2 in. (3 cm) across. Sepals and petals are apple-green. The recurved lip is flushed and veined with maroon.

REFERENCES: 83, 220, 254, 304, 416, 437, 550.

PHOTOS/DRAWINGS: *83, 304*.

Dendrobium copelandianum F. Mueller and Kränzlin

AKA: Schlechter (ref. 437) considered this a doubtful species.

ORIGIN/HABITAT: Papua New Guinea. Plants grow along the southeast section of Bartle Bay near the eastern tip of the island on the south coast. Elevation and habitat information were not given, so the following temperatures should be used with caution.

CLIMATE: Station #94075, Samarai, Sideia Island, Papua New Guinea, Lat. 10.6°S, Long. 150.7°E, at 20 ft. (6 m). Record extreme temperatures are 104°F (40°C) and 64°F (18°C).

Cultural Recommendations

LIGHT: 2500–3000 fc.

TEMPERATURES: Throughout the year, days average 81–88°F (27–31°C), and nights average 73–77°F (23–25°C), with a diurnal range of 7–11°F (4–6°C).

HUMIDITY: Information is not available for this location. However, records from nearby locations indicate that humidity probably averages 70–80% year-round.

WATER: Rainfall is very heavy all year. Cultivated plants should be kept moist but not soggy.

FERTILIZER: ¼–½ recommended strength. A balanced fertilizer should be applied weekly to biweekly throughout the year.

REST PERIOD: Growing conditions should be maintained year-round. In the habitat, winter rainfall is high; but water and fertilizer should be reduced somewhat for cultivated plants, especially those grown in the dark, short-day conditions in temperate latitudes. Plants should never be allowed to dry out completely, however. In the habitat, seasonal light variation is minor.

GROWING MEDIA: Plants may be mounted on tree-fern or cork slabs if humidity is high and plants are watered at least once daily in summer. When plants are potted, any open, fast-draining medium may be used. Repotting may be done anytime new roots are growing.

Plant and Flower Information

PLANT SIZE AND TYPE: A sympodial epiphyte of unreported size.

PSEUDOBULB: The slender, somewhat flattened stems were described as "not tall," from an incomplete specimen.

LEAVES: Many. The leaves are about 2.4 in. (6 cm) long and papery with an ovate base and pointed tip.

INFLORESCENCE: Several racemes emerge from the upper part of the stem.

FLOWERS: Few per inflorescence. The flowers are 1 in. (2.5 cm) across. Blossoms have ovate-lanceolate sepals and somewhat small, lanceolate petals. Segments are pointed at the tip. The lip has a kidney-shaped midlobe, which is uneven along the margin, and a disk with 3 elevated keels and several smaller lines.

REFERENCES: 218, 254, 437.

Dendrobium coplandii (F. M. Bailey) Rupp. Now considered a synonym of *Diplocaulobium coplandii* (F. M. Bailey) P. F. Hunt. REFERENCES: 212, 227.

Dendrobium corallorhizon J. J. Smith

AKA: Sometimes spelled *D. corallorhiza*.

ORIGIN/HABITAT: Central east Borneo. Plants have been collected along the West Koetai (Mahakam) River, at about 5250 ft. (1600 m). They grow on trees in primeval forest at slightly higher elevations than *D. endertii* J. J. Smith.

CLIMATE: Station #96633, Balikpapan, Borneo, Indonesia, Lat. 1.3°S, Long. 116.9°E, at 10 ft. (3 m). Temperatures are calculated for an elevation of 5250 ft. (1600 m), resulting in probable extremes of 75°F (24°C) and 43°F (6°C).

N/HEMISPHERE	JAN	FEB	MAR	APR	MAY	JUN	JUL	AUG	SEP	OCT	NOV	DEC
°F AVG MAX	66	67	67	68	68	68	68	69	69	68	68	67
°F AVG MIN	56	57	57	57	56	56	56	56	56	56	57	57
DIURNAL RANGE	10	10	10	11	12	12	12	13	13	12	11	10
RAIN/INCHES	7.1	6.4	5.5	5.2	6.6	8.1	7.9	8.9	9.1	8.2	9.1	7.6
HUMIDITY/%	82	80	77	78	80	79	82	81	81	82	83	82
BLOOM SEASON				*								
DAYS CLR @ 8AM	4	2	3	3	3	3	2	3	4	4	2	5
DAYS CLR @ 2PM	6	4	5	5	3	1	2	1	2	3	4	5
RAIN/MM	180	163	140	132	168	206	201	226	231	208	231	193
°C AVG MAX	18.7	19.3	19.3	19.8	19.8	19.8	19.8	20.4	20.4	19.8	19.8	19.3
°C AVG MIN	13.2	13.7	13.7	13.7	13.2	13.2	13.2	13.2	13.2	13.2	13.7	13.7
DIURNAL RANGE	5.5	5.6	5.6	6.1	6.6	6.6	6.6	7.2	7.2	6.6	6.1	5.6
S/HEMISPHERE	JUL	AUG	SEP	OCT	NOV	DEC	JAN	FEB	MAR	APR	MAY	JUN

Cultural Recommendations

LIGHT: 1800–2500 fc.

TEMPERATURES: Throughout the year, days average 66–69°F (19–20°C), and nights average 56–57°F (13–14°C), with a diurnal range of 10–13°F (6–7°C). Due to the effects of microclimate, maximum temperatures in the habitat may actually be 8–10°F (4–6°C) warmer than indicated.

HUMIDITY: Near 80% year-round.

WATER: Rainfall is moderate to heavy throughout the year. Cultivated plants should be kept moist but not soggy with only slight drying allowed between waterings.

FERTILIZER: ¼–½ recommended strength. A balanced fertilizer should be applied weekly to biweekly throughout the year.

REST PERIOD: Growing temperatures should be maintained year-round. Water should be reduced somewhat in winter, especially for plants grown in the dark, short-day conditions common in temperate latitudes; but they should never be allowed to dry out completely. Fertilizer should be reduced or eliminated if water is reduced. In the habitat, seasonal light variation is minor.

GROWING MEDIA: Plants may be mounted on tree-fern or cork slabs if humidity is high and plants are watered at least once daily in summer. When plants are potted, any open, fast-draining medium may be used. Repotting may be done anytime new roots are growing.

MISCELLANEOUS NOTES: The bloom season shown in the climate table is based on reports from the habitat. The plant was described in 1931 in *Bul. Jard. Bot. Buit.* 3rd sér. 9:140.

Plant and Flower Information

PLANT SIZE AND TYPE: A 16 in. (40 cm) sympodial epiphyte.

PSEUDOBULB: 16 in. (40 cm) long. The clustered stems arise from a short rhizome.

LEAVES: The deciduous leaves are 3–5 in. (8–13 cm) long. They are ovate-lanceolate, spreading to suberect, and somewhat twisted at the base.

INFLORESCENCE: Short. Inflorescences arise from nodes on leafless stems.

FLOWERS: 2–3 per inflorescence. The flowers are 1 in. (2.5 cm) long. Blossoms are nearly white, but the spur is suffused with rose, and the tip of the column is yellow.

REFERENCES: 225, 286.

Dendrobium cordinatum. See *D. ordinatum* J. J. Smith.

REFERENCES: 223, 443.

Dendrobium corniculatum Swartz. Now considered a synonym of *Pleurothallis corniculata* Lindley. REFERENCES: 216, 254.

Dendrobium cornutum Hooker f. See *D. hasseltii* (Blume) Lindley not Rchb. f. REFERENCES: 75, 200, 202, 218, 254, 402, 437, 445, 455, 469.

Dendrobium correllianum A. Hawkes and A. H. Heller

AKA: *D. tricolor* Kränzlin.

ORIGIN/HABITAT: Papua New Guinea near Mita in Milne Bay province. Plants grow at 2150–2600 ft. (650–800 m).

CLIMATE: Station #94075, Samarai, Sideia Island, Papua New Guinea, Lat. 10.6°S, Long. 150.7°E, at 20 ft. (6 m). Temperatures are calculated for an elevation of 2300 ft. (700 m), resulting in probable extremes of 96°F (36°C) and 56°F (14°C).

N/HEMISPHERE	JAN	FEB	MAR	APR	MAY	JUN	JUL	AUG	SEP	OCT	NOV	DEC
°F AVG MAX	73	73	74	75	77	79	79	80	79	78	76	74
°F AVG MIN	66	65	66	66	67	68	69	69	68	67	67	66
DIURNAL RANGE	7	8	8	9	10	11	10	11	11	11	9	8
RAIN/INCHES	8.1	8.6	10.1	8.7	8.4	6.1	7.0	7.8	10.0	9.8	12.0	11.3
HUMIDITY/%	N/A											
BLOOM SEASON									*			
DAYS CLR	N/A											
RAIN/MM	206	218	257	221	213	155	178	198	254	249	305	287
°C AVG MAX	23.0	23.0	23.6	24.2	25.3	26.4	26.4	26.9	26.4	25.8	24.7	23.6
°C AVG MIN	19.2	18.6	19.2	19.2	19.7	20.3	20.8	20.8	20.3	19.7	19.7	19.2
DIURNAL RANGE	3.8	4.4	4.4	5.0	5.6	6.1	5.6	6.1	6.1	6.1	5.0	4.4
S/HEMISPHERE	JUL	AUG	SEP	OCT	NOV	DEC	JAN	FEB	MAR	APR	MAY	JUN

Cultural Recommendations

LIGHT: 2500–3000 fc.

TEMPERATURES: Throughout the year, days average 73–80°F (23–27°C), and nights average 65–69°F (19–21°C), with a diurnal range of 7–11°F (4–6°C).

HUMIDITY: Information is not available for this location. However, records from nearby stations indicate that humidity is probably 70–80% year-round.

WATER: Rainfall is very heavy year-round. Cultivated plants should be kept moist but not soggy with only slight drying allowed between waterings.

FERTILIZER: ¼–½ recommended strength. A balanced fertilizer should be applied weekly to biweekly throughout the year.

REST PERIOD: Growing conditions should be maintained year-round. In the habitat, winter rainfall is high; but water and fertilizer should be reduced somewhat for cultivated plants, especially those grown in the dark, short-day conditions in temperate-latitude winters. Plants should never be allowed to dry out completely, however. In the habitat, seasonal light variation is minor.

GROWING MEDIA: Plants may be mounted on tree-fern or cork slabs if humidity is high and plants are watered at least once daily in summer. When plants are potted, any open, fast-draining medium may be used. Repotting may be done anytime new roots are growing.

MISCELLANEOUS NOTES: The bloom season shown in the climate table is based on reports from the habitat.

Plant and Flower Information

PLANT SIZE AND TYPE: A 28–32 in. (70–80 cm) sympodial epiphyte.

PSEUDOBULB: 28–32 in. (70–80 cm) long.

LEAVES: Many. The ovate to oblong leaves are 1.0–2.6 in. (2.5–6.5 cm) long and minutely bilobed at the tip. The leaf sheaths are brownish.

INFLORESCENCE: Described as "not long," the racemes are white.

FLOWERS: Few per inflorescence. The fleshy flowers are 1 in. (2.5 cm) long. The oblong-lanceolate sepals and twisted petals are white. The lip is yellow in the middle with brownish violet. It has toothed sidelobes. The toothed, wavy margins on the midlobe are rolled back along the edge. The disk is densely bearded. The describer indicated that blossoms may open in succession.

REFERENCES: 191, 229, 254.

Dendrobium corrugatilobum J. J. Smith

ORIGIN/HABITAT: Endemic and uncommon in west Java. Plants grow in humid forests at about 3300 ft. (1000 m).

CLIMATE: Station #96755, Bogor, Indonesia, at Lat. 6.5°S, Long. 106.8°E, at 558 ft. (170 m). Temperatures are calculated for an elevation of 3000 ft. (914 m), resulting in probable extremes of 88°F (31°C) and 58°F (14°C).

N/HEMISPHERE	JAN	FEB	MAR	APR	MAY	JUN	JUL	AUG	SEP	OCT	NOV	DEC
°F AVG MAX	78	79	80	80	79	77	76	76	77	78	79	78
°F AVG MIN	65	65	65	66	66	66	66	66	66	67	67	66
DIURNAL RANGE	13	14	15	14	13	11	10	10	11	11	12	12
RAIN/INCHES	2.1	1.0	0.5	5.0	8.1	18.8	23.7	20.2	14.4	12.0	11.9	3.4
HUMIDITY/%	72	68	65	66	74	79	84	84	81	79	77	75
BLOOM SEASON							*					
DAYS CLR @ 7AM	14	14	14	11	5	3	1	2	4	6	10	12
DAYS CLR @ 1PM	9	10	8	5	1	1	0	0	1	3	7	
RAIN/MM	53	25	13	127	206	478	602	513	366	305	302	86
°C AVG MAX	25.5	26.1	26.6	26.6	26.1	25.0	24.4	24.4	25.0	25.5	26.1	25.5
°C AVG MIN	18.3	18.3	18.3	18.9	18.9	18.9	18.9	18.9	18.9	19.4	19.4	18.9
DIURNAL RANGE	7.2	7.8	8.3	7.7	7.2	6.1	5.5	5.5	6.1	6.1	6.7	6.6
S/HEMISPHERE	JUL	AUG	SEP	OCT	NOV	DEC	JAN	FEB	MAR	APR	MAY	JUN

Cultural Recommendations

LIGHT: 1800–2400 fc. Diffused or dappled light is recommended. Direct sunlight should be avoided.

TEMPERATURES: Through the year, days average 76–80°F (24–27°C), and nights average 65–67°F (18–19°C), with a diurnal range of 10–15°F (6–8°C). The warmest weather occurs in spring. The extremes vary only slightly from the average growing temperatures, indicating that plants may not tolerate wide temperature fluctuations.

HUMIDITY: 80–85% in summer, dropping to about 65% in winter. Excellent air circulation may be particularly important for plants from this habitat.

WATER: Rainfall is very heavy from spring into autumn, but conditions are very dry for 1–2 months in winter. During the growing season, plants should never be allowed to dry out completely, but water should be gradually reduced in late autumn.

FERTILIZER: ¼–½ recommended strength, applied weekly. A high-nitrogen fertilizer is beneficial from spring to midsummer, but a fertilizer high in phosphates should be used in late summer and autumn.

REST PERIOD: Growing conditions should be maintained all year, but winter rainfall is very low for 1–2 months. In cultivation, water should be reduced and the plants allowed to dry out between waterings, but they should not remain dry for prolonged periods. Fertilizer may be reduced or eliminated anytime the plant is not actively growing. In the habitat, light is highest in winter.

GROWING MEDIA: Plants may be mounted on tree-fern or cork slabs if humidity is high and plants are watered at least once daily in summer. When plants are potted, any open medium that retains moisture may be used. Repotting may be done anytime new roots are growing.

MISCELLANEOUS NOTES: The bloom season shown in the climate table is based on collection records.

Plant and Flower Information

PLANT SIZE AND TYPE: A 14 in. (35 cm) sympodial epiphyte.

PSEUDOBULB: 14 in. (35 cm) long. The stems are yellow.

LEAVES: Many. The leaves, which may reach a length of 7 in. (18 cm), are smallest at the apex and base. They are held at right angles to the stem. The apex has 2 rounded lobes.

INFLORESCENCE: Short. Inflorescences emerge laterally from nodes on leafy stems.

FLOWERS: 2–3 per inflorescence. The brownish flowers are 0.4 in. (1 cm) long from the tip of the spur to the apex of the lip. The dorsal sepal is ovate and pointed, and lateral sepals are oblong, with spoon-shaped, pointed petals. The lip is narrow in the center with triangular sidelobes. The rounded midlobe has 2 prominent ribs at the base.

REFERENCES: 25, 75, 223, 445.

Dendrobium corticola Schlechter

ORIGIN/HABITAT: Papua New Guinea in the Bismarck Mountains on forest trees at 4600–5250 ft. (1400–1600 m).

CLIMATE: Station #94010, Goroka, Papua New Guinea, Lat. 6.1°S, Long. 145.4°E, at 5141 ft. (1567 m). Record extreme temperatures are 87°F (31°C) and 43°F (6°C).

N/HEMISPHERE	JAN	FEB	MAR	APR	MAY	JUN	JUL	AUG	SEP	OCT	NOV	DEC
°F AVG MAX	76	77	78	79	79	78	79	78	78	78	79	77
°F AVG MIN	56	57	57	57	58	59	59	59	60	59	59	57
DIURNAL RANGE	20	20	21	22	21	19	20	19	18	19	20	20
RAIN/INCHES	2.1	2.8	4.6	5.9	6.6	9.3	9.1	10.1	10.7	8.3	4.6	2.0
HUMIDITY/%	70	67	67	67	67	71	72	73	74	71	70	70
BLOOM SEASON			*	*	*							
DAYS CLR	N/A											
RAIN/MM	54	70	118	151	167	236	230	256	271	211	116	52
°C AVG MAX	24.7	25.1	25.6	26.3	26.2	25.7	25.8	25.6	25.5	25.6	25.9	25.1
°C AVG MIN	13.5	13.8	14.0	14.0	14.2	14.8	15.0	15.2	15.3	15.1	14.7	13.7
DIURNAL RANGE	11.2	11.3	11.6	12.3	12.0	10.9	10.8	10.4	10.2	10.5	11.2	11.4
S/HEMISPHERE	JUL	AUG	SEP	OCT	NOV	DEC	JAN	FEB	MAR	APR	MAY	JUN

Cultural Recommendations

LIGHT: 2500–3000 fc.

TEMPERATURES: Throughout the year, days average 76–79°F (25–26°C), and nights average 56–60°F (14–15°C), with a diurnal range of 18–20°F (10–11°C).

HUMIDITY: 70–75% most of the year, dropping to near 65% in late winter and spring.

WATER: Rainfall is moderate to heavy most of the year, but conditions are slightly drier for 3 months in winter. The high relative humidity and wide temperature range cause frequent heavy deposits of dew. Additional moisture is available as mist from fog and low clouds. Cultivated plants should be kept moist and never be allowed to dry completely. In summer, daily watering may be necessary during hot, dry weather. Additional early morning mistings may be beneficial, especially on bright, sunny days.

FERTILIZER: ¼–½ recommended strength. A balanced fertilizer should be applied weekly to biweekly throughout the year.

REST PERIOD: Growing temperatures should be maintained all year. Water should be reduced in winter, especially for plants grown in the dark, short-day conditions common in temperate latitudes; but plants should never be allowed to dry completely. Fertilizer should be reduced or eliminated until spring. In the habitat, light is probably highest in winter.

GROWING MEDIA: Plants may be mounted on tree-fern or cork slabs if humidity is high and plants are watered at least once daily in summer. When plants are potted, any open, fast-draining medium may be used. Repotting is best done in early spring when new roots are growing.

MISCELLANEOUS NOTES: The bloom season shown in the climate table is based on collection reports.

Plant and Flower Information

PLANT SIZE AND TYPE: A compact, 8–12 in. (20–30 cm) sympodial epiphyte.

PSEUDOBULB: 8–12 in. (20–30 cm) long. Stems are flattened and do not branch.

LEAVES: Many. The linear leaves are usually 1.6–2.0 in. (4–5 cm) long. Each growth is densely leafy.

FLOWERS: 1 per inflorescence. The flowers are 0.3 in. (0.8 cm) across. The sulfur yellow blossoms are inverted and do not open fully.

REFERENCES: 221, 437, 445.

PHOTOS/DRAWINGS: 437.

Dendrobium courtauldii Summerhayes ex J. J. Wood

ORIGIN/HABITAT: Alor Island, which is located just north of Timor, in the Lesser Sunda Islands. Habitat elevation was not reported. Alor is very mountainous with several peaks above 4000 ft. (1220 m), so plants may grow at higher elevations and require much cooler temperatures than shown in the climate data. Habitat elevation is estimated, so the following climate data should be used with caution.

CLIMATE: Station #97320, Kutawang, Pulau Alor, Indonesia, Lat. 8.2°S, Long. 124.5°E, at 56 ft. (17 m). Record extreme temperatures are not available for this location.

N/HEMISPHERE	JAN	FEB	MAR	APR	MAY	JUN	JUL	AUG	SEP	OCT	NOV	DEC
°F AVG MAX	85	86	87	89	89	88	86	85	86	87	88	86
°F AVG MIN	74	75	76	80	80	80	79	77	77	78	77	74
DIURNAL RANGE	11	11	11	9	9	8	7	8	9	9	11	12
RAIN/INCHES	0.4	0.3	0.6	0.7	2.9	4.7	9.2	10.3	4.8	2.3	1.3	0.4
HUMIDITY/%	N/A											
BLOOM SEASON			*		*							
DAYS CLR	N/A											
RAIN/MM	10	7	15	17	75	120	233	261	121	58	34	11
°C AVG MAX	29.6	30.0	30.7	31.5	31.9	31.0	30.3	29.6	30.2	30.8	31.0	30.2
°C AVG MIN	23.2	23.6	24.6	26.4	26.6	26.5	25.9	25.2	25.2	25.4	25.0	23.6
DIURNAL RANGE	6.4	6.4	6.1	5.1	5.3	4.5	4.4	4.4	5.0	5.4	6.0	6.6
S/HEMISPHERE	JUL	AUG	SEP	OCT	NOV	DEC	JAN	FEB	MAR	APR	MAY	JUN

Cultural Recommendations

LIGHT: 2000–3500 fc. Plants may easily tolerate, or possibly require, high light. Records from other stations in the region indicate a large number of days with clear skies during the long dry season. Some shading may be required in summer, but light should be as high as possible, short of burning the leaves.

TEMPERATURES: Throughout the year, days average 85–89°F (30–32°C), and nights average 74–80°F (23–27°C), with a diurnal range of 7–12°F (4–7°C).

HUMIDITY: Information is not available for this location. However, records from other stations in the region indicate that averages are probably 75–80% from summer to early autumn, dropping to near 55% in winter and early spring.

WATER: Rainfall is moderate to heavy from late spring into autumn, but conditions are very dry in the long winter dry season. Cultivated plants should be kept moist while actively growing, but water should be gradually reduced in autumn.

FERTILIZER: ¼–½ recommended strength. A balanced fertilizer should be applied weekly to biweekly throughout the growing season.

REST PERIOD: Growing temperatures should be maintained all year. Rainfall is low in winter, and humidity is so low that even moisture from morning dew is uncommon. Water should be reduced for cultivated plants in winter. Plants should be allowed to dry out between waterings, but they should not remain completely dry for extended periods. Fertilizer should be eliminated until water is increased in spring.

GROWING MEDIA: Plants may be mounted on tree-fern or cork slabs or potted in small pots filled with any open, fast-draining medium. Repotting is best done in early spring at the end of the dry season when new roots begin to grow.

MISCELLANEOUS NOTES: The bloom season shown in the climate table is based on reports from the habitat.

Plant and Flower Information

PLANT SIZE AND TYPE: A 14 in. (35 cm) sympodial epiphyte.

PSEUDOBULB: 11 in. (28 cm) long. The stems are covered with pale brown or greenish brown sheaths.

LEAVES: Several. The thin, narrowly elliptical leaves are 2.8–3.2 in. (7–8 cm) long.

INFLORESCENCE: 0.8–2.4 in. (2–6 cm) long.

FLOWERS: 1–6 per inflorescence. The flowers are 1.6–2.0 in. (4–5 cm) across. Blossoms are normally pure white, but occasionally the sepals are tinged with yellow at the tips. The white lip, which has yellow in the center of the disk, is marked with 2 orange-yellow to brick-pink lines at the base. Blossoms are odorless.

REFERENCES: 234, 584.

PHOTOS/DRAWINGS: *584*.

Dendrobium coxii F. M. Bailey. See *D. inaequale* Rolfe not Finet. REFERENCES: 26, 67, 220, 254.

Dendrobium crabro Ridley

ORIGIN/HABITAT: Sarawak, Borneo, near Matang. Habitat location and elevation is unavailable, so the following climate data should be used with caution.

CLIMATE: Station #96413, Kuching, Sarawak, Lat. 1.5°N, Long. 110.3°E, at 85 ft. (26 m). Record extreme temperatures are 97°F (36°C) and 64°F (18°C).

N/HEMISPHERE	JAN	FEB	MAR	APR	MAY	JUN	JUL	AUG	SEP	OCT	NOV	DEC
°F AVG MAX	88	88	89	90	91	91	91	92	90	90	90	88
°F AVG MIN	72	72	72	72	72	73	72	72	72	72	72	72
DIURNAL RANGE	16	16	17	18	19	18	19	20	18	18	18	16
RAIN/INCHES	27.1	19.7	14.2	9.7	9.0	8.5	6.9	8.8	9.5	12.6	13.1	20.1
HUMIDITY/%	89	88	86	85	85	83	82	83	84	85	87	88
BLOOM SEASON							*					
DAYS CLR @ 7AM	1	0	1	2	3	2	4	1	2	1	1	1
DAYS CLR @ 1PM	0	0	0	0	1	1	1	0	0	0	0	0
RAIN/MM	688	500	361	246	229	216	175	224	241	320	333	511
°C AVG MAX	31.1	31.1	31.7	32.2	32.8	32.8	32.8	33.3	32.2	32.2	32.2	31.1
°C AVG MIN	22.2	22.2	22.2	22.2	22.2	22.8	22.2	22.2	22.2	22.2	22.2	22.2
DIURNAL RANGE	8.9	8.9	9.5	10.0	10.6	10.0	10.6	11.1	10.0	10.0	10.0	8.9
S/HEMISPHERE	JUL	AUG	SEP	OCT	NOV	DEC	JAN	FEB	MAR	APR	MAY	JUN

Cultural Recommendations

LIGHT: 2000–3000 fc.

TEMPERATURES: Throughout the year, days average 88–91°F (31–33°C), and nights average 72–73°F (22–23°C), with a diurnal range of 18–20°F (10–11°C). The diurnal range is unusually large for a habitat with so little seasonal variation. Average highs fluctuate only 4°F (2°C) and lows vary only 1°F (1°C) during the year.

HUMIDITY: 80–90% year-round.

WATER: Rainfall is very heavy all year. Cultivated plants should be kept moist. Warm water may be beneficial.

FERTILIZER: ¼–½ recommended strength. A balanced fertilizer should be applied weekly to biweekly throughout the year.

REST PERIOD: Growing conditions should be maintained all year. The record low is only 10°F (6°C) below the average lows. Although rainfall remains heavy in winter, water should be reduced for cultivated plants grown in the dark, short-day conditions common in temperate latitudes. Plants should not be allowed to dry out completely, however.

Dendrobium crassicaule

GROWING MEDIA: Plants may be mounted on tree-fern or cork slabs or potted in small pots filled with any open, fast-draining medium. Repotting may be done any time new roots are growing.

MISCELLANEOUS NOTES: The bloom season shown in the climate table is based on records from the habitat.

Plant and Flower Information

PLANT SIZE AND TYPE: A 12–24 in. (30–60 cm) sympodial epiphyte.

PSEUDOBULB: 12–24 in. (30–60 cm) long. The cylindrical stems are largest near the apex.

LEAVES: The elliptic leaves are 3 in. (7.6 cm) long.

INFLORESCENCE: Short. Inflorescences are borne on the upper nodes of leafless stems.

FLOWERS: 1 per inflorescence. The flowers are 0.8 in. (2 cm) long. Sepals and petals have a green tinge and red veins. The fan-shaped lip and column are white. The mentum narrows and then becomes dilated at the tip, resembling the abdomen of a wasp.

REFERENCES: 220, 286, 295, 398.

Dendrobium crassicaule Schlechter

ORIGIN/HABITAT: New Caledonia. Plants grow on tree trunks on the slopes of Mt. Humboldt at about 3950 ft. (1200 m).

CLIMATE: Station #91592, Noumea, New Caledonia, Lat. 22.3°S, Long. 166.5°E, at 246 ft. (75 m). Temperatures are calculated for an elevation of 3500 ft. (1070 m), resulting in probable extremes of 88°F (31°C) and 41°F (5°C).

N/HEMISPHERE	JAN	FEB	MAR	APR	MAY	JUN	JUL	AUG	SEP	OCT	NOV	DEC
°F AVG MAX	65	65	67	69	72	75	75	74	74	72	68	66
°F AVG MIN	51	50	52	54	57	59	61	62	61	59	55	53
DIURNAL RANGE	14	15	15	15	15	16	14	12	13	13	13	13
RAIN/INCHES	3.6	2.6	2.5	2.0	2.4	2.6	3.7	5.1	5.7	5.2	4.4	3.7
HUMIDITY/%	73	70	69	67	68	69	71	74	75	76	73	73
BLOOM SEASON					**	**		*	*			
DAYS CLR @ 11AM	7	9	9	15	12	10	7	6	7	7	7	7
DAYS CLR @ 5PM	7	11	6	11	7	6	5	4	4	5	3	7
RAIN/MM	91	66	64	51	61	66	94	130	145	132	112	94
°C AVG MAX	18.5	18.5	19.6	20.7	22.4	24.0	24.0	23.5	23.5	22.4	20.1	19.0
°C AVG MIN	10.7	10.1	11.3	12.4	14.0	15.1	16.3	16.8	16.3	15.1	12.9	11.8
DIURNAL RANGE	7.8	8.4	8.3	8.3	8.4	8.9	7.7	6.7	7.2	7.3	7.2	7.2
S/HEMISPHERE	JUL	AUG	SEP	OCT	NOV	DEC	JAN	FEB	MAR	APR	MAY	JUN

Cultural Recommendations

LIGHT: 1800–3000 fc. Days are frequently clear, particularly in winter and spring, indicating relatively high light. However, the humid forest microclimate suggests lower light.

TEMPERATURES: Summer days average 74–75°F (24°C), and nights average 59–62°F (15–17°C), with a diurnal range of 12–16°F (7–9°C).

HUMIDITY: 70–75% year-round.

WATER: Rainfall is relatively low and consistent throughout the year, with the greatest amounts falling in late summer and early autumn. More moisture may be available in the mountain habitat than the climate records indicate. However, in this region, rain normally falls as heavy showers, and plants might be healthiest if they are thoroughly saturated and then allowed to become almost dry before being watered again. Plants should be kept moist while actively growing, but the medium should not be soggy.

FERTILIZER: ¼–½ recommended strength, applied weekly. A high-nitrogen fertilizer is beneficial from spring to midsummer, but a fertilizer high in phosphates should be used in late summer and autumn.

REST PERIOD: Winter days average 65–67°F (19–20°C), and nights average 50–53°F (10–12°C), with a diurnal range of 13–15°F (7–8°C). Day and night temperatures decline simultaneously, resulting in little change in the diurnal range. Rainfall is somewhat lower in late winter and spring. In cultivation, water and fertilizer should be reduced and the plants allowed to dry even more between waterings than in summer. They should not dry out completely or remain dry for long periods, however. In the habitat, light is highest in winter.

GROWING MEDIA: Plants may be mounted on tree-fern or cork slabs if humidity is high and plants are watered at least once daily in summer. When plants are potted, any open, fast-draining medium may be used. Repotting is best done immediately after blooming when new roots begin growing.

MISCELLANEOUS NOTES: The bloom season shown in the climate table is based on reports from the habitat.

Plant and Flower Information

PLANT SIZE AND TYPE: A 12–24 in. (30–60 cm) sympodial epiphyte.

PSEUDOBULB: 12–24 in. (30–60 cm) long. The clustered pseudobulbs are erect and arise from a very short rhizome.

LEAVES: 9–11 on the upper portion of the stem. The linear leaves are arranged in 2 rows. They are spreading, leathery, deeply and unequally bilobed, and 1.2–2.0 in. (3–5 cm) long.

INFLORESCENCE: 4 in. (10 cm) long. The blossoms are held well beyond the tips of the leaves.

FLOWERS: 3–9 per inflorescence. The flowers are 0.7 in. (1.8 cm) long and remain rather closed. They are greenish with violet margins on the petals and at the base of the lip. The sepals and smaller petals are pointed. The lip has 3 ridges that do not extend to the tip. The sidelobes are small.

REFERENCES: 173, 220, 254, 432, 437.

PHOTOS/DRAWINGS: 173.

Dendrobium crassiflorum J. J. Smith

ORIGIN/HABITAT: Irian Jaya (western New Guinea). Plants grow on trees in primary forests along the Lorentz and upper Eilanden Rivers. They were cultivated in the botanical garden at Bogor, Java, suggesting a low to moderate elevation.

CLIMATE: Station #97876, Tanahmerah, Irian Jaya, Lat. 6.1°S, Long. 140.3°E, at 75 ft. (23 m). Temperatures are calculated for an elevation of 500 ft. (150 m), resulting in probable extremes of 97°F (36°C) and 63°F (17°C).

N/HEMISPHERE	JAN	FEB	MAR	APR	MAY	JUN	JUL	AUG	SEP	OCT	NOV	DEC
°F AVG MAX	83	84	86	89	90	89	89	88	89	88	86	84
°F AVG MIN	71	70	70	71	72	73	72	72	72	72	73	72
DIURNAL RANGE	12	14	16	18	18	16	17	16	17	16	13	12
RAIN/INCHES	11.5	12.1	14.7	13.2	14.4	15.9	14.5	15.8	17.4	17.3	15.5	11.9
HUMIDITY/%	N/A											
BLOOM SEASON			*									
DAYS CLR	N/A											
RAIN/MM	292	307	373	335	366	404	368	401	442	439	394	302
°C AVG MAX	28.1	28.7	29.8	31.4	32.0	31.4	31.4	30.9	31.4	30.9	29.8	28.7
°C AVG MIN	21.4	20.9	20.9	21.4	22.0	22.6	22.0	22.0	22.0	22.0	22.6	22.0
DIURNAL RANGE	6.7	7.8	8.9	10.0	10.0	8.8	9.4	8.9	9.4	8.9	7.2	6.7
S/HEMISPHERE	JUL	AUG	SEP	OCT	NOV	DEC	JAN	FEB	MAR	APR	MAY	JUN

Cultural Recommendations

LIGHT: 2000–3000 fc.

TEMPERATURES: Throughout the year, days average 83–90°F (28–32°C), and nights average 70–73°F (21–23°C), with a diurnal range of 12–18°F (7–10°C).

HUMIDITY: Information is not available for this location. However, records

from nearby locations indicate that humidity probably averages near 85% year-round.

WATER: Rainfall is very heavy all year. Cultivated plants should be kept evenly moist and never be allowed to dry out completely.

FERTILIZER: ¼–½ recommended strength. A balanced fertilizer should be applied weekly to biweekly throughout the year.

REST PERIOD: Growing conditions should be maintained year-round. Water and fertilizer might be reduced slightly in winter, especially for plants cultivated in the dark, short-day conditions common in temperate latitudes, but they should never be allowed dry completely between waterings.

GROWING MEDIA: Because plants must be kept moist, they are easier to manage when potted. Any open medium that retains moisture may be used. Repotting may be done anytime new roots are growing.

MISCELLANEOUS NOTES: The bloom season shown in the climate table is based on reports from the habitat. The plant was described in 1911 in *Bul. Dep. Agric. Indes Neerl.* 45:4.

Plant and Flower Information

PLANT SIZE AND TYPE: A sympodial plant of unreported size.

PSEUDOBULB: The stem is elongated.

LEAVES: Many. The lanceolate leaves are 2.4–4.0 in. (6–10 cm) long.

INFLORESCENCE: Short.

FLOWERS: 2 per inflorescence. The sepals and petals are 0.5 in. (1.3 cm) long. They are pale yellow with red dots. The lip is decorated with orange. It is dark purple on the front margin of the midlobe.

REFERENCES: 221, 437, 445, 470.

Dendrobium crassifolium Schlechter

ORIGIN/HABITAT: Endemic to New Caledonia. *D. crassifolium* grows near Ou Hinna high on trees in humid, mountain forests. Collections are reported as low as 100 ft. (30 m) and as high as 2950 ft. (900 m).

CLIMATE: Station #91583, Poindimie, New Caledonia, Lat. 20.9°S, Long. 165.3°E, at 36 ft. (11 m). Temperatures are calculated for an elevation of 2100 ft. (640 m). Record extreme temperatures are not available for this location.

N/HEMISPHERE	JAN	FEB	MAR	APR	MAY	JUN	JUL	AUG	SEP	OCT	NOV	DEC
°F AVG MAX	67	67	68	70	72	74	76	76	75	74	70	69
°F AVG MIN	57	56	58	60	63	65	66	68	67	65	61	59
DIURNAL RANGE	10	11	10	10	9	9	10	8	8	9	9	10
RAIN/INCHES	3.4	3.0	2.6	4.2	7.5	7.7	11.4	10.4	9.3	5.7	6.7	4.6
HUMIDITY/%	N/A											
BLOOM SEASON				*			*					
DAYS CLR	N/A											
RAIN/MM	87	75	67	108	190	194	290	264	237	145	169	116
°C AVG MAX	19.5	19.5	20.1	21.2	22.3	23.4	24.5	24.5	24.0	23.4	21.2	20.7
°C AVG MIN	14.0	13.4	14.5	15.7	17.3	18.4	19.0	20.1	19.5	18.4	16.2	15.1
DIURNAL RANGE	5.5	6.1	5.6	5.5	5.0	5.0	5.5	4.4	4.5	5.0	5.0	5.6
S/HEMISPHERE	JUL	AUG	SEP	OCT	NOV	DEC	JAN	FEB	MAR	APR	MAY	JUN

Cultural Recommendations

LIGHT: 3000–4000 fc. Some shading should be provided when conditions are hot and bright.

TEMPERATURES: Summer days average 74–76°F (23–25°C), and nights average 65–68°F (18–20°C), with a diurnal range of 8–10°F (4–6°C).

HUMIDITY: Information is not available for this location. However, records from nearby locations indicate that humidity probably averages 70–75% year-round. Averages may be even greater in the mountain forest habitat.

WATER: Rainfall is moderate to heavy for most of the year with a short drier period in winter. Cultivated plants should be kept moist and never be allowed to dry out completely.

FERTILIZER: ¼–½ recommended strength, applied weekly. A high-nitrogen fertilizer is beneficial from spring to midsummer, but a fertilizer high in phosphates should be used in late summer and autumn.

REST PERIOD: Winter days average 67–69°F (20–21°C), and nights average 56–59°F (13–15°C), with a diurnal range of 10–11°F (6°C). Water should be reduced somewhat in winter, so that plants are kept barely moist.

GROWING MEDIA: Plants may be mounted on tree-fern or cork slabs if humidity is high and plants are watered at least once daily in summer. When plants are potted, any open, fast-draining medium may be used. Repotting is best done in early spring when new roots are growing.

MISCELLANEOUS NOTES: The bloom season shown in the climate table is based on reports from the habitat. A plant cultivated at Noumea bloomed in midsummer and midwinter. Plants have been collected in late spring and early summer.

Plant and Flower Information

PLANT SIZE AND TYPE: An erect, 8–12 in. (20–30 cm) sympodial epiphyte.

PSEUDOBULB: 8–12 in. (20–30 cm) long. Growths are clustered and arise from a very short rhizome.

LEAVES: 6–8. The unequally bilobed leaves are 1.6–2.8 in. (4–7 cm) long. They are leathery and appear to twist at the base to face one direction. Stems are leafy near the apex.

INFLORESCENCE: Short. Inflorescences emerge opposite the base of the leaves.

FLOWERS: 1–2 per inflorescence. The fragrant flowers are 0.5 in. (1.3 cm) long. All segments are pale yellow with orange-yellow on the midvein keel of the lip and at the base of the column-foot. The midlobe is covered with protuberances.

HYBRIDIZING NOTES: Chromosome count is 2n = 38 (ref. 153, 273).

REFERENCES: 153, 173, 220, 254, 273, 432.

PHOTOS/DRAWINGS: 173.

Dendrobium crassimarginatum L. O. Williams

ORIGIN/HABITAT: The Philippines. Plants grow near Jaro on Leyte Island in forests at about 1950 ft. (600 m).

CLIMATE: Station #98550, Tacloban, Leyte, Philippines, Lat. 11.3°N, Long. 125.0°E, at 52 ft. (16 m). Temperatures are calculated for an elevation of 2000 ft. (610 m). Record extreme temperatures are not available for this location.

N/HEMISPHERE	JAN	FEB	MAR	APR	MAY	JUN	JUL	AUG	SEP	OCT	NOV	DEC
°F AVG MAX	77	79	80	82	83	83	81	82	81	81	80	78
°F AVG MIN	67	67	68	69	71	71	70	70	69	69	69	67
DIURNAL RANGE	10	12	12	13	12	12	11	12	12	12	11	11
RAIN/INCHES	9.0	6.2	4.4	3.3	5.8	7.8	6.9	5.7	8.3	9.1	11.4	8.5
HUMIDITY/%	N/A											
BLOOM SEASON											*	
DAYS CLR	N/A											
RAIN/MM	229	157	112	84	147	198	175	145	211	231	290	216
°C AVG MAX	24.8	25.9	26.4	27.5	28.1	28.1	27.0	27.5	27.0	27.0	26.4	25.3
°C AVG MIN	19.2	19.2	19.8	20.3	21.4	21.4	20.9	20.9	20.3	20.3	20.3	19.2
DIURNAL RANGE	5.6	6.7	6.6	7.2	6.7	6.7	6.1	6.6	6.7	6.7	6.1	6.1
S/HEMISPHERE	JUL	AUG	SEP	OCT	NOV	DEC	JAN	FEB	MAR	APR	MAY	JUN

Cultural Recommendations

LIGHT: 2500–3500 fc.

TEMPERATURES: Throughout the year, days average 77–83°F (25–28°C),

and nights average 67–71°F (19–21°C), with a diurnal range of 10–13°F (6–7°C). Average winter temperatures are only 3–4°F (2°C) cooler than summer values.

HUMIDITY: Information is not available for this location. However, records from nearby stations indicate that humidity probably averages 80–85% most of the year, dropping to 75–80% in late winter and early spring.

WATER: Rainfall is moderate to heavy most of the year with a slightly drier period in late winter and early spring. Cultivated plants should be kept evenly moist with only slight drying between waterings.

FERTILIZER: ¼–½ recommended strength. A balanced fertilizer should be applied weekly to biweekly throughout the year.

REST PERIOD: Growing conditions should be maintained all year. In the habitat, a brief rest may occur during the slightly drier period in late winter and early spring. Water may be reduced for about 2 months for cultivated plants. They should dry out slightly between waterings, but should not remain dry for long periods. Fertilizer should be limited anytime water is reduced. In the habitat, seasonal light variation is minor.

GROWING MEDIA: Plants may be mounted on tree-fern or cork slabs if humidity is high and plants are watered at least once daily in summer. When plants are potted, any open, fast-draining medium may be used. Repotting may be done anytime new roots are growing.

MISCELLANEOUS NOTES: The bloom season shown in the climate table is based on collection reports.

Plant and Flower Information

PLANT SIZE AND TYPE: A 12 in. (30 cm) sympodial epiphyte.

PSEUDOBULB: 12 in. (30 cm) long. The yellow stems are jointed, rigid, and do not branch. Younger parts of the stem are covered with leaf sheaths.

LEAVES: Many. The lanceolate leaves are usually 1.2–1.6 in. (3–4 cm) long and have 5 veins. They are slightly bilobed. Leaves are deciduous.

INFLORESCENCE: Short. Inflorescences arise at or near the apex of leafless stems.

FLOWERS: 2–5 per inflorescence. The pink and white flowers are 0.7 in. (1.8 cm) long. Sepals are lanceolate. The nearly elliptic petals are broad above the middle. The simple lip is wavy, pointed, and toothed along the margin with an inconspicuous callus.

REFERENCES: 226, 536.

Dendrobium crassinervium J. J. Smith

ORIGIN/HABITAT: Irian Jaya (western New Guinea). Plants grow on the north-facing slopes of the Gautier Range at about 1650–2000 ft. (500–610 m).

CLIMATE: Station #97690, Sentani/Jayapura, Irian Jaya, Lat. 2.7°S, Long. 140.5°E, at 289 ft. (88 m). Temperatures are calculated for an estimated elevation of 2000 ft. (610 m), resulting in probable extremes of 91°F (33°C) and 62°F (17°C).

N/HEMISPHERE	JAN	FEB	MAR	APR	MAY	JUN	JUL	AUG	SEP	OCT	NOV	DEC
°F AVG MAX	81	83	83	84	84	83	83	82	83	84	84	83
°F AVG MIN	66	66	66	67	67	67	67	67	67	68	67	67
DIURNAL RANGE	15	17	17	17	17	16	16	15	16	16	17	16
RAIN/INCHES	4.1	3.9	5.3	2.9	6.7	7.0	8.3	8.3	8.5	4.6	2.4	5.2
HUMIDITY/%	81	80	80	79	81	81	79	80	80	80	81	80
BLOOM SEASON				*	*							
DAYS CLR @ 9AM	5	3	4	3	2	1	1	0	1	2	2	5
DAYS CLR @ 3PM	4	3	3	3	2	1	3	0	1	2	2	3
RAIN/MM	104	99	135	74	170	178	211	211	216	117	61	132
°C AVG MAX	27.4	28.5	28.5	29.1	29.1	28.5	28.5	28.0	28.5	29.1	29.1	28.5
°C AVG MIN	19.1	19.1	19.1	19.6	19.6	19.6	19.6	19.6	19.6	20.2	19.6	19.6
DIURNAL RANGE	8.3	9.4	9.4	9.5	9.5	8.9	8.9	8.4	8.9	8.9	9.5	8.9
S/HEMISPHERE	JUL	AUG	SEP	OCT	NOV	DEC	JAN	FEB	MAR	APR	MAY	JUN

Cultural Recommendations

LIGHT: 2000–3000 fc.

TEMPERATURES: Throughout the year, days average 81–84°F (27–29°C), and nights average 66–68°F (19–20°C), with a diurnal range of 15–17°F (8–10°C).

HUMIDITY: Near 80% year-round.

WATER: Rainfall is heavy all year with brief semidry periods in spring and autumn. Cultivated plants should be kept evenly moist with only slight drying allowed between waterings.

FERTILIZER: ¼–½ recommended strength. A balanced fertilizer should be applied weekly to biweekly throughout the year.

REST PERIOD: Growing conditions should be maintained year-round. Water may be reduced somewhat for cultivated plants in winter, especially those grown in the dark, short-day conditions common in temperate latitudes. They should never be allowed to dry out completely, however. In the habitat, light is slightly higher in winter.

GROWING MEDIA: Plants may be mounted on tree-fern or cork slabs if humidity is high and plants are watered at least once daily in summer. When plants are potted, any open, fast-draining medium may be used. Repotting may be done anytime new roots are growing.

MISCELLANEOUS NOTES: The bloom season shown in the climate table is based on reports from the habitat.

Plant and Flower Information

PLANT SIZE AND TYPE: A sympodial epiphyte of unreported size.

PSEUDOBULB: The stems are very flattened. The internodes, which are 0.5–0.8 in. (1.3–1.7 cm) long, are enlarged at the base.

LEAVES: Many. The slender, oblong leaves are 1.8 in. (4.5 cm) long. They are chopped off at the tip.

INFLORESCENCE: Short. The inflorescences perforate the leaf bases and emerge along the stem.

FLOWERS: 1 per inflorescence. The blossoms are inverted. The dorsal sepal is 0.5 in. (1.3 cm) long. The sepals are ovate, and the rounded petals are oblong. The 3-lobed lip is recurved with a hairy, nearly round midlobe.

REFERENCES: 221, 470, 476.

Dendrobium crassinode Benson and Rchb. f. See *D. pendulum* Roxburgh. The International Orchid Commission (ref. 236) registers hybrids under the name *D. crassinode*. REFERENCES: 25, 38, 46, 72, 151, 154, 187, 188, 190, 200, 216, 236, 245, 247, 254, 369, 389, 430, 445, 447, 448, 454, 460, 504, 541, 557, 570, 580. PHOTOS/DRAWINGS: 72, *133*, *245*, *247*, *541*.

Dendrobium crassulaefolium A. Cunningham. Sometimes listed a synonym of *Bulbophyllum crassulifolium*, Clements (ref. 67) considers it an invalid name. REFERENCES: 67, 105, 216, 254.

Dendrobium crassulum (Schlechter) J. J. Smith

AKA: *Cadetia crassula* Schlechter. When J. J. Smith moved *C. crassula* to the genus *Dendrobium* he left the spelling as *D. crassula*. *Cadetia* is now considered a valid genus by some botanists, so this plant may again be considered a *Cadetia*.

ORIGIN/HABITAT: Papua New Guinea. The orchids grow in the Finisterre Mountains at about 4250 ft. (1300 m).

CLIMATE: Station #94010, Goroka, Papua New Guinea, Lat. 6.1°S, Long. 145.4°E, at 5141 ft. (1567 m). Temperatures are calculated for an elevation of 4000 ft. (1220 m), resulting in probable extremes of 90°F (32°C) and 46°F (8°C).

N/HEMISPHERE	JAN	FEB	MAR	APR	MAY	JUN	JUL	AUG	SEP	OCT	NOV	DEC
°F AVG MAX	80	81	82	83	83	82	83	82	82	82	83	81
°F AVG MIN	60	61	61	61	62	63	63	63	64	63	63	61
DIURNAL RANGE	20	20	21	22	21	19	20	19	18	19	20	20
RAIN/INCHES	2.1	2.8	4.6	5.9	6.6	9.3	9.1	10.1	10.7	8.3	4.6	2.0
HUMIDITY/%	70	67	67	67	67	71	72	73	74	71	70	70
BLOOM SEASON							*					
DAYS CLR	N/A											
RAIN/MM	53	71	117	150	168	236	231	257	272	211	117	51
°C AVG MAX	26.5	27.1	27.6	28.2	28.2	27.6	28.2	27.6	27.6	27.6	28.2	27.1
°C AVG MIN	15.4	16.0	16.0	16.0	16.5	17.1	17.1	17.1	17.6	17.1	17.1	16.0
DIURNAL RANGE	11.1	11.1	11.6	12.2	11.7	10.5	11.1	10.5	10.0	10.5	11.1	11.1
S/HEMISPHERE	JUL	AUG	SEP	OCT	NOV	DEC	JAN	FEB	MAR	APR	MAY	JUN

Cultural Recommendations

LIGHT: 2000–3000 fc.

TEMPERATURES: Throughout the year, days average 80–83°F (27–28°C), and nights average 60–64°F (15–18°C), with a diurnal range of 18–22°F (10–12°C).

HUMIDITY: Near 70–75% most of the year, dropping to near 65% in late winter and spring.

WATER: Rainfall is moderate to heavy most of the year but is relatively low for 2–3 months in winter. However, additional moisture is available from dew, fog, and mist, even during periods when rainfall is low. Cultivated plants should be kept moist but not soggy. Additional early morning mistings between waterings are often beneficial, especially on warm, bright, sunny days.

FERTILIZER: ¼–½ recommended strength. A balanced fertilizer should be applied weekly to biweekly throughout the year.

REST PERIOD: Growing temperatures should be maintained all year. Water should be reduced in winter. Plants should dry slightly between waterings, but they should never be allowed to dry out completely. Fertilizer should be reduced or eliminated until water is increased in spring. In the habitat, winter light may be slightly higher.

GROWING MEDIA: Plants may be mounted on tree-fern or cork slabs or potted in small pots filled with any open, fast-draining medium. Repotting may be done anytime new roots are growing.

MISCELLANEOUS NOTES: The bloom season shown in the climate table is based on collection reports.

Plant and Flower Information

PLANT SIZE AND TYPE: A 0.4–0.8 in. (1–2 cm) sympodial epiphyte.

PSEUDOBULB: 0.2–0.8 in. (0.4–2.0 cm) long. The dense pseudobulbs are borne on a very short rhizome.

LEAVES: 1 per growth. The oblong to oval leaves are 0.2–0.5 in. (0.5–1.2 cm) long. They are smooth and leathery.

INFLORESCENCE: Very short. The short inflorescence emerges at the apex of the pseudobulb, holding the flower at the base of the leaf.

FLOWERS: 1 per inflorescence. The yellowish white flowers are 0.2 in. (0.4 cm) long and remain rather closed. Sepals and petals are pointed. The simple lip is rounded with a point in the center.

REFERENCES: 221, 437, 472

Dendrobium crenatifolium J. J. Smith

ORIGIN/HABITAT: Irian Jaya (western New Guinea). Plants grow on Mt. Goliath, near the summit of Mt. Wichmann in the Hubrecht Mountains, and near Lake Habbema. They are common at 10,000–11,300 ft. (3050–3450 m). The orchids grow in alpine heath or grasslands on rocks covered with mossy humus.

CLIMATE: Station #97686, Wamena, Irian Jaya, Lat. 4.1°S, Long. 139.0°E at 5446 ft. (1660 m). Temperatures are calculated for a habitat elevation of 10,000 ft. (3050 m). Record extreme temperatures are not available for this location.

N/HEMISPHERE	JAN	FEB	MAR	APR	MAY	JUN	JUL	AUG	SEP	OCT	NOV	DEC
°F AVG MAX	60	61	62	61	62	61	62	61	61	64	63	59
°F AVG MIN	45	45	47	47	48	49	48	47	48	50	50	46
DIURNAL RANGE	15	16	15	14	14	12	14	14	13	14	13	13
RAIN/INCHES	3.0	1.9	2.2	4.0	4.6	3.3	2.8	4.2	6.9	3.9	5.4	4.9
HUMIDITY/%	N/A											
BLOOM SEASON		*							*		*	
DAYS CLR	N/A											
RAIN/MM	76	48	56	102	117	84	71	107	175	99	137	124
°C AVG MAX	15.5	16.1	16.7	16.1	16.7	16.1	16.7	16.1	16.1	17.8	17.2	15.0
°C AVG MIN	7.2	7.2	8.3	8.3	8.9	9.4	8.9	8.3	8.9	10.0	10.0	7.8
DIURNAL RANGE	8.3	8.9	8.4	7.8	7.8	6.7	7.8	7.8	7.2	7.8	7.2	7.2
S/HEMISPHERE	JUL	AUG	SEP	OCT	NOV	DEC	JAN	FEB	MAR	APR	MAY	JUN

Cultural Recommendations

LIGHT: 1500–2500 fc. Plants from this habitat may tolerate higher light levels, especially early in the morning.

TEMPERATURES: Throughout the year, days average 59–64°F (15–18°C), and nights average 45–50°F (7–10°C), with a diurnal range of 12–16°F (7–9°C). In the habitat, the warmest temperatures of the day occur in late morning, when skies are clear. Because of microclimate effects, actual maximum temperatures may be somewhat warmer than indicated. Reports from the habitat indicate a sharp contrast between day and night temperatures.

HUMIDITY: Information is not available for this location. However, records from nearby stations indicate that humidity probably averages near 80% year-round. High humidity and excellent air circulation are particularly important if temperatures are warm. Placing the plants in front of an evaporative cooler or near a fine mist is very beneficial.

WATER: Rainfall is moderate to heavy through most of the year. In the higher-elevation habitat, rainfall may be greater than indicated in the climate table. In addition, large amounts of water are available from mist and heavy dew, even during periods of reduced rainfall. Cultivated plants should be misted several times daily on the hottest days, but the foliage should always be dry before evening.

FERTILIZER: ¼–½ recommended strength, applied weekly throughout the year. The Royal Botanic Garden in Edinburgh uses a seaweed-based fertilizer for high-elevation plants from New Guinea.

REST PERIOD: Growing conditions should be maintained all year. Seasonal temperatures vary 5°F (3°C) or less. Rainfall is moderate throughout the year, with a month or so of drier conditions in late winter and a secondary drier period in summer. In cultivation, water may be decreased somewhat in winter, but plants should never be allowed to dry out completely. In the habitat, light may be slightly higher in winter.

GROWING MEDIA: Plants may be mounted on tree-fern or cork slabs if humidity is high and plants are watered at least once daily in summer. When plants are potted, any open moisture-retaining medium may be used. Repotting may be done anytime new roots are growing.

MISCELLANEOUS NOTES: The bloom season shown in the climate table is based on collection reports.

Plant and Flower Information

PLANT SIZE AND TYPE: An 8–20 in. (20–50 cm) sympodial epiphyte.

PSEUDOBULB: 8–20 in. (20–50 cm) long. The stems are stiff and many-noded.

LEAVES: Many. The ovate-lanceolate leaves are erect, somewhat wavy, and 0.6–2.1 in. (1.5–5.3 cm) long.

INFLORESCENCE: 0.3 in. (0.8 cm) long. The erect inflorescences emerge near the apex of the stem.

FLOWERS: 1–4 per inflorescence. The flowers are 0.8–1.2 in. (2–3 cm) long and do not open fully. Blossoms are violet to purple to red shading to orange and yellow. The lip is orange with a purple margin and purple markings.

REFERENCES: 221, 445, 470, 538.

PHOTOS/DRAWINGS: 538.

Dendrobium crenatilabre J. J. Smith

ORIGIN/HABITAT: Irian Jaya (western New Guinea) and Seram. Plants are found on the eastern slopes of the Cyclops Mountains, where they grow on trees in forests at 6550 ft. (2000 m). *D. crenatilabre* var. *seranicum* J. J. Smith grows in the mountains of Seram at 3300–3950 ft. (1000–1200 m), and requires temperatures about 10°F (6°C) warmer than those indicated below.

CLIMATE: Station #97690, Sentani/Jayapura, Irian Jaya, Lat. 2.7°S, Long. 140.5°E, at 289 ft. (88 m). Temperatures are calculated for an elevation of 6550 ft. (2000 m), resulting in probable extremes of 76°F (25°C) and 47°F (9°C).

N/HEMISPHERE	JAN	FEB	MAR	APR	MAY	JUN	JUL	AUG	SEP	OCT	NOV	DEC
°F AVG MAX	66	68	68	69	69	68	68	67	68	69	69	68
°F AVG MIN	51	51	51	52	52	52	52	52	52	53	52	52
DIURNAL RANGE	15	17	17	17	17	16	16	15	16	16	17	16
RAIN/INCHES	4.1	3.9	5.3	2.9	6.7	7.0	8.3	8.3	8.5	4.6	2.4	5.2
HUMIDITY/%	81	80	80	79	81	81	79	80	80	80	81	80
BLOOM SEASON											*	**
DAYS CLR @ 9AM	5	3	4	3	2	1	1	0	1	2	2	5
DAYS CLR @ 3PM	4	3	3	3	2	1	3	0	1	2	2	3
RAIN/MM	104	99	135	74	170	178	211	211	216	117	61	132
°C AVG MAX	19.1	20.2	20.2	20.7	20.7	20.2	20.2	19.6	20.2	20.7	20.7	20.2
°C AVG MIN	10.7	10.7	10.7	11.3	11.3	11.3	11.3	11.3	11.3	11.9	11.3	11.3
DIURNAL RANGE	8.4	9.5	9.5	9.4	9.4	8.9	8.9	8.3	8.9	8.9	8.8	9.4	8.9
S/HEMISPHERE	JUL	AUG	SEP	OCT	NOV	DEC	JAN	FEB	MAR	APR	MAY	JUN

Cultural Recommendations

LIGHT: 1500–2500 fc.

TEMPERATURES: Throughout the year, days average 66–69°F (19–21°C), and nights average 51–53°F (11–12°C), with a diurnal range of 15–17°F (8–10°C). Because of microclimate effects, actual maximum temperatures may be somewhat warmer than indicated.

HUMIDITY: Near 80% year-round.

WATER: Rainfall is heavy all year with brief semidry periods in spring and autumn. Cultivated plants should be kept evenly moist with only slight drying allowed between waterings.

FERTILIZER: ¼–½ recommended strength. A balanced fertilizer should be applied weekly to biweekly throughout the year.

REST PERIOD: Growing conditions should be maintained year-round. Water may be reduced somewhat for cultivated plants in winter, especially those grown in the dark, short-day conditions common in temperate latitudes. They should never be allowed to dry out completely, however. In the habitat, light is slightly higher in winter.

GROWING MEDIA: Plants may be mounted on tree-fern or cork slabs if humidity is high and plants are watered at least once daily in summer. When plants are potted, any open, fast-draining medium may be used. Repotting may be done anytime new roots are growing.

MISCELLANEOUS NOTES: The bloom season shown in the climate table is based on reports from the habitat.

Plant and Flower Information

PLANT SIZE AND TYPE: A sympodial epiphyte of unreported size.

PSEUDOBULB: Stems are elongated and flattened.

LEAVES: Many. The linear leaves are 2–3 in. (5–8 cm) long. They are bilobed at the apex. The leaf bases are wrinkled.

INFLORESCENCE: Short.

FLOWERS: 1 per inflorescence. The flowers are about 0.4 in. (1 cm) across. Sepals and petals are pale yellowish rose-red. The oblong lip, which is irregularly ruffled, is yellow along the front margin with violet patches at the base. It has no sidelobes.

REFERENCES: 221, 437, 445, 470.

Dendrobium crenicristatum Ridley. Now considered a synonym of *Flickingeria crenicristata* (Ridley) J. J. Wood. REFERENCES: 213, 221, 230, 235, 286, 295, 399, 449, 590.

Dendrobium crenulatum J. J. Smith. Now considered a synonym of *Diplocaulobium crenulatum* (J. J. Smith) Kränzlin. REFERENCES: 111, 220, 254, 437, 445, 470.

Dendrobium crepidatum Griffith not Lindley and Paxton. Status unknown. Index Kewensis (ref. 216) lists it is a doubtful species. We suspect that the following references should apply to *D. crepidatum* Lindley and Paxton. Chromosome counts of 2n = 38 are reported (ref. 273) under this name; Kumar and Sasidharan (ref. 255) indicate that it comes from the southern peninsular region of Kerala in southern India; Bose and Bhattacharjee (ref. 46) indicate that it is widespread through India at up to 3950 ft. (1200 m); and Bhattacharjee (ref. 38) includes it as an Indian species. REFERENCES: 38, 46, 153, 157, 216, 254, 255, 273, 278. PHOTOS/DRAWINGS: 38, 46.

Dendrobium crepidatum Lindley and Paxton not Griffith

AKA: Seidenfaden (ref. 454) includes the synonyms *Dendrobium actinomorphum* Blatter and Hallberg, *D. lawanum (lawianum)* Lindley, and *Dendrochilum roseum* Dalzell. Santapau and Kapadia (ref. 424) consider *Dendrobium actinomorphum* Blatter and Hallberg to be a synonym of *D. lawanum (lawianum)* Lindley.

ORIGIN/HABITAT: Widespread in India and Southeast Asia. The habitat extends from the southern peninsula of India through the lower Himalayan area including the Garhwal and Mussorie regions of northern India, Nepal, Sikkim, Bhutan, and the Khasi (Khasia) Hills of the Meghalaya region of northeastern India. Distribution extends eastward through Burma, the mountain regions of mainland Thailand, Laos, and Yunnan Province in China. Plants usually grow on tree trunks at 1950–6900 ft. (600–2100 m).

CLIMATE: Station #48327, Chiang Mai, Thailand, Lat. 18.8°N, Long. 99.0°E, at 1100 ft. (335 m). Temperatures are calculated for a habitat elevation of 3500 ft. (1070 m), resulting in probable extremes of 101°F (38°C) and 30°F (−1°C).

N/HEMISPHERE	JAN	FEB	MAR	APR	MAY	JUN	JUL	AUG	SEP	OCT	NOV	DEC
°F AVG MAX	77	82	87	88	86	82	81	79	80	81	78	76
°F AVG MIN	48	49	54	62	66	66	66	67	65	63	58	49
DIURNAL RANGE	29	33	33	26	20	16	15	12	15	18	20	27
RAIN/INCHES	0.3	0.4	0.6	2.0	5.5	6.1	7.4	8.7	11.5	4.9	1.5	0.4
HUMIDITY/%	73	65	58	62	73	78	80	83	83	81	79	76
BLOOM SEASON		*	**	***	***		*					*
DAYS CLR @ 7AM	5	5	2	2	1	0	0	0	0	1	3	3
DAYS CLR @ 1PM	9	8	4	2	0	0	0	0	0	0	1	3
RAIN/MM	8	10	15	51	140	155	188	221	292	124	38	10
°C AVG MAX	25.0	27.8	30.6	31.2	30.0	27.8	27.3	26.2	26.7	27.3	25.6	24.5
°C AVG MIN	8.9	9.5	12.3	16.7	18.9	18.9	18.9	19.5	18.4	17.3	14.5	9.5
DIURNAL RANGE	16.1	18.3	18.3	14.5	11.1	8.9	8.4	6.7	8.3	10.0	11.1	15.0
S/HEMISPHERE	JUL	AUG	SEP	OCT	NOV	DEC	JAN	FEB	MAR	APR	MAY	JUN

Cultural Recommendations

LIGHT: 3500–4500 fc. Cultivated plants need bright light and strong air movement. As much light as possible, short of burning the foliage, should be provided all year.

TEMPERATURES: Summer days average 77–80°F (25–27°C), and nights average 64–65°F (18–19°C), with a diurnal range of 12–16°F (7–9°C). The warmest weather occurs in spring. Days average 86–88°F (30–31°C), and nights average 54–66°F (12–19°C), with a diurnal range of 20–33°F (11–18°C). Both highs and lows are more moderate after the start of the summer wet season.

HUMIDITY: 75–85% during most of the year, dropping to near 60% for 2 months in late winter and early spring.

WATER: Rainfall is heavy while plants are actively growing from spring to early autumn. During this season, cultivated plants should be kept moist with little if any drying allowed between waterings. However, water should be gradually reduced after new growths mature in autumn.

FERTILIZER: ¼–½ recommended strength, applied weekly. A high-nitrogen fertilizer is beneficial from spring to midsummer, but a fertilizer high in phosphates should be used in late summer and autumn.

REST PERIOD: Winter days average 76–82°F (25–28°C), and nights average 48–49°F (9–10°C), with a diurnal range of 27–33°F (15–18°C). Growers report that *D. crepidatum* tolerates light frost. During very cold weather, a plant's chance of surviving with minimal damage is better if it is dry when temperatures are low. In the habitat, rainfall averages are very low for 4–5 months in winter; but during the early part of the season, the high relative humidity indicates that additional moisture is available from frequent fog, mist, and heavy deposits of dew. Growers sometimes recommend eliminating water in winter, but plants are healthiest if for most of the winter they are allowed to become somewhat dry between waterings but do not remain dry for extended periods. For 1–2 months in late winter, however, conditions are clear, warm, and dry, with humidity so low that even the moisture from morning dew is uncommon. Plants should be allowed to dry out completely between waterings and remain dry longer during this time. Occasional early morning mistings between waterings may help keep the plants from becoming too dry. Fertilizer should be greatly reduced or eliminated until water is increased in spring. In the habitat, light is slightly higher in winter, but increased light may not be critical in cultivation. The dry season, low night temperatures, or wide diurnal range may be necessary to initiate blooming.

GROWING MEDIA: Mounting plants on tree-fern or cork slabs accommodates their pendulous growth habit. However, humidity must be high and plants must be watered at least once a day in summer. If plants cannot be mounted, hanging baskets, filled with an open, fast-draining medium, are suggested. Repotting may be done anytime new roots are actively growing.

MISCELLANEOUS NOTES: The bloom season shown in the climate table is based on cultivation records. The bloom season can be delayed by extending the cool, dry rest period. In the habitat, blooming occurs in early spring at the end of the dry season.

Growers indicate that plants are difficult to keep alive in Singapore and that they rarely bloom.

Plant and Flower Information

PLANT SIZE AND TYPE: A 2–18 in. (5–45 cm) sympodial epiphyte.

PSEUDOBULB: 2–18 in. (5–45 cm) long. Size is variable, but cultivated plants are usually about 10 in. (25 cm) long. Stems are suberect to pendulous, thicker toward the apex, and curved in one direction. The greenish-yellow stems have many nodes that are not swollen. They may be marked with white or purple lines. The leaf sheaths are marked with white stripes and cover the stems.

LEAVES: 5–9 per growth. The deciduous leaves are usually 2–5 in. (5–13 cm) long. They are linear-lanceolate to oblong, pointed at the tip, and distichous.

INFLORESCENCE: Short. The purple inflorescences arise from nodes near the apex of 1-year old leafless stems.

FLOWERS: 1–4 per inflorescence. The shiny, waxy flowers are 1.0–1.8 in. (2.5–4.6 cm) across. The sepals and wider petals are white with pinkish lilac tint, especially at the tips. The large, round to heart-shaped lip is shallowly cupped. It may be white, cream, or pinkish with a yellow or orange stain near the base. Plants from India often have smaller, usually self-pollinating flowers that do not open fully. Reports on flower life vary from 8–10 days to 3 weeks. Cool temperatures lengthen flower life. Blossoms are delicately fragrant and extremely variable in size, form, and color.

HYBRIDIZING NOTES: Chromosome count is n = 19 (ref. 154) and 2n = 38 (ref. 153, 154, 504, 542). As *D. lawanum* the count was 2n = 38 (ref. 504).

REFERENCES: 32, 36, 102, 153, 154, 157, 179, 190, 196, 202, 208, 210, 216, 245, 247, 254, 266, 267, 278, 317, 359, 368, 369, 371, 374, 376, 389, 424, 430, 445, 447, 448, 454, 504, 528, 541, 542, 547, 557, 570, 577, 580.

PHOTOS/DRAWINGS: 32, 36, 102, *134*, 210, *245, 247, 267*, 359, 368, 369, *371, 389, 430, 454*.

Dendrobium crepidiferum J. J. Smith

ORIGIN/HABITAT: The Molucca Islands. On Ternate Island, plants grow in old forests at about 3950 ft. (1200 m). They are reported at higher elevations on Halmahera Island.

CLIMATE: Station #97430, Ternate Island, Indonesia, Lat. 0.8°N, Long. 127.4°E, at 75 ft. (23 m). Temperatures are calculated for an elevation of 3950 ft. (1200 m). Record extreme temperatures are not available for this location.

N/HEMISPHERE	JAN	FEB	MAR	APR	MAY	JUN	JUL	AUG	SEP	OCT	NOV	DEC
°F AVG MAX	72	72	73	73	74	73	74	73	73	74	74	73
°F AVG MIN	64	63	64	64	64	63	62	62	63	64	64	64
DIURNAL RANGE	8	9	9	9	10	10	12	11	10	10	10	9
RAIN/INCHES	5.3	6.1	6.7	6.6	9.4	8.4	4.6	2.1	3.1	3.2	7.2	8.2
HUMIDITY/%	N/A											
BLOOM SEASON					*			*				
DAYS CLR	N/A											
RAIN/MM	135	155	170	168	239	213	117	53	79	81	183	208
°C AVG MAX	22.3	22.3	22.9	22.9	23.5	22.9	23.5	22.9	22.9	23.5	23.5	22.9
°C AVG MIN	17.9	17.3	17.9	17.9	17.9	17.3	16.8	16.8	17.3	17.9	17.9	17.9
DIURNAL RANGE	4.4	5.0	5.0	5.0	5.6	5.6	6.7	6.1	5.6	5.6	5.6	5.0
S/HEMISPHERE	JUL	AUG	SEP	OCT	NOV	DEC	JAN	FEB	MAR	APR	MAY	JUN

Cultural Recommendations

LIGHT: 2000–3000 fc.

TEMPERATURES: Throughout the year, days average 72–74°F (22–24°C), and nights average 62–64°F (17–18°C), with a diurnal range of 8–12°F (4–7°C). The warmest days and coolest nights occur simultaneously in summer.

HUMIDITY: Information is not available for this location. However, records from nearby locations indicate that humidity probably averages near 85% year-round.

WATER: Rainfall is moderate to heavy most of the year. For 2–3 months in late summer and autumn, conditions are somewhat drier. Cultivated plants should be kept moist with only slight drying allowed between waterings through most of the year. For 1–3 months in late summer and early autumn, however, plants should become moderately dry between waterings, but they should not remain dry for long periods.

FERTILIZER: ¼–½ recommended strength. A balanced fertilizer should be applied weekly to biweekly throughout the year.

REST PERIOD: Growing temperatures should be maintained all year. Water may be reduced somewhat in winter, especially for plants grown in the dark, short-day conditions in temperate latitudes. They should never dry out completely, however. In the habitat, seasonal light variation is minor.

GROWING MEDIA: Mounting plants on tree-fern or cork slabs accommodates their pendulous growth habit. However, humidity must be high and plants must be watered at least once a day in summer. If plants cannot be mounted, hanging baskets filled with an open, fast-draining medium are recommended. Repotting or mounting may be done anytime new roots are actively growing.

MISCELLANEOUS NOTES: The bloom season shown in the climate table is based on collection reports. The plant was described in 1917 in *Bul. Jard. Bot. Buit.* 3rd sér. 5:89.

Plant and Flower Information

PLANT SIZE AND TYPE: A 39 in. (100 cm) sympodial epiphyte.

PSEUDOBULB: 39 in. (100 cm) long. The stems are pendent.

LEAVES: Many. The lanceolate leaves are 4 in. (10 cm) long and papery when dry. The leaf bases are covered with dark spots.

INFLORESCENCE: Short. Inflorescences emerge from nodes on leafless stems.

FLOWERS: 3–10 per inflorescence. The lovely flowers are 1.9 in. (4.8 cm) long and sparkle in the light. The blossoms have lanceolate petals and dorsal sepal and triangular lateral sepals. The sepals and petals are violet. The lip is red.

REFERENCES: 223.

Dendrobium cretaceum Lindley

AKA: Stewart and Schlepe (ref. 430) include *D. cretaceum* Lindley as a synonym of *D. polyanthum* Lindley. However, Seidenfaden in 1992 *Opera Botanica* #114 discusses the confusion surrounding the specimens associated with the name *D. polyanthum* Lindley. He suggests retaining the name *D. cretaceum* until the confusion is resolved.

ORIGIN/HABITAT: The Himalayan region of northern India from the Garhwal area near Dehra Dun to the Lushai Hills along the Burma border. Distribution extends eastward through Burma and Thailand, with questionable reports from Cambodia, Laos, and Vietnam. Plants are also reported on the Andaman Islands. Plants known as *D. cretaceum* usually grow at 3300–5900 ft. (1000–1800 m).

CLIMATE: Station #42147, Mukteswar, India, Lat. 29.5°N, Long. 79.7°E, at 7592 ft. (2314 m). Temperatures are calculated for an elevation of 4000 ft. (1220 m), resulting in probable extremes of 102°F (39°C) and 33°F (1°C).

N/HEMISPHERE	JAN	FEB	MAR	APR	MAY	JUN	JUL	AUG	SEP	OCT	NOV	DEC
°F AVG MAX	63	66	73	81	87	87	81	81	80	77	73	67
°F AVG MIN	48	50	56	64	69	71	71	70	68	62	56	51
DIURNAL RANGE	15	16	17	17	18	16	10	11	12	15	17	16
RAIN/INCHES	1.0	2.1	1.7	1.0	0.3	4.6	11.4	12.8	4.6	3.5	0.3	0.2
HUMIDITY/%	61	55	50	39	44	67	91	93	93	66	55	56
BLOOM SEASON		*	*	*	*							
DAYS CLR	17	17	15	18	18	12	1	1	6	25	26	21
RAIN/MM	25	53	43	25	8	117	290	325	117	89	8	5
°C AVG MAX	17.1	18.8	22.7	27.1	30.5	30.5	27.1	27.1	26.6	24.9	22.7	19.4
°C AVG MIN	8.8	9.9	13.3	17.7	20.5	21.6	21.6	21.0	19.9	16.6	13.3	10.5
DIURNAL RANGE	8.3	8.9	9.4	9.4	10.0	8.9	5.5	6.1	6.7	8.3	9.4	8.9
S/HEMISPHERE	JUL	AUG	SEP	OCT	NOV	DEC	JAN	FEB	MAR	APR	MAY	JUN

Cultural Recommendations

LIGHT: 2500–3500 fc.

TEMPERATURES: Summer days average 81–87°F (27–31°C), and nights average 70–71°F (21–22°C), with a diurnal range of 10–16°F (6–9°C).

HUMIDITY: Near 90% in summer, decreasing to 55–60% for most of the winter. In spring, just before the rainy season begins, humidity drops to near 40% for 2 months.

WATER: Rainfall is moderate to heavy 5 months in summer. The wet season is followed immediately by 5–7 very dry months from autumn through spring. Several months are so dry that even morning dew is uncommon. Cultivated plants should be kept moist while actively growing, but water should be gradually reduced after growths mature in autumn.

FERTILIZER: ¼–½ recommended strength, applied weekly. A high-nitrogen fertilizer is beneficial from spring to midsummer, but a fertilizer high in phosphates should be used in late summer and autumn.

REST PERIOD: Winter days average 63–67°F (17–19°C), and nights average 48–51°F (9–11°C), with a diurnal range of 15–16°F (8–9°C). Water should be reduced for cultivated plants in winter. They should be allowed to dry out between waterings but should not remain dry for more than a few weeks. An occasional early morning misting on bright, sunny days may help keep plants from becoming too dry. Fertilizer should be reduced or eliminated while water is reduced. In the habitat, winter is the brightest season, so light for cultivated plants should be as high as possible, short of burning the foliage.

GROWING MEDIA: Mounting plants on tree-fern or cork slabs accommodates their pendulous growth habit. However, humidity must be high and plants must be watered at least once a day in summer. If plants cannot be mounted, hanging baskets, filled with an open, fast-draining medium, are recommended. Repotting may be done anytime new roots are actively growing.

MISCELLANEOUS NOTES: The bloom season shown in the climate table is based on cultivation reports. Plants grow but flower poorly in the warm, uniform climate in Singapore.

Plant and Flower Information

PLANT SIZE AND TYPE: A 6–12 in. (15–30 cm) sympodial epiphyte.

PSEUDOBULB: 6–12 in. (15–30 cm) long, rarely to 30 in. (76 cm). The clustered pseudobulbs are whitish with purple stripes. The curved, pendent stems are ridged.

LEAVES: 6 per growth. The oblong-lanceolate leaves are leathery, 2–4 in. (5–10 cm) long, uneven along the margin, and deciduous.

INFLORESCENCE: 0.5 in. (1.3 cm) long. Inflorescences emerge opposite the leaves from each node of both leafy and leafless stems.

FLOWERS: 1 per inflorescence, rarely more. The flowers are 1.2–2.0 in. (3–5 cm) across. Sepals and petals may be flat-white to creamy white, often with yellow at the tips. The almost round lip is pale yellow with scarlet stripes and a white margin. It is pubescent, undulate, and fringed on the edge. The fragrant blossoms last 6 weeks.

HYBRIDIZING NOTES: Chromosome count is $2n = 38+1f$ (ref. 504) as *D. cretaceum* (ref. 580).

REFERENCES: 38, 157, 179, 190, 200, 202, 216, 254, 266, 317, 430, 447, 454, 504, 541, 570, 580.

PHOTOS/DRAWINGS: *430*.

Dendrobium criniferum Lindley.

Now considered as synonym of *Flickingeria comata* (Blume) A. Hawkes. REFERENCES: 67, 75, 105, 200, 211, 213, 216, 220, 230, 254, 270, 271, 286, 317, 395, 445, 454, 469, 493.

Dendrobium crispatum (Forster) Swartz not Seem.

AKA: *Epidendrum crispatum* Forster. Specimens collected as *D. crispatum* in New Guinea were later identified as *D. polycladium* Rchb. f. and *D. sylvanum* Rchb. f.

ORIGIN/HABITAT: The Society Islands. On Tahiti, plants grow on the south slopes of Mr. Orohena at 3950 ft. (1200 m) and on Mt. Aorai at 3580 ft. (1090 m). In some references, distribution includes the Fiji Islands, but Kores (ref. 466) did not include it. Schlechter (ref. 432) indicated *D. crispatum* occurs in New Caledonia, but Hallé (ref. 173) disagreed, stating that the plant had been incorrectly identified.

CLIMATE: Station #91938, Tahiti, Society Islands, Lat. 17.5°S, Long. 149.6°W, at 7 ft. (2 m). Temperatures are calculated for an elevation of 3750 ft. (1140 m), resulting in probable extremes of 81°F (27°C) and 49°F (9°C).

N/HEMISPHERE	JAN	FEB	MAR	APR	MAY	JUN	JUL	AUG	SEP	OCT	NOV	DEC
°F AVG MAX	74	74	74	75	76	76	77	77	77	77	75	74
°F AVG MIN	56	56	57	58	59	60	60	60	60	60	58	57
DIURNAL RANGE	18	18	17	17	17	16	17	17	17	17	17	17
RAIN/INCHES	2.6	1.9	2.3	3.4	6.5	11.9	13.2	11.5	6.5	6.8	4.9	3.2
HUMIDITY/%	80	81	79	78	79	80	80	80	81	82	81	82
BLOOM SEASON			*	*							*	
DAYS CLR @ 2PM	13	11	9	8	2	3	4	3	4	6	8	11
RAIN/MM	66	48	58	86	165	302	335	292	165	173	124	81
°C AVG MAX	23.1	23.1	23.1	23.7	24.2	24.2	24.8	24.8	24.8	24.8	23.7	23.1
°C AVG MIN	13.1	13.1	13.7	14.2	14.8	15.4	15.4	15.4	15.4	15.4	14.2	13.7
DIURNAL RANGE	10.0	10.0	9.4	9.5	9.4	8.8	9.4	9.4	9.4	9.4	9.5	9.4
S/HEMISPHERE	JUL	AUG	SEP	OCT	NOV	DEC	JAN	FEB	MAR	APR	MAY	JUN

Cultural Recommendations

LIGHT: 2000–3000 fc.

TEMPERATURES: Throughout the year, days average 74–77°F (23–25°C), and nights average 56–60°F (13–15°C), with a diurnal range of 16–18°F (9–10°C).

HUMIDITY: Near 80% year-round.

WATER: Rainfall is heavy from spring into autumn, with a 2–3 month semi-dry period in winter. Cultivated plants should be kept evenly moist while actively growing, but water should be gradually reduced in autumn.

FERTILIZER: ¼–½ recommended strength. A balanced fertilizer should be applied weekly to biweekly throughout the year.

REST PERIOD: Growing conditions should be maintained all year. In the habitat, rainfall is less in winter, but additional moisture is available from frequent heavy dew. Water should be reduced for cultivated plants in winter. They should dry out slightly between waterings but should not remain dry for long periods. Fertilizer should be reduced or eliminated anytime water is reduced. In the habitat, light is highest in winter.

GROWING MEDIA: The creeping, pendulous growth habit suggests that plants are more easily managed when mounted on tree-fern or cork slabs, providing humidity is high and plants are watered at least once daily in summer. If plants must be potted, any open, fast-draining medium may be used. Repotting is best done in early spring when new roots are growing.

MISCELLANEOUS NOTES: The bloom season shown in the climate table is based on collection reports.

Plant and Flower Information

PLANT SIZE AND TYPE: A creeping, 47–59 in. (120–150 cm) sympodial epiphyte.

PSEUDOBULB: 47–59 in. (120–150 cm) long. The slender, pendulous stems emerge from an elongated, often branched, angled rhizome. Also, numerous lateral branches are produced along the stems.

LEAVES: 1 at the apex of each growth. The fleshy, elongated leaves are slender, terete, and pointed. They are 4–6 in. (10–15 cm) long. The leaves are quickly deciduous.

INFLORESCENCE: 1.2–2.8 in. (3–7 cm) long. Inflorescences emerge laterally from the side of the stem.

FLOWERS: 2–5 per inflorescence. The fragrant flowers are 0.7 in. (1.8 cm) across and may be either open or rather closed. White or yellow while open, the flowers close after 1 day and become rosy-purple. The lip is ruffled and crisped.

REFERENCES: 52, 216, 224, 254, 277, 353, 432.

Dendrobium crispatum Seem. not (Forster) Swartz. See *D. vagans* Schlechter 1911 not 1923. REFERENCES: 252, 434, 466.

Dendrobium crispilinguum Cribb

ORIGIN/HABITAT: Papua New Guinea, including the Western Highlands, Chimbu, Eastern Highlands, Enga, and Morobe Provinces. Plants commonly grow in mountain rainforests at 3600–5250 ft. (1100–1600 m), but in Enga Province, they are found as high as 5900 ft. (1800 m).

CLIMATE: Station #94010, Goroka, Papua New Guinea, Lat. 6.1°S, Long. 145.4°E, at 5141 ft. (1567 m). Temperatures are calculated for an elevation of 4600 ft. (1400 m), resulting in probable extremes of 89°F (32°C) and 45°F (7°C).

N/HEMISPHERE	JAN	FEB	MAR	APR	MAY	JUN	JUL	AUG	SEP	OCT	NOV	DEC
°F AVG MAX	78	79	80	81	81	80	81	80	80	80	81	79
°F AVG MIN	58	59	59	59	60	61	61	61	62	61	61	59
DIURNAL RANGE	20	20	21	22	21	19	20	19	18	19	20	20
RAIN/INCHES	2.1	2.8	4.6	5.9	6.6	9.3	9.1	10.1	10.7	8.3	4.6	2.0
HUMIDITY/%	70	67	67	67	71	72	73	74	71	70	70
BLOOM SEASON								*	*	*	*	
DAYS CLR	N/A
RAIN/MM	53	71	117	150	168	236	231	257	272	211	117	51
°C AVG MAX	25.4	26.0	26.5	27.1	27.1	26.5	27.1	26.5	26.5	26.5	27.1	26.0
°C AVG MIN	14.3	14.9	14.9	14.9	15.4	16.0	16.0	16.0	16.5	16.0	16.0	14.9
DIURNAL RANGE	11.1	11.1	11.6	12.2	11.7	10.5	11.1	10.5	10.0	10.5	11.1	11.1
S/HEMISPHERE	JUL	AUG	SEP	OCT	NOV	DEC	JAN	FEB	MAR	APR	MAY	JUN

Cultural Recommendations

LIGHT: 2500–3000 fc.

TEMPERATURES: Throughout the year, days average 78–81°F (25–27°C), and nights average 58–62°F (14–17°C), with a diurnal range of 18–22°F (10–12°C).

HUMIDITY: 70–75% from summer into autumn, dropping to 65–70% in winter and spring. Plants require excellent air movement.

WATER: Rainfall is moderate to heavy most of the year, with slightly drier conditions for 3 months in winter. Cultivated plants should be kept moist but not soggy. Occasional early morning mistings may be beneficial, especially on bright, sunny days.

FERTILIZER: ¼–½ recommended strength. A balanced fertilizer should be applied weekly to biweekly throughout the year.

REST PERIOD: Growing temperatures should be maintained all year. In the habitat, rainfall is lowest in winter, but dew and mist from fog and low clouds are common. Water and fertilizer should be reduced somewhat for cultivated plants, especially those grown in the dark, short-day conditions common during temperate-latitude winters. Plants should be kept on the dry side, but they should never be allowed to dry out completely. In the habitat, light is higher in winter.

GROWING MEDIA: Plants may be mounted on tree-fern or cork slabs if humidity is high and plants are watered at least once daily in summer. When plants are potted, any open, fast-draining medium may be used. Repotting is best done in early spring when new roots are growing.

MISCELLANEOUS NOTES: The bloom season shown in the climate table is based on reports from the habitat. Plants may rarely bloom in spring. Growers indicate that excellent air circulation around the roots is critically important to a healthy plant.

Plant and Flower Information

PLANT SIZE AND TYPE: An erect, 35–79 in. (90–200 cm) sympodial epiphyte.

PSEUDOBULB: 35 in. (90 cm) long, rarely to 79 in. (200 cm). The slender, canelike pseudobulbs are swollen at the base. They turn orange when dry.

LEAVES: 8–10 at the apex of each growth. The leaves are 3–5 in. (8–13 cm) long, ovate-lanceolate, leathery, and suberect.

INFLORESCENCE: 16 in. (41 cm) long. Numerous suberect or spreading inflorescences emerge through the leaf bases at the upper leaf nodes.

FLOWERS: 18–20 per inflorescence. The slender flowers are 1.6 in. (4 cm) across. Sepals and petals are cream, yellowish, or greenish white. The linear petals are twisted 1–3 times. The lip is white or greenish and heavily suffused with lilac or purple. The lip midlobe is wavy and ruffled along the margin with 5 ridges on the callus. The 3-lobed lip is not recurved.

HYBRIDIZING NOTES: Chromosome count is 2n = 38 (ref. 152, 243). As a parent, *D. crispilinguum* imparts color, a high degree of cold tolerance, and attractive, erect flowers. Plants are known to hybridize with *D. lineale* Rolfe and *D. tangerinum* Cribb.

REFERENCES: 80, 84, 95, 152, 179, 196, 233, 243, 345, 379, 526, 551, 554.

PHOTOS/DRAWINGS: *80, 84,* 345.

Dendrobium crispilobum J. J. Smith. See *D. pruinosum* Teijsm. and Binn. REFERENCES: 221, 470.

Dendrobium crispulum Kimura and Migo. See *D. moniliforme* (Linn.) Swartz. REFERENCES: 208, 226, 528, 547.

Dendrobium crispum Dalzell. See *D. microbulbon* A. Richard. REFERENCES: 216, 254, 369, 424.

Dendrobium critae-rubrae Guillaumin. See *D. austrocaledonicum* Schlechter. REFERENCES: 229, 270, 271.

Dendrobium crocatum Hooker f.

AKA: *D. pyropum* Ridley.

ORIGIN/HABITAT: Malaya and the southern peninsula of Thailand. Plants are widely distributed in the lowlands especially along rivers.

CLIMATE: Station #48625, Ipoh, Malaya, Lat. 4.6°N, Long. 101.1°E, at 123 ft. (37 m). Record extreme temperatures are 99°F (37°C) and 64°F (18°C).

N/HEMISPHERE	JAN	FEB	MAR	APR	MAY	JUN	JUL	AUG	SEP	OCT	NOV	DEC
°F AVG MAX	90	92	93	92	92	92	91	91	90	89	89	89
°F AVG MIN	72	72	73	73	74	73	72	72	73	72	72	72
DIURNAL RANGE	18	20	20	19	18	19	19	19	17	17	17	17
RAIN/INCHES	7.9	3.1	7.6	8.4	6.2	3.6	7.2	6.9	8.8	11.0	13.0	8.9
HUMIDITY/%	76	74	76	78	78	75	76	77	79	82	82	81
BLOOM SEASON									*			
DAYS CLR @ 7AM	3	3	3	1	1	2	1	1	0	0	1	2
DAYS CLR @ 1PM	2	2	2	1	1	1	1	1	0	0	0	2
RAIN/MM	201	79	193	213	157	91	183	175	224	279	330	226
°C AVG MAX	32.2	33.3	33.9	33.3	33.3	33.3	32.8	32.8	32.2	31.7	31.7	31.7
°C AVG MIN	22.2	22.2	22.8	22.8	23.3	22.8	22.2	22.2	22.8	22.2	22.2	22.2
DIURNAL RANGE	10.0	11.1	11.1	10.5	10.0	10.5	10.6	10.6	9.4	9.5	9.5	9.5
S/HEMISPHERE	JUL	AUG	SEP	OCT	NOV	DEC	JAN	FEB	MAR	APR	MAY	JUN

Cultural Recommendations

LIGHT: 1500–3000 fc.

TEMPERATURES: Throughout the year, days average 89–93°F (32–34°C), and nights average 72–74°F (22–23°C), with a diurnal range of 17–20°F (9–11°C). Highs fluctuate only 4°F (2°C) through the year, and lows vary only 2°F (1°C).

HUMIDITY: 75–80% year-round.

WATER: Rainfall is heavy most of the year. The heaviest rainfall occurs in autumn with a secondary maximum in spring. Brief semidry periods occur in midwinter and midsummer. Cultivated plants should be kept evenly moist with only slight drying allowed between waterings.

FERTILIZER: ¼–½ recommended strength. A balanced fertilizer should be applied weekly to biweekly throughout the year.

REST PERIOD: Growing conditions should be maintained year-round. Water should be reduced somewhat in winter for plants cultivated in the dark, short-day conditions common in temperate latitudes. They should never be allowed to dry out completely, however. Fertilizer may be reduced when the plant is not actively growing or when water is reduced. In the habitat, light is slightly higher in winter.

GROWING MEDIA: Mounting plants on tree-fern or cork slabs accommodates their pendent growth habit, but humidity must be high and the plants must be watered at least once daily in summer. When plants are potted, any open, fast-draining medium may be used. Repotting may be done anytime new roots are growing.

MISCELLANEOUS NOTES: The bloom season shown in the climate table is based on reports from the habitat.

Plant and Flower Information

PLANT SIZE AND TYPE: A 6–35 in. (15–90 cm) sympodial epiphyte.

PSEUDOBULB: 6–35 in. (15–90 cm) long. The pendent stems are narrowed at the base.

LEAVES: Many per growth. The leaves are 3–4 in. (8–10 cm) long, bright green, and lanceolate. They are spaced 1 in. (2.5 cm) apart.

INFLORESCENCE: 0.5 in. (1.3 cm). Racemes emerge laterally on leafless stems.

FLOWERS: 2–3 per inflorescence. The bright orange flowers are 1.6–2.0 in. (4–5 cm) long. The base of the lip is decorated with red specks on both sides of the ruffled, finely-toothed margin.

REFERENCES: 200, 202, 203, 218, 254, 395, 402, 445, 454, 455.

PHOTOS/DRAWINGS: 203, 454, 455.

Dendrobium croceocentrum J. J. Smith

ORIGIN/HABITAT: Western Sumatra. Plants were originally found on trees growing on the crater walls of Lake Manindjau, just west of Bukittinggi, at 1950–2600 ft. (600–800 m).

CLIMATE: Station #96163, Padang, Sumatra, Indonesia, Lat. 0.9°S, Long. 100.4°E, at 19 ft. (6 m). Temperatures are calculated for an elevation of 2500 ft. (760 m), resulting in probable extremes of 86°F (30°C) and 60°F (16°C).

N/HEMISPHERE	JAN	FEB	MAR	APR	MAY	JUN	JUL	AUG	SEP	OCT	NOV	DEC
°F AVG MAX	79	79	78	78	78	78	79	79	79	79	80	79
°F AVG MIN	66	66	66	66	66	66	66	66	66	67	67	66
DIURNAL RANGE	13	13	12	12	12	12	13	13	13	12	13	13
RAIN/INCHES	10.9	13.7	6.0	19.5	20.4	18.9	13.8	10.2	12.1	14.3	12.4	12.1
HUMIDITY/%	81	82	82	84	85	84	81	81	82	83	81	81
BLOOM SEASON	N/A											
DAYS CLR @ 7AM	5	1	1	0	0	2	2	1	2	2	3	5
DAYS CLR @ 1PM	5	2	2	1	1	3	3	4	3	3	6	5
RAIN/MM	277	348	152	495	518	480	351	259	307	363	315	307
°C AVG MAX	26.0	26.0	25.5	25.5	25.5	25.5	26.0	26.0	26.0	26.0	26.6	26.0
°C AVG MIN	18.8	18.8	18.8	18.8	18.8	18.8	18.8	18.8	18.8	19.3	19.3	18.8
DIURNAL RANGE	7.2	7.2	6.7	6.7	6.7	6.7	7.2	7.2	7.2	6.7	7.3	7.2
S/HEMISPHERE	JUL	AUG	SEP	OCT	NOV	DEC	JAN	FEB	MAR	APR	MAY	JUN

Cultural Recommendations

LIGHT: 2000–2500 fc.

TEMPERATURES: Throughout the year, days average 78–80°F (26–27°C), and nights average 66–67°F (19°C), with a diurnal range of 12–13°F (7°C). Probable extremes vary only a few degrees from the averages indicating that plants probably cannot tolerate wide temperature fluctuations.

HUMIDITY: 80–85% year-round.

WATER: Rainfall is heavy all year. Cultivated plants should be constantly moist but not soggy.

FERTILIZER: ¼–½ recommended strength. A balanced fertilizer should be applied weekly to biweekly throughout the year.

REST PERIOD: Growing conditions should be maintained year-round. Water may be reduced somewhat for cultivated plants in winter, especially those grown in the dark, short-day conditions common in temperate latitudes; but they should never be allowed to dry out completely.

GROWING MEDIA: Mounting plants on tree-fern or cork slabs accommodates their pendulous growth habit. However, humidity must be high and plants must be watered at least once a day in summer. If plants cannot be mounted, hanging baskets, filled with an open, fast-draining medium, are recommended. Repotting may be done anytime new roots are actively growing.

MISCELLANEOUS NOTES: The plant was described in 1917 in *Bul. Jard. Bot. Buit.* 3rd sér. 2:75.

Plant and Flower Information

PLANT SIZE AND TYPE: A 21 in. (53 cm) sympodial epiphyte.

PSEUDOBULB: 21 in. (53 cm) long. The stems are clustered, pendulous, and taper at each end. They are pale green when young, developing dirty purple stripes that darken with age.

LEAVES: Many. The lanceolate-linear leaves are 2.8–4.0 in. (7–10 cm) long. They are smallest near the apex. The foliage, which is normally dark green, is often flushed with purple when young. The leaf sheaths may be pale green or yellow-green with a violet suffusion.

INFLORESCENCE: Short. The pale green and purple inflorescences emerge from nodes on leafless stems.

FLOWERS: 1 per inflorescence. The flowers are 1.0 in. (2.5 cm) across. They are white with a purplish suffusion. The margin of the ovate sepals is uneven at the apex. The very wavy petals have an uneven margin. The lip is simple with 2 longitudinal lines.

REFERENCES: 222.

Dendrobium crucilabre J. J. Smith

ORIGIN/HABITAT: Central east Borneo. Plants are found on Mt. Kemoel in West Koetai (Kalimantan). They grow on trees in primeval forests on mountain ridges at about 3950 ft. (1200 m).

CLIMATE: Station #96633, Balikpapan, Borneo, Indonesia, Lat. 1.3°S, Long. 116.9°E, at 10 ft. (3 m). Temperatures are calculated for an elevation of 3950 ft. (1200 m), resulting in probable extremes of 79°F (26°C) and 47°F (8°C).

N/HEMISPHERE	JAN	FEB	MAR	APR	MAY	JUN	JUL	AUG	SEP	OCT	NOV	DEC
°F AVG MAX	70	71	71	72	72	72	72	73	73	72	72	71
°F AVG MIN	60	61	61	61	60	60	60	60	60	60	61	61
DIURNAL RANGE	10	10	10	11	12	12	12	13	13	12	11	10
RAIN/INCHES	7.1	6.4	5.5	5.2	6.6	8.1	7.9	8.9	9.1	8.2	9.1	7.6
HUMIDITY/%	82	80	77	78	80	79	82	81	81	82	83	82
BLOOM SEASON			*			*						
DAYS CLR @ 8AM	4	2	3	3	3	3	2	3	3	4	2	5
DAYS CLR @ 2PM	6	4	5	5	3	1	2	1	2	3	4	5
RAIN/MM	180	163	140	132	168	206	201	226	231	208	231	193
°C AVG MAX	21.1	21.7	21.7	22.2	22.2	22.2	22.2	22.8	22.8	22.2	22.2	21.7
°C AVG MIN	15.6	16.1	16.1	16.1	15.6	15.6	15.6	15.6	15.6	15.6	16.1	16.1
DIURNAL RANGE	5.5	5.6	5.6	6.1	6.6	6.6	6.6	7.2	7.2	6.6	6.1	5.6
S/HEMISPHERE	JUL	AUG	SEP	OCT	NOV	DEC	JAN	FEB	MAR	APR	MAY	JUN

Cultural Recommendations

LIGHT: 1800–2500 fc.

TEMPERATURES: Throughout the year, days average 70–73°F (21–23°C), and nights average 60–61°F (16°C), with a diurnal range of 10–13°F (6–7°C). Seasonal temperature variations are minor, suggesting that plants may not tolerate wide temperature fluctuations.

HUMIDITY: Near 80% year-round.

WATER: Rainfall is heavy all year, but conditions are slightly drier for 2 months in late winter or early spring. Cultivated plants should be kept moist with only slight drying allowed between waterings.

FERTILIZER: ¼–½ recommended strength. A balanced fertilizer should be applied weekly to biweekly throughout the year.

REST PERIOD: Growing temperatures should be maintained year-round. Water should be reduced somewhat in winter, especially for plants cultivated in the dark, short-day conditions common in temperate latitudes; but they should never be allowed to dry out completely. Fertilizer should be reduced or eliminated if water is reduced. In the habitat, seasonal light variation is minor.

GROWING MEDIA: Plants may be mounted on tree-fern or cork slabs if humidity is high and plants are watered at least once daily in summer. When plants are potted, any open, fast-draining medium may be used. Repotting may be done anytime new roots are growing.

MISCELLANEOUS NOTES: The bloom season shown in the climate table is based on reports from the habitat. The plant was described in 1931 in *Bul. Jard. Bot. Buit.* 3rd sér. 7:55.

Plant and Flower Information

PLANT SIZE AND TYPE: An 18 in. (45 cm) sympodial epiphyte.

PSEUDOBULB: 18 in. (45 cm) long. The flattened, snaky stems are slender above the base. They turn yellow when dry.

LEAVES: Many. The erect, lanceolate leaves, which are 1.6–1.8 in. (4.0–4.5 cm) long, are equally spaced along the stem.

INFLORESCENCE: Short. Inflorescences emerge from nodes along the lower part of leafy stems.

FLOWERS: Several per inflorescence. Blossoms open in succession. The flowers are 0.3 in. (0.7 cm) long. Sepals and petals are white with longitudinal purple markings. The yellowish, 3-lobed lip is covered with minute warts. The triangular sidelobes are fringed. The small midlobe is incurved along the side margin.

REFERENCES: 224, 286, 445.

Dendrobium cruentum Rchb. f.

ORIGIN/HABITAT: Thailand. Plants grow along the west coast of peninsular Thailand as far south as Setul. They are usually found on small trees in open forests at low elevations.

CLIMATE: Station #48564, Phuket, Thailand, Lat. 8.0°N, Long. 98.4°E, at 100 ft. (30 m). Temperatures are calculated for an elevation of 1500 ft. (460 m), resulting in probable extremes of 95°F (35°C) and 57°F (14°C).

N/HEMISPHERE	JAN	FEB	MAR	APR	MAY	JUN	JUL	AUG	SEP	OCT	NOV	DEC
°F AVG MAX	83	85	86	86	84	84	82	82	81	82	82	82
°F AVG MIN	70	70	70	72	71	71	71	71	70	70	70	70
DIURNAL RANGE	13	15	16	14	13	13	11	11	11	12	12	12
RAIN/INCHES	1.4	1.2	2.6	5.9	11.0	11.8	11.1	10.9	12.9	14.3	8.1	2.7
HUMIDITY/%	73	72	73	78	82	81	81	81	83	83	81	77
BLOOM SEASON			*	*	*	*	*	*				
DAYS CLR @ 7AM	13	10	10	3	1	2	4	2	2	3	6	12
DAYS CLR @ 1PM	13	13	14	3	1	3	3	1	2	1	6	10
RAIN/MM	36	30	66	150	279	300	282	277	328	363	206	69
°C AVG MAX	28.5	29.7	30.2	30.2	29.1	29.1	28.0	28.0	27.4	28.0	28.0	28.0
°C AVG MIN	21.3	21.3	21.3	22.4	21.9	21.9	21.9	21.9	21.3	21.3	21.3	21.3
DIURNAL RANGE	7.2	8.4	8.9	7.8	7.2	7.2	6.1	6.1	6.1	6.7	6.7	6.7
S/HEMISPHERE	JUL	AUG	SEP	OCT	NOV	DEC	JAN	FEB	MAR	APR	MAY	JUN

Dendrobium crumenatum

Cultural Recommendations

LIGHT: 2500–3500 fc.

TEMPERATURES: Throughout the year, days average 81–86°F (27–30°C), and nights average 70–72°F (21–22°C), with a diurnal range of 11–16°F (6–9°C). Temperatures are warmest and the diurnal range is greatest in spring.

HUMIDITY: 80–85% most of the year, dropping to 70–75% in winter.

WATER: Rainfall is heavy from spring through early autumn. Conditions are drier in winter. Cultivated plants should be kept evenly moist from spring to autumn, but water should be reduced in late autumn.

FERTILIZER: 1/4–1/2 recommended strength, applied weekly. A high-nitrogen fertilizer is beneficial from spring to midsummer, but a fertilizer high in phosphates should be used in late summer and autumn.

REST PERIOD: Growing temperatures should be maintained all year. However, growers report that plants tolerate winter minimum temperatures of 59°F (15°C). In the habitat, rainfall is reduced for 3–4 months in winter, and humidity is so low that even moisture from morning dew is uncommon. Cultivated plants should be allowed to dry out between waterings, but they should not remain dry for extended periods. Fertilizer should be reduced or eliminated anytime water is reduced. In the habitat, light is much higher in winter, and light should be as high as possible for cultivated plants, short of burning the foliage.

GROWING MEDIA: Plants may be mounted on tree-fern or cork slabs if humidity is high and plants are watered at least once daily in summer. When plants are potted, any open, fast-draining medium may be used. Repotting is best done in early spring when new roots are growing.

MISCELLANEOUS NOTES: The bloom season shown in the climate table is based on cultivation records. Growers report that *D. cruentum* grows well and blooms almost continuously in Bangkok, where temperatures are several degrees warmer than indicated in the climate data.

Plant and Flower Information

PLANT SIZE AND TYPE: A 12–14 in. (30–35 cm) sympodial epiphyte.

PSEUDOBULB: 10–12 in. (25–30 cm) long. The erect pseudobulbs are swollen at the base. Leaf sheaths are covered with small black hairs.

LEAVES: Many. The deciduous leaves are elliptic-oblong, leathery, and hairy on the backside. They are 2–5 in. (5–13 cm) long. Leaves are spaced all along the stem.

INFLORESCENCE: Short. Inflorescences emerge opposite the leaves from the upper nodes of mature stems.

FLOWERS: 1–3 per inflorescence. The flowers are 1.6–2.4 in. (4–6 cm) across and faintly fragrant. The heavily textured blossoms last a month or more. Sepals and narrow petals are pale green with deeper green longitudinal veins. The lip may be white or yellowish green. The sidelobes and margins are marked with red and the large center crest has 3 red ridges. Smaller flowered plants reportedly originate in Borneo. The column is green with red along the edges.

HYBRIDIZING NOTES: Chromosome counts are 2n = 38 (ref. 580), 2n = 38+1B (ref. 150), and 2n = 40 (ref. 504).

REFERENCES: 150, 157, 179, 190, 196, 200, 202, 216, 245, 254, 371, 389, 395, 402, 429, 430, 445, 454, 504, 510, 541, 570, 580, 581.

PHOTOS/DRAWINGS: *245, 350, 371, 389, 430, 454, 581.*

Dendrobium crumenatum Swartz

AKA: Seidenfaden (ref. 454) includes *Onychium crumenatum* Blume, *Dendrobium caninum* Merrill, *D. kwashotense* Hayata, *D. schmidtianum* Kränzlin, and *D. cumulatum* as used by Kränzlin not Lindley as synonyms. He also includes *D. ceraia* Lindley and *D. simplicissimum* (Loureiro) Kränzlin as possible synonyms.

ORIGIN/HABITAT: Widely distributed. The habitat extends from India and Sri Lanka (Ceylon) eastward into China to as far north as Taiwan. Distribution includes Indochina, peninsular Thailand, Malaya, Indonesia, New Guinea, Borneo, and the Philippine Islands. *D. crumenatum* normally grows on trees and the tops of tree branches in moderately exposed, semishaded locations near wet, lowland areas, sometimes immediately along the seashore. However, Schlechter (ref. 435) reported collecting plants at about 2600 ft. (800 m) near Padang-Pandjang, Sumatra; and in Borneo they are found in Sabah in hill forests at 2300–2950 ft. (700–900 m). In Malaya, plants are common on orchard and roadside trees all over the peninsula. It is common and widespread in the Philippines, where it grows from sea level to about 1650 ft. (500 m), usually on coconut or other palms. Plants have been reported in Sulawesi and Ambon, with collections recorded as far east as Bougainville Island. Kores (ref. 466) reports that *D. crumenatum* was introduced into Fiji as an ornamental and has been naturalized in coastal areas near Suva.

CLIMATE: Station #48551, Surat (Ban Don), Thailand, Lat. 9.1°N, Long. 99.3°E, at 10 ft. (3 m). Temperatures are calculated for an elevation of 800 ft. (240 m), resulting in probable extremes of 102°F (39°C) and 44°F (7°C).

N/HEMISPHERE	JAN	FEB	MAR	APR	MAY	JUN	JUL	AUG	SEP	OCT	NOV	DEC
°F AVG MAX	85	89	92	92	90	88	87	88	87	86	84	83
°F AVG MIN	66	66	67	70	71	71	71	71	70	70	69	68
DIURNAL RANGE	19	23	25	22	19	17	16	17	17	16	15	15
RAIN/INCHES	1.0	0.3	0.4	2.5	6.6	4.5	6.9	5.8	7.1	8.1	12.1	4.0
HUMIDITY/%	82	78	75	79	83	82	82	82	84	87	87	86
BLOOM SEASON			*	*	*	*	*	*	*	*		
DAYS CLR @ 7AM	4	3	3	2	1	1	1	1	1	1	1	2
DAYS CLR @ 1PM	2	2	2	1	1	0	0	0	0	0	1	1
RAIN/MM	25	8	10	64	168	114	175	147	180	206	307	102
°C AVG MAX	29.6	31.8	33.5	33.5	32.4	31.3	30.7	31.3	30.7	30.2	29.1	28.5
°C AVG MIN	19.1	19.1	19.6	21.3	21.8	21.8	21.8	21.8	21.3	21.3	20.7	20.2
DIURNAL RANGE	10.5	12.7	13.9	12.2	10.6	9.5	8.9	9.5	9.4	8.9	8.4	8.3
S/HEMISPHERE	JUL	AUG	SEP	OCT	NOV	DEC	JAN	FEB	MAR	APR	MAY	JUN

Cultural Recommendations

LIGHT: 3500–4500 fc.

TEMPERATURES: Throughout the year, days average 85–92°F (30–34°C), and nights average 66–71°F (19–22°C), with a diurnal range of 15–25°F (8–14°C). The warmest season is early spring.

HUMIDITY: 80–85% most of the year, dropping to 75–80% for 3 months in winter.

WATER: Rainfall is moderate to heavy from late spring through autumn. Conditions are drier in winter. Cultivated plants should be kept moist from late spring into autumn, with only slight drying allowed between waterings. Water should be gradually reduced in late autumn.

FERTILIZER: 1/4–1/2 recommended strength. A balanced fertilizer should be applied weekly to biweekly throughout the year.

REST PERIOD: Growing temperatures should be maintained year-round. Because of the wide distribution and large range in habitat elevation, however, plants should easily adapt to winter minimum temperatures 8–10°F (4–6°C) cooler than indicated in the climate data. Growers report that plants tolerate winter minimum temperatures of 59°F (15°C). Winter rainfall is low for 2–3 months, but additional moisture is available from frequent heavy dew. Water and fertilizer should be reduced and the plants allowed to dry somewhat between waterings. They should not remain dry for long periods, however. In the habitat, light is slightly higher in winter.

GROWING MEDIA: Plants may be mounted on tree-fern or cork slabs if humidity is high and plants are watered at least once daily in summer.

When plants are potted, any open, fast-draining medium may be used. New vegetative growth begins when the rains resume after the dry period, and new roots begin emerging after the new growths are partially mature. Repotting is best done as soon as possible after new roots begin to grow.

MISCELLANEOUS NOTES: The bloom season shown in the climate table is based on cultivation records. Plants bloom about once a month during warm dry weather when evaporation from a sudden rain shower (or greenhouse sprinkling) causes a 10°F (6°C) temperature drop. Buds develop to a specific stage and wait for the temperatures to suddenly drop, after which the flowers open in about 9 days. The boiled stems are used for earaches.

Plant and Flower Information

PLANT SIZE AND TYPE: A variable, sympodial epiphyte or lithophyte. Plants from Sri Lanka (Ceylon) may be as small as 2–3 in. (5–8 cm), but plants from other regions are frequently 24–36 in. (60–92 cm) long and may reach a length of 60 in. (152 cm).

PSEUDOBULB: Variable. The whiplike pseudobulbs often branch. They are spindle shaped, swollen for a few nodes above the base, ridged, and yellow when mature.

LEAVES: 4–10 or more per growth. The leaves are 2–3 in. (5–8 cm) long, thick and leathery, and 2-ranked on the middle of the stem. They are eventually deciduous.

INFLORESCENCE: Short. Inflorescences emerge from several upper nodes on leafless stems.

FLOWERS: 1–5 per inflorescence, many per plant. The number of blossoms is partially dependent on how long since the last blooming. The flowers, which are short-lived, may be only slightly fragrant or fill the air with fragrance. They are normally 1–2 in. (2.5–5.0 cm) long, but size is extremely variable. The white blossoms glisten in the light and may have a bluish or pinkish tinge. The lip is decorated with 5 bright yellow keels.

HYBRIDIZING NOTES: Chromosome counts are 2n = 38 (ref. 151, 152, 154, 187, 188, 243, 504, 580), 2n = 38+1B (ref. 542), 2n = 38±1f (ref. 187, 504, 580), 2n = 38+0−2B (ref. 154), 2n = 40 (ref. 280, 504, 580). As *D. kwashotense*, the count is 2n = 38 (ref. 504, 580). Johansen (ref. 239) indicates that plants are self-sterile and that flowers dropped 4–7 days after self-pollination.

REFERENCES: 12, 25, 61, 67, 75, 97, 98, 111, 148, 151, 152, 154, 157, 179, 187, 188, 190, 193, 200, 202, 208, 210, 216, 239, 243, 254, 266, 274, 279, 280, 286, 296, 297, 310, 317, 369, 371, 373, 389, 394, 395, 402, 430, 435, 436, 445, 447, 448, 454, 455, 458, 466, 468, 469, 474, 497, 504, 509, 510, 516, 524, 528, 536, 542, 570, 580, 592.

PHOTOS/DRAWINGS: 75, 97, 98, 122, *148*, 210, 254, *274*, 279, *371*, *389*, *430*, 454, 455, 458, 466, 469, 497, *510*.

Dendrobium cruttwellii T. M. Reeve

AKA: *Sayeria paradoxa* Kränzlin, *Dendrobium sayeria* Schlechter 1912 not *D. sayeri* Schlechter 1907.

ORIGIN/HABITAT: Eastern Papua New Guinea. Plants usually grow low on tree trunks, seldom more than 10 ft. (3 m) above the ground, and on the small branches of shrubs. They are found in primary mountain forests as well as secondary regrowth at 4900–8050 ft. (1500–2450 m).

CLIMATE: Station #94010, Goroka, Papua New Guinea, Lat. 6.1°S, Long. 145.4°E, at 5141 ft. (1567 m). Temperatures are calculated for an elevation of 6550 ft. (2000 m), resulting in probable extremes of 82°F (28°C) and 38°F (4°C).

N/HEMISPHERE	JAN	FEB	MAR	APR	MAY	JUN	JUL	AUG	SEP	OCT	NOV	DEC
°F AVG MAX	71	72	73	74	74	73	74	73	73	73	74	72
°F AVG MIN	51	52	52	52	53	54	54	54	55	54	54	52
DIURNAL RANGE	20	20	21	22	21	19	20	19	18	19	20	20
RAIN/INCHES	2.1	2.8	4.6	5.9	6.6	9.3	9.1	10.1	10.7	8.3	4.6	2.0
HUMIDITY/%	70	67	67	67	67	71	72	73	74	71	70	70
BLOOM SEASON							*	*	*			
DAYS CLR	N/A											
RAIN/MM	53	71	117	150	168	236	231	257	272	211	117	51
°C AVG MAX	21.8	22.4	23.0	23.5	23.5	23.0	23.5	23.0	23.0	23.0	23.5	22.4
°C AVG MIN	10.7	11.3	11.3	11.3	11.8	12.4	12.4	12.4	13.0	12.4	12.4	11.3
DIURNAL RANGE	11.1	11.1	11.7	12.2	11.7	10.6	11.1	10.6	10.0	10.6	11.1	11.1
S/HEMISPHERE	JUL	AUG	SEP	OCT	NOV	DEC	JAN	FEB	MAR	APR	MAY	JUN

Cultural Recommendations

LIGHT: 2500–3000 fc.

TEMPERATURES: Throughout the year, days average 71–74°F (22–24°C), and nights average 51–55°F (11–13°C), with a diurnal range of 18–22°F (10–12°C). Plants are unlikely to tolerate continuous high temperatures, especially warm nights.

HUMIDITY: 70–75% from summer into autumn. Humidity declines to 65–70% in winter and spring. Growers indicate that other plants from this habitat require a delicate balance between air movement, moisture, and drainage.

WATER: Rainfall is moderate to heavy most of the year, but conditions are slightly drier for 3 months in winter. Cultivated plants should be kept moist. In summer, daily water may be necessary during hot, dry weather. In addition, early morning mistings may be beneficial, especially on bright, sunny days.

FERTILIZER: ¼–½ recommended strength. A balanced fertilizer should be applied weekly to biweekly throughout the year.

REST PERIOD: Growing conditions must be cool year-round. In the habitat, rainfall is lowest in winter, but dew, fog, and mist from low clouds are common. Water should be reduced for cultivated plants, especially those grown in the dark, short-day conditions common in temperate latitudes; but they should never be allowed to dry out completely. Fertilizer should be reduced or eliminated until water is increased in spring. In the habitat, seasonal light variation is minor.

GROWING MEDIA: Mounting plants on tree-fern or cork slabs accommodates their pendulous growth habit. However, humidity must be high and plants must be watered at least once a day in summer. If plants cannot be mounted, small pots or hanging baskets may be filled with an open, fast-draining medium. Repotting may be done anytime new roots are actively growing.

MISCELLANEOUS NOTES: The bloom season shown in the climate table is based on cultivation records. Plants growing in the wild bloom any time of year.

Plant and Flower Information

PLANT SIZE AND TYPE: A pendent, 3–11 in. (8–28 cm) sympodial epiphyte.

PSEUDOBULB: 0.8–5.0 in. (2–13 cm) long. The shiny pseudobulbs become red-brown when dry. They are erect.

LEAVES: 2–3 per growth. The oblong-lanceolate leaves are 2–6 in. (5–16 cm) long.

INFLORESCENCE: 8 in. (20 cm) long. The very slender inflorescences may be arching or pendent. They emerge from nodes near the apex of the pseudobulb.

FLOWERS: 2–12 per inflorescence. The pendulous flowers are 0.8–1.2 in. (2–3 cm) across and last 3–4 weeks. Blossoms may be whitish to pale green with red spots. The lip is apple green.

HYBRIDIZING NOTES: Chromosome count is 2n = 38 (ref. 152).

REFERENCES: 83, 95, 152, 179, 233, 243, 550.

Dendrobium crystallinum

PHOTOS/DRAWINGS: *83, 95*.

Dendrobium crystallinum Rchb. f.

ORIGIN/HABITAT: Widespread. The habitat extends from northeastern India across Burma and Thailand into Cambodia, Laos, and Vietnam. Plants most often grow on small trees in exposed locations at 3000–5600 ft. (910–1700 m).

CLIMATE: Station #48327, Chiang Mai, Thailand, Lat. 18.8°N, Long. 99.0°E, at 1100 ft. (335 m). Temperatures are calculated for an elevation of 4000 ft. (1219 m), resulting in probable extremes of 99°F (38°C) and 28°F (−2°C).

N/HEMISPHERE	JAN	FEB	MAR	APR	MAY	JUN	JUL	AUG	SEP	OCT	NOV	DEC
°F AVG MAX	75	80	85	86	84	80	79	77	78	79	76	74
°F AVG MIN	46	47	52	60	64	64	64	65	63	61	56	47
DIURNAL RANGE	29	33	33	26	20	16	15	12	15	18	20	27
RAIN/INCHES	0.3	0.4	0.6	2.0	5.5	6.1	7.4	8.7	11.5	4.9	1.5	0.4
HUMIDITY/%	73	65	58	62	73	78	80	83	83	81	79	76
BLOOM SEASON			*	*	**	**	*	*	*	*		
DAYS CLR @ 7AM	5	5	2	2	1	0	0	0	0	1	3	3
DAYS CLR @ 1PM	9	8	4	2	0	0	0	0	0	0	1	3
RAIN/MM	8	10	15	51	140	155	188	221	292	124	38	10
°C AVG MAX	24.1	26.9	29.7	30.2	29.1	26.9	26.4	25.2	25.8	26.4	24.7	23.6
°C AVG MIN	8.0	8.6	11.3	15.8	18.0	18.0	18.0	18.6	17.5	16.4	13.6	8.6
DIURNAL RANGE	16.1	18.3	18.4	14.4	11.1	8.9	8.4	6.6	8.3	10.0	11.1	15.0
S/HEMISPHERE	JUL	AUG	SEP	OCT	NOV	DEC	JAN	FEB	MAR	APR	MAY	JUN

Cultural Recommendations

LIGHT: 1500–2400 fc. Direct sunlight should be avoided. In the habitat, clear summer days are exceedingly rare.

TEMPERATURES: Summer days average 77–80°F (25–27°C), and nights average 64–65°F (18–19°C), with a diurnal range of 12–16°F (7–9°C). The warmest weather occurs in spring. Days average 84–86°F (29–30°C), and nights average 52–64°F (11–18°C), with a diurnal range of 20–33°F (11–18°C). Both highs and lows are more moderate after the start of the summer wet season.

HUMIDITY: 75–85% during most of the year, dropping to near 60% for 2 months in late winter and early spring.

WATER: Rainfall is heavy while plants are actively growing from spring to early autumn. During this season, cultivated plants should be kept moist with little if any drying allowed between waterings. However, water should be gradually reduced after new growths mature in autumn.

FERTILIZER: ¼–½ recommended strength, applied weekly. A high-nitrogen fertilizer is beneficial from spring to midsummer, but a fertilizer high in phosphates should be used in late summer and autumn. Some growers report good success alternating applications of fish emulsion with their regular fertilizer.

REST PERIOD: Winter days average 74–80°F (24–27°C), and nights average 46–47°F (8–9°C), with a diurnal range of 27–33°F (15–18°C). Overnight lows are below 50°F (10°C) for 3 months. Plants should be able to tolerate temperatures a few degrees below freezing for short periods, but extremes should be avoided in cultivation. During very cold weather, a plant's chance of surviving with minimal damage is better if it is dry when temperatures are low. In the habitat, rainfall averages are very low for 4–5 months in winter; but during the early part of the season, the high relative humidity indicates that additional moisture is available from frequent fog, mist, and heavy deposits of dew. Plants are healthiest if for most of the winter they are allowed to become somewhat dry between waterings but do not remain dry for extended periods. For 1–2 months in late winter, however, conditions are clear, warm, and dry with humidity so low that even the moisture from morning dew is uncommon. Plants should be allowed to dry out completely between waterings and remain dry longer during this time. Occasional early morning mistings between waterings may help keep the plants from becoming too dry. Fertilizer should be greatly reduced or eliminated until water is increased in spring. A cool, dry rest is essential for cultivated plants and should be continued until new growth starts in spring. In the habitat, light is highest in winter.

GROWING MEDIA: Mounting plants on tree-fern or cork slabs accommodates their pendent growth habit. However, humidity must be high and plants must be watered at least once daily in summer. If plants must be potted, hanging pots or baskets may be filled with any open, fast-draining medium. Repotting is best done in early spring when new roots are growing.

MISCELLANEOUS NOTES: The bloom season shown in the climate table is based on cultivation records.

Plant and Flower Information

PLANT SIZE AND TYPE: An 18 in. (45 cm) sympodial epiphyte. Plants may form large clumps.

PSEUDOBULB: 18 in. (45 cm) long. The slender pseudobulbs, which are marked with lines, do not have nodes. They may be erect or pendulous and are described as cascading.

LEAVES: 2–4 per growth. The linear-lanceolate leaves are soft-textured, 6 in. (15 cm) long, distichous, and deciduous.

INFLORESCENCE: Very short. Inflorescences emerge near the apex of the most recently matured pseudobulbs.

FLOWERS: 1–3 per inflorescence, but on well-grown, mature plants, numerous inflorescences result in many blossoms per cane and hundreds of flowers per plant. Blossoms all open at the same time. The delicately textured flowers are 1.6–2.0 in. (4–5 cm) across. They are described as distinct and beautiful. Sepals and petals are white. A magenta blotch is always present on the tips of the petals and sometimes on the tips of the sepals. The lip, which is white or yellow with a white border, is orange at the base with an amethyst or magenta blotch at the apex. The very fragrant blossoms perfume an entire greenhouse.

HYBRIDIZING NOTES: Chromosome count is 2n = 38 (ref. 153, 273, 504, 580). Johansen (ref. 239) indicates that some clones of *D. crystallinum* may be self-fertile, while others were self-sterile. He also indicated that an individual plant may be self-sterile sometimes and self-fertile at other times. When seed was produced, the capsule opened in 361 days and about 49% of the seed germinated. When crossed with *D. secundum* (Blume) Lindley, capsules formed but no seed was produced.

REFERENCES: 25, 38, 46, 153, 157, 179, 190, 196, 202, 210, 216, 235, 239, 245, 254, 266, 273, 389, 430, 445, 447, 448, 454, 504, 507, 541, 557, 570, 580.

PHOTOS/DRAWINGS: 210, *245, 350, 389, 430, 454*.

Dendrobium ctenoglossum Schlechter. See *D. strongylanthum* Rchb. f. REFERENCES: 208, 223, 454.

Dendrobium cucullatum R. Brown. See *D. aphyllum* (Roxburgh) C. Fischer. REFERENCES: 190, 211, 216, 254, 317, 430, 454.

Dendrobium cuculliferum J. J. Smith

ORIGIN/HABITAT: Irian Jaya (western New Guinea). Common in the Arfak Mountains, plants grow on trees which are rooted in decomposed granite soil at 4500–5900 ft. (1400–1800 m).

CLIMATE: Station #97530, Manokwari, Irian Jaya, Lat. 0.9°S, Long. 134.1°E, at 10 ft. (3 m). Temperatures are calculated for an elevation of 5000 ft. (1520 m), resulting in probable extremes of 77°F (25°C) and 52°F (11°C).

N/HEMISPHERE	JAN	FEB	MAR	APR	MAY	JUN	JUL	AUG	SEP	OCT	NOV	DEC
°F AVG MAX	70	69	71	71	72	70	70	70	70	70	70	69
°F AVG MIN	58	59	58	58	58	59	57	57	58	58	58	58
DIURNAL RANGE	12	10	13	13	14	11	13	13	12	12	12	11
RAIN/INCHES	5.4	5.6	5.0	4.7	4.5	10.3	12.0	9.4	13.2	11.1	7.8	7.3
HUMIDITY/%	87	87	86	84	85	86	86	85	86	86	86	85
BLOOM SEASON									*			
DAYS CLR @ 9AM	4	3	3	5	3	3	3	1	1	2	3	7
DAYS CLR @ 3PM	2	2	2	3	1	1	1	1	0	1	0	2
RAIN/MM	137	142	127	119	114	262	305	239	335	282	198	185
°C AVG MAX	20.9	20.3	21.4	21.4	22.0	20.9	20.9	20.9	20.9	20.9	20.9	20.3
°C AVG MIN	14.2	14.7	14.2	14.2	14.2	14.7	13.6	13.6	14.2	14.2	14.2	14.2
DIURNAL RANGE	6.7	5.6	7.2	7.2	7.8	6.2	7.3	7.3	6.7	6.7	6.7	6.1
S/HEMISPHERE	JUL	AUG	SEP	OCT	NOV	DEC	JAN	FEB	MAR	APR	MAY	JUN

Cultural Recommendations

LIGHT: 2000–3000 fc.

TEMPERATURES: Throughout the year, days average 69–72°F (20–22°C), and nights average 57–59°F (14–15°C), with a diurnal range of 10–14°F (6–8°C). Because of microclimate effects, actual maximum temperatures in the habitat may be as much as 10°F (6°C) warmer than indicated.

HUMIDITY: Near 85% year-round.

WATER: Rainfall is moderate to very heavy all year. Cultivated plants should be kept moist with only slight drying allowed between waterings.

FERTILIZER: ¼–½ recommended strength. A balanced fertilizer should be applied weekly to biweekly throughout the year.

REST PERIOD: Growing conditions should be maintained year-round. Water and fertilizer may be reduced somewhat in winter, especially for plants grown in the dark, short-day conditions common in temperate latitudes; but they should never be allowed to dry out completely.

GROWING MEDIA: Plants may be mounted on tree-fern or cork slabs if humidity is high and plants are watered at least once daily in summer. When plants are potted, any open, fast-draining medium may be used. Repotting may be done anytime new roots are growing.

MISCELLANEOUS NOTES: The bloom season shown in the climate table is based on reports from the habitat.

Plant and Flower Information

PLANT SIZE AND TYPE: A 35 in. (90 cm) sympodial epiphyte.

PSEUDOBULB: 35 in. (90 cm) long. The stems are flexuous near the apex. They are very branching.

LEAVES: The lanceolate leaves, which are 0.8–3.4 in. (2.1–8.6 cm) long with a long point at the apex, are minutely toothed along the margin. They are often tinged with violet.

INFLORESCENCE: Short.

FLOWERS: 3–10 per inflorescence. The flowers are 1.1 in. (2.9 cm) long. Blossoms are pink to violet-red. They have ovate dorsal sepals and obliquely triangular lateral sepals. The elliptical to oblong petals have uneven margins that appear to have been gnawed. The lip is shorter than the column.

REFERENCES: 221, 470, 476.

Dendrobium cucullitepalum J. J. Smith

ORIGIN/HABITAT: Molucca Islands. Plants were originally found near sea level on Ambon Island.

CLIMATE: Station #97724, Ambon/Pattimura, Indonesia, Lat. 3.7°S, Long. 128.1°E, at an elevation of 33 ft. (10 m). Record extreme temperatures are 96°F (36°C) and 66°F (19°C).

N/HEMISPHERE	JAN	FEB	MAR	APR	MAY	JUN	JUL	AUG	SEP	OCT	NOV	DEC
°F AVG MAX	81	81	83	85	88	88	88	88	88	86	84	82
°F AVG MIN	74	74	74	74	75	76	76	76	76	76	75	74
DIURNAL RANGE	7	7	9	11	13	12	12	12	12	10	9	8
RAIN/INCHES	23.7	15.8	9.5	6.1	4.5	5.2	5.0	4.7	5.3	11.0	20.3	25.1
HUMIDITY/%	83	82	81	80	79	78	78	77	79	82	83	84
BLOOM SEASON									*			
DAYS CLR @ 9AM	1	1	1	6	7	3	3	5	5	3	3	
DAYS CLR @ 3PM	1	1	2	5	6	1	1	1	2	3	1	3
RAIN/MM	602	401	241	155	114	132	127	119	135	279	516	638
°C AVG MAX	27.2	27.2	28.3	29.4	31.1	31.1	31.1	31.1	31.1	30.0	28.9	27.8
°C AVG MIN	23.3	23.3	23.3	23.3	23.9	24.4	24.4	24.4	24.4	24.4	23.9	23.3
DIURNAL RANGE	3.9	3.9	5.0	6.1	7.2	6.7	6.7	6.7	6.7	5.6	5.0	4.5
S/HEMISPHERE	JUL	AUG	SEP	OCT	NOV	DEC	JAN	FEB	MAR	APR	MAY	JUN

Cultural Recommendations

LIGHT: 2500–3500 fc.

TEMPERATURES: Throughout the year, days average 81–88°F (27–31°C), and nights average 74–76°F (23–24°C), with a diurnal range of 7–13°F (4–7°C).

HUMIDITY: 80–85% year-round.

WATER: Rainfall is moderate to heavy all year, but conditions are slightly drier in late spring and summer. Cultivated plants should be kept evenly moist with only slight drying allowed between waterings.

FERTILIZER: ¼–½ recommended strength. A balanced fertilizer should be applied weekly to biweekly throughout the year.

REST PERIOD: Growing conditions should be maintained all year. In the habitat, rainfall is heaviest in winter, but water and fertilizer should be reduced somewhat for cultivated plants, especially those grown in the dark, short-day conditions common in temperate latitudes. Plants should never be allowed to dry completely, however. In the habitat, light is highest in spring.

GROWING MEDIA: Plants may be mounted on tree-fern or cork slabs if humidity is high and plants are watered daily at least once a day in summer. When plants are potted, any open, fast-draining medium may be used. Repotting may be done anytime new roots are growing.

MISCELLANEOUS NOTES: The bloom season shown in the climate table is based on reports from the habitat. The plant was described in 1928 in *Bul. Jard. Bot. Buit.* 3rd sér. 10:145.

Plant and Flower Information

PLANT SIZE AND TYPE: An 87 in. (220 cm) sympodial epiphyte.

PSEUDOBULB: 87 in. (220 cm) long. The stems do not branch.

LEAVES: Many. The lanceolate leaves are 5 in. (13 cm) long.

INFLORESCENCE: Short. Inflorescences emerge from nodes along the stem.

FLOWERS: 2 per inflorescence. The warty flowers are about 0.8 in. (2 cm) across. Blossoms have yellow sepals and petals and a black lip.

REFERENCES: 224.

Dendrobium cucumerinum W. McLeay ex Lindley

ORIGIN/HABITAT: Southeastern Australia from near Sydney to just north of Brisbane. *D. cucumerinum* was once common along rivers of northern New South Wales, but is now sparsely distributed inland from the coast. Plants normally grow in high light on trees in river valleys, usually hanging over the streams. While they are found at considerable distances inland, the habitat does not extend to the western slopes of the Great Dividing Range.

CLIMATE: Station #94568, Ipswich, Australia, Lat. 27.7°S, Long. 152.7°E, at 87 ft. (27 m). Record extreme temperatures are 109°F (43°C) and 25°F (−4°C).

Dendrobium cultratum

N/HEMISPHERE	JAN	FEB	MAR	APR	MAY	JUN	JUL	AUG	SEP	OCT	NOV	DEC
°F AVG MAX	69	71	76	81	86	89	88	86	85	81	75	70
°F AVG MIN	42	44	49	57	61	65	67	68	66	59	50	47
DIURNAL RANGE	27	27	27	24	25	24	21	18	19	22	25	23
RAIN/INCHES	6.8	5.0	4.7	10.5	6.8	14.6	10.6	8.3	3.4	2.8	3.7	3.0
HUMIDITY/%	72	69	69	70	68	70	73	77	73	72	72	73
BLOOM SEASON			*		*	*		*				
DAYS CLR @ 4AM	3	3	2	2	3	3	3	3	4	3	3	5
DAYS CLR @ 10AM	17	22	19	12	12	9	7	5	10	15	18	16
RAIN/MM	173	127	119	267	173	371	269	211	86	71	94	76
°C AVG MAX	20.6	21.7	24.4	27.2	30.0	31.7	31.1	30.0	29.4	27.2	23.9	21.1
°C AVG MIN	5.6	6.7	9.4	13.9	16.1	18.3	19.4	20.0	18.9	15.0	10.0	8.3
DIURNAL RANGE	15.0	15.0	15.0	13.3	13.9	13.4	11.7	10.0	10.5	12.2	13.9	12.8
S/HEMISPHERE	JUL	AUG	SEP	OCT	NOV	DEC	JAN	FEB	MAR	APR	MAY	JUN

Cultural Recommendations

LIGHT: 1500–2500 fc. Growers recommend bright shade. In the habitat, skies are frequently clear by 10 a.m. after early morning fog or low clouds dissipate. Growers indicate that strong air movement is critically important.

TEMPERATURES: Summer days average 86–89°F (30–32°C), and nights average 65–68°F (18–20°C), with a diurnal range of 18–24°F (10–13°C). Plants are healthiest with a wide diurnal temperature range.

HUMIDITY: Near 70% most of the year, increasing to near 75% in summer.

WATER: Rainfall is moderate to heavy from spring through summer. In addition to rainfall, plants usually receive heavy dew and early morning mist, even during the dry season; but conditions in the habitat allow quick drying during the day. The primary dry season occurs in autumn, with a short secondary dry season in late winter or early spring. Plants should be kept moist in spring and summer, but water should be reduced in autumn. Some growers recommend additional misting in the evening during hot weather.

FERTILIZER: ¼–½ recommended strength, applied weekly. A high-nitrogen fertilizer is beneficial from spring to midsummer, but a fertilizer high in phosphates should be used in late summer and autumn.

REST PERIOD: Winter days average 69–71°F (21–22°C), and nights average 42–47°F (6–8°C), with a diurnal range of 23–27°F (13–15°C). Growers indicate that plants tolerate winter lows near 32°F (0°C). Cultivated plants tolerate cold temperatures, but they grow better if the winter conditions are not as long or as severe as indicated in the climate data. The record lows indicate that plants in the wild survive below freezing temperatures. These extreme conditions should be avoided in cultivation; but if exposed, the plant's chance of surviving is better if it is dry at the time. Rainfall in the habitat is moderate during winter. Water should be reduced somewhat for cultivated plants, but they should not be allowed to dry out completely or to remain dry for long periods. Some growers indicate that plants should be dry in winter, but others feel that early morning misting followed by rapid drying more closely resembles conditions in the habitat. Water should not be allowed to stand on the plants for long periods, however. Strong air movement helps promote rapid drying during the day. Fertilizer should be reduced anytime water is reduced. In the habitat, light is highest in winter.

GROWING MEDIA: *D. cucumerinum* never produces many roots and is very difficult to establish. The stems are extremely brittle, and the plants tend to break into small pieces when disturbed. The resulting small pieces are seldom viable. Growers indicate that a plant is more easily established and grows best if it is very tightly mounted to rough-barked cork or hardwood. Plants tend to grow with the leaves pointing downward. Even if mounted with the leaves pointing upward, the next year or so will be spent getting new growths turned around so they end up pointing down. Plants should be divided or remounted only when absolutely necessary and only when new roots are actively growing.

MISCELLANEOUS NOTES: The bloom season shown in the climate table is based on cultivation records. In the habitat, plants bloom erratically between spring and autumn. Many growers consider *D. cucumerinum* difficult to cultivate, but others indicate that once established, it is easy to grow, providing cultural requirements are met.

Plant and Flower Information

PLANT SIZE AND TYPE: A miniature, 0.6–1.4 in. (1.5–3.6 cm) sympodial epiphyte or lithophyte.

PSEUDOBULB: None. Growths arise from a wandering, branching rhizome.

LEAVES: 1 per growth. The flat leaves are 0.6–1.4 in. (1.5–3.6 cm) long. They are dark or matte green, oval, and covered with cucumberlike warts.

INFLORESCENCE: 1 in. (2.5 cm) long. Inflorescences emerge from the base of the gherkin-like leaf. The flowers are held just above the leaves.

FLOWERS: 2–10 per inflorescence. The flowers, which do not open fully, are 0.6–1.0 in. (1.5–2.5 cm) across. The faintly fragrant blossoms are cream to greenish yellow with wine-red spots, streaks, or stripes near the base of the ruffled lip. Sepals and petals are very narrow, almost wispy and twisted.

HYBRIDIZING NOTES: Chromosome count is 2n = 38 (ref. 151, 154, 187, 188).

REFERENCES: 23, 67, 105, 151, 154, 179, 187, 188, 190, 210, 216, 240, 254, 291, 317, 325, 326, 330, 352, 371, 390, 421, 458, 495, 527, 533.

PHOTOS/DRAWINGS: *105*, 210, 240, 254, *291*, 325, *371*, 458, *533*.

Dendrobium cultratum Schlechter

AKA: *D. atropurpureum* Ames, *D. sinuatum* Schlechter.

ORIGIN/HABITAT: Widespread through Southeast Asia. *D. cultratum* grows throughout the Philippines, Borneo, the Malaya peninsula, and Burma. It is also reported in New Guinea, Sulawesi (Celebes), and Hainan Island. Plants usually grow on forest trees from sea level to 500 ft. (0–150 m), but they may also be found at somewhat higher elevations.

CLIMATE: Station #98836, Zamboanga, Philippines, Lat. 6.9°N, Long. 122.1°E, at 17 ft. (5 m). Record extreme temperatures are 96°F (36°C) and 60°F (16°C).

N/HEMISPHERE	JAN	FEB	MAR	APR	MAY	JUN	JUL	AUG	SEP	OCT	NOV	DEC
°F AVG MAX	89	89	90	90	89	88	88	88	88	88	89	88
°F AVG MIN	71	71	72	73	74	74	73	73	73	73	72	71
DIURNAL RANGE	18	18	18	17	15	14	15	15	15	15	17	17
RAIN/INCHES	2.1	2.2	1.5	2.0	3.5	4.2	4.9	4.0	4.7	5.6	4.2	3.4
HUMIDITY/%	78	76	76	77	79	80	80	80	80	81	80	79
BLOOM SEASON	*										*	*
DAYS CLR @ 8AM	6	6	8	7	3	1	3	2	4	7	6	5
DAYS CLR @ 2PM	4	3	5	3	1	1	1	2	2	2	2	3
RAIN/MM	53	56	38	51	89	107	124	102	119	142	107	86
°C AVG MAX	31.7	31.7	32.2	32.2	31.7	31.1	31.1	31.1	31.1	31.1	31.7	31.1
°C AVG MIN	21.7	21.7	22.2	22.8	23.3	23.3	22.8	22.8	22.8	22.8	22.2	21.7
DIURNAL RANGE	10.0	10.0	10.0	9.4	8.4	7.8	8.3	8.3	8.3	8.3	9.5	9.4
S/HEMISPHERE	JUL	AUG	SEP	OCT	NOV	DEC	JAN	FEB	MAR	APR	MAY	JUN

Cultural Recommendations

LIGHT: 2500–3500 fc.

TEMPERATURES: Throughout the year, days average 88–90°F (31–32°C), and nights average 71–74°F (22–23°C), with a diurnal range of 14–18°F (8–10°C).

HUMIDITY: Near 80% most of the year, falling to near 75% in winter and early spring.

WATER: Rainfall is moderate most of the year. Cultivated plants should be allowed to dry slightly between waterings from late spring into autumn. Water should be gradually reduced in late autumn and early winter.

FERTILIZER: ¼–½ recommended strength. A balanced fertilizer should be applied weekly to biweekly throughout the year.

REST PERIOD: Warm growing temperatures should be maintained year-round. Water and fertilizer should be reduced slightly in winter. Plants should be allowed to dry out between waterings, but they should not remain dry for long periods.

GROWING MEDIA: Mounting plants on tree-fern or cork slabs accommodates their pendulous growth habit. However, humidity must be high and plants must be watered at least once a day in summer. If plants cannot be mounted, small pots or hanging baskets may be filled with an open, fast-draining medium. Repotting may be done anytime new roots are actively growing.

MISCELLANEOUS NOTES: The bloom season shown in the climate table is based on collection reports.

Plant and Flower Information

PLANT SIZE AND TYPE: A 2.4–12.0 in. (6–30 cm) sympodial epiphyte.

PSEUDOBULB: 1.6–6.0 in. (4–15 cm) long. The branching pendent growths are very close together.

LEAVES: Many. Leaves are linear, fleshy, pointed, and 0.8–2.0 in. (2–5 cm) long. They are densely 2-ranked all along each growth.

INFLORESCENCE: 0.4–0.8 in. (1–2 cm) long. Inflorescences emerge from bracts near the apex of the stem.

FLOWERS: 1–2. The blossoms are 0.2 in. (0.5 cm) across. Normally dark purple, flower color is extremely variable. The lip is fleshy, fringed, and broadest in the middle.

REFERENCES: 12, 221 296, 436, 454, 536.

Dendrobium cultrifolium Schlechter

ORIGIN/HABITAT: New Guinea. Collections are reported from both Irian Jaya (western New Guinea) and Papua New Guinea. In Papua, plants grow in the Waria District and near the border with Irian Jaya at about 4250 ft. (1300 m).

CLIMATE: Station #200192, Garaina, Papua New Guinea, Lat. 7.9°S, Long. 147.1°E, at 2350 ft. (716 m). Temperatures are calculated for an elevation of 4250 ft. (1300 m), resulting in probable extremes of 88°F (31°C) and 40°F (4°C).

N/HEMISPHERE	JAN	FEB	MAR	APR	MAY	JUN	JUL	AUG	SEP	OCT	NOV	DEC
°F AVG MAX	74	76	77	78	79	79	79	79	78	78	77	75
°F AVG MIN	57	57	57	58	57	58	59	59	59	58	58	57
DIURNAL RANGE	17	19	20	20	22	21	20	20	19	20	19	18
RAIN/INCHES	5.8	6.5	8.7	11.1	11.8	11.9	8.9	11.7	11.5	9.9	7.7	5.2
HUMIDITY/%	84	82	82	81	80	80	81	81	82	83	84	84
BLOOM SEASON	N/A											
DAYS CLR	N/A											
RAIN/MM	147	165	221	282	300	302	226	297	292	251	196	132
°C AVG MAX	23.1	24.3	24.8	25.4	25.9	25.9	25.9	25.9	25.4	25.4	24.8	23.7
°C AVG MIN	13.7	13.7	13.7	14.3	13.7	14.3	14.8	14.8	14.8	14.3	14.3	13.7
DIURNAL RANGE	9.4	10.6	11.1	11.1	12.2	11.6	11.1	11.1	10.6	11.1	10.5	10.0
S/HEMISPHERE	JUL	AUG	SEP	OCT	NOV	DEC	JAN	FEB	MAR	APR	MAY	JUN

Cultural Recommendations

LIGHT: 2000–3000 fc.

TEMPERATURES: Throughout the year, days average 74–79°F (23–26°C), and nights average 57–59°F (14–15°C), with a diurnal range of 17–22°F (9–12°C).

HUMIDITY: 80–85% year-round.

WATER: Rainfall is heavy all year. Conditions are slightly drier in winter. Cultivated plants should be kept moist but not soggy.

FERTILIZER: ¼–½ recommended strength. A balanced fertilizer should be applied weekly to biweekly throughout the year.

REST PERIOD: Growing conditions should be maintained all year. In the habitat, rainfall is slightly lower in winter. Water and fertilizer should be reduced somewhat for cultivated plants, especially those grown in the dark, short-day conditions common during temperate-latitude winters. They should never be allowed to dry out completely, however. In the habitat, seasonal light variation is minor.

GROWING MEDIA: Plants may be mounted on tree-fern or cork slabs if humidity is high and plants are watered daily in summer. When plants are potted, any open, fast-draining medium may be used. Repotting may be done anytime new roots are growing.

MISCELLANEOUS NOTES: Schlechter described this plant in 1919 in Fedde's *Repert. Sp. Nov.* 16:111.

Plant and Flower Information

PLANT SIZE AND TYPE: A 28 in. (70 cm) sympodial epiphyte.

PSEUDOBULB: 28 in. (70 cm) long. The flattened stems arise from a very short rhizome.

LEAVES: Many. The curved, lanceolate leaves are 3.5 in. (9 cm) long. The upper part of each growth is leafy.

INFLORESCENCE: Short. Clusters of flowers emerge along the upper, leafless part of the stem.

FLOWERS: Many per inflorescence. The smooth flowers are 0.8 in. (2 cm) long. The blossoms have a concave, oblong dorsal sepal, obliquely triangular lateral sepals, and oblong petals. The curved lip, which appears 4-lobed, is wavy along the margin.

REFERENCES: 222.

Dendrobium cultriforme J. J. Smith. See *D. sumatranum* A. Hawkes and A. H. Heller. REFERENCES: 220, 229, 254, 445.

Dendrobium cultriforme Thouars. Now considered a synonym of *Polystachya cultrata* Lindley. REFERENCES: 100, 216, 254.

Dendrobium cumulatum Kränzlin. See *D. crumenatum* Swartz. REFERENCES: 296, 536.

Dendrobium cumulatum Lindley

AKA: *D. eoum* Ridley.

ORIGIN/HABITAT: Widespread in India and Southeast Asia. The habitat includes Nepal, Sikkim, Assam, Bhutan, and the Khasi (Khasia) Hills in the Meghalaya district of northeastern India, and extends eastward through Burma, Thailand, Cambodia, Laos and Vietnam. Plants usually grow at 1000–3300 ft. (300–1000 m). In Sabah, Borneo, they are found in the lower mountain forests of Mt. Kinabalu, at about 4900 ft. (1500 m). The Philippines is sometimes included in the habitat, but Ames (ref. 12) specifically excludes it.

CLIMATE: Station #42410, Gauhati, India, Lat. 26.1°N, Long. 91.6°E, at 158 ft. (48 m). Temperatures are calculated for a habitat elevation of 2000 ft. (610 m), resulting in probable extremes of 98°F (37°C) and 35°F (2°C).

N/HEMISPHERE	JAN	FEB	MAR	APR	MAY	JUN	JUL	AUG	SEP	OCT	NOV	DEC
°F AVG MAX	70	72	80	82	82	83	84	84	83	81	75	70
°F AVG MIN	45	48	54	62	66	71	72	72	70	65	55	47
DIURNAL RANGE	25	24	26	20	16	12	12	12	13	16	20	23
RAIN/INCHES	0.4	1.2	2.0	5.7	9.3	12.3	12.3	10.3	6.6	2.8	0.6	0.2
HUMIDITY/%	79	72	64	71	82	85	85	86	84	84	83	82
BLOOM SEASON	*	*			*	*	*				*	*
DAYS CLR @ 6AM	6	12	16	11	3	0	1	3	7	6	3	
DAYS CLR @ 12PM	17	16	18	15	6	1	0	0	2	11	17	19
RAIN/MM	10	30	51	145	236	312	312	262	168	71	15	5
°C AVG MAX	21.1	22.2	26.6	27.7	27.7	28.3	28.8	28.8	28.3	27.7	23.8	21.1
°C AVG MIN	7.2	8.8	12.2	16.6	18.8	21.6	22.2	22.2	21.1	18.3	12.7	8.3
DIURNAL RANGE	13.9	13.4	14.4	11.1	8.9	6.7	6.6	6.6	7.2	8.9	11.1	12.8
S/HEMISPHERE	JUL	AUG	SEP	OCT	NOV	DEC	JAN	FEB	MAR	APR	MAY	JUN

Dendrobium cuneatipetalum

Cultural Recommendations

LIGHT: 2500–3500 fc.

TEMPERATURES: Summer days average 83–84°F (28–29°C), and nights average 71–72°F (22°C), with a diurnal range of 12°F (7°C).

HUMIDITY: 80–85% most of the year, falling to 65–70% in late winter and early spring.

WATER: Rainfall is heavy from spring through summer but decreases rapidly in autumn with a 1–2 month transition into the winter dry season. Cultivated plants need to be moist while actively growing, but water should be gradually reduced after new growths mature in autumn.

FERTILIZER: ¼–½ recommended strength, applied weekly. A high-nitrogen fertilizer is beneficial from spring to midsummer, but a fertilizer high in phosphates should be used in late summer and autumn.

REST PERIOD: Winter days average 70–72°F (21–22°C), and nights average 45–48°F (7–9°C), with a diurnal range of 23–25°F (13–14°C). While actual minimum temperatures do not appear to be critical, the increased diurnal range in winter is common throughout the habitat. Although rainfall is low for 4–5 winter months, high humidity and the large temperature range indicate that additional moisture from heavy dew is common. Therefore, while water should be greatly reduced and cultivated plants allowed to dry out between waterings from late autumn into early spring, they should not remain dry for extended periods. Occasional mistings between waterings during bright, sunny weather may help prevent the plants from becoming too dry. Fertilizer should be reduced or eliminated until active growth resumes and water is increased in spring. In the habitat, light is brightest in winter.

GROWING MEDIA: Mounting plants on tree-fern or cork slabs accommodates their pendulous growth habit. However, humidity must be high and plants must be watered at least once a day in summer. If plants must be potted, hanging pots or baskets may be filled with any open, fast-draining medium. Repotting may be done anytime new roots are actively growing.

MISCELLANEOUS NOTES: The bloom season shown in the climate table is based on cultivation records. In the habitat, plants bloom in summer.

Plant and Flower Information

PLANT SIZE AND TYPE: An 18–24 in. (45–60 cm) sympodial epiphyte.

PSEUDOBULB: 15–20 in. (38–50 cm) long. Pseudobulbs are pendulous, narrow at the base, and laterally flattened.

LEAVES: 4–6 per growth. The leaves are 3–4 in. (8–10 cm) long.

INFLORESCENCE: 4 in. (10 cm) long. Racemes are reddish purple and emerge from lateral nodes on both leafy and leafless stems.

FLOWERS: 3–6 per inflorescence. The nearly transparent flowers are 1.2–1.6 in. (3–4 cm) across. The sepals and wider petals may be white or pale rosy purple sometimes suffused with white. The clawed lip is white with yellow at the base. It is sometimes marked with a pink patch at the notched tip, suffused with purple or rose freckles, or marked with red longitudinal lines. Flower color is variable. The callus is smooth, elongated, and grooved. Blossoms have a vanillalike fragrance.

HYBRIDIZING NOTES: Chromosome count is 2n = 40 (ref. 152).

REFERENCES: 12, 38, 46, 152, 157, 179, 202, 210, 216, 254, 286, 317, 369, 376, 394, 395, 430, 445, 447, 448, 454, 541, 592.

PHOTOS/DRAWINGS: 46, 210, *369*, *430*, *454*, *592*.

Dendrobium cuneatipetalum J. J. Smith

ORIGIN/HABITAT: The Moluccas. Plants grow on Ambon Island at about 2150 ft. (650 m) on Mt. Salhoetoe. They are also reported in the Bengkulu district of western Sumatra.

CLIMATE: Station #97724, Ambon Island, Indonesia, Lat. 3.7°S, Long. 128.1°E, at 33 ft. (10 m). Temperatures are calculated for an elevation of 2150 ft. (650 m), resulting in probable extremes of 89°F (32°C) and 59°F (15°C).

N/HEMISPHERE	JAN	FEB	MAR	APR	MAY	JUN	JUL	AUG	SEP	OCT	NOV	DEC
°F AVG MAX	74	74	76	78	81	81	81	81	81	79	77	75
°F AVG MIN	67	67	67	67	68	69	69	69	69	69	68	67
DIURNAL RANGE	7	7	9	11	13	12	12	12	12	10	9	8
RAIN/INCHES	23.7	15.8	9.5	6.1	4.5	5.2	5.0	4.7	5.3	11.0	20.3	25.1
HUMIDITY/%	83	82	81	80	79	78	78	77	79	82	83	84
BLOOM SEASON	N/A											
DAYS CLR @ 9AM	1	1	1	6	7	4	3	3	5	5	3	3
DAYS CLR @ 3PM	1	1	2	5	6	1	1	1	2	3	1	3
RAIN/MM	602	401	241	155	114	132	127	119	135	279	516	638
°C AVG MAX	23.3	23.3	24.5	25.6	27.2	27.2	27.2	27.2	27.2	26.1	25.0	23.9
°C AVG MIN	19.5	19.5	19.5	19.5	20.0	20.6	20.6	20.6	20.6	20.6	20.0	19.5
DIURNAL RANGE	3.8	3.8	5.0	6.1	7.2	6.6	6.6	6.6	6.6	5.5	5.0	4.4
S/HEMISPHERE	JUL	AUG	SEP	OCT	NOV	DEC	JAN	FEB	MAR	APR	MAY	JUN

Cultural Recommendations

LIGHT: 2500–3500 fc.

TEMPERATURES: Throughout the year, days average 74–81°F (23–27°C), and nights average 67–69°F (20–21°C), with a diurnal range of 7–13°F (4–7°C). Record extreme temperatures are only a few degrees above and below the averages, indicating that plants may not tolerate wide temperature fluctuations.

HUMIDITY: 80–85% most of the year, dropping to 75–80% in summer.

WATER: Rainfall is moderate to heavy all year, but conditions are slightly drier in late spring and summer. Cultivated plants should be kept evenly moist all year with only slight drying allowed between waterings.

FERTILIZER: ¼–½ recommended strength. A balanced fertilizer should be applied weekly to biweekly throughout the year.

REST PERIOD: Growing conditions should be maintained all year. In the habitat, a brief, semidry period occurs in late spring. Rainfall is heaviest in winter, but water and fertilizer should be reduced for plants cultivated in the dark, short-day conditions common in temperate-latitude winters. Plants should never be allowed to dry completely, however. In the habitat, light is highest in spring.

GROWING MEDIA: Plants may be mounted on tree-fern or cork slabs or potted in small pots filled with any open, fast-draining medium. Repotting may be done anytime new roots are actively growing.

MISCELLANEOUS NOTES: The plant was described in 1927 in *Bul. Jard. Bot. Buit.* 3rd sér. 9:145.

Plant and Flower Information

PLANT SIZE AND TYPE: A 6 in. (15 cm) sympodial epiphyte.

PSEUDOBULB: 6 in. (15 cm) long. The suberect stems, which are flattened, rigid, and unbranched, are slender at the base and somewhat swollen above. They arise from a branching rhizome.

LEAVES: Many. The flattened, alternating leaves, which are about 1.2 in. (3 cm) long, are arranged in 2 rows. They have a pale green margin.

INFLORESCENCE: Inflorescences emerge from the side and apex of the stem.

FLOWERS: The flowers are 0.3 in. (0.8 cm) across. The fleshy blossoms are pale yellow-green with dirty purple streaks. The tips of the sepals are suffused with purple.

REFERENCES: 224.

Dendrobium cuneatum Schlechter

ORIGIN/HABITAT: The Molucca Islands. Plants were collected on Mt. Api, on Banda Island. Habitat elevation is not available, so the following temperatures should be used with caution.

CLIMATE: Station #49620, Amahai, Seram, Indonesia, Lat. 3.3°S, Long. 128.9°E, at 10 ft. (3 m). Record extreme temperatures are 96°F (36°C) and 66°F (19°C).

N/HEMISPHERE	JAN	FEB	MAR	APR	MAY	JUN	JUL	AUG	SEP	OCT	NOV	DEC
°F AVG MAX	81	81	83	85	88	88	88	88	88	86	84	82
°F AVG MIN	74	74	74	74	75	76	76	76	76	76	75	74
DIURNAL RANGE	7	7	9	11	13	12	12	12	12	10	9	8
RAIN/INCHES	23.7	15.8	9.5	6.1	4.5	5.2	5.0	4.7	5.3	11.0	20.3	25.1
HUMIDITY/%	83	82	81	80	79	78	78	77	79	82	83	84
BLOOM SEASON				*								
DAYS CLR @ 9AM	1	1	1	6	7	4	3	3	5	5	3	3
DAYS CLR @ 3PM	1	1	2	5	6	1	1	1	2	3	1	3
RAIN/MM	602	401	241	155	114	132	127	119	135	279	516	638
°C AVG MAX	27.2	27.2	28.3	29.4	31.1	31.1	31.1	31.1	31.1	30.0	28.9	27.8
°C AVG MIN	23.3	23.3	23.3	23.3	23.9	24.4	24.4	24.4	24.4	24.4	23.9	23.3
DIURNAL RANGE	3.9	3.9	5.0	6.1	7.2	6.7	6.7	6.7	6.7	5.6	5.0	4.5
S/HEMISPHERE	JUL	AUG	SEP	OCT	NOV	DEC	JAN	FEB	MAR	APR	MAY	JUN

Cultural Recommendations

LIGHT: 2000–3000 fc.

TEMPERATURES: Throughout the year, days average 81–88°F (27–31°C), and nights average 74–76°F (23–24°C), with a diurnal range of 7–13°F (4–7°C).

HUMIDITY: 75–80% most of the year, increasing to near 85% in winter.

WATER: Rainfall is moderate to heavy throughout the year, with a slightly drier season in spring and summer. Cultivated plants should be kept moist but not soggy. Only slight drying should be allowed between waterings.

FERTILIZER: ¼–½ recommended strength. A balanced fertilizer should be applied weekly to biweekly year-round.

REST PERIOD: Growing conditions should be maintained all year. In the habitat, winter is the wettest season; but water should be reduced for plants cultivated in the dark, short-day conditions common in temperate-latitude winters. Plants should never be allowed to dry out completely between waterings, however. Fertilizer should be reduced or eliminated anytime water is reduced. In the habitat, light is highest in early spring.

GROWING MEDIA: The prostrate growth habit suggests that plants are best mounted on a tree-fern or cork rafts. If plants must be potted, the container may be filled with any open, fast-draining medium. Repotting may be done anytime new roots are actively growing.

MISCELLANEOUS NOTES: The bloom season shown in the climate table is based on reports from the habitat.

Plant and Flower Information

PLANT SIZE AND TYPE: A 24 in. (60 cm) sympodial epiphyte.

PSEUDOBULB: 24 in. (60 cm) long. The prostrate stems rarely branch.

LEAVES: Many. The distichous, somewhat sickle-shaped leaves are 1.2–1.8 in. (3.0–4.5 cm) long, pointed, and leathery.

INFLORESCENCE: Inflorescences are distichous and emerge from nodes on upper part of the stem.

FLOWERS: 2 per inflorescence. The flowers are less than 0.3 in. (0.8 cm) across. Blossoms are yellowish-white with violet lines or streaks. The small flowers have an ovate dorsal sepal, somewhat sickle-shaped lateral sepals with very broadly triangular bases, spoon-shaped petals, and a simple lip which is minutely toothed.

REFERENCES: 220, 254, 433.

Dendrobium cuneilabium (Schlechter) J. J. Smith.

Although not correctly transferred, Schlechter (ref. 443) considered this name to be a synonym of *Cadetia cuneilabia* Schlechter. REFERENCES: 223, 225, 443, 445, 486.

Dendrobium cuneilabrum J. J. Smith

AKA: *D. utriculariopsis* Kränzlin.

ORIGIN/HABITAT: Endemic to Sulawesi (Celebes). *D. cuneilabrum* is very abundant in Minahassa on Mt. Masarang and Mt. Sopoetan. Plants grow on forest trees and in coffee plantations at 3300–3950 ft. (1000–1200 m).

CLIMATE: Station #97014, Manado, Sulawesi, Indonesia, Lat. 1.5°N, Long. 124.9°E, at 264 ft. (80 m). Temperatures are calculated for an elevation of 3600 ft. (1100 m), resulting in probable extremes of 86°F (30°C) and 54°F (12°C).

N/HEMISPHERE	JAN	FEB	MAR	APR	MAY	JUN	JUL	AUG	SEP	OCT	NOV	DEC
°F AVG MAX	74	74	74	75	76	76	76	78	78	78	76	75
°F AVG MIN	62	62	62	62	63	62	62	62	62	61	62	63
DIURNAL RANGE	12	12	12	13	13	14	14	16	16	17	14	12
RAIN/INCHES	18.6	13.8	12.2	8.0	6.4	6.5	4.8	4.0	3.4	4.9	8.9	14.7
HUMIDITY/%	84	83	83	83	81	80	75	72	75	77	82	83
BLOOM SEASON			*		*					*		
DAYS CLR @ 8AM	4	3	6	11	11	12	12	14	17	12	8	
DAYS CLR @ 2PM	1	1	1	2	1	3	3	4	4	4	1	1
RAIN/MM	472	351	310	203	163	165	122	102	86	124	226	373
°C AVG MAX	23.3	23.3	23.3	23.9	24.4	24.4	24.4	25.5	25.5	25.5	24.4	23.9
°C AVG MIN	16.6	16.6	16.6	16.6	17.2	16.6	16.6	16.6	16.6	16.1	16.6	17.2
DIURNAL RANGE	6.7	6.7	6.7	7.3	7.2	7.8	7.8	8.9	8.9	9.4	7.8	6.7
S/HEMISPHERE	JUL	AUG	SEP	OCT	NOV	DEC	JAN	FEB	MAR	APR	MAY	JUN

Cultural Recommendations

LIGHT: 2000–3000 fc. Plants grow in shady forest habitats, so low to intermediate diffused light is suggested. In the habitat, light is brightest during the frequent clear mornings from spring into autumn. Afternoons are generally cloudy all year.

TEMPERATURES: Throughout the year, days average 74–78°F (23–26°C), and nights average 61–63°F (16–17°C), with a diurnal range of 12–17°F (7–9°C). Extremes vary less than 10°F (6°C) from average growing temperatures, indicating that plants probably cannot tolerate wide temperature fluctuations.

HUMIDITY: 80–85% most of the year, dropping to 70–75% in summer and early autumn.

WATER: Rainfall is moderate to heavy all year. The driest weather occurs in late summer when temperatures are warm. Cultivated plants should be kept moist but not soggy. Warm water might be beneficial.

FERTILIZER: ¼–½ recommended strength. A balanced fertilizer should be applied weekly to biweekly throughout the year.

REST PERIOD: Growing temperatures should be maintained all year. The plants may rest during the 1–2 month drier period which occurs in late summer and coincides with the period of greatest diurnal range. Cultivated plants should dry out slightly during this period, but they should never remain dry for long. The heaviest rainfall in the habitat occurs in winter, but water should not be increased for cultivated plants. In fact, water should be reduced somewhat for plants grown in the dark, short-day conditions common in temperate latitudes, but they should not be allowed to dry out completely.

GROWING MEDIA: Mounting plants on tree-fern or cork slabs accommodates their pendent growth habit, but humidity must be high and plants need daily watering in summer. Plants may be potted in hanging pots or baskets filled with any open, fast-draining medium. Repotting may be done anytime new roots are growing.

MISCELLANEOUS NOTES: The bloom times shown in the climate table are based on reports from the habitat. Plants that produce flowers which last a single day commonly bloom several times during the year. Flowering usually occurs 7–14 days after a sudden 10°F (6°C) drop in daytime temperatures.

Dendrobium cunninghamii

Plant and Flower Information

PLANT SIZE AND TYPE: A 12–14 in. (30–35 cm) sympodial epiphyte. Plants occasionally reach a length of 33 in. (84 cm).

PSEUDOBULB: 12–14 in. (30–35 cm) long. *D. cuneilabrum* propagates vegetatively by developing rooting keikis on old stems so that the stems appear to branch. The clustered stems, which are very slender at the base, have 2 swollen nodes above the base that are approximately 0.6 in. (1.5 cm) long. Above the swelling, the stems are again slender. They are pendent and dirty green with pointed terete leaves that appear to be an extension of the stem.

LEAVES: 4–7 per growth. The terete leaves are 2.8–3.2 in. (7–8 cm) long, round, and fleshy. They are held at an acute angle to the stem.

INFLORESCENCE: Short. Inflorescences emerge above several of the upper leaf nodes.

FLOWERS: 1, rarely more per inflorescence. The white flowers have fine pink lines on the inside. They are 1.1 in. (2.8 cm) long and last a single day. As with most other ephemeral species, all blossoms open on the same day.

REFERENCES: 220, 254, 436, 471.

Dendrobium cunninghamii Lindley not Steudel

AKA: *D. biflorum* A. Richard, *D. lessonii* Colenso.

ORIGIN/HABITAT: Widely distributed in New Zealand. The habitat includes the Hawke Bay District on the southeast side of North Island and the Palliser Bay (Cape Turakirae) region at the southern end of North Island. The range extends southward to Stewart Island, which makes *D. cunninghamii* the most southerly *Dendrobium*. Plants commonly grow in coastal areas at low elevations, but they also occur in higher-elevation forests. They are usually found in bright situations on well-lit tree trunks and branches.

CLIMATE: Station #93844, Invercagrill, New Zealand, Lat. 46.4°S, Long. 163.3°E, at 5 ft. (2 m). Record extreme temperatures are 90°F (32°C) and 19°F (−7°C).

N/HEMISPHERE	JAN	FEB	MAR	APR	MAY	JUN	JUL	AUG	SEP	OCT	NOV	DEC
°F AVG MAX	49	52	56	60	61	64	66	66	64	59	54	50
°F AVG MIN	34	37	39	42	44	47	48	48	46	43	39	36
DIURNAL RANGE	15	15	17	18	17	17	18	18	18	16	15	14
RAIN/INCHES	3.2	3.2	3.2	4.1	4.2	4.0	4.2	3.3	4.0	4.1	4.4	3.6
HUMIDITY/%	87	84	82	80	81	80	81	80	83	85	87	89
BLOOM SEASON	*				**	*	*	*				
DAYS CLR @ 11AM	6	6	5	4	3	3	4	4	4	4	5	5
DAYS CLR @ 5PM	6	7	7	7	4	5	6	7	5	5	6	5
RAIN/MM	81	81	81	104	107	102	107	84	102	104	112	91
°C AVG MAX	9.4	11.1	13.3	15.6	16.1	17.8	18.9	18.9	17.8	15.0	12.2	10.0
°C AVG MIN	1.1	2.8	3.9	5.6	6.7	8.3	8.9	8.9	7.8	6.1	3.9	2.2
DIURNAL RANGE	8.3	8.3	9.4	10.0	9.4	9.5	10.0	10.0	10.0	8.9	8.3	7.8
S/HEMISPHERE	JUL	AUG	SEP	OCT	NOV	DEC	JAN	FEB	MAR	APR	MAY	JUN

Cultural Recommendations

LIGHT: 2500–3500 fc. Strong air movement is recommended.

TEMPERATURES: Summer days average 64–66°F (18–19°C), and nights average 47–48°F (8–9°C), with a diurnal range of 17–18°F (10°C). The preceding climate data represents the coldest conditions likely to occur in the habitat. Temperatures in warmer areas are 6–10°F (3–6°C) warmer than indicted in the climate table.

HUMIDITY: 80–85% most of the year, increasing to 85–90% in winter.

WATER: The moderate rainfall is evenly distributed throughout the year, although amounts are somewhat less in winter. Cultivated plants should be kept evenly moist but not soggy.

FERTILIZER: ¼–½ recommended strength, applied weekly. A high-nitrogen fertilizer is beneficial from spring to midsummer, but a fertilizer high in phosphates should be used in late summer and autumn. New Zealand growers indicate that *D. cunninghamii* grows most actively in late summer and autumn.

REST PERIOD: Winter days average 49–56°F (9–13°C), and nights average 34–39°F (1–4°C), with a diurnal range of 14–17°F (8–9°C). Water should be reduced for cultivated plants, but they should never be allowed to dry out completely. Fertilizer should be eliminated.

GROWING MEDIA: Slabs, hanging pots, or baskets best accommodate the rambling growth habit. Growers in New Zealand recommend using a pot or basket filled with a potting medium appropriate for cymbidiums such as fine fir bark mixed with 10% charcoal and 10% perlite. Repotting may be done anytime new roots are growing.

MISCELLANEOUS NOTES: The bloom season shown in the climate table is based on cultivation records and reports from the habitat. Growers often consider *D. cunninghamii* difficult to grow and bloom in cultivation, so careful attention should be given to its cultural requirements.

Plant and Flower Information

PLANT SIZE AND TYPE: A rambling, 30–59 in. (75–150 cm) sympodial plant that often reaches an overall length of 118 in. (300 cm). Plants are normally epiphytic or lithophytic, but they are occasionally terrestrial.

PSEUDOBULB: 30–59 in. (75–150 cm) long. The shiny, bright yellow stems are wiry, woody, and brittle. They branch repeatedly, often forming large tangled masses. The branches are carried at such a wide angle to the primary stem that they often droop. The pseudobulbs are sometimes thickened at the base. They arise from a stemlike rhizome with branched roots.

LEAVES: Several. The glossy, linear leaves, which are 2–5 in. (5–13 cm) long, are held at the tip of each new cane. The leaf sheaths are covered with very small hairs.

INFLORESCENCE: Short. The slender inflorescences emerge laterally a few nodes back from the leafy branch tips.

FLOWERS: 2–6 per inflorescence. The white flowers are 1 in. (2.5 cm) across and may be marked with a yellow flush in the throat. The 3-lobed lip and column may have rose-pink to purplish or green markings. The small sidelobes are often rose-red.

HYBRIDIZING NOTES: Chromosome count is $2n = 38$ (ref. 152, 243).

REFERENCES: 152, 179, 190, 216, 243, 254, 289, 316, 317, 371, 389, 390, 430, 527.

PHOTOS/DRAWINGS: 24, 289, *389, 390, 430.*

Dendrobium cunninghamii Steudel not Lindley.
Considered a synonym of *D. caleyi* A. Cunningham, which is now considered a synonym of *Bulbophyllum exiguum*. REFERENCES: 67, 216.

Dendrobium cupreum Herbert.
See *D. moschatum* (Buch.-Ham.) Swartz. REFERENCES: 190, 216, 254, 430, 454.

Dendrobium curranii Ames.
Status unknown. This name was used by Löve and Solbrig (ref. 280) in a list of IOPB chromosome counts. Later writers have used this information in their lists of chromosome counts, but we have found no other use of the name. Because we can find no original description of this plant, we suspect that these references should have applied to *Dendrochilum curranii* Ames. REFERENCES: 280, 504, 580.

Dendrobium curtisii Rchb. f.
Kränzlin (ref. 254) lists this species as imperfectly described. It was reported to have originated in Borneo, but without more precise habitat information, climate data cannot

be selected. The first recorded blooming occurred in Europe in July after the plant was imported. Reichenbach described it as having stems 30 in. (75 cm) long that resembled *D. devonianum* Paxton. Leaves were not described. He indicated that clusters of amethyst-colored flowers arise from nearly every joint. The lip is pointed, tongue-shaped, white with orange in the middle and amethyst near the tip. REFERENCES: 216, 254, 286, 295.

Dendrobium curvicaule (F. M. Bailey) M. Clements and D. Jones

AKA: Considered by most botanists to be part of the *D. speciosum* alliance. See discussion at *D. speciosum* J. E. Smith. Clements (ref. 67) considers it a separate species and includes as synonyms *D. speciosum* var. *capricornicum* Clemesha, *D. speciosum* var. *curvicaule* Clemesha, and *D. speciosum* var. *fragrans* R. Brown (in part).

ORIGIN/HABITAT: Australia, including the northern and central parts of eastern Queensland from Mt. Amos, south of Cooktown, to southwest of Sarina. *D. curvicaule* was originally collected from volcanic rocks near a disused quarry. It is found near the Tropic of Capricorn from just south of Rockhampton (23.5°S) to near Thornton's Peak (16.2°S). The habitat also extends southwestward to Carnarvon Gorge, about 280 mi. (450 km) inland. Plants are found both near the coast and in the highlands but are most common at higher elevations. They often grow in moderately exposed locations on sandstone rockfaces near creeks and waterfalls, usually in narrow gorges. One plant, collected near Tully Falls, was growing on rock in open forest in nearly full sun.

CLIMATE: Station #94295, Ingham, Australia, Lat. 18.7°S, Long. 146.2°E, at an elevation of 45 ft. (14 m). Temperatures are calculated for a habitat elevation of 3000 ft. (910 m), resulting in probable extremes of 100°F (38°C) and 29°F (−2°C).

N/HEMISPHERE	JAN	FEB	MAR	APR	MAY	JUN	JUL	AUG	SEP	OCT	NOV	DEC
°F AVG MAX	65	67	70	73	75	77	77	77	76	74	71	67
°F AVG MIN	49	51	56	61	64	66	66	65	63	60	55	51
DIURNAL RANGE	16	16	14	12	11	11	11	12	13	14	16	16
RAIN/INCHES	0.6	0.5	0.7	1.3	1.9	5.4	10.9	11.2	7.2	3.3	1.3	1.4
HUMIDITY/%	61	61	62	64	66	70	72	71	70	64	63	63
BLOOM SEASON	*	*										
DAYS CLR @ 10AM	16	18	15	10	7	7	5	5	9	13	14	15
DAYS CLR @ 4PM	16	18	20	20	17	15	8	5	7	11	14	15
RAIN/MM	15	13	18	33	48	137	277	284	183	84	33	36
°C AVG MAX	18.5	19.6	21.2	22.9	24.0	25.1	25.1	25.1	24.6	23.5	21.8	19.6
°C AVG MIN	9.6	10.7	13.5	16.2	17.9	19.0	19.0	18.5	17.4	15.7	12.9	10.7
DIURNAL RANGE	8.9	8.9	7.7	6.7	6.1	6.1	6.1	6.6	7.2	7.8	8.9	8.9
S/HEMISPHERE	JUL	AUG	SEP	OCT	NOV	DEC	JAN	FEB	MAR	APR	MAY	JUN

Cultural Recommendations

LIGHT: 3000–4000 fc. Light levels should be relatively high.

TEMPERATURES: Summer days average 77°F (25°C), and nights average near 65–66°F (19°C), with a diurnal range of 11–12°F (6–7°C).

HUMIDITY: Near 70% for 4 months during summer and early autumn, dropping to near 60% in winter. Humidity is probably greater than indicated at higher elevations, however.

WATER: Rainfall is moderate to heavy in summer and early autumn, but conditions are much drier from late autumn to spring. Cultivated plants should be kept moist while actively growing, but pot grown plants should be allowed to dry out slightly between waterings. Water should be gradually reduced in autumn.

FERTILIZER: ¼–½ recommended strength, applied weekly. A high-nitrogen fertilizer is beneficial from spring to midsummer, but a fertilizer high in phosphates should be used in late summer and autumn.

REST PERIOD: Winter days average 65–67°F (19–20°C), and nights average 49–51°F (10–11°C), with a diurnal range of 16°F (9°C). Although rainfall is lower in winter, some water is available from heavy dew and mist in the high elevation habitat throughout the year. Cultivated plants should be allowed to dry out between waterings, but they should never remain dry for long periods. Occasional early morning mistings between waterings may be beneficial. Fertilizer should be reduced or eliminated unless plants are actively growing.

GROWING MEDIA: Plants may be mounted on tree-fern or cork slabs if humidity is high and plants are watered at least once daily in summer. When plants are potted, any open, fast-draining medium may be used. They may be repotted anytime new roots are growing.

MISCELLANEOUS NOTES: The bloom season shown in the climate table is based on records from the habitat.

Plant and Flower Information

PLANT SIZE AND TYPE: A 43 in. (110 cm) sympodial lithophyte.

PSEUDOBULB: 31 in. (80 cm) long. Although the plant name means curved stems, the stems are normally straight. They are covered with sheaths.

LEAVES: 4 per growth. The large, leathery leaves are 12 in. (30 cm) long. Young leaves are often purplish.

INFLORESCENCE: Several. The pendulous inflorescences often appear simultaneously from nodes near the apex of the stem. The densely flowered inflorescences may be suberect or pendent.

FLOWERS: Many per inflorescence. The flowers are 1.2 in. (3 cm) across. Blossoms have short, stout segments that are normally cream-colored but may be white to pale yellow. The lip, which is not notched at the apex, has red markings.

HYBRIDIZING NOTES: *D. curvicaule* hybridizes naturally with *D. gracilicaule* F. Mueller and *D. jonesii* Rendle. Cross pollinations between *D. curvicaule* and *D. jonesii* produce the hybrid *D.* × *ruppiosum* S. C. Clemsha. Although members of the *D. speciosum* J. E. Smith alliance are seldom self-fertile, Adams (ref. 4) indicates that seed is commonly produced when different clones of the same variety and different varieties are cross-pollinated.

REFERENCES: 4, 67, 240.

PHOTOS/DRAWINGS: 240.

Dendrobium curviflorum Rolfe

ORIGIN/HABITAT: Burma. Plants were originally found near Maymyo at about 4000 ft. (1220 m). A single collection has been reported from northern Thailand. No additional habitat information could be found.

CLIMATE: Station #48035, Lashio, Burma, Lat. 23.0°N, Long. 97.8°E, at 2450 ft. (747 m). Temperatures are calculated for an elevation of 4000 ft. (1220 m), resulting in probable extremes of 99°F (37°C) and 26°F (−3°C).

N/HEMISPHERE	JAN	FEB	MAR	APR	MAY	JUN	JUL	AUG	SEP	OCT	NOV	DEC
°F AVG MAX	69	73	80	84	82	79	78	77	78	77	72	68
°F AVG MIN	41	44	51	57	62	65	65	65	64	59	52	44
DIURNAL RANGE	28	29	29	27	20	14	13	12	14	18	20	24
RAIN/INCHES	0.2	0.4	0.5	2.2	6.7	10.1	11.7	12.8	7.9	5.6	2.9	0.9
HUMIDITY/%	75	66	59	60	71	78	83	85	81	83	80	78
BLOOM SEASON							*					
DAYS CLR @ 7AM	1	12	15	13	7	2	0	0	0	0	0	2
DAYS CLR @ 1PM	20	21	22	12	4	0	0	0	2	4	12	18
RAIN/MM	5	10	13	56	170	257	297	325	201	142	74	23
°C AVG MAX	20.5	22.7	26.6	28.8	27.7	26.0	25.5	24.9	25.5	24.9	22.2	19.9
°C AVG MIN	4.9	6.6	10.5	13.8	16.6	18.3	18.3	18.3	17.7	14.9	11.0	6.6
DIURNAL RANGE	15.6	16.1	16.1	15.0	11.1	7.7	7.2	6.6	7.8	10.0	11.2	13.3
S/HEMISPHERE	JUL	AUG	SEP	OCT	NOV	DEC	JAN	FEB	MAR	APR	MAY	JUN

Cultural Recommendations

LIGHT: 2500–3500 fc. In the habitat, light is low from spring to early autumn because of heavy, persistent cloud cover. Conditions are brightest in late winter and early spring when many days are clear, especially during afternoons. In cultivation, as much light as possible, short of burning the foliage, should be provided.

TEMPERATURES: Summer days average 77–79°F (25–26°C), and nights average 65°F (18°C), with a diurnal range of 12–14°F (7–8°C). The warmest weather occurs in spring. Days average 80–84°F (27–29°C), and nights warm from 51–62°F (11–17°C), with a diurnal range of 20–29°F (11–16°C).

HUMIDITY: 80–85% in summer and autumn, dropping to near 75% in early winter. Humidity is lowest during clear, dry weather in early spring when it averages 60% for about 2 months.

WATER: Rainfall is heavy while plants are actively growing from late spring to early autumn. During this season, cultivated plants should be kept moist, with little if any drying allowed between waterings. Water should be gradually reduced after new growths mature in autumn.

FERTILIZER: ¼–½ recommended strength, applied weekly. A high-nitrogen fertilizer is beneficial from spring to midsummer, but a fertilizer high in phosphates should be used in late summer and autumn.

REST PERIOD: Winter days average 68–73°F (20–23°C), and nights average 41–44°F (5–7°C), with a diurnal range of 24–29°F (13–16°C). Plants should be able to tolerate temperatures a few degrees below freezing for short periods, but extremes should be avoided in cultivation. During very cold weather, a plant's chance of surviving with minimal damage is better if it is dry when temperatures are low. In the habitat, winter rainfall is low for 4–5 months, and humidity falls to near 60% in late winter and early spring, indicating distinctly reduced moisture. During the early part of the dry season, additional moisture is available from dew and as mist from fog and low clouds. For most of the winter, cultivated plants should be allowed to dry out between waterings, but they should not remain dry for extended periods. For 1–2 months in spring, however, weather in the habitat is clear, warm, and dry. Humidity is so low that even moisture from morning dew is uncommon. In cultivation, water should be further reduced to only an occasional early morning misting for 1–2 months. In the habitat, light is slightly higher in winter, but increased light may not be critical in cultivation. Low night temperatures or wide diurnal range may be necessary to initiate blooming.

GROWING MEDIA: Plants may be mounted on tree-fern or cork slabs if humidity is high and plants are watered at least once daily in summer. When plants are potted, any open, fast-draining medium may be used. Repotting is best done in early spring when new roots are growing.

MISCELLANEOUS NOTES: Bloom season in climate table based on cultivation records.

Plant and Flower Information

PLANT SIZE AND TYPE: A sympodial plant of unreported size.

PSEUDOBULB: Seidenfaden (ref. 454) indicates that the 6 in. (15 cm) stem measurement was for an incomplete specimen.

LEAVES: Many per growth. The leaves are usually 1.6–2.0 in. (4–5 cm) long. The pointed leaves are fleshy and distichous.

FLOWERS: Few. The 1.2 in. (3 cm) flowers are white suffused with rose. They do not open fully.

REFERENCES: 179, 218, 254, 454.

PHOTOS/DRAWINGS: 454.

Dendrobium curviflorum Thwaites. This name was used by Pradhan (ref. 369), but all listed references refer to *D. haemoglossum* Thwaites. REFERENCES: 369.

Dendrobium curvimentum J. J. Smith

ORIGIN/HABITAT: Irian Jaya (western New Guinea). Plants grow in the Arfak Mountains on the Vogelkop Peninsula. They are usually found in mountain forests at 7200–9350 ft. (2200–2850 m).

CLIMATE: Station #97530, Manokwari, Irian Jaya, Lat. 0.9°S, Long. 134.1°E, at 10 ft. (3 m). Temperatures are calculated for an elevation of 8200 ft. (2500 m), resulting in probable extremes of 66°F (19°C) and 41°F (5°C).

N/HEMISPHERE	JAN	FEB	MAR	APR	MAY	JUN	JUL	AUG	SEP	OCT	NOV	DEC
°F AVG MAX	59	58	60	60	61	59	59	59	59	59	59	58
°F AVG MIN	47	48	47	47	47	48	46	46	47	47	47	47
DIURNAL RANGE	12	10	13	13	14	11	13	13	12	12	12	11
RAIN/INCHES	5.4	5.6	5.0	4.7	4.5	10.3	12.0	9.4	13.2	11.1	7.8	7.3
HUMIDITY/%	87	87	86	84	85	86	86	85	86	86	86	85
BLOOM SEASON					*							
DAYS CLR @ 9AM	4	3	3	5	3	3	3	1	1	2	3	7
DAYS CLR @ 3PM	2	2	2	3	1	1	1	1	0	1	0	2
RAIN/MM	137	142	127	119	114	262	305	239	335	282	198	185
°C AVG MAX	15.0	14.4	15.5	15.5	16.1	15.0	15.0	15.0	15.0	15.0	15.0	14.4
°C AVG MIN	8.3	8.9	8.3	8.3	8.3	8.9	7.8	7.8	8.3	8.3	8.3	8.3
DIURNAL RANGE	6.7	5.5	7.2	7.2	7.8	6.1	7.2	7.2	6.7	6.7	6.7	6.1
S/HEMISPHERE	JUL	AUG	SEP	OCT	NOV	DEC	JAN	FEB	MAR	APR	MAY	JUN

Cultural Recommendations

LIGHT: 2000–3000 fc.

TEMPERATURES: Throughout the year, days average 58–61°F (14–16°C), and nights average 46–48°F (8–9°C), with a diurnal range of 11–14°F (6–8°C). Due to the effects of the microclimate, actual temperatures in the habitat may be as much as 10°F (6°C) warmer than indicated, especially the day-time maximums.

HUMIDITY: Near 85% year-round.

WATER: Rainfall is moderate to very heavy all year. Cultivated plants should be kept moist but not soggy.

FERTILIZER: ¼–½ recommended strength. A balanced fertilizer should be applied weekly to biweekly throughout the year.

REST PERIOD: Growing conditions should be maintained year-round. Water and fertilizer should be reduced somewhat in winter, especially for plants grown in the dark, short-day conditions in temperate latitudes, but they should never be allowed to dry out completely.

GROWING MEDIA: Plants may be mounted on tree-fern or cork slabs if humidity is high and plants are watered at least once daily in summer. When plants are potted, any open, fast-draining medium may be used. Repotting may be done anytime new roots are growing.

MISCELLANEOUS NOTES: The bloom season shown in the climate table is based on the collection record. Plants are known only from the type collection.

Plant and Flower Information

PLANT SIZE AND TYPE: An 8 in. (20 cm) or less sympodial epiphyte.

PSEUDOBULB: 8 in. (20 cm) long. The stems, which have 5 nodes below the leaves, become orange-yellow when dry.

LEAVES: 3 per growth. The pointed leaves are 2.0–2.6 in. (5.0–6.5 cm) long, leathery, and lanceolate.

INFLORESCENCE: 2.8–3.3 in. (7.0–8.5 cm) long. The erect inflorescences emerge at or near the apex of the stem.

FLOWERS: 15 or less per inflorescence. The small green flowers are 0.25 in. (0.6 cm) across. Blossoms glitter in the light.

REFERENCES: 83, 144, 222.

Dendrobium curvisepalum Ridley

ORIGIN/HABITAT: Irian Jaya (western New Guinea). Plants were found near the Noord River, inland from the south coast, at about 3100 ft. (950 m).

CLIMATE: Station #97796, Kokenau (Kokonau), Irian Jaya, Lat. 4.7°S, Long. 135.4°E, at 10 ft. (3 m). Temperatures are calculated for an elevation of 3000 ft. (910 m). Record extreme temperatures are not available for this location.

N/HEMISPHERE	JAN	FEB	MAR	APR	MAY	JUN	JUL	AUG	SEP	OCT	NOV	DEC
°F AVG MAX	73	73	76	78	80	79	79	79	80	78	77	74
°F AVG MIN	63	63	64	64	64	65	64	64	64	64	64	63
DIURNAL RANGE	10	10	12	14	16	14	15	15	16	14	13	11
RAIN/INCHES	18.4	15.8	18.9	11.6	9.7	10.6	11.5	15.7	11.6	11.6	16.0	19.9
HUMIDITY/%	N/A											
BLOOM SEASON	N/A											
DAYS CLR	N/A											
RAIN/MM	467	401	480	295	246	269	292	399	295	295	406	505
°C AVG MAX	22.9	22.9	24.5	25.6	26.7	26.2	26.2	26.2	26.7	25.6	25.1	23.4
°C AVG MIN	17.3	17.3	17.9	17.9	17.9	18.4	17.9	17.9	17.9	17.9	17.9	17.3
DIURNAL RANGE	5.6	5.6	6.6	7.7	8.8	7.8	8.3	8.3	8.8	7.7	7.2	6.1
S/HEMISPHERE	JUL	AUG	SEP	OCT	NOV	DEC	JAN	FEB	MAR	APR	MAY	JUN

Cultural Recommendations

LIGHT: 2500–3500 fc.

TEMPERATURES: Throughout the year, days average 73–80°F (23–27°C), and nights average 63–65°F (17–18°C), with a diurnal range of 10–16°F (6–9°C).

HUMIDITY: Information is not available for this location. However, average humidity at other stations in the region indicates probable values near 80% year-round.

WATER: Rainfall is very heavy year-round. Cultivated plants should be kept evenly moist but not soggy.

FERTILIZER: ¼–½ recommended strength. A balanced fertilizer should be applied weekly to biweekly throughout the year.

REST PERIOD: Growing conditions should be maintained year-round. Water and fertilizer might be reduced slightly in winter, especially for plants cultivated in the dark, short-day conditions common in temperate latitudes. Plants should never be allowed to dry out completely, however.

GROWING MEDIA: Plants may be mounted on tree-fern or cork slabs or potted in small pots filled with any open, fast-draining medium. Repotting may be done anytime new roots are growing.

Plant and Flower Information

PLANT SIZE AND TYPE: A sympodial epiphyte of unreported size.

PSEUDOBULB: The stems are slender.

LEAVES: Many. The ovate-lanceolate leaves are 2.2 in. (5.5 cm) long.

INFLORESCENCE: Short.

FLOWERS: 2 per inflorescence. The flowers are 2.4 in. (6 cm) across the spread lateral sepals. The sepals are curved. Petals are linear or lanceolate. The lip is fleshy and rounded at the apex. Blossoms were described as "fleshy and apparently white."

REFERENCES: 222, 400.

Dendrobium curvum Ridley

ORIGIN/HABITAT: Sumatra and near Quop, Sarawak, Borneo. In Sumatra, plants grow near Barong Bharu on the west side of the Barisan Range at 4000 ft. (1920 m).

CLIMATE: Station #96163, Padang, Sumatra, Indonesia, Lat. 0.9°S, Long. 100.4°E, at 19 ft. (6 m). Temperatures are calculated for an elevation of 4000 ft. (1220 m), resulting in probable extremes of 81°F (27°C) and 55°F (13°C).

N/HEMISPHERE	JAN	FEB	MAR	APR	MAY	JUN	JUL	AUG	SEP	OCT	NOV	DEC
°F AVG MAX	74	74	73	73	73	73	74	74	74	74	75	74
°F AVG MIN	61	61	61	61	61	61	61	61	61	62	62	61
DIURNAL RANGE	13	13	12	12	12	12	13	13	13	12	13	13
RAIN/INCHES	10.9	13.7	6.0	19.5	20.4	18.9	13.8	10.2	12.1	14.3	12.4	12.1
HUMIDITY/%	81	82	82	84	85	84	81	81	82	83	81	81
BLOOM SEASON	N/A											
DAYS CLR @ 7AM	5	1	1	0	0	2	2	1	2	2	3	5
DAYS CLR @ 1PM	5	2	2	1	1	3	3	4	3	3	6	5
RAIN/MM	277	348	152	495	518	480	351	259	307	363	315	307
°C AVG MAX	23.3	23.3	22.8	22.8	22.8	22.8	23.3	23.3	23.3	23.3	23.9	23.3
°C AVG MIN	16.1	16.1	16.1	16.1	16.1	16.1	16.1	16.1	16.1	16.7	16.7	16.1
DIURNAL RANGE	7.2	7.2	6.7	6.7	6.7	6.7	7.2	7.2	7.2	6.6	7.2	7.2
S/HEMISPHERE	JUL	AUG	SEP	OCT	NOV	DEC	JAN	FEB	MAR	APR	MAY	JUN

Cultural Recommendations

LIGHT: 2000–3000 fc. Clear days are rare, so light is naturally diffused.

TEMPERATURES: Throughout the year, days average 73–75°F (23–24°C), and nights average 61–62°F (16–17°C), with a diurnal range of 12–13°F (7°C). Probable extremes vary only a few degrees from the averages indicating that plants from this habitat may not tolerate wide temperature fluctuations.

HUMIDITY: 80–85% year-round.

WATER: Rainfall is heavy all year. Cultivated plants should be constantly moist but not soggy.

FERTILIZER: ¼–½ recommended strength. A balanced fertilizer should be applied weekly to biweekly throughout the year.

REST PERIOD: Growing conditions should be maintained year-round. Water might be reduced somewhat in winter, especially for plants grown in the dark, short-day conditions common in temperate latitudes. Plants should never be allowed to dry out completely, however. In the habitat, light is somewhat brighter for 2–3 months in winter as indicated by the increased number of clear afternoons.

GROWING MEDIA: Mounting plants on tree-fern or cork slabs accommodates their pendulous growth habit. However, humidity must be high and plants must be watered at least once a day in summer. If plants cannot be mounted, small pots or hanging baskets may be filled with an open, fast-draining medium. Repotting may be done anytime new roots are actively growing.

Plant and Flower Information

PLANT SIZE AND TYPE: A 9 in. (23 cm) sympodial epiphyte.

PSEUDOBULB: 3 in. (8 cm) long. The stem consists of internodes about 1.2 in. (3 cm) long.

LEAVES: The pointed, broadly lanceolate leaves are 6 in. (15 cm) long.

INFLORESCENCE: 4 in. (10 cm) long. The inflorescence emerges below the apex of the stem.

FLOWERS: 5 per inflorescence. Sepals are 0.9 in. (2.4 cm) long. Blossoms are white with orange markings on the lip. Sepals and petals are acutely lanceolate. The oblong lip is rounded at the apex. The spur is curved into a semicircle.

REFERENCES: 222, 401.

Dendrobium cuspidatum Kränzlin not Lindley. See *D. pseudocalceolum* J. J. Smith. REFERENCES: 437.

Dendrobium cuspidatum Lindley 1830 not 1858

AKA: *D. sarcanthum* Lindley.

ORIGIN/HABITAT: The Tenasserim region of Burma and the mountains of northwestern Thailand. In Thailand, plants were found north of Mae Sot at about 750 ft. (230 m).

Dendrobium cuspidatum

CLIMATE: Station #48375, Ban Mae Sot, Thailand, Lat. 16.7°N, Long. 98.5°E, at 742 ft. (226 m). Record extreme temperatures are 106°F (41°C) and 39°F (4°C).

N/HEMISPHERE	JAN	FEB	MAR	APR	MAY	JUN	JUL	AUG	SEP	OCT	NOV	DEC
°F AVG MAX	89	93	97	99	94	87	85	85	88	90	89	87
°F AVG MIN	58	61	67	73	75	75	74	75	74	72	67	60
DIURNAL RANGE	31	32	30	26	19	12	11	10	14	18	22	27
RAIN/INCHES	0.2	0.2	0.2	1.5	5.7	8.8	13.6	16.0	7.8	4.1	0.7	0.1
HUMIDITY/%	67	64	58	63	75	84	86	87	85	81	76	74
BLOOM SEASON	N/A											
DAYS CLR @ 7AM	2	1	2	5	1	0	0	0	0	2	2	2
DAYS CLR @ 1PM	20	19	17	10	1	0	0	0	0	2	7	13
RAIN/MM	5	5	5	38	145	224	345	406	198	104	18	3
°C AVG MAX	31.7	33.9	36.1	37.2	34.4	30.6	29.4	29.4	31.1	32.2	31.7	30.6
°C AVG MIN	14.4	16.1	19.4	22.8	23.9	23.9	23.3	23.9	23.3	22.2	19.4	15.6
DIURNAL RANGE	17.3	17.8	16.7	14.4	10.5	6.7	6.1	5.5	7.8	10.0	12.3	15.0
S/HEMISPHERE	JUL	AUG	SEP	OCT	NOV	DEC	JAN	FEB	MAR	APR	MAY	JUN

Cultural Recommendations

LIGHT: 1800–2400 fc. Diffused light is recommended. In nature, winter is the brightest season, having a large number of clear afternoons.

TEMPERATURES: Summer days average 85–87°F (29–31°C), and nights average 74–75°F (23–24°C), with a diurnal range of 10–12°F (6–7°C). The heavy cloud cover associated with summer monsoon results in the coolest daytime temperatures of the year. The warmest season occurs during the clear, dry weather in late winter and early spring. Days average 94–99°F (34–37°C), and nights average 67–75°F (19–24°C), with a diurnal range of 19–30°F (11–17°C).

HUMIDITY: Near 85% in summer, dropping to 60–65% for 3–4 months in winter.

WATER: Rainfall is heavy while plants are actively growing from late spring to early autumn. During this season, cultivated plants should be kept moist, with little if any drying allowed between waterings. However, water should be gradually reduced after new growths mature in autumn.

FERTILIZER: ¼–½ recommended strength, applied weekly. A high-nitrogen fertilizer is beneficial from spring to midsummer, but a fertilizer high in phosphates should be used in late summer and autumn.

REST PERIOD: Winter days average 87–93°F (31–34°C), and nights average 58–61°F (14–16°C), with a diurnal range of 27–32°F (15–18°C). The increased diurnal range results from warmer days and cooler nights during clear winter weather. In the habitat, winter rainfall is low for 4–5 months, and humidity falls to near 60% in late winter and early spring. During the early part of the dry season, additional moisture is available from dew and as mist from fog and low clouds. For most of the winter, cultivated plants should be allowed to dry out between waterings, but they should not remain dry for extended periods. For 1–2 months in late winter, however, weather in the habitat is clear, warm, and dry. Humidity is so low that even moisture from morning dew is uncommon. In cultivation, water should be further reduced to only an occasional early morning misting for 1–2 months. In the habitat, light is higher in winter, but increased light may not be critical in cultivation. The dry rest or the wide diurnal temperature range may be necessary to initiate blooming.

GROWING MEDIA: Plants may be mounted on tree-fern or cork slabs if humidity is high and plants are watered at least once daily in summer. When plants are potted, any open, fast-draining medium may be used. Repotting is best done in early spring when new roots are growing.

Plant and Flower Information

PLANT SIZE AND TYPE: A 2–6 in. (5–15 cm) sympodial epiphyte.

PSEUDOBULB: 1–4 in. (2.5–10.0 cm) long. The short, stout pseudobulbs taper at the tip.

LEAVES: 3–5 per growth. The linear-oblong leaves are 1.2–2.0 in. (3–5 cm) long.

INFLORESCENCE: 0.8–1.2 in. (2–3 cm) long. Many inflorescences arise near the apex of new growths. Flowers are clustered at the tip of the inflorescence.

FLOWERS: 3–6 per inflorescence. The flowers are 0.5–0.7 in. (1.3–1.8 cm) across. The pointed sepals and petals are white often with a faint greenish tinge. The lip is light green with purple stripes on the sidelobes and yellow-green at the base of the throat.

REFERENCES: 157, 202, 216, 254, 437, 454.

PHOTOS/DRAWINGS: 454.

Dendrobium cuspidatum Lindley 1858 not 1830. See *D. nathanielis* Rchb. f. REFERENCES: 216, 254, 278, 369, 454.

Dendrobium cuthbertsonii F. Mueller

AKA: Reeve and Woods (ref. 385) include the synonyms *D. agathodaemonis* J. J. Smith, *D. asperifolium* J. J. Smith, *D. atromarginatum* J. J. Smith, *D. carstensziense* J. J. Smith, *D. coccinellum* Ridley, *D. euphues* Ridley, *D. fulgidum* Ridley, *D. laetum* Schlechter, *D. lichenicola* J. J. Smith, *D. sophronites* Schlechter, and *D. trachyphyllum* Schlechter.

ORIGIN/HABITAT: New Guinea. Plants grow at high elevations on moss-covered trees, mossy rocks near streams, and cliff faces and east-facing road cuts, where the roots attach to the clay soil beneath the covering of moss, lichens, and other small plants. They are found in shady places as well as on exposed mountain peaks in typical alpine habitat, where they are exposed to breezes. Plants have been reported from elevations as low as 2450 ft. (750 m), but they are more often found at 6550–11,500 ft. (2000–3500 m). Schlechter (ref. 437) indicated that the high alpine species require "much moisture for their cultivation and under no circumstances will they tolerate high, continuous heat. Where they occur, particularly in the mornings during their growth periods, the temperature drops to 41°F (5°C) and below."

CLIMATE: Botanical garden records, Laiagam, Papua New Guinea, Lat. 5.5°S, Long. 143.5°E, at 7218 ft. (2200 m). Temperatures are calculated for an elevation of 8500 ft. (2600 m), resulting in probable extremes of 87°F (30°C) and 28°F (−2°C).

N/HEMISPHERE	JAN	FEB	MAR	APR	MAY	JUN	JUL	AUG	SEP	OCT	NOV	DEC
°F AVG MAX	72	73	74	72	74	74	78	73	72	74	74	72
°F AVG MIN	51	50	51	51	52	52	51	52	54	53	52	52
DIURNAL RANGE	21	23	23	21	22	22	27	21	18	21	22	20
RAIN/INCHES	4.0	4.8	6.1	7.8	8.5	9.1	8.4	9.6	9.5	8.9	6.3	4.0
HUMIDITY/%	N/A											
BLOOM SEASON	*	*	*	*	*	*	*	*	*	*	*	*
DAYS CLR	N/A											
RAIN/MM	102	122	155	198	216	231	213	244	241	226	160	102
°C AVG MAX	22.1	22.6	23.2	22.1	23.2	23.2	25.4	22.6	22.1	23.2	23.2	22.1
°C AVG MIN	10.4	9.9	10.4	10.4	11.0	11.0	10.4	11.0	12.1	11.5	11.0	11.0
DIURNAL RANGE	11.7	12.7	12.8	11.7	12.2	12.2	15.0	11.6	10.0	11.7	12.2	11.1
S/HEMISPHERE	JUL	AUG	SEP	OCT	NOV	DEC	JAN	FEB	MAR	APR	MAY	JUN

Cultural Recommendations

LIGHT: 1500–3000 fc. *D. cuthbertsonii* may tolerate higher light levels, especially during mornings. Growers indicate that plants need more light than they often receive in cultivation.

TEMPERATURES: Throughout the year, days average 72–78°F (22–25°C), and nights average 50–54°F (10–12°C), with a diurnal range of 18–27°F (10–15°C). In the habitat, the warmest temperatures of the day occur in late morning when skies are clear. Clouds and mist develop near noon and continue through the afternoon, thus preventing additional warming. Reports from the habitat indicate a sharp contrast between day and night temperatures. Because plants are found over a wide range of elevations, they should adapt to temperatures 6–8°F (3–4°C) warmer or cooler than indicated above.

HUMIDITY: Information is not available for this location. However, humidity in mistforest habitats normally exceeds 80% year-round. In cultivation, high humidity and excellent air circulation are particularly important if temperatures are warm. Placing the plants in front of an evaporative cooler or near a fine mist is very beneficial.

WATER: Rainfall is heavy throughout the year, but for 3–4 months in winter, conditions are slightly drier. Cultivated plants should be kept moist, with little if any drying allowed between waterings.

FERTILIZER: ¼–½ recommended strength. A balanced fertilizer should be applied weekly to biweekly throughout the year. *D. cuthbertsonii* requires little or no fertilizer if grown in live sphagnum moss. In any medium, fertilizer should be very weak. The Royal Botanic Garden in Edinburgh uses a dilute, seaweed-based fertilizer.

REST PERIOD: Growing conditions should be maintained year-round. Water and fertilizer may be reduced somewhat in winter, especially for plants grown in the dark, short-day conditions common in temperate latitudes, but they should never be allowed to dry out completely. Occasional early morning mistings between waterings may be beneficial, particularly on bright, sunny days. In the habitat, light may be slightly higher in winter.

GROWING MEDIA: In our experience and that of the Australian Orchid Foundation, who raised 5000 seedlings, the greatest success is achieved when plants are potted in New Zealand sphagnum moss. Roots grow better and remain healthier in this medium. Plants may be mounted on tree-fern slabs, but they must be misted frequently. *D. cuthbertsonii* should never be allowed to dry out. Some growers use a small layer of osmunda over broken crock or chopped tree-fern. However, the Australian Orchid Foundation found that tree fern becomes sour in about 2 years. Repotting is best done in early spring when conditions are most conducive to active growth. Plants grown in sphagnum moss should be repotted at least once a year. They should not be divided into small clumps, as the divisions seldom survive unless growing conditions are ideal.

MISCELLANEOUS NOTES: The bloom season shown in the climate table is based on cultivation records. Growers report that *D. cuthbertsonii* generally grows well in conditions appropriate for cool-growing Masdevallias. High humidity and excellent air movement are essential. However, it has a reputation for being difficult to grow, and even successful growers indicate they sometimes lose a plant after growing it successfully for years. Speculation regarding cause includes the possibility that the plant's life-span may be short or that plants may bloom themselves to death. The practice of removing the first blossom on seedlings soon after it opens allows the plant to build additional reserves and is highly recommended. Plants grown in Scotland have grown slowly on cork or tree-fern slabs for more than 17 years. Plants usually bloom within 5 years from seed, but some have been reported to bloom only 1–2 years out of flask. Roots may be white, pinkish, or purplish when wet, but the growing tips are green.

Plant and Flower Information

PLANT SIZE AND TYPE: A 0.8–3.2 in. (2–8 cm) sympodial epiphyte, lithophyte, or terrestrial.

PSEUDOBULB: 0.2–3.2 in. (0.5–8.0 cm) long. Pseudobulbs are variable, and may be ovoid, spheroid, or stemlike. They may sometimes even branch. Growths normally arise from a short rhizome. Observers indicate that plants grow on most moss-covered surfaces and often form clumps that reach a circumference of 5 in. (13 cm). Plants exposed to high light tend to be tufted and form clumps, however, those grown in lower light or in competition with mosses tend to develop a branching, elongated growth habit. If conditions change, plants modify their growth habits.

LEAVES: 1–5 per growth. The green to blackish green leaves are 0.2–1.6 in. (0.5–4.2 cm) long. They may be linear to broadly elliptic. The upper leaf surface may be smooth, but it is normally rough with a dense covering of small warts.

INFLORESCENCE: 0.1 in. (0.25 cm) long. Inflorescences emerge from the apex of the plant. In rare instances, inflorescences are lateral. Flowers tend to hang or flop, due to the weight of the blossom, resulting in the lip usually being uppermost or horizontal.

FLOWERS: 1 per inflorescence. The flowers are 0.9–1.6 in. (2.2–4.0 cm), rarely to 2.0 in. (5 cm) across. In the sunlight, they are glittering and luminous. The sepals and petals, which are normally scarlet- to crimson-red, may be purple, pink, orange, yellow, or white. Rarely, flowers with bicolored segments are found. The lip is often paler with dark, reddish brown markings near the apex. Flower size and shape are variable. Blossoms last up to 10 months.

HYBRIDIZING NOTES: Chromosome counts as *D. sophronites* Schlechter are 2n = 38 (ref. 151, 154, 187, 188) and 2n = about 80 (ref. 187, 504, 580). As *D. cuthbertsonii* F. Mueller, the count is 2n = 76 (ref. 153, 273).

REFERENCES: 36, 49, 91, 95, 144, 151, 153, 154, 179, 187, 188, 196, 218, 254, 273, 304, 305, 318, 332, 333, 371, 378, 379, 385, 400, 430, 437, 498, 504, 525, 549, 554, 556, 580, 598.

PHOTOS/DRAWINGS: *47, 49, 91, 95, 115, 124, 126, 273, 304, 305, 318, 321, 332, 333, 371, 378, 379, 385, 430, 437, 498, 519, 554, 556.*

Dendrobium cyananthum L. O. Williams. See *D. hellwigianum* Kränzlin. REFERENCES: 227, 385.

Dendrobium cyanocentrum Schlechter

AKA: *D. flavispiculum* J. J. Smith, *D. lapeyrouseoides* Schlechter.

ORIGIN/HABITAT: The mountain regions of New Guinea. Plants grow in rainforests, forest clearings, and on trees along river banks. They are normally found at 2600–4250 ft. (800–1300 m), but they sometimes grow as low as 350 ft. (100 m). Plants have also been collected in the Solomon Islands.

CLIMATE: Station #94010, Goroka, Papua New Guinea, Lat. 6.1°S, Long. 145.4°E, at 5141 ft. (1567 m). Temperatures are calculated for an elevation of 3300 ft. (1000 m), resulting in probable extremes of 93°F (34°C) and 49°F (10°C).

N/HEMISPHERE	JAN	FEB	MAR	APR	MAY	JUN	JUL	AUG	SEP	OCT	NOV	DEC
°F AVG MAX	82	83	84	85	85	84	85	84	84	84	85	83
°F AVG MIN	62	63	63	63	64	65	65	65	66	65	65	63
DIURNAL RANGE	20	20	21	22	21	19	20	19	18	19	20	20
RAIN/INCHES	2.1	2.8	4.6	5.9	6.6	9.3	9.1	10.1	10.7	8.3	4.6	2.0
HUMIDITY/%	70	67	67	67	67	71	72	73	74	71	70	70
BLOOM SEASON	*											
DAYS CLR	N/A											
RAIN/MM	53	71	117	150	168	236	231	257	272	211	117	51
°C AVG MAX	27.9	28.4	29.0	29.5	29.5	29.0	29.5	29.0	29.0	29.0	29.5	28.4
°C AVG MIN	16.7	17.3	17.3	17.3	17.9	18.4	18.4	18.4	19.0	18.4	18.4	17.3
DIURNAL RANGE	11.2	11.1	11.7	12.2	11.6	10.6	11.1	10.6	10.0	10.6	11.1	11.1
S/HEMISPHERE	JUL	AUG	SEP	OCT	NOV	DEC	JAN	FEB	MAR	APR	MAY	JUN

Cultural Recommendations

LIGHT: 1000–1800 fc. Growers recommend shady conditions.

TEMPERATURES: Throughout the year, days average 82–85°F (28–30°C), and nights average 62–66°F (17–19°C), with a diurnal range of 19–22°F (11–12°C). Average highs and lows vary only slightly during the year, indicating that plants are unlikely to be healthy under widely fluctuating temperatures.

HUMIDITY: 70–75% in summer and autumn, dropping to 65–70% in winter and spring.

WATER: Rainfall is moderate to heavy most of the year but is relatively low for 2–3 months in winter. However, additional moisture is available from dew, fog, and mist, even during periods when rainfall is low. Cultivated plants should be kept moist but not soggy. Additional early morning mistings between waterings are often beneficial, especially on warm, bright, sunny days.

FERTILIZER: ¼–½ recommended strength. A balanced fertilizer should be applied weekly to biweekly throughout the year.

Dendrobium cyanopterum

REST PERIOD: Growing temperatures should be maintained all year. Water should be reduced in winter. Plants should dry slightly between waterings, but they should never be allowed to dry out completely. Fertilizer should be reduced or eliminated until water is increased in spring. In the habitat, winter light may be slightly higher.

GROWING MEDIA: Plants may be mounted on tree-fern or cork slabs if humidity is high and plants are watered at least once daily in summer. Plants adhere firmly to tree bark. When plants are potted, any open, fast-draining medium may be used. Repotting may be done anytime new roots are growing.

MISCELLANEOUS NOTES: The bloom season shown in the climate table is based on collection records. Cultivation records indicate that blooming occurs every season of the year. Growers consider this species easy to cultivate.

Plant and Flower Information

PLANT SIZE AND TYPE: A 0.6–3.2 in. (1.5–8.0 cm) sympodial epiphyte. Plants may be erect or semipendulous. They grow in colonies and may form clumps 4.8 in. (12 cm) across.

PSEUDOBULB: 0.3–2.5 in. (0.8–6.4 cm) long. The ovoid to cylindrical pseudobulbs vary from greenish, to greenish yellow, to reddish.

LEAVES: 2–4 at the apex of each growth. The leaves are 0.4–2.4 in. (1–6 cm) long, slender, rough, and twisted. They may be pale yellowish to dark green with purplish red on the underside.

INFLORESCENCE: Short. Flowers tend to be hidden in the leaves. Inflorescences arise at the apex of leafy and leafless pseudobulbs.

FLOWERS: 1, rarely 2 per inflorescence. Shaped like a shooting star, the flowers are 0.6 in. (1.5 cm) across. Sepals and petals are strongly reflexed. They are white to greenish white overlaid with pink, blue, or violet stripes. Color is darkest near the base of the segments and along the veins. The lip is often purplish brown, but it may be purple, yellowish brown, orange, yellow, or green. The anther may be blue, violet, green, or yellow.

HYBRIDIZING NOTES: Chromosome count is 2n = 38 (ref. 153, 273).

REFERENCES: 92, 153, 179, 219, 254, 273, 305, 318, 330, 385, 437, 444, 445, 470, 476, 516, 549, 554.

PHOTOS/DRAWINGS: 24, *318, 385*, 437, *549*.

Dendrobium cyanopterum Kränzlin

ORIGIN/HABITAT: Papua New Guinea. Plants were collected at Bartle Bay, which is on the south coast near the eastern tip of the island. Additional habitat information is not available, so the following temperatures should be used with caution.

CLIMATE: Station #94075, Samarai, Sideia Island, Papua New Guinea, Lat. 10.6°S, Long. 150.7°E, at 20 ft. (6 m). Record extreme temperatures are 104°F (40°C) and 64°F (18°C).

N/HEMISPHERE	JAN	FEB	MAR	APR	MAY	JUN	JUL	AUG	SEP	OCT	NOV	DEC
°F AVG MAX	81	81	82	83	85	87	87	88	87	86	84	82
°F AVG MIN	74	73	74	74	75	76	77	77	76	75	75	74
DIURNAL RANGE	7	8	8	9	10	11	10	11	11	11	9	8
RAIN/INCHES	8.1	8.6	10.1	8.7	8.4	6.1	7.0	7.8	10.0	9.8	12.0	11.3
HUMIDITY/%	N/A											
BLOOM SEASON	N/A											
DAYS CLR	N/A											
RAIN/MM	206	218	257	221	213	155	178	198	254	249	305	287
°C AVG MAX	27.2	27.2	27.8	28.3	29.4	30.6	30.6	31.1	30.6	30.0	28.9	27.8
°C AVG MIN	23.3	22.8	23.3	23.3	23.9	24.4	25.0	25.0	24.4	23.9	23.9	23.3
DIURNAL RANGE	3.9	4.4	4.5	5.0	5.5	6.2	5.6	6.1	6.2	6.1	5.0	4.5
S/HEMISPHERE	JUL	AUG	SEP	OCT	NOV	DEC	JAN	FEB	MAR	APR	MAY	JUN

Cultural Recommendations

LIGHT: 2500–3000 fc.

TEMPERATURES: Throughout the year, days average 81–88°F (27–31°C), and nights average 73–77°F (23–25°C), with a diurnal range of 7–11°F (4–6°C).

HUMIDITY: Information is not available for this location. However, records from nearby stations indicate that humidity is probably 70–80% year-round.

WATER: Rainfall is very heavy year-round. Cultivated plants should be kept moist but not soggy.

FERTILIZER: ¼–½ recommended strength. A balanced fertilizer should be applied weekly to biweekly throughout the year.

REST PERIOD: Growing conditions should be maintained year-round. In the habitat, winter rainfall is high; but water and fertilizer should be reduced for cultivated plants, especially those grown in the dark, short-day conditions in temperate-latitude winters. Plants should never be allowed to dry out completely, however. In the habitat, seasonal light variation is minor.

GROWING MEDIA: Plants may be mounted on tree-fern or cork slabs if humidity is high and plants are watered at least once daily in summer. When plants are potted, any open, fast-draining medium may be used. Repotting may be done anytime new roots are growing.

Plant and Flower Information

PLANT SIZE AND TYPE: A sympodial epiphyte of unreported size.

PSEUDOBULB: The stems are flattened. The plant was described from an incomplete specimen 10 in. (25 cm) long.

LEAVES: Many. The linear leaves are 4 in. (10 cm) long, papery, and pointed. The leaf sheaths are slightly scaly.

INFLORESCENCE: Short.

FLOWERS: 2 per inflorescence. The flowers are 0.5 in. (1.3 cm) long. They are pale yellow with blue on the lip sidelobes. The blossoms have a lanceolate, pointed dorsal sepal, linear-lanceolate petals, and sickle-shaped lateral sepals that are somewhat triangular. The disk is covered with hairs.

REFERENCES: 220, 254.

Dendrobium cyatheicola P. van Royen. See *D. brevicaule* Rolfe. REFERENCES: 233, 385, 538. PHOTOS/DRAWINGS: 538.

Dendrobium cyclobulbon Schlechter. Now considered a synonym of *Diplocaulobium cyclobulbon* (Schlechter) A. Hawkes. REFERENCES: 87, 92, 191, 221, 229, 271, 437, 445, 470.

Dendrobium cyclolobum Schlechter

ORIGIN/HABITAT: Northern Papua New Guinea near Madang. Plants grow along the upper Djamu River, a tributary of the Mindjim (Minjem) River, in mountain forests at about 1650 ft. (500 m).

CLIMATE: Station #200187, Erap, Papua New Guinea, Lat. 6.6°S, Long. 146.7°E, at 850 ft. (260 m). Temperatures are calculated for an elevation of 1950 ft. (600 m), resulting in probable extremes of 98°F (37°C) and 49°F (10°C).

N/HEMISPHERE	JAN	FEB	MAR	APR	MAY	JUN	JUL	AUG	SEP	OCT	NOV	DEC
°F AVG MAX	84	84	85	86	89	89	89	89	89	88	86	86
°F AVG MIN	65	65	65	66	68	69	68	68	69	67	70	66
DIURNAL RANGE	19	19	20	20	21	20	21	21	20	21	16	20
RAIN/INCHES	3.9	3.9	2.7	3.0	3.0	5.3	5.9	5.9	7.0	3.4	2.4	3.1
HUMIDITY/%	82	81	81	79	75	74	74	74	77	76	80	80
BLOOM SEASON					*							
DAYS CLR	N/A											
RAIN/MM	99	99	69	76	76	135	150	150	178	86	61	79
°C AVG MAX	29.1	29.1	29.6	30.2	31.8	31.8	31.8	31.8	31.8	31.3	30.2	30.2
°C AVG MIN	18.5	18.5	18.5	19.1	20.2	20.7	20.2	20.2	20.7	19.6	21.3	19.1
DIURNAL RANGE	10.6	10.6	11.1	11.1	11.6	11.1	11.6	11.6	11.1	11.7	8.9	11.1
S/HEMISPHERE	JUL	AUG	SEP	OCT	NOV	DEC	JAN	FEB	MAR	APR	MAY	JUN

Cultural Recommendations

LIGHT: 2500–3000 fc.

TEMPERATURES: Throughout the year, days average 84–89°F (29–32°C), and nights average 65–70°F (19–21°C), with a diurnal range of 16–21°F (9–12°C).

HUMIDITY: Near 75–80% year-round. The habitat may be quite dry for a few hours during hot afternoons, however.

WATER: Rainfall is moderate most of the year, but conditions are a little drier from late autumn to spring. However, the high relative humidity and the large diurnal temperature range indicate additional water is available from frequent heavy deposits of dew. Cultivated plants should be allowed to dry slightly between waterings, but they should not remain dry for extended periods.

FERTILIZER: ¼–½ recommended strength. A balanced fertilizer should be applied weekly to biweekly throughout the year.

REST PERIOD: Growing temperatures should be maintained all year. Water should be reduced somewhat for cultivated plants, especially those grown in the dark, short-day conditions common in temperate-latitude winters, but they should not be allowed to dry out completely. Fertilizer should be reduced in winter.

GROWING MEDIA: Plants may be mounted on tree-fern or cork slabs if humidity is high and plants are watered at least once daily in summer. When plants are potted, any open, fast-draining medium may be used. Repotting may be done anytime new roots are growing.

MISCELLANEOUS NOTES: The bloom season shown in the climate table is based on the collection report. Plants that produce flowers which last a single day commonly bloom several times during the year. Flowering usually occurs 7–14 days after a sudden 10°F (5°C) drop in daytime temperatures.

Plant and Flower Information

PLANT SIZE AND TYPE: A 20 in. (50 cm) sympodial epiphyte.

PSEUDOBULB: 20 in. (50 cm) long. Pseudobulbs are somewhat flattened and do not branch.

LEAVES: Many. The spreading, oblong leaves are 2.4–3.1 in. (6–8 cm) long. Growths are densely leafy.

INFLORESCENCE: Short. Inflorescences emerge from leaf axils.

FLOWERS: 2 per inflorescence. The flowers, which last a single day, are 0.6 in. (1.4 cm) across. Blossoms are creamy yellow with a violet column foot marked with an orange-red spot.

REFERENCES: 221, 437, 445.

PHOTOS/DRAWINGS: 437.

Dendrobium cyclopense J. J. Smith. Although not correctly transferred, Schlechter (ref. 443) considered this name to be a synonym of *Cadetia cyclopensis* (J. J. Smith) Schlechter. REFERENCES: 221, 223, 443, 445, 470.

Dendrobium cylindricum J. J. Smith

ORIGIN/HABITAT: Irian Jaya (western New Guinea). *D. cylindricum* grows on mountain peaks in the Arfak Range at about 6250 ft. (1900 m). It is epiphytic in open moss-covered forests.

CLIMATE: Station #97530, Manokwari, Irian Jaya, Lat. 0.9°S, Long. 134.1°E, at 10 ft. (3 m). Temperatures are calculated for an elevation of 6250 ft. (1900 m), resulting in probable extremes of 72°F (22°C) and 47°F (9°C).

N/HEMISPHERE	JAN	FEB	MAR	APR	MAY	JUN	JUL	AUG	SEP	OCT	NOV	DEC
°F AVG MAX	65	64	66	66	67	65	65	65	65	65	65	64
°F AVG MIN	53	54	53	53	53	54	52	52	53	53	53	53
DIURNAL RANGE	12	10	13	13	14	11	13	13	12	12	12	11
RAIN/INCHES	5.4	5.6	5.0	4.7	4.5	10.3	12.0	9.4	13.2	11.1	7.8	7.3
HUMIDITY/%	87	87	86	84	85	86	86	85	86	86	86	85
BLOOM SEASON												
DAYS CLR @ 9AM	4	3	3	5	3	3	3	1	1	2	3	7
DAYS CLR @ 3PM	2	2	2	3	1	1	1	1	0	1	0	2
RAIN/MM	137	142	127	119	114	262	305	239	335	282	198	185
°C AVG MAX	18.6	18.0	19.1	19.1	19.7	18.6	18.6	18.6	18.6	18.6	18.6	18.0
°C AVG MIN	11.9	12.4	11.9	11.9	11.9	12.4	11.3	11.3	11.9	11.9	11.9	11.9
DIURNAL RANGE	6.7	5.6	7.2	7.2	7.8	6.2	7.3	7.3	6.7	6.7	6.7	6.1
S/HEMISPHERE	JUL	AUG	SEP	OCT	NOV	DEC	JAN	FEB	MAR	APR	MAY	JUN

Cultural Recommendations

LIGHT: 2000–3000 fc.

TEMPERATURES: Throughout the year, days average 64–67°F (18–20°C), and nights average 52–54°F (11–12°C), with a diurnal range of 11–14°F (6–8°C). Due to the effects of microclimate, the actual day-time high temperatures may be as much as 10°F (6°C) warmer than indicated.

HUMIDITY: Near 85% year-round.

WATER: Rainfall is moderate to very heavy all year. Cultivated plants should be kept moist with only slight drying allowed between waterings.

FERTILIZER: ¼–½ recommended strength. A balanced fertilizer should be applied weekly to biweekly throughout the year.

REST PERIOD: Growing conditions should be maintained year-round. Water and fertilizer may be reduced somewhat in winter, especially for plants grown in the dark, short-day conditions common in temperate latitudes. Plants should never be allowed to dry out completely, however.

GROWING MEDIA: Plants may be mounted on tree-fern or cork slabs if humidity is high and plants are watered at least once daily in summer. When plants are potted, any open, fast-draining medium may be used. Repotting may be done anytime new roots are growing.

MISCELLANEOUS NOTES: The bloom season shown in the climate table is based on reports from the habitat.

Plant and Flower Information

PLANT SIZE AND TYPE: A 28 in. (70 cm) sympodial epiphyte.

PSEUDOBULB: 28 in. (70 cm) long. The unbranched stems are terete, flexuous, and angled on the upper part.

LEAVES: Many. The pale green leaves are 1.4–3.0 in. (3.5–7.5 cm) long. They are pointed, ovate to lanceolate, and minutely serrated.

INFLORESCENCE: Short. Inflorescences emerge near the apex of the stem.

FLOWERS: 9 per inflorescence. The orange flowers are 1 in. (2.5 cm) across. They have an ovate dorsal sepal, obliquely triangular lateral sepals, and lanceolate petals. The concave lip has no callus.

REFERENCES: 221, 470, 476.

Dendrobium cymatoleguum Schlechter

AKA: *D. schinzianum* Kränzlin.

ORIGIN/HABITAT: New Caledonia. *D. cymatoleguum* roots in river rubble along the banks of the Ngoye River at about 164 ft. (50 m).

CLIMATE: Station #91592, Noumea, New Caledonia, Lat. 22.3°S, Long. 166.5°E, at 246 ft. (75 m). Record extreme temperatures are 99°F (37°C) and 52°F (11°C).

Dendrobium cymbidioides

N/HEMISPHERE	JAN	FEB	MAR	APR	MAY	JUN	JUL	AUG	SEP	OCT	NOV	DEC
°F AVG MAX	76	76	78	80	83	86	86	85	85	83	79	77
°F AVG MIN	62	61	63	65	68	70	72	73	72	70	66	64
DIURNAL RANGE	14	15	15	15	15	16	14	12	13	13	13	13
RAIN/INCHES	3.6	2.6	2.5	2.0	2.4	2.6	3.7	5.1	5.7	5.2	4.4	3.7
HUMIDITY/%	73	70	69	67	68	69	71	74	75	76	73	73
BLOOM SEASON	*	*	*	*	*							
DAYS CLR @ 11AM	7	9	9	15	12	10	7	6	7	7	7	7
DAYS CLR @ 5PM	7	11	6	11	7	6	5	4	4	5	3	7
RAIN/MM	91	66	64	51	61	66	94	130	145	132	112	94
°C AVG MAX	24.4	24.4	25.6	26.7	28.3	30.0	30.0	29.4	29.4	28.3	26.1	25.0
°C AVG MIN	16.7	16.1	17.2	18.3	20.0	21.1	22.2	22.8	22.2	21.1	18.9	17.8
DIURNAL RANGE	7.7	8.3	8.4	8.4	8.3	8.9	7.8	6.6	7.2	7.2	7.2	7.2
S/HEMISPHERE	JUL	AUG	SEP	OCT	NOV	DEC	JAN	FEB	MAR	APR	MAY	JUN

Cultural Recommendations

LIGHT: 1500–2500 fc.

TEMPERATURES: Summer days average 85–86°F (29–30°C), and nights average 70–73°F (21–23°C), with a diurnal range of 12–16°F (7–9°C).

HUMIDITY: 70–75% most of the year, dropping to near 65% for 1–2 months in spring.

WATER: Rainfall is moderate to heavy year-round. Cultivated plants should be allowed to dry slightly between waterings.

FERTILIZER: 1/4–1/2 recommended strength. A balanced fertilizer should be applied weekly to biweekly throughout the year.

REST PERIOD: Winter days average 76–78°F (24–26°C), and nights average 61–64°F (16–18°C), with a diurnal range of 13–15°F (7–8°C). High and low temperatures decline simultaneously, resulting in little change in the diurnal range. In the habitat, rainfall is somewhat lower in late winter and spring. In cultivation, water and fertilizer should be reduced and the plants allowed to dry even more between waterings than in summer. They should not dry out completely or remain dry for long periods, however. In the habitat, light is highest in winter.

GROWING MEDIA: Plants may be mounted on tree-fern or cork slabs if humidity is high and plants are watered at least once daily in summer. When plants are potted, any open, fast-draining medium may be used. Repotting may be done anytime new roots are growing.

MISCELLANEOUS NOTES: The bloom season shown in the climate table is based on reports from the habitat.

Plant and Flower Information

PLANT SIZE AND TYPE: A 20–35 in. (50–90 cm) sympodial terrestrial.

PSEUDOBULB: 20–35 in. (50–90 cm) long.

LEAVES: Many. The unequally bilobed leaves, which are 1.6–2.0 in. (4–5 cm) long, are held in 2 rows.

INFLORESCENCE: 1.6–2.0 in. (4–5 cm) long. Inflorescences emerge opposite the base of most leaves, so they are also arranged in 2 rows.

FLOWERS: 3–6 per inflorescence. The flowers are 0.2 in. (0.6 cm) long and remain rather closed. All segments are brown with white crests on the lip. The 3-keeled lip is deeply ruffled along the margin of the midlobe.

REFERENCES: 173, 220, 254, 432.

PHOTOS/DRAWINGS: 173.

Dendrobium cymbidioides (Blume) Lindley.

Now considered a synonym of *Epigeneium cymbidioides* (Blume) Summerhayes. REFERENCES: 25, 75, 151, 154, 187, 188, 190, 213, 216, 229, 254, 277, 298, 310, 317, 445, 469, 499, 541. PHOTOS/DRAWINGS: 469.

Dendrobium cymbiforme Rolfe.

Plants originated in Sumatra. Habitat and elevation are unavailable, so climate data cannot be selected. The plant is a sympodial epiphyte with erect stems 6–12 in. (15–30 cm) long. The oblong-lanceolate leaves are 1.0–1.5 in. (2.5–3.8 cm) long. Short inflorescences emerge from the side of the stem and carry 2 blossoms. The flowers are 1 in. (2.5 cm) across. The petals are somewhat whiter than the straw yellow sepals. Each segment is decorated with 5 purple stripes. The purple lines on the lip are near the apex. The ovate-oblong sepals and slightly shorter petals are less than 0.5 in. (1.2 cm) long. The lip is nearly twice as wide as it is long. The wavy midlobe appears chopped-off at the recurved tip. The callus is boat-shaped. REFERENCES: 254, 411.

Dendrobium cymboglossum J. J. Wood and A. Lamb

ORIGIN/HABITAT: Borneo. Plants have been collected in northeast Borneo near Tawao (Tawau), Sabah, in the Sepilok Forest Reserve near Sandakan, and at Taman Tawao. Habitat elevation was not reported, but plants were cultivated at the Poring Orchid Garden near Ranau, which is at about 1800 ft. (550 m). Therefore, we have calculated temperatures based on the elevation at Ranau, but the resulting values should be used with caution.

CLIMATE: Station #96491, Sandakan, Sabah, Lat. 5.9°N, Long. 118.1°E, at 38 ft. (12 m). Temperatures are calculated for an elevation of 1800 ft. (550 m), resulting in probable extremes of 93°F (34°C) and 64°F (18°C).

N/HEMISPHERE	JAN	FEB	MAR	APR	MAY	JUN	JUL	AUG	SEP	OCT	NOV	DEC
°F AVG MAX	79	80	81	83	83	83	83	83	83	82	81	80
°F AVG MIN	68	68	69	70	70	69	69	69	69	69	69	68
DIURNAL RANGE	11	12	12	13	13	14	14	14	14	13	12	12
RAIN/INCHES	19.0	10.9	8.6	4.5	6.2	7.4	6.7	7.9	9.3	10.2	14.5	18.5
HUMIDITY/%	84	83	83	81	81	81	80	80	79	81	84	84
BLOOM SEASON							*					
DAYS CLR @ 8AM	1	1	2	3	2	3	2	2	2	1	1	1
DAYS CLR @ 2PM	0	1	3	3	1	1	1	0	0	1	0	0
RAIN/MM	483	277	218	114	157	188	170	201	236	259	368	470
°C AVG MAX	26.1	26.7	27.2	28.3	28.3	28.5	28.4	28.3	28.3	27.8	27.2	26.7
°C AVG MIN	20.0	20.1	20.7	21.2	21.2	20.7	20.7	20.7	20.7	20.7	20.7	20.1
DIURNAL RANGE	6.1	6.6	6.5	7.1	7.1	7.8	7.7	7.6	7.6	7.1	6.5	6.6
S/HEMISPHERE	JUL	AUG	SEP	OCT	NOV	DEC	JAN	FEB	MAR	APR	MAY	JUN

Cultural Recommendations

LIGHT: 1800–2500 fc.

TEMPERATURES: Throughout the year, days average 79–83°F (26–29°C), and nights average 68–70°F (20–21°C), with a diurnal range of 11–14°F (6–8°C).

HUMIDITY: 80–85% year-round.

WATER: Rainfall is moderate to heavy all year. Cultivated plants should be kept moist but not soggy.

FERTILIZER: 1/4–1/2 recommended strength. A balanced fertilizer should be applied weekly to biweekly throughout the year.

REST PERIOD: Growing temperatures should be maintained all year. Water and fertilizer should be reduced for plants cultivated in the dark, short-day conditions common in temperate-latitude winters. But they should never be allowed to dry out completely. In the habitat, light is slightly lower in winter.

GROWING MEDIA: Plants may be mounted on tree-fern or cork slabs if humidity is high and plants are watered at least once daily in summer. When plants are potted, any open, fast-draining medium may be used. Repotting is best done in early spring when new roots begin to grow.

MISCELLANEOUS NOTES: The bloom season shown in the climate table is based on collection records.

Plant and Flower Information

PLANT SIZE AND TYPE: A 12–40 in. (30–100 cm) sympodial epiphyte.

PSEUDOBULB: 12–40 in. (30–100 cm) long. The slender, somewhat erect stems emerge from a clustered base. They frequently produce keikis from the nodes.

LEAVES: Several along the upper portion of the stem. The narrowly elliptic leaves are about 4.5 in. (11–12 cm) long and pointed at the tip.

INFLORESCENCE: 1.4–2.2 in. (3.5–5.5 cm) long. Pendant inflorescences emerge from nodes along the stem.

FLOWERS: 8 per inflorescence. The flowers are 1.4 in. (3.5 cm) across. Sepals are cream to yellowish with a dense covering of purple-red streaks on the backside. They are up to 1.2 in. (3 cm) long, slightly hooded, narrowly elliptic, and pointed at the tip. Lateral sepals, which are fused to the column foot, are not symmetrical. The spur is 0.5–0.8 in. (1.3–2.0 cm) long and strongly hooked at the tip. Petals are cream to whitish-yellow with a pink flush. They are elliptic and pointed at the tip. The lip is 1 in. (2.5 cm) long, oblong-elliptic, deeply concave, smooth along the margins. It is yellow to whitish with pinkish spots near the tip and an orange flush on the sides near the base. The thornlike callus is upcurved, fleshy, triangular, and acute. It is yellow with dark orange banding on the front of the disc.

REFERENCES: Wood, J. J. and P. Cribb. 1994. A checklist of the orchids of Borneo. Royal Botanic Gardens, Kew.

PHOTOS/DRAWINGS: Wood, J. J. and P. Cribb. 1994. A checklist of the orchids of Borneo. Royal Botanic Gardens, Kew.

Dendrobium cymbulipes J. J. Smith

ORIGIN/HABITAT: Borneo. Plants grow in Sarawak, in central east Borneo in primeval forests near Mt. Kemoel at about 4900 ft. (1500 m), and in Sabah on the lower slopes of Mt. Kinabalu at 2950–7850 ft. (900–2400 m).

CLIMATE: Station #96633, Balikpapan, Borneo, Lat. 1.3°S, Long. 116.9°E, at 10 ft. (3 m). Temperatures are calculated for an elevation of 4500 ft. (1370 m), resulting in probable extremes of 77°F (25°C) and 45°F (7°C).

N/HEMISPHERE	JAN	FEB	MAR	APR	MAY	JUN	JUL	AUG	SEP	OCT	NOV	DEC
°F AVG MAX	68	69	69	70	70	70	70	71	71	70	70	69
°F AVG MIN	58	59	59	59	58	58	58	58	58	58	59	59
DIURNAL RANGE	10	10	10	11	12	12	12	13	13	12	11	10
RAIN/INCHES	7.1	6.4	5.5	5.2	6.6	8.1	7.9	8.9	9.1	8.2	9.1	7.6
HUMIDITY/%	82	80	77	78	80	79	82	81	81	82	83	82
BLOOM SEASON				*		*						
DAYS CLR @ 8AM	4	2	3	3	3	3	2	3	4	4	2	5
DAYS CLR @ 2PM	6	4	5	5	3	1	2	1	2	3	4	5
RAIN/MM	180	163	140	132	168	206	201	226	231	208	231	193
°C AVG MAX	20.1	20.7	20.7	21.2	21.2	21.2	21.2	21.8	21.8	21.2	21.2	20.7
°C AVG MIN	14.5	15.1	15.1	15.1	14.5	14.5	14.5	14.5	14.5	14.5	15.1	15.1
DIURNAL RANGE	5.6	5.6	5.6	6.1	6.7	6.7	6.7	7.3	7.3	6.7	6.1	5.6
S/HEMISPHERE	JUL	AUG	SEP	OCT	NOV	DEC	JAN	FEB	MAR	APR	MAY	JUN

Cultural Recommendations

LIGHT: 1800–2500 fc.

TEMPERATURES: Throughout the year, days average 68–71°F (20–22°C), and nights average 58–59°F (15°C), with a diurnal range of 10–13°F (6–7°C).

HUMIDITY: Near 80% year-round.

WATER: Rainfall is heavy all year, but conditions are slightly drier for 2 months in late winter or early spring. Cultivated plants should be kept mist with only slight drying allowed between waterings.

FERTILIZER: ¼–½ recommended strength. A balanced fertilizer should be applied weekly to biweekly throughout the year.

REST PERIOD: Growing temperatures should be maintained year-round. Water may be reduced somewhat in winter, especially for plants cultivated in the dark, short day conditions common in temperate latitudes. Plants should never be allowed to dry out completely, however. Fertilizer should be reduced or eliminated when water is reduced.

GROWING MEDIA: Plants may be mounted on tree-fern or cork slabs or potted in small pots filled with any open, fast-draining medium. Repotting may be done anytime new roots are growing.

MISCELLANEOUS NOTES: The bloom season shown in the climate table is based on reports from the habitat.

Plant and Flower Information

PLANT SIZE AND TYPE: A 16 in. (40 cm) sympodial epiphyte.

PSEUDOBULB: 16 in. (40 cm) long. The stems, which are swollen above the base, form a many-angled pseudobulb. Above the pseudobulb, the branching stems are leafy, flattened, and slender.

LEAVES: Many. The linear-lanceolate leaves are 2.4–3.5 in. (6–9 cm) long. They are folded, slightly twisted at the base, and 2-toothed at the apex. The leaves are papery and spotted when dried.

INFLORESCENCE: Short. Inflorescences emerge from nodes on mature stems.

FLOWERS: Few per inflorescence. The flowers are 0.7 in. (1.8 cm) long. Sepals and petals may be white or light yellow. The upper half of the lip is orange and the lower half is marked with red dots. The lip is uneven and ruffled along the margin.

REFERENCES: 224, 286, 445, 586, 592.

PHOTOS/DRAWINGS: 592.

Dendrobium cyperifolium Schlechter. See *D. violaceum* Kränzlin. REFERENCES: 223, 385, 443.

Dendrobium cyrtolobum Schlechter

ORIGIN/HABITAT: The Morobe District of northeastern Papua New Guinea. *D. cyrtolobum* grows along the upper Waria River on moss-free, mountain forest trees close to 2600 ft. (800 m).

CLIMATE: Station #200192, Garaina, Papua New Guinea, Lat. 7.9°S, Long. 147.1°E, at 2350 ft. (716 m). Record extreme temperatures are 94°F (34°C) and 46°F (8°C).

N/HEMISPHERE	JAN	FEB	MAR	APR	MAY	JUN	JUL	AUG	SEP	OCT	NOV	DEC
°F AVG MAX	80	82	83	84	85	85	85	85	84	84	83	81
°F AVG MIN	63	63	63	64	63	64	65	65	64	64	64	63
DIURNAL RANGE	17	19	20	20	22	21	20	20	20	20	19	18
RAIN/INCHES	5.8	6.5	8.7	11.1	11.8	11.9	8.9	11.7	11.5	9.9	7.7	5.2
HUMIDITY/%	84	82	82	81	80	80	81	81	82	83	84	84
BLOOM SEASON											*	
DAYS CLR	N/A											
RAIN/MM	148	166	220	282	300	303	227	296	291	251	195	131
°C AVG MAX	26.8	27.5	28.2	28.6	29.3	29.3	29.4	29.4	29.1	28.7	28.2	27.2
°C AVG MIN	16.9	16.9	17.4	17.6	17.4	18.0	18.1	18.2	18.4	17.7	17.7	17.1
DIURNAL RANGE	9.9	10.6	10.8	11.0	11.9	11.3	11.3	11.2	10.7	11.0	10.5	10.1
S/HEMISPHERE	JUL	AUG	SEP	OCT	NOV	DEC	JAN	FEB	MAR	APR	MAY	JUN

Cultural Recommendations

LIGHT: 2500–3500 fc.

TEMPERATURES: Throughout the year, days average 80–85°F (27–29°C), and nights average 63–65°F (17–18°C), with a diurnal range of 17–22°F (10–12°C).

HUMIDITY: 80–85% year-round.

WATER: Rainfall is heavy all year. Conditions are slightly drier in winter. Cultivated plants should be kept moist but not soggy.

FERTILIZER: ¼–½ recommended strength. A balanced fertilizer should be applied weekly to biweekly throughout the year.

REST PERIOD: Growing conditions should be maintained all year. In the habitat, rainfall is slightly lower in winter. Water and fertilizer should be reduced somewhat for cultivated plants, especially those grown in the dark, short-day conditions common during temperate-latitude winters. They should never be allowed to dry out completely, however. In the habitat, seasonal light variation is minor.

GROWING MEDIA: Plants may be mounted on tree-fern or cork slabs if humidity is high and plants are watered at least once daily in summer. When plants are potted, any open, fast-draining medium may be used. Repotting may be done anytime new roots are growing.

MISCELLANEOUS NOTES: The bloom season shown in the climate table is based on reports from the habitat.

Plant and Flower Information

PLANT SIZE AND TYPE: A 24 in. (60 cm) sympodial epiphyte.

PSEUDOBULB: 24 in. (60 cm) long.

LEAVES: Many. The erect to spreading leaves are 2.4–3.5 in. (6–9 cm) long.

INFLORESCENCE: 3.5 in. (9 cm) long.

FLOWERS: 3–7 per inflorescence. The flowers are 0.4 in. (0.9 cm) across. Blossoms are greenish white with red dots on the sepals.

REFERENCES: 221, 437, 445.

PHOTOS/DRAWINGS: 437.

Dendrobium cyrtosepalum Schlechter

ORIGIN/HABITAT: The northeastern coast of New Ireland, Papua New Guinea, Bougainville, and the Solomon Islands. Plants are often found on trees near sea level, but they also grow in rainforests to 2950 ft. (900 m).

CLIMATE: Station #94076, Kavieng, New Ireland, Papua New Guinea, Lat. 2.6°S, Long. 150.8°E, at 15 ft. (5 m). Record extreme temperatures are 99°F (37°C) and 66°F (19°C).

N/HEMISPHERE	JAN	FEB	MAR	APR	MAY	JUN	JUL	AUG	SEP	OCT	NOV	DEC
°F AVG MAX	88	88	89	90	90	89	88	88	87	88	88	88
°F AVG MIN	73	73	73	73	74	74	75	75	75	74	74	74
DIURNAL RANGE	15	15	16	17	16	15	13	13	12	14	14	14
RAIN/INCHES	10.7	11.2	7.8	8.0	9.7	10.7	12.2	11.1	11.6	12.5	10.0	9.9
HUMIDITY/%	78	76	76	75	77	78	80	79	79	80	79	79
BLOOM SEASON												*
DAYS CLR	N/A											
RAIN/MM	272	284	198	203	246	272	310	282	295	318	254	251
°C AVG MAX	31.1	31.1	31.7	32.2	32.2	31.7	31.1	31.1	30.6	31.1	31.1	31.1
°C AVG MIN	22.8	22.8	22.8	22.8	23.3	23.3	23.9	23.9	23.9	23.3	23.3	23.3
DIURNAL RANGE	8.3	8.3	8.9	9.4	8.9	8.4	7.2	7.2	6.7	7.8	7.8	7.8
S/HEMISPHERE	JUL	AUG	SEP	OCT	NOV	DEC	JAN	FEB	MAR	APR	MAY	JUN

Cultural Recommendations

LIGHT: 2000–3000 fc.

TEMPERATURES: Throughout the year, days average 87–90°F (31–32°C), and nights average 73–75°F (23–24°C), with a diurnal range of 12–17°F (7–9°C).

HUMIDITY: 75–80% year-round.

WATER: Rainfall is very heavy all year. Cultivated plants should be kept evenly moist but not soggy.

FERTILIZER: ¼–½ recommended strength. A balanced fertilizer should be applied weekly to biweekly throughout the year.

REST PERIOD: Growing conditions should be maintained year-round. In the habitat, rainfall is heavy in winter; but water and fertilizer may be reduced somewhat for cultivated plants, especially those grown in the dark, short-day conditions common in temperate latitudes. Plants should never be allowed dry out completely, however. In the habitat, seasonal light variation is minor.

GROWING MEDIA: Plants may be mounted on tree-fern or cork slabs if humidity is high and plants are watered at least once daily in summer. When plants are potted, any open, fast-draining medium may be used. Repotting may be done anytime new roots are growing.

MISCELLANEOUS NOTES: The bloom season shown in the climate table is based on collection records. Lewis and Cribb (ref. 271) indicate that specimens collected from the Pacific Islands differ slightly from those collected in New Guinea.

Plant and Flower Information

PLANT SIZE AND TYPE: A 12–16 in. (30–40 cm) sympodial epiphyte. Plants occasionally reach a length of 28 in. (71 cm).

PSEUDOBULB: 12–16 in. (30–40 cm) long, rarely to 28 in. (71 cm). Stems are many-jointed with internodes which are 0.8 in. (2 cm) long.

LEAVES: The ovate-lanceolate leaves are 4 in. (10 cm) long.

INFLORESCENCE: Short.

FLOWERS: 2 per inflorescence. Flowers last a single day. Sepals and petals are white. The lip is yellow with an orange-red crest.

REFERENCES: 219, 254, 271, 437, 444, 445, 516.

PHOTOS/DRAWINGS: 271, 437.

Dendrobium cystopoides J. J. Smith. Now considered a synonym of *Flickingeria appendiculata* (Blume) A. Hawkes. REFERENCES: 25, 75, 213, 225, 449.

Dendrobium dactyliferum Rchb. f. Originally described without origin, so climate data cannot be selected. REFERENCES: 216, 219, 254.

Dendrobium dactylodes Rchb. f.

AKA: Kores (ref. 466) includes *D. biflorum* Kränzlin not Swartz, *D. cheesmanae* Guillaumin, *D. everardii* Rolfe, *D. involutum* Kränzlin not Lindley, and *D. vaupelianum* Kränzlin as synonyms. Lewis and Cribb (ref. 270), however, list *D. cheesmanae* Guillaumin as a synonym of *D. involutum*. In addition, Schlechter (ref. 434) included *D. lepidochilum* Kränzlin as a synonym of *D. vaupelianum* Kränzlin.

ORIGIN/HABITAT: Islands of the South Pacific. Plants are found near Nandarivatu on Viti Levu in Fiji, at various locations in Vanuatu (New Hebrides), and in Samoa where they are common. They grow in open forest or on isolated trees from sea level to 2950 ft. (0–900 m).

CLIMATE: Station #91683, Nausori, Vitu Levu, Fiji, Lat. 18.1°S, Long. 178.6°E, at 19 ft. (6 m). Temperatures are calculated for an elevation of 2000 ft. (610 m), resulting in probable extremes of 91°F (33°C) and 48°F (9°C).

N/HEMISPHERE	JAN	FEB	MAR	APR	MAY	JUN	JUL	AUG	SEP	OCT	NOV	DEC
°F AVG MAX	72	72	73	74	76	78	79	79	79	77	75	73
°F AVG MIN	61	61	62	63	64	66	67	67	67	66	64	62
DIURNAL RANGE	11	11	11	11	12	12	12	12	12	11	11	11
RAIN/INCHES	4.9	8.3	7.7	8.3	9.8	12.5	11.4	10.7	14.5	12.2	10.1	6.7
HUMIDITY/%	77	77	76	75	75	76	76	78	79	79	81	78
BLOOM SEASON	*	*						*	*	*	*	
DAYS CLR @ 12PM	3	1	0	0	1	1	2	0	0	0	1	0
RAIN/MM	124	211	196	211	249	318	290	272	368	310	257	170
°C AVG MAX	22.5	22.5	23.0	23.6	24.7	25.8	26.4	26.4	26.4	25.3	24.1	23.0
°C AVG MIN	16.4	16.4	16.9	17.5	18.0	19.1	19.7	19.7	19.7	19.1	18.0	16.9
DIURNAL RANGE	6.1	6.1	6.1	6.1	6.7	6.7	6.7	6.7	6.7	6.2	6.1	6.1
S/HEMISPHERE	JUL	AUG	SEP	OCT	NOV	DEC	JAN	FEB	MAR	APR	MAY	JUN

Cultural Recommendations

LIGHT: 2500–3500 fc. Strong air movement is very important for cultivated plants.

TEMPERATURES: Summer days average 78–79°F (26°C), and nights average 66–67°F (19–20°C), with a diurnal range of 12°F (7°C).

HUMIDITY: 75–80% year-round.

WATER: Rainfall is moderate to heavy all year. Cultivated plants should be kept moist.

FERTILIZER: ¼–½ recommended strength. A balanced fertilizer should be applied weekly to biweekly throughout the year.

REST PERIOD: Winter days average 72–73°F (23°C), and nights average 61–62°F (16–17°C), with a diurnal range of 11°F (6°C). Temperatures are slightly cooler in winter and rainfall is somewhat lower, but basic growing conditions should be maintained year-round. While rainfall in the habitat remains high, water should be reduced somewhat for plants cultivated in the dark, short-days of temperate-latitude winters. They should never be allowed to dry out completely, however. Fertilizer should be reduced or eliminated if water is reduced.

GROWING MEDIA: Plants may be grown on slabs or rafts if humidity is high. Mounted plants should be misted several times a day when weather is hot and dry. If plants are potted, the smallest possible pot may be filled with any open, rapidly draining medium. Plants are healthiest when they are watered frequently but do not stay wet. Repotting is best done immediately after flowering, or as soon as new roots begin to grow.

MISCELLANEOUS NOTES: The bloom season shown in the climate table is based on reports from the habitat. Plants that produce flowers which last a single day commonly bloom several times during the year. Flowering usually occurs 7–14 days after a sudden 10°F (5°C) drop in daytime temperatures.

Plant and Flower Information

PLANT SIZE AND TYPE: A 59 in. (150 cm) sympodial epiphyte.

PSEUDOBULB: 15–55 in. (38–140 cm) long. The slender stems, which are hard and reedlike, are clustered on a short rhizome.

LEAVES: Many. The leaves are 1.4–3.2 in. (3.5–8.0 cm) long and somewhat leathery. They form near the apex of new growths.

INFLORESCENCE: Short. Inflorescences arise from nodes opposite leaves.

FLOWERS: 2 per inflorescence. Flowers are 1.2–2.0 in. (3–5 cm) across. The slender sepals and petals may be dark yellow or pale yellowish white. Blossoms last 1–2 days.

REFERENCES: 216, 252, 254, 270, 353, 417, 434, 466.

Dendrobium daenikerianum Kränzlin. See *D. sylvanum* Rchb. f. REFERENCES: 173, 224.

Dendrobium dahlemense Schlechter. Transferred to *Ephemerantha dahlemense* (Schlechter) Hunt and Summerhayes, which is now considered synonymous with *Flickingeria*. REFERENCES: 214, 222, 231, 449.

Dendrobium dalatense Gagnepain

ORIGIN/HABITAT: Vietnam. Plants were originally found in the Lang-bian region near Dalat.

CLIMATE: Station #48881, Dalat, Vietnam, Lat. 11.1°N, Long. 108.1°E, at 3156 ft. (962 m). Record extreme temperatures are 93°F (34°C) and 43°F (6°C).

N/HEMISPHERE	JAN	FEB	MAR	APR	MAY	JUN	JUL	AUG	SEP	OCT	NOV	DEC
°F AVG MAX	80	82	84	85	84	81	81	80	80	80	79	79
°F AVG MIN	56	57	59	62	65	65	65	65	65	63	60	58
DIURNAL RANGE	24	25	25	23	19	16	16	15	15	17	19	21
RAIN/INCHES	0.2	0.9	1.6	4.6	9.1	6.1	7.7	8.2	10.1	9.7	2.7	1.3
HUMIDITY/%	68	64	65	71	78	81	82	83	84	82	76	73
BLOOM SEASON	N/A											
DAYS CLR @ 7AM	13	13	13	9	5	3	2	2	2	5	7	10
DAYS CLR @ 1PM	8	8	8	2	0	0	0	0	0	1	3	4
RAIN/MM	5	23	41	117	231	155	196	208	257	246	69	33
°C AVG MAX	26.7	27.8	28.9	29.4	28.9	27.2	27.2	26.7	26.7	26.7	26.1	26.1
°C AVG MIN	13.3	13.9	15.0	16.7	18.3	18.3	18.3	18.3	18.3	17.2	15.6	14.4
DIURNAL RANGE	13.4	13.9	13.9	12.7	10.6	8.9	8.9	8.4	8.4	9.5	10.5	11.7
S/HEMISPHERE	JUL	AUG	SEP	OCT	NOV	DEC	JAN	FEB	MAR	APR	MAY	JUN

Cultural Recommendations

LIGHT: 2000–2500 fc.

TEMPERATURES: Summer days average 80–81°F (27°C), and nights average 65°F (18°C), with a diurnal range of 15–16°F (8–9°C). The warmest season is spring. Days average 84–85°F (29°C), and nights average 59–65°F (15–18°C), with a diurnal range of 19–25°F (11–14°C).

HUMIDITY: 80–85% in summer, dropping to 65–70% in winter.

WATER: Rainfall is moderate to heavy from spring into autumn with a 2–3 month winter dry season. Cultivated plants should be kept moist while growing, but water should be gradually reduced after new growths mature in autumn.

FERTILIZER: ¼–½ recommended strength, applied weekly. A high-nitrogen fertilizer is beneficial from spring to midsummer, but a fertilizer high in phosphates should be used in late summer and autumn.

REST PERIOD: Winter days average 79–82°F (26–28°C), and nights average 56–58°F (13–14°C), with a diurnal range of 21–25°F (12–14°C). Rainfall is low for 3–4 months in winter; and for 1–2 months, conditions are so dry that even moisture from dew is uncommon. For cultivated plants, water and fertilizer should be reduced for 2–3 months.

Dendrobium d'albertisii

Plants should be allowed to dry out between waterings, but they should not remain dry for extended periods. In the habitat, light is highest in winter.

GROWING MEDIA: Plants may be mounted on tree-fern or cork slabs or potted in small pots filled with any open, fast-draining medium. Repotting may be done anytime new roots are growing.

MISCELLANEOUS NOTES: The plant and flower are pictured by Seidenfaden in 1992 *Opera Botanica* 114.

Plant and Flower Information

PLANT SIZE AND TYPE: A 12 in. (30 cm) sympodial epiphyte.

PSEUDOBULB: 12 in. (30 cm) long. The stems are somewhat compressed.

LEAVES: Many. The distichous leaves are 2.4 in. (6 cm) long, folded, and widely spaced.

INFLORESCENCE: Short. Flowers emerge from the leafless, apical portion of the stem.

FLOWERS: 1 per inflorescence. The flowers are 0.2 in. (0.5 cm) across. They may be white or pale yellow. The dorsal sepal and petals are similar. The large lateral sepals form a broad cone. The lip sometimes has a small, brownish purple cushion near the apical notch with reddish purple margins on the sides.

REFERENCES: 136, 224, 266, 448.

Dendrobium d'albertisii Rchb. f. Sometimes spelled *D. d'albertsii*, see *D. antennatum* Lindley. The International Orchid Commission (ref. 236) registers hybrids under both *D. d'albertisii* and *D. antennatum*. REFERENCES: 25, 67, 84, 105, 179, 190, 196, 216, 236, 254, 271, 430, 437, 470, 504, 533, 568, 570, 580.

Dendrobium dalhousieanum Wallich. Sometimes spelled *D. dalhouseanum* or *D. dalhousianum*, see *D. pulchellum* Roxburgh ex Lindley. REFERENCES: 25, 38, 46, 190, 196, 200, 202, 216, 236, 245, 254, 266, 278, 317, 369, 395, 402, 430, 448, 454, 541, 557, 570. PHOTOS/DRAWINGS: 541, 557.

Dendrobium d'alleizettii Gagnepain. An old spelling for *D. alleizettei*, see *D. sociale* J. J. Smith. REFERENCES: 137, 227, 448, Seidenfaden 1992 *Opera Botanica* #114.

Dendrobium dalzelli Hooker. Now considered a synonym of *Eria dalzelli* Lindley. REFERENCES: 216, 254, 424.

Dendrobium dammerboerii J. J. Smith. See *D. strebloceras* Rchb. f. REFERENCES: 25, 84, 190, 223.

Dendrobium daoensis Gagnepain. See *D. henryi* Schlechter. REFERENCES: 137, 227, 448.

Dendrobium dantaniense Guillaumin

AKA: Seidenfaden, in a 1994 personal communication, stated that *D. alterum* Seidenfaden is conspecific with *D. dantaniense*.

ORIGIN/HABITAT: Thailand and Vietnam. In Thailand, plants were collected near Mae Sot at 2400 ft. (730 m), Phu Luang Loei at 4450 ft. (1350 m), and Doi Chik Chong at 5900 ft. (1800 m). They are also reported on Doi Suthep, the mountain near Chiang Mai. In Vietnam, plants were originally found at Dantania, near Dalat.

CLIMATE: Station #48375, Ban Mae Sot, Thailand, Lat. 16.7°N, Long. 98.5°E, at 742 ft. (226 m). Temperatures are calculated for an elevation of 2400 ft. (730 m), resulting in probable extremes of 100°F (38°C) and 34°F (1°C).

N/HEMISPHERE	JAN	FEB	MAR	APR	MAY	JUN	JUL	AUG	SEP	OCT	NOV	DEC
°F AVG MAX	84	88	92	94	89	82	80	80	83	85	84	82
°F AVG MIN	53	56	62	68	70	70	69	70	69	67	62	55
DIURNAL RANGE	31	32	30	26	19	12	11	10	14	18	22	27
RAIN/INCHES	0.2	0.2	0.2	1.5	5.7	8.8	13.6	16.0	7.8	4.1	0.7	0.1
HUMIDITY/%	67	64	58	63	75	84	86	87	85	81	76	74
BLOOM SEASON						*	*					
DAYS CLR @ 7AM	2	1	2	5	1	0	0	0	0	0	2	2
DAYS CLR @ 1PM	20	19	17	10	1	0	0	0	0	2	7	13
RAIN/MM	5	5	5	38	145	224	345	406	198	104	18	3
°C AVG MAX	28.6	30.8	33.1	34.2	31.4	27.5	26.4	26.4	28.1	29.2	28.6	27.5
°C AVG MIN	11.4	13.1	16.4	19.7	20.8	20.8	20.3	20.8	20.3	19.2	16.4	12.5
DIURNAL RANGE	17.2	17.7	16.7	14.5	10.6	6.7	6.1	5.6	7.8	10.0	12.2	15.0
S/HEMISPHERE	JUL	AUG	SEP	OCT	NOV	DEC	JAN	FEB	MAR	APR	MAY	JUN

Cultural Recommendations

LIGHT: 2000–2500 fc. Diffused light is recommended. In the habitat, clear summer days are rare.

TEMPERATURES: Summer days average 80–82°F (26–28°C), and nights average 69–70°F (20–21°C), with a diurnal range of 10–12°F (6–7°C). The warmest season is spring. Days average 89–94°F (31–34°C), and nights average 62–70°F (16–21°C), with a diurnal range of 19–30°F (11–17°C). *D. dantaniense* is found over a wide range of elevations, so cultivated plants may adapt to conditions as much as 10°F (6°C) cooler than indicated.

HUMIDITY: 75–85% during the growing season, dropping to 60–65% in winter and early spring.

WATER: Rainfall is moderate to heavy for 6 months from late spring through early autumn. Conditions are dry the balance of the year. Cultivated plants should be kept moist while actively growing, but water should be gradually reduced in autumn after new growths mature.

FERTILIZER: ¼–½ recommended strength, applied weekly. A high-nitrogen fertilizer is beneficial from spring to midsummer, but a fertilizer high in phosphates should be used in late summer and autumn.

REST PERIOD: Winter days average 82–88°F (28–31°C), and nights average 53–56°F (11–13°C), with a diurnal range of 27–32°F (15–18°C). The large increase in the diurnal range is the result of warmer days and cooler nights during clear winter weather. In the habitat, rainfall is low for 4–6 months, but except for 1–2 months in late winter, additional moisture is available from dew, fog, and morning mist. For cultivated plants, water should be reduced and the plants allowed to dry out somewhat between waterings for most of the winter; but they should not remain dry for extended periods. For 1–2 months in late winter, however, plants should be allowed to dry out completely. A light watering or early morning misting may be given if plants start to shrivel or show other signs of stress. Fertilizer should be reduced or eliminated anytime the plants are not actively growing. In the habitat, light is highest in winter.

GROWING MEDIA: Plants may be mounted on tree-fern or cork slabs if humidity is high and plants are watered at least once daily in summer. When plants are potted, any open, fast-draining medium may be used. Repotting is best done in early spring when new roots begin growing.

MISCELLANEOUS NOTES: The bloom season shown in the climate table is based on collection reports.

Plant and Flower Information

PLANT SIZE AND TYPE: A 7–22 in. (17–55 cm) sympodial epiphyte. Plants from Thailand are usually 10–12 in. (25–30 cm) long.

PSEUDOBULB: 4–18 in. (10–45 cm) long. The stems are erect and clustered. They consist of nodes 0.6–0.8 in. (1.5–2.0 cm) long. The pseudobulbs are narrowest at the base and somewhat swollen above.

LEAVES: 4–6 per growth. The oblong to lanceolate leaves are 2.4–4.0 in. (6–10 cm) long.

INFLORESCENCE: Short. The spikes of tightly clustered flowers emerge at the apex and laterally from nodes near the apex of the pseudobulbs after leaves drop.

FLOWERS: 3–6 per inflorescence. The tiny, fleshy flowers are 0.2–0.4 in. (0.5–1.0 cm) across. Blossoms have an ovate lanceolate dorsal sepal, rhomboid, pointed lateral sepals, and ovate petals. The dorsal sepal and petals are somewhat cupped, causing the flower to appear less than fully open. Sepals and petals are off-white, dirty yellow, or whitish orange with mauve to maroon spots which form contrasting broken lines. The lip is yellow with upcurved sides and a recurved midlobe. The broad, wavy lip is orange and white. Flower color is variable.

HYBRIDIZING NOTES: Johansen (ref. 239) indicates that plants known as *D. alterum* are self-sterile. The flowers dropped 5–11 days after self-pollination.

REFERENCES: 166, 229, 234, 239, 448, 454.

PHOTOS/DRAWINGS: *454.*

Dendrobium darjeelingensis U. C. Pradhan

ORIGIN/HABITAT: India. Plants were found near Darjeeling at 6550 ft. (2000 m).

CLIMATE: Station #42398, Baghdogra, India, Lat. 26.7°N, Long. 88.3°E, at 412 ft. (126 m). Temperatures are calculated for an elevation of 5900 ft. (1800 m), resulting in probable extremes of 86°F (30°C) and 18°F (−8°C).

N/HEMISPHERE	JAN	FEB	MAR	APR	MAY	JUN	JUL	AUG	SEP	OCT	NOV	DEC
°F AVG MAX	56	59	67	72	72	71	71	71	70	69	64	59
°F AVG MIN	32	36	42	50	55	58	59	59	58	52	42	35
DIURNAL RANGE	24	23	25	22	17	13	12	12	12	17	22	24
RAIN/INCHES	0.3	0.7	1.3	3.7	11.8	25.9	32.2	25.3	21.2	5.6	0.5	0.2
HUMIDITY/%	73	68	57	58	74	84	86	85	85	79	75	76
BLOOM SEASON	N/A											
DAYS CLR @ 6AM	21	18	15	11	5	0	1	1	4	13	23	19
DAYS CLR @ 12PM	23	16	16	11	2	2	0	1	2	10	21	18
RAIN/MM	8	18	33	94	300	658	818	643	538	142	13	5
°C AVG MAX	13.3	14.9	19.4	22.2	22.2	21.6	21.6	21.6	21.0	20.5	17.7	14.9
°C AVG MIN	0.0	2.2	5.5	9.9	12.7	14.4	14.9	14.9	14.4	11.0	5.5	1.6
DIURNAL RANGE	13.3	12.7	13.9	12.3	9.5	7.2	6.7	6.7	6.6	9.5	12.2	13.3
S/HEMISPHERE	JUL	AUG	SEP	OCT	NOV	DEC	JAN	FEB	MAR	APR	MAY	JUN

Cultural Recommendations

LIGHT: 2000–3000 fc. Strong air movement is important at all times. The heavy cloud cover during the summer monsoon indicates that summer light is low. Cultivated plants need some shading during the warmest, brightest time of year, but light should be as high as the plant can tolerate, short of burning the foliage.

TEMPERATURES: Summer days average 71°F (22°C), and nights average 58–59°F (14–15°C), with a diurnal range of 12–13°F (7°C). Due to the effects of the microclimate, actual temperatures in the habitat may be 6–8°F (3–4°C) warmer than indicated.

HUMIDITY: Near 85% in summer and early autumn. Humidity decreases to 70–75% in early winter, but the driest season occurs in late winter and early spring, when averages drop below 60% for 2 months.

WATER: Rainfall is extremely heavy in summer, but conditions are much drier in winter. More moisture is available at higher elevations than is recorded at the weather station. Cultivated plants should be kept wet but not soggy from spring to early autumn. Water should be gradually reduced in late autumn after new growths mature.

FERTILIZER: ½–¾ recommended strength, applied weekly. A high-nitrogen fertilizer is beneficial from spring to midsummer, but a fertilizer high in phosphates should be used in late summer and autumn.

REST PERIOD: Winter days average 56–69°F (13–15°C), and nights average 32–36°F (0–2°C), with a diurnal range of 23–25°F (13–14°C). Growers are cautioned that the calculated winter minimum temperatures may be too low. Observed temperatures at high-elevation stations in nearby regions suggest that average night temperatures may be 6–8°F (3–4°C) warmer than indicated. However, plants should tolerate freezing temperatures, at least for short periods, if they are dry at the time; but extremes should be avoided in cultivation. In the habitat, the dry period is 4–5 months long, but for 3 months, the high humidity indicates that some additional moisture is available from heavy dew. Therefore, conditions are extremely dry for only 1–2 months. Cultivated plants should be allowed to dry out between waterings in winter, but they should not remain dry for extended periods. Occasional early morning mistings between waterings, especially on warm, sunny days, may help prevent the plants from becoming too dry. Fertilizer should be eliminated until water is increased in spring. In the habitat, light is much higher in winter. The rest period is essential for healthy growth and flowering, but it may not need to be quite as long or as severe as indicated by the climate data.

GROWING MEDIA: Plants may be mounted on tree-fern or cork slabs if humidity is high and plants are watered at least once daily in summer. When plants are potted, any open, fast-draining medium may be used. Repotting is best done in early spring when new roots are growing.

Plant and Flower Information

PLANT SIZE AND TYPE: A 3 in. (7.6 cm) sympodial epiphyte.

PSEUDOBULB: 3 in. (7.6 cm) long. Pseudobulbs are erect and tightly clustered. They are covered with sheaths.

LEAVES: 3–5 per growth. The leaves are deciduous, pale green, and 1.6 in. (4 cm) long.

INFLORESCENCE: 1.6 in. (4 cm) long. Up to 8 erect scapes emerge from upper nodes of leafy growths. Plants bloom on partially mature new growths.

FLOWERS: 4–6 per inflorescence. The pale green flowers are 0.5 in. (1.3 cm) across if spread, but they usually remain rather closed. Sepals and petals are pointed. The lip midlobe is uneven along the margin with 3 raised keels.

REFERENCES: 233, 369, 454.

Dendrobium dartoisianum Wildeman. Now considered a variety of *D. tortile* Lindley. REFERENCES: 211, 220, 254, 445, 454.

Dendrobium dayanum Boxall ex Naves. Listed as an invalid name by Kränzlin (ref. 254) and Merrill (ref. 296). REFERENCES: 216, 254, 296, 298.

Dendrobium dearei Rchb. f.

ORIGIN/HABITAT: Widespread in the Philippines. Plants are found on Luzon, Mindoro, Leyte, Samar, Mindanao, and the small islands off the coast of Mindanao. The habitat is usually about 200 ft. (60 m).

CLIMATE: Station #98548, Catbalogan, Samar Island, Philippines, Lat. 11.8°N, Long. 125.9°E, at 16 ft. (5 m). Record extreme temperatures are not available for this location.

N/HEMISPHERE	JAN	FEB	MAR	APR	MAY	JUN	JUL	AUG	SEP	OCT	NOV	DEC
°F AVG MAX	85	86	88	91	91	90	89	90	89	88	87	85
°F AVG MIN	74	73	74	77	78	79	77	79	78	77	76	75
DIURNAL RANGE	11	13	14	14	13	11	12	11	11	11	11	10
RAIN/INCHES	12.3	8.3	6.1	5.8	5.9	8.3	10.4	7.7	10.6	11.6	14.2	15.5
HUMIDITY/%	86	83	84	81	82	81	82	81	86	85	86	88
BLOOM SEASON	*	*	*	*	***	*	***	**	**	**	**	*
DAYS CLR @ 8AM	6	4	5	8	5	4	4	1	2	4	4	2
DAYS CLR @ 2PM	2	2	2	2	2	0	1	1	1	0	2	1
RAIN/MM	312	211	155	147	150	211	264	196	269	295	361	394
°C AVG MAX	29.4	30.0	31.1	32.8	32.8	32.2	31.7	32.2	31.7	31.1	30.6	29.4
°C AVG MIN	23.3	22.8	23.3	25.0	25.6	26.1	25.0	26.1	25.6	25.0	24.4	23.9
DIURNAL RANGE	6.1	7.2	7.8	7.8	7.2	6.1	6.7	6.1	6.1	6.1	6.2	5.5
S/HEMISPHERE	JUL	AUG	SEP	OCT	NOV	DEC	JAN	FEB	MAR	APR	MAY	JUN

Cultural Recommendations

LIGHT: 2500–3500 fc.

TEMPERATURES: Throughout the year, days average 85–91°F (29–33°C), and nights average 73–79°F (23–26°C), with a diurnal range of 10–14°F (6–8°C).

HUMIDITY: 81–88% year-round.

WATER: Rainfall is very heavy year-round, and cultivated plants should never be allowed to dry out completely.

FERTILIZER: ¼–½ recommended strength. A balanced fertilizer should be applied weekly to biweekly throughout the year.

REST PERIOD: Growing conditions may be maintained year-round, but plants are adaptable. Some growers report that plants are healthy with winter lows of 55–59°F (13–15°C). Although rainfall is heavy throughout the year, water and fertilizer should be reduced for plants grown with cooler temperatures or in the dark, short-day conditions common in temperate-latitude winters. Growers suggest a 3-week drier, cooler rest after flowering. Some growers indicate that high winter light is necessary to initiate blooms, but others report that plants bloom regularly in areas where winter skies are commonly overcast.

GROWING MEDIA: Plants are best potted in an open, fast-draining medium, but they may be mounted on tree-fern or cork slabs if humidity is high and plants are watered at least once daily in summer. Repotting is best done in early spring when new roots are growing.

MISCELLANEOUS NOTES: The bloom season shown in the climate table is based on cultivation records. In a warm environment, *D. dearei* may bloom several times a year. Apparently each new growth blooms as it matures. When grown under cool conditions, the plants may not bloom until the growth is fully mature, which may take more than one growing season.

D. dearei grows in a warm habitat in nature. It is much more adaptable in cultivation than *D. schuetzei* Rolfe, although collectors indicate that the 2 species often grow together in lush forests at 1000–3000 ft. (300–910 m) in Surigao and Agusan Provinces on Mindanao.

Plant and Flower Information

PLANT SIZE AND TYPE: A 12–35 in. (30–90 cm) sympodial epiphyte.

PSEUDOBULB: 12–35 in. (30–90 cm) long. The canelike stems may be swollen at the base. They are covered by persistent leaf bases.

LEAVES: Many. The light green leaves are glossy when young, distichous, leathery, and 2–3 in. (5–8 cm) long. They persist for 2 years or more. Leaf sheaths are covered with inconspicuous brownish hairs. The upper ⅓–½ of the stem is leafy.

INFLORESCENCE: 12–15 in. (31–38 cm) long. Arching inflorescences emerge from the uppermost nodes of both old and new canes. Several inflorescences may be produced on each growth. Mature growths commonly produce inflorescences for several years.

FLOWERS: 6–18 per inflorescence. The showy flowers are 2–3 in. (5–8 cm) across. All segments are white, but the ruffled lip is decorated with a lime-green or yellow patch at the base. Flowers often last many months when conditions are cool. When grown under warm conditions flowers are shorter-lived, but *D. dearei* may bloom several times a year.

HYBRIDIZING NOTES: Hybridizers indicate that *D. dearei* is receptive to pollen from most *Dendrobium* species.

REFERENCES: 12, 25, 36, 98, 179, 190, 196, 200, 216, 254, 293, 296, 326, 371, 373, 389, 429, 430, 445, 458, 524, 536, 541, 557, 570.

PHOTOS/DRAWINGS: *36*, 98, *371*, *389*, *430*, 458, 541.

Dendrobium debile Schlechter

ORIGIN/HABITAT: Northern Papua New Guinea. Plants grow in the forests of the Kani and Finisterre Ranges. They are usually found on tall trees at 3600–3950 ft. (1100–1200 m).

CLIMATE: Station #200187, Erap, Papua New Guinea, Lat. 6.6°S, Long. 146.7°E, at 850 ft. (260 m). Temperatures are calculated for an elevation of 3600 ft. (1100 m), resulting in probable extremes of 93°F (34°C) and 44°F (7°C).

N/HEMISPHERE	JAN	FEB	MAR	APR	MAY	JUN	JUL	AUG	SEP	OCT	NOV	DEC
°F AVG MAX	79	79	80	81	84	84	84	84	84	83	81	81
°F AVG MIN	60	60	60	61	63	64	63	63	64	62	65	61
DIURNAL RANGE	19	19	20	20	21	20	21	21	20	21	16	20
RAIN/INCHES	3.9	3.9	2.7	3.0	3.0	5.3	5.9	5.9	7.0	3.4	2.4	3.1
HUMIDITY/%	82	81	81	79	75	74	74	74	77	76	80	80
BLOOM SEASON			*				*					
DAYS CLR	N/A											
RAIN/MM	99	99	69	76	76	135	150	150	178	86	61	79
°C AVG MAX	26.1	26.1	26.7	27.2	28.9	29.1	29.0	28.9	28.9	28.3	27.2	27.2
°C AVG MIN	15.6	15.5	15.5	16.1	17.2	17.7	17.2	17.2	17.7	16.6	18.3	16.1
DIURNAL RANGE	10.5	10.6	11.2	11.1	11.7	11.4	11.8	11.7	11.2	11.7	8.9	11.1
S/HEMISPHERE	JUL	AUG	SEP	OCT	NOV	DEC	JAN	FEB	MAR	APR	MAY	JUN

Cultural Recommendations

LIGHT: 2500–3500 fc.

TEMPERATURES: Throughout the year, days average 79–84°F (26–29°C), and nights average 60–65°F (16–18°C), with a diurnal range of 16–21°F (9–12°C).

HUMIDITY: 75–80% year-round. Despite high average humidity, the habitat may be quite dry during hot afternoons.

WATER: Rainfall is moderate most of the year, but conditions are wetter for 4–5 months in summer and early autumn. Cultivated plants should be thoroughly saturated then allowed to dry slightly between waterings.

FERTILIZER: ¼–½ recommended strength. A balanced fertilizer should be applied weekly to biweekly throughout the year.

REST PERIOD: Growing temperatures should be maintained all year. In the habitat, rainfall is lowest in winter, but the high humidity indicates that additional moisture is frequently available from heavy dew. Cultivated plants should be allowed to dry for somewhat longer between waterings, but should not remain dry for extended periods. Fertilizer should be reduced until water is increased in spring. In the habitat, seasonal light variation is minor.

GROWING MEDIA: Plants may be mounted on tree-fern or cork slabs if humidity is high and plants are watered at least once daily in summer. When plants are potted, any open, fast-draining medium may be used. Repotting is best done in early spring when new roots are growing.

MISCELLANEOUS NOTES: The bloom season shown in the climate table is based on reports from the habitat. Plants that produce very short-lived flowers commonly bloom several times during the year. Flowering usually occurs 7–14 days after a sudden 10°F (5°C) drop in daytime temperatures.

Plant and Flower Information

PLANT SIZE AND TYPE: A lax, somewhat snaky sympodial epiphyte of unreported size.

LEAVES: Few. Growths are sparsely leafy. The linear leaves are usually 1.4–2.0 in. (3.5–5.0 cm) long.

INFLORESCENCE: Short. The inflorescences emerge from the side of the pseudobulbs. The blossoms are held opposite each other.

FLOWERS: 2 per inflorescence. The flowers are 0.6 in. (1.4 cm) across and last a single day. The pale yellow sepals and petals are narrow and project forward. The hairy, ruffled lip is whitish with a dark red margin.

REFERENCES: 221, 437, 445.

PHOTOS/DRAWINGS: 437.

Dendrobium decumbens Schlechter

ORIGIN/HABITAT: Northern Papua New Guinea. In the Kani Range, plants grow on the moss-covered branches of mistforest trees at about 3300 ft. (1000 m).

CLIMATE: Station #94010, Goroka, Papua New Guinea, Lat. 6.1°S, Long. 145.4°E, at 5141 ft. (1567 m). Temperatures are calculated for an elevation of 3300 ft. (1000 m), resulting in probable extremes of 93°F (34°C) and 49°F (10°C).

N/HEMISPHERE	JAN	FEB	MAR	APR	MAY	JUN	JUL	AUG	SEP	OCT	NOV	DEC
°F AVG MAX	82	83	84	85	85	84	85	84	84	84	85	83
°F AVG MIN	62	63	63	63	64	65	65	65	66	65	65	63
DIURNAL RANGE	20	20	21	22	21	19	20	19	18	19	20	20
RAIN/INCHES	2.1	2.8	4.6	5.9	6.6	9.3	9.1	10.1	10.7	8.3	4.6	2.0
HUMIDITY/%	70	67	67	67	67	71	72	73	74	71	70	70
BLOOM SEASON				*				*				
DAYS CLR	N/A											
RAIN/MM	53	71	117	150	168	236	231	257	272	211	117	51
°C AVG MAX	27.9	28.4	29.0	29.5	29.5	29.0	29.5	29.0	29.0	29.0	29.5	28.4
°C AVG MIN	16.7	17.3	17.3	17.3	17.9	18.4	18.4	18.4	19.0	18.4	18.4	17.3
DIURNAL RANGE	11.2	11.1	11.7	12.2	11.6	10.6	11.1	10.6	10.0	10.6	11.1	11.1
S/HEMISPHERE	JUL	AUG	SEP	OCT	NOV	DEC	JAN	FEB	MAR	APR	MAY	JUN

Cultural Recommendations

LIGHT: 2500–3000 fc.

TEMPERATURES: Throughout the year, days average 82–85°F (28–30°C), and nights average 62–66°F (17–19°C), with a diurnal range of 19–22°F (11–12°C). Average highs and lows vary only slightly during the year, indicating that plants are unlikely to be healthy under widely fluctuating temperatures.

HUMIDITY: 70–75% in summer and autumn, dropping to 65–70% in winter and spring.

WATER: Rainfall is moderate to heavy most of the year but is relatively low for 2–3 months in winter. However, additional moisture is available from dew, fog, and mist, even during periods when rainfall is low. Cultivated plants should be kept moist but not soggy. Additional early morning mistings between waterings are often beneficial, especially on warm, bright, sunny days.

FERTILIZER: ¼–½ recommended strength. A balanced fertilizer should be applied weekly to biweekly throughout the year.

REST PERIOD: Growing temperatures should be maintained all year. Water should be reduced in winter. Plants should dry slightly between waterings, but they should never be allowed to dry out completely. Fertilizer should be reduced or eliminated until water is increased in spring. In the habitat, winter light may be slightly higher.

GROWING MEDIA: Plants may be mounted on tree-fern or cork slabs or potted in small pots filled with any open, fast-draining medium. Repotting may be done anytime new roots are growing.

MISCELLANEOUS NOTES: The bloom season shown in the climate table is based on reports from the habitat. Plants that produce very short-lived flowers commonly bloom several times during the year. Flowering usually occurs 7–14 days after a sudden 10°F (5°C) drop in daytime temperatures.

Plant and Flower Information

PLANT SIZE AND TYPE: An 8 in. (20 cm) sympodial epiphyte.

PSEUDOBULB: 8 in. (20 cm) long. The curved pseudobulbs are erect to ascending.

LEAVES: Many. The linear leaves are erect to spreading and 0.4–0.8 in. (1–2 cm) long. Growths are densely leafy.

INFLORESCENCE: Very short.

FLOWERS: 1 per inflorescence. The tiny, white flowers are 0.2 in. (0.5 cm) across. The lip is uppermost and marked with red at the front. Blossoms are very short lived, but they commonly last more than 1 day.

REFERENCES: 92, 221, 437, 445.

PHOTOS/DRAWINGS: 437.

Dendrobium deflexum Ridley

ORIGIN/HABITAT: Irian Jaya (western New Guinea). Plants were collected in mountain forests at 8300–11,000 ft. (2530–3360 m) on Mt. Jaya (Mt. Carstensz), the highest peak on New Guinea.

CLIMATE: Station #97686, Wamena, Irian Jaya, Lat. 4.1°S, Long. 139.0°E, at 5446 ft. (1660 m). Temperatures are calculated for an elevation of 8500 ft. (2600 m). Record extreme temperatures are not available for this location.

N/HEMISPHERE	JAN	FEB	MAR	APR	MAY	JUN	JUL	AUG	SEP	OCT	NOV	DEC
°F AVG MAX	65	66	67	66	67	66	67	66	66	69	68	64
°F AVG MIN	50	50	52	52	53	54	53	52	53	55	55	51
DIURNAL RANGE	15	16	15	14	14	12	14	14	13	14	13	13
RAIN/INCHES	3.0	1.9	2.2	4.0	4.6	3.3	2.8	4.2	6.9	3.9	5.4	4.9
HUMIDITY/%	N/A											
BLOOM SEASON								*				
DAYS CLR	N/A											
RAIN/MM	76	48	56	102	117	84	71	107	175	99	137	124
°C AVG MAX	18.2	18.8	19.3	18.8	19.3	18.8	19.3	18.8	18.8	20.5	19.9	17.7
°C AVG MIN	9.9	9.9	11.0	11.0	11.6	12.1	11.6	11.0	11.6	12.7	12.7	10.5
DIURNAL RANGE	8.3	8.9	8.3	7.8	7.7	6.7	7.7	7.8	7.2	7.8	7.2	7.2
S/HEMISPHERE	JUL	AUG	SEP	OCT	NOV	DEC	JAN	FEB	MAR	APR	MAY	JUN

Cultural Recommendations

LIGHT: 1500–2000 fc.

TEMPERATURES: Throughout the year, days average 64–69°F (18–21°C), and nights average 50–55°F (10–13°C), with a diurnal range of 12–16°F (7–9°C). The warmest temperatures of the day occur in late morning when skies are clear. Clouds and mist develop near noon and continue through the afternoon, thus preventing additional warming. Due to the effects of the microclimate, actual maximum temperatures may be somewhat warmer than indicated. Reports from the habitat indicate a sharp contrast between day and night temperatures.

HUMIDITY: Information is not available for this location. However, average humidity in mistforest habitats normally exceeds 80% year-round. High humidity and excellent air circulation are particularly important if temperatures are excessively warm. Placing the plants in front of an evaporative cooler or near a fine mist is very beneficial.

WATER: Rainfall is moderate to heavy through most of the year. In the higher-elevation habitat, rainfall amounts may be greater than indicated in the climate table. In addition, large amounts of water are available from mist and heavy dew, even during periods of reduced rainfall. Cultivated plants should be misted several times daily on the hottest days, but the foliage should always be dry before evening.

FERTILIZER: ¼–½ recommended strength. A balanced fertilizer should be applied weekly to biweekly throughout the year. The Royal Botanic Garden in Edinburgh uses a dilute, seaweed-based fertilizer.

REST PERIOD: Growing conditions should be maintained all year. Cultivated plants often grow year-round. Rainfall is moderate throughout the year with a month or so of drier conditions in late winter. In cultivation, water may be decreased somewhat in winter, but plants should never be allowed to dry out completely. In the habitat, light may be slightly higher in winter.

GROWING MEDIA: Plants may be mounted on tree-fern or cork slabs if humidity is high and plants are watered at least once daily in summer. When plants are potted, any open, fast-draining medium may be used. Repotting is best done in early spring when new roots are growing.

MISCELLANEOUS NOTES: The bloom season shown in the climate table is based on collection reports.

Dendrobium dekockii

Plant and Flower Information

PLANT SIZE AND TYPE: A 1.4–10.0 in. (3.6–25.0 cm) sympodial epiphyte.

PSEUDOBULB: 0.7–0.9 in. (1.8–2.3 cm) long. Stems are erect and branching.

LEAVES: Many. The small, deflexed leaves are usually 0.7–0.9 in. (1.8–2.3 cm) long, thick, and ovate. Larger clones may have larger leaves.

INFLORESCENCE: 4 in. (10 cm) long. The raceme arises at the apex of the stem.

FLOWERS: 1–2 per inflorescence. The flowers are 1 in. (2.5 cm) across. Sepals may be elliptical or ovate. The smaller petals are ovate. The deep orange blossoms are very large compared to the tiny leaves.

REFERENCES: 222, 400, 538.

PHOTOS/DRAWINGS: 538.

Dendrobium dekockii J. J. Smith

AKA: Reeve and Woods (ref. 385) list the following synonyms: *D. cedricola* P. van Royen, *D. chrysornis* Ridley, *D. erythrocarpum* J. J. Smith, *D. gaudens* P. van Royen, *D. kerewense* P. van Royen, *D. montigenum* Ridley.

ORIGIN/HABITAT: New Guinea. In the high mountains, plants grow epiphytically at the tips of branches on mossy trees, in alpine shrubbery, and along forest margins at 8850–12,450 ft. (2700–3800 m).

CLIMATE: Botanical garden records, Laiagam, Papua New Guinea, Lat. 5.5°S, Long. 143.5°E, at 7218 ft. (2200 m). Temperatures are calculated for an elevation of 9500 ft. (2900 m), resulting in probable extremes of 83°F (29°C) and 24°F (–4°C).

N/HEMISPHERE	JAN	FEB	MAR	APR	MAY	JUN	JUL	AUG	SEP	OCT	NOV	DEC
°F AVG MAX	68	69	70	68	70	70	74	69	68	70	70	68
°F AVG MIN	47	46	47	47	48	48	47	48	50	49	48	48
DIURNAL RANGE	21	23	23	21	22	22	27	21	18	21	22	20
RAIN/INCHES	4.0	4.8	6.1	7.8	8.5	9.1	8.4	9.6	9.5	8.9	6.3	4.0
HUMIDITY/%	M/A											
BLOOM SEASON	*	*	*		*			*	*	*		
DAYS CLR	N/A											
RAIN/MM	102	122	155	198	216	231	213	244	241	226	160	102
°C AVG MAX	20.2	20.8	21.4	20.2	21.4	21.4	23.6	20.8	20.2	21.4	21.4	20.2
°C AVG MIN	8.6	8.0	8.6	8.6	9.1	9.1	8.6	9.1	10.2	9.7	9.1	9.1
DIURNAL RANGE	11.6	12.8	12.8	11.6	12.3	12.3	15.0	11.7	10.0	11.7	12.3	11.1
S/HEMISPHERE	JUL	AUG	SEP	OCT	NOV	DEC	JAN	FEB	MAR	APR	MAY	JUN

Cultural Recommendations

LIGHT: 2000–3000 fc.

TEMPERATURES: Throughout the year, days average 68–74°F (20–24°C), and nights average 46–50°F (8–10°C), with a diurnal range of 18–27°F (10–15°C). In the habitat, the warmest temperatures of the day occur during late morning when skies are usually clear. Clouds and mist develop near noon, thus preventing additional warming.

HUMIDITY: Information is not available for this location. However, records from other stations in the region indicate that values are probably 70–80% year-round.

WATER: Rainfall is heavy throughout the year, but conditions are slightly drier for 3–4 months in winter. Cultivated plants should be kept moist.

FERTILIZER: ¼–½ recommended strength. A balanced fertilizer should be applied weekly to biweekly throughout the year.

REST PERIOD: Growing conditions should be maintained all year. Water and fertilizer should be reduced somewhat in winter, especially when plants are grown in the dark, short-day conditions common in temperate latitudes. Plants should dry slightly between waterings, but they should never be allowed to dry out completely. Water and fertilizer should be gradually increased when plants begin growing in spring.

GROWING MEDIA: Most successful growers pot in live sphagnum moss and indicate that it is good for the roots, but others use a small layer of osmunda over broken crock or tree-fern slabs. Mounted plants must be watered at least once a day in summer. Repotting may be done anytime new roots are growing.

MISCELLANEOUS NOTES: The bloom reports shown in the climate table are based on cultivation records, but Reeve and Woods (ref. 385) report that *D. dekockii* is difficult to flower in cultivation.

Plant and Flower Information

PLANT SIZE AND TYPE: A 0.8–3.2 in. (2–8 cm) sympodial epiphyte. Plants may reach a length of 6 in. (15 cm).

PSEUDOBULB: 0.1–1.0 in. (0.2–2.5 cm) long, rarely as large as 2 in. (5 cm). Pseudobulbs, which take a variety of shapes, are often distinctly constricted at a central node. Growths may be tightly clustered or arise from a branching rhizome. They may be erect or semipendulous. Roots are purplish pink.

LEAVES: 3–4, rarely 1 at the apex of each growth. The long-linear to short-lanceolate leaves, which have a sharp point at the tip, are 0.2–2.4 in. (0.5–6.0 cm) long. They may be green, dark purple, or red.

INFLORESCENCE: Short. Inflorescences arise from the terminal node of leafy pseudobulbs.

FLOWERS: 1–2, rarely 3 per inflorescence. The bright orange flowers are 0.6–1.1 in. (1.4–2.8 cm), rarely to 1.3 in. (3.2 cm) long. The long-lasting, somewhat fan-shaped blossoms vary in size. The lip is sharply pointed. Unlike the very similar *D. brevicaule* Rolfe, *D. dekockii* does not have a purplish black anther cap.

HYBRIDIZING NOTES: Reeve and Woods (ref. 385) indicate that some collections appear intermediate between *D. dekockii* and *D. brevicaule*, suggesting that the 2 species may hybridize naturally.

REFERENCES: 95, 179, 221, 385, 400, 445, 470, 538, 556.

PHOTOS/DRAWINGS: 385, 538, 556.

Dendrobium delacourii Guillaumin

AKA: Hunt (ref. 211) includes the synonyms *D. ciliatum* Parish ex Hooker not Persoon and *D. ciliferum* Bakhuizen. Seidenfaden (ref. 454) includes as synonyms *D. ciliatum* as used by some, not (Ruiz and Pavon) Persoon or Parish ex Hooker f., and *D. ciliatum* var. *breve*. Rchb. f. He considers *D. rupicola* var. *breve* (Rchb. f.) Atwood to be an invalid name.

ORIGIN/HABITAT: Widespread in Southeast Asia. In Thailand, plants grow in deciduous forests, often exposed to full sun, at 800–4250 ft. (250–1300 m). The habitat extends westward into Burma and eastward through Cambodia, Laos, and Vietnam.

CLIMATE: Station #48327, Chiang Mai, Thailand, Lat. 18.8°N, Long. 99.0°E, at 1100 ft. (335 m). Temperatures are calculated for an elevation of 2500 ft. (760 m), resulting in probable extremes of 104°F (40°C) and 33°F (1°C).

N/HEMISPHERE	JAN	FEB	MAR	APR	MAY	JUN	JUL	AUG	SEP	OCT	NOV	DEC
°F AVG MAX	80	85	90	91	89	85	84	82	83	84	81	79
°F AVG MIN	51	52	57	65	69	69	69	70	68	66	61	52
DIURNAL RANGE	29	33	33	26	20	16	15	12	15	18	20	27
RAIN/INCHES	0.3	0.4	0.6	2.0	5.5	6.1	7.4	8.7	11.5	4.9	1.5	0.4
HUMIDITY/%	73	65	58	62	73	78	80	83	83	81	79	76
BLOOM SEASON				**	**	*	*					
DAYS CLR @ 7AM	5	5	2	2	1	0	0	0	0	1	3	3
DAYS CLR @ 1PM	9	8	4	2	0	0	0	0	0	0	1	3
RAIN/MM	8	10	15	51	140	155	188	221	292	124	38	10
°C AVG MAX	26.9	29.7	32.4	33.0	31.9	29.7	29.1	28.0	28.5	29.1	27.4	26.3
°C AVG MIN	10.8	11.3	14.1	18.5	20.8	20.8	20.8	21.3	20.2	19.1	16.3	11.3
DIURNAL RANGE	16.1	18.4	18.3	14.5	11.1	8.9	8.3	6.7	8.3	10.0	11.1	15.0
S/HEMISPHERE	JUL	AUG	SEP	OCT	NOV	DEC	JAN	FEB	MAR	APR	MAY	JUN

Cultural Recommendations

LIGHT: 3000–4000 fc. Bright light and strong air movement are recommended. Light should be as high as the plant can tolerate, short of burning the foliage. In the habitat, heavy cloud cover during the rainy season reduces summer light levels.

TEMPERATURES: Summer days average 82–85°F (28–30°C), and nights average 69–70°F (21°C), with a diurnal range of 12–16°F (7–9°C). Spring, before the start of the summer rainy season, is the warmest time of the year. Days average 89–91°F (32–33°C), and nights average 57–69°F (14–21°C), with a diurnal range of 20–33°F (11–18°C).

HUMIDITY: Near 80% most of the year, dropping to near 60% in late winter and early spring.

WATER: Rainfall is moderate to heavy from late spring through early autumn, but conditions are much drier in winter. Cultivated plants should be kept moist while actively growing, but water should be gradually reduced after new growths mature in autumn.

FERTILIZER: ½ recommended strength, applied weekly. *D. delacourii* is healthiest if encouraged to grow rapidly during the summer. A high-nitrogen fertilizer is beneficial from spring to midsummer, but a fertilizer high in phosphates should be used in late summer and autumn.

REST PERIOD: Winter days average 79–85°F (26–30°C), and nights average 51–52°F (11°C), with a diurnal range of 27–33°F (15–18°C). Some growers report that the plants tolerate light frost, and others indicate that plants grow well in an intermediate to warm greenhouse with only a short dry period in winter. In the habitat, rainfall averages are very low for 4–5 months in winter, but during the early part of the season the high relative humidity indicates that additional moisture is available from frequent fog, mist, and heavy deposits of dew. Growers sometimes recommend eliminating water in winter, but plants are healthiest if for most of the winter they are allowed to become somewhat dry between waterings but do not remain dry for extended periods. For 1–2 months in late winter, however, conditions are clear, warm, and dry, with humidity so low that even the moisture from morning dew is uncommon. Plants should be allowed to dry out completely between waterings and remain dry longer during this time. Occasional early morning mistings between waterings may help keep the plants from becoming too dry. Fertilizer should be greatly reduced or eliminated until water is increased in spring. A cool, dry rest is essential for cultivated plants and should be continued until new growth starts in spring. In the habitat, light is highest in winter.

GROWING MEDIA: Plants are best mounted on slabs of cork or tree-fern fiber if humidity is high and plants are watered at least once daily in summer. If plants are potted, a very open, fast-draining media is recommended. Undersized pots that are barely large enough to hold the roots should be used. Repotting should be done as seldom as possible. When necessary, repotting is best done in early spring when new root growth starts.

MISCELLANEOUS NOTES: The bloom season shown in the climate table is based on reports from the habitat. Cultivated plants usually bloom in late summer. Growers indicate that *D. delacourii* is very difficult to flower in warm, uniform climates. Flowers are very similar of to those of *D. venustum*, but Seidenfaden (ref. 454) indicates that *D. venustum* Teijsm. and Binn. has longer cilia on its midlobe than *D. delacourii*.

Plant and Flower Information

PLANT SIZE AND TYPE: A 1.2–3.2 in. (3–8 cm) sympodial epiphyte.

PSEUDOBULB: 0.8–1.6 in. (2–4 cm) long. The short, yellowish stems are tightly clustered. Cultivated plants sometimes reach a length of 4 in. (10 cm).

LEAVES: 2–4 per growth. The pale- to mid-green leaves, which are usually 0.8–1.2 in. (2–3 cm) long, have a papery texture. They are deciduous in early winter.

INFLORESCENCE: 0.8–1.2 in. (2–3 cm) long. The erect inflorescences arise from the most recent growths. They emerge below the apex of the stem after the leaves form. Each new growth may produce up to 5 inflorescences.

FLOWERS: 1–10 per inflorescence. The flowers are 0.6–1.0 in. (1.6–2.5 cm) across. They may be pale greenish white to clear yellow. The oblong, pointed sepals and petals are widest at the tip. The cream to golden brown lip is fringed at the tip of the midlobe and marked with dark reddish purple ridges on the sidelobes. The fringe, which may be white, golden yellow, or orange, is formed by elongation of the veins which are enlarged at the tip. Blossoms last about a month.

HYBRIDIZING NOTES: Chromosome counts are n = 20 (ref. 151) and 2n = 40 (ref. 151, 153, 187, 273, 504), and 2n = 38 (ref. 187).

REFERENCES: 36, 151, 153, 179, 187, 200, 210, 223, 245, 273, 291, 330, 371, 430, 447, 448, 454, 504, 524, 568, 580.

PHOTOS/DRAWINGS: *36, 210, 245, 291, 330, 371, 430, 454, 568*.

Dendrobium delicatulum Kränzlin 1892 not F. Mueller and Kränzlin 1894

AKA: Reeve and Woods (ref. 385) divided *D. delicatulum* into 3 subspecies; subsp. *delicatulum*, which has been known as *D. minutum* Schlechter and *D. nanarauticolum* Fukuyama; subsp. *huliorum* Reeve and Woods; and subsp. *parvulum* (Rolfe) Reeve and Woods, which has been known as *D. parvulum* Rolfe.

ORIGIN/HABITAT: Widespread. *D. delicatulum* subsp. *delicatulum* grows in Vanuatu, Bougainville, the Solomon Islands, Fiji, Ponape, and northern Papua New Guinea. It is epiphytic on the mossy, horizontal branches of mistforest trees at 1950–8700 ft. (600–2650 m).

D. delicatulum subsp. *huliorum* grows in eastern New Guinea at 4600–5900 ft. (1400–1800 m).

D. delicatulum subsp. *parvulum* grows on Mt. Klabat, on the Minahassa Peninsula in northern Sulawesi (Celebes), at 2950–3950 ft. (900–1200 m). This variety also grows on Waigeo Island, just off the tip of western New Guinea. The average lows for this variety are 4–8°F (2–4°C) warmer than indicated in the following climate table, but average highs are similar.

CLIMATE: Station #94010, Goroka, Papua New Guinea, Lat. 6.1°S, Long. 145.4°E, at 5141 ft. (1567 m). Record extreme temperatures are 87°F (31°C) and 43°F (6°C).

N/HEMISPHERE	JAN	FEB	MAR	APR	MAY	JUN	JUL	AUG	SEP	OCT	NOV	DEC
°F AVG MAX	76	77	78	79	79	78	79	78	78	78	79	77
°F AVG MIN	56	57	57	57	58	59	59	59	60	59	59	57
DIURNAL RANGE	20	20	21	22	21	19	20	19	18	19	20	20
RAIN/INCHES	2.1	2.8	4.6	5.9	6.6	9.3	9.1	10.1	10.7	8.3	4.6	2.0
HUMIDITY/%	70	67	67	67	67	71	72	73	74	71	70	70
BLOOM SEASON	*			*								
DAYS CLR	N/A											
RAIN/MM	54	70	118	151	167	236	230	256	271	211	116	52
°C AVG MAX	24.7	25.1	25.6	26.3	26.2	25.7	25.8	25.6	25.5	25.6	25.9	25.1
°C AVG MIN	13.5	13.8	14.0	14.0	14.2	14.8	15.0	15.2	15.3	15.1	14.7	13.7
DIURNAL RANGE	11.2	11.3	11.6	12.3	12.0	10.9	10.8	10.4	10.2	10.5	11.2	11.4
S/HEMISPHERE	JUL	AUG	SEP	OCT	NOV	DEC	JAN	FEB	MAR	APR	MAY	JUN

Cultural Recommendations

LIGHT: 2500–3000 fc.

TEMPERATURES: Throughout the year, days average 76–79°F (25–26°C), and nights average 56–60°F (14–15°C), with a diurnal range of 18–22°F (10–12°C).

HUMIDITY: 70–75% in summer and autumn, dropping to 65–75% in winter and spring.

WATER: Rainfall is moderate to heavy most of the year, but conditions are

somewhat drier for 2–3 months in winter. However, additional moisture from dew, fog, and mist is usually available, even during periods when rainfall is low. Cultivated plants should be kept moist but not soggy. Additional early morning mistings between waterings are often beneficial, especially on warm, bright, sunny days.

FERTILIZER: ¼–½ recommended strength. A balanced fertilizer should be applied weekly to biweekly throughout the year.

REST PERIOD: Growing temperatures should be maintained all year. Water should be reduced in winter. Plants should dry slightly between waterings, but they should never be allowed to dry out completely. Fertilizer should be reduced or eliminated until water is increased in spring. In the habitat, winter light may be slightly higher.

GROWING MEDIA: Plants may be mounted on tree-fern or cork slabs if humidity is high and plants are watered at least once daily in summer. Plants may be potted in shallow pots or baskets filled with any open, fast-draining medium. Repotting may be done anytime new roots are growing.

MISCELLANEOUS NOTES: The bloom season shown in the climate table is based on collection reports. Cultivated plants may bloom at any time.

Plant and Flower Information

PLANT SIZE AND TYPE: A creeping, 1.8 in. (4.6 cm) sympodial epiphyte, which rarely grows terrestrially. Plants form mats may which reach a diameter of 39 in. (100 cm) and cover a tree trunk.

PSEUDOBULB: 0.1–0.6 in. (0.2–1.5 cm) long. The variable pseudobulbs, which often grow at an oblique angle, may be round, ellipsoid, or ovoid. They are yellow, usually tinged with green or red.

LEAVES: 2 per growth. The ovate to elliptic leaves are 0.1–0.6 in. (0.3–1.5 cm) long. They are green with a purplish tinge on the underside.

INFLORESCENCE: Short. The apical inflorescences arise from between the leaves or leaf nodes of both leafy and leafless stems.

FLOWERS: 1–3 per inflorescence. The small flowers are 0.3–0.6 in. (0.7–1.5 cm) long. Subsp. *huliorum*, with its large yellow pseudobulbs, has small, whitish yellow blossoms that are usually self-pollinating, sometimes before the flowers open. The following 2 subspecies are seldom self-pollinating and both have small, reddish stems. Subsp. *delicatulum* has red, pinkish purple, violet, or blue flowers. Subsp. *parvulum* has violet-pink blossoms with bright orange-red at the apex of the lip. Blossoms cover the plant making a carpet of color. The ovaries have 5 wings.

REFERENCES: 95, 135, 179, 189, 218, 220, 234, 254, 270, 271, 384, 385, 436, 437, 445, 466, 516, 556.

PHOTOS/DRAWINGS: *270, 271, 384, 385, 437.*

Dendrobium delicatulum F. Mueller and Kränzlin 1894 not Kränzlin 1892.

An invalid name. Reportedly collected from Dinner Island, Papua New Guinea, plants were cultivated at Moreton Bay near Brisbane, Australia. Kränzlin (ref. 254) included the plants in the section *Stachyobium*. They were 12 in. (30 cm) sympodial epiphytes with 2-edged stems, 5–6 papery, linear-lanceolate leaves, and several pendulous inflorescences. Each inflorescence carried several small flowers with oblong sepals and spathulate petals. The lip was somewhat fiddle-shaped with a heart-shaped midlobe and uneven margins. We found no indication where this plant should be referred. REFERENCES: 253, 254.

Dendrobium × delicatum (F. M. Bailey) F. M. Bailey.

A natural hybrid between *D. kingianum* Bidwill ex Lindley and *D. tarberi* M. Clements and D. Jones *(D. speciosum* var. *hillii* Masters). *D. × delicatum* has been known as *D. × kestevenii* Rupp, *D. speciosum* J. E. Smith var. *album* B. S. Williams, *D. speciosum* J. E. Smith var. *delicatum* F. M. Bailey, and *D. speciosum* J. E. Smith var. *nitidum* F. M. Bailey. Many growers consider *D. × delicatum* difficult to grow. The climate data for *D. kingianum* Bidwill ex Lindley suggests that winter conditions should be cooler and much drier than in summer. HYBRIDIZING NOTES: Chromosome counts are 2n = 38 (ref. 152, 153, 243) and 2n = about 57 (ref. 504, 580). Pollen from the same plant seldom produces pods, but seeds are regularly produced when pollen from another plant is used. REFERENCES: 23, 67, 105, 152, 153, 230, 240, 243, 254, 262, 273, 325, 390, 421, 430, 504, 522, 533, 580. PHOTOS/DRAWINGS: 105, *240, 325, 390, 533.*

Dendrobium deliense Schlechter

ORIGIN/HABITAT: Northern Sumatra. Plants grow in the forests of Bandar-Baroe, near Medan, at about 2300 ft. (700 m).

CLIMATE: Station #96035, Medan, Sumatra, Indonesia, Lat. 3.6°N, Long. 98.7°E, at 87 ft. (27 m). Temperatures are calculated for an elevation of 2300 ft. (700 m), resulting in probable extremes of 92°F (33°C) and 53°F (12°C).

N/HEMISPHERE	JAN	FEB	MAR	APR	MAY	JUN	JUL	AUG	SEP	OCT	NOV	DEC
°F AVG MAX	78	80	81	82	82	82	82	82	81	79	79	78
°F AVG MIN	64	64	65	66	66	65	65	65	65	65	65	65
DIURNAL RANGE	14	16	16	16	16	17	17	17	16	14	14	13
RAIN/INCHES	5.4	3.6	4.1	5.2	6.9	5.2	5.3	7.0	8.3	10.2	9.7	9.0
HUMIDITY/%	80	79	78	78	79	78	79	79	81	83	83	82
BLOOM SEASON				*								
DAYS CLR @ 7AM	4	2	2	2	2	2	2	0	0	0	1	1
DAYS CLR @ 1PM	0	1	0	0	1	0	2	1	0	0	0	0
RAIN/MM	137	91	104	132	175	132	135	178	211	259	246	229
°C AVG MAX	25.4	26.5	27.1	27.6	27.6	27.6	27.6	27.6	27.1	25.9	25.9	25.4
°C AVG MIN	17.6	17.6	18.2	18.7	18.7	18.2	18.2	18.2	18.2	18.2	18.2	18.2
DIURNAL RANGE	7.8	8.9	8.9	8.9	8.9	9.4	9.4	9.4	8.9	7.7	7.7	7.2
S/HEMISPHERE	JUL	AUG	SEP	OCT	NOV	DEC	JAN	FEB	MAR	APR	MAY	JUN

Cultural Recommendations

LIGHT: 2000–3000 fc.

TEMPERATURES: Throughout the year, days average 78–82°F (25–28°C), and nights average 64–66°F (18–19°C), with a diurnal range of 13–17°F (7–9°C).

HUMIDITY: 75–80% most of the year, increasing to near 85% in autumn.

WATER: Rainfall is moderate to heavy all year with a brief slightly drier period in winter. Cultivated plants should be kept moist with only slight drying allowed between waterings.

FERTILIZER: ¼–½ recommended strength. A balanced fertilizer should be applied weekly to biweekly throughout the year.

REST PERIOD: Growing conditions should be maintained all year. Water may be reduced somewhat in winter for plants grown in the dark, short-day conditions common in temperate latitudes, but they should never be allowed to dry out completely. In the habitat, light is slightly higher for about 3 months in winter.

GROWING MEDIA: Plants may be mounted on tree-fern or cork slabs or potted in small pots filled with any open, fast-draining medium. Repotting is best done when new roots are beginning to grow.

MISCELLANEOUS NOTES: The bloom season shown in the climate table is based on reports from the habitat. Schlechter described this plant in 1912 in *Fedde's Repert. Sp. Nov.* 11:143.

Plant and Flower Information

PLANT SIZE AND TYPE: A 9 in. (23 cm) sympodial epiphyte.

PSEUDOBULB: 9 in. (23 cm) long. The nearly erect stems do not branch. Growths are spaced 0.4–0.6 in. (1.0–1.5 cm) apart.

LEAVES: Many. The stems are densely leafy. The lanceolate, knifelike leaves are smooth, leathery, and 1.2–1.6 in. (3–4 cm) long.

INFLORESCENCE: Short. Inflorescences are clustered at the apex of the stem.

FLOWERS: 1 per inflorescence. The dark purple flowers are 0.2 in. (0.6 cm) long. The blossoms have an ovate dorsal sepal, somewhat triangular lateral sepals, and oblong, pointed petals. The lip, which is larger than the sepals and petals, is nearly round with a hairy, lightly wavy margin.

REFERENCES: 221.

Dendrobium delphinioides R. S. Rogers

ORIGIN/HABITAT: Papua New Guinea. Plants grow on tree trunks near Laruni in the Owen Stanley Range at 5000 ft. (1520 m).

CLIMATE: Station #200192, Garaina, Papua New Guinea, Lat. 7.9°S, Long. 147.1°E, at 2350 ft. (716 m). Temperatures are calculated for an elevation of 5000 ft. (1520 m), resulting in probable extremes of 85°F (30°C) and 37°F (3°C).

N/HEMISPHERE	JAN	FEB	MAR	APR	MAY	JUN	JUL	AUG	SEP	OCT	NOV	DEC
°F AVG MAX	71	73	74	75	76	76	76	76	75	75	74	72
°F AVG MIN	54	54	54	55	54	55	56	56	56	55	55	54
DIURNAL RANGE	17	19	20	20	22	21	20	20	19	20	19	18
RAIN/INCHES	5.8	6.5	8.7	11.1	11.8	11.9	8.9	11.7	11.5	9.9	7.7	5.2
HUMIDITY/%	84	82	82	81	80	80	81	81	82	83	84	84
BLOOM SEASON	N/A											
DAYS CLR	N/A											
RAIN/MM	147	165	221	282	300	302	226	297	292	251	196	132
°C AVG MAX	21.8	22.9	23.5	24.0	24.6	24.6	24.6	24.6	24.0	24.0	23.5	22.4
°C AVG MIN	12.4	12.4	12.4	12.9	12.4	12.9	13.5	13.5	13.5	12.9	12.9	12.4
DIURNAL RANGE	9.4	10.5	11.1	11.1	12.2	11.7	11.1	11.1	10.5	11.1	10.6	10.0
S/HEMISPHERE	JUL	AUG	SEP	OCT	NOV	DEC	JAN	FEB	MAR	APR	MAY	JUN

Cultural Recommendations

LIGHT: 2000–3000 fc.

TEMPERATURES: Throughout the year, days average 71–76°F (22–25°C), and nights average 54–56°F (12–14°C), with a diurnal range of 17–22°F (10–12°C).

HUMIDITY: 80–85% year-round. Values drop to 65–70% for a few hours each afternoon.

WATER: Rainfall is heavy most of the year, but conditions are slightly drier in winter. Cultivated plants should never be allowed to dry out completely.

FERTILIZER: ¼–½ recommended strength. A balanced fertilizer should be applied weekly to biweekly throughout the year. The Royal Botanic Garden in Edinburgh uses a seaweed-based fertilizer for plants from high-elevation habitats in New Guinea.

REST PERIOD: Growing conditions should be maintained all year. In the habitat, rainfall is slightly lower in winter. Water should be reduced for cultivated plants, especially those grown in the dark, short-day conditions common in temperate-latitude winters. Fertilizer should be reduced or eliminated anytime water is reduced. In the habitat, light may be slightly higher in winter.

GROWING MEDIA: Plants may be mounted on tree-fern or cork slabs if humidity is high and plants are watered at least once daily in summer. When plants are potted, any open, fast-draining medium may be used. They may be repotted anytime new roots are growing.

Plant and Flower Information

PLANT SIZE AND TYPE: A 12 in. (30 cm) sympodial epiphyte.

PSEUDOBULB: 12 in. (30 cm) long. The unbranched stems, which are slender and grooved, are covered by leaf-sheaths.

LEAVES: Many. The ovate-lanceolate leaves are 1.6–2.6 in. (4.0–6.5 cm) long. They are semitwisted at the base. Leaves are thin and papery when dry.

INFLORESCENCE: Very short. Inflorescences emerge laterally from nodes along the stem.

FLOWERS: Few per inflorescence. The red flowers are 1.1–1.3 in. (2.7–3.3 cm) across. Blossoms have ovate to oblong sepals and small, erect petals. The lip is erect.

REFERENCES: 223, 406.

Dendrobium deltatum Seidenfaden

ORIGIN/HABITAT: Endemic to eastern Thailand, where plants are reported as far south as Prachinburi. Habitat elevation is estimated at about 2000 ft. (610 m) based on comments by Seidenfaden (ref. 454) regarding its relationship with *D. oligophyllum* Gagnepain, but the following climate data should be used with caution.

CLIMATE: Station #49000, Ban Ta Khli, Thailand, Lat. 15.3°N, Long. 100.3°E, at 100 ft. (30 m). Temperatures are calculated for an elevation of 2000 ft. (610 m), resulting in probable extremes of 106°F (42°C) and 37°F (3°C).

N/HEMISPHERE	JAN	FEB	MAR	APR	MAY	JUN	JUL	AUG	SEP	OCT	NOV	DEC
°F AVG MAX	83	88	93	94	91	88	86	85	83	83	83	82
°F AVG MIN	57	64	68	71	71	70	70	69	69	68	64	58
DIURNAL RANGE	26	24	25	23	20	18	16	16	14	15	19	24
RAIN/INCHES	0.1	0.7	1.4	3.4	5.1	5.4	5.5	6.3	11.2	6.2	1.4	0.1
HUMIDITY/%	60	61	60	72	64	75	80	83	85	83	78	68
BLOOM SEASON	N/A											
DAYS CLR @ 7AM	5	2	4	4	3	0	0	0	0	2	4	5
DAYS CLR @ 1PM	12	7	7	4	1	0	0	0	0	1	3	7
RAIN/MM	3	18	36	86	130	137	140	160	284	157	36	3
°C AVG MAX	28.2	31.0	33.7	34.3	32.6	31.0	29.9	29.3	28.2	28.2	28.2	27.6
°C AVG MIN	13.7	17.6	19.9	21.5	21.5	21.0	21.0	20.4	20.4	19.9	17.6	14.3
DIURNAL RANGE	14.5	13.4	13.8	12.8	11.1	10.0	8.9	8.9	7.8	8.3	10.6	13.3
S/HEMISPHERE	JUL	AUG	SEP	OCT	NOV	DEC	JAN	FEB	MAR	APR	MAY	JUN

Cultural Recommendations

LIGHT: 3000–3500 fc.

TEMPERATURES: Summer days average 85–88°F (29–31°C), and nights average 69–70°F (20–21°C), with a diurnal range of 16–18°F (9–10°C). The warmest weather occurs in spring. Days average 91–94°F (33–34°C), and nights average 68–71°F (20–22°C), with a diurnal range of 20–25°F (11–14°C).

HUMIDITY: 75–85% in summer and autumn, decreasing to about 60% in winter.

WATER: Rainfall is moderate to heavy for 7 months from late spring into autumn. The wet season changes rapidly into a 4–5 month dry period that extends from late autumn to spring. Cultivated plants should be kept moist during the growing season, but water should be reduced after new growths mature in autumn.

FERTILIZER: ¼–½ recommended strength. A balanced fertilizer should be applied weekly to biweekly throughout the growing season.

REST PERIOD: Winter days average 82–88°F (28–31°C), and nights average 57–64°F (14–18°C), with a diurnal range of 24–26°F (13–15°C). In the habitat, rainfall is low in winter, and humidity is so low that even morning dew is uncommon. In cultivation, water should be reduced to an occasional light misting for 2–3 months. Fertilizer should be eliminated until water is increased in spring.

GROWING MEDIA: Plants may be mounted on tree-fern or cork slabs if humidity is high and plants are watered at least once daily in summer. When plants are potted, any open, fast-draining medium may be used. Repotting is best done in early spring when new roots are growing.

Plant and Flower Information

PLANT SIZE AND TYPE: A 2.4–3.2 in. (6–8 cm) sympodial epiphyte. Plants grow in tufts.

Dendrobium delumbe

PSEUDOBULB: 1.2–2.0 in. (3–5 cm) long. Pseudobulbs are covered by leaf-sheaths.

LEAVES: 4–5, rarely up to 8 per growth. The ovate to lanceolate leaves are usually 1.2–2.0 in. (3–5 cm) long with a thin texture.

INFLORESCENCE: Short. Inflorescences are lateral and emerge from nodes along the side of the pseudobulb. Blossoms are held near the base of the leaves.

FLOWERS: 2–3 per inflorescence. The flowers, which open in succession, are 0.4–0.6 in. (1.0–1.5 cm) across. All segments are greenish white. The lip is marked with red-brown spots on the keels and sometimes elsewhere.

REFERENCES: 234, 454.

PHOTOS/DRAWINGS: 454.

Dendrobium delumbe Kränzlin. See *D. polycladium* Rchb. f.
REFERENCES: 173, 224.

Dendrobium demissum D. Don. Sometimes listed as a synonym of *Panisea demissa* (D. Don) Pfitz, but in 1982, Seidenfaden in *Opera Botanica* #62 discusses the confusion regarding this name and it's relationship to *D. muscicola* Lindley. REFERENCES: 32, 216, 254, 369.

Dendrobium demmenii J. J. Smith. See *D. bicaudatum* Reinwardt ex Lindley. REFERENCES: 25, 84, 200, 222.

Dendrobium dempoense J. J. Smith. Originally spelled *D. dempoënse*, it is now considered a synonym of *Epigeneium dempoense* (J. J. Smith) Summerhayes. REFERENCES: 222, 229, 499.

Dendrobium dendrocolla J. J. Smith. Now considered a synonym of *Diplocaulobium dendrocolla* (J. J. Smith) Kränzlin. REFERENCES: 111, 219, 220, 254, 445, 468.

Dendrobium dendrocolloides J. J. Smith

AKA: *D. incurvilabium* Schlechter.

ORIGIN/HABITAT: Irian Jaya (western New Guinea), between the Arfak Range and Angi Lake. Plants usually grow on trees in open forests on heath-like mountain ridges at 5900–10,150 ft. (1800–3100 m).

CLIMATE: Station #97530, Manokwari, Irian Jaya, Lat. 0.9°S, Long. 134.1°E, at 10 ft. (3 m). Temperatures are calculated for an elevation of 8200 ft. (2500 m), resulting in probable extremes of 66°F (19°C) and 41°F (5°C).

N/HEMISPHERE	JAN	FEB	MAR	APR	MAY	JUN	JUL	AUG	SEP	OCT	NOV	DEC
°F AVG MAX	59	58	60	60	61	59	59	59	59	59	59	58
°F AVG MIN	47	48	47	47	47	48	46	46	47	47	47	47
DIURNAL RANGE	12	10	13	13	14	11	13	13	12	12	12	11
RAIN/INCHES	5.4	5.6	5.0	4.7	4.5	10.3	12.0	9.4	13.2	11.1	7.8	7.3
HUMIDITY/%	87	87	86	84	85	86	86	85	86	86	86	85
BLOOM SEASON									*			
DAYS CLR @ 9AM	4	3	3	5	3	3	3	1	1	2	3	7
DAYS CLR @ 3PM	2	2	2	3	1	1	1	0	1	0	0	2
RAIN/MM	137	142	127	119	114	262	305	239	335	282	198	185
°C AVG MAX	15.0	14.4	15.5	15.5	16.1	15.0	15.0	15.0	15.0	15.0	15.0	14.4
°C AVG MIN	8.3	8.9	8.3	8.3	8.3	8.9	7.8	7.8	8.3	8.3	8.3	8.3
DIURNAL RANGE	6.7	5.5	7.2	7.2	7.8	6.1	7.2	7.2	6.7	6.7	6.7	6.1
S/HEMISPHERE	JUL	AUG	SEP	OCT	NOV	DEC	JAN	FEB	MAR	APR	MAY	JUN

Cultural Recommendations

LIGHT: 2000–3000 fc.

TEMPERATURES: Throughout the year, days average 58–61°F (14–16°C), and nights average 46–48°F (8–9°C), with a diurnal range of 11–14°F (6–8°C). Due to the effects of the microclimate, actual day-time maximum temperatures may be as much as 10°F (6°C) warmer than indicated.

HUMIDITY: Near 85% year-round.

WATER: Rainfall is moderate to very heavy all year. Cultivated plants should be kept moist but not soggy.

FERTILIZER: ¼–½ recommended strength. A balanced fertilizer should be applied weekly to biweekly throughout the year.

REST PERIOD: Growing conditions should be maintained year-round. In cultivation, water and fertilizer may be reduced in winter, especially for plants grown in the dark, short-day conditions common in temperate latitudes. However, plants should never be allowed to dry out completely.

GROWING MEDIA: Plants may be mounted on tree-fern or cork slabs if humidity is high and plants are watered at least once daily in summer. When plants are potted, any open, fast-draining medium may be used. Repotting may be done anytime new roots are growing.

MISCELLANEOUS NOTES: The bloom season shown in the climate table is based on reports from the habitat. In the habitat, blooming plants also carried fruit.

Plant and Flower Information

PLANT SIZE AND TYPE: A variably sized, 6–18 in. (15–45 cm) sympodial epiphyte.

PSEUDOBULB: 2–13 in. (5–33 cm) long. The orange or red-brown stems have 3–5 nodes below the leaves.

LEAVES: 2–3 per growth. The elliptic-lanceolate leaves are about 3 in. (8 cm) long.

INFLORESCENCE: 2–3 in. (5–8 cm) long. Inflorescences may be arching or suberect.

FLOWERS: 8 or less per inflorescence. The fleshy blossoms are 0.3–0.4 in. (0.8–1.0 cm) across but do not open fully. They are self-pollinating. Sepals and petals may be white or greenish with purple dots. The midlobe of the erect lip is purple with white at the base. The sidelobes are green.

REFERENCES: 83, 221, 470, 476.

PHOTOS/DRAWINGS: 83.

Dendrobium denigratum J. J. Smith. Now considered as synonym of *Flickingeria denigrata* (J. J. Smith) J. J. Wood. REFERENCES: 213, 222, 230, 235, 286, 449, 590.

Dendrobium denneanum Kerr. See *D. chryseum* Rolfe. REFERENCES: 19, 32, 61, 102, 153, 154, 179, 210, 225, 236, 430, 447, 448, 454, 528, 547. PHOTOS/DRAWINGS: 210.

Dendrobium densiflorum Lindley

AKA: Wallich is sometimes listed as the describer of this species. Synonyms include *D. clavatum* Roxburgh not Lindley, *D. griffithianum* Lindley var. *guibertii* (Carriere) Veitch, and *D. guibertii* Carriere. Seidenfaden (ref. 454) discusses the confusion surrounding the use of the name *D. densiflorum*. He indicates that *D. thyrsiflorum* is frequently listed as a synonym of *D. densiflorum*, but he considers them separate species. He states that *D. densiflorum* var. *alboluteum* Hooker f. is synonymous with *D. thyrsiflorum* Rchb. f. and reports that plants which are actually *D. palpebrae* are frequently called *D. densiflorum*. Kränzlin (ref. 254) and Hawkes (ref. 190) include *D. schroderi* Hort. as a synonym. The International Orchid Commission (ref. 236) lists *D. thyrsiflorum* Rchb. f. as a synonym but registers hybrids under that name.

ORIGIN/HABITAT: Widespread. The habitat includes Nepal, where plants were first collected, Bhutan, Sikkim, Assam, and the Khasi (Khasia) Hills of northeastern India. Distribution continues eastward across Burma, northwest Thailand, Laos, and southwest China. Plants usually grow on the moss-covered trunks and branches of trees at 3300–6000 ft. (1000–1830 m) but are also found on rocks. Seidenfaden (ref. 454) indicates that a number of different species have been incorrectly identified as *D. densiflorum*, resulting in confusing habitat reports.

CLIMATE: Station #42147, Mukteswar, India, Lat. 29.5°N, Long. 79.7°E, at 7592 ft. (2314 m). Temperatures are calculated for an elevation of 4000 ft. (1220 m), resulting in probable extremes of 102°F (39°C) and 33°F (1°C).

N/HEMISPHERE	JAN	FEB	MAR	APR	MAY	JUN	JUL	AUG	SEP	OCT	NOV	DEC
°F AVG MAX	63	66	73	81	87	87	81	81	80	77	73	67
°F AVG MIN	48	50	56	64	69	71	71	70	68	62	56	51
DIURNAL RANGE	15	16	17	17	18	16	10	11	12	15	17	16
RAIN/INCHES	1.0	2.1	1.7	1.0	0.3	4.6	11.4	12.8	4.6	3.5	0.3	0.2
HUMIDITY/%	61	55	50	39	44	67	91	93	83	66	55	56
BLOOM SEASON		*	**	***	***	**	*	*				
DAYS CLR @ 5PM	17	17	15	18	18	12	1	1	6	25	26	21
RAIN/MM	25	53	43	25	8	117	290	325	117	89	8	5
°C AVG MAX	17.1	18.8	22.7	27.1	30.5	30.5	27.1	27.1	26.6	24.9	22.7	19.4
°C AVG MIN	8.8	9.9	13.3	17.7	20.5	21.6	21.6	21.0	19.9	16.6	13.3	10.5
DIURNAL RANGE	8.3	8.9	9.4	9.4	10.0	8.9	5.5	6.1	6.7	8.3	9.4	8.9
S/HEMISPHERE	JUL	AUG	SEP	OCT	NOV	DEC	JAN	FEB	MAR	APR	MAY	JUN

Cultural Recommendations

LIGHT: 2500–3500 fc.

TEMPERATURES: Summer days average 81–87°F (27–31°C), and nights average 70–71°F (21–22°C), with a diurnal range of 10–16°F (6–9°C).

HUMIDITY: Near 90% in summer, decreasing to 55–60% most of the winter. Spring is driest season, when humidity drops to near 40% for 2 months.

WATER: Rainfall is moderate to heavy for 5 months in summer. The wet season is followed immediately by 7 very dry months from autumn through spring. Several months are so dry that even morning dew is uncommon. In parts of the habitat, however, the rainy season may be somewhat longer and the dry season not quite as long as indicated by the climate data. Cultivated plants should be kept moist while actively growing, but they should be allowed to dry out after growths mature in autumn.

FERTILIZER: ½ recommended strength, applied weekly. From spring to midsummer, a high-nitrogen fertilizer is beneficial to encourage maximum vegetative growth, but a fertilizer high in phosphates should be used in late summer and autumn.

REST PERIOD: Winter days average 63–67°F (17–19°C), and nights average 48–51°F (9–11°C), with a diurnal range of 15–16°F (8–9°C). In cultivation, water should be greatly reduced and the plants allowed to dry out between waterings. They should not remain dry for extended periods, however. Occasional early morning mistings on bright, sunny days may be beneficial and help keep the plants from becoming too dry. Fertilizer should be eliminated anytime water is reduced. Plants should be watered liberally in spring and summer, but watering should not be increased until flower buds swell or new growth begins. In the habitat, light is highest during clear winter weather.

GROWING MEDIA: Plants are best grown in a pot filled with an open, fast-draining medium, but they may be mounted on tree-fern or cork slabs if humidity is high and plants are watered at least once daily in summer. Repotting is best done in early spring when new roots are growing.

MISCELLANEOUS NOTES: The bloom season shown in the climate table is based on cultivation records. Plants may be encouraged to bloom earlier by raising temperatures earlier in the spring.

D. densiflorum requires an extended rest. Plants are often quite late starting a new growth, which then grows rapidly. Some growers report that an exceptionally long, cool, dry, rest period is necessary to initiate blooming, and that plants do not bloom well in warm uniform climates. Other growers report that *D. densiflorum* is free-flowering, grows all year, and does not require a rest period. We suspect that this results from incorrect identification of closely related plants and suggest that a prudent approach would be to slightly reduce water and temperatures in autumn. If a mature plant does not bloom under those conditions, it may be a true *D. densiflorum* and a longer, more definite rest should be imposed the following year, as indicated in the climate table.

Plant and Flower Information

PLANT SIZE AND TYPE: A compact, 12–18 in. (30–45 cm) sympodial epiphyte. Plants grow in tufts.

PSEUDOBULB: 12–18 in. (30–45 cm) long. The usually erect tufts of club-shaped pseudobulbs may grow sideways or hang upside down. Pseudobulbs are many-angled, club-shaped, and swollen at the internodes.

LEAVES: 3–5 per growth. The evergreen leaves are usually 6 in. (15 cm) long and close together on the pseudobulb. They are satiny when young, but with age, they become leathery.

INFLORESCENCE: 7–10 in. (18–25 cm) long. Numerous, pendent inflorescences emerge from nodes along the upper half of the pseudobulb. Each is densely covered with many flowers. Mature specimen plants have carried 100 inflorescences.

FLOWERS: 50–100 blossoms per inflorescence is not uncommon. The showy flowers are 1.2–2.0 in. (3–5 cm) across. The sepals and petals are semi-transparent with a crystalline texture that reflects the light. They are commonly rich, butter yellow but may be a pale yellow. The ruffled lip is orange with a pale orange margin. It is covered with soft, downy hairs. The lip and petals are finely toothed. The delicately fragrant blossoms last 1–2 weeks.

HYBRIDIZING NOTES: Chromosome counts are n = 20 (ref. 150, 187, 542), n = 20+0−2B (ref. 154, 542), n = 20+1−2B (ref. 187, 504, 580), 2n = 38 (ref. 150, 152, 187, 542), 2n = 40 (ref. 152, 154, 187, 542), 2n = 40+1f (ref. 151, 154, 187, 188), 2n = 40+3f (ref. 152), 2n = 40+2f, (ref. 187, 504, 580), and 2n = 42 (ref. 150, 154, 542). Growers indicate that a pure white form found near Darjeeling in Sikkim is self-sterile.

REFERENCES: 6, 25, 32, 36, 38, 46, 71, 150, 151, 152, 153, 154, 157, 179, 187, 188, 190, 196, 200, 202, 210, 216, 229, 236, 245, 247, 254, 266, 277, 278, 317, 326, 358, 365, 367, 369, 376, 428, 430, 445, 447, 448, 452, 454, 458, 461, 504, 523, 528, 541, 542, 557, 569, 570, 580, 581.

PHOTOS/DRAWINGS: 6, 19, 32, *36*, 46, 210, *245, 247, 299, 365, 369, 428, 430,* 454, 458, *569,* 570, *581.*

Dendrobium densifolium Schlechter

ORIGIN/HABITAT: Northeastern Papua New Guinea. At the mouth of the Waria River, plants grow near sea level on coastal forest trees.

CLIMATE: Station #94048, Finschhafen, Papua New Guinea, Lat. 6.6°S, Long. 147.9°E, at 25 ft. (8 m). Record extreme temperatures are 93°F (34°C) and 68°F (20°C).

N/HEMISPHERE	JAN	FEB	MAR	APR	MAY	JUN	JUL	AUG	SEP	OCT	NOV	DEC
°F AVG MAX	84	83	83	84	86	88	89	89	87	86	84	84
°F AVG MIN	73	72	72	71	71	72	74	74	74	74	73	73
DIURNAL RANGE	11	11	11	13	15	16	15	15	13	12	11	11
RAIN/INCHES	25.8	22.4	20.9	15.8	11.7	8.9	5.5	3.7	5.3	11.9	18.3	23.2
HUMIDITY/%	88	87	86	86	84	85	84	85	86	88	88	88
BLOOM SEASON	*											
DAYS CLR	N/A											
RAIN/MM	655	568	531	402	297	227	140	95	135	301	464	589
°C AVG MAX	28.9	28.3	28.3	28.9	30.0	31.1	31.7	31.7	30.6	30.0	28.9	28.9
°C AVG MIN	22.8	22.2	22.2	21.7	21.7	22.2	23.3	23.3	23.3	23.3	22.8	22.8
DIURNAL RANGE	6.1	6.1	6.1	7.2	8.3	8.9	8.4	8.4	7.3	6.7	6.1	6.1
S/HEMISPHERE	JUL	AUG	SEP	OCT	NOV	DEC	JAN	FEB	MAR	APR	MAY	JUN

Dendrobium dentatum

Cultural Recommendations

LIGHT: 2500–3000 fc.

TEMPERATURES: Throughout the year, days average 83–89°F (28–32°C), and nights average 71–74°F (22–23°C), with a diurnal range of 11–16°F (6–9°C).

HUMIDITY: 84–88% year-round.

WATER: Rainfall is very heavy most of the year, with a 3–4 month somewhat drier period in summer. Cultivated plants should dry slightly between waterings but never be allowed to dry out completely.

FERTILIZER: ¼–½ recommended strength. A balanced fertilizer should be applied weekly to biweekly throughout the year.

REST PERIOD: Growing conditions should be maintained year-round. While rainfall in the habitat is heaviest in winter, water and fertilizer should be reduced somewhat if plants are cultivated in the dark, short-day conditions common in temperate-latitude winters.

GROWING MEDIA: Plants may be mounted on tree-fern or cork slabs if humidity is high and plants are watered at least once daily in summer. When plants are potted, any open, fast-draining medium may be used. Repotting may be done anytime new roots are growing.

MISCELLANEOUS NOTES: The bloom season shown in the climate table is based on collection reports. Plants that produce flowers which last a single day commonly bloom several times during the year. Flowering usually occurs 7–14 days after a sudden 10°F (5°C) drop in daytime temperatures.

Plant and Flower Information

PLANT SIZE AND TYPE: A 20–24 in. (50–60 cm) sympodial epiphyte.

PSEUDOBULB: 20–24 in. (50–60 cm) long. The rigid stems do not branch.

LEAVES: Many. The leaves are oval, erect-spreading, and 2–3 in. (5–8 cm) long.

INFLORESCENCE: Short. Numerous, flattened inflorescences emerge from the side of the pseudobulb.

FLOWERS: 2 per inflorescence. The flowers are 0.9 in. (2.3 cm) across. The spreading sepals and petals may be white or yellow. The notched and scalloped lip is sulfur yellow with brown markings and an orange-red crest. The column is white with orange-red at the tip. Blossoms last a single day.

REFERENCES: 221, 437, 445.

PHOTOS/DRAWINGS: 437.

Dendrobium dentatum Seidenfaden

AKA: Plants were originally thought to be *D. tenellum* (Blume) Lindley.

ORIGIN/HABITAT: Vietnam. Plants have been collected near Dalat, Camly, Tonkin, Kontum, Quang Nam, and Dong Tho. Habitat elevation is unavailable, so the following climate data should be used with caution.

CLIMATE: Station #48881, Dalat, Vietnam, Lat. 11.1°N, Long. 108.1°E, at 3156 ft. (962 m). Record extreme temperatures are 93°F (34°C) and 43°F (6°C).

N/HEMISPHERE	JAN	FEB	MAR	APR	MAY	JUN	JUL	AUG	SEP	OCT	NOV	DEC
°F AVG MAX	80	82	84	85	84	81	81	80	80	80	79	79
°F AVG MIN	56	57	59	62	65	65	65	65	65	63	60	58
DIURNAL RANGE	24	25	25	23	19	16	16	15	15	17	19	21
RAIN/INCHES	0.2	0.9	1.6	4.6	9.1	6.1	7.7	8.2	10.1	9.7	2.7	1.3
HUMIDITY/%	68	64	65	71	78	81	82	83	84	82	76	73
BLOOM SEASON	N/A											
DAYS CLR @ 7AM	13	13	13	9	5	3	2	2	2	5	7	10
DAYS CLR @ 1PM	8	8	8	2	0	0	0	0	0	1	3	4
RAIN/MM	5	23	41	117	231	155	196	208	257	246	69	33
°C AVG MAX	26.7	27.8	28.9	29.4	28.9	27.2	27.2	26.7	26.7	26.7	26.1	26.1
°C AVG MIN	13.3	13.9	15.0	16.7	18.3	18.3	18.3	18.3	18.3	17.2	15.6	14.4
DIURNAL RANGE	13.4	13.9	13.9	12.7	10.6	8.9	8.9	8.4	8.4	9.5	10.5	11.7
S/HEMISPHERE	JUL	AUG	SEP	OCT	NOV	DEC	JAN	FEB	MAR	APR	MAY	JUN

Cultural Recommendations

LIGHT: 2000–3000 fc.

TEMPERATURES: Summer days average 80–81°F (27°C), and nights average 65°F (18°C), with a diurnal range of 15–16°F (8–9°C). The warmest temperatures occur in late winter and spring. Days average 84–85°F (29°C), and nights average 59–65°F (15–18°C), and the diurnal range averages 19–25°F (11–14°C).

HUMIDITY: 80–85% in summer, dropping to near 65% in late winter.

WATER: Rainfall is moderate to heavy in summer but is very light for 2 months in winter. Cultivated plants should be kept moist while growing, but water should be gradually reduced after new growths mature in autumn.

FERTILIZER: ¼–½ recommended strength, applied weekly. A high-nitrogen fertilizer is beneficial from spring to midsummer, but a fertilizer high in phosphates should be used in late summer and autumn.

REST PERIOD: Winter days average 79–82°F (26–28°C), and nights average 56–58°F (13–14°C), with a diurnal range of 21–25°F (12–14°C). The increased diurnal range results from warmer days and cooler nights. Rainfall is low for 3–4 months, and for 1–2 months, conditions are so dry that even moisture from dew is uncommon. For cultivated plants, water and fertilizer should be reduced for 2–3 months. Plants should be allowed to dry out between waterings, but they should not remain dry for extended periods. In the habitat, light is highest in winter.

GROWING MEDIA: Plants may be mounted on tree-fern or cork slabs if humidity is high and plants are watered at least once daily in summer. When plants are potted, any open, fast-draining medium may be used. Repotting may be done anytime new roots are growing.

Plant and Flower Information

PLANT SIZE AND TYPE: A 16–24 in. (40–60 cm) sympodial epiphyte.

PSEUDOBULB: 16–24 in. (40–60 cm) long. The straight, thin stems are clustered and occasionally branch. A single, enlarged node, approximately 0.4 in. (1 cm) above the base, forms a pseudobulbous swelling 0.8–1.2 in. (2–3 cm) long.

LEAVES: Many. The terete leaves are 1.6–4.0 in. (4–10 cm) long. New stems are leafy.

INFLORESCENCE: Inflorescences are spaced 0.4–0.8 in. (1–2 cm) apart on the upper, leafless portion of the stem. They emerge from tufts of small bracts.

FLOWERS: 1 per inflorescence. The white flowers are 0.4 in. (1 cm) across. The petals are lanceolate. The sepals are broadly triangular. The fan-shaped, ruffled lip, which is truncate at the apex, is toothed along the front margin.

REFERENCES: 234, 450.

PHOTOS/DRAWINGS: 450.

Dendrobium denudans D. Don

ORIGIN/HABITAT: India, Nepal, and Sikkim. In the Garhwal district of northwestern India, plants grow at 3300–6550 ft. (1000–2000 m). They commonly grow at the base of trees where they receive ample moisture and protection from extreme temperature fluctuations. In deforested areas, plants may grow lithophytically.

CLIMATE: Station #42147, Mukteswar, India, Lat. 29.5°N, Long. 79.7°E, at 7592 ft. (2314 m). Temperatures are calculated for an elevation of 4000 ft. (1220 m), resulting in probable extremes of 102°F (39°C) and 33°F (1°C).

N/HEMISPHERE	JAN	FEB	MAR	APR	MAY	JUN	JUL	AUG	SEP	OCT	NOV	DEC
°F AVG MAX	63	66	73	81	87	87	81	81	80	77	73	67
°F AVG MIN	48	50	56	64	69	71	71	70	68	62	56	51
DIURNAL RANGE	15	16	17	17	18	16	10	11	12	15	17	16
RAIN/INCHES	1.0	2.1	1.7	1.0	0.3	4.6	11.4	12.8	4.6	3.5	0.3	0.2
HUMIDITY/%	61	55	50	39	44	67	91	93	83	66	55	56
BLOOM SEASON						*	*	*	*			
DAYS CLR @ 5PM	17	17	15	18	18	12	1	1	6	25	26	21
RAIN/MM	25	53	43	25	8	117	290	325	117	89	8	5
°C AVG MAX	17.1	18.8	22.7	27.1	30.5	30.5	27.1	27.1	26.6	24.9	22.7	19.4
°C AVG MIN	8.8	9.9	13.3	17.7	20.5	21.6	21.6	21.0	19.9	16.6	13.3	10.5
DIURNAL RANGE	8.3	8.9	9.4	9.4	10.0	8.9	5.5	6.1	6.7	8.3	9.4	8.9
S/HEMISPHERE	JUL	AUG	SEP	OCT	NOV	DEC	JAN	FEB	MAR	APR	MAY	JUN

Cultural Recommendations

LIGHT: 2500–3500 fc.

TEMPERATURES: Summer days average 81–87°F (27–31°C), and nights average 70–71°F (21–22°C), with a diurnal range of 10–16°F (6–9°C).

HUMIDITY: Near 90% in summer, decreasing to 55–60% most of the winter. In spring, at the end of the dry season, humidity drops to near 40% for 2 months.

WATER: Rainfall is moderate to heavy for 5 months in summer. The wet season is followed immediately by 7 very dry months from autumn through spring. Several months are so dry that even morning dew is uncommon. Cultivated plants should be kept moist while growing, but they should be allowed to dry out after growths mature in autumn.

FERTILIZER: ¼–½ recommended strength, applied weekly. A high-nitrogen fertilizer is beneficial from spring to midsummer, but a fertilizer high in phosphates should be used in late summer and autumn.

REST PERIOD: Winter days average 63–67°F (17–19°C), and nights average 48–51°F (9–11°C), with a diurnal range of 15–16°F (8–9°C). In cultivation, water should be greatly reduced and the plants allowed to dry out between waterings. They should not remain dry for extended periods, however. Occasional early morning mistings on bright, sunny days, may be beneficial and help keep the plants from becoming too dry. Fertilizer should be eliminated anytime water is reduced. Water should not be increased until flower buds swell and new growth begins in spring. In the habitat, light is highest during clear winter weather.

GROWING MEDIA: Mounting plants on tree-fern or cork slabs accommodates their pendent growth habit. If plants cannot be mounted, small pots or hanging baskets may be filled with any open, fast-draining medium. Repotting may be done anytime new roots are actively growing.

MISCELLANEOUS NOTES: The bloom season shown in the climate table is based on cultivation records and reports from the habitat.

Plant and Flower Information

PLANT SIZE AND TYPE: A pendent, 3–12 in. (8–30 cm) sympodial epiphyte.

PSEUDOBULB: 3–10 in. (8–25 cm) long. The delicate yellow stems are suberect and taper from the base toward the apex.

LEAVES: Many. The linear to oblong leaves are 2–4 in. (5–10 cm) long. They are thin-textured and deciduous at flowering.

INFLORESCENCE: 4–6 in. (10–15 cm) long. The pendent inflorescences emerge opposite the leaves from nodes near the tip of the stem. Each stem usually produces 3–4 slender inflorescences. Plants often begin blooming when stems are about 2.4 in. (6 cm) long.

FLOWERS: 10–15 per inflorescence. The spidery flowers are 0.6–1.0 in. (1.5–2.5 cm) across, which is large for the plant size. The long, slender sepals and petals are creamy white often tinged with green or yellow. They do not open fully. The lip is usually green, but it may be white or yellowish. It is ruffled and marked with reddish veins. The edges of the 3-lobed lip are toothed and ruffled.

HYBRIDIZING NOTES: Chromosome counts are n = 20 (ref. 150, 154, 187, 542) and 2n = 40 (ref. 151, 154, 187, 188, 504, 542, 580). Johansen (ref. 239) indicates that plants are self-sterile and that flowers dropped 12–14 days after self-pollination.

REFERENCES: 32, 36, 102, 150, 151, 154, 179, 187, 188, 202, 203, 210, 216, 239, 254, 278, 294, 317, 330, 369, 376, 445, 454, 504, 542, 580.

PHOTOS/DRAWINGS: 102, 203, 210, *454*.

Dendrobium denudans Wallich. See *D. monticola* Hunt and Summerhayes. REFERENCES: 38, 46, 254. PHOTOS/DRAWINGS: 46.

Dendrobium deplanchei Rchb. f.

ORIGIN/HABITAT: New Caledonia. These uncommon plants grow at 2300–3300 ft. (700–1000 m) along mountain foot paths in the litter found on the border of humid forests.

CLIMATE: Station #91583, Poindimie, New Caledonia, Lat. 20.9°S, Long. 165.3°E, at 36 ft. (11 m). Temperatures are calculated for an elevation of 3000 ft. (910 m). Record extreme temperatures are not available for this location.

N/HEMISPHERE	JAN	FEB	MAR	APR	MAY	JUN	JUL	AUG	SEP	OCT	NOV	DEC
°F AVG MAX	64	64	65	67	69	71	73	73	72	71	67	66
°F AVG MIN	54	53	55	57	60	62	63	65	64	62	58	56
DIURNAL RANGE	10	11	10	10	9	9	10	8	8	9	9	10
RAIN/INCHES	3.4	3.0	2.6	4.2	7.5	7.7	11.4	10.4	9.3	5.7	6.7	4.6
HUMIDITY/%	N/A											
BLOOM SEASON					*		*		*		*	
DAYS CLR	N/A											
RAIN/MM	86	76	66	107	190	196	290	264	236	145	170	117
°C AVG MAX	17.9	17.9	18.5	19.6	20.7	21.8	22.9	22.9	22.3	21.8	19.6	19.0
°C AVG MIN	12.3	11.8	12.9	14.0	15.7	16.8	17.3	18.5	17.9	16.8	14.6	13.5
DIURNAL RANGE	5.6	6.1	5.6	5.6	5.0	5.0	5.6	4.4	4.4	5.0	5.0	5.5
S/HEMISPHERE	JUL	AUG	SEP	OCT	NOV	DEC	JAN	FEB	MAR	APR	MAY	JUN

Cultural Recommendations

LIGHT: 2500–3000 fc.

TEMPERATURES: Summer days average 71–73°F (22–23°C), and nights average 62–65°F (17–19°C), with a diurnal range of 8–10°F (4–6°C).

HUMIDITY: Information is not available for this location. However, records from nearby locations indicate that humidity probably averages 70–80% year-round.

WATER: Rainfall is moderate to heavy most of the year, but conditions are somewhat drier for 3 months in winter. Cultivated plants should be kept moist and not be allowed to dry completely.

FERTILIZER: ¼–½ recommended strength, applied weekly. A high-nitrogen fertilizer is beneficial from spring to midsummer, but a fertilizer high in phosphates should be used in late summer and autumn.

REST PERIOD: Winter days average 64–66°F (18–19°C), and nights average 53–56°F (12–14°C), with a diurnal range of 10–11°F (6°C). Water should be reduced for cultivated plants in winter, but they should never be allowed to dry out completely. Reduce or eliminate fertilizer when water is restricted.

GROWING MEDIA: *D. deplanchei* is terrestrial, but it is probably best potted in a small to medium fir-bark mix. Depending on watering practices, moisture retaining materials such as Perlite or chopped sphagnum moss may be added as needed to keep the medium moist. However, the mix should be open and drain rapidly. Repotting is best done in early spring when new roots are growing.

MISCELLANEOUS NOTES: The bloom season shown in the climate table is based on reports from the habitat.

Dendrobium derryi

Plant and Flower Information

PLANT SIZE AND TYPE: An extremely large, 118–197 in. (300–500 cm) sympodial terrestrial.

PSEUDOBULB: 118–197 in. (300–500 cm) long. The bamboolike stems, which sometimes branch, are swollen at the base. The stems are covered by the clasping leaf bases.

LEAVES: Many. The brownish to olive-green leaves are 4–6 in. (10–15 cm) long. Stems are densely leafy.

INFLORESCENCE: Long. Inflorescences emerge opposite the leaves.

FLOWERS: 6–15 per inflorescence. The flowers are 0.8 in. (2 cm) long and remain rather closed. The lanceolate sepals and petals are pointed at the tip. The dorsal sepal is recurved. The lip has 3 raised keels. The sides of the midlobe curve inward and touch at the center.

HYBRIDIZING NOTES: *D. deplanchei* is reported to be self-sterile.

REFERENCES: 173, 216, 254.

PHOTOS/DRAWINGS: 173.

Dendrobium derryi Ridley

ORIGIN/HABITAT: Borneo and the Taiping Hills of Malaya, where plants are rare. Habitat elevation is estimated at 3500 ft. (1070 m), so the following climate data should be used with caution.

CLIMATE: Station #48625, Ipoh, Malaya, Lat. 4.6°N, Long. 101.1°E, at 123 ft. (37 m). Temperatures are calculated for an estimated elevation of 3500 ft. (1070 m), resulting in probable extremes of 88°F (31°C) and 53°F (12°C).

N/HEMISPHERE	JAN	FEB	MAR	APR	MAY	JUN	JUL	AUG	SEP	OCT	NOV	DEC
°F AVG MAX	79	81	82	81	81	81	80	80	79	78	78	78
°F AVG MIN	61	61	62	62	63	62	61	61	62	61	61	61
DIURNAL RANGE	18	20	20	19	18	19	19	19	17	17	17	17
RAIN/INCHES	7.9	3.1	7.6	8.4	6.2	3.6	7.2	6.9	8.8	11.0	13.0	8.9
HUMIDITY/%	76	74	76	78	78	75	76	77	79	82	82	81
BLOOM SEASON	N/A											
DAYS CLR @ 7AM	3	3	3	1	1	2	1	1	0	0	1	2
DAYS CLR @ 1PM	2	2	2	1	1	1	1	1	0	0	0	2
RAIN/MM	201	79	193	213	157	91	183	175	224	279	330	226
°C AVG MAX	26.0	27.1	27.7	27.1	27.1	27.1	26.6	26.6	26.0	25.5	25.5	25.5
°C AVG MIN	16.0	16.0	16.6	16.6	17.1	16.6	16.0	16.0	16.6	16.0	16.0	16.0
DIURNAL RANGE	10.0	11.1	11.1	10.5	10.0	10.5	10.6	10.6	9.4	9.5	9.5	9.5
S/HEMISPHERE	JUL	AUG	SEP	OCT	NOV	DEC	JAN	FEB	MAR	APR	MAY	JUN

Cultural Recommendations

LIGHT: 2500–3500 fc.

TEMPERATURES: Throughout the year, days average 78–82°F (26–28°C), and nights average 61–63°F (16–17°C), with a diurnal range of 17–20°F (9–11°C).

HUMIDITY: Near 75–80% year-round.

WATER: Rainfall is heavy most of the year. The heaviest rainfall occurs in autumn with a secondary maximum in spring. Brief semidry periods occur in midwinter and midsummer. Cultivated plants should be kept evenly moist with only slight drying allowed between waterings.

FERTILIZER: ¼–½ recommended strength. A balanced fertilizer should be applied weekly to biweekly throughout the year.

REST PERIOD: Growing conditions should be maintained year-round. Water should be reduced somewhat in winter for plants cultivated in the dark, short-day conditions common in temperate latitudes. They should never be allowed to dry out completely, however. Fertilizer may be reduced when the plant is not actively growing or when water is reduced. In the habitat, light is slightly higher in winter.

GROWING MEDIA: Plants may be mounted on tree-fern or cork slabs if humidity is high and plants are watered at least once daily in summer. When plants are potted, any open, fast-draining medium may be used. Repotting may be done anytime new roots are growing.

Plant and Flower Information

PLANT SIZE AND TYPE: An 8–14 in. (20–35 cm) sympodial plant.

PSEUDOBULB: 6–10 in. (15–25 cm) long.

LEAVES: Many. The leaves, which are spaced 1 in. (2.5 cm) apart along the stem, are 3–4 in. (8–10 cm) long.

INFLORESCENCE: Short. The inflorescences emerge from nodes along the stem and blossoms are held close to the stem. Inflorescences are produced on old stems.

FLOWERS: 1–2 per inflorescence. The flowers are 0.8–1.2 in. (2.0–3.0 cm) across. The blossoms have pale yellowish sepals and petals and a white lip which has no sidelobes. The flat anther is orange.

REFERENCES: 200, 220, 254, 286, 295, 402, 454, 455.

PHOTOS/DRAWINGS: 455.

Dendrobium desmotrichoides J. J. Smith

ORIGIN/HABITAT: Irian Jaya (western New Guinea). Plants grow along the Merauke River. Habitat elevation is not available, so the following climate data should be used with caution.

CLIMATE: Station #97980, Merauke, Irian Jaya, Lat. 8.5°S, Long. 140.4°E, at 10 ft. (3 m). Record extreme temperatures are 97°F (36°C) and 58°F (14°C).

N/HEMISPHERE	JAN	FEB	MAR	APR	MAY	JUN	JUL	AUG	SEP	OCT	NOV	DEC
°F AVG MAX	84	85	87	89	91	89	89	87	88	88	87	85
°F AVG MIN	70	71	69	71	73	74	74	74	74	74	73	71
DIURNAL RANGE	14	14	18	18	18	15	15	13	14	14	14	14
RAIN/INCHES	1.3	0.7	1.1	1.6	3.0	7.4	10.3	9.0	10.0	7.2	4.9	1.7
HUMIDITY/%	88	85	85	85	79	87	89	91	88	88	85	88
BLOOM SEASON	N/A											
DAYS CLR	N/A											
RAIN/MM	33	18	28	41	76	188	262	229	254	183	124	43
°C AVG MAX	28.9	29.4	30.6	31.7	32.8	31.7	31.7	30.6	31.1	31.1	30.6	29.4
°C AVG MIN	21.1	21.7	20.6	21.7	22.8	23.3	23.3	23.3	23.3	23.3	22.8	21.7
DIURNAL RANGE	7.8	7.7	10.0	10.0	10.0	8.4	8.4	7.3	7.8	7.8	7.8	7.7
S/HEMISPHERE	JUL	AUG	SEP	OCT	NOV	DEC	JAN	FEB	MAR	APR	MAY	JUN

Cultural Recommendations

LIGHT: 2000–3000 fc during the growing season.

TEMPERATURES: Throughout the year, days average 84–91°F (29–33°C), and nights average 69–74°F (21–23°C), with a diurnal range of 13–18°F (7–10°C). The warmest season is spring, at the end of the winter dry season.

HUMIDITY: 85–90% year-round.

WATER: Rainfall is moderate to heavy from summer through autumn, followed by a 4–5 month winter dry season. Cultivated plants should be kept evenly moist while actively growing, but water should be gradually reduced in autumn.

FERTILIZER: ¼–½ recommended strength. A balanced fertilizer should be applied weekly to biweekly throughout the year.

REST PERIOD: Growing temperatures should be maintained all year. Winter rainfall is low, but humidity remains high, and additional moisture is available from the frequent heavy dews. For cultivated plants, water should be reduced in winter. They should be allowed to dry out somewhat between waterings but should never remain dry for long periods. Occasional early morning mistings between waterings, especially on bright sunny days, may be beneficial. In the habitat, light is brightest during the winter dry season. Fertilizer should be reduced anytime water is restricted or plants are not actively growing, especially if light is low or temperatures are cool.

GROWING MEDIA: Plants may be mounted on tree-fern or cork slabs or potted in small pots filled with any open, fast-draining medium. Repotting may be done anytime new roots are actively growing.

Plant and Flower Information

PLANT SIZE AND TYPE: A 2.0–2.4 in. (5–6 cm) sympodial epiphyte.

PSEUDOBULB: 0.5 in. (1.3 cm) long. The branching stems arise from a creeping branching rhizome.

LEAVES: 1 per growth. Each lanceolate leaf is 1.6–2.0 in. (4–5 cm) long, fleshy, and rigid.

INFLORESCENCE: Short.

FLOWERS: 1–2 per inflorescence. The fragrant flowers are 0.6 in. (1.5 cm) across. Sepals and petals are pale yellow-green with red dots. The lip is yellow with red stripes.

REFERENCES: 220, 254, 437, 445, 470.

Dendrobium devonianum Paxton

AKA: *D. brevifolium* Hort. ex Lindley, *D. pictum* Griffith, *D. pulchellum* as used by Lindley not Loddiges or Roxburgh, *D. pulchellum* Lindley var. *devonianum* (Paxton) Rchb. f.

ORIGIN/HABITAT: The Himalayan region. The habitat extends eastward from Sikkim through northeastern India, Burma, the mountains of northern Thailand, Laos, near Chapa in northern Vietnam, and into southwest China and Taiwan. Plants usually grow at 3300–6550 ft. (1000–2000 m), but they are sometimes found as low as 1800 ft. (550 m).

CLIMATE: Station #42410, Gauhati, India, Lat. 26.1°N, Long. 91.6°E, at 158 ft. (48 m). Temperatures are calculated for an elevation of 4600 ft. (1400 m), resulting in probable extremes of 89°F (32°C) and 26°F (−3°C).

N/HEMISPHERE	JAN	FEB	MAR	APR	MAY	JUN	JUL	AUG	SEP	OCT	NOV	DEC
°F AVG MAX	61	63	71	73	73	74	75	75	74	72	66	61
°F AVG MIN	36	39	45	53	57	62	63	63	61	56	46	38
DIURNAL RANGE	25	24	26	20	16	12	12	12	13	16	20	23
RAIN/INCHES	0.4	1.2	2.0	5.7	9.3	12.3	12.3	10.3	6.6	2.8	0.6	0.2
HUMIDITY/%	79	72	64	71	82	85	85	86	84	84	83	82
BLOOM SEASON		*	*	***	***	*	*					
DAYS CLR @ 6AM	6	12	16	11	3	0	0	1	3	7	6	3
DAYS CLR @ 12PM	17	16	18	15	6	1	0	0	2	11	17	19
RAIN/MM	10	30	51	145	236	312	312	262	168	71	15	5
°C AVG MAX	16.3	17.4	21.9	23.0	23.0	23.5	24.1	24.1	23.5	22.4	19.1	16.3
°C AVG MIN	2.4	4.1	7.4	11.9	14.1	16.9	17.4	17.4	16.3	13.5	8.0	3.5
DIURNAL RANGE	13.9	13.3	14.5	11.1	8.9	6.6	6.7	6.7	7.2	8.9	11.1	12.8
S/HEMISPHERE	JUL	AUG	SEP	OCT	NOV	DEC	JAN	FEB	MAR	APR	MAY	JUN

Cultural Recommendations

LIGHT: 2500–3500 fc. In the habitat, summer light is relatively low because clouds are heavy during the rainy season. Light increases by midautumn when about half of the afternoons are clear each month. Light should be as high as possible, short of burning the leaves, from autumn into early spring.

TEMPERATURES: Summer days average 74–75°F (24°C), and nights average 62–63°F (17°C), with a diurnal range of 12°F (7°C). Due to microclimate effects, actual temperatures may be 6–8°F (3–4°C) warmer than indicated.

HUMIDITY: Near 85% in summer, dropping to 65–70% for 2–3 months in late winter and early spring.

WATER: Rainfall is heavy from spring through summer but decreases rapidly in autumn with a 1–2 month transition into the winter dry season. Cultivated plants should be kept moist while actively growing, but water should be gradually reduced after new growths mature in autumn.

FERTILIZER: ¼–½ recommended strength, applied weekly. A high-nitrogen fertilizer is beneficial from spring to midsummer, but a fertilizer high in phosphates should be used in late summer and autumn.

REST PERIOD: Winter days average 61–63°F (16–17°C), and nights average 36–39°F (2–4°C), with a diurnal range of 23–25°F (13–14°C). Although rainfall is low for 4–5 winter months, high humidity and the large temperature range indicate that additional moisture from heavy dew is common. Therefore, while water should be greatly reduced and cultivated plants allowed to dry out between waterings from late autumn into early spring, they should not remain dry for extended periods. Occasional mistings between waterings during bright, sunny weather may help prevent the plants from becoming too dry. Fertilizer should be reduced or eliminated until active growth resumes and water is increased in spring.

GROWING MEDIA: Growers often recommend mounting plants on tree-fern slabs to accommodate the pendent growth habit. They often place a pad of sphagnum moss between the mount and the plant. If plants are mounted, summer humidity must be high, and plants should be watered at least once a day in summer. If plants cannot be mounted, hanging pots or baskets may be filled with any open, rapidly draining medium. Containers should be barely large enough to hold the roots. Mounts or baskets reduce the risk of the slender new canes becoming kinked under their own weight. Repotting is best done in spring, immediately after flowering.

MISCELLANEOUS NOTES: The bloom season shown in the climate table is based on cultivation records. Growers indicate that *D. devonianum* is difficult to grow and is extremely susceptible to spider mites. Plants are healthier and cultural problems less severe when the plants receive a cool, dry rest. Growers also state that plants flower only rarely in warm, uniform climates, indicating that a rest period is necessary to initiate blooming.

Plant and Flower Information

PLANT SIZE AND TYPE: A 35–59 in. (90–150 cm) sympodial epiphyte.

PSEUDOBULB: 35–59 in. (90–150 cm) long. The purplish stems are slender, often branching, and bend under the weight of numerous blossoms.

LEAVES: Many. The pale green, distichous leaves are about 4 in. (10 cm) long and grow from each node along the stem. They are quickly deciduous and drop before blooming occurs.

INFLORESCENCE: 1 in. (2.5 cm) long. Inflorescences arise from nearly every node along the upper 50–75% of 1-year-old stems. Each node blooms only once.

FLOWERS: 1–3 per inflorescence, rarely more. The flowers are 2–3 in. (5–8 cm) across. Sepals and petals are creamy white, often tinged with pink or lavender, and suffused with pink at the tip of each segment, especially on the petals. On some clones, the petals and lip may be lemon-yellow. The petals have a row of hairs along the margin. The heart-shaped lip is very open, white along the edge, with a large pink to lavender blotch at the tip and purple lines in the throat. It is decorated with 2 orange-yellow blotches on each side of the center line. The edge is deeply fringed and portions of the fringe may branch. Blossoms last about 2 weeks.

HYBRIDIZING NOTES: Chromosome counts are n = 19 (ref. 504, 580), 2n = 38 (ref. 504). Seeds are sufficiently mature for green-pod culture in about 186 days but time ranges from 160–250 days. Plantlets are easy to maintain in flask. Johansen (ref. 239) found *D. devonianum* to be self-sterile, with blossoms dropping 5–18 days after self-pollination. *D. devonianum* and *D. crystallinum* Rchb. f. produced viable seed. However, when crossed with *D. aphyllum* (Roxburgh) C. Fischer, capsules formed but no seed was produced.

REFERENCES: 2, 38, 46, 153, 157, 179, 190, 196, 200, 202, 208, 210, 216, 239, 245, 247, 254, 266, 278, 369, 376, 425, 430, 445, 447, 448, 454, 504, 512, 523, 528, 541, 557, 570, 580.

PHOTOS/DRAWINGS: 210, *245*, *247*, *369*, *430*, *454*, 512, 523, 541, 557.

Dendrobium devosianum J. J. Smith

AKA: Cribb (ref. 84) suggests that since these were cultivated plants, they may have been hybrids.

ORIGIN/HABITAT: The Moluccas. Habitat location and elevation are not available, so the following climate data should be used with caution. Backer and Brink (ref. 25) indicate that plants have been cultivated in Java and were reportedly cultivated in Irian Jaya (western New Guinea).

CLIMATE: Station #97690, Sentani/Jayapura, Irian Jaya, Lat. 2.7°S, Long. 140.5°E, at 289 ft. (88 m). Record extreme temperatures are 97°F (36°C) and 68°F (20°C).

N/HEMISPHERE	JAN	FEB	MAR	APR	MAY	JUN	JUL	AUG	SEP	OCT	NOV	DEC
°F AVG MAX	87	89	89	90	90	89	89	88	89	90	90	89
°F AVG MIN	72	72	72	73	73	73	73	73	73	74	73	73
DIURNAL RANGE	15	17	17	17	17	16	16	15	16	16	17	16
RAIN/INCHES	4.1	3.9	5.3	2.9	6.7	7.0	8.3	8.3	8.5	4.6	2.4	5.2
HUMIDITY/%	81	80	80	79	81	81	79	80	80	80	81	80
BLOOM SEASON	N/A											
DAYS CLR @ 9AM	5	3	4	3	2	1	1	0	1	2	2	5
DAYS CLR @ 3PM	4	3	3	3	2	1	3	0	1	2	2	3
RAIN/MM	104	99	135	74	170	178	211	211	216	117	61	132
°C AVG MAX	30.6	31.7	31.7	32.2	32.2	31.7	31.7	31.1	31.7	32.2	32.2	31.7
°C AVG MIN	22.2	22.2	22.2	22.8	22.8	22.8	22.8	22.8	22.8	23.3	22.8	22.8
DIURNAL RANGE	8.3	9.4	9.4	9.4	9.4	8.9	8.9	8.3	8.9	8.9	9.4	8.9
S/HEMISPHERE	JUL	AUG	SEP	OCT	NOV	DEC	JAN	FEB	MAR	APR	MAY	JUN

Cultural Recommendations

LIGHT: 1500–2000 fc.

TEMPERATURES: Throughout the year, days average 87–90°F (31–32°C), and nights average 72–74°F (22–23°C), with a diurnal range of 15–17°F (8–9°C).

HUMIDITY: Near 80% year-round.

WATER: Rainfall is heavy all year, with brief semidry periods in spring and autumn. Cultivated plants should be kept evenly moist with only slight drying allowed between waterings.

FERTILIZER: 1/4–1/2 recommended strength. A balanced fertilizer should be applied weekly to biweekly throughout the year.

REST PERIOD: Growing conditions should be maintained year-round. Water may be reduced somewhat for cultivated plants in winter, especially those grown in the dark, short-day conditions common in temperate latitudes. They should never be allowed to dry out completely, however. In the habitat, light is slightly higher in winter.

GROWING MEDIA: Plants may be mounted on tree-fern or cork slabs if humidity is high and plants are watered at least once daily in summer. When plants are potted, any open, fast-draining medium may be used. Repotting may be done anytime new roots are growing.

Plant and Flower Information

PLANT SIZE AND TYPE: A 12–16 in. (30–40 cm) sympodial epiphyte.

PSEUDOBULB: 12–16 in. (30–40 cm) long. Plants were described as having a growth habit similar to *D. antennatum* Lindley.

LEAVES: Several per growth. The oblong leaves are 3–5 in. (8–13 cm) long, spreading, recurved, and concave.

INFLORESCENCE: 12–13 in. (31–34 cm) long. The erect or ascending inflorescences are borne laterally from nodes near the apex of the stem.

FLOWERS: 12–16 per inflorescence. The fleshy blossoms are about 1.8 in. (4.5 cm) long. Flowers are whitish with dark purple stripes on the upper surface. The dorsal sepal is linear-lanceolate, acute, slightly wavy, and recurved near the apex. Lateral sepals somewhat triangular, pointed at the tip, and slightly wavy. The diverging petals, which are purple with a green margin, are suberect and twisted twice. The 3-lobed lip is yellow with green sidelobes and an uneven margin.

REFERENCES: 25, 84, 225, 226, 485.

PHOTOS/DRAWINGS: *84*.

Dendrobium diaphanum Schlechter

ORIGIN/HABITAT: Endemic to northern Sulawesi (Celebes). Plants grow on forest trees on the Minahassa Peninsula near Mt. Klabat at 1650–1950 ft. (500–600 m).

CLIMATE: Station #97014, Manado, Sulawesi, Indonesia, Lat. 1.5°N, Long. 124.9°E, at 264 ft. (80 m). Temperatures are calculated for an elevation of 1800 ft. (550 m), resulting in probable extremes of 92°F (33°C) and 60°F (16°C).

N/HEMISPHERE	JAN	FEB	MAR	APR	MAY	JUN	JUL	AUG	SEP	OCT	NOV	DEC
°F AVG MAX	80	80	80	81	82	82	82	84	84	84	82	81
°F AVG MIN	68	68	68	68	69	68	68	68	68	67	68	69
DIURNAL RANGE	12	12	12	13	13	14	14	16	16	17	14	12
RAIN/INCHES	18.6	13.8	12.2	8.0	6.4	6.5	4.8	4.0	3.4	4.9	8.9	14.7
HUMIDITY/%	84	83	83	83	81	80	75	72	75	77	82	83
BLOOM SEASON						**						
DAYS CLR @ 8AM	4	3	6	11	11	12	12	12	14	17	12	8
DAYS CLR @ 2PM	1	1	1	2	1	3	3	4	4	4	1	1
RAIN/MM	472	351	310	203	163	165	122	102	86	124	226	373
°C AVG MAX	26.6	26.6	26.6	27.2	27.7	27.7	27.7	28.9	28.9	28.9	27.7	27.2
°C AVG MIN	20.0	20.0	20.0	20.0	20.5	20.0	20.0	20.0	20.0	19.4	20.0	20.5
DIURNAL RANGE	6.6	6.6	6.6	7.2	7.2	7.7	7.7	8.9	8.9	9.5	7.7	6.7
S/HEMISPHERE	JUL	AUG	SEP	OCT	NOV	DEC	JAN	FEB	MAR	APR	MAY	JUN

Cultural Recommendations

LIGHT: 2500–4000 fc. In the habitat, summer skies are frequently clear in the morning and cloudy in the afternoon.

TEMPERATURES: Throughout the year, days average 80–84°F (27–29°C), and nights average 67–69°F (19–21°C), with a diurnal range of 12–17°F (7–10°C).

HUMIDITY: 80–85% most of the year, dropping to 70–75% in summer and early autumn.

WATER: Rainfall is moderate to heavy year-round. The driest weather occurs in summer and autumn. Cultivated plants should be kept moist while actively growing, with only slight drying allowed between waterings. Ample water should be provided for 6 months, then water should be reduced slightly for 6 months. Warm water might be beneficial.

FERTILIZER: 1/4–1/2 recommended strength. A balanced fertilizer should be applied weekly to biweekly throughout the year.

REST PERIOD: Growing temperatures should be maintained all year. In the habitat, the average highs, lows, and diurnal range fluctuate only slightly during the year. The plants may rest during the drier period, which occurs in late summer and coincides with a period of highest diurnal range. The heaviest rainfall occurs in winter, but if cultivated plants are kept moist, water should not be increased.

GROWING MEDIA: Mounting plants on tree-fern or cork slabs accommodates their pendulous growth habit. If plants cannot be mounted, small pots or hanging baskets may be filled with any open, fast-draining medium. Repotting may be done anytime new roots are actively growing.

MISCELLANEOUS NOTES: The bloom season shown in the climate table is based on collection reports.

Plant and Flower Information

PLANT SIZE AND TYPE: A 12–20 in. (30–50 cm) sympodial epiphyte.

PSEUDOBULB: 12–20 in. (30–50 cm) long. The flattened stems are pendulous with narrow leaves to the tip of each growth. They arise from a very short rhizome.

LEAVES: Many. The pointed, linear leaves, which are 2–3 in. (5–8 cm) long, are smooth and leathery.

INFLORESCENCE: Short. Inflorescences emerge opposite the leaves in simple clusters near the apex of the stem.

FLOWERS: The flowers are 0.6 in. (1.6 cm) across. Sepals and petals are yellowish with red veins. Blossom have an ovate-lanceolate dorsal sepal, somewhat triangular lateral sepals, and tongue-shaped petals. The bi-lobed lip is yellowish with 3 raised, dark yellow ridges at the front.

REFERENCES: 220, 436.

Dendrobium diceras Schlechter

ORIGIN/HABITAT: Northern Papua New Guinea. Plants grow near the coast in West Sepik Province close to Vanimo. Habitat elevation is estimated at 2000 ft. (610 m), so the following temperatures should be used with caution.

CLIMATE: Station #97690, Sentani/Jayapura, Irian Jaya, Lat. 2.7°S, Long. 140.5°E, at 289 ft. (88 m). Temperatures are calculated for an estimated elevation of 2000 ft. (610 m), resulting in probable extremes of 91°F (33°C) and 62°F (17°C).

N/HEMISPHERE	JAN	FEB	MAR	APR	MAY	JUN	JUL	AUG	SEP	OCT	NOV	DEC
°F AVG MAX	81	83	83	84	84	83	83	82	83	84	84	83
°F AVG MIN	66	66	66	67	67	67	67	67	67	68	67	67
DIURNAL RANGE	15	17	17	17	17	16	16	15	16	16	17	16
RAIN/INCHES	4.1	3.9	5.3	2.9	6.7	7.0	8.3	8.3	8.5	4.6	2.4	5.2
HUMIDITY/%	81	80	80	79	81	81	79	80	80	80	81	80
BLOOM SEASON	N/A											
DAYS CLR @ 9AM	5	3	4	3	2	1	1	0	1	2	2	5
DAYS CLR @ 3PM	4	3	3	3	2	1	3	0	1	2	2	3
RAIN/MM	104	99	135	74	170	178	211	211	216	117	61	132
°C AVG MAX	27.4	28.5	28.5	29.1	29.1	28.5	28.5	28.0	28.5	29.1	29.1	28.5
°C AVG MIN	19.1	19.1	19.1	19.6	19.6	19.6	19.6	19.6	19.6	20.2	19.6	19.6
DIURNAL RANGE	8.3	9.4	9.4	9.5	9.5	8.9	8.9	8.4	8.9	8.9	9.5	8.9
S/HEMISPHERE	JUL	AUG	SEP	OCT	NOV	DEC	JAN	FEB	MAR	APR	MAY	JUN

Cultural Recommendations

LIGHT: 2000–3000 fc.

TEMPERATURES: Throughout the year, days average 81–84°F (27–29°C), and nights average 66–68°F (19–20°C), with a diurnal range of 15–17°F (8–9°C).

HUMIDITY: Near 80% year-round.

WATER: Rainfall is heavy all year with brief semidry periods in spring and autumn. Cultivated plants should be kept evenly moist with only slight drying allowed between waterings.

FERTILIZER: 1/4–1/2 recommended strength. A balanced fertilizer should be applied weekly to biweekly throughout the year.

REST PERIOD: Growing conditions should be maintained year-round. Water may be reduced somewhat for cultivated plants in winter, especially those grown in the dark, short-day conditions common in temperate latitudes. They should never be allowed to dry out completely, however. In the habitat, light is slightly higher in winter.

GROWING MEDIA: Plants may be mounted on tree-fern or cork slabs if humidity is high and plants are watered at least once daily in summer. When plants are potted, any open, fast-draining medium may be used. Repotting may be done anytime new roots are growing.

MISCELLANEOUS NOTES: Cribb (ref. 83) indicates that this species is known only from the type collection. Unless rediscovered, it is not available for cultivation.

Plant and Flower Information

PLANT SIZE AND TYPE: A 16–18 in. (40–45 cm) sympodial epiphyte.

PSEUDOBULB: 15 in. (38 cm) long. The slender stems are grooved.

LEAVES: 3 per growth. The erect to spreading leaves are 4–5 in. (10–13 cm) long. The leaves are held at the apex of each growth.

INFLORESCENCE: 5–6 in. (13–15 cm) long. Inflorescences are laxly flowered.

FLOWERS: 5–7 per inflorescence. The smooth, fleshy flowers are 2.8–3.2 in. (7–8 cm) across. Sepals are oblong. The sickle-shaped petals are slightly dilated at the apex. The 3-lobed lip has a fleshy callus and 3 raised keels. The midlobe, which is somewhat triangular, is smaller than the sidelobes.

REFERENCES: 83, 222.

Dendrobium dichaeoides Schlechter

AKA: Sometimes spelled *D. dichaeiodes*.

ORIGIN/HABITAT: Northern Papua New Guinea. Plants are common in mountain forests at 4900–8200 ft. (1500–2500 m). They usually grow on moss-covered branches of large trees. In Irian Jaya (western New Guinea), plants were collected in the Jabi Mountains along the south coast of Geelvink Bay near Wape and in the Arfak Range near Angi Lake at about 6200 ft. (1900 m).

CLIMATE: Station #94010, Goroka, Papua New Guinea, Lat. 6.1°S, Long. 145.4°E, at 5141 ft. (1567 m). Temperatures are calculated for an elevation of 6550 ft. (2000 m), resulting in probable extremes of 82°F (28°C) and 38°F (4°C).

N/HEMISPHERE	JAN	FEB	MAR	APR	MAY	JUN	JUL	AUG	SEP	OCT	NOV	DEC
°F AVG MAX	71	72	73	74	74	73	74	73	73	73	74	72
°F AVG MIN	51	52	52	52	53	54	54	54	55	54	54	52
DIURNAL RANGE	20	20	21	22	21	19	20	19	18	19	20	20
RAIN/INCHES	2.1	2.8	4.6	5.9	6.6	9.3	9.1	10.1	10.7	8.3	4.6	2.0
HUMIDITY/%	70	67	67	67	69	71	72	73	74	71	70	70
BLOOM SEASON	*	*	*				*			*		*
DAYS CLR	N/A											
RAIN/MM	53	71	117	150	168	236	231	257	272	211	117	51
°C AVG MAX	21.8	22.4	23.0	23.5	23.5	23.0	23.5	23.0	23.0	23.0	23.5	22.4
°C AVG MIN	10.7	11.3	11.3	11.3	11.8	12.4	12.4	12.4	13.0	12.4	12.4	11.3
DIURNAL RANGE	11.1	11.1	11.7	12.2	11.7	10.6	11.1	10.6	10.0	10.6	11.1	11.1
S/HEMISPHERE	JUL	AUG	SEP	OCT	NOV	DEC	JAN	FEB	MAR	APR	MAY	JUN

Cultural Recommendations

LIGHT: 1500–2500 fc.

TEMPERATURES: Throughout the year, days average 71–74°F (22–24°C), and nights average 51–55°F (11–13°C), with a diurnal range of 18–22°F (10–12°C).

HUMIDITY: 70–75% most of the year, dropping to near 65% in late winter and early spring. Growers indicate that other plants from this habitat require a delicate balance between air movement, moisture, and drainage.

WATER: Rainfall is moderate to heavy most of the year, but conditions are slightly drier for 3 months in winter. Cultivated plants should be kept moist. In summer, daily water may be necessary during hot, dry weather. In addition, early morning mistings may be beneficial, especially on bright, sunny days.

FERTILIZER: 1/4 recommended strength. A balanced fertilizer should be applied weekly to biweekly throughout the year. Plants require little or no fertilizer if grown in live sphagnum. In any medium, fertilizer should be very weak. The Royal Botanic Garden in Edinburgh uses a weak, seaweed-based fertilizer for plants from this habitat.

REST PERIOD: Growing conditions must be cool year-round. In the habitat, rainfall is lowest in winter, but dew, fog, and low clouds are common. Water should be reduced in winter, especially for plants grown in the dark, short-day conditions common in temperate latitudes, but they should never be allowed to dry out completely. Fertilizer should be reduced or eliminated until water is increased in spring. In the habitat, seasonal light variation is minor.

GROWING MEDIA: Plants may be mounted on tree-fern or cork slabs if

humidity is high and plants are watered at least once daily in summer. When plants are potted, any open, fast-draining medium may be used. Repotting is best done in early spring, after blooming when new roots start growing.

MISCELLANEOUS NOTES: The bloom season shown in the climate table is based on collection records and reports from the habitat.

Plant and Flower Information

PLANT SIZE AND TYPE: A miniature, 0.8–2.0 in. (2–5 cm) sympodial epiphyte. Plants form a dense, tangled mat.

PSEUDOBULB: 1.2–4.7 in. (3–12 cm) long. The soft, slender stems normally creep along and attach to the substrate. However, if they don't attach, individual stems or even the entire mat may be pendulous. Plants are often very small, but they occasionally reach a length of 20 in. (50 cm).

LEAVES: Many. The tiny, overlapping leaves are usually 0.4–0.5 in. (1.0–1.3 cm) long. They are distichous, closely set, held at right angles to the stem, and all face forward. The leaves are bluish green often with a slight crimson tinge.

INFLORESCENCE: Short. The pendent inflorescences are densely flowered and arise from the leafless, apical portion of the stem.

FLOWERS: 4–10 per inflorescence. The long-lasting flowers are 0.25 in. (0.6 cm) across. Blossoms are bright rose-purple. The narrow flowers resemble a hanging fan.

HYBRIDIZING NOTES: Chromosome count is 2n = 38 (ref. 153, 273).

REFERENCES: 79, 95, 146, 153, 179, 196, 221, 273, 304, 305, 330, 437, 445, 470, 552.

PHOTOS/DRAWINGS: 79, *304, 305, 330,* 437, *552.*

Dendrobium dichroma Schlechter. See *D. subclausum* Rolfe.
REFERENCES: 146, 221, 437, 445, 486, 588.

Dendrobium dichrotropis Schlechter. Now considered a synonym of *Diplocaulobium dichrotropis* (Schlechter) A. Hawkes. REFERENCES: 221, 229, 437, 445.

Dendrobium dickasonii L. O. Williams

AKA: Seidenfaden, in a 1994 personal communication, states that *D. seidenfadenii* K. Senghas and L. Bockemühl and *D. arachnites* Rchb. f. are synonyms.

ORIGIN/HABITAT: Burma, India, and Thailand. Originally found near Haka in western Burma, plants grow on rhododendron bushes at about 5900 ft. (1800 m). They are found in the Mandalay region as well as the Chin Hills. In northern Thailand, plants grow near Chiang Mai at about 5250 ft. (1600 m). They occur in northeast India near Manipur and the Lushai Hills at about 5000 ft. (1520 m).

CLIMATE: Station #48327, Chiang Mai, Thailand, Lat. 18.8°N, Long. 99.0°E, at 1100 ft. (335 m). Temperatures are calculated for an elevation of 5000 ft. (1520 m), resulting in probable extremes of 96°F (36°C) and 25°F (–4°C).

N/HEMISPHERE	JAN	FEB	MAR	APR	MAY	JUN	JUL	AUG	SEP	OCT	NOV	DEC
°F AVG MAX	72	77	82	83	81	77	76	74	75	76	73	71
°F AVG MIN	43	44	49	57	61	61	61	62	60	58	53	44
DIURNAL RANGE	29	33	33	26	20	16	15	12	15	18	20	27
RAIN/INCHES	0.3	0.4	0.6	2.0	5.5	6.1	7.4	8.7	11.5	4.9	1.5	0.4
HUMIDITY/%	73	65	58	62	73	78	80	83	83	81	79	76
BLOOM SEASON	*	*	*	**	***	**	*					
DAYS CLR @ 7AM	5	5	2	2	1	0	0	0	0	0	3	5
DAYS CLR @ 1PM	9	8	4	2	0	0	0	0	0	0	1	3
RAIN/MM	8	10	15	51	140	155	188	221	292	124	38	10
°C AVG MAX	22.3	25.1	27.9	28.4	27.3	25.1	24.5	23.4	24.0	24.5	22.9	21.7
°C AVG MIN	6.2	6.7	9.5	14.0	16.2	16.2	16.2	16.7	15.6	14.5	11.7	6.7
DIURNAL RANGE	16.1	18.4	18.4	14.4	11.1	8.9	8.3	6.7	8.4	10.0	11.2	15.0
S/HEMISPHERE	JUL	AUG	SEP	OCT	NOV	DEC	JAN	FEB	MAR	APR	MAY	JUN

Cultural Recommendations

LIGHT: 2500–3500 fc. Bright light and strong air movement are recommended. The heavy summer cloud cover indicates that some shading is needed from spring through autumn, but light should be as high as the plant can tolerate, short of burning the leaves.

TEMPERATURES: Summer days average 74–77°F (23–25°C), and nights average 61–62°F (16–17°C), with a diurnal range of 12–16°F (7–9°C). The warmest temperatures occur in spring. Days average 81–83°F (27–28°C), and nights are 49–61°F (10–16°C), with a diurnal range of 20–33°F (11–18°C).

HUMIDITY: 75–85% from late spring through autumn, dropping to near 60% in late winter and early spring.

WATER: Rainfall is moderate to heavy from late spring through early autumn, but conditions are very dry in winter. Cultivated plants should be kept moist while actively growing, but water should be gradually reduced after new growths mature in autumn.

FERTILIZER: 1/4–1/2 recommended strength, applied weekly. A high-nitrogen fertilizer is beneficial from spring to midsummer, but a fertilizer high in phosphates should be used in late summer and autumn.

REST PERIOD: Winter days average 71–77°F (22–25°C), and nights average 43–44°F (6–7°C), with a diurnal range of 27–33°F (15–18°C). The average low temperatures are below 50°F (10°C) for 3 months and then warm rapidly in spring. Plants should be able to tolerate temperatures a few degrees below freezing, but extremes should be avoided in cultivation. During very cold weather, a plant's chance of surviving with minimal damage is better if it is dry. In the habitat, rainfall averages are very low for 4–5 months in winter, but during the early part of the season the high relative humidity indicates that additional moisture is available from frequent fog, mist, and heavy deposits of dew. Growers sometimes recommend eliminating water in winter, but plants are healthiest if for most of the winter they are allowed to become somewhat dry between waterings but do not remain dry for extended periods. For 1–2 months in late winter, however, conditions are clear, warm, and dry, with humidity so low that even the moisture from morning dew is uncommon. Plants should be allowed to dry out completely between waterings and remain dry longer during this time. Occasional early morning mistings between waterings may help keep the plants from becoming too dry. Fertilizer should be greatly reduced or eliminated until water is increased in spring. A cool, dry rest is essential for cultivated plants and should be continued until new growth starts in spring. In the habitat, light is highest in winter, but increased light may not be critical in cultivation.

GROWING MEDIA: Plants may be mounted on tree-fern or cork slabs or potted in small pots filled with any open, fast-draining medium. Repotting is best done in early spring when new roots are growing.

MISCELLANEOUS NOTES: The bloom season shown in the climate table is based on cultivation records. Growers often consider this a problem plant, so careful attention should be paid to cultural needs.

Plant and Flower Information

PLANT SIZE AND TYPE: A small, 2.6–6.0 in. (6.5–15 cm) sympodial epiphyte.

PSEUDOBULB: 2–4 in. (5–10 cm) long. A miniature plant with a dwarf, dense growth habit. The spindle-shaped pseudobulbs, which may be slender or swollen, consist 4–5 nodes with somewhat swollen apical nodes. The glossy stems may be honey-yellow or purplish brown.

LEAVES: 2–8 per growth. The leaves are 1.2–2.6 in. (3.0–6.5 cm) long, linear- to elliptic-lanceolate, and glossy.

INFLORESCENCE: 0.8–1.2 in. (2–3 cm) long. Numerous inflorescences emerge laterally from nodes near the apex of older, mature stems.

FLOWERS: 1–2, rarely 3 per inflorescence. The flowers are 2.0–2.4 in. (5–6 cm) across the lateral sepals when spread, but the segments tend to recurve. Large for the plant, the orange flowers are distinctive, showy, and brilliantly colored. Sepals and petals may be cinnabar-red to flame colored. Sepals are narrow and may have darker spotting, but the petals are paler. The large lip has wavy margins with darker veins. The anther is white.

HYBRIDIZING NOTES: Chromosome count is 2n = 38 (ref. 280, 504) as *D. arachnites* Rchb. f.

REFERENCES: 36, 157, 179, 190, 196, 202, 226, 233, 245, 254, 280, 369, 452, 454, 504, 541, 568, 570, 572, 580, 582.

PHOTOS/DRAWINGS: 454.

Dendrobium dicuphum F. Mueller. See *D. affine* (Decaisne) Steudel.

REFERENCES: 44, 67, 105, 151, 154, 179, 187, 216, 240, 254, 262, 325, 351, 389, 390, 421, 430, 504, 526, 533, 580. PHOTOS/DRAWINGS: 105, *262, 350, 351, 389, 390*.

Dendrobium dielsianum Schlechter

ORIGIN/HABITAT: Northern Sumatra. Plants were found near Medan in the forests of Bandar-Baroe at about 2300 ft. (700 m).

CLIMATE: Station #96035, Medan, Sumatra, Indonesia, Lat. 3.6°N, Long. 98.7°E, at 87 ft. (27 m). Temperatures are calculated for an elevation of 2300 ft. (700 m), resulting in probable extremes of 92°F (33°C) and 53°F (12°C).

N/HEMISPHERE	JAN	FEB	MAR	APR	MAY	JUN	JUL	AUG	SEP	OCT	NOV	DEC
°F AVG MAX	78	80	81	82	82	82	82	82	81	79	79	78
°F AVG MIN	64	64	65	66	66	65	65	65	65	65	65	65
DIURNAL RANGE	14	16	16	16	16	17	17	17	16	14	14	13
RAIN/INCHES	5.4	3.6	4.1	5.2	6.9	5.2	5.3	7.0	8.3	10.2	9.7	9.0
HUMIDITY/%	80	79	78	78	79	78	79	79	81	83	83	82
BLOOM SEASON				*								
DAYS CLR @ 7AM	4	2	2	2	2	2	2	0	0	0	1	1
DAYS CLR @ 1PM	0	1	0	0	1	0	2	1	0	0	0	0
RAIN/MM	137	91	104	132	175	132	135	178	211	259	246	229
°C AVG MAX	25.4	26.5	27.1	27.6	27.6	27.6	27.6	27.6	27.1	25.9	25.9	25.4
°C AVG MIN	17.6	17.6	18.2	18.7	18.7	18.2	18.2	18.2	18.2	18.2	18.2	18.2
DIURNAL RANGE	7.8	8.9	8.9	8.9	8.9	9.4	9.4	9.4	8.9	7.7	7.7	7.2
S/HEMISPHERE	JUL	AUG	SEP	OCT	NOV	DEC	JAN	FEB	MAR	APR	MAY	JUN

Cultural Recommendations

LIGHT: 2000–3000 fc.

TEMPERATURES: Throughout the year, days average 78–82°F (25–28°C), and nights average 64–66°F (18–19°C), with a diurnal range of 13–17°F (7–9°C).

HUMIDITY: 75–80% most of the year, increasing to near 85% in autumn.

WATER: Rainfall is moderate to heavy year-round with the greatest amounts falling from late spring through autumn. Cultivated plants should be kept moist with only slight drying allowed between waterings. Warm water might be beneficial.

FERTILIZER: ¼–½ recommended strength. A balanced fertilizer should be applied weekly to biweekly throughout the year.

REST PERIOD: Growing conditions should be maintained all year. Water and fertilizer should be reduced somewhat for plants cultivated in the dark, short-day conditions common in temperate-latitude winters, but they should never be allowed to dry out completely.

GROWING MEDIA: Plants may be mounted on tree-fern or cork slabs if humidity is high and plants are watered at least once daily in summer. When plants are potted, any open, fast-draining medium may be used. Repotting may be done anytime new roots are growing.

MISCELLANEOUS NOTES: The bloom season shown in the climate table is based on reports from the habitat. Other plants from this habitat are reportedly difficult to maintain in Singapore. Overall climatic conditions are similar at the 2 locations, but average night temperatures in Singapore are about 5°F (3°C) warmer, and the diurnal range averages about 6°F (3°C) less.

Plant and Flower Information

PLANT SIZE AND TYPE: A 20 in. (50 cm) sympodial epiphyte.

PSEUDOBULB: 20 in. (50 cm) long. The nonbranching, slender stems arise from a very short rhizome.

LEAVES: Many. The lanceolate to oblong lanceolate leaves are 3.5–4.7 in. (9–12 cm) long.

INFLORESCENCE: Short. Inflorescences are densely flowered.

FLOWERS: 8–15 per inflorescence. The flowers are 0.8 in. (2 cm) across. The blossoms are waxy white, and the backside is sparsely covered with scales. Sepals and petals are somewhat elliptical. The oblong to ovate lip is concave and the apical part is covered with short hairs.

REFERENCES: 223, 443.

Dendrobium diffusum L. O. Williams

ORIGIN/HABITAT: The Philippines. Plants grow on Mindoro Island and on Mt. Apo in Davao Province in southern Mindanao. Habitat elevation is estimated, so the following temperatures should be used with caution.

CLIMATE: Station #98754, Davao, Philippines, Lat. 7.1°N, Long. 125.6°E, at 88 ft. (27 m). Temperatures are calculated for an estimated elevation of 3000 ft. (910 m), resulting in probable extremes of 87°F (31°C) and 55°F (13°C).

N/HEMISPHERE	JAN	FEB	MAR	APR	MAY	JUN	JUL	AUG	SEP	OCT	NOV	DEC
°F AVG MAX	77	78	80	81	80	78	78	78	78	79	79	78
°F AVG MIN	62	62	62	63	64	63	63	63	63	63	63	62
DIURNAL RANGE	15	16	18	18	16	15	15	15	15	16	16	16
RAIN/INCHES	4.8	4.5	5.2	5.8	9.2	9.1	6.5	6.5	6.7	7.9	5.3	6.1
HUMIDITY/%	81	82	78	79	82	83	84	83	83	82	82	82
BLOOM SEASON							*					
DAYS CLR @ 8AM	5	7	9	9	6	4	5	4	5	7	6	6
DAYS CLR @ 2PM	3	1	3	4	2	2	3	2	2	2	2	2
RAIN/MM	122	114	132	147	234	231	165	165	170	201	135	155
°C AVG MAX	25.2	25.8	26.9	27.4	26.9	25.8	25.8	25.8	25.8	26.3	26.3	25.8
°C AVG MIN	16.9	16.9	16.9	17.4	18.0	17.4	17.4	17.4	17.4	17.4	17.4	16.9
DIURNAL RANGE	8.3	8.9	10.0	10.0	8.9	8.4	8.4	8.4	8.4	8.9	8.9	8.9
S/HEMISPHERE	JUL	AUG	SEP	OCT	NOV	DEC	JAN	FEB	MAR	APR	MAY	JUN

Cultural Recommendations

LIGHT: 1500–2400 fc. In the habitat, clear days are rare, and direct sunlight should be avoided.

TEMPERATURES: Throughout the year, days average 77–81°F (25–27°C), and nights average 62–64°F (17–18°C), with a diurnal range of 15–18°F (8–10°C). The narrow seasonal range with extreme temperatures that are only a few degrees different than the averages indicate that plants may not tolerate wide temperature fluctuations.

HUMIDITY: 80–85% year-round.

WATER: Rainfall is moderate to heavy all year, and amounts may be even greater in the mountain habitat. Cultivated plants should be kept moist with only slight drying allowed between waterings.

FERTILIZER: ¼–½ recommended strength. A balanced fertilizer should be applied weekly to biweekly throughout the year.

REST PERIOD: Growing temperatures should be maintained year-round. Water should be reduced somewhat in winter, especially for plants cultivated in the dark, short-day conditions common in temperate latitudes. Fertilizer should be reduced, but plants should be kept moist all winter.

GROWING MEDIA: Plants may be mounted on tree-fern or cork slabs or potted in small pots filled with any open, fast-draining medium. Repotting may be done anytime new roots are actively growing.

Dendrobium dilatatocolle

MISCELLANEOUS NOTES: The bloom season shown in the climate table is based on collection reports.

Plant and Flower Information

PLANT SIZE AND TYPE: A sympodial epiphyte of unreported size.

PSEUDOBULB: The stems all arise from a common base, but often branch repeatedly.

LEAVES: The lanceolate leaves, which have many veins, are 0.8–2.4 in. (2–6 cm) long.

INFLORESCENCE: Short. The blossoms are pendulous.

FLOWERS: 1–2 per inflorescence. The creamy white flowers are 0.6 in. (1.5 cm) across.

REFERENCES: 226, 536.

Dendrobium dilatatocolle J. J. Smith. Now considered a synonym of *Diplocaulobium dilatatocolle* (J. J. Smith) Kränzlin. REFERENCES: 111, 219, 220, 254, 445.

Dendrobium dillonianum A. Hawkes and A. H. Heller

AKA: Sometimes spelled *D. dillonionum*. *D. sacculiferum* J. J. Smith 1929 not 1922.

ORIGIN/HABITAT: Irian Jaya (western New Guinea). Plants were found on a ridge to Mt. Doorman at about 4600 ft. (1410 m). They grow on trees in thin, moss-covered *Vaccinium* forests.

CLIMATE: Station #97686, Wamena, New Guinea, Lat. 4.1°S, Long. 139.0°E, at 5446 ft. (1660 m). Temperatures are calculated for an elevation of 4400 ft. (1340 m). Record extreme temperatures are not available for this location.

N/HEMISPHERE	JAN	FEB	MAR	APR	MAY	JUN	JUL	AUG	SEP	OCT	NOV	DEC
°F AVG MAX	78	79	80	79	80	79	80	79	79	82	81	77
°F AVG MIN	63	63	65	65	66	67	66	65	66	68	68	64
DIURNAL RANGE	15	16	15	14	14	12	14	14	13	14	13	13
RAIN/INCHES	3.0	1.9	2.2	4.0	4.6	3.3	2.8	4.2	6.9	3.9	5.4	4.9
HUMIDITY/%	N/A											
BLOOM SEASON				*								
DAYS CLR	N/A											
RAIN/MM	76	48	56	102	117	84	71	107	175	99	137	124
°C AVG MAX	25.8	26.4	26.9	26.4	26.9	26.4	26.9	26.4	26.4	28.0	27.5	25.3
°C AVG MIN	17.5	17.5	18.6	18.6	19.1	19.7	19.1	18.6	19.1	20.3	20.3	18.0
DIURNAL RANGE	8.3	8.9	8.3	7.8	7.8	6.7	7.8	7.8	7.3	7.7	7.2	7.3
S/HEMISPHERE	JUL	AUG	SEP	OCT	NOV	DEC	JAN	FEB	MAR	APR	MAY	JUN

Cultural Recommendations

LIGHT: 1500–3000 fc.

TEMPERATURES: Throughout the year, days average 77–82°F (25–28°C), and nights average 63–68°F (18–20°C), with a diurnal range of 12–16°F (7–9°C). The warmest temperatures of the day occur during late morning when skies are clear. Clouds and mist develop near noon and continue through the afternoon, thus preventing additional warming.

HUMIDITY: Information is not available for this location. However, average humidity in mistforest habitats normally exceeds 80% year-round.

WATER: Rainfall is light to moderate through most of the year, but large amounts of water are usually available from mist and heavy dew, even during periods of lower rainfall. Cultivated plants should be kept moist with only slight drying allowed between waterings. Good air movement is critically important and should be maintained at all times.

FERTILIZER: ¼–½ recommended strength. A balanced fertilizer should be applied weekly to biweekly throughout the year.

REST PERIOD: Growing conditions should be maintained all year. Conditions are slightly drier for 1–2 months in winter. In cultivation, water may be decreased somewhat, but plants should never be allowed to dry out completely or remain dry for long periods. In the habitat, light is slightly higher in winter.

GROWING MEDIA: Mounting plants on tree-fern or cork slabs accommodates their pendulous growth habit. However, humidity must be high and plants must be watered at least once a day in summer. If plants cannot be mounted, small pots or hanging baskets may be filled with an open, fast-draining medium. Repotting may be done anytime new roots are actively growing.

MISCELLANEOUS NOTES: The bloom season shown in the climate table is based on collection reports. Cultivation reports show blooming in autumn. Warren (ref. 549) reports that *D. dillonianum* seedlings are very difficult to successfully grow to flowering.

Plant and Flower Information

PLANT SIZE AND TYPE: A 13 in. (33 cm) sympodial epiphyte.

PSEUDOBULB: 13 in. (33 cm) long. Each slender branching stem is pendulous with roots all along the stem. It becomes grooved and angled with age.

LEAVES: Many. The small leaves are bright green, oblong to ovate, and less than 0.4 in. (1.0 cm) long. They are somewhat twisted at the base. The leaf sheaths are warty.

INFLORESCENCE: Short. Blossoms are borne laterally along leafless stems.

FLOWERS: 1 per inflorescence. The flowers are 0.8 in. (2 cm) long. They are dark red with bluish violet at the tip of the column. The backsides of the sepals are covered with scalelike dots.

HYBRIDIZING NOTES: Chromosome count is $2n = 38$ (ref. 153, 273).

REFERENCES: 95, 153, 179, 191, 224, 229, 273, 470, 549, 553.

Dendrobium dimorphum J. J. Smith. Transferred to *Ephemerantha denigrata* (J. J. Smith) Hunt and Summerhayes, which is now considered a synonym of *Flickingeria*. REFERENCES: 105, 213, 224, 230.

Dendrobium diodon Rchb. f.

AKA: *D. albidulum* Thwaites ex Trimen.

ORIGIN/HABITAT: Endemic to Sri Lanka (Ceylon). Near Hakgalle, plants usually grow on *Eurya* trees in subtropical mountain forests. They are also found on Adam's Peak and in other mountain areas. Habitat elevation was not reported, so the following climate data should be used with caution.

CLIMATE: Station #43466, Colombo, Sri Lanka, Lat. 6.9°N, Long. 79.9°E, at 27 ft. (8 m). Temperatures are calculated for an estimated elevation of 5000 ft. (1520 m), resulting in probable extremes of 83°F (28°C) and 43°F (6°C).

N/HEMISPHERE	JAN	FEB	MAR	APR	MAY	JUN	JUL	AUG	SEP	OCT	NOV	DEC
°F AVG MAX	70	71	68	72	71	69	69	69	69	69	69	69
°F AVG MIN	56	56	58	60	62	61	61	61	61	59	57	56
DIURNAL RANGE	14	15	10	12	9	8	8	8	8	10	12	13
RAIN/INCHES	3.5	2.7	5.8	9.1	14.6	8.8	5.3	4.3	6.3	13.7	12.4	5.8
HUMIDITY/%	70	69	69	72	77	79	78	77	76	77	76	72
BLOOM SEASON	*	*	*	*								
DAYS CLR @ 5PM	11	10	9	6	3	2	2	2	1	2	4	7
RAIN/MM	89	69	147	231	371	224	135	109	160	348	315	147
°C AVG MAX	20.9	21.4	19.8	22.0	21.4	20.3	20.3	20.3	20.3	20.3	20.3	20.3
°C AVG MIN	13.1	13.1	14.2	15.3	16.4	15.9	15.9	15.9	15.9	14.8	13.7	13.1
DIURNAL RANGE	7.8	8.3	5.6	6.7	5.0	4.4	4.4	4.4	4.4	5.5	6.6	7.2
S/HEMISPHERE	JUL	AUG	SEP	OCT	NOV	DEC	JAN	FEB	MAR	APR	MAY	JUN

Cultural Recommendations

LIGHT: 1200–2400 fc. Diffused or barely dappled light is recommended. Direct sunlight should be avoided.

TEMPERATURES: Summer days average 69°F (20°C), and nights average 61°F (16°C), with a diurnal range of 8°F (4°C). Reports from the habitat indicate that midsummer highs may average 79°F (26°C) while average lows may drop to 30°F (−1°C). Therefore, highs are probably warmer than indicated in the climate table and lows may be considerably cooler.

HUMIDITY: 70–80% year-round.

WATER: Rainfall is moderate to heavy most of the year but is lowest in winter with a secondary minimum in late summer. For cultivated plants, the medium should be kept wet but not soggy with only slight drying allowed between waterings.

FERTILIZER: ¼–½ recommended strength, applied weekly. A high-nitrogen fertilizer is beneficial from spring to midsummer, but a fertilizer high in phosphates should be used in late summer and autumn.

REST PERIOD: Winter days average 68–71°F (20–21°C), and nights average 56–58°F (13–14°C), with a diurnal range of 10–15°F (6–8°C). The increased diurnal range results from slightly warmer days and cooler nights. In the habitat, clear days occur much more frequently in winter, indicating that winter light is highest. Water and fertilizer should be reduced somewhat, but plants should never be allowed to dry out completely.

GROWING MEDIA: Plants may be mounted on tree-fern or cork slabs or potted in small pots filled with any open, fast-draining medium. Repotting may be done anytime new roots are growing.

MISCELLANEOUS NOTES: The bloom season shown in the climate table is based on reports from the habitat.

Plant and Flower Information

PLANT SIZE AND TYPE: A dwarf, 1.4–2.0 in. (3.6–5.0 cm) sympodial epiphyte.

PSEUDOBULB: 1.4–2.0 in. (3.6–5.0 cm) long. Pseudobulbs have 5 nodes and are covered with sheaths when young. They are crowded, ovoid, wrinkled, and arise from a slender rhizome.

LEAVES: 2–4 per growth. The linear-oblong leaves, which are slightly twisted at the base, are 1.2–1.6 in. (3–4 cm) long.

INFLORESCENCE: 1.0–1.4 in. (2.5–3.6 cm) long. 1–2 racemes arise from the apex of immature growths.

FLOWERS: Few per inflorescence. The white flowers are 0.4 in. (1 cm) across. Sepals are lanceolate, and the somewhat sickle-shaped petals are linear-oblong. The lip has short, pointed sidelobes and a ruffled, wavy margin on the midlobe.

REFERENCES: 97, 202, 216, 235, 254.

PHOTOS/DRAWINGS: 97.

Dendrobium dionaeoides J. J. Smith

ORIGIN/HABITAT: Irian Jaya (western New Guinea). Plants were collected in mountain forests of the Jabi Range near Wape on south coast of Geelvink Bay.

CLIMATE: Station #97682, Nabire, Irian Jaya, Lat. 3.3°S, Long. 135.5°E, at 10 ft. (3 m). Record extreme temperatures are not available for this location.

N/HEMISPHERE	JAN	FEB	MAR	APR	MAY	JUN	JUL	AUG	SEP	OCT	NOV	DEC
°F AVG MAX	86	86	86	86	87	87	86	86	87	87	87	87
°F AVG MIN	75	75	76	77	77	76	77	75	75	76	76	76
DIURNAL RANGE	11	11	10	9	10	11	9	11	12	11	11	11
RAIN/INCHES	7.4	11.1	8.5	8.5	7.5	9.0	9.2	10.6	12.1	11.3	10.2	9.8
HUMIDITY/%	N/A											
BLOOM SEASON												
DAYS CLR	N/A											
RAIN/MM	190	283	217	217	192	228	233	270	308	286	259	248
°C AVG MAX	30.1	29.9	30.1	30.3	30.5	30.6	30.0	30.0	30.5	30.5	30.3	30.3
°C AVG MIN	24.0	24.0	24.3	24.7	24.9	24.5	24.8	24.0	23.8	24.6	24.3	24.2
DIURNAL RANGE	6.1	5.9	5.8	5.6	5.6	6.1	5.2	6.0	6.7	5.9	6.0	6.1
S/HEMISPHERE	JUL	AUG	SEP	OCT	NOV	DEC	JAN	FEB	MAR	APR	MAY	JUN

Cultural Recommendations

LIGHT: 2000–3000 fc.

TEMPERATURES: Throughout the year, days average 86–87°F (30–31°C), and nights average 75–77°F (24–25°C), with a diurnal range of 9–12°F (6–7°C).

HUMIDITY: Information is not available for this location. However, reports from nearby areas indicate that humidity probably averages near 85% year-round.

WATER: Rainfall is heavy all year. Cultivated plants should be kept evenly moist and never be allowed to dry out completely.

FERTILIZER: ¼–½ recommended strength. A balanced fertilizer should be applied weekly to biweekly throughout the year.

REST PERIOD: Growing conditions should be maintained year-round. Water and fertilizer might be reduced slightly in winter, especially for plants cultivated in the dark, short-day conditions common in temperate latitudes, but they should never be allowed dry out completely.

GROWING MEDIA: Plants may be mounted on tree-fern or cork slabs if humidity is high and plants are watered at least once daily in summer. When plants are potted, any open, fast-draining medium may be used. Repotting may be done anytime new roots are growing.

MISCELLANEOUS NOTES: The bloom season shown in the climate table is based on reports from the habitat.

Plant and Flower Information

PLANT SIZE AND TYPE: A 59 in. (150 cm) sympodial epiphyte.

PSEUDOBULB: 59 in. (150 cm) long. The shiny stems are elongated, slender, and flattened. They are elliptical in cross-section.

LEAVES: Many. The linear, grasslike leaves are 2–3 in. (5–8 cm) long. They are papery when dry.

INFLORESCENCE: Short. Numerous inflorescences are borne along the stem.

FLOWERS: 2 per inflorescence. The flowers are 1.3 in. (3.3 cm) long. The collector described the flowers as "corolla red, tip yellow, and lip white," but J. J. Smith indicated that the preserved flowers had sepals and petals marked with violet at the base, lip with a black-violet margin, and column black-violet. The blossoms have sepals that are dilated at the base, and linear petals. The 3-lobed lip is recurved with conspicuous veins and short, rough points near the base. The triangular sidelobes have soft bristles on the inside.

REFERENCES: 221, 470, 478.

Dendrobium discerptum J. J. Smith

ORIGIN/HABITAT: Irian Jaya (western New Guinea). Plants grow on trees in the lowlands along the Noord River.

CLIMATE: Station #97796, Kokenau (Kokonau), Irian Jaya, Lat. 4.7°S, Long. 136.4°E, at 10 ft. (3 m). Record extreme temperatures are not available for this location.

N/HEMISPHERE	JAN	FEB	MAR	APR	MAY	JUN	JUL	AUG	SEP	OCT	NOV	DEC
°F AVG MAX	83	83	86	88	90	89	89	89	90	88	87	84
°F AVG MIN	73	73	74	74	74	75	74	74	74	74	74	73
DIURNAL RANGE	10	10	12	14	16	14	15	15	16	14	13	11
RAIN/INCHES	18.4	15.8	18.9	11.6	9.7	10.6	11.5	15.7	11.6	11.6	16.0	19.9
HUMIDITY/%	N/A											
BLOOM SEASON			*									
DAYS CLR	N/A											
RAIN/MM	467	401	479	295	245	269	293	400	294	296	407	506
°C AVG MAX	28.6	28.4	30.2	31.1	32.1	31.9	31.9	31.7	32.0	31.4	30.7	28.7
°C AVG MIN	22.7	22.6	23.3	23.4	23.5	23.7	23.6	23.5	23.4	23.4	23.5	23.0
DIURNAL RANGE	5.9	5.8	6.9	7.7	8.6	8.2	8.3	8.2	8.6	8.0	7.2	5.7
S/HEMISPHERE	JUL	AUG	SEP	OCT	NOV	DEC	JAN	FEB	MAR	APR	MAY	JUN

Cultural Recommendations

LIGHT: 2500–3500 fc.

Dendrobium dischorense

TEMPERATURES: Throughout the year, days average 83–90°F (28–32°C), and nights average 73–75°F (23–24°C), with a diurnal range of 10–16°F (6–9°C).

HUMIDITY: Information is not available for this location. However, records from nearby locations indicate that humidity probably averages near 85% year-round.

WATER: Rainfall is very heavy all year. Cultivated plants should be kept evenly moist, with only slight drying allowed between waterings.

FERTILIZER: ¼–½ recommended strength. A balanced fertilizer should be applied weekly to biweekly throughout the year.

REST PERIOD: Growing conditions should be maintained year-round. Water and fertilizer may be reduced slightly in winter, especially for plants cultivated in the dark, short-day conditions common in the temperate latitudes, but they should never be allowed to dry out completely.

GROWING MEDIA: Plants are best potted in small containers. The pots may be filled with any open, fast-draining medium if water is applied frequently. If humidity is low or watering is irregular, the medium should retain some moisture, but it should never be soggy. Repotting may be done anytime new roots are growing.

MISCELLANEOUS NOTES: The bloom season shown in the climate table is based on reports from the habitat.

Plant and Flower Information

PLANT SIZE AND TYPE: A sympodial plant of unreported size.

PSEUDOBULB: The slender growths are elliptical in cross-section.

LEAVES: Many. The linear leaves are usually 4 in. (10 cm) long.

FLOWERS: 2 per inflorescence. Flowers are 0.8 in. (2 cm) across. They were described as white and brown striped.

REFERENCES: 220, 254, 445, 470.

Dendrobium dischorense Schlechter. See *D. millarae* A. Hawkes. REFERENCES: 191, 221, 437, 445.

Dendrobium dischorense (Schlechter) J. J. Smith

AKA: *Cadetia dischorense* Schlechter. *Cadetia* is again considered a valid genus by some botanists, so this plant probably belongs with the genus *Cadetia*.

ORIGIN/HABITAT: Northern Papua New Guinea. Plants grow on moss-covered mistforest trees of the Dischore Range at 4000–6000 ft. (1220–1830 m).

CLIMATE: Station #200192, Garaina, Papua New Guinea, Lat. 7.9°S, Long. 147.1°E, at 2350 ft. (716 m). Temperatures are calculated for an elevation of 4250 ft. (1300 m), resulting in probable extremes of 88°F (31°C) and 40°F (4°C).

N/HEMISPHERE	JAN	FEB	MAR	APR	MAY	JUN	JUL	AUG	SEP	OCT	NOV	DEC
°F AVG MAX	74	76	77	78	79	79	79	79	78	78	77	75
°F AVG MIN	57	57	57	58	57	58	59	59	59	58	58	57
DIURNAL RANGE	17	19	20	20	22	21	20	20	19	20	19	18
RAIN/INCHES	5.8	6.5	8.7	11.1	11.8	11.9	8.9	11.7	11.5	9.9	7.7	5.2
HUMIDITY/%	84	82	82	81	80	80	81	81	82	83	84	84
BLOOM SEASON	N/A											
DAYS CLR	N/A											
RAIN/MM	147	165	221	282	300	302	226	297	292	251	196	132
°C AVG MAX	23.1	24.3	24.8	25.4	25.9	25.9	25.9	25.9	25.4	25.4	24.8	23.7
°C AVG MIN	13.7	13.7	13.7	14.3	13.7	14.3	14.8	14.8	14.8	14.3	14.3	13.7
DIURNAL RANGE	9.4	10.6	11.1	11.1	12.2	11.6	11.1	11.1	10.6	11.1	10.5	10.0
S/HEMISPHERE	JUL	AUG	SEP	OCT	NOV	DEC	JAN	FEB	MAR	APR	MAY	JUN

Cultural Recommendations

LIGHT: 2000–3000 fc.

TEMPERATURES: Throughout the year, days average 74–79°F (23–26°C), and nights average 57–59°F (14–15°C), with a diurnal range of 17–22°F (9–12°C).

HUMIDITY: 80–85% year-round.

WATER: Rainfall is moderate to heavy all year. Conditions are slightly drier in winter. Cultivated plants should be kept moist but not soggy.

FERTILIZER: ¼–½ recommended strength. A balanced fertilizer should be applied weekly to biweekly throughout the year.

REST PERIOD: Growing conditions vary only slightly during the year. In the habitat, rainfall is slightly lower in winter. Water should be reduced somewhat for cultivated plants, especially those grown in the dark, short-day conditions common in temperate-latitude winters, but they should never be allowed to dry out completely. Fertilizer should be reduced or eliminated anytime water is reduced.

GROWING MEDIA: Plants may be mounted on tree-fern or cork slabs, but high humidity must be maintained and plants given water at least once daily in summer. When plants are potted, any open, fast-draining medium may be used. Repotting may be done anytime new roots are growing.

Plant and Flower Information

PLANT SIZE AND TYPE: A 1.2–2.4 in. (3–6 cm) sympodial epiphyte.

PSEUDOBULB: 0.4–1.2 in. (1–3 cm) long.

LEAVES: 1 per growth. The somewhat linear leaves are 0.4–1.1 in. (1.0–2.7 cm) long.

INFLORESCENCE: Very short.

FLOWERS: 1 per inflorescence. The pure white flowers are 0.2 in. (0.6 cm) long.

REFERENCES: 221, 227, 472, 574.

Dendrobium discocaulon Schlechter

ORIGIN/HABITAT: Northern Papua New Guinea. Plants grow on forest trees in the Kani Range at about 2600 ft. (800 m) and near the mouth of the Waria River at 800 ft. (250 m).

CLIMATE: Station #200192, Garaina, Papua New Guinea, Lat. 7.9°S, Long. 147.1°E, at 2350 ft. (716 m). Record extreme temperatures are 94°F (34°C) and 46°F (8°C).

N/HEMISPHERE	JAN	FEB	MAR	APR	MAY	JUN	JUL	AUG	SEP	OCT	NOV	DEC
°F AVG MAX	80	82	83	84	85	85	85	85	84	84	83	81
°F AVG MIN	63	63	63	64	63	64	65	65	65	64	64	63
DIURNAL RANGE	17	19	20	20	22	21	20	20	19	20	19	18
RAIN/INCHES	5.8	6.5	8.7	11.1	11.8	11.9	8.9	11.7	11.5	9.9	7.7	5.2
HUMIDITY/%	84	82	82	81	80	80	81	81	82	83	84	84
BLOOM SEASON	*								*	*	*	
DAYS CLR	N/A											
RAIN/MM	148	166	220	282	300	303	227	296	291	251	195	131
°C AVG MAX	26.8	27.5	28.2	28.6	29.3	29.3	29.4	29.4	29.1	28.7	28.2	27.2
°C AVG MIN	16.9	16.9	17.4	17.6	17.4	18.0	18.1	18.2	18.4	17.7	17.7	17.1
DIURNAL RANGE	9.9	10.6	10.8	11.0	11.9	11.3	11.3	11.2	10.7	11.0	10.5	10.1
S/HEMISPHERE	JUL	AUG	SEP	OCT	NOV	DEC	JAN	FEB	MAR	APR	MAY	JUN

Cultural Recommendations

LIGHT: 2500–3500 fc.

TEMPERATURES: Throughout the year, days average 80–85°F (27–29°C), and nights average 63–65°F (17–18°C), with a diurnal range of 17–22°F (10–12°C).

HUMIDITY: 80–85% year-round.

WATER: Rainfall is moderate to heavy all year, but conditions are slightly drier in winter. Cultivated plants should be kept moist but not soggy.

FERTILIZER: ¼–½ recommended strength. A balanced fertilizer should be applied weekly to biweekly throughout the year.

REST PERIOD: Growing conditions vary only slightly during the year. In the habitat, rainfall is slightly lower in winter. Water should be reduced somewhat for cultivated plants, especially those grown in the dark, short-day conditions common in temperate-latitude winters, but they should never be allowed to dry out completely. Fertilizer should be reduced or eliminated anytime water is reduced.

GROWING MEDIA: Plants may be mounted on tree-fern or cork slabs if humidity is high and plants are watered least once daily in summer. When plants are potted, any open, fast-draining medium may be used. Repotting may be done anytime new roots are growing.

MISCELLANEOUS NOTES: The bloom season shown in the climate table is based on reports from the habitat.

Plant and Flower Information

PLANT SIZE AND TYPE: An 8–16 in. (20–40 cm) sympodial epiphyte.

PSEUDOBULB: 4–12 in. (10–30 cm) long. Pseudobulbs are swollen at the base.

LEAVES: 3–7 per growth. The elliptic-lanceolate leaves may be erect or spreading and usually measure 3–5 in. (8–13 cm) long. They are quickly deciduous.

INFLORESCENCE: 3 in. (8 cm) long. The inflorescence arises from the apex of the pseudobulb.

FLOWERS: 3–5 per inflorescence. The flowers are 0.7 in. (1.7 cm) deep. The lip is scalloped.

REFERENCES: 221, 437, 445.

PHOTOS/DRAWINGS: 437.

Dendrobium discolor Lindley

AKA: *D. undulans* Bakhuizen f. is sometimes listed as a synonym of *D. undulatum* R. Brown, which is now considered a synonym of *D. discolor* var. *discolor*. Hunt (ref. 211) includes *D. undulatum* R. Brown and *D. undulans* Bakhuizen. The International Orchid Commission (ref. 236) registers hybrids under the name *D. undulatum*. Clements (ref. 67) recognizes the following 4 varieties of *D. discolor* and lists synonyms as follows.

D. discolor var. *broomfieldii* (Fitzgerald) M. Clements and D. Jones has been known as *D. broomfieldii* (Fitzgerald) Fitzgerald, *D. discolor* Lindley forma *broomfieldii* (Fitzgerald) Dockrill, and *D. undulatum* R. Brown var. *carterae* Bailey.

D. discolor var. *discolor* Edward's Bot. Reg. 27 has been known as *D. arachnanthe* Kränzlin, *D. elobatum* Rupp, and *D. undulatum* R. Brown not Persoon.

Some authors consider the preceding varieties to be part of an alliance that should be grouped under the name *D. discolor* var. *discolor*.

D. discolor var. *fimbrilabium* (Rchb. f.) Dockrill has been known as *D. undulatum* R. Brown var. *fimbrilabium* Rchb. f.

D. discolor var. *fuscum* (Fitzgerald) Dockrill has been known as *D. fuscum* Fitzgerald.

A new variety was recently described as *D. discolor* var. *incurvata* D. J. Liddle and P. I. Forster.

ORIGIN/HABITAT: Northeastern Australia and New Guinea. The habitat extends from near Rockhampton to the tip of the Cape York Peninsula and includes the islands of the Torres Striates and the lowlands of southern New Guinea, particularly the region near Merauke, Irian Jaya. Plants grow on trees and rocks in exposed situations. They often grow on trees in coastal swamps where they tolerate salt spray, but plants are also found on cliffs and rock faces from sea level to 1800 ft. (0–550 m). In the western part of the habitat, conditions are hot and dry.

CLIMATE: Station #94287, Cairns, Australia, Lat. 16.9°S, Long. 145.8°E, at 7 ft. (2 m). Record extreme temperatures are 110°F (43°C) and 43°F (6°C).

N/HEMISPHERE	JAN	FEB	MAR	APR	MAY	JUN	JUL	AUG	SEP	OCT	NOV	DEC
°F AVG MAX	78	80	83	86	88	90	90	89	87	85	81	79
°F AVG MIN	61	62	64	68	70	73	74	74	73	70	66	64
DIURNAL RANGE	17	18	19	18	18	17	16	15	14	15	15	15
RAIN/INCHES	1.6	1.7	1.7	2.1	3.9	8.7	16.6	15.7	18.1	11.3	4.4	2.9
HUMIDITY/%	69	67	65	65	65	68	72	72	74	73	73	72
BLOOM SEASON	*	*	***	*	*	*	*	*	*	*	*	*
DAYS CLR @ 10AM	9	11	13	11	6	4	5	6	7	11	10	
DAYS CLR @ 4PM	8	10	12	16	10	7	3	4	6	9	10	
RAIN/MM	41	43	43	53	99	221	422	399	460	287	112	74
°C AVG MAX	25.6	26.7	28.3	30.0	31.1	32.2	32.2	31.7	30.6	29.4	27.2	26.1
°C AVG MIN	16.1	16.7	17.8	20.0	21.1	22.8	23.3	23.3	22.8	21.1	18.9	17.8
DIURNAL RANGE	9.5	10.0	10.5	10.0	10.0	9.4	8.9	8.4	7.8	8.3	8.3	8.3
S/HEMISPHERE	JUL	AUG	SEP	OCT	NOV	DEC	JAN	FEB	MAR	APR	MAY	JUN

Cultural Recommendations

LIGHT: 3000–4500 fc. High light is essential for *D. discolor* to flower well. Strong air movement and high relative humidity are especially important for orchids grown with high light.

TEMPERATURES: Summer days average 89–90°F (32°C), and nights average 73–74°F (23°C), with a diurnal range of 15–17°F (8–9°C).

HUMIDITY: 65–75% year-round. In cloudforest habitats, humidity probably averages 10% more than indicated in the climate table. Cultivated plants are healthiest with high humidity and strong air movement all year.

WATER: Rainfall is heavy from late spring into autumn, with much drier conditions in winter. Cultivated plants should be kept moist from late spring into autumn, but water should be gradually reduced in late autumn. Growers indicate that mounted plants should be misted frequently and never be allowed to remain completely dry for any length of time.

FERTILIZER: ¼–½ recommended strength. A balanced fertilizer should be applied weekly to biweekly throughout the growing season.

REST PERIOD: Winter days average 78–83°F (26–28°C), and nights average 61–64°F (16–18°C), with a diurnal range of 15–19°F (8–11°C). Growers recommend that winter lows be kept above 59°F (15°C). For cultivated plants, water should be reduced for 4–5 months from late autumn into early spring. The medium should be kept on the dry side, but it should never be allowed to dry out completely. Light, humidity, and air movement should be maintained. Fertilizer may be reduced to an occasional weak application until water is increased in spring.

GROWING MEDIA: Plants grow well mounted on large slabs of cork bark if humidity is high and plants are watered at least once daily in summer. If plants are potted, a very open, fast-draining medium should be used with an undersized pot that is only large enough to hold the roots. Repotting is best done in early spring when new roots are growing.

MISCELLANEOUS NOTES: The bloom season shown in the climate table is based on cultivation records.

Although plants are primarily warm growing, they tolerate winter minimum temperatures down to 43°F (6°C), or even colder if the roots are dry. Plants growing on the islands in the Torres Strait receive little if any rainfall for 6–7 months in winter, but some moisture is available from morning dew.

Plant and Flower Information

PLANT SIZE AND TYPE: A highly variable, 16–197 in. (40–500 cm) sympodial epiphyte, lithophyte, or terrestrial that forms large clumps. Plant growth habit resembles that of *D. odoardi* Kränzlin.

PSEUDOBULB: 12–197 in. (30–500 cm) long. The yellowish canes, which are ringed with old leaf scars, are shorter and heavier in higher light. New vegetative plants are often produced at the nodes of old canes, and these keikis often break off, propagating the plant vegetatively.

LEAVES: Many. Growths are typically leafy on the upper 60% of the stem. Leaves are usually 2–8 in. (5–20 cm) long. Leaf size and number vary tremendously depending on plant size. The ovate leaves are leathery, often yellowish, and at least some of the leaves are persistent.

Dendrobium discrepans

INFLORESCENCE: 8–24 in. (20–60 cm) long. Most often gracefully arching, inflorescences may be pendent or horizontal. Blossoms are closely spaced and face all directions. Inflorescences emerge from upper nodes of older stems as the new growths develop. Canes frequently produce 1–6 inflorescences, but have been known to produce as many as 18 flowering stems.

FLOWERS: 20–80 per inflorescence. The flowers are commonly 2.0–2.4 in. (5–6 cm) across, but they range from 1.2–3.2 in. (3–8 cm) across. The extremely long-lived blossoms may last more than 3 months. They have a spicy, honey fragrance. The glossy, waxy flowers are often dingy yellow, but they may be any combination of creamy yellow to orange suffused with brown, bronze, or violet. Many shades and combinations are known. The blossoms tend to turn reddish with age. All segments are wavy and ruffled along the margin, and, in addition, the somewhat limp petals are extremely twisted. Petals may each be 1.5 in. (4 cm) long. The lip is marked with purple spots and has 5 white keels on a white to bright yellow background. *D. discolor* is highly variable and many cultivars are recognized.

HYBRIDIZING NOTES: Chromosome counts are n = 19 (ref. 580) and 2n = 38 (ref. 580) as *D. undulatum* and *D. undulatum* var. *broomfieldii* (ref. 504, 580). When used as a parent, *D. discolor* contributes heavy substance, improved yellows, and a complex, frilly shape to the flower segments. *D. discolor* Lindley hybridizes naturally with *D. bigibbum* Lindley producing *D.* × *superbiens* Rchb. f.

REFERENCES: 24, 25, 36, 67, 84, 105, 179, 190, 196, 200, 211, 216, 235, 236, 240, 254, 262, 263, 264, 301, 302, 304, 317, 325, 326, 342, 347, 351, 371, 389, 390, 421, 430, 454, 470, 504, 510, 526, 533, 537, 551, 568, 580.

PHOTOS/DRAWINGS: *36, 84,* 105, 240, *262,* 300, 301, *304,* 325, *342, 347, 351, 371, 389, 390, 430, 533, 551, 568.*

Dendrobium discrepans J. J. Smith. See *D. puniceum* Ridley.
REFERENCES: 221, 385, 470, 476.

Dendrobium discreptum J. J. Smith. This name is mentioned by Schlechter (ref. 437) as a member of the section *Grastidium*, no other mention of a species by this name was found. REFERENCES: 437.

Dendrobium disoides Schlechter

ORIGIN/HABITAT: Northern Papua New Guinea. Plants grow on moss-covered mistforest trees in the Kani Range at about 3300 ft. (1000 m).

CLIMATE: Station #94010, Goroka, Papua New Guinea, Lat. 6.1°S, Long. 145.4°E, at 5141 ft. (1567 m). Temperatures are calculated for an elevation of 3300 ft. (1000 m), resulting in probable extremes of 93°F (34°C) and 49°F (10°C).

N/HEMISPHERE	JAN	FEB	MAR	APR	MAY	JUN	JUL	AUG	SEP	OCT	NOV	DEC
°F AVG MAX	82	83	84	85	85	84	85	84	84	84	85	83
°F AVG MIN	62	63	63	63	64	65	65	65	66	65	65	63
DIURNAL RANGE	20	20	21	22	21	19	20	19	18	19	20	20
RAIN/INCHES	2.1	2.8	4.6	5.9	6.6	9.3	9.1	10.1	10.7	8.3	4.6	2.0
HUMIDITY/%	70	67	67	67	67	71	72	73	74	71	70	70
BLOOM SEASON												
DAYS CLR	N/A											
RAIN/MM	53	71	117	150	168	236	231	257	272	211	117	51
°C AVG MAX	27.9	28.4	29.0	29.5	29.5	29.0	29.5	29.0	29.0	29.0	29.5	28.4
°C AVG MIN	16.7	17.3	17.3	17.3	17.9	18.4	18.4	18.4	19.0	18.4	18.4	17.3
DIURNAL RANGE	11.2	11.1	11.7	12.2	11.6	10.6	11.1	10.6	10.0	10.6	11.1	11.1
S/HEMISPHERE	JUL	AUG	SEP	OCT	NOV	DEC	JAN	FEB	MAR	APR	MAY	JUN

Cultural Recommendations

LIGHT: 2000–3000 fc.

TEMPERATURES: Throughout the year, days average 82–85°F (28–30°C), and nights average 62–65°F (17–18°C), with a diurnal range of 18–22°F (10–12°C). Average highs and lows vary only slightly during the year, indicating that plants may not tolerate wide seasonal fluctuations.

HUMIDITY: 70–75% in summer and autumn, dropping to 65–70% in winter and spring.

WATER: Rainfall is moderate to heavy most of the year but is relatively low for 2–3 months in winter. However, additional moisture is available from dew, fog, and mist, even during periods when rainfall is low. Cultivated plants should be kept moist but not soggy. Additional early morning mistings between waterings are often beneficial, especially on warm, bright, sunny days.

FERTILIZER: ¼–½ recommended strength. A balanced fertilizer should be applied weekly to biweekly throughout the year.

REST PERIOD: Growing temperatures should be maintained all year. Water should be reduced in winter. Plants should dry slightly between waterings, but they should never be allowed to dry out completely. Fertilizer should be reduced or eliminated until water is increased in spring. In the habitat, winter light may be slightly higher.

GROWING MEDIA: Plants may be mounted on tree-fern or cork slabs if humidity is high and plants are watered at least once daily in summer. When plants are potted, any open, fast-draining medium may be used. Repotting may be done anytime new roots are growing.

MISCELLANEOUS NOTES: The bloom season shown in the climate table is based on collection reports.

Plant and Flower Information

PLANT SIZE AND TYPE: A 14 in. (35 cm) sympodial epiphyte.

PSEUDOBULB: 14 in. (35 cm) long. The pseudobulb, which is somewhat limply erect, does not branch.

LEAVES: Each growth is densely leafy. The leaves are usually 0.4–0.8 in. (1–2 cm) long. They are erect-spreading, somewhat fleshy, shiny, and nearly transparent.

INFLORESCENCE: Short. Flowers emerge from nodes at the side of the pseudobulb.

FLOWERS: 1 per inflorescence. The tiny flowers are 0.2 in. (0.5 cm) long and last only a few days. Sepals and petals are pure white while the lip is marked with red. The blossoms are inverted with the lip uppermost. The lateral sepals are joined, forming a hood over the lip.

REFERENCES: 92, 221, 437, 445.

PHOTOS/DRAWINGS: 437.

Dendrobium dissitifolium Ridley

ORIGIN/HABITAT: Irian Jaya (western New Guinea). Plants were collected on the south side of Mt. Jaya (Mt. Carstensz) at about 5500 ft. (1680 m).

CLIMATE: Station #97796, Kokenau (Kokonau), Irian Jaya, Lat. 4.7°S, Long. 135.4°E, at 10 ft. (3 m). Temperatures are calculated for an elevation of 5500 ft. (1680 m). Record extreme temperatures are not available for this location.

N/HEMISPHERE	JAN	FEB	MAR	APR	MAY	JUN	JUL	AUG	SEP	OCT	NOV	DEC
°F AVG MAX	65	65	68	70	72	71	71	71	72	70	69	66
°F AVG MIN	55	55	56	56	56	57	56	56	56	56	56	55
DIURNAL RANGE	10	10	12	14	16	14	15	15	16	14	13	11
RAIN/INCHES	18.4	15.8	18.9	11.6	9.7	10.6	11.5	15.7	11.6	11.6	16.0	19.9
HUMIDITY/%	N/A											
BLOOM SEASON	N/A											
DAYS CLR	N/A											
RAIN/MM	467	401	480	295	246	269	292	399	295	295	406	505
°C AVG MAX	18.3	18.3	19.9	21.0	22.2	21.6	21.6	21.6	22.2	21.0	20.5	18.8
°C AVG MIN	12.7	12.7	13.3	13.3	13.3	13.8	13.3	13.3	13.3	13.3	13.3	12.7
DIURNAL RANGE	5.6	5.6	6.6	7.7	8.9	7.8	8.3	8.3	8.9	7.7	7.2	6.1
S/HEMISPHERE	JUL	AUG	SEP	OCT	NOV	DEC	JAN	FEB	MAR	APR	MAY	JUN

Cultural Recommendations

LIGHT: 2500–3500 fc.

TEMPERATURES: Throughout the year, days average 65–72°F (18–22°C),

and nights average 55–57°F (13–14°C), with a diurnal range of 10–16°F (6–9°C).

HUMIDITY: Information is not available for this location. However, records from nearby locations indicate that humidity probably averages near 85% year-round.

WATER: Rainfall is very heavy all year. Cultivated plants should be kept evenly moist but not soggy.

FERTILIZER: ¼–½ recommended strength. A balanced fertilizer should be applied weekly to biweekly throughout the year.

REST PERIOD: Growing conditions should be maintained year-round. Water and fertilizer may be reduced slightly in winter, especially for plants cultivated in the dark, short-day conditions common in temperate latitudes, but they should never be allowed to dry out completely.

GROWING MEDIA: Plants may be mounted on tree-fern or cork slabs or potted in any open, fast-draining medium. Repotting may be done anytime new roots are growing.

Plant and Flower Information

PLANT SIZE AND TYPE: A 16 in. (40 cm) sympodial epiphyte.

PSEUDOBULB: At least 16 in. (40 cm) long.

LEAVES: Several per growth. The lanceolate leaves, which are 0.4 in. (1 cm) long, are widely spaced along the stem.

INFLORESCENCE: 2 in. (5 cm) long. Racemes emerge through the leaf sheaths.

FLOWERS: 2 per inflorescence. The yellow flowers are 0.5 in. (1.2 cm) long. The dorsal sepal is oval, and lateral sepals are triangular. The lip is minutely toothed along the margin.

REFERENCES: 222, 400.

Dendrobium distachyum Lindley

AKA: Also spelled *D. distachyon*. Synonyms include *D. appendiculiforme* Kränzlin and *D. distichum* Miquel.

ORIGIN/HABITAT: Southwest Borneo. Plants grow in Sarawak, near Pontianak in Kalimantan, and in the Natuna Islands. Habitat elevation is estimated, so the following climate data should be used with caution.

CLIMATE: Station #96583, Pontianak, Borneo, Lat. 0.0°N, Long. 109.3°E, at 13 ft. (4 m) elevation. Temperatures are calculated for an elevation of 500 ft. (152 m), resulting in probable extremes of 94°F (35°C) and 66°F (19°C).

N/HEMISPHERE	JAN	FEB	MAR	APR	MAY	JUN	JUL	AUG	SEP	OCT	NOV	DEC
°F AVG MAX	85	87	87	87	88	88	87	88	88	87	86	85
°F AVG MIN	72	74	73	73	73	73	72	72	73	73	73	72
DIURNAL RANGE	13	13	14	14	15	15	15	16	15	14	13	13
RAIN/INCHES	10.8	8.2	9.5	10.9	11.1	8.7	6.5	8.0	9.0	14.4	15.3	12.7
HUMIDITY/%	85	85	84	84	82	81	79	82	83	87	86	87
BLOOM SEASON					*							
DAYS CLR @ 7AM	1	1	1	3	2	4	5	1	2	1	1	2
DAYS CLR @ 1PM	0	0	1	0	0	0	1	1	1	0	1	0
RAIN/MM	274	208	241	277	282	221	165	203	229	366	389	323
°C AVG MAX	29.7	30.8	30.8	30.8	31.3	31.3	30.8	31.3	31.3	30.8	30.2	29.7
°C AVG MIN	22.4	23.6	23.0	23.0	23.0	23.0	22.4	22.4	23.0	23.0	23.0	22.4
DIURNAL RANGE	7.3	7.2	7.8	7.8	8.3	8.3	8.4	8.9	8.3	7.8	7.2	7.3
S/HEMISPHERE	JUL	AUG	SEP	OCT	NOV	DEC	JAN	FEB	MAR	APR	MAY	JUN

Cultural Recommendations

LIGHT: 2000–3000 fc.

TEMPERATURES: Throughout the year, days average 85–88°F (30–31°C), and nights average 72–74°F (22–24°C), with a diurnal range of 13–16°F (7–9°C).

HUMIDITY: 80–85% year-round.

WATER: Rainfall is very heavy all year. Cultivated plants should be kept moist but not soggy. High humidity and constant air movement are highly recommended.

FERTILIZER: ¼–½ recommended strength. A balanced fertilizer should be applied weekly to biweekly throughout the year.

REST PERIOD: Growing conditions should be maintained all year. The plants should not be subjected to wide temperature fluctuations. Water and fertilizer may be reduced slightly in winter, especially for plants grown in the darker, short-day conditions common in temperate-latitude winters, but they should not be allowed to dry out completely.

GROWING MEDIA: Plants may be mounted on tree-fern or cork slabs if humidity is high and plants are watered daily in summer months. When plants are potted, any open, fast-draining medium may be used. Repotting may be done anytime new roots are growing.

MISCELLANEOUS NOTES: The bloom season shown in the climate table is based on reports from the habitat.

Plant and Flower Information

PLANT SIZE AND TYPE: A 10 in. (25 cm) sympodial epiphyte.

PSEUDOBULB: 10 in. (25 cm) long. Stems are densely clustered.

LEAVES: Many per growth. The distichous leaves are 0.6–1.2 in. (1.5–3.0 cm) long.

INFLORESCENCE: Short. Inflorescences emerge from the leaf axils.

FLOWERS: 1–2 per inflorescence. The small, white flowers are 0.4 in. (1 cm) across. The lip is linear.

REFERENCES: 216, 254, 278, 286, 394.

Dendrobium distichophyllum A. Hawkes and A. H. Heller. See *D. rupicolum* Ridley. REFERENCES: 191, 200, 211, 229, 454.

Dendrobium distichum Miquel. See *D. distachyum* Lindley. REFERENCES: 286, 295.

Dendrobium distichum (Presl) Rchb. f.

AKA: *Schizmoceras disticha* Presl, *Dendrobium indivisum* Naves.

ORIGIN/HABITAT: Widespread in the Philippines. Plants grow on Luzon Island in Zambales Province and on Mt. Makiling in Laguna Province. They also occur on Mindanao Island, the Polillo Islands, and islands of the Sulu Archipelago. Plants usually grow in swamps and mangroves from sea level to 2950 ft. (0–900 m).

CLIMATE: Station #98427, Manila, Philippines, Lat. 14.5°N, Long. 121.0°E, at 85 ft. (26 m). Temperatures are calculated for 800 ft. (240 m), resulting in probable extremes of 99°F (37°C) and 56°F (13°C).

N/HEMISPHERE	JAN	FEB	MAR	APR	MAY	JUN	JUL	AUG	SEP	OCT	NOV	DEC
°F AVG MAX	84	86	89	91	91	89	86	85	86	86	85	84
°F AVG MIN	67	67	69	71	73	73	73	73	73	72	70	68
DIURNAL RANGE	17	19	20	20	18	16	13	12	13	14	15	16
RAIN/INCHES	0.9	0.5	0.7	1.3	5.1	10.0	17.0	16.6	14.0	7.6	5.7	2.6
HUMIDITY/%	77	73	70	68	71	81	84	86	87	84	82	89
BLOOM SEASON		*	*	*	*	*	*	*	*	*		
DAYS CLR @ 8AM	6	9	14	14	10	3	2	1	1	6	7	6
DAYS CLR @ 2PM	3	6	10	10	8	2	1	1	0	2	2	3
RAIN/MM	23	13	18	33	130	254	432	422	356	193	145	66
°C AVG MAX	28.7	29.8	31.4	32.6	32.6	31.4	29.8	29.2	29.8	29.8	29.2	28.7
°C AVG MIN	19.2	19.2	20.3	21.4	22.6	22.6	22.6	22.6	22.6	22.0	20.9	19.8
DIURNAL RANGE	9.5	10.6	11.1	11.2	10.0	8.8	7.2	6.6	7.2	7.8	8.3	8.9
S/HEMISPHERE	JUL	AUG	SEP	OCT	NOV	DEC	JAN	FEB	MAR	APR	MAY	JUN

Cultural Recommendations

LIGHT: 1800–2500 fc in summer.

TEMPERATURES: Throughout the year, days average 84–91°F (29–33°C), and nights average 67–73°F (19–23°C), with a diurnal range of 12–20°F (7–11°C). The warmest days occur in spring.

Dendrobium ditschiense

HUMIDITY: 80–90% in summer and autumn, dropping to near 70% at the end of the winter dry season.

WATER: Rainfall is heavy from late spring through autumn, but conditions are dry for 3–4 months in winter. Cultivated plants should be kept moist while actively growing, but water should be gradually reduced in late autumn.

FERTILIZER: ¼–½ recommended strength, applied weekly. A high-nitrogen fertilizer is beneficial from spring to midsummer, but a fertilizer high in phosphates should be used in late summer and autumn.

REST PERIOD: Growing temperatures should be maintained all year. Rainfall is low for 3–4 months in winter, but additional moisture is available from frequent heavy dew. In cultivation, water should be reduced and the plants allowed to dry out between waterings. They should not remain dry for extended periods, however. Fertilizer should also be reduced or eliminated anytime water is reduced. In the habitat, light is highest in winter.

GROWING MEDIA: Mounting plants on tree-fern or cork slabs accommodates their pendulous growth habit. However, humidity must be high and plants must be watered at least once a day in summer. If plants cannot be mounted, small pots or hanging baskets may be filled with an open, fast-draining medium. Repotting may be done anytime new roots are actively growing.

MISCELLANEOUS NOTES: The bloom season shown in the climate table is based on cultivation records. Reports from the habitat indicate that in the wild, plants bloom Mar.–Dec. (Sep.–Jun.).

Plant and Flower Information

PLANT SIZE AND TYPE: A pendent, 6–16 in. (15–40 cm) sympodial epiphyte.

PSEUDOBULB: 6–16 in. (15–40 cm) long.

LEAVES: Many. The leaves are thick, rigid, and swordlike.

INFLORESCENCE: Inflorescences emerge from a cushion of fibrous scales at nodes opposite rudimentary leaves at the apex of the stem.

FLOWERS: The small flowers are slightly fragrant. Sepals and petals are greenish yellow on the outer surface and marked with lavender-red streaks on the upper surface. The lip is creamy white with reddish stripes on the outer edge.

HYBRIDIZING NOTES: Chromosome counts are n = 19 (ref. 151), and n = variable (ref. 187), 2n = 38 (ref. 151, 154, 187, 188, 280, 504, 580), and 2n = 57 (ref. 151, 187, 504, 580). Johansen (ref. 239) reports that pods dropped 18–21 days after self-pollination.

REFERENCES: 12, 51, 98, 151, 154, 179, 187, 188, 216, 239, 254, 280, 296, 373, 504, 536, 580.

PHOTOS/DRAWINGS: 350.

Dendrobium ditschiense J. J. Smith. Now considered a synonym of *Diplocaulobium ditschiense* (J. J. Smith) Hunt and Summerhayes. REFERENCES: 213, 225, 230, 486.

Dendrobium dixanthum Rchb. f.

AKA: *D. moulmeinense* Parish ex Hooker f. is sometimes listed as a synonym, but Seidenfaden (ref. 454) expresses reservations regarding this synonymy.

ORIGIN/HABITAT: Burma and northern Thailand. Plants grow in deciduous forests, usually near the tops of tall trees, at about 2500 ft. (760 m). In Burma, they grow with *D. albosanguineum* Lindley in Moulmein.

CLIMATE: Station #48327, Chiang Mai, Thailand, Lat. 18.8°N, Long. 99.0°E, at 1100 ft. (335 m). Temperatures are calculated for an elevation of 2500 ft. (760 m), resulting in probable extremes of 104°F (40°C) and 33°F (1°C).

N/HEMISPHERE	JAN	FEB	MAR	APR	MAY	JUN	JUL	AUG	SEP	OCT	NOV	DEC
°F AVG MAX	80	85	90	91	89	85	84	82	83	84	81	79
°F AVG MIN	51	52	57	65	69	69	69	70	68	66	61	52
DIURNAL RANGE	29	33	33	26	20	16	15	12	15	18	20	27
RAIN/INCHES	0.3	0.4	0.6	2.0	5.5	6.1	7.4	8.7	11.5	4.9	1.5	0.4
HUMIDITY/%	73	65	58	62	73	78	80	83	83	81	79	76
BLOOM SEASON	*	*	*	**	***	*		*				
DAYS CLR @ 7AM	5	5	2	2	1	0	0	0	0	1	3	3
DAYS CLR @ 1PM	9	8	4	2	0	0	0	0	0	1	3	
RAIN/MM	8	10	15	51	140	155	188	221	292	124	38	10
°C AVG MAX	26.9	29.7	32.4	33.0	31.9	29.7	29.1	28.0	28.5	29.1	27.4	26.3
°C AVG MIN	10.8	11.3	14.1	18.5	20.8	20.8	20.8	21.3	20.2	19.1	16.3	11.3
DIURNAL RANGE	16.1	18.4	18.3	14.5	11.1	8.9	8.3	6.7	8.3	10.0	11.1	15.0
S/HEMISPHERE	JUL	AUG	SEP	OCT	NOV	DEC	JAN	FEB	MAR	APR	MAY	JUN

Cultural Recommendations

LIGHT: 2500–3500 fc. Bright light and strong air movement should be provided. In the habitat, cloud cover during the rainy season results in reduced summer light. Cultivated plants need as much light as possible, short of burning the foliage.

TEMPERATURES: Summer days average 82–85°F (28–30°C), and nights average 69–70°F (21°C), with a diurnal range of 12–16°F (7–9°C). Spring, before the start of the summer rainy season, is the warmest time of the year. Days average 89–91°F (32–33°C), and nights average 57–69°F (14–21°C), with a diurnal range of 20–33°F (11–18°C).

HUMIDITY: Near 80% most of the year, dropping to near 60% in late winter and early spring.

WATER: Rainfall is moderate to heavy from late spring through early autumn, but conditions are much drier in winter. Cultivated plants should be kept moist while actively growing, but water should be gradually reduced after new growths mature in autumn.

FERTILIZER: ¼–½ recommended strength, applied weekly. A high-nitrogen fertilizer is beneficial from spring to midsummer, but a fertilizer high in phosphates should be used in late summer and autumn.

REST PERIOD: Winter days average 79–85°F (26–30°C), and nights average 51–52°F (11°C), with a diurnal range of 27–33°F (15–18°C). In the habitat, rainfall averages are very low for 4 months in winter, but during the early part of the season the high relative humidity indicates that additional moisture is available from frequent fog, mist, and heavy deposits of dew. Growers sometimes recommend eliminating water in winter, but plants are healthiest if for most of the winter they are allowed to become dry between waterings but do not remain dry for extended periods. For 1–2 months in early spring, however, conditions in the habitat are clear, warm, and dry; and humidity is so low that even the moisture from morning dew is uncommon. During a corresponding time for cultivated plants, water should be limited to an occasional early morning misting if the pseudobulbs start to shrivel, or if an extended period of bright, sunny weather is expected. Fertilizer should be eliminated in winter, and resumed only when water is increased in spring. In the habitat, light is highest in winter.

GROWING MEDIA: Mounting plants on tree-fern or cork slabs accommodates their pendulous growth habit. However, humidity must be high and plants must be watered at least once a day in summer. If plants cannot be mounted, small pots or hanging baskets may be filled with an open, fast-draining medium. Repotting may be done anytime new roots are actively growing.

MISCELLANEOUS NOTES: The bloom season shown in the climate table is based on cultivation records. Growers indicate that the plant grows freely and blooms abundantly in most greenhouses.

Plant and Flower Information

PLANT SIZE AND TYPE: A 19–48 in. (48–122 cm) sympodial epiphyte.

PSEUDOBULB: 18–40 in. (46–102 cm) long. The slender stems turn yellowish with age.

LEAVES: 4. The grass-green leaves are 3–7 in. (8–18 cm) long. They are pointed, narrowly linear, and deciduous before blooming. Leaves are held at the apex of each growth.

INFLORESCENCE: 2 in. (5 cm) long. The racemes emerge at the upper leaf nodes of 1-year old, leafless stems.

FLOWERS: 2–5 per node with many per cane. The thin-textured flowers are 1.6 in. (4 cm) across. Sepals and petals may be pale lemon-yellow to bright buttercup-yellow. The large, conspicuous lip is usually a darker shade of yellow with an even deeper tint on the disk. The lip has no dark blotches, but it is often greenish at the base. The margins of the nearly circular lip are finely fringed.

HYBRIDIZING NOTES: Chromosome counts are 2n = 40 (ref. 152, 187, 504, 580), 2n = 40+2f (ref. 151, 154, 187, 188), 2n = 40+4f (ref. 152), and 2n = 41 (ref. 187, 504, 580).

REFERENCES: 25, 36, 151, 152, 154, 157, 179, 187, 188, 202, 210, 216, 245, 254, 266, 359, 430, 445, 448, 454, 504, 541, 568, 570, 580.

PHOTOS/DRAWINGS: 36, 210, 245, 430, 454.

Dendrobium dixonianum Rolfe ex Downie

ORIGIN/HABITAT: Endemic to northwest Thailand. Plants grow on Mt. Chiengdao at 5400–5900 ft. (1650–1800 m).

CLIMATE: Station #48327, Chiang Mai, Thailand, Lat. 18.8°N, Long. 99.0°E, at 1100 ft. (335 m). Temperatures are calculated for an elevation of 5600 ft. (1710 m), resulting in probable extremes of 94°F (35°C) and 23°F (−5°C).

N/HEMISPHERE	JAN	FEB	MAR	APR	MAY	JUN	JUL	AUG	SEP	OCT	NOV	DEC
°F AVG MAX	70	75	80	81	79	75	74	72	73	74	71	69
°F AVG MIN	41	42	47	55	59	59	59	60	58	56	51	42
DIURNAL RANGE	29	33	33	26	20	16	15	12	15	18	20	27
RAIN/INCHES	0.3	0.4	0.6	2.0	5.5	6.1	7.4	8.7	11.5	4.9	1.5	0.4
HUMIDITY/%	73	65	58	62	73	78	80	83	83	81	79	76
BLOOM SEASON	N/A											
DAYS CLR @ 7AM	5	5	2	2	1	0	0	0	0	1	3	3
DAYS CLR @ 1PM	9	8	4	2	0	0	0	0	0	0	1	3
RAIN/MM	8	10	15	51	140	155	188	221	292	124	38	10
°C AVG MAX	21.2	24.0	26.8	27.3	26.2	24.0	23.4	22.3	22.9	23.4	21.8	20.6
°C AVG MIN	5.1	5.6	8.4	12.9	15.1	15.1	15.1	15.6	14.5	13.4	10.6	5.6
DIURNAL RANGE	16.1	18.4	18.4	14.4	11.1	8.9	8.3	6.7	8.4	10.0	11.2	15.0
S/HEMISPHERE	JUL	AUG	SEP	OCT	NOV	DEC	JAN	FEB	MAR	APR	MAY	JUN

Cultural Recommendations

LIGHT: 1800–2400 fc. Diffused light is suggested.

TEMPERATURES: Summer days average 72–75°F (22–24°C), and nights average 59–60°F (15–16°C), with a diurnal range of 12–16°F (7–9°C). The warmest temperatures and widest diurnal range occur in spring. Days average 79–81°F (26–27°C), and nights average 47–59°F (8–15°C), with a diurnal range of 20–33°F (11–18°C).

HUMIDITY: 75–85% most of the year. Humidity drops to near 60% for 2–3 months in late winter and early spring.

WATER: Rainfall is moderate to heavy from late spring through early autumn, but conditions are very dry in winter. Cultivated plants should be kept moist while actively growing, but water should be gradually reduced after new growths mature in autumn.

FERTILIZER: ¼–½ recommended strength, applied weekly. A high-nitrogen fertilizer is beneficial from spring to midsummer, but a fertilizer high in phosphates should be used in late summer and autumn.

REST PERIOD: Winter days average 69–80°F (21–27°C), and nights average 41–47°F (5–8°C), with a diurnal range of 27–33°F (15–18°C). The average low temperatures are below 50°F (10°C) for 4 months and then warm rapidly in spring. Plants should be able to tolerate temperatures a few degrees below freezing, but extremes should be avoided in cultivation. During very cold weather, a plant's chance of surviving with minimal damage is better if it is dry. In the habitat, rainfall averages are very low for 4–5 months in winter; but during the early part of the season, the high relative humidity indicates that additional moisture is available from frequent fog, mist, and heavy deposits of dew. Growers sometimes recommend eliminating water in winter, but plants are healthiest if for most of the winter they are allowed to become somewhat dry between waterings but do not remain dry for extended periods. For 1–2 months in late winter, however, conditions are clear, warm, and dry with humidity so low that even the moisture from morning dew is uncommon. Plants should be allowed to dry out completely between waterings and remain dry longer during this time. Occasional early morning mistings between waterings may help keep the plants from becoming too dry. Fertilizer should be greatly reduced or eliminated until water is increased in spring. A cool, dry rest is essential for cultivated plants and should be continued until new growth starts in spring. In the habitat, light is highest in winter, but increased light may not be critical in cultivation.

GROWING MEDIA: Plants may be mounted on tree-fern or cork slabs if humidity is high and plants are watered at least once daily in summer. When plants are potted, any open, fast-draining medium may be used. Repotting is best done in early spring when new roots begin growing.

Plant and Flower Information

PLANT SIZE AND TYPE: A 1.6–2.4 in. (4–6 cm) sympodial epiphyte or lithophyte.

PSEUDOBULB: 0.4–1.2 in. (1–3 cm) long. The growths are tightly clustered.

LEAVES: 4 per growth. Leaves are about 1.2 in. (3 cm) long.

INFLORESCENCE: 1.2–2.0 in. (3–5 cm) long. The inflorescence arises at the apex of the pseudobulb.

FLOWERS: 5–13 per inflorescence. Flowers are 0.4 in. (1 cm) across, which is large for the plant size, but they do not open fully. Blossoms are greenish-white. The yellow lip is marked with 3 dark lines.

REFERENCES: 223, 266, 418, 448, 454.

PHOTOS/DRAWINGS: 454.

Dendrobium dixsonii F. M. Bailey, also spelled *D. dixsoni*, see *D. bracteosum* Rchb. f. REFERENCES: 190, 254, 437, 470.

Dendrobium djamuense Schlechter

ORIGIN/HABITAT: Northern Papua New Guinea. Plants grow on forest trees along the upper Djamu River at about 1150 ft. (350 m).

CLIMATE: Station #200187, Erap, Papua New Guinea, Lat. 6.6°S, Long. 146.7°E, at 850 ft. (260 m). Record extreme temperatures are 102°F (39°C) and 53°F (12°C).

N/HEMISPHERE	JAN	FEB	MAR	APR	MAY	JUN	JUL	AUG	SEP	OCT	NOV	DEC
°F AVG MAX	88	88	89	90	93	93	93	93	93	92	90	90
°F AVG MIN	69	69	69	70	72	73	72	72	73	71	74	70
DIURNAL RANGE	19	19	20	20	21	20	21	21	20	21	16	20
RAIN/INCHES	3.9	3.9	2.7	3.0	3.0	5.3	5.9	5.9	7.0	3.4	2.4	3.1
HUMIDITY/%	82	81	81	79	75	74	74	74	77	76	80	80
BLOOM SEASON					*							
DAYS CLR	N/A											
RAIN/MM	98	99	68	77	76	135	149	149	179	87	60	78
°C AVG MAX	30.9	30.9	31.7	32.3	34.0	33.9	33.8	33.9	34.0	33.6	32.3	32.0
°C AVG MIN	20.4	20.5	20.7	21.1	22.0	22.5	22.1	22.4	22.5	21.7	23.3	20.9
DIURNAL RANGE	10.5	10.4	11.0	11.2	12.0	11.4	11.7	11.5	11.5	11.9	9.0	11.1
S/HEMISPHERE	JUL	AUG	SEP	OCT	NOV	DEC	JAN	FEB	MAR	APR	MAY	JUN

Cultural Recommendations

LIGHT: 2000–3000 fc.

TEMPERATURES: Throughout the year, days average 88–93°F (31–34°C), and nights average 69–74°F (20–23°C), with a diurnal range of 16–21°F (9–12°C).

Dendrobium dolichocaulon

HUMIDITY: 75–80% year-round. Despite high average humidity, the habitat may be quite dry during hot afternoons.

WATER: Rainfall is moderate most of the year, but for 4–5 months in summer and early autumn, conditions are somewhat wetter. Cultivated plants should be thoroughly saturated, then allowed to dry slightly between waterings in summer and early autumn. Water should be gradually reduced in autumn.

FERTILIZER: ¼–½ recommended strength. A balanced fertilizer should be applied weekly to biweekly throughout the year.

REST PERIOD: Growing temperatures should be maintained all year. In the habitat, rainfall is lowest in winter, but the high humidity indicates that additional moisture is frequently available from heavy dew. Cultivated plants should be allowed to dry for somewhat longer between waterings, but should not remain dry for extended periods. Fertilizer should be reduced until water is increased in spring. In the habitat, seasonal light variation is minor.

GROWING MEDIA: Plants may be mounted on tree-fern or cork slabs if humidity is high and plants are watered at least once daily in summer. When plants are potted, any open, fast-draining medium may be used. Repotting may be done anytime new roots are growing.

MISCELLANEOUS NOTES: The bloom season shown in the climate table is based on collection reports. Plants that produce flowers which last a single day commonly bloom several times during the year. Flowering usually occurs 7–14 days after a sudden 10°F (5°C) drop in daytime temperatures.

Plant and Flower Information

PLANT SIZE AND TYPE: A 16–24 in. (40–60 cm) sympodial epiphyte.

PSEUDOBULB: The non-branching stems are densely leafy.

LEAVES: Many. The leaves are usually 3.5–4.3 in. (9–11 cm) long.

INFLORESCENCE: Short. Inflorescences emerge from nodes along the side of the stem.

FLOWERS: 2 per inflorescence. The flowers are 1 in. (2.6 cm) across and last a single day. Sepals and petals all point up. Blossoms are red-brown with white in the center of the recurved lip. The center of the midlobe, which comes to a sharp point, is decorated with hairlike protuberances.

REFERENCES: 92, 221, 437, 445.

PHOTOS/DRAWINGS: 437.

Dendrobium dolichocaulon Schlechter

ORIGIN/HABITAT: Papua New Guinea. Plants were found in the Sepik River region at 2300–2800 ft. (700–850 m).

CLIMATE: Station #200004, Ambunti, Papua New Guinea, Lat. 4.2°S, Long. 142.8°E, at 164 ft. (50 m). Temperatures are calculated for an elevation of 2500 ft. (760 m), resulting in probable extremes of 91°F (33°C) and 44°F (7°C).

N/HEMISPHERE	JAN	FEB	MAR	APR	MAY	JUN	JUL	AUG	SEP	OCT	NOV	DEC
°F AVG MAX	80	82	82	82	83	82	82	82	82	82	82	81
°F AVG MIN	64	65	66	65	65	65	64	65	65	65	65	66
DIURNAL RANGE	16	17	16	17	18	17	18	17	17	17	17	15
RAIN/INCHES	6.4	7.4	7.7	8.5	9.2	9.4	10.9	10.2	12.2	10.4	8.3	5.2
HUMIDITY/%	N/A											
BLOOM SEASON			*		*							
DAYS CLR	N/A											
RAIN/MM	163	188	196	216	234	239	277	259	310	264	211	132
°C AVG MAX	26.8	27.9	27.9	27.9	28.5	27.9	27.9	27.9	27.9	27.9	27.9	27.4
°C AVG MIN	17.9	18.5	19.1	18.5	18.5	18.5	17.9	18.5	18.5	18.5	18.5	19.1
DIURNAL RANGE	8.9	9.4	8.8	9.4	10.0	9.4	10.0	9.4	9.4	9.4	9.4	8.3
S/HEMISPHERE	JUL	AUG	SEP	OCT	NOV	DEC	JAN	FEB	MAR	APR	MAY	JUN

Cultural Recommendations

LIGHT: 2000–3000 fc.

TEMPERATURES: Throughout the year, days average 80–83°F (27–29°C), and nights average 64–66°F (18–19°C), with a diurnal range of 15–18°F (8–10°C).

HUMIDITY: Information is not available for this location. However, records from nearby locations indicate that humidity probably averages near 85% year-round.

WATER: Rainfall is heavy year-round. The greatest amounts fall in summer and early autumn. Cultivated plants should be kept moist but not soggy.

FERTILIZER: ¼–½ recommended strength. A balanced fertilizer should be applied weekly to biweekly throughout the year.

REST PERIOD: Growing conditions should be maintained all year. Water and fertilizer should be reduced somewhat in winter, especially for plants grown in the dark, short-day conditions common in temperate latitudes. They should never be allowed to dry out completely, however.

GROWING MEDIA: Plants may be mounted on cork or tree-fern slabs if humidity is high and plants are watered at least once daily in summer. When plants are potted, any open, fast-draining medium may be used, but fir bark is preferred by most growers. Repotting may be done anytime new roots are growing.

MISCELLANEOUS NOTES: The bloom season shown in the climate table is based on reports from the habitat.

Plant and Flower Information

PLANT SIZE AND TYPE: A 79 in. (200 cm) sympodial epiphyte.

PSEUDOBULB: 79 in. (200 cm) long. Stems emerge from a very short rhizome.

LEAVES: Many. The linear leaves are 6–9 in. (16–23 cm) long, leathery, and smooth.

INFLORESCENCE: Short. Inflorescences emerge from the side of the stem.

FLOWERS: The smooth, white flowers are 0.6 in. (1.5 cm) long. The dorsal sepal is somewhat lanceolate with a rounded tip. The ovate-triangular lateral sepals are sickle-shaped and pointed at the tips. Petals are tongue-shaped. The lip is oval and trilobed near the apex. The kidney-shaped midlobe has a densely-warty, wrinkled surface.

REFERENCES: 223, 436, 443.

Dendrobium dolichocentrum Koorders. See *D. furcatum* Reinwardt ex Lindley. REFERENCES: 436.

Dendrobium dolichocentrum Schlechter. Included by Koorders in his 1914 list *Syst. Verz.* 3:23, but Schlechter (ref. 436) indicates that he never described a plant by that name. REFERENCES: 436.

Dendrobium dolichophyllum D. Jones and M. Clements.

AKA: Jones and Clements (ref. 67) include the following names as synonyms of their new species. *D. teretifolium* R. Brown var. *album* C. White, *D. teretifolium* R. Brown var. *aureum* F. M. Bailey, and *D. teretifolium* R. Brown var. *fairfaxii* Fitzgerald ex F. Mueller f. *aureum* (Bailey) Clemsha. Only time will tell whether this becomes generally accepted as an independent species.

ORIGIN/HABITAT: Eastern Australia. The small habitat extends from near Nambour in southern Queensland to near the Richmond River in northern New South Wales. Plants grow on rocks and trees in damp, shady rainforests. They are usually found at 2600–3950 ft. (800–1200 m).

CLIMATE: Station #94576, Brisbane, Australia, Lat. 27.4°S, Long. 153.1°E, at 17 ft. (5 m). Temperatures are calculated for an elevation of 3000 ft.

(910 m), resulting in probable extremes of 100°F (38°C) and 25°F (−4°C).

N/HEMISPHERE	JAN	FEB	MAR	APR	MAY	JUN	JUL	AUG	SEP	OCT	NOV	DEC
°F AVG MAX	58	61	66	70	72	75	75	75	72	69	64	59
°F AVG MIN	39	40	45	50	54	57	59	58	56	51	46	41
DIURNAL RANGE	19	21	21	20	18	18	16	17	16	18	18	18
RAIN/INCHES	2.2	1.9	1.9	2.5	3.7	5.0	6.4	6.3	5.7	3.7	2.8	2.6
HUMIDITY/%	62	59	58	57	59	59	63	65	66	64	64	64
BLOOM SEASON			*	*	*							
DAYS CLR @ 10AM	17	20	18	11	12	9	5	9	14	18	16	
DAYS CLR @ 4PM	15	16	15	12	14	12	8	5	8	10	14	14
RAIN/MM	56	48	48	64	94	127	163	160	145	94	71	66
°C AVG MAX	14.5	16.2	19.0	21.2	22.3	24.0	24.0	24.0	22.3	20.6	17.9	15.1
°C AVG MIN	4.0	4.5	7.3	10.1	12.3	14.0	15.1	14.5	13.4	10.6	7.9	5.1
DIURNAL RANGE	10.5	11.7	11.7	11.1	10.0	10.0	8.9	9.5	8.9	10.0	10.0	10.0
S/HEMISPHERE	JUL	AUG	SEP	OCT	NOV	DEC	JAN	FEB	MAR	APR	MAY	JUN

Cultural Recommendations

LIGHT: 1500–2500 fc. In the habitat, more than half the days are clear each month except during the summer rainy season, when skies are clear approximately 30% of the time. Plants usually grow in shady habitats, but light should be as high as the plant can tolerate, short of burning the leaves. Plants may be adaptable, as the smallest forms are found in open forests exposed to high light; however, more robust forms tend to grow in shadier habitats.

TEMPERATURES: Summer days average near 75°F (24°C), and nights average 57–59°F (14–15°C), with a diurnal range of 16–18°F (9–10°C). *D. dolichophyllum* also grows in the lowlands where temperatures are 5–7°F (3–4°C) warmer than indicated.

HUMIDITY: Near 65% most of the year, dropping to near 60% in winter and spring. However, values are probably greater in the moist, shady, habitat. Growers recommend strong air circulation.

WATER: Rainfall is moderate in summer and autumn but is somewhat lower in winter and early spring. However, more water is probably available in the rainforest habitat than is indicated by the climate from the low elevation weather station. Cultivated plants should be allowed to dry only slightly between waterings from late spring into early autumn. Water should be gradually reduced in late autumn.

FERTILIZER: ¼–½ recommended strength, applied weekly. A high-nitrogen fertilizer is beneficial from spring to midsummer, but a fertilizer high in phosphates should be used in late summer and autumn.

REST PERIOD: Winter days average 58–66°F (15–19°C), and nights average 39–45°F (4–7°C), with a diurnal range of 18–21°F (10–12°C). In cultivation, water should be reduced so that the plants are kept only barely moist until growth resumes in spring. Fertilizer should be reduced or eliminated. Growers indicate that distinct seasonal variation is essential for plant health.

GROWING MEDIA: Mounting plants on cork or a rough-barked hardwood slabs accommodates their pendent growth habit, but humidity must be high and the plants must be watered at least once daily in summer. If plants are potted, the smallest possible pot or hanging basket should be filled with a rapidly draining medium. Growers report that clay pots are preferable to plastic ones. Repotting is best done immediately after flowering.

MISCELLANEOUS NOTES: The spring bloom season shown in the climate table is based on reports from the habitat. Plants are easy to grow on a slab of tree-fern fiber, hardwood, or cork. *D. dolichophyllum* needs shade, high humidity, and excellent air movement.

Plant and Flower Information

PLANT SIZE AND TYPE: A highly variable, 2–118 in. (5–300 cm) sympodial epiphyte or lithophyte.

PSEUDOBULB: 2–118 in. (5–300 cm) long. The dark green or yellowish stems are commonly pendulous. They are tough, very slender, and branch only rarely.

LEAVES: Several. The linear or terete leaves are 8–40 in. (20–102 cm) long. They are dull dark green and pendulous.

INFLORESCENCE: 1.2–3.2 in. (3–8 cm) long, with up to 3 per stem.

FLOWERS: 1–7 per inflorescence. The fragrant flowers are 1.6–2.0 in. (4–5 cm) across and open fully. Sepals and petals may be greenish or golden yellow, but they are always marked with dark striations near the center of the blossom. Individual flowers last 10–20 days, but a plant may be in bloom for 6 to 8 weeks.

REFERENCES: 67, 68, 235, 240.

PHOTOS/DRAWINGS: 68.

Dendrobium donacoides Ridley

ORIGIN/HABITAT: Irian Jaya (western New Guinea). Plants were collected south of Mt. Jaya (Mt. Carstensz) at about 700 ft. (210 m).

CLIMATE: Station #97796, Kokenau (Kokonau), Irian Jaya, Lat. 4.7°S, Long. 135.4°E, at 10 ft. (3 m). Temperatures are calculated for an elevation of 500 ft. (150 m). Record extreme temperatures are not available for this location.

N/HEMISPHERE	JAN	FEB	MAR	APR	MAY	JUN	JUL	AUG	SEP	OCT	NOV	DEC
°F AVG MAX	81	81	84	86	88	87	87	87	88	86	85	82
°F AVG MIN	71	71	72	72	72	73	72	72	72	72	72	71
DIURNAL RANGE	10	10	12	14	16	14	15	15	16	14	13	11
RAIN/INCHES	18.4	15.8	18.9	11.6	9.7	10.6	11.5	15.7	11.6	11.6	16.0	19.9
HUMIDITY/%	N/A											
BLOOM SEASON	N/A											
DAYS CLR	N/A											
RAIN/MM	467	401	480	295	246	269	292	399	295	295	406	505
°C AVG MAX	27.4	27.4	29.1	30.2	31.3	30.8	30.8	30.8	31.3	30.2	29.7	28.0
°C AVG MIN	21.9	21.9	22.4	22.4	22.4	23.0	22.4	22.4	22.4	22.4	22.4	21.9
DIURNAL RANGE	5.5	5.5	6.7	7.8	8.9	7.8	8.4	8.4	8.9	7.8	7.3	6.1
S/HEMISPHERE	JUL	AUG	SEP	OCT	NOV	DEC	JAN	FEB	MAR	APR	MAY	JUN

Cultural Recommendations

LIGHT: 2500–3500 fc.

TEMPERATURES: Throughout the year, days average 81–88°F (27–31°C), and nights average 71–73°F (22–23°C), with a diurnal range of 10–16°F (6–9°C).

HUMIDITY: Information is not available for this location. However, records from nearby stations indicate that humidity probably averages near 85% year-round.

WATER: Rainfall is very heavy all year. Cultivated plants should be kept evenly moist.

FERTILIZER: ¼–½ recommended strength. A balanced fertilizer should be applied weekly to biweekly throughout the year.

REST PERIOD: Growing conditions should be maintained year-round. Water and fertilizer may be reduced slightly in winter, especially for plants grown in the dark, short-day conditions common in temperate latitudes, but they should never be allowed to dry out completely.

GROWING MEDIA: Plants may be mounted on tree-fern or cork slabs or potted in small pots filled with any open, fast-draining medium. Repotting may be done anytime new roots are growing.

Plant and Flower Information

PLANT SIZE AND TYPE: A sympodial epiphyte of unreported size.

PSEUDOBULB: The canelike stems resemble bamboo.

LEAVES: Many. The slender, lanceolate leaves are 4.3 in. (11 cm) long.

INFLORESCENCE: Short.

FLOWERS: 2 per inflorescence. The highly variable flowers are 0.4–3.2 in.

(1–8 cm) long. The linear sepals are long, but the petals are much smaller at 0.7 in. (1.7 cm). The lip is 0.4 in. (1 cm) long with short sidelobes. The midlobe has a dense yellow disk with elevated lines. The disk and midlobe are covered with yellow hairs.

REFERENCES: 222, 400.

Dendrobium donnaiense Gagnepain.

Now considered a synonym of *Eria donnaiensis* (Gagnepain) Seidenfaden. REFERENCES: 137, 227, 448, Seidenfaden 1992 *Opera Botanica* #114.

Dendrobium × *donnesiae* Hort.

Probably a natural hybrid between *D. formosum* Roxburgh ex Lindley and *D. infundibulum* Lindley, but Schelpe (ref. 429) included *D. donnesiae* as a synonym of *D. infundibulum*. REFERENCES: 254, 429.

Dendrobium doormanii J. J. Smith

ORIGIN/HABITAT: Irian Jaya (western New Guinea). Plants were collected on a mountain ridge 44 mi. (70 km) north of the Carstensz Mountains at 2600–2950 ft. (800–900 m).

CLIMATE: Station #97686, Wamena, Irian Jaya, Lat. 4.1°S, Long. 139.0°E, at 5446 ft. (1660 m). Temperatures are calculated for an elevation of 2950 ft. (900 m). Record extreme temperatures are not available for this location.

N/HEMISPHERE	JAN	FEB	MAR	APR	MAY	JUN	JUL	AUG	SEP	OCT	NOV	DEC
°F AVG MAX	83	84	85	84	85	84	85	84	84	87	86	82
°F AVG MIN	68	68	70	70	71	72	71	70	71	73	73	69
DIURNAL RANGE	15	16	15	14	14	12	14	14	13	14	13	13
RAIN/INCHES	3.0	1.9	2.2	4.0	4.6	3.3	2.8	4.2	6.9	3.9	5.4	4.9
HUMIDITY/%	N/A											
BLOOM SEASON				*								
DAYS CLR	N/A											
RAIN/MM	76	48	56	102	117	84	71	107	175	99	137	124
°C AVG MAX	28.5	29.0	29.6	29.0	29.6	29.0	29.6	29.0	29.0	30.7	30.1	27.9
°C AVG MIN	20.1	20.1	21.2	21.2	21.8	22.4	21.8	21.2	21.8	22.9	22.9	20.7
DIURNAL RANGE	8.4	8.9	8.4	7.8	7.8	6.6	7.8	7.8	7.2	7.8	7.2	7.2
S/HEMISPHERE	JUL	AUG	SEP	OCT	NOV	DEC	JAN	FEB	MAR	APR	MAY	JUN

Cultural Recommendations

LIGHT: 1800–3000 fc.

TEMPERATURES: Throughout the year, days average 82–87°F (28–31°C), and nights average 68–73°F (20–23°C), with a diurnal range of 12–16°F (7–9°C). In the habitat, the warmest temperatures of the day occur in late morning when skies are clear. Clouds and mist develop near noon, thus preventing additional warming.

HUMIDITY: Information is not available for this location. However, humidity at other locations in the region normally exceeds 80% year-round.

WATER: Rainfall is moderate through most of the year with a short, semidry period in late winter. Cultivated plants should be kept moist with only slight drying allowed between waterings through most of the year.

FERTILIZER: ¼–½ recommended strength. A balanced fertilizer should be applied weekly to biweekly throughout the year.

REST PERIOD: Growing conditions should be maintained all year. In the habitat, winter rainfall is reduced. For cultivated plants, water should be reduced and the plants kept just barely moist for 2–3 months. However, plants should not be allowed to dry out completely.

GROWING MEDIA: Plants may be mounted on tree-fern or cork slabs if humidity is high and plants are watered at least once daily in summer. When plants are potted, any open, fast-draining medium may be used. Repotting is best done in early spring when new roots are growing.

MISCELLANEOUS NOTES: The bloom season shown in the climate table is based on reports from the habitat.

Plant and Flower Information

PLANT SIZE AND TYPE: A 6 in. (15 cm) sympodial epiphyte.

PSEUDOBULB: 3.0–3.5 in. (7.5–9.0 cm) long. The clustered, somewhat club-shaped stems are flattened near the apex. They are erect and emerge from a short rhizome.

LEAVES: 1 per growth. The ovate-lanceolate leaf is 3 in. (8 cm) long with 2 teeth at the apex.

INFLORESCENCE: Short. Inflorescences emerge below the leaf. Flowers open in succession.

FLOWERS: 1 at a time. The flowers are less than 0.3 in. (0.8 cm) across. Blossoms are white with a violet spot on the lip. The dorsal sepal is sparsely marked with scalelike dots. The erect lip is recurved. Floral segments are incurved along the margins.

REFERENCES: 224, 445, 470.

Dendrobium doreyanum (Linn.) Linden.

Listed as an invalid name by Kränzlin. REFERENCES: 218, 254.

Dendrobium draconis Rchb. f.

AKA: *D. andersonii* J. Scott, *D. eburneum* "Rchb. f." ex Bateman.

ORIGIN/HABITAT: Widespread from India through Southeast Asia. The habitat extends from the Manipur district of northeastern India, through the Tenasserim region of Burma, into the mountains of northern Thailand. Distribution continues eastward into Cambodia, Laos, and Vietnam. Plants usually grow at 2600–4250 ft. (800–1300 m), but they have been reported as low as 650 ft. (200 m) and as high as 6550 ft. (2000 m). It is one of the most common dendrobiums.

CLIMATE: Station #48327, Chiang Mai, Thailand, Lat. 18.8°N, Long. 99.0°E, at 1100 ft. (335 m). Temperatures have been calculated for a habitat elevation of 3500 ft. (1070 m), resulting in probable extremes of 101°F (38°C) and 30°F (–1°C).

N/HEMISPHERE	JAN	FEB	MAR	APR	MAY	JUN	JUL	AUG	SEP	OCT	NOV	DEC
°F AVG MAX	77	82	87	88	86	82	81	79	80	81	78	76
°F AVG MIN	48	49	54	62	66	66	66	67	65	63	58	49
DIURNAL RANGE	29	33	33	26	20	16	15	12	15	18	20	27
RAIN/INCHES	0.3	0.4	0.6	2.0	5.5	6.1	7.4	8.7	11.5	4.9	1.5	0.4
HUMIDITY/%	73	65	58	62	73	78	80	83	83	81	79	76
BLOOM SEASON			**	**								
DAYS CLR @ 7AM	5	5	2	2	1	0	0	0	0	1	3	3
DAYS CLR @ 1PM	9	8	4	2	0	0	0	0	0	1	0	3
RAIN/MM	8	10	15	51	140	155	188	221	292	124	38	10
°C AVG MAX	25.0	27.8	30.6	31.2	30.0	27.8	27.3	26.2	26.7	27.3	25.6	24.5
°C AVG MIN	8.9	9.5	12.3	16.7	18.9	18.9	18.9	19.5	18.4	17.3	14.5	9.5
DIURNAL RANGE	16.1	18.3	18.3	14.5	11.1	8.9	8.4	6.7	8.3	10.0	11.1	15.0
S/HEMISPHERE	JUL	AUG	SEP	OCT	NOV	DEC	JAN	FEB	MAR	APR	MAY	JUN

Cultural Recommendations

LIGHT: 3000–4000 fc. Cultivated plants need bright light and brisk air movement, especially if temperatures are high. The heavy summer cloud cover indicates that some shading is needed from spring through autumn, but light should be as high as the plants can tolerate, short of burning the foliage.

TEMPERATURES: Summer days average 77–80°F (25–27°C), and nights average 64–65°F (18–19°C), with a diurnal range of 12–16°F (7–9°C). The warmest weather occurs in spring. Days average 86–88°F (30–31°C), and nights average 54–66°F (12–19°C), with a diurnal range of 20–33°F (11–18°C). Both highs and lows are more moderate after the start of the summer wet season.

HUMIDITY: 80–85% from summer into autumn, dropping to near 60% for 2–3 months in late winter and early spring.

WATER: Rainfall is heavy while plants are actively growing from spring to early autumn. During this season, cultivated plants should be kept moist, with little if any drying allowed between waterings. However, water should be gradually reduced after new growths mature in autumn.

FERTILIZER: ½ to full recommended strength, applied weekly. A high-nitrogen fertilizer is beneficial from spring to midsummer, but a fertilizer high in phosphates should be used in late summer and autumn.

REST PERIOD: Winter days average 76–82°F (25–28°C), and nights average 48–49°F (9–10°C), with a diurnal range of 27–33°F (15–18°C). Growers indicate that plants from this habitat tolerate light frost if they are dry when temperatures are low. In the habitat, rainfall averages are very low for 4–5 months in winter, but during the early part of the season the high relative humidity indicates that additional moisture is available from frequent fog, mist, and heavy deposits of dew. Growers sometimes recommend eliminating water in winter, but plants are healthiest if for most of the winter they are allowed to become somewhat dry between waterings but do not remain dry for extended periods. For 1–2 months in late winter, however, conditions are clear, warm, and dry, with humidity so low that even the moisture from morning dew is uncommon. Plants should be allowed to dry out completely between waterings and remain dry longer during this time. Occasional early morning mistings between waterings may help keep the plants from becoming too dry. Fertilizer should be greatly reduced or eliminated until water is increased in spring. A cool, dry rest is essential for cultivated plants and should be continued until new growth starts in spring. In the habitat, light is highest in winter, but increased light may not be critical in cultivation.

GROWING MEDIA: Plants may be mounted on slabs of cork or tree-fern fiber if humidity is high and water is applied at least once a day in summer. If plants are potted, undersized pots that are barely large enough to hold the roots may be filled with a very open, fast-draining medium. Repotting should be done as seldom as possible. When necessary, repotting is best done as soon as new root growth starts, or immediately after flowering.

MISCELLANEOUS NOTES: The bloom season shown in the climate table is based on reports from the habitat. Cultivated plants may bloom anytime in spring or summer, but they most often flower in May–Jun. (Nov.–Dec.). *D. draconis* sometimes grows with *D. williamsonii* Day and Rchb. f.

Plant and Flower Information

PLANT SIZE AND TYPE: A 9–22 in. (23–56 cm) sympodial epiphyte.

PSEUDOBULB: 6–18 in. (15–45 cm) long. Stems consist of 8–9 nodes. The sheaths covering the pseudobulb are covered with short, black, deciduous hairs.

LEAVES: Many. The leaves are 2.4–4.0 in. (6–10 cm) long. They are dark green, lanceolate, leathery, and persist for 2 seasons.

INFLORESCENCE: Very short. Inflorescences emerge from opposite leaves on upper nodes of the stem.

FLOWERS: 2–5 per inflorescence. The flowers are 1.6–2.4 in. (4–6 cm) across with waxy, ivory-white sepals and petals. The white lip is decorated with crimson, red-orange, or gold lines at the base of the oblong midlobe. The lip apex is pointed with ruffled, wavy margins. The long spur is slender and tubular. Highly aromatic, the fragrance resembles tangerines. Individual blooms last 3 weeks, but they do not all open at the same time, so plants are often in flower for 6 weeks.

HYBRIDIZING NOTES: Chromosome count is 2n = 38 (ref. 152, 504, 580). Johansen (ref. 239) indicates that plants are self-sterile and that flowers drop 18–21 days after self-pollination. *D. draconis* hybridizes with *D. cariniferum* Rchb. f. when either is used as the female or pollen parent.

REFERENCES: 25, 36, 152, 157, 179, 190, 196, 200, 202, 210, 216, 239, 243, 245, 254, 266, 366, 369, 371, 429, 430, 445, 447, 448, 454, 504, 541, 557, 568, 570, 580.

PHOTOS/DRAWINGS: 36, 210, 245, 366, 371, 430, 454, 568.

Dendrobium drake-castilloi Kränzlin. See *D. macropus* (Endl.) Rchb. f. ex Lindley.
REFERENCES: 173, 224, 270.

Dendrobium dryadum Schlechter. See *D. violaceum* Kränzlin.
REFERENCES: 92, 179, 221, 304, 330, 385, 430, 437, 445.

Dendrobium dubium (Schlechter) J. J. Smith

AKA: Schlechter (ref. 437) originally described the plant as *Cadetia crenulata*, and J. J. Smith (ref. 470) transferred it to *Dendrobium*. However, *Cadetia* is again considered a valid genus by some botanists.

ORIGIN/HABITAT: New Guinea. Plants grow on forest trees and shrubs near Jaduna along the Waria River at 1150–1950 ft. (350–600 m).

CLIMATE: Station #200192, Garaina, Papua New Guinea, Lat. 7.9°S, Long. 147.1°E, at 2350 ft. (716 m). Temperatures are calculated for an elevation of 1500 ft. (460 m), resulting in probable extremes of 97°F (36°C) and 49°F (9°C).

N/HEMISPHERE	JAN	FEB	MAR	APR	MAY	JUN	JUL	AUG	SEP	OCT	NOV	DEC
°F AVG MAX	83	85	86	87	88	88	88	88	87	87	86	84
°F AVG MIN	66	66	66	67	66	67	68	68	68	67	67	66
DIURNAL RANGE	17	19	20	20	22	21	20	20	19	20	19	18
RAIN/INCHES	5.8	6.5	8.7	11.1	11.8	11.9	8.9	11.7	11.5	9.9	7.7	5.2
HUMIDITY/%	84	82	82	81	80	80	81	81	82	83	84	84
BLOOM SEASON									*	*		
DAYS CLR	N/A											
RAIN/MM	147	165	221	282	300	302	226	297	292	251	196	132
°C AVG MAX	28.2	29.3	29.9	30.4	31.0	31.0	31.0	31.0	30.4	30.4	29.9	28.8
°C AVG MIN	18.8	18.8	18.8	19.3	18.8	19.3	19.9	19.9	19.9	19.3	19.3	18.8
DIURNAL RANGE	9.4	10.5	11.1	11.1	12.2	11.7	11.1	11.1	10.5	11.1	10.6	10.0
S/HEMISPHERE	JUL	AUG	SEP	OCT	NOV	DEC	JAN	FEB	MAR	APR	MAY	JUN

Cultural Recommendations

LIGHT: 2500–3500 fc.

TEMPERATURES: Throughout the year, days average 83–88°F (28–31°C), and nights average 66–68°F (19–20°C), with a diurnal range of 17–22°F (9–12°C).

HUMIDITY: 80–85% year-round.

WATER: Rainfall is moderate to heavy year-round. Conditions are slightly drier in winter. Cultivated plants should be kept moist but not soggy.

FERTILIZER: ¼–½ recommended strength. A balanced fertilizer should be applied weekly to biweekly throughout the year.

REST PERIOD: Growing conditions vary only slightly during the year. In the habitat, rainfall is slightly lower in winter. Water should be reduced somewhat for cultivated plants in winter, especially those grown in the dark, short-day conditions common in temperate latitudes, but they should not be allowed to dry out completely. Fertilizer should be reduced or eliminated anytime water is reduced.

GROWING MEDIA: Plants may be mounted on tree-fern or cork slabs if humidity is high and plants are watered at least once daily in summer. When plants are potted, any open, fast-draining medium may be used. Repotting may be done anytime new roots are growing.

MISCELLANEOUS NOTES: The bloom season shown in the climate table is based on reports from the habitat.

Plant and Flower Information

PLANT SIZE AND TYPE: A 4–7 in. (10–18 cm) sympodial epiphyte.

PSEUDOBULB: 1.2–3.2 in. (3–8 cm) long. Growths emerge from a very short rhizome.

LEAVES: 1 per growth. The erect, somewhat tongue-shaped leaf is 2–4 in. (5–10 cm) long.

Dendrobium dulce

INFLORESCENCE: Very short.

FLOWERS: Several per inflorescence, but only a single blossom opens at a time. The flowers, which are 0.2 in. (0.6 cm) long, are whitish with yellow on the midlobe of the lip.

REFERENCES: 92, 221, 437, 470, 472.

PHOTOS/DRAWINGS: 437.

Dendrobium dulce J. J. Smith

ORIGIN/HABITAT: Irian Jaya (western New Guinea) and the Admiralty Islands. Plants have recently been rediscovered in the Admiralty Islands, where they grow in partial shade at 2450 ft. (740 m).

CLIMATE: Station #94044, Momote, Admiralty Islands, Lat. 2.1°S, Long. 147.4°E, at 12 ft. (4 m). Temperatures are calculated for an elevation of 2450 ft. (750 m), resulting in probable extremes of 88°F (31°C) and 55°F (13°C).

N/HEMISPHERE	JAN	FEB	MAR	APR	MAY	JUN	JUL	AUG	SEP	OCT	NOV	DEC
°F AVG MAX	77	77	78	78	78	78	78	78	78	78	79	78
°F AVG MIN	68	68	68	68	68	67	68	68	68	68	69	69
DIURNAL RANGE	9	9	10	10	10	11	10	10	10	10	10	9
RAIN/INCHES	13.1	11.5	10.1	9.1	9.4	12.2	10.6	10.2	12.0	11.3	8.5	12.1
HUMIDITY/%	84	84	84	83	84	86	86	85	86	86	84	84
BLOOM SEASON	N/A											
DAYS CLR	N/A											
RAIN/MM	333	292	257	231	239	310	269	259	305	287	216	307
°C AVG MAX	25.0	25.0	25.6	25.6	25.6	25.7	25.6	25.6	25.6	25.6	26.1	25.6
°C AVG MIN	20.0	20.0	20.0	20.0	20.0	19.4	20.0	20.0	20.0	20.0	20.5	20.5
DIURNAL RANGE	5.0	5.0	5.6	5.6	5.6	6.3	5.6	5.6	5.6	5.6	5.6	5.1
S/HEMISPHERE	JUL	AUG	SEP	OCT	NOV	DEC	JAN	FEB	MAR	APR	MAY	JUN

Cultural Recommendations

LIGHT: 1200–2400 fc.

TEMPERATURES: Throughout the year, days average 77–79°F (25–26°C), and nights average 67–69°F (19–21°C), with a diurnal range of 9–11°F (5–6°C).

HUMIDITY: Near 85% year-round.

WATER: Rainfall is heavy all year. Cultivated plants should be kept moist but not soggy.

FERTILIZER: ¼–½ recommended strength. A balanced fertilizer should be applied weekly to biweekly throughout the year.

REST PERIOD: Growing conditions should be maintained all year. For cultivated plants, water and fertilizer may be reduced somewhat in winter, especially if plants are grown in the dark, short-day conditions common in temperate latitudes. They should never be allowed to dry out completely, however.

GROWING MEDIA: Plants may be mounted on tree-fern or cork slabs if humidity is high and plants are watered at least once daily in summer. When plants are potted, any open, fast-draining medium may be used. Repotting is best done in spring when new growth starts.

MISCELLANEOUS NOTES: One plant grew for many years at the botanical garden in Bogor, Java, but it did not flower. Plants that produce flowers which last a single day commonly bloom several times during the year. Flowering usually occurs 7–14 days after a sudden 10°F (5°C) drop in daytime temperatures.

Plant and Flower Information

PLANT SIZE AND TYPE: A 24–28 in. (60–70 cm) sympodial epiphyte, terrestrial, or lithophyte.

PSEUDOBULB: 24–28 in. (60–70 cm) long. The erect, grasslike growths, which normally do not branch, consist of many internodes.

LEAVES: Many. The leaves are 4–6 in. (10–15 cm) long, linear, and papery.

INFLORESCENCE: Short. Flowers are borne between brown bracts.

FLOWERS: 2 per inflorescence. Blossoms are about 2.4 in. (6 cm) long. The grooved dorsal sepal is slender and linear, becoming threadlike at the tip. Lateral sepals are 2 in. (5 cm) long. Sepals and petals are yellowish with a purplish or greenish yellow tinge at the tip. The erect lip may be white or yellowish with an apricot-orange callus. It is often flushed with purple near the apex. The midlobe is densely fringed along the margin. Blossoms last a single day, but plants produce many, sweetly fragrant blossoms. The fragrance is similar to *Galium verum* Linn.

REFERENCES: 220, 254, 445, 470, 583.

PHOTOS/DRAWINGS: 583.

Dendrobium durum J. J. Smith. Now considered a synonym of *Flickingeria dura* (J. J. Smith) A. Hawkes. REFERENCES: 25, 75, 213, 219, 220, 230, 231, 254, 469. PHOTOS/DRAWINGS: 469.

Dendrobium eboracense Kränzlin

AKA: J. J. Smith (ref. 470) indicates that *D. eboracense* Kränzlin should be a synonym of *D. macfarlanei* F. Mueller not Rchb. f. We found no recent use of this synonymy so both species are included. Schlechter (ref. 437) includes *D. macfarlanei* Schlechter not F. Mueller and *D. podagraria* Kränzlin as synonyms.

ORIGIN/HABITAT: New Britain island off the northeastern coast of New Guinea. Plants were collected along the beach near Ralum and between Massawa and Cape Lambert at 50 ft. (20 m).

CLIMATE: Station #94085, Rabaul, Papua New Guinea, Lat. 4.2°S, Long. 152.2°E, at 28 ft. (9 m). Record extreme temperatures are 100°F (38°C) and 65°F (18°C).

N/HEMISPHERE	JAN	FEB	MAR	APR	MAY	JUN	JUL	AUG	SEP	OCT	NOV	DEC
°F AVG MAX	89	89	91	92	91	90	90	90	90	90	90	90
°F AVG MIN	73	72	73	73	73	73	73	73	73	73	73	73
DIURNAL RANGE	16	17	18	19	18	17	17	17	17	17	17	17
RAIN/INCHES	5.4	3.7	3.5	5.1	7.1	10.1	14.8	10.4	10.2	10.0	5.2	3.3
HUMIDITY/%	74	73	69	70	73	76	77	76	77	77	75	74
BLOOM SEASON					*	*						
DAYS CLR	N/A											
RAIN/MM	137	94	89	130	180	257	376	264	259	254	132	84
°C AVG MAX	31.7	31.7	32.8	33.3	32.8	32.2	32.2	32.2	32.2	32.2	32.2	32.2
°C AVG MIN	22.8	22.2	22.8	22.8	22.8	22.8	22.8	22.8	22.8	22.8	22.8	22.8
DIURNAL RANGE	8.9	9.5	10.0	10.5	10.0	9.4	9.4	9.4	9.4	9.4	9.4	9.4
S/HEMISPHERE	JUL	AUG	SEP	OCT	NOV	DEC	JAN	FEB	MAR	APR	MAY	JUN

Cultural Recommendations

LIGHT: 2500–3000 fc.

TEMPERATURES: Throughout the year, days average 89–92°F (32–33°C), and nights average 72–73°F (22–23°C), with a diurnal range of 16–19°F (9–11°C).

HUMIDITY: Near 75% most of the year. Humidity rises to near 100% at night, but during the dry season, it may decline to 35% at midday.

WATER: Rainfall is heavy most of the year, but conditions are slightly drier for 2 months in late winter. Cultivated plants should be kept moist, with only slight drying allowed between waterings.

FERTILIZER: ¼–½ recommended strength. A balanced fertilizer should be applied weekly to biweekly throughout the year.

REST PERIOD: Growing conditions should be maintained all year. Water should be reduced for cultivated plants in winter, especially those grown in the dark, short-day conditions common in temperate latitudes. They should never be allowed to dry out completely, however. Fertilizer may be reduced or eliminated until plants begin to grow in spring.

GROWING MEDIA: Plants may be mounted on tree-fern or cork slabs if humidity is high and plants are watered at least once daily in summer. When plants are potted, any open, fast-draining medium may be used. Repotting may be done anytime new roots are growing.

MISCELLANEOUS NOTES: The bloom season shown in the climate table is based collection reports. Plants that produce flowers which last a single day commonly bloom several times during the year. Flowering usually occurs 7–14 days after a sudden 10°F (5°C) drop in daytime temperatures. Buds form and hold on the plant until the temperature drop occurs, following which the blossoms open simultaneously.

Plant and Flower Information

PLANT SIZE AND TYPE: A 35 in. (88 cm) sympodial epiphyte.

PSEUDOBULB: 31 in. (80 cm) long. The shiny, yellow stems are clustered and narrow at the base. The upper half of the stem is leafy.

LEAVES: Many. The deciduous leaves are 3.1 in. (8 cm) long, lanceolate, and rigid.

INFLORESCENCE: Short.

FLOWERS: Few per inflorescence. The flowers are 0.4 in. (1 cm) across. Sepals and petals are pale yellow with red longitudinal veins. The lip is whitish to pale yellow with purple markings and a bright yellow disk. Flowers last a single day.

REFERENCES: 218, 254, 437, 445, 470.

PHOTOS/DRAWINGS: 437.

Dendrobium eboracense F. Mueller and Kränzlin. Schlechter (ref. 437) includes this name in a discussion of *D. macfarlanei* F. Mueller. REFERENCES: 437.

Dendrobium eburneum "Rchb. f." ex Bateman. See *D. draconis* Rchb. f. REFERENCES: 25, 190, 216, 254, 430, 445, 454.

Dendrobium echinocarpum (Schlechter) J. J. Smith

AKA: *Cadetia echinocarpa* Schlechter. Schlechter (ref. 437) originally described the plant as *Cadetia crenulata*, but J. J. Smith (ref. 470) transferred it to the genus *Dendrobium*. However, the species name *D. crenulata* was already used for a different plant, so J. J. Smith assigned the name *D. echinocarpum*. *Cadetia* is again considered a valid genus by some botanists, so this plant may again be *Cadetia crenulata*.

ORIGIN/HABITAT: New Guinea. Plants grow at about 150 ft. (50 m) near Madang along the Maijen River.

CLIMATE: Station #94014, Madang, Papua New Guinea, Lat. 5.2°S, Long. 145.8°E, at 13 ft. (4 m). Record extreme temperatures are 98°F (37°C) and 62°F (17°C).

N/HEMISPHERE	JAN	FEB	MAR	APR	MAY	JUN	JUL	AUG	SEP	OCT	NOV	DEC
°F AVG MAX	83	83	85	85	85	85	85	85	85	87	87	84
°F AVG MIN	77	78	78	78	77	77	77	77	77	76	77	78
DIURNAL RANGE	6	5	7	7	8	8	8	8	8	11	10	6
RAIN/INCHES	4.0	3.4	3.2	8.5	11.2	11.1	10.1	11.3	9.4	11.3	10.5	6.7
HUMIDITY/%	88	87	86	86	86	86	86	85	85	87	88	89
BLOOM SEASON	*											
DAYS CLR	N/A											
RAIN/MM	102	86	81	216	284	282	257	287	239	287	267	170
°C AVG MAX	28.3	28.3	29.4	29.4	29.4	29.4	29.4	29.4	29.4	30.6	30.6	28.9
°C AVG MIN	25.0	25.6	25.6	25.6	25.0	25.0	25.0	25.0	25.0	24.4	25.0	25.6
DIURNAL RANGE	3.3	2.7	3.8	3.8	4.4	4.4	4.4	4.4	4.4	6.2	5.6	3.3
S/HEMISPHERE	JUL	AUG	SEP	OCT	NOV	DEC	JAN	FEB	MAR	APR	MAY	JUN

Cultural Recommendations

LIGHT: 2000–3000 fc. is suggested initially.

TEMPERATURES: Throughout the year, days average 83–87°F (28–31°C), and nights average 76–78°F (24–26°C), with a diurnal range of 5–11°F (3–6°C). The warmest highs, the coolest lows, and the greatest diurnal range occur in autumn.

HUMIDITY: 85–90% year-round.

WATER: Rainfall is heavy from spring into autumn, but conditions are somewhat drier for 3 months in winter. Cultivated plants should be kept evenly moist but not soggy.

FERTILIZER: ¼–½ recommended strength. A balanced fertilizer should be applied weekly to biweekly throughout the year.

REST PERIOD: Growing conditions should be maintained year-round. Growers report that plants from this habitat do poorly if they are subjected to temperatures below 55°F (13°C). In the habitat, rainfall decreases somewhat for 3 months in winter. Water should be reduced for cultivated plants, especially those grown in the dark, short-day conditions common in temperate-latitude winters. However, these plants should never be allowed to dry out completely. Fertilizer may be reduced or eliminated if plants are not actively growing. In the habitat, winter light may be slightly higher.

Dendrobium ecolle

GROWING MEDIA: Plants may be mounted on tree-fern or cork slabs if humidity is high and plants are watered at least once daily in summer. When plants are potted, any open, fast-draining medium may be used. Repotting may be done anytime new roots are growing.

MISCELLANEOUS NOTES: The bloom season shown in the climate table is based on reports from the habitat.

Plant and Flower Information

PLANT SIZE AND TYPE: A 2.8–5.0 in. (7–13 cm) sympodial epiphyte.

PSEUDOBULB: 0.8–2.8 in. (2–7 cm) long. The erect growths are connected to a very short rhizome.

LEAVES: 1. The erect leaves are 1.6–2.0 in. (4–5 cm) long and somewhat tongue-shaped.

INFLORESCENCE: Short.

FLOWERS: The flowers are 0.2 in. (0.5 cm) long. The blossoms are white with yellow markings on the hairy front lobe of the lip.

REFERENCES: 92, 221, 437, 472.

PHOTOS/DRAWINGS: 437.

Dendrobium ecolle J. J. Smith. Now considered a synonym of *Diplocaulobium ecolle* (J. J. Smith) Kränzlin. REFERENCES: 111, 219, 220, 254, 445, 468.

Dendrobium egertoniae Lindley. See *D. amoenum* Wallich ex Lindley. REFERENCES: 190, 216, 254, 317.

Dendrobium eitapense Schlechter. See *D. bracteosum* Rchb. f. REFERENCES: 221, 437, 445.

Dendrobium elatum Schlechter

ORIGIN/HABITAT: Northern Papua New Guinea. Plants grow on forest trees at about 2600 ft. (800 m) in the Torricelli Range.

CLIMATE: Station #94004, Wewak, Papua New Guinea, Lat. 3.6°N, Long. 143.7°E, at 16 ft. (5 m). Temperatures are calculated for an elevation of 2600 ft. (800 m), resulting in probable extremes of 89°F (32°C) and 53°F (12°C).

N/HEMISPHERE	JAN	FEB	MAR	APR	MAY	JUN	JUL	AUG	SEP	OCT	NOV	DEC
°F AVG MAX	79	79	79	79	79	79	78	77	78	79	79	79
°F AVG MIN	65	65	65	66	66	66	66	66	65	65	66	65
DIURNAL RANGE	14	14	14	13	13	13	12	11	13	14	13	14
RAIN/INCHES	7.6	4.8	5.3	10.0	13.3	14.5	12.1	11.9	14.9	16.9	15.1	10.8
HUMIDITY/%	80	79	79	78	79	81	82	82	81	82	81	80
BLOOM SEASON			*									
DAYS CLR	N/A											
RAIN/MM	193	122	135	254	338	368	307	302	378	429	384	274
°C AVG MAX	26.3	26.3	26.3	26.3	26.3	26.3	25.8	25.2	25.8	26.3	26.3	26.3
°C AVG MIN	18.6	18.6	18.6	19.1	19.1	19.1	19.1	19.1	18.6	18.6	19.1	18.6
DIURNAL RANGE	7.7	7.7	7.7	7.2	7.2	7.2	6.7	6.1	7.2	7.7	7.2	7.7
S/HEMISPHERE	JUL	AUG	SEP	OCT	NOV	DEC	JAN	FEB	MAR	APR	MAY	JUN

Cultural Recommendations

LIGHT: 2000–2500 fc.

TEMPERATURES: Throughout the year, days average 77–79°F (25–26°C), and nights average 65–66°F (19°C), with a diurnal range of 11–14°F (6–8°C).

HUMIDITY: Near 80% year-round.

WATER: Rainfall is heavy all year, but conditions are slightly drier for 1–2 months in winter. Cultivated plants should be kept evenly moist and never be allowed to dry out completely.

FERTILIZER: ¼–½ recommended strength. A balanced fertilizer should be applied weekly to biweekly throughout the year.

REST PERIOD: Growing conditions should be maintained year-round, but water should be reduced somewhat if plants are grown in the dark, short-day conditions common in temperate-latitude winters. Fertilizer should also be reduced until water is increased in spring.

GROWING MEDIA: A very open and fast-draining medium should be used with baskets or small pots. Repotting may be done anytime new roots are growing.

MISCELLANEOUS NOTES: The bloom season shown in the climate table is based on collection reports. Plants that produce flowers which last a single day commonly bloom several times during the year. Flowering usually occurs 7–14 days after a sudden 10°F (5°C) drop in daytime temperatures.

Plant and Flower Information

PLANT SIZE AND TYPE: A robust, 39 in. (100 cm) sympodial epiphyte.

PSEUDOBULB: 39 in. (100 cm) long. The unbranched canes are somewhat flattened, straight, and erect.

LEAVES: The oblong-lanceolate leaves are erect to spreading, 5–6 in. (12–16 cm) long, smooth, and nearly transparent.

INFLORESCENCE: Short. Inflorescences emerge from nodes along the sides of the stems.

FLOWERS: 2 per inflorescence. The flowers are 1.7 in. (4.3 cm) long and do not open fully. The golden yellow sepals and petals are long and pointed. The lip crest and column are orange-yellow. Blossoms last a single day.

REFERENCES: 221, 437, 445.

PHOTOS/DRAWINGS: 437.

Dendrobium elegans H. B. and K. Now considered a synonym of *Pleurothallis elegans* Lindley. REFERENCES: 45, 190, 216, 254.

Dendrobium elephantinum Finet

ORIGIN/HABITAT: Western Borneo. Plants were reported to have originated in Sarawak. Habitat location and elevation details are not available, so the following temperatures should be used with caution.

CLIMATE: Station #96413, Kuching, Sarawak, Lat. 1.5°N, Long. 110.3°E, at 85 ft. (26 m). Record extreme temperatures are 97°F (36°C) and 64°F (18°C).

N/HEMISPHERE	JAN	FEB	MAR	APR	MAY	JUN	JUL	AUG	SEP	OCT	NOV	DEC
°F AVG MAX	88	88	89	90	91	91	91	92	90	90	90	88
°F AVG MIN	72	72	72	72	72	73	72	72	72	72	72	72
DIURNAL RANGE	16	16	17	18	19	18	19	20	18	18	18	16
RAIN/INCHES	27.1	19.7	14.2	9.7	9.0	8.5	6.9	8.8	9.5	12.6	13.1	20.1
HUMIDITY/%	89	88	86	85	85	83	82	83	84	85	87	88
BLOOM SEASON							*					
DAYS CLR @ 7AM	1	0	1	2	3	2	4	1	2	1	1	1
DAYS CLR @ 1PM	0	0	0	0	1	1	1	0	0	0	0	0
RAIN/MM	688	500	361	246	229	216	175	224	241	320	333	511
°C AVG MAX	31.1	31.1	31.7	32.2	32.8	32.8	32.8	33.3	32.2	32.2	32.2	31.1
°C AVG MIN	22.2	22.2	22.2	22.2	22.2	22.8	22.2	22.2	22.2	22.2	22.2	22.2
DIURNAL RANGE	8.9	8.9	9.5	10.0	10.6	10.0	10.6	11.1	10.0	10.0	10.0	8.9
S/HEMISPHERE	JUL	AUG	SEP	OCT	NOV	DEC	JAN	FEB	MAR	APR	MAY	JUN

Cultural Recommendations

LIGHT: 2500–3000 fc.

TEMPERATURES: Throughout the year, days average 88–92°F (31–33°C), and nights average 72–73°F (22–23°C), with a diurnal range of 16–20°F (9–11°C). The diurnal range is unusually large for a habitat with so little seasonal variation.

HUMIDITY: 85–90% most of the year, dropping to near 80% for a short period in summer. High humidity and excellent air circulation are important for cultivated plants.

WATER: Rainfall is very heavy all year. Cultivated plants should be kept moist, with only slight drying allowed between waterings. Warm water may be beneficial.

FERTILIZER: ¼–½ recommended strength. A balanced fertilizer should be applied weekly to biweekly throughout the year.

REST PERIOD: Growing conditions should be maintained all year. The record low is only 10°F (6°C) below the average lows. Although rainfall remains heavy in winter, water may be reduced somewhat for cultivated plants, especially those grown in the dark, short-day conditions common in temperate latitudes. They should never be allowed to dry out completely, however. In the habitat, light is highest in winter.

GROWING MEDIA: Plants may be mounted on tree-fern or cork slabs if humidity is high and plants are watered at least once daily in summer. When plants are potted, any open, fast-draining medium may be used. They may be repotted anytime new roots are growing.

MISCELLANEOUS NOTES: The bloom season shown in the climate table is based on reports from the habitat.

Plant and Flower Information

PLANT SIZE AND TYPE: A 16–24 in. (40–60 cm) sympodial epiphyte.

PSEUDOBULB: 16–24 in. (40–60 cm) long.

LEAVES: Many. The distichous, oblong leaves are 3.2 in. (8 cm) long.

INFLORESCENCE: Short. Numerous inflorescence emerge laterally from nodes along the stem.

FLOWERS: 1–4 per inflorescence. The flowers are 0.9 in. (2.2 cm) across. Blossoms are milk-white with an orange lip. The ovate sepals are pointed. The petals are oblong-lanceolate with an uneven, ruffled margin. The 3-lobed lip has 3 raised, hairy lines.

REFERENCES: 118, 219, 254, 286, 295, 445.

Dendrobium eleutheroglossum Schlechter. See *D. closterium* Rchb. f. REFERENCES: 173, 220, 254, 432, 437.

Dendrobium ellipsophyllum T. Tang and F. T. Wang

AKA: *D. revolutum* as sometimes used not Lindley.

ORIGIN/HABITAT: Widespread throughout much of Southeast Asia. Plants grow near Moulmein, Burma, across much of Thailand, Cambodia, Laos, the region near Dalat, Vietnam, and Yunnan Province in southwest China. In Thailand, plants are found at 1000–3300 ft. (300–1000 m).

CLIMATE: Station #48353, Loei, Thailand, Lat. 17.5°N, Long. 101.5°E, at 817 ft. (249 m). Temperatures are calculated for an elevation of 2500 ft. (760 m), resulting in probable extremes of 100°F (38°C) and 28°F (−2°C).

N/HEMISPHERE	JAN	FEB	MAR	APR	MAY	JUN	JUL	AUG	SEP	OCT	NOV	DEC
°F AVG MAX	79	83	88	91	87	85	84	83	82	81	81	78
°F AVG MIN	46	52	59	64	67	68	68	68	67	63	58	50
DIURNAL RANGE	33	31	29	27	20	17	16	15	15	18	23	28
RAIN/INCHES	0.2	0.8	1.4	3.6	6.9	6.8	5.0	8.3	8.8	4.3	0.8	0.1
HUMIDITY/%	62	60	59	62	75	77	77	79	82	79	74	69
BLOOM SEASON	N/A											
DAYS CLR @ 7AM	1	1	1	2	1	0	1	0	0	1	1	1
DAYS CLR @ 1PM	22	14	8	5	2	0	0	1	1	5	11	15
RAIN/MM	5	20	36	91	175	173	127	211	224	109	20	3
°C AVG MAX	26.4	28.6	31.4	33.0	30.8	29.7	29.1	28.6	28.0	27.5	27.5	25.8
°C AVG MIN	8.0	11.4	15.2	18.0	19.7	20.2	20.2	20.2	19.7	17.5	14.7	10.2
DIURNAL RANGE	18.4	17.2	16.2	15.0	11.1	9.5	8.9	8.4	8.3	10.0	12.8	15.6
S/HEMISPHERE	JUL	AUG	SEP	OCT	NOV	DEC	JAN	FEB	MAR	APR	MAY	JUN

Cultural Recommendations

LIGHT: 1800–2500 fc. Diffused or barely dappled light is recommended. Direct sunlight should be avoided.

TEMPERATURES: Summer days average 83–85°F (29–30°C), and nights average 68°F (20°C), with a 15–17°F (8–10°C) diurnal range. In the habitat, the warmest season is spring. Days average 87–91°F (31–33°C), and nights average 59–67°F (15–20°C), with a diurnal range of 20–29°F (11–16°C). Probable extreme temperatures indicate a tolerance of both summer heat and winter cold.

HUMIDITY: 75–80% from late spring through autumn, dropping to near 60% in winter and early spring.

WATER: Rainfall is moderate to heavy from late spring through summer, but conditions are quite dry in winter. Cultivated plants should be watered often while actively growing, with only sight drying allowed between waterings. Water should be gradually reduced after new growths mature in autumn.

FERTILIZER: ¼–½ recommended strength, applied weekly. A high-nitrogen fertilizer is beneficial from spring to midsummer, but a fertilizer high in phosphates should be used in late summer and autumn.

REST PERIOD: Winter days average 78–83°F (26–29°C), and nights average 46–52°F (8–11°C), with a diurnal range of 28–33°F (16–18°C). While the record low temperatures in the habitat are below freezing, such extremes should be avoided for cultivated plants. Rainfall is low for 3–5 months in winter, but additional moisture is available from heavy dew, fog, and mist during most of the season. In cultivation, water should be reduced and the plants allowed to dry out between waterings. They should not remain completely dry for extended periods, however. Occasional early morning mistings between waterings may help keep the plants from becoming too dry. Fertilizer should be eliminated until water is increased in spring. In the habitat, light is highest in winter.

GROWING MEDIA: Plants may be mounted on tree-fern or cork slabs if humidity is high and plants are watered at least once daily in summer. When plants are potted, any open, fast-draining medium may be used. Repotting may be done anytime new roots are growing.

Plant and Flower Information

PLANT SIZE AND TYPE: A 12–20 in. (30–50 cm) sympodial epiphyte.

PSEUDOBULB: 12–20 in. (30–50 cm) long. The canelike pseudobulbs are ridged along their entire length. They turn brown with age.

LEAVES: 14–18 per growth. The bilobed leaves are elliptic and 1.2–1.6 in. (3–4 cm) long. They are distichous and twisted at the base so they all face one direction.

INFLORESCENCE: Short. Inflorescences arise opposite the leaves near the apex of leafy stems.

FLOWERS: 1 per inflorescence. The flowers are 0.8 in. (2 cm) across. The snow white sepals and petals are curled back. The gold lip, which is decorated with 3, reddish brown, longitudinal streaks, is curled lengthwise.

HYBRIDIZING NOTES: Johansen (ref. 239) indicates that plants are self-sterile and that flowers dropped 3–4 days after self-pollination.

REFERENCES: 228, 239, 454, 505.

PHOTOS/DRAWINGS: *454*.

Dendrobium elmeri Ames

ORIGIN/HABITAT: Widespread on Luzon Island in the Philippines. Plants grow at about 2700 ft. (820 m) in the provinces of Cagayan, Quezon, and Laguna. The orchids are also reported on Mindoro and Mindanao Islands.

CLIMATE: Station #98427, Manila, Philippines, Lat. 14.5°N, Long. 121.0°E, at 74 ft. (23 m). Temperatures are calculated for an elevation of 2450 ft. (750 m), resulting in probable extremes of 93°F (34°C) and 50°F (10°C).

Dendrobium elobatum

N/HEMISPHERE	JAN	FEB	MAR	APR	MAY	JUN	JUL	AUG	SEP	OCT	NOV	DEC
°F AVG MAX	78	80	83	85	83	83	80	79	80	80	79	78
°F AVG MIN	61	61	63	65	67	67	67	67	67	66	64	62
DIURNAL RANGE	17	19	20	20	18	16	13	12	13	14	15	16
RAIN/INCHES	0.9	0.5	0.7	1.3	5.1	10.0	17.0	16.6	14.0	7.6	5.7	2.6
HUMIDITY/%	77	73	70	68	71	81	84	86	87	84	82	79
BLOOM SEASON	*	*	*	*	*	*			*	*	*	*
DAYS CLR @ 8AM	6	9	14	14	10	3	2	1	1	6	7	6
DAYS CLR @ 2PM	3	6	10	10	8	2	1	1	0	2	2	3
RAIN/MM	23	13	18	33	130	254	432	422	356	193	145	66
°C AVG MAX	25.6	26.7	28.4	29.5	29.5	28.4	26.7	26.2	26.7	26.7	26.2	25.6
°C AVG MIN	16.2	16.2	17.3	18.4	19.5	19.5	19.5	19.5	19.5	19.0	17.8	16.7
DIURNAL RANGE	9.4	10.5	11.1	11.1	10.0	8.9	7.2	6.7	7.2	7.7	8.4	8.9
S/HEMISPHERE	JUL	AUG	SEP	OCT	NOV	DEC	JAN	FEB	MAR	APR	MAY	JUN

Cultural Recommendations

LIGHT: 1800–3000 fc. In the habitat, light is highest in the morning during most of the year.

TEMPERATURES: Throughout the year, days average 78–85°F (26–30°C), and nights average 61–67°F (16–20°C), with a diurnal range of 12–20°F (7–11°C).

HUMIDITY: 80–85% in summer and autumn, dropping to about 70% in winter and spring.

WATER: Rainfall is heavy from late spring through autumn, but conditions are dry for 3–4 months in winter. Cultivated plants should be kept moist while actively growing, but water should be gradually reduced in late autumn.

FERTILIZER: ¼–½ recommended strength, applied weekly. A high-nitrogen fertilizer is beneficial from spring to midsummer, but a fertilizer high in phosphates should be used in late summer and autumn.

REST PERIOD: Growing temperatures should be maintained all year. Rainfall is low for 3–4 months in winter, but additional moisture is available from frequent heavy dew. In cultivation, water should be reduced and the plants allowed to dry out between waterings. They should not remain dry for extended periods, however. Fertilizer should also be reduced or eliminated anytime water is reduced. In the habitat, light is highest in winter.

GROWING MEDIA: Mounting plants on tree-fern slabs accommodates their pendent growth habit, but humidity must be high and the plants need daily watering in summer. Plants may be potted in hanging pots or baskets filled with any open, fast-draining medium. Repotting is best done after flowering when new root growth begins in early spring.

MISCELLANEOUS NOTES: The bloom season shown in the climate table is based on collection reports.

Plant and Flower Information

PLANT SIZE AND TYPE: An 8–24 in. (20–60 cm) sympodial epiphyte.

PSEUDOBULB: 6–22 in. (15–56 cm) long. The pseudobulb is pendulous, stemlike, and flexible.

LEAVES: Many. The dark green leaves are linear-lanceolate, feathery, and 2.0–2.4 in. (5–6 cm) long. They are arranged in 2 rows along the stem.

INFLORESCENCE: 0.6 in. (1.5 cm) long. Many inflorescences arise laterally from bracts near the apex of the stem.

FLOWERS: 1 per inflorescence. The very small flowers are 0.2 in. (0.5 cm) across. The rigid blossoms have an oblong dorsal sepal, triangular lateral sepals, and smaller, oblong petals. The lip is broad above the middle with a minutely hairy margin and a warty tip.

REFERENCES: 12, 98, 222, 296, 536.

Dendrobium elobatum Rupp. See *D. discolor* Lindley. REFERENCES: 67, 84, 105, 228, 533.

Dendrobium elongaticolle Schlechter. Now considered a synonym of *Diplocaulobium elongaticolle* (Schlechter) A. Hawkes. REFERENCES: 223, 228, 441.

Dendrobium elongatum (Blume) Lindley. J. J. Smith (ref. 469) considered this species to be a probable synonym of *Dendrobium cymbidioides* (Blume) Lindley, which is now considered a synonym of *Epigeneium cymbidioides* (Blume) Summerhayes. Hunt and Summerhayes (ref. 213) included *Epigeneium cymbidioides* as a synonym of *Epigeneium elongatum* (Blume) Summerhayes. However, Comber (ref. 75) includes *Desmotrichum elongatum* Blume [*Dendrobium elongatum* (Blume) Lindley] and *Dendrobium elongatum* Lindley var. *orientale* J. J. Smith as synonyms of *Epigeneium triflorum* (Blume) Summerhayes. REFERENCES: 25, 75, 213, 216, 229, 254, 277, 310, 469, 499.

Dendrobium elongatum A. Cunningham. See *D. gracilicaule* F. Mueller not Kränzlin and discussion at *D. macropus* (Endl.) Rchb. f. ex Lindley. REFERENCES: 67, 105, 216, 254, 533.

Dendrobium emarginatum J. W. Moore

ORIGIN/HABITAT: Society Islands. Near Raiatea in the Avera Valley, plants grow on tree branches at about 800 ft. (250 m).

CLIMATE: Station #91938, Tahiti, Society Islands, Lat. 17.5°S, Long. 149.6°W, at 7 ft. (2 m). Temperatures are calculated for an elevation of 800 ft. (240 m), resulting in probable extremes of 90°F (32°C) and 58°F (15°C).

N/HEMISPHERE	JAN	FEB	MAR	APR	MAY	JUN	JUL	AUG	SEP	OCT	NOV	DEC
°F AVG MAX	83	83	83	84	85	85	86	86	86	86	84	83
°F AVG MIN	65	65	66	67	68	69	69	69	69	69	67	66
DIURNAL RANGE	18	18	17	17	17	16	17	17	17	17	17	17
RAIN/INCHES	2.6	1.9	2.3	3.4	6.5	11.9	13.2	11.5	6.5	6.8	4.9	3.2
HUMIDITY/%	80	81	79	78	79	80	80	80	81	82	81	82
BLOOM SEASON						*						
DAYS CLE @ 2PM	13	11	9	8	2	3	4	3	4	6	8	11
RAIN/MM	66	48	58	86	165	302	335	292	165	173	124	81
°C AVG MAX	28.5	28.5	28.5	29.1	29.7	29.7	30.2	30.2	30.2	30.2	29.1	28.5
°C AVG MIN	18.5	18.5	19.1	19.7	20.2	20.8	20.8	20.8	20.8	20.8	19.7	19.1
DIURNAL RANGE	10.0	10.0	9.4	9.4	9.5	8.9	9.4	9.4	9.4	9.4	9.4	9.4
S/HEMISPHERE	JUL	AUG	SEP	OCT	NOV	DEC	JAN	FEB	MAR	APR	MAY	JUN

Cultural Recommendations

LIGHT: 2000–3000 fc.

TEMPERATURES: Throughout the year, days average 83–86°F (29–30°C), and nights average 65–69°F (19–21°C), with a diurnal range of 16–18°F (9–10°C).

HUMIDITY: Near 80% year-round.

WATER: Rainfall is heavy from spring into autumn, with a 2–3 month semi-dry period in winter. Cultivated plants should be kept evenly moist while actively growing, but water should be gradually reduced in autumn.

FERTILIZER: ¼–½ recommended strength. A balanced fertilizer should be applied weekly to biweekly throughout the year.

REST PERIOD: Growing conditions should be maintained all year. In the habitat, rainfall is less in winter, but additional moisture is available from frequent heavy dew. Water should be reduced for cultivated plants in winter. They should dry out slightly between waterings but should not remain dry for long periods. Fertilizer should be reduced or eliminated anytime water is reduced. In the habitat, light is highest in winter.

GROWING MEDIA: Plants may be mounted on tree-fern or cork slabs or potted in small pots filled with any open, fast-draining medium. Repotting may be done anytime new roots are growing.

MISCELLANEOUS NOTES: The bloom season shown in the climate table is based on reports from the habitat.

Plant and Flower Information

PLANT SIZE AND TYPE: A 35 in. (90 cm) sympodial epiphyte.

PSEUDOBULB: 35 in. (90 cm) long. The stems have dark streaks. The internodes are 0.4–1.0 in. (1.0–2.5 cm) long.

LEAVES: Many. The leaves, which are 2.8 in. (7 cm) long, are notched not pointed at the apex.

INFLORESCENCE: Short. Racemes emerge through the leaf sheaths from nodes along the stem.

FLOWERS: 2 per inflorescence. The flowers are 0.8–1.2 in. (2–3 cm) long. Sepals and petals are lanceolate. The spur is short. The small lip has a triangular midlobe that is lacerated and fringed. Flower color was not included in the original description.

REFERENCES: 225, 315.

Dendrobium endertii J. J. Smith

ORIGIN/HABITAT: Central eastern Borneo. Plants grow epiphytically in primeval forests along the upper Mahakam River at 3300–3600 ft. (1000–1100 m).

CLIMATE: Station #96633, Balikpapan, Borneo, Indonesia, Lat. 1.3°S, Long. 116.9°E, at 10 ft. (3 m). Temperatures are calculated for an elevation of 3500 ft. (1070 m), resulting in probable extremes of 80°F (27°C) and 48°F (9°C).

N/HEMISPHERE	JAN	FEB	MAR	APR	MAY	JUN	JUL	AUG	SEP	OCT	NOV	DEC
°F AVG MAX	71	72	72	73	73	73	73	74	74	73	73	72
°F AVG MIN	61	62	62	62	61	61	61	61	61	61	62	62
DIURNAL RANGE	10	10	10	11	12	12	12	13	13	12	11	10
RAIN/INCHES	7.1	6.4	5.5	5.2	6.6	8.1	7.9	8.9	9.1	8.2	9.1	7.6
HUMIDITY/%	82	80	77	78	80	79	82	81	81	82	83	82
BLOOM SEASON			*	*								
DAYS CLR @ 8AM	4	2	3	3	3	3	2	3	4	4	2	5
DAYS CLR @ 2PM	6	4	5	5	3	1	2	1	2	3	4	5
RAIN/MM	180	163	140	132	168	206	201	226	231	208	231	193
°C AVG MAX	21.9	22.5	22.5	23.0	23.0	23.0	23.0	23.6	23.6	23.0	23.0	22.5
°C AVG MIN	16.4	16.9	16.9	16.9	16.4	16.4	16.4	16.4	16.4	16.4	16.9	16.9
DIURNAL RANGE	5.5	5.6	5.6	6.1	6.6	6.6	6.6	7.2	7.2	6.6	6.1	5.6
S/HEMISPHERE	JUL	AUG	SEP	OCT	NOV	DEC	JAN	FEB	MAR	APR	MAY	JUN

Cultural Recommendations

LIGHT: 1800–2500 fc.

TEMPERATURES: Throughout the year, days average 71–74°F (22–24°C), and nights average 61–62°F (16–17°C), with a diurnal range of 10–13°F (6–7°C).

HUMIDITY: Near 80% year-round.

WATER: Rainfall is heavy all year. Cultivated plants should be kept moist.

FERTILIZER: ¼–½ recommended strength. A balanced fertilizer should be applied weekly to biweekly throughout the year.

REST PERIOD: Growing conditions should be maintained year-round. Water and fertilizer should be reduced somewhat in winter, especially for plants cultivated in the dark, short-day conditions common in temperate latitudes. Plants should never be allowed to dry out completely, however. In the habitat, seasonal light variation is minor.

GROWING MEDIA: Plants may be mounted on tree-fern or cork slabs or potted in small pots filled with any open, fast-draining medium. Repotting may be done anytime new roots are growing.

MISCELLANEOUS NOTES: The bloom season shown in the climate table is based on reports from the habitat. *D. endertii* grows at slightly lower elevations than *D. corallorhizon* J. J. Smith. *D. endertii* was described in 1931 in *Bul. Jard. Bot. Buit.* 3rd sér. 11:138.

Plant and Flower Information

PLANT SIZE AND TYPE: A 22 in. (55 cm) sympodial epiphyte.

PSEUDOBULB: 22 in. (55 cm) long. The stems do not branch.

LEAVES: Many. The obliquely lanceolate leaves are about 4 in. (10 cm) long, pointed, and twisted at the base.

INFLORESCENCE: 1 in. (2.5 cm) long. Inflorescences are borne at nodes along the stem.

FLOWERS: 7–9 per inflorescence. The flowers are 1.5 in. (3.8 cm) long. The white sepals and petals have reddish violet in the center and on the tip of the spur. The violet color becomes brick red with age. The lip is very light yellow on the inside.

REFERENCES: 225, 286.

Dendrobium × *endocharis* Rchb. f. An artificial hybrid between *D. heterocarpum* Wallich ex Lindley and *D. moniliforme* (Linn.) Swartz. REFERENCES: 254, 541, 570.

Dendrobium engae T. M. Reeve

ORIGIN/HABITAT: Widespread in the highlands of Papua New Guinea. Plants grow high on large branches of *Nothofagus* (Southern Beech) trees in mountain forests at 6550–8850 ft. (2000–2700 m). They are reported in the provinces of Enga, Chimbu, Eastern Highlands, Western Highlands, and Morobe in the Bismarck Range, but they are becoming rare.

CLIMATE: Botanical garden records, Laiagam, Papua New Guinea, Lat. 5.5°S, Long. 143.5°E, at 7218 ft. (2200 m). Record extreme temperatures are 91°F (33°C) and 32°F (0°C).

N/HEMISPHERE	JAN	FEB	MAR	APR	MAY	JUN	JUL	AUG	SEP	OCT	NOV	DEC
°F AVG MAX	76	77	78	76	78	78	82	77	76	78	78	76
°F AVG MIN	55	54	55	55	56	56	55	56	58	57	56	56
DIURNAL RANGE	21	23	23	21	22	22	27	21	18	21	22	20
RAIN/INCHES	4.0	4.8	6.1	7.8	8.5	9.1	8.4	9.6	9.5	8.9	6.3	4.0
HUMIDITY/%	N/A											
BLOOM SEASON	*					*						
DAYS CLR	N/A											
RAIN/MM	102	121	154	198	217	230	213	243	241	227	159	102
°C AVG MAX	24.4	25.0	25.6	24.4	25.6	25.6	27.8	25.0	24.4	25.6	25.6	24.4
°C AVG MIN	12.8	12.2	12.8	12.8	13.3	13.3	12.8	13.3	14.4	13.9	13.3	13.3
DIURNAL RANGE	11.6	12.8	12.8	11.6	12.3	12.3	15.0	11.7	10.0	11.7	12.3	11.1
S/HEMISPHERE	JUL	AUG	SEP	OCT	NOV	DEC	JAN	FEB	MAR	APR	MAY	JUN

Cultural Recommendations

LIGHT: 2000–3000 fc.

TEMPERATURES: Throughout the year, days average 76–82°F (24–28°C), and nights average 54–58°F (12–14°C), with a diurnal range of 18–27°F (10–15°C).

HUMIDITY: Information is not available for this location. However, records from nearby stations indicate that humidity probably averages near 80% year-round.

WATER: Rainfall is heavy throughout the year, but conditions are slightly drier for 3–4 months in winter. Cultivated plants should be kept moist.

FERTILIZER: ¼–½ recommended strength. A balanced fertilizer should be applied weekly to biweekly throughout the year.

REST PERIOD: Growing conditions should be maintained all year. Water and fertilizer should be reduced somewhat in winter, especially when plants are grown in the dark, short-day conditions common in temperate latitudes. Plants should dry slightly between waterings, but they should never be allowed to dry out completely. Water and fertilizer should be gradually increased when plants begin growing in spring.

GROWING MEDIA: Plants are usually grown in pots or baskets, but they may be mounted on tree-fern or cork slabs if humidity is high and they are watered at least once daily in summer. When plants are potted, any open, fast-draining medium may be used. Growers report that *D. engae* is extremely sensitive to poor drainage. Repotting may be done anytime new roots are growing.

MISCELLANEOUS NOTES: The bloom season shown in the climate table is based on cultivation records.

Plant and Flower Information

PLANT SIZE AND TYPE: A robust, 20 in. (50 cm) sympodial epiphyte.

PSEUDOBULB: 20 in. (50 cm) long. The yellowish pseudobulbs consist of about 10 nodes. They are stout and erect.

LEAVES: 3–5. The spreading to suberect leaves are held at the apex of each growth. They are 2–8 in. (5–21 cm) long, thick, leathery, oblong, glossy, dark green, and rounded at the tip.

INFLORESCENCE: 10 in. (25 cm) long. The inflorescence arises from the apex of the pseudobulb.

FLOWERS: 3–18 per inflorescence. Flowers are 2.4–3.2 in. (6–8 cm) across and open widely. They have a strong, sweet fragrance that is described as distinctive. Segments may be pure white though the sepals eventually turn yellow. In some clones, the sepals are creamy white with greenish white petals and a greenish yellow lip. The recurved lip is heavily spotted with maroon or black on the midlobe. The sidelobes are decorated with maroon veins. Blossoms last about 8 weeks.

HYBRIDIZING NOTES: Chromosome count is 2n = 36 (ref. 152, 153, 154, 188, 273).

REFERENCES: 83, 95, 152, 153, 154, 179, 188, 233, 243, 273, 371, 379, 526, 549, 550, 554.

PHOTOS/DRAWINGS: *83, 95, 308, 371, 379, 549, 554.*

Dendrobium eoum Ridley. See *D. cumulatum* Lindley. REFERENCES: 254, 395, 454.

Dendrobium ephemerum J. J. Smith

AKA: J. J. Smith (ref. 479) includes *Angraecum album minus* Rumph. and *Dendrobium papilioniferum* var. *ephemerum* J. J. Smith.

ORIGIN/HABITAT: The Molucca Islands. Collectors reported that plants were abundant in northern Seram, and they have also been found in the southern and eastern parts of the island between sea level and 350 ft. (0–100 m). Near Leksula on Buru Island, however, plants were found at 2600 ft. (800 m).

CLIMATE: Station #49620, Amahai, Seram, Indonesia, Lat. 3.3°S, Long. 128.9°E, at 10 ft. (3 m). Record extreme temperatures are 96°F (36°C) and 66°F (19°C).

N/HEMISPHERE	JAN	FEB	MAR	APR	MAY	JUN	JUL	AUG	SEP	OCT	NOV	DEC
°F AVG MAX	81	81	83	85	88	88	88	88	88	86	84	82
°F AVG MIN	74	74	74	74	75	76	76	76	76	76	75	74
DIURNAL RANGE	7	7	9	11	13	12	12	12	12	10	9	8
RAIN/INCHES	23.7	15.8	9.5	6.1	4.5	5.2	5.0	4.7	5.3	11.0	20.3	25.1
HUMIDITY/%	83	82	81	80	79	78	78	77	79	82	83	84
BLOOM SEASON			*				*					
DAYS CLR @ 9AM	1	1	1	6	7	4	3	5	5	5	3	3
DAYS CLR @ 3PM	1	1	2	5	6	1	1	5	1	2	3	1	3
RAIN/MM	602	401	241	155	114	132	127	119	135	279	516	638
°C AVG MAX	27.2	27.2	28.3	29.4	31.1	31.1	31.1	31.1	31.1	30.0	28.9	27.8
°C AVG MIN	23.3	23.3	23.3	23.3	23.9	24.4	24.4	24.4	24.4	24.4	23.9	23.3
DIURNAL RANGE	3.9	3.9	5.0	6.1	7.2	6.7	6.7	6.7	6.7	5.6	5.0	4.5
S/HEMISPHERE	JUL	AUG	SEP	OCT	NOV	DEC	JAN	FEB	MAR	APR	MAY	JUN

Cultural Recommendations

LIGHT: 2000–3000 fc. Light is highest in the morning. Little is known about the plant's microclimate, but clear days are uncommon.

TEMPERATURES: Throughout the year, days average 81–88°F (27–31°C), and nights average 74–76°F (23–24°C), with a diurnal range of 7–13°F (4–7°C).

HUMIDITY: 75–80% most of the year, increasing to near 85% in winter.

WATER: Rainfall is moderate to heavy all year with a slightly drier season in spring and summer. Plants should be kept moist with only slight drying allowed between waterings.

FERTILIZER: ¼–½ recommended strength. A balanced fertilizer should be applied weekly to biweekly throughout the year.

REST PERIOD: Growing conditions should be maintained all year. In the habitat, winter is the wettest season, but water should not be increased for cultivated plants. In fact, it should be reduced for plants grown in the dark, short-day conditions common in temperate-latitude winters. Plants should never be allowed to dry out completely, however. Fertilizer should be reduced or eliminated anytime water is reduced. In the habitat, light is highest in early spring.

GROWING MEDIA: Plants may be mounted on tree-fern or cork slabs if humidity is high and plants are watered at least once daily in summer. When plants are potted, any open, fast-draining medium may be used. They may be repotted anytime new roots are growing.

MISCELLANEOUS NOTES: The bloom season shown in the climate table is based on reports from the habitat. Plants that produce flowers which last a single day commonly bloom several times during the year. Flowering usually occurs 7–14 days after a sudden 10°F (5°C) drop in daytime temperatures.

Plant and Flower Information

PLANT SIZE AND TYPE: A 47 in. (120 cm) sympodial epiphyte which has the growth habit of *D. crumenatum* Swartz.

PSEUDOBULB: 47 in. (120 cm) long.

LEAVES: Many. The fleshy, 2-lobed leaves are 4.3 in. (11 cm) long.

INFLORESCENCE: Very short inflorescences emerge from nodes along the stem.

FLOWERS: The fragrant flowers are 1.6 in. (4 cm) across. The normally white blossoms are occasionally yellow with an orange streak on the lip. They last a single day. Sepals and petals are oblong. The 3-lobed lip has a nearly round, warty midlobe. The midlobe, which has 3 yellow keels, is toothed, ruffled, and reflexed along the margin. The sidelobes are marked with purple veins.

REFERENCES: 25, 222, 468, 479.

Dendrobium epidendropsis Kränzlin

ORIGIN/HABITAT: The Philippines Islands, Japan, and Java. In the Philippines, plants grow on tree trunks on the forested slopes of Luzon Island in Bataan, Benguet, and Rizal provinces at about 3000 ft. (910 m).

CLIMATE: Station #98426, Cubi Point NAS, Philippines, Lat. 14.8°N, Long. 120.3°E, at 55 ft. (17 m). Temperatures are calculated for an elevation of 3000 ft. (910 m), resulting in probable extremes of 91°F (33°C) and 52°F (11°C).

N/HEMISPHERE	JAN	FEB	MAR	APR	MAY	JUN	JUL	AUG	SEP	OCT	NOV	DEC
°F AVG MAX	77	78	81	83	82	78	77	76	76	79	78	77
°F AVG MIN	62	62	64	66	67	66	65	65	65	65	65	63
DIURNAL RANGE	15	16	17	17	15	12	12	11	11	14	13	14
RAIN/INCHES	0.1	0.1	0.1	0.8	7.1	25.1	30.5	33.7	29.5	7.8	2.4	0.8
HUMIDITY/%	68	67	68	67	72	82	84	86	86	80	74	71
BLOOM SEASON			*						*	*	*	
DAYS CLR @ 8AM	7	7	8	10	2	1	0	0	4	3	4
DAYS CLR @ 2PM	4	3	4	4	3	1	0	0	0	2	1	2
RAIN/MM	3	3	3	20	180	638	775	856	749	198	61	20
°C AVG MAX	25.2	25.7	27.4	28.5	27.9	25.7	25.2	24.6	24.6	26.3	25.7	25.2
°C AVG MIN	16.8	16.8	17.9	19.0	19.6	19.0	18.5	18.5	18.5	18.5	18.5	17.4
DIURNAL RANGE	8.4	8.9	9.5	9.5	8.3	6.7	6.7	6.1	6.1	7.8	7.2	7.8
S/HEMISPHERE	JUL	AUG	SEP	OCT	NOV	DEC	JAN	FEB	MAR	APR	MAY	JUN

Cultural Recommendations

LIGHT: 2500–3500 fc. In addition to bright, diffused light, brisk air movement should be provided.

TEMPERATURES: Summer days average 76–78°F (25–26°C), and nights average 65–66°F (19°C), with a diurnal range of 11–12°F (6–7°C). The warmest weather occurs in spring before the start of the rainy season. Days average 81–83°F (27–29°C), and nights average 64–67°F (18–20°C), with a diurnal range of 15–17°F (8–10°C).

HUMIDITY: 80–85% in summer and early autumn, dropping to 65–70% in winter and spring.

WATER: Rainfall is very heavy from late spring into autumn, but conditions are very dry in winter. Cultivated plants should be kept evenly moist in summer and autumn, but water should be gradually reduced in late autumn.

FERTILIZER: ¼–½ recommended strength, applied weekly. A high-nitrogen fertilizer is beneficial from spring to midsummer, but a fertilizer high in phosphates should be used in late summer and autumn.

REST PERIOD: Winter days average 77–78°F (25–26°C), and nights average 62–63°F (17°C), with a diurnal range of 14–16°F (8–9°C). In the habitat, rainfall is low for 3–5 months in winter; but high humidity and nightly cooling result in heavy deposits of dew during most of the period. In cultivation, water should be reduced and the plants allowed to dry out between waterings. They should not remain completely dry for extended periods, however. Occasional early morning mistings between waterings may be beneficial, especially on bright, sunny days. Fertilizer should reduced or eliminated. In the habitat, light is highest in winter and spring.

GROWING MEDIA: Plants may be mounted on tree-fern or cork slabs if humidity is high and plants are watered at least once daily in summer. When plants are potted, any open, fast-draining medium may be used. Repotting is best done in early spring when new roots are growing.

MISCELLANEOUS NOTES: The bloom season shown in the climate table is based on collection reports. Cultivation records show that plants bloom in autumn and winter.

Plant and Flower Information

PLANT SIZE AND TYPE: A 24 in. (60 cm) sympodial epiphyte.

PSEUDOBULB: 24 in. (60 cm) long. The slender stems are canelike.

LEAVES: The leaves are oblong-lanceolate, leathery, and 3 in. (8 cm) long.

INFLORESCENCE: 4 in. (10 cm) long. The slender, pendulous raceme emerges near the apex of the stem.

FLOWERS: 15 per inflorescence. The flowers are 2.5 in. (6.4 cm) across. They are waxy, glossy, and showy. The sepals are greenish yellow. Petals are pale green with 3–4 brown stripes from the base to the tip. The large, bright lip is pale green to ochre yellow with a pink-purple tinge. The blossoms are sometimes fragrant.

REFERENCES: 12, 179, 190, 220, 254, 296, 536.

PHOTOS/DRAWINGS: 536.

Dendrobium epiphedum Lindley.
Status unknown. This name was included in lists of chromosome counts (ref. 150, 542). We found no other use of this name. REFERENCES: 150, 542.

Dendrobium equitans Kränzlin

AKA: Valmayor (ref. 536) includes *D. batanense* Ames and Quisumbing. Merrill (ref. 296) indicates that *D. equitans* Kränzlin is a synonym of *D. aporoides* (Lindley) Merrill, which is now considered a synonym of *Eria aporoides* Lindley. He further states, however, that *D. equitans* is known only from Formosa. We found no recent use of this synonymy, so the species is included. This species is considered by Chen and Tang (ref. 61), Liu (ref. 279), Tsi (ref. 528) and Su (ref. 497) to be a synonym of *D. ventricosum* Kränzlin.

ORIGIN/HABITAT: The Philippines Islands. Plants grow in the Batan Island group north of Luzon and on Orchid Island (Lanyu) off the southeast coast of Taiwan at about 1950 ft. (600 m). They are usually found in thickets on forested slopes, often on the branches of *Ficus retusa* trees, frequently mixed with *Dendrobium miyakei*, *Dendrochilum formosanum*, and *Appendicula formosana*.

CLIMATE: Station #98135, Basco, Philippines, Lat. 20.5°N, Long. 122.0°E, at 36 ft. (11 m). Temperatures are calculated for an elevation of 2000 ft. (610 m), resulting in probable extremes of 92°F (33°C) and 47°F (8°C).

N/HEMISPHERE	JAN	FEB	MAR	APR	MAY	JUN	JUL	AUG	SEP	OCT	NOV	DEC
°F AVG MAX	70	72	75	78	82	82	82	82	81	78	75	72
°F AVG MIN	61	63	65	69	71	72	72	71	70	69	67	64
DIURNAL RANGE	9	9	10	9	11	10	10	11	11	9	8	8
RAIN/INCHES	7.9	5.9	4.9	3.8	5.0	11.8	10.3	16.2	14.6	11.8	11.6	11.0
HUMIDITY/%	82	81	81	82	82	84	83	84	84	81	81	81
BLOOM SEASON	*		*		*		*					*
DAYS CLR @ 8AM	1	1	3	2	1	1	1	2	1	1	1	
DAYS CLR @ 2PM	1	2	3	2	2	0	1	0	1	1	1	
RAIN/MM	201	150	124	97	127	300	262	411	371	300	295	279
°C AVG MAX	20.8	22.0	23.6	25.3	27.5	27.5	27.5	27.5	27.0	25.3	23.6	22.0
°C AVG MIN	15.8	17.0	18.1	20.3	21.4	22.0	22.0	21.4	20.8	20.3	19.2	17.5
DIURNAL RANGE	5.0	5.0	5.5	5.0	6.1	5.5	5.5	6.1	6.2	5.0	4.4	4.5
S/HEMISPHERE	JUL	AUG	SEP	OCT	NOV	DEC	JAN	FEB	MAR	APR	MAY	JUN

Cultural Recommendations

LIGHT: 2500–3500 fc. In the usually overcast habitat, *D. equitans* normally grows in bright conditions. Brisk air movement should be maintained at all times.

TEMPERATURES: Summer days average 82°F (28°C), and nights average 71–72°F (21–22°C), with a diurnal range of 10–11°F (6°C).

HUMIDITY: 80–85% year-round.

WATER: Rainfall is moderate to heavy all year, with a 1–2 month slightly drier period in spring. Cultivated plants should be kept moist, with only slight drying allowed between waterings.

FERTILIZER: ¼–½ recommended strength. A balanced fertilizer should be applied weekly to biweekly throughout the year.

REST PERIOD: Winter days average 70–75°F (21–24°C), and nights average 61–65°F (16–18°C), with a diurnal range of 8–10°F (5–6°C). Plants may adjust to cooler winters but are likely to be healthiest in a warmer environment. Growers report that other plants from this habitat survive winter lows of 35°F (2°C) providing they are kept dry at temperatures below 45°F (7°C). Water and fertilizer should be reduced slightly for 1–2 months in early spring, but the plants should not be allowed to dry out completely.

GROWING MEDIA: Plants may be mounted on tree-fern or cork slabs if humidity is high and plants are watered at least once daily in summer. When plants are potted, any open, fast-draining medium may be used. Repotting is best done in early spring when new roots are growing.

MISCELLANEOUS NOTES: The bloom season shown in the climate table is based on cultivation records. These free-flowering plants often bloom throughout the year, and plants cultivated in Manila bloom every month of the year, sometimes twice a month.

Plant and Flower Information

PLANT SIZE AND TYPE: A 5–12 in. (13–30 cm) sympodial epiphyte.

PSEUDOBULB: 3.5–9.5 in. (9–24 cm) long. The angled stems consist of 2–3 internodes. They are erect and densely clustered.

LEAVES: Many. The overlapping leaves are arranged in 2 rows. They are

Dendrobium erectifolium

1.6–2.4 in. (4–6 cm) long, linear-lanceolate, flattened lengthwise, and pointed at the tip.

INFLORESCENCE: Blossoms are borne at nodes along the leafless, apical portion of the stem. Individual flowers open in succession.

FLOWERS: 1 per inflorescence. Very fragrant, the white flowers are 1 in. (2.5 cm) across and do not open fully. The deeply fringed lip is decorated with purple lines on the triangular sidelobes and a deep orange-yellow stain at the base of the throat.

HYBRIDIZING NOTES: Chromosome count is n = 19 (ref. 151) and 2n = 38 (ref. 151) as *D. batanense* var. *superbum* Hort. and 2n = 38 as *D. batanense* (ref. 152, 187) and *D. equitans* (ref. 151, 154, 187, 188).

REFERENCES: 61, 62, 151, 152, 154, 179, 187, 188, 192, 208, 220, 243, 254, 274, 279, 296, 373, 497, 528, 536.

PHOTOS/DRAWINGS: 62, 254, *274.*, 373.

Dendrobium erectifolium J. J. Smith

ORIGIN/HABITAT: Irian Jaya (western New Guinea). Plants grow on trees in primary forests of Mt. Goliath, along the Noord River south of Geluks Hill, on the summit of Resi-Rüken at about 2950 ft. (900 m), along the upper Digul River, and on Nepenthes Hill.

CLIMATE: Station #97876, Tanahmerah, Irian Jaya, Lat. 6.1°S, Long. 140.3°E, at 75 ft. (23 m). Temperatures are calculated for an elevation of 2950 ft. (900 m), resulting in probable extremes of 89°F (31°C) and 55°F (13°C).

N/HEMISPHERE	JAN	FEB	MAR	APR	MAY	JUN	JUL	AUG	SEP	OCT	NOV	DEC
°F AVG MAX	75	76	78	81	82	81	81	80	81	80	78	76
°F AVG MIN	63	62	62	63	64	65	64	64	64	64	65	64
DIURNAL RANGE	12	14	16	18	18	16	17	16	17	16	13	12
RAIN/INCHES	11.5	12.1	14.7	13.2	14.4	15.9	14.5	15.8	17.4	17.3	15.5	11.9
HUMIDITY/%	N/A											
BLOOM SEASON	*	*										*
DAYS CLR	N/A											
RAIN/MM	292	307	373	335	366	404	368	401	442	439	394	302
°C AVG MAX	23.6	24.2	25.3	27.0	27.5	27.0	27.0	26.4	27.0	26.4	25.3	24.2
°C AVG MIN	17.0	16.4	16.4	17.0	17.5	18.1	17.5	17.5	17.5	17.5	18.1	17.5
DIURNAL RANGE	6.6	7.8	8.9	10.0	10.0	8.9	9.5	8.9	9.5	8.9	7.2	6.7
S/HEMISPHERE	JUL	AUG	SEP	OCT	NOV	DEC	JAN	FEB	MAR	APR	MAY	JUN

Cultural Recommendations

LIGHT: 2000–3000 fc.

TEMPERATURES: Throughout the year, days average 75–82°F (24–28°C), and nights average 62–65°F (16–18°C), with a diurnal range of 12–18°F (7–10°C).

HUMIDITY: Information is not available for this location. However, records from nearby locations indicate that humidity probably averages near 85% year-round.

WATER: Rainfall is heavy all year. Cultivated plants should be kept evenly moist, with little if any drying allowed between waterings. During very hot summer weather, plants may be misted several times a day, but the leaves should always be dry before evening. Brisk air movement should be maintained at all times.

FERTILIZER: ¼–½ recommended strength. A balanced fertilizer should be applied weekly to biweekly throughout the year.

REST PERIOD: Growing conditions should be maintained year-round. Water and fertilizer might be reduced slightly in winter for plants grown in the dark, short-day conditions common in temperate latitudes. They should never be allowed to dry out completely, however.

GROWING MEDIA: Plants must be kept moist, so they may be easier to manage when potted. Fir bark or any open, fast-draining medium may be used. Repotting may be done anytime new roots are growing.

MISCELLANEOUS NOTES: The bloom season shown in the climate table is based on reports from the habitat.

Plant and Flower Information

PLANT SIZE AND TYPE: An 8–16 in. (20–40 cm) sympodial epiphyte.

PSEUDOBULB: 8–16 in. (20–40 cm) long. The slender, flattened stems arise from a very short rhizome.

LEAVES: Many. The erect, linear leaves are 2.4–4.0 in. (6–10 cm) long.

INFLORESCENCE: Very short. Inflorescences emerge through the leaf sheaths.

FLOWERS: 1 per inflorescence. The red-brown flowers are 0.6 in. (1.6 cm) across with an ovate, convex dorsal sepal, obliquely triangular lateral sepals, and oblong, convex petals. The fleshy, 3-lobed lip is nearly round.

REFERENCES: 220, 254, 437, 445, 470.

Dendrobium erectopatens J. J. Smith

ORIGIN/HABITAT: The north coast of Irian Jaya (western New Guinea). Plants grow along the upper Mbái River at 150 ft. (40 m) and on the northern slopes of the Gautier Range at about 2950 ft. (900 m). In Papua New Guinea, they are epiphytic on trees near the upper Sepik River at about 750 ft. (225 m).

CLIMATE: Station #97690, Sentani/Jayapura, Irian Jaya, Lat. 2.7°S, Long. 140.5°E, at 289 ft. (88 m). Temperatures are calculated for an elevation of 1000 ft. (300 m), resulting in probable extremes of 95°F (35°C) and 66°F (19°C).

N/HEMISPHERE	JAN	FEB	MAR	APR	MAY	JUN	JUL	AUG	SEP	OCT	NOV	DEC
°F AVG MAX	85	87	87	88	88	87	87	86	87	88	88	87
°F AVG MIN	70	70	70	71	71	71	71	71	71	72	71	71
DIURNAL RANGE	15	17	17	17	17	16	16	15	16	16	17	16
RAIN/INCHES	4.1	3.9	5.3	2.9	6.7	7.0	8.3	8.3	8.5	4.6	2.4	5.2
HUMIDITY/%	81	80	81	79	81	81	79	80	80	80	81	80
BLOOM SEASON	*			*	*				*			
DAYS CLR @ 9AM	5	3	4	3	2	1	1	0	1	2	2	5
DAYS CLR @ 3PM	4	3	3	3	2	1	3	0	1	2	2	3
RAIN/MM	104	99	135	74	170	178	211	211	216	117	61	132
°C AVG MAX	29.3	30.4	30.4	31.0	31.0	30.4	30.4	29.8	30.4	31.0	31.0	30.4
°C AVG MIN	21.0	21.0	21.0	21.5	21.5	21.5	21.5	21.5	21.5	22.1	21.5	21.5
DIURNAL RANGE	8.3	9.4	9.4	9.5	9.5	8.9	8.9	8.3	8.9	8.9	9.5	8.9
S/HEMISPHERE	JUL	AUG	SEP	OCT	NOV	DEC	JAN	FEB	MAR	APR	MAY	JUN

Cultural Recommendations

LIGHT: 2500–3500 fc.

TEMPERATURES: Throughout the year, days average 85–88°F (29–31°C), and nights average 70–72°F (21–22°C), with a diurnal range of 15–17°F (8–9°C).

HUMIDITY: Near 80% year-round.

WATER: Rainfall is heavy all year, with brief semidry periods in spring and autumn. Cultivated plants should be kept moist most of the year, but they should be allowed to become somewhat dry for a few weeks in spring and again in autumn.

FERTILIZER: ¼–½ recommended strength. A balanced fertilizer should be applied weekly to biweekly throughout the year.

REST PERIOD: Growing conditions should be maintained year-round. Water and fertilizer might be reduced slightly in winter, especially for plants grown in the dark, short-day conditions common in temperate latitudes. They should never be allowed to dry completely, however. In the habitat, light is slightly higher in winter.

GROWING MEDIA: Plants may be mounted on tree-fern or cork slabs, if humidity is high and plants are watered at least once daily in summer. When plants are potted, any open, fast-draining medium may be used. Repotting may be done anytime new roots are growing.

MISCELLANEOUS NOTES: The bloom season shown in the climate table is based on collection reports. The plant was described in 1911 in *Bul. Jard. Bot. Buit.* 2nd sér. 2:10.

Plant and Flower Information

PLANT SIZE AND TYPE: A sympodial epiphyte of unreported size.

PSEUDOBULB: The long, slender stems are flattened.

LEAVES: Many. The lanceolate leaves are 1.2–1.6 in. (3–4 cm) long and nearly erect. They are pointed with 2 teeth at the apex. The leaf sheaths are speckled.

FLOWERS: 2 per inflorescence. Blossoms are 0.5 in. (1.3 cm) long. Sepals and petals are yellowish white with pale violet at the base. The lip is darker yellow with shortly lacerated sidelobes and a sharply recurved midlobe. The anther is yellow.

REFERENCES: 221, 445, 470.

Dendrobium erectum Schlechter

ORIGIN/HABITAT: Northern Papua New Guinea. Plants grow on trees in mountain forests at about 2950 ft. (900 m). They were collected on upper Waube Creek, a tributary of the Waria River.

CLIMATE: Station #200192, Garaina, Papua New Guinea, Lat. 7.9°S, Long. 147.1°E, at 2350 ft. (716 m). Record extreme temperatures are 94°F (34°C) and 46°F (8°C).

N/HEMISPHERE	JAN	FEB	MAR	APR	MAY	JUN	JUL	AUG	SEP	OCT	NOV	DEC
°F AVG MAX	80	82	83	84	85	85	85	85	84	84	83	81
°F AVG MIN	63	63	63	64	63	64	65	65	65	64	64	63
DIURNAL RANGE	17	19	20	20	22	21	20	20	19	20	19	18
RAIN/INCHES	5.8	6.5	8.7	11.1	11.8	11.9	8.9	11.7	11.5	9.9	7.7	5.2
HUMIDITY/%	84	82	82	81	80	80	81	81	82	83	84	84
BLOOM SEASON										*		
DAYS CLR	N/A											
RAIN/MM	148	166	220	282	300	303	227	296	291	251	195	131
°C AVG MAX	26.8	27.5	28.2	28.6	29.3	29.3	29.4	29.4	29.1	28.7	28.2	27.2
°C AVG MIN	16.9	16.9	17.4	17.6	17.4	18.0	18.1	18.2	18.4	17.7	17.7	17.1
DIURNAL RANGE	9.9	10.6	10.8	11.0	11.9	11.3	11.3	11.2	10.7	11.0	10.5	10.1
S/HEMISPHERE	JUL	AUG	SEP	OCT	NOV	DEC	JAN	FEB	MAR	APR	MAY	JUN

Cultural Recommendations

LIGHT: 2500–3500 fc.

TEMPERATURES: Throughout the year, days average 80–85°F (27–29°C), and nights average 63–65°F (17–18°C), with a diurnal range of 17–22°F (10–12°C).

HUMIDITY: 80–85% year-round.

WATER: Rainfall is heavy all year with a slightly drier period in winter. Cultivated plants should be kept moist but not soggy.

FERTILIZER: ¼–½ recommended strength. A balanced fertilizer should be applied weekly to biweekly throughout the year.

REST PERIOD: Growing conditions should be maintained all year. In the habitat, rainfall is slightly lower in winter. Water and fertilizer should be reduced somewhat for cultivated plants, especially those grown in the dark, short-day conditions common during temperate-latitude winters. They should never be allowed to dry out completely, however. In the habitat, seasonal light variation is minor.

GROWING MEDIA: Plants may be mounted on tree-fern or cork slabs if humidity is high and plants are watered daily in summer. When plants are potted, any open, fast-draining medium may be used. Repotting may be done anytime new roots are growing.

MISCELLANEOUS NOTES: The bloom season shown in the climate table is based on collection reports. Plants that produce flowers which last a single day commonly bloom several times during the year. Flowering usually occurs 7–14 days after a sudden 10°F (5°C) drop in daytime temperatures.

Plant and Flower Information

PLANT SIZE AND TYPE: An 8–16 in. (20–40 cm) sympodial epiphyte.

PSEUDOBULB: 8–16 in. (20–40 cm) long. The stems are densely leafy.

LEAVES: Many. The lanceolate leaves, which are 1.4–1.8 in. (3.6–4.6 cm) long, may be erect or spreading.

INFLORESCENCE: Short. The flowers are held opposite each other.

FLOWERS: 2 per inflorescence. The flowers, which last 1 day, are 1.1 in. (2.8 cm) across. They are whitish with red spots on the outside and a yellow flush on the inside. Sepals and petals are narrow and project forward. The lip is covered with hairs.

REFERENCES: 221, 437, 445.

PHOTOS/DRAWINGS: 437.

Dendrobium eriae F. Mueller. Kränzlin (ref. 254) considered this a synonym of *Eria eriaeoides,* but Clements (ref. 67) lists it as an invalid name. REFERENCES: 67, 217, 254.

Dendrobium eriaeoides F. M. Bailey. Now considered a synonym of *Eria eriaeoides* (F. M. Bailey) Rolfe. REFERENCES: 67, 105, 217, 218.

Dendrobium eriaeflorum Griffith

AKA: Also spelled *D. eriiflorum,* which is apparently the original spelling. Most recent references, however, spell the name *D. eriaeflorum.*

ORIGIN/HABITAT: Widespread. The habitat includes central Nepal, Sikkim, Bhutan, Manipur, and the Khasi (Khasia) Hills of northeastern India. Plants are also reported from Burma, Malaya, and Sumbawa at 3300–6550 ft. (1000–2000 m). Comber (ref. 75) indicates that plants are common in East Java, especially on Mt. Arjuno, Mt. Wilis, and Mt. Kelud, where they grow on tree branches in high light at 3950–5900 ft. (1200–1800 m).

CLIMATE: Station #42410, Gauhati, India, Lat. 26.1°N, Long. 91.6°E, at 158 ft. (48 m). Temperatures are calculated for an elevation of 4600 ft. (1400 m), resulting in probable extremes of 89°F (32°C) and 26°F (–3°C).

N/HEMISPHERE	JAN	FEB	MAR	APR	MAY	JUN	JUL	AUG	SEP	OCT	NOV	DEC
°F AVG MAX	61	63	71	73	73	74	75	75	74	72	66	61
°F AVG MIN	36	39	45	53	57	62	63	63	61	56	46	38
DIURNAL RANGE	25	24	26	20	16	12	12	12	13	16	20	23
RAIN/INCHES	0.4	1.2	2.0	5.7	9.3	12.3	12.3	10.3	6.6	2.8	0.6	0.2
HUMIDITY/%	79	72	64	71	82	85	86	86	84	84	83	82
BLOOM SEASON								*	*	*	*	
DAYS CLR @ 6AM	6	12	16	11	3	0	0	1	3	7	6	3
DAYS CLR @ 12PM	17	16	18	15	6	1	0	0	2	11	17	19
RAIN/MM	10	30	51	145	236	312	312	262	168	71	15	5
°C AVG MAX	16.3	17.4	21.9	23.0	23.0	23.5	24.1	24.1	23.5	22.4	19.1	16.3
°C AVG MIN	2.4	4.1	7.4	11.9	14.1	16.9	17.4	17.4	16.3	13.5	8.0	3.5
DIURNAL RANGE	13.9	13.3	14.5	11.1	8.9	6.6	6.7	6.7	7.2	8.9	11.1	12.8
S/HEMISPHERE	JUL	AUG	SEP	OCT	NOV	DEC	JAN	FEB	MAR	APR	MAY	JUN

Cultural Recommendations

LIGHT: 2500–3500 fc. In the habitat, summer light is relatively low because clouds are heavy during the rainy season. Light increases by midautumn when about half of the afternoons are clear. From autumn to spring, light should be as high as possible, short of burning the leaves.

TEMPERATURES: Summer days average 74–75°F (24°C), and nights average 62–63°F (17°C), with a diurnal range of 12°F (7°C). These temperatures represent conditions found in the most northerly portion on the plant's range

Dendrobium eriaeoides

In Java, plants grow where temperatures have little seasonal variation. Throughout the year, days averaging 69–71°F (21–23°C), and nights average 52–55°F (11–13°C), with a diurnal range of 12–16°F (7–9°C). Whether plants from different regions can adapt to conditions in other habitats is unknown. The common denominator through most of the range is a very dry season.

HUMIDITY: Near 85% in summer, dropping to 65–70% in late winter and early spring.

WATER: Rainfall is heavy from spring through summer but decreases rapidly in autumn. Cultivated plants should be kept moist while actively growing, but water should be gradually reduced after new growths mature in autumn.

FERTILIZER: ¼–½ recommended strength, applied weekly. A high-nitrogen fertilizer is beneficial from spring to midsummer, but a fertilizer high in phosphates should be used in late summer and autumn.

REST PERIOD: Winter days average 61–63°F (17–22°C), and nights average 36–39°F (2–4°C), with a diurnal range of 23–25°F (13–14°C). Growers are cautioned that these calculated lows may be too cold. Observed temperatures at high-elevation stations in nearby regions suggest that averages may be 4–6°F (2–3°C) warmer than indicated in the table. Plants should survive exposure to freezing if they are dry at the time, but extreme conditions should be avoided in cultivation. Although rainfall is low for 4–5 winter months, high humidity and the large temperature range indicate that additional moisture from heavy dew is common. Therefore, while water should be greatly reduced and cultivated plants allowed to dry out between waterings from late autumn into early spring, they should not remain dry for extended periods. Occasional mistings between waterings during bright, sunny weather may help prevent the plants from becoming too dry. Fertilizer should be reduced or eliminated until active growth resumes and water is increased in spring. In the habitat, light is brightest in winter.

GROWING MEDIA: Fine to medium fir bark with moisture-retaining additives such as perlite is preferred by most growers. Repotting is best done in early spring when new roots are growing.

MISCELLANEOUS NOTES: The bloom season shown in the climate table is based on cultivation records. In the wild, plants bloom at the end of the growing season after leaves drop.

Plant and Flower Information

PLANT SIZE AND TYPE: A 3–12 in. (8–30 cm) sympodial epiphyte.

PSEUDOBULB: 2–10 in. (5–25 cm) long. The clustered, often yellowish stems taper from a thickened basal node. They are erect and fleshy.

LEAVES: 4–9 per growth. The thin, deciduous leaves are linear-lanceolate and 1.6–5.1 in. (4–13 cm) long. They are folded at the base and unequally 2-toothed at the apex.

INFLORESCENCE: 1.6–3.2 in. (4–8 cm) long. Each growth may produce 4–8 inflorescences. The erect to arching inflorescences are laxly flowered. They arise from upper nodes opposite the leaves or opposite where the leaves were attached.

FLOWERS: Commonly 6–8, rarely up to 20 per inflorescence. The upside down blossoms are 0.4–0.6 in. (0.9–1.5 cm) long and open simultaneously. Sepals and petals, which do not open fully, are varying shades of yellow, white, or green. The dorsal sepal is linear-lanceolate. The pointed lateral sepals are oblong-triangular and somewhat curved. The petals are nearly lanceolate, wavy on the lower 30%, and contracted at the base. The yellowish lip and column are veined and lightly spotted with dull purple. The midlobe is broad and undulate. The crested disk has 3 wavy, green keels. Blossoms have a thin texture.

REFERENCES: 36, 38, 46, 75, 179, 190, 200, 202, 203, 216, 224, 254, 278, 369, 376, 402, 437, 445, 482.

PHOTOS/DRAWINGS: 46, 75, 190, 203.

Dendrobium eriaeoides F. M. Bailey. Now considered a synonym *Eria eriaeoides*. REFERENCES: 67, 218, 254, 271.

Dendrobium eriiflorum Griffith. See *D. eriaeflorum* Griffith.
REFERENCES: 190.

Dendrobium eriopexis Schlechter

ORIGIN/HABITAT: Endemic to the island of New Ireland (New Mecklenburg), off the northeastern coast of Papua New Guinea. Plants grow at about 2000 ft. (610 m) on moss-covered trees in the mistforests of the Rossel Range.

CLIMATE: Station #94085, Rabaul, Papua New Guinea, Lat. 4.2°S, Long. 152.2°E, at 28 ft. (9 m). Temperatures are calculated for an elevation of 2000 ft. (610 m), resulting in probable extremes of 93°F (34°C) and 58°F (15°C).

N/HEMISPHERE	JAN	FEB	MAR	APR	MAY	JUN	JUL	AUG	SEP	OCT	NOV	DEC
°F AVG MAX	82	82	84	85	84	83	83	83	83	83	83	83
°F AVG MIN	66	65	66	66	66	66	66	66	66	66	66	66
DIURNAL RANGE	16	17	18	19	18	17	17	17	17	17	17	17
RAIN/INCHES	5.4	3.7	3.5	5.1	7.1	10.1	14.8	10.4	10.2	10.0	5.2	3.3
HUMIDITY/%	74	73	69	70	73	76	77	76	77	77	75	74
BLOOM SEASON	*									*		
DAYS CLR	N/A											
RAIN/MM	137	94	89	130	180	257	376	264	259	254	132	84
°C AVG MAX	28.1	28.1	29.2	29.7	29.2	28.6	28.6	28.6	28.6	28.6	28.6	28.6
°C AVG MIN	19.2	18.6	19.2	19.2	19.2	19.2	19.2	19.2	19.2	19.2	19.2	19.2
DIURNAL RANGE	8.9	9.5	10.0	10.5	10.0	9.4	9.4	9.4	9.4	9.4	9.4	9.4
S/HEMISPHERE	JUL	AUG	SEP	OCT	NOV	DEC	JAN	FEB	MAR	APR	MAY	JUN

Cultural Recommendations

LIGHT: 2500–3000 fc.

TEMPERATURES: Throughout the year, days average 82–85°F (28–30°C), and nights average 65–66°F (19°C), with a diurnal range of 16–18°F (9–11°C). The warmest temperatures and widest diurnal range occur in spring.

HUMIDITY: Near 75% most of the year, dropping to near 70% for 2 months in early spring. Humidity generally increases to 90–100% at night but may drop as low as 35% on hot days in the dry season.

WATER: Rainfall is moderate to heavy most of the year, with 2–3 slightly drier months in winter. Cultivated plants should be kept moist but not soggy.

FERTILIZER: ¼–½ recommended strength. A balanced fertilizer should be applied weekly to biweekly throughout the year.

REST PERIOD: Growing conditions should be maintained all year. Water may be reduced somewhat in winter, especially for plants cultivated in the dark, short-day conditions common in temperate latitudes. These plants should not be allowed to dry out completely, however. Fertilizer may be reduced until water is increased in spring.

GROWING MEDIA: Plants may be mounted on a tree-fern slab or potted in a medium of fir bark or chopped tree-fern mixed with moisture-retaining additives. Repotting may be done anytime new roots are actively growing.

MISCELLANEOUS NOTES: The bloom season shown in the climate table is based on cultivation records and reports from the habitat. Plants that produce flowers which last a single day commonly bloom several times during the year. Flowering usually occurs 7–14 days after a sudden 10°F (5°C) drop in daytime temperatures.

Plant and Flower Information

PLANT SIZE AND TYPE: A pendulous, 20 in. (50 cm) sympodial epiphyte.

PSEUDOBULB: 20 in. (50 cm) long. The many angled pseudobulbs, which are joined by a very short rhizome, are densely leafy.

LEAVES: Many. The oval leaves are 8 in. (20 cm) long, leathery, and somewhat bilobed.

INFLORESCENCE: Short.

FLOWERS: 2 per inflorescence. Blossoms are white and last a single day. The slender sepals, near 1 in. (2.5 cm) long, are much larger than the petals. The lip has a hairy cushion along the center and measures 0.4 in. (1 cm) long. The column foot is accented with golden yellow markings.

REFERENCES: 92, 179, 219, 254, 437, 444, 445.

PHOTOS/DRAWINGS: 437.

Dendrobium erostelle Seidenfaden

ORIGIN/HABITAT: Endemic to Thailand. Plants grow in the foothills of mountains near Ranong. Habitat elevation is estimated at 1500 ft. (460 m). The following climate data should, therefore, be used with caution.

CLIMATE: Station #48532, Ranong, Thailand, Lat. 10.0°N, Long. 98.6°E, at 26 ft. (8 m). Temperatures are calculated for an elevation of 1500 ft. (460 m). Record extreme temperatures are not available for this location.

N/HEMISPHERE	JAN	FEB	MAR	APR	MAY	JUN	JUL	AUG	SEP	OCT	NOV	DEC
°F AVG MAX	86	89	90	89	85	82	82	81	82	83	83	83
°F AVG MIN	65	66	68	71	71	71	70	70	70	69	69	66
DIURNAL RANGE	21	23	22	18	14	11	12	11	12	14	14	17
RAIN/INCHES	0.3	0.4	1.3	5.3	18.0	26.0	25.7	31.4	26.8	14.2	6.8	1.0
HUMIDITY/%	N/A											
BLOOM SEASON	N/A											
DAYS CLR	N/A											
RAIN/MM	8	10	33	135	457	660	653	798	681	361	173	25
°C AVG MAX	30.1	31.7	32.3	31.7	29.5	27.9	27.9	27.3	27.9	28.4	28.4	28.4
°C AVG MIN	18.4	19.0	20.1	21.7	21.7	21.7	21.2	21.2	21.2	20.6	20.6	19.0
DIURNAL RANGE	11.7	12.7	12.2	10.0	7.8	6.2	6.7	6.1	6.7	7.8	7.8	9.4
S/HEMISPHERE	JUL	AUG	SEP	OCT	NOV	DEC	JAN	FEB	MAR	APR	MAY	JUN

Cultural Recommendations

LIGHT: 2000–3000 fc. The rainfall pattern indicates that light is probably lowest in midsummer and highest during the winter dry season.

TEMPERATURES: Summer days average 81–82°F (27–28°C), and nights average 70–71°F (21–22°C), with a diurnal range of 11–12°F (6–7°C). Spring is the warmest season. Days average 89–90°F (32°C), and nights average 68–71°F (20–22°C), and the diurnal range is 18–22°F (10–12°C).

HUMIDITY: Information is not available for this location. However, records from nearby stations indicate that humidity probably averages 85–95% from late spring to autumn, dropping to 75–80% in winter.

WATER: Rainfall is very heavy from spring into autumn, but conditions are much drier during the 3–4 month winter dry season. Cultivated plants should be kept moist during the growing season, but water should be reduced in late autumn.

FERTILIZER: ¼–½ recommended strength, applied weekly. A high-nitrogen fertilizer is beneficial from spring to midsummer, but a fertilizer high in phosphates should be used in late summer and autumn.

REST PERIOD: Winter days average 83–89°F (28–32°C), and nights average 65–66°F (18–19°C), with a diurnal range of 17–23°F (9–13°C). In the habitat, rainfall is low for 4 months and very low for 2 months. Additional moisture is frequently available when high humidity and nightly cooling cause heavy deposits of dew, so conditions are not as dry as they appear during much of the dry season. For cultivated plants, water should be reduced and the plants allowed to dry out between waterings. They should not remain dry for extended periods, however. Fertilizer should be reduced or eliminated anytime water is decreased.

GROWING MEDIA: Plants may be mounted on tree-fern or cork slabs if humidity is high and plants are watered at least once daily in summer. When plants are potted, any open, fast-draining medium may be used. Repotting is best done in early spring when new roots are growing.

MISCELLANEOUS NOTES: Described by Seidenfaden (ref. 454), this species is uncommon and unlikely to be available for cultivation.

Plant and Flower Information

PLANT SIZE AND TYPE: A 3–5 in. (8–13 cm) sympodial plant.

PSEUDOBULB: 1.6 in. (4 cm) long. Nearly cylindrical, the pseudobulbs have 4–5 internodes.

LEAVES: 4–6 per growth. The leaves are 1.6–2.4 in. (4–6 cm) long.

INFLORESCENCE: 1 in. (2.5 cm) long. Inflorescences arise from nodes at the apex and side of the stem.

FLOWERS: 3–4 per inflorescence. The flowers, which are self-pollinating, are 0.2 in. (0.5 cm) across and remain rather closed. All segments are light green with white at the tips. The recurved lip is narrow with wavy margins.

HYBRIDIZING NOTES: Johansen (ref. 239) indicates that "the number of days to capsule maturity could not be determined exactly because of spontaneous self-pollination." Approximately 70% of the seed produced was viable.

REFERENCES: 234, 239, 454.

PHOTOS/DRAWINGS: 454.

Dendrobium erosum (Blume) Lindley

AKA: *Pedilonum erosum* Blume, *Dendrobium aegle* Ridley, *D. aemulans* Schlechter, *D. inopinatum* J. J. Smith.

ORIGIN/HABITAT: The Solomon Islands, Vanuatu, New Guinea, Sulawesi (Celebes), Java, Sumatra, Malaya, and southern Thailand. In Java, plants grow in mountain forests on Mt. Salak, a volcano southwest of Bogor, at about 2050 ft. (620 m); and in Malaya, they are reported in the Taiping (Thaiping) Hills at 2500 ft. (760 m). Some reports indicate that in New Guinea they grow high in trees only in high-mountain cloudforests at about 6550 ft. (2000 m). However, Schlechter collected plants in the Kani Mountains south of Madang at 3300 ft. (1000 m) and in the Torricelli Range west of Wewak at 2300–2950 ft. (700–900 m).

CLIMATE: Station #96755, Bogor, Java, Indonesia, Lat. 6.5°S, Long. 106.8°E, at 558 ft. (170 m). Temperatures are calculated for an elevation of 1800 ft. (550 m), resulting in probable extremes of 92°F (33°C) and 62°F (17°C).

N/HEMISPHERE	JAN	FEB	MAR	APR	MAY	JUN	JUL	AUG	SEP	OCT	NOV	DEC
°F AVG MAX	82	83	84	84	83	81	80	80	81	82	83	82
°F AVG MIN	69	69	69	70	70	70	70	70	70	71	71	70
DIURNAL RANGE	13	14	15	14	13	11	10	10	11	11	12	12
RAIN/INCHES	2.1	1.0	0.5	5.0	8.1	18.8	23.7	20.2	14.4	12.0	11.9	3.4
HUMIDITY/%	72	68	65	66	74	79	84	84	81	79	77	75
BLOOM SEASON											*	
DAYS CLR @ 7AM	14	14	14	11	5	3	1	2	4	6	10	12
DAYS CLR @ 1PM	9	10	8	5	1	1	0	0	1	1	3	7
RAIN/MM	53	25	13	127	206	478	602	513	366	305	302	86
°C AVG MAX	27.7	28.3	28.8	28.8	28.3	27.2	26.6	26.6	27.2	27.7	28.3	27.7
°C AVG MIN	20.5	20.5	20.5	21.1	21.1	21.1	21.1	21.1	21.1	21.6	21.6	21.1
DIURNAL RANGE	7.2	7.8	8.3	7.7	7.2	6.1	5.5	5.5	6.1	6.1	6.7	6.6
S/HEMISPHERE	JUL	AUG	SEP	OCT	NOV	DEC	JAN	FEB	MAR	APR	MAY	JUN

Cultural Recommendations

LIGHT: 1200–2500 fc. Diffused or barely dappled light is preferred, and direct sunlight should be avoided.

Dendrobium erosum

TEMPERATURES: Throughout the year, days average 80–84°F (27–29°C), and nights average 69–71°F (21–22°C), with a diurnal range of 10–15°F (6–8°C). The highest temperatures occur in spring. The average highs fluctuate only 4°F (2°C), and average lows vary even less, indicating that plants may not tolerate wide temperature fluctuations.

HUMIDITY: 80–85% during the growing season, dropping to near 65% for 2 months in winter.

WATER: Rainfall is very heavy from spring to autumn, but conditions are very dry for 2 months in winter. During the growing season, plants should never be allowed to dry out completely, but water should be gradually reduced in late autumn.

FERTILIZER: ¼–½ recommended strength, applied weekly. A high-nitrogen fertilizer is beneficial from spring to midsummer, but a fertilizer high in phosphates should be used in late summer and autumn.

REST PERIOD: Growing conditions should be maintained all year, but rainfall is very low for 2–3 months. In cultivation, water should be reduced and the plants allowed to become somewhat dry between waterings. They should not remain dry for prolonged periods, however. Fertilizer may be reduced or eliminated anytime the plant is not actively growing. In the habitat, light is highest in winter.

GROWING MEDIA: Mounting plants on tree-fern or cork slabs accommodates their pendent growth habit, but humidity must be high and water should be applied at least once daily in summer. If plants must be potted, a hanging pot or basket may be filled with any open fast-draining medium. Repotting is best done in early spring when new roots are growing.

MISCELLANEOUS NOTES: The bloom season shown in the climate table is based on reports from the habitat.

Plant and Flower Information

PLANT SIZE AND TYPE: A 24–31 in. (60–80 cm) sympodial epiphyte.

PSEUDOBULB: 24–31 in. (60–80 cm) long. The pendent, leafy stems are many angled with nodes spaced 1.0–1.2 in. (2.5–3.0 cm) apart. They are clustered and do not branch.

LEAVES: Many. The lanceolate leaves are 2–4 in. (5–10 cm) long.

INFLORESCENCE: Short. Numerous pendent racemes emerge at the nodes on leafless stems.

FLOWERS: 5–10. Blossoms are 1 in. (2.5 cm) across and do not open fully. The white flowers are flushed with rose on the back. Petals are fringed along the margins and especially at the apex. The lip margin is toothed to slashed.

REFERENCES: 86, 92, 75, 200, 216, 254, 271, 277, 304, 310, 395, 402, 444, 455, 469, 486, 516.

PHOTOS/DRAWINGS: 75, 271, *304,* 437, *455.*

Dendrobium erosum Kränzlin not Lindley. See *D. amblyogenium* Schlechter. REFERENCES: 436.

Dendrobium erthroxanthum Rchb. f. See *D. bullenianum* Rchb. f. REFERENCES: 216, 536.

Dendrobium erubescens Schlechter

ORIGIN/HABITAT: Northern Papua New Guinea. Plants grow on forest trees in the Bismarck Range at about 6550 ft. (2000 m).

CLIMATE: Botanical garden records, Laiagam, Papua New Guinea, Lat. 5.5°S, Long. 143.5°E, at 7218 ft. (2200 m). Record extreme temperatures are 91°F (33°C) and 32°F (0°C).

N/HEMISPHERE	JAN	FEB	MAR	APR	MAY	JUN	JUL	AUG	SEP	OCT	NOV	DEC
°F AVG MAX	76	77	78	76	78	78	82	77	76	78	78	76
°F AVG MIN	55	54	55	55	56	56	55	56	58	57	56	56
DIURNAL RANGE	21	23	23	21	22	22	27	21	18	21	22	20
RAIN/INCHES	4.0	4.8	6.1	7.8	8.5	9.1	8.4	9.6	9.5	8.9	6.3	4.0
HUMIDITY/%	N/A											
BLOOM SEASON							*					
DAYS CLR	N/A											
RAIN/MM	102	121	154	198	217	230	213	243	241	227	159	102
°C AVG MAX	24.4	25.0	25.6	24.4	25.6	25.6	27.8	25.0	24.4	25.6	25.6	24.4
°C AVG MIN	12.8	12.2	12.8	12.8	13.3	13.3	12.8	13.3	14.4	13.9	13.3	13.3
DIURNAL RANGE	11.6	12.8	12.8	11.6	12.3	12.3	15.0	11.7	10.0	11.7	12.3	11.1
S/HEMISPHERE	JUL	AUG	SEP	OCT	NOV	DEC	JAN	FEB	MAR	APR	MAY	JUN

Cultural Recommendations

LIGHT: 2000–3000 fc.

TEMPERATURES: Throughout the year, days average 76–82°F (24–28°C), and nights average 54–58°F (12–14°C), with a diurnal range of 18–27°F (10–15°C).

HUMIDITY: Information is not available for this location. However, records from nearby stations indicate that humidity probably averages 70–80% all year.

WATER: Rainfall is moderate to heavy throughout the year, but conditions are driest for 3–4 months in winter. Cultivated plants should be kept evenly moist.

FERTILIZER: ¼–½ recommended strength. A balanced fertilizer should be applied weekly to biweekly throughout the year.

REST PERIOD: Growing conditions should be maintained year-round. Water and fertilizer should be reduced somewhat in winter, especially for plants grown in the dark, short-day conditions common in temperate latitudes. They should never be allowed to dry out completely, however. In the habitat, light is highest in winter.

GROWING MEDIA: Plants may be mounted on tree-fern or cork slabs if humidity is high and plants are watered at least once daily in summer. When plants are potted, any open, fast-draining medium may be used. Repotting may be done anytime new roots are growing.

MISCELLANEOUS NOTES: The bloom season shown in the climate table is based on collection reports. Plants that produce flowers which last a single day commonly bloom several times during the year. Flowering usually occurs 7–14 days after a sudden 10°F (5°C) drop in daytime temperatures.

Plant and Flower Information

PLANT SIZE AND TYPE: A 16 in. (40 cm) sympodial epiphyte.

PSEUDOBULB: 16 in. (40 cm) long. The strictly erect pseudobulbs arise from a very short rhizome. The somewhat flattened stems are densely leafy.

LEAVES: Many. The very narrow leaves are 1.6–2.4 in. (4–6 cm) long, blunt, erect, and leathery.

INFLORESCENCE: Short.

FLOWERS: 2 per inflorescence. The reddish flowers are 0.4 in. (0.9 cm) across. Blossoms remain rather closed and last a single day. When spread, the lip resembles a whales tail.

REFERENCES: 221, 437, 445.

PHOTOS/DRAWINGS: 437.

Dendrobium erythrocarpum J. J. Smith. See *D. dekockii* J. J. Smith. REFERENCES: 224, 385, 445, 538. PHOTOS/DRAWINGS: 538.

Dendrobium erythroglossum Hayata. See *D. falconeri* Hooker. REFERENCES: 61, 62, 179, 193, 208, 221, 274, 279, 445, 454. PHOTOS/DRAWINGS: 62, *274.*

Dendrobium erythropogon Rchb. f.

ORIGIN/HABITAT: Northern Borneo. In the mountains of Sarawak near Labuan, plants grow on forest trees above 3300 ft. (1000 m).

CLIMATE: Station #49613, Tambunan, Sabah (North Borneo), Lat. 5.7°N, Long. 116.4°E, at 1200 ft. (366 m). Temperatures are calculated for an elevation of 4000 ft. (1220 m), resulting in probable extremes of 89°F (32°C) and 45°F (7°C).

N/HEMISPHERE	JAN	FEB	MAR	APR	MAY	JUN	JUL	AUG	SEP	OCT	NOV	DEC
°F AVG MAX	77	78	80	81	81	80	80	80	80	79	78	77
°F AVG MIN	58	56	57	58	59	58	57	57	58	58	58	59
DIURNAL RANGE	19	22	23	23	22	22	23	23	22	21	20	18
RAIN/INCHES	5.8	3.7	5.8	7.5	8.2	7.3	5.1	4.9	6.4	7.0	6.8	6.0
HUMIDITY/%	N/A											
BLOOM SEASON	N/A											
DAYS CLR	N/A											
RAIN/MM	147	94	147	190	208	185	130	124	163	178	173	152
°C AVG MAX	24.9	25.4	26.5	27.1	27.1	26.5	26.5	26.5	26.5	26.0	25.4	24.9
°C AVG MIN	14.3	13.2	13.8	14.3	14.9	14.3	13.8	13.8	14.3	14.3	14.3	14.9
DIURNAL RANGE	10.6	12.2	12.7	12.8	12.2	12.2	12.7	12.7	12.2	11.7	11.1	10.0
S/HEMISPHERE	JUL	AUG	SEP	OCT	NOV	DEC	JAN	FEB	MAR	APR	MAY	JUN

Cultural Recommendations

LIGHT: 2000–3000 fc. Bright, reflected light is recommended.

TEMPERATURES: Throughout the year, days average 77–81°F (25–27°C), and nights average 56–59°F (13–15°C), with a diurnal range of 18–23°F (10–13°C).

HUMIDITY: Information is not available for this location. However, records from nearby locations indicate that humidity probably averages 80–85% year-round.

WATER: Rainfall is moderate to heavy through the year. Cultivated plants should be kept moist, with only slight drying allowed between waterings.

FERTILIZER: ¼–½ recommended strength. A balanced fertilizer should be applied weekly to biweekly throughout the year.

REST PERIOD: Growing conditions vary only slightly through the year. The diurnal range is slightly lower in winter due to somewhat cooler days. In cultivation, water should be reduced somewhat in winter, especially for plants grown in the dark, short-day conditions common in temperate latitudes. Plants should never be allowed to dry out completely, however. Fertilizer should be decreased when water is reduced and when plants are not actively growing.

GROWING MEDIA: Plants may be potted in any open medium that retains moisture, but is not soggy. Repotting may be done anytime new roots are growing.

Plant and Flower Information

PLANT SIZE AND TYPE: A 10–12 in. (25–30 cm) sympodial plant.

PSEUDOBULB: 10–12 in. (25–30 cm) long. It was described as a poor cousin of *D. lowii* Lindley with very similar vegetative growths.

LEAVES: Many. The ovate to oblong leaves, which are 3 in. (8 cm) long, are held near the apex of the stem. Sheaths are covered with black hairs.

INFLORESCENCE: The bracts on the inflorescence are covered with black hairs.

FLOWERS: 4 per inflorescence. The flowers, which resemble small *D. lowii* Lindley, are pale, whitish ochre with oblong, wavy petals. The lip has 7 crimson keels with a crimson flush between the keels. The outside keels have crimson hairs on each side and 2 scarlet spots near the base. The heart-shaped midlobe is wavy with small teeth. The sides of the lip have long, white lacerations with crimson edges.

REFERENCES: 216, 254, 286, 295, 429, 570.

Dendrobium erythroxanthum Rchb. f. See *D. bullenianum* Rchb. f. REFERENCES: 190, 216, 254, 296, 298, 536, 570.

Dendrobium escritorii Ames

ORIGIN/HABITAT: The Philippines. Plants grow on Luzon Island in Quezon and Camarines Provinces and on Mindanao Island in Surigao Province at 100–500 ft. (35–150 m).

CLIMATE: Station #98439, Daet, Philippines, Lat. 14.1°N, Long. 122.9°E, at 36 ft. (11 m). Temperatures are calculated for an elevation of 200 ft. (60 m), resulting in probable extremes of 100°F (38°C) and 59°F (15°C).

N/HEMISPHERE	JAN	FEB	MAR	APR	MAY	JUN	JUL	AUG	SEP	OCT	NOV	DEC
°F AVG MAX	82	83	85	88	90	91	89	89	89	87	85	83
°F AVG MIN	71	71	72	73	74	74	74	74	73	73	73	72
DIURNAL RANGE	11	12	13	15	16	17	15	15	16	14	12	11
RAIN/INCHES	16.2	7.8	7.0	4.9	5.7	5.9	7.9	9.4	10.5	19.3	22.8	21.7
HUMIDITY/%	82	81	81	81	81	80	83	83	84	84	84	84
BLOOM SEASON			*	*							*	*
DAYS CLR @ 8AM	3	4	7	10	8	8	4	4	4	4	3	3
DAYS CLR @ 2PM	3	5	9	10	9	3	1	1	1	3	3	2
RAIN/MM	411	198	178	124	145	150	201	239	267	490	579	551
°C AVG MAX	28.0	28.6	29.7	31.4	32.5	33.0	31.9	31.9	31.9	30.8	29.7	28.6
°C AVG MIN	21.9	21.9	22.5	23.0	23.6	23.6	23.6	23.6	23.0	23.0	23.0	22.5
DIURNAL RANGE	6.1	6.7	7.2	8.4	8.9	9.4	8.3	8.3	8.9	7.8	6.7	6.1
S/HEMISPHERE	JUL	AUG	SEP	OCT	NOV	DEC	JAN	FEB	MAR	APR	MAY	JUN

Cultural Recommendations

LIGHT: 2500–3500 fc.

TEMPERATURES: Summer days average 89–91°F (32–33°C), and nights average 74°F (24°C), with a diurnal range of 15–17°F (8–9°C).

HUMIDITY: 80–85% year-round.

WATER: Rainfall is heavy all year, but winter is the wettest season. Cultivated plants should be kept evenly moist with only slight drying allowed between waterings.

FERTILIZER: ¼–½ recommended strength. A balanced fertilizer should be applied weekly to biweekly throughout the year.

REST PERIOD: Winter days average 82–85°F (28–30°C), and nights average 71–72°F (22–23°C), with a diurnal range of 11–13°F (6–7°C). Although rainfall is greatest in winter, water should not be increased for cultivated plants. In fact, it should be reduced for plants grown in the dark, short-day conditions common in temperate-latitude winters. These plants should never be allowed to dry out completely, however. Fertilizer should be reduced if water is reduced.

GROWING MEDIA: Plants may be mounted on tree-fern or cork slabs if humidity is high and plants are watered at least once daily in summer. When plants are potted, any open, fast-draining medium may be used. Repotting may be done anytime new roots are growing.

MISCELLANEOUS NOTES: The bloom season shown in the climate table is based on collection reports.

Plant and Flower Information

PLANT SIZE AND TYPE: A 12 in. (30 cm) sympodial epiphyte.

PSEUDOBULB: 12 in. (30 cm) long. Pseudobulbs are many-jointed, slender, and leafless near the apex. Stems are leafy at the base.

LEAVES: Many. The leaves are about 1.0 in. (2.5 cm) long and 0.4 in. (1 cm) apart. They are arranged in 2 rows and resemble flat swords.

INFLORESCENCE: 6–8 in. (15–20 cm) long. Inflorescences arise from a cushion of fibrous scales at apical nodes opposite rudimentary leaves.

FLOWERS: The very small flowers are 0.4 in. (1 cm) across and open in succession. Sepals and petals may be white or yellow with dark red lines. The red lip is toothed on the margin and fringed on the margin of the midlobe.

Dendrobium eserre

REFERENCES: 12, 222, 296, 536

Dendrobium eserre Seidenfaden

ORIGIN/HABITAT: Endemic to Thailand. Plants grow in the northwestern mountains at 4900–5600 ft. (1500–1700 m).

CLIMATE: Station #48300, Mae Hong Son, Thailand, Lat. 19.3°N, Long. 97.9°E, at 711 ft. (217 m). Temperatures are calculated for an elevation of 5250 ft. (1600 m), resulting in probable extremes of 93°F (34°C) and 28°F (−2°C).

N/HEMISPHERE	JAN	FEB	MAR	APR	MAY	JUN	JUL	AUG	SEP	OCT	NOV	DEC
°F AVG MAX	71	75	82	83	80	74	72	72	73	75	73	70
°F AVG MIN	42	42	47	57	61	60	59	59	59	57	53	44
DIURNAL RANGE	29	33	35	26	19	14	13	13	14	18	20	26
RAIN/INCHES	0.4	0.2	0.3	1.7	6.1	7.1	9.6	9.9	8.1	3.9	1.2	0.4
HUMIDITY/%	67	60	50	50	68	81	82	83	83	82	75	71
BLOOM SEASON						*	*	*	*			
DAYS CLR @ 7AM	2	8	10	9	3	0	0	0	0	1	1	2
DAYS CLR @ 1PM	20	20	20	13	3	0	0	0	0	3	13	17
RAIN/MM	10	5	8	43	155	180	244	251	206	99	30	10
°C AVG MAX	21.7	23.9	27.8	28.3	26.7	23.3	22.2	22.2	22.8	23.9	22.8	21.1
°C AVG MIN	5.6	5.6	8.3	13.9	16.1	15.6	15.0	15.0	15.0	13.9	11.7	6.7
DIURNAL RANGE	16.1	18.3	19.5	14.4	10.6	7.7	7.2	7.2	7.8	10.0	11.1	14.4
S/HEMISPHERE	JUL	AUG	SEP	OCT	NOV	DEC	JAN	FEB	MAR	APR	MAY	JUN

Cultural Recommendations

LIGHT: 2000–3000 fc. The heavy summer cloud cover indicates that light is low in that habitat and that some shading is needed for cultivated plants from spring through autumn, but light should be as high as the plant can tolerate, short of burning the leaves. The brightest season in the habitat is indicated by the large number of clear afternoons from midautumn into spring. Brisk air movement is important at all times.

TEMPERATURES: Summer days average 72–74°F (22–23°C), and nights average 59–60°F (15–16°C), with a diurnal range of 13–14°F (7–8°C). The warmest season is spring. Days average 80–83°F (27–28°C), and nights average 47–61°F (8–16°C), with a diurnal range of 19–35°F (11–20°C).

HUMIDITY: 80–85% from summer into autumn, decreasing to 60–70% in winter. For 2 months in spring, however, conditions are very dry and averages drop to near 50%.

WATER: Rainfall is very heavy during the growing season, but winters are very dry. Cultivated plants should be kept moist while actively growing, but water should be gradually reduced after new growths mature in autumn.

FERTILIZER: ¼–½ recommended strength, applied weekly. A high nitrogen fertilizer is beneficial from spring to midsummer, but a fertilizer high in phosphates should be used in late summer and autumn.

REST PERIOD: Winter days average 70–75°F (21–24°C), and nights average 42–44°F (6–7°C), with a diurnal range of 26–33°F (14–18°C). In the habitat, rainfall is low for 4–5 months in winter. For 2–3 of these months, high humidity and nightly cooling result in frequent, heavy deposits of dew, with even more moisture available from fog and mist. Therefore, the driest season is only 1–2 months long. For cultivated plants, water should be reduced from late autumn to early spring. During most of the winter, plants should be allowed to dry out between waterings, but they should not remain completely dry for extended periods. Occasional early morning mistings between waterings may help prevent the plants from becoming too dry. For 1–2 months in late winter, however, water should be limited to occasional early morning mistings. Fertilizer should be reduced or eliminated, until new growth starts in spring. In the habitat, the large number of clear, winter afternoons indicates very bright conditions.

GROWING MEDIA: Plants may be mounted on tree-fern or cork slabs if humidity is high and plants are watered at least once daily in summer. When plants are potted, any open, fast-draining medium may be used. Repotting is best done in early spring when new roots are growing.

MISCELLANEOUS NOTES: The bloom season shown in the climate table is based on reports from the habitat.

Plant and Flower Information

PLANT SIZE AND TYPE: A tidy, 5–6 in. (13–15 cm) sympodial plant.

PSEUDOBULB: 3–4 in. (8–10 cm) long. The cylindrical pseudobulbs taper toward the apex.

LEAVES: 5–7 per growth. The leaves are 1.6–2.0 in. (4–5 cm) long.

INFLORESCENCE: 1.6–2.4 in. (4–6 cm) long. Inflorescences arise from the side of the pseudobulb and break through a leaf sheath.

FLOWERS: 10 or less per inflorescence. The flowers, which last several months, are 0.4 in. (1 cm) across. The narrow sepals and petals are white. The lip is pale to strong yellow with a purple tinge and tiny dark purple dots along the veins. The column is light green.

REFERENCES: 234, 454.

PHOTOS/DRAWINGS: 454.

Dendrobium esuriens Rchb. f.
Described in 1860 and thought to originate in Java, but location details were not given. This species is not included in recent literature and is unlikely to be available for cultivation. REFERENCES: 216, 254, 469.

Dendrobium eulophotum Lindley.
See *D. indivisum* (Blume) Miquel. REFERENCES: 75, 157, 202, 216, 254, 278, 286, 295, 310, 394, 395, 402, 454, 469.

Dendrobium eumelinum Schlechter

ORIGIN/HABITAT: Papua New Guinea. Plants grow in the Sepik River region at 3300–6800 ft. (1000–2070 m).

CLIMATE: Station #200004, Ambunti, Papua New Guinea, Lat. 4.2°S, Long. 142.8°E, at 164 ft. (50 m). Temperatures are calculated for an elevation of 5000 ft. (1520 m), resulting in probable extremes of 83°F (28°C) and 36°F (2°C).

N/HEMISPHERE	JAN	FEB	MAR	APR	MAY	JUN	JUL	AUG	SEP	OCT	NOV	DEC
°F AVG MAX	72	74	74	74	75	74	74	74	74	74	74	73
°F AVG MIN	56	57	58	57	57	57	56	57	57	57	57	58
DIURNAL RANGE	16	17	16	17	18	17	18	17	17	17	17	15
RAIN/INCHES	6.4	7.4	7.7	8.5	9.2	9.4	10.9	10.2	12.2	10.4	8.3	5.2
HUMIDITY/%	N/A											
BLOOM SEASON						*					*	
DAYS CLR	N/A											
RAIN/MM	163	188	196	216	234	239	277	259	310	264	211	132
°C AVG MAX	22.2	23.4	23.4	23.4	23.9	23.4	23.4	23.4	23.4	23.4	23.4	22.8
°C AVG MIN	13.4	13.9	14.5	13.9	13.9	13.9	13.4	13.9	13.9	13.9	13.9	14.5
DIURNAL RANGE	8.8	9.5	8.9	9.5	10.0	9.5	10.0	9.5	9.5	9.5	9.5	8.3
S/HEMISPHERE	JUL	AUG	SEP	OCT	NOV	DEC	JAN	FEB	MAR	APR	MAY	JUN

Cultural Recommendations

LIGHT: 2000–3000 fc.

TEMPERATURES: Throughout the year, days average 72–75°F (22–24°C), and nights average 56–58°F (13–15°C), with a diurnal range of 15–18°F (8–10°C).

HUMIDITY: Information is not available for this location. However, records from nearby locations indicate that humidity probably averages near 80% year-round.

WATER: Rainfall is heavy all year with the greatest amounts falling in summer and early autumn. Cultivated plants should be kept moist but not soggy.

FERTILIZER: ¼–½ recommended strength. A balanced fertilizer should be applied weekly to biweekly throughout the year.

REST PERIOD: Growing conditions should be maintained all year. Water and fertilizer should be reduced for plants cultivated in the dark, short-day conditions common during temperate-latitude winters, but the plants should never be allowed to dry out completely.

GROWING MEDIA: Plants may be mounted on cork or tree-fern slabs if humidity is high and plants are watered at least once daily in summer. When plants are potted, any open, fast-draining medium may be used, but fir bark is preferred by most growers. Repotting may be done anytime new roots are growing.

MISCELLANEOUS NOTES: The bloom seasons shown in the climate table is based on collection reports.

Plant and Flower Information

PLANT SIZE AND TYPE: A 12–20 in. (30–50 cm) sympodial epiphyte.

PSEUDOBULB: 12–20 in. (30–50 cm) long. The cylindrical stems occasionally branch. New growths arise from a very short rhizome.

LEAVES: Many. The somewhat lanceolate leaves are 1.4–3.2 in. (3.6–8.0 cm) long, very pointed at the tip, and broad at the base.

INFLORESCENCE: Short.

FLOWERS: The tiny flowers are 0.4–0.6 in. (1.0–1.5 cm) across. Sepals and petals are orange-red. The lip is orange-gold.

REFERENCES: 223, 443.

Dendrobium euphlebium Rchb. f. ex Lindley. See *D. spurium* (Blume) J. J. Smith. REFERENCES: 75, 190, 200, 216, 254, 278, 296, 298, 310, 394, 395, 402, 445, 469.

Dendrobium euphues Ridley. See *D. cuthbertsonii* F. Mueller. REFERENCES: 222, 385, 400.

Dendrobium eurorum Ames. Now considered a synonym of *Flickingeria eurorum* (Ames) A. Hawkes. REFERENCES: 12, 213, 222, 229, 230, 231, 296, 536.

Dendrobium euryanthum Schlechter

ORIGIN/HABITAT: Northern Papua New Guinea. Plants grow in the Torricelli Mountains on moss-covered mistforest trees at 2600–4900 ft. (800–1500 m).

CLIMATE: Station #94004, Wewak, Papua New Guinea, Lat. 3.6°S, Long. 143.7°E, at 16 ft. (5 m). Temperatures are calculated for an elevation of 3800 ft. (1160 m), resulting in probable extremes of 86°F (30°C) and 50°F (10°C).

N/HEMISPHERE	JAN	FEB	MAR	APR	MAY	JUN	JUL	AUG	SEP	OCT	NOV	DEC
°F AVG MAX	76	76	76	76	76	76	75	74	75	76	76	76
°F AVG MIN	62	62	62	63	63	63	63	63	62	62	63	62
DIURNAL RANGE	14	14	14	13	13	13	12	11	13	14	13	14
RAIN/INCHES	7.6	4.8	5.3	10.0	13.3	14.5	12.1	11.9	14.9	16.9	15.1	10.8
HUMIDITY/%	80	79	79	78	79	81	82	82	81	82	81	80
BLOOM SEASON									*			
DAYS CLR	N/A											
RAIN/MM	193	122	135	254	338	368	307	302	378	429	384	274
°C AVG MAX	24.2	24.2	24.2	24.2	24.2	24.2	23.6	23.1	23.6	24.2	24.2	24.2
°C AVG MIN	16.4	16.4	16.4	17.0	17.0	17.0	17.0	17.0	16.4	16.4	17.0	16.4
DIURNAL RANGE	7.8	7.8	7.8	7.2	7.2	7.2	6.6	6.1	7.2	7.8	7.2	7.8
S/HEMISPHERE	JUL	AUG	SEP	OCT	NOV	DEC	JAN	FEB	MAR	APR	MAY	JUN

Cultural Recommendations

LIGHT: 1500–2500 fc.

TEMPERATURES: Throughout the year, days average 74–76°F (23–24°C), and nights average 62–63°F (16–17°C), with a diurnal range of 11–14°F (6–8°C).

HUMIDITY: Near 80% year-round.

WATER: Rainfall is heavy all year. Conditions are slightly drier for 1–2 months in winter. Cultivated plants should be kept moist but not soggy.

FERTILIZER: ¼–½ recommended strength. A balanced fertilizer should be applied weekly to biweekly throughout the year. Growers indicate that many closely related *Dendrobium* from low elevations are heavy feeders.

REST PERIOD: Growing conditions should be maintained year-round, but water should be reduced somewhat if plants are grown in the dark, short-day conditions common in temperate-latitude winters. Plants should never be allowed to dry out completely, however. Fertilizer should also be reduced if water is reduced. In the habitat, light may be slightly higher in winter.

GROWING MEDIA: Any open, fast-draining medium may be used with baskets or small pots. Plants may be mounted on slabs if humidity is high and plants are watered at least once daily in summer. Repotting may be done anytime new roots are growing.

MISCELLANEOUS NOTES: The bloom season shown in the climate table is based on reports from the habitat.

Plant and Flower Information

PLANT SIZE AND TYPE: An 8–10 in. (20–25 cm) sympodial epiphyte.

PSEUDOBULB: 4–5 in. (10–13 cm) long. The slender growths, which may be erect or pendent, are dilated.

LEAVES: 2. The apical leaves are 4 in. (10 cm) long, elliptic, and twisted at the base to lie on a single plane. They are bluish green on the upper surface.

INFLORESCENCE: 3 in. (8 cm) long. Inflorescences are slender and wiry.

FLOWERS: 2–4 per inflorescence. Flowers are 0.8 in. (2 cm) across and sometimes remain rather closed. Sepals and petals off-white, flesh-colored, yellow, or orange. The lip is commonly orange to orange-red with red-brown veins.

REFERENCES: 83, 219, 254, 437, 444, 445.

PHOTOS/DRAWINGS: *83*, 437.

Dendrobium eustachyum Schlechter. See *D. forbesii* Ridley. REFERENCES: 83, 223, 443.

Dendrobium evaginatum Gagnepain. See *D. aphyllum* (Roxburgh) C. Fischer. REFERENCES: 225, 266, 448, Seidenfaden 1992 *Opera Botanica* #114.

Dendrobium everardii Rolfe. See *D. dactylodes* Rchb. f. REFERENCES: 223, 252, 353, 417, 466.

Dendrobium evrardii Gagnepain. See *D. wattii* (Hooker f.) Rchb. f. REFERENCES: 136, 224, 266, 369, 448, 454.

Dendrobium exaltatum Schlechter

ORIGIN/HABITAT: Northern Papua New Guinea. Plants grow on forest trees in the Kani Range at about 3300 ft. (1000 m).

CLIMATE: Station #94010, Goroka, Papua New Guinea, Lat. 6.1°S, Long. 145.4°E, at 5141 ft. (1567 m). Temperatures are calculated for an elevation of 3300 ft. (1000 m), resulting in probable extremes of 93°F (34°C) and 49°F (10°C).

Dendrobium exasperatum

N/HEMISPHERE	JAN	FEB	MAR	APR	MAY	JUN	JUL	AUG	SEP	OCT	NOV	DEC
°F AVG MAX	82	83	84	85	85	84	85	84	84	84	85	83
°F AVG MIN	62	63	63	63	64	65	65	65	66	65	65	63
DIURNAL RANGE	20	20	21	22	21	19	20	19	18	19	20	20
RAIN/INCHES	2.1	2.8	4.6	5.9	6.6	9.3	9.1	10.1	10.7	8.3	4.6	2.0
HUMIDITY/%	70	67	67	67	67	71	72	73	74	71	70	70
BLOOM SEASON									*			
DAYS CLR	N/A											
RAIN/MM	53	71	117	150	168	236	231	257	272	211	117	51
°C AVG MAX	27.9	28.4	29.0	29.5	29.5	29.0	29.5	29.0	29.0	29.0	29.5	28.4
°C AVG MIN	16.7	17.3	17.3	17.3	17.9	18.4	18.4	18.4	19.0	18.4	18.4	17.3
DIURNAL RANGE	11.2	11.1	11.7	12.2	11.6	10.6	11.1	10.6	10.0	10.6	11.1	11.1
S/HEMISPHERE	JUL	AUG	SEP	OCT	NOV	DEC	JAN	FEB	MAR	APR	MAY	JUN

Cultural Recommendations

LIGHT: 2000–3000 fc.

TEMPERATURES: Throughout the year, days average 82–85°F (28–30°C), and nights average 62–65°F (17–18°C), with a diurnal range of 19–22°F (11–12°C).

HUMIDITY: 70–75% from summer into autumn, dropping to 65–70% in winter and spring.

WATER: Rainfall is moderate to heavy most of the year, but conditions are slightly drier for 3 months in winter. Cultivated plants should be kept moist but not soggy. Occasional early morning mistings may be beneficial, especially on bright, sunny days.

FERTILIZER: ¼–½ recommended strength. A balanced fertilizer should be applied weekly to biweekly throughout the year.

REST PERIOD: Growing temperatures should be maintained all year. In the habitat, rainfall is lowest in winter, but dew and mist from fog and low clouds are common. Water and fertilizer should be reduced somewhat for cultivated plants, especially those grown in the darker, short-day conditions common during temperate-latitude winters. Plants should be kept on the dry side, but they should never be allowed to dry out completely. In the habitat, light is higher in winter.

GROWING MEDIA: Plants may be mounted on tree-fern or cork slabs if humidity is high and plants are watered at least once daily in summer. When plants are potted, any open, fast-draining medium may be used. Repotting may be done anytime new roots are growing.

MISCELLANEOUS NOTES: The bloom season shown in the climate table is based on collection reports. Plants producing flowers which last a single day commonly bloom several times during the year. Flowering usually occurs 7–14 days after a sudden 10°F (5°C) drop in daytime temperatures.

Plant and Flower Information

PLANT SIZE AND TYPE: A robust, 36–44 in. (91–112 cm) sympodial epiphyte.

PSEUDOBULB: 36–44 in. (91–112 cm) long. The slightly flattened pseudobulbs are densely leafy.

LEAVES: Many. The leaves are usually 6–7 in. (15–18 cm) long.

INFLORESCENCE: Short. Inflorescences emerge from just above the leaf axils.

FLOWERS: 2 per inflorescence. The flowers, which last a single day, are 0.7 in. (1.8 cm) across. Sepals and petals are creamy white. The cream-colored lip has dark violet markings on the sidelobes. The column is violet and yellow.

REFERENCES: 221, 437, 445.

PHOTOS/DRAWINGS: 437.

Dendrobium exasperatum Schlechter

ORIGIN/HABITAT: Northern Papua New Guinea. Plants grow on forest trees in the Kani Range at about 2950 ft. (900 m).

CLIMATE: Station #94010, Goroka, Papua New Guinea, Lat. 6.1°S, Long. 145.4°E, at 5141 ft. (1567 m). Temperatures are calculated for an elevation of 3300 ft. (1000 m), resulting in probable extremes of 93°F (34°C) and 49°F (10°C).

N/HEMISPHERE	JAN	FEB	MAR	APR	MAY	JUN	JUL	AUG	SEP	OCT	NOV	DEC
°F AVG MAX	82	83	84	85	85	84	85	84	84	84	85	83
°F AVG MIN	62	63	63	63	64	65	65	65	66	65	65	63
DIURNAL RANGE	20	20	21	22	21	19	20	19	18	19	20	20
RAIN/INCHES	2.1	2.8	4.6	5.9	6.6	9.3	9.1	10.1	10.7	8.3	4.6	2.0
HUMIDITY/%	70	67	67	67	67	71	72	73	74	71	70	70
BLOOM SEASON									*			
DAYS CLR	N/A											
RAIN/MM	53	71	117	150	168	236	231	257	272	211	117	51
°C AVG MAX	27.9	28.4	29.0	29.5	29.5	29.0	29.5	29.0	29.0	29.0	29.5	28.4
°C AVG MIN	16.7	17.3	17.3	17.3	17.9	18.4	18.4	18.4	19.0	18.4	18.4	17.3
DIURNAL RANGE	11.2	11.1	11.7	12.2	11.6	10.6	11.1	10.6	10.0	10.6	11.1	11.1
S/HEMISPHERE	JUL	AUG	SEP	OCT	NOV	DEC	JAN	FEB	MAR	APR	MAY	JUN

Cultural Recommendations

LIGHT: 2000–3000 fc.

TEMPERATURES: Throughout the year, days average 82–85°F (28–30°C), and nights average 62–65°F (17–18°C), with a diurnal range of 19–22°F (11–12°C).

HUMIDITY: 70–75% from summer into autumn, dropping to 65–70% in winter and spring.

WATER: Rainfall is moderate to heavy most of the year, but conditions are slightly drier for 3 months in winter. Cultivated plants should be kept moist but not soggy. Occasional early morning mistings may be beneficial, especially on bright, sunny days.

FERTILIZER: ¼–½ recommended strength. A balanced fertilizer should be applied weekly to biweekly throughout the year.

REST PERIOD: Growing temperatures should be maintained all year. In the habitat, rainfall is lowest in winter, but dew and mist from fog and low clouds are common. Water and fertilizer should be reduced somewhat for cultivated plants, especially those grown in the darker, short-day conditions common during temperate-latitude winters. Plants should be kept on the dry side, but they should never be allowed to dry out completely. In the habitat, light is higher in winter.

GROWING MEDIA: Plants may be mounted on tree-fern or cork slabs if humidity is high and plants are watered at least once daily in summer. When plants are potted, any open, fast-draining medium may be used. Repotting may be done anytime new roots are growing.

MISCELLANEOUS NOTES: The bloom season shown in the climate table is based on Schlechter's collection record. Schlechter indicated that he found the plant only once, suggesting that this location may be near one of the limits of its range. Plants producing flowers which last a single day commonly bloom several times during the year. Flowering usually occurs 7–14 days after a sudden 10°F (5°C) drop in daytime temperatures.

Plant and Flower Information

PLANT SIZE AND TYPE: A 31 in. (80 cm) sympodial epiphyte.

PSEUDOBULB: 31 in. (80 cm) long. The stems are densely leafy.

LEAVES: Many. The lanceolate, spreading leaves are 3–4 in. (8–10 cm) long.

INFLORESCENCE: Short. The flowers are subopposite.

FLOWERS: 2 per inflorescence. The small flowers are 0.9 in. (2.2 cm) across. They are pale yellow with red spots. The backs of the sepals are covered with soft prickles. The lip is white in front, fringed, hairy, and recurved.

REFERENCES: 221, 437, 445.

PHOTOS/DRAWINGS: 437.

Dendrobium excavatum (Blume) Miquel

AKA: *Oxystophyllum excavatum* Blume. Seidenfaden (ref. 454) indicates that plants of *Dendrobium excavatum* have sometimes been incorrectly identified and labeled *D. atropurpureum*. Consequently, some discussions of *D. atropurpureum* may actually refer to *D. excavatum*.

ORIGIN/HABITAT: Southeast Asia. In Malaya, plants grow at about 4900 ft. (1500 m) on Penang Hill and in the Cameron Highlands, where they are most often found on old trees. They are also reported in Cambodia, Borneo, and Indonesia from Sumatra to as far east as New Guinea. Comber (ref. 75) reports that in Java, plants are uncommon and found only in West Java at 1950–3950 ft. (600–1200 m).

CLIMATE: Station #48625, Ipoh, Malaya, Lat. 4.6°N, Long. 101.1°E, at 123 ft. (37 m). Temperatures are calculated for an elevation of 4900 ft. (1500 m), resulting in probable extremes of 83°F (28°C) and 48°F (9°C).

N/HEMISPHERE	JAN	FEB	MAR	APR	MAY	JUN	JUL	AUG	SEP	OCT	NOV	DEC
°F AVG MAX	74	76	77	76	76	76	75	75	74	73	73	73
°F AVG MIN	56	56	57	57	58	57	56	56	57	56	56	56
DIURNAL RANGE	18	20	20	19	18	19	19	19	17	17	17	17
RAIN/INCHES	7.9	3.1	7.6	8.4	6.2	3.6	7.2	6.9	8.8	11.0	13.0	8.9
HUMIDITY/%	76	74	78	78	78	75	76	77	79	82	82	81
BLOOM SEASON									*	*	*	*
DAYS CLR @ 7AM	3	3	3	1	1	2	1	1	0	0	1	2
DAYS CLR @ 1PM	2	2	2	1	1	1	1	0	0	0	0	2
RAIN/MM	201	79	193	213	157	91	183	175	224	279	330	226
°C AVG MAX	23.4	24.5	25.1	24.5	24.5	24.5	24.0	24.0	23.4	22.9	22.9	22.9
°C AVG MIN	13.4	13.4	14.0	14.0	14.5	14.0	13.4	13.4	14.0	13.4	13.4	13.4
DIURNAL RANGE	10.0	11.1	11.1	10.5	10.0	10.5	10.6	10.6	9.4	9.5	9.5	9.5
S/HEMISPHERE	JUL	AUG	SEP	OCT	NOV	DEC	JAN	FEB	MAR	APR	MAY	JUN

Cultural Recommendations

LIGHT: 1800–3000 fc. Light should be diffused or dappled, and direct sunlight should be avoided. Clear days are quite rare.

TEMPERATURES: Throughout the year, days average 73–77°F (24–25°C), and nights average 56–58°F (13–15°C), with a diurnal range of 17–20°F (9–11°C). The extreme high does not exceed the warmest average by more than 6°F (3°C), indicating that plants may be sensitive to wide temperature fluctuations.

HUMIDITY: 75–80% year-round.

WATER: Rainfall is heavy most of the year. The heaviest rainfall occurs in autumn with a secondary maximum in spring. Brief semidry periods occur in midwinter and midsummer. Cultivated plants should be kept evenly moist with only slight drying allowed between waterings.

FERTILIZER: ¼–½ recommended strength. A balanced fertilizer should be applied weekly to biweekly throughout the year.

REST PERIOD: Growing conditions should be maintained year-round. Water should be reduced somewhat in winter for plants cultivated in the dark, short-day conditions common in temperate latitudes. They should never be allowed to dry out completely, however. Fertilizer may be reduced when the plant is not actively growing or when water is reduced. In the habitat, light is slightly higher in winter.

GROWING MEDIA: Plants may be mounted on tree-fern or cork slabs if humidity is high and plants are watered at least once daily in summer. When plants are potted, any open, fast-draining medium may be used. Repotting may be done anytime new roots are growing.

MISCELLANEOUS NOTES: Reports from the habitat indicate that blooming occurs during the wet season.

Plant and Flower Information

PLANT SIZE AND TYPE: An 8–20 in. (20–50 cm) sympodial epiphyte.

PSEUDOBULB: 8–20 in. (20–50 cm) long. The stems are completely leaf-covered. They seldom branch.

LEAVES: Many. The leaves are folded, distichous, very pointed, and overlap at the base. They are 1–2 in. (2.5–5.1 cm) long. Seidenfaden (ref. 454) indicates that the leaves are not jointed, a characteristic that distinguishes this species from other very similar species.

INFLORESCENCE: Very short. Inflorescences arise from between the leaves. Individual flowers appear to rest on the centerline of the stem.

FLOWERS: 1 per inflorescence. The tiny flowers are 0.3 in. (0.8 cm) across and remain somewhat closed. Sepals and petals are pale greenish yellow with fine red dots. The lip is yellowish white to pale green, and the inside with violet speckles. Along of the lower 66% of the shiny lip, the margins are papillose. Along the apical part of the lip, there are 4 thickened, red, wavy crests which join together at their apices. The short column is greenish, with dark red at the top. Flowers are sometimes self-pollinating.

REFERENCES: 25, 75, 200, 216, 254, 310, 317, 437, 448, 454, 455, 469.

PHOTOS/DRAWINGS: 454, 455.

Dendrobium excisum Lindley. See *D. bifarium* Lindley. REFERENCES: 216, 254, 317, 454.

Dendrobium exiguum F. Mueller. Now considered a synonym of *Bulbophyllum exiguum* F. Mueller. REFERENCES: 105, 216, 254.

Dendrobium exile Schlechter

AKA: *D. heterocaulon* Guillaumin.

ORIGIN/HABITAT: Northwestern Thailand. Plants grow in the mountains near Chiang Mai at 1000–5650 ft. (300–1700 m). They are also reported near Dalat, Vietnam and in Yunnan Province of southwest China.

CLIMATE: Station #48327, Chiang Mai, Thailand, Lat. 18.8°N, Long. 99.0°E, at 1100 ft. (335 m). Temperatures are calculated for an elevation of 3500 ft. (1070 m), resulting in probable extremes of 101°F (38°C) and 30°F (–1°C).

N/HEMISPHERE	JAN	FEB	MAR	APR	MAY	JUN	JUL	AUG	SEP	OCT	NOV	DEC
°F AVG MAX	77	82	87	88	86	82	81	79	80	81	78	76
°F AVG MIN	48	49	54	62	66	66	66	67	65	63	58	49
DIURNAL RANGE	29	33	33	26	20	16	15	12	15	18	20	27
RAIN/INCHES	0.3	0.4	0.6	2.0	5.5	6.1	7.4	8.7	11.5	4.9	1.5	0.4
HUMIDITY/%	73	65	58	62	73	78	80	83	83	81	79	76
BLOOM SEASON	N/A											
DAYS CLR @ 7AM	5	5	2	2	1	0	0	0	0	1	3	3
DAYS CLR @ 1PM	9	8	4	2	0	0	0	0	0	0	1	3
RAIN/MM	8	10	15	51	140	155	188	221	292	124	38	10
°C AVG MAX	25.0	27.8	30.6	31.2	30.0	27.8	27.3	26.2	26.7	27.3	25.6	24.5
°C AVG MIN	8.9	9.5	12.3	16.7	18.9	18.9	18.9	19.5	18.4	17.3	14.5	9.5
DIURNAL RANGE	16.1	18.3	18.3	14.5	11.1	8.9	8.4	6.7	8.3	10.0	11.1	15.0
S/HEMISPHERE	JUL	AUG	SEP	OCT	NOV	DEC	JAN	FEB	MAR	APR	MAY	JUN

Cultural Recommendations

LIGHT: 3500–4500 fc. The heavy summer cloud cover indicates that some shading is needed from spring through autumn, but light should be as high as the plant can tolerate, short of burning the leaves. Brisk air movement is recommended.

TEMPERATURES: Summer days average 79–82°F (26–28°C), and nights average 66–67°F (19–20°C), with a diurnal range of 12–16°F (7–9°C). Spring, before the start of the summer rainy season, is the warmest time of the year. Days average 86–88°F (30–31°C), and nights average 54–66°F (12–19°C), with a diurnal range of 20–33°F (11–18°C).

HUMIDITY: 78–83% during the growing season, dropping to near 60% in winter and early spring.

WATER: Rainfall is moderate to heavy from late spring through early autumn, but conditions are much drier in winter. Cultivated plants should be kept moist while actively growing, but water should be gradually reduced after new growths mature in autumn.

Dendrobium exilicaule

FERTILIZER: ¼–½ recommended strength, applied weekly. A high-nitrogen fertilizer is beneficial from spring to midsummer, but a fertilizer high in phosphates should be used in late summer and autumn.

REST PERIOD: Winter days average 76–82°F (25–28°C), and nights average 48–49°F (9–10°C), with a diurnal range of 27–33°F (15–18°C). Growers report that the plants tolerate light frost. In the habitat, rainfall averages are very low for 4–5 months in winter; but during the early part of the season, the high relative humidity indicates that additional moisture is available from frequent fog, mist, and heavy deposits of dew. Growers sometimes recommend eliminating water in winter, but plants are healthiest if for most of the winter they are allowed to become somewhat dry between waterings but do not remain dry for extended periods. For 1–2 months in late winter, however, conditions are clear, warm, and dry, with humidity so low that even the moisture from morning dew is uncommon. Plants should be allowed to dry out completely between waterings and remain dry longer during this time. Occasional early morning mistings between waterings may help keep the plants from becoming too dry. Fertilizer should be greatly reduced or eliminated until water is increased in spring. A cool, dry rest is essential for cultivated plants and should be continued until new growth starts in spring. In the habitat, light is highest in winter.

GROWING MEDIA: Plants may be mounted on cork or tree-fern slabs if humidity is high and water is applied at least once daily in summer. If plants are potted, undersized pots that are barely large enough to hold the roots may be filled with a very open, fast-draining medium. Repotting is best done in early spring when new roots are growing.

MISCELLANEOUS NOTES: Cultivated plants reportedly bloom at random times from summer into early winter.

Plant and Flower Information

PLANT SIZE AND TYPE: A 16–20 in. (40–50 cm) sympodial epiphyte.

PSEUDOBULB: 16–20 in. (40–50 cm) long. The stems sometimes branch near the apex. They have a swollen, pseudobulbous enlargement several nodes above the base. The swollen area is sharply angled and about 4 in. (10 cm) long. The dark greenish brown stems are covered with silvery-grey sheaths.

LEAVES: Many. The terete leaves are 1.6–2.0 in. (4–5 cm) long. They are held close to the stem which provides an easy means of differentiating this plant from closely related species when they are not in bloom. The upper 12–16 in. (30–40 cm) of the stem is leafy. Near the apex, the leaves are so clustered the stems almost appear tasseled.

INFLORESCENCE: 1.6–2.0 in. (4–5 cm) long. Flowers are held near the tips of the leaves. Inflorescences arise from apical nodes of mature stems.

FLOWERS: 1 per inflorescence. The white flowers are 1 in. (2.5 cm) across. The lip is marked with yellow in the throat, a yellow disk, and very minute red or orange dots on the inside of the lip. It has numerous long hairs near the back. The fragrance is reminiscent of baby powder.

HYBRIDIZING NOTES: Johansen (ref. 239) found that the seed capsule opened 217 days after self-pollination and 83% of the seed germinated.

REFERENCES: 220, 239, 254, 450, 454, 528.

PHOTOS/DRAWINGS: 450, *454*.

Dendrobium exilicaule Ridley

AKA: *D. tenuicaule* Ridley not Hooker f.

ORIGIN/HABITAT: Malaya. Plants are found on Langkawi Island, just off the northwest coast near the border with Thailand. Habitat elevation is estimated, so the following climate data should be used with caution.

CLIMATE: Station #48603, Alor Setar, Malaya, Lat. 6.2°N, Long. 100.4°E, at 13 ft. (4 m). Temperatures are calculated for an elevation of 1500 ft. (460 m), resulting in probable extremes of 95°F (35°C) and 56°F (13°C).

N/HEMISPHERE	JAN	FEB	MAR	APR	MAY	JUN	JUL	AUG	SEP	OCT	NOV	DEC
°F AVG MAX	85	87	88	88	85	84	83	83	82	82	83	83
°F AVG MIN	66	66	68	69	70	69	69	69	69	69	68	67
DIURNAL RANGE	19	21	20	19	15	15	14	14	13	13	15	16
RAIN/INCHES	2.5	2.2	5.8	9.0	10.7	7.8	7.7	10.4	12.8	11.9	8.1	5.2
HUMIDITY/%	71	66	70	75	79	79	79	79	82	84	83	77
BLOOM SEASON	N/A											
DAYS CLR @ 7AM	5	4	5	2	0	1	1	1	1	1	2	5
DAYS CLR @ 1PM	2	2	2	1	0	1	1	1	0	0	1	2
RAIN/MM	64	56	147	229	272	198	196	264	325	302	206	132
°C AVG MAX	29.5	30.6	31.2	31.2	29.5	28.9	28.4	28.4	27.8	27.8	28.4	28.4
°C AVG MIN	18.9	18.9	20.1	20.6	21.2	20.6	20.6	20.6	20.6	20.6	20.1	19.5
DIURNAL RANGE	10.6	11.7	11.1	10.6	8.3	8.3	7.8	7.8	7.2	7.2	8.3	8.9
S/HEMISPHERE	JUL	AUG	SEP	OCT	NOV	DEC	JAN	FEB	MAR	APR	MAY	JUN

Cultural Recommendations

LIGHT: 1800–2500 fc. The heavy, persistent cloud cover throughout the year indicates relatively low levels of diffused light. Brisk air movement is important for cultivated plants at all times.

TEMPERATURES: Throughout the year, days average 82–88°F (28–31°C), and nights average 66–70°F (19–21°C), with a diurnal range of 13–21°F (7–12°C). The warmest season is spring, near the end of the semidry period.

HUMIDITY: 75–85% most of the year, dropping to 65–70% for 3 months in winter.

WATER: Rainfall is moderate to heavy most of the year, with a short, 2-month semidry period in winter. Cultivated plants should be kept moist while actively growing, but water should be gradually reduced as the new growths mature in autumn.

FERTILIZER: ¼–½ recommended strength, applied weekly. A high-nitrogen fertilizer is beneficial from spring to midsummer, but a fertilizer high in phosphates should be used in late summer and autumn.

REST PERIOD: Growing conditions should be maintained all year. However, winter diurnal range should be increased to about 20°F (11°C). In the habitat, rainfall is reduced, but heavy dew is common, making more water available than is indicated by the rainfall averages. In cultivation, water should be reduced for 1–2 months and the plants allowed to dry slightly between waterings. Fertilizer should be reduced or eliminated until water is increased in spring.

GROWING MEDIA: Plants may be mounted on tree-fern or cork slabs if humidity is high and plants are watered at least once daily in summer. When plants are potted, any open, fast-draining medium may be used. Repotting may be done anytime new roots are growing.

Plant and Flower Information

PLANT SIZE AND TYPE: A 12 in. (30 cm) sympodial epiphyte.

PSEUDOBULB: 12 in. (30 cm) long. The slender stems are weak.

LEAVES: Several. The linear-lanceolate leaves are 3 in. (8 cm) long.

FLOWERS: 1–2 per inflorescence. The flowers are 1.3 in. (3.4 cm) long. Sepals and petals are pink with darker tips. The white lip is marked with pink lines in the center. The lip has an ovate, ruffled midlobe and broad, erect sidelobes.

REFERENCES: 200, 223, 402, 455.

PHOTOS/DRAWINGS: 455.

Dendrobium exilifolium Ames and Schweinfurth

AKA: When describing this plant, Ames and Schweinfurth indicated that it is probably the plant named *Sarcopodium verruciferum* Rolfe var. *pauciflorum* Carr and include it in the section *Sarcopodium*. Most species in this section have now been transferred to the genus *Epigeneium*.

ORIGIN/HABITAT: Western Sumatra. Plants were originally found in virgin jungle at 4100–4500 ft. (1250–1370 m) on the northwest side of Toba Lake.

CLIMATE: Station #96163, Padang, Sumatra, Indonesia, Lat. 0.9°S, Long. 100.4°E, at 19 ft. (6 m). Temperatures are calculated for an elevation of 4300 ft. (1310 m), resulting in probable extremes of 80°F (27°C) and 54°F (12°C).

N/HEMISPHERE	JAN	FEB	MAR	APR	MAY	JUN	JUL	AUG	SEP	OCT	NOV	DEC
°F AVG MAX	73	73	72	72	72	72	73	73	73	73	74	73
°F AVG MIN	60	60	60	60	60	60	60	60	60	61	61	60
DIURNAL RANGE	13	13	12	12	12	12	13	13	13	12	13	13
RAIN/INCHES	10.9	13.7	6.0	19.5	20.4	18.9	13.8	10.2	12.1	14.3	12.4	12.1
HUMIDITY/%	81	82	82	84	85	84	81	81	82	83	81	81
BLOOM SEASON						*						
DAYS CLR @ 7AM	5	1	1	0	0	2	2	1	2	2	3	5
DAYS CLR @ 1PM	5	2	2	1	1	3	3	4	3	3	6	5
RAIN/MM	277	348	152	495	518	480	351	259	307	363	315	307
°C AVG MAX	22.7	22.7	22.2	22.2	22.2	22.2	22.7	22.7	22.7	22.7	23.3	22.7
°C AVG MIN	15.5	15.5	15.5	15.5	15.5	15.5	15.5	15.5	15.5	16.0	16.0	15.5
DIURNAL RANGE	7.2	7.2	6.7	6.7	6.7	6.7	7.2	7.2	7.2	6.7	7.3	7.2
S/HEMISPHERE	JUL	AUG	SEP	OCT	NOV	DEC	JAN	FEB	MAR	APR	MAY	JUN

Cultural Recommendations

LIGHT: 2000–3000 fc. Diffused light is preferred.

TEMPERATURES: Throughout the year, days average 72–74°F (22–23°C), and nights average 60–61°F (16°C), with a diurnal range of 12–13°F (7°C). Probable extremes vary only a few degrees from the averages, indicating that plants from this habitat probably cannot tolerate wide temperature fluctuations.

HUMIDITY: Near 80–85% year-round.

WATER: Rainfall is heavy all year. Cultivated plants should be constantly moist.

FERTILIZER: ¼–½ recommended strength. A balanced fertilizer should be applied weekly to biweekly throughout the year.

REST PERIOD: Growing conditions should be maintained year-round. Water may be reduced somewhat in winter for plants grown in the dark, short-day conditions common in temperate latitudes, but they should never be allowed to dry out completely.

GROWING MEDIA: Plants may be mounted on tree-fern or cork slabs or potted in small pots filled with any open, fast-draining medium. Repotting may be done anytime new roots are actively growing.

MISCELLANEOUS NOTES: The bloom season shown in the climate table is based on collection reports.

Plant and Flower Information

PLANT SIZE AND TYPE: A sympodial epiphyte less than 6 in. (15 cm) tall.

PSEUDOBULB: 1.3 in. (3.3 cm) long. The yellow pseudobulbs, which are connected by a very short rhizome, become deeply grooved with age.

LEAVES: 2. The leathery leaves are 3.0–4.5 in. (8–11 cm) long. They may be linear or tongue-shaped.

INFLORESCENCE: Short. Inflorescences are shorter than the leaf.

FLOWERS: 1–3 per inflorescence. The flowers are 0.7 in. (1.8 cm) across. Sepals are red-green on the outside. Blossoms are yellow on the inside with reddish purple splotches in the throat.

REFERENCES: 225, 298.

Dendrobium eximium Schlechter

AKA: *D. bellum* J. J. Smith, *D. wollastonii* Ridley.

ORIGIN/HABITAT: New Guinea. In northern Papua, plants grow on moss-covered trees on both north- and south-facing slopes of the Torricelli Range at about 2000 ft. (610 m). In Irian Jaya (western New Guinea), they grow in the Went mountains at about 1300 ft. (400 m). Plants cultivated at the botanical garden at Bogor, Java had much smaller flowers. Whether the difference was caused by environmental conditions or a natural variation in flower size is unknown.

CLIMATE: Station #94004, Wewak, Papua New Guinea, Lat. 3.6°S, Long. 143.7°E, at 16 ft. (5 m). Temperatures are calculated for an elevation of 2000 ft. (610 m), resulting in probable extremes of 91°F (33°C) and 55°F (13°C).

N/HEMISPHERE	JAN	FEB	MAR	APR	MAY	JUN	JUL	AUG	SEP	OCT	NOV	DEC
°F AVG MAX	81	81	81	81	81	81	80	79	80	81	81	81
°F AVG MIN	67	67	67	68	68	68	68	68	67	67	68	67
DIURNAL RANGE	14	14	14	13	13	13	12	11	13	14	13	14
RAIN/INCHES	7.6	4.8	5.3	10.0	13.3	14.5	12.1	11.9	14.9	16.9	15.1	10.8
HUMIDITY/%	80	79	79	78	79	81	82	82	81	82	81	80
BLOOM SEASON			*							*		
DAYS CLR	N/A											
RAIN/MM	193	122	135	254	338	368	307	302	378	429	384	274
°C AVG MAX	27.5	27.5	27.5	27.5	27.5	27.5	26.9	26.4	26.9	27.5	27.5	27.5
°C AVG MIN	19.7	19.7	19.7	20.3	20.3	20.3	20.3	20.3	19.7	19.7	20.3	19.7
DIURNAL RANGE	7.8	7.8	7.8	7.2	7.2	7.2	6.6	6.1	7.2	7.8	7.2	7.8
S/HEMISPHERE	JUL	AUG	SEP	OCT	NOV	DEC	JAN	FEB	MAR	APR	MAY	JUN

Cultural Recommendations

LIGHT: 1800–3000 fc.

TEMPERATURES: Throughout the year, days average 79–81°F (26–28°C), and nights average 67–68°F (20°C), with a diurnal range of 11–14°F (6–8°C). Growers indicate that plants grow well in intermediate to cool conditions.

HUMIDITY: Near 80% year-round.

WATER: Rainfall is heavy all year, but conditions are slightly drier for 1–2 months in winter. Cultivated plants should be kept moist, with little if any drying allowed between waterings.

FERTILIZER: ½ recommended strength. A balanced fertilizer should be applied weekly to biweekly throughout the year. Growers indicate that many closely related *Dendrobium* from low elevations are heavy feeders.

REST PERIOD: Growing conditions should be maintained year-round. Water should be reduced somewhat if plants are grown in the dark, short-day conditions common during temperate-latitude winters. Plants should never be allowed to dry out completely, however. Fertilizer should be reduced if water is reduced.

GROWING MEDIA: A very open and fast-draining medium should be used with either baskets or small pots. Repotting is best done in early spring immediately after the short dry rest when new roots begin growing.

MISCELLANEOUS NOTES: The bloom season shown in the climate table is based on reports from the habitat. Growers indicate that plants are easy to grow and bloom while plants are quite small.

Plant and Flower Information

PLANT SIZE AND TYPE: A 11–18 in. (28–45 cm) sympodial epiphyte.

PSEUDOBULB: 8–16 in. (20–40 cm) long. Pseudobulbs have 5 nodes below the leaves. They become orange-yellow when dry.

LEAVES: 2 at the apex of each growth. The oblong, spreading leaves are 6–8 in. (15–20 cm) long.

INFLORESCENCE: 6 in. (15 cm) long. The erect inflorescences arise from nodes near the apex of the stem.

FLOWERS: Few to many per inflorescence. The large flowers are 1.8–3.0 in. (4.5–7.6 cm) across and showy. The white blossoms sometimes have yellow sepals. They are covered with hairs on the back. Petals are very broad. The sidelobes of the recurved lip are decorated with mauve, purple, or red-brown lines. They are incurved around the column.

REFERENCES: 83, 91, 92, 219, 254, 400, 437, 444, 445, 470, 550, 554.

Dendrobium exsculptum

PHOTOS/DRAWINGS: 437.

Dendrobium exsculptum Teijsm. and Binn. See *D. spegidoglossum* Rchb. f. REFERENCES: 25, 75, 216, 254, 454, 469. PHOTOS/DRAWINGS: 469.

Dendrobium extinctorium Lindley. Often listed as a synonym of *Eria extinctoria* Oliver, but in 1982, Seidenfaden in *Opera Botanica* #62 discusses the confusion regarding the names *Dendrobium extinctorium* and *Eria extinctoria*. REFERENCES: 190, 216, 254, 278, 317.

Dendrobium extraaxillare Schlechter

AKA: Sometimes spelled *D. extra-axillare*.

ORIGIN/HABITAT: Northern Papua New Guinea. Plants grow on tall forest trees at about 1000 ft. (300 m) near the village of Kulel, south of Madang.

CLIMATE: Station #94014, Madang, Papua New Guinea, Lat. 5.2°S, Long. 145.8°E, at 13 ft. (4 m). Temperatures are calculated for a habitat elevation of 1000 ft. (300 m), resulting in probable extremes of 95°F (35°C) and 59°F (15°C).

N/HEMISPHERE	JAN	FEB	MAR	APR	MAY	JUN	JUL	AUG	SEP	OCT	NOV	DEC
°F AVG MAX	80	80	82	82	82	82	82	82	82	84	84	81
°F AVG MIN	74	75	75	75	74	74	74	74	74	73	74	75
DIURNAL RANGE	6	5	7	7	8	8	8	8	8	11	10	6
RAIN/INCHES	4.0	3.4	3.2	8.5	11.2	11.1	10.1	11.3	9.4	11.3	10.5	6.7
HUMIDITY/%	88	87	86	86	86	86	86	85	85	87	88	89
BLOOM SEASON			*									
DAYS CLR	N/A											
RAIN/MM	102	86	81	216	284	282	257	287	239	287	267	170
°C AVG MAX	26.6	26.6	27.7	27.7	27.7	27.7	27.7	27.7	27.7	28.8	28.8	27.1
°C AVG MIN	23.2	23.8	23.8	23.8	23.2	23.2	23.2	23.2	23.2	22.7	23.2	23.8
DIURNAL RANGE	3.4	2.8	3.9	3.9	4.5	4.5	4.5	4.5	4.5	6.1	5.6	3.3
S/HEMISPHERE	JUL	AUG	SEP	OCT	NOV	DEC	JAN	FEB	MAR	APR	MAY	JUN

Cultural Recommendations

LIGHT: 2500–3000 fc.

TEMPERATURES: Throughout the year, days average 80–84°F (27–29°C), and nights average 73–75°F (23–24°C), with a diurnal range of 5–11°F (3–6°C). The warmest highs, the coolest lows, and the greatest diurnal range occur in autumn.

HUMIDITY: Near 85–90% year-round.

WATER: Rainfall is heavy during most of the year but is moderate in midwinter. For most of the year, cultivated plants should be kept moist with little if any drying allowed between waterings.

FERTILIZER: ¼–½ recommended strength. A balanced fertilizer should be applied weekly to biweekly most of the year.

REST PERIOD: Growing conditions should be maintained all year. In the habitat, rainfall decreases for 2–3 months in winter. In cultivation, water and fertilizer should be reduced and the plants allowed to dry slightly between waterings. In the habitat, light is somewhat higher in winter.

GROWING MEDIA: Plants may be mounted on tree-fern or cork slabs if humidity is high and plants are watered at least once daily in summer. When plants are potted, any open, fast-draining medium may be used. Repotting is best done in early spring when new roots are growing.

MISCELLANEOUS NOTES: The bloom season shown in the climate table is based on a collection report. Plants that produce flowers which last a single day commonly bloom several times during the year. Flowering usually occurs 7–14 days after a sudden 10°F (5°C) drop in daytime temperatures.

Plant and Flower Information

PLANT SIZE AND TYPE: A 31–35 in. (80–90 cm) sympodial epiphyte.

PSEUDOBULB: 31–35 in. (80–90 cm) long. The stems are densely leafy.

LEAVES: Many. The elliptical leaves are 4–5 in. (10–13 cm) long.

INFLORESCENCE: Short. The inflorescences are flattened.

FLOWERS: 2 per inflorescence. The flowers, which last a single day, are 0.7 in. (1.8 cm) across but do not open fully. Sepals and petals are somewhat whitish on the outside with a dense, red-brown marbling on the inside. The simple lip has no sidelobes. The column is white.

REFERENCES: 221, 437, 445.

PHOTOS/DRAWINGS: 437.

Dendrobium faciferum J. J. Smith

ORIGIN/HABITAT: Malang, Ambon, and Sulawesi (Celebes). Additional habitat information is not available, but plants were cultivated in the botanical garden at Bogor, Java.

CLIMATE: Station #96755, Bogor, Java, Indonesia, Lat. 6.5°S, Long. 106.8°E, at 558 ft. (170 m). Record extreme temperatures are 96°F (36°C) and 66°F (19°C).

N/HEMISPHERE	JAN	FEB	MAR	APR	MAY	JUN	JUL	AUG	SEP	OCT	NOV	DEC
°F AVG MAX	86	87	88	88	87	85	84	84	85	86	87	86
°F AVG MIN	73	73	73	74	74	74	74	74	74	75	75	74
DIURNAL RANGE	13	14	15	14	13	11	10	10	11	11	12	12
RAIN/INCHES	2.1	1.0	0.5	5.0	8.1	18.8	23.7	20.2	14.4	12.0	11.9	3.4
HUMIDITY/%	72	68	65	66	74	79	84	84	81	79	77	75
BLOOM SEASON	N/A											
DAYS CLR @ 7AM	14	14	14	11	5	3	1	2	4	6	10	12
DAYS CLR @ 1PM	9	10	8	5	1	1	0	0	1	1	3	7
RAIN/MM	53	25	13	127	206	478	602	513	366	305	302	86
°C AVG MAX	30.0	30.6	31.1	31.1	30.6	29.4	28.9	28.9	29.4	30.0	30.6	30.0
°C AVG MIN	22.8	22.8	22.8	23.3	23.3	23.3	23.3	23.3	23.3	23.9	23.9	23.3
DIURNAL RANGE	7.2	7.8	8.3	7.8	7.3	6.1	5.6	5.6	6.1	6.1	6.7	6.7
S/HEMISPHERE	JUL	AUG	SEP	OCT	NOV	DEC	JAN	FEB	MAR	APR	MAY	JUN

Cultural Recommendations

LIGHT: 1800–3000 fc.

TEMPERATURES: Throughout the year, days average 84–88°F (29–31°C), and nights average 73–75°F (23–24°C), with a diurnal range of 10–15°F (6–8°C).

HUMIDITY: 80–85% in summer and early autumn, dropping to 65–70% in winter.

WATER: Rainfall is very heavy from spring into autumn, but conditions are very dry for 2 months in winter. During the growing season, plants should never be allowed to dry out completely, but water should be gradually reduced in late autumn.

FERTILIZER: ¼–½ recommended strength, applied weekly. A high-nitrogen fertilizer is beneficial from spring to midsummer, but a fertilizer high in phosphates should be used in late summer and autumn.

REST PERIOD: Growing conditions should be maintained all year, but the diurnal range increases slightly in winter, and rainfall is very low for 2–3 months. In cultivation, water should be reduced and the plants allowed to become dry between waterings. They should not remain dry for prolonged periods, however. Fertilizer may be reduced or eliminated anytime the plant is not actively growing. In the habitat, light is highest in winter.

GROWING MEDIA: Plants may be mounted on tree-fern or cork slabs if humidity is high and plants are watered at least once daily in summer. When plants are potted, any open, fast-draining medium may be used. Repotting is best done in spring when new growth starts.

Plant and Flower Information

PLANT SIZE AND TYPE: A 39 in. (100 cm) sympodial epiphyte.

PSEUDOBULB: 39 in. (100 cm) long. The slender stems are greyish brown with greenish yellow stripes. They arise from a very short rhizome. The upper portion of each stem is branching.

LEAVES: Many. The lanceolate leaves are 3.2–3.5 in. (8–9 cm) long. They are shortly and unequally bilobed at the apex. The fleshy leaves have a very shiny upper surface and a darker underside. Leaf sheaths are dirty violet.

INFLORESCENCE: 1.2–1.4 in. (3.0–3.5 cm) long. Numerous inflorescences are formed on the upper, leafless portion of the stem.

FLOWERS: Many. The densely clustered flowers are 0.5 in. (1.3 cm) long. The brilliantly yellow blossoms have a pointed, oblong-ovate dorsal sepal, triangular lateral sepals, and oblong petals. The spur is long. The 3-lobed lip is dilated at the apex with erect sidelobes.

REFERENCES: 25, 220, 254, 436.

Dendrobium fairchildae Ames and Quisumbing

AKA: H. Wood (ref. 582) suggests that the rules of nomenclature indicate that the name should be spelled *D. fairchildiae*.

ORIGIN/HABITAT: Luzon Island, the Philippines. Plants grow in Rizal, Catanduanes, and Mountain Provinces. Near Bontoc, they grow on exposed rocks.

CLIMATE: Station #98328, Baguio, Philippines, Lat. 16.4°N, Long. 120.6°E, at 4962 ft. (1512 m). Record extreme temperatures are 84°F (29°C) and 46°F (8°C).

N/HEMISPHERE	JAN	FEB	MAR	APR	MAY	JUN	JUL	AUG	SEP	OCT	NOV	DEC
°F AVG MAX	72	73	76	77	76	75	71	71	71	73	74	74
°F AVG MIN	55	56	58	60	61	61	60	60	60	60	59	57
DIURNAL RANGE	17	17	18	17	15	14	11	11	11	13	15	17
RAIN/INCHES	0.9	0.9	1.7	4.3	15.8	17.2	42.3	45.7	28.1	15.0	4.9	2.0
HUMIDITY/%	83	83	83	85	89	90	93	93	92	89	86	84
BLOOM SEASON								*	*	*	*	
DAYS CLR	N/A											
RAIN/MM	23	23	43	109	401	437	1074	1161	714	381	124	51
°C AVG MAX	22.2	22.8	24.4	25.0	24.4	23.9	21.7	21.7	21.7	22.8	23.3	23.3
°C AVG MIN	12.8	13.3	14.4	15.6	16.1	16.1	15.6	15.6	15.6	15.6	15.0	13.9
DIURNAL RANGE	9.4	9.4	10.0	9.4	8.3	7.8	6.1	6.1	6.1	7.2	8.3	9.4
S/HEMISPHERE	JUL	AUG	SEP	OCT	NOV	DEC	JAN	FEB	MAR	APR	MAY	JUN

Cultural Recommendations

LIGHT: 1800–3000 fc. Diffused or dappled light is recommended. Sky-cover records are unavailable, but high elevations are typically cloudy in this region.

TEMPERATURES: Throughout the year, days average 71–77°F (22–25°C), and nights average 55–61°F (13–16°C), with a diurnal range of 11–18°F (6–10°C). Plants from this habitat usually are not heat tolerant and may be difficult to grow when conditions are hot. If cultivated at warm temperatures, buds may drop.

HUMIDITY: 80–90% year-round.

WATER: Rainfall is very heavy from late spring into autumn, but conditions are much drier in winter. Cultivated plants should be kept moist while actively growing, but water should be gradually reduced in autumn.

FERTILIZER: ¼–½ recommended strength, applied weekly. A high-nitrogen fertilizer is beneficial from spring to midsummer, but a fertilizer high in phosphates should be used in late summer and autumn.

REST PERIOD: Growing temperatures should be maintained all year. Rainfall is low for 2–4 months in winter, but the continuing high humidity indicates that additional moisture is frequently available from fog, dew, or mist. Cultivated plants should be allowed to dry somewhat between waterings, but should never remain dry for long periods. In the habitat, light may be highest in winter.

GROWING MEDIA: Any open, fast-draining medium may be used for potting. Repotting may be done anytime new roots are growing.

MISCELLANEOUS NOTES: The bloom season shown in the climate table is based on collection records. Cultivated plants bloom in autumn.

Plant and Flower Information

PLANT SIZE AND TYPE: A 28–35 in. (70–90 cm) sympodial lithophyte.

PSEUDOBULB: 28–35 in. (70–90 cm) long. The clustered stems are slender and terete.

LEAVES: Many. The 2-ranked leaves are 5–6 in. (13–15 cm) long, lanceolate, pointed, and membranelike. They are deciduous on the lower part of the plant.

Dendrobium fairfaxii

INFLORESCENCE: Very short. The flower clusters emerge from nodes along the side of the pseudobulb.

FLOWERS: 6–9 per inflorescence. The flowers are 1.6–2.0 in. (4–5 cm) long. They are crystalline white with a pink or purple flush on the apex of the lip and the tips of the petals. The large, ovate lip, which is pointed at the tip, is narrowed and sharply angled at the base. The sidelobes are erect and broadly rounded. Blossoms are odorless.

REFERENCES: 179, 224, 373, 536, 582.

PHOTOS/DRAWINGS: *373*, 536.

Dendrobium fairfaxii F. Mueller

AKA: *D. teretifolium* R. Brown var. *fairfaxii* (F. Mueller and Fitzgerald) F. M. Bailey, which is the name used by the International Orchid Commission (ref. 236) to register hybrids and the name under which many plants are grown.

ORIGIN/HABITAT: Eastern Australia. The habitat extends from central to northern New South Wales. Plants grow above 2950 ft. (900 m) in rainforests located between the Blue Mountains and the headwater area of the Clarence River.

CLIMATE: Station #94791, Coffs Harbour, Australia, Lat. 30.3°S, Long. 153.1°E, at 14 ft. (4 m). Temperatures are calculated for an elevation of 3000 ft. (910 m), resulting in probable extremes of 96°F (36°C) and 20°F (−7°C).

N/HEMISPHERE	JAN	FEB	MAR	APR	MAY	JUN	JUL	AUG	SEP	OCT	NOV	DEC
°F AVG MAX	55	57	61	64	69	70	70	70	69	67	61	58
°F AVG MIN	34	35	40	45	49	53	55	56	54	49	40	35
DIURNAL RANGE	21	22	21	19	20	17	15	14	15	18	21	23
RAIN/INCHES	3.8	2.1	2.9	3.8	4.0	5.8	6.9	7.7	8.7	7.7	5.7	4.5
HUMIDITY/%	74	72	70	74	72	76	79	83	79	78	75	74
BLOOM SEASON		*	*									
DAYS CLR @ 4AM	8	9	10	10	12	11	9	8	10	7	11	8
DAYS CLR @ 10AM	16	18	18	12	15	11	8	5	10	10	14	15
RAIN/MM	97	53	74	97	102	147	175	196	221	196	145	114
°C AVG MAX	12.9	14.0	16.2	17.9	20.6	21.2	21.2	21.2	20.6	19.5	16.2	14.5
°C AVG MIN	1.2	1.7	4.5	7.3	9.5	11.7	12.9	13.4	12.3	9.5	4.5	1.7
DIURNAL RANGE	11.7	12.3	11.7	10.6	11.1	9.5	8.3	7.8	8.3	10.0	11.7	12.8
S/HEMISPHERE	JUL	AUG	SEP	OCT	NOV	DEC	JAN	FEB	MAR	APR	MAY	JUN

Cultural Recommendations

LIGHT: 1800–2500 fc. Plants are healthiest with brisk air movement and full early morning sun. Filtered light is recommended during the remainder of the day.

TEMPERATURES: Summer days average 70°F (21°C), and nights average 53–56°F (12–13°C), with a diurnal range of 14–17°F (8–10°C).

HUMIDITY: 80–85% year-round. Humidity in the rainforest habitat is higher than indicated for the weather station.

WATER: Rainfall is moderate to heavy most of the year with a 2–3 month period of somewhat drier conditions in winter. Cultivated plants should kept moist and never allowed to dry out completely, but water should be gradually reduced during autumn.

FERTILIZER: ¼–½ recommended strength, applied weekly. A high-nitrogen fertilizer is beneficial from spring to midsummer, but a fertilizer high in phosphates should be used in late summer and autumn. Growers indicate that many closely related *Dendrobium* from low elevations are heavy feeders.

REST PERIOD: Winter days average 55–58°F (13–15°C), and nights average 34–35°F (1–2°C), with a diurnal range of 21–23°F (12–13°C). In cultivation, water should be reduced, and the plants kept just slightly moist for 2–3 months. Reduce fertilizer until water is increased in the spring. Record low temperatures indicate that plants should survive subfreezing temperatures, at least for short periods. However, cultivated plants should not be exposed to these extremes if at all possible; but if they are, their chance of survival is much better if they are dry at the time. In the habitat, light is highest in winter.

GROWING MEDIA: Mounting plants on tree-fern or cork slabs accommodates their pendulous growth habit. Also, growers report that plants are healthiest if grown on slabs or rafts. However, they may be slow to establish, sometimes taking several years, and should therefore be mounted very tightly. If mounted, humidity must be high and plants must be watered at least once a day in summer. If plants cannot be mounted, hanging pots or baskets may be filled with an open, fast-draining medium. Repotting may be done anytime new roots are growing.

MISCELLANEOUS NOTES: The bloom season shown in the climate table is based on cultivation records.

Plant and Flower Information

PLANT SIZE AND TYPE: A branching sympodial epiphyte or lithophyte that may reach a length of 118 in. (300 cm) but is usually much smaller.

PSEUDOBULB: 2–6 in. (5–15 cm) long. The wiry stems are branching and pendent.

LEAVES: 1 per branch. A leaf forms near the tip of each new branch. New branches emanate from nodes behind the leaf. The terete leaves are 4–24 in. (10–61 cm) long, slender, shiny, and smooth.

INFLORESCENCE: 1.6–4.0 in. (4–10 cm) long. Each branch normally produces 1 inflorescence, which results in many blossoms on a mature plant.

FLOWERS: 2, rarely 4, per inflorescence. The waxy flower segments are 0.8–1.6 in. (2–4 cm) long and remain nearly closed. All segments are slender and elongated. They are white or cream and prominently striped with reddish purple on the basal half. The lip is ruffled at the margin of the midlobe, sharply recurved at the very elongated tip, and decorated with 3 reddish purple keels.

REFERENCES: 67, 105, 216, 218, 240, 254, 533.

PHOTOS/DRAWINGS: 240, *533*.

Dendrobium fairfaxii Rolfe. See *D. mooreanum* Lindley. REFERENCES: 83, 211, 218, 254, 270.

Dendrobium falcatum J. J. Smith

ORIGIN/HABITAT: New Guinea. Isolated and rare in Irian Jaya (western New Guinea), plants grow in the hills near Humboldt Bay, as well as near Alkmaar, Rcahmat, and Mt. Goliath at 150–400 ft. (50–150 m). They were also collected along the Noord River, south of Geluks hill. Plants usually grow in the shade on smooth-barked tree trunks in secondary forests.

CLIMATE: Station #97690, Sentani/Jayapura, Irian Jaya, Lat. 2.7°S, Long. 140.5°E, at 289 ft. (88 m). Record extreme temperatures are 97°F (36°C) and 68°F (20°C).

N/HEMISPHERE	JAN	FEB	MAR	APR	MAY	JUN	JUL	AUG	SEP	OCT	NOV	DEC
°F AVG MAX	87	89	89	90	90	89	89	88	89	90	90	89
°F AVG MIN	72	72	72	73	73	73	73	73	73	74	73	73
DIURNAL RANGE	15	17	17	17	17	16	16	15	16	16	17	16
RAIN/INCHES	4.1	3.9	5.3	2.9	6.7	7.0	8.3	8.3	8.5	4.6	2.4	5.2
HUMIDITY/%	81	80	80	79	81	81	79	80	80	80	81	80
BLOOM SEASON			*									
DAYS CLR @ 9AM	5	3	4	3	2	1	1	0	1	2	2	5
DAYS CLR @ 3PM	4	3	3	3	2	1	3	0	1	2	2	3
RAIN/MM	104	99	135	74	170	178	211	211	216	117	61	132
°C AVG MAX	30.6	31.7	31.7	32.2	32.2	31.7	31.7	31.1	31.7	32.2	32.2	31.7
°C AVG MIN	22.2	22.2	22.2	22.8	22.8	22.8	22.8	22.8	22.8	23.3	22.8	22.8
DIURNAL RANGE	8.3	9.4	9.4	9.4	9.4	8.9	8.9	8.3	8.9	8.9	9.4	8.9
S/HEMISPHERE	JUL	AUG	SEP	OCT	NOV	DEC	JAN	FEB	MAR	APR	MAY	JUN

Cultural Recommendations

LIGHT: 1500–2000 fc.

TEMPERATURES: Throughout the year, days average 87–90°F (31–32°C), and nights average 72–74°F (22–23°C), with a diurnal range of 15–17°F (8–9°C).

HUMIDITY: Near 80% year-round.

WATER: Rainfall is heavy all year, with brief semidry periods in spring and autumn. Cultivated plants should be kept evenly moist and only slight drying allowed between waterings.

FERTILIZER: ¼–½ recommended strength. A balanced fertilizer should be applied weekly to biweekly throughout the year.

REST PERIOD: Growing conditions should be maintained year-round. Water may be reduced somewhat for cultivated plants in winter, especially those grown in the dark, short-day conditions common in temperate latitudes. They should never be allowed to dry out completely, however. In the habitat, light is slightly higher in winter.

GROWING MEDIA: Plants may be mounted on tree-fern or cork slabs if humidity is high and plants are watered at least once daily in summer. When plants are potted, any open, fast-draining medium may be used. Repotting may be done anytime new roots are growing.

MISCELLANEOUS NOTES: The bloom season shown in the climate table is based on reports from the habitat. Plants that produce flowers which last a single day commonly bloom several times during the year. Flowering usually occurs 7–14 days after a sudden 10°F (5°C) drop in daytime temperatures.

Plant and Flower Information

PLANT SIZE AND TYPE: An 11–15 in. (28–38 cm) sympodial epiphyte.

PSEUDOBULB: 11–15 in. (28–38 cm) long. The stems are somewhat flattened.

LEAVES: The narrowly ovate-lanceolate leaves are 1.2–1.6 in. (3–4 cm) long, shiny, and pale green. The leaves taper, becoming slender with 2 teeth at the apex.

INFLORESCENCE: Inflorescences emerge through the leaf sheaths opposite the leaves.

FLOWERS: Few per inflorescence. The short-lived flowers are 0.6 in. (1.4 cm) across. The blossoms have an oblong dorsal sepal, somewhat triangular lateral sepals, and nearly linear petals. They are thickened and incurved at the tips. Sepals and petals are white with merging purple spots. The pointed, 3-lobed lip, which is decorated with dense purple stripes at the margin, is sharply recurved at the tip. It has a wartlike middle strip that is orange below and yellow towards the front.

REFERENCES: 220, 254, 437, 445, 470.

Dendrobium falcipetalum Schlechter

ORIGIN/HABITAT: Northern Papua New Guinea. Plants grow on forest trees at the foot of the Bismarck Range at about 1000 ft. (300 m).

CLIMATE: Station #200187, Erap, Papua New Guinea, Lat. 6.6°S, Long. 146.7°E, at 850 ft. (260 m). Record extreme temperatures are 102°F (39°C) and 53°F (12°C).

N/HEMISPHERE	JAN	FEB	MAR	APR	MAY	JUN	JUL	AUG	SEP	OCT	NOV	DEC
°F AVG MAX	88	88	89	90	93	93	93	93	93	92	90	90
°F AVG MIN	69	69	69	70	72	73	72	72	73	71	74	70
DIURNAL RANGE	19	19	20	20	21	20	21	21	20	21	16	20
RAIN/INCHES	3.9	3.9	2.7	3.0	3.0	5.3	5.9	5.9	7.0	3.4	2.4	3.1
HUMIDITY/%	82	81	81	79	75	74	74	74	77	76	80	80
BLOOM SEASON				*								
DAYS CLR	N/A											
RAIN/MM	98	99	68	77	76	135	149	149	179	87	60	78
°C AVG MAX	30.9	30.9	31.7	32.3	34.0	33.9	33.8	33.9	34.0	33.6	32.3	32.0
°C AVG MIN	20.4	20.5	20.7	21.1	22.0	22.5	22.1	22.4	22.5	21.7	23.3	20.9
DIURNAL RANGE	10.5	10.4	11.0	11.2	12.0	11.4	11.7	11.5	11.5	11.9	9.0	11.1
S/HEMISPHERE	JUL	AUG	SEP	OCT	NOV	DEC	JAN	FEB	MAR	APR	MAY	JUN

Cultural Recommendations

LIGHT: 2500–3000 fc.

TEMPERATURES: Throughout the year, days average 88–93°F (31–34°C), and nights average 69–73°F (20–24°C), with a diurnal range of 16–21°F (9–12°C).

HUMIDITY: 75–80% year-round. However, conditions may be quite dry during hot afternoons.

WATER: Rainfall is moderate most of the year, but conditions are somewhat wetter for 4–5 months in summer and early autumn. Cultivated plants should be thoroughly saturated then allowed to dry slightly between waterings in summer and early autumn. Water should be gradually reduced in autumn.

FERTILIZER: ¼–½ recommended strength. A balanced fertilizer should be applied weekly to biweekly throughout the year.

REST PERIOD: Growing temperatures should be maintained all year. In the habitat, rainfall is lowest in winter, but the high humidity indicates that additional moisture is frequently available from heavy dew. Cultivated plants should be allowed to dry for somewhat longer between waterings, but should not remain dry for extended periods. Fertilizer should be reduced until water is increased in spring. In the habitat, seasonal light variation is minor.

GROWING MEDIA: Plants may be mounted on tree-fern or cork slabs if humidity is high and plants are watered at least once daily in summer. When plants are potted, any open, fast-draining medium may be used. Repotting may be done anytime new roots are growing.

MISCELLANEOUS NOTES: The bloom season shown in the climate table is based on collection records. Plants that produce flowers which last a single day commonly bloom several times during the year. Flowering usually occurs 7–14 days after a sudden 10°F (5°C) drop in daytime temperatures.

Plant and Flower Information

PLANT SIZE AND TYPE: An erect, 16 in. (40 cm) sympodial epiphyte.

PSEUDOBULB: 16 in. (40 cm) long. Stems are simple and erect. They gradually become flattened towards the apex.

LEAVES: The oblong leaves, which are erect-spreading, are 2.4–4.3 in. (6–11 cm) long.

INFLORESCENCE: Short. Inflorescences emerge from nodes at the side of the stem.

FLOWERS: 2 per inflorescence. The short-lived flowers are 0.7 in. (1.7 cm) across. All segments are white. In bright contrast, the tip of the column foot and the keel on the lip are orange-red.

REFERENCES: 221, 437, 445.

PHOTOS/DRAWINGS: 437.

Dendrobium falconeri Hooker

AKA: *D. erythroglossum* Hayata.

ORIGIN/HABITAT: Widespread across India and Southeast Asia. The habitat includes Bhutan, Assam, Khasi (Khasia) Hill region of northeastern India, Burma, northern Thailand, and China as far east as Taiwan. Plants usually grow on lightly shaded branches of broad-leaved trees at 3300–5900 ft. (1000–1800 m).

CLIMATE: Station #48327, Chiang Mai, Thailand, Lat. 18.8°N, Long. 99.0°E, at 1100 ft. (335 m). Temperatures are calculated for an elevation of 5000 ft. (1520 m), resulting in probable extremes of 96°F (36°C) and 25°F (–4°C).

Dendrobium falcorostre

N/HEMISPHERE	JAN	FEB	MAR	APR	MAY	JUN	JUL	AUG	SEP	OCT	NOV	DEC
°F AVG MAX	72	77	82	83	81	77	76	74	75	76	73	71
°F AVG MIN	43	44	49	57	61	61	61	62	60	58	53	44
DIURNAL RANGE	29	33	33	26	20	16	15	12	15	18	20	27
RAIN/INCHES	0.3	0.4	0.6	2.0	5.5	6.1	7.4	8.7	11.5	4.9	1.5	0.4
HUMIDITY/%	73	65	58	62	73	78	80	83	83	81	79	76
BLOOM SEASON	*	*	*	**	**	**	*					
DAYS CLR @ 7AM	5	5	2	2	1	0	0	0	0	1	3	3
DAYS CLR @ 1PM	9	8	4	2	0	0	0	0	0	0	1	3
RAIN/MM	8	10	15	51	140	155	188	221	292	124	38	10
°C AVG MAX	22.3	25.1	27.9	28.4	27.3	25.1	24.5	23.4	24.0	24.5	22.9	21.7
°C AVG MIN	6.2	6.7	9.5	14.0	16.2	16.2	16.2	16.7	15.6	14.5	11.7	6.7
DIURNAL RANGE	16.1	18.4	18.4	14.4	11.1	8.9	8.3	6.7	8.4	10.0	11.2	15.0
S/HEMISPHERE	JUL	AUG	SEP	OCT	NOV	DEC	JAN	FEB	MAR	APR	MAY	JUN

Cultural Recommendations

LIGHT: 2500–3500 fc. The heavy summer cloud cover indicates that some shading is needed for cultivated plants from spring through autumn. However, light should be as high as the plant can tolerate, short of burning the leaves. Growers often recommend that plants be hung near the roof of the greenhouse.

TEMPERATURES: Summer days average 74–77°F (23–25°C), and nights average 61–62°F (16–17°C), with a diurnal range of 12–16°F (7–9°C). The warmest temperatures occur in spring. Days average 81–83°F (27–28°C), and nights average 49–61°F (10–16°C), with a diurnal range of 20–33°F (11–18°C).

HUMIDITY: Near 75–80% most of the year. However, averages increase to near 85% in late summer and drop to near 60% in late winter and early spring.

WATER: Rainfall is moderate to heavy from late spring through early autumn, but conditions are very dry in winter. Cultivated plants should be kept moist while actively growing, but water should be gradually reduced after new growths mature in autumn.

FERTILIZER: ¼–½ recommended strength, applied weekly. A high-nitrogen fertilizer is beneficial from spring to midsummer, but a fertilizer high in phosphates should be used in late summer and autumn.

REST PERIOD: Winter days average 71–77°F (22–25°C), and nights average 43–44°F (6–7°C), with a diurnal range of 27–33°F (15–18°C). The average low temperatures are below 50°F (10°C) for 3 months and then warm rapidly in spring. Plants should be able to tolerate temperatures a few degrees below freezing, but extremes should be avoided in cultivation. During very cold weather, a plant's chance of surviving with minimal damage is better if it is dry. In the habitat, rainfall averages are very low for 4–5 months in winter, but during the early part of the season the high relative humidity indicates that additional moisture is available from frequent fog, mist, and heavy deposits of dew. Growers sometimes recommend eliminating water in winter, but plants are healthiest if for most of the winter they are allowed to become somewhat dry between waterings but do not remain dry for extended periods. For 1–2 months in late winter, however, conditions are clear, warm, and dry, with humidity so low that even the moisture from morning dew is uncommon. Plants should be allowed to dry out completely between waterings and remain dry longer during this time. Occasional early morning mistings between waterings may help keep the plants from becoming too dry. Fertilizer should be greatly reduced or eliminated until water is increased in spring. A cool, dry rest is essential for cultivated plants and should be continued until new growth starts in spring. In the habitat, light is highest in winter. Growers report that plants grown in uniformly warm, wet climates gradually deteriorate.

GROWING MEDIA: Mounting plants on tree-fern or cork slabs accommodates their pendulous growth habit. However, humidity must be high and plants must be watered at least once a day in summer. If plants cannot be mounted, small pots or hanging baskets may be filled with an open, fast-draining medium. Repotting may be done anytime new roots are actively growing.

MISCELLANEOUS NOTES: The bloom season shown in the climate table is based on cultivation records. In the habitat, blooming occurs in late winter or spring.

Plant and Flower Information

PLANT SIZE AND TYPE: A 24–47 in. (60–120 cm) sympodial epiphyte.

PSEUDOBULB: 24–47 in. (60–120 cm) long. The soft, slender stems are thin and knotty with numerous branchlets. They are cascading, pendent, and often become densely tangled and interwoven, forming a confused cluster of stems, roots, branches, and leaves. Stems frequently form roots at the nodes.

LEAVES: Few. New growth is leafy at the apex. The linear, grasslike leaves are 1–3 in. (2.5–7.6 cm) long and quickly deciduous.

INFLORESCENCE: Very short. Numerous inflorescences emerge from nodes on older, leafless stems and all along the most recently matured growths.

FLOWERS: 1 per inflorescence. Considered by many to be the loveliest of all *Dendrobium*, the blossoms are commonly described with adjectives ranging from pretty to magnificent. The fragrant flowers are 2–4 in. (5–10 cm) across. They commonly last 10–14 days, but var. *giganteum* is larger and longer lasting. The pointed sepals and petals are white to pinkish white with amethyst-purple at the tips. The white lip is amethyst at the tip with a deep magenta disk at the base of the throat. The disk is surrounded by a yellow stain which extends to the sidelobes.

HYBRIDIZING NOTES: Chromosome counts are 2n = 38 (ref. 151, 153, 154, 187, 188, 542) and 2n = 2x (ref. 187, 504, 580). Johansen (ref. 239) indicates that plants are self-sterile and that flowers dropped 3–4 days after self-pollination.

REFERENCES: 38, 46, 61, 151, 153, 154, 157, 179, 187, 188, 190, 193, 202, 208, 210, 216, 239, 245, 254, 279, 369, 376, 430, 445, 454, 458, 497, 504, 523, 528, 541, 542, 557, 570, 580.

PHOTOS/DRAWINGS: 210, *245*, 279, *369, 430, 454,* 458, 497.

Dendrobium falcorostre Fitzgerald. See *D. falcorostrum* Fitzgerald. REFERENCES: 216.

Dendrobium falcorostrum Fitzgerald

ORIGIN/HABITAT: Eastern Australia. The habitat extends northward from near Newcastle to the McPherson Range, just south of Brisbane. Plants grow in the highlands at 2950–4600 ft. (900–1400 m). They are usually found in the upper branches of Antarctic beech (*Nothofagus moorei*), where they receive strong filtered light, but the tree foliage protects them from the brightest summer sun and winter frosts. The habitat is commonly cool and cloudy, and plants are often in the clouds for several days at a time. Rainfall is heavy, and snow occurs in winter.

CLIMATE: Station #94788, Kempsey, Australia, Lat. 31.1°S, Long. 152.8°E, at 48 ft. (15 m). Temperatures are calculated for an elevation of 4000 ft. (1220 m), resulting in probable extremes of 93°F (34°C) and 17°F (−8°C).

N/HEMISPHERE	JAN	FEB	MAR	APR	MAY	JUN	JUL	AUG	SEP	OCT	NOV	DEC
°F AVG MAX	55	58	64	67	70	72	73	72	70	66	60	55
°F AVG MIN	29	30	34	40	45	48	50	50	48	42	36	31
DIURNAL RANGE	26	28	30	27	25	24	23	22	22	24	24	24
RAIN/INCHES	3.2	2.6	2.3	2.9	3.2	4.0	4.8	5.8	5.1	4.2	3.8	3.6
HUMIDITY/%	74	72	70	74	72	76	79	83	79	78	75	74
BLOOM SEASON			**	*			*					
DAYS CLR @ 10AM	16	18	18	12	15	11	8	5	10	10	14	15
DAYS CLR @ 4PM	15	14	13	12	12	10	8	4	9	9	12	12
RAIN/MM	81	66	58	74	81	102	122	147	130	107	97	91
°C AVG MAX	12.8	14.4	17.8	19.4	21.1	22.2	22.8	22.2	21.1	18.9	15.5	12.8
°C AVG MIN	−1.7	−1.1	1.1	4.4	7.2	8.9	10.0	10.0	8.9	5.5	2.2	−0.6
DIURNAL RANGE	14.5	15.5	16.7	15.0	13.9	13.3	12.8	12.2	12.2	13.4	13.3	13.0
S/HEMISPHERE	JUL	AUG	SEP	OCT	NOV	DEC	JAN	FEB	MAR	APR	MAY	JUN

Cultural Recommendations

LIGHT: 2500–3500 fc. The heavy summer cloud cover indicates that some shading is needed from spring through autumn, but light should be as high as the plant can tolerate, short of burning the leaves.

TEMPERATURES: Summer days average 72–73°F (22–23°C), and nights average 48–50°F (9–10°C), with a diurnal range of 22–24°F (12–13°C). Due to the effects of the microclimate, actual temperatures in the habitat may be 2–4°F (1°C) warmer than indicated.

HUMIDITY: 75–80% in summer and autumn, dropping to near 70% in winter.

WATER: Rainfall is moderate all year, with a 2–3 month slightly drier period in winter. Watering for cultivated plants should be moderate to heavy during the growing season. Plants should be kept evenly moist, and never be allowed to dry out completely, even in winter.

FERTILIZER: ¼–½ recommended strength, applied weekly. A high-nitrogen fertilizer is beneficial from spring to midsummer, but a fertilizer high in phosphates should be used in late summer and autumn. Growers indicate that *D. falcorostrum* requires a richer potting mix or more frequent fertilizing than most Dendrobiums.

REST PERIOD: Winter days average 55–58°F (13–14°C), and nights average 29–31°F (–1 to –2°C), with a diurnal range of 24–28°F (13–16°C). Cultivated plants do not need temperatures to be quite this cold and grow well when lows are slightly above freezing. In the habitat, rainfall is somewhat less during winter, but additional moisture is also available from heavy dew, mist, fog, and low clouds. Cultivated plants need less water during this time, but they should never be allowed to dry out completely. Brisk air movement is recommended at all times. Plants should be watered or misted on bright, sunny days so that any water on the foliage can dry before nightfall. Fertilizer should be reduced or eliminated until light increases and temperatures warm in the spring. In the habitat, light is highest in winter.

GROWING MEDIA: Plants are healthiest grown outdoors in compatible climates. *D. falcorostrum* may be potted in any open, fast-draining medium. Some Australian growers use tree needles, crushed rock, and pine bark; this suggests that plants may require an acid medium. Repotting is best done in early spring, immediately after flowering, when new roots begin to grow.

MISCELLANEOUS NOTES: The bloom season shown in the climate table is based on cultivation records. Growers report that *D. falcorostrum* grows outdoors in Melbourne, Australia. Other growers indicate that it is difficult in cultivation, but they have found that a cool, dry rest initiates blooming.

Plant and Flower Information

PLANT SIZE AND TYPE: A 5–20 in. (13–50 cm) sympodial epiphyte or rarely a lithophyte.

PSEUDOBULB: 5–20 in. (13–50 cm) long. The yellow-green stems, which may be rather slender or relatively thick, taper at each end. Short plants tend to have thick stems, while tall plants are more likely to have slender stems.

LEAVES: 2–5 per growth. The pale green leaves are 2.5–5.5 in. (6–14 cm) long, narrowly obovate, and thin. They are held near the top of the stem.

INFLORESCENCE: 3–6 in. (8–15 cm) long. Plants produce 1–4 drooping inflorescences from nodes near the apex of the stem.

FLOWERS: 5–20 per inflorescence. The large, waxy flowers are 1–2 in. (2.5–5.0 cm) across and open fully. The densely packed masses of blossoms are described as truly beautiful. Sepals and petals are white to cream. The lip is marked with yellow and purple. It is curved to form a long tapering point. They are strongly fragrant during the warmer hours of the day.

HYBRIDIZING NOTES: Australian growers (ref. 563) report that *D. falcorostrum* is difficult to breed because plants rarely hold their capsules to maturity.

REFERENCES: 23, 67, 105, 161, 216, 240, 254, 262, 325, 326, 389, 390, 421, 445, 495, 527, 533, 534, 563.

PHOTOS/DRAWINGS: *105, 240, 325, 389, 390, 495, 533, 534, 563.*

Dendrobium fallax Guillaumin. See *D. pachyglossum* Parish and Rchb. f. **REFERENCES:** 229, 448, 454.

Dendrobium fantasticum L. O. Williams. See *D. amphigenyum* Ridley. **REFERENCES:** 83, 227.

Dendrobium fantasticum P. Taylor and J. J. Wood. See *D. woodsii* Cribb. **REFERENCES:** 83.

Dendrobium fargesii Finet. Now considered a synonym of *Epigeneium fargesii* (Finet) Gagnepain. **REFERENCES:** 118, 208, 213, 219, 220, 225, 254, 445, 449, 499, 505.

Dendrobium fariniferum Schlechter. Now considered a synonym of *Diplocaulobium fariniferum* (Schlechter) Carr. **REFERENCES:** 92, 221, 225, 437, 445.

Dendrobium farmerii Paxton

AKA: Sometimes spelled *D. farmeri*. Synonyms include *D. densiflorum* Lindley var. *farmerii* Regal. Seidenfaden (ref. 454) indicates that plants which should be *D. palpebrae* Lindley are sometimes incorrectly called *D. farmerii*. Some references indicate that *D. palpebrae* may be a variety of *D. farmerii*, but Seidenfaden (ref. 454) retained species status for both.

D. farmerii var. *parviflora* Regal and *D. farmerii* var. *aureoflava* Hooker f. are recognized varieties from Burma. The yellow flowered variety, *D. farmerii* var. *aureoflava*, has also been collected at high elevations in the Khanburi forest of western Thailand.

ORIGIN/HABITAT: Widespread in Nepal, Bhutan, northeastern India, Burma, Thailand, Laos, and Malaya. Plants are usually found at 1000–3300 ft. (300–1000 m). In Malaya, plants grow in primary forests on large trees that overhang rivers.

CLIMATE: Station #42410, Gauhati, India, Lat. 26.1°N, Long. 91.6°E, at 158 ft. (48 m). Temperatures have been calculated for 2000 ft. (610 m), resulting in probable extremes of 98°F (37°C) and 35°F (2°C). This station represents the northern portion of the habitat. In the southern part of the habitat, data for Chanthaburi, Thailand at 3000 ft. (910 m), resulted in probable extremes of 93°F (34°C) and 38°F (3°C).

N/HEMISPHERE	JAN	FEB	MAR	APR	MAY	JUN	JUL	AUG	SEP	OCT	NOV	DEC
°F AVG MAX	70	72	80	82	82	83	84	84	83	81	75	70
°F AVG MIN	45	48	54	62	66	71	72	72	70	65	55	47
DIURNAL RANGE	25	24	26	20	16	12	12	12	13	16	20	23
RAIN/INCHES	0.4	1.2	2.0	5.7	9.3	12.3	12.3	10.3	6.6	2.8	0.6	0.2
HUMIDITY/%	79	72	64	71	82	85	85	86	84	84	83	82
BLOOM SEASON	*	*	**	***	***	**	**					
DAYS CLR @ 6AM	6	12	16	11	3	0	0	1	3	7	6	3
DAYS CLR @ 12PM	17	16	18	15	6	1	0	0	2	11	17	19
RAIN/MM	10	30	51	145	236	312	312	262	168	71	15	5
°C AVG MAX	21.1	22.2	26.6	27.7	27.7	28.3	28.8	28.8	28.3	27.2	23.8	21.1
°C AVG MIN	7.2	8.8	12.2	16.6	18.8	21.6	22.2	22.2	21.1	18.3	12.7	8.3
DIURNAL RANGE	13.9	13.4	14.4	11.1	8.9	6.7	6.6	6.6	7.2	8.9	11.1	12.8
S/HEMISPHERE	JUL	AUG	SEP	OCT	NOV	DEC	JAN	FEB	MAR	APR	MAY	JUN

Dendrobium fasciculatum

Cultural Recommendations

LIGHT: 2000–2500 fc.

TEMPERATURES: Summer days average 83–84°F (28–29°C), and nights average 71–72°F (22°C), with a diurnal range of 12°F (7°C). Plants from the southern part of the habitat may experience temperatures 5–10°F (3–6°C) warmer than indicated.

HUMIDITY: 80–85% most of the year, dropping to 65–70% in winter.

WATER: Rainfall is heavy from spring into autumn but is low for 2–3 months in winter. Cultivated plants should be kept moist while growing, but water should be gradually reduced after new growths mature in autumn.

FERTILIZER: ¼–½ recommended strength, applied weekly. A high nitrogen fertilizer is beneficial from spring to midsummer, but a fertilizer high in phosphates should be used in late summer and autumn.

REST PERIOD: Winter days average 70–72°F (21–22°C), and nights average 45–48°F (7–9°C), with a diurnal range of 23–25°F (13–14°C). The actual temperatures do not appear to be critical, but the increased diurnal range is common throughout the habitat. Although rainfall is low for 4–5 winter months, high humidity and the large temperature range indicate that additional moisture from heavy dew is common. Therefore, while water should be greatly reduced and cultivated plants allowed to dry out between waterings from late autumn into early spring, they should not remain dry for extended periods. Occasional mistings between waterings during bright, sunny weather may help prevent the plants from becoming too dry. Fertilizer should be reduced or eliminated until active growth resumes and water is increased in spring. In the habitat, light is brightest in winter.

GROWING MEDIA: Plants may be mounted on slabs or rafts, if humidity is high. When plants are potted, a container that is small for the size of the plant may be filled with any open, fast-draining medium. Repotting is best done in early spring or immediately after flowering.

MISCELLANEOUS NOTES: The bloom season shown in the climate table is based on cultivation records. In the habitat, plants bloom when temperatures warm and rainfall increases in spring. Growers report that a prolonged dry period is essential to promote flowering.

Growers in Singapore indicate that Burmese plants have relatively solid pseudobulbs and do not bloom in the warm, uniform climate of Singapore, but plants brought to Singapore from the mountains of northern Malaya usually flower once a year.

Plant and Flower Information

PLANT SIZE AND TYPE: A 12–18 in. (30–45 cm) sympodial epiphyte.

PSEUDOBULB: 12–18 in. (30–45 cm) long. Pseudobulbs are spindle-shaped, usually erect, thickened, strongly 4-angled in the upper part, and swollen at the base.

LEAVES: 2–4. The leaves are oval to oblong, 3–6 in. (8–15 cm) long, leathery, evergreen, and pointed at the apex. They appear near the top of the pseudobulb.

INFLORESCENCE: 8–12 in. (20–30 cm) long. The inflorescences are drooping, laxly to densely flowered, and emerge from near the top of both leafy and leafless pseudobulbs. Mature, well-grown plants produce several inflorescences.

FLOWERS: 14–35 loosely arranged flowers per inflorescence. Blossoms are about 2 in. (5 cm) across. The sepals and much broader petals are pink, lilac-mauve, straw-yellow, or white. The large, downy lip is nearly round, egg-yolk to orange-yellow, and often edged with white. Plants sold as *D. farmerii* var. *albiflorum* have flowers with white, crystalline sepals and petals and a bright yellow lip. They last 2 weeks if kept cool.

HYBRIDIZING NOTES: Chromosome counts are 2n = 40 (ref. 151, 152, 187, 504, 580) as *D. farmerii* and 2n = 40 (ref. 150, 504, 580) as *D. farmerii* var. *aureum*. Relatively few hybrids have been produced using *D. farmerii* or closely related species, probably because of sterility factors. Johansen (ref. 239) found *D. farmerii* to be self-sterile and the flowers dropped 4–7 days after self-pollination. However, when plants were pollinated by an unrelated clone of *D. farmerii*, all pollinations produced capsules which opened about 385 days after pollination. Of the seed produced, 95% contained embryos and 84% germinated. When crossed with *D. secundum* (Blume) Lindley, using *D. farmerii* as the female parent, no viable seed was produced. It was also incompatible with *D. linguella* Rchb. f. *D. farmerii* is reported to hybridize naturally with *D. thyrsiflorum* Rchb. f. and cross-pollination occurs easily in the greenhouse

REFERENCES: 6, 25, 32, 36, 38, 46, 150, 151, 152, 157, 179, 187, 190, 196, 200, 202, 210, 216, 239, 243, 245, 254, 266, 326, 365, 369, 371, 376, 389, 395, 428, 430, 445, 447, 448, 454, 455, 458, 504, 510, 523, 541, 557. 568, 570, 580, 581.

PHOTOS/DRAWINGS: 6, *36,* 46, 190, 200, 210, *245, 365, 369, 371, 389, 428, 430, 454, 455,* 458, 541, 557, *581.*

Dendrobium fasciculatum F. M. Bailey.
Now considered a synonym of *Flickingeria comata*. REFERENCES: 67, 219, 254.

Dendrobium faulhaberianum Schlechter

AKA: *D. aduncum* Wallich ex Lindley var. *faulhaberianum* (Schlechter) Tang and Wang, and *D. oxyanthum* Gagnepain. Hu (ref. 208) and Tsi (ref. 528) consider *D. faulhaberianum* a variety of *D. aduncum*, but Seidenfaden (ref. 454) retains it as a separate species. Plants that should have been identified as *D. faulhaberianum* have sometimes been called *D. hercoglossum*.

ORIGIN/HABITAT: Laos, Vietnam, and Hainan Island, China. In Laos, plants were collected 6 mi. (10 km) south of Vang Vieng, Vientiane. In Vietnam, they were found in the Quang Tri region. Habitat elevation is unreported, so the following climate data should be used with caution.

CLIMATE: Station #48940, Vientiane, Laos, Lat. 18.0°N, Long. 102.6°E, at 559 ft. (170 m). Record extreme temperatures are 108°F (42°C) and 37°F (3°C).

N/HEMISPHERE	JAN	FEB	MAR	APR	MAY	JUN	JUL	AUG	SEP	OCT	NOV	DEC
°F AVG MAX	83	87	91	93	90	89	87	87	87	87	85	83
°F AVG MIN	58	63	67	72	75	76	75	75	74	71	66	59
DIURNAL RANGE	25	24	24	21	15	13	12	12	13	16	19	24
RAIN/INCHES	0.3	0.6	1.4	3.8	10.5	11.6	10.1	12.8	12.2	4.1	0.8	0.1
HUMIDITY/%	71	70	67	70	79	83	83	85	85	79	75	73
BLOOM SEASON	N/A											
DAYS CLR @ 7AM	11	5	6	1	1	1	0	1	6	10	11
DAYS CLR @ 1PM	16	16	15	11	2	1	0	0	1	4	7	12
RAIN/MM	8	15	36	97	267	295	257	325	310	104	20	3
°C AVG MAX	28.3	30.6	32.8	33.9	32.2	31.7	30.6	30.6	30.6	30.6	29.4	28.3
°C AVG MIN	14.4	17.2	19.4	22.2	23.9	24.4	23.9	23.9	23.3	21.7	18.9	15.0
DIURNAL RANGE	13.9	13.4	13.4	11.7	8.3	7.3	6.7	6.7	7.3	8.9	10.5	13.3
S/HEMISPHERE	JUL	AUG	SEP	OCT	NOV	DEC	JAN	FEB	MAR	APR	MAY	JUN

Cultural Recommendations

LIGHT: 2000–3000 fc.

TEMPERATURES: Summer days average 87–89°F (31–32°C), and nights average 75–76°F (24°C), with a diurnal range of 12–13°F (7°C). The warmest season is spring, just before the start of the summer rainy season. Days average 90–93°F (32–34°C), and nights average 67–75°F (19–24°C), with a diurnal range of 15–24°F (8–13°C).

HUMIDITY: 80–85% in summer and autumn, decreasing to 70–75% in winter and spring.

WATER: Rainfall is heavy for about 6 months from late spring into autumn. Cultivated plants should be kept moist during this time. They may even need daily watering during very hot weather. However, water should be gradually reduced after new growths mature in autumn.

FERTILIZER: ¼–½ recommended strength, applied weekly. A high-nitrogen fertilizer is beneficial from spring to midsummer, but a fertilizer high in phosphates should be used in late summer and autumn.

REST PERIOD: Winter days average 83–87°F (28–31°C), and nights average 58–63°F (14–17°C), with a diurnal range of 24–25°F (13–14°C). In the habitat, rainfall is very low for 4–5 months in winter, but considerable moisture is available from frequent heavy dew and mist. Water should be reduced for cultivated plants, but not eliminated completely. Plants should be allowed dry out between waterings, but they should not remain dry for extended periods. Occasional early morning mistings on sunny days between waterings may help keep plants from becoming too dry.

GROWING MEDIA: Plants may be mounted on tree-fern or cork slabs if humidity is high and plants are watered at least once daily in summer. When plants are potted, any open, fast-draining medium may be used. Repotting is best done in early spring when new roots are growing.

Plant and Flower Information

PLANT SIZE AND TYPE: A 20–39 in. (50–100 cm) sympodial epiphyte.

PSEUDOBULB: 20–39 in. (50–100 cm) long. Above the pseudobulbous base, the stems have a roughly equal diameter along their entire length.

LEAVES: The leaves are usually 2.4–3.5 in. (6–9 cm) long.

INFLORESCENCE: 2.8 in. (7 cm) long. Inflorescences emerge along the side of the stem.

FLOWERS: 5–8 per inflorescence. The flowers are 0.8–1.2 in. (2–3 cm) across. All segments are pointed and approximately equal in length. The lip, which has a large, glossy central callus, is finely pubescent near the apex and along the midline.

REFERENCES: 61, 136, 208, 221, 266, 448, 454, 528.

PHOTOS/DRAWINGS: 454.

Dendrobium fellowsii F. Mueller

AKA: *D. bairdianum* F. M. Bailey, *D. giddinsii* T. E. Hunt. Plants are frequently cultivated under the name *D. bairdianum*.

ORIGIN/HABITAT: Eastern Queensland, Australia between the Burdekin and Bloomfield Rivers. Plants grow in open forests at 1500–3300 ft. (450–1000 m), which is usually below the level of the highland rainforests but in a zone where plants receive considerable moisture each night from heavy dew and mists. These areas are hot and dry during the day but cool and moist at night. Plants normally grow high on the host trees, where they are beyond the reach of frequent grass fires. Plants often grow with *D. agrostophyllum* F. Mueller.

CLIMATE: Station #94287, Cairns, Australia, Lat. 16.9°S, Long. 145.8°E, at 7 ft. (2 m). Temperatures are calculated for an elevation of 2000 ft. (610 m), resulting in probable extremes of 103°F (40°C) and 36°F (3°C).

N/HEMISPHERE	JAN	FEB	MAR	APR	MAY	JUN	JUL	AUG	SEP	OCT	NOV	DEC
°F AVG MAX	71	73	76	79	81	83	83	82	80	78	74	72
°F AVG MIN	54	55	57	61	63	66	67	67	66	63	59	57
DIURNAL RANGE	17	18	19	18	18	17	16	15	14	15	15	15
RAIN/INCHES	1.6	1.7	1.7	2.1	3.9	8.7	16.6	15.7	18.1	11.3	4.4	2.9
HUMIDITY/%	69	67	65	65	65	68	72	72	74	73	73	72
BLOOM SEASON				*	*	**	**	*				
DAYS CLR @ 10AM	9	11	13	11	6	6	4	5	6	7	11	10
DAYS CLR @ 4PM	8	10	12	16	10	7	4	3	4	6	9	10
RAIN/MM	41	43	43	53	99	221	422	399	460	287	112	74
°C AVG MAX	21.9	23.0	24.7	26.3	27.5	28.6	28.6	28.0	26.9	25.8	23.6	22.5
°C AVG MIN	12.5	13.0	14.1	16.3	17.5	19.1	19.7	19.7	19.1	17.5	15.2	14.1
DIURNAL RANGE	9.4	10.0	10.6	10.0	10.0	9.5	8.9	8.3	7.8	8.3	8.4	8.4
S/HEMISPHERE	JUL	AUG	SEP	OCT	NOV	DEC	JAN	FEB	MAR	APR	MAY	JUN

Cultural Recommendations

LIGHT: 2500–3500 fc. In the habitat, plants receive plenty of bright light.

TEMPERATURES: Summer days average 82–83°F (28–29°C), and nights average 66–67°F (19–20°C), with a diurnal range of 15–17°F (8–9°C).

HUMIDITY: 75–85% year-round. Humidity near cloudforests is probably greater than indicated in the climate table. Cultivated plants are healthiest with high humidity and brisk air movement.

WATER: Rainfall is moderate to heavy from late spring into autumn, with a 4–5 month semidry period in winter and early spring. Cultivated plants should be kept moist and never be allowed to dry out during the growing season, but water should be gradually reduced in autumn

FERTILIZER: ¼–½ recommended strength, applied weekly. A high-nitrogen fertilizer is beneficial from spring to midsummer, but a fertilizer high in phosphates should be used in late summer and autumn.

REST PERIOD: Winter days average 71–76°F (22–25°C), and nights average 54–57°F (13–14°C), with a diurnal range of 15–19°F (8–11°C). In cultivation, water should be reduced for 3–5 months from late autumn into early spring. Plants should be kept somewhat dry, but they should never be allowed to dry out completely. Light, humidity, and air movement should be maintained. Fertilizer should be reduced or eliminated until water is increased in spring.

GROWING MEDIA: Mounting on slabs or rafts produces excellent results providing humidity is high and plants are watered at least once daily in summer. On the hottest days, several waterings may be necessary. If plants are potted, a very open and fast-draining medium is recommended. Undersized pots, barely large enough to hold the roots, should be used. Repotting may be done in very early spring, as soon as new growth begins.

MISCELLANEOUS NOTES: *D. fellowsii* is rather scarce in nature. Australian growers consider it very difficult to grow, so cultural requirements should receive careful attention. The McQueens (ref. 291) state that they lost several plants until they mounted them on small cork or tree fern slabs, hung them high in the greenhouse, and provided a cooler, drier rest.

Plant and Flower Information

PLANT SIZE AND TYPE: A 2–10 in. (5–25 cm) sympodial epiphyte.

PSEUDOBULB: 0.8–6.0 in. (2–15 cm) long. The distinctive pseudobulbs are tufted, slender, constricted at the nodes, dark purple-brown, and ribbed with age. Plants may grow as small clumps or individual plants.

LEAVES: 2–5. Leaves are held at the apex of young growths. They are linear-lanceolate, 1.2–3.5 in. (3–9 cm) long, short-lived, and curved along the margin.

INFLORESCENCE: 0.8–3.2 in. (2–8 cm) long. Surprisingly small plants frequently produce 1 or 2 inflorescences, but more mature plants often produce many. Inflorescences emerge from nodes near the apex of old and new pseudobulbs.

FLOWERS: 2–7 per inflorescence. The flowers are 0.8–1.0 in. (2.0–2.5 cm) across, which is large for the plant size. They open fully. Sepals and petals are uniform pale green or yellow-green, becoming buff-brown with age. The green lip has rich purple-brown markings and a white callus consisting of 2 ridges covered with fine hairs. The column is purplish in front.

HYBRIDIZING NOTES: Chromosome count is $2n = 36$ (ref. 153, 273) as *D. bairdianum* Bailey. Upton (ref. 533) indicates that it was used once with *D. bigibbum*. The resulting hybrids resembled *D. bigibbum* in flower color and size as well as plant form, but the flower shape resembled *D. fellowsii*.

REFERENCES: 67, 153, 179, 216, 240, 254, 262, 263, 273, 291, 325, 533.

PHOTOS/DRAWINGS: *240, 291,* 325, *533.*

Dendrobium ferdinandi Kränzlin

ORIGIN/HABITAT: Papua New Guinea. Plants probably originated from the southern part of the island, but specific location and elevation information is not available, so the following climate information should be used with extreme caution. The plants used for the original description were grown in the botanical garden in Melbourne, Australia.

CLIMATE: Station #94035, Port Moresby, Papua New Guinea, Lat. 9.5°S, Long. 147.2°E, at 126 ft. (38 m). Record extreme temperatures are 98°F (37°C) and 64°F (18°C).

N/HEMISPHERE	JAN	FEB	MAR	APR	MAY	JUN	JUL	AUG	SEP	OCT	NOV	DEC
°F AVG MAX	83	82	84	86	88	90	89	87	88	87	86	84
°F AVG MIN	73	73	74	75	76	76	76	76	76	75	75	74
DIURNAL RANGE	10	9	10	11	12	14	13	11	12	12	11	10
RAIN/INCHES	1.1	0.7	1.0	1.4	1.9	4.4	7.0	7.6	6.7	4.2	2.5	1.3
HUMIDITY/%	78	77	78	76	73	71	71	73	74	75	77	78
BLOOM SEASON	N/A											
DAYS CLR	N/A											
RAIN/MM	28	18	25	36	48	112	178	193	170	107	64	33
°C AVG MAX	28.3	27.8	28.9	30.0	31.1	32.2	31.7	30.6	31.1	30.6	30.0	28.9
°C AVG MIN	22.8	22.8	23.3	23.9	24.4	24.4	24.4	24.4	24.4	23.9	23.9	23.3
DIURNAL RANGE	5.5	5.0	5.6	6.1	6.7	7.8	7.3	6.2	6.7	6.7	6.1	5.6
S/HEMISPHERE	JUL	AUG	SEP	OCT	NOV	DEC	JAN	FEB	MAR	APR	MAY	JUN

Cultural Recommendations

LIGHT: 2500–3000 fc.

TEMPERATURES: Throughout the year, days average 82–90°F (28–32°C), and nights average 73–76°F (23–24°C), with a diurnal range of 9–14°F (5–8°C).

HUMIDITY: 70–75% most of the year, increasing to about 80% in winter.

WATER: Rainfall is moderate from late spring through late autumn, followed by a 5–6 month dry season. Cultivated plants should be kept moist during the summer growing season with only slight drying allowed between waterings. Water should be gradually reduced in autumn.

FERTILIZER: ¼–½ recommended strength. A balanced fertilizer should be applied weekly to biweekly throughout the growing season.

REST PERIOD: Growing conditions should be maintained all year. In the habitat, rainfall is low for 5–6 months in winter. Water and fertilizer should be reduced considerably for cultivated plants. They should be allowed to dry between waterings but should not remain dry for extended periods. Occasional mistings on clear, sunny mornings are usually beneficial. In the habitat, winter light is high.

GROWING MEDIA: Plants may be mounted on tree-fern or cork slabs or potted in small pots filled with any open, fast-draining medium. Repotting may be done anytime new roots are growing.

Plant and Flower Information

PLANT SIZE AND TYPE: A sympodial epiphyte of unreported size.

PSEUDOBULB: The elongated stems are very branching. They are leafless near the tip.

LEAVES: Many. The leaves are 1.2–1.6 in. (3–4 cm) long, pointed, and sickle-shaped.

INFLORESCENCE: Short.

FLOWERS: Few per inflorescence. The flowers are 0.4 in. (1 cm) long. Blossoms have reddish sepals and petals and a purple lip. The dorsal sepal and slightly smaller petals are ovate to oblong and pointed at the tips. The lateral sepals are somewhat triangular at the base and sickle-shaped at the tips. The lip is ruffled and uneven along the margin. The disk is decorated with 3 raised keels.

REFERENCES: 220, 254.

Dendrobium ferox Hasskarl. See *D. macrophyllum* A. Richard.
REFERENCES: 75, 83, 190, 216, 254, 270, 271, 373, 430, 436, 469.

Dendrobium fesselianum M. Wolff. See *D. peguanum* Lindley. REFERENCES: 235.

Dendrobium filicaule Gagnepain

ORIGIN/HABITAT: Vietnam. Plants grow near the summit of mountains south of Hue in moss and forest compost at 4600–4900 ft. (1400–1500 m).

CLIMATE: Station #48855, Da Nang, Vietnam, Lat. 16.0°N, Long. 108.2°E, at 33 ft. (10 m). Temperatures are calculated for an elevation of 4600 ft. (1400 m), resulting in probable extremes of 91°F (33°C) and 35°F (2°C).

N/HEMISPHERE	JAN	FEB	MAR	APR	MAY	JUN	JUL	AUG	SEP	OCT	NOV	DEC
°F AVG MAX	61	64	67	72	76	79	78	78	74	69	66	62
°F AVG MIN	51	52	55	59	61	63	62	62	60	58	56	52
DIURNAL RANGE	10	12	12	13	15	16	16	16	14	11	10	10
RAIN/INCHES	4.5	1.6	1.0	1.2	2.4	2.9	3.0	4.6	15.3	22.4	15.2	8.8
HUMIDITY/%	85	84	81	82	79	76	75	77	82	85	85	85
BLOOM SEASON	N/A											
DAYS CLR @ 7AM	3	3	5	6	5	4	4	5	4	3	4	3	2
DAYS CLR @ 1PM	4	7	12	11	6	2	4	3	2	3	2	2
RAIN/MM	114	41	25	30	61	74	76	117	389	569	386	224
°C AVG MAX	16.1	17.7	19.4	22.2	24.4	26.1	25.5	25.5	23.3	20.5	18.8	16.6
°C AVG MIN	10.5	11.1	12.7	15.0	16.1	17.2	16.6	16.6	15.5	14.4	13.3	11.1
DIURNAL RANGE	5.6	6.6	6.7	7.2	8.3	8.9	8.9	8.9	7.8	6.1	5.5	5.5
S/HEMISPHERE	JUL	AUG	SEP	OCT	NOV	DEC	JAN	FEB	MAR	APR	MAY	JUN

Cultural Recommendations

LIGHT: 1800–3000 fc. Light should be diffused or dappled, and direct sunlight avoided.

TEMPERATURES: Summer days average 78–79°F (26°C), and nights average 62–63°F (17°C), with a diurnal range of 16°F (9°C).

HUMIDITY: Near 75% in summer, increasing to near 85% in autumn and winter.

WATER: Rainfall is moderate in summer, increasing to heavy during the autumn wet season, then becoming very low for 3–4 months in late winter and early spring. Additional moisture is often available from heavy dew, however, even in periods of low rainfall. Cultivated plants should be kept moist in summer and autumn, with only slight drying allowed between waterings. Water should be reduced in winter.

FERTILIZER: ¼–½ recommended strength, applied weekly. A high-nitrogen fertilizer is beneficial from spring to midsummer, but a fertilizer high in phosphates should be used in late summer and autumn.

REST PERIOD: Winter days average 61–67°F (16–19°C), and nights average 51–55°F (11–13°C), with a diurnal range of 10–12°F (6–7°C). Even though rainfall is relatively low in winter, additional water is available from dew, mist, and fog. For cultivated plants, water should be reduced for 3–4 months. Plants should be allowed to dry somewhat between waterings, but they should never remain dry for long periods. Fertilizer should be reduced. In the habitat, light is highest in winter and spring.

GROWING MEDIA: Plants may be potted in any open, fast-draining medium. Moisture-retaining additives may be included as needed to prevent the roots from ever drying out completely. Repotting is best done in early spring when new roots are growing.

MISCELLANEOUS NOTES: Plants are known only from the type specimen.

Plant and Flower Information

PLANT SIZE AND TYPE: An 8–12 in. (20–30 cm) sympodial terrestrial.

PSEUDOBULB: 6–10 in. (15–25 cm) long. Stems are slender and cylindrical.

LEAVES: The grasslike leaves are 2 in. (5 cm) long.

INFLORESCENCE: Short. Inflorescences are borne at the apex of leafless stems.

FLOWERS: 1 per inflorescence. The pale rose flowers are 0.6 in. (1.5 cm) long. The 3-lobed lip is wavy along the margin.

REFERENCES: 137, 227, 448.

Dendrobium filiforme J. J. Smith. Now considered a synonym of *Diplocaulobium filiforme* (J. J. Smith) Kränzlin. REFERENCES: 111, 219, 220, 254, 436, 445.

Dendrobium filiforme Wight. Now considered a synonym of *Eria dalzelli* Lindley. REFERENCES: 216, 244, 254.

Dendrobium fililobum F. Mueller. Now considered a *Diplocaulobium* species. REFERENCES: 216, 220, 254, 434.

Dendrobium fimbriatolabellum Hayata. Now considered a synonym of *Flickingeria fimbriatolabellum* (Hayata) A. Hawkes. REFERENCES: 193, 211, 213, 221, 230, 231, 279, 445, 449, 504, 536.

Dendrobium fimbriatum Dalzell not Duthie or Hooker. Now considered a synonym of *Eria dalzelli* Lindley. REFERENCES: 216, 254, 277, 424.

Dendrobium fimbriatum Duthie not Dalzell or Hooker. See *D. normale* Falconer. REFERENCES: 102.

Dendrobium fimbriatum Hooker not Duthie or Dalzell

ORIGIN/HABITAT: Widespread in southeast Asia. The habitat extends eastward from Nepal and Sikkim and includes the hills of northeastern India, the Moulmein and Tenasserim regions of Burma, Thailand, southwestern China, Laos, and Vietnam. Plants have been reported as far south as Malaya. They usually grow at 1650–5000 ft. (500–1520 m), but in some habitats, plants are found as high as 7850 ft. (2400 m).

CLIMATE: Station #42147, Mukteswar, India, Lat. 29.5°N, Long. 79.7°E, at 7592 ft. (2314 m). Temperatures are calculated for an elevation of 4000 ft. (1220 m), resulting in probable extremes of 102°F (39°C) and 33°F (1°C).

N/HEMISPHERE	JAN	FEB	MAR	APR	MAY	JUN	JUL	AUG	SEP	OCT	NOV	DEC
°F AVG MAX	63	66	73	81	87	87	81	81	80	77	73	67
°F AVG MIN	48	50	56	64	69	71	71	70	68	62	56	51
DIURNAL RANGE	15	16	17	17	18	16	10	11	12	15	17	16
RAIN/INCHES	1.0	2.1	1.7	1.0	0.3	4.6	11.4	12.8	4.6	3.5	0.3	0.2
HUMIDITY/%	61	55	50	39	44	67	91	93	83	66	55	56
BLOOM SEASON	*	*	**	**	**	*	*	*	*			*
DAYS CLR @ 5PM	17	17	15	18	18	12	1	1	6	25	26	21
RAIN/MM	25	53	43	25	8	117	290	325	117	89	8	5
°C AVG MAX	17.1	18.8	22.7	27.1	30.5	30.5	27.1	27.1	26.6	24.9	22.7	19.4
°C AVG MIN	8.8	9.9	13.3	17.7	20.5	21.6	21.6	21.0	19.9	16.6	13.3	10.5
DIURNAL RANGE	8.3	8.9	9.4	9.4	10.0	8.9	5.5	6.1	6.7	8.3	9.4	8.9
S/HEMISPHERE	JUL	AUG	SEP	OCT	NOV	DEC	JAN	FEB	MAR	APR	MAY	JUN

Cultural Recommendations

LIGHT: 2500–3500 fc.

TEMPERATURES: Summer days average 81–87°F (27–31°C), and nights average 70–71°F (21–22°C), with a diurnal range of 10–16°F (6–9°C).

HUMIDITY: Near 90% in summer, dropping to 55–60% in winter. The driest season occurs in spring when humidity drops to near 40% for 2 months.

WATER: Rainfall is moderate to heavy for 5 months in summer. The wet season is followed immediately by 7 very dry months from autumn through spring. Several months are so dry that even morning dew is uncommon. Cultivated plants should be kept moist while actively growing, but water should be gradually reduced after new growths mature in autumn. The dry season is not necessarily as long as indicated in all sections of the area of distribution.

FERTILIZER: ¼–½ recommended strength, applied weekly. A high-nitrogen fertilizer is beneficial from spring to midsummer, but a fertilizer high in phosphates should be used in late summer and autumn.

REST PERIOD: Winter days average 63–67°F (17–19°C), and nights average 48–51°F (9–11°C), with a diurnal range of 15–16°F (8–9°C). Water should be reduced for cultivated plants in winter. They should be allowed to dry out between waterings but should not remain dry for extended periods. Occasional early morning mistings between waterings may be beneficial in keeping plants from becoming too dry. In the habitat, light is highest during clear winter weather. Growers indicate that for many plants from this region, precise winter temperatures are not critical, providing they drop to near 50°F (10°C) and conditions are dry. The cool dry rest is required to initiate blooming.

GROWING MEDIA: Mounting plants on tree-fern or cork slabs accommodates their pendent growth habit. If plants are potted, hanging pots or baskets may be filled with any open, fast-draining medium. Repotting may be done anytime new roots are growing.

MISCELLANEOUS NOTES: The bloom season shown in the climate table is based on cultivation records. In the habitat, blooming occurs in late winter and early spring.

Plant and Flower Information

PLANT SIZE AND TYPE: A 24–47 in. (60–120 cm) sympodial epiphyte. Plants occasionally reach a length of 71 in. (180 cm).

PSEUDOBULB: 24–47 in. (60–120 cm) long. The stout pseudobulbs are stemlike and taper at both ends. They are grooved, slender, and either fleshy or woody. Initially erect, the stems become pendulous from the weight of the inflorescences.

LEAVES: Many. The dark green leaves are 3–6 in. (8–15 cm) long, thin, lanceolate, distichous, and drooping. They last more than a single season.

INFLORESCENCE: 7–8 in. (18–20 cm) long. The pendulous inflorescences emerge from nodes near the apex of mature canes. Stems do not mature and flower until they are 2 years old, but then they produce blossoms for several years. Flowering occurs on leafy and leafless stems.

FLOWERS: 6–15 per inflorescence. The flowers are 1.6–3.0 in. (4.0–7.6 cm) across. Sepals and petals may be pale yellow-green or deep, rich orange-yellow. They are thin and delicate with a sparkling, crystalline texture. The slightly darker lip is nearly round, ruffled, and densely fringed along the margin. It is velvety and commonly has a single orange or red-brown blotch in the center. The markings are variable, however, as some varieties have 2 blotches while others have none. Blossoms last only 7–10 days, even if kept cool, but plants are very floriferous. Hundreds of flowers are possible on a well-grown plant. One cultivated specimen plant carried 123 racemes with 1216 flowers. The fragrance is described as somewhat sour.

HYBRIDIZING NOTES: Chromosome counts are $n = 18$ (ref. 154) and $n = 19$ (ref. 153, 154, 542), $n = 20$ (ref. 504, 542), $2n = 19, 18$ (ref. 542), $2n = 38$ (ref. 187, 504, 547, 580), $2n = 38+2B$ (ref. 150, 187, 542), and $2n = 40$ (ref. 150, 152, 153, 542). When tested as *D. fimbriatum* Hooker var. *oculatum* Hooker, the counts were $2n = 38$ (ref. 151, 504, 542, 580) and $2n = 43$ (ref. 153, 273).

REFERENCES: 6, 25, 36, 38, 46, 150, 151, 152, 153, 154, 157, 161, 179, 187, 190, 196, 200, 202, 208, 210, 216, 245, 247, 254, 266, 273, 317, 326, 358, 369, 371, 376, 389, 426, 430, 445, 447, 448, 454, 458, 504, 505, 528, 541, 542, 547, 557, 568, 569, 570, 577, 580.

PHOTOS/DRAWINGS: 6, *36*, 46, 210, *245*, *247*, *371*, *389*, *426*, *430*, *454*, 458, 541, *569*, 570.

Dendrobium fimbriatum (Blume) Lindley. Now considered a synonym of *Flickingeria fimbriata* (Blume) A. Hawkes. REFERENCES: 75, 76, 213, 216, 254, 395, 436, 449, 469, 536.

Dendrobium fimbrilabium J. J. Smith

ORIGIN/HABITAT: The west coast of Sumatra near Natal. No additional habi-

Dendrobium findlayanum

tat or elevation information is available, so the following climate data should be used with caution.

CLIMATE: Station #96163, Padang, Sumatra, Indonesia, Lat. 0.9°S, Long. 100.4°E, at 19 ft. (6 m). Temperatures are calculated for an elevation of 450 ft. (140 m), resulting in probable extremes of 93°F (34°C) and 67°F (19°C).

N/HEMISPHERE	JAN	FEB	MAR	APR	MAY	JUN	JUL	AUG	SEP	OCT	NOV	DEC
°F AVG MAX	86	86	85	85	85	85	86	86	86	86	87	86
°F AVG MIN	73	73	73	73	73	73	73	73	73	74	74	73
DIURNAL RANGE	13	13	12	12	12	12	13	13	13	12	13	13
RAIN/INCHES	10.9	13.7	6.0	19.5	20.4	18.9	13.8	10.2	12.1	14.3	12.4	12.1
HUMIDITY/%	81	82	82	84	85	84	81	81	82	83	81	81
BLOOM SEASON	N/A											
DAYS CLR @ 7AM	5	1	1	0	0	2	2	1	2	2	3	5
DAYS CLR @ 1PM	5	2	2	1	1	3	3	4	3	3	6	5
RAIN/MM	277	348	152	495	518	480	351	259	307	363	315	307
°C AVG MAX	29.8	29.8	29.2	29.2	29.2	29.2	29.8	29.8	29.8	29.8	30.3	29.8
°C AVG MIN	22.5	22.5	22.5	22.5	22.5	22.5	22.5	22.5	22.5	23.1	23.1	22.5
DIURNAL RANGE	7.3	7.3	6.7	6.7	6.7	6.7	7.3	7.3	7.3	6.7	7.2	7.3
S/HEMISPHERE	JUL	AUG	SEP	OCT	NOV	DEC	JAN	FEB	MAR	APR	MAY	JUN

Cultural Recommendations

LIGHT: 2000–2500 fc. Diffused light is preferred.

TEMPERATURES: Throughout the year, days average 85–87°F (29–30°C), and nights average 73–74°F (23°C), with a diurnal range of 12–13°F (7°C). Probable extremes vary only a few degrees from the averages, indicating that the plant may not tolerate wide temperature fluctuations.

HUMIDITY: 80–85% year-round.

WATER: Rainfall is heavy all year. Cultivated plants should be kept moist but not soggy. Warm water may be beneficial.

FERTILIZER: ¼–½ recommended strength. A balanced fertilizer should be applied weekly to biweekly throughout the year.

REST PERIOD: Growing conditions should be maintained year-round. Water may be reduced somewhat for plants grown in the dark, short-day conditions common in temperate latitudes, but they should never be allowed to dry out completely.

GROWING MEDIA: Plants may be mounted on tree-fern or cork slabs or potted in small pots filled with any open, fast-draining medium. Repotting may be done anytime new roots are growing.

MISCELLANEOUS NOTES: The plant was described in 1920 in *Bul. Jard. Bot. Buit.* 3rd sér. 2:81.

Plant and Flower Information

PLANT SIZE AND TYPE: An 11–13 in. (28–33 cm) sympodial epiphyte.

PSEUDOBULB: 11–13 in. (28–33 cm) long. The stems become violet-reddish brown with age.

LEAVES: Many. The ovate-oblong leaves are about 3 in. (8 cm) long, dark green, deciduous, and unequally 2-toothed at the apex.

INFLORESCENCE: Short. Inflorescences emerge from nodes on leafless stems.

FLOWERS: 3 per inflorescence. The flowers are 1.3 in. (3.4 cm) long. Sepals and petals are light yellowish green, transparent, and shiny. They are decorated with small, faint, brownish purple dots arranged in longitudinal rows. The transparent lip, which is light yellowish green, is shiny near the base. The ovary is dark olive green with tiny, brownish purple dots.

REFERENCES: 222.

Dendrobium findlayanum Parish and Rchb. f.

AKA: Sometimes spelled *D. findleyanum*. The describers intended to name the plant for Mr. James Findlay, but the name was misspelled in the first publication. This spelling has been followed by some later writers.

ORIGIN/HABITAT: Southeast Asia. In Burma, plants have been reported from the regions near Tenasserim, Taunggyi, and Inle Lake. The habitat extends eastward across the mountains of northern Thailand into Laos. Plants usually grow in mixed forests at 3300–5600 ft. (1000–1700 m).

CLIMATE: Station #48300, Mae Hong Son, Thailand, Lat. 19.3°N, Long. 97.9°E, at 711 ft. (217 m). Temperatures are calculated for an elevation of 4000 ft. (1220 m), resulting in probable extremes of 97°F (36°C) and 32°F (0°C).

N/HEMISPHERE	JAN	FEB	MAR	APR	MAY	JUN	JUL	AUG	SEP	OCT	NOV	DEC
°F AVG MAX	75	79	86	87	84	78	76	76	77	79	77	74
°F AVG MIN	46	46	51	61	65	64	63	63	63	61	57	48
DIURNAL RANGE	29	33	35	26	19	14	13	13	14	18	20	26
RAIN/INCHES	0.4	0.2	0.3	1.7	6.1	7.1	9.6	9.9	8.1	3.9	1.2	0.4
HUMIDITY/%	67	60	50	50	68	81	82	83	83	82	75	71
BLOOM SEASON	*	*	***	*	*	*						*
DAYS CLR @ 7AM	2	8	10	9	3	0	0	0	0	1	1	2
DAYS CLR @ 1PM	20	20	20	13	3	0	0	0	0	3	13	17
RAIN/MM	10	5	8	43	155	180	244	251	206	99	30	10
°C AVG MAX	24.0	26.2	30.1	30.6	29.0	25.6	24.5	24.5	25.1	26.2	25.1	23.4
°C AVG MIN	7.9	7.9	10.6	16.2	18.4	17.9	17.3	17.3	17.3	16.2	14.0	9.0
DIURNAL RANGE	16.1	18.3	19.5	14.4	10.6	7.7	7.2	7.2	7.8	10.0	11.1	14.4
S/HEMISPHERE	JUL	AUG	SEP	OCT	NOV	DEC	JAN	FEB	MAR	APR	MAY	JUN

Cultural Recommendations

LIGHT: 2000–3000 fc. The heavy summer cloud cover indicates that some shading is needed from spring through autumn, but light should be as high as the plant can tolerate, short of burning the leaves.

TEMPERATURES: Summer days average 76–78°F (25–26°C), and nights average 63–64°F (17–18°C), with a diurnal range of 13–14°F (7–8°C). The warmest weather occurs in spring. Days average 84–87°F (29–31°C), and nights average 51–65°F (11–18°C), with a diurnal range of 19–35°F (11–20°C).

HUMIDITY: 80–85% from summer into autumn, diminishing to 60–70% in winter. For 2 months in early spring, humidity drops to near 50%.

WATER: Rainfall is very heavy during the growing season, but winters are very dry. Cultivated plants should be kept moist while actively growing, but water should be gradually reduced after new growths mature in autumn.

FERTILIZER: ¼–½ recommended strength, applied weekly. A high-nitrogen fertilizer is beneficial from spring to midsummer, but a fertilizer high in phosphates should be used in late summer and autumn.

REST PERIOD: Winter days average 74–79°F (23–26°C), and nights average 46–48°F (8–9°C), with a greatly increased diurnal range of 26–33°F (14–18°C). In the habitat, rainfall is low for 4–5 months in winter. For 2–3 of these months, high humidity and nightly cooling result in frequent, heavy deposits of dew, with even more moisture available from fog and mist. Therefore, the driest season is only 1–2 months long. For cultivated plants, water should be reduced from late autumn to early spring. During most of the winter, plants should be allowed to dry out between waterings, but they should not remain completely dry for extended periods. Occasional early morning mistings between waterings may help prevent the plants from becoming too dry. For 1–2 months in late winter, however, water should be limited to occasional early morning mistings. Fertilizer should be reduced or eliminated, until new growth starts in spring. In the habitat, the large number of clear afternoons in winter indicates very bright conditions.

GROWING MEDIA: Plants may be mounted on tree-fern or cork slabs if humidity is high and plants are watered at least once daily in summer. When plants are potted, any open, fast-draining medium may be used. Repotting is best done in early spring immediately after flowering when new roots are growing.

MISCELLANEOUS NOTES: The bloom season shown in the climate table is based on cultivation records. *D. findlayanum* is among the first to bloom in late winter. Growers report that plants do not grow or flower in the warm, uniform climate of Singapore.

Plant and Flower Information

PLANT SIZE AND TYPE: A 15–28 in. (38–70 cm) sympodial epiphyte or lithophyte.

PSEUDOBULB: 12–28 in. (30–70 cm) long. The tall, flexuous stems are usually erect with swollen, pear-shaped nodes and narrow internodes. They are glossy green when young, becoming shiny yellow and wrinkled with age.

LEAVES: 3–5 per growth. The bright green leaves are 3–4 in. (8–10 cm) long, oblong-lanceolate, and deciduous.

INFLORESCENCE: 1.6 in. (4 cm) long. Inflorescences emerge from nodes near the apex of the most recently matured, leafless stems.

FLOWERS: 1–3 per inflorescence. The flowers are 2–3 in. (5–8 cm) across. The papery sepals and petals, which often curl back, may be pale to dark violet. They are darkest at the tip with a white suffusion at the base. The finely pubescent lip may be cream to orange-yellow or white tipped with pink. It is often deep yellow at the base with a magenta or blackish red blotch that is edged with pale lilac. The anther is white. The blossoms are fragrant and long-lasting.

HYBRIDIZING NOTES: Chromosome count is 2n = 38 (ref. 151, 154, 187, 188, 504, 580). When used as a parent, the reddish purple flower color is normally dominant.

REFERENCES: 25, 36, 151, 154, 157, 179, 187, 188, 190, 196, 200, 202, 210, 216, 245, 254, 266, 326, 359, 389, 430, 447, 448, 454, 504, 541, 557, 570, 580, 582.

PHOTOS/DRAWINGS: *36, 210, 245, 389, 430, 454, 557.*

Dendrobium findleyanum Parish and Rchb. f. See *D. findlayanum*. REFERENCES: 25, 216, 445, 454.

Dendrobium finetianum Schlechter

ORIGIN/HABITAT: New Caledonia. Plants usually grow in the mountains along forest borders at 1000–1650 ft. (328–500 m), but they are occasionally found at higher and lower elevations.

CLIMATE: Station #91592, Noumea, New Caledonia, Lat. 22.3°S, Long. 166.5°E, at 246 ft. (75 m). Temperatures are calculated for an elevation of 1000 ft. (300 m), resulting in probable extremes of 97°F (36°C) and 50°F (10°C).

N/HEMISPHERE	JAN	FEB	MAR	APR	MAY	JUN	JUL	AUG	SEP	OCT	NOV	DEC
°F AVG MAX	74	74	76	78	81	84	84	83	83	81	77	75
°F AVG MIN	60	59	61	63	66	68	70	71	70	68	64	62
DIURNAL RANGE	14	15	15	15	15	16	14	12	13	13	13	13
RAIN/INCHES	3.6	2.6	2.5	2.0	2.4	2.6	3.7	5.1	5.7	5.2	4.4	3.7
HUMIDITY/%	73	70	69	67	68	69	71	74	75	76	73	73
BLOOM SEASON	*	*	*	*	*	*	*	*	*	*	*	*
DAYS CLR @ 11AM	7	9	9	15	12	10	7	6	7	7	7	7
DAYS CLR @ 5PM	7	11	6	11	7	6	5	4	4	5	3	7
RAIN/MM	91	66	64	51	61	66	94	130	145	132	112	94
°C AVG MAX	23.1	23.1	24.2	25.3	27.0	28.6	28.6	28.1	28.1	27.0	24.7	23.6
°C AVG MIN	15.3	14.7	15.8	17.0	18.6	19.7	20.8	21.4	20.8	19.7	17.5	16.4
DIURNAL RANGE	7.8	8.4	8.4	8.3	8.4	8.9	7.8	6.7	7.3	7.3	7.2	7.2
S/HEMISPHERE	JUL	AUG	SEP	OCT	NOV	DEC	JAN	FEB	MAR	APR	MAY	JUN

Cultural Recommendations

LIGHT: 2000–3000 fc.

TEMPERATURES: Summer days average 83–84°F (28–29°C), and nights average 68–71°F (20–21°C), with a diurnal range of 12–16°F (7–9°C) that fluctuates only 4°F (2°C) during the year.

HUMIDITY: 70–75% most of the year, falling to near 65% in early spring.

WATER: Rainfall is light to moderate year-round, with the wettest period in late summer and early autumn. Cultivated plants should be allowed to become slightly dry between waterings but should not remain dry for extended periods.

FERTILIZER: ¼–½ recommended strength. A balanced fertilizer should be applied weekly to biweekly throughout the year.

REST PERIOD: Winter days average 74–76°F (23–24°C), and nights average 59–62°F (15–16°C), with a diurnal range of 13–15°F (7–8°C). In the habitat, rainfall is somewhat lower in late winter and spring. In cultivation, water and fertilizer should be reduced and the plants allowed to dry even more between waterings than in summer. They should not dry out completely or remain dry for long periods, however. In the habitat, light is highest in winter.

GROWING MEDIA: Plants may be potted in any open, fast-draining medium. They are best repotted when roots are actively growing.

MISCELLANEOUS NOTES: The bloom season shown in the climate table is based on reports from the habitat.

Plant and Flower Information

PLANT SIZE AND TYPE: A 10–16 in. (25–40 cm) sympodial terrestrial.

PSEUDOBULB: 10–16 in. (25–40 cm) long. The tall, woody canes grow in a shrublike, clustered mass. They are slightly zigzag and arise from a very short rhizome.

LEAVES: 8–12. Leaves are held in 2 rows on the upper portion of the stem. They are linear, spreading to erect, bilobed, leathery, and 1.2–2.0 in. (3–5 cm) long.

INFLORESCENCE: 0.8–1.6 in. (2–4 cm) long. Inflorescences are produced opposite the bases of most leaves.

FLOWERS: 5–8 per inflorescence, but plants produce many blossoms. The flowers are 0.4 in. (1 cm) across and open fully. Sepals and petals, which are yellow with brown markings, are slightly cupped at the tips. The ruffled, recurved lip and column are white. The anther is violet. *D. finetianum* is extremely variable, particularly the shape of the lip and the pattern and nature of the protuberances that cover the surface of the lip.

REFERENCES: 173, 220, 254, 432.

PHOTOS/DRAWINGS: 173.

Dendrobium finisterrae Schlechter not (Schlechter) J. J. Smith

AKA: *D. finisterrae* Schlechter var. *polystictum* Schlechter.

ORIGIN/HABITAT: Papua New Guinea. Plants grow in the highland provinces on moss-covered mistforest trees at 4250–6900 ft. (1300–2100 m).

CLIMATE: Station #94010, Goroka, Papua New Guinea, Lat. 6.1°S, Long. 145.4°E, at 5141 ft. (1567 m). Record extreme temperatures are 87°F (31°C) and 43°F (6°C).

N/HEMISPHERE	JAN	FEB	MAR	APR	MAY	JUN	JUL	AUG	SEP	OCT	NOV	DEC
°F AVG MAX	76	77	78	79	79	78	79	78	78	78	79	77
°F AVG MIN	56	57	57	57	58	59	59	59	60	59	59	57
DIURNAL RANGE	20	20	21	22	21	19	20	19	18	19	20	20
RAIN/INCHES	2.1	2.8	4.6	5.9	6.6	9.3	9.1	10.1	10.7	8.3	4.6	2.0
HUMIDITY/%	70	67	67	67	67	71	72	73	74	71	70	70
BLOOM SEASON	*	*	*	*	*	*	*	*	*	*	*	*
DAYS CLR	N/A											
RAIN/MM	54	70	118	151	167	236	230	256	271	211	116	52
°C AVG MAX	24.7	25.1	25.6	26.3	26.2	25.7	25.8	25.6	25.5	25.6	25.9	25.1
°C AVG MIN	13.5	13.8	14.0	14.0	14.2	14.8	15.0	15.2	15.3	15.1	14.7	13.7
DIURNAL RANGE	11.2	11.3	11.6	12.3	12.0	10.9	10.8	10.4	10.2	10.5	11.2	11.4
S/HEMISPHERE	JUL	AUG	SEP	OCT	NOV	DEC	JAN	FEB	MAR	APR	MAY	JUN

Dendrobium finisterrae

Cultural Recommendations

LIGHT: 2000–3000 fc.

TEMPERATURES: Throughout the year, days average 76–79°F (25–26°C), and nights average 56–60°F (14–15°C), with a diurnal range of 18–22°F (10–12°C). Because of the relatively wide range in habitat elevation, plants should adapt to temperatures 4–6°F (2–3°C) cooler than indicated.

HUMIDITY: 70–75% from summer into autumn, dropping to 65–70% in winter and spring.

WATER: Rainfall is moderate to heavy most of the year, but conditions are slightly drier for 3 months in winter. Cultivated plants should be kept moist but not soggy. Occasional early morning mistings may be beneficial, especially on bright, sunny days.

FERTILIZER: ¼–½ recommended strength. A balanced fertilizer should be applied weekly to biweekly throughout the year.

REST PERIOD: Growing temperatures should be maintained all year. In the habitat, rainfall is lowest in winter, but dew and mist from fog and low clouds are common. Water and fertilizer should be reduced somewhat for cultivated plants, especially those grown in the darker, short-day conditions common during temperate-latitude winters. Plants should be kept on the dry side, but they should never be allowed to dry out completely. In the habitat, light is higher in winter.

GROWING MEDIA: Plants may be mounted on tree-fern or cork slabs if humidity is high and plants are watered at least once daily in summer. When plants are potted, any open, fast-draining medium may be used. Repotting is best done in early spring when new roots are growing.

MISCELLANEOUS NOTES: The bloom season shown in the climate table is based on cultivation records.

Plant and Flower Information

PLANT SIZE AND TYPE: A 22–29 in. (56–74 cm) sympodial epiphyte.

PSEUDOBULB: 12–20 in. (30–50 cm) long. The clustered growths are somewhat flattened. They are orange-yellow when dry.

LEAVES: 2–3. The leaves are 6–10 in. (15–25 cm) long, oblong-elliptic, and suberect.

INFLORESCENCE: 10 in. (25 cm) long. The erect, laxly flowered inflorescence arises near the apex of the pseudobulb. The flowers are held just above the tips of the leaves.

FLOWERS: 8–10 per inflorescence. The flowers are 2.4 in. (6 cm) across but do not open fully. They are faintly fragrant. Sepals and petals, which may be whitish green or yellow, are heavily spotted with red or maroon on the backside. The backs of sepals are densely covered with prominent white hairs, but the petals are smooth. The yellow or white lip is marked with violet veins and spots.

HYBRIDIZING NOTES: Chromosome counts are 2n = 38 + 2B (ref. 152, 243) and 2n = 40 (ref. 151, 154, 187, 188).

REFERENCES: 83, 95, 151, 152, 154, 179, 187, 188, 221, 243, 371, 437, 445, 550.

PHOTOS/DRAWINGS: 83, *128, 371*, 437, *508*.

Dendrobium finisterrae (Schlechter) J. J. Smith not Schlechter

AKA: Originally described as *Cadetia finisterrae* Schlechter, it was transferred to the genus *Dendrobium* by J. J. Smith at about the same time that Schlechter described a different plant as *D. finisterrae*. We did not find a transfer to another *Dendrobium* name. Since *Cadetia* is now considered a valid genus by some botanists, this plant may again be considered a *Cadetia*.

ORIGIN/HABITAT: Papua New Guinea. Plants grow in the forests of the Torricelli Range at about 2950 ft. (900 m).

CLIMATE: Station #94004, Wewak, Papua New Guinea, Lat. 3.6°N, Long. 143.7°E, at 16 ft. (5 m). Temperatures are calculated for an elevation of 2600 ft. (800 m), resulting in probable extremes of 89°F (32°C) and 53°F (12°C).

N/HEMISPHERE	JAN	FEB	MAR	APR	MAY	JUN	JUL	AUG	SEP	OCT	NOV	DEC
°F AVG MAX	79	79	79	79	79	79	78	77	78	79	79	79
°F AVG MIN	65	65	65	66	66	66	66	66	65	65	66	65
DIURNAL RANGE	14	14	14	13	13	13	12	11	13	14	13	14
RAIN/INCHES	7.6	4.8	5.3	10.0	13.3	14.5	12.1	11.9	14.9	16.9	15.1	10.8
HUMIDITY/%	80	79	78	78	79	81	82	82	81	82	81	80
BLOOM SEASON			*									
DAYS CLR	N/A											
RAIN/MM	193	122	135	254	338	368	307	302	378	429	384	274
°C AVG MAX	26.3	26.3	26.3	26.3	26.3	26.3	25.8	25.2	25.8	26.3	26.3	26.3
°C AVG MIN	18.6	18.6	18.6	19.1	19.1	19.1	19.1	19.1	18.6	18.6	19.1	18.6
DIURNAL RANGE	7.7	7.7	7.7	7.2	7.2	7.2	6.7	6.1	7.2	7.7	7.2	7.7
S/HEMISPHERE	JUL	AUG	SEP	OCT	NOV	DEC	JAN	FEB	MAR	APR	MAY	JUN

Cultural Recommendations

LIGHT: 2000–2500 fc.

TEMPERATURES: Throughout the year, days average 77–79°F (25–26°C), and nights average 65–66°F (19°C), with a diurnal range of 11–14°F (6–8°C).

HUMIDITY: Near 80% year-round.

WATER: Rainfall is heavy all year, but conditions are slightly drier for 1–2 months in winter. Cultivated plants should be kept moist and never be allowed to dry out completely.

FERTILIZER: ¼–½ recommended strength. A balanced fertilizer should be applied weekly to biweekly throughout the year.

REST PERIOD: Growing conditions should be maintained year-round. Water should be reduced somewhat for plants cultivated in the dark, short-day conditions common during temperate-latitude winters. Fertilizer should also be reduced until water is increased in spring.

GROWING MEDIA: A very open and fast-draining medium should be used with either baskets or small pots. Repotting may be done anytime new roots are growing.

MISCELLANEOUS NOTES: The bloom season shown in the climate table is based on reports from the habitat. Blossoms are self-pollinating.

Plant and Flower Information

PLANT SIZE AND TYPE: A 1.6–2.0 in. (4–5 cm) sympodial epiphyte.

PSEUDOBULB: 0.4–0.8 in. (1–2 cm) long. Stems are borne on a very short rhizome.

LEAVES: 1 per growth. The somewhat linear leaves are 0.7–0.9 in. (1.8–2.2 cm) long.

INFLORESCENCE: Very short. Inflorescences emerge at the apex of the pseudobulb.

FLOWERS: 1 per inflorescence. The flowers are 0.2 in. (0.5 cm) long. The blossom used for the original description was self-pollinating, and flower color was not included.

REFERENCES: 221, 437, 472.

PHOTOS/DRAWINGS: 437.

Dendrobium finniganense D. Jones

ORIGIN/HABITAT: Australia. Habitat is restricted to northeast Queensland where plants are found on Mt. Finnigan, Mt. Pieter Botte, and Thornton's Peak. Plants grow as a terrestrial or lithophyte in open exposed sites among rocks and boulders at about 3600 ft. (1100 m).

CLIMATE: Station #94287, Cairns, Australia, Lat. 16.9°S, Long. 145.8°E, at 7 ft. (2 m). Temperatures are calculated for 4000 ft. (1220 m), resulting in probable extremes of 97°F (36°C) and 30°F (–1°C).

N/HEMISPHERE	JAN	FEB	MAR	APR	MAY	JUN	JUL	AUG	SEP	OCT	NOV	DEC
°F AVG MAX	65	67	70	73	75	77	77	76	74	72	68	66
°F AVG MIN	48	49	51	55	57	60	61	61	60	57	53	51
DIURNAL RANGE	17	18	19	18	18	17	16	15	14	15	15	15
RAIN/INCHES	1.6	1.7	1.7	2.1	3.9	8.7	16.6	15.7	18.1	11.3	4.4	2.9
HUMIDITY/%	69	67	65	65	65	68	72	72	74	73	73	72
BLOOM SEASON				*	*	*						
DAYS CLR @ 10AM	9	11	13	11	6	6	4	5	6	7	11	10
DAYS CLR @ 4PM	8	10	12	16	10	7	4	3	4	6	9	10
RAIN/MM	41	43	43	53	99	221	422	399	460	287	112	74
°C AVG MAX	18.2	19.3	21.0	22.7	23.8	24.9	24.9	24.3	23.2	22.1	19.9	18.8
°C AVG MIN	8.8	9.3	10.5	12.7	13.8	15.5	16.0	16.0	15.5	13.8	11.6	10.5
DIURNAL RANGE	9.4	10.0	10.5	10.0	10.0	9.4	8.9	8.3	7.7	8.3	8.3	8.3
S/HEMISPHERE	JUL	AUG	SEP	OCT	NOV	DEC	JAN	FEB	MAR	APR	MAY	JUN

Cultural Recommendations

LIGHT: 3000–4000 fc. Strong air movement at all times is very important.

TEMPERATURES: Summer days average 76–77°F (24–25°C), and nights average 60–61°F (16°C), with a diurnal range of 15–17°F (8–9°C).

HUMIDITY: 75–85% year-round. In the habitat, humidity probably averages at least 10% more than indicated in the climate table. Cultivated plants are healthier if high humidity and strong air movement are provided all year.

WATER: Rainfall is heavy from late spring into autumn, but conditions are drier in winter. Cultivated plants should be kept moist during the growing season, with only slight drying allowed between waterings.

FERTILIZER: ¼–½ recommended strength, applied weekly. A high-nitrogen fertilizer is beneficial from spring to midsummer, but a fertilizer high in phosphates should be used in late summer and autumn.

REST PERIOD: Winter days average 65–70°F (18–21°C), and nights average 48–51°F (9–11°C), with a diurnal range of 15–19°F (8–11°C). Water should be reduced for 4–5 months from late autumn into early spring. Cultivated plants should be allowed to dry out somewhat between waterings; but they should never be allowed to dry out completely, even in winter. Light, humidity, and air movement should remain constant, but fertilizer should be reduced to a weak application at 2–3 week intervals until water is increased in spring.

GROWING MEDIA: Plants may be grown on slabs or rafts if they are watered at least daily throughout the year. Additional mistings are required on very hot summer days. Undersized pots may be used if needed to keep the roots slightly moist, but a very open, fast-draining medium is suggested. The medium should almost dry out between waterings, but it should never become completely dry. Repotting is best done immediately after flowering when new roots are growing.

MISCELLANEOUS NOTES: The bloom season shown in the climate table is based on reports from the habitat.

Closely related to *D. adae* F. M. Bailey and *D. fleckeri* Rupp and C. T. White, *D. finniganense* can be distinguished from those species by its much larger white flowers and larger growth habit. It grows on rocks in open, exposed situations in the same mountains and at the same altitude as *D. fleckeri*, which grows on rainforest trees in shaded situations. *D. adae* is found on the same mountains but at lower altitudes.

When not in flower, *D. finniganense* may be slightly larger, but it is otherwise indistinguishable from *D. adae* and *D. fleckeri*. If a plant labeled *D. finniganense* does not bloom, it may actually be *D. adae*, which requires higher light, slightly warmer temperatures, and a dry winter rest period. Growers in dry areas often have difficulty maintaining the necessary combination of high humidity, excellent air circulation, and bright light necessary for *D. finniganense*.

Plants tolerate winter temperatures near 32°F (0°C) for short periods without harm, but these extremes should be avoided. In nature, *D. finniganense* colonizes nearby sites by producing large numbers of aerial growths (keikis).

Plant and Flower Information

PLANT SIZE AND TYPE: A 12–13 in. (29–32 cm) sympodial terrestrial or lithophyte that forms extensive branched clumps with numerous aerial growths.

PSEUDOBULB: 9 in. (24 cm) long. The stems are pale green to yellow, swollen at the base then narrowed above, with 3–7 nodes.

LEAVES: 2–3 in. (5–8 cm) long. There are 1–3 dark green, elliptical leaves near the top of each pseudobulb.

INFLORESCENCE: Short. A solitary inflorescence emerges from the apex of mature growths.

FLOWERS: 1–2. The blossoms are 1.0–1.3 in. (2.6–3.4 cm) across and open fully. They are cream to white with yellow and purple markings near the center. The flowers are fragrant.

REFERENCES: 241.

PHOTOS/DRAWINGS: 241.

Dendrobium firmum Steudel. See *D. mutabile* (Blume) Lindley. REFERENCES: 216, 254, 469.

Dendrobium fissum Schlechter

ORIGIN/HABITAT: New Guinea. In northern Papua, plants grow at about 1000 ft. (300 m) on forest trees at the foot of the Bismarck Range. In Irian Jaya (western New Guinea), they are found in the Cyclops Mountains.

CLIMATE: Station #200187, Erap, Papua New Guinea, Lat. 6.6°S, Long. 146.7°E, at 850 ft. (260 m). Record extreme temperatures are 102°F (39°C) and 53°F (12°C).

N/HEMISPHERE	JAN	FEB	MAR	APR	MAY	JUN	JUL	AUG	SEP	OCT	NOV	DEC
°F AVG MAX	88	88	89	90	93	93	93	93	93	92	90	90
°F AVG MIN	69	69	69	70	72	73	72	72	73	71	74	70
DIURNAL RANGE	19	19	20	20	21	20	21	21	20	21	16	20
RAIN/INCHES	3.9	3.9	2.7	3.0	3.0	5.3	5.9	5.9	7.0	3.4	2.4	3.1
HUMIDITY/%	82	81	81	79	75	74	74	74	77	76	80	80
BLOOM SEASON				*			*					
DAYS CLR	N/A											
RAIN/MM	98	99	68	77	76	135	149	149	179	87	60	78
°C AVG MAX	30.9	30.9	31.7	32.3	34.0	33.9	33.8	33.9	34.0	33.6	32.3	32.0
°C AVG MIN	20.4	20.5	20.7	21.1	22.0	22.5	22.1	22.4	22.5	21.7	23.3	20.9
DIURNAL RANGE	10.5	10.4	11.0	11.2	12.0	11.4	11.7	11.5	11.5	11.9	9.0	11.1
S/HEMISPHERE	JUL	AUG	SEP	OCT	NOV	DEC	JAN	FEB	MAR	APR	MAY	JUN

Cultural Recommendations

LIGHT: 2500–3500 fc.

TEMPERATURES: Throughout the year, days average 88–93°F (31–34°C), and nights average 69–73°F (20–24°C), with a diurnal range of 16–21°F (9–12°C).

HUMIDITY: 75–80% year-round. However, the habitat may be quite dry during hot afternoons.

WATER: Rainfall is moderate most of the year, but conditions are somewhat wetter for 4–5 months in summer and early autumn. Cultivated plants should be thoroughly saturated then allowed to dry slightly between waterings in summer and early autumn. Water should be gradually reduced in autumn.

FERTILIZER: ¼–½ recommended strength. A balanced fertilizer should be applied weekly to biweekly throughout the year.

REST PERIOD: Growing temperatures should be maintained all year. In the habitat, rainfall is lowest in winter, but the high humidity indicates that additional moisture is frequently available from heavy dew. Cultivated plants should be allowed to dry for somewhat longer between waterings, but should not remain dry for extended periods. Fertilizer should be reduced until water is increased in spring. In the habitat, seasonal light variation is minor.

Dendrobium fitzgeraldii

GROWING MEDIA: Plants may be mounted on tree-fern or cork slabs if humidity is high and plants are watered at least once daily in summer. When plants are potted, any open, fast-draining medium may be used. Repotting may be done anytime new roots are growing.

MISCELLANEOUS NOTES: The bloom season shown in the climate table is based on collection reports. Plants that produce flowers which last a single day commonly bloom several times during the year. Flowering usually occurs 7–14 days after a sudden 10°F (5°C) drop in daytime temperatures.

Plant and Flower Information

PLANT SIZE AND TYPE: A 24–28 in. (60–70 cm) sympodial epiphyte.

PSEUDOBULB: 22–24 in. (57–62 cm) long.

LEAVES: Many. The erect to spreading leaves are 1.6–3.5 in. (4–9 cm) long.

INFLORESCENCE: Short.

FLOWERS: 2 per inflorescence. The flowers, which last 1 day, are 0.7 in. (1.8 cm) across. Sepals and petals are yellowish white and thickly covered with papillae on the outside. The fringed lip, which has a central yellow crest, is wrinkled and marked with violet. The column foot is marked with orange-yellow.

REFERENCES: 221, 437, 445, 470.

PHOTOS/DRAWINGS: 437.

Dendrobium fitzgeraldii F. Mueller. See *D.* × *superbiens*.
REFERENCES: 67, 105, 190, 216, 254, 262, 533.

Dendrobium flabelliforme Schlechter. Now considered a synonym of *Flickingeria flabelliformis* (Schlechter) A. Hawkes. REFERENCES: 213, 221, 229, 230, 231, 437, 445.

Dendrobium flabelloides J. J. Smith. Now considered a synonym of *Flickingeria flabelloides* (J. J. Smith) J. J. Wood. REFERENCES: 111, 213, 222, 230, 235, 286, 449, 590.

Dendrobium flabellum Rchb. f. Now considered a probable synonym of *Flickingeria fimbriata* (Blume) A. Hawkes. REFERENCES: 25, 75, 213, 216, 254, 286, 295, 435, 436, 445, 449, 469, 470, 536. PHOTOS/DRAWINGS: 469.

Dendrobium flagellum Schlechter

ORIGIN/HABITAT: Northern Papua New Guinea. Plants grow on isolated trees on the hot plains at the foot of the Bismarck Range. They are most often found at about 500 ft. (150 m), where they are exposed to continuous heat and frequent drought.

CLIMATE: Station #200187, Erap, Papua New Guinea, Lat. 6.6°S, Long. 146.7°E, at 850 ft. (260 m). Record extreme temperatures are 102°F (39°C) and 53°F (12°C).

N/HEMISPHERE	JAN	FEB	MAR	APR	MAY	JUN	JUL	AUG	SEP	OCT	NOV	DEC
°F AVG MAX	88	88	89	90	93	93	93	93	93	92	90	90
°F AVG MIN	69	69	69	70	72	73	72	72	73	71	74	70
DIURNAL RANGE	19	19	20	20	21	20	21	21	20	21	16	20
RAIN/INCHES	3.9	3.9	2.7	3.0	3.0	5.3	5.9	5.9	7.0	3.4	2.4	3.1
HUMIDITY/%	82	81	81	79	75	74	74	74	77	76	80	80
BLOOM SEASON				*								
DAYS CLR	N/A											
RAIN/MM	98	99	68	77	76	135	149	149	179	87	60	78
°C AVG MAX	30.9	30.9	31.7	32.3	34.0	33.9	33.8	33.9	34.0	33.6	32.3	32.0
°C AVG MIN	20.4	20.5	20.7	21.1	22.0	22.5	22.1	22.4	22.5	21.7	23.3	20.9
DIURNAL RANGE	10.5	10.4	11.0	11.2	12.0	11.4	11.7	11.5	11.5	11.9	9.0	11.1
S/HEMISPHERE	JUL	AUG	SEP	OCT	NOV	DEC	JAN	FEB	MAR	APR	MAY	JUN

Cultural Recommendations

LIGHT: 3000–4000 fc.

TEMPERATURES: Throughout the year, days average 88–93°F (31–34°C), and nights average 69–73°F (20–24°C), with a diurnal range of 16–21°F (9–12°C).

HUMIDITY: Near 75% in summer and autumn, increasing to near 80% in winter and spring. The habitat may be quite dry during hot afternoons.

WATER: Rainfall is moderate most of the year, but conditions are somewhat wetter for 4–5 months in summer and early autumn. Cultivated plants should be thoroughly saturated then allowed to dry slightly between waterings in summer and early autumn. Water should be gradually reduced in autumn.

FERTILIZER: ¼–½ recommended strength. A balanced fertilizer should be applied weekly to biweekly throughout the year.

REST PERIOD: Growing temperatures should be maintained all year. In the habitat, rainfall is lowest in winter, but the high humidity indicates that additional moisture is frequently available from heavy dew. Cultivated plants should be allowed to dry for somewhat longer between waterings than in summer, but should not remain dry for extended periods. Fertilizer should be reduced until water is increased in spring. In the habitat, seasonal light variation is minor.

GROWING MEDIA: Plants may be mounted on tree-fern or cork slabs if humidity is high and plants are watered at least once daily in summer. Repotting may be done anytime new roots are growing.

MISCELLANEOUS NOTES: The bloom season shown in the climate table is based on collection reports.

Plant and Flower Information

PLANT SIZE AND TYPE: A 20 in. (50 cm) sympodial epiphyte.

PSEUDOBULB: 8 in. (20 cm) long. The branching stems are cylindrical. They are widely spaced on the rhizome.

LEAVES: 1 per growth. The very slender leaf is 12–14 in. (31–36 cm) long.

INFLORESCENCE: 3–5 in. (8–13 cm) long. The pendent inflorescences are somewhat laxly flowered.

FLOWERS: Several per inflorescence. The snow-white flowers are 1.2 in. (3 cm) across. The sepals are oblong-lanceolate, pointed, and smooth. The petals are narrower and smaller. The 3-lobed lip is wavy along the margin with 2 raised keels at the base. The anther is pale yellow.

REFERENCES: 92, 221, 437, 445.

PHOTOS/DRAWINGS: 437.

Dendrobium flammula Schlechter. See *D. subclausum* Rolfe.
REFERENCES: 95, 179, 221, 305, 437, 445, 486, 504, 538, 580, 588. PHOTOS/DRAWINGS: 538.

Dendrobium flavescens Blume. Now considered a synonym of *Eria flavescens* (Blume) Lindley. REFERENCES: 200, 277, 310.

Dendrobium flavescens Lindley. J. J. Smith (ref. 469) and Kränzlin (ref. 254) considered this a synonym of *Polystachya flavescens* J. J. Smith, which Valmayor (ref. 536) listed as a synonym of *Polystachya luteola* J. J. Smith. REFERENCES: 216, 254, 469, 536.

Dendrobium flavicolle Schlechter. Now considered a synonym of *Diplocaulobium flavicolle* (Schlechter) A. Hawkes. REFERENCES: 223, 228, 441.

Dendrobium flavidulum Ridley ex Hooker f. See *D. spegidoglossum* Rchb. f. REFERENCES: 75, 200, 202, 218, 254, 395, 402, 454, 469.

Dendrobium flaviflorum Hayata. See *D. chryseum* Rolfe. REFERENCES: 61, 62, 179, 192, 208, 221, 279, 389, 430, 454, 504. PHOTOS/DRAWINGS: 62, *389*.

Dendrobium flavispiculum J. J. Smith. See *D. cyanocentrum* Schlechter. REFERENCES: 221, 385, 470, 476.

Dendrobium flavum Roxburgh. Listed as an invalid name by Kränzlin. REFERENCES: 216, 254.

Dendrobium fleckeri Rupp and C. T. White

ORIGIN/HABITAT: Northeastern Australia. Plants grow in the southeastern part of the Cape York Peninsula from the Johnstone River to the Annan River. They are usually found in rainforests near mountain tops at 2600–4900 ft. (800–1500 m), where there are breaks in the forest and heavy dew, fog, and low clouds are common. They normally grow in shade on forest trees. Plants growing at higher elevations are usually lithophytic and tend to be small and spindly.

CLIMATE: Station #94287, Cairns, Australia, Lat. 16.9°S, Long. 145.8°E, at 7 ft. (2 m). Temperatures are calculated for 4000 ft. (1220 m), resulting in probable extremes of 97°F (36°C) and 30°F (−1°C).

N/HEMISPHERE	JAN	FEB	MAR	APR	MAY	JUN	JUL	AUG	SEP	OCT	NOV	DEC
°F AVG MAX	65	67	70	73	75	77	77	76	74	72	68	66
°F AVG MIN	48	49	51	55	57	60	61	61	60	57	53	51
DIURNAL RANGE	17	18	19	18	18	17	16	15	14	15	15	15
RAIN/INCHES	1.6	1.7	1.7	2.1	3.9	8.7	16.6	15.7	18.1	11.3	4.4	2.9
HUMIDITY/%	69	67	65	65	65	68	72	72	74	73	73	72
BLOOM SEASON				*	*	***	*	*				
DAYS CLR @ 10AM	9	11	13	11	6	4	5	6	7	11	10	
DAYS CLR @ 4PM	8	10	12	16	10	7	4	3	4	6	9	10
RAIN/MM	41	43	43	53	99	221	422	399	460	287	112	74
°C AVG MAX	18.2	19.3	21.0	22.7	23.8	24.9	24.9	24.3	23.2	22.1	19.9	18.8
°C AVG MIN	8.8	9.3	10.5	12.7	13.8	15.5	16.0	16.0	15.5	13.8	11.6	10.5
DIURNAL RANGE	9.4	10.0	10.5	10.0	10.0	9.4	8.9	8.3	7.7	8.3	8.3	8.3
S/HEMISPHERE	JUL	AUG	SEP	OCT	NOV	DEC	JAN	FEB	MAR	APR	MAY	JUN

Cultural Recommendations

LIGHT: 1800–2500 fc. Strong air movement at all times is very important.

TEMPERATURES: Summer days average 76–77°F (24–25°C), and nights average 60–61°F (16°C), with a diurnal range of 15–17°F (8–9°C).

HUMIDITY: 75–85% year-round. In the cloudforest habitat, humidity probably averages at least 10% more than indicated in the climate table. Cultivated plants are healthier if high humidity and strong air movement are provided all year.

WATER: Rainfall is heavy from late spring into autumn, but conditions are drier in winter. Cultivated plants should be kept moist during the growing season with only slight drying allowed between waterings.

FERTILIZER: ¼–½ recommended strength, applied weekly. A high-nitrogen fertilizer is beneficial from spring to midsummer, but a fertilizer high in phosphates should be used in late summer and autumn.

REST PERIOD: Winter days average 65–70°F (18–21°C), and nights average 48–51°F (9–11°C), with a diurnal range of 15–19°F (8–11°C). Water should be reduced for 4–5 months from late autumn into early spring. Cultivated plants should be allowed to dry out somewhat between waterings; but they should never be allowed to dry out completely, even in winter. Light, humidity, and air movement should remain constant, but fertilizer should be reduced to a weak application at 2–3 week intervals until water is increased in spring.

GROWING MEDIA: Plants may be grown on slabs or rafts if they are watered at least daily throughout the year. Additional mistings are required on very hot summer days. Undersized pots may be used if needed to keep the roots slightly moist, but a very open, fast-draining medium is suggested. The medium should almost dry out between waterings, but it should never become completely dry. Repotting is best done immediately after flowering when new roots are growing.

MISCELLANEOUS NOTES: The bloom season shown in the climate table is based on reports from the habitat. Cultivated plants also bloom in spring.

When not in flower, the plants are indistinguishable from *D. adae* F. M. Bailey. If a plant labeled *D. fleckeri* does not bloom, it may actually be *D. adae*, which requires higher light and a dry winter rest period. Growers in dry areas often have difficulty maintaining the necessary combination of high humidity, excellent air circulation, and moderately bright light necessary for *D. fleckeri*.

Plants are known to tolerate winter temperatures near 32°F (0°C) for short periods without harm, but these extremes should be avoided if at all possible.

Plant and Flower Information

PLANT SIZE AND TYPE: A 4–12 in. (10–30 cm) sympodial epiphyte or lithophyte.

PSEUDOBULB: 4–12 in. (10–30 cm) long. Plants form small to moderate clumps that may be erect to nearly pendulous. Pseudobulbs become grooved with age. Growths are leafy at the apex. Plants are found with 2 distinct vegetative forms. The lithophytic form, found on exposed rock faces, has short, 4 in. (10 cm) pseudobulbs. The epiphytic form, found in shady forests, has taller, often curved pseudobulbs to 12 in. (30 cm) long. When not in bloom, the taller plants are easily confused with *D. gracilicaule* F. Mueller and *D. adae* F. M. Bailey.

LEAVES: 2–3. The thin, ovate leaves, which are 1.2–3.2 in. (3–8 cm) long, may be stiff or limp.

INFLORESCENCE: 0.4–0.8 in. (1–2 cm) long. Inflorescences emerge from nodes at or near the tip of the stem.

FLOWERS: 1–3 per inflorescence. The flowers are 1 in. (2.5 cm) across. Plants do not flower profusely. The broad sepals, somewhat narrow petals, and prominent, densely hairy lip are commonly apricot-yellow to yellowish green. Rare clones are almost brown. The blossoms have a musky or spicy fragrance. At high elevations, plants are smaller but flower size is unaffected and flower color is more intense.

HYBRIDIZING NOTES: Chromosome count is 2n = 38 (ref. 153, 273). When used as a parent, *D. fleckeri* tends to contribute flower color, fragrance, size, shape, and number of blooms. When crossed with *D. speciosum*, hybrids produce up to 9 flowers per inflorescence and may bloom more than once a year. When crossed with *D. bigibbum*, flower shape is intermediate between the parents, but *D. bigibbum* color tends to be dominant. *D. fleckeri* normally contributes temperature tolerance to tropical species.

REFERENCES: 23, 24, 67, 105, 153, 179, 226, 240, 262, 263, 264, 273, 325, 390, 421, 457, 495, 533, 562.

PHOTOS/DRAWINGS: 105, *240, 262, 390, 533, 562*.

Dendrobium × *fleischeri* J. J. Smith. A natural hybrid between *D. bigibbum* Lindley and *D. antennatum* Lindley. REFERENCES: 25, 200, 221, 348, 476.

Dendrobium flexile Ridley

AKA: *D. adpressifolium* J. J. Smith.

ORIGIN/HABITAT: Southern Thailand north of Satul (Satun), Singapore,

Dendrobium flexicaule

Johore state in Malaya, several locations in Sumatra at about 3000 ft. (1000 m), and along the Lawas River in Borneo. Plants often grow low on trees near rivers and in old mangroves.

CLIMATE: Station #48674, Mersing, Malaya, Lat. 2.5°N, Long. 103.8°E, at 151 ft. (46 m). Record extreme temperatures are 99°F (37°C) and 68°F (20°C).

N/HEMISPHERE	JAN	FEB	MAR	APR	MAY	JUN	JUL	AUG	SEP	OCT	NOV	DEC
°F AVG MAX	82	83	86	89	90	89	88	87	87	87	86	82
°F AVG MIN	74	74	74	73	73	72	72	72	72	72	72	73
DIURNAL RANGE	8	9	12	16	17	17	16	15	15	15	14	9
RAIN/INCHES	14.4	6.3	6.1	4.6	7.1	5.1	5.6	6.7	9.3	9.9	13.4	24.3
HUMIDITY/%	82	82	81	82	82	83	84	84	84	84	85	86
BLOOM SEASON	N/A											
DAYS CLR @ 7AM	0	0	1	3	2	2	3	2	1	0	1	1
DAYS CLR @ 1PM	0	0	1	2	1	1	1	0	1	0	0	0
RAIN/MM	366	160	155	117	180	130	142	170	236	251	340	617
°C AVG MAX	27.8	28.3	30.0	31.7	32.2	31.7	31.1	30.6	30.6	30.6	30.0	27.8
°C AVG MIN	23.3	23.3	23.3	22.8	22.8	22.2	22.2	22.2	22.2	22.2	22.2	22.8
DIURNAL RANGE	4.5	5.0	6.7	8.9	9.4	9.5	8.9	8.4	8.4	8.4	7.8	5.0
S/HEMISPHERE	JUL	AUG	SEP	OCT	NOV	DEC	JAN	FEB	MAR	APR	MAY	JUN

Cultural Recommendations

LIGHT: 2000–3000 fc. Direct sun should be avoided.

TEMPERATURES: Throughout the year, days average 82–90°F (28–32°C), and nights average 72–74°F (22–23°C), with a diurnal range of 8–17°F (5–10°C). The diurnal range is greatest in the summer, the result of warmer days rather than cooler nights. Plants are also found at higher elevations, so they should adapt to temperatures 8–10°F (4–6°C) cooler than indicated.

HUMIDITY: 80–85% year-round.

WATER: Rainfall is very heavy all year. Cultivated plants should be kept moist. Warm water might be beneficial.

FERTILIZER: 1/4–1/2 recommended strength. A balanced fertilizer should be applied weekly to biweekly throughout the year.

REST PERIOD: Growing temperatures should be maintained all year. Winters in the habitat are very wet, but water should be reduced somewhat for plants grown in the dark, short-day conditions common in temperate latitudes. They should never be allowed to dry out completely, however. In the habitat, clear days are rare in winter, but seasonal light variation is minor near the equator.

GROWING MEDIA: Mounting plants on tree-fern or cork slabs accommodates their pendulous growth habit. However, humidity must be high and plants must be watered at least once a day in summer. If plants cannot be mounted, small pots or hanging baskets may be filled with an open, fast-draining medium. Repotting may be done anytime new roots are actively growing.

Plant and Flower Information

PLANT SIZE AND TYPE: A 3–8 in. (8–20 cm) sympodial epiphyte.

PSEUDOBULB: 3–8 in. (8–20 cm) long. The nodes on the stemlike pseudobulbs are spaced 0.4 in. (1 cm) apart. The stems are dark yellowish green, slender, flexuous, and pendulous. The lower portion of each stem is leafy.

LEAVES: Many. The fleshy leaves, which are 0.6–1.0 in. (1.5–2.5 cm) long, are slender, acute, and nearly terete. They are held very close to the stem.

INFLORESCENCE: Short. Inflorescences emerge from nodes along the upper, leafless portion of the stem.

FLOWERS: 1 per inflorescence. The white flowers are 0.5–0.6 in. (1.2–1.5 cm) long. They are marked with a strong yellow-orange spot in the center of the recurved lip. The sepals and very narrow petals are sometimes flushed with purple, but they are white along the margin. The lip is barely lobbed.

REFERENCES: 200, 254, 395, 402, 454, 455.

PHOTOS/DRAWINGS: *454*, 455.

Dendrobium flexicaule Z. H. Tsi, S. C. Sun, and L. G. Xu

ORIGIN/HABITAT: China. Collections have been made near Ganluo in southwest Sichuan province, near Shennongjia in northwest Hubei province, and near Nanyue in east-central Hunan province. Plants grow in rocks at 3950–6550 ft. (1200–2000 m).

CLIMATE: Station #57776, Heng-shan, Hunan, China, Lat. 27.3°N, Long. 112.7°E, at 4295 ft. (1309 m). Record extreme temperatures are 88°F (31°C) and 5°F (−15°C).

N/HEMISPHERE	JAN	FEB	MAR	APR	MAY	JUN	JUL	AUG	SEP	OCT	NOV	DEC
°F AVG MAX	38	41	52	60	65	72	77	76	70	60	52	45
°F AVG MIN	27	30	39	47	54	63	67	66	60	50	41	32
DIURNAL RANGE	11	11	13	13	11	9	10	10	10	10	11	13
RAIN/INCHES	1.9	3.3	6.8	8.3	7.8	7.6	10.0	10.0	5.8	6.5	4.3	1.7
HUMIDITY/%	71	82	87	88	88	89	85	87	87	81	83	78
BLOOM SEASON				*		*						
DAYS CLR @ 8AM	9	6	5	4	4	6	7	8	9	8	11	
DAYS CLR @ 2PM	8	7	5	3	2	1	1	2	4	9	10	12
RAIN/MM	48	84	173	211	198	193	254	254	147	165	109	43
°C AVG MAX	3.3	5.0	11.1	15.6	18.3	22.2	25.0	24.4	21.1	15.6	11.1	7.2
°C AVG MIN	−2.8	−1.1	3.9	8.3	12.2	17.2	19.4	18.9	15.6	10.0	5.0	0.0
DIURNAL RANGE	6.1	6.1	7.2	7.3	6.1	5.0	5.6	5.5	5.5	5.6	6.1	7.2
S/HEMISPHERE	JUL	AUG	SEP	OCT	NOV	DEC	JAN	FEB	MAR	APR	MAY	JUN

Cultural Recommendations

LIGHT: 2000–3000 fc. Light is naturally diffused by the frequent cloud cover. Full sun should be avoided. In the habitat, light is brightest in the morning.

TEMPERATURES: Summer days average 72–77°F (22–25°C), and nights average 63–67°F (17–19°C), with a diurnal range of 9–10°F (5–6°C).

HUMIDITY: 80–90% through most of the year, dropping to near 70% for 1–2 months in winter.

WATER: Rainfall is moderate to heavy most of the year, but conditions are semidry for 2 months in winter. Cultivated plants should be kept moist from spring through summer, but water should be gradually reduced during autumn.

FERTILIZER: 1/4–1/2 recommended strength, applied weekly. A high nitrogen fertilizer is beneficial from spring to midsummer, but a fertilizer high in phosphates should be used in late summer and autumn.

REST PERIOD: Winter days average 38–45°F (3–7°C), and nights average 27–32°F (−3–0°C), with a diurnal range of 11–13°F (6–7°C). Water should be reduced in winter and the plants allowed to dry somewhat between waterings. They should not remain dry for long periods, however. In the habitat, winter is the brightest season.

GROWING MEDIA: Plants should be potted using an open, fast-draining medium. The lithophytic growth habit indicates that drainage probably needs to be excellent, but that some moisture is likely retained around the roots. Plants may be repotted anytime new roots are growing.

MISCELLANEOUS NOTES: The bloom season shown in the climate table is based on collection reports.

Plant and Flower Information

PLANT SIZE AND TYPE: A 2.4–4.3 in. (6–11 cm) sympodial epiphyte.

PSEUDOBULB: 2.4–4.3 in. (6–11 cm) long. The clustered, somewhat zigzag stems are dark yellow when dry.

LEAVES: 2–4. The oblong-lanceolate leaves are 1.2 in. (3 cm) long. They are deciduous.

INFLORESCENCE: 0.4–0.8 in. (1–2 cm) long. Inflorescences emerge from nodes near the apex of leafless stems.

FLOWERS: 1–2 per inflorescence. The flowers are 2.0–2.4 in. (5–6 cm) across, with an oblong dorsal sepal, ovate-lanceolate lateral sepals, and elliptical petals. The 3-lobed lip is broadly ovate and smaller than the other segments. Blossoms are yellowish green with purple on the back of the sepals. The yellow lip is marked with purple along the margin and on the large, velvety disk.

REFERENCES: 235, 501.

PHOTOS/DRAWINGS: 501.

Dendrobium flexuosum Griffith. See *D. longicornu* Lindley.
REFERENCES: 190, 216, 254, 369, 454.

Dendrobium floribundum D. Don. Reported to have originated in Nepal, Kränzlin (ref. 254) included this plant name in his list of imperfectly described species. It was described as having linear leaves, inflorescences that were slightly longer than the leafy stem, and light pink flowers which had an oval lip with flat, toothed margins. REFERENCES: 46, 190, 216, 254.

Dendrobium floribundum Rchb. f. See *D. macropus* (Endl.) Rchb. f. ex Lindley. REFERENCES: 216, 254, 270.

Dendrobium floridanum Guillaumin. See *D. goldfinchii* F. Mueller not Kränzlin. REFERENCES: 170, 211, 230, 232.

Dendrobium fluctuosum J. J. Smith. Now considered a synonym of *Cadetia fluctuosa* (J. J. Smith) P. Hunt. REFERENCES: 212, 225, 230, 486.

Dendrobium × foederatum St. Cloud. A natural hybrid between *D. calamiforme* Loddiges and *D. rigidum* R. Brown. REFERENCES: 67, 105, 228, 240, 533. PHOTOS/DRAWINGS: 105, 240.

Dendrobium foelschei F. Mueller

AKA: Clements (ref. 67) reinstated *D. foelschei* F. Mueller as a separate species and includes *D. canaliculatum* R. Brown var. *foelschei* F. Mueller as a synonym.

ORIGIN/HABITAT: Australia. Plants are found in the Northern Territory, primarily in the Darwin and Gulf District. They are widespread in swamps and on the flood plains along rivers, usually growing on *Melaleuca* species.

CLIMATE: Station #94120, Darwin, Australia, Lat. 12.4°S, Long. 130.9°E, at 104 ft. (32 m). Record extreme temperatures are 105°F (41°C) and 55°F (13°C).

N/HEMISPHERE	JAN	FEB	MAR	APR	MAY	JUN	JUL	AUG	SEP	OCT	NOV	DEC
°F AVG MAX	87	89	91	93	94	92	90	90	91	92	91	88
°F AVG MIN	67	70	74	77	78	78	77	77	77	76	73	69
DIURNAL RANGE	20	19	17	16	16	14	13	13	14	16	18	19
RAIN/INCHES	0.0	0.1	0.5	2.0	4.7	9.4	15.2	12.3	10.0	3.8	0.0	0.1
HUMIDITY/%	52	54	57	59	63	69	75	76	73	62	55	54
BLOOM SEASON			*	*	*	*						
DAYS CLR @ 9AM	20	19	17	9	5	3	4	7	6	7	17	17
DAYS CLR @ 3PM	17	19	18	14	6	3	2	1	3	3	13	15
RAIN/MM	0	3	13	51	119	239	386	312	254	97	0	3
°C AVG MAX	30.6	31.7	32.8	33.9	34.4	33.3	32.2	32.2	32.8	33.3	32.8	31.1
°C AVG MIN	19.4	21.1	23.3	25.0	25.6	25.6	25.0	25.0	25.0	24.4	22.8	20.6
DIURNAL RANGE	11.2	10.6	9.5	8.9	8.8	7.7	7.2	7.2	7.8	8.9	10.0	10.5
S/HEMISPHERE	JUL	AUG	SEP	OCT	NOV	DEC	JAN	FEB	MAR	APR	MAY	JUN

Cultural Recommendations

LIGHT: 3500–4500 fc. Light should be as high as possible, short of burning the leaves. Growers recommend placing plants high in the greenhouse for maximum light.

TEMPERATURES: Summer days average 90–92°F (32–33°C), and nights average 77–78°F (25–26°C), with a diurnal range of 13–14°F (7–8°C). The diurnal temperature range and seasonal fluctuations are important. Plants from this habitat are reportedly very difficult to grow in warm, uniform climates.

HUMIDITY: 70–75% in summer, falling to 55–60% from autumn to spring at the weather station. However, the plants grow in swampy or other moist habitats where humidity is higher. Growers indicate that excellent air movement is critically important for cultivated plants.

WATER: Rainfall is heavy during the growing season. The rainfall pattern is wet/dry, with an extended dry season. Cultivated plants should be kept evenly moist while actively growing with only a slight drying between waterings. Water should be gradually reduced after new growths mature in autumn.

FERTILIZER: ¼–½ recommended strength. A balanced fertilizer should be applied weekly to biweekly throughout the growing season.

REST PERIOD: Winter days average 87–91°F (31–33°C), and nights average 67–74°F (19–23°C), with a diurnal range of 17–20°F (9–11°C). Growers report that winter temperatures should not fall below 60°F (16°C). Rainfall is very low from midautumn to early spring. Cultivated plants decline unless given a long dry season, and some growers withhold water completely during the winter rest. Fertilizer should be eliminated until watering is increased in spring. Growers report that heavy summer watering should not be started until roots are actively growing and new growths are about 2 in. (5 cm) tall. Light should be as high as possible short of burning the foliage.

GROWING MEDIA: Plants are healthiest when mounted on cork slabs; but water must be applied at least once a day in summer, and humidity must be high. These plants do not usually grow well in pots, but if they must be potted, the smallest possible pot should be used. Clay pots are preferable to plastic ones, and a rapidly draining medium should be used. Repotting is best done in early spring when new roots begin to grow.

MISCELLANEOUS NOTES: The bloom season shown in the climate table is based on reports from the habitat. Growers indicate that plants in flower should be given just enough water to keep the flowers firm and the pseudobulbs from shriveling too much.

Plant and Flower Information

PLANT SIZE AND TYPE: A 3–10 in. (8–25 cm) sympodial epiphyte.

PSEUDOBULB: 1–2 in. (2.5–5.0 cm) long, rarely to 6 in. (15 cm). The pear-shaped pseudobulbs resemble clumps of 4–7 onions. Growths are densely clustered and form small to medium mats or clumps.

LEAVES: 3–6 per growth. The fleshy, nearly terete leaves are variable. They are usually 2–4 in. (5–10 cm) long, but may reach a length of 8 in. (20 cm). Environmental conditions, particularly the amount of light, strongly influences leaf size, thickness, and shape, which varies from terete to straplike to linear.

INFLORESCENCE: 4–16 in. (10–41 cm) long. The pendent inflorescences emerge from nodes near the apex of each growth. Each growth produces 1 to several flower spikes every year and continues to bloom for several years. Mature, well-grown plants are covered with blossoms.

FLOWERS: 12–15 per inflorescence. The flowers are about 1 in. (2.5 cm) long. The Sepals and somewhat longer petals are cream with variously colored tips. This color is usually brown, but may be green, yellow, gray, or purple. The lip is narrow with a distinctly enlarged midlobe and a point at the tip. All floral segments are narrow and are usually twisted less than once. The blooms have a thin substance and seldom open fully.

REFERENCES: 67, 105, 216, 254, 533.

PHOTOS/DRAWINGS: 533.

Dendrobium foetens Kränzlin

ORIGIN/HABITAT: Endemic to northern Sulawesi (Celebes). Plants were originally found near Tondano at the eastern end of the Minahassa Peninsula. Habitat elevation was not reported, so the following climate data should be used with caution.

CLIMATE: Station #97014, Manado, Indonesia, at Lat. 1.5°N, Long. 124.9°E, at 264 ft. (80 m). Record extreme temperatures are 97°F (36°C) and 65°F (18°C).

N/HEMISPHERE	JAN	FEB	MAR	APR	MAY	JUN	JUL	AUG	SEP	OCT	NOV	DEC
°F AVG MAX	85	85	85	86	87	87	87	89	89	89	87	86
°F AVG MIN	73	73	73	73	74	73	73	73	73	72	73	74
DIURNAL RANGE	12	12	12	13	13	14	14	16	16	17	14	12
RAIN/INCHES	18.6	13.8	12.2	8.0	6.4	6.5	4.8	4.0	3.4	4.9	8.9	14.7
HUMIDITY/%	84	83	83	83	81	80	75	72	75	77	82	83
BLOOM SEASON	N/A											
DAYS CLR @ 8AM	4	3	6	11	11	12	12	12	14	17	12	8
DAYS CLR @ 2PM	1	1	1	2	1	3	3	4	4	4	1	1
RAIN/MM	472	351	310	203	163	165	122	102	86	124	226	373
°C AVG MAX	29.4	29.4	29.4	30.0	30.6	30.6	30.6	31.7	31.7	31.7	30.6	30.0
°C AVG MIN	22.8	22.8	22.8	22.8	23.3	22.8	22.8	22.8	22.8	22.2	22.8	23.3
DIURNAL RANGE	6.6	6.6	6.6	7.2	7.3	7.8	7.8	8.9	8.9	9.5	7.8	6.7
S/HEMISPHERE	JUL	AUG	SEP	OCT	NOV	DEC	JAN	FEB	MAR	APR	MAY	JUN

Cultural Recommendations

LIGHT: 2500–4000 fc. In the habitat, summer skies are frequently clear in the mornings and cloudy in the afternoon.

TEMPERATURES: Throughout the year, days average 85–89°F (29–32°C), and nights average 72–74°F (22–23°C), with a diurnal range of 12–17°F (7–10°C). The record low of 65°F (18°C) is less than 10°F (6°C) below the averages, indicating a probable intolerance to wide temperature fluctuations. The daily range is greater than the seasonal variation.

HUMIDITY: 80–85% most of the year, dropping to 70–75% in summer and early autumn.

WATER: Rainfall is moderate to heavy all year. The driest weather occurs in late summer when temperatures are warmest. Warm water may be beneficial. Cultivated plants should be kept moist for 6 months. Water should then be reduced and plants allowed to dry slightly between waterings for 6 months.

FERTILIZER: ¼–½ recommended strength. A balanced fertilizer should be applied weekly to biweekly throughout the year.

REST PERIOD: Growing conditions should be maintained year-round. In the habitat, the heaviest rainfall occurs in winter, but water should not be increased for cultivated plants. They should be kept moist, however. Fertilizer should be reduced when plants are not actively growing. Light may be increased slightly in autumn.

GROWING MEDIA: Plants may be mounted on tree-fern or cork slabs if humidity is high and plants are watered daily in summer. When plants are potted, any open, fast-draining medium may be used. Repotting may be done anytime new roots are growing.

Plant and Flower Information

PLANT SIZE AND TYPE: A sympodial plant of unreported size.

PSEUDOBULB: The clustered pseudobulbs are club-shaped and taper to a narrow base.

LEAVES: 6–8 per growth. The oblong-lanceolate leaves are 2.4–4.0 in. (6.0–10.0 cm) long, somewhat wavy, bilobed at the apex, and papery when dry.

INFLORESCENCE: 6 in. (15 cm) long. Inflorescences emerge from nodes opposite the leaves.

FLOWERS: 3–4 per inflorescence. Blossoms are 1 in. (2.5 cm) long. The somewhat narrow sepals and broader petals are white. The ruffled, wavy lip is marked with a large, honey-yellow spot on the inside. Flower shape is similar to *D. lamellatum* Lindley. The unpleasant odor is fetid.

REFERENCES: 220, 254, 436.

Dendrobium foliosum Brongniart. Now considered a synonym of *Pseuderia foliosa* (Brogniart) Schlechter. REFERENCES: 216, 221, 254, 437.

Dendrobium forbesii Ridley

AKA: *D. ashworthiae* O'Brien, *D. forbesii* var. *praestans* Schlechter. Cribb (ref. 83) also lists *D. eustachyum* Schlechter as a probable synonym.

ORIGIN/HABITAT: Eastern Papua New Guinea. Plants grow in mountain rainforests and in moist, mossy, open valleys of the highland provinces. They are usually found at 2950–4900 ft. (900–1500 m), but they occasionally grow at higher elevations.

CLIMATE: Station #94010, Goroka, Papua New Guinea, Lat. 6.1°S, Long. 145.4°E, at 5141 ft. (1567 m). Temperatures are calculated for an elevation of 4000 ft. (1220 m), resulting in probable extremes of 90°F (32°C) and 46°F (8°C).

N/HEMISPHERE	JAN	FEB	MAR	APR	MAY	JUN	JUL	AUG	SEP	OCT	NOV	DEC
°F AVG MAX	80	81	82	83	83	82	83	82	82	82	83	81
°F AVG MIN	60	61	61	61	62	63	63	64	63	63	63	61
DIURNAL RANGE	20	20	21	22	21	19	20	19	18	19	20	20
RAIN/INCHES	2.1	2.8	4.6	5.9	6.6	9.3	9.1	10.1	10.7	8.3	4.6	2.0
HUMIDITY/%	70	67	67	67	69	71	72	73	74	71	70	70
BLOOM SEASON	*						*	*	*	*	*	
DAYS CLR	N/A											
RAIN/MM	53	71	117	150	168	236	231	257	272	211	117	51
°C AVG MAX	26.5	27.1	27.6	28.2	28.2	27.6	28.2	27.6	27.6	27.6	28.2	27.1
°C AVG MIN	15.4	16.0	16.0	16.0	16.5	17.1	17.1	17.6	17.1	17.1	17.1	16.0
DIURNAL RANGE	11.1	11.1	11.6	12.2	11.7	10.5	11.1	10.5	10.0	10.5	11.1	11.1
S/HEMISPHERE	JUL	AUG	SEP	OCT	NOV	DEC	JAN	FEB	MAR	APR	MAY	JUN

Cultural Recommendations

LIGHT: 2000–3000 fc.

TEMPERATURES: Throughout the year, days average 80–83°F (27–28°C), and nights average 60–63°F (15–17°C), with a diurnal range of 18–20°F (10–12°C).

HUMIDITY: 70–75% from summer into autumn, dropping to 65–70% in winter and spring. Plants require excellent air movement.

WATER: Rainfall is moderate to heavy most of the year, but conditions are somewhat drier in winter. Cultivated plants should be kept moist while actively growing, but water should be gradually reduced in autumn. Early morning mistings between waterings are often beneficial, especially on warm, sunny days.

FERTILIZER: ¼–½ recommended strength. A balanced fertilizer should be applied weekly to biweekly throughout the year.

REST PERIOD: Growing conditions should be maintained all year. In the habitat, rainfall is lowest in winter, but heavy dew and mist from fog and low clouds are common. Water and fertilizer should be reduced for cultivated plants, especially those grown in the dark, short-day conditions common in temperate-latitude winters. Plants should dry slightly between waterings, but they should never be allowed to dry completely or to remain dry for long periods. In the habitat, light is slightly higher in winter.

GROWING MEDIA: At Laiagam, plants are healthy when potted in charcoal and bark, but other open, fast-draining media may also work. However, plants do not grow well on tree-fern. Repotting is best done as soon as new growth begins after flowering.

MISCELLANEOUS NOTES: The bloom season shown in the climate table is based on cultivation records.

Plant and Flower Information

PLANT SIZE AND TYPE: A 10–14 in. (25–35 cm) sympodial epiphyte.

PSEUDOBULB: 8–12 in. (20–30 cm) long. The yellowish green pseudobulbs, which turn orange when dry, have 4–6 nodes. They are club-shaped on the upper portion and slender at the base. They have strong, fleshy roots that branch repeatedly. Stems are leafy at the apex.

LEAVES: 2. The elliptic-oblong leaves are 3.5–7.5 in. (9–19 cm) long.

INFLORESCENCE: 6–12 in. (15–30 cm) long. An erect inflorescence arises from between the leaves at the apex of each new growth.

FLOWERS: 7–20 per inflorescence. Blossoms are 1.2–2.8 in. (3–7 cm) across. The broad sepals are pure creamy white with a greenish tinge on the outer surface and purple flecks and spots near the base. The sparsely hairy lateral sepals have high keels. The petals are undulate on the margin. The densely hairy ovary is mauve or violet. Blossoms last 5–6 weeks if cool. Plants from the Central Province have a strong honey fragrance, but plants from other areas may have a mild fragrance or none at all. *D. forbesii* is very floriferous and good for cut flowers.

HYBRIDIZING NOTES: Chromosome counts are 2n = 38 + 2B (ref. 152, 243) and 2n = 40 (ref. 187). Plants flower while quite young.

REFERENCES: 83, 92, 95, 152, 179, 187, 190, 196, 210, 218, 243, 254, 304, 371, 393, 430, 437, 445, 526, 550.

PHOTOS/DRAWINGS: 83, 210, *304, 371, 430,* 437, *550.*

Dendrobium forcipatum J. J. Smith.
Now considered a synonym of *Flickingeria appendiculata* (Blume) A. Hawkes. REFERENCES: 111, 213, 222, 230, 231.

Dendrobium formosanum (Rchb. f.) Masamune.
Sometimes spelled *D. formosamum,* see *D. nobile* Lindley. REFERENCES: 61, 208, 279, 454, 504.

Dendrobium formosum Roxburgh ex Lindley

AKA: *D. infundibulum* as used by Rchb. f. not Lindley.

ORIGIN/HABITAT: Widespread in the forests of Nepal, Sikkim, Bhutan, and northeastern India, including Assam and the Khasi (Khasia) Hills. The habitat extends across the mountain regions of Burma and northern Thailand to Dalat, Vietnam. Plants grow at about 4900 ft. (1500 m) in northeastern India and at 6550–7550 ft. (2000–2300 m) in northern Thailand. However, plants known as *D. formosum* var. *giganteum,* a warm growing, larger-flowered variety, grow at low elevations in India and the Ranong Region of southwestern Thailand.

CLIMATE: Station #48327, Chiang Mai, Thailand, Lat. 18.8°N, Long. 99.0°E, at 1100 ft. (335 m). Temperatures are calculated for an elevation of 7250 ft. (2210 m), resulting in probable extremes of 89°F (32°C) and 18°F (−8°C).

N/HEMISPHERE	JAN	FEB	MAR	APR	MAY	JUN	JUL	AUG	SEP	OCT	NOV	DEC
°F AVG MAX	65	70	75	76	74	70	69	67	68	69	66	64
°F AVG MIN	36	37	42	50	54	54	54	55	53	51	46	37
DIURNAL RANGE	29	33	33	26	20	16	15	12	15	18	20	27
RAIN/INCHES	0.3	0.4	0.6	2.0	5.5	6.1	7.4	8.7	11.5	4.9	1.5	0.4
HUMIDITY/%	73	65	58	62	73	78	80	83	83	81	79	76
BLOOM SEASON			*	*	**	*	*	*	***	***	**	*
DAYS CLR @ 7AM	5	5	2	2	1	0	0	0	0	1	3	3
DAYS CLR @ 1PM	9	8	4	2	0	0	0	0	0	0	1	3
RAIN/MM	8	10	15	51	140	155	188	221	292	124	38	10
°C AVG MAX	18.2	20.9	23.7	24.3	23.2	20.9	20.4	19.3	19.8	20.4	18.7	17.6
°C AVG MIN	2.1	2.6	5.4	9.8	12.1	12.1	12.1	12.6	11.5	10.4	7.6	2.6
DIURNAL RANGE	16.1	18.3	18.3	14.5	11.1	8.8	8.3	6.7	8.3	10.0	11.1	15.0
S/HEMISPHERE	JUL	AUG	SEP	OCT	NOV	DEC	JAN	FEB	MAR	APR	MAY	JUN

Cultural Recommendations

LIGHT: 3000–4000 fc. *D. formosum* appreciates high light and does well in nearly full sun after the growths harden.

TEMPERATURES: Caution. See the discussion at Miscellaneous Notes. Summer days average 67–70°F (19–21°C), and nights average 54–55°F (12–13°C), with a diurnal range of 12–16°F (7–9°C). The warmest temperatures occur in spring. Days average 74–76°F (23–24°C), and nights average 42–54°F (5–12°C), with a diurnal range of 20–33°F (11–18°C).

HUMIDITY: 80–85% in summer and autumn, dropping to near 75% in early winter. Averages then fall to near 60% for 2 months in late winter and early spring.

WATER: Rainfall is moderate to heavy from late spring through early autumn, but conditions are much drier in winter. Cultivated plants should be kept moist while actively growing, but water should be gradually reduced after new growths mature in autumn.

FERTILIZER: ¼–½ recommended strength, applied weekly. A high-nitrogen fertilizer is beneficial from spring to midsummer, but a fertilizer high in phosphates should be used in late summer and autumn.

REST PERIOD: Winter days average 64–70°F (18–21°C), and nights average 36–37°F (2–3°C), with a diurnal range of 27–33°F (15–18°C). Growers indicate that plants tolerate winter lows to 53°F (12°C). However, see the following discussion under Miscellaneous Notes. In the habitat, rainfall averages are very low for 4–5 months in winter, but during the early part of the season the high relative humidity indicates that additional moisture is available from frequent fog, mist, and heavy deposits of dew. Growers sometimes recommend eliminating water in winter, but plants are healthiest if for most of the winter they are allowed to become somewhat dry between waterings but do not remain dry for extended periods. For 1–2 months in late winter, however, conditions are clear, warm, and dry, with humidity so low that even the moisture from morning dew is uncommon. Plants should be allowed to dry out completely between waterings and remain dry longer during this time. Occasional early morning mistings between waterings may help keep the plants from becoming too dry. Fertilizer should be greatly reduced or eliminated until water is increased in spring. A cool, dry rest is essential for cultivated plants and should be continued until new growth starts in spring. In the habitat, light is highest in winter.

GROWING MEDIA: Plants may be mounted on tree-fern or cork slabs or placed in baskets if humidity is high and plants are watered at least once daily in summer. If plants must be potted, growers report that plants are very healthy in osmunda. Repotting is best done in early spring when new roots are growing.

MISCELLANEOUS NOTES: The bloom season shown in the climate table is based on cultivation records. In the habitat, plants bloom in late spring.

There appears to be confusion between *D. formosum, D. formosum* var. *giganteum,* and *D. infundibulum* Lindley, not only by growers, but also in the literature. *D. infundibulum* is usually described as very similar to *D. formosum,* but with smaller flowers and growing at higher elevations. However, Seidenfaden (ref. 454) reports that *D. formosum* is found at 6900–7550 ft. (2100–2300 m) in northern Thailand, while *D. infundibulum* is sometimes found near 3950 ft. (1200 m), but it is more common at 5600–6250 ft. (1700–1900 m) in the same region. Therefore, while it appears that *D. infundibulum* does indeed have slightly smaller flowers and grows at higher elevations than *D. formosum* var. *giganteum,* it actually grows at lower elevations and slightly warmer temperatures than *D. formosum.*

Growers report that *D. formosum* var. *giganteum* grows and flowers well in Singapore and the central lowlands of Bangkok. (See climate for *D. leucochlorum* Rchb. f. for temperatures appropriate for *D. formosum* var. *giganteum.*) However, *D. infundibulum* usually withers and dies when brought into the same environment. What happens if attempts are made to grow high-elevation *D. formosum* in a warm environment is unknown, but we assume that it might not survive since it comes from an even cooler habitat than *D. infundibulum.* Because it is nearly impossible for growers to know which plant they have, night temperatures of

60°F (16°C) are recommended initially. If the plant appears stressed or does not bloom, conditions should gradually be changed in the direction indicated in the climate table. Early growers found that plants cultivated in the wrong environments died in 2–3 years.

Plant and Flower Information

PLANT SIZE AND TYPE: A 9–18 in. (23–45 cm) sympodial epiphyte or lithophyte.

PSEUDOBULB: 9–18 in. (23–45 cm) long. The compact, closely set pseudobulbs may be erect or pendulous. They are stout and longitudinally ridged. The sheaths are covered with black hairs. The apical 65% of the stem is leafy.

LEAVES: Many. The spreading, evergreen leaves are 3.5–6.0 in. (9–15 cm) long. They have a thick, leathery texture.

INFLORESCENCE: Short. Racemes emerge from leaf axils at or near the apex of leafy stems.

FLOWERS: 2–5 per inflorescence. Blossoms are 3–6 in. (8–15 cm) across. The showy white flowers have a crystalline texture. Sepals are lanceolate. The rounded petals are nearly as broad as they are long. The white, scoop-shaped lip is marked with a bright yellow to orange blotch in the throat. The front of the lip is tonguelike and reflexed. The delicately scented blossoms last 6 weeks or more. Pradhan (ref. 364) reports that var. *giganteum* is not scented.

HYBRIDIZING NOTES: Chromosome counts are n = 19 and 2n = 38 (ref. 151, 154, 187, 188, 504, 542, 580) as *D. formosum* and *D. formosum* var. *giganteum*. Seeds are sufficiently mature for green-pod culture in about 210 days. In his studies of self-fertility using *D. formosum* var. *giganteum*, Johansen (ref. 239) found that seed capsules opened in 587 days, and while 92% of the resulting seed had visible embryos, none of the seeds germinated. Identical results occurred when *D. formosum* var. *giganteum* was crossed with *D. virgineum* Rchb. f. However, *D. infundibulum* reportedly hybridizes naturally with *D. formosum* (*D.* × *donnesiae* Hort.), suggesting that dry seed may become dormant until some unidentified factor breaks the dormancy.

REFERENCES: 6, 25, 36, 38, 46, 71, 151, 154, 157, 179, 187, 188, 190, 196, 200, 202, 216, 239, 245, 247, 254, 266, 278, 294, 317, 326, 364, 366, 369, 371, 389, 429, 430, 445, 448, 454, 458, 504, 510, 541, 542, 557, 568, 570, 580, 581.

PHOTOS/DRAWINGS: *36*, 38, 46, *245, 247, 364, 366,* 369, *389, 430, 454,* 458, 522, 541, *581*.

Dendrobium fornicatum Schlechter. See *D. concavissimum* J. J. Smith. REFERENCES: 92, 221, 271, 437, 445, 516.

Dendrobium foxii Ridley

ORIGIN/HABITAT: Northwestern Malaya. In Perak, plants grow in the Taiping Hills at 3000–4250 ft. (910–1300 m).

CLIMATE: Station #48602, Butterworth, Malaya, Lat. 5.5°N, Long. 100.4°E, at 8 ft. (2 m). Temperatures are calculated for an elevation of 3000 ft. (910 m), resulting in probable extremes of 86°F (30°C) and 55°F (13°C).

N/HEMISPHERE	JAN	FEB	MAR	APR	MAY	JUN	JUL	AUG	SEP	OCT	NOV	DEC
°F AVG MAX	78	79	79	79	79	78	77	77	77	76	76	77
°F AVG MIN	62	63	64	65	65	64	64	64	64	64	63	63
DIURNAL RANGE	16	16	15	14	14	14	13	13	13	12	13	14
RAIN/INCHES	4.2	4.1	6.3	8.1	7.2	7.9	5.8	8.7	11.5	14.7	11.9	5.4
HUMIDITY/%	80	81	83	86	85	84	84	85	84	86	87	83
BLOOM SEASON	N/A											
DAYS CLR @ 7AM	2	1	2	0	0	1	0	0	0	0	1	1
DAYS CLR @ 1PM	3	2	2	1	1	1	1	0	0	0	1	2
RAIN/MM	107	104	160	206	183	201	147	221	292	373	302	137
°C AVG MAX	25.6	26.2	26.2	26.2	26.2	25.6	25.1	25.1	25.1	24.5	24.5	25.1
°C AVG MIN	16.7	17.3	17.8	18.4	18.4	17.8	17.8	17.8	17.8	17.8	17.3	17.3
DIURNAL RANGE	8.9	8.9	8.4	7.8	7.8	7.8	7.3	7.3	7.3	6.7	7.2	7.8
S/HEMISPHERE	JUL	AUG	SEP	OCT	NOV	DEC	JAN	FEB	MAR	APR	MAY	JUN

Cultural Recommendations

LIGHT: 2000–3000 fc.

TEMPERATURES: Throughout the year, days average 76–79°F (25–26°C), and nights average 62–65°F (17–18°C), with a diurnal range of 12–16°F (7–9°C).

HUMIDITY: 80–85% year-round.

WATER: Rainfall is heavy all year, but conditions are slightly drier in winter. Cultivated plants should be kept moist from spring to autumn, but water should be gradually reduced in late autumn.

FERTILIZER: ¼–½ recommended strength. A balanced fertilizer should be applied weekly when plants are actively growing.

REST PERIOD: Growing conditions should be maintained all year. Winter rainfall is somewhat lower in the habitat. Water should be reduced for cultivated plants. They should be allowed to dry slightly between waterings but should never dry out completely. Fertilizer should be reduced or eliminated.

GROWING MEDIA: Plants may be mounted on tree-fern or cork slabs if humidity is high and plants are watered at least once daily in summer. When plants are potted, any open, fast-draining medium may be used. Repotting may be done anytime new roots are growing.

Plant and Flower Information

PLANT SIZE AND TYPE: A 16–35 in. (40–90 cm) sympodial epiphyte.

PSEUDOBULB: 16–35 in. (40–90 cm) long. The reddish stems are slender.

LEAVES: Several. The delicate leaves are 3–4 in. (8–10 cm) long, lanceolate, shiny, and dark green.

INFLORESCENCE: 0.5–1.0 in. (1.3–2.5 cm) long. The inflorescence is pale rose.

FLOWERS: 3–10 per inflorescence. The pretty flowers are 1.0–1.6 in. (2.5–4.0 cm) across. The petals and lip are white, but the sepals are tinged with rose, especially at the tip. The fiddle-shaped lip is fringed at the margins. The curved spur is dilated near the tip. Plants are free-flowering.

REFERENCES: 200, 254, 396, 402, 455.

PHOTOS/DRAWINGS: 455.

Dendrobium fractiflexum Finet

ORIGIN/HABITAT: New Caledonia. Plants grow in the forests of the Ngoye Valley at about 350 ft. (100 m).

CLIMATE: Station #91592, Noumea, New Caledonia, Lat. 22.3°S, Long. 166.5°E, at 246 ft. (75 m). Record extreme temperatures are 99°F (37°C) and 52°F (11°C).

N/HEMISPHERE	JAN	FEB	MAR	APR	MAY	JUN	JUL	AUG	SEP	OCT	NOV	DEC
°F AVG MAX	76	76	78	80	83	86	86	85	85	83	79	77
°F AVG MIN	62	61	63	65	68	70	72	73	72	70	66	64
DIURNAL RANGE	14	15	15	15	15	16	14	12	13	13	13	13
RAIN/INCHES	3.6	2.6	2.5	2.0	2.4	2.6	3.7	5.1	5.7	5.2	4.4	3.7
HUMIDITY/%	73	70	69	67	68	69	71	74	75	76	73	73
BLOOM SEASON	*		*		*		*		*	*		
DAYS CLR @ 11AM	7	9	9	15	12	10	7	6	7	7	7	7
DAYS CLR @ 5PM	7	11	6	11	7	6	5	4	4	5	3	7
RAIN/MM	91	66	64	51	61	66	94	130	145	132	112	94
°C AVG MAX	24.4	24.4	25.6	26.7	28.3	30.0	30.0	29.4	29.4	28.3	26.1	25.0
°C AVG MIN	16.7	16.1	17.2	18.3	20.0	21.1	22.2	22.8	22.2	21.1	18.9	17.8
DIURNAL RANGE	7.7	8.3	8.4	8.4	8.3	8.9	7.8	6.6	7.2	7.2	7.2	7.2
S/HEMISPHERE	JUL	AUG	SEP	OCT	NOV	DEC	JAN	FEB	MAR	APR	MAY	JUN

Cultural Recommendations

LIGHT: 1500–2500 fc.

TEMPERATURES: Summer days average 85–86°F (29–30°C), and nights average 70–73°F (21–23°C), with a diurnal range of 12–16°F (7–9°C).

HUMIDITY: 70–75% most of the year, falling to near 65% in spring.

WATER: Rainfall is moderate to heavy year-round. Cultivated plants should be watered heavily and then allowed to dry slightly before being watered again.

FERTILIZER: ¼–½ recommended strength, applied weekly. A high-nitrogen fertilizer is beneficial from spring to midsummer, but a fertilizer high in phosphates should be used in late summer and autumn.

REST PERIOD: Winter days average 76–78°F (24–26°C), and nights average 61–64°F (16–18°C), with a diurnal range of 13–15°F (7–8°C). In the habitat, rainfall is somewhat lower in late winter and spring. In cultivation, water and fertilizer should be reduced and the plants allowed to dry even more between waterings than in summer. They should not dry out completely or remain dry for long periods, however. In the habitat, light is highest in winter.

GROWING MEDIA: Plants should be potted in an open, fast-draining medium that retains some moisture. Potting mixtures used for most *Paphiopedilum* should work well. Repotting may be done anytime new roots are growing.

MISCELLANEOUS NOTES: The bloom seasons shown in the climate table is based on reports from the habitat.

Plant and Flower Information

PLANT SIZE AND TYPE: A 20 in. (50 cm) shrublike sympodial terrestrial.

PSEUDOBULB: 20 in. (50 cm) long. The tall, woody canes are bamboolike.

LEAVES: Several per growth. The blue-green leaves are 4 in. (10 cm) long distichous, papery, and congested near the apex of the stem.

INFLORESCENCE: 6 in. (15 cm) long. The pendulous racemes emerge from leaf nodes on the upper portion of the stem.

FLOWERS: 6–7 per inflorescence. The relatively long-lasting flowers are 1.1 in. (2.8 cm) long. They are white, but the lip is marked with pinkish purple. The pointed segments are long and slender. The lip, which has small or no sidelobes, is incurved along the margin with 3 raised lines near the base.

REFERENCES: 118, 173, 219, 254, 432, 445.

PHOTOS/DRAWINGS: 173.

Dendrobium fractum T. M. Reeve

ORIGIN/HABITAT: Papua New Guinea. Plants grow in the Highland Provinces at 6900–9500 ft. (2100–2900 m). They are common on the south slopes of Mt. Giluwe at 8550 ft. (2600 m).

CLIMATE: Station #200265, Wabag, Papua New Guinea, Lat. 5.5°S, Long. 143.7°E, at 6500 ft. (1980 m). Temperatures are calculated for an elevation of 8500 ft. (2590 m), resulting in probable extremes of 77°F (25°C) and 30°F (–1°C).

N/HEMISPHERE	JAN	FEB	MAR	APR	MAY	JUN	JUL	AUG	SEP	OCT	NOV	DEC
°F AVG MAX	64	64	65	65	66	65	65	65	65	65	66	65
°F AVG MIN	44	44	45	45	45	45	46	47	47	45	45	43
DIURNAL RANGE	20	20	20	20	21	20	20	18	18	20	21	22
RAIN/INCHES	5.0	7.6	10.4	10.4	10.3	12.2	11.8	11.9	13.5	11.5	7.8	5.3
HUMIDITY/%	N/A											
BLOOM SEASON					*	*	*					
DAYS CLR	N/A											
RAIN/MM	127	193	264	264	262	310	300	302	343	292	198	135
°C AVG MAX	18.0	18.0	18.6	18.6	19.1	18.6	19.1	18.6	18.6	18.6	19.1	18.6
°C AVG MIN	6.9	6.9	7.4	7.4	7.4	7.4	8.0	8.6	8.6	7.4	7.4	6.3
DIURNAL RANGE	11.1	11.1	11.2	11.2	11.7	11.2	11.1	10.0	10.0	11.2	11.7	12.3
S/HEMISPHERE	JUL	AUG	SEP	OCT	NOV	DEC	JAN	FEB	MAR	APR	MAY	JUN

Cultural Recommendations

LIGHT: 2000–3000 fc. Growers indicate that plants need plenty of shade for good growth.

TEMPERATURES: Throughout the year, days average 64–66°F (18–19°C), and nights average 43–47°F (6–9°C), with a diurnal range of 18–22°F (10–12°C).

HUMIDITY: Information is not available for this location. However, records from nearby stations indicate that humidity is probably 75–80% year-round.

WATER: Rainfall is heavy all year with a slightly drier period in winter. Cultivated plants should be kept moist.

FERTILIZER: ¼–½ recommended strength. A balanced fertilizer should be applied weekly to biweekly throughout the year.

REST PERIOD: Growing conditions should be maintained year-round. Water may be reduced somewhat in winter, especially for plants grown in the dark, short-day conditions common in temperate latitudes; but they should never be allowed to dry completely. If cultivated plants do not bloom, growers might allow plants to dry out somewhat between waterings in winter. In the habitat, light may be slightly higher in winter.

GROWING MEDIA: To accommodate the pendent growth habit, plants are best grown in hanging baskets filled with an open, fast-draining medium. *D. fractum* grows best if the roots are covered, so slab culture is usually not satisfactory. Repotting may be done anytime new roots are actively growing.

MISCELLANEOUS NOTES: The bloom season shown in the climate table is based on cultivation records at Laiagam. Reports from the habitat indicate that plants are seldom seen in bloom, and some suggest that blossoms may be initiated by a marked dry season that occurs occasionally.

Plant and Flower Information

PLANT SIZE AND TYPE: A 4–98 in. (10–250 cm) sympodial epiphyte.

PSEUDOBULB: 4–98 in. (10–250 cm) long. The robust, pendulous canes are yellow to yellowish green with black at the nodes. They are cylindrical, slightly constricted at the nodes, robust, and pendulous. They arise from a very short rhizome. Leafless stems are covered by leaf-sheaths which are also deciduous with time.

LEAVES: Many. The deciduous leaves are 0.8–4.0 in. (2–10 cm) long. They are ovate to elliptic and rounded to unequally bilobed at the apex. They are arranged in 2 rows.

INFLORESCENCE: Short. The densely flowered racemes are borne at nodes on leafless stems.

FLOWERS: Many per inflorescence. The purplish-pink flowers are 0.8 in. (2 cm) long and do not open fully. The white lip is golden yellow on the upper part and lilac at the tip. It is oblong and not lobed.

REFERENCES: 234, 381.

PHOTOS/DRAWINGS: 381.

Dendrobium fragrans Hort. ex Hooker f. See *D. sarmentosum* Rolfe. REFERENCES: 254.

Dendrobium franssenianum J. J. Smith. Now considered a synonym of *Diplocaulobium franssenianum* (J. J. Smith) A. Hawkes. REFERENCES: 213, 221, 229, 445, 470, 478.

Dendrobium fredianum Hort. See *D. longicornu* Lindley. REFERENCES: 190.

Dendrobium friedericksianum Rchb. f.

AKA: Sometimes spelled *D. friedricksianum*.

ORIGIN/HABITAT: Endemic to southeastern Thailand. Plants grow in the low elevation forests of the Chanthaburi district as well as on nearby islands. They are usually found in tall trees about 60 ft. (20 m) above the ground.

CLIMATE: Station #48480, Chanthaburi, Thailand, Lat. 12.6°N, Long. 102.1°E, at 16 ft. (5 m). Record extreme temperatures are 103°F (39°C) and 48°F (9°C).

N/HEMISPHERE	JAN	FEB	MAR	APR	MAY	JUN	JUL	AUG	SEP	OCT	NOV	DEC
°F AVG MAX	91	92	92	93	91	88	87	87	87	89	89	88
°F AVG MIN	67	70	72	74	75	76	75	75	74	73	71	67
DIURNAL RANGE	24	22	20	19	16	12	12	12	13	16	18	21
RAIN/INCHES	0.8	1.4	2.7	4.8	12.4	19.3	19.3	17.9	19.6	9.9	2.8	0.5
HUMIDITY/%	71	75	78	80	85	86	86	87	88	84	77	71
BLOOM SEASON	*	*	*	*								
DAYS CLR @ 7AM	5	1	1	1	0	0	0	0	0	1	5	7
DAYS CLR @ 1PM	7	3	1	1	0	0	0	0	0	0	4	8
RAIN/MM	20	36	69	122	315	490	490	455	498	251	71	13
°C AVG MAX	32.8	33.3	33.3	33.9	32.8	31.1	30.6	30.6	30.6	31.7	31.7	31.1
°C AVG MIN	19.4	21.1	22.2	23.3	23.9	24.4	23.9	23.9	23.3	22.8	21.7	19.4
DIURNAL RANGE	13.4	12.2	11.1	10.6	8.9	6.7	6.7	6.7	7.3	8.9	10.0	11.7
S/HEMISPHERE	JUL	AUG	SEP	OCT	NOV	DEC	JAN	FEB	MAR	APR	MAY	JUN

Cultural Recommendations

LIGHT: 2000–3000 fc.

TEMPERATURES: Summer days average 87–88°F (31°C), and nights average 75–76°F (24°C), with a diurnal range of 12°F (7°C). The warmest season is spring, before the start of the summer rainy season. Days average 91–93°F (33–34°C), and nights average 72–75°F (22–24°C), with a diurnal range of 16–20°F (9–11°C).

HUMIDITY: Near 85% from spring to autumn, dropping to 70–75% in winter.

WATER: Rainfall is very heavy for 6 months from late spring through autumn, with a 3 month winter dry season. Cultivated plants should be kept moist in summer, and daily watering may be necessary during hot, bright weather. Water should be gradually reduced in autumn.

FERTILIZER: ¼–½ recommended strength. A balanced fertilizer should be applied weekly to biweekly throughout the year.

REST PERIOD: Winter days average 88–92°F (31–33°C), and nights average 67–70°F (19–21°C), with a diurnal range of 21–24°F (12–13°C). Although rainfall is low for 2–3 months in winter, considerable moisture is available from frequent heavy dew and morning mists. For cultivated plants, water should be reduced in winter. Plants should be allowed to dry somewhat between waterings, but they should not remain dry for long periods. Occasional early morning mistings between waterings may be beneficial, especially in bright, sunny weather. Fertilizer should be reduced or eliminated until water is increased in spring.

GROWING MEDIA: Plants may be mounted on tree-fern or cork slabs if humidity is high and plants are watered at least once daily in summer. When plants are potted, any open, fast-draining medium may be used. Repotting may be done anytime new roots are growing.

MISCELLANEOUS NOTES: The bloom season shown in the climate table is based on reports from the habitat. Cultivated plants bloom in late spring and summer. *D. friedericksianum* grows and flowers well in lowland tropical climates. It is considered the easiest of the Nobile group to grow in warm, uniform conditions.

Plant and Flower Information

PLANT SIZE AND TYPE: An 18–20 in. (45–50 cm) sympodial epiphyte.

PSEUDOBULB: 18–20 in. (45–50 cm) long. The suberect stems, which are slender at the base, may be cylindrical or club-shaped above. Although uniform green when young, the pseudobulbs become light yellow with age.

LEAVES: Several. The leaves are quickly deciduous.

INFLORESCENCE: Short. Several inflorescences are borne at nodes near the apex of leafless stems.

FLOWERS: 2–4 per inflorescence. The glossy flowers are 1.6–2.0 in. (4–5 cm) across and last 5 weeks. Sepals and petals are pale chrome yellow. The margins of the deeper yellow lip are crisped, and the base of the throat is marked with 2 purple blotches. Blossoms have a nice form and good substance, but color is variable.

HYBRIDIZING NOTES: Chromosome count is 2n = 38 (ref. 151, 152, 154, 187, 188, 504, 580). Growers indicate that including *D. friedericksianum* in a hybrid may increase the warmth tolerance of progeny.

REFERENCES: 151, 152, 154, 179, 187, 188, 190, 200, 218, 243, 245, 254, 266, 430, 448, 454, 504, 568, 580.

PHOTOS/DRAWINGS: *245, 422, 430, 454.*

Dendrobium frigidum Schlechter. See *D. masarangense* Schlechter. REFERENCES: 221, 385, 445, 470.

Dendrobium frigidum J. J. Smith. A synonym of *D. pseudofrigidum* J. J. Smith, which is now considered a synonym of *D. masarangense* Schlechter. REFERENCES: 538.

Dendrobium frimbriatolabellum Hayata. Now considered a synonym of *Flickingeria comata*. REFERENCES: 208, 221, 449.

Dendrobium frostii Hort. Status unknown. No additional information was located. REFERENCES: 226.

Dendrobium frutex Schlechter. Now considered a synonym of *Pseuderia frutex* Schlechter. REFERENCES: 219, 221, 254, 437, 444.

Dendrobium fruticicola J. J. Smith. See *D. subclausum* Rolfe. REFERENCES: 144, 221, 470, 476, 588.

Dendrobium fuerstenbergianum Schlechter

ORIGIN/HABITAT: Endemic to Thailand. Plants grow in the northern mountains at 4250–4600 ft. (1300–1400 m).

CLIMATE: Station #48353, Loei, Thailand, Lat. 17.5°N, Long. 101.5°E, at 817 ft. (249 m). Temperatures are calculated for an elevation of 4500 ft. (1370 m), resulting in probable extremes of 94°F (34°C) and 22°F (−6°C).

N/HEMISPHERE	JAN	FEB	MAR	APR	MAY	JUN	JUL	AUG	SEP	OCT	NOV	DEC
°F AVG MAX	73	77	82	85	81	79	78	77	76	75	75	72
°F AVG MIN	40	46	53	58	61	62	62	62	61	57	52	44
DIURNAL RANGE	33	31	29	27	20	17	16	15	15	18	23	28
RAIN/INCHES	0.2	0.8	1.4	3.6	6.9	6.8	5.0	8.3	8.8	4.3	0.8	0.1
HUMIDITY/%	62	60	59	62	75	77	77	79	82	79	74	69
BLOOM SEASON									*	*	*	
DAYS CLR @ 7AM	1	1	1	2	1	0	1	0	0	1	1	1
DAYS CLR @ 1PM	22	14	8	5	2	0	1	1	1	5	11	15
RAIN/MM	5	20	36	91	175	173	127	211	224	109	20	3
°C AVG MAX	22.7	24.9	27.7	29.4	27.1	26.0	25.5	24.9	24.4	23.8	23.8	22.1
°C AVG MIN	4.4	7.7	11.6	14.4	16.0	16.6	16.6	16.6	16.0	13.8	11.0	6.6
DIURNAL RANGE	18.3	17.2	16.1	15.0	11.1	9.4	8.9	8.3	8.4	10.0	12.8	15.5
S/HEMISPHERE	JUL	AUG	SEP	OCT	NOV	DEC	JAN	FEB	MAR	APR	MAY	JUN

Cultural Recommendations

LIGHT: 1800–2500 fc.

TEMPERATURES: Summer days average 77–79°F (25–26°C), and nights average 62°F (17°C), with a diurnal range of 15–17°F (8–9°C). The warmest season is spring. Days average 81–85°F (27–29°C), and nights average 53–61°F (12–16°C), with a diurnal range of 20–29°F (11–16°C).

HUMIDITY: 75–80% most of the year, decreasing to near 60% in winter and early spring.

WATER: Conditions in the habitat are wet in summer and dry in winter. Cultivated plants need ample moisture and should be kept moist while actively growing, but water should be gradually reduced during autumn.

FERTILIZER: ¼–½ recommended strength, applied weekly. A high-nitrogen fertilizer is beneficial from spring to midsummer, but a fertilizer high in phosphates should be used in late summer and autumn.

REST PERIOD: For about 3 months, winter days average 72–77°F (22–25°C), and nights average 40–46°F (4–8°C), with a diurnal range of 28–33°F (16–18°C). Habitat records indicate that the plant tolerates short periods below freezing, but severe temperatures are best avoided in cultivation. Fertilizer should be eliminated when plants are not actively growing. Although rainfall is low in the habitat, frequent morning fog, dew, and mist provide some moisture in addition to the sparse rainfall. For cultivated plants, water should be reduced for 3–4 months and the plants allowed to become dry between waterings. They should not remain dry for extended periods, however. Occasional early morning mistings between waterings, especially on bright, sunny days, may be beneficial. In the habitat, light is brightest during winter afternoons.

GROWING MEDIA: Plants may be potted in any open, fast-draining medium. Repotting is best done in early spring when new roots begin to grow.

MISCELLANEOUS NOTES: Seidenfaden (ref. 454) suggests that *D. fuerstenbergianum* may perhaps be only a tall form of *D. christyanum* Rchb. f.

Plant and Flower Information

PLANT SIZE AND TYPE: A 6–10 in. (15–25 cm) sympodial epiphyte.

PSEUDOBULB: 6–10 in. (15–25 cm) long. The surface is covered with hairs.

LEAVES: 4–7 per growth. The leaves are 2.0–2.8 in. (5–7 cm) long.

INFLORESCENCE: Very short. Inflorescences are borne on leafy and nearly leafless stems.

FLOWERS: 1 per inflorescence. The flowers are 2 in. (5 cm) across, which is very large for the plant size. All segments are white, with orange and yellow or orange and red markings on the midlobe of the lip.

REFERENCES: 190, 220, 254, 266, 429, 448, 454, 524.

PHOTOS/DRAWINGS: 454.

Dendrobium fugax Rchb. f. not Schlechter. Now considered a synonym of *Flickingeria fugax* (Rchb. f.) Seidenfaden. REFERENCES: 102, 111, 157, 213, 216, 231, 254, 449.

Dendrobium fugax Schlechter not Rchb. f. See *D. hendersonii* A. Hawkes and A. H. Heller. REFERENCES: 56, 190, 200, 220, 254, 286, 295, 433, 454, 455.

Dendrobium fulgens. Cribb and Robbins (ref. 92) listed this species, without describers name, as being present in Herbarium Bogoriense. No additional information was located. REFERENCES: 92.

Dendrobium fulgescens J. J. Smith

ORIGIN/HABITAT: Irian Jaya (western New Guinea). Plants grow in primary forests at low elevations in the hills near the Rouffaer River at about 600 ft. (175 m).

CLIMATE: Station #200004, Ambunti, Papua New Guinea, Lat. 4.2°S, Long. 142.8°E, at 164 ft. (50 m). Temperatures are calculated for an elevation of 1000 ft. (300 m), resulting in probable extremes of 96°F (36°C) and 49°F (10°C).

N/HEMISPHERE	JAN	FEB	MAR	APR	MAY	JUN	JUL	AUG	SEP	OCT	NOV	DEC
°F AVG MAX	85	87	87	87	88	87	87	87	87	87	87	86
°F AVG MIN	69	70	71	70	70	70	69	70	70	70	70	71
DIURNAL RANGE	16	17	16	17	18	17	18	17	17	17	17	15
RAIN/INCHES	6.4	7.4	7.7	8.5	9.2	9.4	10.9	10.2	12.2	10.4	8.3	5.2
HUMIDITY/%	N/A											
BLOOM SEASON			*									
DAYS CLR	N/A											
RAIN/MM	163	188	196	216	234	239	277	259	310	264	211	132
°C AVG MAX	29.6	30.7	30.7	30.7	31.2	30.7	30.7	30.7	30.7	30.7	30.7	30.1
°C AVG MIN	20.7	21.2	21.8	21.2	21.2	21.2	20.7	21.2	21.2	21.2	21.2	21.8
DIURNAL RANGE	8.9	9.5	8.9	9.5	10.0	9.5	10.0	9.5	9.5	9.5	9.5	8.3
S/HEMISPHERE	JUL	AUG	SEP	OCT	NOV	DEC	JAN	FEB	MAR	APR	MAY	JUN

Cultural Recommendations

LIGHT: 2000–3000 fc.

TEMPERATURES: Throughout the year, days average 85–88°F (30–31°C), and nights average 69–71°F (21–22°C), with a diurnal range of 15–18°F (8–10°C).

HUMIDITY: Information is not available for this location. However, records from nearby stations indicate that humidity probably averages near 80% year-round.

WATER: Rainfall is heavy all year with the greatest amounts falling in summer and early autumn. Cultivated plants should be kept moist but not soggy.

FERTILIZER: ¼–½ recommended strength. A balanced fertilizer should be applied weekly to biweekly throughout the year.

REST PERIOD: Growing conditions should be maintained all year. Water and fertilizer should be reduced somewhat in winter, especially for plants grown in the dark, short-day conditions common in temperate latitudes. Plants should never be allowed to dry out completely, however. In the habitat, seasonal light variation is minor.

GROWING MEDIA: Plants may be mounted on cork or tree-fern slabs if humidity is high and plants are watered at least once daily in summer. When plants are potted, any open, fast-draining medium may be used, but fir bark is preferred by most growers. Repotting may be done anytime new roots are growing.

MISCELLANEOUS NOTES: The bloom season shown in the climate table is based on reports from the habitat.

Plant and Flower Information

PLANT SIZE AND TYPE: A 30 in. (75 cm) sympodial epiphyte.

PSEUDOBULB: 30 in. (75 cm) long. The shiny, unbranched stems are flattened.

LEAVES: Many. The elliptic-oblong leaves are 3–5 in. (8–13 cm) long. They are flattened, recurved at the tip, and somewhat twisted at the base.

INFLORESCENCE: Short. Inflorescences emerge along the stem.

FLOWERS: 2 per inflorescence. The flowers are 1.7 in. (4.3 cm) across. Described by the collectors as "fraise," which may indicate a strawberry color. The sepals and petals have white glittering points and a white streak down the center of each segment. The lip is white with dark violet streaks on the sidelobes and 2 orange blotches at the base. The blossoms have a delightful, vanilla fragrance.

REFERENCES: 225, 470.

Dendrobium fulgidum Ridley. See *D. cuthbertsonii* F. Mueller. REFERENCES: 222, 385, 430, 437.

Dendrobium fulgidum Schlechter

ORIGIN/HABITAT: Northern Papua New Guinea. Schlechter (ref. 437) indicated that his original and only collection, which had orange-red flowers, grew in thick moss on mistforest trees on exposed ridges of the Finisterre Range at about 4250 ft. (1300 m). Millar (ref. 304) reports that plants with golden yellow flowers are found in many areas of Papua New Guinea, but the greatest concentration occurs on islands in the Milne Bay region where they grow on tall trees overhanging the beaches. In Irian Jaya (western New Guinea), plants grow on north-facing slopes, sometimes on limestone rocks, in the Gautier Range at about 2950 ft. (900 m). J. Van Bodegom (ref. 537) describes a variety with bright orange flowers from the Vogelkop Peninsula of western Irian Jaya at about 1000 ft. (300 m). He indicated that they were also found in the Arfak Range and in the eastern part of the Cyclops Mountains above Jayapura.

CLIMATE: Station #94075, Samarai, Sideia Island, Papua New Guinea, Lat. 10.6°S, Long. 150.7°E, at 20 ft. (6 m). Record extreme temperatures are 104°F (40°C) and 64°F (18°C).

N/HEMISPHERE	JAN	FEB	MAR	APR	MAY	JUN	JUL	AUG	SEP	OCT	NOV	DEC
°F AVG MAX	81	81	82	83	85	87	87	88	87	86	84	82
°F AVG MIN	74	73	74	74	75	76	77	77	76	75	75	74
DIURNAL RANGE	7	8	8	9	10	11	10	11	11	11	9	8
RAIN/INCHES	8.1	8.6	10.1	8.7	8.4	6.1	7.0	7.8	10.0	9.8	12.0	11.3
HUMIDITY/%	N/A											
BLOOM SEASON	*		*		*					*	*	
DAYS CLR	N/A											
RAIN/MM	206	218	257	221	213	155	178	198	254	249	305	287
°C AVG MAX	27.2	27.2	27.8	28.3	29.4	30.6	30.6	31.1	30.6	30.0	28.9	27.8
°C AVG MIN	23.3	22.8	23.3	23.3	23.9	24.4	25.0	25.0	24.4	23.9	23.9	23.3
DIURNAL RANGE	3.9	4.4	4.5	5.0	5.5	6.2	5.6	6.1	6.2	6.1	5.0	4.5
S/HEMISPHERE	JUL	AUG	SEP	OCT	NOV	DEC	JAN	FEB	MAR	APR	MAY	JUN

Cultural Recommendations

LIGHT: 2500–3000 fc.

TEMPERATURES: Throughout the year, days average 81–88°F (27–31°C), and nights average 73–77°F (23–25°C), with a diurnal range of 7–11°F (4–6°C). Because plants are reported from a variety of locations and elevations, they may adapt to minimum temperatures that are 8–10°F (4–6°C) cooler than indicated along with correspondingly greater diurnal ranges.

HUMIDITY: Information is not available for this location. However, records from nearby locations indicate that humidity probably averages 70–80% year-round.

WATER: Rainfall is very heavy all year. Cultivated plants should be kept moist but not soggy.

FERTILIZER: ¼–½ recommended strength. A balanced fertilizer should be applied weekly to biweekly throughout the year.

REST PERIOD: Maintain growing temperatures all year. In the habitat, winter rainfall is high, but water should be reduced for plants cultivated in the dark, short-day conditions common in temperate latitudes. They should not be allowed to dry out completely, however. Fertilizer should also be reduced until water is increased in spring.

GROWING MEDIA: Plants may be mounted on tree-fern or cork slabs if humidity is high and plants are watered at least once daily in summer. When plants are potted, any open, fast-draining medium may be used. Old canes should not be removed when plants are repotted, as they continue to bloom for years. Repotting may be done anytime new roots are growing.

MISCELLANEOUS NOTES: The bloom season shown in the climate table is based on reports from the habitat.

Plant and Flower Information

PLANT SIZE AND TYPE: A 16–39 in. (40–100 cm) sympodial epiphyte or lithophyte.

PSEUDOBULB: 16–39 in. (40–100 cm) long. The slender, branching canes root at numerous places along the stem.

LEAVES: Many. The alternating leaves are 3 in. (8 cm) long. They are lanceolate, thin, bilobed, and spreading to suberect. They become deciduous as flowering nodes mature.

INFLORESCENCE: 4–6 in. (10–15 cm) long. The somewhat densely flowered inflorescences arise from various nodes on leafless canes.

FLOWERS: 25–35 per inflorescence. The flowers are 0.8–1.0 in. (2.0–2.5 cm) long. They last approximately 4 weeks. Blossoms may be orange-red or bright golden yellow. The lip and lateral sepals are nearly twice as long as the dorsal sepal and petals.

REFERENCES: 221, 304, 400, 437, 445, 470.

PHOTOS/DRAWINGS: *304*, 437, 537.

Dendrobium fuligineum J. J. Smith

ORIGIN/HABITAT: Northen Irian Jaya (western New Guinea). Plants grow in swampy forest at about 650 ft. (200 m).

CLIMATE: Station #97690, Sentani/Jayapura, Irian Jaya, Lat. 2.7°S, Long. 140.5°E, at 289 ft. (88 m). Temperatures are calculated for an elevation of 1000 ft. (300 m), resulting in probable extremes of 95°F (35°C) and 66°F (19°C).

N/HEMISPHERE	JAN	FEB	MAR	APR	MAY	JUN	JUL	AUG	SEP	OCT	NOV	DEC
°F AVG MAX	85	87	87	88	88	87	87	86	87	88	88	87
°F AVG MIN	70	70	70	71	71	71	71	71	71	72	71	71
DIURNAL RANGE	15	17	17	17	17	16	16	15	16	16	17	16
RAIN/INCHES	4.1	3.9	5.3	2.9	6.7	7.0	8.3	8.3	8.5	4.6	2.4	5.2
HUMIDITY/%	81	80	80	79	81	81	79	80	80	80	81	80
BLOOM SEASON			*									
DAYS CLR @ 9AM	5	3	4	3	2	1	1	0	1	2	2	5
DAYS CLR @ 3PM	4	3	3	3	2	1	3	0	1	2	2	3
RAIN/MM	104	99	135	74	170	178	211	211	216	117	61	132
°C AVG MAX	29.3	30.4	30.4	31.0	31.0	30.4	30.4	29.8	30.4	31.0	31.0	30.4
°C AVG MIN	21.0	21.0	21.0	21.5	21.5	21.5	21.5	21.5	21.5	22.1	21.5	21.5
DIURNAL RANGE	8.3	9.4	9.4	9.5	9.5	8.9	8.9	8.3	8.9	8.9	9.5	8.9
S/HEMISPHERE	JUL	AUG	SEP	OCT	NOV	DEC	JAN	FEB	MAR	APR	MAY	JUN

Cultural Recommendations

LIGHT: 2000–3000 fc.

TEMPERATURES: Throughout the year, days average 85–88°F (29–31°C), and nights average 70–72°F (21–22°C), with a diurnal range of 15–17°F (8–9°C). During the year, the average highs fluctuate only 3°F (2°C), while the average lows and the diurnal ranges vary only 2°F (1°C), indicating that plants may not tolerate wide temperature fluctuations.

HUMIDITY: Near 80% year-round.

WATER: Rainfall is heavy all year, with brief semidry periods in spring and autumn.

FERTILIZER: ¼–½ recommended strength. A balanced fertilizer should be applied weekly to biweekly throughout the year.

REST PERIOD: Growing conditions should be maintained year-round. Plants cultivated in the temperate latitudes need less water and fertilizer during the dark, short-day conditions common in winter. However, they should never be allowed to dry out completely. In the habitat, light is slightly higher in winter.

GROWING MEDIA: Plants may be mounted on tree-fern or cork slabs if humidity is high and plants are watered at least once daily in summer. When plants are potted, any open, fast-draining medium may be used. They may be repotted anytime new roots are growing.

MISCELLANEOUS NOTES: The bloom season shown in the climate table is based on reports from the habitat.

Plant and Flower Information

PLANT SIZE AND TYPE: A sympodial epiphyte of unreported size.

PSEUDOBULB: An elongated stem. The portion available to the original describer was 5 in. (13 cm) long.

LEAVES: The lanceolate leaves are 2.8 in. (7 cm) long. They are dark green and papery with very small, scalelike dots. The tip of the leaf is uneven to acutely 2-toothed.

INFLORESCENCE: Short. Inflorescences are borne along the stem.

FLOWERS: 4–6 per inflorescence. The flowers are 0.7 in. (1.8 cm) across. Sepals and petals are white with orange dots on the inside of the petals. The simple lip is concave and rounded at the tip. Flowers are similar to *D. squamiferum* J. J. Smith, but the lip is not hairy.

REFERENCES: 224, 445, 470.

Dendrobium fulminicaule J. J. Smith

ORIGIN/HABITAT: Western Sumatra near Padang. No additional habitat or elevation information is available, but a plant was cultivated in the botanical garden at Bogor, Java, where it grew for several years before it finally bloomed once. The plant may have originated at a higher elevation and required cooler or drier temperatures to bloom. The habitat elevation is estimated at 3000 ft. (910 m), but the following climate data should be used with caution.

CLIMATE: Station #96163, Padang, Sumatra, Indonesia, Lat. 0.9°S, Long. 100.4°E, at 19 ft. (6 m). Temperatures are calculated for an elevation of 3000 ft. (910 m), resulting in probable extremes of 84°F (29°C) and 58°F (15°C).

N/HEMISPHERE	JAN	FEB	MAR	APR	MAY	JUN	JUL	AUG	SEP	OCT	NOV	DEC
°F AVG MAX	77	77	76	76	76	76	77	77	77	77	78	77
°F AVG MIN	64	64	64	64	64	64	64	64	64	65	65	64
DIURNAL RANGE	13	13	12	12	12	12	13	13	13	12	13	13
RAIN/INCHES	10.9	13.7	6.0	19.5	20.4	18.9	13.8	10.2	12.1	14.3	12.4	12.1
HUMIDITY/%	81	82	82	84	85	84	81	81	82	83	81	81
BLOOM SEASON	N/A											
DAYS CLR @ 7AM	5	1	1	0	0	2	2	1	2	2	3	5
DAYS CLR @ 1PM	5	2	2	1	1	3	3	4	3	3	6	5
RAIN/MM	277	348	152	495	518	480	351	259	307	363	315	307
°C AVG MAX	25.1	25.1	24.5	24.5	24.5	24.5	25.1	25.1	25.1	25.1	25.6	25.1
°C AVG MIN	17.9	17.9	17.9	17.9	17.9	17.9	17.9	17.9	17.9	18.4	18.4	17.9
DIURNAL RANGE	7.2	7.2	6.6	6.6	6.6	6.6	7.2	7.2	7.2	6.7	7.2	7.2
S/HEMISPHERE	JUL	AUG	SEP	OCT	NOV	DEC	JAN	FEB	MAR	APR	MAY	JUN

Cultural Recommendations

LIGHT: 2000 fc. Diffused light is preferred.

TEMPERATURES: Throughout the year, days average 76–78°F (25–26°C), and nights average 64–65°F (18°C), with a diurnal range of 12–13°F (7°C). Probable extremes vary only a few degrees from the averages, indicating that plants may not tolerate wide temperature fluctuations.

HUMIDITY: 80–85% year-round.

WATER: Rainfall is heavy all year. Cultivated plants should be constantly moist but not soggy.

FERTILIZER: ¼–½ recommended strength. A balanced fertilizer should be applied weekly to biweekly throughout the year.

REST PERIOD: Growing conditions should be maintained year-round. Water should be reduced somewhat in winter for plants grown in the dark, short-day conditions common in temperate latitudes, but they should never be allowed to dry out completely.

GROWING MEDIA: Plants may be mounted on tree-fern or cork slabs or potted in small pots filled with any open, fast-draining medium. Repotting may be done anytime new roots are growing.

MISCELLANEOUS NOTES: The plant was described in 1917 in *Bul. Jard. Bot. Buit.* 2nd sér. 25:51.

Plant and Flower Information

PLANT SIZE AND TYPE: A 21 in. (53 cm) sympodial epiphyte.

PSEUDOBULB: 21 in. (53 cm) long. The stems, which are strongly flattened, are black to dark green at the base. They are close together, emerging from a short rhizome.

LEAVES: The lanceolate leaves are 3.3 in. (8.5 cm) long, laterally flattened, and unequally bilobed at the apex. They are dark green to blackish.

INFLORESCENCE: Short. Inflorescences are borne on leafless stems.

FLOWERS: 1 per inflorescence. The flowers are 1 in. (2.5 cm) long. They are pale green with large purple spots on the lip. The ovate dorsal sepal is concave, lateral sepals are somewhat triangular, and petals are nearly oblong. The erect lip is recurved with a somewhat warty margin.

REFERENCES: 222.

Dendrobium funiforme Blume.

Now considered a synonym of *Cadetia funiformis* (Blume) Schlechter. REFERENCES: 216, 221, 254, 310, 437, 470.

Dendrobium furcatopedicellatum Hayata

ORIGIN/HABITAT: Endemic to Taiwan. Plants grow in the mountain forests of the central and southern parts of the island. Habitat elevation is estimated at 2600 ft. (800 m), so the following temperatures should be used with caution.

CLIMATE: Station #46766, Taitung, Taiwan, Lat. 22.8°N, Long. 121.2°E, at 31 ft. (9 m). Temperatures are calculated for an elevation of 2600 ft. (800 m), resulting in probable extremes of 92°F (33°C) and 40°F (4°C).

N/HEMISPHERE	JAN	FEB	MAR	APR	MAY	JUN	JUL	AUG	SEP	OCT	NOV	DEC
°F AVG MAX	65	66	70	73	77	79	82	80	78	74	71	67
°F AVG MIN	51	52	55	59	63	65	66	66	65	62	58	54
DIURNAL RANGE	14	14	15	14	14	14	16	14	13	12	13	13
RAIN/INCHES	1.1	1.2	1.1	3.0	5.3	10.0	6.4	11.7	12.4	4.8	5.4	2.3
HUMIDITY/%	77	78	79	81	82	84	80	83	84	80	77	77
BLOOM SEASON								*				
DAYS CLR @ 8AM	4	5	4	6	3	11	8	7	9	7	5	
DAYS CLR @ 2PM	3	3	4	3	3	8	5	5	4	4	4	
RAIN/MM	28	30	28	76	135	254	163	297	315	122	137	58
°C AVG MAX	18.1	18.6	20.8	22.5	24.7	25.8	27.5	26.4	25.3	23.1	21.4	19.2
°C AVG MIN	10.3	10.8	12.5	14.7	17.0	18.1	18.6	18.6	18.1	16.4	14.2	12.0
DIURNAL RANGE	7.8	7.8	8.3	7.8	7.7	7.7	8.9	7.8	7.2	6.7	7.2	7.2
S/HEMISPHERE	JUL	AUG	SEP	OCT	NOV	DEC	JAN	FEB	MAR	APR	MAY	JUN

Cultural Recommendations

LIGHT: 2000–3000 fc.

TEMPERATURES: Summer days average 79–82°F (26–28°C), and nights average 65–66°F (18–19°C), with a diurnal range of 14–16°F (8–9°C).

HUMIDITY: 80–85% in summer and autumn, decreasing to 75–80% in winter and spring.

WATER: Rainfall is moderate to heavy for 6–8 months from spring into autumn. Conditions are drier during a 3 month semidry season in winter. Cultivated plants should be kept moist while actively growing, but water should be gradually reduced in autumn.

FERTILIZER: ¼–½ recommended strength, applied weekly. A high-nitrogen fertilizer is beneficial from spring to midsummer, but a fertilizer high in phosphates should be used in late summer and autumn.

REST PERIOD: Winter days average 65–70°F (18–21°C), and nights average 51–55°F (10–13°C), with a diurnal range of 13–15°F (7–8°C). In the habitat, rainfall is low for 4–6 months in winter, but high humidity and nightly cooling result in frequent, heavy deposits of dew. Consequently, more water is available than the rainfall averages indicate. In cultivation, water should be reduced and the plants allowed to become slightly dry between waterings for 3 months. Occasional early morning mistings during this time may be beneficial. Fertilizer should be reduced or eliminated when water is restricted.

GROWING MEDIA: Plants may be mounted on slabs of cork or tree-fern if humidity is high, and water is applied at least once daily in summer. Repotting is best done in early spring when new roots are growing.

MISCELLANEOUS NOTES: The bloom season shown in the climate table is based on collection reports.

Plant and Flower Information

PLANT SIZE AND TYPE: A 12–16 in. (30–40 cm) sympodial epiphyte.

PSEUDOBULB: 12–16 in. (30–40 cm) long. The stems are erect.

LEAVES: Several. The linear leaves are 4.3 in. (11 cm) long and pointed at the tip.

INFLORESCENCE: Short. Inflorescences emerge from the side of the stem. The blossoms face each other.

FLOWERS: 2 per inflorescence. The flowers are 1.2 in. (3 cm) long and do not open fully. The slender, erect sepals and petals are yellowish with purple dots. The lip margin is fringed and toothed and recurved at the apex. The disk is hairy.

REFERENCES: 61, 193, 208, 221, 279, 445, 528.

PHOTOS/DRAWINGS: 193.

Dendrobium furcatum Reinwardt ex Lindley

AKA: *D. amabile* Schlechter, *D. dolichocentrum* Koorders, *D. sarasinorum* Kränzlin. *D. celebicum* A. Hawkes is considered synonymous with *D. amabile* Schlechter, a synonym of *D. furcatum*.

ORIGIN/HABITAT: Endemic to the Minahassa Peninsula of northeastern Sulawesi (Celebes). Plants grow on forest trees on Mt. Masarang, Mt. Klabat, and Mt. Sopoetan at 2950–5600 ft. (900–1700 m). They also grow on older trees on coffee plantations.

CLIMATE: Station #97014, Manado, Indonesia, Lat. 1.5°N, Long. 124.9°E, at 264 ft. (80 m). Temperatures are calculated for an elevation of 3950 ft. (1200 m), resulting in probable extremes of 85°F (29°C) and 53°F (12°C).

N/HEMISPHERE	JAN	FEB	MAR	APR	MAY	JUN	JUL	AUG	SEP	OCT	NOV	DEC
°F AVG MAX	73	73	73	74	75	75	75	77	77	77	75	74
°F AVG MIN	61	61	61	61	62	61	61	61	61	60	61	62
DIURNAL RANGE	12	12	12	13	13	14	14	16	16	17	14	12
RAIN/INCHES	18.6	13.8	12.2	8.0	6.4	6.5	4.8	4.0	3.4	4.9	8.9	14.7
HUMIDITY/%	84	83	83	83	81	80	75	72	75	77	82	83
BLOOM SEASON			*	*						*	*	*
DAYS CLR @ 8AM	4	3	6	11	11	12	12	12	14	17	12	8
DAYS CLR @ 2PM	1	1	1	2	1	3	3	4	4	4	1	1
RAIN/MM	472	351	310	203	163	165	122	102	86	124	226	373
°C AVG MAX	22.7	22.7	22.7	23.2	23.8	23.8	23.8	24.9	24.9	24.9	23.8	23.2
°C AVG MIN	16.0	16.0	16.0	16.0	16.6	16.0	16.0	16.0	16.0	15.5	16.0	16.6
DIURNAL RANGE	6.7	6.7	6.7	7.2	7.2	7.8	7.8	8.9	8.9	9.4	7.8	6.6
S/HEMISPHERE	JUL	AUG	SEP	OCT	NOV	DEC	JAN	FEB	MAR	APR	MAY	JUN

Cultural Recommendations

LIGHT: 2000–3000 fc. Light is bright during the clear mornings of summer and autumn; but afternoons are cloudy, and plants usually grow in shady forest habitats.

TEMPERATURES: Throughout the year, days average 73–77°F (23–25°C), and nights average 60–62°F (16–17°C), with a diurnal range of 12–17°F (7–9°C). Extremes vary less than 10°F (6°C) from average growing temperatures, indicating a probable intolerance to wide temperature fluctuations.

HUMIDITY: 80–85% most of the year, dropping to 70–75% in late summer and autumn.

WATER: Rainfall is moderate to heavy all year. Cultivated plants should be kept moist most of the year, but they should be allowed to dry slightly between waterings for several months after flowering is completed.

FERTILIZER: ¼–½ recommended strength, applied weekly during periods of active growth.

REST PERIOD: Growing temperatures should be maintained all year. The plants may rest during the 1–2 month drier period which occurs in late summer and coincides with the period of greatest diurnal range. Cultivated plants should dry out slightly during this period, but they should never remain dry for long. The heaviest rainfall in the habitat occurs in winter, but water should not be increased for cultivated plants. In fact, water should be reduced somewhat for plants grown in the dark, short-day conditions common in temperate latitudes, but they should not be allowed to dry out completely.

GROWING MEDIA: Plants may be mounted on tree-fern or cork slabs or potted in small pots filled with any open, fast-draining medium. Repotting may be done anytime new roots are actively growing.

MISCELLANEOUS NOTES: The bloom season shown in the climate table is based on reports from the habitat.

Plant and Flower Information

PLANT SIZE AND TYPE: An 18 in. (45 cm) sympodial epiphyte.

PSEUDOBULB: 18 in. (45 cm) long. The occasionally branching stems arise from a pendent, branching rhizome. The stems are laxly leafy.

LEAVES: Many. The distichous leaves are somewhat widely spaced. They are 0.8–2.0 in. (2–5 cm) long, linear to nearly lanceolate, with 2 unequal teeth at the apex.

INFLORESCENCE: Shorter than the leaves. Erect inflorescences emerge laterally from nodes along the stem. They are sometimes so close to the tip of the stem that they appear to be apical.

FLOWERS: 2–3 per inflorescence. The large, pure white flowers, which are flushed with rose on the backside, are 1.2–1.6 in. (3–4 cm) across. Sepals are oblong, and the smaller petals are rounded at the tip. The lip is incurved along the margin with 3 raised lines in the center.

REFERENCES: 216, 220, 254, 278, 310, 436.

Dendrobium furcillatum J. J. Smith. Now considered a synonym of *Cadetia furcillata* (J. J. Smith) A. Hawkes. REFERENCES: 224, 230, 445.

Dendrobium furfuriferum J. J. Smith

ORIGIN/HABITAT: Irian Jaya (western New Guinea). Plants grow on trees on the forested eastern slopes of the Cyclops Mountains at about 3300 ft. (1000 m).

CLIMATE: Station #97690, Sentani/Jayapura, Irian Jaya, Lat. 2.7°S, Long. 140.5°E, at 289 ft. (88 m). Temperatures are calculated for an elevation of 3000 ft. (910 m), resulting in probable extremes of 88°F (31°C) and 59°F (15°C).

N/HEMISPHERE	JAN	FEB	MAR	APR	MAY	JUN	JUL	AUG	SEP	OCT	NOV	DEC
°F AVG MAX	78	80	80	81	81	80	80	79	80	81	81	80
°F AVG MIN	63	63	63	64	64	64	64	64	64	65	64	64
DIURNAL RANGE	15	17	17	17	17	16	16	15	16	16	17	16
RAIN/INCHES	4.1	3.9	5.3	2.9	6.7	7.0	8.3	8.3	8.5	4.6	2.4	5.2
HUMIDITY/%	81	80	80	79	81	81	79	80	80	80	81	80
BLOOM SEASON												*
DAYS CLR @ 9AM	5	3	4	3	2	1	1	0	1	2	2	5
DAYS CLR @ 3PM	4	3	3	2	1	3	1	0	1	2	2	3
RAIN/MM	104	99	135	74	170	178	211	211	216	117	61	132
°C AVG MAX	25.6	26.7	26.7	27.3	27.3	26.7	26.7	26.1	26.7	27.3	27.3	26.7
°C AVG MIN	17.3	17.3	17.3	17.8	17.8	17.8	17.8	17.8	17.8	18.4	17.8	17.8
DIURNAL RANGE	8.3	9.4	9.4	9.5	9.5	8.9	8.9	8.3	8.9	8.9	9.5	8.9
S/HEMISPHERE	JUL	AUG	SEP	OCT	NOV	DEC	JAN	FEB	MAR	APR	MAY	JUN

Cultural Recommendations

LIGHT: 2000–3000 fc.

TEMPERATURES: Throughout the year, days average 78–81°F (26–27°C), and nights average 63–65°F (17–18°C), with a diurnal range of 15–17°F (8–10°C).

HUMIDITY: Near 80% year-round.

WATER: Rainfall is moderate to heavy all year. Brief semidry periods occur in spring and autumn. Cultivated plants should be allowed to dry only slightly between waterings.

FERTILIZER: ¼–½ recommended strength. A balanced fertilizer should be applied weekly to biweekly throughout the year.

REST PERIOD: Growing conditions should be maintained year-round. Water and fertilizer might be reduced slightly in winter, especially for plants grown in the dark, short-day conditions common in temperate latitudes, but plants should never be allowed to dry completely. In the habitat, light is slightly higher in winter.

GROWING MEDIA: Plants may be mounted on tree-fern or cork slabs if humidity is high and plants are watered at least once daily in summer. When plants are potted, any open, fast-draining medium may be used. Repotting may be done anytime new roots are growing.

MISCELLANEOUS NOTES: The bloom season shown in the climate table is based on reports from the habitat.

Plant and Flower Information

PLANT SIZE AND TYPE: A 12 in. (30 cm) sympodial epiphyte.

PSEUDOBULB: 12 in. (30 cm) long.

LEAVES: The pointed, lanceolate leaves are 6–8 in. (15–20 cm) long. They have 2 unequal teeth at the apex.

INFLORESCENCE: Short. Inflorescences are borne on leafy stems.

FLOWERS: 4–6 per inflorescence. The fleshy flowers are 0.9 in. (2.3 cm) across. Sepals and petals are pure white in the center with dainty brown dots on other parts. The oblong sepals, which touch at their tips, are covered with scales on the backside. The petals are slender, oblong, and toothed on the upper margin. The slender lip is fiddle-shaped with a short fringe on the front margin of the midlobe. It is 3-lobed with an unusual transverse fold in front of the sidelobes. The base of the lip is pale yellow, and the anther is pale violet-pink.

REFERENCES: 221, 470, 476.

Dendrobium fuscatum Lindley. See *D. gibsonii* Lindley. REFERENCES: 190, 208, 216, 254, 278, 430, 445, 454, 541, 570.

Dendrobium fuscescens Griffith. Now considered a synonym of *Epigeneium fuscescens* (Griffith) Summerhayes. REFERENCES: 38, 46, 153, 154, 179, 190, 202, 216, 224, 229, 254, 369, 445, 499. PHOTOS/DRAWINGS: 46.

Dendrobium fuscopilosum Ames and Schweinfurth. See *D. orbiculare* J. J. Smith. REFERENCES: 12, 222, 286, 454.

Dendrobium fuscum Fitzgerald. See *D. discolor* Lindley. REFERENCES: 67, 84, 105, 216, 254, 421.

Dendrobium fusiforme F. M. Bailey not Thouars. See *D. jonesii* Rendle. REFERENCES: 67, 105, 216, 240, 421, 445, 504, 533, 580.

Dendrobium fusiforme Thouars. Now considered a synonym of *Polystachya fusiformis* Lindley. REFERENCES: 100, 216, 254.

Dendrobium fytchianum Bateman

AKA: Sometimes spelled *D. fytcheanum*. *D. barbatulum* Bateman not Lindley is a synonym.

ORIGIN/HABITAT: Moulmein, Burma. Plants grow in exposed positions on trees overhanging rivers. Habitat elevation is estimated, so the following climate data should be used with caution.

CLIMATE: Station #48103, Moulmein, Burma, Lat. 16.4°N, Long. 97.7°E, at 150 ft. (46 m). Temperatures are calculated for an estimated habitat elevation of 2000 ft. (610 m), resulting in probable extremes 96°F (36°C) and 45°F (7°C).

N/HEMISPHERE	JAN	FEB	MAR	APR	MAY	JUN	JUL	AUG	SEP	OCT	NOV	DEC
°F AVG MAX	83	86	88	89	83	79	77	77	79	82	83	81
°F AVG MIN	60	62	67	70	70	69	69	69	69	69	67	62
DIURNAL RANGE	23	24	21	19	13	10	8	8	10	13	16	19
RAIN/INCHES	0.3	0.2	0.4	3.0	20.3	35.6	46.3	43.4	28.1	8.5	2.1	0.1
HUMIDITY/%	66	68	68	70	81	91	92	93	91	81	75	64
BLOOM SEASON			**				*					
DAYS CLR @ 7AM	12	7	5	6	1	0	0	0	0	3	7	12
DAYS CLR @ 1PM	20	13	10	8	3	0	0	0	0	4	12	17
RAIN/MM	8	5	10	76	516	904	1176	1102	714	216	53	3
°C AVG MAX	28.3	29.9	31.1	31.6	28.3	26.1	24.9	24.9	26.1	27.7	28.3	27.2
°C AVG MIN	15.5	16.6	19.4	21.1	21.1	20.5	20.5	20.5	20.5	20.5	19.4	16.6
DIURNAL RANGE	12.8	13.3	11.7	10.5	7.2	5.6	4.4	4.4	5.6	7.2	8.9	10.6
S/HEMISPHERE	JUL	AUG	SEP	OCT	NOV	DEC	JAN	FEB	MAR	APR	MAY	JUN

Cultural Recommendations

LIGHT: 2500–3500 fc. Diffused light is recommended. Although plants normally grow in high light situations on trees that overhang rivers, summer light is lower than might be expected because clear days are rare. Also, cloud cover is extremely heavy during the summer monsoon.

TEMPERATURES: Summer days average 77–79°F (25–26°C), and nights average 69°F (21°C), with a diurnal range of 8–10°F (4–6°C). Weather is warmest in spring, when days average 83–89°F (28–32°C), and nights average 67–70°F (19–21°C), with a diurnal range of 13–21°F (7–12°C).

HUMIDITY: 80–90% from late spring to midautumn, dropping to near 65% in winter.

WATER: Rainfall is very heavy from late spring into autumn but decreases rapidly to a 4-month winter dry season. Cultivated plants should be kept evenly moist while actively growing, but water should be gradually reduced in autumn.

FERTILIZER: ¼–½ recommended strength, applied weekly. A high-nitrogen fertilizer is beneficial from spring to midsummer, but a fertilizer high in phosphates should be used in late summer and autumn.

REST PERIOD: Winter days average 81–86°F (27–30°C), and nights average 60–62°F (16–17°C), with a diurnal range of 19–24°F (11–13°C). The wide diurnal range results from both warmer days and cooler nights. In the habitat, rainfall is low for 4 months, but additional moisture is available from frequent heavy deposits of dew. Cultivated plants should be allowed to dry out between waterings, but they should never remain dry for long periods. Occasional early morning mistings between waterings may help prevent plants from becoming too dry. Fertilizer should be reduced or eliminated. In the habitat, light is highest in winter.

GROWING MEDIA: Plants grow well in baskets or very small pots filled with any rapidly draining medium. Plants may be mounted on slabs of cork or tree-fern if humidity is high and water is applied at least once daily in summer. Repotting is best done in early spring when new roots are growing.

Dendrobium fytchianum

MISCELLANEOUS NOTES: The bloom season shown in the climate table is based on 3 cultivation records. *D. fytchianum* is considered one of the prettiest of the smaller flowered species. It is good for cut flowers.

Plant and Flower Information

PLANT SIZE AND TYPE: A 12–22 in. (30–55 cm) sympodial epiphyte.

PSEUDOBULB: 12–22 in. (30–55 cm) long. Stems are slender, erect, cylindrical, and not swollen at the base. They branch repeatedly. Young stems are leafy.

LEAVES: Many. The deciduous, lance-shaped leaves are 3–4 in. (8–10 cm) long.

INFLORESCENCE: 8 in. (20 cm) long. The erect to arching inflorescences arise from nodes at or near the apex of each stem.

FLOWERS: 5–15 per inflorescence. The flowers are 1.2–2.0 in. (3.0–5.0 cm) across. The narrow sepals and broad petals are white. The heart-shaped lip has a tuft of yellowish hairs at the base. The base of the throat and sidelobes are tinted purple. The blossoms have a nice shape and are described as lovely and long-lasting.

HYBRIDIZING NOTES: The chromosome count is n = 20 (ref. 542).

REFERENCES: 157, 179, 190, 200, 202, 210, 216, 254, 430, 445, 541, 542, 557.

PHOTOS/DRAWINGS: 210, *430*.

Dendrobium gagnepainii
A. Hawkes and A. H. Heller. Now considered a synonym of *Eria eriopsidobulbon* Parish and Rchb. f. REFERENCES: 137, 191, 227, 229, Seidenfaden 1992 *Opera Botanica* #114.

Dendrobium galactanthum
Schlechter. See *D. scabrilingue* Lindley. REFERENCES: 221, 266, 445, 448, 454.

Dendrobium galeatum
Swartz. Now considered a synonym of *Bulbophyllum galeatum* Lindley. REFERENCES: 190, 216, 254.

Dendrobium galliceanum
Linden. See *D. thyrsiflorum* Rchb. f. REFERENCES: 157, 217, 445, 454, 570.

Dendrobium gamblei
King and Pantling. See *D. macrostachyum* Lindley. REFERENCES: 102, 250, 254, 424, 504, 584.

Dendrobium garayanum
A. Hawkes and A. H. Heller. See *D. austrocaledonicum* Schlechter. REFERENCES: 173, 191, 211, 229, 270, 271.

Dendrobium garrettii
Seidenfaden

ORIGIN/HABITAT: Endemic to Thailand. Plants were discovered in the mountains of northwestern Thailand on the southern slope of Mt. Pa Kao. They grow near the summit at about 5900 ft. (1800 m).

CLIMATE: Station #48327, Chiang Mai, Thailand, Lat. 18.8°N, Long. 99.0°E, at 1100 ft. (335 m). Temperatures are calculated for an elevation of 5900 ft. (1800 m), resulting in probable extremes of 93°F (34°C) and 22°F (−6°C).

N/HEMISPHERE	JAN	FEB	MAR	APR	MAY	JUN	JUL	AUG	SEP	OCT	NOV	DEC
°F AVG MAX	69	74	79	80	78	74	73	71	72	73	70	68
°F AVG MIN	40	41	46	54	58	58	58	59	57	55	50	41
DIURNAL RANGE	29	33	33	26	20	16	15	12	15	18	20	27
RAIN/INCHES	0.3	0.4	0.6	2.0	5.5	6.1	7.4	8.7	11.5	4.9	1.5	0.4
HUMIDITY/%	73	65	58	62	73	78	80	83	83	81	79	76
BLOOM SEASON									*			
DAYS CLR @ 7AM	5	5	2	1	0	0	0	0	0	1	3	3
DAYS CLR @ 1PM	9	8	4	2	0	0	0	0	0	0	1	3
RAIN/MM	8	10	15	51	140	155	188	221	292	124	38	10
°C AVG MAX	20.6	23.4	26.2	26.8	25.6	23.4	22.9	21.8	22.3	22.9	21.2	20.1
°C AVG MIN	4.5	5.1	7.9	12.3	14.5	14.5	14.5	15.1	14.0	12.9	10.1	5.1
DIURNAL RANGE	16.1	18.3	18.3	14.5	11.1	8.9	8.4	6.7	8.3	10.0	11.1	15.0
S/HEMISPHERE	JUL	AUG	SEP	OCT	NOV	DEC	JAN	FEB	MAR	APR	MAY	JUN

Cultural Recommendations

LIGHT: 1800–2400 fc. Diffused light is suggested.

TEMPERATURES: Summer days average 71–74°F (22–23°C), and nights average 58–59°F (15°C), with a diurnal range of 12–16°F (7–9°C). Spring is the warmest season. Days average 78–80°F (26–27°C), and nights average 46–58°F (8–15°C), with a diurnal range of 20–33°F (11–18°C). The warm weather occurs with, or immediately follows, the period of widest diurnal range.

HUMIDITY: 75–80% most of the year, dropping to near 60% in late winter and early spring.

WATER: Rainfall is heavy in summer and autumn, but conditions are dry in winter and early spring. Cultivated plants should be kept moist while actively growing, but water should be gradually reduced in autumn after new growths mature.

FERTILIZER: ¼–½ recommended strength, applied weekly. A high-nitrogen fertilizer is beneficial from spring to midsummer, but a fertilizer high in phosphates should be used in late summer and autumn.

REST PERIOD: Winter days average 68–74°F (20–23°C), and nights average 40–41°F (5°C), with a diurnal range of 27–33°F (15–18°C). The average low temperatures are below 50°F (10°C) for 4 months and then warm rapidly in spring. Plants should be able to tolerate temperatures a few degrees below freezing, but extremes should be avoided in cultivation. During very cold weather, a plant's chance of surviving with minimal damage is better if it is dry. In the habitat, rainfall averages are very low for 4–5 months in winter, but during the early part of the season the high relative humidity indicates that additional moisture is available from frequent fog, mist, and heavy deposits of dew. Growers sometimes recommend eliminating water in winter, but plants are healthiest if for most of the winter they are allowed to become somewhat dry between waterings. They should not remain dry for extended periods, however. For 1–2 months in late winter, conditions are clear, warm, and dry, with humidity so low that even the moisture from morning dew is uncommon. Plants should be allowed to dry out completely between waterings and remain dry longer during this time. Occasional early morning mistings between waterings may help keep the plants from becoming too dry. Fertilizer should be greatly reduced or eliminated until water is increased in spring. A cool, dry rest is essential for cultivated plants and should be continued until new growth starts in spring. In the habitat, light is highest in winter.

GROWING MEDIA: Plants may be mounted on tree-fern or cork slabs if humidity is high and plants are watered at least once daily in summer. When plants are potted, any open, fast-draining medium may be used. Repotting is best done in early spring when new roots are growing.

MISCELLANEOUS NOTES: The bloom season shown in the climate table is based on reports from the habitat.

Plant and Flower Information

PLANT SIZE AND TYPE: A small, less than 2 in. (5 cm), sympodial epiphyte.

PSEUDOBULB: 0.5 in. (1.3 cm) long. The nearly conical pseudobulbs are clustered forming a small tuft of growths.

LEAVES: 3 per growth. The ovate-lanceolate leaves are usually less than 1.4 in. (3.6 cm) long.

INFLORESCENCE: 0.8–2.0 in. (2–5 cm) long. Inflorescences emerge near the apex of the pseudobulb.

FLOWERS: 3–9 per inflorescence. The flowers are 0.6–0.8 in. (1.5–2.0 cm) across. The lanceolate sepals and petals are white with fine violet lines. The fringed lip is yellow and green.

REFERENCES: 234, 454.

PHOTOS/DRAWINGS: 454.

Dendrobium gatiense
Schlechter

ORIGIN/HABITAT: Northern Papua New Guinea. On Gati Mountain ridges above the Minjem Valley, plants grow on trees at about 2600 ft. (800 m).

CLIMATE: Station #94014, Madang, Papua New Guinea, Lat. 5.2°S, Long. 145.8°E, at 13 ft. (4 m). Temperatures are calculated for an elevation of 2600 ft. (800 m), resulting in probable extremes of 89°F (32°C) and 53°F (12°C).

N/HEMISPHERE	JAN	FEB	MAR	APR	MAY	JUN	JUL	AUG	SEP	OCT	NOV	DEC
°F AVG MAX	74	74	76	76	76	76	76	76	76	78	78	75
°F AVG MIN	68	69	69	69	68	68	68	68	68	67	68	69
DIURNAL RANGE	6	5	7	7	8	8	8	8	8	11	10	6
RAIN/INCHES	4.0	3.4	3.2	8.5	11.2	11.1	10.1	11.3	9.4	11.3	10.5	6.7
HUMIDITY/%	88	87	86	86	86	86	86	85	85	87	88	89
BLOOM SEASON												*
DAYS CLR	N/A											
RAIN/MM	102	86	81	216	284	282	257	287	239	287	267	170
°C AVG MAX	23.6	23.6	24.7	24.7	24.7	24.7	24.7	24.7	24.7	25.8	25.8	24.1
°C AVG MIN	20.2	20.8	20.8	20.8	20.2	20.2	20.2	20.2	20.2	19.7	20.2	20.8
DIURNAL RANGE	3.4	2.8	3.9	3.9	4.5	4.5	4.5	4.5	4.5	6.1	5.6	3.3
S/HEMISPHERE	JUL	AUG	SEP	OCT	NOV	DEC	JAN	FEB	MAR	APR	MAY	JUN

Dendrobium gaudens

Cultural Recommendations

LIGHT: 2500–3000 fc.

TEMPERATURES: Throughout the year, days average 74–78°F (24–26°C), and nights average 67–69°F (20–21°C), with a diurnal range of 5–11°F (3–6°C). The warmest highs, the coolest lows, and the greatest diurnal range occur in autumn.

HUMIDITY: 85–90% year-round.

WATER: Rainfall is moderate to heavy all year. The driest conditions occur in late winter. Cultivated plants should be kept moist but not soggy.

FERTILIZER: ¼–½ recommended strength. A balanced fertilizer should be applied weekly to biweekly throughout the year.

REST PERIOD: Growing temperatures should be maintained all year. In the habitat, rainfall decreases for 4 months in winter. Water should be reduced somewhat for cultivated plants, but they should not be allowed to dry out completely. Fertilizer should be reduced or eliminated while water is reduced. In the habitat, light is slightly higher in late winter.

GROWING MEDIA: Plants may be mounted on tree-fern or cork slabs if humidity is high and plants are watered at least once daily in summer. When plants are potted, any open, fast-draining medium may be used. Repotting may be done anytime new roots are growing.

MISCELLANEOUS NOTES: The bloom season shown in the climate table is based on reports from the habitat. Plants that produce flowers which last a single day commonly bloom several times during the year. Flowering usually occurs 7–14 days after a sudden 10°F (5°C) drop in daytime temperatures.

Plant and Flower Information

PLANT SIZE AND TYPE: A 16–24 in. (40–60 cm) sympodial epiphyte.

PSEUDOBULB: 13–19 in. (33–48 cm) long. Pseudobulbs are simple, curved, and somewhat flattened.

LEAVES: Many. The leaves are 3–5 in. (8–13 cm) long.

INFLORESCENCE: Short. Inflorescences emerge from the leaf axils.

FLOWERS: 2 per inflorescence. The flowers, which last a single day, are 0.5 in. (1.3 cm) across. The white blossoms are marked with rose-red warts on the midlobe of the lip. The center keel and callus of the lip are yellow.

REFERENCES: 92, 221, 437, 445.

PHOTOS/DRAWINGS: 437.

Dendrobium gaudens P. van Royen. See *D. dekockii* J. J. Smith. REFERENCES: 233, 385, 538. PHOTOS/DRAWINGS: 538.

Dendrobium gazellae Kränzlin. See *D. insigne* (Blume) Rchb. f. ex Miquel. REFERENCES: 218, 254, 270, 437, 445, 470, 533.

Dendrobium gedeanum J. J. Smith. See *D. gracile* (Blume) Lindley. REFERENCES: 75, 220, 254.

Dendrobium geluanum Schlechter. See *D. hellwigianum* Kränzlin. REFERENCES: 223, 385.

Dendrobium gemellum as used by Kränzlin not Lindley. See *D. reineckei* Schlechter. Kränzlin (ref. 254) included *D. gemellum* as both a valid species and as synonym for *D. salaccense* (Blume) Lindley. REFERENCES: 254, 434.

Dendrobium gemellum Lindley not Kränzlin or Ridley

AKA: *Pedilonum biflorum* Blume.

ORIGIN/HABITAT: Sumatra and western Java. Plants grow on trees at 1650–6550 ft. (500–2000 m). *D. gemellum* is uncommon despite the relatively large habitat.

CLIMATE: Station #96755, Bogor, Java, Indonesia, Lat. 6.5°S, Long. 106.8°E, at 558 ft. (170 m). Temperatures are calculated for an elevation of 4000 ft. (1220 m), resulting in probable extremes of 85°F (29°C) and 55°F (13°C).

N/HEMISPHERE	JAN	FEB	MAR	APR	MAY	JUN	JUL	AUG	SEP	OCT	NOV	DEC
°F AVG MAX	75	76	77	77	76	74	73	73	74	75	76	75
°F AVG MIN	62	62	62	63	63	63	63	63	63	64	64	63
DIURNAL RANGE	13	14	15	14	13	11	10	10	11	11	12	12
RAIN/INCHES	2.1	1.0	0.5	5.0	8.1	18.8	23.7	20.2	14.4	12.0	11.9	3.4
HUMIDITY/%	72	68	65	66	74	79	84	84	81	79	77	75
BLOOM SEASON	*					*						
DAYS CLR @ 7AM	14	14	14	11	5	3	1	2	4	6	10	12
DAYS CLR @ 1PM	9	10	8	5	1	1	0	0	1	1	3	7
RAIN/MM	53	25	13	127	206	478	602	513	366	305	302	86
°C AVG MAX	23.7	24.2	24.8	24.8	24.2	23.1	22.6	22.6	23.1	23.7	24.2	23.7
°C AVG MIN	16.5	16.5	16.5	17.0	17.0	17.0	17.0	17.0	17.0	17.6	17.6	17.0
DIURNAL RANGE	7.2	7.7	8.3	7.8	7.2	6.1	5.6	5.6	6.1	6.1	6.6	6.7
S/HEMISPHERE	JUL	AUG	SEP	OCT	NOV	DEC	JAN	FEB	MAR	APR	MAY	JUN

Cultural Recommendations

LIGHT: 2000–3000 fc. Diffused light or dappled shade are recommended.

TEMPERATURES: Throughout the year, days average 73–77°F (23–25°C), and nights average 62–64°F (17–18°C), with a diurnal range of 10–15°F (6–8°C). Night temperatures vary only 2°F (1°C) throughout the year.

HUMIDITY: 75–85% most of the year, dropping to near 65% in winter and spring.

WATER: Rainfall is very heavy from spring into autumn, but conditions are very dry for 1–2 months in winter. During the growing season, plants should never be allowed to dry out completely, but water should be gradually reduced in autumn.

FERTILIZER: ¼–½ recommended strength, applied weekly. A high-nitrogen fertilizer is beneficial from spring to midsummer, but a fertilizer high in phosphates should be used in late summer and autumn.

REST PERIOD: Growing conditions should be maintained all year; but the diurnal range increases slightly in winter, and rainfall is very low for 1–2 months. In cultivation, water should be reduced and the plants allowed to become slightly dry between waterings. They should not remain dry for prolonged periods, however. Fertilizer may be reduced or eliminated anytime the plant is not actively growing. In the habitat, light is highest in winter.

GROWING MEDIA: Plants may be mounted on tree-fern or cork slabs if humidity is high and plants are watered at least once daily in summer. When plants are potted, any open, fast-draining medium may be used. Repotting may be done anytime new roots are growing.

MISCELLANEOUS NOTES: In 1983, *D. gemellum* was considered a lost species. Schlechter (ref. 435) reported collecting it in 1907 from trees near Padang-Pandjang, Sumatra at 2800 ft. (800 m). Plant and flower information is based on Ridley (ref. 402).

Plant and Flower Information

PLANT SIZE AND TYPE: A 14–35 in. (35–90 cm) sympodial epiphyte.

PSEUDOBULB: 14–35 in. (35–90 cm) long. The upper part of the stems are flattened. They do not branch.

LEAVES: The grass-like, linear-lanceolate leaves are about 4 in. (10 cm) long. They have a thin texture and pale green color. Leaf sheaths are wrinkled.

INFLORESCENCE: Very short. Racemes emerge opposite the leaves from the center of the internode and may be enclosed in bracts.

FLOWERS: 2–3 per inflorescence. The yellowish to greenish white flowers are 1.4 in. (3.5 cm) long. They may open fully or remain rather closed. Sepals and petals are pointed at the tip and roughly equal in size. The pointed lip has prominent veins, 3 obscure toothed ridges, and a slightly ruffled margin. The spur equals the length of the dorsal sepal.

REFERENCES: 25, 74, 75, 202, 216, 254, 286, 295, 310, 317, 395, 435, 468, 469.

PHOTOS/DRAWINGS: 74, 469.

Dendrobium gemellum as used by Ridley (ref. 402) not Lindley or Kränzlin. See *D. indragiriense* Schlechter. REFERENCES: 402, 469.

Dendrobium geminatum (Blume) Lindley. Now considered a synonym of *Epigeneium geminatum* (Blume) Summerhayes. REFERENCES: 25, 75, 200, 202, 213, 216, 229, 254, 277, 310, 395, 449, 455, 469, 499. PHOTOS/DRAWINGS: 200, 469.

Dendrobium geminiflorum Schlechter. See *D. violaceum* Kränzlin. REFERENCES: 222, 385.

Dendrobium gemma Schlechter. See *D. masarangense* Schlechter. REFERENCES: 223, 385, 443, 486.

Dendrobium gemmiferum Kränzlin. Schlechter (ref. 436: 1911) included *D. gemmiferum* Kränzlin as a possible synonym of *D. suaveolens* Schlechter, but he later (ref. 436:1925) listed it as a synonym of *D. odoratum* Schlechter. REFERENCES: 220, 254, 436.

Dendrobium geotropum T. M. Reeve

ORIGIN/HABITAT: Papua New Guinea in the provinces of Enga, Morobe, Southern Highlands, and Western Highlands. Plants grow at 6550–9350 ft. (2000–2850 m). The largest plants are found on *Pandanus* trees.

CLIMATE: Station #200243, Mt. Hagen, Papua New Guinea, Lat. 5.8°S, Long. 144.3°E, at 5350 ft. (1630 m). Temperatures are calculated for an elevation of 8200 ft. (2500 m), resulting in probable extremes of 79°F (26°C) and 26°F (–4°C).

N/HEMISPHERE	JAN	FEB	MAR	APR	MAY	JUN	JUL	AUG	SEP	OCT	NOV	DEC
°F AVG MAX	63	64	65	66	67	67	67	67	66	66	67	65
°F AVG MIN	46	46	46	46	46	47	47	47	47	48	47	45
DIURNAL RANGE	17	18	19	20	21	20	20	20	19	18	20	20
RAIN/INCHES	5.2	6.7	8.7	8.7	8.2	10.2	10.4	10.7	11.2	10.0	7.2	4.7
HUMIDITY/%	84	83	82	78	79	81	81	80	82	81	82	82
BLOOM SEASON								*				
DAYS CLR	N/A											
RAIN/MM	132	170	221	221	208	259	264	272	284	254	183	119
°C AVG MAX	17.0	17.6	18.1	18.7	19.2	19.2	19.2	19.2	18.7	18.7	19.2	18.1
°C AVG MIN	7.6	7.6	7.6	7.6	7.6	8.1	8.1	8.1	8.1	8.7	8.1	7.0
DIURNAL RANGE	9.4	10.0	10.5	11.1	11.6	11.1	11.1	11.1	10.6	10.0	11.1	11.1
S/HEMISPHERE	JUL	AUG	SEP	OCT	NOV	DEC	JAN	FEB	MAR	APR	MAY	JUN

Cultural Recommendations

LIGHT: 1800–2500 fc.

TEMPERATURES: Throughout the year, days average 63–67°F (17–19°C), and nights average 45–48°F (7–9°C), with a diurnal range of 17–21°F (9–12°C).

HUMIDITY: Near 80% year-round.

WATER: Rainfall is moderate to heavy all year with a 1–2 month slightly drier period in winter. Cultivated plants should never be allowed to dry out completely.

FERTILIZER: ¼–½ recommended strength, applied weekly during periods of active growth.

REST PERIOD: Growing conditions should be maintained year-round. Water may be reduced somewhat in winter, especially for plants grown in the dark, short-day conditions common in temperate latitudes. Fertilizer should be reduced or eliminated anytime water is reduced. In the habitat, light is higher in winter.

GROWING MEDIA: Mounting plants on tree-fern or cork slabs accommodates their pendulous growth habit. However, humidity must be high and plants must be watered at least once a day in summer. If plants cannot be mounted, hanging pots or baskets may be filled with an open, fast-draining medium. Repotting may be done anytime new roots are actively growing.

MISCELLANEOUS NOTES: The bloom season shown in the climate table is based on reports from the habitat.

Plant and Flower Information

PLANT SIZE AND TYPE: A pendent, 4–24 in. (10–60 cm) sympodial epiphyte.

PSEUDOBULB: 2–11 in. (5–28 cm) long. The yellowish- to dark-brown pseudobulbs are borne on an extremely short rhizome. The club-shaped stems are slender at the base but very swollen at the apex. They become grooved with age.

LEAVES: 1–3, normally 2 per growth. The ovate-elliptic to lanceolate leaves are 2.4–9.4 in. (6–24 cm) long. Normally mid- to dark-green, they are sometimes suffused with purple.

INFLORESCENCE: 1.2–7.1 in. (3–18 cm) long. The pendent inflorescences are often partially enclosed by the leaves. They emerge at the apex of the pseudobulb.

FLOWERS: 3–12 per inflorescence. The green and purple flowers are 0.6–1.0 in. (1.5–2.5 cm) across and may not open fully. Blossoms vary in size and degree of opening. They are fleshy and smooth. Sepals and petals are pale green, but the outside of the sepals are variably spotted or suffused with purple. The sharply contrasting lip is dark purple with a large, 3-ridged, white callus. It is incurved along the margin. The outside of the lip has a white streak on the center-line. The pollinia are golden yellow. Blossoms are odorless and last several weeks or more.

REFERENCES: 95, 234, 380.

PHOTOS/DRAWINGS: 380.

Dendrobium gerlandianum Kränzlin

ORIGIN/HABITAT: Manila, Luzon Island, the Philippines. The plant bloomed in the botanical garden at Erlangen, Germany. Habitat elevation is not available, so the following climate data should be used with caution.

CLIMATE: Station #98427, Manila, Philippines, Lat. 14.5°N, Long. 121.0°E, at 74 ft. (23 m). Record extreme temperatures are 101°F (38°C) and 58°F (14°C).

N/HEMISPHERE	JAN	FEB	MAR	APR	MAY	JUN	JUL	AUG	SEP	OCT	NOV	DEC
°F AVG MAX	86	88	91	93	93	91	88	87	88	88	87	86
°F AVG MIN	69	69	71	73	75	75	75	75	75	74	72	70
DIURNAL RANGE	17	19	20	20	18	16	13	12	13	14	15	16
RAIN/INCHES	0.9	0.5	0.7	1.3	5.1	10.0	17.0	16.6	14.0	7.6	5.7	2.6
HUMIDITY/%	77	73	70	68	71	81	84	86	87	84	82	89
BLOOM SEASON	*											
DAYS CLR @ 8AM	6	9	14	14	10	3	2	1	1	6	7	6
DAYS CLR @ 2PM	3	6	10	10	8	2	1	1	0	2	2	3
RAIN/MM	23	13	18	33	130	254	432	422	356	193	145	66
°C AVG MAX	30.0	31.1	32.8	33.9	33.9	32.8	31.1	30.6	31.1	31.1	30.6	30.0
°C AVG MIN	20.6	20.6	21.7	22.8	23.9	23.9	23.9	23.9	23.9	23.3	22.2	21.1
DIURNAL RANGE	9.4	10.5	11.1	11.1	10.0	8.9	7.2	6.7	7.2	7.8	8.4	8.9
S/HEMISPHERE	JUL	AUG	SEP	OCT	NOV	DEC	JAN	FEB	MAR	APR	MAY	JUN

Cultural Recommendations

LIGHT: 2000–3000 fc.

TEMPERATURES: Throughout the year, days average 86–93°F (30–34°C), and nights average 69–75°F (21–24°C), with a diurnal range of 12–20°F (7–11°C).

HUMIDITY: 80–85% in summer and autumn, dropping to about 70% in winter and spring.

WATER: Rainfall is heavy from late spring through autumn, but conditions

Dendrobium gibbiferum

are dry for 3–4 months in winter. Cultivated plants should be kept moist while actively growing, but water should be gradually reduced in late autumn.

FERTILIZER: ¼–½ recommended strength, applied weekly. A high-nitrogen fertilizer is beneficial from spring to midsummer, but a fertilizer high in phosphates should be used in late summer and autumn.

REST PERIOD: Growing temperatures should be maintained all year. Rainfall is low for 3–4 months in winter, but additional moisture is available from frequent heavy dew. In cultivation, water should be reduced and the plants allowed to dry out between waterings. They should not remain dry for extended periods, however. Fertilizer should also be reduced or eliminated anytime water is reduced. In the habitat, light is highest in winter.

GROWING MEDIA: Plants may be mounted on tree-fern or cork slabs if humidity is high and plants are watered at least once daily in summer. When plants are potted, any open, fast-draining medium may be used. Repotting is best done in early spring at the end of the dry season.

MISCELLANEOUS NOTES: The bloom season shown in the climate table is based on reports from the habitat.

Plant and Flower Information

PLANT SIZE AND TYPE: A 3–4 in. (8–10 cm) sympodial epiphyte, terrestrial, or lithophyte.

PSEUDOBULB: 1.3 in. (3.2 cm) long. Pseudobulbs are swollen at the base and slender above. They taper to a needle point at the tip.

LEAVES: Few. The terete leaves are usually 2.4 in. (6 cm) long. They are not grooved.

INFLORESCENCE: Inflorescences are borne at the tip and upper nodes of the stem.

FLOWERS: 1 per inflorescence. The blossoms are uniformly green. The oblong lip is pointed at the apex and wavy at the margin. It has no side-lobes.

REFERENCES: 220, 254, 296, 536.

Dendrobium gibbiferum J. J. Smith. Now considered a synonym of *Diplocaulobium gibbiferum* (J. J. Smith) A. Hawkes. REFERENCES: 224, 229, 445, 470.

Dendrobium gibbosum A. Gilli

ORIGIN/HABITAT: Papua New Guinea. Plants were collected between Laiagam and Kandep at about 10,150 ft. (3100 m).

CLIMATE: Botanical garden records, Laiagam, Papua New Guinea, Lat. 5.5°S, Long. 143.5°E, at 7218 ft. (2200 m). Temperatures are calculated for an elevation of 10,500 ft. (3200 m), resulting in probable extremes of 80°F (27°C) and 21°F (–6°C).

N/HEMISPHERE	JAN	FEB	MAR	APR	MAY	JUN	JUL	AUG	SEP	OCT	NOV	DEC
°F AVG MAX	65	66	67	65	67	67	71	66	65	67	67	65
°F AVG MIN	44	43	44	44	45	45	44	45	47	46	45	45
DIURNAL RANGE	21	23	23	21	22	22	27	21	18	21	22	20
RAIN/INCHES	4.0	4.8	6.1	7.8	8.5	9.1	8.4	9.6	9.5	8.9	6.3	4.0
HUMIDITY/%	N/A											
BLOOM SEASON							*					
DAYS CLR	N/A											
RAIN/MM	102	122	155	198	216	231	213	244	241	226	160	102
°C AVG MAX	18.4	19.0	19.5	18.4	19.5	19.5	21.8	19.0	18.4	19.5	19.5	18.4
°C AVG MIN	6.8	6.2	6.8	6.8	7.3	7.3	6.8	7.3	8.4	7.9	7.3	7.3
DIURNAL RANGE	11.7	12.8	12.8	11.7	12.2	12.2	15.0	11.7	10.0	11.7	12.2	11.1
S/HEMISPHERE	JUL	AUG	SEP	OCT	NOV	DEC	JAN	FEB	MAR	APR	MAY	JUN

Cultural Recommendations

LIGHT: 2000–3000 fc.

TEMPERATURES: Throughout the year, days average 65–71°F (18–22°C), and nights average 43–47°F (6–8°C), with a diurnal range of 18–27°F (10–15°C).

HUMIDITY: Information is not available for this location. However, records from nearby stations indicate that humidity is probably 80–85% year-round.

WATER: Rainfall is heavy throughout the year. Conditions are slightly drier for 3–4 months in winter. Cultivated plants should be kept moist.

FERTILIZER: ¼–½ recommended strength. A balanced fertilizer should be applied weekly to biweekly throughout the year. The Royal Botanic Garden in Edinburgh uses a seaweed-based fertilizer for plants from this habitat.

REST PERIOD: Growing conditions should be maintained all year. Water and fertilizer should be reduced somewhat in winter, especially when plants are grown in the dark, short-day conditions common in temperate latitudes. Plants should dry slightly between waterings, but they should never be allowed to dry out completely. Water and fertilizer should be gradually increased when plants begin growing in spring.

GROWING MEDIA: Plants may be mounted on tree-fern or cork slabs if humidity is high and plants are watered daily in summer. When plants are potted, any open, fast-draining medium may be used. Repotting may be done anytime new roots are growing.

MISCELLANEOUS NOTES: The bloom season shown in the climate table is based on collection reports.

Plant and Flower Information

PLANT SIZE AND TYPE: An elongated sympodial epiphyte of unreported size.

PSEUDOBULB: The long, slender stems are branching.

LEAVES: Many. The linear-lanceolate leaves are 1.0–2.8 in. (2.5–7.0 cm) long.

INFLORESCENCE: Short.

FLOWERS: 2 per inflorescence. The reddish violet flowers are 1.0–1.2 in. (2.5–3.0 cm) long. The slender sepals and petals are curved down over the lip. The lip midlobe is fringed along the margin.

REFERENCES: 146, 234.

PHOTOS/DRAWINGS: 146.

Dendrobium gibsonii Lindley

AKA: *D. fuscatum* Lindley.

ORIGIN/HABITAT: Widespread across the Himalayan region including Nepal, Sikkim, Bhutan, northeastern India, the mountains of northwestern Thailand, and near Mengtze in Yunnan Province, southwestern China. In Sikkim and the Khasi (Khasia) Hills, plants grow at 2300–5600 ft. (700–1700 m). In Thailand, they are found at 2300–5250 ft. (700–1600 m). In extreme northeastern India, plants are rare in Arunachal Pradesh, where they grow at 650–3300 ft. (200–1000 m). Plants are normally epiphytic, but in deforested areas, they may grow lithophytically.

CLIMATE: Station #42398, Baghdogra/Siliguri, India, Lat. 26.7°N, Long. 88.3°E, at 412 ft. (126 m). Temperatures are calculated for an elevation of 4000 ft. (1220 m), resulting in probable extremes of 92°F (33°C) and 24°F (–4°C).

N/HEMISPHERE	JAN	FEB	MAR	APR	MAY	JUN	JUL	AUG	SEP	OCT	NOV	DEC
°F AVG MAX	62	65	73	78	78	77	77	77	76	75	70	65
°F AVG MIN	38	42	48	56	61	64	65	65	64	58	48	41
DIURNAL RANGE	24	23	25	22	17	13	12	12	12	17	22	24
RAIN/INCHES	0.3	0.7	1.3	3.7	11.8	25.9	32.2	25.3	21.2	5.6	0.5	0.2
HUMIDITY/%	73	68	57	58	74	84	86	85	85	79	75	76
BLOOM SEASON				*	*	**	**	*				
DAYS CLR @ 6AM	21	18	15	11	5	0	1	1	4	13	23	19
DAYS CLR @ 12PM	23	16	16	11	2	2	0	1	2	10	21	18
RAIN/MM	8	18	33	94	300	658	818	643	538	142	13	5
°C AVG MAX	16.8	18.4	22.9	25.6	25.6	25.1	25.1	25.1	24.5	24.0	21.2	18.4
°C AVG MIN	3.4	5.6	9.0	13.4	16.2	17.9	18.4	18.4	17.9	14.5	9.0	5.1
DIURNAL RANGE	13.4	12.8	13.9	12.2	9.4	7.2	6.7	6.7	6.6	9.5	12.2	13.3
S/HEMISPHERE	JUL	AUG	SEP	OCT	NOV	DEC	JAN	FEB	MAR	APR	MAY	JUN

Cultural Recommendations

LIGHT: 2000–3000 fc. Diffused light is suggested. The heavy summer cloud cover indicates that some shading is needed from spring through autumn, but light should be as high as the plant can tolerate, short of burning the leaves.

TEMPERATURES: Summer days average 77°F (25°C), and nights average 64–65°F (18°C), with a diurnal range of 12–13°F (7°C). Due to the effects of the microclimate, actual habitat temperatures may be 6–8°F (3–4°C) warmer than indicated.

HUMIDITY: Near 85% in summer. Humidity decreases to 75–80% in autumn, and to near 60% in late winter and early spring.

WATER: Conditions are very wet for 5 months in summer, very dry for 5 months in winter, with short transition periods in autumn and spring. Cultivated plants should be kept evenly moist from spring to early autumn, but water should be gradually reduced after new growths mature in late autumn.

FERTILIZER: 1/4–1/2 recommended strength, applied weekly. A high-nitrogen fertilizer is beneficial from spring to midsummer, but a fertilizer high in phosphates should be used in late summer and autumn.

REST PERIOD: For 2–4 months in winter, days average 62–65°F (17–18°C), and nights average 38–42°F (3–6°C), with a diurnal range of 23–24°F (13°C). Plants should survive exposure to freezing providing they are dry at the time, but these extreme conditions should be avoided in cultivation. In the habitat, winter rainfall is low but additional moisture is often available from heavy deposits of dew. For about a month in late winter or early spring, however, humidity is so low that even the moisture from dew is uncommon. Cultivated plants should be allowed to dry out between waterings in winter, but they should not remain dry for extended periods. Occasional early morning mistings between waterings, especially on warm, sunny days, may help prevent the plants from becoming too dry. Fertilizer should be eliminated until water is increased in spring. In the habitat, light is highest in winter. The cool, dry rest with increased light may be necessary to initiate blooming.

GROWING MEDIA: Mounting plants on tree-fern or cork slabs accommodates their pendent growth habit, but humidity must be high and plants should be watered at least once daily in summer. Plants may be placed in hanging pots or baskets filled with any open, fast-draining medium. Repotting is best done in early spring as soon as new growth begins.

MISCELLANEOUS NOTES: The bloom season shown in the climate table is based on cultivation records. In the habitat, blooming occurs midsummer.

Plant and Flower Information

PLANT SIZE AND TYPE: A 24–47 in. (60–120 cm) sympodial epiphyte.

PSEUDOBULB: 24–47 in. (60–120 cm) long. The stemlike pseudobulbs are swollen in the center and taper toward the apex. They are pendulous, ribbed, and slightly thickened at the nodes.

LEAVES: 6–10 per growth. The ovate to lanceolate leaves are about 6 in. (15 cm) long and pointed at the tip. Leaves are eventually deciduous.

INFLORESCENCE: 6–8 in. (15–20 cm) long. Somewhat zigzag, the inflorescences are nodding or pendulous and loosely flowered. They arise from nodes on the upper part of older stems opposite the base of fallen leaves.

FLOWERS: 6–15 per inflorescence. The saffron-yellow to orange-yellow flowers are downy, 1.2–2.0 in. (3–5 cm) across, and last 2 weeks. The lip is marked with 2, brownish, crimson, or purple spots. *D. gibsonii* is considered one of the finest yellow-flowered species. It is extremely fragrant.

HYBRIDIZING NOTES: Chromosome counts are n = 19 (ref. 154, 542) and 2n = 38 (ref. 150, 153, 154, 273, 504, 542, 580) and 2n = 40 (ref. 152, 542). Johansen (ref. 239) indicates that some clones of *D. gibsonii* could be self-pollinated while others were self-sterile. The seed capsules opened 178 days after pollination. Of the seed produced, however, none had visible embryos and none germinated.

REFERENCES: 38, 46, 150, 152, 153, 154, 157, 179, 190, 202, 208, 210, 216, 239, 254, 273, 278, 294, 317, 369, 376, 414, 430, 445, 454, 504, 528, 541, 542, 570, 580.

PHOTOS/DRAWINGS: 46, 210, *369, 430, 454.*

Dendrobium giddinsii T. E. Hunt. See *D. fellowsii* F. Mueller.
REFERENCES: 67, 105, 227, 533.

Dendrobium giluwense P. van Royen. See *D. rigidifolium* Rolfe.
REFERENCES: 83, 233, 538. PHOTOS/DRAWINGS: 538.

Dendrobium giriwoense J. J. Smith

ORIGIN/HABITAT: Irian Jaya (western New Guinea). Plants grow on forest trees near the Giriwo River.

CLIMATE: Station #97682, Nabire, Irian Jaya, Lat. 3.3°S, Long. 135.5°E, at 10 ft. (3 m). Record extreme temperatures are not available for this location.

N/HEMISPHERE	JAN	FEB	MAR	APR	MAY	JUN	JUL	AUG	SEP	OCT	NOV	DEC
°F AVG MAX	86	86	86	86	87	87	86	86	87	87	87	87
°F AVG MIN	75	75	76	77	77	76	77	75	75	76	76	76
DIURNAL RANGE	11	11	10	9	10	11	9	11	12	11	11	11
RAIN/INCHES	7.4	11.1	8.5	8.5	7.5	9.0	9.2	10.6	12.1	11.3	10.2	9.8
HUMIDITY/%	N/A											
BLOOM SEASON	*											
DAYS CLR	N/A											
RAIN/MM	190	283	217	217	192	228	233	270	308	286	259	248
°C AVG MAX	30.1	29.9	30.1	30.3	30.5	30.6	30.0	30.0	30.5	30.5	30.3	30.3
°C AVG MIN	24.0	24.0	24.3	24.7	24.9	24.5	24.8	24.0	23.8	24.6	24.3	24.2
DIURNAL RANGE	6.1	5.9	5.8	5.6	5.6	6.1	5.2	6.0	6.7	5.9	6.0	6.1
S/HEMISPHERE	JUL	AUG	SEP	OCT	NOV	DEC	JAN	FEB	MAR	APR	MAY	JUN

Cultural Recommendations

LIGHT: 2000–3000 fc.

TEMPERATURES: Throughout the year, days average 86–87°F (30–31°C), and nights average 75–77°F (24–25°C), with a diurnal range of 9–12°F (5–7°C).

HUMIDITY: Information is not available for this location. However, records from nearby stations indicate that humidity probably averages near 85% year-round.

WATER: Rainfall is heavy year-round. Cultivated plants should be kept evenly moist with only slight drying between waterings. Warm water might be beneficial.

FERTILIZER: 1/4–1/2 recommended strength. A balanced fertilizer should be applied weekly to biweekly throughout the year.

REST PERIOD: Growing conditions should be maintained year-round. Water and fertilizer may be reduced slightly in winter, especially for plants grown in the dark, short-day conditions common in temperate latitudes. Plants should never be allowed to dry completely, however.

GROWING MEDIA: Plants may be mounted on tree-fern or cork slabs or potted in any open, fast-draining medium. Repotting may be done anytime new roots are growing.

MISCELLANEOUS NOTES: The bloom season shown in the climate table is based on reports from the habitat.

Plant and Flower Information

PLANT SIZE AND TYPE: A 22 in. (55 cm) sympodial epiphyte.

Dendrobium giulianettii

PSEUDOBULB: 22 in. (55 cm) long. The unbranched stems are 2-edged on the upper portion.

LEAVES: Many. The oblong-ovate leaves are 0.9–1.7 in. (2.3–4.3 cm) long, rounded at the base, and unequally bilobed at the apex. They are spreading and papery.

INFLORESCENCE: The inflorescences are subspreading and emerge laterally from flat sheaths.

FLOWERS: 2 per inflorescence. The insignificant white flowers are 0.3 in. (0.8 cm) long. The somewhat sickle-shaped petals and pointed dorsal sepal are oblong. The lateral sepals are obliquely triangular. The curved lip is relatively broad with large sidelobes.

REFERENCES: 221, 470, 476.

Dendrobium giulianettii F. M. Bailey. See *D. mirbelianum* Gaudich. REFERENCES: 67, 84, 254, 533.

Dendrobium gjellerupii J. J. Smith

ORIGIN/HABITAT: Irian Jaya (western New Guinea). Plants were collected at about 150 ft. (50 m).

CLIMATE: Station #97690, Sentani/Jayapura, Irian Jaya, Lat. 2.7°S, Long. 140.5°E, at 289 ft. (88 m). Record extreme temperatures are 97°F (36°C) and 68°F (20°C).

N/HEMISPHERE	JAN	FEB	MAR	APR	MAY	JUN	JUL	AUG	SEP	OCT	NOV	DEC
°F AVG MAX	87	89	89	90	90	89	89	88	89	90	90	89
°F AVG MIN	72	72	72	73	73	73	73	73	73	74	73	73
DIURNAL RANGE	15	17	17	17	17	16	16	15	16	16	17	16
RAIN/INCHES	4.1	3.9	5.3	2.9	6.7	7.0	8.3	8.3	8.5	4.6	2.4	5.2
HUMIDITY/%	81	80	80	79	81	81	79	80	80	80	81	80
BLOOM SEASON			*									
DAYS CLR @ 9AM	5	3	4	3	2	1	1	0	1	2	2	5
DAYS CLR @ 3PM	4	3	3	3	2	1	3	0	1	2	2	3
RAIN/MM	104	99	135	74	170	178	211	211	216	117	61	132
°C AVG MAX	30.6	31.7	31.7	32.2	32.2	31.7	31.7	31.1	31.7	32.2	32.2	31.7
°C AVG MIN	22.2	22.2	22.2	22.8	22.8	22.8	22.8	22.8	22.8	23.3	22.8	22.8
DIURNAL RANGE	8.3	9.4	9.4	9.4	9.4	8.9	8.9	8.3	8.9	8.9	9.4	8.9
S/HEMISPHERE	JUL	AUG	SEP	OCT	NOV	DEC	JAN	FEB	MAR	APR	MAY	JUN

Cultural Recommendations

LIGHT: 2000–3000 fc.

TEMPERATURES: Throughout the year, days average 87–90°F (31–32°C), and nights average 72–74°F (22–23°C), with a diurnal range of 15–17°F (8–9°C).

HUMIDITY: Near 80% year-round.

WATER: Rainfall is moderate to heavy most of the year with brief semidry periods in spring and autumn. Cultivated plants should be kept moist.

FERTILIZER: ¼–½ recommended strength. A balanced fertilizer should be applied weekly to biweekly throughout the year.

REST PERIOD: Growing conditions should be maintained year-round. Water and fertilizer may be reduced somewhat for plants grown in the dark, short-day conditions common in temperate-latitude winters, but they should never be allowed to dry out completely.

GROWING MEDIA: Plants may be mounted on tree-fern or cork slabs if humidity is high and plants are watered at least once daily in summer. When plants are potted, any open, fast-draining medium may be used. Repotting may be done anytime new roots are growing.

MISCELLANEOUS NOTES: The bloom season shown in the climate table is based on reports from the habitat. Plants that produce flowers which last a single day commonly bloom several times during the year. Flowering usually occurs 7–14 days after a sudden 10°F (5°C) drop in daytime temperatures. The plant was described in 1911 in *Bul. Dép. Agric. Indes Néerl.* 45:4.

Plant and Flower Information

PLANT SIZE AND TYPE: A long sympodial plant of unreported size.

PSEUDOBULB: The clustered stems are flattened and elongated.

LEAVES: Many. The leaves are 3.3 in. (8.5 cm) long. The lanceolate leaves have warts on the upper surface, as do the leaf sheaths, which terminate in a pronounced tooth.

INFLORESCENCE: The bracts at the base of the inflorescence are covered with warts.

FLOWERS: The round flowers are 0.8 in. (2 cm) long. They may be glistening white with a yellow spot on the lip or yellow-green with a stronger green lip. The backside of the sepals, ovaries, and pedicels are covered with warts. Blossoms last a single day, but plants are showy when in full bloom.

REFERENCES: 221, 445, 470.

Dendrobium glabrum J. J. Smith. Now considered a synonym of *Diplocaulobium glabrum* (J. J. Smith) Kränzlin. REFERENCES: 67, 105, 220, 254, 437, 445, 470.

Dendrobium glaucophyllum Teijsm. and Binn. See *D. rugosum* (Blume) Lindley. REFERENCES: 25, 216, 254, 469.

Dendrobium glaucoviride J. J. Smith

ORIGIN/HABITAT: Irian Jaya (western New Guinea). Plants grow on trees in mossy forests near Angi Lake in the Arfak Range at 6250–8000 ft. (1900–2440 m).

CLIMATE: Station #97530, Manokwari, Irian Jaya, Lat. 0.9°S, Long. 134.1°E, at 10 ft. (3 m). Temperatures are calculated for an elevation of 6250 ft. (1900 m), resulting in probable extremes of 72°F (22°C) and 47°F (9°C).

N/HEMISPHERE	JAN	FEB	MAR	APR	MAY	JUN	JUL	AUG	SEP	OCT	NOV	DEC
°F AVG MAX	65	64	66	66	67	65	65	65	65	65	65	64
°F AVG MIN	53	54	53	53	53	54	52	52	53	53	53	53
DIURNAL RANGE	12	10	13	13	14	11	13	13	12	12	12	11
RAIN/INCHES	5.4	5.6	5.0	4.7	4.5	10.3	12.0	9.4	13.2	11.1	7.8	7.3
HUMIDITY/%	87	87	86	84	85	86	86	85	86	86	86	85
BLOOM SEASON						*						
DAYS CLR @ 9AM	4	3	3	5	3	3	3	1	1	2	3	7
DAYS CLR @ 3PM	2	2	2	3	1	1	1	1	0	1	0	2
RAIN/MM	137	142	127	119	114	262	305	239	335	282	198	185
°C AVG MAX	18.6	18.0	19.1	19.1	19.7	18.6	18.6	18.6	18.6	18.6	18.6	18.0
°C AVG MIN	11.9	12.2	11.9	11.9	11.9	12.4	11.3	11.3	11.9	11.9	11.9	11.9
DIURNAL RANGE	6.7	5.6	7.2	7.2	7.8	6.2	7.3	7.3	6.7	6.7	6.7	6.1
S/HEMISPHERE	JUL	AUG	SEP	OCT	NOV	DEC	JAN	FEB	MAR	APR	MAY	JUN

Cultural Recommendations

LIGHT: 2000–3000 fc.

TEMPERATURES: Throughout the year, days average 64–67°F (18–20°C), and nights average 52–54°F (11–12°C), with a diurnal range of 10–14°F (6–8°C). Because of microclimate effects, actual day-time highs may be as much as 10°F (6°C) warmer than indicated.

HUMIDITY: Near 85% year-round.

WATER: Rainfall is moderate to very heavy all year. Cultivated plants should be kept moist.

FERTILIZER: ¼–½ recommended strength. A balanced fertilizer should be applied weekly to biweekly throughout the year.

REST PERIOD: Growing conditions should be maintained year-round. Water and fertilizer may be reduced somewhat in winter, especially for plants cultivated in the dark, short-day conditions of temperate-latitude winters, but they should never be allowed to dry out completely.

GROWING MEDIA: Plants may be mounted on tree-fern or cork slabs if humidity is high and plants are watered at least once daily in summer.

When plants are potted, any open, fast-draining medium may be used. Repotting may be done anytime new roots are growing.

MISCELLANEOUS NOTES: The bloom season shown in the climate table is based on collection reports.

Plant and Flower Information

PLANT SIZE AND TYPE: A 12 in. (30 cm) sympodial epiphyte.

PSEUDOBULB: 12 in. (30 cm) long. The stems do not branch.

LEAVES: Many. The ovate-lanceolate leaves are 1.3–2.5 in. (3.2–6.4 cm) long. They are toothed with a long point at the tip. They are dark green with a bluish tinge and matte finish. The leaf sheaths are warty.

INFLORESCENCE: Short. The inflorescences emerge on leafless stems.

FLOWERS: 7–11 per inflorescence. Blossoms are 0.9 in. (2.3 cm) long. The flowers have an oval dorsal sepal, obliquely triangular lateral sepals, and somewhat elliptical petals. Sepals and petals are violet to purple-magenta. The short lip is white, hooded, and incurved at the apex. It does not have a callus.

REFERENCES: 144, 221, 470, 476.

Dendrobium glaucum Teijsm. and Binn.
Listed as an invalid name by Kränzlin (ref. 254). REFERENCES: 216, 254, 468.

Dendrobium glebulosum Schlechter

ORIGIN/HABITAT: Northern Papua New Guinea. Plants grow on forest trees in the Finisterre and Bismarck Ranges at 3950–5250 ft. (1200–1600 m).

CLIMATE: Station #94010, Goroka, Papua New Guinea, Lat. 6.1°S, Long. 145.4°E, at 5141 ft. (1567 m). Temperatures are calculated for an elevation of 4600 ft. (1400 m), resulting in probable extremes of 89°F (32°C) and 45°F (7°C).

N/HEMISPHERE	JAN	FEB	MAR	APR	MAY	JUN	JUL	AUG	SEP	OCT	NOV	DEC
°F AVG MAX	78	79	80	81	81	80	81	80	80	80	81	79
°F AVG MIN	58	59	59	59	60	61	61	61	62	61	61	59
DIURNAL RANGE	20	20	21	22	21	19	20	19	18	19	20	20
RAIN/INCHES	2.1	2.8	4.6	5.9	6.6	9.3	9.1	10.1	10.7	8.3	4.6	2.0
HUMIDITY/%	70	67	67	67	67	71	72	73	74	71	70	70
BLOOM SEASON				*		*						
DAYS CLR	N/A											
RAIN/MM	53	71	117	150	168	236	231	257	272	211	117	51
°C AVG MAX	25.4	26.0	26.5	27.1	27.1	26.5	27.1	26.5	26.5	26.5	27.1	26.0
°C AVG MIN	14.3	14.9	14.9	14.9	15.4	16.0	16.0	16.0	16.5	16.0	16.0	14.9
DIURNAL RANGE	11.1	11.1	11.6	12.2	11.7	10.5	11.1	10.5	10.0	10.5	11.1	11.1
S/HEMISPHERE	JUL	AUG	SEP	OCT	NOV	DEC	JAN	FEB	MAR	APR	MAY	JUN

Cultural Recommendations

LIGHT: 2500–3000 fc.

TEMPERATURES: Throughout the year, days average 78–81°F (25–27°C), and nights average 58–62°F (14–17°C), with a diurnal range of 18–22°F (10–12°C).

HUMIDITY: 70–75% from summer into autumn, dropping to near 65% in late winter and spring.

WATER: Rainfall is moderate to heavy most of the year, but conditions are slightly drier for 3 months in winter. Cultivated plants should be kept moist but not soggy. Occasional early morning mistings may be beneficial, especially on bright, sunny days.

FERTILIZER: ¼–½ recommended strength. A balanced fertilizer should be applied weekly to biweekly throughout the year.

REST PERIOD: Growing temperatures should be maintained all year. In the habitat, rainfall is lowest in winter, but dew and mist from fog and low clouds are common. Water and fertilizer should be reduced somewhat for cultivated plants, especially those grown in the darker, short-day conditions common during temperate-latitude winters. Plants should be kept on the dry side, but they should never be allowed to dry out completely. In the habitat, light is higher in winter.

GROWING MEDIA: Plants may be mounted on tree-fern or cork slabs if humidity is high and plants are watered at least once daily in summer. When plants are potted, any open, fast-draining medium may be used. Repotting may be done anytime new roots are growing.

MISCELLANEOUS NOTES: The bloom season shown in the climate table is based on reports from the habitat. Plants that produce flowers which last a single day commonly bloom several times during the year. Flowering usually occurs 7–14 days after a sudden 10°F (5°C) drop in daytime temperatures.

Plant and Flower Information

PLANT SIZE AND TYPE: A 35 in. (90 cm) sympodial epiphyte.

PSEUDOBULB: 35 in. (90 cm) long. The stems are flattened.

LEAVES: The linear-lanceolate leaves are usually 1.6–2.8 in. (4–7 cm) long and sharply reflexed.

INFLORESCENCE: Short.

FLOWERS: 2 per inflorescence. The flowers are 0.7 in. (1.7 cm) across. They are greenish white and lightly flushed with brown on the outside. The lip is recurved, ruffled, and scalloped. The column is yellow. Blossoms last a single day.

REFERENCES: 92, 221, 437, 445.

PHOTOS/DRAWINGS: 437.

Dendrobium globiflorum Schlechter

ORIGIN/HABITAT: Northern Papua New Guinea. Plants grow on moss-covered forest trees in the Kani Range at about 3300 ft. (1000 m).

CLIMATE: Station #94010, Goroka, Papua New Guinea, Lat. 6.1°S, Long. 145.4°E, at 5141 ft. (1567 m). Temperatures are calculated for an elevation of 3300 ft. (1000 m), resulting in probable extremes of 93°F (34°C) and 49°F (10°C).

N/HEMISPHERE	JAN	FEB	MAR	APR	MAY	JUN	JUL	AUG	SEP	OCT	NOV	DEC
°F AVG MAX	82	83	84	85	85	84	85	84	84	84	85	83
°F AVG MIN	62	63	63	63	64	65	65	65	66	65	65	63
DIURNAL RANGE	20	20	21	22	21	19	20	19	18	19	20	20
RAIN/INCHES	2.1	2.8	4.6	5.9	6.6	9.3	9.1	10.1	10.7	8.3	4.6	2.0
HUMIDITY/%	70	67	67	67	67	71	72	73	74	71	70	70
BLOOM SEASON							*					
DAYS CLR	N/A											
RAIN/MM	53	71	117	150	168	236	231	257	272	211	117	51
°C AVG MAX	27.9	28.4	29.0	29.5	29.5	29.0	29.5	29.0	29.0	29.0	29.5	28.4
°C AVG MIN	16.7	17.3	17.3	17.3	17.9	18.4	18.4	18.4	19.0	18.4	18.4	17.3
DIURNAL RANGE	11.2	11.1	11.7	12.2	11.6	10.6	11.1	10.6	10.0	10.6	11.1	11.1
S/HEMISPHERE	JUL	AUG	SEP	OCT	NOV	DEC	JAN	FEB	MAR	APR	MAY	JUN

Cultural Recommendations

LIGHT: 2500–3000 fc.

TEMPERATURES: Throughout the year, days average 82–85°F (28–30°C), and nights average 62–66°F (17–19°C), with a diurnal range of 18–22°F (10–12°C).

HUMIDITY: 70–75% from summer into autumn, dropping to near 65% in late winter and early spring.

WATER: Rainfall is moderate to heavy most of the year, but conditions are slightly drier for 3 months in winter. Cultivated plants should be kept moist but not soggy. Occasional early morning mistings may be beneficial, especially on bright, sunny days.

FERTILIZER: ¼–½ recommended strength. A balanced fertilizer should be applied weekly to biweekly throughout the year.

REST PERIOD: Growing temperatures should be maintained all year. In the habitat, rainfall is lowest in winter, but dew and mist from fog and low clouds are common. Water and fertilizer should be reduced somewhat for cultivated plants, especially those grown in the darker, short-day conditions common during temperate-latitude winters. Plants should be kept on the dry side, but they should never be allowed to dry out completely. In the habitat, light is higher in winter.

- GROWING MEDIA: Plants may be mounted on tree-fern or cork slabs if humidity is high and plants are watered at least once daily in summer. When plants are potted, any open, fast-draining medium may be used. Repotting may be done anytime new roots are growing.
- MISCELLANEOUS NOTES: The bloom season shown in the climate table is based on reports from the habitat. Plants that produce flowers which last a single day commonly bloom several times during the year. Flowering usually occurs 7–14 days after a sudden 10°F (5°C) drop in daytime temperatures.

Plant and Flower Information

- PLANT SIZE AND TYPE: A 35 in. (90 cm) sympodial epiphyte.
- PSEUDOBULB: 35 in. (90 cm) long. Stems arise from a very short rhizome. Stems are densely leafy.
- LEAVES: Many. The leaves are 4–5 in. (10–13 cm) long, elliptic, and sub-erect.
- INFLORESCENCE: Short.
- FLOWERS: 2 per inflorescence. The white flowers are 1.0 in. (2.5 cm) long. The white lip is covered with pointed, hairlike, orange-red papillae. The column is yellow with a darker striped foot. Blossoms last a single day.
- REFERENCES: 221, 437, 445.
- PHOTOS/DRAWINGS: 437.

Dendrobium glomeratum Rolfe ex Veitch

ORIGIN/HABITAT: New Guinea and the Molucca Islands. In Western Province of Papua New Guinea, plants grow at low elevations along swampy rivers. In Irian Jaya, plants were collected along the Noord River.

CLIMATE: Station #94003, Daru, Papua New Guinea, Lat. 9.1°S, Long. 143.2°E, at 20 ft. (6 m). Record extreme temperatures are 98°F (37°C) and 63°F (17°C).

N/HEMISPHERE	JAN	FEB	MAR	APR	MAY	JUN	JUL	AUG	SEP	OCT	NOV	DEC
°F AVG MAX	81	82	83	85	88	88	88	87	87	86	84	82
°F AVG MIN	74	74	74	76	76	76	76	76	76	76	77	75
DIURNAL RANGE	7	8	9	9	12	12	12	11	11	10	7	7
RAIN/INCHES	3.0	2.2	1.8	2.3	4.6	8.1	11.9	10.4	12.5	12.6	9.4	3.8
HUMIDITY/%	94	93	91	88	85	88	85	87	84	88	91	94
BLOOM SEASON	*	*	*	*	*	*	*	*	*	*	*	*
DAYS CLR	N/A											
RAIN/MM	76	56	46	58	117	206	302	264	318	320	239	97
°C AVG MAX	27.2	27.8	28.3	29.4	31.1	31.1	31.1	30.6	30.6	30.0	28.9	27.8
°C AVG MIN	23.3	23.3	23.3	24.4	24.4	24.4	24.4	24.4	24.4	24.4	25.0	23.9
DIURNAL RANGE	3.9	4.5	5.0	5.0	6.7	6.7	6.7	6.2	6.2	5.6	3.9	3.9
S/HEMISPHERE	JUL	AUG	SEP	OCT	NOV	DEC	JAN	FEB	MAR	APR	MAY	JUN

Cultural Recommendations

- LIGHT: 1000–2000 fc. Growers recommend *Phalaenopsis* light levels.
- TEMPERATURES: Throughout the year, days average 81–88°F (27–31°C), and nights average 74–77°F (23–25°C), with a diurnal range of 7–12°F (4–7°C).
- HUMIDITY: 85–90% from spring to autumn, increasing to 90–95% in winter.
- WATER: Rainfall is heavy from late spring through autumn, with a 2–3 month drier season in late winter and early spring. Cultivated plants should be kept wet but not soggy from late spring through early autumn, but water should be gradually reduced in late autumn.
- FERTILIZER: ¼–½ recommended strength. A balanced fertilizer should be applied weekly to biweekly throughout the year.
- REST PERIOD: Growing temperatures should be maintained all year. Rainfall is low for about 5 months, but the driest part of the season lasts only 2–3 months. However, large quantities of water are available from nightly dew. Cultivated plants should be allowed to dry out between waterings, but they should not remain completely dry for long periods. Fertilizer should be reduced or eliminated until water is increased in spring. In the habitat, light is probably greater in winter.
- GROWING MEDIA: Plants may be mounted on tree-fern or cork slabs if humidity is high and plants are watered at least once daily in summer. When plants are potted, any open, fast-draining medium may be used. Growers recommend using a shallow pot. Repotting may be done anytime new roots are growing.
- MISCELLANEOUS NOTES: The bloom season shown in the climate table is based on cultivation records.

Plant and Flower Information

- PLANT SIZE AND TYPE: A 10–20 in. (25–50 cm) sympodial epiphyte.
- PSEUDOBULB: 10–20 in. (25–50 cm) long. Stems are brownish-gray with many nodes.
- LEAVES: The thin, dark green leaves are deciduous. They are present only on the newest growths.
- INFLORESCENCE: Inflorescences arise from the sides of leafless canes. Plants may bloom several times a year, and scattered reports from the habitat indicate that blooming occurs in all seasons. Flowers are arranged in a short, loosely clustered head of flowers.
- FLOWERS: 6–10 per inflorescence. The flowers are 1.2 in. (3 cm) across. Sepals and petals are deep rose-pink, and the lip is bright orange to orange-vermilion. The lip is folded at the apex with a toothed, uneven margin.
- REFERENCES: 179, 218, 254, 302, 304, 352, 407, 445, 470.
- PHOTOS/DRAWINGS: *302, 304*.

Dendrobium glomeriflorum Kränzlin

ORIGIN/HABITAT: Western Samoa, near Apia on Upolu Island. Plants grow close to the edge of the forest at 1000–1300 ft. (300–400 m).

CLIMATE: Station #91762, Apia, Western Samoa, Lat. 13.8°S, Long. 171.8°W, at 7 ft. (2 m). Temperatures are calculated for an elevation of 1300 ft. (400 m), resulting in probable extremes of 89°F (32°C) and 59°F (15°C).

N/HEMISPHERE	JAN	FEB	MAR	APR	MAY	JUN	JUL	AUG	SEP	OCT	NOV	DEC
°F AVG MAX	81	80	80	81	82	81	82	81	82	82	81	81
°F AVG MIN	70	71	70	71	70	71	72	70	71	70	70	70
DIURNAL RANGE	11	9	10	10	12	11	11	9	12	11	11	11
RAIN/INCHES	3.2	3.5	5.2	6.7	10.5	14.6	17.9	15.2	14.1	10.0	6.3	5.1
HUMIDITY/%	76	75	75	77	77	78	81	80	80	78	77	75
BLOOM SEASON									*			
DAYS CLR @ 1PM	9	10	9	6	3	3	4	2	3	5	9	10
DAYS CLR @ 7PM	12	10	11	7	4	3	2	2	2	5	11	8
RAIN/MM	81	89	132	170	267	371	455	386	358	254	160	130
°C AVG MAX	27.1	26.5	26.5	27.1	27.6	27.1	27.6	27.1	27.6	27.6	27.1	27.1
°C AVG MIN	21.0	21.5	21.0	21.5	21.0	21.5	22.1	21.0	21.5	21.0	21.0	21.0
DIURNAL RANGE	6.1	5.0	5.5	5.6	6.6	6.1	5.5	5.0	6.6	6.1	6.1	6.1
S/HEMISPHERE	JUL	AUG	SEP	OCT	NOV	DEC	JAN	FEB	MAR	APR	MAY	JUN

Cultural Recommendations

- LIGHT: 2000–3000 fc.
- TEMPERATURES: Throughout the year, days average 80–82°F (27–28°C), and nights average 70–72°F (21–22°C), with a diurnal range of 9–12°F (5–7°C).
- HUMIDITY: 75–80% year-round.
- WATER: Rainfall is moderate to heavy all year, but conditions are slightly drier for 2–3 months in winter. Cultivated plants should be kept moist with only slight drying allowed between waterings.

FERTILIZER: ¼–½ recommended strength. A balanced fertilizer should be applied weekly to biweekly throughout the year.

REST PERIOD: Growing temperatures should be maintained all year. Water should be reduced somewhat for cultivated plants, especially those grown in the dark, short-day conditions common during temperate-latitude winters; but they should never be allowed to dry out completely. Fertilizer should be reduced or eliminated anytime water is reduced. In the habitat, light is highest in winter.

GROWING MEDIA: Plants may be mounted on tree-fern or cork slabs or potted in small pots filled with any open, fast-draining medium. Repotting may be done anytime new roots are growing.

MISCELLANEOUS NOTES: The bloom season shown in the climate table is based on reports from the habitat. Cultivated plants bloom from spring to early summer.

Plant and Flower Information

PLANT SIZE AND TYPE: A 28 in. (70 cm) sympodial epiphyte.

PSEUDOBULB: 28 in. (70 cm) long. The grooved stems are somewhat zigzag near the apex.

LEAVES: Many. The lanceolate leaves are 0.5 in. (1.3 cm) long.

INFLORESCENCE: Short. Inflorescences emerge from leafless stems.

FLOWERS: Few per inflorescence. The rosy white flowers are 0.4–0.5 in. (1.0–1.3 cm) long. They are held in tightly clustered heads.

REFERENCES: 179, 219, 254.

Dendrobium glossorhynchoides Schlechter

AKA: Originally spelled *D. glossorrhynchoides* (ref. 444), but Schlechter (ref. 437) and Kränzlin (ref. 254) later spelled the name *D. glossorhynchoides*.

ORIGIN/HABITAT: Northern Papua New Guinea. Plants grow on moss-covered trees in the mistforests of the Torricelli Range at 2950–3300 ft. (900–1000 m).

CLIMATE: Station #94004, Wewak, Papua New Guinea, Lat. 3.6°S, Long. 143.7°E, at 16 ft. (5 m). Temperatures are calculated for an elevation of 3300 ft. (1000 m), resulting in probable extremes of 87°F (31°C) and 51°F (11°C).

N/HEMISPHERE	JAN	FEB	MAR	APR	MAY	JUN	JUL	AUG	SEP	OCT	NOV	DEC
°F AVG MAX	77	77	77	77	77	77	76	75	76	77	77	77
°F AVG MIN	63	63	63	64	64	64	64	64	63	63	64	63
DIURNAL RANGE	14	14	14	13	13	13	12	11	13	14	13	14
RAIN/INCHES	7.6	4.8	5.3	10.0	13.3	14.5	12.1	11.9	14.9	16.9	15.1	10.8
HUMIDITY/%	80	79	79	78	79	81	82	82	81	82	81	80
BLOOM SEASON			*						*			
DAYS CLR	N/A											
RAIN/MM	193	122	135	254	338	368	307	302	378	429	384	274
°C AVG MAX	25.1	25.1	25.1	25.1	25.1	25.1	24.6	24.0	24.6	25.1	25.1	25.1
°C AVG MIN	17.3	17.3	17.3	17.9	17.9	17.9	17.9	17.9	17.3	17.3	17.9	17.3
DIURNAL RANGE	7.8	7.8	7.8	7.2	7.2	7.2	6.7	6.1	7.3	7.8	7.2	7.8
S/HEMISPHERE	JUL	AUG	SEP	OCT	NOV	DEC	JAN	FEB	MAR	APR	MAY	JUN

Cultural Recommendations

LIGHT: 2000–2500 fc.

TEMPERATURES: Throughout the year, days average 75–77°F (24–25°C), and nights average 63–64°F (17–18°C), with a diurnal range of 11–14°F (6–8°C). Average high and low temperatures vary only 2°F (1°C) during the year, indicating that plants may not be healthy under widely fluctuating conditions.

HUMIDITY: Near 80% year-round.

WATER: Rainfall is heavy all year, but conditions are slightly drier for 1–2 months in late winter. Cultivated plants should be kept moist and never be allowed to dry out.

FERTILIZER: ¼–½ recommended strength. A balanced fertilizer should be applied weekly to biweekly throughout the year.

REST PERIOD: Growing conditions should be maintained year-round. Water should be reduced for plants cultivated in the dark, short-day conditions common during temperate-latitude winters, but they should still not be allowed to dry out completely. Fertilizer should also be reduced if water is reduced. In the habitat, light may be slightly higher in winter.

GROWING MEDIA: Mounting plants on tree-fern or cork slabs accommodates their pendent growth habit. Potted plants are best placed in baskets or small, hanging pots, which may be filled with any open, fast-draining medium. Repotting may be done anytime new roots are growing.

MISCELLANEOUS NOTES: The bloom season shown in the climate table is based on cultivation records.

Plant and Flower Information

PLANT SIZE AND TYPE: An 8 in. (20 cm) sympodial epiphyte.

PSEUDOBULB: 8 in. (20 cm) long. Stems are pendent, slender, and smooth.

LEAVES: Many. The linear leaves are 0.4–0.6 in. (1.0–1.5 cm) long. They are small, distichous, and quickly deciduous.

INFLORESCENCE: Short.

FLOWERS: 1 per inflorescence. The very small flowers have white sepals and petals. The lateral sepals are joined to form a hood over the lip. The white lip is marked with red or rose. It is uppermost. The apex of the midlobe is scalloped. Sidelobes are large. The short-lived blossoms last only a few days.

REFERENCES: 219, 254, 437, 444, 445.

PHOTOS/DRAWINGS: 437.

Dendrobium glossotis Rchb. f. See *D. catillare* Rchb. f. REFERENCES: 216, 252, 254, 353, 466, Dauncey and Cribb 1993 *Kew Bulletin* 48(3):545–576.

Dendrobium gnomus Ames

ORIGIN/HABITAT: Santa Cruz Islands (New Hebrides). Plants grow in moss in the rainforests on Vanikoro at about 2600 ft. (800 m).

CLIMATE: Station #91551, Ngusui, Vanua Lava, Vanuatu, Lat. 13.8°S, Long. 167.6°E, at 137 ft. (42 m). Temperatures are calculated for an elevation of 2600 ft. (800 m), resulting in probable extremes of 86°F (30°C) and 55°F (13°C).

N/HEMISPHERE	JAN	FEB	MAR	APR	MAY	JUN	JUL	AUG	SEP	OCT	NOV	DEC
°F AVG MAX	74	74	74	75	76	77	78	78	77	77	76	75
°F AVG MIN	65	64	65	66	66	66	65	66	66	66	65	65
DIURNAL RANGE	9	10	9	9	10	11	13	12	11	11	11	10
RAIN/INCHES	8.0	5.6	5.0	8.2	8.1	12.0	10.0	11.9	9.1	14.0	10.8	10.2
HUMIDITY/%	82	82	84	84	84	85	86	87	88	87	86	84
BLOOM SEASON					*							
DAYS CLR @ 5AM	7	5	4	3	7	6	10	6	8	6	7	5
DAYS CLR @ 11AM	5	7	3	5	7	7	6	5	4	6	6	5
RAIN/MM	203	142	127	208	206	305	254	302	231	356	274	259
°C AVG MAX	23.3	23.3	23.3	23.8	24.4	24.9	25.5	25.5	24.9	24.9	24.4	23.8
°C AVG MIN	18.3	17.7	18.3	18.8	18.8	18.8	18.3	18.8	18.8	18.8	18.3	18.3
DIURNAL RANGE	5.0	5.6	5.0	5.0	5.6	6.1	7.2	6.7	6.1	6.1	6.1	5.5
S/HEMISPHERE	JUL	AUG	SEP	OCT	NOV	DEC	JAN	FEB	MAR	APR	MAY	JUN

Cultural Recommendations

LIGHT: 2000–3000 fc.

TEMPERATURES: Throughout the year, days average 74–78°F (23–26°C), and nights average 64–66°F (18–19°C), with a diurnal range of 9–13°F (5–7°C).

HUMIDITY: 82–88% year-round.

WATER: Rainfall is heavy all year with a short, slightly drier period in win-

Dendrobium gobiense

ter. Cultivated plants should be kept evenly moist with only slight drying between waterings.

FERTILIZER: ¼–½ recommended strength. A balanced fertilizer should be applied weekly to biweekly throughout the year.

REST PERIOD: Growing conditions should be maintained year-round. Water may be reduced somewhat if plants are cultivated in the dark, short-day conditions common in temperate-latitude winters, but they should not be allowed to dry out completely.

GROWING MEDIA: Plants may be mounted on tree-fern or cork slabs or potted in small pots filled with any open, fast-draining medium. Repotting may be done anytime new roots are growing.

MISCELLANEOUS NOTES: The bloom season shown in the climate table is based on collection reports.

Plant and Flower Information

PLANT SIZE AND TYPE: Ames (ref. 17) originally described the plant as a 1.4 in. (3.5 cm) sympodial epiphyte; however, Lewis and Cribb (ref. 271) indicate that plants are 12 in. (30 cm) tall.

PSEUDOBULB: 1.4 in. (3.5 cm) long. The densely clustered, yellow stems consist of 4–8 nodes. They develop deep, longitudinal furrows when dry. Stems are covered with the residual fibers from disintegrated leaf sheaths. The white roots are slender, fibrous, and smooth. However, Lewis and Cribb (ref. 271) indicate that the slender stems turn dark purple brown with age.

LEAVES: Many. The linear-oblong leaves, which taper toward each end, are 0.7–0.8 in. (1.7–2.0 cm) long. They are distichous and alternate along the stem. Lewis and Cribb (ref. 271) indicate that the mid-green leaves, which are bilobed at the apex, have sheathing bases covered with brown spots.

INFLORESCENCE: 0.2 in. (0.6 cm) long. Inflorescences emerge laterally from nodes on older leafless stems.

FLOWERS: 2–4 per inflorescence. The flowers are 0.4 in. (1.1 cm) long and do not open fully. Ames described the blossoms as bright purple and very pretty. Lewis and Cribb (ref. 271) describe the blossoms as "pale mauve with the petals glistening silvery white in the light." The exterior of the sepals are covered with brown dots

REFERENCES: 17, 225, 271, 516.

PHOTOS/DRAWINGS: 271.

Dendrobium gobiense Schlechter

ORIGIN/HABITAT: Northern Papua New Guinea, near Gobi. Plants grow low on tree trunks along the Waria River at about 1150 ft. (350 m).

CLIMATE: Station #200192, Garaina, Papua New Guinea, Lat. 7.9°S, Long. 147.1°E, at 2350 ft. (716 m). Temperatures are calculated for an elevation of 1150 ft. (350 m), resulting in probable extremes of 98°F (37°C) and 50°F (10°C).

N/HEMISPHERE	JAN	FEB	MAR	APR	MAY	JUN	JUL	AUG	SEP	OCT	NOV	DEC
°F AVG MAX	84	86	87	88	89	89	89	89	88	88	87	85
°F AVG MIN	67	67	67	68	67	68	69	69	69	68	68	67
DIURNAL RANGE	17	19	20	20	22	21	20	20	19	20	19	18
RAIN/INCHES	5.8	6.5	8.7	11.1	11.8	11.9	8.9	11.7	11.5	9.9	7.7	5.2
HUMIDITY/%	84	82	82	81	80	80	81	81	82	83	84	84
BLOOM SEASON					*				*			
DAYS CLR	N/A											
RAIN/MM	147	165	221	282	300	302	226	297	292	251	196	132
°C AVG MAX	28.9	30.0	30.5	31.1	31.6	31.6	31.6	31.6	31.1	31.1	30.5	29.4
°C AVG MIN	19.4	19.4	19.4	20.0	19.4	20.0	20.5	20.5	20.5	20.0	20.0	19.4
DIURNAL RANGE	9.5	10.6	11.1	11.1	12.2	11.6	11.1	11.1	10.6	11.1	10.5	10.0
S/HEMISPHERE	JUL	AUG	SEP	OCT	NOV	DEC	JAN	FEB	MAR	APR	MAY	JUN

Cultural Recommendations

LIGHT: 2000–3000 fc.

TEMPERATURES: Throughout the year, days average 84–89°F (29–32°C), and nights average 67–69°F (19–21°C), with a diurnal range of 17–22°F (10–12°C). The narrowest diurnal range, which occurs in winter, is due to cooler days, not cooler nights.

HUMIDITY: 80–85% year-round.

WATER: Rainfall is heavy all year. Conditions are slightly drier in winter. Cultivated plants should be kept moist but not soggy.

FERTILIZER: ¼–½ recommended strength. A balanced fertilizer should be applied weekly to biweekly throughout the year.

REST PERIOD: Growing conditions should be maintained all year. In the habitat, rainfall is slightly lower in winter. Water and fertilizer should be reduced somewhat for cultivated plants, especially those grown in the dark, short-day conditions common during temperate-latitude winters. They should never be allowed to dry out completely, however. In the habitat, seasonal light variation is minor.

GROWING MEDIA: Mounting plants on tree-fern or cork slabs accommodates the pendent growth habit, but humidity must be high and the plants watered at least once daily in summer. Plants may be potted in hanging pots or baskets filled with any open, fast-draining medium. Repotting may be done anytime new roots are growing.

MISCELLANEOUS NOTES: The bloom season shown in the climate table is based on reports from the habitat.

Plant and Flower Information

PLANT SIZE AND TYPE: A 39 in. (100 cm) sympodial epiphyte.

PSEUDOBULB: 39 in. (100 cm) long. Robust growths are spreading to pendent. They frequently grow at right angles to the tree trunk or mount. They are densely leafy and become ridged with age.

LEAVES: Many. The oblong-elliptic leaves are 4–6 in. (10–15 cm) long.

INFLORESCENCE: Very short. Inflorescences are densely flowered.

FLOWERS: 4–6 per inflorescence. The flowers are 0.6 in. (1.5 cm) long and barely open. Sepals and petals are yellow on the outside and white on the inside. The lip is decorated with orange-red crests and brown-red pads. The sepals are scaly on the outside.

REFERENCES: 221, 437, 445.

PHOTOS/DRAWINGS: 437.

Dendrobium goldfinchii F. Mueller

AKA: Hunt (ref. 211) includes *D. floridanum* Guillaumin as a synonym, but Lewis and Cribb (ref. 270) do not.

ORIGIN/HABITAT: Many islands in the South Pacific, including Bougainville, the Solomon Islands, the Santa Cruz Islands, Samoa, and the Banks Islands. Plants usually grow where light is high in open, coastal lowlands below 1050 ft. (320 m), but they are also found on rainforest trees at elevations to 2600 ft. (800 m).

CLIMATE: Station #91502, Kieta, Bougainville, Lat. 6.2°S, Long. 155.6°E, at 240 ft. (73 m). Record extreme temperatures are 96°F (36°C) and 64°F (18°C).

N/HEMISPHERE	JAN	FEB	MAR	APR	MAY	JUN	JUL	AUG	SEP	OCT	NOV	DEC
°F AVG MAX	85	85	87	88	88	89	88	88	88	87	87	86
°F AVG MIN	74	74	74	75	75	75	76	75	76	76	75	75
DIURNAL RANGE	11	11	13	13	13	14	12	13	12	11	12	11
RAIN/INCHES	10.9	9.4	8.0	9.8	9.6	9.4	10.5	10.7	11.2	11.7	9.3	9.0
HUMIDITY/%	80	80	79	76	78	76	79	77	78	80	80	82
BLOOM SEASON					*			*				
DAYS CLR	N/A											
RAIN/MM	277	239	203	249	244	239	267	272	284	297	236	229
°C AVG MAX	29.4	29.4	30.6	31.1	31.1	31.7	31.1	31.1	31.1	30.6	30.6	30.0
°C AVG MIN	23.3	23.3	23.3	23.9	23.9	23.9	24.4	23.9	24.4	24.4	23.9	23.9
DIURNAL RANGE	6.1	6.1	7.3	7.2	7.2	7.8	6.7	7.2	6.7	6.2	6.7	6.1
S/HEMISPHERE	JUL	AUG	SEP	OCT	NOV	DEC	JAN	FEB	MAR	APR	MAY	JUN

Cultural Recommendations

LIGHT: 3000–4000 fc. Humidity should be high and air movement strong when light is high.

TEMPERATURES: Throughout the year, days average 85–89°F (29–32°C), and nights average 74–76°F (23–24°C), with a diurnal range of 11–14°F (6–8°C).

HUMIDITY: Near 80% year-round.

WATER: Rainfall is heavy throughout the year. Cultivated plants should be kept moist. Warm water might be beneficial.

FERTILIZER: ¼–½ recommended strength. A balanced fertilizer should be applied weekly to biweekly throughout the year.

REST PERIOD: Growing conditions should be maintained all year. Water may be reduced somewhat in winter, especially for plants growing in the dark, short-day conditions common during temperate latitudes. Plants should never be allowed to dry out completely, however. Fertilizer should be reduced or eliminated until water is increased in spring.

GROWING MEDIA: Mounting plants on slabs accommodates their tendency to be pendent, but humidity must be high and plants need to be watered at least once daily in summer. Plants may be potted in hanging pots or baskets filled with any open, fast-draining medium. Repotting may be done anytime new roots are growing.

MISCELLANEOUS NOTES: The bloom season shown in the climate table is based on cultivation records. Plants that produce flowers which last a single day commonly bloom several times during the year. Flowering usually occurs 7–14 days after a sudden 10°F (5°C) drop in daytime temperatures.

Plant and Flower Information

PLANT SIZE AND TYPE: A 20 in. (50 cm) sympodial terrestrial or epiphyte.

PSEUDOBULB: 20 in. (50 cm) long. The clustered stems, which are zigzag and reddish, may be pendent or erect. Pseudobulbs are narrow at the base and swollen higher on the stem. Stems may have a reddish tinge.

LEAVES: Many. The leaves are 2–3 in. (5–8 cm) long. They are thick, stiff, and bilaterally flattened. They often have a strong red tinge. The leaves alternate along the stem.

INFLORESCENCE: 10 in. (25 cm) long. The inflorescence arises at the apex of the stem.

FLOWERS: 20 per inflorescence with 1–4 from each node on the inflorescence. The delicate flowers are pale yellow-green and measure 0.6 in. (1.5 cm) across. The short-lived blossoms last a single day. The plant called *D. floridanum* had pale rose flowers.

HYBRIDIZING NOTES: Chromosome count is 2n = 38 (ref. 152, 243).

REFERENCES: 16, 152, 170, 179, 211, 216, 243, 254, 270, 271, 437, 516.

PHOTOS/DRAWINGS: *41, 254, 271*.

Dendrobium × goldiei Rchb. f.
Also spelled *D. goldei*, it is now considered a synonym of *D. × superbiens* Rchb. f. REFERENCES: 67, 179, 190, 200, 216, 230, 236, 254, 262, 445, 533, 570.

Dendrobium goldschmidtianum Kränzlin.
Plants were thought to have originated in the Philippines and Taiwan. However, it is excluded by Merrill (ref. 298), not included by Valmayor (ref. 536), and listed as an uncertain species by Liu (ref. 279). It was included in a list of species for a flora of Formosa (ref. 192) but no information was included. Without habitat and elevation, climate data cannot be selected. REFERENCES: 61, 192, 208, 220, 254, 279, 296, 528.

Dendrobium goliathense J. J. Smith.
Now considered a synonym of *Cadetia goliathense* (J. J. Smith) Schlechter. REFERENCES: 221, 437, 445, 470, 538. PHOTOS/DRAWINGS: 538.

Dendrobium gonzalesii Quisumbing

ORIGIN/HABITAT: The Philippines. Plants grow in Albay Province of southeastern Luzon. They are usually found at about 2800 ft. (860 m).

CLIMATE: Station #98444, Legaspi, Luzon, Philippines, Lat. 13.1°N, Long. 123.8°E, at 62 ft. (19 m). Temperatures are calculated for an elevation of 2800 ft. (860 m), resulting in probable extremes of 91°F (33°C) and 53°F (12°C).

N/HEMISPHERE	JAN	FEB	MAR	APR	MAY	JUN	JUL	AUG	SEP	OCT	NOV	DEC
°F AVG MAX	74	75	76	78	80	81	80	80	80	79	77	75
°F AVG MIN	63	64	64	66	67	66	66	66	65	65	65	64
DIURNAL RANGE	11	11	12	12	13	15	14	14	15	14	12	11
RAIN/INCHES	15.4	11.5	7.7	5.9	6.4	7.9	10.2	7.9	10.2	13.7	18.3	20.3
HUMIDITY/%	82	81	81	80	80	80	82	83	83	83	84	84
BLOOM SEASON								*				
DAYS CLR @ 8AM	4	4	6	5	4	3	2	2	4	3	3
DAYS CLR @ 2PM	1	1	4	5	4	1	0	0	1	1	1
RAIN/MM	391	292	196	150	163	201	259	201	259	348	465	516
°C AVG MAX	23.3	23.8	24.4	25.5	26.6	27.2	26.6	26.6	26.6	26.1	24.9	23.8
°C AVG MIN	17.2	17.7	17.7	18.8	19.4	18.8	18.8	18.8	18.3	18.3	18.3	17.7
DIURNAL RANGE	6.1	6.1	6.7	6.7	7.2	8.4	7.8	7.8	8.3	7.8	6.6	6.1
S/HEMISPHERE	JUL	AUG	SEP	OCT	NOV	DEC	JAN	FEB	MAR	APR	MAY	JUN

Cultural Recommendations

LIGHT: 2500–3500 fc. High humidity and strong air movement should be provided.

TEMPERATURES: Summer days average 80–81°F (27°C), and nights average 66°F (19°C), with a diurnal range of 14–15°F (8°C).

HUMIDITY: 80–85% year-round.

WATER: Rainfall is very heavy all year. Cultivated plants should be kept moist but not soggy.

FERTILIZER: ¼–½ recommended strength. A balanced fertilizer should be applied weekly to biweekly throughout the year.

REST PERIOD: Winter days average 74–76°F (23–24°C), and nights average 63–64°F (17–18°C), with a diurnal range of 11–12°F (6–7°C). In the habitat, rainfall is high, but water should be reduced somewhat for plants cultivated in the darker, short-day conditions common in temperate-latitude winters. Plants should never be allowed to dry out completely, however. Fertilizer should be reduced or eliminated anytime plants are not actively growing.

GROWING MEDIA: Mounting plants on tree-fern or cork slabs accommodates their pendulous growth habit. However, humidity must be high and plants must be watered at least once a day in summer. If plants cannot be mounted, hanging pots or baskets may be filled with an open, fast-draining medium. Repotting may be done anytime new roots are actively growing.

MISCELLANEOUS NOTES: The bloom season shown in the climate table is based on collection reports.

Plant and Flower Information

PLANT SIZE AND TYPE: A 16–22 in. (40–55 cm) sympodial epiphyte.

PSEUDOBULB: 16–22 in. (40–55 cm) long. The slender stems are swollen at the nodes. They are clustered, pendulous, and sometimes branching.

LEAVES: 6–10 per growth. The oblong-lanceolate leaves are 2–4 in. (5–10 cm) long.

INFLORESCENCE: 0.5 in. (1.3 cm) long. Inflorescences arise on mature, leafless stems.

FLOWERS: 1–3 per inflorescence. The showy flowers are 2 in. (5 cm) across. Flower color varies from white to pink. The lip is decorated with dark purple lines at the base. Blossoms are not fragrant.

REFERENCES: 226, 373, 536.

PHOTOS/DRAWINGS: *373.*

Dendrobium gordonii S. Moore ex Baker. Occasionally spelled *D. gordoni*, see *D. macrophyllum* A. Richard. REFERENCES: 83, 142, 179, 216, 252, 254, 270, 271, 277, 353, 466, 504, 580.

Dendrobium gouldii Rchb. f.

AKA: *D. gouldii* var. *acutum* Rchb. f., *D. imthurnii* Rolfe, *D. undulatum* R. Brown var. *woodfordianum* Maiden, *D. woodfordianum* (Maiden) Schlechter. Hunt (ref. 211) includes the preceding species names, together with the synonyms included for *D. lineale* Rolfe, as synonyms of *D. gouldii*. However, Cribb (ref. 84) concurs with growers' strong opinions that *D. lineale* and *D. gouldii* should be maintained as separate species. Only time will tell whether taxonomists finally consider *D. lineale* and *D. gouldii* as separate species or simply color variations of a single species. Hunt (ref. 211) recommended that for horticultural purposes *D. gouldii* be used for the brown and yellow flowered forms, and that *D. veratrifolium* be retained (in place of the taxonomically recognized *D. lineale*) for the white and mauve flower forms. Ossian (ref. 346) discusses the names applied to plants from different parts of the habitat.

ORIGIN/HABITAT: The Islands off the east coast of New Guinea from New Ireland southward to Bougainville, the Solomon Islands, and Vanuatu. Plants usually grow in *Pandanus* plains, in open, parklike country, or in clearings and beside roads from sea level to 2300 ft. (0–700 m). Although sometimes included as an Australian species, Clements (ref. 67) indicates that these plants are never found in Australia.

CLIMATE: Station #91520, Honiara, Guadalcanal, Solomon Islands, Lat. 9.4°S, Long. 160.0°E, at 10 ft. (3 m). Temperatures are calculated for an elevation of 1200 ft. (370 m), resulting in probable extremes of 91°F (33°C) and 61°F (16°C).

N/HEMISPHERE	JAN	FEB	MAR	APR	MAY	JUN	JUL	AUG	SEP	OCT	NOV	DEC
°F AVG MAX	82	83	84	84	84	84	84	84	83	84	84	83
°F AVG MIN	68	68	68	68	69	69	70	70	69	69	69	68
DIURNAL RANGE	14	15	16	16	15	15	14	14	14	15	15	15
RAIN/INCHES	6.0	4.4	4.6	7.7	7.7	9.5	14.1	13.3	16.7	10.6	8.1	6.7
HUMIDITY/%	84	82	81	80	81	82	83	83	87	85	85	85
BLOOM SEASON	*	**	*	**	***	***	**	*	*	*	*	*
DAYS CLR @ 5AM	6	7	7	5	6	4	3	3	4	4	8	7
DAYS CLR @ 11AM	3	2	2	1	1	1	1	0	2	2	4	4
RAIN/MM	152	112	117	196	196	241	358	338	424	269	206	170
°C AVG MAX	27.8	28.4	28.9	28.9	28.9	28.9	28.9	28.9	28.4	28.9	28.9	28.4
°C AVG MIN	20.0	20.0	20.0	20.0	20.6	20.6	21.2	21.2	20.6	20.6	20.6	20.0
DIURNAL RANGE	7.8	8.4	8.9	8.9	8.3	8.3	7.7	7.7	7.8	8.3	8.3	8.4
S/HEMISPHERE	JUL	AUG	SEP	OCT	NOV	DEC	JAN	FEB	MAR	APR	MAY	JUN

Cultural Recommendations

LIGHT: 3000–4000 fc.

TEMPERATURES: Throughout the year, days average 82–84°F (28–29°C), and nights average 68–70°F (20–21°C), with a diurnal range of 14–16°F (8–9°C).

HUMIDITY: 80–85% year-round.

WATER: Rainfall is heavy all year, but conditions are slightly drier for 2–3 months in winter. Cultivated plants should be kept moist but not soggy.

FERTILIZER: ¼–½ recommended strength. A balanced fertilizer should be applied weekly to biweekly throughout the year.

REST PERIOD: Growing conditions should be maintained year-round. Water should be reduced somewhat for plants cultivated in the dark, short-day conditions common in temperate-latitude winters, but they should never be allowed to dry out completely.

GROWING MEDIA: Plants may be mounted on tree-fern or cork slabs if humidity is high and plants are watered at least once daily in summer. When plants are potted, any open, fast-draining medium may be used. Repotting may be done anytime new roots are growing.

MISCELLANEOUS NOTES: The bloom season shown in the climate table is based on cultivation records. Growers report that plants are often in bloom much of the year. J. J. Smith indicated that *D. gouldii* was difficult to cultivate at Bogor as were several other related species.

Plant and Flower Information

PLANT SIZE AND TYPE: A 35–83 in. (90–210 cm) sympodial terrestrial.

PSEUDOBULB: 35–83 in. (90–211 cm) long. The sparsely jointed and somewhat canelike pseudobulbs are swollen in the middle.

LEAVES: 3–6. The oblong-elliptic leaves are 5–7 in. (13–18 cm) long, thick, fleshy, rigid, and grooved on the upper surface.

INFLORESCENCE: 12–28 in. (30–70 cm) long. Inflorescences are erect and arise from upper leaf nodes.

FLOWERS: 7–40 per inflorescence. The flowers are 1.6–2.8 in. (4–7 cm) across and open fully. Sepals are white, pale yellow, or yellow and white. The narrow, twisted petals may be white, pale yellow, brown, or blackish violet. The lip is white to yellow with red, lavender, or brownish colored stripes on the keels. Flower size and color are highly variable depending on the place of origin. A cultivated specimen plant had 300 blossoms on 12 spikes. Blossoms are very similar to those of *D. lineale*, except that *D. gouldii* has petals that are more pointed and a longer lip.

HYBRIDIZING NOTES: Chromosome count is 2n = 38 (ref. 152, 154, 188, 504, 580). When used as a parent, *D. gouldii* contributes long-lasting flowers which are also good cut flowers. It tends to increase both the number of spikes and number of flowers per spike and helps round-out flower form.

REFERENCES: 25, 36, 67, 82, 84, 116, 152, 154, 179, 188, 190, 196, 200, 210, 211, 216, 243, 254, 270, 271, 326, 346, 351, 371, 421, 445, 470, 504, 516, 551, 568, 580.

PHOTOS/DRAWINGS: *41, 84, 116,* 210, *271, 346, 351, 371.*

Dendrobium govidjoae Schlechter

ORIGIN/HABITAT: Northeastern Papua New Guinea. In the Dischore Range, plants grow at about 3950 ft. (1200 m) on trees along Govidjoa Creek.

CLIMATE: Station #200192, Garaina, Papua New Guinea, Lat. 7.9°S, Long. 147.1°E, at 2350 ft. (716 m). Temperatures are calculated for an elevation of 4250 ft. (1300 m), resulting in probable extremes of 88°F (31°C) and 40°F (4°C).

N/HEMISPHERE	JAN	FEB	MAR	APR	MAY	JUN	JUL	AUG	SEP	OCT	NOV	DEC
°F AVG MAX	74	76	77	78	79	79	79	79	79	78	78	75
°F AVG MIN	57	57	57	58	57	58	59	59	59	58	58	57
DIURNAL RANGE	17	19	20	20	22	21	20	20	20	20	19	18
RAIN/INCHES	5.8	6.5	8.7	11.1	11.8	11.9	8.9	11.7	11.5	9.9	7.7	5.2
HUMIDITY/%	84	82	82	81	80	80	81	81	82	83	84	84
BLOOM SEASON												*
DAYS CLR	N/A											
RAIN/MM	147	165	221	282	300	302	226	297	292	251	196	132
°C AVG MAX	23.1	24.3	24.8	25.4	25.9	25.9	25.9	25.9	25.4	25.4	24.8	23.7
°C AVG MIN	13.7	13.7	13.7	14.3	13.7	14.3	14.8	14.8	14.8	14.3	14.3	13.7
DIURNAL RANGE	9.4	10.6	11.1	11.1	12.2	11.6	11.1	11.1	10.6	11.1	10.5	10.0
S/HEMISPHERE	JUL	AUG	SEP	OCT	NOV	DEC	JAN	FEB	MAR	APR	MAY	JUN

Cultural Recommendations

LIGHT: 2000–3000 fc.

TEMPERATURES: Throughout the year, days average 74–79°F (23–26°C), and nights average 57–59°F (14–15°C), with a diurnal range of 17–22°F (9–12°C).

HUMIDITY: 80–85% year-round.

WATER: Rainfall is heavy all year. Conditions are slightly drier in winter. Cultivated plants should be kept moist but not soggy.

FERTILIZER: ¼–½ recommended strength. A balanced fertilizer should be applied weekly to biweekly throughout the year.

REST PERIOD: Growing conditions should be maintained all year. In the habitat, rainfall is slightly lower in winter. Water and fertilizer should be reduced somewhat for cultivated plants, especially those grown in the dark, short-day conditions common during temperate-latitude winters. They should never be allowed to dry out completely, however. In the habitat, seasonal light variation is minor.

GROWING MEDIA: Mounting plants on tree-fern or cork slabs accommodates their pendulous growth habit. However, humidity must be high and plants must be watered at least once a day in summer. If plants cannot be mounted, small pots or hanging baskets may be filled with an open, fast-draining medium. Repotting may be done anytime new roots are actively growing.

MISCELLANEOUS NOTES: The bloom season shown in the climate table is based on reports from the habitat.

Plant and Flower Information

PLANT SIZE AND TYPE: A 39 in. (100 cm) sympodial epiphyte.

PSEUDOBULB: 39 in. (100 cm) long. The stems are pendent and occasionally branching. The stems are densely leafy.

LEAVES: Many. The equitant leaves are 0.8–1.6 in. (2–4 cm) long, leathery, and more or less lanceolate.

INFLORESCENCE: Short. Inflorescences arise from both apical and lateral nodes.

FLOWERS: The thick, fleshy flowers are 0.6 in. (1.5 cm) long. They are dark purplish red. The small dorsal sepal and petals are pointed at the tip. Lateral sepals are relatively large. The lip is narrow and blunt with a short point at the apex. It has a center callus that runs almost to the apex of the lip and no sidelobes.

REFERENCES: 221, 437, 445.

PHOTOS/DRAWINGS: 437.

Dendrobium gracile (Blume) Lindley

AKA: *Onychium gracile* Blume, *Dendrobium gedeanum* J. J. Smith. Although *D. tenellum* (Blume) Lindley is sometimes listed as a synonym, Seidenfaden (ref. 450) excludes this synonymy because the type specimens are incomplete and confused.

ORIGIN/HABITAT: Java, Sumatra, and Borneo. In Sumatra, plants grow near Padang-Pandjang at about 2600 ft. (800 m). In Borneo, they are found in Sabah, Sarawak, and Kalimantan and have been collected on the lower slopes of Mt. Kinabalu at 4900–5600 ft. (1500–1700 m). In Java, they are found in the mossy, mountain forests of West Java and on Mt. Gede at 5500–8550 ft. (1680–2600 m).

CLIMATE: Station #96755, Bogor, Java, Indonesia, Lat. 6.5°S, Long. 106.8°E, at 558 ft. (170 m). Temperatures are calculated for an elevation of 7000 ft. (2130 m), resulting in probable extremes of 75°F (24°C) and 45°F (7°C).

N/HEMISPHERE	JAN	FEB	MAR	APR	MAY	JUN	JUL	AUG	SEP	OCT	NOV	DEC
°F AVG MAX	65	66	67	67	66	64	63	63	64	65	66	65
°F AVG MIN	52	52	52	53	53	53	53	53	53	54	54	53
DIURNAL RANGE	13	14	15	14	13	11	10	10	11	11	12	12
RAIN/INCHES	2.1	1.0	0.5	5.0	8.1	18.8	23.7	20.2	14.4	12.0	11.9	3.4
HUMIDITY/%	72	68	65	66	74	79	84	84	81	79	77	75
BLOOM SEASON				*	*							
DAYS CLR @ 7AM	14	14	14	11	5	3	1	2	4	6	10	12
DAYS CLR @ 1PM	9	10	8	5	1	1	0	0	1	1	3	7
RAIN/MM	53	25	13	127	206	478	602	513	366	305	302	86
°C AVG MAX	18.2	18.7	19.3	19.3	18.7	17.6	17.1	17.1	17.6	18.2	18.7	18.2
°C AVG MIN	11.0	11.0	11.0	11.5	11.5	11.5	11.5	11.5	11.5	12.1	12.1	11.5
DIURNAL RANGE	7.2	7.7	8.3	7.8	7.2	6.1	5.6	5.6	6.1	6.1	6.6	6.7
S/HEMISPHERE	JUL	AUG	SEP	OCT	NOV	DEC	JAN	FEB	MAR	APR	MAY	JUN

Cultural Recommendations

LIGHT: 1800–3000 fc. Diffused or barely dappled light is preferred. Direct sunlight should be avoided.

TEMPERATURES: Throughout the year, days average 63–67°F (17–19°C), and nights average 52–54°F (11–12°C), with a diurnal range of 10–15°F (6–8°C). Highs vary only 4°F (2°C) and nights fluctuate even less.

HUMIDITY: 80% during the growing season, dropping to near 65% in winter.

WATER: Rainfall is very heavy from spring to autumn, but conditions are very dry for 2–3 months in winter. During the growing season, plants should never be allowed to dry out completely, but water should be gradually reduced in late autumn.

FERTILIZER: ¼–½ recommended strength, applied weekly. A high-nitrogen fertilizer is beneficial from spring to midsummer, but a fertilizer high in phosphates should be used in late summer and autumn.

REST PERIOD: Growing conditions should be maintained all year, but rainfall is very low for 2–3 winter months. In cultivation, water should be reduced and the plants allowed to become somewhat dry between waterings. They should not remain dry for prolonged periods, however. Fertilizer may be reduced or eliminated anytime the plant is not actively growing. In the habitat, light is highest in winter.

GROWING MEDIA: Plants may be mounted on tree-fern or cork slabs if humidity is high and plants are watered at least once daily in summer. When plants are potted, any open, fast-draining medium may be used. Repotting is best done in spring when new growth starts.

MISCELLANEOUS NOTES: The bloom season shown in the climate table is based on collection reports. Most cultivation records indicate a midwinter bloom season, but other records report a spring bloom season. Plants that produce flowers which last a single day commonly bloom several times during the year. Flowering usually occurs 7–14 days after a sudden 10°F (5°C) drop in daytime temperatures. All plants in a given area normally bloom simultaneously.

Plant and Flower Information

PLANT SIZE AND TYPE: A 24 in. (60 cm) sympodial epiphyte.

PSEUDOBULB: 24 in. (60 cm) long. Clustered stems arise from a creeping, rooting rhizome. Above the base, the stems have a pseudobulbous swelling 0.6–1.2 in. (1.5–3.0 cm) long, but the balance of the stem is slender. Older stems sometimes branch and may be pendent. The upper part of the stems are jumbled and tangled.

LEAVES: Many. The leaves are normally 1.6–2.4 in. (4–6 cm) long, but they become very small at the apex of the stem. They are distichous, persistent, linear, and nearly terete.

INFLORESCENCE: Short. The blossoms appear at the apex of the stem.

FLOWERS: Several per inflorescence, but only a single blossom is open at one time. The fragile flowers are 0.2–0.7 in. (0.5–1.8 cm) across. They

Dendrobium gracilentum

are usually mauve pink and sparkle in the light. Sepals and petals are lanceolate, but the larger lateral sepals are somewhat incurved. The oblong lip has 7 longitudinal red streaks, which may be faint.

REFERENCES: 25, 75, 179, 216, 254, 277, 286, 295, 310, 402, 450, 469, 592.

PHOTOS/DRAWINGS: *75, 450.*

Dendrobium gracilentum Schlechter. Now considered a synonym of *Diplocaulobium gracilentum* (Schlechter) Kränzlin. REFERENCES: 219, 220, 254, 437, 444, 445.

Dendrobium gracilicaule Kränzlin not F. Mueller. See *D. piestocaulon* Schlechter. REFERENCES: 216, 254.

Dendrobium gracilicaule F. Mueller not Kränzlin

AKA: Commonly considered part of the *D. macropus* alliance, Clements (ref. 67) reinstated species status pending conclusion of research currently being conducted in Australia. He includes *D. brisbanense* Rchb. f., *D. elongatum* A. Cunningham not Lindley, *D. macropus* (Endl.) Rchb. f. subsp. *gracilicaule* (F. Mueller) P. Green as synonyms. Also see discussion at *D. macropus* (Endl.) Rchb. f. ex Lindley. Halle (ref. 173) included *D. gracilicaule* F. Mueller as occurring in New Caledonia, but these plants may well end up being considered as synonyms of *D. macropus*.

ORIGIN/HABITAT: Eastern Australia. The habitat extends from near Kiama in southern New South Wales to the just north of Cairns near the Bloomfield River in Queensland. The habitat varies considerably. Plants usually grow on trees in shady rainforests, but they are occasionally found on rocks or in coastal scrub and open forest, frequently in very sunny situations. In the northern part of the habitat, plants are found only in the mountains and on tablelands.

CLIMATE: Station #94576, Brisbane, Australia, Lat. 27.4°S, Long. 153.1°E, at 17 ft. (5 m). Temperatures are calculated for an elevation of 2000 ft. (610 m), resulting in probable extremes of 103°F (40°C) and 28°F (−2°C).

N/HEMISPHERE	JAN	FEB	MAR	APR	MAY	JUN	JUL	AUG	SEP	OCT	NOV	DEC
°F AVG MAX	61	64	69	73	75	78	78	78	75	72	67	62
°F AVG MIN	42	43	48	53	57	60	62	61	59	54	49	44
DIURNAL RANGE	19	21	21	20	18	18	16	17	16	18	18	18
RAIN/INCHES	2.2	1.9	1.9	2.5	3.7	5.0	6.4	6.3	5.7	3.7	2.8	2.6
HUMIDITY/%	62	59	58	57	59	59	63	65	66	64	64	64
BLOOM SEASON	**	***	***	**	*	*	*	**	*	*	*	*
DAYS CLR @ 10AM	17	20	18	11	12	9	5	4	9	14	18	16
DAYS CLR @ 4PM	15	16	15	12	14	12	8	5	8	10	14	14
RAIN/MM	56	48	48	64	94	127	163	160	145	94	71	66
°C AVG MAX	16.4	18.0	20.8	23.0	24.1	25.8	25.8	25.8	24.1	22.5	19.7	16.9
°C AVG MIN	5.8	6.4	9.1	11.9	14.1	15.8	16.9	16.4	15.3	12.5	9.7	6.9
DIURNAL RANGE	10.6	11.6	11.7	11.1	10.0	10.0	8.9	9.4	8.8	10.0	10.0	10.0
S/HEMISPHERE	JUL	AUG	SEP	OCT	NOV	DEC	JAN	FEB	MAR	APR	MAY	JUN

Cultural Recommendations

LIGHT: 2500–4500 fc. Light may be as bright as the plant can tolerate, short of burning the leaves. In the habitat, more than half the days are clear each month, except during the summer rainy season, when skies are clear approximately 30% of the time. The plants may be adaptable, but the smallest forms grow in open forests exposed to high light, while the more robust forms tend to grow in shadier habitats.

TEMPERATURES: Summer days average near 78°F (26°C), and nights average 60–62°F (16–17°C), with a diurnal range of 16–18°F (9–10°C).

HUMIDITY: 60–65% year-round. Growers recommend maximum air circulation.

WATER: Rainfall is moderate in summer and autumn, with slightly drier conditions in winter. In cultivation, the fine roots of the plant deteriorate quickly if overwatered. *D. gracilicaule* must dry out between waterings, and growers indicate that ventilation should be excellent.

FERTILIZER: ¼–½ recommended strength, applied weekly. A high-nitrogen fertilizer is beneficial from spring to midsummer, but a fertilizer high in phosphates should be used in late summer and autumn. Growers report that maximum summer growth should be encouraged.

REST PERIOD: Winter days average 61–69°F (16–21°C), and nights average 42–48°F (6–9°C), with a diurnal range of 19–21°F (11–12°C). Growers indicate that lows should be above 35°F (2°C). In cultivation, water should be greatly reduced from midautumn until growth resumes in spring. Fertilizer should be reduced or eliminated after growths mature in the fall. Growers indicate that *D. gracilicaule* is often considered difficult to grow. Distinct seasonal variation is essential for plant health, and the cool, drier winter conditions are very important.

GROWING MEDIA: Plants are best mounted on cork slabs or a rough-barked hardwood. If plants are mounted, they need daily watering and high humidity in summer. If plants must be potted, the smallest possible shallow pot should be used. A rapidly draining medium is recommended, as excellent drainage is essential. Clay pots are preferable to plastic ones. Repotting is best done immediately after flowering.

MISCELLANEOUS NOTES: The bloom season shown in the climate table is based on cultivation records. Several plant forms are recognized, and variations are sometimes identified by the habitat from which they originate. Thus they may be identified as the ironbark form (with short, chunky, crowded, yellowish stems that may become purplish brown and cream or white flowers); brush box form (with tall slender stems which radiate in a circle); rainforest form (with stout stems); *Casuarina* form (with short, stout, prominently ribbed, dark stems); or *Callitris* form (with slender pseudobulbs and small, greenish cream blossoms).

Plants bloom while quite small, and mature plants are free-flowering.

Plant and Flower Information

PLANT SIZE AND TYPE: A 10–29 in. (25–74 cm) sympodial epiphyte that forms moderately sized clumps.

PSEUDOBULB: 8–24 in. (20–60 cm) long. The erect stems are slender and prominently grooved. They are swollen at the base, contracted for a short distance, then gradually dilated to become cylindrical near the apex.

LEAVES: 3–6 at the apex. The thin, ovate-lanceolate leaves are 2–5 in. (5–13 cm) long.

INFLORESCENCE: 2–5 in. (5–13 cm) long. The drooping raceme emerges at the apex of the pseudobulb.

FLOWERS: 5–40 per inflorescence. The flowers are 0.5–0.8 in. (1.3–2.0 cm) across and crowded on the inflorescence. Sepals and petals are cream- to dull-yellow, usually with considerable red-brown blotching on the sepals. The yellow lip has red-brown markings. It is erect, recurved, and kidney-shaped with 3 keels on the disk. Blossoms are fragrant.

HYBRIDIZING NOTES: Chromosome count is 2n = 38 as *D. gracilicaule* (ref. 152, 243, 580), *D. gracilicaule* var. *gracilicaule* (ref. 504), and *D. gracilicaule* var. *howeanum* (ref. 504, 580). When used as a parent, it unfortunately transmits the tendency for drooping flowers and inflorescences. Plants are rarely self-fertile and pollen from the same plant often does not produce seed, but seeds are regularly produced when pollen from another plant is used. *D. gracilicaule* and its hybrids are easy to propagate in flask. Seedlings as small as 4 in. (10 cm) often bloom in 2–3 years.

REFERENCES: 2, 23, 36, 105, 152, 173, 179, 210, 216, 240, 243, 254, 262, 317, 325, 371, 390, 421, 445, 495, 504, 533, 544, 562, 580.

PHOTOS/DRAWINGS: *36, 105, 210, 240, 325, 371, 390, 531, 562.*

Dendrobium gracilicolle Schlechter. Now considered a synonym of *Diplocaulobium gracilicolle* (Schlechter) W. Kittredge. REFERENCES: 222, 230.

Dendrobium gracilifolium Schlechter. Now considered a synonym of *Diplocaulobium linearifolium* Ridley. Schlechter (ref. 443) used the name *D. gracilifolium* for this species, but he failed to validly publish it. REFERENCES: 223, 400, 443.

Dendrobium gracilipes Burkill

AKA: The current status of this species is unknown. It was not included as either a species or synonym by Holttum (ref. 200) or Seidenfaden and Wood (ref. 455).

ORIGIN/HABITAT: Peninsular Malaya. No habitat location or elevation information was reported, but plants were cultivated in Singapore.

CLIMATE: Station #48698, Singapore, Lat. 1.4°N, Long. 104.0°E, at 10 ft. (3 m). Record extreme temperatures are not available for this location.

N/HEMISPHERE	JAN	FEB	MAR	APR	MAY	JUN	JUL	AUG	SEP	OCT	NOV	DEC
°F AVG MAX	85	88	87	88	88	88	87	87	87	88	87	85
°F AVG MIN	75	76	77	78	79	79	78	79	77	77	76	75
DIURNAL RANGE	10	12	10	10	9	9	9	8	10	11	11	10
RAIN/INCHES	9.0	3.9	6.7	4.4	6.8	5.7	5.8	4.9	6.6	5.3	8.7	11.9
HUMIDITY/%	N/A											
BLOOM SEASON												
DAYS CLR	N/A											
RAIN/MM	229	99	170	112	173	145	147	124	168	135	221	302
°C AVG MAX	29.4	31.1	30.6	31.1	31.1	31.1	30.6	30.6	30.6	31.1	30.6	29.4
°C AVG MIN	23.9	24.4	25.0	25.6	26.1	26.1	25.6	26.1	25.0	25.0	24.4	23.9
DIURNAL RANGE	5.5	6.7	5.6	5.5	5.0	5.0	5.0	4.5	5.6	6.1	6.2	5.5
S/HEMISPHERE	JUL	AUG	SEP	OCT	NOV	DEC	JAN	FEB	MAR	APR	MAY	JUN

Cultural Recommendations

LIGHT: 2500–3500 fc.

TEMPERATURES: Throughout the year, days average 85–88°F (29–31°C), and nights average 75–79°F (24–26°C), with a diurnal range of 8–12°F (5–7°C).

HUMIDITY: Information is not available for this location. However, records from nearby stations indicate that humidity probably averages 80–85% year-round.

WATER: Rainfall is moderate to heavy all year. Cultivated plants should never be allowed to dry out completely.

FERTILIZER: ¼–½ recommended strength. A balanced fertilizer should be applied weekly to biweekly throughout the year.

REST PERIOD: Growing temperatures should be maintained year-round. Water may be reduced somewhat in winter, especially if plants are grown in the dark, short-day conditions common in temperate latitudes.

GROWING MEDIA: Plants may be mounted on tree-fern or cork slabs if humidity is high and plants are watered at least once daily in summer. When plants are potted, any open, fast-draining medium may be used. They may be repotted anytime new roots are growing.

MISCELLANEOUS NOTES: The bloom season shown in the climate table is based on records from the habitat.

Plant and Flower Information

PLANT SIZE AND TYPE: A 7–8 in. (18–20 cm) sympodial epiphyte.

PSEUDOBULB: 1–2 in. (3–5 cm) long. The pseudobulbs arise from an elongated rhizome.

LEAVES: 2 per growth. The smooth leaves are 6 in. (16 cm) long with 2 rounded teeth at the apex.

INFLORESCENCE: 6–7 in. (15–18 cm) long. A single inflorescence arises at the apex of the pseudobulb.

FLOWERS: 2 per inflorescence. The ivory-white flowers are 0.6 in. (1.5 cm) across. The 3-lobed lip is marked with bright yellow in the center and purple on the sidelobes and at the apex. The flower was described as superficially resembling a *Coelogyne*.

REFERENCES: 53, 222.

PHOTOS/DRAWINGS: 53.

Dendrobium × *gracillimum* (Rupp) Leaney.

A natural hybrid between *D. speciosum* J. E. Smith var. *hillii* author unknown (*D. tarberi* M. Clements and D. Jones) and *D. gracilicaule* F. Mueller (*D. macropus* (Endl.) Rchb. f. ex Lindley subsp. *gracilicaule* (F. Mueller) P. S. Green). Synonyms include *D.* × *gracilosum* Clemesha, *D. speciosum* J. E. Smith var. *gracillimum* Rupp, and *D. speciosum* J. E. Smith var. *hillii* author unknown forma *bancroftianum* (Rchb. f.) F. M. Bailey.

HYBRIDIZING NOTES: Plants are self-sterile. REFERENCES: 23, 67, 105, 179, 227, 231, 240, 325, 390, 421, 533. PHOTOS/DRAWINGS: 105, 240, 390.

Dendrobium × *gracilosum* Clemsha. See *D.* × *gracillimum*.

REFERENCES: 67, 533.

Dendrobium gramineum Ridley

ORIGIN/HABITAT: Sarawak, Borneo. Plants were reportedly collected from trees near Matang. Habitat elevation was not reported. We have been unable to locate Matang in Borneo (there is a Matang in northwest Malaya near Taiping). So the following climate data should be used with a great deal of caution.

CLIMATE: Station #96413, Kuching, Sarawak, Lat. 1.5°N, Long. 110.3°E, at 85 ft. (26 m). Record extreme temperatures are 97°F (36°C) and 64°F (18°C).

N/HEMISPHERE	JAN	FEB	MAR	APR	MAY	JUN	JUL	AUG	SEP	OCT	NOV	DEC
°F AVG MAX	88	88	89	90	91	91	91	92	90	90	90	88
°F AVG MIN	72	72	72	72	72	73	72	72	72	72	72	72
DIURNAL RANGE	16	16	17	18	19	18	19	20	18	18	18	16
RAIN/INCHES	27.1	19.7	14.2	9.7	9.0	8.5	6.9	8.8	9.5	12.6	13.1	20.1
HUMIDITY/%	89	88	86	85	85	83	82	83	84	85	87	88
BLOOM SEASON	N/A											
DAYS CLR @ 7AM	1	0	1	2	3	2	4	1	2	1	1	1
DAYS CLR @ 1PM	0	0	0	0	0	1	1	1	0	0	0	0
RAIN/MM	688	500	361	246	229	216	175	224	241	320	333	511
°C AVG MAX	31.1	31.1	31.7	32.2	32.8	32.8	32.8	33.3	32.2	32.2	32.2	31.1
°C AVG MIN	22.2	22.2	22.2	22.2	22.2	22.8	22.2	22.2	22.2	22.2	22.2	22.2
DIURNAL RANGE	8.9	8.9	9.5	10.0	10.6	10.0	10.6	11.1	10.0	10.0	10.0	8.9
S/HEMISPHERE	JUL	AUG	SEP	OCT	NOV	DEC	JAN	FEB	MAR	APR	MAY	JUN

Cultural Recommendations

LIGHT: 2000–3000 fc.

TEMPERATURES: Throughout the year, days average 88–91°F (31–33°C), and nights average 72–73°F (22–23°C), with a diurnal range of 18–20°F (10–11°C). This habitat has essentially no seasonal temperature fluctuations. Average highs fluctuate only 4°F (2°C), and average lows vary only 1°F (.6°C).

HUMIDITY: 80–90% year-round.

WATER: Rainfall is very heavy all year. Cultivated plants should be kept moist and never be allowed to dry out completely. Warm water may be beneficial.

FERTILIZER: ¼–½ recommended strength. A balanced fertilizer should be applied weekly to biweekly throughout the year.

REST PERIOD: Growing conditions should be maintained all year. The

Dendrobium graminifolium

smaller diurnal range in winter results from cooler days, not cooler nights. The record low is only 10°F (6°C) below the average lows. In the habitat, light is highest in winter.

GROWING MEDIA: Plants may be mounted on tree-fern or cork slabs if humidity is high and plants are watered at least once daily in summer. When plants are potted, any open, fast-draining medium may be used. They may be repotted anytime new roots are growing.

MISCELLANEOUS NOTES: The bloom season shown in the climate table is based on records from the habitat.

Plant and Flower Information

PLANT SIZE AND TYPE: A sympodial epiphyte of unreported size.

PSEUDOBULB: The long stems are very slender and flexuous. Individual branches often exceed a length of 6 in. (15 cm).

LEAVES: The linear-lanceolate leaves are 0.5–1.5 in. (1.3–3.8 cm) long and unequally 2-toothed at the apex.

INFLORESCENCE: Short. Flowers are borne at nodes along the stem.

FLOWERS: 1 per inflorescence. The flowers are 0.5 in. (1.3 cm) across.

REFERENCES: 220, 286, 295, 398.

Dendrobium graminifolium Ames not Wight or Willdenow.

This name was used by Löve and Solbrig (ref. 280). Later writers have used this information in their lists of chromosome counts, but we have found no other use of the name. Because we can find no original description of *Dendrobium graminifolium* Ames, we suspect that these references should be applied to *Dendrochilum graminifolium* Ames. REFERENCES: 280, 580.

Dendrobium graminifolium Wight not Ames or Willdenow.

See *D. wightii* A. Hawkes and A. H. Heller. REFERENCES: 31, 38, 46, 119, 202, 216, 230, 244, 254, 317, 369.

Dendrobium graminifolium Willdenow not Ames or Wight.

Now considered a synonym of *Octomeria gramminifolia* R. Brown. REFERENCES: 190, 216, 254.

Dendrobium grande Hooker f.

ORIGIN/HABITAT: Adaman Islands, Malaya, peninsular Thailand, and Sarawak, Borneo. In Thailand, plants usually grow high in very tall trees at about 1650 ft. (500 m). In Borneo, they are found at 2600–3300 ft. (800–1000 m).

CLIMATE: Station #48567, Trang, Thailand, Lat. 7.5°N, Long. 99.7°E, at 39 ft. (12 m). Temperatures are calculated for an elevation of 1650 ft. (500 m), resulting in probable extremes of 99°F (37°C) and 56°F (13°C).

N/HEMISPHERE	JAN	FEB	MAR	APR	MAY	JUN	JUL	AUG	SEP	OCT	NOV	DEC
°F AVG MAX	86	89	91	89	86	84	83	83	83	83	82	83
°F AVG MIN	65	66	67	69	70	69	69	72	69	68	67	66
DIURNAL RANGE	21	23	24	20	16	15	14	11	14	15	15	17
RAIN/INCHES	2.1	1.0	2.6	7.5	9.7	9.8	10.2	11.6	12.8	12.7	9.5	4.4
HUMIDITY/%	73	69	70	75	82	82	83	83	84	85	83	78
BLOOM SEASON	N/A											
DAYS CLR @ 7AM	5	3	2	2	0	1	0	0	0	0	2	3
DAYS CLR @ 1PM	2	2	1	0	0	0	0	0	0	0	0	1
RAIN/MM	53	25	66	190	246	249	259	295	325	323	241	112
°C AVG MAX	29.8	31.5	32.6	31.5	29.8	28.7	28.2	28.2	28.2	28.2	27.6	28.2
°C AVG MIN	18.2	18.7	19.3	20.4	21.0	20.4	20.4	22.1	20.4	19.8	19.3	18.7
DIURNAL RANGE	11.6	12.8	13.3	11.1	8.8	8.3	7.8	6.1	7.8	8.4	8.3	9.5
S/HEMISPHERE	JUL	AUG	SEP	OCT	NOV	DEC	JAN	FEB	MAR	APR	MAY	JUN

Cultural Recommendations

LIGHT: 2500–3500 fc.

TEMPERATURES: Summer days average 83–84°F (28–29°C), and nights average 69–72°F (20–22°C), with a diurnal range of 11–15°F (6–8°C). The warmest season is spring when days average 86–91°F (30–33°C), and nights average 67–70°F (19–21°C), with a diurnal range of 16–24°F (9–13°C).

HUMIDITY: 80–85% from late spring through autumn, dropping to near 70% in winter.

WATER: Rainfall is heavy from spring into early winter, but conditions are drier for 2–3 months in winter. However, high humidity and the large daily temperature range results in frequent heavy deposits of dew. Consequently, the dry season is neither as long or as severe as the rainfall averages alone indicate. Cultivated plants should be kept moist while actively growing, but water should be gradually reduced during late autumn.

FERTILIZER: 1/4–1/2 recommended strength. A balanced fertilizer should be applied weekly to biweekly throughout the year.

REST PERIOD: Winter days average 83–89°F (28–32°C), and nights average 65–66°F (18–19°C), with a diurnal range of 17–23°F (10–13°C). Water should be reduced for 1–2 winter months, but plants should be allowed to dry only slightly between waterings. Fertilizer should be reduced when water is reduced.

GROWING MEDIA: Mounting plants on tree-fern or cork slabs accommodates their pendulous growth habit. However, humidity must be high and plants must be watered at least once a day in summer. If plants cannot be mounted, hanging pots or baskets may be filled with an open, fast-draining medium. Repotting may be done anytime new roots are actively growing.

MISCELLANEOUS NOTES: Plants are seldom found in bloom, and they do not often flower in cultivation.

Plant and Flower Information

PLANT SIZE AND TYPE: A 20–39 in. (50–100 cm) sympodial epiphyte. Plants are occasionally as small as 6 in. (15 cm).

PSEUDOBULB: 6–39 in. (15–100 cm) long. The flattened, pendulous stems are slender, but with the broad, overlapping leaves they may measure 10–20 in. (25–50 cm) across. Stems are leafiest near the apex.

LEAVES: Many. The persistent, pale green leaves are 2.4 in. (6 cm) long. They are laterally flattened and overlap at the base.

INFLORESCENCE: Very short. Blossoms appear to rest on the stem. Inflorescences emerge from between the leaves on the upper portion of the stem.

FLOWERS: 1 per inflorescence. The flowers are 0.4 in. (1 cm) across and open in succession. They are yellowish with red-purple stripes near the base of the sepals and petals. The lip has erect, triangular sidelobes with a yellow callus between the bases of the sidelobes. The rounded midlobe is deeply notched.

HYBRIDIZING NOTES: The chromosome count is $2n = 38$ (ref. 542).

REFERENCES: 200, 202, 216, 254, 286, 295, 394, 395, 402, 445, 454, 455, 542, 592.

PHOTOS/DRAWINGS: 454, 455.

Dendrobium grandiflorum (Blume) Lindley.

Now considered a synonym of *Flickingeria grandiflora* (Blume) A. Hawkes. REFERENCES: 25, 75, 213, 216, 230, 231, 254, 277, 395, 445, 449, 469. PHOTOS/DRAWINGS: 469.

Dendrobium grandiflorum H. B. and K. Now considered a synonym of *Maxillaria grandiflora* Lindley. REFERENCES: 45, 190, 216, 254.

Dendrobium grandiflorum Reinwardt. Now considered a synonym of *Bulbophyllum reinwardtii* Rchb. f. REFERENCES: 216, 254, 310.

Dendrobium grantii C. T. White. See *D. lineale* Rolfe. REFERENCES: 84, 226, 236, 504, 568, 580.

Dendrobium grastidioides J. J. Smith

ORIGIN/HABITAT: Western Sumatra. Plants grow near Padang in shady rainforests on Mt. Singgalang at about 6250 ft. (1900 m) and near Bengkulu on Mt. Dempoe at about 5600 ft. (1700 m).

CLIMATE: Station #96163, Padang, Sumatra, Indonesia, Lat. 0.9°S, Long. 100.4°E, at 19 ft. (6 m). Temperatures are calculated for an elevation of 6250 ft. (1900 m), resulting in probable extremes of 73°F (23°C) and 47°F (9°C).

N/HEMISPHERE	JAN	FEB	MAR	APR	MAY	JUN	JUL	AUG	SEP	OCT	NOV	DEC
°F AVG MAX	66	66	65	65	65	65	66	66	66	66	67	66
°F AVG MIN	53	53	53	53	53	53	53	53	53	54	54	53
DIURNAL RANGE	13	13	12	12	12	12	13	13	13	12	13	13
RAIN/INCHES	10.9	13.7	6.0	19.5	20.4	18.9	13.8	10.2	12.1	14.3	12.4	12.1
HUMIDITY/%	81	82	82	84	85	84	81	81	82	83	81	81
BLOOM SEASON		*										
DAYS CLR @ 7AM	5	1	1	0	0	2	2	1	2	2	3	5
DAYS CLR @ 1PM	5	2	2	1	1	3	3	4	3	3	6	5
RAIN/MM	277	348	152	495	518	480	351	259	307	363	315	307
°C AVG MAX	19.1	19.1	18.6	18.6	18.6	18.6	19.1	19.1	19.1	19.1	19.7	19.1
°C AVG MIN	11.9	11.9	11.9	11.9	11.9	11.9	11.9	11.9	11.9	12.5	12.5	11.9
DIURNAL RANGE	7.2	7.2	6.7	6.7	6.7	6.7	7.2	7.2	7.2	6.6	7.2	7.2
S/HEMISPHERE	JUL	AUG	SEP	OCT	NOV	DEC	JAN	FEB	MAR	APR	MAY	JUN

Cultural Recommendations

LIGHT: 2000–3000 fc. Diffused light is preferred.

TEMPERATURES: Throughout the year, the cool days average 65–67°F (19°C), and nights average 53–54°F (12–13°C), with a diurnal range of 12–13°F (7°C). Probable extremes vary only a few degrees from the averages, indicating that plants may not tolerate wide temperature fluctuations.

HUMIDITY: 80–85% year-round.

WATER: Rainfall is heavy all year. Cultivated plants should be kept moist but not soggy.

FERTILIZER: ¼–½ recommended strength. A balanced fertilizer should be applied weekly to biweekly throughout the year.

REST PERIOD: Growing conditions should be maintained year-round. Water may be reduced somewhat for cultivated plants in winter, especially those grown in the dark, short-day conditions common in temperate latitudes. They should never be allowed to dry out completely, however.

GROWING MEDIA: Plants may be mounted on tree-fern or cork slabs if humidity is high and the plants are watered daily in summer. When plants are potted, any open, fast-draining medium may be used. Repotting may be done anytime new roots are growing.

MISCELLANEOUS NOTES: The bloom season shown in the climate table is based on reports from the habitat. The plant was described in 1920 in *Bul. Jard. Bot. Buit.* 3rd sér. 2:80.

Plant and Flower Information

PLANT SIZE AND TYPE: A 39 in. (100 cm) sympodial epiphyte.

PSEUDOBULB: 39 in. (100 cm) long.

LEAVES: Many. The leaves are 6 in. (15 cm) long, becoming smaller at the tip of the stem. The somewhat linear leaves are papery when dried.

INFLORESCENCE: Short. Inflorescences emerge from nodes along leafless stems.

FLOWERS: 3–4 per inflorescence. The delicate flowers are about 1.6 in. (4 cm) across. Blossoms are white with a yellow blotch on the lip.

REFERENCES: 222.

Dendrobium gratiosissimum Rchb. f.

AKA: Sometimes spelled *D. gratiotissimum*. *D. boxallii* Rchb. f., *D. bullerianum* Bateman.

ORIGIN/HABITAT: Widespread from India to China. The habitat extends from Manipur in northeastern India, across Burma near Moulmein and Bhamo, the mountains of northern Thailand, through Laos, and into Yunnan Province of southwestern China. In Thailand, plants frequently grow at 2900–4600 ft. (850–1400 m).

CLIMATE: Station #48327, Chiang Mai, Thailand, Lat. 18.8°N, Long. 99.0°E, at 1100 ft. (335 m). Temperatures have been calculated for a habitat elevation of 3500 ft. (1070 m), resulting in probable extremes of 101°F (38°C) and 30°F (−1°C).

N/HEMISPHERE	JAN	FEB	MAR	APR	MAY	JUN	JUL	AUG	SEP	OCT	NOV	DEC
°F AVG MAX	77	82	87	88	86	82	81	79	80	81	78	76
°F AVG MIN	48	49	54	62	66	66	66	67	65	63	58	49
DIURNAL RANGE	29	33	33	26	20	16	15	12	15	18	20	27
RAIN/INCHES	0.3	0.4	0.6	2.0	5.5	6.1	7.4	8.7	11.5	4.9	1.5	0.4
HUMIDITY/%	73	65	58	62	73	78	80	83	83	81	79	76
BLOOM SEASON			**	***	**		*					
DAYS CLR @ 7AM	5	5	2	2	1	0	0	0	0	1	3	3
DAYS CLR @ 1PM	9	8	4	2	0	0	0	0	0	0	1	3
RAIN/MM	8	10	15	51	140	155	188	221	292	124	38	10
°C AVG MAX	25.0	27.8	30.6	31.2	30.0	27.8	27.3	26.2	26.7	27.3	25.6	24.5
°C AVG MIN	8.9	9.5	12.3	16.7	18.9	18.9	18.9	19.5	18.4	17.3	14.5	5.0
DIURNAL RANGE	16.1	18.3	18.3	14.5	11.1	8.9	8.4	6.7	8.3	10.0	11.1	15.0
S/HEMISPHERE	JUL	AUG	SEP	OCT	NOV	DEC	JAN	FEB	MAR	APR	MAY	JUN

Cultural Recommendations

LIGHT: 3000–4000 fc. Cultivated plants need bright light and strong air movement. Some shading is needed from spring through autumn, but light should be as bright as the plant can tolerate, short of burning the foliage.

TEMPERATURES: Summer days average 79–82°F (26–28°C), and nights average 66–67°F (19–20°C), with a diurnal range of 12–16°F (7–9°C). Spring is the warmest season. Days average 86–88°F (30–31°C), and nights average 54–66°F (12–19°C), with a diurnal range of 20–33°F (11–18°C).

HUMIDITY: 78–83% during the growing season, dropping to near 60% in late winter and early spring.

WATER: Rainfall is moderate to heavy from late spring through early autumn. Cultivated plants should be kept moist while they are actively growing, but water should be gradually reduced after new growths mature in autumn.

FERTILIZER: ¼–½ recommended strength, applied weekly. A high-nitrogen fertilizer is beneficial from spring to midsummer, but a fertilizer high in phosphates should be used in late summer and autumn.

REST PERIOD: Winter days average 76–82°F (25–28°C), and nights average 48–49°F (9–10°C), with a diurnal range of 27–33°F (15–18°C). Overnight lows are below 50°F (10°C) for 3 months. Plants should be able to tolerate temperatures a few degrees below freezing for short periods, but extremes should be avoided in cultivation. During very cold weather, a plant's chance of surviving with minimal damage is better if

Dendrobium graven-horstii

it is dry when temperatures are low. In the habitat, rainfall averages are very low for 4–5 months in winter, but during the early part of the season the high relative humidity indicates that additional moisture is available from frequent fog, mist, and heavy deposits of dew. Growers sometimes recommend eliminating water in winter, but plants are healthiest if for most of the winter they are allowed to become somewhat dry between waterings but do not remain dry for extended periods. For 1–2 months in late winter, however, conditions are clear, warm, and dry, with humidity so low that even the moisture from morning dew is uncommon. Plants should be allowed to dry out completely between waterings and remain dry longer during this time. Occasional early morning mistings between waterings may help keep the plants from becoming too dry. Fertilizer should be greatly reduced or eliminated until water is increased in spring. A cool, dry rest is essential for cultivated plants and should be continued until new growth starts in spring. In the habitat, light is highest in winter.

GROWING MEDIA: Mounting plants on tree-fern or cork slabs accommodates their pendulous growth habit. However, humidity must be high and plants must be watered at least once a day in summer. If plants cannot be mounted, hanging pots or baskets may be filled with an open, fast-draining medium. Repotting may be done anytime new roots are actively growing.

MISCELLANEOUS NOTES: The bloom season shown in the climate table is based on cultivation records.

Plant and Flower Information

PLANT SIZE AND TYPE: A 12–35 in. (30–90 cm) sympodial epiphyte.

PSEUDOBULB: 12–35 in. (30–90 cm) long. The entire plant is pendulous. The canes are stout, narrow at the base, and swollen at the nodes. Stems are pale yellow with purple stripes and strong white veins.

LEAVES: 8–12 per growth. The deciduous leaves, which may be linear to ovate-lanceolate, are 2.8–6.0 in. (7–15 cm) long. They are leathery with 2 teeth at the apex.

INFLORESCENCE: Short. Purplish inflorescences arise from nearly every node near the apex of leafless stems.

FLOWERS: 1–3 per inflorescence. The flowers are 2.4–2.8 in. (6–7 cm) across. The wavy sepals and lance-shaped petals may be white, pink, or deep lavender. They are usually rose-purple at the tips. The white lip has pink or purple along the toothed, wavy margin. The somewhat boat-shaped lip is decorated with a large, deep yellow disk and red to dark purple lines in the throat.

HYBRIDIZING NOTES: Chromosome count is 2n = 38 (ref. 152, 504, 580). Johansen (ref. 239) indicates that plants are self-sterile and that flowers dropped 9 days after self-pollination.

REFERENCES: 25, 36, 152, 157, 179, 190, 202, 210, 216, 239, 254, 266, 369, 430, 445, 447, 448, 454, 504, 523, 541, 570, 580.

PHOTOS/DRAWINGS: *36*, 210, *369*, *430*, *454*.

Dendrobium graven-horstii J. J. Smith.
Masamune (ref. 286) included this name in his list of Borneo plants, but the plant was described in 1920 in *Bul. Jard. Bot. Buit.* 3rd sér. 2:28 as *Dendrochilum graven-horstii*. REFERENCES: 286.

Dendrobium greenianum Cribb and B. Lewis

ORIGIN/HABITAT: Pentecost Island in Vanuatu (New Hebrides). Plants grow on *Eugenia* trees in light shade at about 1000 ft. (300 m).

CLIMATE: Station #91554, Luganville, Espiritu Santo Island, Vanuatu, Lat. 15.5°S, Long. 167.1°E, at 493 ft. (150 m). Temperatures are calculated for an elevation of 1000 ft. (300 m), resulting in probable extremes of 91°F (33°C) and 59°F (15°C).

N/HEMISPHERE	JAN	FEB	MAR	APR	MAY	JUN	JUL	AUG	SEP	OCT	NOV	DEC
°F AVG MAX	79	79	80	81	81	84	84	85	84	83	81	79
°F AVG MIN	69	69	70	70	71	72	73	72	71	72	71	70
DIURNAL RANGE	10	10	10	11	10	12	11	13	13	11	10	9
RAIN/INCHES	6.4	6.3	4.7	6.3	9.5	9.2	10.6	9.7	10.9	10.1	8.1	6.1
HUMIDITY/%	81	80	83	81	82	81	83	83	88	86	83	80
BLOOM SEASON	*											
DAYS CLR	N/A											
RAIN/MM	163	160	119	160	241	234	269	246	277	257	206	155
°C AVG MAX	26.3	26.3	26.8	27.4	27.4	29.1	29.1	29.6	29.1	28.5	27.4	26.3
°C AVG MIN	20.7	20.7	21.3	21.3	21.8	22.4	23.0	22.4	21.8	22.4	21.8	21.3
DIURNAL RANGE	5.6	5.6	5.5	6.1	5.6	6.7	6.1	7.2	7.3	6.1	5.6	5.0
S/HEMISPHERE	JUL	AUG	SEP	OCT	NOV	DEC	JAN	FEB	MAR	APR	MAY	JUN

Cultural Recommendations

LIGHT: 2000–3000 fc.

TEMPERATURES: Throughout the year, days average 79–84°F (26–29°C), and nights average 69–73°F (21–23°C), with a diurnal range of 9–13°F (5–7°C).

HUMIDITY: 80–83% most of the year, increasing to 85–88% for 2 months in autumn.

WATER: Rainfall is moderate to heavy most of the year. Cultivated plants should be kept moist but not soggy with only slight drying allowed between waterings.

FERTILIZER: ¼–½ recommended strength. A balanced fertilizer should be applied weekly to biweekly throughout the year.

REST PERIOD: Growing conditions should be maintained all year. Water and fertilizer may be reduced somewhat in winter for plants grown in the dark, short-day conditions common in temperate latitudes. They should not be allowed to dry out completely, however.

GROWING MEDIA: Mounting plants on tree-fern or cork slabs accommodates their pendulous growth habit. However, humidity must be high and plants must be watered at least once a day in summer. If plants cannot be mounted, small pots or hanging baskets may be filled with an open, fast-draining medium. Repotting may be done anytime new roots are actively growing.

MISCELLANEOUS NOTES: The bloom season shown in the climate table is based on collection reports. The plant is known only from the type collection.

Plant and Flower Information

PLANT SIZE AND TYPE: A pendent, 24 in. (60 cm) sympodial epiphyte.

PSEUDOBULB: 24 in. (60 cm) long. The stems are slightly flattened.

LEAVES: Many. The leathery, lanceolate leaves are usually 2.0–2.7 in. (5.0–6.8 cm) long. They are distichous and twisted at the base so that all face one direction.

INFLORESCENCE: Very short. Blossoms emerge opposite the leaves through the leaf bases.

FLOWERS: 2 at each node. The small, white to creamy white flowers remain nearly closed. Sepals are more or less oblong. Petals are spatula-shaped. The obscurely 3-lobed lip has transverse ridges and a low raised central callus.

REFERENCES: 90, 235, 270.

PHOTOS/DRAWINGS: 90, 270.

Dendrobium gregulus Seidenfaden

ORIGIN/HABITAT: Endemic to northern and western Thailand. Plants grow on tree branches in open, deciduous mountain forest at 3600–4100 ft. (1100–1250 m).

CLIMATE: Station #48325, Mae Sariang, Thailand, Lat. 18.2°N, Long. 97.8°E, at 1030 ft. (314 m). Temperatures are calculated for an elevation of 3900 ft. (1190 m), resulting in probable extremes of 101°F (39°C) and 32°F (0°C).

N/HEMISPHERE	JAN	FEB	MAR	APR	MAY	JUN	JUL	AUG	SEP	OCT	NOV	DEC
°F AVG MAX	79	83	87	90	85	80	78	78	80	81	80	77
°F AVG MIN	49	48	55	64	67	66	65	65	65	63	59	51
DIURNAL RANGE	30	35	32	26	18	14	13	13	15	18	21	26
RAIN/INCHES	0.3	0.2	0.3	1.9	5.7	9.0	8.4	10.8	8.7	3.7	1.1	0.6
HUMIDITY/%	72	67	57	55	68	83	83	84	83	81	77	75
BLOOM SEASON	*	*	*									
DAYS CLR @ 7AM	1	16	0	3	4	0	0	0	0	0	0	1
DAYS CLR @ 1PM	24	18	9	5	2	0	0	1	1	6	13	20
RAIN/MM	8	5	8	48	145	229	213	274	221	94	28	15
°C AVG MAX	25.8	28.1	30.3	32.0	29.2	26.4	25.3	25.3	26.4	27.0	26.4	24.7
°C AVG MIN	9.2	8.6	12.5	17.5	19.2	18.6	18.1	18.1	18.1	17.0	14.7	10.3
DIURNAL RANGE	16.6	19.5	17.8	14.5	10.0	7.8	7.2	7.2	8.3	10.0	11.7	14.4
S/HEMISPHERE	JUL	AUG	SEP	OCT	NOV	DEC	JAN	FEB	MAR	APR	MAY	JUN

Cultural Recommendations

LIGHT: 3000–4000 fc. Heavy cloud cover in summer reduces light levels considerably during what should be the brightest part of the year. Winter is actually the brightest season in the habitat, as indicated by the large number of clear afternoons. Cultivated plants should be shaded from late spring into autumn, but shading should be reduced or removed in winter to provide as much light as possible, short of burning the leaves. Strong air movement is very important throughout the year.

TEMPERATURES: Summer days average 78–80°F (25–26°C), and nights average 65–66°F (18–19°C), with a diurnal range of 13–14°F (7–8°C). The warmest weather occurs in spring when days average 85–90°F (29–32°C), and nights average 55–67°F (13–19°C), with a diurnal range of 18–32°F (10–18°C).

HUMIDITY: 80–85% from summer into early autumn, dropping to near 55% in late winter and early spring.

WATER: Rainfall is moderate to heavy from late spring through early autumn. Cultivated plants should be kept moist while actively growing, but water should be gradually reduced after new growths mature in autumn.

FERTILIZER: ¼–½ recommended strength, applied weekly. A high-nitrogen fertilizer is beneficial from spring to midsummer, but a fertilizer high in phosphates should be used in late summer and autumn.

REST PERIOD: Winter days average 77–83°F (25–28°C), and nights average 48–51°F (9–10°C), with a diurnal range of 26–35°F (14–20°C). In the habitat, winter rainfall is low for 4–5 months. During the early part of the dry season, overnight fog, low clouds, and very heavy dew results in more available moisture than is indicated by the rainfall averages. For most of the winter dry season, cultivated plants should be allowed to dry out between waterings, but they should not remain dry for extended periods. For 1–2 months in late winter, however, conditions are clear, warm, and dry, with humidity so low that even the moisture from morning dew is uncommon. Cultivated plants should be allowed to remain dry during this time but may be given an occasional early morning misting to keep them from becoming too dry. Fertilizer should be eliminated when plants are dry.

GROWING MEDIA: Plants may be mounted on tree-fern or cork slabs if humidity is high and plants are watered at least once daily in summer. When plants are potted, any open, fast-draining medium may be used. Repotting is best done in early spring when new roots are growing.

MISCELLANEOUS NOTES: The bloom season shown in the climate table is based on reports from the habitat.

Plant and Flower Information

PLANT SIZE AND TYPE: A dwarf, 1.6–2.8 in. (4–7 cm) sympodial epiphyte. Plants form a large cushion.

PSEUDOBULB: 0.4 in. (1 cm) long. The tiny, round pseudobulbs are densely clustered. They are covered with onionlike sheaths.

LEAVES: The leaves are deciduous.

INFLORESCENCE: 1.2–2.4 in. (3–6 cm) long. An inflorescence arises from the apex of the leafless pseudobulb.

FLOWERS: 4–6 per inflorescence. The flowers are 0.6 in. (1.5 cm) across. Sepals and petals are light sulfur yellow. The petals are erect. The lip, which has no distinct sidelobes, is recurved, ruffled along the margin, and marked with a broad, dark yellow callus at its apex. It is decorated with red-purplish veins at the sides near the base.

REFERENCES: 234, 454.

PHOTOS/DRAWINGS: 454.

Dendrobium griffithianum Lindley

AKA: *D. griffithianum* var. *guibertii* (Carriere) Veitch is considered a synonym of *D. densiflorum* Lindley. *D. griffithianum* is sometimes confused with *D. densiflorum*.

ORIGIN/HABITAT: Burma and the mountains of northern and western Thailand. These uncommon plants grow high in trees at about 1600 ft. (490 m).

CLIMATE: Station #48331, Nan, Thailand, Lat. 18.8°N, Long. 100.8°E, at 660 ft. (201 m). Temperatures are calculated for an elevation of 1600 ft. (490 m), resulting in probable extremes of 105°F (41°C) and 38°F (3°C).

N/HEMISPHERE	JAN	FEB	MAR	APR	MAY	JUN	JUL	AUG	SEP	OCT	NOV	DEC
°F AVG MAX	83	88	93	96	93	89	87	86	87	87	85	82
°F AVG MIN	52	56	61	68	72	72	72	72	71	68	63	55
DIURNAL RANGE	31	32	32	28	21	17	15	14	16	19	22	27
RAIN/INCHES	0.3	0.5	0.9	3.3	5.7	4.9	8.1	10.6	8.5	2.2	0.6	0.2
HUMIDITY/%	74	69	65	65	73	79	81	84	84	83	79	78
BLOOM SEASON			*	*	*	**	*					
DAYS CLR @ 7AM	1	1	2	4	2	0	0	0	0	0	1	0
DAYS CLR @ 1PM	18	16	15	11	2	0	0	1	4	9	14	
RAIN/MM	8	13	23	84	145	124	206	269	216	56	15	5
°C AVG MAX	28.3	31.1	33.8	35.5	33.8	31.6	30.5	29.9	30.5	30.5	29.4	27.7
°C AVG MIN	11.1	13.3	16.1	19.9	22.2	22.2	22.2	22.2	21.6	19.9	17.2	12.7
DIURNAL RANGE	17.2	17.8	17.7	15.6	11.6	9.4	8.3	7.7	8.9	10.6	12.2	15.0
S/HEMISPHERE	JUL	AUG	SEP	OCT	NOV	DEC	JAN	FEB	MAR	APR	MAY	JUN

Cultural Recommendations

LIGHT: 2500–3500 fc.

TEMPERATURES: Summer days average 86–89°F (30–32°C), and nights average 72°F (22°C), with a diurnal range of 14–17°F (8–9°C). Spring is the warmest season. Days average 93–96°F (34–36°C), the nights average 61–72°F (16–22°C), with a diurnal range of 21–32°F (12–18°C).

HUMIDITY: 80–85% in summer and autumn, dropping to 65–75% in winter and spring.

WATER: Rainfall is moderate to heavy from late spring through early autumn. Cultivated plants should be kept moist while actively growing, but water should be gradually reduced in autumn after new growths mature.

FERTILIZER: ¼–½ recommended strength, applied weekly. A high-nitrogen fertilizer is beneficial from spring to midsummer, but a fertilizer high in phosphates should be used in late summer and autumn.

REST PERIOD: Winter days average 82–88°F (28–31°C), and nights average 52–56°F (11–13°C), with a diurnal range of 27–32°F (15–18°C). In the habitat, winter rainfall is low for 4–5 months. During most of the dry season, however, overnight fog, mist, and very heavy dew results in more available moisture than is indicated by the rainfall averages. Cultivated plants should be allowed to dry out between waterings, but should not remain dry for extended periods. Fertilizer should be eliminated until water is increased in spring. In the habitat, conditions are brightest in winter.

GROWING MEDIA: Plants may be mounted on tree-fern or cork slabs if humidity is high and plants are watered at least once daily in summer.

When plants are potted, any open, fast-draining medium may be used. Repotting is best done in early spring when new roots begin to grow.

MISCELLANEOUS NOTES: The bloom season shown in the climate table is based on cultivation records.

Plant and Flower Information

PLANT SIZE AND TYPE: A 12–18 in. (30–45 cm) sympodial epiphyte.

PSEUDOBULB: 12–18 in. (30–45 cm) long. The yellow pseudobulbs are stemlike, shiny, and erect. They are furrowed, narrow, and stalklike at the base, and obscurely 4-angled on the upper part. Each stem consists of 5 nodes. The apex of each growth is leafy.

LEAVES: 2–3. The deep green leaves are 3.5–4.0 in. (9–10 cm) long, oblong-lanceolate, and leathery.

INFLORESCENCE: 6–10 in. (15–25 cm) long. Inflorescences emerge from nodes at or near the top of the stem. They are suberect to pendulous and somewhat loosely flowered.

FLOWERS: Few to many per inflorescence. Flowers are 1.6–2.0 in. (4–5 cm) across. Sepals and petals are bright, golden yellow with a deeper yellow lip that becomes nearly orange in the throat. The lip is hairy to fringed along the margin and velvety on the upper surface, except in the center. Plants are often described as glorious when they are in full bloom. Blossoms last about 2 weeks. They are odorless.

HYBRIDIZING NOTES: Chromosome count is 2n = 40 (ref. 152). Johansen (ref. 239) indicates that plants are self-sterile and that flowers dropped 10–12 days after self-pollination.

REFERENCES: 36, 152, 157, 179, 202, 210, 216, 239, 243, 254, 317, 428, 430, 454, 541, 557, 570.

PHOTOS/DRAWINGS: 210, *428, 430*, 454.

Dendrobium × *grimesii* C. T. White and Summerhayes.

A natural hybrid between *D. teretifolium* R. Brown var. *fasciculatum* Rupp (*D. calamiforme* Loddiges) and *D. linguiforme* Swartz var. *nugentii* F. M. Bailey (*D. nugentii* (F. M. Bailey) D. Jones and M. Clements). REFERENCES: 67, 105, 179, 225, 240, 421, 533. PHOTOS/DRAWINGS: 105, 240.

Dendrobium groeneveldtii J. J. Smith

ORIGIN/HABITAT: Western Sumatra. Plants were originally found near Agam near Mt. Ophir. Habitat elevation is estimated at 3000 ft. (910 m), so the following climate data should be used with caution.

CLIMATE: Station #96163, Padang, Sumatra, Indonesia, Lat. 0.9°S, Long. 100.4°E, at 19 ft. (6 m). Temperatures are calculated for an elevation of 3000 ft. (910 m), resulting in probable extremes of 84°F (29°C) and 58°F (15°C).

N/HEMISPHERE	JAN	FEB	MAR	APR	MAY	JUN	JUL	AUG	SEP	OCT	NOV	DEC
°F AVG MAX	77	77	76	76	76	76	77	77	77	77	78	77
°F AVG MIN	64	64	64	64	64	64	64	64	64	65	65	64
DIURNAL RANGE	13	13	12	12	12	12	13	13	13	12	13	13
RAIN/INCHES	10.9	13.7	6.0	19.5	20.4	18.9	13.8	10.2	12.1	14.3	12.4	12.1
HUMIDITY/%	81	82	82	84	85	84	81	81	82	83	81	81
BLOOM SEASON	N/A											
DAYS CLR @ 7AM	5	1	1	0	0	2	2	1	2	2	3	5
DAYS CLR @ 1PM	5	2	2	1	1	3	3	4	3	3	6	5
RAIN/MM	277	348	152	495	518	480	351	259	307	363	315	307
°C AVG MAX	25.1	25.1	24.5	24.5	24.5	24.5	25.1	25.1	25.1	25.1	25.6	25.1
°C AVG MIN	17.9	17.9	17.9	17.9	17.9	17.9	17.9	17.9	17.9	18.4	18.4	17.9
DIURNAL RANGE	7.2	7.2	6.6	6.6	6.6	6.6	7.2	7.2	7.2	6.7	7.2	7.2
S/HEMISPHERE	JUL	AUG	SEP	OCT	NOV	DEC	JAN	FEB	MAR	APR	MAY	JUN

Cultural Recommendations

LIGHT: 2000 fc. Diffused light is preferred.

TEMPERATURES: Throughout the year, days average 76–78°F (25–26°C), and nights average 64–65°F (18°C), with a diurnal range of 12–13°F (7°C). Probable extremes vary only a few degrees from the averages indicating that plants may not tolerate wide temperature fluctuations.

HUMIDITY: 80–85% year-round.

WATER: Rainfall is heavy all year. Cultivated plants should be kept moist but not soggy.

FERTILIZER: ¼–½ recommended strength. A balanced fertilizer should be applied weekly to biweekly throughout the year.

REST PERIOD: Growing conditions should be maintained year-round. Water may be reduced somewhat for cultivated plants in winter, especially those grown in the dark, short-day conditions common in temperate latitudes. They should never be allowed to dry out completely, however.

GROWING MEDIA: Plants may be mounted on tree-fern or cork slabs or potted in small pots filled with any open, fast-draining medium. Repotting may be done anytime new roots are growing.

MISCELLANEOUS NOTES: The plant was described in 1920 in *Bul. Jard. Bot. Buit.* 3rd sér. 2:79.

Plant and Flower Information

PLANT SIZE AND TYPE: A 6–8 in. (15–20 cm) sympodial epiphyte.

PSEUDOBULB: 4–6 in. (10–16 cm) long. The short, dark purple stems are flattened.

LEAVES: The lanceolate, deciduous leaves are 1.8–2.5 in. (4.5–6.5 cm) long. They are dark olive-green with violet on the underside.

INFLORESCENCE: Short. Inflorescences emerge from nodes along leafless stems.

FLOWERS: 1 per inflorescence. The flowers are 0.9 in. (2.3 cm) across. The ovate dorsal sepal and somewhat sickle-shaped lateral sepals may be green or creamy yellow with purple stripes on the backside and light brownish green on the inside. The greenish white petals are palest near the tip. They have uneven margins that are tinged with purple. The blade of the white lip is 2-lobed and may or may not be marked with a purple dot.

REFERENCES: 222.

Dendrobium grootingsii J. J. Smith

ORIGIN/HABITAT: Southern Borneo. Plants were originally collected at 250–650 ft. (80–200 m) near Muaratewe (Moeara Tewe), a town in south-central Kalimantan on the upper Barito River.

CLIMATE: Station #96655, Tengirang, Borneo, Lat. 1.0°S, Long. 114.0°E, at 89 ft. (27 m). Record extreme temperatures are not available for this location.

N/HEMISPHERE	JAN	FEB	MAR	APR	MAY	JUN	JUL	AUG	SEP	OCT	NOV	DEC
°F AVG MAX	88	89	89	90	89	87	87	87	88	89	88	88
°F AVG MIN	73	74	74	75	76	76	75	75	76	77	76	75
DIURNAL RANGE	15	15	15	15	13	11	12	12	12	12	12	13
RAIN/INCHES	2.5	2.2	2.2	5.5	9.8	10.5	7.4	8.7	6.3	7.5	9.3	4.8
HUMIDITY/%	N/A											
BLOOM SEASON	*											
DAYS CLR	N/A											
RAIN/MM	63	55	56	139	249	266	189	222	159	191	237	122
°C AVG MAX	31.2	31.5	31.7	32.0	31.6	30.7	30.6	30.8	31.1	31.8	31.3	31.3
°C AVG MIN	23.0	23.2	23.6	24.0	24.5	24.2	24.0	23.7	24.3	25.0	24.7	24.2
DIURNAL RANGE	8.2	8.3	8.1	8.0	7.1	6.5	6.6	7.1	6.8	6.8	6.6	7.1
S/HEMISPHERE	JUL	AUG	SEP	OCT	NOV	DEC	JAN	FEB	MAR	APR	MAY	JUN

Cultural Recommendations

LIGHT: 2000–3000 fc.

TEMPERATURES: Throughout the year, days average 87–90°F (31–32°C), and nights average 73–77°F (23–25°C), with a diurnal range of 11–15°F (7–8°C).

HUMIDITY: Information is not available for this location. However, records

from nearby locations indicate that humidity probably averages near 80–85% all year.

WATER: Rainfall in moderate to heavy most of the year, but conditions are slightly drier for 3 months in winter. Cultivated plants should never be allowed to dry out completely while actively growing, but water should be gradually reduced in late autumn.

FERTILIZER: ¼–½ recommended strength. A balanced fertilizer should be applied weekly to biweekly throughout the year.

REST PERIOD: Growing conditions should be maintained all year. For cultivated plants, water should be reduced for about 3 months in winter. They should be allowed to become somewhat dry between waterings but should not remain dry for long periods. Fertilizer should be reduced until water is increased in spring.

GROWING MEDIA: Plants may be mounted on tree-fern or cork slabs or placed in small pots filled with any open, fast-draining medium. Repotting may be done anytime new roots are actively growing.

MISCELLANEOUS NOTES: The bloom season shown in the climate table is based on collection reports. The plant was described in 1917 in *Bul. Jard. Bot. Buit.* 2nd sér. 25:33.

Plant and Flower Information

PLANT SIZE AND TYPE: An 8–19 in. (20–48 cm) sympodial epiphyte.

PSEUDOBULB: 8–19 in. (20–48 cm) long. The branching stems arise from a short rhizome. They are club-shaped above the base.

LEAVES: Many. The generally erect leaves are 1.4–2.5 in. (3.6–6.4 cm) long. They are dark green and contracted to a point at the tip.

INFLORESCENCE: Inflorescences emerge through the leaf bases on leafy stems.

FLOWERS: Few per inflorescence. The flowers are 0.5 in. (1.3 cm) long. Sepals and petals are white, but the lip is marked with an ochre blotch. Unlike *D. tenellum* Lindley, a closely related species, the lip is not purple veined. The dorsal sepal is ovate. The lateral sepals are somewhat triangular and taper to a slender point. The erect lip is concave and recurved. The spur in incurved.

REFERENCES: 222, 286, 295.

Dendrobium grossum Schlechter

ORIGIN/HABITAT: Northern Papua New Guinea. Plants grow on forest trees at 3300–4250 ft. (1000–1300 m) in the Finisterre and Bismarck Mountains.

CLIMATE: Station #94010, Goroka, Papua New Guinea, Lat. 6.1°S, Long. 145.4°E, at 5141 ft. (1567 m). Temperatures are calculated for an elevation of 4000 ft. (1220 m), resulting in probable extremes of 90°F (32°C) and 46°F (8°C).

N/HEMISPHERE	JAN	FEB	MAR	APR	MAY	JUN	JUL	AUG	SEP	OCT	NOV	DEC
°F AVG MAX	80	81	82	83	83	82	83	82	82	82	83	81
°F AVG MIN	60	61	61	61	62	63	63	63	64	63	63	61
DIURNAL RANGE	20	20	21	22	21	19	20	19	18	19	20	20
RAIN/INCHES	2.1	2.8	4.6	5.9	6.6	9.3	9.1	10.1	10.7	8.3	4.6	2.0
HUMIDITY/%	70	67	67	67	67	71	72	73	74	71	70	70
BLOOM SEASON	N/A											
DAYS CLR	N/A											
RAIN/MM	53	71	117	150	168	236	231	257	272	211	117	51
°C AVG MAX	26.5	27.1	27.6	28.2	28.2	27.6	28.2	27.6	27.6	27.6	28.2	27.1
°C AVG MIN	15.4	16.0	16.0	16.0	16.5	17.1	17.1	17.1	17.6	17.1	17.1	16.0
DIURNAL RANGE	11.1	11.1	11.6	12.2	11.7	10.5	11.1	10.5	10.0	10.5	11.1	11.1
S/HEMISPHERE	JUL	AUG	SEP	OCT	NOV	DEC	JAN	FEB	MAR	APR	MAY	JUN

Cultural Recommendations

LIGHT: 2000–3000 fc.

TEMPERATURES: Throughout the year, days average 80–83°F (27–28°C), and nights average 60–63°F (15–17°C), with a diurnal range of 18–22°F (10–12°C).

HUMIDITY: 70–75% in summer and autumn, dropping to 65–70% in winter and spring. Plants require excellent air movement.

WATER: Rainfall is moderate to heavy most of the year, but conditions are slightly drier for 3 months in winter. Cultivated plants should be kept moist but not soggy. Occasional early morning mistings may be beneficial, especially on bright, sunny days.

FERTILIZER: ¼–½ recommended strength. A balanced fertilizer should be applied weekly to biweekly throughout the year.

REST PERIOD: Growing temperatures should be maintained all year. In the habitat, rainfall is lowest in winter, but dew and mist from fog and low clouds are common. Water and fertilizer should be reduced somewhat for cultivated plants, especially those grown in the darker, short-day conditions common during temperate-latitude winters. Plants should be kept on the dry side, but they should never be allowed to dry out completely. In the habitat, light is higher in winter.

GROWING MEDIA: Plants may be mounted on tree-fern or cork slabs if humidity is high and plants are watered at least once daily in summer. When plants are potted, any open, fast-draining medium may be used. Repotting is best done in early spring when new roots are growing.

MISCELLANEOUS NOTES: Plants that produce flowers which last a single day commonly bloom several times during the year. Flowering usually occurs 7–14 days after a sudden 10°F (5°C) drop in daytime temperatures.

Plant and Flower Information

PLANT SIZE AND TYPE: A 31 in. (80 cm) sympodial epiphyte. The robust plant is thick and fleshy.

PSEUDOBULB: 31 in. (80 cm) long. The stems are simple, straight, and erect.

LEAVES: The lanceolate leaves, which are 3–5 in. (8–13 cm) long, may be erect or spreading. They are smooth, transparent, and shiny on the upper surface.

INFLORESCENCE: Short. Inflorescences arise from nodes along the side of the pseudobulb. The flowers are held opposite each other.

FLOWERS: 2 per inflorescence. The flowers are 1 in. (2.5 cm) long and remain somewhat closed. Sepals and petals are pale yellow to orange-yellow. The lip is reddish. Blossoms last a single day.

REFERENCES: 92, 221, 437, 445.

PHOTOS/DRAWINGS: 437.

Dendrobium guadalcanalense Guillaumin. Now considered a synonym of *Cadetia hispida* (A. Richard) Schlechter. REFERENCES: 170, 230, 271.

Dendrobium guamense Ames

ORIGIN/HABITAT: Micronesia. Plants grow on the islands of Guam, Tinian, Rota, and Saipan. They may grow on in filtered shade on trees or in full sun on dead trees or coral rocks.

CLIMATE: Station #91212, Agana NAS, Guam, Lat. 13.5°N, Long. 144.8°E, at 298 ft. (91 m). Record extreme temperatures are 94°F (34°C) and 68°F (20°C).

N/HEMISPHERE	JAN	FEB	MAR	APR	MAY	JUN	JUL	AUG	SEP	OCT	NOV	DEC
°F AVG MAX	84	84	85	85	86	86	86	86	86	86	86	85
°F AVG MIN	75	75	76	76	76	77	76	76	76	76	77	76
DIURNAL RANGE	9	9	9	9	10	9	10	10	10	10	9	9
RAIN/INCHES	4.3	3.2	1.8	4.4	5.4	4.8	8.8	12.0	13.9	12.9	8.6	5.5
HUMIDITY/%	81	79	77	79	80	81	83	84	85	84	83	82
BLOOM SEASON						*		*				
DAYS CLR @ 10AM	0	0	1	0	0	0	0	0	0	0	0	0
DAYS CLR @ 4PM	1	1	1	0	0	0	0	0	0	0	1	1
RAIN/MM	109	81	46	112	137	122	224	305	353	328	218	140
°C AVG MAX	28.9	28.9	29.4	29.4	30.0	30.0	30.0	30.0	30.0	30.0	30.0	29.4
°C AVG MIN	23.9	23.9	24.4	24.4	24.4	25.0	24.4	24.4	24.4	24.4	25.0	24.4
DIURNAL RANGE	5.0	5.0	5.0	5.0	5.6	5.0	5.6	5.6	5.6	5.6	5.0	5.0
S/HEMISPHERE	JUL	AUG	SEP	OCT	NOV	DEC	JAN	FEB	MAR	APR	MAY	JUN

Cultural Recommendations

LIGHT: 2000–3000 fc.

TEMPERATURES: Throughout the year, days average 84–86°F (29–30°C), and nights average 75–77°F (24–25°C), with a diurnal range of 9–10°F (5–6°C).

HUMIDITY: 80–85% most of the year, dropping to 75–80% in late winter and spring.

WATER: Rainfall is moderate to heavy most of the year, with a brief 1–2 month semidry period in late winter. Cultivated plants should be kept moist while actively growing, but water should be gradually reduced in late autumn.

FERTILIZER: ¼–½ recommended strength. A balanced fertilizer should be applied weekly to biweekly throughout the year.

REST PERIOD: Growing conditions should be maintained all year. Water should be reduced for a month or so during the brief semidry period in late winter, but plants should never be allowed to dry out completely. Fertilizer should be reduced or eliminated anytime water is reduced.

GROWING MEDIA: Plants may be mounted on tree-fern or cork slabs if humidity is high and plants are watered at least once daily in summer. When plants are potted, any open, fast-draining medium may be used. In the tropics, plants grow well in coconut fiber in shallow, open baskets. Repotting is best done in early spring when new roots begin to grow.

MISCELLANEOUS NOTES: The bloom season shown in the climate table is based on cultivation records. Plants that produce flowers which last a single day commonly bloom several times during the year. Flowering usually occurs 7–14 days after a sudden 10°F (5°C) drop in daytime temperatures.

Plant and Flower Information

PLANT SIZE AND TYPE: A 24–39 in. (60–100 cm) sympodial epiphyte or lithophyte.

PSEUDOBULB: 24–39 in. (60–100 cm) long. The small stems, which are wiry, rigid, and unbranched, are smooth when dry.

LEAVES: Many. The oblong-lanceolate leaves are usually 4 in. (10 cm) long and unequally bilobed at the apex. They are distichous.

INFLORESCENCE: Short. Inflorescences normally appear between the leaves on leafy stems, but they sometimes appear on leafless stems.

FLOWERS: 2 per inflorescence. The flowers are 1.1 in. (2.8 cm) across. They may be either wide-opening or rather closed. The lip midlobe is triangular-lanceolate and pointed. Blossoms have white sepals and petals and a yellow lip. They are fragrant but only last a single day.

REFERENCES: 14, 205, 221, 441.

Dendrobium guangxiense S. J. Cheng and C. Z. Tang

ORIGIN/HABITAT: China. Plants are found in Guangxi, Yunnan, and Geizhou Provinces. Specific habitat location and elevation are unavailable. The following climate data is for a station in the mountain region where the borders of the three provinces intersect. Since specific habitat information is missing, the following climate data should be used with caution.

CLIMATE: Station #57902, Xingran (Hsing-jen), Gweizhou, China, Lat. 25.4°N, Long. 105.3°E, at 4636 ft. (1413 m). Record extreme temperatures are 99°F (37°C) and 23°F (−5°C).

N/HEMISPHERE	JAN	FEB	MAR	APR	MAY	JUN	JUL	AUG	SEP	OCT	NOV	DEC
°F AVG MAX	52	53	67	74	78	78	80	80	76	68	62	55
°F AVG MIN	36	39	48	55	61	63	66	64	60	54	48	41
DIURNAL RANGE	16	14	19	19	17	15	14	16	16	14	14	14
RAIN/INCHES	0.7	1.1	2.3	2.8	5.8	10.5	10.0	7.4	6.0	4.0	1.2	0.8
HUMIDITY/%	77	79	71	69	73	79	82	82	80	83	81	81
BLOOM SEASON					*							
DAYS CLR @ 7AM	5	4	8	8	5	2	2	4	6	3	4	5
DAYS CLR @ 1PM	7	5	12	9	3	1	1	2	3	3	5	7
RAIN/MM	18	28	58	71	147	267	254	188	152	102	30	20
°C AVG MAX	11.1	11.7	19.4	23.3	25.6	25.6	26.7	26.7	24.4	20.0	16.7	12.8
°C AVG MIN	2.2	3.9	8.9	12.8	16.1	17.2	18.9	17.8	15.6	12.2	8.9	5.0
DIURNAL RANGE	8.9	7.8	10.5	10.5	9.5	8.4	7.8	8.9	8.8	7.8	7.8	7.8
S/HEMISPHERE	JUL	AUG	SEP	OCT	NOV	DEC	JAN	FEB	MAR	APR	MAY	JUN

Cultural Recommendations

LIGHT: 2000–3000 fc.

TEMPERATURES: Summer days average 78–80°F (26–27°C), and nights average 63–66°F (17–19°C), with a diurnal range of 14–16°F (8–9°C). The widest diurnal range of the year occurs in spring when slightly cooler days and much cooler nights cause a range of 17–19°F (10–11°C).

HUMIDITY: 80–85% in summer and autumn, dropping to near 70% in late winter and early spring.

WATER: Rainfall is moderate to heavy from late spring into autumn, with a much drier season in winter and early spring. Cultivated plants should be kept moist while actively growing, but water should be gradually reduced in autumn.

FERTILIZER: ¼–½ recommended strength, applied weekly. A high nitrogen fertilizer is beneficial from spring to midsummer, but a fertilizer high in phosphates should be used in late summer and autumn.

REST PERIOD: Winter days average 52–55°F (11–13°C), and nights average 36–41°F (2–5°C), and the diurnal range is 14–16°F (8–9°C). Rainfall is low in the habitat for 3–4 months in winter, but additional moisture is available from heavy dew, mist, and fog for most of this time. Cultivated plants should be allowed to dry slightly between waterings, but should not remain dry for extended periods. Fertilizer should be reduced or eliminated while water is reduced.

GROWING MEDIA: Hanging pots or baskets accommodate the semipendent growth habit. Growers indicate that plants grow well in osmunda mixed with broken brick and charcoal, but any open, rapidly draining medium that retains some moisture should work. Repotting is best done in early spring when new roots are growing.

MISCELLANEOUS NOTES: Plant description, drawing, and photograph are available in *Orchid Digest* 50(3):95–97.

Plant and Flower Information

PLANT SIZE AND TYPE: A 10–24 in. (25–60 cm) sympodial epiphyte.

PSEUDOBULB: 10–24 in. (25–60 cm) long. The stems are slightly zigzag and clustered. They are pendent to suberect.

LEAVES: 6–8 per growth. Oblong-lanceolate leaves are 1.6–2.4 in. (4–6 cm) long. They are dark green, lustrous, and deciduous.

INFLORESCENCE: Short. Inflorescences emerge from nodes on leafless canes.

FLOWERS: 1–2 per inflorescence. The flowers are 1 in. (2.5 cm) across. Sepals and petals are creamy white, sometimes lightly tinged with yellow or pale green at the base. The callus is lemon yellow. The irregularly toothed lip has a white margin around deep red to purplish markings.

HYBRIDIZING NOTES: Chromosome count, 2n = 38 (ref. 153) as *D. guangxiensis*.

REFERENCES: 153, 235.

PHOTOS/DRAWINGS: *130*.

Dendrobium guerreroi Ames and Quisumbing

ORIGIN/HABITAT: Philippines. Plants grow on Dinagat and Mindoro Islands. Little else has been reported about the habitat. The following climate data should be used with caution.

CLIMATE: Station #98653, Surigao, Philippines, Lat. 9.8°N, Long. 125.5°E, at 72 ft. (22 m) elevation. Record extreme temperatures are 99°F (37°C) and 65°F (18°C).

N/HEMISPHERE	JAN	FEB	MAR	APR	MAY	JUN	JUL	AUG	SEP	OCT	NOV	DEC
°F AVG MAX	83	84	85	87	89	89	89	89	89	88	86	84
°F AVG MIN	72	72	73	73	74	74	74	75	75	74	74	73
DIURNAL RANGE	11	12	12	14	15	15	15	14	14	14	12	11
RAIN/INCHES	21.4	14.8	19.9	10.0	6.2	4.9	7.0	5.1	6.6	10.7	16.8	24.4
HUMIDITY/%	91	90	88	85	85	82	83	82	83	84	88	89
BLOOM SEASON	*	*		*							*	*
DAYS CLR @ 8AM	1	1	2	4	2	3	2	2	1	2	1	1
DAYS CLR @ 2PM	1	2	2	6	3	1	2	1	2	3	1	1
RAIN/MM	544	376	505	254	157	124	178	130	168	272	427	620
°C AVG MAX	28.3	28.9	29.4	30.6	31.7	31.7	31.7	31.7	31.7	31.1	30.0	28.9
°C AVG MIN	22.2	22.2	22.8	22.8	23.3	23.3	23.3	23.9	23.9	23.3	23.3	22.8
DIURNAL RANGE	6.1	6.7	6.6	7.8	8.4	8.4	8.4	7.8	7.8	7.8	6.7	6.1
S/HEMISPHERE	JUL	AUG	SEP	OCT	NOV	DEC	JAN	FEB	MAR	APR	MAY	JUN

Cultural Recommendations

LIGHT: 2000–3000 fc.

TEMPERATURES: Throughout the year, days average 83–89°F (28–32°C), and nights average 72–75°F (22–24°C), with a diurnal range of 11–15°F (6–8°C). The widest diurnal range occurs in summer and results from warmer days.

HUMIDITY: 80–90% year-round.

WATER: Rainfall is moderate to very heavy all year. Cultivated plants should be kept moist but not soggy. Warm water, about 70°F (21°C), might be beneficial.

FERTILIZER: ¼–½ recommended strength. A balanced fertilizer should be applied weekly to biweekly throughout the year.

REST PERIOD: Growing conditions should be maintained all year. Wide seasonal temperature fluctuations should be avoided. In the habitat, the heaviest rainfall occurs in winter; but in cultivation, increased water could be detrimental. This is especially true for plants grown in the dark, short-day conditions common in temperate latitudes. Cultivated plants should be kept moist, with only slight drying allowed between waterings. In the habitat, light is lowest in winter.

GROWING MEDIA: Plants may be mounted on tree-fern or cork slabs if humidity is high and plants are watered at least once daily in summer. When plants are potted, any open, fast-draining medium may be used. Repotting is best done in early spring soon after flowering when new roots are growing.

MISCELLANEOUS NOTES: The bloom season shown in the climate table is based on cultivation records.

Plant and Flower Information

PLANT SIZE AND TYPE: A 12–30 in. (30–75 cm) sympodial epiphyte.

PSEUDOBULB: 12–30 in. (30–75 cm) long. The nearly erect canes are narrow at the base.

LEAVES: Many. The deciduous leaves are 2.8–4.0 in. (7–10 cm) long. They are lanceolate to oblong and greenish flushed with purple when young. They are distichous all along the stem.

INFLORESCENCE: 3 in. (8 cm) long. The pendulous raceme is loosely flowered.

FLOWERS: 10–13 per inflorescence. The flowers are 1.2–1.4 in. (3.0–3.6 cm) across. The white to yellowish segments are often flushed with purple. They are odorless.

HYBRIDIZING NOTES: Chromosome count is 2n = 40 (ref. 151, 187).

REFERENCES: 151, 179, 187, 225, 373, 536.

PHOTOS/DRAWINGS: *373*.

Dendrobium guibertii Carriere. See *D. densiflorum* Lindley.

REFERENCES: 179, 216, 445, 454, 541, 570.

Dendrobium guilianetii F. M. Bailey. Schlechter (ref. 437) mentions this name as part of the section *Ceratobium*. No other information was located. REFERENCES: 437.

Dendrobium gunnarii P. S. N. Rao

ORIGIN/HABITAT: North Andaman Island. Plants grow on trees in tropical, mostly evergreen forests and moist deciduous forests where conditions are semishady.

CLIMATE: Station #43333, Port Blair, Andaman Islands, Lat. 11.7°N, Long. 92.7°E, at 259 ft. (79 m). Record extreme temperatures are 99°F (37°C) and 62°F (17°C).

N/HEMISPHERE	JAN	FEB	MAR	APR	MAY	JUN	JUL	AUG	SEP	OCT	NOV	DEC
°F AVG MAX	84	86	88	89	87	84	84	83	83	84	84	84
°F AVG MIN	72	71	72	75	75	75	75	75	74	74	74	73
DIURNAL RANGE	12	15	16	14	12	9	9	8	9	10	10	11
RAIN/INCHES	1.8	1.1	1.1	2.4	15.1	21.8	15.4	16.3	17.4	12.5	10.5	7.9
HUMIDITY/%	79	76	79	79	86	87	87	89	89	86	84	81
BLOOM SEASON											*	*
DAYS CLR @ 6AM	1	5	6	2	0	1	0	0	0	1	5	3
DAYS CLR @ 12PM	1	6	11	2	0	0	0	0	0	0	4	2
RAIN/MM	46	28	28	61	384	554	391	414	442	318	267	201
°C AVG MAX	28.9	30.0	31.1	31.7	30.6	28.9	28.9	28.3	28.3	28.9	28.9	28.9
°C AVG MIN	22.2	21.7	22.2	23.9	23.9	23.9	23.9	23.9	23.3	23.3	23.3	22.8
DIURNAL RANGE	6.7	8.3	8.9	7.8	6.7	5.0	5.0	4.4	5.0	5.6	5.6	6.1
S/HEMISPHERE	JUL	AUG	SEP	OCT	NOV	DEC	JAN	FEB	MAR	APR	MAY	JUN

Cultural Recommendations

LIGHT: 1800–3000 fc.

TEMPERATURES: Throughout the year, days average 83–89°F (28–32°C), and nights average 71–75°F (22–24°C), with a diurnal range of 8–16°F (4–9°C).

HUMIDITY: 85–90% from late spring into autumn, dropping to 75–80% in winter and early spring.

WATER: Rainfall is heavy from late spring through autumn, but conditions are drier for 3–4 months in winter. Cultivated plants should be kept moist while actively growing, but water should be reduced in late autumn.

FERTILIZER: ¼–½ recommended strength. A balanced fertilizer should be applied weekly to biweekly throughout the year.

REST PERIOD: Growing temperatures should be maintained all year. Water and fertilizer should be reduced in winter. Plants should be allowed to dry out somewhat between waterings, but they should not remain dry for extended periods. In the habitat, light is highest in winter.

GROWING MEDIA: Plants are best mounted on tree-fern or cork slabs if humidity is high and plants are watered at least once daily in summer. When plants are potted, any open, fast-draining medium may be used. They may be repotted anytime new roots are growing.

MISCELLANEOUS NOTES: The bloom season shown in the climate table is based on records from the habitat.

Plant and Flower Information

PLANT SIZE AND TYPE: A pendent, 8 in. (20 cm) sympodial epiphyte.

PSEUDOBULB: 5 in. (13 cm) long. The zigzag stems are slender and terete.

Dendrobium guttatum

LEAVES: 5–10 per growth. The linear-lanceolate leaves are 4 in. (10 cm) long and unequally bilobed at the apex. They are distichous.

INFLORESCENCE: Short. Inflorescences are borne opposite the leaves at nodes along leafy stems.

FLOWERS: 1–2 per inflorescence. The flowers are 0.5 in. (1.3 cm) across. The white sepals and petals are ovate to ovate-lanceolate and pointed. The green lip is marked with a dark purple flush near the base. It is 3-lobed, with a notch at the apex of the midlobe, making it appear 4-lobed.

REFERENCES: 377.

PHOTOS/DRAWINGS: 377.

Dendrobium guttatum J. J. Smith. See *D. rigidifolium* Rolfe.
REFERENCES: 83, 221, 445, 470, 538. PHOTOS/DRAWINGS: 538.

Dendrobium guttenbergii J. J. Smith. Transferred to *Ephemerantha guttenbergii* (J. J. Smith) Hunt and Summerhayes, which is now considered synonymous with *Flickingeria*. REFERENCES: 213, 225, 230, 449.

Dendrobium guttulatum Schlechter. Now considered a synonym of *Diplocaulobium guttulatum* (Schlechter) A. Hawkes. REFERENCES: 92, 221, 229, 437, 445.

Dendrobium gynoglottis Carr

ORIGIN/HABITAT: Borneo. Plants were collected near Ulu Koyan at about 2950 ft. (900 m).

CLIMATE: Station #96449, Miri, Sarawak, Borneo, Lat. 4.4°N, Long. 114.0°E, at 13 ft. (4 m). Temperatures are calculated for an elevation of 2950 ft. (900 m), resulting in probable extremes of 85°F (30°C) and 57°F (14°C).

N/HEMISPHERE	JAN	FEB	MAR	APR	MAY	JUN	JUL	AUG	SEP	OCT	NOV	DEC
°F AVG MAX	76	76	77	78	78	78	78	78	77	77	77	77
°F AVG MIN	64	64	64	65	65	65	64	64	64	64	64	64
DIURNAL RANGE	12	12	13	13	13	13	14	14	13	13	13	13
RAIN/INCHES	16.8	6.5	5.5	4.4	8.2	12.0	8.5	8.4	11.8	11.7	14.5	11.3
HUMIDITY/%	86	86	85	83	83	82	81	81	82	83	84	85
BLOOM SEASON							*					
DAYS CLR @ 8AM	1	2	4	4	3	2	3	2	2	1	2	2
DAYS CLR @ 2PM	1	1	3	4	2	5	3	2	3	2	1	1
RAIN/MM	427	165	140	112	208	305	216	213	300	297	368	287
°C AVG MAX	24.6	24.6	25.2	25.7	25.7	25.7	25.7	25.7	25.2	25.2	25.2	25.2
°C AVG MIN	17.9	17.9	17.9	18.5	18.5	18.5	17.9	17.9	17.9	17.9	17.9	17.9
DIURNAL RANGE	6.7	6.7	7.3	7.2	7.2	7.2	7.8	7.8	7.3	7.3	7.3	7.3
S/HEMISPHERE	JUL	AUG	SEP	OCT	NOV	DEC	JAN	FEB	MAR	APR	MAY	JUN

Cultural Recommendations

LIGHT: 2000–3000 fc.

TEMPERATURES: Throughout the year, days average 76–78°F (25–26°C), and nights average 64–65°F (18–19°C), with a diurnal range of 12–14°F (7–8°C).

HUMIDITY: 80–85% year-round.

WATER: Rainfall is heavy to very heavy all year, but conditions are slightly drier in winter. Cultivated plants should be kept moist but not soggy.

FERTILIZER: ¼–½ recommended strength. A balanced fertilizer should be applied weekly to biweekly throughout the year.

REST PERIOD: Growing conditions should be maintained all year. In cultivation, water and fertilizer should be reduced in winter, especially for plants grown in the dark, short-day conditions common in temperate latitudes. They should never be allowed to dry out completely, however. In the habitat, seasonal light variation is minor.

GROWING MEDIA: Plants may be mounted on tree-fern or cork slabs if humidity is high and plants are watered at least once daily in summer. When plants are potted, any open, fast-draining medium may be used. They may be repotted anytime new roots are growing.

MISCELLANEOUS NOTES: The bloom season shown in the climate table is based on collection reports.

Plant and Flower Information

PLANT SIZE AND TYPE: A 22 in. (55 cm) sympodial epiphyte.

PSEUDOBULB: 22 in. (55 cm) long. The slender, clustered stems are slightly flattened at the base, becoming very dilated and flattened above, with some constrictions at the nodes. They are elliptical in cross section. Stems are sometimes leafless near the apex.

LEAVES: Many. The narrowly lanceolate leaves are up to 3.4 in. (8.6 cm) long. They are thin, purplish green, and unequally bilobed at the tip.

INFLORESCENCE: Very short. Inflorescences emerge from tufts of dry scales at the upper nodes.

FLOWERS: 1 per inflorescence. The odorless flowers are 0.6–0.8 in. (1.5–2.0 cm) across. They are white with crimson markings on the outside of the petals. The 3-lobed lip is hairy at the base with 3 pale orange ridges. The base of the spur is marked with pale orange.

REFERENCES: 59, 225, 286.

Dendrobium habbemense P. van Royen

AKA: *D. spathulatilabratum* P. van Royen.

ORIGIN/HABITAT: Papua New Guinea and Irian Jaya (western New Guinea). Plants usually grow as low, pendulous epiphytes in mountain forests at 6900–11,500 ft. (2100–3500 m), but they are also found in alpine shrubs and grasslands on peat-covered ridges.

CLIMATE: Station #200243, Mt. Hagen, Papua New Guinea, Lat. 5.8°S, Long. 144.3°E, at 5350 ft. (1630 m). Temperatures are calculated for an elevation of 9200 ft. (2800 m), resulting in probable extremes of 75°F (24°C) and 22°F (−5°C).

N/HEMISPHERE	JAN	FEB	MAR	APR	MAY	JUN	JUL	AUG	SEP	OCT	NOV	DEC
°F AVG MAX	59	60	61	62	63	63	63	63	62	62	63	61
°F AVG MIN	42	42	42	42	42	43	43	43	43	44	43	41
DIURNAL RANGE	17	18	19	20	21	20	20	20	19	18	20	20
RAIN/INCHES	5.2	6.7	8.7	8.7	8.2	10.2	10.4	10.7	11.2	10.0	7.2	4.7
HUMIDITY/%	84	83	82	78	79	81	81	80	82	81	82	82
BLOOM SEASON	*	*	*								*	*
DAYS CLR	N/A											
RAIN/MM	132	170	221	221	208	259	264	272	284	254	183	119
°C AVG MAX	15.2	15.7	16.3	16.8	17.4	17.4	17.4	17.4	16.8	16.8	17.4	16.3
°C AVG MIN	5.7	5.7	5.7	5.7	5.7	6.3	6.3	6.3	6.3	6.8	6.3	5.2
DIURNAL RANGE	9.5	10.0	10.6	11.1	11.7	11.1	11.1	11.1	10.5	10.0	11.1	11.1
S/HEMISPHERE	JUL	AUG	SEP	OCT	NOV	DEC	JAN	FEB	MAR	APR	MAY	JUN

Cultural Recommendations

LIGHT: 1800–2500 fc.

TEMPERATURES: Throughout the year, days average 59–63°F (15–17°C), and nights average 41–44°F (5–7°C), with a diurnal range of 17–20°F (10–11°C).

HUMIDITY: Near 80% year-round.

WATER: Rainfall is moderate to heavy all year. Cultivated plants should be kept moist with only slight drying allowed between waterings.

FERTILIZER: ¼–½ recommended strength. A balanced fertilizer should be applied weekly to biweekly throughout the year.

REST PERIOD: Growing temperatures should be maintained all year. Water should be reduced somewhat in winter for plants grown in the dark, short-day conditions common in temperate latitudes. They should never be allowed to dry out completely, however. Fertilizer should be reduced or eliminated when water is reduced.

GROWING MEDIA: Mounting plants on tree-fern or cork slabs accommodates their pendulous growth habit. However, humidity must be high and plants must be watered at least once a day in summer. If plants cannot be mounted, small pots or hanging baskets may be filled with an open, fast-draining medium. Repotting may be done anytime new roots are actively growing.

MISCELLANEOUS NOTES: The bloom season shown in the climate table is based on reports from the habitat.

Plant and Flower Information

PLANT SIZE AND TYPE: A 10–24 in. (25–60 cm) sympodial epiphyte or terrestrial.

PSEUDOBULB: 8–20 in. (20–50 cm) long. The slender, pendulous stems have many thickened nodes. They often branch at apical nodes which makes the plants appear somewhat bushy.

LEAVES: 5–8 per growth. The linear leaves are 1.6–3.5 in. (4–9 cm) long. They are light yellowish green.

INFLORESCENCE: 0.4–1.2 in. (1–3 cm) long. 2–5 inflorescences are borne at nodes near the apex of leafy stems.

FLOWERS: 1 per inflorescence. The flowers are 1.0–1.2 in. (2.5–3.0 cm) long. They are brilliant orange-red, flat, waxy, and somewhat fan-shaped.

REFERENCES: 95, 233, 385, 538, 556.

PHOTOS/DRAWINGS: *385*, 538.

Dendrobium haeckeanum Steudel.
Sometimes spelled *D. haenkeanum*, it is generally considered a synonym of *Geodorum densiflorum* (Lamarck) Schlechter. REFERENCES: 67, 139, 298, 373.

Dendrobium haemoglossum Thwaites

AKA: *D. haemoglossum* is sometimes listed as a synonym of *D. salaccense* (Blume) Lindley.

ORIGIN/HABITAT: Southern Deccan in India and the Matele and Dolosbagey districts of Sri Lanka (Ceylon). Plants grow at about 3000 ft. (1000 m).

CLIMATE: Station #43296, Bangalore-Hindustan, India, Lat. 13.0°N, Long. 77.7°E, at 2937 ft. (895 m). Record extreme temperatures are 102°F (39°C) and 46°F (8°C).

N/HEMISPHERE	JAN	FEB	MAR	APR	MAY	JUN	JUL	AUG	SEP	OCT	NOV	DEC
°F AVG MAX	80	86	90	93	91	84	81	81	82	82	79	78
°F AVG MIN	57	60	65	69	69	67	66	66	65	65	62	58
DIURNAL RANGE	23	26	25	24	22	17	15	15	17	17	17	20
RAIN/INCHES	0.2	0.3	0.4	1.6	4.2	2.9	3.8	5.0	6.7	5.9	2.7	0.4
HUMIDITY/%	64	57	55	59	63	73	80	79	79	79	81	74
BLOOM SEASON										*	*	*
DAYS CLR @ 11AM	11	14	18	10	4	1	0	0	0	0	9	9
DAYS CLR @ 5PM	14	13	13	3	1	0	0	1	1	5	8	
RAIN/MM	5	8	10	41	107	74	97	127	170	150	69	10
°C AVG MAX	26.7	30.0	32.2	33.9	32.8	28.9	27.2	27.2	27.8	27.8	26.1	25.6
°C AVG MIN	13.9	15.6	18.3	20.6	20.6	19.4	18.9	18.9	18.3	18.3	16.7	14.4
DIURNAL RANGE	12.8	14.4	13.9	13.3	12.2	9.5	8.3	8.3	9.5	9.5	9.4	11.2
S/HEMISPHERE	JUL	AUG	SEP	OCT	NOV	DEC	JAN	FEB	MAR	APR	MAY	JUN

Cultural Recommendations

LIGHT: 2500–3500 fc.

TEMPERATURES: Summer Days average 81–84°F (27–29°C), and nights average 66–67°F (19°C), with a diurnal range of 15–17°F (8–10°C). Spring is the warmest season. Days average 90–93°F (32–34°C), and nights average 65–69°F (18–21°C), with a diurnal range of 22–25°F (12–14°C). The record high for this station is 102°F (39°C), indicating that plants should be heat tolerant with moderate humidity and good air movement.

HUMIDITY: 70–80% during the growing season, dropping to 55–60% in winter and spring.

WATER: Rainfall is light to moderate most of the year with 4 very dry months in winter. Cultivated plants should be allowed to dry slightly between waterings while growing, but water should be gradually reduced after new growths mature in autumn.

FERTILIZER: ½ recommended strength, applied weekly during the relatively short growing season to produce the best flowering. A high-nitrogen fertilizer is beneficial from spring to midsummer, but a fertilizer high in phosphates should be used in late summer and autumn.

REST PERIOD: Winter days average 78–86°F (26–30°C), and nights average 57–60°F (14–16°C), with a diurnal range of 20–26°F (11–14°C). The record low indicates that plants should be able to tolerate occasional periods of cold temperatures. Rainfall is low in winter, and humidity is so low that even moisture from dew is uncommon. Cultivated plants should dry out between waterings but should not remain completely dry for extended periods. Occasional mistings between waterings may help prevent excessive drying. Fertilizer should be eliminated until new growth begins and watering is increased in spring. In the habitat, light is highest in winter.

GROWING MEDIA: Mounting plants on tree-fern or cork slabs accommodates their pendulous growth habit. However, humidity must be high and plants must be watered at least once a day in summer. If plants can-

Dendrobium haenkeanum

not be mounted, small pots or hanging baskets may be filled with an open, fast-draining medium. Repotting may be done anytime new roots are actively growing.

Plant and Flower Information

PLANT SIZE AND TYPE: A 30 in. (75 cm) sympodial epiphyte.

PSEUDOBULB: 24 in. (60 cm) long. The pendulous stems are elongated and flattened. The vegetative characteristics were described as being so like *D. bambusifolium* [*D. salaccense* (Blume) Lindley] that the 2 species cannot be differentiated when not in bloom.

LEAVES: Many. The leaves are 5 in. (13 cm) long, linear-lanceolate, and leathery.

INFLORESCENCE: Short. Inflorescences emerge opposite the leaves on leafy stems.

FLOWERS: 2 per inflorescence. The tiny flowers are 0.3 in. (0.8 cm) across. The lanceolate sepals and ovate-lanceolate petals are yellow with dark red at the tips. The tongue-shaped, pointed lip is smooth and wavy. It is darker yellow than the other segments and may have a red tinge or red bands. The conical spur is very short.

HYBRIDIZING NOTES: In nature, plants are in fruit until Apr. (Oct.).

REFERENCES: 38, 46, 119, 202, 216, 254, 454, 468.

Dendrobium haenkeanum Steudel. Sometimes spelled *D. haeckeanum*, it is now considered a synonym of *Geodorum densiflorum* (Lamarck) Schlechter. REFERENCES: 216, 254, 536.

Dendrobium hagerupii J. J. Smith

ORIGIN/HABITAT: North central Sumatra. Plants were found originally in Batakland, the region around Lake Toba at about 4750 ft. (1450 m).

CLIMATE: Station #96035, Medan, Sumatra, Indonesia, Lat. 3.6°N, Long. 98.7°E, at 87 ft. (27 m). Temperatures are calculated for an elevation of 4750 ft. (1450 m), resulting in probable extremes of 84°F (29°C) and 45°F (7°C).

N/HEMISPHERE	JAN	FEB	MAR	APR	MAY	JUN	JUL	AUG	SEP	OCT	NOV	DEC
°F AVG MAX	70	72	73	74	74	74	74	74	73	71	71	70
°F AVG MIN	56	56	57	58	58	57	57	57	57	57	57	57
DIURNAL RANGE	14	16	16	16	16	17	17	17	16	14	14	13
RAIN/INCHES	5.4	3.6	4.1	5.2	6.9	5.2	5.3	7.0	8.3	10.2	9.7	9.0
HUMIDITY/%	80	79	78	78	79	78	79	79	81	83	83	82
BLOOM SEASON	N/A											
DAYS CLR @ 7AM	4	2	2	2	2	2	2	0	0	0	1	1
DAYS CLR @ 1PM	0	1	0	1	0	2	1	0	0	0	0	0
RAIN/MM	137	91	104	132	175	132	135	178	211	259	246	229
°C AVG MAX	20.9	22.0	22.6	23.1	23.1	23.1	23.1	23.1	22.6	21.5	21.5	20.9
°C AVG MIN	13.1	13.1	13.7	14.2	14.2	13.7	13.7	13.7	13.7	13.7	13.7	13.7
DIURNAL RANGE	7.8	8.9	8.9	8.9	8.9	9.4	9.4	9.4	8.9	7.8	7.8	7.2
S/HEMISPHERE	JUL	AUG	SEP	OCT	NOV	DEC	JAN	FEB	MAR	APR	MAY	JUN

Cultural Recommendations

LIGHT: 2000–3000 fc.

TEMPERATURES: Throughout the year, days average 70–74°F (21–23°C), and nights average 56–58°F (13–14°C), with a diurnal range of 13–17°F (7–9°C). Average lows vary only 2°F (1°C) during the year.

HUMIDITY: 75–80% year-round.

WATER: Rainfall is moderate to heavy all year, with a brief slightly drier period in winter. Cultivated plants should be kept moist, and only slight drying allowed between waterings.

FERTILIZER: ¼–½ recommended strength. A balanced fertilizer should be applied weekly to biweekly throughout the year.

REST PERIOD: Growing conditions should be maintained all year. Water may be reduced somewhat in winter for plants grown in the dark, short-day conditions common in temperate latitudes, but they should never be allowed to dry out completely. In the habitat, light is slightly higher for about 3 months in winter.

GROWING MEDIA: Plants may be mounted on tree-fern or cork slabs or potted in small pots filled with any open, fast-draining medium. Repotting may be done anytime new roots are growing.

MISCELLANEOUS NOTES: The plant was described in 1922 in *Bul. Jard. Bot. Buit.* 3rd sér. 5:78.

Plant and Flower Information

PLANT SIZE AND TYPE: A 7–9 in. (18–23 cm) sympodial epiphyte.

PSEUDOBULB: 7–9 in. (18–23 cm) long. The flattened stems, which are densely leafy, are borne on a branching rhizome.

LEAVES: Many. The leaves are about 1 in. (2.5 cm) long, but they are smaller near the apex of the stem. They are flattened, fleshy, and triangular.

INFLORESCENCE: 0.4 in. (1 cm) long. Inflorescences emerge all along the stem as well as at the apex.

FLOWERS: Several. The fleshy, dark red flowers are 0.4 in. (1 cm) long. The lip callus is large.

REFERENCES: 223.

Dendrobium hainanense Masamune and Hayata not Rolfe. See *D. miyakei* Schlechter. REFERENCES: 279, 528.

Dendrobium hainanense Rolfe. See *D. parciflorum* Rchb. f. ex Lindley not Kränzlin. REFERENCES: 208, 254, 266, 410, 414, 448, 528. PHOTOS/DRAWINGS: 130.

Dendrobium hallieri J. J. Smith

ORIGIN/HABITAT: Borneo. Plants were originally collected on Mt. Kelam in northwestern Kalimantan, but habitat elevation was not given. The plants were taken to the low elevation Buitenzorg Botanic Garden in Java where they bloomed and then died. Therefore, we have estimated a higher elevation habitat, but the following temperatures should be used with caution.

CLIMATE: Station #96583, Pontianak, Kalimantan, Borneo, Lat. 0.0°N, Long. 109.3°E, at 13 ft. (4 m). Temperatures are calculated for an elevation of 4100 ft. (1250 m), resulting in probable extremes of 83°F (28°C) and 55°F (13°C).

N/HEMISPHERE	JAN	FEB	MAR	APR	MAY	JUN	JUL	AUG	SEP	OCT	NOV	DEC
°F AVG MAX	74	76	76	76	77	77	76	77	77	76	75	74
°F AVG MIN	61	63	62	62	62	62	61	61	62	62	62	61
DIURNAL RANGE	13	13	14	14	15	15	15	16	15	14	13	13
RAIN/INCHES	10.8	8.2	9.5	10.9	11.1	8.7	6.5	8.0	9.0	14.4	15.3	12.7
HUMIDITY/%	85	85	84	84	82	81	79	82	83	87	86	87
BLOOM SEASON	N/A											
DAYS CLR @ 7AM	1	1	1	3	2	4	5	1	2	1	1	2
DAYS CLR @ 1PM	0	0	1	0	0	0	1	1	1	0	1	0
RAIN/MM	274	208	241	277	282	221	165	203	229	366	389	323
°C AVG MAX	23.1	24.2	24.2	24.2	24.7	24.7	24.2	24.7	24.7	24.2	23.6	23.1
°C AVG MIN	15.8	17.0	16.4	16.4	16.4	16.4	15.8	15.8	16.4	16.4	16.4	15.8
DIURNAL RANGE	7.3	7.2	7.8	7.8	8.3	8.3	8.4	8.9	8.3	7.8	7.2	7.3
S/HEMISPHERE	JUL	AUG	SEP	OCT	NOV	DEC	JAN	FEB	MAR	APR	MAY	JUN

Cultural Recommendations

LIGHT: 2000–3000 fc. The heavy cloud cover indicates that some shading is needed, but light should be as high as the plant can tolerate, short of burning the leaves.

TEMPERATURES: Throughout the year, days average 74–77°F (23–25°C), and nights average 61–63°F (16–17°C), with a diurnal range of 13–16°F

(7–9°C). Average highs fluctuate only 3°F (1°C), and average lows vary 2°F (1°C), indicating that plants may not tolerate wide temperature fluctuations.

HUMIDITY: 80–85% year-round.

WATER: Rainfall is moderate to heavy all year. Cultivated plants should be kept moist, with only slight drying allowed between waterings. Constant air movement is highly recommended. Warm water may be beneficial.

FERTILIZER: ¼–½ recommended strength. A balanced fertilizer should be applied weekly to biweekly year-round.

REST PERIOD: Growing conditions should be maintained all year. Water may be reduced somewhat in winter, especially for plants grown in the dark, short-day conditions common in temperate latitudes. They should never be allowed to dry out completely, however. Fertilizer should be reduced if water is reduced. In the habitat, seasonal light variation is minor.

GROWING MEDIA: Plants may be mounted on tree-fern or cork slabs or potted in small pots filled with any open, fast-draining medium. Repotting may be done anytime new roots are growing.

Plant and Flower Information

PLANT SIZE AND TYPE: A 12 in. (30 cm) sympodial epiphyte.

PSEUDOBULB: 12 in. (30 cm) long. The stems are rigidly erect but still flexuous. They are covered with black hairs. The clustered pseudobulbs arise from a short rhizome.

LEAVES: Many. The oblong leaves are 2–5 in. (5–13 cm) long and covered with black hairs.

INFLORESCENCE: 0.4–1.0 in. (1.0–2.5 cm) long. Inflorescences emerge through the base of the leaf sheaths.

FLOWERS: 2–7 per inflorescence. The pale yellow flowers are 1 in. (2.5 cm) across. The dorsal sepal is recurved, and lateral sepals are decurved. The wavy petals are recurved at the apex. The lip, which is marked with red lines, is densely covered with small wartlike growths except on the midlobe.

REFERENCES: 221, 286, 295, 429, 473.

Dendrobium halmaheirense J. J. Smith

ORIGIN/HABITAT: Molucca Islands. Plants were originally found on Halmahera Island (Gilolo). They were cultivated at the botanical garden in Bogor, Java. Habitat elevation is estimated, so the following climate data should be used with caution.

CLIMATE: Station #97406, Galela, Halmahera Island, Indonesia, Lat. 1.8°N, Long. 127.8°E, at 180 ft. (55 m). Record extreme temperatures are not available for this location.

N/HEMISPHERE	JAN	FEB	MAR	APR	MAY	JUN	JUL	AUG	SEP	OCT	NOV	DEC
°F AVG MAX	86	86	86	88	87	86	86	87	87	88	88	87
°F AVG MIN	76	74	76	76	77	75	73	75	76	77	77	76
DIURNAL RANGE	10	12	10	12	10	11	13	12	11	11	11	11
RAIN/INCHES	5.3	6.4	7.4	4.1	10.0	7.1	8.1	9.3	5.2	6.9	7.0	11.4
HUMIDITY/%	N/A											
BLOOM SEASON	N/A											
DAYS CLR	N/A											
RAIN/MM	134	163	188	104	254	180	205	236	132	175	177	289
°C AVG MAX	30.1	30.0	29.8	30.9	30.2	30.0	30.5	30.7	31.4	31.2	30.5
°C AVG MIN	24.3	23.6	24.6	24.6	24.9	23.9	22.9	23.7	24.2	24.9	25.2	24.6
DIURNAL RANGE	5.8	6.4	5.2	6.3	5.7	6.3	7.1	6.8	6.5	6.5	6.0	5.9
S/HEMISPHERE	JUL	AUG	SEP	OCT	NOV	DEC	JAN	FEB	MAR	APR	MAY	JUN

Cultural Recommendations

LIGHT: 2000–3000 fc.

TEMPERATURES: Throughout the year, days average 86–88°F (30–31°C), and nights average 73–77°F (23–25°C), with a diurnal range of 10–13°F (5–7°C).

HUMIDITY: Information is not available for this location. However, average humidity at other stations in the region is near 80% year-round.

WATER: Rainfall is moderate to heavy all year. Cultivated plants should be allowed to dry only slightly between waterings.

FERTILIZER: ¼–½ recommended strength. A balanced fertilizer should be applied weekly to biweekly throughout the year.

REST PERIOD: Growing conditions should be maintained year-round. Water should be reduced slightly in winter, especially for plants grown in the dark, short-day conditions common in temperate latitudes. Fertilizer should be reduced or eliminated when plants are not actively growing.

GROWING MEDIA: Plants may be mounted on tree-fern or cork slabs or potted in small pots filled with any open, fast-draining medium. Repotting may be done anytime new roots are actively growing.

MISCELLANEOUS NOTES: The plant was described in 1914 in *Bul. Jard. Bot. Buit.* 2nd sér. 13:15.

Plant and Flower Information

PLANT SIZE AND TYPE: A 9–14 in. (23–35 cm) sympodial epiphyte.

PSEUDOBULB: 9–14 in. (23–35 cm) long. The erect stems are grooved, shiny, dirty olive, and quadrangular at the apex. They emerge from a creeping, rooting rhizome.

LEAVES: 2 per growth. The leaves are 6.5 in. (17 cm) long, spreading, lanceolate, and shiny green.

INFLORESCENCE: Short. Inflorescences emerge from nodes along the stem.

FLOWERS: 2–3 per inflorescence. The shiny flowers are 2.4–3.5 in. (6–9 cm) long, pendulous, short-lived, and odorless. Sepals and petals are slender and pointed. All segments are white, but the lip is decorated with yellow-orange to cinnamon dots.

REFERENCES: 221.

Dendrobium hamadryas Schlechter

ORIGIN/HABITAT: Northern Papua New Guinea. Plants grow in mountain forests close to the Minjim River at about 2600 ft. (800 m).

CLIMATE: Station #94014, Madang, Papua New Guinea, Lat. 5.2°S, Long. 145.8°E, at 13 ft. (4 m). Temperatures are calculated for an elevation of 2600 ft. (800 m), resulting in probable extremes of 89°F (32°C) and 53°F (12°C).

N/HEMISPHERE	JAN	FEB	MAR	APR	MAY	JUN	JUL	AUG	SEP	OCT	NOV	DEC
°F AVG MAX	74	74	76	76	76	76	76	76	76	78	78	75
°F AVG MIN	68	69	69	69	68	68	68	68	68	67	68	69
DIURNAL RANGE	6	5	7	7	8	8	8	8	8	11	10	6
RAIN/INCHES	4.0	3.4	3.2	8.5	11.2	11.1	10.1	11.3	9.4	11.3	10.5	6.7
HUMIDITY/%	88	87	86	86	86	86	86	85	85	87	88	89
BLOOM SEASON									*			
DAYS CLR	N/A											
RAIN/MM	102	86	81	216	284	282	257	287	239	287	267	170
°C AVG MAX	23.6	23.6	24.7	24.7	24.7	24.7	24.7	24.7	24.7	25.8	25.8	24.1
°C AVG MIN	20.2	20.8	20.8	20.8	20.2	20.2	20.2	20.2	20.2	19.7	20.2	20.8
DIURNAL RANGE	3.4	2.8	3.9	3.9	4.5	4.5	4.5	4.5	4.5	6.1	5.6	3.3
S/HEMISPHERE	JUL	AUG	SEP	OCT	NOV	DEC	JAN	FEB	MAR	APR	MAY	JUN

Cultural Recommendations

LIGHT: 2500–3000 fc.

TEMPERATURES: Throughout the year, days average 74–78°F (24–26°C), and nights average 67–69°F (20–21°C), with a diurnal range of 5–11°F (3–6°C). The warmest highs, the coolest lows, and the widest diurnal range occur in autumn.

HUMIDITY: 85–90% year-round.

Dendrobium hamaticalcar

WATER: Rainfall is heavy most of the year, but conditions are slightly drier in winter. Cultivated plants should be kept moist with only slight drying allowed between waterings.

FERTILIZER: ¼–½ recommended strength. A balanced fertilizer should be applied weekly to biweekly throughout the year.

REST PERIOD: Growing temperatures should be maintained all year. Water should be reduced somewhat in winter, especially for plants grown in the dark, short-day conditions common in temperate latitudes. However, plants should not be allowed to dry out completely. Fertilizer should be reduced if water is reduced. In the habitat, light is highest in winter.

GROWING MEDIA: Mounting plants on tree-fern or cork slabs accommodates their pendulous growth habit. However, humidity must be high and plants must be watered at least once a day in summer. If plants cannot be mounted, small pots or hanging baskets may be filled with an open, fast-draining medium. Repotting may be done anytime new roots are actively growing.

MISCELLANEOUS NOTES: The bloom season shown in the climate table is based on reports from the habitat. Plants that produce flowers which last a single day commonly bloom several times during the year. Flowering usually occurs 7–14 days after a sudden 10°F (5°C) drop in daytime temperatures.

Plant and Flower Information

PLANT SIZE AND TYPE: A 31–39 in. (80–100 cm) sympodial epiphyte.

PSEUDOBULB: 31–39 in. (80–100 cm) long. The pendulous stems are simple, curved, and leafy.

LEAVES: Many. The leaves are 3.5–4.7 in. (9–12 cm) long, smooth, lanceolate, and pointed.

INFLORESCENCE: Very short.

FLOWERS: 2 per inflorescence. The flowers are 0.4 in. (1 cm) across. Sepals and petals are spreading, incurved, and somewhat thickened at the tip. They are densely covered with brownish red spots. The small yellow lip is covered with hairs, and the sidelobes are marked with red-brown spots. Blossoms last a single day.

REFERENCES: 92, 221, 437, 445.

PHOTOS/DRAWINGS: 437.

Dendrobium hamaticalcar J. J. Wood and Dauncey

ORIGIN/HABITAT: Sabah, Borneo. Plants grow in the lowlands and the foothills of Mt. Trus Madi near Kaingaran at 1300–2950 ft. (400–900 m).

CLIMATE: Station #49613, Tambunan, Sabah, Borneo, Lat. 5.7°N, Long. 116.4°E, at 1200 ft. (366 m). Temperatures are calculated for an elevation of 2500 ft. (760 m), resulting in probable extremes of 94°F (34°C) and 50°F (10°C).

N/HEMISPHERE	JAN	FEB	MAR	APR	MAY	JUN	JUL	AUG	SEP	OCT	NOV	DEC
°F AVG MAX	82	83	85	86	86	85	85	85	85	84	83	82
°F AVG MIN	63	61	62	63	64	63	62	62	63	63	63	64
DIURNAL RANGE	19	22	23	23	22	22	23	23	22	21	20	18
RAIN/INCHES	5.8	3.7	5.8	7.5	8.2	7.3	5.1	4.9	6.4	7.0	6.8	6.0
HUMIDITY/%	N/A											
BLOOM SEASON							*					
DAYS CLR	N/A											
RAIN/MM	147	94	147	191	208	185	130	124	163	178	173	152
°C AVG MAX	27.8	28.3	29.4	30.0	30.0	29.6	29.5	29.4	29.4	28.9	28.3	27.8
°C AVG MIN	17.2	16.0	16.5	17.1	17.6	17.1	16.5	16.5	17.1	17.1	17.1	17.6
DIURNAL RANGE	10.6	12.3	12.9	12.9	12.4	12.5	13.0	12.9	12.3	11.8	11.2	10.2
S/HEMISPHERE	JUL	AUG	SEP	OCT	NOV	DEC	JAN	FEB	MAR	APR	MAY	JUN

Cultural Recommendations

LIGHT: 2000–2500 fc.

TEMPERATURES: Throughout the year, days average 82–86°F (28–30°C), and nights average 61–64°F (16–18°C), with a diurnal range of 18–23°F (10–13°C).

HUMIDITY: Information is not available for this location. However, records from nearby locations indicate that humidity probably averages 80–85% year-round.

WATER: Rainfall is moderate to heavy all year with a brief, slightly drier period in winter. Cultivated plants should be allowed to dry only slightly between waterings.

FERTILIZER: ¼–½ recommended strength. A balanced fertilizer should be applied weekly to biweekly throughout the year.

REST PERIOD: Growing conditions should be maintained all year. Water should be reduced slightly in winter, but the plants should never be allowed to dry out completely. Fertilizer should be reduced anytime plants are not actively growing.

GROWING MEDIA: Plants may be mounted on tree-fern or cork slabs if humidity is high and plants are watered at least once daily in summer. When plants are potted, any open, fast-draining medium may be used. Repotting is best done in early spring when new roots begin to grow.

MISCELLANEOUS NOTES: The bloom season shown in the climate table is based on cultivation records.

Plant and Flower Information

PLANT SIZE AND TYPE: A 24–40 in. (60–102 cm) sympodial epiphyte.

PSEUDOBULB: 24–40 in. (60–102 cm) long. The arching stems are slightly thicker toward the apex. They are covered with violet flushed sheaths. The apical portion of the stem is leafy.

LEAVES: 2.6–4.0 in. (6–10 cm) long. The broad, ovate leaves are pointed at the tip. They have several nerves and a thin texture.

INFLORESCENCE: 0.8–1.8 in. (2–4 cm) long. The pendulous inflorescences emerge from the nodes of leafy and leafless stems.

FLOWERS: 4–9 per inflorescence. The flowers are 1.0–1.4 in. (2.4–3.6 cm) long. They are pale yellow and not shiny, darker on the backside The yellow lip has magenta veins and a yellow callus.

REFERENCES: 592.

PHOTOS/DRAWINGS: 592.

Dendrobium hamatum Rolfe.

A single collection originated in southern Vietnam (Cochinchina); but without additional habitat information, climate data cannot be selected. The plant bloomed in spring after being imported to France. *D. hamatum* is a pendulous, sympodial epiphyte with slender stems 24 in. (60 cm) long. The leaves are oblong to lanceolate, 4 in. (10 cm) long, and pointed at the tip. They are alternate up the stem in 2 rows. The pendulous inflorescences are few-flowered with blossoms 1.2–1.4 in. (3.0–3.5 cm) across. The flowers are whitish yellow with broad stripes of purple dots that more or less merge. The rounded petals are uneven along the margins. The sepals are pointed and smooth along the margin. The fiddle-shaped lip is light yellow with a faint purple stain. It is wavy and uneven along the front margin. REFERENCES: 218, 254, 266, 408, Seidenfaden 1992 *Opera Botanica* #114.

Dendrobium hamiferum Cribb

ORIGIN/HABITAT: Irian Jaya (western New Guinea) and Papua New Guinea. In the Lagaip Valley, Engae Province, Papua New Guinea, plants grow in open mountain forests and in humus collected in rock slides at 3600–5900 ft. (1100–1800 m).

CLIMATE: Station #200243, Mt. Hagen, Papua New Guinea, Lat. 5.8°S, Long. 144.3°E, at 5350 ft. (1630 m). Record extreme temperatures are 88°F (31°C) and 35°F (2°C).

N/HEMISPHERE	JAN	FEB	MAR	APR	MAY	JUN	JUL	AUG	SEP	OCT	NOV	DEC

°F AVG MAX	72	73	74	75	76	76	76	76	75	75	76	74
°F AVG MIN	55	55	55	55	55	56	56	56	56	57	56	54
DIURNAL RANGE	17	18	19	20	21	20	20	20	19	18	20	20
RAIN/INCHES	5.2	6.7	8.7	8.7	8.2	10.2	10.4	10.7	11.2	10.0	7.2	4.7
HUMIDITY/%	84	83	82	78	79	81	81	80	82	81	82	82
BLOOM SEASON	N/A											
DAYS CLR	N/A											
RAIN/MM	131	171	221	221	208	258	264	271	285	253	184	119
°C AVG MAX	22.4	22.7	23.2	23.9	24.3	24.2	24.2	24.4	23.8	23.9	24.3	23.1
°C AVG MIN	12.5	12.7	12.6	12.5	12.7	13.3	13.4	13.3	13.4	13.7	13.4	12.4
DIURNAL RANGE	9.9	10.0	10.6	11.4	11.6	10.9	10.8	11.1	10.4	10.2	10.9	10.7
S/HEMISPHERE	JUL	AUG	SEP	OCT	NOV	DEC	JAN	FEB	MAR	APR	MAY	JUN

Cultural Recommendations

LIGHT: 1800–2500 fc.

TEMPERATURES: Throughout the year, days average 72–76°F (22–24°C), and nights average 54–57°F (12–14°C), with a diurnal range of 17–20°F (10–11°C).

HUMIDITY: Near 80% year-round.

WATER: Rainfall is moderate to heavy all year. Cultivated plants should be kept moist with only slight drying allowed between waterings.

FERTILIZER: ¼–½ recommended strength. A balanced fertilizer should be applied weekly to biweekly throughout the year.

REST PERIOD: Growing temperatures should be maintained all year. Water should be reduced somewhat in winter for plants grown in the dark, short-day conditions common in temperate latitudes. They should never be allowed to dry out completely, however. Fertilizer should be reduced or eliminated when water is reduced.

GROWING MEDIA: Plants may be mounted on tree-fern or cork slabs if humidity is high and plants are watered at least once daily in summer. When plants are potted, any open, fast-draining medium may be used. Repotting may be done anytime new roots are growing.

Plant and Flower Information

PLANT SIZE AND TYPE: A 14–43 in. (35–110 cm) sympodial epiphyte or lithophyte.

PSEUDOBULB: 14–43 in. (35–110 cm) long. The slender, canelike stems are somewhat flattened. They are narrowest at the base. New growths are spaced 0.4–0.8 in. (1–2 cm) on a creeping rhizome.

LEAVES: 6–10. The leaves are 2.4–3.2 in. (6–8 cm) long, narrowly oblong, flat, and suberect. Leaves are held near the apex of each growth.

INFLORESCENCE: 6–7 in. (15–18 cm) long. The laxly flowered inflorescences arise from nodes at or near the apex of the stem. They may be erect or spreading.

FLOWERS: Few per inflorescence. The small flowers are cream with purple on the back side near the tips. The white lip is delicately marked with purple. The sepals are incurved. The petals are twisted up to 3 times.

REFERENCES: 24, 81, 84, 95, 234, 551.

PHOTOS/DRAWINGS: 81, *84, 95*.

Dendrobium hanburyanum Rchb. f. See *D. lituiflorum* Lindley. REFERENCES: 190, 216, 254, 369, 445, 454.

Dendrobium hancockii Rolfe

AKA: *D. odiosum* Finet.

ORIGIN/HABITAT: China. Near Mengtze (Mong-tsè) in Yunnan Province, plants grow on rocks at 6000–7000 ft. (1850–2150 m). They are also found near Kangting in Szechuan Province at about 5250 ft. (1600 m).

CLIMATE: Station #56985, Mengtze, China, Lat. 23.3°N, Long. 103.4°E, at 4262 ft. (1299 m). Temperatures are calculated for an elevation of 6500 ft. (1980 m), resulting in probable extremes of 90°F (32°C) and 21°F (−6°C).

N/HEMISPHERE	JAN	FEB	MAR	APR	MAY	JUN	JUL	AUG	SEP	OCT	NOV	DEC
°F AVG MAX	58	60	70	76	78	75	75	74	74	68	66	60
°F AVG MIN	38	42	48	54	59	60	61	59	56	52	47	40
DIURNAL RANGE	20	18	22	22	19	15	14	15	18	16	19	20
RAIN/INCHES	0.2	1.0	1.2	1.5	5.4	6.9	10.2	9.3	2.9	2.7	2.2	0.5
HUMIDITY/%	68	69	62	61	64	74	78	79	74	74	71	70
BLOOM SEASON	N/A											
DAYS CLR @ 6AM	13	11	13	11	7	2	2	3	5	4	12	14
DAYS CLR @ 12PM	12	10	10	11	3	1	1	1	2	2	7	13
RAIN/MM	5	25	30	38	137	175	259	236	74	69	56	13
°C AVG MAX	14.4	15.6	21.1	24.4	25.6	24.1	23.9	23.3	23.3	20.0	18.9	15.6
°C AVG MIN	3.3	5.3	8.7	12.0	14.8	15.3	15.9	14.8	13.1	10.9	8.1	4.2
DIURNAL RANGE	11.1	10.3	12.4	12.4	10.8	8.8	8.0	8.5	10.2	9.1	10.8	11.4
S/HEMISPHERE	JUL	AUG	SEP	OCT	NOV	DEC	JAN	FEB	MAR	APR	MAY	JUN

Cultural Recommendations

LIGHT: 3500–4000 fc. Dappled light is recommended.

TEMPERATURES: Summer days average 74–75°F (23–24°C), and nights average 59–61°F (15–16°C), with a diurnal range of 14–15°F (8–9°C).

HUMIDITY: 75–80% in summer, dropping to near 60% for 2 months in late winter.

WATER: Rainfall is moderate to heavy through most of the year but is considerably lower in winter. However, additional moisture is provided by dew, fog, and mist during the period of low rainfall. Cultivated plants should be kept moist in late spring and summer, but water should be gradually reduced in autumn after new growths mature.

FERTILIZER: ¼–½ recommended strength, applied weekly. A high-nitrogen fertilizer is beneficial from spring to midsummer, but a fertilizer high in phosphates should be used in late summer and autumn.

REST PERIOD: Winter days average 58–70°F (14–21°C), and nights average 38–48°F (3–9°C), with a diurnal range of 18–22°F (10–12°C). In cultivation, water should be reduced and the plants allowed to dry between waterings. They should not remain dry for extended periods, however. Fertilizer should be reduced or eliminated while water is reduced.

GROWING MEDIA: Plants may be mounted on tree-fern or cork slabs if humidity is high and plants are watered at least once daily in summer. When plants are potted, any open, fast-draining medium may be used. Repotting is best done in early spring when new roots are growing.

MISCELLANEOUS NOTES: Collected plants are dried and used in Chinese medicine.

Plant and Flower Information

PLANT SIZE AND TYPE: A 6–12 in. (15–30 cm) sympodial lithophyte.

PSEUDOBULB: 6–12 in. (15–30 cm) long. The slender stems occasionally branch.

LEAVES: The linear leaves are 2–3 in. (5–8 cm) long. They are unequally 2-toothed at the apex.

INFLORESCENCE: Short. Inflorescences emerge from leaf axils.

FLOWERS: 1–2 per inflorescence. The yellow flowers are 0.8 in. (2 cm) long. The oblong sepals and petals are pointed. The 3-lobed lip is short, broad, wavy, and velvety with rounded sidelobes and a kidney-shaped midlobe. The blossoms are strongly fragrant with a sweet odor reminiscent of honey.

HYBRIDIZING NOTES: Chromosome count is $2n = 40$ (ref. 153).

REFERENCES: 61, 118, 153, 208, 219, 254, 414, 528.

PHOTOS/DRAWINGS: 254.

Dendrobium haniffii Ridley. See *D. tortile* Lindley. REFERENCES: 38, 46, 190, 223, 402, 454, 455.

Dendrobium harrisoniae Hooker. Now considered a synonym of *Bifrenaria harrisoniae* Rchb. f. REFERENCES: 190, 216, 254, 445.

Dendrobium harveyanum Rchb. f.

ORIGIN/HABITAT: Rare in Burma, Thailand, Vietnam, and Yunnan Province in southwest China. Plants grow on the slopes of Doi Suthep in Thailand and near Dalat in Vietnam. Habitat elevation is estimated, so the following climate data should be used with caution.

CLIMATE: Station #48327, Chiang Mai, Thailand, Lat. 18.8°N, Long. 99.0°E, at 1100 ft. (335 m). Temperatures are calculated for an elevation of 2500 ft. (760 m), resulting in probable extremes of 104°F (40°C) and 33°F (1°C).

N/HEMISPHERE	JAN	FEB	MAR	APR	MAY	JUN	JUL	AUG	SEP	OCT	NOV	DEC
°F AVG MAX	80	85	90	91	89	85	84	82	83	84	81	79
°F AVG MIN	51	52	57	65	69	69	69	70	68	66	61	52
DIURNAL RANGE	29	33	33	26	20	16	15	12	15	18	20	27
RAIN/INCHES	0.3	0.4	0.6	2.0	5.5	6.1	7.4	8.7	11.5	4.9	1.5	0.4
HUMIDITY/%	73	65	58	62	73	78	80	83	83	81	79	76
BLOOM SEASON		*	*	**								
DAYS CLR @ 7AM	5	5	2	2	1	0	0	0	0	1	3	3
DAYS CLR @ 1PM	9	8	4	2	0	0	0	0	0	1	3	3
RAIN/MM	8	10	15	51	140	155	188	221	292	124	38	10
°C AVG MAX	26.9	29.7	32.4	33.0	31.9	29.7	29.1	28.0	28.5	29.1	27.4	26.3
°C AVG MIN	10.8	11.3	14.1	18.5	20.8	20.8	20.8	21.3	20.2	19.1	16.3	11.3
DIURNAL RANGE	16.1	18.4	18.3	14.5	11.1	8.9	8.3	6.7	8.3	10.0	11.1	15.0
S/HEMISPHERE	JUL	AUG	SEP	OCT	NOV	DEC	JAN	FEB	MAR	APR	MAY	JUN

Cultural Recommendations

LIGHT: 2500–3500 fc. Bright light and strong air movement should be provided. The heavy summer cloud cover indicates that some shading is needed from spring through autumn, but light should be as high as the plant can tolerate, short of burning the leaves.

TEMPERATURES: Summer days average 82–85°F (28–30°C), and nights average 69–70°F (21°C), with a diurnal range of 12–16°F (7–9°C). Spring, before the start of the summer rainy season, is the warmest time of the year. Days average 89–91°F (32–33°C), and nights average 57–69°F (14–21°C), with a diurnal range of 20–33°F (11–18°C).

HUMIDITY: 78–83% most of the year, dropping to near 60% in late winter and early spring.

WATER: Rainfall is moderate to heavy from late spring through early autumn, but conditions are very dry in winter. Cultivated plants should be kept moist while actively growing, but water should be gradually reduced after new growths mature in autumn.

FERTILIZER: ¼–½ recommended strength, applied weekly. A high-nitrogen fertilizer is beneficial from spring to midsummer, but a fertilizer high in phosphates should be used in late summer and autumn.

REST PERIOD: Winter days average 79–85°F (26–30°C), and nights average 51–52°F (11°C), with a diurnal range of 27–33°F (15–18°C). Growers indicate that plants need a prolonged winter rest. In the habitat, rainfall averages are very low for 4–5 months in winter, but during the early part of the season the high relative humidity indicates that additional moisture is available from frequent fog, mist, and heavy deposits of dew. Growers sometimes recommend eliminating water in winter, but plants are healthiest if for most of the winter they are allowed to become somewhat dry between waterings but do not remain dry for extended periods. For 1–2 months in late winter, however, conditions are clear, warm, and dry, with humidity so low that even the moisture from morning dew is uncommon. Plants should be allowed to dry out completely between waterings and remain dry longer during this time. Occasional early morning mistings between waterings may help keep the plants from becoming too dry. Fertilizer should be greatly reduced or eliminated until water is increased in spring. A cool, dry rest is essential for cultivated plants and should be continued until new growth starts in spring. In the habitat, light is highest in winter.

GROWING MEDIA: Plants may be mounted on cork or tree-fern slabs if humidity is high and water is applied at least once daily in summer. If plants are potted, undersized pots that are barely large enough to hold the roots may be filled with a very open, fast-draining media. Repotting is best done in early spring when new roots begin growing.

MISCELLANEOUS NOTES: The bloom season shown in the climate table is based on cultivation records. Although smaller, the flowers are similar to those of *D. brymerianum* Rchb. f.

Plant and Flower Information

PLANT SIZE AND TYPE: A 6–9 in. (15–23 cm) sympodial epiphyte.

PSEUDOBULB: 6–9 in. (15–23 cm) long. The spindle-shaped pseudobulbs are deeply furrowed. Newer growths are leafy at the apex.

LEAVES: 2–3. The deciduous leaves are 3–4 in. (8–10 cm) long, ovate-oblong, and leathery.

INFLORESCENCE: 6 in. (15 cm) long. The lax inflorescences emerge from the uppermost nodes on older, leafless stems.

FLOWERS: 3–6 per inflorescence. The flowers are 2 in. (5 cm) across. Sepals and petals may be bright chrome to canary yellow or nearly coppery red. The unique petals have long hairs on the margins. The lip is circular and densely fringed. The blossoms have a honey fragrance.

REFERENCES: 157, 179, 190, 202, 216, 254, 371, 430, 445, 448, 454, 541.

PHOTOS/DRAWINGS: *133, 371, 430, 454.*

Dendrobium hasseltii (Blume) Lindley not Rchb. f.

AKA: *Pedilonum hasseltii* Blume, *D. cornutum* Hooker f. J. J. Smith (ref. 469), Holttum (ref. 200), and Comber (ref. 75) consider *D. cornutum* to be a synonym of *D. hasseltii*, but Seidenfaden and Woods (ref. 455) list *D. hasseltii* as a possible synonym of *D. cornutum*.

ORIGIN/HABITAT: Java, Sumatra on Mt. Kerintji, and Peninsular Malaya. Throughout Java, plants are common on ridges in high mountain moss-forests at 4900–9850 ft. (1500–3000 m).

CLIMATE: Station #96755, Bogor, Java, Indonesia, Lat. 6.5°S, Long. 106.8°E, at 558 ft. (170 m). Temperatures are calculated for an elevation of 7000 ft. (2130 m), resulting in probable extremes of 75°F (24°C) and 45°F (7°C).

N/HEMISPHERE	JAN	FEB	MAR	APR	MAY	JUN	JUL	AUG	SEP	OCT	NOV	DEC
°F AVG MAX	65	66	67	67	66	64	63	63	64	65	66	65
°F AVG MIN	52	52	52	53	53	53	53	53	53	54	54	53
DIURNAL RANGE	13	14	15	14	13	11	10	10	11	11	12	12
RAIN/INCHES	2.1	1.0	0.5	5.0	8.1	18.8	23.7	20.2	14.4	12.0	11.9	3.4
HUMIDITY/%	72	68	65	66	74	79	84	84	81	79	77	75
BLOOM SEASON								*	*			
DAYS CLR @ 7AM	14	14	14	11	5	3	1	2	4	6	10	12
DAYS CLR @ 1PM	9	10	8	5	1	0	0	1	1	3	7	
RAIN/MM	53	25	13	127	206	478	602	513	366	305	302	86
°C AVG MAX	18.2	18.7	19.3	19.3	18.7	17.6	17.1	17.1	17.6	18.2	18.7	18.2
°C AVG MIN	11.0	11.0	11.0	11.5	11.5	11.5	11.5	11.5	11.5	12.1	12.1	11.5
DIURNAL RANGE	7.2	7.7	8.3	7.8	7.2	6.1	5.6	5.6	6.1	6.1	6.6	6.7
S/HEMISPHERE	JUL	AUG	SEP	OCT	NOV	DEC	JAN	FEB	MAR	APR	MAY	JUN

Cultural Recommendations

LIGHT: 2500–4000 fc. Diffused or barely dappled light is preferred. Direct sunlight should be avoided.

TEMPERATURES: Throughout the year, days average 63–67°F (17–19°C),

and nights average 52–54°F (11–12°C), with a diurnal range of 10–15°F (6–8°C). The average highs vary only 4°F (2°C), and average lows fluctuate even less, suggesting that plants from this habitat may not tolerate wide temperature fluctuations.

HUMIDITY: 80% in summer, dropping to 65% in late winter and early spring.

WATER: Rainfall is very heavy from spring to autumn, but conditions are dry for 2–3 months in winter. During the growing season, plants should never be allowed to dry out completely, but water should be gradually reduced in late autumn.

FERTILIZER: 1/4–1/2 recommended strength, applied weekly. A high-nitrogen fertilizer is beneficial from spring to midsummer, but a fertilizer high in phosphates should be used in late summer and autumn.

REST PERIOD: Growing conditions should be maintained all year, but rainfall is low for 2–3 winter months. In cultivation, water should be reduced and the plants allowed to become somewhat dry between waterings. They should not remain dry for prolonged periods, however. Fertilizer may be reduced or eliminated anytime the plant is not actively growing. In the habitat, light is highest in winter.

GROWING MEDIA: Mounting plants on tree-fern or cork slabs accommodates their sometimes pendulous growth habit. However, humidity must be high and plants must be watered at least once a day in summer. If plants cannot be mounted, small pots or hanging baskets may be filled with an open, fast-draining medium. Repotting may be done anytime new roots are actively growing.

MISCELLANEOUS NOTES: The bloom season in the climate table is based on cultivation records. In western Java, plants bloom throughout the year; but in eastern Java, which has a longer, more severe dry season, *D. hasseltii* blooms about a month after the rains start.

Plant and Flower Information

PLANT SIZE AND TYPE: An 8–24 in. (20–61 cm) sympodial epiphyte.

PSEUDOBULB: 8–24 in. (20–61 cm) long. The slender, somewhat zigzag stems may vary from 3–32 in. (8–81 cm) in length. The smallest forms are often found at higher elevations. The stems are short and erect when grown in high light, but they are long and pendulous when grown in shade.

LEAVES: Many. The thin, lanceolate leaves are 0.6–2.7 in. (1.5–7.0 cm) long.

INFLORESCENCE: Short. Several racemes arise from nodes on the leafless part of mature stems.

FLOWERS: 2–4 per inflorescence. Flowers are 1 in. (2.5 cm) across. They are normally deep pink to dark purple with an orange blotch on the lip. The lip has 2 notches at the tip.

REFERENCES: 25, 73, 75, 179, 180, 190, 200, 202, 216, 254, 310, 395, 402, 445, 455, 469.

PHOTOS/DRAWINGS: 73, 75, 469.

Dendrobium hasseltii Rchb. f. not (Blume) Lindley.
Listed as a synonym of *Ephemerantha angulata* (Blume) P. F. Hunt and Summerhayes, which is now considered a synonym of *Flickingeria*. REFERENCES: 213, 216, 455, 449, 469.

Dendrobium hastatum Persoon.
Now considered a synonym of *Maxillaria hastata* Ruiz and Pavón. REFERENCES: 216, 254.

Dendrobium hastilabium Kränzlin

ORIGIN/HABITAT: Irian Jaya (western New Guinea). Plants were originally found at Andai, on the north coast of the Vogelkop Peninsula, just south of Manokawri. Habitat elevation is not available, so the following temperatures should be used with caution.

CLIMATE: Station #97530, Manokwari, Irian Jaya, Lat. 0.9°S, Long. 134.1°E, at 10 ft. (3 m). Record extreme temperatures are 93°F (34°C) and 68°F (20°C).

N/HEMISPHERE	JAN	FEB	MAR	APR	MAY	JUN	JUL	AUG	SEP	OCT	NOV	DEC
°F AVG MAX	86	85	87	87	88	86	86	86	86	86	86	85
°F AVG MIN	74	75	74	74	74	75	73	73	74	74	74	74
DIURNAL RANGE	12	10	13	13	14	11	13	13	12	12	12	11
RAIN/INCHES	5.4	5.6	5.0	4.7	4.5	10.3	12.0	9.4	13.2	11.1	7.8	7.3
HUMIDITY/%	87	87	86	84	85	86	86	85	86	86	86	85
BLOOM SEASON	N/A											
DAYS CLR @ 9AM	4	3	3	5	3	3	3	1	1	2	3	7
DAYS CLR @ 3PM	2	2	2	3	1	1	1	1	0	1	0	2
RAIN/MM	137	142	127	119	114	262	305	239	335	282	198	185
°C AVG MAX	30.0	29.4	30.6	30.6	31.1	30.0	30.0	30.0	30.0	30.0	30.0	29.4
°C AVG MIN	23.3	23.9	23.3	23.3	23.3	23.9	22.8	22.8	23.3	23.3	23.3	23.3
DIURNAL RANGE	6.7	5.5	7.3	7.3	7.8	6.1	7.2	7.2	6.7	6.7	6.7	6.1
S/HEMISPHERE	JUL	AUG	SEP	OCT	NOV	DEC	JAN	FEB	MAR	APR	MAY	JUN

Cultural Recommendations

LIGHT: 2000–3000 fc.

TEMPERATURES: Throughout the year, days average 85–88°F (29–31°C), and nights average 73–75°F (23–24°C), with a diurnal range of 10–14°F (6–8°C).

HUMIDITY: Near 85% year-round.

WATER: Rainfall is moderate to very heavy all year. Cultivated plants should be kept moist with only slight drying between waterings.

FERTILIZER: 1/4–1/2 recommended strength. A balanced fertilizer should be applied weekly to biweekly throughout the year.

REST PERIOD: Growing conditions should be maintained year-round. Water and fertilizer may be reduced somewhat in winter, especially for plants cultivated in the dark, short-day conditions common in temperate latitudes, but they should never be allowed to dry out completely.

GROWING MEDIA: Plants may be mounted on tree-fern or cork slabs if humidity is high and plants are watered at least once daily in summer. When plants are potted, any open, fast-draining medium may be used. Repotting may be done anytime new roots are growing.

MISCELLANEOUS NOTES: The bloom season shown in the climate table is based on reports from the habitat.

Plant and Flower Information

PLANT SIZE AND TYPE: A 31 in. (80 cm) sympodial epiphyte.

PSEUDOBULB: 31 in. (80 cm) long. The stems are densely leafy above the leafless base.

LEAVES: Many. The acute, oblong leaves are 2.0–3.0 in. (5.0–7.5 cm) long and somewhat twisted at the apex.

FLOWERS: 1–12 per inflorescence. The flowers are 0.6 in. (1.5 cm) across. The yellow blossoms are marked with purple spots. The lip sidelobes are suffused with violet. Blossoms have a pointed, oblong dorsal sepal and ovate lateral sepals. The tongue-shaped petals are wavy along the margin. The lip has no sidelobes.

REFERENCES: 220, 254.

Dendrobium hawkesii A. H. Heller.
See *D. fimbriatum* Hooker. REFERENCES: 138, 191, 229.

Dendrobium hedyosmum Bateman.
See *D. scabrilingue* Lindley. REFERENCES: 190, 216, 254, 445, 454, 570.

Dendrobium heishanense Hayata.
See *D. moniliforme* (Linn.) Swartz. REFERENCES: 61, 193, 208, 221, 279, 445, 504.

Dendrobium helenae Chadim. See *D. rigidifolium* Rolfe. REFERENCES: 83, 231.

Dendrobium helix Cribb

AKA: Plants are commonly cultivated and have been hybridized as *Dendrobium* 'pomio brown'. Cribb (ref. 80) indicates plants sold as *D. talasea* (a lime-yellow form) have not been described as an independent species and based on herbarium specimens, he is unable to differentiate between them.

ORIGIN/HABITAT: Papua New Guinea, near the coast on eastern and western New Britain Island. Plants grow on exposed branches in forest trees.

CLIMATE: Station #94085, Rabul, New Britain Is., Papua New Guinea, Lat. 4.2°S, Long. 152.2°E, at 28 ft. (9 m). Record extreme temperatures are 100°F (38°C) and 65°F (18°C).

N/HEMISPHERE	JAN	FEB	MAR	APR	MAY	JUN	JUL	AUG	SEP	OCT	NOV	DEC
°F AVG MAX	89	89	91	92	91	90	90	90	90	90	90	90
°F AVG MIN	73	72	73	73	73	73	73	73	73	73	73	73
DIURNAL RANGE	16	17	18	19	18	17	17	17	17	17	17	17
RAIN/INCHES	5.4	3.7	3.5	5.1	7.1	10.1	14.8	10.4	10.2	10.0	5.2	3.3
HUMIDITY/%	74	73	69	70	73	76	77	76	77	77	75	74
BLOOM SEASON					*	*	*					*
DAYS CLR	N/A											
RAIN/MM	137	94	89	130	180	257	376	264	259	254	132	84
°C AVG MAX	31.7	31.7	32.8	33.3	32.8	32.2	32.2	32.2	32.2	32.2	32.2	32.2
°C AVG MIN	22.8	22.2	22.8	22.8	22.8	22.8	22.8	22.8	22.8	22.8	22.8	22.8
DIURNAL RANGE	8.9	9.5	10.0	10.5	10.0	9.4	9.4	9.4	9.4	9.4	9.4	9.4
S/HEMISPHERE	JUL	AUG	SEP	OCT	NOV	DEC	JAN	FEB	MAR	APR	MAY	JUN

Cultural Recommendations

LIGHT: 2500–3000 fc.

TEMPERATURES: Throughout the year, days average 89–92°F (32–33°C), and nights average 72–73°F (22–23°C), with a diurnal range of 16–19°F (9–11°C).

HUMIDITY: Near 75% most of the year. Humidity usually rises to 90–100% at night, but during the dry season, it may drop to as low as 35% in midday.

WATER: Rainfall is heavy most of the year, but conditions are slightly drier for 2 months in late winter. Cultivated plants should be kept moist but not soggy.

FERTILIZER: ¼–½ recommended strength. A balanced fertilizer should be applied weekly to biweekly throughout the year.

REST PERIOD: Growing conditions should be maintained all year. Water and fertilizer should be reduced somewhat in winter. Plants should dry slightly between waterings, but they should never be allowed to dry completely. In the habitat, light may be slightly higher in winter.

GROWING MEDIA: Plants may be mounted on tree-fern or cork slabs if humidity is high and plants are watered at least once daily in summer. When plants are potted, any open, fast-draining medium may be used. Repotting is best done in early spring when new roots are growing.

MISCELLANEOUS NOTES: The bloom season shown in the climate table is based on cultivation reports.

Plant and Flower Information

PLANT SIZE AND TYPE: A 39–79 in. (100–200 cm) sympodial epiphyte.

PSEUDOBULB: 39–79 in. (100–200 cm) long. The canes are clustered, swollen at the base, and taper toward the tip. Stems become yellow-orange when dry.

LEAVES: Many. The elliptic to ovate-elliptic leaves are up to 6 in. (16 cm) long, but they are usually smallest near the apex of the stem.

INFLORESCENCE: 5.5 in. (14 cm) long. One or more inflorescences emerge through the leaf sheaths at the upper leaf nodes. They may be erect, ascending, or horizontal. Inflorescences are laxly flowered.

FLOWERS: 20 per inflorescence. The erect or nodding flowers are 1.6–2.0 in. (4–5 cm) long, which is one of the largest of several closely related species. The attractive blossoms are often rich chocolate-brown but may be yellow or pinkish. They have a maroon or pink center with violet veins on the lip. The dorsal sepal curls in a spiral. Lateral sepals are recurved and inrolled. The erect petals are twisted 2–4 times. The 3-lobed lip is oblong, pointed, and recurved, with 3 low longitudinal ridges on the midlobe. Flower color and the extent of petal twisting are variable characteristics.

HYBRIDIZING NOTES: Chromosome count is 2n = 38 (ref. 152) for both the yellow and brown forms. When used in hybridizing, many clones contribute bright colors to the progeny.

REFERENCES: 80, 84, 152, 179, 233, 243, 347, 430, 526, 551.

PHOTOS/DRAWINGS: *80, 84, 347, 430.*

Dendrobium hellerianum A. Hawkes

AKA: *D. inflatum* Schlechter.

ORIGIN/HABITAT: Java and northern Papua New Guinea. In New Guinea, plants grow on moss-covered mistforest trees in the Dischore Range (Waria District) at about 3950 ft. (1200 m).

CLIMATE: Station #200192, Garaina, Papua New Guinea, Lat. 7.9°S, Long. 147.1°E, at 2350 ft. (716 m). Temperatures are calculated for an elevation of 3950 ft. (1200 m), resulting in probable extremes of 89°F (32°C) and 41°F (5°C).

N/HEMISPHERE	JAN	FEB	MAR	APR	MAY	JUN	JUL	AUG	SEP	OCT	NOV	DEC
°F AVG MAX	75	77	78	79	80	80	80	80	79	79	78	76
°F AVG MIN	58	58	58	59	58	59	60	60	60	59	59	58
DIURNAL RANGE	17	19	20	20	22	21	20	20	19	20	19	18
RAIN/INCHES	5.8	6.5	8.7	11.1	11.8	11.9	8.9	11.7	11.5	9.9	7.7	5.2
HUMIDITY/%	84	82	82	81	80	80	81	81	82	83	84	84
BLOOM SEASON					*							
DAYS CLR	N/A											
RAIN/MM	147	165	221	282	300	302	226	297	292	251	196	132
°C AVG MAX	23.8	24.9	25.4	26.0	26.5	26.5	26.5	26.5	26.0	26.0	25.4	24.3
°C AVG MIN	14.3	14.3	14.3	14.9	14.3	14.9	15.4	15.4	15.4	14.9	14.9	14.3
DIURNAL RANGE	9.5	10.6	11.1	11.1	12.2	11.6	11.1	11.1	10.6	11.1	10.5	10.0
S/HEMISPHERE	JUL	AUG	SEP	OCT	NOV	DEC	JAN	FEB	MAR	APR	MAY	JUN

Cultural Recommendations

LIGHT: 2000–3000 fc.

TEMPERATURES: Throughout the year, days average 75–80°F (24–27°C), and nights average 58–60°F (14–15°C), with a diurnal range of 17–22°F (10–12°C).

HUMIDITY: 80–85% year-round.

WATER: Rainfall is heavy all year, but conditions are slightly drier in winter. Cultivated plants should be kept moist but not soggy.

FERTILIZER: ¼–½ recommended strength. A balanced fertilizer should be applied weekly to biweekly throughout the year.

REST PERIOD: Growing conditions should be maintained all year. In the habitat, rainfall is slightly lower in winter. Water and fertilizer should be reduced somewhat for cultivated plants, especially those grown in the dark, short-day conditions common during temperate-latitude winters. They should never be allowed to dry out completely, however. In the habitat, seasonal light variation is minor.

GROWING MEDIA: Plants may be mounted on tree-fern or cork slabs if humidity is high and plants are watered at least once daily in summer. When plants are potted, any open, fast-draining medium may be used. Repotting may be done anytime new roots are growing.

MISCELLANEOUS NOTES: The bloom season shown in the climate table is based on collection records. Plants that produce flowers which last a single day commonly bloom several times during the year. Flowering usually occurs 7–14 days after a sudden 10°F (5°C) drop in daytime temperatures.

Plant and Flower Information

PLANT SIZE AND TYPE: A 24–31 in. (60–80 cm) sympodial epiphyte.

PSEUDOBULB: 24–31 in. (60–80 cm) long. The flattened stems arise from a very short rhizome.

LEAVES: Many. The oval leaves are 4–5 in. (10–13 cm) long.

INFLORESCENCE: Short.

FLOWERS: 2 per inflorescence. The short-lived flowers are 0.9 in. (2.2 cm) long and do not open fully. Sepals and petals are white with a light pink flush inside. The lip has an orange-red beard at the base. The column is yellow with orange-yellow at the foot. The mentum has small yellow warts on the inside.

REFERENCES: 191, 229, 437.

PHOTOS/DRAWINGS: 437.

Dendrobium hellwigianum Kränzlin

AKA: *D. cyananthum* L. O. Williams, *D. geluanum* Schlechter, *D. rhaphiotes* Schlechter. Plants have been cultivated under the incorrect name *D. coerulescens*.

ORIGIN/HABITAT: Papua New Guinea. Plants are very common and widespread in the uplands of most of the mainland provinces. They usually grow on the horizontal branches of mistforest trees at 4600–8850 ft. (1400–2700 m).

CLIMATE: Station #94010, Goroka, Papua New Guinea, Lat. 6.1°S, Long. 145.4°E, at 5141 ft. (1567 m). Temperatures are calculated for an elevation of 6550 ft. (2000 m), resulting in probable extremes of 82°F (28°C) and 38°F (4°C).

N/HEMISPHERE	JAN	FEB	MAR	APR	MAY	JUN	JUL	AUG	SEP	OCT	NOV	DEC
°F AVG MAX	71	72	73	74	74	73	74	73	73	73	74	72
°F AVG MIN	51	52	52	52	53	54	54	54	55	54	54	52
DIURNAL RANGE	20	20	21	22	21	19	20	19	18	19	20	20
RAIN/INCHES	2.1	2.8	4.6	5.9	6.6	9.3	9.1	10.1	10.7	8.3	4.6	2.0
HUMIDITY/%	70	67	67	67	67	71	72	73	74	71	70	70
BLOOM SEASON										**	**	
DAYS CLR	N/A											
RAIN/MM	53	71	117	150	168	236	231	257	272	211	117	51
°C AVG MAX	21.8	22.4	23.0	23.5	23.5	23.0	23.5	23.0	23.0	23.0	23.5	22.4
°C AVG MIN	10.7	11.3	11.3	11.3	11.8	12.4	12.4	12.4	13.0	12.4	12.4	11.3
DIURNAL RANGE	11.1	11.1	11.7	12.2	11.7	10.6	11.1	10.6	10.0	10.6	11.1	11.1
S/HEMISPHERE	JUL	AUG	SEP	OCT	NOV	DEC	JAN	FEB	MAR	APR	MAY	JUN

Cultural Recommendations

LIGHT: 2000–3000 fc.

TEMPERATURES: Throughout the year, days average 71–74°F (22–24°C), and nights average 51–55°F (11–13°C), with a diurnal range of 18–22°F (10–12°C). Plants are unlikely to tolerate continuous high temperatures, especially warm nights.

HUMIDITY: 70–75% from summer into autumn, dropping to 65–70% in winter and spring.

WATER: Rainfall is moderate to heavy most of the year, but conditions are slightly drier for 3 months in winter. Cultivated plants should be kept moist but not soggy. Occasional early morning mistings may be beneficial, especially on bright, sunny days.

FERTILIZER: ¼–½ recommended strength. A balanced fertilizer should be applied weekly to biweekly throughout the year.

REST PERIOD: Growing temperatures should be maintained all year. In the habitat, rainfall is lowest in winter, but dew and mist from fog and low clouds are common. Water and fertilizer should be reduced somewhat for cultivated plants, especially those grown in the darker, short-day conditions common during temperate-latitude winters. Plants should be kept on the dry side, but they should never be allowed to dry out completely. In the habitat, light is higher in winter.

GROWING MEDIA: Plants may be mounted on tree-fern or cork slabs if humidity is high and plants are watered at least once daily in summer. When plants are potted, any open, fast-draining medium may be used. Repotting may be done anytime new roots are growing.

MISCELLANEOUS NOTES: The primary bloom season shown in the climate table is based on cultivation records. However, plants may bloom any month of the year.

Plant and Flower Information

PLANT SIZE AND TYPE: A 10 in. (25 cm) sympodial plant that is normally epiphytic but occasionally grows terrestrially.

PSEUDOBULB: 0.4–3.2 in. (1–8 cm) long. Pseudobulbs are tufted and sometimes branching.

LEAVES: 1–5 at the apex of each stem. The fleshy, nearly terete leaves are 0.8–6.3 in. (2–16 cm) long. They resemble dwarf garden chives.

INFLORESCENCE: Very short. The apical inflorescences are borne on both leafy and leafless stems. The blossoms are nestled amongst the leaves.

FLOWERS: 1–3 per inflorescence. The flowers, which last for 4–6 months, are large for the plant size and resemble those of *D. violaceum* Kränzlin. They open fully and measure 0.7–1.3 in. (1.7–3.2 cm) long. Several color forms are found, including pink, pinkish purple, greyish blue, and creamy yellow varieties. Plants originally described as *D. cyananthum* have a deep red lip and a purplish pink tube.

HYBRIDIZING NOTES: Chromosome count, 2n = 38 (ref. 152, 243). *D. hellwigianum* and *D. violaceum* Kränzlin are known to hybridize naturally.

REFERENCES: 91, 95, 152, 196, 218, 243, 254, 318, 385, 525, 549, 556, 574.

PHOTOS/DRAWINGS: *91, 318, 385, 549.*

Dendrobium helvolum J. J. Smith

ORIGIN/HABITAT: Endemic to Borneo. Plants were reportedly found in southern Borneo near Kwaru and Hayup growing in mangroves. Because we have been unable to find either of these locations, the following climate data should be used with caution.

CLIMATE: Station #96583, Pontianak, Borneo, Lat. 0.0°N, Long. 109.3°E, at 13 ft. (4 m). Temperatures are calculated for an elevation of 1000 ft. (328 m), resulting in probable extremes of 93°F (34°C) and 65°F (18°C).

N/HEMISPHERE	JAN	FEB	MAR	APR	MAY	JUN	JUL	AUG	SEP	OCT	NOV	DEC
°F AVG MAX	84	86	86	86	87	87	86	87	87	86	85	84
°F AVG MIN	71	73	72	72	72	72	71	71	72	72	72	71
DIURNAL RANGE	13	13	14	14	15	15	15	16	15	14	13	13
RAIN/INCHES	10.8	8.2	9.5	10.9	11.1	8.7	6.5	8.0	9.0	14.4	15.3	12.7
HUMIDITY/%	85	85	84	84	82	81	79	82	83	87	86	87
BLOOM SEASON	*											*
DAYS CLR @ 7AM	1	1	1	3	2	4	5	2	2	1	1	2
DAYS CLR @ 1PM	0	0	1	0	0	0	1	1	1	0	1	0
RAIN/MM	274	208	241	277	282	221	165	203	229	366	389	323
°C AVG MAX	28.7	29.9	29.9	29.9	30.4	30.4	29.9	30.4	30.4	29.9	29.3	28.7
°C AVG MIN	21.5	22.6	22.1	22.1	22.1	22.1	21.5	21.5	22.1	22.1	22.1	21.5
DIURNAL RANGE	7.2	7.3	7.8	7.8	8.3	8.3	8.4	8.9	8.3	7.8	7.2	7.2
S/HEMISPHERE	JUL	AUG	SEP	OCT	NOV	DEC	JAN	FEB	MAR	APR	MAY	JUN

Cultural Recommendations

LIGHT: 2000–3000 fc.

TEMPERATURES: Throughout the year, days average 84–87°F (29–30°C),

and nights average 71–73°F (22–23°C), with a diurnal range of 13–16°F (7–9°C). The probable extreme temperatures are near the averages, indicating that plants probably cannot tolerate wide temperature fluctuations.

HUMIDITY: 80–85% year-round. Air circulation should be excellent.

WATER: Rainfall is heavy all year. Cultivated plants should receive year-round moisture and never be allowed to dry out completely. Constant air movement is highly recommended. Plants from this habitat are often very sensitive to cold water, which may cause bud blast and cellular damage.

FERTILIZER: ¼–½ recommended strength. A balanced fertilizer should be applied weekly to biweekly throughout the year.

REST PERIOD: Growing conditions should be maintained all year. In the habitat, the heaviest rainfall occurs in winter; but water may be reduced somewhat for cultivated plants, especially those grown in the dark, short-day conditions common in temperate latitudes. Fertilizer should be reduced if water is reduced.

GROWING MEDIA: Plants may be mounted on tree-fern or cork slabs if humidity is high and plants are watered at least once daily in summer. When plants are potted, any open, fast-draining medium may be used. They may be repotted anytime new roots are growing.

MISCELLANEOUS NOTES: The bloom season shown in the climate table is based on collection reports.

Plant and Flower Information

PLANT SIZE AND TYPE: A 2.4 in. (6 cm) sympodial epiphyte.

PSEUDOBULB: 2.4 in. (6 cm) long. The stems are clustered.

LEAVES: 7–9 per growth. The linear-lanceolate leaves are 1.3 in. (3.3 cm) long, and laterally compressed. They are arranged in 2 rows.

INFLORESCENCE: Short. Inflorescences emerge from the side and at the apex of the stem.

FLOWERS: The fleshy flowers are 0.3 in. (0.7 cm) long. The erect lip has short, slender protrusions on the midlobe. Flower color was not included in the original description.

REFERENCES: 221, 286, 295, 474.

Dendrobium hemimelanoglossum Guillaumin

ORIGIN/HABITAT: Near Dalat, Vietnam. Habitat elevation is not available, so the following temperatures should be used with caution.

CLIMATE: Station #48881, Dalat, Vietnam, Lat. 11.1°N, Long. 108.1°E, at 3156 ft. (962 m). Record extreme temperatures are 93°F (34°C) and 43°F (6°C).

N/HEMISPHERE	JAN	FEB	MAR	APR	MAY	JUN	JUL	AUG	SEP	OCT	NOV	DEC
°F AVG MAX	80	82	84	85	84	81	81	80	80	80	79	79
°F AVG MIN	56	57	59	62	65	65	65	65	65	63	60	58
DIURNAL RANGE	24	25	25	23	19	16	16	15	15	17	19	21
RAIN/INCHES	0.2	0.9	1.6	4.6	9.1	6.1	7.7	8.2	10.1	9.7	2.7	1.3
HUMIDITY/%	68	64	65	71	78	81	82	83	84	82	76	73
BLOOM SEASON	N/A											
DAYS CLR @ 7AM	13	13	13	9	5	3	2	2	2	5	7	10
DAYS CLR @ 1PM	8	8	8	2	0	0	0	0	0	1	3	4
RAIN/MM	5	23	41	117	231	155	196	208	257	246	69	33
°C AVG MAX	26.7	27.8	28.9	29.4	28.9	27.2	27.2	26.7	26.7	26.7	26.1	26.1
°C AVG MIN	13.3	13.9	15.0	16.7	18.3	18.3	18.3	18.3	18.3	17.2	15.6	14.4
DIURNAL RANGE	13.4	13.9	13.9	12.7	10.6	8.9	8.9	8.4	8.4	9.5	10.5	11.7
S/HEMISPHERE	JUL	AUG	SEP	OCT	NOV	DEC	JAN	FEB	MAR	APR	MAY	JUN

Cultural Recommendations

LIGHT: 2000–2500 fc initially. The deciduous forest and semishade habitats indicate that summer light should be low, but optimal cultivation levels are unknown.

TEMPERATURES: Summer days average 80–81°F (27°C), and nights average 65°F (18°C), with a diurnal range of 15–16°F (8–9°C). Spring is the warmest season. Days average 84–85°F (29°C), and nights average 59–65°F (15–18°C), with a diurnal range of 19–25°F (11–14°C).

HUMIDITY: 80–85% in summer and autumn, dropping to near 65% in midwinter.

WATER: Rainfall is moderate to heavy from late spring into autumn, but conditions are much drier in winter and early spring. Cultivated plants should be kept moist while growing, but water should be gradually reduced in autumn.

FERTILIZER: ¼–½ recommended strength, applied weekly. A high-nitrogen fertilizer is beneficial from spring to midsummer, but a fertilizer high in phosphates should be used in late summer and autumn.

REST PERIOD: Winter days average 79–82°F (26–28°C), and nights average 56–58°F (13–14°C), with a diurnal range of 21–25°F (12–14°C). The increased diurnal range results from warmer days and cooler nights. Rainfall is low for 3–4 months. For 1–2 of these months, conditions are so dry that even moisture from dew is uncommon. For cultivated plants, water and fertilizer should be reduced for 2–3 months. Plants should be allowed to dry out between waterings, but they should not remain dry for extended periods. In the habitat, light is highest in winter.

GROWING MEDIA: Plants may be mounted on tree-fern or cork slabs if humidity is high and plants are watered at least once daily in summer. When plants are potted, any open, fast-draining medium may be used. Repotting is best done in early spring when new roots are growing.

Plant and Flower Information

PLANT SIZE AND TYPE: An 8 in. (20 cm) sympodial epiphyte.

PSEUDOBULB: 8 in. (20 cm) long. Older, leafless stems become wrinkled and grooved with age.

LEAVES: 4–5 per growth. The thin, linear-lanceolate leaves are 2.8 in. (7 cm) long. They are deciduous.

INFLORESCENCE: 8 in. (20 cm) long. The long, hanging racemes emerge at the tips of new, pendent stems.

FLOWERS: The very thin flowers are 0.4 in. (1 cm) long. The dorsal sepal and petals are spreading, with 3–4 violet nerves. Lateral sepals are curved to sickle-shaped. The 3-lobed lip is green with dark violet near the tip. The midlobe is longer than the sepals and petals. It is wavy along the margin with 3 raised keels that are rounded and swollen near the tip. Near the base of the lip, the keels are thin, erect, and irregular. The anther is yellow-green.

REFERENCES: 165, 229, 448, Seidenfaden 1992 *Opera Botanica* #114.

PHOTOS/DRAWINGS: Seidenfaden 1992 *Opera Botanica* #114.

Dendrobium hendersonii A. Hawkes and A. H. Heller

AKA: *D. fugax* Schlechter not Rchb. f., *D. ridleyanum* Kerr, *D. rudolphii* A. Hawkes and A. H. Heller. Seidenfaden and Wood (ref. 455) include only *D. fugax* as a synonym.

ORIGIN/HABITAT: Peninsular Thailand, Malaya, Borneo and Sumatra. In Malaya, plants grow in the states of Tembeling, Terengganu, Pahang, Johore, and Perak. They are found on trees in evergreen forests and usually grow in protected places, often near waterfalls. Habitat elevation was reported as about 650 ft. (200 m).

CLIMATE: Station #48551, Surat (Ban Don), Thailand, Lat. 9.1°N, Long. 99.3°E, at 10 ft. (3 m). Temperatures are calculated for an elevation of 800 ft. (250 m), resulting in probable extremes of 102°F (39°C) and 44°F (7°C).

N/HEMISPHERE	JAN	FEB	MAR	APR	MAY	JUN	JUL	AUG	SEP	OCT	NOV	DEC
°F AVG MAX	85	89	92	92	90	88	87	88	87	86	84	83
°F AVG MIN	66	66	67	70	71	71	71	71	70	70	69	68
DIURNAL RANGE	19	23	25	22	19	17	16	17	17	16	15	15
RAIN/INCHES	1.0	0.3	0.4	2.5	6.6	4.5	6.9	5.8	7.1	8.1	12.1	4.0
HUMIDITY/%	82	78	75	79	83	82	82	82	84	87	87	86
BLOOM SEASON				*								
DAYS CLR @ 7AM	4	3	3	2	1	1	1	1	1	1	1	2
DAYS CLR @ 1PM	2	2	2	1	1	0	0	0	0	0	1	1
RAIN/MM	25	8	10	64	168	114	175	147	180	206	307	102
°C AVG MAX	29.6	31.8	33.5	33.5	32.4	31.3	30.7	31.3	30.7	30.2	29.1	28.5
°C AVG MIN	19.1	19.1	19.6	21.3	21.8	21.8	21.8	21.8	21.3	21.3	20.7	20.2
DIURNAL RANGE	10.5	12.7	13.9	12.2	10.6	9.5	8.9	9.5	9.4	8.9	8.4	8.3
S/HEMISPHERE	JUL	AUG	SEP	OCT	NOV	DEC	JAN	FEB	MAR	APR	MAY	JUN

Cultural Recommendations

LIGHT: 2500–3000 fc.

TEMPERATURES: Throughout the year, days average 83–92°F (29–34°C), and nights average 66–71°F (19–22°C), with a diurnal range of 15–25°F (8–14°C). The warmest season is early spring, before the start of the summer monsoon.

HUMIDITY: 80–85% most of the year, dropping to 75–80% for 3 months in winter.

WATER: Rainfall is moderate to heavy from late spring through autumn. Conditions are drier in winter. Cultivated plants should be kept moist from late spring into autumn, with only slight drying allowed between waterings. Water should be gradually reduced in late autumn.

FERTILIZER: ¼–½ recommended strength, applied weekly. A high-nitrogen fertilizer is beneficial from spring to midsummer, but a fertilizer high in phosphates should be used in late summer and autumn.

REST PERIOD: Growing temperatures should be maintained year-round. Winter rainfall is low for 2–3 months, but additional moisture is available from frequent heavy dew. For cultivated plants, water and fertilizer should be reduced and the plants allowed to dry somewhat between waterings. They should not remain dry for long periods, however. In the habitat, light is slightly higher in winter.

GROWING MEDIA: Plants may be mounted on tree-fern or cork slabs if humidity is high and plants are watered at least once daily in summer. When plants are potted, any open, fast-draining medium may be used. Repotting is best done in early spring when new roots are growing.

MISCELLANEOUS NOTES: The bloom season shown in the climate table is based on collection reports. Plants that produce flowers which last a single day commonly bloom several times during the year. Flowering usually occurs 7–14 days after a sudden 10°F (5°C) drop in daytime temperatures.

Plant and Flower Information

PLANT SIZE AND TYPE: An 8–24 in. (20–60 cm) sympodial epiphyte.

PSEUDOBULB: 8–24 in. (20–60 cm) long. The stems are closely spaced, swollen near the base, flattened, and 4-angled on the pseudobulbous part especially when young.

LEAVES: 8–10 per growth. The lanceolate leaves are 1.6–3.2 in. (4–8 cm) long. When young, the leaves and sheaths are tinged with purple.

INFLORESCENCE: Very short. Inflorescences emerge from nodes on the apical, leafless portion of the pseudobulbs.

FLOWERS: 1–2 per inflorescence. The white flowers are 1 in. (2.5 cm) long and remain rather closed. The blossoms may be flushed and speckled with pink markings. The lip has 2 yellow ridges at the base of the fringed, triangular midlobe. It is striped with rose with a yellow spot at the apex. The extremely fragile blossoms are short-lived.

HYBRIDIZING NOTES: Chromosome count is 2n = 38 (ref. 504, 580). Johansen (ref. 239) indicates that plants are self-sterile and that flowers dropped 5 days after self-pollination. Most cross-pollinated blossoms produced capsules which opened 105 days after pollination. Of these, 77% of the seeds contained visible embryos and 91% germinated.

REFERENCES: 56, 190, 191, 200, 229, 239, 249, 286, 295, 433, 454, 455, 504, 580.

PHOTOS/DRAWINGS: 200, *454, 455*.

Dendrobium henanense J. L. Lu and L. X. Gao

ORIGIN/HABITAT: China. Plants were recently found in the mountains of northwest Henan province. Collections were made near Xixia at 2250 ft. (680 m) and near Lingbao at 4050 ft. (1240 m). The type of habitat was not described.

CLIMATE: Station #57067, Lushi, Henan, China, Lat. 34.0°N, Long. 111.0°E, at 2421 ft. (738 m). Record extreme temperatures are 104°F (40°C) and 1°F (–17°C).

N/HEMISPHERE	JAN	FEB	MAR	APR	MAY	JUN	JUL	AUG	SEP	OCT	NOV	DEC
°F AVG MAX	42	51	59	69	77	88	90	86	78	68	55	46
°F AVG MIN	20	26	36	46	54	64	71	68	57	47	36	25
DIURNAL RANGE	22	25	23	23	23	24	19	18	21	21	19	21
RAIN/INCHES	0.3	0.6	1.0	0.8	2.5	2.5	7.2	7.3	2.3	1.3	1.2	0.7
HUMIDITY/%	57	55	61	62	65	61	72	76	73	70	75	68
BLOOM SEASON			*	*								
DAYS CLR @ 7AM	14	9	9	8	9	10	7	9	11	10	9	13
DAYS CLR @ 1PM	15	10	9	7	7	7	6	8	10	11	10	14
RAIN/MM	8	15	25	20	64	64	183	185	58	33	30	18
°C AVG MAX	5.6	10.6	15.0	20.6	25.0	31.1	32.2	30.0	25.6	20.0	12.8	7.8
°C AVG MIN	-6.7	-3.3	2.2	7.8	12.2	17.8	21.7	20.0	13.9	8.3	2.2	-3.9
DIURNAL RANGE	12.3	13.9	12.8	12.8	12.8	13.3	10.5	10.0	11.7	11.7	10.6	11.7
S/HEMISPHERE	JUL	AUG	SEP	OCT	NOV	DEC	JAN	FEB	MAR	APR	MAY	JUN

Cultural Recommendations

LIGHT: 2500–3500 fc.

TEMPERATURES: Summer days average 86–90°F (30–32°C), and nights average 64–71°F (18–22°C), with a diurnal range of 18–24°F (10–13°C).

HUMIDITY: 70–75% from summer into autumn, dropping to 55–60% from winter through spring.

WATER: Rainfall is light to moderate from late spring to early autumn. This is followed by a 6–7 month dry season in winter and spring. Cultivated plants should be kept moist while actively growing, with only slight drying allowed between waterings. Water should be gradually reduced in autumn.

FERTILIZER: ¼–½ recommended strength. A balanced fertilizer should be applied weekly to biweekly throughout the growing season.

REST PERIOD: Winters are very cold and dry. Winter days average 42–51°F (6–11°C), and nights average 20–26°F (–7 to –3°C), with a diurnal range of 21–25°F (12–14°C). Rainfall is low for 6–7 months, with conditions so dry that even dew is uncommon in the coldest months. Cultivated plants should be allowed to dry out in winter, but they should not remain completely dry for extended periods. We do not know if the below freezing temperatures are merely tolerated, or if they are necessary to induce blooming. A relatively long, cool, dry rest is indicated.

GROWING MEDIA: Plants may be mounted on tree-fern or cork slabs if humidity is high and plants are watered at least once daily in summer. When plants are potted, any open, fast-draining medium may be used. They may be repotted anytime new roots are growing.

MISCELLANEOUS NOTES: The bloom season shown in the climate table is based on records from the habitat.

Plant and Flower Information

PLANT SIZE AND TYPE: A 1.2–3.1 in. (3–8 cm) sympodial epiphyte.

Dendrobium henryi

PSEUDOBULB: 1.2–3.1 in. (3–8 cm) long. The clustered stems are dark yellow when dry.

LEAVES: 2–4 per growth. The oblong-lanceolate leaves are 0.6–1.0 in. (1.4–2.6 cm) long. The leaf bases are persistent.

INFLORESCENCE: 1 in. (2.5 cm) long. Inflorescences are borne near the apex of leafless pseudobulbs.

FLOWERS: 1, rarely 2 per inflorescence. The white flowers, which open fully, are 0.8–1.2 in. (2–3 cm) across. Sepals and petals are more or less oblong. The 3-lobed lip is ovate-triangular with a purple disk and very short hairs along the margin of the midlobe.

REFERENCES: 235, 282.

PHOTOS/DRAWINGS: 282.

Dendrobium henryi Schlechter

AKA: Seidenfaden, in a 1994 personal communication, stated that *D. daoense* (*D. daoensis*) Gagnepain is a synonym of *D. henryi*.

ORIGIN/HABITAT: Northern Vietnam and southwest China. Plants grow near Cha-pa, Vietnam at about 4900 ft. (1500 m), and near Szemao, Yunnan Province, China at about 4000 ft. (1220 m). They also have been found growing as low as 1950 ft. (600 m). In northern Vietnam, *D. daoensis* was originally found on Tam-dao Mountain in the Tonkin region.

CLIMATE: Station #48802, Cha Pa, Vietnam, Lat. 22.3°N, Long. 103.8°E, at 5381 ft. (1640 m). Record extreme temperatures are 91°F (33°C) and 28°F (–2°C).

N/HEMISPHERE	JAN	FEB	MAR	APR	MAY	JUN	JUL	AUG	SEP	OCT	NOV	DEC
°F AVG MAX	52	54	65	70	73	73	74	73	72	66	63	57
°F AVG MIN	41	44	52	56	61	63	64	63	61	56	51	46
DIURNAL RANGE	11	10	13	14	12	10	10	10	11	10	12	11
RAIN/INCHES	1.6	2.8	4.7	7.0	14.6	14.0	18.9	18.9	12.6	7.5	4.7	1.6
HUMIDITY/%	86	92	86	82	85	88	88	89	87	93	90	88
BLOOM SEASON	N/A											
DAYS CLR @ 7AM	7	4	6	5	1	2	1	3	5	5	9	7
DAYS CLR @ 1PM	8	3	9	7	2	1	0	0	1	1	3	7
RAIN/MM	41	71	119	178	371	356	480	480	320	190	119	41
°C AVG MAX	11.1	12.2	18.3	21.1	22.8	22.8	23.3	22.8	22.2	18.9	17.2	13.9
°C AVG MIN	5.0	6.7	11.1	13.3	16.1	17.2	17.8	17.2	16.1	13.3	10.6	7.8
DIURNAL RANGE	6.1	5.5	7.2	7.8	6.7	5.6	5.5	5.6	6.1	5.6	6.6	6.1
S/HEMISPHERE	JUL	AUG	SEP	OCT	NOV	DEC	JAN	FEB	MAR	APR	MAY	JUN

Cultural Recommendations

LIGHT: 2000–3000 fc. Diffused light is suggested.

TEMPERATURES: Summer days average 73–74°F (23°C), and nights average 63–64°F (17–18°C), with a diurnal range of 10°F (6°C).

HUMIDITY: 85–93% year-round.

WATER: Rainfall is heavy from spring into autumn, but conditions are much drier in winter. Cultivated plants should be constantly moist while actively growing, but water should be gradually reduced after new growths mature in autumn.

FERTILIZER: ¼–½ recommended strength, applied weekly. A high-nitrogen fertilizer is beneficial from spring to midsummer, but a fertilizer high in phosphates should be used in late summer and autumn.

REST PERIOD: For 2–3 months in winter, days average 52–57°F (11–14°C), and nights average 41–46°F (5–8°C), with a diurnal range of 10–11°F (6°C). Little change occurs in the diurnal range, as high and low temperatures decline simultaneously. In the habitat, light may be somewhat higher in winter. Although rainfall is low in winter, the unusually high winter humidity indicates that additional moisture is available from frequent early morning dew, fog, and mist. In cultivation, water should be reduced and the plants allowed to dry somewhat between waterings, but they should never be allowed to dry out completely. Fertilizer should be reduced or eliminated when the plants are not actively growing.

GROWING MEDIA: Plants may be mounted on tree-fern or cork slabs if humidity is high and plants are watered at least daily in summer. When plants are potted, any open, fast-draining medium may be used. Repotting is best done in early spring when new roots are growing.

Plant and Flower Information

PLANT SIZE AND TYPE: A 12–32 in. (30–80 cm) sympodial epiphyte or terrestrial.

PSEUDOBULB: 12–32 in. (30–80 cm) long. The cylindrical stems are angled at each node.

LEAVES: Many. The deciduous leaves are 2.4–4.0 in. (6–10 cm) long, oblong to oblong-lanceolate, pointed at the tip, and somewhat distichous. They have a very thin, membrane-like texture.

INFLORESCENCE: 0.8–2.0 in. (2.0–5.0 cm) long. The very slender inflorescences emerge laterally from nodes along leafless stems.

FLOWERS: 1–3 per inflorescence. The yellow blossoms are 2.0–2.4 in. (5–6 cm) across. The lanceolate-oblong sepals and petals are smooth and somewhat pointed. The nearly round lip is concave with a minutely serrated margin. Above the base, it is densely covered with short, stiff hairs. It has a transverse, ornamental thickening near the apex. The blossoms are fragrant.

REFERENCES: 208, 223, 227, 528.

Dendrobium henshalli Rchb. f. See *D. transparens* Wallich.

REFERENCES: 190, 216, 254, 570.

Dendrobium hepaticum J. J. Smith

ORIGIN/HABITAT: Western Borneo. Plants were originally reported from Mt. Kelam in northwestern Kalimantan, but no additional elevation or habitat information is available. Habitat elevation is estimated, so the following climate data should be used with caution. Plants were cultivated in the botanical garden at Bogor, Java.

CLIMATE: Station #96633, Balikpapan, Borneo, Indonesia, Lat. 1.3°S, Long. 116.9°E, at 10 ft. (3 m). Temperatures are calculated for an elevation of 1800 ft. (550 m), resulting in probable extremes of 86°F (30°C) and 54°F (12°C).

N/HEMISPHERE	JAN	FEB	MAR	APR	MAY	JUN	JUL	AUG	SEP	OCT	NOV	DEC
°F AVG MAX	77	78	78	79	79	79	79	80	80	79	79	78
°F AVG MIN	67	68	68	68	67	67	67	67	67	67	68	68
DIURNAL RANGE	10	10	10	11	12	12	12	13	13	12	11	10
RAIN/INCHES	7.1	6.4	5.5	5.2	6.6	8.1	7.9	8.9	9.1	8.2	9.1	7.6
HUMIDITY/%	82	80	77	78	80	79	82	81	81	82	83	82
BLOOM SEASON	N/A											
DAYS CLR @ 8AM	4	2	3	3	3	3	3	4	4	4	2	5
DAYS CLR @ 2PM	6	4	5	3	1	2	1	2	4	3	4	5
RAIN/MM	180	163	140	132	168	206	201	226	231	208	231	193
°C AVG MAX	25.1	25.6	25.6	26.2	26.2	26.2	26.2	26.7	26.7	26.2	26.2	25.6
°C AVG MIN	19.5	20.1	20.1	20.1	19.5	19.5	19.5	19.5	19.5	19.5	20.1	20.1
DIURNAL RANGE	5.6	5.5	5.5	6.1	6.7	6.7	6.7	7.2	7.2	6.7	6.1	5.5
S/HEMISPHERE	JUL	AUG	SEP	OCT	NOV	DEC	JAN	FEB	MAR	APR	MAY	JUN

Cultural Recommendations

LIGHT: 2500–3000 fc.

TEMPERATURES: Throughout the year, days average 77–80°F (25–27°C), and nights average 67–68°F (20°C), with a diurnal range of 10–13°F (6–7°C).

HUMIDITY: Near 80% year-round.

WATER: Rainfall is heavy most of the year, but conditions are slightly drier for 2 months in late winter or early spring. Cultivated plants should be kept moist but not soggy with only slight drying allowed between waterings.

FERTILIZER: ¼–½ recommended strength. A balanced fertilizer should be applied weekly to biweekly throughout the year.

REST PERIOD: Growing temperatures should be maintained year-round. Water should be reduced somewhat in winter, especially for plants cultivated in the dark, short-day conditions common in temperate latitudes. They should never be allowed to dry out completely, however. Fertilizer should be reduced or eliminated if water is reduced. In the habitat, seasonal light variation is minor.

GROWING MEDIA: Plants may be mounted on tree-fern or cork slabs or potted in small pots filled with any open, fast-draining medium. Repotting is best done in spring when new growth starts.

MISCELLANEOUS NOTES: The plant was described in 1917 in *Bul. Jard. Bot. Buit.* 2nd sér. 25:48.

Plant and Flower Information

PLANT SIZE AND TYPE: A 28 in. (70 cm) sympodial epiphyte.

PSEUDOBULB: 28 in. (70 cm) long. The 4-sided stems are rigid and close together.

LEAVES: Many. The oblong to oval leaves, which are 1.2–1.6 in. (3–4 cm) long, are bilobed at the apex. They are fleshy and dark green.

INFLORESCENCE: Short. Numerous inflorescences emerge from nodes along the stem.

FLOWERS: 1 per inflorescence. The flowers are 1 in. (2.5 cm) long and nearly as wide. Sepals and petals have dark and light stripes with white near the center. They are somewhat twisted. The dorsal sepal is oval, petals are oblong, and the fleshy lip is 3-lobed.

REFERENCES: 222, 286, 295.

Dendrobium herbaceum Lindley

AKA: *D. ramosissimum* Wight.

ORIGIN/HABITAT: India, including Western Ghats and the hills of the Bihar region. Plants usually grow at 2300–4250 ft. (700–1300 m).

CLIMATE: Station #43314, Calicut, India, Lat. 11.3°N, Long. 75.8°E, at 17 ft. (5 m). Temperatures are calculated for an elevation of 3300 ft. (1000 m), resulting in probable extremes of 88°F (31°C) and 46°F (8°C).

N/HEMISPHERE	JAN	FEB	MAR	APR	MAY	JUN	JUL	AUG	SEP	OCT	NOV	DEC
°F AVG MAX	77	78	79	80	79	74	71	72	73	75	76	77
°F AVG MIN	60	62	65	67	67	64	63	63	64	64	63	60
DIURNAL RANGE	17	16	14	13	12	10	8	9	9	11	13	17
RAIN/INCHES	0.4	0.2	0.7	3.6	9.3	33.1	32.5	17.2	7.9	10.3	5.5	1.0
HUMIDITY/%	71	73	73	74	82	87	91	91	87	85	77	74
BLOOM SEASON		*	*	*								
DAYS CLR @ 5AM	19	18	21	12	5	4	2	2	4	4	19	20
DAYS CLR @ 11AM	16	18	23	15	5	3	0	1	6	5	12	14
RAIN/MM	10	5	18	91	236	841	826	437	201	262	140	25
°C AVG MAX	25.1	25.7	26.2	26.8	26.2	23.5	21.8	22.4	22.9	24.0	24.6	25.1
°C AVG MIN	15.7	16.8	18.5	19.6	19.6	17.9	17.4	17.4	17.9	17.9	17.4	15.7
DIURNAL RANGE	9.4	8.9	7.7	7.2	6.6	5.6	4.4	5.0	5.0	6.1	7.2	9.4
S/HEMISPHERE	JUL	AUG	SEP	OCT	NOV	DEC	JAN	FEB	MAR	APR	MAY	JUN

Cultural Recommendations

LIGHT: 3000–4000 fc. The heavy summer cloud cover indicates that some shading is needed from spring through autumn, but light should be as high as the plant can tolerate, short of burning the leaves.

TEMPERATURES: Summer days average 71–74°F (22–24°C), and nights average 63–64°F (17–18°C), with a diurnal range of 8–10°F (4–6°C). Spring is the warmest season. Days average 79–80°F (26–27°C), and nights average 65–67°F (19–20°C), with a diurnal range of 12–14°F (7–8°C).

HUMIDITY: 85–90% in summer, dropping to 70–75% in winter.

WATER: Rainfall is extremely heavy in summer, but conditions are much drier for 3–4 months in winter. Cultivated plants should be kept moist while actively growing, but water should be gradually reduced in autumn.

FERTILIZER: ¼–½ recommended strength. A balanced fertilizer should be applied weekly to biweekly throughout the growing season.

REST PERIOD: Winter days average 77–78°F (25–26°C), and nights average 60–62°F (16–17°C), with a diurnal range of 16–17°F (9°C). For cultivated plants, water should be greatly reduced for 3–4 months. Plants should be allowed to dry out between waterings, but they should not remain dry for extended periods. Occasional early morning mistings between waterings may prevent plants from becoming too dry. Fertilizer should be greatly reduced or eliminated until plants begin actively growing. In the habitat, light is highest in winter.

GROWING MEDIA: Plants may be mounted on tree-fern or cork slabs if humidity is high and plants are watered at least once daily in summer. When plants are potted, any open, fast-draining medium may be used. They may be repotted anytime new roots are growing.

MISCELLANEOUS NOTES: The bloom season shown in the climate table is based on reports from the habitat. Cultivated plants may bloom in autumn.

Plant and Flower Information

PLANT SIZE AND TYPE: A 12–35 in. (30–90 cm) sympodial epiphyte.

PSEUDOBULB: 12–35 in. (30–90 cm) long. The clustered growths arise from an indistinct rhizome. The erect stems, which branch and rebranch, are narrowest at the base. The lower part of the stem is dark, smooth, shiny, and leafless. Stems become grooved with age.

LEAVES: 1–3 at the apex of each branch. The linear-lanceolate leaves are about 5 in. (13 cm) long.

INFLORESCENCE: Short. Inflorescences emerge at the apex of each leafy branch.

FLOWERS: 2–5 per inflorescence. The tiny flowers are 0.2–0.3 in. (0.5–0.8 cm) across and do not open fully. Sepals and petals may be greenish white to yellow. The oblong lip has obscure sidelobes. It is contracted near the apex, forming a round to triangular apical lobe.

HYBRIDIZING NOTES: Chromosome count is n = 20 (ref. 542) and 2n = 38 (ref. 151, 154, 542).

REFERENCES: 38, 46, 119, 151, 154, 179, 202, 216, 244, 254, 255, 317, 369, 424, 542.

PHOTOS/DRAWINGS: 244.

Dendrobium hercoglossum Rchb. f.

AKA: *D. poilanei* Guillaumin, *D. vexans* Dammer, *D. wangii* Tso. Seidenfaden (ref. 454) reports that the name *D. linguella* has sometimes been erroneously applied to plants that should have been called *D. hercoglossum*. He believes the 2 species are separate entities. The International Orchid Commission (ref. 236) lists *D. linguella* as a synonym of *D. hercoglossum*, but registers hybrids under both names.

ORIGIN/HABITAT: Sumatra, Malaya, Burma, Thailand, Laos, Vietnam, China, and the Philippines. In China, plants grow in Kwangtung, Hainan and Hong Kong at 1950–4150 ft. (600–1260 m). In Sumatra, Schlechter collected a single plant from a tree near Padang at about 100 ft. (30 m). Plants often grow on trees near streams.

CLIMATE: Station #48881, Dalat, Vietnam, Lat. 11.1°N, Long. 108.1°E, at 3156 ft. (962 m). Record extreme temperatures are 93°F (34°C) and 43°F (6°C).

Dendrobium herpetophytum

N/HEMISPHERE	JAN	FEB	MAR	APR	MAY	JUN	JUL	AUG	SEP	OCT	NOV	DEC
°F AVG MAX	80	82	84	85	84	81	81	80	80	80	79	79
°F AVG MIN	56	57	59	62	65	65	65	65	65	63	60	58
DIURNAL RANGE	24	25	25	23	19	16	16	15	15	17	19	21
RAIN/INCHES	0.2	0.9	1.6	4.6	9.1	6.1	7.7	8.2	10.1	9.7	2.7	1.3
HUMIDITY/%	68	64	65	71	78	81	82	83	84	82	76	73
BLOOM SEASON				*	**	**	**	*		*		*
DAYS CLR @ 7AM	13	13	13	9	5	3	2	2	2	5	7	10
DAYS CLR @ 1PM	8	8	8	2	0	0	0	0	0	1	3	4
RAIN/MM	5	23	41	117	231	155	196	208	257	246	69	33
°C AVG MAX	26.7	27.8	28.9	29.4	28.9	27.2	27.2	26.7	26.7	26.7	26.1	26.1
°C AVG MIN	13.3	13.9	15.0	16.7	18.3	18.3	18.3	18.3	18.3	17.2	15.6	14.4
DIURNAL RANGE	13.4	13.9	13.9	12.7	10.6	8.9	8.9	8.4	8.4	9.5	10.5	11.7
S/HEMISPHERE	JUL	AUG	SEP	OCT	NOV	DEC	JAN	FEB	MAR	APR	MAY	JUN

Cultural Recommendations

LIGHT: 2000–3000 fc.

TEMPERATURES: Summer days average 80–81°F (27°C), and nights average 65°F (18°C), with a diurnal range of 15–16°F (8–9°C). Spring is the warmest season. Days average 84–85°F (29°C), and nights average 59–65°F (15°C to 18°C), with a diurnal range of 19–25°F (11–14°C).

HUMIDITY: 80–85% in summer and autumn, dropping to near 65% in midwinter.

WATER: Rainfall is moderate to heavy from late spring into autumn, but conditions are much drier in winter and early spring. Cultivated plants should be kept moist while growing, but water should be gradually reduced in autumn.

FERTILIZER: ¼–½ recommended strength, applied weekly. A high-nitrogen fertilizer is beneficial from spring to midsummer, but a fertilizer high in phosphates should be used in late summer and autumn.

REST PERIOD: Winter days average 79–82°F (26–28°C), and nights average 56–58°F (13–14°C), with a diurnal range of 21–25°F (12–14°C). The increased diurnal range results from warmer days and cooler nights. Rainfall is low for 3–4 months. For 1–2 of these months, conditions are so dry that even moisture from dew is uncommon. For cultivated plants, water and fertilizer should be reduced for 2–3 months. Plants should be allowed to dry out between waterings, but they should not remain dry for extended periods. In the habitat, light is highest in winter.

GROWING MEDIA: Plants may be mounted on tree-fern or cork slabs if humidity is high and plants are watered at least once daily in summer. When plants are potted, any open, fast-draining medium may be used. Repotting is best done in early spring when new roots are growing.

MISCELLANEOUS NOTES: The bloom season shown in the climate table is based on cultivation records. The extremely wide-ranging and varied habitat suggests that *D. hercoglossum* is probably adaptable to a variety of conditions in cultivation. Collected plants are dried and used in Chinese medicine.

Plant and Flower Information

PLANT SIZE AND TYPE: A 10–18 in. (25–45 cm) sympodial epiphyte.

PSEUDOBULB: 8–14 in. (20–35 cm) long. The stems are slender at the base and somewhat swollen at the apex. They are sometimes pendulous.

LEAVES: 4–6 per growth. The distichous leaves are 2–4 in. (5–10 cm) long. They are narrowly linear, thin, and pointed.

INFLORESCENCE: 1.6 in. (4 cm) long. Inflorescences arise from many apical nodes on the most recently matured growths. They often emerge before the leaves drop.

FLOWERS: 2–8 per inflorescence. The waxy flowers are 1 in. (2.5 cm) across. They are dainty, flat, showy, and well-shaped. Sepals and petals may be rosy pink, bright magenta, or white at the base with light mauve at the apex. The white lip, which is shorter than the sepals, is tinged with green or cream and marked with a bright magenta at the apex. The inner surface of the midlobe is finely pubescent except at the pointed apex. The anther is dark purple.

HYBRIDIZING NOTES: Chromosome counts are 2n = 38 (ref. 152, 153, 243, 547) as *D. wangii* and 2n = 57 (ref. 153) as *D. hercoglossum*.

REFERENCES: 36, 152, 153, 179, 200, 202, 208, 210, 218, 223, 234, 236, 243, 245, 254, 266, 296, 395, 402, 435, 447, 448, 454, 455, 507, 528, 536, 547.

PHOTOS/DRAWINGS: *36*, 210, *245, 454, 455*.

Dendrobium herpetophytum Schlechter

AKA: Spelled *D. herpetophytum* in the original description, but sometimes spelled *D. herpethophytum* in later writings.

ORIGIN/HABITAT: Papua New Guinea. In the Bismarck Mountains, plants grow on moss-covered tree branches in the mistforests at 4900–5900 ft. (1500–1800 m).

CLIMATE: Station #94010, Goroka, Papua New Guinea, Lat. 6.1°S, Long. 145.4°E, at 5141 ft. (1567 m). Record extreme temperatures are 87°F (31°C) and 43°F (6°C).

N/HEMISPHERE	JAN	FEB	MAR	APR	MAY	JUN	JUL	AUG	SEP	OCT	NOV	DEC
°F AVG MAX	76	77	78	79	79	78	78	78	78	78	79	77
°F AVG MIN	56	57	57	57	58	59	59	59	60	59	59	57
DIURNAL RANGE	20	20	21	22	21	19	19	19	18	19	20	20
RAIN/INCHES	2.1	2.8	4.6	5.9	6.6	9.3	9.1	10.1	10.7	8.3	4.6	2.0
HUMIDITY/%	70	67	67	67	67	71	72	73	74	71	70	70
BLOOM SEASON									*			*
DAYS CLR	N/A											
RAIN/MM	54	70	118	151	167	236	230	256	271	211	116	52
°C AVG MAX	24.7	25.1	25.6	26.3	26.2	25.7	25.8	25.6	25.5	25.6	25.9	25.1
°C AVG MIN	13.5	13.8	14.0	14.0	14.2	14.8	15.0	15.2	15.3	15.1	14.7	13.7
DIURNAL RANGE	11.2	11.3	11.6	12.3	12.0	10.9	10.8	10.4	10.2	10.5	11.2	11.4
S/HEMISPHERE	JUL	AUG	SEP	OCT	NOV	DEC	JAN	FEB	MAR	APR	MAY	JUN

Cultural Recommendations

LIGHT: 2000–3000 fc.

TEMPERATURES: Throughout the year, days average 76–79°F (25–26°C), and nights average 56–59°F (14–15°C), with a diurnal range of 18–22°F (10–12°C).

HUMIDITY: Near 70–75% in summer and autumn, dropping to near 65% in winter and spring.

WATER: Rainfall is moderate to heavy most of the year, but conditions are slightly drier for 3 months in winter. Cultivated plants should be kept moist but not soggy. Occasional early morning mistings may be beneficial, especially on bright, sunny days.

FERTILIZER: ¼–½ recommended strength. A balanced fertilizer should be applied weekly to biweekly throughout the year.

REST PERIOD: Growing temperatures should be maintained all year. In the habitat, rainfall is lowest in winter, but dew and mist from fog and low clouds are common. Water and fertilizer should be reduced somewhat for cultivated plants, especially those grown in the darker, short-day conditions common during temperate-latitude winters. Plants should be kept on the dry side, but they should never be allowed to dry out completely. In the habitat, light is higher in winter.

GROWING MEDIA: Mounting plants on tree-fern or cork slabs accommodates their pendent growth habit, but humidity must be high and plants should be watered at least once daily in summer. Plants may be potted in hanging pots or baskets filled with any open, fast-draining medium. Repotting may be done anytime new roots are growing.

MISCELLANEOUS NOTES: The bloom season shown in the climate table is based on reports from the habitat.

Plant and Flower Information

PLANT SIZE AND TYPE: A pendent sympodial epiphyte of unreported size.

PSEUDOBULB: The elongated, many angled stems are pendulous. They branch and rebranch.

LEAVES: The leaves are 0.4 in. (1 cm) long.

INFLORESCENCE: Short. Inflorescences are flattened.

FLOWERS: 1–2 per inflorescence. The very tiny, short-lived flowers are 0.2 in. (0.4 cm) long. The blossoms are white or rose with a rose-red lip. Lateral sepals are joined to form a hood over the lip. The lip is uppermost. The disk has 3 elevated lines.

REFERENCES: 92, 219, 254, 437, 444, 445.

PHOTOS/DRAWINGS: 437.

Dendrobium heterobulbum Schlechter. Transferred to *Ephemerantha heterobulba* (Schlechter) Hunt and Summerhayes which is now considered synonymous with *Flickingeria*. REFERENCES: 213, 220, 230, 436, 449.

Dendrobium heterocarpum Wallich ex Lindley

AKA: *D. atractodes* Ridley, *D. aureum* Lindley, *D. hildebrandii* Kränzlin not Rolfe, *D. minahassae* Kränzlin, *D. rhombeum* Lindley. Seidenfaden and Wood (ref. 455) list only *D. aureum*. The International Orchid Commission (ref. 236) registers hybrids under the name *D. aureum*.

ORIGIN/HABITAT: One of the most widely distributed of all *Dendrobium* species. The habitat includes southwest India and the Himalayan region from northwestern India to southwestern China, including the tropical valleys of Sikkim and Assam and the Patkai and Khasi (Khasia) Hills. Distribution extends across Burma, Thailand, Cambodia, Laos, Vietnam, and into the Philippines, where plants grow on Luzon at 4250–4900 ft. (1300–1500 m). To the south, the habitat continues through Malaya, Sumatra, Java, and northern Sulawesi (Celebes), as well as Sri Lanka and the Sunda Islands. In Thailand, plants grow at 1970–5580 ft. (600–1700 m). In India, they are found as low as 350 ft. (100 m) in cooler regions, but in warmer areas they may grow as high as 4250 ft. (1300 m). Plants usually grow on trees in forest clearings.

CLIMATE: Station #48300, Mae Hong Son, Thailand, Lat. 19.3°N, Long. 97.9°E, at 711 ft. (217 m). Temperatures are calculated for an elevation of 4000 ft. (1220 m), resulting in probable extremes of 97°F (36°C) and 32°F (0°C).

N/HEMISPHERE	JAN	FEB	MAR	APR	MAY	JUN	JUL	AUG	SEP	OCT	NOV	DEC
°F AVG MAX	75	79	86	87	84	78	76	76	77	79	77	74
°F AVG MIN	46	46	51	61	65	64	63	63	63	61	57	48
DIURNAL RANGE	29	33	35	26	19	14	13	13	14	18	20	26
RAIN/INCHES	0.4	0.2	0.3	1.7	6.1	7.1	9.6	9.9	8.1	3.9	1.2	0.4
HUMIDITY/%	67	60	50	50	68	81	82	83	83	82	75	71
BLOOM SEASON	**	**	**	*	*			*	*	*		*
DAYS CLR @ 7AM	2	8	10	9	3	0	0	0	0	1	1	2
DAYS CLR @ 1PM	20	20	20	13	3	0	0	0	0	3	13	17
RAIN/MM	10	5	8	43	155	180	244	251	206	99	30	10
°C AVG MAX	24.0	26.2	30.1	30.6	29.0	25.6	24.5	24.5	25.1	26.2	25.1	23.4
°C AVG MIN	7.9	7.9	10.6	16.2	18.4	17.9	17.3	17.3	17.3	16.2	14.0	9.0
DIURNAL RANGE	16.1	18.3	19.5	14.4	10.6	7.7	7.2	7.2	7.8	10.0	11.1	14.4
S/HEMISPHERE	JUL	AUG	SEP	OCT	NOV	DEC	JAN	FEB	MAR	APR	MAY	JUN

Cultural Recommendations

LIGHT: 3000–4000 fc. The heavy summer cloud cover indicates that light is naturally filtered from spring through autumn, but it should be as high as the plant can tolerate, short of burning the leaves.

TEMPERATURES: Summer days average 76–78°F (25–26°C), and nights average 63–64°F (17–18°C), with a diurnal range of 13–14°F (7–8°C). The warmest season is spring. Days average 84–87°F (29–31°C), and nights average 51–65°F (11–18°C), with a diurnal range of 19–35°F (11–20°C).

HUMIDITY: 80–85% from summer into autumn, decreasing to 60–70% in winter. For 2 months in spring, however, conditions are very dry and averages drop to near 50%.

WATER: Rainfall is very heavy during the growing season, but winters are very dry. Cultivated plants should be kept moist while actively growing, but water should be gradually reduced after new growths mature in autumn.

FERTILIZER: ¼–½ recommended strength, applied weekly. A high-nitrogen fertilizer is beneficial from spring to midsummer, but a fertilizer high in phosphates should be used in late summer and autumn.

REST PERIOD: Winter days average 74–86°F (23–30°C), and nights average 46–51°F (8–11°C), with a diurnal range of 26–35°F (14–20°C). In the habitat, rainfall is low for 4–5 months in winter. For 2–3 of these months, high humidity and nightly cooling result in frequent, heavy deposits of dew, with even more moisture available from fog and mist. Therefore, the driest season is only 1–2 months long. For cultivated plants, water should be reduced from late autumn to early spring. During most of the winter, plants should be allowed to dry out between waterings, but they should not remain completely dry for extended periods. Occasional early morning mistings between waterings may help prevent the plants from becoming too dry. For 1–2 months in late winter, however, water should be limited to occasional early morning mistings. Fertilizer should be reduced or eliminated, until new growth starts in spring. In the habitat, the large number of clear, winter afternoons indicates very bright conditions.

GROWING MEDIA: Plants are frequently pendent, so they are more easily managed when mounted on tree-fern or cork slabs or grown in small hanging pots or baskets. When plants are potted, any open, fast-draining medium may be used. Repotting is best done in early spring when new roots are growing. Blooms may be produced on 3-year-old canes, so they should not be removed when repotting.

MISCELLANEOUS NOTES: The bloom season shown in the climate table is based on cultivation records. Cultivated plants are free-flowering and may bloom anytime of year except early summer. In the Sulawesi habitat, plants bloom in late fall and early winter. Reports from other areas indicate that plants also bloom in spring. In most regions, *D. heterocarpum* is one of the first *Dendrobium* to bloom in spring. It normally blooms when the light is very high before the host trees leaf-out. It is an adaptable and popularly grown plant.

Growers in the Philippines indicate that plants gathered from higher elevations do not survive cultivation in the warm lowlands around Manila.

Plant and Flower Information

PLANT SIZE AND TYPE: A 6–60 in. (15–150 cm) sympodial epiphyte. Cultivated plants are frequently about 12 in. (30 cm) tall, but plants originating from the Philippines may be larger.

PSEUDOBULB: 6–60 in. (15–150 cm) long. The yellow stems are erect or pendulous, depending on length. They are thickened near the tip. The stems become ridged or ribbed except for the lowest 2 nodes.

LEAVES: Many. The leathery leaves are 4–5 in. (10–13 cm) long. They are oblong- to linear-lanceolate. Leaves are usually deciduous at the end of the rainy season.

INFLORESCENCE: Short. The lateral inflorescences emerge from nodes on 1-, 2-, or 3-year-old, leafless stems.

FLOWERS: 2–6 per inflorescence, often with hundreds per plant. Flowers are 1.4–3.0 in. (3.5–8.0 cm) across. The sepals are slender, but the lip and petals are much broader. The beautiful blossoms may be white, pale yellow, or amber. The narrow, wavy lip, which is pointed at the tip, is obscurely 3-lobed. It is golden brown on the inside with red- or brown-veins. The disk is velvety and becomes deep golden yellow with age. Blossoms last several weeks. The sweet fragrance reminds some growers of violets or primroses, but others describe the odor as fetid.

Comber (ref. 75) indicates that flowers vary considerably and are quite distinct in different habitats. Borneo plants have smaller flowers than plants from many other areas. Lindley felt that the plants included under this species name should be separated into several separate species, and some botanists still support this view.

HYBRIDIZING NOTES: Chromosome counts are n = 20 (ref. 150, 542), 2n = 36 (ref. 150, 187), and 2n = 38 (ref. 151, 152, 154, 187, 188, 243, 280, 504, 580) all as *D. heterocarpum*. When used as a parent, the yellow flowers with markings resembling a veined eye tend to be dominant. Johansen (ref. 239) found that seed capsules matured in 441 days and that 94% of the seed had visible embryos and 97% of the seed germinated.

REFERENCES: 6, 12, 25, 36, 38, 46, 75, 97, 98, 102, 119, 150, 151, 152, 154, 179, 187, 188, 190, 196, 200, 202, 210, 216, 218, 239, 243, 245, 254, 266, 277, 280, 293, 296, 326, 367, 369, 373, 376, 389, 402, 430, 436, 445, 447, 448, 454, 455, 458, 461, 469, 504, 511, 524, 528, 536, 542, 557, 568, 569, 577, 580.

PHOTOS/DRAWINGS: 6, 12, *36*, 46, *75*, 97, 98, 102, 157, 190, 210, *245*, 367, *389, 430, 454, 455*, 458, 469, 511, *569*.

Dendrobium heterocaulon Guillaumin. See *D. exile* Schlechter. REFERENCES: 230, 448, 454.

Dendrobium heterochromum (Schlechter) J. J. Smith

AKA: *Cadetia heterochroma* Schlechter. *Cadetia* is now considered a valid genus by some botanists, so this plant may again be a *Cadetia*.

ORIGIN/HABITAT: Papua New Guinea. In the Eitape District, plants grow on forest trees along the Garup River at about 150 ft. (50 m).

CLIMATE: Station #94004, Wewak, Papua New Guinea, Lat. 3.6°S, Long. 143.7°E, at 16 ft. (5 m). Record extreme temperatures are 98°F (37°C) and 62°F (17°C).

N/HEMISPHERE	JAN	FEB	MAR	APR	MAY	JUN	JUL	AUG	SEP	OCT	NOV	DEC
°F AVG MAX	88	88	88	88	88	88	87	86	87	88	88	88
°F AVG MIN	74	74	74	75	75	75	75	75	74	74	75	74
DIURNAL RANGE	14	14	14	13	13	13	12	11	13	14	13	14
RAIN/INCHES	7.6	4.8	5.3	10.0	13.3	14.5	12.1	11.9	14.9	16.9	15.1	10.8
HUMIDITY/%	80	79	79	78	79	81	82	82	81	82	81	80
BLOOM SEASON			*									
DAYS CLR	N/A											
RAIN/MM	193	122	135	254	338	368	307	302	378	429	384	274
°C AVG MAX	31.1	31.1	31.1	31.1	31.1	31.1	30.6	30.0	30.6	31.1	31.1	31.1
°C AVG MIN	23.3	23.3	23.3	23.9	23.9	23.9	23.9	23.9	23.3	23.3	23.9	23.3
DIURNAL RANGE	7.8	7.8	7.8	7.2	7.2	7.2	6.7	6.1	7.3	7.8	7.2	7.8
S/HEMISPHERE	JUL	AUG	SEP	OCT	NOV	DEC	JAN	FEB	MAR	APR	MAY	JUN

Cultural Recommendations

LIGHT: 2500–3500 fc.

TEMPERATURES: Throughout the year, days average 86–88°F (30–31°C), and nights average 74–75°F (23–24°C), with a diurnal range of 11–14°F (6–8°C).

HUMIDITY: Near 80% year-round.

WATER: Rainfall is heavy all year, but conditions are slightly drier for 1–2 months in winter. Cultivated plants should be kept moist but not soggy.

FERTILIZER: ¼–½ recommended strength. A balanced fertilizer should be applied weekly to biweekly year-round.

REST PERIOD: Growing temperatures should be maintained year-round. Water should be reduced somewhat for plants cultivated in the dark, short-day conditions common during temperate-latitude winters, but the plants should never be allowed to dry out completely. Fertilizer should also be reduced if water is reduced.

GROWING MEDIA: Baskets or small pots may be filled with any open, fast-draining medium. Repotting may be done anytime new roots are growing.

MISCELLANEOUS NOTES: The bloom season shown in the climate table is based on collection reports.

Plant and Flower Information

PLANT SIZE AND TYPE: A 4–6 in. (10–15 cm) sympodial epiphyte.

PSEUDOBULB: 2–3 in. (5–8 cm) long. The erect, flattened stems are connected by a very short rhizome.

LEAVES: 1 per growth. The broadly oblong leaves are 2–3 in. (5–8 cm) long, flexible, and smooth.

INFLORESCENCE: Inflorescences are borne at the apex of the stem.

FLOWERS: The flowers are 0.2 in. (0.5 cm) long. Sepals and petals are dark red with yellow at the tips of the sepals. The lip is white.

REFERENCES: 221, 437, 472.

Dendrobium heteroglossum Schlechter

ORIGIN/HABITAT: Northeastern Papua New Guinea. In the Waria District, plants grow on forest trees in the Maboro Mountains at about 3950 ft. (1200 m).

CLIMATE: Station #200192, Garaina, Papua New Guinea, Lat. 7.9°S, Long. 147.1°E, at 2350 ft. (716 m). Temperatures are calculated for an elevation of 3950 ft. (1200 m), resulting in probable extremes of 89°F (32°C) and 41°F (5°C).

N/HEMISPHERE	JAN	FEB	MAR	APR	MAY	JUN	JUL	AUG	SEP	OCT	NOV	DEC
°F AVG MAX	75	77	78	79	80	80	80	80	79	79	78	76
°F AVG MIN	58	58	58	59	58	59	60	60	60	59	59	58
DIURNAL RANGE	17	19	20	20	22	21	20	20	19	20	19	18
RAIN/INCHES	5.8	6.5	8.7	11.1	11.8	11.9	8.9	11.7	11.5	9.9	7.7	5.2
HUMIDITY/%	84	82	82	81	80	80	81	81	82	83	84	84
BLOOM SEASON					*							*
DAYS CLR	N/A											
RAIN/MM	147	165	221	282	300	302	226	297	292	251	196	132
°C AVG MAX	23.8	24.9	25.4	26.0	26.5	26.5	26.5	26.5	26.0	26.0	25.4	24.3
°C AVG MIN	14.3	14.3	14.3	14.9	14.3	14.9	15.4	15.4	15.4	14.9	14.9	14.3
DIURNAL RANGE	9.5	10.6	11.1	11.1	12.2	11.6	11.1	11.1	10.6	11.1	10.5	10.0
S/HEMISPHERE	JUL	AUG	SEP	OCT	NOV	DEC	JAN	FEB	MAR	APR	MAY	JUN

Cultural Recommendations

LIGHT: 2000–3000 fc.

TEMPERATURES: Throughout the year, days average 75–80°F (24–27°C), and nights average 58–60°F (14–15°C), with a diurnal range of 17–22°F (10–12°C).

HUMIDITY: 80–85% year-round.

WATER: Rainfall is heavy year-round, but conditions are slightly drier in winter. Cultivated plants should be kept moist but not soggy.

FERTILIZER: ¼–½ recommended strength. A balanced fertilizer should be applied weekly to biweekly throughout the year. The Royal Botanic Garden in Edinburgh uses a seaweed-based fertilizer for high-elevation plants from New Guinea.

REST PERIOD: Growing conditions vary only slightly all year. In the habitat, rainfall is slightly lower in winter. Water should be reduced for plants cultivated in the dark, short-day conditions common during temperate-latitude winters, but they should not be allowed to dry out completely. Fertilizer should be reduced or eliminated anytime water is reduced. In the habitat, light is slightly higher in winter.

GROWING MEDIA: Plants may be mounted on tree-fern or cork slabs if

humidity is high and plants are watered at least once daily in summer. When plants are potted, any open, fast-draining medium may be used. Repotting may be done anytime new roots are growing.

MISCELLANEOUS NOTES: The bloom season shown in the climate table is based on collection records. Sparse cultivation records indicate autumn blooming. Plants that produce flowers which last a single day commonly bloom several times during the year. Flowering usually occurs 7–14 days after a sudden 10°F (5°C) drop in daytime temperatures.

Plant and Flower Information

PLANT SIZE AND TYPE: A 20–24 in. (50–60 cm) sympodial epiphyte.

PSEUDOBULB: 16–20 in. (40–50 cm) long.

LEAVES: Many. The smooth, elliptic leaves are 4–5 in. (10–13 cm) long.

INFLORESCENCE: Short.

FLOWERS: 2 per inflorescence. The flowers are 1 in. (2.5 cm) across. Sepals and petals are dark purple and nearly erect. The lip is pale yellow with dark purple markings on the sidelobes. It is hairy at the recurved tip. The strongly fragrant blossoms last a single day.

REFERENCES: 179, 221, 437, 445.

PHOTOS/DRAWINGS: 437.

Dendrobium heteroideum Blume. Now considered a synonym of *Cadetia heteroidea* (Blume) Schlechter. REFERENCES: 216, 221, 254, 310, 437, 470.

Dendrobium heterostigma Rchb. f. See *D. secundum* (Blume) Lindley. REFERENCES: 216, 254, 454, 469.

Dendrobium hexadesmia Rchb. f. The origin was not known when the species was described and has not been reported since. The rod-like pseudobulbs were described as similar to *Hexadesmiae crurigerae*. The small, greenish yellow flowers had an arched, oblong dorsal sepal, and ovate, pointed lateral sepals, with a linear, tongue-shaped lip. The lip was dilated at the front, slightly bilobed, and marked with yellow at the tip. REFERENCES: 216, 254.

Dendrobium heyneanum Lindley

ORIGIN/HABITAT: The Western Ghats region of southwest India. Plants grow at 4800–5300 ft. (1460–1620 m).

CLIMATE: Station #43314, Calicut, India, Lat. 11.3°N, Long. 75.8°E, at 17 ft. (5 m). Temperatures are calculated for an elevation of 5000 ft. (1520 m), resulting in probable extremes of 83°F (28°C) and 41°F (5°C).

N/HEMISPHERE	JAN	FEB	MAR	APR	MAY	JUN	JUL	AUG	SEP	OCT	NOV	DEC
°F AVG MAX	72	73	74	75	74	69	66	67	68	70	71	72
°F AVG MIN	55	57	60	62	62	59	58	58	59	59	58	55
DIURNAL RANGE	17	16	14	13	12	10	8	9	9	11	13	17
RAIN/INCHES	0.4	0.2	0.7	3.6	9.3	33.1	32.5	17.2	7.9	10.3	5.5	1.0
HUMIDITY/%	71	73	73	74	82	87	91	91	87	85	77	74
BLOOM SEASON				*	*		*	*				
DAYS CLR @ 5AM	19	18	21	12	5	4	2	2	4	4	19	20
DAYS CLR @ 11AM	16	18	23	15	5	3	0	1	6	5	12	14
RAIN/MM	10	5	18	91	236	841	826	437	201	262	140	25
°C AVG MAX	22.0	22.5	23.1	23.6	23.1	20.3	18.6	19.2	19.8	20.9	21.4	22.0
°C AVG MIN	12.5	13.6	15.3	16.4	16.4	14.8	14.2	14.2	14.8	14.8	14.2	12.5
DIURNAL RANGE	9.5	8.9	7.8	7.2	6.7	5.5	4.4	5.0	5.0	6.1	7.2	9.5
S/HEMISPHERE	JUL	AUG	SEP	OCT	NOV	DEC	JAN	FEB	MAR	APR	MAY	JUN

Cultural Recommendations

LIGHT: 3000–4000 fc. The heavy summer cloud cover indicates that some shading is needed for cultivated plants from spring through autumn, but light should be as high as the plant can tolerate, short of burning the leaves.

TEMPERATURES: Summer days average 66–69°F (19–20°C), and nights average 58–59°F (14–15°C), with a diurnal range of 8–10°F (4–6°C). Spring is the warmest season. Days average 74–75°F (23–24°C), and nights average 60–62°F (15–16°C), with a diurnal range of 12–14°F (7–8°C).

HUMIDITY: 85–90% in summer and early autumn, dropping to 70–75% in winter.

WATER: Rainfall is heavy to extremely heavy most of the year, but conditions are very dry for 3–4 months in winter. Cultivated plants should be watered liberally in summer, as often several times a week during bright, hot weather. Water should be gradually reduced through autumn, greatly reduced in winter, then gradually increased in spring when new growth starts.

FERTILIZER: ¼–½ recommended strength, applied weekly. A high-nitrogen fertilizer is beneficial from spring to midsummer, but a fertilizer high in phosphates should be used in late summer and autumn.

REST PERIOD: Winter days average 72–73°F (22–23°C), and nights average 55–57°F (13–14°C), with a diurnal range of 16–17°F (9–10°C). Rainfall is low for 3–4 months, but some additional moisture from dew and mist remains available. For cultivated plants, water should be greatly reduced for 3–4 months. Plants should be allowed to dry out between waterings, but they should not remain completely dry for extended periods. Occasional early morning mistings between waterings may be beneficial, especially on warm, sunny days. Fertilizer should be greatly reduced or eliminated until water is increased in spring. In the habitat, light is highest in winter.

GROWING MEDIA: Growers recommend mounting plants on tree-fern slabs if humidity is high and if they can be watered at least once daily in summer. If plants are potted, any open, fast-draining medium may be used. Repotting is best done in late spring when new roots begin to grow.

MISCELLANEOUS NOTES: The bloom season shown in the climate table is based on cultivation records. Plants may bloom at various times of year. In the wild, the primary bloom season varies depending on conditions in the habitat.

Plant and Flower Information

PLANT SIZE AND TYPE: A 7–12 in. (18–30 cm) sympodial epiphyte.

PSEUDOBULB: 4–8 in. (10–20 cm) long. The tufted stems are erect, flexuous, and consist of several nodes. Growths are connected by a short rhizome.

LEAVES: 3–6 per growth. The leaves are 3–4 in. (8–10 cm) long, linear-lanceolate, and pointed. The leaves are deciduous, but the leaf sheaths persist for a longer period.

INFLORESCENCE: 2–4 in. (5–10 cm) long. Inflorescences are semierect and very slender. They are usually longer than the leaves so that flowers are held at or above the leaf tips. Inflorescences may arise at the apex or from nodes on along the side of leafy stems.

FLOWERS: 5–9 per inflorescence. The white flowers are 0.6 in. (1.5 cm) across. Sepals and petals are ovate-lanceolate. The distinctly 3-lobed lip, which is greenish yellow streaked with pink or violet, is ruffled along the margin of the rounded midlobe. The disk is warty. Blossoms are odorless and last 10–14 days.

REFERENCES: 38, 46, 119, 179, 202, 216, 244, 254, 255, 277, 317, 369, 445, 541, 570.

PHOTOS/DRAWINGS: 244.

Dendrobium hildebrandii Kränzlin not Rolfe. Sometimes spelled *D. hildebrandi,* see *D. heterocarpum* Lindley. REFERENCES: 75, 296, 436, 536.

Dendrobium hildebrandii Rolfe not Kränzlin. See *D. signatum* Rchb. f. REFERENCES: 153, 157, 187, 190, 210, 218, 254, 359, 389, 408, 445, 447, 448, 454, 505, 568. PHOTOS/DRAWINGS: 210, *389*.

Dendrobium hillii Hooker not F. Mueller. See *D. tarberi* M. Clements and D. Jones and discussion at *D. speciosum* J. E. Smith. REFERENCES: 67, 105, 190, 216, 254, 445, 533.

Dendrobium hillii F. Mueller not Hooker. Now considered a synonym of *Sarcochilus hillii*. REFERENCES: 67, 105, 173, 190, 216, 254.

Dendrobium hippocrepiferum Schlechter

ORIGIN/HABITAT: Papua New Guinea. Plants grow on moss-covered trees in the mistforests of the Bismarck Range at about 8200 ft. (2500 m).

CLIMATE: Station #200243, Mt. Hagen, Papua New Guinea, Lat. 5.8°S, Long. 144.3°E, at 5350 ft. (1630 m). Temperatures are calculated for an elevation of 8200 ft. (2500 m), resulting in probable extremes of 79°F (26°C) and 26°F (−4°C).

N/HEMISPHERE	JAN	FEB	MAR	APR	MAY	JUN	JUL	AUG	SEP	OCT	NOV	DEC
°F AVG MAX	63	64	65	66	67	67	67	67	66	66	67	65
°F AVG MIN	46	46	46	46	46	47	47	47	47	48	47	45
DIURNAL RANGE	17	18	19	20	21	20	20	20	19	18	20	20
RAIN/INCHES	5.2	6.7	8.7	8.7	8.2	10.2	10.4	10.7	11.2	10.0	7.2	4.7
HUMIDITY/%	84	83	82	78	79	81	81	80	82	81	82	82
BLOOM SEASON					*							
DAYS CLR	N/A											
RAIN/MM	132	170	221	221	208	259	264	272	284	254	183	119
°C AVG MAX	17.0	17.6	18.1	18.7	19.2	19.2	19.2	19.2	18.7	18.7	19.2	18.1
°C AVG MIN	7.6	7.6	7.6	7.6	7.6	8.1	8.1	8.1	8.1	8.8	8.7	8.1
DIURNAL RANGE	9.4	10.0	10.5	11.1	11.6	11.1	11.1	11.1	10.6	10.0	11.1	11.1
S/HEMISPHERE	JUL	AUG	SEP	OCT	NOV	DEC	JAN	FEB	MAR	APR	MAY	JUN

Cultural Recommendations

LIGHT: 1800–2500 fc.

TEMPERATURES: Throughout the year, days average 63–67°F (17–19°C), and nights average 45–48°F (7–9°C), with a diurnal range of 17–21°F (9–12°C).

HUMIDITY: Near 80% year-round.

WATER: Rainfall is moderate to heavy all year with a 1–2 month slightly drier period in winter. Cultivated plants should never be allowed to dry out completely.

FERTILIZER: ¼–½ recommended strength. A balanced fertilizer should be applied weekly to biweekly throughout the year.

REST PERIOD: Growing conditions should be maintained year-round. Water may be reduced somewhat in winter, especially for plants cultivated in the dark, short-day conditions common in temperate latitudes. Fertilizer should be reduced or eliminated anytime water is reduced. In the habitat, light is higher in winter.

GROWING MEDIA: Plants may be mounted on tree-fern or cork slabs if humidity is high and plants are watered at least once daily in summer. When plants are potted, any open, fast-draining medium may be used. Repotting may be done anytime new roots are growing.

MISCELLANEOUS NOTES: The bloom season shown in the climate table is based on reports from the habitat. Plants that produce flowers which are very short-lived often bloom several times a year. Blooming usually occurs 7–14 days after a sudden 10°F (5°C) drop in daytime temperatures.

Plant and Flower Information

PLANT SIZE AND TYPE: A 20 in. (50 cm) sympodial epiphyte.

PSEUDOBULB: 20 in. (50 cm) long. The nearly erect stems may produce aerial roots. Stems are densely leafy.

LEAVES: Many. The erect, lanceolate leaves are 0.7–1.2 in. (1.7–3.0 cm) long.

INFLORESCENCE: Short. Inflorescences arise from the side of the stem.

FLOWERS: 1 per inflorescence. The tiny, inverted flowers are 0.3 in. (0.7 cm) across. The lateral sepals join to form a hood over the lip. All segments are white, but the lip is marked with red.

REFERENCES: 221, 437, 445.

PHOTOS/DRAWINGS: 437.

Dendrobium hirsutum Griffith. See *D. longicornu* Lindley. REFERENCES: 190, 216, 254, 369.

Dendrobium hirtulum Rolfe

ORIGIN/HABITAT: Burma? Habitat information was not available when *D. hirtulum* was described and has not been reported since. The plant was imported with a shipment of *D. infundibulum* Lindley, so the climate for that species is included as a possible starting point. However, the following information on conditions should be used with extreme caution.

CLIMATE: Station #48327, Chiang Mai, Thailand, Lat. 18.8°N, Long. 99.0°E, at 1100 ft. (335 m). Temperatures are calculated for an elevation of 5600 ft. (1710 m), resulting in probable extremes of 94°F (35°C) and 23°F (−5°C).

N/HEMISPHERE	JAN	FEB	MAR	APR	MAY	JUN	JUL	AUG	SEP	OCT	NOV	DEC
°F AVG MAX	70	75	80	81	79	75	74	72	73	74	71	69
°F AVG MIN	41	42	47	55	59	59	59	60	58	56	51	42
DIURNAL RANGE	29	33	33	26	20	16	15	12	15	18	20	27
RAIN/INCHES	0.3	0.4	0.6	2.0	5.5	6.1	7.4	8.7	11.5	4.9	1.5	0.4
HUMIDITY/%	73	65	58	62	73	78	80	83	83	81	79	76
BLOOM SEASON			*									
DAYS CLR @ 7AM	5	5	2	2	1	0	0	0	0	1	3	3
DAYS CLR @ 1PM	9	8	4	2	0	0	0	0	0	0	1	3
RAIN/MM	8	10	15	51	140	155	188	221	292	124	38	10
°C AVG MAX	21.2	24.0	26.8	27.3	26.2	24.0	23.4	22.3	22.9	23.4	21.8	20.6
°C AVG MIN	5.1	5.6	8.4	12.9	15.1	15.1	15.1	15.6	14.5	13.4	10.6	5.6
DIURNAL RANGE	16.1	18.4	18.4	14.4	11.1	8.9	8.3	6.7	8.4	10.0	11.2	15.0
S/HEMISPHERE	JUL	AUG	SEP	OCT	NOV	DEC	JAN	FEB	MAR	APR	MAY	JUN

Cultural Recommendations

LIGHT: 1800–3000 fc. Diffused light is suggested.

TEMPERATURES: Summer days average 72–75°F (22–24°C), and nights average 59–60°F (15–16°C), with a diurnal range of 12–16°F (7–9°C). The warmest temperatures and widest diurnal range occur in spring. Days average 79–81°F (26–27°C), and nights average 47–59°F (8–15°C), with a diurnal range of 20–33°F (11–18°C).

HUMIDITY: 75–80% in summer, dropping to near 60% for 2 months in winter.

WATER: Rainfall is moderate to heavy in summer. Conditions become quite dry in winter. Cultivated plants should be kept moist while actively growing, but water should be gradually reduced after new growths mature in autumn.

FERTILIZER: ¼–½ recommended strength, applied weekly. A high-nitrogen fertilizer is beneficial from spring to midsummer, but a fertilizer high in phosphates should be used in late summer and autumn.

REST PERIOD: Winter days average 69–75°F (21–24°C), and nights average 41–42°F (5–6°C), with a diurnal range of 27–33°F (15–18°C). Plants should be able to tolerate temperatures a few degrees below freezing for short periods, but extremes should be avoided in cultivation. During very cold weather, a plant's chance of surviving with minimal damage is better if it is dry when temperatures are low. In the habitat, rainfall averages are very low for 4–5 months in winter, but during the early part of the season the high relative humidity indicates that additional moisture is available from frequent fog, mist, and heavy deposits of dew. Growers sometimes recommend eliminating water in winter, but plants are healthiest if for most of the winter they are allowed to become somewhat dry between waterings but do not remain dry for extended periods. For 1–2 months in late winter, however, conditions are clear, warm, and dry with humidity so low that even the moisture from morning dew is uncommon. Plants should be allowed to dry out completely between waterings and remain dry longer during this time. Occasional early morning mistings between waterings may help keep the plants from becoming too dry. Fertilizer should be greatly reduced or eliminated until water is increased in spring. A cool, dry rest is essential for cultivated plants and should be continued until new growth starts in spring. In the habitat, light is highest in winter.

GROWING MEDIA: Plants may be mounted on tree-fern or cork slabs if humidity is high and plants are watered at least once daily in summer. When plants are potted, any open, fast-draining medium may be used. Repotting is best done in early spring when new roots are growing.

MISCELLANEOUS NOTES: The bloom season shown in the climate table is based on bloom reports for a plant imported to England.

Plant and Flower Information

PLANT SIZE AND TYPE: A 9–13 in. (23–33 cm) sympodial epiphyte.

PSEUDOBULB: 9–13 in. (23–33 cm) long. The stem is somewhat thickened.

LEAVES: The leaves are 1.5–2.5 in. (3.8–6.4 cm) long.

INFLORESCENCE: Short. Inflorescences emerge from between the leaves along the side of the stem.

FLOWERS: 2–4 per inflorescence. The flowers are 0.5 in. (1.2 cm) across. They are bright yellow with red–brown streaks on the sides of the lip. Lateral sepals are somewhat sickle-shaped, the dorsal sepal is linear-oblong, and petals are ovate-oblong. The disk is covered with long straight hairs. Blossoms are borne on a bright yellow flower stalk.

REFERENCES: 254, 411.

Dendrobium hispidum F. Mueller.
Now considered a synonym of *Cadetia maideniana* (Schlechter) Schlechter. *D. hispidum* var. *taylori* (F. Mueller) Bailey is now considered a synonym of *Cadetia taylori* (F. Mueller) Schlechter. REFERENCES: 67, 105.

Dendrobium hispidum A. Richard.
Now considered a synonym of *Cadetia hispida* (A. Richard) Schlechter. REFERENCES: 216, 221, 254, 271, 317, 437, 466, 516.

Dendrobium histrionicum Schlechter.
See *D. brymerianum* Rchb. f. REFERENCES: 190, 221, 442.

Dendrobium hodgkinsonii Rolfe

AKA: Some botanists speculate that this may be a natural hybrid between *D. spectabile* (Blume) Miquel and *D. atroviolaceum* Rolfe, but this has not been confirmed.

ORIGIN/HABITAT: Eastern Papua New Guinea. Cribb (ref. 83) indicated that the plants have not been rediscovered since their original collection when a few plants were imported in a consignment of *D. spectabile*. Nothing else is known of its habitat, so the following temperatures, based on those required for *D. spectabile*, should be used with caution.

CLIMATE: Station #200187, Erap, Papua New Guinea, Lat. 6.6°S, Long. 146.7°E, at 850 ft. (260 m). Temperatures are calculated for an elevation of 1950 ft. (600 m), resulting in probable extremes of 98°F (37°C) and 49°F (10°C).

N/HEMISPHERE	JAN	FEB	MAR	APR	MAY	JUN	JUL	AUG	SEP	OCT	NOV	DEC
°F AVG MAX	84	84	85	86	89	89	89	89	89	88	86	86
°F AVG MIN	65	65	65	66	68	69	68	68	69	67	70	66
DIURNAL RANGE	19	19	20	20	21	20	21	21	20	21	16	20
RAIN/INCHES	3.9	3.9	2.7	3.0	3.0	5.3	5.9	5.9	7.0	3.4	2.4	3.1
HUMIDITY/%	82	81	81	79	75	74	74	74	77	76	80	80
BLOOM SEASON		*	*									*
DAYS CLR	N/A											
RAIN/MM	99	99	69	76	76	135	150	150	178	86	61	79
°C AVG MAX	29.1	29.1	29.6	30.2	31.8	31.8	31.8	31.8	31.8	31.3	30.2	30.2
°C AVG MIN	18.5	18.5	18.5	19.1	20.2	20.7	20.2	20.2	20.7	19.6	21.3	19.1
DIURNAL RANGE	10.6	10.6	11.1	11.1	11.6	11.1	11.6	11.6	11.1	11.7	8.9	11.1
S/HEMISPHERE	JUL	AUG	SEP	OCT	NOV	DEC	JAN	FEB	MAR	APR	MAY	JUN

Cultural Recommendations

LIGHT: 1800–3000 fc. Growers report that these plants often tolerate full sun, providing it is introduced gradually. Strong air movement should be provided all year.

TEMPERATURES: Throughout the year, days average 84–89°F (29–32°C), and nights average 65–70°F (19–21°C), with a diurnal range of 16–21°F (9–12°C).

HUMIDITY: Near 75–80% year-round. The habitat may be quite dry for a few hours during hot afternoons, however.

WATER: Rainfall is moderate most of the year, but conditions are a little drier from late autumn to spring. However, the high relative humidity and the large diurnal temperature range indicate additional water is available from frequent heavy deposits of dew. Cultivated plants should be allowed to dry slightly between waterings, but they should not remain dry for extended periods.

FERTILIZER: ¼–½ recommended strength. A balanced fertilizer should be applied weekly to biweekly throughout the year.

REST PERIOD: Growing temperatures should be maintained all year. Water should be reduced somewhat for cultivated plants, especially those grown in the dark, short-day conditions common in temperate-latitude winters, but they should not be allowed to dry out completely. Fertilizer should be reduced in winter.

GROWING MEDIA: Plants may be mounted on tree-fern or cork slabs if humidity is high and plants are watered at least once daily in summer. If plants are potted, any open, fast-draining medium may be used. Repotting is best done in early spring soon after flowering when new roots are growing.

MISCELLANEOUS NOTES: The bloom season shown in the climate table is based on cultivation records for specimens at the Royal Botanic Gardens, Kew.

Plant and Flower Information

PLANT SIZE AND TYPE: A 7–19 in. (18–48 cm) sympodial epiphyte.

PSEUDOBULB: 3.5–12.0 in. (9–31 cm) long. The yellow stems have 4–5 nodes below the leaves. The apex of each growth is leafy.

LEAVES: 2–3 per growth. The bright green leaves are 4–7 in. (10–18 cm) long. They are elliptic to ovate and nearly erect.

INFLORESCENCE: 6–8 in. (15–20 cm) long. Inflorescences emerge from nodes at or near the apex of the stem. The flowers nod on the stem.

FLOWERS: 2–7, normally 5 per inflorescence. The flowers are 1.6–2.0 in. (4–5 cm) across. The slender sepals may be yellowish or pale green. The white petals are wavy at the margin. The yellow lip is marked with radiating purple veins.

REFERENCES: 36, 83, 179, 210, 220, 254, 445.

PHOTOS/DRAWINGS: 210.

Dendrobium hollandianum J. J. Smith

ORIGIN/HABITAT: Irian Jaya (western New Guinea) on Humboldt Bay near Hollandia. Plants are found on forest trees that grow on rocky slopes near the sea, usually below 50 ft. (10 m).

CLIMATE: Station #97690, Sentani/Jayapura, Irian Jaya, Lat. 2.7°S, Long. 140.5°E, at 289 ft. (88 m). Record extreme temperatures are 97°F (36°C) and 68°F (20°C).

N/HEMISPHERE	JAN	FEB	MAR	APR	MAY	JUN	JUL	AUG	SEP	OCT	NOV	DEC
°F AVG MAX	87	89	89	90	90	89	89	88	89	90	90	89
°F AVG MIN	72	72	72	73	73	73	73	73	73	74	73	73
DIURNAL RANGE	15	17	17	17	17	16	16	15	16	16	17	16
RAIN/INCHES	4.1	3.9	5.3	2.9	6.7	7.0	8.3	8.3	8.5	4.6	2.4	5.2
HUMIDITY/%	81	80	80	79	81	81	79	80	80	80	81	80
BLOOM SEASON									*			
DAYS CLR @ 9AM	5	3	4	3	2	1	1	0	1	2	2	5
DAYS CLR @ 3PM	4	3	3	3	2	1	3	0	1	2	2	3
RAIN/MM	104	99	135	74	170	178	211	211	216	117	61	132
°C AVG MAX	30.6	31.7	31.7	32.2	32.2	31.7	31.7	31.1	31.7	32.2	32.2	31.7
°C AVG MIN	22.2	22.2	22.2	22.8	22.8	22.8	22.8	22.8	22.8	23.3	22.8	22.8
DIURNAL RANGE	8.4	9.5	9.5	9.4	9.4	8.9	8.9	8.3	8.9	8.9	9.4	8.9
S/HEMISPHERE	JUL	AUG	SEP	OCT	NOV	DEC	JAN	FEB	MAR	APR	MAY	JUN

Cultural Recommendations

LIGHT: 3000–4000 fc.

TEMPERATURES: Throughout the year, days average 87–90°F (31–32°C), and nights average 72–74°F (22–23°C), with a diurnal range of 15–17°F (8–10°C).

HUMIDITY: Near 80% year-round.

WATER: Rainfall is heavy all year, with brief, semidry periods in spring and autumn. Cultivated plants should be kept moist but not soggy with only slight drying allowed between waterings.

FERTILIZER: ¼–½ recommended strength. A balanced fertilizer should be applied weekly to biweekly throughout the year.

REST PERIOD: Growing temperatures should be maintained year-round. Water and fertilizer should be reduced somewhat in winter, especially for plants cultivated in the dark, short-day conditions common in temperate latitudes. They should never be allowed to dry out completely, however. In the habitat, light is higher in winter.

GROWING MEDIA: Plants may be mounted on tree-fern or cork slabs if humidity is high and plants are watered at least once daily in summer. When plants are potted, any open, fast-draining medium may be used. Repotting may be done anytime new roots are growing.

MISCELLANEOUS NOTES: The bloom season shown in the climate table is based on reports from the habitat.

Plant and Flower Information

PLANT SIZE AND TYPE: A 39 in. (100 cm) sympodial epiphyte.

PSEUDOBULB: 39 in. (100 cm) long.

LEAVES: Many. The linear-lanceolate leaves are 3.5–4.0 in. (9–10 cm) long with 2 unequal teeth at the apex.

INFLORESCENCE: Inflorescences emerge laterally from flat sheaths.

FLOWERS: 2 per inflorescence. The fleshy flowers are about 0.6 in. (1.5 cm) long. They are yellowish white to creamy yellow. The dorsal sepal is oblong, lateral sepals are obliquely triangular, and the petals are somewhat sickle-shaped. The extremely recurved lip has small lateral lobes and a V-shaped yellow spot at the base. The column foot is marked with blue-violet. The anther is pale yellow. Blossoms are sweetly fragrant.

REFERENCES: 221, 470, 476.

Dendrobium hollrungii Kränzlin

AKA: Schlechter (ref. 437) includes *D. kaernbachii* Kränzlin, *D. pachyceras* F. Mueller, and *D. smilliae* Kränzlin not F. Mueller as synonyms. J. J. Smith (ref. 470) specifically disagreed, listing the same species as synonyms of *D. smilliae* F. Mueller. However, we found no recent use of J. J. Smith's synonymy. *D. hollrungii* Kränzlin var. *australiense* Rendle is considered a synonym of *D. smilliae* F. Mueller.

ORIGIN/HABITAT: Northern Papua New Guinea. Plants grow on tall trees in the coastal forests near Madang and Paub. They are found near sea level, often exposed to glaring sun and hot temperatures.

CLIMATE: Station #94004, Wewak, Papua New Guinea, Lat. 3.6°S, Long. 143.7°E, at 16 ft. (5 m). Record extreme temperatures are 98°F (37°C) and 62°F (17°C).

N/HEMISPHERE	JAN	FEB	MAR	APR	MAY	JUN	JUL	AUG	SEP	OCT	NOV	DEC
°F AVG MAX	88	88	88	88	88	88	87	86	87	88	88	88
°F AVG MIN	74	74	74	75	75	75	75	74	75	74	75	74
DIURNAL RANGE	14	14	14	13	13	13	12	11	13	14	13	14
RAIN/INCHES	7.6	4.8	5.3	10.0	13.3	14.5	12.1	11.9	14.9	16.9	15.1	10.8
HUMIDITY/%	80	79	79	78	79	81	82	82	81	82	81	80
BLOOM SEASON		*										
DAYS CLR	N/A											
RAIN/MM	193	122	135	254	338	368	307	302	378	429	384	274
°C AVG MAX	31.1	31.1	31.1	31.1	31.1	31.1	30.6	30.0	30.6	31.1	31.1	31.1
°C AVG MIN	23.3	23.3	23.3	23.9	23.9	23.9	23.9	23.9	23.9	23.3	23.9	23.3
DIURNAL RANGE	7.8	7.8	7.8	7.2	7.2	7.2	6.7	6.1	7.3	7.8	7.2	7.8
S/HEMISPHERE	JUL	AUG	SEP	OCT	NOV	DEC	JAN	FEB	MAR	APR	MAY	JUN

Cultural Recommendations

LIGHT: 3000–4500 fc.

TEMPERATURES: Throughout the year, days average 86–88°F (30–31°C), and nights average 74–75°F (23–24°C), with a diurnal range of 11–14°F (6–8°C).

HUMIDITY: Near 80% year-round.

WATER: Rainfall is heavy all year, but conditions are slightly drier for 1–2 months in winter. Cultivated plants should dry slightly between waterings.

FERTILIZER: ¼–½ recommended strength. A balanced fertilizer should be applied weekly to biweekly throughout the year.

REST PERIOD: Growing conditions should be maintained year-round, but water should be reduced somewhat if plants are grown in the dark, short-day conditions common during temperate-latitude winters. Plants should never be allowed to dry out completely, however. Fertilizer should be reduced until plants begin actively growing and water is increased in spring.

GROWING MEDIA: A very open and fast-draining medium should be used with either baskets or small pots. Repotting may be done anytime new roots are growing.

MISCELLANEOUS NOTES: The bloom season shown in the climate table is based on reports from the habitat.

Plant and Flower Information

PLANT SIZE AND TYPE: A 30 in. (75 cm) sympodial epiphyte.

PSEUDOBULB: 24 in. (60 cm) long. The many-angled stems are yellow. Stems are leafy.

LEAVES: Many. The ovate-lanceolate leaves are 6 in. (15 cm) long.

INFLORESCENCE: Up to 3 inflorescences are borne on the upper portion of older, leafless stems. Inflorescences are densely flowered.

FLOWERS: Many. The flowers are 0.8 in. (2 cm) long. They may be sulfur yellow to yellowish white with a reddish tinge. The apex of the lip is dark green.

REFERENCES: 67, 105, 218, 254, 421, 437, 445, 470, 533.

PHOTOS/DRAWINGS: 437.

Dendrobium holochilum Schlechter

ORIGIN/HABITAT: Northeastern Papua New Guinea. The plant was collected from a forest tree in the Maboro Range at about 3300 ft. (1000 m).

CLIMATE: Station #200192, Garaina, Papua New Guinea, Lat. 7.9°S, Long. 147.1°E, at 2350 ft. (716 m). Temperatures are calculated for an elevation of 3300 ft. (1000 m), resulting in probable extremes of 91°F (33°C) and 43°F (6°C).

N/HEMISPHERE	JAN	FEB	MAR	APR	MAY	JUN	JUL	AUG	SEP	OCT	NOV	DEC
°F AVG MAX	77	79	80	81	82	82	82	82	81	81	80	78
°F AVG MIN	60	60	60	61	60	61	62	62	62	61	61	60
DIURNAL RANGE	17	19	20	20	22	21	20	20	19	20	19	18
RAIN/INCHES	5.8	6.5	8.7	11.1	11.8	11.9	8.9	11.7	11.5	9.9	7.7	5.2
HUMIDITY/%	84	82	82	81	80	80	81	81	82	83	84	84
BLOOM SEASON											*	
DAYS CLR	N/A											
RAIN/MM	147	165	221	282	300	302	226	297	292	251	196	132
°C AVG MAX	25.0	26.1	26.6	27.2	27.7	27.7	27.7	27.7	27.2	27.2	26.6	25.5
°C AVG MIN	15.5	15.5	15.5	16.1	15.5	16.1	16.6	16.6	16.6	16.1	16.1	15.5
DIURNAL RANGE	9.5	10.6	11.1	11.1	12.2	11.6	11.1	11.1	10.6	11.1	10.5	10.0
S/HEMISPHERE	JUL	AUG	SEP	OCT	NOV	DEC	JAN	FEB	MAR	APR	MAY	JUN

Cultural Recommendations

LIGHT: 2000–3000 fc.

TEMPERATURES: Throughout the year, days average 77–82°F (25–28°C), and nights average 60–62°F (16–17°C), with a diurnal range of 17–22°F (10–12°C). Average highs vary only 5°F (3°C), and average lows fluctuate only 2°F (1°C).

HUMIDITY: 80–85% year-round.

WATER: Rainfall is heavy all year. Conditions are slightly drier in winter. Cultivated plants should be kept moist but not soggy.

FERTILIZER: ¼–½ recommended strength. A balanced fertilizer should be applied weekly to biweekly throughout the year.

REST PERIOD: Growing conditions should be maintained all year. In the habitat, rainfall is slightly lower in winter. Water and fertilizer should be reduced somewhat for cultivated plants, especially those grown in the dark, short-day conditions common during temperate-latitude winters. They should never be allowed to dry out completely, however. In the habitat, seasonal light variation is minor.

GROWING MEDIA: Plants may be mounted on tree-fern or cork slabs if humidity is high and plants are watered at least once daily in summer. When plants are potted, any open, fast-draining medium may be used. Repotting may be done anytime new roots are growing.

MISCELLANEOUS NOTES: The bloom season shown in the climate table is based on reports from the habitat. Plants that produce flowers which last a single day commonly bloom several times each year. Flowering usually occurs 7–14 days after a sudden 10°F (5°C) drop in daytime temperatures.

Plant and Flower Information

PLANT SIZE AND TYPE: An 8–12 in. (20–30 cm) sympodial epiphyte.

PSEUDOBULB: 8–12 in. (20–30 cm) long. The densely leafy stems may be erect or suberect.

LEAVES: Many. The leaves are 0.8–1.4 in. (2.0–3.6 cm) long, erect-spreading, and lanceolate.

INFLORESCENCE: Very short.

FLOWERS: 2 per inflorescence. The short, blunt flowers are 0.6 in. (1.5 cm) across. The whitish sepals and petals project forward. The yellow lip has sulfur yellow at the tip. It is fringed, hairy, and recurved. Blossoms last a single day.

REFERENCES: 221, 437, 445.

PHOTOS/DRAWINGS: 437.

Dendrobium holttumianum A. Hawkes and A. H. Heller.
See *D. cinnabarinum* Rchb. f. REFERENCES: 191, 211, 229.

Dendrobium homochromum J. J. Smith.
Although not correctly transferred, Schlechter (ref. 443) considered this plant to be a synonym of *Cadetia homochroma* (J. J. Smith) Schlechter. REFERENCES: 221, 223, 443, 445, 470, 475, 486.

Dendrobium homoglossum Schlechter.
Now considered a synonym of *Flickingeria homoglossa* (Schlechter) A. Hawkes. REFERENCES: 221, 229, 230, 231, 437, 445.

Dendrobium homonymum Steudel.
Listed as a synonym of *Ephemerantha angulata* (Blume) P. F. Hunt and Summerhayes, which is now considered synonymous with *Flickingeria*. REFERENCES: 213, 216, 254, 469.

Dendrobium hookerianum Lindley

AKA: Sometimes spelled *D. hookeranum*. *D. chrysotis* Rchb. f. is a synonym. Kränzlin (ref. 254) considered *D. brachystachyum* Rchb. f. a variety of *D. hookerianum*.

ORIGIN/HABITAT: Central Nepal, northeastern India, and Yunnan Province, China. In China, plants grow on lava rocks west of Tengyueh at 4000 ft. (1220 m). In the Sikkim and Assam regions of India, plants grow on trees in warm valleys at 3300–6550 ft. (1000–2000 m).

CLIMATE: Station #42398, Baghdogra, India, Lat. 26.7°N, Long. 88.3°E, at 412 ft. (126 m). Temperatures are calculated for an elevation of 5000 ft. (1520 m), resulting in probable extremes of 89°F (32°C) and 21°F (–6°C).

N/HEMISPHERE	JAN	FEB	MAR	APR	MAY	JUN	JUL	AUG	SEP	OCT	NOV	DEC
°F AVG MAX	59	62	70	75	75	74	74	74	73	72	67	62
°F AVG MIN	35	39	45	53	58	61	62	62	61	55	45	38
DIURNAL RANGE	24	23	25	22	17	13	12	12	12	17	22	24
RAIN/INCHES	0.3	0.7	1.3	3.7	11.8	25.9	32.2	25.3	21.2	5.6	0.5	0.2
HUMIDITY/%	73	68	57	58	74	84	86	85	85	79	75	76
BLOOM SEASON					*		*	*	*	*		
DAYS CLR @ 6AM	21	18	15	11	5	0	1	1	4	13	23	19
DAYS CLR @ 12PM	23	16	16	11	2	2	0	1	2	10	21	18
DAYS CLR @ 6PM	15	14	13	10	7	3	1	1	2	14	17	14
RAIN/MM	8	18	33	94	300	658	818	643	538	142	13	5
°C AVG MAX	14.9	16.6	21.0	23.8	23.8	23.3	23.3	23.3	22.7	22.1	19.4	16.6
°C AVG MIN	1.6	3.8	7.1	11.6	14.4	16.0	16.6	16.6	16.0	12.7	7.1	3.3
DIURNAL RANGE	13.3	12.8	13.9	12.2	9.4	7.3	6.7	6.7	6.7	9.4	12.3	13.3
S/HEMISPHERE	JUL	AUG	SEP	OCT	NOV	DEC	JAN	FEB	MAR	APR	MAY	JUN

Cultural Recommendations

LIGHT: 2000–3000 fc. Diffused light is suggested.

TEMPERATURES: Summer days average 74°F (23°C), and nights average 61–62°F (16–17°C), with a diurnal range of 12–13°F (7°C). Microclimate effects may cause actual summer high temperatures to be 6–8°F (3–4°C) warmer than indicated.

HUMIDITY: 75–85% from late spring through autumn, dropping below 60% for 2 months in late winter and early spring.

WATER: Conditions are very wet for 5 months in summer, very dry for 5 months in winter, with short transition periods in autumn and spring. Cultivated plants should be kept evenly moist from spring to early autumn, but water should be gradually reduced after new growths mature in late autumn.

FERTILIZER: ¼–½ recommended strength, applied weekly. A high-nitro-

Dendrobium hornei

gen fertilizer is beneficial from spring to midsummer, but a fertilizer high in phosphates should be used in late summer and autumn.

REST PERIOD: Winter days average 59–70°F (15–21°C), and nights average 35–45°F (2–7°C), with a diurnal range of 23–25°F (13–14°C). Because of microclimate effects, actual winter low temperatures in the habitat may be 6–8°F (3–4°C) warmer than indicated. The temperatures in the climate table may represent the coolest part of the habitat, so cultivated plants may not require temperatures as cool as indicated. Plants should survive exposure to freezing temperatures, providing they are dry at the time, but these extremes should be avoided in cultivation. In the habitat, winter rainfall is low but additional moisture is often available from heavy deposits of dew. For about a month in late winter or early spring, however, humidity is so low that even the moisture from dew is uncommon. Cultivated plants should be allowed to dry out between waterings in winter, but they should not remain dry for extended periods. Occasional early morning mistings between waterings, especially on warm, sunny days, may help prevent plants from becoming too dry. Fertilizer should be eliminated until water is increased in spring. In the habitat, light is highest in winter. The cool, dry rest is essential and increased light may be necessary to initiate blooming.

GROWING MEDIA: Mounting plants on tree-fern or cork slabs accommodates their pendulous growth habit. However, humidity must be high and plants must be watered at least once a day in summer. If plants cannot be mounted, hanging pots or baskets may be filled with an open, fast-draining medium. Repotting may be done anytime new roots are actively growing.

MISCELLANEOUS NOTES: The bloom season shown in the climate table is based on cultivation records. Many growers consider *D. hookerianum* very difficult to bring to bloom, and others indicate that it does not grow or bloom in a warm uniform climate.

Plant and Flower Information

PLANT SIZE AND TYPE: A 39–96 in. (100–245 cm) sympodial epiphyte.

PSEUDOBULB: 39–96 in. (100–245 cm) long, but cultivated plants may be as small as 8 in. (20 cm). The yellowish, rodlike stems have small pseudobulbous swellings at the base. They are pendulous to arching and continue to elongate for years.

LEAVES: Several. The dark green leaves are 7–12 in. (18–30 cm) long and persist for several years. They are oblong-lanceolate with wavy margins and a papery texture.

INFLORESCENCE: 6 in. (15 cm) long. Slender, drooping inflorescences are borne near the apex of the prior year's growth.

FLOWERS: Small groups of 2–4 for a total of 9–12 per inflorescence. The golden yellow flowers are 2–4 in. (5–10 cm) across. They are the largest yellow-flowered dendrobium. Sepals and petals are nearly equal. The large, round, velvety lip has long, shaggy fringe on the margin. It is usually a deep apricot yellow and may be marked with 2 oblique maroon or dark purple patches. The blossoms are fragrant.

HYBRIDIZING NOTES: Chromosome counts are n = 20 (ref. 152, 154, 542) and 2n = 40 (ref. 150, 151, 152, 154, 504, 542, 580).

REFERENCES: 19, 38, 46, 61, 150, 151, 152, 154, 179, 190, 200, 202, 208, 210, 216, 254, 278, 369, 376, 445, 454, 489, 504, 528, 541, 542, 557, 580.

PHOTOS/DRAWINGS: 46, 210, 369, 454.

Dendrobium hornei Horne

AKA: The describer's name is sometimes given as Baker (ref. 254), Horne (ref. 466), S. Moore ex Baker (ref. 84), or S. Moore (ref. 252, 353). The plant was originally discussed by the collector, J. Horne, in his book *A Year in Fiji*. J. Baker (ref. 30) indicates that the plant was examined and characterized by S. Moore in 1879.

ORIGIN/HABITAT: Rambi Island in the Fiji Islands. Only the type collection is known. The habitat was given as "on trees on the shore," but Cribb (ref. 84) indicates reservations regarding this report. If the plants are rediscovered, additional habitat information should be available.

CLIMATE: Station #91661, Savusavu, Fiji Islands, Lat. 16.8°S, Long. 179.3°E, at 10 ft. (3 m). Record extreme temperatures are 98°F (37°C) and 55°F (13°C).

N/HEMISPHERE	JAN	FEB	MAR	APR	MAY	JUN	JUL	AUG	SEP	OCT	NOV	DEC
°F AVG MAX	79	79	80	81	83	85	86	86	86	84	82	80
°F AVG MIN	68	68	69	70	71	73	74	74	74	73	71	69
DIURNAL RANGE	11	11	11	11	12	12	12	12	12	11	11	11
RAIN/INCHES	4.9	8.3	7.7	8.3	9.8	12.5	11.4	10.7	14.5	12.2	10.1	6.7
HUMIDITY/%	77	77	76	75	75	76	76	78	79	79	81	78
BLOOM SEASON	N/A											
DAYS CLR @ 12PM	1	4	1	1	2	1	1	0	0	1	1	2
RAIN/MM	124	211	196	211	249	318	290	272	368	310	257	170
°C AVG MAX	26.1	26.1	26.7	27.2	28.3	29.4	30.0	30.0	30.0	28.9	27.8	26.7
°C AVG MIN	20.0	20.0	20.6	21.1	21.7	22.8	23.3	23.3	23.3	22.8	21.7	20.6
DIURNAL RANGE	6.1	6.1	6.1	6.1	6.6	6.6	6.7	6.7	6.7	6.1	6.1	6.1
S/HEMISPHERE	JUL	AUG	SEP	OCT	NOV	DEC	JAN	FEB	MAR	APR	MAY	JUN

Cultural Recommendations

LIGHT: 2500–3500 fc.

TEMPERATURES: Throughout the year, days average 79–86°F (26–30°C), and nights average 68–74°F (20–23°C), with a diurnal range of 11–12°F (6–7°C).

HUMIDITY: Near 75–80% year-round.

WATER: Rainfall is moderate to heavy all year with a brief, slightly drier period in winter. Cultivated plants should be kept moist, with only slight drying allowed between waterings.

FERTILIZER: ¼–½ recommended strength. A balanced fertilizer should be applied weekly to biweekly throughout the year.

REST PERIOD: Growing conditions should be maintained all year. Cultivated plants should never be allowed to dry out completely, but water should be reduced slightly in winter, especially for plants grown in the dark, short-day conditions common in temperate latitudes.

GROWING MEDIA: Plants may be mounted on tree-fern or cork slabs if humidity is high and plants are watered at least once daily in summer. When plants are potted, any open, fast-draining medium may be used. Repotting may be done anytime new roots are growing.

MISCELLANEOUS NOTES: This species is known only from the type collection and is unlikely to be available for cultivation.

Plant and Flower Information

PLANT SIZE AND TYPE: An 18 in. (45 cm) sympodial epiphyte.

PSEUDOBULB: 14 in. (35 cm) long. The stems are swollen at the base. Stems are leafy at the apex. New growths arise from a short rhizome.

LEAVES: Many. The leaves are 4 in. (10 cm) long.

INFLORESCENCE: 10 in. (25 cm) long. Inflorescences arise from upper nodes.

FLOWERS: 9 per inflorescence. Probably greenish or yellowish, the flowers are approximately 1 in. (2.5 cm) long but do not open fully.

REFERENCES: 30, 82, 84, 216, 252, 254, 353, 466.

Dendrobium horstii J. J. Smith

ORIGIN/HABITAT: Irian Jaya (western New Guinea). Plants grow along the upper Digul River as well as between Geelvink Bay and the MacCluer Gulf. They were cultivated in the botanical garden at Bogor, Java.

CLIMATE: Station #97876, Tanahmerah, Irian Jaya, Lat. 6.1°S, Long. 140.3°E, at 75 ft. (23 m). Temperatures are calculated for an elevation of 500 ft. (150 m), resulting in probable extremes of 97°F (36°C) and 63°F (17°C).

N/HEMISPHERE	JAN	FEB	MAR	APR	MAY	JUN	JUL	AUG	SEP	OCT	NOV	DEC
°F AVG MAX	83	84	86	89	90	89	89	88	89	88	86	84
°F AVG MIN	71	70	70	71	72	73	72	72	72	72	73	72
DIURNAL RANGE	12	14	16	18	18	16	17	16	17	16	13	12
RAIN/INCHES	11.5	12.1	14.7	13.2	14.4	15.9	14.5	15.8	17.4	17.3	15.5	11.9
HUMIDITY/%	N/A											
BLOOM SEASON							*					
DAYS CLR	N/A											
RAIN/MM	292	307	373	335	366	404	368	401	442	439	394	302
°C AVG MAX	28.1	28.7	29.8	31.4	32.0	31.4	31.4	30.9	31.4	30.9	29.8	28.7
°C AVG MIN	21.4	20.9	20.9	21.4	22.0	22.6	22.0	22.0	22.0	22.0	22.6	22.0
DIURNAL RANGE	6.7	7.8	8.9	10.0	10.0	8.8	9.4	8.9	9.4	8.9	7.2	6.7
S/HEMISPHERE	JUL	AUG	SEP	OCT	NOV	DEC	JAN	FEB	MAR	APR	MAY	JUN

Cultural Recommendations

LIGHT: 2000–3000 fc.

TEMPERATURES: Throughout the year, days average 83–90°F (28–32°C), and nights average 70–73°F (21–23°C), with a diurnal range of 12–18°F (7–10°C).

HUMIDITY: Information is not available for this location. However, records from other stations in the region indicate that humidity probably averages near 85% year-round.

WATER: Rainfall is very heavy all year. Cultivated plants should be kept evenly moist.

FERTILIZER: ¼–½ recommended strength. A balanced fertilizer should be applied weekly to biweekly throughout the year.

REST PERIOD: Growing conditions should be maintained year-round. Water and fertilizer might be reduced slightly in winter, especially for plants cultivated in the dark, short-day conditions common in temperate latitudes. They should never be allowed to dry out completely, however.

GROWING MEDIA: Because plants must be kept moist, they are easier to manage when potted. Fir bark or any open, fast-draining medium may be used. Repotting may be done anytime new roots are growing.

MISCELLANEOUS NOTES: The bloom season shown in the climate table is based on collection reports.

Plant and Flower Information

PLANT SIZE AND TYPE: A 27 in. (69 cm) sympodial epiphyte.

PSEUDOBULB: 27 in. (69 cm) long. The stems are erect, somewhat flattened, and arise from a short, creeping rhizome.

LEAVES: Many. The lanceolate leaves are 5.5 in. (14 cm) long. They are folded at the base and unequally bilobed at the apex.

INFLORESCENCE: 1.6 in. (4 cm) long. Racemes emerge through the leaf bases from nodes along the stem.

FLOWERS: 2 per inflorescence. The flowers are 1 in. (2.5 cm) across. Sepals and petals are orange-yellow. The lip has a golden yellow midlobe and dark violet sidelobes.

REFERENCES: 220, 254, 445, 470.

Dendrobium hosei Ridley

AKA: J. J. Wood (ref. 583) included *D. multicostatum* J. J. Smith and *D. pluricostatum* Schlechter as synonyms. Seidenfaden and Wood (ref. 455) include only *D. hosei* Ridley var. *pelor* Carr.

ORIGIN/HABITAT: Borneo, Malaya, New Guinea, and the Admiralty Islands. In Borneo, plants were found on Boekit Lesoeng (Bukit Lesung) in central Kalimantan. In Malaya, plants grow on trees by rivers in Pahang State. In New Guinea, plants known as *D. pluricostatum* grow on mountain trees at 1500–3300 ft. (450–1000 m). They are found in hill country as well as mistforest zones. In the Admiralty Islands, plants grow at 2450 ft. (740 m) in mossy, ridge-top forests, where they occur on mossy tree trunks in partial shade.

CLIMATE: Station #200192, Garaina, Papua New Guinea, Lat. 7.9°S, Long. 147.1°E, at 2350 ft. (716 m). Temperatures are calculated for an elevation of 3300 ft. (1000 m), resulting in probable extremes of 91°F (33°C) and 43°F (6°C).

N/HEMISPHERE	JAN	FEB	MAR	APR	MAY	JUN	JUL	AUG	SEP	OCT	NOV	DEC
°F AVG MAX	77	79	80	81	82	82	82	82	81	81	80	78
°F AVG MIN	60	60	60	61	62	61	62	62	62	61	61	60
DIURNAL RANGE	17	19	20	20	22	21	20	20	19	20	19	18
RAIN/INCHES	5.8	6.5	8.7	11.1	11.8	11.9	8.9	11.7	11.5	9.9	7.7	5.2
HUMIDITY/%	84	82	82	81	80	80	81	81	82	83	84	84
BLOOM SEASON		*							*			*
DAYS CLR	N/A											
RAIN/MM	147	165	221	282	300	302	226	297	292	251	196	132
°C AVG MAX	25.0	26.1	26.6	27.2	27.7	27.7	27.7	27.7	27.2	27.2	26.6	25.5
°C AVG MIN	15.5	15.5	15.5	16.1	15.5	16.6	16.6	16.6	16.1	16.1	16.1	15.5
DIURNAL RANGE	9.5	10.6	11.1	11.1	12.2	11.6	11.1	11.1	10.6	11.1	10.5	10.0
S/HEMISPHERE	JUL	AUG	SEP	OCT	NOV	DEC	JAN	FEB	MAR	APR	MAY	JUN

Cultural Recommendations

LIGHT: 2000–3000 fc.

TEMPERATURES: Throughout the year, days average 77–82°F (25–28°C), and nights average 60–62°F (16–17°C), with a diurnal range of 17–22°F (10–12°C).

HUMIDITY: 80–85% year-round.

WATER: Rainfall is heavy all year, but conditions are slightly drier in winter. Cultivated plants should be kept moist but not soggy, with only slight drying allowed between waterings.

FERTILIZER: ¼–½ recommended strength. A balanced fertilizer should be applied weekly to biweekly throughout the year.

REST PERIOD: Growing conditions should be maintained all year. In the habitat, rainfall is slightly lower in winter. In cultivation, water and fertilizer should be reduced somewhat, especially for plants grown in the dark, short-day conditions common during temperate-latitude winters. Plants should not be allowed to dry out completely, however. In the habitat, seasonal light variation is minor.

GROWING MEDIA: Plants may be mounted on tree-fern or cork slabs if humidity is high and plants are watered at least once daily in summer. If plants are potted, any open, fast-draining medium may be used. Repotting may be done anytime new roots are growing.

MISCELLANEOUS NOTES: The bloom season shown in the climate table is based on reports from the habitat.

Plant and Flower Information

PLANT SIZE AND TYPE: A 20–28 in. (50–70 cm) sympodial epiphyte.

PSEUDOBULB: 20–28 in. (50–70 cm) long. The stems consist of many nodes that are spaced every 0.6–0.8 in. (1.5–2.0 cm). They are elongated, quadrangular, and dirty yellow with longitudinal grooves. Plants from higher elevations are smaller.

LEAVES: Many. The linear-lanceolate leaves are 2.4–4.0 in. (6–10 cm) long. They are dark green, very unequally bilobed, and distichous.

INFLORESCENCE: 0.8 in. (2 cm) long. Racemes emerge laterally from the base of internodes.

FLOWERS: 1–4 per inflorescence. The flowers are 0.3–1.0 in. (0.7–2.5 cm) across. Sepals and petals may be white or greenish and turn pale yellow with age. Some clones have a brownish flush. The lip may be white or yellow with orange-yellow veining. The wavy margin on the kidney-shaped midlobe is ciliate with 3, parallel brown nerves and a very short point at the apex. The sidelobes, which are white with brown veins, are short, blunt, and deflexed. Blossoms may be marked with yellow, red, or orange. Some plants, which have an additional anther on each side of the normal anther, are self-pollinating.

Dendrobium hughii

REFERENCES: 92, 200, 218, 220, 254, 286, 295, 394, 395, 402, 437, 445, 455, 583.

PHOTOS/DRAWINGS: 437, 455, 583.

Dendrobium hughii Rchb. f.

AKA: *D. hymenopterum* as used by Ridley not Hooker f., *D. lepidum* Ridley.

ORIGIN/HABITAT: Malaya. Plants are endemic but relatively common at 4000–5500 ft. (1220–1680 m) on Kedah Peak, Frazer's Hill, and other mountains across northern and central Malaya. They grow low on tree trunks.

CLIMATE: Station #48625, Ipoh, Malaya, Lat. 4.6°N, Long. 101.1°E, at 123 ft. (37 m). Temperatures are calculated for an estimated elevation of 4000 ft. (1220 m), resulting in probable extremes of 86°F (30°C) and 51°F (11°C).

N/HEMISPHERE	JAN	FEB	MAR	APR	MAY	JUN	JUL	AUG	SEP	OCT	NOV	DEC
°F AVG MAX	77	79	80	79	79	79	78	78	77	76	76	76
°F AVG MIN	59	59	60	60	61	60	59	59	60	59	59	59
DIURNAL RANGE	18	20	20	19	18	19	19	19	17	17	17	17
RAIN/INCHES	7.9	3.1	7.6	8.4	6.2	3.6	7.2	6.9	8.8	11.0	13.0	8.9
HUMIDITY/%	76	74	76	78	78	75	76	77	79	82	82	81
BLOOM SEASON					*							
DAYS CLR @ 7AM	3	3	3	1	1	2	1	1	0	0	1	2
DAYS CLR @ 1PM	2	2	2	1	1	1	1	0	0	0	0	2
RAIN/MM	201	79	193	213	157	91	183	175	224	279	330	226
°C AVG MAX	25.1	26.2	26.8	26.2	26.2	26.2	25.7	25.7	25.1	24.6	24.6	24.6
°C AVG MIN	15.1	15.1	15.7	15.7	16.2	15.7	15.1	15.1	15.7	15.1	15.1	15.1
DIURNAL RANGE	10.0	11.1	11.1	10.5	10.0	10.5	10.6	10.6	9.4	9.5	9.5	9.5
S/HEMISPHERE	JUL	AUG	SEP	OCT	NOV	DEC	JAN	FEB	MAR	APR	MAY	JUN

Cultural Recommendations

LIGHT: 1500–2500 fc. Light should be diffused or dappled, and direct sunlight should be avoided. Clear days are rare.

TEMPERATURES: Throughout the year, days average 76–80°F (25–27°C), and nights average 59–61°F (15–16°C), with a diurnal range of 17–20°F (9–11°C). The extreme high does not exceed the warmest average by more than 6°F (3°C), indicating that plants may not be able to tolerate wide temperature fluctuations. Although temperatures are uniform all year, the diurnal range is surprising large.

HUMIDITY: 75–80% year-round.

WATER: Rainfall is heavy most of the year. The heaviest rainfall occurs in autumn with a secondary maximum in spring. Brief semidry periods occur in midwinter and midsummer. Cultivated plants should be kept evenly moist with only slight drying allowed between waterings.

FERTILIZER: ¼–½ recommended strength. A balanced fertilizer should be applied weekly to biweekly throughout the year.

REST PERIOD: Growing conditions should be maintained year-round. Water should be reduced somewhat in winter for plants cultivated in the dark, short-day conditions common in temperate latitudes. They should never be allowed to dry out completely, however. Fertilizer may be reduced when the plant is not actively growing or when water is reduced. In the habitat, light is slightly higher in winter.

GROWING MEDIA: Plants may be mounted on tree-fern or cork slabs if humidity is high and plants are watered at least once daily in summer. When plants are potted, any open, fast-draining medium may be used. Repotting may be done anytime new roots are growing.

MISCELLANEOUS NOTES: The bloom season shown in the climate table is based on cultivation records.

Plant and Flower Information

PLANT SIZE AND TYPE: A 12 in. (30 cm) sympodial epiphyte.

PSEUDOBULB: 12 in. (30 cm) long. The purplish stems are somewhat zigzag near the tip.

LEAVES: Several. The linear leaves, which may be closely or widely spaced along the stem, are 2.8–3.5 in. (7–9 cm) long. They alternate along the stem in 2 rows.

INFLORESCENCE: 1.2 in. (3 cm) long. Inflorescences arise from nodes on leafless stems.

FLOWERS: 1 per inflorescence. The decorative flowers are 1.4 in. (3.5 cm) across. Sepals and petals are white, sometimes with a pale pink suffusion and yellow dots. The petals are wider than the sepals. The lip, which is broadly rounded at the apex, has no sidelobes.

REFERENCES: 179, 200, 216, 254, 395, 402, 454, 455.

PHOTOS/DRAWINGS: 455.

Dendrobium humboldtense J. J. Smith

ORIGIN/HABITAT: Irian Jaya (western New Guinea). Plants were found near Humboldt Bay at about 150 ft. (50 m). They grow on forest trees in the coastal hills. They were cultivated in the botanical garden at Bogor, Java.

CLIMATE: Station #97690, Sentani/Jayapura, Irian Jaya, Lat. 2.7°S, Long. 140.5°E, at 289 ft. (88 m). Record extreme temperatures are 97°F (36°C) and 68°F (20°C).

N/HEMISPHERE	JAN	FEB	MAR	APR	MAY	JUN	JUL	AUG	SEP	OCT	NOV	DEC
°F AVG MAX	87	89	89	90	90	89	89	88	89	90	90	89
°F AVG MIN	72	72	72	73	73	73	73	73	73	74	73	73
DIURNAL RANGE	15	17	17	17	17	16	16	15	16	16	17	16
RAIN/INCHES	4.1	3.9	5.3	2.9	6.7	7.0	8.3	8.3	8.5	4.6	2.4	5.2
HUMIDITY/%	81	80	80	79	81	81	79	80	80	80	81	80
BLOOM SEASON												
DAYS CLR @ 9AM	5	3	4	3	2	1	1	0	1	2	2	5
DAYS CLR @ 3PM	4	3	3	3	2	1	3	0	1	2	2	3
RAIN/MM	104	99	135	74	170	178	211	211	216	117	61	132
°C AVG MAX	30.6	31.7	31.7	32.2	32.2	31.7	31.7	31.1	31.7	32.2	32.2	31.7
°C AVG MIN	22.2	22.2	22.2	22.8	22.8	22.8	22.8	22.8	22.8	23.3	22.8	22.8
DIURNAL RANGE	8.3	9.4	9.4	9.4	9.4	8.9	8.9	8.3	8.9	8.9	9.4	8.9
S/HEMISPHERE	JUL	AUG	SEP	OCT	NOV	DEC	JAN	FEB	MAR	APR	MAY	JUN

Cultural Recommendations

LIGHT: 2000–3000 fc.

TEMPERATURES: Throughout the year, days average 87–90°F (31–32°C), and nights average 72–74°F (22–23°C), with a diurnal range of 15–17°F (8–9°C).

HUMIDITY: Near 80% year-round.

WATER: Rainfall is heavy all year with brief, semidry periods in spring and autumn. Cultivated plants should be kept moist with only slight drying allowed between waterings.

FERTILIZER: ¼–½ recommended strength. A balanced fertilizer should be applied weekly to biweekly throughout the year.

REST PERIOD: Growing conditions should be maintained year-round. Cultivated plants should never be allowed to dry out completely; but water and fertilizer should be reduced somewhat for plants cultivated in the dark, short-day conditions common in temperate-latitude winters.

GROWING MEDIA: Plants may be mounted on tree-fern or cork slabs if humidity is high and plants are watered at least once daily in summer. When plants are potted, any open, fast-draining medium may be used. Repotting may be done anytime new roots are growing.

MISCELLANEOUS NOTES: The bloom season shown in the climate table is based on reports from the habitat.

Plant and Flower Information

PLANT SIZE AND TYPE: A sympodial epiphyte of unreported size.

PSEUDOBULB: The elongated stems are flattened.

LEAVES: Many. The leaves are 1.8 in. (4.6 cm) long, lanceolate, and laterally flattened. They are smaller at the apex of the stem.

INFLORESCENCE: 0.7 in. (1.9 cm) long. Inflorescences emerge on the upper part of the stem.

FLOWERS: The flowers are 0.7 in. (1.9 cm) long. J. J. Smith (ref. 470) described the flowers as quite similar to those of *D. macfarlanei* F. Mueller, but the margins of the sepals and petals are distinctly curled back.

REFERENCES: 221, 470.

Dendrobium humicolle Schlechter.
Schlechter (ref. 443) used the name *Dendrobium humicolle* for *Diplocaulobium humile* Ridley, but he did not validly publish this use. REFERENCES: 223, 230, 400, 443.

Dendrobium humifusum Kränzlin
AKA: *D. reptans* Ridley not Swartz.

ORIGIN/HABITAT: Papua New Guinea. Plants were collected near Sogeri (Sogere) at 1750 ft. (530 m).

CLIMATE: Station #94035, Port Moresby, Papua New Guinea, Lat. 9.5°S, Long. 147.2°E, at 126 ft. (38 m). Temperatures are calculated for an elevation of 1800 ft. (550 m), resulting in probable extremes of 92°F (34°C) and 58°F (15°C).

N/HEMISPHERE	JAN	FEB	MAR	APR	MAY	JUN	JUL	AUG	SEP	OCT	NOV	DEC
°F AVG MAX	77	76	78	80	82	84	83	81	82	81	80	78
°F AVG MIN	67	67	68	69	70	70	70	70	70	69	69	68
DIURNAL RANGE	10	9	10	11	12	14	13	11	12	12	11	10
RAIN/INCHES	1.1	0.7	1.0	1.4	1.9	4.4	7.0	7.6	6.7	4.2	2.5	1.3
HUMIDITY/%	78	77	78	76	73	71	71	73	74	75	77	78
BLOOM SEASON	N/A											
DAYS CLR	N/A											
RAIN/MM	28	18	25	36	48	112	178	193	170	107	64	33
°C AVG MAX	25.3	24.7	25.8	26.9	28.0	29.2	28.6	27.5	28.0	27.5	26.9	25.8
°C AVG MIN	19.7	19.7	20.3	20.8	21.4	21.4	21.4	21.4	21.4	20.8	20.8	20.3
DIURNAL RANGE	5.6	5.0	5.5	6.1	6.6	7.8	7.2	6.1	6.6	6.7	6.1	5.5
S/HEMISPHERE	JUL	AUG	SEP	OCT	NOV	DEC	JAN	FEB	MAR	APR	MAY	JUN

Cultural Recommendations

LIGHT: 2000–3000 fc. High light and strong air movement are recommended. Light should be as high as the plant can tolerate, short of burning the leaves.

TEMPERATURES: Throughout the year, days average 76–84°F (25–29°C), and nights average 67–70°F (20–21°C), with a diurnal range of 9–14°F (5–8°C).

HUMIDITY: 70–75% most of the year, increasing to near 80% in winter.

WATER: Rainfall is moderate for 5 months in summer, but conditions are dry in winter. Cultivated plants should dry slightly between waterings from spring to early autumn, but water should be gradually reduced in late autumn.

FERTILIZER: ¼–½ recommended strength. A balanced fertilizer should be applied weekly to biweekly throughout the growing season.

REST PERIOD: Growing conditions should be maintained all year. In the habitat, rainfall is low for 6–7 months in winter. Water and fertilizer should be reduced considerably in winter. Plants should be allowed to dry between waterings but should not remain dry for extended periods. Occasional mistings on clear, sunny mornings are usually beneficial. In the habitat, winter light is high.

GROWING MEDIA: Plants may be mounted on tree-fern or cork slabs if humidity is high and plants are watered at least once daily in summer. When plants are potted, any open, fast-draining medium may be used. They may be repotted anytime new roots are growing.

Plant and Flower Information

PLANT SIZE AND TYPE: A 1.5 in. (4.0 cm) sympodial epiphyte.

PSEUDOBULB: 0.2–0.5 in. (0.5–1.3 cm) long. Numerous slender pseudobulbs, which become yellow when dry, are borne on a woody, creeping rhizome. Each growth produces a single leaf.

LEAVES: 1 in. (2.5 cm) long. Each lanceolate leaf is rounded at the apex.

INFLORESCENCE: 1.3 in. (3.3 cm) long.

FLOWERS: 1. The delicate, white flowers are 0.2 in. (0.6 cm) long, with a lanceolate dorsal sepal, somewhat triangular lateral sepals, and linear petals. The obscurely 3-lobed lip is orange in the center with lilac spots along the margin of the sidelobes. It is rounded at the apex. The orange column is marked with violet.

REFERENCES: 220, 254, 393.

Dendrobium humile Smith.
Now considered a synonym of *Coelogyne humilis* Lindley. REFERENCES: 216, 254.

Dendrobium humile Wight.
See *D. microbolbon* A. Richard. REFERENCES: 216, 244, 254, 369, 424, 445.

Dendrobium huoshanense G. Z. Tang and S. J. Cheng

ORIGIN/HABITAT: China. Plants were collected near Huoshan in southwest Anhui Province. They grow in rocky places in forests at 1650 ft. (500 m).

CLIMATE: Station #58314, Huoshan, Anhui, China, Lat. 31.3°N, Long. 116.4°E, at 164 ft. (50 m). Temperatures are calculated for an elevation of 1650 ft. (500 m), resulting in probable extremes of 101°F (38°C) and 2°F (−17°C).

N/HEMISPHERE	JAN	FEB	MAR	APR	MAY	JUN	JUL	AUG	SEP	OCT	NOV	DEC
°F AVG MAX	42	48	57	67	74	82	89	85	76	67	55	47
°F AVG MIN	23	26	37	45	54	63	70	67	59	46	37	28
DIURNAL RANGE	19	22	20	22	20	19	19	18	17	21	18	19
RAIN/INCHES*	1.4	1.4	4.7	2.0	3.9	3.4	3.9	3.6	4.3	1.5	1.5	1.3
HUMIDITY/%	69	70	74	76	77	79	77	83	83	77	80	76
BLOOM SEASON	N/A											
DAYS CLR @ 8AM	14	10	9	7	9	9	9	8	13	9	13	
DAYS CLR @ 2PM	14	10	8	5	7	4	5	7	13	10	13	
RAIN/MM	13	0	0	0	0	0	0	0	0	0	0	0
°C AVG MAX	5.6	8.9	13.9	19.5	23.4	27.8	31.7	29.5	24.5	19.5	12.8	8.4
°C AVG MIN	−4.9	−3.3	2.8	7.3	12.3	17.3	21.2	19.5	15.1	7.8	2.8	−2.2
DIURNAL RANGE	10.5	12.2	11.1	12.2	11.1	10.5	10.5	10.0	9.4	11.7	10.0	10.6
S/HEMISPHERE	JUL	AUG	SEP	OCT	NOV	DEC	JAN	FEB	MAR	APR	MAY	JUN

*Rainfall records are not available for this location. The rainfall values in the table are taken from the nearby station #58321 at Hefei.

Cultural Recommendations

LIGHT: 2000–3000 fc. In the habitat, winter is the brightest season.

TEMPERATURES: Summer days average 82–89°F (28–32°C), and nights average 63–70°F (17–21°C), with a diurnal range of 18–19°F (10–11°C).

HUMIDITY: Near 80% from summer into autumn, dropping to 70–75% in winter and spring.

WATER: Rainfall in the region, as indicated by the records from Hefei, is light to moderate throughout the year. The driest season is a 4–5 month period in winter. However, the high humidity and large diurnal temperature range results in heavy dews most of the year. Cultivated plants should be watered frequently while actively growing, being allowed to dry only slightly between waterings.

FERTILIZER: ¼–½ recommended strength, applied weekly. A high nitrogen fertilizer is beneficial from spring to midsummer, but a fertilizer high in phosphates should be used in late summer and autumn.

REST PERIOD: Winter days average 42–48°F (6–9°C), and nights average 23–28°F (−5 to −3°C), with a diurnal range of 19–22°F (11–12°C). We do not know whether *D. huoshanense* merely tolerates the below freezing temperatures or whether the extremely low temperatures are required to initiate blooms. Water should be reduced for cultivated plants, but they should not be allowed to become completely dry unless exposed to below freezing temperatures. Fertilizer should be reduced or eliminated until new growth starts in the spring.

Dendrobium huttoni

GROWING MEDIA: Plants may be mounted on tree-fern or cork slabs if humidity is high and plants are watered at least once daily in summer. When plants are potted, any open, fast-draining medium may be used. They may be repotted anytime new roots are growing.

Plant and Flower Information

PLANT SIZE AND TYPE: A 2–4 in. (5–10 cm) sympodial lithophyte.

PSEUDOBULB: 1.2–2.8 in. (3–7 cm) long. Plants usually consist of 4–5, tightly clustered canes.

LEAVES: 2, at the apex of each growth. The oblong to oblong-lanceolate leaves are 0.8–1.2 in. (2–3 cm) long.

INFLORESCENCE: 1.2 in. (2.9 cm) long. An erect inflorescence is borne at the apex of leafless pseudobulbs.

FLOWERS: 1 per inflorescence. The fleshy flowers are 0.7 in. (1.9 cm) across. They have an oblong-ovate dorsal sepal, ovate-falcate lateral sepals, and elliptical petals that narrow at the base. Segments are cream-white with darker veins and a green tinge at the tips. The erect, recurved lip is obscurely 3-lobed. It has numerous brownish hairs especially at the base and along the veins. Blossoms are fragrant.

REFERENCES: 234, 507.

PHOTOS/DRAWINGS: 507.

Dendrobium huttoni Rchb. f.

ORIGIN/HABITAT: Timor Island in the Malaysian Archipelago. Habitat elevation is unavailable, so the following temperatures should be used with caution.

CLIMATE: Station #97372, Kupang/Penfui, Timor Island, Indonesia, Lat. 10.2°S, Long. 123.7°E, at 335 ft. (102 m). Record extreme temperatures are 101°F (38°C) and 58°F (14°C).

N/HEMISPHERE	JAN	FEB	MAR	APR	MAY	JUN	JUL	AUG	SEP	OCT	NOV	DEC
°F AVG MAX	88	89	91	92	92	88	87	87	87	89	89	88
°F AVG MIN	70	70	71	72	74	75	75	75	74	72	72	71
DIURNAL RANGE	18	19	20	20	18	13	12	12	13	17	17	17
RAIN/INCHES	0.2	0.1	0.1	0.7	3.5	9.7	15.3	14.4	8.7	2.5	1.1	0.4
HUMIDITY/%	56	53	53	56	61	74	78	79	78	68	61	59
BLOOM SEASON					*							
DAYS CLR @ 8AM	19	22	25	15	10	5	5	2	6	14	14	18
DAYS CLR @ 2PM	13	16	18	12	8	2	1	1	2	6	10	10
RAIN/MM	5	3	3	18	89	246	389	366	221	64	28	10
°C AVG MAX	31.1	31.7	32.8	33.3	33.3	31.1	30.6	30.6	30.6	31.7	31.7	31.1
°C AVG MIN	21.1	21.1	21.7	22.2	23.3	23.9	23.9	23.9	23.3	22.2	22.2	21.7
DIURNAL RANGE	10.0	10.6	11.1	11.1	10.0	7.2	6.7	6.7	7.3	9.5	9.5	9.4
S/HEMISPHERE	JUL	AUG	SEP	OCT	NOV	DEC	JAN	FEB	MAR	APR	MAY	JUN

Cultural Recommendations

LIGHT: 2500–3500 fc.

TEMPERATURES: Throughout the year, days average 87–92°F (31–33°C), and nights average 70–75°F (21–24°C), with a diurnal range of 12–20°F (7–11°C). The warmest temperatures occur in spring before the rainy season starts.

HUMIDITY: 75–80% during the growing season, dropping to 55–60% from midautumn through spring.

WATER: Rainfall is heavy during the growing season, but there is a long dry season in winter and spring. Cultivated plants should not be allowed to dry out completely while actively growing, but water should be gradually reduced in autumn.

FERTILIZER: ¼–½ recommended strength, applied weekly. A high-nitrogen fertilizer is beneficial from spring to midsummer, but a fertilizer high in phosphates should be used in late summer and autumn.

REST PERIOD: Growing temperatures should be maintained all year. In the habitat, the dry season lasts 5–6 months from late autumn into spring. Not only is rainfall low, but humidity is so low that even moisture from dew is uncommon. Cultivated plants should be allowed to dry out in winter. Water should be limited to an occasional misting until spring. Fertilizer should be eliminated until water is increased. In the habitat, light is highest in winter.

GROWING MEDIA: Plants may be mounted on tree-fern or cork slabs if humidity is high and plants are watered at least once daily in summer. When plants are potted, any open, fast-draining medium may be used. Repotting is best done in early spring when new roots are growing.

MISCELLANEOUS NOTES: The bloom season shown in the climate table is based on cultivation records.

Plant and Flower Information

PLANT SIZE AND TYPE: A 20–30 in. (50–75 cm) sympodial epiphyte.

PSEUDOBULB: 20–30 in. (50–75 cm) long. Stems are leafy on the upper half.

LEAVES: Many. The linear-lanceolate leaves are 2.8–3.1 in. (7–8 cm) long.

INFLORESCENCE: Short. Inflorescences arise from uppermost nodes.

FLOWERS: 1–2 per inflorescence. Flower size is unavailable. All segments are white with a purple suffusion along the margin. The margin of the lip may be red or deeper purple than the borders on the sepals and petals.

REFERENCES: 216, 254, 541.

Dendrobium hydrophilum J. J. Smith.

Sometimes spelled *D. hydrophyllum*, it is now considered a synonym of *Diplocaulobium hydrophilum* (J. J. Smith) Kränzlin. REFERENCES: 213, 220, 254, 445, 470, 537.

Dendrobium hymenanthum Hooker f. not Rchb. f.

See *D. hymenopterum* Hooker f. REFERENCES: 202, 218, 254, 395, 454.

Dendrobium hymenanthum Rchb. f. not Hooker f.

AKA: *D. micholitzii* Rolfe, *D. quadrangulare* Parish and Rchb. f. Seidenfaden (ref. 454) discusses the possibility of the preceding synonymy, and in a 1994 personal communication, he stated that plants must be called *D. hymenanthum*. Merrill (ref. 296) includes the name *Dendrochilum hymenanthum* Vidal as a synonym, but Valmayor (ref. 536) includes the synonym as *Dendrobium hymenanthum* Vidal.

ORIGIN/HABITAT: Widespread and common in many areas. The habitat includes western Thailand, the Tenasserim region of Burma, Peninsular Thailand, Malaya, Borneo, and the Philippines. In the Philippines, plants grow near sea level on Luzon Island in the provinces of Bataan, Quezon, and Rizal. They are also found on the Polillo Islands, a group of small islands off the east coast of Luzon.

CLIMATE: Station #98427, Manila, Philippines, Lat. 14.5°N, Long. 121.0°E, at 74 ft. (23 m). Record extreme temperatures are 101°F (38°C) and 58°F (14°C).

N/HEMISPHERE	JAN	FEB	MAR	APR	MAY	JUN	JUL	AUG	SEP	OCT	NOV	DEC
°F AVG MAX	86	88	91	93	93	91	88	87	88	88	87	86
°F AVG MIN	69	69	71	73	75	75	75	75	75	74	72	70
DIURNAL RANGE	17	19	20	20	18	16	13	12	13	14	15	16
RAIN/INCHES	0.9	0.5	0.7	1.3	5.1	10.0	17.0	16.6	14.0	7.6	5.7	2.6
HUMIDITY/%	77	73	70	68	71	81	84	86	87	84	82	89
BLOOM SEASON					*	*		*				*
DAYS CLR @ 8AM	6	9	14	14	10	3	2	1	1	6	7	6
DAYS CLR @ 2PM	3	6	10	10	8	2	1	1	0	2	2	3
RAIN/MM	23	13	18	33	130	254	432	422	356	193	145	66
°C AVG MAX	30.0	31.1	32.8	33.9	33.9	32.8	31.1	30.6	31.1	31.1	30.6	30.0
°C AVG MIN	20.6	20.6	21.7	22.8	23.9	23.9	23.9	23.9	23.9	23.3	22.2	21.1
DIURNAL RANGE	9.4	10.5	11.1	11.1	10.0	8.9	7.2	6.7	7.2	7.8	8.4	8.9
S/HEMISPHERE	JUL	AUG	SEP	OCT	NOV	DEC	JAN	FEB	MAR	APR	MAY	JUN

Cultural Recommendations

LIGHT: 2500–3500 fc.

TEMPERATURES: Throughout the year, days average 86–93°F (30–34°C), and nights average 69–75°F (21–24°C), with a diurnal range of 12–20°F (7–11°C).

HUMIDITY: 80–85% in summer and autumn, dropping to about 70% in late winter and spring.

WATER: Rainfall is heavy from late spring through autumn, but conditions are dry for 3–4 months in winter. Cultivated plants should be kept moist while actively growing, but water should be gradually reduced in autumn.

FERTILIZER: ¼–½ recommended strength, applied weekly. A high-nitrogen fertilizer is beneficial from spring to midsummer, while a fertilizer high in phosphates should be used in late summer and autumn.

REST PERIOD: Growing temperatures should be maintained all year, with occasional drops to 60–65°F (16–18°C). In the habitat, winter rainfall is low, but additional moisture is usually available from heavy deposits of dew. For 3–4 months in winter, water should be reduced for cultivated plants. They should be allowed to dry slightly between waterings, but should not remain dry for extended periods. Fertilizer should be eliminated when plants are not actively growing. For many plants from this habitat, the winter dry season is necessary to initiate blooms. In the habitat, light is highest for about 2 months in winter.

GROWING MEDIA: Plants may be mounted on tree-fern or cork slabs if humidity is high and plants are watered at least once daily in summer. When plants are potted, any open, fast-draining medium may be used. Repotting is best done in early spring when new roots are growing.

MISCELLANEOUS NOTES: The bloom season shown in the climate table is based on collection reports. Cultivated plants bloom for about 36 hours every 6–8 weeks. Plants that produce flowers which last a single day commonly bloom several times during the year. Flowering usually occurs 7–14 days after a sudden 10°F (5°C) drop in daytime temperatures.

Plant and Flower Information

PLANT SIZE AND TYPE: A 4 in. (10 cm) sympodial epiphyte.

PSEUDOBULB: 1.2–3.0 in. (3–8 cm) long. The yellow stems, which are sharply 4-angled on the upper part, are clustered, slender, rigid, and erect. Plants consist of numerous stems.

LEAVES: 2 per growth. The leaves are 0.8–1.2 in. (2–3 cm) long, oblong, and leathery.

INFLORESCENCE: Short. One or more inflorescences arise from between the leaves at the apex of the stem. Inflorescences are usually produced one after another so that each flowering stem has a pair of blossoms. Occasionally, however, several inflorescences are produced at the same time. Cultivated plants are often covered with blossoms.

FLOWERS: 1 per inflorescence. The blossoms, which are shaped like a half-open fan, are 0.4–0.8 in. (1–2 cm) long. The sepals and linear petals are white to yellowish white with a thin texture. The lip is marked with yellow and purple at the base. It has a small hairy crest near the apex and 2 small keels near the middle. Blossoms are short-lived and open in succession. Blossoms are fragrant.

REFERENCES: 12, 56, 157, 200, 202, 216, 254, 286, 295, 296, 317, 448, 454, 455, 524, 536.

PHOTOS/DRAWINGS: 455.

Dendrobium hymenanthum Vidal. See *D. hymenanthum* Rchb. f. REFERENCES: 536.

Dendrobium hymenocentrum Schlechter

AKA: Lewis and Cribb (ref. 271) indicate that *D. hymenocentrum* is similar to *D. macfarlanei* F. Mueller and suggest that their relationship needs reassessment.

ORIGIN/HABITAT: Bougainville and northern Papua New Guinea. Plants grow in coastal forests at about 50 ft. (15 m). They were originally found near Aitape, New Guinea.

CLIMATE: Station #94004, Wewak, Papua New Guinea, Lat. 3.6°S, Long. 143.7°E, at 16 ft. (5 m). Record extreme temperatures are 98°F (37°C) and 62°F (17°C).

N/HEMISPHERE	JAN	FEB	MAR	APR	MAY	JUN	JUL	AUG	SEP	OCT	NOV	DEC
°F AVG MAX	88	88	88	88	88	88	87	86	87	88	88	88
°F AVG MIN	74	74	74	75	75	75	75	75	74	74	75	74
DIURNAL RANGE	14	14	14	13	13	13	12	11	13	14	13	14
RAIN/INCHES	7.6	4.8	5.3	10.0	13.3	14.5	12.1	11.9	14.9	16.9	15.1	10.8
HUMIDITY/%	80	79	79	78	79	81	82	82	81	82	81	80
BLOOM SEASON			*									
DAYS CLR	N/A											
RAIN/MM	193	122	135	254	338	368	307	302	378	429	384	274
°C AVG MAX	31.1	31.1	31.1	31.1	31.1	31.1	30.6	30.0	30.6	31.1	31.1	31.1
°C AVG MIN	23.3	23.3	23.3	23.9	23.9	23.9	23.9	23.9	23.3	23.3	23.9	23.3
DIURNAL RANGE	7.8	7.8	7.8	7.2	7.2	7.2	6.7	6.1	7.3	7.8	7.2	7.8
S/HEMISPHERE	JUL	AUG	SEP	OCT	NOV	DEC	JAN	FEB	MAR	APR	MAY	JUN

Cultural Recommendations

LIGHT: 2500–3500 fc.

TEMPERATURES: Throughout the year, days average 86–88°F (30–31°C), and nights average 74–75°F (23–24°C), with a diurnal range of 11–14°F (6–8°C).

HUMIDITY: Near 80% year-round.

WATER: Rainfall is heavy all year, but conditions are slightly drier for 1–2 months in late winter. Cultivated plants should be kept moist and never be allowed to dry out.

FERTILIZER: ¼–½ recommended strength. A balanced fertilizer should be applied weekly to biweekly throughout the year.

REST PERIOD: Growing conditions should be maintained year-round. Water should be reduced for plants cultivated in the dark, short-day conditions common during temperate-latitude winters, but they should still not be allowed to dry out completely. Fertilizer should also be reduced if water is reduced. In the habitat, light may be slightly higher in winter.

GROWING MEDIA: A very open and fast-draining medium may be used with either baskets or small pots. Repotting may be done anytime new roots are growing.

MISCELLANEOUS NOTES: The bloom season shown in the climate table is based on reports from the habitat. Plants that produce flowers which last a single day commonly bloom several times each year. Flowering usually occurs 7–14 days after a sudden 10°F (5°C) drop in daytime temperatures.

Plant and Flower Information

PLANT SIZE AND TYPE: A 24 in. (60 cm) sympodial epiphyte.

PSEUDOBULB: 24 in. (60 cm) long. Stems are slender, rigid, wiry, and swollen at the base.

LEAVES: Many. The lanceolate leaves are 1–2 in. (2.5–5.1 cm) long.

INFLORESCENCE: Short. Inflorescences emerge from the side of the pseudobulb.

FLOWERS: Many. The flowers are somewhat fan-shaped with recurved tips. The sepals and petals are greenish white with red veins. The white lip has a green midline crest and red veins at the base. Blossoms last a single day.

Dendrobium hymenopetalum Schlechter

REFERENCES: 92, 221, 271, 437, 445.

PHOTOS/DRAWINGS: 437.

ORIGIN/HABITAT: Sumatra, near Bukit Tinggi (Fort de Kock). Plants grow on the trunks of palms at about 3300 ft. (1000 m).

CLIMATE: Station #96163, Padang, Sumatra, Indonesia, Lat. 0.9°S, Long. 100.4°E, at 19 ft. (6 m). Temperatures are calculated for an elevation of 2950 ft. (900 m), resulting in probable extremes of 84°F (29°C) and 58°F (15°C).

N/HEMISPHERE	JAN	FEB	MAR	APR	MAY	JUN	JUL	AUG	SEP	OCT	NOV	DEC
°F AVG MAX	77	77	76	76	76	76	77	77	77	77	78	77
°F AVG MIN	64	64	64	64	64	64	64	64	64	65	65	64
DIURNAL RANGE	13	13	12	12	12	12	13	13	13	12	13	13
RAIN/INCHES	10.9	13.7	6.0	19.5	20.4	18.9	13.8	10.2	12.1	14.3	12.4	12.1
HUMIDITY/%	81	82	82	84	85	84	81	81	82	83	81	81
BLOOM SEASON	*											
DAYS CLR @ 7AM	5	1	1	0	0	2	2	2	2	2	3	5
DAYS CLR @ 1PM	5	2	2	1	1	3	3	4	3	3	6	5
RAIN/MM	277	348	152	495	518	480	351	259	307	363	315	307
°C AVG MAX	25.2	25.2	24.6	24.6	24.6	24.6	25.2	25.2	25.2	25.2	25.7	25.2
°C AVG MIN	18.0	18.0	18.0	18.0	18.0	18.0	18.0	18.0	18.0	18.5	18.5	18.0
DIURNAL RANGE	7.2	7.2	6.6	6.6	6.6	6.6	7.2	7.2	7.2	6.7	7.2	7.2
S/HEMISPHERE	JUL	AUG	SEP	OCT	NOV	DEC	JAN	FEB	MAR	APR	MAY	JUN

Cultural Recommendations

LIGHT: 2000–3000 fc. Diffused light is preferred.

TEMPERATURES: Throughout the year, days average 76–78°F (25–26°C), and nights average 64–65°F (18–19°C), with a diurnal range of 12–13°F (7°C). Extremes vary only a few degrees from the averages, indicating that the plant may not tolerate wide temperature fluctuations.

HUMIDITY: 80–85% year-round.

WATER: Rainfall is heavy all year. Cultivated plants should be kept moist but not soggy.

FERTILIZER: ¼–½ recommended strength. A balanced fertilizer should be applied weekly to biweekly throughout the year.

REST PERIOD: Growing conditions should be maintained year-round. Water may be reduced somewhat for cultivated plants in winter, especially those grown in the dark, short-day conditions common in temperate latitudes. They should never be allowed to dry out completely, however.

GROWING MEDIA: Plants may be mounted on tree-fern or cork slabs if humidity is high and plants are watered at least once daily in summer. When plants are potted, any open, fast-draining medium may be used. Repotting may be done anytime new roots are growing.

MISCELLANEOUS NOTES: The bloom season shown in the climate table is based on reports from the habitat.

Plant and Flower Information

PLANT SIZE AND TYPE: A 4–10 in. (10–25 cm) sympodial epiphyte.

PSEUDOBULB: 4–10 in. (10–25 cm) long. The stems are slender, terete, somewhat angled and often curved. They are laxly leafy. Growths are connected by a very short rhizome.

LEAVES: Few. The leaves are 0.6–1.2 in. (1.5–3.0 cm) long. They are curved, erect to spreading, and evenly spaced. The leaves are quickly deciduous.

INFLORESCENCE: Very short. The flowers, which open in succession, are arranged in loose clusters on the upper, leafless part of the stem.

FLOWERS: Few per inflorescence. The transparent flowers are 0.4 in. (1 cm) long. The wavy lip is bilobed in front. Blossoms open in succession. Schlechter (ref. 435) described the flowers as similar to *D. teloense* J. J. Smith.

Dendrobium hymenophyllum Lindley

REFERENCES: 221, 435, 454.

ORIGIN/HABITAT: Sumatra and West and Central Java. Plants usually grow in moist, dark, primary forests in the foothills at 2950–4100 ft. (900–1250 m) and have been found on Mt. Salak near Bogor, Java. They seldom grow in areas with a long dry season.

CLIMATE: Station #96755, Bogor, Java, Lat. 6.5°S, Long. 106.8°E, at 558 ft. (170 m). Temperatures are calculated for an elevation of 3500 ft. (1070 m), resulting in probable extremes of 86°F (30°C) and 56°F (13°C).

N/HEMISPHERE	JAN	FEB	MAR	APR	MAY	JUN	JUL	AUG	SEP	OCT	NOV	DEC
°F AVG MAX	76	77	78	78	77	75	74	74	75	76	77	76
°F AVG MIN	63	63	63	64	64	64	64	64	64	65	65	64
DIURNAL RANGE	13	14	15	14	13	11	10	10	11	11	12	12
RAIN/INCHES	2.1	1.0	0.5	5.0	8.1	18.8	23.7	20.2	14.4	12.0	11.9	3.4
HUMIDITY/%	72	68	65	66	74	79	84	84	81	79	77	75
BLOOM SEASON					*							*
DAYS CLR @ 7AM	14	14	14	11	9	3	1	2	4	6	10	12
DAYS CLR @ 1PM	9	10	8	5	1	1	0	0	1	1	3	7
RAIN/MM	53	25	13	127	206	478	602	513	366	305	302	86
°C AVG MAX	24.6	25.2	25.7	25.7	25.2	24.1	23.5	23.5	24.1	24.6	25.2	24.6
°C AVG MIN	17.4	17.4	17.4	17.9	17.9	17.9	17.9	17.9	17.9	18.5	18.5	17.9
DIURNAL RANGE	7.2	7.8	8.3	7.8	7.3	6.2	5.6	5.6	6.2	6.1	6.7	6.7
S/HEMISPHERE	JUL	AUG	SEP	OCT	NOV	DEC	JAN	FEB	MAR	APR	MAY	JUN

Cultural Recommendations

LIGHT: 1800–2500 fc.

TEMPERATURES: Throughout the year, days average 74–78°F (24–26°C), and nights average 63–65°F (17–19°C), with a diurnal range of 10–15°F (6–8°C). Night temperatures vary only 2°F (1°C) throughout the year. The diurnal range is lowest in summer when the frequently overcast skies prevent daytime heating.

HUMIDITY: 75–85% most of the year, dropping to near 65% for 2 months in winter.

WATER: Rainfall is very heavy from spring into autumn, but conditions are very dry for 2 months in winter. Cultivated plants should be kept moist during the growing season, but water should be gradually reduced in late autumn.

FERTILIZER: ¼–½ recommended strength, applied weekly. A high-nitrogen fertilizer is beneficial from spring to midsummer, but a fertilizer high in phosphates should be used in late summer and autumn.

REST PERIOD: Growing conditions should be maintained all year, but rainfall is very low for 2–3 winter months. In cultivation, water should be reduced and the plants allowed to become somewhat dry between waterings. They should not remain dry for prolonged periods, however. Fertilizer may be reduced or eliminated anytime the plant is not actively growing. In the habitat, light is highest in winter.

GROWING MEDIA: Plants may be mounted on tree-fern or cork slabs if humidity is high and plants are watered at least once daily in summer. When plants are potted, any open, fast-draining medium may be used. Repotting is best done in early spring when new roots are growing.

MISCELLANEOUS NOTES: The bloom season shown in the climate table is based on reports from the habitat.

Plant and Flower Information

PLANT SIZE AND TYPE: A 30 in. (75 cm) sympodial epiphyte.

PSEUDOBULB: 30 in. (75 cm) long. Young stems are horizontal but they droop as they become older. They are clustered at the base.

LEAVES: Many. The leaves, which are 4–5 in. (10–13 cm) long, are spaced 1.2 in. (3 cm) apart. They are lanceolate, papery, and wavy along the margin. The upper surfaces of the leaves are dark green, but the sheaths and underside of the leaves are reddish.

INFLORESCENCE: 1.2 in. (3 cm) long. Several pendulous inflorescences emerge from nodes on the apical half of stems, usually after leaves have fallen. The clustered flowers are held away from the stem on a relatively short inflorescence.

FLOWERS: 7–14 per inflorescence. The shiny flowers are 0.6 in. (1.5 cm) across and open fully. They were described as interesting but not beautiful. The recurved sepals and minutely toothed petals are fan-shaped. They may be pale greenish, yellowish, reddish, purplish, or brownish, variably flushed with dark red. Blossoms have an unusually long, fat, curved spur. The lip is greenish-yellow and sharply recurved at the tip. The thick column is white. Var. *sumatranum* J. J. Smith is intensely purple.

REFERENCES: 25, 74, 75, 216, 254, 277, 310, 454, 469

PHOTOS/DRAWINGS: *74, 75,* 469.

Dendrobium hymenopterum Hooker f. not Ridley

AKA: *D. hymenanthum* Hooker f. not Rchb. f., *D. singalanense* Kränzlin.

ORIGIN/HABITAT: Southeastern Thailand, Malaya, and Sumatra. In Thailand, plants are found at 3950 ft. (1200 m). In Malaya, where they are very rare, the orchids were collected on Mt. Batu Puteh (Batu Pateh or Putih) in Perak at 3600 ft. (1100 m). In Sumatra, plants grow at 5600 ft. (1700 m).

CLIMATE: Station #48625, Ipoh, Malaya, Lat. 4.6°N, Long. 101.1°E, at 123 ft. (37 m). Temperatures are calculated for an elevation of 3500 ft. (1070 m), resulting in probable extremes of 88°F (31°C) and 53°F (12°C).

N/HEMISPHERE	JAN	FEB	MAR	APR	MAY	JUN	JUL	AUG	SEP	OCT	NOV	DEC
°F AVG MAX	79	81	82	81	81	81	80	80	79	78	78	78
°F AVG MIN	61	61	62	62	63	62	61	61	62	61	61	61
DIURNAL RANGE	18	20	20	19	18	19	19	19	17	17	17	17
RAIN/INCHES	7.9	3.1	7.6	8.4	6.2	3.6	7.2	6.9	8.8	11.0	13.0	8.9
HUMIDITY/%	76	74	76	78	78	75	76	77	79	82	82	81
BLOOM SEASON					*							
DAYS CLR @ 7AM	3	3	3	1	2	1	2	1	1	0	1	2
DAYS CLR @ 1PM	2	2	2	1	1	1	1	1	1	0	0	2
RAIN/MM	201	79	193	213	157	91	183	175	224	279	330	226
°C AVG MAX	26.0	27.1	27.7	27.1	27.1	27.1	26.6	26.6	26.0	25.5	25.5	25.5
°C AVG MIN	16.0	16.0	16.6	16.6	17.1	16.6	16.0	16.0	16.6	16.0	16.0	16.0
DIURNAL RANGE	10.0	11.1	11.1	10.5	10.0	10.5	10.6	10.6	9.4	9.5	9.5	9.5
S/HEMISPHERE	JUL	AUG	SEP	OCT	NOV	DEC	JAN	FEB	MAR	APR	MAY	JUN

Cultural Recommendations

LIGHT: 2500–3500 fc.

TEMPERATURES: Throughout the year, days average 78–82°F (26–28°C), and nights average 61–63°F (16–17°C), with a diurnal range of 17–20°F (9–11°C).

HUMIDITY: 75–80% year-round.

WATER: Rainfall is heavy most of the year. The heaviest rainfall occurs in autumn, with a secondary maximum in spring. Brief semidry periods occur in midwinter and midsummer. Cultivated plants should be kept evenly moist with only slight drying allowed between waterings.

FERTILIZER: ¼–½ recommended strength. A balanced fertilizer should be applied weekly to biweekly throughout the year.

REST PERIOD: Growing conditions should be maintained year-round. Water should be reduced somewhat in winter for plants cultivated in the dark, short-day conditions common in temperate latitudes. They should never be allowed to dry out completely, however. Fertilizer may be reduced when the plant is not actively growing or when water is reduced. In the habitat, light is slightly higher in winter.

GROWING MEDIA: Plants may be mounted on tree-fern or cork slabs if humidity is high and plants are watered at least once daily in summer. When plants are potted, any open, fast-draining medium may be used. Repotting may be done anytime new roots are growing.

MISCELLANEOUS NOTES: The bloom season shown in the climate table is based on collection records. Plants are unlikely to be in cultivation.

Plant and Flower Information

PLANT SIZE AND TYPE: A 9–16 in. (23–40 cm) sympodial epiphyte.

PSEUDOBULB: 8–14 in. (20–35 cm) long. The flexuous stems may be slender or moderately stout.

LEAVES: 5–6 per growth. The leathery, broadly lanceolate leaves are 3–6 in. (8–15 cm) long.

INFLORESCENCE: Inflorescences emerge from the side of leafless pseudobulbs.

FLOWERS: 1–3, rarely 5 per inflorescence. The flowers are 0.5–1.0 in. (1.3–2.5 cm) across. The lateral sepals are broadly triangular. Sepals and petals are white tinted with rose and green. The lip, which is rounded at the apex, is not lobed. The spur is long, curved, and clubbed.

REFERENCES: 200, 202, 218, 254, 395, 402, 445, 454, 455.

PHOTOS/DRAWINGS: 454, 455.

Dendrobium hymenopterum as used by Ridley not Hooker f. See *D. hughii* Rchb. f. REFERENCES: 402.

Dendrobium hyperanthiflorum Kränzlin. A misspelling for *D. lyperanthiflorum,* see *D. insigne* (Blume) Rchb. f. ex Miquel. REFERENCES: 218, 253.

Dendrobium hypodon Schlechter

AKA: Schlechter (ref. 436) included *D. capitellatum* Kränzlin as a synonym. Heller (ref. 191) later transferred *D. capitellatum* Kränzlin to *D. christianae* A. H. Heller, so apparently both names are synonyms.

ORIGIN/HABITAT: Endemic to Sulawesi (Celebes). Plants grow on the Minahassa Peninsula near Tondano (Tomohon) and Langean (Langawan). Plants are usually found on trees at 2600–3000 ft. (800–910 m).

CLIMATE: Station #97014, Manado, Sulawesi, Lat. 1.5°N, Long. 124.9°E, at 264 ft. (80 m). Temperatures are calculated for an elevation of 3000 ft. (910 m), resulting in probable extremes of 88°F (31°C) and 56°F (13°C).

N/HEMISPHERE	JAN	FEB	MAR	APR	MAY	JUN	JUL	AUG	SEP	OCT	NOV	DEC
°F AVG MAX	76	76	76	77	78	78	78	80	80	80	78	77
°F AVG MIN	64	64	64	64	65	64	64	64	64	63	64	65
DIURNAL RANGE	12	12	12	13	13	14	14	16	16	17	14	12
RAIN/INCHES	18.6	13.8	12.2	8.0	6.4	6.5	4.8	4.0	3.4	4.9	8.9	14.7
HUMIDITY/%	84	83	83	83	81	80	75	72	75	77	82	83
BLOOM SEASON									*		*	
DAYS CLR @ 8AM	4	3	6	11	11	12	12	12	14	17	12	8
DAYS CLR @ 2PM	1	1	1	2	1	3	3	4	4	4	1	1
RAIN/MM	472	351	310	203	163	165	122	102	86	124	226	373
°C AVG MAX	24.4	24.4	24.4	25.0	25.5	25.5	25.5	26.7	26.7	26.7	25.5	25.0
°C AVG MIN	17.8	17.8	17.8	17.8	18.3	17.8	17.8	17.8	17.8	17.2	17.8	18.3
DIURNAL RANGE	6.6	6.6	6.6	7.2	7.2	7.7	7.7	8.9	8.9	9.5	7.7	6.7
S/HEMISPHERE	JUL	AUG	SEP	OCT	NOV	DEC	JAN	FEB	MAR	APR	MAY	JUN

Cultural Recommendations

LIGHT: 2000–3000 fc. The habitat is usually overcast in the afternoon.

TEMPERATURES: Throughout the year, days average 76–80°F (24–27°C), and nights average 63–65°F (17–18°C), with a diurnal range of 12–17°F (7–10°C). Record extreme temperatures are only a few degrees above and below the average temperatures, indicating that plants may not be able to tolerate wide temperature fluctuations.

HUMIDITY: 80–85% most of the year, dropping to 70–75% in late summer and autumn.

WATER: Rainfall is moderate to heavy all year. The driest weather occurs in

Dendrobium hypopogon

late summer when temperatures are warm. Cultivated plants should be kept moist but not soggy. Warm water might be beneficial.

FERTILIZER: ¼–½ recommended strength. A balanced fertilizer should be applied weekly to biweekly throughout the year.

REST PERIOD: Growing temperatures should be maintained all year. The plants may rest during the 1–2 month drier period which occurs in late summer and coincides with the period of greatest diurnal range. Cultivated plants should dry out slightly during this period, but they should never remain dry for long. The heaviest rainfall in the habitat occurs in winter, but water should not be increased for cultivated plants. In fact, water should be reduced somewhat for plants grown in the dark, short-day conditions common in temperate latitudes, but they should not be allowed to dry out completely.

GROWING MEDIA: Plants may be mounted on tree-fern or cork slabs if humidity is high and plants are watered at least once daily in summer. When plants are potted, any open, fast-draining medium may be used. Repotting may be done anytime new roots are growing.

MISCELLANEOUS NOTES: The bloom season shown in the climate table is based on reports from the habitat.

Plant and Flower Information

PLANT SIZE AND TYPE: An 8–10 in. (20–25 cm) sympodial epiphyte.

PSEUDOBULB: 6–8 in. (15–20 cm) long. The clustered stems are erect to suberect. They do not branch.

LEAVES: Many. The lanceolate leaves are 2.4 in. (6 cm) long, pointed, and rigidly leathery.

INFLORESCENCE: Blossoms are held in clusters at the apex of the inflorescence.

FLOWERS: Many per inflorescence. The sepals and petals are about 0.2 in. (0.5 cm) long. Blossoms may be dark purple or nearly purplish black.

REFERENCES: 12, 191, 220, 254, 436, 454.

Dendrobium hypopogon Kränzlin

ORIGIN/HABITAT: Sumatra. Plants grow near Singaloan in Padang Province at about 450 ft. (140 m).

CLIMATE: Station #96163, Padang, Sumatra, Indonesia, Lat. 0.9°S, Long. 100.4°E, at 19 ft. (6 m). Temperatures are calculated for an elevation of 450 ft. (140 m), resulting in probable extremes of 93°F (34°C) and 67°F (19°C).

N/HEMISPHERE	JAN	FEB	MAR	APR	MAY	JUN	JUL	AUG	SEP	OCT	NOV	DEC
°F AVG MAX	86	86	85	85	85	85	86	86	86	86	87	86
°F AVG MIN	73	73	73	73	73	73	73	73	73	74	74	73
DIURNAL RANGE	13	13	12	12	12	12	13	13	13	12	13	13
RAIN/INCHES	10.9	13.7	6.0	19.5	20.4	18.9	13.8	10.2	12.1	14.3	12.4	12.1
HUMIDITY/%	81	82	82	84	85	84	81	81	82	83	81	81
BLOOM SEASON	N/A											
DAYS CLR @ 7AM	5	1	1	0	0	2	2	1	2	2	3	5
DAYS CLR @ 1PM	5	2	2	1	1	3	3	4	3	3	6	5
RAIN/MM	277	348	152	495	518	480	351	259	307	363	315	307
°C AVG MAX	29.8	29.8	29.2	29.2	29.2	29.2	29.8	29.8	29.8	29.8	30.3	29.8
°C AVG MIN	22.5	22.5	22.5	22.5	22.5	22.5	22.5	22.5	22.5	23.1	23.1	22.5
DIURNAL RANGE	7.3	7.3	6.7	6.7	6.7	6.7	7.3	7.3	7.3	6.7	7.2	7.3
S/HEMISPHERE	JUL	AUG	SEP	OCT	NOV	DEC	JAN	FEB	MAR	APR	MAY	JUN

Cultural Recommendations

LIGHT: 2000–3000 fc. Diffused light is preferred.

TEMPERATURES: Throughout the year, days average 85–87°F (29–30°C), and nights average 73–74°F (23°C), with a diurnal range of 12–13°F (7°C). Extremes vary only a few degrees from the averages, indicating that the plant may not tolerate wide temperature fluctuations.

HUMIDITY: 80–85% year-round.

WATER: Rainfall is heavy all year. Cultivated plants should be kept moist but not soggy.

FERTILIZER: ¼–½ recommended strength. A balanced fertilizer should be applied weekly to biweekly throughout the year.

REST PERIOD: Growing conditions should be maintained year-round. Water may be reduced somewhat for cultivated plants in winter, especially those grown in the dark, short-day conditions common in temperate latitudes. They should never be allowed to dry out completely, however.

GROWING MEDIA: Plants may be mounted on tree-fern or cork slabs or potted in small pots filled with any open, fast-draining medium. Repotting may be done anytime new roots are actively growing.

Plant and Flower Information

PLANT SIZE AND TYPE: A sympodial epiphyte of unreported size.

PSEUDOBULB: The stems are sparsely leafy.

LEAVES: The leaves are 4 in. (10 cm) long, curved, and very slender.

FLOWERS: 1 per inflorescence. The flowers are 0.6 in. (1.6 cm) long. Sepals and petals are yellowish, and the lip is white.

REFERENCES: 220, 254.

Dendrobium iboense Schlechter. Now considered a synonym of *Diplocaulobium iboense* (Schlechter) A. Hawkes. Blossoms last a single day. REFERENCES: 221, 229, 437, 445.

Dendrobium igneoniveum J. J. Smith

ORIGIN/HABITAT: Western Sumatra near Sipirok. Additional habitat information is not available. Elevation is estimated at 2950 ft. (900 m), so the following temperatures should be used with caution.

CLIMATE: Station #96163, Padang, Sumatra, Indonesia, Lat. 0.9°S, Long. 100.4°E, at 19 ft. (6 m). Temperatures are calculated for an elevation of 2950 ft. (900 m), resulting in probable extremes of 84°F (29°C) and 58°F (15°C).

N/HEMISPHERE	JAN	FEB	MAR	APR	MAY	JUN	JUL	AUG	SEP	OCT	NOV	DEC
°F AVG MAX	77	77	76	76	76	76	77	77	77	77	78	77
°F AVG MIN	64	64	64	64	64	64	64	64	64	65	65	64
DIURNAL RANGE	13	13	12	12	12	12	13	13	13	12	13	13
RAIN/INCHES	10.9	13.7	6.0	19.5	20.4	18.9	13.8	10.2	12.1	14.3	12.4	12.1
HUMIDITY/%	81	82	82	84	85	84	81	81	82	83	81	81
BLOOM SEASON	N/A											
DAYS CLR @ 7AM	5	1	1	0	0	2	2	1	2	2	3	5
DAYS CLR @ 1PM	5	2	2	1	1	3	3	4	3	3	6	5
RAIN/MM	277	348	152	495	518	480	351	259	307	363	315	307
°C AVG MAX	25.2	25.2	24.6	24.6	24.6	24.6	25.2	25.2	25.2	25.2	25.7	25.2
°C AVG MIN	18.0	18.0	18.0	18.0	18.0	18.0	18.0	18.0	18.0	18.5	18.5	18.0
DIURNAL RANGE	7.2	7.2	6.6	6.6	6.6	6.6	7.2	7.2	7.2	6.7	7.2	7.2
S/HEMISPHERE	JUL	AUG	SEP	OCT	NOV	DEC	JAN	FEB	MAR	APR	MAY	JUN

Cultural Recommendations

LIGHT: 2000–2500 fc. Diffused light is preferred.

TEMPERATURES: Throughout the year, days average 76–78°F (25–26°C), and nights average 64–65°F (18–19°C), with a diurnal range of 12–13°F (7°C). Probable extremes vary only a few degrees from the averages, indicating that plants may not tolerate wide temperature fluctuations.

HUMIDITY: Near 80–85% year-round.

WATER: Rainfall is heavy all year. Cultivated plants should be kept moist but not soggy.

FERTILIZER: ¼–½ recommended strength. A balanced fertilizer should be applied weekly to biweekly throughout the year.

REST PERIOD: Growing conditions should be maintained year-round. Water may be reduced somewhat for cultivated plants in winter, especially those grown in the dark, short-day conditions common in temperate latitudes. They should never be allowed to dry out completely, however.

GROWING MEDIA: Plants may be mounted on tree-fern or cork slabs if humidity is high and plants are watered at least once daily in summer. When plants are potted, any open, fast-draining medium may be used. They may be repotted anytime new roots are growing.

MISCELLANEOUS NOTES: The plant was described in 1927 in *Bul. Jard. Bot. Buit.* 3rd sér. 9:161.

Plant and Flower Information

PLANT SIZE AND TYPE: A 16 in. (40 cm) sympodial epiphyte.

PSEUDOBULB: 16 in. (40 cm) long. The stems are grooved and hairless.

LEAVES: Many. The dark green, oblong leaves are 2.0–2.4 in. (5–6 cm) long. They are smaller near the base of the stem. The leaf sheaths are covered with dark hairs.

INFLORESCENCE: Short. Inflorescences emerge from nodes along the stem.

FLOWERS: 3–5 per inflorescence. The conspicuous flowers are 2 in. (5 cm) long. Sepals and petals are white. The lip has orange-red markings on the sidelobes and an orange red blotch at the base of the midlobe.

REFERENCES: 224.

Dendrobium igneoviolaceum J. J. Smith. See *D. violaceum* Kränzlin. REFERENCES: 224, 385, 445.

Dendrobium igneum J. J. Smith

AKA: J. J. Smith (ref. 475) suggested *D. patentissimum* might prove to be a variety of *D. igneum* J. J. Smith.

ORIGIN/HABITAT: Irian Jaya (western New Guinea). Along the Noord River at the base of Nepenthes Hill, plants grow on trees in *Pandanus* and *Metroxylon* swamps. On Geluks Hill, the plants grow in primary forests.

CLIMATE: Station #97796, Kokenau (Kokonau), Irian Jaya, Lat. 4.7°S, Long. 136.4°E, at 10 ft. (3 m). Record extreme temperatures are not available for this location.

N/HEMISPHERE	JAN	FEB	MAR	APR	MAY	JUN	JUL	AUG	SEP	OCT	NOV	DEC
°F AVG MAX	83	83	86	88	90	89	89	89	90	88	87	84
°F AVG MIN	73	73	74	74	74	75	74	74	74	74	74	73
DIURNAL RANGE	10	10	12	14	16	14	15	15	16	14	13	11
RAIN/INCHES	18.4	15.8	18.9	11.6	9.7	10.6	11.5	15.7	11.6	11.6	16.0	19.9
HUMIDITY/%	N/A											
BLOOM SEASON		*										
DAYS CLR	N/A											
RAIN/MM	467	401	479	295	245	269	293	400	294	296	407	506
°C AVG MAX	28.6	28.4	30.2	31.1	32.1	31.9	31.9	31.7	32.0	31.4	30.7	28.7
°C AVG MIN	22.7	22.6	23.3	23.4	23.5	23.7	23.6	23.5	23.4	23.4	23.5	23.0
DIURNAL RANGE	5.9	5.8	6.9	7.7	8.6	8.2	8.3	8.2	8.6	8.0	7.2	5.7
S/HEMISPHERE	JUL	AUG	SEP	OCT	NOV	DEC	JAN	FEB	MAR	APR	MAY	JUN

Cultural Recommendations

LIGHT: 2500–3500 fc.

TEMPERATURES: Throughout the year, days average 83–90°F (28–32°C), and nights average 73–75°F (23–24°C), with a diurnal range of 10–16°F (6–9°C).

HUMIDITY: Information is not available for this location. However, records from nearby locations indicate that humidity probably averages near 85% year-round.

WATER: Rainfall is very heavy year-round. Cultivated plants should be kept moist.

FERTILIZER: ¼–½ recommended strength. A balanced fertilizer should be applied weekly to biweekly throughout the year.

REST PERIOD: Growing conditions should be maintained year-round. Water and fertilizer might be reduced slightly in winter for plants cultivated in the dark, short-day conditions common in the temperate latitudes, but they should never be allowed to dry out completely.

GROWING MEDIA: Because plants must be kept moist, they are easier to manage when potted. Fir bark or any open, fast-draining medium may be used. Repotting may be done anytime new roots are growing.

MISCELLANEOUS NOTES: The bloom season shown in the climate table is based on reports from the habitat.

Plant and Flower Information

PLANT SIZE AND TYPE: A 12–16 in. (30–40 cm) sympodial epiphyte.

PSEUDOBULB: 12–16 in. (30–40 cm) long. The somewhat flattened stems are close together. The small internodes are 0.2–0.3 in. (0.5–0.7 cm).

LEAVES: Many. The leaves are 0.6–1.3 in. (1.5–3.2 cm) long.

INFLORESCENCE: Very short.

FLOWERS: 2 per inflorescence, but plants may produce numerous flowers. The orange flowers are 0.6 in. (1.5 cm) long. The erect lip is 3-lobed with an uneven, toothed margin.

REFERENCES: 220, 254, 445, 470, 475.

Dendrobium imbricatum J. J. Smith

ORIGIN/HABITAT: Irian Jaya (western New Guinea). Plants grow along the upper Digul River. They were cultivated in the botanical garden at Bogor, Java.

CLIMATE: Station #97876, Tanahmerah, Irian Jaya, Lat. 6.1°S, Long. 140.3°E, at 75 ft. (23 m). Temperatures are calculated for an elevation of 500 ft. (150 m), resulting in probable extremes of 97°F (36°C) and 63°F (17°C).

N/HEMISPHERE	JAN	FEB	MAR	APR	MAY	JUN	JUL	AUG	SEP	OCT	NOV	DEC
°F AVG MAX	83	84	86	89	90	89	89	88	89	88	86	84
°F AVG MIN	71	70	70	71	72	73	72	72	72	72	73	72
DIURNAL RANGE	12	14	16	18	18	16	17	16	17	16	13	12
RAIN/INCHES	11.5	12.1	14.7	13.2	14.4	15.9	14.5	15.8	17.4	17.3	15.5	11.9
HUMIDITY/%	N/A											
BLOOM SEASON								*				
DAYS CLR	N/A											
RAIN/MM	292	307	373	335	366	404	368	401	442	439	394	302
°C AVG MAX	28.1	28.7	29.8	31.4	32.0	31.4	31.4	30.9	31.4	30.9	29.8	28.7
°C AVG MIN	21.4	20.9	20.9	21.4	22.0	22.6	22.0	22.0	22.0	22.0	22.6	22.0
DIURNAL RANGE	6.7	7.8	7.9	10.0	10.0	8.8	9.4	8.9	9.4	8.9	7.2	6.7
S/HEMISPHERE	JUL	AUG	SEP	OCT	NOV	DEC	JAN	FEB	MAR	APR	MAY	JUN

Cultural Recommendations

LIGHT: 2000–3000 fc.

TEMPERATURES: Throughout the year, days average 83–90°F (28–32°C), and nights average 70–73°F (21–23°C), with a diurnal range of 12–18°F (7–10°C).

HUMIDITY: Information is not available for this location. However, records from nearby locations indicate that humidity probably averages near 85% year-round.

WATER: Rainfall is very heavy year-round. Cultivated plants should be kept evenly moist but not soggy.

FERTILIZER: ¼–½ recommended strength. A balanced fertilizer should be applied weekly to biweekly throughout the year.

REST PERIOD: Growing conditions should be maintained year-round. Water and fertilizer might be reduced slightly in winter, especially for plants cultivated in the dark, short-day conditions common in temperate latitudes. However, plants should never be allowed dry out completely.

GROWING MEDIA: Because plants must be kept moist, they are easier to manage when potted. Fir bark or any open, fast-draining medium may be used. Repotting may be done anytime new roots are growing.

MISCELLANEOUS NOTES: The bloom season shown in the climate table is based on reports from the habitat. Plants that produce very short-lived flowers commonly bloom several times during the year. Flowering usually occurs 7–14 days after a sudden 10°F (5°C) drop in daytime temperatures.

Plant and Flower Information

PLANT SIZE AND TYPE: A 39 in. (100 cm) sympodial plant.

PSEUDOBULB: 39 in. (100 cm) long. The shiny stems are stiffly erect, clustered, robust, and densely leafy.

LEAVES: Many. The ovate leaves are 1.0–2.6 in. (2.5–6.5 cm) long, thick, roundly bilobed at the apex, and glaucous blue. They become smaller toward the tip of the stem.

INFLORESCENCE: Short. Numerous inflorescences emerge through the leaf sheaths.

FLOWERS: 2 per inflorescence. The shiny yellow flowers are 0.8 in. (2 cm) across. They are thick and fleshy. The small, 3-lobed lip is membrane-like and pale yellow. The small, somewhat triangular midlobe is recurved. It has an uneven margin. The fragrant blossoms are very short lived.

REFERENCES: 220, 254, 445, 470.

Dendrobium imitans Schlechter

ORIGIN/HABITAT: Northern Sulawesi (Celebes). Plants grow on trees on the Minahassa Peninsula near Lansot at 1650–2300 ft. (500–700 m).

CLIMATE: Station #97014, Manado, Sulawesi, Indonesia, Lat. 1.5°N, Long. 124.9°E, at 264 ft. (80 m). Temperatures are calculated for an elevation of 2300 ft. (700 m), resulting in probable extremes of 90°F (32°C) and 58°F (15°C).

N/HEMISPHERE	JAN	FEB	MAR	APR	MAY	JUN	JUL	AUG	SEP	OCT	NOV	DEC
°F AVG MAX	78	78	78	79	80	80	80	82	82	82	80	79
°F AVG MIN	66	66	66	66	67	66	66	66	66	65	66	67
DIURNAL RANGE	12	12	12	13	13	14	14	16	16	17	14	12
RAIN/INCHES	18.6	13.8	12.2	8.0	6.4	6.5	4.8	4.0	3.4	4.9	8.9	14.7
HUMIDITY/%	84	83	83	83	81	80	75	72	75	77	82	83
BLOOM SEASON									*	*	*	
DAYS CLR @ 8AM	4	3	6	11	11	12	12	12	14	17	12	8
DAYS CLR @ 2PM	1	1	1	2	1	3	3	4	4	4	1	1
RAIN/MM	472	351	310	203	163	165	122	102	86	124	226	373
°C AVG MAX	25.7	25.7	25.7	26.3	26.8	26.8	26.8	27.9	27.9	27.9	26.8	26.3
°C AVG MIN	19.0	19.0	19.0	19.0	19.6	19.0	19.0	19.0	19.0	18.5	19.0	19.6
DIURNAL RANGE	6.7	6.7	6.7	7.3	7.2	7.8	7.8	8.9	8.9	9.4	7.8	6.7
S/HEMISPHERE	JUL	AUG	SEP	OCT	NOV	DEC	JAN	FEB	MAR	APR	MAY	JUN

Cultural Recommendations

LIGHT: 2000–3000 fc. The habitat is usually overcast in the afternoon.

TEMPERATURES: Throughout the year, days average 78–82°F (26–28°C), and nights average 65–67°F (19–20°C), with a diurnal range of 12–17°F (8–9°C). The record high is only a few degrees above the average highs.

HUMIDITY: 80–85% most of the year, dropping to 70–75% in late summer and autumn.

WATER: Rainfall is moderate to heavy all year. The driest weather occurs in late summer when temperatures are warm. Cultivated plants should be kept moist but not soggy. Warm water might be beneficial.

FERTILIZER: ¼–½ recommended strength. A balanced fertilizer should be applied weekly to biweekly throughout the year.

REST PERIOD: Growing temperatures should be maintained all year. The plants may rest during the 1–2 month drier period which occurs in late summer and coincides with the period of greatest diurnal range. Cultivated plants should dry out slightly during this period, but they should never remain dry for long. The heaviest rainfall in the habitat occurs in winter, but water should not be increased for cultivated plants. In fact, water should be reduced somewhat for plants grown in the dark, short-day conditions common in temperate latitudes, but they should not be allowed to dry out completely.

GROWING MEDIA: Plants may be mounted on tree-fern or cork slabs if humidity is high and plants are watered at least once daily in summer. When plants are potted, any open, fast-draining medium may be used. Repotting may be done anytime new roots are growing.

MISCELLANEOUS NOTES: The bloom season shown in the climate table is based on collection reports.

Plant and Flower Information

PLANT SIZE AND TYPE: A 39 in. (100 cm) sympodial epiphyte.

PSEUDOBULB: 39 in. (100 cm) long. The rigid stems are erect to spreading and connected by a very short rhizome.

LEAVES: Many. The leaves are 3–4 in. (8–10 cm) long, erect to spreading, and linear.

INFLORESCENCE: Short. Racemes arise from nodes along the stem.

FLOWERS: 2 per inflorescence. The whitish yellow flowers are 0.5 in. (1.3 cm) long. The smooth, oblong midlobe is bilobed with a short point at the apex.

REFERENCES: 221, 436.

Dendrobium imperatrix Kränzlin. See *D. lineale* Rolfe. REFERENCES: 84, 190, 211, 217, 254, 437.

Dendrobium implicatum Fukuyama

ORIGIN/HABITAT: Caroline Islands. On Ponape, plants grow on the trunks of hardwood trees at about 1700 ft. (520 m) on Mt. Tolenkiup and Mt. Tolotom. They are also found in the Palau Islands.

CLIMATE: Station #91348, Ponape, Caroline Islands, Lat. 7.0°N, Long. 158.2°E, at 121 ft. (37 m). Temperatures are calculated for an elevation of 1500 ft. (450 m). Record extreme temperatures are not available for this location.

N/HEMISPHERE	JAN	FEB	MAR	APR	MAY	JUN	JUL	AUG	SEP	OCT	NOV	DEC
°F AVG MAX	82	82	83	84	84	83	83	84	84	84	84	83
°F AVG MIN	73	73	73	73	72	72	71	70	71	71	71	72
DIURNAL RANGE	9	9	10	11	12	11	12	14	13	13	13	11
RAIN/INCHES	13.7	9.4	11.2	12.6	15.2	23.8	22.9	17.1	17.4	15.7	17.0	16.7
HUMIDITY/%	N/A											
BLOOM SEASON							*					
DAYS CLR	N/A											
RAIN/MM	348	239	284	320	386	605	582	434	442	399	432	424
°C AVG MAX	27.5	27.5	28.1	28.6	28.6	28.1	28.1	28.6	28.6	28.6	28.6	28.1
°C AVG MIN	22.5	22.5	22.5	22.5	22.0	22.0	21.4	20.8	21.4	21.4	21.4	22.0
DIURNAL RANGE	5.0	5.0	5.6	6.1	6.6	6.1	6.7	7.8	7.2	7.2	7.2	6.1
S/HEMISPHERE	JUL	AUG	SEP	OCT	NOV	DEC	JAN	FEB	MAR	APR	MAY	JUN

Cultural Recommendations

LIGHT: 2000–3000 fc.

TEMPERATURES: Throughout the year, days average 82–84°F (28–29°C), and nights average 70–73°F (21–23°C), with a diurnal range of 9–14°F (5–8°C).

HUMIDITY: Information is not available for this location. However, records from nearby locations indicate that humidity probably averages near 80% year-round.

WATER: Rainfall is heavy all year. Cultivated plants should be kept moist but not soggy.

FERTILIZER: ¼–½ recommended strength. A balanced fertilizer should be applied weekly to biweekly throughout the year.

REST PERIOD: Growing conditions vary only slightly all year. Water should be reduced somewhat for plants cultivated in the dark, short-day conditions common in temperate-latitude winters, but they should never be allowed to dry out completely. Fertilizer should be reduced or eliminated anytime water is reduced.

GROWING MEDIA: Plants may be mounted on tree-fern or cork slabs if humidity is high and plants are watered at least once daily in summer. When plants are potted, any open, fast-draining medium may be used. Repotting may be done anytime new roots are growing.

MISCELLANEOUS NOTES: The bloom season shown in the climate table is based on reports from the habitat.

Plant and Flower Information

PLANT SIZE AND TYPE: A 24 in. (60 cm) sympodial epiphyte.

PSEUDOBULB: 24 in. (60 cm) long. The erect, rigid growths are clustered.

LEAVES: Many. The lanceolate leaves are 3.5–4.3 in. (9–11 cm) long.

INFLORESCENCE: Very short. Inflorescences emerge from nodes along the side of the stem.

FLOWERS: 2 per inflorescence. The flowers are 0.8–1.8 in. (2.0–4.5 cm) long. Blossoms may be pale green or pale pink with darker spots or blotches.

REFERENCES: 135, 189, 226.

Dendrobium imthurnii Rolfe. See *D. gouldii* Rchb. f. REFERENCES: 84, 221, 270, 271, 445.

Dendrobium inaequale Finet not Rolfe. See *D. austrocaledonicum* Schlechter not Rolfe. REFERENCES: 118, 173, 211, 219, 254, 270, 271, 432, 470.

Dendrobium inaequale Rolfe not Finet

AKA: Sometimes spelled *D. inequale. D. coxii* F. M. Bailey. Schlechter (ref. 437) listed *D. purissimum* Kränzlin as a synonym. Kränzlin (ref. 254) and Clements (ref. 67) indicate that *D. coxii* Bailey may be a synonym of *D. inaequale*, in which case the name *D. coxii* would have priority. However, Clements states that the type specimen for *D. coxii* lacks floral material and the description lacks information regarding origin.

ORIGIN/HABITAT: New Guinea. In Irian Jaya (western New Guinea), plants were collected near Jayapura (Hollandia). In Papua New Guinea, they are widespread in the Waria District where they normally grow at 1500–2950 ft. (450–900 m). They are also found in the forests of the Kani Range at about 2000 ft. (600 m). Only rarely are they found at lower elevations. Plants usually grow near the tips of branches on very tall forest trees.

CLIMATE: Station #200192, Garaina, Papua New Guinea, Lat. 7.9°S, Long. 147.1°E, at 2350 ft. (716 m). Record extreme temperatures are 94°F (34°C) and 46°F (8°C).

N/HEMISPHERE	JAN	FEB	MAR	APR	MAY	JUN	JUL	AUG	SEP	OCT	NOV	DEC
°F AVG MAX	80	82	83	84	85	85	85	85	84	84	83	81
°F AVG MIN	63	63	63	64	63	64	65	65	65	64	64	63
DIURNAL RANGE	17	19	20	20	22	21	20	20	19	20	19	18
RAIN/INCHES	5.8	6.5	8.7	11.1	11.8	11.9	8.9	11.7	11.5	9.9	7.7	5.2
HUMIDITY/%	84	82	82	81	80	80	81	81	82	83	84	84
BLOOM SEASON									*	*	*	*
DAYS CLR	N/A											
RAIN/MM	148	166	220	282	300	303	227	296	291	251	195	131
°C AVG MAX	26.8	27.5	28.2	28.6	29.3	29.3	29.4	29.4	29.1	28.7	28.2	27.2
°C AVG MIN	16.9	16.9	17.4	17.6	17.4	18.0	18.1	18.2	18.4	17.7	17.7	17.1
DIURNAL RANGE	9.9	10.6	10.8	11.0	11.1	11.3	11.3	11.2	10.7	11.0	10.5	10.1
S/HEMISPHERE	JUL	AUG	SEP	OCT	NOV	DEC	JAN	FEB	MAR	APR	MAY	JUN

Cultural Recommendations

LIGHT: 2500–3500 fc.

TEMPERATURES: Throughout the year, days average 80–85°F (27–29°C), and nights average 63–65°F (17–18°C), with a diurnal range of 17–22°F (10–12°C).

HUMIDITY: 80–85% year-round.

WATER: Rainfall is heavy all year, with a slightly drier period in winter. Cultivated plants should be kept moist but not soggy.

FERTILIZER: ¼–½ recommended strength. A balanced fertilizer should be applied weekly to biweekly throughout the year.

REST PERIOD: Growing conditions vary only slightly during the year. In the habitat, rainfall is lowest in winter. Water should be reduced somewhat, especially for plants grown in the dark, short-day conditions common during temperate-latitude winters, but they should never be allowed to dry out completely. Fertilizer should be reduced or eliminated anytime water is reduced. In the habitat, light is slightly higher in winter.

GROWING MEDIA: Plants may be mounted on tree-fern or cork slabs if humidity is high and plants are watered at least once daily in summer. When plants are potted, any open, fast-draining medium may be used. Repotting is best done in early spring when new roots are growing.

MISCELLANEOUS NOTES: The bloom season shown in the climate table is based on collection reports. Plants that produce flowers which last a single day commonly bloom several times each year. Flowering

Dendrobium inamoenum

usually occurs 7–14 days after a sudden 10°F (5°C) drop in daytime temperatures.

Plant and Flower Information

PLANT SIZE AND TYPE: A small, 8–12 in. (20–30 cm) sympodial epiphyte.

PSEUDOBULB: 4–8 in. (10–20 cm) long. The dark, quadrangular pseudobulbs have several joints. The edges are flattened and very sharp. Stems are clustered and emerge from a shortly branched, rooting, creeping rhizome. They are swollen in the middle and taper at each end.

LEAVES: 2–5 at the apex of each growth. The lanceolate leaves are 4–8 in. (10–20 cm) long, dark green, and leathery.

INFLORESCENCE: Inflorescences emerge from cavities of alternate nodes on the 2 adjacent exterior faces of the pseudobulb.

FLOWERS: 1–4 per inflorescence. The short-lived flowers are 1.0–1.4 in. (2.5–3.5 cm) across. They may be cupped, nearly forming a small round ball, or open fully to a star-shaped blossom. Sepals and petals may be white or deep cream. The lip is bright yellow with brown or purple veins at the apex. The midlobe has 5 raised cinnamon-brown ribs and a brown margin. The callus is yellow with brown spots.

REFERENCES: 67, 92, 210, 219, 254, 304, 413, 437, 445, 470, 537.

PHOTOS/DRAWINGS: 210, 254, *304*, 437.

Dendrobium inamoenum Kränzlin

ORIGIN/HABITAT: Papua New Guinea. Plants are found at 8850–9850 ft. (2700–3000 m).

CLIMATE: Station #200243, Mt. Hagen, Papua New Guinea, Lat. 5.8°S, Long. 144.3°E, at 5350 ft. (1630 m). Temperatures are calculated for an elevation of 9200 ft. (2800 m), resulting in probable extremes of 75°F (24°C) and 22°F (–5°C).

N/HEMISPHERE	JAN	FEB	MAR	APR	MAY	JUN	JUL	AUG	SEP	OCT	NOV	DEC
°F AVG MAX	59	60	61	62	63	63	63	63	62	62	63	61
°F AVG MIN	42	42	42	42	42	43	43	43	43	44	43	41
DIURNAL RANGE	17	18	19	20	21	20	20	20	19	18	20	20
RAIN/INCHES	5.2	6.7	8.7	8.7	8.2	10.2	10.4	10.7	11.2	10.0	7.2	4.7
HUMIDITY/%	84	83	82	78	79	81	81	80	82	81	82	82
BLOOM SEASON	N/A											
DAYS CLR	N/A											
RAIN/MM	132	170	221	221	208	259	264	272	284	254	183	119
°C AVG MAX	15.2	15.7	16.3	16.8	17.4	17.4	17.4	17.4	16.8	16.8	17.4	16.3
°C AVG MIN	5.7	5.7	5.7	5.7	5.7	6.3	6.3	6.3	6.3	6.8	6.3	5.2
DIURNAL RANGE	9.5	10.0	10.6	11.1	11.7	11.1	11.1	11.1	10.5	10.0	11.1	11.1
S/HEMISPHERE	JUL	AUG	SEP	OCT	NOV	DEC	JAN	FEB	MAR	APR	MAY	JUN

Cultural Recommendations

LIGHT: 1800–2500 fc.

TEMPERATURES: Throughout the year, days average 59–63°F (15–17°C), and nights average 41–44°F (5–7°C), with a diurnal range of 17–20°F (10–11°C).

HUMIDITY: Near 80% year-round.

WATER: Rainfall is moderate to heavy all year. Cultivated plants should be kept moist but not soggy.

FERTILIZER: ¼–½ recommended strength. A balanced fertilizer should be applied weekly to biweekly throughout the year.

REST PERIOD: Growing temperatures should be maintained all year. Water should be reduced for plants cultivated in the dark, short-day conditions common during temperate-latitude winters, but they should never be allowed to dry out completely. Fertilizer should be reduced or eliminated when water is reduced. In the habitat, light is slightly higher in winter.

GROWING MEDIA: Plants may be mounted on tree-fern or cork slabs if humidity is high and plants are watered at least once daily in summer. When plants are potted, any open, fast-draining medium may be used. Repotting may be done anytime new roots are growing.

MISCELLANEOUS NOTES: The plant was described in 1909 in *Bul. Dép. Agric. Indes. Néerl.* 19:17.

Plant and Flower Information

PLANT SIZE AND TYPE: A sympodial epiphyte of unreported size.

PSEUDOBULB: The apical part of the stem is leafy.

LEAVES: Many. The linear-lanceolate leaves are about 2.4 in. (6 cm) long.

INFLORESCENCE: 0.8 in. (2 cm) long. Inflorescences arise from nodes near the apex of older, leafless stems.

FLOWERS: 3–5 per inflorescence. The yellow flowers are 0.5 in. (1.2 cm) long. The sepals and much smaller petals resemble a flared fan. The lip, which is narrow and cupped at the apex, has an uneven front edge.

REFERENCES: 220, 254.

PHOTOS/DRAWINGS: 254.

Dendrobium inauditum Rchb. f. Now considered a synonym of *Diplocaulobium inauditum* (Rchb. f.) Kränzlin. REFERENCES: 179, 218, 220, 254, 445.

Dendrobium inconcinnum Ridley. See note at *D. podagraria* Hooker f. REFERENCES: 254, 395, 454.

Dendrobium inconspicuiflorum J. J. Smith. See *D. indragiriense* Schlechter. REFERENCES: 56, 222, 286, 295, 445, 454.

Dendrobium inconspicuum J. J. Smith

ORIGIN/HABITAT: Irian Jaya (western New Guinea). Plants are common on Biak in the Schouten Islands where they grow on strand trees.

CLIMATE: Station #97560 Mokmer, Biak Island, Irian Jaya, Lat. 1.2°S, Long. 136.1°E, at 46 ft. (14 m). Record extreme temperatures are 91°F (33°C) and 70°F (21°C).

N/HEMISPHERE	JAN	FEB	MAR	APR	MAY	JUN	JUL	AUG	SEP	OCT	NOV	DEC
°F AVG MAX	85	86	86	87	87	86	86	85	86	86	87	87
°F AVG MIN	74	75	74	75	75	75	74	74	75	75	75	75
DIURNAL RANGE	11	11	12	12	12	11	12	11	11	11	12	12
RAIN/INCHES	11.3	11.2	7.0	6.1	7.3	12.5	11.0	8.2	11.7	8.3	8.6	10.5
HUMIDITY/%	85	84	83	83	84	85	84	85	86	85	87	86
BLOOM SEASON	*											
DAYS CLR @ 9AM	2	2	4	1	2	1	2	1	2	1	2	3
DAYS CLR @ 3PM	3	3	3	3	2	1	2	1	2	2	1	2
RAIN/MM	287	284	178	155	185	318	279	208	297	211	218	267
°C AVG MAX	29.4	30.0	30.0	30.6	30.6	30.0	30.0	29.4	30.0	30.0	30.6	30.6
°C AVG MIN	23.3	23.9	23.3	23.9	23.9	23.9	23.3	23.3	23.9	23.9	23.9	23.9
DIURNAL RANGE	6.1	6.1	6.7	6.7	6.7	6.1	6.7	6.1	6.1	6.1	6.7	6.7
S/HEMISPHERE	JUL	AUG	SEP	OCT	NOV	DEC	JAN	FEB	MAR	APR	MAY	JUN

Cultural Recommendations

LIGHT: 2500–3500 fc. The heavy summer cloud cover indicates that some shading is needed from spring through autumn, but light should be as high as the plant can tolerate, short of burning the leaves. Strong air movement is recommended all year.

TEMPERATURES: Throughout the year, days average 85–87°F (29–31°C), and nights average 74–75°F (23–24°C), with a diurnal range of 11–12°F (6–7°C).

HUMIDITY: Near 85% year-round.

WATER: Rainfall is heavy all year with no real dry season. Cultivated plants should be kept moist but not soggy. Warm water might be beneficial.

FERTILIZER: ¼–½ recommended strength. A balanced fertilizer should be applied weekly to biweekly throughout the year.

REST PERIOD: Growing temperatures should be maintained year-round. In the habitat, rainfall is heavy; but water and fertilizer might be reduced for plants grown in the dark, short-day conditions common in temperate-latitude winters. They should never be allowed to dry out completely, however. In the habitat, seasonal light variation is minor.

GROWING MEDIA: Plants may be mounted on tree-fern or cork slabs if humidity is high and plants are watered at least once daily in summer. When plants are potted, any open, fast-draining medium may be used. They may be repotted anytime new roots are growing.

MISCELLANEOUS NOTES: The bloom season shown in the climate table is based on records from the habitat.

Plant and Flower Information

PLANT SIZE AND TYPE: A 30 in. (75 cm) sympodial epiphyte. Plant size is based on an incomplete specimen.

PSEUDOBULB: 30 in. (75 cm) long. The shiny stems are elongated, branched, and flattened.

LEAVES: Many. The widely spaced leaves are 2 in. (5 cm) long. They are lanceolate-linear, erect-spreading, and flattened.

INFLORESCENCE: Short. Inflorescences are borne at nodes on the upper part of the stem.

FLOWERS: 1 per inflorescence. The very tiny yellow flowers are 0.1 in. (0.3 cm) across.

REFERENCES: 144, 222, 445.

Dendrobium inconstans J. J. Smith. Now considered a synonym of *Diplocaulobium inconstans* (J. J. Smith) Kränzlin. REFERENCES: 220, 254, 445, 470.

Dendrobium incrassatum (Blume) Miquel. See *D. indivisum* (Blume) Miquel. REFERENCES: 75, 216, 310, 448, 454, 469

Dendrobium incumbens Schlechter

ORIGIN/HABITAT: Northern Papua New Guinea. Plants grow on forest trees at 130 ft. (40 m) along the coast near Alexishafen. They are also found along the Waria River near Jaduna at about 500 ft. (150 m).

CLIMATE: Station #94014, Madang, Papua New Guinea, Lat. 5.2°S, Long. 145.8°E, at 13 ft. (4 m). Record extreme temperatures are 98°F (37°C) and 62°F (17°C).

N/HEMISPHERE	JAN	FEB	MAR	APR	MAY	JUN	JUL	AUG	SEP	OCT	NOV	DEC
°F AVG MAX	83	83	85	85	85	85	85	85	85	87	87	84
°F AVG MIN	77	78	78	78	77	77	77	77	77	76	77	78
DIURNAL RANGE	6	5	7	7	8	8	8	8	8	11	10	6
RAIN/INCHES	4.0	3.4	3.2	8.5	11.2	11.1	10.1	11.3	9.4	11.3	10.5	6.7
HUMIDITY/%	88	87	86	86	86	86	86	85	85	87	88	89
BLOOM SEASON			*	*								
DAYS CLR	N/A											
RAIN/MM	102	86	81	216	284	282	257	287	239	287	267	170
°C AVG MAX	28.3	28.3	29.4	29.4	29.4	29.4	29.4	29.4	29.4	30.6	30.6	28.9
°C AVG MIN	25.0	25.6	25.6	25.6	25.0	25.0	25.0	25.0	25.0	24.4	25.0	25.6
DIURNAL RANGE	3.3	2.7	3.8	3.8	4.4	4.4	4.4	4.4	4.4	6.2	5.6	3.3
S/HEMISPHERE	JUL	AUG	SEP	OCT	NOV	DEC	JAN	FEB	MAR	APR	MAY	JUN

Cultural Recommendations

LIGHT: 2000–3000 fc. is suggested initially.

TEMPERATURES: Throughout the year, days average 83–87°F (28–31°C), and nights average 76–78°F (24–26°C), with a diurnal range of 5–11°F (3–6°C). The warmest highs, the coolest lows, and the greatest diurnal range occur in autumn.

HUMIDITY: 85–90% year-round.

WATER: Rainfall is moderate to heavy all year. The driest conditions occur in late winter. Cultivated plants should be kept moist but not soggy.

FERTILIZER: ¼–½ recommended strength. A balanced fertilizer should be applied weekly to biweekly throughout the year.

REST PERIOD: Growing temperatures should be maintained all year. In the habitat, rainfall decreases for 4 months in winter. Water should be reduced for cultivated plants, but they should not be allowed to dry out completely. Fertilizer should be reduced or eliminated while water is reduced. In the habitat, light is slightly higher in late winter.

GROWING MEDIA: Plants may be mounted on tree-fern or cork slabs if humidity is high and plants are watered at least once daily in summer. When plants are potted, any open, fast-draining medium may be used. Repotting may be done anytime new roots are growing.

MISCELLANEOUS NOTES: The bloom season shown in the climate table is based on cultivation records. Plants that produce flowers which last a single day commonly bloom several times during the year. Flowering usually occurs 7–14 days after a sudden 10°F (5°C) drop in daytime temperatures.

Plant and Flower Information

PLANT SIZE AND TYPE: A 16–20 in. (40–50 cm) sympodial epiphyte.

PSEUDOBULB: 16–20 in. (40–50 cm) long.

LEAVES: Many. The linear leaves are 1.6–3.2 in. (4–8 cm) long.

FLOWERS: 2 per inflorescence. The tiny flowers are 0.25 in. (0.6 cm) long. Sepals and petals are pale yellow. They do not open fully but form a deep pouch. They last a single day.

REFERENCES: 221, 437, 445.

PHOTOS/DRAWINGS: 437.

Dendrobium incurvatum Schlechter

ORIGIN/HABITAT: Northern Papua New Guinea. In the Torricelli Range, plants grow on forest trees at about 2600 ft. (800 m).

CLIMATE: Station #94004, Wewak, Papua New Guinea, Lat. 3.6°S, Long. 143.7°E, at 16 ft. (5 m). Temperatures are calculated for an elevation of 2600 ft. (800 m), resulting in probable extremes of 89°F (32°C) and 53°F (12°C).

N/HEMISPHERE	JAN	FEB	MAR	APR	MAY	JUN	JUL	AUG	SEP	OCT	NOV	DEC
°F AVG MAX	79	79	79	79	79	79	78	77	78	79	79	79
°F AVG MIN	65	65	65	66	66	66	66	66	65	65	66	65
DIURNAL RANGE	14	14	14	13	13	13	12	11	13	14	13	14
RAIN/INCHES	7.6	4.8	5.3	10.0	13.3	14.5	12.1	11.9	14.9	16.9	15.1	10.8
HUMIDITY/%	80	79	79	78	79	81	82	82	81	82	81	80
BLOOM SEASON									*			
DAYS CLR	N/A											
RAIN/MM	193	122	135	254	338	368	307	302	378	429	384	274
°C AVG MAX	26.3	26.3	26.3	26.3	26.3	26.3	25.8	25.2	25.8	26.3	26.3	26.3
°C AVG MIN	18.6	18.6	18.6	19.1	19.1	19.1	19.1	19.1	18.6	18.6	19.1	18.6
DIURNAL RANGE	7.7	7.7	7.7	7.2	7.2	7.2	6.7	6.1	7.2	7.7	7.2	7.7
S/HEMISPHERE	JUL	AUG	SEP	OCT	NOV	DEC	JAN	FEB	MAR	APR	MAY	JUN

Cultural Recommendations

LIGHT: 2000–3000 fc.

TEMPERATURES: Throughout the year, days average 77–79°F (25–26°C), and nights average 65–66°F (19°C), with a diurnal range of 11–14°F (6–8°C).

HUMIDITY: Near 80% year-round.

WATER: Rainfall is heavy all year, but conditions are slightly drier for 1–2 months in winter. Cultivated plants should be kept moist but not soggy.

FERTILIZER: ¼–½ recommended strength. A balanced fertilizer should be applied weekly to biweekly throughout the year.

Dendrobium incurvilabium

- REST PERIOD: Growing conditions should be maintained year-round. Water should be reduced somewhat for plants cultivated in the dark, short-day conditions common during temperate-latitude winters. They should never be allowed to dry out completely, however. Fertilizer should be reduced anytime water is reduced. In the habitat, light is slightly higher in winter.
- GROWING MEDIA: A very open and fast-draining medium should be used with either baskets or small pots. Repotting may be done anytime new roots are growing.
- MISCELLANEOUS NOTES: The bloom season shown in the climate table is based on collection reports.

Plant and Flower Information

- PLANT SIZE AND TYPE: A 12–16 in. (30–40 cm) sympodial epiphyte.
- PSEUDOBULB: 12–16 in. (30–40 cm) long. The leafy stems are curved and unbranched.
- LEAVES: Many. The lanceolate, spreading leaves are 1.4–2.2 in. (3.6–5.5 cm) long.
- INFLORESCENCE: Very short. Inflorescences emerge from nodes at the side of the pseudobulb. The blossoms are nearly opposite each other on the inflorescence.
- FLOWERS: 2 per inflorescence. The flowers are 0.6 in. (1.5 cm) long. The blossoms are spreading but do not open fully. They are densely covered with violet-red spots. The sepals are so incurved that they are almost curly.
- REFERENCES: 221, 437, 445.
- PHOTOS/DRAWINGS: 437.

Dendrobium incurvilabium Schlechter. See *D. dendrocolloides* J. J. Smith. REFERENCES: 83, 222.

Dendrobium incurvociliatum J. J. Smith

- ORIGIN/HABITAT: Central east Borneo. Plants were originally found along the upper Mahakam (Koetai) River. They grew on trees in primeval forests on mountain ridges at about 4900 ft. (1500 m).
- CLIMATE: Station #96633, Balikpapan, Borneo, Lat. 1.3°S, Long. 116.9°E, at 10 ft. (3 m). Temperatures are calculated for an elevation of 4500 ft. (1370 m), resulting in probable extremes of 77°F (25°C) and 45°F (7°C).

N/HEMISPHERE	JAN	FEB	MAR	APR	MAY	JUN	JUL	AUG	SEP	OCT	NOV	DEC
°F AVG MAX	68	69	69	70	70	70	70	71	71	70	70	69
°F AVG MIN	58	59	59	59	58	58	58	58	58	58	59	59
DIURNAL RANGE	10	10	10	11	12	12	12	13	13	12	11	10
RAIN/INCHES	7.1	6.4	5.5	5.2	6.6	8.1	7.9	8.9	9.1	8.2	9.1	7.6
HUMIDITY/%	82	80	77	78	80	79	82	81	81	82	83	82
BLOOM SEASON				*								
DAYS CLR @ 8AM	4	2	3	3	3	3	2	3	4	4	2	5
DAYS CLR @ 2PM	6	4	5	5	3	1	2	1	2	3	4	5
RAIN/MM	180	163	140	132	168	206	201	226	231	208	231	193
°C AVG MAX	20.1	20.7	20.7	21.2	21.2	21.2	21.2	21.8	21.8	21.2	21.2	20.7
°C AVG MIN	14.5	15.1	15.1	15.1	14.5	14.5	14.5	14.5	14.5	14.5	15.1	15.1
DIURNAL RANGE	5.6	5.6	5.6	6.1	6.7	6.7	6.7	7.3	7.3	6.7	6.1	5.6
S/HEMISPHERE	JUL	AUG	SEP	OCT	NOV	DEC	JAN	FEB	MAR	APR	MAY	JUN

Cultural Recommendations

- LIGHT: 2500–3500 fc. The habitat on mountain ridges indicates that high light and strong air movement may be required
- TEMPERATURES: Throughout the year, days average 68–71°F (20–22°C), and nights average 58–59°F (15°C), with a diurnal range of 10–13°F (6–7°C).
- HUMIDITY: Near 80% year-round.
- WATER: Rainfall is heavy most of the year. Conditions are slightly drier for 2 months in late winter or early spring. Cultivated plants should be kept moist while actively growing, with only slight drying allowed between waterings.
- FERTILIZER: ¼–½ recommended strength. A balanced fertilizer should be applied weekly to biweekly throughout the year.
- REST PERIOD: Growing temperatures should be maintained year-round. Water may be reduced somewhat in winter, especially for plants cultivated in the dark, short-day conditions common in temperate latitudes. Plants should never be allowed to dry out completely, however. Fertilizer should be reduced or eliminated if water is reduced. In the habitat, light is slightly higher in winter.
- GROWING MEDIA: Plants may be mounted on tree-fern or cork slabs or potted in small pots filled with any open, fast-draining medium. Repotting may be done anytime new roots are actively growing.
- MISCELLANEOUS NOTES: The bloom season shown in the climate table is based on reports from the habitat. The plant was described in 1931 in *Bul. Jard. Bot. Buit.* 3rd sér. 11:137.

Plant and Flower Information

- PLANT SIZE AND TYPE: A 9–13 in. (23–33 cm) sympodial epiphyte.
- PSEUDOBULB: 9–13 in. (23–33 cm) long. The flattened pseudobulbs are swollen near the base.
- LEAVES: Many. The linear leaves are 0.2 in. (0.5 cm) long, rigidly papery, and unequally bilobed at the apex.
- INFLORESCENCE: Short. Clusters of blossoms appear from nodes along the upper, leafless portion of the stem.
- FLOWERS: Several per inflorescence. The flowers are 0.6 in. (1.5 cm) long. Sepals and petals are light yellow. The somewhat erect lip is triangular, concave, marked with transverse brown streaks, with a very long fringe along the margin.
- REFERENCES: 225, 286.

Dendrobium incurvum Lindley

- AKA: *D. aclinia* Lindley not Rchb. f. Seidenfaden and Wood (ref. 455) indicate that the name *D. eriaeflorum* is sometimes erroneously applied to this plant.
- ORIGIN/HABITAT: Burma near Mergui in the Tenasserim Region. The habitat includes peninsular Thailand and extends into the northern part of Kedah state in Malaya. In Vietnam, plants grow near Bao Loc. Habitat elevation is unavailable, so the following temperatures should be used with caution.
- CLIMATE: Station #48110, Mergui, Burma, Lat. 12.4°N, Long. 98.6°E, at 75 ft. (23 m). Record extreme temperatures are 99°F (37°C) and 53°F (12°C).

N/HEMISPHERE	JAN	FEB	MAR	APR	MAY	JUN	JUL	AUG	SEP	OCT	NOV	DEC
°F AVG MAX	87	89	90	91	89	85	84	84	84	86	87	87
°F AVG MIN	69	71	73	75	75	74	73	73	73	73	71	69
DIURNAL RANGE	18	18	17	16	14	11	11	11	11	13	16	18
RAIN/INCHES	1.0	2.1	3.1	4.9	16.7	30.0	32.9	30.0	24.9	12.1	3.8	0.8
HUMIDITY/%	73	75	78	79	86	91	93	94	92	86	79	75
BLOOM SEASON	N/A											
DAYS CLR @ 7AM	9	3	4	2	0	0	0	0	0	1	4	8
DAYS CLR @ 1PM	11	7	4	2	0	0	0	0	0	1	4	9
RAIN/MM	25	53	79	124	424	762	836	762	632	307	97	20
°C AVG MAX	30.6	31.7	32.2	32.8	31.7	29.4	28.9	28.9	28.9	30.0	30.6	30.6
°C AVG MIN	20.6	21.7	22.8	23.9	23.9	23.3	22.8	22.8	22.8	22.8	21.7	20.6
DIURNAL RANGE	10.0	10.0	9.4	8.9	7.8	6.1	6.1	6.1	6.1	7.2	8.9	10.0
S/HEMISPHERE	JUL	AUG	SEP	OCT	NOV	DEC	JAN	FEB	MAR	APR	MAY	JUN

Cultural Recommendations

- LIGHT: 2000–3000 fc.

TEMPERATURES: Throughout the year, days average 84–91°F (29–33°C), and nights average 69–75°F (21–24°C), with a diurnal range of 11–18°F (6–10°C).

HUMIDITY: 85–95% in summer and autumn, dropping to near 75% in winter and spring.

WATER: Rainfall is very heavy for 6 months during summer and early autumn, but is reduced considerably for 2–3 months in winter. Cultivated plants should be kept moist while actively growing, but water should be gradually reduced in autumn.

FERTILIZER: ¼–½ recommended strength. A balanced fertilizer should be applied weekly to biweekly throughout the year.

REST PERIOD: Growing conditions should be maintained all year. Rainfall is lower for 2–3 months in winter, but high humidity and nightly cooling cause frequent, heavy dew. Therefore, considerable moisture is available and the dry season is neither as long or as severe as indicated by the rainfall averages. Water should be reduced and cultivated plants allowed to dry out between waterings, but they should not remain dry for long periods. Fertilizer should be reduced or eliminated anytime water is reduced. In the habitat, light is highest in winter.

GROWING MEDIA: Plants may be mounted on tree-fern or cork slabs if humidity is high and plants are watered at least once daily in summer. When plants are potted, any open, fast-draining medium may be used. Repotting is best done in early spring when new roots are growing.

MISCELLANEOUS NOTES: Plants that produce flowers which last a single day commonly bloom several times each year. Flowering usually occurs 7–14 days after a sudden 10°F (5°C) drop in daytime temperatures.

Plant and Flower Information

PLANT SIZE AND TYPE: A 5–6 in. (13–15 cm) sympodial epiphyte. The growth habit is similar to that of *D. eriaeflorum*.

PSEUDOBULB: 3–6 in. (8–15 cm) long. Each stem consists of many internodes.

LEAVES: 3 or more per growth. The linear-oblong leaves are 2–3 in. (5–8 cm) long. They are notched at the apex.

INFLORESCENCE: 1.0–1.5 in. (2.5–3.8 cm) long. Inflorescences emerge from nodes opposite the leaves below the apex of the pseudobulb.

FLOWERS: 4–8 per inflorescence. The greenish yellow flowers are 0.4 in. (1 cm) long and do not open fully. Sepals and petals are narrow. The lip is oblong, concave, and ruffled. It is greenish with purple lines. One form has abnormal flowers with the lip the same shape as the sepals and petals. Blossoms last a single day.

REFERENCES: 157, 202, 216, 254, 278, 452, 454, 455.

PHOTOS/DRAWINGS: 454, 455.

Dendrobium indivisum (Blume) Miquel

AKA: *Aporum indivisum* Blume, *Dendrobium eulophotum* Lindley, *D. incrassatum* (Blume) Miquel. Seidenfaden (ref. 454) discussed the problems surrounding the taxonomy of these plants and considered them a variable alliance. He included *D. porphyrophyllum* Guillaumin as a synonym of *D. indivisum* var. *lampangense* Rolfe, (*D. neolampangense* L. V. Aver'yanov). However, in 1992 *Opera Botanica* 114, Seidenfaden included *D. porphyrophyllum* as a separate species with *D. indivisum* var. *lampangense* and *D. neolampangense* as synonyms. The species are considered together in this work, as the differences do not alter the way the plants are grown.

ORIGIN/HABITAT: The Tenasserim region of Burma, northern Thailand, Laos, Malaya, Sumatra, Java, Borneo, and the Molucca Islands. In Malaya, plants grow in exposed locations and low on Mangrove trees. In Borneo, plants are found in the lower hill forests of Sabah at about 1950 ft. (600 m); and in Java, they are very common on trees from sea level to 5250 ft. (0–1600 m). Plants known as *D. porphyrophyllum* grow near Vientiane, Laos and Dalat, Vietnam.

CLIMATE: Station #48375, Ban Mae Sot, Thailand, Lat. 16.7°N, Long. 98.5°E, at 742 ft. (800 m). Temperatures are calculated for an elevation of 2600 ft. (800 m), resulting in probable extremes of 100°F (38°C) and 32°F (0°C).

N/HEMISPHERE	JAN	FEB	MAR	APR	MAY	JUN	JUL	AUG	SEP	OCT	NOV	DEC
°F AVG MAX	83	87	91	93	88	81	79	79	82	84	83	81
°F AVG MIN	52	55	61	67	69	69	68	69	68	66	61	54
DIURNAL RANGE	31	32	30	26	19	12	11	10	14	18	22	27
RAIN/INCHES	0.2	0.2	0.2	1.5	5.7	8.8	13.6	16.0	7.8	4.1	0.7	0.1
HUMIDITY/%	67	64	58	63	75	84	86	87	85	81	76	74
BLOOM SEASON						*	*	*	*	*	*	*
DAYS CLR @ 7AM	2	1	2	5	1	0	0	0	0	2	2	2
DAYS CLR @ 1PM	20	19	17	10	1	0	0	0	0	2	7	13
RAIN/MM	5	5	5	38	145	224	345	406	198	104	18	3
°C AVG MAX	28.2	30.4	32.7	33.8	31.0	27.1	26.0	26.0	27.7	28.8	28.2	27.1
°C AVG MIN	11.0	12.7	16.0	19.3	20.4	20.4	19.9	20.4	19.9	18.8	16.0	12.1
DIURNAL RANGE	17.2	17.7	16.7	14.5	10.6	6.7	6.1	5.6	7.8	10.0	12.2	15.0
S/HEMISPHERE	JUL	AUG	SEP	OCT	NOV	DEC	JAN	FEB	MAR	APR	MAY	JUN

Cultural Recommendations

LIGHT: 1800–2500 fc. Diffused light is recommended. In nature, clear days in summer are rare.

TEMPERATURES: Summer days average 79–81°F (26–27°C), and nights average 68–69°F (20°C), with a diurnal range of 10–12°F (6–7°C). The warmest season is spring. Days average 88–93°F (31–34°C), and nights average 61–69°F (16–20°C), with a diurnal range of 19–30°F (11–17°C).

HUMIDITY: 75–85% during the growing season, dropping to near 60–65% in winter and early spring.

WATER: Rainfall is moderate to heavy for 6 months from late spring through early autumn. Conditions are dry the balance of the year. Cultivated plants should be kept moist while actively growing, but water should be gradually reduced in autumn after new growths mature.

FERTILIZER: ¼–½ recommended strength, applied weekly. A high-nitrogen fertilizer is beneficial from spring to midsummer, but a fertilizer high in phosphates should be used in late summer and autumn.

REST PERIOD: In Thailand, winter days average 81–87°F (27–30°C), and nights average 52–55°F (11–13°C), with a diurnal range of 27–32°F (15–18°C). The increased diurnal range results from warmer days and cooler nights during clear winter weather. In other habitats, winter temperatures may be warmer and the diurnal range less extreme than in the Thailand habitat. Whether plants from one region can adapt to the very different conditions found in other parts of the habitat is not known.

In the Thailand habitat, rainfall is low for 4–6 months, but except for 1–2 months in late winter, additional moisture is often available from dew, fog, and morning mist. For cultivated plants, water should be reduced and the plants allowed to dry out somewhat between waterings for most of the winter; but they should not remain dry for extended periods. For 1–2 months in late winter, however, plants should be allowed to dry out completely. A light watering or early morning misting may be given if plants start to shrivel or show other signs of stress. Fertilizer should be reduced or eliminated anytime the plants are not actively growing. In the habitat, light is highest in winter.

GROWING MEDIA: Plants may be mounted on tree-fern or cork slabs if humidity is high and plants are watered at least once daily in summer. When plants are potted, any open, fast-draining medium may be used. Repotting is best done in early spring when new roots are growing.

MISCELLANEOUS NOTES: The bloom season shown in the climate table is based on cultivation records. Ridley (ref. 395) indicated that low-elevation plants flower all year.

Dendrobium indivisum

Plant and Flower Information

PLANT SIZE AND TYPE: A 4–16 in. (10–40 cm) sympodial epiphyte.

PSEUDOBULB: 4–16 in. (10–40 cm) long. The stems are covered by the overlapping leaf bases.

LEAVES: Many. The leaves are 0.5–1.0 in. (1.2–2.5 cm) long. They are normally thick, folded, flattened, distichous, and overlapping at the base. Leaf shape is variable. They persist for several seasons.

INFLORESCENCE: Very short. Inflorescences emerge near the bases of numerous leaves. The blossoms are held at all angles, so that the lip may be uppermost.

FLOWERS: 1 per inflorescence. The tiny, fan-shaped flowers are 0.1–0.4 in. (0.3–0.9 cm) long. They open simultaneously. Sepals and petals are pale greenish to greenish yellow with few to many crimson or purple veins and longitudinal streaks. The 3-lobed lip is white with a pink flush. It is variably heart-shaped with rounded, uneven sidelobes. Flower color and lip shape take many intermediate forms. The plant known as *D. porphyrophyllum* has small, earlike sidelobes. *D. indivisum* var. *pallidum* Seidenfaden has no purple stripes.

HYBRIDIZING NOTES: Chromosome count is n = 19 (ref. 504) as *D. porphyrophyllum*. Johansen (ref. 239) indicates that *D. indivisum* var. *pallidum* is self-sterile and that flowers dropped 4–10 days after self-pollination.

REFERENCES: 25, 75, 179, 200, 202, 216, 234, 239, 254, 266, 278, 286, 295, 310, 394, 395, 402, 418, 435, 447, 448, 454, 455, 469, 504, 510, 580, 592.

PHOTOS/DRAWINGS: 75, *454*, 455, 469, *510*.

Dendrobium indivisum Naves. See *D. distichum* (Presl) Rchb. f. REFERENCES: 296, 298, 536.

Dendrobium indochinense A. Hawkes and A. H. Heller.
Now considered a synonym of *Eria corneri* Rchb. f. REFERENCES: 138, 191, 227, 229, Seidenfaden 1992 *Opera Botanica* #114.

Dendrobium indragiriense Schlechter

AKA: Sometimes spelled *D. intragiriense*. Synonyms include *D. gemellum* as used by Ridley (ref. 402), *D. inconspicuiflorum* J. J. Smith, and *D. isomerum* Schlechter.

ORIGIN/HABITAT: South Andaman Island, peninsular Thailand, Malaya, Sumatra, and Borneo. In Sumatra, plants grow at about 2950 ft. (900 m) near Pariaman, Padang Pandjang.

CLIMATE: Station #96163, Padang, Sumatra, Indonesia, Lat. 0.9°S, Long. 100.4°E, at 19 ft. (6 m). Temperatures are calculated for an elevation of 2950 ft. (900 m), resulting in probable extremes of 84°F (29°C) and 58°F (15°C).

N/HEMISPHERE	JAN	FEB	MAR	APR	MAY	JUN	JUL	AUG	SEP	OCT	NOV	DEC
°F AVG MAX	77	77	76	76	76	76	77	77	77	77	78	77
°F AVG MIN	64	64	64	64	64	64	64	64	64	65	65	64
DIURNAL RANGE	13	13	12	12	12	12	13	13	13	12	13	13
RAIN/INCHES	10.9	13.7	6.0	19.5	20.4	18.9	13.8	10.2	12.1	14.3	12.4	12.1
HUMIDITY/%	81	82	82	84	85	84	81	81	82	83	81	81
BLOOM SEASON	N/A											
DAYS CLR @ 7AM	5	1	1	0	0	2	2	1	2	2	3	5
DAYS CLR @ 1PM	5	2	2	1	1	3	3	4	3	3	6	5
RAIN/MM	277	348	152	495	518	480	351	259	307	363	315	307
°C AVG MAX	25.2	25.2	24.6	24.6	24.6	24.6	25.2	25.2	25.2	25.2	25.7	25.2
°C AVG MIN	18.0	18.0	18.0	18.0	18.0	18.0	18.0	18.0	18.0	18.5	18.5	18.0
DIURNAL RANGE	7.2	7.2	6.6	6.6	6.6	6.6	7.2	7.2	7.2	6.7	7.2	7.2
S/HEMISPHERE	JUL	AUG	SEP	OCT	NOV	DEC	JAN	FEB	MAR	APR	MAY	JUN

Cultural Recommendations

LIGHT: 2000–3000 fc.

TEMPERATURES: Throughout the year, days average 76–78°F (25–26°C), and nights average 64–65°F (18–19°C), with a diurnal range of 12–13°F (7°C). Probable extremes vary only a few degrees from the averages, indicating that the plant may not tolerate wide temperature fluctuations.

HUMIDITY: 80–85% year-round.

WATER: Rainfall is heavy all year. Cultivated plants should be kept moist but not soggy.

FERTILIZER: ¼–½ recommended strength. A balanced fertilizer should be applied weekly to biweekly throughout the year.

REST PERIOD: Growing conditions should be maintained year-round. Water may be reduced somewhat for cultivated plants in winter, especially those grown in the dark, short-day conditions common in temperate latitudes. They should never be allowed to dry out completely, however.

GROWING MEDIA: Plants may be mounted on tree-fern or cork slabs if humidity is high and plants are watered at least once daily in summer. When plants are potted, any open, fast-draining medium may be used. Repotting may be done anytime new roots are growing.

MISCELLANEOUS NOTES: *D. indragiriense* produces flowers which last a single day and blooms nearly every month of the year. Flowering usually occurs 7–14 days after a sudden 10°F (5°C) drop in daytime temperatures.

Plant and Flower Information

PLANT SIZE AND TYPE: A 39 in. (100 cm) sympodial epiphyte.

PSEUDOBULB: 39 in. (100 cm) long. The very slender stems consist of many nodes about 0.8 in. (2 cm) apart. The stems are leafy along their entire length.

LEAVES: Many. The narrow leaves are 4–5 in. (10–13 cm) long. They are dark green, papery, linear, and somewhat twisted at the base. The leaves and flowers hang from the stem.

INFLORESCENCE: Short. Numerous inflorescences emerge through the leaf bases from nodes along the leafy stems.

FLOWERS: 2 per inflorescence. The pale yellow flowers are less than 0.5 in. (1.3 cm) long. The blossoms have somewhat incurved lateral sepals and erect, lanceolate petals. The lip has a raised orange band down the center of the slightly crisped, 3-lobed lip. The lip is concave and minutely toothed at the apex. It has no sidelobes.

REFERENCES: 56, 57, 200, 221, 286, 295, 402, 435, 454, 455.

PHOTOS/DRAWINGS: 200, *454*, 455.

Dendrobium inflatum Rolfe

ORIGIN/HABITAT: Common throughout Java at 3000–4000 ft. (920–1220 m). Plants also grow on Bali. In both habitats, they frequently grow on roadside trees in high light.

CLIMATE: Station #96853, Jogjakarta, Java, Indonesia, Lat. 7.8°S, Long. 110.4°E, at 350 ft. (107 m). Temperatures are calculated for an elevation of 3500 ft. (1070 m), resulting in probable extremes of 85°F (29°C) and 52°F (11°C).

N/HEMISPHERE	JAN	FEB	MAR	APR	MAY	JUN	JUL	AUG	SEP	OCT	NOV	DEC
°F AVG MAX	75	76	77	78	76	75	74	74	75	77	76	76
°F AVG MIN	59	59	61	62	62	62	62	62	62	62	62	60
DIURNAL RANGE	16	17	16	16	14	13	12	12	13	15	14	16
RAIN/INCHES	1.6	1.0	1.2	3.7	9.0	13.4	13.9	13.2	12.2	8.3	5.0	3.5
HUMIDITY/%	74	71	69	73	77	82	82	82	81	78	77	74
BLOOM SEASON					*							
DAYS CLR @ 7AM	9	8	7	8	4	2	2	5	7	8	12	
DAYS CLR @ 1PM	6	6	3	3	2	0	1	1	1	2	3	5
RAIN/MM	41	25	30	94	229	340	353	335	310	211	127	89
°C AVG MAX	23.7	24.2	24.8	25.3	24.2	23.7	23.1	23.1	23.7	24.8	24.2	24.2
°C AVG MIN	14.8	14.8	15.9	16.4	16.4	16.4	16.4	16.4	16.4	16.4	16.4	15.3
DIURNAL RANGE	8.9	9.4	8.9	8.9	7.8	7.3	6.7	6.7	7.3	8.4	7.8	8.9
S/HEMISPHERE	JUL	AUG	SEP	OCT	NOV	DEC	JAN	FEB	MAR	APR	MAY	JUN

Cultural Recommendations

LIGHT: 3000–4500 fc. Light should be as high as the plant can tolerate, short of burning the foliage.

TEMPERATURES: Throughout the year, days average 75–78°F (24–25°C), and nights average 59–62°F (15–16°C), with a diurnal range of 12–17°F (7–9°C). The warmest weather occurs in spring.

HUMIDITY: Near 80% in summer and early autumn, dropping to near 70% in winter.

WATER: Rainfall is moderate to heavy from spring through autumn. This is followed by a winter dry season which lasts about 3 months. Cultivated plants should be kept moist from late spring into autumn, but water should be gradually reduced in late autumn, greatly reduced in winter, then gradually increased in spring when new growth starts.

FERTILIZER: ¼–½ recommended strength. A balanced fertilizer should be applied weekly to biweekly throughout the growing sseason.

REST PERIOD: Growing conditions should be maintained all year. Winter nights are somewhat cooler and the diurnal range is slightly larger, but the differences are not critical in cultivation. For 2–3 months, water should be greatly reduced for cultivated plants. They should be allowed to dry between waterings, but should not remain dry for extended periods. The dry rest is important to plant health. Fertilizer should be greatly reduced or eliminated until water is increased in spring. In the habitat, light is highest in winter.

GROWING MEDIA: Plants may be mounted on tree-fern or cork slabs if humidity is high and plants are watered at least once daily in summer. When plants are potted, any open, fast-draining medium may be used. Repotting may be done anytime new roots are growing.

MISCELLANEOUS NOTES: The bloom season shown in the climate table is based on reports from the habitat. Comber (ref. 75) indicates that plants grown in high light are smaller but are more floriferous.

Plant and Flower Information

PLANT SIZE AND TYPE: A 14 in. (35 cm) sympodial epiphyte.

PSEUDOBULB: 14 in. (35 cm) long. The stems are slender at the base, somewhat thickened along most of their length, but they are thickest in the middle.

LEAVES: Many. The closely spaced, oblong leaves are 0.8 in. (2 cm) long. Leaves may be larger if plants grow in the shade.

INFLORESCENCE: Short. Inflorescences normally emerge on leafless stems.

FLOWERS: 2–4 per inflorescence. The white flowers are 0.8 in. (2 cm) long. They have a thin texture and do not open fully. The nearly transparent lip is wavy along the margin. The center of the midlobe has a green or yellow spot with faint red speckles at the base.

REFERENCES: 25, 75, 218, 254, 469.

PHOTOS/DRAWINGS: 75.

Dendrobium inflatum Schlechter. See *D. hellerianum* A. Hawkes. REFERENCES: 221, 229, 437, 445.

Dendrobium inflexum Teijsm. and Binn. Considered an invalid name by Kränzlin and J. J. Smith. REFERENCES: 216, 254, 469.

Dendrobium informe J. J. Smith

ORIGIN/HABITAT: The north coast of Irian Jaya (western New Guinea). Plants are found in the Gautier Mountains at about 1000 ft. (300 m). They grow on forest trees on limestone and basalt hills. Plants were cultivated in the botanical garden at Bogor, Java.

CLIMATE: Station #97690, Sentani/Jayapura, Irian Jaya, Lat. 2.7°S, Long. 140.5°E, at 289 ft. (88 m). Temperatures are calculated for an elevation of 1000 ft. (300 m), resulting in probable extremes of 95°F (35°C) and 66°F (19°C).

N/HEMISPHERE	JAN	FEB	MAR	APR	MAY	JUN	JUL	AUG	SEP	OCT	NOV	DEC
°F AVG MAX	85	87	87	88	88	87	87	86	87	88	88	87
°F AVG MIN	70	70	70	71	71	71	71	71	71	72	71	71
DIURNAL RANGE	15	17	17	17	17	16	16	15	16	16	17	16
RAIN/INCHES	4.1	3.9	5.3	2.9	6.7	7.0	8.3	8.3	8.5	4.6	2.4	5.2
HUMIDITY/%	81	80	80	79	81	81	79	80	80	80	81	80
BLOOM SEASON					*							
DAYS CLR @ 9AM	5	3	4	3	2	1	1	0	1	2	2	5
DAYS CLR @ 3PM	4	3	3	3	2	1	3	0	1	2	2	3
RAIN/MM	104	99	135	74	170	178	211	211	216	117	61	132
°C AVG MAX	29.3	30.4	30.4	31.0	31.0	30.4	30.4	29.8	30.4	31.0	31.0	30.4
°C AVG MIN	21.0	21.0	21.0	21.5	21.5	21.5	21.5	21.5	21.5	22.1	21.5	21.5
DIURNAL RANGE	8.3	9.4	9.4	9.5	9.5	8.9	8.9	8.3	8.9	8.9	9.5	8.9
S/HEMISPHERE	JUL	AUG	SEP	OCT	NOV	DEC	JAN	FEB	MAR	APR	MAY	JUN

Cultural Recommendations

LIGHT: 2000–3000 fc.

TEMPERATURES: Throughout the year, days average 85–88°F (29–31°C), and nights average 70–72°F (21–22°C), with a diurnal range of 15–17°F (8–10°C).

HUMIDITY: Near 80% year-round.

WATER: Rainfall is heavy most of the year with brief semidry periods in spring and autumn. Cultivated plants should be kept moist most of the year, but they should be allowed to become somewhat dry for a few weeks in spring and again in autumn.

FERTILIZER: ¼–½ recommended strength. A balanced fertilizer should be applied weekly to biweekly throughout the year.

REST PERIOD: Growing conditions should be maintained year-round. Water and fertilizer might be reduced slightly in winter, especially for plants grown in the dark, short-day conditions common in temperate latitudes. They should never be allowed to dry out completely, however. In the habitat, light is slightly higher in winter.

GROWING MEDIA: Plants may be mounted on tree-fern or cork slabs if humidity is high and plants are watered at least once daily in summer. When plants are potted, any open, fast-draining medium may be used. Repotting may be done anytime new roots are growing.

MISCELLANEOUS NOTES: The bloom season shown in the climate table is based on reports from the habitat.

Plant and Flower Information

PLANT SIZE AND TYPE: A 16 in. (40 cm) sympodial epiphyte.

PSEUDOBULB: 8 in. (20 cm) long. The elliptical stems are elongated, club-shaped, and very grooved.

LEAVES: 1 at the apex of each growth. The leaves are 9 in. (23 cm) long, rigid, folded, lanceolate, and pointed.

INFLORESCENCE: 2.0–2.4 in. (5–6 cm) long.

FLOWERS: 9 per inflorescence. The fleshy flowers are 0.4 in. (1 cm) across and do not open fully. The white to yellowish segments are covered with blackish brown spots on the backs of the petals. The apical 30% of the lip is recurved. The lip has no callus.

HYBRIDIZING NOTES: Blossoms are self-pollinating.

REFERENCES: 83, 221, 470, 476.

Dendrobium infortunatum J. J. Smith

AKA: *Cadetia potamophila* Schlechter. *Dendrobium potamophilum* (Schlechter) J. J. Smith. *Cadetia* is now considered a valid genus by some botanists, so this plant may again be a *Cadetia*. Schlechter (ref. 437) described this species as a *Cadetia*. J. J. Smith (ref. 470) moved it

Dendrobium infractum

to *Dendrobium potamophilum*. At about the same time, Schlechter described a new plant as *Dendrobium potamophilum*. It was then necessary to assign a new name to the original *Cadetia potamophila*. J. J. Smith did so when he renamed it *D. infortunatum* J. J. Smith.

ORIGIN/HABITAT: New Guinea. In the forests near Kelel along the Minjem River, plants grow at 650–800 ft. (200–250 m).

CLIMATE: Station #94014, Madang, Papua New Guinea, Lat. 5.2°S, Long. 145.8°E, at 13 ft. (4 m). Temperatures are calculated for an elevation of 1000 ft. (300 m), resulting in probable extremes of 95°F (35°C) and 59°F (15°C).

N/HEMISPHERE	JAN	FEB	MAR	APR	MAY	JUN	JUL	AUG	SEP	OCT	NOV	DEC
°F AVG MAX	80	80	82	82	82	82	82	82	82	84	84	81
°F AVG MIN	74	75	75	75	74	74	74	74	74	73	74	75
DIURNAL RANGE	6	5	7	7	8	8	8	8	8	11	10	6
RAIN/INCHES	4.0	3.4	3.2	8.5	11.2	11.1	10.1	11.3	9.4	11.3	10.5	6.7
HUMIDITY/%	88	87	86	86	86	86	86	85	85	87	88	89
BLOOM SEASON												*
DAYS CLR	N/A											
RAIN/MM	102	86	81	216	284	282	257	287	239	287	267	170
°C AVG MAX	26.6	26.6	27.7	27.7	27.7	27.7	27.7	27.7	27.7	28.8	28.8	27.1
°C AVG MIN	23.2	23.8	23.8	23.8	23.2	23.2	23.2	23.2	23.2	22.7	23.2	23.8
DIURNAL RANGE	3.4	2.8	3.9	3.9	4.5	4.5	4.5	4.5	4.5	6.1	5.6	3.3
S/HEMISPHERE	JUL	AUG	SEP	OCT	NOV	DEC	JAN	FEB	MAR	APR	MAY	JUN

Cultural Recommendations

LIGHT: 2500–3000 fc.

TEMPERATURES: Throughout the year, days average 80–84°F (27–29°C), and nights average 73–75°F (23–24°C), with a diurnal range of 5–11°F (3–6°C). The warmest highs, the coolest lows, and the greatest diurnal range occur in autumn.

HUMIDITY: 85–90% year-round.

WATER: Rainfall is heavy during the growing season but decreases to moderate in midwinter. Cultivated plants should be kept evenly moist while actively growing, but water should be gradually reduced in late autumn.

FERTILIZER: ¼–½ recommended strength. A balanced fertilizer should be applied weekly to biweekly throughout the year.

REST PERIOD: Growing conditions should be maintained all year. In the habitat, rainfall decreases somewhat for 2–3 months in winter. In cultivation, water and fertilizer should be reduced. Plants should dry slightly between waterings, but they should not be allowed to dry out completely. In the habitat, light is somewhat higher in winter.

GROWING MEDIA: Plants may be mounted on tree-fern or cork slabs if humidity is high and the plant is watered daily in summer. If plants are potted, any open, fast-draining medium may be used. Repotting may be done anytime new roots are growing.

MISCELLANEOUS NOTES: The bloom season shown in the climate table is based on reports from the habitat.

Plant and Flower Information

PLANT SIZE AND TYPE: A 2–3 in. (5–8 cm) sympodial epiphyte.

PSEUDOBULB: 0.6–1.6 in. (1.5–4.0 cm) long. Growths are connected by a very short rhizome.

LEAVES: 1 per growth. The erect, linear leaves are 1–2 in. (2.5–5.0 cm) long. They are rounded at the apex with a sharp point at the tip.

INFLORESCENCE: Short.

FLOWERS: 1 at a time on each flowering growth. The tiny flowers are 0.1 in. (0.3 cm) long. Floral segments are white with yellow on the lip. The column is red at the tip.

REFERENCES: 92, 224, 437, 470, 472, 486.

Dendrobium infractum J. J. Smith. See *D. subclausum* Rolfe.
REFERENCES: 144, 221, 470, 476, 588.

Dendrobium infundibulum Lindley not Rchb. f.

AKA: Williams (ref. 570) includes the synonym *D. moulmeinense* Hort. Low ex Warner and Williams. Seidenfaden (ref. 454) lists *D. jamesianum* Rchb. f. as a synonym. Schelpe (ref. 429) considered *D.* × *donnesiae* Hort. to be a synonym.

ORIGIN/HABITAT: Widespread throughout Southeast Asia. The habitat includes northeastern India, Burma, northern Thailand, Cambodia, Laos, and Vietnam. Plants usually grow in deciduous or partly deciduous forests at 3300–7550 ft. (1000–2300 m). In some locations, plants may grow as low as 650 ft. (200 m).

CLIMATE: Station #48327, Chiang Mai, Thailand, Lat. 18.8°N, Long. 99.0°E, at 1100 ft. (335 m). Temperatures are calculated for an elevation of 5600 ft. (1710 m), resulting in probable extremes of 94°F (35°C) and 23°F (−5°C).

N/HEMISPHERE	JAN	FEB	MAR	APR	MAY	JUN	JUL	AUG	SEP	OCT	NOV	DEC
°F AVG MAX	70	75	80	81	79	75	74	72	73	74	71	69
°F AVG MIN	41	42	47	55	59	59	59	60	58	56	51	42
DIURNAL RANGE	29	33	33	26	20	16	15	12	15	18	20	27
RAIN/INCHES	0.3	0.4	0.6	2.0	5.5	6.1	7.4	8.7	11.5	4.9	1.5	0.4
HUMIDITY/%	73	65	58	62	73	78	80	83	83	81	79	76
BLOOM SEASON	*	*	**	**	**	*	*	*	*	*		*
DAYS CLR @ 7AM	5	5	2	2	1	0	0	0	0	1	3	3
DAYS CLR @ 1PM	9	8	4	2	0	0	0	0	0	0	1	3
RAIN/MM	8	10	15	51	140	155	188	221	292	124	38	10
°C AVG MAX	21.2	24.0	26.8	27.3	26.2	24.0	23.4	22.3	22.9	23.4	21.8	20.6
°C AVG MIN	5.1	5.6	8.4	12.9	15.1	15.1	15.1	15.6	14.5	13.4	10.6	5.6
DIURNAL RANGE	16.1	18.4	18.4	14.4	11.1	8.9	8.3	6.7	8.4	10.0	11.2	15.0
S/HEMISPHERE	JUL	AUG	SEP	OCT	NOV	DEC	JAN	FEB	MAR	APR	MAY	JUN

Cultural Recommendations

LIGHT: 2500–3500 fc. Diffused light is suggested.

TEMPERATURES: Summer days average 72–75°F (22–24°C), and nights average 59–60°F (15–16°C), with a diurnal range of 12–16°F (7–9°C). The warmest temperatures and widest diurnal range occur in spring. Days average 79–81°F (26–27°C), and nights average 47–59°F (8–15°C), with a diurnal range of 20–33°F (11–18°C).

HUMIDITY: 75–80% in summer, dropping to near 60% for 2 months in winter.

WATER: Rainfall is moderate to heavy in summer. Conditions become quite dry in winter. Cultivated plants should be kept moist while actively growing, but water should be gradually reduced after new growths mature in autumn.

FERTILIZER: ¼–½ recommended strength, applied weekly. A high-nitrogen fertilizer is beneficial from spring to midsummer, but a fertilizer high in phosphates should be used in late summer and autumn.

REST PERIOD: Winter days average 69–75°F (21–24°C), and nights average 41–42°F (5–6°C), with a diurnal range of 27–33°F (15–18°C). Plants should be able to tolerate temperatures a few degrees below freezing for short periods, but extremes should be avoided in cultivation. During very cold weather, a plant's chance of surviving with minimal damage is better if it is dry when temperatures are low. In the habitat, rainfall averages are very low for 4–5 months in winter, but during the early part of the season the high relative humidity indicates that additional moisture is available from frequent fog, mist, and heavy deposits of dew. Growers sometimes recommend eliminating water in winter, but plants are healthiest if for most of the winter they are allowed to become somewhat dry between waterings but do not remain dry for extended periods. For 1–2 months in late winter, however, conditions are clear, warm, and dry, with humidity so low that even the moisture from morning dew is uncommon. Plants should be allowed to dry out completely between waterings and remain dry longer during this time. Occasional early morning mistings between waterings may help keep the plants from becoming too dry. Fertilizer should be greatly reduced or eliminated until water is increased in spring. A cool, dry rest is essential for cultivated plants and should be continued until new growth starts in spring. In the habitat, light is highest in winter.

GROWING MEDIA: Growers recommend potting plants in an open medium that can be kept moist during the growing season. Growers indicate that plants are healthiest if conditions are appropriate for moss. Plants should be mounted on tree-fern or cork slabs only if humidity is high and plants are watered at least once daily in summer. Repotting is best done in early spring when new roots are growing.

MISCELLANEOUS NOTES: The bloom season shown in the climate table is based on cultivation records. In the habitat, plants may bloom anytime in spring, depending on temperatures. Mature plants in full bloom are spectacular. Growers indicate that if the plants are watered in winter their blossoms tend to open sporadically rather than opening simultaneously. The plants reportedly wither and die when brought down to the lowlands of Malaya and Thailand and would be unlikely to survive in any warm, uniform climate. Growers report that *D. infundibulum* tolerates the coolest *Cattleya* temperatures but is healthier in even cooler conditions.

Plant and Flower Information

PLANT SIZE AND TYPE: A 12–39 in. (30–100 cm) sympodial epiphyte or lithophyte.

PSEUDOBULB: 12–39 in. (30–100 cm) long. The slender, erect stems are densely covered with black hairs. They are normally cylindrical, but plants that grow on rocks develop pseudobulbous stems.

LEAVES: 10 per growth. The leaves are 3–5 in. (8–13 cm) long. They are thin and flexible, oblong-lanceolate, and appear all along the new growths. They are persistent near the apex.

INFLORESCENCE: Short. During the first blooming on prior year's growth, inflorescences emerge near the apex of the stem, but with subsequent flowerings, they emerge lower on the stem.

FLOWERS: 3–5 per inflorescence, many per plant. The flowers are 3–4 in. (8–10 cm) across. Sepals and large round petals are pristine ivory white. The base of the lateral sepals form a long, funnel-shaped spur. The white lip is marked with a large orange or golden yellow blotch and scarlet or yellow lines at the base. The large midlobe is wavy along the serrated margin. Var. *jamesianum* is deeply stained with cinnabar-red. Individual blossoms last 1–3 months. They have a soft, papery texture but keep well as cut flowers.

HYBRIDIZING NOTES: Chromosome counts are n = 19 (ref. 150, 154, 187, 542), n = 20 (ref. 187, 504, 580), 2n = 38 (ref. 151, 153, 154, 187, 188, 273, 504, 542, 580), and 2n = 40 (ref. 187, 504, 580). As *D. infundibulum* var. *jamesianum* the count is 2n = 38 (ref. 504, 580). Johansen (ref. 239) indicates that some clones could be self-pollinated, while others were self-sterile. Seed capsules opened 350 days after pollination and 53% contained visible embryos.

REFERENCES: 6, 25, 36, 38, 46, 150, 151, 153, 154, 157, 179, 187, 188, 190, 196, 200, 202, 210, 216, 236, 239, 245, 247, 251, 254, 266, 273, 278, 317, 326, 364, 366, 369, 371, 389, 429, 430, 445, 447, 448, 454, 458, 461, 504, 541, 542, 557, 569, 570, 580.

PHOTOS/DRAWINGS: 6, *36, 125,* 210, *245, 247, 251, 364, 366, 369, 371, 389, 430, 454,* 458, 557, *569,* 570.

Dendrobium infundibulum Rchb. f. not Lindley. See *D. formosum* Roxburgh ex Lindley. REFERENCES: 254, 430.

Dendrobium ingratum J. J. Smith

ORIGIN/HABITAT: Irian Jaya (western New Guinea). Near Seka, plants grow on trees close to sea level at the mouth of the Tami River.

CLIMATE: Station #97690, Sentani/Jayapura, Irian Jaya, Lat. 2.7°S, Long. 140.5°E, at 289 ft. (88 m). Record extreme temperatures are 97°F (36°C) and 68°F (20°C).

N/HEMISPHERE	JAN	FEB	MAR	APR	MAY	JUN	JUL	AUG	SEP	OCT	NOV	DEC
°F AVG MAX	87	89	89	90	90	89	89	88	89	90	90	89
°F AVG MIN	72	72	72	73	73	73	73	73	73	74	73	73
DIURNAL RANGE	15	17	17	17	17	16	16	15	16	16	17	16
RAIN/INCHES	4.1	3.9	5.3	2.9	6.7	7.0	8.3	8.3	8.5	4.6	2.4	5.2
HUMIDITY/%	81	80	80	79	81	81	79	80	80	80	81	80
BLOOM SEASON	*											
DAYS CLR @ 9AM	5	3	4	3	2	1	1	0	1	2	2	5
DAYS CLR @ 3PM	4	3	3	3	2	1	3	0	1	2	2	3
RAIN/MM	104	99	135	74	170	178	211	211	216	117	61	132
°C AVG MAX	30.6	31.7	31.7	32.2	32.2	31.7	31.7	31.1	31.7	32.2	32.2	31.7
°C AVG MIN	22.2	22.2	22.2	22.8	22.8	22.8	22.8	22.8	22.8	23.3	22.8	22.8
DIURNAL RANGE	8.3	9.4	9.4	9.4	9.4	8.9	8.9	8.3	8.9	8.9	9.4	8.9
S/HEMISPHERE	JUL	AUG	SEP	OCT	NOV	DEC	JAN	FEB	MAR	APR	MAY	JUN

Cultural Recommendations

LIGHT: 2500–3500 fc.

TEMPERATURES: Throughout the year, days average 87–89°F (31–32°C), and nights average 72–74°F (22–23°C), with a diurnal range of 15–17°F (8–9°C).

HUMIDITY: Near 80% year-round.

WATER: Rainfall is heavy all year, with brief semidry periods in spring and autumn. Cultivated plants should be kept moist most of the year, but they should be allowed to become somewhat dry for a few weeks in spring and again in autumn.

FERTILIZER: ¼–½ recommended strength. A balanced fertilizer should be applied weekly to biweekly throughout the year.

REST PERIOD: Growing conditions should be maintained year-round. Water and fertilizer might be reduced slightly in winter, especially for plants grown in the dark, short-day conditions common in temperate latitudes. They should never be allowed to dry completely, however. In the habitat, light is slightly higher in winter.

GROWING MEDIA: Plants may be mounted on tree-fern or cork slabs if humidity is high and plants are watered at least once daily in summer. When plants are potted, any open, fast-draining medium may be used. Repotting may be done anytime new roots are growing.

MISCELLANEOUS NOTES: The bloom season shown in the climate table is based on reports from the habitat. The plant was described in 1912 in *Bul. Jard. Bot. Buit.* 2nd sér. 3:72.

Plant and Flower Information

PLANT SIZE AND TYPE: A 31 in. (80 cm) sympodial epiphyte.

PSEUDOBULB: 31 in. (80 cm) long. The flattened stems, which are yellow-green when immature, become pale brown with age.

LEAVES: The broadly linear leaves, which are 1.1–1.8 in. (2.8–4.7 cm) long, are held close to the stem. They are pale green, thin, and leathery.

INFLORESCENCE: Short.

FLOWERS: 2 per inflorescence. The flowers are 0.5 in. (1.3 cm) long. They may be greenish yellow or brownish yellow. The lip is marked with a pale brown, longitudinal stripe. The column is greenish white. The blossoms were described by J. J. Smith as smelling like "putrid horse urine."

REFERENCES: 221, 445, 470.

Dendrobium inopinatum J. J. Smith. See *D. erosum* (Blume) Lindley. REFERENCES: 75, 223, 270, 271, 454.

Dendrobium insigne (Blume) Rchb. f. ex Miquel

AKA: Schlechter (ref. 437) included *Dichopus insignis* Blume, *Dendrobium gazellae* Kränzlin, *D. lyperanthiflorum* Kränzlin, *D. obcuneatum* F. M. Bailey, and *D. pentactis* Kränzlin as synonyms. However, Clements (ref. 67) and Lewis and Cribb (ref. 271) include only *Dichopus insignis* Blume and *D. pentactis* Kränzlin as synonyms. Clements indicates that *D. obcuneatum* F. M. Bailey should be retained as a separate species, but the other synonyms included by Schlechter are not mentioned.

ORIGIN/HABITAT: Widespread in lowland New Guinea, Vanuatu, the Solomon Islands, New Britain, New Ireland, and the islands of the Torres Straits. Plants grow on the tips of small branches on mangrove trees from sea level to 1950 ft. (0–600 m). Schlechter collected plants along the beach near Aitape, along the upper reaches of the Ramu River at about 500 ft. (150 m), and near the mouth of the Waria River at about 50 ft. (10 m). On Santa Ana Island, plants grow on the outer edges of tufts of wet sphagnum moss, sedges, and ferns near freshwater lagoons.

CLIMATE: Station #94004, Wewak, Papua New Guinea, Lat. 3.6°S, Long. 143.7°E, at 16 ft. (5 m). Record extreme temperatures are 98°F (37°C) and 62°F (17°C).

N/HEMISPHERE	JAN	FEB	MAR	APR	MAY	JUN	JUL	AUG	SEP	OCT	NOV	DEC
°F AVG MAX	88	88	88	88	88	88	87	86	87	88	88	88
°F AVG MIN	74	74	74	75	75	75	75	75	74	74	75	74
DIURNAL RANGE	14	14	14	13	13	13	12	11	13	14	13	14
RAIN/INCHES	7.6	4.8	5.3	10.0	13.3	14.5	12.1	11.9	14.9	16.9	15.1	10.8
HUMIDITY/%	80	79	79	78	79	81	82	82	81	82	81	80
BLOOM SEASON			*		*			*				
DAYS CLR	N/A											
RAIN/MM	193	122	135	254	338	368	307	302	378	429	384	274
°C AVG MAX	31.1	31.1	31.1	31.1	31.1	31.1	30.6	30.0	30.6	31.1	31.1	31.1
°C AVG MIN	23.3	23.3	23.3	23.9	23.9	23.9	23.9	23.9	23.3	23.3	23.9	23.3
DIURNAL RANGE	7.8	7.8	7.8	7.2	7.2	7.2	6.7	6.1	7.3	7.8	7.2	7.8
S/HEMISPHERE	JUL	AUG	SEP	OCT	NOV	DEC	JAN	FEB	MAR	APR	MAY	JUN

Cultural Recommendations

LIGHT: 2500–4000 fc. Plants often grow fully exposed to direct sun and must have bright light to flower.

TEMPERATURES: Throughout the year, days average 86–88°F (30–31°C), and nights average 74–75°F (23–24°C), with a diurnal range of 11–14°F (6–8°C). The plants are able to tolerate the heat of direct sun.

HUMIDITY: Near 80% year-round.

WATER: Rainfall is heavy all year, but conditions are slightly drier for 1–2 months in late winter. Cultivated plants should be kept moist with only slight drying allowed between waterings.

FERTILIZER: ¼–½ recommended strength. A balanced fertilizer should be applied weekly to biweekly throughout the year.

REST PERIOD: Growing conditions should be maintained year-round. Water should be reduced somewhat in winter, especially for plants grown in the dark, short-day conditions common in temperate latitudes. They should not be allowed to dry out completely, however. Fertilizer should also be reduced if water is reduced. In the habitat, light may be slightly higher in winter.

GROWING MEDIA: Growers report that *D. insigne* grows poorly if overpotted but grows well when mounted on a slab if adequate moisture is available. If not mounted, a very open and fast-draining medium should be used with either baskets or small pots. Plants should be repotted every 2 years, anytime new roots are growing.

MISCELLANEOUS NOTES: The bloom season shown in the climate table is based on cultivation records. In the habitat, plants bloom several times a year. Flowering occurs 9 days after a sudden 10°F (5°C) drop in daytime temperatures.

Plant and Flower Information

PLANT SIZE AND TYPE: A 10–24 in. (25–60 cm) sympodial epiphyte. Plants form large, untidy clumps.

PSEUDOBULB: 10–24 in. (25–60 cm) long. The stems are woody and brittle.

LEAVES: Many. The leaf size varies considerably on each stem with the smallest near the apex of the stem.

INFLORESCENCE: Very short. Inflorescences emerge from nodes along the stem.

FLOWERS: 2 per inflorescence. The flowers, which last 1–3 days, are 0.5–1.0 in. (1.5–2.5 cm) across and open fully. They are very fragrant. The pointed sepals and petals may be bright or dull yellow with reddish orange or purplish red markings. The lip is white to cream with glistening keels that are covered with soft hairs. The lip may be marked with yellow-brown spots or intense purple-red markings. The midlobe has deep cuts along the margin.

HYBRIDIZING NOTES: Chromosome count is 2n = 36+2f (ref. 151, 153, 154, 187, 188, 273).

REFERENCES: 25, 67, 92, 111, 151, 153, 154, 179, 187, 188, 216, 240, 254, 262, 270, 271, 273, 302, 304, 310, 318, 437, 444, 445, 470, 516, 533, 537.

PHOTOS/DRAWINGS: 240, 254, *262, 304, 318*, 437, *533*.

Dendrobium insulare Steudel. Now considered a synonym of *Flickingeria fimbriata* (Blume) A. Hawkes. REFERENCES: 213, 216, 254, 449.

Dendrobium integrilabium J. J. Smith. Now considered a synonym of *Flickingeria integrilabia* (J. J. Smith) A. Hawkes. REFERENCES: 25, 75, 213, 219, 229, 230, 231, 254, 445, 469. PHOTOS/DRAWINGS: 469.

Dendrobium integrum Schlechter

ORIGIN/HABITAT: Papua New Guinea. Plants grow on forest trees in the Bismarck Range at about 5900 ft. (1800 m).

CLIMATE: Station #94010, Goroka, Papua New Guinea, Lat. 6.1°S, Long. 145.4°E, at 5141 ft. (1567 m). Temperatures are calculated for an elevation of 5900 ft. (1800 m), resulting in probable extremes of 84°F (29°C) and 40°F (5°C).

N/HEMISPHERE	JAN	FEB	MAR	APR	MAY	JUN	JUL	AUG	SEP	OCT	NOV	DEC
°F AVG MAX	73	74	75	76	76	75	76	75	75	75	76	74
°F AVG MIN	53	54	54	54	55	56	56	56	57	56	56	54
DIURNAL RANGE	20	20	21	22	21	19	20	19	18	19	20	20
RAIN/INCHES	2.1	2.8	4.6	5.9	6.6	9.3	9.1	10.1	10.7	8.3	4.6	2.0
HUMIDITY/%	70	67	67	67	67	71	72	73	74	71	70	70
BLOOM SEASON					*							
DAYS CLR	N/A											
RAIN/MM	53	71	117	150	168	236	231	257	272	211	117	51
°C AVG MAX	23.0	23.6	24.1	24.7	24.7	24.1	24.7	24.1	24.1	24.1	24.7	23.6
°C AVG MIN	11.9	12.5	12.5	12.5	13.0	13.6	13.6	13.6	14.1	13.6	13.6	12.5
DIURNAL RANGE	11.1	11.1	11.6	12.2	11.7	10.5	11.1	10.5	10.0	10.5	11.1	11.1
S/HEMISPHERE	JUL	AUG	SEP	OCT	NOV	DEC	JAN	FEB	MAR	APR	MAY	JUN

Cultural Recommendations

LIGHT: 2500–3500 fc.

TEMPERATURES: Throughout the year, days average 73–76°F (23–25°C), and nights average 53–57°F (12–14°C), with a diurnal range of 18–22°F (10–12°C).

HUMIDITY: 70–75% most of the year, dropping to near 65% in late winter and early spring.

WATER: Rainfall is moderate to heavy most of the year, but conditions are slightly drier for 3 months in winter. Cultivated plants should be kept moist but not soggy. Occasional early morning mistings may be beneficial, especially on bright, sunny days.

FERTILIZER: ¼–½ recommended strength. A balanced fertilizer should be applied weekly to biweekly throughout the year.

REST PERIOD: Growing temperatures should be maintained all year. In the habitat, rainfall is lowest in winter, but dew and mist from fog and low clouds are common. Water and fertilizer should be reduced somewhat for cultivated plants, especially those grown in the darker, short-day conditions common during temperate-latitude winters. Plants should be kept on the dry side, but they should never be allowed to dry out completely. In the habitat, light is higher in winter.

GROWING MEDIA: Plants may be mounted on tree-fern or cork slabs if humidity is high and plants are watered at least once daily in summer. When plants are potted, any open, fast-draining medium may be used. Repotting may be done anytime new roots are growing.

MISCELLANEOUS NOTES: The bloom season shown in the climate table is based on reports from the habitat.

Plant and Flower Information

PLANT SIZE AND TYPE: A 12–20 in. (30–50 cm) sympodial epiphyte.

PSEUDOBULB: 12–20 in. (30–50 cm) long. The flattened stems, which do not branch, arise from a very short rhizome.

LEAVES: Many. The stiffly erect leaves are 1.4–2.2 in. (3.5–5.5 cm) long. They are narrow, pointed, and dagger-like.

INFLORESCENCE: Short.

FLOWERS: 1 per inflorescence. The tiny inverted flowers are 0.3 in. (0.8 cm) across. The blossoms are golden yellow with a dark red column.

REFERENCES: 221, 437, 445.

PHOTOS/DRAWINGS: 437.

Dendrobium interjectum Ames.
Now considered a synonym of *Flickingeria interjecta* (Ames) A. Hawkes. REFERENCES: 12, 213, 222, 229, 230, 231, 296, 536.

Dendrobium intermedium Ridley not Schlechter or Teijsm. and Binn.
In Merrill (ref. 295), Ames changed the name to *Dendrobium ridleyi* Ames. However, the plant was originally described as a *Dendrochilum* not a *Dendrobium*. REFERENCES: 295, 398.

Dendrobium × intermedium Schlechter not Ridley or Teijsm. and Binn.
See *D. × von-paulsenianum* A. Hawkes. REFERENCES: 191, 221, 229, 437.

Dendrobium intermedium Teijsm. and Binn. not Ridley or Schlechter.
See *D. salaccense* (Blume) Lindley. REFERENCES: 216, 254, 310, 317, 454, 469.

Dendrobium interruptum J. J. Smith.
Now considered a synonym of *Epigeneium verruciferum* (Rolfe) Summerhayes. REFERENCES: 221, 286, 499.

Dendrobium intricatum Gagnepain

AKA: *D. uniflorum* Finet ex Gagnepain not Griffith or Teijsm. and Binnend. Seidenfaden (ref. 454) discusses the confusion surrounding the use of this plant name.

ORIGIN/HABITAT: Thailand, Cambodia, and Vietnam. Plants have been collected near Trat and Kho Kuap in southeastern Thailand, near Cam Chay in Cambodia, and near Phu Quoc, Bao Lo, and Dalat in Vietnam. Habitat elevation is not available, so the following climate data should be used with caution.

CLIMATE: Station #48881, Dalat, Vietnam, Lat. 11.1°N, Long. 108.1°E, at 3156 ft. (962 m). Record extreme temperatures are 93°F (34°C) and 43°F (6°C).

N/HEMISPHERE	JAN	FEB	MAR	APR	MAY	JUN	JUL	AUG	SEP	OCT	NOV	DEC
°F AVG MAX	80	82	84	85	84	81	81	80	80	80	79	79
°F AVG MIN	56	57	59	62	65	65	65	65	65	63	60	58
DIURNAL RANGE	24	25	25	23	19	16	16	15	15	17	19	21
RAIN/INCHES	0.2	0.9	1.6	4.6	9.1	6.1	7.7	8.2	10.1	9.7	2.7	1.3
HUMIDITY/%	68	64	65	71	78	81	82	83	84	82	76	73
BLOOM SEASON	N/A											
DAYS CLR @ 7AM	13	13	13	9	5	3	2	2	2	5	7	10
DAYS CLR @ 1PM	8	8	8	2	0	0	0	0	0	1	3	4
RAIN/MM	5	23	41	117	231	155	196	208	257	246	69	33
°C AVG MAX	26.7	27.8	28.9	29.4	28.9	27.2	27.2	26.7	26.7	26.7	26.1	26.1
°C AVG MIN	13.3	13.9	15.0	16.7	18.3	18.3	18.3	18.3	18.3	17.2	15.6	14.4
DIURNAL RANGE	13.4	13.9	13.9	12.7	10.6	8.9	8.9	8.4	8.4	9.5	10.5	11.7
S/HEMISPHERE	JUL	AUG	SEP	OCT	NOV	DEC	JAN	FEB	MAR	APR	MAY	JUN

Cultural Recommendations

LIGHT: 2000–3000 fc.

TEMPERATURES: Summer days average 80–81°F (27°C), and nights average 65°F (18°C), with a diurnal range of 15–16°F (8–9°C). The warmest temperatures occur in late winter and spring. Days average 84–85°F (29°C), and nights average 59–65°F (15–18°C), with a diurnal range of 19–25°F (11–14°C).

HUMIDITY: 80–85% in summer, dropping to near 65% in late winter.

WATER: Rainfall is moderate to heavy in summer but is very light for 2 months in winter. Cultivated plants should be kept moist while growing, but water should be gradually reduced after new growths mature in autumn.

FERTILIZER: ¼–½ recommended strength, applied weekly. A high-nitrogen fertilizer is beneficial from spring to midsummer, but a fertilizer high in phosphates should be used in late summer and autumn.

REST PERIOD: Winter days average 79–82°F (26–28°C), and nights average 56–58°F (13–14°C), with a diurnal range of 21–25°F (12–14°C). The increased diurnal range results from warmer days and cooler nights. Rainfall is low for 3–4 months. For 1–2 of these months, conditions are so dry that even moisture from dew is uncommon. For cultivated plants, water and fertilizer should be reduced for 2–3 months. Plants should be allowed to dry out between waterings, but they should not remain dry for extended periods. In the habitat, light is highest in winter.

GROWING MEDIA: Plants may be mounted on tree-fern or cork slabs if humidity is high and plants are watered at least once daily in summer. When plants are potted, any open, fast-draining medium may be used. Repotting is best done in early spring when new roots are growing.

Plant and Flower Information

PLANT SIZE AND TYPE: A sympodial epiphyte of unreported size.

PSEUDOBULB: The clustered, flattened stems are swollen at the base and thinner toward the tip.

LEAVES: 5–7 per growth. The leaves are 3–4 in. (8–10 cm) long, deciduous, and linear-lanceolate.

INFLORESCENCE: Very short. Numerous inflorescences are borne at nodes near the apex of leafless stems.

FLOWERS: 2–5 per inflorescence. The flowers are 0.8–1.2 in. (2–3 cm) across. Sepals and petals are purplish pink. The lip is toothed along the margin. The spur curves forward. It is longer than the dorsal sepal.

Dendrobium involutum

REFERENCES: 136, 169, 224, 225, 266, 448, 454.

PHOTOS/DRAWINGS: 454.

Dendrobium involutum Kränzlin. See *D. dactylodes* Rchb. f.
REFERENCES: 434.

Dendrobium involutum Lindley

AKA: Lewis and Cribb (ref. 270) include *D. cheesmanae* Guillaumin as a synonym, but indicate that leaf shape is variable and several species may be combined under the name *D. involutum*. However, Kores (ref. 466) includes *D. cheesmanae* Guillaumin as a synonym of *D. dactylodes* Rchb. f.

ORIGIN/HABITAT: Numerous Pacific Islands including Vanuatu, the Society Islands, and the Santa Cruz Islands. Plants grow in rainforests below 1650 ft. (500 m).

CLIMATE: Station #91554, Luganville, Espiritu Santo Island, Vanuatu, Lat. 15.5°S, Long. 167.1°E, at 493 ft. (150 m). Record extreme temperatures are 93°F (34°C) and 61°F (16°C).

N/HEMISPHERE	JAN	FEB	MAR	APR	MAY	JUN	JUL	AUG	SEP	OCT	NOV	DEC
°F AVG MAX	81	81	82	83	83	86	86	87	86	85	83	81
°F AVG MIN	71	71	72	72	73	74	75	74	73	74	73	72
DIURNAL RANGE	10	10	10	11	10	12	11	13	13	11	10	9
RAIN/INCHES	6.4	6.3	4.7	6.3	9.5	9.2	10.6	9.7	10.9	10.1	8.1	6.1
HUMIDITY/%	81	80	83	81	82	81	83	83	88	86	83	80
BLOOM SEASON			*							*		
DAYS CLR	N/A											
RAIN/MM	163	160	119	160	241	234	269	246	277	257	206	155
°C AVG MAX	27.2	27.2	27.8	28.3	28.3	30.0	30.0	30.6	30.0	29.4	28.3	27.2
°C AVG MIN	21.7	21.7	22.2	22.2	22.8	23.3	23.9	23.3	22.8	23.3	22.8	22.2
DIURNAL RANGE	5.5	5.5	5.6	6.1	5.5	6.7	6.1	7.3	7.2	6.1	5.5	5.0
S/HEMISPHERE	JUL	AUG	SEP	OCT	NOV	DEC	JAN	FEB	MAR	APR	MAY	JUN

Cultural Recommendations

LIGHT: 2000–3000 fc.

TEMPERATURES: Throughout the year, days average 81–87°F (27–31°C), and nights average 71–75°F (22–24°C), with a diurnal range of 9–13°F (5–7°C).

HUMIDITY: 80–85% year-round.

WATER: Rainfall is moderate to heavy most of the year. Cultivated plants should be kept moist but not soggy with only slight drying allowed between waterings.

FERTILIZER: ¼–½ recommended strength. A balanced fertilizer should be applied weekly to biweekly throughout the year.

REST PERIOD: Growing conditions should be maintained all year. Water and fertilizer may be reduced somewhat in winter for plants grown in the dark, short-day conditions common in temperate latitudes. They should not be allowed to dry out completely, however.

GROWING MEDIA: Mounting plants on tree-fern or cork slabs accommodates their pendulous growth habit. However, humidity must be high and plants must be watered at least once a day in summer. If plants cannot be mounted, small pots or hanging baskets may be filled with an open, fast-draining medium. Repotting may be done anytime new roots are actively growing.

MISCELLANEOUS NOTES: The bloom season shown in the climate table is based on collection reports.

Plant and Flower Information

PLANT SIZE AND TYPE: A 31 in. (80 cm) sympodial epiphyte.

PSEUDOBULB: 31 in. (80 cm) long. The clustered, pendent stems are covered with fibers from old leaf sheaths.

LEAVES: The thick, lanceolate leaves are 2–3 in. (5–8 cm) long.

INFLORESCENCE: Inflorescences emerge from nodes along the stem.

FLOWERS: 2 per inflorescence. The flowers are 0.4 in. (1 cm) long. Sepals and petals are creamy yellow-orange. The lip is creamy yellow with an orange-yellow midlobe and radiating purple-red lines on the sidelobes.

REFERENCES: 52, 216, 224, 254, 270, 278, 466.

Dendrobium ionoglossum Schlechter. See *D. nindii* W. Hill.
REFERENCES: 67, 84, 105, 179, 221, 236, 437, 445, 533, 537.

Dendrobium ionopus Rchb. f.

Seidenfaden (ref. 454) indicates that Kränzlin's (ref. 254) inclusion of *D. serpens* Hooker f. and *D. panduriferum* Hooker f. var. *serpens* Hooker f. as synonyms was incorrect. The plant was thought to have been found in Malaya or Burma, but even the country of origin is not certain. Without habitat location and elevation, climate data cannot be selected. No information regarding the vegetative characteristics is available, since only the blossoms were available when the plant was described. The inflorescences were short with unusually small bracts. Blossoms were yellow with 2 red or purple blotches near the back of the lip. The sepals and petals were triangular.

REFERENCES: 157, 202, 216, 254.

Dendrobium irayense Ames and Quisumbing. See *D. miyakei* Schlechter.
REFERENCES: 61, 225, 373, 536. PHOTOS/DRAWINGS: *373*.

Dendrobium ischnopetalum Schlechter.
Now considered a synonym of *Diplocaulobium ischnopetalum* (Schlechter) Kränzlin.
REFERENCES: 219, 220, 254, 437, 444, 445.

Dendrobium ischnophyton Schlechter.
Now considered a synonym of *Diplocaulobium ischnophyton* (Schlechter) A. Hawkes.
REFERENCES: 223, 230, 443.

Dendrobium isochiloides Kränzlin

AKA: J. J. Smith (ref. 470) suggests the possibility that *D. isochiloides* Kränzlin and *D. koordersii* J. J. Smith may belong with *D. bilobum* Lindley. *D. isochiloides* Kränzlin var. *pumilum* J. J. Smith is considered a synonym of *D. poneroides* Schlechter.

ORIGIN/HABITAT: New Guinea. In Papua, plants grow near sea level at Port Praslin and Port Carteret on New Ireland. Plants have also been found on New Britain Island and at about 1950 ft. (600 m) in the Torricelli mountains on the mainland. In Irian Jaya (western New Guinea), plants grow on trees on the coastal plain and along the upper Digul River.

CLIMATE: Station #94085, Rabul, New Britain Is., Papua New Guinea, Lat. 4.2°S, Long. 152.2°E, at 28 ft. (9 m). Record extreme temperatures are 100°F (38°C) and 65°F (18°C).

N/HEMISPHERE	JAN	FEB	MAR	APR	MAY	JUN	JUL	AUG	SEP	OCT	NOV	DEC
°F AVG MAX	89	89	91	92	91	90	90	90	90	90	90	90
°F AVG MIN	73	72	73	73	73	73	73	73	73	73	73	73
DIURNAL RANGE	16	17	18	19	18	17	17	17	17	17	17	17
RAIN/INCHES	5.4	3.7	3.5	5.1	7.1	10.1	14.8	10.4	10.2	10.0	5.2	3.3
HUMIDITY/%	74	73	69	70	73	76	77	76	77	77	75	74
BLOOM SEASON	*	*	*	*								
DAYS CLR	N/A											
RAIN/MM	137	94	89	130	180	257	376	264	259	254	132	84
°C AVG MAX	31.7	31.7	32.8	33.3	32.8	32.2	32.2	32.2	32.2	32.2	32.2	32.2
°C AVG MIN	22.8	22.2	22.8	22.8	22.8	22.8	22.8	22.8	22.8	22.8	22.8	22.8
DIURNAL RANGE	8.9	9.5	10.0	10.5	10.0	9.4	9.4	9.4	9.4	9.4	9.4	9.4
S/HEMISPHERE	JUL	AUG	SEP	OCT	NOV	DEC	JAN	FEB	MAR	APR	MAY	JUN

Cultural Recommendations

LIGHT: 2500–3000 fc.

TEMPERATURES: Throughout the year, days average 89–92°F (32–33°C), and nights average 72–73°F (22–23°C), with a diurnal range of 16–19°F (9–11°C). Because plants are also found at higher elevations in other parts of the habitat, they should adapt to temperatures 6–8°F (3–4°C) cooler than indicated above.

HUMIDITY: 70–80% most of the year. Humidity increases to 90–100% at night but may drop as low as 35% during hot afternoons.

WATER: Rainfall is heavy most of the year, but conditions are slightly drier for 2 months in late winter. Cultivated plants should be kept moist but not soggy.

FERTILIZER: ¼–½ recommended strength. A balanced fertilizer should be applied weekly to biweekly throughout the year.

REST PERIOD: Growing conditions should be maintained all year. Water and fertilizer should be reduced somewhat in winter. Plants should dry slightly between waterings, but they should never be allowed to dry completely. In the habitat, light may be slightly higher in winter.

GROWING MEDIA: Plants grow well mounted on tree-fern or cork slabs if humidity is high and plants are watered at least once daily in summer. When plants are potted, any open, fast-draining medium may be used. Repotting may be done anytime new roots are growing.

MISCELLANEOUS NOTES: The bloom season shown in the climate table is based on reports from the habitat.

Plant and Flower Information

PLANT SIZE AND TYPE: A 16–20 in. (40–50 cm) sympodial epiphyte.

PSEUDOBULB: 16–20 in. (40–50 cm) long. The stems are densely leafy.

LEAVES: Many. The linear leaves are 1.2 in. (3 cm) long.

INFLORESCENCE: Short.

FLOWERS: 1 per inflorescence. The greenish yellow flowers are 0.2 in. (0.6 cm) across. The lip is red-brown or purplish. It is sometimes marked with green at the tip.

REFERENCES: 218, 253, 254, 437, 445, 470.

Dendrobium isomerum Schlechter. See *D. indragiriense* Schlechter. REFERENCES: 221, 435, 454.

Dendrobium isthmiferum J. J. Smith. Now considered a synonym of *Diplocaulobium isthmiferum* (J. J. Smith) Hunt and Summerhayes. REFERENCES: 213, 225, 230, 470.

Dendrobium iteratum J. J. Smith

ORIGIN/HABITAT: Irian Jaya (western New Guinea). Plants were originally found in the Weyland Range (Weijland Range) at about 4600 ft. (1400 m).

CLIMATE: Station #97682, Nabire, Irian Jaya, Lat. 3.3°S, Long. 135.5°E, at 10 ft. (3 m). Temperatures are calculated for an elevation of 4600 ft. (1400 m). Record extreme temperatures are not available for this location.

N/HEMISPHERE	JAN	FEB	MAR	APR	MAY	JUN	JUL	AUG	SEP	OCT	NOV	DEC
°F AVG MAX	71	71	71	71	72	72	71	71	72	72	72	72
°F AVG MIN	60	60	61	62	62	61	62	60	60	61	61	61
DIURNAL RANGE	11	11	10	9	10	11	9	11	12	11	11	11
RAIN/INCHES	7.4	11.1	8.5	8.5	7.5	9.0	9.2	10.6	12.1	11.3	10.2	9.8
HUMIDITY/%	N/A											
BLOOM SEASON					*							
DAYS CLR	N/A											
RAIN/MM	188	282	216	216	190	229	234	269	307	287	259	249
°C AVG MAX	21.6	21.6	21.6	21.6	22.1	22.1	21.6	21.6	22.1	22.1	22.1	22.1
°C AVG MIN	15.5	15.5	16.0	16.6	16.6	16.0	16.6	15.5	15.5	16.0	16.0	16.0
DIURNAL RANGE	6.1	6.1	5.6	5.0	5.5	6.1	5.0	6.1	6.6	6.1	6.1	6.1
S/HEMISPHERE	JUL	AUG	SEP	OCT	NOV	DEC	JAN	FEB	MAR	APR	MAY	JUN

Cultural Recommendations

LIGHT: 2000–3000 fc.

TEMPERATURES: Throughout the year, days average 71–72°F (22°C), and nights average 60–62°F (16–17°C), with a diurnal range of 9–12°F (5–7°C).

HUMIDITY: Information is not available for this location. However, records from nearby locations indicate that humidity probably averages near 85% year-round.

WATER: Rainfall is heavy all year. Cultivated plants should be kept evenly moist.

FERTILIZER: ¼–½ recommended strength. A balanced fertilizer should be applied weekly to biweekly throughout the year.

REST PERIOD: Growing conditions should be maintained year-round. Water and fertilizer might be reduced slightly in winter, especially for plants grown in the dark, short-day conditions common in temperate latitudes. They should never be allowed to dry out completely, however.

GROWING MEDIA: Plants may be mounted on tree-fern or cork slabs or potted in small pots filled with any open, fast-draining medium. Repotting may be done anytime new roots are actively growing.

MISCELLANEOUS NOTES: The bloom season shown in the climate table is based on reports from the habitat.

Plant and Flower Information

PLANT SIZE AND TYPE: A 9–13 in. (24–32 cm) sympodial epiphyte.

PSEUDOBULB: 9–13 in. (24–32 cm) long.

LEAVES: Many. The grasslike leaves are 5–7 in. (13–18 cm) long, linear, and papery. They have 2 teeth at the apex.

INFLORESCENCE: Short.

FLOWERS: 2 per inflorescence. The flowers are 0.7 in. (1.7 cm) long. The dorsal sepal is oblong, concave and incurved. The lateral sepals are somewhat oblong-triangular and recurved along the margins. The petals are oblong. The curved, 3-lobed lip is concave.

REFERENCES: 225, 486.

Dendrobium jabiense J. J. Smith

ORIGIN/HABITAT: Irian Jaya (western New Guinea), along the south coast of Teluk Cenderawasih (Teluk Sareba) (Geelvink Bay). Plants grow on forest trees near the village of Wape in the Jabi Range.

CLIMATE: Station #97682, Nabire, Irian Jaya, Lat. 3.3°S, Long. 135.5°E, at 10 ft. (3 m). Record extreme temperatures are not available for this location.

N/HEMISPHERE	JAN	FEB	MAR	APR	MAY	JUN	JUL	AUG	SEP	OCT	NOV	DEC
°F AVG MAX	86	86	86	86	87	87	86	86	87	87	87	87
°F AVG MIN	75	75	76	77	77	76	77	75	75	76	76	76
DIURNAL RANGE	11	11	10	9	10	11	9	11	12	11	11	11
RAIN/INCHES	7.4	11.1	8.5	8.5	7.5	9.0	9.2	10.6	12.1	11.3	10.2	9.8
HUMIDITY/%	N/A											
BLOOM SEASON												
DAYS CLR	N/A											
RAIN/MM	190	283	217	217	192	228	233	270	308	286	259	248
°C AVG MAX	30.1	29.9	30.1	30.3	30.5	30.6	30.0	30.0	30.5	30.5	30.3	30.3
°C AVG MIN	24.0	24.0	24.3	24.7	24.9	24.5	24.8	24.0	23.8	24.6	24.3	24.2
DIURNAL RANGE	6.1	5.9	5.8	5.6	5.6	6.1	5.2	6.0	6.7	5.9	6.0	6.1
S/HEMISPHERE	JUL	AUG	SEP	OCT	NOV	DEC	JAN	FEB	MAR	APR	MAY	JUN

Cultural Recommendations

LIGHT: 2000–3000 fc.

TEMPERATURES: Throughout the year, days average 86–87°F (30–31°C), and nights average 75–77°F (24–25°C), with a diurnal range of 9–12°F (6–7°C).

HUMIDITY: Information is not available for this location. However, records from nearby locations indicate that humidity probably averages near 85% year-round.

WATER: Rainfall is heavy all year. Cultivated plants should be kept evenly moist.

FERTILIZER: ¼–½ recommended strength. A balanced fertilizer should be applied weekly to biweekly throughout the year.

REST PERIOD: Growing conditions should be maintained year-round. Water and fertilizer might be reduced slightly in winter, especially for plants grown in the dark, short-day conditions common in temperate latitudes. They should never be allowed to dry out completely, however.

GROWING MEDIA: Plants may be mounted on tree-fern or cork slabs if humidity is high and plants are watered at least once daily in summer. When plants are potted, any open, fast-draining medium may be used. Repotting may be done anytime new roots are growing.

MISCELLANEOUS NOTES: The bloom season shown in the climate table is based on reports from the habitat.

Plant and Flower Information

PLANT SIZE AND TYPE: A 9 in. (23 cm) sympodial epiphyte.

PSEUDOBULB: 9 in. (23 cm) long. Stems are clustered and branching.

LEAVES: Many. The pointed, ovate-lanceolate leaves are 1.2–1.8 in. (3.0–4.5 cm) long, with minute teeth at the apex.

INFLORESCENCE: Short.

FLOWERS: 6 per inflorescence. The flowers are 1 in. (2.5 cm) long. The blossoms are orange-yellow with orange margins. Blossoms have an oval-ovate dorsal sepal, obliquely triangular lateral sepals, and oblong-obovate petals. The erect lip has no callus. The somewhat rectangular midlobe is lacerated at the apex.

REFERENCES: 221, 470, 478.

Dendrobium jacobsonii J. J. Smith

ORIGIN/HABITAT: Endemic eastern Java. Plants grow in the high mountain mistforests on Mt. Lawu and Mt. Semeru at 7550–9850 ft. (2300–3000 m), but Comber (ref. 73) states that he has never found the plant below 8850 ft. (2700 m). Plants usually grow on small exposed trees in areas where mists are common.

CLIMATE: Station #96881, Madiun, Java, Indonesia, Lat. 7.6°S, Long. 111.4°E, at 361 ft. (110 m). Temperatures are calculated for an elevation of 8700 ft. (2650 m), resulting in probable extremes of 67°F (20°C) and 34°F (1°C).

N/HEMISPHERE	JAN	FEB	MAR	APR	MAY	JUN	JUL	AUG	SEP	OCT	NOV	DEC
°F AVG MAX	57	58	59	60	58	57	56	56	57	59	58	58
°F AVG MIN	41	41	43	44	44	44	44	44	44	44	44	42
DIURNAL RANGE	16	17	16	16	14	13	12	12	13	15	14	16
RAIN/INCHES	1.3	0.8	1.2	2.9	7.6	10.2	11.9	10.9	10.4	8.8	5.1	3.2
HUMIDITY/%	60	54	52	52	64	72	77	78	78	74	70	64
BLOOM SEASON				*								
DAYS CLR @ 7AM	18	22	21	16	8	4	2	2	3	6	9	16
DAYS CLR @ 1PM	15	17	14	9	4	2	1	1	1	3	6	11
RAIN/MM	33	20	30	74	193	259	302	277	264	224	130	81
°C AVG MAX	14.2	14.7	15.3	15.8	14.7	14.2	13.6	13.6	14.2	15.3	14.7	14.7
°C AVG MIN	5.3	5.3	6.4	6.9	6.9	6.9	6.9	6.9	6.9	6.9	6.9	5.8
DIURNAL RANGE	8.9	9.4	8.9	8.9	7.8	7.3	6.7	6.7	7.3	8.4	7.8	8.9
S/HEMISPHERE	JUL	AUG	SEP	OCT	NOV	DEC	JAN	FEB	MAR	APR	MAY	JUN

Cultural Recommendations

LIGHT: 2500–3500 fc.

TEMPERATURES: Throughout the year, days average 56–60°F (14–16°C), and nights average 41–44°F (5–7°C), with a diurnal range of 12–17°F (7–9°C). Because of microclimate effects, actual daytime temperatures may be 6–10°F (3–6°C) warmer than indicated by the temperatures in the climate table.

HUMIDITY: 70–80% much of the year, dropping to near 50% in winter. In the cloudforest habitat, however, humidity is probably greater than records at the weather station indicate.

WATER: At the weather station, rainfall is heavy from spring through autumn, followed by a 2–3 month winter dry season. During the dry season, humidity is so low that even moisture from dew is uncommon. Rainfall is much heavier in the high-elevation cloudforest, however, and moisture from mist, fog, and dew is usually available. Therefore, cultivated plants should be watered frequently while actively growing and should not be allowed to dry completely. Water should be reduced in late autumn.

FERTILIZER: ¼–½ recommended strength. A balanced fertilizer should be applied weekly to biweekly throughout the year.

REST PERIOD: Growing conditions should be maintained year-round. Water and fertilizer should be reduced in winter. Plants should be allowed to dry somewhat between waterings, but they should not remain dry for long periods. In the habitat, light may be higher in winter.

GROWING MEDIA: Plants may be mounted on tree-fern or cork slabs or potted in small pots filled with any open, fast-draining medium. Repotting may be done anytime new roots are growing.

MISCELLANEOUS NOTES: The bloom season shown in the climate table is based on reports from the habitat. Comber (ref. 75) reports that when brought to lower elevations the flower color is much paler, but that plants brought to lower elevations do not survive for long, even at 2800 ft. (850 m).

Plant and Flower Information

PLANT SIZE AND TYPE: A 12 in. (30 cm) sympodial epiphyte.

PSEUDOBULB: 12 in. (30 cm) long. The stems are clustered in a tight clump. Keikis often form on the sides of the pseudobulbs.

LEAVES: Many. The leaves are 0.4–0.7 in. (1.0–1.8 cm) long. They are carried along 2 sides of the stem. The lower leaves drop quickly but the upper leaves are more persistent.

INFLORESCENCE: Short. Blossoms emerge at various locations on both leafy and leafless mature stems.

FLOWERS: 1, rarely 2 per inflorescence. The flowers are 1.1 in. (2.8 cm) across and hang straight down from the stem. Uniformly bright, shiny, vivid orange to scarlet-red, all segments are pointed at the tip. The lateral sepals are broader than the other segments. The lip is thickened near the tip.

REFERENCES: 25, 73, 75, 222, 445.

PHOTOS/DRAWINGS: 73, 75.

Dendrobium jadunae Schlechter. Now considered a synonym of *Diplocaulobium jadunae* (Schlechter) A. Hawkes. REFERENCES: 221, 229, 437, 445.

Dendrobium jamesianum Rchb. f. See *D. infundibulum* Lindley. REFERENCES: 190, 196, 216, 236, 254, 369, 389, 429, 430, 445, 454, 504, 541, 570, 580.

Dendrobium janowskii J. J. Smith. Now considered a synonym of *Diplocaulobium janowskii* (J. J. Smith) Hunt and Summerhayes. REFERENCES: 213, 221, 230, 470, 475.

Dendrobium japonicum Lindley. See *D. moniliforme* (Linn.) Swartz. REFERENCES: 139, 190, 208, 216, 236, 254, 430, 445, 541, 570.

Dendrobium javanicum Korthals ex Blume. Now considered a synonym of *Plocoglottis acuminata* Blume. REFERENCES: 75, 190, 216, 228, 254.

Dendrobium javanicum Miquel. Miquel (ref. 310) and J. J. Smith (ref. 469) list the describer's name as Lindley. It is now considered a synonym of *Sarcostoma javanica* Blume. REFERENCES: 75, 216, 254, 310, 445, 469.

Dendrobium javanicum Swartz. In 1982 Seidenfaden in *Opera Botanica* #62 indicates that *D. javanicum* is a synonym of *Eria javanica* (Swartz) Blume. REFERENCES: 57, 200, 216, 254, 275, 436, 469, 536.

Dendrobium jenkinsi Lindley 1859 not *D. jenkinsii* Wallich ex Lindley 1839. See *D. parciflorum* Rchb. f. ex Lindley. Kränzlin (ref. 254) listed the name as *D. jenkinsii* Griffith. REFERENCES: 216, 254.

Dendrobium jenkinsii Wallich ex Lindley 1839 not *D. jenkinsi* Lindley.

AKA: Seidenfaden (ref. 454) includes *D. aggregatum* Roxburgh var. *jenkinsii* (Wallich ex Lindley) King and Pantling, and *D. marseillei* Gagnepain as synonyms.

ORIGIN/HABITAT: Widespread in India and Southeast Asia. The habitat extends eastward from northeastern India to include Sikkim, Bhutan, Assam, Burma, northern Thailand, Laos, and Yunnan Province of southwestern China. Plants usually grow on trunks and branches of deciduous trees. Habitat elevation varies from as low as 1650 ft. (500 m) in northeastern India to as high as 6550 ft. (2000 m) in the more southerly regions.

CLIMATE: Station #42398, Baghdogra, India, Lat. 26.7°N, Long. 88.3°E, at 412 ft. (126 m). Temperatures have been calculated for a habitat elevation of 2000 ft. (610 m), resulting in probable extremes of 99°F (37°C) and 31°F (−1°C).

N/HEMISPHERE	JAN	FEB	MAR	APR	MAY	JUN	JUL	AUG	SEP	OCT	NOV	DEC
°F AVG MAX	69	72	80	85	85	84	84	84	83	82	77	72
°F AVG MIN	45	49	55	63	68	71	72	72	71	65	55	48
DIURNAL RANGE	24	23	25	22	17	13	12	12	12	17	22	24
RAIN/INCHES	0.3	0.7	1.3	3.7	11.8	25.9	32.2	25.3	21.2	5.6	0.5	0.2
HUMIDITY/%	73	68	57	58	74	84	86	85	85	79	75	76
BLOOM SEASON	*		**	**	**	*						*
DAYS CLR @ 6AM	21	18	15	11	5	0	1	1	4	13	23	19
DAYS CLR @ 12PM	23	16	16	11	2	2	0	1	2	10	21	18
RAIN/MM	8	18	33	94	300	658	818	643	538	142	13	5
°C AVG MAX	20.4	22.1	26.5	29.3	29.3	28.8	28.8	28.8	28.2	27.6	24.9	22.1
°C AVG MIN	7.1	9.3	12.6	17.1	19.9	21.5	22.1	22.1	21.5	18.2	12.6	8.8
DIURNAL RANGE	13.3	12.8	13.9	12.2	9.4	7.3	6.7	6.7	6.7	9.4	12.3	13.3
S/HEMISPHERE	JUL	AUG	SEP	OCT	NOV	DEC	JAN	FEB	MAR	APR	MAY	JUN

Cultural Recommendations

LIGHT: 2500–3500 fc. Light is lowest in summer when cloud cover is very heavy.

TEMPERATURES: Summer days average 84°F (29°C), and nights average 71–72°F (22°C), with a diurnal range of 12–13°F (7°C). The climate table represents the warmest part of the habitat. Temperatures at higher elevations may be 6–10°F (3–6°C) cooler than indicated.

HUMIDITY: Near 85% in summer, dropping to 70–80% in autumn and early winter, then decreasing to 55–60% in late winter and early spring.

WATER: Conditions are very wet for 5 months in summer, very dry for 5 months in winter, with short transition periods in autumn and spring. Cultivated plants should be kept evenly moist from spring to early autumn, but water should be gradually reduced after new growths mature in late autumn.

FERTILIZER: ¼–½ recommended strength, applied weekly. A high-nitrogen fertilizer is beneficial from spring to midsummer, while a fertilizer high in phosphates should be used in late summer and autumn. Summer growth should be rapid to improve flowering the following year.

REST PERIOD: Winter days average 69–72°F (20–22°C), and nights average 45–49°F (7–9°C), with a diurnal range of 23–24°F (13°C). In the habitat, winter rainfall is low, but additional moisture is often available from heavy deposits of dew. For about a month in late winter or early spring, however, humidity is so low that even the moisture from dew is uncommon. Cultivated plants should be allowed to dry out between waterings in winter, but they should not remain completely dry for extended periods. Occasional early morning mistings between waterings, especially on warm, sunny days, may help prevent the plants from becoming too dry. Fertilizer should be eliminated until water is increased in spring. In the habitat, light is highest in winter. The cool, dry rest with increased light may be necessary to initiate blooming.

GROWING MEDIA: Plants are best mounted on wood, cork, or tree-fern slabs if humidity is high and plants are watered at least once daily in summer. When plants must be potted, any open, fast-draining medium may be used. Repotting is best done in early spring when new roots are growing.

MISCELLANEOUS NOTES: The bloom season shown in the climate table is based on cultivation records. Many growers consider *D. jenkinsii* difficult to grow, so careful attention should be paid to the rest-period conditions.

Plant and Flower Information

PLANT SIZE AND TYPE: A 2.4–4.0 in. (6–10 cm) sympodial epiphyte.

PSEUDOBULB: 1.2–2.0 in. (3–5 cm) long. The ovoid pseudobulbs are flattened, grooved, and erect. They grow crowded together in a dense mat.

LEAVES: 1 per growth. The ovate leaves are 1.2–2.0 in. (3–5 cm) long, thick, and shiny. They persist for several seasons.

INFLORESCENCE: Short. The drooping inflorescences arise from the base of leafy pseudobulbs. The blossoms are held just above the leaves.

FLOWERS: 1–2 per inflorescence. The gold flowers are 1.2 in. (3 cm) across, which is very large for the plant size. Blossoms from closely related species last up to 3 weeks. The broad petals are much wider than the narrow sepals. *D. jenkinsii* has a heart-shaped lip that is wholly pubescent. Flowers are similar to *D. lindleyi* Steudel, which has numerous flowers per inflorescence and a lip that is not pubescent along the border. In other aspects, the blossoms are extremely similar.

HYBRIDIZING NOTES: Chromosome counts are 2n = 38 as *D. jenkinsii* (ref. 504, 580) and *D. aggregatum* var. *jenkinsii* (ref. 152).

REFERENCES: 25, 152, 179, 190, 216, 238, 254, 317, 369, 376, 428, 430, 445, 447, 448, 452, 454, 493, 504, 524, 528, 541, 547, 557, 570, 580.

PHOTOS/DRAWINGS: *130, 238, 428, 430, 454, 493.*

Dendrobium jennyanum Kränzlin.

Northern New Guinea is considered the probable point of origin, but without habitat information, climate data cannot be selected. Ossian (ref. 344) indicates that this may not be a valid species. *D. jennyanum* was described as a sympodial epiphyte 63 in. (160 cm) long with numerous leaves 4–5 in. (10–13 cm) long. The elongated inflorescences were somewhat laxly flowered, with 25–30 per inflorescence. The blossoms were described as yellow on the outside and leather brown on the inside. The fleshy lip was violet at the base and white near the tip. Sepals were 1.2 in. (3 cm) long, and the somewhat twisted petals were 1.6 in. (4 cm) long. REFERENCES: 84, 254, 344.

Dendrobium jerdonianum Wight. See *D. nutans* Lindley.

REFERENCES: 179, 202, 211, 216, 244, 254, 369, 445.

Dendrobium jocosum Rchb. f. See *D. closterium* Rchb. f.

REFERENCES: 173, 216, 254.

Dendrobium jofftii F. M. Bailey.

A misspelling of *D. tofftii* F. M. Bailey, which is now considered a synonym of *D. nindii* W. Hill. REFERENCES: 105.

Dendrobium jofftii Durand and B. D. Jackson.

An invalid name. REFERENCES: 67, 218, 219.

Dendrobium johannis Rchb. f.

AKA: *D. undulatum* R. Brown var. *johannis* (Rchb. f.) F. M. Bailey. Clements (ref. 67) indicates that some specimens labeled *D. johannis* are actually *D. trilamellatum* J. J. Smith. *D. johannis* Rchb. f. var. *semifuscum* Rchb. f. is now considered a synonym of *D. trilamellatum* J. J. Smith.

ORIGIN/HABITAT: Northeastern Australia and New Guinea. Distribution extends northward from near Coen on the eastern Cape York Peninsula to the Torres Strait Islands and across to Papua New Guinea. Plants grow along the edges of rainforests, in swampy areas where winter rainfall is low, and in moderately open forests where light is high.

CLIMATE: Station #94175, Thursday Island, Australia, Lat. 10.6°S, Long. 142.2°E, at 200 ft. (61 m). Record extreme temperatures are 98°F (37°C) and 64°F (18°C).

N/HEMISPHERE	JAN	FEB	MAR	APR	MAY	JUN	JUL	AUG	SEP	OCT	NOV	DEC
°F AVG MAX	82	82	84	86	88	89	87	87	87	86	85	84
°F AVG MIN	73	73	74	76	77	78	77	77	77	77	76	74
DIURNAL RANGE	9	9	10	10	11	11	10	10	10	9	9	10
RAIN/INCHES	0.4	0.2	0.1	0.3	1.5	7.0	18.2	15.8	13.9	8.0	1.6	0.5
HUMIDITY/%	75	72	71	70	69	72	79	80	79	77	75	75
BLOOM SEASON	*		*						*			
DAYS CLR @ 9AM	3	4	3	2	3	1	0	0	1	4	9	5
DAYS CLR @ 3PM	4	5	6	8	7	2	0	1	1	4	8	6
RAIN/MM	10	5	3	8	38	178	462	401	353	203	41	13
°C AVG MAX	27.8	27.8	28.9	30.0	31.1	31.7	30.6	30.6	30.6	30.0	29.4	28.9
°C AVG MIN	22.8	22.8	23.3	24.4	25.0	25.6	25.0	25.0	25.0	25.0	24.4	23.3
DIURNAL RANGE	5.0	5.0	5.6	5.6	6.1	6.1	5.6	5.6	5.6	5.0	5.0	5.6
S/HEMISPHERE	JUL	AUG	SEP	OCT	NOV	DEC	JAN	FEB	MAR	APR	MAY	JUN

Cultural Recommendations

LIGHT: 3000–4000 fc. The heavy summer cloud cover indicates that some shading is needed from spring through autumn, but light should be as high as the plant can tolerate, short of burning the leaves. Strong air movement should be provided year-round.

TEMPERATURES: Throughout the year, days average 82–89°F (28–32°C), and nights average 73–78°F (23–26°C), with a diurnal range of 9–11°F (5–6°C).

HUMIDITY: 70–80% year-round.

WATER: Rainfall in very heavy for 5 months in summer and early autumn. The wet season is followed almost immediately by a 5–6 month very dry season in winter and spring. Cultivated plants should be kept moist while growing, but water should be reduced in autumn.

FERTILIZER: ¼–½ recommended strength, applied weekly. A high-nitrogen fertilizer is beneficial from spring to midsummer, but a fertilizer high in phosphates should be used in late summer and autumn.

REST PERIOD: Temperatures should be maintained year-round, but a long, dry winter rest is required. Cultivated plants should be allowed to dry out between waterings but should not remain completely dry for extended periods. An occasional light misting between waterings may help keep plants from becoming too dry. Some growers have reported success with winter minimum temperatures near 60°F (15°C). It should be noted, however, that this is near the record lows in the habitat. Plants are probably healthier if not subjected to these extremes for extended periods, but seed-grown plants are somewhat adaptable. Cultural instructions in some recent literature have indicated that these plants need winter minimum temperatures near 50°F (10°C), but we have not found anything in the climate data that reflects this need. Australian growers recommend hanging plants high in the greenhouse and almost forgetting them for 2–3 months in winter. Fertilizer should be eliminated until watering is resumed in spring. In the habitat, light may be slightly higher in winter.

GROWING MEDIA: Plants may be mounted or potted. If plants are potted, the medium should be very open and fast draining. Repotting is best done when the new growth is 2–3 in. (5–7 cm) high and new root growth is evident.

MISCELLANEOUS NOTES: The bloom season shown in the climate table is based on cultivation records. The plants do not survive a uniformly moist climate such as occurs in Singapore. Rentoul (ref. 390) indicates that while plants are somewhat adaptable, they still require very warm conditions and should be tried only if these conditions can be provided.

The blossoms are very similar to those of *D. trilamellatum*. The most easily identifiable difference is that in nature *D. johannis* blooms most heavily in autumn and usually has a deep purple spur. *D. trilamellatum*, on the other hand, blooms heaviest in spring and usually has a yellow to dark brown spur.

Plant and Flower Information

PLANT SIZE AND TYPE: A 4–24 in. (10–60 cm) sympodial epiphyte. Cultivated plants are normally 6–12 in. (15–30 cm) tall.

PSEUDOBULB: 2–18 in. (5–46 cm) long. The brownish pseudobulbs are densely clustered. They are unevenly swollen. Leaves are held on the apical 25% of the stem.

LEAVES: 3–8 per growth. The lanceolate leaves are 4–6 in. (10–15 cm) long. They are dark green, tough, thick, and sharply pointed at the tip.

INFLORESCENCE: 6–20 in. (15–51 cm) long. Inflorescences arise from upper nodes of leafy and leafless pseudobulbs.

FLOWERS: 2–20 per inflorescence. The flowers are 1.2–2.4 in. (3–6 cm) across. They are glossy and appear heavily waxed. The erect, evenly twisted petals and curly sepals are usually dark brown with purple lines on the front. They are often paler at the base. The lip is usually clear, but—

ter yellow with a darker crest. Plant size and flower color are highly variable. The blossoms are long-lasting and have a spicy, honey fragrance that some growers find too strong to be pleasant.

HYBRIDIZING NOTES: Chromosome count is n = 19 (ref. 504, 580). When used in hybridizing, *D. johannis* contributes the tendency toward spikes with numerous flowers, short canes, improved flower substance, and twisted floral segments.

REFERENCES: 25, 67, 84, 105, 179, 190, 196, 200, 210, 216, 240, 254, 262, 302, 304, 325, 345, 351, 390, 421, 430, 445, 504, 533, 580.

PHOTOS/DRAWINGS: *84, 105,* 210, 240, *262, 304, 308,* 325, *345, 351, 390, 430, 533.*

Dendrobium johansoniae F. M. Bailey. See *D. johnsoniae* F. Mueller. REFERENCES: 105.

Dendrobium johnsoniae F. Mueller

AKA: *D. johansoniae* F. M. Bailey, *D. macfarlanei* Rchb. f. not F. Mueller, *D. monodon* Kränzlin, *D. niveum* Rolfe.

ORIGIN/HABITAT: Bougainville Island, Guadalcanal, and New Guinea. In Irian Jaya (western New Guinea), plants are found on Yapen (Japen) Island, the Vogelkop Peninsula and near Jayapura. In Papua, plants grow along the north coast from near the border with Irian Jaya to the eastern tip of the island. They usually grow in high light, and in many locations, they are exposed to full sun for at least part of the day. Plants are often found on *Casuarina* trees along water courses and in gullies at 1650–3950 ft. (500–1200 m). In Guadalcanal, plants grow on *Calophyllum* trees near the summit of Mt. Austen at about 1750 ft. (530 m).

CLIMATE: Station #94048, Finschhafen, Papua New Guinea, Lat. 6.6°S, Long. 147.9°E, at 25 ft. (8 m). Temperatures are calculated for a habitat elevation of 2950 ft. (900 m), resulting in probable extremes of 83°F (29°C) and 58°F (15°C).

N/HEMISPHERE	JAN	FEB	MAR	APR	MAY	JUN	JUL	AUG	SEP	OCT	NOV	DEC
°F AVG MAX	74	73	73	74	76	78	79	79	77	76	74	74
°F AVG MIN	63	62	62	61	61	62	64	64	64	64	63	63
DIURNAL RANGE	11	11	11	13	15	16	15	15	13	12	11	11
RAIN/INCHES	25.8	22.4	20.9	15.8	11.7	8.9	5.5	3.7	5.3	11.9	18.3	23.2
HUMIDITY/%	88	87	86	86	84	85	84	85	86	88	88	88
BLOOM SEASON	**	*	*	*	*	*	*	*	*	**	**	**
DAYS CLR	N/A											
RAIN/MM	655	568	531	402	297	227	140	95	135	301	464	589
°C AVG MAX	23.5	23.0	23.0	23.5	24.6	25.7	26.3	26.3	25.2	24.6	23.5	23.5
°C AVG MIN	17.4	16.9	16.9	16.3	16.3	16.9	18.0	18.0	18.0	18.0	17.4	17.4
DIURNAL RANGE	6.1	6.1	6.1	7.2	8.3	8.8	8.3	8.3	7.2	6.6	6.1	6.1
S/HEMISPHERE	JUL	AUG	SEP	OCT	NOV	DEC	JAN	FEB	MAR	APR	MAY	JUN

Cultural Recommendations

LIGHT: 3000–4000 fc.

TEMPERATURES: Throughout the year, days average 73–79°F (23–26°C), and nights average 61–64°F (16–18°C), with a diurnal range of 11–16°F (6–9°C).

HUMIDITY: 85–90% year-round.

WATER: Rainfall is very heavy most of the year, but conditions are somewhat drier for 3–4 months in summer. Cultivated plants should be kept moist with only slight drying allowed between waterings. During hot weather, plants may need to be watered at least once daily.

FERTILIZER: ½ recommended strength. A balanced fertilizer should be applied weekly to biweekly throughout the year. Growers indicate that many closely related *Dendrobium* from low elevations are heavy feeders.

REST PERIOD: Growing conditions should be maintained year-round. In the habitat, rainfall is heaviest in winter. However, water and fertilizer should be reduced somewhat for cultivated plants, especially those grown in the dark, short-day conditions common in temperate latitudes. Plants should never be allowed to dry out completely, however.

GROWING MEDIA: Because plants must be kept moist, they are difficult to grow when mounted. However, potted plants must be placed in a medium that retains moisture but is open and fast draining. The roots should never be allowed to become wet and soggy. Growers indicate that these are surface-rooting plants with moisture-sensitive roots and recommend using small, well-drained pots that are barely large enough to hold the roots. Repotting is best done yearly when new root growth begins.

MISCELLANEOUS NOTES: The bloom season shown in the climate table is based on cultivation records. Cruttwell (ref. 95) states that these plants grow well at Goroka at 4900 ft. (1500 m). Minimum temperatures at this location are 56–60°F (13–16°C) year-round.

Plant and Flower Information

PLANT SIZE AND TYPE: An 8–16 in. (20–40 cm) sympodial epiphyte. Plants often form large clumps.

PSEUDOBULB: 5–12 in. (13–30 cm) long. The ascending stems are cylindrical with 4–6 nodes below the leaves. They may be green or purplish-brown.

LEAVES: 2–5 per growth. The thin leaves are usually 3–4 in. (8–10 cm) long but may reach a length of 6 in. (15 cm). The texture ranges from leathery to brittle.

INFLORESCENCE: 3–8 in. (8–20 cm), rarely 16 in. (41 cm) long. 1–2 inflorescences emerge from leaf axils near the apex of leafy and leafless stems. Flowers are usually held above the leaf tips on erect inflorescences. Plants produce inflorescences while very small.

FLOWERS: 6, rarely 12 per inflorescence. Considered among the finest of the genus, the fragrant flowers are 2.5–5.0 in. (6.5–12.5 cm) across and open fully. The petals, which are wavy along the margin, are wider and longer than the sepals. The pointed sepals and petals are white and glisten in the light. The lip is decorated with purple lines in the throat and on the sidelobes of the fiddle-shaped lip. The blossoms commonly last 2 months.

HYBRIDIZING NOTES: Chromosome count is 2n = 38 (ref. 153, 273). Hereditary influences include the lip and flower shape. When crossed with *D. bigibbum* Lindley, the white color is recessive.

REFERENCES: 25, 36, 67, 83, 92, 95, 105, 153, 179, 190, 196, 240, 254, 262, 271, 273, 304, 307, 371, 430, 437, 445, 516, 526, 533, 537, 541, 550, 570.

PHOTOS/DRAWINGS: 36, 83, 105, *271, 304, 307, 371,* 430, 437, 533.

Dendrobium jonesii Rendle

AKA: Most botanists still consider these plants to be part of the *D. speciosum* alliance. See discussion at *D. speciosum* J. E. Smith.

Clements (ref. 67), however, considers *D. jonesii* to be a valid species and divides it into the following subspecies.

D. jonesii subsp. *jonesii* has been known as *D. fusiforme* F. M Bailey not Thouars, *D. ruppianum* A. Hawkes, *D. speciosum* var. *fusiforme* F. M. Bailey. It grows along the Johnstone River and in the Cairns Range in Queensland, Australia.

D. jonesii subsp. *bancroftianum* (Rchb. f.) M. Clements and D. Jones has been known as *D. fusiforme* (F. M. Bailey) F. M. Bailey forma *magnifica* Dockrill, *D. ruppianum* A. Hawkes forma *magnificum* (Dockrill) Dockrill, *D. speciosum* var. *bancroftianum* Rchb. f., *D. speciosum* var. *hillii* F. M. Bailey forma *bancroftianum* (Rchb. f.) F. M. Bailey. Plants are found in northern Queensland, Bellenden Ker, and the Cairns Range. In parts of their habitat, they are exposed to freezing conditions.

D. jonesii subsp. *blackburnii* (Nicholls) M. Clements and D. Jones has been known as *D. fusiforme* F. M Bailey var. *blackburnii* Nicholls and *D. ruppianum* A. Hawkes var. *blackburnii* (Nicholls) Dockrill. Plants are found west of Port Douglas, Queensland, Australia at 16° 39′S and 145° 08′E in an isolated pocket of rainforest on the western side of the great divide.

ORIGIN/HABITAT: Northeastern Australia. Plants grow in the mountains northwest of Mackay northward to near the Iron Range on the Cape York Peninsula. They are found in the highlands and in lowland gorges at 500–4600 ft. (150–1400 m). The healthiest plants are usually found above 2300–2950 ft. (700–900 m). Plants grow in high light in open forests on the outskirts of rainforests, but they are also found high in rainforest trees.

CLIMATE: Station #94287, Cairns, Australia, Lat. 16.9°S, Long. 145.8°E, at 7 ft. (2 m). Temperatures are calculated for an elevation of 3000 ft. (910 m), resulting in probable extremes of 100°F (38°C) and 33°F (1°C).

N/HEMISPHERE	JAN	FEB	MAR	APR	MAY	JUN	JUL	AUG	SEP	OCT	NOV	DEC
°F AVG MAX	68	70	73	76	78	80	80	79	77	75	71	69
°F AVG MIN	51	52	54	58	60	63	64	64	63	60	56	54
DIURNAL RANGE	17	18	19	18	18	17	16	15	14	15	15	15
RAIN/INCHES	1.6	1.7	1.7	2.1	3.9	8.7	16.6	15.7	18.1	11.3	4.4	2.9
HUMIDITY/%	69	67	65	65	65	68	72	72	74	73	73	72
BLOOM SEASON	*	*	*	*								
DAYS CLR @ 10AM	9	11	13	11	6	6	4	5	6	7	11	10
DAYS CLR @ 4PM	8	10	12	16	10	7	4	3	4	6	9	10
RAIN/MM	41	43	43	53	99	221	422	399	460	287	112	74
°C AVG MAX	20.1	21.2	22.8	24.5	25.6	26.7	26.7	26.2	25.1	24.0	21.7	20.6
°C AVG MIN	10.6	11.2	12.3	14.5	15.6	17.3	17.8	17.8	17.3	15.6	13.4	12.3
DIURNAL RANGE	9.5	10.0	10.5	10.0	10.0	9.4	8.9	8.4	7.8	8.4	8.3	8.3
S/HEMISPHERE	JUL	AUG	SEP	OCT	NOV	DEC	JAN	FEB	MAR	APR	MAY	JUN

Cultural Recommendations

LIGHT: 3000–4000 fc.

TEMPERATURES: Summer days average 79–80°F (26–27°C), and nights average 63–64°F (17–18°C), with a diurnal range of 15–17°F (8–9°C). Growers indicate that temperatures greater than 86°F (30°C) are extremely detrimental.

HUMIDITY: Near 75–85% year-round. In the habitat, relative humidity probably averages at least 10% more than the values recorded at the low elevation weather station. Cultivated plants thrive if high humidity and strong air movement are provided throughout the year.

WATER: Rainfall is heavy from late spring into autumn, but is greatly reduced in winter. Cultivated plants should be kept moist while actively growing, but water should be gradually reduced in autumn.

FERTILIZER: ¼–½ recommended strength, applied weekly. A high-nitrogen fertilizer is beneficial from spring to midsummer, but a fertilizer high in phosphates should be used in late summer and autumn.

REST PERIOD: Winter days average 68–73°F (20–23°C), and nights average 51–54°F (11–12°C), with a diurnal range of 15–19°F (8–11°C). Growers report that winter lows should not fall below 46°F (8°C). Water should be reduced for 4–5 months from late autumn to early spring. In winter, the medium must be kept on the dry side, but humidity should be high enough that the plants do not become desiccated. Light levels, humidity, and air movement should be maintained. Fertilizer may be reduced or eliminated until water is increased in spring. Growers in Sydney report that plants grow well if they are hung high in the greenhouse in winter so that light is high and the plants are easily kept dry.

GROWING MEDIA: Plants are best mounted on large slabs of cork or tree-fern. This species is extremely intolerant of a soggy medium, especially in winter. However, mounted plants require high humidity and daily watering in summer. When plants must be potted, a small pot may be filled with any open, fast-draining medium. Repotting is best done in early spring, immediately after flowering, when new roots begin growing.

MISCELLANEOUS NOTES: The bloom season shown in the climate table is based on reports from the habitat. Cultivated plants bloom mostly in late winter and early spring. Some growers indicate that plants often do poorly in a greenhouse environment, but others indicate that plants are healthy if they have high light and if they are kept dry in winter. Growers indicate the plants tend to produce new growths throughout the year. In nature, the root system is strong and extensive. Plants from elevations higher than 2950 ft. (900 m) are more robust, flower later in the season, and produce larger flowers.

Plant and Flower Information

PLANT SIZE AND TYPE: A 12–20 in. (30–50 cm) sympodial epiphyte or lithophyte. Epiphytic clumps may exceed 100 stems, but lithophytic clumps are usually much smaller.

PSEUDOBULB: 8–12 in. (20–30 cm) long, rarely as small as 6 in. (15 cm). The dark swollen stems are grooved with a pseudobulbous swelling at the base.

LEAVES: 2–7 per growth. The ovate leaves, which are crowded at the apex, are 2–6 in. (5–15 cm) long. They have a thin texture.

INFLORESCENCE: 6–14 in. (15–36 cm) long. 1–4 inflorescences may be produced on each stem. The racemes may be erect or arching and carry many, densely packed blossoms.

FLOWERS: 30 or more per inflorescence. The flowers, which do not open fully, are 0.6–0.8 in. (1.5–2.0 cm) long. All segments are white to cream and become yellow with age. The lip is irregularly marked with purple stripes. Some clones, which may be cultivated as *D. ruppianum* var. *ruppianum* forma *magnificum* or *D. fusiforme* var. *fusiforme* forma *magnificum*, have blooms that are longer than 3.1–3.5 in. (8–9 cm). Blossoms last 10 days. On warm, sunny days, blossoms have a long-lasting spicy fragrance that is considered too strong by some growers.

HYBRIDIZING NOTES: Chromosome count is 2n = 38 as *D. ruppianum* (ref. 151, 152, 154, 187, 243) and as *D. fusiforme* (ref. 504, 580). When used in hybridizing, vegetative characteristics are recessive, but the number of flowers, number of inflorescences, and the densely clustered flowers tend to be dominant characteristics. Although members of the *D. speciosum* alliance are seldom self-fertile, Adams (ref. 4) indicates that pollinations between different clones of the same variety and between different varieties commonly produce seed.

REFERENCES: 4, 36, 67, 151, 152, 154, 179, 187, 219, 235, 240, 243, 254, 262, 263, 389, 390, 421, 495, 504, 533, 580.

PHOTOS/DRAWINGS: 240, *263, 390, 533.*

Dendrobium junceum Lindley

ORIGIN/HABITAT: The Philippines, including Bucas Grande Island, Quezon and Rizal Provinces on Luzon, and Surigao Province on Mindanao. Mueller (ref. 317) and Hooker (ref. 202) indicated that *D. junceum* originated in Singapore and Borneo, but these reports are now considered doubtful.

CLIMATE: Station #98427, Manila, Philippines, Lat. 14.5°N, Long. 121.0°E, at 85 ft. (26 m). Temperatures are calculated for 800 ft. (240 m), resulting in probable extremes of 99°F (37°C) and 56°F (13°C).

N/HEMISPHERE	JAN	FEB	MAR	APR	MAY	JUN	JUL	AUG	SEP	OCT	NOV	DEC
°F AVG MAX	84	86	89	91	91	89	86	85	86	86	85	84
°F AVG MIN	67	67	69	71	73	73	73	73	73	72	70	68
DIURNAL RANGE	17	19	20	20	18	16	13	12	13	14	15	16
RAIN/INCHES	0.9	0.5	0.7	1.3	5.1	10.0	17.0	16.6	14.0	7.6	5.7	2.6
HUMIDITY/%	77	73	70	68	71	81	84	86	87	84	82	89
BLOOM SEASON					*		*	*	*			
DAYS CLR @ 8AM	6	9	14	14	10	3	2	1	1	6	7	6
DAYS CLR @ 2PM	3	6	10	10	8	2	1	1	0	2	2	3
RAIN/MM	23	13	18	33	130	254	432	422	356	193	145	66
°C AVG MAX	28.7	29.8	31.4	32.6	32.6	31.4	29.8	29.2	29.8	29.8	29.2	28.7
°C AVG MIN	19.2	19.2	20.3	21.4	22.6	22.6	22.6	22.6	22.6	22.0	20.9	19.8
DIURNAL RANGE	9.5	10.6	11.1	11.2	10.0	8.8	7.2	6.6	7.2	7.8	8.3	8.9
S/HEMISPHERE	JUL	AUG	SEP	OCT	NOV	DEC	JAN	FEB	MAR	APR	MAY	JUN

Cultural Recommendations

LIGHT: 2000–3000 fc in summer.

TEMPERATURES: Throughout the year, days average 84–91°F (29–33°C), and nights average 67–73°F (19–23°C), with a diurnal range of 12–20°F (7–11°C).

HUMIDITY: 80–90% during most of the year, dropping to near 70% in late winter and spring.

WATER: Rainfall is very heavy from late spring into autumn, but conditions are much drier in winter and early spring. Cultivated plants should be kept moist while actively growing, but water should be gradually reduced in autumn.

FERTILIZER: ¼–½ recommended strength, applied weekly. A high-nitrogen fertilizer is beneficial from spring to midsummer, but a fertilizer high in phosphates should be used in late summer and autumn.

REST PERIOD: Growing temperatures should be maintained all year. Rainfall is low for 2–3 months in winter; but humidity remains high, indicating additional moisture from frequent heavy dew. In winter, cultivated plants should be allowed to dry out between waterings, but they should not remain completely dry for extended periods. Fertilizer should be reduced or eliminated when plants are not actively growing. In the habitat, light is highest in winter.

GROWING MEDIA: Plants may be mounted on tree-fern or cork slabs if humidity is high and plants are watered at least once daily in summer. When plants are potted, any open, fast-draining medium may be used. Repotting is best done in early spring after blooming when new roots begin growing.

MISCELLANEOUS NOTES: The bloom season shown in the climate table is based on cultivation records. In the habitat, collections have been made in late spring–early summer, suggesting that plants may have been blooming at that time.

Plant and Flower Information

PLANT SIZE AND TYPE: A 45 in. (115 cm) sympodial epiphyte.

PSEUDOBULB: 45 in. (115 cm) long. The slender stems are pseudobulbous at the base, slightly swollen at the middle, and taper at each end. They may be greenish olive or reddish brown. They are conspicuously ridged and branch sparingly near the apex.

LEAVES: The dark green leaves are 3–6 in. (8–15 cm) long. They are nearly terete and taper to a threadlike point.

INFLORESCENCE: 1.2–1.6 in. (3–4 cm). Flowers arise from tufts of bracts at the uppermost leaf axils of leafy or leafless branches.

FLOWERS: 1–2 per inflorescence. The blossoms are 1.2–1.6 in. (3–4 cm) across. Sepals and petals are white to yellow with cream at the tips. The large lip is notched at the apex and minutely ruffled along the margin. The midlobe and disc are chartreuse yellow, and the white sidelobes are marked with purple or violet stripes. The blooms appear sprinkled here and there, usually on scraggly clumps of slender, leafless stems. The very fragrant blossoms last several days.

REFERENCES: 179, 202, 216, 225, 254, 286, 295, 317, 373, 395, 454, 536.

PHOTOS/DRAWINGS: 373.

Dendrobium juncifolium Schlechter

ORIGIN/HABITAT: Endemic to Sulawesi (Celebes). Plants grow near sea level on trees along the Lampasioe and Kuala Besaar Rivers in the Tolitoli district.

CLIMATE: Station #97028, Tolitoli, Sulawesi, Indonesia, Lat. 1.0°N, Long. 120.8°E, at 7 ft. (2 m). Record extreme temperatures are not available for this location.

N/HEMISPHERE	JAN	FEB	MAR	APR	MAY	JUN	JUL	AUG	SEP	OCT	NOV	DEC
°F AVG MAX	84	83	85	86	86	86	85	86	86	86	86	85
°F AVG MIN	76	74	76	78	78	76	76	77	77	77	78	77
DIURNAL RANGE	8	9	9	8	8	10	9	9	9	9	8	8
RAIN/INCHES	6.3	4.9	7.4	3.8	6.4	6.3	5.5	4.1	4.9	4.7	4.0	4.3
HUMIDITY/%	N/A											
BLOOM SEASON	*											
DAYS CLR	N/A											
RAIN/MM	161	125	187	98	162	160	139	103	125	120	101	110
°C AVG MAX	28.7	28.5	29.3	29.9	30.1	30.1	29.7	30.1	30.2	30.2	30.0	29.5
°C AVG MIN	24.5	23.6	24.3	25.3	25.3	24.4	24.4	24.8	24.7	25.2	25.3	25.0
DIURNAL RANGE	4.2	4.9	5.0	4.6	4.8	5.7	5.3	5.3	5.5	5.0	4.7	4.5
S/HEMISPHERE	JUL	AUG	SEP	OCT	NOV	DEC	JAN	FEB	MAR	APR	MAY	JUN

Cultural Recommendations

LIGHT: 2500–3500 fc.

TEMPERATURES: Throughout the year, days average 83–86°F (29–30°C), and nights average 74–78°F (24–25°C), with a diurnal range of 8–10°F (4–6°C).

HUMIDITY: Information is not available for this location. However, records from nearby locations indicate that humidity probably averages 75–85% year-round.

WATER: Rainfall is moderate to heavy throughout the year. Cultivated plants should be allowed to dry slightly between waterings, but they should never dry out completely.

FERTILIZER: ¼–½ recommended strength. A balanced fertilizer should be applied weekly to biweekly throughout the year.

REST PERIOD: Growing conditions should be maintained all year. However, water should be reduced for plants cultivated in the dark, short-day conditions common during temperate-latitude winters, but they should not remain dry for extended periods. Fertilizer should be reduced or eliminated anytime water is reduced.

GROWING MEDIA: Plants may be mounted on tree-fern or cork slabs if humidity is high and plants are watered at least once daily in summer. When plants are potted, any open, fast-draining medium may be used. Repotting may be done anytime new roots are growing.

MISCELLANEOUS NOTES: The bloom season shown in the climate table is based on reports from the habitat.

Plant and Flower Information

PLANT SIZE AND TYPE: An 8–24 in. (20–60 cm) sympodial epiphyte.

PSEUDOBULB: 8–24 in. (20–60 cm) long. The stems are erect, slender, and 4-angled, and leafless at the base and apex. They arise from a short rhizome and do not branch.

LEAVES: 5–8 per growth. The terete, very slender leaves resemble the leaves of rushes and are 1.6–5.0 in. (4–13 cm) long.

INFLORESCENCE: Inflorescences carry bunches of flowers at or near the apex of the stem.

FLOWERS: Many per inflorescence. The white flowers, which have a yellow spot on the lip, are delicate, erect, spreading, and 0.4 in. (1 cm) long. The lateral sepals are triangular, and the petals somewhat sickle-shaped. The trilobed lip has a kidney-shaped midlobe that is wavy along the margin. It is moderately recurved at the apex.

REFERENCES: 221, 436.

Dendrobium juncoideum P. van Royen

ORIGIN/HABITAT: Northeastern Papua New Guinea. Plants grow Mt. Albert Edward on subalpine shrubbery at 8850–10,500 ft. (2700–3200 m).

CLIMATE: Station #200192, Garaina, Papua New Guinea, Lat. 7.9°S, Long. 147.1°E, at 2350 ft. (716 m). Temperatures are calculated for an elevation of 10,150 ft. (3100 m), resulting in probable extremes of 68°F (20°C) and 20°F (−7°C).

N/HEMISPHERE	JAN	FEB	MAR	APR	MAY	JUN	JUL	AUG	SEP	OCT	NOV	DEC
°F AVG MAX	54	56	57	58	59	59	59	59	58	58	57	55
°F AVG MIN	37	37	37	38	37	38	39	39	39	38	38	37
DIURNAL RANGE	17	19	20	20	22	21	20	20	19	20	19	18
RAIN/INCHES	5.8	6.5	8.7	11.1	11.8	11.9	8.9	11.7	11.5	9.9	7.7	5.2
HUMIDITY/%	84	82	82	81	80	80	81	81	82	83	84	84
BLOOM SEASON		*										
DAYS CLR	N/A											
RAIN/MM	147	165	221	282	300	302	226	297	292	251	196	132
°C AVG MAX	12.3	13.4	14.0	14.6	15.1	15.1	15.1	15.1	14.6	14.6	14.0	12.9
°C AVG MIN	2.9	2.9	2.9	3.4	2.9	3.4	4.0	4.0	4.0	3.4	3.4	2.9
DIURNAL RANGE	9.4	10.5	11.1	11.2	12.2	11.7	11.1	11.1	10.6	11.2	10.6	10.0
S/HEMISPHERE	JUL	AUG	SEP	OCT	NOV	DEC	JAN	FEB	MAR	APR	MAY	JUN

Cultural Recommendations

LIGHT: 2000–3000 fc.

TEMPERATURES: Throughout the year, days average 54–59°F (12–15°C), and nights average 37–39°F (3–4°C), with a diurnal range of 17–22°F (9–12°C).

HUMIDITY: 80–85% year-round.

WATER: Rainfall is heavy year-round, with a slightly drier period in winter. Cultivated plants should be kept moist but not soggy.

FERTILIZER: ¼–½ recommended strength. A balanced fertilizer should be applied weekly to biweekly throughout the year.

REST PERIOD: Growing conditions vary only slightly all year. In the habitat, rainfall is slightly lower in winter. Water should be reduced somewhat for cultivated plants, especially those grown in the dark, short-day conditions common during temperate-latitude winters. They should never be allowed to dry out completely, however. Fertilizer should be reduced or eliminated anytime water is reduced. In the habitat, light is slightly higher in winter.

GROWING MEDIA: Plants may be mounted on tree-fern or cork slabs if humidity is high and plants are watered at least once daily in summer. When plants are potted, any open, fast-draining medium may be used. Repotting may be done anytime new roots are growing.

MISCELLANEOUS NOTES: The bloom season shown in the climate table is based on reports from the habitat.

Plant and Flower Information

PLANT SIZE AND TYPE: A 28–39 in. (70–100 cm) sympodial epiphyte.

PSEUDOBULB: 28–39 in. (70–100 cm) long. Plants are pendulous if growing in shade, but they are stunted and as short 4 in. (10 cm) if grown in the open on exposed tree ferns and exposed to full sun.

LEAVES: 2 per growth. The linear-lanceolate leaves are 1.0–2.2 in. (2.5–5.5 cm) long.

INFLORESCENCE: 0.4 in. (1 cm) long. Inflorescences arise from nodes on leafless stems.

FLOWERS: 1–5 per inflorescence. The flowers are 1.3 in. (3.3 cm) across. They are somewhat fan-shaped with rich, purplish pink sepals and petals and an orange lip.

REFERENCES: 24, 233, 538.

PHOTOS/DRAWINGS: 538.

Dendrobium juniperinum Schlechter

ORIGIN/HABITAT: Northern Papua New Guinea. Plants grow on forest trees in the Finisterre Range at about 4100 ft. (1250 m).

CLIMATE: Station #94010, Goroka, Papua New Guinea, Lat. 6.1°S, Long. 145.4°E, at 5141 ft. (1567 m). Temperatures are calculated for an elevation of 4000 ft. (1220 m), resulting in probable extremes of 90°F (32°C) and 46°F (8°C).

N/HEMISPHERE	JAN	FEB	MAR	APR	MAY	JUN	JUL	AUG	SEP	OCT	NOV	DEC
°F AVG MAX	80	81	82	83	83	82	83	82	82	82	83	81
°F AVG MIN	60	61	61	61	62	63	63	63	64	63	63	61
DIURNAL RANGE	20	20	21	22	21	19	20	19	18	19	20	20
RAIN/INCHES	2.1	2.8	4.6	5.9	6.6	9.3	9.1	10.1	10.7	8.3	4.6	2.0
HUMIDITY/%	70	67	67	67	67	71	72	73	74	71	70	70
BLOOM SEASON		*										
DAYS CLR	N/A											
RAIN/MM	53	71	117	150	168	236	231	257	272	211	117	51
°C AVG MAX	26.5	27.1	27.6	28.2	28.2	27.6	28.2	27.6	27.6	27.6	28.2	27.1
°C AVG MIN	15.4	16.0	16.0	16.0	16.5	17.1	17.1	17.1	17.6	17.1	17.1	16.0
DIURNAL RANGE	11.1	11.1	11.6	12.2	11.7	10.5	11.1	10.5	10.0	10.5	11.1	11.1
S/HEMISPHERE	JUL	AUG	SEP	OCT	NOV	DEC	JAN	FEB	MAR	APR	MAY	JUN

Cultural Recommendations

LIGHT: 2500–3500 fc.

TEMPERATURES: Throughout the year, days average 80–83°F (27–28°C), and nights average 60–64°F (15–18°C), with a diurnal range of 18–22°F (11–12°C). The diurnal range is unusually large for a habitat with such constant temperatures.

HUMIDITY: 70–75% from summer into autumn, dropping to 65–70% in winter and spring. Plants require excellent air movement.

WATER: Rainfall is moderate to heavy most of the year, but conditions are slightly drier for 3 months in winter. Cultivated plants should be kept moist but not soggy. Occasional early morning mistings may be beneficial, especially on bright, sunny days.

FERTILIZER: ¼–½ recommended strength. A balanced fertilizer should be applied weekly to biweekly throughout the year.

REST PERIOD: Growing temperatures should be maintained all year. In the habitat, rainfall is lowest in winter, but dew and mist from fog and low clouds are common. Water and fertilizer should be reduced somewhat for cultivated plants, especially those grown in the darker, short-day conditions common during temperate-latitude winters. Plants should be kept on the dry side, but they should never be allowed to dry out completely. In the habitat, light is higher in winter.

GROWING MEDIA: Plants may be mounted on tree-fern or cork slabs if humidity is high and plants are watered at least once daily in summer. When plants are potted, any open, fast-draining medium may be used. Repotting may be done anytime new roots are growing.

MISCELLANEOUS NOTES: The bloom season shown in the climate table is based on reports from the habitat. Plants that produce flowers which last a single day commonly bloom several times during the year. Flowering usually occurs 7–14 days after a sudden 10°F (5°C) drop in daytime temperatures.

Plant and Flower Information

PLANT SIZE AND TYPE: A 16–20 in. (40–50 cm) sympodial epiphyte. Schlechter (ref. 437) indicated that the plant resembled a small, branched juniper bush.

PSEUDOBULB: 16–20 in. (40–50 cm) long. The branching, densely leafy stems are rigid and erect. They arise from an elongated rhizome.

LEAVES: Many. The linear leaves are 0.8–1.0 in. (2.0–2.5 cm) long, pointed, and rigid.

INFLORESCENCE: Short.

FLOWERS: 2 per inflorescence. The flowers are 0.4 in. (1 cm) across. Sepals and petals are pale pink. The fringed and scalloped lip is yellowish white. Blossoms last a single day.

REFERENCES: 221, 437, 445.

PHOTOS/DRAWINGS: 437.

Dendrobium junzaingense J. J. Smith. See *D. subacaule* Reinwardt ex Lindley. REFERENCES: 225, 385, 486.

Dendrobium kaernbachii Kränzlin. Sometimes spelled *D. kärnbachii*, see *D. hollrungii* Kränzlin. REFERENCES: 218, 253, 254, 437, 470.

Dendrobium kajewskii Ames. See *D. conanthum* Schlechter. REFERENCES: 16, 84, 225, 270, 271, 516.

Dendrobium kanakorum Kränzlin. Kränzlin (ref. 254) indicated that this species originated in New Caledonia. However, Hallé (ref. 173) states that it is not found there. Without habitat location, climate data cannot be selected. Plants were 12–16 in. (30–40 cm) tall with leafy, somewhat flattened stems that become grooved when dry. Several inflorescences emerge from the upper part of the stem. The pale rose-violet blossoms were 0.2 in. (0.5 cm) long. The extremely small blossoms, which do not open fully, have oblong sepals and tongue-shaped petals. The obscurely 3-lobed lip is stalked at the base becoming broad then tapering to a sharp point at the tip. The margins are wavy and uneven. REFERENCES: 173, 220, 254. PHOTOS/DRAWINGS: 254.

Dendrobium kanburiense Seidenfaden

ORIGIN/HABITAT: Endemic to Thailand. Plants are found at several locations in the Kanburi region west of Bangkok.

CLIMATE: Station #48450, Kanchanaburi, Thailand, Lat. 14.0°N, Long. 99.5°E, at 92 ft. (28 m). Temperatures are calculated for an elevation of 800 ft. (240 m), resulting in probable extremes of 107°F (42°C) and 40°F (4°C).

N/HEMISPHERE	JAN	FEB	MAR	APR	MAY	JUN	JUL	AUG	SEP	OCT	NOV	DEC
°F AVG MAX	89	94	98	98	94	91	90	89	89	87	86	86
°F AVG MIN	61	67	71	75	75	74	73	73	72	71	67	61
DIURNAL RANGE	28	27	27	23	19	17	17	16	17	16	19	25
RAIN/INCHES	0.1	0.6	1.2	2.8	5.1	3.5	4.4	3.8	7.5	7.1	2.5	0.2
HUMIDITY/%	61	61	58	58	72	74	73	75	79	80	75	67
BLOOM SEASON					*		*	*	*			
DAYS CLR @ 7AM	8	4	6	3	1	1	0	0	0	2	4	6
DAYS CLR @ 1PM	13	6	5	5	1	0	0	0	1	2	3	7
RAIN/MM	3	15	30	71	130	89	112	97	190	180	64	5
°C AVG MAX	31.5	34.3	36.5	36.5	34.3	32.6	32.0	31.5	31.5	30.4	29.8	29.8
°C AVG MIN	15.9	19.3	21.5	23.7	23.7	23.1	22.6	22.6	22.0	21.5	19.3	15.9
DIURNAL RANGE	15.6	15.0	15.0	12.8	10.6	9.5	9.4	8.9	9.5	8.9	10.5	13.9
S/HEMISPHERE	JUL	AUG	SEP	OCT	NOV	DEC	JAN	FEB	MAR	APR	MAY	JUN

Cultural Recommendations

LIGHT: 2000–3000 fc.

TEMPERATURES: Summer days average 89–91°F (32–33°C), and nights average 73–74°F (23°C), with a diurnal range of 16–17°F (9–10°C). The warmest season is spring, before the start of the rainy season. Days average 94–98°F (34–37°C), and nights average 71–75°F (22–24°C), with a diurnal range of 19–27°F (11–15°C).

HUMIDITY: 75–80% in summer and autumn, dropping to near 60% for 4 months in winter and early spring.

WATER: Rainfall is low to moderate most of the year, but conditions are very dry for 3–4 months in winter. During the growing season, cultivated plants should be watered heavily and then allowed to dry out somewhat between waterings. Water should be gradually reduced in autumn.

FERTILIZER: ¼–½ recommended strength, applied weekly. A high-nitrogen fertilizer is beneficial from spring to midsummer, but a fertilizer high in phosphates should be used in late summer and autumn.

REST PERIOD: Winter days average 86–94°F (30–34°C), and nights average 61–67°F (16–19°C), with a diurnal range of 25–28°F (14–16°C). Other orchids from this area regularly survive temperatures of 45°F (7°C) when they are dry. Rainfall is low for 3–4 months in winter, and conditions are so dry that even moisture from dew is uncommon. Cultivated plants should be allowed to dry out between waterings, but they should not remain completely dry for extended periods. Occasional mistings between waterings may help prevent excessive desiccation. In the habitat, light is highest in winter.

GROWING MEDIA: Plants may be mounted on tree-fern or cork slabs if humidity is high and plants are watered at least once daily in summer. When plants are potted, any open, fast-draining medium may be used. Repotting is best done in early spring when new roots are growing.

MISCELLANEOUS NOTES: The bloom season shown in the climate table is based on reports from the habitat.

Plant and Flower Information

PLANT SIZE AND TYPE: A 1.4–1.6 in. (3.5–4.0 cm) sympodial epiphyte.

PSEUDOBULB: 0.6 in. (1.5 cm) long. The fat pseudobulbs are nearly conical.

LEAVES: 3–4 per growth. The broad leaves are 0.8–1.0 in. (2.0–2.5 cm) long and unequally bilobed at the apex.

INFLORESCENCE: 1.2 in. (3 cm) long. 1–2 inflorescences arise from nodes at or near the apex of new stems. They emerge at the same time as the new leaves.

FLOWERS: 6–10 per inflorescence. The greenish yellow flowers are 0.2 in. (0.5 cm) long. The lip is a stronger green with 3 rounded keels. The edges are uneven but not wavy.

REFERENCES: 234, 454.

PHOTOS/DRAWINGS: 454.

Dendrobium kandarianum Kränzlin. Now considered a synonym of *Eria kandariana* (Kränzlin) Schlechter. REFERENCES: 25, 220, 254.

Dendrobium kaniense Schlechter

ORIGIN/HABITAT: Northern Papua New Guinea. Plants grow low on the trunks of mistforest trees in the Kani Range at about 3300 ft. (1000 m).

CLIMATE: Station #94010, Goroka, Papua New Guinea, Lat. 6.1°S, Long. 145.4°E, at 5141 ft. (1567 m). Temperatures are calculated for an elevation of 3300 ft. (1000 m), resulting in probable extremes of 93°F (34°C) and 49°F (10°C).

N/HEMISPHERE	JAN	FEB	MAR	APR	MAY	JUN	JUL	AUG	SEP	OCT	NOV	DEC
°F AVG MAX	82	83	84	85	85	84	85	84	84	84	85	83
°F AVG MIN	62	63	63	63	64	65	65	65	66	65	65	63
DIURNAL RANGE	20	20	21	22	21	19	20	19	18	19	20	20
RAIN/INCHES	2.1	2.8	4.6	5.9	6.6	9.3	9.1	10.1	10.7	8.3	4.6	2.0
HUMIDITY/%	70	67	67	67	67	71	72	73	74	71	70	70
BLOOM SEASON									*			
DAYS CLR	N/A											
RAIN/MM	53	71	117	150	168	236	231	257	272	211	117	51
°C AVG MAX	27.9	28.4	29.0	29.5	29.5	29.0	29.5	29.0	29.0	29.0	29.5	28.4
°C AVG MIN	16.7	17.3	17.3	17.3	17.9	18.4	18.4	18.4	19.0	18.4	18.4	17.3
DIURNAL RANGE	11.2	11.1	11.7	12.2	11.6	10.6	11.1	10.6	10.0	10.6	11.1	11.1
S/HEMISPHERE	JUL	AUG	SEP	OCT	NOV	DEC	JAN	FEB	MAR	APR	MAY	JUN

Cultural Recommendations

LIGHT: 2500–3500 fc.

TEMPERATURES: Throughout the year, days average 82–85°F (28–30°C), and nights average 62–66°F (17–19°C), with a diurnal range of 18–22°F (10–12°C).

HUMIDITY: 70–75% from summer into autumn, dropping to near 65% in winter and spring.

WATER: Rainfall is moderate to heavy most of the year, but conditions are

Dendrobium karoense

slightly drier for 3 months in winter. Cultivated plants should be kept moist but not soggy. Occasional early morning mistings may be beneficial, especially on bright, sunny days.

FERTILIZER: ¼–½ recommended strength. A balanced fertilizer should be applied weekly to biweekly throughout the year.

REST PERIOD: Growing temperatures should be maintained all year. In the habitat, rainfall is lowest in winter, but dew and mist from fog and low clouds are common. Water and fertilizer should be reduced somewhat for cultivated plants, especially those grown in the darker, short-day conditions common during temperate-latitude winters. Plants should be kept on the dry side, but they should never be allowed to dry out completely. In the habitat, light is higher in winter.

GROWING MEDIA: Plants may be mounted on tree-fern or cork slabs if humidity is high and plants are watered at least once daily in summer. When plants are potted, any open, fast-draining medium may be used. Repotting may be done anytime new roots are growing.

MISCELLANEOUS NOTES: The bloom season shown in the climate table is based on reports from the habitat.

Plant and Flower Information

PLANT SIZE AND TYPE: A 12–20 in. (30–50 cm) sympodial epiphyte.

PSEUDOBULB: 12–20 in. (30–50 cm) long. The stems are densely leafy.

LEAVES: Many. The lanceolate leaves may be erect or spreading. They are 3–5 in. (8–13 cm) long.

INFLORESCENCE: Short. Flowers are held in a dense cluster.

FLOWERS: 4–6 per inflorescence. The flowers, which remain nearly closed, are 0.5 in. (1.3 cm) long. Sepals and petals are yellowish on the outside and white inside. The lip is golden yellow in the center.

REFERENCES: 221, 437, 445.

PHOTOS/DRAWINGS: 437.

Dendrobium karoense Schlechter. Now considered a synonym of *Cadetia karoense* (Schlechter) Schlechter. REFERENCES: 179, 219, 221, 254, 437, 444.

Dendrobium katherinae A. Hawkes

AKA: *D. pachyanthum* Schlechter 1912 not 1911.

ORIGIN/HABITAT: Northern Papua New Guinea. Plants grow on forest trees at about 1300 ft. (400 m) near Pema on the Waria River.

CLIMATE: Station #200192, Garaina, Papua New Guinea, Lat. 7.9°S, Long. 147.1°E, at 2350 ft. (716 m). Temperatures are calculated for an elevation of 1150 ft. (350 m), resulting in probable extremes of 98°F (37°C) and 50°F (10°C).

N/HEMISPHERE	JAN	FEB	MAR	APR	MAY	JUN	JUL	AUG	SEP	OCT	NOV	DEC
°F AVG MAX	84	86	87	88	89	89	89	89	88	88	87	85
°F AVG MIN	67	67	67	68	67	68	69	69	69	68	68	67
DIURNAL RANGE	17	19	20	20	22	21	20	20	19	20	19	18
RAIN/INCHES	5.8	6.5	8.7	11.1	11.8	11.9	8.9	11.7	11.5	9.9	7.7	5.2
HUMIDITY/%	84	82	82	81	80	80	81	81	82	83	84	84
BLOOM SEASON												*
DAYS CLR	N/A											
RAIN/MM	147	165	221	282	300	302	226	297	292	251	196	132
°C AVG MAX	28.9	30.0	30.5	31.1	31.6	31.6	31.6	31.6	31.1	31.1	30.5	29.4
°C AVG MIN	19.4	19.4	19.4	20.0	19.4	20.0	20.5	20.5	20.5	20.0	20.0	19.4
DIURNAL RANGE	9.5	10.6	11.1	11.1	12.2	11.6	11.1	11.1	10.6	11.1	10.5	10.0
S/HEMISPHERE	JUL	AUG	SEP	OCT	NOV	DEC	JAN	FEB	MAR	APR	MAY	JUN

Cultural Recommendations

LIGHT: 2000–3000 fc.

TEMPERATURES: Throughout the year, days average 84–89°F (29–32°C), and nights average 67–69°F (19–21°C), with a diurnal range of 17–22°F (10–12°C).

HUMIDITY: 80–85% year-round.

WATER: Rainfall is moderate to heavy all year, but conditions are slightly drier in winter. Cultivated plants should be kept moist but not soggy.

FERTILIZER: ¼–½ recommended strength. A balanced fertilizer should be applied weekly to biweekly throughout the year.

REST PERIOD: Growing conditions should be maintained all year. In the habitat, rainfall is slightly lower in winter. Water should be reduced somewhat for cultivated plants, especially those grown in the dark, short-day conditions common in temperate latitudes, but they should never be allowed to dry out completely. Fertilizer should be reduced or eliminated anytime water is reduced. In the habitat, light is higher in winter.

GROWING MEDIA: Plants may be mounted on tree-fern or cork slabs if humidity is high and plants are watered at least once daily in summer. When plants are potted, any open, fast-draining medium may be used. Repotting may be done anytime new roots are growing.

MISCELLANEOUS NOTES: The bloom season shown in the climate table is based on reports from the habitat. Plants that produce flowers which last a single day commonly bloom several times each year. Flowering usually occurs 7–14 days after a sudden 10°F (5°C) drop in daytime temperatures.

Plant and Flower Information

PLANT SIZE AND TYPE: A sympodial epiphyte of unreported size.

PSEUDOBULB: The leafy stems are unbranched.

LEAVES: Many. The elliptic leaves are 5–7 in. (13–18 cm) long.

INFLORESCENCE: Very short. Inflorescences emerge from nodes at the side of the stem. The flowers are subopposite.

FLOWERS: 2 per inflorescence. The short-lived flowers are 0.6 in. (1.5 cm) long. Sepals and petals, which make a ¾ curl at the tips, are yellow with red-brown spots on the inside. The small lip is nearly hidden. The base of the column is marked with orange-red.

REFERENCES: 191, 229, 437.

PHOTOS/DRAWINGS: 437.

Dendrobium kaudernii J. J. Smith

ORIGIN/HABITAT: Sulawesi (Celebes) near Bolaäng Mongondou. No specific habitat information or elevation is available, so the following climate data should be used with caution.

CLIMATE: Station #97096, Poso, Sulawesi, Indonesia, Lat. 1.4°S, Long. 120.7°E, elevation 7 ft. (2 m). Record extreme temperatures are not available for this location.

N/HEMISPHERE	JAN	FEB	MAR	APR	MAY	JUN	JUL	AUG	SEP	OCT	NOV	DEC
°F AVG MAX	87	88	88	88	87	86	86	86	87	86	87	88
°F AVG MIN	74	75	73	75	76	75	75	75	74	75	76	75
DIURNAL RANGE	13	13	15	13	11	11	11	11	13	11	11	13
RAIN/INCHES	5.9	4.0	2.7	5.6	7.2	5.6	6.3	6.9	8.4	7.5	9.2	4.8
HUMIDITY/%	N/A											
BLOOM SEASON	N/A											
DAYS CLR	N/A											
RAIN/MM	151	100	70	143	183	142	160	176	212	189	234	123
°C AVG MAX	30.7	31.3	31.2	31.0	30.6	30.1	30.1	29.8	30.4	30.0	30.6	31.1
°C AVG MIN	23.4	23.7	22.6	24.0	24.2	23.9	23.7	23.6	23.5	24.0	24.2	24.0
DIURNAL RANGE	7.3	7.6	8.6	7.0	6.4	6.2	6.4	6.2	6.9	6.0	6.4	7.1
S/HEMISPHERE	JUL	AUG	SEP	OCT	NOV	DEC	JAN	FEB	MAR	APR	MAY	JUN

Cultural Recommendations

LIGHT: 2000–3000 fc.

TEMPERATURES: Throughout the year, days average 86–88°F (30–31°C), and nights average 73–76°F (23–24°C), with a diurnal range of 11–15°F (6–9°C).

HUMIDITY: Information is not available for this location. However, records from nearby locations indicate that humidity probably averages 75–85% year-round.

WATER: Rainfall is moderate to heavy throughout the year, with a brief, one-month drier period in winter. Cultivated plants should be kept moist with only slight drying allowed between waterings.

FERTILIZER: 1/4–1/2 recommended strength. A balanced fertilizer should be applied weekly to biweekly throughout the year.

REST PERIOD: Growing conditions should be maintained all year. Water should be reduced for plants cultivated in the dark, short-day conditions common during temperate-latitude winters, but they should never be allowed to dry out completely. Fertilizer should be reduced or eliminated when water is reduced.

GROWING MEDIA: Plants may be mounted on tree-fern or cork slabs if humidity is high and plants are watered at least once daily in summer. When plants are potted, any open, fast-draining medium may be used. They may be repotted anytime new roots are growing.

Plant and Flower Information

PLANT SIZE AND TYPE: An 18 in. (45 cm) sympodial epiphyte.

PSEUDOBULB: 18 in. (45 cm) long. The elongated, branched stems are laterally flattened.

LEAVES: Many. The leaves are oblong-triangular, flattened, pointed, and 1 in. (2.5 cm) long.

INFLORESCENCE: Short. Numerous, branching inflorescences are borne along the side of the stem.

FLOWERS: 1 per branch. The flowers are 0.3 in. (0.8 cm) across. They are fleshy and dark purple. The erect, recurved lip is minutely fringed along the margin.

REFERENCES: 224, 483.

Dendrobium kauldorumii T. M. Reeve

AKA: Sometimes spelled *D. kauldorumi*.

ORIGIN/HABITAT: Papua New Guinea. Plants grow on *Nothofagus* trees in a very restricted area in Chimbu and Eastern Highland Provinces at 5900–7200 ft. (1800–2200 m).

CLIMATE: Station #94010, Goroka, Papua New Guinea, Lat. 6.1°S, Long. 145.4°E, at 5141 ft. (1567 m). Temperatures are calculated for an elevation of 6550 ft. (2000 m), resulting in probable extremes of 82°F (28°C) and 38°F (4°C).

N/HEMISPHERE	JAN	FEB	MAR	APR	MAY	JUN	JUL	AUG	SEP	OCT	NOV	DEC
°F AVG MAX	71	72	73	74	74	73	74	73	73	73	74	72
°F AVG MIN	51	52	52	52	53	54	54	54	55	54	54	52
DIURNAL RANGE	20	20	21	22	21	19	20	19	18	19	20	20
RAIN/INCHES	2.1	2.8	4.6	5.9	6.6	9.3	9.1	10.1	10.7	8.3	4.6	2.0
HUMIDITY/%	70	67	67	67	67	71	72	73	74	71	70	70
BLOOM SEASON				•								
DAYS CLR	N/A											
RAIN/MM	53	71	117	150	168	236	231	257	272	211	117	51
°C AVG MAX	21.8	22.4	23.0	23.5	23.5	23.0	23.5	23.0	23.0	23.0	23.5	22.4
°C AVG MIN	10.7	11.3	11.3	11.3	11.8	12.4	12.4	12.4	13.0	12.4	12.4	11.3
DIURNAL RANGE	11.1	11.1	11.7	12.2	11.7	10.6	11.1	10.6	10.0	10.6	11.1	11.1
S/HEMISPHERE	JUL	AUG	SEP	OCT	NOV	DEC	JAN	FEB	MAR	APR	MAY	JUN

Cultural Recommendations

LIGHT: 2500–3500 fc.

TEMPERATURES: Throughout the year, days average 71–74°F (22–24°C), and nights average 51–55°F (11–13°C), with a diurnal range of 18–22°F (10–12°C).

HUMIDITY: 70–75% most of the year, dropping to near 65% in late winter and spring.

WATER: Rainfall is moderate to heavy most of the year. Conditions are slightly drier for 3 months in winter. Cultivated plants should be kept moist with only slight drying allowed between waterings. Daily water may be necessary during hot weather. In addition, early morning mistings are often beneficial, especially on bright, sunny days.

FERTILIZER: 1/4–1/2 recommended strength. A balanced fertilizer should be applied weekly to biweekly throughout the year.

REST PERIOD: Growing temperatures should be maintained all year. In the habitat, rainfall is lowest in winter, but dew and mist from fog and low clouds are common. Water and fertilizer should be reduced somewhat for cultivated plants, especially those grown in the darker, short-day conditions common during temperate-latitude winters. Plants should be kept on the dry side, but they should never be allowed to dry out completely. In the habitat, light is higher in winter.

GROWING MEDIA: Plants may be mounted on tree-fern or cork slabs if humidity is high and plants are watered at least once daily in summer. When plants are potted, any open, fast-draining medium may be used. Repotting may be done anytime new roots are growing.

MISCELLANEOUS NOTES: The bloom season shown in the climate table is based on collection reports. However, reports from the habitat indicate that blooming is not seasonal, and some plants bloom several times a year.

Plant and Flower Information

PLANT SIZE AND TYPE: An 8–18 in. (20–45 cm) sympodial epiphyte.

PSEUDOBULB: 8–18 in. (20–45 cm) long. The clustered stems, which arise from an extremely short rhizome, are slightly swollen at the base. When young, the stout pseudobulbs are purple to brown and nearly covered by papery sheaths. They become orange-yellow when dried.

LEAVES: 2–3. The spreading leaves are 3 in. (8 cm) long. They are held at the apex of the growth. The green leaves are often suffused with purplish red, especially at the base.

INFLORESCENCE: 8 in. (20 cm) long. Inflorescences arise at or below the apex of the stem. The nodding flowers are laxly arranged on an erect spike.

FLOWERS: 3–15 per inflorescence. The flowers are 0.8 in. (2 cm) across. Sepals and petals are white. The lip is pale green with darker green veins. Blossoms normally last 3–4 weeks, but they are sometimes self-pollinating.

HYBRIDIZING NOTES: Chromosome counts are 2n = 36 (ref. 152) and 2n = about 36 (ref. 153, 187, 243). Seed pods mature in 4 months.

REFERENCES: 83, 95, 152, 153, 187, 234, 243, 273.

PHOTOS/DRAWINGS: 83.

Dendrobium keffordii F. M. Bailey. See *D. baileyi* F. Mueller.
REFERENCES: 67, 105, 216, 254, 421, 533.

Dendrobium keithii Ridley

ORIGIN/HABITAT: Endemic to Thailand. Plants grow in the southeastern mainland regions as well as several areas along the southern peninsula.

CLIMATE: Station #48430, Prachin Buri, Thailand, Lat. 14.1°N, Long. 101.4°E, at 16 ft. (5 m). Record extreme temperatures are not available for this location.

Dendrobium keisallii

N/HEMISPHERE	JAN	FEB	MAR	APR	MAY	JUN	JUL	AUG	SEP	OCT	NOV	DEC
°F AVG MAX	91	94	97	97	95	91	90	90	90	89	90	89
°F AVG MIN	69	74	76	78	78	78	77	77	77	76	74	68
DIURNAL RANGE	22	20	21	19	17	13	13	13	13	13	16	21
RAIN/INCHES	1.0	1.0	1.2	4.0	8.3	10.3	11.5	13.9	11.8	6.9	1.6	0.3
HUMIDITY/%	N/A											
BLOOM SEASON	N/A											
DAYS CLR	N/A											
RAIN/MM	25	25	30	102	211	262	292	353	300	175	41	8
°C AVG MAX	32.8	34.4	36.1	36.1	35.0	32.8	32.2	32.2	32.2	31.7	32.2	31.7
°C AVG MIN	20.6	23.3	24.4	25.6	25.6	25.6	25.0	25.0	25.0	24.4	23.3	20.0
DIURNAL RANGE	12.2	11.1	11.7	10.5	9.4	7.2	7.2	7.2	7.2	7.3	8.9	11.7
S/HEMISPHERE	JUL	AUG	SEP	OCT	NOV	DEC	JAN	FEB	MAR	APR	MAY	JUN

Cultural Recommendations

LIGHT: 2000–3000 fc.

TEMPERATURES: Summer days average 90–91°F (32–33°C), and nights average 77–78°F (25–26°C), with a diurnal range of 13°F (7°C). The warmest weather occurs in spring when days average 95–97°F (35–36°C), and nights average 76–78°F (24–26°C), with a diurnal range of 17–21°F (9–12°C).

HUMIDITY: Information is not available for this location. However, records from nearby locations indicate that humidity probably averages 80–85% year-round.

WATER: Rainfall is heavy from spring through early autumn. Cultivated plants should be kept moist while actively growing, but water should be gradually reduced in autumn. Watering may be necessary several times a week during the warmest and brightest part of the year.

FERTILIZER: ¼–½ recommended strength, applied weekly. A high-nitrogen fertilizer is beneficial from spring to midsummer, but a fertilizer high in phosphates should be used in late summer and autumn.

REST PERIOD: Winter days average 89–94°F (32–34°C), and nights average 68–74°F (20–23°C), with a diurnal range of 20–22°F (11–12°C). In the habitat, rainfall is low for 4–5 months from late autumn into early spring, but the nightly cooling and high humidity results in frequent, heavy deposits of dew. Water should be reduced for cultivated plants. They should be allowed to dry slightly between waterings but should not remain dry for extended periods. Fertilizer should also be reduced when less water is used. In the habitat, light is highest in winter.

GROWING MEDIA: Plants may be mounted on tree-fern or cork slabs if humidity is high and plants are watered at least once daily in summer. When plants are potted, any open, fast-draining medium may be used. Repotting is best done in early spring when new roots are growing.

Plant and Flower Information

PLANT SIZE AND TYPE: A 16 in. (40 cm) sympodial epiphyte.

PSEUDOBULB: 16 in. (40 cm) long. The erect to pendulous stems are flattened, slender, and curving.

LEAVES: Many. The fleshy, pointed leaves are 0.6–2.0 in. (1.5–5.0 cm) long. They are flat, overlapping, and held on a single plane.

INFLORESCENCE: Short. Inflorescences arise from the overlapping leaf bases on one side of the stem. The blossoms are held on top of the leaves, forming a row of flowers down the centerline of the stem.

FLOWERS: 1 per inflorescence. The flowers are nearly spherical. They are 0.4 in. (1.0 cm) across. Sepals and petals may be pale yellow or dull purplish green. The lip is greenish yellow with a bright pink edge. The midlobe is notched at the apex and obscurely toothed along the margin. It has no callus but is thickened and fleshier at the tip.

HYBRIDIZING NOTES: Johansen (ref. 239) indicates that plants are self-sterile and that flowers dropped 4–5 days after self-pollination. All cross-pollinated flowers produced capsules which opened 92–98 days after pollination. The seeds contained 91–93% visible embryos and 93–95% germinated.

REFERENCES: 239, 254, 395, 454.

PHOTOS/DRAWINGS: *454.*

Dendrobium kelsallii Ridley.

Now considered a synonym of *Flickingeria angustifolia* (Blume) A. Hawkes. REFERENCES: 75, 111, 200, 213, 222, 223, 230, 231, 254, 395, 449, 455, 469. PHOTOS/DRAWINGS: 200.

Dendrobium kempterianum Schlechter

ORIGIN/HABITAT: Northern Papua New Guinea. Plants grow in hillside forests along the Minjem and upper Djamu Rivers. They are usually found close to the ground on the trunks of forest trees at 1000–1650 ft. (300–500 m).

CLIMATE: Station #94014, Madang, Papua New Guinea, Lat. 5.2°S, Long. 145.8°E, at 13 ft. (4 m). Temperatures are calculated for a habitat elevation of 1150 ft. (350 m), resulting in probable extremes of 94°F (35°C) and 58°F (15°C).

N/HEMISPHERE	JAN	FEB	MAR	APR	MAY	JUN	JUL	AUG	SEP	OCT	NOV	DEC
°F AVG MAX	79	79	81	81	81	81	81	81	81	83	83	80
°F AVG MIN	73	74	74	74	73	73	73	73	73	72	73	74
DIURNAL RANGE	6	5	7	7	8	8	8	8	8	11	10	6
RAIN/INCHES	4.0	3.4	3.2	8.5	11.2	11.1	10.1	11.3	9.4	11.3	10.5	6.7
HUMIDITY/%	88	87	86	86	86	86	86	85	86	87	88	89
BLOOM SEASON		*						*				
DAYS CLR	N/A											
RAIN/MM	102	86	81	216	284	282	257	287	239	287	267	170
°C AVG MAX	26.2	26.2	27.4	27.4	27.4	27.4	27.4	27.4	27.4	28.5	28.5	26.8
°C AVG MIN	22.9	23.5	23.5	23.5	22.9	22.9	22.9	22.9	22.9	22.4	22.9	23.5
DIURNAL RANGE	3.3	2.7	3.9	3.9	4.5	4.5	4.5	4.5	4.5	6.1	5.6	3.3
S/HEMISPHERE	JUL	AUG	SEP	OCT	NOV	DEC	JAN	FEB	MAR	APR	MAY	JUN

Cultural Recommendations

LIGHT: 2000–3000 fc.

TEMPERATURES: Throughout the year, days average 79–83°F (26–29°C), and nights average 72–74°F (22–24°C), with a diurnal range of 5–11°F (3–6°C). The warmest highs, the coolest lows, and the greatest diurnal range occur in autumn.

HUMIDITY: 85–90% year-round.

WATER: Rainfall is moderate to heavy all year. The driest conditions occur in late winter. Cultivated plants should be kept moist but not soggy.

FERTILIZER: ¼–½ recommended strength. A balanced fertilizer should be applied weekly to biweekly throughout the year.

REST PERIOD: Growing temperatures should be maintained all year. In the habitat, rainfall decreases for 4 months in winter. Water should be reduced for cultivated plants, but they should not be allowed to dry out completely. Fertilizer should be reduced or eliminated while water is reduced. In the habitat, light is slightly higher in late winter.

GROWING MEDIA: Mounting plants on tree-fern or cork slabs accommodates their pendulous growth habit. However, humidity must be high and plants must be watered at least once a day in summer. If plants cannot be mounted, small pots or hanging baskets may be filled with an open, fast-draining medium. Repotting may be done anytime new roots are actively growing.

MISCELLANEOUS NOTES: The bloom season shown in the climate table is based on reports from the habitat.

Plant and Flower Information

PLANT SIZE AND TYPE: A 31 in. (80 cm) sympodial epiphyte.

PSEUDOBULB: 31 in. (80 cm) long. The stems become ridged with age. They stand at right angles to or hang down the tree trunks.

LEAVES: Many. The leaves are 3.1–5.5 in. (8–14 cm) long.

INFLORESCENCE: Short.

FLOWERS: 5–10 per inflorescence. The flowers are 0.5 in. (1.3 cm) long and do not open fully. Sepals and petals are yellowish on the outside and white on the inside. The sepals are scaly on the outside. The lip is sulfur yellow with an orange center.

REFERENCES: 221, 437, 445.

PHOTOS/DRAWINGS: 437.

Dendrobium kenejianum Schlechter

ORIGIN/HABITAT: Northern Papua New Guinea. Plants grow along the upper Ramu River at about 500 ft. (150 m).

CLIMATE: Station #200187, Erap, Papua New Guinea, Lat. 6.6°S, Long. 146.7°E, at 850 ft. (260 m). Record extreme temperatures are 102°F (39°C) and 53°F (12°C).

N/HEMISPHERE	JAN	FEB	MAR	APR	MAY	JUN	JUL	AUG	SEP	OCT	NOV	DEC
°F AVG MAX	88	88	89	90	93	93	93	93	93	92	90	90
°F AVG MIN	69	69	69	70	72	73	72	72	73	71	74	70
DIURNAL RANGE	19	19	20	20	21	20	21	21	20	21	16	20
RAIN/INCHES	3.9	3.9	2.7	3.0	3.0	5.3	5.9	5.9	7.0	3.4	2.4	3.1
HUMIDITY/%	82	81	81	79	75	74	74	74	77	76	80	80
BLOOM SEASON				*								
DAYS CLR	N/A											
RAIN/MM	98	99	68	77	76	135	149	149	179	87	60	78
°C AVG MAX	30.9	30.9	31.7	32.3	34.0	33.9	33.8	33.9	34.0	33.6	32.3	32.0
°C AVG MIN	20.4	20.5	20.7	21.1	22.0	22.5	22.1	22.4	22.5	21.7	23.3	20.9
DIURNAL RANGE	10.5	10.4	11.0	11.2	12.0	11.4	11.7	11.5	11.5	11.9	9.0	11.1
S/HEMISPHERE	JUL	AUG	SEP	OCT	NOV	DEC	JAN	FEB	MAR	APR	MAY	JUN

Cultural Recommendations

LIGHT: 2500–3500 fc.

TEMPERATURES: Throughout the year, days average 88–93°F (31–34°C), and nights average 69–74°F (20–23°C), with a diurnal range of 16–21°F (9–12°C).

HUMIDITY: 75–80% year-round. In the habitat, humidity may be quite low during hot afternoons.

WATER: Rainfall is moderate most of the year, but conditions are somewhat wetter for 4–5 months in summer and early autumn. Cultivated plants should be thoroughly saturated then allowed to dry slightly between waterings in summer and early autumn. Water should be gradually reduced in autumn.

FERTILIZER: ¼–½ recommended strength. A balanced fertilizer should be applied weekly to biweekly throughout the year.

REST PERIOD: Growing temperatures should be maintained all year. In the habitat, rainfall is lowest in winter, but the high humidity indicates that additional moisture is frequently available from heavy dew. Cultivated plants should be allowed to dry for somewhat longer between waterings, but should not remain dry for extended periods. Fertilizer should be reduced until water is increased in spring. In the habitat, seasonal light variation is minor.

GROWING MEDIA: Plants may be mounted on tree-fern or cork slabs if humidity is high and plants are watered at least once daily in summer. When plants are potted, any open, fast-draining medium may be used. Repotting may be done anytime new roots are growing.

MISCELLANEOUS NOTES: The bloom season shown in the climate table is based on reports from the habitat. Plants that produce flowers which last a single day commonly bloom several times each year. Flowering usually occurs 7–14 days after a sudden 10°F (5°C) drop in daytime temperatures.

Plant and Flower Information

PLANT SIZE AND TYPE: A 39 in. (100 cm) sympodial epiphyte that eventually climbs the host tree.

PSEUDOBULB: 16 in. (40 cm) long. The erect stems are simple and flattened. They arise from an elongated rhizome.

LEAVES: The leaves are 1.4–2.0 in. (3.5–5.0 cm) long.

INFLORESCENCE: Short.

FLOWERS: 2 per inflorescence. The flowers are 0.3 in. (0.8 cm) across. Sepals and petals are golden yellow. The lip is marked with a broad, central band of yellow-brown. The lip is deeply veined and shaped like a whale's tail. Blossoms last a single day.

REFERENCES: 221, 437, 445.

PHOTOS/DRAWINGS: 437.

Dendrobium kenepaiense J. J. Smith

ORIGIN/HABITAT: Southwestern Borneo. Plants were originally found on Mt. Kenepai. No additional habitat or elevation information was given with the original description, so the following climate data should be used with caution.

CLIMATE: Station #96413, Kuching, Sarawak, Lat. 1.5°N, Long. 110.3°E, at 85 ft. (26 m). Temperatures are calculated for an elevation of 1750 ft. (530 m), resulting in probable extremes of 92°F (33°C) and 59°F (15°C).

N/HEMISPHERE	JAN	FEB	MAR	APR	MAY	JUN	JUL	AUG	SEP	OCT	NOV	DEC
°F AVG MAX	83	83	84	85	86	86	86	87	85	85	85	83
°F AVG MIN	67	67	67	67	68	67	67	67	67	67	67	67
DIURNAL RANGE	16	16	17	18	19	18	19	20	18	18	18	16
RAIN/INCHES	27.1	19.7	14.2	9.7	9.0	8.5	6.9	8.8	9.5	12.6	13.1	20.1
HUMIDITY/%	89	88	86	85	85	83	82	83	84	85	87	88
BLOOM SEASON	N/A											
DAYS CLR @ 7AM	1	0	1	2	3	2	4	2	1	2	1	1
DAYS CLR @ 1PM	0	0	0	0	1	1	1	0	0	0	0	0
RAIN/MM	688	500	361	246	229	216	175	224	241	320	333	511
°C AVG MAX	28.1	28.1	28.6	29.2	29.7	29.7	29.7	30.3	29.2	29.2	29.2	28.1
°C AVG MIN	19.2	19.2	19.2	19.2	19.7	19.7	19.2	19.2	19.2	19.2	19.2	19.2
DIURNAL RANGE	8.9	8.9	9.4	10.0	10.5	10.0	10.5	11.1	10.0	10.0	10.0	8.9
S/HEMISPHERE	JUL	AUG	SEP	OCT	NOV	DEC	JAN	FEB	MAR	APR	MAY	JUN

Cultural Recommendations

LIGHT: 2000–3000 fc.

TEMPERATURES: Throughout the year, days average 83–87°F (28–30°C), and nights average 67–68°F (19–20°C), with a diurnal range of 16–20°F (9–11°C). This habitat has essentially no seasonal temperature fluctuations.

HUMIDITY: 85–90% year-round.

WATER: Rainfall is very heavy all year. Plants should be kept moist but not soggy. Warm water may be beneficial.

FERTILIZER: ¼–½ recommended strength. A balanced fertilizer should be applied weekly to biweekly throughout the year.

REST PERIOD: Growing conditions should be maintained all year. The record low is only 10°F (6°C) below the average lows, indicating that plants may not tolerate wide temperature fluctuations. Although rainfall remains heavy in winter, water may be reduced somewhat for cultivated plants, especially those grown in the dark, short-day conditions common in temperate latitudes. They should never be allowed to dry out completely, however. In the habitat, light is highest in winter.

GROWING MEDIA: Plants may be mounted on tree-fern or cork slabs if humidity is high and plants are watered at least once daily in summer. When plants are potted, any open, fast-draining medium may be used. Repotting may be done anytime new roots are growing.

MISCELLANEOUS NOTES: The plant was described in 1918 in *Bul. Jard. Bot. Buit.* 2nd sér. 24:46.

Dendrobium kennedyi

Plant and Flower Information

PLANT SIZE AND TYPE: An 8 in. (20 cm) sympodial epiphyte.

PSEUDOBULB: 8 in. (20 cm) long. The quadrangular stems are densely leafy.

LEAVES: Many. The oval leaves are 0.8–1.2 in. (2–3 cm) long, unequally bilobed, rigid, and dark on the upper surface.

INFLORESCENCE: Short.

FLOWERS: The blossoms are 0.4 in. (1 cm) long. The dorsal sepal is ovate, and the lateral sepals are somewhat triangular. The lanceolate petals are reflexed with an uneven margin.

REFERENCES: 222, 286, 295.

Dendrobium kennedyi Schlechter. Cribb (ref. 84) lists *D. kennedyi* Schlechter as a possible synonym of *D. sylvanum* Rchb. f. REFERENCES: 84, 223.

Dendrobium kentrochilum Hooker f.

ORIGIN/HABITAT: Malaya. This uncommon plant was collected in the state of Perak, in the Batang Padang (Balang Padung) Valley, at about 2000 ft. (610 m).

CLIMATE: Station #48625, Ipoh, Malaya, Lat. 4.6°N, Long. 101.1°E, at 123 ft. (37 m). Temperatures are calculated for an elevation of 2000 ft. (610 m), resulting in probable extremes of 93°F (34°C) and 58°F (14°C).

N/HEMISPHERE	JAN	FEB	MAR	APR	MAY	JUN	JUL	AUG	SEP	OCT	NOV	DEC
°F AVG MAX	84	86	87	86	86	86	85	85	84	83	83	83
°F AVG MIN	66	66	67	67	68	67	66	66	67	66	66	66
DIURNAL RANGE	18	20	20	19	18	19	19	19	17	17	17	17
RAIN/INCHES	7.9	3.1	7.6	8.4	6.2	3.6	7.2	6.9	8.8	11.0	13.0	8.9
HUMIDITY/%	76	74	76	78	78	75	76	77	79	82	82	81
BLOOM SEASON	N/A											
DAYS CLR @ 7AM	3	3	3	1	1	2	1	1	0	0	1	2
DAYS CLR @ 1PM	2	2	2	1	1	1	1	1	0	0	0	2
RAIN/MM	201	79	193	213	157	91	183	175	224	279	330	226
°C AVG MAX	28.8	29.9	30.4	29.9	29.9	29.9	29.3	29.3	28.8	28.2	28.2	28.2
°C AVG MIN	18.8	18.8	19.3	19.3	19.9	19.3	18.8	18.8	19.3	18.8	18.8	18.8
DIURNAL RANGE	10.0	11.1	11.1	10.6	10.0	10.6	10.5	10.5	9.5	9.4	9.4	9.4
S/HEMISPHERE	JUL	AUG	SEP	OCT	NOV	DEC	JAN	FEB	MAR	APR	MAY	JUN

Cultural Recommendations

LIGHT: 2500–3500 fc.

TEMPERATURES: Throughout the year, days average 83–87°F (28–30°C), and nights average 66–68°F (19–20°C), with a diurnal range of 17–20°F (9–11°C).

HUMIDITY: 75–80% year-round.

WATER: Rainfall is heavy most of the year. The heaviest rainfall occurs in autumn with a secondary maximum in spring. Brief semidry periods occur in midwinter and midsummer. Cultivated plants should be kept evenly moist with only slight drying allowed between waterings.

FERTILIZER: ¼–½ recommended strength. A balanced fertilizer should be applied weekly to biweekly throughout the year.

REST PERIOD: Growing conditions should be maintained year-round. Water should be reduced somewhat in winter for plants cultivated in the dark, short-day conditions common in temperate latitudes. They should never be allowed to dry out completely, however. Fertilizer may be reduced when the plant is not actively growing or when water is reduced. In the habitat, light is slightly higher in winter.

GROWING MEDIA: Plants may be mounted on tree-fern or cork slabs or potted in small pots filled with any open, fast-draining medium. Repotting may be done anytime new roots are growing.

MISCELLANEOUS NOTES: Seidenfaden and Wood (ref. 455) indicate that *D. kentrochilum* may be a form of *D. sanguinolentum* Lindley.

Plant and Flower Information

PLANT SIZE AND TYPE: A 12–15 in. (30–38 cm) sympodial epiphyte.

PSEUDOBULB: 12 in. (30 cm) long. The stout, flexuous stems are somewhat flattened.

LEAVES: The leathery leaves are 3–6 in. (8–15 cm) long and very narrow at the base. They may be oblong to broadly elliptical with 2 unequal points at the apex. Leaves are deciduous.

INFLORESCENCE: Short. Inflorescences emerge from nodes along the side of leafless stems.

FLOWERS: 1–2 per inflorescence. The white to cream flowers are 1 in. (2.5 cm) across. Blossoms have ovate to oblong sepals, nearly round petals, and a broad, nearly fan-shaped lip.

REFERENCES: 202, 218, 254, 395, 402, 445, 454, 455.

PHOTOS/DRAWINGS: 455.

Dendrobium kentrophyllum Hooker f.

AKA: Sometimes spelled *D. kentrophylem*. *D. albicolor* Ridley. Holttum (ref. 200) includes *D. capitellatum* J. J. Smith as a synonym. Seidenfaden (ref. 454) includes it as a possible synonym, but Seidenfaden and Wood (ref. 455) do not mention it. Earlier writers suggested that *D. kentrophyllum* Hooker f. and *D. parciflorum* Rchb. f. were conspecific. However, Seidenfaden (ref. 454) considers them separate species.

ORIGIN/HABITAT: Peninsular Thailand, Malaya, Sabah in Borneo, and the Padang region of Sumatra. In Malaya, these uncommon plants have been collected from Fraser's Hill, the Taiping Hills, and the Cameron Heights at about 4000 ft. (1220 m). In Sumatra, plants grow at the jungle's edge between Kabajakan and Tretet at 3500–5000 ft. (1070–1520 m); and in Borneo, they are found in Sabah, Sarawak, and Kalimantan in hill forests at 1950–3950 ft. (600–1200 m).

CLIMATE: Station #48625, Ipoh, Malaya, Lat. 4.6°N, Long. 101.1°E, at 123 ft. (37 m). Temperatures are calculated for an estimated elevation of 4000 ft. (1220 m), resulting in probable extremes of 86°F (30°C) and 51°F (11°C).

N/HEMISPHERE	JAN	FEB	MAR	APR	MAY	JUN	JUL	AUG	SEP	OCT	NOV	DEC
°F AVG MAX	77	79	80	79	79	79	78	78	77	76	76	76
°F AVG MIN	59	59	60	60	61	60	59	59	60	59	59	59
DIURNAL RANGE	18	20	20	19	18	19	19	19	17	17	17	17
RAIN/INCHES	7.9	3.1	7.6	8.4	6.2	3.6	7.2	6.9	8.8	11.0	13.0	8.9
HUMIDITY/%	76	74	76	78	78	75	76	77	79	82	82	81
BLOOM SEASON									*	*	*	
DAYS CLR @ 7AM	3	3	3	1	1	2	1	1	0	0	1	2
DAYS CLR @ 1PM	2	2	2	1	1	1	1	1	0	0	0	2
RAIN/MM	201	79	193	213	157	91	183	175	224	279	330	226
°C AVG MAX	25.1	26.2	26.8	26.2	26.2	26.2	25.7	25.7	25.1	24.6	24.6	24.6
°C AVG MIN	15.1	15.1	15.7	15.7	16.2	15.7	15.1	15.1	15.7	15.1	15.1	15.1
DIURNAL RANGE	10.0	11.1	11.1	10.5	10.0	10.5	10.6	10.6	9.4	9.5	9.5	9.5
S/HEMISPHERE	JUL	AUG	SEP	OCT	NOV	DEC	JAN	FEB	MAR	APR	MAY	JUN

Cultural Recommendations

LIGHT: 2000–3000 fc. Light should be diffused or dappled, and direct sunlight should be avoided. Clear days are quite rare.

TEMPERATURES: Throughout the year, days average 76–80°F (25–27°C), and nights average 59–61°F (15–16°C), with a diurnal range of 17–20°F (9–11°C). Although temperatures are uniform all year, the diurnal range is surprising large.

HUMIDITY: Near 75–80% year-round.

WATER: Rainfall is heavy most of the year. The heaviest rainfall occurs in autumn with a secondary maximum in spring. Brief semidry periods occur in midwinter and midsummer. Cultivated plants should be kept evenly moist with only slight drying allowed between waterings.

FERTILIZER: ¼–½ recommended strength. A balanced fertilizer should be applied weekly to biweekly throughout the year.

REST PERIOD: Growing conditions should be maintained year-round. Water should be reduced somewhat in winter for plants cultivated in the dark, short-day conditions common in temperate latitudes. They should never be allowed to dry out completely, however. Fertilizer may be reduced when the plant is not actively growing or when water is reduced. In the habitat, light is slightly higher in winter.

GROWING MEDIA: Plants may be mounted on tree-fern or cork slabs if humidity is high and plants are watered at least once daily in summer. When plants are potted, a fast-draining medium should be used. Repotting is best done in early spring.

MISCELLANEOUS NOTES: The bloom season shown in the climate table is based on cultivation records.

Plant and Flower Information

PLANT SIZE AND TYPE: A 4–8 in. (10–20 cm) sympodial epiphyte.

PSEUDOBULB: 4–8 in. (10–20 cm) long. The angled, stemlike growths may be thin or stout. They are leafy to the tip.

LEAVES: Many. The nearly terete leaves are 0.5–1.4 in. (1.3–3.6 cm) long. They are flattened, pointed, and curve outward slightly. They are held on a single plane.

INFLORESCENCE: Short. Inflorescences are borne at or near the apex of the stem. Several inflorescences may arise in a small cluster on nearly leafless stems.

FLOWERS: 1 per inflorescence. The waxy flowers, which do not open fully, are less than 0.8 in. (2 cm) across. Sepals and petals are pale greenish-yellow flushed with pink on the outside. The lip is marked with a median yellow band. It has no sidelobes. The ruffled margin is notched at the apex. The Sumatra plant had white sepals and petals that were marked with lilac flecks and a slightly ruffled, cream-colored lip.

REFERENCES: 190, 197, 200, 202, 218, 254, 395, 402, 435, 445, 448, 454, 455, 592.

PHOTOS/DRAWINGS: 197, *454*, 455.

Dendrobium kerewense P. van Royen. See *D. dekockii* J. J. Smith. REFERENCES: 233, 385, 538. PHOTOS/DRAWINGS: 538.

Dendrobium kerstingianum Schlechter. Now considered a *Flickingeria*. REFERENCES: 221, 441, 449.

Dendrobium × *kestevenii* Rupp. A natural hybrid between *D. kingianum* Bidwill ex Lindley and *D. speciosum* J. E. Smith. *D.* × *kestevenii* is often considered synonymous with *D.* × *delicatum* (F. M. Bailey) F. M. Bailey. REFERENCES: 67, 105, 179, 225, 240, 421, 533. PHOTOS/DRAWINGS: 533.

Dendrobium keysseri Schlechter. See *D. nebularum* Schlechter. REFERENCES: 222, 385.

Dendrobium keytsianum J. J. Smith

ORIGIN/HABITAT: Common in Irian Jaya (western New Guinea). Plants grow at about 6250 ft. (1900 m) in the Johannes Keyts Range.

CLIMATE: Station #97686, Wamena, Irian Jaya, Lat. 4.1°S, Long. 139.0°E, at 5446 ft. (1660 m). Temperatures are calculated for an elevation of 6400 ft. (1950 m). Record extreme temperatures are not available for this location.

N/HEMISPHERE	JAN	FEB	MAR	APR	MAY	JUN	JUL	AUG	SEP	OCT	NOV	DEC
°F AVG MAX	72	73	74	73	74	73	74	73	73	76	75	71
°F AVG MIN	57	57	59	59	60	61	60	59	60	62	62	58
DIURNAL RANGE	15	16	15	14	14	12	14	14	13	14	13	13
RAIN/INCHES	3.0	1.9	2.2	4.0	4.6	3.3	2.8	4.2	6.9	3.9	5.4	4.9
HUMIDITY/%	N/A											
BLOOM SEASON							*					
DAYS CLR	N/A											
RAIN/MM	76	48	56	102	117	84	71	107	175	99	137	124
°C AVG MAX	22.1	22.7	23.3	22.7	23.3	22.7	23.3	22.7	22.7	24.4	23.8	21.6
°C AVG MIN	13.8	13.8	14.9	14.9	15.5	16.0	15.5	14.9	15.5	16.6	16.6	14.4
DIURNAL RANGE	8.3	8.9	8.4	7.8	7.8	6.7	7.8	7.8	7.2	7.8	7.2	7.2
S/HEMISPHERE	JUL	AUG	SEP	OCT	NOV	DEC	JAN	FEB	MAR	APR	MAY	JUN

Cultural Recommendations

LIGHT: 2000–2500 fc. In the habitat, light is highest in the morning.

TEMPERATURES: Throughout the year, days average 71–76°F (22–24°C), and nights average 57–62°F (14–17°C), with a diurnal range of 12–16°F (7–9°C). In the habitat the warmest temperatures of the day occur in late morning when skies are clear. Clouds and mist develop near noon and continue through the afternoon, thus preventing additional warming.

HUMIDITY: Information is not available for this location. However, records from nearby stations indicate that humidity probably averages near 80% year-round. High humidity and excellent air circulation are particularly important if temperatures are warm. Placing the plants in front of an evaporative cooler or near a fine mist may be very beneficial on especially warm days.

WATER: Rainfall is light to moderate most of the year but is probably greater in the higher-elevation habitat than indicated in the climate table. In addition, large amounts of water are available from mist and heavy dews, even during periods when rainfall is reduced. Cultivated plants should be kept moist but not soggy.

FERTILIZER: ¼–½ recommended strength. A balanced fertilizer should be applied weekly to biweekly throughout the year.

REST PERIOD: Growing conditions should be maintained all year. Seasonal high and low temperatures vary about 5°F (3°C). Conditions are slightly drier for 1–2 months in winter. In cultivation, water may be decreased somewhat, but plants should never be allowed to dry out completely. In the habitat, light is slightly higher in winter.

GROWING MEDIA: Plants may be mounted on tree-fern or cork slabs if humidity is high and plants are watered at least once daily in summer. When plants are potted, any open, fast-draining medium may be used. Repotting may be done anytime new roots are growing.

MISCELLANEOUS NOTES: The bloom season shown in the climate table is based on reports from the habitat.

Plant and Flower Information

PLANT SIZE AND TYPE: A sympodial epiphyte of unreported size.

PSEUDOBULB: The terete stems are elongated.

LEAVES: The linear-lanceolate leaves are 4 in. (10 cm) long. They are minutely fringed with a sharp point at the apex. The leaf sheaths are covered with warts.

INFLORESCENCE: Short.

FLOWERS: 3 per inflorescence. The yellow and orange flowers are 1.4 in. (3.5 cm) long. The dorsal sepal and petals are ovate, and the obliquely triangular lateral sepals are drooping. The apical third of the lip is recurved.

REFERENCES: 221, 470, 476.

Dendrobium khasianum N. C. Deori

ORIGIN/HABITAT: India. Plants grow in the Pongtong forest of the Khasia

Dendrobium kiauense

hills in Meghalaya. Habitat elevation is estimated so the following climate data should be used with caution.

CLIMATE: Station #42410, Gauhati, India, Lat. 26.1°N, Long. 91.6°E, at 158 ft. (44 m). Temperatures are calculated for a habitat elevation of 3000 ft. (910 m), resulting in probable extremes of 95°F (35°C) and 32°F (0°C).

N/HEMISPHERE	JAN	FEB	MAR	APR	MAY	JUN	JUL	AUG	SEP	OCT	NOV	DEC
°F AVG MAX	67	69	77	79	79	80	81	81	80	72	72	67
°F AVG MIN	42	45	51	59	63	68	69	69	67	62	52	44
DIURNAL RANGE	25	24	26	20	16	12	12	12	13	16	20	23
RAIN/INCHES	0.4	1.2	2.0	5.7	9.3	12.3	12.3	10.3	6.6	2.8	0.6	0.2
HUMIDITY/%	69	72	64	71	82	85	85	86	84	84	83	82
BLOOM SEASON				•	•							
DAYS CLR @ 6AM	6	12	16	11	3	0	0	1	3	7	6	3
DAYS CLR @ 12PM	17	16	18	15	6	1	0	0	2	11	17	19
RAIN/MM	10	30	51	145	236	312	312	262	168	71	15	5
°C AVG MAX	19.2	20.3	24.8	25.9	25.9	26.5	27.0	27.0	26.5	25.3	22.0	19.2
°C AVG MIN	5.3	7.0	10.3	14.8	17.0	19.8	20.3	20.3	19.2	16.5	10.9	6.5
DIURNAL RANGE	13.9	13.3	14.5	11.1	8.9	6.7	6.7	6.7	7.3	8.8	11.1	12.7
S/HEMISPHERE	JUL	AUG	SEP	OCT	NOV	DEC	JAN	FEB	MAR	APR	MAY	JUN

Cultural Recommendations

LIGHT: 2500–3500 fc. Cultivated plants need as much light as possible without burning the foliage during autumn and winter.

TEMPERATURES: Summer days average 80–81°F (27°C), and nights average 68–69°F (20°C), with a diurnal range of 12°F (7°C).

HUMIDITY: 80–85% most of the year, dropping to 65–70% for 3 months in late winter and spring.

WATER: Rainfall is heavy from spring through summer but decreases rapidly in autumn, with a 1–2 month transition into the winter dry season. Cultivated plants should be kept moist while actively growing, then water should be gradually reduced after new growths mature in autumn.

FERTILIZER: ¼–½ recommended strength, applied weekly. A high nitrogen fertilizer is beneficial from spring to midsummer, but a fertilizer high in phosphates should be used in late summer and autumn.

REST PERIOD: Winder days average 67–69°F (19–20°C), and nights average 42–45°F (5–7°C), with an increased diurnal range of 23–25°F (13–14°C). Although rainfall is low for 4–5 winter months, high humidity and the large temperature range indicate that additional moisture from heavy dew is common. Therefore, while water should be greatly reduced and cultivated plants allowed to dry out between waterings from late autumn into early spring, they should not remain dry for extended periods. Occasional mistings between waterings during bright, sunny weather may help prevent the plants from becoming too dry. Fertilizer should be reduced or elimated until active growth resumes and water is increased in spring.

GROWING MEDIA: Plants may be mounted on tree-fern or cork slabs if humidity is high and plants are watered at least once daily in summer. When plants are potted, any open, fast-draining medium may be used. Repotting is best done in early spring when new roots are growing.

MISCELLANEOUS NOTES: The bloom season shown in the climate table is based on reports from the habitat.

Plant and Flower Information

PLANT SIZE AND TYPE: A 20 in. (51 cm) sympodial epiphyte.

PSEUDOBULB: 20 in. (51 cm) long. The uniformly slender stems are zigzag near the apex. They are covered with striped sheaths.

LEAVES: 4.7 in. (12 cm) long. The deciduous leaves are narrowly lanceolate, pointed, and unequally bilobed at the tip.

INFLORESCENCE: Short. Inflorescences emerge from the upper nodes of leafless stems.

FLOWERS: 2–3 per inflorescence. The golden yellow flowers are 2.4 in. (6 cm) across. Blossoms are thick with keels along the back of the oblong dorsal sepal and lanceolate lateral sepals. The ovate petals are rounded at the apex and fringed along the margin. The nearly round lip has a dark brown blotch on the disk. The beard along the margin of the lip is about 0.4 in. (1 cm) long and occasionally branches. Blossoms are fragrant.

REFERENCES: 235, *J. Orchid Soc. India* 2 (1–2):73–75 (1988).

PHOTOS/DRAWINGS: *J. Orchid Soc. India* 2 (1–2):73–75 (1988).

Dendrobium kiauense Ames and Schweinfurth

ORIGIN/HABITAT: Borneo. Plants are found in Kalimantan and in Sabah in the lower mountain forests of the Mt. Kinabalu region at 2600–4900 ft. (800–1500 m).

CLIMATE: Station #49613, Tambuan, Sabah (North Borneo), Lat. 5.7°N, Long. 116.4°E, at 1200 ft. (366 m). Temperatures are calculated for an elevation of 3000 ft. (910 m), resulting in probable extremes of 92°F (33°C) and 48°F (9°C).

N/HEMISPHERE	JAN	FEB	MAR	APR	MAY	JUN	JUL	AUG	SEP	OCT	NOV	DEC
°F AVG MAX	80	81	83	84	84	83	83	83	83	82	81	80
°F AVG MIN	61	59	60	61	62	61	60	60	61	61	61	62
DIURNAL RANGE	19	22	23	23	22	22	23	23	22	21	20	18
RAIN/INCHES	5.8	3.7	5.8	7.5	8.2	7.3	5.1	4.9	6.4	7.0	6.8	6.0
HUMIDITY/%	N/A											
BLOOM SEASON	N/A											
DAYS CLR	N/A											
RAIN/MM	147	94	147	190	208	185	130	124	163	178	173	152
°C AVG MAX	26.7	27.3	28.4	28.9	28.9	28.4	28.4	28.4	28.4	27.8	27.3	26.7
°C AVG MIN	16.1	15.0	15.6	16.1	16.7	16.1	15.6	15.6	16.1	16.1	16.1	16.7
DIURNAL RANGE	10.6	12.3	12.8	12.8	12.2	12.3	12.8	12.8	12.3	11.7	11.2	10.0
S/HEMISPHERE	JUL	AUG	SEP	OCT	NOV	DEC	JAN	FEB	MAR	APR	MAY	JUN

Cultural Recommendations

LIGHT: 2000–2500 fc.

TEMPERATURES: Throughout the year, days average 80–84°F (27–29°C), and nights average 59–62°F (15–17°C), with a diurnal range of 18–23°F (10–13°C).

HUMIDITY: Information is not available for this location. However, records from nearby stations indicate that averages are probably 80–85% year-round.

WATER: Rainfall is moderate to heavy most of the year with a brief slightly drier period in winter.

FERTILIZER: ¼–½ recommended strength. A balanced fertilizer should be applied weekly to biweekly throughout the year.

REST PERIOD: Growing conditions should be maintained all year. Water may be reduced for cultivated plants in winter, especially those grown in the dark, short-day conditions common in temperate latitudes. They should never be allowed to dry out completely, however. Fertilizer should be reduced until water is increased in the spring.

GROWING MEDIA: Plants may be mounted on tree-fern or cork slabs or potted in small pots filled with any open, fast-draining medium. Repotting may be done anytime new roots are growing.

Plant and Flower Information

PLANT SIZE AND TYPE: A 14 in. (35 cm) sympodial epiphyte.

PSEUDOBULB: 14 in. (35 cm) long. The shiny yellow pseudobulbs are stout and usually less than fully erect. The stems are almost completely covered by leaf sheaths.

LEAVES: Many. The distichous leaves are 1.6–2.4 in. (4–6 cm) long, pointed, incurved, and nearly erect. They are gradually smaller toward the apex.

INFLORESCENCE: Inflorescences emerge near the leaf bases.

FLOWERS: 1 at a time per inflorescence. Blossoms open in succession. The flowers are 0.4–0.6 in. (1.0–1.5 cm) across. Sepals and petals are ovate to broadly ovate. Sepals may be pointed or rounded, but petals are pointed. They are cream and yellow with purple stripes. The 3-lobed lip has erect sidelobes and a smaller, reflexed midlobe. The transverse callus is fleshy and 2-lobed.

REFERENCES: 12, 222, 286, 592.

PHOTOS/DRAWINGS: 592.

Dendrobium kietaense Schlechter

AKA: *D. malaitense* Rolfe.

ORIGIN/HABITAT: Bougainville, the Solomon Islands, and Vanuatu. On Bougainville, plants grow below 1000 ft. (300 m) in rainforest near the beach at Kieta Bay.

CLIMATE: Station #91502, Kieta, Bougainville Island, Lat. 6.2°S, Long. 155.6°E, at 240 ft. (73 m). Record extreme temperatures are 96°F (36°C) and 64°F (18°C).

N/HEMISPHERE	JAN	FEB	MAR	APR	MAY	JUN	JUL	AUG	SEP	OCT	NOV	DEC
°F AVG MAX	85	85	87	88	88	89	88	88	88	87	87	86
°F AVG MIN	74	74	74	75	75	75	76	75	76	76	75	75
DIURNAL RANGE	11	11	13	13	13	14	12	13	12	11	12	11
RAIN/INCHES	10.9	9.4	8.0	9.8	9.6	9.4	10.5	10.7	11.2	11.7	9.3	9.0
HUMIDITY/%	80	80	79	76	78	76	79	77	78	80	80	82
BLOOM SEASON			*	*								
DAYS CLR	N/A											
RAIN/MM	277	239	203	249	244	239	267	272	284	297	236	229
°C AVG MAX	29.4	29.4	30.6	31.1	31.1	31.7	31.1	31.1	31.1	30.6	30.6	30.0
°C AVG MIN	23.3	23.3	23.3	23.9	23.9	23.9	24.4	23.9	24.4	24.4	23.9	23.9
DIURNAL RANGE	6.1	6.1	7.3	7.2	7.2	7.8	6.7	7.2	6.7	6.2	6.7	6.1
S/HEMISPHERE	JUL	AUG	SEP	OCT	NOV	DEC	JAN	FEB	MAR	APR	MAY	JUN

Cultural Recommendations

LIGHT: 2500–3500 fc. Humidity should be high and air movement strong when light is high.

TEMPERATURES: Throughout the year, days average 85–88°F (29–31°C), and nights average 74–76°F (23–24°C), with a diurnal range of 11–14°F (6–8°C).

HUMIDITY: 75–80% year-round.

WATER: Rainfall is heavy all year. Cultivated plants should be kept moist but not soggy. Warm water might be beneficial.

FERTILIZER: ¼–½ recommended strength. A balanced fertilizer should be applied weekly to biweekly throughout the year.

REST PERIOD: Growing conditions should be maintained all year. In cultivation, water should be reduced somewhat in winter, especially for plants grown in the dark, short-day conditions common in temperate latitudes. However, plants should never be allowed to dry out completely. Fertilizer should be reduced or eliminated until water is increased in spring.

GROWING MEDIA: Mounting plants on tree-fern or cork slabs accommodates their pendulous growth habit. However, humidity must be high and plants must be watered at least once a day in summer. If plants cannot be mounted, small pots or hanging baskets may be filled with an open, fast-draining medium. Repotting may be done anytime new roots are actively growing.

MISCELLANEOUS NOTES: The bloom season shown in the climate table is based on reports from the habitat. Plants that produce flowers which last a single day commonly bloom several times each year. Flowering usually occurs 7–14 days after a sudden 10°F (5°C) drop in daytime temperatures, but in this case, the records indicate that the bloom time was the same for several collections.

Plant and Flower Information

PLANT SIZE AND TYPE: A 59 in. (150 cm) sympodial epiphyte.

PSEUDOBULB: 59 in. (150 cm) long. The slender, pendent stems are clustered.

LEAVES: Many. The light green leaves are 3.5–7.0 in. (9–18 cm) long, distichous, lanceolate, rough, and wrinkled. They have 2 unequal teeth at the apex.

INFLORESCENCE: Short. The blossoms emerge from flattened sheaths at the side of the stem.

FLOWERS: 2 per inflorescence. The flowers are about 0.6 in. (1.5 cm) long and do not open fully. The fleshy blossoms may be white or yellow. They have elliptic petals, an oblong dorsal sepal, and oblong-sickle-shaped lateral sepals. The 3-lobed lip is fiddle-shaped with crescent-shaped sidelobes. They are very easily detached and last a single day.

REFERENCES: 221, 270, 271, 417, 437, 440, 445, 516.

PHOTOS/DRAWINGS: 271, 437, 440.

Dendrobium kinabaluense Ridley.

Now considered a synonym of *Epigeneium kinabaluense* (Ridley) Summerhayes. REFERENCES: 12, 218, 229, 254, 286, 394, 499.

Dendrobium kingianum Bidwill ex Lindley

AKA: Clements (ref. 67) indicates that this highly variable species requires additional study. In the meantime, he includes all described varieties and subvarieties as synonyms.

ORIGIN/HABITAT: Eastern Australia. The habitat extends from the Hunter River in New South Wales to near the Tropic of Capricorn. Plants also occur in Carnarvon Gorge, about 280 mi. (50 km) inland at 25.0°S. Plants often grow in areas with high humidity, strong air movement, and full sun for much of the day, but they are also found in more shaded areas. Plants are found in pockets of leaf-mold on rocks in open forests or on cliff faces between sea level and 3950 ft. (0–1200 m). They are usually found on rocks but occasionally may also grow on trees.

CLIMATE: Station #94576, Brisbane, Australia, Lat. 27.4°S, Long. 153.1°E, at 17 ft. (5 m). Temperatures are calculated for an elevation of 3000 ft. (910 m), resulting in probable extremes of 100°F (38°C) and 25°F (–4°C).

N/HEMISPHERE	JAN	FEB	MAR	APR	MAY	JUN	JUL	AUG	SEP	OCT	NOV	DEC
°F AVG MAX	58	61	66	70	72	75	75	75	72	69	64	59
°F AVG MIN	39	40	45	50	54	57	59	58	56	51	46	41
DIURNAL RANGE	19	21	21	20	18	18	16	17	16	18	18	18
RAIN/INCHES	2.2	1.9	1.9	2.5	3.7	5.0	6.4	6.3	5.7	3.7	2.8	2.6
HUMIDITY/%	62	59	58	57	59	59	63	65	66	64	64	64
BLOOM SEASON	*	**	***	**	**	*						
DAYS CLR @ 10AM	17	20	18	11	12	9	5	9	9	14	18	16
DAYS CLR @ 4PM	15	16	15	12	14	12	8	5	8	10	14	14
RAIN/MM	56	48	48	64	94	127	163	160	145	94	71	66
°C AVG MAX	14.5	16.2	19.0	21.2	22.3	24.0	24.0	24.0	22.3	20.6	17.9	15.1
°C AVG MIN	4.0	4.5	7.3	10.1	12.3	14.0	15.1	14.5	13.4	10.6	7.9	5.1
DIURNAL RANGE	10.5	11.7	11.7	11.1	10.0	10.0	8.9	9.5	8.9	10.0	10.0	10.0
S/HEMISPHERE	JUL	AUG	SEP	OCT	NOV	DEC	JAN	FEB	MAR	APR	MAY	JUN

Cultural Recommendations

LIGHT: 2500–4000 fc. Some growers recommend bright *Phalaenopsis* light, but others indicate that light must be intense. At optimum light levels, the leaves have a slight reddish or purplish tinge. In the habitat, more than half the days are clear each month except during the summer rainy season, when skies are clear approximately 30% of the time. Plants usually grow in open, high light conditions. Growers using artificial lights recommend 14–16 hours of light.

TEMPERATURES: Summer days average near 75°F (24°C), and nights average 57–59°F (14–15°C), with a diurnal range of 16–18°F (9–10°C). Growers indicate that plants survive daily summer highs warmer than 100°F (38°C).

HUMIDITY: 60–65% year-round. Growers recommend maximum air circulation.

WATER: Rainfall is moderate in summer and autumn, but conditions are somewhat drier from late autumn into early spring. As a rock dweller, the plant is accustomed to rapid drying. Cultivated plants should be watered often while actively growing, but the roots should be allowed to dry between waterings. Water should be gradually reduced in autumn.

FERTILIZER: ½ recommended strength, applied weekly during periods of active growth. In addition to regular fertilizer, some Australian growers recommend sprinkling manure or blood and bone meal on top of the medium 2–3 times each growing season.

REST PERIOD: Winter days average 58–66°F (15–19°C), and nights average 39–45°F (4–7°C), with a diurnal range of 18–21°F (10–12°C). Some growers indicate that winter nights at least as cool as 50°F (10°C) are necessary to initiate blooms and that plants tolerate lows to 36°F (2°C). Plants tolerate winter days of 86°F (30°C). In cultivation, water should be greatly reduced from midautumn until growth resumes in spring. Plants should be allowed to dry out between waterings, but they should not remain dry for prolonged periods. Australian growers recommend just enough water in winter so the pseudobulbous stems do not become shriveled. Fertilizer should be reduced or eliminated when water is reduced. Growers indicate that distinct seasonal variation is essential for plant health.

GROWING MEDIA: Plants are best potted in a fibrous medium that drains rapidly. Plants may be mounted if they are watered daily and humidity is high in summer, but mounted plants usually do not grow well. If plants are potted, the smallest possible pot with room for no more than 2 years' growth should be used. Growers report that clay pots are preferable to plastic ones and shallow pots are preferable to deep containers. High humidity and excellent air movement are essential to plant health. Plants are very susceptible to root rot if they are overwatered or are in pots that are too large. Repotting is best done immediately after flowering when roots and new leads are beginning to grow. Plants may be divided into clumps with 3–4 growths.

MISCELLANEOUS NOTES: The bloom season shown in the climate table is based on cultivation records. Widely and popularly grown, *D. kingianum* is considered by many to be the easiest Australian *Dendrobium* to grow. Growers report that plants do not grow vigorously if they are overpotted, have wet feet, or if the medium is stale.

Some clones are considered reluctant bloomers, but whether the plants have been given a dry cool rest is unknown. *D. kingianum* commonly produces many keikis, especially when overwatered in winter. In nature, these aerial offshoots drop off as they mature to form new individuals. In cultivation, plants produce mostly keikis instead of flowering unless they have a dry winter rest. Mother plants flower better if keikis are removed and potted as soon as roots develop. While plants will not bloom unless they are given a cool dry rest, latent buds may all develop and bloom after the necessary rest conditions are finally provided, even after several years. This may result in a spectacular floral display.

Plant and Flower Information

PLANT SIZE AND TYPE: A 3–26 in. (8–65 cm) sympodial lithophyte. Plants occasionally grow epiphytically or terrestrially, but terrestrial plants are usually smaller than lithophytic plants. Plants form a large, thick mat.

PSEUDOBULB: 2–22 in. (5–55 cm) long. Plant size is highly variable. The slender pseudobulbs are dilated at the base and taper toward the apex. They may be green, yellowish, or reddish.

LEAVES: 2–9 at the apex of each growth. The persistent leaves are 1.2–4.0 in. (3–10 cm) long. They are oblong-lanceolate and thin-textured. They may be light green or dark reddish-green.

INFLORESCENCE: 5–7 in. (13–18 cm) long. The racemes may be erect to pendulous, but they are most often arching. The extent of drooping is apparently determined by the number and size of the blossoms. Inflorescences emerge from between the leaves near the apex of each growth. Each growth may produce 1–3 inflorescences.

FLOWERS: 2–15, commonly 3–7 per inflorescence. The highly variable flowers are 0.5–1.2 in. (1.3–3.0 cm) across. The sepals and petals are most often pink to deep mauve, but white clones are occasionally found. The lip may be snow white or heavily decorated with red or dark purple. Nearly every combination and permutation of these colors may be found, and growers indicate that no 2 plants have flowers that are precisely alike. Individual blossoms last nearly a month. The flowers may be faintly fragrant or very sweetly scented.

HYBRIDIZING NOTES: Chromosome counts are $2n = 38$ (ref. 580), $2n = 76$ (ref. 151, 187, 504, 580), $2n = 112–114$ (ref. 580). When tested as *D. kingianum* var. *kingianum* the counts were highly variable including $2n = 38$ (ref. 187, 504), $2n = 57$ (ref. 504), $2n = 76$ (ref. 187, 504, 580), and $2n = 112–114$ (ref. 187, 504). When *D. kingianum* var. *album* was tested, the counts were $2n = $ about 57 (ref. 504, 580) and $2n = 76$ (ref. 504). *D. kingianum* var. *silcockii* had a chromosome count of $2n = $ about 76 (ref. 504, 580). Adams (ref. 5) showed that not only do triploids occasionally occur, but they are common in some areas and in some red breeding lines. Tetraploids, however, are very rare. He found no correlation between chromosome number and plant habit, cane length, leaf size or shape, flower color, or any other characteristic.

D. kingianum seeds are normally mature enough for green-pod culture in 64 days. They are sometimes self-fertile, but some clones are never self-fertile. Growers report that older pollen often has a higher success rate. Pods are regularly produced when pollen from another plant was used.

When used in hybridizing, each clone of the variable *D. kingianum* is usually dominant for plant growth habit as well as flower size, shape, and color, often for several generations. White clones, however, are generally recessive. The tendency for the inflorescence to droop is a dominant characteristic.

REFERENCES: 2, 5, 23, 36, 105, 129, 151, 158, 161, 179, 187, 190, 196, 210, 216, 240, 254, 272, 291, 309, 317, 325, 326, 352, 371, 389, 390, 421, 430, 445, 461, 464, 492, 495, 504, 527, 533, 534, 541, 559, 570, 580, 598.

PHOTOS/DRAWINGS: 1, *5, 27, 36,* 105, *129, 158, 161, 184,* 210, *240, 291, 323,* 325, *371, 389, 390, 430, 492, 520, 533, 534, 559, 560, 566, 598.*

Dendrobium kirchianum A. Hawkes and A. H. Heller. Now considered a synonym of *Diplocaulobium kirchianum* (A. Hawkes and A. H. Heller) Hunt and Summerhayes. REFERENCES: 191, 213, 229, 230, 273.

Dendrobium kjellbergii J. J. Smith

ORIGIN/HABITAT: Central Sulawesi (Celebes). Plants grow at sea level near Malili at the north end of Bone Bay.

CLIMATE: Station #97146, Kendari, Sulawesi, Indonesia, Lat. 4.1°S, Long. 122.4°E, at 164 ft. (50 m). Record extreme temperatures are not available for this location.

N/HEMISPHERE	JAN	FEB	MAR	APR	MAY	JUN	JUL	AUG	SEP	OCT	NOV	DEC
°F AVG MAX	85	86	88	90	90	89	88	87	88	86	86	84
°F AVG MIN	70	71	70	72	74	75	75	74	74	74	74	72
DIURNAL RANGE	15	15	18	18	16	14	13	13	14	12	12	12
RAIN/INCHES	5.7	4.0	2.3	2.5	6.0	7.7	7.9	7.3	8.4	8.2	9.9	9.1
HUMIDITY/%	86	80	76	73	76	82	80	81	82	83	85	84
BLOOM SEASON			*									
DAYS CLR @ 8AM	3	10	10	14	8	5	1	2	2	3	2	4
DAYS CLR @ 2PM	0	0	1	2	1	0	1	0	0	0	0	0
RAIN/MM	144	102	58	63	152	197	201	186	213	208	252	231
°C AVG MAX	29.2	29.9	31.0	32.3	32.4	31.8	31.1	30.7	30.9	29.9	30.1	28.8
°C AVG MIN	21.3	21.5	21.1	22.4	23.6	24.0	24.0	23.4	23.4	23.6	23.4	22.3
DIURNAL RANGE	7.9	8.4	9.9	9.9	8.8	7.8	7.1	7.3	7.5	6.3	6.7	6.5
S/HEMISPHERE	JUL	AUG	SEP	OCT	NOV	DEC	JAN	FEB	MAR	APR	MAY	JUN

Cultural Recommendations

LIGHT: 2000–3000 fc.

TEMPERATURES: Throughout the year, days average 84–90°F (29–32°C), and nights average 70–75°F (21–24°C), with a diurnal range of 12–18°F (6–10°C).

HUMIDITY: 80–85% most of the year, dropping to near 75% in spring.

WATER: Rainfall is moderate to heavy most of the year with a 2–3 month slightly drier season in late winter and early spring. Cultivated plants should be kept moist but not soggy.

FERTILIZER: ¼–½ recommended strength. A balanced fertilizer should be applied weekly to biweekly throughout the year.

REST PERIOD: Growing conditions should be maintained all year. Winter low temperatures drop about 5°F (3°C) below summer levels. In cultivation, water should be reduced for 2–3 months. Plants should dry slightly between waterings, but they should not remain dry for extended periods. Occasional mistings on bright, sunny days between waterings may be beneficial. Fertilizer should be reduced or eliminated anytime water is reduced. In the habitat, mornings are frequently clear in late winter and spring.

GROWING MEDIA: Plants may be mounted on tree-fern or cork slabs or potted in small pots filled with any open, fast-draining medium. Repotting may be done anytime new roots are growing.

MISCELLANEOUS NOTES: The bloom season shown in the climate table is based on reports from the habitat. The plant was described in 1933 in *Engler's Bot. Jahrb.* 65:489.

Plant and Flower Information

PLANT SIZE AND TYPE: A 5–10 in. (13–25 cm) sympodial epiphyte.

PSEUDOBULB: 5–10 in. (13–25 cm) long. The slender stems become dark yellow with age. They are borne on a short, branching rhizome. The lower part of the stem is leafy. The upper half of the stem has only rudimentary leaves.

LEAVES: Many. The linear leaves are 0.9–1.1 in. (2.3–2.9 cm) long, spreading, and flattened. They are quickly deciduous. The leaves may be erect or recurved.

INFLORESCENCE: Short. Inflorescences are borne on the upper, leafless part of the stem.

FLOWERS: 1 per inflorescence. The delicate flowers are 0.4 in. (1 cm) across. The blossoms have a somewhat triangular, erect dorsal sepal, very slender lateral sepals, and an erect lip. Blossoms are white with gold flecks on the lip.

REFERENCES: 225.

Dendrobium klabatense Schlechter

ORIGIN/HABITAT: Endemic to Sulawesi (Celebes). Plants grow on trees at about 1650 ft. (500 m) on Mt. Klabat, which is located near the eastern tip of the Minahassa Peninsula.

CLIMATE: Station #97014, Manado, Sulawesi, Indonesia, Lat. 1.5°N, Long. 124.9°E, at 264 ft. (80 m). Temperatures are calculated for an elevation of 1650 ft. (500 m), resulting in probable extremes of 92°F (34°C) and 60°F (16°C).

N/HEMISPHERE	JAN	FEB	MAR	APR	MAY	JUN	JUL	AUG	SEP	OCT	NOV	DEC
°F AVG MAX	80	80	80	81	82	82	82	84	84	84	82	81
°F AVG MIN	68	68	68	68	69	68	68	68	68	67	68	69
DIURNAL RANGE	12	12	12	13	13	14	14	16	16	17	14	12
RAIN/INCHES	18.6	13.8	12.2	8.0	6.4	6.5	4.8	4.0	3.4	4.9	8.9	14.7
HUMIDITY/%	84	83	83	83	81	80	75	72	75	77	82	83
BLOOM SEASON												*
DAYS CLR @ 8AM	4	3	6	11	11	12	12	12	14	17	12	8
DAYS CLR @ 2PM	1	1	1	2	1	3	3	4	4	4	1	1
RAIN/MM	472	351	310	203	163	165	122	102	86	124	226	373
°C AVG MAX	26.9	26.9	26.9	27.5	28.0	28.0	28.0	29.1	29.1	29.1	28.0	27.5
°C AVG MIN	20.2	20.2	20.2	20.2	20.8	20.2	20.2	20.2	20.2	19.7	20.2	20.8
DIURNAL RANGE	6.7	6.7	6.7	7.3	7.2	7.8	7.8	8.9	8.9	9.4	7.8	6.7
S/HEMISPHERE	JUL	AUG	SEP	OCT	NOV	DEC	JAN	FEB	MAR	APR	MAY	JUN

Cultural Recommendations

LIGHT: 2000–3000 fc. The habitat is usually overcast in the afternoon.

TEMPERATURES: Throughout the year, days average 80–84°F (27–29°C), and nights average 67–69°F (20–21°C), with a diurnal range of 12–17°F (7–9°C). Extreme temperatures are within 10°F (6°C) of the averages, indicating that plants may not tolerant large seasonal temperature fluctuations. The daily temperature range is greater than the seasonal variation.

HUMIDITY: 80–85% most of the year, dropping to 70–75% in late summer and early autumn.

WATER: Rainfall is moderate to heavy all year. The driest weather occurs in late summer, which is the warmest season. Cultivated plants should be kept moist but not soggy. Warm water might be beneficial.

FERTILIZER: ¼–½ recommended strength. A balanced fertilizer should be applied weekly to biweekly throughout the year.

REST PERIOD: Growing temperatures should be maintained all year. The plants may rest during the semidry period in late summer and autumn, which is also the period of greatest diurnal range. Cultivated plants should be allowed to dry slightly during this time but should not remain dry for extended periods. Plants should be kept moist the rest of the year.

GROWING MEDIA: Plants may be mounted on tree-fern or cork slabs if humidity is high and plants are watered at least once daily in summer. When plants are potted, any open, fast-draining medium may be used. Repotting may be done anytime new roots are growing.

MISCELLANEOUS NOTES: The bloom season shown in the climate table is based on reports from the habitat.

Plant and Flower Information

PLANT SIZE AND TYPE: A 12 in. (30 cm) sympodial epiphyte.

PSEUDOBULB: 12 in. (30 cm) long. The grooved, slender stems occasionally branch.

LEAVES: Many. The lanceolate leaves are 1.2–2.0 in. (3–5 cm) long, with a pointed, unequally 2-toothed apex.

INFLORESCENCE: Very short. Inflorescences emerge from nodes along the stem.

FLOWERS: 2 per inflorescence. Blossoms are 1.0–1.2 in. (2.5–3.0 cm) across. The fan-shaped flowers have pale violet-pink sepals and petals, a yellowish spur, and yellow anther. The fiddle-shaped lip is finely toothed or serrated along the apical margin.

REFERENCES: 220, 436.

Dendrobium klossii Ridley

ORIGIN/HABITAT: Irian Jaya (western New Guinea). Plants were collected south of Mt. Jaya (Mt. Carstensz) at about 500 ft. (150 m).

CLIMATE: Station #97796, Kokenau (Kokonau), Irian Jaya, Lat. 4.7°S, Long. 135.4°E, at 10 ft. (3 m). Temperatures are calculated for an elevation of 500 ft. (150 m). Record extreme temperatures are not available for this location.

N/HEMISPHERE	JAN	FEB	MAR	APR	MAY	JUN	JUL	AUG	SEP	OCT	NOV	DEC
°F AVG MAX	81	81	84	86	88	87	87	87	88	86	85	82
°F AVG MIN	71	71	72	72	72	73	72	72	72	72	72	71
DIURNAL RANGE	10	10	12	14	16	14	15	15	16	14	13	11
RAIN/INCHES	18.4	15.8	18.9	11.6	9.7	10.6	11.5	15.7	11.6	11.6	16.0	19.9
HUMIDITY/%	N/A											
BLOOM SEASON	N/A											
DAYS CLR	N/A											
RAIN/MM	467	401	480	295	246	269	292	399	295	295	406	505
°C AVG MAX	27.4	27.4	29.1	30.2	31.3	30.8	30.8	30.8	31.3	30.2	29.7	28.0
°C AVG MIN	21.9	21.9	22.4	22.4	22.4	23.0	22.4	22.4	22.4	22.4	22.4	21.9
DIURNAL RANGE	5.5	5.5	6.7	7.8	8.9	7.8	8.4	8.4	8.9	7.8	7.3	6.1
S/HEMISPHERE	JUL	AUG	SEP	OCT	NOV	DEC	JAN	FEB	MAR	APR	MAY	JUN

Cultural Recommendations

LIGHT: 2500–3500 fc.

TEMPERATURES: Throughout the year, days average 81–88°F (27–31°C), and nights average 71–73°F (22–23°C), with a diurnal range of 10–16°F (6–9°C).

HUMIDITY: Information is not available for this location. However, records from nearby locations indicate that humidity probably averages near 85% year-round.

WATER: Rainfall is very heavy all year. Cultivated plants should be kept evenly moist but not soggy.

FERTILIZER: ¼–½ recommended strength. A balanced fertilizer should be applied weekly to biweekly throughout the year.

REST PERIOD: Growing conditions should be maintained year-round. For cultivated plants, water and fertilizer may be reduced slightly in winter, especially for plants grown in the dark, short-day conditions common in temperate latitudes. They should never be allowed to dry out completely, however.

GROWING MEDIA: Plants may be mounted on tree-fern or cork slabs or potted in small pots filled with any open, fast-draining medium. Repotting may be done anytime new roots are growing.

Plant and Flower Information

PLANT SIZE AND TYPE: An 8 in. (20 cm) sympodial epiphyte.

PSEUDOBULB: 8 in. (20 cm) long.

LEAVES: Many. The elongated lanceolate leaves, which are papery when dried, are 6 in. (15 cm) long. They are held very close to the stem.

INFLORESCENCE: Short.

FLOWERS: 2 per inflorescence. The flowers are 0.8–1.2 in. (2–3 cm) across when spread. The sickle-shaped sepals are linear, fleshy, and papillose. They become threadlike at the tips. Petals are oblong. The lip is short, curved, papillose, and channeled. Flower color was not included in the description.

REFERENCES: 222, 400.

Dendrobium koeteianum Schlechter

AKA: *D. koeteianum* is sometimes listed as a synonym of *D. aciculare* Lindley, but Seidenfaden (ref. 450) expresses strong reservations regarding this synonymy.

ORIGIN/HABITAT: Koetai State, near Samarinda, Borneo. Additional habitat information is unavailable, so the following climate data should be used with caution.

CLIMATE: Station #96633, Balikpapan, Borneo, Lat. 1.3°S, Long. 116.9°E, at 10 ft. (3 m). Record extreme temperatures are 92°F (33°C) and 60°F (16°C).

N/HEMISPHERE	JAN	FEB	MAR	APR	MAY	JUN	JUL	AUG	SEP	OCT	NOV	DEC
°F AVG MAX	83	84	84	85	85	85	85	86	86	85	85	84
°F AVG MIN	73	74	74	74	73	73	73	73	73	73	74	74
DIURNAL RANGE	10	10	10	11	12	12	12	13	13	12	11	10
RAIN/INCHES	7.1	6.4	5.5	5.2	6.6	8.1	7.9	8.9	9.1	8.2	9.1	7.6
HUMIDITY/%	82	80	77	78	80	79	82	81	81	82	83	82
BLOOM SEASON	N/A											
DAYS CLR @ 8AM	4	2	3	3	3	3	2	3	4	4	2	5
DAYS CLR @ 2PM	6	4	5	3	1	2	1	2	3	4	5	
RAIN/MM	180	163	140	132	168	206	201	226	231	208	231	193
°C AVG MAX	28.3	28.9	28.9	29.4	29.4	29.4	29.4	30.0	30.0	29.4	29.4	28.9
°C AVG MIN	22.8	23.3	23.3	23.3	22.8	22.8	22.8	22.8	22.8	22.8	23.3	23.3
DIURNAL RANGE	5.5	5.6	5.6	6.1	6.6	6.6	6.6	7.2	7.2	6.6	6.1	5.6
S/HEMISPHERE	JUL	AUG	SEP	OCT	NOV	DEC	JAN	FEB	MAR	APR	MAY	JUN

Cultural Recommendations

LIGHT: 2000–3000 fc.

TEMPERATURES: Throughout the year, days average 83–86°F (28–30°C), and nights average 73–74°F (23°C), with a diurnal range of 10–13°F (6–7°C).

HUMIDITY: Near 80% year-round.

WATER: Rainfall is heavy all year. Cultivated plants should be kept moist.

FERTILIZER: ¼–½ recommended strength. A balanced fertilizer should be applied weekly to biweekly throughout the year.

REST PERIOD: Growing conditions should be maintained year-round. Water and fertilizer should be reduced somewhat in winter, especially for plants cultivated in the dark, short-day conditions common in temperate latitudes. Plants should never be allowed to dry out completely, however. In the habitat, seasonal light variation is minor.

GROWING MEDIA: Plants may be mounted on tree-fern or cork slabs or potted in small pots filled with any open, fast-draining medium. Repotting may be done anytime new roots are growing.

Plant and Flower Information

PLANT SIZE AND TYPE: A 12 in. (30 cm) sympodial epiphyte.

PSEUDOBULB: 12 in. (30 cm) long. The erect stems are ovoid above the base. They arise from a very short rhizome.

LEAVES: The smooth leaves are 1.2–2.0 in. (3–5 cm) long, erect-spreading, and rigidly-fleshy

INFLORESCENCE: Short. Inflorescences emerge from nodes along the side and especially at apex of the stem.

FLOWERS: Few per inflorescence. The white flowers are 0.4 in. (1 cm) across. The 3-lobed lip is toothed along the margin with 3 parallel lines at the base of the midlobe.

REFERENCES: 220, 254, 286, 433, 450.

Dendrobium kohlmeyerianum Teijsm. and Binn. See *D. tricuspe* (Blume) Lindley. REFERENCES: 216, 254, 469.

Dendrobium kontumense Gagnepain. See *D. virgineum* Rchb. f. REFERENCES: 225, 266, 448, 454.

Dendrobium koordersii J. J. Smith

AKA: J. J. Smith (ref. 470) suggests the possibility that *D. isochiloides* Kränzlin and *D. koordersii* J. J. Smith may belong with *D. bilobum* Lindley.

ORIGIN/HABITAT: Sulawesi (Celebes) and Ambon Island. On Sulawesi, plants grow on trees near Tomohon on the Minahasssa Peninsula at about 3000 ft. (910 m). They are also found in primary forests on Mt. Lolomboelan.

CLIMATE: Station #97014, Manado, Sulawesi, Lat. 1.5°N, Long. 124.9°E, at 264 ft. (80 m). Temperatures are calculated for an elevation of 3000 ft. (910 m), resulting in probable extremes of 88°F (31°C) and 56°F (13°C).

N/HEMISPHERE	JAN	FEB	MAR	APR	MAY	JUN	JUL	AUG	SEP	OCT	NOV	DEC
°F AVG MAX	76	76	76	77	78	78	78	80	80	80	78	77
°F AVG MIN	64	64	64	64	65	64	64	64	64	63	64	65
DIURNAL RANGE	12	12	12	13	13	14	14	16	16	17	14	12
RAIN/INCHES	18.6	13.8	12.2	8.0	6.4	6.5	4.8	4.0	3.4	4.9	8.9	14.7
HUMIDITY/%	84	83	83	83	81	80	75	72	75	77	82	83
BLOOM SEASON		*	*	*							*	
DAYS CLR @ 8AM	4	3	6	11	11	12	12	12	14	17	12	8
DAYS CLR @ 2PM	1	1	1	2	1	3	3	4	4	4	1	1
RAIN/MM	472	351	310	203	163	165	122	102	86	124	226	373
°C AVG MAX	24.4	24.4	24.4	25.0	25.5	25.5	25.5	26.7	26.7	26.7	25.5	25.0
°C AVG MIN	17.8	17.8	17.8	17.8	18.3	17.8	17.8	17.8	17.8	17.2	17.8	18.3
DIURNAL RANGE	6.6	6.6	6.6	7.2	7.2	7.7	7.7	8.9	8.9	9.5	7.7	6.7
S/HEMISPHERE	JUL	AUG	SEP	OCT	NOV	DEC	JAN	FEB	MAR	APR	MAY	JUN

Cultural Recommendations

LIGHT: 2000–3000 fc. In the habitat, morning light is highest as skies are usually overcast by afternoon.

TEMPERATURES: Throughout the year, days average 76–80°F (24–27°C), and nights average 63–65°F (17–18°C), with a diurnal range of 12–17°F (7–10°C). The extreme temperatures are only a few degrees above and below the averages, indicating that plants may not tolerate wide temperature fluctuations.

HUMIDITY: 80–85% most of the year, dropping to 70–75% in late summer and autumn.

WATER: Rainfall is moderate to heavy all year. The driest weather occurs in late summer, which is the warmest season. Cultivated plants should be kept moist but not soggy. Warm water might be beneficial.

FERTILIZER: ¼–½ recommended strength. A balanced fertilizer should be applied weekly to biweekly throughout the year.

REST PERIOD: Growing temperatures should be maintained all year. The plants may rest during the semidry period in late summer and autumn, which is also the period of greatest diurnal range. Cultivated plants should be allowed to dry slightly during this time but should not remain dry for extended periods. Plants should be kept moist the rest of the year.

GROWING MEDIA: Plants may be mounted on tree-fern or cork slabs if humidity is high and plants are watered at least once daily in summer. When plants are potted, any open, fast-draining medium may be used. Repotting may be done anytime new roots are growing.

MISCELLANEOUS NOTES: The bloom season shown in the climate table is based on reports from the habitat.

Plant and Flower Information

PLANT SIZE AND TYPE: A 12 in. (30 cm) sympodial epiphyte.

PSEUDOBULB: 12 in. (30 cm) long. Stems are clustered.

LEAVES: Many. The linear, bilobed leaves are 2–3 in. (5–8 cm) long.

INFLORESCENCE: Short and few.

FLOWERS: 1 per inflorescence. The flowers are 0.2 in. (0.5 cm) long. Sepals and petals are pale greenish white. The lip, which is uppermost, is green with dark red spots.

REFERENCES: 219, 254, 436, 468, 470.

Dendrobium korinchense Ridley

ORIGIN/HABITAT: Sumatra. Plants were found near Sungei Kumbang at about 4500 ft. (1370 m).

CLIMATE: Station #96163, Padang, Sumatra, Indonesia, Lat. 0.9°S, Long. 100.4°E, at 19 ft. (6 m). Temperatures are calculated for an elevation of 4600 ft. (1400 m), resulting in probable extremes of 79°F (26°C) and 53°F (12°C).

N/HEMISPHERE	JAN	FEB	MAR	APR	MAY	JUN	JUL	AUG	SEP	OCT	NOV	DEC
°F AVG MAX	72	72	71	71	71	71	72	72	72	72	73	72
°F AVG MIN	59	59	59	59	59	59	59	59	59	60	60	59
DIURNAL RANGE	13	13	12	12	12	12	13	13	13	12	13	13
RAIN/INCHES	10.9	13.7	6.0	19.5	20.4	18.9	13.8	10.2	12.1	14.3	12.4	12.1
HUMIDITY/%	81	82	82	84	85	84	81	81	82	83	81	81
BLOOM SEASON	N/A											
DAYS CLR @ 7AM	5	1	1	0	0	2	2	1	2	2	3	5
DAYS CLR @ 1PM	5	2	2	1	1	3	3	4	3	3	6	5
RAIN/MM	277	348	152	495	518	480	351	259	307	363	315	307
°C AVG MAX	22.2	22.2	21.6	21.6	21.6	21.6	22.2	22.2	22.2	22.2	22.7	22.2
°C AVG MIN	14.9	14.9	14.9	14.9	14.9	14.9	14.9	14.9	14.9	15.5	15.5	14.9
DIURNAL RANGE	7.3	7.3	6.7	6.7	6.7	6.7	7.3	7.3	7.3	6.7	7.2	7.3
S/HEMISPHERE	JUL	AUG	SEP	OCT	NOV	DEC	JAN	FEB	MAR	APR	MAY	JUN

Cultural Recommendations

LIGHT: 2000–3000 fc. Clear summer days are rare.

TEMPERATURES: Throughout the year, days average 71–73°F (22–23°C), and nights average 59–60°F (15–16°C), with a diurnal range of 12–13°F (7°C). Probable extremes vary only a few degrees from the averages indicating that plants from this habitat may not tolerate wide temperature fluctuations.

HUMIDITY: 80–85% year-round.

WATER: Rainfall is heavy all year. Cultivated plants should be kept moist but not soggy.

FERTILIZER: ¼–½ recommended strength. A balanced fertilizer should be applied weekly to biweekly throughout the year.

REST PERIOD: Growing conditions should be maintained year-round. Water may be reduced somewhat for cultivated plants in winter, especially those grown in the dark, short-day conditions common in temperate latitudes. They should never be allowed to dry out completely, however.

GROWING MEDIA: Mounting plants on tree-fern or cork slabs accommodates their pendulous growth habit. However, humidity must be high and plants must be watered at least once a day in summer. If plants cannot be mounted, small pots or hanging baskets may be filled with an open, fast-draining medium. Repotting may be done anytime new roots are actively growing.

Plant and Flower Information

PLANT SIZE AND TYPE: A 24 in. (60 cm) sympodial epiphyte.

PSEUDOBULB: 24 in. (60 cm) long. The stems consist of internodes 1.2 in. (3 cm) long.

LEAVES: The pointed, lanceolate leaves are 3.3 in. (8.5 cm) long. They are leathery and unequally bilobed at the apex.

INFLORESCENCE: Short.

FLOWERS: The flowers are 0.5 in. (1.3 cm) long. The dorsal sepal is lanceolate, and petals are linear-oblong. The linear-oblong lip is papillose at the base.

REFERENCES: 222, 401.

Dendrobium korthalsii J. J. Smith

ORIGIN/HABITAT: Southeastern and the central part of eastern Borneo. Plants were originally collected in mangrove swamps near sea level close to Martapura (Martapoera), a small town east of Bandjarmasin, Borneo.

CLIMATE: Station #96685, Bandjarmasin, Borneo, Lat. 3.4°S, Long. 114.8°E, at 66 ft. (20 m). Record extreme temperatures are not available for this location.

Dendrobium kosepangii

N/HEMISPHERE	JAN	FEB	MAR	APR	MAY	JUN	JUL	AUG	SEP	OCT	NOV	DEC
°F AVG MAX	88	89	91	90	87	86	86	86	87	89	88	88
°F AVG MIN	74	73	74	76	76	76	76	75	75	77	77	76
DIURNAL RANGE	14	16	17	14	11	10	10	11	12	12	11	12
RAIN/INCHES	3.5	3.2	3.9	5.1	8.5	12.2	12.7	11.7	11.9	8.5	6.2	5.6
HUMIDITY/%	78	77	73	75	81	84	84	83	82	81	80	79
BLOOM SEASON									*			*
DAYS CLR @ 8AM	12	12	13	8	5	3	1	2	3	6	9	11
DAYS CLR @ 2PM	3	2	2	3	1	0	0	0	1	2	2	3
RAIN/MM	89	81	99	130	216	310	323	297	302	216	157	142
°C AVG MAX	31.0	31.9	32.7	32.4	30.7	29.9	29.8	30.0	30.6	31.4	30.9	31.1
°C AVG MIN	23.2	23.0	23.4	24.2	24.3	24.2	24.2	24.1	24.1	24.9	24.9	24.2
DIURNAL RANGE	7.8	8.9	9.3	8.2	6.4	5.7	5.6	5.9	6.5	6.5	6.0	6.9
S/HEMISPHERE	JUL	AUG	SEP	OCT	NOV	DEC	JAN	FEB	MAR	APR	MAY	JUN

Cultural Recommendations

LIGHT: 2000–3000 fc.

TEMPERATURES: Throughout the year, days average 86–91°F (30–33°C), and nights average 73–77°F (23–25°C), with a diurnal range of 10–17°F (6–9°C).

HUMIDITY: 80–85% from late spring through autumn, dropping to about 75% in winter and early spring.

WATER: Rainfall is moderate to heavy all year, but conditions are slightly drier for 3 months in winter. Plants should be kept evenly moist from spring into autumn, but water should be gradually reduced in late autumn. Warm water might be beneficial.

FERTILIZER: ¼–½ recommended strength. A balanced fertilizer should be applied weekly to biweekly throughout the year.

REST PERIOD: Growing conditions should be maintained all year. Water and fertilizer should be reduced somewhat in winter, especially for plants cultivated in the dark, short-day conditions common in temperate latitudes. Plants should be allowed to dry slightly between waterings, but they should not remain dry for long periods. In the habitat, light is highest in winter.

GROWING MEDIA: Plants may be mounted on tree-fern or cork slabs or potted in small pots filled with any open, fast-draining medium. Repotting may be done anytime new roots are growing.

MISCELLANEOUS NOTES: The bloom season shown in the climate table is based on collection reports. The plant was described in 1917 in *Bul. Jard. Bot. Buit.* 2nd sér. 25:40.

Plant and Flower Information

PLANT SIZE AND TYPE: A 20 in. (50 cm) sympodial epiphyte.

PSEUDOBULB: 20 in. (50 cm) long. The flattened stems are branching.

LEAVES: Many. The lanceolate-triangular leaves are 0.7–1.1 in. (1.8–2.9 cm) long and laterally flattened.

INFLORESCENCE: Short. Inflorescences emerge from nodes along the stem.

FLOWERS: 1 per inflorescence. The tiny flowers are 0.2 in. (0.5 cm) across. They are greenish-yellow with violet stripes near the base. The spur is violet.

REFERENCES: 222, 286, 295.

Dendrobium kosepangii Tso. See *D. wilsonii* Rolfe. REFERENCES: 208, 225, 528.

Dendrobium kosterianum Vermeulen. Probably an invalid name. This plant was imported from New Guinea to The Netherlands. However, no Latin description or type specimen information was included. REFERENCES: Vermeulen 1975 *Orchideen* 37(4):119.

Dendrobium kraemeri Schlechter

AKA: In 1993 Dauncey and Cribb in *Kew Bulletin* 48(3) listed *D. pseudokraemeri* Fukuyama as a possible synonym.

ORIGIN/HABITAT: The Caroline Islands. Plants are found on the islands of Koror and Palau at 50–1000 ft. (20–300 m). They grow on trees in parklike cultivated land, in scrub forest strips on rocky land, and in dense intermediate forests. They are often found on ridges.

CLIMATE: Station #91408, Koror Is., Caroline Islands, Lat. 7.3°N, Long. 134.5°E, at 108 ft. (33 m). Temperatures are calculated for an elevation of 650 ft. (200 m), resulting in probable extremes of 91°F (33°C) and 67°F (20°C).

N/HEMISPHERE	JAN	FEB	MAR	APR	MAY	JUN	JUL	AUG	SEP	OCT	NOV	DEC
°F AVG MAX	84	85	85	86	86	86	85	85	85	86	86	85
°F AVG MIN	73	73	73	74	74	73	73	73	73	74	74	73
DIURNAL RANGE	11	12	12	12	12	13	12	12	12	12	12	12
RAIN/INCHES	12.6	6.8	7.7	9.7	16.3	14.6	16.8	16.8	15.4	13.4	10.8	12.7
HUMIDITY/%	86	85	84	85	87	87	87	86	86	85	86	86
BLOOM SEASON		*	*									
DAYS CLR @ 9AM	0	0	0	0	0	0	0	0	0	1	0	0
DAYS CLR @ 3PM	0	0	0	0	0	0	0	0	0	0	0	0
RAIN/MM	320	173	196	246	414	371	427	427	391	340	274	323
°C AVG MAX	29.0	29.6	29.6	30.1	30.1	30.1	29.6	29.6	29.6	30.1	30.1	29.6
°C AVG MIN	22.9	22.9	22.9	23.5	23.5	22.9	22.9	22.9	22.9	23.5	23.5	22.9
DIURNAL RANGE	6.1	6.7	6.7	6.6	6.6	7.2	6.7	6.7	6.7	6.6	6.6	6.7
S/HEMISPHERE	JUL	AUG	SEP	OCT	NOV	DEC	JAN	FEB	MAR	APR	MAY	JUN

Cultural Recommendations

LIGHT: 2000–3000 fc.

TEMPERATURES: Throughout the year, days average 84–86°F (29–30°C), and nights average 73–74°F (23–24°C), with a diurnal range of 11–13°F (6–7°C).

HUMIDITY: Near 85% year-round.

WATER: Rainfall is heavy all year. Cultivated plants should be kept moist but not soggy.

FERTILIZER: ¼–½ recommended strength. A balanced fertilizer should be applied weekly to biweekly throughout the year.

REST PERIOD: Growing conditions should be maintained all year. Water should be reduced somewhat in winter for plants grown in the dark, short-day conditions common in temperate latitudes. They should never be allowed to dry out completely, however. Fertilizer should be reduced or eliminated anytime water is reduced.

GROWING MEDIA: Plants may be mounted on tree-fern or cork slabs if humidity is high and plants are watered at least once daily in summer. When plants are potted, any open, fast-draining medium may be used. Repotting may be done anytime new roots are growing.

MISCELLANEOUS NOTES: The bloom season shown in the climate table is based on reports from the habitat. Collection reports indicate that plants were in bloom and in fruit at the same time.

Plant and Flower Information

PLANT SIZE AND TYPE: A 16–32 in. (40–80 cm) sympodial epiphyte.

PSEUDOBULB: 16–32 in. (40–80 cm) long. The cylindrical, fleshy stems become longitudinally grooved when dry. They are uniformly leafy. The internodes are somewhat rectangular.

LEAVES: Many. The leaves are elliptic-lanceolate to lanceolate-linear, rounded at the unequally bilobed tip, and contracted at the base. They have a thin texture. The leaves are attached to the pseudobulb by means of a distinct sheath.

INFLORESCENCE: Normally 1.0–1.4 in. (2.5–3.5 cm) long, rarely to 2 in. (5.2 cm) long. The cylindrical, densely flowered racemes emerge laterally. Inflorescences are most often borne on leafless stems.

FLOWERS: 10–26 per inflorescence. The smooth flowers are 1.0–1.4 in. (2.5–3.5 cm) long. The sepals and petals are white or pink-white with green at the tips. The elliptical sepals and lanceolate-elliptic petals are pointed. The length of the mentum equals the length of the free portion of the lateral sepals. The edges near the apex of the lip and along the upper margin of the petals are minutely toothed. The 3-lobed lip has yellow lamina and a half moon-shaped transverse callus.

REFERENCES: 221, 441.

PHOTOS/DRAWINGS: Dauncey and Cribb 1993 *Kew Bulletin* 48(3):545–576.

Dendrobium kraenzlinii L. O. Williams

AKA: *D. vitiense* Kränzlin not Rolfe. The plant name is sometimes spelled *D. kränzlinii*.

ORIGIN/HABITAT: Endemic and uncommon in Fiji. On Vanua Levu and Viti Levu, plants are found in the mountains near Lautoka and along the southern base of Mathusta Range north of Natua. They grow on trees in dense and open forests at 350–1950 ft. (100–600 m).

CLIMATE: Station #91680, Nadi, Vitu Levu, Fiji, Lat. 17.8°S, Long. 177.4°E, at 63 ft. (19 m). Temperatures are calculated for an elevation of 1300 ft. (400 m), resulting in probable extremes of 91°F (33°C) and 51°F (11°C).

N/HEMISPHERE	JAN	FEB	MAR	APR	MAY	JUN	JUL	AUG	SEP	OCT	NOV	DEC
°F AVG MAX	79	81	81	82	82	83	85	84	84	84	82	79
°F AVG MIN	60	62	63	64	65	67	68	68	69	67	64	61
DIURNAL RANGE	19	19	18	18	17	16	17	16	15	17	18	18
RAIN/INCHES	0.5	1.4	3.7	3.5	2.8	4.7	12.7	10.0	15.1	6.8	5.3	4.3
HUMIDITY/%	74	73	73	75	73	78	80	80	83	82	78	78
BLOOM SEASON							*					
DAYS CLR @ 12PM	10	15	7	9	8	5	5	3	3	6	9	11
DAYS CLR @ 6PM	12	10	4	6	3	2	1	1	3	6	8	
RAIN/MM	13	36	94	89	71	119	323	254	384	173	135	109
°C AVG MAX	26.1	27.2	27.2	27.7	27.7	28.3	29.4	28.8	28.8	28.8	27.7	26.1
°C AVG MIN	15.5	16.6	17.2	17.7	18.3	19.4	20.0	20.0	20.5	19.4	17.7	16.1
DIURNAL RANGE	10.6	10.6	10.0	10.0	9.4	8.9	9.4	8.8	8.3	9.4	10.0	10.0
S/HEMISPHERE	JUL	AUG	SEP	OCT	NOV	DEC	JAN	FEB	MAR	APR	MAY	JUN

Cultural Recommendations

LIGHT: 1500–3000 fc.

TEMPERATURES: Summer days average 82–85°F (28–29°C), and nights average 67–69°F (19–21°C), with a diurnal range of 16–17°F (9–10°C).

HUMIDITY: Near 80% in summer and early autumn, dropping to about 75% in winter and spring.

WATER: Rainfall is moderate to heavy from spring through autumn. Conditions are significantly drier for 2–3 months in winter. Cultivated plants should be kept evenly moist while in actively growing, but water should be gradually reduced in autumn.

FERTILIZER: ¼–½ recommended strength, applied weekly. A high-nitrogen fertilizer is beneficial from spring to midsummer, but a fertilizer high in phosphates should be used in late summer and autumn.

REST PERIOD: Winter days average 79–81°F (26–27°C), and nights average 60–63°F (16–17°C), with a diurnal range of 18–19°F (10–11°C). In cultivation, water should be reduced for 2–3 months and plants allowed to become somewhat dry between waterings. They should not remain dry for extended periods, however. Fertilizer should be reduced until growth resumes in spring, especially for plants grown in areas with short days or low light.

GROWING MEDIA: Plants may be mounted on tree-fern or cork slabs or potted in small pots filled with any open, fast-draining medium. Repotting is best done in early spring when new roots are growing.

MISCELLANEOUS NOTES: The bloom season shown in the climate table is based on collection reports.

Plant and Flower Information

PLANT SIZE AND TYPE: A 79 in. (200 cm) sympodial epiphyte. Plants are often smaller.

PSEUDOBULB: 71 in. (180 cm) long. The slender, reedlike stems are hard and shiny. They emerge from a short, stout rhizome. The apex of each growth is leafy.

LEAVES: Many. The narrowly lanceolate leaves are 4–7 in. (10–18 cm) long. They taper toward the apex.

INFLORESCENCE: Short. Racemes emerge opposite the leaves on the upper portion of the stem. The blossoms are crowded together.

FLOWERS: 2 per inflorescence. The flowers are 0.8–1.2 in. (2–3 cm) across the lateral sepals. They may be white or pale yellow with bright green markings at the base of the column. The lip is somewhat wavy along the margin and recurved at the tip.

REFERENCES: 224, 226, 252, 353, 466.

PHOTOS/DRAWINGS: 466.

Dendrobium kratense Kerr

ORIGIN/HABITAT: Endemic to Thailand. Plants grow in the foothills of the southwestern peninsular region and the southeastern mainland. Habitat elevation was reported as less than 50 ft. (20 m).

CLIMATE: Station #48480, Chanthaburi, Thailand, Lat. 12.6°N, Long. 102.1°E, at 16 ft. (5 m). Record extreme temperatures are 103°F (39°C) and 48°F (9°C).

N/HEMISPHERE	JAN	FEB	MAR	APR	MAY	JUN	JUL	AUG	SEP	OCT	NOV	DEC
°F AVG MAX	91	92	92	93	91	88	87	87	87	89	89	88
°F AVG MIN	67	70	72	74	75	76	75	75	74	73	71	67
DIURNAL RANGE	24	22	20	19	16	12	12	12	13	16	18	21
RAIN/INCHES	0.8	1.4	2.7	4.8	12.4	19.3	19.3	17.9	19.6	9.9	2.8	0.5
HUMIDITY/%	71	75	78	80	85	86	86	87	88	84	77	71
BLOOM SEASON										*		
DAYS CLR @ 7AM	5	1	1	1	0	0	0	0	0	1	5	7
DAYS CLR @ 1PM	7	3	1	1	0	0	0	0	0	0	4	8
RAIN/MM	20	36	69	122	315	490	490	455	498	251	71	13
°C AVG MAX	32.8	33.3	33.3	33.9	32.8	31.1	30.6	30.6	30.6	31.7	31.7	31.1
°C AVG MIN	19.4	21.1	22.2	23.3	23.9	24.4	23.9	23.9	23.3	22.8	21.7	19.4
DIURNAL RANGE	13.4	12.2	11.1	10.6	8.9	6.7	6.7	6.7	7.3	8.9	10.0	11.7
S/HEMISPHERE	JUL	AUG	SEP	OCT	NOV	DEC	JAN	FEB	MAR	APR	MAY	JUN

Cultural Recommendations

LIGHT: 2000–3000 fc.

TEMPERATURES: Summer days average 87–88°F (31°C), and nights average 75–76°F (24°C), with a diurnal range of 12°F (7°C). The warmest season is spring, before the start of the summer rainy season. Spring days average 91–93°F (33–34°C), and nights average 72–75°F (22–24°C), with a diurnal range of 16–20°F (9–11°C)

HUMIDITY: Near 85% in summer and autumn, dropping to about 70% in winter.

WATER: Rainfall is very heavy for 6 months from late spring through autumn, but amounts are much lower for 2–3 months in winter. Cultivated plants should be kept moist from late spring to early autumn. Daily watering may be necessary during bright, hot weather. Water should be gradually reduced after new growths mature in autumn.

FERTILIZER: ¼–½ recommended strength, applied weekly. A high-nitrogen fertilizer is beneficial from spring to midsummer, but a fertilizer high in phosphates should be used in late summer and autumn.

REST PERIOD: Winter days average 88–92°F (31–33°C), and nights average 67–70°F (19–21°C), with a diurnal range of 21–24°F (12–13°C). In the habitat, rainfall is low for 2–3 months in winter, but considerable additional moisture is available from nightly deposits of dew. Water should be reduced for cultivated plants in winter. They should be allowed to become almost dry between waterings, but should never remain dry for long periods. Fertilizer should be reduced or eliminated until water is increased in spring. In the habitat, light is much higher in winter.

GROWING MEDIA: Plants may be mounted on tree-fern or cork slabs if humidity is high and plants are watered at least once daily in summer. When plants are potted, any open, fast-draining medium may be used. Repotting is best done in early spring when new roots are growing.

MISCELLANEOUS NOTES: The bloom season shown in the climate table is based on reports from the habitat.

Plant and Flower Information

PLANT SIZE AND TYPE: A 6 in. (15 cm) sympodial epiphyte.

PSEUDOBULB: 6 in. (15 cm) long. The stems are often shorter.

LEAVES: Few per stem. The leaves are 1.2–2.0 in. (3–5 cm) long.

INFLORESCENCE: Many. Inflorescences are carried from upper nodes, usually when some leaves are present.

FLOWERS: 4–6 per inflorescence. The white flowers are 0.4 in. (1 cm) across. The lip is narrow, deeply ruffled, and decorated with bright, grass-green veins. Sidelobes are absent or very small. Blossoms are fragrant.

REFERENCES: 224, 249, 266, 448, 454.

PHOTOS/DRAWINGS: 454.

Dendrobium kruiense J. J. Smith

ORIGIN/HABITAT: Sumatra. Plants were originally found at Liwa, near Kroie, in the Bengkulu district. Additional habitat information is unavailable, so the following climate data should be used with caution. Plants were cultivated at botanical garden in Bogor, Java.

CLIMATE: Station #96253, Bengkulu, Sumatra, Indonesia, Lat. 3.9°S, Long. 102.3°E, at 49 ft. (15 m). Record extreme temperatures are not available for this location.

N/HEMISPHERE	JAN	FEB	MAR	APR	MAY	JUN	JUL	AUG	SEP	OCT	NOV	DEC
°F AVG MAX	88	87	87	87	87	87	88	88	88	88	89	88
°F AVG MIN	72	72	72	73	73	73	73	72	73	74	73	73
DIURNAL RANGE	16	15	15	14	14	14	15	16	15	14	16	15
RAIN/INCHES	6.9	6.8	9.1	13.9	16.0	12.7	16.0	11.5	12.0	8.3	8.4	8.4
HUMIDITY/%	77	78	77	77	79	80	78	76	77	79	77	78
BLOOM SEASON	N/A											
DAYS CLR @ 7AM	5	1	1	1	0	0	2	1	1	1	2	3
DAYS CLR @ 1PM	5	4	3	1	2	3	2	2	2	3	7	5
RAIN/MM	176	173	231	354	405	322	407	291	304	211	215	213
°C AVG MAX	30.8	30.8	30.7	30.7	30.5	30.8	30.8	31.3	31.2	31.2	31.4	31.3
°C AVG MIN	22.1	22.0	22.3	22.6	22.7	22.7	22.7	22.5	22.8	23.2	23.1	22.6
DIURNAL RANGE	8.9	8.3	8.3	7.8	7.8	7.8	8.3	8.9	8.3	7.8	8.9	8.3
S/HEMISPHERE	JUL	AUG	SEP	OCT	NOV	DEC	JAN	FEB	MAR	APR	MAY	JUN

Cultural Recommendations

LIGHT: 2000–3000 fc.

TEMPERATURES: Throughout the year, days average 87–89°F (31°C), and nights average 72–74°F (22–23°C), with a diurnal range of 14–16°F (8–9°C).

HUMIDITY: 75–80% year-round.

WATER: Rainfall is heavy all year, but winter is slightly drier than summer. Cultivated plants should be kept moist but not soggy. Warm water may be beneficial.

FERTILIZER: ¼–½ recommended strength. A balanced fertilizer should be applied weekly to biweekly throughout the year.

REST PERIOD: Growing conditions should be maintained year-round. Water and fertilizer may be reduced somewhat in winter, especially for plants grown in the dark, short-day conditions common in temperate latitudes. They should never be allowed to dry out completely between waterings, however. In the habitat, light is highest in winter.

GROWING MEDIA: Plants may be mounted on tree-fern or cork slabs or potted in small pots filled with any open, fast-draining medium. Repotting may be done anytime new roots are growing.

MISCELLANEOUS NOTES: The plant was described in 1926 in *Bul. Jard. Bot. Buit.* 3rd sér. 8:56.

Plant and Flower Information

PLANT SIZE AND TYPE: A 22 in. (55 cm) sympodial epiphyte.

PSEUDOBULB: 22 in. (55 cm) long. The stems are clustered.

INFLORESCENCE: Short. Inflorescences emerge from nodes on leafless stems.

FLOWERS: 1 per inflorescence. The flowers are 1 in. (2.5 cm) across. They are white with a purplish suffusion on the dorsal sepal. The lip, which has a yellowish-green suffusion, is nearly equally trilobed at the apex.

REFERENCES: 224.

Dendrobium kryptocheilum A. Gilli

ORIGIN/HABITAT: Papua New Guinea. Plants were originally found in the hills north of Fatima at about 7200 ft. (2190 m).

CLIMATE: Station #200192, Garaina, Papua New Guinea, Lat. 7.9°S, Long. 147.1°E, at 2350 ft. (716 m). Temperatures are calculated for an elevation of 7200 ft. (2190 m), resulting in probable extremes of 78°F (26°C) and 30°F (−1°C).

N/HEMISPHERE	JAN	FEB	MAR	APR	MAY	JUN	JUL	AUG	SEP	OCT	NOV	DEC
°F AVG MAX	64	66	67	68	69	69	69	69	68	68	67	65
°F AVG MIN	47	47	47	48	47	48	49	49	49	48	48	47
DIURNAL RANGE	17	19	20	20	22	21	20	20	19	20	19	18
RAIN/INCHES	5.8	6.5	8.7	11.1	11.8	11.9	8.9	11.7	11.5	9.9	7.7	5.2
HUMIDITY/%	84	82	82	81	80	80	81	81	82	83	84	84
BLOOM SEASON								*				
DAYS CLR	N/A											
RAIN/MM	147	165	221	282	300	302	226	297	292	251	196	132
°C AVG MAX	17.8	18.9	19.4	20.0	20.6	20.6	20.6	20.6	20.0	20.0	19.4	18.3
°C AVG MIN	8.3	8.3	8.3	8.9	8.3	8.9	9.4	9.4	9.4	8.9	8.9	8.3
DIURNAL RANGE	9.5	10.6	11.1	11.1	12.3	11.7	11.2	11.2	10.6	11.1	10.5	10.0
S/HEMISPHERE	JUL	AUG	SEP	OCT	NOV	DEC	JAN	FEB	MAR	APR	MAY	JUN

Cultural Recommendations

LIGHT: 2000–3000 fc.

TEMPERATURES: Throughout the year, days average 64–69°F (18–21°C), and nights average 47–49°F (8–9°C), with a diurnal range of 17–22°F (10–12°C).

HUMIDITY: 80–85% year-round.

WATER: Rainfall is heavy all year, but conditions are slightly drier in winter. Cultivated plants should be kept moist but not soggy.

FERTILIZER: ¼–½ recommended strength. A balanced fertilizer should be applied weekly to biweekly throughout the year.

REST PERIOD: Growing conditions should be maintained all year. In the habitat, rainfall is slightly lower in winter. Water and fertilizer should be reduced somewhat for cultivated plants, especially those grown in the dark, short-day conditions common during temperate-latitude winters. They should never be allowed to dry out completely, however. In the habitat, seasonal light variation is minor.

GROWING MEDIA: Plants may be mounted on tree-fern or cork slabs or potted in small pots filled with any open, fast-draining medium. Repotting may be done anytime new roots are growing.

MISCELLANEOUS NOTES: The bloom season shown in the climate table is based on reports from the habitat.

Plant and Flower Information

PLANT SIZE AND TYPE: A 20 in. (50 cm) sympodial epiphyte.

PSEUDOBULB: 20 in. (50 cm) long. The grooved stems do not branch.

LEAVES: The broadly lanceolate leaves are about 3.5 in. (9 cm) long.

INFLORESCENCE: 4 in. (10 cm) long. The curved racemes emerge laterally from the side of the stem.

FLOWERS: 8–10 per inflorescence. The flowers are 0.4 in. (1 cm) long. On the front side, the ovate-lanceolate sepals and lanceolate petals are yellow with obscure red stripes. The backside is green with a dark purplish suffusion. The lip midlobe is notched at the apex and decorated with red stripes. The small sidelobes are marked with red dots.

REFERENCES: 146, 234.

PHOTOS/DRAWINGS: 146.

Dendrobium kuhlii (Blume) Lindley

AKA: *Pedilonum kuhlii* Blume, *D. thyrsodes* Rchb. f.

ORIGIN/HABITAT: Western Java. Plants grow in open, mossy forests along ridge tops on Mt. Gede at 2500–8200 ft. (760–2500 m). *D. kuhlii* grows with but is less common than *D. hasseltii* (Blume) Lindley not Rchb. f.

CLIMATE: Station #96755, Bogor, Indonesia, Lat. 6.5°S, Long. 106.8°E, at 558 ft. (170 m). Temperatures are calculated for an elevation of 5000 ft. (1520 m), resulting in probable extremes of 81°F (27°C) and 51°F (11°C).

N/HEMISPHERE	JAN	FEB	MAR	APR	MAY	JUN	JUL	AUG	SEP	OCT	NOV	DEC
°F AVG MAX	71	72	73	73	72	70	69	69	70	71	72	71
°F AVG MIN	58	58	58	59	59	59	59	59	59	60	60	59
DIURNAL RANGE	13	14	15	14	13	11	10	10	11	11	12	12
RAIN/INCHES	2.1	1.0	0.5	5.0	8.1	18.8	23.7	20.2	14.4	12.0	11.9	3.4
HUMIDITY/%	72	68	65	66	74	79	84	84	81	79	77	75
BLOOM SEASON				*	*	*						
DAYS CLR @ 7AM	14	14	14	11	5	3	1	2	4	6	10	12
DAYS CLR @ 1PM	9	10	8	5	1	1	0	0	1	1	3	7
RAIN/MM	53	25	13	127	206	478	602	513	366	305	302	86
°C AVG MAX	21.9	22.4	23.0	23.0	22.4	21.3	20.7	20.7	21.3	21.9	22.4	21.9
°C AVG MIN	14.6	14.6	14.6	15.2	15.2	15.2	15.2	15.2	15.2	15.7	15.7	15.2
DIURNAL RANGE	7.3	7.8	8.4	7.8	7.2	6.1	5.5	5.5	6.1	6.2	6.7	6.7
S/HEMISPHERE	JUL	AUG	SEP	OCT	NOV	DEC	JAN	FEB	MAR	APR	MAY	JUN

Cultural Recommendations

LIGHT: 1200–2500 fc. Plants grow in deep shade and full sun. Clear summer days are rare, however, and light levels below 3000 fc are probably appropriate. Plants may require brighter morning light from autumn into spring. Also, the ridge-top habitat indicates that strong air movement may be very important for the overall plant health.

TEMPERATURES: Throughout the year, days average 69–73°F (21–23°C), and nights average 58–60°F (15–16°C), with a diurnal range of 10–15°F (6–8°C). The average lows vary only 2°F (1°C) all year. Plants may not tolerate hot summer weather or wide seasonal fluctuations.

HUMIDITY: 75–85% most of the year, dropping to near 65% in late winter and early spring.

WATER: Rainfall is very heavy from spring to autumn, but conditions are very dry for 2–3 months in winter. During the growing season, plants should never be allowed to dry out completely, but water should be gradually reduced in late autumn.

FERTILIZER: ¼–½ recommended strength, applied weekly. A high-nitrogen fertilizer is beneficial from spring to midsummer, but a fertilizer high in phosphates should be used in late summer and autumn.

REST PERIOD: Growing conditions should be maintained all year, but rainfall is very low for 2–3 winter months. In cultivation, water should be reduced and the plants allowed to become somewhat dry between waterings. They should not remain dry for prolonged periods, however. Fertilizer may be reduced or eliminated anytime the plant is not actively growing. In the habitat, light is highest in winter.

GROWING MEDIA: Mounting plants on tree-fern or cork slabs accommodates their pendulous growth habit. However, humidity must be high and plants must be watered at least once a day in summer. If plants cannot be mounted, small pots or hanging baskets may be filled with an open, fast-draining medium. Repotting may be done anytime new roots are actively growing.

MISCELLANEOUS NOTES: The bloom season shown in the climate table is based on reports from the habitat.

Plant and Flower Information

PLANT SIZE AND TYPE: A 39 in. (100 cm) sympodial epiphyte, but cultivated plants may be smaller.

PSEUDOBULB: 39 in. (100 cm) long. The curved, pendent stems are many angled. They are densely covered with leaves.

LEAVES: Many. The lanceolate leaves are 1.6–2.4 in. (4–6 cm) long, thin, and deciduous.

INFLORESCENCE: Short. Usually 3 inflorescences emerge from nodes near the apex of leafless, mature stems.

FLOWERS: 3–12 per inflorescence. The flowers are 1 in. (2.5 cm) long. Often intensely colored, blossoms may be pale or deep violet-red with darker veins or longitudinal lines. Lateral sepals are more than twice the length of the very small dorsal sepal and petals. The lip is marked with a square orange blotch. The long spur is slender and curved.

REFERENCES: 25, 73, 75, 180, 190, 216, 254, 277, 310, 317, 445, 469.

PHOTOS/DRAWINGS: *73, 75.*

Dendrobium kunstleri Hooker f. Now considered a synonym of *Flickingeria fimbriata* (Blume) A. Hawkes. REFERENCES: 202, 213, 218, 220, 230, 231, 254, 286, 295, 394, 395, 424, 436, 445, 449, 469, 536.

Dendrobium kuyperi J. J. Smith

ORIGIN/HABITAT: Indonesia in Palembang, Sumatra. No additional habitat information or elevation was given, so the following climate data should be used with caution.

CLIMATE: Station #96221, Palembang, Sumatra, Indonesia, Lat. 2.9°S, Long. 104.7°E, at 33 ft. (10 m). Record extreme temperatures are not available for this location.

N/HEMISPHERE	JAN	FEB	MAR	APR	MAY	JUN	JUL	AUG	SEP	OCT	NOV	DEC
°F AVG MAX	89	89	90	90	88	87	86	87	88	89	89	89
°F AVG MIN	74	74	74	74	74	74	74	74	74	75	76	75
DIURNAL RANGE	15	15	16	16	14	13	12	13	14	14	13	14
RAIN/INCHES	3.8	4.1	4.3	8.0	11.1	12.7	11.3	9.7	12.2	11.2	7.2	4.8
HUMIDITY/%	79	76	73	76	78	81	81	81	81	80	80	79
BLOOM SEASON	N/A											
DAYS CLR @ 7AM	3	2	2	2	1	1	1	0	1	2	2	3
DAYS CLR @ 1PM	1	1	1	0	0	0	0	0	0	0	0	1
RAIN/MM	97	104	109	203	282	323	287	246	310	284	183	122
°C AVG MAX	31.4	31.8	32.1	32.0	31.4	30.5	30.1	30.7	31.3	31.6	31.4	31.8
°C AVG MIN	23.3	23.1	23.1	23.4	23.5	23.5	23.5	23.4	23.4	24.0	24.4	23.8
DIURNAL RANGE	8.1	8.7	9.0	8.5	7.9	7.0	6.6	7.3	7.9	7.6	7.0	8.1
S/HEMISPHERE	JUL	AUG	SEP	OCT	NOV	DEC	JAN	FEB	MAR	APR	MAY	JUN

Cultural Recommendations

LIGHT: 2000–3000 fc.

TEMPERATURES: Throughout the year, days average 87–90°F (31–32°C), and nights average 74–76°F (23–24°C), with a diurnal range of 12–16°F (7–9°C).

Dendrobium kwangtungense

HUMIDITY: Near 80% most of the year, dropping to about 75% in late winter and early spring.

WATER: Rainfall is moderate to heavy most of the year. Conditions are slightly drier in winter, but cultivated plants should be kept moist year-round.

FERTILIZER: ¼–½ recommended strength. A balanced fertilizer should be applied weekly to biweekly throughout the year.

REST PERIOD: Growing conditions should be maintained all year. Water should be reduced somewhat for cultivated plants in winter, especially those grown in the dark, short-day conditions common in temperate latitudes. Plants should dry slightly between waterings but should not be allowed to dry out completely. Fertilizer should be reduced if water is reduced. In the habitat, light is higher in winter.

GROWING MEDIA: Plants may be mounted on tree-fern or cork slabs or potted in small pots filled with any open, fast-draining medium. Repotting may be done anytime new roots are growing.

MISCELLANEOUS NOTES: The plant was described in 1914 in *Bul. Jard. Bot. Buit.* 2nd sér. 13:10.

Plant and Flower Information

PLANT SIZE AND TYPE: An 8–10 in. (20–25 cm) sympodial epiphyte.

PSEUDOBULB: 8–10 in. (20–25 cm) long. The shiny, flattened stems emerge from a short, creeping rhizome. They may be erect, ascending, or pendent. The lower part of the stem is exceptionally leafy, but the upper part has only rudimentary leaves.

LEAVES: Many. The linear-lanceolate leaves are 1.6–2.0 in. (4–5 cm) long and laterally compressed. They are rigid, fleshy, and curved along the upper surface.

INFLORESCENCE: Short. Inflorescences are borne at nodes on the upper part of the stem.

FLOWERS: 1 per inflorescence. The yellowish flowers are 0.4 in. (1 cm) across. The sepals, which have purple stripes on the backs, are somewhat triangular. Petals are linear-lanceolate. The curved, concave lip is incurved along the apical margin. It is yellow with purple stripes. The delicate blossoms are fragrant.

REFERENCES: 221.

Dendrobium kwangtungense Tso. See *D. wilsonii* Rolfe.
REFERENCES: 208, 225, 528.

Dendrobium kwashotense Hayata. See *D. crumenatum* Swartz.
REFERENCES: 61, 67, 193, 208, 221, 279, 445, 454, 504, 580.

Dendrobium labangense J. J. Smith. Sometimes spelled *D. labangensis,* it is now considered a synonym of *Flickingeria labangense* (J. J. Smith) J. J. Wood. REFERENCES: 213, 222, 230, 235, 286, 449.

Dendrobium labuanum Lindley. Now considered a synonym of *Epigeneium labuanum* (Lindley) Summerhayes. REFERENCES: 216, 229, 254, 278, 286, 310, 394, 449, 499.

Dendrobium laceratum Schlechter

ORIGIN/HABITAT: Northeastern Papua New Guinea. Plants grow on forest trees of the Maboro Range in the Waria District at about 3950 ft. (1200 m).

CLIMATE: Station #200192, Garaina, Papua New Guinea, Lat. 7.9°S, Long. 147.1°E, at 2350 ft. (716 m). Temperatures are calculated for an elevation of 3950 ft. (1200 m), resulting in probable extremes of 89°F (32°C) and 41°F (5°C).

N/HEMISPHERE	JAN	FEB	MAR	APR	MAY	JUN	JUL	AUG	SEP	OCT	NOV	DEC
°F AVG MAX	75	77	78	79	80	80	80	80	79	79	78	76
°F AVG MIN	58	58	58	59	58	59	60	60	60	59	59	58
DIURNAL RANGE	17	19	20	20	22	21	20	20	19	20	19	18
RAIN/INCHES	5.8	6.5	8.7	11.1	11.8	11.9	8.9	11.7	11.5	9.9	7.7	5.2
HUMIDITY/%	84	82	82	81	80	80	81	81	82	83	84	84
BLOOM SEASON												*
DAYS CLR	N/A											
RAIN/MM	147	165	221	282	300	302	226	297	292	251	196	132
°C AVG MAX	23.8	24.9	25.4	26.0	26.5	26.5	26.5	26.5	26.0	26.0	25.4	24.3
°C AVG MIN	14.3	14.3	14.3	14.9	14.3	14.9	15.4	15.4	15.4	14.9	14.9	14.3
DIURNAL RANGE	9.5	10.6	11.1	11.1	12.2	11.6	11.1	11.1	10.6	11.1	10.5	10.0
S/HEMISPHERE	JUL	AUG	SEP	OCT	NOV	DEC	JAN	FEB	MAR	APR	MAY	JUN

Cultural Recommendations

LIGHT: 2000–3000 fc.

TEMPERATURES: Throughout the year, days average 75–80°F (24–27°C), and nights average 58–60°F (14–15°C), with a diurnal range of 17–22°F (10–12°C).

HUMIDITY: 80–85% year-round.

WATER: Rainfall is heavy all year, but conditions are slightly drier in winter. Cultivated plants should be kept moist but not soggy.

FERTILIZER: ¼–½ recommended strength. A balanced fertilizer should be applied weekly to biweekly throughout the year. The Royal Botanic Garden in Edinburgh uses a seaweed based fertilizer for high elevation plants from New Guinea.

REST PERIOD: Growing conditions should be maintained all year. In the habitat, rainfall is slightly lower in winter. Water and fertilizer should be reduced somewhat for cultivated plants, especially those grown in the dark, short-day conditions common during temperate-latitude winters. They should never be allowed to dry out completely, however. In the habitat, seasonal light variation is minor.

GROWING MEDIA: Plants may be mounted on tree-fern or cork slabs if humidity is high and plants are watered at least once daily in summer. When plants are potted, any open, fast-draining medium may be used. Repotting may be done anytime new roots are growing.

MISCELLANEOUS NOTES: The bloom season shown in the climate table is based on collection reports. Plants that produce flowers which last a single day commonly bloom several times during the year. Flowering usually occurs 7–14 days after a sudden 10°F (5°C) drop in daytime temperatures.

Plant and Flower Information

PLANT SIZE AND TYPE: A 16–20 in. (40–50 cm) sympodial epiphyte. The growth habit is described as similar to *D. camaridiorum* Rchb. f. from New Caledonia.

PSEUDOBULB: 16–20 in. (40–50 cm) long. The leafy growths emerge from a very short rhizome.

LEAVES: Many. The leaves are 2.8–4.0 in. (7–10 cm) long, linear, pointed, and smooth.

INFLORESCENCE: Short.

FLOWERS: 2 per inflorescence. The flowers are 1 in. (2.5 cm) long. They are yellowish white with orange-yellow at the tip of the column. The elongated sepals and petals are very narrow. The 3-lobed lip is lacerated along the front margin of the midlobe and toothed near the back. Blossoms last a single day.

REFERENCES: 221, 437, 445.

PHOTOS/DRAWINGS: 437.

Dendrobium laciniosum Ridley. Now considered a synonym of *Flickingeria laciniosa* (Ridley) A. Hawkes. REFERENCES: 179, 200, 213, 220, 230, 231, 254, 395, 449, 455. PHOTOS/DRAWINGS: 200.

Dendrobium lacteum Kränzlin

ORIGIN/HABITAT: Papua New Guinea. Plants grow near Port Praslin on New Ireland Island (New Mecklenburg).

CLIMATE: Station #94085, Rabul, New Britain Is., Papua New Guinea, Lat. 4.2°S, Long. 152.2°E, at 28 ft. (9 m). Record extreme temperatures are 100°F (38°C) and 65°F (18°C).

N/HEMISPHERE	JAN	FEB	MAR	APR	MAY	JUN	JUL	AUG	SEP	OCT	NOV	DEC
°F AVG MAX	89	89	91	92	91	90	90	90	90	90	90	90
°F AVG MIN	73	72	73	73	73	73	73	73	73	73	73	73
DIURNAL RANGE	16	17	18	19	18	17	17	17	17	17	17	17
RAIN/INCHES	5.4	3.7	3.5	5.1	7.1	10.1	14.8	10.4	10.2	10.0	5.2	3.3
HUMIDITY/%	74	73	69	70	73	76	77	76	77	77	75	74
BLOOM SEASON						*						
DAYS CLR	N/A											
RAIN/MM	137	94	89	130	180	257	376	264	259	254	132	84
°C AVG MAX	31.7	31.7	32.8	33.3	32.8	32.2	32.2	32.2	32.2	32.2	32.2	32.2
°C AVG MIN	22.8	22.2	22.8	22.8	22.8	22.8	22.8	22.8	22.8	22.8	22.8	22.8
DIURNAL RANGE	8.9	9.5	10.0	10.5	10.0	9.4	9.4	9.4	9.4	9.4	9.4	9.4
S/HEMISPHERE	JUL	AUG	SEP	OCT	NOV	DEC	JAN	FEB	MAR	APR	MAY	JUN

Cultural Recommendations

LIGHT: 2500–3000 fc.

TEMPERATURES: Throughout the year, days average 89–92°F (32–33°C), and nights average 72–73°F (22–23°C), with a diurnal range of 16–19°F (9–11°C).

HUMIDITY: Near 75% most of the year, dropping to near 70% in late winter and early spring. Humidity usually rises to 90–100% at night, but during the dry season, it may drop to as low as 35% in midday.

WATER: Rainfall is moderate to heavy most of the year, but conditions are slightly drier for 2 months in late winter. Cultivated plants should be kept moist in spring and summer, but water should be gradually reduced in autumn.

FERTILIZER: ¼–½ recommended strength. A balanced fertilizer should be applied weekly to biweekly throughout the year.

REST PERIOD: Growing conditions should be maintained all year. Water and fertilizer should be reduced somewhat in winter. Plants should dry slightly between waterings, but they should never be allowed to dry completely. In the habitat, light may be slightly higher in winter.

GROWING MEDIA: Plants may be mounted on tree-fern or cork slabs if humidity is high and plants are watered at least once daily in summer. When plants are potted, any open, fast-draining medium may be used. Repotting may be done anytime new roots are growing.

MISCELLANEOUS NOTES: The bloom season shown in the climate table is based on reports from the habitat. Plants that produce flowers which last a single day commonly bloom several times during the year. Flowering usually occurs 7–14 days after a sudden 10°F (5°C) drop in daytime temperatures.

Plant and Flower Information

PLANT SIZE AND TYPE: A 20 in. (50 cm) sympodial epiphyte.

PSEUDOBULB: 20 in. (50 cm) long. The densely clustered stems are obscurely quadrangular. The apex of each stem has about 3 leaves.

LEAVES: Few. The stalked, pointed leaves are papery.

FLOWERS: 2–3 per inflorescence. The flowers are 2 in. (5 cm) long. They are milk-white with yellow-orange markings on the oblong lip. The disc is marked with radiating, elevated lines. Blossoms last a single day.

REFERENCES: 218, 253, 254, 437.

Dendrobium lactiflorum (Schlechter) J. J. Smith. Although not correctly transferred, Schlechter (ref. 443) considered this plant to be a synonym of *Cadetia lactiflora* Schlechter. REFERENCES: 223, 225, 443, 486.

Dendrobium lacustre Schlechter

AKA: *D. conostalix* Kränzlin not Rchb. f.

ORIGIN/HABITAT: Endemic to Sulawesi (Celebes). Plants grow in the central section on the south shore of Lake Poso. Habitat elevation is estimated based on topographical maps of the region, so the following temperatures should be used with caution.

CLIMATE: Station #97096, Poso, Sulawesi, Indonesia, Lat. 1.4°S, Long. 120.7°E, at 7 ft. (2 m). Temperatures are calculated for an estimated elevation of 2000 ft. (610 m). Record extreme temperatures are not available for this location.

N/HEMISPHERE	JAN	FEB	MAR	APR	MAY	JUN	JUL	AUG	SEP	OCT	NOV	DEC
°F AVG MAX	80	81	81	81	80	79	79	79	80	79	80	81
°F AVG MIN	67	68	66	68	69	68	68	68	67	68	69	68
DIURNAL RANGE	13	13	15	13	11	11	11	11	13	11	11	13
RAIN/INCHES	5.9	4.0	2.7	5.6	7.2	5.6	6.3	6.9	8.4	7.5	9.2	4.8
HUMIDITY/%	N/A											
BLOOM SEASON							*					
DAYS CLR	N/A											
RAIN/MM	150	102	69	142	183	142	160	175	213	190	234	122
°C AVG MAX	26.9	27.5	27.5	27.5	26.9	26.3	26.3	26.3	26.9	26.3	26.9	27.5
°C AVG MIN	19.7	20.2	19.1	20.2	20.8	20.2	20.2	20.2	19.7	20.2	20.8	20.2
DIURNAL RANGE	7.2	7.3	8.4	7.3	6.1	6.1	6.1	6.1	7.2	6.1	6.1	7.3
S/HEMISPHERE	JUL	AUG	SEP	OCT	NOV	DEC	JAN	FEB	MAR	APR	MAY	JUN

Cultural Recommendations

LIGHT: 2500–3500 fc.

TEMPERATURES: Throughout the year, days average 79–81°F (26–28°C), and nights average 66–69°F (19–21°C), with a diurnal range of 11–15°F (6–8°C).

HUMIDITY: Information is not available for this location. However, records from nearby locations indicate that humidity probably averages 75–85% year-round.

WATER: Rainfall is moderate to heavy all year, but conditions are slightly drier for about a month in late winter. Cultivated plants should be kept evenly moist.

FERTILIZER: ¼–½ recommended strength. A balanced fertilizer should be applied weekly to biweekly throughout the year.

REST PERIOD: Growing conditions should be maintained all year. Water should be reduced somewhat in winter for cultivated plants, especially those grown in the dark, short-day conditions common in temperate latitudes. They should never be allowed to dry out completely, however. Fertilizer should be reduced or eliminated anytime water is reduced.

GROWING MEDIA: Plants may be mounted on tree-fern or cork slabs if humidity is high and plants are watered at least once daily in summer. When plants are potted, any open, fast-draining medium may be used. Repotting may be done anytime new roots are growing.

MISCELLANEOUS NOTES: The bloom season shown in the climate table is based on reports from the habitat.

Plant and Flower Information

PLANT SIZE AND TYPE: A 28–30 in. (70–75 cm) sympodial epiphyte, lithophyte, or terrestrial.

PSEUDOBULB: 28–30 in. (70–75 cm) long. The slender stems are erect and nearly woody.

LEAVES: The erect, linear leaves are 1.8–2.4 in. (4.5–6.0 cm) long. The leaf sheaths are hirsute and spotted. The 3-lobed lip has a large, slightly ruffled margin with 2 fleshy, parallel ridges, and small, pointed, triangular sidelobes.

INFLORESCENCE: Very short.

FLOWERS: 1–2 per inflorescence. The white flowers are 0.3 in. (0.7 cm) long and do not open fully. The sepals are pointed. The margins on the pointed petals are very slightly toothed.

REFERENCES: 223, 436.

Dendrobium laetum Schlechter. See *D. cuthbertsonii* F. Mueller. REFERENCES: 223, 385.

Dendrobium laevifolium Stapf

AKA: *D. occultum* Ames.

ORIGIN/HABITAT: Widespread on islands of the southwest Pacific. Plants grow on Bougainville, Guadalcanal, Santa Isabel, the Santa Cruz Islands, Vanuatu, and in Papua New Guinea on Rossel and Misima Islands in the Louisiade Archipelago. On Misima, plants grow on moss-covered branches, twigs, and rocks in areas with a dense groundcover of mosses, begonias, ferns, and small creepers. Collections were made on the steep ridge of a forested gully at about 3100 ft. (950 m). Reports from other parts of the habitat indicate that plants grow at 1200–7700 ft. (360–2340 m). They usually grow in thick moss near the base of trees, on moss covered saplings, or in deep lichen and moss on the trunks of elfin forest trees in areas normally saturated with cold mist or light rain with brief bursts of very hot sunshine.

CLIMATE: Station #91520, Honiara, Guadalcanal Island, Lat. 9.4°S, Long. 160.0°E, at 10 ft. (3 m). Temperatures are calculated for an elevation of 5000 ft. (1520 m), resulting in probable extremes of 79°F (26°C) and 49°F (9°C).

N/HEMISPHERE	JAN	FEB	MAR	APR	MAY	JUN	JUL	AUG	SEP	OCT	NOV	DEC
°F AVG MAX	70	71	72	72	72	72	72	72	71	72	72	71
°F AVG MIN	56	56	56	56	57	57	58	58	57	57	57	56
DIURNAL RANGE	14	15	16	16	15	15	14	14	14	15	15	15
RAIN/INCHES	6.0	4.4	4.6	7.7	7.7	9.5	14.1	13.3	16.7	10.6	8.1	6.7
HUMIDITY/%	84	82	81	80	81	82	83	83	87	85	85	85
BLOOM SEASON	*	*				*	*	*				*
DAYS CLR @ 5AM	6	7	7	5	6	4	3	3	4	4	8	7
DAYS CLR @ 11AM	3	2	2	1	1	1	0	2	2	4	4	4
RAIN/MM	152	112	117	196	196	241	358	338	424	269	206	170
°C AVG MAX	21.1	21.7	22.2	22.2	22.2	22.2	22.4	22.3	21.7	22.2	22.2	21.7
°C AVG MIN	13.3	13.1	13.1	13.1	13.6	13.6	14.2	14.2	13.6	13.6	13.6	13.1
DIURNAL RANGE	7.8	8.6	9.1	9.1	8.6	8.8	8.1	8.0	8.1	8.6	8.6	8.6
S/HEMISPHERE	JUL	AUG	SEP	OCT	NOV	DEC	JAN	FEB	MAR	APR	MAY	JUN

Cultural Recommendations

LIGHT: 2000–3000 fc.

TEMPERATURES: Throughout the year, days average 70–72°F (21–22°C), and nights average 56–58°F (13–14°C), with a diurnal range of 14–16°F (8–9°C). Because plants are found over a wide range of elevation, they should adapt to conditions 6–8°F (3–4°C) warmer or cooler than indicated.

HUMIDITY: 80–85% year-round.

WATER: Rainfall is heavy all year, but conditions are slightly drier for 2–3 months in winter. Cultivated plants should be kept moist but not soggy.

FERTILIZER: 1/4–1/2 recommended strength. A balanced fertilizer should be applied weekly to biweekly throughout the year.

REST PERIOD: Growing conditions should be maintained all year. Water may be reduced somewhat for plants cultivated in the dark, short-day conditions common in temperate-latitude winters. They should never be allowed to dry out completely, however.

GROWING MEDIA: Plants may be mounted on tree-fern or cork slabs if humidity is high and plants are watered at least once daily in summer. When plants are potted, any open, fast-draining medium may be used. Repotting may be done anytime new roots are growing.

MISCELLANEOUS NOTES: The bloom season shown in the climate table is based on cultivation records. Growers indicate that *D. laevifolium* is easy to grow and flower, providing it is never allowed to dry out.

Plant and Flower Information

PLANT SIZE AND TYPE: A 1.2–7.0 in. (3–18 cm) sympodial epiphyte.

PSEUDOBULB: 0.4–2.0 in. (1–5 cm) long. The stems may be club-shaped or taper at each end. They arise from a very short rhizome.

LEAVES: 2. Rarely a third very small leaf may be present. The deciduous, linear leaves are 2.4–6.0 in. (6–15 cm) long. They vary from medium- to deep-green and may be suffused with purple along the midline and margins.

INFLORESCENCE: Short. The nearly stemless flowers arise from the apex or upper nodes of leafless stems. In nature, the blossoms tend to be hidden in the moss where the plants grow.

FLOWERS: 1–2, rarely 4 per inflorescence. The flowers are 0.8–1.8 in. (2.0–4.5 cm) long. Color is variable. Sepals and petals are usually cream, frequently overlaid with mauve or other shades of red, purple, or pink. The lip is most often a paler shade of the same color, but on rare occasions, it may be a contrasting orange. Blossom resemble an open fan. Plants from the Santa Cruz Islands produce blossoms with a yellow margin on the lip.

REFERENCES: 17, 95, 179, 210, 223, 269, 270, 271, 305, 385, 445, 516, 526, 556.

PHOTOS/DRAWINGS: 210, *269, 270, 271, 385, 519.*

Dendrobium lagarum Seidenfaden

ORIGIN/HABITAT: Northeastern Thailand. Habitat elevation is unavailable, so the following temperatures should be used with caution.

CLIMATE: Station #48354, Udon Thani, Thailand, Lat. 17.4°N, Long. 102.8°E, at 585 ft. (178 m). Record extreme temperatures are 111°F (44°C) and 37°F (3°C).

N/HEMISPHERE	JAN	FEB	MAR	APR	MAY	JUN	JUL	AUG	SEP	OCT	NOV	DEC
°F AVG MAX	87	91	96	98	94	92	91	90	89	89	88	86
°F AVG MIN	57	63	69	74	75	76	75	75	75	71	65	59
DIURNAL RANGE	30	28	27	24	19	16	16	15	14	18	23	27
RAIN/INCHES	0.3	0.8	1.5	3.8	8.8	8.6	7.8	9.7	10.4	3.5	0.6	0.2
HUMIDITY/%	63	64	62	63	74	78	78	81	81	76	71	66
BLOOM SEASON	N/A											
DAYS CLR @ 7AM	1	2	1	2	2	1	1	0	1	5	4	3
DAYS CLR @ 1PM	16	10	8	7	2	0	0	0	1	5	9	13
RAIN/MM	8	20	38	97	224	218	198	246	264	89	15	5
°C AVG MAX	30.6	32.8	35.6	36.7	34.4	33.3	32.8	32.2	31.7	31.7	31.1	30.0
°C AVG MIN	13.9	17.2	20.6	23.3	23.9	24.4	23.9	23.9	23.9	21.7	18.3	15.0
DIURNAL RANGE	16.7	15.6	15.0	13.4	10.5	8.9	8.9	8.3	7.8	10.0	12.8	15.0
S/HEMISPHERE	JUL	AUG	SEP	OCT	NOV	DEC	JAN	FEB	MAR	APR	MAY	JUN

Cultural Recommendations

LIGHT: 2000–3000 fc. The heavy summer cloud cover indicates that some shading is needed from spring through autumn, but light should be as high as the plant can tolerate, short of burning the leaves.

TEMPERATURES: Summer days average 90–92°F (32–33°C), and nights average 75–76°F (24°C), with a diurnal range of 15–16°F (8–9°C). The warmest temperatures occur in spring. Days average 94–98°F (34–37°C), and nights average 69–75°F (21–24°C), with a diurnal range of 19–27°F (11–15°C).

HUMIDITY: Near 80% in summer, dropping to 60–65% in winter and early spring.

WATER: Rainfall is heavy from late spring to early autumn. The rainy season is followed by 4–5 very dry winter months. Cultivated plants should be kept evenly moist while actively growing, but water should be gradually reduced in autumn after new growths mature.

FERTILIZER: 1/4–1/2 recommended strength, applied weekly. A high-nitrogen fertilizer is beneficial from spring to midsummer, but a fertilizer high in phosphates should be used in late summer and autumn.

REST PERIOD: Winter days average 86–91°F (30–33°C), and nights average 57–63°F (14–17°C), with a diurnal range of 27–30°F (15–17°C). In the habitat, winter rainfall is low, but additional moisture is available from dew and as mist from fog and low clouds. In cultivation, water should be reduced. Plants should be allowed to dry out between waterings but should not remain completely dry for extended periods. Occasional early morning mistings on sunny mornings between waterings may be beneficial and keep the plants from becoming too dry. Fertilizer should be eliminated until water is increased in spring. In the habitat, light is highest in winter and spring.

GROWING MEDIA: Plants may be mounted on tree-fern or cork slabs if humidity is high and plants are watered at least once daily in summer. When plants are potted, any open, fast-draining medium may be used. Repotting is best done in early spring when new roots are growing.

MISCELLANEOUS NOTES: Plants are unlikely to be available for cultivation.

Plant and Flower Information

PLANT SIZE AND TYPE: A 14–20 in. (35–50 cm) sympodial epiphyte.

PSEUDOBULB: 14–20 in. (35–50 cm) long. The apical and basal portions of the tightly clustered stems are leafless. The lower part of the stem is covered by grayish sheaths, but the thin upper stem is dull green with brownish sheaths. Stems are not swollen during the dry season.

LEAVES: 4–6 per growth. The widely spaced, terete leaves are 2–3 in. (5–8 cm) long.

INFLORESCENCE: Short. Inflorescences emerge at nodes near the apex of the stem.

FLOWERS: 1–4. The blooms open one at a time on each inflorescence. The flowers are 0.4–0.6 in. (1.0–1.5 cm) across and do not open fully. Sepals and petals are white with a purple tint on the outside. They are pointed and curl slightly at the tips. The lip is yellow-orange on the midline with many papillae, especially along the 3 median veins. The margin on the pointed midlobe and the front of the sidelobes is uneven.

REFERENCES: 234, 454.

PHOTOS/DRAWINGS: *454.*

Dendrobium lageniforme J. J. Smith. Now considered a synonym of *Diplocaulobium lageniforme* (J. J. Smith) Kränzlin. REFERENCES: 219, 220, 254, 445, 470.

Dendrobium lagorum P. van Royen

AKA: Seidenfaden (personal communication) indicates that this is no longer considered a *Dendrobium,* but no transfer was found.

Dendrobium lambii

ORIGIN/HABITAT: Endemic to Irian Jaya (western New Guinea). Plants were collected northeast of Lake Habbema, where they grew on a log in open, subalpine forest at about 10,170 ft. (3100 m).

CLIMATE: Station #97686, Wamena, Irian Jaya, Lat. 4.1°S, Long. 139.0°E at 5446 ft. (1660 m). Temperatures are calculated for an elevation of 10,000 ft. (3050 m). Record extreme temperatures are not available for this location.

N/HEMISPHERE	JAN	FEB	MAR	APR	MAY	JUN	JUL	AUG	SEP	OCT	NOV	DEC
°F AVG MAX	60	61	62	61	62	61	62	61	61	64	63	59
°F AVG MIN	45	45	47	47	48	49	48	47	48	50	50	46
DIURNAL RANGE	15	16	15	14	14	12	14	14	13	14	13	13
RAIN/INCHES	3.0	1.9	2.2	4.0	4.6	3.3	2.8	4.2	6.9	3.9	5.4	4.9
HUMIDITY/%	N/A											
BLOOM SEASON				*								
DAYS CLR	N/A											
RAIN/MM	76	48	56	102	117	84	71	107	175	99	137	124
°C AVG MAX	15.5	16.1	16.7	16.1	16.7	16.1	16.7	16.1	16.1	17.8	17.2	15.0
°C AVG MIN	7.2	7.2	8.3	8.3	8.9	9.4	8.9	8.3	8.9	10.0	10.0	7.8
DIURNAL RANGE	8.3	8.9	8.3	7.8	7.8	6.7	7.8	7.8	7.2	7.8	7.2	7.2
S/HEMISPHERE	JUL	AUG	SEP	OCT	NOV	DEC	JAN	FEB	MAR	APR	MAY	JUN

Cultural Recommendations.

LIGHT: 2000–2500 fc.

TEMPERATURES: Throughout the year, days average 59–62°F (15–17°C), and nights average 45–50°F (7–10°C), with a diurnal range of 12–16°F (7–9°C). In the habitat, the warmest temperatures of the day occur during late morning, when skies are usually clear. Clouds and mist develop near noon, thus preventing additional warming. Because of microclimate effects, actual maximum temperatures may be somewhat warmer than indicated. Reports from the habitat indicate a sharp contrast between day and night temperatures.

HUMIDITY: Information is not available for this location. However, records from nearby stations indicate that humidity probably averages near 80% year-round. High humidity and excellent air circulation are particularly important if temperatures are warm. Placing the plants in front of an evaporative cooler or near a fine mist may be very beneficial on especially warm days.

WATER: Rainfall is moderate through most of the year. In the higher-elevation habitat, rainfall amounts may be greater than indicated in the climate table. In addition, large amounts of water are available from mist and heavy dew, even during periods of reduced rainfall. Cultivated plants should be kept moist, with only slight drying allowed between waterings. They should be misted several times daily on the hottest days, but the foliage should always be dry before evening. Good air movement is critically important and should be maintained at all times.

FERTILIZER: ¼–½ recommended strength. A balanced fertilizer should be applied weekly to biweekly throughout the year. The Royal Botanic Garden in Edinburgh uses a seaweed-based fertilizer for plants from this habitat.

REST PERIOD: Growing conditions should be maintained all year. Rainfall averages are somewhat lower for a month or so in winter and again in midsummer. In cultivation, water may be decreased, but plants should never be allowed to dry out completely. In the habitat, light is slightly higher in winter.

GROWING MEDIA: Plants may be mounted on tree-fern or cork slabs if humidity is high and plants are watered at least once daily in summer. When plants are potted, any open, fast-draining medium may be used. Repotting may be done anytime new roots are growing.

MISCELLANEOUS NOTES: The bloom season shown in the climate table is based on reports in the habitat.

Plant and Flower Information

PLANT SIZE AND TYPE: A 1.2–1.8 in. (3.0–4.6 cm) sympodial epiphyte.

PSEUDOBULB: 0.3–0.6 in. (0.8–1.4 cm) long. The smooth, cylindrical stems are tightly clustered.

LEAVES: 1 per growth. The erect leaves are 0.6–0.7 in. (1.5–1.8 cm) long. They are V-shaped in cross-section with extremely rolled margins.

INFLORESCENCE: 1.6–4.0 in. (4–10 cm) long. 1 or 2 inflorescences are produced at the apex of the pseudobulb.

FLOWERS: 1 per inflorescence. The erect, white flowers are 0.2–0.3 in. (0.6–0.7 cm) long. They are shaped like a flared tube. The tips of the ovate sepals and petals are curled. The 3-lobed lip is uneven and slightly ruffled along the margin with a deep, wide notch at the apex of the midlobe and smaller notches on the side of the midlobe. The center of the midlobe has a raised, V-shaped area.

REFERENCES: 233, 538.

PHOTOS/DRAWINGS: 538.

Dendrobium lambii J. J. Wood

ORIGIN/HABITAT: Sabah, Borneo. Plants were collected from a ridge on Mt. Alab above Sinsuron, along the crest of the Crocker Range. They grow on *Dacrydium* in lightly moss-covered forests at 5250–5900 ft. (1600–1800 m).

CLIMATE: Station #49613, Tambunan, Sabah (North Borneo), Lat. 5.7°N, Long. 116.4°E, at 1200 ft. (366 m). Temperatures are calculated for an elevation of 5400 ft. (1640 m), resulting in probable extremes of 85°F (30°C) and 42°F (5°C).

N/HEMISPHERE	JAN	FEB	MAR	APR	MAY	JUN	JUL	AUG	SEP	OCT	NOV	DEC
°F AVG MAX	73	74	76	77	77	76	76	76	76	75	74	73
°F AVG MIN	54	52	53	54	55	54	53	53	54	54	54	55
DIURNAL RANGE	19	22	23	23	22	22	23	23	22	21	20	18
RAIN/INCHES	5.8	3.7	5.8	7.5	8.2	7.3	5.1	4.9	6.4	7.0	6.8	6.0
HUMIDITY/%	N/A											
BLOOM SEASON			*	*								
DAYS CLR	N/A											
RAIN/MM	147	94	147	190	208	185	130	124	163	178	173	152
°C AVG MAX	23.0	23.6	24.7	25.3	25.3	24.7	24.7	24.7	24.7	24.1	23.6	23.0
°C AVG MIN	12.5	11.4	11.9	12.5	13.0	12.5	11.9	11.9	12.5	12.5	12.5	13.0
DIURNAL RANGE	10.5	12.2	12.8	12.8	12.3	12.2	12.8	12.8	12.2	11.6	11.1	10.0
S/HEMISPHERE	JUL	AUG	SEP	OCT	NOV	DEC	JAN	FEB	MAR	APR	MAY	JUN

Cultural Recommendations

LIGHT: 2000–2500 fc.

TEMPERATURES: Throughout the year, days average 73–77°F (23–25°C), and nights average 52–55°F (11–13°C), with a diurnal range of 18–23°F (10–13°C). Plants are unlikely to tolerate hot weather, as the probable extreme high is 85°F (30°C).

HUMIDITY: 75–80% year-round.

WATER: Rainfall is moderate to heavy through the year. Cultivated plants should be kept moist, with only slight drying allowed between waterings.

FERTILIZER: ¼–½ recommended strength. A balanced fertilizer should be applied weekly to biweekly throughout the year.

REST PERIOD: Growing conditions vary only slightly through the year. The diurnal range is slightly lower in winter due to somewhat cooler days. In cultivation, water should be reduced somewhat in winter, especially for plants grown in the dark, short-day conditions common in temperate latitudes. Plants should never be allowed to dry out completely, however. Fertilizer should be decreased when water is reduced and when plants are not actively growing.

GROWING MEDIA: Plants may be mounted on tree-fern or cork slabs if humidity is high and plants are watered at least once daily in summer. When plants are potted, any open, fast-draining medium may be used. Repotting may be done anytime new roots are growing.

MISCELLANEOUS NOTES: The bloom season shown in the climate table is based on collection reports.

Plant and Flower Information

PLANT SIZE AND TYPE: A 26 in. (65 cm) sympodial epiphyte.

PSEUDOBULB: 26 in. (65 cm) long. Stems are completely covered by wrinkled gray-brown leaf sheaths.

LEAVES: Many. The curved, distichous leaves are 2.4–3.5 in. (6–9 cm) long.

INFLORESCENCE: Very short. Inflorescences emerge between the 2 rows of leaves. They are so short that the blossoms appear to rest on the centerline of the stem.

FLOWERS: 1 per inflorescence. The long-lasting flowers are 1.2 in. (3 cm) across. All segments twist or recurve at the tip. Sepals and petals are white shading to cinnamon brown and olive green. As they age, the blossoms become a shade of orange, apricot, or salmon pink. The lip is uppermost and notched at the apex. They are not fragrant.

REFERENCES: 234, 585.

PHOTOS/DRAWINGS: 585, 589.

Dendrobium lambusiforme Schlechter

ORIGIN/HABITAT: Papua New Guinea. Plants grow in the Sepik River region. Schlechter (ref. 443) indicates that the plant grows at 19,700 ft. (6000 m); however, since that part of New Guinea has no mountains that high, we are assuming that the elevation given was a typographical error and that it should read 1970 ft. (600 m). Because this is an assumption, temperature data should be used with caution.

CLIMATE: Station #200004, Ambunti, Papua New Guinea, Lat. 4.2°S, Long. 142.8°E, at 164 ft. (50 m). Temperatures are calculated for an elevation of 2000 ft. (610 m), resulting in probable extremes of 93°F (34°C) and 46°F (8°C).

N/HEMISPHERE	JAN	FEB	MAR	APR	MAY	JUN	JUL	AUG	SEP	OCT	NOV	DEC
°F AVG MAX	82	84	84	84	85	84	84	84	84	84	84	83
°F AVG MIN	66	67	68	67	67	67	66	67	67	67	67	68
DIURNAL RANGE	16	17	16	17	18	17	18	17	17	17	17	15
RAIN/INCHES	6.4	7.4	7.7	8.5	9.2	9.4	10.9	10.2	12.2	10.4	8.3	5.2
HUMIDITY/%	N/A											
BLOOM SEASON					*							
DAYS CLR	N/A											
RAIN/MM	163	188	196	216	234	239	277	259	310	264	211	132
°C AVG MAX	27.7	28.9	28.9	28.9	29.4	28.9	28.9	28.9	28.9	28.9	28.9	28.3
°C AVG MIN	18.9	19.4	20.0	19.4	19.4	19.4	18.9	19.4	19.4	19.4	19.4	20.0
DIURNAL RANGE	8.8	9.5	8.9	9.5	10.0	9.5	10.0	9.5	9.5	9.5	9.5	8.3
S/HEMISPHERE	JUL	AUG	SEP	OCT	NOV	DEC	JAN	FEB	MAR	APR	MAY	JUN

Cultural Recommendations

LIGHT: 2000–3000 fc.

TEMPERATURES: Throughout the year, days average 82–85°F (28–29°C), and nights average 66–68°F (19–20°C), with a diurnal range of 15–18°F (8–10°C).

HUMIDITY: Information is not available for this location. However, records from nearby locations indicate that humidity probably averages near 80% year-round.

WATER: Rainfall is heavy year-round with the greatest amounts falling in summer and early autumn. Cultivated plants should be moist but not soggy.

FERTILIZER: ¼–½ recommended strength. A balanced fertilizer should be applied weekly to biweekly throughout the year.

REST PERIOD: Growing conditions should be maintained all year. Water and fertilizer should be reduced for plants cultivated in the dark, short-day conditions common in temperate-latitude winters, but they should never be allowed to dry out completely. In the habitat, seasonal light variation is minor.

GROWING MEDIA: Mounting plants on tree-fern or cork slabs accommodates their pendulous growth habit. However, humidity must be high and plants must be watered at least once a day in summer. If plants cannot be mounted, hanging pots or baskets may be filled with an open, fast-draining medium. Repotting may be done anytime new roots are actively growing.

MISCELLANEOUS NOTES: The bloom season shown in the climate table is based on reports from the habitat.

Plant and Flower Information

PLANT SIZE AND TYPE: A 79 in. (200 cm) sympodial epiphyte.

PSEUDOBULB: 79 in. (200 cm) long. The pendent stems are unbranched.

LEAVES: Many. The lanceolate leaves are 5–7 in. (13–18 cm) long.

INFLORESCENCE: Racemes are oblong and flattened.

FLOWERS: 2 per inflorescence. The smooth, fleshy flowers are 0.8 in. (2 cm) long. Blossoms are yellowish with wine-red spots. The tongue-shaped sepals are larger than the curved lip, which is round and wavy at the front of the midlobe. The midlobe is decorated with wartlike protuberances.

REFERENCES: 223, 443.

Dendrobium lamellatum (Blume) Lindley

AKA: *Onychium lamellatum* Blume. Seidenfaden (ref. 454) includes *Dendrobium compressum* Lindley as a synonym, and Valmayor (ref. 536) includes *D. platycaulon* Rolfe. Merrill (ref. 296) indicates that Kränzlin's use of *D. lamellatum* should refer to *D. platycaulon*.

ORIGIN/HABITAT: Southeast Asia. Distribution extends from Laos to Moulmein, Burma southward through peninsular Thailand, to Malaya, Sumatra, and western Java and northward into Borneo and the Philippines. Plants grow on trees in sheltered places at 1500–2000 ft. (460–610 m). Although found over a large region, the plant is uncommon.

CLIMATE: Station #48567, Trang, Thailand, Lat. 7.5°N, Long. 99.7°E, at 39 ft. (12 m). Temperatures are calculated for an elevation of 1650 ft. (500 m), resulting in probable extremes of 99°F (37°C) and 56°F (13°C).

N/HEMISPHERE	JAN	FEB	MAR	APR	MAY	JUN	JUL	AUG	SEP	OCT	NOV	DEC
°F AVG MAX	86	89	91	89	86	84	83	83	83	83	82	83
°F AVG MIN	65	66	67	69	70	69	69	72	69	68	67	66
DIURNAL RANGE	21	23	24	20	16	15	14	11	14	15	15	17
RAIN/INCHES	2.1	1.0	2.6	7.5	9.7	9.8	10.2	11.6	12.8	12.7	9.5	4.4
HUMIDITY/%	73	69	70	75	82	82	83	83	84	85	83	78
BLOOM SEASON	*	*	*	*	*	*				*		*
DAYS CLR @ 7AM	5	3	2	2	0	1	0	0	0	0	2	3
DAYS CLR @ 1PM	2	2	1	0	0	0	0	0	0	0	0	1
RAIN/MM	53	25	66	190	246	249	259	295	325	323	241	112
°C AVG MAX	29.8	31.5	32.6	31.5	29.8	28.7	28.2	28.2	28.2	28.2	27.6	28.2
°C AVG MIN	18.2	18.7	19.3	20.4	21.0	20.4	20.4	22.1	20.4	19.8	19.3	18.7
DIURNAL RANGE	11.6	12.8	13.3	11.1	8.8	8.3	7.8	6.1	7.8	8.4	8.3	9.5
S/HEMISPHERE	JUL	AUG	SEP	OCT	NOV	DEC	JAN	FEB	MAR	APR	MAY	JUN

Cultural Recommendations

LIGHT: 1500–2500 fc.

TEMPERATURES: Summer days average 83–84°F (28–29°C), and nights average 69–72°F (20–22°C), with a diurnal range of 11–15°F (6–8°C). The warmest season of the year is spring when days average 86–91°F (30–33°C), and nights average 67–70°F (19–21°C), with a diurnal range of 16–24°F (9–13°C).

HUMIDITY: 80–85% from late spring through autumn, dropping to near 70% in winter.

WATER: Rainfall is heavy from spring into early winter, but conditions are drier for 2–3 months in winter. However, high humidity and the large daily temperature range results in frequent heavy deposits of dew. Consequently, the dry season is neither as long or as severe as the rainfall averages alone indicate. Cultivated plants should be kept moist while actively growing, but water should be gradually reduced during late autumn.

FERTILIZER: ¼–½ recommended strength, applied weekly. A high-nitrogen fertilizer is beneficial from spring to midsummer, but a fertilizer high in phosphates should be used in late summer and autumn.

REST PERIOD: Winter days average 83–89°F (28–32°C), and nights average 65–66°F (18–19°C), with a diurnal range of 17–23°F (10–13°C). Water should be reduced for 1–2 winter months and plants allowed to dry somewhat between waterings. They should not remain dry for long periods, however. Some growers report that cultivated plants are healthiest in a warm, humid environment with constant moisture year-round, but a 1–3 month winter dry period is common in most areas where the plant is found. Fertilizer should be reduced if water is reduced.

GROWING MEDIA: Plants may be mounted on tree-fern slabs if humidity is high and plants are watered at least once daily in summer. When plants are potted, any open, fast-draining medium may be used. Growers report good results from tree-fern chunks. Repotting is best done in early spring when new roots are growing.

MISCELLANEOUS NOTES: The bloom season shown in the climate table is based on cultivation records. From a grower's vantage point, H. Wood (ref. 582) expresses strong reservations regarding the synonymy given above. He indicates that *D. platycaulon* from the Philippines has a narrow tubular lip and yellow flowers; *D. platygastrium* Rchb. f. from Fiji, which is usually self-pollinating before it opens, has a flat lip when it does open; and *D. lamellatum* from Thailand has an inverted lip. Only time and additional study can clarify these differences of opinion.

Plant and Flower Information

PLANT SIZE AND TYPE: A 2–8 in. (5–20 cm) sympodial epiphyte.

PSEUDOBULB: 2–5 in. (5–13 cm) long. The green stems, which resemble smooth cactus leaves, are broad, thin, very flat, and somewhat curved or cupped. They may be nearly as wide as they are tall. The plant is very branched and each flat branch consists of 3–4 nodes.

LEAVES: 1–3 per growth. The oval leaves are carried at upper nodes of young stems. They are 1.5–3.0 in. (3.8–7.6 cm) long.

INFLORESCENCE: Short. The arching to pendulous racemes emerge at the apex of the stem.

FLOWERS: 2–6 per inflorescence. The pendulous flowers are 0.9 in. (2.2 cm) across and do not open fully. The blossoms are shaped like a flared funnel. Sepals and petals are creamy yellow to greenish white when fresh and become yellow with age. The lip, which is narrow at the base and broad at the tip, is green with a dirty orange cast at the center. It is reflexed along the margin with 3–5 rounded keels in the center.

HYBRIDIZING NOTES: Johansen (ref. 239) indicates that plants are self-sterile and that flowers dropped 7–15 days after self-pollination.

REFERENCES: 12, 25, 75, 157, 179, 190, 200, 202, 216, 239, 254, 280, 286, 291, 295, 296, 310, 317, 326, 395, 402, 445, 454, 455, 469, 504, 536, 570, 592.

PHOTOS/DRAWINGS: 75, 200, *291, 454, 455,* 469

Dendrobium lamelluliferum J. J. Smith

ORIGIN/HABITAT: Western Borneo. Plants grow in forests of western Kalimantan near Lebang Hara at 500 ft. (150 m). Collections have also been made in northern Sarawak near Mt. Dulit at 4050 ft. (1230 m) and in Sabah in the lower mountain forests on Mt. Kinabalu at 3950–7200 ft. (1200–2200 m).

CLIMATE: Station #96449, Miri, Sarawak, Lat. 4.4°N, Long. 114.0°E, at 13 ft. (4 m). Temperatures are calculated for an elevation of 4000 ft. (1220 m), resulting in probable extremes of 82°F (28°C) and 54°F (12°C).

N/HEMISPHERE	JAN	FEB	MAR	APR	MAY	JUN	JUL	AUG	SEP	OCT	NOV	DEC
°F AVG MAX	73	73	74	75	75	75	75	75	74	74	74	74
°F AVG MIN	61	61	61	62	62	62	61	61	61	61	61	61
DIURNAL RANGE	12	12	13	13	13	13	14	14	13	13	13	13
RAIN/INCHES	16.8	6.5	5.5	4.4	8.2	12.0	8.5	8.4	11.8	11.7	14.5	11.3
HUMIDITY/%	86	86	85	83	83	82	81	81	82	83	84	85
BLOOM SEASON					*				*			
DAYS CLR @ 8AM	1	2	4	4	3	2	3	2	2	1	2	2
DAYS CLR @ 2PM	1	1	3	4	2	5	3	2	3	2	1	1
RAIN	427	165	140	112	208	305	216	213	300	297	368	287
°C AVG MAX	22.7	22.7	23.2	23.8	23.8	23.8	23.8	23.8	23.2	23.2	23.2	23.2
°C AVG MIN	16.0	16.0	16.0	16.6	16.6	16.6	16.0	16.0	16.0	16.0	16.0	16.0
DIURNAL RANGE	6.7	6.7	7.2	7.2	7.2	7.2	7.8	7.8	7.2	7.2	7.2	7.2
S/HEMISPHERE	JUL	AUG	SEP	OCT	NOV	DEC	JAN	FEB	MAR	APR	MAY	JUN

Cultural Recommendations

LIGHT: 2000–3000 fc.

TEMPERATURES: Throughout the year, days average 73–75°F (23–24°C), and nights average 61–62°F (16–17°C), with a diurnal range of 12–14°F (7–8°C).

HUMIDITY: 80–85% year-round.

WATER: Rainfall is heavy most of the year, but conditions are slightly drier in late winter and early spring. Cultivated plants should be kept moist but not soggy.

FERTILIZER: ¼–½ recommended strength. A balanced fertilizer should be applied weekly to biweekly throughout the year.

REST PERIOD: Growing conditions should be maintained all year. In cultivation, water and fertilizer should be reduced in winter, especially for plants grown in the dark, short-day conditions common in temperate latitudes. Plants should never be allowed to dry out completely, however.

GROWING MEDIA: Plants may be mounted on tree-fern or cork slabs if humidity is high and plants are watered at least once daily in summer. When plants are potted, any open, fast-draining medium may be used. They may be repotted anytime new roots are growing.

MISCELLANEOUS NOTES: The bloom season shown in the climate table is based on collection reports. The plant was described in 1927 in *Mitt. Inst. Bot. Hamburg* 7:52.

Plant and Flower Information

PLANT SIZE AND TYPE: A 12 in. (30 cm) sympodial epiphyte.

PSEUDOBULB: 12 in. (30 cm) long. The flattened, slender stems are swollen above the base, forming a small, elliptical pseudobulb. They become slender again above the pseudobulb. They are greenish-yellow when dry. Carr (ref. 59) described plants as having brown stems and ribbed, chestnut brown pseudobulbs.

LEAVES: 9–12 per growth. The lanceolate leaves are 1.2–1.6 in. (3–4 cm) long.

INFLORESCENCE: 1.5–2.0 in. (3.8–5.0 cm) long. Inflorescences emerge from nodes on the upper part of the stem.

FLOWERS: Few per inflorescence. Blossoms open in succession. The flowers are 0.2 in. (0.6 cm) long. They may be white or creamy yellow. The tip of the column is bright yellow. The concave lip is sharply pointed at the tip of the small, triangular midlobe.

REFERENCES: 59, 224, 286, 445, 592.

Dendrobium lamii J. J. Smith

ORIGIN/HABITAT: Irian Jaya (western New Guinea). Plants were collected on a ridge near Mt. Doorman at 8350–9350 ft. (2550–2850 m), where they grow in a protected valley in moss-covered, light forest.

CLIMATE: Station #97686, Wamena, New Guinea, Lat. 4.1°S, Long. 139.0°E, at 5446 ft. (1660 m). Temperatures are calculated for an elevation of 8500 ft. (2590 m). Record extreme temperatures are not available for this location.

N/HEMISPHERE	JAN	FEB	MAR	APR	MAY	JUN	JUL	AUG	SEP	OCT	NOV	DEC
°F AVG MAX	65	66	67	66	67	66	67	66	66	69	68	64
°F AVG MIN	50	50	52	52	53	54	53	52	53	55	55	51
DIURNAL RANGE	15	16	15	14	14	12	14	14	13	14	13	13
RAIN/INCHES	3.0	1.9	2.2	4.0	4.6	3.3	2.8	4.2	6.9	3.9	5.4	4.9
HUMIDITY/%	N/A											
BLOOM SEASON			*	*								
DAYS CLR	N/A											
RAIN/MM	76	48	56	102	117	84	71	107	175	99	137	124
°C AVG MAX	18.2	18.8	19.3	18.8	19.3	18.8	19.3	18.8	18.8	20.5	19.9	17.7
°C AVG MIN	9.9	9.9	11.0	11.0	11.6	12.1	11.6	11.0	11.6	12.7	12.7	10.5
DIURNAL RANGE	8.3	8.9	8.3	7.8	7.7	6.7	7.7	7.8	7.2	7.8	7.2	7.2
S/HEMISPHERE	JUL	AUG	SEP	OCT	NOV	DEC	JAN	FEB	MAR	APR	MAY	JUN

Cultural Recommendations

LIGHT: 2500–3500 fc.

TEMPERATURES: Throughout the year, days average 64–69°F (18–21°C), and nights average 50–55°F (10–13°C), with a diurnal range of 12–16°F (7–9°C). In the habitat, the warmest temperatures of the day occur in late morning, when skies are clear. Clouds and mist develop near noon and continue through the afternoon, thus preventing additional warming. Because of microclimate effects, actual maximum temperatures may be somewhat warmer than indicated. Reports from the habitat indicate a sharp contrast between day and night temperatures.

HUMIDITY: Information is not available for this location. However, records from nearby locations indicate that humidity probably averages near 80% year-round. High humidity and excellent air circulation are particularly important if temperatures are warm. Placing the plants in front of an evaporative cooler or near a fine mist may be very beneficial.

WATER: Rainfall is moderate through most of the year. In the higher-elevation habitat, rainfall amounts may be greater than indicated in the climate table. In addition, large amounts of water are available from mist and heavy dew, even during periods of reduced rainfall. Cultivated plants should be kept moist with only slight drying allowed between waterings. They should be misted several times daily on the hottest days, but the foliage should always be dry before evening. Good air movement is critically important and should be maintained at all times.

FERTILIZER: ¼–½ recommended strength. A balanced fertilizer should be applied weekly to biweekly throughout the year. The Royal Botanic Garden in Edinburgh uses a dilute, seaweed-based fertilizer.

REST PERIOD: Growing conditions should be maintained all year. Rainfall averages are somewhat lower for a month or so in winter and again in midsummer. In cultivation, water may be decreased, but plants should never be allowed to dry out completely. In the habitat, light is slightly higher in winter. Cultivated plants often grow year-round.

GROWING MEDIA: Plants may be mounted on tree-fern or cork slabs if humidity is high and plants are watered daily in summer. When plants are potted, any open, fast-draining medium may be used. Repotting may be done anytime new roots are growing.

MISCELLANEOUS NOTES: The bloom season shown in the climate table is based on reports from the habitat.

Plant and Flower Information

PLANT SIZE AND TYPE: An 18 in. (45 cm) sympodial epiphyte.

PSEUDOBULB: 18 in. (45 cm) long. The branching stems are elongated.

LEAVES: Many. The lanceolate to ovate-lanceolate leaves are 0.4 in. (1 cm) long. They are dark green on the upper surface and light green on the underside.

INFLORESCENCE: Short. Inflorescences emerge from nodes along leafless stems.

FLOWERS: 1–2 per inflorescence. The somewhat flattened flowers are 0.8 in. (2 cm) long. Sepals and petals may be bluish violet to dark violet. Lateral sepals are dilated at the base. The erect lip is very dark violet at the tip. It has no callus. The column is dirty rose with a salmon colored tip.

REFERENCES: 224, 445, 470.

Dendrobium lamonganense Rchb. f. Sometimes spelled *D. lamorganense*, it is now considered a synonym of *Eria pilifera* Ridley. REFERENCES: 25, 75, 216, 254, 469.

Dendrobium lampongense J. J. Smith

ORIGIN/HABITAT: Malaya, Sabah, and Sumatra. In Sumatra, plants grow at the eastern tip of Lampong Province. In Malaya, plants grow in the lowlands of Negeri Sembilan and probably the lowlands of Kedah. Habitat elevation is not available, so the following climate data should be used with caution.

CLIMATE: Station #48665, Melaka (Malacca), Malaya, Lat. 2.3°N, Long. 102.3°E, at 40 ft. (12 m). Temperatures are calculated for an elevation of 1000 ft. (300 m), resulting in probable extremes of 96°F (36°C) and 58°F (14°C).

N/HEMISPHERE	JAN	FEB	MAR	APR	MAY	JUN	JUL	AUG	SEP	OCT	NOV	DEC
°F AVG MAX	85	86	86	86	86	85	85	85	85	85	85	85
°F AVG MIN	69	69	69	70	70	70	69	69	69	69	69	69
DIURNAL RANGE	16	17	17	16	16	15	16	16	16	16	16	16
RAIN/INCHES	3.9	3.7	4.9	7.4	6.8	7.9	7.8	10.3	8.8	10.1	8.7	6.5
HUMIDITY/%	79	79	82	85	85	83	84	84	84	84	84	82
BLOOM SEASON	N/A											
DAYS CLR @ 7AM	1	1	1	1	1	1	2	1	1	1	0	1
DAYS CLR @ 1PM	1	1	1	1	1	1	1	1	1	1	0	0
RAIN/MM	99	94	124	188	173	201	198	262	224	257	221	165
°C AVG MAX	29.4	29.9	29.9	29.9	29.9	29.4	29.4	29.4	29.4	29.4	29.4	29.4
°C AVG MIN	20.5	20.5	20.5	21.0	21.0	21.0	20.5	20.5	20.5	20.5	20.5	20.5
DIURNAL RANGE	8.9	9.4	9.4	8.9	8.9	8.4	8.9	8.9	8.9	8.9	8.9	8.9
S/HEMISPHERE	JUL	AUG	SEP	OCT	NOV	DEC	JAN	FEB	MAR	APR	MAY	JUN

Cultural Recommendations

LIGHT: 2000–3000 fc.

TEMPERATURES: Throughout the year, days average 85–86°F (29–30°C), and nights average 69–70°F (21°C), with a diurnal range of 15–17°F (8–9°C).

HUMIDITY: 80–85% year-round.

WATER: Rainfall is moderate to heavy all year, but conditions are slightly drier for about 2 months in winter. Cultivated plants should be kept moist, with only slight drying allowed between waterings.

FERTILIZER: ¼–½ recommended strength. A balanced fertilizer should be applied weekly to biweekly throughout the year.

REST PERIOD: Growing conditions should be maintained all year. Water and fertilizer may be reduced somewhat in winter, especially for plants cultivated in the dark, short-day conditions common in the temperate latitudes. Plants should never be allowed to dry out completely, however. In the habitat, seasonal light variation is minor.

GROWING MEDIA: Plants may be mounted on tree-fern or cork slabs if humidity is high and plants are watered at least once daily in summer. When plants are potted, any open, fast-draining medium may be used. They may be repotted anytime new roots are growing.

MISCELLANEOUS NOTES: The bloom season shown in the climate table is based on records from the habitat.

Plant and Flower Information

PLANT SIZE AND TYPE: A 26 in. (65 cm) sympodial epiphyte.

PSEUDOBULB: 26 in. (65 cm) long. The stemlike pseudobulbs consist of numerous nodes.

Dendrobium lamprocaulon

LEAVES: Many. The lanceolate leaves are 4.3 in. (11 cm) long. They are deciduous.

INFLORESCENCE: Inflorescences emerge from nodes along leafless stems.

FLOWERS: 3–7 per inflorescence. The flowers are 1.6–1.9 in. (4.2–4.8 cm) across. Sepals and petals are pale yellow with a purplish tint on the backside. The base of the light yellow lip is marked with 4–8 brownish lines. The wavy to ruffled midlobe may be rounded or notched. Sidelobes are usually small and triangular, but they may be missing.

REFERENCES: 220, 254, 455.

PHOTOS/DRAWINGS: 455.

Dendrobium lamprocaulon Schlechter

AKA: Kränzlin (ref. 253, 254) lists *D. lamprocaulon* Schlechter as a synonym of *D. platygastrium* Rchb. f., but we found no recent use of this synonymy.

ORIGIN/HABITAT: New Ireland Island (New Mecklenburg) off Papua New Guinea. Plants grow on forest trees near Punam at about 1950 ft. (600 m).

CLIMATE: Station #94076, Kavieng, New Ireland Island, Papua New Guinea, Lat. 2.6°S, Long. 150.8°E, at 15 ft. (5 m). Temperatures are calculated for an elevation of 1800 ft. (550 m), resulting in probable extremes of 93°F (34°C) and 60°F (16°C).

N/HEMISPHERE	JAN	FEB	MAR	APR	MAY	JUN	JUL	AUG	SEP	OCT	NOV	DEC
°F AVG MAX	82	82	83	84	84	83	82	82	81	82	82	82
°F AVG MIN	67	67	67	67	68	68	69	69	69	68	68	68
DIURNAL RANGE	15	15	16	17	16	15	13	13	12	14	14	14
RAIN/INCHES	10.7	11.2	7.8	8.0	9.7	10.7	12.2	11.1	11.6	12.5	10.0	9.9
HUMIDITY/%	78	76	76	75	77	78	80	79	79	80	79	79
BLOOM SEASON	*											
DAYS CLR	N/A											
RAIN/MM	272	284	198	203	246	272	310	282	295	318	254	251
°C AVG MAX	27.8	27.8	28.4	28.9	28.9	28.4	27.8	27.8	27.3	27.8	27.8	27.8
°C AVG MIN	19.5	19.5	19.5	19.5	20.1	20.1	20.6	20.6	20.6	20.1	20.1	20.1
DIURNAL RANGE	8.3	8.3	8.9	9.4	8.8	8.3	7.2	7.2	6.7	7.7	7.7	7.7
S/HEMISPHERE	JUL	AUG	SEP	OCT	NOV	DEC	JAN	FEB	MAR	APR	MAY	JUN

Cultural Recommendations

LIGHT: 2000–3000 fc.

TEMPERATURES: Throughout the year, days average 81–84°F (27–29°C), and nights average 67–69°F (20–21°C), with a diurnal range of 12–17°F (7–9°C).

HUMIDITY: 75–80% year-round.

WATER: Rainfall is very heavy all year. Plants should be kept evenly moist.

FERTILIZER: ¼–½ recommended strength. A balanced fertilizer should be applied weekly to biweekly throughout the year.

REST PERIOD: Growing conditions should be maintained year-round. In the habitat, winter rainfall is very heavy, but water and fertilizer should be reduced somewhat for cultivated plants, especially those grown in the dark, short-day conditions common in temperate latitudes. Plants should never be allowed dry out completely, however.

GROWING MEDIA: Plants may be mounted on tree-fern or cork slabs if humidity is high and plants are watered at least once daily in summer. When plants are potted, any open, fast-draining medium may be used. Repotting may be done anytime new roots are growing.

MISCELLANEOUS NOTES: The bloom season shown in the climate table is based on reports from the habitat.

Plant and Flower Information

PLANT SIZE AND TYPE: A 4–7 in. (10–18 cm) sympodial epiphyte. The plant habit strongly resembles that of *D. lamellatum*.

PSEUDOBULB: 2–3 in. (5–8 cm) long. The clustered growths arise from a very short rhizome. The shiny stems are elliptic to oblong.

LEAVES: 3–4 per growth. The oblong leaves are 2.0–2.8 in. (5–7 cm) long and quickly deciduous. They are smooth and unequally bilobed at the apex.

INFLORESCENCE: 1.0–1.4 in. (2.5–3.5 cm) long. Inflorescences are laxly flowered.

FLOWERS: 2–3 per inflorescence. The flowers, which do not open fully, are 0.4–0.5 in. (1.0–1.3 cm) long. Sepals and petals are oblong; the base of the lateral sepals is dilated. The lip is obscurely trilobed with 2 raised lines on the midlobe. The sidelobes are broadly triangular. The blossoms are white flushed with rose-red.

REFERENCES: 219, 253, 254, 437, 444, 445.

PHOTOS/DRAWINGS: 437.

Dendrobium lamproglossum Schlechter

ORIGIN/HABITAT: Papua New Guinea. Plants grow on forest trees in the Bismarck Mountains at about 4600 ft. (1400 m).

CLIMATE: Station #94010, Goroka, Papua New Guinea, Lat. 6.1°S, Long. 145.4°E, at 5141 ft. (1567 m). Temperatures are calculated for an elevation of 4600 ft. (1400 m), resulting in probable extremes of 89°F (32°C) and 45°F (7°C).

N/HEMISPHERE	JAN	FEB	MAR	APR	MAY	JUN	JUL	AUG	SEP	OCT	NOV	DEC
°F AVG MAX	78	79	80	81	81	80	81	80	80	80	81	79
°F AVG MIN	58	59	59	59	60	61	61	61	62	61	61	59
DIURNAL RANGE	20	20	21	22	21	19	20	19	18	19	20	20
RAIN/INCHES	2.1	2.8	4.6	5.9	6.6	9.3	9.1	10.1	10.7	8.3	4.6	2.0
HUMIDITY/%	70	67	67	67	71	72	73	74	71	70	70	70
BLOOM SEASON			*									
DAYS CLR	N/A											
RAIN/MM	53	71	117	150	168	236	231	257	272	211	117	51
°C AVG MAX	25.4	26.0	26.5	27.1	27.1	26.5	27.1	26.5	26.5	26.5	27.1	26.0
°C AVG MIN	14.3	14.9	14.9	14.9	15.4	16.0	16.0	16.0	16.5	16.0	16.0	14.9
DIURNAL RANGE	11.1	11.1	11.6	12.2	11.7	10.5	11.1	10.5	10.0	10.5	11.1	11.1
S/HEMISPHERE	JUL	AUG	SEP	OCT	NOV	DEC	JAN	FEB	MAR	APR	MAY	JUN

Cultural Recommendations

LIGHT: 1800–3000 fc.

TEMPERATURES: Throughout the year, days average 78–81°F (25–27°C), and nights average 58–62°F (14–17°C), with a diurnal range of 18–22°F (10–12°C).

HUMIDITY: 70–75% from summer into autumn, dropping to 65–70% in winter and spring. Plants from this habitat require excellent air movement.

WATER: Rainfall is moderate to heavy most of the year, but conditions are slightly drier for 3 months in winter. Cultivated plants should be kept moist but not soggy. Occasional early morning mistings may be beneficial, especially on bright, sunny days.

FERTILIZER: ¼–½ recommended strength. A balanced fertilizer should be applied weekly to biweekly throughout the year.

REST PERIOD: Growing temperatures should be maintained all year. In the habitat, rainfall is lowest in winter, but dew and mist from fog and low clouds are common. Water and fertilizer should be reduced somewhat for cultivated plants, especially those grown in the darker, short-day conditions common during temperate-latitude winters. Plants should be kept on the dry side, but they should never be allowed to dry out completely. In the habitat, light is higher in winter.

GROWING MEDIA: Plants may be mounted on tree-fern or cork slabs if humidity is high and plants are watered at least once daily in summer. When plants are potted, any open, fast-draining medium may be used. Repotting may be done anytime new roots are growing.

MISCELLANEOUS NOTES: The bloom season shown in the climate table is based on reports from the habitat.

Plant and Flower Information

PLANT SIZE AND TYPE: A 14–18 in. (35–45 cm) sympodial epiphyte.

PSEUDOBULB: 14–18 in. (35–45 cm) long. The unbranched, flattened stems arise from a very short rhizome. The stems are densely leafy.

LEAVES: Many. The leaves are 2–3 in. (5–8 cm) long, erect, and linear.

FLOWERS: 1 per inflorescence. The flowers are 0.4 in. (1.1 cm) long and barely open. The sepals and petals are dark red on the outside and white on the inside. The glossy, circular-oblong lip is thickly covered with red spots. It is decorated with 4 transverse lines on the front of the midlobe and a large callus at the back.

REFERENCES: 92, 221, 437, 445.

PHOTOS/DRAWINGS: 437.

Dendrobium lanceola Swartz.
Now considered a synonym of *Pleurothallis lanceola* Sprengel. REFERENCES: 216, 254, 445.

Dendrobium lanceolatum Gaudich.
Reportedly from the Molucca Islands, Kränzlin included it in his list of imperfectly described species. REFERENCES: 216, 254.

Dendrobium lancifolium A. Richard

AKA: *D. lilacinum* Teijsm. and Binn. not Rchb. f., *D. vulcanicum* Schlechter.

ORIGIN/HABITAT: Widespread throughout eastern Indonesia, including the Molucca Islands and the Banda Island group south of Seram. On Ambon, plants grow on the ground in forest litter along dry water courses at 250–500 ft. (70–150 m). On Sulawesi (Celebes), plants are found at 1250–1950 ft. (380–600 m). In Irian Jaya (western New Guinea), the plants have been reported on trees in mountain forests in the Arfak Range at about 6250 ft. (1900 m) and on limestone soils and limestone rocks on Waigeo Island, Biak Island, and near Jayapura (Hollandia). On Buru (Boeroe) Island, about 10 miles (16 km) from Leksoela, plants grow on barren, conglomerate rocks. In other locations, they grow among grass on dry calcareous ground, or under shrubs on open, sunny, eastern slopes.

CLIMATE: Station #97724, Ambon Island, Moluccas, Indonesia, Lat. 3.7°S, Long. 128.1°E, at 33 ft. (10 m). Temperatures are calculated for an elevation of 500 ft. (150 m), resulting in probable extremes of 94°F (35°C) and 64°F (18°C).

N/HEMISPHERE	JAN	FEB	MAR	APR	MAY	JUN	JUL	AUG	SEP	OCT	NOV	DEC
°F AVG MAX	79	79	81	83	86	86	86	86	86	84	82	80
°F AVG MIN	72	72	72	72	73	74	74	74	74	74	73	72
DIURNAL RANGE	7	7	9	11	13	12	12	12	12	10	9	8
RAIN/INCHES	23.7	15.8	9.5	6.1	4.5	5.2	5.0	4.7	5.3	11.0	20.3	25.1
HUMIDITY/%	83	82	81	80	79	78	78	78	77	79	82	83	84
BLOOM SEASON	*		*		*			*	*			
DAYS CLR @ 9AM	1	1	1	6	7	4	3	3	5	5	3	3
DAYS CLR @ 3PM	1	1	2	5	6	1	1	1	2	3	1	3
RAIN/MM	602	401	241	155	114	132	127	119	135	279	516	638
°C AVG MAX	26.4	26.4	27.5	28.6	30.3	30.3	30.3	30.3	30.3	29.1	28.0	26.9
°C AVG MIN	22.5	22.5	22.5	22.5	23.0	23.6	23.6	23.6	23.6	23.6	23.0	22.5
DIURNAL RANGE	3.9	3.9	5.0	6.1	7.3	6.7	6.7	6.7	6.7	5.5	5.0	4.4
S/HEMISPHERE	JUL	AUG	SEP	OCT	NOV	DEC	JAN	FEB	MAR	APR	MAY	JUN

Cultural Recommendations

LIGHT: 2500–3500 fc.

TEMPERATURES: Throughout the year, days average 79–86°F (26–30°C), and nights average 72–74°F (23–24°C), with a diurnal range of 7–13°F (4–7°C). Plants collected at very high elevations in Irian Jaya (western New Guinea) could require temperatures 15–20°F (8–11°C) cooler than indicated by the climate table.

HUMIDITY: 80–85% year-round.

WATER: Rainfall is moderate to heavy all year, but conditions are slightly drier in late spring and summer. Cultivated plants should be kept evenly moist, with only slight drying allowed between waterings.

FERTILIZER: ¼–½ recommended strength. A balanced fertilizer should be applied weekly to biweekly throughout the year.

REST PERIOD: Growing conditions should be maintained all year. In the habitat, rainfall is heaviest in winter, but water and fertilizer should be reduced for cultivated plants, especially those grown in the dark, short-day conditions common in temperate latitudes. However, plants should never be allowed to dry completely. In the habitat, light is highest in spring.

GROWING MEDIA: Growers report that plants grow easily in a somewhat humus-rich, well-drained soil mix. The pot and base of the plant should be kept shaded. Repotting may be done anytime new roots are growing.

MISCELLANEOUS NOTES: The bloom season shown in the climate table is based on reports from the habitat.

Plant and Flower Information

PLANT SIZE AND TYPE: A 12–18 in. (30–45 cm) sympodial terrestrial. Var. *papuanum* J. J. Smith is also lithophytic.

PSEUDOBULB: 12–18 in. (30–45 cm) long. The tall, branching stems are purplish and somewhat zigzag. They are erect, smooth, leafy, and emerge from a very short rhizome.

LEAVES: Many. The papery leaves are 4–5 in. (10–13 cm) long, alternating, deciduous, and linear-lanceolate.

INFLORESCENCE: Racemes emerge from nodes along leafless stems.

FLOWERS: 1–4 per inflorescence. The handsome, crystalline blossoms are 0.8–1.6 in. (2–4 cm) long. They are rose-red with purple on the front of the lip and violet along the margin. The extent of purple markings is variable. Plants collected from Ambon had pale lilac to pure white blossoms which sometimes had pink-lilac at the tip of the lip and on the column. Blossoms have an ovate dorsal sepal, broad, oblong-elliptic petals, and lateral sepals that are dilated at the base. The lip has a V-shaped callus.

REFERENCES: 25, 177, 216, 254, 317, 433, 436, 468, 470, 479, 483, 537.

Dendrobium lancilabium J. J. Smith

ORIGIN/HABITAT: Irian Jaya (western New Guinea). Plants were originally collected in the Wondiwoi Range at about 6500 ft. (1980 m). They usually grow in mossy forests on the trunks of *Nothofagus* at 5100–6500 ft. (1550–1980 m).

CLIMATE: Station #97682, Nabire, Irian Jaya, Lat. 3.3°S, Long. 135.5°E, at 10 ft. (3 m). Temperatures are calculated for an elevation of 6500 ft. (1980 m). Record extreme temperatures are not available for this location.

N/HEMISPHERE	JAN	FEB	MAR	APR	MAY	JUN	JUL	AUG	SEP	OCT	NOV	DEC
°F AVG MAX	65	65	65	65	66	66	65	65	66	66	66	66
°F AVG MIN	54	54	55	56	56	55	54	54	54	55	55	55
DIURNAL RANGE	11	11	10	9	10	11	9	11	12	11	11	11
RAIN/INCHES	7.4	11.1	8.5	8.5	7.5	9.0	9.2	10.6	12.1	11.3	10.2	9.8
HUMIDITY/%	N/A											
BLOOM SEASON	*											
DAYS CLR	N/A											
RAIN/MM	188	282	216	216	190	229	234	269	307	287	259	249
°C AVG MAX	18.1	18.1	18.1	18.1	18.7	18.7	18.1	18.1	18.7	18.7	18.7	18.7
°C AVG MIN	12.0	12.0	12.5	13.1	13.1	12.5	13.1	12.0	12.0	12.5	12.5	12.5
DIURNAL RANGE	6.1	6.1	5.6	5.0	5.6	6.2	5.0	6.1	6.7	6.2	6.2	6.2
S/HEMISPHERE	JUL	AUG	SEP	OCT	NOV	DEC	JAN	FEB	MAR	APR	MAY	JUN

Cultural Recommendations

LIGHT: 2000–3000 fc.

TEMPERATURES: Throughout the year, days average 65–66°F (18–19°C),

and nights average 54–56°F (12–13°C), with a diurnal range of 9–12°F (5–7°C).

HUMIDITY: Information is not available for this location. However, records from nearby locations indicate that humidity probably averages near 85% year-round.

WATER: Rainfall is heavy all year. Cultivated plants should be kept evenly moist.

FERTILIZER: 1/4–1/2 recommended strength. A balanced fertilizer should be applied weekly to biweekly throughout the year.

REST PERIOD: Growing conditions should be maintained year-round. Water and fertilizer might be reduced slightly in winter, especially for plants cultivated in the dark, short-day conditions common in temperate latitudes. However, plants should never be allowed to dry out completely.

GROWING MEDIA: Plants may be mounted on tree-fern or cork slabs or potted in small pots filled with any open, fast-draining medium. Repotting may be done anytime new roots are growing.

MISCELLANEOUS NOTES: The bloom season shown in the climate table is based on reports from the habitat. While plants are reportedly common in the habitat, none are currently known to be in cultivation.

Plant and Flower Information

PLANT SIZE AND TYPE: A 2.8 in. (7 cm) sympodial epiphyte.

PSEUDOBULB: 2.8 in. (7 cm) long.

LEAVES: 4 per growth. The oval to oblong leaves are 1.2 in. (3 cm) long.

INFLORESCENCE: Short. Inflorescences are apparently borne on leafless stems.

FLOWERS: 2 per inflorescence. The blood red flowers are 1.4 in. (3.6 cm) long and laterally flattened. The dorsal sepal and petals are wider than the lateral sepals. The erect lip is incurved along the margin.

REFERENCES: 198, 225, 385, 486, 556.

PHOTOS/DRAWINGS: 385.

Dendrobium lancilobum J. J. Wood.

ORIGIN/HABITAT: Sabah (North Borneo). Plants were collected in the Sipitand District east of the trail from Long Pa Sia to Long Miau at about 3600 ft. (1100 m) and near the Maga River at about 4150 ft. (1260 m). They are found in very open kerangas forest and lower montane forest.

CLIMATE: Station #49613, Tambunan, Sabah (North Borneo), Lat. 5.7°N, Long. 116.4°E, at 1200 ft. (366 m). Temperatures are calculated for an elevation of 4000 ft. (1220 m), resulting in probable extremes of 89°F (32°C) and 45°F (7°C).

N/HEMISPHERE	JAN	FEB	MAR	APR	MAY	JUN	JUL	AUG	SEP	OCT	NOV	DEC
°F AVG MAX	77	78	80	81	81	80	80	80	80	79	78	77
°F AVG MIN	58	56	57	58	59	58	57	57	58	58	58	59
DIURNAL RANGE	19	22	23	23	22	22	23	23	22	21	20	18
RAIN/INCHES	5.8	3.7	5.8	7.5	8.2	7.3	5.1	4.9	6.4	7.0	6.8	6.0
HUMIDITY/%	N/A											
BLOOM SEASON											*	*
DAYS CLR	N/A											
RAIN/MM	147	94	147	190	208	185	130	124	163	178	173	152
°C AVG MAX	24.9	25.4	26.5	27.1	27.1	26.5	26.5	26.5	26.5	26.0	25.4	24.9
°C AVG MIN	14.3	13.2	13.8	14.3	14.9	14.3	13.8	13.8	14.3	14.3	14.3	14.9
DIURNAL RANGE	10.6	12.2	12.7	12.8	12.2	12.2	12.7	12.7	12.2	11.7	11.1	10.0
S/HEMISPHERE	JUL	AUG	SEP	OCT	NOV	DEC	JAN	FEB	MAR	APR	MAY	JUN

Cultural Recommendations

LIGHT: 3000–4000 fc.

TEMPERATURES: Throughout the year, days average 77–81°F (25–27°C), and nights average 56–59°F (13–15°C), with a diurnal range of 18–23°F (10–13°C).

HUMIDITY: Information is not available for this location. However, records from nearby locations indicate that humidity probably averages 80–85% year-round.

WATER: Rainfall is moderate to heavy through the year. Cultivated plants should be kept moist, with only slight drying allowed between waterings.

FERTILIZER: 1/4–1/2 recommended strength. A balanced fertilizer should be applied weekly to biweekly throughout the year.

REST PERIOD: Growing conditions vary only slightly through the year. The diurnal range is slightly lower in winter due to somewhat cooler days. In cultivation, water should be reduced somewhat in winter, especially for plants grown in the dark, short-day conditions common in temperate latitudes. Plants should never be allowed to dry out completely, however. Fertilizer should be decreased when water is reduced and when plants are not actively growing.

GROWING MEDIA: Plants may be mounted on tree-fern or cork slabs or potted in small pots filled with any open, fast-draining medium. Repotting may be done anytime new roots are growing.

MISCELLANEOUS NOTES: The bloom season shown in the climate table is based on collection reports. Plants that produce flowers which last a single day commonly bloom several times during the year. Flowering usually occurs 7–14 days after a sudden 10°F (5°C) drop in daytime temperatures.

Plant and Flower Information

PLANT SIZE AND TYPE: An 8–14 in. (20–35 cm) sympodial epiphyte.

PSEUDOBULB: 8–14 in. (20–35 cm) long. The stems are flattened, straw yellow, and shiny. They may branch at the rooting nodes. Near the base of the stem, 1–4 of the lower nodes form a pseudobulbous swelling 0.8–1.4 in. (2.0–3.5 cm) long.

LEAVES: 4–8 per branch. The leaves are 0.7–1.8 in. (1.8–4.5 cm) long, thin, linear, and deciduous.

INFLORESCENCE: Very short. Inflorescences emerge from clumps of chaff-like bracts at nodes along the side of upper branches of leafless stems.

FLOWERS: 1 per inflorescence. The tiny, very short-lived flowers are 0.2 in. (0.5 cm) across. Sepals and petals may be whitish or pale apricot but are sometimes darker at the base. The lip is pale yellow.

REFERENCES: 235, 590.

PHOTOS/DRAWINGS: 590.

Dendrobium lane-poolei R. S. Rogers

ORIGIN/HABITAT: Papua New Guinea. Plants were collected between Adai and Naro at 6000–7000 ft. (1830–2130 m). They are common on mossy tree trunks in the forests of the Owen Stanley Range.

CLIMATE: Station #200192, Garaina, Papua New Guinea, Lat. 7.9°E, Long. 147.1°E, at 2350 ft. (716 m). Temperatures are calculated for an elevation of 6500 ft. (1980 m), resulting in probable extremes of 80°F (27°C) and 32°F (0°C).

N/HEMISPHERE	JAN	FEB	MAR	APR	MAY	JUN	JUL	AUG	SEP	OCT	NOV	DEC
°F AVG MAX	66	68	69	70	71	71	71	71	70	70	69	67
°F AVG MIN	49	49	49	50	49	50	51	51	51	50	50	49
DIURNAL RANGE	17	19	20	20	22	21	20	20	19	20	19	18
RAIN/INCHES	5.8	6.5	8.7	11.1	11.8	11.9	8.9	11.7	11.5	9.9	7.7	5.2
HUMIDITY/%	84	82	82	81	80	80	81	81	82	83	84	84
BLOOM SEASON		*										
DAYS CLR	N/A											
RAIN/MM	147	165	221	282	300	302	226	297	292	251	196	132
°C AVG MAX	19.1	20.2	20.7	21.3	21.8	21.8	21.8	21.8	21.3	21.3	20.7	19.6
°C AVG MIN	9.6	9.6	9.6	10.2	9.6	10.2	10.7	10.7	10.7	10.2	10.2	9.6
DIURNAL RANGE	9.5	10.6	11.1	11.1	12.2	11.6	11.1	11.1	10.6	11.1	10.5	10.0
S/HEMISPHERE	JUL	AUG	SEP	OCT	NOV	DEC	JAN	FEB	MAR	APR	MAY	JUN

Cultural Recommendations

LIGHT: 2000–3000 fc.

TEMPERATURES: Throughout the year, days average 66–71°F (19–22°C),

and nights average 49–51°F (10–11°C), with a diurnal range of 17–22°F (10–12°C).

HUMIDITY: 80–85% year-round.

WATER: Rainfall is heavy most of the year, but conditions are slightly drier in winter. Cultivated plants should kept evenly moist.

FERTILIZER: ¼–½ recommended strength. A balanced fertilizer should be applied weekly to biweekly throughout the year. The Royal Botanic Garden in Edinburgh uses a seaweed-based fertilizer for plants from high-elevation habitats in New Guinea.

REST PERIOD: Growing conditions should be maintained all year. In the habitat, rainfall is only slightly lower in winter. Water may be reduced somewhat for cultivated plants, especially those grown in the dark, short-day conditions common in temperate-latitude winters; but they should never be allowed to dry out completely. Fertilizer should be reduced or eliminated anytime water is reduced. In the habitat, light may be slightly higher in winter.

GROWING MEDIA: Plants may be mounted on tree-fern or cork slabs if humidity is high and plants are watered at least once daily in summer. When plants are potted, any open, fast-draining medium may be used. They may be repotted anytime new roots are growing.

MISCELLANEOUS NOTES: The bloom season shown in the climate table is based on records from the habitat.

Plant and Flower Information

PLANT SIZE AND TYPE: A 12 in. (30 cm) sympodial epiphyte.

PSEUDOBULB: 12 in. (30 cm) long. The branched stems are slender, ribbed, and covered by leaf-sheaths. The ribbed leaf-sheaths are covered with hairy dots.

LEAVES: Many. The pointed, lanceolate leaves are 1–2 in. (2.5–5.0 cm) long. They are rigid but rather papery.

INFLORESCENCE: Very short racemes.

FLOWERS: 5–6 per inflorescence. The orange-yellow flowers are 0.8 in. (2 cm) long, pendent and cone-shaped

REFERENCES: 223, 406.

Dendrobium langbianense Gagnepain

AKA: Seidenfaden (ref. 454) indicates that *D. monticola* Hunt and Summerhayes may prove to be a synonym of *D. langbianense*.

ORIGIN/HABITAT: Vietnam. Plants have been found on the Langbian Plateau near Dalat and Camly. Habitat elevation is estimated, so the following temperatures should be used with caution.

CLIMATE: Station #48881, Dalat, Vietnam, Lat. 11.1°N, Long. 108.1°E, at 3156 ft. (962 m). Record extreme temperatures are 93°F (34°C) and 43°F (6°C).

N/HEMISPHERE	JAN	FEB	MAR	APR	MAY	JUN	JUL	AUG	SEP	OCT	NOV	DEC
°F AVG MAX	80	82	84	85	84	81	81	80	80	80	79	79
°F AVG MIN	56	57	59	62	65	65	65	65	65	63	60	58
DIURNAL RANGE	24	25	25	23	19	16	16	15	15	17	19	21
RAIN/INCHES	0.2	0.9	1.6	4.6	9.1	6.1	7.7	8.2	10.1	9.7	2.7	1.3
HUMIDITY/%	68	64	65	71	78	81	82	83	84	82	76	73
BLOOM SEASON	N/A											
DAYS CLR @ 7AM	13	13	13	9	5	3	2	2	2	5	7	10
DAYS CLR @ 1PM	8	8	8	2	0	0	0	0	0	1	3	4
RAIN/MM	5	23	41	117	231	155	196	208	257	246	69	33
°C AVG MAX	26.7	27.8	28.9	29.4	28.9	27.2	27.2	26.7	26.7	26.7	26.1	26.1
°C AVG MIN	13.3	13.9	15.0	16.7	18.3	18.3	18.3	18.3	18.3	17.2	15.6	14.4
DIURNAL RANGE	13.4	13.9	13.9	12.7	10.6	8.9	8.9	8.4	8.4	9.5	10.5	11.7
S/HEMISPHERE	JUL	AUG	SEP	OCT	NOV	DEC	JAN	FEB	MAR	APR	MAY	JUN

Cultural Recommendations

LIGHT: 2000–3000 fc.

TEMPERATURES: Summer days average 80–81°F (27°C), and nights average 65°F (18°C), with a diurnal range of 15–16°F (8–9°C). The warmest temperatures occur in late winter and spring. Days average 84–85°F (29°C), and nights average 59–65°F (15°C to 18°C), with a diurnal range of 19–25°F (11–14°C).

HUMIDITY: 80–85% in summer, dropping to near 65% in midwinter.

WATER: Rainfall is moderate to heavy in summer but is very light for 2 months in winter. Cultivated plants should be kept moist while growing, but water should be gradually reduced after new growths mature in autumn.

FERTILIZER: ¼–½ recommended strength, applied weekly. A high-nitrogen fertilizer is beneficial from spring to midsummer, but a fertilizer high in phosphates should be used in late summer and autumn.

REST PERIOD: Winter days average 79–82°F (26–28°C), and nights average 56–58°F (13–14°C), with a diurnal range of 21–25°F (12–14°C). The increased diurnal range results from warmer days and cooler nights. Rainfall is low for 3–4 months. For 1–2 of these months, conditions are so dry that even moisture from dew is uncommon. For cultivated plants, water and fertilizer should be reduced for 2–3 months. Plants should be allowed to dry out between waterings, but they should not remain dry for extended periods. In the habitat, light is highest in winter.

GROWING MEDIA: Plants may be mounted on tree-fern or cork slabs if humidity is high and plants are watered at least once daily in summer. When plants are potted, any open, fast-draining medium may be used. Repotting is best done in early spring when new roots are growing.

Plant and Flower Information

PLANT SIZE AND TYPE: A 1.2–2.0 in. (3–5 cm) sympodial epiphyte.

PSEUDOBULB: 0.4 in. (1 cm) long. Pseudobulbs are covered with leaf bases.

LEAVES: 3–6 per growth. The leaves are 0.8 in. (2 cm) long.

INFLORESCENCE: 0.8 in. (2 cm) long. Up to 3 inflorescences emerge from the upper part of leafy pseudobulbs.

FLOWERS: 4–9 per inflorescence. The flowers are 0.2–0.3 in. (0.5–0.7 cm) across. The pointed midlobe of the lip is ruffled with deeply toothed margins and a callus along the centerline. The spur and the apex of the lip curve toward each other. Blossoms were described as pale.

REFERENCES: 136, 224, 448, 454.

PHOTOS/DRAWINGS: 454.

Dendrobium lankaviense Ridley

AKA: Also spelled *D. lankawiense,* which is the commonly used spelling. However, Seidenfaden and Wood (ref. 455) report that the plant was originally described as *D. lankaviense*.

ORIGIN/HABITAT: Langkawi Island off the extreme northwest coast of Malaya. Habitat elevation was not given, but topographical maps indicate that 2900 ft. (880 m) is the highest elevation on the island. Habitat elevation is estimated, so the following temperatures should be used with caution.

CLIMATE: Station #48603, Alor Setar, Malaya, Lat. 6.2°N, Long. 100.4°E, at 13 ft. (4 m). Temperatures are calculated for an elevation of 1500 ft. (460 m), resulting in probable extremes of 95°F (35°C) and 56°F (13°C).

N/HEMISPHERE	JAN	FEB	MAR	APR	MAY	JUN	JUL	AUG	SEP	OCT	NOV	DEC
°F AVG MAX	85	87	88	88	85	84	83	83	82	82	83	83
°F AVG MIN	66	66	68	69	70	69	69	69	69	69	68	67
DIURNAL RANGE	19	21	20	19	15	15	14	14	13	13	15	16
RAIN/INCHES	2.5	2.2	5.8	9.0	10.7	7.8	7.7	10.4	12.8	11.9	8.1	5.2
HUMIDITY/%	71	66	70	75	79	79	79	79	82	84	83	77
BLOOM SEASON										*		
DAYS CLR @ 7AM	5	4	5	2	1	1	1	1	1	1	2	5
DAYS CLR @ 1PM	2	2	2	1	0	1	1	0	0	0	1	2
RAIN/MM	64	56	147	229	272	198	196	264	325	302	206	132
°C AVG MAX	29.5	30.6	31.2	31.2	29.5	28.9	28.4	28.4	27.8	27.8	28.4	28.4
°C AVG MIN	18.9	18.9	20.1	20.6	21.2	20.6	20.6	20.6	20.6	20.6	20.1	19.5
DIURNAL RANGE	10.6	11.7	11.1	10.6	8.3	8.3	7.8	7.8	7.2	7.2	8.3	8.9
S/HEMISPHERE	JUL	AUG	SEP	OCT	NOV	DEC	JAN	FEB	MAR	APR	MAY	JUN

Dendrobium lankawiense

Cultural Recommendations

LIGHT: 2000–3000 fc.

TEMPERATURES: Throughout the year, days average 82–88°F (28–31°C), and nights average 66–70°F (19–21°C), with a diurnal range of 13–21°F (7–12°C). The warmest days, the coolest nights, and the greatest diurnal ranges occur in late winter and spring during the dry season.

HUMIDITY: 80–85% most of the year, dropping to 65–70% in late winter and spring.

WATER: Rainfall is moderate to heavy most of the year, but conditions are semidry for 2 months in winter. Cultivated plants should be kept moist while actively growing, but water should be gradually reduced in late autumn.

FERTILIZER: ¼–½ recommended strength. A balanced fertilizer should be applied weekly to biweekly throughout the year.

REST PERIOD: Growing conditions should be maintained all year. In the habitat, rainfall is lower in winter, but heavy dew is common. For 1–2 months, water should be reduced and plants allowed to dry slightly between waterings; but they should not remain dry for long periods. Fertilizer should be reduced until water is increased in spring. In the habitat, light is highest in winter.

GROWING MEDIA: Plants may be mounted on tree-fern or cork slabs if humidity is high and plants are watered at least once daily in summer. When plants are potted, any open, fast-draining medium may be used. Repotting is best done in early spring when new roots are growing.

MISCELLANEOUS NOTES: The bloom season shown in the climate table is based on collection records. Two plants have been collected.

Plant and Flower Information

PLANT SIZE AND TYPE: A 12 in. (30 cm) sympodial epiphyte.

PSEUDOBULB: 12 in. (30 cm) long. The tufted pseudobulbs are very slender with a slight thickening above. They are red when young but turn grey with age.

LEAVES: The leaves are 2 in. (5 cm) long. They are linear to lanceolate and pointed at the apex.

INFLORESCENCE: Short. Inflorescences arise from leafless stems.

FLOWERS: 1 per inflorescence. The flowers are 0.6–0.8 in. (1.5–2.0 cm) across. All segments are deep purple, but the color is darkest at the apex of the lip.

REFERENCES: 200, 221, 399, 455.

PHOTOS/DRAWINGS: 455.

Dendrobium lankawiense Ridley. See *D. lankaviense* Ridley. *D. lankawiense* is the common spelling, but the plant was originally described as *D. lankaviense*. REFERENCES: 200, 399, 455.

Dendrobium lapeyrouseoides Schlechter. Sometimes spelled *D. lapeyrouseoides*, see *D. cyanocentrum* Schlechter. REFERENCES: 221, 385, 437, 445.

Dendrobium lasianthera J. J. Smith

AKA: *D. stueberi* Hort., *D. ostrinoglossum* Rupp. The name is sometimes spelled *D. lasiantherum*. Millar (ref. 304) referred to the red form as May River red, and the lavender form as Sepik blue. The International Orchid Commission (ref. 236) registers hybrids under both *D. ostrinoglossum* and *D. lasianthera*.

ORIGIN/HABITAT: New Guinea. Plants grow on tall trees below 330 ft. (100 m) in very humid habitats near rivers, streams, and in swamp forests. In Papua, plants grow along the May River, a tributary of the Sepik River, near the border between Papua and Irian Jaya. In Irian Jaya, plants are found near Jayapura and in the south along the Pulau (Eilanden) River. They were once thought to grow with roots in water, and seasonal flooding may actually submerge their roots for short periods without causing damage.

CLIMATE: Station #200004, Ambunti, Papua New Guinea, Lat. 4.2°S, Long. 142.8°E, at 164 ft. (50 m). Record extreme temperatures are 99°F (37°C) and 52°F (11°C).

N/HEMISPHERE	JAN	FEB	MAR	APR	MAY	JUN	JUL	AUG	SEP	OCT	NOV	DEC
°F AVG MAX	88	90	90	90	91	90	90	90	90	90	90	89
°F AVG MIN	72	73	74	73	73	73	72	73	73	73	73	74
DIURNAL RANGE	16	17	16	17	18	17	18	17	17	17	17	15
RAIN/INCHES	6.4	7.4	7.7	8.5	9.2	9.4	10.9	10.2	12.2	10.4	8.3	5.2
HUMIDITY/%	N/A											
BLOOM SEASON			*		*		*	*				
DAYS CLR	N/A											
RAIN/MM	163	187	196	217	233	240	277	260	311	265	211	132
°C AVG MAX	31.2	32.2	32.4	32.1	32.6	32.2	32.3	31.9	32.1	31.9	31.9	31.7
°C AVG MIN	22.4	22.8	23.2	22.8	23.0	22.8	22.4	22.5	22.7	22.8	22.9	23.1
DIURNAL RANGE	8.8	9.4	9.2	9.3	9.6	9.4	9.9	9.4	9.4	9.1	9.0	8.6
S/HEMISPHERE	JUL	AUG	SEP	OCT	NOV	DEC	JAN	FEB	MAR	APR	MAY	JUN

Cultural Recommendations

LIGHT: 2500–3000 fc.

TEMPERATURES: Throughout the year, days average 88–91°F (31–33°C), and nights average 72–74°F (22–23°C), with a diurnal range of 15–18°F (9–10°C).

HUMIDITY: Information is not available for this location. The habitat is always described as being near water, so humidity probably averages 80–85% year-round.

WATER: Rainfall is heavy year-round, with the greatest amounts falling in summer and early autumn. Cultivated plants should be kept moist but not soggy.

FERTILIZER: ¼–½ recommended strength. A balanced fertilizer should be applied weekly to biweekly throughout the year.

REST PERIOD: Growing conditions should be maintained all year. Growers suggest that winter lows should be kept above 59°F (15°C), but this is considerably cooler than indicated by the climate data. Water and fertilizer should be reduced somewhat for plants cultivated in the dark, short-day conditions common in temperate-latitude winters; but they should never be allowed to dry out completely.

GROWING MEDIA: Plants may be mounted on tree-fern or cork slabs if humidity is high and plants are watered at least once daily in summer. When plants are potted, any open, fast-draining medium may be used. Repotting may be done anytime new roots are growing.

MISCELLANEOUS NOTES: The bloom season shown in the climate table is based on cultivation records. A specimen at Kew grows on a tree branch overhanging a pond. High humidity, warm temperatures, and strong air movement should be provided for cultivated plants. The plant is reportedly difficult to maintain in Singapore, but no specific horticultural problem was given. Overall climatic conditions are similar to the habitat, but average night temperatures in Singapore are about 5°F (3°C) warmer, and the diurnal range averages about 6°F (3°C) less. In nature, some plants are nearly always in bloom.

Plant and Flower Information

PLANT SIZE AND TYPE: A large, strong sympodial epiphyte. Cultivated plants may be as small as 10 in. (25 cm). In nature, however, plants may reach a length of 118 in. (300 cm). The plant resembles *D. discolor* Lindley when not in bloom.

PSEUDOBULB: 10–118 in. (25–300 cm) long. The jointed stems are usually erect. The leaves are primarily on the upper 50% of the stem.

LEAVES: Many. The dark green leaves are 1.4–5.5 in. (3.5–14.0 cm) long, ovate to elliptic, and leathery. They last 2–3 years.

INFLORESCENCE: 12–24 in. (30–60 cm) long. Inflorescences arise from leaf nodes near the apex of leafy stems. Flowers tend to hang down and are not well displayed on the inflorescence.

FLOWERS: 10–15, rarely to 30 per inflorescence. The flowers are 2.6–3.2 in. (6.5–8.0 cm) across. Often described with numerous superlatives, the glossy blossoms are large and showy. Color is variable. Flowers may be predominately brown, orange-red, rose-purple, lavender, or maroon. The sepals, which are most often yellow-brown, are darker brown toward the apex and white or yellow at the base and along the margin. They twist once. The long, spiraled petals are the same color as the sepals. The brownish to golden yellow lip may be suffused with purple with a yellow margin on the midlobe. The blossoms last up to 6 months.

HYBRIDIZING NOTES: Chromosome count is 2n = 38 (ref. 151, 152, 154, 187, 188, 243). As a parent, *D. lasianthera* contributes the tendency toward numerous, long-lasting flowers and increases the frequency of blooming. The 'antelope' flower shape with the twisted, stiffly erect petals persists for several generations.

REFERENCES: 25, 36, 84, 151, 152, 154, 179, 187, 188, 190, 200, 225, 236, 243, 301, 303, 304, 306, 343, 351, 371, 430, 510, 526, 537, 551.

PHOTOS/DRAWINGS: *36, 84,* 301, *303, 304, 306, 343, 351, 371, 430, 496, 551.*

Dendrobium lasioglossum Rchb. f.

AKA: Sometimes spelled *D. lassioglossum.*

ORIGIN/HABITAT: Burma. Plants reportedly grow in the forests, and that is everything we have been able to find about habitat type, location, and elevation. Without detailed habitat information, the selection of the following climate data was based on estimations, assumptions, suppositions, and conjecture and should, therefore, be used with extreme caution.

CLIMATE: Station #48103, Moulmein, Burma, Lat. 16.4°N, Long. 97.7°E, at 150 ft. (46 m). Temperatures are calculated for an estimated habitat elevation of 2000 ft. (610 m), resulting in probable extremes of 96°F (36°C) and 45°F (7°C).

N/HEMISPHERE	JAN	FEB	MAR	APR	MAY	JUN	JUL	AUG	SEP	OCT	NOV	DEC
°F AVG MAX	83	86	88	89	83	79	77	77	79	82	83	81
°F AVG MIN	60	62	67	70	70	69	69	69	69	69	67	62
DIURNAL RANGE	23	24	21	19	13	10	8	8	10	13	16	19
RAIN/INCHES	0.3	0.2	0.4	3.0	20.3	35.6	46.3	43.4	28.1	8.5	2.1	0.1
HUMIDITY/%	66	68	68	70	81	91	92	93	91	81	75	64
BLOOM SEASON				*								
DAYS CLR @ 7AM	12	7	5	6	1	0	0	0	0	3	7	12
DAYS CLR @ 1PM	20	13	10	8	3	0	0	0	0	4	12	17
RAIN/MM	8	5	10	76	516	904	1176	1102	714	216	53	3
°C AVG MAX	28.3	29.9	31.1	31.6	28.3	26.1	24.9	24.9	26.1	27.7	28.3	27.2
°C AVG MIN	15.5	16.6	19.4	21.1	21.1	20.5	20.5	20.5	20.5	20.5	19.4	16.6
DIURNAL RANGE	12.8	13.3	11.7	10.5	7.2	5.6	4.4	4.4	5.6	7.2	8.9	10.6
S/HEMISPHERE	JUL	AUG	SEP	OCT	NOV	DEC	JAN	FEB	MAR	APR	MAY	JUN

Cultural Recommendations

LIGHT: 2000–3000 fc.

TEMPERATURES: Summer days average 77–79°F (25–26°C), and nights average 69°F (21°C), with a diurnal range of 8–10°F (4–6°C). Weather is warmest in spring. Days average 83–89°F (28–32°C), and nights average 67–70°F (19–21°C), with a diurnal range of 13–21°F (7–12°C).

HUMIDITY: 80–90% from late spring to midautumn, dropping to 65–70% in winter and early spring.

WATER: Rainfall is very heavy from late spring to autumn, but amounts are greatly reduced in winter. Cultivated plants require frequent and heavy watering while actively growing, but they must be able to dry rapidly after watering. Water should be gradually reduced after new growths mature in autumn.

FERTILIZER: ¼–½ recommended strength, applied weekly. A high-nitrogen fertilizer is beneficial from spring to midsummer, but a fertilizer high in phosphates should be used in late summer and autumn.

REST PERIOD: Winter days average 81–86°F (27–30°C), and nights average 60–62°F (16–17°C), with a diurnal range of 19–24°F (11–13°C). In the habitat, rainfall is very low for 4 months, but the high humidity and the large temperature range result in frequent, heavy deposits of dew. Cultivated plants should be allowed to dry somewhat between waterings, but they should not remain dry for long periods. Fertilizer should be reduced or eliminated while water is reduced. In the habitat, light is highest in winter.

GROWING MEDIA: Mounting plants on tree-fern or cork slabs accommodates their drooping to pendent growth habit, but humidity must be high and water should be applied daily in summer. Repotting may be done anytime new roots are actively growing.

MISCELLANEOUS NOTES: The bloom season shown in the climate table is based on cultivation records.

Plant and Flower Information

PLANT SIZE AND TYPE: A 10–24 in. (25–60 cm) sympodial epiphyte.

PSEUDOBULB: 10–24 in. (25–60 cm) long. The stems are slender, drooping, and branched with internodes at 1–2 in. (2.5–5.0 cm) intervals.

LEAVES: The flat, lanceolate leaves are 1–2 in. (2.5–5.0 cm) long.

INFLORESCENCE: Inflorescences arise opposite the leaves from the uppermost nodes of leafy stems.

FLOWERS: 1–4 per inflorescence. The flowers are 1.6–2.0 in. (4–5 cm) across. The lateral sepals are longer than the dorsal sepal and petals. Sepals and ovate petals are white. The funnel-shaped lip may have purplish veins with a few reddish streaks on the large sidelobes. The short midlobe is wavy along margin. The hairy disk may be greenish-yellow to orange-yellow.

REFERENCES: 157, 179, 202, 210, 216, 254, 445, 541, 570.

PHOTOS/DRAWINGS: 210.

Dendrobium latelabellatum A. Gilli

ORIGIN/HABITAT: Papua New Guinea. Plants were found originally in grasslands near Lakai. We were unable to find this location but have assumed it is merely a different spelling of Lakei, which is located on the south coast of New Britain Island. Habitat elevation is unavailable, so the following climate data should be used with caution.

CLIMATE: Station #94085, Rabul, New Britain Island, Papua New Guinea, Lat. 4.2°S, Long. 152.2°E, at 28 ft. (9 m). Record extreme temperatures are 100°F (38°C) and 65°F (18°C).

N/HEMISPHERE	JAN	FEB	MAR	APR	MAY	JUN	JUL	AUG	SEP	OCT	NOV	DEC
°F AVG MAX	89	89	91	92	91	90	90	90	90	90	90	90
°F AVG MIN	73	72	73	73	73	73	73	73	73	73	73	73
DIURNAL RANGE	16	17	18	19	18	17	17	17	17	17	17	17
RAIN/INCHES	5.4	3.7	3.5	5.1	7.1	10.1	14.8	10.4	10.2	10.0	5.2	3.3
HUMIDITY/%	74	73	69	70	73	76	77	76	77	77	75	74
BLOOM SEASON								*				
DAYS CLR	N/A											
RAIN/MM	137	94	89	130	180	257	376	264	259	254	132	84
°C AVG MAX	31.7	31.7	32.8	33.3	32.8	32.2	32.2	32.2	32.2	32.2	32.2	32.2
°C AVG MIN	22.8	22.2	22.8	22.8	22.8	22.8	22.8	22.8	22.8	22.8	22.8	22.8
DIURNAL RANGE	8.9	9.5	10.0	10.5	10.0	9.4	9.4	9.4	9.4	9.4	9.4	9.4
S/HEMISPHERE	JUL	AUG	SEP	OCT	NOV	DEC	JAN	FEB	MAR	APR	MAY	JUN

Cultural Recommendations

LIGHT: 2500–3000 fc.

Dendrobium laterale

TEMPERATURES: Throughout the year, days average 89–92°F (32–33°C), and nights average 72–73°F (22–23°C), with a diurnal range of 16–19°F (9–11°C).

HUMIDITY: Near 75% most of the year. Humidity usually rises 90–100% at night, but it may drop to as low as 35% at midday during the winter dry season.

WATER: Rainfall is heavy most of the year. Conditions are slightly drier for 2 months in late winter. Cultivated plants should be kept evenly moist.

FERTILIZER: ¼–½ recommended strength. A balanced fertilizer should be applied weekly to biweekly throughout the year.

REST PERIOD: Growing conditions should be maintained all year. For cultivated plants, water may be reduced somewhat in winter, especially for plants grown in the dark, short-day conditions common in temperate latitudes. They should never be allowed to dry out completely, however. Fertilizer should be reduced if water is reduced. In the habitat, light is highest in winter.

GROWING MEDIA: Plants may be mounted on tree-fern or cork slabs if humidity is high and the plants are watered at least once daily in summer. When plants are potted, medium to coarse fir bark or any open, fast-draining medium may be used. Repotting may be done anytime new roots are growing.

MISCELLANEOUS NOTES: The bloom season shown in the climate table is based on collection reports.

Plant and Flower Information

PLANT SIZE AND TYPE: A 20 in. (50 cm) sympodial terrestrial.

PSEUDOBULB: 20 in. (50 cm) long. The erect stems, which do not branch, are moderately thick, grooved, and round in cross-section.

LEAVES: The broadly lanceolate leaves are 1.5–2.5 in. (4.0–6.4 cm) long. They are leathery and taper to a point at the tip.

INFLORESCENCE: 0.8–1.2 in. (2–3 cm) long. Inflorescences emerge from nodes along the side of the stem.

FLOWERS: 3–7 per inflorescence. The flowers are 0.4 in. (1 cm) long. Sepals and petals are pale green with yellow at the base. The lip is yellow and white. The midlobe has a small, unusual third lobe at the apex of the divided midlobe making it appear 3-lobed.

REFERENCES: 146, 234.

PHOTOS/DRAWINGS: 146.

Dendrobium laterale L. O. Williams

ORIGIN/HABITAT: Western Burma. Plants are relatively common on trees in the mountains near Haka at 5500–7600 ft. (1700–2320 m).

CLIMATE: Station #48042, Mandalay, Burma. Lat. 21.9°N, Long. 96.1°E, at 252 ft. (77 m). Temperatures are calculated for an elevation of 6500 ft. (1980 m), resulting in probable extremes of 93°F (34°C) and 21°F (–6°C).

N/HEMISPHERE	JAN	FEB	MAR	APR	MAY	JUN	JUL	AUG	SEP	OCT	NOV	DEC
°F AVG MAX	61	67	75	79	77	72	72	71	70	68	64	60
°F AVG MIN	35	39	47	56	58	58	58	57	56	54	47	38
DIURNAL RANGE	26	28	28	23	19	14	14	14	14	14	17	22
RAIN/INCHES	0.1	0.2	0.2	1.4	5.9	6.0	2.9	4.0	5.8	5.0	2.5	0.4
HUMIDITY/%	68	57	47	47	64	70	70	73	78	80	76	72
BLOOM SEASON				*								
DAYS CLR @ 6AM	21	20	23	16	6	1	1	0	1	3	12	16
DAYS CLR @ 12PM	22	22	24	20	7	0	0	0	0	2	14	19
RAIN/MM	3	5	5	36	150	152	74	102	147	127	64	10
°C AVG MAX	16.3	19.7	24.1	26.3	25.2	22.4	22.4	21.9	21.3	20.2	18.0	15.8
°C AVG MIN	1.9	4.1	8.5	13.4	14.7	14.7	14.7	14.1	13.5	12.4	8.5	3.5
DIURNAL RANGE	14.4	15.6	15.6	12.8	10.5	7.7	7.7	7.8	7.8	7.8	9.5	12.3
S/HEMISPHERE	JUL	AUG	SEP	OCT	NOV	DEC	JAN	FEB	MAR	APR	MAY	JUN

Cultural Recommendations

LIGHT: 2000–3000 fc.

TEMPERATURES: Summer days average 71–72°F (22°C), and nights average 57–58°F (14–15°C), with a diurnal range of 14°F (8°C). Spring is the warmest season. Days average 75–79°F (24–26°C), and nights average 47–58°F (9–15°C), with a diurnal range of 19–28°F (11–16°C).

HUMIDITY: In the mountains, humidity is probably greater than shown in the climate table. However, we found no weather records from stations in the western mountains. We estimate that summer humidity averages near 80%, but may drop to 50–60% in winter and early spring.

WATER: Rainfall is probably greater in the mountain habitat than is indicated in the climate table. The seasonal pattern would be similar, however. Cultivated plants should be kept moist from summer through early autumn, but water should be gradually reduced after new growths mature in autumn.

FERTILIZER: ¼–½ recommended strength, applied weekly. A high-nitrogen fertilizer is beneficial from spring to midsummer, but a fertilizer high in phosphates should be used in late summer and autumn.

REST PERIOD: Winter days average 60–67°F (16–20°C), and nights average 35–39°F (2–4°C), with a diurnal range of 22–28°F (12–16°C). Rainfall amounts are significantly less for 4–5 months in winter and early spring. Water should be reduced for cultivated plants and the medium allowed to dry out between waterings. Plants should not remain completely dry for extended periods, however. Fertilizer should be reduced or eliminated until water is increased in spring. In the habitat, light is highest in winter.

GROWING MEDIA: Plants may be mounted on tree-fern or cork slabs or potted in small pots filled with any open, fast-draining medium. Repotting may be done anytime new roots are actively growing.

MISCELLANEOUS NOTES: The bloom season shown in the climate table is based on collection reports.

Plant and Flower Information

PLANT SIZE AND TYPE: A mat-forming, 2 in. (5 cm) sympodial epiphyte.

PSEUDOBULB: 0.4 in. (1 cm) long. The ovoid pseudobulbs are covered with membranelike sheaths that disintegrate with age.

INFLORESCENCE: Flowers are held above the tips of the pseudobulbs. The raceme arises from the base of newer, leafless pseudobulbs.

FLOWERS: Few per inflorescence. The flowers are about 1 in. (2.5 cm) long, which is large for the plant size. Sepals and petals may be pink or lavender. The lip is red with yellow markings on the inside. It is 3-lobed with a raised, lobed callus. Blossoms are not fragrant.

REFERENCES: 227, 573.

PHOTOS/DRAWINGS: 573.

Dendrobium lateriflorum Ridley. See *D. puniceum* Ridley.

REFERENCES: 222, 385, 400.

Dendrobium latifolium H. B. and K. Now considered a synonym of *Maxillaria latifolia* Lindley. REFERENCES: 216, 254.

Dendrobium latifrons J. J. Smith

ORIGIN/HABITAT: New Guinea. Plants grow in marshy ground in the Angi Lakes District at 7000 ft. (2150 m).

CLIMATE: Station #97530, Manokwari, Irian Jaya, Lat. 0.9°S, Long. 134.1°E, at 10 ft. (3 m). Temperatures are calculated for an elevation of 7000 ft. (2130 m), resulting in probable extremes of 70°F (21°C) and 45°F (7°C).

N/HEMISPHERE	JAN	FEB	MAR	APR	MAY	JUN	JUL	AUG	SEP	OCT	NOV	DEC
°F AVG MAX	63	62	64	64	65	63	63	63	63	63	63	62
°F AVG MIN	51	52	51	51	51	52	50	50	51	51	51	51
DIURNAL RANGE	12	10	13	13	14	11	13	13	12	12	12	11
RAIN/INCHES	5.4	5.6	5.0	4.7	4.5	10.3	12.0	9.4	13.2	11.1	7.8	7.3
HUMIDITY/%	87	87	86	84	85	86	86	85	86	86	86	85
BLOOM SEASON					*							
DAYS CLR @ 6AM	4	3	3	3	3	3	3	1	1	2	3	7
DAYS CLR @ 12PM	2	2	2	3	1	1	1	1	0	1	0	2
RAIN/MM	137	142	127	119	114	262	305	239	335	282	198	185
°C AVG MAX	17.2	16.7	17.8	17.8	18.3	17.4	17.3	17.2	17.2	17.2	17.2	16.7
°C AVG MIN	10.6	11.1	10.5	10.5	10.5	11.1	10.0	10.0	10.5	10.5	10.5	10.5
DIURNAL RANGE	6.6	5.6	7.3	7.3	7.8	6.3	7.3	7.2	6.7	6.7	6.7	6.2
S/HEMISPHERE	JUL	AUG	SEP	OCT	NOV	DEC	JAN	FEB	MAR	APR	MAY	JUN

Cultural Recommendations

LIGHT: 2000–3000 fc.

TEMPERATURES: Throughout the year, days average 62–65°F (17–18°C), and nights average 50–52°F (10–11°C), with a diurnal range of 10–14°F (6–8°C). Due to the effects of the microclimate, actual high temperatures may be as much as 10°F (6°C) warmer than indicated.

HUMIDITY: Near 85% year-round.

WATER: Rainfall is moderate to very heavy all year. In the habitat, plants grow in marshy ground, so cultivated plants should be kept very moist.

FERTILIZER: ¼–½ recommended strength. A balanced fertilizer should be applied weekly to biweekly throughout the year.

REST PERIOD: Growing conditions should be maintained year-round. Water and fertilizer may be reduced somewhat in winter, especially for plants cultivated in the dark, short-day conditions common in temperate latitudes. However, these plants should never be allowed to dry out completely. In the habitat, light is highest in winter.

GROWING MEDIA: An acidic medium that retains moisture is needed. Live sphagnum moss may be the most reasonable starting point. Information regarding the use of live sphagnum is included in Chapter 1. Another alternative might be a medium which growers have used for wet-growing *Phragmipedium,* which consists of a mixture of sand, loam, chopped tree-fern, and garden compost.

MISCELLANEOUS NOTES: The bloom season shown in the climate table is based on collection reports. Terrestrial plants from high elevation marshes are often particularly difficult to maintain in cultivation.

Plant and Flower Information

PLANT SIZE AND TYPE: A 19 in. (47 cm) sympodial terrestrial.

PSEUDOBULB: 19 in. (47 cm) long. The elongated, unbranched stems are connected by a short rhizome.

LEAVES: 2.2 in. (5.5 cm) long. The leaves are oblong and spreading with 2 pointed teeth at the apex. When dry, the leaf margin is recurved.

INFLORESCENCE: 1.2–2.0 in. (3–5 cm) long. Inflorescences emerge along the stem through the leaf bases. The blossoms on each inflorescence face in all directions.

FLOWERS: 3–5 per inflorescence. The yellow flowers are 0.6–0.8 in. (1.5–2.0 cm) across. They have broadly triangular sepals and nearly oval petals. The short 3-lobed lip is curved and concave above the base. The midlobe appears 2-lobed. It is hairy on the inside and irregularly ruffled along the margin.

REFERENCES: 144, 222.

Dendrobium latilabre J. J. Smith. See *D. tenellum* (Blume) Lindley. REFERENCES: 25, 445.

Dendrobium latoureoides (Schlechter) J. J. Smith. Although not correctly transferred, Schlechter (ref. 443) considered this name to be a synonym of *Cadetia latoureoides* Schlechter. REFERENCES: 223, 225, 443, 486.

Dendrobium laurensii J. J. Smith

ORIGIN/HABITAT: The Molucca Islands. Plants have been found east of Ternate Island on Halmaheira Island.

CLIMATE: Station #97430, Ternate, Indonesia, Lat. 0.8°N, Long.127.4°E, at 75 ft. (23 m). Record extreme temperatures are not available for this station.

N/HEMISPHERE	JAN	FEB	MAR	APR	MAY	JUN	JUL	AUG	SEP	OCT	NOV	DEC
°F AVG MAX	85	85	86	86	87	86	87	86	86	87	87	86
°F AVG MIN	77	76	77	77	77	76	75	75	76	77	77	77
DIURNAL RANGE	8	9	9	9	10	10	12	11	10	10	10	9
RAIN/INCHES	5.3	6.1	6.7	6.6	9.4	8.4	4.6	2.1	3.1	3.2	7.2	8.2
HUMIDITY/%	N/A											
BLOOM SEASON	N/A											
DAYS CLR	N/A											
RAIN/MM	135	155	170	168	239	213	117	53	79	81	183	208
°C AVG MAX	29.4	29.4	30.0	30.0	30.6	30.0	30.6	30.0	30.0	30.6	30.6	30.0
°C AVG MIN	25.0	24.4	25.0	25.0	25.0	24.4	23.9	23.9	24.4	25.0	25.0	25.0
DIURNAL RANGE	4.4	5.0	5.0	5.0	5.6	5.6	6.7	6.1	5.6	5.6	5.6	5.0
S/HEMISPHERE	JUL	AUG	SEP	OCT	NOV	DEC	JAN	FEB	MAR	APR	MAY	JUN

Cultural Recommendations

LIGHT: 2500–3500 fc.

TEMPERATURES: Throughout the year, days average 85–87°F (29–31°C), and nights average 75–77°F (24–25°C), with a diurnal range of 8–12°F (4–7°C). The warmest days and coolest nights occur in early summer.

HUMIDITY: Information is not available for this location. However, records from nearby locations indicate that humidity probably averages near 80% year-round.

WATER: Rainfall is moderate to heavy most of the year, but conditions are somewhat drier for 2–3 months in late summer and autumn. Cultivated plants should be kept moist with only slight drying allowed between waterings during most of the year. Plants should become moderately dry between waterings in late summer and early autumn; however, but they should not remain dry for long periods.

FERTILIZER: ¼–½ recommended strength. A balanced fertilizer should be applied weekly to biweekly throughout the year.

REST PERIOD: Growing temperatures should be maintained all year. Water may be reduced somewhat in winter, especially for plants grown in the dark, short-day conditions in temperate latitudes. They should not be allowed to dry out completely, however. In the habitat, seasonal light variation is minor.

GROWING MEDIA: Plants may be mounted on tree-fern or cork slabs if humidity is high and plants are watered at least once daily in summer. When plants are potted, any open, fast-draining medium may be used. Repotting may be done anytime new roots are growing.

Plant and Flower Information

PLANT SIZE AND TYPE: A 5–7 in. (13–18 cm) sympodial epiphyte.

PSEUDOBULB: 5–7 in. (13–18 cm) long. The pale green stems usually consist of 5–9 nodes.

LEAVES: 1 at the apex of each growth. The shiny, light green leaves are 7 in. (18 cm) long. They are lanceolate and may be fleshy or leathery.

INFLORESCENCE: 0.4 in. (1 cm) long. Inflorescences emerge from nodes at the side of the pseudobulb.

FLOWERS: 2–4 per inflorescence. The waxy flowers are 0.8 in. (2 cm) across. Sepals and petals are white with yellow at the base. The sepals are spotted with dark brown on the outer surface. The lip is very fleshy with a concave, broad, nearly triangular midlobe. The triangular, erect to incurved sidelobes have purple veins. Blossoms are slightly fragrant.

REFERENCES: 83, 222.

Dendrobium laurifolium (Kränzlin) J. J. Smith. Now considered a synonym of *Epigeneium laurifolium* (Kränzlin) Summerhayes.
REFERENCES: 225, 229, 254, 499.

Dendrobium lauterbachianum A. Hawkes

AKA: *D. obtusum* Schlechter.

ORIGIN/HABITAT: Northern Papua New Guinea. Plants grow on forest trees in the Torricelli Range at about 3800 ft. (1160 m).

CLIMATE: Station #94004, Wewak, Papua New Guinea, Lat. 3.6°S, Long. 143.7°E, at 16 ft. (5 m). Temperatures are calculated for an elevation of 3800 ft. (1160 m), resulting in probable extremes of 86°F (30°C) and 50°F (10°C).

N/HEMISPHERE	JAN	FEB	MAR	APR	MAY	JUN	JUL	AUG	SEP	OCT	NOV	DEC
°F AVG MAX	76	76	76	76	76	76	75	74	75	76	76	76
°F AVG MIN	62	62	62	63	63	63	63	63	62	62	63	62
DIURNAL RANGE	14	14	14	13	13	13	12	11	13	14	13	14
RAIN/INCHES	7.6	4.8	5.3	10.0	13.3	14.5	12.1	11.9	14.9	16.9	15.1	10.8
HUMIDITY/%	80	79	79	78	79	81	82	82	81	82	81	80
BLOOM SEASON							*					
DAYS CLR	N/A											
RAIN/MM	193	122	135	254	338	368	307	302	378	429	384	274
°C AVG MAX	24.2	24.2	24.2	24.2	24.2	24.2	23.6	23.1	23.6	24.2	24.2	24.2
°C AVG MIN	16.4	16.4	16.4	17.0	17.0	17.0	17.0	17.0	16.4	16.4	17.0	16.4
DIURNAL RANGE	7.8	7.8	7.8	7.2	7.2	7.2	6.6	6.1	7.2	7.8	7.2	7.8
S/HEMISPHERE	JUL	AUG	SEP	OCT	NOV	DEC	JAN	FEB	MAR	APR	MAY	JUN

Cultural Recommendations

LIGHT: 2000–3000 fc.

TEMPERATURES: Throughout the year, days average 74–76°F (23–24°C), and nights average 62–63°F (16–17°C), with a diurnal range of 11–14°F (6–8°C).

HUMIDITY: Near 80% year-round.

WATER: Rainfall is heavy all year, but conditions are slightly drier for 1–2 months in late winter. Cultivated plants should be kept moist with only slight drying allowed between waterings.

FERTILIZER: ¼–½ recommended strength. A balanced fertilizer should be applied weekly to biweekly throughout the year.

REST PERIOD: Growing conditions should be maintained year-round. Water should be reduced for plants cultivated in the dark, short-day conditions common during temperate-latitude winters, but they should not be allowed to dry out completely. Fertilizer should also be reduced if water is reduced. In the habitat, light may be slightly higher in winter.

GROWING MEDIA: Plants may be mounted on tree-fern or cork slabs or potted in small pots or baskets filled with any open, fast-draining medium. Repotting may be done anytime new roots are growing.

MISCELLANEOUS NOTES: The bloom season shown in the climate table is based on reports from the habitat.

Plant and Flower Information

PLANT SIZE AND TYPE: A 20 in. (50 cm) sympodial epiphyte.

PSEUDOBULB: 20 in. (50 cm) long. The stems, which arise from a very short rhizome, are usually sparsely branched.

LEAVES: Many. The lanceolate to oblong leaves are 1.0–1.4 in. (2.5–3.5 cm) long, smooth, and flexible.

INFLORESCENCE: Short. Clumps of flowers emerge from nodes along the side of the stem.

FLOWERS: 12–18 per inflorescence. The blossoms are 0.5 in. (1.3 cm) long. The ovate to obtuse sepals and petals are pale rose-violet. The lip is oblong with incurved margins.

REFERENCES: 231, 437, 444.

Dendrobium × lavarackianum M. Clements. A natural hybrid thought to be a back cross between *D. bigibbum* Lindley and *D. × superbiens* Rchb. f. The hybrid has also been known as *D. bigibbum* var. *venosum* F. M. Bailey, *D. bigibbum* forma *venosum* (Bailey) Bailey, and *D. bigibbum* var. *georgei* C. White. REFERENCES: 67, 235.

Dendrobium lawanum Lindley. Often spelled *D. lawianum*, see *D. crepidatum* Lindley. REFERENCES: 38, 102, 190, 216, 254, 278, 369, 454, 504.

Dendrobium lawesii F. Mueller

AKA: *D. mohlianum* as used by Kränzlin not Rchb. f., *D. pseudomohlianum* Kränzlin, *D. warburgianum* Kränzlin.

ORIGIN/HABITAT: Bougainville Island and Northern Papua New Guinea. Plants grow on the underside of mistforest tree branches or low on tree trunks in deep shade. In New Guinea, the orchids are found in the Finisterre, Ibo, and Bismarck Ranges at 2600–4900 ft. (800–1500 m). On Bougainville Island, they grow at 2950–6550 ft. (900–2000 m).

CLIMATE: Station #94010, Goroka, Papua New Guinea, Lat. 6.1°S, Long. 145.4°E, at 5141 ft. (1567 m). Temperatures are calculated for an elevation of 4000 ft. (1220 m), resulting in probable extremes of 90°F (32°C) and 46°F (8°C).

N/HEMISPHERE	JAN	FEB	MAR	APR	MAY	JUN	JUL	AUG	SEP	OCT	NOV	DEC
°F AVG MAX	80	81	82	83	83	82	83	82	82	82	83	81
°F AVG MIN	60	61	61	61	62	63	63	63	64	63	63	61
DIURNAL RANGE	20	20	21	22	21	19	20	19	18	19	20	20
RAIN/INCHES	2.1	2.8	4.6	5.9	6.6	9.3	9.1	10.1	10.7	8.3	4.6	2.0
HUMIDITY/%	70	67	67	67	67	71	72	73	74	71	70	70
BLOOM SEASON	*	*	**	**	**	**	**	**	**	**	**	**
DAYS CLR	N/A											
RAIN/MM	53	71	117	150	168	236	231	257	272	211	117	51
°C AVG MAX	26.5	27.1	27.6	28.2	28.2	27.6	28.2	27.6	27.6	27.6	28.2	27.1
°C AVG MIN	15.4	16.0	16.0	16.0	16.5	17.1	17.1	17.1	17.6	17.1	17.1	16.0
DIURNAL RANGE	11.1	11.1	11.6	12.2	11.7	10.5	11.1	10.5	10.0	10.5	11.1	11.1
S/HEMISPHERE	JUL	AUG	SEP	OCT	NOV	DEC	JAN	FEB	MAR	APR	MAY	JUN

Cultural Recommendations

LIGHT: 1200–2500 fc.

TEMPERATURES: Throughout the year, days average 80–83°F (27–28°C), and nights average 60–64°F (15–18°C), with a diurnal range of 18–22°F (10–12°C). The diurnal range is unusually large for a habitat with such constant temperatures. Growers indicate that plants grow well in cool to intermediate temperatures.

HUMIDITY: 70–75% from summer into autumn, dropping to 65–70% in winter and spring. Plants require strong air movement.

WATER: Rainfall is moderate to heavy most of the year, but conditions are slightly drier for 3 months in winter. Cultivated plants should be kept moist but not soggy. Occasional early morning mistings may be beneficial, especially on bright, sunny days.

FERTILIZER: ¼–½ recommended strength. A balanced fertilizer should be applied weekly to biweekly throughout the year.

REST PERIOD: Growing conditions should be maintained all year. Growers indicate that winter temperatures should be kept above 50°F (10°C). In the habitat, rainfall is lowest in winter, but dew and mist from fog and low clouds are common. Water and fertilizer should be reduced somewhat for cultivated plants, especially those grown in the dark, short-day conditions common in temperate latitudes. Plants should be kept on the dry side, but they should not be allowed to remain dry for long periods. Fertilizer should be reduced or eliminated until water is increased in spring. In the habitat, light is higher in winter. Growers indicate that a drier rest period is needed to induce flowering and that restricting water and fertilizer after stems are mature helps encourage blooming.

GROWING MEDIA: Hanging pots or baskets best accommodate the pendulous growth habit of the plants and permit the excellent air movement that is essential. Plants may be potted in any open, fast-draining medium. Growers indicate that although plants are pendulous, they are nearly impossible to grow when mounted unless the plants are very small when they are attached to the mount. Repotting may be done anytime new roots are growing.

MISCELLANEOUS NOTES: The bloom season shown in the climate table is based on cultivation records. Warren (ref. 553) indicates that plants often bloom twice a year when conditions are cool. He also states (ref. 549) that *D. lawesii* seedlings are among the easiest of all seedlings to successfully grow to flowering.

Plant and Flower Information

PLANT SIZE AND TYPE: A 10–18 in. (25–45 cm) sympodial epiphyte.

PSEUDOBULB: 10–18 in. (25–45 cm) long. The slender stems are generally pendulous.

LEAVES: Many. The leaves, which are 2.6 in. (6.5 cm) long, may be dark or light green. They are persistent and distichous.

INFLORESCENCE: Inflorescences bear successive clusters of flowers at the ends of old and new stems.

FLOWERS: 5–8, rarely 1–2 per inflorescence. The flowers are 0.6 in. (1.5 cm) across and 0.8–2.0 in. (2–5 cm) long. They are showy, bell-shaped, and highly variable. Sepals and petals are usually a bright, clear color sometimes tipped with white. They may be red, orange, mauve, purple, salmon, yellow, or white, and some forms are bicolored. The upturned lip is often whitish.

HYBRIDIZING NOTES: Chromosome count 2n = 38 (ref. 152, 243). *D. lawesii* is known to hybridize naturally with *D. flammula* Schlechter, creating *D.* × *von-paulsenianum* A. Hawkes. Growers indicate that plants often bloom 18 months out of flask.

REFERENCES: 36, 92, 95, 152, 179, 196, 216, 243, 254, 271, 304, 305, 371, 389, 430, 437, 444, 445, 486, 516, 526, 548, 549, 553, 554.

PHOTOS/DRAWINGS: *36, 271, 304, 305, 371, 389, 430, 437, 548, 553.*

Dendrobium lawianum Lindley.

Seidenfaden (ref. 454) spells the name *D. lawanum*, see *D. crepidatum* Lindley. REFERENCES: 216, 454, 504.

Dendrobium lawiense J. J. Smith

ORIGIN/HABITAT: Borneo. Plants were found in northern Sarawak at Batu Lawi, near Limbang, which is just southeast of Brunei/Muara, Brunei.

CLIMATE: Station #96315, Brunei/Muara, Brunei, Lat. 4.9°N, Long. 114.9°E, at 10 ft. (3 m). Record extreme temperatures are 95°F (35°C) and 67°F (19°C).

N/HEMISPHERE	JAN	FEB	MAR	APR	MAY	JUN	JUL	AUG	SEP	OCT	NOV	DEC
°F AVG MAX	86	86	87	88	88	88	88	88	87	87	87	87
°F AVG MIN	74	74	74	75	75	75	74	74	74	74	74	74
DIURNAL RANGE	12	12	13	13	13	13	14	14	13	13	13	13
RAIN/INCHES	16.8	6.5	5.5	4.4	8.2	12.0	8.5	8.4	11.8	11.7	14.5	11.3
HUMIDITY/%	86	86	85	83	83	82	81	81	82	83	84	85
BLOOM SEASON				*								
DAYS CLR @ 8AM	1	2	4	4	3	2	3	2	2	1	2	2
DAYS CLR @ 2PM	1	1	3	4	2	5	3	2	3	2	1	1
RAIN/MM	427	165	140	112	208	305	216	213	300	297	368	287
°C AVG MAX	30.0	30.0	30.6	31.1	31.1	31.1	31.1	31.1	30.6	30.6	30.6	30.6
°C AVG MIN	23.3	23.3	23.3	23.9	23.9	23.9	23.3	23.3	23.3	23.3	23.3	23.3
DIURNAL RANGE	6.7	6.7	7.3	7.2	7.2	7.2	7.8	7.8	7.3	7.3	7.3	7.3
S/HEMISPHERE	JUL	AUG	SEP	OCT	NOV	DEC	JAN	FEB	MAR	APR	MAY	JUN

Cultural Recommendations

LIGHT: 2000–3000 fc.

TEMPERATURES: Throughout the year, days average 86–88°F (30–31°C), and nights average 74–75°F (23–24°C), with a diurnal range of 12–14°F (7–8°C).

HUMIDITY: 80–85% year-round.

WATER: Rainfall is very heavy most of the year, but conditions are slightly drier for 3 months in late winter and early spring. Cultivated plants should be kept moist with only slight drying allowed between waterings.

FERTILIZER: ¼–½ recommended strength. A balanced fertilizer should be applied weekly to biweekly throughout the year.

REST PERIOD: Growing conditions should be maintained all year. Water may be reduced somewhat in winter, especially for plants grown in the dark, short-day conditions common in temperate latitudes. They should never be allowed to dry out completely, however. Fertilizer should be reduced if water is reduced.

GROWING MEDIA: Plants may be mounted on tree-fern or cork slabs or potted in small pots filled with any open, fast-draining medium. Repotting may be done anytime new roots are actively growing.

MISCELLANEOUS NOTES: The bloom season shown in the climate table is based on reports from the habitat. The plant was described in 1912 in *Bul. Jard. Bot. Buit.* 2nd sér. 3:60.

Plant and Flower Information

PLANT SIZE AND TYPE: A 10–22 in. (25–55 cm) sympodial epiphyte.

PSEUDOBULB: 10–22 in. (25–55 cm) long. The stems are swollen above the base and near the apex.

LEAVES: Many. The rigid, linear leaves are 1.5–2.5 in. (3.8–6.4 cm) long and unequally bilobed at the tip. They are densely and prominently nerved.

INFLORESCENCE: Inflorescences emerge from nodes along the upper part of the stem.

FLOWERS: Few per inflorescence. The short-lived flowers are 1 in. (2.5 cm) across. The dorsal sepal is lanceolate, but lateral sepals and petals are oblong to lanceolate. The lateral sepals form a short, flattened spur. The basal third of the lip is hairy. The sidelobes are irregularly toothed. The apex of the lip is somewhat triangular, ruffled, and wavy. Flower color was not included in the description.

REFERENCES: 221, 286, 295.

Dendrobium laxiflorum J. J. Smith

ORIGIN/HABITAT: The Molucca Islands. Plants have been found only on Halmaheira Island, which is located east of Ternate Island. Habitat elevation is unavailable, so the following temperatures should be used with caution.

CLIMATE: Station #97430, Ternate, Indonesia, Lat. 0.8°N, Long. 127.4°E, at 75 ft. (23 m). Record extreme temperatures are not available for this location.

N/HEMISPHERE	JAN	FEB	MAR	APR	MAY	JUN	JUL	AUG	SEP	OCT	NOV	DEC
°F AVG MAX	85	85	86	86	87	86	87	86	86	87	87	86
°F AVG MIN	77	76	77	77	77	76	75	75	76	77	77	77
DIURNAL RANGE	8	9	9	9	10	10	12	11	10	10	10	9
RAIN/INCHES	5.3	6.1	6.7	6.6	9.4	8.4	4.6	2.1	3.1	3.2	7.2	8.2
HUMIDITY/%	N/A											
BLOOM SEASON	N/A											
DAYS CLR	N/A											
RAIN/MM	135	155	170	168	239	213	117	53	79	81	183	208
°C AVG MAX	29.4	29.4	30.0	30.0	30.6	30.0	30.6	30.0	30.0	30.6	30.6	30.0
°C AVG MIN	25.0	24.4	25.0	25.0	25.0	24.4	23.9	23.9	24.4	25.0	25.0	25.0
DIURNAL RANGE	4.4	5.0	5.0	5.0	5.6	5.6	6.7	6.1	5.6	5.6	5.6	5.0
S/HEMISPHERE	JUL	AUG	SEP	OCT	NOV	DEC	JAN	FEB	MAR	APR	MAY	JUN

Cultural Recommendations

LIGHT: 2000–3000 fc.

Dendrobium laxum

TEMPERATURES: Throughout the year, days average 85–87°F (29–31°C), and nights average 75–77°F (24–25°C), with a diurnal range of 8–12°F (4–7°C). The warmest days and coolest nights occur in summer.

HUMIDITY: Information is not available for this location. However, records from nearby locations indicate that humidity probably averages near 80% year-round.

WATER: Rainfall is moderate to heavy most of the year, but conditions are somewhat drier for 2–3 months in late summer and autumn. Cultivated plants should be kept moist with only slight drying allowed between waterings during most of the year. Plants should become moderately dry between waterings in late summer and early autumn, however, but they should not remain dry for long periods.

FERTILIZER: ¼–½ recommended strength. A balanced fertilizer should be applied weekly to biweekly throughout the year.

REST PERIOD: Growing temperatures should be maintained all year. Water may be reduced somewhat in winter, especially for plants grown in the dark, short-day conditions in temperate latitudes. They should not be allowed to dry out completely, however. In the habitat, seasonal light variation is minor.

GROWING MEDIA: Plants may be mounted on tree-fern or cork slabs if humidity is high and plants are watered at least once daily in summer. When plants are potted, any open, fast-draining medium may be used. Repotting may be done anytime new roots are growing.

MISCELLANEOUS NOTES: *D. laxiflorum* is not commonly cultivated.

Plant and Flower Information

PLANT SIZE AND TYPE: A 39 in. (100 cm) sympodial epiphyte.

PSEUDOBULB: 39 in. (100 cm) long. Stems are canelike with nodes about 2 in. (5 cm) apart.

LEAVES: The lanceolate leaves are 5.1–5.5 in. (13–14 cm) long.

INFLORESCENCE: 18 in. (45 cm) long. The lax, brittle inflorescences emerge from below the leaves.

FLOWERS: 10–14 per inflorescence. The flowers are 2.8 in. (7 cm) across. The blossoms are light green with twisted petals. The lip is white with beautiful dark violet keels and violet spots on the sidelobes. They were described as "deliciously fragrant."

REFERENCES: 25, 84, 200, 225.

Dendrobium laxum Swartz. Now considered a synonym of *Pleurothallis laxa* Lindley. REFERENCES: 216, 254.

Dendrobium ledifolium J. J. Smith. Now considered a synonym of *Cadetia ledifolia* (J. J. Smith) W. Kittredge. REFERENCES: 225, 470.

Dendrobium × *leeanum* O'Brien. This plant is included in *Sander's List of Orchid Hybrids* as a hybrid of *D. phalaenopsis* Fitzgerald and *D.* × *superbiens* Rchb. f. REFERENCES: 25, 200, 218, 254, 348, 570. PHOTOS/DRAWINGS: 570.

Dendrobium legareiense J. J. Smith. Although not correctly transferred, Schlechter (ref. 443) considered this plant to be *Cadetia legareiensis* (J. J. Smith) Schlechter. REFERENCES: 221, 223, 443, 470, 475.

Dendrobium leonis (Lindley) Rchb. f.

AKA: *Aporum leonis* Lindley not Blume. Seidenfaden in 1992 *Opera Botanica* #114 includes *D. leonis* var. *strictum* Finet as a synonym of *D. terminale* Parish and Rchb. f.

ORIGIN/HABITAT: Widespread in Southeast Asia. The habitat includes Borneo, Cambodia, Laos, Malaya, Sumatra, northeastern and peninsular Thailand, and Vietnam. Plants are common lowland epiphytes that are occasionally found as high as 4750 ft. (1450 m). In Sarawak, plants grow on limestone rocks. In Malaya, they are found low on orchard trees, in dry forests, and open places.

CLIMATE: Station #48665, Melaka (Malacca), Malaya, Lat. 2.3°N, Long. 102.3°E, at 40 ft. (12 m). Record extreme temperatures are 99°F (37°C) and 61°F (16°C).

N/HEMISPHERE	JAN	FEB	MAR	APR	MAY	JUN	JUL	AUG	SEP	OCT	NOV	DEC
°F AVG MAX	88	89	89	89	89	88	88	88	88	88	88	88
°F AVG MIN	72	72	72	73	73	73	72	72	72	72	72	72
DIURNAL RANGE	16	17	17	16	16	15	16	16	16	16	16	16
RAIN/INCHES	3.9	3.7	4.9	7.4	6.8	7.9	7.8	10.3	8.8	10.1	8.7	6.5
HUMIDITY/%	79	79	82	85	85	83	84	84	84	84	84	82
BLOOM SEASON			*			*			*		*	
DAYS CLR @ 7AM	1	1	1	1	1	1	2	1	1	1	0	1
DAYS CLR @ 1PM	1	1	1	1	1	1	1	1	1	1	0	0
RAIN/MM	99	94	124	188	173	201	198	262	224	257	221	165
°C AVG MAX	31.1	31.7	31.7	31.7	31.7	31.1	31.1	31.1	31.1	31.1	31.1	31.1
°C AVG MIN	22.2	22.2	22.2	22.8	22.8	22.8	22.2	22.2	22.2	22.2	22.2	22.2
DIURNAL RANGE	8.9	9.5	9.5	8.9	8.9	8.3	8.9	8.9	8.9	8.9	8.9	8.9
S/HEMISPHERE	JUL	AUG	SEP	OCT	NOV	DEC	JAN	FEB	MAR	APR	MAY	JUN

Cultural Recommendations

LIGHT: 2000–3000 fc.

TEMPERATURES: Throughout the year, days average 88–89°F (31–32°C), and nights average 72–73°F (22–23°C), with a diurnal range of 15–17°F (8–10°C). Because plants are found over a wide range of elevations, they should adapt to conditions 8–10°F (4–6°C) cooler than indicated.

HUMIDITY: Near 85% from spring through autumn, dropping to about 80% in winter.

WATER: Rainfall is heavy throughout the year, but conditions are slightly drier for 2 months in winter. Cultivated plants should be kept evenly moist, with only slight drying allowed between waterings.

FERTILIZER: ¼–½ recommended strength. A balanced fertilizer should be applied weekly to biweekly throughout the year.

REST PERIOD: Growing conditions should be maintained all year. Some growers indicate that plants should have winter minimum temperatures of 59°F (15°C). Water and fertilizer should be reduced slightly in winter, especially for plants grown in the dark, short-day conditions common in temperate latitudes. Plants should not be allowed to dry out completely, however.

GROWING MEDIA: Mounting plants on tree-fern or cork slabs accommodates their pendulous growth habit. However, humidity must be high and plants must be watered at least once a day in summer. If plants cannot be mounted, small pots or hanging baskets may be filled with an open, fast-draining medium. Repotting may be done anytime new roots are actively growing.

MISCELLANEOUS NOTES: The bloom season shown in the climate table is based on cultivation records. Blooming may occur at any time, and plants are often in bloom most of the year.

Plant and Flower Information

PLANT SIZE AND TYPE: A 4–10 in. (10–25 cm) sympodial epiphyte that may be lithophytic in some regions. Plants are usually pendent, growing from the bottom of branches on forest trees. They resemble a fleshy *Lockhartia* plant.

PSEUDOBULB: 4–9 in. (10–23 cm) long. The clustered, leafy stems are thin and flattened. The upper parts have a fanlike or circular arrangement.

LEAVES: Many. The distichous, alternating leaves are triangular, overlapping, succulent, and 0.6–1.0 in. (1.5–2.5 cm) long. The lower edge is straight and the upper edge is curved. They are dark, dull green.

INFLORESCENCE: Short. Inflorescences are borne from upper leaf axils near the tips of branches.

FLOWERS: 1–2 per inflorescence. The fleshy blossoms are 0.6–0.8 in. (1.5–2.0 cm) long. Sepals and petals are dull creamy yellow or pale green streaked or flushed with pink or dull purple on the backside. Sepals and petals are narrow, rounded, and point forward. The rounded, oblong lip is shorter than the sepals. It normally has an orange-yellow center bar ending in a small callus with a purple patch just below the swollen area and a white hairy patch near the tip. The short yellow column has an orange spot at the base. Blossoms have a strong, pleasant, vanilla fragrance.

HYBRIDIZING NOTES: Chromosome counts are n = 19 (ref. 187), 2n = 38 (ref. 151, 154, 187, 188), and 2n = 40 (ref. 187, 504, 580). Johansen (ref. 239) indicates that plants are self-sterile and that flowers dropped 5–8 days after self-pollination. None of his attempts to cross-pollinate produced capsules. Wilfret and Hashimoto (ref. 568) did not get seed when they tried to cross *D. leonis* with *D. bigibbum* Lindley.

REFERENCES: 36, 151, 154, 179, 187, 188, 196, 200, 202, 203, 210, 216, 239, 254, 286, 291, 295, 317, 330, 371, 394, 395, 402, 430, 445, 447, 448, 454, 455, 504, 510, 568, 580.

PHOTOS/DRAWINGS: *36, 200, 203, 210, 291, 371, 430, 454, 455, 568.*

Dendrobium leontoglossum (Ridley) Schlechter

AKA: *Trichoglottis leontoglossa* Ridley.

ORIGIN/HABITAT: New Guinea. Plants were collected at 2000 ft. (610 m) near Sogeri (Sogere).

CLIMATE: Station #94035, Port Moresby, Papua New Guinea, Lat. 9.5°S, Long. 147.2°E, at 126 ft. (38 m). Temperatures are calculated for an elevation of 1800 ft. (550 m), resulting in probable extremes of 92°F (34°C) and 58°F (15°C).

N/HEMISPHERE	JAN	FEB	MAR	APR	MAY	JUN	JUL	AUG	SEP	OCT	NOV	DEC
°F AVG MAX	77	76	78	80	82	84	83	81	82	81	80	78
°F AVG MIN	67	67	68	69	70	70	70	70	70	69	69	68
DIURNAL RANGE	10	9	10	11	12	14	13	11	12	12	11	10
RAIN/INCHES	1.1	0.7	1.0	1.4	1.9	4.4	7.0	7.6	6.7	4.2	2.5	1.3
HUMIDITY/%	78	77	78	76	73	71	71	73	74	75	77	78
BLOOM SEASON	N/A											
DAYS CLR	N/A											
RAIN/MM	28	18	25	36	48	112	178	193	170	107	64	33
°C AVG MAX	25.3	24.7	25.8	26.9	28.0	29.2	28.6	27.5	28.0	27.5	26.9	25.8
°C AVG MIN	19.7	19.7	20.3	20.8	21.4	21.4	21.4	21.4	21.4	20.8	20.8	20.3
DIURNAL RANGE	5.6	5.0	5.5	6.1	6.6	7.8	7.2	6.1	6.6	6.7	6.1	5.5
S/HEMISPHERE	JUL	AUG	SEP	OCT	NOV	DEC	JAN	FEB	MAR	APR	MAY	JUN

Cultural Recommendations

LIGHT: 2000–3000 fc. High light and strong air movement are recommended. Light should be as high as the plant can tolerate, short of burning the leaves.

TEMPERATURES: Throughout the year, days average 76–84°F (25–29°C), and nights average 67–70°F (20–21°C), with a diurnal range of 9–14°F (5–8°C).

HUMIDITY: 70–75% most of the year, increasing to near 80% in winter.

WATER: Rainfall is moderate for 5 months in summer, but conditions are dry in winter. Cultivated plants should dry slightly between waterings from spring to early autumn, but water should be gradually reduced in late autumn.

FERTILIZER: ¼–½ recommended strength. A balanced fertilizer should be applied weekly to biweekly throughout the growing season.

REST PERIOD: Growing conditions should be maintained all year. In the habitat, rainfall is low for 6–7 months in winter. Water and fertilizer should be reduced considerably in winter. Plants should be allowed to dry between waterings but should not remain dry for extended periods. Occasional mistings on clear, sunny mornings are usually beneficial. In the habitat, winter light is high.

GROWING MEDIA: Plants may be mounted on tree-fern or cork slabs if humidity is high and plants are watered at least once daily in summer. When plants are potted, any open, fast-draining medium may be used. They may be repotted anytime new roots are growing.

Plant and Flower Information

PLANT SIZE AND TYPE: A 6 in. (15 cm) sympodial epiphyte.

PSEUDOBULB: 6 in. (15 cm) long. The stems are covered by persistent strands of old leaf sheaths.

LEAVES: The lanceolate leaves are 1 in. (2.5 cm) long and bilobed at the tip.

INFLORESCENCE: Short. Blossoms emerge from the leaf sheaths.

FLOWERS: 1–2 per inflorescence. The small, fleshy flowers are yellow with purple markings. The sepals 0.2 in. (0.5 cm) long with much shorter petals. The lip is trilobed with a hairy disc on the rounded tongue-shaped midlobe.

REFERENCES: 221, 393, 437.

Dendrobium leopardinum Schlechter. See *D. schweinfurthianum* A. Hawkes and A. H. Heller. REFERENCES: 92, 221, 229, 437, 445, 486.

Dendrobium leopardinum Wallich. Now considered a synonym of *Bulbophyllum leopardinum* Lindley. REFERENCES: 102, 190, 216, 254, 369.

Dendrobium lepidochilum Kränzlin. See *D. dactylodes* Rchb. f. REFERENCES: 220, 254, 434.

Dendrobium lepidum Ridley. See *D. hughii* Rchb. f. REFERENCES: 201, 220, 223, 402, 454, 455

Dendrobium lepoense Schlechter

ORIGIN/HABITAT: Endemic to southeastern Sulawesi (Celebes). The plants were originally collected near Lepo-lepo, which is close to Kendari. Habitat elevation was not given, so the following temperatures should be used with caution.

CLIMATE: Station #97146, Kendari, Sulawesi, Indonesia, Lat. 4.1°S, Long. 122.4°E, at 164 ft. (50 m). Record extreme temperatures are not available for this location.

N/HEMISPHERE	JAN	FEB	MAR	APR	MAY	JUN	JUL	AUG	SEP	OCT	NOV	DEC
°F AVG MAX	85	86	88	90	90	89	88	87	88	86	86	84
°F AVG MIN	70	71	70	72	74	75	75	74	74	74	74	72
DIURNAL RANGE	15	15	18	18	16	14	13	13	14	12	12	12
RAIN/INCHES	5.7	4.0	2.3	2.5	6.0	7.7	7.9	7.3	8.4	8.2	9.9	9.1
HUMIDITY/%	86	80	76	73	76	82	80	81	82	83	85	84
BLOOM SEASON	*											
DAYS CLR @ 8AM	3	10	10	14	8	5	1	2	2	3	2	4
DAYS CLR @ 2PM	0	0	1	2	1	0	1	0	0	0	0	0
RAIN/MM	144	102	58	63	152	197	201	186	213	208	252	231
°C AVG MAX	29.2	29.9	31.0	32.3	32.4	31.8	31.1	30.7	30.9	29.9	30.1	28.8
°C AVG MIN	21.3	21.5	21.1	22.4	23.6	24.0	24.0	23.4	23.4	23.6	23.4	22.3
DIURNAL RANGE	7.9	8.4	9.9	9.9	8.8	7.8	7.1	7.3	7.5	6.3	6.7	6.5
S/HEMISPHERE	JUL	AUG	SEP	OCT	NOV	DEC	JAN	FEB	MAR	APR	MAY	JUN

Cultural Recommendations

LIGHT: 2000–3000 fc.

TEMPERATURES: Throughout the year, days average 84–90°F (29–32°C), and nights average 70–75°F (21–24°C), with a diurnal range of 12–18°F (6–10°C).

Dendrobium leporinum

HUMIDITY: 80–85% most of the year, dropping to near 75% in spring.

WATER: Rainfall in moderate to heavy most of the year, but conditions are somewhat drier for 2–3 months in late winter and early spring. Cultivated plants should be kept moist while actively growing, with only slight drying allowed between waterings.

FERTILIZER: ¼–½ recommended strength. A balanced fertilizer should be applied weekly to biweekly throughout the year.

REST PERIOD: Growing conditions should be maintained all year. Winter temperatures drop about 5°F (3°C) below summer levels. In cultivation, water should be reduced for 2–3 months and plants allowed to dry somewhat between waterings. They should not remain dry for extended periods, however. Fertilizer should be reduced or eliminated anytime water is reduced. In the habitat, light is highest in late winter and spring.

GROWING MEDIA: Plants may be mounted on tree-fern or cork slabs or potted in small pots filled with any open, fast-draining medium. Repotting may be done anytime new roots are growing.

MISCELLANEOUS NOTES: The bloom season shown in the climate table is based on reports from the habitat.

Plant and Flower Information

PLANT SIZE AND TYPE: A 5–7 in. (13–17 cm) sympodial epiphyte.

PSEUDOBULB: 5–7 in. (13–17 cm) long. The flattened, erect to suberect stems arise from a very short rhizome.

LEAVES: Several. The leaves are 1.2–1.8 in. (3.0–4.5 cm) long. They are smooth, fleshy or leathery, narrowly lanceolate, and widely spaced.

INFLORESCENCE: Short. Inflorescences emerge from several bracts. Blossoms are held in a short head at the apex of the inflorescence.

FLOWERS: Several per inflorescence. The fleshy flowers are 0.2 in. (0.4 cm) long. The sepals are very short. The margins of the petals are irregular and slightly wavy. The somewhat oblong lip is distinctively blunt and minutely toothed along the margin. Flower color was not available at the time the plant was described.

REFERENCES: 221, 436.

Dendrobium leporinum J. J. Smith

ORIGIN/HABITAT: Halmaheira Island in the Moluccas and the northern part of Irian Jaya (western New Guinea). Habitat elevation is unavailable, so the following climate data should be used with caution.

CLIMATE: Station #97430, Ternate, Indonesia, Lat. 0.8°N, Long. 127.4°E, at 75 ft. (23 m). Record extreme temperatures are not available for this location.

N/HEMISPHERE	JAN	FEB	MAR	APR	MAY	JUN	JUL	AUG	SEP	OCT	NOV	DEC
°F AVG MAX	85	85	86	86	87	86	87	86	86	87	87	86
°F AVG MIN	77	76	77	77	77	76	75	75	76	77	77	77
DIURNAL RANGE	8	9	9	9	10	10	12	11	10	10	10	9
RAIN/INCHES	5.3	6.1	6.7	6.6	9.4	8.4	4.6	2.1	3.1	3.2	7.2	8.2
HUMIDITY/%	N/A											
BLOOM SEASON	N/A											
DAYS CLR	N/A											
RAIN/MM	135	155	170	168	239	213	117	53	79	81	183	208
°C AVG MAX	29.4	29.4	30.0	30.0	30.6	30.0	30.6	30.0	30.0	30.6	30.6	30.0
°C AVG MIN	25.0	24.4	25.0	25.0	25.0	24.4	23.9	23.9	24.4	25.0	25.0	25.0
DIURNAL RANGE	4.4	5.0	5.0	5.0	5.6	5.6	6.7	6.1	5.6	5.6	5.6	5.0
S/HEMISPHERE	JUL	AUG	SEP	OCT	NOV	DEC	JAN	FEB	MAR	APR	MAY	JUN

Cultural Recommendations

LIGHT: 2000–3000 fc.

TEMPERATURES: Throughout the year, days average 85–87°F (29–31°C), and nights average 75–77°F (24–25°C), with a diurnal range of 8–12°F (4–7°C). The warmest days and coolest nights occur in early summer.

HUMIDITY: Information is not available for this location. However, records from nearby locations indicate that humidity probably averages near 80% year-round.

WATER: Rainfall is moderate to heavy most of the year, but conditions are somewhat drier for 2–3 months in late summer and autumn. Cultivated plants should be kept moist, with only slight drying allowed between waterings during most of the year. Plants should become moderately dry between waterings in late summer and early autumn, but they should not remain dry for long periods.

FERTILIZER: ¼–½ recommended strength. A balanced fertilizer should be applied weekly to biweekly throughout the year.

REST PERIOD: Growing temperatures should be maintained all year. Water may be reduced somewhat in winter, especially for plants grown in the dark, short-day conditions in temperate latitudes. They should not be allowed to dry out completely, however. In the habitat, seasonal light variation is minor.

GROWING MEDIA: Plants may be mounted on tree-fern or cork slabs if humidity is high and plants are watered at least once daily in summer. When plants are potted, any open, fast-draining medium may be used. Repotting may be done anytime new roots are growing.

Plant and Flower Information

PLANT SIZE AND TYPE: A 12–33 in. (30–85 cm) sympodial epiphyte.

PSEUDOBULB: 12–33 in. (30–85 cm) long. The canelike stem is shiny yellow-green and 4-angled. Growths are spaced 1.2–2.0 in. (3–5 cm) apart on the creeping rhizome.

LEAVES: Many. The shiny, lanceolate leaves are 2–3 in. (5–8 cm) long.

INFLORESCENCE: 5–7 in. (13–19 cm) long. The scapes are suberect and emerge from below the leaves.

FLOWERS: 3–6 per inflorescence. The large, showy flowers are 2.2–2.4 in. (5.5–6.2 cm) long. Sepals are white, often with purple veins and a pale mauve suffusion. They are commonly crisped along the edges. The narrow petals, which are very twisted, may be suberect or stiffly erect. They are often 1.6 in. (4 cm) long. The petals may be violet or dark purple sometimes with greenish tips. The lip has a white midlobe with purple veins and greenish sidelobes.

REFERENCES: 25, 84, 190, 200, 220, 254, 445, 470.

PHOTOS/DRAWINGS: 84.

Dendrobium leptocladum Hayata

AKA: *D. tenuicaule* Hayata not Hooker f.

ORIGIN/HABITAT: Endemic to Taiwan. Plants grow at relatively low elevations in the mountain forests of the central and southern parts of the island. They are reported near Taitung at about 2600 ft. (800 m).

CLIMATE: Station #46766, Taitung, Taiwan, Lat. 22.8°N, Long. 121.2°E, at 31 ft. (9 m). Temperatures are calculated for an elevation of 2600 ft. (800 m), resulting in probable extremes of 92°F (33°C) and 40°F (4°C).

N/HEMISPHERE	JAN	FEB	MAR	APR	MAY	JUN	JUL	AUG	SEP	OCT	NOV	DEC
°F AVG MAX	65	66	70	73	77	79	82	80	78	74	71	67
°F AVG MIN	51	52	55	59	63	65	66	66	65	62	58	54
DIURNAL RANGE	14	14	15	14	14	14	16	14	13	12	13	13
RAIN/INCHES	1.1	1.2	1.1	3.0	5.3	10.0	6.4	11.7	12.4	4.8	5.4	2.3
HUMIDITY/%	77	78	79	81	82	84	80	83	84	80	77	77
BLOOM SEASON							*					
DAYS CLR @ 8AM	4	5	4	5	6	9	11	8	7	9	7	5
DAYS CLR @ 2PM	3	3	3	4	3	3	8	5	5	4	4	4
RAIN/MM	28	30	28	76	135	254	163	297	315	122	137	58
°C AVG MAX	18.1	18.6	20.8	22.5	24.7	25.8	27.5	26.4	25.3	23.1	21.4	19.2
°C AVG MIN	10.3	10.8	12.5	14.7	17.0	18.1	18.6	18.6	18.1	16.4	14.2	12.0
DIURNAL RANGE	7.8	7.8	8.3	7.8	7.7	7.7	8.9	7.8	7.2	6.7	7.2	7.2
S/HEMISPHERE	JUL	AUG	SEP	OCT	NOV	DEC	JAN	FEB	MAR	APR	MAY	JUN

Cultural Recommendations

LIGHT: 2000–3000 fc.

TEMPERATURES: Summer days average 79–82°F (26–28°C), and nights average 65–66°F (18–19°C), with a diurnal range of 14–16°F (8–9°C).

HUMIDITY: 80–85% in summer and autumn, decreasing to 75–80% in winter and spring.

WATER: Rainfall is moderate to heavy for 6–8 months from spring to autumn, but is relatively light in winter. Cultivated plants should be kept moist while actively growing, but water should be gradually reduced in autumn.

FERTILIZER: 1/4–1/2 recommended strength, applied weekly. A high-nitrogen fertilizer is beneficial from spring to midsummer, but a fertilizer high in phosphates should be used in late summer and autumn.

REST PERIOD: Winter days average 65–70°F (18–21°C), and nights average 51–55°F (10–13°C), with a diurnal range of 13–15°F (7–8°C). In the habitat, rainfall is low for 3–4 months in winter, but high humidity and nightly cooling result in frequent, heavy deposits of dew which makes more water available than the rainfall averages indicate. In winter, cultivated plants should be allowed to become somewhat dry between waterings, but they should not remain dry for long periods.

GROWING MEDIA: Plants may be mounted on slabs of cork or tree-fern fiber if high humidity can be maintained, and if water can be applied at least daily during the summer. Repotting is best done in early spring when new roots are growing.

MISCELLANEOUS NOTES: The bloom season shown in the climate table is based on reports from the habitat.

Plant and Flower Information

PLANT SIZE AND TYPE: A 16–20 in. (40–50 cm) sympodial epiphyte.

PSEUDOBULB: 16–20 in. (40–50 cm) long. The stems are very slender.

LEAVES: 4–6. The persistent leaves are 2.4 in. (6 cm) long, linear, and pointed at the apex. They are widely spaced at the apex of the stem.

INFLORESCENCE: 0.6 in. (1.5 cm) long. Inflorescences emerge laterally from nodes along the side of the stem.

FLOWERS: 1–2 per inflorescence. The tiny flowers are 0.6 in. (1.5 cm) long. Sepals and petals are nearly equal in length. The obscurely 3-lobed lip is rhomboid, abruptly pointed, and wavy. The margin is hairy and the apex appears fringed. The disk is covered with curly hairs. Blossoms are white with brown or reddish brown spots and blotches on the white lip.

REFERENCES: 61, 192, 193, 208, 221, 274, 279, 528.

PHOTOS/DRAWINGS: 274.

Dendrobium lessonii Colenso. See *D. cunninghamii* Lindley not Steudel. REFERENCES: 190, 216, 254.

Dendrobium leucanthum J. J. Smith

AKA: *Dendrobium chamaephytum* as used by J. J. Smith not Schlechter, *Cadetia leucantha* Schlechter. *Cadetia* is again considered a valid genus by some botanists, so this plant may again be a *Cadetia*.

ORIGIN/HABITAT: Irian Jaya (western New Guinea). Plants were collected in southern Irian Jaya at the summit of Resi-Rüken from trees in primary forests at 2950 ft. (900 m).

CLIMATE: Station #97796, Kokenau (Kokonau), Irian Jaya, Lat. 4.7°S, Long. 135.4°E, at 10 ft. (3 m). Temperatures are calculated for an elevation of 3000 ft. (910 m). Record extreme temperatures are not available for this location.

N/HEMISPHERE	JAN	FEB	MAR	APR	MAY	JUN	JUL	AUG	SEP	OCT	NOV	DEC
°F AVG MAX	73	73	76	78	80	79	79	79	80	78	77	74
°F AVG MIN	63	63	64	64	64	65	64	64	64	64	64	63
DIURNAL RANGE	10	10	12	14	16	14	15	15	16	14	13	11
RAIN/INCHES	18.4	15.8	18.9	11.6	9.7	10.6	11.5	15.7	11.6	11.6	16.0	19.9
HUMIDITY/%	N/A											
BLOOM SEASON		*										
DAYS CLR	N/A											
RAIN/MM	467	401	480	295	246	269	292	399	295	295	406	505
°C AVG MAX	22.9	22.9	24.5	25.6	26.7	26.2	26.2	26.2	26.7	25.6	25.1	23.4
°C AVG MIN	17.3	17.3	17.9	17.9	17.9	18.4	17.9	17.9	17.9	17.9	17.9	17.3
DIURNAL RANGE	5.6	5.6	6.6	7.7	8.8	7.8	8.3	8.3	8.8	7.7	7.2	6.1
S/HEMISPHERE	JUL	AUG	SEP	OCT	NOV	DEC	JAN	FEB	MAR	APR	MAY	JUN

Cultural Recommendations

LIGHT: 2500–3500 fc.

TEMPERATURES: Throughout the year, days average 73–80°F (23–27°C), and nights average 63–65°F (17–18°C), with a diurnal range of 10–16°F (6–9°C).

HUMIDITY: Information is not available for this location. However, average humidity at other stations in the region indicates probable values near 80% year-round.

WATER: Rainfall is very heavy year-round. Cultivated plants should be kept evenly moist but not soggy.

FERTILIZER: 1/4–1/2 recommended strength. A balanced fertilizer should be applied weekly to biweekly throughout the year.

REST PERIOD: Growing conditions should be maintained year-round. Water and fertilizer might be reduced slightly in winter, especially for plants cultivated in the dark, short-day conditions common in temperate latitudes. Plants should never be allowed to dry out completely, however.

GROWING MEDIA: Plants may be mounted on tree-fern or cork slabs or potted in small pots filled with any open, fast-draining medium. Repotting may be done anytime new roots are growing.

MISCELLANEOUS NOTES: The bloom season shown in the climate table is based on reports from the habitat.

Plant and Flower Information

PLANT SIZE AND TYPE: A 0.4–0.9 in. (1.0–2.3 cm) sympodial epiphyte.

PSEUDOBULB: 0.2–0.4 in. (0.4–1.1 cm) long. The stems are 3 grooved. They are densely clustered on a very short rhizome.

LEAVES: 1 per growth. The ovate-oblong leaves are 0.5 in. (1.3 cm) long with 3 small teeth at the apex.

INFLORESCENCE: Short. Inflorescences emerge at the apex of the pseudobulb.

FLOWERS: 1 per inflorescence. The white flowers are 0.2 in. (0.5 cm) across. The ovate petals are ruffled along the margin. The ovate dorsal sepal is erect and incurved. Lateral sepals are parallel, slender, and shortly pointed. The 3-lobed lip has an ovate midlobe that is fleshy and convex along the center and short sidelobes.

REFERENCES: 221, 437, 470, 472.

Dendrobium leuchophotum Rchb. f. See *D. affine* (Decaisne) Steudel. REFERENCES: 67, 216.

Dendrobium leucochlorum Rchb. f.

ORIGIN/HABITAT: The Tenasserim region of Burma. Plants were collected near Moulmein. Habitat elevation is unavailable, so the following temperatures should be used with caution.

CLIMATE: Station #48103, Moulmein, Burma, Lat. 16.4°N, Long. 97.7°E, at 150 ft. (46 m). Record extreme temperatures are 103°F (39°C) and 52°F (11°C).

Dendrobium leucochysum

N/HEMISPHERE	JAN	FEB	MAR	APR	MAY	JUN	JUL	AUG	SEP	OCT	NOV	DEC
°F AVG MAX	89	92	94	95	89	85	83	83	85	88	89	87
°F AVG MIN	66	68	73	76	76	75	75	75	75	75	73	68
DIURNAL RANGE	23	24	21	19	13	10	8	8	10	13	16	19
RAIN/INCHES	0.3	0.2	0.4	3.0	20.3	35.6	46.3	43.4	28.1	8.5	2.1	0.1
HUMIDITY/%	66	68	68	70	81	91	92	93	91	81	75	64
BLOOM SEASON					*							
DAYS CLR @ 7AM	12	7	5	6	1	0	0	0	0	3	7	12
DAYS CLR @ 1PM	20	13	10	8	3	0	0	0	0	4	12	17
RAIN/MM	8	5	10	76	516	904	1176	1102	714	216	53	3
°C AVG MAX	31.7	33.3	34.4	35.0	31.7	29.4	28.3	28.3	29.4	31.1	31.7	30.6
°C AVG MIN	18.9	20.0	22.8	24.4	24.4	23.9	23.9	23.9	23.9	23.9	22.8	20.0
DIURNAL RANGE	12.8	13.3	11.6	10.6	7.3	5.5	4.4	4.4	5.5	7.2	8.9	10.6
S/HEMISPHERE	JUL	AUG	SEP	OCT	NOV	DEC	JAN	FEB	MAR	APR	MAY	JUN

Cultural Recommendations

LIGHT: 2000–3000 fc.

TEMPERATURES: Summer days average 83–85°F (28–29°C), and nights average 75°F (24°C), with a diurnal range of 8–10°F (4–6°C). Plants should be heat tolerant, as the warmest weather occurs during clear, dry periods in spring. Days average 89–94°F (32–34°C), and nights average 73–76°F (23–24°C), with a diurnal range of 13–21°F (7–12°C).

HUMIDITY: 80–90% from late spring to early autumn, dropping to near 65% for 2 months in winter.

WATER: Rainfall is very heavy from late spring into autumn, but conditions are much drier in winter. Cultivated plants should be kept evenly moist while actively growing, but water should be gradually reduced in autumn after new growths mature.

FERTILIZER: ¼–½ recommended strength, applied weekly. A high-nitrogen fertilizer is beneficial from spring to midsummer, but a fertilizer high in phosphates should be used in late summer and autumn.

REST PERIOD: Winter days average 87–92°F (31–33°C), and nights average 66–68°F (19–20°C), with a diurnal range of 19–24°F (11–13°C). The larger diurnal range results from both warmer days and cooler nights. In the habitat, rainfall is low for 4 months, but additional moisture is available from frequent heavy deposits of dew. Cultivated plants should be allowed to dry out between waterings, but they should never remain dry for extended periods. Occasional early morning mistings between waterings may help prevent plants from becoming too dry. Fertilizer should be reduced or eliminated. In the habitat, light is highest in winter.

GROWING MEDIA: Plants may be mounted on tree-fern or cork slabs if humidity is high and plants are watered at least once daily in summer. When plants are potted, any open, fast-draining medium may be used. Repotting is best done in early spring when new roots are growing.

MISCELLANEOUS NOTES: The bloom season shown in the climate table is based on reports from the habitat.

Plant and Flower Information

PLANT SIZE AND TYPE: A sympodial epiphyte of unreported size.

PSEUDOBULB: The grooved stems are nearly cylindrical.

INFLORESCENCE: Flowers are carried on a short raceme.

FLOWERS: 1–2 per inflorescence. The flowers are 0.7 in. (1.8 cm) across. The triangular sepals and oblong petals are white. The white lip is yellow-green on the back with purple lines on the sidelobes.

REFERENCES: 157, 216, 254.

Dendrobium leucochysum Schlechter. See *D. bracteosum* Rchb. f. REFERENCES: 223, 443.

Dendrobium leucocyanum T. M. Reeve

ORIGIN/HABITAT: Northern Papua New Guinea. Plants grow in Enga Province near Laiagam at 7000–8500 ft. (2130–2590 m). They grow on a variety of host trees.

CLIMATE: Botanical garden records, Laiagam, Papua New Guinea, Lat. 5.5°S, Long. 143.5°E, at 7218 ft. (2200 m). Temperatures are calculated for an elevation of 8000 ft. (2440 m), resulting in probable extremes of 88°F (31°C) and 29°F (–1°C).

N/HEMISPHERE	JAN	FEB	MAR	APR	MAY	JUN	JUL	AUG	SEP	OCT	NOV	DEC
°F AVG MAX	73	74	75	73	75	75	79	74	73	75	75	73
°F AVG MIN	52	51	52	52	53	53	52	53	55	54	53	53
DIURNAL RANGE	21	23	23	21	22	22	27	21	18	21	22	20
RAIN/INCHES	4.0	4.8	6.1	7.8	8.5	9.1	8.4	9.6	9.5	8.9	6.3	4.0
HUMIDITY/%	N/A											
BLOOM SEASON	*											*
DAYS CLR	N/A											
RAIN/MM	102	122	155	198	216	231	213	244	241	226	160	102
°C AVG MAX	23.0	23.6	24.1	23.0	24.1	24.1	26.3	23.6	23.0	24.1	24.1	23.0
°C AVG MIN	11.3	10.8	11.3	11.3	11.9	11.9	11.3	11.9	13.0	12.5	11.9	11.9
DIURNAL RANGE	11.7	12.8	12.8	11.7	12.2	12.2	15.0	11.7	10.0	11.6	12.2	11.1
S/HEMISPHERE	JUL	AUG	SEP	OCT	NOV	DEC	JAN	FEB	MAR	APR	MAY	JUN

Cultural Recommendations

LIGHT: 2000–3000 fc.

TEMPERATURES: Throughout the year, days average 73–79°F (23–26°C), and nights average 51–55°F (11–13°C), with a diurnal range of 18–27°F (10–15°C). The climate table represents the lower, therefore warmer, portion of the habitat, so plants should easily adapt to conditions that are 5–7°F (3–4°C) cooler than indicated.

HUMIDITY: Information is not available for this location. However, records from nearby stations indicate that averages are probably near 80% year-round.

WATER: Rainfall is moderate to heavy all year, but conditions are slightly drier for 3–4 months in winter. Rain falls as heavy showers most afternoons. Skies clear by early evening. Low clouds and mist develop during the evening and continue until midmorning the next day. The mist is so heavy that trees and shrubs drip moisture soon after the clouds form. Cultivated plants should be kept moist but not soggy.

FERTILIZER: ¼–½ recommended strength. A balanced fertilizer should be applied weekly to biweekly throughout the year. The Royal Botanic Garden in Edinburgh uses a seaweed-based fertilizer for high-elevation plants from New Guinea.

REST PERIOD: Growing conditions should be maintained year-round. Water and fertilizer should be reduced somewhat in winter, especially for plants grown in the dark, short-day conditions common in temperate latitudes. They should never be allowed to dry out completely, however. In the habitat, light is highest in winter.

GROWING MEDIA: Plants may be mounted on tree-fern slabs if humidity is high and plants are watered at least once daily in summer. When plants are potted, any open, fast-draining medium may be used. Repotting is best done in early spring when new roots are growing.

MISCELLANEOUS NOTES: The bloom season shown in the climate table is based on cultivation records, but in the habitat blooming is not seasonal. Growers indicate that this species is easier to cultivate than many high altitude species.

Plant and Flower Information

PLANT SIZE AND TYPE: A creeping, mat-forming, 2 in. (5 cm) sympodial epiphyte.

PSEUDOBULB: 0.2–0.5 in. (0.5–1.3 cm) diameter. The spherical pseudobulbs are tightly clustered, and the plant has a neat creeping habit. They are green and covered with sheaths when young, but they turn brown to reddish brown with age.

LEAVES: 2, rarely 3, at the apex of new pseudobulbs. The ovate-elliptic leaves are 1.5 in. (3.8 cm) long. They are soft, wavy, and sometimes suffused with purplish maroon.

INFLORESCENCE: Very short. The inflorescences emerge at the apex of leafless pseudobulbs. The tight clusters of blossoms are 0.8 in. (2 cm) across.

FLOWERS: 5–25 per inflorescence. The small, elongated flowers are 0.3–0.4 in. (0.8–1.1 cm) long, are formed in tight clusters, and last about 2 months. The translucent sepals and petals may be pale blue to blue-gray, sometimes with a violet tinge and green at the tips, or uniformly greenish. The lip is whitish with green at the apex.

HYBRIDIZING NOTES: Chromosome count is 2n = 38 (ref. 153, 273). *D. leucocyanum* is known to hybridize naturally with *D. alaticaulinum* P. van Royen, producing *D.* × *yengiliense* T. M. Reeve.

REFERENCES: 79, 95, 153, 179, 234, 273, 318, 381, 554.

PHOTOS/DRAWINGS: *318*, 381.

Dendrobium leucohybos Schlechter

AKA: Cribb (ref. 83) includes *D. leucohybos* var. *leucanthum* Schlechter as a synonym.

ORIGIN/HABITAT: Northern Papua New Guinea. Plants grow on moss-covered mistforest trees of the Kani and Finisterre Mountains at 2950–7850 ft. (900–2400 m).

CLIMATE: Station #94010, Goroka, Papua New Guinea, Lat. 6.1°S, Long. 145.4°E, at 5141 ft. (1567 m). Temperatures are calculated for an elevation of 5900 ft. (1800 m), resulting in probable extremes of 84°F (29°C) and 40°F (5°C).

N/HEMISPHERE	JAN	FEB	MAR	APR	MAY	JUN	JUL	AUG	SEP	OCT	NOV	DEC
°F AVG MAX	73	74	75	76	76	75	76	75	75	75	76	74
°F AVG MIN	53	54	54	54	55	56	56	56	57	56	56	54
DIURNAL RANGE	20	20	21	22	21	19	20	19	18	19	20	20
RAIN/INCHES	2.1	2.8	4.6	5.9	6.6	9.3	9.1	10.1	10.7	8.3	4.6	2.0
HUMIDITY/%	70	67	67	67	67	71	72	73	74	71	70	70
BLOOM SEASON	*				*			*				
DAYS CLR	N/A											
RAIN/MM	53	71	117	150	168	236	231	257	272	211	117	51
°C AVG MAX	23.0	23.6	24.1	24.7	24.7	24.1	24.7	24.1	24.1	24.1	24.7	23.6
°C AVG MIN	11.9	12.5	12.5	12.5	13.0	13.6	13.6	13.6	14.1	13.6	13.6	12.5
DIURNAL RANGE	11.1	11.1	11.6	12.2	11.7	10.5	11.1	10.5	10.0	10.5	11.1	11.1
S/HEMISPHERE	JUL	AUG	SEP	OCT	NOV	DEC	JAN	FEB	MAR	APR	MAY	JUN

Cultural Recommendations

LIGHT: 1800–3000 fc.

TEMPERATURES: Throughout the year, days average 73–76°F (23–25°C), and nights average 53–57°F (12–14°C), with a diurnal range of 18–22°F (10–12°C). Growers report that plants from this habitat do not survive continuous high temperatures.

HUMIDITY: 70–75% most of the year, dropping to near 65% in late winter and spring.

WATER: Rainfall is moderate to heavy most of the year, but conditions are slightly drier for 3 months in winter. Cultivated plants should be kept moist but not soggy. Occasional early morning mistings may be beneficial, especially on bright, sunny days.

FERTILIZER: ¼–½ recommended strength. A balanced fertilizer should be applied weekly to biweekly throughout the year.

REST PERIOD: Growing temperatures should be maintained all year. In the habitat, rainfall is lowest in winter, but dew and mist from fog and low clouds are common. Water and fertilizer should be reduced somewhat for cultivated plants, especially those grown in the darker, short-day conditions common during temperate-latitude winters. Plants should be kept on the dry side, but they should never be allowed to dry out completely. In the habitat, light is higher in winter.

GROWING MEDIA: Plants may be mounted on tree-fern or cork slabs if humidity is high and plants are watered at least once daily in summer. When plants are potted, any open, fast-draining medium may be used. Repotting may be done anytime new roots are growing.

MISCELLANEOUS NOTES: The bloom season shown in the climate table is based on collection reports.

Plant and Flower Information

PLANT SIZE AND TYPE: An 8–12 in. (20–30 cm) sympodial epiphyte.

PSEUDOBULB: 4–7 in. (10–17 cm) long. The clustered, cylindrical stems may be erect or pendent. The upper portion of each stem is swollen.

LEAVES: 2 at the apex of each growth. The narrow leaves, which are elliptic-lanceolate, are 4–7 in. (10–18 cm) long. They are twisted at the base to lie on a single plane.

INFLORESCENCE: 4 in. (10 cm) long. Inflorescences are borne from terminal and the uppermost lateral nodes from below the leaves.

FLOWERS: 3–5 per inflorescence. The fleshy blossoms are 0.6–0.8 in. (1.5–2.0 cm) across. Sepals and petals are white to pale apricot. The obovate lip is obscurely 3-lobed. It may be orange or white or intermediate shades. The callus is 3-ridged at the apex.

HYBRIDIZING NOTES: Chromosome count is 2n = 38 (ref. 273).

REFERENCES: 83, 92, 153, 221, 273, 437, 445.

PHOTOS/DRAWINGS: 437.

Dendrobium leucolophotum Rchb. f. See *D. affine* (Decaisne) Steudel. REFERENCES: 179, 216, 254, 445, 470, 533, 541, 570.

Dendrobium leucorhodum Schlechter. See *D. anosmum* Lindley. REFERENCES: 190, 221, 296, 437, 445, 454, 470, 504, 580.

Dendrobium levatii Kränzlin. Status unknown. Supposedly from the New Hebrides (Vanuatu), but Lewis and Cribb (ref. 270) do not include this name in the *Orchids of Vanuatu*. REFERENCES: 162, 224.

Dendrobium leytense Ames

ORIGIN/HABITAT: The Philippines. Plants grow on Leyte Island on extremely tall trees at 200–1650 ft. (60–500 m).

CLIMATE: Station #98550, Tacloban, Leyte, Philippines, Lat. 11.3°N, Long. 125.0°E, at 52 ft. (16 m). Temperatures are calculated for an elevation of 1000 ft. (300 m). Record extreme temperatures are not available for this location.

N/HEMISPHERE	JAN	FEB	MAR	APR	MAY	JUN	JUL	AUG	SEP	OCT	NOV	DEC
°F AVG MAX	80	82	83	85	86	86	84	85	84	84	83	81
°F AVG MIN	70	70	71	72	74	74	73	73	72	72	72	70
DIURNAL RANGE	10	12	12	13	12	12	11	12	12	12	11	11
RAIN/INCHES	9.4	6.2	4.4	3.3	5.8	7.8	6.9	5.7	8.3	9.1	11.4	8.5
HUMIDITY/%	N/A											
BLOOM SEASON	*			*				*				
DAYS CLR	N/A											
RAIN/MM	239	157	112	84	147	198	175	145	211	231	290	216
°C AVG MAX	26.6	27.7	28.3	29.4	29.9	29.9	28.8	29.4	28.8	28.8	28.3	27.2
°C AVG MIN	21.0	21.0	21.6	22.2	23.3	23.3	22.7	22.7	22.2	22.2	22.2	21.0
DIURNAL RANGE	5.6	6.7	6.7	7.2	6.6	6.6	6.1	6.7	6.6	6.6	6.1	6.2
S/HEMISPHERE	JUL	AUG	SEP	OCT	NOV	DEC	JAN	FEB	MAR	APR	MAY	JUN

Cultural Recommendations

LIGHT: 2500–3500 fc.

TEMPERATURES: Throughout the year, days average 80–86°F (27–30°C), and nights average 70–74°F (21–23°C), with a diurnal range of 10–13°F (6–7°C).

Dendrobium lichenastrum

HUMIDITY: Information is not available for this location. However, records from nearby locations indicate that humidity probably averages 80–85% most of the year, dropping to 75–80% in late winter and early spring.

WATER: Rainfall is moderate to heavy most of the year. Conditions are slightly drier for 2–3 months in late winter and early spring. Cultivated plants should be kept moist but not soggy.

FERTILIZER: ¼–½ recommended strength. A balanced fertilizer should be applied weekly to biweekly throughout the year.

REST PERIOD: Growing temperatures should be maintained all year. A brief rest may occur in late winter or early spring when conditions are slightly drier. In cultivation, water and fertilizer should be reduced for 1–2 months and plants allowed to dry slightly between waterings. They should not remain dry for long periods, however.

GROWING MEDIA: Plants may be mounted on tree-fern or cork slabs if humidity is high and plants are watered at least once daily in summer. When plants are potted, any open, fast-draining medium may be used. Repotting may be done anytime new roots are growing.

MISCELLANEOUS NOTES: The bloom season shown in the climate table is based on collection reports.

Plant and Flower Information

PLANT SIZE AND TYPE: A 12 in. (30 cm) sympodial epiphyte.

PSEUDOBULB: 12 in. (30 cm) long. The jointed stems arise from a short rhizome.

LEAVES: Many. The oblong-lanceolate leaves are 2 in. (5 cm) long, greenish yellow, and nearly erect.

INFLORESCENCE: Short. The bracts from which the inflorescences emerge nearly conceal the flowers.

FLOWERS: 2 per inflorescence. The very small flowers are 0.4 in. (1 cm) across. They are greenish yellow with a pale purple tinge on the lip. The triangular lateral sepals taper to a slender point. The dorsal sepal is lanceolate, acute, and concave. The petals are linear. The 3-lobed lip is wedge-shaped with a triangular midlobe and round, slightly scalloped sidelobes.

REFERENCES: 12, 222, 296, 536.

Dendrobium lichenastrum (F. Mueller) Kränzlin

AKA: *Bulbophyllum lichenastrum* F. Mueller. Clements (ref. 67) includes *D. lichenastrum* (F. Mueller) Kränzlin var. *prenticei* (F. Mueller) Dockrill as a synonym of *D. prenticei* (F. Mueller) Nicholls.

ORIGIN/HABITAT: Northeastern Australia. Plants are found in Queensland from Mackay to just north of Cairns. They grow on trees and rocks in both open forests and dense rainforests from sea level to 1950 ft. (0–600 m).

CLIMATE: Station #94294, Townsville, Australia, Lat. 19.3°S, Long. 146.8°E, at 18 ft. (5 m). Temperatures are calculated for an elevation of 1950 ft. (600 m), resulting in probable extremes of 103°F (40°C) and 33°F (1°C).

N/HEMISPHERE	JAN	FEB	MAR	APR	MAY	JUN	JUL	AUG	SEP	OCT	NOV	DEC
°F AVG MAX	69	71	74	77	79	81	81	81	80	78	75	71
°F AVG MIN	53	55	60	65	68	70	70	69	67	64	59	55
DIURNAL RANGE	16	16	14	12	11	11	11	12	13	14	16	16
RAIN/INCHES	0.6	0.5	0.7	1.3	1.9	5.4	10.9	11.2	7.2	3.3	1.3	1.4
HUMIDITY/%	61	61	62	64	66	70	72	71	70	64	63	63
BLOOM SEASON									***	***		
DAYS CLR @ 10AM	16	18	15	10	7	7	5	5	9	13	14	15
DAYS CLR @ 4PM	16	18	20	20	17	15	8	5	7	11	14	15
RAIN/MM	15	13	18	33	48	137	277	284	183	84	33	36
°C AVG MAX	20.3	21.4	23.1	24.8	25.9	27.0	27.0	27.0	26.4	25.3	23.6	21.4
°C AVG MIN	11.4	12.5	15.3	18.1	19.8	20.9	20.9	20.3	19.2	17.5	14.8	12.5
DIURNAL RANGE	8.9	8.9	7.8	6.7	6.1	6.1	6.1	6.7	7.2	7.8	8.8	8.9
S/HEMISPHERE	JUL	AUG	SEP	OCT	NOV	DEC	JAN	FEB	MAR	APR	MAY	JUN

Cultural Recommendations

LIGHT: 2500–3500 fc. Cultivated plants require about 50% shade in summer.

TEMPERATURES: Summer days average 81°F (27°C), and nights average 69–70°F (20–21°C), with a diurnal range of 11–12°F (6–7°C).

HUMIDITY: Near 70% at lower elevations. However, in the habitat, values may be closer to 80–85% year-round.

WATER: Rainfall is moderate to heavy for 5 months during the summer wet season, followed by a 6–7 month dry season. Additional water is available in the rainforest habitat from heavy dew and mist from fog and low clouds, however. Successful growers report that orchids from this habitat require "lots of water," and that they must never be allowed to dry out.

FERTILIZER: ¼–½ recommended strength, applied weekly. A high-nitrogen fertilizer is beneficial from spring to midsummer, but a fertilizer high in phosphates should be used in late summer and autumn.

REST PERIOD: Winter days average 69–71°F (20–21°C), and nights average 53–55°F (11–13°C), with a diurnal range of 16°F (9°C). Some growers indicate that lows should be kept above 43°F (6°C); but record lows in the habitat are near freezing, and other growers indicate that plants will tolerate temperatures down to 28°F (–2°C) if they are dry. Water and humidity may be reduced somewhat, especially for plants grown in the dark, short-day conditions common in temperate-latitude winters. However, plants should never be allowed to dry out completely. Occasional morning mistings between waterings may be beneficial, especially on bright, sunny days. Fertilizer should be reduced or eliminated until water is increased in spring. In the habitat, light is highest in winter.

GROWING MEDIA: Plants are healthiest mounted on cork or tree-fern slabs. Some growers layer sphagnum moss between 2 thin pieces of tree-fern. Plants are then mounted on this sandwich. This mount retains more moisture than a regular slab, but still allows free air movement around the roots. *D. lichenastrum* is a slow growing species and is difficult to establish. Remounting is best avoided whenever possible. When it must be done, however, it is best done in early spring when new roots are growing.

MISCELLANEOUS NOTES: The bloom season shown in the climate table is based on reports from the habitat. Cultivated plants are reported to bloom in every month, and plants may be in almost continuous bloom.

Plant and Flower Information

PLANT SIZE AND TYPE: A tiny sympodial epiphyte that forms a nearly solid mat.

PSEUDOBULB: None.

LEAVES: Leaves arise directly from the rhizome. The oval to round leaves are 0.2–0.6 in. (0.5–1.5 cm) long, densely crowded, 0.1 in. (0.2 cm) apart, and alternate on either side of the rhizome. Leaves may be green to reddish, depending on light levels.

INFLORESCENCE: 0.2–0.6 in. (0.5–1.5 cm) long. Inflorescences arise directly from the rhizome near the base of the leaf.

FLOWERS: 1 per inflorescence. The tiny, cupped flowers are 0.2–0.3 in. (0.5–0.7 cm) across. Blossoms are normally pink with red stripes, but they may be dingy white or creamy yellow. The tonguelike lip may be yellow or orange. The highly variable flowers are fairly insignificant on the matted foliage. They last about 2 weeks.

HYBRIDIZING NOTES: Chromosome counts are $2n = 40$ (ref. 151, 187) and $2n = 38$ (ref. 152) and $2n = 38$ as *D. lichenastrum* var. *lichenastrum* and *D. lichenastrum* var. *prenticei* (ref. 243). Plants are not self-fertile, but seeds are regularly produced when pollen from another plant is used.

REFERENCES: 23, 36, 67, 105, 151, 152, 179, 187, 216, 228, 240, 242, 243, 254, 260, 262, 263, 291, 325, 330, 332, 333, 371, 390, 421, 527, 533.

PHOTOS/DRAWINGS: 105, *240, 242, 291*, 325, *330, 333, 371, 390, 533*.

Dendrobium lichenicola J. J. Smith. See *D. cuthbertsonii* F. Mueller. REFERENCES: 224, 385, 445.

Dendrobium ligulatum Persoon. Now considered a synonym of *Maxillaria ligulata* Ruiz and Pavón. REFERENCES: 216, 254.

Dendrobium lilacinum Rchb. f. not Teijsm. and Binn. See *D. swartzii* A. Hawkes and A. H. Heller. REFERENCES: 229, 254, 286, 295, 394, 445.

Dendrobium lilacinum Teijsm. and Binn. not Rchb. f. See *D. lancifolium* A. Richard. REFERENCES: 216, 254, 436, 470.

Dendrobium limii J. J. Wood

ORIGIN/HABITAT: Borneo. Details of habitat location and elevation were not reported. Therefore, we are unable to select representative climate data or suggest cultural requirements.

MISCELLANEOUS NOTES: The plant was described from a single flower and a keiki preserved in alcohol.

Plant and Flower Information

PLANT SIZE AND TYPE: An 8–24 in. (20–60 cm) sympodial epiphyte.

PSEUDOBULB: 8–24 in. (20–60 cm) long. The slender stems are swollen at the lowest node.

LEAVES: Several on the central portion of the stem. The slender, terete leaves are 1.8–4.7 in. (4.5–12.0 cm) long, smooth, and ungrooved.

INFLORESCENCE: 0.2 in. (0.6 cm) long. Flowers emerge one at a time from small clusters of chaffy bracts at nodes on the leafless apical portion of the stem.

FLOWERS: 1 per inflorescence. The very short lived blossoms are 0.6 in. (1.5 cm) long. Sepals are translucent white with a pink suffusion at the tips of the lateral sepals. The oblong petals, which have uneven margins near the chopped-off tip, are white with a pink suffusion at the base. The curved, conical spur is 0.6 in. (1.5 cm) long. The white lip has 2 purple spots at the base and a small, notched midlobe. The wavy margins of the midlobe overlap the large sidelobes. The anther cap is minutely hairy.

REFERENCES: Wood, J. J. and P. Cribb. 1994. A checklist of the orchids of Borneo. Royal Botanic Gardens, Kew.

PHOTOS/DRAWINGS: Wood, J. J. and P. Cribb. 1994. A checklist of the orchids of Borneo. Royal Botanic Gardens, Kew.

Dendrobium linawianum Rchb. f.

AKA: *D. alboviride* Hayata, *D. moniliforme* Lindley not Swartz.

ORIGIN/HABITAT: Taiwan and China. Plants have been found only in the Wulai district south of Taipei on Taiwan Island and in Kwangsi Province in southern China. They usually grow in broadleaf forests below 3300 ft. (1000 m).

CLIMATE: Station #46696, Taipei, Taiwan, Lat. 25.1°N, Long. 121.5°E, at 21 ft. (6 m). Temperatures are calculated for an elevation of 2000 ft. (610 m), resulting in probable extremes of 92°F (34°C) and 26°F (–3°C).

N/HEMISPHERE	JAN	FEB	MAR	APR	MAY	JUN	JUL	AUG	SEP	OCT	NOV	DEC
°F AVG MAX	59	60	64	70	77	81	85	84	81	73	68	62
°F AVG MIN	46	48	51	57	62	66	69	69	67	61	56	51
DIURNAL RANGE	13	12	13	13	15	15	16	15	14	12	12	11
RAIN/INCHES	3.8	5.3	4.3	5.3	6.9	8.8	8.8	8.7	8.2	5.5	4.2	2.9
HUMIDITY/%	84	86	86	85	85	85	82	82	83	84	84	84
BLOOM SEASON		*	*	*								
DAYS CLR @ 8AM	1	1	1	2	3	2	4	4	4	4	3	2
DAYS CLR @ 2PM	4	4	4	3	2	1	2	4	5	4	5	4
RAIN/MM	97	135	109	135	175	224	224	221	208	140	107	74
°C AVG MAX	15.3	15.8	18.0	21.4	25.3	27.5	29.7	29.1	27.5	23.0	20.3	16.9
°C AVG MIN	8.0	9.1	10.8	14.1	16.9	19.1	20.8	20.8	19.7	16.4	13.6	10.8
DIURNAL RANGE	7.3	6.7	7.2	7.3	8.4	8.4	8.9	8.3	7.8	6.6	6.7	6.1
S/HEMISPHERE	JUL	AUG	SEP	OCT	NOV	DEC	JAN	FEB	MAR	APR	MAY	JUN

Cultural Recommendations

LIGHT: 1500–2500 fc. Clear days in the habitat are rare, and the plants usually grow in deep to partial shade; this indicates that direct, summer sun and bright light should be avoided. Growers note that light shade may be adequate.

TEMPERATURES: Summer days average 81–85°F (28–30°C), and nights average 66–69°F (19–21°C), with a diurnal range of 15–16°F (8–9°C). The widest diurnal range occurs in summer.

HUMIDITY: 80–85% year-round.

WATER: Rainfall is heavy from late spring through early autumn but decreases to moderate the remainder of the year. Cultivated plants should be kept moist while actively growing, but water should be gradually reduced in autumn.

FERTILIZER: ¼–½ recommended strength, applied weekly. A high-nitrogen fertilizer is beneficial from spring to midsummer, but a fertilizer high in phosphates should be used in late summer and autumn.

REST PERIOD: Winter days average 59–64°F (15–18°C), and nights average 46–51°F (8–11°C), with a diurnal range of 11–13°F (6–7°C). Rainfall is somewhat lower for 1–2 months in winter. However, frequent heavy deposits of dew along with mist from fog and low clouds result in more available moisture than is indicated by the rainfall averages. Water should be reduced for cultivated plants, but they should never be allowed to dry out completely. Fertilizer should be greatly reduced or eliminated until spring.

GROWING MEDIA: Plants are best mounted on tree-fern or cork slabs if humidity is high and plants are watered at least once daily in summer. When plants are potted, any open, fast-draining medium may be used. They may be repotted anytime new roots are growing.

MISCELLANEOUS NOTES: The bloom season shown in the climate table is based on reports from the habitat. Cultivated plants bloom in the same season. Collected plants are dried and used in Chinese medicine.

Plant and Flower Information

PLANT SIZE AND TYPE: A 12–16 in. (30–40 cm) sympodial epiphyte.

PSEUDOBULB: 12–16 in. (30–40 cm) long. The somewhat flattened stems are erect, clustered, and branching. They are slightly swollen on the upper part with a pseudobulbous swelling at the base. Nodes are 1.2–1.6 in. (3–4 cm) apart.

LEAVES: 6–7. The leaves are 1.6–2.8 in. (4–7 cm) long and narrowly elliptical to oblong. They are arranged in 2 rows. Foliage is sometimes described as deciduous and other times evergreen, depending on growing conditions.

INFLORESCENCE: Inflorescences are borne from the upper nodes of leafless stems.

FLOWERS: 2–3 per inflorescence. The large, showy flowers are 1.6–2.0 in. (4–5 cm) across. The pointed, elliptical sepals and rounded, oval petals are white in the center with varying amounts of purple near the tips. The oblong lip is white with a purple band along the front margin and 2 purple spots on the central disc. The basal disc is covered with short hairs.

HYBRIDIZING NOTES: Chromosome counts, 2n = 38 (ref. 153), 2n = 40 (ref. 153), and 2n = 76 (ref. 153).

REFERENCES: 61, 153, 179, 192, 208, 210, 216, 254, 274, 279, 317, 414, 430, 445, 497, 528, 541, 557, 570.

PHOTOS/DRAWINGS: 38, 210, *274*, 279, *430, 497*.

Dendrobium lindleyanum Griffith. See *D. nobile* Lindley.
REFERENCES: 190, 216, 254, 278, 445, 454.

Dendrobium lindleyi Steudel

AKA: *D. aggregatum* Roxburgh not H. B. and K. The International Orchid Commission (ref. 236) registers hybrids under the name *D. aggregatum*. Seidenfaden (ref. 454) disscusses the massive confusion surrounding the use of the name *D. aggregatum*.

ORIGIN/HABITAT: Widespread across southeast Asia, including Sikkim, Bhutan, northeastern India, Burma, Thailand, Laos, Vietnam, and southwestern China. In Thailand, plants commonly grow in the northern mountains at 2150–4600 ft. (650–1400 m), but they are also reported in the southern and south-central regions. Plants usually grow on the trunks and branches of deciduous trees.

CLIMATE: Station #48327, Chiang Mai, Thailand, Lat. 18.8°N, Long. 99.0°E, at 1100 ft. (335 m). Temperatures are calculated for an elevation of 3500 ft. (1070 m), resulting in probable extremes of 101°F (38°C) and 30°F (−1°C).

N/HEMISPHERE	JAN	FEB	MAR	APR	MAY	JUN	JUL	AUG	SEP	OCT	NOV	DEC
°F AVG MAX	77	82	87	88	86	82	81	79	80	81	78	76
°F AVG MIN	48	49	54	62	66	66	66	67	65	63	58	49
DIURNAL RANGE	29	33	33	26	20	16	15	12	15	18	20	27
RAIN/INCHES	0.3	0.4	0.6	2.0	5.5	6.1	7.4	8.7	11.5	4.9	1.5	0.4
HUMIDITY/%	73	65	58	62	73	78	80	83	83	81	79	76
BLOOM SEASON	*	*	***	***	***	*	*					
DAYS CLR @ 7AM	5	5	2	2	1	0	0	0	0	1	3	3
DAYS CLR @ 1PM	9	8	4	2	0	0	0	0	0	0	1	3
RAIN/MM	8	10	15	51	140	155	188	221	292	124	38	10
°C AVG MAX	25.0	27.8	30.6	31.2	30.0	27.8	27.3	26.2	26.7	27.3	25.6	24.5
°C AVG MIN	8.9	9.5	12.3	16.7	18.9	18.9	18.9	19.5	18.4	17.3	14.5	9.5
DIURNAL RANGE	16.1	18.3	18.3	14.5	11.1	8.9	8.4	6.7	8.3	10.0	11.1	15.0
S/HEMISPHERE	JUL	AUG	SEP	OCT	NOV	DEC	JAN	FEB	MAR	APR	MAY	JUN

Cultural Recommendations

LIGHT: 3500–4500 fc. Cultivated plants need bright light and strong air movement. The heavy summer cloud cover indicates that some shading is needed from spring through autumn, but light should be as high as the plant can tolerate, short of burning the leaves. The increased number of clear days in winter and the deciduous nature of the trees in the habitat indicate that light should be very bright in winter. Growers indicate that it is possible to grow and flower *D. lindleyi* on a bright window sill, but that it is nearly impossible to bloom under lights.

TEMPERATURES: Summer days average 79–82°F (26–28°C), and nights average 66–67°F (19–20°C), with a diurnal range of 12–16°F (7–9°C). Spring is the warmest time of the year. Days average 86–88°F (30–31°C), and nights average 54–66°F (12–19°C), with a diurnal range of 20–33°F (11–18°C).

HUMIDITY: Near 80–85% during the growing season, dropping to 60–65% in winter and early spring.

WATER: Rainfall is moderate to heavy from late spring through early autumn, but conditions are very dry in winter. Cultivated plants should be kept moist while actively growing, but water should be gradually reduced after new growths mature in autumn.

FERTILIZER: ½ to full recommended strength, applied weekly. A high-nitrogen fertilizer with trace elements is beneficial from spring to midsummer, but a fertilizer high in phosphates should be used in late summer and autumn.

REST PERIOD: Winter days average 76–82°F (25–28°C), and nights average 48–49°F (9–10°C), with a diurnal range of 27–33°F (15–18°C). Growers report that plants tolerate light frost, but extreme temperatures should be avoided in cultivation. Growers also indicate that *D. lindleyi* will still bloom with 60°F (16°C) winter nights if a dry rest is provided, but plants are healthiest if temperatures are closer to 50°F (10°C). The cool dry rest is needed to initiate blooms. Plants that do not receive a rest may produce keikis instead of flowers.

In the habitat, rainfall averages are very low for 4–5 months in winter, but during the early part of the season the high relative humidity indicates that additional moisture is available from frequent fog, mist, and heavy dew. Growers report that several months of winter drought is essential to promote flowering. Some even recommend eliminating water in winter; but plants are healthiest if, for most of the winter, they are allowed to become somewhat dry between waterings but do not remain dry for extended periods. For 1–2 months in late winter, however, conditions are clear, warm, and dry with humidity so low that even the moisture from morning dew is uncommon. Plants should be allowed to dry out completely between waterings and remain dry longer during this time. Occasional early morning mistings between waterings may help keep the plants from becoming too dry. Some growers recommend misting only enough to prevent severe pseudobulb shriveling. The pseudobulbs normally shrivel, however, so growers are cautioned to use care when using the amount of shriveling to indicate the need for additional water. The dry rest should be continued until new flower spikes are about 1 in. (2.5 cm) long. Fertilizer should be eliminated until heavier watering is resumed. Winter light should be as high as possible.

GROWING MEDIA: Mounting plants on bare wood or tree-fern slabs accommodates the rambling growth habit. Growers often place a pad of sphagnum moss between the mount and the plant. If plants are mounted, summer humidity must be high, and plants should be watered at least once a day in summer. If plants cannot be mounted, hanging pots or baskets may be filled with any open, rapidly draining medium. Containers should be barely large enough to hold the roots. Mounts or baskets reduce the risk of the slender new canes becoming kinked under their own weight. Repotting should be avoided as long as possible, but it must be done before the medium starts to break down. Plants should not be divided into clumps smaller than 3–4 growths. When necessary, repotting is best done immediately after blooming.

MISCELLANEOUS NOTES: The bloom season shown in the climate table is based on cultivation records, but in the habitat, plants also bloom in spring. Growers often consider *D. lindleyi* a problem plant so careful attention should be paid to its cultural needs.

Plant and Flower Information

PLANT SIZE AND TYPE: A 4–8 in. (10–20 cm) sympodial epiphyte.

PSEUDOBULB: 2–4 in. (5–10 cm) long. The grooved stems are clustered. They may lie flat against the host or point all different directions. Canes are slightly tapered at both ends.

LEAVES: 1 per growth. The gray-green leaves are usually 3 in. (7.6 cm) long. They are rigidly leathery and persistent.

INFLORESCENCE: 6–12 in. (15–30 cm) long. The wiry racemes, which are longer than the plant is tall, are arching to pendent. They arise from nodes near the middle of the cane.

FLOWERS: 10–14 per inflorescence. The highly variable flowers are 1.0–2.0 in. (2.5–5.0 cm) across, which is large for the plant size. The round, flat sepals and petals may be nearly white to deep orange, but they are normally a shade of yellow. Color tends to deepen with age. The lip, which is commonly orange-yellow, is darkest near the base. It may be highly colored even when the sepals and petals are pale. Unlike *D. jenkinsii* Wallich ex Lindley 1839 not *D. jenkinsi* Lindley, whose lip is wholly pubescent, the borders of the lip on *D. lindleyi* are not pubescent. In other respects they are extremely similar. The fragile blossoms, which have a honey fragrance, last 2–3 weeks when kept cool and dry.

HYBRIDIZING NOTES: Chromosome counts as *D. aggregatum* are n = 19 (ref. 504, 580), 2n = 32–37 (ref. 542), 2n = 38 (ref. 152, 504, 580), 2n = 32–35 (ref. 504, 580); as *D. lindleyi*, 2n = 38 (ref. 152, 153, 154, 243, 504, 542, 580); as *D. aggregatum.* var. *majus* Rolfe, 2n = 38 (ref. 151, 154, 187, 188, 580). Johansen (ref. 239) indicates that plants are self-sterile and that flowers dropped 7–8 days after self-pollination. None of his attempts to cross-pollinate produced capsules. Viable seeds were produced when *D. lindleyi* was crossed with *D. thyrsiflorum* Rchb. f.

REFERENCES: 6, 36, 38, 46, 71, 151, 152, 153, 154, 157, 179, 187, 188, 190, 196, 202, 208, 210, 214, 216, 232, 236, 239, 243, 245, 254, 266, 317, 326, 356, 359, 369, 371, 376, 395, 402, 414, 428, 430, 446, 447, 448, 452, 454, 458, 461, 504, 523, 541, 542, 557, 568, 570, 580.

PHOTOS/DRAWINGS: 6, 38, *71*, 210, *356, 369, 371, 428, 430, 446, 454*, 458, 461, 523, *539, 568*.

Dendrobium lineale Rolfe

AKA: *D. augustae-victoriae* Kränzlin, *D. cogniauxianum* Kränzlin (in part), *D. grantii* C. T. White, *D. imperatrix* Kränzlin, *D. veratrifolium* Lindley not Roxburgh, Kränzlin, or Naves, *D. veratroides* Bakhuizen f. In his analysis of *D. gouldii*, Hunt (ref. 211) included the preceding names and *D. lineale* as synonyms, but he excluded *D. grantii*. Cribb (ref. 84), however, concurs with growers' strong opinions that *D. lineale* and *D. gouldii* should be maintained as separate species. Only time will tell whether botanists finally consider *D. lineale* and *D. gouldii* as separate species or simply color variations of a single species. Hunt recommended that for horticultural purposes *D. gouldii* be used for the brown and yellow flowered forms, and that *D. veratrifolium* be retained (in lieu of the taxonomically correct *D. lineale*) for the white and mauve flower forms.

ORIGIN/HABITAT: Widespread throughout northern Papua New Guinea, Irian Jaya (western New Guinea), and adjacent islands. Plants grow on coastal forest trees and on rocks on shoreline cliffs from sea level to 2600 ft. (0–800 m). Plants tolerate ocean spray. They were cultivated in the botanical garden at Bogor, Java.

CLIMATE: Station #94004, Wewak, Papua New Guinea, Lat. 3.6°S, Long. 143.7°E, at 16 ft. (5 m). Temperatures are calculated for an elevation of 2000 ft. (610 m), resulting in probable extremes of 91°F (33°C) and 55°F (13°C).

N/HEMISPHERE	JAN	FEB	MAR	APR	MAY	JUN	JUL	AUG	SEP	OCT	NOV	DEC
°F AVG MAX	81	81	81	81	81	81	80	79	80	81	81	81
°F AVG MIN	67	67	67	68	68	68	68	68	67	67	68	67
DIURNAL RANGE	14	14	14	13	13	13	12	11	13	14	13	14
RAIN/INCHES	7.6	4.8	5.3	10.0	13.3	14.5	12.1	11.9	14.9	16.9	15.1	10.8
HUMIDITY/%	80	79	79	78	79	81	82	82	81	82	81	80
BLOOM SEASON			*	*	*	*	*	*	*	*		
DAYS CLR	N/A											
RAIN/MM	193	122	135	254	338	368	307	302	378	429	384	274
°C AVG MAX	27.5	27.5	27.5	27.5	27.5	27.5	26.9	26.4	26.9	27.5	27.5	27.5
°C AVG MIN	19.7	19.7	19.7	20.3	20.3	20.3	20.3	20.3	19.7	19.7	20.3	19.7
DIURNAL RANGE	7.8	7.8	7.8	7.2	7.2	7.2	6.6	6.1	7.2	7.8	7.2	7.8
S/HEMISPHERE	JUL	AUG	SEP	OCT	NOV	DEC	JAN	FEB	MAR	APR	MAY	JUN

Cultural Recommendations

LIGHT: 2500–4000 fc. Plants can tolerate full sun, but they grow better in light shade.

TEMPERATURES: Throughout the year, days average 79–81°F (26–28°C), and nights average 67–68°F (20°C), with a diurnal range of 11–14°F (6–8°C).

HUMIDITY: Near 80% year-round.

WATER: Rainfall is heavy all year, but conditions are slightly drier for 1–2 months in winter. Cultivated plants should be kept moist but not soggy.

FERTILIZER: ¼–½ recommended strength. A balanced fertilizer should be applied weekly to biweekly throughout the year.

REST PERIOD: Growing temperatures should be maintained year-round. Rainfall is lowest in winter. Water should be reduced somewhat for cultivated plants, especially those grown in the dark, short-day conditions common in temperate-latitude winters, but they should never be allowed to dry out completely. Fertilizer should be reduced until water is increased in spring. In the habitat, light is highest in winter.

GROWING MEDIA: Plants may be mounted on tree-fern or cork slabs if humidity is high and plants are watered at least once daily in summer. When well-grown, however, mounted plants can become too large and unwieldy to move. When plants are potted, a roomy pot with any open, fast-draining medium may be used. Repotting may be done anytime new roots are growing.

MISCELLANEOUS NOTES: A free-flowering species, the bloom season shown in the climate table is based on reports from the habitat. Sparse cultivation records report blooming from spring through summer. *D. lineale* is often confused with *D. gouldii* from the Solomon Islands which normally has yellow flowers.

Plant and Flower Information

PLANT SIZE AND TYPE: A 39–126 in. (100–320 cm) sympodial epiphyte or lithophyte. In nature, plants are normally large, but cultivated plants tend to be smaller.

PSEUDOBULB: 39–126 in. (100–320 cm) long. The erect, canelike stems arise from a short rhizome. The upper 65% of the stem is leafy.

LEAVES: Many. The oblong or lanceolate leaves are 3–6 in. (8–15 cm) long. They are rigidly leathery and persistent. The leaves are normally dark green when mature, but they often have a purple tinge when young.

INFLORESCENCE: 10–30 in. (25–75 cm) long. The arching inflorescences, which may be densely or laxly flowered, are borne from nodes at or near the apex of older pseudobulbs.

FLOWERS: 17–35 per inflorescence. The flowers are 1.4–3.2 in. (3.5–8.0 cm) long. The rounded segments are wavy with a heavy texture. Sepals and petals are usually white, but some clones are lavender, pink, or pale yellow. The sepals are recurved and slightly twisted. The erect, twisted petals are ruffled along the margin. They may be lavender, pink, yellow, or white. The wavy-margined lip is marked with violet or purplish veins and 5 raised keels. Blossoms are fragrant and long-lived.

HYBRIDIZING NOTES: Chromosome count is 2n = 38 (ref. 152, 243) as *D. lineale* and as *D. grantii* (ref. 504, 580). *D. lineale* is thought to hybridize naturally with *D. antennatum* Lindley. The free-flowering characteristic is usually passed on to its progeny.

REFERENCES: 25, 84, 152, 179, 190, 196, 200, 211, 218, 236, 243, 254, 304, 306, 310, 317, 326, 346, 371, 437, 444, 470, 504, 510, 516, 537, 551, 568, 580.

PHOTOS/DRAWINGS: *84, 304, 306, 346, 371*, 437, *551*.

Dendrobium linearifolium Teijsm. and Binn.

AKA: *D. gracile* Kränzlin not Lindley.

ORIGIN/HABITAT: Sumatra, Java, and Bali. Plants are common in Central and East Java, where they grow at 2300–5900 ft. (700–1800 m). They

Dendrobium lineatum

are often found on roadside trees and may grow on dead trees in full sun.

CLIMATE: Station #96881, Madium, Java, Indonesia, Lat. 7.6°S, Long. 111.4°E, at 361 ft. (110 m). Temperatures are calculated for an elevation of 4100 ft. (1250 m), resulting in probable extremes of 83°F (28°C) and 50°F (10°C).

N/HEMISPHERE	JAN	FEB	MAR	APR	MAY	JUN	JUL	AUG	SEP	OCT	NOV	DEC
°F AVG MAX	73	74	75	76	74	73	72	72	73	75	74	74
°F AVG MIN	57	57	59	60	60	60	60	60	60	60	60	58
DIURNAL RANGE	16	17	16	16	14	13	12	12	13	15	14	16
RAIN/INCHES	1.3	0.8	1.2	2.9	7.6	10.2	11.9	10.9	10.4	8.8	5.1	3.2
HUMIDITY/%	60	54	52	52	64	72	77	78	78	74	70	64
BLOOM SEASON			*									
DAYS CLR @ 7AM	18	22	21	16	8	4	2	2	3	6	9	11
DAYS CLR @ 1PM	15	17	14	9	4	2	1	1	3	6	11	
RAIN/MM	33	20	30	74	193	259	302	277	264	224	130	81
°C AVG MAX	22.6	23.1	23.7	24.3	23.1	22.6	22.0	22.0	22.6	23.7	23.1	23.1
°C AVG MIN	13.7	13.7	14.8	15.4	15.4	15.4	15.4	15.4	15.4	15.4	15.4	14.3
DIURNAL RANGE	8.9	9.4	8.9	8.9	7.7	7.2	6.6	6.6	7.2	8.3	7.7	8.8
S/HEMISPHERE	JUL	AUG	SEP	OCT	NOV	DEC	JAN	FEB	MAR	APR	MAY	JUN

Cultural Recommendations

LIGHT: 3000–4000 fc.

TEMPERATURES: Throughout the year, days average 72–76°F (22–24°C), and nights average 57–60°F (14–15°C), with a diurnal range of 12–17°F (7–9°C). In the microclimate, highs may be 6–10°F (3–6°C) warmer than indicated in the climate table.

HUMIDITY: Near 70–80% in summer, dropping to near 50–55% for 3 months in winter and spring.

WATER: Rainfall is heavy from spring through autumn, followed by a 2–3 month winter dry season when humidity is so low that even moisture from dew is uncommon. Cultivated plants should be kept moist from spring into autumn, but water should be gradually reduced in late autumn.

FERTILIZER: ¼–½ recommended strength. A balanced fertilizer should be applied weekly to biweekly throughout the growing season.

REST PERIOD: Growing temperatures should be maintained all year, but conditions are dry in winter. For cultivated plants, water and fertilizer should be reduced and the plants allowed to dry out between waterings. They should not remain dry for extended periods, however.

GROWING MEDIA: Plants may be potted in any open, fast-draining medium. Repotting may be done anytime new roots are growing.

MISCELLANEOUS NOTES: The bloom season shown in the climate table is based on reports from the habitat. Plants that produce very short-lived flowers commonly bloom several times during the year. Flowering usually occurs 7–14 days after a sudden 10°F (5°C) drop in daytime temperatures.

Plant and Flower Information

PLANT SIZE AND TYPE: A 28 in. (70 cm) sympodial epiphyte.

PSEUDOBULB: 28 in. (70 cm) long. The swollen portion at the base of the stem is 1.4 in. (3.5 cm) long, oval, and shiny. It is red when the plants grow in high light. The balance of the stem is slender and often branches.

LEAVES: Many. The linear leaves, which are 2.4 in. (6 cm) long, are spaced 1.1 in. (2.8 cm) apart along the entire length of the stem.

INFLORESCENCE: Short. Many inflorescences arise all along mature stems.

FLOWERS: 1–2 per inflorescence. The flowers are 0.7 in. (1.8 cm) across. Sepals are white with green at the base and red veins. Petals are uniformly white. The lip, which is notched in the center, has a broad, raised yellow band in the center with red veins at the back. The front margin is wavy. Blossoms last 2–3 days.

REFERENCES: 25, 75, 190, 216, 254, 435, 445, 469.

PHOTOS/DRAWINGS: 75, 469.

Dendrobium lineatum Teijsm. and Binn. Kränzlin (ref. 254) considered this an invalid name, and J. J. Smith (ref. 469) considered it synonymous with *D. linearifolium* Teijsm. and Binn. REFERENCES: 216, 254, 469.

Dendrobium linguaeforme Swartz. See *D. linguiforme* Swartz. REFERENCES: 216.

Dendrobium linguella Rchb. f.

AKA: The International Orchid Commission (ref. 236) lists *D. linguella* as a synonym of *D. hercoglossum* but registers hybrids under both names. However, Seidenfaden (ref. 454) indicates that the name *D. linguella* has been erroneously applied to plants that should have been identified as *D. hercoglossum,* and he maintains the plants as separate species.

ORIGIN/HABITAT: Burma, Thailand, Vietnam, Sumatra, Borneo, and southern Malaya. In Borneo, plants are found in the lowlands and hill forests of Sabah at 1000–2950 ft. (300–900 m). In Thailand, plants grow in the foothills on the peninsula near Trang.

CLIMATE: Station #48567, Trang, Thailand, Lat. 7.5°N, Long. 99.7°E, at 39 ft. (12 m). Temperatures are calculated for an elevation of 1650 ft. (500 m), resulting in probable extremes of 99°F (37°C) and 56°F (13°C).

N/HEMISPHERE	JAN	FEB	MAR	APR	MAY	JUN	JUL	AUG	SEP	OCT	NOV	DEC
°F AVG MAX	86	89	91	89	86	84	83	83	83	83	82	83
°F AVG MIN	65	66	67	69	70	69	69	72	69	68	67	66
DIURNAL RANGE	21	23	24	20	16	15	14	11	14	15	15	17
RAIN/INCHES	2.1	1.0	2.6	7.5	9.7	9.8	10.2	11.6	12.8	12.7	9.5	4.4
HUMIDITY/%	73	69	70	75	82	82	83	83	84	85	83	78
BLOOM SEASON			*									
DAYS CLR @ 7AM	5	3	2	0	1	0	0	0	0	0	2	3
DAYS CLR @ 1PM	2	2	1	0	0	0	0	0	0	0	0	1
RAIN/MM	53	25	66	190	246	249	259	295	325	323	241	112
°C AVG MAX	29.8	31.5	32.6	31.5	29.8	28.7	28.2	28.2	28.2	28.2	27.6	28.2
°C AVG MIN	18.2	18.7	19.3	20.4	21.0	20.4	20.4	22.1	20.4	19.8	19.3	18.7
DIURNAL RANGE	11.6	12.8	13.3	11.1	8.8	8.3	7.8	6.1	7.8	8.4	8.3	9.5
S/HEMISPHERE	JUL	AUG	SEP	OCT	NOV	DEC	JAN	FEB	MAR	APR	MAY	JUN

Cultural Recommendations

LIGHT: 2000–3000 fc.

TEMPERATURES: Summer days average 83–84°F (28–29°C), and nights average 69–72°F (20–22°C), with a diurnal range of 11–15°F (6–8°C). Spring is the warmest season. Days average 86–91°F (30–33°C), and nights average 67–70°F (19–21°C), with a diurnal range of 16–24°F (9–13°C).

HUMIDITY: 80–85% from late spring through autumn, dropping to 70–75% in winter.

WATER: Rainfall is heavy from spring through autumn, but conditions are drier for 2–3 months in winter. Cultivated plants should be kept moist but not soggy while actively growing, but water should be reduced gradually in late autumn.

FERTILIZER: ¼–½ recommended strength, applied weekly. A high-nitrogen fertilizer is beneficial from spring to midsummer, but a fertilizer high in phosphates should be used in late summer and autumn.

REST PERIOD: Winter days average 83–89°F (28–32°C), and nights average 65–66°F (18–19°C), with a diurnal range of 17–23°F (9–13°C). The increased diurnal range results from warmer days and cooler nights. Growers indicate that plants tolerate winter minimums of 55–60°F (13–16°C). Water should be reduced for 1–2 winter months and plants allowed to dry somewhat between waterings. They should not remain dry for long periods, however. Fertilizer should be reduced anytime water is reduced. In the habitat, light is highest in winter.

GROWING MEDIA: Plants may be mounted on tree-fern or cork slabs if humidity is high and plants are watered at least once daily in summer. When plants are potted, any open, fast-draining medium may be used. Repotting is best done in early spring when new roots are growing.

MISCELLANEOUS NOTES: The bloom season shown in the climate table is based on collection reports from the Batu Islands.

Plant and Flower Information

PLANT SIZE AND TYPE: A 20–24 in. (50–60 cm) sympodial epiphyte. Plants closely resemble *D. aduncum* Wallich ex Lindley when not in bloom.

PSEUDOBULB: 20–24 in. (50–60 cm) long. The soft-caned stems are uniformly slender and erect. The upper 60% of each growth is leafy.

LEAVES: Many. The deciduous leaves are about 4 in. (10 cm) long and very pointed.

INFLORESCENCE: 1.2 in. (3 cm) long. Clusters of blossoms arise from the uppermost nodes of leafless stems. They are held at right angles to the pseudobulb.

FLOWERS: 4–6 per inflorescence. The waxy flowers are 0.8–1.6 in. (2–4 cm) across. Sepals and petals are rose to pink. The lateral sepals are broad at the base. The petals are smaller than the sepals. The cupped lip is light yellowish pink. It is pubescent at the apex and along the median line with a large, glossy callus in the center. The anther cap is dark purple.

HYBRIDIZING NOTES: Chromosome count is 2n = 38 (ref. 152, 243, 504, 580) as *D. linguella*. Johansen (ref. 239) indicates that plants are self-sterile and that flowers dropped 5–13 days after self-pollination. When cross-pollinated, all blossoms produced capsules, which opened 613 days after pollination; 98% of the seed contained visible embryos and 97% germinated. *D. linguella* is incompatible with *D. acinaciforme* Roxburgh, *D. aphyllum* (Roxburgh) C. Fischer, *D. panduriferum* Hooker f., *D. primulinum* Lindley, *D. salaccense* (Blume) Lindley, *D. secundum* (Blume) Lindley, and *D. thyrsiflorum* Rchb. f., but it produces viable seed when crossed with *D. bilobulatum* Seidenfaden, *D. heterocarpum* Wallich ex Lindley, and *D. unicum* Seidenfaden. *D. linguella* produced a few seeds with visible embryos when crossed with *D. farmerii* Paxton but none germinated.

REFERENCES: 152, 200, 216, 236, 239, 243, 254, 448, 454, 455, 504, 568, 580, 592.

PHOTOS/DRAWINGS: 200, *454, 455, 592.*

Dendrobium linguiforme Swartz

AKA: Sometimes spelled *D. linguaeforme*. Hawkes (ref. 190) indicates that the originally spelling was *D. linguaeforme*, but in recent literature the spelling is usually *D. linguiforme*. Clements (ref. 67) includes *D. linguiforme* Swartz var. *huntianum* Rupp as a synonym. He considers *D. linguiforme* var. *nugentii* F. M. Bailey as a synonym of *D. nugentii* (F. M. Bailey) D. Jones and M. Clements.

ORIGIN/HABITAT: Australia and New Caledonia. In Australia, distribution extends along the east coast from near Narooma in southeastern New South Wales northward to near Cooktown in Queensland. Although plants usually grow near the coast, they have been found as far as 155 mi. (250 km) inland near Coolah, New South Wales. The habitat is extremely varied. Plants may grow on rocks in full sun, in open forest, or on trees in the dense shade of rainforests. They grow from near sea level to at least 3600 ft. (0–1100 m). In the more northerly (warmer) locations, they are usually found in the highlands.

CLIMATE: Station #94791, Coffs Harbour, Australia, Lat. 30.3°S, Long. 153.1°E, at 14 ft. (4 m). Temperatures are calculated for an elevation of 3000 ft. (910 m), resulting in probable extremes of 96°F (36°C) and 20°F (–7°C).

N/HEMISPHERE	JAN	FEB	MAR	APR	MAY	JUN	JUL	AUG	SEP	OCT	NOV	DEC
°F AVG MAX	55	57	61	64	69	70	70	70	69	67	61	58
°F AVG MIN	34	35	40	45	49	53	55	56	54	49	40	35
DIURNAL RANGE	21	22	21	19	20	17	15	14	15	18	21	23
RAIN/INCHES	3.8	2.1	2.9	3.8	4.0	5.8	6.9	7.7	8.7	7.7	5.7	4.5
HUMIDITY/%	74	72	70	74	72	76	79	83	79	78	75	74
BLOOM SEASON	*	**	***	**	*	*			*			
DAYS CLR @ 4AM	8	9	10	10	12	11	9	8	10	7	11	8
DAYS CLR @ 10AM	16	18	18	12	15	11	8	5	10	10	14	15
RAIN/MM	97	53	74	97	102	147	175	196	221	196	145	114
°C AVG MAX	12.9	14.0	16.2	17.9	20.6	21.2	21.2	21.2	20.6	19.5	16.2	14.5
°C AVG MIN	1.2	1.7	4.5	7.3	9.5	11.7	12.9	13.4	12.3	9.5	4.5	1.7
DIURNAL RANGE	11.7	12.3	11.7	10.6	11.1	9.5	8.3	7.8	8.3	10.0	11.7	12.8
S/HEMISPHERE	JUL	AUG	SEP	OCT	NOV	DEC	JAN	FEB	MAR	APR	MAY	JUN

Cultural Recommendations

LIGHT: 2000–4000 fc. Growers indicate that plants adapt to a variety of light levels. Plants are healthiest with brisk air movement and full early morning sun. Filtered light is recommended during the remainder of the day. Plants become reddish-purple under high light and flower profusely.

TEMPERATURES: Summer days average 70°F (21°C), and nights average 53–56°F (12–13°C), with a diurnal range of 14–17°F (8–9°C).

HUMIDITY: 75–80% through summer and autumn, dropping to near 70% in winter.

WATER: Rainfall is moderate to heavy most of the year, but in winter, conditions are somewhat drier for 2–3 months. Cultivated plants should kept moist while growing, but water should be gradually reduced in autumn. The plants are very drought-resistant, however. Growers recommend that mounted plants be watered every evening in summer and in the mornings in winter.

FERTILIZER: ¼–½ recommended strength, applied weekly. A high-nitrogen fertilizer is beneficial from spring to midsummer, but a fertilizer high in phosphates should be used in late summer and autumn.

REST PERIOD: Winter days average 55–58°F (13–15°C), and nights average 34–35°F (1–2°C), with a diurnal range of 21–23°F (12–13°C). Growers indicate that minimums of at least 55°F (13°C) are critically important. While plants in the wild survive below freezing temperatures, these extremes should be avoided for cultivated plants. However, if plants are exposed to cold conditions, their chance of survival is better if they are dry at the time. In winter, water should be reduced and the plants allowed to become dry between waterings, but they should not remain dry for extended periods. Occasional early morning mistings on bright, sunny days may be beneficial. Many growers withhold water until the flower spikes begin to show. Fertilizer should be eliminated until water is increased in spring. In the habitat, light is highest in winter.

GROWING MEDIA: Plants grow well on hardwood or cork slabs, or attached to garden trees in areas where the climate allows year-round outdoor growing. If plants are grown outside, however, they must be protected from heavy winter rains. If plants must be potted, clay pots may be filled with a very open and fast-draining medium. Pot-grown plants should be watered carefully and sparingly. Once established, plants should be disturbed as little as possible, so a long-lasting mount or potting medium is advisable. When the medium must be changed, repotting is best done in spring when new roots begin to grow.

MISCELLANEOUS NOTES: The bloom season shown in the climate table is based on cultivation records and corresponds to the early spring bloom season in the habitat. Flowering is apparently initiated by the cool winter temperatures, as blossoms open when conditions are the driest. *D. linguiforme* is vary hardy. Growers indicate that plants can be grown under a variety of conditions, such as high light to deep shade, and a dry winter rest to no winter rest.

Plant and Flower Information

PLANT SIZE AND TYPE: A miniature sympodial epiphyte or lithophyte. Plants resemble a matlike cactus. The entire plant hugs the substratum.

PSEUDOBULB: Very small. The tiny pseudobulbs are carried on a very short, creeping rhizome. The rhizome branches freely and forms a dense mat. Each branch is 0.4–1.6 in. (1–4 cm) long.

LEAVES: 1 per growth. The oval to tongue-shaped leaves are 1–2 in. (2.5–5.0 cm) long. They alternate along the rhizome. The growths may be close together (in dry areas) or widely spaced (in wet habitats). The smooth leaves are very thick, fleshy. They are dull green with a purplish tinge or reddish blotches when light is high.

INFLORESCENCE: 2–6 in. (5–15 cm) long. The erect to arching inflorescences are held away from the leaf. They emerge from nodes below the leaf bases, especially near the growing tip. The mass of flowers point all directions, making the inflorescences appear feathery. Plants are extremely floriferous.

FLOWERS: 5–30, occasionally more per inflorescence. The spidery flowers are 0.8–1.2 in. (2–3 cm) long and do not open fully. They are white to cream with pink to purple markings on the lip. The recurved lip is uppermost. Blossoms are fragrant.

HYBRIDIZING NOTES: Chromosome count is 2n = 38 (ref. 151, 152, 154, 187, 188, 504, 580). Plants are normally self-sterile. Pollen from the same flower rarely produces pods, but pollen from a different flower on the same plant sometimes produces pods. Seeds are regularly produced when pollen from another plant is used. *D. calamiforme* Loddiges (*D. teretifolium* R. Brown var. *fasciculatum* Rupp) is known to hybridize naturally with *D. linguiforme*, forming *D.* × *grimesii* C. T. White and Summerhayes.

REFERENCES: 23, 36, 67, 105, 151, 152, 154, 161, 173, 179, 187, 188, 190, 196, 210, 216, 240, 243, 254, 260, 262, 291, 317, 325, 326, 330, 333, 352, 390, 421, 430, 445, 495, 504, 527, 533, 544, 546, 580.

PHOTOS/DRAWINGS: 65, 105, *161*, 173, 210, 240, 254, *291*, 325, 330, *390*, *430*, *463*, *465*, *533*, *544*, *546*.

Dendrobium listeroglossum Kränzlin. See *D. parcum* Rchb. f. REFERENCES: 218, 254, 445, 454.

Dendrobium lithocola D. Jones and M. Clements

AKA: Clements (ref. 67) includes *D. bigibbum* Lindley var. *phalaenopsis* (Fitzgerald) F. M. Bailey forma *compactum* (C. White) G. L. Piper, *D. bigibbum* Lindley forma *compactum* (C. White) St. Cloud, *D. bigibbum* Lindley subvar. *compactum* (C. White) St. Cloud, *D. bigibbum* Lindley var. *superbum* Hort. ex Rchb. f. subvar. *compactum* (C. White) Dockrill, *D. phalaenopsis* Lindley var. *compactum* C. White. See discussion at *D. bigibbum* Lindley.

ORIGIN/HABITAT: Australia. Plants grow on cliffs in the coastal mountains between the Barron River at 16.8°S and the Mossman River at 16.5°S. They are usually found on bare rock, often in almost full sun, at 1000–1950 ft. (300–600 m). Plants are sometimes found in the lower parts of trees, usually no more than 10 ft. (3 m) above the ground.

CLIMATE: Station #94287, Cairns, Australia, Lat. 16.9°S, Long. 145.8°E, at 7 ft. (2 m). Temperatures are calculated for an elevation of 2000 ft. (610 m), resulting in probable extremes of 103°F (40°C) and 36°F (3°C).

N/HEMISPHERE	JAN	FEB	MAR	APR	MAY	JUN	JUL	AUG	SEP	OCT	NOV	DEC
°F AVG MAX	71	73	76	79	81	83	83	82	80	78	74	72
°F AVG MIN	54	55	57	61	63	66	67	67	66	63	59	57
DIURNAL RANGE	17	18	19	18	18	17	16	15	14	15	15	15
RAIN/INCHES	1.6	1.7	1.7	2.1	3.9	8.7	16.6	15.7	18.1	11.3	4.4	2.9
HUMIDITY/%	69	67	65	65	65	68	72	72	74	73	73	72
BLOOM SEASON	**	*	*	*			*	*	**	**	**	**
DAYS CLR @ 10AM	9	11	13	11	6	6	4	5	6	7	11	10
DAYS CLR @ 4PM	8	10	12	16	10	7	4	3	4	6	9	10
RAIN/MM	41	43	43	53	99	221	422	399	460	287	112	74
°C AVG MAX	21.9	23.0	24.7	26.3	27.5	28.6	28.6	28.0	26.9	25.8	23.6	22.5
°C AVG MIN	12.5	13.0	14.1	16.3	17.5	19.1	19.7	19.7	19.1	17.5	15.2	14.1
DIURNAL RANGE	9.4	10.0	10.6	10.0	10.0	9.5	8.9	8.3	7.8	8.3	8.4	8.4
S/HEMISPHERE	JUL	AUG	SEP	OCT	NOV	DEC	JAN	FEB	MAR	APR	MAY	JUN

Cultural Recommendations

LIGHT: 3000–4500 fc.

TEMPERATURES: Summer days average 82–83°F (28–29°C), and nights average 66–67°F (19–20°C), with a diurnal range of 15–17°F (8–10°C).

HUMIDITY: Near 75% summer through autumn, dropping to about 65% in winter and spring.

WATER: Rainfall is heavy from late spring into autumn, but conditions are quite dry in winter. Cultivated plants should be kept moist while actively growing, but water should be gradually reduced in late autumn after the new growths mature.

FERTILIZER: ¼–½ recommended strength, applied weekly. A high-nitrogen fertilizer is beneficial from spring to midsummer, while a fertilizer high in phosphates should be used in late summer and autumn.

REST PERIOD: Winter days average 71–73°F (22–23°C), and nights average 54–57°F (13–14°C), with a diurnal range of 15–18°F (8–10°C). Water and fertilizer should be reduced for 4–5 months from late autumn into early spring. Cultivated plants should be kept somewhat dry, but they should not be allowed to dry out completely. In the habitat, light is highest in winter.

GROWING MEDIA: Mounting plants on tree-fern or cork slabs accommodates their pendulous growth habit. However, humidity must be high and plants must be watered at least once a day in summer. If plants cannot be mounted, small pots or hanging baskets may be filled with an open, fast-draining medium. Repotting may be done anytime new roots are actively growing.

MISCELLANEOUS NOTES: The bloom season shown in the climate table is based on cultivation records. Because new growths are very susceptible to infection and rot, care should be exercised to keep water from them until they are 2–3 in. (5–8 cm) tall.

Plant and Flower Information

PLANT SIZE AND TYPE: A 2–10 in. (5–25 cm) sympodial lithophyte.

PSEUDOBULB: 2–10 in. (5–25 cm) long, normally 4–5 in. (10–13 cm) long. The short, stout stems are purplish when light is high.

LEAVES: 5–7 per inflorescence. The oblong-lanceolate leaves are 3–6 in. (8–15 cm) long. They are purplish-bronze in high light.

INFLORESCENCE: Inflorescences are borne at or near the apex of old and new growths.

FLOWERS: 3–10. The highly variable flowers are 1.2–2.0 in. (3–5 cm) across. The sepals are relatively narrow and pointed, but the petals are very broad and rounded. The sepals and petals are overlapping. Blossoms are normally violet, but they may be white or white with a purple lip. Petals tend to droop more than on blossoms of other closely related plants and the lip is narrower.

HYBRIDIZING NOTES: Chromosome counts are 2n = 38 (ref. 154) and 2n = about 57 (ref. 504, 580) as *D. bigibbum* Lindley var. *compactum* C. T. White.

REFERENCES: 67, 154, 235, 504, 533, 580.

PHOTOS/DRAWINGS: 533.

Dendrobium litorale Schlechter

AKA: H. Wood (ref. 582) indicates that from a grower's vantage point he found plants halfway between *D. litorale* and *D. macfarlanei* F. Mueller in the Ymas Lake region of Papua New Guinea, suggesting that these plants may be part of a variable alliance.

ORIGIN/HABITAT: Northern Papua New Guinea. Plants are found on trees along the beach near Morobe (Adolfhaven) and at the mouth of the Waria River. This species was recently found in Australia on the islands of the Torres Straits.

CLIMATE: Station #94048, Finschhafen, Papua New Guinea, Lat. 6.6°S, Long. 147.9°E, at 25 ft. (8 m). Record extreme temperatures are 93°F (34°C) and 68°F (20°C).

N/HEMISPHERE	JAN	FEB	MAR	APR	MAY	JUN	JUL	AUG	SEP	OCT	NOV	DEC
°F AVG MAX	84	83	83	84	86	88	89	89	87	86	84	84
°F AVG MIN	73	72	72	71	71	72	74	74	74	74	73	73
DIURNAL RANGE	11	11	11	13	15	16	15	15	13	12	11	11
RAIN/INCHES	25.8	22.4	20.9	15.8	11.7	8.9	5.5	3.7	5.3	11.9	18.3	23.2
HUMIDITY/%	88	87	86	86	84	85	84	85	86	88	88	88
BLOOM SEASON	*						*	*	*			
DAYS CLR	N/A											
RAIN/MM	655	568	531	402	297	227	140	95	135	301	464	589
°C AVG MAX	28.9	28.3	28.3	28.9	30.0	31.1	31.7	31.7	30.6	30.0	28.9	28.9
°C AVG MIN	22.8	22.2	22.2	21.7	21.7	22.2	23.3	23.3	23.3	23.3	22.8	22.8
DIURNAL RANGE	6.1	6.1	6.1	7.2	8.3	8.9	8.4	8.4	7.3	6.7	6.1	6.1
S/HEMISPHERE	JUL	AUG	SEP	OCT	NOV	DEC	JAN	FEB	MAR	APR	MAY	JUN

Cultural Recommendations

LIGHT: 2000–3000 fc.

TEMPERATURES: Throughout the year, days average 83–89°F (28–32°C), and nights average 71–74°F (22–23°C), with a diurnal range of 11–16°F (6–9°C).

HUMIDITY: 85–90% year-round.

WATER: Rainfall is very heavy most of the year. In the habitat, conditions are slightly drier for 3–4 months in summer, but cultivated plants should be kept evenly moist with only slight drying allowed between waterings.

FERTILIZER: ¼–½ recommended strength. A balanced fertilizer should be applied weekly to biweekly throughout the year.

REST PERIOD: Growing conditions should be maintained year-round. Winter rainfall is heaviest in the habitat, but water and fertilizer may be reduced somewhat for cultivated plants, especially those grown in the dark, short-day conditions common in temperate-latitude winters. These plants should never be allowed to dry out completely, however.

GROWING MEDIA: Plants may be mounted on tree-fern or cork slabs if humidity is high and plants are watered at least once daily in summer. When plants are potted, any open, fast-draining medium may be used. Repotting may be done anytime new roots are growing.

MISCELLANEOUS NOTES: The bloom season shown in the climate table is based on reports from the habitat. Sparse cultivation records indicate blooming in late summer. Plants that produce flowers which last a single day commonly bloom several times during the year. Flowering usually occurs 7–14 days after a sudden 10°F (5°C) drop in daytime temperatures.

Plant and Flower Information

PLANT SIZE AND TYPE: A 24 in. (60 cm) sympodial epiphyte.

PSEUDOBULB: 24 in. (60 cm) long. The slightly flattened stems, which may have 4–6 angles, are swollen for 2–4 nodes, then become slender for the remainder of their length. The center part of the stem is leafy.

LEAVES: Many. The smooth leaves are 2.0–2.4 in. (5–6 cm) long, nearly linear, pointed, and equally spaced.

INFLORESCENCE: Short. Inflorescences emerge from nodes at the side of the stem.

FLOWERS: The fan-shaped flowers are 0.4 in. (1 cm) long. They are pale yellow with red veins. The ovate lateral sepals are dilated at the base. The very small petals are oblong. The 3-lobed lip is deeply notched at the apex and uneven along the margin. The callus extends from the base of the lip to the notch on the midlobe. The blossoms open simultaneously and last a single day.

REFERENCES: 67, 179, 221, 437, 445, 582.

PHOTOS/DRAWINGS: 437.

Dendrobium litoreum F. M. Bailey

ORIGIN/HABITAT: Papua New Guinea. Plants were originally collected near Cape Nelson on the north coast near the eastern end of the island. They grow at low elevations in mangrove forests.

CLIMATE: Station #94075, Samarai, Sideia Island, Papua New Guinea, Lat. 10.6°S, Long. 150.7°E, at 20 ft. (6 m). Record extreme temperatures are 104°F (40°C) and 64°F (18°C).

N/HEMISPHERE	JAN	FEB	MAR	APR	MAY	JUN	JUL	AUG	SEP	OCT	NOV	DEC
°F AVG MAX	81	81	82	83	85	87	87	88	87	86	84	82
°F AVG MIN	74	73	74	74	75	76	77	77	76	75	75	74
DIURNAL RANGE	7	8	8	9	10	11	10	11	11	11	9	8
RAIN/INCHES	8.1	8.6	10.1	8.7	8.4	6.1	7.0	7.8	10.0	9.8	12.0	11.3
HUMIDITY/%	N/A											
BLOOM SEASON	N/A											
DAYS CLR	N/A											
RAIN/MM	206	218	257	221	213	155	178	198	254	249	305	287
°C AVG MAX	27.2	27.2	27.8	28.3	29.4	30.6	30.6	31.1	30.6	30.0	28.9	27.8
°C AVG MIN	23.3	22.8	23.3	23.3	23.9	24.4	25.0	25.0	24.4	23.9	23.9	23.3
DIURNAL RANGE	3.9	4.4	4.5	5.0	5.5	6.2	5.6	6.1	6.2	6.1	5.0	4.5
S/HEMISPHERE	JUL	AUG	SEP	OCT	NOV	DEC	JAN	FEB	MAR	APR	MAY	JUN

Cultural Recommendations

LIGHT: 2500–3000 fc.

TEMPERATURES: Throughout the year, days average 81–88°F (27–31°C), and nights average 73–77°F (23–25°C), with a diurnal range of 7–11°F (4–6°C).

HUMIDITY: Information is not available for this location. However, records from nearby locations indicate that humidity probably averages near 80% year-round.

WATER: Rainfall is very heavy all year. Cultivated plants should be kept moist but not soggy.

FERTILIZER: ¼–½ recommended strength. A balanced fertilizer should be applied weekly to biweekly throughout the year.

REST PERIOD: Growing conditions should be maintained year-round. In the habitat, winter rainfall is high, but water may be reduced somewhat for cultivated plants, especially those grown in the dark, short-day conditions in temperate-latitude winters. These plants should not be allowed to dry out completely, however. Fertilizer should also be reduced until water is increased in spring.

GROWING MEDIA: Plants may be mounted on tree-fern or cork slabs if humidity is high and plants are watered at least once daily in summer. When plants are potted, any open, fast-draining medium may be used. Repotting may be done anytime new roots are growing.

Plant and Flower Information

PLANT SIZE AND TYPE: A 6 in. (15 cm) sympodial epiphyte.

PSEUDOBULB: 4–5 in. (10–13 cm) long.

LEAVES: Many. The distichous leaves are 1.2 in. (3 cm) long, sickle-shaped, and lanceolate.

INFLORESCENCE: Short. The blossoms are held in a dense cluster. Inflorescences emerge from nodes near the apex of the stem.

FLOWERS: Several. The blossoms are 1 in. (2.5 cm) across. They are white with yellow raised areas on the midlobe of the lip. The lip and lateral sepals are nearly 3 times the length of the petals and dorsal sepal.

REFERENCES: 26, 220, 254.

Dendrobium lituiflorum Lindley

AKA: *D. hanburyanum* Rchb. f.

ORIGIN/HABITAT: Southeast Asia. The habitat includes northeastern India, Burma, northern Thailand, Laos, and southwestern China. Plants often densely cover tree tops. In Thailand, plants grow at 1300–2600 ft. (400–800 m). Bhattacharjee (ref. 38) reports that in Assam and Manipur in northeastern India, plants grow at about 5600 ft. (1700 m), but Rao (ref. 376) indicates they grow at 650–1650 ft. (200–500 m). Tsi (ref. 528) reports they grow in China at 3600–5600 ft. (1100–1700 m).

CLIMATE: Station #48353, Loei, Thailand, Lat. 17.5°N, Long. 101.5°E, at 817 ft. (249 m). Temperatures are calculated for an elevation of 2500 ft. (760 m), resulting in probable extremes of 100°F (38°C) and 28°F (–2°C).

N/HEMISPHERE	JAN	FEB	MAR	APR	MAY	JUN	JUL	AUG	SEP	OCT	NOV	DEC
°F AVG MAX	79	83	88	91	87	85	84	83	82	81	81	78
°F AVG MIN	46	52	59	64	67	68	68	68	67	63	58	50
DIURNAL RANGE	33	31	29	27	20	17	16	15	15	18	23	28
RAIN/INCHES	0.2	0.8	1.4	3.6	6.9	6.8	5.0	8.3	8.8	4.3	0.8	0.1
HUMIDITY/%	62	60	59	62	75	77	77	79	82	79	74	69
BLOOM SEASON		*	***	***	***	**	*		*			
DAYS CLR @ 7AM	1	1	1	2	1	0	1	0	0	1	1	1
DAYS CLR @ 1PM	22	14	8	5	2	0	0	1	1	5	11	15
RAIN/MM	5	20	36	91	175	173	127	211	224	109	20	3
°C AVG MAX	26.4	28.6	31.4	33.0	30.8	29.7	29.1	28.6	28.0	27.5	27.5	25.8
°C AVG MIN	8.0	11.4	15.2	18.0	19.7	20.2	20.2	20.2	19.7	17.5	14.7	10.2
DIURNAL RANGE	18.4	17.2	16.2	15.0	11.1	9.5	8.9	8.4	8.3	10.0	12.8	15.6
S/HEMISPHERE	JUL	AUG	SEP	OCT	NOV	DEC	JAN	FEB	MAR	APR	MAY	JUN

Cultural Recommendations

LIGHT: 3000–4500 fc.

TEMPERATURES: Summer days average 83–85°F (29–30°C), and nights average 68°F (20°C), with a 15–17°F (8–10°C) diurnal range. Spring is the warmest season. Days average 87–91°F (31–33°C), and nights average 59–67°F (15–20°C), with a diurnal range of 20–29°F (11–16°C). The probable extreme temperatures indicate a tolerance of both summer heat and winter cold.

HUMIDITY: 75–80% from spring through autumn, dropping to near 60% in winter and early spring.

WATER: Rainfall is moderate to heavy from late spring through early autumn, but conditions are much drier the rest of the year. Cultivated plants should be watered often from spring into autumn, with only slight drying allowed between waterings. Water should be gradually reduced after new growths mature in autumn. Growers indicate that plants should be constantly moist while actively growing.

FERTILIZER: ½ recommended strength, applied weekly. A high-nitrogen fertilizer is beneficial from spring to midsummer, but a fertilizer high in phosphates should be used in late summer and autumn.

REST PERIOD: Winter days average 78–83°F (26–29°C), and nights average 46–52°F (8–11°C), with a diurnal range of 28–33°F (16–18°C). The calculated record low is below freezing, but such extremes should be avoided in cultivation. Rainfall is low for 3–5 months in winter, but additional moisture is available from heavy dew, fog, and mist during most of the season. Cultivated plants need to dry out between waterings, but they should not remain completely dry for extended periods. Occasional early morning mistings between waterings may help keep the plants from becoming too dry. Fertilizer should be eliminated until water is increased in spring. In the habitat, light is highest in winter.

GROWING MEDIA: Mounting plants on tree-fern or cork slabs accommodates their usually pendulous growth habit. However, humidity must be high and plants must be watered at least once a day in summer. If plants cannot be mounted, small pots or hanging baskets may be filled with an open, fast-draining medium. Repotting may be done anytime new roots are actively growing.

MISCELLANEOUS NOTES: The bloom season shown in the climate table is based on cultivation reports. In the habitat, plants bloom in late winter and spring, usually about the time new growths start. *D. lituiflorum* does not grow or flower well in the uniform Singapore climate.

Plant and Flower Information

PLANT SIZE AND TYPE: A 12–24 in. (30–60 cm) sympodial epiphyte.

PSEUDOBULB: 12–24 in. (30–60 cm) long, rarely to 35 in. (90 cm). The slender, reedlike stems are usually pendent. They are greyish white or yellow with a swollen knob at the base. Plants often produce several new growths each season.

LEAVES: Many. The distichous, oblong leaves are 3–5 in. (8–13 cm) long. They are fleshy but fragile and drop quickly in autumn.

INFLORESCENCE: Short. Inflorescences arise from nearly every node along the entire length of leafless pseudobulbs. Plants are free-flowering.

FLOWERS: 2–5 per inflorescence. The flowers are 2.4–4.0 in. (6–10 cm) across. They are described as charming. Blossoms vary from white to deep, bright amethyst-purple which usually fades to a lighter shade in the center. The trumpet-shaped lip may be white or dark violet-purple with a white margin. The maroon or purple disk is edged with a yellow or white velvety band. The lip is sometimes marked with transverse purple stripes. Blossoms are fragrant and last about 2 weeks.

HYBRIDIZING NOTES: Chromosome count is n = 19 and 2n = 38 (ref. 150, 154, 504, 542, 580). Sauleda (ref. 425) reports that seeds of *D. lituifolium* Lindley are ready for green-pod culture in 160-250 (186) days. We found no description for a *D. lituifolium* Lindley and suspect that the information applies to *D. lituiflorum* Lindley.

REFERENCES: 36, 38, 46, 150, 154, 157, 179, 190, 196, 200, 202, 210, 216, 245, 254, 361, 369, 376, 389, 395, 425, 430, 445, 447, 448, 454, 504, 523, 528, 541, 542, 557, 568, 569, 570, 577, 580.

PHOTOS/DRAWINGS: *36,* 38, 210, *245,* 361, 369, *389, 430, 454, 569.*

Dendrobium lividum Teijsm. and Binn. This name is considered invalid. REFERENCES: 216, 254.

Dendrobium lobatum (Blume) Miquel

AKA: *Aporum lobatum* Blume, *Dendrobium rhizophoreti* Ridley. Kränzlin (ref. 254) and J. J. Smith (ref. 486) included *D. bicornutum* Schlechter as a synonym, but this has not been followed by current authors.

ORIGIN/HABITAT: Sumatra, Java, Borneo, and lowland Malaya. Plants grow on mangroves or on trees near rivers. In West Java, collections are recorded at about 2450 ft. (750 m), but the plant is uncommon. It is more common in Sumatra and Peninsular Malaysia, where plants are found in mangroves near sea level.

CLIMATE: Station #48674, Mersing, Malaya, Lat. 2.5°N, Long. 103.8°E, at 151 ft. (46 m). Record extreme temperatures are 99°F (37°C) and 68°F (20°C).

N/HEMISPHERE	JAN	FEB	MAR	APR	MAY	JUN	JUL	AUG	SEP	OCT	NOV	DEC
°F AVG MAX	82	83	86	89	90	89	88	87	87	87	86	82
°F AVG MIN	74	74	74	73	73	72	72	72	72	72	72	73
DIURNAL RANGE	8	9	12	16	17	17	16	15	15	15	14	9
RAIN/INCHES	14.4	6.3	6.1	4.6	7.1	5.1	5.6	6.7	9.3	9.9	13.4	24.3
HUMIDITY/%	82	82	81	82	82	83	84	84	84	84	85	86
BLOOM SEASON	*											
DAYS CLR @ 7AM	0	0	1	3	2	2	3	2	0	0	1	1
DAYS CLR @ 1PM	0	0	1	2	1	1	1	0	1	0	0	0
RAIN/MM	366	160	155	117	180	130	142	170	236	251	340	617
°C AVG MAX	27.8	28.3	30.0	31.7	32.2	31.7	31.1	30.6	30.6	30.6	30.0	27.8
°C AVG MIN	23.3	23.3	23.3	22.8	22.8	22.2	22.2	22.2	22.2	22.2	22.2	22.8
DIURNAL RANGE	4.5	5.0	6.7	8.9	9.4	9.5	8.9	8.4	8.4	8.4	7.8	5.0
S/HEMISPHERE	JUL	AUG	SEP	OCT	NOV	DEC	JAN	FEB	MAR	APR	MAY	JUN

Cultural Recommendations

LIGHT: 2000–3000 fc.

TEMPERATURES: Throughout the year, days average 82–90°F (28–32°C), and nights average 72–74°F (22–23°C), with a diurnal range of 8–17°F (5–10°C). The diurnal range is greatest in the summer, the result of warmer days rather than cooler nights.

HUMIDITY: 80–85% year-round.

WATER: Rainfall is moderate to heavy all year. Cultivated plants should be kept moist, with only slight drying allowed between waterings.

FERTILIZER: ¼–½ recommended strength. A balanced fertilizer should be applied weekly to biweekly anytime the plants are actively growing.

REST PERIOD: Growing conditions should be maintained all year. Lows vary only 2°F (1°C) throughout the year, but winter days are noticeably cooler. Winters are very wet, but excess moisture is harmful in cultivation, particularly if light is low, days are short, or temperatures are cool. Water should be reduced for cultivated plants, but they should not be allowed to dry out completely. In the habitat, clear days are rare in winter; but near the equator, seasonal light variations are minor.

GROWING MEDIA: Mounting plants on tree-fern or cork slabs accommodates their pendent growth habit. However, humidity must be high and plants must be watered at least once a day in summer. If plants cannot be mounted, small pots or hanging baskets may be filled with an open, fast-draining medium. Repotting may be done anytime new roots are actively growing.

MISCELLANEOUS NOTES: The bloom season shown in the climate table is based on cultivation records. Plants often bloom more than once a year.

Plant and Flower Information

PLANT SIZE AND TYPE: A 12–39 in. (30–100 cm) sympodial epiphyte. Plants are often smaller.

PSEUDOBULB: 12–39 in. (30–100 cm) long. The stems become pendulous as they mature and branch.

LEAVES: Many. The somewhat widely spaced leaves are 0.8–1.2 in. (2–3 cm) long. They are flushed with purple when young.

INFLORESCENCE: Very short. Inflorescences emerge from nodes all along the stem.

FLOWERS: Few per inflorescence. Blossoms are 0.3 in. (0.8 cm) across and open in succession. They are pale greenish yellow flushed with purple near the center. The small linear petals have a red line down the center. The lip, which is shaped like a whale's tail, is uppermost.

REFERENCES: 25, 75, 190, 200, 216, 254, 286, 295, 310, 395, 402, 445, 454, 455, 469, 486.

PHOTOS/DRAWINGS: 200, 455, 469.

Dendrobium lobbii Lindley not Teijsm. and Binn. See *D. aloifolium* (Blume) Rchb. f. REFERENCES: 216, 254, 278, 286, 295, 310, 454.

Dendrobium lobbii Teijsm. and Binn. not Lindley

AKA: Seidenfaden and Wood (ref. 455) include *D. calcaratum* Lindley and *D. conostalix* Rchb. f. Other authors include *D. paludicola* Schlechter and *D. teijsmannii (teysmannii)* Miquel. Seidenfaden (ref. 454) and Clements (ref. 67) include *D. paludicola* Schlechter as a possible synonym.

ORIGIN/HABITAT: Borneo, Malaya, Sumatra, Thailand, Vietnam, New Guinea, Santa Ana Island in the Solomons, and the northeast coast of Cape York Peninsula in Australia. Plants usually grow in the leaf-mold that overlies sandy soil through which water is continuously seeping. They are normally found along streams, in areas subject to seasonal flooding, in swampy habitats, or in shallow water in ditches. Plants are frequently found in bright light, but the roots are shaded from full sun by tall grasses and reeds. In Australia, plants were first found south of Cairns at Rockingham Bay. They have also been found in swampland from Cape York to the McIlwraith Range, but have not been found in the 300 miles. (500 km) between these locations.

CLIMATE: Station #48665, Melaka (Malacca), Malaya, Lat. 2.3°N, Long. 102.3°E, at 40 ft. (12 m). Record extreme temperatures are 99°F (37°C) and 61°F (16°C).

N/HEMISPHERE	JAN	FEB	MAR	APR	MAY	JUN	JUL	AUG	SEP	OCT	NOV	DEC
°F AVG MAX	88	89	89	89	89	88	88	88	88	88	88	88
°F AVG MIN	72	72	72	73	73	72	72	72	72	72	72	72
DIURNAL RANGE	16	17	17	16	16	15	16	16	16	16	16	16
RAIN/INCHES	3.9	3.7	4.9	7.4	6.8	7.9	7.8	10.3	8.8	10.1	8.7	6.5
HUMIDITY/%	79	79	82	85	85	83	84	84	84	84	84	82
BLOOM SEASON	*	*	*									
DAYS CLR @ 7AM	1	1	1	1	1	2	1	1	1	1	0	1
DAYS CLR @ 1PM	1	1	1	1	1	1	1	1	1	0	0	0
RAIN/MM	99	94	124	188	173	201	198	262	224	257	221	165
°C AVG MAX	31.1	31.7	31.7	31.7	31.7	31.1	31.1	31.1	31.1	31.1	31.1	31.1
°C AVG MIN	22.2	22.2	22.2	22.8	22.8	22.8	22.2	22.2	22.2	22.2	22.2	22.2
DIURNAL RANGE	8.9	9.5	9.5	8.9	8.9	8.3	8.9	8.9	8.9	8.9	8.9	8.9
S/HEMISPHERE	JUL	AUG	SEP	OCT	NOV	DEC	JAN	FEB	MAR	APR	MAY	JUN

Cultural Recommendations

LIGHT: 2000–3000 fc.

TEMPERATURES: Throughout the year, days average 88–89°F (31–32°C), and nights average 72–73°F (22–23°C), with a diurnal range of 15–17°F (8–10°C). Australian growers recommend winter minimum temperatures of 54°F (12°C).

HUMIDITY: Near 80–85% year-round.

WATER: Rainfall is heavy all year. Conditions are slightly drier for 2–3 months in winter, but *D. lobbii* always grows in wet microclimates, so it should be kept constantly moist.

FERTILIZER: ¼–½ recommended strength. A balanced fertilizer should be applied weekly to biweekly throughout the year.

REST PERIOD: Growing conditions should be maintained all year. Water and fertilizer may be reduced somewhat in winter, especially for plants cultivated in the dark, short-day conditions common in the temperate latitudes. Plants should never be allowed to dry out completely, however. In the habitat, seasonal light variation is minor.

GROWING MEDIA: Plants may be potted in a mixture of coarse sand, leaf-mold, and peat moss. Place the pot on pebbles in a tray of water, with the water just touching the bottom of the pot, keeping the mixture barely moist. The water in the tray should be changed frequently. It should never be allowed to become stagnant. Repotting may be done anytime new roots are growing, but immediately after blooming is probably best.

MISCELLANEOUS NOTES: The primary bloom season shown in the climate table is based on Australian cultivation records. *D. lobbii*, like many swamp plants, could be very difficult to cultivate unless conditions similar to those found in the habitat can be provided.

Dendrobium lobulatum

Plant and Flower Information

PLANT SIZE AND TYPE: A 10–36 in. (25–94 cm) sympodial terrestrial. Some speculate that plants may be epiphytic on the roots of the herbs with which they always grow.

PSEUDOBULB: 10–36 in. (25–94 cm) long. The slender stems are dry and wiry with nodes at 1 in. (2.5 cm) intervals. The lowermost nodes may be slightly swollen. The stems are covered with coarse, black to rust-brown hairs. They are densely clustered and arise from a very short rhizome.

LEAVES: Many. The stiffly erect leaves are 0.8–2.4 in. (2–6 cm) long. They are narrowly linear and unequally bilobed at the tip. They are held at a very narrow angle to the stem. The leaf sheaths, which clasp the stem, are spotted and hairy.

INFLORESCENCE: Many. The slender inflorescences, which are produced at the same time, emerge through the leaf sheaths. The flowers face down.

FLOWERS: 1–2 per inflorescence. The flowers are 0.4–0.6 in. (1.0–1.5 cm) across. They may open widely or remain rather closed. The buds are green. Sepals and narrower petals may be pale brownish, yellow, greenish yellow, or yellowish white. They are marked with orange veins. The erect, fleshy lip is almost white with 2 keels, a toothed, notched midlobe, and small toothlike sidelobes.

REFERENCES: 24, 67, 92, 105, 200, 202, 216, 240, 254, 262, 263, 264, 266, 271, 278, 286, 310, 317, 395, 402, 437, 444, 445, 448, 454, 455, 533.

PHOTOS/DRAWINGS: 105, 200, 240, 437, 454, 455, *533*.

Dendrobium lobulatum Rolfe and J. J. Smith

ORIGIN/HABITAT: West Java, Sumatra, Borneo, and possibly Ambon Island and Sulawesi. Plants are common on trees at 1650–3300 ft. (500–1000 m).

CLIMATE: Station #96755, Bogor, Java, Indonesia, Lat. 6.5°S, Long. 106.8°E, at 558 ft. (170 m). Temperatures are calculated for an elevation of 2600 ft. (790 m), resulting in probable extremes of 89°F (32°C) and 59°F (15°C).

N/HEMISPHERE	JAN	FEB	MAR	APR	MAY	JUN	JUL	AUG	SEP	OCT	NOV	DEC
°F AVG MAX	79	80	81	81	80	78	77	77	78	79	80	79
°F AVG MIN	66	66	66	67	67	67	67	67	67	68	68	67
DIURNAL RANGE	13	14	15	14	13	11	10	10	11	11	12	12
RAIN/INCHES	2.1	1.0	0.5	5.0	8.1	18.8	23.7	20.2	14.4	12.0	11.9	3.4
HUMIDITY/%	72	68	65	66	74	79	84	84	81	79	77	75
BLOOM SEASON					*					*		
DAYS CLR @ 7AM	14	14	14	11	5	3	1	2	4	6	10	12
DAYS CLR @ 1PM	9	10	8	5	1	1	0	0	1	3	3	7
RAIN/MM	53	25	13	127	206	478	602	513	366	305	302	86
°C AVG MAX	26.3	26.8	27.4	27.4	26.8	25.7	25.2	25.2	25.7	26.3	26.8	26.3
°C AVG MIN	19.1	19.1	19.1	19.6	19.6	19.6	19.6	19.6	19.6	20.2	20.2	19.6
DIURNAL RANGE	7.2	7.7	8.3	7.8	7.2	6.1	5.6	5.6	6.1	6.1	6.6	6.7
S/HEMISPHERE	JUL	AUG	SEP	OCT	NOV	DEC	JAN	FEB	MAR	APR	MAY	JUN

Cultural Recommendations

LIGHT: 1800–3000 fc.

TEMPERATURES: Throughout the year, days average 77–81°F (25–27°C), and nights average 66–68°F (19–20°C), with a diurnal range of 10–15°F (6–8°C). Uniform temperatures may be critical for plant health.

HUMIDITY: 75–85% most of the year, dropping to near 65% for 2–3 months in late winter and early spring. Excellent air circulation may be particularly important for plants from this habitat.

WATER: Rainfall is very heavy from spring into autumn, but conditions are very dry for 2 months in winter. During the growing season, cultivated plants should be kept moist with only slight drying allowed between waterings. Growers indicate that plants from this habitat are healthiest if they are saturated with water and then allowed to dry rapidly even in summer. Warm water, about 65°F (18°C), is highly recommended.

FERTILIZER: ¼–½ recommended strength, applied weekly. A high-nitrogen fertilizer is beneficial from spring to midsummer, but a fertilizer high in phosphates should be used in late summer and autumn.

REST PERIOD: Growing conditions should be maintained all year, but the diurnal range increases slightly in winter, and rainfall is very low for 2–3 months. In cultivation, water should be reduced and the plants allowed to become dry between waterings. They should not remain dry for prolonged periods, however. Fertilizer may be reduced or eliminated anytime the plant is not actively growing. In the habitat, light is highest in winter.

GROWING MEDIA: Mounting plants on tree-fern or cork slabs accommodates their pendent growth habit. However, humidity must be high and plants must be watered at least once a day in summer. If plants cannot be mounted, small pots or hanging baskets may be filled with an open, fast-draining medium. Repotting may be done anytime new roots are actively growing.

MISCELLANEOUS NOTES: The bloom season shown in the climate table is based on reports from the habitat.

Plant and Flower Information

PLANT SIZE AND TYPE: A 20 in. (50 cm) sympodial epiphyte.

PSEUDOBULB: 20 in. (50 cm) long. Stems are pendulous and very flattened. They are leafy on the apical portion of the stem.

LEAVES: Many. The triangular leaves are 1 in. (2.5 cm) long. They are pointed, stiff, fleshy, and either dull green or dirty purplish green. The leaves are largest near the base of the stem and smallest near the apex.

INFLORESCENCE: Very short. Inflorescences arise from the upper, nearly leafless apical portion of the stem.

FLOWERS: Several per inflorescence, but the blossoms open 1 or a few at a time. The clustered flowers open fully and measure 0.3 in. (0.7 cm) across. They are somewhat fan-shaped. The white sepals and petals are suffused with pink. The decorative red veins extend the length of each segment. The dorsal sepal is nearly round, but the lateral sepals and smaller petals are oblong. The lip is white with a bright yellow blotch in the center and a red or orange claw.

REFERENCES: 25, 75, 219, 254, 286, 295, 445, 468, 469.

PHOTOS/DRAWINGS: 75, 469.

Dendrobium lockhartioides Schlechter

AKA: *D. atropurpureum* Kränzlin.

ORIGIN/HABITAT: The Minahassa Peninsula of northern Sulawesi. Plants grow on trees above Kakaskassen on Mt. Lokon at about 3300 ft. (1000 m).

CLIMATE: Station #97014, Manado, Sulawesi, Lat. 1.5°N, Long. 124.9°E, at 264 ft. (80 m). Temperatures are calculated for an elevation of 3000 ft. (910 m), resulting in probable extremes of 88°F (31°C) and 56°F (13°C).

N/HEMISPHERE	JAN	FEB	MAR	APR	MAY	JUN	JUL	AUG	SEP	OCT	NOV	DEC
°F AVG MAX	76	76	76	77	78	78	78	80	80	80	78	77
°F AVG MIN	64	64	64	64	65	64	64	64	64	63	64	65
DIURNAL RANGE	12	12	12	13	13	14	14	16	16	17	14	12
RAIN/INCHES	18.6	13.8	12.2	8.0	6.4	6.5	4.8	4.0	3.4	4.9	8.9	14.7
HUMIDITY/%	84	83	83	83	81	80	75	72	75	77	82	83
BLOOM SEASON										*	*	*
DAYS CLR @ 8AM	4	3	6	11	12	12	12	14	17	12	6	8
DAYS CLR @ 2PM	1	1	1	2	1	3	3	4	4	4	1	1
RAIN/MM	472	351	310	203	163	165	122	102	86	124	226	373
°C AVG MAX	24.4	24.4	24.4	25.0	25.5	25.5	25.5	26.7	26.7	26.7	25.5	25.0
°C AVG MIN	17.8	17.8	17.8	17.8	18.3	17.8	17.8	17.8	17.8	17.2	17.8	18.3
DIURNAL RANGE	6.6	6.6	6.6	7.2	7.2	7.7	7.7	8.9	8.9	9.5	7.7	6.7
S/HEMISPHERE	JUL	AUG	SEP	OCT	NOV	DEC	JAN	FEB	MAR	APR	MAY	JUN

Cultural Recommendations

LIGHT: 2000–3000 fc. The habitat is usually overcast in the afternoon.

TEMPERATURES: Throughout the year, days average 76–80°F (24–27°C),

and nights average 63–65°F (17–18°C), with a diurnal range of 12–17°F (7–10°C). The record temperatures are only a few degrees above and below the averages, indicating that plants may not be able to tolerate wide temperature fluctuations.

HUMIDITY: 80–85% most of the year, dropping to 70–75% in summer.

WATER: Rainfall is moderate to heavy all year. The driest period occurs in late summer and early autumn. Cultivated plants should be kept moist but not soggy.

FERTILIZER: ¼–½ recommended strength. A balanced fertilizer should be applied weekly to biweekly throughout the year.

REST PERIOD: Growing conditions should be maintained all year. In the habitat, rainfall is greatest in winter. In cultivation, water may be reduced somewhat, especially if plants are grown in the dark, short-day conditions common in temperate-latitude winters. They should never be allowed to dry out completely, however. In the habitat, light is lowest in winter.

GROWING MEDIA: Plants may be mounted on tree-fern or cork slabs if humidity is high and plants are watered at least once daily in summer. When plants are potted, any open, fast-draining medium may be used. They may be repotted anytime new roots are growing.

MISCELLANEOUS NOTES: The bloom season shown in the climate table is based on reports from the habitat.

Plant and Flower Information

PLANT SIZE AND TYPE: A 16 in. (40 cm) sympodial epiphyte.

PSEUDOBULB: 16 in. (40 cm) long. The tightly clustered stems are elongated and branching. They are densely leafy.

LEAVES: Many. The leaves are 0.6–1.2 in. (1.5–3.0 cm) long, lanceolate, and fleshy but flexible.

INFLORESCENCE: Short. Blossoms are borne in clusters. Inflorescences emerge from nodes near the apex of the stem.

FLOWERS: Few per inflorescence. The flowers are 0.1 in. (0.3 cm) across. Sepals are yellowish with red suffusion. Petals are pink. The wine-red lip is darkest on the inside.

REFERENCES: 220, 436.

Dendrobium loddigesii Rolfe

AKA: *D. pulchellum* Loddiges not Roxburgh, *D. seidelianum* Rchb. f.

ORIGIN/HABITAT: Laos, southwestern China, and Hong Kong. In Laos, the plants are found in the Xieng Khouang region. Plants are usually found at 3300–4900 ft. (1000–1500 m) but have been found as low as 1300 ft. (400 m). The habitat in China includes Yunnan Province, where plants grow in the eastern mountains at about 4500 ft. (1370 m), Hainan Island, and Kwangtung Province, where plants grow on rocks 150 miles (240 km) southwest of Canton. Near Hong Kong, plants grow at about 3300 ft. (1000 m).

CLIMATE: Station #45007, Hong Kong, Lat. 22.3°N, Long. 114.2°E, at 15 ft. (5 m). Temperatures are calculated for an elevation of 3300 ft. (1000 m), resulting in probable extremes of 86°F (30°C) and 21°F (–6°C).

N/HEMISPHERE	JAN	FEB	MAR	APR	MAY	JUN	JUL	AUG	SEP	OCT	NOV	DEC
°F AVG MAX	53	52	56	65	71	74	76	76	74	70	63	57
°F AVG MIN	45	44	49	56	63	67	67	67	66	62	54	48
DIURNAL RANGE	8	8	7	9	8	7	9	9	8	8	9	9
RAIN/INCHES	1.3	1.8	2.9	5.4	11.5	15.5	15.0	14.2	10.1	4.5	1.7	1.2
HUMIDITY/%	72	78	79	82	83	82	82	82	78	69	67	69
BLOOM SEASON		*	**	***	**	*						
DAYS CLR @ 8AM	7	3	2	2	2	1	1	3	4	9	8	8
DAYS CLR @ 2PM	10	5	4	2	2	1	2	4	4	11	10	11
RAIN/MM	33	46	74	137	292	394	381	361	257	114	43	30
°C AVG MAX	11.8	11.2	13.5	18.5	21.8	23.5	24.6	24.6	23.5	21.2	17.3	14.0
°C AVG MIN	7.3	6.8	9.6	13.5	17.3	19.6	19.6	19.6	19.0	16.8	12.3	9.0
DIURNAL RANGE	4.5	4.4	3.9	5.0	4.5	3.9	5.0	5.0	4.5	4.4	5.0	5.0
S/HEMISPHERE	JUL	AUG	SEP	OCT	NOV	DEC	JAN	FEB	MAR	APR	MAY	JUN

Cultural Recommendations

LIGHT: 2000–3000 fc. Light should be diffused or dappled, and direct sunlight should be avoided, particularly when temperatures are high. Growers indicate that *D. loddigesii* is difficult to bring to bloom when grown under florescent lights.

TEMPERATURES: Summer days average 74–76°F (24–25°C), and nights average 67°F (20°C), with a diurnal range of 7–9°F (4–5°C). The warmest weather coincides with the period of heaviest rainfall. Growers indicate that plants cannot tolerate hot summer weather.

HUMIDITY: 80% most of the year, dropping to about 70% in autumn and early winter.

WATER: Rainfall is moderate to heavy from spring into autumn, but conditions are much drier in winter. Cultivated plants should be kept moist during the growing season, but water should be gradually reduced after new growths mature in autumn.

FERTILIZER: ¼–½ recommended strength, applied weekly. A high-nitrogen fertilizer is beneficial from spring to midsummer, but a fertilizer high in phosphates should be used in late summer and autumn.

REST PERIOD: Winter days average 52–57°F (11–14°C), and nights average 44–49°F (7–10°C), with a diurnal range of 7–9°F (4–5°C). Day and night temperatures decline simultaneously, resulting in a consistent diurnal range year-round. In the habitat, plants are occasionally subjected to outbreaks of cold air which cause temperatures to drop dramatically. The record low is 21°F (–6°C), but these extremes should be avoided for cultivated plants. Some growers indicate that *D. loddigesii* grows well with Cattleyas most of the year but needs a cool 50°F (10°C) dry rest to initiate blooms. Other growers provide intermediate to warm temperatures all year. If winter temperatures are cool, water should be reduced and the plants allowed to dry slightly between waterings. They should not remain dry for long periods, however. Most growers indicate that plants should be allowed to dry between waterings in winter. The prevailing winter temperatures should dictate the amount of water given. The cooler the temperatures, the less water. Fertilizer should be reduced or eliminated. In the habitat, light is highest in winter.

GROWING MEDIA: Mounting plants on tree-fern slabs accommodates their creeping, pendent growth habit. One grower tied a plant to a ball of chicken wire and allowed the plant to cover the ball. When exhibited, the plant reportedly carried nearly 1000 flowers that covered the hanging ball. If plants must be potted, a shallow pan may be filled with any open, fast-draining medium. Repotting is best done in early spring when new roots are growing.

MISCELLANEOUS NOTES: The bloom season shown in the climate table is based on cultivation records. Collected plants are dried and used in Chinese medicine. Growers indicate that *D. loddigesii* is sometimes difficult to bloom and speculate that low light may be the cause. However, if a plant does not bloom, a cool, dry rest should induce flowering

Plant and Flower Information

PLANT SIZE AND TYPE: A 4–7 in. (10–18 cm) sympodial lithophyte.

PSEUDOBULB: 3–6 in. (8–15 cm) long. The slender stems, which resemble a goose quill, are prostrate or pendent. They branch freely, with new roots forming on each branch as it develops. New growths arise from a creeping rhizome.

LEAVES: Many. The deciduous leaves are 1.6–2.4 in. (4–6 cm) long. They are fleshy, glossy, oblong-lanceolate, and alternate along the stem.

INFLORESCENCE: 1.5–2.0 in. (3.8–5.0 cm) long. Inflorescences arise from leaf nodes after the leaves have dropped.

FLOWERS: 1 per inflorescence. The flowers are about 2 in. (5 cm) across, which is very large for the plant size. Blossoms have pale rose-purple sepals and lilac petals. The downy lip is round and fringed along the edge. The rose-purple lip has a yellow-orange disk and a white edge. They are delicately fragrant and long-lived if kept cool.

HYBRIDIZING NOTES: Chromosome counts are 2n = 38 (ref. 152, 153, 243, 504, 580) and 2n = 40 (ref. 504, 580).

REFERENCES: 6, 36, 152, 153, 161, 179, 190, 196, 208, 209, 210, 218, 243, 254, 266, 326, 354, 371, 389, 414, 430, 445, 448, 461, 504, 505, 524, 528, 541, 543, 557, 580.

PHOTOS/DRAWINGS: *35, 36, 209,* 210, 354, *371, 389, 430, 503,* 557, *581.*

Dendrobium loesenerianum Schlechter

ORIGIN/HABITAT: Northern Papua New Guinea. Plants grow on mistforest trees in the Torricelli Range at about 3300 ft. (1000 m).

CLIMATE: Station #94004, Wewak, Papua New Guinea, Lat. 3.6°S, Long. 143.7°E, at 16 ft. (5 m). Temperatures are calculated for an elevation of 3300 ft. (1000 m), resulting in probable extremes of 87°F (31°C) and 51°F (11°C).

N/HEMISPHERE	JAN	FEB	MAR	APR	MAY	JUN	JUL	AUG	SEP	OCT	NOV	DEC
°F AVG MAX	77	77	77	77	77	77	76	75	76	77	77	77
°F AVG MIN	63	63	63	64	64	64	64	64	63	63	64	63
DIURNAL RANGE	14	14	14	13	13	13	12	11	13	14	13	14
RAIN/INCHES	7.6	4.8	5.3	10.0	13.3	14.5	12.1	11.9	14.9	16.9	15.1	10.8
HUMIDITY/%	80	79	79	78	79	81	82	82	81	82	81	80
BLOOM SEASON			*									
DAYS CLR	N/A											
RAIN/MM	193	122	135	254	338	368	307	302	378	429	384	274
°C AVG MAX	25.1	25.1	25.1	25.1	25.1	25.1	24.6	24.0	24.6	25.1	25.1	25.1
°C AVG MIN	17.3	17.3	17.3	17.9	17.9	17.9	17.9	17.9	17.3	17.3	17.9	17.3
DIURNAL RANGE	7.8	7.8	7.8	7.2	7.2	7.2	6.7	6.1	7.3	7.8	7.2	7.8
S/HEMISPHERE	JUL	AUG	SEP	OCT	NOV	DEC	JAN	FEB	MAR	APR	MAY	JUN

Cultural Recommendations

LIGHT: 2000–2500 fc.

TEMPERATURES: Throughout the year, days average 75–77°F (24–25°C), and nights average 63–64°F (17–18°C), with a diurnal range of 11–14°F (6–8°C). Average high and low temperatures vary only 2°F (1°C) during the year, indicating that plants may not be healthy with large seasonal changes.

HUMIDITY: Near 80% year-round.

WATER: Rainfall is heavy all year, but conditions are slightly drier for 1–2 months in winter. Cultivated plants should be kept moist but not soggy.

FERTILIZER: ¼–½ recommended strength. A balanced fertilizer should be applied weekly to biweekly throughout the year.

REST PERIOD: Growing conditions should be maintained year-round. Water should be reduced for plants growing in the dark, short-day conditions common during temperate-latitude winters, but they should never be allowed to dry out completely. Fertilizer should be reduced until water is increased in spring. In the habitat, light is highest in winter.

GROWING MEDIA: A very open and fast-draining medium should be used with either baskets or small pots. Repotting may be done anytime new roots are growing.

MISCELLANEOUS NOTES: The bloom season shown in the climate table is based on reports from the habitat.

Plant and Flower Information

PLANT SIZE AND TYPE: A 24 in. (60 cm) sympodial epiphyte.

PSEUDOBULB: 24 in. (60 cm) long.

LEAVES: Many. The lanceolate leaves are 2.4–3.1 in. (6–8 cm) long. They are erect to suberect.

INFLORESCENCE: Very short.

FLOWERS: 3–8 per inflorescence. The flowers are 0.8 in. (2 cm) long. They do not open fully. All segments are salmon with purple-red veins. The anther is violet.

REFERENCES: 92, 221, 437, 445.

PHOTOS/DRAWINGS: 437.

Dendrobium loherianum Kränzlin

ORIGIN/HABITAT: The Philippines, probably on Luzon Island. No additional habitat information is available, so the following climate should be used cautiously to indicate seasonal patterns only.

CLIMATE: Station #98427, Manila, Philippines, Lat. 14.5°N, Long. 121.0°E, at 74 ft. (23 m). Record extreme temperatures are 101°F (38°C) and 58°F (14°C).

N/HEMISPHERE	JAN	FEB	MAR	APR	MAY	JUN	JUL	AUG	SEP	OCT	NOV	DEC
°F AVG MAX	86	88	91	93	93	91	88	87	88	88	87	86
°F AVG MIN	69	69	71	73	75	75	75	75	75	74	72	70
DIURNAL RANGE	17	19	20	20	18	16	13	12	13	14	15	16
RAIN/INCHES	0.9	0.5	0.7	1.3	5.1	10.0	17.0	16.6	14.0	7.6	5.7	2.6
HUMIDITY/%	77	73	70	68	71	81	84	86	87	84	82	89
BLOOM SEASON	N/A											
DAYS CLR @ 8AM	6	9	14	14	10	3	2	1	1	6	7	6
DAYS CLR @ 2PM	3	6	10	10	8	2	1	1	0	2	2	3
RAIN/MM	23	13	18	33	130	254	432	422	356	193	145	66
°C AVG MAX	30.0	31.1	32.8	33.9	33.9	32.8	31.1	30.6	31.1	31.1	30.6	30.0
°C AVG MIN	20.6	20.6	21.7	22.8	23.9	23.9	23.9	23.9	23.9	23.3	22.2	21.1
DIURNAL RANGE	9.4	10.5	11.1	11.1	10.0	8.9	7.2	6.7	7.2	7.8	8.4	8.9
S/HEMISPHERE	JUL	AUG	SEP	OCT	NOV	DEC	JAN	FEB	MAR	APR	MAY	JUN

Cultural Recommendations

LIGHT: 2000–3000 fc.

TEMPERATURES: Throughout the year, days average 86–93°F (30–34°C), and nights average 69–75°F (21–24°C), with a diurnal range of 12–20°F (7–11°C).

HUMIDITY: 80–85% in summer and autumn, dropping to near 70% in late winter and spring.

WATER: Rainfall is heavy from late spring into autumn, but conditions are much drier in winter. Cultivated plants should be kept moist while actively growing, but water should be gradually reduced in autumn.

FERTILIZER: ¼–½ recommended strength, applied weekly. A high-nitrogen fertilizer is beneficial from spring to midsummer, but a fertilizer high in phosphates should be used in late summer and autumn.

REST PERIOD: Growing temperatures should be maintained all year. Rainfall is low for 3–4 months in winter, but additional moisture is available from heavy dew. For cultivated plants, water should be reduced and the plants allowed to dry slightly between waterings. They should not remain dry for long periods, however. Fertilizer should be eliminated anytime plants are not actively growing. For many plants from this habitat, the winter dry season is necessary to initiate blooms. In the habitat, light is highest in winter.

GROWING MEDIA: Plants may be mounted on tree-fern or cork slabs if humidity is high and plants are watered at least once daily in summer. When plants are potted, any open, fast-draining medium may be used. Repotting may be done anytime new roots are growing.

MISCELLANEOUS NOTES: *D. loherianum* is unlikely to be available for general cultivation.

Plant and Flower Information

PLANT SIZE AND TYPE: A 7 in. (18 cm) sympodial epiphyte.

PSEUDOBULB: 5 in. (13 cm) long. New growths arise from a short, branching rhizome. The stems have a thick ovoid swelling at the base, above which they are slender and slightly flattened.

LEAVES: 1 per growth. The leaves are 2.4 in. (6 cm) long. They are pointed, ovate, and leathery.

INFLORESCENCE: 0.6 in. (1.5 cm) long. Inflorescences emerge from the axils of young leaves.

FLOWERS: The flowers, which open in succession, are 0.8–1.2 in. (2–3 cm) across. Sepals and petals are pale yellow. The white lip is suffused with rose at the base and sides. It is nearly round, wavy, notched and rolled in front, and twisted at the margins. The sidelobes are suffused with dark rose. The raised lip callus is yellow.

REFERENCES: 222, 296, 536.

Dendrobium lohohense T. Tang and F. T. Wang

ORIGIN/HABITAT: Southwest China in Kwangsi Province near Loh Hoh Tsuen and Ling Yün Hsien. Plants were found on rocks in a rocky valley at 3750 ft. (1150 m).

CLIMATE: Station #59211, Pose (Pai-se), Kwangsi, China, Lat. 23.9°N, Long. 106.5°E, at 650 ft. (198 m). Temperatures are calculated for an elevation of 3750 ft. (1150 m), resulting in probable extremes of 99°F (37°C) and 27°F (–3°C).

N/HEMISPHERE	JAN	FEB	MAR	APR	MAY	JUN	JUL	AUG	SEP	OCT	NOV	DEC
°F AVG MAX	56	59	67	77	82	82	83	83	81	74	67	60
°F AVG MIN	38	42	50	58	63	66	67	66	62	56	49	42
DIURNAL RANGE	18	17	17	19	19	16	16	17	19	18	18	18
RAIN/INCHES	0.1	0.7	1.8	2.4	6.3	8.2	11.7	8.0	2.6	4.1	2.5	0.5
HUMIDITY/%	70	72	72	68	69	75	79	81	79	76	77	76
BLOOM SEASON												*
DAYS CLR @ 7AM	3	4	5	5	5	3	2	4	8	6	5	6
DAYS CLR @ 1PM	8	6	8	9	5	3	1	3	8	8	9	11
RAIN/MM	3	18	46	61	160	208	297	203	66	104	64	13
°C AVG MAX	13.3	15.0	19.4	25.0	27.8	28.0	28.4	28.3	27.2	23.3	19.4	15.6
°C AVG MIN	3.3	5.4	9.9	14.3	17.1	18.8	19.3	18.8	16.5	13.2	9.3	5.4
DIURNAL RANGE	10.0	9.6	9.5	10.7	10.7	9.2	9.1	9.5	10.7	10.1	10.1	10.2
S/HEMISPHERE	JUL	AUG	SEP	OCT	NOV	DEC	JAN	FEB	MAR	APR	MAY	JUN

Cultural Recommendations

LIGHT: 2000–3000 fc.

TEMPERATURES: Summer days average 82–83°F (28°C), and nights average 66–67°F (19°C), with a diurnal range of 16–17°F (9–10°C).

HUMIDITY: 75–80% in summer and autumn, dropping to near 70% in winter and spring.

WATER: Rainfall is moderate to heavy from late spring into autumn but is very low for 3–4 months in winter. Plants should be kept moist while actively growing, but water should be gradually reduced after new growths mature in late autumn.

FERTILIZER: 1/4–1/2 recommended strength, applied weekly. A high nitrogen fertilizer is beneficial from spring to midsummer, but a fertilizer high in phosphates should be used in late summer and autumn.

REST PERIOD: Winter days average 56–60°F (13–16°C), and nights average 38–42°F (3–5°C), with a diurnal range of 17–18°F (10°C). Rainfall is reduced in winter, but additional moisture is available from dew and as mist from morning fog and low clouds. Water should be reduced for cultivated plants. They should be allowed to become somewhat dry between waterings but should not remain completely dry for extended periods.

GROWING MEDIA: Plants may be mounted on tree-fern or cork slabs if humidity is high and plants are watered at least once daily in summer. When plants are potted, any open, fast-draining medium may be used. Repotting is best done in early spring when new roots begin to grow.

MISCELLANEOUS NOTES: The bloom season shown in the climate table is based on records from the habitat. Plants are collected and used in Chinese medicine.

Plant and Flower Information

PLANT SIZE AND TYPE: A 10–11 in. (25–28 cm) sympodial lithophyte.

PSEUDOBULB: 8 in. (20 cm) long. The slender pseudobulbs may develop a few branches.

LEAVES: Many. The elliptic-oblong leaves are 1.4–2.4 in. (3.6–6.1 cm) long, pointed at the tip, and contracted at the base. They are distichous.

INFLORESCENCE: Short. The erect inflorescences emerge from nodes at the apex of the stem.

FLOWERS: 1 per inflorescence. The yellow flowers are 1 in. (2.5 cm) long. The smooth, elliptical sepals and petals are rounded at the apex. The petals are nearly as broad as the dorsal sepal. The lip is concave and irregularly toothed along the margin. On the front of the midlobe, the callus is fleshy and papillose.

HYBRIDIZING NOTES: Chromosome count is 2n = 38 (ref. 153).

REFERENCES: 153, 208, 228, 505, 528, 547.

Dendrobium lomatochilum Seidenfaden

ORIGIN/HABITAT: Vietnam. Plants were originally collected near Nha Trang on Mt. Co Inh at about 3450 ft. (1050 m).

CLIMATE: Station #48877, Nha Trang, Vietnam, Lat. 12.2°N, Long. 109.2°E, at 19 ft. (6 m). Temperatures are calculated for an elevation of 3450 ft. (1050 m), resulting in probable extremes of 92°F (33°C) and 43°F (6°C).

N/HEMISPHERE	JAN	FEB	MAR	APR	MAY	JUN	JUL	AUG	SEP	OCT	NOV	DEC
°F AVG MAX	71	73	75	78	80	81	80	80	78	75	73	71
°F AVG MIN	58	58	60	63	65	65	65	65	64	63	61	60
DIURNAL RANGE	13	15	15	15	15	16	15	15	14	12	12	11
RAIN/INCHES	1.8	0.7	1.2	1.5	2.4	1.8	1.6	2.1	6.5	12.7	14.3	7.0
HUMIDITY/%	77	78	79	80	77	77	77	77	80	83	81	78
BLOOM SEASON	N/A											
DAYS CLR @ 7AM	2	3	6	6	5	4	4	3	2	3	1	1
DAYS CLR @ 1PM	3	4	9	8	5	2	3	2	2	1	1	1
RAIN/MM	46	18	30	38	61	46	41	53	165	323	363	178
°C AVG MAX	21.5	22.6	23.7	25.4	26.5	27.0	26.5	26.5	25.4	23.7	22.6	21.5
°C AVG MIN	14.3	14.3	15.4	17.0	18.2	18.2	18.2	18.2	17.6	17.0	15.9	15.4
DIURNAL RANGE	7.2	8.3	8.3	8.4	8.3	8.8	8.3	8.3	7.8	6.7	6.7	6.1
S/HEMISPHERE	JUL	AUG	SEP	OCT	NOV	DEC	JAN	FEB	MAR	APR	MAY	JUN

Cultural Recommendations

LIGHT: 2000–3000 fc.

TEMPERATURES: Summer days average 80–81°F (27°C), and nights average 65°F (18°C), with a diurnal range of 15–16°F (8–9°C).

HUMIDITY: 75–80% most of the year, increasing to near 85% for a brief period in autumn.

WATER: Rainfall is light to moderate most of the year but is heavy for 4 months in autumn. Records from nearby high-elevation stations indicate that rainfall is probably greater in the habitat than is indicated by the climate data for this station. Rain falls as showers, so cultivated plants should be watered heavily and then allowed to dry between waterings. They should not remain dry for extended periods, however.

FERTILIZER: 1/4–1/2 recommended strength, applied weekly. A high-nitrogen fertilizer is beneficial from spring to midsummer, but a fertilizer high in phosphates should be used in late summer and autumn.

REST PERIOD: Winter days average 71–75°F (22–24°C), and nights average 58–60°F (14–15°C), with a diurnal range of 11–15°F (6–8°C). Rainfall is low in winter, but nightly cooling results in heavy deposits of dew during much of the year. For cultivated plants, water should be reduced somewhat in winter; but they should still not remain dry for long periods. Fertilizer should be reduced until water is increased in spring.

GROWING MEDIA: Plants may be mounted on tree-fern or cork slabs or potted in small pots filled with any open, fast-draining medium. Repotting may be done anytime new roots are actively growing.

Plant and Flower Information

PLANT SIZE AND TYPE: A 12–14 in. (30–35 cm) sympodial epiphyte.

PSEUDOBULB: 12–14 in. (30–35 cm) long. The pseudobulbous swelling at the base of the stem is 2 internodes long. Rooting keikis may develop on the stems.

LEAVES: Many. The leaves are about 4 in. (10 cm) long.

INFLORESCENCE: Inflorescences arise at the apex of the stem.

FLOWERS: 1 per inflorescence. The white flowers are 0.8 in. (2 cm) long. The squared apex of the lip has a long fringe at the front edge.

REFERENCES: 234, 450.

PHOTOS/DRAWINGS: 450.

Dendrobium lompobatangense J. J. Smith

ORIGIN/HABITAT: Sulawesi (Celebes). Plants were originally found in the southwest on Mt. Lompobatang at 5250–7200 ft. (1600–2200 m).

CLIMATE: Station #97180, Makassar, Sulawesi, Indonesia, Lat. 5.1°S, Long. 119.6°E, at 46 ft. (14 m). Temperatures are calculated for an elevation of 6200 ft. (1890 m), resulting in probable extremes of 75°F (24°C) and 38°F (3°C).

N/HEMISPHERE	JAN	FEB	MAR	APR	MAY	JUN	JUL	AUG	SEP	OCT	NOV	DEC
°F AVG MAX	66	67	67	67	66	64	64	64	65	66	67	66
°F AVG MIN	50	49	50	52	54	54	54	55	54	54	54	52
DIURNAL RANGE	16	18	17	15	12	10	10	9	11	12	13	14
RAIN/INCHES	1.3	0.4	0.5	1.6	6.7	23.2	28.3	20.9	16.7	6.5	3.6	2.7
HUMIDITY/%	72	67	64	70	77	84	84	85	84	80	79	76
BLOOM SEASON												•
DAYS CLR @ 8AM	14	17	15	14	8	4	4	1	4	8	8	11
DAYS CLR @ 2PM	7	7	11	13	9	3	1	1	1	2	6	7
RAIN/MM	33	10	13	41	170	589	719	531	424	165	91	69
°C AVG MAX	18.7	19.3	19.3	19.3	18.7	17.6	17.6	17.6	18.2	18.7	19.3	18.7
°C AVG MIN	9.8	9.3	9.8	10.9	12.1	12.1	12.1	12.6	12.1	12.1	12.1	10.9
DIURNAL RANGE	8.9	10.0	9.5	8.4	6.6	5.5	5.5	5.0	6.1	6.6	7.2	7.8
S/HEMISPHERE	JUL	AUG	SEP	OCT	NOV	DEC	JAN	FEB	MAR	APR	MAY	JUN

Cultural Recommendations

LIGHT: 2500–3500 fc. In the habitat, clear summer days are rare.

TEMPERATURES: Summer days average 64°F (18°C), and nights average 54–55°F (12–13°C), with a diurnal range of 9–10°F (5–6°C).

HUMIDITY: Near 85% in summer and early autumn, decreasing to 65–70% in winter.

WATER: Rainfall is heavy from late spring to autumn, but conditions are much drier in winter. Cultivated plants should be kept moist from spring into early autumn, but water should be gradually reduced in late autumn.

FERTILIZER: ¼–½ recommended strength, applied weekly. A high-nitrogen fertilizer is beneficial from spring to midsummer, but a fertilizer high in phosphates should be used in late summer and autumn.

REST PERIOD: Winter days average 66–67°F (19°C), and nights average 49–52°F (9–11°C), with a diurnal range of 14–18°F (8–10°C). In the habitat, winter rainfall is very low for about 4 months. Conditions become so dry that even dew is uncommon for about 2 months. Water should be reduced for cultivated plants. They should be allowed to dry out between waterings, but should not remain dry for extended periods. Occasional early morning mistings on bright, sunny days is suggested to prevent excessive drying. Reduce or eliminate fertilizer anytime water is reduced. The large number of clear winter and spring mornings in the habitat indicate that light should be as high as the plant can tolerate, short of burning the leaves.

GROWING MEDIA: Plants may be mounted on tree-fern or cork slabs or potted in small pots filled with any open, fast-draining medium. Repotting may be done anytime new roots are actively growing.

MISCELLANEOUS NOTES: The bloom season shown in the climate table is based on reports from the habitat. The plant was described in 1928 in *Bul. Jard. Bot. Buit.* 3rd sér. 10:15.

Plant and Flower Information

PLANT SIZE AND TYPE: A 13–22 in. (33–56 cm) sympodial epiphyte.

PSEUDOBULB: 13–22 in. (33–56 cm) long. The stems are very branching.

LEAVES: Many. The linear-lanceolate leaves are 1.2–2.4 in. (3–6 cm) long. They are wavy along the margin.

INFLORESCENCE: Short. The erect inflorescences are very densely flowered. They are borne near the apex of leafy stems.

FLOWERS: 9–10 per inflorescence. The violet flowers are 0.6 in. (1.5 cm) long. They have a somewhat ovate dorsal sepal and very slender lateral sepals. The erect, lanceolate petals are minutely toothed along the apical margin. They are held nearly parallel to the dorsal sepal. The lip is simple.

REFERENCES: 224.

Dendrobium lonchigerum Schlechter. Transferred to *Ephemerantha lonchigera* (Schlechter) P. F. Hunt, which is now considered synonymous with *Flickingeria*. REFERENCES: 212, 223, 229, 232, 443, 449.

Dendrobium lonchophyllum Hooker f. Now considered a synonym of *Flickingeria xantholeucha* (Rchb. f.) A. Hawkes. REFERENCES: 75, 200, 202, 213, 218, 220, 230, 231, 254, 395, 445, 449, 455.

Dendrobium longicalcaratum Hayata. See *D. chameleon* Ames. REFERENCES: 61, 62, 193, 208, 221, 279, 445, 504, 536. PHOTOS/DRAWINGS: 62.

Dendrobium longicaule Schlechter. See *D. neo-guineënse* A. Hawkes and A. H. Heller. REFERENCES: 223, 229, 443.

Dendrobium longicaule J. J. Smith

ORIGIN/HABITAT: Southern Irian Jaya (western New Guinea). Habitat and elevation are unavailable, so the following climate data should be used with caution. Plants were cultivated at the botanical garden in Bogor, Java.

CLIMATE: Station #97876, Tanahmerah, Irian Jaya, Lat. 6.1°S, Long. 140.3°E, at 75 ft. (23 m). Record extreme temperatures are 98°F (37°C) and 64°F (18°C).

N/HEMISPHERE	JAN	FEB	MAR	APR	MAY	JUN	JUL	AUG	SEP	OCT	NOV	DEC
°F AVG MAX	84	85	87	90	91	90	90	89	90	89	87	85
°F AVG MIN	72	71	71	72	73	74	73	73	73	73	74	73
DIURNAL RANGE	12	14	16	18	18	16	17	16	17	16	13	12
RAIN/INCHES	11.5	12.1	14.7	13.2	14.4	15.9	14.5	15.8	17.4	17.3	15.5	11.9
HUMIDITY/%	N/A											
BLOOM SEASON	N/A											
DAYS CLR	N/A											
RAIN/MM	292	307	373	335	366	404	368	401	442	439	394	302
°C AVG MAX	28.9	29.4	30.6	32.2	32.8	32.2	32.2	31.7	32.2	31.7	30.6	29.4
°C AVG MIN	22.2	21.7	21.7	22.2	22.8	23.3	22.8	22.8	22.8	22.8	23.3	22.8
DIURNAL RANGE	6.7	7.7	8.9	10.0	10.0	8.9	9.4	8.9	9.4	8.9	7.3	6.6
S/HEMISPHERE	JUL	AUG	SEP	OCT	NOV	DEC	JAN	FEB	MAR	APR	MAY	JUN

Cultural Recommendations

LIGHT: 2000–3000 fc.

TEMPERATURES: Throughout the year, days average 84–91°F (29–33°C), and nights average 71–74°F (22–23°C), with a diurnal range of 12–18°F (7–10°C).

HUMIDITY: Information is not available for this location. However, records from nearby locations indicate that humidity probably averages near 85% year-round.

WATER: Rainfall is very heavy year-round. Cultivated plants should be kept evenly moist.

FERTILIZER: ¼–½ recommended strength. A balanced fertilizer should be applied weekly to biweekly throughout the year.

REST PERIOD: Growing conditions should be maintained year-round. Water and fertilizer might be reduced slightly in winter, especially for plants cultivated in the dark, short-day conditions common in temperate latitudes. However, cultivated plants should never be allowed to dry completely between waterings.

GROWING MEDIA: Plants are best potted, as they must be kept moist. Fir bark or any open, fast-draining medium may be used. Repotting may be done anytime new roots are growing.

MISCELLANEOUS NOTES: The plant was described in 1910 in *Bul. Dép. Agric. Indes. Néerl.* 39:9.

Plant and Flower Information

PLANT SIZE AND TYPE: A sympodial plant of unreported size.

PSEUDOBULB: The robust stems are elongated.

LEAVES: Many. The leathery leaves are 1.6–4.0 in. (4–10 cm) long. They may be oblong to lanceolate-elliptic.

FLOWERS: 2 per inflorescence. The flowers are 0.6 in. (1.5 cm) long. They are yellow with brown markings. Sepals and petals are broadest at the tip. The ruffled, wavy lip, which has large side lobes and a small midlobe, is covered with warts.

REFERENCES: 220, 254, 470.

Dendrobium longicolle Lindley.
Now considered a synonym of *Diplocaulobium longicolle* (Lindley) Kränzlin. REFERENCES: 12, 179, 200, 202, 216, 220, 239, 254, 286, 295, 296, 317, 395, 455. PHOTOS/DRAWINGS: 200.

Dendrobium longicornu Lindley

AKA: *D. bulleyi* Rolfe, *D. flexuosum* Griffith, *D. hirsutum* Griffith. Hawkes (ref. 190) also includes *D. fredianum* Hort. Schelpe (ref. 429) notes that although the overall lip shape of *D. bulleyi* is similar, the sidelobes are more oblong and the midlobe is much more coarsely hairy.

ORIGIN/HABITAT: Central Nepal, Sikkim, the Khasi (Khasia) and Naga Hills of northeastern India, Burma, northern Vietnam near Cha-pa, and Yunnan Province in southwest China. Plants grow on mossy trees at 3950–9500 ft. (1200–2900 m), often with *Coelogyne cristata*. Plants known as *D. bulleyi* were found on dry shady banks in pine woods at 8000–9000 ft. (2440–2740 m), where temperatures are cooler than indicated below. Plants commonly grow at the base of trees in lower forests where they receive ample moisture and high light. However, in mistforest zones they are found on ridge-tops where light is high and plants can dry.

CLIMATE: Station #42398, Baghdogra, India, Lat. 26.7°N, Long. 88.3°E, at 412 ft. (126 m). Temperatures are calculated for an elevation of 5900 ft. (1800 m), resulting in probable extremes of 86°F (30°C) and 18°F (–8°C).

N/HEMISPHERE	JAN	FEB	MAR	APR	MAY	JUN	JUL	AUG	SEP	OCT	NOV	DEC
°F AVG MAX	56	59	67	72	72	71	71	71	70	69	64	59
°F AVG MIN	32	36	42	50	55	58	59	59	58	52	42	35
DIURNAL RANGE	24	23	25	22	17	13	12	12	12	17	22	24
RAIN/INCHES	0.3	0.7	1.3	3.7	11.8	25.9	32.2	25.3	21.2	5.6	0.5	0.2
HUMIDITY/%	73	68	57	58	74	84	86	85	85	79	75	76
BLOOM SEASON									**	**	**	
DAYS CLR @ 6AM	21	18	15	11	5	0	1	1	4	13	23	19
DAYS CLR @ 12PM	23	16	16	11	2	2	0	1	2	10	21	18
RAIN/MM	8	18	33	94	300	658	818	643	538	142	13	5
°C AVG MAX	13.3	14.9	19.4	22.2	22.2	21.6	21.6	21.6	21.0	20.5	17.7	14.9
°C AVG MIN	0.0	2.2	5.5	9.9	12.7	14.4	14.9	14.9	14.4	11.0	5.5	1.6
DIURNAL RANGE	13.3	12.7	13.9	12.3	9.5	7.2	6.7	6.7	6.6	9.5	12.2	13.3
S/HEMISPHERE	JUL	AUG	SEP	OCT	NOV	DEC	JAN	FEB	MAR	APR	MAY	JUN

Cultural Recommendations

LIGHT: 2000–3000 fc. Strong air movement is important at all times. The heavy summer cloud cover indicates that some shading is needed from spring through autumn, but light should be as high as the plant can tolerate, short of burning the leaves.

TEMPERATURES: Summer days average 71°F (22°C), and nights average 58–59°F (14–15°C), with a diurnal range of 12–13°F (7°C). Because of microclimate effects, the actual summer highs and winter lows may be 6–8°F (3–4°C) warmer than indicated in the table. Also, because the habitat extends over a wide range of elevation, plants may adapt to temperatures that are somewhat cooler than indicated.

HUMIDITY: Near 85% in summer and early autumn, decreasing to 60–70% in winter and spring.

WATER: Rainfall is very heavy from late spring to early autumn, but conditions are much drier in winter. Cultivated plants should be kept moist. Some growers recommend placing the pot in a saucer of water during this period to meet the plant's heavy water requirement. Water should be gradually reduced in autumn after new growths mature.

FERTILIZER: ½ recommended strength, applied weekly. A high-nitrogen fertilizer is beneficial from spring to midsummer, but a fertilizer high in phosphates should be used in late summer and autumn. Maximum growth should be encouraged during the relatively short growing season.

REST PERIOD: Winter days average 56–59°F (13–15°C), and nights average 32–36°F (0–2°C), with a diurnal range of 23–24°F (13°C). In the habitat, rainfall is low for 4–5 months; but for 2–3 of these months, additional water is available from frequent, heavy deposits of dew as well as mist from fog and low clouds. Consequently, the driest part of the season only lasts 1–2 months. Growers indicate that a dry rest lasting 2 months meets the plant's requirements and that temperatures need not drop very low. Fertilizer should be reduced, or even eliminated, until water is increased in spring. The cool, dry rest is essential for healthy growth and flowering, but it need not be quite as long or as severe as indicated by the climate data. Growers indicate that *D. longicornu* is difficult to grow without the rest period.

GROWING MEDIA: Plants may be mounted on tree-fern or cork slabs if humidity is high and plants are watered at least once daily in summer. When plants are potted, any open, fast-draining medium may be used. Repotting may be done anytime new roots are growing.

MISCELLANEOUS NOTES: The bloom season shown in the climate table is based on reports from the habitat. Cultivation records indicate blooming in every season.

Plant and Flower Information

PLANT SIZE AND TYPE: A 6–12 in. (15–30 cm) sympodial epiphyte. Plants may reach a height of 24 in. (60 cm). They are described as a less vigorous than *D. formosum* Roxburgh ex Lindley.

PSEUDOBULB: 6–24 in. (15–60 cm) long. The clustered pseudobulbs grow in all directions. They are slender, erect, and somewhat zigzag. The lower nodes are covered with black, hairy leaf-bases.

Dendrobium longifolium

LEAVES: 5–11 at the apex of each growth. The linear to ovate leaves are 1.2–4.0 in. (3–10 cm) long. The dull green leaves are arranged in 2 rows. In nature, they are quickly deciduous, but growers indicate that the leaves of cultivated plants may last more than one season.

INFLORESCENCE: 0.4 in. (1 cm) long. The very short inflorescences arise at the apex or along the side of leafy and leafless stems.

FLOWERS: 1–3 per inflorescence. The fragrant flowers are 1.6 in. (4 cm) across and do not open fully. They are long-lasting if kept cool. Sepals and petals are pure transparent white. The funnel-shaped lip has a central band that may be yellow, pale brown, or orange-red. It is marked with darker streaks and veins. The lip margins are fringed. The blossoms have a long spur.

HYBRIDIZING NOTES: Chromosome counts are n = 19 (ref. 150, 151, 154, 504, 542), 2n = 38 (ref. 152, 154, 504, 542, 580), and 2n = 43 as *D. longicornu* var. *java* (ref. 151, 187).

REFERENCES: 36, 38, 46, 150, 151, 152, 154, 179, 187, 190, 202, 208, 216, 247, 254, 266, 278, 294, 317, 364, 366, 367, 369, 376, 429, 430, 448, 454, 504, 528, 541, 542, 570, 577, 580.

PHOTOS/DRAWINGS: *36*, 38, 46, *247*, *364*, *366*, *430*, 454.

Dendrobium longifolium H. B. and K.
Different sources refer this species to a variety of genera, but Hawkes (ref. 190) considers it a synonym of *Eulophia alta*. REFERENCES: 190, 216, 254.

Dendrobium longipecten J. J. Smith

ORIGIN/HABITAT: Indonesia. Plants were found on the west coast of Sumatra in the Benkulu district. Habitat elevation is not available, so the following temperatures should be used with caution.

CLIMATE: Station #96253, Bengkulu, Sumatra, Indonesia, Lat. 3.9°S, Long. 102.3°E, at 49 ft. (15 m). Record extreme temperatures are not available for this location.

N/HEMISPHERE	JAN	FEB	MAR	APR	MAY	JUN	JUL	AUG	SEP	OCT	NOV	DEC
°F AVG MAX	88	87	87	87	87	87	88	88	88	88	89	88
°F AVG MIN	72	72	72	73	73	73	73	72	73	74	73	73
DIURNAL RANGE	16	15	15	14	14	14	15	16	15	14	16	15
RAIN/INCHES	6.9	6.8	9.1	13.9	16.0	12.7	16.0	11.5	12.0	8.3	8.4	8.4
HUMIDITY/%	77	78	77	77	79	80	78	76	77	79	77	78
BLOOM SEASON	*											
DAYS CLR @ 7AM	5	1	1	1	0	0	2	1	1	1	2	3
DAYS CLR @ 1PM	5	4	3	1	2	3	2	2	2	3	7	5
RAIN/MM	176	173	231	354	405	322	407	291	304	211	215	213
°C AVG MAX	30.8	30.8	30.7	30.7	30.5	30.8	30.8	31.3	31.2	31.2	31.4	31.3
°C AVG MIN	22.1	22.0	22.3	22.6	22.7	22.7	22.7	22.5	22.8	23.2	23.1	22.6
DIURNAL RANGE	8.9	8.3	8.3	7.8	7.8	7.8	8.3	8.9	8.3	7.8	8.9	8.3
S/HEMISPHERE	JUL	AUG	SEP	OCT	NOV	DEC	JAN	FEB	MAR	APR	MAY	JUN

Cultural Recommendations

LIGHT: 2000–3000 fc.

TEMPERATURES: Throughout the year, days average 87–89°F (31°C), and nights average 72–74°F (22–23°C), with a diurnal range of 14–16°F (8–9°C). Plants may be moved to a cooler location if they show signs of stress.

HUMIDITY: 75–80% year-round.

WATER: Rainfall is moderate to heavy throughout the year. Winter is only slightly drier than summer. Cultivated plants should be kept moist and never be allowed to dry out completely. Warm water may be beneficial.

FERTILIZER: ¼–½ recommended strength. A balanced fertilizer should be applied weekly to biweekly throughout the year.

REST PERIOD: Growing conditions should be maintained year-round. Water may be reduced somewhat for plants grown in the dark, short-day conditions common in temperate-latitude winters, but cultivated plants should never be allowed to dry completely between waterings. In the habitat, light is slightly higher in winter.

GROWING MEDIA: Plants may be mounted on tree-fern or cork slabs or potted in small pots filled with any open, fast-draining medium. Repotting may be done anytime new roots are growing.

MISCELLANEOUS NOTES: The bloom season shown in the climate table is based on collection reports. The plant was described in 1928 in *Bul. Jard. Bot. Buit.* 3rd sér. 10:61.

Plant and Flower Information

PLANT SIZE AND TYPE: An 19 in. (48 cm) sympodial epiphyte.

PSEUDOBULB: 19 in. (48 cm) long. The branching stems are slender.

LEAVES: Many. The somewhat oblong-triangular leaves are about 1 in. (2.5 cm) long. They are distinctly curved and pointed at the tip.

INFLORESCENCE: Short. Clusters of inflorescences emerge from nodes along the stem.

FLOWERS: The fleshy blossoms are less than 0.4 in. (1 cm) long. The sepals and petals are brownish purple. The basal half of the recurved lip is also brownish purple with dark purple on the front half. The bracts and ovary are purplish brown.

REFERENCES: 224.

Dendrobium longipes Hooker f.
Now considered a synonym of *Epigeneium longipes* (Hooker f.) Summerhayes. REFERENCES: 200, 202, 218, 229, 254, 395, 445, 449, 455, 499.

Dendrobium longipetalum Persoon.
Now considered a synonym of *Maxillaria longipetala* Ruiz and Pavón. REFERENCES: 216, 254.

Dendrobium longirepens Ames and Schweinfurth.
Now considered a synonym of *Epigeneium longirepens* (Ames and Schweinfurth) Seidenfaden. REFERENCES: 12, 213, 222, 228, 229, 230, 449.

Dendrobium longispicatum. Status unknown.
This name was used by Löve and Solbrig (ref. 280) in a list chromosome counts. Later writers have used this information in their lists of chromosome counts. However, we found no source or original description, so we suspect that these references should have applied to *Dendrochilum longispicatum* Ames. REFERENCES: 280, 504, 580.

Dendrobium longissimum Schlechter

ORIGIN/HABITAT: Northeastern Papua New Guinea. Plants grow on tall trees in forests of the Maboro Range in the Waria District at about 3950 ft. (1200 m).

CLIMATE: Station #200192, Garaina, Papua New Guinea, Lat. 7.9°S, Long. 147.1°E, at 2350 ft. (716 m). Temperatures are calculated for an elevation of 3950 ft. (1200 m), resulting in probable extremes of 89°F (32°C) and 41°F (5°C).

N/HEMISPHERE	JAN	FEB	MAR	APR	MAY	JUN	JUL	AUG	SEP	OCT	NOV	DEC
°F AVG MAX	75	77	78	79	80	80	80	80	79	79	78	76
°F AVG MIN	58	58	58	59	58	59	60	60	60	59	59	58
DIURNAL RANGE	17	19	20	20	22	21	20	20	19	20	19	18
RAIN/INCHES	5.8	6.5	8.7	11.1	11.8	11.9	8.9	11.7	11.5	9.9	7.7	5.2
HUMIDITY/%	84	82	82	81	80	80	81	81	82	83	84	84
BLOOM SEASON											*	
DAYS CLR	N/A											
RAIN/MM	147	165	221	282	300	302	226	297	292	251	196	132
°C AVG MAX	23.8	24.9	25.4	26.0	26.5	26.5	26.5	26.5	26.0	26.0	25.4	24.3
°C AVG MIN	14.3	14.3	14.3	14.9	14.3	14.9	15.4	15.4	15.4	14.9	14.9	14.3
DIURNAL RANGE	9.5	10.6	11.1	11.1	12.2	11.6	11.1	11.1	10.6	11.1	10.5	10.0
S/HEMISPHERE	JUL	AUG	SEP	OCT	NOV	DEC	JAN	FEB	MAR	APR	MAY	JUN

Cultural Recommendations

LIGHT: 2000–3000 fc.

TEMPERATURES: Throughout the year, days average 75–80°F (24–27°C),

and nights average 58–60°F (14–15°C), with a diurnal range of 17–22°F (10–12°C).

HUMIDITY: 80–85% year-round.

WATER: Rainfall is moderate to heavy all year. Cultivated plants should be kept moist but not soggy.

FERTILIZER: 1/4–1/2 recommended strength. A balanced fertilizer should be applied weekly to biweekly throughout the year. The Royal Botanic Garden in Edinburgh uses a seaweed-based fertilizer for high elevation plants from New Guinea.

REST PERIOD: Growing conditions vary only slightly during the year. In the habitat, rainfall is slightly lower in winter. Water should be reduced somewhat for cultivated plants, especially those grown in the dark, short-day conditions common in temperate latitudes. They should never be allowed to dry out completely, however. Fertilizer should be reduced or eliminated anytime water is reduced. In the habitat, light is slightly higher in winter.

GROWING MEDIA: Mounting plants on tree-fern or cork slabs accommodates their pendulous growth habit. However, humidity must be high and plants must be watered at least once a day in summer. If plants cannot be mounted, small pots or hanging baskets may be filled with an open, fast-draining medium. Repotting may be done anytime new roots are actively growing.

MISCELLANEOUS NOTES: The bloom season shown in the climate table is based on reports from the habitat. Plants that produce flowers which last a single day commonly bloom several times during the year. Flowering usually occurs 7–14 days after a sudden 10°F (5°C) drop in daytime temperatures.

Plant and Flower Information

PLANT SIZE AND TYPE: An 79 in. (200 cm) sympodial epiphyte.

PSEUDOBULB: 79 in. (200 cm) long. The stems are long, simple, and densely leafy. They are pendent and sway in the wind.

LEAVES: Many. The leaves are 5–9 in. (13–23 cm) long.

INFLORESCENCE: Very short.

FLOWERS: 2 per inflorescence. The creamy yellow flowers are 0.6 in. (1.6 cm) across. The round sepals and petals are incurved, cupped, and thickened at the tip. The tiny lip, which has an orange-yellow keel, is nearly hidden. The pointed midlobe is wavy to scalloped along the margin with protuberances near the back. The erect sidelobes have brown veins and margins. The highly fragrant blossoms last a single day.

REFERENCES: 221, 437, 445.

PHOTOS/DRAWINGS: 437.

Dendrobium lowii Lindley

ORIGIN/HABITAT: Sarawak in northwestern Borneo. Plants grow on trees in exposed mountain locations at about 3300 ft. (1000 m).

CLIMATE: Station #49613, Tambunan, Sabah (North Borneo), Lat. 5.7°N, Long. 116.4°E, at 1200 ft. (366 m). Temperatures are calculated for an elevation of 4000 ft. (1220 m), resulting in probable extremes of 89°F (32°C) and 45°F (7°C).

N/HEMISPHERE	JAN	FEB	MAR	APR	MAY	JUN	JUL	AUG	SEP	OCT	NOV	DEC
°F AVG MAX	77	78	80	81	81	80	80	80	80	79	78	77
°F AVG MIN	58	56	57	58	59	58	57	57	58	58	58	59
DIURNAL RANGE	19	22	23	23	22	22	23	23	22	21	20	18
RAIN/INCHES	5.8	3.7	5.8	7.5	8.2	7.3	5.1	4.9	6.4	7.0	6.8	6.0
HUMIDITY/%	N/A											
BLOOM SEASON	*	*	*	*	*	**	**	*	*	*	*	*
DAYS CLR	N/A											
RAIN/MM	147	94	147	190	208	185	130	124	163	178	173	152
°C AVG MAX	24.9	25.4	26.5	27.1	27.1	26.5	26.5	26.5	26.5	26.0	25.4	24.9
°C AVG MIN	14.3	13.2	13.8	14.3	14.9	14.3	13.8	13.8	14.3	14.3	14.3	14.9
DIURNAL RANGE	10.6	12.2	12.7	12.8	12.2	12.2	12.7	12.7	12.2	11.7	11.1	10.0
S/HEMISPHERE	JUL	AUG	SEP	OCT	NOV	DEC	JAN	FEB	MAR	APR	MAY	JUN

Cultural Recommendations

LIGHT: 2500–3500 fc. Bright, reflected light is recommended.

TEMPERATURES: Throughout the year, days average 77–81°F (25–27°C), and nights average 56–59°F (13–15°C), with a diurnal range of 18–23°F (10–13°C).

HUMIDITY: Information is not available for this location. However, records from nearby locations indicate that humidity probably averages 80–85% year-round.

WATER: Rainfall is moderate to heavy all year with a brief slightly drier period in winter. Cultivated plants should be kept moist with only slight drying allowed between waterings.

FERTILIZER: 1/4–1/2 recommended strength, applied weekly. A high-nitrogen fertilizer is beneficial from spring to midsummer, but a fertilizer high in phosphates should be used in late summer and autumn.

REST PERIOD: Growing temperatures should be maintained all year. Water should be reduced somewhat for cultivated plants in winter, especially those grown in the dark, short-day conditions common in temperate latitudes. They should never be allowed to dry out completely, however. Fertilizer should be reduced or eliminated anytime water is reduced.

GROWING MEDIA: Plants may be potted in any open, well drained media that remains moist but is not soggy. Fine- or medium-grade fir bark mixed with perlite or other moisture-retaining additives is preferred by many growers. Chopped sphagnum moss is sometimes added to the mix, especially in drier areas with low humidity. Repotting is best done in early spring when new roots begin growing.

MISCELLANEOUS NOTES: The bloom season shown in the climate table is based on cultivation records. Blooming may occur any time of year, and plants sometimes bloom twice a year. Growers indicate that *D. lowii* is easy to grow in an intermediate greenhouse with bright light and excellent air movement.

Plant and Flower Information

PLANT SIZE AND TYPE: A 12–19 in. (30–48 cm) sympodial epiphyte.

PSEUDOBULB: 10–16 in. (25–40 cm) long. The erect stems have 9 nodes. The leaf sheaths are covered with brown or black hairs.

LEAVES: 6 at the apex. The ovate-oblong leaves are 2–3 in. (5–8 cm) long. The underside is covered with black or brown hairs.

INFLORESCENCE: Short. Dense racemes are borne from the uppermost nodes of leafy stems.

FLOWERS: 2–7 per inflorescence. The funnel-shaped flowers are 1.5–2.0 in. (3.8–5.0 cm) across. The sepals and wider petals may be buff- or deep-yellow. The petals and reflexed lip are wavy along the margin. The lip is decorated with 3–6 orange-red keels, which are toothed and covered with long hairs. The spur is long and straight. Blossoms are fragrant and long-lasting.

HYBRIDIZING NOTES: Chromosome count is 2n = 38 (ref. 542) as *D. lowianum* Lindley.

REFERENCES: 36, 179, 190, 196, 200, 210, 216, 254, 286, 295, 394, 429, 430, 445, 541, 542, 557. 570.

PHOTOS/DRAWINGS: 210, *430*.

Dendrobium lubbersianum Rchb. f. See *D. williamsonii*

Day and Rchb. f. REFERENCES: 157, 202, 216, 454.

Dendrobium lucae F. Mueller. Kränzlin (ref. 254) lists *D. lucae* as a synonym of *D. gordonii* S. Moore which Lewis and Cribb (ref. 270) include as a synonym of *D. macrophyllum* A. Richard. REFERENCES: 220, 254, 270, 504.

Dendrobium lucens Rchb. f.

AKA: Sometimes spelled *D. lucenti* or *D. lucentis*.

ORIGIN/HABITAT: Endemic to Borneo. Plants grow near Tawau on small trees in humid forests. Habitat elevation is estimated, so the following climate data should be used with caution.

CLIMATE: Station #49609, Tawau, North Borneo, Lat. 4.3°N, Long. 117.9°E, at 58 ft. (18 m). Temperatures are calculated for an elevation of 1200 ft. (370 m), resulting in probable extremes of 93°F (34°C) and 57°F (14°C).

N/HEMISPHERE	JAN	FEB	MAR	APR	MAY	JUN	JUL	AUG	SEP	OCT	NOV	DEC
°F AVG MAX	85	85	85	86	85	84	85	84	85	86	85	85
°F AVG MIN	67	67	67	68	67	67	67	67	67	67	67	67
DIURNAL RANGE	18	18	18	18	18	17	18	17	18	19	18	18
RAIN/INCHES	4.8	3.8	3.9	5.0	7.0	7.4	7.7	7.6	6.0	5.8	6.7	6.2
HUMIDITY/%	N/A											
BLOOM SEASON	N/A											
DAYS CLR	N/A											
RAIN/MM	122	97	99	127	178	188	196	193	152	147	170	157
°C AVG MAX	29.6	29.6	29.6	30.1	29.6	29.0	29.6	29.0	29.6	30.1	29.6	29.6
°C AVG MIN	19.6	19.6	19.6	20.1	19.6	19.6	19.6	19.6	19.6	19.6	19.6	19.6
DIURNAL RANGE	10.0	10.0	10.0	10.0	10.0	9.4	10.0	9.4	10.0	10.5	10.0	10.0
S/HEMISPHERE	JUL	AUG	SEP	OCT	NOV	DEC	JAN	FEB	MAR	APR	MAY	JUN

Cultural Recommendations

LIGHT: 1800–3000 fc.

TEMPERATURES: Throughout the year, days average 84–86°F (29–30°C), and nights average 67–68°F (20°C), with a diurnal range of 17–19°F (9–11°C). Because the probable extremes are only about 10°F (6°C) above and below average highs and lows and there is no seasonal variation in temperatures, plants probably cannot tolerate wide temperature fluctuations.

HUMIDITY: Information is not available for this location. However, records from nearby locations indicate that humidity probably averages 80–85% year-round.

WATER: Rainfall is moderate all year. Cultivated plants should be kept moist, and only slight drying allowed between waterings.

FERTILIZER: ¼–½ recommended strength. A balanced fertilizer should be applied weekly to biweekly throughout the year.

REST PERIOD: Growing conditions should be maintained all year. Rainfall is somewhat lower for 2–3 months in winter, and water should be reduced for cultivated plants. They should be allowed to dry slightly between waterings, but should not remain dry for long periods.

GROWING MEDIA: Plants may be mounted on tree-fern or cork slabs or potted in small pots filled with any open, fast-draining medium. Repotting may be done anytime new roots are actively growing.

MISCELLANEOUS NOTES: Vegetative plant parts were not available when the blossom was described.

Plant and Flower Information

PLANT SIZE AND TYPE: A sympodial plant of unreported size. The plant was described on the basis of just the flower.

FLOWERS: The flowers are 1.2 in. (3 cm) long. The wide, oval sepals and oblong petals are white with yellowish on the backside of the sepals. The dorsal sepal is marked with brownish-purple on the backside. Lateral sepals each have 2 streaks. The white lip has an orange disk.

REFERENCES: 216, 254, 286, 295, 297, 394, 445.

Dendrobium lucidum Schlechter not J. J. Smith

ORIGIN/HABITAT: Northeastern Papua New Guinea. Plants grow on moss-covered mistforest trees in the Dischore Range at about 3950 ft. (1200 m).

CLIMATE: Station #200192, Garaina, Papua New Guinea, Lat. 7.9°S, Long. 147.1°E, at 2350 ft. (716 m). Temperatures are calculated for an elevation of 3950 ft. (1200 m), resulting in probable extremes of 89°F (32°C) and 41°F (5°C).

N/HEMISPHERE	JAN	FEB	MAR	APR	MAY	JUN	JUL	AUG	SEP	OCT	NOV	DEC
°F AVG MAX	75	77	78	79	80	80	80	80	79	79	78	76
°F AVG MIN	58	58	58	59	58	59	60	60	60	59	59	58
DIURNAL RANGE	17	19	20	20	22	21	20	20	19	20	19	18
RAIN/INCHES	5.8	6.5	8.7	11.1	11.8	11.9	8.9	11.7	11.5	9.9	7.7	5.2
HUMIDITY/%	84	82	82	81	80	80	81	81	82	83	84	84
BLOOM SEASON												*
DAYS CLR	N/A											
RAIN/MM	147	165	221	282	300	302	226	297	292	251	196	132
°C AVG MAX	23.8	24.9	25.4	26.0	26.5	26.5	26.5	26.5	26.0	26.0	25.4	24.3
°C AVG MIN	14.3	14.3	14.3	14.9	14.3	14.9	15.4	15.4	15.4	14.9	14.9	14.3
DIURNAL RANGE	9.5	10.6	11.1	11.1	12.2	11.6	11.1	11.1	10.6	11.1	10.5	10.0
S/HEMISPHERE	JUL	AUG	SEP	OCT	NOV	DEC	JAN	FEB	MAR	APR	MAY	JUN

Cultural Recommendations

LIGHT: 2000–3000 fc.

TEMPERATURES: Throughout the year, days average 75–80°F (24–27°C), and nights average 58–60°F (14–15°C), with a diurnal range of 17–22°F (10–12°C).

HUMIDITY: 80–85% year-round.

WATER: Rainfall is moderate to heavy all year. Conditions are only slightly drier in winter. Cultivated plants should be kept moist but not soggy.

FERTILIZER: ¼–½ recommended strength. A balanced fertilizer should be applied weekly to biweekly throughout the year.

REST PERIOD: Growing conditions vary only slightly during the year. Water should be reduced somewhat for plants grown in the dark, short-day conditions common during temperate-latitude winters, but they should never be allowed to dry out completely. Fertilizer should be reduced or eliminated anytime water is reduced. In the habitat, light is highest in winter.

GROWING MEDIA: Plants may be mounted on tree-fern or cork slabs if humidity is high and plants are watered at least once daily in summer. When plants are potted, any open, fast-draining medium may be used. Repotting may be done anytime new roots are growing.

MISCELLANEOUS NOTES: The bloom season shown in the climate table is based on collection reports.

Plant and Flower Information

PLANT SIZE AND TYPE: A 4–6 in. (10–15 cm) sympodial epiphyte.

PSEUDOBULB: 4–6 in. (10–15 cm) long. The erect or spreading stems arise from a short, decumbent rhizome. The stems are densely leafy.

LEAVES: Many. The tongue-shaped leaves are 0.5–0.9 in. (1.3–2.3 cm) long. They are shiny, somewhat fleshy, and nearly transparent.

INFLORESCENCE: Inflorescences arise from nodes along the side of the stem.

FLOWERS: 1 per inflorescence. The tiny white flowers are 0.1 in. (0.3 cm) across and only last a few days. The lip, which is marked with red, is uppermost. Schlechter (ref. 437) considered this plant to be the smallest flowered species in the genus.

REFERENCES: 92, 221, 437, 445.

PHOTOS/DRAWINGS: 437.

Dendrobium lucidum (Schlechter) J. J. Smith

AKA: *Cadetia lucida* Schlechter. Originally described as a *Cadetia* and transferred to the genus *Dendrobium* by J. J. Smith at the same time that a different plant was described as a *Dendrobium lucidum*. Since *Cadetia* is now accepted as a valid genus by some botanists, this plant may again be considered a *Cadetia*.

ORIGIN/HABITAT: Northern Papua New Guinea. Plants grow in the forests near Danip at about 350 ft. (100 m).

CLIMATE: Station #94014, Madang, Papua New Guinea, Lat. 5.2°S, Long. 145.8°E, at 13 ft. (4 m). Temperatures are calculated for an elevation of 500 ft. (150 m), resulting in probable extremes of 96°F (36°C) and 60°F (16°C).

N/HEMISPHERE	JAN	FEB	MAR	APR	MAY	JUN	JUL	AUG	SEP	OCT	NOV	DEC
°F AVG MAX	81	81	83	83	83	83	83	83	83	85	85	82
°F AVG MIN	75	76	76	76	75	75	75	75	75	74	75	76
DIURNAL RANGE	6	5	7	7	8	8	8	8	8	11	10	6
RAIN/INCHES	4.0	3.4	3.2	8.5	11.2	11.1	10.1	11.3	9.4	11.3	10.5	6.7
HUMIDITY/%	88	87	86	86	86	86	86	85	85	87	88	89
BLOOM SEASON									*			
DAYS CLR	N/A											
RAIN/MM	102	86	81	216	284	282	257	287	239	287	267	170
°C AVG MAX	27.4	27.4	28.6	28.6	28.6	28.6	28.6	28.6	28.6	29.7	29.7	28.0
°C AVG MIN	24.1	24.7	24.7	24.7	24.1	24.1	24.1	24.1	24.1	23.6	24.1	24.7
DIURNAL RANGE	3.3	2.7	3.9	3.9	4.5	4.5	4.5	4.5	4.5	6.1	5.6	3.3
S/HEMISPHERE	JUL	AUG	SEP	OCT	NOV	DEC	JAN	FEB	MAR	APR	MAY	JUN

Cultural Recommendations

LIGHT: 2000–3000 fc.

TEMPERATURES: Throughout the year, days average 81–85°F (27–30°C), and nights average 74–76°F (24–25°C), with a diurnal range of 5–11°F (3–6°C). The warmest highs, the coolest lows, and the greatest diurnal range occur in autumn.

HUMIDITY: Near 85–90% year-round.

WATER: Rainfall is heavy during the growing season and moderate in midwinter. Cultivated plants should be kept moist.

FERTILIZER: ¼–½ recommended strength. A balanced fertilizer should be applied weekly to biweekly throughout the year.

REST PERIOD: Growing temperatures should be maintained all year. In the habitat, rainfall decreases for 4 months in winter. Water should be reduced for cultivated plants until light increases in spring. Fertilizer should be eliminated or reduced to once every 3–4 weeks. In the habitat, light is slightly higher in winter.

GROWING MEDIA: Plants may be mounted on tree-fern or cork slabs or potted in small pots filled with any open, fast-draining medium. Repotting may be done anytime new roots are growing.

MISCELLANEOUS NOTES: The bloom season shown in the climate table is based on reports from the habitat.

Plant and Flower Information

PLANT SIZE AND TYPE: A 4–5 in. (10–13 cm) sympodial epiphyte.

PSEUDOBULB: 1.4–2.4 in. (3.5–6.0 cm) long. The obscurely quadrangular stems are densely clustered on a very short rhizome.

LEAVES: 1 per growth. The oblong leaves are 1.6–2.2 in. (4.0–5.5 cm) long, shiny, and erect.

INFLORESCENCE: Short. Inflorescences emerge at the apex of the pseudobulb.

FLOWERS: 1 per inflorescence. The white flowers are 0.4 in. (1 cm) across. The oblong dorsal sepal and narrow petals arch over the lip. The broad, keeled lateral sepals are held below the lip. The 3-lobed lip has elongated sidelobes and broad midlobe divided into 2 distinct lobes with a point in the center notch.

REFERENCES: 221, 437, 472.

PHOTOS/DRAWINGS: 437.

Dendrobium luebbersianum Rchb. f. See *D. williamsonii* Day and Rchb. f. REFERENCES: 216, 254, 429.

Dendrobium lueckelianum H. Fessel and M. Wolff

ORIGIN/HABITAT: Thailand. Seidenfaden (ref. 454) indicated that a plant similar to this was collected near Phu Krading at 3950–4250 ft. (1200–1300 m). Specific habitat information is unavailable, so the following climate data should be used with caution.

CLIMATE: Station #48353, Loei, Thailand, Lat. 17.5°N, Long. 101.5°E, at 817 ft. (249 m). Temperatures are calculated for an estimated elevation of 3500 ft. (1070 m), resulting in probable extremes of 97°F (36°C) and 25°F (−4°C).

N/HEMISPHERE	JAN	FEB	MAR	APR	MAY	JUN	JUL	AUG	SEP	OCT	NOV	DEC
°F AVG MAX	76	80	85	88	84	82	81	80	79	78	78	75
°F AVG MIN	43	49	56	61	64	65	65	65	64	60	55	47
DIURNAL RANGE	33	31	29	27	20	17	16	15	15	18	23	28
RAIN/INCHES	0.2	0.8	1.4	3.6	6.9	6.8	5.0	8.3	8.8	4.3	0.8	0.1
HUMIDITY/%	62	60	59	62	75	77	77	79	82	79	74	69
BLOOM SEASON		*	*	*								
DAYS CLR @ 7AM	1	1	1	2	1	0	1	0	0	1	1	1
DAYS CLR @ 1PM	22	14	8	5	2	0	0	1	1	5	11	15
RAIN/MM	5	20	36	91	175	173	127	211	224	109	20	3
°C AVG MAX	24.5	26.7	29.5	31.2	29.0	27.9	27.3	26.7	26.2	25.6	25.6	24.0
°C AVG MIN	6.2	9.5	13.4	16.2	17.9	18.4	18.4	18.4	17.9	15.6	12.9	8.4
DIURNAL RANGE	18.3	17.2	16.1	15.0	11.1	9.5	8.9	8.3	8.3	10.0	12.7	15.6
S/HEMISPHERE	JUL	AUG	SEP	OCT	NOV	DEC	JAN	FEB	MAR	APR	MAY	JUN

Cultural Recommendations

LIGHT: 2000–3000 fc. Diffused or barely dappled light is recommended. Direct sunlight should be avoided.

TEMPERATURES: Summer days average 80–82°F (27–28°C), and nights average 65°F (18°C), with a diurnal range of 15–17°F (8–10°C). The warmest temperatures occur in early spring. Days average 84–88°F (29–31°C), and nights average 56–64°F (13–18°C), with a diurnal range of 20–29°F (11–16°C).

HUMIDITY: Near 75–80% most of the year, dropping to about 60% for 4 months in winter and early spring.

WATER: Rainfall is heavy from late spring into autumn, but conditions are quite dry in winter. Cultivated plants should be kept evenly moist while actively growing, but water should be gradually reduced in autumn.

FERTILIZER: ¼–½ recommended strength, applied weekly. A high-nitrogen fertilizer is beneficial from spring to midsummer, but a fertilizer high in phosphates should be used in late summer and autumn.

REST PERIOD: Winter days average 75–80°F (24–27°C), and nights average 43–49°F (6–10°C), with a diurnal range of 28–33°F (16–18°C). For 3–5 months in winter, rainfall is low, but additional moisture is available from dew as well as mist from fog and low clouds. Cultivated plants need to dry out between waterings, but they should not remain completely dry for extended periods. Fertilizer should be eliminated. In the habitat, light is highest in winter.

GROWING MEDIA: Plants may be mounted on tree-fern or cork slabs if humidity is high and plants are watered at least once daily in summer. When plants are potted, any open, fast-draining medium may be used. They may be repotted anytime new roots are growing.

MISCELLANEOUS NOTES: Seidenfaden indicates that plants bloom late winter and early spring in nature, but imported plants bloomed in late summer and early autumn. Fessel, in *Die Orchidee* 41(2):37 (1990), describes this plant and includes photographs of the other closely related species *D. bellatulum* Rolfe, *D. fuerstenbergianum* Schlechter, and *D. christyanum* Rchb. f.

Plant and Flower Information

PLANT SIZE AND TYPE: A 6 in. (15 cm) sympodial epiphyte.

PSEUDOBULB: 3.5 in. (9 cm) long. The clustered stems are club-shaped. They are dark green with brownish markings.

Dendrobium lunatum

LEAVES: 5–8 per growth. The narrow leaves, which are 2.6 in. (6.5 cm) long, are arranged in 2 loose rows.

INFLORESCENCE: Short. Inflorescences emerge laterally from nodes on the stem.

FLOWERS: 1–2 per inflorescence. The cream-white flowers are 2 in. (5 cm) across. The 3-lobed lip has large sidelobes that come together above the column and a deeply notched midlobe with 3 prominent ridges. The center ridge becomes abruptly warty. In addition to the prominent ridges, there are 2 obscure ridges. The lip is marked with red and orange. The markings are darkest near the apex.

REFERENCES: 235, 454.

PHOTOS/DRAWINGS: See Miscellaneous Notes.

Dendrobium lunatum Lindley

ORIGIN/HABITAT: The Philippines. Plants grow on Palawan Island between sea level and 1650 ft. (0–500 m).

CLIMATE: Station #98618, Puerto Princesa, Palawan Island, Philippines, Lat. 9.7°N, Long. 118.8°E, at 20 ft. (6 m). Temperatures are calculated for an elevation of 1000 ft. (300 m), resulting in probable extremes of 93°F (34°C) and 62°F (17°C).

N/HEMISPHERE	JAN	FEB	MAR	APR	MAY	JUN	JUL	AUG	SEP	OCT	NOV	DEC
°F AVG MAX	84	85	86	88	87	85	84	84	84	85	85	84
°F AVG MIN	70	70	71	72	73	72	71	71	71	71	71	71
DIURNAL RANGE	14	15	15	16	14	13	13	13	13	14	14	13
RAIN/INCHES	1.4	1.0	2.2	1.5	5.7	6.7	7.3	7.8	7.8	7.6	7.5	5.2
HUMIDITY/%	84	82	82	81	84	87	87	88	87	87	87	86
BLOOM SEASON				*	*	*			*			
DAYS CLR @ 8AM	8	6	11	10	6	4	3	4	6	6	6	
DAYS CLR @ 2PM	5	4	6	8	4	1	1	1	1	2	2	3
RAIN/MM	35	25	56	38	146	170	185	199	197	192	190	133
°C AVG MAX	28.8	29.3	29.9	31.0	30.4	29.3	28.8	28.8	28.8	29.3	29.3	28.8
°C AVG MIN	21.0	21.0	21.5	22.1	22.6	22.1	21.5	21.5	21.5	21.5	21.5	21.5
DIURNAL RANGE	7.8	8.3	8.4	8.9	7.8	7.2	7.3	7.3	7.3	7.8	7.8	7.3
S/HEMISPHERE	JUL	AUG	SEP	OCT	NOV	DEC	JAN	FEB	MAR	APR	MAY	JUN

Cultural Recommendations

LIGHT: 2500–3500 fc.

TEMPERATURES: Throughout the year, days average 84–88°F (29–31°C), and nights average 70–73°F (21–23°C), with a diurnal range of 13–16°F (7–9°C). The average lows vary only 3°F (2°C) and the probable extremes are about 10°F (6°C) above and below the averages, thus suggesting that plants may not tolerate wide seasonal temperature fluctuations.

HUMIDITY: 80–90% year-round.

WATER: Rainfall is moderate most of the year, but conditions are relatively dry in winter and early spring. Cultivated plants should be kept moist while actively growing, but water should be gradually reduced in late autumn.

FERTILIZER: ¼–½ recommended strength. A balanced fertilizer should be applied weekly to biweekly throughout the year.

REST PERIOD: Growing temperatures should be maintained all year. Winter rainfall is somewhat lower in the habitat, and water should be reduced for cultivated plants. They should dry slightly between waterings, but they should not remain dry for long periods. Fertilizer should be reduced or eliminated. In the habitat, light is highest in winter.

GROWING MEDIA: Plants may be mounted on tree-fern or cork slabs if humidity is high and plants are watered at least once daily in summer. When plants are potted, any open, fast-draining medium may be used. Repotting may be done anytime new roots are growing.

MISCELLANEOUS NOTES: The bloom season shown in the climate table is based on collection reports.

Plant and Flower Information

PLANT SIZE AND TYPE: A 3.5–11.4 in. (9–29 cm) sympodial epiphyte.

PSEUDOBULB: 2.4–9.8 in. (6–25 cm) long. The rigid stems are pendulous and flattened.

LEAVES: Many. The dark green leaves are 1.2–1.6 in. (3–4 cm) long. They are rigid, lanceolate, and flattened.

INFLORESCENCE: Up to 11 inflorescences are produced from cushions of fibrous scales that cover nodes opposite rudimentary leaves on the upper part of the stem.

FLOWERS: Few per inflorescence. The clustered flowers are 0.2 in. (0.5 cm) across. They are white or pale yellow with purple markings especially at the base of the lip. The lateral sepals are very large, but the petals are very small.

REFERENCES: 12, 216, 254, 278, 296, 310, 536.

Dendrobium luteocilium Rupp

ORIGIN/HABITAT: Papua New Guinea and the northeast coast of Australia. In Australia, distribution extends northward from near the Tully River to the tip of the Cape York Peninsula. Plants are common in most lowland areas of Papua New Guinea, especially in Milne Bay Province. Plants grow in humid locations on rocks and trees in lowland rainforests and in mangrove swamps as well as in open areas. They are occasionally found at moderate elevations.

CLIMATE: Station #94003, Daru, Papua New Guinea, Lat. 9.1°S, Long. 143.2°E, at 20 ft. (6 m). Record extreme temperatures are 98°F (37°C) and 63°F (17°C).

N/HEMISPHERE	JAN	FEB	MAR	APR	MAY	JUN	JUL	AUG	SEP	OCT	NOV	DEC
°F AVG MAX	81	82	83	85	88	88	88	87	87	86	84	82
°F AVG MIN	74	74	74	76	76	76	76	76	76	76	77	75
DIURNAL RANGE	7	8	9	9	12	12	12	11	11	10	7	7
RAIN/INCHES	3.0	2.2	1.8	2.3	4.6	8.1	11.9	10.4	12.5	12.6	9.4	3.8
HUMIDITY/%	94	93	91	88	85	88	85	87	84	88	91	94
BLOOM SEASON		*		*		*	*	*	*			
DAYS CLR	N/A											
RAIN/MM	76	56	46	58	117	206	302	264	318	320	239	97
°C AVG MAX	27.2	27.8	28.3	29.4	31.1	31.1	31.1	30.6	30.6	30.0	28.9	27.8
°C AVG MIN	23.3	23.3	23.3	24.4	24.4	24.4	24.4	24.4	24.4	24.4	25.0	23.9
DIURNAL RANGE	3.9	4.5	5.0	5.0	6.7	6.7	6.7	6.2	6.2	5.6	3.9	3.9
S/HEMISPHERE	JUL	AUG	SEP	OCT	NOV	DEC	JAN	FEB	MAR	APR	MAY	JUN

Cultural Recommendations

LIGHT: 2500–3500 fc. Cultivated plants need about 50% shade in summer.

TEMPERATURES: Throughout the year, days average 81–88°F (27–31°C), and nights average 74–77°F (23–25°C), with a diurnal range of 7–12°F (4–7°C).

HUMIDITY: 85–90% from spring to autumn, increasing to 90–95% in winter.

WATER: Rainfall is moderate to heavy from late spring through autumn, with a 2–3 month drier season in late winter and early spring. Cultivated plants should be kept moist while actively growing, but water should be gradually reduced in late autumn.

FERTILIZER: ¼–½ recommended strength. A balanced fertilizer should be applied weekly to biweekly throughout the year.

REST PERIOD: Growing conditions should be maintained all year. Plants are healthiest with high humidity, good light, and strong air movement. Rainfall is relatively low for 2–3 months. However, winter humidity exceeds 90%, so large quantities of water are available from nightly dew. Cultivated plants should be allowed to dry slightly between waterings, but should not remain dry for long periods. Growers indicate that plants from this habitat are usually healthiest when kept moist year-round, but they do not do well with wet feet or stale, soggy medium.

Fertilizer should be reduced until water is increased in spring. In the habitat, light is probably higher in winter.

GROWING MEDIA: Plants may be potted in a any open medium that retains moderate amounts of moisture. Repotting may be done anytime new roots are growing.

MISCELLANEOUS NOTES: The bloom season shown in the climate table is based on reports from the habitat. Blooming may occur anytime in spring and summer. Plants that produce flowers which last a single day commonly bloom several times during the year. Flowering usually occurs 7–14 days after a sudden 10°F (5°C) drop in daytime temperatures. *D. luteocilium* grows quickly and begins blooming while very young.

Plant and Flower Information

PLANT SIZE AND TYPE: A 24–71 in. (60–180 cm) sympodial epiphyte or lithophyte. Plants slowly form massive clumps of 100 or more stems that are so heavy a man cannot move them, but cultivated plants remain manageable for many years.

PSEUDOBULB: 24–71 in. (60–180 cm) long. Plants may consist of a few woody stems, or they may form a large clump. Although normally erect, the often yellowish stems may droop when long.

LEAVES: Many. The ovate leaves are 1.6–5.0 in. (4–13 cm) long and alternate along most of the stem. They are dark green, thick, stiff, and unequally bilobed.

INFLORESCENCE: 0.2–0.4 in. (0.5–1.0 cm) long. Inflorescences arise opposite the leaves from nodes along the upper portion of the stem. Larger plants may have 6–12 flowering stems.

FLOWERS: 2 per inflorescence, hundreds per plant. The paired flowers, which face each other and remain rather closed, are 0.6–0.8 in. (1.5–2.0 cm) across. Blossoms are dull yellow or greenish yellow with orange, gold, or brown markings on the lip. Sepals and petals are rather narrow and bluntly pointed. They often last only a few hours, but during that time, they perfume the entire area with a honey fragrance.

HYBRIDIZING NOTES: Blossoms are self-pollinating.

REFERENCES: 24, 67, 105, 145, 227, 228, 240, 262, 263, 264, 302, 304, 352, 421, 533.

PHOTOS/DRAWINGS: 105, *145,* 240, *304, 533.*

Dendrobium luteolum Bateman

ORIGIN/HABITAT: Burma. Plants grow near Moulmein along streams at low elevations. The habitat was once thought to include peninsular Malaysia, but Seidenfaden and Wood (ref. 455) do not include *D. luteolum* as coming from that region.

CLIMATE: Station #48103, Moulmein, Burma, Lat. 16.4°N, Long. 97.7°E, at 150 ft. (46 m). Record extreme temperatures are 103°F (39°C) and 52°F (11°C).

N/HEMISPHERE	JAN	FEB	MAR	APR	MAY	JUN	JUL	AUG	SEP	OCT	NOV	DEC
°F AVG MAX	89	92	94	95	89	85	83	83	85	88	89	87
°F AVG MIN	66	68	73	76	76	75	75	75	75	75	73	68
DIURNAL RANGE	23	24	21	19	13	10	8	8	10	13	16	19
RAIN/INCHES	0.3	0.2	0.4	3.0	20.3	35.6	46.3	43.4	28.1	8.5	2.1	0.1
HUMIDITY/%	66	68	68	70	81	91	92	93	91	81	75	64
BLOOM SEASON		*	*	*	*							
DAYS CLR @ 7AM	12	7	5	6	1	0	0	0	0	3	7	12
DAYS CLR @ 1PM	20	13	10	8	3	0	0	0	0	4	12	17
RAIN/MM	8	5	10	76	516	904	1176	1102	714	216	53	3
°C AVG MAX	31.7	33.3	34.4	35.0	31.7	29.4	28.3	28.3	29.4	31.1	31.7	30.6
°C AVG MIN	18.9	20.0	22.8	24.4	24.4	23.9	23.9	23.9	23.9	23.9	22.8	20.0
DIURNAL RANGE	12.8	13.3	11.6	10.6	7.3	5.5	4.4	4.4	5.5	7.2	8.9	10.6
S/HEMISPHERE	JUL	AUG	SEP	OCT	NOV	DEC	JAN	FEB	MAR	APR	MAY	JUN

Cultural Recommendations

LIGHT: 2000–3000 fc.

TEMPERATURES: Summer days average 83–85°F (28–29°C), and nights average 75°F (24°C), with a diurnal range of 8–10°F (4–6°C). Spring is the warmest season. Days average 89–95°F (32–35°C), and nights average 73–76°F (23–24°C), with a diurnal range of 13–21°F (7–12°C). Plants should be heat tolerant.

HUMIDITY: 80% or more in summer, dropping to 65–70% in winter and early spring.

WATER: Rainfall is extremely heavy for 5 months in summer, but conditions become quite dry for 4 months in winter. From late spring into autumn, cultivated plants should be kept moist but not soggy. Water should be gradually reduced after new growths mature in autumn. Warm water is highly recommended. Good air circulation and excellent drainage are particularly important.

FERTILIZER: ¼–½ recommended strength, applied weekly. A high-nitrogen fertilizer is beneficial from spring to midsummer, but a fertilizer high in phosphates should be used in late summer and autumn.

REST PERIOD: Winter days average 87–92°F (31–33°C), and nights average 66–68°F (19–20°C), with a diurnal range of 19–24°F (11–13°C). The larger winter diurnal range results from warmer days and cooler nights. Rainfall is low for 3–4 winter months in the habitat, but growers report that a 1-month dry rest may be sufficient to induce flowering. In cultivation, water should be reduced and the plants allowed to dry out between waterings. They should not remain completely dry for extended periods, however. In the habitat, light is highest in winter.

GROWING MEDIA: Plants may be mounted on tree-fern or cork slabs if humidity is high and plants are watered at least once daily in summer. When plants are potted, any open, fast-draining medium may be used. Repotting may be done anytime new roots are growing.

MISCELLANEOUS NOTES: The bloom season shown in the climate table is based on cultivation records. In Burma, blooming usually occurs in winter.

Plant and Flower Information

PLANT SIZE AND TYPE: A 13–22 in. (33–56 cm) sympodial epiphyte.

PSEUDOBULB: 10–18 in. (25–46 cm) long. The erect stems are grayish white, often with dull purple stripes. The stems become furrowed with age.

LEAVES: The leaves are 3–4 in. (8–10 cm) long, linear to lanceolate, and leathery.

INFLORESCENCE: Short. Many inflorescences are produced from upper nodes of leafy stems.

FLOWERS: 2–4 per inflorescence. Described as distinct and desirable, the fragrant flowers are 2.0–2.4 in. (5–6 cm) across. They have a heavy texture and last several weeks. The sepals and petals are uniformly pale primrose-yellow. The yellow lip is marked with reddish veins between the sidelobes. The downy, deeper yellow disk has 3–5 ridges. The variety known as *D. luteolum* var. *chlorocentrum* Rchb. f., which has greenish hairs on the lip, is said to have larger flowers with heavier substance.

REFERENCES: 107, 157, 179, 190, 202, 210, 216, 254, 445, 541, 570.

PHOTOS/DRAWINGS: *107,* 210, 541, 570.

Dendrobium luxurians J. J. Smith. Now considered a synonym of *Flickingeria luxurians* (J. J. Smith) A. Hawkes. REFERENCES: 25, 75, 111, 200, 213, 216, 223, 230, 231, 286, 445, 449, 455.

Dendrobium luzonense Lindley

AKA: *D. alagense* Ames.

Dendrobium lycopodioides

ORIGIN/HABITAT: The Philippine Islands. Plants grow on Luzon, Mindanao, Mindoro, and Leyte Islands. They are found on trees between sea level and 4250 ft. (0–1300 m).

CLIMATE: Station #98439, Daet, Luzon, Philippines, Lat. 14.1°N, Long. 122.9°E, at 36 ft. (11 m). Temperatures are calculated for an elevation of 2300 ft. (700 m), resulting in probable extremes of 94°F (34°C) and 53°F (11°C).

N/HEMISPHERE	JAN	FEB	MAR	APR	MAY	JUN	JUL	AUG	SEP	OCT	NOV	DEC
°F AVG MAX	76	77	79	82	84	85	83	83	83	81	79	77
°F AVG MIN	65	65	66	67	68	68	68	68	67	67	67	66
DIURNAL RANGE	11	12	13	15	16	17	15	15	16	14	12	11
RAIN/INCHES	16.2	7.8	7.0	4.9	5.7	5.9	7.9	9.4	10.5	19.3	22.8	21.7
HUMIDITY/%	82	81	81	81	81	80	83	83	84	84	84	84
BLOOM SEASON				*	*				*	*	*	*
DAYS CLR @ 8AM	3	4	7	10	8	8	4	4	4	4	3	3
DAYS CLR @ 2PM	3	5	9	10	9	3	1	1	1	3	3	2
RAIN/MM	411	198	178	124	145	150	201	239	267	490	579	551
°C AVG MAX	24.2	24.7	25.8	27.5	28.6	29.2	28.1	28.1	28.1	27.0	25.8	24.7
°C AVG MIN	18.1	18.1	18.6	19.2	19.7	19.7	19.7	19.7	19.2	19.2	19.2	18.6
DIURNAL RANGE	6.1	6.6	7.2	8.3	8.9	9.5	8.4	8.4	8.9	7.8	6.6	6.1
S/HEMISPHERE	JUL	AUG	SEP	OCT	NOV	DEC	JAN	FEB	MAR	APR	MAY	JUN

Cultural Recommendations

LIGHT: 2500–3500 fc.

TEMPERATURES: Summer days average 83–85°F (28–29°C), and nights average 68°F (20°C), with a diurnal range of 15–17°F (8–10°C).

HUMIDITY: 80–85% year-round.

WATER: Rainfall is moderate to heavy all year. Cultivated plants should be kept evenly moist.

FERTILIZER: ¼–½ recommended strength. A balanced fertilizer should be applied weekly to biweekly throughout the year.

REST PERIOD: Winter days average 76–79°F (24–26°C), and nights average 65–66°F (18–19°C), with a diurnal range of 11–13°F (6–7°C). Warm growing conditions should be maintained year-round with only a slight decrease in temperatures during winter. Cultivated plants should be kept moist, but water should be reduced slightly in winter, especially for plants grown in the dark, short-day conditions common in temperate latitudes. Plants should never be allowed to dry out completely, however. Fertilizer should be reduced if water is reduced. In the habitat, light is highest in spring.

GROWING MEDIA: Plants may be mounted on tree-fern or cork slabs if humidity is high and plants are watered at least once daily in summer. When plants are potted, any open, fast-draining medium may be used. Repotting may be done anytime new roots are growing.

MISCELLANEOUS NOTES: The bloom season shown in the climate table is based on collection reports.

Plant and Flower Information

PLANT SIZE AND TYPE: A 24 in. (60 cm) sympodial epiphyte.

PSEUDOBULB: 24 in. (60 cm) long. The stems are smooth.

LEAVES: The pointed, grasslike leaves are 5.5 in. (14 cm) long. They are distichous and closely set.

INFLORESCENCE: Inflorescences arise opposite the leaves from bracts on the stem.

FLOWERS: 2 per inflorescence. The flowers are 0.8 in. (2 cm) across. Sepals and petals are a pale straw color sometimes with a greenish tinge. The 3-lobed lip has raised longitudinal veins, small sidelobes, and a rounded midlobe.

REFERENCES: 12, 216, 254, 296, 317, 445, 536.

Dendrobium lycopodioides Lindley

ORIGIN/HABITAT: The forests of Sarawak, Borneo. Elevation was not included with the original description, so the following climate data should be used with caution.

CLIMATE: Station #96413, Kuching, Sarawak, Lat. 1.5°N, Long. 110.3°E, at 85 ft. (26 m). Record extreme temperatures are 97°F (36°C) and 64°F (18°C).

N/HEMISPHERE	JAN	FEB	MAR	APR	MAY	JUN	JUL	AUG	SEP	OCT	NOV	DEC
°F AVG MAX	88	88	89	90	91	91	91	92	90	90	90	88
°F AVG MIN	72	72	72	72	72	73	72	72	72	72	72	72
DIURNAL RANGE	16	16	17	18	19	18	19	20	18	18	18	16
RAIN/INCHES	27.1	19.7	14.2	9.7	9.0	8.5	6.9	8.8	9.5	12.6	13.1	20.1
HUMIDITY/%	89	88	86	85	85	83	82	83	84	85	87	88
BLOOM SEASON	N/A											
DAYS CLR @ 7AM	1	0	1	2	3	2	4	1	2	1	1	1
DAYS CLR @ 1PM	0	0	0	0	1	1	1	0	0	0	0	0
RAIN/MM	688	500	361	246	229	216	175	224	241	320	333	511
°C AVG MAX	31.1	31.1	31.7	32.2	32.8	32.8	32.8	33.3	32.2	32.2	32.2	31.1
°C AVG MIN	22.2	22.2	22.2	22.2	22.2	22.8	22.2	22.2	22.2	22.2	22.2	22.2
DIURNAL RANGE	8.9	8.9	9.5	10.0	10.6	10.0	10.6	11.1	10.0	10.0	10.0	8.9
S/HEMISPHERE	JUL	AUG	SEP	OCT	NOV	DEC	JAN	FEB	MAR	APR	MAY	JUN

Cultural Recommendations

LIGHT: 2000–3000 fc.

TEMPERATURES: Throughout the year, days average 88–92°F (31–33°C), and nights average 72–73°F (22–23°C), with a diurnal range of 16–20°F (9–11°C). The diurnal range is unusually large for a habitat with so little seasonal variation.

HUMIDITY: 80–90% year-round. High humidity and excellent air circulation are important for cultivated plants.

WATER: Rainfall is very heavy all year. Plants should be kept very moist but not soggy. Warm water may be beneficial.

FERTILIZER: ¼–½ recommended strength. A balanced fertilizer should be applied weekly to biweekly throughout the year.

REST PERIOD: Growing conditions should be maintained all year. The lower diurnal range in winter results from cooler days, not cooler nights. The record low is only 10°F (6°C) below the average lows. Water may be reduced for cultivated plants, especially those grown in the dark, short-day conditions common in temperate-latitude winters. They should not be allowed to dry out completely, however. In the habitat, light is highest in winter.

GROWING MEDIA: Plants may be mounted on tree-fern or cork slabs if humidity is high and plants are watered at least once daily in summer. However, pot culture is recommended because of the large water requirement. When plants are potted, any open, fast-draining medium may be used. They may be repotted anytime new roots are growing.

Plant and Flower Information

PLANT SIZE AND TYPE: A 3 in. (8 cm) sympodial epiphyte.

PSEUDOBULB: 3 in. (8 cm) long. The densely leafy stems are branching.

LEAVES: Many. The distichous leaves are 0.6 in. (1.5 cm) long. They are linear-lanceolate.

INFLORESCENCE: Short.

FLOWERS: 1 per inflorescence. The nearly round flowers are less than 0.2 in. (0.5 cm) across. The lip is nearly covered by 2 fleshy, parallel plates. Flower color was not included in the original description.

REFERENCES: 216, 254, 278, 286, 295, 310, 394.

Dendrobium lyonii Ames

AKA: Now considered to be *Epigeneium lyonii*, but plants are commonly sold, cultivated, and shown as *Dendrobium lyonii*. Synonyms include *Epigeneium lyonii* (Ames) Summerhayes, *Dendrobium acuminatum* Lyon var. *lyonii* (Ames) Kränzlin, *Sarcopodium lyonii* (Ames) Rolfe, S.

acuminatum var. *lyonii* (Ames) Kränzlin, and *Katherinea acuminata* var. *lyonii* (Ames) A. Hawkes.

ORIGIN/HABITAT: The Philippines. On Luzon Island, the plants grow in the provinces of Bataan, Benquet, Kalinga-Apayao, Quezon, and Rizal at 1950–3600 ft. (600–1100 m).

CLIMATE: Station #98427, Manila, Luzon, Philippines, Lat. 14.5°N, Long. 121.0°E, at 74 ft. (23 m). Temperatures are calculated for an elevation of 3000 ft. (914 m), resulting in probable extremes of 91°F (33°C) and 48°F (9°C).

N/HEMISPHERE	JAN	FEB	MAR	APR	MAY	JUN	JUL	AUG	SEP	OCT	NOV	DEC
°F AVG MAX	76	78	81	83	83	81	78	77	78	78	77	76
°F AVG MIN	59	59	61	63	65	65	65	65	65	64	62	60
DIURNAL RANGE	17	19	20	20	18	16	13	12	13	14	15	16
RAIN/INCHES	0.9	0.5	0.7	1.3	5.1	10.0	17.0	16.6	14.0	7.6	5.7	2.6
HUMIDITY/%	77	73	70	68	71	81	84	86	87	84	82	79
BLOOM SEASON			*	*	**	*	**	*				
DAYS CLR @ 8AM	6	9	14	14	10	3	2	1	1	6	7	6
DAYS CLR @ 2PM	3	6	10	10	8	2	1	1	0	2	2	3
RAIN/MM	23	13	18	33	130	254	432	422	356	193	145	66
°C AVG MAX	24.6	25.7	27.4	28.5	28.5	27.4	25.7	25.2	25.7	25.2	25.2	24.6
°C AVG MIN	15.2	15.2	16.3	17.4	18.5	18.5	18.5	18.5	18.5	18.0	16.9	15.7
DIURNAL RANGE	9.4	10.5	11.1	11.1	10.0	8.9	7.2	6.7	7.2	7.7	8.3	8.9
S/HEMISPHERE	JUL	AUG	SEP	OCT	NOV	DEC	JAN	FEB	MAR	APR	MAY	JUN

Cultural Recommendations

LIGHT: 2500–3000 fc.

TEMPERATURES: Summer days average 77–81°F (25–27°C), and nights average 65°F (19°C), with a diurnal range of 12–16°F (7–9°C).

HUMIDITY: Near 80–85% from summer through autumn. Humidity drops to 70–75% in winter and spring.

WATER: Rainfall is heavy from late spring into autumn, but amounts are much lower in winter. Cultivated plants should be kept evenly moist while actively growing, but water should be gradually reduced in autumn.

FERTILIZER: ¼–½ recommended strength, applied weekly. A high-nitrogen fertilizer is beneficial from spring to midsummer, but a fertilizer high in phosphates should be used in late summer and autumn.

REST PERIOD: Winter days average 76–81°F (25–27°C), and nights average 59–61°F (15–16°C), with a diurnal range of 16–20°F (9–11°C). Although rainfall is low for 4 months in winter, the high humidity and nightly cooling result in frequent and heavy deposits of dew. For cultivated plants, water should be reduced and the plants allowed to dry slightly between waterings. They should not remain dry for long periods, however. Fertilizer should be reduced or eliminated when water is reduced. In the habitat, light is highest in late winter and spring.

GROWING MEDIA: Plants are usually grown in pots or baskets filled with an open, fast-draining medium. Varying amounts of water-retaining additives such as perlite or chopped sphagnum moss may be combined with a base material of fine to medium sized fir bark or tree-fern fiber. Another popular medium consists of chopped tree-fern fiber mixed with about 10% fine charcoal, 10% perlite or sponge rock, and 10% chopped sphagnum moss or Amazon orchid moss. Growers report good success using a basket made from ¼ in. (6 mm) mesh hardware cloth lined with a layer of coconut fiber. If the plant outgrows the basket, it can be moved en masse and placed in a larger basket without disturbing the roots. This can be an important consideration because these plants often respond very slowly after being divided or repotted. When repotting is necessary, it should be done only when a flush of new root growth is just starting. This allows the plant to become established as rapidly as possible.

MISCELLANEOUS NOTES: The bloom season shown in the climate table is based on cultivation records. Growers indicate that plants do not survive cultivation in Manila for more than 2 years, but grow well in Honolulu, which is about 10°F (6°C) cooler.

Plant and Flower Information

PLANT SIZE AND TYPE: An 9–13 in. (22–33 cm) sympodial epiphyte.

PSEUDOBULB: 2–3 in. (5–7 cm) long. The squat, ovoid pseudobulbs, which are 4-angled, shiny, and greenish yellow, have a papery sheath at the base. They become minutely pitted when dry.

LEAVES: 2 per growth. The bilobed leaves are 7–10 in. (17–25 cm) long, oblong to elliptical, and leathery. They arise from the top of each pseudobulb.

INFLORESCENCE: 10–20 in. (25–50 cm) long. Inflorescences emerge from the base of the pseudobulb. They may be arching or pendant.

FLOWERS: 6–8, rarely as many as 20 per inflorescence. The large flowers are usually 2.5–3.0 in. (6.4–7.5 cm) across, but they may be as large as 5 in. (12.5 cm). They open fully. They are star-shaped, fragrant, and well spaced along the inflorescence. The lance-shaped sepals and petals are whitish with greenish-yellow at the tips and purplish-red at the base. The lip is maroon at the base and on the sidelobes, but the slender, pointed tip is whitish.

HYBRIDIZING NOTES: Chromosome count is 2n = 40 (ref. 151, 187, 504).

REFERENCES: 12, 36, 98, 151, 187, 190, 196, 220, 229, 296, 373, 445, 499, 504, 536.

PHOTOS/DRAWINGS: 98, 373, 536.

Dendrobium lyperanthiflorum Kränzlin. See *D. insigne* (Blume) Rchb. f. ex Miquel. REFERENCES: 220, 253, 270, 437, 444, 445, 470, 533.

Dendrobium mabelae Gammie

ORIGIN/HABITAT: Endemic to India, including Western Ghats and the northern portions of Kanara and Karnataka provinces. In the southern peninsular region of Kerala, plants are endangered or extinct. Habitat elevation is estimated, so the following climate data should be used with caution.

CLIMATE: Station #43371, Trivandrum, India, Lat. 8.5°N, Long. 76.9°E, at 15 ft. (5 m). Temperatures are calculated for an elevation of 4000 ft. (1220 m), resulting in probable extremes of 87°F (31°C) and 48°F (9°C).

N/HEMISPHERE	JAN	FEB	MAR	APR	MAY	JUN	JUL	AUG	SEP	OCT	NOV	DEC
°F AVG MAX	71	73	75	75	74	70	69	70	70	70	70	70
°F AVG MIN	59	61	64	65	65	63	62	62	62	62	61	60
DIURNAL RANGE	12	12	11	10	9	7	7	8	8	8	9	10
RAIN/INCHES	0.8	0.8	1.5	4.5	8.8	13.2	7.8	4.7	4.5	10.7	7.0	2.5
HUMIDITY/%	70	73	73	79	84	87	88	87	85	85	81	76
BLOOM SEASON						*	*	*				
DAYS CLR @ 5AM	5	8	9	6	3	2	1	3	2	1	7	7
DAYS CLR @ 11AM	11	6	8	2	0	0	0	0	1	1	4	7
RAIN/MM	20	20	38	114	224	335	198	119	114	272	178	64
°C AVG MAX	21.6	22.7	23.8	23.8	23.2	21.0	20.5	21.0	21.0	21.0	21.0	21.0
°C AVG MIN	14.9	16.0	17.7	18.2	18.2	17.1	16.6	16.6	16.6	16.6	16.0	15.5
DIURNAL RANGE	6.7	6.7	6.1	5.6	5.0	3.9	3.9	4.4	4.4	4.4	5.0	5.5
S/HEMISPHERE	JUL	AUG	SEP	OCT	NOV	DEC	JAN	FEB	MAR	APR	MAY	JUN

Cultural Recommendations

LIGHT: 2000–3000 fc. The heavy summer cloud cover indicates that some shading is needed from spring through autumn. However, light should be as high as the plant can tolerate short of burning the leaves.

TEMPERATURES: Throughout the year, days average 69–75°F (21–24°C), and nights average 59–65°F (15–18°C), with a diurnal range of 7–12°F (4–7°C).

HUMIDITY: Near 85% from late spring into autumn, dropping to 70–75% in winter.

WATER: Rainfall is moderate to heavy from spring through autumn. The winter dry season lasts 2–3 months. Cultivated plants should be kept moist from spring into autumn. Water should be gradually reduced in late autumn.

FERTILIZER: ¼–½ recommended strength. A balanced fertilizer should be applied weekly to biweekly throughout the growing season.

REST PERIOD: Growing conditions should be maintained all year. The warmest days and the coolest nights occur in winter, but the variations are minor. In cultivation, water should be reduced in winter. Plants should be allowed to dry between waterings, but they should not remain completely dry for extended periods. Cultivated plants usually benefit from an occasional early morning misting between waterings, especially on bright, sunny days. Fertilizer should be reduced or eliminated anytime water is reduced. In the habitat, light is highest in winter.

GROWING MEDIA: Plants may be mounted on tree-fern or cork slabs if humidity is high and plants are watered at least once daily in summer. When plants are potted, any open, fast-draining medium may be used. Repotting may be done anytime new roots are growing.

MISCELLANEOUS NOTES: The bloom season shown in the climate table is based on cultivation records. In nature, plants commonly bloom in late summer, but they may bloom as late as midwinter.

Plant and Flower Information

PLANT SIZE AND TYPE: A 2.4–3.5 in. (6–9 cm) sympodial epiphyte.

PSEUDOBULB: 0.6 in. (1.5 cm) long. The yellowish-green pseudobulbs may be ovoid or cone-shaped.

LEAVES: 2–4 per growth. The leaves are 1.6–3.1 in. (4–8 cm) long, oblong-lanceolate, and deciduous.

INFLORESCENCE: 2–5 in. (5–13 cm) long. Sometimes more than 1 inflorescence emerges from between the leaves at the apex of leafy (the northern form) or leafless (the southern form) pseudobulbs. They are somewhat zigzag. Blossoms face up on the inflorescence.

FLOWERS: 3–7 per inflorescence. The white flowers are 0.4–0.6 in. (1.0–1.5 cm) across. The obscurely 3-lobed lip is marked with reddish brown veins on the sidelobes and the pale yellow or yellowish green midlobe is suffused with pink. The margins of the nearly round midlobe have 2 rows of stiff glandular hairs along the margin. Santapau and Kapadia (ref. 424) indicate that plants take 2 forms. Plants from North Kanara have smaller flowers with pure white sepals and petals and a yellow lip. They bloom from leafless pseudobulbs.

HYBRIDIZING NOTES: Chromosome count is 2n = 38 (ref. 151, 542). In nature, plants are in fruit Oct.–Apr. (Apr.–Oct.).

REFERENCES: 38, 46, 151, 179, 219, 254, 255, 369, 424, 542.

PHOTOS/DRAWINGS: 424.

Dendrobium maboroense Schlechter. See *D. undatialatum* Schlechter. REFERENCES: 221, 385, 437.

Dendrobium maccarthiae Pfitz. See *D. maccarthiae* Thwaites. REFERENCES: 218.

Dendrobium maccarthiae Thwaites

AKA: *D. maccarthiae* Pfitz.

ORIGIN/HABITAT: Southern Sri Lanka (Ceylon). Plants were found near Ratuapoora, toward Point de Galle. An uncommon species, plants hang from tree trunks in wet, tropical, evergreen forests. Plants grow in areas where summer days are warmer than 80°F (27°C) and annual rainfall is more than 150 in. (3810 mm).

CLIMATE: Station #43497, Hambantota, Sri Lanka, Lat. 6.1°N, Long. 81.1°E, at 66 ft. (20 m). Temperatures are calculated for an elevation of 2000 ft. (610 m), resulting in probable extremes of 93°F (34°C) and 56°F (13°C).

N/HEMISPHERE	JAN	FEB	MAR	APR	MAY	JUN	JUL	AUG	SEP	OCT	NOV	DEC
°F AVG MAX	79	81	82	83	82	81	82	82	81	81	80	79
°F AVG MIN	66	66	67	69	71	70	70	69	69	69	67	66
DIURNAL RANGE	13	15	15	14	11	11	12	13	12	12	13	13
RAIN/INCHES	3.5	1.5	2.5	3.5	3.5	2.3	1.6	1.3	2.5	4.6	6.7	5.4
HUMIDITY/%	81	78	79	80	82	80	78	78	79	81	83	82
BLOOM SEASON		*		*		*		*		*		
DAYS CLR @ 5PM	4	8	8	4	6	1	5	2	4	5	5	4
RAIN/MM	89	38	64	89	89	58	41	33	64	117	170	137
°C AVG MAX	25.9	27.0	27.6	28.1	27.6	27.0	27.6	27.6	27.0	27.0	26.5	25.9
°C AVG MIN	18.7	18.7	19.2	20.3	21.5	20.9	20.9	20.3	20.3	20.3	19.2	18.7
DIURNAL RANGE	7.2	8.3	8.4	7.8	6.1	6.1	6.7	7.3	6.7	6.7	7.3	7.2
S/HEMISPHERE	JUL	AUG	SEP	OCT	NOV	DEC	JAN	FEB	MAR	APR	MAY	JUN

Cultural Recommendations

LIGHT: 2500–3500 fc. Reports from the habitat indicate that plants grow in 30–60% of full sun. Consequently, shading is required in summer to prevent burning the foliage. Strong, constant air movement is important.

TEMPERATURES: Throughout the year, days average 79–83°F (26–28°C), and nights average 66–71°F (19–22°C), with a diurnal range of 11–15°F (6–8°C).

HUMIDITY: Near 80% year-round.

WATER: Rainfall is much heavier in the habitat than indicated by the climate data for a low level, coastal station. However, the rainfall pattern should be similar for the higher elevation habitat. The rainfall pattern consists of 2 wet seasons, spring and autumn, and 2 somewhat drier seasons, late winter and late summer. Cultivated plants should be kept moist most of the year; but during the brief dry seasons, water should be reduced so that plants dry slightly between waterings. It is not known whether a double wet/dry rainfall pattern is important for *D. maccarthiae*, but this water pattern is needed to initiate flowers in many plants.

FERTILIZER: ¼–½ recommended strength. A balanced fertilizer should be applied weekly to biweekly throughout the year.

REST PERIOD: Growing temperatures should be maintained year-round. In the habitat, rainfall is slightly lower in winter. Water should be reduced for cultivated plants, especially those grown in the dark, short-day conditions common during temperate-latitude winters; but the plants should dry only slightly between waterings and should not remain dry for long periods. Fertilizer should be reduced or eliminated anytime water is reduced.

GROWING MEDIA: Mounting plants on tree-fern or cork slabs accommodates their pendulous growth habit. However, humidity must be high and plants must be watered at least once a day in summer. If plants cannot be mounted, small pots or hanging baskets may be filled with an open, fast-draining medium. Repotting may be done anytime new roots are actively growing.

MISCELLANEOUS NOTES: The bloom season shown in the climate table is based on cultivation records. *D. maccarthiae* is apparently very slow growing. Veitch (ref. 541) reported that it was difficult to grow because plants are short-lived and new growths often failed to mature before winter. Watson and Bean (ref. 557) recommend keeping the plants actively growing until midwinter, then giving a 2-month drier rest. They indicate that plants should be hung high in the greenhouse with maximum light, heat, and humidity. They also report that the plants were very scarce in their habitat.

Plant and Flower Information

PLANT SIZE AND TYPE: A 6–24 in. (15–60 cm) sympodial epiphyte.

PSEUDOBULB: 6–24 in. (15–60 cm) long. The green to grayish white stems have crimson spots and blackish joints. They are swollen at the base. Above the base, the very slender, quill-like stems are terete and pendulous.

LEAVES: Few, at the apex of each growth. The linear-lanceolate leaves are 1.6–4.0 in. (4–10 cm) long.

INFLORESCENCE: 3.5–4.3 in. (9–11 cm) long. The racemes are pendulous.

FLOWERS: 2–5 per inflorescence. The flowers, which do not open widely, are 3–4 in. (8–10 cm) long. All segments are pointed. The sepals and petals are pale rosy mauve and white. The tongue-shaped lip is mauve or purple with purple stripes and a deep purple and maroon disk which is surrounded by a white zone. The lip is the same length as the sepals and petals. The spur is long. Blossoms last 6–8 weeks.

REFERENCES: 97, 179, 190, 202, 210, 216, 218, 254, 317, 445, 541, 557, 568, 570.

PHOTOS/DRAWINGS: 97, 210, 541, 557.

Dendrobium macfarlanei F. Mueller not Rchb. f. or Schlechter

AKA: J. J. Smith (ref. 470) included *D. eboracense* Kränzlin and *D. podagraria* Kränzlin not Hooker as synonyms. However, Schlechter (ref. 437) includes *D. podagraria* Kränzlin as a synonym of *D. odoratum* Schlechter. When the botanical work is done, it may be that all 3 species are synonyms of *D. macfarlanei*.

Lewis and Cribb (ref. 271) state that *D. hymenocentrum* Schlechter is very similar to *D. macfarlanei* and that the relationship between the 2 species needs reassessment.

H. Wood (ref. 582) reports that he found plants halfway between *D. litorale* Schlechter and *D. macfarlanei* F. Mueller in the Ymas Lake region of Papua New Guinea, suggesting that these plants may be part of a variable alliance.

ORIGIN/HABITAT: New Guinea, the Kei Islands, and Banda Island. In northern Papua, plants grow on isolated trees along Schibruba Creek in the Kenejia Valley at the foot of the Bismarck Range. They are usually found at about 650 ft. (200 m) in areas where they receive at least some full sun during the day. In Irian Jaya (western New Guinea), plants grow between Geelvink Bay and the MacCluer Gulf and along the Merauke River.

CLIMATE: Station #200187, Erap, Papua New Guinea, Lat. 6.6°S, Long. 146.7°E, at 850 ft. (260 m). Record extreme temperatures are 102°F (39°C) and 53°F (12°C).

N/HEMISPHERE	JAN	FEB	MAR	APR	MAY	JUN	JUL	AUG	SEP	OCT	NOV	DEC
°F AVG MAX	88	88	89	90	93	93	93	93	93	92	90	90
°F AVG MIN	69	69	69	70	72	73	72	72	73	71	74	70
DIURNAL RANGE	19	19	20	20	21	20	21	21	20	21	16	20
RAIN/INCHES	3.9	3.9	2.7	3.0	3.0	5.3	5.9	5.9	7.0	3.4	2.4	3.1
HUMIDITY/%	82	81	81	79	75	74	74	74	77	76	80	80
BLOOM SEASON				*		*	*					
DAYS CLR	N/A											
RAIN/MM	98	99	68	77	76	135	149	149	179	87	60	78
°C AVG MAX	30.9	30.9	31.7	32.3	34.0	33.9	33.8	33.9	34.0	33.6	32.3	32.0
°C AVG MIN	20.4	20.5	20.7	21.1	22.0	22.5	22.1	22.4	22.5	21.7	23.3	20.9
DIURNAL RANGE	10.5	10.4	11.0	11.2	12.0	11.4	11.7	11.5	11.5	11.9	9.0	11.1
S/HEMISPHERE	JUL	AUG	SEP	OCT	NOV	DEC	JAN	FEB	MAR	APR	MAY	JUN

Cultural Recommendations

LIGHT: 2500–3500 fc.

TEMPERATURES: Throughout the year, days average 88–93°F (31–34°C), and nights average 69–74°F (20–23°C), with a diurnal range of 16–21°F (9–12°C).

HUMIDITY: 75–80% year-round. However, the habitat may be quite dry during hot afternoons.

WATER: Rainfall is moderate most of the year, but conditions are somewhat wetter for 4–5 months in summer and early autumn. Cultivated plants should be thoroughly saturated then allowed to dry slightly between waterings in summer and early autumn. Water should be gradually reduced in autumn.

FERTILIZER: ¼–½ recommended strength. A balanced fertilizer should be applied weekly to biweekly throughout the year.

REST PERIOD: Growing temperatures should be maintained all year. In the habitat, rainfall is lowest in winter, but the high humidity indicates that additional moisture is frequently available from heavy dew. Cultivated plants should be allowed to dry for somewhat longer between waterings than in summer, but they should not remain dry for extended periods. Fertilizer should be reduced until water is increased in spring. In the habitat, seasonal light variation is minor.

GROWING MEDIA: Plants may be mounted on tree-fern or cork slabs if humidity is high and plants are watered at least once daily in summer. When plants are potted, any open, fast-draining medium may be used. Repotting may be done anytime new roots are growing.

MISCELLANEOUS NOTES: The bloom season shown in the climate table is based on collection reports. Plants that produce flowers that last a single day commonly bloom several times during the year. Flowering usually occurs 7–14 days after a sudden 10°F (5°C) drop in daytime temperatures.

Plant and Flower Information

PLANT SIZE AND TYPE: A 24–33 in. (60–85 cm) sympodial epiphyte.

PSEUDOBULB: 24–33 in. (60–85 cm) long. The shiny stems become dark

Dendrobium macfarlanei

with age. They are swollen at the base, forming a pseudobulb with 4–5 sides. Above the swelling, they are branching, somewhat flattened, rigid, and wiry.

LEAVES: Many. The linear-lanceolate leaves are about 3 in. (8 cm) long. They are folded, distichous, and spaced about 1.2 in. (3 cm) apart.

INFLORESCENCE: Short. Inflorescences emerge from the side of the stem.

FLOWERS: 1–2 per inflorescence. The flowers are about 0.5 in. (1.3 cm) across. Sepals and petals are yellowish white with red veins. The lip is yellow with a yellow-green central band. The blossoms last a single day.

REFERENCES: 216, 254, 271, 436, 437, 445, 470, 582.

PHOTOS/DRAWINGS: 437.

Dendrobium macfarlanei Rchb. f. not F. Mueller or Schlechter.
See *D. johnsoniae* F. Mueller. REFERENCES: 25, 83, 105, 190, 216, 254, 271, 430, 533, 541, 570. PHOTOS/DRAWINGS: 541, 570.

Dendrobium macfarlanei Schlechter not F. Mueller or Rchb. f.
Schlechter (ref. 437) considers *D. macfarlanei* Schlechter to be a synonym of *D. eboracense* Kränzlin, which J. J. Smith listed as a synonym of *D. macfarlanei* F. Mueller. REFERENCES: 437, 444, 470.

Dendrobium macgregorii Ames.
Sometimes spelled *D. mcgregorii*, see *D. quisumbingii* A. Hawkes and A. H. Heller. REFERENCES: 12, 221, 296, 536.

Dendrobium macgregorii F. Mueller and Kränzlin

AKA: Sometimes spelled *D. mac gregorii*.

ORIGIN/HABITAT: Papua New Guinea and Louisiade Archipelago. Habitat elevation is unavailable, so the following climate data should be used with caution.

CLIMATE: Station #94075, Samarai, Sideia Island, Papua New Guinea, Lat. 10.6°S, Long. 150.7°E, at 20 ft. (6 m). Record extreme temperatures are 104°F (40°C) and 64°F (18°C).

N/HEMISPHERE	JAN	FEB	MAR	APR	MAY	JUN	JUL	AUG	SEP	OCT	NOV	DEC
°F AVG MAX	81	81	82	83	85	87	87	88	87	86	84	82
°F AVG MIN	74	73	74	74	75	76	77	77	76	75	75	74
DIURNAL RANGE	7	8	8	9	10	11	10	11	11	11	9	8
RAIN/INCHES	8.1	8.6	10.1	8.7	8.4	6.1	7.0	7.8	10.0	9.8	12.0	11.3
HUMIDITY/%	N/A											
BLOOM SEASON	N/A											
DAYS CLR	N/A											
RAIN/MM	206	218	257	221	213	155	178	198	254	249	305	287
°C AVG MAX	27.2	27.2	27.8	28.3	29.4	30.6	30.6	31.1	30.6	30.0	28.9	27.8
°C AVG MIN	23.3	22.8	23.3	23.3	23.9	24.4	25.0	25.0	24.4	23.9	23.9	23.3
DIURNAL RANGE	3.9	4.4	4.5	5.0	5.5	6.2	5.6	6.1	6.2	6.1	5.0	4.5
S/HEMISPHERE	JUL	AUG	SEP	OCT	NOV	DEC	JAN	FEB	MAR	APR	MAY	JUN

Cultural Recommendations

LIGHT: 2000–3000 fc.

TEMPERATURES: Throughout the year, days average 81–88°F (27–31°C), and nights average 73–77°F (23–25°C), with a diurnal range of 7–11°F (4–6°C).

HUMIDITY: Information is not available for this location. However, records from nearby stations indicate that humidity is probably near 70–80% year-round.

WATER: Rainfall is very heavy all year. Cultivated plants should be kept moist but not soggy.

FERTILIZER: ¼–½ recommended strength. A balanced fertilizer should be applied weekly to biweekly throughout the year.

REST PERIOD: Growing conditions should be maintained year-round. In the habitat, winter rainfall is high, but water and fertilizer should be reduced for plants cultivated in the dark, short-day conditions in temperate latitudes. They should never be allowed to dry out completely, however. In the habitat, seasonal light variation is minor.

GROWING MEDIA: Plants may be mounted on tree-fern or cork slabs if humidity is high and plants are watered at least once daily in summer. When plants are potted, any open, fast-draining medium may be used. They may be repotted anytime new roots are growing.

Plant and Flower Information

PLANT SIZE AND TYPE: An 8 in. (20 cm) sympodial epiphyte.

PSEUDOBULB: 8 in. (20 cm) long. The stems are nearly tetragon-shaped.

LEAVES: 2–3 per growth. The moderately sized leaves are oblong-lanceolate.

INFLORESCENCE: Longer than the leaves.

FLOWERS: 3–4 per inflorescence. The flowers were described as similar to a well-developed *D. bigibbum* Lindley. The sepals are white, with numerous rose-purple blotches. The petals are large and spreading with a rose-purple line. The lip sidelobes are very deep red-purple. The kidney-shaped midlobe is yellow or orange with purplish veins.

REFERENCES: 218, 253, 254.

Dendrobium machostachyum Lindley.
See *D. macrostachyum* Lindley. REFERENCES: 38.

Dendrobium macraei as used by Rendle.
Now considered a synonym of *Flickingeria nativitatis*. REFERENCES: 67.

Dendrobium macraei as used by Ames.
Considered a synonym of *D. plicatile* Lindley which is now considered a synonym of *Flickingeria fimbriata* (Blume) A. Hawkes. REFERENCES: 12, 25, 75, 296, 469.

Dendrobium macraei Lindley.
Now considered a synonym of *Flickingeria macraei* (Lindley) Seidenfaden. REFERENCES: 38, 46, 111, 150, 151, 154, 157, 187, 188, 190, 202, 213, 216, 230, 231, 254, 277, 278, 395, 424, 445, 448, 449, 469, 504, 580. PHOTOS/DRAWINGS: 46, 469.

Dendrobium macranthum de Vriese ex Lindley not Hooker or A. Richard.
Now considered a synonym of *Eria elongata* Lindley. REFERENCES: 216, 254.

Dendrobium macranthum Hooker not de Vriese ex Lindley or A. Richard.
See *D. anosmum* Lindley. REFERENCES: 216, 254, 296, 430, 454, 470.

Dendrobium macranthum Miquel.
See *D. anosmum* Lindley. REFERENCES: 216, 436.

Dendrobium macranthum A. Richard

AKA: *D. arachnostachyum* Rchb. f., *D. pseudotokai* Kränzlin, *D. tokai* Rchb. f. var. *crassinerve* Finet.

ORIGIN/HABITAT: New Caledonia, Vanuatu (New Hebrides), Samoa, and the Santa Cruz Islands. Plants are common in coastal and lowland rainforests and on mangroves near the sea.

CLIMATE: Station #91592, Noumea, New Caledonia, Lat. 22.3°S, Long. 166.5°E, at 246 ft. (75 m). Record extreme temperatures are 99°F (37°C) and 52°F (11°C).

N/HEMISPHERE	JAN	FEB	MAR	APR	MAY	JUN	JUL	AUG	SEP	OCT	NOV	DEC
°F AVG MAX	76	76	78	80	83	86	86	85	85	83	79	77
°F AVG MIN	62	61	63	65	68	70	72	73	72	70	66	64
DIURNAL RANGE	14	15	15	15	15	16	14	12	13	13	13	13
RAIN/INCHES	3.6	2.6	2.5	2.0	2.4	2.6	3.7	5.1	5.7	5.2	4.4	3.7
HUMIDITY/%	73	70	69	67	68	69	71	74	75	76	73	73
BLOOM SEASON				*	*	*	*	*				
DAYS CLR @ 11AM	7	9	9	15	12	10	7	6	7	7	7	7
DAYS CLR @ 5PM	7	11	6	11	7	6	5	4	4	5	3	7
RAIN/MM	91	66	64	51	61	66	94	130	145	132	112	94
°C AVG MAX	24.4	24.4	25.6	26.7	28.3	30.0	30.0	29.4	29.4	28.3	26.1	25.0
°C AVG MIN	16.7	16.1	17.2	18.3	20.0	21.1	22.2	22.8	22.2	21.1	18.9	17.8
DIURNAL RANGE	7.7	8.3	8.4	8.4	8.3	8.9	7.8	6.6	7.2	7.2	7.2	7.2
S/HEMISPHERE	JUL	AUG	SEP	OCT	NOV	DEC	JAN	FEB	MAR	APR	MAY	JUN

Cultural Recommendations

LIGHT: 2000–3000 fc.

TEMPERATURES: Summer days average 85–86°F (29–30°C), and nights average 70–73°F (21–23°C), with a diurnal range of 12–16°F (7–9°C).

HUMIDITY: 70–75% year-round.

WATER: Rainfall is moderate to heavy year-round. Cultivated plants should be watered heavily and then allowed to dry slightly before being watered again.

FERTILIZER: ¼–½ recommended strength, applied weekly. A high-nitrogen fertilizer is beneficial from spring to midsummer, but a fertilizer high in phosphates should be used in late summer and autumn.

REST PERIOD: Winter days average 76–78°F (24–26°C), and nights average 61–64°F (16–18°C), with a diurnal range of 13–15°F (7–8°C). High and low temperatures decline simultaneously, resulting in little change in the diurnal range. In the habitat, rainfall is somewhat lower in late winter and spring. Water and fertilizer should be reduced, and plants allowed to dry even more between waterings than in summer. They should not dry out completely or remain dry for long periods, however. In the habitat, light is highest in winter.

GROWING MEDIA: Plants may be mounted on tree-fern or cork slabs if humidity is high and plants are watered at least once daily in summer. When plants are potted, any open, fast-draining medium may be used. Repotting is best done in early spring when new roots are growing.

MISCELLANEOUS NOTES: The bloom season shown in the climate table is based on reports from the habitat.

Plant and Flower Information

PLANT SIZE AND TYPE: A 16–39 in. (40–100 cm) sympodial epiphyte.

PSEUDOBULB: 13–37 in. (33–94 cm) long. The canelike stems are erect and clustered. They are swollen near the base and taper toward the apex.

LEAVES: Many. The oblong to elliptic leaves are 3–6 in. (8–15 cm) long.

INFLORESCENCE: 8–12 in. (20–30 cm) long. Inflorescences emerge through the leaf sheaths near the apex of the stem. They may be erect or suberect. The flowers are clustered at the apex of the inflorescence.

FLOWERS: 15–25 per inflorescence. The large flowers are 2–3 in. (5–8 cm) across. The narrow, pointed sepals and petals may be any shade of yellow, greenish yellow, or straw-yellow. The flared lip may be yellowish green, dusky green, or dirty white with violet or purple veins and keels. Although related to the Antelope dendrobiums, none of the segments are twisted.

HYBRIDIZING NOTES: Chromosome count is 2n = 38 (ref. 152, 243). In the Solomon Islands, *D. macranthum* is known to hybridize naturally with *D. conanthum* Schlechter.

REFERENCES: 16, 82, 84, 152, 162, 216, 243, 254, 269, 270, 271, 317, 344, 445, 516.

PHOTOS/DRAWINGS: *84, 269, 271, 344, 540.*

Dendrobium macraporum J. J. Smith

ORIGIN/HABITAT: Endemic to Sulawesi (Celebes). Plants were found near Enrekang in the Masenrempoeloe District in central Sulawesi. Habitat elevation was not reported, so the following climate data should be used with caution.

CLIMATE: Station #97180, Makassar, Sulawesi, Indonesia, Lat. 5.1°S, Long. 119.6°E, at 46 ft. (14 m). Record extreme temperatures are 95°F (35°C) and 58°F (14°C).

N/HEMISPHERE	JAN	FEB	MAR	APR	MAY	JUN	JUL	AUG	SEP	OCT	NOV	DEC
°F AVG MAX	86	87	87	87	86	84	84	84	85	86	87	86
°F AVG MIN	70	69	70	72	74	74	74	75	74	74	74	72
DIURNAL RANGE	16	18	17	15	12	10	10	9	11	12	13	14
RAIN/INCHES	1.3	0.4	0.5	1.6	6.7	23.2	28.3	20.9	16.7	6.5	3.6	2.7
HUMIDITY/%	72	67	64	70	77	84	84	85	84	80	79	76
BLOOM SEASON		*										
DAYS CLR @ 8AM	14	17	15	14	8	4	4	1	4	8	8	11
DAYS CLR @ 2PM	7	7	11	13	9	3	1	1	1	2	6	7
RAIN/MM	33	10	13	41	170	589	719	531	424	165	91	69
°C AVG MAX	30.0	30.6	30.6	30.6	30.0	28.9	28.9	28.9	29.4	30.0	30.6	30.0
°C AVG MIN	21.1	20.6	21.1	22.2	23.3	23.3	23.3	23.9	23.3	23.3	23.3	22.2
DIURNAL RANGE	8.9	10.0	9.5	8.4	6.7	5.6	5.6	5.0	6.1	6.7	7.3	7.8
S/HEMISPHERE	JUL	AUG	SEP	OCT	NOV	DEC	JAN	FEB	MAR	APR	MAY	JUN

Cultural Recommendations

LIGHT: 2500–3500 fc. Clear summer days are rare. Light is reduced by the cloud cover associated with the summer rainy season.

TEMPERATURES: Throughout the year, days average 84–87°F (29–31°C), and nights average 69–75°F (21–24°C), with a diurnal range of 9–18°F (5–10°C).

HUMIDITY: Near 85% in summer and early autumn, dropping to 65–70% in winter.

WATER: Rainfall is heavy from late spring to autumn. The rainy season is followed by a 2–3 month winter dry season. Cultivated plants should be kept moist, but not soggy while actively growing, but water should be gradually reduced in autumn.

FERTILIZER: ¼–½ recommended strength, applied weekly. A high-nitrogen fertilizer is beneficial from spring to midsummer, but a fertilizer high in phosphates should be used in late summer and autumn.

REST PERIOD: Growing temperatures should be maintained all year. In the habitat, rainfall is low for 4 months in winter, and conditions become so dry that even dew is uncommon for 2–3 months. Water should be reduced for cultivated plants and the medium allowed to dry out between waterings. Plants should not remain completely dry for long periods, however. Reduce or eliminate fertilizer anytime water is reduced. In the habitat, light is highest in winter.

GROWING MEDIA: Mounting plants on tree-fern or cork slabs accommodates their pendulous growth habit. However, humidity must be high and plants must be watered at least once a day in summer. If plants cannot be mounted, small pots or hanging baskets may be filled with an open, fast-draining medium. Repotting may be done anytime new roots are actively growing.

MISCELLANEOUS NOTES: The bloom season shown in the climate table is based on botanical garden records.

Plant and Flower Information

PLANT SIZE AND TYPE: A 24–51 in. (60–130 cm) sympodial plant.

PSEUDOBULB: 24–51 in. (60–130 cm) long. The olive-green stems are rigid, pendulous, and very flattened.

LEAVES: Many. The linear-lanceolate leaves, which are somewhat sickle-shaped, are 4–5 in. (10–13 cm) long and laterally flattened.

INFLORESCENCE: Short. Inflorescences are borne from upper nodes.

FLOWERS: 1 per inflorescence. The flowers are 1 in. (2.6 cm) long with a conspicuously long spur. They are large when compared to other closely related plants. Blossoms are yellowish green, becoming pale golden-yellow with age. The sepals and petals are marked with dark purple stripes. The erect dorsal sepal is ovate. The lateral sepals are somewhat triangular and very recurved at the tips. The nearly erect petals are ovate-elliptic and pointed at the tip. They have dark purple along the branching nerves and the lower part of the margin. The lip is erect, 3-lobed, curved, and wavy.

REFERENCES: 221, 436, 473.

Dendrobium macrifolium J. J. Smith

ORIGIN/HABITAT: Irian Jaya (western New Guinea) along the Rouffaer River. Plants grow high in the trees of primeval forests at about 800 ft. (250 m).

CLIMATE: Station #200004, Ambunti, Papua New Guinea, Lat. 4.2°S, Long. 142.8°E, at 164 ft. (50 m). Temperatures are calculated for an elevation of 1000 ft. (300 m), resulting in probable extremes of 96°F (36°C) and 49°F (10°C).

N/HEMISPHERE	JAN	FEB	MAR	APR	MAY	JUN	JUL	AUG	SEP	OCT	NOV	DEC
°F AVG MAX	85	87	87	87	88	87	87	87	87	87	87	86
°F AVG MIN	69	70	71	70	70	70	69	70	70	70	70	71
DIURNAL RANGE	16	17	16	17	18	17	18	17	17	17	17	15
RAIN/INCHES	6.4	7.4	7.7	8.5	9.2	9.4	10.9	10.2	12.2	10.4	8.3	5.2
HUMIDITY/%	N/A											
BLOOM SEASON			*									
DAYS CLR	N/A											
RAIN/MM	163	188	196	216	234	239	277	259	310	264	211	132
°C AVG MAX	29.6	30.7	30.7	30.7	31.2	30.7	30.7	30.7	30.7	30.7	30.7	30.1
°C AVG MIN	20.7	21.2	21.8	21.2	21.2	21.2	20.7	21.2	21.2	21.2	21.2	21.8
DIURNAL RANGE	8.9	9.5	8.9	9.5	10.0	9.5	10.0	9.5	9.5	9.5	9.5	8.3
S/HEMISPHERE	JUL	AUG	SEP	OCT	NOV	DEC	JAN	FEB	MAR	APR	MAY	JUN

Cultural Recommendations

LIGHT: 2000–3000 fc.

TEMPERATURES: Throughout the year, days average 85–88°F (30–31°C), and nights average 69–71°F (21–22°C), with a diurnal range of 15–18°F (8–10°C).

HUMIDITY: Information is not available for this location. However, records from nearby locations indicate that humidity probably averages near 80% year-round.

WATER: Rainfall is heavy year-round, with the greatest amounts falling in summer and early autumn. Cultivated plants should be moist but not soggy.

FERTILIZER: ¼–½ recommended strength. A balanced fertilizer should be applied weekly to biweekly throughout the year.

REST PERIOD: Growing conditions should be maintained all year. Water and fertilizer should be reduced for plants cultivated in the dark, short-day conditions common in temperate-latitude winters, but they should never be allowed to dry out completely. In the habitat, seasonal light variation is minor.

GROWING MEDIA: Plants may be mounted on tree-fern or cork slabs if humidity is high and plants are watered at least once daily in summer. When plants are potted, any open, fast-draining medium may be used. They may be repotted anytime new roots are growing.

MISCELLANEOUS NOTES: The bloom season shown in the climate table is based on reports from the habitat.

Plant and Flower Information

PLANT SIZE AND TYPE: An 11 in. (28 cm) sympodial epiphyte.

PSEUDOBULB: 11 in. (28 cm) long. The slender stems are borne on a short, very branching rhizome.

LEAVES: Many. The linear leaves are 0.8–1.2 in. (2–3 cm) long. They are rigid, channeled, and somewhat spreading.

INFLORESCENCE: Short. Inflorescences emerge along the stem.

FLOWERS: 1–2 per inflorescence. The flowers are less than 0.3 in. (0.8 cm) long. Sepals and petals are light green. The darker lip is bright green. Dorsal sepal is recurved. The oblong lateral sepals are incised along the margin. The petals are spreading and recurved. The 3-lobed lip is linear-oblong.

REFERENCES: 225, 470.

Dendrobium macrocarpum A. Richard. Schlechter (ref. 441) mentioned this name when discussing *D. palawense* Schlechter, but we were unable to locate a description or any additional information.

REFERENCES: 441.

Dendrobium macrogenium Schlechter

ORIGIN/HABITAT: Northeastern Papua New Guinea. In the Waria district, plants grow on mistforest trees of the Dischore Range at about 3950 ft. (1200 m).

CLIMATE: Station #200192, Garaina, Papua New Guinea, Lat. 7.9°S, Long. 147.1°E, at 2350 ft. (716 m). Temperatures are calculated for an elevation of 3950 ft. (1200 m), resulting in probable extremes of 89°F (32°C) and 41°F (5°C).

N/HEMISPHERE	JAN	FEB	MAR	APR	MAY	JUN	JUL	AUG	SEP	OCT	NOV	DEC
°F AVG MAX	75	77	78	79	80	80	80	80	79	79	78	76
°F AVG MIN	58	58	58	59	58	59	60	60	60	59	59	58
DIURNAL RANGE	17	19	20	20	22	21	20	20	19	20	19	18
RAIN/INCHES	5.8	6.5	8.7	11.1	11.8	11.9	8.9	11.7	11.5	9.9	7.7	5.2
HUMIDITY/%	84	82	82	81	80	80	81	81	82	83	84	84
BLOOM SEASON								*	*			
DAYS CLR	N/A											
RAIN/MM	147	165	221	282	300	302	226	297	292	251	196	132
°C AVG MAX	23.8	24.9	25.4	26.0	26.5	26.5	26.5	26.5	26.0	26.0	25.4	24.3
°C AVG MIN	14.3	14.3	14.3	14.9	14.3	14.9	15.4	15.4	15.4	14.9	14.9	14.3
DIURNAL RANGE	9.5	10.6	11.1	11.1	12.2	11.6	11.1	11.1	10.6	11.1	10.5	10.0
S/HEMISPHERE	JUL	AUG	SEP	OCT	NOV	DEC	JAN	FEB	MAR	APR	MAY	JUN

Cultural Recommendations

LIGHT: 2000–3000 fc.

TEMPERATURES: Throughout the year, days average 75–80°F (24–27°C), and nights average 58–60°F (14–15°C), with a diurnal range of 17–22°F (10–12°C).

HUMIDITY: 80–85% year-round.

WATER: Rainfall is heavy all year, but conditions are slightly drier in winter. Cultivated plants should be kept moist, but not soggy.

FERTILIZER: ¼–½ recommended strength. A balanced fertilizer should be applied weekly to biweekly throughout the year. The Royal Botanic Garden in Edinburgh uses a seaweed-based fertilizer for high elevation plants from New Guinea.

REST PERIOD: Growing conditions should be maintained all year. In the habitat, rainfall is slightly lower in winter. Water and fertilizer should be reduced somewhat for cultivated plants, especially those grown in the dark, short-day conditions common during temperate-latitude winters. They should never be allowed to dry out completely, however. In the habitat, seasonal light variation is minor.

GROWING MEDIA: Plants may be mounted on tree-fern or cork slabs if humidity is high and plants are watered at least once daily in summer. When plants are potted, any open, fast-draining medium may be used. Repotting is best done in early spring when new roots are growing.

MISCELLANEOUS NOTES: The bloom season shown in the climate table is based on cultivation records. In the habitat, blooming is reported in autumn.

Plant and Flower Information

PLANT SIZE AND TYPE: A 24 in. (60 cm) sympodial epiphyte.

PSEUDOBULB: 24 in. (60 cm) long.

LEAVES: Many. The lanceolate leaves are 2.8–3.3 in. (7.0–8.5 cm) long. They may be erect or spreading.

INFLORESCENCE: Short. The densely flowered inflorescences may be erect or spreading. They emerge laterally.

FLOWERS: The flowers are 1 in. (2.5 cm) long and shaped like a long, curved cone formed by the large lateral sepals that are joined for most of their length. The dorsal sepal and petals are small. Sepals and petals are bright red with darker veins. The long, narrow lip is whitish with violet markings. The column and anther are violet and white.

REFERENCES: 221, 437, 445.

PHOTOS/DRAWINGS: 437.

Dendrobium macrogerion Schlechter. Listed by Thorne and Cribb (ref. 516), but we found no other reference to this species.

REFERENCES: 516.

Dendrobium macrolobum (Schlechter) J. J. Smith

AKA: *Cadetia macroloba* Schlechter. *Cadetia* is now considered a valid genus by some botanists, so this plant may again become a *Cadetia*.

ORIGIN/HABITAT: Irian Jaya (western New Guinea). Plants were collected on the south side of Mt. Jaya (Mt. Carstensz) at 5500–8300 ft. (1680–2530 m) and on Mt. Goliath at 10,650 ft. (3250 m).

CLIMATE: Station #97796, Kokenau (Kokonau), Irian Jaya, Lat. 4.7°S, Long. 135.4°E, at 10 ft. (3 m). Temperatures are calculated for an elevation of 7000 ft. (2130 m). Record extreme temperatures are not available for this location.

N/HEMISPHERE	JAN	FEB	MAR	APR	MAY	JUN	JUL	AUG	SEP	OCT	NOV	DEC
°F AVG MAX	60	60	63	65	67	66	66	66	67	65	64	61
°F AVG MIN	50	50	51	51	51	52	51	51	51	51	51	50
DIURNAL RANGE	10	10	12	14	16	14	15	16	16	14	13	11
RAIN/INCHES	18.4	15.8	18.9	11.6	9.7	10.6	11.5	15.7	11.6	11.6	16.0	19.9
HUMIDITY/%	N/A											
BLOOM SEASON						*	*					
DAYS CLR	N/A											
RAIN/MM	467	401	480	295	246	269	292	399	295	295	406	505
°C AVG MAX	15.5	15.5	17.2	18.3	19.4	18.9	18.9	18.9	19.4	18.3	17.7	16.1
°C AVG MIN	10.0	10.0	10.5	10.5	10.5	11.1	10.5	10.5	10.5	10.5	10.5	10.0
DIURNAL RANGE	5.5	5.5	6.7	7.8	8.9	7.8	8.4	8.4	8.9	7.8	7.2	6.1
S/HEMISPHERE	JUL	AUG	SEP	OCT	NOV	DEC	JAN	FEB	MAR	APR	MAY	JUN

Cultural Recommendations

LIGHT: 2500–3500 fc.

TEMPERATURES: Throughout the year, days average 60–67°F (16–19°C), and nights average 50–52°F (10–11°C), with a diurnal range of 10–16°F (6–9°C). Due to the effects of the microclimate, actual day-time temperatures may average 3–7°F (2–4°C) warmer than indicated.

HUMIDITY: Information is not available for this location. However, records from nearby locations indicate that humidity probably averages near 85% year-round.

WATER: Rainfall is very heavy all year. Cultivated plants should be kept evenly moist but not soggy.

FERTILIZER: ¼–½ recommended strength. A balanced fertilizer should be applied weekly to biweekly throughout the year.

REST PERIOD: Growing temperatures should be maintained year-round. The smallest diurnal range occurs in winter. Water and fertilizer might be reduced somewhat in winter, especially for plants cultivated in the dark, short-day conditions common in the temperate latitudes. They should never be allowed to dry out completely, however. In the habitat, seasonal light variation is minor.

GROWING MEDIA: Plants may be mounted on tree-fern or cork slabs or potted in small pots filled with any open, fast-draining medium. Repotting may be done anytime new roots are actively growing.

MISCELLANEOUS NOTES: The bloom season shown in the climate table is based on reports from the habitat.

Plant and Flower Information

PLANT SIZE AND TYPE: An erect, 3.5 in. (9 cm) sympodial terrestrial.

PSEUDOBULB: 0.6–1.3 in. (1.5–3.2 cm) long. The stems are clustered, erect, cylindrical, and 4-angled.

LEAVES: 1 per growth. The oblong or elliptic-oblong leaves are 0.8–1.0 in. (2–2.5 cm) long, smooth, and leathery.

INFLORESCENCE: 0.7–1.1 in. (1.8–2.8 cm) long. 1 or 2 inflorescences emerge near the base of the leaf at the top of the stem.

FLOWERS: 1 per inflorescence. The white flowers are 0.8 in. (2 cm) long. Sepals and petals are curled at the tips. The lip extends well forward of the other flower segments.

REFERENCES: 221, 400, 437, 445, 470, 538.

PHOTOS/DRAWINGS: 538.

Dendrobium macrophyllum Ames not Lindley or A. Richard. Merrill (ref. 296) and Valmayor (ref. 536) list *D. macrophyllum* Ames as a synonym of *D. ternatense* J. J. Smith, which Cribb (ref. 83) in turn includes as a synonym of *D. macrophyllum* A. Richard. REFERENCES: 83, 296, 536.

Dendrobium macrophyllum Lindley not Ames or A. Richard. See *D. anosmum* Lindley. REFERENCES: 98, 216, 254, 296, 430, 436, 445, 454, 470.

Dendrobium macrophyllum A. Richard not Lindley or Ames

AKA: *D. brachythecum* F. Mueller and Kränzlin, *D. ferox* Hasskarl, *D. gordonii* S. Moore ex Baker, *D. macrophyllum* var. *giganteum* Hort., *D. macrophyllum* var. *malaccense* Hort., *D. macrophyllum* var. *pallidum* Hort., *D. macrophyllum* var. *subvelutinum* J. J. Smith, *D. macrophyllum* var. *veitchianum* (Lindley) Hooker f., *D. musciferum* Schlechter, *D. psyche* Kränzlin, *D. setigerum* Ames ined., *D. ternatense* J. J. Smith, *D. tomohonense* Kränzlin, *D. veitchianum* Lindley.

Cribb (ref. 83) includes *D. sarcostoma* Teijsm. and Binn. as a synonym, but Hawkes (ref. 190) lists the name as *D. sarcostemma* Teijsm. and Binn.

Kränzlin (ref. 254) included *D. lucae* F. Mueller as a synonym of *D. gordonii* S. Moore ex Baker, which is now considered a synonym of *D. macrophyllum*.

Christianson 1992 *Lindleyana* 7(2):90 added *D. palawense* Schlechter to the list of synonyms.

A recently awarded plant from the Philippines was registered under the name *D. ternatense*.

D. macrophyllum var. *stenopterum* Rchb. f. is now considered a synonym of *D. polysema* Schlechter.

ORIGIN/HABITAT: Widespread in the Pacific Islands, including Java, Ambon, Ternate Island, Sulawesi (Celebes), Borneo, the Philippines,

Dendrobium macropodum

Palau, Irian Jaya (western New Guinea), the Solomon and Santa Cruz Islands, Vanuatu, New Caledonia, Fiji, and Samoa. Plants usually grow on trees in hot jungles from near sea level to about 3950 ft. (1200 m); but in some areas, they are found as high as 5600 ft. (1700 m). They usually grow about half way up large tree trunks in primary forests in light to moderate shade.

CLIMATE: Station #97724, Ambon Island, Indonesia, Lat. 3.7°S, Long. 128.1°E, at 33 ft. (10 m). Temperatures are calculated for an elevation of 2500 ft. (760 m), resulting in probable extremes of 88°F (31°C) and 58°F (14°C).

N/HEMISPHERE	JAN	FEB	MAR	APR	MAY	JUN	JUL	AUG	SEP	OCT	NOV	DEC
°F AVG MAX	73	73	75	77	80	80	80	80	80	78	76	74
°F AVG MIN	66	66	66	66	67	68	68	68	68	68	67	66
DIURNAL RANGE	7	7	9	11	13	12	12	12	12	10	9	8
RAIN/INCHES	23.7	15.8	9.5	6.1	4.5	5.2	5.0	4.7	5.3	11.0	20.3	25.1
HUMIDITY/%	83	82	81	80	79	78	78	77	79	82	83	84
BLOOM SEASON									*	*	*	
DAYS CLR @ 9AM	1	1	1	6	7	4	3	3	5	5	3	3
DAYS CLR @ 3PM	1	1	2	5	6	1	1	1	2	3	1	3
RAIN/MM	602	401	241	155	114	132	127	119	135	279	516	638
°C AVG MAX	22.7	22.7	23.8	24.9	26.6	26.6	26.6	26.6	26.6	25.5	24.4	23.3
°C AVG MIN	18.8	18.8	18.8	18.8	19.4	19.9	19.9	19.9	19.9	19.9	19.4	18.8
DIURNAL RANGE	3.9	3.9	5.0	6.1	7.2	6.7	6.7	6.7	6.7	5.6	5.0	4.5
S/HEMISPHERE	JUL	AUG	SEP	OCT	NOV	DEC	JAN	FEB	MAR	APR	MAY	JUN

Cultural Recommendations

LIGHT: 2500–3500 fc.

TEMPERATURES: Throughout the year, days average 73–80°F (23–27°C), and nights average 66–68°F (19–20°C), with a diurnal range of 7–12°F (4–7°C). Because the plants are found over a wide region with such a large range in habitat elevation, they may adapt to conditions 6–8°F (3–4°C) cooler than indicated above.

HUMIDITY: 80–85% year-round.

WATER: Rainfall is moderate to heavy all year, but conditions are slightly drier in late spring and summer. Cultivated plants should be kept evenly moist, with only slight drying allowed between waterings.

FERTILIZER: ¼–½ recommended strength. A balanced fertilizer should be applied weekly to biweekly throughout the year.

REST PERIOD: Growing conditions should be maintained all year. In the habitat, rainfall is heaviest in winter, but water and fertilizer may be reduced somewhat for cultivated plants, especially those grown in the dark, short-day conditions common in temperate latitudes. They should never be allowed to dry completely, however. In the habitat, light is highest in spring.

GROWING MEDIA: Plants may be mounted on tree-fern or cork slabs if humidity is high and plants are watered at least once daily in summer. When plants are potted, medium or coarse fir bark or any open, fast-draining medium may be used. Repotting is best done in late spring immediately after blooming when new roots are growing.

MISCELLANEOUS NOTES: The bloom season shown in the climate table is based on reports from the habitat. Sparse cultivation reports indicate that blooming occurs in spring and late summer. In Singapore, plants grow and bloom in light shade.

Plant and Flower Information

PLANT SIZE AND TYPE: A 15–25 in. (38–64 cm) sympodial epiphyte. *D. macrophyllum* is robust and may form clumps of 100 canes weighing up to 33 lbs. (15 kg).

PSEUDOBULB: 6–16 in. (15–40 cm) long. The canes are ribbed, slightly flattened, thin at the base, becoming broader on the upper 60%. They are pale green to yellow-green flushed with purple-brown.

LEAVES: 2–4. The large leaves are 9–13 in. (23–33 cm) long and grow close together at the apex of each growth. They may be greenish white or yellow-green. The underside is purple and the upper surface often has a purple flush. Depending on growing conditions, the leaves may be evergreen or at least last several seasons.

INFLORESCENCE: 12 in. (30 cm) long. Several inflorescences arise successively from between the upper leaves. The ovaries and pedicels are covered with coarse, rough hairs.

FLOWERS: 4–30, commonly 15–20 per inflorescence. The highly variable flowers are 1.6–2.4 in. (4–6 cm) across. Initially the sepals are yellow-green, but they become deeper yellow with age. They usually have red or violet spots on the backside and are covered with coarse hairs. The hairless petals, which are purple on the backside, may be dirty white or strong yellow. The large lip may be pale green or yellow-green decorated with red or purple stripes, veins, or spots. The large sidelobes are incurved and meet above the column. The midlobe is somewhat less dramatically striped but the tip has a darker patch. Whether or not this species should be considered beautiful is strictly in the eye of the beholder. Descriptions include "one of the finest," "a curious species," and "striking when in full bloom but hardly beautiful." The very long-lived blossoms have a strong fragrance that is often described as somewhat sour smelling. Schlechter described *D. palawense* as having whitish flowers which are among the largest *Dendrobium* flowers in Micronesia. The sepals were sparsely covered with soft bristles. The dorsal sepal was lanceolate, lateral sepals were oblique, and petals somewhat tongue-shaped. The lip sidelobes were marked with red.

HYBRIDIZING NOTES: Chromosome counts are 2n = 38 (ref. 151, 152, 154, 187, 188, 243, 504, 580), 2n = 38+2f (ref. 153, 273) as *D. lohohense*, 2n = 38 as *D. gordonii* (ref. 504, 580), and 2n = 40 as *D. musciferum* (ref. 152).

REFERENCES: 6, 12, 16, 25, 75, 83, 142, 151, 152, 153, 154, 173, 179, 187, 188, 190, 196, 200, 210, 216, 221, 241, 243, 252, 254, 270, 271, 273, 302, 304, 307, 310, 317, 318, 326, 353, 371, 373, 390, 400, 430, 436, 437, 445, 466, 468, 469, 470, 482, 483, 504, 510, 516, 536, 537, 541, 550, 568, 570, 580.

PHOTOS/DRAWINGS: *75, 83, 173, 200, 210, 271, 304, 307, 318, 371, 373, 390, 430, 437, 466, 469, 536, 540, 568.*

Dendrobium macropodum Hooker f. Now considered a synonym of *Epigeneium macropodum* (Hooker f.) Summerhayes. REFERENCES: 200, 202, 216, 229, 254, 395, 445, 449, 455, 499.

Dendrobium macropus Bentham and Hooker. Included in Index Kewensis (ref. 216), the plant reportedly originated on Norfolk Island. We suspect it refers to the following species. REFERENCES: 216.

Dendrobium macropus (Endl.) Rchb. f. ex Lindley

AKA: *Thelychiton macropus* Endl. The taxonomic work currently being done with this alliance of plants may be the perfect example of today's achievement becoming tomorrow's confusion.

Some botanists and Upton (ref. 533) divide *D. macropus* into 3 subspecies.

D. macropus subsp. *gracilicaule* (F. Mueller) P. S. Green, for which he included the synonyms *D. elongatum* A. Cunningham, *D. brisbanensis* Rchb. f., and *D. comptonii* Rendle.

D. macropus subsp. *howeanum* (Maiden) P. S. Green, for which he included the synonym *D. gracilicaule* F. Mueller var. *howeanum* Maiden.

D. macropus subsp. *macropus* (Endl.) P. S. Green, for which he included the synonym *D. brachypus* (Endl.) Rchb. f.

Lewis and Cribb (ref. 270) include *D. comptonii* Rendle, *D. drake-castilloi* Kränzlin, *D. gracilicaule* F. Mueller, *D. gracilicaule* var. *howeanum* Maiden, *D. floribundum* Rchb. f. not D. Don, and *D. oscari* A. Hawkes and A. H. Heller as synonyms.

Kores (ref. 466) includes *D. comptonii* Rendle, *D. drake-castilloi* Kränzlin, *D. gracilicaule* F. Mueller var. *vitiense* Rolfe ex Hallé as synonyms.

Clements (ref. 67) chose to treat the following plants as independent species pending conclusion of the research currently being conducted on this *Dendrobium* alliance. He assigns the synonyms as follows.

D. brachypus (Endl.) Rchb. f., for which he includes the synonym *Thelychiton brachypus* (Endl.) Rchb. f.

D. comptonii Rendle, for which he includes the synonyms *D. drake-castilloi* Kränzlin and *D. macropus* subsp. *howeanum*.

D. gracilicaule F. Mueller not Kränzlin, for which he includes the synonyms *D. elongatum* A. Cunningham not Lindley, *D. brisbanense* Rchb. f., and *D. macropus* (Endl.) Rchb. f. ex Lindley subsp. *gracilicaule* (F. Mueller) P. Green.

D. macropus (Endl.) Rchb. f. ex Lindley, for which he includes the synonym *Thelychiton macropus* Endl.

ORIGIN/HABITAT: Some botanists consider *D. macropus* endemic to Norfolk Island, but others indicate that its distribution includes Australia, Lord Howe Island, Norfolk Island, the Kermadec Islands, New Caledonia, Vanuatu (New Hebrides), and Fiji. Plants usually grow on trees at about 1000 ft. (300 m), but they occasionally grow on rocks in heavily wooded areas. Plants are common in forests of the Mt. Pitt Reserve and uncommon in other parts of the island.

CLIMATE: Station #94996, Norfolk Island, Australia, Lat. 29.1°S, Long. 167.9°E, at 370 ft. (113 m). Temperatures are calculated for an elevation of 500 ft. (150 m), resulting in probable extremes of 89°F (31°C) and 43°F (6°C).

N/HEMISPHERE	JAN	FEB	MAR	APR	MAY	JUN	JUL	AUG	SEP	OCT	NOV	DEC
°F AVG MAX	65	65	67	69	72	75	78	77	76	73	69	67
°F AVG MIN	57	56	57	60	62	65	67	68	67	65	61	60
DIURNAL RANGE	8	9	10	9	10	10	11	9	9	8	8	7
RAIN/INCHES	6.1	5.4	3.7	3.7	2.6	3.4	3.3	4.3	3.7	5.0	5.7	5.5
HUMIDITY/%	80	83	82	82	82	82	82	85	82	82	83	82
BLOOM SEASON	**	**	**	**								
DAYS CLR @ 5AM	5	6	7	5	5	3	4	3	4	5	5	6
DAYS CLR @ 11AM	4	5	5	5	5	4	4	2	3	3	3	3
RAIN/MM	155	137	94	94	66	86	84	109	94	127	145	140
°C AVG MAX	18.1	18.1	19.2	20.3	22.0	23.7	25.3	24.8	24.2	22.5	20.3	19.2
°C AVG MIN	13.7	13.1	13.7	15.3	16.4	18.1	19.2	19.8	19.2	18.1	15.9	15.3
DIURNAL RANGE	4.4	5.0	5.5	5.0	5.6	5.6	6.1	5.0	5.0	4.4	4.4	3.9
S/HEMISPHERE	JUL	AUG	SEP	OCT	NOV	DEC	JAN	FEB	MAR	APR	MAY	JUN

Cultural Recommendations

LIGHT: 2500–3500 fc. *D. macropus* requires about 50% shade in summer, and strong air movement is important throughout the year.

TEMPERATURES: Summer days average 75–78°F (24–25°C), and nights average 65–68°F (18–20°C), with a diurnal range of 9–11°F (5–6°C).

HUMIDITY: 80–85% year-round.

WATER: Rainfall is moderate all year, with a short, slightly drier period in late spring. Cultivated plants require a delicate balance between too much and too little water. They are healthiest if allowed to dry out between waterings, as the fine roots are quickly lost if plants are overwatered or if the medium is allowed to become stale. However, adequate moisture is critically important to the production of blossoms, and the plants should not be allowed to remain dry for long periods.

FERTILIZER: ¼–½ recommended strength, applied weekly. A high-nitrogen fertilizer is beneficial from spring to midsummer, but a fertilizer high in phosphates should be used in late summer and autumn.

REST PERIOD: Winter days average 65–67°F (18–19°C), and nights average 56–60°F (13–15°C), with a diurnal range of 7–10°F (4–6°C). While winter rainfall is heavy in the habitat, water and fertilizer should be reduced for cultivated plants, especially those grown in the dark, short-day conditions common during temperate-latitude winters. Australian growers report that the roots deteriorate quickly if overwatered, particularly in winter. The plants must be allowed to dry out between waterings. Growers indicate that severe frosts cause leaf damage, but plants recover quickly.

GROWING MEDIA: Plants may be mounted on tree-fern or cork slabs or potted in small pots filled with any open, fast-draining medium. Repotting may be done anytime new roots are growing.

MISCELLANEOUS NOTES: The bloom season shown in the climate table is based on cultivation records, but plants may bloom at any time. Growers indicate that *D. macropus* is easy to grow and quickly becomes a specimen plant.

Plant and Flower Information

PLANT SIZE AND TYPE: A 5–10 in. (12–25 cm) sympodial epiphyte or lithophyte.

PSEUDOBULB: 5–10 in. (12–25 cm) long. The stems are usually yellowish green with longitudinal grooves.

LEAVES: 3–6. The ovate leaves, which are usually 2–6 in. (5–15 cm) long, are crowded at the apex of each growth. They have a thin texture.

INFLORESCENCE: 2–5 in. (5–13 cm) long. The raceme is usually produced at the apex of the stem. The blossoms may be nearly hidden by the leaves.

FLOWERS: 8–10 per inflorescence. The flowers are 0.5 in. (1.3 cm) across. They are yellow-green or cream. The sepals are slightly broader than the petals. The lip is indistinguishable from the petals. The flowers do not open fully and often appear to be self-pollinating.

HYBRIDIZING NOTES: Chromosome count is 2n = 38 for *D. gracilicaule* (ref. 152). Plants are not usually self-fertile, but pods are regularly produced when pollen from another plant is used.

REFERENCES: 36, 66, 67, 152, 179, 235, 237, 243, 254, 270, 466, 504, 527, 533.

PHOTOS/DRAWINGS: 237, 270, 466, 533.

Dendrobium macrostachyum Lindley

AKA: Sometimes spelled *D. machostachyum*. *D. gamblei* King and Pantling.

ORIGIN/HABITAT: India and Sri Lanka (Ceylon). In India, plants are found in the Garhwal region of the northwestern Himalayas at about 2600 ft. (800 m), but they usually grow below 7550 ft. (2300 m) in the southern and central regions and near the coast of West Ghats. In Sri Lanka (Ceylon), plants are common and widely distributed in wet and dry jungles at about 4000 ft. (1220 m).

CLIMATE: Station #43314, Calicut, India, Lat. 11.3°N, Long. 75.8°E, at 17 ft. (5 m). Temperatures are calculated for an elevation of 4000 ft. (1220 m), resulting in probable extremes of 86°F (30°C) and 44°F (7°C).

N/HEMISPHERE	JAN	FEB	MAR	APR	MAY	JUN	JUL	AUG	SEP	OCT	NOV	DEC
°F AVG MAX	75	76	77	78	77	72	69	70	71	73	74	75
°F AVG MIN	58	60	63	65	65	62	61	61	62	62	61	58
DIURNAL RANGE	17	16	14	13	12	10	8	9	9	11	13	17
RAIN/INCHES	0.4	0.2	0.7	3.6	9.3	33.1	32.5	17.2	7.9	10.3	5.5	1.0
HUMIDITY/%	71	73	73	74	82	87	91	91	87	85	77	74
BLOOM SEASON			*			**	**	**	*			
DAYS CLR @ 5AM	19	18	21	12	5	4	2	2	4	4	19	20
DAYS CLR @ 11AM	16	18	23	15	5	3	0	1	6	5	12	14
RAIN/MM	10	5	18	91	236	841	826	437	201	262	140	25
°C AVG MAX	23.8	24.4	24.9	25.5	24.9	22.1	20.5	21.0	21.6	22.7	23.3	23.8
°C AVG MIN	14.4	15.5	17.1	18.3	18.3	16.6	16.0	16.0	16.6	16.6	16.0	14.4
DIURNAL RANGE	9.4	8.9	7.8	7.2	6.6	5.5	4.5	5.0	5.0	6.1	7.3	9.4
S/HEMISPHERE	JUL	AUG	SEP	OCT	NOV	DEC	JAN	FEB	MAR	APR	MAY	JUN

Cultural Recommendations

LIGHT: 3000–4000 fc. The heavy summer cloud cover indicates that some shading is needed from spring through autumn, but light should be as high as the plant can tolerate, short of burning the leaves.

TEMPERATURES: Throughout the year, days average 69–78°F (21–26°C), and nights average 58–65°F (14–18°C), with a diurnal range of 8–17°F (5–9°C). The warmest weather occurs in spring.

HUMIDITY: 85–90% during summer and early autumn, decreasing to 70–75% in winter and spring.

WATER: Rainfall is extremely heavy from late spring into autumn, but conditions are much drier in winter. Cultivated plants should be watered liberally in summer. They should never be allowed to dry out while actively growing. Water should be gradually reduced during autumn, greatly reduced in winter, then gradually increased in spring when new growth starts.

FERTILIZER: ¼–½ recommended strength, applied weekly. A high-nitrogen fertilizer is beneficial from spring to midsummer, but a fertilizer high in phosphates should be used in late summer and autumn.

REST PERIOD: Growing temperatures should be maintained all year. However, the slightly warmer days and slightly cooler nights which occur in winter double the summer diurnal range. The winter dry period lasts 3–4 months, and for 1–2 of these months, conditions are so dry that even dew is uncommon. For cultivated plants, water should be greatly reduced for 3–4 months. Plants should be allowed to dry out between waterings but should not remain dry for extended periods. Occasional early morning mistings between waterings may be beneficial, especially on bright, sunny days. Fertilizer should be reduced or eliminated until water is increased in spring. In the habitat, light is highest in winter.

GROWING MEDIA: Mounting plants on tree-fern or cork slabs accommodates their pendent growth habit. However, humidity must be high and plants must be watered at least once a day in summer. If plants cannot be mounted, small pots or hanging baskets may be filled with an open, fast-draining medium. Repotting may be done anytime new roots are actively growing.

MISCELLANEOUS NOTES: The bloom season shown in the climate table is based on cultivation records.

Plant and Flower Information

PLANT SIZE AND TYPE: A 12–24 in. (30–60 cm) sympodial epiphyte.

PSEUDOBULB: 12–24 in. (30–60 cm) long. The stems are slender, pendulous, and dark purple-brown.

LEAVES: Many. The ovate to oblong-lanceolate leaves are 1.6–5.0 in. (4–13 cm) long, somewhat curved, and pointed at the tip. They are thick, distichous, and variably deciduous depending on conditions.

INFLORESCENCE: Long. Often longer than the canes, the inflorescences emerge laterally from nodes on older, leafless pseudobulbs.

FLOWERS: 2–4 per inflorescence. The flowers are 0.7–1.0 in. (1.8–2.5 cm) across. The oblong sepals and linear petals are usually pale green, becoming creamy yellow with a pink tinge when mature. The hairy lip is fringed and ruffled along the margins with red, purple, or brownish veins. The disk has 3 narrow ridges and 5 veins. Blossoms are sometimes fragrant.

HYBRIDIZING NOTES: Chromosome counts are n = 19 (ref. 542), n = 20 (ref. 504, 542) and 2n = 38 (ref. 151, 504, 542, 580), 2n = 2x (ref. 504, 580) as *D. gamblei*.

REFERENCES: 38, 46, 97, 102, 119, 151, 179, 190, 202, 216, 244, 250, 254, 255, 277, 317, 369, 424, 445, 504, 542, 568, 580.

PHOTOS/DRAWINGS: 97, 102, 244, 424.

Dendrobium macrostigma J. J. Smith

ORIGIN/HABITAT: Molucca Islands. Plants were found near Wai Kaba in southern Seram and north of Wai Kawa in western Seram. Plants grow on banks or sandstone rocks in forests at 350–1300 ft. (100–400 m).

CLIMATE: Station #49620, Amahai, Seram, Indonesia, Lat. 3.3°S, Long. 128.9°E, at 10 ft. (3 m). Temperatures are calculated for an elevation of 1200 ft. (370 m), resulting in probable extremes of 92°F (33°C) and 62°F (17°C).

N/HEMISPHERE	JAN	FEB	MAR	APR	MAY	JUN	JUL	AUG	SEP	OCT	NOV	DEC
°F AVG MAX	77	77	79	81	84	84	84	84	84	82	80	78
°F AVG MIN	70	70	70	70	71	72	72	72	72	72	71	70
DIURNAL RANGE	7	7	9	11	13	12	12	12	12	10	9	8
RAIN/INCHES	23.7	15.8	9.5	6.1	4.5	5.2	5.0	4.7	5.3	11.0	20.3	25.1
HUMIDITY/%	83	82	81	80	79	78	78	77	79	82	83	84
BLOOM SEASON				*	*							
DAYS CLR @ 9AM	1	1	1	6	7	4	3	3	5	5	3	3
DAYS CLR @ 3PM	1	1	2	5	6	1	1	1	2	3	1	3
RAIN/MM	602	401	241	155	114	132	127	119	135	279	516	638
°C AVG MAX	25.0	25.0	26.2	27.3	28.9	28.9	28.9	28.9	28.9	27.8	26.7	25.6
°C AVG MIN	21.2	21.2	21.2	21.2	21.7	22.3	22.3	22.3	22.3	22.3	21.7	21.2
DIURNAL RANGE	3.8	3.8	5.0	6.1	7.2	6.6	6.6	6.6	6.6	5.5	5.0	4.4
S/HEMISPHERE	JUL	AUG	SEP	OCT	NOV	DEC	JAN	FEB	MAR	APR	MAY	JUN

Cultural Recommendations

LIGHT: 2000–3000 fc. In the habitat, clear days are rare.

TEMPERATURES: Throughout the year, days average 77–84°F (25–29°C), and nights average 70–72°F (21–22°C), with a diurnal range of 7–13°F (4–7°C).

HUMIDITY: 75–80% from late spring through summer, increasing to 80–85% in autumn and winter.

WATER: Rainfall is moderate to extremely heavy all year. Conditions are driest in spring and summer. Cultivated plants should be kept moist but not soggy. Only slight drying should be allowed between waterings.

FERTILIZER: ¼–½ recommended strength. A balanced fertilizer should be applied weekly to biweekly throughout the year.

REST PERIOD: Growing temperatures should be maintained all year. In the habitat, winter is the wettest season, but water should not be increased for cultivated plants. In fact, water should be reduced somewhat for plants grown in the dark, short-day conditions common in temperate latitudes, but they should never be allowed to dry out completely. Fertilizer should be reduced or eliminated anytime water is reduced. In the habitat, light is lowest in winter and highest in spring.

GROWING MEDIA: Plants may be mounted on tree-fern or cork slabs or potted in small pots filled with any open, fast-draining medium. Repotting is best done in early spring when new roots are growing.

MISCELLANEOUS NOTES: The bloom season shown in the climate table is based on reports from the habitat. The plant was described in 1928 in *Bul. Jard. Bot. Buit.* 3rd. sér. 10:146.

Plant and Flower Information

PLANT SIZE AND TYPE: A 26–44 in. (66–112 cm) sympodial lithophyte or terrestrial.

PSEUDOBULB: 26–44 in. (66–112 cm) long. The shiny stems are straw yellow.

LEAVES: Many. The linear-lanceolate leaves are 5–6 in. (13–16 cm) long. They are papery and twisted at the base.

INFLORESCENCE: Short. Numerous Inflorescences emerge between the nodes along the stem.

FLOWERS: The fleshy, fragrant flowers are 0.7 in. (1.9 cm) long. Sepals and petals are white, sometimes with pale rose at the apex.

REFERENCES: 224.

Dendrobium macrum Schlechter

AKA: Kränzlin (ref. 254) listed *D. macrum* as a synonym of *D. isochiloides* Kränzlin, but Schlechter (ref. 437) contended that each was a distinct species.

ORIGIN/HABITAT: Northern Papua New Guinea. Plants grow on forest trees in the Torricelli Range at 1950–2600 ft. (600–800 m).

CLIMATE: Station #94004, Wewak, Papua New Guinea, Lat. 3.6°S, Long. 143.7°E, at 16 ft. (5 m). Temperatures are calculated for an elevation of 2000 ft. (610 m), resulting in probable extremes of 91°F (33°C) and 55°F (13°C).

N/HEMISPHERE	JAN	FEB	MAR	APR	MAY	JUN	JUL	AUG	SEP	OCT	NOV	DEC
°F AVG MAX	81	81	81	81	81	81	80	79	80	81	81	81
°F AVG MIN	67	67	67	68	68	68	68	68	67	67	68	67
DIURNAL RANGE	14	14	14	13	13	13	12	11	13	14	13	14
RAIN/INCHES	7.6	4.8	5.3	10.0	13.3	14.5	12.1	11.9	14.9	16.9	15.1	10.8
HUMIDITY/%	80	79	79	78	79	81	82	82	81	82	81	80
BLOOM SEASON			*							*		
DAYS CLR	N/A											
RAIN/MM	193	122	135	254	338	368	307	302	378	429	384	274
°C AVG MAX	27.5	27.5	27.5	27.5	27.5	27.5	26.9	26.4	26.9	27.5	27.5	27.5
°C AVG MIN	19.7	19.7	19.7	20.3	20.3	20.3	20.3	20.3	19.7	19.7	20.3	19.7
DIURNAL RANGE	7.8	7.8	7.8	7.2	7.2	7.2	6.6	6.1	7.2	7.8	7.2	7.8
S/HEMISPHERE	JUL	AUG	SEP	OCT	NOV	DEC	JAN	FEB	MAR	APR	MAY	JUN

Cultural Recommendations

LIGHT: 2000–3000 fc.

TEMPERATURES: Throughout the year, days average 79–81°F (26–28°C), and nights average 67–68°F (20°C), with a diurnal range of 11–14°F (6–8°C).

HUMIDITY: Near 80% year-round.

WATER: Rainfall is heavy all year, but conditions are slightly drier for 1–2 months in winter. Cultivated plants should be kept evenly moist.

FERTILIZER: ¼–½ recommended strength. A balanced fertilizer should be applied weekly to biweekly throughout the year.

REST PERIOD: Growing temperatures should be maintained year-round. Rainfall is lowest in winter, and water should be reduced somewhat for cultivated plants, especially those grown in the dark, short-day conditions common in temperate latitudes. Plants should never be allowed to dry out completely, however. Fertilizer should be reduced until water is increased in spring. In the habitat, light is highest in winter.

GROWING MEDIA: A very open and fast-draining medium should be used with either baskets or small pots. Repotting may be done anytime new roots are growing.

MISCELLANEOUS NOTES: The bloom season shown in the climate table is based on collection reports.

Plant and Flower Information

PLANT SIZE AND TYPE: A 6–8 in. (15–20 cm) sympodial epiphyte.

PSEUDOBULB: 6–8 in. (15–20 cm) long. The erect stems, which do not branch, arise from a very short rhizome.

LEAVES: Many. The papery leaves are 1.2–1.6 in. (3–4 cm) long. They are grasslike and distichous.

INFLORESCENCE: Short. Inflorescences arise laterally from nodes along the stem.

FLOWERS: 1 per inflorescence. The flowers are 0.3 in. (0.8 cm) across. They are whitish with dense red speckling on the lower half of the lip. The petals are small relative to the sepals. The 3-lobed lip has a rounded midlobe with a recurved point at the center. The sidelobes are large.

REFERENCES: 92, 219, 254, 437, 444, 445.

PHOTOS/DRAWINGS: 437.

Dendrobium maculatum H. B. and K. Now considered a synonym of *Maxillaria maculata* Lindley. **REFERENCES:** 45, 216, 254.

Dendrobium maculosum J. J. Smith. Now considered a synonym of *Flickingeria maculosa* (J. J. Smith) Hunt and Summerhayes. **REFERENCES:** 111, 213, 222, 230, 449.

Dendrobium madonnae Rolfe. See *D. rhodostictum* F. Mueller and Kränzlin. **REFERENCES:** 32, 83, 179, 190, 219, 220, 254, 271, 430, 445.

Dendrobium madrasense A. Hawkes. See *D. aphyllum* (Roxburgh) C. Fischer. **REFERENCES:** 211, 454.

Dendrobium magistratus Cribb

ORIGIN/HABITAT: New Georgia Island in the Solomon Islands and Papua New Guinea. In the Solomon Islands, plants grow in lowland rainforests. In West Highlands Province of New Guinea, they grow on trees in mountain forests at 4250–4900 ft. (1300–1500 m).

CLIMATE: Station #200243, Mt. Hagen, Papua New Guinea, Lat. 5.8°S, Long. 144.3°E, at 5350 ft. (1630 m). Temperatures are calculated for an elevation of 4900 ft. (1500 m), resulting in probable extremes of 89°F (32°C) and 36°F (2°C).

N/HEMISPHERE	JAN	FEB	MAR	APR	MAY	JUN	JUL	AUG	SEP	OCT	NOV	DEC
°F AVG MAX	73	74	75	76	77	77	77	77	76	76	77	75
°F AVG MIN	56	56	56	56	56	57	57	57	57	58	57	55
DIURNAL RANGE	17	18	19	20	21	20	20	20	19	18	20	20
RAIN/INCHES	5.2	6.7	8.7	8.7	8.2	10.2	10.4	10.7	11.2	10.0	7.2	4.7
HUMIDITY/%	84	83	82	78	79	81	81	80	82	81	82	82
BLOOM SEASON	N/A											
DAYS CLR	N/A											
RAIN/MM	132	170	221	221	208	259	264	272	284	254	183	119
°C AVG MAX	22.8	23.3	23.9	24.4	25.0	25.2	25.1	25.0	24.4	24.4	25.0	23.9
°C AVG MIN	13.3	13.6	13.6	13.6	13.6	14.2	14.2	14.2	14.2	14.7	14.2	13.0
DIURNAL RANGE	9.5	9.7	10.3	10.8	11.4	11.0	10.9	10.8	10.2	9.7	10.8	10.9
S/HEMISPHERE	JUL	AUG	SEP	OCT	NOV	DEC	JAN	FEB	MAR	APR	MAY	JUN

Cultural Recommendations

LIGHT: 1800–2500 fc.

TEMPERATURES: Throughout the year, days average 73–77°F (23–25°C), and nights average 55–58°F (13–15°C), with a diurnal range of 17–21°F (10–12°C). The preceding temperatures represent the coolest conditions in which *D. magistratus* should be grown. Plants introduced into the botanical sanctuary at 6550 ft. (2000 m), where it is a few degrees cooler, do not bloom. Because of the difference in habitat elevation, plants from the Solomon Islands may require temperatures 8–10°F (4–6°C) warmer than indicated above.

HUMIDITY: Near 80% year-round.

WATER: Rainfall is moderate to heavy all year. Cultivated plants should be kept moist with only slight drying allowed between waterings.

FERTILIZER: ¼–½ recommended strength. A balanced fertilizer should be applied weekly to biweekly throughout the year.

REST PERIOD: Growing temperatures should be maintained all year. Water should be reduced somewhat in winter for plants grown in the dark, short-day conditions common in temperate latitudes. They should never be allowed to dry out completely, however. Fertilizer should be reduced or eliminated when water is reduced.

GROWING MEDIA: Plants may be mounted on tree-fern or cork slabs if humidity is high and plants are watered at least once daily in summer. When plants are potted, any open, fast-draining medium may be used. Repotting may be done anytime new roots are growing.

Dendrobium magnificum

Plant and Flower Information

PLANT SIZE AND TYPE: A 24 in. (60 cm) sympodial epiphyte.

PSEUDOBULB: 24 in. (60 cm) long. The clustered, canelike stems are swollen at the base and taper toward the apex.

LEAVES: 15 or more. The distichous leaves are elliptic, flat, and 4 in. (10 cm) long.

INFLORESCENCE: 5.5 in. (14 cm) long. Several inflorescences emerge through the base of the leaf sheaths near the apex of the stem. The flowers are arranged in a clustered spiral.

FLOWERS: Few to many per inflorescence. The flowers are about 1.3 in. (3.3 cm) long. Sepals and petals are creamy white. The petals are linear, somewhat spreading, and twist 1–3 times. The lip is yellow with red-orange veins. Plants from the Solomon Islands do not have red veins on the lip.

REFERENCES: 81, 84, 95, 234, 271, 551.

PHOTOS/DRAWINGS: 81, *84, 271.*

Dendrobium magnificum Schlechter. See *D. terrestre* J. J. Smith. REFERENCES: 83, 221, 236, 437, 445.

Dendrobium maidenianum Schlechter. Now considered a synonym of *Cadetia maideniana* Schlechter. REFERENCES: 67, 105, 437.

Dendrobium maierae J. J. Smith

ORIGIN/HABITAT: Bali in the Sunda Islands. Habitat elevation is not available, so the following climate data should be used with caution. Plants were cultivated in the botanical garden at Bogor, Java.

CLIMATE: Station #97230, Bali, Indonesia, Lat. 8.7°S, Long. 115.2°E, at 16 ft. (5 m). Record extreme temperatures are 97°F (36°C) and 63°F (17°C).

N/HEMISPHERE	JAN	FEB	MAR	APR	MAY	JUN	JUL	AUG	SEP	OCT	NOV	DEC
°F AVG MAX	87	86	88	89	91	90	90	89	90	91	90	88
°F AVG MIN	68	71	71	71	72	71	73	73	73	72	72	70
DIURNAL RANGE	19	15	17	18	19	19	17	16	17	19	18	18
RAIN/INCHES	3.8	1.5	0.4	4.8	7.9	14.7	15.9	8.4	8.1	5.0	1.6	2.0
HUMIDITY/%	74	72	72	72	73	76	76	78	77	75	76	75
BLOOM SEASON	N/A											
DAYS CLR @ 8AM	8	7	9	8	5	4	6	3	3	10	8	9
DAYS CLR @ 2PM	13	14	16	10	6	2	5	3	5	10	12	12
RAIN/MM	97	38	10	122	201	373	404	213	206	127	41	51
°C AVG MAX	30.6	30.0	31.1	31.7	32.8	32.2	32.2	31.7	32.2	32.8	32.2	31.1
°C AVG MIN	20.0	21.7	21.7	21.7	22.2	21.7	22.8	22.8	22.8	22.2	22.2	21.1
DIURNAL RANGE	10.6	8.3	9.4	10.0	10.6	10.5	9.4	8.9	9.4	10.6	10.0	10.0
S/HEMISPHERE	JUL	AUG	SEP	OCT	NOV	DEC	JAN	FEB	MAR	APR	MAY	JUN

Cultural Recommendations

LIGHT: 2000–3000 fc.

TEMPERATURES: Throughout the year, days average 86–91°F (30–33°C), and nights average 68–73°F (20–23°C), with a diurnal range of 15–19°F (8–11°C).

HUMIDITY: Near 75% most of the year, dropping to near 70% in late winter and early spring.

WATER: Rainfall is very heavy in summer, but conditions are quite dry for 1–2 months in late winter. Cultivated plants should be kept moist while actively growing, but water should be gradually reduced in autumn.

FERTILIZER: ¼–½ recommended strength. A balanced fertilizer should be applied weekly to biweekly throughout the year.

REST PERIOD: Growing temperatures should be maintained all year. For cultivated plants, water and fertilizer should be reduced in winter. The plants should be allowed to dry slightly between waterings, but they should not remain dry for long periods. In the habitat, light is somewhat higher in winter.

GROWING MEDIA: Plants may be mounted on tree-fern or cork slabs or potted in small pots filled with any open, fast-draining medium. Repotting may be done anytime new roots are growing.

MISCELLANEOUS NOTES: The plant was described in 1920 in *Bul. Jard. Bot. Buit.* 3rd. sér. 2:76.

Plant and Flower Information

PLANT SIZE AND TYPE: A 20 in. (51 cm) sympodial epiphyte.

PSEUDOBULB: 20 in. (51 cm) long. The green stems are clustered, pendulous, and grooved. They taper at the apex and base.

LEAVES: Many. The lanceolate leaves are 3.5–4.5 in. (9.0–11.4 cm) long, dark green, and deciduous. They are twisted at the base and recurved along the margin. They have prominent nerves and numerous scalelike dots.

INFLORESCENCE: Short. Inflorescences are borne at nodes on leafless stems.

FLOWERS: 2 per inflorescence. The flowers are 1.0–1.3 in. (2.6–3.3 cm) across. They are white to pale yellow or yellowish brown. The broad, 3-lobed lip is greenish yellow. The reproductive organs are marked with pale purple dots.

REFERENCES: 222.

Dendrobium majus (Schlechter) J. J. Smith

AKA: *Cadetia major* Schlechter. *Cadetia* is now accepted as a valid genus by some botanists, so this plant may again be considered a *Cadetia*.

ORIGIN/HABITAT: Papua New Guinea. Plants grow on isolated trees in open areas of the Finisterre Mountains at 2600–4900 ft. (800–1500 m).

CLIMATE: Station #94010, Goroka, Papua New Guinea, Lat. 6.1°S, Long. 145.4°E, at 5141 ft. (1567 m). Temperatures are calculated for an elevation of 4000 ft. (1220 m), resulting in probable extremes of 90°F (32°C) and 46°F (8°C).

N/HEMISPHERE	JAN	FEB	MAR	APR	MAY	JUN	JUL	AUG	SEP	OCT	NOV	DEC
°F AVG MAX	80	81	82	83	83	82	83	82	82	82	83	81
°F AVG MIN	60	61	61	61	62	63	63	63	64	63	63	61
DIURNAL RANGE	20	20	21	22	21	19	20	19	18	19	20	20
RAIN/INCHES	2.1	2.8	4.6	5.9	6.6	9.3	9.1	10.1	10.7	8.3	4.6	2.0
HUMIDITY/%	70	67	67	67	67	71	72	73	74	71	70	70
BLOOM SEASON									*			
DAYS CLR	N/A											
RAIN/MM	53	71	117	150	168	236	231	257	272	211	117	51
°C AVG MAX	26.5	27.1	27.6	28.2	28.2	27.6	28.2	27.6	27.6	27.6	28.2	27.1
°C AVG MIN	15.4	16.0	16.0	16.0	16.5	17.1	17.1	17.1	17.6	17.1	17.1	16.0
DIURNAL RANGE	11.1	11.1	11.6	12.2	11.7	10.5	11.1	10.5	10.0	10.5	11.1	11.1
S/HEMISPHERE	JUL	AUG	SEP	OCT	NOV	DEC	JAN	FEB	MAR	APR	MAY	JUN

Cultural Recommendations

LIGHT: 2500–3500 fc.

TEMPERATURES: Throughout the year, days average 80–83°F (27–28°C), and nights average 60–64°F (15–18°C), with a diurnal range of 18–22°F (10–12°C). The diurnal range is unusually large for a habitat with such constant temperatures.

HUMIDITY: 70–75% from summer into autumn, dropping to 65–70% in winter and spring. Plants require excellent air movement.

WATER: Rainfall is moderate to heavy most of the year, with a 3-month drier period in winter. The high relative humidity and large diurnal temperature range result in frequent heavy deposits of dew, with additional moisture available from mist, fog, and low clouds. Cultivated plants should be kept moist, but not soggy. In addition, early morning mistings between waterings are usually beneficial, especially on bright, sunny days.

FERTILIZER: ¼–½ recommended strength. A balanced fertilizer should be applied weekly to biweekly throughout the year.

REST PERIOD: Growing temperatures should be maintained all year. For cultivated plants, water should be reduced and the medium allowed to dry slightly between waterings. Plants should never be allowed to dry out completely, however. Fertilizer should be reduced or eliminated until water is increased in spring. In the habitat, light is higher in winter.

GROWING MEDIA: Plants may be mounted on tree-fern or cork slabs if humidity is high and plants are watered at least once daily in summer. When plants are potted, any open, fast-draining medium may be used. Repotting may be done anytime new roots are growing.

MISCELLANEOUS NOTES: The bloom season shown in the climate table is based on reports from the habitat.

Plant and Flower Information

PLANT SIZE AND TYPE: A 6–8 in. (15–20 cm) sympodial epiphyte.

PSEUDOBULB: 2.8–5.0 in. (7–13 cm) long. The slender stems are clustered and obscurely angled. They arise from a very short rhizome.

LEAVES: 1 per growth. The linear leaves are 2.4–3.1 in. (6–8 cm) long. They are minutely cut at the apex.

FLOWERS: 1 per inflorescence. The flowers are 0.6 in. (1.5 cm) across. They are snow-white with yellow-green in the center of the lip. The dorsal sepal is erect. The linear petals are recurved at the tips. The midlobe is deeply notched at the apex.

REFERENCES: 221, 437, 472, 486.

Dendrobium malacanthum Kränzlin

ORIGIN/HABITAT: Bourawari, Papua New Guinea. Plants grow on *Ficus* at about 2550 ft. (780 m). We were unable to find this location and assume that it is probably the same as the Boroai district referred to by Schlechter. Climate data was selected based on this assumption. Because of this uncertainty, the following data should be used with caution.

CLIMATE: Station #200187, Erap, Papua New Guinea, Lat. 6.6°S, Long. 146.7°E, at 850 ft. (260 m). Temperatures are calculated for an elevation of 1950 ft. (600 m), resulting in probable extremes of 98°F (37°C) and 49°F (10°C).

N/HEMISPHERE	JAN	FEB	MAR	APR	MAY	JUN	JUL	AUG	SEP	OCT	NOV	DEC
°F AVG MAX	84	84	85	86	89	89	89	89	89	88	86	86
°F AVG MIN	65	65	65	66	68	69	68	68	69	67	70	66
DIURNAL RANGE	19	19	20	20	21	20	21	21	20	21	16	20
RAIN/INCHES	3.9	3.9	2.7	3.0	3.0	5.3	5.9	5.9	7.0	3.4	2.4	3.1
HUMIDITY/%	82	81	81	79	75	74	74	74	77	76	80	80
BLOOM SEASON	N/A											
DAYS CLR	N/A											
RAIN/MM	99	99	69	76	76	135	150	150	178	86	61	79
°C AVG MAX	29.1	29.1	29.6	30.2	31.8	31.8	31.8	31.8	31.8	31.3	30.2	30.2
°C AVG MIN	18.5	18.5	18.5	19.1	20.2	20.7	20.2	20.2	20.7	19.6	21.3	19.1
DIURNAL RANGE	10.6	10.6	11.1	11.1	11.6	11.1	11.6	11.6	11.1	11.7	8.9	11.1
S/HEMISPHERE	JUL	AUG	SEP	OCT	NOV	DEC	JAN	FEB	MAR	APR	MAY	JUN

Cultural Recommendations

LIGHT: 2000–3000 fc.

TEMPERATURES: Throughout the year, days average 84–89°F (29–32°C), and nights average 65–70°F (19–21°C), with a diurnal range of 16–21°F (9–12°C).

HUMIDITY: 75–80% year-round. The habitat may be quite dry during hot afternoons.

WATER: Rainfall is relatively light most of the year. However, for 4–5 months in summer and early autumn, conditions are much wetter. Cultivated plants should be thoroughly saturated then allowed to dry slightly between waterings.

FERTILIZER: ¼–½ recommended strength. A balanced fertilizer should be applied weekly to biweekly throughout the year.

REST PERIOD: Growing temperatures should be maintained all year. In the habitat, rainfall is lowest in winter, but moisture is available from fog and mist. Cultivated plants should dry slightly between waterings, but they should not remain completely dry for extended periods. Additional early morning mistings between waterings may be beneficial, especially on bright, sunny days. Fertilizer should be reduced in winter. In the habitat, seasonal light variation is minor.

GROWING MEDIA: Mounting plants on tree-fern or cork slabs accommodates their pendulous growth habit. However, humidity must be high and plants must be watered at least once a day in summer. If plants cannot be mounted, small pots or hanging baskets may be filled with an open, fast-draining medium. Repotting may be done anytime new roots are actively growing.

Plant and Flower Information

PLANT SIZE AND TYPE: A 16–18 in. (41–46 cm) sympodial epiphyte.

PSEUDOBULB: 16–18 in. (41–46 cm) long. The stems are limp and pendulous.

LEAVES: Many. The widely spaced leaves are 2.4–3.5 in. (6–9 cm) long, ovate-lanceolate, and bilobed. They have a thin papery texture.

INFLORESCENCE: Inflorescences emerge from nodes above the middle of the stem.

FLOWERS: 2 per inflorescence. The dirty pink flowers are 2 in. (5 cm) across. All segments are elongated to a slender point. The lip margins are deeply cut along the sides of the midlobe with the cuts extending almost to the centerline. The lateral sepals are sickle-shaped. The disk is somewhat scaly.

REFERENCES: 220, 254, 445.

PHOTOS/DRAWINGS: 254.

Dendrobium malaitense Rolfe. See *D. kietaense* Schlechter.

REFERENCES: 55, 223, 271, 417, 516.

Dendrobium malbrownii Dockrill

ORIGIN/HABITAT: New Guinea and northeastern Australia. In Australia, plants grow only in the McIlwraith Range on the Cape York Peninsula. They are usually found in high light near the forest edge or along creeks. The plants are most often in the upper branches of rainforest trees above 1300 ft. (400 m). The orchids are common on mainland New Guinea and offshore islands, where they grow near sea level on tree branches overhanging the beach, but they are also found as high as 4900 ft. (1500 m).

CLIMATE: Station #94185, Coen, Australia, Lat. 14.0°S, Long. 143.2°E, at 633 ft. (193 m). Temperatures are calculated for an elevation of 2000 ft. (610 m). Record extreme temperatures are not available for this location.

N/HEMISPHERE	JAN	FEB	MAR	APR	MAY	JUN	JUL	AUG	SEP	OCT	NOV	DEC
°F AVG MAX	69	70	71	75	77	78	76	76	76	77	75	69
°F AVG MIN	61	62	64	67	70	71	70	70	70	69	67	60
DIURNAL RANGE	8	8	7	8	7	7	6	6	6	8	8	9
RAIN/INCHES	0.2	0.1	0.1	0.4	1.0	2.7	7.4	7.4	4.7	2.2	1.4	0.6
HUMIDITY/%	N/A											
BLOOM SEASON							*	*	*			
DAYS CLR	N/A											
RAIN/MM	5	3	3	10	25	69	188	188	119	56	36	15
°C AVG MAX	20.6	21.1	21.7	23.9	25.0	25.5	24.4	24.4	24.4	25.0	23.9	20.6
°C AVG MIN	16.1	16.9	18.0	19.7	21.4	21.9	21.4	21.4	21.4	20.8	19.7	15.8
DIURNAL RANGE	4.5	4.2	3.7	4.2	3.6	3.6	3.0	3.0	3.0	4.2	4.2	4.8
S/HEMISPHERE	JUL	AUG	SEP	OCT	NOV	DEC	JAN	FEB	MAR	APR	MAY	JUN

Dendrobium maleolens

Cultural Recommendations

LIGHT: 3000–4500 fc. Plants require high light with strong air movement year-round. About 40–50% shading is needed from spring through autumn, but light should be as high as the plant can tolerate, short of burning the leaves.

TEMPERATURES: Summer days average 76–78°F (24–26°C), and nights average 70–71°F (21–22°C), with a diurnal range of 6–7°F (3–4°C).

HUMIDITY: Information is not available for this location. However, average humidity normally exceeds 70–75% at other stations in the region and may be even greater in rainforests.

WATER: Rainfall is moderate during the 5-month summer wet season. However, more moisture is available year-round in the rainforest habitat than is indicated by the rainfall averages at the lower elevation weather station. Cultivated plants should be watered frequently especially in very hot weather. They should be allowed to dry only slightly between waterings.

FERTILIZER: ¼–½ recommended strength, applied weekly. A high-nitrogen fertilizer is beneficial from spring to midsummer, while a fertilizer high in phosphates should be used in late summer and autumn.

REST PERIOD: Winter days average 69–71°F (21–22°C), and nights average 60–64°F (16–18°C), with a diurnal range of 7–9°F (4–5°C). Growers indicate that winter temperatures should not fall below 50°F (10°C). The dry season is long and severe, but mist and heavy dew provide additional moisture in the rainforest habitat. Water should be reduced in winter for cultivated plants, but they should never be allowed to dry completely. Fertilizer should be reduced or eliminated until new growth begins in spring. In the habitat, light is highest in winter.

GROWING MEDIA: Plants are best mounted on tree-fern or cork slabs if humidity is high and plants are watered at least once daily in summer. If plants must be potted, undersized pots that are barely large enough to hold the roots, should be filled with a very open, fast-draining medium. Repotting may be done anytime new roots are growing.

MISCELLANEOUS NOTES: The bloom season shown in the climate table is based on cultivation records. Some plants may have a few blossoms open most of the year.

Plant and Flower Information

PLANT SIZE AND TYPE: A 5–14 in. (13–36 cm) sympodial epiphyte. Plants may form clumps to 12 in. (31 cm) across.

PSEUDOBULB: 5–14 in. (13–36 cm) long. The thin, wiry stems are leafy on the upper half.

LEAVES: 10–20. The leaves are 1.2–2.4 in. (3–6 cm) long, thin, linear, and light olive-green. They persist for several years, and when they do fall, they drop gradually, falling first from the lower part of the stem.

INFLORESCENCE: Short. Flowers are held close to the stem. The inflorescences emerge from nodes on the upper portion of the stem.

FLOWERS: 1 per inflorescence. The flowers are 0.4 in. (1 cm) across and open fully. The sepals and tiny petals are creamy white tinged with yellow-green at the tips. The lip is uppermost. It is shiny red with a yellow midlobe. The column is flushed with deep purple. The blossoms are short-lived, seldom lasting more than 2 days.

REFERENCES: 67, 105, 231, 240, 262, 304, 533.

PHOTOS/DRAWINGS: *105, 240, 304,* 533.

Dendrobium maleolens Kränzlin

ORIGIN/HABITAT: The southeast region of Sulawesi (Celebes). Plants were collected near Lepo-lepo, just southwest of Kendari (Kandari).

CLIMATE: Station #97146, Kendari, Sulawesi, Indonesia, Lat. 4.1°S, Long. 122.4°E, at 164 ft. (50 m). Record extreme temperatures are not available for this location.

N/HEMISPHERE	JAN	FEB	MAR	APR	MAY	JUN	JUL	AUG	SEP	OCT	NOV	DEC
°F AVG MAX	85	86	88	90	90	89	88	87	88	86	86	84
°F AVG MIN	70	71	70	72	74	75	75	74	74	74	74	72
DIURNAL RANGE	15	15	18	18	16	14	13	13	14	12	12	12
RAIN/INCHES	5.7	4.0	2.3	2.5	6.0	7.7	7.9	7.3	8.4	8.2	9.9	9.1
HUMIDITY/%	86	80	76	73	76	82	80	81	82	83	85	84
BLOOM SEASON	*											
DAYS CLR @ 8AM	3	10	10	14	8	5	1	2	2	3	2	4
DAYS CLR @ 2PM	0	0	1	2	1	0	1	0	0	0	0	0
RAIN/MM	144	102	58	63	152	197	201	186	213	208	252	231
°C AVG MAX	29.2	29.9	31.0	32.3	32.4	31.8	31.1	30.7	30.9	29.9	30.1	28.8
°C AVG MIN	21.3	21.5	21.1	22.4	23.6	24.0	24.0	23.4	23.4	23.6	23.4	22.3
DIURNAL RANGE	7.9	8.4	9.9	9.9	8.8	7.8	7.1	7.3	7.5	6.3	6.7	6.5
S/HEMISPHERE	JUL	AUG	SEP	OCT	NOV	DEC	JAN	FEB	MAR	APR	MAY	JUN

Cultural Recommendations

LIGHT: 2000–3000 fc.

TEMPERATURES: Throughout the year, days average 84–90°F (29–32°C), and nights average 70–75°F (21–24°C), with a diurnal range of 12–18°F (6–10°C).

HUMIDITY: 80–85% most of the year, dropping to near 75% in spring.

WATER: Rainfall is moderate to heavy most of the year, but conditions are slightly drier for 2–3 months in late winter and early spring. Plants should be kept evenly moist while actively growing.

FERTILIZER: ¼–½ recommended strength. A balanced fertilizer should be applied weekly to biweekly throughout the year.

REST PERIOD: Growing temperatures should be maintained all year. For cultivated plants, water should be reduced for 2–3 months and the plants allowed to dry slightly between waterings. They should not remain dry for long periods, however. Fertilizer should be reduced or eliminated anytime water is reduced. In the habitat, light is highest in late winter and spring.

GROWING MEDIA: Plants may be mounted on tree-fern or cork slabs if humidity is high and plants are watered at least once daily in summer. When plants are potted, any open, fast-draining medium may be used. Repotting may be done anytime new roots are growing.

MISCELLANEOUS NOTES: The bloom season shown in the climate table is based on collection reports.

Plant and Flower Information

PLANT SIZE AND TYPE: A 32 in. (81 cm) sympodial epiphyte.

PSEUDOBULB: 32 in. (81 cm) long. The stems are very branching.

LEAVES: Many. The variable leaves, which are 0.8–3.1 in. (2–8 cm) long, may be oblong, ovate, or linear. They face in all directions. The leaves are smallest near the apex of the stem.

INFLORESCENCE: Racemes are clustered on upper part of the stem.

FLOWERS: 2–4 per inflorescence. The flowers are 2.4 in. (6 cm) across. Blossoms are white suffused with rose and open at different times. The petals have violet veins. The 3-lobed lip has erect, rounded sidelobes. The heart-shaped midlobe is ruffled along the uneven margin.

REFERENCES: 220, 254.

Dendrobium maliliense J. J. Smith

AKA: This plant was originally described as part of the section *Cadetia*, which is now considered a separate genus.

ORIGIN/HABITAT: Central Sulawesi (Celebes). Plants were found at sea level near Malili at the north end of Bone Bay.

CLIMATE: Station #97146, Kendari, Sulawesi, Indonesia, Lat. 4.1°S, Long.

122.4°E, at 164 ft. (50 m). Record extreme temperatures are not available for this location.

N/HEMISPHERE	JAN	FEB	MAR	APR	MAY	JUN	JUL	AUG	SEP	OCT	NOV	DEC
°F AVG MAX	85	86	88	90	90	89	88	87	88	86	86	84
°F AVG MIN	70	71	70	72	74	75	75	74	74	74	74	72
DIURNAL RANGE	15	15	18	18	16	14	13	13	14	12	12	12
RAIN/INCHES	5.7	4.0	2.3	2.5	6.0	7.7	7.9	7.3	8.4	8.2	9.9	9.1
HUMIDITY/%	86	80	76	73	76	82	80	81	82	83	85	84
BLOOM SEASON			*									
DAYS CLR @ 8AM	3	10	10	14	8	5	1	2	2	3	2	4
DAYS CLR @ 2PM	0	0	1	2	1	0	1	0	0	0	0	0
RAIN/MM	144	102	58	63	152	197	201	186	213	208	252	231
°C AVG MAX	29.2	29.9	31.0	32.3	32.4	31.8	31.1	30.7	30.9	29.9	30.1	28.8
°C AVG MIN	21.3	21.5	21.1	22.4	23.6	24.0	24.0	23.4	23.4	23.6	23.4	22.3
DIURNAL RANGE	7.9	8.4	9.9	9.9	8.8	7.8	7.1	7.3	7.5	6.3	6.7	6.5
S/HEMISPHERE	JUL	AUG	SEP	OCT	NOV	DEC	JAN	FEB	MAR	APR	MAY	JUN

Cultural Recommendations

LIGHT: 2000–3000 fc.

TEMPERATURES: Throughout the year, days average 84–90°F (29–32°C), and nights average 70–75°F (21–24°C), with a diurnal range of 12–18°F (6–10°C).

HUMIDITY: 80–85% most of the year, dropping to near 75% in spring.

WATER: Rainfall is moderate to heavy most of the year, but conditions are slightly drier for 2–3 months in late winter and early spring. Plants should be kept evenly moist while actively growing.

FERTILIZER: ¼–½ recommended strength. A balanced fertilizer should be applied weekly to biweekly throughout the year.

REST PERIOD: Growing temperatures should be maintained all year. For cultivated plants, water should be reduced for 2–3 months and the plants allowed to dry slightly between waterings. They should not remain dry for long periods, however. Fertilizer should be reduced or eliminated anytime water is reduced. In the habitat, light is highest in late winter and spring.

GROWING MEDIA: Plants may be mounted on tree-fern or cork slabs or potted in small pots filled with any open, fast-draining medium. Repotting may be done anytime new roots are growing.

MISCELLANEOUS NOTES: The bloom season shown in the climate table is based on reports from the habitat. The plant was described in 1933 in *Engler's Bot. Jahrb.* 65:487.

Plant and Flower Information

PLANT SIZE AND TYPE: A tiny, 0.8 in. (2.0 cm) sympodial epiphyte.

PSEUDOBULB: 0.2–0.3 in. (0.5–0.8 cm) long. The clustered, oblong stems are grooved lengthwise. They are held at an angle to the short, branching rhizome.

LEAVES: 1 per growth. The fleshy, oblong leaves are 0.5 in. (1.2 cm) long.

INFLORESCENCE: Short.

FLOWERS: The tiny, white flowers are 0.1–0.2 in. (0.3–0.5 cm) across.

REFERENCES: 225.

Dendrobium maluense (Schlechter) J. J. Smith

AKA: *Cadetia quadriquetra* Schlechter. *Cadetia* is now considered a valid genus by some botanists, so this plant may again become a *Cadetia*.

ORIGIN/HABITAT: Northwest Papua New Guinea. Plants were found along the Sepik River at 150–350 ft. (50–100 m).

CLIMATE: Station #200004, Ambunti, Papua New Guinea, Lat. 4.2°S, Long. 142.8°E, at 164 ft. (50 m). Record extreme temperatures are 99°F (37°C) and 52°F (11°C).

N/HEMISPHERE	JAN	FEB	MAR	APR	MAY	JUN	JUL	AUG	SEP	OCT	NOV	DEC
°F AVG MAX	88	90	90	90	91	90	90	90	90	90	90	89
°F AVG MIN	72	73	74	73	73	73	72	73	73	73	73	74
DIURNAL RANGE	16	17	16	17	18	17	18	17	17	17	17	15
RAIN/INCHES	6.4	7.4	7.7	8.5	9.2	9.4	10.9	10.2	12.2	10.4	8.3	5.2
HUMIDITY/%	N/A											
BLOOM SEASON	*											
DAYS CLR	N/A											
RAIN/MM	163	187	196	217	233	240	277	260	311	265	211	132
°C AVG MAX	31.2	32.2	32.4	32.1	32.6	32.2	32.3	31.9	32.1	31.9	31.9	31.7
°C AVG MIN	22.4	22.8	23.2	22.8	23.0	22.8	22.4	22.5	22.7	22.8	22.9	23.1
DIURNAL RANGE	8.8	9.4	9.2	9.3	9.6	9.4	9.9	9.4	9.4	9.1	9.0	8.6
S/HEMISPHERE	JUL	AUG	SEP	OCT	NOV	DEC	JAN	FEB	MAR	APR	MAY	JUN

Cultural Recommendations

LIGHT: 2000–3000 fc.

TEMPERATURES: Throughout the year, days average 88–91°F (31–33°C), and nights average 72–74°F (22–23°C), with a diurnal range of 15–18°F (9–10°C).

HUMIDITY: Information is not available for this location. Reports from other stations in the region suggest that humidity probably averages 80–85% year-round.

WATER: Rainfall is heavy year-round. The wettest weather occurs in summer and early autumn. Cultivated plants should be kept moist.

FERTILIZER: ¼–½ recommended strength. A balanced fertilizer should be applied weekly to biweekly throughout the year.

REST PERIOD: Growing conditions should be maintained all year. Water and fertilizer should be reduced for plants cultivated in the dark, short-day conditions common in temperate-latitude winters. These plants should never be allowed to dry out completely, however.

GROWING MEDIA: Plants may be mounted on tree-fern or cork slabs if humidity is high and plants are watered at least once daily in summer. When plants are potted, medium to coarse fir bark or any open, fast-draining medium may be used. Repotting may be done anytime new roots are growing.

MISCELLANEOUS NOTES: The bloom season shown in the climate table is based on reports from the habitat.

Plant and Flower Information

PLANT SIZE AND TYPE: A 4–7 in. (11–17 cm) sympodial epiphyte.

PSEUDOBULB: 1.6–4.0 in. (4–10 cm) long. The tiny, square stems are clustered on a very short rhizome.

LEAVES: 1 per growth. The leaf is 1.9–2.4 in. (4.7–6.0 cm) long.

INFLORESCENCE: Short.

FLOWERS: 1 per inflorescence. The sepals are 0.2 in. (0.5 cm) long. Blossoms are white with a carmine-red margin.

REFERENCES: 225, 443, 486.

Dendrobium malvicolor Ridley

ORIGIN/HABITAT: Eastern Java and Sumatra. In Java, plants are found on Mt. Lawu and Mt. Tengger at 5200–6500 ft. (1590–1980 m), where they grow on stunted trees. Comber (ref. 75) indicates that the more common Sumatra plants grow at about the same elevations, but collections are also reported from Kerinci (Korinchi) Peak at 7300–10,000 ft. (2230–3050 m).

CLIMATE: Station #96881, Madiun, Java, Indonesia, Lat. 7.6°S, Long. 111.4°E, at 361 ft. (110m). Temperatures are calculated for an elevation of 5900 ft. (1800 m), resulting in probable extremes of 77°F (25°C) and 44°F (7°C).

Dendrobium mamberamense

N/HEMISPHERE	JAN	FEB	MAR	APR	MAY	JUN	JUL	AUG	SEP	OCT	NOV	DEC
°F AVG MAX	67	68	69	70	68	67	66	66	67	69	68	68
°F AVG MIN	51	51	53	54	54	54	54	54	54	54	54	52
DIURNAL RANGE	16	17	16	16	14	13	12	12	13	15	14	16
RAIN/INCHES	1.3	0.8	1.2	2.9	7.6	10.2	11.9	10.9	10.4	8.8	5.1	3.2
HUMIDITY/%	60	54	52	52	64	72	77	78	78	74	70	64
BLOOM SEASON												*
DAYS CLR @ 7AM	18	22	21	16	8	4	2	2	3	6	9	16
DAYS CLR @ 1PM	15	17	14	9	4	2	1	1	1	3	6	11
RAIN/MM	33	20	30	74	193	259	302	277	264	224	130	81
°C AVG MAX	19.3	19.8	20.4	21.0	19.8	19.3	18.7	18.7	19.3	20.4	19.8	19.8
°C AVG MIN	10.4	10.4	11.5	12.1	12.1	12.1	12.1	12.1	12.1	12.1	12.1	11.0
DIURNAL RANGE	8.9	9.4	8.9	8.9	7.7	7.2	6.6	6.6	7.2	8.3	7.7	8.8
S/HEMISPHERE	JUL	AUG	SEP	OCT	NOV	DEC	JAN	FEB	MAR	APR	MAY	JUN

Cultural Recommendations

LIGHT: 2500–3500 fc.

TEMPERATURES: Throughout the year, days average 66–70°F (19–21°C), and nights average 51–54°F (10–12°C), with a diurnal range of 12–17°F (7–9°C). Due to the effects of the microclimate, maximum temperatures may be 6–10°F (3–6°C) warmer than indicated in the preceding table.

HUMIDITY: 75–80% in summer, dropping to 50–55% for 3 months in winter and spring. However, in the high-elevation habitat, values may be higher.

WATER: At the weather station, rainfall is heavy from spring through autumn, followed by a 2–3 month winter dry season when humidity is so low that even moisture from dew is uncommon. Rainfall is much heavier in the high-elevation forests, however, and moisture from mist, fog, and dew is often available, even during periods of low rainfall. Cultivated plants should be kept moist but not soggy while growing, but water should be gradually reduced in autumn.

FERTILIZER: ¼–½ recommended strength. A balanced fertilizer should be applied weekly to biweekly throughout the year.

REST PERIOD: Growing temperatures should be maintained. In the habitat, winter conditions are drier. Cultivated plants need less water and fertilizer for 2–3 months. Plants should be allowed to dry slightly between waterings, but they should not remain dry for long periods. In the habitat, light is much higher in winter.

GROWING MEDIA: Plants may be mounted on tree-fern or cork slabs or potted in small pots filled with any open, fast-draining medium. Repotting may be done anytime new roots are growing.

MISCELLANEOUS NOTES: The bloom season shown in the climate table is based on reports from the habitat.

Plant and Flower Information

PLANT SIZE AND TYPE: A 2.0–2.4 in. (5–6 cm) sympodial epiphyte.

PSEUDOBULB: 1.2–1.6 in. (3–4 cm) long. The crowded stems are thin and wiry at the base, but the upper portion is swollen. They become wrinkled with age.

LEAVES: 6 per growth. The leaves are 0.8 in. (2 cm) long.

INFLORESCENCE: Short. 1–2 inflorescences arise near the apex of mature, normally leafless stems.

FLOWERS: 3–4 per inflorescence. The flowers are 0.8 in. (2 cm) long. Blossoms are white. Some have a pale mauve tinge, or they may be pale magenta with orange at the base of the lip. The lateral sepals are triangular. The lip and petals are lanceolate. Floral segments are pointed at the tips. The anther cap is marked with 2 dark violet spots.

REFERENCES: 73, 75, 222, 401.

PHOTOS/DRAWINGS: 73, 75.

Dendrobium mamberamense J. J. Smith.
Now considered a synonym of *Diplocaulobium mamberamense* (J. J. Smith) A. Hawkes. REFERENCES: 224, 229, 445, 470.

Dendrobium manillense Schauer.
Sometimes spelled *D. manilense*, it is now considered a synonym of *Appendicula cornuta* Blume. REFERENCES: 216, 296, 469, 536.

Dendrobium mannii Ridley

AKA: Seidenfaden and Wood (ref. 455) indicate that some clones of *D. mannii* have been incorrectly classified as *D. terminale* Parish and Rchb. f. In 1992 *Opera Botanica* 114, Seidenfaden indicates that in Indochina a similar problem exists for plants identified as *D. mannii* and *D. nathanielis* Rchb. f.

ORIGIN/HABITAT: India and Southeast Asia. In northeast India, plants grow near Darjeeling in Sikkim and in the Khasi (Khasia) Hills at 1000–2300 ft. (300–700 m). The habitat includes Burma, Thailand, Malaya, Laos, and Vietnam. In Malaya, collections have been made on Mt. Ophir and along the Sedili River in Johore State. In Vietnam, plants are reported near Dalat at about 2950 ft. (900 m).

CLIMATE: Station #42410, Gauhati, India, Lat. 26.1°N, Long. 91.6°E, at 158 ft. (48 m). Temperatures have been calculated for a habitat elevation of 2000 ft. (610 m), resulting in probable extremes of 98°F (37°C) and 35°F (2°C).

N/HEMISPHERE	JAN	FEB	MAR	APR	MAY	JUN	JUL	AUG	SEP	OCT	NOV	DEC
°F AVG MAX	70	72	80	82	82	83	84	84	83	81	75	70
°F AVG MIN	45	48	54	62	66	71	72	72	70	65	55	47
DIURNAL RANGE	25	24	26	20	16	12	12	12	13	16	20	23
RAIN/INCHES	0.4	1.2	2.0	5.7	9.3	12.3	12.3	10.3	6.6	2.8	0.6	0.2
HUMIDITY/%	79	72	64	71	82	85	85	86	84	84	83	82
BLOOM SEASON									*	*		
DAYS CLR @ 6AM	6	12	16	11	3	0	0	1	3	7	6	3
DAYS CLR @ 12PM	17	16	18	15	6	1	0	0	2	11	17	19
RAIN/MM	10	30	51	145	236	312	312	262	168	71	15	5
°C AVG MAX	21.1	22.2	26.6	27.7	27.7	28.3	28.8	28.8	28.3	27.2	23.8	21.1
°C AVG MIN	7.2	8.8	12.2	16.6	18.8	21.6	22.2	22.2	21.1	18.3	12.7	8.3
DIURNAL RANGE	13.9	13.4	14.4	11.1	8.9	6.7	6.6	6.6	7.2	8.9	11.1	12.8
S/HEMISPHERE	JUL	AUG	SEP	OCT	NOV	DEC	JAN	FEB	MAR	APR	MAY	JUN

Cultural Recommendations

LIGHT: 2500–3500 fc.

TEMPERATURES: Summer days average 83–84°F (28–29°C), and nights average 71–72°F (22°C), with a diurnal range of 12°F (7°C).

HUMIDITY: 80–85% most of the year, dropping to 65–70% for 3 months in late winter and early spring.

WATER: Rainfall is heavy from spring through summer but decreases rapidly in autumn with a 1–2 month transition into the winter dry season. Cultivated plants should be kept moist while actively growing, but water should be gradually reduced after new growths mature in autumn.

FERTILIZER: ¼–½ recommended strength, applied weekly. A high-nitrogen fertilizer is beneficial from spring to midsummer, but a fertilizer high in phosphates should be used in late summer and autumn.

REST PERIOD: Winter days average 70–72°F (21–22°C), and nights average 45–48°F (7–9°C), with a diurnal range of 23–25°F (13–14°C). Actual winter temperatures do not appear to be critical, but the increased diurnal range is common throughout the habitat. Although rainfall is low for 4–5 winter months, high humidity and the large temperature range indicate that additional moisture from heavy dew is common. Therefore, while water should be greatly reduced and cultivated plants allowed to dry out between waterings from late autumn into early spring, they should not remain dry for extended periods. Occasional mistings between waterings during bright, sunny weather may help prevent the plants from becoming too dry. Fertilizer should be reduced or eliminated until active growth resumes and water is increased in spring. In the habitat, light is brightest in winter.

GROWING MEDIA: Plants may be mounted on tree-fern or cork slabs if humidity is high and plants are watered at least once daily in summer. When plants are potted, any open, fast-draining medium may be used. Repotting is best done in early spring when new roots are growing.

MISCELLANEOUS NOTES: The bloom season shown in the climate table is based on reports from the habitat. Cultivated plants may bloom any time of year.

Plant and Flower Information

PLANT SIZE AND TYPE: A 4–6 in. (10–15 cm) sympodial epiphyte.

PSEUDOBULB: 4–6 in. (10–15 cm) long. The stems are thin at the base becoming expanded and flattened above.

LEAVES: 10–12 per growth. The distichous leaves are 0.4–0.8 in. (1–2 cm) long, fleshy, triangular, and deciduous. The leaf sheaths are persistent.

INFLORESCENCE: Short. The clustered flowers arise from apical and lateral nodes, usually after the leaves have fallen.

FLOWERS: 1–2 per inflorescence. The flowers are 0.4 in. (1 cm) across. Blossoms may be pale yellowish, greenish yellow, or white with weak pink to purple stripes, especially on the backside. The whitish petals are small relative to the sepals. The fan-shaped lip is narrow at the base and widest at the apex. It has a deep yellow or orange patch on the disk. It is notched at the apex but has no sidelobes.

HYBRIDIZING NOTES: Chromosome count is 2n = 38 (ref. 154, 188). Johansen (ref. 239) indicates that plants are self-sterile and that flowers dropped 6–7 days after self-pollination.

REFERENCES: 154, 188, 200, 239, 254, 395, 402, 447, 448, 454, 455.

PHOTOS/DRAWINGS: *454*, *455*.

Dendrobium maraiparense J. J. Wood and C. L. Chan

AKA: The plant description is in publication and was not yet available.

ORIGIN/HABITAT: Borneo. The plant is endemic to Sabah, where it grows in the lower mountain forests of Mt. Kinabalu at 3950–6550 ft. (1200–2000 m).

CLIMATE: Station #49613, Tambunan, Sabah, Borneo, Lat. 5.7°N, Long. 116.4°E, at 1200 ft. (366 m). Temperatures are calculated for an elevation of 4800 ft. (1460 m), resulting in probable extremes of 86°F (30°C) and 42°F (6°C).

N/HEMISPHERE	JAN	FEB	MAR	APR	MAY	JUN	JUL	AUG	SEP	OCT	NOV	DEC
°F AVG MAX	74	75	77	78	78	77	77	77	77	76	75	74
°F AVG MIN	55	53	54	55	56	55	54	54	55	55	55	56
DIURNAL RANGE	19	22	23	23	22	22	23	23	22	21	20	18
RAIN/INCHES	5.8	3.7	5.8	7.5	8.2	7.3	5.1	4.9	6.4	7.0	6.8	6.0
HUMIDITY/%	N/A											
BLOOM SEASON	N/A											
DAYS CLR	N/A											
RAIN/MM	147	94	147	190	208	185	130	124	163	178	173	152
°C AVG MAX	23.4	24.0	25.1	25.6	25.6	25.1	25.1	25.1	25.1	24.5	24.0	23.4
°C AVG MIN	12.8	11.7	12.3	12.8	13.4	12.8	12.3	12.3	12.8	12.8	12.8	13.4
DIURNAL RANGE	10.6	12.3	12.8	12.8	12.2	12.3	12.8	12.8	12.3	11.7	11.2	10.0
S/HEMISPHERE	JUL	AUG	SEP	OCT	NOV	DEC	JAN	FEB	MAR	APR	MAY	JUN

Cultural Recommendations

LIGHT: 2000–3000 fc.

TEMPERATURES: Throughout the year, days average 74–78°F (23–26°C), and nights average 53–56°F (12–13°C), with a diurnal range of 18–23°F (10–13°C).

HUMIDITY: Information is not available for this location. However, records from nearby locations indicate that humidity probably averages 80–85% year-round.

WATER: Rainfall is moderate to heavy all year with a brief, slightly drier period in winter. Cultivated plants should be kept moist, with only slight drying allowed between waterings.

FERTILIZER: ¼–½ recommended strength. A balanced fertilizer should be applied weekly to biweekly throughout the year.

REST PERIOD: Growing temperatures should be maintained all year. Water should be reduced for cultivated plants, especially those grown in the dark, short-day conditions common in temperate-latitude winters, but they should never be allowed to dry out completely. Fertilizer should be reduced or eliminated until water is increased in spring.

GROWING MEDIA: Plants may be mounted on tree-fern or cork slabs if humidity is high and plants are watered at least once daily in summer. When plants are potted, any open, fast-draining medium may be used. Repotting is best done in early spring when new roots begin to grow.

Plant and Flower Information

Plant and flower information is unavailable.

REFERENCES: 592.

Dendrobium margaretae T. M. Reeve

AKA: Sometimes spelled *D. margaretiae*.

ORIGIN/HABITAT: Papua New Guinea, including Enga, Southern Highlands, and Eastern Highlands Provinces. Plants most often grow on *Castanopsis acuminatissima*, the New Guinea oak tree, at 4900–6550 ft. (1500–2000 m).

CLIMATE: Station #94010, Goroka, Papua New Guinea, Lat. 6.1°S, Long. 145.4°E, at 5141 ft. (1567 m). Temperatures are calculated for an elevation of 5900 ft. (1800 m), resulting in probable extremes of 84°F (29°C) and 40°F (5°C).

N/HEMISPHERE	JAN	FEB	MAR	APR	MAY	JUN	JUL	AUG	SEP	OCT	NOV	DEC
°F AVG MAX	73	74	75	76	76	75	76	75	75	75	76	74
°F AVG MIN	53	54	54	54	55	56	56	56	57	56	56	54
DIURNAL RANGE	20	20	21	22	21	19	20	19	18	19	20	20
RAIN/INCHES	2.1	2.8	4.6	5.9	6.6	9.3	9.1	10.1	10.7	8.3	4.6	2.0
HUMIDITY/%	70	67	67	67	67	71	72	73	74	71	70	70
BLOOM SEASON	*				*				*			
DAYS CLR	N/A											
RAIN/MM	53	71	117	150	168	236	231	257	272	211	117	51
°C AVG MAX	23.0	23.6	24.1	24.7	24.1	24.1	24.7	24.1	24.1	24.1	24.7	23.6
°C AVG MIN	11.9	12.5	12.5	12.5	13.0	13.6	13.6	13.6	14.1	13.6	13.6	12.5
DIURNAL RANGE	11.1	11.1	11.6	12.2	11.7	10.5	11.1	10.5	10.0	10.5	11.1	11.1
S/HEMISPHERE	JUL	AUG	SEP	OCT	NOV	DEC	JAN	FEB	MAR	APR	MAY	JUN

Cultural Recommendations

LIGHT: 2500–3500 fc.

TEMPERATURES: Throughout the year, days average 73–76°F (23–25°C), and nights average 53–57°F (12–14°C), with a diurnal range of 18–22°F (10–12°C).

HUMIDITY: 70–75% most of the year, falling to near 65% in late winter and spring.

WATER: Rainfall is moderate to heavy most of the year, but conditions are slightly drier for 3 months in winter. Cultivated plants should be kept moist but not soggy. Occasional early morning mistings may be beneficial, especially on bright, sunny days.

FERTILIZER: ¼–½ recommended strength. A balanced fertilizer should be applied weekly to biweekly throughout the year.

REST PERIOD: Growing temperatures should be maintained all year. In the habitat, rainfall is lowest in winter, but dew and mist from fog and low clouds are common. Water and fertilizer should be reduced somewhat

Dendrobium margaritaceum

for cultivated plants, especially those grown in the darker, short-day conditions common during temperate-latitude winters. Plants should be kept on the dry side, but they should never be allowed to dry out completely. In the habitat, light is higher in winter.

GROWING MEDIA: Plants are best mounted on a tree-fern slab to accommodate their mat-forming growth habit, but humidity must be high and plants must be watered daily in summer. If plants must be potted, small pots or baskets may be filled with any open, moisture-retaining medium. Repotting may be done anytime new roots are growing.

MISCELLANEOUS NOTES: The bloom season shown in the climate table is based on collection times.

Plant and Flower Information

PLANT SIZE AND TYPE: A creeping, 1.2 in. (3 cm) sympodial epiphyte.

PSEUDOBULB: 0.2 in. (0.5 cm) long. The greenish to brown pseudobulbs, which are ellipsoid to nearly oblong, become approximately 5-angled with age. Growths arise 0.2–0.6 in. (0.5–1.5 cm) apart on a branching, mat-forming rhizome. Roots are white with green tips.

LEAVES: 1 per growth. The ovate to elliptic leaves are 0.2–0.6 in. (0.6–1.6 cm) long. They may be mid- to dark-green, sometimes with a purplish tinge.

INFLORESCENCE: 0.1 in. (0.3 cm) long. Two single-flowered inflorescences emerge in succession near the base of the leaf.

FLOWERS: 1 per inflorescence. The yellow flowers are 0.3–0.4 in. (0.7–1.1 cm) across. The lip is maroon with a dark yellow apex. The ovary may be greenish or maroon. Blossoms last 10–18 days.

REFERENCES: 234, 382.

PHOTOS/DRAWINGS: 382.

Dendrobium margaritaceum Finet. See *D. christyanum* Rchb. f. REFERENCES: 36, 50, 118, 179, 196, 198, 219, 245, 254, 266, 291, 330, 332, 333, 429, 430, 445, 448, 454. PHOTOS/DRAWINGS: *36, 50, 198, 245, 291, 330.*

Dendrobium marginatum Bateman. See *D. xanthophlebium* Lindley. REFERENCES: 190, 216, 254, 445, 454.

Dendrobium marginatum Teijsm. and Binn. Now considered a synonym of *Epigeneium cymbidioides* (Blume) Summerhayes. REFERENCES: 213, 216, 254, 310, 317, 469, 499.

Dendrobium maritimum J. J. Smith

ORIGIN/HABITAT: Irian Jaya (western New Guinea). Originally collected near Wari on Biak Island, which is in the Schouten Islands just off the north coast. Plants grow near the ocean.

CLIMATE: Station #97560, Mokmer, Biak Island, Irian Jaya, Lat. 1.2°S, Long. 136.1°E, at 46 ft. (14 m). Record extreme temperatures are 91°F (33°C) and 70°F (21°C).

N/HEMISPHERE	JAN	FEB	MAR	APR	MAY	JUN	JUL	AUG	SEP	OCT	NOV	DEC
°F AVG MAX	85	86	86	87	87	86	86	85	86	86	87	87
°F AVG MIN	74	75	74	75	75	75	74	74	75	75	75	75
DIURNAL RANGE	11	11	12	12	12	11	12	11	11	11	12	12
RAIN/INCHES	11.3	11.2	7.0	6.1	7.3	12.5	11.0	8.2	11.7	8.3	8.6	10.5
HUMIDITY/%	85	84	83	83	84	85	84	85	86	85	87	86
BLOOM SEASON			*									
DAYS CLR @ 9AM	2	2	4	1	2	1	2	1	1	2	2	3
DAYS CLR @ 3PM	3	3	3	3	2	1	2	1	2	2	1	2
RAIN/MM	287	284	178	155	185	318	279	208	297	211	218	267
°C AVG MAX	29.4	30.0	30.0	30.6	30.6	30.0	30.0	29.4	30.0	30.0	30.6	30.6
°C AVG MIN	23.3	23.9	23.3	23.9	23.9	23.9	23.3	23.3	23.9	23.9	23.9	23.9
DIURNAL RANGE	6.1	6.1	6.7	6.7	6.7	6.1	6.7	6.1	6.1	6.1	6.7	6.7
S/HEMISPHERE	JUL	AUG	SEP	OCT	NOV	DEC	JAN	FEB	MAR	APR	MAY	JUN

Cultural Recommendations

LIGHT: 2500–3500 fc. About 50% summer shading should be provided. Strong air movement is recommended year-round.

TEMPERATURES: Throughout the year, days average 85–87°F (29–31°C), and nights average 74–75°F (23–24°C), with a diurnal range of 11–12°F (6–7°C).

HUMIDITY: Near 85% year-round.

WATER: Rainfall is heavy all year. Cultivated plants should be kept moist, especially when actively growing.

FERTILIZER: 1/4–1/2 recommended strength. A balanced fertilizer should be applied weekly to biweekly throughout the year.

REST PERIOD: Growing temperatures should be maintained year-round. Water may be reduced somewhat in winter, especially for plants grown in the dark, short-day conditions common in temperate latitudes. Plants should dry slightly between waterings when not actively growing, but they should never be allowed to dry out completely. Fertilizer should be reduced or eliminated if water is reduced.

GROWING MEDIA: Plants may be mounted on tree-fern or cork slabs or potted in small pots filled with any open, fast-draining medium. Repotting may be done anytime new roots are growing.

MISCELLANEOUS NOTES: The bloom season shown in the climate table is based on reports from the habitat.

Plant and Flower Information

PLANT SIZE AND TYPE: A 14 in. (35 cm) sympodial epiphyte.

PSEUDOBULB: 14 in. (35 cm) long. The elongated stems are flexuous.

LEAVES: Many. The lanceolate leaves are about 1 in. (2.5 cm) long.

INFLORESCENCE: Short. Inflorescences emerge from nodes on leafless stems.

FLOWERS: 1–7 per inflorescence. The orange flowers are 0.8 in. (2 cm) long. The petals and dorsal sepal are erect. Lateral sepals are slashed along the margin. The oblong, concave lip is simple with a U-shaped thickening in the center.

REFERENCES: 224, 445, 470.

Dendrobium marivelense Ames

AKA: *D. parciflorum* Kränzlin not Rchb. f. ex Lindley.

ORIGIN/HABITAT: The Philippine Islands. On Luzon Island, plants grow on Mt. Mariveles in Bataan Province. They are also found on Mindanao Island, where they grow in Surigao Province and on Mt. Hilonghilong in Agusan Province.

CLIMATE: Station #98426, Cubi Point NAS, Luzon Island, Philippines, Lat. 14.8°N, Long. 120.3°E, at 55 ft. (17 m). Temperatures are calculated for an elevation of 3000 ft. (910 m), resulting in probable extremes of 91°F (33°C) and 52°F (11°C).

N/HEMISPHERE	JAN	FEB	MAR	APR	MAY	JUN	JUL	AUG	SEP	OCT	NOV	DEC
°F AVG MAX	77	78	81	83	82	78	77	76	76	79	78	77
°F AVG MIN	62	62	64	66	67	66	65	65	65	65	65	63
DIURNAL RANGE	15	16	17	17	15	12	12	11	11	14	13	14
RAIN/INCHES	0.1	0.1	0.1	0.8	7.1	25.1	30.5	33.7	29.5	7.8	2.4	0.8
HUMIDITY/%	68	67	68	67	72	82	84	86	86	80	74	71
BLOOM SEASON			*	*	*	*	*	*				
DAYS CLR @ 8AM	7	7	8	10	6	2	1	0	0	4	3	4
DAYS CLR @ 2PM	4	3	4	4	3	1	0	0	0	2	1	2
RAIN/MM	3	3	3	20	180	638	775	856	749	198	61	20
°C AVG MAX	25.2	25.7	27.4	28.5	27.9	25.7	25.2	24.6	24.6	26.3	25.7	25.2
°C AVG MIN	16.8	16.8	17.9	19.0	19.6	19.0	18.5	18.5	18.5	18.5	18.5	17.4
DIURNAL RANGE	8.4	8.9	9.5	9.5	8.3	6.7	6.7	6.1	6.1	7.8	7.2	7.8
S/HEMISPHERE	JUL	AUG	SEP	OCT	NOV	DEC	JAN	FEB	MAR	APR	MAY	JUN

Cultural Recommendations

LIGHT: 2500–3500 fc. Strong air movement is recommended.

TEMPERATURES: Summer days average 76–78°F (25–26°C), and nights average 65–66°F (19°C), with a diurnal range of 11–12°F (6–7°C). The warmest weather occurs in spring before the start of the rainy season. Days average 81–83°F (27–29°C), and nights average 64–67°F (18–20°C), with a diurnal range of 15–17°F (8–10°C).

HUMIDITY: 80–85% in summer and early autumn, dropping to 65–70% in winter and spring.

WATER: Rainfall is very heavy during the growing season from spring into autumn but is very low in winter. High relative humidity and nightly cooling result in some additional moisture from dew and mist, however. Cultivated plants should be kept evenly moist from late spring to early autumn, but water should be gradually reduced in late autumn after new growths mature. Daily watering or morning mistings might be beneficial when weather is hot and dry.

FERTILIZER: ¼–½ recommended strength, applied weekly. A high-nitrogen fertilizer is beneficial from spring to midsummer, but a fertilizer high in phosphates should be used in late summer and autumn.

REST PERIOD: Winter days average 77–78°F (25–26°C), and nights average 62–63°F (17°C), with a diurnal range of 14–16°F (8–9°C). For cultivated plants, water should be reduced and the plants allowed to dry out between waterings. They should not remain completely dry for extended periods, however. Occasional early morning mistings may be beneficial and keep the plants from becoming too dry. Fertilizer should be reduced or eliminated until water is increased in the spring. Light should be as high as possible, short of burning the foliage.

GROWING MEDIA: Plants may be mounted on tree-fern or cork slabs if humidity is high and plants are watered at least once daily in summer. When plants are potted, any open, fast-draining medium may be used. Repotting may be done anytime new roots are growing.

MISCELLANEOUS NOTES: The bloom season shown in the climate table is based on collection reports. Cultivated plants frequently bloom in early spring.

Plant and Flower Information

PLANT SIZE AND TYPE: A 10 in. (25 cm) sympodial epiphyte.

PSEUDOBULB: 10 in. (25 cm) long.

LEAVES: 6 or more per growth. The slender, terete leaves are 0.6–1.2 in. (1.5–3.0 cm) long. They are laterally flattened. At first glance, the leaves look like sedum foliage.

INFLORESCENCE: 0.4–0.8 in. (1–2 cm) long. Inflorescences arise from the leaf bracts near the apex of both young and old stems.

FLOWERS: 1 per inflorescence. The white flowers are 0.8–1.2 in. (2–3 cm) across. The petals and dorsal sepal are smaller than the lateral sepals. Sepals and petals are recurved at the tip. The ruffled lip has an uneven margin, central callus, and colored markings.

REFERENCES: 12, 220, 254, 296, 373, 445, 536.

PHOTOS/DRAWINGS: 12, 373.

Dendrobium marmoratum Rchb. f.

The species was reported to originate in Burma, but because habitat location and elevation are not available, climate data cannot be selected. A sympodial epiphyte. The stems are covered with sheaths that are mottled with gray bars on a whitish background. Inflorescences, which carry 2 blossoms, are borne at nodes along leafless stems. Sepals and petals are white with purple tips. The back of the lip is tinged with purple and densely covered with short hairs. The front of the lip is purple. The entire margin of the lip is ciliate. The spur is very short and blunt. REFERENCES: 157, 202, 216, 254.

Dendrobium marseillei Gagnepain. See *D. jenkinsii* Wallich ex Lindley. REFERENCES: 225, 447, 448, 454.

Dendrobium masarangense Schlechter

AKA: Lewis and Cribb (ref. 270, 271) and Kores (ref. 466) list only *D. pumilio* Schlechter as a synonym.

Reeve and Woods (ref. 385), in their review of the section *Oxyglossum* consider *D. masarangense* as a variable alliance and compiled the following list of synonyms.

For *D. masarangense* subsp. *masarangense* (white flowered), they include the synonym *D. pumilio* Schlechter.

For *D. masarangense* subsp. *theionanthum* (Schlechter) Reeve and Woods var. *theionanthum* (flowers colored, ovary smooth or with short protuberances), they include the synonyms *D. caespitificum* Ridley, *D. frigidum* Schlechter, *D. gemma* Schlechter, *D. monogrammoides* J. J. Smith, *D. pseudofrigidum* J. J. Smith, and *D. theionanthum* Schlechter.

For *D. masarangense* subsp. *theionanthum* var. *chlorinum* (Ridley) Reeve and Woods (flowers colored, ovary hairy), they include the synonym *D. chlorinum* Ridley.

ORIGIN/HABITAT: *D. masarangense* subsp. *masarangense* is distributed over a wide area from Sulawesi to Fiji, including many provinces in New Guinea, New Britain Island, Bougainville, Guadalcanal in the Solomon Islands, Vanuatu, New Caledonia, and Viti Levu in Fiji. Plants usually grow on trees in lowland forests at 980–3950 ft. (300–1200 m).

D. masarangense subsp. *theionanthum* var. *theionanthum* grows in the mountains throughout New Guinea. The habitat includes the Vogelkop Peninsula, Mt. Jaya (Mt. Carstensz), Mt. Doorman, and Mt. Wilhelmina in Irian Jaya (western New Guinea), most provinces of Papua, and Goodenough Island. Plants usually grow on the twigs of trees and shrubs or among young secondary regrowth. They are found on steep, exposed ridges and summits where light is high and air movement is strong. Habitat extends from 2600–10,660 ft. (800–3250 m), but plants usually grow above 4900 ft. (1500 m), and most collections are made at 6550–8200 ft. (2000–2500 m).

D. masarangense subsp *theionanthum* var. *chlorinum* grows only in Irian Jaya (western New Guinea) near Mt. Jaya (Mt. Carstensz) at about 3950 ft. (1200 m).

CLIMATE: Station #94010, Goroka, Papua New Guinea, Lat. 6.1°S, Long. 145.4°E, at 5141 ft. (1567 m). Temperatures are calculated for an elevation of 4000 ft. (1220 m), resulting in probable extremes of 90°F (32°C) and 46°F (8°C).

N/HEMISPHERE	JAN	FEB	MAR	APR	MAY	JUN	JUL	AUG	SEP	OCT	NOV	DEC
°F AVG MAX	80	81	82	83	83	82	83	82	82	82	83	81
°F AVG MIN	60	61	61	61	62	63	63	63	64	63	63	61
DIURNAL RANGE	20	20	21	22	21	19	20	19	18	19	20	20
RAIN/INCHES	2.1	2.8	4.6	5.9	6.6	9.3	9.1	10.1	10.7	8.3	4.6	2.0
HUMIDITY/%	70	67	67	67	67	71	72	73	74	71	70	70
BLOOM SEASON					**							
DAYS CLR	N/A											
RAIN/MM	53	71	117	150	168	236	231	257	272	211	117	51
°C AVG MAX	26.5	27.1	27.6	28.2	28.2	27.6	28.2	27.6	27.6	27.6	28.2	27.1
°C AVG MIN	15.4	16.0	16.0	16.0	16.5	17.1	17.1	17.1	17.6	17.1	17.1	16.0
DIURNAL RANGE	11.1	11.1	11.6	12.2	11.7	10.5	11.1	10.5	10.0	10.5	11.1	11.1
S/HEMISPHERE	JUL	AUG	SEP	OCT	NOV	DEC	JAN	FEB	MAR	APR	MAY	JUN

Cultural Recommendations

LIGHT: 2000–3000 fc.

TEMPERATURES: Throughout the year, days average 80–83°F (27–28°C),

Dendrobium masonii

and nights average 60–64°F (15–18°C), with a diurnal range of 18–22°F (10–12°C). Temperatures in the primary habitat of *D. masarangense* subsp. *theionanthum* var. *theionanthum* are 8–10°F (4–6°C) cooler than indicated.

HUMIDITY: 70–75% from summer into autumn, dropping to 65–70% in winter and spring. Plants require excellent air movement.

WATER: Rainfall is moderate to heavy most of the year, but conditions are slightly drier for 3 months in winter. Cultivated plants should be kept moist but not soggy. Occasional early morning mistings may be beneficial, especially on bright, sunny days.

FERTILIZER: ¼–½ recommended strength. A balanced fertilizer should be applied weekly to biweekly throughout the year.

REST PERIOD: Growing temperatures should be maintained all year. In the habitat, rainfall is lowest in winter, but dew and mist from fog and low clouds are common. Water and fertilizer should be reduced somewhat for cultivated plants, especially those grown in the darker, short-day conditions common during temperate-latitude winters. Plants should be kept on the dry side, but they should never be allowed to dry out completely. In the habitat, light is higher in winter.

GROWING MEDIA: Plants may be mounted on tree-fern or cork slabs if humidity is high and plants are watered at least once daily in summer. When plants are potted, any open, fast-draining medium may be used. Repotting may be done anytime new roots are growing.

MISCELLANEOUS NOTES: The bloom season shown in the climate table is based on reports from the habitat. Cultivation records also show spring blooming.

Plant and Flower Information

PLANT SIZE AND TYPE: A 0.6–2.8 in. (1.5–7.0 cm) sympodial epiphyte.

PSEUDOBULB: 0.1–0.8 in. (0.2–2.0 cm) long. Growths are normally clustered on a very short rhizome, but the rhizome sometimes creeps and branches.

LEAVES: 2–4 per growth. The linear-lanceolate leaves are 0.4–2.4 in. (1–6 cm) long.

INFLORESCENCE: Short. The blossoms arise directly from the apex of leafy stems. They are held just below the tips of the leaves.

FLOWERS: 1–3 per inflorescence. The flowers are 0.3–0.7 in. (0.8–1.7 cm) across, rarely larger. They open fully and last about 6 months. The green lip usually has yellow, orange, or red-orange near the apex. Subsp. *masarangense* has white sepals and petals with a citron-yellow tip on the lip. Subsp. *theionanthum* has orange, yellow, or green sepals and petals with orange at the apex of the lip.

REFERENCES: 94, 95, 179, 221, 235, 252, 270, 271, 304, 305, 385, 400, 436, 437, 466, 486, 549, 554.

PHOTOS/DRAWINGS: 94, 271 *304*, *385*, 437, 466, *549, 554, 555*.

Dendrobium masonii Rupp.
Now considered a synonym of *Diplocaulobium masonii* (Rupp) Dockrill. REFERENCES: 67, 105, 228, 230.

Dendrobium mastersianum F. Mueller and Kränzlin

ORIGIN/HABITAT: Papua New Guinea. Plants were reportedly found near Dogura and on the islands of Bartle Bay.

CLIMATE: Station #94075, Samarai, Sideia Island, Papua New Guinea, Lat. 10.6°S, Long. 150.7°E, at 20 ft. (6 m). Record extreme temperatures are 104°F (40°C) and 64°F (18°C).

N/HEMISPHERE	JAN	FEB	MAR	APR	MAY	JUN	JUL	AUG	SEP	OCT	NOV	DEC
°F AVG MAX	81	81	82	83	85	87	87	88	87	86	84	82
°F AVG MIN	74	73	74	74	75	76	77	77	76	75	75	74
DIURNAL RANGE	7	8	8	9	10	11	10	11	11	11	9	8
RAIN/INCHES	8.1	8.6	10.1	8.7	8.4	6.1	7.0	7.8	10.0	9.8	12.0	11.3
HUMIDITY/%	N/A											
BLOOM SEASON									•			
DAYS CLR	N/A											
RAIN/MM	206	218	257	221	213	155	178	198	254	249	305	287
°C AVG MAX	27.2	27.2	27.8	28.3	29.4	30.6	30.6	31.1	30.6	30.0	28.9	27.8
°C AVG MIN	23.3	22.8	23.3	23.3	23.9	24.4	25.0	25.0	24.4	23.9	23.9	23.3
DIURNAL RANGE	3.9	4.4	4.5	5.0	5.5	6.2	5.6	6.1	6.2	6.1	5.0	4.5
S/HEMISPHERE	JUL	AUG	SEP	OCT	NOV	DEC	JAN	FEB	MAR	APR	MAY	JUN

Cultural Recommendations

LIGHT: 2500–3000 fc.

TEMPERATURES: Throughout the year, days average 81–88°F (27–31°C), and nights average 73–77°F (23–25°C), with a diurnal range of 7–11°F (4–6°C).

HUMIDITY: Information is not available for this location. However, records from nearby stations indicate that humidity is probably 70–80% year-round.

WATER: Rainfall is very heavy year-round. Cultivated plants should be kept moist but not soggy.

FERTILIZER: ¼–½ recommended strength. A balanced fertilizer should be applied weekly to biweekly throughout the year.

REST PERIOD: Growing conditions should be maintained year-round. In the habitat, winter rainfall is high; but water and fertilizer should be reduced for cultivated plants, especially those grown in the dark, short-day conditions in temperate-latitude winters. Plants should never be allowed to dry out completely, however. In the habitat, seasonal light variation is minor.

GROWING MEDIA: Plants may be mounted on tree-fern or cork slabs if humidity is high and plants are watered at least once daily in summer. When plants are potted, any open, fast-draining medium may be used. Repotting may be done anytime new roots are growing.

MISCELLANEOUS NOTES: The bloom season shown in the climate table is based on reports from the habitat.

Plant and Flower Information

PLANT SIZE AND TYPE: A sympodial epiphyte of unreported size. Kränzlin (ref. 253) described the vegetation as similar to *D. cretaceum* Lindley and indicated that the flower was similar to *D. nobile* Lindley.

PSEUDOBULB: The stems are covered with white membranelike sheaths.

INFLORESCENCE: Short. Racemes emerge from upper nodes.

FLOWERS: 1–3 per inflorescence. The flowers are 2.4–2.8 in. (6–7 cm) across. They are white with large purple spots and lines.

REFERENCES: 220, 254.

Dendrobium mattangianum Kränzlin.
Considered a synonym of *D. bicostatum* J. J. Smith, which is now considered a synonym of *Flickingeria bicostatum* (J. J. Smith) A. Hawkes. REFERENCES: 220, 254, 437.

Dendrobium mayandyi T. M. Reeve and J. Renz

AKA: Sometimes spelled *D. myandii* or *D. myandyii*.

ORIGIN/HABITAT: Eastern Papua New Guinea and the islands of New Britain and New Ireland. Plants grow on mossy trees at 5900–10,150 ft. (1800–3100 m).

CLIMATE: Botanical garden records, Laiagam, Papua New Guinea, Lat. 5.5°S, Long. 143.5°E, at 7218 ft. (2200 m). Record extreme temperatures are 91°F (33°C) and 32°F (0°C).

N/HEMISPHERE	JAN	FEB	MAR	APR	MAY	JUN	JUL	AUG	SEP	OCT	NOV	DEC
°F AVG MAX	76	77	78	76	78	78	82	77	76	78	78	76
°F AVG MIN	55	54	55	55	56	56	55	56	58	57	56	56
DIURNAL RANGE	21	23	23	21	22	22	27	21	18	21	22	20
RAIN/INCHES	4.0	4.8	6.1	7.8	8.5	9.1	8.4	9.6	9.5	8.9	6.3	4.0
HUMIDITY/%	N/A											
BLOOM SEASON							**	**		*		
DAYS CLR	N/A											
RAIN/MM	102	121	154	198	217	230	213	243	241	227	159	102
°C AVG MAX	24.4	25.0	25.6	24.4	25.6	25.6	27.8	25.0	24.4	25.6	25.6	24.4
°C AVG MIN	12.8	12.2	12.8	12.8	13.3	13.3	12.8	13.3	14.4	13.9	13.3	13.3
DIURNAL RANGE	11.6	12.8	12.8	11.6	12.3	12.3	15.0	11.7	10.0	11.7	12.3	11.1
S/HEMISPHERE	JUL	AUG	SEP	OCT	NOV	DEC	JAN	FEB	MAR	APR	MAY	JUN

Cultural Recommendations

LIGHT: 2000–3000 fc.

TEMPERATURES: Throughout the year, days average 76–82°F (24–28°C), and nights average 54–58°F (12–14°C), with a diurnal range of 18–27°F (10–15°C).

HUMIDITY: Information is not available for this location. However, records from nearby locations indicate that humidity probably averages 70–80% year-round.

WATER: Rainfall is moderate to heavy throughout the year, but conditions are driest for 3–4 months in winter. Cultivated plants should be kept evenly moist.

FERTILIZER: ¼–½ recommended strength. A balanced fertilizer should be applied weekly to biweekly throughout the year.

REST PERIOD: Growing conditions should be maintained year-round. Water and fertilizer should be reduced somewhat in winter, especially for plants grown in the dark, short-day conditions common in temperate latitudes. They should never be allowed to dry out completely, however. In the habitat, light is highest in winter.

GROWING MEDIA: Mounting plants on tree-fern or cork slabs accommodates their normally pendulous growth habit. However, humidity must be high and plants must be watered at least once a day in summer. If plants cannot be mounted, small pots or hanging baskets may be filled with an open, fast-draining medium. Repotting may be done anytime new roots are actively growing.

MISCELLANEOUS NOTES: The bloom season shown in the climate table is based on cultivation records.

Plant and Flower Information

PLANT SIZE AND TYPE: A 2.4–12.0 in. (6–30 cm) sympodial epiphyte.

PSEUDOBULB: 2.4–12.0 in. (6–30 cm) long. The slender, clustered stems are usually pendulous. They become red, orange, or yellow when dry.

LEAVES: 2–4 at the apex of each growth. The elliptic-lanceolate leaves are 2.4–4.3 in. (6–11 cm) long.

INFLORESCENCE: 3–4 in. (8–10 cm) long. One to several inflorescences emerge through the leaf bases near the apex of the stem. They may be erect or arching.

FLOWERS: 5–7 per inflorescence. The very fleshy flowers are 0.8 in. (2 cm) across. Sepals and petals, which are off-white, green, or pale yellow, are sometimes marked with maroon or purple spots. The lip is green. Blossoms often turn bright salmon-pink as they age.

HYBRIDIZING NOTES: Chromosome count is 2n = 36 (ref. 152).

REFERENCES: 83, 95, 152, 179, 234, 243, 554.

PHOTOS/DRAWINGS: 83.

Dendrobium mayrii J. J. Smith.
Now considered a synonym of *Cadetia mayrii* (J. J. Smith) P. Hunt. REFERENCES: 212, 225, 230, 486.

Dendrobium mega Kränzlin.
See *D. pandaneti* Ridley. REFERENCES: 75, 220, 254, 454.

Dendrobium megaceras Hooker f.

ORIGIN/HABITAT: Malaya. Only 3 collections are recorded, 1 each in the states of Melaka (Malacca), Perak, and southeastern Johore. Habitat elevation is unavailable, so the following climate data should be used cautiously.

CLIMATE: Station #48665, Melaka (Malacca), Malaya, Lat. 2.3°N, Long. 102.3°E, at 40 ft. (12 m). Record extreme temperatures are 99°F (37°C) and 61°F (16°C).

N/HEMISPHERE	JAN	FEB	MAR	APR	MAY	JUN	JUL	AUG	SEP	OCT	NOV	DEC
°F AVG MAX	88	89	89	89	89	88	88	88	88	88	88	88
°F AVG MIN	72	72	72	73	73	73	72	72	72	72	72	72
DIURNAL RANGE	16	17	17	16	16	15	16	16	16	16	16	16
RAIN/INCHES	3.9	3.7	4.9	7.4	6.8	7.9	7.8	10.3	8.8	10.1	8.7	6.5
HUMIDITY/%	79	79	82	85	85	83	84	84	84	84	84	82
BLOOM SEASON	N/A											
DAYS CLR @ 7AM	1	1	1	1	1	1	2	1	1	1	0	1
DAYS CLR @ 1PM	1	1	1	1	1	1	1	1	1	0	0	0
RAIN/MM	99	94	124	188	173	201	198	262	224	257	221	165
°C AVG MAX	31.1	31.7	31.7	31.7	31.7	31.1	31.1	31.1	31.1	31.1	31.1	31.1
°C AVG MIN	22.2	22.2	22.2	22.8	22.8	22.8	22.2	22.2	22.2	22.2	22.2	22.2
DIURNAL RANGE	8.9	9.5	9.5	8.9	8.9	8.3	8.9	8.9	8.9	8.9	8.9	8.9
S/HEMISPHERE	JUL	AUG	SEP	OCT	NOV	DEC	JAN	FEB	MAR	APR	MAY	JUN

Cultural Recommendations

LIGHT: 2000–3000 fc.

TEMPERATURES: Throughout the year, days average 88–89°F (31–32°C), and nights average 72–73°F (22–23°C), with a diurnal range of 15–17°F (8–10°C).

HUMIDITY: 80–85% year-round.

WATER: Rainfall is moderate to heavy all year, but conditions are slightly drier for 2 months in winter. Cultivated plants should be kept moist but not soggy, with only slight drying allowed between waterings.

FERTILIZER: ¼–½ recommended strength. A balanced fertilizer should be applied weekly to biweekly throughout the year.

REST PERIOD: Growing conditions should be maintained all year. Water and fertilizer may be reduced slightly in winter. Plants cultivated in the dark, short-day conditions common in temperate latitudes need less water, but they should never be allowed to dry out completely.

GROWING MEDIA: Plants may be mounted on tree-fern or cork slabs if humidity is high and plants are watered at least once daily in summer. When plants are potted, any open, fast-draining medium may be used. Repotting is best done in early spring when new roots are growing.

MISCELLANEOUS NOTES: Plants are unlikely to be available for cultivation.

Plant and Flower Information

PLANT SIZE AND TYPE: A 20–24 in. (50–60 cm) sympodial epiphyte.

PSEUDOBULB: 20–24 in. (50–60 cm) long. The slender stems consist of internodes spaced about 1 in. (2.5 cm) apart.

LEAVES: Many. The lanceolate leaves are 3.5–4.0 in. (9–10 cm) long, membranelike, and pointed at the tip. They are spaced 1.2 in. (3 cm) apart along the stem.

INFLORESCENCE: 1.4 in. (3.5 cm) long.

FLOWERS: 6 per inflorescence. The flowers are 1 in. (2.5 cm) across. Sepals and petals may be white or pale, dull yellowish green with pink veins. The 3-lobed lip, which is bent upwards, has a small, round, ruffled midlobe and triangular sidelobes marked with brown veins. It is narrow at the base, broad at the apex with a sharp point at the tip. The margins are minutely toothed. The spur is pinkish.

Dendrobium megalanthum

REFERENCES: 200, 202, 216, 254, 402, 445, 455.

PHOTOS/DRAWINGS: 455.

Dendrobium megalanthum Schlechter. Schlechter (ref. 443) used the name *D. megalanthum* for *Diplocaulobium grandiflorum* Ridley, but he did not validly publish it. REFERENCES: 223, 400, 443.

Dendrobium megalorhizum Kränzlin. See *D. sarcochilus* Finet. REFERENCES: 173, 224.

Dendrobium mekynosepalum Schlechter. Now considered a synonym of *Diplocaulobium mekynosepalum* (Schlechter) Kränzlin. REFERENCES: 87, 219, 220, 254, 271, 437, 444, 445.

Dendrobium melaleucaphilum M. Clements and D. Jones

AKA: These plants are commonly considered part of the *D. tetragonum* alliance.

ORIGIN/HABITAT: Eastern Australia. Plants grow in the coastal districts of northeastern New South Wales, mostly near Grafton, but they may be found as far south as the Blue Mountains west of Sydney. They are usually found on rocks, swamp oak, or *Melaleuca* (prickly paperbark) trees below 1300 ft. (400 m). The largest, healthiest plants are found on *Melaleuca styphelioides*.

CLIMATE: Station #94791, Coffs Harbour, Australia, Lat. 30.3°S, Long. 153.1°E, at 14 ft. (4 m). Temperatures are calculated for an elevation of 1000 ft. (300 m), resulting in probable extremes of 102°F (39°C) and 27°F (−3°C).

N/HEMISPHERE	JAN	FEB	MAR	APR	MAY	JUN	JUL	AUG	SEP	OCT	NOV	DEC
°F AVG MAX	62	64	68	71	76	77	77	77	76	74	68	65
°F AVG MIN	41	42	47	52	56	60	62	63	61	56	47	42
DIURNAL RANGE	21	22	21	19	20	17	15	14	15	18	21	23
RAIN/INCHES	3.8	2.1	2.9	3.8	4.0	5.8	6.9	7.7	8.7	7.7	5.7	4.5
HUMIDITY/%	74	72	70	74	72	76	79	83	79	78	75	74
BLOOM SEASON			*	*	*							
DAYS CLR @ 4AM	8	9	10	10	12	11	9	8	10	7	11	8
DAYS CLR @ 10AM	16	18	18	12	15	11	8	5	10	10	14	15
RAIN/MM	97	53	74	97	102	147	175	196	221	196	145	114
°C AVG MAX	16.5	17.6	19.9	21.5	24.3	24.9	24.9	24.9	24.3	23.2	19.9	18.2
°C AVG MIN	4.9	5.4	8.2	11.0	13.2	15.4	16.5	17.1	16.0	13.2	8.2	5.4
DIURNAL RANGE	11.6	12.2	11.7	10.5	11.1	9.5	8.4	7.8	8.3	10.0	11.7	12.8
S/HEMISPHERE	JUL	AUG	SEP	OCT	NOV	DEC	JAN	FEB	MAR	APR	MAY	JUN

Cultural Recommendations

LIGHT: 2000–3000 fc. Plants are healthiest with brisk air movement and full early morning sun. Filtered light is recommended during the remainder of the day.

TEMPERATURES: Summer days average 77°F (25°C), and nights average 60–63°F (15–17°C), with a diurnal range of 14–17°F (8–10°C).

HUMIDITY: 70–80% year-round.

WATER: Rainfall is moderate to heavy most of the year, but conditions are somewhat drier for 2–3 months in winter. Cultivated plants should be kept moist with only slight drying allowed between waterings.

FERTILIZER: ¼–½ recommended strength, applied weekly. A high-nitrogen fertilizer is beneficial from spring to midsummer, but a fertilizer high in phosphates should be used in late summer and autumn.

REST PERIOD: Winter days average 62–65°F (17–18°C), and nights average 41–42°F (5°C), with a diurnal range of 21–23°F (12–13°C). For cultivated plants, water and fertilizer should be reduced for 2–3 months. Plants should be just slightly moist. Record low temperatures indicate that plants should survive subfreezing temperatures, at least for short periods. However, these extremes should be avoided if possible. A plant's chance of survival is much better if it is dry when exposed to cold temperatures. In the habitat, light is highest in winter.

GROWING MEDIA: Plants are best mounted on tree-fern or cork slabs if humidity is high and plants are watered at least once daily in summer. When plants are potted, any open, fast-draining medium may be used. Repotting is best done in early spring when new roots are growing.

MISCELLANEOUS NOTES: The bloom season shown in the climate table is based on reports from the habitat.

Plant and Flower Information

PLANT SIZE AND TYPE: A 12 in. (30 cm) sympodial epiphyte.

PSEUDOBULB: 12 in. (30 cm) long. The greenish brown stems may be perpendicular or semipendulous. They are slender near the base becoming swollen and 4-angled on the upper portion. Plants may form large clumps.

LEAVES: 2–4 per growth. The thin, tough leaves are 3.5 in. (9 cm) long, ovate, and dark green.

INFLORESCENCE: 1.2 in. (3 cm) long. Inflorescences are wiry.

FLOWERS: 2–8 per inflorescence. The flowers are 4 in. (10 cm) across and open fully. The slender sepals and petals may be yellow or light green with reddish brown markings. The cream-colored lip is marked with reddish brown bars. It has a prominently flared midlobe. The plants are very floriferous.

REFERENCES: 67, 68, 235, 240, 564.

PHOTOS/DRAWINGS: 68, *564*.

Dendrobium melananthum (Describer not listed.) This name was once listed as a synonym of *D. pendulum* Roxburgh, but Hooker (ref. 202) indicates that it is a hybrid between *D. pendulum* Roxburgh and *D. wardianum* Warner. REFERENCES: 202.

Dendrobium melanochlamys Holttum. Holttum (ref. 200) indicates that his plant is a synonym of *D. villosulum* Wallich ex Hooker not Lindley. However, Seidenfaden and Wood (ref. 455) consider it a synonym of *D. villosulum* Lindley. REFERENCES: 200, 227, 455, 586.

Dendrobium melanolasium A. Gilli

ORIGIN/HABITAT: Pompobus, Papua New Guinea. Plants were found in forests at about 7200 ft. (2200 m). We have been unable to find this location, so the following climate data should be used with caution.

CLIMATE: Botanical garden records, Laiagam, Papua New Guinea, Lat. 5.5°S, Long. 143.5°E, at 7218 ft. (2200 m). Record extreme temperatures are 91°F (33°C) and 32°F (0°C).

N/HEMISPHERE	JAN	FEB	MAR	APR	MAY	JUN	JUL	AUG	SEP	OCT	NOV	DEC
°F AVG MAX	76	77	78	76	78	78	82	77	76	78	78	76
°F AVG MIN	55	54	55	55	56	56	55	56	58	57	56	56
DIURNAL RANGE	21	23	23	21	22	22	27	21	18	21	22	20
RAIN/INCHES	4.0	4.8	6.1	7.8	8.5	9.1	8.4	9.6	9.5	8.9	6.3	4.0
HUMIDITY/%	N/A											
BLOOM SEASON	N/A											
DAYS CLR	N/A											
RAIN/MM	102	121	154	198	217	230	213	243	241	227	159	102
°C AVG MAX	24.4	25.0	25.6	24.4	25.6	25.6	27.8	25.0	24.4	25.6	25.6	24.4
°C AVG MIN	12.8	12.2	12.8	12.8	13.3	13.3	12.8	13.3	14.4	13.9	13.3	13.3
DIURNAL RANGE	11.7	12.8	12.8	11.7	12.2	12.2	15.0	11.7	10.0	11.7	12.2	11.1
S/HEMISPHERE	JUL	AUG	SEP	OCT	NOV	DEC	JAN	FEB	MAR	APR	MAY	JUN

Cultural Recommendations

LIGHT: 2000–3000 fc.

TEMPERATURES: Throughout the year, days average 76–82°F (24–28°C),

and nights average 54–58°F (12–14°C), with a diurnal range of 18–27°F (10–15°C).

HUMIDITY: Information is not available for this location. However, records from nearby stations indicate that averages are probably near 70–80% year-round.

WATER: Rainfall is moderate to heavy throughout the year, but conditions are driest for 3–4 months in winter. Cultivated plants should be kept evenly moist.

FERTILIZER: ¼–½ recommended strength. A balanced fertilizer should be applied weekly to biweekly throughout the year.

REST PERIOD: Growing conditions should be maintained year-round. Water and fertilizer should be reduced somewhat in winter, especially for plants grown in the dark, short-day conditions common in temperate latitudes. They should never be allowed to dry out completely, however. In the habitat, light is highest in winter.

GROWING MEDIA: Plants may be mounted on tree-fern or cork slabs if humidity is high and plants are watered at least once daily in summer. When plants are potted, any open, fast-draining medium may be used. They may be repotted anytime new roots are growing.

Plant and Flower Information

PLANT SIZE AND TYPE: An 8 in. (20 cm) sympodial epiphyte.

PSEUDOBULB: 8 in. (20 cm) long. The dark pseudobulbs are angled with long hairs at the joints. They are swollen at the base and slender above.

LEAVES: 2 per growth. The broadly lanceolate leaves are 5–6 in. (13–16 cm) long.

INFLORESCENCE: 5–8 in. (13–20 cm) long. The erect, laxly flowered inflorescence is borne at the apex of the stem.

FLOWERS: Few. The yellow flowers are 1.0–1.4 in. (2.5–3.5 cm) long. The ovary and backs of the sepals are covered with dark hairs. The yellow lip has dark violet markings. The broad midlobe has a tiny third lobe at the apex between the normal, larger lobes, making it appear 3-lobed. It has kidney-shaped sidelobes.

REFERENCES: 146, 234.

PHOTOS/DRAWINGS: 146.

Dendrobium melanophthalmum Rchb. f. See *D. pendulum* Roxburgh. REFERENCES: 218, 254, 454, 570.

Dendrobium melanostictum Schlechter

ORIGIN/HABITAT: Northern Papua New Guinea, Irian Jaya (western New Guinea), and the Santa Cruz Islands. In New Guinea, plants grow near the ground on mistforest trees in the Torricelli Range at about 3600 ft. (1100 m).

CLIMATE: Station #94004, Wewak, Papua New Guinea, Lat. 3.6°S, Long. 143.7°E, at 16 ft. (5 m). Temperatures are calculated for an elevation of 3300 ft. (1000 m), resulting in probable extremes of 87°F (31°C) and 51°F (11°C).

N/HEMISPHERE	JAN	FEB	MAR	APR	MAY	JUN	JUL	AUG	SEP	OCT	NOV	DEC
°F AVG MAX	77	77	77	77	77	77	76	75	76	77	77	77
°F AVG MIN	63	63	63	64	64	64	64	63	63	64	63	63
DIURNAL RANGE	14	14	14	13	13	13	12	11	13	13	14	14
RAIN/INCHES	7.6	4.8	5.3	10.0	13.3	14.5	12.1	11.9	14.9	16.9	15.1	10.8
HUMIDITY/%	80	79	79	78	79	81	82	82	81	82	81	80
BLOOM SEASON										*	*	
DAYS CLR	N/A											
RAIN/MM	193	122	135	254	338	368	307	302	378	429	384	274
°C AVG MAX	25.1	25.1	25.1	25.1	25.1	25.1	24.6	24.0	24.6	25.1	25.1	25.1
°C AVG MIN	17.3	17.3	17.3	17.9	17.9	17.9	17.9	17.3	17.3	17.9	17.3	17.3
DIURNAL RANGE	7.8	7.8	7.8	7.2	7.2	7.2	6.7	6.1	7.3	7.3	7.8	7.8
S/HEMISPHERE	JUL	AUG	SEP	OCT	NOV	DEC	JAN	FEB	MAR	APR	MAY	JUN

Cultural Recommendations

LIGHT: 1500–2500 fc.

TEMPERATURES: Throughout the year, days average 75–77°F (24–25°C), and nights average 63–64°F (17–18°C), with a diurnal range of 11–14°F (6–8°C).

HUMIDITY: Near 80% year-round.

WATER: Rainfall is heavy all year. Cultivated plants should be kept moist.

FERTILIZER: ¼–½ recommended strength. A balanced fertilizer should be applied weekly to biweekly throughout the year.

REST PERIOD: Growing conditions should be maintained year-round. Water should be reduced somewhat for plants grown in the dark, short-day conditions common in temperate-latitude winters. They should never be allowed to dry out completely, however. Fertilizer should be reduced until water is increased in spring.

GROWING MEDIA: Plants may be mounted on tree-fern or cork slabs if humidity is high and plants are watered at least once daily in summer. When plants are potted, any open, fast-draining medium may be used. They may be repotted anytime new roots are growing.

MISCELLANEOUS NOTES: The bloom season shown in the climate table is based on collection reports.

Plant and Flower Information

PLANT SIZE AND TYPE: A 24 in. (60 cm) sympodial epiphyte.

PSEUDOBULB: 24 in. (60 cm) long. The canelike stems are fleshy and close together. They were originally described as pendent, but Lewis and Cribb (ref. 271) described them as erect.

LEAVES: Many. The leaves are 3–4 in. (8–10 cm) long, lanceolate, and papery. They are borne on the upper half of the stem.

INFLORESCENCE: Short. The raceme emerges from nodes along older stems.

FLOWERS: 2–6 per inflorescence. The flowers are 0.5 in. (1.3 cm) long and do not open fully. Sepals and petals are white inside and yellowish outside. The outside of the sepals is covered with scales. The lip is sulfur yellow with orange-yellow in the center. The midlobe is densely hairy, toothed along the margin, and fleshy at the apex.

REFERENCES: 219, 254, 271, 437, 444, 445, 470.

PHOTOS/DRAWINGS: 271, 437.

Dendrobium melanotrichum Schlechter

ORIGIN/HABITAT: New Guinea. Plants grow on mistforest trees in the Torricelli Range at about 2950 ft. (900 m).

CLIMATE: Station #94004, Wewak, Papua New Guinea, Lat. 3.6°S, Long. 143.7°E, at 16 ft. (5 m). Temperatures are calculated for an elevation of 2600 ft. (800 m), resulting in probable extremes of 89°F (32°C) and 53°F (12°C).

N/HEMISPHERE	JAN	FEB	MAR	APR	MAY	JUN	JUL	AUG	SEP	OCT	NOV	DEC
°F AVG MAX	79	79	79	79	79	79	78	77	78	79	79	79
°F AVG MIN	65	65	65	66	66	66	66	66	65	65	66	65
DIURNAL RANGE	14	14	14	13	13	13	12	11	13	14	13	14
RAIN/INCHES	7.6	4.8	5.3	10.0	13.3	14.5	12.1	11.9	14.9	16.9	15.1	10.8
HUMIDITY/%	80	79	79	78	79	81	82	82	81	82	81	80
BLOOM SEASON			**									
DAYS CLR	N/A											
RAIN/MM	193	122	135	254	338	368	307	302	378	429	384	274
°C AVG MAX	26.3	26.3	26.3	26.3	26.3	26.3	25.8	25.2	25.8	26.3	26.3	26.3
°C AVG MIN	18.6	18.6	18.6	19.1	19.1	19.1	19.1	19.1	18.6	18.6	19.1	18.6
DIURNAL RANGE	7.7	7.7	7.7	7.2	7.2	7.2	6.7	6.1	7.2	7.7	7.2	7.7
S/HEMISPHERE	JUL	AUG	SEP	OCT	NOV	DEC	JAN	FEB	MAR	APR	MAY	JUN

Cultural Recommendations

LIGHT: 2000–3000 fc.

Dendrobium melinanthum

TEMPERATURES: Throughout the year, days average 77–79°F (25–26°C), and nights average 65–66°F (19°C), with a diurnal range of 11–14°F (6–8°C).

HUMIDITY: Near 80% year-round.

WATER: Rainfall is heavy all year. Cultivated plants should be kept moist.

FERTILIZER: ¼–½ recommended strength. A balanced fertilizer should be applied weekly to biweekly throughout the year.

REST PERIOD: Growing conditions should be maintained year-round. Water should be reduced somewhat for plants grown in the dark, short-day conditions common in temperate-latitude winters. They should never be allowed to dry out completely, however. Fertilizer should be reduced until water is increased in spring.

GROWING MEDIA: A very open and fast-draining medium should be used with either baskets or small pots. Repotting may be done anytime new roots are growing.

MISCELLANEOUS NOTES: The bloom season shown in the climate table is based on collection reports.

Plant and Flower Information

PLANT SIZE AND TYPE: A 12–16 in. (30–40 cm) sympodial epiphyte.

PSEUDOBULB: 12–16 in. (30–40 cm) long. The stems become ridged with age.

LEAVES: Many. The lanceolate-oblong leaves are 0.6–1.2 in. (1.5–3.0 cm) long. The leaf sheaths are covered with black bristles.

INFLORESCENCE: Short. Inflorescences emerge from nodes along the side of the stem.

FLOWERS: 1, rarely 2 per inflorescence. The flowers are 0.6 in. (1.6 cm) long. They are yellowish with pale brown veins. The dorsal sepal and petals are erect, but the lip and lateral sepals jut forward. The lip is scalloped.

REFERENCES: 221, 437, 445.

PHOTOS/DRAWINGS: 437.

Dendrobium melinanthum Schlechter

ORIGIN/HABITAT: Northern Papua New Guinea. Plants grow on mistforest trees in the Finisterre Range at about 3950 ft. (1200 m).

CLIMATE: Station #94010, Goroka, Papua New Guinea, Lat. 6.1°S, Long. 145.4°E, at 5141 ft. (1567 m). Temperatures are calculated for an elevation of 4000 ft. (1220 m), resulting in probable extremes of 90°F (32°C) and 46°F (8°C).

N/HEMISPHERE	JAN	FEB	MAR	APR	MAY	JUN	JUL	AUG	SEP	OCT	NOV	DEC
°F AVG MAX	80	81	82	83	83	82	83	82	82	82	83	81
°F AVG MIN	60	61	61	61	62	63	63	63	64	63	63	61
DIURNAL RANGE	20	20	21	22	21	19	20	19	18	19	20	20
RAIN/INCHES	2.1	2.8	4.6	5.9	6.6	9.3	9.1	10.1	10.7	8.3	4.6	2.0
HUMIDITY/%	70	67	67	67	67	71	72	73	74	71	70	70
BLOOM SEASON			*				*					
DAYS CLR	N/A											
RAIN/MM	53	71	117	150	168	236	231	257	272	211	117	51
°C AVG MAX	26.5	27.1	27.6	28.2	28.2	27.6	28.2	27.6	27.6	27.6	28.2	27.1
°C AVG MIN	15.4	16.0	16.0	16.0	16.5	17.1	17.1	17.1	17.6	17.1	17.1	16.0
DIURNAL RANGE	11.1	11.1	11.6	12.2	11.7	10.5	11.1	10.5	10.0	10.5	11.1	11.1
S/HEMISPHERE	JUL	AUG	SEP	OCT	NOV	DEC	JAN	FEB	MAR	APR	MAY	JUN

Cultural Recommendations

LIGHT: 2500–3500 fc.

TEMPERATURES: Throughout the year, days average 80–83°F (27–28°C), and nights average 60–64°F (15–18°C), with a diurnal range of 19–22°F (11–12°C).

HUMIDITY: 70–75% from summer into autumn, dropping to 65–70% in winter and spring. Plants require excellent air movement.

WATER: Rainfall is moderate to heavy most of the year, but conditions are slightly drier for 3 months in winter. Cultivated plants should be kept moist but not soggy. Occasional early morning mistings may be beneficial, especially on bright, sunny days.

FERTILIZER: ¼–½ recommended strength. A balanced fertilizer should be applied weekly to biweekly throughout the year.

REST PERIOD: Growing temperatures should be maintained all year. In the habitat, rainfall is lowest in winter, but dew and mist from fog and low clouds are common. Water and fertilizer should be reduced somewhat for cultivated plants, especially those grown in the darker, short-day conditions common during temperate-latitude winters. Plants should be kept on the dry side, but they should never be allowed to dry out completely. In the habitat, light is higher in winter.

GROWING MEDIA: Plants may be mounted on tree-fern or cork slabs if humidity is high and plants are watered at least once daily in summer. When plants are potted, any open, fast-draining medium may be used. Repotting may be done anytime new roots are growing.

MISCELLANEOUS NOTES: The bloom season shown in the climate table is based on cultivation records and reports from the habitat.

Plant and Flower Information

PLANT SIZE AND TYPE: A 20 in. (50 cm) sympodial epiphyte.

PSEUDOBULB: 20 in. (50 cm) long. The densely leafy stems are spreading.

LEAVES: Many. The erect, fleshy leaves are 2 in. (5 cm) long, smooth, pointed, and elliptical to lanceolate.

INFLORESCENCE: Short. Inflorescences are densely flowered.

FLOWERS: Many per inflorescence. The cinnabar red flowers are 0.4 in. (1 cm) across. They are smooth with oval sepals and pointed, elliptical to spatula-shaped petals. The lip is truncated with an evenly serrated comb like margin.

REFERENCES: 221, 437, 445.

PHOTOS/DRAWINGS: 437.

Dendrobium meliodorum Schlechter

ORIGIN/HABITAT: Northern Papua New Guinea. Plants grow on mistforest trees on the lower slopes of the Kani Range at about 1950 ft. (600 m).

CLIMATE: Station #200187, Erap, Papua New Guinea, Lat. 6.6°S, Long. 146.7°E, at 850 ft. (260 m). Temperatures are calculated for an elevation of 1950 ft. (600 m), resulting in probable extremes of 98°F (37°C) and 49°F (10°C).

N/HEMISPHERE	JAN	FEB	MAR	APR	MAY	JUN	JUL	AUG	SEP	OCT	NOV	DEC
°F AVG MAX	84	84	85	86	89	89	89	89	89	88	86	86
°F AVG MIN	65	65	65	66	68	69	68	68	69	67	70	66
DIURNAL RANGE	19	19	20	20	21	20	21	21	20	21	16	20
RAIN/INCHES	3.9	3.9	2.7	3.0	3.0	5.3	5.9	5.9	7.0	3.4	2.4	3.1
HUMIDITY/%	82	81	81	79	75	74	74	74	77	76	80	80
BLOOM SEASON												*
DAYS CLR	N/A											
RAIN/MM	99	99	69	76	76	135	150	150	178	86	61	79
°C AVG MAX	29.1	29.1	29.6	30.2	31.8	31.8	31.8	31.8	31.8	31.3	30.2	30.2
°C AVG MIN	18.5	18.5	18.5	19.1	20.2	20.7	20.2	20.2	20.7	19.6	21.3	19.1
DIURNAL RANGE	10.6	10.6	11.1	11.1	11.6	11.1	11.6	11.6	11.1	11.7	8.9	11.1
S/HEMISPHERE	JUL	AUG	SEP	OCT	NOV	DEC	JAN	FEB	MAR	APR	MAY	JUN

Cultural Recommendations

LIGHT: 2500–3500 fc.

TEMPERATURES: Throughout the year, days average 84–89°F (29–32°C), and nights average 65–70°F (19–21°C), with a diurnal range of 16–21°F (9–12°C).

HUMIDITY: 75–80% year-round. The habitat may be quite dry during hot afternoons.

WATER: Rainfall is moderate most of the year, but conditions are somewhat wetter for 4–5 months in summer and early autumn. Cultivated plants should be thoroughly saturated then allowed to dry slightly between waterings in summer and early autumn. Water should be gradually reduced in autumn.

FERTILIZER: ¼–½ recommended strength. A balanced fertilizer should be applied weekly to biweekly throughout the year.

REST PERIOD: Growing temperatures should be maintained all year. In the habitat, rainfall is lowest in winter, but the high humidity indicates that additional moisture is frequently available from heavy dew. Cultivated plants should be allowed to dry somewhat longer between waterings than in summer, but they should not remain dry for extended periods. Fertilizer should be reduced until water is increased in spring. In the habitat, seasonal light variation is minor.

GROWING MEDIA: Plants may be mounted on tree-fern or cork slabs if humidity is high and plants are watered at least once daily in summer. When plants are potted, any open, fast-draining medium may be used. Repotting may be done anytime new roots are growing.

MISCELLANEOUS NOTES: The bloom season shown in the climate table is based on reports from the habitat. Plants that produce flowers that last a single day commonly bloom several times during the year. Flowering usually occurs 7–14 days after a sudden 10°F (5°C) drop in daytime temperatures.

Plant and Flower Information

PLANT SIZE AND TYPE: A 48 in. (122 cm) sympodial epiphyte.

PSEUDOBULB: 48 in. (122 cm) long.

LEAVES: Many. The leaves are 4.0–5.5 in. (10–14 cm) long. They are linear and may be erect or spreading.

INFLORESCENCE: Short.

FLOWERS: 2 per inflorescence. The flowers, which are 1.8 in. (4.6 cm) across, are held nearly opposite each other. Sepals and petals are linear and very elongated, becoming threadlike at the tips. They are white with a light red flush on the outside. The lip midlobe is yellow with a fringe along the hairy margin. Blossoms have a sweet, honeylike fragrance and last a single day.

REFERENCES: 221, 437.

Dendrobium mellicolor J. J. Smith

ORIGIN/HABITAT: The west coast of Sumatra near Solok, which is close to Padang. Habitat elevation is not available, so the following climate data should be used with caution.

CLIMATE: Station #96163, Padang, Sumatra, Indonesia, Lat. 0.9°S, Long. 100.4°E, at 19 ft. (6 m). Temperatures are calculated for an elevation of 450 ft. (140 m), resulting in probable extremes of 93°F (34°C) and 67°F (19°C).

N/HEMISPHERE	JAN	FEB	MAR	APR	MAY	JUN	JUL	AUG	SEP	OCT	NOV	DEC
°F AVG MAX	86	86	85	85	85	85	86	86	86	86	87	86
°F AVG MIN	73	73	73	73	73	73	73	73	73	74	74	73
DIURNAL RANGE	13	13	12	12	12	12	13	13	13	12	13	13
RAIN/INCHES	10.9	13.7	6.0	19.5	20.4	18.9	13.8	10.2	12.1	14.3	12.4	12.1
HUMIDITY/%	81	82	82	84	85	84	81	81	82	83	81	81
BLOOM SEASON	N/A											
DAYS CLR @ 7AM	5	1	1	0	0	2	2	1	2	2	3	5
DAYS CLR @ 1PM	5	2	2	1	1	3	3	4	3	3	6	5
RAIN/MM	277	348	152	495	518	480	351	259	307	363	315	307
°C AVG MAX	29.8	29.8	29.2	29.2	29.2	29.2	29.8	29.8	29.8	29.8	30.3	29.8
°C AVG MIN	22.5	22.5	22.5	22.5	22.5	22.5	22.5	22.5	22.5	23.1	23.1	22.5
DIURNAL RANGE	7.3	7.3	6.7	6.7	6.7	6.7	7.3	7.3	7.3	6.7	7.2	7.3
S/HEMISPHERE	JUL	AUG	SEP	OCT	NOV	DEC	JAN	FEB	MAR	APR	MAY	JUN

Cultural Recommendations

LIGHT: 1800–3000 fc. Diffused light is preferred.

TEMPERATURES: Throughout the year, days average 85–87°F (29–30°C), and nights average 73–74°F (23°C), with a diurnal range of 12–13°F (7°C). Probable extremes vary only a few degrees from the averages, indicating that plants may not tolerate wide temperature fluctuations.

HUMIDITY: 80–85% year-round.

WATER: Rainfall is heavy all year. Cultivated plants should be constantly moist but not soggy.

FERTILIZER: ¼–½ recommended strength. A balanced fertilizer should be applied weekly to biweekly throughout the year.

REST PERIOD: Growing conditions should be maintained year-round. Water may be reduced somewhat for plants grown in the dark, short-day conditions common in temperate-latitude winters, but they should not be allowed to dry out completely.

GROWING MEDIA: Plants may be mounted on tree-fern or cork slabs or potted in small pots filled with any open, fast-draining medium. Repotting may be done anytime new roots are growing.

MISCELLANEOUS NOTES: The plant was described in 1927 in *Bul. Jard. Bot. Buit.* 3rd. sér. 9:160.

Plant and Flower Information

PLANT SIZE AND TYPE: A 16 in. (40 cm) sympodial epiphyte.

PSEUDOBULB: 16 in. (40 cm) long. The elongated stems are dark, channeled, and nearly terete.

LEAVES: Many. The linear-lanceolate leaves are about 2.4 in. (6 cm) long. They are rigid, leathery, and minutely ruffled along the margin. They may be sparsely or densely hairy.

INFLORESCENCE: Short. Inflorescences emerge from nodes along the stem.

FLOWERS: 6–7 per inflorescence. The flowers are 0.5 in. (1.3 cm) across. The segments are light yellowish brown with somewhat greenish tips on the sepals and petals.

REFERENCES: 224.

Dendrobium mellitum Ridley. See *D. clavator* Ridley. REFERENCES: 219, 254, 454.

Dendrobium meltkeanum Kränzlin. See *D. mettkeanum* Kränzlin. REFERENCES: 218.

Dendrobium mendoncanum Hawkes. See *D. austrocaledonicum* Schlechter. REFERENCES: 173, 211, 230, 270, 271.

Dendrobium mentosum Schlechter. Now considered a synonym of *Flickingeria fimbriata* (Blume) A. Hawkes. REFERENCES: 213, 221, 436, 449, 536.

Dendrobium merrillii Ames

AKA: *D. aloifolium* Rchb. f. as used by Kränzlin. Merrill (ref. 296) and Valmayor (ref. 536), who cite Ames, include *D. aloifolium* Rchb. f. as a synonym.

ORIGIN/HABITAT: The Philippines. Plants grow on Mindoro, Samar, and Luzon Islands. On Luzon, they are found in forests at about 1150 ft. (350 m) in the provinces of Ifugao, Pangasinan, Quezon, and Rizal.

CLIMATE: Station #98427, Manila, Luzon, Philippines, Lat. 14.5°N, Long. 121.0°E, at 74 ft. (23 m). Temperatures are calculated for an elevation of 1150 ft. (350 m), resulting in probable extremes of 97°F (36°C) and 54°F (13°C).

Dendrobium masochlorum

N/HEMISPHERE	JAN	FEB	MAR	APR	MAY	JUN	JUL	AUG	SEP	OCT	NOV	DEC
°F AVG MAX	82	84	87	89	89	87	84	83	84	84	83	82
°F AVG MIN	65	65	67	69	71	71	71	71	71	70	68	66
DIURNAL RANGE	17	19	20	20	18	16	13	12	13	14	15	16
RAIN/INCHES	0.9	0.5	0.7	1.3	5.1	10.0	17.0	16.6	14.0	7.6	5.7	2.6
HUMIDITY/%	77	73	70	68	71	81	84	86	87	84	82	79
BLOOM SEASON		*	*			*	*			*		
DAYS CLR @ 8AM	6	9	14	14	10	3	2	1	1	6	7	6
DAYS CLR @ 2PM	3	6	10	10	8	2	1	1	0	2	2	3
RAIN/MM	23	13	18	33	130	254	432	422	356	193	145	66
°C AVG MAX	28.0	29.1	30.8	31.9	31.9	30.8	29.1	28.6	29.1	29.1	28.6	28.0
°C AVG MIN	18.6	18.6	19.7	20.8	21.9	21.9	21.9	21.9	21.9	21.4	20.2	19.1
DIURNAL RANGE	9.4	10.5	11.1	11.1	10.0	8.9	7.2	6.7	7.2	7.7	8.4	8.9
S/HEMISPHERE	JUL	AUG	SEP	OCT	NOV	DEC	JAN	FEB	MAR	APR	MAY	JUN

Cultural Recommendations

LIGHT: 1800–3000 fc.

TEMPERATURES: Summer days average 83–87°F (29–31°C), and nights average 71°F (22°C), with a diurnal range of 12–16°F (7–9°C). The warmest days and widest diurnal range occur in early spring.

HUMIDITY: 80–85% in summer and autumn, dropping to near 70% in winter and spring.

WATER: Rainfall is moderate to heavy most of the year, but averages are much lower in winter. Cultivated plants should be kept moist while actively growing, but water should be gradually reduced in late autumn.

FERTILIZER: 1/4–1/2 recommended strength, applied weekly. A high-nitrogen fertilizer is beneficial from spring to midsummer, but a fertilizer high in phosphates should be used in late summer and autumn.

REST PERIOD: Winter days average 82–84°F (28–29°C), and nights average 65–66°F (19°C), with a diurnal range of 16–19°F (9–11°C). Rainfall is low for 3–4 months in winter, but additional moisture is available from frequent heavy dew. In cultivation, water should be reduced and the plants allowed to dry out between waterings. They should not remain dry for extended periods, however. Fertilizer should also be reduced or eliminated anytime water is reduced. In the habitat, light is highest in winter.

GROWING MEDIA: Plants may be mounted on tree-fern or cork slabs if humidity is high and plants are watered at least once daily in summer. When plants are potted, any open, fast-draining medium may be used. Repotting is best done in early spring when new roots are growing.

MISCELLANEOUS NOTES: The bloom season shown in the climate table is based on collection reports.

Plant and Flower Information

PLANT SIZE AND TYPE: An 8–17 in. (20–43 cm) sympodial epiphyte. Plants may be as small as 4 in. (10 cm).

PSEUDOBULB: 4–10 in. (10–25 cm) long. The stems are flattened.

LEAVES: Many. The folded leaves may be as small as 0.8 in. (2 cm), or they may reach a length of 4–7 in. (10–18 cm). The 2-ranked leaves alternate up the stem.

INFLORESCENCE: Inflorescences emerge from a cushion of fibrous scales opposite rudimentary leaves near the apex of the stem.

FLOWERS: The flowers are 0.2 in. (0.4 cm) across, tiny, and insignificant. Sepals and petals are white with darker veins. The 3-lobed lip has a small rounded midlobe and obscure, hairy sidelobes.

REFERENCES: 12, 220, 254, 296, 373, 445, 536.

PHOTOS/DRAWINGS: 12.

Dendrobium mesochlorum Lindley. See *D. amoenum* Wallich ex Lindley. REFERENCES: 190, 216, 254, 317, 445, 541.

Dendrobium metachilinum Rchb. f.

AKA: *D. rorulentum* Teijsm. and Binn.

ORIGIN/HABITAT: Thailand, Malaya, Singapore, Sumatra, and Sarawak in Borneo. In Malaya, plants are found in the states of Melaka (Malacca), Perak, Johore, and Pahang, but they are rare in the southern lowlands. The grow in the tops of tall trees.

CLIMATE: Station #48665, Melaka (Malacca), Malaya, Lat. 2.3°N, Long. 102.3°E, at 40 ft. (12 m). Record extreme temperatures are 99°F (37°C) and 61°F (16°C).

N/HEMISPHERE	JAN	FEB	MAR	APR	MAY	JUN	JUL	AUG	SEP	OCT	NOV	DEC
°F AVG MAX	88	89	89	89	89	88	88	88	88	88	88	88
°F AVG MIN	72	72	72	73	73	73	72	72	72	72	72	72
DIURNAL RANGE	16	17	17	16	16	15	16	16	16	16	16	16
RAIN/INCHES	3.9	3.7	4.9	7.4	6.8	7.9	7.8	10.3	8.8	10.1	8.7	6.5
HUMIDITY/%	79	79	82	85	85	83	84	84	84	84	84	82
BLOOM SEASON						**						
DAYS CLR @ 7AM	1	1	1	1	1	1	2	1	1	1	0	1
DAYS CLR @ 1PM	1	1	1	1	1	1	1	1	1	1	0	0
RAIN/MM	99	94	124	188	173	201	198	262	224	257	221	165
°C AVG MAX	31.1	31.7	31.7	31.7	31.7	31.1	31.1	31.1	31.1	31.1	31.1	31.1
°C AVG MIN	22.2	22.2	22.2	22.8	22.8	22.8	22.2	22.2	22.2	22.2	22.2	22.2
DIURNAL RANGE	8.9	9.5	9.5	8.9	8.9	8.3	8.9	8.9	8.9	8.9	8.9	8.9
S/HEMISPHERE	JUL	AUG	SEP	OCT	NOV	DEC	JAN	FEB	MAR	APR	MAY	JUN

Cultural Recommendations

LIGHT: 2000–3000 fc.

TEMPERATURES: Throughout the year, days average 88–89°F (31–32°C), and nights average 72–73°F (22–23°C), with a diurnal range of 15–17°F (8–10°C).

HUMIDITY: Near 85% year-round.

WATER: Rainfall is moderate to heavy all year, but conditions are slightly drier for 2 months in winter. Cultivated plants should be kept moist but not soggy, with only slight drying allowed between waterings.

FERTILIZER: 1/4–1/2 recommended strength. A balanced fertilizer should be applied weekly to biweekly throughout the year.

REST PERIOD: Growing conditions should be maintained all year. Water and fertilizer may be reduced slightly in winter. Plants need less water during the dark, short-days common to temperate-latitude winters. Plants should never be allowed to dry out completely, however.

GROWING MEDIA: Plants may be mounted on tree-fern or cork slabs if humidity is high and plants are watered at least once daily in summer. When plants are potted, any open, fast-draining medium may be used. Repotting may be done anytime new roots are growing.

MISCELLANEOUS NOTES: The bloom season shown in the climate table is based on cultivation records.

Plant and Flower Information

PLANT SIZE AND TYPE: An 8–14 in. (20–35 cm) sympodial epiphyte.

PSEUDOBULB: 8–14 in. (20–35 cm) long. The stout, rooting stems run along the ground and then become erect. They are somewhat tapering and deeply grooved when dry. Internodes are about 0.4 in. (1 cm) long.

LEAVES: 11–13 along the apical 60% of the stem. The leaves are about 2.8 in. (7 cm) long. They may be linear or oblong and are stiffly spreading.

INFLORESCENCE: Very short. Many inflorescences arise opposite the upper leaves on leafy pseudobulbs.

FLOWERS: 2–4 per inflorescence. The flowers are 0.6–1.2 in. (1.5–3.0 cm) across. The pointed sepals and petals may be dirty yellow, greenish, pale dull orange, or burnt sienna. They are marked with darker brown lines or veins. The narrow, fleshy lip may be brown or light yellow. It is marked with 2 grass-green keels that are covered with a mealy powder. The sidelobes are toothlike. The front margin has a broad warty edge.

REFERENCES: 57, 200, 202, 216, 254, 296, 317, 395, 402, 454, 455.

PHOTOS/DRAWINGS: *454*, 455.

Dendrobium metrium Kränzlin

AKA: *D. modestum* Ridley not Rchb. f.

ORIGIN/HABITAT: Very rare in Malaya. Plants were collected on a grassy bank on Buket Bendera, Pinang (Penang) at about 2000 ft. (610 m).

CLIMATE: Station #48601, Penang, Malaya, Lat. 5.3°N, Long. 100.3°E, at 8 ft. (2 m). Temperatures are calculated for an elevation of 2000 ft. (610 m), resulting in probable extremes of 91°F (33°C) and 60°F (16°C).

N/HEMISPHERE	JAN	FEB	MAR	APR	MAY	JUN	JUL	AUG	SEP	OCT	NOV	DEC
°F AVG MAX	83	84	85	84	83	83	83	82	81	82	81	82
°F AVG MIN	66	66	67	68	67	67	67	66	66	66	66	66
DIURNAL RANGE	17	18	18	16	16	16	16	16	15	16	15	16
RAIN/INCHES	3.7	3.1	5.6	7.4	10.7	7.7	7.5	11.6	15.8	16.9	11.9	5.8
HUMIDITY/%	76	77	81	84	84	84	85	85	85	87	86	81
BLOOM SEASON			*									
DAYS CLR @ 7AM	2	1	2	0	0	1	1	0	0	0	1	1
DAYS CLR @ 1PM	3	2	2	1	1	1	1	0	0	0	1	2
RAIN/MM	94	79	142	188	272	196	190	295	401	429	302	147
°C AVG MAX	28.6	29.1	29.7	29.1	28.6	28.6	28.6	28.0	27.5	28.0	27.5	28.0
°C AVG MIN	19.1	19.1	19.7	20.2	19.7	19.7	19.7	19.1	19.1	19.1	19.1	19.1
DIURNAL RANGE	9.5	10.0	10.0	8.9	8.9	8.9	8.9	8.9	8.4	8.9	8.4	8.9
S/HEMISPHERE	JUL	AUG	SEP	OCT	NOV	DEC	JAN	FEB	MAR	APR	MAY	JUN

Cultural Recommendations

LIGHT: 3000–3500 fc.

TEMPERATURES: Throughout the year, days average 81–85°F (28–30°C), nights average 66–68°F (19–20°C), with a diurnal range of 15–18°F (8–10°C).

HUMIDITY: 80–85% most of the year, dropping to near 75% for 2 months in winter.

WATER: Rainfall is moderate to heavy most of the year, but conditions are somewhat drier for 2 months in winter. Cultivated plants should be kept moist and never be allowed to dry out completely.

FERTILIZER: ¼–½ recommended strength, applied weekly during periods of active growth.

REST PERIOD: Growing conditions should be maintained all year. Water should be reduced in winter and slight drying allowed between waterings. Plants should not remain dry for long periods, however. Fertilizer should be reduced until water is increased in spring. In the habitat, seasonal light variation is minor.

GROWING MEDIA: Plants should be potted in small containers filled with any open, fast-draining medium. Repotting may be done anytime new roots are growing.

MISCELLANEOUS NOTES: The bloom season shown in the climate table is based on reports from the habitat.

Plant and Flower Information

PLANT SIZE AND TYPE: An 8 in. (20 cm) sympodial terrestrial.

PSEUDOBULB: 7 in. (18 cm) long. The slender stems are purplish with white stripes. Plants consist of a few stems that are leafy except at the base of the stem.

LEAVES: Many. The leaves are 1.0–2.2 in. (2.5–5.5 cm) long, linear-lanceolate, and thin.

INFLORESCENCE: Very short. Racemes emerge from nodes on leafy stems.

FLOWERS: 2 per inflorescence. Blossoms are about 0.4 in. (1 cm) long. The lanceolate sepals and shorter linear-oblong petals are white suffused with rose. The pointed ovate lip, which is covered with short hairs, is marked with violet stripes.

REFERENCES: 200, 220, 254, 402, 455.

PHOTOS/DRAWINGS: 455.

Dendrobium mettkeanum Kränzlin.

Sometimes spelled *D. meltkeanum*. Now considered a synonym of *Diplocaulobium nitidissimum* (Rchb. f.) Kränzlin. REFERENCES: 87, 190, 216, 254, 271, 583.

Dendrobium mexicanum Presl.

Now considered a synonym of an unspecified *Govenia* species. REFERENCES: 216, 254, 445.

Dendrobium × micans Rchb. f.

A natural hybrid between *D. wardianum* Warner and *D. lituiflorum* Lindley. REFERENCES: Reichenbach 1879 *Gardeners' Chronicle I*, p. 332.

Dendrobium micholitzii Rolfe.

See *D. hymenanthum* Rchb. f. REFERENCES: 219, 254, 437, 445, 454. PHOTOS/DRAWINGS: 254, 437.

Dendrobium micranthum (Griffith) Lindley not Swartz.

See *D. aloifolium* (Blume) Rchb. f. REFERENCES: 75, 216, 254, 278, 317, 454, 469.

Dendrobium micranthum Swartz not (Griffith) Lindley.

Now considered a synonym of *Stelis micrantha* Swartz. REFERENCES: 190, 216, 254.

Dendrobium microblepharum Schlechter.

See *D. vexillarius* J. J. Smith. REFERENCES: 223, 385, 443.

Dendrobium microbulbon A. Richard

AKA: Sometimes spelled *D. microbolbon*. Synonyms include *D. crispum* Dalzell and *D. humile* Wight.

ORIGIN/HABITAT: Western India, including the Konkan, West Ghats, Deccan, and North Kanara regions. Specific habitat information is not available. Elevation is estimated at 4000 ft. (1220 m), so the following climate data should be used with caution.

CLIMATE: Station #43314, Calicut, India, Lat. 11.3°N, Long. 75.8°E, at 17 ft. (5 m). Temperatures are calculated for an elevation of 4000 ft. (1220 m), resulting in probable extremes of 86°F (30°C) and 44°F (7°C).

N/HEMISPHERE	JAN	FEB	MAR	APR	MAY	JUN	JUL	AUG	SEP	OCT	NOV	DEC
°F AVG MAX	75	76	77	78	77	72	69	70	71	73	74	75
°F AVG MIN	58	60	63	65	65	62	61	61	62	62	61	58
DIURNAL RANGE	17	16	14	13	12	10	8	9	9	11	13	17
RAIN/INCHES	0.4	0.2	0.7	3.6	9.3	33.1	32.5	17.2	7.9	10.3	5.5	1.0
HUMIDITY/%	71	73	73	74	82	87	91	91	87	85	77	74
BLOOM SEASON	**					*		*				**
DAYS CLR @ 5AM	19	18	21	12	5	4	2	2	4	4	19	20
DAYS CLR @ 11AM	16	18	23	15	5	3	0	1	6	5	12	14
RAIN/MM	10	5	18	91	236	841	826	437	201	262	140	25
°C AVG MAX	23.8	24.4	24.9	25.5	24.9	22.1	20.5	21.0	21.6	22.7	23.3	23.8
°C AVG MIN	14.4	15.5	17.1	18.3	18.3	16.6	16.0	16.0	16.6	16.6	16.0	14.4
DIURNAL RANGE	9.4	8.9	7.8	7.2	6.6	5.5	4.5	5.0	5.0	6.1	7.3	9.4
S/HEMISPHERE	JUL	AUG	SEP	OCT	NOV	DEC	JAN	FEB	MAR	APR	MAY	JUN

Cultural Recommendations

LIGHT: 3000–4000 fc. Plants need some shading from spring through autumn. However, light should be as high as the plant can tolerate, short of burning the leaves.

TEMPERATURES: Throughout the year, days average 69–78°F (21–26°C), and nights average 58–65°F (14–18°C), with a diurnal range of 8–17°F (4–9°C). Spring is the warmest season.

HUMIDITY: 85–90% in summer, dropping to 71–74% in winter.

WATER: Rainfall is extremely heavy from late spring into autumn. The winter dry season lasts 3–4 months. Cultivated plants should be watered liberally and kept moist from spring to early autumn. Water should be gradually reduced through autumn, greatly reduced in winter, then gradually increased in spring when new growth starts.

FERTILIZER: ¼–½ recommended strength, applied weekly. A high-nitrogen fertilizer is beneficial from spring to midsummer, but a fertilizer high in phosphates should be used in late summer and autumn.

REST PERIOD: Growing temperatures should be maintained all year. However, the slightly warmer days and slightly cooler nights double the summer diurnal range. In the winter dry period, conditions are so dry that even moisture from dew is uncommon for 2–3 months. Water should be greatly reduced for cultivated plants. They should be allowed to dry out between waterings but should not remain completely dry for extended periods. Occasional early morning mistings may be given between waterings, especially on warm, sunny days. Fertilizer should be greatly reduced or eliminated until water is increased in spring. In the habitat, light is highest in winter.

GROWING MEDIA: Growers recommend mounting on tree-fern slabs if humidity is high and plants can be watered at least once daily in summer. If plants are potted, any open, fast-draining medium may be used. Repotting is best done in late spring when new roots begin to grow.

MISCELLANEOUS NOTES: The bloom season shown in the climate table is based on reports from the habitat. Cultivated plants bloom in early winter.

Plant and Flower Information

PLANT SIZE AND TYPE: A 1.6–2.8 in. (4–7 cm) sympodial epiphyte.

PSEUDOBULB: 0.4–0.8 in. (1–2 cm) long. The conical to ovoid pseudobulbs are purplish brown, crowded, and covered with sheaths that leave a network of fibers when they deteriorate. Immediately before flowering, the tiny pseudobulbs elongate.

LEAVES: 2 per growth. The leaves are 3.0–5.5 in. (7.5–14.0 cm) long. They may be thick or thin, linear, oblong, or lanceolate.

INFLORESCENCE: 0.8–4.0 in. (2–10 cm) long. Inflorescences are slender, erect, and branching. One or more emerge at or near the apex of leafless, elongated pseudobulbs.

FLOWERS: 3–10 per inflorescence. The flowers are 0.2–0.6 in. (0.5–1.5 cm) across. Sepals and petals may be white, greenish yellow with pink tips, or pale, purplish green with darker purple lines. The 3-lobed lip may be white or pink with darker, pinkish purple veins or 2 small red spots in the throat. The nearly round midlobe is irregularly ruffled. The spur is long and incurved. Blossoms last for many weeks. They may be faintly or strongly fragrant.

HYBRIDIZING NOTES: Chromosome count is n = 19 (ref. 154) and 2n = 38 (ref. 151, 542).

REFERENCES: 38, 46, 119, 151, 154, 179, 202, 216, 244, 254, 278, 317, 369, 424, 445, 522, 524, 542.

PHOTOS/DRAWINGS: 244.

Dendrobium microchilum Ames.
Status unknown. This name was used by Löve and Solbrig (ref. 280) in their list of chromosome counts. Later writers have used this information in other lists of chromosome counts, but we have found no other use of the name. We can find no original description of this plant and suspect that this information actually applies to *Dendrochilum microchilum* Ames. REFERENCES: 280, 504, 580.

Dendrobium microchilum Dalzell.
Also spelled *D. microchilos*, it is now considered a synonym of *Eria dalzelli* Lindley. REFERENCES: 216, 254.

Dendrobium microglaphys Rchb. f.

AKA: *D. callibotrys* Ridley.

ORIGIN/HABITAT: Southern Malaya, Singapore, and Borneo. Plants usually grow low on tree trunks near the forest floor at low elevations in mangrove swamps. In Sabah, they are found in hill forests at about 2600 ft. (800 m).

Station #49613, Tambunan, Sabah, Borneo, Lat. 5.7°N, Long. 116.4°E, at 1200 ft. (366 m). Temperatures are calculated for an elevation of 2500 ft. (760 m), resulting in probable extremes of 94°F (34°C) and 50°F (10°C).

N/HEMISPHERE	JAN	FEB	MAR	APR	MAY	JUN	JUL	AUG	SEP	OCT	NOV	DEC
°F AVG MAX	82	83	85	86	86	85	85	85	85	84	83	82
°F AVG MIN	63	61	62	63	64	63	62	62	63	63	63	64
DIURNAL RANGE	19	22	23	23	22	22	23	23	22	21	20	18
RAIN/INCHES	5.8	3.7	5.8	7.5	8.2	7.3	5.1	4.9	6.4	7.0	6.8	6.0
HUMIDITY/%	N/A											
BLOOM SEASON		*	*	*	**	*	*	*	*	*	*	
DAYS CLR	N/A											
RAIN/MM	147	94	147	191	208	185	130	124	163	178	173	152
°C AVG MAX	27.8	28.3	29.4	30.0	30.0	29.6	29.5	29.4	29.4	28.9	28.3	27.8
°C AVG MIN	17.2	16.0	16.5	17.1	17.6	17.1	16.5	16.5	17.1	17.1	17.1	17.6
DIURNAL RANGE	10.6	12.3	12.9	12.9	12.4	12.5	13.0	12.9	12.3	11.8	11.2	10.2
S/HEMISPHERE	JUL	AUG	SEP	OCT	NOV	DEC	JAN	FEB	MAR	APR	MAY	JUN

Cultural Recommendations

LIGHT: 1500–2500 fc.

TEMPERATURES: Throughout the year, days average 82–86°F (28–30°C), and nights average 61–64°F (16–18°C), with a diurnal range of 18–23°F (10–13°C).

HUMIDITY: Information is not available for this location. However, records from nearby locations indicate that humidity probably averages 80–85% year-round.

WATER: Rainfall is moderate to heavy all year with a brief, slightly drier period in winter. Cultivated plants should be allowed to dry only slightly between waterings.

FERTILIZER: ¼–½ recommended strength. A balanced fertilizer should be applied weekly to biweekly throughout the year.

REST PERIOD: Growing conditions should be maintained all year. Water should be reduced slightly in winter, but the plants should never be allowed to dry out completely. Fertilizer should be reduced anytime plants are not actively growing.

GROWING MEDIA: Plants may be mounted on tree-fern or cork slabs if humidity is high and plants are watered at least once a day in summer. When plants are potted, any open, fast-draining medium may be used. Repotting may be done anytime new roots are growing.

MISCELLANEOUS NOTES: The bloom season shown in the climate table is based on cultivation records.

Plant and Flower Information

PLANT SIZE AND TYPE: A 9–28 in. (23–70 cm) sympodial epiphyte or terrestrial.

PSEUDOBULB: 6–24 in. (15–60 cm) long. The grooved stems may be slender or swollen in the middle and taper at each end.

LEAVES: 2–10 at the apex of each growth. The oblong leaves, which are 3–4 in. (8–10 cm) long, have 6 nerves.

INFLORESCENCE: 0.2–1 in. (0.5–2.5 cm) long. Racemes emerge laterally from nodes near the apex of the stem. The blossoms are densely clustered on the inflorescence.

FLOWERS: 6–12 per inflorescence. The flowers are 1 in. (2.5 cm) across. They have a broadly ovate upper sepal, sickle-shaped lateral sepals, and lanceolate petals. Sepals and petals are white. The ovate lip is light yellow with 5 or more red to orange streaks. It is inversely wedge-shaped. Blossoms have a fragrance that resembles the grass *Anthoxanthum odoratum*.

REFERENCES: 216, 254, 286, 295, 394, 395, 402, 455, 589, 592.

PHOTOS/DRAWINGS: 455.

Dendrobium microglossum Schlechter

ORIGIN/HABITAT: Northeastern Papua New Guinea. In the Waria District of the Maboro Range, plants grow on trees at about 3300 ft. (1000 m).

CLIMATE: Station #200192, Garaina, Papua New Guinea, Lat. 7.9°S, Long. 147.1°E, at 2350 ft. (716 m). Temperatures are calculated for an elevation of 3300 ft. (1000 m), resulting in probable extremes of 91°F (33°C) and 43°F (6°C).

N/HEMISPHERE	JAN	FEB	MAR	APR	MAY	JUN	JUL	AUG	SEP	OCT	NOV	DEC
°F AVG MAX	77	79	80	81	82	82	82	82	81	81	80	78
°F AVG MIN	60	60	60	61	60	61	62	62	62	61	61	60
DIURNAL RANGE	17	19	20	20	22	21	20	20	19	20	19	18
RAIN/INCHES	5.8	6.5	8.7	11.1	11.8	11.9	8.9	11.7	11.5	9.9	7.7	5.2
HUMIDITY/%	84	82	82	81	80	80	81	81	82	83	84	84
BLOOM SEASON							*					
DAYS CLR	N/A											
RAIN/MM	147	165	221	282	300	302	226	297	292	251	196	132
°C AVG MAX	25.0	26.1	26.6	27.2	27.7	27.7	27.7	27.7	27.2	27.2	26.6	25.5
°C AVG MIN	15.5	15.5	15.5	16.1	15.5	16.1	16.6	16.6	16.6	16.1	16.1	15.5
DIURNAL RANGE	9.5	10.6	11.1	11.1	12.2	11.6	11.1	11.1	10.6	11.1	10.5	10.0
S/HEMISPHERE	JUL	AUG	SEP	OCT	NOV	DEC	JAN	FEB	MAR	APR	MAY	JUN

Cultural Recommendations

LIGHT: 2000–3000 fc.

TEMPERATURES: Throughout the year, days average 77–82°F (25–28°C), and nights average 60–62°F (16–17°C), with a diurnal range of 17–22°F (10–12°C).

HUMIDITY: 80–85% year-round.

WATER: Rainfall is heavy all year, but conditions are slightly drier in winter. Cultivated plants should be kept moist.

FERTILIZER: ¼–½ recommended strength. A balanced fertilizer should be applied weekly to biweekly throughout the year.

REST PERIOD: Growing conditions vary only slightly during the year. In the habitat, rainfall is slightly lower in winter. Water and fertilizer should be reduced. Plants need less water when cultivated in the dark, short-day conditions common during temperate-latitude winters. Plants should never be allowed to dry out completely, however. In the habitat, light is slightly higher in winter.

GROWING MEDIA: Plants may be mounted on tree-fern or cork slabs if humidity is high and plants are watered at least once daily in summer. When plants are potted, any open, fast-draining medium may be used. Repotting may be done anytime new roots are growing.

MISCELLANEOUS NOTES: The bloom season shown in the climate table is based on collection reports. Plants that produce flowers that last a single day commonly bloom several times during the year. Flowering usually occurs 7–14 days after a sudden 10°F (5°C) drop in daytime temperatures.

Plant and Flower Information

PLANT SIZE AND TYPE: A 20 in. (50 cm) sympodial epiphyte.

PSEUDOBULB: 20 in. (50 cm) long. The stem becomes flattened.

LEAVES: The elliptic leaves are 2.0–3.5 in. (5–9 cm) long. They may be erect or spreading.

INFLORESCENCE: Very short. Inflorescences arise from nodes at the side of the pseudobulb.

FLOWERS: 2 per inflorescence. The flowers are 1 in. (2.6 cm) across. Sepals and petals are cream. The fringed, hairy lip, which is recurved at the tip, is creamy white with an orange-yellow crest. The sickle-shaped side-lobes are toothed along the lower margin. They extend nearly to the tip of the midlobe. The column has orange-yellow markings. Blossoms last a single day.

REFERENCES: 221, 437, 445.

PHOTOS/DRAWINGS: 437.

Dendrobium micronephelium J. J. Smith.

Although not correctly transferred, Schlechter (ref. 443) considered this name to be a synonym of *Cadetia micronephelia* (J. J. Smith) Schlechter. REFERENCES: 221, 223, 443, 445, 470, 475.

Dendrobium microphyton L. O. Williams.

Now considered a synonym of *Cadetia microphyton* (L. O. Williams) E. A Christianson. REFERENCES: 226, 536, Christianson 1992 Lindleyana 7(2):89–90.

Dendrobium millarae Hawkes

AKA: *D. dischorense* Schlechter 1912 not 1910.

ORIGIN/HABITAT: Northern Papua New Guinea. Plants grow on moss-covered mistforest trees of the Dischore Range at about 3950 ft. (1200 m).

CLIMATE: Station #200192, Garaina, Papua New Guinea, Lat. 7.9°S, Long. 147.1°E, at 2350 ft. (716 m). Temperatures are calculated for an elevation of 3950 ft. (1200 m), resulting in probable extremes of 89°F (32°C) and 41°F (5°C).

N/HEMISPHERE	JAN	FEB	MAR	APR	MAY	JUN	JUL	AUG	SEP	OCT	NOV	DEC
°F AVG MAX	75	77	78	79	80	80	80	80	79	79	78	76
°F AVG MIN	58	58	58	59	58	59	60	60	60	59	59	58
DIURNAL RANGE	17	19	20	20	22	21	20	20	19	20	19	18
RAIN/INCHES	5.8	6.5	8.7	11.1	11.8	11.9	8.9	11.7	11.5	9.9	7.7	5.2
HUMIDITY/%	84	82	82	81	80	80	81	81	82	83	84	84
BLOOM SEASON												*
DAYS CLR	N/A											
RAIN/MM	147	165	221	282	300	302	226	297	292	251	196	132
°C AVG MAX	23.8	24.9	25.4	26.0	26.5	26.5	26.5	26.5	26.0	26.0	25.4	24.3
°C AVG MIN	14.3	14.3	14.3	14.9	14.3	14.9	15.4	15.4	15.4	14.9	14.9	14.3
DIURNAL RANGE	9.5	10.6	11.1	11.1	12.2	11.6	11.1	11.1	10.6	11.1	10.5	10.0
S/HEMISPHERE	JUL	AUG	SEP	OCT	NOV	DEC	JAN	FEB	MAR	APR	MAY	JUN

Cultural Recommendations

LIGHT: 2000–3000 fc.

TEMPERATURES: Throughout the year, days average 75–80°F (24–27°C), and nights average 58–60°F (14–15°C), with a diurnal range of 17–22°F (10–12°C).

HUMIDITY: 80–85% year-round.

WATER: Rainfall is heavy all year, but conditions are slightly drier in winter. Cultivated plants should be kept moist but not soggy.

FERTILIZER: ¼–½ recommended strength. A balanced fertilizer should be applied weekly to biweekly throughout the year. The Royal Botanic Garden in Edinburgh uses a seaweed-based fertilizer for high elevation plants from New Guinea.

REST PERIOD: Growing conditions vary only slightly during the year. In the habitat, rainfall is slightly lower in winter. Water and fertilizer should be reduced. Plants need less water when cultivated in the darker, short-day conditions common in temperate-latitude winters. Plants should never be allowed to dry out completely, however. In the habitat, light is slightly higher in winter.

GROWING MEDIA: Plants may be mounted on tree-fern or cork slabs if humidity is high and plants are watered at least once daily in summer.

Dendrobium milligani

When plants are potted, any open, fast-draining medium may be used. Repotting may be done anytime new roots are growing.

MISCELLANEOUS NOTES: The bloom season shown in the climate table is based on cultivation records.

Plant and Flower Information

PLANT SIZE AND TYPE: An 8–12 in. (20–30 cm) sympodial epiphyte.

PSEUDOBULB: 8–12 in. (20–30 cm) long. The somewhat flattened, leafy stems may be simple or branched. They arise from a short rhizome.

LEAVES: Many. The leaves are 0.6–1.0 in. (1.5–2.5 cm) long, lanceolate to elliptical, and shiny with a very thin texture. They are erect to spreading.

INFLORESCENCE: Inflorescences emerge from nodes along the side of the stems.

FLOWERS: 1 per inflorescence. The tiny flowers are 0.2 in. (0.5 cm) across. Blossoms are white with red markings on the lip. The lateral sepals are joined, forming a hood over the lip, which is uppermost. The very short lived blossoms only last a few days.

REFERENCES: 191, 229, 437

PHOTOS/DRAWINGS: 437.

Dendrobium milligani F. Mueller. Sometimes spelled *D. milliganii*, see *D. striolatum* Rchb. f. not F. M. Bailey. REFERENCES: 67, 105, 190, 216, 254, 445, 533.

Dendrobium mimiense Schlechter

AKA: In 1993 Dauncey and Cribb in *Kew Bulletin* 48(3) consider *D. mimiense* a possible synonym of *D. constrictum* J. J. Smith.

ORIGIN/HABITAT: Northeastern Papua New Guinea. On Mt. Mimi in the Waria District, plants grow on moss-covered trees below the mistforest zone at about 2300 ft. (700 m).

CLIMATE: Station #200192, Garaina, Papua New Guinea, Lat. 7.9°S, Long. 147.1°E, at 2350 ft. (716 m). Record extreme temperatures are 94°F (34°C) and 46°F (8°C).

N/HEMISPHERE	JAN	FEB	MAR	APR	MAY	JUN	JUL	AUG	SEP	OCT	NOV	DEC
°F AVG MAX	80	82	83	84	85	85	85	85	84	84	83	81
°F AVG MIN	63	63	63	64	63	64	65	65	65	64	64	63
DIURNAL RANGE	17	19	20	20	22	21	20	20	19	20	19	18
RAIN/INCHES	5.8	6.5	8.7	11.1	11.8	11.9	8.9	11.7	11.5	9.9	7.7	5.2
HUMIDITY/%	84	82	82	81	80	80	81	81	82	83	84	84
BLOOM SEASON											**	
DAYS CLR	N/A											
RAIN/MM	148	166	220	282	300	303	227	296	291	251	195	131
°C AVG MAX	26.8	27.5	28.2	28.6	29.3	29.3	29.4	29.4	29.1	28.7	28.2	27.2
°C AVG MIN	16.9	16.9	17.4	17.6	17.4	18.0	18.1	18.2	18.4	17.7	17.7	17.1
DIURNAL RANGE	9.9	10.6	10.8	11.0	11.9	11.3	11.3	11.2	10.7	11.0	10.5	10.1
S/HEMISPHERE	JUL	AUG	SEP	OCT	NOV	DEC	JAN	FEB	MAR	APR	MAY	JUN

Cultural Recommendations

LIGHT: 1000–2000 fc. Growers recommend *Phalaenopsis* light levels.

TEMPERATURES: Throughout the year, days average 80–85°F (27–29°C), and nights average 63–65°F (17–18°C), with a diurnal range of 17–22°F (11–12°C).

HUMIDITY: 80–85% year-round.

WATER: Rainfall is heavy year-round, but conditions are slightly drier in winter. Cultivated plants should be kept moist but not soggy.

FERTILIZER: ¼–½ recommended strength. A balanced fertilizer should be applied weekly to biweekly throughout the year.

REST PERIOD: Growing conditions vary only slightly during the year. In the habitat, rainfall is slightly lower in winter. Water and fertilizer should be reduced somewhat, especially for plants cultivated in the darker, short-day conditions common in temperate-latitude winters. Plants should never be allowed to dry out completely, however. In the habitat, light is slightly higher in winter.

GROWING MEDIA: Mounting plants on tree-fern or cork slabs accommodates their growth habit. However, humidity must be high and plants must be watered at least once a day in summer. If plants cannot be mounted, small pots or hanging baskets may be filled with an open, fast-draining medium. Repotting may be done anytime new roots are actively growing.

MISCELLANEOUS NOTES: The bloom season shown in the climate table is based on collection reports.

Plant and Flower Information

PLANT SIZE AND TYPE: A 6–10 in. (15–25 cm) sympodial epiphyte.

PSEUDOBULB: 2–4 in. (5–10 cm) long. The stems are suberect.

LEAVES: 3–6 per growth. The leaves are 4.0–5.5 in. (10–14 cm) long.

INFLORESCENCE: 1.2–1.4 in. (3.0–3.6 cm) long. The blossoms are carried on a densely flowered raceme.

FLOWERS: Many per inflorescence. The pure white flowers are 0.3 in. (0.8 cm) long and do not open fully. Sepals and petals are pointed. The lip is fringed along the margin.

REFERENCES: 92, 221, 352, 437, 445.

PHOTOS/DRAWINGS: 437.

Dendrobium minahassae Kränzlin. See *D. heterocarpum* Lindley. Listed in Comber (ref. 75) as *D. minhassae*. REFERENCES: 75, 190, 220, 254, 296, 436, 445, 454.

Dendrobium minax Rchb. f. See *D. bicaudatum* Reinwardt ex Lindley. The International Orchid Commission (ref. 236) registers hybrids under the name *D. minax*. REFERENCES: 36, 84, 179, 196, 216, 236, 254, 445.

Dendrobium mindanaense Ames

ORIGIN/HABITAT: The Philippine Islands of Mindanao, Leyte, Polillo, Luzon, Negros Occidental, Palawan, and Culion. On Luzon, plants grow in Quezon and Rizal Provinces, and on Mindanao, they are found in the provinces of Surigao, Agusan, Cotabato, and Zamboanga. Plants usually grow at low elevations on the underside of limbs of large trees in mangrove swamps.

CLIMATE: Station #98746, Cotabato, Mindanao, Philippines, Lat. 7.2°N, Long. 124.3°E, at 56 ft. (17 m). Record extreme temperatures are 99°F (37°C) and 61°F (16°C).

N/HEMISPHERE	JAN	FEB	MAR	APR	MAY	JUN	JUL	AUG	SEP	OCT	NOV	DEC
°F AVG MAX	91	91	93	93	92	90	90	89	90	90	91	90
°F AVG MIN	70	71	71	72	73	72	72	72	72	72	72	71
DIURNAL RANGE	21	20	22	21	19	18	18	17	18	18	19	19
RAIN/INCHES	2.5	3.4	3.6	5.1	9.3	8.8	9.0	12.9	9.8	10.0	7.0	3.7
HUMIDITY/%	83	82	80	81	84	86	86	86	86	86	85	84
BLOOM SEASON			*		*		*		*			
DAYS CLR @ 8AM	4	3	8	6	2	2	2	1	3	2	3	3
DAYS CLR @ 2PM	2	1	3	5	2	2	1	1	2	1	1	1
RAIN/MM	64	86	91	130	236	224	229	328	249	254	178	94
°C AVG MAX	32.8	32.8	33.9	33.9	33.3	32.2	32.2	31.7	32.2	32.2	32.8	32.2
°C AVG MIN	21.1	21.7	21.7	22.2	22.8	22.2	22.2	22.2	22.2	22.2	22.2	21.7
DIURNAL RANGE	11.7	11.1	12.2	11.7	10.5	10.0	10.0	9.5	10.0	10.0	10.6	10.5
S/HEMISPHERE	JUL	AUG	SEP	OCT	NOV	DEC	JAN	FEB	MAR	APR	MAY	JUN

Cultural Recommendations

LIGHT: 2000–3000 fc.

TEMPERATURES: Throughout the year, days average 89–93°F (32–34°C), nights average 70–73°F (21–23°C), with a diurnal range of 17–22°F (10–12°C).

HUMIDITY: 80–85% year-round.

WATER: Rainfall is moderate to heavy all year, but conditions are slightly drier for 3–4 months in winter. Cultivated plants should be kept moist but not soggy while growing, but water should be gradually reduced in autumn.

FERTILIZER: ¼–½ recommended strength. A balanced fertilizer should be applied weekly to biweekly throughout the year.

REST PERIOD: Growing temperatures should be maintained year-round. Water should be reduced somewhat for 3–4 months in winter, especially for plants cultivated in dark, short-day conditions common in temperate latitudes. Plants should dry slightly between waterings but never remain dry for long periods. Fertilizer should be reduced or eliminated anytime water is restricted. In the habitat, light is highest in winter.

GROWING MEDIA: Mounting plants on tree-fern or cork slabs accommodates their pendent growth habit. However, humidity must be high and plants must be watered at least once a day in summer. If plants cannot be mounted, small pots or hanging baskets may be filled with an open, fast-draining medium. Repotting may be done anytime new roots are actively growing.

MISCELLANEOUS NOTES: The bloom season shown in the climate table is based on collection reports.

Plant and Flower Information

PLANT SIZE AND TYPE: A 4–20 in. (10–50 cm) sympodial epiphyte.

PSEUDOBULB: 4–20 in. (10–50 cm) long. The variably sized plants grow in pendent tufts. The stems are slender, jointed, and curved upward. They are yellowish at the base and green on the leaf-bearing, apical portion.

LEAVES: Several. The terete leaves, which are curved, deep green, and rigid, are 0.7 in. (1.8 cm) long.

INFLORESCENCE: Each inflorescence carries a single pendent flower.

FLOWERS: 1 per inflorescence. The blossoms, which are 0.4 in. (1 cm) long, are white or pale mauve with faint purplish streaks. The flowers have an oblong dorsal sepal, triangular lateral sepals, and linear-oblong petals. The lip is simple. Blossoms are not fragrant.

REFERENCES: 12, 13, 221, 296, 373, 536.

Dendrobium minimiflorum A. Gilli

ORIGIN/HABITAT: Kompiam, Papua New Guinea. Plants grow on tree limbs in forests at about 8700 ft. (2650 m).

CLIMATE: Botanical garden records, Laiagam, Papua New Guinea, Lat. 5.5°S, Long. 143.5°E, at 7218 ft. (2200 m). Temperatures are calculated for an elevation of 8500 ft. (2600 m), resulting in probable extremes of 87°F (30°C) and 28°F (−2°C).

N/HEMISPHERE	JAN	FEB	MAR	APR	MAY	JUN	JUL	AUG	SEP	OCT	NOV	DEC
°F AVG MAX	72	73	74	72	74	74	78	73	72	74	74	72
°F AVG MIN	51	50	51	51	52	52	51	52	54	53	52	52
DIURNAL RANGE	21	23	23	21	22	22	27	21	18	21	22	20
RAIN/INCHES	4.0	4.8	6.1	7.8	8.5	9.1	8.4	9.6	9.5	8.9	6.3	4.0
HUMIDITY/%	N/A											
BLOOM SEASON	N/A											
DAYS CLR	N/A											
RAIN/MM	102	122	155	198	216	231	213	244	241	226	160	102
°C AVG MAX	22.1	22.6	23.2	22.1	23.2	23.2	25.4	22.6	22.1	23.2	23.2	22.1
°C AVG MIN	10.4	9.9	10.4	10.4	11.0	11.0	10.4	11.0	12.1	11.5	11.0	11.0
DIURNAL RANGE	11.7	12.7	12.8	11.7	12.2	12.2	15.0	11.6	10.0	11.7	12.2	11.1
S/HEMISPHERE	JUL	AUG	SEP	OCT	NOV	DEC	JAN	FEB	MAR	APR	MAY	JUN

Cultural Recommendations

LIGHT: 2000–3000 fc.

TEMPERATURES: Throughout the year, days average 72–78°F (22–25°C), and nights average 50–54°F (10–12°C), with a diurnal range of 18–27°F (10–15°C).

HUMIDITY: Information is not available for this location. However, records from nearby stations indicate that averages are probably near 70–80% year-round.

WATER: Rainfall is moderate to heavy throughout the year, but conditions are driest for 3–4 months in winter. Cultivated plants should be kept evenly moist.

FERTILIZER: ¼–½ recommended strength. A balanced fertilizer should be applied weekly to biweekly throughout the year.

REST PERIOD: Growing conditions should be maintained year-round. Water and fertilizer should be reduced somewhat in winter, especially for plants grown in the dark, short-day conditions common in temperate latitudes. They should never be allowed to dry out completely, however. In the habitat, light is highest in winter.

GROWING MEDIA: Plants may be mounted on tree-fern or cork slabs if humidity is high and plants are watered at least once daily in summer. When plants are potted, any open, fast-draining medium may be used. They may be repotted anytime new roots are growing.

Plant and Flower Information

PLANT SIZE AND TYPE: A sympodial epiphyte of unreported size.

PSEUDOBULB: The elongated, pendent stems are flattened, branching, and covered with roots.

LEAVES: The linear-lanceolate leaves are 0.5–1.2 in. (1.3–3.0 cm) long.

INFLORESCENCE: Inflorescences emerge from nodes along the stem.

FLOWERS: 1 per inflorescence. The white flowers, which do not open fully, are 0.2 in. (0.5 cm) long. The lip is a somewhat ovate parallelogram with 3 points along the front margin.

REFERENCES: 146, 234.

PHOTOS/DRAWINGS: 146.

Dendrobium minimum Ames and Schweinfurth

ORIGIN/HABITAT: Borneo. Plants grow in Sabah in the lower mountain forests on the Marei Parei Spur of Mt. Kinabalu at 3950–6550 ft. (1200–2000 m).

CLIMATE: Station #49613, Tambunan, Sabah, Borneo, Lat. 5.7°N, Long. 116.4°E, at 1200 ft. (366 m). Temperatures are calculated for an elevation of 6000 ft. (1830 m), resulting in probable extremes of 82°F (28°C) and 38°F (3°C).

N/HEMISPHERE	JAN	FEB	MAR	APR	MAY	JUN	JUL	AUG	SEP	OCT	NOV	DEC
°F AVG MAX	70	71	73	74	74	73	73	73	73	72	71	70
°F AVG MIN	51	49	50	51	52	51	50	50	51	51	51	52
DIURNAL RANGE	19	22	23	23	22	22	23	23	22	21	20	18
RAIN/INCHES	5.8	3.7	5.8	7.5	8.2	7.3	5.1	4.9	6.4	7.0	6.8	6.0
HUMIDITY/%	N/A											
BLOOM SEASON	N/A											
DAYS CLR	N/A											
RAIN/MM	147	94	147	190	208	185	130	124	163	178	173	152
°C AVG MAX	21.2	21.8	22.9	23.4	23.4	22.9	22.9	22.9	22.9	22.3	21.8	21.2
°C AVG MIN	10.6	9.5	10.1	10.6	11.2	10.6	10.1	10.1	10.6	10.6	10.6	11.2
DIURNAL RANGE	10.6	12.3	12.8	12.8	12.2	12.3	12.8	12.8	12.3	11.7	11.2	10.0
S/HEMISPHERE	JUL	AUG	SEP	OCT	NOV	DEC	JAN	FEB	MAR	APR	MAY	JUN

Cultural Recommendations

LIGHT: 1800–2500 fc.

Dendrobium minjemense

TEMPERATURES: Throughout the year, days average 70–74°F (21–23°C), and nights average 49–52°F (10–11°C), with a diurnal range of 18–23°F (10–13°C). The daily temperature range is much greater than seasonal temperature fluctuations.

HUMIDITY: Information is not available for this location. However, reports from nearby stations indicate that humidity is probably 80–85% year-round. Excellent air circulation should be provided.

WATER: Rainfall is moderate to heavy all year. Cultivated plants should be kept moist with only slight drying allowed between waterings.

FERTILIZER: ¼–½ recommended strength. A balanced fertilizer should be applied weekly to biweekly throughout the year.

REST PERIOD: Growing conditions vary only slightly through the year. The diurnal range is slightly lower in winter because of somewhat cooler days. In cultivation, water should be reduced somewhat in winter, especially for plants grown in the dark, short-day conditions common in temperate latitudes. Plants should never be allowed to dry out completely, however. Fertilizer should be decreased when plants are not actively growing.

GROWING MEDIA: Plants may be mounted on tree-fern or cork slabs if humidity is high and plants are watered at least once daily in summer. When plants are potted, any open, fast-draining medium may be used. They may be repotted anytime new roots are growing.

Plant and Flower Information

PLANT SIZE AND TYPE: An 18 in. (45 cm) sympodial epiphyte.

PSEUDOBULB: 18 in. (45 cm) long. The stems, which have 2–3 swollen, flattened nodes just above the base, are slender above. They are shiny, yellow, erect, and longitudinally grooved.

LEAVES: Several at the apex of each stem. The leaves are 3.3 in. (8.5 cm) long, linear, and grasslike.

INFLORESCENCE: Short. Inflorescences emerge from the uppermost nodes opposite the leaves.

FLOWERS: 1 per inflorescence. The minute flowers are 0.2 in. (0.4 cm) long. They may be white or white and yellow. The sepals and petals are translucent when dry. The papilose lip, which has no sidelobes, is broadly truncate and uneven along the margin.

REFERENCES: 12, 222, 286, 445.

PHOTOS/DRAWINGS: 12.

Dendrobium minjemense Schlechter.

Now considered a synonym of *Diplocaulobium minjemense* (Schlechter) A. Hawkes. REFERENCES: 92, 179, 221, 229, 437, 445.

Dendrobium minutiflorum Gagnepain.

Now considered a synonym of *Eria eriopsidobulbon* Parish and Rchb. f. REFERENCES: 137, 227, 229, 448, Seidenfaden 1992 *Opera Botanica* #114.

Dendrobium minutiflorum Kränzlin.

Although Kränzlin (ref. 254) described this species as originating in New Caledonia, N. Hallé (ref. 173) excluded it. REFERENCES: 173, 221.

Dendrobium minutiflorum S. C. Chen and Z. H. Tsi

ORIGIN/HABITAT: China. Plants were discovered in Yunnan province growing in trees near Menghai Xian at 3950 ft. (1200 m).

CLIMATE: Station #56959, Meng-lun, Yunnan, China, Lat. 21.9°N, Long. 101.1°E, at 1814 ft. (553 m). Temperatures are calculated for an elevation of 3950 ft. (1200 m), resulting in probable extremes of 97°F (36°C) and 30°F (−1°C).

N/HEMISPHERE	JAN	FEB	MAR	APR	MAY	JUN	JUL	AUG	SEP	OCT	NOV	DEC
°F AVG MAX	71	77	82	85	82	81	80	80	80	77	72	68
°F AVG MIN	46	46	51	58	62	66	66	66	64	60	55	48
DIURNAL RANGE	25	31	31	27	20	15	14	14	16	17	17	20
RAIN/INCHES	0.4	0.5	0.7	1.2	5.0	5.5	7.3	7.9	6.4	2.5	3.4	0.7
HUMIDITY/%	85	83	69	65	72	83	85	86	85	88	87	87
BLOOM SEASON									*			
DAYS CLR @ 7AM	1	6	12	10	9	1	0	0	0	0	0	0
DAYS CLR @ 1PM	13	16	20	16	8	2	1	3	6	4	16	17
RAIN/MM	10	13	18	30	127	140	185	201	163	64	86	18
°C AVG MAX	21.6	25.0	27.8	29.4	27.8	27.2	26.6	26.6	26.6	25.0	22.2	20.0
°C AVG MIN	7.8	7.8	10.5	14.4	16.6	18.9	18.9	18.9	17.8	15.5	12.8	8.9
DIURNAL RANGE	13.8	17.2	17.3	15.0	11.2	8.3	7.7	7.7	8.8	9.5	9.4	11.1
S/HEMISPHERE	JUL	AUG	SEP	OCT	NOV	DEC	JAN	FEB	MAR	APR	MAY	JUN

Cultural Recommendations

LIGHT: 2500–3500 fc. In the habitat, light is naturally filtered by the heavy cloud cover in summer and autumn.

TEMPERATURES: Summer days average 80–81°F (27°C), and nights average 66°F (19°C), with a diurnal range of 14–15°F (8°C).

HUMIDITY: 80–90% most of the year, dropping to 65–70% for 3 months in spring.

WATER: Rainfall is moderate to heavy from spring to autumn, but conditions are much drier during the 4–5 month winter dry season. Cultivated plants should be kept moist while actively growing, but water should be gradually reduced in autumn.

FERTILIZER: ¼–½ recommended strength, applied weekly. A high nitrogen fertilizer is beneficial from spring to midsummer, but a fertilizer high in phosphates should be used in late summer and autumn.

REST PERIOD: Winter days average 68–77°F (20–25°C), and nights average 46–48°F (8–9°C), with a diurnal range of 20–31°F (11–17°C). While rainfall is low in winter, additional moisture is available through most of the dry season from deposits of heavy dew, mist, and fog. For cultivated plants, water should be reduced and the plants kept barely moist. They may be allowed to dry out somewhat between waterings but should not remain dry for long periods. Fertilizer should also be reduced while water is reduced. In the habitat, the brightest conditions occur during the clear afternoons common in winter and early spring.

GROWING MEDIA: Plants may be mounted on tree-fern or cork slabs if humidity is high and plants are watered at least once daily in summer. When plants are potted, any open, fast-draining medium may be used. They may be repotted anytime new roots are growing.

MISCELLANEOUS NOTES: The bloom season shown in the climate table is based on collection reports.

Plant and Flower Information

PLANT SIZE AND TYPE: A 1–3 in. (2.5–7.6 cm) sympodial epiphyte.

PSEUDOBULB: 0.6–1.2 in. (1.5–3.0 cm) long. The clustered stems, which consist of 3–4 nodes, are slightly swollen in the middle and taper at each end.

LEAVES: 2–3 per growth. The oblong leaves are 0.6–2.2 in. (1.5–5.5 cm) long. The rounded apex is unequally bilobed.

INFLORESCENCE: 0.8–1.6 in. (2–4 cm) long. Two-three inflorescences are borne at or near the apex of the stem.

FLOWERS: The greenish white flowers are 0.4 in. (1 cm) across. Blossoms have an ovate dorsal sepal, ovate-triangular lateral sepals, and oblong petals. The oblong lip is rounded and lightly ruffled at the apex.

REFERENCES: 235, 529.

Dendrobium minutigibbum J. J. Smith

ORIGIN/HABITAT: Sumatra. The original collection was reported from Mt.

Gompong in the Padang region. Habitat elevation was not included with the description, so the following climate data should be used with caution.

CLIMATE: Station #96163, Padang, Sumatra, Indonesia, Lat. 0.9°S, Long. 100.4°E, at 19 ft. (6 m). Temperatures are calculated for an estimated elevation of 3000 ft. (910 m), resulting in probable extremes of 84°F (29°C) and 58°F (15°C).

N/HEMISPHERE	JAN	FEB	MAR	APR	MAY	JUN	JUL	AUG	SEP	OCT	NOV	DEC
°F AVG MAX	77	77	76	76	76	76	77	77	77	77	78	77
°F AVG MIN	64	64	64	64	64	64	64	64	64	65	65	64
DIURNAL RANGE	13	13	12	12	12	12	13	13	13	12	13	13
RAIN/INCHES	10.9	13.7	6.0	19.5	20.4	18.9	13.8	10.2	12.1	14.3	12.4	12.1
HUMIDITY/%	81	82	82	84	85	84	81	81	82	83	81	81
BLOOM SEASON	N/A											
DAYS CLR @ 7AM	5	1	1	0	0	2	2	1	2	2	3	5
DAYS CLR @ 1PM	5	2	2	1	1	3	3	4	3	3	6	5
RAIN/MM	277	348	152	495	518	480	351	259	307	363	315	307
°C AVG MAX	25.1	25.1	24.5	24.5	24.5	24.5	25.1	25.1	25.1	25.1	25.6	25.1
°C AVG MIN	17.9	17.9	17.9	17.9	17.9	17.9	17.9	17.9	17.9	18.4	18.4	17.9
DIURNAL RANGE	7.2	7.2	6.6	6.6	6.6	6.6	7.2	7.2	7.2	6.7	7.2	7.2
S/HEMISPHERE	JUL	AUG	SEP	OCT	NOV	DEC	JAN	FEB	MAR	APR	MAY	JUN

Cultural Recommendations

LIGHT: 2000–3000 fc.

TEMPERATURES: Throughout the year, days average 76–78°F (25–26°C), and nights average 64–65°F (18°C), with a diurnal range of 12–13°F (7°C). Probable extremes vary only a few degrees from the averages, indicating that plants may not tolerate wide temperature fluctuations.

HUMIDITY: 80–85% year-round.

WATER: Rainfall is heavy all year. Cultivated plants should be constantly moist but not soggy.

FERTILIZER: ¼–½ recommended strength. A balanced fertilizer should be applied weekly to biweekly throughout the year.

REST PERIOD: Growing conditions should be maintained year-round. For cultivated plants, water may be reduced somewhat in winter, especially for plants grown in the dark, short-day conditions common in temperate latitudes. They should never be allowed to dry out completely, however. In the habitat, light is highest in winter.

GROWING MEDIA: Plants may be mounted on tree-fern or cork slabs if humidity is high and plants are watered at least once daily in summer. When plants are potted, any open, fast-draining medium may be used. They may be repotted anytime new roots are growing.

MISCELLANEOUS NOTES: The plant was described in 1917 in *Bul. Jard. Bot. Buit.* 2nd sér. 13:13.

Plant and Flower Information

PLANT SIZE AND TYPE: An 8–16 in. (20–40 cm) sympodial epiphyte.

PSEUDOBULB: 8–16 in. (20–40 cm) long. Stems are rigid, dark green, flattened, unbranched, and densely leafy. They arise from a branching, rooting rhizome.

LEAVES: Many. The linear-lanceolate leaves are 1.2 in. (3 cm) long. They are pale green, fleshy, and flattened. The leaves are arranged in 2 overlapping rows.

INFLORESCENCE: Short. The branching inflorescences emerge laterally at or near the apex of the stem.

FLOWERS: 4–6 per inflorescence. The fleshy, dark purple flowers are 0.4 in. (1 cm) across. They have an oval dorsal sepal, concave, obliquely triangular lateral sepals, and oblong petals. The erect lip is shiny, recurved, convex, and covered with hairs. The margin is incurved with minute hairs along the margin. Blossoms open simultaneously.

REFERENCES: 221.

Dendrobium minutissimum F. Mueller.
Now considered a synonym of *Bulbophyllum minutissimum*. REFERENCES: 67, 105, 216, 254.

Dendrobium minutum Schlechter.
See *D. delicatulum* Kränzlin. REFERENCES: 221, 270, 271, 384, 385, 437, 445, 516.

Dendrobium mirandum Schlechter.
Now considered a synonym of *Flickingeria miranda* (Schlechter) F. G. Brieger. REFERENCES: 220, 234, 436.

Dendrobium mirbelianum Gaudich not J. J. Smith

AKA: Cribb (ref. 84) includes *Callista mirbeliana* Gaudich, *Dendrobium aruanum* Kränzlin, *D. buluense* Schlechter, *D. buluense* var. *kauloense* Schlechter, *D. giulianettii* F. M. Bailey, *D. polycarpum* Rchb. f., *D. rosenbergii* Teijsm. and Binn., and *D. wilkianum* Rupp as synonyms. Clements (ref. 67) indicates that he follows Cribb but also includes Schlechter's use of *D. prionochilum* F. Mueller and Kränzlin as a synonym. Cribb suggests that *D. bandaense* Schlechter may be conspecific with *D. mirbelianum*.

ORIGIN/HABITAT: The Molucca Islands, New Guinea, the Bismarck Archipelago, the Solomon Islands, and northeastern Australia from south of Cooktown to Innisfail. Plants are usually found in lowland forests and coastal swamps in areas with strong light and high humidity.

CLIMATE: Station #97690, Sentani/Jayapura, Irian Jaya, Lat. 2.7°S, Long. 140.5°E, at 289 ft. (88 m). Record extreme temperatures are 97°F (36°C) and 68°F (20°C).

N/HEMISPHERE	JAN	FEB	MAR	APR	MAY	JUN	JUL	AUG	SEP	OCT	NOV	DEC
°F AVG MAX	87	89	89	90	90	89	89	88	89	90	90	89
°F AVG MIN	72	72	72	73	73	73	73	73	73	74	73	73
DIURNAL RANGE	15	17	17	17	17	16	16	15	16	16	17	16
RAIN/INCHES	4.1	3.9	5.3	2.9	6.7	7.0	8.3	8.3	8.5	4.6	2.4	5.2
HUMIDITY/%	81	80	80	79	81	81	79	80	80	80	81	80
BLOOM SEASON	*	*	*	*					*			
DAYS CLR @ 9AM	5	3	4	3	2	1	1	0	1	2	2	5
DAYS CLR @ 3PM	4	3	3	3	2	1	3	0	1	2	2	3
RAIN/MM	104	99	135	74	170	178	211	211	216	117	61	132
°C AVG MAX	30.6	31.7	31.7	32.2	32.2	31.7	31.7	31.1	31.7	32.2	32.2	31.7
°C AVG MIN	22.2	22.2	22.2	22.8	22.8	22.8	22.8	22.8	22.8	23.3	22.8	22.8
DIURNAL RANGE	8.4	9.5	9.5	9.4	9.4	8.9	8.9	8.3	8.9	8.9	9.4	8.9
S/HEMISPHERE	JUL	AUG	SEP	OCT	NOV	DEC	JAN	FEB	MAR	APR	MAY	JUN

Cultural Recommendations

LIGHT: 3000–4500 fc. Plants are often found in full sun.

TEMPERATURES: Throughout the year, days average 87–90°F (31–32°C), and nights average 72–74°F (22–23°C), with a diurnal range of 15–17°F (8–10°C).

HUMIDITY: Near 80% year-round.

WATER: Rainfall is heavy all year. Brief semidry periods occur in spring and autumn. Cultivated plants should be kept moist most of the year, but they should be allowed to become somewhat dry for a few weeks in spring and again in autumn.

FERTILIZER: ¼–½ recommended strength. A balanced fertilizer should be applied weekly to biweekly throughout the year.

REST PERIOD: Growing conditions should be maintained year-round. Water and fertilizer might be reduced slightly in winter, especially for plants grown in the dark, short-day conditions common in temperate latitudes. They should never be allowed to dry completely, however. In the habitat, light is slightly higher in winter. Growers report that plants are in almost continuous growth, but they seem to benefit from a brief rest in winter, when they should be kept slightly dry. Australian plants reportedly tolerate winter temperatures as low as 54°F (12°C).

GROWING MEDIA: Plants may be mounted on tree-fern or cork slabs or potted in pots filled with any open, fast-draining medium. Repotting may be done anytime new roots are growing.

MISCELLANEOUS NOTES: The bloom season shown in the climate table is based on cultivation reports. Individual plants frequently bloom several times a year. *D. mirbelianum* grows and flowers well in Singapore. Plants may bloom when they are as small as 4 in. (10 cm).

Plant and Flower Information

PLANT SIZE AND TYPE: A 12–118 in. (30–300 cm) sympodial epiphyte. The smallest plants come from the southern (cooler) part of the range and the largest plants are found in the northern (warmer) part of the habitat.

PSEUDOBULB: 24–48 in. (60–122 cm) long. The stems are swollen at the base, becoming canelike and leafy above. Although normally in the size range given, the stems may vary from 12–118 in. (30–300 cm). The robust plant is erect and stately.

LEAVES: Many. The oval to ovate leaves are 5–6 in. (13–15 cm) long. The thick, leathery leaves are dark green, often with purple stripes or a red suffusion.

INFLORESCENCE: 2–20 in. (5–51 cm) long. Up to 3 horizontal or arching inflorescences are produced from leaf axils near the apex of both old and new stems.

FLOWERS: 4–30 per inflorescence. The flowers are 1.4–2.2 in. (3.6–5.5 cm) across and sometimes remain rather closed. Flower size and quality are highly variable. All segments may be wavy and twisted with recurving tips. The sepals, which tend to thrust forward, and the erect, slightly twisted petals are normally green to yellow with purple-brown spots. Some forms are clear green or greenish-yellow with red veins at the base of the sepals and petals. The ruffled lip may be green or yellow with white in the center and red or brown veins. The midlobe is ovate-elliptic and pointed at the tip with callus ridges that disappear near the middle of the lip. The sidelobes are broad. Blossoms are sometimes self-pollinating, but they may last 2–3 weeks

HYBRIDIZING NOTES: Chromosome count is 2n = 38 (ref. 504, 580). When used in hybridizing, *D. mirbelianum* contributes several desirable characteristics to the offspring. They tend to have long-lasting, full flowers with good flower substance and thus make good cut flowers. As a parent, *D. mirbelianum* tends to increase the number of flowers on a spike as well as increase the number of spikes. Flower color tends to be dominant, especially yellows, greens, and "blues."

REFERENCES: 25, 67, 84, 88, 105, 179, 190, 196, 200, 216, 236, 240, 253, 254, 262, 263, 271, 302, 304, 317, 345, 346, 421, 430, 437, 445, 468, 470, 486, 504, 510, 516, 526, 533, 537, 551, 580.

PHOTOS/DRAWINGS: *84*, 240, *271*, *304*, 345, *346*, *430*, 437, *533*, *551*.

Dendrobium mirbelianum Rchb. f. Status unknown.

Schlechter (ref. 437) mentioned this species in a discussion of the section *Ceratobium,* but we found no original description or any other reference to this species. REFERENCES: 437.

Dendrobium mirbelianum J. J. Smith not Gaudich. See *D. calophyllum* Rchb. f. REFERENCES: 254, 468.

Dendrobium mischobulbon Schlechter. Now considered a synonym of *Diplocaulobium mischobulbon* (Schlechter) A. Hawkes. REFERENCES: 92, 221, 229, 437, 445.

Dendrobium miserum Rchb. f.

ORIGIN/HABITAT: The Assam region of northeast India. Precise habitat information is unavailable. Habitat elevation is estimated, so the following temperatures should be used with caution.

CLIMATE: Station #42410, Gauhati, India, Lat. 26.1°N, Long. 91.6°E, at 158 ft. (48 m). Temperatures have been calculated for a habitat elevation of 2000 ft. (610 m), resulting in probable extremes of 98°F (37°C) and 35°F (2°C).

N/HEMISPHERE	JAN	FEB	MAR	APR	MAY	JUN	JUL	AUG	SEP	OCT	NOV	DEC
°F AVG MAX	70	72	80	82	82	83	84	84	83	81	75	70
°F AVG MIN	45	48	54	62	66	71	72	72	70	65	55	47
DIURNAL RANGE	25	24	26	20	16	12	12	12	13	16	20	23
RAIN/INCHES	0.4	1.2	2.0	5.7	9.3	12.3	12.3	10.3	6.6	2.8	0.6	0.2
HUMIDITY/%	79	72	64	71	82	85	85	86	84	84	83	82
BLOOM SEASON			*									
DAYS CLR @ 6AM	6	12	16	11	3	0	0	1	3	7	6	3
DAYS CLR @ 12PM	17	16	18	15	6	1	0	0	2	11	17	19
RAIN/MM	10	30	51	145	236	312	312	262	168	71	15	5
°C AVG MAX	21.1	22.2	26.6	27.7	27.7	28.3	28.8	28.8	28.3	27.2	23.8	21.1
°C AVG MIN	7.2	8.8	12.2	16.6	18.8	21.6	22.2	22.2	21.1	18.3	12.7	8.3
DIURNAL RANGE	13.9	13.4	14.4	11.1	8.9	6.7	6.6	6.6	7.2	8.9	11.1	12.8
S/HEMISPHERE	JUL	AUG	SEP	OCT	NOV	DEC	JAN	FEB	MAR	APR	MAY	JUN

Cultural Recommendations

LIGHT: 2500–3500 fc.

TEMPERATURES: Summer days average 83–84°F (28–29°C), and nights average 71–72°F (22°C), with a diurnal range of 12°F (7°C).

HUMIDITY: 80–85% most of the year, dropping to 65–70% for 2–3 months in winter.

WATER: Rainfall is heavy in spring and summer, but conditions are much drier in late autumn and winter. Cultivated plants should be kept moist while growing, but water should be gradually reduced after new growths mature in autumn.

FERTILIZER: ¼–½ recommended strength, applied weekly. A high-nitrogen fertilizer is beneficial from spring to midsummer, but a fertilizer high in phosphates should be used in late summer and autumn.

REST PERIOD: Winter days average 70–72°F (21–22°C), and nights average 45–48°F (7–9°C), with a diurnal range of 23–25°F (13–14°C). Although rainfall is low for 4–5 winter months, high humidity and the large temperature range indicate that additional moisture from heavy dew is common. Therefore, while water should be greatly reduced and cultivated plants allowed to dry out between waterings from late autumn into early spring, they should not remain dry for extended periods. Occasional mistings between waterings during bright, sunny weather may help prevent the plants from becoming too dry. Fertilizer should be reduced or eliminated until active growth resumes and water is increased in spring. In the habitat, light is brightest in winter.

GROWING MEDIA: Plants may be mounted on tree-fern or cork slabs if humidity is high and plants are watered at least once daily in summer. When plants are potted, any open, fast-draining medium may be used. Repotting may be done anytime new roots are growing.

MISCELLANEOUS NOTES: The bloom season shown in the climate table is based on cultivation records.

Plant and Flower Information

PLANT SIZE AND TYPE: A 2.8 in. (7 cm) sympodial epiphyte.

PSEUDOBULB: 2 in. (5 cm) long. The pseudobulbs taper at each end.

LEAVES: 2 per growth. The leaves are 0.8 in. (2 cm) long. They are linear-lanceolate and minutely toothed at the tip.

INFLORESCENCE: The inflorescence arises at or near the apex of the stem.

FLOWERS: 3 per inflorescence. The flowers are 0.3–0.4 in. (0.8–1.0 cm) across. Sepals and petals are yellow-green. The upper surface of the serrated, undulate lip is blackish-purple.

REFERENCES: 38, 46, 179, 202, 216, 254, 369, 454.

Dendrobium mitriferum J. J. Smith

AKA: J. J. Wood (ref. 588) considers *D. mitriferum* f. *alpinum* J. J. Smith to be a synonym of *D. subclausum* Rolfe var. *subclausum*.

ORIGIN/HABITAT: Common in Irian Jaya (western New Guinea). Plants grow on Mt. Goliath at about 9850 ft. (3000 m), at the summit and on the slopes of the Hellwig Mountains, the Treub Mountains, the summit of Mt. Erica at about 4800 ft. (1460 m), and Mt. Doorman. Plants grow in grasslands at 980–9350 ft. (300–2850 m) and in the shade of rocks covered with mossy humus.

CLIMATE: Station #97686, Wamena, Irian Jaya, Lat. 4.1°S, Long. 139.0°E, at 5446 ft. (1660 m). Temperatures are calculated for an elevation of 6400 ft. (1950 m). Record extreme temperatures are not available for this location.

N/HEMISPHERE	JAN	FEB	MAR	APR	MAY	JUN	JUL	AUG	SEP	OCT	NOV	DEC
°F AVG MAX	72	73	74	73	74	73	74	73	73	76	75	71
°F AVG MIN	57	57	59	59	60	61	60	59	60	62	62	58
DIURNAL RANGE	15	16	15	14	14	12	14	14	13	14	13	13
RAIN/INCHES	3.0	1.9	2.2	4.0	4.6	3.3	2.8	4.2	6.9	3.9	5.4	4.9
HUMIDITY/%	N/A											
BLOOM SEASON	*	*	*	*	*				*	*	*	*
DAYS CLR	N/A											
RAIN/MM	76	48	56	102	117	84	71	107	175	99	137	124
°C AVG MAX	22.1	22.7	23.3	22.7	23.3	22.7	23.3	22.7	22.7	24.4	23.8	21.6
°C AVG MIN	13.8	13.8	14.9	14.9	15.5	16.0	15.5	14.9	15.5	16.6	16.6	14.4
DIURNAL RANGE	8.3	8.9	8.4	7.8	7.8	6.7	7.8	7.8	7.2	7.8	7.2	7.2
S/HEMISPHERE	JUL	AUG	SEP	OCT	NOV	DEC	JAN	FEB	MAR	APR	MAY	JUN

Cultural Recommendations

LIGHT: 2000–3000 fc. Morning is usually the brightest part of the day.

TEMPERATURES: Throughout the year, days average 71–76°F (22–24°C), and nights average 57–62°F (14–17°C), with a diurnal range of 12–16°F (7–9°C). In the habitat, the warmest temperatures of the day occur during late morning when skies are clear. Clouds and mist develop near noon and continue through the afternoon, preventing additional warming.

HUMIDITY: Information is not available for this location. However, records from nearby locations indicate that humidity probably averages near 80% year-round. High humidity and excellent air circulation are particularly important if temperatures are warm. Placing the plants in front of an evaporative cooler or near a fine mist may be very beneficial on especially warm days.

WATER: Rainfall is light to moderate through most of the year, but large amounts of water are usually available from mist and heavy dew, even during periods of lower rainfall. In addition, rainfall amounts are probably greater in the higher-elevation habitat than indicated by the climate data. Cultivated plants should be kept moist and only slight drying allowed between waterings. Good air movement is critically important and should be maintained at all times.

FERTILIZER: ¼–½ recommended strength. A balanced fertilizer should be applied weekly to biweekly throughout the year.

REST PERIOD: Growing conditions should be maintained all year. Conditions in the habitat are slightly drier for 1–2 months in winter. In cultivation, water may be decreased somewhat, but plants should never be allowed to dry out completely or remain dry for long periods. In the habitat, light is slightly higher in winter.

GROWING MEDIA: Plants may be mounted on tree-fern or cork slabs if humidity is high and plants are watered at least once daily in summer. When plants are potted, any open, fast-draining medium may be used. Repotting may be done anytime new roots are growing.

MISCELLANEOUS NOTES: The bloom season shown in the climate table is based on reports from the habitat.

Plant and Flower Information

PLANT SIZE AND TYPE: A 20 in. (50 cm) sympodial epiphyte that may grow terrestrially.

PSEUDOBULB: 20 in. (50 cm) long.

LEAVES: Several at the apex of each growth. The ovate-lanceolate leaves are 1.0–3.3 in. (2.5–8.5 cm) long, but may be as small as 0.8 in. (2 cm). They are fringed and toothed at the apex.

INFLORESCENCE: Very short. The inflorescences are carried at nodes on leafless stems.

FLOWERS: 2–3 per inflorescence. The flowers are 0.8–1.0 in. (2.0–2.5 cm) long. Sepals and petals are red shading into orange and yellow, but they are sometimes a brilliant orange-red. The lip is orange-red at the tip. Ridley indicates that the sepals and petals are pink, and the lip is white with yellow at the tip.

REFERENCES: 220, 254, 400, 445, 470, 538, 588.

PHOTOS/DRAWINGS: 538.

Dendrobium miyakei Schlechter

AKA: *D. hainanense* Masamune and Hayata not Rolfe, *D. irayense* Ames and Quisumbing, *D. pseudo-hainense* Masamune, *D. victoriae-reginae* Loher var. *miyakei* (Schlechter) Liu and Su. H. Wood (ref. 582) believes that *D. miyakei* and *D. irayense* are separate entities.

ORIGIN/HABITAT: Taiwan and the Philippine Islands. Plants grow on Mt. Iraya on Batan Island and on Botel Tobago and Lu-Tao Islands, which are located approximately 60 mi. (97 km) southeast of Taiwan. Plants are usually found in semishade on the branches of *Ficus retusa* in banyan jungles at about 1000 ft. (300 m).

CLIMATE: Station #98135, Basco, Batan Island, Philippines, Lat. 20.5°N, Long. 122.0°E, at 36 ft. (11 m). Temperatures are calculated for an elevation of 1000 ft. (300 m), resulting in probable extremes of 95°F (35°C) and 50°F (10°C).

N/HEMISPHERE	JAN	FEB	MAR	APR	MAY	JUN	JUL	AUG	SEP	OCT	NOV	DEC
°F AVG MAX	73	75	78	81	85	85	85	85	84	81	78	75
°F AVG MIN	64	66	68	72	74	75	75	74	73	72	70	67
DIURNAL RANGE	9	9	10	9	11	10	10	11	11	9	8	8
RAIN/INCHES	7.9	5.9	4.9	3.8	5.0	11.8	10.3	16.2	14.6	11.8	11.6	11.0
HUMIDITY/%	82	81	81	82	82	84	83	84	84	81	81	81
BLOOM SEASON	*	*	**				*	*	*	*	*	*
DAYS CLR @ 8AM	1	1	3	2	2	1	1	1	2	1	1	1
DAYS CLR @ 2PM	1	2	3	2	2	0	1	0	1	1	1	1
RAIN/MM	201	150	124	97	127	300	262	411	371	300	295	279
°C AVG MAX	22.7	23.8	25.5	27.1	29.3	29.3	29.3	29.3	28.8	27.1	25.5	23.8
°C AVG MIN	17.7	18.8	19.9	22.1	23.2	23.8	23.8	23.2	22.7	22.1	21.0	19.3
DIURNAL RANGE	5.0	5.0	5.6	5.0	6.1	5.5	5.5	6.1	6.1	5.0	4.5	4.5
S/HEMISPHERE	JUL	AUG	SEP	OCT	NOV	DEC	JAN	FEB	MAR	APR	MAY	JUN

Cultural Recommendations

LIGHT: 1800–3000 fc. The habitat is usually overcast.

TEMPERATURES: Summer days average 85°F (29°C), and nights average 74–75°F (23–24°C), with a diurnal range of 10–11°F (6°C).

HUMIDITY: 80–85% year-round.

WATER: Rainfall is moderate to heavy all year with a 1–2 month slightly drier period in spring. Cultivated plants should be kept moist. Warm water may be beneficial.

FERTILIZER: ¼–½ recommended strength, applied weekly. A high-nitrogen fertilizer is beneficial from spring to midsummer, but a fertilizer high in phosphates should be used in late summer and autumn.

REST PERIOD: Winter days average 73–78°F (23–26°C), and nights average 64–68°F (18–20°C), with a diurnal range of 8–10°F (5–6°C). Water and fertilizer may be reduced somewhat in winter, especially for plants grown in the dark, short-day conditions common in temperate latitudes; but plants should not be allowed to dry out completely. Growers indicate that plants tolerate intermediate to cool growing temperatures. However, growing plants under these conditions should be approached cautiously and the plants kept somewhat dry when temperatures are cool.

GROWING MEDIA: Mounting plants on tree-fern or cork slabs accommodates their sometimes pendent growth habit. However, humidity must be high and plants must be watered at least once a day in summer. If plants cannot be mounted, small pots or hanging baskets may be filled with an open, fast-draining medium. Repotting may be done anytime new roots are actively growing.

MISCELLANEOUS NOTES: The bloom season shown in the climate table is based on cultivation records.

Plant and Flower Information

PLANT SIZE AND TYPE: A 12–36 in. (30–91 cm) sympodial epiphyte.

PSEUDOBULB: 12–36 in. (30–91 cm) long. The canelike stems, which are clustered and unbranched, may be pendulous or erect. The nodes are swollen.

LEAVES: Many. The deciduous leaves are 3–4 in. (8–10 cm) long, linear-lanceolate, and pointed.

INFLORESCENCE: Short. The flowers are borne in clusters that emerge from the nodes of leafless stems. The floral bracts are purple.

FLOWERS: 4–8 per inflorescence. The small, odorless flowers are 0.4–0.7 in. (1.0–1.8 cm) across. They are arranged in a showy cluster. The floral segments are vivid purple to magenta with dark streaking. The blossoms have ovate lateral sepals, an ovate-lanceolate dorsal sepal, and lanceolate-elliptic petals. The simple lip is oblanceolate with a horseshoe shaped callus at the base.

HYBRIDIZING NOTES: Chromosome count is 2n = 38 (ref. 151, 154, 187, 188, 504) as *D. miyakei* and n = 19 as *D. victoriae-reginae* var. *miyakei* (ref. 154).

REFERENCES: 61, 62, 151, 154, 179, 187, 188, 196, 208, 221, 236, 274, 279, 373, 430, 497, 504, 524, 528, 536, 582.

PHOTOS/DRAWINGS: 62, *274*, *279*, 357, *430*, *497*.

Dendrobium miyasakii Ames and Quisumbing

ORIGIN/HABITAT: The Philippines. In the provinces of Pampanga and Zambales on Luzon Island, plants grow on rocks or in forest soil at about 1950 ft. (600 m). The status of this species since the eruption of Mt. Pinatubo is unknown, but the habitat is the region near the volcano.

CLIMATE: Station #98327, Clark Air Base, Luzon, Philippines, Lat. 15.2°N, Long. 120.6°E, at 478 ft. (146 m). Temperatures are calculated for an elevation of 1950 ft. (600 m), resulting in probable extremes of 94°F (35°C) and 56°F (13°C).

N/HEMISPHERE	JAN	FEB	MAR	APR	MAY	JUN	JUL	AUG	SEP	OCT	NOV	DEC
°F AVG MAX	80	82	85	87	87	84	82	81	81	82	81	80
°F AVG MIN	65	65	68	70	71	70	69	69	69	69	68	66
DIURNAL RANGE	15	17	17	17	16	14	13	12	12	13	13	14
RAIN/INCHES	0.8	0.7	0.9	1.5	3.9	10.8	12.6	16.1	13.1	4.9	2.0	0.9
HUMIDITY/%	67	65	64	63	68	79	81	83	84	76	72	70
BLOOM SEASON	*	*	*								*	*
DAYS CLR @ 8AM	5	5	7	9	6	1	0	0	0	3	3	4
DAYS CLR @ 2PM	2	1	2	2	1	0	0	0	0	1	1	1
RAIN/MM	20	18	23	38	99	274	320	409	333	124	51	23
°C AVG MAX	26.7	27.8	29.5	30.6	30.6	28.9	27.8	27.3	27.3	27.8	27.3	26.7
°C AVG MIN	18.4	18.4	20.0	21.2	21.7	21.2	20.6	20.6	20.6	20.6	20.0	18.9
DIURNAL RANGE	8.3	9.4	9.5	9.4	8.9	7.7	7.2	6.7	6.7	7.2	7.3	7.8
S/HEMISPHERE	JUL	AUG	SEP	OCT	NOV	DEC	JAN	FEB	MAR	APR	MAY	JUN

Cultural Recommendations

LIGHT: 2500–3500 fc.

TEMPERATURES: Throughout the year, days average 80–87°F (27–31°C), and nights average 65–71°F (18–22°C), with a diurnal range of 12–17°F (7–10°C). The warmest days of the year occur in spring before the rainy season starts.

HUMIDITY: 80–85% in summer, dropping to 70–75% in autumn, then falling to near 65% in late winter and spring.

WATER: Rainfall is heavy for 4 months in summer, but conditions are dry in winter. Cultivated plants should be kept moist from late spring to early autumn, but water should be gradually reduced after new growths mature.

FERTILIZER: ¼–½ recommended strength, applied weekly. A high-nitrogen fertilizer is beneficial from spring to midsummer, but a fertilizer high in phosphates should be used in late summer and autumn.

REST PERIOD: Growing temperatures should be maintained all year. Not only is rainfall low for 4 months in winter, but even moisture from dew is uncommon. Water should be reduced for cultivated plants. They should be allowed to dry out between waterings, but should not remain completely dry for extended periods. Occasional mistings on bright sunny mornings may help keep plants from becoming too dry. Fertilizer should be reduced or eliminated until water is increased in spring. In the habitat, light is highest in winter.

GROWING MEDIA: Plants may be mounted on cork or tree-fern slabs if water can be applied daily during the summer and if high humidity levels can be maintained. If plants are potted, a rapidly draining medium is recommended. Repotting is best done in early spring immediately after blooming when new roots begin growing.

MISCELLANEOUS NOTES: The bloom season shown in the climate table is based on reports from the habitat.

Plant and Flower Information

PLANT SIZE AND TYPE: A 30 in. (75 cm) sympodial lithophyte or terrestrial.

PSEUDOBULB: 30 in. (75 cm) long. The erect stems are deeply furrowed. They are slender, dark purple, and seldom branch. Each plant consists of a few stems.

LEAVES: The linear-lanceolate leaves are 2.4–3.1 in. (6–8 cm) long.

INFLORESCENCE: Pendulous inflorescences emerge near the apex of leafless stems.

FLOWERS: 1 per inflorescence. The flowers are 1.8–2.2 in. (4.6–5.6 cm) across. The sepals are white suffused with pink on the basal half. Petals are pinkish purple with scalloped margins. The simple lip is purple at the apex with 3 purple lines extending to the base. Blossoms are not fragrant.

REFERENCES: 225, 373, 536.

PHOTOS/DRAWINGS: *373*.

Dendrobium modestissimum Kränzlin

ORIGIN/HABITAT: Sarawak, Borneo. Details on habitat location and elevation are not available, so the following climate data should be used with caution.

CLIMATE: Station #96413, Kuching, Sarawak, Lat. 1.5°N, Long. 110.3°E, at 85 ft. (26 m). Record extreme temperatures are 97°F (36°C) and 64°F (18°C).

N/HEMISPHERE	JAN	FEB	MAR	APR	MAY	JUN	JUL	AUG	SEP	OCT	NOV	DEC
°F AVG MAX	88	88	89	90	91	91	92	90	90	90	90	88
°F AVG MIN	72	72	72	72	72	73	72	72	72	72	72	72
DIURNAL RANGE	16	16	17	18	19	18	20	18	18	18	18	16
RAIN/INCHES	27.1	19.7	14.2	9.7	9.0	8.5	6.9	8.8	9.5	12.6	13.1	20.1
HUMIDITY/%	89	88	86	85	85	83	82	83	84	85	87	88
BLOOM SEASON	N/A											
DAYS CLR @ 7AM	1	0	1	2	3	2	4	2	1	2	1	1
DAYS CLR @ 1PM	0	0	0	0	1	1	1	0	0	0	0	0
RAIN/MM	688	500	361	246	229	216	175	224	241	320	333	511
°C AVG MAX	31.1	31.1	31.7	32.2	32.8	32.8	33.3	32.2	32.2	32.2	31.1	
°C AVG MIN	22.2	22.2	22.2	22.2	22.2	22.8	22.2	22.2	22.2	22.2	22.2	22.2
DIURNAL RANGE	8.9	8.9	9.5	10.0	10.6	10.0	10.6	11.1	10.0	10.0	10.0	8.9
S/HEMISPHERE	JUL	AUG	SEP	OCT	NOV	DEC	JAN	FEB	MAR	APR	MAY	JUN

Cultural Recommendations

LIGHT: 2000–3000 fc.

TEMPERATURES: Throughout the year, days average 88–92°F (31–33°C), and nights average 72–73°F (22–23°C), with a diurnal range of 16–20°F (9–11°C). The diurnal range is unusually large for a habitat with so little seasonal variation.

HUMIDITY: 80–90% year-round.

WATER: Rainfall is very heavy all year. Cultivated plants should be kept moist but not soggy. Warm water may be beneficial.

FERTILIZER: ¼–½ recommended strength. A balanced fertilizer should be applied weekly to biweekly throughout the growing season

REST PERIOD: Growing conditions should be maintained all year. The smaller diurnal range results from cooler days, not cooler nights. Although rainfall remains heavy in winter, water may be reduced somewhat for cultivated plants, especially those grown in the dark, short-day conditions common in temperate latitudes. They should never be allowed to dry out completely, however. In the habitat, light is highest in winter.

GROWING MEDIA: Plants may be mounted on tree-fern or cork slabs if humidity is high and plants are watered at least once daily in summer. When plants are potted, any open, fast-draining medium may be used. They may be repotted anytime new roots are growing.

MISCELLANEOUS NOTES: Plants were cultivated in the botanical garden in Heidelberg.

Plant and Flower Information

PLANT SIZE AND TYPE: A 10–16 in. (25–40 cm) sympodial epiphyte.

PSEUDOBULB: 10–16 in. (25–40 cm) long. The stem is leafy on the lower part and completely naked on the upper part.

LEAVES: Many. The distichous leaves are 0.8–1.0 in. (2.0–2.5 cm) long, oblong-lanceolate, and pointed.

INFLORESCENCE: Short.

FLOWERS: The tiny, globe-shaped flowers are less than 0.2 in. (0.5 cm) long. Blossoms were thought to be pale yellow.

REFERENCES: 220, 254, 286, 295.

Dendrobium modestum Rchb. f.

ORIGIN/HABITAT: The Philippines, including the Polillo Islands, Rizal Province on Luzon, Coron Island in the Calamian Group, and Palawan Island. Plants usually grow on small trees on cliffs near the shore.

CLIMATE: Station #98526, Coron, Philippines, Lat. 12.0°N, Long. 120.2°E, at 48 ft. Record extreme temperatures are 99°F (37°C) and 61°F (16°C).

N/HEMISPHERE	JAN	FEB	MAR	APR	MAY	JUN	JUL	AUG	SEP	OCT	NOV	DEC
°F AVG MAX	89	89	90	92	91	88	87	86	87	88	89	88
°F AVG MIN	73	73	74	76	77	75	73	74	74	74	74	73
DIURNAL RANGE	16	16	16	16	14	13	14	12	13	14	15	15
RAIN/INCHES	1.3	0.2	0.2	1.0	6.9	16.4	18.6	20.4	18.9	11.4	5.5	4.9
HUMIDITY/%	81	77	75	74	74	84	88	87	86	84	80	80
BLOOM SEASON			*									*
DAYS CLR @ 8AM	12	11	14	11	7	3	2	2	3	7	9	8
DAYS CLR @ 2PM	8	7	14	11	6	2	1	1	3	6	6	6
RAIN/MM	33	5	5	25	175	417	472	518	480	290	140	124
°C AVG MAX	31.7	31.7	32.2	33.3	32.8	31.1	30.6	30.0	30.6	31.1	31.7	31.1
°C AVG MIN	22.8	22.8	23.3	24.4	25.0	23.9	22.8	23.3	23.3	23.3	23.3	22.8
DIURNAL RANGE	8.9	8.9	8.9	8.9	7.8	7.2	7.8	6.7	7.3	7.8	8.4	8.3
S/HEMISPHERE	JUL	AUG	SEP	OCT	NOV	DEC	JAN	FEB	MAR	APR	MAY	JUN

Cultural Recommendations

LIGHT: 2000–3000 fc.

TEMPERATURES: Throughout the year, days average 86–92°F (30–33°C), and nights average 73–77°F (23–25°C), with a diurnal range of 12–16°F (7–9°C). Summer is the coolest season, and spring is the warmest.

HUMIDITY: 80–90% most of the year, dropping to near 75% for 4 months in late winter and spring.

WATER: Rainfall is very heavy from late spring through autumn. Cultivated plants should be kept moist while growing, but water should be gradually reduced in late autumn.

FERTILIZER: ¼–½ recommended strength. A balanced fertilizer should be applied weekly to biweekly throughout the growing season.

REST PERIOD: Growing temperatures should be maintained all year. The dry season lasts about 4 months; 2 of those months are so dry that even moisture from dew is uncommon. Cultivated plants should be allowed to dry out between waterings in winter; but for most of that period, they should not remain completely dry for long. For about 2 months in late winter, however, water should be limited to occasional light mistings. Fertilizer should be reduced or eliminated until water is increased in spring. In the habitat, light is highest in winter.

GROWING MEDIA: Plants may be mounted on tree-fern or cork slabs if humidity is high and plants are watered at least once daily in summer. When plants are potted, any open, fast-draining medium may be used. Repotting is best done in early spring when new roots are growing.

MISCELLANEOUS NOTES: The bloom season shown in the climate table is based on collection reports.

Plant and Flower Information

PLANT SIZE AND TYPE: A 9–22 in. (23–55 cm) sympodial epiphyte.

PSEUDOBULB: 7–18 in. (19–45 cm) long. The stems, which are flushed with purple, are slender and flexuous. The pseudobulbous base is angled and thickened for 3 internodes.

LEAVES: The terete leaves are 2–4 in. (5–10 cm) long, pointed, nearly erect, smooth, fleshy, and rigid. They are green with a brownish purple flush.

INFLORESCENCE: Inflorescences emerge opposite the leaves at the apex of the stem.

FLOWERS: 1 to a few per inflorescence. The flowers are 0.4–0.6 in. (1.0–1.5 cm) across. They are pinkish yellow or pale purple with 3 purple lines on the disk. The 3-lobed lip is toothed along the margin. Blossoms are odorless.

REFERENCES: 12, 216, 225, 254, 296, 317, 373, 454, 455, 536.

PHOTOS/DRAWINGS: *373*.

Dendrobium modestum Ridley. See *D. metrium* Kränzlin.

REFERENCES: 200, 402.

Dendrobium mohlianum Rchb. f.

AKA: Kores (ref. 466) includes only *D. neo-ebudanum* Schlechter, but Lewis and Cribb (ref. 270) also include *D. vitellianum* Kränzlin.

ORIGIN/HABITAT: South Pacific Islands. In Vanuatu (New Hebrides), the habitat includes the islands of Anatom, Epi, Erromango, Espiritu Santo, Malekula, and Tanna, where they grow in mountain forests at 1400–3100 ft. (430–950 m). In the Solomon Islands, plants are found in mountain forests and cloudforests at 2600–7050 ft. (800–2150 m). In Fiji, they are abundant on the crests and ridges of hills, at 1000–4250 ft. (300–1300 m), but they are most common at the higher elevations. Plants also grow in Samoa.

CLIMATE: Station #91554, Luganville, Espiritu Santo Island, Vanuatu, Lat. 15.5°S, Long. 167.1°E, at 493 ft. (150 m). Temperatures are calculated for an elevation of 2300 ft. (700 m), resulting in probable extremes of 87°F (31°C) and 55°F (13°C).

Dendrobium moirianum

N/HEMISPHERE	JAN	FEB	MAR	APR	MAY	JUN	JUL	AUG	SEP	OCT	NOV	DEC
°F AVG MAX	75	75	76	77	77	80	80	81	80	79	77	75
°F AVG MIN	65	65	66	66	67	68	69	68	67	68	67	66
DIURNAL RANGE	10	10	10	11	10	12	11	13	13	11	10	9
RAIN/INCHES	6.4	6.3	4.7	6.3	9.5	9.2	10.6	9.7	10.9	10.1	8.1	6.1
HUMIDITY/%	81	80	83	81	82	81	83	83	88	86	83	80
BLOOM SEASON		**	**	**	**	*	*					
DAYS CLR	N/A											
RAIN/MM	163	160	119	160	241	234	269	246	277	257	206	155
°C AVG MAX	23.9	23.9	24.5	25.0	25.0	26.7	26.7	27.2	26.7	26.1	25.0	23.9
°C AVG MIN	18.4	18.4	18.9	18.9	19.5	20.0	20.6	20.0	19.5	20.0	19.5	18.9
DIURNAL RANGE	5.5	5.5	5.6	6.1	5.5	6.7	6.1	7.2	7.2	6.1	5.5	5.0
S/HEMISPHERE	JUL	AUG	SEP	OCT	NOV	DEC	JAN	FEB	MAR	APR	MAY	JUN

Cultural Recommendations

LIGHT: 2000–3000 fc.

TEMPERATURES: Throughout the year, days average 75–81°F (24–27°C), and nights average 65–69°F (18–21°C), with a diurnal range of 9–13°F (5–7°C). Plants from higher elevations in the Solomon Islands and Fiji commonly experience night-time temperatures of 50–55°F (10–13°C), so cultivated plants should adapt to conditions ranging from cool to warm.

HUMIDITY: 80–85% most of the year.

WATER: Rainfall is moderate to heavy year-round. Conditions are slightly drier for 2 months in late winter or early spring. Cultivated plants should be kept moist, but not soggy. The crest and ridge-line habitat suggests that plants may need excellent air circulation.

FERTILIZER: ¼–½ recommended strength. A balanced fertilizer should be applied weekly to biweekly throughout the year.

REST PERIOD: Growing conditions should be maintained all year. Water should be reduced for plants grown in the dark, short-day conditions common in temperate-latitude winters, but they should never be allowed to dry out completely. Fertilizer should be reduced until growth resumes in spring.

GROWING MEDIA: The spreading to pendent growth habit suggests that plants may be easier to manage when mounted on tree-fern or cork slabs if appropriate conditions can be provided. Repotting may be done anytime new roots are growing.

MISCELLANEOUS NOTES: The bloom season shown in the climate table is based on cultivation records. Reports from Fiji indicate that plants may bloom any time of year. The plants are in fruit from autumn to early spring. *D. mohlianum* is pollinated by birds.

Plant and Flower Information

PLANT SIZE AND TYPE: A 20–28 in. (50–70 cm) sympodial epiphyte.

PSEUDOBULB: 16–24 in. (40–60 cm) long. The slender, clustered stems may be spreading or pendent. They are slightly swollen at the base and leafy on the upper part of the stem. Stems become ribbed with age.

LEAVES: Many. The leaves are 2.4–5.1 in. (6–13 cm) long, distichous, and lanceolate.

INFLORESCENCE: Short. Inflorescences, which may be 1.8 in. (4.5 cm) long, are borne laterally from the upper nodes of older, leafless stems.

FLOWERS: 4–6 per inflorescence. Blossoms are 0.4–1.2 in. (1–3 cm) long. The flowers are commonly orange to bright red, but rare clones are yellow. Reports from the habitat indicate that flowers from higher altitudes are redder than those from lower elevations. The lip is sometimes marked with purple lines. The column is white.

HYBRIDIZING NOTES: Chromosome count is 2n = 38 (ref. 152, 243) with the name listed as *D. mohlianum* Kränzlin. We found no other reference to a plant with this describer, so we assume the information should apply to *D. mohlianum* Rchb. f.

REFERENCES: 17, 142, 152, 179, 216, 243, 252, 254, 269, 270, 271, 353, 371, 430, 433, 434, 445, 462, 466, 516, 553.

PHOTOS/DRAWINGS: *269, 270, 271, 430, 462, 466, 540, 553.*

Dendrobium moirianum A. Hawkes and A. H. Heller. See *D. rutriferum* Rchb. f. REFERENCES: 191, 229, 254, 271, 381.

Dendrobium molle J. J. Smith

ORIGIN/HABITAT: Irian Jaya (western New Guinea). Plants were collected along the Noord River south of Geluks Hill and on the north slopes of the Gautier Range. They grow on trees in primary forests. Plants were cultivated in the botanical garden at Bogor, Java.

CLIMATE: Station #97796, Kokenau (Kokonau), Irian Jaya, Lat. 4.7°S, Long. 136.4°E, at 10 ft. (3 m). Record extreme temperatures are not available for this location.

N/HEMISPHERE	JAN	FEB	MAR	APR	MAY	JUN	JUL	AUG	SEP	OCT	NOV	DEC
°F AVG MAX	83	83	86	88	90	89	89	89	90	88	87	84
°F AVG MIN	73	73	74	74	74	75	74	74	74	74	74	73
DIURNAL RANGE	10	10	12	14	16	14	15	15	16	14	13	11
RAIN/INCHES	18.4	15.8	18.9	11.6	9.7	10.6	11.5	15.7	11.6	11.6	16.0	19.9
HUMIDITY/%	N/A											
BLOOM SEASON	*										*	
DAYS CLR	N/A											
RAIN/MM	467	401	479	295	245	269	293	400	294	296	407	506
°C AVG MAX	28.6	28.4	30.2	31.1	32.1	31.9	31.9	31.7	32.0	31.4	30.7	28.7
°C AVG MIN	22.7	22.6	23.3	23.4	23.5	23.7	23.6	23.5	23.4	23.4	23.5	23.0
DIURNAL RANGE	5.9	5.8	6.9	7.7	8.6	8.2	8.3	8.2	8.6	8.0	7.2	5.7
S/HEMISPHERE	JUL	AUG	SEP	OCT	NOV	DEC	JAN	FEB	MAR	APR	MAY	JUN

Cultural Recommendations

LIGHT: 2500–3500 fc.

TEMPERATURES: Throughout the year, days average 83–90°F (29–32°C), and nights average 73–75°F (23–24°C), with a diurnal range of 10–16°F (6–9°C).

HUMIDITY: Information is not available for this location. However, records from nearby locations indicate that humidity probably averages near 85% year-round.

WATER: Rainfall is very heavy all year. Cultivated plants should be kept moist.

FERTILIZER: ¼–½ recommended strength. A balanced fertilizer should be applied weekly to biweekly throughout the year.

REST PERIOD: Growing conditions should be maintained year-round. Water and fertilizer should be reduced for plants grown in the dark, short-day conditions common in temperate-latitude winters, but they should never be allowed to dry out completely.

GROWING MEDIA: Plants are best placed in small pots filled with any open, fast-draining medium. Repotting may be done anytime new roots are growing.

MISCELLANEOUS NOTES: The bloom season shown in the climate table is based on reports from the habitat.

Plant and Flower Information

PLANT SIZE AND TYPE: A 12 in. (30 cm) sympodial epiphyte.

PSEUDOBULB: 12 in. (30 cm) long. The stems are elongated.

LEAVES: Many. The lanceolate leaves are 3–5 in. (8–13 cm) long.

INFLORESCENCE: Short. The densely flowered racemes are covered with short, erect hairs.

FLOWERS: Several per inflorescence. The small, glossy blossoms are 0.5 in. (1.3 cm) across. They may be white or pale yellowish. All segments are covered with short, erect hairs. The linear lip is ovate, concave, and pointed with an inconspicuous V-shaped callus.

REFERENCES: 220, 254, 437, 445, 470.

Dendrobium moluccense J. J. Smith

AKA: *D. atropurpureum* J. J. Smith not Miquel.

ORIGIN/HABITAT: The Moluccas. Plants were collected from *Calophyllum* trees near sea level on Ambon Island.

CLIMATE: Station #97724, Ambon/Pattimura, Indonesia, Lat. 3.7°S, Long. 128.1°E, at 33 ft. (10 m). Record extreme temperatures are 96°F (36°C) and 66°F (19°C).

N/HEMISPHERE	JAN	FEB	MAR	APR	MAY	JUN	JUL	AUG	SEP	OCT	NOV	DEC
°F AVG MAX	81	81	83	85	88	88	88	88	88	86	84	82
°F AVG MIN	74	74	74	74	75	76	76	76	76	76	75	74
DIURNAL RANGE	7	7	9	11	13	12	12	12	12	10	9	8
RAIN/INCHES	23.7	15.8	9.5	6.1	4.5	5.2	5.0	4.7	5.3	11.0	20.3	25.1
HUMIDITY/%	83	82	81	80	79	78	78	77	79	82	83	84
BLOOM SEASON						*						
DAYS CLR @ 9AM	1	1	1	6	7	4	3	3	5	5	3	3
DAYS CLR @ 3PM	1	1	2	5	6	1	1	1	2	3	1	3
RAIN/MM	602	401	241	155	114	132	127	119	135	279	516	638
°C AVG MAX	27.2	27.2	28.3	29.4	31.1	31.1	31.1	31.1	31.1	30.0	28.9	27.8
°C AVG MIN	23.3	23.3	23.3	23.3	23.9	24.4	24.4	24.4	24.4	24.4	23.9	23.3
DIURNAL RANGE	3.9	3.9	5.0	6.1	7.2	6.7	6.7	6.7	6.7	5.6	5.0	4.5
S/HEMISPHERE	JUL	AUG	SEP	OCT	NOV	DEC	JAN	FEB	MAR	APR	MAY	JUN

Cultural Recommendations

LIGHT: 2500–3500 fc.

TEMPERATURES: Throughout the year, days average 81–88°F (27–31°C), and nights average 74–76°F (23–24°C), with a diurnal range of 7–13°F (4–7°C).

HUMIDITY: 80–85% year-round.

WATER: Rainfall is moderate to heavy all year, but conditions are slightly drier in late spring and summer. Cultivated plants should be kept moist year-round.

FERTILIZER: ¼–½ recommended strength. A balanced fertilizer should be applied weekly to biweekly throughout the year.

REST PERIOD: Growing conditions should be maintained all year. Although rainfall is heaviest in winter, water should be reduced somewhat for cultivated plants, especially those grown in the dark, short-day conditions common in temperate latitudes. The plants should never be allowed to dry out completely, however. Fertilizer should be reduced if water is reduced. In the habitat, light is highest in spring.

GROWING MEDIA: Plants may be mounted on tree-fern or cork slabs or potted in small pots filled with an open, fast-draining medium. Repotting may be done anytime new roots are actively growing.

MISCELLANEOUS NOTES: The bloom season shown in the climate table is based on collection reports.

Plant and Flower Information

PLANT SIZE AND TYPE: A 7–8 in. (18–20 cm) sympodial epiphyte.

PSEUDOBULB: 5–6 in. (13–16 cm) long. Numerous unbranched stems arise from a creeping, branching rhizome. The stems are green, flattened, and densely leafy. They are contracted at the base of each internode, becoming swollen before the next node.

LEAVES: Many. The fleshy, very flattened leaves are 2.0–2.4 in. (5–6 cm) long. They are arranged in 2 overlapping rows.

INFLORESCENCE: Branching inflorescences emerge from the leaf axils near the apex of the stem.

FLOWERS: Many per inflorescence. The fleshy flowers are 0.3 in. (0.8 cm) long. They are very dark purplish-red. Blossoms have ovate-triangular sepals and small, oblong petals. The erect lip is wavy, inconspicuously 3-lobed, and concave. The margin is irregular.

REFERENCES: 221, 445, 479.

Dendrobium monanthum Teijsm. and Binn. See note at *D. prostratum* Ridley. REFERENCES: 216, 254, 454, 455.

Dendrobium monile (Thunberg) Kränzlin. See *D. moniliforme* (Linn.) Swartz. REFERENCES: 139, 151, 154, 187, 190, 208, 220, 236, 254, 430, 445, 568, 580. PHOTOS/DRAWINGS: 568.

Dendrobium moniliforme Lindley not Swartz. See *D. linawianum* Rchb. f. REFERENCES: 254, 277.

Dendrobium moniliforme (Linn.) Swartz

AKA: Originally described as *Epidendrum moniliforme* Linn., this species has been specified as the type species for the genus. Other names considered synonymous are *Epidendrum monile* Thunberg, *E. moniliferum* Panzer, *Dendrobium castum* Bateman, *D. catenatum* Lindley, and *D. japonicum* (Blume) Lindley. Chen and Tang (ref. 61) also include *D. heishanense* Hayata. Tsi (ref. 528) includes *D. crispulum* Kimura and Migo, *D. heishanense* Hayata, *D. nienkui* Tso, *D. yunnanense* Finet, and *D. zonatum* Rolfe. The International Orchid Commission (ref. 236) lists *D. japonicum* and *D. moniliforme* without describers names as synonyms for *D. monile*, but registers hybrids under the name *D. moniliforme*.

ORIGIN/HABITAT: The Far East. Plants grow on forest trees on Okinawa, the Ryukyu Islands, the Japanese islands of Honshu, Shikoku, and Kyushu, and on numerous small islands off the southern Japanese coast and between Japan and Korea. The habitat extends west to Korea and China. Plants are usually found at 2600–8000 ft. (800–2500 m) but have been reported from as high as 9850 ft. (3000 m). In the central mountains of Taiwan, plants are found in subtropical and temperate habitats at 6000–7000 ft. (1830–2130 m), where they grow on rocks or sunlit tree branches in broadleaf forests.

CLIMATE: Station #46753, Ali-Shaw, Taiwan, Lat. 23.5°N, Long. 120.9°E, at 7891 ft. (2405 m). Temperatures are calculated for an elevation of 6500 ft. (1980 m), resulting in probable extremes of 80°F (26°C) and 24°F (−5°C).

N/HEMISPHERE	JAN	FEB	MAR	APR	MAY	JUN	JUL	AUG	SEP	OCT	NOV	DEC
°F AVG MAX	58	58	63	65	67	69	70	71	71	69	65	60
°F AVG MIN	40	41	45	49	52	56	54	55	52	50	45	42
DIURNAL RANGE	18	17	18	16	15	13	16	16	19	19	20	18
RAIN/INCHES	3.7	3.3	3.0	12.9	35.9	28.2	25.3	29.9	8.5	6.4	3.8	1.8
HUMIDITY/%	78	84	82	86	90	91	90	92	89	87	79	80
BLOOM SEASON	*	*	**	*	*	*						
DAYS CLR @ 8AM	15	13	15	6	10	4	5	9	14	16	16	15
DAYS CLR @ 2PM	7	3	2	0	0	0	0	0	0	1	4	7
RAIN/MM	94	84	76	328	912	716	643	759	216	163	97	46
°C AVG MAX	14.2	14.2	17.0	18.1	19.2	20.3	20.9	21.4	21.4	20.3	18.1	15.3
°C AVG MIN	4.2	4.8	7.0	9.2	10.9	13.1	12.0	12.6	10.9	9.8	7.0	5.3
DIURNAL RANGE	10.0	9.4	10.0	8.9	8.3	7.2	8.9	8.8	10.5	10.5	11.1	10.0
S/HEMISPHERE	JUL	AUG	SEP	OCT	NOV	DEC	JAN	FEB	MAR	APR	MAY	JUN

Cultural Recommendations

LIGHT: 2500–3500 fc. Bright morning light throughout the year is recommended. In summer, the heavy afternoon cloud cover indicates that some shading is needed from spring through autumn, but light should be as high as the plant can tolerate, short of burning the leaves.

TEMPERATURES: Summer days average 69–71°F (20–21°C), and nights average 54–56°F (12–13°C), with a diurnal range of 13–16°F (7–9°C).

HUMIDITY: 80–90% year-round.

WATER: Rainfall is heavy most of the year, with a brief semidry period in winter. Cultivated plants should be kept moist while actively growing, but water should be gradually decreased in autumn.

Dendrobium moniliforme

FERTILIZER: ¼–½ recommended strength, applied weekly. If growing temperatures are cool, a high-nitrogen fertilizer may be used from spring to midsummer, and a fertilizer high in phosphates is best in late summer and autumn. If growing temperatures are warm all year, a balanced fertilizer may be applied weekly to biweekly throughout the year.

REST PERIOD: Winter days average 58–60°F (14–15°C), and nights average 40–42°F (4–5°C), with a diurnal range of 17–18°F (9–10°C). Water should be reduced in winter, but plants should never be allowed to dry out completely. Fertilizer should be reduced or eliminated until temperatures warm and plants are actively growing. The winter low temperatures shown in the climate table are warmer than in most of the habitat. *D. moniliforme* is unusually cold tolerant with the rest period lasting 3–4 months. Freezing winter temperatures are common in the Japanese and Korean habitats, even near sea level. Some growers indicate that a cool, dry season of several months is necessary to initiate blooms; but others indicate that temperatures do not need to be below 50°F (10°C). Plants will apparently also tolerate even warmer conditions, as they reportedly grow and flower well in Hawaii. When conditions are cool and wet, air circulation must be excellent. In the habitat, light is highest during mornings from autumn to spring.

GROWING MEDIA: Plants may be mounted on cork or tree-fern slabs if humidity is high and plants are watered at least once daily in summer. If plants are potted, undersized pots barely large enough to hold the roots should be filled with a very open, fast-draining medium. Repotting is best done in early spring or anytime new roots are growing.

MISCELLANEOUS NOTES: The bloom season shown in the climate table is based on cultivation records. Collected plants are dried and used in Chinese medicine.

Plant and Flower Information

PLANT SIZE AND TYPE: A 2–20 in. (5–50 cm) epiphyte or lithophyte. Cultivated plants are usually 6–12 in. (15–30 cm) tall.

PSEUDOBULB: 2–18 in. (5–45 cm) long. The erect or pendant pseudobulbs are covered by a tight sheath. They are clustered on a short connecting rhizome. Stems are round and slender with many irregular nodes. Stems are purplish green when young becoming yellow with age.

LEAVES: Several per pseudobulb. The leaves are 2–5 in. (5–13 cm) long, glossy, and lanceolate-linear. Usually deciduous, they may last for 2 years, especially if cultivation conditions are less severe that those found in the habitat. *D. moniliforme* var. *variegata* has attractive leaves with alternating green and white stripes. If this color break is or was originally caused by a virus, it is not contagious.

INFLORESCENCE: Very short. The inflorescences arise from nearly every upper node of mature, 2- and 3-year-old pseudobulbs.

FLOWERS: 1–2 per inflorescence. The spreading, star-shaped flowers are 1.0–1.5 in. (2.5–3.8 cm) across. They are white, sometimes with a pink suffusion, and marked with purple or reddish purple spots inside the greenish tube of the lip. Blossoms are fragrant and relatively long-lasting.

HYBRIDIZING NOTES: Chromosome counts as *D. moniliforme* are n = 38 (ref. 153), 2n = 38 (ref. 151, 152, 187, 243, 504, 547, 580), 2n = about 38 (ref. 504), and 2n = 38 + 1–3f (ref. 504, 580). The count as *D. heishanense* was 2n = 38 (ref. 504); as *D. monile* the count was 2n = 38 (ref. 154, 187, 188); as *D. moniliforme* 'Pink Flower' the count was 2n = 48 (ref. 504, 580).

D. moniliforme is used to miniaturize larger nobile *Dendrobium* and to increase the number of flowers. The small plant and flower size and the fragrance tend to be dominant characteristics.

REFERENCES: 36, 61, 62, 117, 139, 151, 152, 153, 154, 179, 187, 188, 190, 193, 201, 208, 210, 216, 236, 243, 254, 274, 279, 317, 338, 371, 389, 414, 430, 445, 454, 497, 504, 524, 528, 541, 547, 568, 570, 580, 596.

PHOTOS/DRAWINGS: *36, 62, 210, 274, 279, 371, 389, 430, 497, 568.*

Dendrobium moniliforme McLeay ex F. Mueller. Clements (ref. 67) indicates that this is an invalid name. REFERENCES: 67, 232.

Dendrobium monodon Kränzlin. See *D. johnsoniae* F. Mueller. REFERENCES: 83, 105, 190, 219, 220, 254, 430, 437, 444, 533.

Dendrobium monogrammoides J. J. Smith. See *D. masarangense* Schlechter. REFERENCES: 224, 385, 445.

Dendrobium monophyllum R. Brown. Schlechter (ref. 437) used this name in his discussion of the section *Dendrocoryne*. We found no other reference. REFERENCES: 437.

Dendrobium monophyllum F. Mueller

AKA: *D. tortile* A. Cunningham not Lindley.

ORIGIN/HABITAT: Eastern Australia. The habitat extends from northeastern New South Wales to the Cape York Peninsula (Grafton to Cooktown). Plants grow on exposed rock faces, in open forests, and on the outer branches of rainforest trees. They are always found where light is high and air movement is strong. Those from the southern (cooler) part of the range are larger. The elevation varies from coastal swamps to the mountains. In the warmer part of the habitat, where plants are usually smaller, they are generally found above 2000 ft. (600 m). In cooler areas, plants are found at sea level to 3300 ft. (0–1000 m). In portions of the habitat, plants are exposed to nearly continuous sea spray.

CLIMATE: Station #94576, Brisbane, Australia, Lat. 27.4°S, Long. 153.1°E, at 17 ft. (5 m). Record extreme temperatures are 110°F (43°C) and 35°F (2°C).

N/HEMISPHERE	JAN	FEB	MAR	APR	MAY	JUN	JUL	AUG	SEP	OCT	NOV	DEC
°F AVG MAX	68	71	76	80	82	85	85	85	82	79	74	69
°F AVG MIN	49	50	55	60	64	67	69	68	66	61	56	51
DIURNAL RANGE	19	21	21	20	18	18	16	17	16	18	18	18
RAIN/INCHES	2.2	1.9	1.9	2.5	3.7	5.0	6.4	6.3	5.7	3.7	2.8	2.6
HUMIDITY/%	62	59	58	57	59	59	63	65	66	64	64	64
BLOOM SEASON			*	*	*							
DAYS CLR @ 10AM	17	20	18	11	12	9	5	4	9	14	18	16
DAYS CLR @ 4PM	15	16	15	12	14	12	8	5	8	10	14	14
RAIN/MM	56	48	48	64	94	127	163	160	145	94	71	66
°C AVG MAX	20.0	21.7	24.4	26.7	27.8	29.4	29.4	29.4	27.8	26.1	23.3	20.6
°C AVG MIN	9.4	10.0	12.8	15.6	17.8	19.4	20.6	20.0	18.9	16.1	13.3	10.6
DIURNAL RANGE	10.6	11.7	11.6	11.1	10.0	10.0	8.8	9.4	8.9	10.0	10.0	10.0
S/HEMISPHERE	JUL	AUG	SEP	OCT	NOV	DEC	JAN	FEB	MAR	APR	MAY	JUN

Cultural Recommendations

LIGHT: 3500–4500 fc. In the habitat, more than half the days are clear each month, except during the summer rainy season when skies are clear about 30% of the time. Growers recommend using 40–50% shade cloth. High light is required to initiate blooms. Light should be as high as the plant can tolerate, short of burning the leaves. Excellent air movement should be provided year-round.

TEMPERATURES: Summer days average 85°F (29°C), and nights average 67–69°F (19–21°C), with a diurnal range of 16–18°F (9–10°C). Because plants also grow in the mountains at higher elevations, they should adapt to temperatures 6–8°F (3–4°C) cooler than indicated above.

HUMIDITY: 60–65% year-round. Values are probably greater in the coastal swamp and rainforest habitats.

WATER: Rainfall is moderate in summer and autumn, but conditions are somewhat drier in winter. Cultivated plants should be watered frequently during the growing season, but they should be allowed to dry quickly between waterings. Water should be gradually reduced in autumn.

FERTILIZER: ¼–½ recommended strength, applied weekly. A high-nitrogen fertilizer is beneficial from spring to midsummer, but a fertilizer high in phosphates should be used in late summer and autumn.

REST PERIOD: Winter days average 68–71°F (20–22°C), and nights average 49–51°F (9–11°C), with a diurnal range of 18–21°F (10–12°C). Australian growers recommend that winter lows be kept above 35°F (2°C). Rainfall is relatively low in winter. In cultivation, water should be reduced and the plants allowed to dry somewhat between waterings, but they should not remain dry for long periods. Plants should remain somewhat dry when flowering. Fertilizer should be reduced or eliminated. Plants from this habitat usually require distinct seasonal variation to be healthy.

GROWING MEDIA: Plants are best mounted on slabs of cork, tree-fern, or rough-barked hardwood with a thin pad of moss between the rhizome and the mount. They need to dry out quickly after watering. Mounted plants need daily watering and high humidity in summer. Growers recommend summering the plants outside through autumn and indicate that it is almost impossible to overwater plants in summer. If plants are potted, the smallest possible pot should be used, and growers report that clay pots are preferable to plastic ones. Pots should be filled with a rapidly draining medium. Repotting should be avoided, but when needed it is best done when new roots are beginning to grow. *D. monophyllum* is difficult to establish, as the roots are short, strong, and thick. They tend to dry-off where they contact the mount.

MISCELLANEOUS NOTES: The bloom season shown in the climate table is based on reports from the habitat. Cultivated plants tend to bloom sporadically with scattered reports all seasons. Plants may be in bloom most of the year. Growers indicate that plants are generally slow growing.

Plant and Flower Information

PLANT SIZE AND TYPE: A 3–9 in. (8–23 cm) sympodial epiphyte or lithophyte.

PSEUDOBULB: 0.8–4.0 in. (2–10 cm) long. The erect stems arise from a creeping, mat-forming rhizome which may overgrow itself and form several layers. Pseudobulbs are yellow to yellow-brown in high light and become ridged with age. Larger plants tend to grow in cooler temperatures.

LEAVES: 1, rarely 2 per growth. The oval leaves are thin, dark green, and 2–5 in. (5–13 cm) long.

INFLORESCENCE: 2–8 in. (5–20 cm) long. The erect inflorescences emerge from the apex of the most recently matured pseudobulbs. The blossoms all face one direction.

FLOWERS: 3–20 per inflorescence. The cream to buttercup-yellow flowers are 0.2–0.4 in. (0.5–1.0 cm) across. The nodding, bell-shaped blossoms resemble lily-of-the-valley. The lip has 2 ridges on the midlobe. The blossoms are long lasting with a delightfully sweet fragrance.

HYBRIDIZING NOTES: Chromosome count is 2n = 38 as *D. monophyllum* F. Mueller (ref. 152, 154, 188, 243). Pollen from the same plant seldom produces pods, but seeds are regularly produced when pollen from another plant is used. As a parent it helps produce longer lasting flowers in the progeny.

REFERENCES: 23, 67, 105, 152, 154, 179, 188, 216, 240, 243, 254, 262, 291, 325, 330, 390, 421, 445, 527, 533.

PHOTOS/DRAWINGS: 24, 105, 240, *291*, 325, *390*, *533*.

Dendrobium montanum J. J. Smith

ORIGIN/HABITAT: Endemic to western and central Java. Plants are found on Mt. Gede and Mt. Slamet. They grow low on tree trunks at the edge of mossy forests at 4600–6550 ft. (1400–2000 m).

CLIMATE: Station #96853, Jogjakarta, Java, Lat. 7.8°S, Long. 110.4°E, at 350 ft. (107 m). Temperatures are calculated for an elevation of 5500 ft. (1680 m), resulting in probable extremes of 78°F (26°C) and 45°F (7°C).

N/HEMISPHERE	JAN	FEB	MAR	APR	MAY	JUN	JUL	AUG	SEP	OCT	NOV	DEC
°F AVG MAX	68	69	70	71	69	68	67	67	68	70	69	69
°F AVG MIN	52	52	54	55	55	55	55	55	55	55	55	53
DIURNAL RANGE	16	17	16	16	14	13	12	12	13	15	14	16
RAIN/INCHES	1.6	1.0	1.2	3.7	9.0	13.4	13.9	13.2	12.2	8.3	5.0	3.5
HUMIDITY/%	74	71	69	73	77	82	82	82	81	78	77	74
BLOOM SEASON			*									
DAYS CLR @ 7AM	9	8	7	8	4	2	2	3	5	7	8	12
DAYS CLR @ 1PM	6	6	3	3	2	0	1	1	1	2	3	5
RAIN/MM	41	25	30	94	229	340	353	335	310	211	127	89
°C AVG MAX	20.0	20.6	21.1	21.7	20.6	20.0	19.4	19.4	20.0	21.1	20.6	20.6
°C AVG MIN	11.1	11.1	12.2	12.8	12.8	12.8	12.8	12.8	12.8	12.8	12.8	11.7
DIURNAL RANGE	8.9	9.5	8.9	8.9	7.8	7.2	6.6	6.6	7.2	8.3	7.8	8.9
S/HEMISPHERE	JUL	AUG	SEP	OCT	NOV	DEC	JAN	FEB	MAR	APR	MAY	JUN

Cultural Recommendations

LIGHT: 3000–4000 fc. Light should be as high as the plant can tolerate, short of burning the leaves.

TEMPERATURES: Throughout the year, days average 68–71°F (20–22°C), and nights average 52–55°F (11–13°C), with a diurnal range of 12–17°F (7–10°C). Spring is the warmest time of year, before the summer rainy season starts.

HUMIDITY: Near 80% in summer and early autumn, dropping to 70% in winter.

WATER: Rainfall is very heavy for 6 months from spring into autumn, but conditions are relatively dry for 3 months in winter. Cultivated plants should be kept moist from spring to early autumn, but water should be gradually reduced through autumn.

FERTILIZER: 1/4–1/2 recommended strength, applied weekly. A high-nitrogen fertilizer is beneficial from spring to midsummer, but a fertilizer high in phosphates should be used in late summer and autumn.

REST PERIOD: Growing temperatures should be maintained all year. A dry, winter rest is important to plant health, and water should be greatly reduced for 3 months. Plants should be allowed to dry out between waterings, but they should not remain dry for extended periods. Fertilizer should be greatly reduced or eliminated until plants begin actively growing in spring. In the habitat, light is highest in winter.

GROWING MEDIA: Plants may be mounted on tree-fern or cork slabs if humidity is high and plants are watered at least once daily in summer. When plants are potted, any open, fast-draining medium may be used. Repotting should be done between flowerings as soon as possible after new roots begin growing.

MISCELLANEOUS NOTES: Reports from the habitat indicate that plants bloom during the dry season. *D. montanum* is described as spectacular when blooming.

Plant and Flower Information

PLANT SIZE AND TYPE: A 24 in. (60 cm) sympodial epiphyte.

PSEUDOBULB: 24 in. (60 cm) long. The stems normally point down when mature.

LEAVES: Many. The leaves are 2.8 in. (7 cm) long, but they are smaller near the tip of the stem. They are spaced 0.8 in. (2 cm) apart and are reddish when young. The underside stays dark red, but the upper surface becomes green as the leaf ages.

INFLORESCENCE: Short. Many inflorescences emerge from nodes along the upper portion of mature, almost leafless, stems.

FLOWERS: 3–6 per inflorescence. The flowers are about 1.4 in. (3.5 cm) across. The white sepals and petals are sometimes tinged with violet. They are lanceolate, open fully, and overlap at the base. The petals are slightly wavy along the margin. The white lip, which has a yellow blotch near the base, is broadest at the tip. The lip margin has a rough edge.

REFERENCES: 25, 74, 75, 219, 254, 445, 469.

PHOTOS/DRAWINGS: *74*, *75*, 469.

Dendrobium montedeakinense F. M. Bailey. Papua New Guinea.
Plants were originally collected on Mt. Deakin, but we have been unable to find this location. Without details of habitat location and elevation, climate data cannot be selected. Plants were described as 10–12 in. (25–30 cm) long. The numerous linear leaves are 1–2 in. (2.5–5.0 cm) long. Blossoms are borne singly on a very short inflorescence. The very small flowers are 0.2 in. (0.5 cm) across. REFERENCES: 219, 254.

Dendrobium monticola P. F. Hunt and Summerhayes

AKA: Hunt (ref. 211) includes *D. alpestre* Royle not Swartz and *D. roylei* A. Hawkes and A. H. Heller. Seidenfaden (ref. 454) also includes *D. pusillum* D. Don, *D. roylei* Hawkes, and *D. roylei* Hiroe. He discusses the possibility that *D. monticola* may prove to be a synonym of *D. langbianense* Gagnepain.

ORIGIN/HABITAT: The northwestern Himalayas. The habitat includes Manipur in eastern India, Sikkim, central Nepal, and the Dehra Dun and Garhwal regions in northern India. Plants grow at 4900–6550 ft. (1500–2000 m). Chen and Tang (ref. 61) list *D. mondicola* (probably *D. monticola*) as occurring in Tibet at about 7550 ft. (2300 m). Tsi (ref. 528) indicates the plants grow in China at 5750–7800 ft. (1750–2380 m).

CLIMATE: Station #42147, Mukteswar, India, Lat. 29.5°N, Long. 79.7°E, at 7592 ft. (2314 m). Temperatures are calculated for an elevation of 5900 ft. (1800 m), resulting in probable extremes of 97°F (36°C) and 27°F (−3°C).

N/HEMISPHERE	JAN	FEB	MAR	APR	MAY	JUN	JUL	AUG	SEP	OCT	NOV	DEC
°F AVG MAX	57	60	67	75	81	81	75	75	74	71	67	61
°F AVG MIN	42	44	50	58	63	65	65	64	62	56	50	45
DIURNAL RANGE	15	16	17	17	18	16	10	11	12	15	17	16
RAIN/INCHES	1.0	2.1	1.7	1.0	0.3	4.6	11.4	12.8	4.6	3.5	0.3	0.2
HUMIDITY/%	61	55	50	39	44	67	91	93	83	66	55	56
BLOOM SEASON							**	**				
DAYS CLR @ 5PM	17	17	15	18	18	12	1	1	6	25	26	21
RAIN/MM	25	53	43	25	8	117	290	325	117	89	8	5
°C AVG MAX	13.7	15.3	19.2	23.7	27.0	27.0	23.7	23.7	23.1	21.4	19.2	15.9
°C AVG MIN	5.3	6.4	9.8	14.2	17.0	18.1	18.1	17.5	16.4	13.1	9.8	7.0
DIURNAL RANGE	8.4	8.9	9.4	9.5	10.0	8.9	5.6	6.2	6.7	8.3	9.4	8.9
S/HEMISPHERE	JUL	AUG	SEP	OCT	NOV	DEC	JAN	FEB	MAR	APR	MAY	JUN

Cultural Recommendations

LIGHT: 2500–3500 fc.

TEMPERATURES: Summer days average 75–81°F (24–27°C), and nights average 64–65°F (18°C), with a diurnal range of 10–16°F (6–9°C).

HUMIDITY: Above 90% in midsummer. Humidity decreases to 55–60% for most of the rest of the year but drops to near 40% for 2 months in spring.

WATER: Rainfall is moderate to heavy for 5 months in summer and early autumn. The other 7 months of the year are very dry. In fact, several months are so dry that even morning dew is uncommon. Cultivated plants should be kept moist while actively growing, but water should be reduced and the plants allowed to dry out after new growths mature in autumn.

FERTILIZER: ¼–½ recommended strength, applied weekly. A high-nitrogen fertilizer is beneficial from spring to midsummer, but a fertilizer high in phosphates should be used in late summer and autumn.

REST PERIOD: Winter days average 57–61°F (14–16°C), and nights average 42–45°F (5–7°C), with a diurnal range of 15–16°F (8–9°C). Water should be reduced for cultivated plants in winter. They should be allowed to dry out between waterings, but should not remain completely dry for extended periods. Occasional early morning mistings between waterings may be beneficial. Fertilizer should be eliminated until plants begin to grow in the spring. In the habitat, light is highest in winter.

GROWING MEDIA: Plants may be mounted on tree-fern or cork slabs if humidity is high and plants are watered at least once daily in summer. When plants are potted, any open, fast-draining medium may be used. Repotting is best done in early spring when new roots are growing.

MISCELLANEOUS NOTES: The bloom season shown in the climate table is based on cultivation records. In the habitat, blooming usually occurs in autumn.

Plant and Flower Information

PLANT SIZE AND TYPE: A 1.2–7.5 in. (3–19 cm) sympodial epiphyte.

PSEUDOBULB: 0.8–1.6 in. (2–4 cm) long. The pseudobulbs taper toward the apex. They form a dense clump.

LEAVES: 2–4 at the apex of each growth. The thin, linear-lanceolate leaves are 1.2–6.0 in. (3–15 cm) long.

INFLORESCENCE: 2–6 in. (5–15 cm) long. Inflorescences are slightly longer than the leaves, so blossoms are held at the tip of the foliage. Inflorescences are erect and slender. They may be terminal or arise opposite the leaves from nodes near the apex of the stem.

FLOWERS: 3–8 per inflorescence. The flowers are 0.6–1.0 in. (1.5–2.5 cm) across. The sepals and small petals are pointed. They may be green or white with red veins. The 3-lobed lip is yellowish-green with dark purple lines. It is deeply incised and serrated with a recurved midlobe.

HYBRIDIZING NOTES: Chromosome count is n = 20 as *D. alpestre* (ref. 150, 153, 504, 580). As *D. monticola,* counts are n = 19 (ref. 542) and n = 20 (ref. 542).

REFERENCES: 38, 102, 150, 153, 179, 190, 202, 211, 230, 254, 317, 369, 374, 454, 504, 528, 542, 580.

PHOTOS/DRAWINGS: 102, 190, 454.

Dendrobium montigenum Ridley. See *D. dekockii* J. J. Smith.
REFERENCES: 222, 385, 400, 538. PHOTOS/DRAWINGS: 538.

Dendrobium montis-movi Kränzlin.
Now considered a synonym of *Glossorhyncha macdonaldii* Schlechter. REFERENCES: 173, 224, 270, 271.

Dendrobium montis-sellae Kränzlin

ORIGIN/HABITAT: Papua New Guinea. Plants were collected near Sattelberg at about 3000 ft. (910 m).

CLIMATE: Station #94048, Finschhafen, Papua New Guinea, Lat. 6.6°S, Long. 147.9°E, at 25 ft. (8 m). Temperatures are calculated for an elevation of 3000 ft. (910 m), resulting in probable extremes of 83°F (29°C) and 58°F (15°C).

N/HEMISPHERE	JAN	FEB	MAR	APR	MAY	JUN	JUL	AUG	SEP	OCT	NOV	DEC
°F AVG MAX	74	73	73	74	76	78	79	79	77	76	74	74
°F AVG MIN	63	62	62	61	61	62	64	64	64	64	63	63
DIURNAL RANGE	11	11	11	13	15	16	15	15	13	12	11	11
RAIN/INCHES	25.8	22.4	20.9	15.8	11.7	8.9	5.5	3.7	5.3	11.9	18.3	23.2
HUMIDITY/%	88	87	86	86	84	85	84	85	86	88	88	88
BLOOM SEASON	N/A											
DAYS CLR	N/A											
RAIN/MM	655	568	531	402	297	227	140	95	135	301	464	589
°C AVG MAX	23.5	23.0	23.0	23.5	24.6	25.7	26.3	26.3	25.2	24.6	23.5	23.5
°C AVG MIN	17.4	16.9	16.6	16.3	16.3	16.9	18.0	18.0	18.0	18.0	17.4	17.4
DIURNAL RANGE	6.1	6.1	6.1	7.2	8.3	8.8	8.3	8.3	7.2	6.6	6.1	6.1
S/HEMISPHERE	JUL	AUG	SEP	OCT	NOV	DEC	JAN	FEB	MAR	APR	MAY	JUN

Cultural Recommendations

LIGHT: 2000–3000 fc.

TEMPERATURES: Throughout the year, days average 73–79°F (23–26°C), and nights average 61–64°F (16–18°C), with a diurnal range of 11–16°F (6–9°C).

HUMIDITY: 85–90% year-round.

WATER: Rainfall is very heavy most of the year but is only moderate for 3 months in summer. Cultivated plants should be kept evenly moist, with only slight drying allowed between waterings.

FERTILIZER: ½ recommended strength. A balanced fertilizer should be applied weekly to biweekly throughout the year.

REST PERIOD: Growing conditions should be maintained year-round. In the habitat, rainfall is heaviest in winter. Water and fertilizer may be reduced somewhat for cultivated plants, especially those grown in the dark, short-day conditions common in temperate latitudes. Plants should never be allowed to dry completely, however.

GROWING MEDIA: This plant may be difficult to grow on a slab unless humidity is very high and it is watered frequently. When plants are potted, small pots, barely large enough to hold the roots, may be filled with any open and fast-draining medium. The medium should be kept moist, but not soggy. Repotting is best done annually when new roots are growing.

Plant and Flower Information

PLANT SIZE AND TYPE: A 20 in. (50 cm) sympodial epiphyte.

PSEUDOBULB: 17 in. (43 cm) long.

LEAVES: Many. The lanceolate leaves are 3 in. (8 cm) long.

INFLORESCENCE: Inflorescences emerge opposite the leaves.

FLOWERS: 1 per inflorescence. The flowers are 0.3 in. (0.8 cm) across. Sepals and petals are yellow with purple spots. The purple lip has serrated margins and is decorated with raised diverging lines.

REFERENCES: 220, 254.

Dendrobium montistellare P. van Royen. See *D. brevicaule* Rolfe. REFERENCES: 233, 385, 538. PHOTOS/DRAWINGS: 538.

Dendrobium montis-yulei Kränzlin. Schlechter (ref. 437) lists *D. montis-yulei* as a doubtful species. Cribb (ref. 83) excludes *D. montis-yulei* for lack of a type specimen and suggests that it may have been closely related to or conspecific with *D. terrestre* J. J. Smith. REFERENCES: 83, 220, 254, 437.

Dendrobium mooreanum Lindley

AKA: Hunt (ref. 211) includes *D. fairfaxii* Rolfe and *D. priscillae* Hawkes. Lewis and Cribb (ref. 270) also include *D. petri* Rchb. f. and *D. quaifei* Rolfe ex Ames.

ORIGIN/HABITAT: Common on most of the islands of Vanuatu (New Hebrides). Plants grow in lowland and mountain forests at 1000–3600 ft. (300–1100 m). Ames (ref. 17) indicates that *D. quaifei* was collected on Santo Peak at 4500 ft. (1370 m). Plants are also reported from Fiji.

CLIMATE: Station #91554, Luganville, Espiritu Santo Island, Vanuatu, Lat. 15.5°S, Long. 167.1°E, at 493 ft. (150 m). Temperatures are calculated for an elevation of 2300 ft. (700 m), resulting in probable extremes of 87°F (31°C) and 55°F (13°C).

N/HEMISPHERE	JAN	FEB	MAR	APR	MAY	JUN	JUL	AUG	SEP	OCT	NOV	DEC
°F AVG MAX	75	75	76	77	77	80	80	81	80	79	77	75
°F AVG MIN	65	65	66	66	67	68	69	68	67	68	67	66
DIURNAL RANGE	10	10	10	11	10	12	11	13	13	11	10	9
RAIN/INCHES	6.4	6.3	4.7	6.3	9.5	9.2	10.6	9.7	10.9	10.1	8.1	6.1
HUMIDITY/%	81	80	83	81	82	81	83	83	88	86	83	80
BLOOM SEASON	N/A											
DAYS CLR	N/A											
RAIN/MM	163	160	119	160	241	234	269	246	277	257	206	155
°C AVG MAX	23.9	23.9	24.5	25.0	25.0	26.7	26.7	27.2	26.7	26.1	25.0	23.9
°C AVG MIN	18.4	18.4	18.9	18.9	19.5	20.0	20.6	20.0	19.5	20.0	19.5	18.9
DIURNAL RANGE	5.5	5.5	5.6	6.1	5.5	6.7	6.1	7.2	7.2	6.1	5.5	5.0
S/HEMISPHERE	JUL	AUG	SEP	OCT	NOV	DEC	JAN	FEB	MAR	APR	MAY	JUN

Cultural Recommendations

LIGHT: 2000–3000 fc.

TEMPERATURES: Throughout the year, days average 75–81°F (24–27°C), and nights average 65–69°F (18–21°C), with a diurnal range of 9–13°F (5–7°C).

HUMIDITY: 80–85% year-round.

WATER: Rainfall is moderate to heavy year-round, with a short, slightly drier period in late winter or early spring. Cultivated plants should be kept moist.

FERTILIZER: ¼–½ recommended strength. A balanced fertilizer should be applied weekly to biweekly throughout the year.

REST PERIOD: Growing conditions should be maintained all year. If plants are cultivated in the dark, short-day conditions common in temperate-latitude winters, water and fertilizer should be reduced until light increases in spring. Plants should never be allowed to dry out completely, however. In the habitat, light may be slightly higher in winter.

GROWING MEDIA: Plants may be mounted on tree-fern or cork slabs if humidity is high and plants are watered at least once daily in summer. When plants are potted, any open, fast-draining medium may be used. Repotting may be done anytime new roots are growing.

MISCELLANEOUS NOTES: Lewis and Cribb (ref. 270) indicate that *D. mooreanum* resembles *D. ruginosum* Ames from Bougainville and other Pacific Islands.

Plant and Flower Information

PLANT SIZE AND TYPE: A 10 in. (25 cm) sympodial epiphyte.

PSEUDOBULB: 7 in. (18 cm) long. The stems are yellow, erect, and clustered. They consist of 3–4 nodes.

LEAVES: 2–4 at the apex of each growth. The ovate-lanceolate leaves are 3.3 in. (8.5 cm) long. They are spreading, leathery, and pointed at the tip.

INFLORESCENCE: 7 in. (18 cm) long. One or several erect inflorescences emerge from nodes near the apex of the pseudobulb.

FLOWERS: Few per inflorescence. The flowers are 1.2–1.6 in. (3–4 cm) across. Sepals and petals are normally white with a pink tinge, but some clones are primarily pink with white tips. Petals are recurved. The lip may be greenish with purple veins or white with green veins.

HYBRIDIZING NOTES: Chromosome count is 2n = 36 (ref. 153, 273).

REFERENCES: 17, 83, 153, 211, 216, 254, 269, 270, 273, 353.

PHOTOS/DRAWINGS: 269, 270, 540.

Dendrobium moorei F. Mueller

ORIGIN/HABITAT: Australia, only on Lord Howe Island. Plants grow on rocks, tree ferns, scrub, figs, and palms, as well as in the soil. They are most often found low on trees where light is relatively high. Although plants are more common above 1000 ft. (300 m), some are reported as low as 100 ft. (30 m). Collectors indicate that the best plants grow on tree ferns.

CLIMATE: Station #94995, Lord Howe Island, Lat. 31.5°S, Long. 159.1°E, at 35 ft. (11 m). Temperatures are calculated for an elevation of 1000 ft. (300 m), resulting in probable extremes of 86°F (30°C) and 40°F (4°C).

N/HEMISPHERE	JAN	FEB	MAR	APR	MAY	JUN	JUL	AUG	SEP	OCT	NOV	DEC
°F AVG MAX	62	62	65	67	70	73	75	75	74	71	67	64
°F AVG MIN	52	52	53	56	58	61	64	64	63	60	57	54
DIURNAL RANGE	10	10	12	11	12	12	11	11	11	11	10	10
RAIN/INCHES	7.7	5.3	5.3	5.2	4.5	4.9	4.9	4.2	5.0	6.7	6.2	7.7
HUMIDITY/%	72	70	70	71	72	72	71	69	69	71	71	70
BLOOM SEASON							*	*	*	*		
DAYS CLR @ 5AM	5	8	6	7	5	6	6	9	7	7	5	
DAYS CLR @ 11AM	4	4	5	5	7	6	5	3	5	6	4	3
RAIN/MM	196	135	135	132	114	124	124	107	127	170	157	196
°C AVG MAX	16.6	16.6	18.3	19.4	21.0	22.7	23.8	23.8	23.3	21.6	19.4	17.7
°C AVG MIN	11.0	11.0	11.6	13.3	14.4	16.0	17.7	17.7	17.2	15.5	13.8	12.2
DIURNAL RANGE	5.6	5.6	6.7	6.1	6.6	6.7	6.1	6.1	6.1	6.1	5.6	5.5
S/HEMISPHERE	JUL	AUG	SEP	OCT	NOV	DEC	JAN	FEB	MAR	APR	MAY	JUN

Dendrobium moquetteanum

Cultural Recommendations

LIGHT: 3000–4000 fc. Cultivated plants require strong air movement.

TEMPERATURES: Summer days average 73–75°F (23–24°C), and nights average 61–64°F (16–18°C), with a diurnal range of 11–12°F (6–7°C).

HUMIDITY: Near 70% year-round.

WATER: Rainfall is moderate all year. Plants are healthiest if they are allowed to dry between waterings. The fine roots deteriorate quickly if plants are overwatered or if the medium becomes stale. Overwatering causes plants to produce numerous aerial growths (keikis), which are not formed as readily if the plant is allowed to dry between waterings.

FERTILIZER: ¼–½ recommended strength, applied weekly. A high-nitrogen fertilizer is beneficial from spring to midsummer, but a fertilizer high in phosphates should be used in late summer and autumn.

REST PERIOD: Winter days average 62–65°F (17–18°C), and nights average 52–54°F (11–12°C), with a diurnal range of 10–12°F (6–7°C). Water and fertilizer should be reduced for cultivated plants, especially those grown in the dark, short-day conditions common in temperate-latitude winters. Plants should never remain completely dry for long periods, however. Growers report that some clones are reluctant to bloom unless winter minimums are kept above 54°F (12°C).

GROWING MEDIA: Australian growers indicate that plants are healthiest when potted, but they also grow well on tree-fern slabs if humidity is high and if plants are watered daily in summer. Repotting is best done in early spring when new roots are growing.

MISCELLANEOUS NOTES: The primary bloom season shown in the climate table is based on cultivation records. A well-grown plant is usually in bloom. Plants normally produce numerous aerial growths (keikis), but excessive keiki production may reduce flowering.

Plant and Flower Information

PLANT SIZE AND TYPE: A 6–12 in. (15–30 cm) sympodial epiphyte, lithophyte, or terrestrial.

PSEUDOBULB: 3–10 in. (8–25 cm) long. The stems, which are sometimes thickened at the base, are angled and furrowed.

LEAVES: 2–6 near the apex of each growth. The leaves are 2–4 in. (5–10 cm) long. They are oval to lanceolate, leathery, and thin-textured.

INFLORESCENCE: Inflorescences arise from between the leaves near the apex of the stem. The blossoms are held above the tips of the leaves. Upton (ref. 533) indicates that racemes need 4 months to mature from the time they first emerge.

FLOWERS: 6–10 per inflorescence. The flowers are 0.8 in. (2 cm) across and do not open fully. They are snow-white, waxy, and glisten in the light to appear almost frosted. Rare clones are tinged with purple. The slender sepals and petals are recurved at the tips. They are sweetly fragrant like hyacinths.

HYBRIDIZING NOTES: When used as a parent, *D. moorei* tends to contribute the glistening flower texture and lip shape.

REFERENCES: 67, 179, 190, 216, 240, 254, 325, 326, 330, 390, 445, 533, 541.

PHOTOS/DRAWINGS: 240, 325, *533*.

Dendrobium moquetteanum J. J. Smith

ORIGIN/HABITAT: Borneo. Habitat location and elevation are not available. The following climate data are for Bogor, Java, where plants were cultivated in the botanical garden. However, data are not necessarily representative of conditions in the habitat and should be used with caution.

CLIMATE: Station #96755, Bogor, Indonesia, Lat. 6.5°S, Long. 106.8°E, at 558 ft. (170 m). Record extreme temperatures are 96°F (36°C) and 66°F (19°C).

N/HEMISPHERE	JAN	FEB	MAR	APR	MAY	JUN	JUL	AUG	SEP	OCT	NOV	DEC
°F AVG MAX	86	87	88	88	87	85	84	84	85	86	87	86
°F AVG MIN	73	73	73	74	74	74	74	74	74	75	75	74
DIURNAL RANGE	13	14	15	14	13	11	10	10	11	11	12	12
RAIN/INCHES	2.1	1.0	0.5	5.0	8.1	18.8	23.7	20.2	14.4	12.0	11.9	3.4
HUMIDITY/%	72	68	65	66	74	79	84	84	81	79	77	75
BLOOM SEASON	N/A											
DAYS CLR @ 7AM	14	14	14	11	5	3	1	2	4	6	10	12
DAYS CLR @ 1PM	9	10	8	5	1	1	0	0	1	1	3	7
RAIN/MM	53	25	13	127	206	478	602	513	366	305	302	86
°C AVG MAX	30.0	30.6	31.1	31.1	30.6	29.4	28.9	28.9	29.4	30.0	30.6	30.0
°C AVG MIN	22.8	22.8	22.8	23.3	23.3	23.3	23.3	23.3	23.3	23.9	23.9	23.3
DIURNAL RANGE	7.2	7.8	8.3	7.8	7.3	6.1	5.6	5.6	6.1	6.1	6.7	6.7
S/HEMISPHERE	JUL	AUG	SEP	OCT	NOV	DEC	JAN	FEB	MAR	APR	MAY	JUN

Cultural Recommendations

LIGHT: 2500–3000 fc.

TEMPERATURES: Throughout the year, days average 84–88°F (29–31°C), and nights average 73–75°F (23–24°C), with a diurnal range of 10–15°F (6–8°C). Cultivated plants may not be able to tolerate wide temperature fluctuations. Temperatures at higher elevations are a few degrees cooler, with a similar diurnal range and limited seasonal fluctuation.

HUMIDITY: 80–85% in summer, dropping to near 65% for 2–3 months in late winter and early spring.

WATER: Rainfall is heavy from spring to autumn, but conditions are very dry for 2–3 months in winter. During the growing season, plants should kept moist, with only slight drying allowed between waterings, but water should be gradually reduced in late autumn.

FERTILIZER: ¼–½ recommended strength, applied weekly. A high-nitrogen fertilizer is beneficial from spring to midsummer, but a fertilizer high in phosphates should be used in late summer and autumn.

REST PERIOD: Growing conditions should be maintained all year; but the diurnal range increases slightly in winter, and rainfall is very low for 2–3 months. In cultivation, water should be reduced and the plants allowed to dry out between waterings. They should not remain dry for prolonged periods, however. Fertilizer may be reduced or eliminated anytime the plant is not actively growing. In the habitat, light is highest in winter.

GROWING MEDIA: Plants may be mounted on tree-fern or cork slabs or potted in small pots filled with any open, fast-draining medium. Repotting may be done anytime new roots are growing.

Plant and Flower Information

PLANT SIZE AND TYPE: A 30 in. (75 cm) sympodial epiphyte.

PSEUDOBULB: 30 in. (75 cm) long. The pale, yellow-green stems are spaced 1.6–2.4 in. (4–6 cm) apart. They emerge from an elongated rhizome.

LEAVES: Many. The linear leaves are 2–3 in. (5–8 cm) long, leathery, bilobed at the apex, and somewhat twisted at the base. They are usually dark green with pale nerves.

INFLORESCENCE: Inflorescences arise from nodes along the stem.

FLOWERS: 1 per inflorescence. The flowers are bright, snow-white with a yellowish brown lip. The dorsal sepal is oval-ovate, but lateral sepals taper to a slender point. The fleshy, 3-lobed lip has 3 pale ridges.

REFERENCES: 222, 286, 295, 455.

Dendrobium morotaiense J. J. Smith

ORIGIN/HABITAT: Morotai in the northern Molucca Islands. Additional information on habitat and elevation is not available. Plants were cultivated at the botanical garden in Bogor, Java. The following climate data should be used with caution.

CLIMATE: Station #97406, Galela, Halmahera Island, Indonesia, Lat. 1.8°N,

Long. 127.8°E, at 180 ft. (55 m). Record extreme temperatures are not available for this location.

N/HEMISPHERE	JAN	FEB	MAR	APR	MAY	JUN	JUL	AUG	SEP	OCT	NOV	DEC
°F AVG MAX	86	86	86	88	87	86	86	87	87	88	88	87
°F AVG MIN	76	74	76	76	77	75	73	75	76	77	77	76
DIURNAL RANGE	10	12	10	12	10	11	13	12	11	11	11	11
RAIN/INCHES	5.3	6.4	7.4	4.1	10.0	7.1	8.1	9.3	5.2	6.9	7.0	11.4
HUMIDITY/%	N/A											
BLOOM SEASON							*					
DAYS CLR	N/A											
RAIN/MM	134	163	188	104	254	180	205	236	132	175	177	289
°C AVG MAX	30.1	30.0	29.8	30.9	30.6	30.2	30.0	30.5	30.7	31.4	31.2	30.5
°C AVG MIN	24.3	23.6	24.6	24.6	24.9	23.9	22.9	23.7	24.2	24.9	25.2	24.6
DIURNAL RANGE	5.8	6.4	5.2	6.3	5.7	6.3	7.1	6.8	6.5	6.5	6.0	5.9
S/HEMISPHERE	JUL	AUG	SEP	OCT	NOV	DEC	JAN	FEB	MAR	APR	MAY	JUN

Cultural Recommendations

LIGHT: 2000–3000 fc.

TEMPERATURES: Throughout the year, days average 86–88°F (30–31°C), and nights average 73–77°F (23–25°C), with a diurnal range of 10–13°F (5–7°C).

HUMIDITY: Information is not available for this location. However, records from nearby locations indicate that humidity probably averages near 80% year-round.

WATER: Rainfall is moderate to heavy all year. Cultivated plants should be kept moist, with only slight drying allowed between waterings.

FERTILIZER: 1/4–1/2 recommended strength. A balanced fertilizer should be applied weekly to biweekly throughout the year.

REST PERIOD: Growing conditions should be maintained year-round. Water should be reduced slightly in winter, especially for plants grown in the dark, short-day conditions common in temperate latitudes. Plants should never be allowed to dry out completely, however. Fertilizer should be reduced or eliminated if water is reduced.

GROWING MEDIA: Plants may be mounted on tree-fern or cork slabs or potted in small pots filled with any open, fast-draining medium. Repotting may be done anytime new roots are growing.

MISCELLANEOUS NOTES: The bloom season shown in the climate table is based on reports from the habitat. The plant was described in 1937 in *Bul. Jard. Bot. Buit.* 3rd sér. 14:163.

Plant and Flower Information

PLANT SIZE AND TYPE: A sympodial epiphyte of unreported size.

PSEUDOBULB: The elongated stems are flattened and elliptical in cross-section.

LEAVES: Many. The lanceolate leaves are about 4 in. (10 cm) long.

INFLORESCENCE: Short. Inflorescences emerge through the leaf sheaths.

FLOWERS: 2 per inflorescence. The flowers are 1 in. (2.5 cm) long. Sepals and petals are uniformly dark brown. The lip, spur, and ovary are canary yellow. The blossoms have S-shaped petals and dorsal sepal, with sickle-shaped lateral sepals. The 3-lobed lip is very recurved with a ruffled margin which is slashed to uneven along the edge.

REFERENCES: 226.

Dendrobium morrisonii Schlechter

AKA: Commonly listed as a synonym of *D. purpureum* Roxburgh, but in 1993 Dauncy and Cribb in *Kew Bulletin* 48(3) reinstated it to species status.

ORIGIN/HABITAT: The islands of Vanuatu including Ambae, Anatom, Efate, Espiritu Santo, Malekula, Paama, and Sheperd Island (Tongoa). Plants grow on trees in mixed forests, where they are often found on ridges at 800–2950 ft. (250–900 m).

CLIMATE: Station #91554, Luganville, Espiritu Santo Island, Vanuatu, Lat. 15.5°S, Long. 167.1°E, at 493 ft. (150 m). Temperatures are calculated for an elevation of 2300 ft. (700 m), resulting in probable extremes of 87°F (31°C) and 55°F (13°C).

N/HEMISPHERE	JAN	FEB	MAR	APR	MAY	JUN	JUL	AUG	SEP	OCT	NOV	DEC
°F AVG MAX	75	75	76	77	77	80	80	81	80	79	77	75
°F AVG MIN	65	65	66	66	67	68	69	68	67	68	67	66
DIURNAL RANGE	10	10	10	11	10	12	11	13	13	11	10	9
RAIN/INCHES	6.4	6.3	4.7	6.3	9.5	9.2	10.6	9.7	10.9	10.1	8.1	6.1
HUMIDITY/%	81	80	83	81	82	81	83	83	88	86	83	80
BLOOM SEASON											*	
DAYS CLR	N/A											
RAIN/MM	163	160	119	160	241	234	269	246	277	257	206	155
°C AVG MAX	23.9	23.9	24.5	25.0	25.0	26.7	26.7	27.2	26.7	26.1	25.0	23.9
°C AVG MIN	18.4	18.4	18.9	18.9	19.5	20.0	20.6	20.0	19.5	20.0	19.5	18.9
DIURNAL RANGE	5.5	5.5	5.6	6.1	5.5	6.7	6.1	7.2	7.2	6.1	5.5	5.0
S/HEMISPHERE	JUL	AUG	SEP	OCT	NOV	DEC	JAN	FEB	MAR	APR	MAY	JUN

Cultural Recommendations

LIGHT: 2000–3000 fc.

TEMPERATURES: Throughout the year, days average 75–81°F (24–27°C) and nights average 65–69°F (18–21°C), with a diurnal range of 9–13°F (5–7°C).

HUMIDITY: 80–85% year-round.

WATER: Rainfall is moderate to heavy year-round, with a short, slightly drier period in late winter or early spring. Cultivated plants should be kept moist.

FERTILIZER: 1/4–1/2 recommended strength. A balanced fertilizer should be applied weekly to biweekly throughout the year.

REST PERIOD: Growing conditions should be maintained all year. If plants are cultivated in the dark, short-day conditions common in temperate-latitude winters, water and fertilizer should be reduced until light increases in spring. Plants should never be allowed to dry out completely, however. In the habitat, light may be slightly higher in winter.

GROWING MEDIA: Plants may be mounted on tree-fern or cork slabs if humidity is high and plants are watered at least once daily in summer. When plants are potted, any open, fast-draining medium may be used. Repotting may be done anytime new roots are growing.

MISCELLANEOUS NOTES: The bloom season shown in the climate table is based on collection records.

Plant and Flower Information

PLANT SIZE AND TYPE: A 14–35 in. (35–90 cm) sympodial epiphyte.

PSEUDOBULB: 14–35 in. (35–90 cm) long. The pendent stems consist of many nodes which are slightly constricted at the base. The yellow-green stems become purple with age. They are curved, spreading, and covered with persistent, papery white leaf-sheaths.

LEAVES: 2.8–5.5 in. (7–14 cm) long. The silky leaves are elliptic-lanceolate to oblong-lanceolate. They may be pale or dark green.

INFLORESCENCE: 0.4 in. (1 cm) long. Normally about 10 inflorescences arise from leafless stems, but they occasionally emerge from leafy stems. The large green floral bracts are sometimes tinged with purple.

FLOWERS: 10–20 per inflorescence. The smooth flowers are 0.4–0.6 in. (1.1–1.7 cm) long and do not open widely. They are normally purple to rose-purple, but plants with all white or pink and white blossoms are known. Flowers have an incurved, pointed dorsal sepal, recurved petals, and a wide, cylindrical mentum. The pointed lip and slender, lanceolate petals have an uneven margin near the apex. The blade of the lip has straight sides before tapering to a point. The ovary is curved. Although similar to *D. catillare*, the ovary on *D. morrisonii* lacks prominent wings.

Dendrobium mortii

REFERENCES: 220, 254, 270, 433.

PHOTOS/DRAWINGS: Dauncey and Cribb 1993 *Kew Bulletin* 48(3):545–576.

Dendrobium mortii as used by Dockrill not Bentham or F. Mueller. See *D. bowmanii* Bentham. REFERENCES: 67, 216, 533.

Dendrobium mortii Bentham not F. Mueller. See *D. schoeninum* Lindley. REFERENCES: 105, 254, 533.

Dendrobium mortii F. Mueller not Bentham

AKA: *D. robertsii* F. Mueller ex Rupp, *D. tenuissimum* Rupp.

ORIGIN/HABITAT: Eastern Australia at 1000–2950 ft. (300–900 m). The habitat extends from the southern foothills of Barrington Tops in New South Wales to the mountains of southeast Queensland. Plants usually grow on the uppermost branches of moss-covered trees in rainforests, where mist and dew are common. They are occasionally found in more open forests.

CLIMATE: Station #94791, Coffs Harbour, Australia, Lat. 30.3°S, Long. 153.1°E, at 14 ft. (4 m). Temperatures are calculated for an elevation of 2000 ft. (610 m), resulting in probable extremes of 99°F (38°C) and 23°F (−5°C).

N/HEMISPHERE	JAN	FEB	MAR	APR	MAY	JUN	JUL	AUG	SEP	OCT	NOV	DEC
°F AVG MAX	58	60	64	67	72	73	73	73	72	70	64	61
°F AVG MIN	37	38	43	48	52	56	58	59	57	52	43	38
DIURNAL RANGE	21	22	21	19	20	17	15	14	15	18	21	23
RAIN/INCHES	3.8	2.1	2.9	3.8	4.0	5.8	6.9	7.7	8.7	7.7	5.7	4.5
HUMIDITY/%	74	72	70	74	72	76	79	83	79	78	75	74
BLOOM SEASON				*	*	*						
DAYS CLR @ 4AM	8	9	10	10	12	11	9	8	10	7	11	8
DAYS CLR @ 10AM	16	18	18	12	15	11	8	5	10	10	14	15
RAIN/MM	97	53	74	97	102	147	175	196	221	196	145	114
°C AVG MAX	14.7	15.8	18.0	19.7	22.5	23.0	23.0	23.0	22.5	21.4	18.0	16.4
°C AVG MIN	3.0	3.6	6.4	9.1	11.4	13.6	14.7	15.2	14.1	11.4	6.4	3.6
DIURNAL RANGE	11.7	12.2	11.6	10.6	11.1	9.4	8.3	7.8	8.4	10.0	11.6	12.8
S/HEMISPHERE	JUL	AUG	SEP	OCT	NOV	DEC	JAN	FEB	MAR	APR	MAY	JUN

Cultural Recommendations

LIGHT: 2500–3000 fc. Plants are healthiest with brisk air movement.

TEMPERATURES: Summer days average 73°F (23°C), and nights average 56–59°F (14–15°C), with a diurnal range of 14–17°F (8–9°C).

HUMIDITY: 75–80% in summer and autumn, dropping to near 70% in winter. Humidity may be somewhat greater in the rainforest habitat, however.

WATER: Rainfall is moderate to heavy most of the year, but conditions are slightly drier for 2–3 months in winter. *D. mortii* usually grows in areas with frequent mist and heavy dew, so cultivated plants should kept moist but not soggy, with only slight drying allowed between waterings. If plants are mounted, misting may be necessary several times a day during the hottest periods, and a light misting on hot evenings is usually beneficial. New leaves must be kept dry, however, because rot starts easily if water is allowed to stand on the tender new growth.

FERTILIZER: ¼–½ recommended strength, applied weekly. A high-nitrogen fertilizer is beneficial from spring to midsummer, but a fertilizer high in phosphates should be used in late summer and autumn.

REST PERIOD: Winter days average 58–64°F (15–18°C), and nights average 37–43°F (3–6°C), with a diurnal range of 21–23°F (12–13°C). For 2–3 months in winter, cultivated plants should be kept just barely moist; but they should never be allowed to dry out completely. Fertilizer should be reduced until water is increased in spring. In the habitat, the probable extreme low is 23°F (−5°C), thus indicating that plants probably survive below freezing temperatures. These extremes should be avoided for cultivated plants. If conditions become severe, the plant is more likely to survive if it is dry when temperatures are cold.

GROWING MEDIA: Mounting plants on tree-fern or cork slabs accommodates their pendulous growth habit. However, humidity must be high and plants must be watered at least once a day in summer. Hanging baskets filled with an open, fast-draining medium may also be used. Repotting is best done in early spring when new roots are growing.

MISCELLANEOUS NOTES: The bloom season shown in the climate table is based on reports from the habitat.

Plant and Flower Information

PLANT SIZE AND TYPE: A 1.2–6.0 in. (3–15 cm) sympodial epiphyte.

PSEUDOBULB: 0.4–1.6 in. (1–4 cm) long. The pendulous stems are wiry almost hairlike, cylindrical, flexible, and branching.

LEAVES: 1 per node. The fleshy leaf is normally 0.8–3.5 in. (2–9 cm) long, but leaves may reach a length of 6 in. (15 cm).

INFLORESCENCE: Very short. Inflorescences emerge at the base of the leaf.

FLOWERS: 1–3 per inflorescence, few per plant. The fragrant flowers are 0.8 in. (2 cm) across and open fully. Sepals and petals are recurved. Sepals may be dark purple-green to light green. The green petals are narrower than the sepals. The lip is white with yellow-green keels.

HYBRIDIZING NOTES: Chromosome count is 2n = 38 as *D. mortii* (ref. 153, 273) and *D. tenuissimum* Rupp (ref. 153, 273).

REFERENCES: 23, 67, 105, 153, 216, 240, 254, 273, 325, 390, 421, 533.

PHOTOS/DRAWINGS: 105, *240*, 325, *390, 533*.

Dendrobium moschatum Griffith not (Buch.-Ham.) Swartz or Wallich ex. D. Don. *Index Kewensis* (ref. 216) includes this name as a synonym of *D. pulchellum* without an author's name. REFERENCES: 216.

Dendrobium moschatum (Buch.-Ham.) Swartz not Griffith or Wallich ex. D. Don

AKA: Seidenfaden (ref. 454) includes *Epidendrum moschatum* Buch.-Ham., *Cymbidium moschatum* (Buch.-Ham.) Willdenow, *Dendrobium calceolaria* Carey ex Hooker, and *D. cupreum* Herbert. Several current references list the describers as (Willdenow) Swartz.

ORIGIN/HABITAT: Northwestern Himalayas, including the Dehra Dun region in northern India, Nepal, Sikkim, Bhutan, and the Assam region in the northeast India. Plants grow at 1000–6550 ft. (300–2000 m). They are also found at moderate to high elevations in lower Burma, Thailand, and Laos; and plants have been reported in Yunnan Province of southwest China. Plants usually grow at the tops of tall deciduous trees in high light and brisk air movement.

CLIMATE: Station #42147, Mukteswar, India, Lat. 29.5°N, Long. 79.7°E, at 7592 ft. (2314 m). Temperatures are calculated for an elevation of 4000 ft. (1220 m), resulting in probable extremes of 102°F (39°C) and 33°F (1°C).

N/HEMISPHERE	JAN	FEB	MAR	APR	MAY	JUN	JUL	AUG	SEP	OCT	NOV	DEC
°F AVG MAX	63	66	73	81	87	87	81	81	80	77	73	67
°F AVG MIN	48	50	56	64	69	71	71	70	68	62	56	51
DIURNAL RANGE	15	16	17	17	18	16	10	11	12	15	17	16
RAIN/INCHES	1.0	2.1	1.7	1.0	0.3	4.6	11.4	12.8	4.6	3.5	0.3	0.2
HUMIDITY/%	61	55	50	39	44	67	91	93	83	66	55	56
BLOOM SEASON				*	**	**	**	**	*	*		
DAYS CLR @ 5PM	17	17	15	18	18	12	1	1	6	25	26	21
RAIN/MM	25	53	43	25	8	117	290	325	117	89	8	5
°C AVG MAX	17.1	18.8	22.7	27.1	30.5	30.5	27.1	27.1	26.6	24.9	22.7	19.4
°C AVG MIN	8.8	9.9	13.3	17.7	20.5	21.6	21.6	21.0	19.9	16.6	13.3	10.5
DIURNAL RANGE	8.3	8.9	9.4	9.4	10.0	8.9	5.5	6.1	6.7	8.3	9.4	8.9
S/HEMISPHERE	JUL	AUG	SEP	OCT	NOV	DEC	JAN	FEB	MAR	APR	MAY	JUN

Cultural Recommendations

LIGHT: 3000–4000 fc. Some shading is needed from spring through autumn, but conditions in the habitat are very bright from autumn through winter and spring. In cultivation, light should be as high as the plant can tolerate, short of burning the leaves.

TEMPERATURES: Summer days average 81–87°F (27–31°C), and nights average 70–71°F (21–22°C), with a diurnal range of 10–16°F (6–9°C).

HUMIDITY: Near 90% in summer, decreasing to 55–60% most of the winter. In spring, at the end of the long dry season, humidity drops to near 40% for 2 months.

WATER: Rainfall is moderate to heavy for 5 months from summer into autumn. Cultivated plants should be kept moist while actively growing, but water should be gradually reduced as growths mature in autumn.

FERTILIZER: ¼–½ recommended strength, applied weekly. A high-nitrogen fertilizer is beneficial from spring to midsummer, while a fertilizer high in phosphates should be used in late summer and autumn.

REST PERIOD: Winter days average 63–67°F (17–19°C), and nights average 48–51°F (9–11°C), with a diurnal range of 15–16°F (8–9°C). Some growers indicate that winter lows should be kept above 43°F (6°C), but others state that plants will tolerate a few degrees of frost. Cultivated plants should be allowed to dry between waterings after growths mature in autumn, but they should not remain dry for more than a few weeks. Occasional early morning mistings between waterings may be beneficial, especially when several days of clear weather are expected. Fertilizer should be eliminated anytime water is reduced.

GROWING MEDIA: Mounting plants on tree-fern or cork slabs accommodates their pendulous growth habit. However, humidity must be high and plants must be watered at least once a day in summer. If plants cannot be mounted, large hanging pots or baskets may be filled with any open, fast-draining medium. Repotting may be done anytime new roots are actively growing.

MISCELLANEOUS NOTES: The bloom season shown in the climate table is based on cultivation records. In the habitat, plants growing in the hot plains and lower valleys experience a very hot, dry period in spring prior to new growth'ss emerging. Growers indicate that plants grow well in Singapore but flower only occasionally in that uniform climate.

Plant and Flower Information

PLANT SIZE AND TYPE: A 35–96 in. (90–245 cm) sympodial epiphyte.

PSEUDOBULB: 35–96 in. (90–245 cm) long. Initially erect to arching, the cylindrical stems become pendulous as they lengthen. Young canes are purplish with green spots, but older stems are dark brown. Stems are leafy, especially near the apex. Plants are free-rooting.

LEAVES: Many. The oblong-lanceolate leaves are 3–6 in. (8–15 cm) long, thin, smooth, and glossy. They turn purple during the dry season. The leaves alternate along the entire length of the stem. The leaves last 2 years.

INFLORESCENCE: 4–12 in. (10–30 cm) long. The pendulous inflorescences arise from upper nodes of older leafy and leafless stems. The racemes are laxly flowered.

FLOWERS: 5–15 per inflorescence. The flowers are normally 1.0–1.6 in. (2.5–4.0 cm) across, but some are as large as 3 in. (8 cm). Sepals and much broader petals may be white, pale or bright yellow, apricot with lilac tips, or uniformly purplish. The slipper-shaped lip, which is a deeper shade of the same color as the sepals and petals, is marked with 2 maroon blotches. It is downy on both surfaces. The fragrance is described as resembling musk, rhubarb, or sweet woodruff. Blossoms last about a week.

HYBRIDIZING NOTES: Chromosome counts are n = 19 (ref. 150, 154, 187, 542), 2n = 38 (ref. 151, 154, 187, 188, 504, 542, 580), 2n = 39 (ref. 187, 504, 580), and 2n = 40 (ref. 150, 187, 504, 542, 580), and counts for *D. moschatum* var. *cupreum* without describer's name are 2n = 38 (ref. 504, 542) and 2n = 38+3f (ref. 504, 580). Chromosome count as *D. moschatum* Wallich is 2n = 40 (ref. 152).

Johansen (ref. 239) indicates that plants are self-sterile and that flowers dropped 7–9 days after self-pollination. When cross-pollinated, half of the blossoms produced capsules which opened 327 days after pollination. Of the seed produced, 87% contained visible embryos and 52% germinated. When crossed with *D. secundum* (Blume) Lindley, capsules formed but no viable seed was produced.

REFERENCES: 25, 36, 46, 102, 150, 151, 152, 154, 161, 179, 187, 188, 190, 196, 200, 202, 210, 216, 238, 239, 245, 247, 254, 266, 278, 317, 326, 369, 371, 376, 389, 430, 445, 447, 448, 454, 455, 458, 504, 507, 524, 541, 542, 557, 568, 570, 577, 580, 581.

PHOTOS/DRAWINGS: *36,* 102, 210, 238, *245, 247, 369, 371, 389, 430, 454,* 455, 458, *577, 581.*

Dendrobium moschatum Wallich ex D. Don.
A synonym of *D. calceolaria* Carey ex Hooker, which is now considered a synonym of *D. moschatum* (Buch.-Ham.) Swartz. REFERENCES: 46, 152, 216, 278, 317, 541.

Dendrobium mouanum Guillaumin.
Now considered a synonym of *Glossorhyncha macdonaldii* Schlechter. REFERENCES: 173, 227, 270, 271.

Dendrobium moulmeinense Hort., Low ex Warner and Williams.
See *D. infundibulum* Lindley. REFERENCES: 190, 218.

Dendrobium moulmeinense Parish ex Hooker f.
The type specimen reportedly originated in Moulmein, Burma, but habitat elevation was not reported. Kränzlin (ref. 254) included *D. moulmeinense* as a synonym of *D. dixanthum* Rchb. f., but Seidenfaden (ref. 454) expressed reservations regarding this synonymy and indicated that fresh material needed to be studied. Climate data were not selected because of uncertainties regarding the status of this species and the elevation of the habitat. Plant and flower information is not available, as the plant was unavailable to the original describer. The blossom had plumose-fimbriate edges on the lip, and the margins of the petals were toothed. REFERENCES: 157, 202, 218, 254, 445, 454.

Dendrobium mucronatum Seidenfaden

ORIGIN/HABITAT: Endemic to Thailand. The single collection was made north of Khao Luang, Khun Yuan at about 5250 ft. (1600 m).

CLIMATE: Station #48300, Mae Hong Son, Thailand, Lat. 19.3°N, Long. 97.9°E, at 711 ft. (217 m). Temperatures are calculated for an elevation of 5250 ft. (1600 m), resulting in probable extremes of 93°F (34°C) and 28°F (−2°C).

N/HEMISPHERE	JAN	FEB	MAR	APR	MAY	JUN	JUL	AUG	SEP	OCT	NOV	DEC
°F AVG MAX	71	75	82	83	80	74	72	72	73	75	73	70
°F AVG MIN	42	42	47	57	61	60	59	59	59	57	53	44
DIURNAL RANGE	29	33	35	26	19	14	13	13	14	18	20	26
RAIN/INCHES	0.4	0.2	0.3	1.7	6.1	7.1	9.6	9.9	8.1	3.9	1.2	0.4
HUMIDITY/%	67	60	50	50	68	81	82	83	83	82	75	71
BLOOM SEASON				*								
DAYS CLR @ 7AM	2	8	10	9	3	0	0	0	0	1	1	2
DAYS CLR @ 1PM	20	20	20	13	3	0	0	0	0	3	13	17
RAIN/MM	10	5	8	43	155	180	244	251	206	99	30	10
°C AVG MAX	21.7	23.9	27.8	28.3	26.7	23.3	22.2	22.2	22.8	23.9	22.8	21.1
°C AVG MIN	5.6	5.6	8.3	13.9	16.1	15.6	15.0	15.0	15.0	13.9	11.7	6.7
DIURNAL RANGE	16.1	18.3	19.5	14.4	10.6	7.7	7.2	7.2	7.8	10.0	11.1	14.4
S/HEMISPHERE	JUL	AUG	SEP	OCT	NOV	DEC	JAN	FEB	MAR	APR	MAY	JUN

Dendrobium mucronulatum

Cultural Recommendations

LIGHT: 2000–3000 fc. The heavy summer cloud cover indicates that some shading is needed from spring through autumn, but light should be as high as the plant can tolerate, short of burning the leaves. Brisk air movement is important at all times.

TEMPERATURES: Summer days average 72–74°F (22–23°C), and nights average 59–60°F (15–16°C), with a diurnal range of 13–14°F (7–8°C). The warmest weather occurs in spring, when days average 80–83°F (27–28°C) and nights average 47–61°F (8–16°C), with a diurnal range of 19–35°F (11–20°C).

HUMIDITY: Near 80–85% in summer and autumn, dropping to 60–70% most other months. However, averages fall to 50% for 2 months in early spring.

WATER: Rainfall is very heavy during the growing season, but winters are very dry. Cultivated plants should be kept moist while actively growing, but water should be gradually reduced after new growths mature in autumn.

FERTILIZER: ¼–½ recommended strength, applied weekly. A high-nitrogen fertilizer is beneficial from spring to midsummer, but a fertilizer high in phosphates should be used in late summer and autumn.

REST PERIOD: Winter days average 70–75°F (21–24°C), and nights average 42–44°F (6–7°C), with a diurnal range of 26–33°F (14–18°C). The winter diurnal range is nearly 3 times the summer values. In the habitat, rainfall is low for 4–5 months in winter. For 2–3 of these months, high humidity and nightly cooling result in frequent, heavy deposits of dew, with even more moisture available from fog and mist. Therefore, the driest season is only 1–2 months long. For cultivated plants, water should be reduced from late autumn to early spring. During most of the winter, plants should be allowed to dry out between waterings, but they should not remain completely dry for extended periods. Occasional early morning mistings between waterings may help prevent the plants from becoming too dry. For 1–2 months in late winter, however, water should be limited to occasional early morning mistings. Fertilizer should be reduced or eliminated until new growth starts in spring. In the habitat, the large number of clear, winter afternoons indicates very bright conditions.

GROWING MEDIA: Plants may be mounted on tree-fern or cork slabs if humidity is high and plants are watered at least once daily in summer. When plants are potted, any open, fast-draining medium may be used. Repotting is best done in early spring when new roots are growing.

MISCELLANEOUS NOTES: The bloom season shown in the climate table is based on the collection report.

Plant and Flower Information

PLANT SIZE AND TYPE: A 1.6–2.0 in. (4–5 cm) sympodial epiphyte.

PSEUDOBULB: 0.7 in. (1.8 cm) long. The glossy green stems arise in a straight line.

LEAVES: 3 per growth. The leaves are 1.2 in. (3 cm) long with a strong purple tint.

INFLORESCENCE: 1.6–2.0 in. (4–5 cm) long. The purple, laxly flowered inflorescences emerge at or near the apex of leafy pseudobulbs.

FLOWERS: 8–10 per inflorescence. The flowers are 0.2 in. (0.5 cm) across and do not open fully. Sepals and petals are light greenish yellow. The sepals have a purple keel that forms a distinct point at the tip. The green lip, which has no sidelobes, is recurved at the base.

HYBRIDIZING NOTES: Johansen (ref. 239) indicates that plants are self-sterile and that flowers dropped 10–15 days after self-pollination.

REFERENCES: 234, 239, 454.

PHOTOS/DRAWINGS: *454*.

Dendrobium mucronulatum Planchon. Listed as an invalid name by Kränzlin (ref. 254). REFERENCES: 216, 254.

Dendrobium muellerianum Schlechter. See *D. agrostophyllum* F. Mueller. REFERENCES: 67, 105, 220, 254, 533.

Dendrobium multicaule Teijsm. and Binn. Now considered a synonym of *Eria muscicola* Lindley. REFERENCES: 216, 254.

Dendrobium multicostatum J. J. Smith. See *D. hosei* Ridley. REFERENCES: 220, 254, 286, 295, 437.

Dendrobium multiflorum Parish and Rchb. f. See *D. nathanielis* Rchb. f. REFERENCES: 216, 220, 254, 445, 454.

Dendrobium multiflorum Ridley. See *D. sarawakense* Merrill. REFERENCES: 220, 223, 286, 398.

Dendrobium multifolium Schlechter

ORIGIN/HABITAT: Northern Papua New Guinea. Plants grow on forest trees in the Torricelli Range at 2600 ft. (800 m). Collections are also reported from Bougainville and the Solomon Islands.

CLIMATE: Station #94004, Wewak, Papua New Guinea, Lat. 3.6°S, Long. 143.7°E, at 16 ft. (5 m). Temperatures are calculated for an elevation of 2600 ft. (800 m), resulting in probable extremes of 89°F (32°C) and 53°F (12°C).

N/HEMISPHERE	JAN	FEB	MAR	APR	MAY	JUN	JUL	AUG	SEP	OCT	NOV	DEC
°F AVG MAX	79	79	79	79	79	79	78	77	78	79	79	79
°F AVG MIN	65	65	65	66	66	66	66	66	65	66	66	65
DIURNAL RANGE	14	14	14	13	13	13	12	11	13	13	13	14
RAIN/INCHES	7.6	4.8	5.3	10.0	13.3	14.5	12.1	11.9	14.9	16.9	15.1	10.8
HUMIDITY/%	80	79	79	78	79	81	82	82	81	82	81	80
BLOOM SEASON			*									
DAYS CLR	N/A											
RAIN/MM	193	122	135	254	338	368	307	302	378	429	384	274
°C AVG MAX	26.3	26.3	26.3	26.3	26.3	26.3	25.8	25.2	25.8	26.3	26.3	26.3
°C AVG MIN	18.6	18.6	18.6	19.1	19.1	19.1	19.1	19.1	18.6	18.6	19.1	18.6
DIURNAL RANGE	7.7	7.7	7.7	7.2	7.2	7.2	6.7	6.1	7.2	7.7	7.2	7.7
S/HEMISPHERE	JUL	AUG	SEP	OCT	NOV	DEC	JAN	FEB	MAR	APR	MAY	JUN

Cultural Recommendations

LIGHT: 2000–3000 fc.

TEMPERATURES: Throughout the year, days average 77–79°F (25–26°C), and nights average 65–66°F (19°C), with a diurnal range of 11–14°F (6–8°C).

HUMIDITY: Near 80% year-round.

WATER: Rainfall is heavy all year, but conditions are slightly drier for 1–2 months in late winter. Cultivated plants should be kept moist, with only slight drying allowed between waterings.

FERTILIZER: ¼–½ recommended strength. A balanced fertilizer should be applied weekly to biweekly throughout the year.

REST PERIOD: Growing conditions should be maintained year-round. Water should be reduced for plants cultivated in the dark, short-day conditions common during temperate-latitude winters, but they should not be allowed to dry out completely. Fertilizer should also be reduced if water is reduced. In the habitat, light may be slightly higher in winter.

GROWING MEDIA: A very open and fast-draining medium may be used with baskets or small pots. Repotting may be done anytime new roots are growing.

MISCELLANEOUS NOTES: The bloom season shown in the climate table is based on reports from the habitat. Plants that produce flowers which last a single day commonly bloom several times during the year. Flowering usually occurs 7–14 days after a sudden 10°F (5°C) drop in daytime temperatures.

Plant and Flower Information

PLANT SIZE AND TYPE: A 24 in. (60 cm) sympodial epiphyte.

PSEUDOBULB: 24 in. (60 cm) long. The somewhat flattened canes do not branch. They are very densely leafy.

LEAVES: Many. The lanceolate leaves are 3.2–4.3 in. (8–11 cm) long.

INFLORESCENCE: Very short.

FLOWERS: 2 per inflorescence. The flowers are 0.6 in. (1.4 cm) across. Creamy yellow sepals are incurved at their thickened tips. The lip is orange-yellow, 3-lobed, and slightly indented at the broad apex. Blossoms last a single day.

REFERENCES: 221, 437, 445, 516.

PHOTOS/DRAWINGS: 437.

Dendrobium multilineatum Kerr

ORIGIN/HABITAT: Laos. Plants grow near Phu Bia, in the mountains of the Xieng Khouang region, at about 6250 ft. (1900 m).

CLIMATE: Station #48935, Xieng Khouang, Laos, Lat. 19.4°N, Long. 103.1°E, at 3445 ft. (1050 m). Temperatures are calculated for an elevation of 6250 ft. (1900 m), resulting in probable extremes of 90°F (32°C) and 19°F (–7°C).

N/HEMISPHERE	JAN	FEB	MAR	APR	MAY	JUN	JUL	AUG	SEP	OCT	NOV	DEC
°F AVG MAX	67	71	71	76	75	72	66	70	70	69	65	62
°F AVG MIN	37	42	47	53	58	59	58	59	57	52	47	38
DIURNAL RANGE	30	29	24	23	17	13	8	11	13	17	18	24
RAIN/INCHES	0.0	0.4	1.2	3.7	4.2	6.4	12.9	11.4	6.0	1.5	0.3	0.0
HUMIDITY/%	68	67	68	69	76	79	82	84	80	72	69	67
BLOOM SEASON				**								
DAYS CLR @ 6AM	7	5	5	10	2	1	1	1	1	6	5	3
DAYS CLR @ 12PM	19	13	10	5	1	0	0	0	1	5	7	18
RAIN/MM	0	10	30	94	107	163	328	290	152	38	8	0
°C AVG MAX	19.4	21.7	21.7	24.4	23.9	22.4	18.9	21.1	21.1	20.6	18.3	16.7
°C AVG MIN	2.8	5.4	8.2	11.5	14.3	14.9	14.3	14.9	13.7	11.0	8.2	3.2
DIURNAL RANGE	16.6	16.3	13.5	12.9	9.6	7.5	4.6	6.2	7.4	9.6	10.1	13.5
S/HEMISPHERE	JUL	AUG	SEP	OCT	NOV	DEC	JAN	FEB	MAR	APR	MAY	JUN

Cultural Recommendations

LIGHT: 2500–3500 fc.

TEMPERATURES: Summer days average 66–72°F (19–22°C), and nights average 58–59°F (14–15°C), with a diurnal range of 8–13°F (5–8°C). The warmest temperatures occur in spring, when days average 71–76°F (22–24°C) and nights average 47–58°F (8–14°C), with a diurnal range of 17–24°F (10–14°C).

HUMIDITY: 80–85% in summer and early autumn, dropping to near 70% from late autumn into spring.

WATER: Rainfall is moderate to heavy from late spring through summer, but conditions are quite dry in winter. Cultivated plants should be watered often while actively growing, with only sight drying allowed between waterings. Water should be gradually reduced after new growths mature in autumn.

FERTILIZER: ¼–½ recommended strength, applied weekly. A high-nitrogen fertilizer is beneficial from spring to midsummer, but a fertilizer high in phosphates should be used in late summer and autumn.

REST PERIOD: Winter days average 62–71°F (17–22°C), and nights average 37–42°F (3–5°C), with a diurnal range of 24–30°F (14–17°C). A less severe rest, however, might prove sufficient in cultivation. Rainfall is low for 4–6 months in late autumn and winter, but additional moisture is available from heavy dew, fog, and mist during most of the season. In cultivation, water should be reduced and the plants allowed to dry out between waterings. They should not remain completely dry for extended periods, however. Occasional early morning mistings between waterings may help keep the plants from becoming too dry. Fertilizer should be eliminated until water is increased in spring. In the habitat, light is highest in winter.

GROWING MEDIA: Plants may be mounted on tree-fern or cork slabs or potted in small pots filled with any open, fast-draining medium. Repotting is best done in early spring when new roots are growing.

MISCELLANEOUS NOTES: The bloom season shown in the climate table is based on reports from the habitat.

Plant and Flower Information

PLANT SIZE AND TYPE: A 6–8 in. (15–20 cm) sympodial epiphyte.

PSEUDOBULB: 6–8 in. (15–20 cm) long. The hairy, clustered stems are often angled at the internodes.

LEAVES: 4 per growth. The notched leaves, which are 1.2–2.0 in. (3–5 cm) long, are covered with hairs.

INFLORESCENCE: Very short. Inflorescences emerge from nodes near the apex of leafy and leafless pseudobulbs.

FLOWERS: 1 per inflorescence. The flowers are 2.0–2.4 in. (5–6 cm) across. The pointed sepals and rounded petals are white. The 3-lobed lip is white with reddish brown markings and many keels on the notched midlobe.

REFERENCES: 225, 447, 448, 454.

PHOTOS/DRAWINGS: 454.

Dendrobium multilobatum Guillaumin. See *D. oppositifolium* (Kränzlin) Hallé. REFERENCES: 173, 230.

Dendrobium multiramosum Ames

ORIGIN/HABITAT: The Philippines. Plants grow in Benguet and Rizal provinces on Luzon Island at 350–650 ft. (100–200 m).

CLIMATE: Station #98427, Manila, Luzon, Philippines, Lat. 14.5°N, Lat. 121.0°E, at 74 ft. (23 m). Temperatures are calculated for an elevation of 500 ft. (150 m), resulting in probable extremes of 100°F (38°C) and 57°F (14°C).

N/HEMISPHERE	JAN	FEB	MAR	APR	MAY	JUN	JUL	AUG	SEP	OCT	NOV	DEC
°F AVG MAX	85	87	90	92	92	90	87	86	87	87	86	85
°F AVG MIN	68	68	70	72	74	74	74	74	74	73	71	69
DIURNAL RANGE	17	19	20	20	18	16	13	12	13	14	15	16
RAIN/INCHES	0.9	0.5	0.7	1.3	5.1	10.0	17.0	16.6	14.0	7.6	5.7	2.6
HUMIDITY/%	77	73	70	68	71	81	84	86	87	84	82	79
BLOOM SEASON	*				*							
DAYS CLR @ 8AM	6	9	14	14	10	3	2	1	1	6	7	6
DAYS CLR @ 2PM	3	6	10	10	8	2	1	1	0	2	2	3
RAIN/MM	23	13	18	33	130	254	432	422	356	193	145	66
°C AVG MAX	29.2	30.3	32.0	33.1	33.1	32.0	30.3	29.8	30.3	30.3	29.8	29.2
°C AVG MIN	19.8	19.8	20.9	22.0	23.1	23.1	23.1	23.1	23.1	22.6	21.4	20.3
DIURNAL RANGE	9.4	10.5	11.1	11.1	10.0	8.9	7.2	6.7	7.2	7.7	8.4	8.9
S/HEMISPHERE	JUL	AUG	SEP	OCT	NOV	DEC	JAN	FEB	MAR	APR	MAY	JUN

Cultural Recommendations

LIGHT: 2000–3000 fc.

TEMPERATURES: Throughout the year, days average 85–92°F (29–33°C), and nights average 68–74°F (20–23°C), with a diurnal range of 12–20°F (7–11°C).

HUMIDITY: 80–85% in summer and autumn, dropping to near 70% for 3–4 months in late winter and spring.

WATER: Rainfall is heavy in summer and autumn, but conditions are dry in winter. Cultivated plants should be kept moist during the growing season, but water should be gradually reduced in autumn.

FERTILIZER: ¼–½ recommended strength. A balanced fertilizer should be applied weekly to biweekly throughout the growing season

REST PERIOD: Growing temperatures should be maintained all year. Rainfall is low for 3–4 months in winter, but additional moisture is available from frequent heavy dew. In cultivation, water should be reduced and the plants allowed to dry out between waterings. They should not remain dry for extended periods, however. Fertilizer should also be reduced or eliminated anytime water is reduced. In the habitat, light is highest in winter.

GROWING MEDIA: Plants may be mounted on tree-fern or cork slabs if humidity is high and plants are watered at least once daily in summer. When plants are potted, any open, fast-draining medium may be used. Repotting may be done anytime new roots are growing.

MISCELLANEOUS NOTES: The bloom season shown in the climate table is based on reports from the habitat. Plants that produce flowers which last a single day commonly bloom several times during the year. Flowering usually occurs 7–14 days after a sudden 10°F (5°C) drop in daytime temperatures.

Plant and Flower Information

PLANT SIZE AND TYPE: A 16 in. (40 cm) sympodial epiphyte.

PSEUDOBULB: 16 in. (40 cm) long. The very slender stems are thickened at the base with deep grooves and furrows. They are covered with thin, grayish sheaths. Rooting branches form every 1.2–1.6 in. (3–4 cm).

LEAVES: The widely spaced leaves are 1.6–3.5 in. (4–9 cm) long. They are linear, terete, and rigid.

INFLORESCENCE: The branching inflorescences emerge from the leafless apical portion of the stem.

FLOWERS: 1 on each of 3 branches. The flowers are 0.8 in. (2 cm) across. They are greenish-yellow with orange in the center of the scalloped lip. The triangular lateral sepals are pointed and hood-shaped at the apex. The dorsal sepal is elliptic. Petals are elliptical and rounded at the tip. The 3-lobed lip is wedge-shaped. The sidelobes have red stripes. Blossoms last a single day.

REFERENCES: 12, 222, 296, 536.

Dendrobium multistriatum J. J. Smith

ORIGIN/HABITAT: Irian Jaya (western New Guinea). Plants were collected along the Noord River and south of Geluks Hill.

CLIMATE: Station #97796, Kokenau (Kokonau), Irian Jaya, Lat. 4.7°S, Long. 136.4°E, at 10 ft. (3 m). Record extreme temperatures are not available for this location.

N/HEMISPHERE	JAN	FEB	MAR	APR	MAY	JUN	JUL	AUG	SEP	OCT	NOV	DEC
°F AVG MAX	83	83	86	88	90	89	89	89	90	88	87	84
°F AVG MIN	73	73	74	74	74	75	74	74	74	74	74	73
DIURNAL RANGE	10	10	12	14	16	14	15	15	16	14	13	11
RAIN/INCHES	18.4	15.8	18.9	11.6	9.7	10.6	11.5	15.7	11.6	11.6	16.0	19.9
HUMIDITY/%	N/A											
BLOOM SEASON	N/A											
DAYS CLR	N/A											
RAIN/MM	467	401	479	295	245	269	293	400	294	296	407	506
°C AVG MAX	28.6	28.4	30.2	31.1	32.1	31.9	31.9	31.7	32.0	31.4	30.7	28.7
°C AVG MIN	22.7	22.6	23.3	23.4	23.5	23.7	23.6	23.5	23.4	23.4	23.5	23.0
DIURNAL RANGE	5.9	5.8	6.9	7.7	8.6	8.2	8.3	8.2	8.6	8.0	7.2	5.7
S/HEMISPHERE	JUL	AUG	SEP	OCT	NOV	DEC	JAN	FEB	MAR	APR	MAY	JUN

Cultural Recommendations

LIGHT: 2500–3500 fc.

TEMPERATURES: Throughout the year, days average 83–90°F (29–32°C), and nights average 73–75°F (23–24°C), with a diurnal range of 10–16°F (6–9°C).

HUMIDITY: Information is not available for this location. However, records from nearby locations indicate that humidity probably averages near 85% year-round.

WATER: Rainfall is very heavy all year. Cultivated plants should be kept evenly moist but not soggy. Warm water might be beneficial.

FERTILIZER: ¼–½ recommended strength. A balanced fertilizer should be applied weekly to biweekly throughout the year.

REST PERIOD: Growing conditions should be maintained year-round. Water and fertilizer may be reduced somewhat in winter, especially for plants cultivated in the dark, short-day conditions common in temperate latitudes. They should never be allowed to dry out completely, however.

GROWING MEDIA: Plants may be placed in small pots filled with any open medium that can be kept moist but does not become soggy. Repotting may be done anytime new roots are growing.

Plant and Flower Information

PLANT SIZE AND TYPE: A sympodial epiphyte of unreported size.

PSEUDOBULB: The elongated stems are flattened.

LEAVES: Each oblong-ovate leaf is 3.5–4.0 in. (9–10 cm) long with 2 teeth at the apex.

FLOWERS: 2 per inflorescence. The flowers are 0.7 in. (1.8 cm) long. They are covered with dots. Flower color was not included in the original description. The dorsal sepal and petals are linear. The lateral sepals are incurved and somewhat triangular. The curved lip is 3-lobed with a longitudinal row of hairs.

REFERENCES: 220, 254, 445, 470.

Dendrobium munificum (Finet) Hallé

AKA: *D. muricatum* Finet var. *munificum* Finet. The name *D. munificum* was first mentioned by Schlechter (ref. 437), but he did not execute a formal transfer.

ORIGIN/HABITAT: New Caledonia. Plants grow on the southern half of the island northeast of Conception near Mt. Mou at 650–2300 ft. (200–700 m). They are frequently found near streams as high as 50 ft. (15 m) above the ground on the trunks and branches of moss-covered trees in shady, humid forests.

CLIMATE: Station #91590, La Tontouta, New Caledonia, Lat. 22.0°S, Long. 166.2°E, at 52 ft. (16 m). Temperatures are calculated for an elevation of 1650 ft. (500 m), resulting in probable extremes of 90°F (32°C) and 42°F (5°C).

N/HEMISPHERE	JAN	FEB	MAR	APR	MAY	JUN	JUL	AUG	SEP	OCT	NOV	DEC
°F AVG MAX	69	70	72	75	79	81	82	82	79	75	73	71
°F AVG MIN	53	53	54	56	59	62	65	65	65	61	56	54
DIURNAL RANGE	16	17	18	19	20	19	17	17	14	14	17	17
RAIN/INCHES	3.6	2.6	2.5	2.0	2.4	2.6	3.7	5.1	5.7	5.2	4.4	3.7
HUMIDITY/%	78	76	74	71	67	72	72	75	81	79	78	76
BLOOM SEASON					*			*				
DAYS CLR @ 11AM	8	7	7	11	10	6	4	3	5	7	6	7
DAYS CLR @ 5PM	8	9	5	9	8	3	3	1	2	3	4	6
RAIN/MM	91	66	64	51	61	66	94	130	145	132	112	94
°C AVG MAX	20.4	21.0	22.1	23.8	26.0	27.1	27.6	27.6	26.0	23.8	22.6	21.5
°C AVG MIN	11.5	11.5	12.1	13.2	14.9	16.5	18.2	18.2	18.2	16.0	13.2	12.1
DIURNAL RANGE	8.9	9.5	10.0	10.6	11.1	10.6	9.4	9.4	7.8	7.8	9.4	9.4
S/HEMISPHERE	JUL	AUG	SEP	OCT	NOV	DEC	JAN	FEB	MAR	APR	MAY	JUN

Cultural Recommendations

LIGHT: 1500–2500 fc.

TEMPERATURES: Summer days average 81–82°F (27–28°C), and nights average 62–65°F (17–18°C), with a diurnal range of 17–19°F (9–11°C).

HUMIDITY: 70–80% year-round at the weather station, but values in the humid habitat are probably greater.

WATER: At the weather station, rainfall is relatively low and consistent all year, but rainfall amounts may be greater in the higher elevation habitat. However, rain in this region normally falls as heavy showers, and plants might be healthiest if they are thoroughly saturated, then allowed to dry slightly before being watered again.

FERTILIZER: ¼–½ recommended strength, applied weekly. A high-nitrogen fertilizer is beneficial from spring to midsummer, but a fertilizer high in phosphates should be used in late summer and autumn.

REST PERIOD: Winter days average 69–72°F (20–22°C), and nights average 53–54°F (12°C), with a diurnal range of 16–18°F (9–10°C). High and low temperatures decline simultaneously, resulting in little change in the diurnal range. Conditions in the habitat are a little drier in winter, and water should be reduced somewhat for cultivated plants. Plants should be allowed to become a little drier between waterings in winter than in summer but should never dry out completely. In the habitat, light is highest in winter.

GROWING MEDIA: Plants may be mounted on tree-fern or cork slabs if humidity is high and plants are watered at least once daily in summer. When plants are potted, any open, fast-draining medium may be used. Repotting is best done in early spring when new roots are growing.

MISCELLANEOUS NOTES: The bloom season shown in the climate table is based on reports from the habitat.

Plant and Flower Information

PLANT SIZE AND TYPE: A 20 in. (50 cm) sympodial epiphyte. Although similar, *D. munificum* is more vigorous and larger in all parts than *D. muricatum*.

PSEUDOBULB: 6 in. (15 cm) long. The pseudobulbs have long fibers at the nodes. The roots, which have a rough outer surface, may reach a length of 39 in. (100 cm).

LEAVES: 2–3 at the apex of each growth. The dark green, ovate leaves are 8–14 in. (20–36 cm) long. They are thick, fleshy, and persistent.

INFLORESCENCE: 12 in. (30 cm) long. The lateral inflorescences emerge from nodes below the apex of the stem. They are pendent and branching. Up to 3 inflorescences may be produced by each of several pseudobulbs.

FLOWERS: Up to 150 per inflorescence. The large, showy flowers are 1.0–1.4 in. (2.5–3.5 cm) across. Sepals and petals are greenish yellow with dark red blotches. The lip is very dark red with bright yellow at the tip. It is uppermost, ruffled, and rounded at the apex of the midlobe. The blossoms close at night and reopen in the morning.

REFERENCES: 37, 54, 118, 173, 210, 221, 233, 437, 445.

PHOTOS/DRAWINGS: *37,* 173, 210.

Dendrobium muricatum Finet

AKA: Hallé (ref. 173) includes *D. muricatum* Finet var. *munificum* Finet as a synonym of *D. munificum* (Finet) Hallé.

ORIGIN/HABITAT: New Caledonia. This uncommon plant grows on trees in sunny locations at 1300–4250 ft. (400–1300 m) in the humid, mountain forests of the Northern District near Oubatche.

CLIMATE: Station #91592, Noumea, New Caledonia, Lat. 22.3°S, Long. 166.5°E, at 246 ft. (75 m). Temperatures are calculated for an elevation of 3000 ft. (910 m), resulting in probable extremes of 90°F (32°C) and 43°F (6°C).

N/HEMISPHERE	JAN	FEB	MAR	APR	MAY	JUN	JUL	AUG	SEP	OCT	NOV	DEC
°F AVG MAX	67	67	69	71	74	77	77	76	76	74	70	68
°F AVG MIN	53	52	54	56	59	61	63	64	63	61	57	55
DIURNAL RANGE	14	15	15	15	15	16	14	12	13	13	13	13
RAIN/INCHES	3.6	2.6	2.5	2.0	2.4	2.6	3.7	5.1	5.7	5.2	4.4	3.7
HUMIDITY/%	73	70	69	67	68	69	71	74	75	76	73	73
BLOOM SEASON	*					*			*	*	*	*
DAYS CLR @ 11AM	7	9	9	15	12	10	7	6	7	7	7	7
DAYS CLR @ 5PM	7	11	6	11	7	6	5	4	4	5	3	7
RAIN/MM	91	66	64	51	61	66	94	130	145	132	112	94
°C AVG MAX	19.4	19.4	20.5	21.6	23.3	25.0	25.0	24.4	24.4	23.3	21.1	20.0
°C AVG MIN	11.6	11.1	12.2	13.3	15.0	16.1	17.2	17.7	17.2	16.1	13.8	12.7
DIURNAL RANGE	7.8	8.3	8.3	8.3	8.3	8.9	7.8	6.7	7.2	7.2	7.3	7.3
S/HEMISPHERE	JUL	AUG	SEP	OCT	NOV	DEC	JAN	FEB	MAR	APR	MAY	JUN

Cultural Recommendations

LIGHT: 2500–3500 fc. Days are frequently clear, indicating relatively high light.

TEMPERATURES: Summer days average 76–77°F (24–25°C), and nights average 61–64°F (16–18°C), with a diurnal range of 12–16°F (7–9°C). The diurnal range fluctuates only 4°F (2°C) throughout the year.

HUMIDITY: 70–75% year-round.

WATER: At the weather station, rainfall is relatively low and consistent all year, but rainfall amounts may be greater in the higher elevation habitat. However, rain in this region normally falls as heavy showers, and plants might be healthiest if they are thoroughly saturated, then allowed to dry slightly before being watered again.

FERTILIZER: ¼–½ recommended strength, applied weekly. A high-nitrogen fertilizer is beneficial from spring to midsummer, but a fertilizer high in phosphates should be used in late summer and autumn.

REST PERIOD: Winter days average 67–70°F (19–21°C), and nights average 52–59°F (11–15°C), with a diurnal range of 13–15°F (7–8°C). Day and night temperatures decline simultaneously, resulting in little change in the diurnal range. Conditions in the habitat are a little drier in winter, and water should be reduced somewhat for cultivated plants. Plants should be allowed to become a little drier between waterings than in summer but should never dry out completely. In the habitat, light is highest in winter.

GROWING MEDIA: Plants may be mounted on tree fern or cork slabs if humidity is high and plants are watered at least once daily in summer. When plants are potted, any open, fast-draining medium may be used. Repotting is best done in early spring when new roots are growing.

MISCELLANEOUS NOTES: The bloom season shown in the climate table is based on reports from the habitat. Cultivated plants bloom in late summer. Reports indicate that *D. muricatum* blooms before *D. munificum*.

Plant and Flower Information

PLANT SIZE AND TYPE: A 12 in. (30 cm) sympodial epiphyte. The plant is described as very similar to *D. munificum* but smaller in all parts.

PSEUDOBULB: 3 in. (8 cm) long. The pseudobulbs, which consist of about 10 short nodes, have numerous long fibers.

LEAVES: 2 per growth. The elliptic leaves are usually 8–10 in. (20–25 cm) long. They are somewhat coarse with heavy ribs.

INFLORESCENCE: 12 in. (30 cm) long. The slender inflorescences emerge from nodes below the apex of the pseudobulb. They are branched and somewhat densely flowered on the upper portion of each branch.

FLOWERS: 8–25 per inflorescence. The flowers are 0.5 in. (1.3 cm) across. They are purplish with maroon or rouge markings on the lip. Sepals and petals are narrowly lanceolate and, except for the dorsal sepal, they are somewhat sickle-shaped. The lip is uppermost with a thickened, ruffled margin. Blossoms close at night and reopen in the morning.

REFERENCES: 118, 173, 179, 190, 219, 254, 432, 445.

Dendrobium murkelense

PHOTOS/DRAWINGS: 173, 254.

Dendrobium murkelense J. J. Smith. See *D. nebularum* Schlechter. REFERENCES: 224, 385.

Dendrobium muscicola Lindley. Often considered a synonym of *Eria muscicola* Lindley. In 1982, Seidenfaden in *Opera Botanica* #62 discussed the confusion regarding the name *D. muscicola*. REFERENCES: 102, 190, 216, 254, 277.

Dendrobium musciferum Schlechter. See *D. macrophyllum* A. Richard. REFERENCES: 83, 152, 179, 221, 270, 271, 304, 307, 430, 437, 445.

Dendrobium mutabile (Blume) Lindley

AKA: *Onchium mutabile* Blume, *O. rigidum* Blume. Other synonyms include *Dendrobium rigescens* Miquel, *D. rigidum* Lindley, *D. sclerophyllum* Lindley, and *D. triadenium* Lindley. The name is sometimes spelled *D. mutable*. In addition to the preceding synonyms, Kränzlin (ref. 254) includes *D. firmum* Steudel.

ORIGIN/HABITAT: Western Java and Sumatra. Plants usually grow on isolated trees along mountain roads. They are found on Mt. Halimun, just below 3300 ft. (1000 m). In Java, plants are rather common at 1650–5900 ft. (500–1800 m) on trees or rocks in lava-streams on Mt. Guntur. Comber (ref. 75) indicates that the habitat is limited to Java and Sumatra, but Bose and Bhattacharjee (ref. 46) reported it in southern India, where it flowers throughout the year.

CLIMATE: Station #96755, Bogor, Java, Indonesia, at Lat. 6.5°S, Long. 106.8°E, at 558 ft. (170 m). Temperatures are calculated for an elevation of 3000 ft. (910 m), resulting in probable extremes of 88°F (31°C) and 58°F (14°C).

N/HEMISPHERE	JAN	FEB	MAR	APR	MAY	JUN	JUL	AUG	SEP	OCT	NOV	DEC
°F AVG MAX	78	79	80	80	79	77	76	76	77	78	79	78
°F AVG MIN	65	65	65	66	66	66	66	66	66	67	67	66
DIURNAL RANGE	13	14	15	14	13	11	10	10	11	11	12	12
RAIN/INCHES	2.1	1.0	0.5	5.0	8.1	18.8	23.7	20.2	14.4	12.0	11.9	3.4
HUMIDITY/%	72	68	65	66	74	79	84	84	81	79	77	75
BLOOM SEASON					*	*	*	*	*			
DAYS CLR @ 7AM	14	14	14	11	5	3	1	2	4	6	10	12
DAYS CLR @ 1PM	9	10	8	5	1	1	0	0	1	1	3	7
RAIN/MM	53	25	13	127	206	478	602	513	366	305	302	86
°C AVG MAX	25.5	26.1	26.6	26.6	26.1	25.0	24.4	24.4	25.0	25.5	26.1	25.5
°C AVG MIN	18.3	18.3	18.3	18.9	18.9	18.9	18.9	18.9	18.9	19.4	19.4	18.9
DIURNAL RANGE	7.2	7.8	8.3	7.7	7.2	6.1	5.5	5.5	6.1	6.1	6.7	6.6
S/HEMISPHERE	JUL	AUG	SEP	OCT	NOV	DEC	JAN	FEB	MAR	APR	MAY	JUN

Cultural Recommendations

LIGHT: 1800–2400 fc. Direct sunlight should be avoided.

TEMPERATURES: Throughout the year, days average 76–80°F (24–27°C), and nights average 65–67°F (18–19°C), with a diurnal range of 10–15°F (6–8°C). The warmest temperatures occur in spring. Because extremes are very close to the average highs and lows, plants may not tolerate wide temperature fluctuations.

HUMIDITY: 75–85% year-round.

WATER: Rainfall is very heavy from spring to autumn, but conditions are very dry for 2–3 months in winter. During the growing season, plants should never be allowed to dry out completely, but water should be gradually reduced in late autumn.

FERTILIZER: ¼–½ recommended strength, applied weekly. A high-nitrogen fertilizer is beneficial from spring to midsummer, but a fertilizer high in phosphates should be used in late summer and autumn.

REST PERIOD: Growing conditions should be maintained all year, but rainfall is very low for 2–3 winter months. In cultivation, water should be reduced and the plants allowed to dry out between waterings. They should not remain dry for prolonged periods, however. Fertilizer may be reduced or eliminated anytime the plant is not actively growing. In the habitat, light is highest in winter.

GROWING MEDIA: Plants may be mounted on tree-fern or cork slabs if humidity is high and plants are watered at least once daily in summer. When plants are potted, any open, fast-draining medium may be used. Repotting may be done anytime new roots are growing.

MISCELLANEOUS NOTES: The bloom season shown in the climate table is based on cultivation records. Growers indicate that *D. mutabile* often blooms more than once a year. Although it is closely related to *D. spathilingue* J. J. Smith, which is found only in the eastern part of Java, Comber (ref. 75) notes that *D. mutabile* is found only in the western and central part of the island. The habitats of the 2 species do not overlap.

Plant and Flower Information

PLANT SIZE AND TYPE: An 8–12 in. (20–30 cm) sympodial epiphyte or lithophyte. Plants sometimes reach a length of 36 in. (91 cm).

PSEUDOBULB: 8–12 in. (20–30 cm) long. The slender, crowded stems, which are somewhat thickened in the middle, are erect to drooping. They frequently branch, and each branch develops roots. Canes are striped with red and become furrowed with age.

LEAVES: 3–10 along each branch. The evergreen leaves are 2–4 in. (5–10 cm) long. They are lanceolate, blunt at the apex, and tinged with violet on the underside.

INFLORESCENCE: 7 in. (18 cm) long. Inflorescences are borne from leafless nodes at the apex of the stem. The racemes are usually erect and often branch. The blossoms are crowded on the inflorescence.

FLOWERS: 4–15 per inflorescence. The flowers, which have a nice full form, are approximately 1.2 in. (3 cm) across. The sepals are pointed. The round petals have wavy margins. Segments may be white, sometimes with a rose flush, or almost completely violet. The white lip has a raised yellow crest and a deep notch on the margin of the midlobe. The spur is short. Color is somewhat variable. The blossoms last about 2 weeks. They are not fragrant.

HYBRIDIZING NOTES: Chromosome counts as *D. mutabile* are $2n = 2x$ (ref. 504, 580) and $2n = 40$ (ref. 152, 243).

REFERENCES: 25, 46, 74, 75, 152, 179, 180, 190, 210, 216, 243, 254, 277, 310, 317, 445, 469, 504, 541, 570, 580.

PHOTOS/DRAWINGS: 74, 75, 210, 469.

Dendrobium myosurus (Forst. f.) Swartz. Now considered a synonym of *Octarrhena myosurus* (G. Forster) P. F. Hunt [*Oberonia myosurus* (G. Forster) Lindley]. REFERENCES: 211, 216, 254, 369.

Dendrobium myrticola Kränzlin. See *D. closterium* Rchb. f. REFERENCES: 173, 224.

Dendrobium mystroglossum Schlechter

ORIGIN/HABITAT: Papua New Guinea. Plants grow in the Sepik River region at 3300–4900 ft. (1000–1500 m).

CLIMATE: Station #200004, Ambunti, Papua New Guinea, Lat. 4.2°S, Long. 142.8°E, at 164 ft. (50 m). Temperatures are calculated for an elevation of 4000 ft. (1220 m), resulting in probable extremes of 86°F (30°C) and 39°F (4°C).

Dendrobium mystroglossum

N/HEMISPHERE	JAN	FEB	MAR	APR	MAY	JUN	JUL	AUG	SEP	OCT	NOV	DEC
°F AVG MAX	75	77	77	77	78	77	77	77	77	77	77	76
°F AVG MIN	59	60	61	60	60	60	59	60	60	60	60	61
DIURNAL RANGE	16	17	16	17	18	17	18	17	17	17	17	15
RAIN/INCHES	6.4	7.4	7.7	8.5	9.2	9.4	10.9	10.2	12.2	10.4	8.3	5.2
HUMIDITY/%	N/A											
BLOOM SEASON	*	*										*
DAYS CLR	N/A											
RAIN/MM	163	188	196	216	234	239	277	259	310	264	211	132
°C AVG MAX	24.1	25.2	25.2	25.2	25.7	25.2	25.2	25.2	25.2	25.2	25.2	24.6
°C AVG MIN	15.2	15.7	16.3	15.7	15.7	15.7	15.2	15.7	15.7	15.7	15.7	16.3
DIURNAL RANGE	8.9	9.5	8.9	9.5	10.0	9.5	10.0	9.5	9.5	9.5	9.5	8.3
S/HEMISPHERE	JUL	AUG	SEP	OCT	NOV	DEC	JAN	FEB	MAR	APR	MAY	JUN

Cultural Recommendations

LIGHT: 2000–3000 fc.

TEMPERATURES: Throughout the year, days average 75–78°F (24–26°C), and nights average 59–61°F (15–16°C), with a diurnal range of 15–18°F (8–10°C).

HUMIDITY: Information is not available for this location. However, records from nearby locations indicate that humidity probably averages near 80% year-round.

WATER: Rainfall is heavy all year, with the greatest amounts falling in summer and early autumn. Cultivated plants should be kept moist.

FERTILIZER: ¼–½ recommended strength. A balanced fertilizer should be applied weekly to biweekly throughout the year.

REST PERIOD: Growing conditions should be maintained all year. Water and fertilizer should be reduced somewhat for plants cultivated in the dark, short-day conditions common in temperate-latitude winters, but they should never be allowed to dry out completely.

GROWING MEDIA: Plants may be mounted on cork or tree-fern slabs if humidity is high and plants are watered at least once daily in summer. When plants are potted, any open, fast-draining medium may be used. Repotting may be done anytime new roots are growing.

MISCELLANEOUS NOTES: The bloom season shown in the climate table is based on collection reports.

Plant and Flower Information

PLANT SIZE AND TYPE: A 12–20 in. (30–50 cm) sympodial epiphyte.

PSEUDOBULB: 12–20 in. (30–50 cm) long. The slender, cylindrical stems emerge from a very short rhizome.

LEAVES: The leaves are 1.8–3.1 in. (4.5–8.0 cm) long.

INFLORESCENCE: Short.

FLOWERS: The flowers are about 0.8 in. (2 cm) across. They may be orange-red or red-brown. Blossoms have oblong-elliptic sepals and somewhat oblong petals. The lip is more or less obovate, with a serrated, incurved margin.

REFERENCES: 223, 443.

Dendrobium nabawanense J. J. Wood and A. Lamb

ORIGIN/HABITAT: Borneo. Plants were found at 1750–2300 ft. (540–700 m) near Nabawan in Sabah, and on Gunung Nicola in the Lahad Datu District. This species usually grows on the lower branches of trees which occur on infertile, acid, sandstone soils. Other plants in the vicinity include Rhododendron, ferns, and other orchids.

CLIMATE: Station #49613, Tabunan, Sabah, Borneo, Lat. 5.7°N, Long. 116.4°E, at 1200 ft. (366 m). Temperatures are calculated for an elevation of 2000 ft. (610 m), resulting in probable extremes of 95°F (35°C) and 51°F (11°C).

N/HEMISPHERE	JAN	FEB	MAR	APR	MAY	JUN	JUL	AUG	SEP	OCT	NOV	DEC
°F AVG MAX	83	84	86	87	87	86	86	86	86	85	84	83
°F AVG MIN	64	62	63	64	65	64	63	63	64	64	64	65
DIURNAL RANGE	19	22	23	23	22	22	23	23	22	21	20	18
RAIN/INCHES	5.8	3.7	5.8	7.5	8.2	7.3	5.1	4.9	6.4	7.0	6.8	6.0
HUMIDITY/%	N/A											
BLOOM SEASON		*			*			*				
DAYS CLR	N/A											
RAIN/MM	147	94	147	191	208	185	130	124	163	178	173	152
°C AVG MAX	28.3	28.9	30.0	30.6	30.6	30.2	30.1	30.0	30.0	29.4	28.9	28.3
°C AVG MIN	17.8	16.9	17.4	18.0	18.5	18.0	17.4	17.4	18.0	18.0	18.0	18.5
DIURNAL RANGE	10.5	12.0	12.6	12.6	12.1	12.2	12.7	12.6	12.0	11.4	10.9	9.8
S/HEMISPHERE	JUL	AUG	SEP	OCT	NOV	DEC	JAN	FEB	MAR	APR	MAY	JUN

Cultural Recommendations

LIGHT: 2000–3000 fc.

TEMPERATURES: Throughout the year, days average 83–87°F (28–31°C), and nights average 62–65°F (17–19°C), with a diurnal range of 18–23°F (10–13°C). Growers indicate that plants grow well at 60°F (16°C) nights.

HUMIDITY: Information is not available for this location. However, records from nearby locations indicate that humidity is probably 80–85% year-round.

WATER: Rainfall is moderate to heavy all year with a brief, slightly drier period in winter. Cultivated plants should be allowed to dry slightly between waterings.

FERTILIZER: ¼–½ recommended strength. A balanced fertilizer should be applied weekly to biweekly throughout the year.

REST PERIOD: Growing conditions should be maintained all year. Water should be reduced slightly in winter, but plants should never be allowed to dry out completely. Fertilizer should be reduced anytime plants are not actively growing. In the habitat, seasonal light variation is minor.

GROWING MEDIA: Plants may be mounted on tree-fern or cork slabs if humidity is high and plants are watered at least once daily in summer. When plants are potted, any open, fast-draining medium may be used. Repotting is best done in early spring when new roots begin to grow.

MISCELLANEOUS NOTES: The bloom season shown in the climate table is based on collection times.

Plant and Flower Information

PLANT SIZE AND TYPE: A 9.5–17.7 in. (24–45 cm) sympodial terrestrial or epiphyte which occasionally grows to a height of 38 in. (60 cm).

PSEUDOBULB: 9.5–38.0 in. (24–60 cm) long. The erect stems are slightly zig zag.

LEAVES: Several to many on the apical portion of the stems. Leaves are usually 2.4–3.1 in. (6–8 cm) long but may be as small as 1.4 in. (3.5 cm). They are held at right angles and arranged in 2 rows on opposite sides of the stem. The blades are linear-lanceolate, unequally bilobed, and narrowly pointed at the tips. New sheaths have a black, flattened, scalelike covering that disintegrates with age.

INFLORESCENCE: 0.4 in (1 cm) long. Flowers appear to rest on the stem. Inflorescences, which may be horizontal to nearly erect, emerge from the base of the scale-covered sheaths opposite the leaves.

FLOWERS: 1 per inflorescence. The white flowers are 0.8 in. (2 cm) across with stiff sepals and petals that open widely. Blossoms are not fragrant. The dorsal sepal is ovate-elliptic, pointed, and recurved. Lateral sepals are triangular-ovate. The straight spur, which is 0.2 in. (0.5 cm) long, is white with salmon-pink veins. The narrower, tongue-shaped petals, which are recurved at the tip, are uneven along the margin except near the base. The lip is fleshy, waxy, and fiddle-shaped. It is white with ochre-brown veins on the inside and scattered hairs along either side of the center line near the base. The midlobe, which is kidney-shaped and shallowly notched at the apex, is flushed with apricot yellow. The rather flat, 3-ribbed disc is smooth, shiny, and pale ochre-brown.

REFERENCES: Wood, J. J. and P. Cribb. 1994. A checklist of the orchids of Borneo. Royal Botanic Gardens, Kew.

PHOTOS/DRAWINGS: Wood, J. J. and P. Cribb. 1994. A checklist of the orchids of Borneo. Royal Botanic Gardens, Kew.

Dendrobium nakaharaei Schlechter

AKA: Sometimes spelled *D. nakaharai,* it is now considered a synonym of *Epigeneium nakaharaei* (Schlechter) Summerhayes; but plants are commonly sold and grown as *Dendrobium*.

ORIGIN/HABITAT: Endemic to Taiwan. Plants grow on tree trunks and large tree limbs. They are usually found in moist, semishady, broad-leaved forests at 3300–6550 ft. (1000–2000 m).

CLIMATE: Station #46766, Taitung, Taiwan, Lat. 22.8°N, Long. 121.2°E, at 31 ft. (9 m). Temperatures are calculated for an elevation of 3300 ft. (1000 m), resulting in probable extremes of 89°F (32°C) and 37°F (3°C).

N/HEMISPHERE	JAN	FEB	MAR	APR	MAY	JUN	JUL	AUG	SEP	OCT	NOV	DEC
°F AVG MAX	62	63	67	70	74	76	79	77	75	71	68	64
°F AVG MIN	48	49	52	56	60	62	63	63	62	59	55	51
DIURNAL RANGE	14	14	15	14	14	14	16	14	13	12	13	13
RAIN/INCHES	1.1	1.2	1.1	3.0	5.3	10.0	6.4	11.7	12.4	4.8	5.4	2.3
HUMIDITY/%	77	78	79	81	82	84	80	83	84	80	77	77
BLOOM SEASON										*	*	*
DAYS CLR @ 8AM	4	5	4	5	6	3	11	8	7	9	7	5
DAYS CLR @ 2PM	3	3	4	4	3	3	8	5	4	4	4	4
RAIN/MM	28	30	28	76	135	254	163	297	315	122	137	58
°C AVG MAX	16.8	17.4	19.6	21.3	23.5	24.6	26.3	25.2	24.0	21.8	20.2	17.9
°C AVG MIN	9.0	9.6	11.3	13.5	15.7	16.8	17.4	17.4	16.8	15.2	12.9	10.7
DIURNAL RANGE	7.8	7.8	8.3	7.8	7.8	7.8	8.9	7.8	7.2	6.6	7.3	7.2
S/HEMISPHERE	JUL	AUG	SEP	OCT	NOV	DEC	JAN	FEB	MAR	APR	MAY	JUN

Cultural Recommendations

LIGHT: 2000–3000 fc.

TEMPERATURES: Summer days average 76–79°F (25–26°C), and nights average 62–63°F (17°C), with a diurnal range of 14–16°F (8–9°C). These temperatures represent the lowest elevations, and therefore the warmest part, of the habitat. Plants should easily adapt to conditions 10°F (6°C) cooler than indicated.

HUMIDITY: 80–85% during summer and autumn, decreasing to 75–80% during winter and spring.

WATER: Rainfall is moderate to heavy in summer and autumn, but conditions are much drier in winter. Cultivated plants should be kept moist while actively growing, but water should be gradually reduced in autumn.

FERTILIZER: ¼–½ recommended strength, applied weekly. A high nitrogen fertilizer is beneficial from spring to midsummer, but a fertilizer high in phosphates should be used in late summer and autumn.

REST PERIOD: Winter days average 62–64°F (17–18°C), and nights average 48–51°F (9–11°C), with a diurnal range of 13–14°F (7–8°C). Again, these values represent the warmest conditions found in the habitat, and plants will adapt to conditions 10°F (6°C) cooler than indicated in the table. In the habitat, rainfall is low in winter, but heavy dew is common. Cultivated plants should be allowed to dry slightly between waterings, but they should not remain dry for extended periods. Water is most beneficial when bright, sunny weather is expected.

GROWING MEDIA: Plants may be mounted on slabs of cork or tree-fern fiber if humidity is high and if water is applied at least daily during the summer. However, most growers prefer to use baskets or shallow bulb pans which are large enough to accommodate the creeping growth habit. If potted, a very open, fast-draining medium is recommended. A mixture of tree-fern fiber and sphagnum produces excellent results. Plants do not tolerate stale medium around the roots, but once established, plants do not like to be disturbed. Therefore, a medium that breaks down very slowly should be used. Repotting is best done only when absolutely necessary. To allow the plant to reestablish as soon as possible, repotting should be done when a flush of new root growth is just starting.

MISCELLANEOUS NOTES: The bloom season shown in the climate table is based on records from the habitat.

Plant and Flower Information

PLANT SIZE AND TYPE: A miniature, mat-forming epiphyte that may be less than 2 in. (5 cm) tall.

PSEUDOBULB: 1 in. (2–3 cm) long. Growths are somewhat widely spaced along a creeping rhizome.

LEAVES: 1. The leaves are about 1.6 (4 cm) long, rigid, and oval-elliptic. A single leaf emerges from the apex of each pseudobulb.

INFLORESCENCE: Short. Inflorescences emerge from the apex of the most recently matured pseudobulbs.

FLOWERS: 1 per inflorescence. The showy, waxy flowers are 1 in. (2.5 cm) across, very large relative to the plant size. The star-shaped blossoms are yellowish with a violet-brown tinge. They have a triangular-ovate dorsal sepal, oblique lateral sepals, and lanceolate petals. The dorsal sepal and petals are lanceolate and nearly erect. The orange-brown lip is shiny. It is recurved at the notched apex with a basal disk and 2 elevated keels. The sidelobes are small and erect.

HYBRIDIZING NOTES: Chromosome count is 2n = 40 (ref. 152, 154, 188).

REFERENCES: 61, 62, 152, 154, 179, 188, 192, 208, 220, 229, 254, 274, 279, 330, 497, 499.

PHOTOS/DRAWINGS: 62, 274, 279, 330, 497.

Dendrobium nanarauticolum Fukuyama.
Sometimes spelled as *D. nanarauticola*, see *D. delicatulum* Kränzlin. REFERENCES: 135, 189, 226, 384, 385.

Dendrobium nanum Hooker f.

ORIGIN/HABITAT: Southern India. Plants grow in the hills of Mysore, Kerala, and Tamil Nadu at 6550–8200 ft. (2000–2500 m).

CLIMATE: Station #43314, Calicut, India, Lat. 11.3°N, Long. 75.8°E, at 17 ft. (5 m). Temperatures are calculated for an elevation of 7000 ft. (2130 m), resulting in probable extremes of 76°F (24°C) and 34°F (1°C).

N/HEMISPHERE	JAN	FEB	MAR	APR	MAY	JUN	JUL	AUG	SEP	OCT	NOV	DEC
°F AVG MAX	65	66	67	68	67	62	59	60	61	63	64	65
°F AVG MIN	48	50	53	55	55	52	51	51	52	52	51	48
DIURNAL RANGE	17	16	14	13	12	10	8	9	9	11	13	17
RAIN/INCHES	0.4	0.2	0.7	3.6	9.3	33.1	32.5	17.2	7.9	10.3	5.5	1.0
HUMIDITY/%	71	73	73	74	82	87	91	91	87	85	77	74
BLOOM SEASON						*	*					
DAYS CLR @ 5AM	19	18	21	12	5	4	2	2	4	4	19	20
DAYS CLR @ 11AM	16	18	23	15	5	3	0	1	6	5	12	14
RAIN/MM	10	5	18	91	236	841	826	437	201	262	140	25
°C AVG MAX	18.3	18.9	19.4	20.0	19.4	16.6	15.0	15.5	16.1	17.2	17.8	18.3
°C AVG MIN	8.9	10.0	11.6	12.8	12.8	11.1	10.5	10.5	11.1	11.1	10.5	8.9
DIURNAL RANGE	9.4	8.9	7.8	7.2	6.6	5.5	4.5	5.0	5.0	6.1	7.3	9.4
S/HEMISPHERE	JUL	AUG	SEP	OCT	NOV	DEC	JAN	FEB	MAR	APR	MAY	JUN

Cultural Recommendations

LIGHT: 3000–4000 fc. The heavy summer cloud cover indicates that some shading is needed from spring through autumn, but light should be as high as the plant can tolerate, short of burning the leaves.

TEMPERATURES: Summer days average 59–62°F (15–17°C), and nights average 51–52°F (11°C), with a diurnal range of 8–10°F (5–6°C). Spring, before the start of the summer monsoon, is the warmest season. Days average 67–68°F (19–20°C), and nights average 53–55°F (12–13°C), with a diurnal range of 12–14°F (7–8°C).

HUMIDITY: 85–90% in summer, decreasing to 70–75% in winter and spring.

WATER: Rainfall is heavy to extremely heavy most of the year, but conditions are very dry for 3–4 months in winter. Cultivated plants should be watered liberally in summer, as often as several times a week during bright, hot weather. Water should be gradually reduced through autumn, greatly reduced in winter, then gradually increased in spring when new growth starts.

FERTILIZER: 1/4–1/2 recommended strength, applied weekly. A high-nitrogen fertilizer is beneficial from spring to midsummer, but a fertilizer high in phosphates should be used in late summer and autumn.

REST PERIOD: Winter days average 65–66°F (18–19°C), and nights average 48–50°F (9–10°C), with a diurnal range of 16–17°F (9°C). For cultivated plants, water should be greatly reduced for 3–4 months. Plants should be allowed to dry out between waterings, but they should not remain completely dry for extended periods. Occasional early morning mistings between waterings may be beneficial, especially on warm, sunny days. Fertilizer should be greatly reduced or eliminated until water is increased in spring. In the habitat, light is highest in winter.

GROWING MEDIA: Growers recommend mounting plants on tree-fern slabs if humidity is high and if plants are watered at least once daily during hot weather. If plants are potted, any open, fast-draining medium may be used. Repotting is best done in late spring when new roots begin to grow.

MISCELLANEOUS NOTES: The bloom season shown in the climate table is based on reports from the habitat.

Plant and Flower Information

PLANT SIZE AND TYPE: A 1.2–3.2 in. (3–8 cm) sympodial epiphyte.

PSEUDOBULB: 0.2–0.8 in. (0.5–2.0 cm) long. Pseudobulbs are ovoid and have a single node.

LEAVES: 2, rarely up to 4 per growth. The oblong-lanceolate leaves are 1.0–2.5 in. (2.5–6.4 cm) long. They are very thick.

INFLORESCENCE: 1.4–3.0 in. (3.5–7.5 cm) long. The racemes arise from the apex of leafy pseudobulbs.

FLOWERS: 6–10 per inflorescence. The flowers are 0.3–0.6 in. (0.8–1.5 cm) across. The sepals and petals are white. The smooth, nearly round lip is ruffled along the margin. It is green with 2 pinkish purple patches and turns yellow with age. The column is green. The margins of the small sidelobes are serrated.

REFERENCES: 46, 119, 202, 218, 244, 254, 255, 369, 445.

PHOTOS/DRAWINGS: 244.

Dendrobium nardoides Schlechter

AKA: Reeve and Woods (ref. 385) include *D. oligoblepharon* Schlechter as a possible synonym.

ORIGIN/HABITAT: Northern Papua New Guinea. Plants grow in the mistforests of the Bismarck Range at 6550–10,500 ft. (2000–3200 m), usually in clumps of epiphytic mosses on horizontal tree branches. *D. oligoblepharon* was collected at about 3950 ft. (1200 m), which is much lower than other specimens.

Dendrobium nareshbahadurii

CLIMATE: Station #94010, Goroka, Papua New Guinea, Lat. 6.1°S, Long. 145.4°E, at 5141 ft. (1567 m). Temperatures are calculated for an elevation of 8000 ft. (2440 m), resulting in probable extremes of 78°F (25°C) and 34°F (1°C).

N/HEMISPHERE	JAN	FEB	MAR	APR	MAY	JUN	JUL	AUG	SEP	OCT	NOV	DEC
°F AVG MAX	67	68	69	70	70	69	70	69	69	69	70	68
°F AVG MIN	47	48	48	48	49	50	50	50	51	50	50	48
DIURNAL RANGE	20	20	21	22	21	19	20	19	18	19	20	20
RAIN/INCHES	2.1	2.8	4.6	5.9	6.6	9.3	9.1	10.1	10.7	8.3	4.6	2.0
HUMIDITY/%	70	67	67	67	67	71	72	73	74	71	70	70
BLOOM SEASON			*		*		*		*			
DAYS CLR	N/A											
RAIN/MM	53	71	117	150	168	236	231	257	272	211	117	51
°C AVG MAX	19.2	19.8	20.3	20.9	20.9	20.3	20.9	20.3	20.3	20.3	20.9	19.8
°C AVG MIN	8.1	8.6	8.6	8.6	9.2	9.8	9.8	9.8	10.3	9.8	9.8	8.6
DIURNAL RANGE	11.1	11.2	11.7	12.3	11.7	10.5	11.1	10.5	10.0	10.5	11.1	11.2
S/HEMISPHERE	JUL	AUG	SEP	OCT	NOV	DEC	JAN	FEB	MAR	APR	MAY	JUN

Cultural Recommendations

LIGHT: 2000–3000 fc.

TEMPERATURES: Throughout the year, days average 67–70°F (19–21°C), and nights average 47–51°F (8–10°C), with a diurnal range of 18–22°F (10–12°C). In the habitat, the warmest temperatures of the day occur during late morning when skies are clear. Clouds and mist develop near noon and continue through the afternoon, preventing additional warming.

HUMIDITY: 70–75% from summer into autumn, decreasing to 65–70% in winter and spring. Averages in the mistforest habitat are probably greater than indicated, however.

WATER: Rainfall is moderate to heavy most of the year, but conditions are slightly drier for 3 months in winter. Cultivated plants should be kept moist, with only slight drying allowed between waterings. In addition, early morning mistings are often beneficial, especially on bright, sunny days.

FERTILIZER: ¼–½ recommended strength. A balanced fertilizer should be applied weekly to biweekly throughout the year.

REST PERIOD: Growing temperatures should be maintained all year. In the habitat, rainfall is lowest in winter, but dew and mist from fog and low clouds are common. Water and fertilizer should be reduced somewhat for cultivated plants, especially those grown in the darker, short-day conditions common during temperate-latitude winters. Plants should be kept on the dry side, but they should never be allowed to dry out completely. In the habitat, light is higher in winter.

GROWING MEDIA: Plants may be mounted on tree-fern or cork slabs if humidity is high and plants are watered at least once daily in summer. When plants are potted, any open, fast-draining medium may be used. Repotting may be done anytime new roots are growing.

MISCELLANEOUS NOTES: The bloom season shown in the climate table is based on cultivation records.

Plant and Flower Information

PLANT SIZE AND TYPE: A 0.4–2.8 in. (1–7 cm) sympodial epiphyte.

PSEUDOBULB: 0.2–1.0 in. (0.5–2.5 cm) long. The cylindrical stems form clumps that may be 8 in. (20 cm) across. They have a whitish brown covering.

LEAVES: 2–3 per growth. The tufts of grasslike leaves are 0.4–2.4 in. (1–6 cm) long. They are linear, rigid, channeled, and pointed at the tip.

INFLORESCENCE: 0.4 in. (1 cm) long. The short inflorescence arises from the apex of both leafy and leafless pseudobulbs.

FLOWERS: 1–2 per inflorescence. The flowers are 0.4–0.8 in. (1–2 cm) long but do not open fully. The brightly colored sepals and much smaller petals are purplish pink, keeled, and pointed. The lip is also purplish pink, often with carmine at the tip and white at the base. The linear mid-lobe terminates in a toothlike tip.

REFERENCES: 92, 95, 179, 221, 385, 437, 445, 549, 556.

PHOTOS/DRAWINGS: *385*, *437*, *549*.

Dendrobium nareshbahadurii H. B. Naithani

ORIGIN/HABITAT: Northern India. Plants were found in the Kameng district of western Arunachal Pradish at 1950 ft. (600 m).

CLIMATE: Station #42415, Tezpur, India, Lat. 26.7°N, Long. 92.8°E, at 240 ft. (73 m). Temperatures are calculated for an elevation of 1950 ft. (590 m), resulting in probable extremes of 95°F (35°C) and 34°F (1°C).

N/HEMISPHERE	JAN	FEB	MAR	APR	MAY	JUN	JUL	AUG	SEP	OCT	NOV	DEC
°F AVG MAX	68	70	78	79	81	82	83	83	83	80	75	69
°F AVG MIN	47	50	56	62	66	71	72	72	71	65	56	48
DIURNAL RANGE	21	20	22	17	15	11	11	11	12	15	19	21
RAIN/INCHES	0.6	1.1	1.9	6.0	10.7	12.1	13.7	13.0	8.3	4.1	0.9	0.3
HUMIDITY/%	81	75	66	71	79	83	84	85	86	83	83	84
BLOOM SEASON									*			
DAYS CLR @ 6PM	24	19	17	10	9	5	4	7	9	17	21	24
RAIN/MM	15	28	48	152	272	307	348	330	211	104	23	8
°C AVG MAX	20.2	21.3	25.8	26.3	27.4	28.0	28.5	28.5	28.5	26.9	24.1	20.8
°C AVG MIN	8.5	10.2	13.5	16.9	19.1	21.9	22.4	22.4	21.9	18.5	13.5	9.1
DIURNAL RANGE	11.7	11.1	12.3	9.4	8.3	6.1	6.1	6.1	6.6	8.4	10.6	11.7
S/HEMISPHERE	JUL	AUG	SEP	OCT	NOV	DEC	JAN	FEB	MAR	APR	MAY	JUN

Cultural Recommendations

LIGHT: 2500–3500 fc. The brightest conditions in the habitat occur during the clear afternoons common in autumn and winter.

TEMPERATURES: Summer days average 82–83°F (28–29°C), and nights average 71–72°F (22°C), with a diurnal range of 11°F (6°C).

HUMIDITY: 80–85% most of the year, dropping to 65–70% for 2–3 months in early spring.

WATER: Rainfall is moderate to heavy from early spring into autumn. Cultivated plants should be watered heavily while actively growing, but water should be gradually reduced after new growths mature in autumn.

FERTILIZER: ¼–½ recommended strength, applied weekly. A high nitrogen fertilizer is beneficial from spring to midsummer, but a fertilizer high in phosphates should be used in late summer and autumn.

REST PERIOD: Winter days average 68–70°F (20–21°C), and nights average 47–50°F (9–10°C), with an increased diurnal range of 20–21°F (11–12°C). In the habitat, the wet season is followed abruptly by 2–4 dry months in autumn and winter when rainfall is low. For part of the period, however, additional moisture is available from heavy dew, mist, and fog, so the driest conditions last only 1–2 months. Cultivated plants need to dry out somewhat between waterings, but they should not remain dry for extended periods.

GROWING MEDIA: Plants may be mounted on tree-fern or cork slabs if humidity is high and plants are watered at least once daily in summer. When plants are potted, any open, fast-draining medium may be used. Plants may be repotted anytime new roots are growing.

MISCELLANEOUS NOTES: The bloom season shown in the climate table is based on collection records.

Plant and Flower Information

PLANT SIZE AND TYPE: An 8–11 in. (20–28 cm) sympodial epiphyte.

PSEUDOBULB: 6–8 in. (15–20 cm) long.

LEAVES: 4 near the apex of the stem. The leaves are 2.4–2.8 in. (6–7 cm) long. They are narrowly oblong, suberect, and thinly leathery.

INFLORESCENCE: 4–6 in. (10–15 cm) long. Racemes emerge from between the leaves at nodes near the apex of the stem. They are slender and pendulous.

FLOWERS: 3–10 per inflorescence. Blossoms are 1.0–1.4 in. (2.5–3.5 cm) across. The white sepals and petals are lanceolate and taper to a very slender point. The dark purple lip is pointed, recurved at the tip, and toothed along the edges of the sidelobes and the side of the midlobe. The lip is folded lengthwise.

REFERENCES: 235, 320.

PHOTOS/DRAWINGS: 320.

Dendrobium nathanielis Rchb. f.

AKA: *D. cuspidatum* Lindley 1858 not 1828, *D. multiflorum* Parish and Rchb. f. In 1992 *Opera Botanica* 114, Seidenfaden indicates that in Indochina some clones have been incorrectly identified as *D. mannii* Ridley.

ORIGIN/HABITAT: Southeast Asia. Plants grow in the Assam region of northeastern India, the northern Shan States and Tenasserim regions of Burma, throughout much of eastern and southern Thailand, as well as Cambodia, Laos, and near Dalat in Vietnam. In northeastern Thailand, plants are reported in the Nongkhai region at about 600 ft. (180 m).

CLIMATE: Station #48354, Udon Thani, Thailand, Lat. 17.4°N, Long. 102.8°E, at 585 ft. (178 m). Record extreme temperatures are 111°F (44°C) and 37°F (3°C).

N/HEMISPHERE	JAN	FEB	MAR	APR	MAY	JUN	JUL	AUG	SEP	OCT	NOV	DEC
°F AVG MAX	87	91	96	98	94	92	91	90	89	89	88	86
°F AVG MIN	57	63	69	74	75	76	75	75	75	71	65	59
DIURNAL RANGE	30	28	27	24	19	16	16	15	14	18	23	27
RAIN/INCHES	0.3	0.8	1.5	3.8	8.8	8.6	7.8	9.7	10.4	3.5	0.6	0.2
HUMIDITY/%	63	64	62	63	74	78	78	81	81	76	71	66
BLOOM SEASON	N/A											
DAYS CLR @ 7AM	1	2	1	2	2	1	0	1	5	4	3	
DAYS CLR @ 1PM	16	10	8	7	2	0	0	1	5	9	13	
RAIN/MM	8	20	38	97	224	218	198	246	264	89	15	5
°C AVG MAX	30.6	32.8	35.6	36.7	34.4	33.3	32.8	32.2	31.7	31.7	31.1	30.0
°C AVG MIN	13.9	17.2	20.6	23.3	23.9	24.4	23.9	23.9	23.9	21.7	18.3	15.0
DIURNAL RANGE	16.7	15.6	15.0	13.4	10.5	8.9	8.9	8.3	7.8	10.0	12.8	15.0
S/HEMISPHERE	JUL	AUG	SEP	OCT	NOV	DEC	JAN	FEB	MAR	APR	MAY	JUN

Cultural Recommendations

LIGHT: 2000–3000 fc. The heavy summer cloud cover indicates that some shading is needed from spring through autumn, but light should be as high as the plant can tolerate, short of burning the leaves.

TEMPERATURES: Summer days average 90–92°F (32–33°C), and nights average 75–76°F (24°C), with a diurnal range of 15–16°F (8–9°C). The warmest weather occurs in spring. Days average 94–98°F (34–37°C), and nights average 69–75°F (21–24°C), with a diurnal range of 19–27°F (11–15°C).

HUMIDITY: Near 80% in summer, dropping to 60–65% in winter and early spring.

WATER: Rainfall is heavy from late spring to early autumn. The rainy season is followed by 4–5 dry months in winter. Cultivated plants should be kept evenly moist while actively growing, but water should be gradually reduced in autumn.

FERTILIZER: ¼–½ recommended strength, applied weekly. A high-nitrogen fertilizer is beneficial from spring to midsummer, but a fertilizer high in phosphates should be used in late summer and autumn.

REST PERIOD: Winter days average 86–91°F (30–33°C), and nights average 57–63°F (14–17°C), with a diurnal range of 27–30°F (15–17°C). In the habitat, winter rainfall is low, but additional moisture is available from dew and as mist from fog and low clouds. In cultivation, water should be reduced. Plants should be allowed to dry out between waterings but should not remain dry for extended periods. Occasional early morning mistings between waterings, especially on sunny mornings, may be beneficial and keep the plants from becoming too dry. Fertilizer should be eliminated until water is increased in spring. In the habitat, light is highest in winter and spring.

GROWING MEDIA: Plants may be mounted on tree-fern or cork slabs if humidity is high and plants are watered at least once daily in summer. When plants are potted, any open, fast-draining medium may be used. Repotting may be done anytime new roots are growing.

Plant and Flower Information

PLANT SIZE AND TYPE: A 6–10 in. (15–25 cm) sympodial epiphyte.

PSEUDOBULB: 6–10 in. (15–25 cm) long, rarely shorter. The leafy stems are curved and stout.

LEAVES: Many. The leaves are 1.6 in. (4 cm) long. They are lanceolate, overlapping, distichous, and lay flat on a single plane.

INFLORESCENCE: Short. Inflorescences emerge from leaf axils.

FLOWERS: 1–5 per inflorescence. The flowers are 0.2–0.4 in. (0.5–1.0 cm) across. The sepals and smaller, earlike petals are white, sometimes flushed with pink. They are nearly erect. The lip is ruffled along the margin and notched at the apex with a warty patch in the center and 2 hairy lines in the back of the throat. It has no sidelobes. It is white with yellow markings in the throat.

HYBRIDIZING NOTES: Johansen (ref. 239) indicates that some clones of *D. nathanielis* could be self-pollinated, while others were self-sterile. Even when capsules developed from self-pollinations, however, no viable seed was produced. When crossed with *D. aloifolium* (Blume) Rchb. f. and *D. secundum* (Blume) Lindley, capsules formed but no viable seed was produced. Seed capsules opened 144 days after pollination.

REFERENCES: 46, 157, 202, 216, 239, 254, 266, 278, 317, 369, 447, 448, 454.

PHOTOS/DRAWINGS: *454.*

Dendrobium nativitatis Ridley. Now considered a synonym of *Flickingeria nativitatis* (Ridley) J. J. Wood. REFERENCES: 67, 75, 220, 234.

Dendrobium navicula Kränzlin

ORIGIN/HABITAT: Milne Bay, Papua New Guinea. Habitat elevation is unavailable. However, Schlechter (ref. 437) indicates that other closely related species grow in the higher mountains and are never found below the mistforest zone. Habitat elevation is estimated, so the following climate data should be used with caution.

CLIMATE: Station #94075, Samarai, Sideia Island, Papua New Guinea, Lat. 10.6°S, Long. 150.7°E, at 20 ft. (6 m). Temperatures are calculated for an elevation of 3300 ft. (1000 m), resulting in probable extremes of 93°F (34°C) and 53°F (12°C).

N/HEMISPHERE	JAN	FEB	MAR	APR	MAY	JUN	JUL	AUG	SEP	OCT	NOV	DEC
°F AVG MAX	70	70	71	72	74	76	76	77	76	75	73	71
°F AVG MIN	63	62	63	63	64	65	66	66	65	64	64	63
DIURNAL RANGE	7	8	8	9	10	11	10	11	11	11	9	8
RAIN/INCHES	8.1	8.6	10.1	8.7	8.4	6.1	7.0	7.8	10.0	9.8	12.0	11.3
HUMIDITY/%	N/A											
BLOOM SEASON									*			
DAYS CLR	N/A											
RAIN/MM	206	218	257	221	213	155	178	198	254	249	305	287
°C AVG MAX	21.2	21.2	21.8	22.3	23.4	24.5	24.5	25.1	24.5	24.0	22.9	21.8
°C AVG MIN	17.3	16.8	17.3	17.3	17.9	18.4	19.0	19.0	18.4	17.9	17.9	17.3
DIURNAL RANGE	3.9	4.4	4.5	5.0	5.5	6.1	5.5	6.1	6.1	6.1	5.0	4.5
S/HEMISPHERE	JUL	AUG	SEP	OCT	NOV	DEC	JAN	FEB	MAR	APR	MAY	JUN

Cultural Recommendations

LIGHT: 2500–3000 fc.

TEMPERATURES: Throughout the year, days average 70–77°F (21–25°C),

and nights average 62–66°F (17–19°C), with a diurnal range of 7–11°F (4–6°C).

HUMIDITY: Information is not available for this location. However, records at other locations in the region indicate that averages are probably 70–80% all year.

WATER: Rainfall is heavy all year. Cultivated plants should be kept moist, with only slight drying allowed between waterings.

FERTILIZER: ¼–½ recommended strength. A balanced fertilizer should be applied weekly to biweekly throughout the year.

REST PERIOD: Growing conditions should be maintained year-round. In the habitat, winter rainfall is high; but water and fertilizer should be reduced for cultivated plants, especially those grown in the dark, short-day conditions in temperate-latitude winters. Plants should never be allowed to dry out completely, however. In the habitat, seasonal light variation is minor.

GROWING MEDIA: Plants may be mounted on tree-fern or cork slabs if humidity is high and plants are watered at least once daily in summer. When plants are potted, any open, fast-draining medium may be used. Repotting may be done anytime the roots are actively growing.

MISCELLANEOUS NOTES: The bloom season shown in the climate table is based on reports from the habitat.

Plant and Flower Information

PLANT SIZE AND TYPE: An 8–12 in. (20–30 cm) sympodial epiphyte.

PSEUDOBULB: 8–12 in. (20–30 cm) long.

LEAVES: The oblong to oblong-lanceolate leaves are 2.0–2.4 in. (5–6 cm) long.

INFLORESCENCE: The racemes are very short.

FLOWERS: Up to 8 per inflorescence. The flowers are 1.4 in. (3.5 cm) long. Sepals and petals are rose colored. The dorsal sepal and petals are oblong-lanceolate. Lateral sepals are very large and broadly triangular. The boat-shaped lip has a toothed margin. It is shorter than the column.

REFERENCES: 220, 254, 437, 470.

Dendrobium nebularum Schlechter

AKA: *D. murkelense* J. J. Smith, *D. palustre* L. O. Williams, *D. tumidulum* Schlechter. Reeve and Woods (ref. 385) also list *D. keysseri* Schlechter as a possible synonym.

ORIGIN/HABITAT: From the eastern end of Seram Island in the Moluccas to the misty mountain forests of eastern New Guinea at 4600–9200 ft. (1400–2800 m). Although widely distributed, the plants are uncommon and only a few are found in any single location. They usually grow on *Nothofagus* (southern Beech) trees but are occasionally found on the surface of the ground.

CLIMATE: Station #94010, Goroka, Papua New Guinea, Lat. 6.1°S, Long. 145.4°E, at 5141 ft. (1567 m). Temperatures are calculated for an elevation of 6550 ft. (2000 m), resulting in probable extremes of 82°F (28°C) and 38°F (4°C).

N/HEMISPHERE	JAN	FEB	MAR	APR	MAY	JUN	JUL	AUG	SEP	OCT	NOV	DEC
°F AVG MAX	71	72	73	74	74	73	74	73	73	73	74	72
°F AVG MIN	51	52	52	52	53	54	54	54	55	54	54	52
DIURNAL RANGE	20	20	21	22	21	19	20	19	18	19	20	20
RAIN/INCHES	2.1	2.8	4.6	5.9	6.6	9.3	9.1	10.1	10.7	8.3	4.6	2.0
HUMIDITY/%	70	67	67	67	67	71	72	73	74	71	70	70
BLOOM SEASON	*	*	*	*		*				*	*	
DAYS CLR	N/A											
RAIN/MM	53	71	117	150	168	236	231	257	272	211	117	51
°C AVG MAX	21.8	22.4	23.0	23.5	23.5	23.0	23.5	23.0	23.0	23.0	23.5	22.4
°C AVG MIN	10.7	11.3	11.3	11.3	11.8	12.4	12.4	12.4	13.0	12.4	12.4	11.3
DIURNAL RANGE	11.1	11.1	11.7	12.2	11.7	10.6	11.1	10.6	10.0	10.6	11.1	11.1
S/HEMISPHERE	JUL	AUG	SEP	OCT	NOV	DEC	JAN	FEB	MAR	APR	MAY	JUN

Cultural Recommendations

LIGHT: 2000–3000 fc.

TEMPERATURES: Throughout the year, days average 71–74°F (22–24°C), and nights average 51–55°F (11–13°C), with a diurnal range of 18–22°F (10–12°C).

HUMIDITY: About 70% year-round, although values are probably greater in the mistforest habitat.

WATER: Rainfall is moderate to heavy most of the year. Conditions are slightly drier for 3 months in winter. Cultivated plants should be kept evenly moist, but water should be gradually reduced in autumn. Placing plants in front of drifting mist may be beneficial.

FERTILIZER: ¼ recommended strength. A balanced fertilizer should be applied weekly to biweekly throughout the year. Plants require little or no fertilizer if grown in live sphagnum. In any medium, fertilizer should be very weak. The Royal Botanic Garden in Edinburgh uses a weak, seaweed-based fertilizer for plants from this habitat.

REST PERIOD: Growing temperatures should be maintained all year. In the habitat, rainfall is lowest in winter, but dew and mist from fog and low clouds are common. Water and fertilizer should be reduced somewhat for cultivated plants, especially those grown in the darker, short-day conditions common during temperate-latitude winters. Plants should be kept on the dry side, but they should never be allowed to dry out completely. In the habitat, light is higher in winter.

GROWING MEDIA: Plants may be mounted on tree-fern slabs if humidity is high and plants are watered at least once daily in summer. When plants are potted, any open, fast-draining medium may be used. Repotting may be done anytime new roots are growing. The roots have orange tips.

MISCELLANEOUS NOTES: The variable bloom season shown in the climate table is based on cultivation records.

Plant and Flower Information

PLANT SIZE AND TYPE: A 3.2–8.0 in. (8–20 cm) sympodial epiphyte.

PSEUDOBULB: 0.6–6.0 in. (1.5–15.0 cm) long. The variable pseudobulbs arise from a short rhizome.

LEAVES: 1–3, rarely 4 per growth. The persistent leaves are 0.6–5.5 in. (1.5–14.0 cm) long. They are pale green and striped with red.

INFLORESCENCE: 0.6 in. (1.6 cm) long. Inflorescences arise from the upper nodes of leafy and leafless pseudobulbs. Blossoms are held near the base of the leaves.

FLOWERS: 2–5 per inflorescence. The flowers, which do not open fully, are 0.7–1.3 in. (1.9–3.2 cm) long. The blossoms are usually pale greenish white to yellow, and they may be marked with purple lines. A few purplish red forms have been collected. The narrow lip is commonly yellow, but it may be white. All segments are pointed.

HYBRIDIZING NOTES: Chromosome count is 2n = 38 (ref. 153, 273).

REFERENCES: 95, 153, 179, 221, 273, 385, 437, 443, 445, 574.

PHOTOS/DRAWINGS: 385, 437.

Dendrobium neglectum Gagnepain. Now considered a synonym of *Eria dacrydium* Gagnepain. REFERENCES: 137, 227, 448, Seidenfaden 1992 *Opera Botanica* #114.

Dendrobium nemorale L. O. Williams

ORIGIN/HABITAT: The Philippines. Plants grow in Rizal Province on Luzon Island. Habitat elevation was not reported, so the following climate data should be used with caution.

CLIMATE: Station #98427, Manila, Philippines, Lat. 14.5°N, Long. 121.0°E, at 74 ft. (23 m). Record extreme temperatures are 101°F (38°C) and 58°F (14°C).

N/HEMISPHERE	JAN	FEB	MAR	APR	MAY	JUN	JUL	AUG	SEP	OCT	NOV	DEC
°F AVG MAX	86	88	91	93	93	91	88	87	88	88	87	86
°F AVG MIN	69	69	71	73	75	75	75	75	75	74	72	70
DIURNAL RANGE	17	19	20	20	18	16	13	12	13	14	15	16
RAIN/INCHES	0.9	0.5	0.7	1.3	5.1	10.0	17.0	16.6	14.0	7.6	5.7	2.6
HUMIDITY/%	77	73	70	68	71	81	84	86	87	84	82	89
BLOOM SEASON				*								
DAYS CLR @ 8AM	6	9	14	14	10	3	2	1	1	6	7	6
DAYS CLR @ 2PM	3	6	10	10	8	2	1	1	0	2	2	3
RAIN/MM	23	13	18	33	130	254	432	422	356	193	145	66
°C AVG MAX	30.0	31.1	32.8	33.9	33.9	32.8	31.1	30.6	31.1	31.1	30.6	30.0
°C AVG MIN	20.6	20.6	21.7	22.8	23.9	23.9	23.9	23.9	23.9	23.3	22.2	21.1
DIURNAL RANGE	9.4	10.5	11.1	11.1	10.0	8.9	7.2	6.7	7.2	7.8	8.4	8.9
S/HEMISPHERE	JUL	AUG	SEP	OCT	NOV	DEC	JAN	FEB	MAR	APR	MAY	JUN

Cultural Recommendations

LIGHT: 2500–3000 fc.

TEMPERATURES: Throughout the year, days average 86–93°F (30–34°C), and nights average 69–75°F (21–24°C), with a diurnal range of 12–20°F (7–11°C). Plants are healthiest if humidity is high and air circulation is excellent.

HUMIDITY: 80–85% in summer and autumn, dropping to near 70% in winter and spring.

WATER: Rainfall is heavy in summer and autumn, but conditions are dry in winter. Cultivated plants should be kept moist during the growing season, but water should be gradually reduced in autumn.

FERTILIZER: ¼–½ recommended strength, applied weekly. A high-nitrogen fertilizer is beneficial from spring to midsummer, but a fertilizer high in phosphates should be used in late summer and autumn.

REST PERIOD: Growing temperatures should be maintained all year. Rainfall is low for 3–4 months, but humidity remains high enough to indicate that some moisture is available from dew. In cultivation, water should be reduced and the plants allowed to dry out between waterings. They should not remain dry for extended periods, however. Fertilizer may be reduced or eliminated when plants are not actively growing. In the habitat, light is highest in winter.

GROWING MEDIA: Plants may be mounted on tree-fern or cork slabs if humidity is high and plants are watered at least once daily in summer. When plants are potted, any open, fast-draining medium may be used. Repotting is best done in early spring when new roots are growing.

MISCELLANEOUS NOTES: The bloom season shown in the climate table is based on collection reports.

Plant and Flower Information

PLANT SIZE AND TYPE: A 12 in. (30 cm) sympodial epiphyte.

PSEUDOBULB: 12 in. (30 cm) long. The compact stems are jointed and deeply grooved.

LEAVES: The thin leaves are 1.0–1.8 in. (2.5–4.5 cm) long and unequally notched at the tip. They have 3–5 veins.

INFLORESCENCE: Short.

FLOWERS: 1–2 per inflorescence. The flowers are 0.6–0.8 in. (1.5–2.0 cm) across. Blossoms are white or ivory with lateral sepals that join, forming a sack at the base, a lanceolate dorsal sepal, and oblong-lanceolate petals. The 3-lobed lip has prominent sidelobes and a transversely oval midlobe.

REFERENCES: 226, 445, 536.

Dendrobium neo-ebudanum Schlechter.

Sometimes spelled *D. neoebudanum*, see *D. mohlianum* Rchb. f. REFERENCES: 220, 252, 254, 270, 271, 433, 466.

Dendrobium neo-guineënse A. Hawkes and A. H. Heller

AKA: *D. longicaule* Schlechter.

ORIGIN/HABITAT: Papua New Guinea. Plants grow in the Sepik River region at 4600–4900 ft. (1400–1500 m).

CLIMATE: Station #200004, Ambunti, Papua New Guinea, Lat. 4.2°S, Long. 142.8°E, at 164 ft. (50 m). Temperatures are calculated for an elevation of 4600 ft. (1400 m), resulting in probable extremes of 84°F (29°C) and 37°F (3°C).

N/HEMISPHERE	JAN	FEB	MAR	APR	MAY	JUN	JUL	AUG	SEP	OCT	NOV	DEC
°F AVG MAX	73	75	75	75	76	75	75	75	75	75	75	74
°F AVG MIN	57	58	59	58	58	58	57	58	58	58	58	59
DIURNAL RANGE	16	17	16	17	18	17	18	17	17	17	17	15
RAIN/INCHES	6.4	7.4	7.7	8.5	9.2	9.4	10.9	10.2	12.2	10.4	8.3	5.2
HUMIDITY/%	N/A											
BLOOM SEASON			*									
DAYS CLR	N/A											
RAIN/MM	163	188	196	216	234	239	277	259	310	264	211	132
°C AVG MAX	23.0	24.1	24.1	24.1	24.6	24.1	24.1	24.1	24.1	24.1	24.1	23.5
°C AVG MIN	14.1	14.6	15.2	14.6	14.6	14.6	14.1	14.6	14.6	14.6	14.6	15.2
DIURNAL RANGE	8.9	9.5	8.9	9.5	10.0	9.5	10.0	9.5	9.5	9.5	9.5	8.3
S/HEMISPHERE	JUL	AUG	SEP	OCT	NOV	DEC	JAN	FEB	MAR	APR	MAY	JUN

Cultural Recommendations

LIGHT: 2000–3000 fc.

TEMPERATURES: Throughout the year, days average 73–76°F (23–25°C), and nights average 57–59°F (14–15°C), with a diurnal range of 15–18°F (8–10°C).

HUMIDITY: Information is not available for this location. However, records from other stations in the region indicate that averages are probably near 80% year-round.

WATER: Rainfall is heavy all year, with the greatest amounts falling in summer and early autumn. Cultivated plants should be kept moist but not soggy.

FERTILIZER: ¼–½ recommended strength. A balanced fertilizer should be applied weekly to biweekly throughout the year.

REST PERIOD: Growing conditions should be maintained all year. However, water and fertilizer should be reduced for plants grown in the dark, short-day conditions common in temperate-latitude winters. These plants should never be allowed to dry out completely, however.

GROWING MEDIA: Plants may be mounted on cork or tree-fern slabs if humidity is high and plants are watered at least once daily in summer. When plants are potted, any open, fast-draining medium may be used, but fir bark is preferred by most growers. Repotting may be done anytime new roots are growing.

MISCELLANEOUS NOTES: The bloom season shown in the climate table is based on reports from the habitat.

Plant and Flower Information

PLANT SIZE AND TYPE: A 59 in. (150 cm) sympodial epiphyte.

PSEUDOBULB: 59 in. (150 cm) long. The erect stems do not branch.

LEAVES: Many. The somewhat linear, grasslike leaves, which are 2.4–3.1 in. (6–8 cm) long, are unequally bilobed at the apex. They are smooth and leathery.

INFLORESCENCE: Short. Inflorescences are flattened.

FLOWERS: 2 per inflorescence. The snow-white flowers are about 2 in. (5 cm) across. Sepals are oblong and pointed, and petals are obliquely elliptical. The 3-lobed lip has small sidelobes and a broadly oval midlobe. It is decorated with raised lines in the center.

REFERENCES: 191, 223, 229, 443.

Dendrobium neolampangense L. V. Aver'yanov.

See note at *D. indivisum* Rolfe ex Downie. REFERENCES: 235.

Dendrobium nephrolepidis Schlechter

ORIGIN/HABITAT: Northern Papua New Guinea. A lowland species that grows near sea level on forest trees in the Eitape District.

CLIMATE: Station #94004, Wewak, Papua New Guinea, Lat. 3.6°S, Long. 143.7°E, at 16 ft. (5 m). Record extreme temperatures are 98°F (37°C) and 62°F (17°C).

N/HEMISPHERE	JAN	FEB	MAR	APR	MAY	JUN	JUL	AUG	SEP	OCT	NOV	DEC
°F AVG MAX	88	88	88	88	88	88	87	86	87	88	88	88
°F AVG MIN	74	74	74	75	75	75	75	75	74	74	75	74
DIURNAL RANGE	14	14	14	13	13	13	12	11	13	14	13	14
RAIN/INCHES	7.6	4.8	5.3	10.0	13.3	14.5	12.1	11.9	14.9	16.9	15.1	10.8
HUMIDITY/%	80	79	79	78	79	81	82	82	81	82	81	80
BLOOM SEASON			*									
DAYS CLR	N/A											
RAIN/MM	193	122	135	254	338	368	307	302	378	429	384	274
°C AVG MAX	31.1	31.1	31.1	31.1	31.1	31.1	30.6	30.0	30.6	31.1	31.1	31.1
°C AVG MIN	23.3	23.3	23.3	23.9	23.9	23.9	23.9	23.9	23.3	23.3	23.9	23.3
DIURNAL RANGE	7.8	7.8	7.8	7.2	7.2	7.2	6.7	6.1	7.3	7.8	7.2	7.8
S/HEMISPHERE	JUL	AUG	SEP	OCT	NOV	DEC	JAN	FEB	MAR	APR	MAY	JUN

Cultural Recommendations

LIGHT: 2000–3000 fc.

TEMPERATURES: Throughout the year, days average 86–88°F (30–31°C), and nights average 74–75°F (23–24°C), with a diurnal range of 11–14°F (6–8°C).

HUMIDITY: Near 80% year-round.

WATER: Rainfall is heavy all year, but conditions are slightly drier for 1–2 months in winter. Cultivated plants should be kept evenly moist with only slight drying allowed between waterings.

FERTILIZER: ¼–½ recommended strength. A balanced fertilizer should be applied weekly to biweekly throughout the year.

REST PERIOD: Growing temperatures should be maintained year-round. Rainfall is lowest in winter. Water should be reduced somewhat for cultivated plants, especially those grown in the dark, short-day conditions common in temperate latitudes. Plants should never be allowed to dry out completely, however. Fertilizer should be reduced until water is increased in spring. In the habitat, light is highest in winter.

GROWING MEDIA: A very open and fast-draining medium may be used with either baskets or small pots. Repotting may be done anytime new roots are growing.

MISCELLANEOUS NOTES: The bloom season shown in the climate table is based on reports from the habitat. Plants that produce flowers which last a single day commonly bloom several times during the year. Flowering usually occurs 7–14 days after a sudden 10°F (5°C) drop in daytime temperatures.

Plant and Flower Information

PLANT SIZE AND TYPE: A 39 in. (100 cm) sympodial epiphyte.

PSEUDOBULB: 39 in. (100 cm) long. The stems are densely leafy.

LEAVES: Many. The leaves are 1.0–1.4 in. (2.5–3.5 cm) long, elliptical, and spreading.

INFLORESCENCE: Inflorescences arise from leaf axils.

FLOWERS: The flowers are 0.4 in. (1.1 cm) across. They are somewhat cupped and do not open fully. The small sepals and petals are greenish white and rounded at the tip. The 3-lobed lip is greenish. It has an irregularly toothed margin and a sparsely hairy midlobe with a raised centerline and an odd triangular point at the apex. The column is violet at the foot and orange-yellow at the tip. Blossoms last a single day.

REFERENCES: 221, 437.

PHOTOS/DRAWINGS: 437.

Dendrobium neuroglossum Schlechter

ORIGIN/HABITAT: Northern Papua New Guinea. Plants grow on forest trees at about 3300 ft. (1000 m) in the Kani, Ibo, and Finisterre Ranges. In the Bismarck Range, plants have been collected at about 4250 ft. (1300 m).

CLIMATE: Station #94010, Goroka, Papua New Guinea, Lat. 6.1°S, Long. 145.4°E, at 5141 ft. (1567 m). Temperatures are calculated for an elevation of 4000 ft. (1220 m), resulting in probable extremes of 90°F (32°C) and 46°F (8°C).

N/HEMISPHERE	JAN	FEB	MAR	APR	MAY	JUN	JUL	AUG	SEP	OCT	NOV	DEC
°F AVG MAX	80	81	82	83	83	82	83	82	82	82	83	81
°F AVG MIN	60	61	61	61	62	63	63	63	64	63	63	61
DIURNAL RANGE	20	20	21	22	21	19	20	19	18	19	20	20
RAIN/INCHES	2.1	2.8	4.6	5.9	6.6	9.3	9.1	10.1	10.7	8.3	4.6	2.0
HUMIDITY/%	70	67	67	67	67	71	72	73	74	71	70	70
BLOOM SEASON									*	*		
DAYS CLR	N/A											
RAIN/MM	53	71	117	150	168	236	231	257	272	211	117	51
°C AVG MAX	26.5	27.1	27.6	28.2	28.2	27.6	28.2	27.6	27.6	27.6	28.2	27.1
°C AVG MIN	15.4	16.0	16.0	16.0	16.5	17.1	17.1	17.1	17.6	17.1	17.1	16.0
DIURNAL RANGE	11.1	11.1	11.6	12.2	11.7	10.5	11.1	10.5	10.0	10.5	11.1	11.1
S/HEMISPHERE	JUL	AUG	SEP	OCT	NOV	DEC	JAN	FEB	MAR	APR	MAY	JUN

Cultural Recommendations

LIGHT: 2000–3000 fc.

TEMPERATURES: Throughout the year, days average 80–83°F (27–28°C), and nights average 60–64°F (15–18°C), with a diurnal range of 18–22°F (10–12°C).

HUMIDITY: 70–75% from summer into autumn, dropping to 65–70% in winter and spring. Plants require excellent air movement.

WATER: Rainfall is moderate to heavy most of the year, but conditions are slightly drier for 3 months in winter. Cultivated plants should be kept moist but not soggy. Occasional early morning mistings may be beneficial, especially on bright, sunny days.

FERTILIZER: ¼–½ recommended strength. A balanced fertilizer should be applied weekly to biweekly throughout the year.

REST PERIOD: Growing temperatures should be maintained all year. In the habitat, rainfall is lowest in winter, but dew and mist from fog and low clouds are common. Water and fertilizer should be reduced somewhat for cultivated plants, especially those grown in the darker, short-day conditions common during temperate-latitude winters. Plants should be kept on the dry side, but they should never be allowed to dry out completely. In the habitat, light is higher in winter.

GROWING MEDIA: Mounting plants on tree-fern or cork slabs accommodates their pendulous growth habit. However, humidity must be high and plants must be watered at least once a day in summer. If plants cannot be mounted, small pots or hanging baskets may be filled with an open, fast-draining medium. Repotting may be done anytime new roots are actively growing.

MISCELLANEOUS NOTES: The bloom season shown in the climate table is based on reports from the habitat.

Plant and Flower Information

PLANT SIZE AND TYPE: A 24–28 in. (60–70 cm) sympodial epiphyte.

PSEUDOBULB: 24–28 in. (60–70 cm) long. The cylindrical stems, which emerge from a short rhizome, are pendulous. They are laxly leafy.

LEAVES: Several. The oblong leaves are 2.8–3.5 in. (7–9 cm) long. They have a thin texture.

INFLORESCENCE: Short. A few flattened racemes are produced.

FLOWERS: 2 per inflorescence. The flowers are 0.5 in. (1.3 cm) long. Sepals and petals are broad at the apex with cupped, incurved tips. They are yellowish with dense brown spots on the inside. The small, unlobed lip is pointed and recurved at the tip with a wavy area where sidelobes would normally be found. It is muddy violet. The column is marked with violet at the base.

REFERENCES: 92, 219, 254, 437, 444, 445.

PHOTOS/DRAWINGS: 437.

Dendrobium ngoyense Schlechter

ORIGIN/HABITAT: Southern New Caledonia. Plants frequently grow on trees in the hills near the Ngoye River at 350–650 ft. (100–200 m), but they have also been collected as high as 1950–2300 ft. (600–700 m).

CLIMATE: Station #91592, Noumea, New Caledonia, Lat. 22.3°S, Long. 166.5°E, at 246 ft. (75 m). Temperatures are calculated for an elevation of 650 ft. (200 m), resulting in probable extremes of 98°F (36°C) and 51°F (10°C).

N/HEMISPHERE	JAN	FEB	MAR	APR	MAY	JUN	JUL	AUG	SEP	OCT	NOV	DEC
°F AVG MAX	75	75	77	79	82	85	85	84	84	82	78	76
°F AVG MIN	61	60	62	64	67	69	71	72	71	69	65	63
DIURNAL RANGE	14	15	15	15	15	16	14	12	13	13	13	13
RAIN/INCHES	3.6	2.6	2.5	2.0	2.4	2.6	3.7	5.1	5.7	5.2	4.4	3.7
HUMIDITY/%	73	70	69	67	68	69	71	74	75	76	73	73
BLOOM SEASON	*	*	*						*	*		
DAYS CLR @ 11AM	7	9	9	15	12	10	7	6	7	7	7	7
DAYS CLR @ 5PM	7	11	6	11	7	6	5	4	4	5	3	7
RAIN/MM	91	66	64	51	61	66	94	130	145	132	112	94
°C AVG MAX	23.7	23.7	24.8	25.9	27.6	29.2	29.2	28.7	28.7	27.6	25.3	24.2
°C AVG MIN	15.9	15.3	16.4	17.6	19.2	20.3	21.4	22.0	21.4	20.3	18.1	17.0
DIURNAL RANGE	7.8	8.4	8.4	8.3	8.4	8.9	7.8	6.7	7.3	7.3	7.2	7.2
S/HEMISPHERE	JUL	AUG	SEP	OCT	NOV	DEC	JAN	FEB	MAR	APR	MAY	JUN

Cultural Recommendations

LIGHT: 2000–3000 fc.

TEMPERATURES: Summer days average 84–85°F (29°C), and nights average 69–72°F (20–22°C), with a diurnal range of 12–16°F (7–9°C). Plants from higher-elevation habitats should adapt to temperatures that are several degrees cooler than indicated in the climate table.

HUMIDITY: 70–75% year-round.

WATER: Rainfall is moderate most of the year, with even greater amounts falling in the mountains. Cultivated plants should be watered heavily and then allowed to dry slightly before being watered again.

FERTILIZER: ¼–½ recommended strength, applied weekly. A high-nitrogen fertilizer is beneficial from spring to midsummer, but a fertilizer high in phosphates should be used in late summer and autumn.

REST PERIOD: Winter days average 75–77°F (24–25°C), and nights average 60–63°F (15–17°C), with a diurnal range of 13–15°F (7–8°C). High and low temperatures decline simultaneously, resulting in little change in the diurnal range. In the habitat, rainfall is somewhat lower in late winter and spring. In cultivation, water and fertilizer should be reduced and the plants allowed to dry even more between waterings than in summer. They should not dry out completely or remain dry for long periods, however. In the habitat, light is highest in winter.

GROWING MEDIA: Plants may be mounted on tree-fern or cork slabs if humidity is high and plants are watered at least once daily in summer. When plants are potted, any open, fast-draining medium may be used. Repotting may be done anytime new roots are growing.

MISCELLANEOUS NOTES: The bloom season shown in the climate table is based on reports from the habitat.

Plant and Flower Information

PLANT SIZE AND TYPE: A 1.6–2.8 in. (4–7 cm) sympodial epiphyte.

PSEUDOBULB: 0.4–0.8 in. (1–2 cm) long. The pseudobulbs, which may be oblong, ovoid, or cylindrical, are lightly grooved. They arise from a very short rhizome.

LEAVES: 2–3 at the apex of each growth. The oblong leaves are erect-spreading and 0.6–1.6 in. (1.5–4.0 cm) long.

INFLORESCENCE: Short. The inflorescence emerges from the apex of the pseudobulb. Blossoms are below the tips of the leaves.

FLOWERS: 1–3 per inflorescence. The flowers are 0.5 in. (1.2 cm) across, a size large relative to the plant size. They are yellowish with brownish-red or brownish-violet speckles on the lip. The dorsal sepal and petals tend to project forward, but the lateral sepals are sharply recurved near the base. The 3-lobed lip has small sidelobes and a flaring, deeply notched, recurved midlobe. The lip is decorated with 2 parallel lines that extend from the base and become wavy near the apex.

REFERENCES: 173, 220, 432.

PHOTOS/DRAWINGS: 173.

Dendrobium nhatrangense Gagnepain. See *D. sociale* J. J. Smith. REFERENCES: 136, 169, 224, 266, 448, 454.

Dendrobium nidificum Kränzlin. See *D. piestocaulon* Schlechter. REFERENCES: 220, 254, 437.

Dendrobium nienkui Tso. See *D. moniliforme* (Linn.) Swartz.
REFERENCES: 208, 225, 528.

Dendrobium nieuwenhuisii J. J. Smith. Borneo. Plants were found at Soengei Merase and Boekit Mili. We have been unable to locate either of these collection sites, so climate data cannot be selected. Plants are 39 in. (100 cm) sympodial epiphytes with very slender, leafy stems 39 in. (100 cm) long. They are pendulous, with nodes every 1.2–1.6 in. (3–4 cm). The very dark green leaves are 4 in. (10 cm) long, oblong, wavy along the margin, and unequally bilobed at the tip. Inflorescences are 1.4 in. (3.5 cm) long, pendulous, and laxly flowered. They emerge on leafless stems and carry about 6 blossoms. The pendulous flowers are 1.1 in. (2.9 cm) long and do not open widely. The oblong sepals are pale yellow-green with dense purple spotting which is often arranged in lines. The oblong dorsal sepal is concave. The oblong lateral sepals are somewhat triangular at the base. The recurved, oblong petals have 6–8 lines of spots. The lip is also yellow-green with a pale apex and orange-red or rust colored spots. REFERENCES: 220, 254, 286, 295, 445, 471.

Dendrobium nigricans Schlechter

ORIGIN/HABITAT: Northeastern Papua New Guinea. Plants grow on moss-covered tree branches in the mistforests of the Dischore Range at about 3950 ft. (1200 m).

CLIMATE: Station #200192, Garaina, Papua New Guinea, Lat. 7.9°S, Long. 147.1°E, at 2350 ft. (716 m). Temperatures are calculated for an elevation of 3950 ft. (1200 m), resulting in probable extremes of 89°F (32°C) and 41°F (5°C).

N/HEMISPHERE	JAN	FEB	MAR	APR	MAY	JUN	JUL	AUG	SEP	OCT	NOV	DEC
°F AVG MAX	75	77	78	79	80	80	80	80	79	79	78	76
°F AVG MIN	58	58	58	59	58	59	60	60	60	59	59	58
DIURNAL RANGE	17	19	20	20	22	21	20	20	19	20	19	18
RAIN/INCHES	5.8	6.5	8.7	11.1	11.8	11.9	8.9	11.7	11.5	9.9	7.7	5.2
HUMIDITY/%	84	82	82	81	80	80	81	81	82	83	84	84
BLOOM SEASON											*	
DAYS CLR	N/A											
RAIN/MM	147	165	221	282	300	302	226	297	292	251	196	132
°C AVG MAX	23.8	24.9	25.4	26.0	26.5	26.5	26.5	26.5	26.0	26.0	25.4	24.3
°C AVG MIN	14.3	14.3	14.3	14.9	14.3	14.9	15.4	15.4	15.4	14.9	14.9	14.3
DIURNAL RANGE	9.5	10.6	11.1	11.1	12.2	11.6	11.1	11.1	10.6	11.1	10.5	10.0
S/HEMISPHERE	JUL	AUG	SEP	OCT	NOV	DEC	JAN	FEB	MAR	APR	MAY	JUN

Cultural Recommendations

LIGHT: 2000–3000 fc.

TEMPERATURES: Throughout the year, days average 75–80°F (24–27°C), and nights average 58–60°F (14–15°C), with a diurnal range of 17–22°F (10–12°C).

HUMIDITY: 80–85% year-round.

WATER: Rainfall is heavy all year, but conditions are slightly drier in winter. Cultivated plants should be kept moist but not soggy.

FERTILIZER: 1/4–1/2 recommended strength. A balanced fertilizer should be applied weekly to biweekly throughout the year. The Royal Botanic Garden in Edinburgh uses a seaweed-based fertilizer for high-elevation plants from New Guinea.

REST PERIOD: Growing conditions should be maintained all year. In the habitat, rainfall is lower in winter. Water should be reduced somewhat for cultivated plants, especially those grown in the dark, short-day conditions common during temperate-latitude winters. They should not be allowed to dry out completely, however. Fertilizer should be reduced or eliminated anytime water is reduced.

GROWING MEDIA: Plants may be mounted on tree-fern or cork slabs if humidity is high and plants are watered at least once daily in summer. When plants are potted, any open, fast-draining medium may be used. Repotting may be done anytime new roots are growing.

MISCELLANEOUS NOTES: The bloom season shown in the climate table is based on collection reports.

Plant and Flower Information

PLANT SIZE AND TYPE: An 8 in. (20 cm) sympodial epiphyte.

PSEUDOBULB: 8 in. (20 cm) long. The erect, densely leafy stems become black as they dry.

LEAVES: Many. The leaves are 0.5–0.8 in. (1.2–2.0 cm) long.

INFLORESCENCE: Inflorescences emerge from nodes on the side of the stem.

FLOWERS: 1 per inflorescence. The yellowish white flowers are small and remain rather closed. The yellowish white lip is uppermost. It is marked with 2 red spots in front with a yellow claw. The lateral sepals are joined and form a hood over the lip. The lip is shaped like a scalloped whale's tail and decorated with a spindle-shaped callus. Blossoms last a few days at most.

REFERENCES: 221, 437, 445.

PHOTOS/DRAWINGS: 437.

Dendrobium nimium J. J. Smith

ORIGIN/HABITAT: Irian Jaya (western New Guinea), in the Schouten Island group on the north coast of Biak Island near Warsa. Plants grow in full sun.

CLIMATE: Station #97560 Mokmer, Biak Island, Irian Jaya, Lat. 1.2°S, Long. 136.1°E, at 46 ft. (14 m). Record extreme temperatures are 91°F (33°C) and 70°F (21°C).

N/HEMISPHERE	JAN	FEB	MAR	APR	MAY	JUN	JUL	AUG	SEP	OCT	NOV	DEC
°F AVG MAX	85	86	86	87	87	86	86	85	86	86	87	87
°F AVG MIN	74	75	74	75	75	75	74	74	75	75	75	75
DIURNAL RANGE	11	11	12	12	12	11	12	11	11	11	12	12
RAIN/INCHES	11.3	11.2	7.0	6.1	7.3	12.5	11.0	8.2	11.7	8.3	8.6	10.5
HUMIDITY/%	85	84	83	83	84	85	84	85	86	85	87	86
BLOOM SEASON	N/A											
DAYS CLR @ 9AM	2	2	4	1	2	1	2	1	1	2	2	3
DAYS CLR @ 3PM	3	3	3	3	2	1	2	1	2	2	1	2
RAIN/MM	287	284	178	155	185	318	279	208	297	211	218	267
°C AVG MAX	29.4	30.0	30.0	30.6	30.6	30.0	30.0	29.4	30.0	30.0	30.6	30.6
°C AVG MIN	23.3	23.9	23.3	23.9	23.9	23.9	23.3	23.3	23.9	23.9	23.9	23.9
DIURNAL RANGE	6.1	6.1	6.7	6.7	6.7	6.1	6.7	6.1	6.1	6.1	6.7	6.7
S/HEMISPHERE	JUL	AUG	SEP	OCT	NOV	DEC	JAN	FEB	MAR	APR	MAY	JUN

Cultural Recommendations

LIGHT: 2500–3500 fc. Shading should be provided in summer. Strong air movement is recommended year-round.

TEMPERATURES: Throughout the year, days average 85–87°F (29–31°C), and nights average 74–75°F (23–24°C), with a diurnal range of 11–12°F (6–7°C).

HUMIDITY: Near 85% year-round.

WATER: Rainfall is heavy all year. Cultivated plants should be kept moist.

FERTILIZER: 1/4–1/2 recommended strength. A balanced fertilizer should be applied weekly to biweekly throughout the year.

REST PERIOD: Growing temperatures should be maintained year-round. In cultivation, water may be reduced somewhat, especially for plants grown in the dark, short-day conditions common in temperate-latitude winters. They should never be allowed to dry out completely, however. Fertilizer should be reduced or eliminated when water is reduced.

GROWING MEDIA: Plants may be mounted on tree-fern or cork slabs or potted in small pots filled with any open, fast-draining medium. Repotting may be done anytime new roots are actively growing.

Plant and Flower Information

PLANT SIZE AND TYPE: A sympodial epiphyte that was described from an incomplete specimen.

PSEUDOBULB: The upper part of the elongated stem is leafless.

LEAVES: Many. The oblong-ovate leaves are 1.3 in. (3.3 cm) long. They are deciduous.

INFLORESCENCE: Short. The flattened inflorescences emerge through 2 leaf bases on leafy stems.

FLOWERS: 2 per inflorescence. The flowers are about 1 in. (2.5 cm) long. The blossoms have a narrowly oblong dorsal sepal, somewhat tubular lateral sepals, and linear petals. The erect, recurved, 3-lobed lip ends in a long threadlike projection which differentiates this plant from other closely related species. Flower color was not included in the description.

REFERENCES: 224, 445, 470.

Dendrobium nindii W. Hill

AKA: *D. ionoglossum* Schlechter, *D. ionoglossum* Schlechter var. *potamophilum* Schlechter, *D. tofftii (toftii)* F. M. Bailey.

ORIGIN/HABITAT: Northeastern Australia on the Cape York Peninsula with sporadic distribution in many parts of New Guinea. Although plants are sometimes found in rainforests, they generally grow between sea level and 660 ft. (0–200 m) in coastal swamps. The orchids are usually found in mangroves, often in full sun or other high-light situations such as overhanging streams. The steamy swamps, which are infested with crocodiles and pythons, are hot and slimy and smell of rotting vegetation.

CLIMATE: Station #94003, Daru, Papua New Guinea, Lat. 9.1°S, Long. 143.2°E, at 20 ft. (6 m). Record extreme temperatures are 98°F (37°C) and 63°F (17°C).

N/HEMISPHERE	JAN	FEB	MAR	APR	MAY	JUN	JUL	AUG	SEP	OCT	NOV	DEC
°F AVG MAX	81	82	83	85	88	88	88	87	87	86	84	82
°F AVG MIN	74	74	74	76	76	76	76	76	76	76	77	75
DIURNAL RANGE	7	8	9	9	12	12	12	11	11	10	7	7
RAIN/INCHES	3.0	2.2	1.8	2.3	4.6	8.1	11.9	10.4	12.5	12.6	9.4	3.8
HUMIDITY/%	94	93	91	88	85	88	85	87	84	88	91	94
BLOOM SEASON							**	**	**	*		
DAYS CLR	N/A											
RAIN/MM	76	56	46	58	117	206	302	264	318	320	239	97
°C AVG MAX	27.2	27.8	28.3	29.4	31.1	31.1	31.1	30.6	30.6	30.0	28.9	27.8
°C AVG MIN	23.3	23.3	23.3	24.4	24.4	24.4	24.4	24.4	24.4	24.4	25.0	23.9
DIURNAL RANGE	3.9	4.5	5.0	5.0	6.7	6.7	6.7	6.2	6.2	5.6	3.9	3.9
S/HEMISPHERE	JUL	AUG	SEP	OCT	NOV	DEC	JAN	FEB	MAR	APR	MAY	JUN

Cultural Recommendations

LIGHT: 4000–5000 fc. Plants need unusually high light, but the roots should be shaded.

TEMPERATURES: Throughout the year, days average 81–88°F (27–31°C), and nights average 74–77°F (23–25°C), with a diurnal range of 7–12°F (4–7°C).

HUMIDITY: 85–90% from spring to autumn, increasing to 90–95% in winter.

WATER: Rainfall is heavy from late spring through autumn, with a 2–3 month drier season in late winter and early spring. Cultivated plants grow best when kept evenly moist, but they do not grow well with stale, soggy medium. Water should be reduced when inflorescences are present, but the plants must never be allowed to dry out.

FERTILIZER: ¼–½ recommended strength. A balanced fertilizer should be applied weekly to biweekly throughout the year.

REST PERIOD: Growing conditions should be maintained all year. Growers indicate that 59°F (15°C) should be considered a minimum winter temperature. Rainfall is somewhat lower for about 5 months, but the driest part of the season lasts 2–3 months. During this time, however, large quantities of water are available in the form of nightly dew. For cultivated plants, water should be reduced and the plants kept just barely moist.

GROWING MEDIA: Plants are best mounted on slabs if humidity is high. But the roots must be shaded and kept moist. Mounted plants should be watered at least once daily in summer. Growers suggest using a pad of moss or osmunda over the roots to help the plant establish as quickly as possible. When plants must be potted, any open, fast-draining medium may be used. Repotting may be done anytime new roots are growing.

MISCELLANEOUS NOTES: The bloom season shown in the climate table is based on cultivation records. *D. nindii* is very difficult to grow, even in the tropics, unless it receives full sun.

Plant and Flower Information

PLANT SIZE AND TYPE: A 39–79 in. (100–200 cm) sympodial epiphyte that sometimes reaches a length of 118 in. (300 cm).

PSEUDOBULB: 39–79 in. (100–200 cm) long. Cultivated plants are usually about 59 in. (150 cm) long. The stems are somewhat swollen at the base and in the middle but taper toward the apex. They are blackish brown with purple stripes.

LEAVES: 5–15 on the upper half of each growth. The dark green leaves are 2–6 in. (5–15 cm) long. The foliage is distichous and alternates up the stem. The elliptic to ovate leaves are erect to spreading and relatively rigid.

INFLORESCENCE: 14–18 in. (35–45 cm) long. The erect inflorescences occasionally reach a height of 24 in. (61 cm). Each growth may produce 1–4 spikes from upper nodes. Blossoms are attractively arranged on all sides of the spike.

FLOWERS: 8–25, rarely to 50 per inflorescence. The flowers are 1.6–2.4 in. (4–6 cm) long. Sepals and petals are off-white or mauve with darker veins. The sepal shape varies, and the segments may become twisted as the blossoms mature. The petals are stiffly spreading and often twisted 3 times. The large lip is ruffled and frilled with 3 crests in the center. It has a small, broadly oval midlobe and large sidelobes. The lip may be white to dark purple-lavender with darker stripes. White and mauve are the most common colors, but pink and rosy hues are known. The attractive blossoms open fully, and many consider *D. nindii* to be one of the region's loveliest orchids. The blossoms are fragrant.

HYBRIDIZING NOTES: Chromosome count is 2n = 38 as *D. tofftii* (ref. 504, 580). When used as a parent, *D. nindii* tends to contribute bright colors, a large, full mauve lip, and improved flower substance. It is usually dominant for both plant and flower size.

REFERENCES: 25, 67, 84, 105, 179, 196, 228, 236, 240, 262, 263, 302, 304, 325, 342, 347, 390, 421, 437, 504, 533, 537, 580.

PHOTOS/DRAWINGS: 24, 40, *84*, 105, 240, *262*, *302*, *304*, 325, *342*, *347*, 437, *533*.

Dendrobium nitidicolle J. J. Smith.
Now considered a synonym of *Diplocaulobium nitidicolle* (J. J. Smith) Hunt and Summerhayes.

REFERENCES: 111, 213, 221, 230, 436, 482.

Dendrobium nitidiflorum J. J. Smith

ORIGIN/HABITAT: The southern region of Irian Jaya (western New Guinea). Plants were cultivated in the botanical garden at Bogor, Java. Habitat elevation is unavailable so the following climate data should be used with caution.

CLIMATE: Station #97876, Tanahmerah, Irian Jaya, Lat. 6.1°S, Long. 140.3°E, at 75 ft. (23 m). Record extreme temperatures are 98°F (37°C) and 64°F (18°C).

N/HEMISPHERE	JAN	FEB	MAR	APR	MAY	JUN	JUL	AUG	SEP	OCT	NOV	DEC
°F AVG MAX	84	85	87	90	91	90	90	89	90	89	87	85
°F AVG MIN	72	71	71	72	73	74	73	73	73	73	74	73
DIURNAL RANGE	12	14	16	18	18	16	17	16	17	16	13	12
RAIN/INCHES	11.5	12.1	14.7	13.2	14.4	15.9	14.5	15.8	17.4	17.3	15.5	11.9
HUMIDITY/%	N/A											
BLOOM SEASON										*		
DAYS CLR	N/A											
RAIN/MM	292	307	373	335	366	404	368	401	442	439	394	302
°C AVG MAX	28.9	29.4	30.6	32.2	32.8	32.2	32.2	31.7	32.2	31.7	30.6	29.4
°C AVG MIN	22.2	21.7	21.7	22.2	22.8	23.3	22.8	22.8	22.8	22.8	23.3	22.8
DIURNAL RANGE	6.7	7.7	8.9	10.0	10.0	8.9	9.4	8.9	9.4	8.9	7.3	6.6
S/HEMISPHERE	JUL	AUG	SEP	OCT	NOV	DEC	JAN	FEB	MAR	APR	MAY	JUN

Cultural Recommendations

LIGHT: 2000–3000 fc.

TEMPERATURES: Throughout the year, days average 84–91°F (29–33°C), and nights average 71–74°F (22–23°C), with a diurnal range of 12–18°F (7–10°C).

HUMIDITY: Information is not available for this location. However, records from nearby stations indicate that humidity probably averages near 85% year-round.

WATER: Rainfall is very heavy all year. Cultivated plants should be kept evenly moist.

FERTILIZER: ¼–½ recommended strength. A balanced fertilizer should be applied weekly to biweekly throughout the year.

REST PERIOD: Growing conditions should be maintained year-round. Slightly cooler winter days are the primary difference between winter and summer. Water and fertilizer should be reduced slightly, especially for plants cultivated in the dark, short-day conditions common in temperate-latitude winters. Plants should never be allowed to dry out completely, however.

GROWING MEDIA: Because plants must be kept moist, they are easier to manage when potted. Fir bark or any open, fast-draining medium may be used. Repotting may be done anytime new roots are growing.

MISCELLANEOUS NOTES: The bloom season shown in the climate table is based on reports from the habitat.

Plant and Flower Information

PLANT SIZE AND TYPE: A 9 in. (23 cm) sympodial epiphyte.

PSEUDOBULB: 9 in. (23 cm) long. The flattened, branching stems consist of numerous, very short internodes.

LEAVES: Many. The erect-spreading leaves are 0.6–0.8 in. (1.6–2.1 cm) long. They are lanceolate-triangular and pointed.

INFLORESCENCE: Short. Inflorescences emerge from numerous bracts at nodes along the stem.

FLOWERS: 1 per inflorescence. The thick, fleshy flowers are 0.3 in. (0.8 cm) long. They are pale green and shiny. The dorsal sepal is ovate-triangular and pointed, and lateral sepals are obliquely triangular. The petals are oblong-ovate. The lip is oblong and somewhat recurved. The midlobe is smooth and shiny with a hairy margin. The callus is marked with red and shaped like an inverted V.

REFERENCES: 221, 470, 477.

Dendrobium nitidissimum Rchb. f.
Now considered a synonym of *Diplocaulobium nitidissimum* (Rchb. f.) Kränzlin. REFERENCES: 87, 173, 190, 216, 220, 254, 271, 445, 583.

Dendrobium × nitidum (F. M. Bailey) M. Clements and D. Jones.
Thought to be a natural hybrid between *D. pedunculatum* (Clemesha) D. Jones and M. Clements and *D. macropus* (Endl.) Rchb. f. ex Lindley *(D. gracilicaule)* F. Mueller not Kränzlin, this plant has also been known as *D. speciosum* Smith var. *nitidum* F. M. Bailey. REFERENCES: 67, 235.

Dendrobium niveopurpureum J. J. Smith

ORIGIN/HABITAT: Thought have originated on New Guinea, the description was based on a plant grown in the botanical garden at Bogor, Java. Specific habitat location and elevation are not available, so the following climate data should be used with caution.

CLIMATE: Station #96755, Bogor, Indonesia, Lat. 6.5°S, Long. 106.8°E, at 558 ft. (170 m). Record extreme temperatures are 96°F (36°C) and 66°F (19°C).

N/HEMISPHERE	JAN	FEB	MAR	APR	MAY	JUN	JUL	AUG	SEP	OCT	NOV	DEC
°F AVG MAX	86	87	88	88	87	85	84	84	85	86	87	86
°F AVG MIN	73	73	73	74	74	74	74	74	74	75	75	74
DIURNAL RANGE	13	14	15	14	13	11	10	10	11	11	12	12
RAIN/INCHES	2.1	1.0	0.5	5.0	8.1	18.8	23.7	20.2	14.4	12.0	11.9	3.4
HUMIDITY/%	72	68	65	66	74	79	84	84	81	79	77	75
BLOOM SEASON	N/A											
DAYS CLR @ 7AM	14	14	14	11	5	3	1	2	4	6	10	12
DAYS CLR @ 1PM	9	10	8	5	1	1	0	0	1	3	3	7
RAIN/MM	53	25	13	127	206	478	602	513	366	305	302	86
°C AVG MAX	30.0	30.6	31.1	31.1	30.6	29.4	28.9	28.9	29.4	30.0	30.6	30.0
°C AVG MIN	22.8	22.8	22.8	23.3	23.3	23.3	23.3	23.3	23.3	23.9	23.9	23.3
DIURNAL RANGE	7.2	7.8	8.3	7.8	7.3	6.1	5.6	5.6	6.1	6.1	6.7	6.7
S/HEMISPHERE	JUL	AUG	SEP	OCT	NOV	DEC	JAN	FEB	MAR	APR	MAY	JUN

Cultural Recommendations

LIGHT: 2500–3500 fc.

TEMPERATURES: Throughout the year, days average 84–88°F (29–31°C), and nights average 73–75°F (23–24°C), with a diurnal range of 10–15°F (6–8°C). Average highs vary only 4°F (2°C) all year, and nights fluctuate even less. Temperatures at higher elevations are a few degrees cooler, but the diurnal range and limited seasonal fluctuation are similar. Cultivated plants may not be able to tolerate wide temperature fluctuations.

HUMIDITY: 80–85% in summer, dropping to 65–70% in winter and spring.

WATER: Rainfall is very heavy from spring to autumn, but conditions are very dry for 2–3 months in winter. During the growing season, plants should never be allowed to dry out completely, but water should be gradually reduced in late autumn.

FERTILIZER: ¼–½ recommended strength, applied weekly. A high-nitrogen fertilizer is beneficial from spring to midsummer, but a fertilizer high in phosphates should be used in late summer and autumn.

REST PERIOD: Growing temperatures should be maintained all year, but rainfall is very low for 2–3 winter months. In cultivation, water should be reduced and the plants allowed to become somewhat dry between waterings. They should not remain dry for prolonged periods, however. Fertilizer may be reduced or eliminated anytime the plant is not actively growing. In the habitat, light is highest in winter.

GROWING MEDIA: Plants may be mounted on tree-fern or cork slabs if humidity is high and plants are watered at least once daily in summer. When plants are potted, any open, fast-draining medium may be used. Repotting may be done anytime new roots are growing.

MISCELLANEOUS NOTES: Plants that produce flowers which last a single day commonly bloom several times each year. Flowering usually occurs 7–14 days after a sudden 10°F (5°C) drop in daytime temperatures.

Plant and Flower Information

PLANT SIZE AND TYPE: A 20 in. (50 cm) sympodial epiphyte. Plants are often larger.

PSEUDOBULB: 20 in. (50 cm) long. The pale green stems are shiny and very flattened.

LEAVES: Many. The curved, somewhat oblong leaves are 4.3 in. (11 cm) long. They are recurved along the margin.

INFLORESCENCE: Short. Inflorescences emerge through the overlapping leaf sheaths along the side of the stem.

FLOWERS: 2 per inflorescence. The shiny, fleshy flowers are 0.7 in. (1.7 cm) across. They have an oblong, concave dorsal sepal with strongly incurved margins, somewhat triangular, concave lateral sepals, and elliptical, very concave petals. The margin of the 3-lobed lip is warty and edged with purple. The callus is elevated and hairy. J. J. Smith (ref. 470), who was exceptionally frugal with his superlatives, described the flowers as follows, "It is to be regretted that the flowers last only one day, the snow-white of the sepals and petals contrasting really exquisitely with the beautiful purple of the lip."

REFERENCES: 224, 445, 470.

Dendrobium niveum Rolfe.
See *D. johnsoniae* F. Mueller. REFERENCES: 83, 105, 190, 218, 254, 430, 533.

Dendrobium njongense Schlechter

AKA: Sometimes spelled *D. njangense*.

ORIGIN/HABITAT: Northern Papua New Guinea. Plants grow on forest trees along Njonge Creek near Ambo in the Finisterre Range at 1950 ft. (600 m) and near Toliba in the Saki River Valley at about 1650 ft. (500 m).

CLIMATE: Station #200187, Erap, Papua New Guinea, Lat. 6.6°S, Long. 146.7°E, at 850 ft. (260 m). Temperatures are calculated for an elevation of 1950 ft. (600 m), resulting in probable extremes of 98°F (37°C) and 49°F (10°C).

N/HEMISPHERE	JAN	FEB	MAR	APR	MAY	JUN	JUL	AUG	SEP	OCT	NOV	DEC
°F AVG MAX	84	84	85	86	89	89	89	89	89	88	86	86
°F AVG MIN	65	65	65	66	68	69	68	68	69	67	70	66
DIURNAL RANGE	19	19	20	20	21	20	21	21	20	21	16	20
RAIN/INCHES	3.9	3.9	2.7	3.0	3.0	5.3	5.9	5.9	7.0	3.4	2.4	3.1
HUMIDITY/%	82	81	81	79	75	74	74	74	77	76	80	80
BLOOM SEASON			*									
DAYS CLR	N/A											
RAIN/MM	99	99	69	76	76	135	150	150	178	86	61	79
°C AVG MAX	29.1	29.1	29.6	30.2	31.8	31.8	31.8	31.8	31.8	31.3	30.2	30.2
°C AVG MIN	18.5	18.5	18.5	19.1	20.2	20.7	20.2	20.2	20.7	19.6	21.3	19.1
DIURNAL RANGE	10.6	10.6	11.1	11.1	11.6	11.1	11.6	11.6	11.1	11.7	8.9	11.1
S/HEMISPHERE	JUL	AUG	SEP	OCT	NOV	DEC	JAN	FEB	MAR	APR	MAY	JUN

Cultural Recommendations

LIGHT: 2500–3500 fc.

TEMPERATURES: Throughout the year, days average 84–89°F (29–32°C), and nights average 65–70°F (19–21°C), with a diurnal range of 16–21°F (9–12°C).

HUMIDITY: 75–80% year-round. The habitat may be quite dry during hot afternoons.

WATER: Rainfall is moderate most of the year, but conditions are somewhat wetter for 4–5 months in summer and early autumn. Cultivated plants should be thoroughly saturated then allowed to dry slightly between waterings in summer and early autumn. Water should be gradually reduced in autumn.

FERTILIZER: ¼–½ recommended strength. A balanced fertilizer should be applied weekly to biweekly throughout the year.

REST PERIOD: Growing temperatures should be maintained all year. In the habitat, rainfall is lowest in winter, but the high humidity indicates that additional moisture is frequently available from heavy dew. Cultivated plants should be allowed to dry for somewhat longer between waterings than in summer, but they should not remain dry for extended periods. Fertilizer should be reduced until water is increased in spring. In the habitat, seasonal light variation is minor.

GROWING MEDIA: Plants may be mounted on tree-fern or cork slabs, if humidity is high and plants are watered at least once daily in summer. When plants are potted, any open, fast-draining medium may be used. Repotting may be done anytime new roots are growing.

MISCELLANEOUS NOTES: The bloom season shown in the climate table is based on reports from the habitat. Plants that produce flowers which last a single day commonly bloom several times each year. Flowering usually occurs 7–14 days after a sudden 10°F (5°C) drop in daytime temperatures.

Plant and Flower Information

PLANT SIZE AND TYPE: A 28 in. (70 cm) sympodial epiphyte.

PSEUDOBULB: 26 in. (65 cm) long. The stems are curved and do not branch. They are densely leafy.

LEAVES: Many. The lanceolate, pointed leaves are 1.6–2.4 in. (4–6 cm) long. They may be erect or spreading.

INFLORESCENCE: Inflorescences emerge from the leaf axils.

FLOWERS: 2 per inflorescence. The flowers are 0.4 in. (1 cm) long and do not open fully. Sepals and petals are snow-white. The lip has a broadly ovate midlobe and small, triangular sidelobes which are marked with pale yellow. The column is red and orange-yellow. Blossoms last a single day.

REFERENCES: 221, 437, 445.

PHOTOS/DRAWINGS: 437.

Dendrobium nobile Lindley

AKA: *D. coerulescens* Wallich, *D. formosanum* (Rchb. f.) Masamune, *D. lindleyanum* Griffith. The name *D. friedericksianum* is sometimes used for plants which are actually *D. nobile*. *D. nobile* var. *pallidiflora* Hooker is considered a synonym of *D. primulinum* Lindley.

ORIGIN/HABITAT: Southeast Asia, including Nepal, Sikkim, Bhutan, northeastern India, Burma, Thailand, Laos, Vietnam, and much of southern China. In India, plants grow at 650–6550 ft. (200–2000 m). They are widespread in northern Thailand at 1950–4900 ft. (600–1500 m).

CLIMATE: Station #48327, Chiang Mai, Thailand, Lat. 18.8°N, Long. 99.0°E, at 1100 ft. (335 m). Temperatures are calculated for an elevation of 3500 ft. (1070 m), resulting in probable extremes of 101°F (38°C) and 30°F (−1°C).

N/HEMISPHERE	JAN	FEB	MAR	APR	MAY	JUN	JUL	AUG	SEP	OCT	NOV	DEC
°F AVG MAX	77	82	87	88	86	82	81	79	80	81	78	76
°F AVG MIN	48	49	54	62	66	66	66	67	65	63	58	49
DIURNAL RANGE	29	33	33	26	20	16	15	12	15	18	20	27
RAIN/INCHES	0.3	0.4	0.6	2.0	5.5	6.1	7.4	8.7	11.5	4.9	1.5	0.4
HUMIDITY/%	73	65	58	62	73	78	80	83	83	81	79	76
BLOOM SEASON	**	***	***	***	**	*	*	*	*	*	*	*
DAYS CLR @ 7AM	5	5	2	2	1	0	0	0	0	1	3	3
DAYS CLR @ 1PM	9	8	4	2	0	0	0	0	0	0	1	3
RAIN/MM	8	10	15	51	140	155	188	221	292	124	38	10
°C AVG MAX	25.0	27.8	30.6	31.2	30.0	27.8	27.3	26.2	26.7	27.3	25.6	24.5
°C AVG MIN	8.9	9.5	12.3	16.7	18.9	18.9	18.9	19.5	18.4	17.3	14.5	9.5
DIURNAL RANGE	16.1	18.3	18.3	14.5	11.1	8.9	8.4	6.7	8.3	10.0	11.1	15.0
S/HEMISPHERE	JUL	AUG	SEP	OCT	NOV	DEC	JAN	FEB	MAR	APR	MAY	JUN

Cultural Recommendations

LIGHT: 3500–4500 fc. The heavy summer cloud cover indicates that some shading is needed from spring through autumn, but light should be as high as the plant can tolerate, short of burning the leaves. Growers report that *D. nobile* tolerates full sun when grown outdoors if acclimated early in spring and if air movement is excellent. Growers indicate that light is high enough when leaves are slightly yellow.

TEMPERATURES: Summer days average 79–82°F (26–28°C), and nights average 66–67°F (19–20°C), with a diurnal range of 12–16°F (7–9°C). Spring is the warmest time of the year. Days average 86–88°F (30–31°C), and nights average 54–66°F (12–19°C), with a diurnal range of 20–33°F (11–18°C). Growers indicate that plants do well outdoors providing night temperatures are near 50°F (10°C).

HUMIDITY: Near 80% in summer, dropping to near 60% in winter.

WATER: Rainfall is moderate to heavy from late spring through early autumn, but conditions are much drier in winter. Cultivated plants should be kept moist while actively growing, but water should be gradually reduced after new growths mature in autumn.

FERTILIZER: ½ to full strength, applied weekly while plants are actively growing. A high-nitrogen fertilizer is beneficial from spring to midsummer, but a fertilizer high in phosphates should be used in late summer and autumn. Neptune (ref. 322) reports that he obtains better flowering, more uniform growth, and a minimum of keikis by using a 10–30–20 fertilizer mixed at 1 tsp. per gal. (1.3 ml per liter) once a week from spring through midsummer. In late summer and autumn, he uses a 0–44–0 fertilizer at the same dilution rate. Water and fertilizer are then withheld until the following spring.

REST PERIOD: Winter days average 76–82°F (25–28°C), and nights average 48–49°F (9–10°C), with a diurnal range of 27–33°F (15–18°C). Overnight lows are below 50°F (10°C) for 3 months. Plants should be able to tolerate temperatures a few degrees below freezing for short periods, but such extremes should be avoided in cultivation. During very cold weather, a plant's chance of surviving with minimal damage is better if it is dry when temperatures are low. Growers report that the plants from this habitat do tolerate light frost. In the habitat, rainfall averages are very low for 4–5 months in winter, but during the early part of the season the high relative humidity indicates that additional moisture is available from frequent fog, mist, and heavy deposits of dew. Growers sometimes recommend eliminating water in winter, but plants are healthiest if for most of the winter they are allowed to become somewhat dry between waterings but do not remain dry for extended periods. For 1–2 months in late winter, however, conditions are clear, warm, and dry, with humidity so low that even the moisture from morning dew is uncommon. Plants should be allowed to dry out completely between waterings and remain dry longer during this time. Occasional early morning mistings between waterings may help keep the plants from becoming too dry. Fertilizer should be greatly reduced or eliminated until water is increased in spring. A cool, dry rest is essential for cultivated plants and should be continued until new growth starts in spring. In the habitat, light is highest in winter.

Dendrobium nodatum

GROWING MEDIA: Plants may be mounted on cork or tree-fern slabs if humidity is high and plants are watered least once daily in summer. Large plants are best potted in an open, fast-draining media. Growers indicate that the medium is not critical but that using an undersized clay pot which is barely large enough to hold the roots and allow room for 2 year's growth is very important. Repotting should be avoided until the medium starts to break down. When necessary, repotting is best done when new root growth starts or as soon after flowering as possible.

MISCELLANEOUS NOTES: The bloom season shown in the climate table is based on cultivation records. Although considered difficult by many growers, *D. nobile* is one of the most commonly cultivated *Dendrobium* species. It flowers profusely if fertilized regularly while growing and given a cool, dry rest with high light to initiate blooms. A single specimen plant was reported to have produced more than 1000 flowers at one blooming. Bloom time may be delayed by maintaining cool, dry conditions and low light until close to the time the blooms are wanted.

Growers without greenhouses grow *D. nobile* outdoors in spring and summer and bring it indoors in autumn. This suggests that high winter light is not critical.

Plants may be propagated vegetatively by potting keikis and by placing 8–10 in. (20–25 cm) sections of old canes on damp sphagnum. The sections of old canes sometimes root and sometimes produce keikis.

Collected stems are dried and used in Chinese medicine.

Plant and Flower Information

PLANT SIZE AND TYPE: A 24–35 in. (60–90 cm) sympodial epiphyte.

PSEUDOBULB: 24–35 in. (60–90 cm) long. The stems are swollen at the apex and taper to a narrower base. They are clustered on a short connecting rhizome. The canes are often yellowish, somewhat zigzag, round in cross-section, and become furrowed with age. The nodes are usually thickened and flattened.

LEAVES: 6–7. The leaves are distichous, 3–4 in. (7–10 cm) long, oblong to strap-shaped, softly leathery, and deciduous after 2 years.

INFLORESCENCE: Short. Many inflorescences emerge simultaneously from the upper nodes of both leafy and older leafless canes.

FLOWERS: 1–4 per inflorescence. The blossoms are 2.4–4.0 in. (6–10 cm) across, and have a waxy, heavy texture. The oval sepals and much wider, wavy-margined petals are normally white with rose tips. The lip, which is tubular at the base, is downy, cream-white with rose at the apex and deep crimson or crimson-purple markings in the throat. It is occasionally pure white. The flowers are highly variable, however, and even pure white blossoms occur occasionally. The many horticultural variants are based primarily on differences in color. The very fragrant blossoms last 3–6 weeks or longer if conditions are cool and light is low. Specimen plants have carried as many as 200 blooms. Recognized varieties include var. *formosanum* Rchb. f., var. *nobilis* Burbidge, and var. *pallidiflorum* Hooker.

HYBRIDIZING NOTES: Chromosome counts are n = 19 (ref. 154, 187, 504, 542, 580), n = about 20 (ref. 187, 504, 580), 2n = 38 (ref. 150, 151, 152, 153, 154, 187, 188, 243, 504, 542, 547, 580), 2n = 40 (ref. 152, 187, 504, 542, 580), 2n = 57 (ref. 580). When tested as *D. nobile* var. *nobile* the counts were 2n = 19 (ref. 504), 2n = 38 (ref. 504), and 2n = 57 (ref. 187). *D. nobile* var. *cooksonianum* produced counts of n = 19 (ref. 504, 580) and 2n = 38 (ref. 243, 504, 580), and *D. nobile* var. *nobilius* had counts of n = 19 (ref. 504) and 2n = about 57 (ref. 504). *D. nobile* var. *pendulum* 2n = 38 (ref. 504), *D. nobile* var. *sanderianum* was 2n = 38–40 (ref. 504, 580), and *D. nobile* var. *virginale* was 2n = 57 (ref. 504, 580). *D. nobile* var. *wallichianum* was 2n = 38 (ref. 504, 580), *D. nobile* 'King George' was n = 38 (ref. 504, 580), and 2n = 76 (ref. 504, 580). *D. formosanum* had a count of 2n = 38 (ref. 504). *D. nobile* 'Sir F. Moore' had twice the normal count at 2n = 76 (ref. 243).

Seeds are ready for green-pod culture in 150–180 days. They are easy to maintain in flask. *D. nobile* has been widely used in hybridization. Offspring usually have numerous flowers with the size and thick texture of the *D. nobile* parent.

D. nobile is known to hybridize naturally with *D. primulinum* Lindley, producing *D.* × *pitcheranum* Rchb. f.

REFERENCES: 25, 32, 36, 38, 46, 61, 150, 151, 152, 153, 154, 157, 161, 179, 187, 188, 190, 196, 200, 202, 208, 216, 232, 235, 243, 245, 247, 254, 266, 277, 278, 294, 317, 322, 326, 367, 369, 371, 376, 389, 414, 425, 430, 445, 447, 448, 454, 458, 461, 495, 504, 523, 528, 541, 542, 547, 557, 569, 570, 580, 596.

PHOTOS/DRAWINGS: 32, *36*, 55, *245*, *247*, *275*, *322*, *369*, *371*, *389*, *430*, *454*, 458, 461, 541, 557, *569*, 570.

Dendrobium nodatum Lindley. See *D. aphrodite* Rchb. f.

REFERENCES: 190, 216, 254, 445, 570.

Dendrobium nodosum Dalzell. Now considered a synonym

Flickingeria nodosa (Dalzell) Seidenfaden. REFERENCES: 213, 216, 233, 254, 449, 469, 505.

Dendrobium noesae J. J. Smith. Now considered a synonym of

Diplocaulobium noesae. REFERENCES: 25, 75, 220.

Dendrobium non-pommeranicum Schlechter

ORIGIN/HABITAT: New Britain Island. Plants grow at the north end of the Gazelle Peninsula.

CLIMATE: Station #94085, Rabaul, New Britain Is., Papua New Guinea, Lat. 4.2°S, Long. 152.2°E, at 28 ft. (9 m). Record extreme temperatures are 100°F (38°C) and 65°F (18°C).

N/HEMISPHERE	JAN	FEB	MAR	APR	MAY	JUN	JUL	AUG	SEP	OCT	NOV	DEC
°F AVG MAX	89	89	91	92	91	90	90	90	90	90	90	90
°F AVG MIN	73	72	73	73	73	73	73	73	73	73	73	73
DIURNAL RANGE	16	17	18	19	18	17	17	17	17	17	17	17
RAIN/INCHES	5.4	3.7	3.5	5.1	7.1	10.1	14.8	10.4	10.2	10.0	5.2	3.3
HUMIDITY/%	74	73	69	70	73	76	77	76	77	77	75	74
BLOOM SEASON										*		
DAYS CLR	N/A											
RAIN/MM	137	94	89	130	180	257	376	264	259	254	132	84
°C AVG MAX	31.7	31.7	32.8	33.3	32.8	32.2	32.2	32.2	32.2	32.2	32.2	32.2
°C AVG MIN	22.8	22.2	22.8	22.8	22.8	22.8	22.8	22.8	22.8	22.8	22.8	22.8
DIURNAL RANGE	8.9	9.5	10.0	10.5	10.0	9.4	9.4	9.4	9.4	9.4	9.4	9.4
S/HEMISPHERE	JUL	AUG	SEP	OCT	NOV	DEC	JAN	FEB	MAR	APR	MAY	JUN

Cultural Recommendations

LIGHT: 1500–2500 fc.

TEMPERATURES: Throughout the year, days average 89–92°F (32–33°C), and nights average 72–73°F (22–23°C), with a diurnal range of 16–19°F (9–11°C). Average highs and lows vary less than 3°F (2°C) all year, indicating that plants may not tolerate wide temperature fluctuations.

HUMIDITY: 70–80% most of the year. Humidity increases to 90–100% at night, dropping as low as 35% during the day in hot weather.

WATER: Rainfall is moderate to heavy most of the year, but conditions are slightly drier for 2 months in late winter. Cultivated plants should be kept moist in spring and summer, but water should be gradually reduced in autumn.

FERTILIZER: ¼–½ recommended strength. A balanced fertilizer should be applied weekly to biweekly throughout the year.

REST PERIOD: Growing conditions should be maintained all year. Water and fertilizer should be reduced somewhat in winter. Plants should dry slightly between waterings, but they should never be allowed to dry completely. In the habitat, light may be slightly higher in winter.

GROWING MEDIA: Plants may be mounted on tree-fern or cork slabs if humidity is high and plants are watered at least once daily in summer.

When plants are potted, any open, fast-draining medium may be used. They may be repotted anytime new roots are growing.

MISCELLANEOUS NOTES: The bloom season shown in the climate table is based on records from the habitat.

Plant and Flower Information

PLANT SIZE AND TYPE: An 8–18 in. (20–45 cm) sympodial epiphyte.

PSEUDOBULB: 8–18 in. (20–45 cm) long. The erect to spreading stems are swollen at the base and 4–6 angled. They are carried on a very short rhizome. The pseudobulbs occasionally branch.

LEAVES: Many. The leaves, which grow evenly spaced along the stem, were missing from the specimen used for the original description.

INFLORESCENCE: Very short. Inflorescences are borne from nodes along the leafless, upper part of the stem.

FLOWERS: 1–2 per inflorescence. The flowers are 0.4 in. (1 cm) long. The oval sepals and petals are pointed at the tips. The lateral sepals are somewhat triangular. The wavy, erect lip is recurved at the apex. It has 3 parallel lines.

REFERENCES: 222, 440.

PHOTOS/DRAWINGS: 440.

Dendrobium normale Falconer

AKA: *D. fimbriatum* Duthie not Hooker f.

ORIGIN/HABITAT: The northwestern Himalayas of India in the Garhwal and Uttar Pradesh districts. Plants are common near Dehra Dun and Mussoorie at 3300–6550 ft. (1000–2000 m).

CLIMATE: Station #42147, Mukteswar, India, Lat. 29.5°N, Long. 79.7°E, at 7592 ft. (2314 m). Temperatures are calculated for an elevation of 5000 ft. (1520 m), resulting in probable extremes of 100°F (38°C) and 30°F (−1°C).

N/HEMISPHERE	JAN	FEB	MAR	APR	MAY	JUN	JUL	AUG	SEP	OCT	NOV	DEC
°F AVG MAX	60	63	70	78	84	84	78	78	77	74	70	64
°F AVG MIN	45	47	53	61	66	68	68	67	65	59	53	48
DIURNAL RANGE	15	16	17	17	18	16	10	11	12	15	17	16
RAIN/INCHES	1.0	2.1	1.7	1.0	0.3	4.6	11.4	12.8	4.6	3.5	0.3	0.2
HUMIDITY/%	61	55	50	39	44	67	91	93	83	66	55	56
BLOOM SEASON				*	*				*			
DAYS CLR @ 5PM	17	17	15	18	18	12	1	1	6	25	26	21
RAIN/MM	25	53	43	25	8	117	290	325	117	89	8	5
°C AVG MAX	15.3	17.0	20.9	25.3	28.6	28.6	25.3	25.3	24.8	23.1	20.9	17.5
°C AVG MIN	7.0	8.1	11.4	15.9	18.6	19.8	19.8	19.2	18.1	14.8	11.4	8.6
DIURNAL RANGE	8.3	8.9	9.5	9.4	10.0	8.8	5.5	6.1	6.7	8.3	9.5	8.9
S/HEMISPHERE	JUL	AUG	SEP	OCT	NOV	DEC	JAN	FEB	MAR	APR	MAY	JUN

Cultural Recommendations

LIGHT: 2000–3000 fc. Some shading is needed from spring through autumn, but light should be as high as the plant can tolerate, short of burning the leaves. Strong air movement should be provided.

TEMPERATURES: Summer days average 78–84°F (25–29°C), and nights average 67–68°F (19–20°C), with a diurnal range of 10–16°F (6–9°C).

HUMIDITY: Near 90% in summer, decreasing to 55–60% for most of the rest of the year. At the end of the spring dry season, however, averages drop to near 40% for 2 months.

WATER: Rainfall is moderate to heavy for 5 months in summer and very light most of the rest of the year. Cultivated plants should be kept moist while actively growing, but water should be reduced in autumn.

FERTILIZER: ¼–½ recommended strength, applied weekly. A high-nitrogen fertilizer is beneficial from spring to midsummer, but a fertilizer high in phosphates should be used in late summer and autumn.

REST PERIOD: Winter days average 60–64°F (15–18°C), and nights average 45–48°F (7–9°C), with a diurnal range of 15–16°F (8–9°C). In cultivation, water should be reduced and the plants allowed to dry out between waterings. They should not remain dry for extended periods, however. In late spring, water should be withheld until flower buds swell and new growth begins. Fertilizer should be eliminated until water is increased in spring. In the habitat, light is highest during clear winter weather.

GROWING MEDIA: Plants may be mounted on tree-fern or cork slabs if humidity is high and plants are watered at least once daily in summer. When plants are potted, any open, fast-draining medium may be used. Repotting is best done in early spring when new roots are growing.

MISCELLANEOUS NOTES: The bloom season shown in the climate table is based on reports from the habitat.

Plant and Flower Information

PLANT SIZE AND TYPE: A 12 in. (30 cm) sympodial epiphyte.

PSEUDOBULB: 12 in. (30 cm) long. The terete stems are erect with nodes spaced 1.0–1.4 in. (2.5–3.6 cm) apart.

LEAVES: Several per growth. The shiny leaves are 3–5 in. (8–13 cm) long. They are thin, may be linear or lanceolate, and resemble those of *D. chrysanthum* Wallich ex Lindley.

INFLORESCENCE: 1.0–1.4 in. (2.5–3.6 cm) long. Inflorescences emerge near the tip of leafless stems, although a few leaves may be present when plants are flowering.

FLOWERS: 3–4, rarely 1 per inflorescence. The flowers are 1.8–2.6 in. (4.6–6.5 cm) across. They may be pale yellow or golden-yellow. The wavy lip is marked with a dark brown patch in the center. It has fringed or serrated margins. Sterile flowers are occasionally produced, and they are quite different from the normal shape. Blossoms are sweetly fragrant.

HYBRIDIZING NOTES: Chromosome count is 2n = 38 (ref. 150, 154, 542).

REFERENCES: 102, 150, 154, 202, 216, 254, 278, 369, 374, 445, 542.

PHOTOS/DRAWINGS: 102.

Dendrobium nothofagicola T. M. Reeve

ORIGIN/HABITAT: Papua New Guinea, in the central mountain range. Plants were originally discovered in the Wabag District of Enga Province at 7850 ft. (2400 m). They have since been found in the provinces of Enga, Southern Highlands, Western Highlands, Chimbu, and Central (near Woitape). Although widespread, plants are not common. They usually grow epiphytically in *Nothofagus* forests at 5900–9200 ft. (1800–2800 m).

CLIMATE: Station #200265, Wabag, Papua New Guinea, Lat. 5.5°S, Long. 143.7°E, at 6500 ft. (1980 m). Temperatures are calculated for an elevation of 7850 ft. (2400 m), resulting in probable extremes of 80°F (26°C) and 33°F (1°C).

N/HEMISPHERE	JAN	FEB	MAR	APR	MAY	JUN	JUL	AUG	SEP	OCT	NOV	DEC
°F AVG MAX	67	67	68	68	69	68	69	68	68	68	69	68
°F AVG MIN	47	47	48	48	48	48	49	50	50	48	48	46
DIURNAL RANGE	20	20	20	20	21	20	20	18	18	20	21	22
RAIN/INCHES	5.0	7.6	10.4	10.4	10.3	12.2	11.8	11.9	13.5	11.5	7.8	5.3
HUMIDITY/%	N/A											
BLOOM SEASON	N/A											
DAYS CLR	N/A											
RAIN/MM	127	193	264	264	262	310	300	302	343	292	198	135
°C AVG MAX	19.2	19.2	19.7	19.7	20.3	19.7	20.3	19.7	19.7	19.7	20.3	19.7
°C AVG MIN	8.1	8.1	8.6	8.6	8.6	8.6	9.2	9.7	9.7	8.6	8.6	7.5
DIURNAL RANGE	11.1	11.1	11.1	11.1	11.7	11.1	11.1	10.0	10.0	11.1	11.7	12.2
S/HEMISPHERE	JUL	AUG	SEP	OCT	NOV	DEC	JAN	FEB	MAR	APR	MAY	JUN

Cultural Recommendations

LIGHT: 2000–3000 fc.

TEMPERATURES: Throughout the year, days average 67–69°F (19–20°C), and nights average 46–50°F (8–10°C), with a diurnal range of 18–22°F (10–12°C).

HUMIDITY: Information is not available for this location. However, records

Dendrobium novae-hiberniae

from nearby stations indicate that humidity is probably 75–80% year-round.

WATER: Rainfall is heavy all year. A slightly drier period occurs in winter. Cultivated plants should be kept moist.

FERTILIZER: ¼–½ recommended strength. A balanced fertilizer should be applied weekly to biweekly throughout the year.

REST PERIOD: Growing conditions should be maintained year-round. Water may be reduced somewhat in winter, especially for plants grown in the dark, short-day conditions common in temperate latitudes. Cultivated plants should never be allowed to dry out completely, however. In the habitat, light may be slightly higher in winter.

GROWING MEDIA: Plants are best mounted on tree-fern slabs if humidity is high and they are watered at least once daily in summer. They should be mounted at the top of the slab as they grow down. They may be repotted anytime new roots are growing.

MISCELLANEOUS NOTES: Reeve (ref. 381) indicates that cultivated plants seldom bloom. He suggests that they may need to be dried out to initiate flowering. Reeve states that dried flowers are extremely similar to *D. rutriferum* Rchb. f. but that growth habits are totally different.

Plant and Flower Information

PLANT SIZE AND TYPE: A relatively small, creeping, sympodial epiphyte that usually grows downward.

PSEUDOBULB: 0.3–2.6 in. (0.8–6.5 cm) long. The wrinkled pseudobulbs are spherical to oblong-ovoid. They are normally brown to reddish brown, but some are yellowish green. Stems emerge from a distinct rhizome.

LEAVES: 1 at the apex of each new growth. The elliptic leaves are very thick, leathery, and 0.8–4.3 in. (2–11 cm) long. They may be tessellated on the upper surface and tinged with purple on the underside.

INFLORESCENCE: Very short. Inflorescences are borne at the apex of both leafy and leafless stems.

FLOWERS: 3–20 per inflorescence. The tubelike flowers are 0.4–0.6 in. (1.1–1.5 cm) long. Blossoms are yellow with an orange spur. Sepals and petals are ovate. The unlobed lip is toothed along the margin and infolded at the apex.

REFERENCES: 234, 381.

PHOTOS/DRAWINGS: 381.

Dendrobium novae-hiberniae Kränzlin. See *D. bracteosum* Rchb. f. REFERENCES: 190, 218, 254, 437, 444, 445, 470.

Dendrobium nubigenum Schlechter

AKA: Sometimes spelled *D. nubigena*.

ORIGIN/HABITAT: Northern Papua New Guinea. Plants grow on mistforest trees in the Bismarck Range at about 7550 ft. (2300 m).

CLIMATE: Botanical garden records, Laiagam, Papua New Guinea, Lat. 5.5°S, Long. 143.5°E, at 7218 ft. (2200 m). Record extreme temperatures are 91°F (33°C) and 32°F (0°C).

N/HEMISPHERE	JAN	FEB	MAR	APR	MAY	JUN	JUL	AUG	SEP	OCT	NOV	DEC
°F AVG MAX	76	77	78	76	78	78	82	77	76	78	78	76
°F AVG MIN	55	54	55	55	56	56	55	56	58	57	56	56
DIURNAL RANGE	21	23	23	21	22	22	27	21	18	21	22	20
RAIN/INCHES	4.0	4.8	6.1	7.8	8.5	9.1	8.4	9.6	9.5	8.9	6.3	4.0
HUMIDITY/%	N/A											
BLOOM SEASON					*							
DAYS CLR	N/A											
RAIN/MM	102	121	154	198	217	230	213	243	241	227	159	102
°C AVG MAX	24.4	25.0	25.6	24.4	25.6	25.6	27.8	25.0	24.4	25.6	25.6	24.4
°C AVG MIN	12.8	12.2	12.8	12.8	13.3	13.3	12.8	13.3	14.4	13.9	13.3	13.3
DIURNAL RANGE	11.6	12.8	12.8	11.6	12.3	12.3	15.0	11.7	10.0	11.7	12.3	11.1
S/HEMISPHERE	JUL	AUG	SEP	OCT	NOV	DEC	JAN	FEB	MAR	APR	MAY	JUN

Cultural Recommendations

LIGHT: 2000–3000 fc.

TEMPERATURES: Throughout the year, days average 76–82°F (24–28°C), and nights average 54–58°F (12–14°C), with a diurnal range of 18–27°F (10–15°C).

HUMIDITY: Information is not available for this location. However, records from nearby locations indicate that humidity probably averages near 80% year-round.

WATER: Rainfall is moderate to heavy throughout the year, but conditions are slightly drier for 3–4 months in winter. Cultivated plants should be kept moist.

FERTILIZER: ¼–½ recommended strength. A balanced fertilizer should be applied weekly to biweekly throughout the year.

REST PERIOD: Growing conditions should be maintained all year. For cultivated plants, water and fertilizer should be reduced somewhat in winter, especially for plants grown in the dark, short-day conditions common in temperate latitudes. They should never be allowed to dry out completely, however. An occasional early morning misting may be given on clear days between waterings.

GROWING MEDIA: Plants may be mounted on tree-fern or cork slabs if humidity is high and plants are watered at least once daily in summer. When plants are potted, any open, fast-draining medium may be used. Repotting may be done anytime new roots are growing.

MISCELLANEOUS NOTES: The bloom season shown in the climate table is based on reports from the habitat.

Plant and Flower Information

PLANT SIZE AND TYPE: A 5–6 in. (13–15 cm) sympodial epiphyte. The plant is compact and low growing.

PSEUDOBULB: 5–6 in. (13–15 cm) long. The erect to suberect stems are densely leafy.

LEAVES: Many. The leaves are 0.6–0.8 in. (1.5–2.0 cm) long, oblong, smooth, and rigid.

INFLORESCENCE: Very short. The flowers are clustered.

FLOWERS: Few per inflorescence. The flowers are 0.6 in. (1.5 cm) long. They are violet-pink with orange-red on the lip and column. Blossoms have oval sepals and oblong petals. The lip is narrow with parallel margins at the base. Near the apex it flares with a very small, rounded projection at the apex. The callus, which runs the entire length of the lip, has a rounded tip.

REFERENCES: 221, 437, 445.

PHOTOS/DRAWINGS: 437.

Dendrobium nudum (Blume) Lindley

AKA: *Onychium nudum* Blume. Ames (ref. 12) reports that J. J. Smith includes *Dendrobium aureoroseum* Rchb. f. as a synonym but that Kränzlin doubts that synonymy.

ORIGIN/HABITAT: Java and Sumatra. Plants have been found southwest of Bogor in the forests of Mt. Salak at 3950–6550 ft. (1200–2000 m), but they are common on nearly every large mountain in Java. Although they always grow in the shade, they are found in both wet and dry areas.

CLIMATE: Station #96755, Bogor, Indonesia, Lat. 6.5°S, Long. 106.8°E, at 558 ft. (170 m). Temperatures are calculated for an elevation of 5000 ft. (1520 m), resulting in probable extremes of 81°F (27°C) and 51°F (11°C).

N/HEMISPHERE	JAN	FEB	MAR	APR	MAY	JUN	JUL	AUG	SEP	OCT	NOV	DEC
°F AVG MAX	71	72	73	73	72	70	69	69	70	71	72	71
°F AVG MIN	58	58	58	59	59	59	59	59	59	60	60	59
DIURNAL RANGE	13	14	15	14	13	11	10	10	11	11	12	12
RAIN/INCHES	2.1	1.0	0.5	5.0	8.1	18.8	23.7	20.2	14.4	12.0	11.9	3.4
HUMIDITY/%	72	68	65	66	74	79	84	84	81	79	77	75
BLOOM SEASON					*	*						
DAYS CLR @ 7AM	14	14	14	11	5	3	1	2	4	6	10	12
DAYS CLR @ 1PM	9	10	8	5	1	1	0	0	1	1	3	7
RAIN/MM	53	25	13	127	206	478	602	513	366	305	302	86
°C AVG MAX	21.9	22.4	23.0	23.0	22.4	21.3	20.7	20.7	21.3	21.9	22.4	21.9
°C AVG MIN	14.6	14.6	14.6	15.2	15.2	15.2	15.2	15.2	15.2	15.7	15.7	15.2
DIURNAL RANGE	7.3	7.8	8.4	7.8	7.2	6.1	5.5	5.5	6.1	6.2	6.7	6.7
S/HEMISPHERE	JUL	AUG	SEP	OCT	NOV	DEC	JAN	FEB	MAR	APR	MAY	JUN

Cultural Recommendations

LIGHT: 1500–2300 fc. Clear summer days are rare, indicating that light is relatively low.

TEMPERATURES: Throughout the year, days average 69–73°F (21–23°C), and nights average 58–60°F (15–16°C), with a diurnal range of 10–15°F (6–8°C).

HUMIDITY: 75–85% most of the year, dropping to near 65% in late winter and early spring.

WATER: Rainfall is very heavy from spring to autumn, but conditions are very dry for 2–3 months in winter. During the growing season, plants should never be allowed to dry out completely, but water should be gradually reduced in late autumn.

FERTILIZER: ¼–½ recommended strength, applied weekly. A high-nitrogen fertilizer is beneficial from spring to midsummer, but a fertilizer high in phosphates should be used in late summer and autumn.

REST PERIOD: Growing conditions should be maintained all year, but rainfall is very low for 2–3 winter months. In cultivation, water should be reduced and the plants allowed to become somewhat dry between waterings. They should not remain dry for prolonged periods, however. Fertilizer may be reduced or eliminated anytime the plant is not actively growing. In the habitat, light is highest in winter.

GROWING MEDIA: Plants may be mounted on tree-fern or cork slabs if humidity is high and plants are watered at least once daily in summer. When plants are potted, any open, fast-draining medium may be used. Repotting may be done anytime new roots are growing.

MISCELLANEOUS NOTES: The bloom season shown in the climate table is based on cultivation records. Collection records show the same bloom season, but reports from the habitat indicate that it blooms throughout the year.

Plant and Flower Information

PLANT SIZE AND TYPE: A 16 in. (40 cm) sympodial epiphyte. Plants sometimes reach a length of 39 in. (100 cm).

PSEUDOBULB: 16 in. (40 cm) long. The stems are slender at the base, nodding, and close together.

LEAVES: 5 per growth. The linear-lanceolate leaves are 2.4–4.0 in. (6–10 cm) long. They are 0.8 in. (2 cm) apart and become progressively smaller near the apex of the stem. The leaf sheaths are marked with dark speckles.

INFLORESCENCE: Short. Racemes are normally produced at nodes near the apex of leafless stems.

FLOWERS: 2–4 per inflorescence. The flowers are 1.0–1.4 in. (2.5–3.6 cm) across. Sepals and petals spread about 45°. They may be cream or pale yellowish brown, sometimes suffused with violet dots. The sepals are often pink at the tips and suffused with pink on the backside. The broadly tongue-shaped lip has a greenish yellow blotch in the center surrounded by a wide, wavy margin of rose-pink or violet speckles. It is notched at the apex.

REFERENCES: 12, 25, 75, 179, 216, 254, 277, 310, 317, 445, 469.

PHOTOS/DRAWINGS: 75, 469.

Dendrobium nugentii (F. M. Bailey) D. Jones and M. Clements

AKA: Clements (ref. 67) advocates species status for *D. linguiforme* Swartz var. *nugentii* F. M. Bailey, but many botanists still consider it a variety of *D. linguiforme*.

ORIGIN/HABITAT: Northeastern Queensland, Australia. Plants are found in the mountains and tablelands from south of Townsville at about 20.0°S to near Cooktown at 15.5° S. The orchids usually grow on trees near dry creeks, but they also grow on trees near rainforests and on rocks and trees in open forests.

CLIMATE: Station #94287, Cairns, Australia, Lat. 16.9°S, Long. 145.8°E, at 7 ft. (2 m). Temperatures are calculated for an elevation of 2000 ft. (610 m), resulting in probable extremes of 103°F (40°C) and 36°F (3°C).

N/HEMISPHERE	JAN	FEB	MAR	APR	MAY	JUN	JUL	AUG	SEP	OCT	NOV	DEC
°F AVG MAX	71	73	76	79	81	83	83	82	80	78	74	72
°F AVG MIN	54	55	57	61	63	66	67	67	66	63	59	57
DIURNAL RANGE	17	18	19	18	18	17	16	15	14	15	15	15
RAIN/INCHES	1.6	1.7	1.7	2.1	3.9	8.7	16.6	15.7	18.1	11.3	4.4	2.9
HUMIDITY/%	69	67	65	65	65	68	72	72	74	73	73	72
BLOOM SEASON	*	*										*
DAYS CLR @ 10AM	9	11	13	11	6	6	4	5	6	7	11	10
DAYS CLR @ 4PM	8	10	12	16	10	7	4	3	4	6	9	10
RAIN/MM	41	43	43	53	99	221	422	399	460	287	112	74
°C AVG MAX	21.9	23.0	24.7	26.3	27.5	28.6	28.6	28.0	26.9	25.8	23.6	22.5
°C AVG MIN	12.5	13.0	14.1	16.3	17.5	19.1	19.7	19.7	19.1	17.5	15.2	14.1
DIURNAL RANGE	9.4	10.0	10.6	10.0	10.0	9.5	8.9	8.3	7.8	8.3	8.4	8.4
S/HEMISPHERE	JUL	AUG	SEP	OCT	NOV	DEC	JAN	FEB	MAR	APR	MAY	JUN

Cultural Recommendations

LIGHT: 2500–3500 fc.

TEMPERATURES: Summer days average 82–83°F (28–29°C), and nights average 66–67°F (19–20°C), with a diurnal range of 15–17°F (8–10°C).

HUMIDITY: Near 75% in summer and autumn, dropping to about 65% in winter and spring.

WATER: Rainfall is moderate to heavy from late spring into autumn, but conditions are quite dry in winter. Mounted plants should be watered daily in summer, but Australian growers indicate that potted plants should be watered sparingly. Plants should be kept moist while actively growing, but water should be gradually reduced in autumn.

FERTILIZER: ¼–½ recommended strength, applied weekly. A high-nitrogen fertilizer is beneficial from spring to midsummer, but a fertilizer high in phosphates should be used in late summer and autumn.

REST PERIOD: Winter days average 71–76°F (22–25°C), and nights average 54–57°F (13–14°C), with a diurnal range of 15–19°F (8–11°C). Water and fertilizer should be reduced for 4–5 months from late autumn into early spring. Cultivated plants should be kept on the dry side, but they should not be allowed to dry out completely. In the habitat, light is highest in winter.

GROWING MEDIA: Plants are best mounted on hardwood or cork slabs, or attached to garden trees in areas where the climate allows year-round outdoor growing. If plants are grown outside, however, they must be protected from heavy winter rains. Mounted plants should be watered at least once daily in summer. Growers indicate that plants are healthiest when watered each evening in summer and in the mornings in winter. If plants must be potted, clay pots may be filled with a very open and fast-draining medium. Cultivated plants should be watered carefully and sparingly. Once established, plants should be disturbed as little as possible. The rhizome is very brittle, so a long-lasting mount is advisable. Repotting is best done after flowering, when new roots begin to grow.

Dendrobium nummularia

MISCELLANEOUS NOTES: The bloom season shown in the climate table is based on records from the habitat. Growers recommend purchasing an established plant, as small pieces are very difficult to establish.

Plant and Flower Information

PLANT SIZE AND TYPE: A miniature sympodial epiphyte or lithophyte.

PSEUDOBULB: Very small. The tiny pseudobulbs are carried on a very short, creeping rhizome. Each branch is 0.4–1.6 in. (1–4 cm) long. The rhizome branches freely and forms a large, dense, cactuslike mat. The entire plant hugs the substratum.

LEAVES: 1 per growth. The thick, coarsely textured leaves are 0.8–1.6 in. (2–4 cm) long, which is larger than other plants that are considered varieties of *D. linguiforme*. They may be broadly ovate to nearly round with pronounced longitudinal and transverse furrows that make the roughened surface feel like sandpaper. They are prostrate and appear to emerge directly from the creeping rhizome. They tend to alternate along the rhizome. Leaves are often tinged with red.

INFLORESCENCE: 3–8 in. (8–20 cm) long. The erect to arching inflorescences are held away from the leaf. They emerge below the leaf bases, especially near the growing tip. Extremely floriferous, the mass of flowers point in all directions. Blossoms are evenly spaced on the raceme.

FLOWERS: 6–20 per inflorescence. The white to cream flowers are 0.8–1.2 in. (2–3 cm) across and may not open fully. The lip, which is usually uppermost, may have faint purple markings. The fragrant blossoms have shorter, rounder segments than other plants that are considered varieties of *D. linguiforme*. The fragrant blossoms turn yellow with age, and they often age quickly.

HYBRIDIZING NOTES: Hybrids tend to be very floriferous.

REFERENCES: 67, 105, 235, 291, 533, 546.

PHOTOS/DRAWINGS: 105, *291, 533, 546*.

Dendrobium nummularia Schlechter

AKA: *D. prorepens* Schlechter.

ORIGIN/HABITAT: Northern Papua New Guinea. Plants grow on mistforest trees in the Torricelli Range at about 2600 ft. (800 m). Near Jaduna in the Waria District, they have been found below the mistforest zone at about 1500 ft. (450 m). Plants have not been collected recently.

CLIMATE: Station #94004, Wewak, Papua New Guinea, Lat. 3.6°S, Long. 143.7°E, at 16 ft. (5 m). Temperatures are calculated for an elevation of 2600 ft. (800 m), resulting in probable extremes of 89°F (32°C) and 53°F (12°C).

N/HEMISPHERE	JAN	FEB	MAR	APR	MAY	JUN	JUL	AUG	SEP	OCT	NOV	DEC
°F AVG MAX	79	79	79	79	79	79	78	77	78	79	79	79
°F AVG MIN	65	65	65	66	66	66	66	66	65	65	66	65
DIURNAL RANGE	14	14	14	13	13	13	12	11	13	14	13	14
RAIN/INCHES	7.6	4.8	5.3	10.0	13.3	14.5	12.1	11.9	14.9	16.9	15.1	10.8
HUMIDITY/%	80	79	79	78	79	81	82	82	81	82	81	80
BLOOM SEASON				*					*			
DAYS CLR	N/A											
RAIN/MM	193	122	135	254	338	368	307	302	378	429	384	274
°C AVG MAX	26.3	26.3	26.3	26.3	26.3	26.3	25.8	25.2	25.8	26.3	26.3	26.3
°C AVG MIN	18.6	18.6	18.6	19.1	19.1	19.1	19.1	19.1	18.6	18.6	19.1	18.6
DIURNAL RANGE	7.7	7.7	7.7	7.2	7.2	7.2	6.7	6.1	7.2	7.7	7.2	7.7
S/HEMISPHERE	JUL	AUG	SEP	OCT	NOV	DEC	JAN	FEB	MAR	APR	MAY	JUN

Cultural Recommendations

LIGHT: 2000–3000 fc.

TEMPERATURES: Throughout the year, days average 77–79°F (25–26°C), and nights average 65–66°F (19°C), with a diurnal range of 11–14°F (6–8°C).

HUMIDITY: Near 80% year-round.

WATER: Rainfall is heavy all year, but conditions are slightly drier for 1–2 months in winter. Cultivated plants should be kept evenly moist.

FERTILIZER: ¼–½ recommended strength. A balanced fertilizer should be applied weekly to biweekly throughout the year.

REST PERIOD: Growing conditions should be maintained year-round. Water and fertilizer should be reduced somewhat in winter, especially for plants grown in the dark, short-day conditions common in temperate latitudes. Plants should not be allowed to dry out completely, however. Fertilizer should be reduced if water is reduced. In the habitat, light is highest in winter.

GROWING MEDIA: Plants are best mounted on a tree-fern slab to accommodate their mat-forming growth habit, but humidity must be high and plants must be watered daily in summer. If plants are potted, small pots or baskets may be filled with any open, moisture-retaining medium. Repotting may be done anytime new roots are growing.

MISCELLANEOUS NOTES: The bloom season shown in the climate table is based on reports from the habitat.

Plant and Flower Information

PLANT SIZE AND TYPE: A creeping, 1.2 in. (3 cm) sympodial epiphyte.

PSEUDOBULB: 0.1–0.3 in. (0.3–0.7 cm) long. The pseudobulbs are said to resemble a string of beads.

LEAVES: 1 per growth. The tiny leaf, which may be ovate, oblong, or elliptic, is 0.2–0.3 in. (0.5–0.8 cm) long.

INFLORESCENCE: A single inflorescence arises from the apex of the pseudobulb.

FLOWERS: 1 per inflorescence. The flowers are 0.4–0.5 in. (0.9–1.2 cm) across. They are dark violet with yellow at the tips of all segments. Blossoms have an ovate dorsal sepal, small, distinctly spreading petals, and somewhat triangular lateral sepals. The lip is sharply recurved at the minutely hairy tip. The apex is deeply lobed with a small, pointed projection between the 2 rounded lobes.

REFERENCES: 221, 382, 437, 445.

PHOTOS/DRAWINGS: 382, 437.

Dendrobium nummulifolium R. King. Now considered a synonym of *Bulbophyllum minutissimum* F. Mueller. REFERENCES: 216, 254.

Dendrobium nutans Lindley not Presl

AKA: Hunt (ref. 211) includes the synonyms *D. jerdonianum* Wight, *D. nutantiflorum* A. Hawkes and A. H. Heller, and *D. villosulum* Lindley not Wallich or Rchb. f.; but *D. nutantiflorum* is still used in some publications.

ORIGIN/HABITAT: Southern India, Sri Lanka, and Borneo. Considered endangered in India, plants are found in Western Ghats, Kerala, and Tamil Nadu, where they usually grow on rhododendron plants at 2600–6550 ft. (800–2000 m). *D. nutans* is relatively common in Sri Lanka (Ceylon). Plants may grow in a variety of climatic conditions on many different host plants, but they are most common at 4000–6000 ft. (1220–1830 m). Plants collected as *D. villosulum* in Sarawak, Borneo, were found at 3950–8550 ft. (1200–2600 m) on Mt. Dulit. They grow in moss on the edge of a rock in dripping water under a waterfall and in rock crevices in a mossforest.

CLIMATE: Station #43473, Nuwara Eliya, Sri Lanka, Lat. 7.0°N, Long. 80.8°E, at 6168 ft. (1880 m). Temperatures are calculated for an elevation of 5000 ft. (1520 m). Record extreme temperatures are not available for this location.

N/HEMISPHERE	JAN	FEB	MAR	APR	MAY	JUN	JUL	AUG	SEP	OCT	NOV	DEC
°F AVG MAX	71	75	76	77	77	73	70	70	70	72	71	71
°F AVG MIN	54	54	55	58	63	65	60	59	59	58	57	57
DIURNAL RANGE	17	21	21	19	14	8	10	11	11	14	14	14
RAIN/INCHES	3.9	2.4	3.2	6.4	5.7	4.3	4.6	5.8	6.4	6.8	7.7	6.5
HUMIDITY/%	N/A											
BLOOM SEASON				*			*	*	*			
DAYS CLR	N/A											
RAIN/MM	99	61	81	163	145	109	117	147	163	173	196	165
°C AVG MAX	21.6	23.8	24.4	24.9	24.9	22.7	21.0	21.0	21.0	22.1	21.6	21.6
°C AVG MIN	12.1	12.1	12.7	14.4	17.1	18.3	15.5	14.9	14.9	14.4	13.8	13.8
DIURNAL RANGE	9.5	11.7	11.7	10.5	7.8	4.4	5.5	6.1	6.1	7.7	7.8	7.8
S/HEMISPHERE	JUL	AUG	SEP	OCT	NOV	DEC	JAN	FEB	MAR	APR	MAY	JUN

Cultural Recommendations

LIGHT: 2000–3000 fc. Shading is needed from spring through autumn, but light should be as high as the plant can tolerate, short of burning the leaves. Strong air movement should be provided year-round.

TEMPERATURES: Summer days average 70–73°F (21–23°C), and nights average 59–65°F (15–18°C), with a diurnal range of 8–11°F (4–6°C). Spring is the warmest season. Days average 76–77°F (24–25°C), and nights average 55–63°F (13–17°C), with a diurnal range of 14–21°F (8–12°C).

HUMIDITY: Information is not available for this location. However, records from nearby stations indicate that humidity probably averages 70–80% year-round.

WATER: Rainfall is moderate to heavy through most of the year, with a 2–3 month semidry period in winter. Conditions in the mountain habitat are probably much wetter year-round than indicated by the climate data, however. Cultivated plants should be kept moist while actively growing, but water should be gradually reduced in late autumn.

FERTILIZER: ¼–½ recommended strength, applied weekly. A high-nitrogen fertilizer is beneficial from spring to midsummer, but a fertilizer high in phosphates should be used in late summer and autumn.

REST PERIOD: Winter days average 71–75°F (22–24°C), and nights average 54–57°F (12–14°C), with a diurnal range of 14–21°F (8–12°C). The increased diurnal range results from cooler nights. Water should be reduced, especially for plants cultivated in the dark, short-day conditions common in temperate-latitude winters. Plants should dry slightly between waterings but should never be allowed to dry out completely. Fertilizer should be reduced or eliminated anytime water is reduced. In the habitat, light is highest in winter.

GROWING MEDIA: Plants may be mounted on tree-fern or cork slabs if humidity is high and plants are watered at least once daily in summer. When plants are potted, any open, fast-draining medium may be used. Repotting is best done in early spring when new roots are growing.

MISCELLANEOUS NOTES: The bloom season shown in the climate table is based on cultivation records. In the habitat, blooming occurs in late autumn or early winter.

Plant and Flower Information

PLANT SIZE AND TYPE: A 4–12 in. (10–30 cm) sympodial epiphyte.

PSEUDOBULB: 4–10 in. (10–25 cm) long. The grooved stems, which are swollen on the upper part, may be slightly zigzag with few or many angles. The internodes are approximately the length of the leaves. The yellowish pseudobulbs are covered with black hairs.

LEAVES: 3–6 per growth. The distichous leaves are 1–3 in. (3–8 cm) long. They are succulent, stiffly leathery, dark green, and forked at the apex. Leaves may be linear-lanceolate to linear-oblong.

INFLORESCENCE: Short. Growths usually produce 2–3 inflorescences, which appear on leafy stems from opposite and above the leaf axils.

FLOWERS: 2–4 per inflorescence. The flowers are 1.2 in. (3 cm) long. Individual clones may be buff-yellow, deep orange, yellow, pink, or greenish white. Sepals and petals are slender and pointed. The fleshy, pointed, 3-lobed lip is ruffled and wavy along the margin of the elongated linear midlobe. It may be the same color as the sepals and petals or it may be pink with purple markings. The sidelobes are rounded. The disk has 3 ridges along the center.

HYBRIDIZING NOTES: In the habitat, plants carry seed capsules until just before the next bloom season.

REFERENCES: 38, 46, 59, 97, 119, 179, 202, 203, 210, 211, 216, 229, 244, 254, 255, 317, 369, 445.

PHOTOS/DRAWINGS: 97, 203, 210, 244, *369*.

Dendrobium nutans Presl not Lindley.

Sometimes listed as a synonym of *Geodorum densiflorum* Lindley, but Clements (ref. 67) indicates reservations regarding this synonymy. In his list of Philippine species, Merrill (ref. 296) included it as a synonym of *Geodorum nutans* (Presl) Ames. REFERENCES: 67, 139, 216, 254, 296, 373, 445, 536.

Dendrobium nutantiflorum A. Hawkes and A. H. Heller.

See *D. nutans* Lindley not Presl. REFERENCES: 191, 211, 454.

Dendrobium nycteridoglossum Rchb. f.

AKA: *D. platyphyllum* Schlechter.

ORIGIN/HABITAT: Sabah (North Borneo). Plants grew in the gardens on Labuan Island near the north side of Brunei Bay.

CLIMATE: Station #96465, Labuan, Sabah (North Borneo), Lat. 5.3°N, Long. 115.2°E at 98 ft. (30 m). Record extreme temperatures are 99°F (37°C) and 59°F (15°C).

N/HEMISPHERE	JAN	FEB	MAR	APR	MAY	JUN	JUL	AUG	SEP	OCT	NOV	DEC
°F AVG MAX	86	86	87	89	89	88	88	88	87	87	87	86
°F AVG MIN	76	76	76	76	76	76	77	76	76	76	76	76
DIURNAL RANGE	10	10	11	13	13	12	11	12	11	11	11	10
RAIN/INCHES	4.4	4.6	5.9	11.7	13.6	13.8	12.5	11.7	16.4	18.3	16.5	11.2
HUMIDITY/%	83	84	83	82	82	82	82	79	80	81	81	82
BLOOM SEASON					**							
DAYS CLR @ 8AM	1	3	3	4	3	0	1	2	1	2	1	2
DAYS CLR @ 2PM	3	5	5	5	2	2	4	3	1	3	1	1
RAIN/MM	112	117	150	297	345	351	318	297	417	465	419	284
°C AVG MAX	30.0	30.0	30.6	31.7	31.7	31.1	31.1	31.1	30.6	30.6	30.6	30.0
°C AVG MIN	24.4	24.4	24.4	24.4	24.4	24.4	25.0	24.4	24.4	24.4	24.4	24.4
DIURNAL RANGE	5.6	5.6	6.2	7.3	7.3	6.7	6.1	6.7	6.2	6.2	6.2	5.6
S/HEMISPHERE	JUL	AUG	SEP	OCT	NOV	DEC	JAN	FEB	MAR	APR	MAY	JUN

Cultural Recommendations

LIGHT: 2000–3000 fc.

TEMPERATURES: Throughout the year, days average 86–89°F (30–32°C), and nights average 76–77°F (24–25°C), with a diurnal range of 10–13°F (6–7°C).

HUMIDITY: 80–85% year-round.

WATER: Rainfall is moderate to heavy all year. Cultivated plants should be kept moist.

FERTILIZER: ¼–½ recommended strength. A balanced fertilizer should be applied weekly to biweekly throughout the year.

REST PERIOD: Growing temperatures should be maintained year-round. Water and fertilizer should be reduced slightly in winter, particularly for plants grown in the dark, short-day conditions in temperate latitudes. Plants should not be allowed to dry out completely, however. In the habitat, light is highest in winter.

GROWING MEDIA: Plants may be mounted on tree-fern or cork slabs if humidity is high and plants are watered at least once daily in summer.

Dendrobium nycteridoglossum

When plants are potted, any open, fast-draining medium may be used. Repotting may be done anytime new roots are growing.

MISCELLANEOUS NOTES: The bloom season shown in the climate table is based on reports from the habitat.

Plant and Flower Information

PLANT SIZE AND TYPE: A 39 in. (100 cm) sympodial epiphyte.

PSEUDOBULB: 39 in. (100 cm) long. The flattened stems are clustered and arise from a very short rhizome. Part of the stem is leafy, but the apex is leafless.

LEAVES: Many. The ovate-lanceolate leaves are 1.6–2.0 in. (4–5 cm) long.

INFLORESCENCE: Short. Clusters of flowers emerge from nodes on the upper, leafless part of the stem.

FLOWERS: Several per inflorescence. The flowers are 0.3 in. (0.7 cm) across. The dorsal sepal is ovate, and lateral sepals are conspicuously dilated. Petals are elliptical. All segments are smooth. The wedge-shaped lip is 3-lobed.

REFERENCES: 218, 254, 286, 295, 433.

Dendrobium obcordatum J. J. Smith

ORIGIN/HABITAT: Molucca Islands. Plants are common along the coast of Seram, usually below 350 ft. (100 m).

CLIMATE: Station #49620, Amahai, Seram, Indonesia, Lat. 3.3°S, Long. 128.9°E, at 10 ft. (3 m). Temperatures are calculated for an elevation of 300 ft. (90 m), resulting in probable extremes of 95°F (35°C) and 65°F (18°C).

N/HEMISPHERE	JAN	FEB	MAR	APR	MAY	JUN	JUL	AUG	SEP	OCT	NOV	DEC
°F AVG MAX	80	80	82	84	87	87	87	87	87	85	83	81
°F AVG MIN	73	73	73	73	74	75	75	75	75	75	74	73
DIURNAL RANGE	7	7	9	11	13	12	12	12	12	10	9	8
RAIN/INCHES	23.7	15.8	9.5	6.1	4.5	5.2	5.0	4.7	5.3	11.0	20.3	25.1
HUMIDITY/%	83	82	81	80	79	78	78	77	79	82	83	84
BLOOM SEASON				*				*				
DAYS CLR @ 9AM	1	1	1	6	7	4	3	3	5	5	3	3
DAYS CLR @ 3PM	1	1	2	5	6	1	1	1	2	3	1	3
RAIN/MM	602	401	241	155	114	132	127	119	135	279	516	638
°C AVG MAX	26.7	26.7	27.8	28.9	30.6	30.6	30.6	30.6	30.6	29.5	28.4	27.2
°C AVG MIN	22.8	22.8	22.8	22.8	23.4	23.9	23.9	23.9	23.9	23.9	23.4	22.8
DIURNAL RANGE	3.9	3.9	5.0	6.1	7.2	6.7	6.7	6.7	6.7	5.6	5.0	4.4
S/HEMISPHERE	JUL	AUG	SEP	OCT	NOV	DEC	JAN	FEB	MAR	APR	MAY	JUN

Cultural Recommendations

LIGHT: 2000–3000 fc. In the habitat, clear days are rare.

TEMPERATURES: Throughout the year, days average 80–87°F (27–31°C), and nights average 73–75°F (23–24°C), with a diurnal range of 7–13°F (4–7°C).

HUMIDITY: 75–80% most of the year, increasing to near 85% in winter.

WATER: Rainfall is moderate to heavy year-round, but conditions are slightly drier in spring and summer. Cultivated plants should be allowed to dry slightly between waterings, but they should never be allowed to dry completely.

FERTILIZER: ¼–½ recommended strength. A balanced fertilizer should be applied weekly to biweekly throughout the year.

REST PERIOD: Growing conditions should be maintained all year. In the habitat, winter is the wettest season; but water should not be increased for cultivated plants, especially those grown in the dark, short-day conditions common in temperate latitudes. In fact, water should be reduced slightly; but the plants should never be allowed to dry out completely. Fertilizer should be reduced anytime water is reduced. In the habitat, light is highest in early spring.

GROWING MEDIA: Plants may be mounted on tree-fern or cork slabs or potted in small pots filled with any open, fast-draining medium. Repotting may be done anytime new roots are growing.

MISCELLANEOUS NOTES: The bloom season shown in the climate table is based on reports from the habitat. Plants that produce very short-lived flowers commonly bloom several times during the year. Flowering usually occurs 7–14 days after a sudden 10°F (5°C) drop in daytime temperatures. The plant was described in 1928 in *Bul. Jard. Bot. Buit.* 3rd, sér. 10:142.

Plant and Flower Information

PLANT SIZE AND TYPE: A 44 in. (112 cm) sympodial epiphyte.

PSEUDOBULB: 44 in. (112 cm) long. The very branching stems are swollen above the base. Above the swelling, they are shiny, dark yellow, and very flattened. The stem is leafy above the pseudobulb and below the leafless apex of the stem.

LEAVES: Many. Leaves are 2.5 in. (6.4 cm) long, but only rudimentary leaves develop at the apex of the stem.

INFLORESCENCE: Short. Inflorescences emerge from nodes on the leafless, apical portion of the stem.

FLOWERS: 1 per inflorescence. The flowers are 0.4 in. (1.1 cm) long. They may be white or yellow with red or brown streaks or white with red streaks and a yellow lip. The dorsal sepal is ovate-triangular, concave, and recurved. Lateral sepals are obliquely triangular with a convex, recurved apex and a concave base. The oblong petals are diverging. The apical 40% of the lip is rounded and recurved with a wavy margin. The lip has 3 ridges. Blossoms last a single day.

REFERENCES: 224.

Dendrobium obcuneatum F. M. Bailey

AKA: Schlechter (ref. 437), Lewis and Cribb (ref. 270), and Upton (ref. 533) include *D. obcuneatum* as a synonym of *D. insigne* (Blume) Rchb. f. ex Miquel, but Clements (ref. 67) maintains them as separate species.

ORIGIN/HABITAT: The east coast of Papua New Guinea. Plants are often found at low elevations near the beach.

CLIMATE: Station #94014, Madang, Papua New Guinea, Lat. 5.2°S, Long. 145.8°E, at 13 ft. (4 m). Temperatures are calculated for an elevation of 500 ft. (150 m), resulting in probable extremes of 96°F (36°C) and 60°F (16°C).

N/HEMISPHERE	JAN	FEB	MAR	APR	MAY	JUN	JUL	AUG	SEP	OCT	NOV	DEC
°F AVG MAX	81	81	83	83	83	83	83	83	83	85	85	82
°F AVG MIN	75	76	76	76	75	75	75	75	75	74	75	76
DIURNAL RANGE	6	5	7	7	8	8	8	8	8	11	10	6
RAIN/INCHES	4.0	3.4	3.2	8.5	11.2	11.1	10.1	11.3	9.4	11.3	10.5	6.7
HUMIDITY/%	88	87	86	86	86	86	86	85	85	87	88	89
BLOOM SEASON	*		*	*								
DAYS CLR	N/A											
RAIN/MM	102	86	81	216	284	282	257	287	239	287	267	170
°C AVG MAX	27.4	27.4	28.6	28.6	28.6	28.6	28.6	28.6	28.6	29.7	29.7	28.0
°C AVG MIN	24.1	24.7	24.7	24.7	24.1	24.1	24.1	24.1	24.1	23.6	24.1	24.7
DIURNAL RANGE	3.3	2.7	3.9	3.9	4.5	4.5	4.5	4.5	4.5	6.1	5.6	3.3
S/HEMISPHERE	JUL	AUG	SEP	OCT	NOV	DEC	JAN	FEB	MAR	APR	MAY	JUN

Cultural Recommendations

LIGHT: 2000–3000 fc.

TEMPERATURES: Throughout the year, days average 81–85°F (27–30°C), and nights average 74–76°F (24–25°C), with a diurnal range of 5–11°F (3–6°C). The warmest highs, the coolest lows, and the greatest diurnal range occur in autumn.

HUMIDITY: 85–90% year-round.

WATER: Rainfall is heavy most of the year, but conditions are somewhat drier in winter. Cultivated plants should be kept moist, with only slight drying allowed between waterings.

FERTILIZER: ¼–½ recommended strength. A balanced fertilizer should be applied weekly to biweekly throughout the year.

REST PERIOD: Growing temperatures should be maintained all year. In the habitat, rainfall decreases for 2–3 months in winter. Water and fertilizer should be reduced slightly for cultivated plants, but they should not be allowed to dry out completely. In the habitat, light is slightly higher in winter.

GROWING MEDIA: Plants may be mounted on tree-fern or cork slabs or potted in small pots filled with any open, fast-draining medium. Repotting may be done anytime new roots are actively growing.

MISCELLANEOUS NOTES: The bloom season shown in the climate table is based on collection records.

Plant and Flower Information

PLANT SIZE AND TYPE: A sympodial epiphyte of unreported size. Clements (ref. 67) did not indicate that plant size was different than *D. insigne* (Blume) Rchb. f. ex Miquel, which is up to 24 in. (60 cm) long.

Dendrobium obliquum

PSEUDOBULB: The stem is flattened. The piece of stem available at the time of the original description was 7 in. (18 cm) long.

LEAVES: Many. The leaves are 2.0–2.4 in. (5–6 cm) long. They are distichous, oblong, and uneven along the apical margin.

INFLORESCENCE: Short.

FLOWERS: 1–2 per inflorescence. The white flowers are 0.7–0.8 in. (1.8–2.0 cm) long. Clements (ref. 67) states that "Flowers are smaller than *D. insigne* with obovate rather than sickle-shaped tepals. It also lacks a column appendage as well as the heavy orange markings found on the inside of the tepals in *D. insigne*."

REFERENCES: 67, 220, 254, 270, 533.

Dendrobium obliquum Schlechter 1912

AKA: This is not the plant originally described as *Cadetia obliqua* Schlechter and transferred to *Dendrobium obliquum* by J. J. Smith. See following species.

ORIGIN/HABITAT: Northern Papua New Guinea. Plants grow on forest trees near the Malia River at about 1000 ft. (300 m) in the foothills of the Bismarck Range.

CLIMATE: Station #200187, Erap, Papua New Guinea, Lat. 6.6°S, Long. 146.7°E, at 850 ft. (260 m). Record extreme temperatures are 102°F (39°C) and 53°F (12°C).

N/HEMISPHERE	JAN	FEB	MAR	APR	MAY	JUN	JUL	AUG	SEP	OCT	NOV	DEC
°F AVG MAX	88	88	89	90	93	93	93	93	93	92	90	90
°F AVG MIN	69	69	69	70	72	73	72	72	73	71	74	70
DIURNAL RANGE	19	19	20	20	21	20	21	21	20	21	16	20
RAIN/INCHES	3.9	3.9	2.7	3.0	3.0	5.3	5.9	5.9	7.0	3.4	2.4	3.1
HUMIDITY/%	82	81	81	79	75	74	74	74	77	76	80	80
BLOOM SEASON					*							
DAYS CLR	N/A											
RAIN/MM	98	99	68	77	76	135	149	149	179	87	60	78
°C AVG MAX	30.9	30.9	31.7	32.3	34.0	33.9	33.8	33.9	34.0	33.6	32.3	32.0
°C AVG MIN	20.4	20.5	20.7	21.1	22.0	22.5	22.1	22.4	22.5	21.7	23.3	20.9
DIURNAL RANGE	10.5	10.4	11.0	11.2	12.0	11.4	11.7	11.5	11.5	11.9	9.0	11.1
S/HEMISPHERE	JUL	AUG	SEP	OCT	NOV	DEC	JAN	FEB	MAR	APR	MAY	JUN

Cultural Recommendations

LIGHT: 3000–4000 fc.

TEMPERATURES: Throughout the year, days average 88–93°F (31–34°C), and nights average 69–74°F (20–23°C), with a diurnal range of 16–21°F (9–12°C).

HUMIDITY: 75–80% year-round. However, the habitat may be quite dry during hot afternoons.

WATER: Rainfall is moderate most of the year, but for 4–5 months in summer and early autumn, conditions are somewhat wetter. Cultivated plants should be thoroughly saturated then allowed to dry slightly between waterings in summer and early autumn. Water should be gradually reduced in autumn.

FERTILIZER: ¼–½ recommended strength. A balanced fertilizer should be applied weekly to biweekly throughout the year.

REST PERIOD: Growing temperatures should be maintained all year. In the habitat, rainfall is lowest in winter, but the high humidity indicates that additional moisture is frequently available from heavy dew. Cultivated plants should be allowed to dry for somewhat longer between waterings, but should not remain dry for extended periods. Fertilizer should be reduced until water is increased in spring. In the habitat, seasonal light variation is minor.

GROWING MEDIA: Plants may be mounted on tree-fern or cork slabs if humidity is high and plants are watered at least once daily in summer. When plants are potted, any open, fast-draining medium may be used. Repotting may be done anytime new roots are growing.

MISCELLANEOUS NOTES: The bloom season shown in the climate table is based on collection reports. Plants that produce flowers which last a single day commonly bloom several times each year. Flowering usually occurs 7–14 days after a sudden 10°F (5°C) drop in daytime temperatures.

Plant and Flower Information

PLANT SIZE AND TYPE: A 12–16 in. (30–40 cm) sympodial epiphyte.

PSEUDOBULB: 12–16 in. (30–40 cm) long. The slightly flattened stems do not branch. They are densely leafy.

LEAVES: Many. The elliptical leaves are 2–3 in. (5–8 cm) long.

INFLORESCENCE: Short. Inflorescences arise from the leaf axils.

FLOWERS: 2 per inflorescence. The flowers are 0.7 in. (1.7 cm) long and remain rather closed. They are yellowish white with orange-yellow marking on the column foot. Sepals and petals are pointed. The lip side-lobes are square at the tip, with 3 teeth. The broadly oval midlobe is rounded along the sides with a point in the apex. The center of the midlobe has a cluster of protuberances. Blossoms are short-lived.

REFERENCES: 221, 437, 445.

PHOTOS/DRAWINGS: 437.

Dendrobium obliquum (Schlechter) J. J. Smith

AKA: *Cadetia obliqua* Schlechter. This plant was transferred from *Cadetia* to *Dendrobium* at the same time that Schlechter described a different plant under the name *D. obliquum*. *Cadetia* is now considered a valid genus by some botanists, so this plant may be redesignated a *Cadetia*.

ORIGIN/HABITAT: Northern Papua New Guinea. Plants were collected near Peso in the Eitape District at about 150 ft. (50 m).

CLIMATE: Station #94004, Wewak, Papua New Guinea, Lat. 3.6°S, Long. 143.7°E, at 16 ft. (5 m). Record extreme temperatures are 98°F (37°C) and 62°F (17°C).

N/HEMISPHERE	JAN	FEB	MAR	APR	MAY	JUN	JUL	AUG	SEP	OCT	NOV	DEC
°F AVG MAX	88	88	88	88	88	88	87	86	87	88	88	88
°F AVG MIN	74	74	74	75	75	75	75	75	74	74	75	74
DIURNAL RANGE	14	14	14	13	13	13	12	11	13	14	13	14
RAIN/INCHES	7.6	4.8	5.3	10.0	13.3	14.5	12.1	11.9	14.9	16.9	15.1	10.8
HUMIDITY/%	80	79	79	78	79	81	82	82	81	82	81	80
BLOOM SEASON		*										
DAYS CLR	N/A											
RAIN/MM	193	122	135	254	338	368	307	302	378	429	384	274
°C AVG MAX	31.1	31.1	31.1	31.1	31.1	31.1	30.6	30.0	30.6	31.1	31.1	31.1
°C AVG MIN	23.3	23.3	23.3	23.9	23.9	23.9	23.9	23.9	23.3	23.3	23.9	23.3
DIURNAL RANGE	7.8	7.8	7.8	7.2	7.2	7.2	6.7	6.1	7.3	7.8	7.2	7.8
S/HEMISPHERE	JUL	AUG	SEP	OCT	NOV	DEC	JAN	FEB	MAR	APR	MAY	JUN

Cultural Recommendations

LIGHT: 2000–3000 fc.

TEMPERATURES: Throughout the year, days average 86–88°F (30–31°C), and nights average 74–75°F (23–24°C), with a diurnal range of 11–14°F (6–8°C). Average highs vary only 2°F (1°C) and average lows fluctuate even less.

HUMIDITY: Near 80% year-round.

WATER: Rainfall is heavy all year, but conditions are slightly drier for 1–2 months in late winter. Cultivated plants should be kept moist with only slight drying allowed between waterings.

FERTILIZER: ¼–½ recommended strength. A balanced fertilizer should be applied weekly to biweekly throughout the year.

REST PERIOD: Growing conditions should be maintained year-round. Water should be reduced for plants cultivated in the dark, short-day conditions common during temperate-latitude winters, but plants should not be allowed to dry out completely. Fertilizer should also be reduced if water is reduced. In the habitat, light may be slightly higher in winter.

GROWING MEDIA: A very open and fast-draining medium should be used with either baskets or small pots. Repotting may be done anytime new roots are growing.

MISCELLANEOUS NOTES: The bloom season shown in the climate table is based on reports from the habitat.

Plant and Flower Information

PLANT SIZE AND TYPE: A 6–8 in. (15–20 cm) sympodial epiphyte.

PSEUDOBULB: 2.4–4.3 in. (6–11 cm) long. Pseudobulbs are acutely 4-angled. They are borne on a very short rhizome.

LEAVES: 1 per growth. The oblong, almost sickle-shaped leaves are 2.4–3.1 in. (6–8 cm) long, broad, blunt, and smooth.

INFLORESCENCE: Very short.

FLOWERS: 1 per inflorescence. The flower is 0.2 in. (0.5 cm) long. Sepals and petals are white. The lip has red sidelobes and a red margin on the midlobe. The dorsal sepal and petals are erect to flaring back. The lip has large, oval sidelobes with a notched midlobe. The lip is marked with 5 separate raised lines. The centerline is longest. The base of the lip has a cluster of hairs.

REFERENCES: 221, 437, 472.

PHOTOS/DRAWINGS: 437.

Dendrobium oblongimentum Hosokawa and Fukuyama

ORIGIN/HABITAT: Rota Island in the Mariana Island group north of Guam. Habitat information and elevation are unavailable, so the following climate data should be used with caution.

CLIMATE: Station #91218, Anderson AFB, Guam, Lat. 12.6°N, Long. 144.9°E, at 605 ft. (184 m). Record extreme temperatures are 94°F (34°C) and 66°F (19°C).

N/HEMISPHERE	JAN	FEB	MAR	APR	MAY	JUN	JUL	AUG	SEP	OCT	NOV	DEC
°F AVG MAX	81	81	81	83	83	84	84	84	83	83	83	82
°F AVG MIN	75	74	75	76	76	77	76	76	75	76	77	76
DIURNAL RANGE	6	7	6	7	7	7	8	8	8	7	6	6
RAIN/INCHES	4.2	4.6	2.4	4.9	5.7	4.6	8.0	11.7	13.5	15.4	6.8	6.7
HUMIDITY/%	82	82	81	82	83	83	84	86	87	87	84	82
BLOOM SEASON							N/A					
DAYS CLR @ 10AM	1	1	1	2	1	0	0	0	0	0	1	0
DAYS CLR @ 4PM	1	2	1	2	1	1	0	0	0	1	1	2
RAIN/MM	107	117	61	124	145	117	203	297	343	391	173	170
°C AVG MAX	27.2	27.2	27.2	28.3	28.3	28.9	28.9	28.9	28.3	28.3	28.3	27.8
°C AVG MIN	23.9	23.3	23.9	24.4	24.4	25.0	24.4	24.4	23.9	24.4	25.0	24.4
DIURNAL RANGE	3.3	3.9	3.3	3.9	3.9	3.9	4.5	4.5	4.4	3.9	3.3	3.4
S/HEMISPHERE	JUL	AUG	SEP	OCT	NOV	DEC	JAN	FEB	MAR	APR	MAY	JUN

Cultural Recommendations

LIGHT: 1800–2500 fc.

TEMPERATURES: Throughout the year, days average 81–84°F (27–29°C), and nights average 74–77°F (23–25°C), with a diurnal range of 6–8°F (3–5°C). Average high and low temperatures vary only 3°F (2°C) all year.

HUMIDITY: Near 80–85% year-round.

WATER: Rainfall is moderate to heavy most of the year, with a brief, semi-dry period in late winter. Cultivated plants should be kept moist while actively growing, but water should be gradually reduced in late autumn.

FERTILIZER: ¼–½ recommended strength. A balanced fertilizer should be applied weekly to biweekly throughout the year.

REST PERIOD: Growing conditions should be maintained year-round. Water should be reduced somewhat in winter, especially for plants grown in the dark, short-day conditions common in temperate-latitude winters. Plants should never dry out completely, however. Fertilizer should be reduced anytime water is reduced. In the habitat, light is slightly higher in winter.

GROWING MEDIA: Plants may be mounted on tree-fern or cork slabs or potted in small pots filled with any open, fast-draining medium. Repotting may be done anytime new roots are actively growing.

Plant and Flower Information

PLANT SIZE AND TYPE: An 8–10 in. (20–25 cm) sympodial epiphyte.

PSEUDOBULB: 6–8 in. (15–20 cm) long. They do not branch. The lower part of the stem is swollen and leafless.

LEAVES: Many. The distichous leaves are 2.8 in. (7 cm) long. They are terete, swollen, and sharply pointed.

INFLORESCENCE: Short. Inflorescences emerge from nodes on the upper part of the stem.

FLOWERS: 1 per inflorescence. The white flowers are 0.6 in. (1.6 cm) long. The sepals are deltoid. The petals are much smaller than the sepals. The recurved lip has no sidelobes.

REFERENCES: 205, 227.

PHOTOS/DRAWINGS: 205.

Dendrobium oblongum Ames and Schweinfurth

ORIGIN/HABITAT: Borneo. Plants were originally found on Mt. Kinabalu but are now known to occur in Sabah, Sarawak and Kalimantan. They grow in hill forests and lower mountain forests at 3600–5600 ft. (1100–1700 m).

CLIMATE: Station #49613, Tambunan, Sabah, Borneo, Lat. 5.7°N, Long. 116.4°E, at 1200 ft. (366 m). Temperatures are calculated for an elevation of 4800 ft. (1460 m), resulting in probable extremes of 86°F (30°C) and 42°F (6°C).

N/HEMISPHERE	JAN	FEB	MAR	APR	MAY	JUN	JUL	AUG	SEP	OCT	NOV	DEC
°F AVG MAX	74	75	77	78	78	77	77	77	77	76	75	74
°F AVG MIN	55	53	54	55	56	55	54	54	55	55	55	56
DIURNAL RANGE	19	22	23	23	22	22	23	23	22	21	20	18
RAIN/INCHES	5.8	3.7	5.8	7.5	8.2	7.3	5.1	4.9	6.4	7.0	6.8	6.0
HUMIDITY/%	N/A											
BLOOM SEASON												*
DAYS CLR	N/A											
RAIN/MM	147	94	147	190	208	185	130	124	163	178	173	152
°C AVG MAX	23.4	24.0	25.1	25.6	25.6	25.1	25.1	25.1	25.1	24.5	24.0	23.4
°C AVG MIN	12.8	11.7	12.3	12.8	13.4	12.8	12.3	12.3	12.8	12.8	12.8	13.4
DIURNAL RANGE	10.6	12.3	12.8	12.8	12.2	12.3	12.8	12.8	12.3	11.7	11.2	10.0
S/HEMISPHERE	JUL	AUG	SEP	OCT	NOV	DEC	JAN	FEB	MAR	APR	MAY	JUN

Cultural Recommendations

LIGHT: 2000–2500 fc.

TEMPERATURES: Throughout the year, days average 74–78°F (23–26°C), and nights average 53–56°F (12–13°C), with a diurnal range of 18–23°F (10–13°C).

HUMIDITY: Information is not available for this location. However, records from nearby locations indicate that humidity probably averages 80–85% year-round.

WATER: Rainfall is moderate to heavy all year with a brief, slightly drier period in winter. Cultivated plants should be kept moist, with only slight drying allowed between waterings.

FERTILIZER: ¼–½ recommended strength. A balanced fertilizer should be applied weekly to biweekly throughout the year.

REST PERIOD: Growing temperatures should be maintained all year. Water should be reduced for cultivated plants, especially those grown in the dark, short-day conditions common in temperate-latitude winters, but they should never be allowed to dry out completely. Fertilizer should be reduced or eliminated until water is increased in spring.

Dendrobium obovatum

GROWING MEDIA: Plants may be mounted on tree-fern or cork slabs or potted in small pots filled with any open, fast-draining medium. Repotting may be done anytime new roots are growing.

MISCELLANEOUS NOTES: The bloom season shown in the climate table is based on collection reports. The plant was described in 1927 in *Mitt. Inst. Bot. Hamburg* 7:54.

Plant and Flower Information

PLANT SIZE AND TYPE: A stout sympodial epiphyte of unreported size.

PSEUDOBULB: The stems usually have 1 or more rooting branches. It is entirely hidden by the leaf sheaths.

LEAVES: Many. The distichous leaves are 2.8 in. (7 cm) long, linear, and pointed.

INFLORESCENCE: Short. Inflorescences emerge at the base of middle or upper leaves.

FLOWERS: 1 per inflorescence. The conspicuous flowers are 0.4–0.6 in. (1.0–1.5 cm) across. The blossoms of one collection were greenish yellow with red spots and red dots on the lip, but another collection was described as brownish red. The lip is broader at the base and the apex, and has hairy side margins and an uneven, ruffled apical margin.

REFERENCES: 12, 222, 286, 592.

PHOTOS/DRAWINGS: 592.

Dendrobium obovatum Schlechter

ORIGIN/HABITAT: Northern Papua New Guinea. Plants grow on forest trees in the Kani Range at about 3300 ft. (1000 m).

CLIMATE: Station #94010, Goroka, Papua New Guinea, Lat. 6.1°S, Long. 145.4°E, at 5141 ft. (1567 m). Temperatures are calculated for an elevation of 3300 ft. (1000 m), resulting in probable extremes of 93°F (34°C) and 49°F (10°C).

N/HEMISPHERE	JAN	FEB	MAR	APR	MAY	JUN	JUL	AUG	SEP	OCT	NOV	DEC
°F AVG MAX	82	83	84	85	85	84	85	84	84	84	85	83
°F AVG MIN	62	63	63	63	64	65	65	65	66	65	65	63
DIURNAL RANGE	20	20	21	22	21	19	20	19	18	19	20	20
RAIN/INCHES	2.1	2.8	4.6	5.9	6.6	9.3	9.1	10.1	10.7	8.3	4.6	2.0
HUMIDITY/%	70	67	67	67	67	71	72	73	74	71	70	70
BLOOM SEASON				**	**							
DAYS CLR	N/A											
RAIN/MM	53	71	117	150	168	236	231	257	272	211	117	51
°C AVG MAX	27.9	28.4	29.0	29.5	29.5	29.0	29.5	29.0	29.0	29.0	29.5	28.4
°C AVG MIN	16.7	17.3	17.3	17.3	17.9	18.4	18.4	18.4	19.0	18.4	18.4	17.3
DIURNAL RANGE	11.2	11.1	11.7	12.2	11.6	10.6	11.1	10.6	10.0	10.6	11.1	11.1
S/HEMISPHERE	JUL	AUG	SEP	OCT	NOV	DEC	JAN	FEB	MAR	APR	MAY	JUN

Cultural Recommendations

LIGHT: 2500–3500 fc.

TEMPERATURES: Throughout the year, days average 82–85°F (28–30°C), and nights average 62–66°F (17–19°C), with a diurnal range of 18–22°F (10–12°C).

HUMIDITY: 70–75% from summer into autumn, dropping to 65–70% in winter and spring.

WATER: Rainfall is moderate to heavy most of the year, but conditions are slightly drier for 3 months in winter. Cultivated plants should be kept moist and only slight drying allowed between waterings. Occasional early morning mistings may be beneficial, especially on bright, sunny days.

FERTILIZER: ¼–½ recommended strength. A balanced fertilizer should be applied weekly to biweekly throughout the year.

REST PERIOD: Growing temperatures should be maintained all year. In the habitat, rainfall is lowest in winter, but dew and mist from fog and low clouds are common. Water and fertilizer should be reduced somewhat for cultivated plants, especially those grown in the darker, short-day conditions common during temperate-latitude winters. Plants should be kept on the dry side, but they should never be allowed to dry out completely. In the habitat, light is higher in winter.

GROWING MEDIA: Plants may be mounted on tree-fern or cork slabs if humidity is high and plants are watered at least once daily in summer. When plants are potted, any open, fast-draining medium may be used. Repotting may be done anytime new roots are growing.

MISCELLANEOUS NOTES: The bloom season shown in the climate table is based on reports from the habitat.

Plant and Flower Information

PLANT SIZE AND TYPE: A 6–8 in. (15–20 cm) sympodial epiphyte. Plants consist of many stems.

PSEUDOBULB: 6–8 in. (15–20 cm) long. The densely leafy stems are simple, curved, and flattened. They arise from a very short rhizome.

LEAVES: Many. The nearly linear leaves are 0.5–1.0 in. (1.3–2.5 cm) long, smooth, and unequally bilobed at the apex.

FLOWERS: 1 per inflorescence. The flowers, which are 0.2 in. (0.5 cm) across, are shaped like a flared fan. The oblong sepals and somewhat linear petals are yellow. The fleshy lip is brown with a rounded midlobe. When describing the plant, Schlechter (ref. 437) indicated that the easiest way to separate this species from other, closely related species was that the front of the lip is nearly equal in width to the back of the lip.

REFERENCES: 221, 437, 445.

PHOTOS/DRAWINGS: 437.

Dendrobium obrienianum Kränzlin

AKA: *D. striatum* Hort. Originally spelled *D. O'brienianum* Kränzlin.

ORIGIN/HABITAT: Endemic to Luzon Island in the Philippines. Plants grow in Quezon Province. Habitat elevation is unavailable, so the following climate data should be used with caution.

CLIMATE: Station #98427, Manila, Philippines, Lat. 14.5°N, Long. 121.0°E, at 74 ft. (23 m). Record extreme temperatures are 101°F (38°C) and 58°F (14°C).

N/HEMISPHERE	JAN	FEB	MAR	APR	MAY	JUN	JUL	AUG	SEP	OCT	NOV	DEC
°F AVG MAX	86	88	91	93	93	91	88	87	88	88	87	86
°F AVG MIN	69	69	71	73	75	75	75	75	75	74	72	70
DIURNAL RANGE	17	19	20	20	18	16	13	12	13	14	15	16
RAIN/INCHES	0.9	0.5	0.7	1.3	5.1	10.0	17.0	16.6	14.0	7.6	5.7	2.6
HUMIDITY/%	77	73	70	68	71	81	84	86	87	84	82	89
BLOOM SEASON			*	*	*		*					
DAYS CLR @ 8AM	6	9	14	14	10	3	2	1	1	6	7	6
DAYS CLR @ 2PM	3	6	10	10	8	2	1	1	0	2	2	3
RAIN/MM	23	13	18	33	130	254	432	422	356	193	145	66
°C AVG MAX	30.0	31.1	32.8	33.9	33.9	32.8	31.1	30.6	31.1	31.1	30.6	30.0
°C AVG MIN	20.6	20.6	21.7	22.8	23.9	23.9	23.9	23.9	23.9	23.3	22.2	21.1
DIURNAL RANGE	9.4	10.6	11.1	11.1	10.0	8.9	7.2	6.7	7.2	7.8	8.3	8.9
S/HEMISPHERE	JUL	AUG	SEP	OCT	NOV	DEC	JAN	FEB	MAR	APR	MAY	JUN

Cultural Recommendations

LIGHT: 2000–3000 fc.

TEMPERATURES: Throughout the year, days average 86–93°F (30–34°C), and nights average 69–75°F (21–24°C), with a diurnal range of 12–20°F (7–11°C). Plants are healthiest if humidity is high and air circulation is excellent.

HUMIDITY: 80–85% in summer and autumn, dropping to near 70% in winter and spring.

WATER: Rainfall is heavy from late spring through autumn, but conditions are dry in winter. Cultivated plants should be kept moist while actively growing, but water should be gradually reduced in late autumn.

FERTILIZER: ¼–½ recommended strength, applied weekly. A high-nitrogen fertilizer is beneficial from spring to midsummer, but a fertilizer high in phosphates should be used in late summer and autumn.

REST PERIOD: Growing temperatures should be maintained all year. Rainfall is low for 3–4 months in winter, but additional moisture is available from frequent heavy dew. In cultivation, water should be reduced and the plants allowed to dry out between waterings. They should not remain dry for extended periods, however. Fertilizer should also be reduced or eliminated anytime water is reduced. In the habitat, light is highest in winter.

GROWING MEDIA: Mounting plants on tree-fern or cork slabs accommodates their pendulous growth habit. However, humidity must be high and plants must be watered at least once a day in summer. If plants cannot be mounted, small pots or hanging baskets may be filled with an open, fast-draining medium. Repotting may be done anytime new roots are actively growing.

MISCELLANEOUS NOTES: The bloom season shown in the climate table is based on cultivation records.

Plant and Flower Information

PLANT SIZE AND TYPE: A 12–18 in. (30–45 cm) sympodial epiphyte.

PSEUDOBULB: 12–18 in. (30–45 cm) long. The reddish stems are canelike, pendulous, and slightly club-shaped. They have a pseudobulbous swelling at the base and taper toward the tip.

LEAVES: The oblong-lanceolate leaves are 4–5 in. (10–13 cm) long. They are papery and quickly deciduous.

INFLORESCENCE: 5–8 in. (13–20 cm) long. Racemes emerge laterally from upper nodes on the stem. Inflorescences are pendulous and not densely flowered.

FLOWERS: 20 per inflorescence. The flowers are 0.8–1.2 in. (2–3 cm) across. Blossoms are greenish yellow with white at the base. The lip is white sometimes with purple lines or dirty-looking red streaks. Blossoms have an ovate-oblong dorsal sepal, semielliptic lateral sepals, and elliptic petals. The spur is long and bent at the tip. The very long lip is linear and gradually dilating. It is finely serrated along the margin.

REFERENCES: 12, 25, 36, 98, 179, 218, 254, 296, 373, 445, 536.

PHOTOS/DRAWINGS: 12.

Dendrobium obscureauriculatum A. Gilli

AKA: Sometimes spelled *D. obscure-auriculatum*.

ORIGIN/HABITAT: Papua New Guinea. Plants were originally collected in Pandamus forests north of Mingende at about 6900 ft. (2100 m).

CLIMATE: Station #200243, Mt. Hagen, Papua New Guinea, Lat. 5.8°S, Long. 144.3°E, at 5350 ft. (1630 m). Temperatures are calculated for an elevation of 6900 ft. (2100 m), resulting in probable extremes of 83°F (28°C) and 30°F (–1°C).

N/HEMISPHERE	JAN	FEB	MAR	APR	MAY	JUN	JUL	AUG	SEP	OCT	NOV	DEC
°F AVG MAX	67	68	69	70	71	71	71	71	70	70	71	69
°F AVG MIN	50	50	50	50	50	51	51	51	51	52	51	49
DIURNAL RANGE	17	18	19	20	21	20	20	20	19	18	20	20
RAIN/INCHES	5.2	6.7	8.7	8.7	8.2	10.2	10.4	10.7	11.2	10.0	7.2	4.7
HUMIDITY/%	84	83	82	78	79	81	81	80	82	81	82	82
BLOOM SEASON	N/A											
DAYS CLR	N/A											
RAIN/MM	132	170	221	221	208	259	264	272	284	254	183	119
°C AVG MAX	19.4	19.9	20.5	21.0	21.6	21.6	21.6	21.6	21.0	21.0	21.6	20.5
°C AVG MIN	9.9	9.9	9.9	9.9	9.9	10.5	10.5	10.5	10.5	11.0	10.5	9.4
DIURNAL RANGE	9.5	10.0	10.6	11.1	11.7	11.1	11.1	11.1	10.5	10.0	11.1	11.1
S/HEMISPHERE	JUL	AUG	SEP	OCT	NOV	DEC	JAN	FEB	MAR	APR	MAY	JUN

Cultural Recommendations

LIGHT: 1800–2500 fc.

TEMPERATURES: Throughout the year, days average 67–71°F (19–22°C), and nights average 49–52°F (9–11°C), with a diurnal range of 17–21°F (10–12°C).

HUMIDITY: Near 80% year-round.

WATER: Rainfall is moderate to heavy all year. Conditions are slightly drier for 1–2 months in winter. Cultivated plants should be kept moist, with only slight drying allowed between waterings.

FERTILIZER: ¼–½ recommended strength. A balanced fertilizer should be applied weekly to biweekly throughout the year.

REST PERIOD: Growing temperatures should be maintained year-round. Water should be reduced in winter, especially for plants cultivated in the dark, short-day conditions common in temperate latitudes. Plants should never be allowed to dry out completely, however. Fertilizer should be reduced or eliminated when water is reduced. In the habitat, light is higher in winter.

GROWING MEDIA: Plants may be mounted on tree-fern or cork slabs or potted in small pots filled with any open, fast-draining medium. Repotting may be done anytime new roots are actively growing.

Plant and Flower Information

PLANT SIZE AND TYPE: An 8–12 in. (20–30 cm) sympodial epiphyte.

PSEUDOBULB: 8–12 in. (20–30 cm) long. The flattened stems, which do not branch, are connected by a very short rhizome. They alternate dark and light due to the difference in color between the stem and the leaf sheaths. The upper part of the stem is densely leafy.

LEAVES: Many. The ovate-lanceolate leaves are 2–4 in. (5–10 cm) long, smooth, leathery, and unequally bilobed at the tip.

INFLORESCENCE: Short.

FLOWERS: The yellow flowers are 0.6 in. (1.5 cm) long and remain rather closed. The lip is yellow with reddish markings and has small, earlike sidelobes that fold over the midlobe.

REFERENCES: 146, 234.

PHOTOS/DRAWINGS: 146.

Dendrobium obtusa Rchb. f. Transferred to *Dendrocolla obtusa* Rchb. f., which is now considered a synonym of *Trixspermum obtusa*. REFERENCES: 216, 254.

Dendrobium obtusipetalum J. J. Smith. See *D. obtusisepalum* J. J. Smith. REFERENCES: 221, 437, 538.

Dendrobium obtusisepalum J. J. Smith

AKA: *D. obtusipetalum* J. J. Smith.

ORIGIN/HABITAT: New Guinea. Plants are common at high elevations. They grow on rocks in the shady, mossy humus of mountain forests and on sub-alpine shrubs at 6050–10,700 ft. (1850–3260 m).

CLIMATE: Botanical garden records, Laiagam, Papua New Guinea, Lat. 5.5°S, Long. 143.5°E, at 7218 ft. (2200 m). Record extreme temperatures are 91°F (33°C) and 32°F (0°C).

N/HEMISPHERE	JAN	FEB	MAR	APR	MAY	JUN	JUL	AUG	SEP	OCT	NOV	DEC
°F AVG MAX	76	77	78	76	78	78	82	77	76	78	78	76
°F AVG MIN	55	54	55	55	56	56	55	56	58	57	56	56
DIURNAL RANGE	21	23	23	21	22	22	27	21	18	21	22	20
RAIN/INCHES	4.0	4.8	6.1	7.8	8.5	9.1	8.4	9.6	9.5	8.9	6.3	4.0
HUMIDITY/%	N/A											
BLOOM SEASON	*	*							*	*	*	
DAYS CLR	N/A											
RAIN/MM	102	121	154	198	217	230	213	243	241	227	159	102
°C AVG MAX	24.4	25.0	25.6	24.4	25.6	25.6	27.8	25.0	24.4	25.6	25.6	24.4
°C AVG MIN	12.8	12.2	12.8	12.8	13.3	13.3	12.8	13.3	14.4	13.9	13.3	13.3
DIURNAL RANGE	11.6	12.8	12.8	11.6	12.3	12.3	15.0	11.7	10.0	11.7	12.3	11.1
S/HEMISPHERE	JUL	AUG	SEP	OCT	NOV	DEC	JAN	FEB	MAR	APR	MAY	JUN

Dendrobium obtusum

Cultural Recommendations

LIGHT: 2000–3000 fc.

TEMPERATURES: Throughout the year, days average 76–82°F (24–28°C), and nights average 54–58°F (12–14°C), with a diurnal range of 18–27°F (10–15°C).

HUMIDITY: Information is not available for this location. However, records from nearby locations indicate that humidity probably averages near 80% year-round.

WATER: Rainfall is moderate to heavy throughout the year, but conditions are slightly drier for 3–4 months in winter. Cultivated plants should be kept evenly moist.

FERTILIZER: ¼–½ recommended strength. A balanced fertilizer should be applied weekly to biweekly throughout the year.

REST PERIOD: Growing conditions should be maintained year-round. Water and fertilizer should be reduced somewhat in winter, especially for plants grown in the dark, short-day conditions common in temperate latitudes. They should never be allowed to dry out completely, however. In the habitat, light is highest in winter.

GROWING MEDIA: Mounting plants on tree-fern or cork slabs accommodates their frequently pendulous growth habit. However, humidity must be high and plants must be watered at least once a day in summer. If plants cannot be mounted, small pots or hanging baskets may be filled with an open, fast-draining medium. Repotting may be done anytime new roots are actively growing.

MISCELLANEOUS NOTES: The bloom season shown in the climate table is based on reports from the habitat.

Plant and Flower Information

PLANT SIZE AND TYPE: A 39 in. (100 cm) sympodial epiphyte.

PSEUDOBULB: 39 in. (100 cm) long. The many-angled stems are abundantly branched and often pendulous.

LEAVES: Many. The leaves are 1.4–2.4 in. (3.5–6.0 cm) long, thin, ovate, and mid- to dark-green. They are often twisted to lie on a single plane. They are smooth with very fine bumps on the apical part of the margin.

INFLORESCENCE: 2–8 in. (5–20 cm) long. Several inflorescences emerge from nodes near the apex of newer branches.

FLOWERS: 2–5 per inflorescence. The flowers are 0.8 in. (2 cm) across. Sepals and petals may be orange, with or without a red tinge or, rarely, they are yellow tinged with red. The lip is fuzzy at the tip. The ovate dorsal sepal and much larger lateral sepals have fine bumps near the tip of the midrib and along the margins. The oblong petals are bumpy along the apical half of the margin. The smooth, widely obovate lip has 2 V-shaped structures in the center and an uneven to toothed or fringed margin.

REFERENCES: 221, 445, 470, 538.

PHOTOS/DRAWINGS: 538.

Dendrobium obtusum Schlechter. See *D. lauterbachianum* A. Hawkes. REFERENCES: 219, 231, 254, 437, 444.

Dendrobium occultum Ames. See *D. laevifolium* Stapf. REFERENCES: 17, 225, 270, 271, 385, 516.

Dendrobium ochraceum Wildeman

ORIGIN/HABITAT: Northern Vietnam. These plants were first found in Tonkin, a region that included most of what is now northern Vietnam. They were growing at about 1650 ft. (500 m). Because habitat location is not exact, the following climate data should be used with caution.

CLIMATE: Station #48831, Thai Nguyen, Vietnam, Lat. 21.6°N, Long. 105.8°E, at 134 ft. (41 m). Temperatures are calculated for an estimated elevation of 2000 ft. (610 m), resulting in probable extremes of 96°F (36°C) and 31°F (–1°C).

N/HEMISPHERE	JAN	FEB	MAR	APR	MAY	JUN	JUL	AUG	SEP	OCT	NOV	DEC
°F AVG MAX	61	62	67	73	82	85	84	84	82	79	73	65
°F AVG MIN	47	52	59	64	70	72	72	71	69	64	59	52
DIURNAL RANGE	14	10	8	9	12	13	12	13	13	15	14	13
RAIN/INCHES	0.7	1.8	2.5	4.1	10.5	14.0	17.4	17.1	8.3	4.0	1.7	0.9
HUMIDITY/%	75	82	85	86	82	80	84	86	85	82	82	80
BLOOM SEASON				*								
DAYS CLR @ 7AM	6	2	0	1	1	3	1	2	5	7	5	6
DAYS CLR @ 1PM	8	4	3	1	1	2	0	1	4	4	4	5
RAIN/MM	18	46	64	104	267	356	442	434	211	102	43	23
°C AVG MAX	16.0	16.6	19.4	22.7	27.7	29.4	28.8	28.8	27.7	26.0	22.7	18.2
°C AVG MIN	8.2	11.0	14.9	17.7	21.0	22.1	22.1	21.6	20.5	17.7	14.9	11.0
DIURNAL RANGE	7.8	5.6	4.5	5.0	6.7	7.3	6.7	7.2	7.2	8.3	7.8	7.2
S/HEMISPHERE	JUL	AUG	SEP	OCT	NOV	DEC	JAN	FEB	MAR	APR	MAY	JUN

Cultural Recommendations

LIGHT: 2000–3000 fc.

TEMPERATURES: Summer days average 84–85°F (29°C), and nights average 71–72°F (22°C), with a diurnal range of 12–13°F (7°C).

HUMIDITY 80–85% most of the year, dropping to near 75% for a month or so in early winter.

WATER: Rainfall is heavy from spring to early autumn, but conditions are relatively dry for 2–3 months in winter. Cultivated plants should be kept moist while actively growing, but water should be gradually reduced in autumn after new growths mature.

FERTILIZER: ¼–½ recommended strength, applied weekly. A high-nitrogen fertilizer is beneficial from spring to midsummer, but a fertilizer high in phosphates should be used in late summer and autumn.

REST PERIOD: Winter days average 61–65°F (16–18°C), and nights average 47–52°F (8–11°C), with a diurnal range of 10–14°F (6–8°C). While rainfall is low in winter, additional moisture is available from mist and heavy deposits of dew. Cultivated plants should be allowed to dry out somewhat between waterings, but they should not remain dry for long periods.

GROWING MEDIA: Plants may be mounted on tree-fern or cork slabs or potted in small pots filled with any open, fast-draining medium. Repotting may be done anytime new roots are growing.

MISCELLANEOUS NOTES: The bloom season shown in the climate table is based on reports from the habitat.

Plant and Flower Information

PLANT SIZE AND TYPE: A 12 in. (30 cm) sympodial epiphyte.

PSEUDOBULB: 12 in. (30 cm) long.

LEAVES: Several per growth. The oblong leaves, which are unequally bilobed at the tip, are 3 in. (7.6 cm) long. They are arranged on one side of the stem. The leaf sheaths are sparsely covered with brown hairs.

INFLORESCENCE: 1.2–2.0 in. (3–5 cm) long. Inflorescences emerge opposite the leaves from nodes along the stem.

FLOWERS: 2–3 per inflorescence. Flowers are 1.2 in. (3 cm) across. The lanceolate sepals are recurved and pointed at the tip. Smaller, pointed petals are sometimes wavy on the margin. The broad, nearly square lip is wavy and ruffled and the center is decorated with 5 radiating lines. All segments are yellowish white.

REFERENCES: 103, 220, 254, 454.

PHOTOS/DRAWINGS: 454.

Dendrobium ochranthum Schlechter

ORIGIN/HABITAT: New Ireland Island (New Mecklenburg), Papua New

Guinea. Plants grow on forest trees near Punam at about 1950 ft. (600 m).

CLIMATE: Station #94076, Kavieng, New Ireland, Papua New Guinea, Lat. 2.6°S, Long. 150.8°E, at 15 ft. (5 m). Temperatures are calculated for an elevation of 1800 ft. (550 m), resulting in probable extremes of 93°F (34°C) and 60°F (16°C).

N/HEMISPHERE	JAN	FEB	MAR	APR	MAY	JUN	JUL	AUG	SEP	OCT	NOV	DEC
°F AVG MAX	82	82	83	84	84	83	82	82	81	82	82	82
°F AVG MIN	67	67	67	67	68	68	69	69	69	68	68	68
DIURNAL RANGE	15	15	16	17	16	15	13	13	12	14	14	14
RAIN/INCHES	10.7	11.2	7.8	8.0	9.7	10.7	12.2	11.1	11.6	12.5	10.0	9.9
HUMIDITY/%	78	76	76	75	77	78	80	79	79	80	79	79
BLOOM SEASON	*											
DAYS CLR	N/A											
RAIN/MM	272	284	198	203	246	272	310	282	295	318	254	251
°C AVG MAX	27.8	27.8	28.4	28.9	28.9	28.4	27.8	27.8	27.3	27.8	27.8	27.8
°C AVG MIN	19.5	19.5	19.5	19.5	20.1	20.1	20.6	20.6	20.6	20.1	20.1	20.1
DIURNAL RANGE	8.3	8.3	8.9	9.4	8.8	8.3	7.2	7.2	6.7	7.7	7.7	7.7
S/HEMISPHERE	JUL	AUG	SEP	OCT	NOV	DEC	JAN	FEB	MAR	APR	MAY	JUN

Cultural Recommendations

LIGHT: 1500–2500 fc.

TEMPERATURES: Throughout the year, days average 81–84°F (27–29°C), and nights average 67–69°F (20–21°C), with a diurnal range of 12–17°F (7–9°C).

HUMIDITY: 75–80% year-round.

WATER: Rainfall is heavy all year. Plants should be kept evenly moist and never be allowed to dry out completely.

FERTILIZER: ¼–½ recommended strength. A balanced fertilizer should be applied weekly to biweekly throughout the year.

REST PERIOD: Growing conditions should be maintained year-round. Water and fertilizer should be reduced somewhat in winter for cultivated plants, especially those grown in the dark, short-day conditions common in temperate latitudes. Plants should never be allowed dry out completely, however.

GROWING MEDIA: Mounting plants on tree-fern or cork slabs accommodates their pendulous growth habit. However, humidity must be high and plants must be watered at least once a day in summer. If plants can not be mounted, hanging pots or baskets may be filled with an open, fast-draining medium. Repotting may be done anytime new roots are actively growing.

MISCELLANEOUS NOTES: The bloom season shown in the climate table is based on reports from the habitat. Plants that produce flowers which last a single day commonly bloom several times during the year. Flowering usually occurs 7–14 days after a sudden 10°F (5°C) drop in daytime temperatures.

Plant and Flower Information

PLANT SIZE AND TYPE: A sympodial epiphyte of unreported size.

PSEUDOBULB: The pendulous stems arise from a brief rhizome. They are many angled and somewhat flattened at the tip.

LEAVES: Many. Leaf shape is variable. The leaves are 4–5 in. (10–13 cm) long, densely arranged, spreading, and horizontal on a single plane.

INFLORESCENCE: Short.

FLOWERS: 2 per inflorescence. The short-lived flowers are 0.8 in. (2 cm) across. The pointed sepals and petals are pale yellow with incurled margins at the tip of the lateral sepals. The fiddle-shaped lip has a red margin and a broad indentation at the apex. The sickle-shaped sidelobes are blackish red.

REFERENCES: 219, 254, 437, 444, 445.

PHOTOS/DRAWINGS: 437.

Dendrobium ochreatum Lindley

AKA: *D. cambridgeanum* Paxton.

ORIGIN/HABITAT: Burma, the Khasi (Khasia) Hills of northeastern India, and northern Thailand. Plants usually grow at 3950–5250 ft. (1200–1600 m).

CLIMATE: Station #48327, Chiang Mai, Thailand, Lat. 18.8°N, Long. 99.0°E, at 1100 ft. (335 m). Temperatures are calculated for an elevation of 5000 ft. (1520 m), resulting in probable extremes of 96°F (36°C) and 25°F (−4°C).

N/HEMISPHERE	JAN	FEB	MAR	APR	MAY	JUN	JUL	AUG	SEP	OCT	NOV	DEC
°F AVG MAX	72	77	82	83	81	77	76	74	75	76	73	71
°F AVG MIN	43	44	49	57	61	61	61	62	60	58	53	44
DIURNAL RANGE	29	33	33	26	20	16	15	12	15	18	20	27
RAIN/INCHES	0.3	0.4	0.6	2.0	5.5	6.1	7.4	8.7	11.5	4.9	1.5	0.4
HUMIDITY/%	73	65	58	62	73	78	80	83	83	81	79	76
BLOOM SEASON		*	**	**	**	*				*		
DAYS CLR @ 7AM	5	5	2	2	1	0	0	0	0	1	3	3
DAYS CLR @ 1PM	9	8	4	2	0	0	0	0	0	0	1	3
RAIN/MM	8	10	15	51	140	155	188	221	292	124	38	10
°C AVG MAX	22.3	25.1	27.9	28.4	27.3	25.1	24.5	23.4	24.0	24.5	22.9	21.7
°C AVG MIN	6.2	6.7	9.5	14.0	16.2	16.2	16.2	16.7	15.6	14.5	11.7	6.7
DIURNAL RANGE	16.1	18.4	18.4	14.4	11.1	8.9	8.3	6.7	8.4	10.0	11.2	15.0
S/HEMISPHERE	JUL	AUG	SEP	OCT	NOV	DEC	JAN	FEB	MAR	APR	MAY	JUN

Cultural Recommendations

LIGHT: 3500–4500 fc. Cultivated plants need bright light and strong air movement. The heavy summer cloud cover indicates that some shading is needed from spring through autumn, but light should be as high as the plants can tolerate, short of burning the foliage. Growers suggest suspending the plant high in the greenhouse for maximum light.

TEMPERATURES: Summer days average 74–77°F (23–25°C), and nights average 61–62°F (16–17°C), with a diurnal range of 12–16°F (7–9°C). The warmest temperatures occur in spring. Days average 81–83°F (27–28°C), and nights average 49–61°F (10–16°C), with a diurnal range of 20–33°F (11–18°C).

HUMIDITY: 75–85% from late spring through autumn, dropping to near 60% in late winter and early spring.

WATER: Rainfall is moderate to heavy from late spring through early autumn, but conditions are very dry in winter. Cultivated plants should be kept moist while actively growing, but water should be gradually reduced after new growths mature in autumn.

FERTILIZER: ¼–½ recommended strength, applied weekly. A high-nitrogen fertilizer is beneficial from spring to midsummer, but a fertilizer high in phosphates should be used in late summer and autumn. See following discussion under Miscellaneous Notes.

REST PERIOD: Winter days average 71–77°F (22–25°C), and nights average 43–44°F (6–7°C), with a diurnal range of 27–33°F (15–18°C). The average low temperatures are below 50°F (10°C) for 3 months and then warm rapidly in spring. Plants should be able to tolerate temperatures a few degrees below freezing, but extremes should be avoided in cultivation. During very cold weather, a plant's chance of surviving with minimal damage is better if it is dry. In the habitat, rainfall averages are very low for 4–5 months in winter, but during the early part of the season the high relative humidity indicates that additional moisture is available from frequent fog, mist, and heavy deposits of dew. Growers sometimes recommend eliminating water in winter, but plants are healthiest if for most of the winter they are allowed to become dry between waterings but do not remain dry for extended periods. For 1–2 months in late winter, however, conditions are clear, warm, and dry, with humidity so low that even the moisture from morning dew is uncommon. Plants should be allowed to dry out completely between waterings and remain dry longer during this time. Occasional early morning mistings between waterings may help keep the plants from becoming too dry. Fertilizer should be greatly reduced or eliminated until water is increased in spring. Growers indicate that a cool, dry rest is essential for cultivated plants and should be continued until new growth starts in spring. In the habitat, light is highest in winter, but increased light may not be critical in cultivation.

GROWING MEDIA: Plants are usually potted in tree-fern or mounted on tree-fern slabs. They should be kept moist in summer and allowed to dry in winter. Plants need not be repotted frequently, but growers suggest replacing the top layer of medium each year. Repotting is best done in early spring when new roots are growing.

MISCELLANEOUS NOTES: The bloom season shown in the climate table is based on cultivation records. Growers report that plants grow freely, but they are difficult to bloom. Some growers indicate that plants should not be over-fertilized, as new stems may not bloom if they grow too rapidly. *D. ochreatum* is one of the few *Dendrobium* to produce blossoms before the stems are fully mature.

Plant and Flower Information

PLANT SIZE AND TYPE: A 6–30 in. (15–76 cm) sympodial epiphyte or lithophyte.

PSEUDOBULB: 6–30 in. (15–76 cm) long. The stems are short, drooping, curved, and swollen at the nodes. They have red streaks and spots. The plant is very close to and often confused with *D. chrysanthum*.

LEAVES: 15 per growth. The leaves are 2–5 in. (5–13 cm) long, ovate-lanceolate, and thin. They are deciduous each fall.

INFLORESCENCE: Very short. Many inflorescences emerge simultaneously with the leaves from every node of young pseudobulbs.

FLOWERS: 1–3 per inflorescence. The flowers are 2.0–2.8 in. (5–7 cm) across. The pointed sepals and petals may be bright orange or rich golden yellow. The pointed lip is golden yellow with a large, dark maroon or purple blotch near the base. The pubescent lip has a short fringe at the apex. The back side is densely hairy on the front margin. A single specimen plant produced 180 blooms. Blossoms are fragrant and last 2 weeks.

HYBRIDIZING NOTES: Chromosome counts are 2n = 38 (ref. 153, 154, 542), 2n = 40 (ref. 152, 542), and 2n = 2x (ref. 504, 580).

REFERENCES: 38, 46, 152, 153, 154, 179, 190, 196, 202, 210, 216, 254, 278, 317, 369, 430, 445, 454, 504, 541, 542, 557, 570, 580.

PHOTOS/DRAWINGS: 28, 46, 78, 210, *369, 430, 454.*

Dendrobium ochroleucum Teijsm. and Binn. Kränzlin (ref. 254) and J. J. Smith (ref. 469) suggest that *D. ochroleucum* may be a form of *D. heterocarpum* Wallich ex Lindley. Although Teijsm. and Binn. indicated that the plant originated from Mt. Salak, Java, it is only included as a questionable species by J. J. Smith (ref. 469) and is not included by Backer and Bakhuizen Van Den Brink (ref. 25) or Comber (ref. 75). REFERENCES: 216, 254, 310, 317, 469.

Dendrobium oculatum Hort. See *D. fimbriatum* Hooker f. var. *oculatum* Hooker. REFERENCES: 190.

Dendrobium odiosum Finet. See *D. hancockii* Rolfe. REFERENCES: 118, 208, 219, 254, 445.

Dendrobium odoardi Kränzlin

AKA: Sometimes spelled *D. odoardii*.

ORIGIN/HABITAT: The north coast of Irian Jaya (western New Guinea). Plants collected near Jayapura on Humboldt Bay were cultivated in the botanic garden at Bogor, Java.

CLIMATE: Station #97690, Sentani/Jayapura, Irian Jaya, Lat. 2.7°S, Long. 140.5°E, at 289 ft. (88 m). Record extreme temperatures are 97°F (36°C) and 68°F (20°C).

N/HEMISPHERE	JAN	FEB	MAR	APR	MAY	JUN	JUL	AUG	SEP	OCT	NOV	DEC
°F AVG MAX	87	89	89	90	90	89	89	88	89	90	90	89
°F AVG MIN	72	72	72	73	73	73	73	73	73	74	73	73
DIURNAL RANGE	15	17	17	17	17	16	16	15	16	16	17	16
RAIN/INCHES	4.1	3.9	5.3	2.9	6.7	7.0	8.3	8.3	8.5	4.6	2.4	5.2
HUMIDITY/%	81	80	80	79	81	81	79	80	80	80	81	80
BLOOM SEASON					*	*	*	*				
DAYS CLR @ 9AM	5	3	4	3	2	1	1	0	1	2	2	5
DAYS CLR @ 3PM	4	3	3	3	2	1	3	0	1	2	2	3
RAIN/MM	104	99	135	74	170	178	211	211	216	117	61	132
°C AVG MAX	30.6	31.7	31.7	32.2	32.2	31.7	31.7	31.1	31.7	32.2	32.2	31.7
°C AVG MIN	22.2	22.2	22.2	22.8	22.8	22.8	22.8	22.8	22.8	23.3	22.8	22.8
DIURNAL RANGE	8.4	9.5	9.5	9.4	9.4	8.9	8.9	8.3	8.9	8.9	9.4	8.9
S/HEMISPHERE	JUL	AUG	SEP	OCT	NOV	DEC	JAN	FEB	MAR	APR	MAY	JUN

Cultural Recommendations

LIGHT: 2000–3000 fc.

TEMPERATURES: Throughout the year, days average 87–90°F (31–32°C), and nights average 72–74°F (22–23°C), with a diurnal range of 15–17°F (8–10°C).

HUMIDITY: Near 80% year-round.

WATER: Rainfall is heavy, with brief semidry periods in spring and autumn. Cultivated plants should be kept moist most of the year, but they should be allowed to become somewhat dry for a few weeks in spring and again in autumn.

FERTILIZER: ¼–½ recommended strength. A balanced fertilizer should be applied weekly to biweekly throughout the year.

REST PERIOD: Growing conditions should be maintained year-round. Water and fertilizer might be reduced slightly in winter, especially for plants grown in the dark, short-day conditions common in temperate latitudes. They should never be allowed to dry out completely, however. In the habitat, light is slightly higher in winter.

GROWING MEDIA: Plants may be mounted on tree-fern or cork slabs or potted in any open, fast-draining medium if humidity is high and plants are watered at least once daily in summer. Repotting may be done anytime new roots are growing.

MISCELLANEOUS NOTES: The bloom season shown in the climate table is based on cultivation records. Although *D. odoardi* is not in general cultivation, it is an interesting species with lovely coloring.

Plant and Flower Information

PLANT SIZE AND TYPE: A 12 in. (30 cm) sympodial epiphyte. Plant habit resembles that of *D. discolor* Lindley.

PSEUDOBULB: 12 in. (30 cm) long. Canelike stems are slightly flattened to oval near the tip.

LEAVES: Many. The ovate to oblong leaves are 6 in. (15 cm) long. The smooth, shiny leaves may be leathery or fleshy.

INFLORESCENCE: 8 in. (20 cm) long. The laxly flowered inflorescences emerge from among the upper leaves. They are dark yellow with lighter yellow spots.

FLOWERS: 18–22 per inflorescence. The waxy flowers are 1.6 in. (4 cm) across. Sepals curve backward. They are lemon yellow suffused with chestnut brown on the upper surface and white on the backside. The erect, twisted petals are shiny brown suffused with yellow. The yellow lip has brown veins, a pale green or lemon-yellow margin, and a purple callus. It has 3–5 ridges. The center ridge is raised and wavy. The midlobe is somewhat deltoid.

HYBRIDIZING NOTES: When used as a parent, *D. odoardi* improves flower color and substance.

REFERENCES: 25, 84, 190, 200, 220, 254, 347, 437, 445.

PHOTOS/DRAWINGS: 347.

Dendrobium odontochilum Rchb. f.

ORIGIN/HABITAT: Endemic to New Caledonia. Plants grow in humid forests throughout the island at 350–3300 ft. (100–1000 m). They are adaptable, and have been found growing on trees, rocks, and the surface of the ground.

CLIMATE: Station #91592, Noumea, New Caledonia, Lat. 22.3°S, Long. 166.5°E, at 246 ft. (75 m). Temperatures are calculated for an elevation of 3000 ft. (910 m), resulting in probable extremes of 90°F (32°C) and 43°F (6°C).

N/HEMISPHERE	JAN	FEB	MAR	APR	MAY	JUN	JUL	AUG	SEP	OCT	NOV	DEC
°F AVG MAX	67	67	69	71	74	77	77	76	76	74	70	68
°F AVG MIN	53	52	54	56	59	61	63	64	63	61	57	55
DIURNAL RANGE	14	15	15	15	15	16	14	12	13	13	13	13
RAIN/INCHES	3.6	2.6	2.5	2.0	2.4	2.6	3.7	5.1	5.7	5.2	4.4	3.7
HUMIDITY/%	73	70	69	67	68	69	71	74	75	76	73	73
BLOOM SEASON							*	**	**	**	**	*
DAYS CLR @ 11AM	7	9	9	15	12	10	7	6	7	7	7	7
DAYS CLR @ 5PM	7	11	6	11	7	6	5	4	4	5	3	7
RAIN/MM	91	66	64	51	61	66	94	130	145	132	112	94
°C AVG MAX	19.4	19.4	20.5	21.6	23.3	25.0	25.0	24.4	24.4	23.3	21.1	20.0
°C AVG MIN	11.6	11.1	12.2	13.3	15.0	16.1	17.2	17.7	17.2	16.1	13.8	12.7
DIURNAL RANGE	7.8	8.3	8.3	8.3	8.3	8.9	7.8	6.7	7.2	7.2	7.3	7.3
S/HEMISPHERE	JUL	AUG	SEP	OCT	NOV	DEC	JAN	FEB	MAR	APR	MAY	JUN

Cultural Recommendations

LIGHT: 1800–3000 fc. Days are frequently clear, but the humid forest microclimate suggests that plants may need lower light. Light should be raised gradually until it is as high as the plants can tolerate short of burning the leaves.

TEMPERATURES: Summer days average 76–77°F (24–25°C), and nights average 61–64°F (16–18°C), with a diurnal range of 12–16°F (7–9°C). The diurnal range fluctuates only 4°F (2°C) throughout the year.

HUMIDITY: 70–75% most of the year, dropping to 65–70% in late winter and early spring.

WATER: Rainfall is relatively low and consistent most of the year. The driest season is in late winter and spring, and the heaviest rain falls in late summer and early autumn. Moisture may be more available in the humid forest habitat than the climate records indicate. Rain in this region normally falls as heavy showers, however, and plants might be healthiest if they are allowed to become somewhat dry between waterings.

FERTILIZER: ¼–½ recommended strength, applied weekly. A high-nitrogen fertilizer is beneficial from spring to midsummer, but a fertilizer high in phosphates should be used in late summer and autumn.

REST PERIOD: Winter days average 67–69°F (19–21°C), and nights average 52–55°F (11–13°C), with a diurnal range of 13–15°F (7–8°C). Day and night temperatures decline simultaneously, resulting in little change in the diurnal range. In the habitat, rainfall is somewhat lower in late winter and spring. In cultivation, water and fertilizer should be reduced and the plants allowed to dry even more between waterings than in summer. They should not dry out completely or remain dry for long periods, however. In the habitat, light is highest in winter.

GROWING MEDIA: Plants may be mounted on tree-fern or cork slabs if humidity is high and plants are watered at least once daily in summer. When plants are potted, any open, fast-draining medium may be used. Repotting is best done in early spring when new roots are growing.

MISCELLANEOUS NOTES: The bloom season shown in the climate table is based on reports from the habitat. The preceding temperatures represent the coolest conditions found in the habitat. Because of the wide range of habitat elevation, plants should adapt to temperatures 6–8°F (3–4°C) warmer than indicated.

Plant and Flower Information

PLANT SIZE AND TYPE: A 2.4–18.1 in. (6–46 cm) sympodial epiphyte.

PSEUDOBULB: 2.4–18.1 in. (6–46 cm) long. The slender, canelike stems may have 2–6 nodes. They root only at the base.

LEAVES: 2–3 at the apex. The oblong, pointed leaves are 1.6 in. (4 cm) long.

INFLORESCENCE: Usually longer than the leaves, 1–2 inflorescences emerge from between the leaves at the apex of the stem.

FLOWERS: 1–10 per inflorescence. The variable flowers are 1 in. (2.5 cm) across. The slender sepals and petals are white sometimes with a rosy tinge. The lip is pink or rose with a yellow callus. Hallé (ref. 173) indicates that blossoms take 2 forms. In one form, the sepals curl back, and the lip has toothed sidelobes which curve into the midlobe and a single raised centerline that is zigzag near the apex. The other form has pointed sidelobes with notches between the midlobe and sidelobes, and the straighter centerline is bracketed by 2 smaller lines along the side. Blossoms open in succession and reportedly have an unpleasant fragrance.

HYBRIDIZING NOTES: Collector's notes indicate that fruits are rare in nature.

REFERENCES: 173, 216, 254, 445.

PHOTOS/DRAWINGS: 173, 254.

Dendrobium odontopus Schlechter

ORIGIN/HABITAT: Northern Papua New Guinea. Plants grow on forest trees in the Kani Range at about 3000 ft. (1000 m).

CLIMATE: Station #94010, Goroka, Papua New Guinea, Lat. 6.1°S, Long. 145.4°E, at 5141 ft. (1567 m). Temperatures are calculated for an elevation of 3300 ft. (1000 m), resulting in probable extremes of 93°F (34°C) and 49°F (10°C).

N/HEMISPHERE	JAN	FEB	MAR	APR	MAY	JUN	JUL	AUG	SEP	OCT	NOV	DEC
°F AVG MAX	82	83	84	85	85	84	85	84	84	84	85	83
°F AVG MIN	62	63	63	63	64	65	65	65	66	65	65	63
DIURNAL RANGE	20	20	21	22	21	19	20	19	18	19	20	20
RAIN/INCHES	2.1	2.8	4.6	5.9	6.6	9.3	9.1	10.1	10.7	8.3	4.6	2.0
HUMIDITY/%	70	67	67	67	67	71	72	73	74	71	70	70
BLOOM SEASON							*					
DAYS CLR	N/A											
RAIN/MM	53	71	117	150	168	236	231	257	272	211	117	51
°C AVG MAX	27.9	28.4	29.0	29.5	29.5	29.0	29.5	29.0	29.0	29.0	29.5	28.4
°C AVG MIN	16.7	17.3	17.3	17.3	17.9	18.4	18.4	18.4	19.0	18.4	18.4	17.3
DIURNAL RANGE	11.2	11.1	11.7	12.2	11.6	10.6	11.1	10.6	10.0	10.6	11.1	11.1
S/HEMISPHERE	JUL	AUG	SEP	OCT	NOV	DEC	JAN	FEB	MAR	APR	MAY	JUN

Cultural Recommendations

LIGHT: 2500–3500 fc.

TEMPERATURES: Throughout the year, days average 82–85°F (28–30°C), and nights average 62–66°F (17–19°C), with a diurnal range of 18–22°F (10–12°C).

HUMIDITY: 70–75% from summer into autumn, dropping to 65–70% in winter and spring.

WATER: Rainfall is moderate to heavy most of the year, but conditions are slightly drier for 3 months in winter. Cultivated plants should be kept moist but not soggy. Occasional early morning mistings may be beneficial, especially on bright, sunny days.

FERTILIZER: ¼–½ recommended strength. A balanced fertilizer should be applied weekly to biweekly throughout the year.

REST PERIOD: Growing temperatures should be maintained all year. In the habitat, rainfall is lowest in winter, but dew and mist from fog and low clouds are common. Water and fertilizer should be reduced somewhat for cultivated plants, especially those grown in the darker, short-day conditions common during temperate-latitude winters. Plants should be kept on the dry side, but they should never be allowed to dry out completely. In the habitat, light is higher in winter.

Dendrobium odoratum

GROWING MEDIA: Plants may be mounted on tree-fern or cork slabs if humidity is high and plants are watered at least once daily in summer. When plants are potted, any open, fast-draining medium may be used. Repotting may be done anytime new roots are growing.

MISCELLANEOUS NOTES: The bloom season shown in the climate table is based on reports from the habitat. Plants that produce flowers which last a single day commonly bloom several times each year. Flowering usually occurs 7–14 days after a sudden 10°F (5°C) drop in daytime temperatures.

Plant and Flower Information

PLANT SIZE AND TYPE: A 24 in. (60 cm) sympodial epiphyte.

PSEUDOBULB: 24 in. (60 cm) long. The densely leafy stems are simple, curved, and spreading.

LEAVES: Many. The pointed, linear leaves are 2.4–3.5 in. (6–9 cm) long.

INFLORESCENCE: Very short. Inflorescences are borne above the leaf axils.

FLOWERS: 2 per inflorescence. The yellowish white flowers are 0.4 in. (1 cm) long and remain rather closed. Sepals and petals tend to cup at the tips. The 3-lobed lip is somewhat fiddle-shaped with long, narrow side-lobes. The blossoms are very short-lived.

REFERENCES: 92, 221, 437, 445.

PHOTOS/DRAWINGS: 437.

Dendrobium odoratum Schlechter

AKA: At different times, Schlechter (ref. 436) included *D. eboracense* Kränzlin, *D. podagraria* Kränzlin not Hooker f., and *D. gemmiferum* Kränzlin as synonyms.

ORIGIN/HABITAT: Endemic to Sulawesi (Celebes). Plants grow on trees near Tondano (Tomohon) on the Minahassa Peninsula at 2600–3000 ft. (800–910 m).

CLIMATE: Station #97014, Manado, Sulawesi, Lat. 1.5°N, Long. 124.9°E, at 264 ft. (80 m). Temperatures are calculated for an elevation of 3000 ft. (910 m), resulting in probable extremes of 88°F (31°C) and 56°F (13°C).

N/HEMISPHERE	JAN	FEB	MAR	APR	MAY	JUN	JUL	AUG	SEP	OCT	NOV	DEC
°F AVG MAX	76	76	76	77	78	78	78	80	80	80	78	77
°F AVG MIN	64	64	64	64	65	64	64	64	64	63	64	65
DIURNAL RANGE	12	12	12	13	13	14	14	16	16	17	14	12
RAIN/INCHES	18.6	13.8	12.2	8.0	6.4	6.5	4.8	4.0	3.4	4.9	8.9	14.7
HUMIDITY/%	84	83	83	83	81	80	75	72	75	77	82	83
BLOOM SEASON			*							*		*
DAYS CLR @ 8AM	4	3	6	11	11	12	12	12	14	17	12	8
DAYS CLR @ 2PM	1	1	1	2	1	3	4	4	4	1	1	1
RAIN/MM	472	351	310	203	163	165	122	102	86	124	226	373
°C AVG MAX	24.4	24.4	24.4	25.0	25.5	25.5	25.5	26.7	26.7	26.7	25.5	25.0
°C AVG MIN	17.8	17.8	17.8	17.8	18.3	17.8	17.8	17.8	17.8	17.2	17.8	18.3
DIURNAL RANGE	6.6	6.6	6.6	7.2	7.2	7.7	7.7	8.9	8.9	9.5	7.7	6.7
S/HEMISPHERE	JUL	AUG	SEP	OCT	NOV	DEC	JAN	FEB	MAR	APR	MAY	JUN

Cultural Recommendations

LIGHT: 2000–3000 fc. In the habitat, morning light is highest. Skies are usually overcast by afternoon.

TEMPERATURES: Throughout the year, days average 76–80°F (24–27°C), and nights average 63–65°F (17–18°C), with a diurnal range of 12–17°F (7–10°C). Wide seasonal changes should be avoided because average highs vary only 4°F (2°C), average lows fluctuate only 2°F (1°C), and the extreme temperatures are only a few degrees above and below the averages.

HUMIDITY: 80–85% most of the year, dropping to 70–75% in summer.

WATER: Rainfall is moderate to heavy all year. The driest weather occurs in late summer when temperatures are warm. Cultivated plants should be kept moist but not soggy. Warm water might be beneficial.

FERTILIZER: ¼–½ recommended strength. A balanced fertilizer should be applied weekly to biweekly throughout the year.

REST PERIOD: Growing temperatures should be maintained all year. The plants may rest during the 1–2 month drier period which occurs in late summer and coincides with the period of greatest diurnal range. Cultivated plants should dry out slightly during this period, but they should never remain dry for long. The heaviest rainfall in the habitat occurs in winter, but water should not be increased for cultivated plants. In fact, water should be reduced somewhat for plants grown in the dark, short-day conditions common in temperate latitudes, but they should not be allowed to dry out completely.

GROWING MEDIA: Plants may be mounted on tree-fern or cork slabs if humidity is high and plants are watered at least once daily in summer. When plants are potted, any open, fast-draining medium may be used. Repotting may be done anytime new roots are growing.

MISCELLANEOUS NOTES: The bloom season shown in the climate table is based on reports from the habitat.

Plant and Flower Information

PLANT SIZE AND TYPE: A 31 in. (80 cm) sympodial epiphyte.

PSEUDOBULB: 31 in. (80 cm) long. The grooved, erect stems emerge from a very short rhizome. They have a spindle-shaped swelling near the base, occasionally branch, and are leafless at the apex.

LEAVES: Many. The somewhat oblong leaves are 2–3 in. (5–8 cm) long, smooth, and leathery.

INFLORESCENCE: Inflorescences emerge from nodes along the stem.

FLOWERS: Several. The clustered flowers are 0.8 in. (2 cm) long. They are snow-white with red veins and a swollen, golden-yellow longitudinal stripe on the lip. Blossoms have a fragrance reminiscent of hyacinths.

REFERENCES: 25, 220, 436.

Dendrobium officinale Kimura and Migo. See *D. candidum* Wallich ex Lindley. REFERENCES: 208, 226, 547.

Dendrobium okabeanum Tuyama

ORIGIN/HABITAT: The Caroline Islands. Plants were found on Truk near Trowasi (Natusima) at 300 ft. (90 m) on Mt. Tonoman.

CLIMATE: Station #91334, Truk, Caroline Islands, Lat. 7.5°N, Long. 151.8°E, at 6 ft. (2 m). Temperatures are calculated for an elevation of 300 ft. (90 m), resulting in probable extremes of 96°F (36°C) and 69°F (21°C).

N/HEMISPHERE	JAN	FEB	MAR	APR	MAY	JUN	JUL	AUG	SEP	OCT	NOV	DEC
°F AVG MAX	84	85	85	85	85	86	86	86	86	86	86	85
°F AVG MIN	77	77	76	76	76	76	75	75	75	75	76	76
DIURNAL RANGE	7	8	9	9	9	10	11	11	11	11	10	9
RAIN/INCHES	9.6	6.7	7.5	15.3	17.1	12.5	13.9	12.5	13.4	13.0	12.0	14.5
HUMIDITY/%	81	79	80	82	84	84	84	84	83	84	84	84
BLOOM SEASON			*									
DAYS CLR @ 10AM	0	0	0	0	0	0	0	0	0	0	0	0
DAYS CLR @ 4PM	1	0	0	0	1	0	0	0	1	0	0	0
RAIN/MM	244	170	190	389	434	318	353	318	340	330	305	368
°C AVG MAX	28.9	29.5	29.5	29.5	29.5	30.0	30.0	30.0	30.0	30.0	30.0	29.5
°C AVG MIN	25.0	25.0	24.5	24.5	24.5	24.5	23.9	23.9	23.9	23.9	24.5	24.5
DIURNAL RANGE	3.9	4.5	5.0	5.0	5.0	5.5	6.1	6.1	6.1	6.1	5.5	5.0
S/HEMISPHERE	JUL	AUG	SEP	OCT	NOV	DEC	JAN	FEB	MAR	APR	MAY	JUN

Cultural Recommendations

LIGHT: 2000–3000 fc.

TEMPERATURES: Throughout the year, days average 84–86°F (29–30°C), and nights average 75–77°F (24–25°C), with a diurnal range of 7–10°F (4–6°C).

HUMIDITY: 80–85% year-round.

WATER: Rainfall is heavy all year. Cultivated plants should be kept moist and never be allowed to dry out completely.

FERTILIZER: ¼–½ recommended strength. A balanced fertilizer should be applied weekly to biweekly throughout the year.

REST PERIOD: Growing conditions should be maintained all year. In the habitat, conditions are slightly drier in winter. Water should be reduced somewhat for cultivated plants, especially those grown in the dark, short-day conditions common in temperate latitudes. They should never be allowed to dry out completely, however.

GROWING MEDIA: Plants may be mounted on tree-fern or cork slabs if humidity is high and plants are watered at least once daily in summer. When plants are potted, any open, fast-draining medium may be used. They may be repotted anytime new roots are growing.

MISCELLANEOUS NOTES: The bloom season shown in the climate table is based on records from the habitat.

Plant and Flower Information

PLANT SIZE AND TYPE: A 33 in. (85 cm) sympodial epiphyte.

PSEUDOBULB: 33 in. (85 cm) long. The shiny stems are olive to yellow-green with a dark yellow, ovoid swelling at the base. Growths arise from a very short rhizome.

LEAVES: The oval to ovate-oblong leaves are 4.0–5.5 in. (10–14 cm) long. They are leathery, shiny, and unequally bilobed at the tip.

INFLORESCENCE: 16 in. (40 cm) long. The many flowered racemes may be erect or spreading. They emerge from nodes near the tip of the stem.

FLOWERS: 25 per inflorescence. The flowers are 0.8–1.6 in. (2–4 cm) long. The linear-oblong dorsal sepal is ruffled at the base. It is greenish yellow to olive with 7 dark purple lines and violet spots. The lateral sepals are triangular. The twisted petals are olive and dark violet. The midlobe is very undulate and minutely toothed.

REFERENCES: 227, 530.

PHOTOS/DRAWINGS: 530.

Dendrobium okinawense Hatusima and Ida

ORIGIN/HABITAT: Okinawa. Plants grow on Mt. Yonaha at about 1300 ft. (400 m) and are known to be cultivated in the city of Fukuoka.

CLIMATE: Station #47931, Kadena Air Base, Okinawa, Ryukyu Islands, Lat. 26.3°N, Long. 127.8°E, at 142 ft. (43 m). Temperatures are calculated for an elevation of 1300 ft. (400 m), resulting in probable extremes of 90°F (32°C) and 37°F (3°C).

N/HEMISPHERE	JAN	FEB	MAR	APR	MAY	JUN	JUL	AUG	SEP	OCT	NOV	DEC
°F AVG MAX	61	62	66	71	76	80	84	83	82	77	71	65
°F AVG MIN	51	52	56	61	67	71	75	74	73	67	61	56
DIURNAL RANGE	10	10	10	10	9	9	9	9	9	10	10	9
RAIN/INCHES	4.0	4.8	5.1	5.6	8.3	10.8	7.4	8.8	10.4	6.1	4.7	4.4
HUMIDITY/%	73	75	78	81	84	85	82	83	82	76	74	73
BLOOM SEASON						N/A						
DAYS CLR @ 9AM	3	4	3	2	1	0	1	2	4	5	3
DAYS CLR @ 3PM	2	2	2	2	1	0	1	1	3	2	2
RAIN/MM	102	122	130	142	211	274	188	224	264	155	119	112
°C AVG MAX	16.2	16.8	19.0	21.8	24.5	26.8	29.0	28.4	27.9	25.1	21.8	18.4
°C AVG MIN	10.7	11.2	13.4	16.2	19.5	21.8	24.0	23.4	22.9	19.5	16.2	13.4
DIURNAL RANGE	5.5	5.6	5.6	5.6	5.0	5.0	5.0	5.0	5.0	5.6	5.6	5.0
S/HEMISPHERE	JUL	AUG	SEP	OCT	NOV	DEC	JAN	FEB	MAR	APR	MAY	JUN

Cultural Recommendations

LIGHT: 2000–3000 fc.

TEMPERATURES: Summer days average 80–84°F (27–29°C), and nights average 71–75°F (22–24°C), with a diurnal range of 9°F (5°C).

HUMIDITY: 80–85% in spring and summer, dropping to near 75% in autumn and winter.

WATER: Rainfall is moderate to heavy year-round. Summer is the wettest season. Cultivated plants should be kept evenly moist with only slight drying allowed between waterings.

FERTILIZER: ¼–½ recommended strength, applied weekly. A high-nitrogen fertilizer is beneficial from spring to midsummer, but a fertilizer high in phosphates should be used in late summer and autumn.

REST PERIOD: Winter days average 61–66°F (16–19°C), and nights average 51–56°F (11–13°C), with a diurnal range of 9–10°F (5–6°C). Day and night temperatures decline simultaneously, resulting in little change in the diurnal range. Water should be reduced somewhat in winter, especially for plants cultivated in the dark, short-day conditions common in temperate latitudes. Plants should never be allowed to dry out completely, however. Fertilizer should be reduced or eliminated anytime water is reduced. In the habitat, light is slightly higher in winter.

GROWING MEDIA: Mounting plants on tree-fern or cork slabs accommodates their pendulous growth habit. However, humidity must be high and plants must be watered at least once a day in summer. If plants cannot be mounted, small pots or hanging baskets may be filled with an open, fast-draining medium. Repotting may be done anytime new roots are actively growing.

Plant and Flower Information

PLANT SIZE AND TYPE: A 28 in. (70 cm) sympodial epiphyte.

PSEUDOBULB: 28 in. (70 cm) long. The pendulous stems consist of nodes spaced 1.6–2.0 in. (4–5 cm) apart.

LEAVES: Many. The linear-lanceolate leaves are 5 in. (13 cm) long.

INFLORESCENCE: Inflorescences emerge from the upper nodes of the stem.

FLOWERS: 1–2 per inflorescence. The white or pale rose flowers are about 3 in. (8 cm) across with pointed, linear-oblong to linear-lanceolate sepals and petals. The linear-oblong lip is boat-shaped at the base with a 2-keeled disk. The keels are covered with soft hairs.

REFERENCES: 139, 231.

Dendrobium oligadenium Schlechter

ORIGIN/HABITAT: Endemic to Sulawesi (Celebes). Plants grow on trees at very low elevations near Tolitoli.

CLIMATE: Station #97028, Tolitoli, Sulawesi, Indonesia, Lat. 1.0°N, Long. 120.8°E, at 7 ft. (2 m). Record extreme temperatures are not available for this location.

N/HEMISPHERE	JAN	FEB	MAR	APR	MAY	JUN	JUL	AUG	SEP	OCT	NOV	DEC
°F AVG MAX	84	83	85	86	86	86	85	86	86	86	86	85
°F AVG MIN	76	74	76	78	78	76	76	77	77	77	78	77
DIURNAL RANGE	8	9	9	8	8	10	9	9	9	9	8	8
RAIN/INCHES	6.3	4.9	7.4	3.8	6.4	6.3	5.5	4.1	4.9	4.7	4.0	4.3
HUMIDITY/%	N/A											
BLOOM SEASON	*											
DAYS CLR	N/A											
RAIN/MM	161	125	187	98	162	160	139	103	125	120	101	110
°C AVG MAX	28.7	28.5	29.3	29.9	30.1	30.1	29.7	30.1	30.2	30.2	30.0	29.5
°C AVG MIN	24.5	23.6	24.3	25.3	25.3	24.4	24.4	24.8	24.7	25.2	25.3	25.0
DIURNAL RANGE	4.2	4.9	5.0	4.6	4.8	5.7	5.3	5.3	5.5	5.0	4.7	4.5
S/HEMISPHERE	JUL	AUG	SEP	OCT	NOV	DEC	JAN	FEB	MAR	APR	MAY	JUN

Cultural Recommendations

LIGHT: 2500–3500 fc.

TEMPERATURES: Throughout the year, days average 83–86°F (29–30°C), and nights average 74–78°F (24–25°C), with a diurnal range of 8–10°F (4–6°C).

HUMIDITY: Information is not available for this location. However, records from nearby locations indicate that humidity probably averages 75–85% year-round.

WATER: Rainfall is moderate to heavy all year. Cultivated plants should be

Dendrobium oliganthum

allowed to dry out slightly between waterings but should not dry out completely.

FERTILIZER: ¼–½ recommended strength. A balanced fertilizer should be applied weekly to biweekly throughout the year.

REST PERIOD: Growing temperatures should be maintained all year. Water and fertilizer should be reduced somewhat for cultivated plants in winter, especially those grown in the dark, short-day conditions common in temperate latitudes. They should be allowed to dry out slightly between waterings but should not remain dry for long periods.

GROWING MEDIA: Plants may be mounted if humidity is high and plants are watered at least once daily in summer. When plants are potted, any open, fast-draining medium may be used. Repotting may be done anytime new roots are growing.

MISCELLANEOUS NOTES: The bloom season shown in the climate table is based on reports from the habitat.

Plant and Flower Information

PLANT SIZE AND TYPE: A 6–8 in. (15–20 cm) sympodial epiphyte.

PSEUDOBULB: 6 in. (15 cm) long. The erect to spreading stems are covered with many, evenly spaced leaves. They arise from a short, prostrate rhizome that is densely covered with sheaths.

LEAVES: Many. The lanceolate, somewhat sickle-shaped leaves are 2.2 in. (5.5 cm) long, which is shorter than most closely related species.

INFLORESCENCE: Inflorescences emerge from nodes near the apex of the stem. Blossoms are arranged in a clustered head at the apex of the inflorescence.

FLOWERS: Many per inflorescence. The dark purple flowers are 0.1–0.2 in. (3–5 cm) long. The petals have an irregular, slightly toothed margin. The short lip is bilobed in the front with a finely serrated, uneven margin.

REFERENCES: 220, 436.

Dendrobium oliganthum Schlechter

ORIGIN/HABITAT: Sulawesi (Celebes). Schlechter (ref. 436) described this species from a plant cultivated in a hotel garden in Makassar (Macassar). He indicated that the plant was in deplorable condition and was reputed to come from the interior. This suggests that it probably grew at higher elevations, and we estimated the habitat elevation to be 3300 ft. (1000 m). Because the elevation is estimated, the following climate data should be used with caution.

CLIMATE: Station #97180, Makassar, Sulawesi, Indonesia, Lat. 5.1°S, Long. 119.6°E, at 46 ft. (14 m). Temperatures are calculated for an elevation of 3300 ft. (1000 m), resulting in probable extremes of 84°F (29°C) and 47°F (9°C).

N/HEMISPHERE	JAN	FEB	MAR	APR	MAY	JUN	JUL	AUG	SEP	OCT	NOV	DEC
°F AVG MAX	75	76	76	76	75	73	73	73	74	75	76	75
°F AVG MIN	59	58	59	61	63	63	63	64	63	63	63	61
DIURNAL RANGE	16	18	17	15	12	10	10	9	11	12	13	14
RAIN/INCHES	1.3	0.4	0.5	1.6	6.7	23.2	28.3	20.9	16.7	6.5	3.6	2.7
HUMIDITY/%	72	67	64	70	77	84	84	85	84	80	79	76
BLOOM SEASON	N/A											
DAYS CLR @ 8AM	14	17	15	14	8	4	4	1	4	8	8	11
DAYS CLR @ 2PM	7	7	11	13	9	3	1	1	2	6	7	7
RAIN/MM	33	10	13	41	170	589	719	531	424	165	91	69
°C AVG MAX	24.0	24.6	24.6	24.6	24.0	22.9	22.9	22.9	23.5	24.0	24.6	24.0
°C AVG MIN	15.1	14.6	15.1	16.3	17.4	17.4	17.4	17.9	17.4	17.4	17.4	16.3
DIURNAL RANGE	8.9	10.0	9.5	8.3	6.6	5.5	5.5	5.0	6.1	6.6	7.2	7.7
S/HEMISPHERE	JUL	AUG	SEP	OCT	NOV	DEC	JAN	FEB	MAR	APR	MAY	JUN

Cultural Recommendations

LIGHT: 2500–3500 fc. In the habitat, clear summer days are rare because of the cloud cover associated with the summer rainy season.

TEMPERATURES: Summer days average 73°F (23°C), and nights average 63–64°F (17–18°C), with a diurnal range of 9–10°F (5–6°C).

HUMIDITY: Near 85% in summer and early autumn, dropping to 65–70% in winter and early spring.

WATER: Rainfall is heavy from late spring to autumn, but conditions are much drier for 2–3 months in winter. Cultivated plants should be kept moist but not soggy while growing, but water should be gradually reduced in autumn.

FERTILIZER: ¼–½ recommended strength, applied weekly. A high-nitrogen fertilizer is beneficial from spring to midsummer, but a fertilizer high in phosphates should be used in late summer and autumn.

REST PERIOD: Winter days average 75–76°F (24–25°C), and nights average 58–61°F (15–16°C), with a diurnal range of 14–18°F (8–10°C). Rainfall is much lower for 3–4 months in winter. Conditions become so dry that even dew is uncommon for about 2 months. Water should be reduced for cultivated plants. Plants should be allowed to dry out between waterings but should not remain dry for extended periods. Fertilizer should be reduced anytime water is reduced. In the habitat, light is highest in winter.

GROWING MEDIA: Plants may be mounted on tree-fern or cork slabs if humidity is high and plants are watered at least once daily in summer. When plants are potted, any open, fast-draining medium may be used. Repotting is best done in early spring when new roots are growing.

Plant and Flower Information

PLANT SIZE AND TYPE: An 8–10 in. (20–25 cm) sympodial epiphyte.

PSEUDOBULB: 8–10 in. (20–25 cm) long. The unbranched stems are suberect and longitudinally ridged. They arise from a very short rhizome.

LEAVES: Many. The leaves are 1.2–1.4 in. (3.0–3.6 cm) long, linear, thin, and spreading.

INFLORESCENCE: 0.7 in. (1.7 cm) long. Inflorescences emerge along the upper, leafless portion of the stem.

FLOWERS: 1–2 per inflorescence. The smooth, rose-red flowers are 0.4 in. (1 cm) long. The lip is obscurely 3-lobed with a nearly round, ruffled, and wavy midlobe. Blossoms are very similar to *D. lancifolium* A. Richard.

REFERENCES: 223, 436.

Dendrobium oligoblepharon Schlechter. See *D. nardoides* Schlechter. REFERENCES: 221, 385, 437, 445.

Dendrobium oligophyllum Gagnepain

AKA: *D. tixieri* Guillaumin.

ORIGIN/HABITAT: Vietnam and the south central and southeastern regions of Thailand. Plants grow at about 2200 ft. (660 m).

CLIMATE: Station #49000, Ban Ta Khli, Thailand, Lat. 15.3°N, Long. 100.3°E, at 100 ft. (30 m). Temperatures are calculated for an elevation of 2000 ft. (610 m), resulting in probable extremes of 106°F (42°C) and 37°F (3°C).

N/HEMISPHERE	JAN	FEB	MAR	APR	MAY	JUN	JUL	AUG	SEP	OCT	NOV	DEC
°F AVG MAX	83	88	93	94	91	88	86	85	83	83	83	82
°F AVG MIN	57	64	68	71	71	70	70	69	69	68	64	58
DIURNAL RANGE	26	24	25	23	20	18	16	16	14	15	19	24
RAIN/INCHES	0.1	0.7	1.4	3.4	5.1	5.4	5.5	6.3	11.2	6.2	1.4	0.1
HUMIDITY/%	60	61	60	72	64	75	80	83	85	83	78	68
BLOOM SEASON		*		*		*		*		*	*	*
DAYS CLR @ 7AM	5	2	4	4	3	0	0	0	0	2	4	5
DAYS CLR @ 1PM	12	7	7	4	1	0	0	0	0	1	3	7
RAIN/MM	3	18	36	86	130	137	140	160	284	157	36	3
°C AVG MAX	28.2	31.0	33.7	34.3	32.6	31.0	29.9	29.3	28.2	28.2	28.2	27.6
°C AVG MIN	13.7	17.6	19.9	21.5	21.5	21.0	21.0	20.4	20.4	19.9	17.6	14.3
DIURNAL RANGE	14.5	13.4	13.8	12.8	11.1	10.0	8.9	8.9	7.8	8.3	10.6	13.3
S/HEMISPHERE	JUL	AUG	SEP	OCT	NOV	DEC	JAN	FEB	MAR	APR	MAY	JUN

Cultural Recommendations

LIGHT: 3000–3500 fc.

TEMPERATURES: Summer days average 85–88°F (29–31°C), and nights average 69–70°F (20–21°C), with a diurnal range of 16–18°F (9–10°C). Spring is the warmest season. Days average 91–94°F (33–34°C), and nights average 68–71°F (20–22°C), with a diurnal range of 20–25°F (11–14°C).

HUMIDITY: 75–85% from summer into late autumn, decreasing to about 60% in winter.

WATER: Rainfall is moderate to heavy for 7 months from late spring to autumn. The wet season changes rapidly into a 4–5 month dry period that extends from late autumn to spring. During most of the dry season, average humidity is so low that even morning dew is uncommon. Cultivated plants should be kept moist with only slight drying allowed between waterings from spring into autumn, but water should be reduced in late autumn after new growths mature.

FERTILIZER: ¼–½ recommended strength, applied weekly. A high-nitrogen fertilizer is beneficial from spring to midsummer, but a fertilizer high in phosphates should be used in late summer and autumn.

REST PERIOD: Winter days average 82–88°F (28–31°C), and nights average 57–64°F (14–18°C), with a diurnal range of 24–26°F (13–15°C). Conditions in the habitat are dry for 4–5 months. Cultivated plants should be allowed to dry out between waterings. They should be given only enough water to keep pseudobulbs and leaves from shriveling. An occasional misting on bright, sunny mornings is usually sufficient. The dry season may not need to be as long or as severe as indicated, however, and some growers even indicate that plants should be kept moist all year. Fertilizer should be eliminated anytime plants are not actively growing. In the habitat, light is highest in winter.

GROWING MEDIA: Plants are best mounted on tree-fern or cork slabs if humidity is high and plants are watered at least once daily in summer. Growers recommend hanging plants just above eye level, where blossoms can be seen to best advantage. When plants are potted, any open, fast-draining medium may be used. Remounting is best done in early spring when new roots are growing.

MISCELLANEOUS NOTES: Cultivated plants often bloom several times a year, but in spring, plants are covered with blossoms. The bloom season shown in the climate is based on cultivation records for *D. tixieri*.

Plant and Flower Information

PLANT SIZE AND TYPE: A 2.4–4.0 in. (6–10 cm) sympodial epiphyte.

PSEUDOBULB: 1.2–1.6 in. (3–4 cm) long. The cylindrical stems are clustered. The upper portion of the stem is leafy.

LEAVES: 2–8. The distichous leaves are 1.2–2.0 in. (3–5 cm) long with 2 points at the apex.

INFLORESCENCE: 1.2–2.4 in. (3–6 cm) long. Several inflorescences emerge opposite the leaves on leafy stems.

FLOWERS: 1–4 per inflorescence. The flowers are less than 1 in. (2.5 cm) across. The pointed sepals and petals may be white, cream-yellow, or greenish white. They are erect. The 3-lobed lip is similarly colored with dark green stripes in the throat. It has large, roundly pointed sidelobes. The midlobe is uneven along the margin with a slight notch at the apex and 3 raised lines in the center. Plants bloom while very young, even while still in flask. Blossoms are long-lasting.

REFERENCES: 137, 167, 169, 227, 448, 454, 524.

PHOTOS/DRAWINGS: *454, 524.*

Dendrobium olivaceum J. J. Smith

ORIGIN/HABITAT: Borneo. The plant is found in Sabah and Kalimantan. In Sabah, it grows in the lower mountain forests on Mt. Kinabalu at 4900–5250 ft. (1500–1600 m).

CLIMATE: Station #49613, Tambunan, Sabah, Borneo, Lat. 5.7°N, Long. 116.4°E, at 1200 ft. (366 m). Temperatures are calculated for an elevation of 4800 ft. (1460 m), resulting in probable extremes of 86°F (30°C) and 42°F (6°C).

N/HEMISPHERE	JAN	FEB	MAR	APR	MAY	JUN	JUL	AUG	SEP	OCT	NOV	DEC
°F AVG MAX	74	75	77	78	78	77	77	77	77	76	75	74
°F AVG MIN	55	53	54	55	56	55	54	54	55	55	55	56
DIURNAL RANGE	19	22	23	23	22	22	23	23	22	21	20	18
RAIN/INCHES	5.8	3.7	5.8	7.5	8.2	7.3	5.1	4.9	6.4	7.0	6.8	6.0
HUMIDITY/%	N/A											
BLOOM SEASON					*							
DAYS CLR	N/A											
RAIN/MM	147	94	147	190	208	185	130	124	163	178	173	152
°C AVG MAX	23.4	24.0	25.1	25.6	25.6	25.1	25.1	25.1	25.1	24.5	24.0	23.4
°C AVG MIN	12.8	11.7	12.3	12.8	13.4	12.8	12.3	12.3	12.8	12.8	12.8	13.4
DIURNAL RANGE	10.6	12.3	12.8	12.8	12.2	12.3	12.8	12.8	12.3	11.7	11.2	10.0
S/HEMISPHERE	JUL	AUG	SEP	OCT	NOV	DEC	JAN	FEB	MAR	APR	MAY	JUN

Cultural Recommendations

LIGHT: 2000–3000 fc.

TEMPERATURES: Throughout the year, days average 74–78°F (23–26°C), and nights average 53–56°F (12–13°C), with a diurnal range of 18–23°F (10–13°C).

HUMIDITY: Information is not available for this location. However, records from nearby locations indicate that humidity probably averages 80–85% year-round.

WATER: Rainfall is moderate to heavy all year with a brief, slightly drier period in winter. Cultivated plants should be kept moist with only slight drying allowed between waterings.

FERTILIZER: ¼–½ recommended strength. A balanced fertilizer should be applied weekly to biweekly throughout the year.

REST PERIOD: Growing temperatures should be maintained all year. Water should be reduced for cultivated plants, especially those grown in the dark, short-day conditions common in temperate-latitude winters, but they should never be allowed to dry out completely. Fertilizer should be reduced or eliminated until water is increased in spring.

GROWING MEDIA: Plants may be mounted on tree-fern or cork slabs if humidity is high and plants are watered at least once daily in summer. When plants are potted, any open, fast-draining medium may be used. Plants may be repotted anytime new roots are growing.

MISCELLANEOUS NOTES: The bloom season shown in the climate table is based on cultivation records.

Plant and Flower Information

PLANT SIZE AND TYPE: A 59 in. (150 cm) sympodial epiphyte.

PSEUDOBULB: 59 in. (150 cm) long. The clustered stems are rigid and quadrangular in cross-section.

LEAVES: Many. The broadly lanceolate leaves are about 4 in. (11 cm) long. They are unequally 2-toothed at the apex.

INFLORESCENCE: Short. Inflorescences emerge at nodes on leafy stems.

FLOWERS: The fleshy flowers are 1.2 in. (3 cm) across. They are shiny on the backside. The dorsal sepal is oblong-ovate, and lateral sepals are somewhat triangular. Flowers are pointed and light olive-green with white at the base. The lanceolate petals are pale green with white at the base. The 3-lobed lip is brownish, white, and olive with dense warts and white hairs. The large, erect sidelobes are triangular and incurved. The midlobe is roundly truncated.

REFERENCES: 179, 221, 286, 295, 429, 473, 592.

PHOTOS/DRAWINGS: *592.*

Dendrobium opacifolium

Dendrobium opacifolium J. J. Smith. Although not correctly transferred, Schlechter (ref. 443) considered this plant to be a synonym of *Cadetia opacifolia* (J. J. Smith) Schlechter. REFERENCES: 222, 223, 443, 445, 470.

Dendrobium ophioglossoides Seibert. Now considered a synonym of *Pleurothallis floribunda* Lindley. REFERENCES: 216, 254.

Dendrobium ophioglossoides Swartz. Now considered a synonym of *Stelis ophioglossoides* Swartz. REFERENCES: 190, 216, 254.

Dendrobium ophioglossum Rchb. f. See *D. smillieae* F. Mueller. REFERENCES: 24, 67, 105, 151, 179, 187, 216, 254, 262, 390, 421, 430, 533.

Dendrobium opilionites Schlechter. Now considered a synonym of *Diplocaulobium opilionites* (Schlechter) A. Hawkes. REFERENCES: 223, 230, 443.

Dendrobium oppositifolium (Kränzlin) Hallé

AKA: *Eria oppositifolia* Kränzlin, *Dendrobium multilobatum* Guillaumin.

ORIGIN/HABITAT: Endemic to New Caledonia. Plants are found at 1000–3300 ft. (300–1000 m) in the central mountains throughout the length of the island.

CLIMATE: Station #91592, Noumea, New Caledonia, Lat. 22.3°S, Long. 166.5°E, at 246 ft. (75 m). Temperatures are calculated for an elevation of 2200 ft. (670 m), resulting in probable extremes of 93°F (34°C) and 46°F (8°C).

N/HEMISPHERE	JAN	FEB	MAR	APR	MAY	JUN	JUL	AUG	SEP	OCT	NOV	DEC
°F AVG MAX	70	70	72	74	77	80	80	79	79	77	73	71
°F AVG MIN	56	55	57	59	62	64	66	67	66	64	60	58
DIURNAL RANGE	14	15	15	15	15	16	14	12	13	13	13	13
RAIN/INCHES	3.6	2.6	2.5	2.0	2.4	2.6	3.7	5.1	5.7	5.2	4.4	3.7
HUMIDITY/%	73	70	69	67	68	69	71	74	75	76	73	73
BLOOM SEASON	**	**	*									**
DAYS CLR @ 11AM	7	9	9	15	12	10	7	6	7	7	7	7
DAYS CLR @ 5PM	7	11	6	11	7	6	5	4	4	5	3	7
RAIN/MM	91	66	64	51	61	66	94	130	145	132	112	94
°C AVG MAX	20.9	20.9	22.0	23.1	24.8	26.4	26.4	25.9	25.9	24.8	22.5	21.4
°C AVG MIN	13.1	12.5	13.6	14.8	16.4	17.5	18.6	19.2	18.6	17.5	15.3	14.2
DIURNAL RANGE	7.8	8.4	8.4	8.3	8.4	8.9	7.8	6.7	7.3	7.3	7.2	7.2
S/HEMISPHERE	JUL	AUG	SEP	OCT	NOV	DEC	JAN	FEB	MAR	APR	MAY	JUN

Cultural Recommendations

LIGHT: 3000–3500 fc. Days are frequently clear, indicating moderately high light.

TEMPERATURES: Summer days average 79–80°F (26°C), and nights average 64–67°F (18–19°C), with a diurnal range of 12–16°F (7–9°C). The diurnal range fluctuates only 4°F (2°C) all year.

HUMIDITY: 70–75% year-round.

WATER: Rainfall is relatively low and consistent throughout the year, but amounts may be greater than indicated in the mountains. The greatest rainfall occurs in late summer and early autumn. Rain in this region normally falls as heavy showers, and plants might be healthiest if they are thoroughly saturated and then allowed to almost dry before being watered again. Plants should be kept moist but not soggy while actively growing.

FERTILIZER: ¼–½ recommended strength, applied weekly. A high-nitrogen fertilizer is beneficial from spring to midsummer, but a fertilizer high in phosphates should be used in late summer and autumn.

REST PERIOD: Winter days average 70–72°F (21–22°C), and nights average 55–58°F (13–14°C), with a diurnal range of 13–15°F (7–8°C). Day and night temperatures decline simultaneously, resulting in little change in the diurnal range. In cultivation, water and fertilizer should be reduced in winter and spring. Plants should dry slightly between waterings, but should never remain dry for long periods.

GROWING MEDIA: Plants may be mounted on tree-fern or cork slabs if humidity is high and plants are watered at least once daily in summer. When plants are potted, any open, fast-draining medium may be used. They may be repotted anytime new roots are growing.

MISCELLANEOUS NOTES: The bloom season shown in the climate table is based on records from the habitat.

Plant and Flower Information

PLANT SIZE AND TYPE: A 1.2–3.1 in. (3–8 cm) sympodial epiphyte.

PSEUDOBULB: 0.8–1.6 in. (2–4 cm) long. Stems are bright orange when dry.

LEAVES: 2 at the apex of each stem. The erect to spreading leaves are 0.8–2.0 in. (2–5 cm) long, dark green, and oval with 2 small, unequal lobes at the apex.

INFLORESCENCE: 5 in. (13 cm) long. The branching inflorescences emerge from nodes below the leaves. They may be erect or arching.

FLOWERS: 2–12 per inflorescence. The flowers are 2.0–2.8 in. (5–7 cm) across. They may be yellow, pale yellow, or greenish yellow. The lip may be purple, rouge, or violet, sometimes with white. The slender sepals and petals open fully. The lip has a large midlobe that is notched at the apex and covered with small protuberances except along the margin. The sidelobes are small and pointed.

REFERENCES: 173, 233.

PHOTOS/DRAWINGS: 173.

Dendrobium orbiculare J. J. Smith

AKA: *D. fuscopilosum* Ames and Schweinfurth.

ORIGIN/HABITAT: Borneo. Plants are found in Sabah, Sarawak, and Kalimantan. In Sabah, they grow in the lower mountain forests on Mt. Kinabalu at 2950–5600 ft. (900–1700 m). In western Kalimantan, they are found in forests near Bidang Menabai at 2150 ft. (660 m).

CLIMATE: Station #49613, Tambunan, Sabah, Borneo, Lat. 5.7°N, Long. 116.4°E, at 1200 ft. (366 m). Temperatures are calculated for an elevation of 4800 ft. (1460 m), resulting in probable extremes of 86°F (30°C) and 42°F (6°C).

N/HEMISPHERE	JAN	FEB	MAR	APR	MAY	JUN	JUL	AUG	SEP	OCT	NOV	DEC
°F AVG MAX	74	75	77	78	78	77	77	77	77	76	75	74
°F AVG MIN	55	53	54	55	56	55	54	54	55	55	55	56
DIURNAL RANGE	19	22	23	23	22	22	23	23	22	21	20	18
RAIN/INCHES	5.8	3.7	5.8	7.5	8.2	7.3	5.1	4.9	6.4	7.0	6.8	6.0
HUMIDITY/%	N/A											
BLOOM SEASON												*
DAYS CLR	N/A											
RAIN/MM	147	94	147	190	208	185	130	124	163	178	173	152
°C AVG MAX	23.4	24.0	25.1	25.6	25.6	25.1	25.1	25.1	25.1	24.5	24.0	23.4
°C AVG MIN	12.8	11.7	12.3	12.8	13.4	12.8	12.3	12.3	12.8	12.8	12.8	13.4
DIURNAL RANGE	10.6	12.3	12.8	12.8	12.2	12.3	12.8	12.8	12.3	11.7	11.2	10.0
S/HEMISPHERE	JUL	AUG	SEP	OCT	NOV	DEC	JAN	FEB	MAR	APR	MAY	JUN

Cultural Recommendations

LIGHT: 2000–3000 fc.

TEMPERATURES: Throughout the year, days average 74–78°F (23–26°C), and nights average 53–56°F (12–13°C), with a diurnal range of 18–23°F (10–13°C).

HUMIDITY: Information is not available for this location. However, records from nearby locations indicate that humidity probably averages 80–85% year-round.

WATER: Rainfall is moderate to heavy all year with a brief, slightly drier period in winter. Cultivated plants should be kept moist, with only slight drying allowed between waterings.

FERTILIZER: ¼–½ recommended strength. A balanced fertilizer should be applied weekly to biweekly throughout the year.

REST PERIOD: Growing temperatures should be maintained all year. Water should be reduced for cultivated plants, especially those grown in the dark, short-day conditions common in temperate-latitude winters, but they should never be allowed to dry out completely. Fertilizer should be reduced or eliminated until water is increased in spring.

GROWING MEDIA: Plants may be mounted on tree-fern or cork slabs or potted in small pots filled with any open, fast-draining medium. Repotting may be done anytime new roots are growing.

MISCELLANEOUS NOTES: The bloom season shown in the climate table is based on collection reports.

Plant and Flower Information

PLANT SIZE AND TYPE: A 15 in. (38 cm) sympodial epiphyte.

PSEUDOBULB: 15 in. (38 cm) long. The slender, slightly snaky stems are longitudinally grooved and covered with reddish brown hairs.

LEAVES: Many. The distichous leaves are about 1.8 in. (4.6 cm) long. They are narrowly lanceolate with 2 sharp, pointed teeth at the tip.

INFLORESCENCE: Short. Inflorescences emerge from nodes on the upper portion of the stem.

FLOWERS: The flowers are 0.6 in. (1.5 cm) across. One collection was described as having cream-to-white, broad, oblong sepals and linear petals and a purple 3-lobed lip. The erect sidelobes are toothlike triangles. The nearly round midlobe is covered with bumps and pointed at the tip. Another collection described the blossoms as white with reddish brown nerves and a white lip.

REFERENCES: 12, 221, 286, 295, 454, 592.

PHOTOS/DRAWINGS: 592.

Dendrobium ordinatum J. J. Smith

AKA: Although not correctly transferred, Schlechter (ref. 443) discussed a *Cadetia cordinata* (J. J. Smith) Schlechter. We found no original description for a *D. cordinatum* and assume he was probably referring to *D. ordinatum*.

ORIGIN/HABITAT: Irian Jaya (western New Guinea), on the east side of Kajo Bay. Plants grow epiphytically in coastal forests and lithophytically on marine rocks.

CLIMATE: Station #97690, Sentani/Jayapura, Irian Jaya, Lat. 2.7°S, Long. 140.5°E, at 289 ft. (88 m). Record extreme temperatures are 97°F (36°C) and 68°F (20°C).

N/HEMISPHERE	JAN	FEB	MAR	APR	MAY	JUN	JUL	AUG	SEP	OCT	NOV	DEC
°F AVG MAX	87	89	89	90	90	89	89	88	89	90	90	89
°F AVG MIN	72	72	72	73	73	73	73	73	73	74	73	73
DIURNAL RANGE	15	17	17	17	17	16	16	15	16	16	17	16
RAIN/INCHES	4.1	3.9	5.3	2.9	6.7	7.0	8.3	8.3	8.5	4.6	2.4	5.2
HUMIDITY/%	81	80	80	79	81	81	79	80	80	80	81	80
BLOOM SEASON	*											
DAYS CLR @ 9AM	5	3	4	3	2	1	1	0	1	2	2	5
DAYS CLR @ 3PM	4	3	3	3	2	1	3	0	1	2	2	3
RAIN/MM	104	99	135	74	170	178	211	211	216	117	61	132
°C AVG MAX	30.6	31.7	31.7	32.2	32.2	31.7	31.7	31.1	31.7	32.2	32.2	31.7
°C AVG MIN	22.2	22.2	22.2	22.8	22.8	22.8	22.8	22.8	22.8	23.3	22.8	22.8
DIURNAL RANGE	8.4	9.5	9.5	9.4	9.4	8.9	8.9	8.3	8.9	8.9	9.4	8.9
S/HEMISPHERE	JUL	AUG	SEP	OCT	NOV	DEC	JAN	FEB	MAR	APR	MAY	JUN

Cultural Recommendations

LIGHT: 2000–3000 fc.

TEMPERATURES: Throughout the year, days average 87–90°F (31–32°C), and nights average 72–74°F (22–23°C), with a diurnal range of 15–17°F (8–9°C).

HUMIDITY: Near 80% year-round.

WATER: Rainfall is heavy all year, with brief semidry periods in spring and autumn. Cultivated plants should be kept moist most of the year, but they should be allowed to become somewhat dry for a few weeks in spring and again in autumn.

FERTILIZER: ¼–½ recommended strength. A balanced fertilizer should be applied weekly to biweekly throughout the year.

REST PERIOD: Growing conditions should be maintained year-round. Water and fertilizer might be reduced slightly in winter, especially for plants grown in the dark, short-day conditions common in temperate latitudes. They should never be allowed to dry completely, however. In the habitat, light is slightly higher in winter.

GROWING MEDIA: Plants may be mounted on tree-fern or cork slabs if humidity is high and plants are watered at least once daily in summer. When plants are potted, any open, fast-draining medium may be used. Repotting may be done anytime new roots are growing.

Plant and Flower Information

PLANT SIZE AND TYPE: A 0.8–1.0 in. (2.0–2.5 cm) sympodial epiphyte.

PSEUDOBULB: 0.3 in. (0.8 cm) long. The very small pseudobulbs are about 0.1 in. (0.2 cm) apart and arranged in 2 rows. They are shaped like an elongated cone and become grooved with age.

LEAVES: 1 per growth. The oblong to lanceolate leaves are 0.4–0.6 in. (1.1–1.5 cm) long. They are fleshy, contracted at the base, and 2-toothed at the apex.

INFLORESCENCE: Short. A single inflorescence is borne in front of the leaf.

FLOWERS: 1 per inflorescence. The tiny white flowers are 0.2 in. (0.6 cm) long. Blossoms have ovate-triangular lateral sepals and pointed, lanceolate petals. The concave, 3-lobed lip has a nearly round midlobe. The anther is green.

REFERENCES: 221, 445, 470, 475.

Dendrobium oreocharis Schlechter. See *D. subacaule* Reinwardt ex Lindley. REFERENCES: 179, 221, 271, 304, 385, 437, 445.

Dendrobium oreodoxa Schlechter

ORIGIN/HABITAT: Northern Papua New Guinea. Plants grow on mistforest trees in the Bismarck Range at about 6550 ft. (2000 m).

CLIMATE: Station #94010, Goroka, Papua New Guinea, Lat. 6.1°S, Long. 145.4°E, at 5141 ft. (1567 m). Temperatures are calculated for an elevation of 6550 ft. (2000 m), resulting in probable extremes of 82°F (28°C) and 38°F (4°C).

N/HEMISPHERE	JAN	FEB	MAR	APR	MAY	JUN	JUL	AUG	SEP	OCT	NOV	DEC
°F AVG MAX	71	72	73	74	74	73	74	73	73	73	74	72
°F AVG MIN	51	52	52	52	53	54	54	54	55	54	54	52
DIURNAL RANGE	20	20	21	22	21	19	20	19	18	19	20	20
RAIN/INCHES	2.1	2.8	4.6	5.9	6.6	9.3	9.1	10.1	10.7	8.3	4.6	2.0
HUMIDITY/%	70	67	67	67	67	71	72	73	74	71	70	70
BLOOM SEASON						*						
DAYS CLR	N/A											
RAIN/MM	53	71	117	150	168	236	231	257	272	211	117	51
°C AVG MAX	21.8	22.4	23.0	23.5	23.5	23.0	23.5	23.0	23.0	23.0	23.5	22.4
°C AVG MIN	10.7	11.3	11.3	11.3	11.8	12.4	12.4	12.4	13.0	12.4	12.4	11.3
DIURNAL RANGE	11.1	11.1	11.7	12.2	11.7	10.6	11.1	10.6	10.0	10.6	11.1	11.1
S/HEMISPHERE	JUL	AUG	SEP	OCT	NOV	DEC	JAN	FEB	MAR	APR	MAY	JUN

Cultural Recommendations

LIGHT: 2500–3000 fc.

TEMPERATURES: Throughout the year, days average 71–74°F (22–24°C),

Dendrobium oreogenum

and nights average 51–55°F (11–13°C), with a diurnal range of 18–22°F (10–12°C).

HUMIDITY: 70–75% most of the year, dropping to near 65% in late winter and spring.

WATER: Rainfall is moderate to heavy most of the year, but conditions are slightly drier for 3 months in winter. Cultivated plants should be kept moist. Early morning mistings between waterings are often beneficial, especially on bright, sunny days.

FERTILIZER: ¼ recommended strength. A balanced fertilizer should be applied weekly to biweekly throughout the year. Plants require little or no fertilizer if grown in live sphagnum. In any medium, fertilizer should be very weak. The Royal Botanic Garden in Edinburgh uses a weak, seaweed-based fertilizer for plants from this habitat.

REST PERIOD: Growing temperatures should be maintained all year. In the habitat, rainfall is lowest in winter, but dew and mist from fog and low clouds are common. Water and fertilizer should be reduced somewhat for cultivated plants, especially those grown in the darker, short-day conditions common during temperate-latitude winters. Plants should be kept on the dry side, but they should never be allowed to dry out completely. In the habitat, light is higher in winter.

GROWING MEDIA: Plants may be mounted on tree-fern or cork slabs if humidity is high and plants are watered at least once daily in summer. When plants are potted, any open, fast-draining medium may be used. Repotting may be done anytime new roots are growing.

MISCELLANEOUS NOTES: The bloom season shown in the climate table is based on reports from the habitat.

Plant and Flower Information

PLANT SIZE AND TYPE: A 20 in. (50 cm) sympodial epiphyte.

PSEUDOBULB: 20 in. (50 cm) long. The plants are wide-spreading.

LEAVES: Many at the apex. Lanceolate and spreading, the leaves are 1.0–2.4 in. (2.5–6.0 cm) long.

INFLORESCENCE: Very short.

FLOWERS: 1–3 per inflorescence. The small flowers are 0.7 in. (1.7 cm) long. Sepals and petals are scarlet-red and shaped like a flared cone. The lip is orange-red. Blossoms have a broadly oval dorsal sepal, somewhat triangular lateral sepals, and a narrow, rounded lip that gradually expands near the apex.

HYBRIDIZING NOTES: Chromosome count 2n = 38 (ref. 152).

REFERENCES: 92, 152, 221, 243, 437, 445.

PHOTOS/DRAWINGS: 437.

Dendrobium oreogenum Schlechter

ORIGIN/HABITAT: Papua New Guinea. Plants grow on trees in forests of the Torricelli Range at about 1950 ft. (600 m).

CLIMATE: Station #94004, Wewak, Papua New Guinea, Lat. 3.6°S, Long. 143.7°E, at 16 ft. (5 m). Temperatures are calculated for an elevation of 2000 ft. (610 m), resulting in probable extremes of 91°F (33°C) and 55°F (13°C).

N/HEMISPHERE	JAN	FEB	MAR	APR	MAY	JUN	JUL	AUG	SEP	OCT	NOV	DEC
°F AVG MAX	81	81	81	81	81	81	80	79	80	81	81	81
°F AVG MIN	67	67	67	68	68	68	68	68	67	67	68	67
DIURNAL RANGE	14	14	14	13	13	13	12	11	13	14	13	14
RAIN/INCHES	7.6	4.8	5.3	10.0	13.3	14.5	12.1	11.9	14.9	16.9	15.1	10.8
HUMIDITY/%	80	79	79	78	79	81	82	82	81	82	81	80
BLOOM SEASON				*								
DAYS CLR	N/A											
RAIN/MM	193	122	135	254	338	368	307	302	378	429	384	274
°C AVG MAX	27.5	27.5	27.5	27.5	27.5	27.5	26.9	26.4	26.9	27.5	27.5	27.5
°C AVG MIN	19.7	19.7	19.7	20.3	20.3	20.3	20.3	20.3	19.7	19.7	20.3	19.7
DIURNAL RANGE	7.8	7.8	7.8	7.2	7.2	7.2	6.6	6.1	7.2	7.8	7.2	7.8
S/HEMISPHERE	JUL	AUG	SEP	OCT	NOV	DEC	JAN	FEB	MAR	APR	MAY	JUN

Cultural Recommendations

LIGHT: 2000–2500 fc.

TEMPERATURES: Throughout the year, days average 79–81°F (26–28°C), and nights average 67–68°F (20°C), with a diurnal range of 11–14°F (6–8°C).

HUMIDITY: Near 80% year-round.

WATER: Rainfall is heavy all year, but conditions are slightly drier for 1–2 months in winter. Cultivated plants should be kept moist but not soggy.

FERTILIZER: ¼–½ recommended strength. A balanced fertilizer should be applied weekly to biweekly throughout the year.

REST PERIOD: Growing conditions should be maintained year-round. Water should be reduced for plants cultivated in the dark, short-day conditions common during temperate-latitude winters, but they should not be allowed to dry out completely. Fertilizer should also be reduced if water is reduced. In the habitat, light may be slightly higher in winter.

GROWING MEDIA: Any open and fast-draining medium may be used with baskets or small pots. Repotting is best done in early spring when new roots are growing.

MISCELLANEOUS NOTES: The bloom season shown in the climate table is based on collection reports.

Plant and Flower Information

PLANT SIZE AND TYPE: A 12 in. (30 cm) sympodial epiphyte.

PSEUDOBULB: 12 in. (30 cm) long. The smooth, clustered stems are swollen in the middle and taper at each end.

LEAVES: Several at the apex of the stem. The lanceolate leaves are 3 in. (8 cm) long.

INFLORESCENCE: Short. Clusters of flowers are borne on leafless stems.

FLOWERS: The flowers are 0.6 in. (1.5 cm) long. They are scarlet- to purple-red, often with white at the apex. The ovary is rose to rose-white. Flowers were described as similar to *D. lawesii* F. Mueller but smaller. The unlobed lip is narrow at the base and rounded at the apex. The margin is smooth with a fringe inside the edge.

REFERENCES: 92, 219, 254, 437, 444, 445.

PHOTOS/DRAWINGS: 437.

Dendrobium orientale J. J. Smith

ORIGIN/HABITAT: Ambon Island, without specific habitat information. Since habitat elevation is unavailable, the following climate data should be used with caution.

CLIMATE: Station #97724, Ambon/Pattimura, Indonesia, Lat. 3.7°S, Long. 128.1°E, at 33 ft. (10 m). Record extreme temperatures are 96°F (36°C) and 66°F (19°C).

N/HEMISPHERE	JAN	FEB	MAR	APR	MAY	JUN	JUL	AUG	SEP	OCT	NOV	DEC
°F AVG MAX	81	81	83	85	88	88	88	88	88	86	84	82
°F AVG MIN	74	74	74	74	75	76	76	76	76	76	75	74
DIURNAL RANGE	7	7	9	11	13	12	12	12	12	10	9	8
RAIN/INCHES	23.7	15.8	9.5	6.1	4.5	5.2	5.0	4.7	5.3	11.0	20.3	25.1
HUMIDITY/%	83	82	81	80	79	78	78	77	79	82	83	84
BLOOM SEASON	N/A											
DAYS CLR @ 9AM	1	1	1	6	7	4	3	3	5	5	3	3
DAYS CLR @ 3PM	1	1	2	5	6	1	1	1	2	3	1	3
RAIN/MM	602	401	241	155	114	132	127	119	135	279	516	638
°C AVG MAX	27.2	27.2	28.3	29.4	31.1	31.1	31.1	31.1	31.1	30.0	28.9	27.8
°C AVG MIN	23.3	23.3	23.3	23.3	23.9	24.4	24.4	24.4	24.4	24.4	23.9	23.3
DIURNAL RANGE	3.9	3.9	5.0	6.1	7.2	6.7	6.7	6.7	6.7	5.6	5.0	4.5
S/HEMISPHERE	JUL	AUG	SEP	OCT	NOV	DEC	JAN	FEB	MAR	APR	MAY	JUN

Cultural Recommendations

LIGHT: 2000–3000 fc.

TEMPERATURES: Throughout the year, days average 81–88°F (27–31°C), and nights average 74–76°F (23–24°C), with a diurnal range of 7–13°F (4–7°C).

HUMIDITY: 80–85% year-round.

WATER: Rainfall is moderate to heavy all year, but conditions are slightly drier in late spring and summer. Cultivated plants should be kept evenly moist with only slight drying allowed between waterings.

FERTILIZER: 1/4–1/2 recommended strength. A balanced fertilizer should be applied weekly to biweekly throughout the year.

REST PERIOD: Growing conditions should be maintained all year. In the habitat, rainfall is heaviest in winter; but water and fertilizer may be reduced somewhat for cultivated plants, especially those grown in the dark, short-day conditions common in temperate latitudes. They should never be allowed to dry completely, however. In the habitat, light is highest in spring.

GROWING MEDIA: Plants may be mounted on tree-fern or cork slabs if humidity is high and plants are watered at least once daily in summer. When plants are potted, any open, fast-draining medium may be used. Repotting may be done anytime new roots are growing.

Plant and Flower Information

PLANT SIZE AND TYPE: A 39 in. (100 cm) sympodial epiphyte.

PSEUDOBULB: 39 in. (100 cm) long. The elongated stems are slender.

LEAVES: 2 per growth. The broadly linear leaves are 4.3 in. (11 cm) long and unequally bilobed.

INFLORESCENCE: Short. Numerous inflorescences emerge from nodes along the stem.

FLOWERS: The pale yellow flowers are 0.5 in. (1.3 cm) across. Blossoms have an ovate dorsal sepal, 3-angled lateral sepals, and oblong petals. The pale green lip is 3-lobed. It is very small with spreading sidelobes and a dilated midlobe that appears 2-lobed.

REFERENCES: 219, 254, 468.

Dendrobium ornithoflorum Ames

ORIGIN/HABITAT: The Philippines. The habitat includes Misamis Province on Mindanao Island where plants grow at 5700–6250 ft. (1740–1900 m) on Mt. Malindang. They are also found on eastern Negros Island near Dumaquete and on Luzon Island in the provinces of Quezon and Albay.

CLIMATE: Station #98747, Cagayan De Oro, Mindanao Island, Philippines, Lat. 8.4°N, Long. 124.6°E, at 610 ft. (186 m). Temperatures are calculated for an elevation of 5700 ft. (1740 m), resulting in probable extremes of 80°F (27°C) and 44°F (7°C).

N/HEMISPHERE	JAN	FEB	MAR	APR	MAY	JUN	JUL	AUG	SEP	OCT	NOV	DEC
°F AVG MAX	70	71	72	74	75	74	73	74	74	73	73	71
°F AVG MIN	53	54	54	55	57	56	55	55	55	55	55	54
DIURNAL RANGE	17	17	18	19	18	18	18	19	19	18	18	17
RAIN/INCHES	3.7	2.3	1.4	1.3	4.9	8.6	8.9	7.9	8.5	7.8	4.8	4.2
HUMIDITY/%	84	83	81	78	80	81	81	82	82	81	81	82
BLOOM SEASON					*		*					
DAYS CLR @ 8AM	5	3	9	11	7	5	6	4	5	7	7	6
DAYS CLR @ 2PM	2	3	5	5	2	1	1	1	1	2	2	3
RAIN/MM	94	58	36	33	124	218	226	201	216	198	122	107
°C AVG MAX	21.2	21.8	22.3	23.4	24.0	23.4	22.9	23.4	23.4	22.9	22.9	21.8
°C AVG MIN	11.8	12.3	12.3	12.9	14.0	13.4	12.9	12.9	12.9	12.9	12.9	12.3
DIURNAL RANGE	9.4	9.5	10.0	10.5	10.0	10.0	10.0	10.5	10.5	10.0	10.0	9.5
S/HEMISPHERE	JUL	AUG	SEP	OCT	NOV	DEC	JAN	FEB	MAR	APR	MAY	JUN

Cultural Recommendations

LIGHT: 2000–3000 fc.

TEMPERATURES: Throughout the year, days average 70–75°F (21–24°C), and nights average 53–57°F (12–14°C), with a diurnal range of 17–19°F (9–11°C).

HUMIDITY: 80–85% year-round.

WATER: Rainfall is moderate to heavy most of the year, with a 2–3 month semidry season in late winter and early spring. Cultivated plants should be kept moist while growing, but water should be gradually reduced in late autumn.

FERTILIZER: 1/4–1/2 recommended strength. A balanced fertilizer should be applied weekly to biweekly throughout the year.

REST PERIOD: Growing temperatures should be maintained all year. In the habitat, winter rainfall is low, but the high relative humidity and large temperature range cause heavy dew to form most nights. For cultivated plants, water should be reduced for 2–3 months in winter. Plants should be allowed to dry slightly between waterings but should not remain dry for long periods. Fertilizer should be reduced or eliminated anytime water is reduced. In the habitat, light is highest in winter.

GROWING MEDIA: Plants may be mounted on tree-fern or cork slabs or potted in small pots filled with any open, fast-draining medium. Repotting may be done anytime new roots are growing.

MISCELLANEOUS NOTES: The bloom season shown in the climate table is based on collection reports. Plants that produce very short-lived flowers commonly bloom several times during the year. Flowering usually occurs 7–14 days after a sudden 10°F (5°C) drop in daytime temperatures.

Plant and Flower Information

PLANT SIZE AND TYPE: A 24 in. (60 cm) sympodial epiphyte.

PSEUDOBULB: 24 in. (60 cm) long. The graceful plant branches profusely. New growths rise from a climbing rhizome. Young stems are covered by leaf sheaths, but with age, the rigid stems become yellow and appear polished.

LEAVES: Many. The grasslike leaves are 1–4 in. (2.5–10.0 cm) long, narrow, and pointed.

INFLORESCENCE: 0.4 in. (1 cm) long. The short inflorescences emerge from bracts at the leaf axils of younger branches.

FLOWERS: 2 per inflorescence. The small flowers are yellowish white and may not open. The dorsal sepal and petals are linear-lanceolate. Lateral sepals are triangular. The lip is 3-lobed with somewhat sickle-shaped sidelobes and a pointed midlobe which is serrated along the margin. Blossoms last a single day.

REFERENCES: 12, 220, 296, 445, 536.

PHOTOS/DRAWINGS: 12.

Dendrobium oscari A. Hawkes and A. H. Heller. See *D. macropus* (Endl.) Rchb. f. ex Lindley. REFERENCES: 191, 229, 270.

Dendrobium osmophytopsis Kränzlin

ORIGIN/HABITAT: Sarawak, western Borneo. Plants were originally found near Mt. Mattau, but habitat elevation was not reported. Habitat elevation is estimated, so the following climate data should be used with caution.

CLIMATE: Station #96421, Sibu, Sarawak, Borneo, Lat. 2.3°N, Long. 111.8°E, at 22 ft. (7 m). Temperatures are calculated for an estimated elevation of 500 ft. (150 m), resulting in probable extremes of 97°F (36°C) and 61°F (16°C).

Dendrobium ostrinoglossum

N/HEMISPHERE	JAN	FEB	MAR	APR	MAY	JUN	JUL	AUG	SEP	OCT	NOV	DEC
°F AVG MAX	84	84	85	86	86	88	86	88	85	85	86	85
°F AVG MIN	72	72	71	72	72	72	72	71	71	71	71	72
DIURNAL RANGE	12	12	14	14	14	16	14	17	14	14	15	13
RAIN/INCHES	15.2	10.9	11.2	8.1	9.0	7.3	7.0	6.3	10.9	9.2	10.2	12.2
HUMIDITY/%	88	90	90	85	88	81	81	87	90	88	87	89
BLOOM SEASON					*							
DAYS CLR @ 7AM	0	1	1	1	3	3	2	1	0	1	1	1
DAYS CLR @ 1PM	0	0	1	3	3	2	1	1	0	1	1	1
RAIN/MM	386	277	284	206	229	185	178	160	277	234	259	310
°C AVG MAX	29.1	29.1	29.7	30.2	30.2	31.3	30.2	31.3	29.7	29.7	30.2	29.7
°C AVG MIN	22.5	22.5	21.9	22.5	22.5	22.5	22.5	21.9	21.9	21.9	21.9	22.5
DIURNAL RANGE	6.6	6.6	7.8	7.7	7.7	8.8	7.7	9.4	7.8	7.8	8.3	7.2
S/HEMISPHERE	JUL	AUG	SEP	OCT	NOV	DEC	JAN	FEB	MAR	APR	MAY	JUN

Cultural Recommendations

LIGHT: 2000–3000 fc.

TEMPERATURES: Throughout the year, days average 84–88°F (29–31°C), and nights average 71–72°F (22–23°C), with a diurnal range of 12–17°F (7–9°C).

HUMIDITY: 80–90% year-round. Averages this high are probably not essential in cultivation, but humidity should exceed 60% with excellent air movement.

WATER: Rainfall is very heavy year-round. Cultivated plants should be kept moist, with only slight drying allowed between waterings.

FERTILIZER: ¼–½ recommended strength. A balanced fertilizer should be applied weekly to biweekly throughout the year.

REST PERIOD: Growing conditions should be maintained year-round. Although rainfall in the habitat is greatest in winter, water should be decreased somewhat for plants grown in the dark, short-day conditions common in temperate latitudes. They should never dry out completely, however. In the habitat, light is higher in winter.

GROWING MEDIA: Plants may be mounted on tree-fern or cork slabs if humidity is high and plants are watered at least once daily in summer. When plants are potted, any open, fast-draining medium may be used. They may be repotted anytime new roots are growing.

MISCELLANEOUS NOTES: The bloom season shown in the climate table is based on collection reports.

Plant and Flower Information

PLANT SIZE AND TYPE: A 16 in. (40 cm) sympodial epiphyte.

PSEUDOBULB: 16 in. (40 cm) long. The stems are slender above the round, pseudobulbous swelling at the base.

LEAVES: Many. The distichous leaves are 1.6 in. (4 cm) long. They are bilobed, strap-shaped, and somewhat twisted at the base.

INFLORESCENCE: 0.8 in. (2 cm) long.

FLOWERS: 2 per inflorescence. The flowers are 0.6 in. (1.5 cm) across. They are white when dry. Blossoms have a pointed, oblong dorsal sepal, with pointed, ovate petals, and broadly oblong lateral sepals. The 3-lobed lip has small, oblong sidelobes and a broadly obovate midlobe. The lip is decorated 2 heavy lines. The margin is ruffled.

REFERENCES: 220, 254, 286, 295.

Dendrobium ostrinoglossum Rupp. See *D. lasianthera* J. J. Smith.

The International Orchid Commission (ref. 236) registers hybrids under both *D. ostrinoglossum* and *D. lasianthera* J. J. Smith.
REFERENCES: 84, 228, 236, 301, 303, 430. PHOTOS/DRAWINGS: 301, *303*, *496*.

Dendrobium ostrinum J. J. Smith

ORIGIN/HABITAT: New Guinea, Kei Islands, and Ambon. In Irian Jaya (western New Guinea), plants grow along the Noord River on trees in primary forests at low elevations. They were also collected south of Geluks Hill. *D. ostrinum* var. *ochroleucum* J. J. Smith was collected along the upper Sepik River in the central mountains at 800 ft. (250 m). It grew epiphytically in open forests along streams. Plants were cultivated at the botanical garden at Bogor, Java.

CLIMATE: Station #97796, Kokenau (Kokonau), Irian Jaya, Lat. 4.7°S, Long. 136.4°E, at 10 ft. (3 m). Record extreme temperatures are not available for this location.

N/HEMISPHERE	JAN	FEB	MAR	APR	MAY	JUN	JUL	AUG	SEP	OCT	NOV	DEC
°F AVG MAX	83	83	86	88	90	89	89	89	90	88	87	84
°F AVG MIN	73	73	74	74	74	75	74	74	74	74	74	73
DIURNAL RANGE	10	10	12	14	16	14	15	15	16	14	13	11
RAIN/INCHES	18.4	15.8	18.9	11.6	9.7	10.6	11.5	15.7	11.6	11.6	16.0	19.9
HUMIDITY/%	N/A											
BLOOM SEASON			*						*			
DAYS CLR	N/A											
RAIN/MM	467	401	479	295	245	269	293	400	294	296	407	506
°C AVG MAX	28.6	28.4	30.2	31.1	32.1	31.9	31.9	31.7	32.0	31.4	30.7	28.7
°C AVG MIN	22.7	22.6	23.3	23.4	23.5	23.7	23.6	23.5	23.4	23.4	23.5	23.0
DIURNAL RANGE	5.9	5.8	6.9	7.7	8.6	8.2	8.3	8.2	8.6	8.0	7.2	5.7
S/HEMISPHERE	JUL	AUG	SEP	OCT	NOV	DEC	JAN	FEB	MAR	APR	MAY	JUN

Cultural Recommendations

LIGHT: 2500–3500 fc.

TEMPERATURES: Throughout the year, days average 83–90°F (28–32°C), and nights average 73–75°F (23–24°C), with a diurnal range of 10–16°F (6–9°C).

HUMIDITY: Information is not available for this location. However, records from nearby stations indicate that humidity probably averages near 85% year-round.

WATER: Rainfall is very heavy all year. Cultivated plants should be kept evenly moist but not soggy. Warm water might be beneficial.

FERTILIZER: ¼–½ recommended strength. A balanced fertilizer should be applied weekly to biweekly throughout the year.

REST PERIOD: Growing conditions should be maintained year-round. The smallest diurnal range occurs in winter. Water and fertilizer might be reduced slightly, especially for plants cultivated in the dark, short-day conditions common in temperate latitudes. Plants should never be allowed to dry out completely, however.

GROWING MEDIA: Plants are best potted in small pots filled with any open, fast-draining medium. Plants should be kept moist, but not soggy. Repotting may be done anytime new roots are actively growing.

MISCELLANEOUS NOTES: The bloom season shown in the climate table is based on reports from the habitat. Plants that produce very short-lived flowers commonly bloom several times during the year. Flowering usually occurs 7–14 days after a sudden 10°F (5°C) drop in daytime temperatures.

Plant and Flower Information

PLANT SIZE AND TYPE: A sympodial epiphyte of unreported size.

PSEUDOBULB: The stems are elliptical in cross-section.

LEAVES: Many. The oblong leaves, which are 2.2–2.8 in. (5.5–7.0 cm) long, are bilobed.

INFLORESCENCE: Short.

FLOWERS: 2 per inflorescence. The flowers are 0.7 in. (1.7 cm) long. They are purple-violet, a very unusual color among the closely related plants. Blossoms have lanceolate petals and pointed, lanceolate sepals. The lateral sepals are somewhat sickle-shaped. The 3-lobed lip has lanceolate sidelobes and a curled, triangular midlobe that is lacerated to the disk. Blossoms last a single day.

REFERENCES: 220, 254, 445, 470.

Dendrobium otaguroanum A. Hawkes

AKA: *D. chloroleucum* Schlechter.

ORIGIN/HABITAT: Northern mainland New Guinea. Plants usually grow epiphytically on moss-covered branches in the rainforests, but they are also found in exposed locations with high light such as high cliff faces and road cuts at 4900–7200 ft. (1500–2200 m).

CLIMATE: Station #200192, Garaina, Papua New Guinea, Lat. 7.9°S, Long. 147.1°E, at 2350 ft. (1828 m). Temperatures are calculated for an elevation of 6000 ft. (1830 m), resulting in probable extremes of 82°F (28°C) and 34°F (1°C).

N/HEMISPHERE	JAN	FEB	MAR	APR	MAY	JUN	JUL	AUG	SEP	OCT	NOV	DEC
°F AVG MAX	68	70	71	72	73	73	73	73	72	72	71	69
°F AVG MIN	51	51	51	52	51	52	53	53	53	52	52	51
DIURNAL RANGE	17	19	20	20	22	21	20	20	19	20	19	18
RAIN/INCHES	5.8	6.5	8.7	11.1	11.8	11.9	8.9	11.7	11.5	9.9	7.7	5.2
HUMIDITY/%	84	82	82	81	80	80	81	81	82	83	84	84
BLOOM SEASON							*					
DAYS CLR	N/A											
RAIN/MM	147	165	221	282	300	302	226	297	292	251	196	132
°C AVG MAX	20.0	21.1	21.6	22.2	22.8	22.8	22.8	22.8	22.2	22.2	21.6	20.5
°C AVG MIN	10.5	10.5	10.5	11.1	10.5	11.1	11.6	11.6	11.6	11.1	11.1	10.5
DIURNAL RANGE	9.5	10.6	11.1	11.1	12.3	11.7	11.2	11.2	10.6	11.1	10.5	10.0
S/HEMISPHERE	JUL	AUG	SEP	OCT	NOV	DEC	JAN	FEB	MAR	APR	MAY	JUN

Cultural Recommendations

LIGHT: 2500–3500 fc.

TEMPERATURES: Throughout the year, days average 68–73°F (20–23°C), and nights average 51–53°F (11–12°C), with a diurnal range of 17–22°F (10–12°C).

HUMIDITY: 80–85% year-round.

WATER: Rainfall is heavy all year, but conditions are slightly drier in winter. Cultivated plants should be kept moist but not soggy.

FERTILIZER: ¼–½ recommended strength. A balanced fertilizer should be applied weekly to biweekly throughout the year.

REST PERIOD: Growing conditions should be maintained all year. In the habitat, rainfall is slightly lower in winter. Water and fertilizer should be reduced somewhat for cultivated plants, especially those grown in the dark, short-day conditions common during temperate-latitude winters. They should never be allowed to dry out completely, however. In the habitat, seasonal light variation is minor.

GROWING MEDIA: Plants may be mounted on tree-fern or cork slabs if humidity is high and plants are watered at least once daily in summer. When plants are potted, any open, fast-draining medium may be used. Repotting may be done anytime new roots are growing.

MISCELLANEOUS NOTES: The bloom season shown in the climate table is based on cultivation records.

Plant and Flower Information

PLANT SIZE AND TYPE: A 4–10 in. (10–25 cm) sympodial epiphyte.

PSEUDOBULB: 4–10 in. (10–25 cm) long. Stems are clustered, yellow, and erect. The pseudobulbs have 3–4 nodes below the leaves.

LEAVES: 2–4 per growth. The leaves are 2.0–2.8 in. (5–7 cm) long. They may be narrowly lanceolate or ovate.

INFLORESCENCE: 1.0–2.6 in. (2.5–6.7 cm) long. The erect inflorescences are laxly flowered.

FLOWERS: 2–6 per inflorescence. The flowers are 1.2–1.6 in. (3–4 cm) across and open fully. Blossoms are white with yellowish green veins. The petals are narrow at the base, becoming broad at the apex before abruptly contracting to a sharp point. They are wavy near the base along one margin. The oblong sepals are pointed at the tip. The lip is quadrate-rhomboid with a notch at the apex. Blossoms last 4–6 weeks.

REFERENCES: 83, 92, 95, 179, 191, 229, 304, 437.

PHOTOS/DRAWINGS: 83, *304*, 437.

Dendrobium ouhinnae Schlechter. Originally spelled *D. ou-hinnae*, it is now considered a synonym of *Diplocaulobium ouhinnae* (Schlechter) Kränzlin. REFERENCES: 173, 220, 254, 270, 432.

Dendrobium ovatifolium Ridley

ORIGIN/HABITAT: Northern Sarawak, near Bentang Lupar. Plants were recently found in Sarawak near Mt. Mulu in mixed lower forests at about 330 ft. (100 m).

CLIMATE: Station #96449, Miri, Sarawak, Borneo, Lat. 4.4°N, Long. 114.0°E, at 14 ft. (4 m). Temperatures are calculated for an elevation of 350 ft. (110 m), resulting in probable extremes of 94°F (34°C) and 66°F (19°C).

N/HEMISPHERE	JAN	FEB	MAR	APR	MAY	JUN	JUL	AUG	SEP	OCT	NOV	DEC
°F AVG MAX	85	85	86	87	87	87	87	87	86	86	86	86
°F AVG MIN	73	73	73	74	74	74	73	73	73	73	73	73
DIURNAL RANGE	12	12	13	13	13	13	14	14	13	13	13	13
RAIN/INCHES	16.8	6.5	5.5	4.4	8.2	12.0	8.5	8.4	11.8	11.7	14.5	11.3
HUMIDITY/%	86	86	85	83	83	82	81	81	82	83	84	85
BLOOM SEASON	N/A											
DAYS CLR @ 8AM	1	2	4	4	3	2	3	2	2	1	2	2
DAYS CLR @ 2PM	1	1	3	4	2	5	3	2	3	2	1	1
RAIN/MM	427	165	140	112	208	305	216	213	300	297	368	287
°C AVG MAX	29.4	29.4	29.9	30.5	30.5	30.5	30.5	30.5	29.9	29.9	29.9	29.9
°C AVG MIN	22.7	22.7	22.7	23.3	23.3	23.3	22.7	22.7	22.7	22.7	22.7	22.7
DIURNAL RANGE	6.7	6.7	7.2	7.2	7.2	7.2	7.8	7.8	7.2	7.2	7.2	7.2
S/HEMISPHERE	JUL	AUG	SEP	OCT	NOV	DEC	JAN	FEB	MAR	APR	MAY	JUN

Cultural Recommendations

LIGHT: 2000–3000 fc.

TEMPERATURES: Throughout the year, days average 85–87°F (29–31°C), and nights average 73–74°F (23°C), with a diurnal range of 12–14°F (7–8°C).

HUMIDITY: 80–85% year-round.

WATER: Rainfall is heavy to very heavy all year, but conditions are slightly drier in winter. Cultivated plants should be kept moist but not soggy.

FERTILIZER: ¼–½ recommended strength. A balanced fertilizer should be applied weekly to biweekly throughout the year.

REST PERIOD: Growing conditions should be maintained all year. In cultivation, water and fertilizer should be reduced somewhat in winter, especially if plants are grown in the dark, short-day conditions common in temperate latitudes. Plants should never be allowed to dry out completely, however. In the habitat, seasonal light variation is minor.

GROWING MEDIA: Plants may be mounted on tree-fern or cork slabs if humidity is high and plants are watered daily in summer. When plants are potted, any open, fast-draining medium may be used. Repotting may be done anytime new roots are growing.

Plant and Flower Information

PLANT SIZE AND TYPE: A 35 in. (90 cm) sympodial epiphyte.

PSEUDOBULB: 35 in. (90 cm) long. The leafy stems are 4-angled when dry.

LEAVES: Many. The small, leathery leaves are 1.6 in. (4 cm) long. The upper leaves are ovate, while the lower leaves are lanceolate. They are unequally bilobed at the apex.

INFLORESCENCE: Very short.

FLOWERS: The large, fleshy flowers are 1.4 in. (3.5 cm) long. The narrow, spreading petals and ovate sepals are pointed at the tip. The long, 3-lobed lip is rounded at the apex and uneven along the margin. The oblong sidelobes are curved out. *D. ovatifolium* was originally placed in the section *Grastidium*, suggesting that blossoms may be short-lived.

REFERENCES: 254, 286, 295, 394, 586.

Dendrobium ovatipetalum J. J. Smith

ORIGIN/HABITAT: Halmahera Island in the Moluccas. Habitat information and elevation were not included in the original plant description, but plants were cultivated at the botanical garden in Bogor, Java. The following climate data should be used with caution.

CLIMATE: Station #97406, Galela, Halmahera Island, Indonesia, Lat. 1.8°N, Long. 127.8°E, at 180 ft. (55 m). Record extreme temperatures are not available for this location.

N/HEMISPHERE	JAN	FEB	MAR	APR	MAY	JUN	JUL	AUG	SEP	OCT	NOV	DEC
°F AVG MAX	86	86	86	88	87	86	86	87	87	88	88	87
°F AVG MIN	76	74	76	76	77	75	73	75	76	77	77	76
DIURNAL RANGE	10	12	10	12	10	11	13	12	11	11	11	11
RAIN/INCHES	5.3	6.4	7.4	4.1	10.0	7.1	8.1	9.3	5.2	6.9	7.0	11.4
HUMIDITY/%	N/A											
BLOOM SEASON	N/A											
DAYS CLR	N/A											
RAIN/MM	134	163	188	104	254	180	205	236	132	175	177	289
°C AVG MAX	30.1	30.0	29.8	30.9	30.6	30.2	30.0	30.5	30.7	31.4	31.2	30.5
°C AVG MIN	24.3	23.6	24.6	24.6	24.9	23.9	22.9	23.7	24.2	24.9	25.2	24.6
DIURNAL RANGE	5.8	6.4	5.2	6.3	5.7	6.3	7.1	6.8	6.5	6.5	6.0	5.9
S/HEMISPHERE	JUL	AUG	SEP	OCT	NOV	DEC	JAN	FEB	MAR	APR	MAY	JUN

Cultural Recommendations

LIGHT: 2000–3000 fc.

TEMPERATURES: Throughout the year, days average 86–88°F (30–31°C), and nights average 73–77°F (23–25°C), with a diurnal range of 10–13°F (5–7°C).

HUMIDITY: Information is not available for this location. However, records from nearby locations indicate that humidity probably averages near 80% year-round.

WATER: Rainfall is moderate to heavy all year. Cultivated plants should be kept moist and allowed to dry only slightly between waterings.

FERTILIZER: ¼–½ recommended strength. A balanced fertilizer should be applied weekly to biweekly throughout the year.

REST PERIOD: Growing conditions should be maintained year-round. Water may be reduced slightly in winter, especially for plants grown in the dark, short-day conditions common in temperate latitudes, but plants should never be allowed to dry out completely. Fertilizer should be reduced or eliminated anytime water is reduced.

GROWING MEDIA: Plants may be mounted on tree-fern or cork slabs or potted in small pots filled with any open, fast-draining medium. Repotting may be done anytime new roots are growing.

MISCELLANEOUS NOTES: The plant was described in 1932 in *Bul. Jard. Bot. Buit.* 3rd sér. 12:134.

Plant and Flower Information

PLANT SIZE AND TYPE: A 55–65 in. (140–165 cm) sympodial epiphyte.

PSEUDOBULB: 55–65 in. (140–165 cm) long. The slender stems are swollen for a few nodes above the base.

LEAVES: Many. The oblong leaves are 2.8–3.1 in. (7–8 cm) long. On the upper part of the stem, the leaves are rudimentary. They are rigidly leathery when dry.

INFLORESCENCE: Inflorescences emerge from scalelike bracts. Blossoms are carried in simple clusters.

FLOWERS: The flowers are often up to 2 in. (4 cm) across. The more or less triangular sepals and broad, somewhat ovate petals are pure white. The 3-lobed lip is decorated with 3 raised, yellow keels. It has erect, incurved sidelobes and an oval midlobe that is recurved at the apex. Blossoms are fragrant.

REFERENCES: 225.

Dendrobium ovatum (Linn.) Kränzlin

AKA: Commonly listed as *D. ovatum* (Willdenow) Kränzlin. However, G. C. Druce in the *Supplement to the Botanical Exchange Club Report* for 1913 (see ref. 221), indicates that *Epidendrum ovatum* Linn. not *Cymbidium ovatum* Willdenow is the original description for this plant. Kränzlin (ref. 254) includes *Cymbidium ovatum* Willdenow, *Dendrobium barbatulum* as used by Wight not Lindley, and *D. chlorops* Lindley as synonyms.

ORIGIN/HABITAT: Endemic to southern India. Plants are widely distributed in the Mysore and West Ghats regions at 150–5000 ft. (50–1520 m).

CLIMATE: Station #43314, Calicut, India, Lat. 11.3°N, Long. 75.8°E, at 17 ft. (5 m). Temperatures are calculated for an elevation of 4000 ft. (1220 m), resulting in probable extremes of 86°F (30°C) and 44°F (7°C).

N/HEMISPHERE	JAN	FEB	MAR	APR	MAY	JUN	JUL	AUG	SEP	OCT	NOV	DEC
°F AVG MAX	75	76	77	78	77	72	69	70	71	73	74	75
°F AVG MIN	58	60	63	65	65	62	61	61	62	62	61	58
DIURNAL RANGE	17	16	14	13	12	10	8	9	9	11	13	17
RAIN/INCHES	0.4	0.2	0.7	3.6	9.3	33.1	32.5	17.2	7.9	10.3	5.5	1.0
HUMIDITY/%	71	73	73	74	82	87	91	91	87	85	77	74
BLOOM SEASON									**	**	**	
DAYS CLR @ 5AM	19	18	21	12	5	4	2	2	4	4	19	20
DAYS CLR @ 11AM	16	18	23	15	5	3	0	1	6	5	12	16
RAIN/MM	10	5	18	91	236	841	826	437	201	262	140	25
°C AVG MAX	23.8	24.4	24.9	25.5	24.9	22.1	20.5	21.0	21.6	22.7	23.3	23.8
°C AVG MIN	14.4	15.5	17.1	18.3	18.3	16.6	16.0	16.0	16.6	16.6	16.0	14.4
DIURNAL RANGE	9.4	8.9	7.8	7.2	6.6	5.5	4.5	5.0	5.0	6.1	7.3	9.4
S/HEMISPHERE	JUL	AUG	SEP	OCT	NOV	DEC	JAN	FEB	MAR	APR	MAY	JUN

Cultural Recommendations

LIGHT: 3000–4000 fc. The heavy summer cloud cover indicates that some shading is needed from spring through autumn, but light should be as high as the plant can tolerate, short of burning the leaves.

TEMPERATURES: Summer days average 69–72°F (21–22°C), and nights average 61–62°F (16–17°C), with a diurnal range of 8–10°F (5–6°C). Spring is the warmest season. Days average 77–78°F (25–26°C), and nights average 63–65°F (17–18°C), with a diurnal range of 12–14°F (7–8°C).

HUMIDITY: 85–90% in summer and early autumn, decreasing to 70–75% in winter and early spring.

WATER: Rainfall is extremely heavy in summer, but conditions are dry for 3–4 months in winter. Cultivated plants should be watered liberally from spring into autumn. They should not be allowed to dry out completely while actively growing, but water should be reduced after new growths mature in autumn.

FERTILIZER: ¼–½ recommended strength, applied weekly. A high-nitrogen fertilizer is beneficial from spring to midsummer, but a fertilizer high in phosphates should be used in late summer and autumn.

REST PERIOD: Winter days average 75–76°F (24°C), and nights average 58–60°F (14–16°C), with a diurnal range of 16–17°F (9°C). The slightly warmer days and slightly cooler nights double the summer diurnal range. The winter dry period lasts 3–4 months. Water should be greatly reduced for cultivated plants. They should be allowed to dry out between waterings but should not remain dry for extended periods. Fertilizer should be greatly reduced or eliminated until water is increased in spring. In the habitat, light is highest in winter.

GROWING MEDIA: Growers recommend mounting plants on tree-fern slabs if humidity is high and plants receive daily watering in midsummer. If plants are potted, any open, fast-draining medium may be used. Repotting should be done in late spring when new roots begin to grow.

MISCELLANEOUS NOTES: The bloom season shown in the climate table is based on cultivation records.

Plant and Flower Information

PLANT SIZE AND TYPE: A 4–20 in. (10–50 cm) sympodial epiphyte.

PSEUDOBULB: 12–20 in. (30–50 cm) long. The leafy stems may be as small as 4 in. (10 cm). The mauve-brown pseudobulbs are sometimes very stout.

LEAVES: Many. The deciduous leaves are oblong-lanceolate, 1–4 in. (2.5–10.0 cm) long, and alternate along the stem.

INFLORESCENCE: 6 in. (15 cm) long. Inflorescences emerge from the side and the apex of leafless stems.

FLOWERS: Several to many per inflorescence. The flowers are 0.6–0.8 in. (1.5–2.0 cm) across. The sepals and much broader petals may be cream-white, greenish, or yellowish. The base of the 3-lobed lip is pale pea-green. The midlobe is less than twice the length of the sidelobes. The disk has a tuft of short hairs and a channeled ridge. Flowers are variable in size and color.

HYBRIDIZING NOTES: Chromosome counts are n = 20 (ref. 542), 2n = 38 (ref. 154), and 2n = 40 (ref. 151, 504, 542, 580) as *D. ovatum*.

REFERENCES: 38, 46, 119, 151, 154, 179, 202, 220, 221, 236, 254, 255, 317, 369, 424, 504, 542, 580.

PHOTOS/DRAWINGS: 424.

Dendrobium ovipostoriferum J. J. Smith

AKA: Sometimes spelled *D. ovipositoriferum*. *D. takahashii* Carr.

ORIGIN/HABITAT: Collected during stopovers at Sungei Tarik and Kwaru Islands off Borneo. We have not be able to find these locations, but the plants collected as *D. takahashii* were found near Banjermasin in south Borneo, where they grew on rather thinly spaced and stunted trees at about 350 ft. (100 m).

CLIMATE: Station #96685, Bandjarmasin, Borneo, Lat. 3.4°S, Long. 114.8°E, at 66 ft. (20 m). Record extreme temperatures are not available for this location.

N/HEMISPHERE	JAN	FEB	MAR	APR	MAY	JUN	JUL	AUG	SEP	OCT	NOV	DEC
°F AVG MAX	88	89	91	90	87	86	86	86	87	89	88	88
°F AVG MIN	74	73	74	76	76	76	76	75	75	77	77	76
DIURNAL RANGE	14	16	17	14	11	10	10	11	12	12	11	12
RAIN/INCHES	3.5	3.2	3.9	5.1	8.5	12.2	12.7	11.7	11.9	8.5	6.2	5.6
HUMIDITY/%	78	77	73	75	81	84	84	83	82	81	80	79
BLOOM SEASON					*		*					
DAYS CLR @ 8AM	12	12	13	8	5	3	1	2	3	6	9	11
DAYS CLR @ 2PM	3	2	2	3	1	0	0	0	1	2	2	3
RAIN/MM	89	81	99	130	216	310	323	297	302	216	157	142
°C AVG MAX	31.0	31.9	32.7	32.4	30.7	29.9	29.8	30.0	30.6	31.4	30.9	31.1
°C AVG MIN	23.2	23.0	23.4	24.2	24.3	24.2	24.2	24.1	24.1	24.9	24.9	24.2
DIURNAL RANGE	7.8	8.9	9.3	8.2	6.4	5.7	5.6	5.9	6.5	6.5	6.0	6.9
S/HEMISPHERE	JUL	AUG	SEP	OCT	NOV	DEC	JAN	FEB	MAR	APR	MAY	JUN

Cultural Recommendations

LIGHT: 3000–4000 fc.

TEMPERATURES: Throughout the year, days average 86–91°F (30–33°C), and nights average 73–77°F (23–25°C), with a diurnal range of 10–17°F (6–9°C).

HUMIDITY: 80–85% from late spring through autumn, dropping to about 75% in winter and spring.

WATER: Rainfall is moderate to heavy all year, but conditions are slightly drier for 3 months in winter. Cultivated plants should be kept moist during the growing season. Warm water might be beneficial.

FERTILIZER: ¼–½ recommended strength. A balanced fertilizer should be applied weekly to biweekly throughout the year.

REST PERIOD: Growing conditions should be maintained all year. Water and fertilizer may be reduced somewhat in winter, especially for plants cultivated in the dark, short-day conditions common in temperate latitudes. Plants should be allowed to dry slightly between waterings, but they should never dry out completely. In the habitat, light is highest in winter.

GROWING MEDIA: Plants may be mounted on tree-fern or cork slabs if humidity is high and plants are watered at least once daily in summer. When plants are potted, any open, fast-draining medium may be used. They may be repotted anytime new roots are growing.

MISCELLANEOUS NOTES: The bloom season shown in the climate table is based on cultivation records. Reports from the habitat indicate blooming in late summer. In Singapore, plants grow well in light shade, but they are not vigorous.

Plant and Flower Information

PLANT SIZE AND TYPE: A 9–20 in. (23–50 cm) sympodial epiphyte.

PSEUDOBULB: 9–20 in. (23–50 cm) long. The clustered stems have a diameter of about 0.4 in. (1 cm). Internodes are about 1.4 in. (3.6 cm) long.

LEAVES: The leaves are 1.6–3.0 in. (4.0–7.5 cm) long. They are covered with deciduous hairs that are usually dark.

INFLORESCENCE: Short. 6 or more inflorescences arise from nodes near the apex of the stem.

FLOWERS: 1–4 per inflorescence. The flowers are 2.4 in. (6 cm) across. Sepals and petals are white. The lip midlobe is deep golden yellow, sometimes with broad snow-white margins, while the sidelobes are pale yellow with red veins at the base. The dorsal sepal is oblong, lateral sepals are lanceolate-triangular, and the petals are ovate. The wavy, nearly round lip is covered with warts and a few hairs. Holttum (ref. 200) indicates that the flowers, while similar to *D. formosum* Roxburgh ex Lindley, are smaller with much better color.

HYBRIDIZING NOTES: A cross with *D. formosum* was registered in 1949.

REFERENCES: 25, 58, 179, 200, 221, 225, 245, 286, 295, 429, 474.

PHOTOS/DRAWINGS: 58, 200.

Dendrobium oxyanthum Gagnepain. See *D. faulhaberianum* Schlechter. REFERENCES: 136, 224, 266, 448, 454.

Dendrobium oxychilum Schlechter

ORIGIN/HABITAT: Northeastern Papua New Guinea. Plants were collected on Mt. Gomadjidji along the Waria River. They were growing in deep moss on the large branches of mistforest trees at about 1300 ft. (400 m).

CLIMATE: Station #200192, Garaina, Papua New Guinea, Lat. 7.9°S, Long. 147.1°E, at 2350 ft. (716 m). Temperatures are calculated for an elevation of 1150 ft. (350 m), resulting in probable extremes of 98°F (37°C) and 50°F (10°C).

N/HEMISPHERE	JAN	FEB	MAR	APR	MAY	JUN	JUL	AUG	SEP	OCT	NOV	DEC
°F AVG MAX	84	86	87	88	89	89	89	89	88	88	87	85
°F AVG MIN	67	67	67	68	67	68	69	69	69	68	68	67
DIURNAL RANGE	17	19	20	20	22	21	20	20	19	20	19	18
RAIN/INCHES	5.8	6.5	8.7	11.1	11.8	11.9	8.9	11.7	11.5	9.9	7.7	5.2
HUMIDITY/%	84	82	82	81	80	80	81	81	82	83	84	84
BLOOM SEASON										*		*
DAYS CLR	N/A											
RAIN/MM	147	165	221	282	300	302	226	297	292	251	196	132
°C AVG MAX	28.9	30.0	30.5	31.1	31.6	31.6	31.6	31.6	31.1	31.1	30.5	29.4
°C AVG MIN	19.4	19.4	19.4	20.0	19.4	20.0	20.5	20.5	20.5	20.0	20.0	19.4
DIURNAL RANGE	9.5	10.6	11.1	11.1	12.2	11.6	11.1	11.1	10.6	11.1	10.5	10.0
S/HEMISPHERE	JUL	AUG	SEP	OCT	NOV	DEC	JAN	FEB	MAR	APR	MAY	JUN

Dendrobium oxyphyllum

Cultural Recommendations

LIGHT: 2000–3000 fc.

TEMPERATURES: Throughout the year, days average 84–89°F (29–32°C), and nights average 67–69°F (20–21°C), with a diurnal range of 17–22°F (10–12°C). The smallest diurnal range, which occurs in winter, is due to cooler days not cooler nights.

HUMIDITY: 80–85% year-round.

WATER: Rainfall is heavy all year, but conditions are slightly drier in winter. Cultivated plants should be kept moist but not soggy.

FERTILIZER: ¼–½ recommended strength. A balanced fertilizer should be applied weekly to biweekly throughout the year.

REST PERIOD: Growing conditions should be maintained all year. In the habitat, rainfall is slightly lower in winter. Water and fertilizer should be reduced somewhat for cultivated plants, especially those grown in the dark, short-day conditions common during temperate-latitude winters. They should never be allowed to dry out completely, however. In the habitat, seasonal light variation is minor.

GROWING MEDIA: Mounting plants on tree-fern or cork slabs accommodates their rambling growth habit. However, humidity must be high and plants must be watered at least once a day in summer. If plants cannot be mounted, hanging pots or baskets may be filled with an open, fast-draining medium. Repotting may be done anytime new roots are actively growing.

MISCELLANEOUS NOTES: The bloom season shown in the climate table is based on reports from the habitat. Plants that produce very short-lived flowers commonly bloom several times during the year. Flowering usually occurs 7–14 days after a sudden 10°F (5°C) drop in daytime temperatures.

Plant and Flower Information

PLANT SIZE AND TYPE: A 12 in. (30 cm) sympodial epiphyte.

PSEUDOBULB: 12 in. (30 cm) long. The slender stems are branching and leafy. They arise from the very elongated rhizome. The plant rambles horizontally.

LEAVES: Many. The lanceolate, closely set leaves are 0.5–0.9 in. (1.2–2.3 cm) long, shiny, and pointed at the tip.

INFLORESCENCE: Inflorescences emerge laterally.

FLOWERS: 1 per inflorescence. The tiny, white flowers are 0.2 in. (0.5 cm) long and remain rather closed. Sepals and petals are sharply pointed. The white lip has red markings. It is uppermost. The midlobe is toothed along the front edge and tapers to a sharp, elongated point. Blossoms last a single day.

REFERENCES: 221, 437, 445.

PHOTOS/DRAWINGS: 437.

Dendrobium oxyphyllum Gagnepain. See *D. aphyllum* (Roxburgh) C. Fischer. REFERENCES: 137, 227.

Dendrobium paathii J. J. Smith

ORIGIN/HABITAT: Borneo. Plants grow in the hills of western Kalimantan near Singkawang at about 1000 ft. (300 m).

CLIMATE: Station #96583, Pontianak, Borneo, Lat. 0.0°N, Long. 109.3°E, at 13 ft. (4 m). Temperatures are calculated for an elevation of 1000 ft. (300 m), resulting in probable extremes of 93°F (34°C) and 65°F (18°C).

N/HEMISPHERE	JAN	FEB	MAR	APR	MAY	JUN	JUL	AUG	SEP	OCT	NOV	DEC
°F AVG MAX	84	86	86	86	87	87	86	87	87	86	85	84
°F AVG MIN	71	73	72	72	72	72	71	71	72	72	72	71
DIURNAL RANGE	13	13	14	14	15	15	15	16	15	14	13	13
RAIN/INCHES	10.8	8.2	9.5	10.9	11.1	8.7	6.5	8.0	9.0	14.4	15.3	12.7
HUMIDITY/%	85	85	84	84	82	81	79	82	83	87	86	87
BLOOM SEASON				*								
DAYS CLR @ 7AM	1	1	1	3	2	4	5	1	2	1	1	2
DAYS CLR @ 1PM	0	0	1	0	0	0	1	1	1	0	1	0
RAIN/MM	274	208	241	277	282	221	165	203	229	366	389	323
°C AVG MAX	28.7	29.9	29.9	29.9	30.4	30.4	29.9	30.4	30.4	29.9	29.3	28.7
°C AVG MIN	21.5	22.6	22.1	22.1	22.1	22.1	21.5	21.5	22.1	22.1	22.1	21.5
DIURNAL RANGE	7.2	7.3	7.8	7.8	8.3	8.3	8.4	8.9	8.3	7.8	7.2	7.2
S/HEMISPHERE	JUL	AUG	SEP	OCT	NOV	DEC	JAN	FEB	MAR	APR	MAY	JUN

Cultural Recommendations

LIGHT: 2000–3000 fc.

TEMPERATURES: Throughout the year, days average 84–87°F (29–30°C), and nights average 71–73°F (22–23°C), with a diurnal range of 13–16°F (7–9°C). The probable extreme temperatures are near the averages. Thus, plants may not tolerate wide temperature fluctuations.

HUMIDITY: 80–85% year-round. Air circulation should be excellent.

WATER: Rainfall is heavy all year. Cultivated plants should be kept moist. Warm water is highly recommended. Plants from this habitat are often very sensitive to cold water, which may cause bud blast and cellular damage.

FERTILIZER: ¼–½ recommended strength. A balanced fertilizer should be applied weekly to biweekly throughout the year.

REST PERIOD: Growing conditions should be maintained all year. In the habitat, the heaviest rainfall occurs in winter; but water should be reduced somewhat for cultivated plants, especially those grown in the dark, short-day conditions common in temperate-latitude winters. Plants should never be allowed to dry out completely, however.

GROWING MEDIA: Mounting plants on tree-fern or cork slabs accommodates their pendulous growth habit. However, humidity must be high and plants must be watered at least once a day in summer. If plants cannot be mounted, hanging pots or baskets may be filled with an open, fast-draining medium. Repotting may be done anytime new roots are actively growing.

MISCELLANEOUS NOTES: The bloom season shown in the climate table is based on reports from the habitat.

Plant and Flower Information

PLANT SIZE AND TYPE: A sympodial epiphyte of unreported size. Plants resemble *D. anosmum* Lindley in growth habit.

LEAVES: The elliptical leaves are 1.4 in. (3.6 cm) long.

INFLORESCENCE: Short.

FLOWERS: Many. The trumpetlike flowers are 0.8 in. (2 cm) across. They have shiny, white sepals and petals. The lateral sepals are protruding. The yellow, 3-lobed lip is decorated with orange stripes. The midlobe is broader than the sidelobes. Plants are very floriferous.

REFERENCES: 25, 225, 286, 340, 487.

Dendrobium pachyanthum Schlechter 1911 not 1912

ORIGIN/HABITAT: Borneo. Plants are found in Sarawak in the forests near Kuching, and in Sabah in the Mt. Kinabalu region. They grow in lower mountain forests at 1950–3950 ft. (600–1200 m).

CLIMATE: Station #49613, Tambuan, Sabah (North Borneo), Lat. 5.7°N, Long. 116.4°E, at 1200 ft. (366 m). Temperatures are calculated for an elevation of 3000 ft. (910 m), resulting in probable extremes of 92°F (33°C) and 48°F (9°C).

N/HEMISPHERE	JAN	FEB	MAR	APR	MAY	JUN	JUL	AUG	SEP	OCT	NOV	DEC
°F AVG MAX	80	81	83	84	84	83	83	83	83	82	81	80
°F AVG MIN	61	59	60	61	62	61	60	60	61	61	61	62
DIURNAL RANGE	19	22	23	23	22	22	23	23	22	21	20	18
RAIN/INCHES	5.8	3.7	5.8	7.5	8.2	7.3	5.1	4.9	6.4	7.0	6.8	6.0
HUMIDITY/%	N/A											
BLOOM SEASON							*					
DAYS CLR	N/A											
RAIN/MM	147	94	147	190	208	185	130	124	163	178	173	152
°C AVG MAX	26.7	27.3	28.4	28.9	28.9	28.4	28.4	28.4	28.4	27.8	27.3	26.7
°C AVG MIN	16.1	15.0	15.6	16.1	16.7	16.1	15.6	15.6	16.1	16.1	16.1	16.7
DIURNAL RANGE	10.6	12.3	12.8	12.8	12.2	12.3	12.8	12.8	12.3	11.7	11.2	10.0
S/HEMISPHERE	JUL	AUG	SEP	OCT	NOV	DEC	JAN	FEB	MAR	APR	MAY	JUN

Cultural Recommendations

LIGHT: 2000–3000 fc.

TEMPERATURES: Throughout the year, days average 80–84°F (27–29°C), and nights average 59–62°F (15–17°C), with a diurnal range of 18–23°F (10–13°C).

HUMIDITY: Information is not available for this location. However, records from nearby locations indicate that humidity probably averages 80–85% year-round.

WATER: Rainfall is moderate to heavy all year with a brief, slightly drier period in winter. Cultivated plants should be allowed to dry only slightly between waterings.

FERTILIZER: ¼–½ recommended strength. A balanced fertilizer should be applied weekly to biweekly throughout the year.

REST PERIOD: Growing temperatures should be maintained all year. Water should be reduced for cultivated plants, especially those grown in the dark, short-day conditions common in temperate-latitude winters, but they should never be allowed to dry out completely. Fertilizer should be reduced or eliminated until water is increased in spring.

GROWING MEDIA: Plants may be mounted on tree-fern or cork slabs if humidity is high and plants are watered at least once daily in summer. When plants are potted, any open, fast-draining medium may be used. They may be repotted anytime new roots are growing.

MISCELLANEOUS NOTES: The bloom season shown in the climate table is based on reports from the habitat.

Plant and Flower Information

PLANT SIZE AND TYPE: A 16 in. (40 cm) sympodial epiphyte.

PSEUDOBULB: 16 in. (40 cm) long. The cylindrical stems are borne on a short rhizome. They are densely leafy, longitudinally grooved, and somewhat curved.

LEAVES: Many. The oblong leaves are 1.4–2.0 in. (3.5–5.0 cm) long. They are smooth, leathery, and arranged in 2 rows.

INFLORESCENCE: Short. Inflorescences are borne along the side of the stem.

FLOWERS: 1 per inflorescence. The flowers are 0.4 in. (1.1 cm) long. Blossoms are white, sometimes with a brownish tinge. The oblong sepals are smooth, spreading, and pointed. The smooth, somewhat oblong petals are more rounded than the sepals. The 3-lobed lip is smooth with ovate-triangular sidelobes and a nearly round midlobe which is wavy along the margin.

REFERENCES: 221, 286, 295, 445, 592.

Dendrobium pachyanthum Schlechter 1912 not 1911. See *D. katherinae* A. Hawkes. REFERENCES: 191, 221, 437.

Dendrobium pachyceras F. Mueller and Kränzlin. See *D. hollrungii* Kränzlin. REFERENCES: 218, 253, 254, 437, 445, 470.

Dendrobium pachyglossum Parish and Rchb. f.

AKA: *D. abietinum* Ridley, *D. fallax* Guillaumin.

ORIGIN/HABITAT: Southeast Asia. Distribution includes the Taiping Hills, Kedah Peak, and Langkawi Island in northwestern Malaya. The habitat extends through peninsular Thailand, the Tenasserim, Maymyo, and Mandalay regions of Burma, south central and eastern Thailand, Laos, and into Vietnam, where plants are found near Dalat and Blao. They grow low on trees and mossy rocks in dense, mountain forests at 2000–4000 ft. (610–1220 m).

CLIMATE: Station #48601, Penang, Malaya, Lat. 5.3°N, Long. 100.3°E, at 8 ft. (2 m). Temperatures are calculated for an elevation of 3000 ft. (910 m), resulting in probable extremes of 88°F (31°C) and 57°F (14°C).

N/HEMISPHERE	JAN	FEB	MAR	APR	MAY	JUN	JUL	AUG	SEP	OCT	NOV	DEC
°F AVG MAX	80	81	82	81	80	80	80	79	78	79	78	79
°F AVG MIN	63	63	64	65	64	64	64	63	63	63	63	63
DIURNAL RANGE	17	18	18	16	16	16	16	16	15	16	15	16
RAIN/INCHES	3.7	3.1	5.6	7.4	10.7	7.7	7.5	11.6	15.8	16.9	11.9	5.8
HUMIDITY/%	76	77	81	84	84	84	85	85	85	87	86	81
BLOOM SEASON	N/A											
DAYS CLR @ 7AM	2	1	2	0	0	1	1	0	0	0	1	1
DAYS CLR @ 1PM	3	2	2	1	1	1	1	0	0	0	1	2
RAIN/MM	94	79	142	188	272	196	190	295	401	429	302	147
°C AVG MAX	26.7	27.3	27.8	27.3	26.7	26.7	26.7	26.2	25.6	26.2	25.6	26.2
°C AVG MIN	17.3	17.3	17.8	18.4	17.8	17.8	17.8	17.3	17.3	17.3	17.3	17.3
DIURNAL RANGE	9.4	10.0	10.0	8.9	8.9	8.9	8.9	8.9	8.3	8.9	8.3	8.9
S/HEMISPHERE	JUL	AUG	SEP	OCT	NOV	DEC	JAN	FEB	MAR	APR	MAY	JUN

Cultural Recommendations

LIGHT: 3000–3500 fc.

TEMPERATURES: Throughout the year, days average 78–82°F (26–28°C), and nights average 63–65°F (17–18°C), with a diurnal range of 15–18°F (8–10°C).

HUMIDITY: 80–85% for most of the year, dropping to near 75% for 2 months in winter.

WATER: Rainfall is moderate to heavy all year, but conditions are slightly drier for 2 months in winter. Cultivated plants should be kept moist.

FERTILIZER: ¼–½ recommended strength. A balanced fertilizer should be applied weekly to biweekly throughout the year.

REST PERIOD: Growing conditions should be maintained year-round. Water should be reduced somewhat for cultivated plants in winter, but they should never be allowed to dry out completely. In the habitat, light is highest in winter.

GROWING MEDIA: Mounting plants on tree-fern or cork slabs accommodates their somewhat pendulous growth habit. However, humidity must be high and plants must be watered at least once a day in summer. If plants cannot be mounted, small pots or hanging baskets may be filled with an open, fast-draining medium. Repotting may be done anytime new roots are actively growing.

Plant and Flower Information

PLANT SIZE AND TYPE: A 6–20 in. (15–50 cm) sympodial epiphyte or lithophyte. The stems of epiphytic plants occasionally reach a length of 40 in. (102 cm). *D. pachyglossum* was described as very like *D. attenuatum* Lindley.

PSEUDOBULB: 6–20 in. (15–50 cm) long. Stems are somewhat pendulous, slender, and narrowest at the base and apex. They are clustered together. The nodes are spaced 0.6–1.0 in. (1.5–2.5 cm) apart.

LEAVES: Many. The grasslike, linear leaves are 4 in. (10 cm) long. They are held at a wide angle to the stem. The leaf sheaths are covered with black hairs.

INFLORESCENCE: Very short. Lateral racemes arise from the center of the leaf cluster.

FLOWERS: 1–2, rarely more per inflorescence. The smallest forms may have 3–4 blossoms per inflorescence. Individual flowers are 0.5 in. (1.3 cm) across. Flower color is variable. The erect sepals and petals may be white, yellowish, or greenish with red, yellow-orange, or brown longitudinal stripes. Some clones have pinkish segments with light purplish veins. The fleshy lip, which has 2 keels and very small sidelobes, may be pale yellow-green or nearly white edged with yellowish green. The lip is marked with brown streaks.

HYBRIDIZING NOTES: Johansen (ref. 239) indicates that plants are self-sterile and that flowers dropped 8–10 days after self-pollination.

REFERENCES: 157, 200, 202, 203, 216, 239, 254, 395, 402, 445, 447, 448, 454, 455.

PHOTOS/DRAWINGS: 203, *454*, 455.

Dendrobium pachyphyllum (Kuntze) Bakhuizen f.

AKA: *Callista pachyphylla* Kuntze. *Dendrobium borneense* Finet, *D. carnosum* Teijsm. and Binn., *D. perpusillum* Balakrishnan, *D. pisibulbum* Guillaumin, *D. pumilum* Roxburgh, *D. pusillum* (Blume) Lindley. The name *D. quadrangulare* Ridley not Parish and Rchb. f. is sometimes erroneously applied to plants belonging to *D. pachyphyllum*. Seidenfaden (ref. 454) discusses the confusion in the names and synonyms for this plant. However, Seidenfaden and Woods (ref. 455) include only *D. pumilum* Roxburgh as a synonym.

ORIGIN/HABITAT: Common and widespread throughout Southeast Asia. Distribution extends from northeastern India southward through the peninsula region of Burma and Thailand, into Malaya, Sumatra, Java, and Borneo. Plants are also reported near Dalat, Vietnam. Other than *D. crumenatum* Swartz, *D. pachyphyllum* is considered the most common orchid on the Thai Islands in the Andaman Sea. In Java, the plants grow from sea level to 3300 ft. (0–1000 m); and in Borneo, they are reported at 1950–6900 ft. (600–2100 m). They are found low on tree trunks in swamps, orchards, open country, and along the roadside. The orchids rarely grow in primary forests and never where light is low.

CLIMATE: Station #48110, Mergui, Burma, Lat. 12.4°N, Long. 98.6°E, at 75 ft. (23 m). Record extreme temperatures are 99°F (37°C) and 53°F (12°C).

N/HEMISPHERE	JAN	FEB	MAR	APR	MAY	JUN	JUL	AUG	SEP	OCT	NOV	DEC
°F AVG MAX	87	89	90	91	89	85	84	84	84	86	87	87
°F AVG MIN	69	71	73	75	75	74	73	73	73	73	71	69
DIURNAL RANGE	18	18	17	16	14	11	11	11	11	13	16	18
RAIN/INCHES	1.0	2.1	3.1	4.9	16.7	30.0	32.9	30.0	24.9	12.1	3.8	0.8
HUMIDITY/%	73	75	78	79	86	91	93	94	92	86	79	75
BLOOM SEASON			**	**	**							
DAYS CLR @ 7AM	9	3	4	2	0	0	0	0	0	1	4	8
DAYS CLR @ 1PM	11	7	4	2	0	0	0	0	0	1	4	9
RAIN/MM	25	53	79	124	424	762	836	762	632	307	97	20
°C AVG MAX	30.6	31.7	32.2	32.8	31.7	29.4	28.9	28.9	28.9	30.0	30.6	30.6
°C AVG MIN	20.6	21.7	22.8	23.9	23.9	23.3	22.8	22.8	22.8	22.8	21.7	20.6
DIURNAL RANGE	10.0	10.0	9.4	8.9	7.8	6.1	6.1	6.1	6.1	7.2	8.9	10.0
S/HEMISPHERE	JUL	AUG	SEP	OCT	NOV	DEC	JAN	FEB	MAR	APR	MAY	JUN

Cultural Recommendations

LIGHT: 2500–3500 fc.

TEMPERATURES: Throughout the year, days average 84–91°F (29–33°C), and nights average 69–75°F (21–24°C), with a diurnal range of 11–18°F

(6–10°C). Because of the wide range of habitat elevation, plants should adapt to temperatures 15–18°F (8–10°C) cooler than indicated.

HUMIDITY: 85–95% in summer and autumn, dropping to 70–75% in winter and spring.

WATER: Rainfall is very heavy for 6 months from spring to early autumn, but conditions are much drier in winter. Cultivated plants should be kept moist while actively growing, but water should be gradually reduced after new growths mature in autumn.

FERTILIZER: ¼–½ recommended strength. A balanced fertilizer should be applied weekly to biweekly throughout the year.

REST PERIOD: Growing conditions should be maintained all year. Rainfall is low for 2–3 months in winter, but high humidity and nightly cooling cause frequent heavy deposits of dew. Therefore, the dry season is neither as long or as severe as indicated by the rainfall averages. In cultivation, water should be reduced in winter, especially for plants grown in the darker, short-day conditions common in temperate latitudes. Plants should dry somewhat between waterings, but they should not remain dry for long periods. Fertilizer should be reduced or eliminated anytime water is reduced. In the habitat, light is highest in winter.

GROWING MEDIA: Mounting plants on tree-fern or cork slabs accommodates their freely branching growth habit. However, humidity must be high and plants must be watered at least once a day in summer. If plants cannot be mounted, small pots or hanging baskets may be filled with an open, fast-draining medium. Repotting may be done anytime new roots are actively growing.

MISCELLANEOUS NOTES: The bloom season indicated in the climate table is based on cultivation reports. Some reports indicate that blooming occurs in spring in the habitat, but others state that blooming occurs sporadically throughout the year. The blossom initiator is unknown. Growers speculate that sudden temperature changes may cause bud formation, but this explanation has not been confirmed. Plants bloom during both the wet and dry seasons. The roots are boiled and used medicinally for dropsy.

Plant and Flower Information

PLANT SIZE AND TYPE: A 4 in. (10 cm) sympodial epiphyte. Plants are occasionally as small as 1.6 in. (4 cm).

PSEUDOBULB: 0.4–2.0 in. (1–5 cm) long, rarely as long as 3.2 in. (8 cm). The glossy, highly variable stems are usually wiry at the base and swollen at the upper nodes. They are often tufted and stick out in all directions. Growths arise from a creeping, freely branching rhizome that becomes firmly attached to the host.

LEAVES: 2 per growth. The leaves usually equal the length of the pseudobulb. The nearly succulent leaves are thick, fleshy, oblong, and glossy yellow-green with red tips.

INFLORESCENCE: Short. The inflorescences emerge from between the leaves and blossoms are held just above the leaves. Inflorescences may appear successively, thereby extending the bloom season. However, they may also appear 2–3 at a time so that flowers bloom simultaneously.

FLOWERS: 1, rarely 2 per inflorescence. The flowers, which may not open fully, are approximately equal the size of the pseudobulbs or leaves. The broad sepals and linear petals may be white, cream, or yellow, usually with purple lines. The lip is normally cream-colored. It may have red veins and a dark spot at the apex of the midlobe, or it may be white with a greenish yellow spot at the center. The very fragrant blossoms last a single day.

HYBRIDIZING FLOWERS: Johansen (ref. 239) indicates that plants are self-sterile and that flowers dropped 3–6 days after self-pollination. When crossed with *D. devonianum* Paxton, capsules formed but no viable seed was produced.

REFERENCES: 25, 31, 38, 75, 118, 157, 169, 200, 202, 230, 231, 239, 254, 286, 291, 295, 310, 317, 395, 402, 435, 454, 455, 469, 589, 592.

PHOTOS/DRAWINGS: 75, 291, 454, 455.

Dendrobium pachystele Schlechter

AKA: Cribb (ref. 83) includes *D. pachystele* var. *homeoglossum* Schlechter as a synonym.

ORIGIN/HABITAT: Northern Papua New Guinea, the Solomon Islands, and possibly on Palau in the Caroline Islands. Plants grow on trees in lower mountain forests at 80–2600 ft. (25–800 m). They are usually found in cool, shady locations, often in moss near cascading creeks and rivers.

CLIMATE: Station #91520, Honiara, Guadalcanal, Solomon Islands, Lat. 9.4°S, Long. 160.0°E, at 10 ft. (3 m). Temperatures are calculated for an elevation of 1200 ft. (370 m), resulting in probable extremes of 91°F (33°C) and 61°F (16°C).

N/HEMISPHERE	JAN	FEB	MAR	APR	MAY	JUN	JUL	AUG	SEP	OCT	NOV	DEC
°F AVG MAX	82	83	84	84	84	84	84	84	83	84	84	83
°F AVG MIN	68	68	68	68	69	69	70	70	69	69	69	68
DIURNAL RANGE	14	15	16	16	15	15	14	14	14	15	15	15
RAIN/INCHES	6.0	4.4	4.6	7.7	7.7	9.5	14.1	13.3	16.7	10.6	8.1	6.7
HUMIDITY/%	84	82	81	80	81	82	83	83	87	85	85	85
BLOOM SEASON							**					
DAYS CLR @ 5AM	6	7	7	5	6	4	3	3	4	4	4	7
DAYS CLR @ 11AM	3	2	2	1	1	1	1	0	2	2	4	4
RAIN/MM	152	112	117	196	196	241	358	338	424	269	206	170
°C AVG MAX	27.8	28.4	28.9	28.9	28.9	28.9	28.9	28.9	28.4	28.9	28.9	28.4
°C AVG MIN	20.0	20.0	20.0	20.0	20.6	20.6	21.2	21.2	20.6	20.6	20.6	20.0
DIURNAL RANGE	7.8	8.4	8.9	8.9	8.3	8.3	7.7	7.7	7.8	8.3	8.3	8.4
S/HEMISPHERE	JUL	AUG	SEP	OCT	NOV	DEC	JAN	FEB	MAR	APR	MAY	JUN

Cultural Recommendations

LIGHT: 1800–2500 fc.

TEMPERATURES: Throughout the year, days average 82–84°F (28–29°C), and nights average 68–70°F (20–21°C), with a diurnal range of 14–16°F (8–9°C).

HUMIDITY: 80–85% year-round.

WATER: Rainfall is heavy all year, but conditions are slightly drier for 2–3 months in winter. Cultivated plants should be kept moist, with only slight drying allowed between waterings.

FERTILIZER: ¼–½ recommended strength. A balanced fertilizer should be applied weekly to biweekly throughout the year.

REST PERIOD: Growing conditions should be maintained year-round. Water and fertilizer may be reduced somewhat for cultivated plants in winter, especially those grown in the dark, short-day conditions common in temperate latitudes. Plants should never be allowed to dry out completely, however.

GROWING MEDIA: Plants may be mounted on tree-fern or cork slabs if humidity is high and plants are watered at least once daily in summer. When plants are potted, any open, fast-draining medium may be used. They may be repotted anytime new roots are growing.

MISCELLANEOUS NOTES: The bloom season shown in the climate table is based on cultivation records.

Plant and Flower Information

PLANT SIZE AND TYPE: An 11–22 in. (28–55 cm) sympodial epiphyte.

PSEUDOBULB: 4–10 in. (10–25 cm) long. The slender stems are usually slightly swollen near the top.

LEAVES: 1 at the apex of each growth. The lanceolate leaves are 7–12 in. (18–30 cm) long.

INFLORESCENCE: 2 in. (5 cm) long. Inflorescences emerge laterally, often from nodes low on the pseudobulb.

Dendrobium pachythrix

FLOWERS: 3–6 per inflorescence. The flowers are 0.8 in. (2 cm) across. The whitish or creamy blossoms are fleshy. The dorsal sepal is ovate, lateral sepals are somewhat triangular, and petals are oblong-elliptic. The elliptic-obovate lip is obscurely 3-lobed and may be without sidelobes. It is recurved. The 2-ridged callus covers half the length of the lip.

REFERENCES: 83, 179, 221, 271, 437, 445, 516.

PHOTOS/DRAWINGS: 437.

Dendrobium pachythrix T. M. Reeve and P. Woods

ORIGIN/HABITAT: Papua New Guinea. Plants were first found near Yengis in the Koipapalu Mountains of northeastern Enga Province at 4900 ft. (1500 m). They have since been found near Mt. Hagen in the Western Highlands Province at 5600 ft. (1700 m).

CLIMATE: Station #200265, Wabag, Papua New Guinea, Lat. 5.5°S, Long. 143.7°E, at 6500 ft. (1980 m). Temperatures are calculated for an elevation of 5300 ft. (1620 m), resulting in probable extremes of 88°F (31°C) and 41°F (5°C).

N/HEMISPHERE	JAN	FEB	MAR	APR	MAY	JUN	JUL	AUG	SEP	OCT	NOV	DEC
°F AVG MAX	75	75	76	76	77	76	77	76	76	76	77	76
°F AVG MIN	55	55	56	56	56	56	57	58	58	56	56	54
DIURNAL RANGE	20	20	20	20	21	20	20	18	18	20	21	22
RAIN/INCHES	5.0	7.6	10.4	10.4	10.3	12.2	11.8	11.9	13.5	11.5	7.8	5.3
HUMIDITY/%	N/A											
BLOOM SEASON	N/A											
DAYS CLR	N/A											
RAIN/MM	127	193	264	264	262	310	300	302	343	292	198	135
°C AVG MAX	23.9	23.9	24.4	24.4	25.0	24.4	25.0	24.4	24.4	24.4	25.0	24.4
°C AVG MIN	12.8	12.8	13.3	13.3	13.3	13.3	13.9	14.4	14.4	13.3	13.3	12.2
DIURNAL RANGE	11.1	11.1	11.1	11.1	11.7	11.1	11.1	10.0	10.0	11.1	11.7	12.2
S/HEMISPHERE	JUL	AUG	SEP	OCT	NOV	DEC	JAN	FEB	MAR	APR	MAY	JUN

Cultural Recommendations

LIGHT: 2000–3000 fc.

TEMPERATURES: Throughout the year, days average 75–77°F (24–25°C), and nights average 54–58°F (12–14°C), with a diurnal range of 18–22°F (10–12°C).

HUMIDITY: Information is not available for this location. However, records from nearby stations indicate that humidity is probably 75–80% year-round.

WATER: Rainfall is heavy all year. A slightly drier period occurs in winter. Cultivated plants should be kept moist.

FERTILIZER: ¼–½ recommended strength. A balanced fertilizer should be applied weekly to biweekly throughout the year.

REST PERIOD: Growing conditions should be maintained year-round. Water may be reduced somewhat in winter, especially for plants grown in the dark, short-day conditions common in temperate-latitude winters. Plants should never be allowed to dry completely, however. In the habitat, light may be slightly higher in winter.

GROWING MEDIA: Plants may be mounted on tree-fern or cork slabs or potted in small pots filled with any open, fast-draining medium. Repotting may be done anytime new roots are growing.

Plant and Flower Information

PLANT SIZE AND TYPE: A 0.4–1.2 in. (1–3 cm) sympodial epiphyte or terrestrial.

PSEUDOBULB: 0.2–0.5 in. (0.4–1.2 cm) long. The reddish pseudobulbs may be round or club-shaped. They are densely clustered, usually erect, and emerge from a very short rhizome.

LEAVES: 1–2 per growth. The lanceolate leaves are 0.2–0.5 in. (0.5–1.2 cm) long. They are green on the upper side, often with a purplish flush, while the underside is purplish.

INFLORESCENCE: Very short. The apical inflorescence normally emerges on leafy stems.

FLOWERS: 2–3 per inflorescence. The flowers are 0.4–0.7 in. (1.1–1.7 cm) long. The blossoms have red sepals and petals. The orange lip is pale red at the tip. The backs of the sepals, the ovary, and the column are covered with long, thick hairs that sometimes branch. Blossoms are long-lasting.

REFERENCES: 235, 385.

PHOTOS/DRAWINGS: *385*.

Dendrobium padangense Schlechter. Now considered a synonym of *Flickingeria forcipata* (Kränzlin) A. Hawkes. REFERENCES: 200, 213, 222, 231, 435, 449, 455. PHOTOS/DRAWINGS: 200.

Dendrobium pahangense Carr

ORIGIN/HABITAT: Malaya. Plants have been found only on Frazer's Hill and on Mt. Tahan at about 4000 ft. (1220 m).

CLIMATE: Station #49630, Temerloh, Malaya, Lat. 3.5°N, Long. 102.4°E, at 163 ft. (50 m). Temperatures are calculated for an elevation of 4000 ft. (1220 m), resulting in probable extremes of 84°F (29°C) and 51°F (11°C).

N/HEMISPHERE	JAN	FEB	MAR	APR	MAY	JUN	JUL	AUG	SEP	OCT	NOV	DEC
°F AVG MAX	72	75	77	78	78	77	77	77	77	76	74	73
°F AVG MIN	58	58	59	60	60	60	59	59	59	60	60	59
DIURNAL RANGE	14	17	18	18	18	17	18	18	18	16	14	14
RAIN/INCHES	7.8	3.9	6.0	7.6	6.6	4.3	3.4	5.6	6.5	9.3	9.7	10.1
HUMIDITY/%	87	83	84	85	86	86	84	85	86	87	89	88
BLOOM SEASON	N/A											
DAYS CLR @ 7AM	0	0	2	1	1	0	2	2	2	0	0	0
DAYS CLR @ 1PM	1	1	2	1	1	1	0	1	1	0	0	0
RAIN/MM	198	99	152	193	168	109	86	142	165	236	246	257
°C AVG MAX	22.4	24.1	25.2	25.7	25.7	25.2	25.2	25.2	25.2	24.6	23.5	23.0
°C AVG MIN	14.6	14.6	15.2	15.7	15.7	15.7	15.2	15.2	15.2	15.7	15.7	15.2
DIURNAL RANGE	7.8	9.5	10.0	10.0	10.0	9.5	10.0	10.0	10.0	8.9	7.8	7.8
S/HEMISPHERE	JUL	AUG	SEP	OCT	NOV	DEC	JAN	FEB	MAR	APR	MAY	JUN

Cultural Recommendations

LIGHT: 2500–3500 fc.

TEMPERATURES: Throughout the year, days average 72–78°F (22–26°C), and nights average 58–60°F (15–16°C), with a diurnal range of 14–18°F (8–10°C).

HUMIDITY: 85–90% year-round.

WATER: Rainfall is moderate to heavy all year with brief, 1–2 month, slightly drier periods in winter and summer. Cultivated plants should be kept moist, with only slight drying allowed between waterings.

FERTILIZER: ¼–½ recommended strength. A balanced fertilizer should be applied weekly to biweekly throughout the year.

REST PERIOD: Growing conditions should be maintained all year. However, water should be reduced for a month or so in summer, and again in late winter. Plants should be allowed to become somewhat drier between waterings, but they should never dry out completely. Fertilizer should be reduced or eliminated while water is reduced.

GROWING MEDIA: Plants may be mounted on tree-fern or cork slabs if humidity is high and plants are watered at least once daily in summer. When plants are potted, any open, fast-draining medium may be used. Repotting may be done anytime new roots are growing.

Plant and Flower Information

PLANT SIZE AND TYPE: A 9 in. (23 cm) sympodial epiphyte.

PSEUDOBULB: 8 in. (20 cm) long. The nodes are less than 0.4 in. (1 cm) apart.

LEAVES: 1–2. The leaves are 0.8–3.5 in. (2–9 cm) long.

FLOWERS: 1 per inflorescence. The flowers are 0.4–0.6 in. (1.0–1.5 cm) across. The white sepals and petals curl back. The pale yellow lip is marked with orange keels extending to the apex of the lip. The sidelobes are small and rounded. The rounded midlobe, which has a very short point, curls up along the wavy edges.

REFERENCES: 200, 224, 445, 455.

PHOTOS/DRAWINGS: 455.

Dendrobium palawense Schlechter. Now considered a synonym of *D. macrophyllum* A. Richard. REFERENCES: Chrisianson 1992 *Lindleyana* 7(2):89–90.

Dendrobium pallens Ridley. Now considered a synonym of *Flickingeria pallens* (Ridley) A. Hawkes. REFERENCES: 213, 230, 231, 254, 279, 395, 449.

Dendrobium pallidiflorum Ridley. Sometimes spelled *pallideflorum*, it is now considered a synonym of *Flickingeria xantholeucha* (Rchb. f.) A. Hawkes. REFERENCES: 75, 213, 254, 395, 449, 469.

Dendrobium palmerstoniae Schlechter. See *D. adae* F. M. Bailey. REFERENCES: 67, 105, 220, 254, 533.

Dendrobium palmifolium Swartz. Now considered a synonym of *Maxillaria palmifolium*. REFERENCES: 190, 216, 254, 445.

Dendrobium palpebrae Lindley

AKA: Sometimes spelled *D. palpaebrae*. Seidenfaden (ref. 454) indicates that plants which should be called *D. palpebrae* are frequently called *D. densiflorum* or *D. farmeri*.

ORIGIN/HABITAT: Widespread across southeast Asia. The habitat includes India, Yunnan Province in southwest China, the Bhamo and Moulmein districts of Burma, Thailand, Laos, and Vietnam. Plants grow near Dalat, Vietnam at about 2600 ft. (800 m). In India, they are found in the Teesta Valley and rarely in Arunachal Pradesh at 6550–8200 ft. (2000–2500 m).

CLIMATE: Station #48881, Dalat, Vietnam, Lat. 11.1°N, Long. 108.1°E, at 3156 ft. (962 m). Record extreme temperatures are 93°F (34°C) and 43°F (6°C).

N/HEMISPHERE	JAN	FEB	MAR	APR	MAY	JUN	JUL	AUG	SEP	OCT	NOV	DEC
°F AVG MAX	80	82	84	85	84	81	81	80	80	80	79	79
°F AVG MIN	56	57	59	62	65	65	65	65	65	63	60	58
DIURNAL RANGE	24	25	25	23	19	16	16	15	15	17	19	21
RAIN/INCHES	0.2	0.9	1.6	4.6	9.1	6.1	7.7	8.2	10.1	9.7	2.7	1.3
HUMIDITY/%	68	64	65	71	78	81	82	83	84	82	76	73
BLOOM SEASON				*	*	*	*	*	*			
DAYS CLR @ 7AM	13	13	13	9	5	3	2	2	2	5	7	10
DAYS CLR @ 1PM	8	8	8	2	0	0	0	0	0	1	3	4
RAIN/MM	5	23	41	117	231	155	196	208	257	246	69	33
°C AVG MAX	26.7	27.8	28.9	29.4	28.9	27.2	27.2	26.7	26.7	26.7	26.1	26.1
°C AVG MIN	13.3	13.9	15.0	16.7	18.3	18.3	18.3	18.3	18.3	17.2	15.6	14.4
DIURNAL RANGE	13.4	13.9	13.9	12.7	10.6	8.9	8.9	8.4	8.4	9.5	10.5	11.7
S/HEMISPHERE	JUL	AUG	SEP	OCT	NOV	DEC	JAN	FEB	MAR	APR	MAY	JUN

Cultural Recommendations

LIGHT: 2000–3000 fc.

TEMPERATURES: Summer days average 80–81°F (27°C), and nights average 65°F (18°C), with a diurnal range of 15–16°F (8–9°C). The warmest temperatures occur in late winter and spring. Days average 84–85°F (29°C), and nights average 59–65°F (15–18°C), with a diurnal range of 19–25°F (11–14°C).

HUMIDITY: 80–85% in summer, dropping to near 65% in late winter.

WATER: Rainfall is moderate to heavy in summer but is very light for 2 months in winter. Cultivated plants should be kept moist while growing, but water should be gradually reduced after new growths mature in autumn.

FERTILIZER: ¼–½ recommended strength, applied weekly. A high-nitrogen fertilizer is beneficial from spring to midsummer, but a fertilizer high in phosphates should be used in late summer and autumn.

REST PERIOD: Winter days average 79–82°F (26–28°C), and nights average 56–58°F (13–14°C), with a diurnal range of 21–25°F (12–14°C). The increased diurnal range results from warmer days and cooler nights. Rainfall is low for 3–4 months. For 1–2 of these months, conditions are so dry that even moisture from dew is uncommon. For cultivated plants, water and fertilizer should be reduced for 2–3 months. Plants should be allowed to dry out between waterings, but they should not remain dry for extended periods. Growers indicate that conditions should be drier once the growths mature. In the habitat, light is highest in winter.

GROWING MEDIA: Plants may be mounted on tree-fern or cork slabs if humidity is high and plants are watered at least once daily in summer. When plants are potted, any open, fast-draining medium may be used. Repotting may be done anytime new roots are growing.

MISCELLANEOUS NOTES: The bloom season shown in the climate table is based on cultivation records. Reports from the habitat indicate spring blooming.

Plant and Flower Information

PLANT SIZE AND TYPE: A 6–20 in. (15–50 cm) sympodial epiphyte.

PSEUDOBULB: 6–20 in. (15–50 cm) long. The cylindrical stems are 4-angled and grooved. They are clustered and often curved.

LEAVES: 3–5 per stem. The leaves are 4–6 in. (10–15 cm) long, oblong-lanceolate, and pointed at the tip.

INFLORESCENCE: 3–6 in. (8–15 cm) long. Pendulous inflorescences emerge from nodes immediately below the leaves. Blossoms are carried in loose racemes.

FLOWERS: 6–15 per inflorescence. The flowers are 1.4–2.4 in. (3.5–6.0 cm) across. Sepals and petals are most often white, but they may be dark rose or any of the intermediate shades. The petals are nearly round with a finely toothed margin. The lip is white along the margin with an orange disk and a row of eyelash-like hairs at the base. The entire midlobe and the margins of the sidelobes are covered with soft hairs. Blossoms are showy and long-lived with a fragrance similar to apples or hawthorn.

HYBRIDIZING NOTES: Chromosome count is 2n = 40 (ref. 154, 188, 504, 580).

REFERENCES: 25, 36, 38, 46, 154, 157, 179, 188, 190, 196, 202, 203, 208, 210, 216, 247, 254, 266, 317, 376, 445, 447, 448, 454, 504, 541, 580.

PHOTOS/DRAWINGS: 203, 210, *247, 454*.

Dendrobium paludicola Schlechter. See *D. lobbii* Teijsm. and Binn. REFERENCES: 67, 92, 219, 254, 437, 444, 445, 454.

Dendrobium palustre L. O. Williams. See *D. nebularum* Schlechter. REFERENCES: 227, 385.

Dendrobium pandaneti Ridley

AKA: Often spelled *D. pandanetii*. *D. mega* Kränzlin is a synonym.

ORIGIN/HABITAT: Southeast Asia, including Sumatra, Borneo, Java, Thailand, and Malaya. In Java, plants grow from sea level to 2000 ft. (0–610 m); and in Borneo, they are found at about 1300 ft. (400 m). They have been collected near Trang in peninsular Thailand. In Malaya, they grow

Dendrobium panduratum

on the southern part of the peninsula and in northwestern Perak State, usually on the trunks of palms and pandans.

CLIMATE: Station #48665, Melaka (Malacca), Malaya, Lat. 2.3°N, Long. 102.3°E, at 40 ft. (12 m). Record extreme temperatures are 99°F (37°C) and 61°F (16°C).

N/HEMISPHERE	JAN	FEB	MAR	APR	MAY	JUN	JUL	AUG	SEP	OCT	NOV	DEC
°F AVG MAX	88	89	89	89	89	88	88	88	88	88	88	88
°F AVG MIN	72	72	72	73	73	73	72	72	72	72	72	72
DIURNAL RANGE	16	17	17	16	16	15	16	16	16	16	16	16
RAIN/INCHES	3.9	3.7	4.9	7.4	6.8	7.9	7.8	10.3	8.8	10.1	8.7	6.5
HUMIDITY/%	79	79	82	85	85	83	84	84	84	84	84	82
BLOOM SEASON				**								
DAYS CLR @ 7AM	1	1	1	1	1	1	2	1	1	1	0	1
DAYS CLR @ 1PM	1	1	1	1	1	1	1	1	1	0	0	0
RAIN/MM	99	94	124	188	173	201	198	262	224	257	221	165
°C AVG MAX	31.1	31.7	31.7	31.7	31.7	31.1	31.1	31.1	31.1	31.1	31.1	31.1
°C AVG MIN	22.2	22.2	22.2	22.8	22.8	22.8	22.2	22.2	22.2	22.2	22.2	22.2
DIURNAL RANGE	8.9	9.5	9.5	8.9	8.9	8.3	8.9	8.9	8.9	8.9	8.9	8.9
S/HEMISPHERE	JUL	AUG	SEP	OCT	NOV	DEC	JAN	FEB	MAR	APR	MAY	JUN

Cultural Recommendations

LIGHT: 2000–3000 fc.

TEMPERATURES: Throughout the year, days average 88–89°F (31–32°C), and nights average 72–73°F (22–23°C), with a diurnal range of 15–17°F (8–10°C).

HUMIDITY: 80–85% year-round.

WATER: Rainfall is moderate to heavy all year, but conditions are slightly drier for 2–3 months in winter. Cultivated plants should be kept moist but not soggy.

FERTILIZER: ¼–½ recommended strength, applied weekly. A high-nitrogen fertilizer is beneficial from spring to midsummer, but a fertilizer high in phosphates should be used in late summer and autumn.

REST PERIOD: Growing conditions should be maintained all year. Water and fertilizer should be reduced for cultivated plants in winter, especially those grown in the dark short-day conditions common in temperate latitudes. Plants should never be allowed to dry out completely, however.

GROWING MEDIA: Mounting plants on tree-fern or cork slabs accommodates their creeping, climbing growth habit. Repotting may be done anytime new roots are growing.

MISCELLANEOUS NOTES: The bloom season shown in the climate table is based on reports from the habitat. The blossoms are often self-pollinating.

Plant and Flower Information

PLANT SIZE AND TYPE: A 16–18 in. (40–45 cm) sympodial epiphyte.

PSEUDOBULB: 14 in. (35 cm) long. The shiny, green or yellow stems are cylindrical, smooth, and often branching. They arise from a creeping rhizome that climbs a considerable distance up the host tree. The nodes are spaced 0.8 in. (2 cm) apart.

LEAVES: 10–13 per growth. The linear-oblong leaves, which are thin, shiny, and pale green, are 2–4 in. (5–10 cm) long. They are held close to the stem in two rows. The bases of the smooth, pale sheaths overlap.

INFLORESCENCE: 0.3 in. (0.8 cm) long. Several racemes are borne at the upper leaf axils.

FLOWERS: 2–3 per inflorescence, with up to 15 blossoms open at a time. The flowers are 0.8–1.0 in. (2.0–2.5 cm) across and open fully. The oblong sepals and narrower petals are white. The lip midlobe is fleshy. It is dull orange-red with 3 orange keels on the disk. All parts are pointed and recurved. Flowers are self-pollinating.

REFERENCES: 25, 75, 200, 220, 254, 395, 402, 437, 445, 454, 455, 469, 592.

PHOTOS/DRAWINGS: 75, 200, 454, *455*, 469.

Dendrobium panduratum Lindley

ORIGIN/HABITAT: Sri Lanka (Ceylon) and near Chemboti, Palghat District, Kerala, India. In Sri Lanka, plants were collected in tropical lower mountain forests and evergreen rainforests at about 6000 ft. (1830 m).

CLIMATE: Station #43473, Nuwara Eliya, Sri Lanka, Lat. 7.0°N, Long. 80.8°E, at 6168 ft. (1880 m). Record extreme temperatures are not available for this location.

N/HEMISPHERE	JAN	FEB	MAR	APR	MAY	JUN	JUL	AUG	SEP	OCT	NOV	DEC
°F AVG MAX	67	71	72	73	73	69	66	66	66	68	67	67
°F AVG MIN	50	50	51	54	59	61	56	55	55	54	53	53
DIURNAL RANGE	17	21	21	19	14	8	10	11	11	14	14	14
RAIN/INCHES	3.9	2.4	3.2	6.4	5.7	4.3	4.6	5.8	6.4	6.8	7.7	6.5
HUMIDITY/%	N/A											
BLOOM SEASON					*	*	**	*	*	*		
DAYS CLR	N/A											
RAIN/MM	100	62	80	162	144	109	116	146	163	172	194	166
°C AVG MAX	19.6	21.4	22.2	22.6	23.0	20.7	18.8	19.0	19.1	20.0	19.6	19.2
°C AVG MIN	10.2	10.0	10.6	12.2	14.8	15.9	13.3	12.9	12.9	12.2	11.9	11.6
DIURNAL RANGE	9.4	11.4	11.6	10.4	8.2	4.8	5.5	6.1	6.2	7.8	7.7	7.6
S/HEMISPHERE	JUL	AUG	SEP	OCT	NOV	DEC	JAN	FEB	MAR	APR	MAY	JUN

Cultural Recommendations

LIGHT: 2000–3000 fc. Shading is needed from spring through autumn, but light should be as high as the plant can tolerate, short of burning the leaves. Strong air movement should be provided year-round.

TEMPERATURES: Summer days average 66–69°F (19–21°C), and nights average 55–61°F (13–16°C), with a diurnal range of 8–11°F (4–6°C). Spring is the warmest season. Days average 72–73°F (22–23°C), and nights average 51–59°F (11–15°C), with a diurnal range of 14–21°F (8–12°C).

HUMIDITY: Information is not available for this location. However, records from nearby stations indicate that humidity probably averages 70–80% year-round.

WATER: Rainfall is moderate to heavy most of the year, but conditions are slightly drier for 2–3 months in winter. Cultivated plants should be kept moist while actively growing with only slight drying allowed between waterings.

FERTILIZER: ¼–½ recommended strength, applied weekly. A high-nitrogen fertilizer is beneficial from spring to midsummer, but a fertilizer high in phosphates should be used in late summer and autumn.

REST PERIOD: Winter days average 67–71°F (19–21°C), and nights average 50–53°F (10–12°C), with a diurnal range of 14–21°F (8–12°C). The increased diurnal range results from cooler nights. For cultivated plants, water should be reduced in winter, especially for plants grown in the dark, short-day conditions common in temperate latitudes. Plants should dry slightly between waterings, but they should never be allowed to dry out completely. Fertilizer should be reduced or eliminated anytime water is reduced. In the habitat, light is highest in winter.

GROWING MEDIA: Plants may be mounted on tree-fern or cork slabs if humidity is high and plants are watered at least once daily in summer. When plants are potted, any open, fast-draining medium may be used. Repotting is best done in early spring when new roots are growing.

MISCELLANEOUS NOTES: The bloom season shown in the climate table is based on reports from the habitat.

Plant and Flower Information

PLANT SIZE AND TYPE: A 3–5 in. (8–13 cm) sympodial epiphyte.

PSEUDOBULB: 2–4 in. (5–10 cm) long. The tufted stems have ovoid, pseudobulbous swellings about 0.4 in. (1 cm) long.

LEAVES: 2–4 per growth. The distichous leaves are 1–2 in. (2.5–5.0 cm) long, linear-oblong, and pointed at the tip.

INFLORESCENCE: 1–3 in. (2.5–7.5 cm) long. Erect, slender inflorescences emerge from between the leaves near the apex of the stem.

FLOWERS: 2–6. The flowers are 0.5 in. (1.3 cm) across and may not open fully. The pointed sepals and rounded petals are white with a pink or purple tinge. The fiddle-shaped lip is rounded and ruffled along the margin of the oblong midlobe. It has 3 elevated lines on the disk. The sidelobes are broadly triangular and curve out. Blossoms are short-lived.

REFERENCES: 97, 156, 202, 216, 254, 255, 278, 283.

PHOTOS/DRAWINGS: 97, 156, 283.

Dendrobium panduriferum Hooker f.

AKA: *D. panduriferum* Hooker f. var. *serpens* Hooker f., *D. serpens* (Hooker f.) Hooker f., *D. virescens* Ridley.

ORIGIN/HABITAT: The Moulmein region of Burma and peninsular Thailand, where plants grow at about 800 ft. (250 m). In northern Malaya, they are found near Ipoh in Perak, near Taiping, and on an island in the Kertai River. Plants also grow in Sabah, Borneo at about 1950 ft. (600 m). The orchids usually grow high in trees.

CLIMATE: Station #48625, Ipoh, Malaya, Lat. 4.6°N, Long. 101.1°E, at 123 ft. (37 m). Temperatures are calculated for an elevation of 1000 ft. (300 m), resulting in probable extremes of 96°F (36°C) and 61°F (16°C).

N/HEMISPHERE	JAN	FEB	MAR	APR	MAY	JUN	JUL	AUG	SEP	OCT	NOV	DEC
°F AVG MAX	87	89	90	89	89	89	88	88	87	86	86	86
°F AVG MIN	69	69	70	70	71	70	69	69	70	69	69	69
DIURNAL RANGE	18	20	20	19	18	19	19	19	17	17	17	17
RAIN/INCHES	7.9	3.1	7.6	8.4	6.2	3.6	7.2	6.9	8.8	11.0	13.0	8.9
HUMIDITY/%	76	74	76	78	78	75	76	77	79	82	82	81
BLOOM SEASON					*							
DAYS CLR @ 7AM	3	3	3	1	2	1	2	1	1	0	0	1	2
DAYS CLR @ 1PM	2	2	2	1	1	1	1	1	0	0	0	2
RAIN/MM	201	79	193	213	157	91	183	175	224	279	330	226
°C AVG MAX	30.6	31.7	32.3	31.7	31.7	31.7	31.2	31.2	30.6	30.1	30.1	30.1
°C AVG MIN	20.6	20.6	21.2	21.2	21.7	21.2	20.6	20.6	21.2	20.6	20.6	20.6
DIURNAL RANGE	10.0	11.1	11.1	10.5	10.0	10.5	10.6	10.6	9.4	9.5	9.5	9.5
S/HEMISPHERE	JUL	AUG	SEP	OCT	NOV	DEC	JAN	FEB	MAR	APR	MAY	JUN

Cultural Recommendations

LIGHT: 2500–3500 fc.

TEMPERATURES: Throughout the year, days average 86–90°F (30–32°C), and nights average 69–71°F (21–22°C), with a diurnal range of 17–20°F (9–11°C).

HUMIDITY: 75–80% year-round.

WATER: Rainfall is moderate to heavy most of the year. Cultivated plants should be kept evenly moist, with little if any drying between waterings. The heaviest rainfall occurs in autumn with a secondary maximum in spring. Short, semidry periods occur in midwinter and early summer.

FERTILIZER: ¼–½ recommended strength. A balanced fertilizer should be applied weekly to biweekly throughout the year.

REST PERIOD: Growing conditions should be maintained all year. Water and fertilizer might be reduced somewhat during the short, semidry periods, but the plants should never be allowed to dry out completely.

GROWING MEDIA: Plants may be mounted on tree-fern or cork slabs if humidity is high and plants are watered at least once daily in summer. When plants are potted, any open, fast-draining medium may be used. Repotting may be done anytime new roots are growing.

MISCELLANEOUS NOTES: The bloom season shown in the climate table is based on cultivation records.

Plant and Flower Information

PLANT SIZE AND TYPE: A 24–35 in. (60–90 cm) sympodial epiphyte.

PSEUDOBULB: 24–35 in. (60–90 cm) long. The weak, flexuous stems often root at the nodes. They are grooved, cylindrical, and narrow at the base. Rooting keikis are often present.

LEAVES: 10 per growth. The thin lanceolate-elliptic leaves are 2–4 in. (5–10 cm) long and pointed at the tip. They are present only on young stems.

INFLORESCENCE: 1–2 in. (2.5–5.0 cm) long. The lax inflorescences emerge from the sides of leafless stems.

FLOWERS: 6–12 per inflorescence. The flowers are 1–2 in. (2.5–5.0 cm) long. The broad, pointed sepals and narrower, rounded petals may be greenish to orange-yellow with streaks of red dots along numerous nerves. The small lip has a semicircular callus and a slightly wavy front margin. The midlobe may be squared off or rounded at the apex. Sidelobes are triangular with a fold between the sidelobes and midlobe. The green spur may be streaked with red. Although the extremely long spur is usually very straight, it may be incurved or slightly thickened near the base. Flowers from plants originally known as *D. virescens* lack the crimson veins.

HYBRIDIZING NOTES: Johansen (ref. 239) indicates that plants are self-sterile and that flowers dropped 6–7 days after self-pollination. When crossed with *D. secundum* (Blume) Lindley, capsules formed but no viable seed was produced.

REFERENCES: 157, 200, 202, 203, 218, 239, 254, 395, 402, 445, 450, 454, 455, 592.

PHOTOS/DRAWINGS: 203, *454*, *455*, 589, *592*.

Dendrobium paniculatum Persoon. Now considered a synonym of *Maxillaria paniculata* Ruiz and Pavón. REFERENCES: 216, 254.

Dendrobium paniculatum Swartz. Now considered a synonym of *Polystachya paniculata* Rolfe. REFERENCES: 216, 254, 277.

Dendrobium paniferum J. J. Smith

AKA: Holttum (ref. 200) indicates that *D. paniferum* J. J. Smith may be a synonym of *D. sinuatum* (Lindley) Lindley ex Rchb. f.

ORIGIN/HABITAT: Endemic to East and West Java. Plants grow in forests at 2500–3300 ft. (760–1000 m).

CLIMATE: Station #96755, Bogor, Indonesia, at Lat. 6.5°S, Long. 106.8°E, at 558 ft. (170 m). Temperatures are calculated for an elevation of 3000 ft. (910 m), resulting in probable extremes of 88°F (31°C) and 58°F (14°C).

N/HEMISPHERE	JAN	FEB	MAR	APR	MAY	JUN	JUL	AUG	SEP	OCT	NOV	DEC
°F AVG MAX	78	79	80	80	79	77	76	76	77	78	79	78
°F AVG MIN	65	65	65	66	66	66	66	66	66	67	67	66
DIURNAL RANGE	13	14	15	14	13	11	10	10	11	11	12	12
RAIN/INCHES	2.1	1.0	0.5	5.0	8.1	18.8	23.7	20.2	14.4	12.0	11.9	3.4
HUMIDITY/%	72	68	65	66	74	79	84	84	81	79	75
BLOOM SEASON					*							
DAYS CLR @ 7AM	14	14	14	11	5	3	1	2	4	6	10	12
DAYS CLR @ 1PM	9	10	8	5	1	1	0	0	1	1	3	7
RAIN/MM	53	25	13	127	206	478	602	513	366	305	302	86
°C AVG MAX	25.5	26.1	26.6	26.6	26.1	25.0	24.4	24.4	25.0	25.5	26.1	25.5
°C AVG MIN	18.3	18.3	18.3	18.9	18.9	18.9	18.9	18.9	18.9	19.4	19.4	18.9
DIURNAL RANGE	7.2	7.8	8.3	7.7	7.2	6.1	5.5	5.5	6.1	6.1	6.7	6.6
S/HEMISPHERE	JUL	AUG	SEP	OCT	NOV	DEC	JAN	FEB	MAR	APR	MAY	JUN

Cultural Recommendations

LIGHT: 1800–2500 fc. Direct sunlight should be avoided.

TEMPERATURES: Throughout the year, days average 76–80°F (24–27°C), and nights average 65–67°F (18–19°C), with a diurnal range of 10–15°F (6–8°C). The warmest temperatures occur in spring. Plants are unlikely to tolerate wide temperature fluctuations, since probable extremes are very close to the average highs and lows.

Dendrobium pantherinum

HUMIDITY: 75–85% most of the year, dropping to about 65% in late winter and early spring.

WATER: Rainfall is very heavy from spring into autumn, but conditions are dry for 2 months in winter. Cultivated plants should be kept moist from late spring to midautumn, with only slight drying allowed between waterings. Water should then be gradually reduced in late autumn.

FERTILIZER: ¼–½ recommended strength, applied weekly. A high-nitrogen fertilizer is beneficial from spring to midsummer, but a fertilizer high in phosphates should be used in late summer and autumn.

REST PERIOD: Growing conditions should be maintained all year, but rainfall is very low for 2–3 months in winter. In cultivation, water should be reduced and the plants allowed to become dry between waterings. They should not remain dry for prolonged periods, however. Fertilizer may be reduced or eliminated anytime the plant is not actively growing. In the habitat, light is highest in winter.

GROWING MEDIA: Plants may be mounted on tree-fern or cork slabs if humidity is high and plants are watered at least once daily in summer. When plants are potted, any open, fast-draining medium may be used. Repotting may be done anytime new roots are growing.

MISCELLANEOUS NOTES: The bloom season shown in the climate table is based on reports from the habitat.

Plant and Flower Information

PLANT SIZE AND TYPE: A 20 in. (50 cm) sympodial epiphyte.

PSEUDOBULB: 20 in. (50 cm) long. The folded leaves are arranged in 2 rows, making the stem appear flattened. Young stems are leafy.

LEAVES: Many. The leaves are 1.4 in. (3.5 cm) long, triangular, pointed, and dull green.

INFLORESCENCE: Short. Inflorescences are borne all along the stem.

FLOWERS: 1 per inflorescence. The flowers are 0.4 in. (1 cm) across and open fully. Sepals and petals are usually yellow-brown but may be reddish. The dark red-brown lip is shiny in the center with a very rough area near the broader apex.

REFERENCES: 25, 75, 200, 221, 454.

PHOTOS/DRAWINGS: 75.

Dendrobium pantherinum Schlechter

ORIGIN/HABITAT: Northern Papua New Guinea. Plants grow on isolated trees at about 3600 ft. (1100 m) on the slopes of the Finisterre Range.

CLIMATE: Station #200187, Erap, Papua New Guinea, Lat. 6.6°S, Long. 146.7°E, at 850 ft. (260 m). Temperatures are calculated for an elevation of 3300 ft. (1000 m), resulting in probable extremes of 94°F (34°C) and 45°F (7°C).

N/HEMISPHERE	JAN	FEB	MAR	APR	MAY	JUN	JUL	AUG	SEP	OCT	NOV	DEC
°F AVG MAX	80	80	81	82	85	85	85	85	85	84	82	82
°F AVG MIN	61	61	61	62	64	65	64	64	65	63	66	62
DIURNAL RANGE	19	19	20	20	21	20	21	21	20	21	16	20
RAIN/INCHES	3.9	3.9	2.7	3.0	3.0	5.3	5.9	5.9	7.0	3.4	2.4	3.1
HUMIDITY/%	82	81	81	79	75	74	74	74	77	76	80	80
BLOOM SEASON	*											
DAYS CLR	N/A											
RAIN/MM	99	99	69	76	76	135	150	150	178	86	61	79
°C AVG MAX	26.7	26.7	27.2	27.8	29.4	29.4	29.4	29.4	29.4	28.9	27.8	27.8
°C AVG MIN	16.1	16.1	16.1	16.7	17.8	18.3	17.8	17.8	18.3	17.2	18.9	16.7
DIURNAL RANGE	10.6	10.6	11.1	11.1	11.6	11.1	11.6	11.6	11.1	11.7	8.9	11.1
S/HEMISPHERE	JUL	AUG	SEP	OCT	NOV	DEC	JAN	FEB	MAR	APR	MAY	JUN

Cultural Recommendations

LIGHT: 3000–4000 fc. Growers report that plants from this habitat often tolerate full sun.

TEMPERATURES: Throughout the year, days average 80–85°F (27–29°C), and nights average 61–66°F (16–19°C), with a diurnal range of 16–21°F (9–12°C).

HUMIDITY: 75–80% all year. Despite high average humidity, the habitat may be quite dry during hot afternoons.

WATER: Rainfall is moderate most of the year, but conditions are somewhat wetter for 4–5 months in summer and early autumn. Cultivated plants should be thoroughly saturated then allowed to dry slightly between waterings in summer and early autumn. Water should be gradually reduced in autumn.

FERTILIZER: ¼–½ recommended strength. A balanced fertilizer should be applied weekly to biweekly throughout the year.

REST PERIOD: Growing temperatures should be maintained all year. In the habitat, rainfall is lowest in winter, but the high humidity indicates that additional moisture is frequently available from heavy dew. Cultivated plants should be allowed to dry for somewhat longer between waterings than in summer, but they should not remain dry for extended periods. Fertilizer should be reduced until water is increased in spring. In the habitat, seasonal light variation is minor.

GROWING MEDIA: Plants may be mounted on tree-fern or cork slabs or potted in small pots filled with any open, fast-draining medium. Repotting may be done anytime new roots are growing.

MISCELLANEOUS NOTES: The bloom season shown in the climate table is based on collection reports. Plants that produce flowers which last a single day commonly bloom several times during the year. Flowering usually occurs 7–14 days after a sudden 10°F (5°C) drop in daytime temperatures.

Plant and Flower Information

PLANT SIZE AND TYPE: A 40–48 in. (102–122 cm) sympodial epiphyte. Although the plant is larger, it is similar to *D. leopardinum* Schlechter.

PSEUDOBULB: 40–48 in. (102–122 cm) long. The flattened, leafy stems do not branch.

LEAVES: Many. The leaves are 5–6 in. (13–15 cm) long. They are linear and may be erect or spreading.

INFLORESCENCE: 0.8 in. (2 cm) long.

FLOWERS: 2 per inflorescence. The flowers are 3.2 in. (8 cm) long and do not open fully. The long slender sepals and petals are pale yellow with dark red dots. The 3-lobed lip is white with a yellow crest. It is uneven along the margin with a hairy patch that covers most of the midlobe except the margins. The apex of the midlobe is notched and the hairy patch forms a point that extends into the notch. The sidelobes are elongated. The column is yellow. Described as magnificent, the blossoms are very short-lived.

REFERENCES: 92, 221, 437, 445.

PHOTOS/DRAWINGS: 437.

Dendrobium papilio Loher

AKA: *D. vanoverberghii* Ames.

ORIGIN/HABITAT: The Philippines. On Luzon Island, plants are reported in Albay and Benguet Provinces. On Mindanao, they are found in Davao and Surigao Provinces. They are also found on Negros in Negros Oriental. These plants grow on mossy, forest trees at 4600–7200 ft. (1400–2200 m).

CLIMATE: Station #98754, Davao, Mindanao, Philippines, Lat. 7.1°N, Long. 125.6°E, at 88 ft. (27 m). Temperatures are calculated for an elevation of 6000 ft. (1830 m), resulting in probable extremes of 77°F (25°C) and 45°F (8°C).

N/HEMISPHERE	JAN	FEB	MAR	APR	MAY	JUN	JUL	AUG	SEP	OCT	NOV	DEC
°F AVG MAX	67	68	70	71	70	68	68	68	68	69	69	68
°F AVG MIN	52	52	52	53	54	53	53	53	53	53	53	52
DIURNAL RANGE	15	16	18	18	16	15	15	15	15	16	16	16
RAIN/INCHES	4.8	4.5	5.2	5.8	9.2	9.1	6.5	6.5	6.7	7.9	5.3	6.1
HUMIDITY/%	81	82	78	79	82	83	84	83	83	82	82	82
BLOOM SEASON			*	*	*	*	*					
DAYS CLR @ 8AM	5	7	9	9	6	4	5	4	5	7	6	6
DAYS CLR @ 2PM	3	1	3	4	2	2	3	2	2	2	2	2
RAIN/MM	122	114	132	147	234	231	165	165	170	201	135	155
°C AVG MAX	19.7	20.3	21.4	21.9	21.4	20.3	20.3	20.3	20.3	20.8	20.8	20.3
°C AVG MIN	11.4	11.4	11.4	11.9	12.5	11.9	11.9	11.9	11.9	11.9	11.9	11.4
DIURNAL RANGE	8.3	8.9	10.0	10.0	8.9	8.4	8.4	8.4	8.4	8.9	8.9	8.9
S/HEMISPHERE	JUL	AUG	SEP	OCT	NOV	DEC	JAN	FEB	MAR	APR	MAY	JUN

Cultural Recommendations

LIGHT: 2000–3000 fc. In the habitat, clear days are rare, so direct sunlight should be avoided for cultivated plants.

TEMPERATURES: Throughout the year, days average 67–71°F (20–22°C), and nights average 52–54°F (11–13°C), with a diurnal range of 15–18°F (8–10°C). Because of microclimatic effects, actual maximum temperatures may be several degrees warmer than indicated.

HUMIDITY: 80–85% year-round.

WATER: Rainfall is moderate to heavy all year. Amounts may be even greater in the mountain habitat. Cultivated plants should be kept moist.

FERTILIZER: 1/4–1/2 recommended strength. A balanced fertilizer should be applied weekly to biweekly throughout the year.

REST PERIOD: Growing conditions should be maintained year-round. In the habitat, lows occasionally drop below 50°F (10°C). Water should be reduced in winter, especially for plants cultivated in the dark, short-day conditions common in temperate latitudes. Plants should never be allowed to dry out completely, however. Fertilizer should be reduced until water is increased in spring.

GROWING MEDIA: Plants may be mounted on tree-fern or cork slabs if humidity is high and plants are watered at least once daily in summer. When plants are potted, any open, fast-draining medium may be used. Repotting may be done anytime new roots are growing.

MISCELLANEOUS NOTES: The bloom season shown in the climate table is based on collection reports. Cultivation records (ref. 179) indicate blooming at about the same time shown in the table, but other growers report that plants flower several times a year from midwinter to midsummer.

Plant and Flower Information

PLANT SIZE AND TYPE: A 12–18 in. (30–45 cm) sympodial epiphyte.

PSEUDOBULB: 12–18 in. (30–45 cm) long. The stems, which may branch a few times, are marked with black spots. They are slender, nearly erect, and many-jointed. The apex of the stem is leafy.

LEAVES: Few to many. The short, grasslike leaves are 1.5–2.0 in. (4–5 cm) long. They are arranged in 2 rows.

INFLORESCENCE: Inflorescences emerge from nodes along the side of the stem.

FLOWERS: 1, rarely more per inflorescence. The variable flowers are 1.5–2.8 in. (4–7 cm) across. The oblong sepals and ovate petals are white, often with a pinkish tinge. The large, purple lip is minutely wavy along the margin. It is broadly ovate. The slightly fragrant blossoms last 4–5 days. They resemble a butterfly.

HYBRIDIZING NOTES: Chromosome count, 2n = 40 (ref. 152).

REFERENCES: 12, 13, 98, 152, 179, 254, 296, 373, 445, 536.

PHOTOS/DRAWINGS: 13, 98.

Dendrobium papiliolabratum P. van Royen

ORIGIN/HABITAT: Irian Jaya (western New Guinea). Near Lake Habbema, plants were found at about 10,900 ft. (3300 m) on patches of sandy soil on a sterile limestone slope.

CLIMATE: Station #97686, Wamena, Irian Jaya, Lat. 4.1°S, Long. 139.0°E, at 5446 ft. (1660 m). Temperatures are calculated for an elevation of 10,000 ft. (3050 m). Record extreme temperatures are not available for this location.

N/HEMISPHERE	JAN	FEB	MAR	APR	MAY	JUN	JUL	AUG	SEP	OCT	NOV	DEC
°F AVG MAX	60	61	62	61	62	61	62	61	61	64	63	59
°F AVG MIN	45	45	47	47	48	49	48	47	48	50	50	46
DIURNAL RANGE	15	16	15	14	14	12	14	14	13	14	13	13
RAIN/INCHES	3.0	1.9	2.2	4.0	4.6	3.3	2.8	4.2	6.9	3.9	5.4	4.9
HUMIDITY/%	N/A											
BLOOM SEASON		*										
DAYS CLR	N/A											
RAIN/MM	76	48	56	102	117	84	71	107	175	99	137	124
°C AVG MAX	15.5	16.1	16.7	16.1	16.7	16.1	16.7	16.1	16.1	17.8	17.2	15.0
°C AVG MIN	7.2	7.2	8.3	8.3	8.9	9.4	8.9	8.3	8.9	10.0	10.0	7.8
DIURNAL RANGE	8.3	8.9	8.4	7.8	7.8	6.7	7.8	7.8	7.2	7.8	7.2	7.2
S/HEMISPHERE	JUL	AUG	SEP	OCT	NOV	DEC	JAN	FEB	MAR	APR	MAY	JUN

Cultural Recommendations.

LIGHT: 2500–3500 fc.

TEMPERATURES: Throughout the year, days average 59–64°F (15–18°C), and nights average 45–50°F (7–10°C), with a diurnal range of 12–16°F (7–9°C). The warmest temperatures occur in autumn. In the habitat, the warmest temperatures of the day occur in late morning when skies are clear. Clouds and mist develop near noon and continue through the afternoon, thus preventing additional warming.

HUMIDITY: Information is not available for this location. However, average humidity in similar habitats normally exceeds 80% year-round.

WATER: Rainfall is moderate most of the year. Rainfall in the higher-elevation habitat is probably greater than indicated in the climate table. In addition, large amounts of water are available from mist and heavy dew, even during periods of low rainfall. Cultivated plants should be allowed to dry slightly between waterings, but should never remain dry for long periods. Plants are healthiest with strong air movement.

FERTILIZER: 1/4–1/2 recommended strength. A balanced fertilizer should be applied weekly to biweekly throughout the year. The Royal Botanic Garden in Edinburgh uses a seaweed-based fertilizer for other plants from this habitat.

REST PERIOD: Growing conditions should be maintained all year. There is a month or so of slightly drier conditions in winter, with a secondary drier period in midsummer. In cultivation, water may be decreased slightly, but plants should never be allowed to dry completely.

GROWING MEDIA: Plants may be mounted on tree-fern or cork slabs if humidity is high and plants are watered at least once daily in summer. When plants are potted, fir bark or any open, fast-draining medium may be used. Repotting may be done anytime new roots are growing.

MISCELLANEOUS NOTES: The bloom season shown in the climate table is based on collection reports.

Plant and Flower Information

PLANT SIZE AND TYPE: A 24 in. (60 cm) sympodial terrestrial.

PSEUDOBULB: 24 in. (60 cm) long. The erect, bushy stems are leafy at the apex. The internodes are flattened.

LEAVES: 6–8. The ovate-lanceolate leaves are 1.4–2.6 in. (3.5–6.5 cm) long, smooth, and leathery. They have 2, unequal, rounded lobes at the tip. The thin margin is slightly wavy or bumpy. The upper surface is patterned.

Dendrobium papilioniferum

INFLORESCENCE: Very short. Inflorescences arise from leaf nodes near the lower leaves.

FLOWERS: 1 per inflorescence. The flowers are 0.4 in. (1 cm) across. They are deep yellow. The blossoms have an ovate-oblong dorsal sepal, and ovate-triangular lateral sepals, with rounded, slightly sickle-shaped petals. The backside of the sepals is rough. The lip is deeply notched at the apex, with 2 raised lines in the center.

REFERENCES: 233, 538.

PHOTOS/DRAWINGS: 538.

Dendrobium papilioniferum J. J. Smith

AKA: *D. papilioniferum* var. *ephemerum (ephemeranthum)* J. J. Smith is now considered a synonym of *D. ephemerum* J. J. Smith. Kränzlin (ref. 254) listed *D. papilioniferum* as *D. crumenatum* Swartz var. *papilioniferum* Kränzlin, but this synonymy is not found in other references.

ORIGIN/HABITAT: Widespread through the islands of Indonesia. Plants are found on Ambon, the Moluccas, and the Kei Islands. On southeastern Sulawesi (Celebes), they grow near Lepolepo, south of Kendari. In the north, they grow in primary forest near Kajuwatu (Kajoewatoe) near the eastern end of the Minahassa Peninsula. Plants were collected from *Sonneratia* trees near sea level.

CLIMATE: Station #97146, Kendari, Sulawesi, Indonesia, Lat. 4.1°S, Long. 122.4°E, at 164 ft. (50 m). Record extreme temperatures are not available for this location.

N/HEMISPHERE	JAN	FEB	MAR	APR	MAY	JUN	JUL	AUG	SEP	OCT	NOV	DEC
°F AVG MAX	85	86	88	90	90	89	88	87	88	86	86	84
°F AVG MIN	70	71	70	72	74	75	75	74	74	74	74	72
DIURNAL RANGE	15	15	18	18	16	14	13	13	14	12	12	12
RAIN/INCHES	5.7	4.0	2.3	2.5	6.0	7.7	7.9	7.3	8.4	8.2	9.9	9.1
HUMIDITY/%	86	80	76	73	76	82	80	81	82	83	85	84
BLOOM SEASON				*					*	*		
DAYS CLR @ 8AM	3	10	10	14	8	5	1	2	2	3	2	4
DAYS CLR @ 2PM	0	0	1	2	1	0	1	0	0	0	0	0
RAIN/MM	144	102	58	63	152	197	201	186	213	208	252	231
°C AVG MAX	29.2	29.9	31.0	32.3	32.4	31.8	31.1	30.7	30.9	29.9	30.1	28.8
°C AVG MIN	21.3	21.5	21.1	22.4	23.6	24.0	24.0	23.4	23.4	23.6	23.4	22.3
DIURNAL RANGE	7.9	8.4	9.9	9.9	8.8	7.8	7.1	7.3	7.5	6.3	6.7	6.5
S/HEMISPHERE	JUL	AUG	SEP	OCT	NOV	DEC	JAN	FEB	MAR	APR	MAY	JUN

Cultural Recommendations

LIGHT: 2000–3000 fc.

TEMPERATURES: Throughout the year, days average 84–90°F (29–32°C), and nights average 70–75°F (21–24°C), with a diurnal range of 12–18°F (6–10°C).

HUMIDITY: 80–85% most of the year, dropping to near 75% in spring.

WATER: Rainfall is moderate to heavy most of the year. Conditions are driest for 2–3 months in late winter and early spring. Cultivated plants should be kept moist.

FERTILIZER: ¼–½ recommended strength. A balanced fertilizer should be applied weekly to biweekly throughout the year.

REST PERIOD: Growing temperatures should be maintained all year. Water should be reduced somewhat in winter. For 2–3 months, plants should be allowed to dry out somewhat between waterings, but they should not remain dry for long periods. Fertilizer should be reduced or eliminated anytime water is reduced. In the habitat, light is highest in late winter and spring.

GROWING MEDIA: Plants may be mounted on tree-fern or cork slabs if humidity is high and plants are watered at least once daily in summer. When plants are potted, any open, fast-draining medium may be used. Repotting may be done anytime new roots are growing.

MISCELLANEOUS NOTES: The bloom season shown in the climate table is based on reports from the habitat. Plants that produce flowers which last a single day commonly bloom several times during the year. Flowering usually occurs 8 days after a sudden 10°F (5°C) drop in daytime temperatures.

Plant and Flower Information

PLANT SIZE AND TYPE: A 43 in. (110 cm) sympodial plant.

PSEUDOBULB: 43 in. (110 cm) long. The elongated stems consist of numerous nodes.

LEAVES: Many. The leaves were not available when the plant was described.

INFLORESCENCE: Inflorescences emerge at nodes along the stem.

FLOWERS: The flowers are 1.6 in. (4 cm) across. The oblong sepals and petals are reflexed at the pointed tips. They may be snow white, or the tips may be pale lilac. The frontlobe of the lip may be violet-red with a white margin, or the lip may be white below the constriction with lilac beyond. It has a yellow thickening on the center of the margin. Blossoms are fragrant.

REFERENCES: 25, 42, 111, 219, 222, 254, 436, 445, 468, 479, 537.

Dendrobium papillilabium J. J. Smith.

Now considered a synonym of *Diplocaulobium papillilabium* (J. J. Smith) Hunt and Summerhayes. REFERENCES: 213, 224, 230.

Dendrobium papuanum J. J. Smith

ORIGIN/HABITAT: Irian Jaya (western New Guinea). Plants grow in a lakeside forest in the Angi Lakes region of the Arfak Mountains at 7000 ft. (2140 m).

CLIMATE: Station #97530, Manokwari, Irian Jaya, Lat. 0.9°S, Long. 134.1°E, at 10 ft. (3 m). Temperatures are calculated for an elevation of 7000 ft. (2140 m), resulting in probable extremes of 70°F (21°C) and 45°F (7°C).

N/HEMISPHERE	JAN	FEB	MAR	APR	MAY	JUN	JUL	AUG	SEP	OCT	NOV	DEC
°F AVG MAX	63	62	64	64	65	63	63	63	63	63	63	62
°F AVG MIN	51	52	51	51	51	52	50	50	51	51	51	51
DIURNAL RANGE	12	10	13	13	14	11	13	13	12	12	12	11
RAIN/INCHES	5.4	5.6	5.0	4.7	4.5	10.3	12.0	9.4	13.2	11.1	7.8	7.3
HUMIDITY/%	87	87	86	84	85	86	86	85	86	86	86	85
BLOOM SEASON												*
DAYS CLR @ 9AM	4	3	3	5	3	3	3	1	1	2	3	7
DAYS CLR @ 3PM	2	2	2	3	1	1	1	1	0	1	0	2
RAIN/MM	137	142	127	119	114	262	305	239	335	282	198	185
°C AVG MAX	17.2	16.6	17.7	17.7	18.3	17.2	17.2	17.2	17.2	17.2	17.2	16.6
°C AVG MIN	10.5	11.1	10.5	10.5	10.5	11.1	10.0	10.0	10.5	10.5	10.5	10.5
DIURNAL RANGE	6.7	5.5	7.2	7.2	7.8	6.1	7.2	7.2	6.7	6.7	6.7	6.1
S/HEMISPHERE	JUL	AUG	SEP	OCT	NOV	DEC	JAN	FEB	MAR	APR	MAY	JUN

Cultural Recommendations

LIGHT: 2000–3000 fc.

TEMPERATURES: Throughout the year, days average 62–65°F (17–18°C), and nights average 50–52°F (10–11°C), with a diurnal range of 10–14°F (6–8°C). Because of the effects of the microclimate, actual maximum temperatures may be 8–10°F (4–6°C) warmer than indicated.

HUMIDITY: Near 85% year-round.

WATER: Rainfall is moderate to heavy all year. Cultivated plants should be kept moist but not soggy.

FERTILIZER: ¼–½ recommended strength. A balanced fertilizer should be applied weekly to biweekly throughout the year.

REST PERIOD: Growing conditions should be maintained year-round. Water and fertilizer may be reduced somewhat in winter, especially for plants cultivated in the dark, short-day conditions common in temperate latitudes. Plants should never be allowed to dry out completely, however. In the habitat, light is highest in winter.

GROWING MEDIA: Plants may be mounted on tree-fern or cork slabs if humidity is high and plants are watered at least once daily in summer. When plants are potted, any open, fast-draining medium may be used. They may be repotted anytime new roots are growing.

MISCELLANEOUS NOTES: The bloom season shown in the climate table is based on records from the habitat.

Plant and Flower Information

PLANT SIZE AND TYPE: An 18 in. (45 cm) sympodial epiphyte.

PSEUDOBULB: 18 in. (45 cm) long. The leafy, stemlike pseudobulbs are clustered.

LEAVES: Many. The deciduous leaves are 2.4–3.2 in. (6–8 cm) long. They are long, sharply pointed, and semitwisted at the base.

INFLORESCENCE: Short. Inflorescences are borne at nodes on leafless stems.

FLOWERS: 4 per inflorescence. The flowers are 0.6 in. (1.5 cm) long. They are pink to purple. The nearly oval dorsal sepal and oblong petals are concave. Lateral sepals are ovate-triangular. The broad lip has no callus, the primary characteristic that separates it from *D. roseicolor* A. Hawkes and A. H. Heller.

REFERENCES: 144, 222.

Dendrobium papyraceum J. J. Smith

ORIGIN/HABITAT: Irian Jaya (western New Guinea). Plants grow along the upper Eilanden River. They were cultivated in the botanical garden at Bogor, Java.

CLIMATE: Station #97876, Tanahmerah, Irian Jaya, Lat. 6.1°S, Long. 140.3°E, at 75 ft. (23 m). Temperatures are calculated for an elevation of 500 ft. (150 m), resulting in probable extremes of 97°F (36°C) and 63°F (17°C).

N/HEMISPHERE	JAN	FEB	MAR	APR	MAY	JUN	JUL	AUG	SEP	OCT	NOV	DEC
°F AVG MAX	83	84	86	89	90	89	89	88	89	88	86	84
°F AVG MIN	71	70	70	71	72	73	72	72	72	72	73	72
DIURNAL RANGE	12	14	16	18	18	16	17	16	17	16	13	12
RAIN/INCHES	11.5	12.1	14.7	13.2	14.4	15.9	14.5	15.8	17.4	17.3	15.5	11.9
HUMIDITY/%	N/A											
BLOOM SEASON							*					
DAYS CLR	N/A											
RAIN/MM	292	307	373	335	366	404	368	401	442	439	394	302
°C AVG MAX	28.1	28.7	29.8	31.4	32.0	31.4	31.4	30.9	31.4	30.9	29.8	28.7
°C AVG MIN	21.4	20.9	20.9	21.4	22.0	22.6	22.0	22.0	22.0	22.0	22.6	22.0
DIURNAL RANGE	6.7	7.8	8.9	10.0	10.0	8.8	9.4	8.9	9.4	8.9	7.2	6.7
S/HEMISPHERE	JUL	AUG	SEP	OCT	NOV	DEC	JAN	FEB	MAR	APR	MAY	JUN

Cultural Recommendations

LIGHT: 2000–3000 fc.

TEMPERATURES: Throughout the year, days average 83–90°F (28–32°C), and nights average 70–73°F (21–23°C), with a diurnal range of 12–18°F (7–10°C).

HUMIDITY: Information is not available for this location. However, records from nearby stations indicate that humidity probably averages near 85% year-round.

WATER: Rainfall is very heavy all year. Cultivated plants should be kept evenly moist but not soggy.

FERTILIZER: ¼–½ recommended strength. A balanced fertilizer should be applied weekly to biweekly throughout the year.

REST PERIOD: Growing conditions should be maintained year-round. Water and fertilizer might be reduced slightly in winter, especially for plants grown in the dark, short-day conditions common in temperate latitudes; but plants should never be allowed to dry completely.

GROWING MEDIA: Because plants must be kept moist, they are easier to manage when potted. Fir bark or any open, fast-draining medium may be used. Repotting may be done anytime new roots are growing.

MISCELLANEOUS NOTES: The bloom season shown in the climate table is based on reports from the habitat.

Plant and Flower Information

PLANT SIZE AND TYPE: A 16 in. (40 cm) sympodial epiphyte.

PSEUDOBULB: 16 in. (40 cm) long. The rigid stems are elliptical in cross-section.

LEAVES: Many. The narrowly lanceolate leaves usually exceed a length of 2.2 in. (5.6 cm). They are shaped as though they should end in a long tapering point but, instead, the apex ends abruptly in 2, unequal, toothed lobes. They are erect-spreading.

INFLORESCENCE: Short. Inflorescences emerge laterally from flat sheaths.

FLOWERS: 2 per inflorescence. The pale yellow flowers are 0.5–1.0 in. (1.2–2.6 cm) across. The dorsal sepal is oblong, lateral sepals are obliquely triangular, and the petals are oblong. The smooth lip is short and wavy. It is marked with orange lines. The midlobe is violet along the margin.

REFERENCES: 221, 470, 476.

Dendrobium paradoxum Teijsm. and Binn.

ORIGIN/HABITAT: Sumatra. Plants were originally found near a waterfall on the Singalong River, but elevation was not given. We have estimated habitat elevation at 3000 ft. (910 m), so the following climate data should be used with caution.

CLIMATE: Station #96163, Padang, Sumatra, Indonesia, Lat. 0.9°S, Long. 100.4°E, at 19 ft. (6 m). Temperatures are calculated for an elevation of 3000 ft. (910 m), resulting in probable extremes of 84°F (29°C) and 58°F (15°C).

N/HEMISPHERE	JAN	FEB	MAR	APR	MAY	JUN	JUL	AUG	SEP	OCT	NOV	DEC
°F AVG MAX	77	77	76	76	76	76	77	77	77	77	78	77
°F AVG MIN	64	64	64	64	64	64	64	64	64	65	65	64
DIURNAL RANGE	13	13	12	12	12	12	13	13	13	12	13	13
RAIN/INCHES	10.9	13.7	6.0	19.5	20.4	18.9	13.8	10.2	12.1	14.3	12.4	12.1
HUMIDITY/%	81	82	82	84	85	84	81	81	82	83	81	81
BLOOM SEASON	N/A											
DAYS CLR @ 7AM	5	1	1	0	0	2	2	1	2	2	3	5
DAYS CLR @ 1PM	5	2	2	1	1	3	4	3	3	6	5	
RAIN/MM	277	348	152	495	518	480	351	259	307	363	315	307
°C AVG MAX	25.1	25.1	24.5	24.5	24.5	24.5	25.1	25.1	25.1	25.1	25.6	25.1
°C AVG MIN	17.9	17.9	17.9	17.9	17.9	17.9	17.9	17.9	17.9	18.4	18.4	17.9
DIURNAL RANGE	7.2	7.2	6.6	6.6	6.6	6.6	7.2	7.2	7.2	6.7	7.2	7.2
S/HEMISPHERE	JUL	AUG	SEP	OCT	NOV	DEC	JAN	FEB	MAR	APR	MAY	JUN

Cultural Recommendations

LIGHT: 2000–3000 fc.

TEMPERATURES: Throughout the year, days average 76–78°F (25–26°C), and nights average 64–65°F (18°C), with a diurnal range of 12–13°F (7°C). Probable extremes vary only a few degrees from the averages, indicating that wide temperature fluctuations should be avoided for cultivated plants.

HUMIDITY: 80–85% year-round.

WATER: Rainfall is heavy all year. Cultivated plants should be constantly moist but not soggy.

FERTILIZER: ¼–½ recommended strength. A balanced fertilizer should be applied weekly to biweekly throughout the year.

REST PERIOD: Growing conditions should be maintained year-round. Water may be reduced somewhat in winter, especially for plants grown in the dark, short-day conditions common in temperate latitudes. Plants should not be allowed to dry out completely, however. In the habitat, light is highest in winter.

Dendrobium paravalum

GROWING MEDIA: Plants may be mounted on tree-fern or cork slabs or potted in small pots filled with any open, fast-draining medium. Repotting may be done anytime new roots are growing.

Plant and Flower Information

PLANT SIZE AND TYPE: A 12 in. (30 cm) sympodial epiphyte.

PSEUDOBULB: 12 in. (30 cm) long. The stems are erect, flattened, and clustered.

LEAVES: 2 per growth. The leaves are 1.6 in. (4 cm) long, oblong, and unequally pointed at the tip.

FLOWERS: 1 per inflorescence. The green flowers are 1 in. (2.5 cm) long. The linear sepals and petals are nearly transparent. The lip is shorter than the other segments and has a feltlike surface.

REFERENCES: 216, 254.

Dendrobium paravalum Pfitz.
This name was used by Löve and Solbrig (ref. 280) in a list of chromosome counts. Later writers have included this information in their compilations of chromosome counts, but we have found no other use of the name. We can find no original description of this plant, so we suspect that these references referred to *Dendrochilum paravalum* Pfitz. REFERENCES: 280, 504, 580.

Dendrobium parciflorum Kränzlin not Rchb. f. ex Lindley.
Status unknown. Merrill (ref. 296) and Valmayor (ref. 536) include this name as a synonym of *D. marivelense* Ames. However, Schlechter (ref. 436) and J. J. Smith (ref. 470) included *D. parciflorum* Kränzlin as a synonym of *D. confusum* Schlechter. REFERENCES: 254, 278, 296, 436, 445, 470, 536.

Dendrobium parciflorum Rchb. f. ex Lindley not Kränzlin

AKA: *D. jenkinsi* Lindley not *D. jenkinsii* Wallich. In 1992 *Opera Botanica* 114, Seidenfaden includes *D. hainanense* Rolfe as a synonym.

ORIGIN/HABITAT: The Assam region of northeastern India, northern Thailand, Laos, and Vietnam. In Thailand, plants grow in the Nan district and near Huay Gok. In Vietnam, they grow near Dalat and Blao. In China, plants have been collected in Hong Kong, Taiwan, Yunnan Province, and on Hainan Island near Lingmen and Hongting.

CLIMATE: Station #48331, Nan, Thailand, Lat. 18.8°N, Long. 100.8°E, at 660 ft. (201 m). Temperatures are calculated for an elevation of 1600 ft. (490 m), resulting in probable extremes of 105°F (41°C) and 38°F (3°C).

N/HEMISPHERE	JAN	FEB	MAR	APR	MAY	JUN	JUL	AUG	SEP	OCT	NOV	DEC
°F AVG MAX	83	88	93	96	93	89	87	86	87	87	85	82
°F AVG MIN	52	56	61	68	72	72	72	72	71	68	63	55
DIURNAL RANGE	31	32	32	28	21	17	15	14	16	19	22	27
RAIN/INCHES	0.3	0.5	0.9	3.3	5.7	4.9	8.1	10.6	8.5	2.2	0.6	0.2
HUMIDITY/%	74	69	65	65	73	79	81	84	84	83	79	78
BLOOM SEASON									*			
DAYS CLR @ 7AM	1	1	2	4	2	0	0	0	0	0	1	0
DAYS CLR @ 1PM	18	16	15	11	2	0	0	0	1	4	9	14
RAIN/MM	8	13	23	84	145	124	206	269	216	56	15	5
°C AVG MAX	28.3	31.1	33.8	35.5	33.8	31.6	30.5	29.9	30.5	30.5	29.4	27.7
°C AVG MIN	11.1	13.3	16.1	19.9	22.2	22.2	22.2	22.2	21.6	19.9	17.2	12.7
DIURNAL RANGE	17.2	17.8	17.7	15.6	11.6	9.4	8.3	7.7	8.9	10.6	12.2	15.0
S/HEMISPHERE	JUL	AUG	SEP	OCT	NOV	DEC	JAN	FEB	MAR	APR	MAY	JUN

Cultural Recommendations

LIGHT: 2500–3500 fc.

TEMPERATURES: Summer days average 86–89°F (30–32°C), and nights average 72°F (22°C), with a diurnal range of 14–17°F (8–9°C). Spring is the warmest season. Days average 93–96°F (34–36°C), and nights average 61–72°F (16–22°C), with a diurnal range of 21–32°F (12–18°C).

HUMIDITY: 80–85% in summer and autumn, dropping to 65–75% in winter and spring.

WATER: Rainfall is heavy for 5–6 months from late spring to autumn. The rainy season ends abruptly and is followed by 5 months with very low rainfall. Cultivated plants should be kept moist while actively growing, but water should be gradually reduced after new growths mature in autumn.

FERTILIZER: ¼–½ recommended strength, applied weekly. A high-nitrogen fertilizer is beneficial from spring to midsummer, but a fertilizer high in phosphates should be used in late summer and autumn.

REST PERIOD: Winter days average 82–88°F (28–31°C), and nights average 52–56°F (11–13°C), with a diurnal range of 27–32°F (15–18°C). Even though rainfall is low in winter and spring, considerable moisture is available for most of the dry season from frequent heavy dew and as mist from late night fog and low clouds. For cultivated plants, water should be reduced but not eliminated completely. Plants should be allowed to dry between waterings, but they should not remain dry for extended periods. In the habitat, light is highest in winter. Mornings are usually cloudy, but winter afternoons are frequently clear.

GROWING MEDIA: Plants may be mounted on tree-fern or cork slabs if humidity is high and plants are watered at least once daily in summer. When plants are potted, any open, fast-draining medium may be used. Repotting is best done in early spring when new roots are growing.

MISCELLANEOUS NOTES: The bloom season shown in the climate table is based on reports from the habitat for *D. hainanense*.

Plant and Flower Information

PLANT SIZE AND TYPE: An 8–18 in. (20–45 cm) sympodial epiphyte.

PSEUDOBULB: 8–18 in. (20–45 cm) long. The slender stems are very closely spaced on a creeping, rooting rhizome. The upper portion of the stem is leafy.

LEAVES: Many. The linear leaves are 1.2–2.0 in. (3–5 cm) long, narrow, fleshy, and nearly terete. They are distichous, widely spaced, and somewhat flattened.

INFLORESCENCE: Short. Inflorescences emerge from the side or apex of leafy or leafless stems.

FLOWERS: 1 per inflorescence. The flowers are 0.2–1.3 in. (0.5–3.3 cm) across. Blossoms open in succession. They are white with a deep yellow spot on the lip. The dorsal sepal is ovate, and lateral sepals are ovate-triangular. The petals are small. The lip is notched at the apex. It is uneven along the margin.

REFERENCES: 169, 202, 208, 216, 254, 266, 278, 410, 414, 448, 454, 528.

PHOTOS/DRAWINGS: *130, 454*.

Dendrobium parcoides Guillaumin. See *D. parcum* Rchb. f.
REFERENCES: 164, 228, 448, 504, 580.

Dendrobium parcum Rchb. f.

AKA: *D. listeroglossum* Kränzlin, *D. parcoides* Guillaumin.

ORIGIN/HABITAT: The Tenasserim region of Burma, the Langbian region of Vietnam, and the mountains of northern and eastern Thailand. Plants grow at 2450–4750 ft. (750–1450 m).

CLIMATE: Station #48300, Mae Hong Son, Thailand, Lat. 19.3°N, Long. 97.9°E, at 711 ft. (217 m). Temperatures are calculated for an elevation of 4000 ft. (1220 m), resulting in probable extremes of 97°F (36°C) and 32°F (0°C).

N/HEMISPHERE	JAN	FEB	MAR	APR	MAY	JUN	JUL	AUG	SEP	OCT	NOV	DEC
°F AVG MAX	75	79	86	87	84	78	76	76	77	79	77	74
°F AVG MIN	46	46	51	61	65	64	63	63	63	61	57	48
DIURNAL RANGE	29	33	35	26	19	14	13	13	14	18	20	26
RAIN/INCHES	0.4	0.2	0.3	1.7	6.1	7.1	9.6	9.9	8.1	3.9	1.2	0.4
HUMIDITY/%	67	60	50	50	68	81	82	83	83	82	75	71
BLOOM SEASON			*		*							
DAYS CLR @ 7AM	2	8	10	9	3	0	0	0	0	1	1	2
DAYS CLR @ 1PM	20	20	20	13	3	0	0	0	0	3	13	17
RAIN/MM	10	5	8	43	155	180	244	251	206	99	30	10
°C AVG MAX	24.0	26.2	30.1	30.6	29.0	25.6	24.5	24.5	25.1	26.2	25.1	23.4
°C AVG MIN	7.9	7.9	10.6	16.2	18.4	17.9	17.3	17.3	17.3	16.2	14.0	9.0
DIURNAL RANGE	16.1	18.3	19.5	14.4	10.6	7.7	7.2	7.2	7.8	10.0	11.1	14.4
S/HEMISPHERE	JUL	AUG	SEP	OCT	NOV	DEC	JAN	FEB	MAR	APR	MAY	JUN

Cultural Recommendations

LIGHT: 2000–3000 fc. The heavy summer cloud cover indicates that some shading is needed from spring through autumn, but light should be as high as the plant can tolerate, short of burning the leaves. Strong air movement is important at all times.

TEMPERATURES: Summer days average 76–78°F (25–26°C), and nights average 63–64°F (17–18°C), with a diurnal range of 13–14°F (7–8°C). The warmest season is spring. Days average 84–87°F (29–31°C), and nights average 51–65°F (11–18°C), with a diurnal range of 19–35°F (11–20°C).

HUMIDITY: 80–85% from summer into autumn, dropping to 60–70% for most of the other months. However, for about 2 months in spring, conditions are very dry and humidity drops to 50%.

WATER: Rainfall is moderate to heavy from late spring into autumn, but is very low in winter and spring. Cultivated plants should be kept moist while actively growing, but water should be gradually reduced after new growths mature in autumn.

FERTILIZER: ¼–½ recommended strength, applied weekly. A high-nitrogen fertilizer is beneficial from spring to midsummer, but a fertilizer high in phosphates should be used in late summer and autumn.

REST PERIOD: Winter days average 74–79°F (23–26°C), and nights average 46–48°F (8–9°C), with a diurnal range of 26–33°F (14–18°C). In the habitat, rainfall is low for 4–5 months in winter. For 2–3 of these months, high humidity and nightly cooling result in frequent, heavy deposits of dew with even more moisture available from fog and mist. Therefore, the driest season is only 1–2 months long. For cultivated plants, water should be reduced from late autumn to early spring. During most of the winter, plants should be allowed to dry out between waterings, but they should not remain completely dry for extended periods. Occasional early morning mistings between waterings may help prevent the plants from becoming too dry. For 1–2 months in late winter, however, water should be limited to occasional early morning mistings. Fertilizer should be reduced or eliminated, until new growth starts in spring. In the habitat, the large number of clear, winter afternoons indicates very bright conditions.

GROWING MEDIA: Plants may be mounted on tree-fern or cork slabs if humidity is high and plants are watered at least once daily in summer. When plants are potted, any open, fast-draining medium may be used. Repotting is best done in early spring when new roots are growing.

MISCELLANEOUS NOTES: The bloom season shown in the climate table is based on cultivation records.

Plant and Flower Information

PLANT SIZE AND TYPE: A 20 in. (50 cm) sympodial epiphyte.

PSEUDOBULB: 13–18 in. (33–45 cm) long. The thin, purple stems are branching and become furrowed with age. The leaves are held at the apex of the stem and branches.

LEAVES: 4–6 per growth. The linear-lanceolate leaves are 2.4 in. (6 cm) long.

INFLORESCENCE: Short. The inflorescences are normally scattered along leafless stems, but cultivated plants sometimes bloom from leafy stems.

FLOWERS: 2–5 per inflorescence. The flowers, which resemble a flared tube, are less than 0.4 in. (1 cm) long. Sepals and petals may be cream, light green, or dull yellow. The lip is yellow and green with or without dark purple spots. It is notched at the apex and has no sidelobes.

HYBRIDIZING NOTES: Chromosome count is n = 20 as *D. parcoides* (ref. 504, 580). Johansen (ref. 239) indicates that plants are self-sterile and that flowers dropped 8–10 days after self-pollination.

REFERENCES: 157, 164, 179, 202, 203, 216, 228, 239, 254, 266, 445, 448, 454, 504, 580.

PHOTOS/DRAWINGS: 203, *454*.

Dendrobium pardalinum Rchb. f. Now considered a synonym of *Flickingeria pardalina* (Rchb. f.) Seidenfaden. REFERENCES: 213, 216, 233, 254, 449, 469.

Dendrobium parietiforme J. J. Smith. Now considered a synonym of *Flickingeria parietiformis* (J. J. Smith) A. Hawkes. REFERENCES: 213, 219, 230, 231, 254, 436, 445, 449, 483.

Dendrobium parishii Rchb. f.

AKA: Seidenfaden (ref. 454) indicates that he sees no difference between *D. parishii* and *D. rhodopterygium* Rchb. f. However, he left both as separate species, as he was unable to study the type specimen.

ORIGIN/HABITAT: Southeast Asia. Plants are widespread in the eastern Himalayas from the Manipur region of northeastern India through the Tenasserim, Maymyo, and Chin Hills regions of Burma, across northern and eastern Thailand, through Laos and Vietnam, and into Yunnan and Gweizhou Provinces of southwest China. In Thailand, plants grow in dry deciduous forests at 800–5600 ft. (250–1700 m).

CLIMATE: Station #48300, Mae Hong Son, Thailand, Lat. 19.3°N, Long. 97.9°E, at 711 ft. (217 m). Temperatures are calculated for an elevation of 4000 ft. (1220 m), resulting in probable extremes of 97°F (36°C) and 32°F (0°C).

N/HEMISPHERE	JAN	FEB	MAR	APR	MAY	JUN	JUL	AUG	SEP	OCT	NOV	DEC
°F AVG MAX	75	79	86	87	84	78	76	76	77	79	77	74
°F AVG MIN	46	46	51	61	65	64	63	63	63	61	57	48
DIURNAL RANGE	29	33	35	26	19	14	13	13	14	18	20	26
RAIN/INCHES	0.4	0.2	0.3	1.7	6.1	7.1	9.6	9.9	8.1	3.9	1.2	0.4
HUMIDITY/%	67	60	50	50	68	81	82	83	83	82	75	71
BLOOM SEASON		*	*	*	***	**	**		*			
DAYS CLR @ 7AM	2	8	10	9	3	0	0	0	0	1	1	2
DAYS CLR @ 1PM	20	20	20	13	3	0	0	0	0	3	13	17
RAIN/MM	10	5	8	43	155	180	244	251	206	99	30	10
°C AVG MAX	24.0	26.2	30.1	30.6	29.0	25.6	24.5	24.5	25.1	26.2	25.1	23.4
°C AVG MIN	7.9	7.9	10.6	16.2	18.4	17.9	17.3	17.3	17.3	16.2	14.0	9.0
DIURNAL RANGE	16.1	18.3	19.5	14.4	10.6	7.7	7.2	7.2	7.8	10.0	11.1	14.4
S/HEMISPHERE	JUL	AUG	SEP	OCT	NOV	DEC	JAN	FEB	MAR	APR	MAY	JUN

Cultural Recommendations

LIGHT: 2000–3000 fc. The heavy summer cloud cover indicates that some shading is needed from spring through autumn, but light should be as high as the plant can tolerate, short of burning the leaves. Strong air movement is important at all times.

TEMPERATURES: Summer days average 76–78°F (25–26°C), and nights average 63–64°F (17–18°C), with a diurnal range of 13–14°F (7–8°C). The warmest season is spring. Days average 84–87°F (29–31°C), and nights average 51–65°F (11–18°C), with a diurnal range of 19–35°F (11–20°C).

HUMIDITY: 80–85% from summer into autumn, dropping to 60–70% for most of the other months. However, for about 2 months in spring, conditions are very dry and humidity drops to 50%.

Dendrobium parryae

WATER: Rainfall is very heavy during the growing season, but winters are very dry. Cultivated plants should be kept moist while actively growing, but water should be gradually reduced after new growths mature in autumn.

FERTILIZER: ¼–½ recommended strength, applied weekly. A high-nitrogen fertilizer is beneficial from spring to midsummer, but a fertilizer high in phosphates should be used in late summer and autumn.

REST PERIOD: Winter days average 74–79°F (23–26°C), and nights average 46–48°F (8–9°C), with a diurnal range of 26–33°F (14–18°C). In the habitat, rainfall is low for 4–5 months in winter. For 2–3 of these months, high humidity and nightly cooling result in frequent, heavy deposits of dew with even more moisture available from fog and mist. Therefore, the driest season is only 1–2 months long. For cultivated plants, water should be reduced from late autumn to early spring. During most of the winter, plants should be allowed to dry out between waterings, but they should not remain completely dry for extended periods. Occasional early morning mistings between waterings may help prevent the plants from becoming too dry. For 1–2 months in late winter, however, water should be limited to occasional early morning mistings. Fertilizer should be reduced or eliminated, until new growth starts in spring. In the habitat, the large number of clear, winter afternoons indicates very bright conditions.

GROWING MEDIA: Growers indicate that plants do well in pots, baskets, or mounted on tree-fern slabs. When plants are potted, any open, fast-draining medium may be used. Repotting is best done in early spring when new roots are growing.

MISCELLANEOUS NOTES: The bloom season shown in the climate table is based on cultivation records. In the habitat, blooming occurs Feb.–May (Aug.–Nov.). The cool, dry rest is necessary to initiate blooming. Growers indicate that plants rarely flower when grown in the tropical lowlands, but with a rest, the plants are very free-flowering.

Plant and Flower Information

PLANT SIZE AND TYPE: A 6–24 in. (15–60 cm) sympodial epiphyte. Plants become very desirable specimen plants. Plant growth habit is highly variable.

PSEUDOBULB: 6–24 in. (15–60 cm) long. The stems are fleshy, yellowish, curved downward, and knotty at the numerous nodes. They may be stout or elongated depending on growing conditions. Plants from drier regions with high light are usually shorter with upright growth habit. However, the stems of plants from shady, humid areas tend to be longer and may be pendulous.

LEAVES: Several per growth. The oblong-lanceolate leaves are usually 2–6 in. (5–15 cm) long. They are stiff, leathery, and deciduous.

INFLORESCENCE: Short. Inflorescences arise from nodes along more than 50% the length of 2-year-old stems after the leaves have fallen.

FLOWERS: 2–4, rarely 1 per inflorescence. The flowers are 1.6–2.4 in. (4–6 cm) across. Flower color is highly variable. Sepals and petals are often dark rose fading to white near the center. The petals are finely toothed. The dark-rose lip, which is hairy on the upper surface, is marked with rich purple on the inside and 2 deep purple blotches on each side of the throat. It is shorter than the sepals and petals. The column is white. The long-lived blossoms have good substance. They are highly scented. Their fragrance has been variously described as like rhubarb or raspberries.

HYBRIDIZING NOTES: Chromosome counts are 2n = 38 (ref. 151, 153, 154, 187, 188, 273, 504, 542, 580), 2n = 40 (ref. 150, 187, 504, 580), and 2n = 76 (ref. 154, 542). Johansen (ref. 239) indicates that plants are self-sterile and that flowers dropped 7 days after self-pollination. All cross-pollinations produced capsules which opened after 387 days. 93% of the seed contained visible embryos and 96% germinated.

REFERENCES: 25, 36, 38, 46, 150, 151, 153, 154, 157, 165, 179, 187, 188, 190, 196, 200, 202, 210, 216, 239, 245, 247, 254, 266, 273, 326, 361, 369, 371, 389, 430, 445, 447, 448, 454, 458, 504, 507, 528, 541, 542, 557, 568, 570, 580.

PHOTOS/DRAWINGS: *36*, 46, 210, *245, 247, 369, 371, 389, 423, 430, 454,* 458.

Dendrobium parryae Summerhayes ex Parry.

An invalid name. One specimen labeled with this name was actually *Eria muscicola*. REFERENCES: 225, 454.

Dendrobium parthenium Rchb. f.

AKA: *D. sanderianum* Rolfe. Schelpe (ref. 429) suggested that after additional study *D. revolutum* Lindley not Hooker f. may prove to be a synonym of *D. parthenium*.

ORIGIN/HABITAT: Borneo. Plants are endemic to the Mt. Kinabalu region in Sabah. They have been reported from along the Labuk River at about 1500 ft. (450 m) and from other areas at 1950–2950 ft. (600–900 m).

CLIMATE: Station #49613, Tambunan, Sabah, Borneo, Lat. 5.7°N, Long. 116.4°E, at 1200 ft. (366 m). Temperatures are calculated for an elevation of 2000 ft. (610 m), resulting in probable extremes of 95°F (35°C) and 51°F (11°C).

N/HEMISPHERE	JAN	FEB	MAR	APR	MAY	JUN	JUL	AUG	SEP	OCT	NOV	DEC
°F AVG MAX	83	84	86	87	87	86	86	86	86	85	84	83
°F AVG MIN	64	62	63	64	65	64	63	63	64	64	64	65
DIURNAL RANGE	19	22	23	23	22	22	23	23	22	21	20	18
RAIN/INCHES	5.8	3.7	5.8	7.5	8.2	7.3	5.1	4.9	6.4	7.0	6.8	6.0
HUMIDITY/%	N/A											
BLOOM SEASON									*	*		
DAYS CLR	N/A											
RAIN/MM	147	94	147	191	208	185	130	124	163	178	173	152
°C AVG MAX	28.3	28.9	30.0	30.6	30.6	30.2	30.1	30.0	30.0	29.4	28.9	28.3
°C AVG MIN	17.8	16.9	17.4	18.0	18.5	18.0	17.4	17.4	18.0	18.0	18.0	18.5
DIURNAL RANGE	10.5	12.0	12.6	12.6	12.1	12.2	12.7	12.6	12.0	11.4	10.9	9.8
S/HEMISPHERE	JUL	AUG	SEP	OCT	NOV	DEC	JAN	FEB	MAR	APR	MAY	JUN

Cultural Recommendations

LIGHT: 2000–3000 fc.

TEMPERATURES: Throughout the year, days average 83–87°F (28–31°C), and nights average 62–65°F (17–19°C), with a diurnal range of 18–23°F (10–13°C). Growers indicate that plants grow well at 60°F (16°C) nights.

HUMIDITY: Information is not available for this location. However, records from nearby locations indicate that humidity is probably 80–85% year-round.

WATER: Rainfall is moderate to heavy all year with a brief, slightly drier period in winter. Cultivated plants should be allowed to dry slightly between waterings.

FERTILIZER: ¼–½ recommended strength. A balanced fertilizer should be applied weekly to biweekly throughout the year.

REST PERIOD: Growing conditions should be maintained all year. Water should be reduced slightly in winter, but plants should never be allowed to dry out completely. Fertilizer should be reduced anytime plants are not actively growing. In the habitat, seasonal light variation is minor.

GROWING MEDIA: Plants may be mounted on tree-fern or cork slabs if humidity is high and plants are watered at least once daily in summer. When plants are potted, any open, fast-draining medium may be used. Repotting may be done anytime new roots are growing.

MISCELLANEOUS NOTES: The autumn bloom season shown in the climate table is based on the flowering record for an imported plant.

Plant and Flower Information

PLANT SIZE AND TYPE: A 24–35 in. (60–90 cm) sympodial epiphyte.

PSEUDOBULB: Variable. The erect stem continues to grow and may eventually exceed a length of 35 in. (90 cm). As it elongates with age, it continues to produce blossoms.

LEAVES: Many. The ovate-oblong leaves, which are 1.7 in. (4.3 cm) long, are distichous. They have 2 tiny teeth at the apex.

INFLORESCENCE: Many. The leafy pedicels are 2 in. (5 cm) long. A succession of inflorescences appear from between the leaves along the side of the stem.

FLOWERS: 2–3 per inflorescence. The flowers are 2.5 in. (6.4 cm) across. They have somewhat triangular sepals, which are pointed at the tip, and nearly round petals, which are elliptical at the apex. The midlobe is notched and wavy. Blossoms have an inflated sac at the base of the spur. All segments are white with a light purple stain at the base of the lip. They are described a beautiful.

REFERENCES: 216, 254, 257, 286, 295, 407, 429, 430, 592.

PHOTOS/DRAWINGS: *430, 592*.

Dendrobium parviflorum D. Don.

Hooker (ref. 202) indicated that he did not recognize this plant and speculated that it might be an *Eria*. Banerje and Pradhan (ref. 32) included only the information given in the original description. The plant reportedly grew in Nepal in tropical valleys in the Himalayas. The small sympodial epiphyte was about 1.5 in. (3.8 cm) long, with pseudobulbs that were 1 in. (2.5 cm) long. The pointed, lanceolate leaves were 0.5 in. (1.3 cm) long. Inflorescences were 0.5–2.0 in. (1.3–5.0 cm) long. The plants produced numerous small, greenish yellow flowers with lanceolate sepals and petals. The oblong lip was concave and ruffled. REFERENCES: 32, 202, 216, 254.

Dendrobium parviflorum Rchb. f.

Rao (ref. 376) included this name as originating in Arunachal Pradesh, India, where it grew below 1650 ft. (500 m) and was considered threatened. This name and describer were found only in his list. We suspect that the name may be a typographical error for *D. parciflorum* Rchb. f. ex Lindley, but we found no additional information. REFERENCES: 376.

Dendrobium parvifolium J. J. Smith

ORIGIN/HABITAT: Irian Jaya (western New Guinea). Plants grow in the Angi Lakes region of the Arfak Mountains at 7000–8000 ft. (2140–2440 m). Plants were found in a lakeside forest patch and on a ridge above the lake.

CLIMATE: Station #97530, Manokwari, Irian Jaya, Lat. 0.9°S, Long. 134.1°E, at 10 ft. (3 m). Temperatures are calculated for an elevation of 7000 ft. (2130 m), resulting in probable extremes of 70°F (21°C) and 45°F (7°C).

N/HEMISPHERE	JAN	FEB	MAR	APR	MAY	JUN	JUL	AUG	SEP	OCT	NOV	DEC
°F AVG MAX	63	62	64	64	65	63	63	63	63	63	63	62
°F AVG MIN	51	52	51	51	51	52	50	50	51	51	51	51
DIURNAL RANGE	12	10	13	13	14	11	13	13	12	12	12	11
RAIN/INCHES	5.4	5.6	5.0	4.7	4.5	10.3	12.0	9.4	13.2	11.1	7.8	7.3
HUMIDITY/%	87	87	85	84	85	86	86	85	86	86	86	85
BLOOM SEASON												*
DAYS CLR @ 9AM	4	3	3	5	3	3	3	1	1	2	3	7
DAYS CLR @ 3PM	2	2	2	3	1	1	1	0	1	0	0	2
RAIN/MM	137	142	127	119	114	262	305	239	335	282	198	185
°C AVG MAX	17.2	16.6	17.7	17.7	18.3	17.2	17.2	17.2	17.2	17.2	17.2	16.8
°C AVG MIN	10.5	11.1	10.5	10.5	10.5	11.1	10.0	10.0	10.5	10.5	10.5	10.5
DIURNAL RANGE	6.7	5.5	7.2	7.2	7.8	6.1	7.2	7.2	6.7	6.7	6.7	6.1
S/HEMISPHERE	JUL	AUG	SEP	OCT	NOV	DEC	JAN	FEB	MAR	APR	MAY	JUN

Cultural Recommendations

LIGHT: 2000–3000 fc.

TEMPERATURES: Throughout the year, days average 62–65°F (17–18°C), and nights average 50–52°F (10–11°C), with a diurnal range of 10–14°F (6–8°C). Due to the effects of the microclimate, actual maximum temperatures may be 8–10°F (4–6°C) warmer than indicated.

HUMIDITY: Near 85% year-round.

WATER: Rainfall is moderate to heavy all year. Cultivated plants should be kept moist but not soggy.

FERTILIZER: ¼–½ recommended strength. A balanced fertilizer should be applied weekly to biweekly throughout the year.

REST PERIOD: Growing conditions should be maintained year-round. Water and fertilizer may be reduced somewhat in winter, especially for plants cultivated in the dark, short-day conditions common in temperate latitudes. However, these plants should never be allowed to dry out completely. In the habitat, light is highest in winter.

GROWING MEDIA: Plants may be mounted on tree-fern or cork slabs if humidity is high and plants are watered at least once daily in summer. When plants are potted, any open, fast-draining medium may be used. They may be repotted anytime new roots are growing.

MISCELLANEOUS NOTES: The bloom season shown in the climate table is based on reports from the habitat. J. J. Smith indicated that the flowers reminded him of *D. angiense* J. J. Smith (*D. subclausum* Rolfe), but the plant growth habit was different.

Plant and Flower Information

PLANT SIZE AND TYPE: A sympodial epiphyte of undetermined size.

PSEUDOBULB: The original, incomplete specimen was 5.3 in. (13.5 cm) long. The slender, leafy stems are branching.

LEAVES: Many. The pointed, oblong-ovate leaves are 0.4 in. (1.1 cm) long.

INFLORESCENCE: Short. Inflorescences are borne on leafy stems.

FLOWERS: 1 per inflorescence. The red flowers are 0.7 in. (1.8 cm) across. The dorsal sepal is ovate, lateral sepals are triangular and sickle-shaped, and the petals are lanceolate. The recurved lip, which has no callus, is serrated to fringed at the blunt apex.

REFERENCES: 144, 221.

Dendrobium parvilobum Schlechter

ORIGIN/HABITAT: Papua New Guinea. Plants grow on trees in the forests of Mt. Gomadjidji in the Maboro Range at about 1500 ft. (460 m).

CLIMATE: Station #200192, Garaina, Papua New Guinea, Lat. 7.9°S, Long. 147.1°E, at 2350 ft. (716 m). Temperatures are calculated for an elevation of 1500 ft. (460 m), resulting in probable extremes of 97°F (36°C) and 49°F (9°C).

N/HEMISPHERE	JAN	FEB	MAR	APR	MAY	JUN	JUL	AUG	SEP	OCT	NOV	DEC
°F AVG MAX	83	85	86	87	88	88	88	88	87	87	86	84
°F AVG MIN	66	66	66	67	66	67	68	68	68	67	67	66
DIURNAL RANGE	17	19	20	20	22	21	20	20	19	20	19	18
RAIN/INCHES	5.8	6.5	8.7	11.1	11.8	11.9	8.9	11.7	11.5	9.9	7.7	5.2
HUMIDITY/%	84	82	82	81	80	80	81	81	82	83	84	84
BLOOM SEASON									*			
DAYS CLR	N/A											
RAIN/MM	147	165	221	282	300	302	226	297	292	251	196	132
°C AVG MAX	28.2	29.3	29.9	30.4	31.0	31.0	31.0	31.0	30.4	30.4	29.9	28.8
°C AVG MIN	18.8	18.8	18.8	19.3	18.8	19.3	19.9	19.9	19.9	19.3	19.3	18.8
DIURNAL RANGE	9.4	10.5	11.1	11.1	12.2	11.7	11.1	11.1	10.5	11.1	10.6	10.0
S/HEMISPHERE	JUL	AUG	SEP	OCT	NOV	DEC	JAN	FEB	MAR	APR	MAY	JUN

Dendrobium parvulum

Cultural Recommendations

LIGHT: 2500–3500 fc.

TEMPERATURES: Throughout the year, days average 83–88°F (28–31°C), and nights average 66–68°F (19–20°C), with a diurnal range of 17–22°F (9–12°C).

HUMIDITY: 80–85% year-round.

WATER: Rainfall is moderate to heavy all year, but conditions are slightly drier in winter. Cultivated plants should be kept moist but not soggy.

FERTILIZER: ¼–½ recommended strength. A balanced fertilizer should be applied weekly to biweekly throughout the year.

REST PERIOD: Growing conditions should be maintained all year. In the habitat, rainfall is slightly lower in winter. Water and fertilizer should be reduced somewhat for cultivated plants, especially those grown in the dark, short-day conditions common during temperate-latitude winters. They should never be allowed to dry out completely, however. In the habitat, seasonal light variation is minor.

GROWING MEDIA: Plants may be mounted on tree-fern or cork slabs if humidity is high and plants are watered at least once daily in summer. When plants are potted, any open, fast-draining medium may be used. Repotting is best done in early spring when new roots are growing.

MISCELLANEOUS NOTES: The bloom season shown in the climate table is based on reports from the habitat. Plants that produce flowers which last a single day commonly bloom several times during the year. Flowering usually occurs 7–14 days after a sudden 10°F (5°C) drop in daytime temperatures.

Plant and Flower Information

PLANT SIZE AND TYPE: A 10–12 in. (25–30 cm) sympodial epiphyte.

PSEUDOBULB: 10–12 in. (25–30 cm) long. The somewhat flattened stems do not branch. They are densely leafy.

LEAVES: Many. The leaves are 1.0–1.4 in. (2.5–3.5 cm) long, oblong, and spreading.

INFLORESCENCE: Short. Inflorescences are borne at the leaf axils.

FLOWERS: 2 per inflorescence. The salmon-yellow flowers are 0.7 in. (1.8 cm) long and do not open widely. The inflated midlobe is indented with a small point in the center of the indentation. The sidelobes are elongated, sickle-shaped, and toothed along the inside margin. They are sparsely bumpy. The lip has a center keel near the base. Blossoms last a single day.

REFERENCES: 221, 437, 445.

PHOTOS/DRAWINGS: 437.

Dendrobium parvulum Rolfe. See *D. delicatulum* Kränzlin.
REFERENCES: 254, 385, 436.

Dendrobium paspalifolium J. J. Smith. See *D. subclausum* Rolfe. REFERENCES: 225, 470, 588.

Dendrobium patentifiliforme Hosokawa

AKA: Sometimes spelled *D. patenti-filiforme*.

ORIGIN/HABITAT: The Caroline Islands, including Palau and the offshore islet of Babeldoab. On Palau, plants grow in mangrove forests along the Ngarmiscan River near Ngaspan Bay.

CLIMATE: Station #91408, Koror Is., Caroline, Islands, Lat. 7.3°N, Long. 134.5°E, at 108 ft. (33 m). Temperatures are calculated for an elevation of 650 ft. (200 m), resulting in probable extremes of 91°F (33°C) and 67°F (20°C).

N/HEMISPHERE	JAN	FEB	MAR	APR	MAY	JUN	JUL	AUG	SEP	OCT	NOV	DEC
°F AVG MAX	84	85	85	86	86	86	85	85	85	86	86	85
°F AVG MIN	73	73	73	74	74	73	73	73	73	74	74	73
DIURNAL RANGE	11	12	12	12	12	13	12	12	12	12	12	12
RAIN/INCHES	12.6	6.8	7.7	9.7	16.3	14.6	16.8	16.8	15.4	13.4	10.8	12.7
HUMIDITY/%	86	85	84	85	87	87	87	86	86	85	86	86
BLOOM SEASON							*					
DAYS CLR @ 9AM	0	0	0	0	0	0	0	0	0	1	0	0
DAYS CLR @ 3PM	0	0	0	0	0	0	0	0	0	0	0	0
RAIN/MM	320	173	196	246	414	371	427	427	391	340	274	323
°C AVG MAX	29.0	29.6	29.6	30.1	30.1	30.1	29.6	29.6	29.6	30.1	30.1	29.6
°C AVG MIN	22.9	22.9	22.9	23.5	23.5	22.9	22.9	22.9	22.9	23.5	23.5	22.9
DIURNAL RANGE	6.1	6.7	6.7	6.6	6.6	7.2	6.7	6.7	6.7	6.6	6.6	6.7
S/HEMISPHERE	JUL	AUG	SEP	OCT	NOV	DEC	JAN	FEB	MAR	APR	MAY	JUN

Cultural Recommendations

LIGHT: 1800–2500 fc. The plants grow in shady situations in deep forest. In the habitat, clear days are rare.

TEMPERATURES: Throughout the year, days average 84–86°F (29–30°C), and nights average 73–74°F (23–24°C), with a diurnal range of 11–13°F (6–7°C).

HUMIDITY: Near 85% year-round.

WATER: Rainfall is heavy all year. Cultivated plants should be kept moist but not soggy.

FERTILIZER: ¼–½ recommended strength. A balanced fertilizer should be applied weekly to biweekly throughout the year.

REST PERIOD: Growing conditions should be maintained all year. Water should be reduced for plants cultivated in the dark, short-day conditions common in temperate-latitude winters, but they should never be allowed to dry out completely. Fertilizer should be reduced or eliminated anytime water is reduced.

GROWING MEDIA: Mounting plants on tree-fern or cork slabs accommodates their pendulous growth habit. However, humidity must be high and plants must be watered at least once a day in summer. If plants cannot be mounted, small pots or hanging baskets may be filled with an open, fast-draining medium. Repotting may be done anytime new roots are actively growing.

MISCELLANEOUS NOTES: The bloom season shown in the climate table is based on reports from the habitat.

Plant and Flower Information

PLANT SIZE AND TYPE: A 28 in. (70 cm) sympodial epiphyte.

PSEUDOBULB: 28 in. (70 cm) long. The stems are slender, pendulous, and laterally flattened.

LEAVES: Many. The lanceolate leaves are 3.5–4.3 in. (9–11 cm) long, recurved, and distichous.

INFLORESCENCE: Short. Inflorescences emerge from nodes on the upper part of the stem.

FLOWERS: 2 per inflorescence. The yellowish white flowers are 2 in. (5 cm) long. Sepals are linear-lanceolate. Petals are narrowly linear. The recurved lip is fringed along the margin and densely hairy on the midlobe.

REFERENCES: 205, 227.

Dendrobium patentilobum Ames and Schweinfurth

AKA: Spelled *D. pathentilobum* in Masamune (ref. 286).

ORIGIN/HABITAT: Borneo, in Sabah in the Mt. Kinabalu region. Plants grow in hill forests at 2600–4900 ft. (800–1500 m).

CLIMATE: Station #49613, Tambunan, Sabah (North Borneo), Lat. 5.7°N, Long. 116.4°E, at 1200 ft. (366 m). Temperatures are calculated for an elevation of 4000 ft. (1220 m), resulting in probable extremes of 89°F (32°C) and 45°F (7°C).

N/HEMISPHERE	JAN	FEB	MAR	APR	MAY	JUN	JUL	AUG	SEP	OCT	NOV	DEC
°F AVG MAX	77	78	80	81	81	80	80	80	80	79	78	77
°F AVG MIN	58	56	57	58	59	58	57	57	58	58	58	59
DIURNAL RANGE	19	22	23	23	22	22	23	23	22	21	20	18
RAIN/INCHES	5.8	3.7	5.8	7.5	8.2	7.3	5.1	4.9	6.4	7.0	6.8	6.0
HUMIDITY/%	N/A											
BLOOM SEASON												*
DAYS CLR	N/A											
RAIN/MM	147	94	147	190	208	185	130	124	163	178	173	152
°C AVG MAX	24.9	25.4	26.5	27.1	27.1	26.5	26.5	26.5	26.5	26.0	25.4	24.9
°C AVG MIN	14.3	13.2	13.8	14.3	14.9	14.3	13.8	13.8	14.3	14.3	14.3	14.9
DIURNAL RANGE	10.6	12.2	12.7	12.8	12.2	12.2	12.7	12.7	12.2	11.7	11.1	10.0
S/HEMISPHERE	JUL	AUG	SEP	OCT	NOV	DEC	JAN	FEB	MAR	APR	MAY	JUN

Cultural Recommendations

LIGHT: 2000–3000 fc.

TEMPERATURES: Throughout the year, days average 77–81°F (25–27°C), and nights average 56–59°F (13–15°C), with a diurnal range of 18–23°F (10–13°C). These temperatures represent conditions in the higher, cooler portions of the habitat. Because plants grow over a wide range of elevations, they should adapt to conditions about 10°F (6°C) warmer than indicated above.

HUMIDITY: Near 80% year-round.

WATER: Rainfall is heavy most of the year, but conditions are slightly drier for 2–3 months in winter. Cultivated plants should be kept moist but not soggy.

FERTILIZER: ¼–½ recommended strength. A balanced fertilizer should be applied weekly to biweekly throughout the year.

REST PERIOD: Growing conditions vary only slightly through the year. The diurnal range is slightly lower in winter due to somewhat cooler days. In cultivation, water should be reduced somewhat in winter, especially for plants grown in the dark, short-day conditions common in temperate latitudes. Plants should never be allowed to dry out completely, however. Fertilizer should be decreased when water is reduced and when plants are not actively growing.

GROWING MEDIA: Plants may be mounted on tree-fern or cork slabs if humidity is high and plants are watered at least once daily in summer. When plants are potted, any open, fast-draining medium may be used. They may be repotted anytime new roots are growing.

MISCELLANEOUS NOTES: The bloom season shown in the climate table is based of collection records. The plant was described as resembling *D. ventricosum* Kränzlin.

Plant and Flower Information

PLANT SIZE AND TYPE: A 17 in. (43 cm) sympodial epiphyte.

PSEUDOBULB: 17 in. (43 cm) long. The leafy stems are yellow, shiny, and erect.

LEAVES: Many. Commonly 3 in. (8 cm) long, the linear leaves are usually smaller at the top and bottom of the stem. They are spaced 0.8–1.2 in. (2–3 cm) apart. The leaves are distichous, spreading, rigid, and decurved.

INFLORESCENCE: Inflorescences arise from nodes along the leafless, upper portion of the stem. Blossoms open successively.

FLOWERS: 1 per inflorescence. The flowers are 0.6 in. (1.5 cm) across. They are white to cream with 3 red to purple stripes on the petals and 5 on the sepals. The lip has very enlarged, spreading sidelobes that are decorated with several reddish lines and a yellow stain, which are more opaque than the other segments. The deeply notched, white midlobe is nearly transparent.

HYBRIDIZING NOTES: Chromosome count is 2n = 38 (ref. 153, 273).

REFERENCES: 12, 153, 221, 273, 286, 592.

PHOTOS/DRAWINGS: 592.

Dendrobium patentissimum J. J. Smith

AKA: When describing this species, J. J. Smith (ref. 470) suggested the possibility that it might prove to be a variety of *D. igneum* J. J. Smith.

ORIGIN/HABITAT: Irian Jaya (western New Guinea). Plants grow on the north-facing slopes of the Gautier Range, where they are epiphytic in the forests that grow on limestone and basalt at about 2950 ft. (900 m).

CLIMATE: Station #97690, Sentani/Jayapura, Irian Jaya, Lat. 2.7°S, Long. 140.5°E, at 289 ft. (88 m). Temperatures are calculated for an elevation of 3000 ft. (910 m), resulting in probable extremes of 88°F (31°C) and 59°F (15°C).

N/HEMISPHERE	JAN	FEB	MAR	APR	MAY	JUN	JUL	AUG	SEP	OCT	NOV	DEC
°F AVG MAX	78	80	80	81	81	80	80	79	80	81	81	80
°F AVG MIN	63	63	63	64	64	64	64	64	64	65	64	64
DIURNAL RANGE	15	17	17	17	17	16	16	15	16	16	17	16
RAIN/INCHES	4.1	3.9	5.3	2.9	6.7	7.0	8.3	8.3	8.5	4.6	2.4	5.2
HUMIDITY/%	81	80	80	79	81	81	79	80	80	80	81	80
BLOOM SEASON		*										
DAYS CLR @ 9AM	5	3	4	3	2	1	1	0	1	2	2	5
DAYS CLR @ 3PM	4	3	3	3	2	1	3	0	1	2	2	3
RAIN/MM	104	99	135	74	170	178	211	211	216	117	61	132
°C AVG MAX	25.6	26.7	26.7	27.3	27.3	26.7	26.7	26.1	26.7	27.3	27.3	26.7
°C AVG MIN	17.3	17.3	17.3	17.8	17.8	17.8	17.8	17.8	17.8	18.4	17.8	17.8
DIURNAL RANGE	8.3	9.4	9.4	9.5	9.5	8.9	8.9	8.3	8.9	8.9	9.5	8.9
S/HEMISPHERE	JUL	AUG	SEP	OCT	NOV	DEC	JAN	FEB	MAR	APR	MAY	JUN

Cultural Recommendations

LIGHT: 2000–3000 fc.

TEMPERATURES: Throughout the year, days average 78–81°F (26–27°C), and nights average 63–65°F (17–18°C), with a diurnal range of 15–17°F (8–10°C).

HUMIDITY: Near 80% year-round.

WATER: Rainfall is moderate to heavy all year. Brief semidry periods occur in spring and autumn. Cultivated plants should be allowed to dry only slightly between waterings.

FERTILIZER: ¼–½ recommended strength. A balanced fertilizer should be applied weekly to biweekly throughout the year.

REST PERIOD: Growing conditions should be maintained year-round. Water and fertilizer might be reduced slightly in winter, especially for plants grown in the dark, short-day conditions common in temperate latitudes, but plants should never be allowed to dry completely. In the habitat, light is slightly higher in winter.

GROWING MEDIA: Plants may be mounted on slabs or potted in bark or any open, fast-draining medium. Repotting may be done anytime new roots are growing.

MISCELLANEOUS NOTES: The bloom season shown in the climate table is based on reports from the habitat.

Plant and Flower Information

PLANT SIZE AND TYPE: A 16 in. (40 cm) sympodial epiphyte.

PSEUDOBULB: 16 in. (40 cm) long. The stems are close together and the upper part of each stem is flattened and leafy.

LEAVES: Many. The ovate leaves are prominently nerved, unequally bilobed, and reach a length of 0.7–1.3 in. (1.9–3.2 cm). They are spreading and overlap each other.

INFLORESCENCE: Inflorescences emerge laterally from flat sheaths.

FLOWERS: 2 per inflorescence. The flowers are 0.6 in. (1.6 cm) across. The dorsal sepal is oblong and pointed at the tip, the lateral sepals are obliquely triangular, while the somewhat elliptical petals are narrow at the base. The 3-lobed lip is short and wavy. It has a triangular disk and an uneven margin on the midlobe.

Dendrobium patulum

REFERENCES: 221, 470, 476.

Dendrobium patulum Schlechter

ORIGIN/HABITAT: Northern Papua New Guinea. Plants grow epiphytically on forest trees in the Finisterre Range at about 3600 ft. (1100 m).

CLIMATE: Station #200187, Erap, Papua New Guinea, Lat. 6.6°S, Long. 146.7°E, at 850 ft. (260 m). Temperatures are calculated for an elevation of 3300 ft. (1000 m), resulting in probable extremes of 94°F (34°C) and 45°F (7°C).

N/HEMISPHERE	JAN	FEB	MAR	APR	MAY	JUN	JUL	AUG	SEP	OCT	NOV	DEC
°F AVG MAX	80	80	81	82	85	85	85	85	85	84	82	82
°F AVG MIN	61	61	61	62	64	65	64	64	65	63	66	62
DIURNAL RANGE	19	19	20	20	21	20	21	21	20	21	16	20
RAIN/INCHES	3.9	3.9	2.7	3.0	3.0	5.3	5.9	5.9	7.0	3.4	2.4	3.1
HUMIDITY/%	82	81	81	79	75	74	74	74	77	76	80	80
BLOOM SEASON							*					
DAYS CLR	N/A											
RAIN/MM	99	99	69	76	76	135	150	150	178	86	61	79
°C AVG MAX	26.7	26.7	27.2	27.8	29.4	29.4	29.4	29.4	29.4	28.9	27.8	27.8
°C AVG MIN	16.1	16.1	16.1	16.7	17.8	18.3	17.8	17.8	18.3	17.2	18.9	16.7
DIURNAL RANGE	10.6	10.6	11.1	11.1	11.6	11.1	11.6	11.6	11.1	11.7	8.9	11.1
S/HEMISPHERE	JUL	AUG	SEP	OCT	NOV	DEC	JAN	FEB	MAR	APR	MAY	JUN

Cultural Recommendations

LIGHT: 2500–3500 fc.

TEMPERATURES: Throughout the year, days average 80–85°F (27–29°C), and nights average 61–66°F (16–19°C), with a diurnal range of 16–21°F (9–12°C).

HUMIDITY: 75–80% year-round. Despite high average humidity, the habitat may be quite dry during hot afternoons.

WATER: Rainfall is relatively light to moderate most of the year, but conditions are somewhat wetter for 4–5 months in summer and early autumn. Cultivated plants should be thoroughly saturated then allowed to dry slightly between waterings in summer and early autumn. Water should be gradually reduced in autumn.

FERTILIZER: ¼–½ recommended strength. A balanced fertilizer should be applied weekly to biweekly throughout the year.

REST PERIOD: Growing temperatures should be maintained all year. In the habitat, rainfall is lowest in winter, but the high humidity indicates that additional moisture is frequently available from heavy dew. Cultivated plants should be allowed to dry somewhat longer between waterings than in summer, but they should not remain dry for extended periods. Fertilizer should be reduced until water is increased in spring. In the habitat, seasonal light variation is minor.

GROWING MEDIA: Plants may be mounted on tree-fern or cork slabs or potted in small pots filled with any open, fast-draining medium. Repotting may be done anytime new roots are growing.

MISCELLANEOUS NOTES: The bloom season shown in the climate table is based on collection reports. Plants that produce flowers which last a single day commonly bloom several times during the year. Flowering usually occurs 7–14 days after a sudden 10°F (5°C) drop in daytime temperatures.

Plant and Flower Information

PLANT SIZE AND TYPE: A 16–24 in. (40–60 cm) sympodial epiphyte.

PSEUDOBULB: 16–24 in. (40–60 cm) long. The curved stems are somewhat flattened and do not branch. Growths emerge from very short rhizome. The canes are densely leafy.

LEAVES: Many. The spreading lanceolate leaves are 1.2–1.6 in. (3–4 cm) long and unequally bilobed at the apex.

INFLORESCENCE: Very short.

FLOWERS: 2 per inflorescence. The tiny flowers are 0.4 in. (1 cm) long and do not open fully. The ovate sepals and oblong elliptic petals are snow white. The 3-lobed lip is brownish violet on the lower half. It has a fleshy basal callus. The sidelobes are sickle-shaped and roundly toothed at the blunt apex. The column foot is marked with violet.

REFERENCES: 221, 437, 445.

PHOTOS/DRAWINGS: 437.

Dendrobium pauciflorum King and Pantling. See *D. praecinctum* Rchb. f. REFERENCES: 38, 46, 153, 154, 179, 217, 254, 369, 376, 445, 454, 542. PHOTOS/DRAWINGS: *369*, 454.

Dendrobium paucifolium (Breda) Reinwardt ex Blume.
Now considered a synonym of *Mitopetalum (Tainia) plicatum*. REFERENCES: 212, 216, 254, 454.

Dendrobium paucilaciniatum J. J. Smith. Now considered a synonym of *Flickingeria paucilaciniata* (J. J. Smith) A. Hawkes. REFERENCES: 213, 219, 230, 231, 254, 296, 445.

Dendrobium paxtonii Lindley not Paxton. See *D. chrysanthum* Wallich ex Lindley. REFERENCES: 190, 216, 254, 369, 445, 454.

Dendrobium paxtonii Paxton not Lindley. See *D. fimbriatum* Hooker. REFERENCES: 190, 216, 254, 454.

Dendrobium pectinatum Finet not Ridley

ORIGIN/HABITAT: New Caledonia. In the south, plants grow at about 2950 ft. (900 m) on trees in the mountains near the Ngoye River. They are also found near Ou Hinna.

CLIMATE: Station #91592, Noumea, New Caledonia, Lat. 22.3°S, Long. 166.5°E, at 246 ft. (75 m). Temperatures are calculated for an elevation of 3000 ft. (910 m), resulting in probable extremes of 90°F (32°C) and 43°F (6°C).

N/HEMISPHERE	JAN	FEB	MAR	APR	MAY	JUN	JUL	AUG	SEP	OCT	NOV	DEC
°F AVG MAX	67	67	69	71	74	77	77	76	76	74	70	68
°F AVG MIN	53	52	54	56	59	61	63	64	63	61	57	55
DIURNAL RANGE	14	15	15	15	15	16	14	12	13	13	13	13
RAIN/INCHES	3.6	2.6	2.5	2.0	2.4	2.6	3.7	5.1	5.7	5.2	4.4	3.7
HUMIDITY/%	73	70	69	67	68	69	71	74	75	76	73	73
BLOOM SEASON	*	*	*	*	*	*			*			
DAYS CLR @ 11AM	7	9	9	15	12	10	7	6	7	7	7	7
DAYS CLR @ 5PM	7	11	6	11	7	6	5	4	4	5	3	7
RAIN/MM	91	66	64	51	61	66	94	130	145	132	112	94
°C AVG MAX	19.4	19.4	20.5	21.6	23.3	25.0	25.0	24.4	24.4	23.3	21.1	20.0
°C AVG MIN	11.6	11.1	12.2	13.3	15.0	16.1	17.2	17.7	17.2	16.1	13.8	12.7
DIURNAL RANGE	7.8	8.3	8.3	8.3	8.3	8.9	7.8	6.7	7.2	7.2	7.3	7.3
S/HEMISPHERE	JUL	AUG	SEP	OCT	NOV	DEC	JAN	FEB	MAR	APR	MAY	JUN

Cultural Recommendations

LIGHT: 1800–3000 fc. Days are frequently clear, suggesting moderately high light. In cultivation, light should be as high as possible, short of burning the leaves.

TEMPERATURES: Summer days average 76–77°F (24–25°C), and nights average 61–64°F (16–18°C), with a diurnal range of 12–16°F (7–9°C). The diurnal range fluctuates only 4°F (2°C) all year.

HUMIDITY: 70–75% year-round with the lower values occurring from late winter to early summer.

WATER: Rainfall is relatively low and consistent most of the year. The driest period is in late winter and spring, and the heaviest rain falls in late summer and early autumn. Cultivated plants should be allowed to become somewhat dry between waterings but should never dry out completely.

FERTILIZER: ¼–½ recommended strength, applied weekly. A high-nitrogen fertilizer is beneficial from spring to midsummer, but a fertilizer high in phosphates should be used in late summer and autumn.

REST PERIOD: Winter days average 67–69°F (19–21°C), and nights average 52–54°F (11–12°C), with a diurnal range of 13–15°F (7–8°C). In the habitat, rainfall is somewhat lower in late winter and spring. In cultivation, water and fertilizer should be reduced and the plants allowed to dry even more between waterings than in summer. They should not dry out completely or remain dry for long periods, however. In the habitat, light is highest in winter.

GROWING MEDIA: Plants may be mounted on tree-fern or cork slabs if humidity is high and plants are watered at least once daily in summer. When plants are potted, any open, fast-draining medium may be used. Repotting is best done in early spring when new roots are growing.

MISCELLANEOUS NOTES: The bloom season shown in the climate table is based on reports from the habitat.

Plant and Flower Information

PLANT SIZE AND TYPE: A 4–20 in. (10–50 cm) sympodial epiphyte.

PSEUDOBULB: 4–20 in. (10–50 cm) long. The 4-angled stems are zigzag above the lowest nodes. They are densely clustered.

LEAVES: Many. The lanceolate leaves are 2.8–6.7 in. (7–17 cm) long. They are very unequally bilobed at the tip.

INFLORESCENCE: Short. Several inflorescences emerge opposite leaves on the upper part of the stem. They all turn to one side of the stem.

FLOWERS: 1–3 per inflorescence. The tiny flowers, which do not open fully, are 0.2 in. (0.5 cm) long. They are normally yellow, pale yellow, or yellowish white but are occasionally white with brown, rose, purple, or brownish orange. The lip, which has no lobes, has a callus that is solid at the base and separates into 3 lines that nearly merge near the tip.

REFERENCES: 118, 173, 219, 254, 432, 445.

PHOTOS/DRAWINGS: 173.

Dendrobium pectinatum Ridley not Finet.
Now considered a synonym of *Flickingeria nativitatis* (Ridley) J. J. Wood. REFERENCES: 67, 75, 213, 220, 230, 449.

Dendrobium peculiare J. J. Smith

ORIGIN/HABITAT: Western Sumatra and Malaya. In Sumatra, plants grow on mountain slopes at 4250–5600 ft. (1300–1700 m). In Malaya, this orchid grows on forest trees in valleys of the Cameron Highlands at about 4000 ft. (1220 m).

CLIMATE: Station #48625, Ipoh, Malaya, Lat. 4.6°N, Long. 101.1°E, at 123 ft. (37 m). Temperatures are calculated for an estimated elevation of 4000 ft. (1220 m), resulting in probable extremes of 86°F (30°C) and 51°F (11°C).

N/HEMISPHERE	JAN	FEB	MAR	APR	MAY	JUN	JUL	AUG	SEP	OCT	NOV	DEC
°F AVG MAX	77	79	80	79	79	79	78	78	77	76	76	76
°F AVG MIN	59	59	60	60	61	60	59	59	60	59	59	59
DIURNAL RANGE	18	20	20	19	18	19	19	19	17	17	17	17
RAIN/INCHES	7.9	3.1	7.6	8.4	6.2	3.6	7.2	6.9	8.8	11.0	13.0	8.9
HUMIDITY/%	76	74	76	78	78	75	76	77	79	82	82	81
BLOOM SEASON			*									
DAYS CLR @ 7AM	3	3	3	1	1	2	1	1	0	0	1	2
DAYS CLR @ 1PM	2	2	2	1	1	1	1	1	0	0	0	2
RAIN/MM	201	79	193	213	157	91	183	175	224	279	330	226
°C AVG MAX	25.1	26.2	26.8	26.2	26.2	26.2	25.7	25.7	25.1	24.6	24.6	24.6
°C AVG MIN	15.1	15.1	15.7	15.7	16.2	15.7	15.1	15.1	15.7	15.1	15.1	15.1
DIURNAL RANGE	10.0	11.1	11.1	10.5	10.0	10.5	10.6	10.6	9.4	9.5	9.5	9.5
S/HEMISPHERE	JUL	AUG	SEP	OCT	NOV	DEC	JAN	FEB	MAR	APR	MAY	JUN

Cultural Recommendations

LIGHT: 1500–2500 fc. Light should be diffused or dappled, and direct sunlight should be avoided. Clear days are quite rare.

TEMPERATURES: Throughout the year, days average 76–80°F (25–27°C), and nights average 59–61°F (15–16°C), with a diurnal range of 17–20°F (9–11°C). The extreme high does not exceed the warmest average by more than 6°F (3°C), and the average low fluctuates only 2°F (1°C), indicating that plants may not be able to tolerate wide temperature fluctuations. Although temperatures are uniform all year, the diurnal range is surprisingly large.

HUMIDITY: 75–80% year-round.

WATER: Rainfall is heavy most of the year. The heaviest rainfall occurs in autumn, with a secondary maximum in spring. Brief semidry periods occur in midwinter and midsummer. Cultivated plants should be kept evenly moist and only slight drying allowed between waterings.

FERTILIZER: ¼–½ recommended strength. A balanced fertilizer should be applied weekly to biweekly throughout the year.

REST PERIOD: Growing conditions should be maintained year-round. Water should be reduced somewhat in winter for plants cultivated in the dark, short-day conditions common in temperate latitudes. They should never be allowed to dry out completely, however. Fertilizer may be reduced when the plant is not actively growing or when water is reduced. In the habitat, light is slightly higher in winter.

GROWING MEDIA: Plants may be mounted on tree-fern or cork slabs if humidity is high and plants are watered at least once daily in summer. When plants are potted, any open, fast-draining medium may be used. Repotting may be done anytime new roots are growing.

MISCELLANEOUS NOTES: The bloom season shown in the climate table is based on reports from the habitat. Plants that produce flowers which last a single day commonly bloom several times during the year. Flowering usually occurs 7–14 days after a sudden 10°F (5°C) drop in daytime temperatures.

Plant and Flower Information

PLANT SIZE AND TYPE: A 12 in. (30 cm) sympodial epiphyte.

PSEUDOBULB: 12 in. (30 cm) long. The base of the stem is swollen for 1–2 nodes. Nodes are spaced 1 in. (2.5 cm) apart on somewhat zigzag stems. New growths arise from a very branching rhizome.

LEAVES: Several, on the upper portion of the stem. The leaves are 3.5 in. (9 cm) long, grooved, and terete.

INFLORESCENCE: Very Short. Inflorescences emerge from the apical nodes of the stem.

FLOWERS: 1 per inflorescence. The flowers are 0.6 in. (1.5 cm) across. All segments are white. The dorsal sepal and petals are small. The very large lateral sepals form the somewhat square mentum. The 3-lobed lip is marked with 3 purplish keels between the erect sidelobes. The midlobe is truncate. The sidelobes are very large relative to the midlobe. Blossoms are very short-lived.

REFERENCES: 200, 224, 450, 455.

PHOTOS/DRAWINGS: 200, 450, *455*.

Dendrobium pedicellatum J. J. Smith

ORIGIN/HABITAT: Western Sumatra. Plants are common in the mountain forests and brushwood at 6550–9400 ft. (2000–2860 m) on Mt. Singalang near Padang. They are also reported on Mt. Dempoe near Bengkulu.

CLIMATE: Station #96163, Padang, Sumatra, Indonesia, Lat. 0.9°S, Long. 100.4°E, at 19 ft. (6 m). Temperatures are calculated for an elevation of 8000 ft. (2440 m), resulting in probable extremes of 68°F (20°C) and 42°F (5°C).

Dendrobium pedilochilum

N/HEMISPHERE	JAN	FEB	MAR	APR	MAY	JUN	JUL	AUG	SEP	OCT	NOV	DEC
°F AVG MAX	61	61	60	60	60	60	61	61	61	61	62	61
°F AVG MIN	48	48	48	48	48	48	48	48	48	49	49	48
DIURNAL RANGE	13	13	12	12	12	12	13	13	13	12	13	13
RAIN/INCHES	10.9	13.7	6.0	19.5	20.4	18.9	13.8	10.2	12.1	14.3	12.4	12.1
HUMIDITY/%	81	82	82	84	85	84	81	81	82	83	81	81
BLOOM SEASON	*	*			*						*	*
DAYS CLR @ 7AM	5	1	1	0	0	2	2	1	2	2	3	5
DAYS CLR @ 1PM	5	2	2	1	1	3	3	4	3	3	6	5
RAIN/MM	277	348	152	495	518	480	351	259	307	363	315	307
°C AVG MAX	15.9	15.9	15.4	15.4	15.4	15.4	15.9	15.9	15.9	15.9	16.5	15.9
°C AVG MIN	8.7	8.7	8.7	8.7	8.7	8.7	8.7	8.7	8.7	9.3	9.3	8.7
DIURNAL RANGE	7.2	7.2	6.7	6.7	6.7	6.7	7.2	7.2	7.2	6.6	7.2	7.2
S/HEMISPHERE	JUL	AUG	SEP	OCT	NOV	DEC	JAN	FEB	MAR	APR	MAY	JUN

Cultural Recommendations

LIGHT: 2000–3000 fc. Diffused light is preferred.

TEMPERATURES: Throughout the year, days average 60–62°F (15–17°C), and nights average 48–49°F (9°C), with a diurnal range of 12–13°F (7°C). Probable extremes vary only a few degrees from the averages, indicating that the plant may not tolerate wide temperature fluctuations. Because of microclimatic effects, actual maximum temperatures in the habitat may be several degrees warmer than indicated above.

HUMIDITY: 80–85% year-round.

WATER: Rainfall is very heavy all year. Cultivated plants should be constantly moist but not soggy.

FERTILIZER: 1/4–1/2 recommended strength. A balanced fertilizer should be applied weekly to biweekly throughout the year.

REST PERIOD: Growing conditions should be maintained year-round. Water may be reduced somewhat in winter for cultivated plants, especially those cultivated in the dark, short-day conditions common in temperate latitudes. Plants should never be allowed to dry out completely, however.

GROWING MEDIA: Plants may be mounted on tree-fern or cork slabs or potted in small pots filled with any open, fast-draining medium. Repotting may be done anytime new roots are actively growing.

MISCELLANEOUS NOTES: The bloom season shown in the climate table is based on collection reports. The plant was described in 1908 in *Bul. Dép. Agric. Indes. Néerl.* 25:13.

Plant and Flower Information

PLANT SIZE AND TYPE: A 24 in. (60 cm) sympodial plant.

PSEUDOBULB: 24 in. (60 cm) long. The elongated stems consist of nodes spaced about 1–2 in. (2.5–5.0 cm) apart.

LEAVES: The lanceolate leaves are 2–5 in. (5.5–12.7 cm) long.

INFLORESCENCE: 0.4–0.6 in. (1.0–1.5 cm) long. Inflorescences emerge along leafless stems.

FLOWERS: 4–12 per inflorescence. Flowers are about 0.5 in. (1.2 cm) long. They are white to violet with a yellow blotch on the lip. The dorsal sepal is oblong. The broadly triangular lateral sepals form a conical shaped spur. The wavy, ruffled lip is 3-lobed, with a roundly triangular midlobe and triangular sidelobes.

REFERENCES: 220, 254.

Dendrobium pedilochilum Schlechter.

AKA: Seidenfaden (ref. 454) indicates that Schlechter's drawing of *D. pedilochilum* is very similar to *D. moschatum* (Buch.-Ham,) Swartz.

ORIGIN/HABITAT: The plant was originally described as originating in Burma. Habitat habitat location and elevation are unavailable, so climate data cannot be selected.

Plant and Flower Information

PLANT SIZE AND TYPE: A 59 in. (150 cm) sympodial epiphyte.

PSEUDOBULB: The cylindrical stems are connected by a very short rhizome.

LEAVES: The ovate leaves, which are smallest near the apex, cover the stems. They are deciduous.

INFLORESCENCE: 7 in. (18 cm) long. The racemes emerge at the apex of leafless pseudobulbs.

FLOWERS: 5–8 per inflorescence. The flowers are 1.4 in. (3.5 cm) long. The orange blossoms are marked with 2 purple spots on the lip. They resemble *D. moschatum*.

REFERENCES: 221, 445, 454.

Dendrobium pedunculatum (Clemesha) D. Jones and M. Clements

AKA: Still considered by most to be part of the *D. speciosum* alliance. Clements (ref. 67) considers it a species and lists *D. speciosum* J. E. Smith var. *pedunculatum* Clemesha as a synonym. He reports that these species are currently being studied in Australia.

ORIGIN/HABITAT: Northeastern Australia and New Guinea. In Australia, the habitat extends from the Palmer River (16.0°S) to north of the Herbert River (18.3°S). Plants are generally found on the western slopes of the dividing range where conditions are very hot and dry for much of the year. They often grow in full sun on rockfaces above dry creek beds. In New Guinea, plants are found in the Owen Stanley Range.

CLIMATE: Station #94275, Georgetown, Australia, Lat. 18.3°S, Long. 143.6° E, at 981 ft. (299 m). Record extreme temperatures are not available for this location.

N/HEMISPHERE	JAN	FEB	MAR	APR	MAY	JUN	JUL	AUG	SEP	OCT	NOV	DEC
°F AVG MAX	81	85	89	93	96	95	92	91	91	89	85	80
°F AVG MIN	60	63	68	73	76	77	77	77	75	71	66	60
DIURNAL RANGE	21	22	21	20	20	18	15	14	16	18	19	20
RAIN/INCHES	0.2	0.2	T	0.8	1.7	3.2	8.5	6.7	2.4	1.3	0.7	0.1
HUMIDITY/%	N/A											
BLOOM SEASON	*	*	*									
DAYS CLR	N/A											
RAIN/MM	6	6	1	19	42	81	215	171	61	32	19	3
°C AVG MAX	27.0	29.2	31.7	34.0	35.4	35.2	33.4	32.5	32.5	31.6	29.5	26.8
°C AVG MIN	15.5	17.3	20.1	22.8	24.4	25.1	25.1	24.8	23.7	21.8	19.1	15.6
DIURNAL RANGE	11.5	11.9	11.6	11.2	11.0	10.1	8.3	7.7	8.8	9.8	10.4	11.2
S/HEMISPHERE	JUL	AUG	SEP	OCT	NOV	DEC	JAN	FEB	MAR	APR	MAY	JUN

Cultural Recommendations

LIGHT: 3500–4500 fc.

TEMPERATURES: Summer days average 91–95°F (33–35°C), and nights average 77°F (25°C), with a diurnal range of 14–18°F (8–10°C).

HUMIDITY: Values are not available for this location. However, records from other stations in the region indicate that averages are probably 40–50% most of the year, increasing to near 65% during the summer rainy season.

WATER: Rainfall is light most of the year with a 4–5 month rainy season from late spring into autumn. Cultivated plants should be kept moist during the summer growing season with only slight drying allowed between waterings. Water should be gradually reduced after new growths mature in autumn.

FERTILIZER: 1/4–1/2 recommended strength, applied weekly. A high nitrogen fertilizer is beneficial from spring to midsummer, but a fertilizer high in phosphates should be used in late summer and autumn.

REST PERIOD: Winter days average 80–85°F (27–29°C), and nights average 60–63°F (16–17°C), with a diurnal range of 20–22°F (11–12°C). In the habitat, the winter dry season is rather long and severe. Not only is rainfall low, but humidity is so low that even moisture from dew is uncommon. For cultivated plants, water should be greatly reduced with only enough given so that the plants do not become desiccated. Fertilizer should be eliminated until water is increased in the spring.

GROWING MEDIA: Plants may be mounted on hardwood or cork slabs if humidity is high and plants are watered at least once daily in summer. They should be attached firmly to the new mount. When plants are potted, a very open, fast-draining medium should be used. Repotting is best done in early spring immediately after flowering. When established, the plants are robust and need frequent repotting. Relatively small pots should be used, however, since growers caution that plants often do not survive when placed in oversized pots.

MISCELLANEOUS NOTES: The bloom season shown in the climate table is based on cultivation records.

Plant and Flower Information

PLANT SIZE AND TYPE: A 3–11 in. (8–28 cm) sympodial lithophyte.

PSEUDOBULB: 2–6 in. (5–16 cm) long. The small pseudobulbs are conical, thick, and erect. They are often purplish.

LEAVES: 2 per growth. The leaves are 1–5 in. (3–13 cm) long, glossy, and often purplish. They are approximately equal to the size of the pseudobulb.

INFLORESCENCE: 6–12 in. (15–30 cm) long. Normally a single, densely-flowered inflorescence is borne from between the leaves at the apex of the pseudobulb. Blossoms are crowded at the top of the purplish inflorescence.

FLOWERS: Many per inflorescence. The fleshy flowers are 0.8–1.5 in. (2.0–3.8 cm) across. They last about 2 weeks. Buds are often purplish, but when the blossoms open, they are white to light yellow, occasionally with a dark purple stain on the sepals. The lip, which is large relative to the sepals and petals, is 3-lobed with mauve-blue markings. The prominent midlobe is notched at the apex. Seed capsules are dark purple. See discussion at *D. speciosum*.

HYBRIDIZING FLOWERS: Although members of the *D. speciosum* alliance are seldom self-fertile, Adams (ref. 4) indicates that these plants produce capsules if the post-pollination conditions are warm, but that they do not if conditions are cool. Cross-pollination between different clones of the same variety and between different varieties commonly produces seed. Upton (ref. 534) indicates that some hybrids with *D. speciosum* often require longer to reach maturity.

REFERENCES: 4, 24, 67, 235, 240, 263, 264, 533, 534.

PHOTOS/DRAWINGS: 240, *533*.

Dendrobium peekelii Schlechter

ORIGIN/HABITAT: New Britain and New Ireland (Bismarck Islands) off the northeast coast of New Guinea. Habitat elevation is unavailable, so the following climate data should be used with caution.

CLIMATE: Station #94085, Rabul, New Britain Is., Papua New Guinea, Lat. 4.2°S, Long. 152.2°E, at 28 ft. (9 m). Record extreme temperatures are 100°F (38°C) and 65°F (18°C).

N/HEMISPHERE	JAN	FEB	MAR	APR	MAY	JUN	JUL	AUG	SEP	OCT	NOV	DEC
°F AVG MAX	89	89	91	92	91	90	90	90	90	90	90	90
°F AVG MIN	73	72	73	73	73	73	73	73	73	73	73	73
DIURNAL RANGE	16	17	18	19	18	17	17	17	17	17	17	17
RAIN/INCHES	5.4	3.7	3.5	5.1	7.1	10.1	14.8	10.4	10.2	10.0	5.2	3.3
HUMIDITY/%	74	73	69	70	73	76	77	76	77	77	75	74
BLOOM SEASON												
DAYS CLR	N/A											
RAIN/MM	137	94	89	130	180	257	376	264	259	254	132	84
°C AVG MAX	31.7	31.7	32.8	33.3	32.8	32.2	32.2	32.2	32.2	32.2	32.2	32.2
°C AVG MIN	22.8	22.2	22.8	22.8	22.8	22.8	22.8	22.8	22.8	22.8	22.8	22.8
DIURNAL RANGE	8.9	9.5	10.0	10.5	10.0	9.4	9.4	9.4	9.4	9.4	9.4	9.4
S/HEMISPHERE	JUL	AUG	SEP	OCT	NOV	DEC	JAN	FEB	MAR	APR	MAY	JUN

Cultural Recommendations

LIGHT: 2500–3000 fc.

TEMPERATURES: Throughout the year, days average 89–92°F (32–33°C), and nights average 72–73°F (22–23°C), with a diurnal range of 16–19°F (9–11°C).

HUMIDITY: 70–80% most of the year. Humidity increases to 90–100% at night but drops as low as 35% during the hot afternoons.

WATER: Rainfall is moderate to heavy most of the year. Conditions are slightly drier for 2 months in late winter. Cultivated plants should be kept moist from spring into autumn, but water should be gradually reduced in late autumn.

FERTILIZER: ¼–½ recommended strength. A balanced fertilizer should be applied weekly to biweekly throughout the year.

REST PERIOD: Growing conditions should be maintained all year. Water and fertilizer should be reduced somewhat in winter, but plants should never be allowed to dry out completely. Fertilizer should be reduced anytime water is reduced. In the habitat, light may be slightly higher in winter.

GROWING MEDIA: Plants may be mounted on tree-fern or cork slabs if humidity is high and plants are watered at least once daily in summer. When plants are potted, any open, fast-draining medium may be used. Repotting may be done anytime new roots are growing.

MISCELLANEOUS NOTES: The bloom season shown in the climate table is based on reports from the habitat.

Plant and Flower Information

PLANT SIZE AND TYPE: A 14 in. (35 cm) sympodial epiphyte.

PSEUDOBULB: 14 in. (35 cm) long. The long, clustered stems do not branch. They are densely leafy.

LEAVES: Many. The shiny, lanceolate leaves are 4.3–5.5 in. (11–14 cm) long.

INFLORESCENCE: Short.

FLOWERS: 2 per inflorescence. The white flowers are 2.0–2.4 in. (5–6 cm) across. The lanceolate sepals and shorter petals taper to elongated points. The 3-lobed lip is shorter than the other segments. The midlobe is ruffled with a dense covering of hairlike appendages and a deeply cut or lacerated margin. The triangular sidelobes are somewhat sickle-shaped at the apex with a slightly toothed margin on the interior.

REFERENCES: 223, 443.

Dendrobium peguanum Lindley

AKA: Hunt (ref. 211) includes *D. pygmaeum* Lindley 1830 not Smith or A. Cunningham, and *D. wallichii* A. Hawkes and A. H. Heller. Seidenfaden, in a 1994 personal communication, states that *D. fesselianum* Wolff is a synonym.

ORIGIN/HABITAT: India and Burma. Plants are widespread in the hills of southwestern and southeastern India and the foothills of Sikkim at 1000–1300 ft. (300–400 m). In India, plants have been found in Orissa, Jaspur, Gujarat (The Dangs), Konkan, West Ghats, and North Kanara. In Burma, the habitat includes the western hills near the Indian border and along the eastern border with Thailand. Plants usually grow on rocks and secondary shrub vegetation near streams in warm, humid, tropical zones. The species has not been found in Thailand, but since it occurs in the Tenasserim region of Burma, Seidenfaden (ref. 454) suspects that it may also occur in the mountains of northwestern Thailand.

CLIMATE: Station #42398, Baghdogra (Shiliguri), India, Lat. 26.7°N, Long. 88.3°E, at 412 ft. (126 m). Temperatures are calculated for an elevation of 1200 ft. (370 m), resulting in probable extremes of 101°F (39°C) and 33°F (1°C).

Dendrobium pemae

N/HEMISPHERE	JAN	FEB	MAR	APR	MAY	JUN	JUL	AUG	SEP	OCT	NOV	DEC
°F AVG MAX	71	74	82	87	87	86	86	86	85	84	79	74
°F AVG MIN	47	51	57	65	70	73	74	74	73	67	57	50
DIURNAL RANGE	24	23	25	22	17	13	12	12	12	17	22	24
RAIN/INCHES	0.3	0.7	1.3	3.7	11.8	25.9	32.2	25.3	21.2	5.6	0.5	0.2
HUMIDITY/%	73	68	57	58	74	84	86	85	85	79	75	76
BLOOM SEASON									*	*		
DAYS CLR @ 6AM	21	18	15	11	5	0	1	1	4	13	23	19
DAYS CLR @ 12PM	23	16	16	11	2	2	0	1	2	10	21	18
RAIN/MM	8	18	33	94	300	658	818	643	538	142	13	5
°C AVG MAX	21.9	23.6	28.0	30.8	30.8	30.2	30.2	30.2	29.7	29.1	26.3	23.6
°C AVG MIN	8.6	10.8	14.1	18.6	21.3	23.0	23.6	23.6	23.0	19.7	14.1	10.2
DIURNAL RANGE	13.3	12.8	13.9	12.2	9.5	7.2	6.6	6.6	6.7	9.4	12.2	13.4
S/HEMISPHERE	JUL	AUG	SEP	OCT	NOV	DEC	JAN	FEB	MAR	APR	MAY	JUN

Cultural Recommendations

LIGHT: 2000–3000 fc. In the habitat, the heavy cloud cover associated with the summer monsoon results in relatively low light. Cultivated plants must be shaded during the brightest part of year, but light should be as high as the plants can tolerate, short of burning the foliage.

TEMPERATURES: Summer days average 86°F (30°C), and nights average 73–74°F (23–24°C), with a diurnal range of 12–13°F (7°C). The warmest weather occurs in spring. Days average 82–87°F (28–31°C), and nights average 57–70°F (14–21°C), with a diurnal range of 17–25°F (9–14°C).

HUMIDITY: Near 85% in summer, dropping to 55–60% in late winter and early spring.

WATER: Conditions are very wet for 5 months in summer, very dry for 5 months in winter, with short transition periods in autumn and spring. Cultivated plants should be kept evenly moist from spring to early autumn, but water should be gradually reduced after new growths mature in late autumn.

FERTILIZER: ¼–½ recommended strength, applied weekly. A high-nitrogen fertilizer is beneficial from spring to midsummer, but a fertilizer high in phosphates should be used in late summer and autumn. Plants from this habitat may be healthiest if given frequent feedings during the short growing season.

REST PERIOD: Winter days average 71–74°F (22–24°C), and nights average 47–51°F (9–11°C), with a diurnal range of 23–24°F (13°C). In the habitat, winter rainfall is low but additional moisture is often available from heavy deposits of dew. For about a month in late winter or early spring, however, humidity is so low that even the moisture from dew is uncommon. Cultivated plants should be allowed to dry out between waterings in winter, but they should not remain dry for extended periods. Occasional early morning mistings between waterings, especially on warm, sunny days, may help prevent the plants from becoming too dry. Fertilizer should be eliminated until water is increased in spring. In the habitat, light is highest in winter. The cool, dry rest with increased light may be necessary to initiate blooming.

GROWING MEDIA: Plants may be mounted on cork or tree-fern slabs if humidity is high and plants are watered at least once daily in summer. Plants may need to be misted several times a day when weather is hot and bright. If plants are potted, the medium must be open and fast draining. Medium-grade fir bark, cork nuggets, or tree-fern fiber are commonly used. Repotting is best done in early spring when new roots are growing.

MISCELLANEOUS NOTES: The bloom season shown in the climate table is based on cultivation records.

Plant and Flower Information

PLANT SIZE AND TYPE: A small, 5 in. (12 cm) sympodial plant.

PSEUDOBULB: 1.4–2.4 in. (3.6–6.0 cm) long. The stout, tufted pseudobulbs are ovoid to oblong-conical.

LEAVES: 2–4. The broadly elliptic to linear-oblong leaves are 1.4–3.0 in. (3.5–7.5 cm) long, leathery, and deciduous. Leaves occur at the apex of the pseudobulbs.

INFLORESCENCE: 1–3 in. (2.5–7.0 cm) long. One or more erect inflorescences emerge near the apex of leafless pseudobulbs shortly after leaf fall. The blossoms are clustered near the apex of the inflorescence.

FLOWERS: 1–3, rarely 7 per inflorescence. The flowers are 0.5 in. (1.2 cm) across. The white sepals and petals are sometimes flushed with purple. Blossoms have an erect dorsal sepal and sickle-shaped lateral sepals, with oblanceolate, somewhat sickle-shaped petals. The 3-lobed lip is tan or light brown with darker brown or purple lines. The deeply ruffled, pointed midlobe is suffused with amethyst or purple. It has a large, fleshy, rod-like callus between the long sidelobes. Blossoms are fragrant.

REFERENCES: 32, 38, 46, 157, 202, 211, 216, 254, 278, 330, 369, 424, 427, 445, 454.

PHOTOS/DRAWINGS: 254, 424, 427, 454.

Dendrobium pemae Schlechter.
Now considered a synonym of *Flickingeria pemae* (Schlechter) A. Hawkes. REFERENCES: 213, 221, 230, 231, 437, 445.

Dendrobium pendulicaule Hayata.
Now considered a synonym of *Thrixspermum pendulicaule* (Hayata) Schlechter. REFERENCES: 193, 208, 221, 275, 279, 445.

Dendrobium pendulum Roxburgh

AKA: *D. crassinode* Benson and Rchb. f., *D. melanophthalmum* Rchb. f. The International Orchid Commission (ref. 236) registers hybrids under the name *D. crassinode*.

ORIGIN/HABITAT: Widespread in Southeast Asia. The habitat includes the Lushai Hills region of northeastern India, the area near Lake Inle in Burma, and the mountains of northwestern Thailand. Plants are also reported in several locations in Laos, including the Vientiane and Xieng Khouang regions. In southwest China, plants grow in Yunnan Province. The orchids usually grow on rocks or tall trees in full sun at 4150–5250 ft. (1260–1600 m), but they have been found as low as 2500 ft. (760 m).

CLIMATE: Station #48300, Mae Hong Son, Thailand, Lat. 19.3°N, Long. 97.9°E, at 711 ft. (217 m). Temperatures are calculated for an elevation of 4000 ft. (1220 m), resulting in probable extremes of 97°F (36°C) and 32°F (0°C).

N/HEMISPHERE	JAN	FEB	MAR	APR	MAY	JUN	JUL	AUG	SEP	OCT	NOV	DEC
°F AVG MAX	75	79	86	87	84	78	76	76	77	79	77	74
°F AVG MIN	46	46	51	61	65	64	63	63	63	61	57	48
DIURNAL RANGE	29	33	35	26	19	14	13	13	14	18	20	26
RAIN/INCHES	0.4	0.2	0.3	1.7	6.1	7.1	9.6	9.9	8.1	3.9	1.2	0.4
HUMIDITY/%	67	60	50	50	68	81	82	83	83	82	75	71
BLOOM SEASON	*	**	**	*	*					*	*	*
DAYS CLR @ 7AM	2	8	10	9	3	0	0	0	0	1	1	2
DAYS CLR @ 1PM	20	20	20	13	3	0	0	0	0	3	13	17
RAIN/MM	10	5	8	43	155	180	244	251	206	99	30	10
°C AVG MAX	24.0	26.2	30.1	30.6	29.0	25.6	24.5	24.5	25.1	26.2	25.1	23.4
°C AVG MIN	7.9	7.9	10.6	16.2	18.4	17.9	17.3	17.3	17.3	16.2	14.0	9.0
DIURNAL RANGE	16.1	18.3	19.5	14.4	10.6	7.7	7.2	7.2	7.8	10.0	11.1	14.4
S/HEMISPHERE	JUL	AUG	SEP	OCT	NOV	DEC	JAN	FEB	MAR	APR	MAY	JUN

Cultural Recommendations

LIGHT: 3000–4000 fc. Plants grow full sun, but summer days are seldom clear, so light is naturally diffused. Growers indicated that plants grown in low light are not healthy and may die. Strong air movement is important.

TEMPERATURES: Summer days average 76–78°F (25–26°C), and nights average 63–64°F (17–18°C), with a diurnal range of 13–14°F (7–8°C). The warmest season is spring. Days average 84–87°F (29–31°C), and nights average 51–65°F (11–18°C), with a diurnal range of 19–35°F (11–20°C).

HUMIDITY: 80–85% from summer into autumn, dropping to 60–70% for most of the other months. However, for about 2 months in spring, conditions are very dry and humidity drops to 50%.

WATER: Rainfall is very heavy during the growing season, but winters are very dry. Cultivated plants should be kept moist while actively growing, but water should be gradually reduced after new growths mature in autumn.

FERTILIZER: ¼–½ recommended strength, applied weekly. A high-nitrogen fertilizer is beneficial from spring to midsummer, but a fertilizer high in phosphates should be used in late summer and autumn.

REST PERIOD: Winter days average 74–79°F (23–26°C), and nights average 46–48°F (8–9°C), with a diurnal range of 26–33°F (14–18°C). In the habitat, rainfall is low for 4–5 months in winter. For 2–3 of these months, high humidity and nightly cooling result in frequent, heavy deposits of dew with even more moisture available from fog and mist. Therefore, the driest season is only 1–2 months long. For cultivated plants, water should be reduced from late autumn to early spring. During most of the winter, plants should be allowed to dry out between waterings, but they should not remain completely dry for extended periods. Occasional early morning mistings between waterings may help prevent the plants from becoming too dry. For 1–2 months in late winter, however, water should be limited to occasional early morning mistings. Fertilizer should be reduced or eliminated, until new growth starts in spring. In the habitat, the large number of clear, winter afternoons indicates very bright conditions.

GROWING MEDIA: Mounting plants on tree-fern or cork slabs accommodates their pendulous growth habit. Growers recommend tree-fern blocks or small baskets. However, high humidity must be maintained, and the plants should be watered at least once daily in summer. When plants are potted or grown in baskets, any open, fast-draining medium may be used. Repotting is best done in early spring when new roots are growing.

MISCELLANEOUS NOTES: The bloom season shown in the climate table is based on cultivation records. In the habitat, plants bloom in late autumn or early winter. Growers indicate that plants do poorly in the tropical lowlands.

Plant and Flower Information

PLANT SIZE AND TYPE: A 6–24 in. (15–60 cm) sympodial epiphyte or lithophyte.

PSEUDOBULB: 6–24 in. (15–60 cm) long. The arching to pendulous stems, which are sometimes branching, often form a tangled mass. They are swollen at each node and resemble a string of inverted golf tees.

LEAVES: Many. The linear-lanceolate leaves are 4–5 in. (10–13 cm) long. They are thin and usually deciduous at the end of the growing season.

INFLORESCENCE: Short. Numerous inflorescences emerge from the upper nodes of old, leafless stems and the most recently matured pseudobulbs.

FLOWERS: 1–3 per inflorescence. The flowers are 1.6–2.8 in. (4–7 cm) across. The narrow sepals and broad petals are normally white with prominent, magenta-purple markings at the tips, but pure white clones with a yellow disk are known. The kidney-shaped lip is hairy on both sides. It is white with yellow on the basal half and amethyst at the tip. It may be marked with purple on each side of the throat. Flower color is variable. Flower substance is variably described as papery to waxy. Blossoms are fragrant and long-lasting.

HYBRIDIZING NOTES: Chromosome counts as *D. pendulum* are 2n = 38 (ref. 152, 243) and 2n = 2x (ref. 504). As *D. crassinode*, counts are 2n = 2x (ref. 187, 580) and 2n = 38 (ref. 151, 154, 187, 188, 504, 580). The plants known as *D. crassinode* and *D. wardianum* Warner hybridize naturally. Johansen (ref. 239) achieved a high percentage of successful self-pollinations. Of the seed produced, 93% contained visible embryos and 89% of the seed germinated. Capsules opened 366 days after pollination.

REFERENCES: 25, 36, 38, 46, 151, 152, 154, 157, 179, 187, 188, 190, 200, 202, 210, 216, 236, 239, 243, 245, 247, 254, 266, 369, 371, 430, 445, 447, 448, 454, 460, 504, 528, 541, 557, 570, 580.

PHOTOS/DRAWINGS: 36, 72, *133,* 210, *245, 247, 371, 430, 454,* 460.

Dendrobium pensile Ridley

AKA: Seidenfaden (ref. 454) reports that Schlechter considered *D. salaccense* (Blume) Lindley conspecific with *D. pensile,* but he questions this synonymy. In 1911 in *Fedde's Rept. Sp. Nov.* 9:286, Schlechter included *D. torquisepalum* Kränzlin as a synonym.

ORIGIN/HABITAT: Singapore, Johore and Pahang in Malaya, Sumatra, and Sabah, Borneo. In Malaya, plants grow on trees overhanging rivers or in old mangroves near the coast. In Sabah, plants grow in hill forests at about 2950 ft. (900 m).

CLIMATE: Station #49613, Tambuan, Sabah (North Borneo), Lat. 5.7°N, Long. 116.4°E, at 1200 ft. (366 m). Temperatures are calculated for an elevation of 3000 ft. (910 m), resulting in probable extremes of 92°F (33°C) and 48°F (9°C).

N/HEMISPHERE	JAN	FEB	MAR	APR	MAY	JUN	JUL	AUG	SEP	OCT	NOV	DEC
°F AVG MAX	80	81	83	84	84	83	83	83	83	82	81	80
°F AVG MIN	61	59	60	61	62	61	60	60	61	61	61	62
DIURNAL RANGE	19	22	23	23	22	22	23	23	22	21	20	18
RAIN/INCHES	5.8	3.7	5.8	7.5	8.2	7.3	5.1	4.9	6.4	7.0	6.8	6.0
HUMIDITY/%	N/A											
BLOOM SEASON	N/A											
DAYS CLR	N/A											
RAIN/MM	147	94	147	190	208	185	130	124	163	178	173	152
°C AVG MAX	26.7	27.3	28.4	28.9	28.9	28.4	28.4	28.4	28.4	27.8	27.3	26.7
°C AVG MIN	16.1	15.0	15.6	16.1	16.7	16.1	15.6	15.6	16.1	16.1	16.1	16.7
DIURNAL RANGE	10.6	12.3	12.8	12.8	12.2	12.3	12.8	12.8	12.3	11.7	11.2	10.0
S/HEMISPHERE	JUL	AUG	SEP	OCT	NOV	DEC	JAN	FEB	MAR	APR	MAY	JUN

Cultural Recommendations

LIGHT: 2000–3000 fc.

TEMPERATURES: Throughout the year, days average 80–84°F (27–29°C), and nights average 59–62°F (15–17°C), with a diurnal range of 18–23°F (10–13°C).

HUMIDITY: Information is not available for this location. However, records from nearby locations indicate that humidity probably averages 80–85% year-round.

WATER: Rainfall is moderate to heavy all year with a brief, slightly drier period in winter. Cultivated plants should be allowed to dry only slightly between waterings.

FERTILIZER: ¼–½ recommended strength. A balanced fertilizer should be applied weekly to biweekly throughout the year.

REST PERIOD: Growing conditions should be maintained all year. Water should be reduced slightly in winter, but the plants should never be allowed to dry out completely. Fertilizer should be reduced anytime plants are not actively growing.

GROWING MEDIA: Mounting plants on tree-fern or cork slabs accommodates their pendulous growth habit. However, humidity must be high and plants must be watered at least once a day in summer. If plants cannot be mounted, small pots or hanging baskets may be filled with an open, fast-draining medium. Repotting may be done anytime new roots are actively growing.

MISCELLANEOUS NOTES: Holttum (ref. 200) indicated that plants rarely bloom. The flowers are very short-lived, often lasting a day or even for only a few hours. Plants that produce flowers which last a single day commonly bloom several times during the year. Flowering usually occurs 7–14 days after a sudden 10°F (5°C) drop in daytime temperatures.

Plant and Flower Information

PLANT SIZE AND TYPE: A 24–47 in. (60–120 cm) sympodial epiphyte.

PSEUDOBULB: 24–47 in. (60–120 cm) long. A large number of hanging stems are covered with thick, fleshy leaves.

LEAVES: Many. The ovate-lanceolate leaves are 2.8–4.0 in. (7–10 cm) long and narrow to a blunt tip. They are fleshy and distichous.

INFLORESCENCE: Very short. Racemes emerge from the middle of an internode.

FLOWERS: 2 per inflorescence. The yellow blossoms, which may not open fully, are about 0.6 in. (1.5 cm) long. The lanceolate sepals curve forward, and the petals curve backward. The pubescent lip is marked with red on the midline. It has triangular sidelobes, a rough surface, and a recurved tip.

REFERENCES: 200, 254, 295, 395, 402, 434, 454, 455, 592.

PHOTOS/DRAWINGS: 455.

Dendrobium pentactis Kränzlin. See *D. insigne* (Blume) Rchb. f. ex Miquel. REFERENCES: 67, 220, 254, 270, 271, 437, 533.

Dendrobium pentagonum Kränzlin. See *D. brevicaule* Rolfe. REFERENCES: 220, 254, 385, 538.

Dendrobium pentanema Schlechter. Now considered a synonym of *Diplocaulobium pentanema* (Schlechter) Kränzlin. REFERENCES: 219, 220, 254, 437, 444, 445.

Dendrobium pentapterum Schlechter

AKA: *D. brevicaule* Kränzlin.

ORIGIN/HABITAT: Northern Papua New Guinea. Plants have a limited distribution that includes West Sepik, Western Highlands, Madang, and Morobe Provinces. They usually grow in lower mountain forests at 2600–6550 ft. (800–2000 m).

CLIMATE: Station #94010, Goroka, Papua New Guinea, Lat. 6.1°S, Long. 145.4°E, at 5141 ft. (1567 m). Record extreme temperatures are 87°F (31°C) and 43°F (6°C).

N/HEMISPHERE	JAN	FEB	MAR	APR	MAY	JUN	JUL	AUG	SEP	OCT	NOV	DEC
°F AVG MAX	76	77	78	79	79	78	79	78	78	78	79	77
°F AVG MIN	56	57	57	57	58	59	59	59	60	59	59	57
DIURNAL RANGE	20	20	21	22	21	19	20	19	18	19	20	20
RAIN/INCHES	2.1	2.8	4.6	5.9	6.6	9.3	9.1	10.1	10.7	8.3	4.6	2.0
HUMIDITY/%	70	67	67	67	67	71	72	73	74	71	70	70
BLOOM SEASON	*	*	*	*	*	*	*	*	*	*	*	*
DAYS CLR	N/A											
RAIN/MM	54	70	118	151	167	236	230	256	271	211	116	52
°C AVG MAX	24.7	25.1	25.6	26.2	26.2	25.7	25.8	25.6	25.5	25.6	25.9	25.1
°C AVG MIN	13.5	13.8	14.0	14.0	14.2	14.8	15.0	15.2	15.3	15.1	14.7	13.7
DIURNAL RANGE	11.2	11.3	11.6	12.3	12.0	10.9	10.8	10.4	10.2	10.5	11.2	11.4
S/HEMISPHERE	JUL	AUG	SEP	OCT	NOV	DEC	JAN	FEB	MAR	APR	MAY	JUN

Cultural Recommendations

LIGHT: 1500–2500 fc.

TEMPERATURES: Throughout the year, days average 76–79°F (25–26°C), and nights average 56–60°F (14–15°C), with a diurnal range of 18–22°F (10–12°C).

HUMIDITY: 70–75% from summer into autumn, dropping to 65–70% in winter and spring. Plants require excellent air movement.

WATER: Rainfall is moderate to heavy most of the year, but conditions are slightly drier for 3 months in winter. Cultivated plants should be kept moist but not soggy. Occasional early morning mistings may be beneficial, especially on bright, sunny days.

FERTILIZER: ¼–½ recommended strength. A balanced fertilizer should be applied weekly to biweekly throughout the year.

REST PERIOD: Growing temperatures should be maintained all year. In the habitat, rainfall is lowest in winter, but dew and mist from fog and low clouds are common. Water and fertilizer should be reduced somewhat for cultivated plants, especially those grown in the darker, short-day conditions common during temperate-latitude winters. Plants should be kept on the dry side, but they should never be allowed to dry out completely. In the habitat, light is higher in winter.

GROWING MEDIA: Plants may be mounted on tree-fern or cork slabs if humidity is high and plants are watered at least once daily in summer. When plants are potted, any open, fast-draining medium may be used. Repotting may be done anytime new roots are growing.

MISCELLANEOUS NOTES: The bloom season shown in the climate table is based on cultivation records. In nature, flowering occurs throughout year; and some plants bloom continuously. The plants grow in colonies, and a single host tree may contain hundreds of specimens.

Plant and Flower Information

PLANT SIZE AND TYPE: A 2.4–8.0 in. (6–20 cm) sympodial epiphyte.

PSEUDOBULB: 1.6–4.0 in. (4–10 cm) long. Stems may be ovoid or somewhat club-shaped. They are often covered with dried, persistent leaf sheaths. Growths emerge from a short, climbing rhizome as well as directly from the lower nodes of older stems.

LEAVES: 1–3 per growth. The linear to elliptic leaves are 0.8–3.7 in. (2.0–9.5 cm) long.

INFLORESCENCE: Short. Inflorescences emerge from apex of the pseudobulb. The flowers are nestled between the leaves.

FLOWERS: 1 per inflorescence, 2–3 per growth. The fan-shaped flowers, which open fully, are 0.8–1.4 in. (2.0–3.5 cm) long. They are pale greenish yellow, becoming creamy white with age. The anther cap and the apex of the greenish lip are marked with bright orange-red. The oblanceolate, pointed lip is obscurely 3-lobed with incurved margins. The apex of the lip is not recurved. Blossoms often last for several months.

REFERENCES: 92, 179, 196, 219, 254, 385, 437, 444, 445, 538, 556.

PHOTOS/DRAWINGS: *181, 385*, 437, 538, 556.

Dendrobium perakense Hooker f. Now considered a synonym of *Eria javanica* (Swartz) Blume. REFERENCES: 200, 202, 218, 254, 395, 445, 499, 536.

Dendrobium percnanthum Rchb. f.

ORIGIN/HABITAT: Seram Island in the Moluccas. Specific habitat location and elevation are not available, so the following climate data should be used with caution.

CLIMATE: Station #49620, Amahai, Seram, Indonesia, Lat. 3.3°S, Long. 128.9°E, at 10 ft. (3 m). Record extreme temperatures are 96°F (36°C) and 66°F (19°C).

N/HEMISPHERE	JAN	FEB	MAR	APR	MAY	JUN	JUL	AUG	SEP	OCT	NOV	DEC
°F AVG MAX	81	81	83	85	88	88	88	88	88	86	84	82
°F AVG MIN	74	74	74	74	75	76	76	76	76	76	75	74
DIURNAL RANGE	7	7	9	11	13	12	12	12	12	10	9	8
RAIN/INCHES	23.7	15.8	9.5	6.1	4.5	5.2	5.0	4.7	5.3	11.0	20.3	25.1
HUMIDITY/%	83	82	81	80	79	78	78	77	79	82	83	84
BLOOM SEASON	N/A											
DAYS CLR @ 9AM	1	1	1	6	7	4	3	3	5	5	3	3
DAYS CLR @ 3PM	1	1	2	5	6	1	1	1	2	3	1	3
RAIN/MM	602	401	241	155	114	132	127	119	135	279	516	638
°C AVG MAX	27.2	27.2	28.3	29.4	31.1	31.1	31.1	31.1	31.1	30.0	28.9	27.8
°C AVG MIN	23.3	23.3	23.3	23.3	23.9	24.4	24.4	24.4	24.4	24.4	23.9	23.3
DIURNAL RANGE	3.9	3.9	5.0	6.1	7.2	6.7	6.7	6.7	6.7	5.6	5.0	4.5
S/HEMISPHERE	JUL	AUG	SEP	OCT	NOV	DEC	JAN	FEB	MAR	APR	MAY	JUN

Cultural Recommendations

LIGHT: 2000–3000 fc. Clear days are rare, indicating that light levels are low.

TEMPERATURES: Throughout the year, days average 81–88°F (27–31°C), and nights average 74–76°F (23–24°C), with a diurnal range of 7–13°F (4–7°C).

HUMIDITY: 75–80% most of the year, increasing to near 85% in winter.

WATER: Rainfall is moderate to heavy all year, but conditions are somewhat drier in spring and summer. Cultivated plants should be kept moist but not soggy, with only slight drying allowed between waterings.

FERTILIZER: 1/4–1/2 recommended strength. A balanced fertilizer should be applied weekly to biweekly throughout the year.

REST PERIOD: Growing conditions should be maintained all year. In the habitat, winter is the wettest season; but water may be reduced somewhat for cultivated plants, especially those grown in the dark, short-day conditions common in temperate-latitude winters. Plants should never dry out completely between waterings, however. Fertilizer should be reduced or eliminated anytime water is reduced. In the habitat, light is highest in early spring.

GROWING MEDIA: Plants should probably be mounted on tree-fern or cork slabs if humidity is high and if the plants are watered at least once daily in summer. Fir bark or any open, fast-draining medium could be used for potting. Repotting may be done anytime new roots are growing.

MISCELLANEOUS NOTES: This species is known only from the type collection. It is unlikely to be available for cultivation.

Plant and Flower Information

PLANT SIZE AND TYPE: A 16 in. (40 cm) sympodial epiphyte that is known only from the type specimen.

PSEUDOBULB: 16 in. (40 cm) long. The shiny, bamboolike stems are grooved near the base.

INFLORESCENCE: About 5 inflorescences are produced on each growth. They are densely flowered.

FLOWERS: Many. The flowers are 0.8 in. (2 cm) or more long. Sepals and petals are sulfur yellow. The linear petals have a half twist. The somewhat fiddle-shaped, 3-lobed lip is white with yellow on the midlobe. The 3-ridged callus is brown with purple markings.

REFERENCES: 84, 218, 254, 348.

PHOTOS/DRAWINGS: 84.

Dendrobium per-dichaeae Kränzlin.
This name was mentioned by Kränzlin (ref. 254) in discussion of *D. pseudodichaea*. No additional information was found. REFERENCES: 254.

Dendrobium pére-fauriei Hayata. See *D. tosaense* Makino.
REFERENCES: 61, 194, 208, 222, 279.

Dendrobium pergracile Ames

ORIGIN/HABITAT: The Philippines. Plants grow near Lake Lanao on Mindanao Island. Habitat elevation is estimated based on topographical maps of the region, so the following climate data should be used with caution.

CLIMATE: Station #98751, Malaybalay, Mindanao, Philippines, Lat. 8.2°N, Long. 125.1°E, at 2106 ft. (642 m). Record extreme temperatures are 93°F (34°C) and 53°F (12°C).

N/HEMISPHERE	JAN	FEB	MAR	APR	MAY	JUN	JUL	AUG	SEP	OCT	NOV	DEC
°F AVG MAX	82	83	85	87	86	83	83	82	83	84	84	83
°F AVG MIN	64	64	64	65	66	66	66	66	66	66	66	65
DIURNAL RANGE	18	19	21	22	20	17	17	16	17	18	18	18
RAIN/INCHES	4.6	3.7	4.0	3.7	10.0	13.0	14.1	13.8	14.2	12.6	7.3	7.0
HUMIDITY/%	85	85	82	79	85	87	87	88	87	86	83	83
BLOOM SEASON			*									
DAYS CLR @ 8AM	5	5	11	17	10	7	7	4	5	9	8	10
DAYS CLR @ 2PM	2	1	3	3	1	1	1	1	2	1	1
RAIN/MM	117	94	102	94	254	330	358	351	361	320	185	178
°C AVG MAX	27.8	28.3	29.4	30.6	30.0	28.3	28.3	27.8	28.3	28.9	28.9	28.3
°C AVG MIN	17.8	17.8	17.8	18.3	18.9	18.9	18.9	18.9	18.9	18.9	18.9	18.3
DIURNAL RANGE	10.0	10.5	11.6	12.3	11.1	9.4	9.4	8.9	9.4	10.0	10.0	10.0
S/HEMISPHERE	JUL	AUG	SEP	OCT	NOV	DEC	JAN	FEB	MAR	APR	MAY	JUN

Cultural Recommendations

LIGHT: 2000–3000 fc.

TEMPERATURES: Throughout the year, days average 82–87°F (28–31°C), and nights average 64–66°F (18–19°C), with a diurnal range of 16–22°F (9–12°C).

HUMIDITY: 85–90% most of the year, falling briefly to near 80% in spring.

WATER: Rainfall is heavy most of the year but is somewhat less heavy in winter and early spring. Cultivated plants should be kept moist but not soggy.

FERTILIZER: 1/4–1/2 recommended strength. A balanced fertilizer should be applied weekly to biweekly throughout the year.

REST PERIOD: Growing temperatures should be maintained all year. Water and fertilizer should be reduced slightly in winter, especially for plants cultivated in the dark, short-day conditions common in temperate latitudes. Plants should dry slightly between waterings, but they should never be allowed to dry out completely. In the habitat, light is highest in winter.

GROWING MEDIA: Plants may be mounted on tree-fern or cork slabs if humidity is high and plants are watered at least once daily in summer. When plants are potted, any open, fast-draining medium may be used. Repotting may be done anytime new roots are growing.

MISCELLANEOUS NOTES: The bloom season shown in the climate table is based on collection reports.

Plant and Flower Information

PLANT SIZE AND TYPE: A 12–24 in. (30–60 cm) sympodial epiphyte.

PSEUDOBULB: 12–24 in. (30–60 cm) long. The unbranched stems are extremely slender.

LEAVES: The grasslike leaves are 5 in. (13 cm) long. They are linear, taper to a point, and have incurved side-margins.

INFLORESCENCE: Short. The racemes emerge from bracts.

FLOWERS: 2 per inflorescence. The small, white flowers are about 0.5 in. (1.3 cm) long. Sepals and petals are linear-lanceolate and taper to a point. The 3-lobed lip is hairy on the inside. It has 2 rough-textured scales at the base. The midlobe is fringed along the margin, but the side-lobe margins are smooth.

REFERENCES: 12, 13, 221.

Dendrobium perlongum Schlechter

ORIGIN/HABITAT: Northern Papua New Guinea. In the Ibo Range, plants grow on tall forest trees at about 3300 ft. (1000 m).

CLIMATE: Station #94010, Goroka, Papua New Guinea, Lat. 6.1°S, Long. 145.4°E, at 5141 ft. (1567 m). Temperatures are calculated for an elevation of 3300 ft. (1000 m). Record extreme temperatures are not available for this location.

N/HEMISPHERE	JAN	FEB	MAR	APR	MAY	JUN	JUL	AUG	SEP	OCT	NOV	DEC
°F AVG MAX	82	83	84	85	85	84	85	84	84	84	85	83
°F AVG MIN	62	63	63	63	64	65	65	65	66	65	65	63
DIURNAL RANGE	20	20	21	22	21	19	20	19	18	19	20	20
RAIN/INCHES	2.1	2.8	4.6	5.9	6.6	9.3	9.1	10.1	10.7	8.3	4.6	2.0
HUMIDITY/%	70	67	67	67	67	71	72	73	74	71	70	70
BLOOM SEASON						*						
DAYS CLR	N/A											
RAIN/MM	53	71	117	150	168	236	231	257	272	211	117	51
°C AVG MAX	27.9	28.4	29.0	29.5	29.5	29.0	29.5	29.0	29.0	29.0	29.5	28.4
°C AVG MIN	16.7	17.3	17.3	17.3	17.9	18.4	18.4	18.4	19.0	18.4	18.4	17.3
DIURNAL RANGE	11.2	11.1	11.7	12.2	11.6	10.6	11.1	10.6	10.0	10.6	11.1	11.1
S/HEMISPHERE	JUL	AUG	SEP	OCT	NOV	DEC	JAN	FEB	MAR	APR	MAY	JUN

Cultural Recommendations

LIGHT: 2500–3500 fc.

TEMPERATURES: Throughout the year, days average 82–85°F (28–30°C), and nights average 62–66°F (17–19°C), with a diurnal range of 18–22°F (10–12°C). The very small seasonal variation indicates that plants are unlikely to be healthy under widely fluctuating temperatures.

HUMIDITY: 70–75% in summer and autumn, dropping to 65–70% in winter and spring.

WATER: Rainfall is moderate to heavy most of the year, but conditions are slightly drier for 3 months in winter. Cultivated plants should be kept moist but not soggy. Occasional early morning mistings may be beneficial, especially on bright, sunny days.

FERTILIZER: ¼–½ recommended strength. A balanced fertilizer should be applied weekly to biweekly throughout the year.

REST PERIOD: Growing temperatures should be maintained all year. In the habitat, rainfall is lowest in winter, but dew and mist from fog and low clouds are common. Water and fertilizer should be reduced somewhat for cultivated plants, especially those grown in the darker, short-day conditions common during temperate-latitude winters. Plants should be kept on the dry side, but they should never be allowed to dry out completely. In the habitat, light is higher in winter.

GROWING MEDIA: Plants may be mounted on tree-fern or cork slabs if humidity is high and plants are watered at least once daily in summer. When plants are potted, any open, fast-draining medium may be used. Repotting may be done anytime new roots are growing.

MISCELLANEOUS NOTES: The bloom season shown in the climate table is based on reports from the habitat. Plants that produce flowers which last a single day commonly bloom several times during the year. Flowering usually occurs 7–14 days after a sudden 10°F (5°C) drop in daytime temperatures.

Plant and Flower Information

PLANT SIZE AND TYPE: A 118 in. (300 cm) sympodial epiphyte.

PSEUDOBULB: 118 in. (300 cm) long. The densely leafy stems do not branch.

LEAVES: Many. The lanceolate leaves are 5–7 in. (13–18 cm) long.

INFLORESCENCE: Long. Pendent inflorescences emerge from nodes at the side of the stem.

FLOWERS: 2 per inflorescence. The flowers are 0.9 in. (2.2 cm) long and do not open fully. The cream-white sepals and petals are oblong, fleshy, incurved, and thickened at the tips. The small, 3-lobed lip is yellowish with an orange-red central band and brownish sidelobes. The pointed tip is recurled. The margin of the midlobe is wavy to scalloped. Blossoms are short-lived.

REFERENCES: 92, 221, 437, 445.

PHOTOS/DRAWINGS: 437.

Dendrobium perpusillum Balakrishnan. Sometimes spelled *D. perusillum*, see *D. pachyphyllum* (Kuntze) Bakhuizen f. REFERENCES: 31, 231, 454.

Dendrobium perula Rchb. f.

ORIGIN/HABITAT: The Assam region of northeastern India. Habitat elevation is estimated, so the following climate data should be used with caution.

CLIMATE: Station #42410, Gauhati, India, Lat. 26.1°N, Long. 91.6°E, at 158 ft. (48 m). Temperatures have been calculated for an estimated habitat elevation of 2000 ft. (610 m), resulting in probable extremes of 98°F (37°C) and 35°F (2°C).

N/HEMISPHERE	JAN	FEB	MAR	APR	MAY	JUN	JUL	AUG	SEP	OCT	NOV	DEC
°F AVG MAX	70	72	80	82	82	83	84	84	83	81	75	70
°F AVG MIN	45	48	54	62	66	71	72	72	70	65	55	47
DIURNAL RANGE	25	24	26	20	16	12	12	12	13	16	20	23
RAIN/INCHES	0.4	1.2	2.0	5.7	9.3	12.3	12.3	10.3	6.6	2.8	0.6	0.2
HUMIDITY/%	79	72	64	71	82	85	85	86	79	84	84	83
BLOOM SEASON	N/A											
DAYS CLR @ 6AM	6	12	16	11	3	0	0	1	3	7	6	3
DAYS CLR @ 12PM	17	16	18	15	6	1	0	0	2	11	17	19
RAIN/MM	10	30	51	145	236	312	312	262	168	71	15	5
°C AVG MAX	21.1	22.2	26.6	27.7	27.7	28.3	28.8	28.8	28.3	27.2	23.8	21.1
°C AVG MIN	7.2	8.8	12.2	16.6	18.8	21.6	22.2	22.2	21.1	18.3	12.7	8.3
DIURNAL RANGE	13.9	13.4	14.4	11.1	8.9	6.7	6.6	6.6	7.2	8.9	11.1	12.8
S/HEMISPHERE	JUL	AUG	SEP	OCT	NOV	DEC	JAN	FEB	MAR	APR	MAY	JUN

Cultural Recommendations

LIGHT: 2500–3500 fc.

TEMPERATURES: Summer days average 83–84°F (28–29°C), and nights average 71–72°F (22°C), with a diurnal range of 12°F (7°C).

HUMIDITY: 80–85% most of the year, dropping to 65–70% for 3 months in winter.

WATER: Rainfall is heavy from spring through summer but decreases rapidly in autumn with a 1–2 month transition into the winter dry season. Cultivated plants should be kept moist while actively growing, but water should be gradually reduced after new growths mature in autumn.

FERTILIZER: ¼–½ recommended strength, applied weekly. A high-nitrogen fertilizer is beneficial from spring to midsummer, but a fertilizer high in phosphates should be used in late summer and autumn.

REST PERIOD: Winter days average 70–72°F (21–22°C), and nights average 45–48°F (7–9°C), with a diurnal range of 23–25°F (13–14°C). Although rainfall is low for 4–5 winter months, high humidity and the large temperature range indicate that additional moisture from heavy dew is common. In cultivation, water should be greatly reduced and the plants allowed to dry out between waterings from late autumn into early spring. They should not remain dry for extended periods, however. Occasional mistings between waterings during bright, sunny weather may help prevent the plants from becoming too dry. Fertilizer should be reduced or eliminated until active growth resumes and water is increased in spring. In the habitat, light is brightest in winter.

GROWING MEDIA: Plants may be mounted on tree-fern or cork slabs if humidity is high and plants are watered at least once daily in summer. When plants are potted, any open, fast-draining medium may be used. Repotting is best done in early spring when new roots are growing.

Plant and Flower Information

PLANT SIZE AND TYPE: A 12 in. (30 cm) sympodial epiphyte.

PSEUDOBULB: 12 in. (30 cm) long. The incurved, cylindrical stems are swollen at the base and thickened above. They may be irregularly zigzag or somewhat twisted. The short internodes are covered with green sheaths.

LEAVES: Several. The oblong-lanceolate leaves are about 3.2 in. (8 cm) long. Leaves are held on the upper part of each stem.

INFLORESCENCE: 1–2 in. (2.5–5.0 cm) long. Several inflorescences emerge below the apical nodes. The rachis is pink, and the ovary is green.

FLOWERS: 2–6 or more per inflorescence. The flowers are 1 in. (2.5 cm) long. Lateral sepals are triangular. The dorsal sepal and petals may be ovate to nearly round. The dark, red-purple and sulfur-yellow flowers have orange veins. The lip midlobe is ruffled. The callus is shaped like a half-moon. The spur is yellow-green with a rounded tip.

REFERENCES: 38, 46, 200, 202, 216, 254, 369.

Dendrobium perulatum Gagnepain

AKA: In 1992 *Opera Botanica* 114, Seidenfaden indicates that *D. perulatum* is very close to *D. bensonae* Rchb. f., but he maintains them as separate species.

ORIGIN/HABITAT: Vietnam. Plants grow near Djiring in Haut-Donnai Province. Habitat elevation is not available, so the following climate data should be used with caution.

CLIMATE: Station #48881, Dalat, Vietnam, Lat. 11.1°N, Long. 108.1°E, at 3156 ft. (962 m). Record extreme temperatures are 93°F (34°C) and 43°F (6°C).

N/HEMISPHERE	JAN	FEB	MAR	APR	MAY	JUN	JUL	AUG	SEP	OCT	NOV	DEC
°F AVG MAX	80	82	84	85	84	81	81	80	80	80	79	79
°F AVG MIN	56	57	59	62	65	65	65	65	65	63	60	58
DIURNAL RANGE	24	25	25	23	19	16	16	15	15	17	19	21
RAIN/INCHES	0.2	0.9	1.6	4.6	9.1	6.1	7.7	8.2	10.1	9.7	2.7	1.3
HUMIDITY/%	68	64	65	71	78	81	82	83	84	82	76	73
BLOOM SEASON	N/A											
DAYS CLR @ 7AM	13	13	13	9	5	3	2	2	2	5	7	10
DAYS CLR @ 1PM	8	8	8	2	0	0	0	0	0	1	3	4
RAIN/MM	5	23	41	117	231	155	196	208	257	246	69	33
°C AVG MAX	26.7	27.8	28.9	29.4	28.9	27.2	27.2	26.7	26.7	26.7	26.1	26.1
°C AVG MIN	13.3	13.9	15.0	16.7	18.3	18.3	18.3	18.3	18.3	17.2	15.6	14.4
DIURNAL RANGE	13.4	13.9	13.9	12.7	10.6	8.9	8.9	8.4	8.4	9.5	10.5	11.7
S/HEMISPHERE	JUL	AUG	SEP	OCT	NOV	DEC	JAN	FEB	MAR	APR	MAY	JUN

Cultural Recommendations

LIGHT: 2000–3000 fc.

TEMPERATURES: Summer days average 80–81°F (27°C), and nights average 65°F (18°C), with a diurnal range of 15–16°F (8–9°C). The warmest temperatures occur in late winter and spring. Days average 84–85°F (29°C), and nights average 59–65°F (15–18°C), with a diurnal range of 19–25°F (11–14°C).

HUMIDITY: 80–85% in summer, dropping to near 65% in late winter.

WATER: Rainfall is moderate to heavy in summer but is very light for 2 months in winter. Cultivated plants should be kept moist while growing, but water should be gradually reduced after new growths mature in autumn.

FERTILIZER: ¼–½ recommended strength, applied weekly. A high-nitrogen fertilizer is beneficial from spring to midsummer, but a fertilizer high in phosphates should be used in late summer and autumn.

REST PERIOD: Winter days average 79–82°F (26–28°C), and nights average 56–58°F (13–14°C), with a diurnal range of 21–25°F (12–14°C). The increased diurnal range results from warmer days and cooler nights. Rainfall is low for 3–4 months. For 1–2 of these months, conditions are so dry that even moisture from dew is uncommon. For cultivated plants, water and fertilizer should be reduced for 2–3 months. Plants should be allowed to dry out between waterings, but they should not remain dry for extended periods. In the habitat, light is highest in winter.

GROWING MEDIA: Plants may be mounted on tree-fern or cork slabs if humidity is high and plants are watered at least once daily in summer. When plants are potted, any open, fast-draining medium may be used. Repotting is best done in early spring when new roots are growing.

Plant and Flower Information

PLANT SIZE AND TYPE: A 12 in. (30 cm) sympodial epiphyte.

PSEUDOBULB: 12 in. (30 cm) long. The nearly cylindrical stems are swollen in the middle or near the apex. They are covered with fibrous sheaths.

LEAVES: The pointed, lanceolate leaves are 4 in. (10 cm) long.

INFLORESCENCE: Short. Inflorescences emerge laterally from leafless stems.

FLOWERS: 2–3 per inflorescence. The white flowers are 1.6–2.0 in. (4–5 cm) across. The lateral sepals are suberect. The large, 3-lobed lip is yellow near the base. The sidelobes are inconspicuous. Flowers are similar to *D. heterocarpum* Wallich ex Lindley, which has a fragrance resembling that of *Primula officinalis*. *D. perulatum*, however, has no fragrance.

REFERENCES: 138, 227, 448.

Dendrobium petiolatum Schlechter

AKA: *D. unifoliatum* Schlechter.

ORIGIN/HABITAT: Widely distributed but not common in Papua New Guinea, New Britain, and the Solomon Islands. Plants usually grow in very shady areas on the mossy horizontal branches of mistforest trees at 2600–7850 ft. (800–2400 m).

CLIMATE: Station #94010, Goroka, Papua New Guinea, Lat. 6.1°S, Long. 145.4°E, at 5141 ft. (1567 m). Temperatures are calculated for an elevation of 6550 ft. (2000 m), resulting in probable extremes of 82°F (28°C) and 38°F (4°C).

N/HEMISPHERE	JAN	FEB	MAR	APR	MAY	JUN	JUL	AUG	SEP	OCT	NOV	DEC
°F AVG MAX	71	72	73	74	74	73	74	73	73	73	74	72
°F AVG MIN	51	52	52	52	53	54	54	54	55	54	54	52
DIURNAL RANGE	20	20	21	22	21	19	20	19	18	19	20	20
RAIN/INCHES	2.1	2.8	4.6	5.9	6.6	9.3	9.1	10.1	10.7	8.3	4.6	2.0
HUMIDITY/%	70	67	67	67	67	71	72	73	74	71	70	70
BLOOM SEASON			*		*	*	*	*	*			
DAYS CLR	N/A											
RAIN/MM	53	71	117	150	168	236	231	257	272	211	117	51
°C AVG MAX	21.8	22.4	23.0	23.5	23.5	23.0	23.5	23.0	23.0	23.0	23.5	22.4
°C AVG MIN	10.7	11.3	11.3	11.3	11.8	12.4	12.4	12.4	13.0	12.4	12.4	11.3
DIURNAL RANGE	11.1	11.1	11.7	12.2	11.7	10.6	11.1	10.6	10.0	10.6	11.1	11.1
S/HEMISPHERE	JUL	AUG	SEP	OCT	NOV	DEC	JAN	FEB	MAR	APR	MAY	JUN

Cultural Recommendations

LIGHT: 1200–2300 fc.

TEMPERATURES: Throughout the year, days average 71–74°F (22–24°C), and nights average 51–55°F (11–13°C), with a diurnal range of 18–22°F (10–12°C).

HUMIDITY: 70–75% most of the year, dropping to near 65% in late winter and spring. Excellent air movement is essential. Growers indicate that *D. petiolatum* requires a delicate balance between air movement, moisture, and drainage.

WATER: Rainfall is moderate to heavy most of the year, but conditions are slightly drier for 3 months in winter. Cultivated plants should be kept

Dendrobium petri

moist but not soggy. Occasional early morning mistings may be beneficial, especially on bright, sunny days.

FERTILIZER: ¼–½ recommended strength. A balanced fertilizer should be applied weekly to biweekly throughout the year.

REST PERIOD: Growing temperatures should be maintained all year. In the habitat, rainfall is lowest in winter, but dew and mist from fog and low clouds are common. Water and fertilizer should be reduced somewhat for cultivated plants, especially those grown in the darker, short-day conditions common during temperate-latitude winters. Plants should be kept on the dry side, but they should never be allowed to dry out completely. In the habitat, light is higher in winter.

GROWING MEDIA: Plants may be mounted on tree-fern or potted in any open, fast-draining medium. If mounted, humidity must be high and the plants should be watered at least once daily in summer. During hot weather, a very fine cooling mist with constant air movement is nearly essential. We pot seedlings of small, high-altitude species in live sphagnum moss over a layer of bark. This medium has produced good top growth and long healthy roots. Repotting may be done anytime new roots are growing.

MISCELLANEOUS NOTES: The bloom season shown in the climate table is based on cultivation records.

Plant and Flower Information

PLANT SIZE AND TYPE: A 4–6 in. (10–15 cm) sympodial epiphyte.

PSEUDOBULB: 0.8–1.2 in. (2–3 cm) long. Pseudobulbs may be larger or smaller. The very low growing plants may be erect or suberect. The pseudobulbs are covered with the fibers of persistent leaf sheaths.

LEAVES: 1 per growth. Small cultivated plants may develop 2 leaves per pseudobulb. The oblong-elliptic leaves are 1.2–2.0 in. (3–5 cm) long. Leaf shape varies with growing conditions. The leaf has a distinct stem.

INFLORESCENCE: Short. The racemes emerge at the apex or from nodes along the side of leafless pseudobulbs. Inflorescences are densely flowered.

FLOWERS: 4–20 per inflorescence, rarely fewer on small cultivated plants. The flowers are 0.6–0.8 in. (1.4–2.1 cm) long and do not open fully. The slender, sharply pointed sepals and petals have distinct keels. They are bright purple. The bright purple lip has yellow or orange at the sharply pointed tip.

HYBRIDIZING NOTES: Chromosome count is 2n = 38 (ref. 153, 273).

REFERENCES: 153, 179, 221, 271, 273, 385, 437, 445, 556.

PHOTOS/DRAWINGS: *385*, 437, *556*.

Dendrobium petri Rchb. f. See *D. mooreanum* Lindley.
REFERENCES: 83, 216, 254, 270.

Dendrobium petrophilum (Kränzlin) Garay ex Hallé.
Now considered a synonym of *Eria petrophila* Rchb. f. REFERENCES: 173, 233.

Dendrobium phaeanthum Schlechter

AKA: Sometimes spelled *D. pheianthum*.

ORIGIN/HABITAT: Northeastern Papua New Guinea. In the Waria District of the Maboro Range, plants grow on forest trees at about 3950 ft. (1200 m).

CLIMATE: Station #200192, Garaina, Papua New Guinea, Lat. 7.9°S, Long. 147.1°E, at 2350 ft. (716 m). Temperatures are calculated for an elevation of 3950 ft. (1200 m), resulting in probable extremes of 89°F (32°C) and 41°F (5°C).

N/HEMISPHERE	JAN	FEB	MAR	APR	MAY	JUN	JUL	AUG	SEP	OCT	NOV	DEC
°F AVG MAX	75	77	78	79	80	80	80	80	79	79	78	76
°F AVG MIN	58	58	58	59	58	59	60	60	60	59	59	58
DIURNAL RANGE	17	19	20	20	22	21	20	20	19	20	19	18
RAIN/INCHES	5.8	6.5	8.7	11.1	11.8	11.9	8.9	11.7	11.5	9.9	7.7	5.2
HUMIDITY/%	84	82	82	81	80	80	81	81	82	83	84	84
BLOOM SEASON												*
DAYS CLR	N/A											
RAIN/MM	147	165	221	282	300	302	226	297	292	251	196	132
°C AVG MAX	23.8	24.9	25.4	26.0	26.5	26.5	26.5	26.5	26.0	26.0	25.4	24.3
°C AVG MIN	14.3	14.3	14.3	14.9	14.3	14.9	15.4	15.4	15.4	14.9	14.9	14.3
DIURNAL RANGE	9.5	10.6	11.1	11.1	12.2	11.6	11.1	11.1	10.6	11.1	10.5	10.0
S/HEMISPHERE	JUL	AUG	SEP	OCT	NOV	DEC	JAN	FEB	MAR	APR	MAY	JUN

Cultural Recommendations

LIGHT: 2000–3000 fc.

TEMPERATURES: Throughout the year, days average 75–80°F (24–27°C), and nights average 58–60°F (14–15°C), with a diurnal range of 17–22°F (10–12°C).

HUMIDITY: 80–85% year-round.

WATER: Rainfall is heavy all year, but conditions are slightly drier in winter. Cultivated plants should be kept moist but not soggy.

FERTILIZER: ¼–½ recommended strength. A balanced fertilizer should be applied weekly to biweekly throughout the year. The Royal Botanic Garden in Edinburgh uses a seaweed based fertilizer for high elevation plants from New Guinea.

REST PERIOD: Growing conditions should be maintained all year. In the habitat, rainfall is slightly lower in winter. Water and fertilizer should be reduced somewhat for cultivated plants, especially those grown in the dark, short-day conditions common during temperate-latitude winters. They should never be allowed to dry out completely, however. In the habitat, seasonal light variation is minor.

GROWING MEDIA: Plants may be mounted on tree-fern or cork slabs if humidity is high and plants are watered at least once daily in summer. When plants are potted, any open, fast-draining medium may be used. Repotting may be done anytime new roots are growing.

MISCELLANEOUS NOTES: The bloom season shown in the climate table is based on reports from the habitat. Plants that produce flowers which last a single day commonly bloom several times during the year. Flowering usually occurs 7–14 days after a sudden 10°F (5°C) drop in daytime temperatures.

Plant and Flower Information

PLANT SIZE AND TYPE: A 16 in. (40 cm) sympodial epiphyte.

PSEUDOBULB: 14 in. (35 cm) long. The erect pseudobulbs are very flattened. They arise from a short, often climbing rhizome.

LEAVES: Many. The erect-spreading leaves are 2–3 in. (5–8 cm) long.

INFLORESCENCE: Short.

FLOWERS: 2 per inflorescence. The flowers are 1 in. (2.5 cm) across and do not open fully. Sepals and petals are brownish. The elongated, lanceolate sepals are bumpy on the backside. The 3-lobed lip is whitish with a tuft of long hairs near the apex and long projections along the front margin of the midlobe. The central keel is somewhat toothed near the apex. The column is pale brown in front with red spots. Blossoms are short-lived.

REFERENCES: 92, 221, 437, 445.

PHOTOS/DRAWINGS: 437.

Dendrobium phalaenopsis Fitzgerald

AKA: Normally considered synonymous with or a variety of *D. bigibbum* Lindley, Clements (ref. 67) includes both *D. phalaenopsis* and *D. bigibbum* as separate species. He includes *D. bigibbum* var. *macranthum* F.

Dendrobium phalaenopsis

M. Bailey, *D. bigibbum* var. *phalaenopsis* (Fitzgerald) F. M. Bailey, and *D. bigibbum* var. *superbum* Hort. ex Rchb. f. as synonyms. Clements considers *D. phalaenopsis* Fitzgerald var. *compactum* C. White to be a synonym of *D. lithocola* D. Jones and M. Clements and *D. phalaenopsis* Fitzgerald var. *statterainum* Hort. ex Sander to be a synonym of *D. bigibbum*. The plants known as *D. phalaenopsis* from the islands off West Irian he refers to *D. striaenopsis* M. Clements and D. Jones. The International Orchid Commission (ref. 236) lists *D. schroederianum* as a synonym and registers hybrids under the name *D. phalaenopsis*.

ORIGIN/HABITAT: Northeast Australia. Plants grow on the Cape York Peninsula in the coastal ranges between Mt. Malloy and the Iron Range. Plants grow in very bright conditions on small trees and rocks in fairly open forests. They are normally found in semiarid regions below 2000 ft. (610 m).

CLIMATE: Station #94283, Cooktown, Australia, Lat. 15.5°S, Long. 145.2°E, at 24 ft. (7 m). Temperatures are calculated for an elevation of 1000 ft. (305 m), resulting in probable extremes of 101°F (39°C) and 43°F (6°C).

N/HEMISPHERE	JAN	FEB	MAR	APR	MAY	JUN	JUL	AUG	SEP	OCT	NOV	DEC
°F AVG MAX	76	77	79	82	85	86	86	85	83	82	79	77
°F AVG MIN	63	64	67	70	72	72	72	72	72	70	67	65
DIURNAL RANGE	13	13	12	12	13	14	14	13	11	12	12	12
RAIN/INCHES	0.9	1.2	0.6	1.0	2.5	6.6	14.4	13.7	15.3	8.8	2.8	2.0
HUMIDITY/%	73	69	68	67	68	71	75	76	77	75	74	75
BLOOM SEASON	*						*	*	*	*	*	*
DAYS CLR	N/A											
RAIN/MM	23	30	15	25	64	168	366	348	389	224	71	51
°C AVG MAX	24.3	24.9	26.0	27.7	29.3	29.9	29.9	29.3	28.2	27.7	26.0	24.9
°C AVG MIN	17.1	17.7	19.3	21.0	22.1	22.1	22.1	22.1	22.1	21.0	19.3	18.2
DIURNAL RANGE	7.2	7.2	6.7	6.7	7.2	7.8	7.8	7.2	6.1	6.7	6.7	6.7
S/HEMISPHERE	JUL	AUG	SEP	OCT	NOV	DEC	JAN	FEB	MAR	APR	MAY	JUN

Cultural Recommendations

LIGHT: 3000–4500 fc. Seasonal light variation is minor at this latitude, but in the habitat, winter light is higher because weather is often clear. For cultivated plants, high light and strong air movement are vitally important year-round.

TEMPERATURES: Summer days average 85–86°F (29–30°C), and nights average 72°F (22°C), with a diurnal range of 13–14°F (7–8°C). The diurnal range varies only 3°F (2°C) all year.

HUMIDITY: Near 70–75% most of the year, dropping to 65–70% in late winter and spring.

WATER: Rainfall is moderate to heavy during summer and early autumn, but conditions are much drier in winter. Cultivated plants should be kept moist while actively growing, but water should be gradually reduced in autumn. Australian growers recommend a daily morning misting in summer, even for pot-grown plants, with evening mistings also given when temperatures are above 91°F (33°C).

FERTILIZER: ¼–½ recommended strength, applied weekly. A high nitrogen fertilizer is beneficial from spring to midsummer, while a fertilizer high in phosphates should be used in late summer and autumn.

REST PERIOD: Winter days average 76–79°F (24–26°C), and nights average 63–67°F (17–19°C), with a diurnal range of 12–13°F (7°C). For 4 months in winter and spring, rainfall is low. The low humidity indicates that even moisture from dew is uncommon. In cultivation, the dry rest should be started after flowering. Plants should be allowed to dry out between waterings, but they should not remain completely dry for extended periods because they are very slow to recover if allowed to shrivel. Occasional early morning mistings between waterings may help keep plants from becoming too dry. After new growth is evident in spring, water should be gradually increased. Because new growths are very susceptible to infection and rot, care must be taken to keep water off of them until they are 2–3 in. (5–8 cm) tall. Light should be as high as possible in winter. Fertilizer should be eliminated or greatly reduced. In the habitat, light is highest in winter.

GROWING MEDIA: Plants may be mounted on tree-fern or cork slabs if humidity is high and plants are watered at least daily in summer. When plants are potted, excellent drainage in necessary, so a very open and fast-draining medium such as medium cork nuggets or fir bark should be used. A small clay pot that appears to be undersized for the plant usually produces better results. Plants tend to be top heavy. Staking the plant helps support new canes. Repotting is best done when flowering is completed or just as new growth starts in late winter or early spring.

MISCELLANEOUS NOTES: The bloom season shown in the climate table is based on records from the habitat. Cultivation records indicate heaviest blooming in autumn. Growers report that plants do poorly in areas with low winter light and that insufficient light causes buds to drop. *D. phalaenopsis* is often considered difficult to grow and bloom because it requires high light, warm winter temperatures, and the winter dry season, a combination that is sometimes difficult to provide in a general collection.

Plant and Flower Information

PLANT SIZE AND TYPE: A slender, 16–48 in. (40–122 cm) sympodial epiphyte or lithophyte that is very similar to *D. bigibbum*. Plants seldom develop into specimen plants as they are very prone to die-back.

PSEUDOBULB: 16–48 in. (40–122 cm) long. The cylindrical stems are slightly swollen at the base. The apical 30% of the stem is leafy. Stems that die back at the base may produce new plants near the apex.

LEAVES: 3–5, rarely 12. The oblong-lanceolate leaves are 3–6 in. (8–15 cm) long. They are leathery, rigid, and flushed with red or purple. Leaves last for 2 years.

INFLORESCENCE: 8–16 in. (20–40 cm) long. Over a period of several years, each growth produces 1–4 inflorescences from nodes near the apex of the pseudobulb even after stems are leafless. The inflorescences are usually arching or horizontal, but they may be pendent. Flowers are nicely spaced along the upper half of the raceme.

FLOWERS: 3–20 per inflorescence. The showy flowers are 1.4–2.8 in. (3.5–7.0 cm) across with broad overlapping sepals and petals and a heavy texture. They are similar to *D. bigibbum,* but *D. phalaenopsis* blossoms are slightly larger with sepals and petals that are recurved only slightly and a lip midlobe that is usually longer and pointed instead of more or less rounded. Flowers are normally deep lilac, but they may be white, pale lilac, magenta, or purple. All colors are bright and rich. The lip is usually a darker shade of the same color as the sepals and petals, with deeper color in the throat and stripes on the oblong, pointed midlobe. The sidelobes are arching. The spur is broad. Blossoms are highly variable in size and color. If they do not become water spotted, flowers last for months, so that plants are in nearly continuous bloom.

HYBRIDIZING NOTES: Chromosome counts are $n = 19$ and $2n = 38$ as *D. phalaenopsis* Fitzgerald (ref. 154, 187, 188, 504, 580) and *D. bigibbum* Lindley var. *superbum* Hort. Named clones of *D. phalaenopsis* had variable counts including $n = 19$ (ref. 580), $n = 38$ (ref. 580), and $n =$ variable (ref. 580), $2n = 38$ (ref. 580), $2n = 76$ (ref. 580), $2n =$ about 76 (ref. 580), and $2n = 76\pm1$ (ref. 504, 580). Johansen (ref. 239) indicates that the seeds produced when *D. phalaenopsis* was self-pollinated contained no visible embryos and no seeds germinated. Capsules opened 197 days after pollination. Seeds are sufficiently mature for green-pod sowing in 120–140 days.

REFERENCES: 6, 25, 36, 43, 44, 67, 69, 105, 112, 116, 151, 154, 172, 179, 187, 188, 190, 196, 200, 216, 236, 239, 254, 272, 311, 326, 351, 355, 389, 405, 421, 425, 430, 445, 458, 504, 510, 526, 533, 541, 557, 568, 570, 580.

PHOTOS/DRAWINGS: *36, 42, 114, 116, 172, 200, 246, 311, 351, 355, 389, 405, 430, 458, 541, 557, 568, 597.*

Dendrobium phalangillum J. J. Smith.
Now considered a synonym of *Diplocaulobium phalangillum* (J. J. Smith) Kränzlin. REFERENCES: 219, 220, 254, 470.

Dendrobium phalangium Schlechter.
Now considered a synonym of *Diplocaulobium phalangium* (Schlechter) Kränzlin. REFERENCES: 219, 220, 254, 437, 444, 445.

Dendrobium philippinense Ames

AKA: *D. aciculare* Lindley is often listed as a synonym, but Seidenfaden (ref. 450) specifically excludes this synonymy.

ORIGIN/HABITAT: Southeast Asia. The habitat extends from Malaya to the northern Philippine Islands, where plants grow at low elevations on Leyte, Luzon, Mindoro, Panay, and the Polillo Islands. The plants are widespread on Luzon Island and are found in the provinces of Bataan, Bulacan, Laguna, Quezon, Rizal, and Zambales. Habitat elevation is estimated, so the following climate data should be used with caution. In northern Guam, plants have become naturalized on trees and cliff-faces.

CLIMATE: Station #98427, Manila, Philippines, Lat. 14.5°N, Long. 121.0°E, at 85 ft. (26 m). Temperatures are calculated for 800 ft. (240 m), resulting in probable extremes of 99°F (37°C) and 56°F (13°C).

N/HEMISPHERE	JAN	FEB	MAR	APR	MAY	JUN	JUL	AUG	SEP	OCT	NOV	DEC
°F AVG MAX	84	86	89	91	91	89	86	85	86	86	85	84
°F AVG MIN	67	67	69	71	73	73	73	73	73	72	70	68
DIURNAL RANGE	17	19	20	20	18	16	13	12	13	14	15	16
RAIN/INCHES	0.9	0.5	0.7	1.3	5.1	10.0	17.0	16.6	14.0	7.6	5.7	2.6
HUMIDITY/%	77	73	70	68	71	81	84	86	87	84	82	89
BLOOM SEASON					*							
DAYS CLR @ 8AM	6	9	14	14	10	3	2	1	1	6	7	6
DAYS CLR @ 2PM	3	6	10	10	8	2	1	1	0	2	2	3
RAIN/MM	23	13	18	33	130	254	432	422	356	193	145	66
°C AVG MAX	28.7	29.8	31.4	32.6	32.6	31.4	29.8	29.2	29.8	29.8	29.2	28.7
°C AVG MIN	19.2	19.2	20.3	21.4	22.6	22.6	22.6	22.6	22.6	22.0	20.9	19.8
DIURNAL RANGE	9.5	10.6	11.1	11.2	10.0	8.8	7.2	6.6	7.2	7.8	8.3	8.9
S/HEMISPHERE	JUL	AUG	SEP	OCT	NOV	DEC	JAN	FEB	MAR	APR	MAY	JUN

Cultural Recommendations

LIGHT: 2500–3500 fc.

TEMPERATURES: Throughout the year, days average 84–91°F (29–33°C), and nights average 67–73°F (19–23°C), with a diurnal range of 12–20°F (7–11°C). Plants from this habitat are healthiest if humidity is high and air circulation is excellent.

HUMIDITY: 80–85% in summer and autumn, dropping to about 70% in winter and spring.

WATER: Rainfall is heavy in summer and autumn, but conditions are dry in winter. Cultivated plants should be kept moist during the growing season, but water should be gradually reduced in autumn.

FERTILIZER: ¼–½ recommended strength, applied weekly. A high-nitrogen fertilizer is beneficial from spring to midsummer, but a fertilizer high in phosphates should be used in late summer and autumn.

REST PERIOD: Growing temperatures should be maintained all year. Rainfall is low for 3–4 months in winter, but additional moisture is available from frequent heavy dew. In cultivation, water should be reduced and the plants allowed to dry out between waterings. They should not remain dry for extended periods, however. Fertilizer should also be reduced or eliminated anytime water is reduced. In the habitat, light is highest in winter.

GROWING MEDIA: Plants may be mounted on tree-fern or cork slabs if humidity is high and plants are watered at least once daily in summer. When plants are potted, any open, fast-draining medium may be used. Repotting is best done in early spring when new roots are growing.

MISCELLANEOUS NOTES: The bloom season shown in the climate table is based on cultivation records. Plants that produce flowers which last a single day commonly bloom several times during the year. Flowering usually occurs 7–14 days after a sudden 10°F (5°C) drop in daytime temperatures.

Plant and Flower Information

PLANT SIZE AND TYPE: An 8–16 in. (20–40 cm) sympodial epiphyte.

PSEUDOBULB: 8–16 in. (20–40 cm) long. The stems are slender and spindle-shaped. The basal nodes are angular and thickened for about 2 in. (5 cm).

LEAVES: Many. The leaves are 2.4–4.0 in. (6–10 cm) long, needlelike, and persistent. They are often held at a 45° angle to the stem and resemble an extension of the stem.

INFLORESCENCE: Short. Inflorescences arise at the leafless apex of the stem.

FLOWERS: 1 per inflorescence. The flowers are 0.4 in. (1 cm) across. Sepals and petals are white to yellow, often with a purplish tint. The white lip, which has a ruffled, uneven margin, is marked with dark purple veins at the base. The oblong-elliptic lip is simple, not lobed, with a small point at the apex. Blossoms are fragrant in the morning. Individual blossoms only last 3–4 days, but plants may be in nearly continuous bloom.

HYBRIDIZING NOTES: Chromosome count is 2n = 38 (ref. 504, 580).

REFERENCES: 12, 13, 25, 221, 254, 296, 373, 450, 504, 536, 580.

Dendrobium phillipsii Ames and Quisumbing

ORIGIN/HABITAT: The Philippine Islands. Plants are reported from Bukidnon Province on Mindanao Island. Habitat elevation is unavailable, so the following climate data should be used with caution.

CLIMATE: Station #98751, Malaybalay, Mindanao, Philippines, Lat. 8.2°N, Long. 125.1°E, at 2106 ft. (642 m). Record extreme temperatures are 93°F (34°C) and 53°F (12°C).

N/HEMISPHERE	JAN	FEB	MAR	APR	MAY	JUN	JUL	AUG	SEP	OCT	NOV	DEC
°F AVG MAX	82	83	85	87	86	83	83	82	83	84	84	83
°F AVG MIN	64	64	64	65	66	66	66	66	66	66	66	65
DIURNAL RANGE	18	19	21	22	20	17	17	16	17	18	18	18
RAIN/INCHES	4.6	3.7	4.0	3.7	10.0	13.0	14.1	13.8	14.2	12.6	7.3	7.0
HUMIDITY/%	85	85	82	79	85	87	87	88	87	86	83	83
BLOOM SEASON		*										
DAYS CLR @ 8AM	5	5	11	17	10	7	7	4	5	9	8	10
DAYS CLR @ 2PM	2	1	3	3	1	1	1	1	1	2	1	1
RAIN/MM	117	94	102	94	254	330	358	351	361	320	185	178
°C AVG MAX	27.8	28.3	29.4	30.6	30.0	28.3	28.3	27.8	28.3	28.9	28.9	28.3
°C AVG MIN	17.8	17.8	17.8	18.3	18.9	18.9	18.9	18.9	18.9	18.9	18.9	18.3
DIURNAL RANGE	10.0	10.5	11.6	12.3	11.1	9.4	9.4	8.9	9.4	10.0	10.0	10.0
S/HEMISPHERE	JUL	AUG	SEP	OCT	NOV	DEC	JAN	FEB	MAR	APR	MAY	JUN

Cultural Recommendations

LIGHT: 2000–3000 fc.

TEMPERATURES: Throughout the year, days average 82–87°F (28–31°C), and nights average 64–66°F (18–19°C), with a diurnal range of 16–22°F (9–12°C).

HUMIDITY: 85–90% most of the year, dropping to 80–85% in late autumn and winter.

WATER: Rainfall is moderate to heavy most of the year, but conditions are somewhat drier in winter. Cultivated plants should be kept moist but not soggy.

FERTILIZER: ¼–½ recommended strength. A balanced fertilizer should be applied weekly to biweekly throughout the year.

REST PERIOD: Growing temperatures should be maintained all year. For cultivated plants, water and fertilizer may be reduced slightly in winter, especially for plants grown in the dark, short-day conditions common in temperate latitudes. Plants should never be allowed to dry out completely, however. In the habitat, light is highest in winter.

GROWING MEDIA: Mounting plants on tree-fern or cork slabs or growing in hanging pots or baskets accommodates their pendent growth habit. When potted, any open, fast-draining medium may be used. Repotting may be done anytime new roots are growing.

MISCELLANEOUS NOTES: The bloom season shown in the climate table is based on collection reports.

Plant and Flower Information

PLANT SIZE AND TYPE: An 18–24 in. (45–60 cm) sympodial epiphyte.

PSEUDOBULB: 18–24 in. (45–60 cm) long. The crowded, pendulous stems are spindle-shaped, smooth, and reddish-brown.

LEAVES: The leaves are 4–5 in. (10–13 cm) long. They are lanceolate, papery, and deciduous.

INFLORESCENCE: 1.2–1.6 in. (3–4 cm) long.

FLOWERS: Few per inflorescence. The flowers are 0.7 in. (1.8 cm) across. They are white with yellow in the throat and on the spur. The dorsal sepal is broadly ovate. Lateral sepals are obliquely triangular-ovate. Petals are broadly oblong and round at the apex. The unlobed lip has a low, transverse ridge.

REFERENCES: 225, 373, 536.

PHOTOS/DRAWINGS: *373*, 536.

Dendrobium phlox Schlechter. See *D. subclausum* Rolfe. REFERENCES: 151–154, 179, 188, 221, 273, 304, 305, 430, 437, 445, 470, 486, 538, 588. PHOTOS/DRAWINGS: 538.

Dendrobium phragmitoides Schlechter

ORIGIN/HABITAT: Endemic to northern Sulawesi (Celebes). Plants grow near Manado at the eastern end of the Minahassa Peninsula at about 3950 ft. (1200 m).

CLIMATE: Station #97014, Manado, Indonesia, Lat. 1.5°N, Long. 124.9°E, at 264 ft. (80 m). Temperatures are calculated for an elevation of 3950 ft. (1200 m), resulting in probable extremes of 85°F (29°C) and 53°F (12°C).

N/HEMISPHERE	JAN	FEB	MAR	APR	MAY	JUN	JUL	AUG	SEP	OCT	NOV	DEC
°F AVG MAX	73	73	73	74	75	75	75	77	77	77	75	74
°F AVG MIN	61	61	61	62	61	61	61	61	61	60	61	62
DIURNAL RANGE	12	12	12	13	13	14	14	16	16	17	14	12
RAIN/INCHES	18.6	13.8	12.2	8.0	6.4	6.5	4.8	4.0	3.4	4.9	8.9	14.7
HUMIDITY/%	84	83	83	83	81	80	75	72	75	77	82	83
BLOOM SEASON												
DAYS CLR @ 8AM	4	3	6	11	11	12	12	14	17	12	8	
DAYS CLR @ 2PM	1	1	1	2	1	3	3	4	4	4	1	1
RAIN/MM	472	351	310	203	163	165	122	102	86	124	226	373
°C AVG MAX	22.7	22.7	22.7	23.2	23.8	23.8	23.8	24.9	24.9	24.9	23.8	23.2
°C AVG MIN	16.0	16.0	16.0	16.0	16.6	16.0	16.0	16.0	16.0	15.5	16.0	16.6
DIURNAL RANGE	6.7	6.7	6.7	7.2	7.2	7.8	7.8	8.9	8.9	9.4	7.8	6.7
S/HEMISPHERE	JUL	AUG	SEP	OCT	NOV	DEC	JAN	FEB	MAR	APR	MAY	JUN

Cultural Recommendations

LIGHT: 2000–3000 fc. Low to intermediate diffused light is suggested. In the habitat, light is bright during the clear summer mornings, but afternoons are cloudy, and plants grow in shady forest habitats.

TEMPERATURES: Throughout the year, days average 73–77°F (23–25°C), and nights average 60–62°F (16–17°C), with a diurnal range of 12–17°F (7–9°C). Extremes vary less than 10°F (6°C) from average temperatures, indicating that plants may not tolerate wide temperature fluctuations.

HUMIDITY: 80–85% most of the year, dropping to 70–75% in late summer and autumn.

WATER: Rainfall is moderate to heavy all year. The driest weather occurs in late summer when temperatures are warm. Cultivated plants should be kept moist but not soggy. Warm water might be beneficial.

FERTILIZER: ¼–½ recommended strength. A balanced fertilizer should be applied weekly to biweekly throughout the year.

REST PERIOD: Growing temperatures should be maintained all year. The plants may rest during the 1–2 month drier period which occurs in late summer and coincides with the period of greatest diurnal range. Cultivated plants should dry out slightly during this period, but they should never remain dry for long. The heaviest rainfall in the habitat occurs in winter, but water should not be increased for cultivated plants. In fact, water should be reduced somewhat for plants grown in the dark, short-day conditions common in temperate latitudes, but they should not be allowed to dry out completely.

GROWING MEDIA: Plants may be mounted on tree-fern or cork slabs or potted in small pots filled with any open, fast-draining medium. Repotting may be done anytime new roots are actively growing.

MISCELLANEOUS NOTES: The bloom season shown in the climate table is based on reports from the habitat. The plant was described in 1933 in Engler's *Bot. Jarhb.* 65:491.

Plant and Flower Information

PLANT SIZE AND TYPE: A 39 in. (100 cm) sympodial epiphyte.

PSEUDOBULB: 39 in. (100 cm) long. The unbranched, densely leafy stems reportedly resemble a short bulrush.

LEAVES: Many. The linear-lanceolate leaves are 7–9 in. (18–23 cm) long with a rounded, contracted base.

INFLORESCENCE: Inflorescences emerge laterally from the side of the stem.

FLOWERS: 6–10 per inflorescence. The white flowers are 0.3 in. (0.8 cm) long. The sepals are ovate-oblong. Petals are smooth and somewhat tongue-shaped. The 3-lobed lip has a roundly elliptical midlobe with 3 fleshy keels and semiobovate sidelobes.

REFERENCES: 223, 436.

Dendrobium pictum Griffith not Lindley or Schlechter. See *D. devonianum* Paxton. REFERENCES: 190, 216, 254, 445, 454.

Dendrobium pictum Lindley not Schlechter or Griffith.
Reported to have originated in Borneo, but habitat location and elevation are not available, so climate data cannot be selected. The plant is sympodial with leafy, somewhat club-shaped stems. The leaves are pointed ovals. Short inflorescences carry 2 blossoms which are 1.4 in. (3.5 cm) across. Sepals are pale rose, while the lip and petals are white with dark crimson veins except at the margin. The lip is 0.8 in. (2 cm) long and wide. REFERENCES: 216, 254, 286, 295, 394.

Dendrobium pictum Schlechter not Griffith or Lindley. See *D. summerhayesianum* A. Hawkes and A. H. Heller. REFERENCES: 221, 229, 437, 470.

Dendrobium pierardii Roxburgh ex Hooker f. See *D. aphyllum* (Roxburgh) C. Fischer. The International Orchid Commission (ref. 236) registers hybrids under *D. pierardii*. REFERENCES: 6, 25, 32, 38, 46, 102, 150, 151, 152, 154, 157, 165, 187, 190, 196, 200, 202, 208, 211, 216, 235, 236, 245, 247, 254, 266, 277, 278, 317, 326, 369, 402, 430, 445, 447, 452, 454, 455, 458, 504, 510, 541, 557, 569, 570, 577. PHOTOS/DRAWINGS: 46, 72, 200, *245, 247*, 458, *569*, 570, 580.

Dendrobium piestobulbon Schlechter. Now considered a synonym of *Flickingeria forcipata* (Schlechter) A. Hawkes. REFERENCES: 213, 221, 230, 234, 435, 449.

Dendrobium piestocaulon Schlechter

AKA: *D. gracilicaule* Kränzlin not F. Mueller. Schlechter (ref. 437) included *D. nidificum* Kränzlin as a synonym.

ORIGIN/HABITAT: New Ireland (Neu Mecklenberg) Island and Papua New Guinea. Plants grow on trees in mountain forests near Punam at about 1800 ft. (550 m). Plants were cultivated in the botanical garden at Bogor, Java.

CLIMATE: Station #94076, Kavieng, New Ireland, Papua New Guinea, Lat. 2.6°S, Long. 150.8°E, at 15 ft. (5 m). Temperatures are calculated for an elevation of 1800 ft. (550 m), resulting in probable extremes of 93°F (34°C) and 60°F (16°C).

N/HEMISPHERE	JAN	FEB	MAR	APR	MAY	JUN	JUL	AUG	SEP	OCT	NOV	DEC
°F AVG MAX	82	82	83	84	84	83	82	82	81	82	82	82
°F AVG MIN	67	67	67	67	68	68	69	69	69	68	68	68
DIURNAL RANGE	15	15	16	17	16	15	13	13	12	14	14	14
RAIN/INCHES	10.7	11.2	7.8	8.0	9.7	10.7	12.2	11.1	11.6	12.5	10.0	9.9
HUMIDITY/%	78	76	76	75	77	78	80	79	79	80	79	79
BLOOM SEASON	*											
DAYS CLR	N/A											
RAIN/MM	272	284	198	203	246	272	310	282	295	318	254	251
°C AVG MAX	27.8	27.8	28.4	28.9	28.9	28.4	27.8	27.8	27.3	27.8	27.8	27.8
°C AVG MIN	19.5	19.5	19.5	19.5	20.1	20.1	20.6	20.6	20.6	20.1	20.1	20.1
DIURNAL RANGE	8.3	8.3	8.9	9.4	8.8	8.3	7.2	7.2	6.7	7.7	7.7	7.7
S/HEMISPHERE	JUL	AUG	SEP	OCT	NOV	DEC	JAN	FEB	MAR	APR	MAY	JUN

Cultural Recommendations

LIGHT: 2000–3000 fc.

TEMPERATURES: Throughout the year, days average 81–84°F (27–29°C), and nights average 67–69°F (20–21°C), with a diurnal range of 12–17°F (7–9°C).

HUMIDITY: 75–80% year-round.

WATER: Rainfall is very heavy all year. Cultivated plants should be kept evenly moist.

FERTILIZER: ¼–½ recommended strength. A balanced fertilizer should be applied weekly to biweekly throughout the year.

REST PERIOD: Growing conditions should be maintained year-round. In the habitat, rainfall is heavy in winter; but water and fertilizer should be reduced somewhat for plants cultivated in the dark, short-day conditions common in temperate latitudes. Plants should never be allowed to dry out completely, however. In the habitat, seasonal light variation is minor.

GROWING MEDIA: Plants may be mounted on tree-fern or cork slabs if humidity is high and plants are watered at least once daily in summer. When plants are potted, any open, fast-draining medium may be used. Repotting may be done anytime new roots are growing.

MISCELLANEOUS NOTES: The bloom season shown in the climate table is based on reports from the habitat.

Plant and Flower Information

PLANT SIZE AND TYPE: A 12–16 in. (30–40 cm) sympodial epiphyte.

PSEUDOBULB: 12–16 in. (30–40 cm) long. The base of the slender stem is flattened and leafless.

LEAVES: Many. The linear to tongue-shaped leaves are 2.4 in. (6 cm) long, leathery, erect to suberect, and unequally bilobed at the apex.

INFLORESCENCE: Short. Inflorescences emerge laterally along the side of the stem.

FLOWERS: 1 per inflorescence. The white flowers are 0.4 in. (1 cm) across. The sepals are ovate, but the lateral sepals are dilated near the apex. The petals are lanceolate to slightly sickle-shaped. The 3-lobed lip is yellowish with small sidelobes. The 2 keels are diverging and somewhat moon-shaped. Schlechter (ref. 437) described *D. piestocaulon* var. *kauloense* Schlechter as having pale yellow sepals and petals and a red-brown lip with yellow in the center.

REFERENCES: 58, 92, 219, 254, 437, 444, 445, 470.

PHOTOS/DRAWINGS: 437.

Dendrobium pililobum J. J. Smith.

Now considered a synonym of *Diplocaulobium pililobum* (J. J. Smith) Hunt and Summerhayes.

REFERENCES: 213, 221, 230, 445, 470, 475.

Dendrobium pinifolium Ridley

ORIGIN/HABITAT: Northeastern coast of Borneo, near Sandakan, Sabah. Habitat elevation was not reported, so the following climate data should be used with caution.

CLIMATE: Station #96491, Sandakan, Sabah (North Borneo), Lat. 5.9°N, Long. 118.1°E, at 38 ft. (12 m). Record extreme temperatures are 99°F (37°C) and 70°F (21°C).

N/HEMISPHERE	JAN	FEB	MAR	APR	MAY	JUN	JUL	AUG	SEP	OCT	NOV	DEC
°F AVG MAX	85	86	87	89	89	89	89	89	89	88	87	86
°F AVG MIN	74	74	75	76	76	75	75	75	75	75	75	74
DIURNAL RANGE	11	12	12	13	13	14	14	14	14	13	12	12
RAIN/INCHES	19.0	10.9	8.6	4.5	6.2	7.4	6.7	7.9	9.3	10.2	14.5	18.5
HUMIDITY/%	84	83	83	81	81	81	80	80	79	81	84	84
BLOOM SEASON	N/A											
DAYS CLR @ 8AM	1	1	2	3	2	3	2	2	2	1	1	1
DAYS CLR @ 2PM	0	1	3	3	1	1	1	1	0	0	1	0
RAIN/MM	483	277	218	114	157	188	170	201	236	259	368	470
°C AVG MAX	29.4	30.0	30.6	31.7	31.7	31.7	31.7	31.7	31.7	31.1	30.6	30.0
°C AVG MIN	23.3	23.3	23.9	24.4	24.4	23.9	23.9	23.9	23.9	23.9	23.9	23.3
DIURNAL RANGE	6.1	6.7	6.7	7.3	7.3	7.8	7.8	7.8	7.8	7.2	6.7	6.7
S/HEMISPHERE	JUL	AUG	SEP	OCT	NOV	DEC	JAN	FEB	MAR	APR	MAY	JUN

Cultural Recommendations

LIGHT: 1800–2500 fc.

TEMPERATURES: Throughout the year, days average 85–89°F (29–32°C), and nights average 74–76°F (23–24°C), with a diurnal range of 11–14°F (6–8°C).

HUMIDITY: 80–85% year-round.

WATER: Rainfall is moderate to heavy all year. Cultivated plants should be kept moist but not soggy.

FERTILIZER: ¼–½ recommended strength. A balanced fertilizer should be applied weekly to biweekly throughout the year.

REST PERIOD: Growing conditions should be maintained all year. Water and fertilizer should be reduced for plants cultivated in the dark, short-day conditions common in temperate-latitude winters, but they should never be allowed to dry out completely. In the habitat, light is slightly lower in winter.

GROWING MEDIA: Plants may be mounted on tree-fern or cork slabs or potted in small pots filled with any open, fast-draining medium. Repotting may be done anytime new roots are actively growing.

Plant and Flower Information

PLANT SIZE AND TYPE: A 6–8 in. (15–20 cm) sympodial epiphyte.

PSEUDOBULB: 6–8 in. (15–20 cm) long. The leafy stems, which are covered with dark hairs, are grooved with brownish internodes.

LEAVES: Many. The fleshy, dark green leaves are linear, pointed, and grooved.

INFLORESCENCE: Short.

FLOWERS: 3 per inflorescence. The flowers are 0.4 in. (1 cm) across. The sepals and petals are flesh-colored, and the lip is white with pale orange markings. The column is rose-colored. Blossoms have lanceolate sepals and linear petals. The lip has a notched, rounded midlobe.

HYBRIDIZING NOTES: Chromosome count is 2n = 40 (ref. 153, 273).

REFERENCES: 153, 254, 273, 286, 295, 394.

Dendrobium piranha C. L. Chan and Cribb

AKA: The plant description is in publication and not yet available.

ORIGIN/HABITAT: Borneo. Plants are endemic to Mt. Kinabalu. They grow in mountain forests and in scrubby woodlands at 4600–7900 ft. (1400–2400 m).

CLIMATE: Station #49613, Tambunan, Sabah, Borneo, Lat. 5.7°N, Long. 116.4°E, at 1200 ft. (366 m). Temperatures are calculated for an elevation of 6000 ft. (1830 m), resulting in probable extremes of 82°F (28°C) and 38°F (3°C).

N/HEMISPHERE	JAN	FEB	MAR	APR	MAY	JUN	JUL	AUG	SEP	OCT	NOV	DEC
°F AVG MAX	70	71	73	74	74	73	73	73	73	72	71	70
°F AVG MIN	51	49	50	51	52	51	50	50	51	51	51	52
DIURNAL RANGE	19	22	23	23	22	22	23	23	22	21	20	18
RAIN/INCHES	5.8	3.7	5.8	7.5	8.2	7.3	5.1	4.9	6.4	7.0	6.8	6.0
HUMIDITY/%	N/A											
BLOOM SEASON	N/A											
DAYS CLR	N/A											
RAIN/MM	147	94	147	190	208	185	130	124	163	178	173	152
°C AVG MAX	21.2	21.8	22.9	23.4	23.4	22.9	22.9	22.9	22.9	22.3	21.8	21.2
°C AVG MIN	10.6	9.5	10.1	10.6	11.2	10.6	10.1	10.1	10.6	10.6	10.6	11.2
DIURNAL RANGE	10.6	12.3	12.8	12.8	12.2	12.3	12.8	12.8	12.3	11.7	11.2	10.0
S/HEMISPHERE	JUL	AUG	SEP	OCT	NOV	DEC	JAN	FEB	MAR	APR	MAY	JUN

Cultural Recommendations

LIGHT: 2000–3000 fc.

TEMPERATURES: Throughout the year, days average 70–74°F (21–23°C), and nights average 49–52°F (10–11°C), with a diurnal range of 18–23°F (10–13°C).

HUMIDITY: Information is not available for this location. However, reports from nearby stations indicate that humidity is probably 80–85% year-round. Excellent air circulation should be provided.

WATER: Rainfall is moderate to heavy all year. Cultivated plants should be kept moist, with only slight drying allowed between waterings.

FERTILIZER: ¼–½ recommended strength. A balanced fertilizer should be applied weekly to biweekly throughout the year.

REST PERIOD: Growing conditions vary only slightly through the year. The diurnal range is slightly lower in winter due to somewhat cooler days. In cultivation, water should be reduced somewhat in winter, especially for plants grown in the dark, short-day conditions common in temperate latitudes. Plants should never be allowed to dry out completely, however. Fertilizer should be decreased when water is reduced and when plants are not actively growing.

GROWING MEDIA: Plants may be mounted on tree-fern or cork slabs if humidity is high and plants are watered at least once daily in summer. When plants are potted, any open, fast-draining medium may be used. Repotting is best done in early spring when new roots begin to grow.

Plant and Flower Information

PLANT SIZE AND TYPE: A sympodial epiphyte or terrestrial.

FLOWERS: 1 per inflorescence. The sepals and lip are mahogany brown on the inside with a paler, speckled outer surface. The white petals and column are a stark contrast. The large lip sidelobes curve inward and nearly touch in the center. The lip has long hairs at the apex. The area extends back from the edge, forming a clump of hairs on each side. The large keels extend to the back edge of the hairy areas.

REFERENCES: 592.

PHOTOS/DRAWINGS: 592.

Dendrobium pisibulbum Guillaumin. See *D. pachyphyllum* (Kuntze) Bakhuizen f. REFERENCES: 169, 230, 448, 454.

Dendrobium × pitcherianum Rchb. f. Sometimes spelled *D. pitcheranum*, it is a natural hybrid between *D. nobile* Lindley and *D. primulinum* Lindley. REFERENCES: 152, 179, 243, 254, 504, 570, 580.

Dendrobium pityphyllum Schlechter. See *D. violaceum* Kränzlin. REFERENCES: 222, 385.

Dendrobium planibulbe Lindley

AKA: Seidenfaden (ref. 454) lists *D. tuberiferum* Hooker f. as a synonym. Confusion exists regarding the status of the plants known as *D. blumei* Lindley and *D. planibulbe*. J. J. Smith (ref. 469) lists *D. planibulbe* Lindley as a synonym of *D. blumei*, but Valmayor (ref. 536) follows Merrill (ref. 296) in listing *D. blumei* as a synonym of *D. planibulbe*. However, Seidenfaden (ref. 454) indicates that the Philippine plant Valmayor refers to as *D. planibulbe* should in fact be *D. blumei*. Although supposedly reported from the Philippines, Seidenfaden writes, "I do not think *Dendrobium planibulbe* is represented in the Philippines and believe that Cuming's label 'Manila' is wrong: we have several cases of the mix-up of 'Manila' and 'Singapore' in Cuming's material."

ORIGIN/HABITAT: Southeast Asia, including Malaya, Thailand, Sumatra, and Borneo. The habitat includes the states of Perak and Terengganu in Malaya; the region near Palembang, Sumatra; part of peninsular Thailand; and eastern Kalimantan in Borneo, where plants are found at about 2300 ft. (700 m).

CLIMATE: Station #48625, Ipoh, Malaya, Lat. 4.6°N, Long. 101.1°E, at 123 ft. (37 m). Temperatures are calculated for an elevation of 2000 ft. (610 m), resulting in probable extremes of 93°F (34°C) and 58°F (14°C).

N/HEMISPHERE	JAN	FEB	MAR	APR	MAY	JUN	JUL	AUG	SEP	OCT	NOV	DEC
°F AVG MAX	84	86	87	86	86	86	85	85	84	83	83	83
°F AVG MIN	66	66	67	67	68	67	66	66	67	66	66	66
DIURNAL RANGE	18	20	20	19	18	19	19	19	17	17	17	17
RAIN/INCHES	7.9	3.1	7.6	8.4	6.2	3.6	7.2	6.9	8.8	11.0	13.0	8.9
HUMIDITY/%	76	74	76	78	78	75	76	77	79	82	82	81
BLOOM SEASON			*	*						*	*	
DAYS CLR @ 7AM	3	3	3	1	1	2	1	1	0	0	1	2
DAYS CLR @ 1PM	2	2	2	1	1	1	1	1	0	0	0	2
RAIN/MM	201	79	193	213	157	91	183	175	224	279	330	226
°C AVG MAX	28.8	29.9	30.4	29.9	29.9	29.9	29.3	29.3	28.8	28.2	28.2	28.2
°C AVG MIN	18.8	18.8	19.3	19.3	19.9	19.3	18.8	18.8	19.3	18.8	18.8	18.8
DIURNAL RANGE	10.0	11.1	11.1	10.6	10.0	10.6	10.5	10.5	9.5	9.4	9.4	9.4
S/HEMISPHERE	JUL	AUG	SEP	OCT	NOV	DEC	JAN	FEB	MAR	APR	MAY	JUN

Cultural Recommendations

LIGHT: 2500–3500 fc.

TEMPERATURES: Throughout the year, days average 83–87°F (28–30°C), and nights average 66–67°F (19°C), with a diurnal range of 17–20°F (9–11°C).

HUMIDITY: 75–80% year-round.

WATER: Rainfall is heavy most of the year. The heaviest rainfall occurs in autumn, with a secondary maximum in spring. Short, semidry periods occur in midwinter and midsummer. Cultivated plants should be kept evenly moist, with little if any drying between waterings.

FERTILIZER: ¼–½ recommended strength. A balanced fertilizer should be applied weekly to biweekly throughout the year.

REST PERIOD: Growing conditions should be maintained all year. Water and fertilizer might be reduced and the plants allowed to dry slightly between waterings during the brief semidry periods. Water should be reduced somewhat in winter for plants cultivated in the dark, short-day conditions common in temperate latitudes. They should never be allowed to dry out completely, however. Fertilizer may be reduced when the plant is not actively growing or when water is reduced. In the habitat, light is slightly higher in winter.

GROWING MEDIA: Plants may be mounted on tree-fern or cork slabs if humidity is high and plants are watered at least once daily in summer. When plants are potted, any open, fast-draining medium may be used. Repotting may be done anytime new roots are growing.

MISCELLANEOUS NOTES: The bloom season shown in the climate table is based on collection reports. Plants that produce flowers which last a single day commonly bloom several times during the year. Flowering usually occurs 7–14 days after a sudden 10°F (5°C) drop in daytime temperatures.

Plant and Flower Information

PLANT SIZE AND TYPE: A 4–24 in. (10–60 cm) sympodial epiphyte.

PSEUDOBULB: 4–24 in. (10–60 cm) long. Plant size is highly variable. The stems are slender at the base, swollen at the basal internode, then slender again. The swollen portion of the stem is 1.6–2.4 in. (4–6 cm) long, angular and flattened, with 4 ridges. Stems may be red or yellowish and often turn down above the lower, leafy part of the stem.

LEAVES: 6–8. The leaves are about 2 in. (5 cm) long. They may be flat or terete and alternate on the stem. The leaves are tinged with purple when young.

INFLORESCENCE: Very short. Inflorescences emerge from nodes on the apical, leafless portion of the stem.

FLOWERS: 1 per inflorescence. The flowers are 0.6 in. (1.5 cm) long and open only slightly. Sepals and petals are white to cream. They are decorated with violet-crimson veins on the inner surface and a violet midline on the outer surface of the petals. The narrow petals are pointed, with a row of tiny hairs along the edge. The lip has large sidelobes and a conspicuous fringe on the front edge of the rounded, narrow, tongue-shaped midlobe. It is marked with a violet-crimson bar. The callus is yellow. Blossoms are short-lived and very fragile.

HYBRIDIZING NOTES: Johansen (ref. 239) indicates that plants are self-sterile and that flowers dropped 4–5 days after self-pollination.

REFERENCES: 12, 190, 200, 216, 239, 254, 286, 296, 317, 402, 454, 455, 469, 536.

PHOTOS/DRAWINGS: *454, 455*.

Dendrobium planicaule Ridley

ORIGIN/HABITAT: Irian Jaya (western New Guinea). Plants were collected on the south side of Mt. Jaya (Mt. Carstensz) at 3900–5500 ft. (1190–1680 m).

CLIMATE: Station #97796, Kokenau (Kokonau), Irian Jaya, Lat. 4.7°S, Long. 135.4°E, at 10 ft. (3 m). Temperatures are calculated for an elevation of 4500 ft. (1370 m). Record extreme temperatures are not available for this location.

N/HEMISPHERE	JAN	FEB	MAR	APR	MAY	JUN	JUL	AUG	SEP	OCT	NOV	DEC
°F AVG MAX	68	68	71	73	75	74	74	74	75	73	72	69
°F AVG MIN	58	58	59	59	59	60	59	59	59	59	59	58
DIURNAL RANGE	10	10	12	14	16	14	15	15	16	14	13	11
RAIN/INCHES	18.4	15.8	18.9	11.6	9.7	10.6	11.5	15.7	11.6	11.6	16.0	19.9
HUMIDITY/%	N/A											
BLOOM SEASON	N/A											
DAYS CLR	N/A											
RAIN/MM	467	401	480	295	246	269	292	399	295	295	406	505
°C AVG MAX	20.1	20.1	21.8	22.9	24.0	23.4	23.4	23.4	24.0	22.9	22.3	20.7
°C AVG MIN	14.5	14.5	15.1	15.1	15.1	15.7	15.1	15.1	15.1	15.1	15.1	14.5
DIURNAL RANGE	5.6	5.6	6.7	7.8	8.9	7.7	8.3	8.3	8.9	7.8	7.2	6.2
S/HEMISPHERE	JUL	AUG	SEP	OCT	NOV	DEC	JAN	FEB	MAR	APR	MAY	JUN

Cultural Recommendations

LIGHT: 2500–3500 fc.

TEMPERATURES: Throughout the year, days average 68–75°F (20–24°C), and nights average 58–60°F (15–16°C), with a diurnal range of 10–16°F (6–9°C).

HUMIDITY: Information is not available for this location. However, records from nearby stations indicate that humidity probably averages near 85% year-round.

WATER: Rainfall is very heavy all year. Cultivated plants should be kept evenly moist but not soggy.

FERTILIZER: ¼–½ recommended strength. A balanced fertilizer should be applied weekly to biweekly throughout the year.

REST PERIOD: Growing conditions should be maintained year-round. Water and fertilizer might be reduced slightly in winter, especially for plants grown in the dark, short-day conditions common in temperate latitudes. Plants should never be allowed to dry out completely, however. In the habitat, seasonal light variation is minor.

GROWING MEDIA: Plants may be potted in small pots filled with any open, fast-draining medium. Repotting may be done anytime new roots are growing.

Plant and Flower Information

PLANT SIZE AND TYPE: A 12 in. (30 cm) sympodial epiphyte.

PSEUDOBULB: 12 in. (30 cm) long or longer. The stems are robust. They are leafy, with the leaves arranged on a single plane.

LEAVES: Many. The distichous leaves, which are 1.6 in. (4 cm) long, are leathery and oblong-linear with a rounded, unequally bilobed tip.

INFLORESCENCE: Short. Inflorescences emerge laterally through the leaf sheaths.

FLOWERS: 1 per inflorescence. The flowers are 0.8 in. (2 cm) across. They have a lanceolate dorsal sepal, and broad, ovate lateral sepals and petals. The short, tongue-shaped lip is recurved and fleshy at the tip. The sidelobes are curved. The fleshy blossoms become black when dry.

REFERENCES: 222, 400.

Dendrobium planum J. J. Smith

AKA: *D. planum* J. J. Smith var. *collinum* J. J. Smith is now considered a variety of *D. collinum* J. J. Smith.

ORIGIN/HABITAT: West Java, Sumatra, and Irian Jaya (western New Guinea). In Java, plants grow but are not common in moist forests at about 3300 ft. (1000 m) near Tjihanjawsar. In Irian Jaya, plants are found at low elevations along the Noord and Lorentz Rivers. They were cultivated in the botanical garden at Bogor, Java.

CLIMATE: Station #96755, Bogor, Indonesia, at Lat. 6.5°S, Long. 106.8°E, at 558 ft. (170 m). Temperatures are calculated for an elevation of 3000 ft. (910 m), resulting in probable extremes of 88°F (31°C) and 58°F (14°C).

N/HEMISPHERE	JAN	FEB	MAR	APR	MAY	JUN	JUL	AUG	SEP	OCT	NOV	DEC
°F AVG MAX	78	79	80	80	79	77	76	76	77	78	79	78
°F AVG MIN	65	65	65	66	66	66	66	66	66	67	67	66
DIURNAL RANGE	13	14	15	14	13	11	10	10	11	11	12	12
RAIN/INCHES	2.1	1.0	0.5	5.0	8.1	18.8	23.7	20.2	14.4	12.0	11.9	3.4
HUMIDITY/%	72	68	65	66	74	79	84	84	81	79	77	75
BLOOM SEASON			*			*						
DAYS CLR @ 7AM	14	14	14	11	5	3	1	2	4	6	10	12
DAYS CLR @ 1PM	9	10	8	5	1	1	0	0	1	1	3	7
RAIN/MM	53	25	13	127	206	478	602	513	366	305	302	86
°C AVG MAX	25.5	26.1	26.6	26.6	26.1	25.0	24.4	24.4	25.0	25.5	26.1	25.5
°C AVG MIN	18.3	18.3	18.3	18.9	18.9	18.9	18.9	18.9	18.9	19.4	19.4	18.9
DIURNAL RANGE	7.2	7.8	8.3	7.7	7.2	6.1	5.5	5.5	6.1	6.1	6.7	6.6
S/HEMISPHERE	JUL	AUG	SEP	OCT	NOV	DEC	JAN	FEB	MAR	APR	MAY	JUN

Cultural Recommendations

LIGHT: 1800–2400 fc. Diffused or barely dappled light is recommended. Direct sunlight should be avoided.

TEMPERATURES: Throughout the year, days average 76–80°F (24–27°C), and nights average 65–67°F (18–19°C), with a diurnal range of 10–15°F (6–8°C). The warmest months occur in spring. The extremes vary only slightly from the average growing temperatures, indicating that plants are unlikely to tolerate wide temperature fluctuations.

HUMIDITY: 75–85% most of the year, dropping to near 65% in late winter and early spring.

WATER: Rainfall is very heavy from spring into autumn, but conditions are very dry for 2 months in winter. During the growing season, plants should never be allowed to dry out completely, but water should be gradually reduced in autumn.

FERTILIZER: ¼–½ recommended strength, applied weekly. A high nitrogen fertilizer is beneficial from spring to midsummer, but a fertilizer high in phosphates should be used in late summer and autumn.

REST PERIOD: Growing conditions should be maintained all year, but the diurnal range increases slightly in winter, and rainfall is very low for 2–3 months. In cultivation, water should be reduced and the plants allowed to become dry between waterings. They should not remain dry for prolonged periods, however. Fertilizer may be reduced or eliminated anytime the plant is not actively growing. In the habitat, light is highest in winter.

GROWING MEDIA: Plants may be mounted on tree-fern or cork slabs or potted in any open medium. Repotting may be done anytime new roots are growing.

MISCELLANEOUS NOTES: The bloom season shown in the climate table is based on reports from the habitat. Plants that produce flowers which last a single day commonly bloom several times during the year. Flowering usually occurs 7–14 days after a sudden 10°F (5°C) drop in daytime temperatures.

Plant and Flower Information

PLANT SIZE AND TYPE: A 10 in. (25 cm) sympodial epiphyte.

PSEUDOBULB: 10 in. (25 cm) long. The erect stems are flattened, shiny, leafy, and yellowish green.

LEAVES: Many. The flattened, oblong leaves are 2 in. (5 cm) long. They are pale green, leathery, widest on the apical half, and unequally bilobed at the tip. The leaves are held at an acute angle to the stem. They are spaced 0.6–0.8 in. (1.5–2.0 cm) apart. They emerge at every node.

INFLORESCENCE: Very short. Inflorescences emerge at the leaf nodes.

FLOWERS: 1 per inflorescence. Shaped like a fan or flor-de-liss, the short-lived flowers are 0.6 in. (1.4 cm) across. They are pale brownish yellow. The sepals are much larger than the very small, linear petals which are incurved and nearly touch at the tips. The white lip is erect then recurved at the tip. It has a pale red or orange-brown crest that is fringed along part of its length. The sidelobes have red margins and veins.

REFERENCES: 25, 75, 219, 254, 445, 469, 470.

PHOTOS/DRAWINGS: 469.

Dendrobium platybasis Ridley

ORIGIN/HABITAT: Irian Jaya (western New Guinea). Plants were collected near sea level south of Mt. Jaya (Mt. Carstensz).

CLIMATE: Station #97796, Kokenau (Kokonau), Irian Jaya, Lat. 4.7°S, Long. 136.4°E, at 10 ft. (3 m). Record extreme temperatures are not available for this location.

N/HEMISPHERE	JAN	FEB	MAR	APR	MAY	JUN	JUL	AUG	SEP	OCT	NOV	DEC
°F AVG MAX	83	83	86	88	90	89	89	89	90	88	87	84
°F AVG MIN	73	73	74	74	74	75	74	74	74	74	74	73
DIURNAL RANGE	10	10	12	14	16	14	15	15	16	14	13	11
RAIN/INCHES	18.4	15.8	18.9	11.6	9.7	10.6	11.5	15.7	11.6	11.6	16.0	19.9
HUMIDITY/%	N/A											
BLOOM SEASON	N/A											
DAYS CLR	N/A											
RAIN/MM	467	401	479	295	245	269	293	400	294	296	407	506
°C AVG MAX	28.6	28.4	30.2	31.1	32.1	31.9	31.9	31.7	32.0	31.4	30.7	28.7
°C AVG MIN	22.7	22.6	23.3	23.4	23.5	23.7	23.6	23.5	23.4	23.4	23.5	23.0
DIURNAL RANGE	5.9	5.8	6.9	7.7	8.6	8.2	8.3	8.2	8.6	8.0	7.2	5.7
S/HEMISPHERE	JUL	AUG	SEP	OCT	NOV	DEC	JAN	FEB	MAR	APR	MAY	JUN

Cultural Recommendations

LIGHT: 2500–3500 fc.

TEMPERATURES: Throughout the year, days average 83–90°F (29–32°C), and nights average 73–75°F (23–24°C), with a diurnal range of 10–16°F (6–9°C).

HUMIDITY: Information is not available for this location. However, records from nearby stations indicate that humidity probably averages near 85% year-round.

WATER: Rainfall is very heavy year-round. Cultivated plants should be kept evenly moist but not soggy. Warm water might be beneficial.

FERTILIZER: ¼–½ recommended strength. A balanced fertilizer should be applied weekly to biweekly throughout the year.

REST PERIOD: Growing temperatures should be maintained year-round. Water and fertilizer might be reduced slightly for plants cultivated in the dark, short-day conditions common in temperate-latitude winters, but plants should never be allowed to dry completely. In the habitat, seasonal light variation is minor.

GROWING MEDIA: Plants are best potted in small pots filled with any open, fast-draining medium. Mounted plants would be difficult to keep adequately moist. Repotting may be done anytime new roots are growing.

Plant and Flower Information

PLANT SIZE AND TYPE: A 12 in. (30 cm) sympodial epiphyte.

PSEUDOBULB: 12 in. (30 cm) long. The base of the yellow stem is dilated, flattened, and thin. The stems have a sharp keel that runs down each of the flattened faces.

LEAVES: Several. The leaves are about 1.6 in. (4 cm) long, curved, and linear.

INFLORESCENCE: Short. The flower clusters emerge from bracts on the leafless, apical part of the stem.

FLOWERS: Several. The flowers are 0.4 in. (1 cm) across. They have an ovate, pointed dorsal sepal, and somewhat triangular lateral sepals, with linear petals. Blossoms are pinkish at the tips. The margin of the broadly triangular-obovate lip is wavy with very small teeth.

REFERENCES: 222, 400.

Dendrobium platycaulon Rolfe.

Lewis and Cribb (ref. 270, 271) include D. platycaulon Rolfe as a synonym of D. platygastrium Rchb. f. However, Valmayor (ref. 536) considers D. platycaulon Rolfe to be a synonym of D. lamellatum (Blume) Lindley, and Merrill (ref. 296) includes D. lamellatum as used by Kränzlin as a synonym of D. platycaulon. See notes at D. lamellatum and D. platygastrium Rchb. f. HYBRIDIZING NOTES: Chromosome count is 2n = 38 (ref. 280). REFERENCES: 12, 218, 254, 270, 271, 280, 296, 504, 516, 536, 580.

Dendrobium platyclinoides J. J. Smith.

Now considered a synonym of *Diplocaulobium platyclinoides* (J. J. Smith) Hunt and Summerhayes. REFERENCES: 213, 221, 230, 470, 475.

Dendrobium platygastrium Rchb. f.

AKA: Kores (ref. 252, 466) includes only *D. camptocentrum* Schlechter and *D. goldfinchii* as used by Kränzlin not F. Mueller as synonyms. Lewis and Cribb (ref. 270) include *D. platycaulon* Rolfe as a synonym. Kränzlin (ref. 254) listed *D. lamprocaulon* Schlechter as a synonym of *D. platygastrium* Rchb. f.

Hallé (ref. 173) does not include *D. platygastrium* as a New Caledonia species, but he discusses *D. platygastrium* in his review of the synonymy of *D. camptocentrum.*

From a grower's vantage point, H. Wood (ref. 582) expresses strong reservations regarding the lumping of these species. He indicates that based on his personal experience, *D. platycaulon* from the Philippines has a narrow tubular lip and yellow flowers, while *D. platygastrium* from Fiji, which is usually self-pollinating before it opens, has a flat lip when it does open. *D. lamellatum* (Blume) Lindley, for which *D. platycaulon* Rolfe is sometimes listed as a synonym, has an upturned lip. To add more confusion, chromosome counts for *D. platycaulon* and *D. platygastrium* are different, as indicated in the Hybridizing Notes.

ORIGIN/HABITAT: New Guinea, the Solomon Islands, Fiji, New Caledonia, and Vanuatu. Plants grow with moss and ferns in open areas of forests below 1000 ft. (300 m). In New Caledonia, they grow in dense, humid forests near rivers and waterfalls from sea level to 650 ft. (0–200 m). Although found over a large area, plants are uncommon.

CLIMATE: Station #91592, Noumea, New Caledonia, Lat. 22.3°S, Long. 166.5°E, at 246 ft. (75 m). Record extreme temperatures are 99°F (37°C) and 52°F (11°C).

N/HEMISPHERE	JAN	FEB	MAR	APR	MAY	JUN	JUL	AUG	SEP	OCT	NOV	DEC
°F AVG MAX	76	76	78	80	83	86	86	85	85	83	79	77
°F AVG MIN	62	61	63	65	68	70	72	73	72	70	66	64
DIURNAL RANGE	14	15	15	15	15	16	14	12	13	13	13	13
RAIN/INCHES	3.6	2.6	2.5	2.0	2.4	2.6	3.7	5.1	5.7	5.2	4.4	3.7
HUMIDITY/%	73	70	69	67	68	69	71	74	75	76	73	73
BLOOM SEASON					*					*		*
DAYS CLR @ 11AM	7	9	9	15	12	10	7	6	7	7	7	7
DAYS CLR @ 5PM	7	11	6	11	7	6	5	4	4	5	3	7
RAIN/MM	91	66	64	51	61	66	94	130	145	132	112	94
°C AVG MAX	24.4	24.4	25.6	26.7	28.3	30.0	30.0	29.4	29.4	28.3	26.1	25.0
°C AVG MIN	16.7	16.1	17.2	18.3	20.0	21.1	22.2	22.8	22.2	21.1	18.9	17.8
DIURNAL RANGE	7.7	8.3	8.4	8.4	8.3	8.9	7.8	6.6	7.2	7.2	7.2	7.2
S/HEMISPHERE	JUL	AUG	SEP	OCT	NOV	DEC	JAN	FEB	MAR	APR	MAY	JUN

Cultural Recommendations

LIGHT: 1500–2500 fc.

TEMPERATURES: Summer days average 85–86°F (29–30°C), and nights average 70–73°F (21–23°C), with a diurnal range of 12–16°F (7–9°C). Temperatures at low elevations in New Guinea may be slightly warmer than those shown in the climate table for New Caledonia.

HUMIDITY: 70–75% year-round. Humidity is greater than indicated in the shady forest habitat, however.

WATER: Rainfall is relatively low and consistent most of the year. The driest season is in late winter and spring, and the heaviest rain falls in late summer and early autumn. Cultivated plants should be allowed to become somewhat dry between waterings but should never dry out completely.

FERTILIZER: ¼–½ recommended strength, applied weekly. A high-nitrogen fertilizer is beneficial from spring to midsummer, but a fertilizer high in phosphates should be used in late summer and autumn.

REST PERIOD: Winter days average 76–78°F (24–26°C), and nights average 61–64°F (16–18°C), with a diurnal range of 13–15°F (7–8°C). High and low temperatures decline simultaneously, resulting in little change in the diurnal range. In the habitat, rainfall is somewhat lower in late winter and spring. In cultivation, water and fertilizer should be reduced and the plants allowed to dry even more between waterings than in summer. They should not dry out completely or remain dry for long periods, however. In the habitat, light is highest in winter.

GROWING MEDIA: Plants may be mounted on tree-fern or cork slabs if humidity is high and plants are watered at least once daily in summer. When plants are potted, any open, fast-draining medium may be used. Repotting may be done anytime new roots are growing. Old canes continue to bloom for years and should not be removed when repotting.

MISCELLANEOUS NOTES: The bloom season shown in the climate table is based on cultivation records. Plants occasionally bloom at other times.

Plant and Flower Information

PLANT SIZE AND TYPE: A 5–9 in. (13–23 cm) sympodial epiphyte. Plants are occasionally lithophytic.

PSEUDOBULB: 4–6 in. (10–15 cm) long. The erect, clustered pseudobulbs are borne on a very short rhizome. The upper part of the stem is flattened and club-shaped. It tapers to a very narrow base before becoming slightly swollen at the roots. It is covered with sheathing leaf bases. Stems become yellow with age.

LEAVES: 2–8 per growth. The sharply pointed, oval leaves are 2.4–4.3 in. (6–11 cm) long. They are thin, medium green, and deciduous after flowering.

INFLORESCENCE: 1.6 in. (4 cm) long. The erect inflorescences emerge from nodes near the apex of both leafy and leafless pseudobulbs. They are laxly flowered.

FLOWERS: 2–4 per inflorescence. The flowers are 0.8–1.0 in. (2.0–2.5 cm) across and remain rather closed. They are ascending with the lip uppermost. Sepals and petals are white or white with a pinkish tinge. They become purplish with age. The erect dorsal sepal is ovate to elliptic-ovate and pointed at the tip. Lateral sepals are weakly spreading, ovate, and inflexed near the pointed tip. The petals are oblong-ovate, erect and rounder at the apex. The lip is white with a deep yellow throat. The midlobe is broadly pointed at the apex with 5 parallel, slightly raised lines. Blossoms may be self-pollinating.

HYBRIDIZING NOTES: Chromosome count is 2n = 40 (ref. 151, 152, 154, 187, 188), but as *D. platycaulon* the count is 2n = 38 (ref. 280, 504, 580).

REFERENCES: 151, 152, 154, 179, 187, 188, 216, 243, 252, 254, 270, 271, 280, 304, 353, 466, 504, 516, 580, 582.

PHOTOS/DRAWINGS: *270, 271, 304,* 466.

Dendrobium platylobum (Schlechter) J. J. Smith.
Although not correctly transferred, Schlechter (ref. 443) considered this plant to be a synonym of *Cadetia platyloba* Schlechter. REFERENCES: 223, 225, 443, 486.

Dendrobium platypetalum Persoon.
Now considered a synonym of *Maxillaria platypetala* Ruiz and Pavón. REFERENCES: 216, 254.

Dendrobium platyphyllum Schlechter.
See *D. nycteridoglossum* Rchb. f. REFERENCES: 220, 254, 286, 295, 433.

Dendrobium plebejum J. J. Smith

ORIGIN/HABITAT: Endemic to Sulawesi (Celebes). Plants grow close to sea level on trees in mangrove swamps near Tolitoli and Gorontalo.

CLIMATE: Station #97028, Tolitoli, Sulawesi, Indonesia, Lat. 1.0°N, Long. 120.8°E, at 7 ft. (2 m). Record extreme temperatures are not available for this location.

N/HEMISPHERE	JAN	FEB	MAR	APR	MAY	JUN	JUL	AUG	SEP	OCT	NOV	DEC
°F AVG MAX	84	83	85	86	86	86	85	86	86	86	86	85
°F AVG MIN	76	74	76	78	78	76	76	77	77	77	78	77
DIURNAL RANGE	8	9	9	8	8	10	9	9	9	9	8	8
RAIN/INCHES	6.3	4.9	7.4	3.8	6.4	6.3	5.5	4.1	4.9	4.7	4.0	4.3
HUMIDITY/%	N/A											
BLOOM SEASON	*										*	
DAYS CLR	N/A											
RAIN/MM	161	125	187	98	162	160	139	103	125	120	101	110
°C AVG MAX	28.7	28.5	29.3	29.9	30.1	30.1	29.7	30.1	30.2	30.2	30.0	29.5
°C AVG MIN	24.5	23.6	24.3	25.3	25.3	24.4	24.4	24.8	24.7	25.2	25.3	25.0
DIURNAL RANGE	4.2	4.9	5.0	4.6	4.8	5.7	5.3	5.3	5.5	5.0	4.7	4.5
S/HEMISPHERE	JUL	AUG	SEP	OCT	NOV	DEC	JAN	FEB	MAR	APR	MAY	JUN

Cultural Recommendations

LIGHT: 2500–3500 fc.

TEMPERATURES: Throughout the year, days average 83–86°F (29–30°C), and nights average 74–78°F (24–25°C), with a diurnal range of 8–10°F (4–6°C).

HUMIDITY: Information is not available for this location. However, records from nearby stations indicate that humidity probably averages 75–85% year-round.

WATER: Rainfall is moderate to heavy year-round. Cultivated plants should be kept moist, with only slight drying allowed between waterings.

FERTILIZER: ¼–½ recommended strength. A balanced fertilizer should be applied weekly to biweekly throughout the year.

REST PERIOD: Growing conditions should be maintained all year. However, water and fertilizer should be reduced somewhat in winter for cultivated plants, especially those grown in the dark, short-day conditions common in temperate latitudes. Plants should be allowed to dry slightly between waterings but should not remain dry for long periods.

GROWING MEDIA: Mounting plants on tree-fern or cork slabs accommodates their pendulous growth habit. However, humidity must be high and plants must be watered at least once a day in summer. If plants cannot be mounted, small pots or hanging baskets may be filled with an open, fast-draining medium. Repotting may be done anytime new roots are actively growing.

MISCELLANEOUS NOTES: The bloom season shown in the climate table is based on reports from the habitat. The plant was described in 1907 in *Bull. Dép. Agric. Indes Néerl.* 5:6.

Plant and Flower Information

PLANT SIZE AND TYPE: A 4 in. (10 cm) sympodial epiphyte.

PSEUDOBULB: 4 in. (10 cm) long. The stems are yellowish and reddish. The lower portion of the stem is swollen while the upper part is somewhat flattened. They are pendent and emerge from a short rhizome.

LEAVES: About 3 on the upper part of the stem. The leaves are 2–3 in. (5–7 cm) long, almost circular, and widely spaced. They are fleshy and held nearly parallel to the stem.

INFLORESCENCE: Short. The inflorescence emerges at the apex of the stem.

FLOWERS: The flowers are 0.4 in. (1 cm) long when measured from the apex of the sepals to the tip of the mentum. They are whitish green and yellow with violet to purple stripes. The dorsal sepal is oblong-ovate, pointed, and convex with 3–5 longitudinal lines. The lateral sepals form a large conical spur. They are pointed, spreading, and broadly triangular at the apex. Petals are lanceolate and pointed with longitudinal stripes. The oblong lip is vaguely 3-lobed, recurved, with an uneven, wavy to ruffled margin and 2 raised lines. Blossoms are pleasantly fragrant.

REFERENCES: 220, 254, 436.

Dendrobium pleianthum Schlechter

ORIGIN/HABITAT: Northern Papua New Guinea and the Solomon Islands. In New Guinea, plants are found on Gati Mountain near the Minjem Valley at about 1650 ft. (500 m) and in the Kani Range at about 2300 ft. (700 m). They grow in the forks of tall trees below the mistforest zone. In the Solomons, plants are found on Guadalcanal where they grow in ridge-top forests at about 2600 ft. (800 m).

CLIMATE: Station #91520, Honiara, Guadalcanal, Solomon Islands, Lat. 9.4°S, Long. 160.0°E, at 10 ft. (3 m). Temperatures are calculated for an elevation of 2600 ft. (790 m), resulting in probable extremes of 86°F (30°C) and 6°F (14°C).

N/HEMISPHERE	JAN	FEB	MAR	APR	MAY	JUN	JUL	AUG	SEP	OCT	NOV	DEC
°F AVG MAX	77	78	79	79	79	79	79	79	78	79	79	78
°F AVG MIN	63	63	63	63	64	64	65	65	64	64	64	63
DIURNAL RANGE	14	15	16	16	15	15	14	14	14	15	15	15
RAIN/INCHES	6.0	4.4	4.6	7.7	7.7	9.5	14.1	13.3	16.7	10.6	8.1	6.7
HUMIDITY/%	84	82	81	80	81	82	83	83	87	85	85	85
BLOOM SEASON			*	*								
DAYS CLR @ 5AM	6	7	7	5	6	3	3	4	4	4	8	7
DAYS CLR @ 11AM	3	2	2	1	1	1	0	2	2	4	4	
RAIN/MM	152	112	117	196	196	241	358	338	424	269	206	170
°C AVG MAX	25.0	25.6	26.1	26.1	26.1	26.3	26.2	26.1	25.6	26.1	26.1	25.6
°C AVG MIN	17.2	17.5	17.5	17.5	18.0	18.0	18.6	18.6	18.0	18.0	18.0	17.5
DIURNAL RANGE	7.8	8.1	8.6	8.6	8.1	8.3	7.6	7.5	7.6	8.1	8.1	8.1
S/HEMISPHERE	JUL	AUG	SEP	OCT	NOV	DEC	JAN	FEB	MAR	APR	MAY	JUN

Cultural Recommendations

LIGHT: 3000–4000 fc.

TEMPERATURES: Throughout the year, days average 77–79°F (25–26°C), and nights average 63–65°F (17–19°C), with a diurnal range of 14–16°F (8–9°C).

HUMIDITY: 80–85% year-round.

WATER: Rainfall is heavy all year, but conditions are slightly drier for 2–3 months in winter. Cultivated plants should be kept moist while actively growing, but water should be gradually reduced in late autumn.

FERTILIZER: ¼–½ recommended strength. A balanced fertilizer should be applied weekly to biweekly throughout the year.

REST PERIOD: Growing conditions should be maintained year-round. Rainfall in the habitat is somewhat lower in winter. Water should be reduced for cultivated plants, especially those grown in the dark, short-day conditions common in temperate latitudes. They should never be allowed to dry out completely, however. In the habitat, light is highest in winter.

GROWING MEDIA: Plants may be mounted on tree-fern or cork slabs if humidity is high and plants are watered at least once daily in summer. When plants are potted, any open, fast-draining medium may be used. Repotting may be done anytime new roots are growing.

MISCELLANEOUS NOTES: The bloom season shown in the climate table is based on reports from the habitat.

Plant and Flower Information

PLANT SIZE AND TYPE: A 36–48 in. (91–122 cm) sympodial epiphyte or terrestrial.

PSEUDOBULB: 34–45 in. (86–114 cm) long. The flattened stems, which do not branch, may be erect or pendulous. They emerge from a very short rhizome.

LEAVES: Many. The linear-lanceolate leaves are 5–8 in. (13–20 cm) long and slightly twisted at the base to all face in one direction. They may be erect or spreading.

INFLORESCENCE: Extremely short. The inflorescences emerge from the middle of nodes along the side of the stem. The blossoms are clumped together. The inflorescences are arranged in 2 rows along the stem.

FLOWERS: 4–10 per inflorescence. The flowers are 0.4 in. (1.1 cm) across. They are pale yellow with a faint red margin on the lip. Blossoms have an oblong-lanceolate dorsal sepal, with sickle-shaped, keeled lateral sepals, and linear petals. The erect, 3-lobed lip is rounded at the apex with a fleshy disk. The sidelobes are obliquely oblong.

REFERENCES: 96, 221, 271, 318, 437, 445, 516.

PHOTOS/DRAWINGS: 271, *318*, 437.

Dendrobium pleiostachyum Rchb. f.
Thought to have originated in Papua New Guinea or perhaps on off-shore islands, but details on habitat location and elevation are not available, so climate data cannot be selected. The plants were described as having flexible and grooved stems with tongue-shaped leaves which were pointed at the tip. Inflorescences were numerous, very short, densely flowered, and were carried on one side of the stem. Many blossoms were carried on each inflorescence. The flowers were described as "probably white." The dorsal sepal was very ruffled, lateral sepals were triangular, petals ovate, and the lip narrowly fiddle-shaped. REFERENCES: 216, 254, 445.

Dendrobium pleurodes Schlechter

ORIGIN/HABITAT: Papua New Guinea. Plants grow in the Morobe District and the Dischore Range on mossy mistforest trees at about 3950 ft. (1200 m).

CLIMATE: Station #200192, Garaina, Papua New Guinea, Lat. 7.9°S, Long. 147.1°E, at 2350 ft. (716 m). Temperatures are calculated for an elevation of 3950 ft. (1200 m), resulting in probable extremes of 89°F (32°C) and 41°F (5°C).

N/HEMISPHERE	JAN	FEB	MAR	APR	MAY	JUN	JUL	AUG	SEP	OCT	NOV	DEC
°F AVG MAX	75	77	78	79	80	80	80	80	79	79	78	76
°F AVG MIN	58	58	58	59	58	59	60	60	60	59	59	58
DIURNAL RANGE	17	19	20	20	22	21	20	20	19	20	19	18
RAIN/INCHES	5.8	6.5	8.7	11.1	11.8	11.9	8.9	11.7	11.5	9.9	7.7	5.2
HUMIDITY/%	84	82	82	81	80	80	81	81	82	83	84	84
BLOOM SEASON				*								
DAYS CLR	N/A											
RAIN/MM	147	165	221	282	300	302	226	297	292	251	196	132
°C AVG MAX	23.8	24.9	25.4	26.0	26.5	26.5	26.5	26.5	26.0	26.0	25.4	24.3
°C AVG MIN	14.3	14.3	14.3	14.9	14.3	14.9	15.4	15.4	15.4	14.9	14.9	14.3
DIURNAL RANGE	9.5	10.6	11.1	11.1	12.2	11.6	11.1	11.1	10.6	11.1	10.5	10.0
S/HEMISPHERE	JUL	AUG	SEP	OCT	NOV	DEC	JAN	FEB	MAR	APR	MAY	JUN

Cultural Recommendations

LIGHT: 2000–3000 fc.

TEMPERATURES: Throughout the year, days average 75–80°F (24–27°C), and nights average 58–60°F (14–15°C), with a diurnal range of 17–22°F (10–12°C).

HUMIDITY: 80–85% year-round.

WATER: Rainfall is heavy all year, but conditions are slightly drier in winter. Cultivated plants should be kept moist but not soggy.

FERTILIZER: ¼–½ recommended strength. A balanced fertilizer should be applied weekly to biweekly throughout the year. The Royal Botanic Garden in Edinburgh uses a seaweed-based fertilizer for high-elevation plants from New Guinea.

REST PERIOD: Growing conditions should be maintained all year. In the habitat, rainfall is slightly lower in winter. For cultivated plants, water and fertilizer should be reduced somewhat, especially for plants grown in the dark, short-day conditions common in temperate latitudes. Plants should never be allowed to dry out completely, however. In the habitat, light is slightly higher in winter.

GROWING MEDIA: Plants may be mounted on tree-fern or cork slabs if humidity is high and plants are watered at least once daily in summer. When plants are potted, any open, fast-draining medium may be used. Repotting may be done anytime new roots are growing.

MISCELLANEOUS NOTES: The bloom season shown in the climate table is based on reports from the habitat. *D. pleurodes* is known only from the type collection.

Plant and Flower Information

PLANT SIZE AND TYPE: A 6–18 in. (16–45 cm) sympodial epiphyte.

PSEUDOBULB: 3–12 in. (8–30 cm) long. The slender stems are clustered. They have 3–5 nodes below the leaf.

LEAVES: 1 at the apex of each growth. The suberect, linear leaves are 3–6 in. (8–15 cm) long.

INFLORESCENCE: Very short.

FLOWERS: 1–2 per inflorescence. The small flowers are 0.4–0.6 in. (1.0–1.5 cm) long. The blossoms have green, ovate sepals, and white, linear petals, with a brown lip marked with a white callus. The lip has large sidelobes that extend beyond the notched midlobe which has a projecting point in the center of the notch.

REFERENCES: 83, 92, 221, 437, 445.

PHOTOS/DRAWINGS: 437.

Dendrobium pleurothalloides Kränzlin.
Now considered a synonym of *Diplocaulobium inauditum* (Rchb. f.) Kränzlin. REFERENCES: 218, 254.

Dendrobium plicatile Lindley.
Now considered a synonym of *Flickingeria fimbriata* (Blume) A. Hawkes. REFERENCES: 12, 25, 75, 98, 151, 179, 190, 200, 208, 213, 216, 231, 254, 296, 317, 373, 445, 449, 455, 577. PHOTOS/DRAWINGS: *373*.

Dendrobium plicatum Dietrich.
Now considered a synonym of *Maxillaria paniculata* Ruiz and Pavón. REFERENCES: 216, 254.

Dendrobium plumilobum J. J. Smith

ORIGIN/HABITAT: Irian Jaya (western New Guinea). Plants grow near the Rouffaer River in primeval forests at about 800 ft. (250 m).

CLIMATE: Station #200004, Ambunti, Papua New Guinea, Lat. 4.2°S, Long. 142.8°E, at 164 ft. (50 m). Temperatures are calculated for an elevation of 1000 ft. (300 m), resulting in probable extremes of 96°F (36°C) and 49°F (10°C).

N/HEMISPHERE	JAN	FEB	MAR	APR	MAY	JUN	JUL	AUG	SEP	OCT	NOV	DEC
°F AVG MAX	85	87	87	87	88	87	87	87	87	87	87	86
°F AVG MIN	69	70	71	70	70	70	69	70	70	70	70	71
DIURNAL RANGE	16	17	16	17	18	17	18	17	17	17	17	15
RAIN/INCHES	6.4	7.4	7.7	8.5	9.2	9.4	10.9	10.2	12.2	10.4	8.3	5.2
HUMIDITY/%	N/A											
BLOOM SEASON			*									
DAYS CLR	N/A											
RAIN/MM	163	188	196	216	234	239	277	259	310	264	211	132
°C AVG MAX	29.6	30.7	30.7	30.7	31.2	30.7	30.7	30.7	30.7	30.7	30.7	30.1
°C AVG MIN	20.7	21.2	21.8	21.2	21.2	21.2	20.7	21.2	21.2	21.2	21.2	21.8
DIURNAL RANGE	8.9	9.5	8.9	9.5	10.0	9.5	10.0	9.5	9.5	9.5	9.5	8.3
S/HEMISPHERE	JUL	AUG	SEP	OCT	NOV	DEC	JAN	FEB	MAR	APR	MAY	JUN

Cultural Recommendations

LIGHT: 2000–3000 fc.

TEMPERATURES: Throughout the year, days average 85–88°F (30–31°C), and nights average 69–71°F (21–22°C), with a diurnal range of 15–18°F (8–10°C).

HUMIDITY: Information is not available for this location. However, records

from nearby stations indicate that humidity probably averages near 80% year-round.

WATER: Rainfall is heavy all year. The greatest amounts fall in summer and early autumn. Cultivated plants be kept moist but not soggy.

FERTILIZER: ¼–½ recommended strength. A balanced fertilizer should be applied weekly to biweekly throughout the year.

REST PERIOD: Growing conditions should be maintained all year. Water and fertilizer should be reduced for plants cultivated in the dark, short-day conditions common in temperate-latitude winters, but they should never be allowed to dry out completely. In the habitat, light is probably highest in winter.

GROWING MEDIA: Plants may be mounted on cork or tree-fern slabs if humidity is high and plants are watered at least once daily in summer. When plants are potted, any open, fast-draining medium may be used. Repotting may be done anytime new roots are growing.

MISCELLANEOUS NOTES: The bloom season shown in the climate table is based on reports from the habitat. The coarse roots are very twisted.

Plant and Flower Information

PLANT SIZE AND TYPE: A 20 in. (50 cm) sympodial epiphyte.

PSEUDOBULB: 20 in. (50 cm) long. The slender stems are rigid, shiny, and unbranched. They are clustered on a short, branching rhizome.

LEAVES: Many. The linear, grasslike leaves are about 3.3 in. (8.5 cm) long, but they are smaller at the apex. Leaves have 2, unequal teeth at the apex.

INFLORESCENCE: Short. Inflorescences emerge through the often overlapping leaf sheaths.

FLOWERS: 2 per inflorescence. The flowers are 0.9 in. (2.3 cm) long. The light yellow sepals and petals taper to a slender point at the tip. The 3-lobed lip is erect and very recurved. The conspicuous midlobe is ovate and recurved, with a hairy midlobe and a lacerated margin. The erect to suberect sidelobes are sparsely dotted with small warts. The margins are lacerated or uneven.

REFERENCES: 225, 470.

Dendrobium pluricostatum Schlechter. See *D. hosei* Ridley. REFERENCES: 92, 221, 437, 445, 470, 583.

Dendrobium podagraria Kränzlin not Hooker f. Schlechter (ref. 437) included *D. podagraria* Kränzlin as a synonym of *D. eboracense* Kränzlin, but in 1911 (ref. 436) he included it as a synonym of *D. odoratum* Schlechter. However, J. J. Smith (ref. 470) lists *D. podagraria* Kränzlin and *D. eboracense* Kränzlin as synonyms of *D. macfarlanei* F. Mueller not Rchb. f. When botanical work is done, it is possible that *D. podagraria* Kränzlin, *D. eboracense* Kränzlin, and *D. odoratum* Schlechter may all be synonyms of *D. macfarlanei* F. Mueller. REFERENCES: 218, 436, 437, 445, 448, 470.

Dendrobium podagraria Hooker f. not Kränzlin

AKA: *D. angulatum* Lindley 1828 not 1830, *D. angulatum* as used by Parish in 1883. Seidenfaden (ref. 454) lists *D. inconcinnum* Ridley as a possible synonym and discusses the taxonomy of this species.

ORIGIN/HABITAT: Widespread in Southeast Asia. In northeastern India, plants grow along the Attran River in the Cachar and Chittagong regions. They also occur in the Mergui, Moulmein, and Tenasserim regions of Burma and in the peninsular region of southwestern Thailand. In Vietnam, plants grow near Dalat, Blao, Lang Khouai, Quangtri, and Hien-le. Habitat elevation is estimated, so the following climate data should be used with caution.

CLIMATE: Station #48110, Mergui, Burma, Lat. 12.4°N, Long. 98.6°E, at 75 ft. (23 m). Temperatures are calculated for an elevation of 3000 ft. (910 m), resulting in probable extremes of 89°F (32°C) and 43°F (6°C).

N/HEMISPHERE	JAN	FEB	MAR	APR	MAY	JUN	JUL	AUG	SEP	OCT	NOV	DEC
°F AVG MAX	77	79	80	81	79	75	74	74	74	76	77	77
°F AVG MIN	59	61	63	65	65	64	63	63	63	63	61	59
DIURNAL RANGE	18	18	17	16	14	11	11	11	11	13	16	18
RAIN/INCHES	1.0	2.1	3.1	4.9	16.7	30.0	32.9	30.0	24.9	12.1	3.8	0.8
HUMIDITY/%	73	75	78	79	86	91	93	94	92	86	79	75
BLOOM SEASON	N/A											
DAYS CLR @ 7AM	9	3	4	2	0	0	0	0	0	1	4	8
DAYS CLR @ 1PM	11	7	4	2	0	0	0	0	0	1	4	9
RAIN/MM	25	53	79	124	424	762	836	762	632	307	97	20
°C AVG MAX	25.0	26.1	26.7	27.2	26.1	24.1	23.4	23.3	23.3	24.4	25.0	25.0
°C AVG MIN	15.0	16.3	17.4	18.5	18.5	18.0	17.4	17.4	17.4	17.4	16.3	15.2
DIURNAL RANGE	10.0	9.8	9.3	8.7	7.6	6.1	6.0	5.9	5.9	7.0	8.7	9.8
S/HEMISPHERE	JUL	AUG	SEP	OCT	NOV	DEC	JAN	FEB	MAR	APR	MAY	JUN

Cultural Recommendations

LIGHT: 2000–3000 fc.

TEMPERATURES: Throughout the year, days average 74–81°F (23–27°C), and nights average 59–65°F (15–19°C), with a diurnal range of 11–18°F (6–10°C).

HUMIDITY: 85–95% from late spring into autumn, dropping to near 75% in winter.

WATER: Rainfall is very heavy for 6 months during summer and early autumn, but conditions are much drier for 2–3 months in winter. Cultivated plants should be kept moist while actively growing, but water should be gradually reduced in autumn.

FERTILIZER: ¼–½ recommended strength. A balanced fertilizer should be applied weekly to biweekly throughout the year.

REST PERIOD: Growing conditions should be maintained all year. In the habitat, rainfall is low for 2–3 months in winter, but additional moisture from dew and mist is common. Consequently, the dry season is neither as long or as severe as indicated by the rainfall averages. Water and fertilizer should be reduced for cultivated plants in winter. They should dry slightly between waterings but should never be allowed to dry completely. In the habitat, light is highest in winter.

GROWING MEDIA: Plants may be mounted on tree-fern or cork slabs if humidity is high and plants are watered at least once daily in summer. When plants are potted, any open, fast-draining medium may be used. Repotting may be done anytime new roots are growing.

Plant and Flower Information

PLANT SIZE AND TYPE: A 12–35 in. (30–90 cm) sympodial epiphyte.

PSEUDOBULB: 12–35 in. (30–90 cm) long. The stems are slender except for a swollen area about 1.5 in. (4 cm) above the base. They sometimes branch.

LEAVES: 3–12 per growth. The widely spaced leaves are 1.6–2.8 in. (4–7 cm) long. They may be linear or oblong.

INFLORESCENCE: Very short. Inflorescences emerge from nodes near the apex opposite the leaves on leafy stems.

FLOWERS: 1 per inflorescence. The flowers are 0.4–0.8 in. (1–2 cm) long. They are white with red or pink veins on the lip. The dorsal sepal and petals curve forward, and the lateral sepals curve out. The circular midlobe is very small with a point in the center and an uneven margin. The very large sidelobes are incurved and the front margins are recurved.

HYBRIDIZING NOTES: Johansen (ref. 239) indicates that plants are self-sterile and that flowers dropped 4–5 days after self-pollination.

REFERENCES: 157, 202, 216, 239, 254, 266, 395, 454.

PHOTOS/DRAWINGS: 254, 454.

Dendrobium podocarpifolium Schlechter

ORIGIN/HABITAT: Papua New Guinea. Plants grow in the Sepik River region at about 4250 ft. (1300 m).

CLIMATE: Station #200004, Ambunti, Papua New Guinea, Lat. 4.2°S, Long. 142.8°E, at 164 ft. (50 m). Temperatures are calculated for an elevation of 4000 ft. (1220 m), resulting in probable extremes of 86°F (30°C) and 39°F (4°C).

N/HEMISPHERE	JAN	FEB	MAR	APR	MAY	JUN	JUL	AUG	SEP	OCT	NOV	DEC
°F AVG MAX	75	77	77	77	78	77	77	77	77	77	77	76
°F AVG MIN	59	60	61	60	60	60	59	60	60	60	60	61
DIURNAL RANGE	16	17	16	17	18	17	18	17	17	17	17	15
RAIN/INCHES	6.4	7.4	7.7	8.5	9.2	9.4	10.9	10.2	12.2	10.4	8.3	5.2
HUMIDITY/%	N/A											
BLOOM SEASON									*			
DAYS CLR	N/A											
RAIN/MM	163	188	196	216	234	239	277	259	310	264	211	132
°C AVG MAX	24.1	25.2	25.2	25.2	25.7	25.2	25.2	25.2	25.2	25.2	25.2	24.6
°C AVG MIN	15.2	15.7	16.3	15.7	15.7	15.7	15.0	15.7	15.7	15.7	15.7	16.3
DIURNAL RANGE	8.9	9.5	8.9	9.5	10.0	9.5	10.0	9.5	9.5	9.5	9.5	8.3
S/HEMISPHERE	JUL	AUG	SEP	OCT	NOV	DEC	JAN	FEB	MAR	APR	MAY	JUN

Cultural Recommendations

LIGHT: 2000–3000 fc.

TEMPERATURES: Throughout the year, days average 75–78°F (24–26°C), and nights average 59–61°F (15–16°C), with a diurnal range of 15–18°F (8–10°C).

HUMIDITY: Information is not available for this location. However, records from nearby locations indicate that humidity probably averages near 80% year-round.

WATER: Rainfall is heavy all year, with the greatest rainfall falling in summer and early autumn. Cultivated plants should be kept moist but not soggy.

FERTILIZER: ¼–½ recommended strength. A balanced fertilizer should be applied weekly to biweekly throughout the year.

REST PERIOD: Growing conditions should be maintained all year. Water and fertilizer should be reduced for plants cultivated in the dark, short-day conditions common in temperate-latitude winters, but they should never be allowed to dry out completely. In the habitat, seasonal light variation is minor.

GROWING MEDIA: Plants may be mounted on cork or tree-fern slabs if humidity is high and plants are watered at least once daily in summer. When plants are potted, any open, fast-draining medium may be used. Repotting may be done anytime new roots are growing.

MISCELLANEOUS NOTES: The bloom season shown in the climate table is based on reports from the habitat.

Plant and Flower Information

PLANT SIZE AND TYPE: A shrublike, 39 in. (100 cm) sympodial epiphyte.

PSEUDOBULB: 39 in. (100 cm) long. The stems are slender, erect, and branching. They become black when dried.

LEAVES: Many. The broadly linear leaves are 1.2–2.4 in. (3–6 cm) long. They are leathery, smooth, and obscurely bilobed.

INFLORESCENCE: Very short.

FLOWERS: 1 per inflorescence. The very tiny, inverted blossoms are white. Sepals and petals are 0.2 in. (0.4 cm) long. The lip is much shorter. It is 3-lobed with a few scattered protuberances. The sidelobes are triangular. The nearly oval midlobe has a wavy margin.

REFERENCES: 223, 443.

Dendrobium podochiloides Schlechter

ORIGIN/HABITAT: Northern Papua New Guinea. Plants grow on tall forest trees in the Kani Range at about 2600 ft. (800 m).

CLIMATE: Station #200187, Erap, Papua New Guinea, Lat. 6.6°S, Long. 146.7°E, at 850 ft. (260 m). Temperatures are calculated for an elevation of 2600 ft. (790 m), resulting in probable extremes of 96°F (36°C) and 47°F (8°C).

N/HEMISPHERE	JAN	FEB	MAR	APR	MAY	JUN	JUL	AUG	SEP	OCT	NOV	DEC
°F AVG MAX	82	82	83	84	87	87	87	87	87	86	84	84
°F AVG MIN	63	63	63	64	66	67	66	66	67	65	68	64
DIURNAL RANGE	19	19	20	20	21	20	21	21	20	21	16	20
RAIN/INCHES	3.9	3.9	2.7	3.0	3.0	5.3	5.9	5.9	7.0	3.4	2.4	3.1
HUMIDITY/%	82	81	81	79	75	74	74	74	77	76	80	80
BLOOM SEASON									*			
DAYS CLR	N/A											
RAIN/MM	99	99	69	76	76	135	150	150	178	86	61	79
°C AVG MAX	27.8	27.8	28.3	28.9	30.6	30.7	30.6	30.6	30.6	30.0	28.9	28.9
°C AVG MIN	17.2	17.3	17.3	17.9	19.0	19.6	19.0	19.0	19.6	18.5	20.1	17.9
DIURNAL RANGE	10.6	10.5	11.0	11.0	11.6	11.1	11.6	11.6	11.0	11.5	8.8	11.0
S/HEMISPHERE	JUL	AUG	SEP	OCT	NOV	DEC	JAN	FEB	MAR	APR	MAY	JUN

Cultural Recommendations

LIGHT: 2500–3500 fc.

TEMPERATURES: Throughout the year, days average 82–87°F (28–31°C), and nights average 63–68°F (17–20°C), with a diurnal range of 16–21°F (9–12°C).

HUMIDITY: 75–80% year-round. The habitat may be quite dry during hot afternoons.

WATER: Rainfall is moderate most of the year, but conditions are somewhat wetter for 4–5 months in summer and early autumn. Cultivated plants should be thoroughly saturated and then allowed to dry slightly between waterings in summer and early autumn. Water should be gradually reduced in autumn.

FERTILIZER: ¼–½ recommended strength. A balanced fertilizer should be applied weekly to biweekly throughout the year.

REST PERIOD: Growing temperatures should be maintained all year. In the habitat, rainfall is lowest in winter, but the high humidity indicates that additional moisture is frequently available from heavy dew. Cultivated plants should be allowed to dry for somewhat longer between waterings than in summer, but they should not remain dry for extended periods. Fertilizer should be reduced until water is increased in spring. In the habitat, seasonal light variation is minor.

GROWING MEDIA: Plants may be mounted on tree-fern or cork slabs, if humidity is high and plants are watered at least once daily in summer. When plants are potted, any open, fast-draining medium may be used. Repotting may be done anytime new roots are growing.

MISCELLANEOUS NOTES: The bloom season shown in the climate table is based on reports from the habitat. Plants that produce flowers which last a single day commonly bloom several times during the year. Flowering usually occurs 7–14 days after a sudden 10°F (5°C) drop in daytime temperatures.

Plant and Flower Information

PLANT SIZE AND TYPE: A 16–24 in. (40–60 cm) sympodial epiphyte.

PSEUDOBULB: 16–24 in. (40–60 cm) long. The curved, spreading stems are slender and unbranched.

LEAVES: Many. The lanceolate leaves are 1.4–2.0 in. (3.5–5.0 cm) long.

INFLORESCENCE: Short. Inflorescences arise from above the leaf axils.

FLOWERS: 2 per inflorescence. The flowers are 0.3 in. (0.9 cm) long and barely open. They are white with a red tinge on the outside. The lip has a yellow crest and violet-red markings. Blossoms are very short-lived.

REFERENCES: 92, 221, 437, 445.

PHOTOS/DRAWINGS: 437.

Dendrobium pogonatherum J. J. Smith

AKA: Sometimes spelled *D. pogonantherum*.

ORIGIN/HABITAT: The low lying Aru Islands off the southwest coast of Irian Jaya (western New Guinea). Habitat elevation is unavailable, so the following climate data should be used with caution. Plants were cultivated in the botanical garden at Bogor, Java.

CLIMATE: Station #97810, Kai Ketjil, Indonesia, Lat. 5.7°S, Long. 132.8°E, at 39 ft. (12 m). Record extreme temperatures are not available for this location.

N/HEMISPHERE	JAN	FEB	MAR	APR	MAY	JUN	JUL	AUG	SEP	OCT	NOV	DEC
°F AVG MAX	83	83	85	88	88	87	85	86	86	86	85	84
°F AVG MIN	75	76	77	76	77	76	76	76	76	76	77	77
DIURNAL RANGE	8	7	8	12	11	11	9	10	10	10	8	7
RAIN/INCHES	3.8	2.8	2.3	1.7	5.6	12.7	14.7	11.4	9.0	6.9	8.3	5.1
HUMIDITY/%	N/A											
BLOOM SEASON	N/A											
DAYS CLR	N/A											
RAIN/MM	96	71	60	43	143	322	374	289	229	176	211	130
°C AVG MAX	28.2	28.4	29.6	30.9	31.2	30.5	29.6	29.8	30.0	30.2	29.5	28.7
°C AVG MIN	24.2	24.2	24.7	24.7	24.8	24.6	24.3	24.3	24.3	24.6	25.0	24.8
DIURNAL RANGE	4.0	4.2	4.9	6.2	6.4	5.9	5.3	5.5	5.7	5.6	4.5	3.9
S/HEMISPHERE	JUL	AUG	SEP	OCT	NOV	DEC	JAN	FEB	MAR	APR	MAY	JUN

Cultural Recommendations

LIGHT: 2500–3500 fc. These are suggested starting levels since little is known about how or where this species grows in nature. Watch new plants carefully for signs of stress or tissue damage from high light levels.

TEMPERATURES: Throughout the year, days average 83–88°F (28–31°C), and nights average 75–77°F (24–25°C), with a diurnal range of 7–12°F (4–6°C).

HUMIDITY: Information is not available for this location. However, records from nearby stations indicate that humidity probably averages 80–90% year-round.

WATER: Rainfall is very heavy from summer into autumn, but conditions are semidry for 3–4 months in winter. Cultivated plants should be kept moist while actively growing, but water should be gradually reduced in in late autumn.

FERTILIZER: ¼–½ recommended strength. A balanced fertilizer should be applied weekly to biweekly throughout the year.

REST PERIOD: Growing temperatures should be maintained year-round. Water should be reduced somewhat in winter. Plants should be allowed to dry slightly between waterings, but they should not remain dry for extended periods. Occasional early morning mistings on bright, sunny days between waterings may prove beneficial. Fertilizer should be reduced anytime water is reduced. In the habitat, light is probably higher in winter.

GROWING MEDIA: Plants may be mounted on tree-fern or cork slabs or potted in small pots filled with any open, fast-draining medium. Repotting may be done anytime new roots are actively growing.

MISCELLANEOUS NOTES: The plant was described in 1907 in *Bull. Dép. Agric. Indes Néerl.* 5:9.

Plant and Flower Information

PLANT SIZE AND TYPE: A 24–39 in. (60–100 cm) sympodial epiphyte.

PSEUDOBULB: 24–39 in. (60–100 cm) long. The dark, flattened stems are clustered.

LEAVES: Many. The linear leaves are 4 in. (10 cm) long. They are pale green.

INFLORESCENCE: Short. Inflorescences emerge through the leaf bases at nodes along the stem.

FLOWERS: 2 per inflorescence. The flowers are 0.6 in. (1.4 cm) across. Sepals and petals are probably white as are the bracts and ovary. The erect lip is pale orange with pale yellow on the hairy midlobe.

REFERENCES: 220, 254.

Dendrobium pogoniates Rchb. f.

ORIGIN/HABITAT: The forests of Sabah (North Borneo). Habitat location and elevation are unavailable, so the selection of the following climate data is based on estimations, assumptions, suppositions, and conjecture. They should be used with extreme caution.

CLIMATE: Station #96465, Labuan, Sabah, Borneo, Lat. 5.3°N, Long. 115.2°E at 98 ft. (30 m). Record extreme temperatures are 99°F (37°C) and 59°F (15°C).

N/HEMISPHERE	JAN	FEB	MAR	APR	MAY	JUN	JUL	AUG	SEP	OCT	NOV	DEC
°F AVG MAX	86	86	87	89	89	88	88	88	87	87	87	86
°F AVG MIN	76	76	76	76	76	76	77	76	76	76	76	76
DIURNAL RANGE	10	10	11	13	13	12	11	12	11	11	11	10
RAIN/INCHES	4.4	4.6	5.9	11.7	13.6	13.8	12.5	11.7	16.4	18.3	16.5	11.2
HUMIDITY/%	83	84	83	82	82	82	82	79	80	81	81	82
BLOOM SEASON	N/A											
DAYS CLR @ 8AM	1	3	3	4	3	0	1	2	1	2	1	2
DAYS CLR @ 2PM	3	5	5	5	2	2	4	3	1	3	1	1
RAIN/MM	112	117	150	297	345	351	318	297	417	465	419	284
°C AVG MAX	30.0	30.0	30.6	31.7	31.7	31.1	31.1	31.1	30.6	30.6	30.6	30.0
°C AVG MIN	24.4	24.4	24.4	24.4	24.4	25.0	24.4	24.4	24.4	24.4	24.4	24.4
DIURNAL RANGE	5.6	5.6	6.2	7.3	7.3	6.7	6.1	6.7	6.2	6.2	6.2	5.6
S/HEMISPHERE	JUL	AUG	SEP	OCT	NOV	DEC	JAN	FEB	MAR	APR	MAY	JUN

Cultural Recommendations

LIGHT: 2000–3000 fc.

TEMPERATURES: Throughout he year, days average 86–89°F (30–32°C), and nights average 76–77°F (24–25°C), with a diurnal range of l0–13°F (6–7°C).

HUMIDITY: 80–85% year-round.

WATER: Rainfall is moderate to heavy all year. Cultivated plants should be kept moist.

FERTILIZER: ¼–½ recommended strength. A balanced fertilizer should be applied weekly to biweekly throughout the year.

REST PERIOD: Growing temperatures should be maintained. Water and fertilizer should be reduced slightly in winter, particularly for plants grown in the dark, short-day conditions common in temperate latitudes. Plants should not be allowed to dry out completely, however. In the habitat, light is highest in winter.

GROWING MEDIA: Plants may be mounted on tree-fern or cork slabs if humidity is high and plants are watered at least once daily in summer. When plants are potted, any open, fast-draining medium may be used. They may be repotted anytime new roots are growing.

Plant and Flower Information

PLANT SIZE AND TYPE: A 12 in. (30 cm) sympodial epiphyte.

PSEUDOBULB: 12 in. (30 cm) long.

LEAVES: The linear-lanceolate leaves are bilobed at the apex.

INFLORESCENCE: Flowers are held in a cluster.

FLOWERS: Few per inflorescence. Sepals and petals are light yellow and minutely toothed at the apex. Lateral sepals are somewhat triangular. The orange lip has no callus. The long, projecting midlobe has long fringes and hairs.

REFERENCES: 218, 254, 286, 295.

Dendrobium poilanei Guillaumin. See *D. hercoglossum* Rchb. f. REFERENCES: 223, 266, 447, 448, 454.

Dendrobium poissonianum Schlechter

ORIGIN/HABITAT: Endemic to northern New Caledonia. Plants are most common in humid scrub-forests at 1300–2950 ft. (400–900 m), where they frequently grow in full sun. They are occasionally found on creek-side *Casuarina* trees near Ou-Hinna as low as 150 ft. (50 m).

CLIMATE: Station #91583, Poindimie, New Caledonia, Lat. 20.9°S, Long. 165.3°E, at 36 ft. (11 m). Temperatures are calculated for an elevation of 2100 ft. (640 m). Record extreme temperatures are not available for this location.

N/HEMISPHERE	JAN	FEB	MAR	APR	MAY	JUN	JUL	AUG	SEP	OCT	NOV	DEC
°F AVG MAX	67	67	68	70	72	74	76	76	75	74	70	69
°F AVG MIN	57	56	58	60	63	65	66	68	67	65	61	59
DIURNAL RANGE	10	11	10	10	9	9	10	8	8	9	9	10
RAIN/INCHES	3.4	3.0	2.6	4.2	7.5	7.7	11.4	10.4	9.3	5.7	6.7	4.6
HUMIDITY/%	N/A											
BLOOM SEASON				*	*	*						
DAYS CLR	N/A											
RAIN/MM	87	75	67	108	190	194	290	264	237	145	169	116
°C AVG MAX	19.5	19.5	20.1	21.2	22.3	23.4	24.5	24.5	24.0	23.4	21.2	20.7
°C AVG MIN	14.0	13.4	14.5	15.7	17.3	18.4	19.0	20.1	19.5	18.4	16.2	15.1
DIURNAL RANGE	5.5	6.1	5.6	5.5	5.0	5.0	5.5	4.4	4.5	5.0	5.0	5.6
S/HEMISPHERE	JUL	AUG	SEP	OCT	NOV	DEC	JAN	FEB	MAR	APR	MAY	JUN

Cultural Recommendations

LIGHT: 3000–4500 fc. Summer shading should be provided.

TEMPERATURES: Summer days average 74–76°F (23–25°C), and nights average 65–68°F (18–20°C), with a diurnal range of 8–10°F (4–6°C).

HUMIDITY: Information is not available for this location. However, records from nearby stations indicate that humidity probably averages 70–75% year-round.

WATER: Rainfall is moderate to heavy most of the year, but conditions are slightly drier in winter. Cultivated plants should be kept moist but not soggy from spring into autumn, but water should be gradually reduced in late autumn.

FERTILIZER: ¼–½ recommended strength, applied weekly. A high-nitrogen fertilizer is beneficial from spring to midsummer, but a fertilizer high in phosphates should be used in late summer and autumn.

REST PERIOD: Winter days average 67–69°F (20–21°C), and nights average 56–59°F (13–15°C), with a diurnal range of 10–11°F (6°C). Water and fertilizer should be reduced in winter. Cultivated plants should be allowed to become somewhat dry between waterings but should never remain dry for long periods. In the habitat, light is highest in winter.

GROWING MEDIA: Plants may be mounted on tree-fern or cork slabs if humidity is high and plants are watered at least once daily in summer. When plants are potted, any open, fast-draining medium may be used. Repotting is best done in early spring when new roots are growing.

MISCELLANEOUS NOTES: The bloom season shown in the climate table is based on reports from the habitat.

Plant and Flower Information

PLANT SIZE AND TYPE: A 3.5–6.0 in. (9–15 cm) sympodial epiphyte.

PSEUDOBULB: 1.2–4.0 in. (3–10 cm) long. Pseudobulbs are nearly cylindrical with a bulbous swelling at the base. They develop in a straight line.

LEAVES: 2–3 per growth. The leaves are 1.4–2.2 in. (3.6–5.5 cm) long. They are unequally 2-lobed at the apex.

INFLORESCENCE: 2–5 in. (5–13 cm) long. Inflorescences, which are zigzag and laxly flowered, emerge near the apex of the stem. Each growth may produce several inflorescences.

FLOWERS: 2–6 per inflorescence. The flowers are 0.8 in. (2 cm) across. The petals and protruding sepals are yellowish. The 3-lobed lip is marked with brownish-red or brownish-violet speckles. It has elongated, oblong sidelobes. The expanded midlobe is notched and smooth at the apex. It has a large, oval area densely covered with bilobed projections. The lip is often uppermost.

REFERENCES: 173, 220, 254, 432.

PHOTOS/DRAWINGS: 173.

Dendrobium polyanthum Lindley. See *D. cretaceum* Lindley. REFERENCES: Seidenfaden 1992 *Opera Botanica* #114.

Dendrobium polycarpum Rchb. f. See *D. mirbelianum* Gaudich. REFERENCES: 67, 84, 216, 254, 533.

Dendrobium polycladium Rchb. f.

AKA: *D. delumbe* Kränzlin.

ORIGIN/HABITAT: New Caledonia. Plants grow in numerous locations at 150–2300 ft. (50–700 m).

CLIMATE: Station #91592, Noumea, New Caledonia, Lat. 22.3°S, Long. 166.5°E, at 246 ft. (75 m). Temperatures are calculated for an elevation of 1000 ft. (300 m), resulting in probable extremes of 97°F (36°C) and 50°F (10°C).

N/HEMISPHERE	JAN	FEB	MAR	APR	MAY	JUN	JUL	AUG	SEP	OCT	NOV	DEC
°F AVG MAX	74	74	76	78	81	84	84	83	83	81	77	75
°F AVG MIN	60	59	61	63	66	68	70	71	70	68	64	62
DIURNAL RANGE	14	15	15	15	15	16	14	12	13	13	13	13
RAIN/INCHES	3.6	2.6	2.5	2.0	2.4	2.6	3.7	5.1	5.7	5.2	4.4	3.7
HUMIDITY/%	73	70	69	67	68	69	71	74	75	76	73	73
BLOOM SEASON		**		*			**					
DAYS CLR @ 11AM	7	9	8	15	12	10	7	6	7	7	7	7
DAYS CLR @ 5PM	7	11	6	11	7	6	5	4	4	5	3	7
RAIN/MM	91	66	64	51	61	66	94	130	145	132	112	94
°C AVG MAX	23.1	23.1	24.2	25.3	27.0	28.6	28.6	28.1	28.1	27.0	24.7	23.6
°C AVG MIN	15.3	14.7	15.8	17.0	18.6	19.7	20.8	21.4	20.8	19.7	17.5	16.4
DIURNAL RANGE	7.8	8.4	8.4	8.3	8.4	8.9	7.8	6.7	7.3	7.3	7.2	7.2
S/HEMISPHERE	JUL	AUG	SEP	OCT	NOV	DEC	JAN	FEB	MAR	APR	MAY	JUN

Cultural Recommendations

LIGHT: 1800–3000 fc.

TEMPERATURES: Summer days average 83–84°F (28–29°C), and nights average 68–71°F (20–21°C), with a diurnal range of 12–16°F (7–9°C). The diurnal range fluctuates only 4°F (2°C) all year.

HUMIDITY: 70–75% most of the year, dropping briefly to near 65% in spring.

WATER: Rainfall is relatively low and consistent most of the year. The driest season is in late winter and spring, and the heaviest rain falls in late summer and early autumn. Cultivated plants should be allowed to become somewhat dry between waterings but should never dry out completely.

FERTILIZER: ¼–½ recommended strength, applied weekly. A high-nitrogen fertilizer is beneficial from spring to midsummer, but a fertilizer high in phosphates should be used in late summer and autumn.

REST PERIOD: Winter days average 74–76°F (23–24°C), and nights average 59–62°F (15–16°C), with a diurnal range of 13–15°F (7–8°C). In the habitat, rainfall is somewhat lower in late winter and spring. In cultivation, water and fertilizer should be reduced and the plants allowed to dry even more between waterings than in summer. They should not remain dry for long periods, however. In the habitat, light is highest in winter.

GROWING MEDIA: Plants may be mounted on cork or tree-fern slabs if humidity is high and plants are watered at least once daily in summer. When plants are potted, any open, fast-draining medium may be used. Repotting is best done in early spring when new roots are growing.

MISCELLANEOUS NOTES: The bloom season shown in the climate table is based on reports from the habitat.

Plant and Flower Information

PLANT SIZE AND TYPE: An 8–40 in. (20–102 cm) sympodial terrestrial.

PSEUDOBULB: 8–40 in. (20–102 cm) long. The slender, bamboolike stems may branch and rebranch.

LEAVES: Many on the upper portion of each stem. The lanceolate leaves are 2.0–2.8 in. (5–7 cm) long and unequally bilobed. They are arranged in 2 rows.

INFLORESCENCE: 0.8–1.2 in. (2–3 cm) long. Inflorescences emerge opposite the leaves.

FLOWERS: 1–5 per inflorescence. The flowers, which do not open fully, are 0.4 in. (1 cm) long. They may be green, greenish yellow, or white. Sepals and petals are pointed. The unlobed lip has an ovate midlobe with 3 raised lines. The center line may extend nearly to the tip of the midlobe or stop in the center. Some plants have self-pollinating flowers.

REFERENCES: 173, 216, 233, 254.

PHOTOS/DRAWINGS: 173.

Dendrobium polypetalum Steudel.
Now considered a synonym of *Maxillaria platypetala* Ruiz and Pavón. REFERENCES: 216, 254.

Dendrobium polyphlebium Rchb. f.
See *D. rhodopterygium* Rchb. f. REFERENCES: 190, 218, 254, 445, 454, 570.

Dendrobium polyphyllum Schlechter

ORIGIN/HABITAT: Papua New Guinea. Plants grow in the Sepik River region at about 4250 ft. (1300 m).

CLIMATE: Station #200004, Ambunti, Papua New Guinea, Lat. 4.2°S, Long. 142.8°E, at 164 ft. (50 m). Temperatures are calculated for an elevation of 4000 ft. (1220 m), resulting in probable extremes of 86°F (30°C) and 39°F (4°C).

N/HEMISPHERE	JAN	FEB	MAR	APR	MAY	JUN	JUL	AUG	SEP	OCT	NOV	DEC
°F AVG MAX	75	77	77	77	78	77	77	77	77	77	77	76
°F AVG MIN	59	60	61	60	60	60	59	60	60	60	60	61
DIURNAL RANGE	16	17	16	17	18	17	18	17	17	17	17	15
RAIN/INCHES	6.4	7.4	7.7	8.5	9.2	9.4	10.9	10.2	12.2	10.4	8.3	5.2
HUMIDITY/%	N/A											
BLOOM SEASON						*				*		
DAYS CLR	N/A											
RAIN/MM	163	188	196	216	234	239	277	259	310	264	211	132
°C AVG MAX	24.1	25.2	25.2	25.2	25.7	25.2	25.2	25.2	25.2	25.2	25.2	24.6
°C AVG MIN	15.2	15.7	16.3	15.7	15.7	15.7	15.2	15.7	15.7	15.7	15.7	16.3
DIURNAL RANGE	8.9	9.5	8.9	9.5	10.0	9.5	10.0	9.5	9.5	9.5	9.5	8.3
S/HEMISPHERE	JUL	AUG	SEP	OCT	NOV	DEC	JAN	FEB	MAR	APR	MAY	JUN

Cultural Recommendations

LIGHT: 2000–3000 fc.

TEMPERATURES: Throughout the year, days average 75–78°F (24–26°C), and nights average 59–61°F (15–16°C), with a diurnal range of 15–18°F (8–10°C).

HUMIDITY: Information is not available for this location. However, records from nearby stations indicate that humidity probably averages near 80% year-round.

WATER: Rainfall is heavy year-round with the greatest amounts falling in summer and early autumn. Cultivated plants should be moist but not soggy.

FERTILIZER: ¼–½ recommended strength. A balanced fertilizer should be applied weekly to biweekly throughout the year.

REST PERIOD: Growing conditions should be maintained all year. Water and fertilizer should be reduced for plants cultivated in the dark, short-day conditions common in temperate-latitude winters, but they should never be allowed to dry out completely. In the habitat, seasonal light variation is minor.

GROWING MEDIA: Plants may be mounted on tree-fern or cork slabs or potted in small pots filled with any open, fast-draining medium. Repotting may be done anytime new roots are growing.

MISCELLANEOUS NOTES: The bloom season shown in the climate table is based on reports from the habitat.

Plant and Flower Information

PLANT SIZE AND TYPE: A 16 in. (40 cm) sympodial epiphyte.

PSEUDOBULB: 16 in. (40 cm) long. The curved, densely leafy stems do not branch.

LEAVES: Many. The leaves are very unequally bilobed, smooth, and lanceolate. The leaf sheaths are covered with small wartlike protrusions.

INFLORESCENCE: Short.

FLOWERS: 2 per inflorescence. The flowers are 1.6 in. (4 cm) long. The collectors described the flowers as brownish red. The sepals and shorter petals are lanceolate at the base, tapering to an elongated point at the apex. The lip is shorter than the sepals and petals. It is 3-lobed with short sidelobes and a rounded, ruffled midlobe.

REFERENCES: 223, 443.

Dendrobium polyschistum Schlechter

ORIGIN/HABITAT: Northern Papua New Guinea. Plants grow on mistforest trees in the Torricelli Range at about 3300 ft. (1000 m).

CLIMATE: Station #94004, Wewak, Papua New Guinea, Lat. 3.6°S, Long. 143.7°E, at 16 ft. (5 m). Temperatures are calculated for an elevation of 3300 ft. (1000 m), resulting in probable extremes of 87°F (31°C) and 51°F (11°C).

N/HEMISPHERE	JAN	FEB	MAR	APR	MAY	JUN	JUL	AUG	SEP	OCT	NOV	DEC
°F AVG MAX	77	77	77	77	77	77	76	75	76	77	77	77
°F AVG MIN	63	63	63	64	64	64	64	64	63	63	64	63
DIURNAL RANGE	14	14	14	13	13	13	12	11	13	14	13	14
RAIN/INCHES	7.6	4.8	5.3	10.0	13.3	14.5	12.1	11.9	14.9	16.9	15.1	10.8
HUMIDITY/%	80	79	79	78	79	81	82	82	81	82	81	80
BLOOM SEASON			*									
DAYS CLR	N/A											
RAIN/MM	193	122	135	254	338	368	307	302	378	429	384	274
°C AVG MAX	25.1	25.1	25.1	25.1	25.1	25.1	24.6	24.0	24.6	25.1	25.1	25.1
°C AVG MIN	17.3	17.3	17.3	17.9	17.9	17.9	17.9	17.9	17.3	17.3	17.9	17.3
DIURNAL RANGE	7.8	7.8	7.8	7.2	7.2	7.2	6.7	6.1	7.3	7.8	7.2	7.8
S/HEMISPHERE	JUL	AUG	SEP	OCT	NOV	DEC	JAN	FEB	MAR	APR	MAY	JUN

Cultural Recommendations

LIGHT: 1200–2500 fc.

TEMPERATURES: Throughout the year, days average 75–77°F (24–25°C), and nights average 63–64°F (17–18°C), with a diurnal range of 11–14°F (6–8°C).

HUMIDITY: Near 80% year-round.

WATER: Rainfall is heavy to very heavy all year. Conditions are slightly drier for 1–2 months in winter. Cultivated plants should be kept moist but not soggy. During hot weather, plants may need to be watered at least once daily.

FERTILIZER: ¼–½ recommended strength. A balanced fertilizer should be applied weekly to biweekly throughout the year.

Dendrobium polysema

REST PERIOD: Growing conditions should be maintained year-round. Water and fertilizer may be reduced somewhat in winter, especially for plants grown in the dark, short-day conditions common in temperate latitudes. Plants should never be allowed to dry out completely, however. In the habitat, light is highest in winter.

GROWING MEDIA: A very open and fast-draining medium may be used with either baskets or small pots. Repotting may be done anytime new roots are growing.

MISCELLANEOUS NOTES: The bloom season shown in the climate table is based on cultivation records. Plants that produce flowers which last a single day commonly bloom several times during the year. Flowering usually occurs 7–14 days after a sudden 10°F (5°C) drop in daytime temperatures.

Plant and Flower Information

PLANT SIZE AND TYPE: A 12–16 in. (30–40 cm) sympodial epiphyte.

PSEUDOBULB: 12–16 in. (30–40 cm) long. The erect to arching stems are slender and sometimes branching.

LEAVES: The linear leaves are 2–3 in. (5–8 cm) long.

INFLORESCENCE: Short.

FLOWERS: 2 per inflorescence. The flowers are 1.2 in. (3 cm) across. The white blossoms are flushed with red on the outside. Sepals and petals are linear. The 3-lobed lip is covered with elongated hairs. It is deeply fringed on the margin of the broadly diamond-shaped, recurved midlobe. It is hairless along the centerline. The sidelobes are sharply pointed. Blossoms are short-lived.

HYBRIDIZING NOTES: Chromosome count is 2n = 38 (ref. 153, 273).

REFERENCES: 92, 153, 221, 273, 437, 445, 486.

PHOTOS/DRAWINGS: 437.

Dendrobium polysema Schlechter

AKA: *D. macrophyllum* A. Richard var. *stenopterum* Rchb. f., *D. polysema* var. *pallidum* Chadim, *D. pulchrum* Schlechter.

ORIGIN/HABITAT: Bougainville Island, the Solomon Islands, the Santa Cruz Islands, Vanuatu, and Papua New Guinea. In New Guinea, plants are found in the Eastern Highlands, Western Highlands, Morobe, and the Northern Provinces. They usually grow on moss-covered mistforest trees at 3950–6250 ft. (1200–1900 m) in New Guinea but are found at 500–2300 ft. (150–700 m) on the other islands.

CLIMATE: Station #200590, Bulolo, Papua New Guinea, Lat. 7.2°S, Long. 146.6°E, at 2440 ft. (745 m). Temperatures are calculated for an elevation of 5250 ft. (1600 m), resulting in probable extremes of 87°F (30°C) and 43°F (6°C).

N/HEMISPHERE	JAN	FEB	MAR	APR	MAY	JUN	JUL	AUG	SEP	OCT	NOV	DEC
°F AVG MAX	74	75	77	77	79	78	78	78	78	78	77	75
°F AVG MIN	56	55	56	57	56	58	57	57	57	56	57	56
DIURNAL RANGE	18	20	21	20	23	20	21	21	21	22	20	19
RAIN/INCHES	4.1	4.4	5.1	5.7	6.1	7.2	5.2	4.9	6.2	5.4	5.0	3.5
HUMIDITY/%	76	74	72	74	71	73	71	72	73	73	75	75
BLOOM SEASON	*	*	*					*	*	*	*	*
DAYS CLR	N/A											
RAIN/MM	104	112	130	145	155	183	132	124	157	137	127	89
°C AVG MAX	23.2	23.7	24.8	24.8	26.0	25.4	25.4	25.4	25.4	25.4	24.8	23.7
°C AVG MIN	13.2	12.6	13.2	13.7	13.2	14.3	13.7	13.7	13.7	13.2	13.7	13.2
DIURNAL RANGE	10.0	11.1	11.6	11.1	12.8	11.1	11.7	11.7	11.7	12.2	11.1	10.5
S/HEMISPHERE	JUL	AUG	SEP	OCT	NOV	DEC	JAN	FEB	MAR	APR	MAY	JUN

Cultural Recommendations

LIGHT: 2000–3000 fc.

TEMPERATURES: Throughout the year, days average 74–78°F (23–25°C), and nights average 55–58°F (13–14°C), with a diurnal range of 18–23°F (10–13°C). Growers indicate that plants do poorly if grown in continuously warm temperatures.

HUMIDITY: 70–75% year-round.

WATER: Rainfall is moderate to heavy throughout the year. Conditions are slightly drier for 1–2 months in winter. Cultivated plants should be allowed to dry slightly between waterings.

FERTILIZER: ¼–½ recommended strength. A balanced fertilizer should be applied weekly to biweekly throughout the year.

REST PERIOD: Growing conditions should be maintained year-round. Water and fertilizer should be reduced somewhat in winter, especially for plants cultivated in the dark, short-day conditions common in temperate latitudes. Cultivated plants should never be allowed to dry completely, however. In the habitat, seasonal light variation is minor.

GROWING MEDIA: Plants may be mounted on tree-fern or cork slabs if humidity is high and plants are watered at least once daily in summer. When plants are potted, fir bark or any open, fast-draining medium may be used. Repotting may be done anytime new roots are growing.

MISCELLANEOUS NOTES: The bloom season shown in the climate table is based on cultivation records. Growers indicate that *D. polysema* is sometimes difficult to bloom and suggest that relatively drier conditions may stimulate flowering.

Plant and Flower Information

PLANT SIZE AND TYPE: An 8–26 in. (20–65 cm) sympodial epiphyte.

PSEUDOBULB: 4–16 in. (10–40 cm) long. The erect pseudobulbs have 3–5 nodes below the leaves. The stems become yellow or orange when dry.

LEAVES: 2 per growth. The elliptic-oblong leaves are 4.0–9.5 in. (10–24 cm) long. They may be erect or spreading.

INFLORESCENCE: 12–18 in. (30–45 cm) long. The erect inflorescence arises from the apex of the pseudobulb. The ovaries and pedicels are roughly hairy.

FLOWERS: 8–12 per inflorescence. The open, flattened flowers are 1.6–2.4 in. (4–6 cm) long. Sepals and petals are sometimes deeply ruffled. The sepals, which are coarsely hairy on the backside, may be yellow or greenish with violet spots. Petals are cream color with maroon spots. The extent of spotting is highly variable. The flared lip is gold with a greenish tinge that ages to deep gold before fading. It is marked with violet dots on the midlobe and violet stripes on the sidelobes. The anther is green. Blossoms are similar to *D. macrophyllum* A. Richard, but *D. polysema* has tapering sidelobes on the lip.

HYBRIDIZING NOTES: Chromosome count is 2n = 38 + B (ref. 152, 243).

REFERENCES: 83, 95, 152, 179, 219, 243, 254, 270, 271, 359, 371, 430, 437, 444, 445, 516, 536, 550.

PHOTOS/DRAWINGS: 83, *270, 271, 371, 430,* 437, *550, 561.*

Dendrobium polystachyon Swartz. Now considered a synonym of *Polystachya luteola* Hooker. REFERENCES: 98, 190, 216, 445, 536.

Dendrobium polystachys Thouars. Sometimes spelled *D. polystachyum*, it is now considered a synonym of *Polystachya mauritiana* Sprengel. REFERENCES: 100, 216, 445.

Dendrobium polytrichum Ames

ORIGIN/HABITAT: The Philippines islands of Mindanao, Mindoro, and Luzon. Plants are widespread on Luzon where they grow in the humid forests in the provinces of Bataan, Cagayan, Isabela, Laguna, Quezon, and Rizal. In Bataan, plants are found on Mt. Mariveles at or below 800 ft. (240 m).

CLIMATE: Station #98426, Cubi Point NAS, Luzon, Philippines, Lat. 14.8°N, Long. 120.3°E, at 55 ft. (17 m). Temperatures are calculated for an elevation of 800 ft. (240 m), resulting in probable extremes of 99°F (37°C) and 60°F (15°C).

N/HEMISPHERE	JAN	FEB	MAR	APR	MAY	JUN	JUL	AUG	SEP	OCT	NOV	DEC
°F AVG MAX	85	86	89	91	90	86	85	84	84	87	86	85
°F AVG MIN	70	70	72	74	75	74	73	73	73	73	73	71
DIURNAL RANGE	15	16	17	17	15	12	12	11	11	14	13	14
RAIN/INCHES	0.1	0.1	0.1	0.8	7.1	25.1	30.5	33.7	29.5	7.8	2.4	0.8
HUMIDITY/%	68	67	68	67	72	82	84	86	86	80	74	71
BLOOM SEASON		*	*	*	*	*				*	*	
DAYS CLR @ 8AM	7	7	8	10	6	2	1	0	0	4	3	4
DAYS CLR @ 2PM	4	3	4	4	3	1	0	0	0	2	1	2
RAIN/MM	3	3	3	20	180	638	775	856	749	198	61	20
°C AVG MAX	29.2	29.7	31.4	32.5	32.0	29.7	29.2	28.6	28.6	30.3	29.7	29.2
°C AVG MIN	20.9	20.9	22.0	23.1	23.6	23.1	22.5	22.5	22.5	22.5	22.5	21.4
DIURNAL RANGE	8.3	8.8	9.4	9.4	8.4	6.6	6.7	6.1	6.1	7.8	7.2	7.8
S/HEMISPHERE	JUL	AUG	SEP	OCT	NOV	DEC	JAN	FEB	MAR	APR	MAY	JUN

Cultural Recommendations

LIGHT: 2500–3500 fc. Bright, diffused light and strong air movement are recommended at all times. The brightest season is spring.

TEMPERATURES: Throughout the year, days average 84–91°F (29–33°C), and nights average 70–75°F (21–24°C), with a diurnal range of 11–17°F (6–9°C). The warmest weather occurs in spring, just before the start of the rainy season.

HUMIDITY: 80–85% in summer and early autumn, dropping to 65–70% in winter and spring.

WATER: Rainfall is very heavy in the growing season from late spring into autumn, but conditions become very dry for 5 months from late autumn through early spring. Cultivated plants should be kept moist in summer and early autumn, but water should be gradually reduced in autumn.

FERTILIZER: 1/4–1/2 recommended strength, applied weekly. A high-nitrogen fertilizer is beneficial from spring to midsummer, but a fertilizer high in phosphates should be used in late summer and autumn.

REST PERIOD: Growing conditions should be maintained all year. Rainfall is very low for 3–5 months in winter and spring, and conditions are so dry that even moisture from dew in uncommon. In cultivation, water should be reduced and the plants allowed to dry out between waterings. Occasional early morning mistings may help prevent the plants from becoming too dry. Fertilizer should be reduced or eliminated anytime water is reduced. In the habitat, light is highest in winter and spring.

GROWING MEDIA: Plants may be mounted on tree-fern or cork slabs if humidity is high and plants are watered at least once daily in summer. When plants are potted, any open, fast-draining medium may be used. Repotting may be done anytime new roots are growing.

MISCELLANEOUS NOTES: The bloom season shown in the climate table is based on collection reports.

Plant and Flower Information

PLANT SIZE AND TYPE: A 12–16 in. (30–40 cm) sympodial epiphyte.

PSEUDOBULB: 12–16 in. (30–40 cm) long. The slender stems, which are thickened at the base, are spaced 2.4–3.1 in. (6–8 cm) apart.

LEAVES: Several per growth. The semiterete leaves are 2.8–4.0 in. (7–10 cm) long.

INFLORESCENCE: Flowers are carried on the leafless, apical portion of the stem.

FLOWERS: Few per inflorescence. The flowers are 1–2 in. (2.5–5.0 cm) across. Sepals and petals are white. The 3-lobed lip has a red-yellow spot halfway down the lip. The oval midlobe is notched and deeply fringed. Sidelobes are rounded. Blossoms vary from fragrant to nearly odorless.

REFERENCES: 12, 220, 254, 296, 536.

Dendrobium ponapense Schlechter

ORIGIN/HABITAT: Ponape in the Caroline Islands. Plants grow on Mt. Sankaku at 1100–1500 ft. (335–450 m). They hang from bird's nest ferns, and all older plants have accumulations of organic material around the roots.

CLIMATE: Station #91348, Ponape, Caroline Islands, Lat. 7.0°N, Long. 158.2°E, at 121 ft. (37 m). Temperatures are calculated for an elevation of 1500 ft. (450 m). Record extreme temperatures are not available for this location.

N/HEMISPHERE	JAN	FEB	MAR	APR	MAY	JUN	JUL	AUG	SEP	OCT	NOV	DEC
°F AVG MAX	82	82	83	84	84	83	83	84	84	84	84	83
°F AVG MIN	73	73	73	73	72	72	71	70	71	71	71	72
DIURNAL RANGE	9	9	10	11	12	11	12	14	13	13	13	11
RAIN/INCHES	13.7	9.4	11.2	12.6	15.2	23.8	22.9	17.1	17.4	15.7	17.0	16.7
HUMIDITY/%	N/A											
BLOOM SEASON									*			
DAYS CLR	N/A											
RAIN/MM	348	239	284	320	386	605	582	434	442	399	432	424
°C AVG MAX	27.5	27.5	28.1	28.6	28.6	28.1	28.1	28.6	28.6	28.6	28.6	28.1
°C AVG MIN	22.5	22.5	22.5	22.5	22.0	22.0	21.4	20.8	21.4	21.4	21.4	22.0
DIURNAL RANGE	5.0	5.0	5.6	6.1	6.6	6.1	6.7	7.8	7.2	7.2	7.2	6.1
S/HEMISPHERE	JUL	AUG	SEP	OCT	NOV	DEC	JAN	FEB	MAR	APR	MAY	JUN

Cultural Recommendations

LIGHT: 2000–3000 fc.

TEMPERATURES: Throughout the year, days average 82–84°F (28–29°C), and nights average 70–73°F (21–23°C), with a diurnal range of 9–14°F (5–8°C).

HUMIDITY: Information is not available for this location. However, records from nearby stations indicate that humidity probably averages near 80% year-round.

WATER: Rainfall is heavy to extremely heavy all year. Cultivated plants should be kept moist but not soggy.

FERTILIZER: 1/4–1/2 recommended strength. A balanced fertilizer should be applied weekly to biweekly throughout the year.

REST PERIOD: Growing conditions should be maintained all year. Water and fertilizer may be reduced somewhat for cultivated plants in winter, especially those grown in the dark, short-day conditions common in temperate latitudes. They should never be allowed to dry out completely, however. In the habitat, seasonal light variation is minor.

GROWING MEDIA: Plants may be mounted on tree-fern or cork slabs if humidity is high and plants are watered at least once daily in summer. When plants are potted, any open, fast-draining medium may be used. Repotting may be done anytime new roots are growing.

MISCELLANEOUS NOTES: The bloom season shown in the climate table is based on reports from the habitat.

Plant and Flower Information

PLANT SIZE AND TYPE: A 39 in. (100 cm) sympodial epiphyte.

PSEUDOBULB: 39 in. (100 cm) long. The densely leafy stems are wiry, rigid, and unbranched. They are smooth when dry. Plants are probably pendant.

LEAVES: Many. The oblong leaves, which are held close to the stem, are 2.4–3.5 in. (6–9 cm) long. They are smooth and leathery.

INFLORESCENCE: Inflorescences emerge laterally along the side of the stem.

FLOWERS: 2 per inflorescence. Relatively small and somewhat fleshy, the flowers are 1.8 in. (4.5 cm) long. Petals are much shorter than the sepals. The lip has 3 nearly equal lobes. Blossoms are white with violet on the inside of the lip and a pale orange strip in the middle.

REFERENCES: 189, 223, 441.

Dendrobium poneroides Schlechter

AKA: *D. isochiloides* Kränzlin var. *pumilum* J. J. Smith.

ORIGIN/HABITAT: New Guinea. Plants grow on trees in mountain forests at 1000 ft. (300 m), near Jaduna on the lower Waria River. In other localities, the habitat may be as low as 250 ft. (75 m). Plants were originally collected along the Noord River in Irian Jaya (western New Guinea) at the base of Nepenthes Hill. In the Gautier Mountains, they grow on north-facing (sunny) slopes at about 2950 ft. (900 m) and in forests where the trees grow on limestone and basalt.

CLIMATE: Station #97796, Kokonau, Irian Jaya, Lat. 4.7°S, Long. 135.4°E, at 10 ft. (3 m). Temperatures are calculated for an elevation of 3000 ft. (910 m). Record extreme temperatures are not available for this location.

N/HEMISPHERE	JAN	FEB	MAR	APR	MAY	JUN	JUL	AUG	SEP	OCT	NOV	DEC
°F AVG MAX	73	73	76	78	80	79	79	79	80	78	77	74
°F AVG MIN	63	63	64	64	64	65	64	64	64	64	64	63
DIURNAL RANGE	10	10	12	14	16	14	15	15	16	14	13	11
RAIN/INCHES	18.4	15.8	18.9	11.6	9.7	10.6	11.5	15.7	11.6	11.6	16.0	19.9
HUMIDITY/%	N/A											
BLOOM SEASON	*			*		*			*			
DAYS CLR	N/A											
RAIN/MM	467	401	480	295	246	269	292	399	295	295	406	505
°C AVG MAX	22.9	22.9	24.5	25.6	26.7	26.2	26.2	26.2	26.7	25.6	25.1	23.4
°C AVG MIN	17.3	17.3	17.9	17.9	17.9	18.4	17.9	17.9	17.9	17.9	17.9	17.3
DIURNAL RANGE	5.6	5.6	6.6	7.7	8.8	7.8	8.3	8.3	8.8	7.7	7.2	6.1
S/HEMISPHERE	JUL	AUG	SEP	OCT	NOV	DEC	JAN	FEB	MAR	APR	MAY	JUN

Cultural Recommendations

LIGHT: 1500–2500 fc. Plants are healthiest in a shady environment.

TEMPERATURES: Throughout the year, days average 73–80°F (23–27°C), and nights average 63–65°F (17–18°C), with a diurnal range of 10–16°F (6–9°C).

HUMIDITY: Information is not available for this location. However, records from nearby stations indicate that humidity is probably near 85% year-round.

WATER: Rainfall is very heavy year-round. Cultivated plants should be kept evenly moist, but not soggy.

FERTILIZER: ¼–½ recommended strength. A balanced fertilizer should be applied weekly to biweekly throughout the year.

REST PERIOD: Growing conditions should be maintained year-round. Water and fertilizer should be reduced slightly in winter for plants cultivated in the dark, short-day conditions common in temperate latitudes, but they should never be allowed to dry out completely. In the habitat, seasonal light variation is minor.

GROWING MEDIA: Plants may be mounted on tree-fern or cork slabs if high humidity can be maintained and if the plant is watered at least once daily in summer. If plants are potted, any open, fast-draining medium may be used. Repotting may be done anytime new roots are growing.

MISCELLANEOUS NOTES: The bloom season shown in the climate table is based on reports from the habitat.

Plant and Flower Information

PLANT SIZE AND TYPE: A 4.3 in. (11 cm) sympodial epiphyte. The plants were described as similar to *D. obovatum* Schlechter.

PSEUDOBULB: 4.3 in. (11 cm) long. The clustered stems are slender and flattened.

LEAVES: Many. The leaves are 0.6–1.0 in. (1.5–2.5 cm) long.

INFLORESCENCE: Short. Inflorescences emerge at nodes through the leaf bases.

FLOWERS: 1 per inflorescence. The flowers are 0.4 in. (0.9 cm) across and do not open fully. Sepals and petals are yellowish green. The 3-lobed lip is brownish red with green at the apex. It is uppermost. The small midlobe is blunt at the apex.

REFERENCES: 92, 221, 437, 439, 445, 470.

PHOTOS/DRAWINGS: 437.

Dendrobium porphyrochilum Lindley

AKA: *D. caespitosum* King and Pantling.

ORIGIN/HABITAT: Southeast Asia. In western and northern Thailand, the plants grow on rocks and trees in the mountains at 2600–6550 ft. (800–2000 m). Distribution extends northward to Yunnan Province in southwest China and westward through Burma, the Khasi (Khasia) Hills region of northeastern India, Bhutan, Sikkim, and Nepal. In Sikkim, plants grow at 5600–7550 ft. (1700–2300 m). The species is considered threatened in some of these areas.

CLIMATE: Station #48327, Chiang Mai, Thailand, Lat. 18.8°N, Long. 99.0°E, at 1100 ft. (335 m). Temperatures are calculated for an elevation of 5000 ft. (1520 m), resulting in probable extremes of 96°F (36°C) and 25°F (–4°C).

N/HEMISPHERE	JAN	FEB	MAR	APR	MAY	JUN	JUL	AUG	SEP	OCT	NOV	DEC
°F AVG MAX	72	77	82	83	81	77	76	74	75	76	73	71
°F AVG MIN	43	44	49	57	61	61	61	62	60	58	53	44
DIURNAL RANGE	29	33	33	26	20	16	15	12	15	18	20	27
RAIN/INCHES	0.3	0.4	0.6	2.0	5.5	6.1	7.4	8.7	11.5	4.9	1.5	0.4
HUMIDITY/%	73	65	58	62	73	78	80	83	83	81	79	76
BLOOM SEASON	*	*										*
DAYS CLR @ 7AM	5	5	2	2	1	0	0	0	0	1	3	3
DAYS CLR @ 1PM	9	8	4	2	0	0	0	0	0	0	1	3
RAIN/MM	8	10	15	51	140	155	188	221	292	124	38	10
°C AVG MAX	22.3	25.1	27.9	28.4	27.3	25.1	24.5	23.4	24.0	24.5	22.9	21.7
°C AVG MIN	6.2	6.7	9.5	14.0	16.2	16.2	16.2	16.7	15.6	14.5	11.7	6.7
DIURNAL RANGE	16.1	18.4	18.4	14.4	11.1	8.9	8.3	6.7	8.4	10.0	11.2	15.0
S/HEMISPHERE	JUL	AUG	SEP	OCT	NOV	DEC	JAN	FEB	MAR	APR	MAY	JUN

Cultural Recommendations

LIGHT: 3500–4500 fc. Cultivated plants need bright light and strong air movement. The heavy summer cloud cover indicates that some shading is needed from spring through autumn, but light should be as high as the plants can tolerate, short of burning the foliage.

TEMPERATURES: Summer days average 74–77°F (23–25°C), and nights average 61–62°F (16–17°C), with a diurnal range of 12–16°F (7–9°C). The warmest temperatures occur in spring. Days average 81–83°F (27–28°C), and nights average 49–61°F (10–16°C), with a diurnal range of 20–33°F (11–18°C).

HUMIDITY: 75–85% from late spring through autumn, dropping to near 60% in late winter and early spring.

WATER: Rainfall is moderate to heavy from late spring through early autumn, but conditions are very dry in winter. Cultivated plants should be kept moist while actively growing, but water should be gradually reduced after new growths mature in autumn.

FERTILIZER: ¼–½ recommended strength, applied weekly. A high-nitrogen fertilizer is beneficial from spring to midsummer, but a fertilizer high in phosphates should be used in late summer and autumn.

REST PERIOD: Winter days average 71–77°F (22–25°C), and nights average 43–44°F (6–7°C), with a diurnal range of 27–33°F (15–18°C). The average low temperatures are below 50°F (10°C) for 3–4 months and then warm rapidly in spring. Plants should be able to tolerate temperatures a few degrees below freezing, but such extremes should be avoided in cultivation. During very cold weather, a plant's chance of surviving with minimal damage is better if it is dry. In the habitat, rainfall averages are very low for 4–5 months in winter, but during the early part of the season the high relative humidity indicates that additional moisture is available from frequent fog, mist, and heavy deposits of dew. Growers sometimes recommend eliminating water in winter, but plants are healthiest if for most of the winter they are allowed to become somewhat dry between waterings but do not remain dry for extended periods. For 1–2 months in late winter, however, conditions are clear, warm, and dry, with humidity so low that even the moisture from morning dew is uncommon. Plants should be allowed to dry out completely between waterings and remain dry longer during this time. Occasional early morning mistings between waterings may help keep the plants from becoming too dry. Fertilizer should be greatly reduced or eliminated until water is increased in spring. A cool, dry rest is essential for cultivated plants and should be continued until new growth starts in spring. In the habitat, light is highest in winter.

GROWING MEDIA: Growers recommend mounting plants on tree-fern slabs if humidity is high and plants are watered at least once daily in summer. When plants are potted, any open, fast-draining medium may be used. Repotting is best done in early spring when new roots are growing.

MISCELLANEOUS NOTES: The bloom season shown in the climate table is based on cultivation records.

Plant and Flower Information

PLANT SIZE AND TYPE: A miniature, 1.2–4.0 in. (3–10 cm) sympodial epiphyte.

PSEUDOBULB: 0.4–1.0 in. (1.0–2.5 cm) long. The pseudobulbs may be conical to cylindrical. They often narrow near the top to become a short stem.

LEAVES: 2 per growth. The oval to nearly linear leaves are 0.8–2.8 in. (2–7 cm) long.

INFLORESCENCE: 1.6–3.1 in. (4–8 cm) long. The inflorescences exceed the length of the leaves so that the blossoms are held above the leaf tips.

FLOWERS: 6–10 per inflorescence. The flowers, which do not open fully, are 0.3–0.4 in. (0.8–1.0 cm) across. Sepals and petals may be cream, pale green, or yellow, often with red nerves and purple blotches. The unlobed lip is brownish purple with a large, raised callus in the center and pale green margins.

HYBRIDIZING NOTES: Chromosome count is n = 19 (ref. 150, 504, 542, 580).

REFERENCES: 32, 38, 46, 150, 179, 202, 208, 216, 228, 254, 278, 330, 369, 376, 445, 454, 489, 504, 528, 542, 580.

PHOTOS/DRAWINGS: 32, 46, 454.

Dendrobium porphyrophyllum Guillaumin. See *D. indivisum* (Blume) Miquel. REFERENCES: 165, 228, 448, 454, 504, 580.

Dendrobium potamophila Schlechter Oct. 1, 1912

ORIGIN/HABITAT: Northern Papua New Guinea. Plants grow on trees along the Minjem River near Wobbe and Kelel at about 1000 ft. (300 m).

CLIMATE: Station #94014, Madang, Papua New Guinea, Lat. 5.2°S, Long. 145.8°E, at 13 ft. (4 m). Temperatures are calculated for an elevation of 1000 ft. (300 m), resulting in probable extremes of 95°F (35°C) and 59°F (15°C).

N/HEMISPHERE	JAN	FEB	MAR	APR	MAY	JUN	JUL	AUG	SEP	OCT	NOV	DEC
°F AVG MAX	80	80	82	82	82	82	82	82	82	84	84	81
°F AVG MIN	74	75	75	75	74	74	74	74	74	73	74	75
DIURNAL RANGE	6	5	7	7	8	8	8	8	8	11	10	6
RAIN/INCHES	4.0	3.4	3.2	8.5	11.2	11.1	10.1	11.3	9.4	11.3	10.5	6.7
HUMIDITY/%	88	87	86	86	86	86	86	85	85	87	88	89
BLOOM SEASON			*	*								
DAYS CLR	N/A											
RAIN/MM	102	86	81	216	284	282	257	287	239	287	267	170
°C AVG MAX	26.6	26.6	27.7	27.7	27.7	27.7	27.7	27.7	27.7	28.8	28.8	27.1
°C AVG MIN	23.2	23.8	23.8	23.8	23.2	23.2	23.2	23.2	23.2	22.7	23.2	23.8
DIURNAL RANGE	3.4	2.8	3.9	3.9	4.5	4.5	4.5	4.5	4.5	6.1	5.6	3.3
S/HEMISPHERE	JUL	AUG	SEP	OCT	NOV	DEC	JAN	FEB	MAR	APR	MAY	JUN

Cultural Recommendations

LIGHT: 2500–3000 fc.

TEMPERATURES: Throughout the year, days average 80–84°F (27–29°C), and nights average 73–75°F (23–24°C), with a diurnal range of 5–11°F (3–6°C).

HUMIDITY: 85–90% year-round.

WATER: Rainfall is heavy most of the year, but conditions are somewhat drier in winter. Cultivated plants should be kept moist but not soggy.

FERTILIZER: ¼–½ recommended strength. A balanced fertilizer should be applied weekly to biweekly throughout the year.

REST PERIOD: Growing temperatures should be maintained all year. In the habitat, rainfall decreases for 2–3 months in winter. Water should be reduced for cultivated plants, but they should not be allowed to dry out completely. Fertilizer should be reduced or eliminated while water is reduced. In the habitat, light is slightly higher in late winter.

GROWING MEDIA: Plants may be mounted on tree-fern or cork slabs if humidity is high and plants are watered at least once daily in summer. If plants are potted, any open, fast-draining medium may be used. Repotting may be done anytime new roots are growing.

MISCELLANEOUS NOTES: The bloom season shown in the climate table is based on reports from the habitat. Plants that produce flowers which last a single day commonly bloom several times during the year. Flowering usually occurs 7–14 days after a sudden 10°F (5°C) drop in daytime temperatures.

Plant and Flower Information

PLANT SIZE AND TYPE: An 8–10 in. (20–25 cm) sympodial epiphyte. Plants have a compact growth habit.

PSEUDOBULB: 6–8 in. (16–20 cm) long. The erect stems arise from a very short rhizome.

LEAVES: The oblong leaves are 1.6–2.8 in. (4–7 cm) long. They may be erect or spreading.

INFLORESCENCE: Short. The blossoms are held opposite each other.

FLOWERS: 2 per inflorescence. The flowers are 1.1 in. (2.8 cm) across. Sepals and petals are white, with yellow papillae along the central crest and midlobe of the 3-lobed lip. The tips of the sidelobes extend to the apex of the midlobe. Blossoms are short-lived.

REFERENCES: 221, 437, 445, 486.

PHOTOS/DRAWINGS: 437.

Dendrobium potamophilum (Schlechter) J. J. Smith Oct. 1912. See *D. infortunatum* J. J. Smith. REFERENCES: 92, 221, 224, 437, 470, 472.

Dendrobium praecinctum Rchb. f.

AKA: Until recently, *D. praecinctum* was considered an imperfectly described species. However, Seidenfaden, in a personal communication, stated that *D. pauciflorum* King and Pantling and *D. sikkimense* A. Hawkes and A. H. Heller must be considered synonyms of *D. praecinctum*.

ORIGIN/HABITAT: Thailand, northeastern India, Sikkim, Bhutan, and Assam. In northeast India, plants are usually found at 2300–4250 ft. (700–1300 m) but may be found as high as 6550 ft. (2000 m). In northern Thailand, they are found at 3600–4900 ft. (1100–1500 m). This orchid is considered threatened in some parts of its habitat. *D. praecinctum* was originally imported to England with *D. devonianum*.

CLIMATE: Station #48300, Mae Hong Son, Thailand, Lat. 19.3°N, Long. 97.9°E, at 711 ft. (217 m). Temperatures are calculated for an elevation

Dendrobium praecox

of 4000 ft. (1220 m), resulting in probable extremes of 97°F (36°C) and 32°F (0°C).

N/HEMISPHERE	JAN	FEB	MAR	APR	MAY	JUN	JUL	AUG	SEP	OCT	NOV	DEC
°F AVG MAX	75	79	86	87	84	78	76	76	77	79	77	74
°F AVG MIN	46	46	51	61	65	64	63	63	63	61	57	48
DIURNAL RANGE	29	33	35	26	19	14	13	13	14	18	20	26
RAIN/INCHES	0.4	0.2	0.3	1.7	6.1	7.1	9.6	9.9	8.1	3.9	1.2	0.4
HUMIDITY/%	67	60	50	50	68	81	82	83	83	82	75	71
BLOOM SEASON						**	**					
DAYS CLR @ 7AM	2	8	10	9	3	0	0	0	0	1	1	2
DAYS CLR @ 1PM	20	20	20	13	3	0	0	0	0	3	13	17
RAIN/MM	10	5	8	43	155	180	244	251	206	99	30	10
°C AVG MAX	24.0	26.2	30.1	30.6	29.0	25.6	24.5	24.5	25.1	26.2	25.1	23.4
°C AVG MIN	7.9	7.9	10.6	16.2	18.4	17.9	17.3	17.3	17.3	16.2	14.0	9.0
DIURNAL RANGE	16.1	18.3	19.5	14.4	10.6	7.7	7.2	7.2	7.8	10.0	11.1	14.4
S/HEMISPHERE	JUL	AUG	SEP	OCT	NOV	DEC	JAN	FEB	MAR	APR	MAY	JUN

Cultural Recommendations

LIGHT: 2000–3000 fc. The heavy summer cloud cover indicates that some shading is needed from spring through autumn, but light should be as high as the plant can tolerate, short of burning the leaves. Strong air movement is important at all times.

TEMPERATURES: Summer days average 76–78°F (25–26°C), and nights average 63–64°F (17–18°C), with a diurnal range of 13–14°F (7–8°C). The warmest season is spring. Days average 84–87°F (29–31°C), and nights average 51–65°F (11–18°C), with a diurnal range of 19–35°F (11–20°C).

HUMIDITY: Near 80–85% in summer and autumn, dropping to 60–70% most other months. However, averages fall to 50% for 2 months in early spring.

WATER: Rainfall is very heavy during the growing season, but winters are very dry. Cultivated plants should be kept moist while actively growing, but water should be gradually reduced after new growths mature in autumn.

FERTILIZER: ¼–½ recommended strength, applied weekly. A high-nitrogen fertilizer is beneficial from spring to midsummer, but a fertilizer high in phosphates should be used in late summer and autumn.

REST PERIOD: Winter days average 74–79°F (23–26°C), and nights average 46–48°F (8–9°C), with a diurnal range of 26–33°F (14–18°C). In the habitat, rainfall is low for 4–5 months in winter. For 2–3 of these months, high humidity and nightly cooling result in frequent, heavy deposits of dew with even more moisture available from fog and mist. Therefore, the driest season is only 1–2 months long. For cultivated plants, water should be reduced from late autumn to early spring. During most of the winter, plants should be allowed to dry out between waterings, but they should not remain completely dry for extended periods. Occasional early morning mistings between waterings may help prevent the plants from becoming too dry. For 1–2 months in late winter, however, water should be limited to occasional early morning mistings. Fertilizer should be reduced or eliminated, until new growth starts in spring. In the habitat, the large number of clear, winter afternoons indicates very bright conditions.

GROWING MEDIA: Mounting plants on tree-fern or cork slabs accommodates their sprawling, pendulous growth habit. However, humidity must be high and plants must be watered at least once a day in summer. If plants cannot be mounted, hanging pots or baskets may be filled with an open, fast-draining medium. Repotting may be done anytime new roots are actively growing.

MISCELLANEOUS NOTES: The bloom season shown in the climate table is based on reports from the habitat. In cultivation, plants bloom in early summer.

Plant and Flower Information

PLANT SIZE AND TYPE: A 24–35 in. (60–90 cm) sympodial epiphyte.

PSEUDOBULB: 24–35 in. (60–90 cm) long. Individual stems may be as short as 6 in. (15 cm). They are pendulous and taper at each end. Stems emerge from a very short rhizome, but new branches arise from nodes near the apex of mature stems, forming a rather sprawling, untidy plant. *D. praecinctum* was originally described as having stems that were erect, slender, dark, and furrowed.

LEAVES: Many per stem, few per branch. The linear-lanceolate leaves are usually 3–4 in. (8–10 cm) long. They are arranged in 2 rows on each branch. *D. praecinctum* was originally described as having 2-toothed leaves.

INFLORESCENCE: Short. Inflorescences emerge laterally from nodes near the apex of both leafy and leafless stems.

FLOWERS: 1–5 per inflorescence. The flowers are 0.5–0.8 in. (1.3–2.0 cm) across. The cupped sepals and petals may be pale ochre to golden yellow with a red or purple edge along the margin. The 3-lobed lip, which may be sulfur yellow, has small, red spots on the midlobe. The entire front margin of the lip has a dense fringe of long hairs. *D. praecinctum* was described as having a sulfur yellow lip marked with orange in front and a velvety central lobe with 3 keels.

HYBRIDIZING NOTES: Chromosome count is 2n = 38 (ref. 153, 154, 542).

REFERENCES: 38, 46, 153, 154, 179, 216, 217, 254, 369, 376, 445, 454, 542.

PHOTOS/DRAWINGS: *369*, 454.

Dendrobium praecox J. E. Smith. Now considered a synonym of *Pleione praecox* (J. E. Smith) D. Don. REFERENCES: 216, 254.

Dendrobium praeustum Kränzlin. See *D. purpureum* Roxburgh. REFERENCES: 220, 254, Dauncey and Cribb 1993 *Kew Bulletin* 48(3):545–576.

Dendrobium prasinum Lindley

AKA: Sometimes spelled *D. praesinum*.

ORIGIN/HABITAT: Endemic to Fiji. Plants were originally collected at 1950 ft. (600 m) in the Mathuata (Nawavi) Mountains on the northern coast of Vanua Levu. They grow in shade on the trunks or in the forks of moss-covered trees in open or dense forests. They are often found near streams and along forested ridges at 1950–3750 ft. (600–1150 m).

CLIMATE: Station #91655, Lambasa, Vanua Levu, Fiji Islands, Lat. 16.5°S, Long. 179.3°E, at 30 ft. (9 m). Temperatures are calculated for an elevation of 3000 ft. (910 m), resulting in probable extremes of 84°F (29°C) and 46°F (8°C).

N/HEMISPHERE	JAN	FEB	MAR	APR	MAY	JUN	JUL	AUG	SEP	OCT	NOV	DEC
°F AVG MAX	74	74	74	75	77	76	77	77	76	76	75	74
°F AVG MIN	57	58	59	60	61	62	63	63	63	61	60	57
DIURNAL RANGE	17	16	15	15	16	14	14	14	13	15	15	17
RAIN/INCHES	1.9	1.8	2.8	3.6	6.0	10.1	13.0	14.4	14.4	8.4	4.8	2.1
HUMIDITY/%	74	73	73	75	73	78	80	80	83	82	78	78
BLOOM SEASON	*	*	*				*	*	*	*	*	*
DAYS CLR @ 12PM	5	8	4	2	2	2	1	2	3	3	4	
RAIN/MM	48	46	71	91	152	257	330	366	366	213	122	53
°C AVG MAX	23.4	23.4	23.4	24.0	25.1	24.6	25.1	25.1	24.6	24.6	24.0	23.4
°C AVG MIN	14.0	14.6	15.1	15.7	16.2	16.8	17.3	17.3	17.3	16.2	15.7	14.0
DIURNAL RANGE	9.4	8.8	8.3	8.3	8.9	7.8	7.8	7.8	7.3	8.4	8.3	9.4
S/HEMISPHERE	JUL	AUG	SEP	OCT	NOV	DEC	JAN	FEB	MAR	APR	MAY	JUN

Cultural Recommendations

LIGHT: 2500–3500 fc. Strong air movement should be provided at all times.

TEMPERATURES: Throughout the year, days average 74–77°F (24–25°C),

and nights average 57–63°F (14–17°C), with a diurnal range of 13–17°F (7–9°C).

HUMIDITY: 80–85% in summer and autumn, dropping to 70–75% in winter and spring.

WATER: Rainfall is heavy from late spring to autumn, but conditions are drier for 2–3 months in winter. Cultivated plants should be kept evenly moist while actively growing, but water should be gradually reduced in autumn.

FERTILIZER: ¼–½ recommended strength, applied weekly. A high-nitrogen fertilizer is beneficial from spring to midsummer, but a fertilizer high in phosphates should be used in late summer and autumn.

REST PERIOD: Growing temperatures should be maintained all year. Although rainfall is low in winter, additional moisture is available from frequent heavy dew. Water and fertilizer should be reduced for cultivated plants in winter. They should be allowed to dry slightly between waterings, but should not remain dry for extended periods. Occasional early morning mistings on bright, sunny days between waterings may help prevent plants from becoming too dry. In the habitat, light is highest in winter.

GROWING MEDIA: Plants may be mounted on tree-fern or cork slabs if humidity is high and plants are watered at least once daily in summer. When plants are potted, any open, fast-draining medium may be used. Repotting may be done anytime new roots are growing.

MISCELLANEOUS NOTES: The bloom season shown in the climate table is based on cultivation records. Growers report that blooming occurs in all seasons except spring. Plants bloom in spring in the habitat.

Plant and Flower Information

PLANT SIZE AND TYPE: A 3–7 in. (8–18 cm) sympodial epiphyte. Plants form clumps to 6 in. (15 cm) across.

PSEUDOBULB: 3–7 in. (8–18 cm) long. The stems are ovoid or cylindrical and narrow at the tip. They are yellow or orange when dry. When stems are young, they are covered with gray leaf sheaths. The sheaths deteriorate in time, leaving numerous fibers attached to each old growth.

LEAVES: 2–3 at the apex of each growth. The oblong-lanceolate leaves are 1.0–5.5 in. (2.5–14.0 cm) long.

INFLORESCENCE: Short. Inflorescences may arise at the tip of the pseudobulb or laterally from nodes near the apex. They are normally borne on leafless stems.

FLOWERS: 2–3, rarely 1 per inflorescence. The flowers are 1.6 in. (4 cm) across. The greenish lip is sometimes uppermost. It is strongly boat-shaped with upcurved margins and a hairy surface. Blossoms last 6–7 weeks and resemble flared fans. They may be white, cream, or pale yellow, often with a greenish tinge. The column is bright green.

REFERENCES: 142, 179, 216, 252, 254, 278, 353, 385, 466, 499, 526, 556.

PHOTOS/DRAWINGS: *385.*

Dendrobium prenticei (F. Mueller) Nicholls

AKA: Originally described as *Bulbophyllum prenticei* F. Mueller, Clements (ref. 67) also includes the following synonyms: *B. lichenastrum* Fitzgerald not F. Mueller, *Dendrobium aurantiaco-purpureum* Nicholls, *D. lichenastrum* (F. Mueller) Kränzlin var. *prenticei* (F. Mueller) Dockrill, *D. lichenastrum* (F. Mueller) Kränzlin var. *prenticei* (F. Mueller) Dockrill forma *aurantiaco-purpureum* (Nicholls) Dockrill, and *D. variabile* Nicholls. However, Dockrill (ref. 105) lists *D. prenticei* (F. Mueller) Nicholls as a synonym of *D. lichenastrum* (F. Mueller) Kränzlin var. *prenticei* (F. Mueller) Dockrill forma *prenticei* Dockrill.

ORIGIN/HABITAT: Northeastern Australia. The habitat extends from the Burdekin River northward to the Annan River. Plants grow from near sea level to moderately high elevations. They are usually found in high light, often on the outer branches of rainforest trees, on moss-covered branches overhanging creeks, or on trees or rocks in moderately open forests.

CLIMATE: Station #94287, Cairns, Australia, Lat. 16.9°S, Long. 145.8°E, at 7 ft. (2 m). Temperatures are calculated for an elevation of 2000 ft. (610 m), resulting in probable extremes of 103°F (40°C) and 36°F (3°C).

N/HEMISPHERE	JAN	FEB	MAR	APR	MAY	JUN	JUL	AUG	SEP	OCT	NOV	DEC
°F AVG MAX	71	73	76	79	81	83	83	82	80	78	74	72
°F AVG MIN	54	55	57	61	63	66	67	67	66	63	59	57
DIURNAL RANGE	17	18	19	18	18	17	16	15	14	15	15	15
RAIN/INCHES	1.6	1.7	1.7	2.1	3.9	8.7	16.6	15.7	18.1	11.3	4.4	2.9
HUMIDITY/%	69	67	65	65	65	68	72	72	74	73	73	72
BLOOM SEASON		*	*	*								
DAYS CLR @ 10AM	9	11	13	11	6	6	4	5	6	7	11	10
DAYS CLR @ 4PM	8	10	12	16	10	7	4	3	4	6	9	10
RAIN/MM	41	43	43	53	99	221	422	399	460	287	112	74
°C AVG MAX	21.9	23.0	24.7	26.3	27.5	28.6	28.6	28.0	26.9	25.8	23.6	22.5
°C AVG MIN	12.5	13.0	14.1	16.3	17.5	19.1	19.7	19.7	19.1	17.5	15.2	14.1
DIURNAL RANGE	9.4	10.0	10.6	10.0	10.0	9.5	8.9	8.3	7.8	8.3	8.4	8.4
S/HEMISPHERE	JUL	AUG	SEP	OCT	NOV	DEC	JAN	FEB	MAR	APR	MAY	JUN

Cultural Recommendations

LIGHT: 3000–4000 fc. Light is relatively high in the open-forest habitat. Growers recommend using 50% summer shade.

TEMPERATURES: Summer days average 82–83°F (28–29°C), and nights average 66–67°F (19–20°C), with a diurnal range of 15–17°F (8–10°C).

HUMIDITY: 70–75% summer through autumn, dropping to about 65% in winter and spring. In the habitat, however, humidity is probably greater than indicated in the climate table. Cultivated plants are healthiest when provided with high humidity and strong air movement.

WATER: Rainfall is heavy from late spring into autumn, but conditions are quite dry in winter. Cultivated plants should be kept moist while actively growing, but water should be gradually reduced in autumn.

FERTILIZER: ¼–½ recommended strength, applied weekly. A high-nitrogen fertilizer is beneficial from spring to midsummer, but a fertilizer high in phosphates should be used in late summer and autumn.

REST PERIOD: Winter days average 71–77°F (22–25°C), and nights average 54–57°F (13–14°C), with a diurnal range of 15–19°F (8–11°C). Growers recommend that winter lows be kept above 43°F (6°C). Water and fertilizer should be reduced for 4–5 months from late autumn into early spring. Cultivated plants should be kept somewhat dry, but they should never be allowed to dry out completely. In the habitat, light is highest in winter.

GROWING MEDIA: Growers indicate that plants are healthiest when mounted. Plants must never be allowed to dry, however, so they should be potted if growing conditions are marginal. Plants may be potted in any open, fast-draining medium. Repotting is best done in early spring immediately after flowering when new roots are growing.

MISCELLANEOUS NOTES: The bloom season shown in the climate table is based on cultivation records. The preceding temperatures represent the coolest conditions found in the habitat. This species also grows closer to sea level, so the plants should tolerate temperatures that are 6–8°F (3–4°C) warmer than indicated in the climate table.

Plant and Flower Information

PLANT SIZE AND TYPE: A 0.8–2.4 in. (2–6 cm) sympodial epiphyte.

PSEUDOBULB: 0.8–2.4 in. (2–6 cm) tall. Growths may be close together or widely spaced.

LEAVES: 1 per growth. The highly variable leaves, which are 0.4–2.4 in. (1–6 cm) long, may be oval, terete, or nearly cylindrical. They may be prostrate or erect.

Dendrobium prianganense

INFLORESCENCE: Short. Inflorescences may arise in close association with a leaf or appear to emerge directly from a growthless part of the rooting, creeping rhizome.

FLOWERS: 1 per inflorescence. The flowers are 0.2–0.4 in. (0.4–0.9 cm) across and vary in size, shape, and color. All segments are translucent. The sepals and petals may be dirty cream to pale, dirty pink, and some have mauve or purple stripes. The sepals and much smaller petals usually open fully and may recurve at the tips, but some clones remain rather closed. The lip may be pale yellow or orange. The musty-smelling blossoms last 2–3 weeks.

REFERENCES: 67, 105, 179, 227, 228, 240, 254, 421, 533.

PHOTOS/DRAWINGS: *36, 240, 533.*

Dendrobium prianganense J. J. Wood and J. B. Comber

ORIGIN/HABITAT: Endemic to West Java. Plants grow in primary forests at about 3100 ft. (950 m). They were collected in a dark, wet valley at Cibarengkok, south of Bandung.

CLIMATE: Station #96781, Bandung, Java, Indonesia, Lat. 6.9°S, Long. 107.6°E, at 2430 ft. (741 m). Temperatures are calculated for an elevation of 3000 ft. (910 m), resulting in probable extremes of 92°F (33°C) and 50°F (10°C).

N/HEMISPHERE	JAN	FEB	MAR	APR	MAY	JUN	JUL	AUG	SEP	OCT	NOV	DEC
°F AVG MAX	80	81	82	82	80	79	79	78	79	80	80	80
°F AVG MIN	61	61	62	63	64	65	65	65	65	65	64	62
DIURNAL RANGE	19	20	20	19	16	14	14	13	14	15	16	18
RAIN/INCHES	2.7	2.2	2.0	6.0	7.9	8.5	9.5	10.0	9.4	5.6	4.6	4.0
HUMIDITY/%	70	66	62	65	73	77	79	78	78	78	75	72
BLOOM SEASON												*
DAYS CLR @ 7AM	9	10	12	9	4	1	1	1	2	4	5	8
DAYS CLR @ 1PM	8	8	7	2	1	0	0	1	1	1	3	6
RAIN/MM	69	56	51	152	201	216	241	254	239	142	117	102
°C AVG MAX	26.7	27.3	27.8	27.8	26.7	26.2	26.2	25.6	26.2	26.7	26.7	26.7
°C AVG MIN	16.2	16.2	16.7	17.3	17.8	18.4	18.4	18.4	18.4	18.4	17.8	16.7
DIURNAL RANGE	10.5	11.1	11.1	10.5	8.9	7.8	7.8	7.2	7.8	8.3	8.9	10.0
S/HEMISPHERE	JUL	AUG	SEP	OCT	NOV	DEC	JAN	FEB	MAR	APR	MAY	JUN

Cultural Recommendations

LIGHT: 1500–3000 fc. Diffused light is preferred because clear days are very rare in the habitat. Plants normally grow on forest trees, but they are also found growing fully exposed to available light.

TEMPERATURES: Throughout the year, days average 78–82°F (26–28°C), and nights average 61–65°F (16–18°C), with a diurnal range of 13–20°F (7–11°C). The diurnal range is lowest in summer, when overcast skies prevent warming. Plants are unlikely to tolerate hot summer weather.

HUMIDITY: 70–80% most of the year, dropping to 60–65% in late winter and early spring.

WATER: Rainfall is moderate to heavy most of the year, but conditions are somewhat drier in winter. Cultivated plants should be kept moist while growing, but water should be gradually reduced in autumn.

FERTILIZER: ¼–½ recommended strength. A balanced fertilizer should be applied weekly to biweekly throughout the year.

REST PERIOD: Growing conditions should be maintained all year. The increased diurnal range results from both warmer days and cooler nights. Water and fertilizer should be reduced for 2–3 months in winter. Plants should be allowed to dry slightly between waterings, but they should not dry out completely. In the habitat, winter light is highest.

GROWING MEDIA: Mounting plants on tree-fern or cork slabs accommodates their rather pendulous growth habit. However, humidity must be high and plants must be watered at least once a day in summer. If plants cannot be mounted, hanging pots or baskets may be filled with an open, fast-draining medium. Repotting may be done anytime new roots are actively growing.

MISCELLANEOUS NOTES: The bloom season shown in the climate table is based on reports from the habitat.

Plant and Flower Information

PLANT SIZE AND TYPE: A 20 in. (50 cm) sympodial epiphyte.

PSEUDOBULB: 20 in. (50 cm) long. The stems are very slender at the base but become enlarged and slightly flattened on the upper 65%. They are about 0.4 in. (1 cm) apart along the rhizome. The stems are erect when young, becoming pendulous with age.

LEAVES: Many. The leaves are 4.3 in. (11 cm) long, thin, lanceolate, and widest at the base.

INFLORESCENCE: Very short. Many inflorescences emerge from nodes on both leafy and leafless stems. The flowers are held back to back.

FLOWERS: 2 per inflorescence. The white flowers are 0.8 in. (2 cm) long. Petals and dorsal sepal are oblong and narrower than the lateral sepals. The white lip is wavy along the margin. It is decorated with 2, somewhat thickened yellow bands that extend from the base to near the tip. The bands are marked with many tiny brown spots.

REFERENCES: 75, 235.

PHOTOS/DRAWINGS: *75.*

Dendrobium × *primulardii* Horridge. A natural hybrid between *D. primulinum* Lindley and *D. pierardii* Roxburgh ex Hooker f. [now *D. aphyllum* (Roxburgh) C. Fischer]. REFERENCES: 204, 222.

Dendrobium primulinum Lindley

AKA: *D. nobile* Lindley var. *pallidiflora* Hooker.

ORIGIN/HABITAT: Widespread in India and Southeast Asia. Distribution extends from near Mussorie in the Garhwal region of northern India, through Nepal, Sikkim, and the Lushai Hills region of northeastern India, the Chin Hills of Burma, the mountains of northern and western Thailand, the Vientiane region of Laos, the Dalat, Blao, and Langbian regions in Vietnam, and Yunnan Province in southwestern China. Plants usually grow on deciduous trees at 1640–5250 ft. (500–1600 m).

CLIMATE: Station #48327, Chiang Mai, Thailand, Lat. 18.8°N, Long. 99.0°E, at 1100 ft. (335 m). Temperatures are calculated for an elevation of 3500 ft. (1070 m), resulting in probable extremes of 101°F (38°C) and 30°F (−1°C).

N/HEMISPHERE	JAN	FEB	MAR	APR	MAY	JUN	JUL	AUG	SEP	OCT	NOV	DEC
°F AVG MAX	77	82	87	88	86	82	81	79	80	81	78	76
°F AVG MIN	48	49	54	62	66	66	66	67	65	63	58	49
DIURNAL RANGE	29	33	33	26	20	16	15	12	15	18	20	27
RAIN/INCHES	0.3	0.4	0.6	2.0	5.5	6.1	7.4	8.7	11.5	4.9	1.5	0.4
HUMIDITY/%	73	65	58	62	73	78	80	83	83	81	79	76
BLOOM SEASON	*	**	**	**	**	*		*				*
DAYS CLR @ 7AM	5	5	2	2	1	0	0	0	0	1	3	3
DAYS CLR @ 1PM	9	8	4	2	0	0	0	0	0	0	1	3
RAIN/MM	8	10	15	51	140	155	188	221	292	124	38	10
°C AVG MAX	25.0	27.8	30.6	31.2	30.0	27.8	27.3	26.2	26.7	27.3	25.6	24.5
°C AVG MIN	8.9	9.5	12.3	16.7	18.9	18.9	18.9	19.5	18.4	17.3	14.5	9.5
DIURNAL RANGE	16.1	18.3	18.3	14.5	11.1	8.9	8.4	6.7	8.3	10.0	11.1	15.0
S/HEMISPHERE	JUL	AUG	SEP	OCT	NOV	DEC	JAN	FEB	MAR	APR	MAY	JUN

Cultural Recommendations

LIGHT: 3000–4000 fc. The heavy summer cloud cover indicates that some shading is needed from spring through autumn, but light should be as high as the plant can tolerate, short of burning the leaves.

TEMPERATURES: Summer days average 79–82°F (26–28°C), and nights average 66–67°F (19–20°C), with a diurnal range of 12–16°F (7–9°C). Spring is the warmest time of the year. Days average 86–88°F (30–31°C), and nights average 54–66°F (12–19°C), with a diurnal range of 20–33°F (11–18°C).

HUMIDITY: Near 80% in summer, dropping to near 60% in winter.

WATER: Rainfall is moderate to heavy from late spring through early autumn, but conditions are much drier in winter. Cultivated plants should be kept moist while actively growing, but water should be gradually reduced after new growths mature in autumn.

FERTILIZER: ½ to full strength, applied weekly while plants are actively growing. A high-nitrogen fertilizer is beneficial from spring to midsummer, but a fertilizer high in phosphates should be used in late summer and autumn.

REST PERIOD: Winter days average 76–82°F (25–28°C), and nights average 48–49°F (9–10°C), with a diurnal range of 27–33°F (15–18°C). Plants will probably tolerate light frost, especially if they are dry at the time. In the habitat, rainfall averages are very low for 4–5 months in winter, but during the early part of the season the high relative humidity indicates that additional moisture is available from frequent fog, mist, and heavy deposits of dew. Growers sometimes recommend eliminating water in winter, but plants are healthiest if for most of the winter they are allowed to become somewhat dry between waterings but do not remain dry for extended periods. For 1–2 months in late winter, however, conditions are clear, warm, and dry, with humidity so low that even the moisture from morning dew is uncommon. Plants should be allowed to dry out completely between waterings and remain dry longer during this time. Occasional early morning mistings between waterings may help keep the plants from becoming too dry. Fertilizer should be greatly reduced or eliminated until water is increased in spring. A cool, dry rest is essential for cultivated plants and should be continued until new growth starts in spring. In the habitat, light is highest in winter, as indicated by the increased number of clear days and the fact that the plants grow on deciduous trees.

GROWING MEDIA: Growers often recommend mounting plants on tree-fern slabs to accommodate the pendent growth habit. They often place a pad of sphagnum moss between the mount and the plant. If plants are mounted, summer humidity must be high, and plants should be watered at least once a day in summer. If plants cannot be mounted, hanging pots or baskets may be filled with any open, rapidly draining medium. Containers should be barely large enough to hold the roots and allow for 2 years' growth. Mounts or baskets reduce the risk of the slender new canes' becoming kinked under their own weight. Repotting is best done in spring, immediately after flowering.

MISCELLANEOUS NOTES: The bloom season shown in the climate table is based on cultivation records. In the habitat, plants bloom in spring. Although considered easy to grow in most seasonal climates, growers indicate that *D. primulinum* is difficult to grow in warm uniform climates or warm greenhouses. The cool, dry rest is essential in order to induce flowering.

Plant and Flower Information

PLANT SIZE AND TYPE: A 10–18 in. (25–45 cm) sympodial epiphyte. Plants that are subjected to shorter, less severe dry seasons tend to be larger.

PSEUDOBULB: 10–18 in. (25–45 cm) long, but sometimes smaller. The slender, gray-green stems may be somewhat erect or pendent. They are clustered and often become furrowed with age. Stems are leafy at the apex of young growths.

LEAVES: Many. The deciduous leaves are 3–5 in. (8–13 cm) long. They are lanceolate to oblong and smallest near the apex.

INFLORESCENCE: Very short. The blossoms arise from nodes near the apex of leafless stems. The plants are free-flowering.

FLOWERS: 1–2 per inflorescence. The very showy flowers are 2–3 in. (4–8 cm) across. The narrow sepals and petals may be purple, mauve, rose-pink, or white with rose at the tips. They contrast sharply with the yellow lip. The large, downy lip is shaped like a flared trumpet with a fringe along the margin. It may be pale cream-yellow or bright primrose-yellow. The throat is tinged with dark red or purple near the base. The strong fragrance reminds some of cowslips. Blossoms last 1–2 weeks.

HYBRIDIZING NOTES: Chromosome counts are n = 19 (ref. 153, 154, 504, 580), 2n = 38 (ref. 150, 153, 154, 273, 504, 542, 580), 2n = 40 (ref. 150), and 2n = 57 (ref. 150, 154, 542). Johansen (ref. 239) indicates that plants are self-sterile and that flowers dropped 9–10 days after self-pollination. However, when crossed with *D. aphyllum* (Roxburgh) C. Fischer, 28–78% of the seeds had visible embryos and 35–43% of the seed germinated. *D. primulinum* is known to hybridize naturally with *D. nobile* Lindley, producing *D.* × *pitcheranum* Rchb. f.

REFERENCES: 25, 32, 36, 38, 46, 71, 102, 150, 153, 154, 157, 179, 190, 196, 200, 202, 210, 239, 245, 247, 254, 266, 273, 278, 326, 360, 369, 376, 388, 430, 445, 447, 448, 454, 458, 461, 504, 507, 523, 541, 557, 568, 570, 580.

PHOTOS/DRAWINGS: 32, *36*, 38, 102, 210, *245, 247*, 360, *369, 388, 430, 454*, 458, 541, 542, *568*.

Dendrobium prionochilum F. Mueller and Kränzlin.

See note at *D. mirbelianum* Gaudich not J. J. Smith and *D. sylvanum* Rchb. f. not Kränzlin. REFERENCES: 67, 84, 190, 218, 253, 254, 437.

Dendrobium priscillae A. Hawkes.

See *D. mooreanum* Lindley. REFERENCES: 83, 191, 211, 229, 270.

Dendrobium pristinum Ames

ORIGIN/HABITAT: The Philippine Islands. Plants are found on Luzon Island near Manila and in Rizal Province near the summit of Mt. Susong Dalaga.

CLIMATE: Station #98427, Manila, Luzon, Philippines, Lat. 14.5°N, Long. 121.0°E, at 74 ft. (23 m). Temperatures are calculated for an elevation of 3000 ft. (910 m), resulting in probable extremes of 91°F (33°C) and 48°F (9°C).

N/HEMISPHERE	JAN	FEB	MAR	APR	MAY	JUN	JUL	AUG	SEP	OCT	NOV	DEC
°F AVG MAX	76	78	81	83	83	81	78	77	78	78	77	76
°F AVG MIN	59	59	61	63	65	65	65	65	65	64	62	60
DIURNAL RANGE	17	19	20	20	18	16	13	12	13	14	15	16
RAIN/INCHES	0.9	0.5	0.7	1.3	5.1	10.0	17.0	16.6	14.0	7.6	5.7	2.6
HUMIDITY/%	77	73	70	68	71	81	84	86	87	84	82	79
BLOOM SEASON					*		*					
DAYS CLR @ 8AM	6	9	14	14	10	3	2	1	1	6	7	6
DAYS CLR @ 2PM	3	6	10	10	8	2	1	1	0	2	2	3
RAIN/MM	23	13	18	33	130	254	432	422	356	193	145	66
°C AVG MAX	24.6	25.7	27.4	28.5	28.5	27.4	25.7	25.2	25.7	25.7	25.2	24.6
°C AVG MIN	15.2	15.2	16.3	17.4	18.5	18.5	18.5	18.5	18.5	18.0	16.9	15.7
DIURNAL RANGE	9.4	10.5	11.1	11.1	10.0	8.9	7.2	6.7	7.2	7.7	8.3	8.9
S/HEMISPHERE	JUL	AUG	SEP	OCT	NOV	DEC	JAN	FEB	MAR	APR	MAY	JUN

Cultural Recommendations

LIGHT: 2000–3000 fc.

TEMPERATURES: Summer days average 77–81°F (25–27°C), and nights average 65°F (19°C), with a diurnal range of 12–16°F (7–9°C). Spring is the warmest season. Days average 81–83°F (27–29°C), and nights average 61–65°F (16–19°C), with a diurnal range of 18–20°F (10–11°C).

HUMIDITY: 80–85% from summer through autumn. Humidity drops to near 75% in winter and falls even further to near 70% in spring.

WATER: Rainfall is heavy from late spring to autumn, but conditions are dry in winter. Cultivated plants should be kept evenly moist while growing, but water should be gradually reduced in autumn.

FERTILIZER: ¼–½ recommended strength, applied weekly. A high-nitrogen fertilizer is beneficial from spring to midsummer, but a fertilizer high in phosphates should be used in late summer and autumn.

Dendrobium procerum

REST PERIOD: Winter days average 76–78°F (25–26°C), and nights average 59–60°F (15–16°C), with a diurnal range of 16–19°F (9–11°C). Rainfall is low for 3–4 months in winter, but additional moisture is available from frequent heavy dew. In cultivation, water should be reduced and the plants allowed to dry out between waterings. They should not remain dry for extended periods, however. Fertilizer should also be reduced or eliminated anytime water is reduced. In the habitat, light is highest in winter.

GROWING MEDIA: Plants may be mounted on slabs of cork or tree-fern fiber if humidity is high and water is applied at least once daily in summer. Plants may be grown in pots or baskets filled with any open, fast-draining medium. Repotting is best done in early spring when new roots are growing.

MISCELLANEOUS NOTES: The bloom season shown in the climate table is based on collection reports.

Plant and Flower Information

PLANT SIZE AND TYPE: A 16 in. (40 cm) sympodial epiphyte.

PSEUDOBULB: 16 in. (40 cm) long. The plants grow in tufted patches of canelike stems.

LEAVES: Many. The oblong-lanceolate leaves are arranged in 2 rows.

INFLORESCENCE: 0.6 in. (1.5 cm) long. The blossoms are held in crowded racemes which emerge from leafless stems.

FLOWERS: 3–5 per inflorescence. The flowers are 0.4 in. (1 cm) long. Sepals and petals may be white, cream, or pale yellow. The keel on each lateral sepal extends beyond the apex. The 3-lobed lip is fringed along the margin. The sidelobes are oblong, and the midlobe is triangular. The spur is mustard yellow. The lip is fringed along the edge.

REFERENCES: 12, 222, 296, 536.

Dendrobium procerum Schlechter

ORIGIN/HABITAT: Northern Papua New Guinea. Plants grow on forest trees in the Kani Range at about 1950 ft. (600 m).

CLIMATE: Station #200187, Erap, Papua New Guinea, Lat. 6.6°S, Long. 146.7°E, at 850 ft. (260 m). Temperatures are calculated for an elevation of 1950 ft. (600 m), resulting in probable extremes of 98°F (37°C) and 49°F (10°C).

N/HEMISPHERE	JAN	FEB	MAR	APR	MAY	JUN	JUL	AUG	SEP	OCT	NOV	DEC
°F AVG MAX	84	84	85	86	89	89	89	89	89	88	86	86
°F AVG MIN	65	65	65	66	68	69	68	68	69	67	70	66
DIURNAL RANGE	19	19	20	20	21	20	21	21	20	21	16	20
RAIN/INCHES	3.9	3.9	2.7	3.0	3.0	5.3	5.9	5.9	7.0	3.4	2.4	3.1
HUMIDITY/%	82	81	81	79	75	74	74	74	77	76	80	80
BLOOM SEASON	*											
DAYS CLR	N/A											
RAIN/MM	99	99	69	76	76	135	150	150	178	86	61	79
°C AVG MAX	29.1	29.1	29.6	30.2	31.8	31.8	31.8	31.8	31.8	31.3	30.2	30.2
°C AVG MIN	18.5	18.5	18.5	19.1	20.2	20.7	20.2	20.2	20.7	19.6	21.3	19.1
DIURNAL RANGE	10.6	10.6	11.1	11.1	11.6	11.1	11.6	11.6	11.1	11.7	8.9	11.1
S/HEMISPHERE	JUL	AUG	SEP	OCT	NOV	DEC	JAN	FEB	MAR	APR	MAY	JUN

Cultural Recommendations

LIGHT: 2500–3500 fc. Growers report that plants from this habitat often tolerate high light, providing it is introduced gradually.

TEMPERATURES: Throughout the year, days average 84–89°F (29–32°C), and nights average 65–70°F (19–21°C), with a diurnal range of 16–21°F (9–12°C).

HUMIDITY: 75–80% year-round, but the habitat may be quite dry during hot afternoons.

WATER: Rainfall is moderate most of the year, but conditions are somewhat wetter for 4–5 months in summer and early autumn. Cultivated plants should be thoroughly saturated, then allowed to dry slightly between waterings in summer and early autumn. Water should be gradually reduced in autumn.

FERTILIZER: ¼–½ recommended strength. A balanced fertilizer should be applied weekly to biweekly throughout the year.

REST PERIOD: Growing temperatures should be maintained all year. In the habitat, rainfall is lowest in winter, but the high humidity indicates that additional moisture is frequently available from heavy dew. Cultivated plants should be allowed to dry for somewhat longer between waterings than in summer, but they should not remain dry for extended periods. Fertilizer should be reduced until water is increased in spring. In the habitat, seasonal light variation is minor.

GROWING MEDIA: Plants may be mounted on tree-fern or cork slabs or potted in small pots filled with any open, fast-draining medium. Repotting may be done anytime new roots are growing.

MISCELLANEOUS NOTES: The bloom season shown in the climate table is based on reports from the habitat.

Plant and Flower Information

PLANT SIZE AND TYPE: A 16 in. (40 cm) sympodial epiphyte.

PSEUDOBULB: 16 in. (40 cm) long. The flattened, curved stems arise from a very short rhizome.

LEAVES: Many. The narrow leaves are 1.6–2.6 in. (4.0–6.5 cm) long and somewhat lax.

FLOWERS: The flowers are 0.2 in. (0.6 cm) across and do not open fully. Blossoms are white with numerous rose-red dots. The 3-lobed lip is covered with brownish red speckles.

REFERENCES: 221, 437, 445.

PHOTOS/DRAWINGS: 437.

Dendrobium procumbens Carr

ORIGIN/HABITAT: Malaya. Plants were collected in the Cameron Highlands at about 4800 ft. (1460 m).

CLIMATE: Station #48625, Ipoh, Perak, Malaya, Lat. 4.6°N, Long. 101.1°E, at 123 ft. (37 m). Temperatures are calculated for an elevation of 4800 ft. (1460 m), resulting in probable extremes of 84°F (29°C) and 49°F (9°C).

N/HEMISPHERE	JAN	FEB	MAR	APR	MAY	JUN	JUL	AUG	SEP	OCT	NOV	DEC
°F AVG MAX	75	77	78	77	77	77	76	76	75	74	74	74
°F AVG MIN	57	57	58	58	59	58	57	57	58	57	57	57
DIURNAL RANGE	18	20	20	19	18	19	19	19	17	17	17	17
RAIN/INCHES	7.9	3.1	7.6	8.4	6.2	3.6	7.2	6.9	8.8	11.0	13.0	8.9
HUMIDITY/%	76	74	76	78	78	75	76	77	79	82	82	81
BLOOM SEASON				*								
DAYS CLR @ 7AM	3	3	3	1	1	2	1	1	0	0	1	2
DAYS CLR @ 1PM	2	2	2	1	1	1	1	1	0	0	0	2
RAIN/MM	201	79	193	213	157	91	183	175	224	279	330	226
°C AVG MAX	23.6	24.8	25.3	24.8	24.8	24.8	24.2	24.2	23.6	23.1	23.1	23.1
°C AVG MIN	13.6	13.6	14.2	14.2	14.8	14.2	13.6	13.6	14.2	13.6	13.6	13.6
DIURNAL RANGE	10.0	11.2	11.1	10.6	10.0	10.6	10.6	10.6	9.4	9.5	9.5	9.5
S/HEMISPHERE	JUL	AUG	SEP	OCT	NOV	DEC	JAN	FEB	MAR	APR	MAY	JUN

Cultural Recommendations

LIGHT: 2000–3000 fc. Light should be diffused or dappled, and direct sunlight should be avoided. Clear days are rare.

TEMPERATURES: Throughout the year, days average 74–78°F (23–25°C), and nights average 57–59°F (14–15°C), with a diurnal range of 17–20°F (9–11°C).

HUMIDITY: 75–80% year-round.

WATER: Rainfall is heavy most of the year. The heaviest rainfall occurs in autumn with a secondary maximum in spring. Brief semidry periods occur in midwinter and midsummer. Cultivated plants should be kept evenly moist, with only slight drying allowed between waterings.

FERTILIZER: ¼–½ recommended strength. A balanced fertilizer should be applied weekly to biweekly throughout the year.

REST PERIOD: Growing conditions should be maintained year-round. Water should be reduced somewhat in winter for plants cultivated in the dark, short-day conditions common in temperate latitudes. They should never be allowed to dry out completely, however. Fertilizer may be reduced when the plant is not actively growing or when water is reduced. In the habitat, light is slightly higher in winter.

GROWING MEDIA: Plants may be mounted on tree-fern or cork slabs if humidity is high and plants are watered at least once daily in summer. When plants are potted, any open, fast-draining medium may be used. They may be repotted anytime new roots are growing.

MISCELLANEOUS NOTES: The bloom season is based on the collection time. Plants that produce flowers which last a single day commonly bloom several times during the year. Flowering usually occurs 7–14 days after a sudden 10°F (5°C) drop in daytime temperatures.

Plant and Flower Information

PLANT SIZE AND TYPE: A 1.8 in. (4.5 cm) sympodial epiphyte.

PSEUDOBULB: 0.8–1.2 in. (2–3 cm) long. The short stems consist of 4 internodes. The 2 lower nodes are slender, but the swollen third node is round or slightly quadrangular. The apical node is very small. The stems alternate along the elongated, creeping rhizome.

LEAVES: 2 at the apex of each growth. The oblong leaves are 0.6–0.9 in. (1.5–2.2 cm) long, fleshy, and unequally bilobed at the apex.

INFLORESCENCE: 0.8 in. (2 cm) long. Blossoms emerge one at a time from a tuft of dry bracts between the leaves near the apex of the stem.

FLOWERS: 1 per inflorescence. The flowers are 0.7–0.8 in. (1.7–2.0 cm) long. The pale yellow sepals and petals have a purplish suffusion near the base and faint purple veins on the back. The unlobed lip is pale yellow, oblong-obovate, ruffled, and very uneven along the margin. The darker, yellow-green warty patch in the center is thickened along the margin. The back of the lip has purple veins. Blossoms last a single day.

REFERENCES: 57, 200, 225, 455.

PHOTOS/DRAWINGS: 455.

Dendrobium profusum Rchb. f.
The Philippine Islands. Habitat location and elevation are not available, so climate data cannot be selected. The leaves are deciduous, suggesting that the habitat has either a cool or a dry period. However, H. Wood (ref. 582) indicated that a plant imported from the Philippines as *D. obrienanum* proved to be *D. profusum*. For a number of years, it grew and flowered for him with winter nights of 55°F (13°C), semishade, and little drying. This sympodial epiphyte has greenish stems about 20 in. (50 cm) long. They are slender and pendulous. The deciduous leaves were not available when the flower was described. Slender inflorescences arise on leafless stems and carry 7 or more blossoms per inflorescence. The pointed, strap-shaped sepals and oblong, finely toothed petals are yellow with pinkish stripes on the front. The fiddle-shaped lip has a long claw. It is bright yellow with a dark spot in the center. The midlobe, which is shaped like an inverted heart, is finely toothed along the margin. REFERENCES: 12, 216, 254, 296, 536, 582.

Dendrobium proliferum Persoon.
Now considered a synonym of *Maxillaria prolifera* Ruiz and Pavón. REFERENCES: 216, 254.

Dendrobium prorepens Schlechter.
See *D. nummularia* Schlechter. REFERENCES: 222, 382.

Dendrobium prostheciglossum Schlechter

ORIGIN/HABITAT: Papua New Guinea, New Britain, New Ireland, the Solomon Islands, and Vanuatu. In New Guinea, plants grow on open slopes of the Finisterre and Dischore Mountains. They are generally found in mountain forests on limestone rocks and at the base of trees at 3600–3950 ft. (1100–1200 m), but plants have been reported on Mt. Hagen at about 5900 ft. (1800 m).

CLIMATE: Station #200192, Garaina, Papua New Guinea, Lat. 7.9°S, Long. 147.1°E, at 2350 ft. (716 m). Temperatures are calculated for an elevation of 3950 ft. (1200 m), resulting in probable extremes of 89°F (32°C) and 41°F (5°C).

N/HEMISPHERE	JAN	FEB	MAR	APR	MAY	JUN	JUL	AUG	SEP	OCT	NOV	DEC
°F AVG MAX	75	77	78	79	80	80	80	80	79	79	78	76
°F AVG MIN	58	58	58	59	58	59	60	60	60	59	59	58
DIURNAL RANGE	17	19	20	20	22	21	20	20	19	20	19	18
RAIN/INCHES	5.8	6.5	8.7	11.1	11.8	11.9	8.9	11.7	11.5	9.9	7.7	5.2
HUMIDITY/%	84	82	82	81	80	80	81	81	82	83	84	84
BLOOM SEASON						*		*				
DAYS CLR	N/A											
RAIN/MM	147	165	221	282	300	302	226	297	292	251	196	132
°C AVG MAX	23.8	24.9	25.4	26.0	26.5	26.5	26.5	26.5	26.0	26.0	25.4	24.3
°C AVG MIN	14.3	14.3	14.3	14.9	14.3	14.9	15.4	15.4	15.4	14.9	14.9	14.3
DIURNAL RANGE	9.5	10.6	11.1	11.1	12.2	11.6	11.1	11.1	10.6	11.1	10.5	10.0
S/HEMISPHERE	JUL	AUG	SEP	OCT	NOV	DEC	JAN	FEB	MAR	APR	MAY	JUN

Cultural Recommendations

LIGHT: 2000–3000 fc.

TEMPERATURES: Throughout the year, days average 75–80°F (24–27°C), and nights average 58–60°F (14–15°C), with a diurnal range of 17–22°F (10–12°C).

HUMIDITY: 80–85% year-round.

WATER: Rainfall is moderate to heavy all year. Conditions are slightly drier in winter. Cultivated plants should be kept moist but not soggy.

FERTILIZER: ¼–½ recommended strength. A balanced fertilizer should be applied weekly to biweekly throughout the year. The Royal Botanic Garden in Edinburgh uses a seaweed-based fertilizer for high-elevation plants from New Guinea.

REST PERIOD: Growing conditions should be maintained all year. In the habitat, rainfall is slightly lower in winter. Water and fertilizer may be reduced somewhat for cultivated plants, especially those grown in the dark, short-day conditions common during temperate-latitude winters. They should never be allowed to dry out completely, however. In the habitat, light is slightly higher in winter.

GROWING MEDIA: Plants may be mounted on tree-fern or cork slabs if humidity is high and plants are watered at least once daily in summer. When plants are potted, any open, fast-draining medium may be used. Repotting may be done anytime new roots are growing.

MISCELLANEOUS NOTES: The bloom season shown in the climate table is based on reports from the habitat. Schlechter also described *D. prostheciglossum* var. *obtusilobum* Schlechter that grew in the Bismarck range at 6550 ft. (2000 m) and bloomed in May (Nov.). The blossoms were the same color as *D. prostheciglossum,* but he indicated that it would probably prove to be a separate species if the differences between the plants were constant.

Plant and Flower Information

PLANT SIZE AND TYPE: A 12–35 in. (30–90 cm) sympodial terrestrial that is occasionally lithophytic or epiphytic.

PSEUDOBULB: 12–35 in. (30–90 cm) long.

LEAVES: The leaves are 2.4–4.7 in. (6–12 cm) long. They may be lanceolate to oblong and erect to spreading.

INFLORESCENCE: 5.5 in. (14 cm) long.

FLOWERS: 4–9 per inflorescence. The flowers are 0.6 in. (1.6 cm) across. Sepals and petals are yellow-green with a red or brown tinge on the back. The 3-lobed lip is white with an inverted, U-shaped callus in the center. The wavy to ruffled midlobe is blunt at the apex and notched in the center. The sidelobes may be sharply pointed or unevenly rounded at the tips.

REFERENCES: 92, 96, 146, 221, 270, 271, 437, 445, 470.

PHOTOS/DRAWINGS: 437.

Dendrobium prostratum Ridley

AKA: Seidenfaden (ref. 454) discusses the confusion surrounding the names *D. xanthoacron* Schlechter and *D. monanthum* Teijsm. and Binn., for which *D. uniflorum* Teijsm. and Binn. is considered a synonym. He indicates that if these plants are the same as *D. prostratum*, then the name *D. monanthum* has priority.

ORIGIN/HABITAT: Borneo, Lampong province in Sumatra, Singapore, and Malaya. Plants grow in woods on tree branches and on old mangrove trees. In Borneo, plants are found in hill forests of Sabah and Sarawak at about 1950 ft. (600 m).

CLIMATE: Station #48674, Mersing, Malaya, Lat. 2.5°N, Long. 103.8°E, at 151 ft. (46 m). Record extreme temperatures are 99°F (37°C) and 68°F (20°C).

N/HEMISPHERE	JAN	FEB	MAR	APR	MAY	JUN	JUL	AUG	SEP	OCT	NOV	DEC
°F AVG MAX	82	83	86	89	90	89	88	87	87	87	86	82
°F AVG MIN	74	74	74	73	73	72	72	72	72	72	72	73
DIURNAL RANGE	8	9	12	16	17	17	16	15	15	15	14	9
RAIN/INCHES	14.4	6.3	6.1	4.6	7.1	5.1	5.6	6.7	9.3	9.9	13.4	24.3
HUMIDITY/%	82	82	81	82	82	83	84	84	84	84	85	86
BLOOM SEASON						*			*			
DAYS CLR @ 7AM	0	0	1	3	2	2	3	2	1	0	1	1
DAYS CLR @ 1PM	0	0	1	2	1	1	1	0	1	0	0	0
RAIN/MM	366	160	155	117	180	130	142	170	236	251	340	617
°C AVG MAX	27.8	28.3	30.0	31.7	32.2	31.7	31.1	30.6	30.6	30.6	30.0	27.8
°C AVG MIN	23.3	23.3	23.3	22.8	22.8	22.2	22.2	22.2	22.2	22.2	22.2	22.8
DIURNAL RANGE	4.5	5.0	6.7	8.9	9.4	9.5	8.9	8.4	8.4	8.4	7.8	5.0
S/HEMISPHERE	JUL	AUG	SEP	OCT	NOV	DEC	JAN	FEB	MAR	APR	MAY	JUN

Cultural Recommendations

LIGHT: 2500–3500 fc. Direct sun should be avoided.

TEMPERATURES: Throughout the year, days average 82–90°F (28–32°C), and nights average 72–74°F (22–23°C), with a diurnal range of 8–17°F (5–10°C). The diurnal range is greatest in summer, the result of warmer days rather than cooler nights.

HUMIDITY: 80–85% year-round.

WATER: Rainfall is moderate to heavy all year. Cultivated plants should be kept moist but not soggy.

FERTILIZER: ¼–½ recommended strength. A balanced fertilizer should be applied weekly to biweekly throughout the year.

REST PERIOD: Growing conditions should be maintained all year. Lows vary only 2°F (1°C) throughout the year. Winters in the habitat are very wet; but water may be reduced somewhat for cultivated plants, especially those grown in the dark, short-day conditions common in temperate latitudes. Plants should not be allowed to dry out completely, however. In the habitat, seasonal light variations are minor.

GROWING MEDIA: Plants may be mounted on tree-fern or cork slabs if humidity is high and plants are watered at least once daily in summer. When plants are potted, any open, fast-draining medium may be used. Repotting may be done anytime new roots are growing.

MISCELLANEOUS NOTES: The bloom season shown in the climate table is based on reports from the habitat.

Plant and Flower Information

PLANT SIZE AND TYPE: A creeping, 1.6–2.4 in. (4–6 cm) sympodial epiphyte. The plant frequently reaches an overall length of 12 in. (30 cm).

PSEUDOBULB: 1.6–2.4 in. (4–6 cm) long. The flat, brownish yellow stems are creeping, rooting, and branching. They resemble a densely leafy *Angraecum distichum*.

LEAVES: Many. The triangular, sickle-shaped leaves are 0.2–0.4 in. (0.5–1.0 cm) long. They are normally dark green but may be tinged with purple.

INFLORESCENCE: Short. Inflorescences are borne near the apex of the stem.

FLOWERS: 1–few per inflorescence. The flowers are 0.4 in. (1 cm) across. They are pale yellow or greenish yellow and occasionally tinged with red. The lip is marked with a small yellow callus. Although smaller, blossoms are described as similar to those of *D. leonis* (Lindley) Rchb. f. They have a vanilla-like fragrance.

HYBRIDIZING NOTES: Chromosome count is 2n = 2x (ref. 504, 580).

REFERENCES: 200, 254, 395, 402, 433, 454, 455, 504, 580, 592.

PHOTOS/DRAWINGS: 455.

Dendrobium proteranthum Seidenfaden

ORIGIN/HABITAT: Endemic to Thailand. Plants grow near Phu Lunag, Loei where they are considered rare.

CLIMATE: Station #48353, Loei, Thailand, Lat. 17.5°N, Long. 101.5°E, at 817 ft. (249 m). Record extreme temperatures are 106°F (41°C) and 34°F (1°C).

N/HEMISPHERE	JAN	FEB	MAR	APR	MAY	JUN	JUL	AUG	SEP	OCT	NOV	DEC
°F AVG MAX	85	89	94	97	93	91	90	89	88	87	87	84
°F AVG MIN	52	58	65	70	73	74	74	74	73	69	64	56
DIURNAL RANGE	33	31	29	27	20	17	16	15	15	18	23	28
RAIN/INCHES	0.2	0.8	1.4	3.6	6.9	6.8	5.0	8.3	8.8	4.3	0.8	0.1
HUMIDITY/%	62	60	59	62	75	77	77	79	82	79	74	69
BLOOM SEASON	*	*										
DAYS CLR @ 7AM	1	1	1	2	0	1	0	0	1	1	1	
DAYS CLR @ 1PM	22	14	8	5	2	0	1	1	5	11	15	
RAIN/MM	5	20	36	91	175	173	127	211	224	109	20	3
°C AVG MAX	29.4	31.7	34.4	36.1	33.9	32.8	32.2	31.7	31.1	30.6	30.6	28.9
°C AVG MIN	11.1	14.4	18.3	21.1	22.8	23.3	23.3	23.3	22.8	20.6	17.8	13.3
DIURNAL RANGE	18.3	17.3	16.1	15.0	11.1	9.5	8.9	8.4	8.3	10.0	12.8	15.6
S/HEMISPHERE	JUL	AUG	SEP	OCT	NOV	DEC	JAN	FEB	MAR	APR	MAY	JUN

Cultural Recommendations

LIGHT: 2000–3000 fc.

TEMPERATURES: Summer days average 89–91°F (32–33°C), and nights average 74°F (23°C), with a diurnal range of 15–17°F (8–10°C). In the habitat, the warmest temperatures occur in spring. Days average 93–97°F (34–46°C), and nights average 65–73°F (18–23°C), with a diurnal range of 20–29°F (11–16°C). The probable extreme temperatures indicate a tolerance of both summer heat and winter cold.

HUMIDITY: 75–80% in summer and autumn, dropping to near 60% for 4 months in winter and spring.

WATER: Rainfall is moderate to heavy from late spring through summer, but conditions are quite dry in winter. Cultivated plants should be watered often while actively growing, with only sight drying allowed between waterings. Water should be gradually reduced after new growths mature in autumn.

FERTILIZER: ¼–½ recommended strength, applied weekly. A high-nitrogen fertilizer is beneficial from spring to midsummer, but a fertilizer high in phosphates should be used in late summer and autumn.

REST PERIOD: Winter days average 84–89°F (29–32°C), and nights average 52–58°F (11–14°C), with a diurnal range of 28–33°F (16–18°C). Rainfall is low for 3–5 months in winter, but additional moisture is available from heavy dew, fog, and mist during most of the season. In cultivation, water should be reduced and the plants allowed to dry out between waterings. They should not remain completely dry for extended periods, however. Occasional early morning mistings between waterings may help keep the plants from becoming too dry. Fertilizer should be eliminated until water is increased in spring. In the habitat, light is highest in winter.

GROWING MEDIA: Plants may be mounted on tree-fern or cork slabs if humidity is high and plants are watered at least once daily in summer. When plants are potted, any open, fast-draining medium may be used. Repotting is best done in early spring when new roots are growing.

MISCELLANEOUS NOTES: The bloom season shown in the climate table is based on reports from the habitat.

Plant and Flower Information

PLANT SIZE AND TYPE: A small sympodial epiphyte.

PSEUDOBULB: 0.5 in. (1.3 cm) long. The globular pseudobulbs are closely spaced. They are covered with sheaths.

INFLORESCENCE: 1 in. (2.5 cm) long. Inflorescences develop on new shoots which emerge from the base of old pseudobulbs. Blooming occurs before the leaves and pseudobulbs develop.

FLOWERS: 4–7 per inflorescence. The flowers are 0.3 in. (0.8 cm) across and do not open fully. All segments project forward. Sepals and petals are light greenish yellow. The small lip, which is bright grass-green at the tip, has purple streaks.

REFERENCES: 234, 454.

PHOTOS/DRAWINGS: 454.

Dendrobium pruinosum Teijsm. and Binn.

AKA: *Dendrobium crispilobum* J. J. Smith.

ORIGIN/HABITAT: Irian Jaya (western New Guinea) between Geelvink Bay and the MacCluer Gulf, the Molucca Islands, Sulawesi (Celebes) near Manado, and Ambon Island. On Ambon, plants grow in brambles below 650 ft. (200 m).

CLIMATE: Station #97724, Ambon/Pattimura, Indonesia, Lat. 3.7°S, Long. 128.1°E, at 33 ft. (10 m). Record extreme temperatures are 96°F (36°C) and 66°F (19°C).

N/HEMISPHERE	JAN	FEB	MAR	APR	MAY	JUN	JUL	AUG	SEP	OCT	NOV	DEC
°F AVG MAX	81	81	83	85	88	88	88	88	88	86	84	82
°F AVG MIN	74	74	74	74	75	76	76	76	76	76	75	74
DIURNAL RANGE	7	7	9	11	13	12	12	12	12	10	9	8
RAIN/INCHES	23.7	15.8	9.5	6.1	4.5	5.2	5.0	4.7	5.3	11.0	20.3	25.1
HUMIDITY/%	83	82	81	80	79	78	78	77	79	82	83	84
BLOOM SEASON									*			
DAYS CLR @ 9AM	1	1	1	6	7	4	3	3	5	5	3	3
DAYS CLR @ 3PM	1	1	2	5	6	1	1	1	2	3	1	3
RAIN/MM	602	401	241	155	114	132	127	119	135	279	516	638
°C AVG MAX	27.2	27.2	28.3	29.4	31.1	31.1	31.1	31.1	31.1	30.0	28.9	27.8
°C AVG MIN	23.3	23.3	23.3	23.3	23.9	24.4	24.4	24.4	24.4	24.4	23.9	23.3
DIURNAL RANGE	3.9	3.9	5.0	6.1	7.2	6.7	6.7	6.7	6.7	5.6	5.0	4.5
S/HEMISPHERE	JUL	AUG	SEP	OCT	NOV	DEC	JAN	FEB	MAR	APR	MAY	JUN

Cultural Recommendations

LIGHT: 2500–3500 fc.

TEMPERATURES: Throughout the year, days average 81–88°F (27–31°C), and nights average 74–76°F (23–24°C), with a diurnal range of 7–13°F (4–7°C).

HUMIDITY: 80–85% year-round.

WATER: Rainfall is moderate to heavy all year, but conditions are slightly drier in late spring and summer. Cultivated plants should be kept evenly moist with only slight drying allowed between waterings.

FERTILIZER: ¼–½ recommended strength. A balanced fertilizer should be applied weekly to biweekly throughout the year.

REST PERIOD: Growing conditions should be maintained all year. In the habitat, rainfall is heaviest in winter, but water and fertilizer may be reduced somewhat for cultivated plants, especially those grown in the dark, short-day conditions common in temperate latitudes. They should never be allowed to dry completely, however. In the habitat, light is highest in spring.

GROWING MEDIA: Plants may be mounted on tree-fern or cork slabs if humidity is high and plants are watered at least once a day in summer. When plants are potted, any open, fast-draining medium may be used. Repotting may be done anytime new roots are growing.

MISCELLANEOUS NOTES: The bloom season shown in the climate table is based on reports from the habitat. Blooming occurs at the end of the semidry season, so some drying may be necessary to initiate flowering. Many plants that produce flowers which last a single day commonly bloom several times during the year. Flowering usually occurs 7–14 days after a sudden 10°F (5°C) drop in daytime temperatures.

Plant and Flower Information

PLANT SIZE AND TYPE: A 39–69 in. (100–175 cm) sympodial epiphyte.

PSEUDOBULB: 39–69 in. (100–175 cm) long. The nodes are spaced 1.0–1.2 in. (2.5–3.0 cm) apart. The stems are densely leafy. Newly formed shoots and half-grown stems are bent-over at the tip.

LEAVES: Many. The oblong leaves are 4 in. (10 cm) long. They are twisted at the base to lay nearly horizontal.

INFLORESCENCE: Short. Many inflorescences emerge through the 2 overlapping leaf sheaths.

FLOWERS: 2 per inflorescence. The citrus yellow flowers are 1 in. (2.5 cm) across. Sepals and petals are slender. The sidelobes are small, triangular, and covered with wartlike protuberances. The pointed, ovate midlobe is recurved at the pointed tip. It has raised lines forming a callus. Blossoms last a single day.

REFERENCES: 216, 437, 445, 468, 470.

Dendrobium pseudaclinia Lindley. See *D. aclinia* Rchb. f. not Lindley. REFERENCES: 12, 216, 254, 278, 296, 454.

Dendrobium pseudoaloifolium J. J. Wood

AKA: *Grastidium salaccense* Blume.

ORIGIN/HABITAT: Borneo, in the 4th division of Sarawak. In Gunung Mulu National Park, plants are found on ridges between Sungai Berar and Sungai Mentawai. They grow on trees in dipterocarp forests (tropical heath forests) at 500–700 ft. (150–220 m).

CLIMATE: Station #49610, Seria, Brunei, Borneo, Lat. 4.6°N, Long. 114.4°E, at 7 ft. (2 m). Temperatures are calculated for an elevation of 600 ft. (180 m), resulting in probable extremes of 93°F (34°C) and 65°F (18°C).

N/HEMISPHERE	JAN	FEB	MAR	APR	MAY	JUN	JUL	AUG	SEP	OCT	NOV	DEC
°F AVG MAX	84	84	85	86	86	86	86	86	85	85	85	85
°F AVG MIN	72	72	72	73	73	73	72	72	72	72	72	72
DIURNAL RANGE	12	12	13	13	13	13	14	14	13	13	13	13
RAIN/INCHES	16.8	6.5	5.5	4.4	8.2	12.0	8.5	8.4	11.8	11.7	14.5	11.3
HUMIDITY/%	86	86	85	83	83	82	81	81	82	83	84	85
BLOOM SEASON			*									
DAYS CLR @ 8AM	2	2	4	4	3	2	3	2	2	1	2	2
DAYS CLR @ 2PM	1	1	3	4	2	5	3	2	3	2	1	1
RAIN/MM	427	165	140	112	208	305	216	213	300	297	368	287
°C AVG MAX	28.9	28.9	29.5	30.0	30.0	30.0	30.0	30.0	29.5	29.5	29.5	29.5
°C AVG MIN	22.2	22.2	22.2	22.8	22.8	22.8	22.2	22.2	22.2	22.2	22.2	22.2
DIURNAL RANGE	6.7	6.7	7.3	7.2	7.2	7.2	7.8	7.8	7.3	7.3	7.3	7.3
S/HEMISPHERE	JUL	AUG	SEP	OCT	NOV	DEC	JAN	FEB	MAR	APR	MAY	JUN

Cultural Recommendations

LIGHT: 2000–3000 fc. Plants should be watched carefully and moved to lower light if stress is shown, or into higher light if plants do not bloom.

TEMPERATURES: Throughout the year, days average 84–86°F (29–30°C), and nights average 72–73°F (22–23°C), with a diurnal range of 12–14°F

(7–8°C). The extreme temperatures are very close to the averages, suggesting that plants may not tolerate wide temperature fluctuations.

HUMIDITY: 80–85% year-round.

WATER: Rainfall is heavy all year, but conditions are slightly drier for 2–3 months in late winter and early spring. Cultivated plants should be kept evenly moist.

FERTILIZER: ¼–½ recommended strength. A balanced fertilizer should be applied weekly to biweekly throughout the year.

REST PERIOD: Growing conditions should be maintained year-round. Water may be reduced somewhat in winter, especially for plants cultivated in the dark, short-day conditions common in temperate latitudes. Plants may dry slightly between waterings, but they should not be allowed to dry out completely. In the habitat, seasonal light variation is minor.

GROWING MEDIA: Plants may be mounted on tree-fern or cork slabs if humidity is high and plants are watered at least once a day in summer. When plants are potted, any open, fast-draining medium may be used. Repotting may be done anytime new roots are growing.

MISCELLANEOUS NOTES: The bloom season shown in the climate table is based on collection reports.

Plant and Flower Information

PLANT SIZE AND TYPE: A 0.6–2.8 in. (1.5–7.0 cm) sympodial epiphyte.

PSEUDOBULB: 0.6–2.8 in. (1.5–7.0 cm) long. The flattened stems are densely leafy.

LEAVES: Many. The distichous leaves are 0.2–0.4 in. (0.6–1.1 cm) long. They become smallest at the apex. The leaves are folded and flattened so as to appear triangular. They alternate along the stem and overlap slightly.

INFLORESCENCE: Very short. Flowers are borne on the upper portion of the stem where leaves are rudimentary.

FLOWERS: 1–3 per inflorescence. The tiny flowers are 0.1–0.2 in. (0.3–0.5 cm) across. Sepals and smaller petals are whitish pink. The pink lip is fleshy, narrowly oblong, curved, with a slightly wavy, thickened ridge near the apex. The unlobed lip has a smooth margin.

REFERENCES: 15, 234, 586, 587.

PHOTOS/DRAWINGS: 587.

Dendrobium pseudoaprinum J. J. Smith

AKA: Sometimes spelled *D. pseudo-aprinum*. The plant was originally placed in the section *Cadetia*. Since *Cadetia* is now considered a valid genus by some botanists, this plant may be transferred to the genus *Cadetia*.

ORIGIN/HABITAT: Irian Jaya (western New Guinea). Plants were collected on a ridge 43 mi. (70 km) north of Mt. Jaya (Mt. Carstenz) at about 5900 ft. (1800 m).

CLIMATE: Station #97686, Wamena, Irian Jaya, Lat.4.1°S, Long. 139.0°E, at 5446 ft. (1660 m). Temperatures are calculated for an elevation of 5900 ft. (1800 m). Record extreme temperatures are not available for this location.

N/HEMISPHERE	JAN	FEB	MAR	APR	MAY	JUN	JUL	AUG	SEP	OCT	NOV	DEC
°F AVG MAX	74	75	76	75	76	75	76	75	75	78	77	73
°F AVG MIN	59	59	61	61	62	63	62	61	62	64	64	60
DIURNAL RANGE	15	16	15	14	14	12	14	14	13	14	13	13
RAIN/INCHES	3.0	1.9	2.2	4.0	4.6	3.3	2.8	4.2	6.9	3.9	5.4	4.9
HUMIDITY/%	N/A											
BLOOM SEASON		*	*									
DAYS CLR	N/A											
RAIN/MM	76	48	56	102	117	84	71	107	175	99	137	124
°C AVG MAX	23.1	23.6	24.2	23.6	24.2	23.6	24.2	23.6	23.6	25.3	24.7	22.5
°C AVG MIN	14.7	14.7	15.8	15.8	16.4	16.9	16.4	15.8	16.4	17.5	17.5	15.3
DIURNAL RANGE	8.4	8.9	8.4	7.8	7.8	6.7	7.8	7.8	7.2	7.8	7.2	7.2
S/HEMISPHERE	JUL	AUG	SEP	OCT	NOV	DEC	JAN	FEB	MAR	APR	MAY	JUN

Cultural Recommendations

LIGHT: 1800–3000 fc. Plants may tolerate higher light levels, especially in the morning.

TEMPERATURES: Throughout the year, days average 73–76°F (23–24°C), and nights average 59–64°F (15–18°C), with a diurnal range of 12–16°F (7–9°C). In the habitat, the warmest temperatures of the day occur during late morning. Clouds and mist develop near noon, thus preventing additional warming.

HUMIDITY: Information is not available for this location. However, humidity in mistforest habitats normally exceeds 80% year-round.

WATER: Rainfall is light to moderate through most of the year, but large amounts of water are usually available from mist and heavy dew, even during periods of lower rainfall. Cultivated plants should be kept moist, with only slight drying allowed between waterings. Good air movement is critically important and should be maintained at all times.

FERTILIZER: ¼–½ recommended strength. A balanced fertilizer should be applied weekly to biweekly throughout the year.

REST PERIOD: Growing conditions should be maintained all year. Conditions are slightly drier for 1–2 months in winter. In cultivation, water may be decreased somewhat, but plants should never be allowed to dry out completely. In the habitat, light is slightly higher in winter.

GROWING MEDIA: Plants may be mounted on tree-fern or cork slabs or potted in small pots filled with any open, fast-draining medium. Repotting may be done anytime new roots are actively growing.

MISCELLANEOUS NOTES: The bloom season shown in the climate table is based on reports from the habitat.

Plant and Flower Information

PLANT SIZE AND TYPE: A 1.2–2.0 in. (3–5 cm) sympodial epiphyte.

PSEUDOBULB: 1.0–1.3 in. (2.6–3.3 cm) long. Pseudobulbs are 1.0–1.6 in. (2–4 cm) apart on the flattened, serpentine rhizome. The rhizome, which is usually about 5.5 in. (14 cm) long, is covered with sheaths marked with dark spots.

LEAVES: 1 per growth. The lanceolate leaf is 1.5–1.8 in. (3.8–4.6 cm) long, coarsely fleshy, and sparsely covered with dark spots. It is recurved with 3 short teeth at the apex.

INFLORESCENCE: Short. The inflorescence emerges at the base of the leaf.

FLOWERS: 1 per inflorescence. The flowers are 0.5 in. (1.2 cm) across. The ovate dorsal sepal and slender lateral sepals are marked with dark spots on the backside. The lanceolate petals are recurved and incurved at the tips. The lip is 3-lobed and 3-nerved with small sidelobes and a wavy, nearly erect midlobe.

REFERENCES: 224, 445, 470.

Dendrobium pseudocalceolum J. J. Smith

ORIGIN/HABITAT: Northern New Guinea. In Irian Jaya, collections were made near Manokwari (Manokoeari) and near Majalabit Bay on Waigeo Island. Collections are reported in Papua at Kelel in the Minjem River Valley. Plants are most often found somewhat inland growing in seasonally dry and semideciduous forests along creeks in hill country at 650–1650 ft. (200–500 m). Plants also grow on tall trees in primary forests and on trees overhanging the sea.

CLIMATE: Station #97530, Manokwari, Irian Jaya, Lat. 0.9°S, Long. 134.1°E, at 10 ft. (3 m). Temperatures are calculated for an elevation of 1000 ft. (300 m), resulting in probable extremes of 90°F (32°C) and 65°F (18°C).

N/HEMISPHERE	JAN	FEB	MAR	APR	MAY	JUN	JUL	AUG	SEP	OCT	NOV	DEC
°F AVG MAX	83	82	84	84	85	83	83	83	83	83	83	82
°F AVG MIN	71	72	71	71	71	72	70	70	71	71	71	71
DIURNAL RANGE	12	10	13	13	14	11	13	13	12	12	12	11
RAIN/INCHES	5.4	5.6	5.0	4.7	4.5	10.3	12.0	9.4	13.2	11.1	7.8	7.3
HUMIDITY/%	87	87	86	84	85	86	86	85	86	86	86	85
BLOOM SEASON				*			*		*	*	*	*
DAYS CLR @ 6AM	4	3	3	5	3	3	3	1	1	2	3	7
DAYS CLR @ 12PM	2	2	2	3	1	1	1	0	1	0	0	2
RAIN/MM	137	142	127	119	114	262	305	239	335	282	198	185
°C AVG MAX	28.3	27.8	28.9	28.9	29.4	28.5	28.4	28.3	28.3	28.3	28.3	27.8
°C AVG MIN	21.7	22.1	21.5	21.5	21.5	22.1	21.0	21.0	21.5	21.5	21.5	21.5
DIURNAL RANGE	6.6	5.7	7.4	7.4	7.9	6.4	7.4	7.3	6.8	6.8	6.8	6.3
S/HEMISPHERE	JUL	AUG	SEP	OCT	NOV	DEC	JAN	FEB	MAR	APR	MAY	JUN

Cultural Recommendations

LIGHT: 2500–3000 fc.

TEMPERATURES: Throughout the year, days average 82–85°F (28–29°C), and nights average 70–72°F (21–22°C), with a diurnal range of 10–14°F (6–8°C).

HUMIDITY: Near 85% year-round.

WATER: Rainfall is very heavy all year, but conditions are driest in winter and spring. Cultivated plants should be kept moist.

FERTILIZER: ¼–½ recommended strength. A balanced fertilizer should be applied weekly to biweekly throughout the year.

REST PERIOD: Growing conditions should be maintained all year. Water and fertilizer may be reduced somewhat in winter, especially for plants cultivated in the dark, short-day conditions common in temperate latitudes. Plants should never be allowed to dry out completely, however. In the habitat, light is slightly higher in winter.

GROWING MEDIA: Mounting plants on tree-fern or cork slabs accommodates their pendulous growth habit. However, humidity must be high and plants must be watered at least once a day in summer. If plants cannot be mounted, small pots or hanging baskets may be filled with an open, fast-draining medium. When mounted, room should be left below the plant for keikis to root. Remounting may be done anytime new roots are growing.

MISCELLANEOUS NOTES: The bloom season shown in the climate table is based on reports from the habitat. *D. pseudocalceolum* produces short-lived flowers but may bloom every few weeks. Flowering usually occurs 12–13 days after a sudden 10°F (5°C) drop in daytime temperatures.

Plant and Flower Information

PLANT SIZE AND TYPE: A large sympodial epiphyte that occasionally roots at the base of trees.

PSEUDOBULB: 24 in. (60 cm) long. The stems consist of slightly curved, conical nodes. They are yellow with a dark ring at each node. Initially suberect, the branching, zigzag stems become pendulous and hang like a tangled, airy curtain which may be 10–13 ft. (3–4 m) across. Growths emerge from the short, creeping rhizome. The elongated stems are flattened and covered with sheaths. They are not swollen at the base. The newest growth is laxly leafy.

LEAVES: Several. The dagger-like leaves are laterally flattened and often curve out from the stem. They are distichous with the smallest leaves near the apex. Leaves may be thin or succulent.

INFLORESCENCE: Short. Inflorescences emerge from dry bracts at the tip of each stem and branch. They are occasionally borne at nodes immediately below the apex.

FLOWERS: 1–3 per inflorescence. The flowers are 0.5–0.8 in. (1.2–2.0 cm) long. They may be mauve or crystalline white with purple stripes. The lip is marked with 2 yellow keels and a yellow spot at the front. It is notched at the apex. Blossoms have a faint, sweet fragrance. They last 2–3 days.

REFERENCES: 92, 220, 336, 437, 445, 470, 486.

PHOTOS/DRAWINGS: 336.

Dendrobium pseudoconanthum J. J. Smith

AKA: Sometimes spelled *D. pseudo-conanthum*.

ORIGIN/HABITAT: Endemic to southern Sulawesi (Celebes) Island. Plants have been collected at Bone, near Pampanoea.

CLIMATE: Station #97146, Kendari, Sulawesi, Indonesia, Lat. 4.1°S, Long. 122.4°E, at 164 ft. (50 m). Record extreme temperatures are not available for this location.

N/HEMISPHERE	JAN	FEB	MAR	APR	MAY	JUN	JUL	AUG	SEP	OCT	NOV	DEC
°F AVG MAX	85	86	88	90	90	89	88	87	88	86	86	84
°F AVG MIN	70	71	70	72	74	75	75	74	74	74	74	72
DIURNAL RANGE	15	15	18	18	16	14	13	13	14	12	12	12
RAIN/INCHES	5.7	4.0	2.3	2.5	6.0	7.7	7.9	7.3	8.4	8.2	9.9	9.1
HUMIDITY/%	86	80	76	73	76	82	80	81	82	83	85	84
BLOOM SEASON		*	*	*	*							
DAYS CLR @ 8AM	3	10	10	14	8	5	1	2	2	3	2	4
DAYS CLR @ 2PM	0	0	1	2	1	0	1	0	0	0	0	0
RAIN/MM	144	102	58	63	152	197	201	186	213	208	252	231
°C AVG MAX	29.2	29.9	31.0	32.3	32.4	31.8	31.1	30.7	30.9	29.9	30.1	28.8
°C AVG MIN	21.3	21.5	21.1	22.4	23.6	24.0	24.0	23.4	23.4	23.6	23.4	22.3
DIURNAL RANGE	7.9	8.4	9.9	9.9	8.8	7.8	7.1	7.3	7.5	6.3	6.7	6.5
S/HEMISPHERE	JUL	AUG	SEP	OCT	NOV	DEC	JAN	FEB	MAR	APR	MAY	JUN

Cultural Recommendations

LIGHT: 2000–3000 fc.

TEMPERATURES: Throughout the year, days average 84–90°F (29–32°C), and nights average 70–75°F (21–24°C), with a diurnal range of 12–18°F (6–10°C).

HUMIDITY: 80–85% most of the year, dropping to near 75% in spring.

WATER: Rainfall is moderate to heavy most of the year, but conditions are drier for 2–3 months in late winter and early spring. Cultivated plants should be kept moist but not soggy while actively growing. They should be allowed to dry only slightly between waterings.

FERTILIZER: ¼–½ recommended strength. A balanced fertilizer should be applied weekly to biweekly throughout the year.

REST PERIOD: Growing temperatures should be maintained all year. Water and fertilizer should be reduced for 2–3 months in late winter. Plants should be allowed to become somewhat dry between waterings, but they should not remain dry for long periods. Occasional morning mistings on sunny days between waterings may be beneficial. In the habitat, light is highest in late winter and spring.

GROWING MEDIA: Plants may be mounted on tree-fern or cork slabs if humidity is high and plants are watered at least once daily in summer. When plants are potted, any open, fast-draining medium may be used. Repotting may be done anytime new roots are growing.

MISCELLANEOUS NOTES: The bloom season shown in the climate table is based on reports from the habitat. Cultivated plants bloom in spring.

Plant and Flower Information

PLANT SIZE AND TYPE: A 79–197 in. (200–500 cm) sympodial epiphyte.

PSEUDOBULB: 79–197 in. (200–500 cm) long. The spindle-shaped pseudobulbs are narrowest at the tip. Nodes are 2.8 in. (7 cm) apart.

LEAVES: Many. The dark green leaves, which are smallest near the tip, are 1.6–3.5 in. (4–9 cm) long. They are thick, shiny, and recurved at the margins.

INFLORESCENCE: 9–12 in. (23–31 cm) long. The inflorescences are laxly flowered and emerge from the upper part of the cane. They may be horizontal or slightly erect.

FLOWERS: 25 or more per inflorescence. The flowers are 1.0–1.2 in. (2.5–3.0 cm) across. The white sepals are suffused with yellow and overlaid with violet dots on the inside near the apex. The similar dorsal sepal is wavy along the margin and strongly recurved. The twisted petals are pale yellow suffused with violet above. The lip is whitish with a conspicuous white callus marked with lines of purple spots. All segments are picoteed with a solid color margin of the base color.

HYBRIDIZING NOTES: When used as a parent, *D. pseudoconanthum* tends to contribute many-flowered spikes of long-lasting blossoms that make good cut flowers. It has been used to contribute yellows, greens, and blue tones to hybrids. The progeny usually have a picoteed edge on the sepals and petals.

REFERENCES: 25, 84, 179, 196, 224, 304, 342, 346.

PHOTOS/DRAWINGS: *304, 342, 346.*

Dendrobium pseudoconvexum Ames. Now considered a synonym of *Flickingeria pseudoconvexa* (Ames) A. Hawkes. REFERENCES: 12, 213, 222, 230, 231, 286, 296, 536.

Dendrobium pseudodichaea Kränzlin

AKA: Sometimes spelled *D. pseudo-dichaea.*

ORIGIN/HABITAT: Sarawak, Borneo. Habitat elevation was not included with the original description, so the following information should be used with caution.

CLIMATE: Station #96413, Kuching, Sarawak, Lat. 1.5°N, Long. 110.3°E, at 85 ft. (26 m). Record extreme temperatures are 97°F (36°C) and 64°F (18°C).

N/HEMISPHERE	JAN	FEB	MAR	APR	MAY	JUN	JUL	AUG	SEP	OCT	NOV	DEC
°F AVG MAX	88	88	89	90	91	91	91	92	90	90	90	88
°F AVG MIN	72	72	72	72	72	73	72	72	72	72	72	72
DIURNAL RANGE	16	16	17	18	19	18	19	20	18	18	18	16
RAIN/INCHES	27.1	19.7	14.2	9.7	9.0	8.5	6.9	8.8	9.5	12.6	13.1	20.1
HUMIDITY/%	89	88	86	85	85	83	82	83	84	85	87	88
BLOOM SEASON	N/A											
DAYS CLR @ 7AM	1	0	1	2	3	2	4	1	2	1	1	1
DAYS CLR @ 1PM	0	0	0	0	0	1	1	1	0	0	0	0
RAIN/MM	688	500	361	246	229	216	175	224	241	320	333	511
°C AVG MAX	31.1	31.1	31.7	32.2	32.8	32.8	32.8	33.3	32.2	32.2	32.2	31.1
°C AVG MIN	22.2	22.2	22.2	22.2	22.2	22.8	22.2	22.2	22.2	22.2	22.2	22.2
DIURNAL RANGE	8.9	8.9	9.5	10.0	10.6	10.0	10.6	11.1	10.0	10.0	10.0	8.9
S/HEMISPHERE	JUL	AUG	SEP	OCT	NOV	DEC	JAN	FEB	MAR	APR	MAY	JUN

Cultural Recommendations

LIGHT: 2000–3000 fc.

TEMPERATURES: Throughout the year, days average 88–92°F (31–33°C), and nights average 72–73°F (22–23°C), with a diurnal range of 16–20°F (9–11°C). The diurnal range is unusually large for a habitat with so little seasonal variation.

HUMIDITY: 80–90% year-round. High humidity and excellent air circulation are important.

WATER: Rainfall is very heavy all year. Plants should be kept very moist. Warm water may be beneficial.

FERTILIZER: ¼–½ recommended strength. A balanced fertilizer should be applied weekly to biweekly throughout the year.

REST PERIOD: Growing conditions should be maintained all year. The smaller diurnal range results from cooler days, not cooler nights. The record low is only 10°F (6°C) below the average lows. Water may be reduced somewhat for cultivated plants in winter, especially those grown in the dark, short-day conditions common in temperate latitudes. They should never dry out completely, however. In the habitat, light is highest in winter.

GROWING MEDIA: Plants may be mounted on tree-fern or cork slabs if humidity is high and plants are watered at least once daily in summer. When plants are potted, any open, fast-draining medium may be used. Repotting may be done anytime new roots are growing.

Plant and Flower Information

PLANT SIZE AND TYPE: A sympodial epiphyte.

PSEUDOBULB: The slender, leafy stems consist of nodes spaced 1.6 in. (4 cm) apart.

LEAVES: Many. The bright green leaves are 3.1 in. (8 cm) long, rectangular, and unequally bilobed. They are widely spaced along the stem.

INFLORESCENCE: Inflorescences emerge opposite the leaves.

FLOWERS: 1–2 per inflorescence. The milk-white flowers are 0.5–0.6 in. (1.2–1.4 cm) across. Blossoms have a pointed, oblong dorsal sepal, triangular lateral sepals, and tongue-shaped petals which are uneven along the margin near the tip. The margin of the 3-lobed lip is ruffled and uneven.

REFERENCES: 220, 254, 286, 295.

Dendrobium pseudofrigidum J. J. Smith. See *D. masarangense* Schlechter. REFERENCES: 179, 224, 304, 330, 385, 445, 538. PHOTOS/DRAWINGS: 538.

Dendrobium pseudoglomeratum J. J. Wood and T. M. Reeve

ORIGIN/HABITAT: New Guinea. Plants usually grow in mistforests at 3000–6000 ft. (910–1830 m), but they are occasionally found near sea level. In Papua, collections are reported along the Ramu River and in the Waria Valley.

CLIMATE: Station #200192, Garaina, Papua New Guinea, Lat. 7.9°S, Long. 147.1°E, at 2350 ft. (716 m). Temperatures are calculated for an elevation of 4250 ft. (1300 m), resulting in probable extremes of 88°F (31°C) and 40°F (4°C).

N/HEMISPHERE	JAN	FEB	MAR	APR	MAY	JUN	JUL	AUG	SEP	OCT	NOV	DEC
°F AVG MAX	74	76	77	78	79	79	79	79	78	78	77	75
°F AVG MIN	57	57	57	58	57	58	59	59	59	58	58	57
DIURNAL RANGE	17	19	20	20	22	21	20	20	19	20	19	18
RAIN/INCHES	5.8	6.5	8.7	11.1	11.8	11.9	8.9	11.7	11.5	9.9	7.7	5.2
HUMIDITY/%	84	82	82	81	80	80	81	81	82	83	84	84
BLOOM SEASON					*							
DAYS CLR	N/A											
RAIN/MM	147	165	221	282	300	302	226	297	292	251	196	132
°C AVG MAX	23.1	24.3	24.8	25.4	25.9	25.9	25.9	25.9	25.4	25.4	24.8	23.7
°C AVG MIN	13.7	13.7	13.7	14.3	13.7	14.3	14.8	14.8	14.8	14.3	14.3	13.7
DIURNAL RANGE	9.4	10.6	11.1	11.1	12.2	11.6	11.1	11.1	10.6	11.1	10.5	10.0
S/HEMISPHERE	JUL	AUG	SEP	OCT	NOV	DEC	JAN	FEB	MAR	APR	MAY	JUN

Cultural Recommendations

LIGHT: 3000–4000 fc. Bright diffused light is recommended.

TEMPERATURES: Throughout the year, days average 74–79°F (23–26°C), and nights average 57–59°F (14–15°C), with a diurnal range of 17–22°F (9–12°C). Growers indicate that plants will tolerate cooler temperatures; but since they are also found near sea level, they should also adapt to warmer conditions.

HUMIDITY: 80–85% year-round.

WATER: Rainfall is moderate to heavy all year, but conditions are slightly drier in winter. Cultivated plants should be kept moist but not soggy.

FERTILIZER: ¼–½ recommended strength. A balanced fertilizer should be applied weekly to biweekly throughout the year. The Royal Botanic Garden in Edinburgh uses a seaweed-based fertilizer for plants from high-elevation New Guinea habitats.

REST PERIOD: Growing conditions should be maintained all year. Growers indicate that plants grow well in warm or intermediate conditions. In the habitat, rainfall is slightly lower in winter. Water and fertilizer may be reduced somewhat, especially for plants grown in the dark, short-day conditions common in temperate latitudes. Plants should not be allowed to dry out completely, however. In the habitat, light is probably higher in winter.

GROWING MEDIA: Growers recommend mounting plants on tree-fern slabs if humidity is high and plants are watered at least once daily in summer. When plants are potted, any open, fast-draining medium may be used. Repotting may be done anytime new roots are growing.

MISCELLANEOUS NOTES: The bloom season shown in the climate table is based on cultivation records. Of the higher elevation New Guinea Dendrobiums, *D. pseudoglomeratum* is one of the easiest to cultivate.

Plant and Flower Information

PLANT SIZE AND TYPE: A 12–39 in. (30–100 cm) sympodial epiphyte.

PSEUDOBULB: 12–39 in. (30–100 cm) long. The canelike stems are semi-erect.

LEAVES: Many on young growths. The leaves are deciduous.

INFLORESCENCE: Very short. Inflorescences arise from uppermost nodes of mature stems, both leafy and leafless. The flowers are arranged in an apical cluster.

FLOWERS: Many. The showy flowers are 0.5–1.6 in. (1.3–4.0 cm) long, but flower size can vary even on a single inflorescence. The flowers are bright, transparent pink to rose-purple. The narrow lip is pinkish- to scarlet-orange and is uppermost. A rare form has a golden yellow lip. Although the blossoms have a thin texture, they last about 5 weeks.

HYBRIDIZING NOTES: Chromosome count is 2n = 38 (ref. 153, 273). Flowers are easily pollinated.

REFERENCES: 79, 95, 153, 179, 234, 273, 371, 508, 549, 552, 554.

PHOTOS/DRAWINGS: *79, 95, 371, 508, 549, 552, 554.*

Dendrobium pseudohainense Masamune.

Sometimes spelled *D. pseudo-hainense*, see *D. miyakei* Schlechter. REFERENCES: 61, 208, 279.

Dendrobium pseudointricatum Guillaumin

AKA: Sometimes spelled *D. pseudo intricatum*.

ORIGIN/HABITAT: Vietnam. Plants were collected near Dalat. Habitat elevation was not given, so the following temperatures should be used with caution.

CLIMATE: Station #48881, Dalat, Vietnam, Lat. 11.1°N, Long. 108.1°E, at 3156 ft. (962 m). Record extreme temperatures are 93°F (34°C) and 43°F (6°C).

N/HEMISPHERE	JAN	FEB	MAR	APR	MAY	JUN	JUL	AUG	SEP	OCT	NOV	DEC
°F AVG MAX	80	82	84	85	84	81	81	80	80	80	79	79
°F AVG MIN	56	57	59	62	65	65	65	65	65	63	60	58
DIURNAL RANGE	24	25	25	23	19	16	16	15	15	17	19	21
RAIN/INCHES	0.2	0.9	1.6	4.6	9.1	6.1	7.7	8.2	10.1	9.7	2.7	1.3
HUMIDITY/%	68	64	65	71	78	81	82	83	84	82	76	73
BLOOM SEASON	N/A											
DAYS CLR @ 7AM	13	13	13	9	5	3	2	2	2	5	7	10
DAYS CLR @ 1PM	8	8	8	2	0	0	0	0	0	1	3	4
RAIN/MM	5	23	41	117	231	155	196	208	257	246	69	33
°C AVG MAX	26.7	27.8	28.9	29.4	28.9	27.2	27.2	26.7	26.7	26.7	26.1	26.1
°C AVG MIN	13.3	13.9	15.0	16.7	18.3	18.3	18.3	18.3	18.3	17.2	15.6	14.4
DIURNAL RANGE	13.4	13.9	13.9	12.7	10.6	8.9	8.9	8.4	8.4	9.5	10.5	11.7
S/HEMISPHERE	JUL	AUG	SEP	OCT	NOV	DEC	JAN	FEB	MAR	APR	MAY	JUN

Cultural Recommendations

LIGHT: 2000–2500 fc.

TEMPERATURES: Summer days average 80–81°F (27°C), and nights average 65°F (18°C), with a diurnal range of 15–16°F (8–9°C). The warmest temperatures occur in late winter and spring. Days average 84–85°F (29°C), and nights average 59–65°F (15–18°C), with a diurnal range of 19–25°F (11–14°C).

HUMIDITY: 80–85% in summer, dropping to near 65% in late winter.

WATER: Rainfall is moderate to heavy in summer but is very light for 2 months in winter. Cultivated plants should be kept moist while growing, but water should be gradually reduced after new growths mature in autumn.

FERTILIZER: ¼–½ recommended strength, applied weekly. A high-nitrogen fertilizer is beneficial from spring to midsummer, but a fertilizer high in phosphates should be used in late summer and autumn.

REST PERIOD: Winter days average 79–82°F (26–28°C), and nights average 56–58°F (13–14°C), with a diurnal range of 21–25°F (12–14°C). The increased diurnal range results from warmer days and cooler nights. Rainfall is low for 3–4 months. For 1–2 of these months, conditions are so dry that even moisture from dew is uncommon. For cultivated plants, water and fertilizer should be reduced for 2–3 months. Plants should be allowed to dry out between waterings, but they should not remain dry for extended periods. In the habitat, light is highest in winter.

GROWING MEDIA: Plants may be mounted on tree-fern or cork slabs if humidity is high and plants are watered at least once daily in summer. When plants are potted, any open, fast-draining medium may be used. Repotting is best done in early spring when new roots are growing.

Plant and Flower Information

PLANT SIZE AND TYPE: A sympodial epiphyte of unreported size.

PSEUDOBULB: The cylindrical stems are slender at the base and slightly larger near the apex.

LEAVES: The lanceolate leaves are 2.4–2.8 in. (6–7 cm) long.

INFLORESCENCE: 0.2 in. (0.5 cm) long. The lateral racemes emerge from nodes along the side of leafy and leafless stems.

FLOWERS: 2 per inflorescence. The flowers are 0.8–1.0 in. (2.0–2.5 cm) across. The ovate sepals and petals are yellow at the tip and paler near the base. The lip is pale rose with darker, nearly orange markings on the midlobe. The large sidelobes are covered with red stripes. The lip margin is minutely toothed.

REFERENCES: 168, 230, 448.

Dendrobium pseudokraemeri Fukuyama

AKA: Sometimes spelled *D. pseudo-kraemeri*. In 1993 Dauncey and Cribb in *Kew Bulletin* 48(3) included *D. pseudokraemeri* as a possible synonym of *D. kraemeri* Schlechter.

ORIGIN/HABITAT: The eastern Caroline Islands including Ponape and Kosrae (Kusai, Kusaie). Plants grow at about 2100 ft. (640 m) near the summit of Mt. Batie.

CLIMATE: Station #91348, Ponape, Caroline Islands, Lat. 7.0°N, Long. 158.2°E, at 121 ft. (37 m). Temperatures are calculated for an elevation of 2100 ft. (640 m). Record extreme temperatures are not available for this location.

N/HEMISPHERE	JAN	FEB	MAR	APR	MAY	JUN	JUL	AUG	SEP	OCT	NOV	DEC
°F AVG MAX	81	82	82	82	82	82	83	82	82	82	82	81
°F AVG MIN	66	65	65	64	64	64	63	62	63	64	64	65
DIURNAL RANGE	15	17	17	18	18	18	20	20	19	18	18	16
RAIN/INCHES	11.1	9.7	14.6	20.0	20.3	16.7	16.2	16.3	15.8	16.0	16.9	18.3
HUMIDITY/%	N/A											
BLOOM SEASON												
DAYS CLR	N/A											
RAIN/MM	282	246	371	508	516	424	411	414	401	406	429	465
°C AVG MAX	27.5	28.0	28.0	28.0	28.0	28.0	28.6	28.0	28.0	28.0	28.0	27.5
°C AVG MIN	19.1	18.6	18.6	18.0	18.0	18.0	17.5	16.9	17.5	18.0	18.0	18.6
DIURNAL RANGE	8.4	9.4	9.4	10.0	10.0	10.0	11.1	11.1	10.5	10.0	10.0	8.9
S/HEMISPHERE	JUL	AUG	SEP	OCT	NOV	DEC	JAN	FEB	MAR	APR	MAY	JUN

Dendrobium pseudomohlianum

Cultural Recommendations

LIGHT: 2000–3000 fc. Although cloud cover records are not available for this location, other stations in the Caroline Islands report less than 3 days with clear skies each year.

TEMPERATURES: Throughout the year, days average 81–83°F (28–29°C), and nights average 62–66°F (17–19°C), with a diurnal range of 15–20°F (8–11°C).

HUMIDITY: Information is not available for this location, but other stations in the island group report averages of 80–85% year-round.

WATER: Rainfall is very heavy all year. Cultivated plants should be evenly moist.

FERTILIZER: ¼–½ recommended strength. A balanced fertilizer should be applied weekly to biweekly throughout the year.

REST PERIOD: Growing conditions should be maintained year-round. Water and fertilizer should be reduced for plants cultivated in the dark, short-day conditions common in temperate-latitude winters, but they should never be allowed to dry out completely.

GROWING MEDIA: Plants may be mounted on tree-fern or cork slabs if humidity is high and plants are watered at least once daily in summer. When plants are potted, any open, fast-draining medium may be used. They may be repotted anytime new roots are growing.

MISCELLANEOUS NOTES: The bloom season shown in the climate table is based on records from the habitat.

Plant and Flower Information

PLANT SIZE AND TYPE: A 16–31 in. (40–80 cm) sympodial epiphyte.

PSEUDOBULB: 16–31 in. (40–80 cm) long. The cylindrical stems are erect to spreading and not branched. They are borne on a short rhizome and become longitudinally ridged with age.

LEAVES: Many. The linear-lanceolate leaves are 3.5–6.0 in. (9–15 cm) long and pointed at the tip.

INFLORESCENCE: 1.0–1.6 in. (2.5–4.0 cm) long. Racemes are borne on leafless stems.

FLOWERS: 10–20 per inflorescence. The flowers are 0.5 in. (1.3 cm) across. The ovate-oblong sepals are rounded at the tip, contracted at the base, and sometimes slightly irregular along the margin. The petals are elliptical, contracted at the base, and pointed at the tips. The lip is small, concave, oblong-lanceolate, and minutely toothed along the margin. Flower color was not included in the original description.

REFERENCES: 135, 226.

PHOTOS/DRAWINGS: 135.

Dendrobium pseudomohlianum Kränzlin. Sometimes spelled *D. pseudo-mohlianum*, see *D. lawesii* F. Mueller not Schlechter.
REFERENCES: 219, 254, 437, 444,

Dendrobium pseudopeloricum J. J. Smith

ORIGIN/HABITAT: Irian Jaya (western New Guinea). Plants grow on moss-covered trees on a ridge leading to Mt. Doorman at about 8550 ft. (2600 m).

CLIMATE: Station #97686, Wamena, New Guinea, Lat. 4.1°S, Long. 139.0°E, at 5446 ft. (1660 m). Temperatures are calculated for an elevation of 8550 ft. (2600 m). Record extreme temperatures are not available for this location.

N/HEMISPHERE	JAN	FEB	MAR	APR	MAY	JUN	JUL	AUG	SEP	OCT	NOV	DEC
°F AVG MAX	65	66	67	66	67	66	67	66	66	69	68	64
°F AVG MIN	50	50	52	52	53	54	53	52	53	55	55	51
DIURNAL RANGE	15	16	15	14	14	12	14	14	13	14	13	13
RAIN/INCHES	3.0	1.9	2.2	4.0	4.6	3.3	2.8	4.2	6.9	3.9	5.4	4.9
HUMIDITY/%	N/A											
BLOOM SEASON							*					
DAYS CLR	N/A											
RAIN/MM	76	48	56	102	117	84	71	107	175	99	137	124
°C AVG MAX	18.2	18.8	19.3	18.8	19.3	18.8	19.3	18.8	18.8	20.5	19.9	17.7
°C AVG MIN	9.9	9.9	11.0	11.0	11.6	12.1	11.6	11.0	11.6	12.7	12.7	10.5
DIURNAL RANGE	8.3	8.9	8.3	7.8	7.7	6.7	7.7	7.8	7.2	7.8	7.2	7.2
S/HEMISPHERE	JUL	AUG	SEP	OCT	NOV	DEC	JAN	FEB	MAR	APR	MAY	JUN

Cultural Recommendations

LIGHT: 1800–2500 fc.

TEMPERATURES: Throughout the year, days average 64–69°F (18–21°C), and nights average 50–55°F (10–13°C), with a diurnal range of 12–16°F (7–9°C). In the habitat, the warmest temperatures of the day occur in late morning when skies are clear. Clouds and mist develop near noon, thus preventing additional warming.

HUMIDITY: Information is not available for this location. However, humidity in mistforest habitats normally exceeds 80% year-round. In hot, dry weather, plants are healthier if placed in front of an evaporative cooler.

WATER: Rainfall is moderate through most of the year. In the higher-elevation habitat, rainfall amounts may be greater than indicated in the climate table. In addition, large amounts of water are available from mist and heavy dew, even during periods of reduced rainfall. Cultivated plants should be kept moist, with only slight drying allowed between waterings. They should be misted several times daily on the hottest days, but the foliage should always be dry before evening. Good air movement is critically important and should be maintained at all times.

FERTILIZER: ¼–½ recommended strength. A balanced fertilizer should be applied weekly to biweekly throughout the year. The Royal Botanic Garden in Edinburgh uses a dilute, seaweed-based fertilizer.

REST PERIOD: Growing conditions should be maintained all year. Rainfall averages are somewhat lower for a month or so in winter and again in midsummer. In cultivation, water may be decreased, but plants should never be allowed to dry out completely. In the habitat, light is slightly higher in winter.

GROWING MEDIA: Plants may be mounted on tree-fern or cork slabs or potted in small pots filled with any open, fast-draining medium. Repotting may be done anytime new roots are growing.

MISCELLANEOUS NOTES: The bloom season shown in the climate table is based on reports from the habitat.

Plant and Flower Information

PLANT SIZE AND TYPE: A 0.8 in. (2 cm) sympodial epiphyte.

PSEUDOBULB: 0.5 in. (1.3 cm) long. The stems, which may be more than 0.5 in. (1.3 cm) apart, are held at an angle to the elongated, ascending rhizome.

LEAVES: 5–6 per growth. The lanceolate-triangular leaves are 0.3 in. (0.8 cm) long, recurved, and channeled. They may be violet to dark red.

INFLORESCENCE: Short. The erect inflorescences emerge from nodes along the stem.

FLOWERS: 1 per inflorescence. The flowers are less than 0.5 in. (1.3 cm) long. Sepals and petals are pale blue at the base, pale dirty greenish in the middle, and pale dirty yellow with a touch of blue at the tips. The petals resemble the hooded lip. The lip has no callus.

REFERENCES: 224, 445, 470.

Dendrobium pseudorevolutum Guillaumin. Now considered a synonym of *Appendiculata cornuta* Blume. REFERENCES: 167, 229.

Dendrobium pseudotenellum Guillaumin

AKA: *D. tenellum* (Blume) Lindley var. *setifolium* Guillaumin.

ORIGIN/HABITAT: Vietnam. Plants grow near Dalat, Langbian, and Nhatrang. Reports from the habitat indicate that plants growing in sheltered places are larger.

CLIMATE: Station #48881, Dalat, Vietnam, Lat. 11.1°N, Long. 108.1°E, at 3156 ft. (962 m). Record extreme temperatures are 93°F (34°C) and 43°F (6°C).

N/HEMISPHERE	JAN	FEB	MAR	APR	MAY	JUN	JUL	AUG	SEP	OCT	NOV	DEC
°F AVG MAX	80	82	84	85	84	81	81	80	80	80	79	79
°F AVG MIN	56	57	59	62	65	65	65	65	65	63	60	58
DIURNAL RANGE	24	25	25	23	19	16	16	15	15	17	19	21
RAIN/INCHES	0.2	0.9	1.6	4.6	9.1	6.1	7.7	8.2	10.1	9.7	2.7	1.3
HUMIDITY/%	68	64	65	71	78	81	82	83	84	82	76	73
BLOOM SEASON	N/A											
DAYS CLR @ 7AM	13	13	13	9	5	3	2	2	2	5	7	10
DAYS CLR @ 1PM	8	8	8	2	0	0	0	0	0	1	3	4
RAIN/MM	5	23	41	117	231	155	196	208	257	246	69	33
°C AVG MAX	26.7	27.8	28.9	29.4	28.9	27.2	27.2	26.7	26.7	26.7	26.1	26.1
°C AVG MIN	13.3	13.9	15.0	16.7	18.3	18.3	18.3	18.3	18.3	17.2	15.6	14.4
DIURNAL RANGE	13.4	13.9	13.9	12.7	10.6	8.9	8.9	8.4	8.4	9.5	10.5	11.7
S/HEMISPHERE	JUL	AUG	SEP	OCT	NOV	DEC	JAN	FEB	MAR	APR	MAY	JUN

Cultural Recommendations

LIGHT: 2000–2500 fc.

TEMPERATURES: Summer days average 80–81°F (27°C), and nights average 65°F (18°C), with a diurnal range of 15–16°F (8–9°C). The warmest temperatures occur in late winter and spring. Days average 84–85°F (29°C), and nights average 59–65°F (15–18°C), with a diurnal range of 19–25°F (11–14°C).

HUMIDITY: 80–85% in summer, dropping to near 65% in late winter.

WATER: Rainfall is moderate to heavy in summer but is very light for 2 months in winter. Cultivated plants should be kept moist while growing, but water should be gradually reduced after new growths mature in autumn.

FERTILIZER: ¼–½ recommended strength, applied weekly. A high-nitrogen fertilizer is beneficial from spring to midsummer, but a fertilizer high in phosphates should be used in late summer and autumn.

REST PERIOD: Winter days average 79–82°F (26–28°C), and nights average 56–58°F (13–14°C), with a diurnal range of 21–25°F (12–14°C). The increased diurnal range results from warmer days and cooler nights. Rainfall is low for 3–4 months. For 1–2 of these months, conditions are so dry that even moisture from dew is uncommon. For cultivated plants, water and fertilizer should be reduced for 2–3 months. Plants should be allowed to dry out between waterings, but they should not remain dry for extended periods. In the habitat, light is highest in winter.

GROWING MEDIA: Plants may be mounted on tree-fern or cork slabs if humidity is high and plants are watered daily in summer. When plants are potted, any open, fast-draining medium may be used. Repotting is best done in early spring when new roots are growing.

Plant and Flower Information

PLANT SIZE AND TYPE: A 2.4–4.7 in. (6–12 cm) sympodial epiphyte.

PSEUDOBULB: 0.4 in. (1 cm) long. The stems form tufts of growths.

LEAVES: 4–6 per growth. The slender leaves, which are 0.4–0.8 in. (1–2 cm) long, are held at a wide angle to the stem.

INFLORESCENCE: Short. Inflorescences are born at the apex of the stem.

FLOWERS: 1 per inflorescence. The white flowers have purple lines on the lip. The dorsal sepal and petals are narrow, but the lateral sepals are broadly triangular. The recurved front edges of the somewhat square lip are coarsely toothed or fringed. The callus is brownish.

REFERENCES: 230, 448, 450.

PHOTOS/DRAWINGS: 450.

Dendrobium pseudotokai Kränzlin. See *D. macranthum* A. Richard. REFERENCES: 84, 162, 179, 224, 270, 271.

Dendrobium pseudoumbellatum J. J. Smith. Sometimes spelled *D. pseudo-umbellatum*, it is now considered a synonym of *Cadetia pseudo-umbellata* (J. J. Smith) Schlechter. REFERENCES: 220, 254, 437.

Dendrobium psyche Kränzlin. See *D. macrophyllum* A. Richard. REFERENCES: 83, 220, 254, 270, 271, 430.

Dendrobium psychrophilum F. Mueller

AKA: Mueller indicated that placing this plant in the family *Dendrobium* was open to question, that it might prove to be a *Bulbophyllum* since the pollinia had dropped from the shrivelled flowers available to him.

ORIGIN/HABITAT: New Guinea. Plants grow in moss near the summit of the Owen Stanley Mountains.

CLIMATE: Station #200192, Garaina, Papua New Guinea, Lat. 7.9°S, Long. 147.1°E, at 2350 ft. (716 m). Temperatures are calculated for an elevation of 7200 ft. (2190 m), resulting in probable extremes of 78°F (26°C) and 30°F (−1°C).

N/HEMISPHERE	JAN	FEB	MAR	APR	MAY	JUN	JUL	AUG	SEP	OCT	NOV	DEC
°F AVG MAX	64	66	67	68	69	69	69	69	68	68	67	65
°F AVG MIN	47	47	47	48	47	48	49	49	49	48	48	47
DIURNAL RANGE	17	19	20	20	22	21	20	20	19	20	19	18
RAIN/INCHES	5.8	6.5	8.7	11.1	11.8	11.9	8.9	11.7	11.5	9.9	7.7	5.2
HUMIDITY/%	84	82	82	81	80	80	81	81	82	83	84	84
BLOOM SEASON	N/A											
DAYS CLR	N/A											
RAIN/MM	147	165	221	282	300	302	226	297	292	251	196	132
°C AVG MAX	17.8	18.9	19.4	20.0	20.6	20.6	20.6	20.6	20.0	20.0	19.4	18.3
°C AVG MIN	8.3	8.3	8.3	8.9	8.3	8.9	9.4	9.4	9.4	8.9	8.9	8.3
DIURNAL RANGE	9.5	10.6	11.1	11.1	12.3	11.7	11.2	11.2	10.6	11.1	10.5	10.0
S/HEMISPHERE	JUL	AUG	SEP	OCT	NOV	DEC	JAN	FEB	MAR	APR	MAY	JUN

Cultural Recommendations

LIGHT: 2000–3000 fc.

TEMPERATURES: Throughout the year, days average 64–69°F (18–21°C), and nights average 47–49°F (8–9°C), with a diurnal range of 17–22°F (10–12°C).

HUMIDITY: 80–85% year-round.

WATER: Rainfall is heavy all year, but conditions are slightly drier in winter. Cultivated plants should be kept moist but not soggy.

FERTILIZER: ¼–½ recommended strength. A balanced fertilizer should be applied weekly to biweekly throughout the year.

REST PERIOD: Growing conditions should be maintained all year. In the habitat, rainfall is slightly lower in winter. Water and fertilizer should be reduced somewhat for cultivated plants, especially those grown in the dark, short-day conditions common during temperate-latitude winters. They should never be allowed to dry out completely, however. In the habitat, seasonal variation in light levels is minor.

Dendrobium pterocarpum

GROWING MEDIA: Plants may be mounted on tree-fern or cork slabs or potted in small pots filled with any open, fast-draining medium. Repotting may be done anytime new roots are growing.

MISCELLANEOUS NOTES: We would like to thank David Jones and Catherine, the librarian at the Australian National Botanical Gardens, who located this description for us, since it was listed incorrectly in *Index Kewensis*.

Plant and Flower Information

PLANT SIZE AND TYPE: A very dwarf sympodial epiphyte that grows in tufts.

PSEUDOBULB: 0.3–0.6 in. (0.8–1.5 cm) long. Pseudobulbs are smooth, without nodes, shortly ovate, and very wrinkled.

LEAVES: 0.7 in. (1.8 cm) long. The small, somewhat channeled leaf was linear-lanceolate on a very short petiole. Only one leaf was available to the describer.

INFLORESCENCE: 2.5 in. (6 cm) long. The very slender inflorescence emerges from the base of the pseudobulb.

FLOWERS: 1. The flowers are white. The papery sepals are broadly lanceolate and somewhat pointed. The ovate-lanceolate petals are about ⅓ the length of the sepals. The ovate lip, which is approximately the same length as the sepals, is longitudinally concave. The summit of the lip is tender and membrane like, ending in a smooth, narrowly elliptic-lanceolate lobe.

REFERENCES: 218, *Transactions Royal Society Victoria* (1889) 1(2):34.

Dendrobium pterocarpum Ames

ORIGIN/HABITAT: The Philippines on Mindanao Island. Plants grow in Davao Province on moss-covered limbs in dense forests on Mt. Apo at about 6800 ft. (2080 m).

CLIMATE: Station #98754, Davao, Mindanao, Philippines, Lat. 7.1°N, Long. 125.6°E, at 88 ft. (27 m). Temperatures are calculated for an elevation of 6800 ft. (2080 m), resulting in probable extremes of 75°F (24°C) and 43°F (6°C).

N/HEMISPHERE	JAN	FEB	MAR	APR	MAY	JUN	JUL	AUG	SEP	OCT	NOV	DEC
°F AVG MAX	65	66	68	69	68	66	66	66	66	67	67	66
°F AVG MIN	50	50	50	51	52	51	51	51	51	51	51	50
DIURNAL RANGE	15	16	18	18	16	15	15	15	15	16	16	16
RAIN/INCHES	4.8	4.5	5.2	5.8	9.2	9.1	6.5	6.5	6.7	7.9	5.3	6.1
HUMIDITY/%	81	82	78	79	82	83	84	83	83	82	82	82
BLOOM SEASON									*			
DAYS CLR @ 8AM	5	7	9	9	6	4	5	4	5	7	6	6
DAYS CLR @ 2PM	3	1	3	4	2	3	2	2	2	2	2	2
RAIN/MM	122	114	132	147	234	231	165	165	170	201	135	155
°C AVG MAX	18.2	18.8	19.9	20.4	19.9	18.8	18.8	18.8	18.8	19.3	19.3	18.8
°C AVG MIN	9.9	9.9	9.9	10.4	11.0	10.4	10.4	10.4	10.4	10.4	10.4	9.9
DIURNAL RANGE	8.3	8.9	10.0	10.0	8.9	8.4	8.4	8.4	8.4	8.9	8.9	8.9
S/HEMISPHERE	JUL	AUG	SEP	OCT	NOV	DEC	JAN	FEB	MAR	APR	MAY	JUN

Cultural Recommendations

LIGHT: 1800–2500 fc. In the habitat, clear days are rare, and direct sunlight should be avoided.

TEMPERATURES: Throughout the year, days average 65–69°F (18–20°C), and nights average 50–52°F (10–11°C), with a diurnal range of 15–18°F (8–10°C). Highs fluctuate only 4°F (2°C), and lows vary only 2°F (1°C) all year.

HUMIDITY: 80–85% year-round.

WATER: Rainfall is moderate to heavy all year. Rainfall amounts may be greater than indicated in the high-elevation habitat. Cultivated plants should be kept moist, with only slight drying allowed between waterings.

FERTILIZER: ¼–½ recommended strength. A balanced fertilizer should be applied weekly to biweekly throughout the year.

REST PERIOD: Growing conditions should be maintained year-round. Water and fertilizer may be reduced somewhat in winter, especially for plants grown in the dark, short-day conditions common in temperate latitudes. They should never be allowed to dry out completely, however. In the habitat, seasonal light variation is minor.

GROWING MEDIA: Plants may be mounted on tree-fern or cork slabs if humidity is high and plants are watered at least once daily in summer. When plants are potted, any open, fast-draining medium may be used. Repotting may be done anytime new roots are growing.

MISCELLANEOUS NOTES: The bloom season shown in the climate table is based on reports from the habitat.

Plant and Flower Information

PLANT SIZE AND TYPE: A 10 in. (25 cm) sympodial epiphyte. Plants are often smaller.

PSEUDOBULB: 6 in. (15 cm) long. The green stems are erect.

LEAVES: 1–4 at the apex of each growth. The leathery leaves, which are linear-lanceolate, are 1.4–4.0 in. (3.5–10.0 cm) long. They are recurved, shiny, and dark green with a lighter underside.

INFLORESCENCE: 1.2 in. (3 cm) long. The racemes are shorter than the leaves. Inflorescences arise from the uppermost leaf axils.

FLOWERS: Few per inflorescence. The pale white flowers are 0.6–1.0 in. (1.5–2.5 cm) across. The triangular lateral sepals are pointed, with a short, folded keel at the apex. The dorsal sepal is lanceolate, hollowed, and pointed. Petals are elliptic-lanceolate with a thickened tip. The lip is narrow at the base with a round front and a triangular, pointed apex. The blossoms are not fragrant.

REFERENCES: 223, 296, 536.

Dendrobium puberulilingue J. J. Smith

ORIGIN/HABITAT: Southwest Borneo. Plants grow in western Kalimantan near Mt. Raja at 4100 ft. (1250 m).

CLIMATE: Station #96583, Pontianak, Kalimantan, Borneo, Lat. 0.0°N, Long. 109.3°E, at 13 ft. (4 m). Temperatures are calculated for an elevation of 4100 ft. (1250 m), resulting in probable extremes of 83°F (28°C) and 55°F (13°C).

N/HEMISPHERE	JAN	FEB	MAR	APR	MAY	JUN	JUL	AUG	SEP	OCT	NOV	DEC
°F AVG MAX	74	76	76	76	77	77	76	77	77	76	75	74
°F AVG MIN	61	63	62	62	62	62	61	61	62	62	62	61
DIURNAL RANGE	13	13	14	14	15	15	15	16	15	14	13	13
RAIN/INCHES	10.8	8.2	9.5	10.9	11.1	8.7	6.5	8.0	9.0	14.4	15.3	12.7
HUMIDITY/%	85	85	84	84	82	81	79	82	83	87	86	87
BLOOM SEASON									*			
DAYS CLR @ 7AM	1	1	1	3	2	4	5	2	2	1	1	2
DAYS CLR @ 1PM	0	0	1	0	0	0	1	1	1	0	1	0
RAIN/MM	274	208	241	277	282	221	165	203	229	366	389	323
°C AVG MAX	23.1	24.2	24.2	24.2	24.7	24.7	24.2	24.7	24.7	24.2	23.6	23.1
°C AVG MIN	15.8	17.0	16.4	16.4	16.4	16.4	15.8	15.8	16.4	16.4	16.4	15.8
DIURNAL RANGE	7.3	7.2	7.8	7.8	8.3	8.3	8.4	8.9	8.3	7.8	7.2	7.3
S/HEMISPHERE	JUL	AUG	SEP	OCT	NOV	DEC	JAN	FEB	MAR	APR	MAY	JUN

Cultural Recommendations

LIGHT: 2000–3000 fc. The heavy cloud cover indicates that some shading is needed, but light should be as high as the plant can tolerate, short of burning the leaves.

TEMPERATURES: Throughout the year, days average 74–77°F (23–25°C), and nights average 61–63°F (16–17°C), with a diurnal range of 13–16°F (7–9°C). Average highs fluctuate only 3°F (1°C), and average lows vary 2°F (1°C), indicating that plants may not tolerate wide temperature fluctuations.

HUMIDITY: 80–85% year-round.

WATER: Rainfall is moderate to heavy all year. Cultivated plants should be kept moist, with only slight drying allowed between waterings. Constant air movement is highly recommended. Warm water may be beneficial.

FERTILIZER: ¼–½ recommended strength. A balanced fertilizer should be applied weekly to biweekly year-round.

REST PERIOD: Growing conditions should be maintained all year. Water may be reduced somewhat in winter, especially for plants grown in the dark, short-day conditions common in temperate latitudes. They should never be allowed to dry out completely, however. Fertilizer should be reduced if water is reduced. In the habitat, seasonal light variation is minor.

GROWING MEDIA: Plants may be mounted on tree-fern or cork slabs or potted in small pots filled with any open, fast-draining medium. Repotting may be done anytime new roots are growing.

MISCELLANEOUS NOTES: The bloom season shown in the climate table is based on collection reports. The plant was described in 1927 in *Mitt. Inst. Bot. Hamburg* 7(1):53.

Plant and Flower Information

PLANT SIZE AND TYPE: A 4 in. (10 cm) sympodial epiphyte.

PSEUDOBULB: 4 in. (10 cm) long. The stem is slender at the base, swollen for 1–2 nodes, then slender again. The pseudobulbous swelling is oblong to lanceolate and flattened.

LEAVES: Many. The linear leaves are 1.0–1.5 in. (2.5–3.8 cm) long with 2 unequal teeth at the apex.

INFLORESCENCE: Short. Inflorescences emerge at the apex of the stem.

FLOWERS: Several per inflorescence. The flowers are 0.2 in. (0.4 cm) long. They open in succession. The dorsal sepal is spreading at the apex. Lateral sepals are broadly triangular. The slender petals are sickle-shaped. The lip has large, triangular sidelobes and a very small midlobe. Blossoms have bright amber-yellow sepals and petals and an orange lip.

REFERENCES: 224, 286, 445.

Dendrobium pubescens Hooker.
Sometimes listed as a synonym of *Eria flava* Lindley, it is more often considered a synonym of *E. pubescens* (Hooker f.) Lindley ex Steudel, but in 1982 Seidenfaden in *Opera Botanica* #62 includes it with a question mark. REFERENCES: 32, 102, 216, 254, 369, 445.

Dendrobium pugioniforme A. Cunningham

AKA: *D. pungentifolium* F. Mueller.

ORIGIN/HABITAT: Eastern Australia. The habitat includes the Illawarra District of New South Wales and the Bunyah Mountains in the north. Plants grow on trees and mossy rocks from the coastal lowlands to cascading mountain ravines in rainforests at about 4250 ft. (1300 m). Plants at lower elevations usually grow on cliffs, but those at higher elevations may grow high on the outer branches of trees. They are most often found in mountain rainforests, where conditions are heavily shaded, damp, and mossy.

CLIMATE: Station #94791, Coffs Harbour, Australia, Lat. 30.3°S, Long. 153.1°E, at 14 ft. (4 m). Temperatures are calculated for an elevation of 3000 ft. (910 m), resulting in probable extremes of 96°F (36°C) and 20°F (−7°C).

N/HEMISPHERE	JAN	FEB	MAR	APR	MAY	JUN	JUL	AUG	SEP	OCT	NOV	DEC
°F AVG MAX	55	57	61	64	69	70	70	70	69	67	61	58
°F AVG MIN	34	35	40	45	49	53	55	56	54	49	40	35
DIURNAL RANGE	21	22	21	19	20	17	15	14	15	18	21	23
RAIN/INCHES	3.8	2.1	2.9	3.8	4.0	5.8	6.9	7.7	8.7	7.7	5.7	4.5
HUMIDITY/%	74	72	70	74	72	76	79	83	79	78	75	74
BLOOM SEASON			*	*	*							
DAYS CLR @ 4AM	8	9	10	10	12	11	9	8	10	7	11	8
DAYS CLR @ 10AM	16	18	18	12	15	11	8	5	10	10	14	15
RAIN/MM	97	53	74	97	102	147	175	196	221	196	145	114
°C AVG MAX	12.9	14.0	16.2	17.9	20.6	21.2	21.2	21.2	20.6	19.5	16.2	14.5
°C AVG MIN	1.2	1.7	4.5	7.3	9.5	11.7	12.9	13.4	12.3	9.5	4.5	1.7
DIURNAL RANGE	11.7	12.3	11.7	10.6	11.1	9.5	8.3	7.8	8.3	10.0	11.7	12.8
S/HEMISPHERE	JUL	AUG	SEP	OCT	NOV	DEC	JAN	FEB	MAR	APR	MAY	JUN

Cultural Recommendations

LIGHT: 1500–2500 fc. Plants are often found growing in a shady environment where vegetative growth is luxurious, but they bloom more profusely in higher light. Plants are healthiest with brisk air movement.

TEMPERATURES: Summer days average 70°F (21°C), and nights average 53–56°F (12–13°C), with a diurnal range of 14–17°F (8–10°C).

HUMIDITY: 75–80% most of the year, dropping to about 70% in winter.

WATER: Rainfall is moderate to heavy most of the year. Conditions are slightly drier for 2–3 months in winter. Cultivated plants should kept moist but not soggy.

FERTILIZER: ¼–½ recommended strength, applied weekly. A high-nitrogen fertilizer is beneficial from spring to midsummer, but a fertilizer high in phosphates should be used in late summer and autumn.

REST PERIOD: Winter days average 55–58°F (13–15°C), and nights average 34–35°F (1–2°C), with a diurnal range of 21–23°F (12–13°C). In the habitat, plants survive temperatures as low as 20°F (−7°C), at least for short periods, but such extremes should be avoided for cultivated plants. If conditions do become severe, however, the plant is more likely to survive if it is dry when temperatures are cold. In cultivation, water and fertilizer should be reduced somewhat in winter. Plants should be kept just slightly moist for 2–3 months.

GROWING MEDIA: Mounting plants on tree-fern or cork slabs accommodates their pendulous growth habit. However, humidity must be high and plants must be kept moist at all times. Plants are slow to establish, sometimes taking several years. They should be mounted very tightly to a long-lasting slab. Remounting should be avoided if at all possible, but if plants must be remounted, it should only be done when new roots are beginning to grow. If plants cannot be mounted, hanging pots or baskets may be filled with an open, fast-draining medium. Repotting may be done anytime new roots are actively growing.

MISCELLANEOUS NOTES: The bloom season shown in the climate table is based on cultivation records. Reports from the habitat indicate that pieces of the plant break off easily, frequently littering the ground.

Plant and Flower Information

PLANT SIZE AND TYPE: A pendent, 72 in. (183 cm) sympodial epiphyte. Cultivated plants are normally much smaller.

PSEUDOBULB: 72 in. (183 cm) long. The apparent stem, which is actually a vinelike rhizome, is straggly and branching. The rhizome roots where it branches.

LEAVES: Many. The round to dagger-shaped leaves are 1–3 in. (2.5–7.5 cm) long. Commonly referred to as the "dagger orchid" because of the leaf shape, they are actually shaped more like a spear blade. They are shiny, flat, smooth, thick, and sharply pointed. The widely spaced leaves are usually small on cultivated plants.

INFLORESCENCE: Short. Inflorescences arise near the apex of new branches.

FLOWERS: 1–3 per inflorescence. Similar to *D. schoeninum* Lindley, the

Dendrobium pulchellum

flowers are 1 in. (2.5 cm) and open fully. The pointed sepals and slender, pointed petals may be white or pale green. The 3-lobed lip is pointed at the apex with 3 raised lines that are wavy at the front. The margin of the midlobe is deeply ruffled. The lip is normally white with red or purple markings. The alba form has green sepals and petals and a snow-white lip. Blossoms are fragrant and last about 2 weeks.

HYBRIDIZING NOTES: Chromosome count is 2n = 38 (ref. 151, 152, 154, 187, 188, 243).

REFERENCES: 23, 36, 67, 105, 151, 152, 154, 179, 187, 188, 216, 243, 254, 325, 330, 390, 421, 445, 495, 527, 533, 544.

PHOTOS/DRAWINGS: *36, 105, 325, 390, 465, 533.*

Dendrobium pulchellum as used by Lindley not Loddiges or Roxburgh ex Lindley. See *D. devonianum* Paxton. REFERENCES: 254, 277, 278, 454.

Dendrobium pulchellum Loddiges not Roxburgh. See *D. loddigesii* Rolfe. REFERENCES: 153, 190, 216, 218, 254, 445, 504.

Dendrobium pulchellum Roxburgh ex Lindley not Loddiges

AKA: *D. brevifolium* Hort. ex Lindley and *D. dalhousieanum* Wallich are often listed as synonyms, but Seidenfaden and Wood (ref. 455) include only *D. dalhousieanum*. *D. pulchellum* var. *devonianum* (Paxton) Rchb. f. is now considered a synonym of *D. devonianum* Paxton. *Index Kewensis* (ref. 216) includes *D. moschatum* Griffith not (Buch.-Ham.) Swartz or Wallich ex. D. Don as a synonym of *D. pulchellum* without a describer's name.

ORIGIN/HABITAT: Widespread across India and Southeast Asia. The habitat includes Nepal, Sikkim, the Assam and Manipur regions, and the Khasi (Khasia) and Naga Hills of northeastern India. Plants grow at 4900–7200 ft. (1500–2200 m). In Burma, plants are found in the Moulmein region, the Kachin Hills, near Toungoo, Mergui, and Inle Lake. In Thailand, plants grow in open, deciduous forests at 750–4600 ft. (230–1400 m). They are also reported in Laos and Vietnam, and a single plant was found in Malaya.

CLIMATE: Station #48325, Mae Sariang, Thailand, Lat. 18.2°N, Long. 97.8°E, at 1030 ft. (314 m). Temperatures are calculated for an elevation of 3000 ft. (910 m), resulting in probable extremes of 104°F (40°C) and 34°F (1°C).

N/HEMISPHERE	JAN	FEB	MAR	APR	MAY	JUN	JUL	AUG	SEP	OCT	NOV	DEC
°F AVG MAX	81	85	89	92	87	82	80	80	82	83	82	79
°F AVG MIN	51	50	57	66	69	68	67	67	67	65	61	53
DIURNAL RANGE	30	35	32	26	18	14	13	13	15	18	21	26
RAIN/INCHES	0.3	0.2	0.3	1.9	5.7	9.0	8.4	10.8	8.7	3.7	1.1	0.6
HUMIDITY/%	72	57	57	55	68	83	83	84	83	81	77	75
BLOOM SEASON		*	*	**	**	**	*	*				
DAYS CLR @ 7AM	1	16	0	3	4	0	0	0	0	0	0	1
DAYS CLR @ 1PM	24	18	9	5	2	0	0	1	1	6	13	20
RAIN/MM	8	5	8	48	145	229	213	274	221	94	28	15
°C AVG MAX	27.5	29.7	31.9	33.6	30.8	28.1	26.9	26.9	28.1	28.6	28.1	26.4
°C AVG MIN	10.8	10.3	14.2	19.2	20.8	20.3	19.7	19.7	19.7	18.6	16.4	11.9
DIURNAL RANGE	16.7	19.4	17.7	14.4	10.0	7.8	7.2	7.2	8.4	10.0	11.7	14.5
S/HEMISPHERE	JUL	AUG	SEP	OCT	NOV	DEC	JAN	FEB	MAR	APR	MAY	JUN

Cultural Recommendations

LIGHT: 3000–4500 fc. The heavy summer cloud cover indicates that some shading is needed from spring through autumn, but light should be as high as the plant can tolerate, short of burning the leaves. Strong air movement is very important all year.

TEMPERATURES: Summer days average 80–82°F (27–28°C), and nights average 67–68°F (20°C), with a diurnal range of 13–14°F (7–8°C). The warmest season is spring. Days average 87–92°F (31–34°C), and nights average 57–69°F (14–21°C), with a diurnal range of 18–32°F (10–19°C).

HUMIDITY: 80–85% in summer through early autumn, dropping to near 55% for 2 months in winter.

WATER: Rainfall is heavy for 6 months from spring into early autumn but is very light in winter and early spring. Cultivated plants should be kept moist while actively growing, but water should be gradually reduced in autumn after new growths mature.

FERTILIZER: $1/4$–$1/2$ recommended strength, applied weekly. A high-nitrogen fertilizer is beneficial from spring to midsummer, but a fertilizer high in phosphates should be used in late summer and autumn.

REST PERIOD: Winter days average 79–85°F (26–30°C), and nights average 50–53°F (10–12°C), with a diurnal range of 26–35°F (15–19°C). Rainfall is light for 5–6 months from autumn into spring; but during the early part of the dry period, considerable moisture is available from heavy dew and as mist from low clouds and fog. For 2 months in spring, however, the weather is clear and dry, with humidity so low that even the moisture from dew is uncommon. During most of the winter dry season, cultivated plants should be allowed to dry out between waterings, but they should not remain dry for long periods. For 1–2 months in late winter, however, water should be further decreased and limited only to occasional early morning mistings. Fertilizer should be eliminated until water is increased in spring. The cool dry rest is necessary to initiate flowering but probably does not need to be as long or as severe as indicated by the climate data. Growers report that the minimum rest period for *D. pulchellum* is 3 weeks. In the habitat, light is highest in winter.

GROWING MEDIA: Mounting plants on tree-fern or cork slabs accommodates their sometimes pendulous growth habit. However, humidity must be high and plants must be watered at least once a day in summer. If plants cannot be mounted, hanging pots or baskets may be filled with an open, fast-draining medium. Repotting may be done anytime new roots are actively growing. Older stems should not be removed during repotting as each stem continues to produce blossoms for up to 3 years.

MISCELLANEOUS NOTES: The bloom season in the climate table is based on cultivation reports. Blooming occurs in spring in the habitat. Plants are reported to grow well in lowland Malaya, where they bloom frequently. A single specimen plant carried 43 inflorescences with 440, 4.5 in. (11 cm) flowers.

Plant and Flower Information

PLANT SIZE AND TYPE: A 24–87 in. (60–220 cm) sympodial epiphyte.

PSEUDOBULB: 24–87 in. (60–220 cm) long. Pseudobulb length is based on records for cultivated plants. The cylindrical canes, which may be erect or pendulous, are streaked and spotted with red or purple lines when young, and they gradually become hard and woody with age.

LEAVES: Many. The linear-oblong leaves are 4–8 in. (10–20 cm) long. They are leathery and may persist for several years if environmental conditions are moderate. The leaf sheaths are marked with purple streaks and spots.

INFLORESCENCE: 4–8 in. (10–20 cm) long. Inflorescences may be as short as 0.8 in. (2 cm) or as long as 12 in. (30 cm). The drooping racemes are borne laterally from nodes near the apex of leafy and leafless stems. Canes continue to bloom for several years. Each year flowers are produced from nodes lower on the stem.

FLOWERS: 2–12 per inflorescence. The handsome, waxy flowers are 3–5 in. (8–13 cm) across. The variable blossoms may be white, lemon-yellow with a rosy tinge, apricot, coppery orange, or reddish. The margins are often edged with a contrasting color. The lip is usually creamy white, sometimes with a crimson tinge. It is cupped, hairy, fringed along the margin, and decorated with 2 large blood-red or maroon blotches in the throat. Plants known as *D. pulchellum* var. *luteum* have no maroon markings. The musk-scented blossoms last 1–2 weeks.

Flower size is highly variable. Notes from the habitat suggest that flower size may be influenced by conditions in the habitat, but this has not been confirmed. Plants from the warmest and coldest parts of the habitat often have the smallest flowers, and plants exposed to moderate rest-period conditions tend to have larger flowers. It is not known whether the influence has become genetic and different populations have different-sized flowers, or whether the flower size of an individual clone can be increased by altering the growing conditions.

HYBRIDIZING NOTES: Chromosome counts are 2n = 2x (ref. 504, 580), 2n = 38 (ref. 504, 580), 2n = 40 (ref. 504, 580). Johansen (ref. 239) indicates that plants are self-sterile and that flowers dropped 7–8 days after self-pollination. Half the cross-pollinations produced capsules which opened 360 days after pollination. 91% of the seeds contained visible embryos, but only 2% germinated.

REFERENCES: 25, 32, 36, 38, 46, 77, 157, 179, 190, 196, 200, 202, 216, 236, 239, 245, 254, 266, 317, 369, 375, 389, 395, 402, 430, 447, 448, 454, 455, 461, 504, 507, 524, 557, 570, 580.

PHOTOS/DRAWINGS: *77, 245, 375, 389, 430, 454, 455, 557.*

Dendrobium pulchrum Schlechter. See *D. polysema* Schlechter.
REFERENCES: 83, 179, 221, 270, 271, 437, 445.

Dendrobium pulleanum J. J. Smith

ORIGIN/HABITAT: Irian Jaya (western New Guinea). Plants grow in primary forests on the lower slopes of Mt. Goliath and along the Lorentz and upper Eilanden Rivers. They were cultivated in the botanical garden at Bogor, Java.

CLIMATE: Station #97876, Tanahmerah, Irian Jaya, Lat. 6.1°S, Long. 140.3°E, at 75 ft. (23 m). Temperatures are calculated for an elevation of 500 ft. (150 m), resulting in probable extremes of 97°F (36°C) and 63°F (17°C).

N/HEMISPHERE	JAN	FEB	MAR	APR	MAY	JUN	JUL	AUG	SEP	OCT	NOV	DEC
°F AVG MAX	83	84	86	89	90	89	89	88	89	88	86	84
°F AVG MIN	71	70	70	71	72	73	72	72	72	72	73	72
DIURNAL RANGE	12	14	16	18	18	16	17	16	17	16	13	12
RAIN/INCHES	11.5	12.1	14.7	13.2	14.4	15.9	14.5	15.8	17.4	17.3	15.5	11.9
HUMIDITY/%	N/A											
BLOOM SEASON					*							
DAYS CLR	N/A											
RAIN/MM	292	307	373	335	366	404	368	401	442	439	394	302
°C AVG MAX	28.1	28.7	29.8	31.4	32.0	31.4	31.4	30.9	31.4	30.9	29.8	28.7
°C AVG MIN	21.4	20.9	20.9	21.4	22.0	22.6	22.0	22.0	22.0	22.0	22.6	22.0
DIURNAL RANGE	6.7	7.8	8.9	10.0	10.0	8.8	9.4	8.9	9.4	8.9	7.2	6.7
S/HEMISPHERE	JUL	AUG	SEP	OCT	NOV	DEC	JAN	FEB	MAR	APR	MAY	JUN

Cultural Recommendations

LIGHT: 2000–3000 fc.

TEMPERATURES: Throughout the year, days average 83–90°F (28–32°C), and nights average 70–73°F (21–23°C), with a diurnal range of 12–18°F (7–10°C).

HUMIDITY: Information is not available for this location. However, records from nearby locations indicate that humidity probably averages near 85% year-round.

WATER: Rainfall is very heavy all year. Cultivated plants should be kept evenly moist with only slight drying allowed between waterings.

FERTILIZER: ¼–½ recommended strength. A balanced fertilizer should be applied weekly to biweekly throughout the year.

REST PERIOD: Growing conditions should be maintained year-round. Water and fertilizer may be reduced slightly in winter, especially for plants cultivated in the dark, short-day conditions common in temperate latitudes; but plants should never be allowed to dry completely.

GROWING MEDIA: Because plants must be kept moist, they are easier to manage when potted. Fir bark or any open, fast-draining medium may be used. Repotting may be done anytime new roots are growing.

MISCELLANEOUS NOTES: The bloom season shown in the climate table is based on reports from the habitat. Plants that produce very short-lived flowers commonly bloom several times during the year. Flowering usually occurs 7–14 days after a sudden 10°F (5°C) drop in daytime temperatures. The plant was described in 1911 in *Bull. Dép. Agric. Indes Néerl.* 15:4

Plant and Flower Information

PLANT SIZE AND TYPE: A 30 in. (75 cm) sympodial epiphyte.

PSEUDOBULB: 30 in. (75 cm) long. The shiny, rigid stems are elliptical in cross-section.

LEAVES: Many. The lanceolate leaves, which are 5 in. (12 cm) long, are pointed with 2 lobes at the apex. They are pale green, especially on the underside, with a violet tinge. They are flexible with prominent nerves.

INFLORESCENCE: Short. Inflorescences emerge from nodes along the stem.

FLOWERS: 2 per inflorescence. The blossoms are 1 in. (2.6 cm) long, large relative to other closely related plants. They are purple with a pale coppery tinge. The dorsal sepal is slender and erect. Lateral sepals are sickle-shaped. Petals are reflexed. The lip is not lobed. Blossoms have a peculiar but not unpleasant fragrance. They are very short lived.

REFERENCES: 221, 445, 470.

Dendrobium pulvilliferum Schlechter. Now considered a synonym of *Diplocaulobium pulvilliferum* (Schlechter) A. Hawkes.
REFERENCES: 179, 221, 229, 437, 445.

Dendrobium pulvinatum Schlechter

ORIGIN/HABITAT: Northern Papua New Guinea. Plants grow on forest trees in the Finisterre Range at about 3950 ft. (1200 m).

CLIMATE: Station #200187, Erap, Papua New Guinea, Lat. 6.6°S, Long. 146.7°E, at 850 ft. (260 m). Temperatures are calculated for an elevation of 3300 ft. (1000 m), resulting in probable extremes of 94°F (34°C) and 45°F (7°C).

N/HEMISPHERE	JAN	FEB	MAR	APR	MAY	JUN	JUL	AUG	SEP	OCT	NOV	DEC
°F AVG MAX	80	80	81	82	85	85	85	85	85	84	82	82
°F AVG MIN	61	61	61	62	64	65	64	64	65	63	66	62
DIURNAL RANGE	19	19	20	20	21	20	21	21	20	21	16	20
RAIN/INCHES	3.9	3.9	2.7	3.0	3.0	5.3	5.9	5.9	7.0	3.4	2.4	3.1
HUMIDITY/%	82	81	81	79	75	74	74	74	77	76	80	80
BLOOM SEASON							*					
DAYS CLR	N/A											
RAIN/MM	99	99	69	76	76	135	150	150	178	86	61	79
°C AVG MAX	26.7	26.7	27.2	27.8	29.4	29.4	29.4	29.4	29.4	28.9	27.8	27.8
°C AVG MIN	16.1	16.1	16.1	16.7	17.8	18.3	17.8	17.8	18.3	17.2	18.9	16.7
DIURNAL RANGE	10.6	10.6	11.1	11.1	11.6	11.1	11.6	11.6	11.1	11.7	8.9	11.1
S/HEMISPHERE	JUL	AUG	SEP	OCT	NOV	DEC	JAN	FEB	MAR	APR	MAY	JUN

Cultural Recommendations

LIGHT: 2500–3500 fc.

TEMPERATURES: Throughout the year, days average 80–85°F (27–29°C), and nights average 61–66°F (16–19°C), with a diurnal range of 16–21°F (9–12°C).

HUMIDITY: 75–80% all year. Despite high average humidity, the habitat may be quite dry during hot afternoons.

WATER: Rainfall is moderate most of the year, but conditions are somewhat wetter for 4–5 months in summer and early autumn. Cultivated plants should be thoroughly saturated then allowed to dry slightly between waterings in summer and early autumn. Water should be gradually reduced in autumn.

Dendrobium pumilio

FERTILIZER: ¼–½ recommended strength. A balanced fertilizer should be applied weekly to biweekly throughout the year.

REST PERIOD: Growing temperatures should be maintained all year. In the habitat, rainfall is lowest in winter, but the high humidity indicates that additional moisture is frequently available from heavy dew. Cultivated plants should be allowed to dry for somewhat longer between waterings than in summer, but they should not remain dry for extended periods. Fertilizer should be reduced until water is increased in spring. In the habitat, seasonal light variation is minor.

GROWING MEDIA: Plants may be mounted on tree-fern or cork slabs or potted in small pots filled with any open, fast-draining medium. Repotting may be done anytime new roots are growing.

MISCELLANEOUS NOTES: The bloom season shown in the climate table is based on reports from the habitat. Plants that produce flowers which last a single day commonly bloom several times during the year. Flowering usually occurs 7–14 days after a sudden 10°F (5°C) drop in daytime temperatures.

Plant and Flower Information

PLANT SIZE AND TYPE: A 20 in. (50 cm) sympodial epiphyte.

PSEUDOBULB: 20 in. (50 cm) long. The stems do not branch.

LEAVES: Many. The oblong, leathery leaves are 1.6–3.5 in. (4–9 cm) long.

INFLORESCENCE: Short. Flattened inflorescences arise from nodes along the side of the stem.

FLOWERS: 2 per inflorescence. The flowers are 1 in. (2.5 cm) across. The dorsal sepal and petals point forward, and the sickle-shaped lateral sepals curve down. Sepals and petals are pale yellow. The 3-lobed lip is scalloped on the margin, hairy in the center of the midlobe, and recurved at the tip. Flowers have small violet tubercles, an orange-red crest, and a violet callus on the lip. They are short-lived.

REFERENCES: 221, 437, 445.

PHOTOS/DRAWINGS: 437.

Dendrobium pumilio Schlechter. See *D. masarangense* Schlechter. REFERENCES: 221, 270, 271, 385, 437, 445, 486.

Dendrobium pumilum Parish and Rchb. f. not Roxburgh or Swartz. See *D. hymenanthum* Rchb. f. REFERENCES: 218.

Dendrobium pumilum Roxburgh not Swartz or Parish and Rchb. f. See *D. pachyphyllum* (Kuntze) Bakhuizen f. Seidenfaden (ref. 454) includes a comprehensive discussion of the errors and confusion surrounding the use of the name *D. pumilum* from the time it was first used in 1805. REFERENCES: 25, 31, 38, 46, 75, 157, 200, 202, 203, 213, 216, 230, 231, 254, 278, 286, 295, 394, 395, 402, 435, 445, 454, 455, 469. PHOTOS/DRAWINGS: 203, 469.

Dendrobium pumilum Swartz not Roxburgh or Parish and Rchb. f. Now considered a synonym of *Genyorchis pumila* (Swartz) Schlechter. REFERENCES: 190, 213, 216.

Dendrobium punamense Schlechter

AKA: *D. waterhousei* Carr.

ORIGIN/HABITAT: Papua New Guinea and the islands of New Ireland, New Britain, Bougainville, Guadalcanal, and Manus. Plants grow in deep shade on the trunks and branches of moss-covered trees in rainforests at 700–3600 ft. (220–1100 m).

CLIMATE: Station #94085, Rabaul, New Britain Island, Lat. 4.2°S, Long. 152.2°E, at 28 ft. (9 m). Temperatures are calculated for an elevation of 1150 ft. (350 m), resulting in probable extremes of 96°F (36°C) and 61°F (16°C).

N/HEMISPHERE	JAN	FEB	MAR	APR	MAY	JUN	JUL	AUG	SEP	OCT	NOV	DEC
°F AVG MAX	85	85	87	88	87	86	86	86	86	86	86	86
°F AVG MIN	69	68	69	69	69	69	69	69	69	69	69	69
DIURNAL RANGE	16	17	18	19	18	17	17	17	17	17	17	17
RAIN/INCHES	5.4	3.7	3.5	5.1	7.1	10.1	14.8	10.4	10.2	10.0	5.2	3.3
HUMIDITY/%	74	73	69	70	73	76	77	76	77	77	75	74
BLOOM SEASON							*					
DAYS CLR	N/A											
RAIN/MM	137	94	89	130	180	257	376	264	259	254	132	84
°C AVG MAX	29.6	29.6	30.7	31.3	30.7	30.2	30.2	30.2	30.2	30.2	30.2	30.2
°C AVG MIN	20.7	20.2	20.7	20.7	20.7	20.7	20.7	20.7	20.7	20.7	20.7	20.7
DIURNAL RANGE	8.9	9.4	10.0	10.6	10.0	9.5	9.5	9.5	9.5	9.5	9.5	9.5
S/HEMISPHERE	JUL	AUG	SEP	OCT	NOV	DEC	JAN	FEB	MAR	APR	MAY	JUN

Cultural Recommendations

LIGHT: 1200–2000 fc.

TEMPERATURES: Throughout the year, days average 85–88°F (30–31°C), and nights average 68–69°F (20–21°C), with a diurnal range of 16–19°F (9–11°C).

HUMIDITY: 70–75% year-round. Humidity is generally 90–100% at night, but during the dry season, values may drop as low as 35% during the day.

WATER: Rainfall is moderate to heavy most of the year, but conditions are slightly drier for 2 months in late winter. Cultivated plants should be kept moist in spring and summer, but water should be gradually reduced in autumn.

FERTILIZER: ¼–½ recommended strength. A balanced fertilizer should be applied weekly to biweekly throughout the year.

REST PERIOD: Growing conditions should be maintained all year. Water should be reduced somewhat in winter, especially for plants grown in the dark, short-day conditions common in temperate latitudes. Plants may be allowed to dry slightly between waterings, but they should never remain dry for long periods. Fertilizer may be reduced or eliminated anytime water is reduced.

GROWING MEDIA: Mounting plants on tree-fern or cork slabs accommodates their sometimes pendulous growth habit. However, humidity must be high and plants must be watered at least once a day in summer. If plants cannot be mounted, hanging pots or baskets may be filled with an open, fast-draining medium. Repotting may be done anytime new roots are actively growing.

MISCELLANEOUS NOTES: The bloom season shown in the climate table is based on reports from the habitat. Cultivated plants bloom in spring.

Plant and Flower Information

PLANT SIZE AND TYPE: A 6–12 in. (15–30 cm) sympodial epiphyte.

PSEUDOBULB: 6–12 in. (15–30 cm) long. Plants may be erect or pendulous. The stems have 3–6 nodes below the leaves. They may be green or olive green when young, becoming yellow when dry.

LEAVES: 2 at the apex of each growth. The oblong-lanceolate leaves are 2–5 in. (5–13 cm) long. They are twisted at the base to lie on a single plane.

INFLORESCENCE: 2–5 in. (5–13 cm) long. Stems often produce 2 inflorescences from nodes near the apex of the pseudobulb.

FLOWERS: Few per inflorescence. The inconspicuous flowers are 0.8 in. (2 cm) across. Blossoms may be flesh colored, creamy white, or pale green. The veins are often green. The dorsal sepal and petals are slender and pointed. Blooms have large, somewhat triangular lateral sepals. The 3-lobed lip has a sharp point in the center of the notched midlobe and a 3-ridged callus. The sidelobes and sides of the midlobe are erect to incurved.

HYBRIDIZING NOTES: Chromosome count is 2n = 38 (ref. 152).

REFERENCES: 83, 152, 179, 219, 243, 254, 271, 437, 444, 445, 516.

PHOTOS/DRAWINGS: *83*, 437.

Dendrobium punctatum J. E. Smith.
Sometimes listed as *D. punctatum* Swartz, it is now considered a synonym of *Dipodium punctatum* R. Brown. REFERENCES: 67, 105, 190, 216, 254.

Dendrobium puncticulosum J. J. Smith.
Now considered a synonym of *Flickingeria puncticulosa* (J. J. Smith) J. J. Wood. REFERENCES: 25, 75, 214, 223, 235, 445, 449.

Dendrobium pungentifolium F. Mueller.
See *D. pugioniforme* A. Cunningham. REFERENCES: 67, 105, 216, 254, 533.

Dendrobium puniceum Ridley not Rolfe

AKA: *D. adolphi* Schlechter, *D. cerasinum* Ridley, *D. discrepans* J. J. Smith, *D. lateriflorum* Ridley, *D. scarlatinum* Schlechter.

ORIGIN/HABITAT: Northeastern Papua New Guinea, the Solomon Islands, and New Britain. In the Dischore Range of New Guinea, plants grow at 3950–5000 ft. (1200–1500 m). In the Waria District, plants usually grow on horizontal tree branches in the mistforests.

CLIMATE: Station #200192, Garaina, Papua New Guinea, Lat. 7.9°S, Long. 147.1°E, at 2350 ft. (716 m). Temperatures are calculated for an elevation of 3950 ft. (1200 m), resulting in probable extremes of 89°F (32°C) and 41°F (5°C).

N/HEMISPHERE	JAN	FEB	MAR	APR	MAY	JUN	JUL	AUG	SEP	OCT	NOV	DEC
°F AVG MAX	75	77	78	79	80	80	80	80	79	79	78	76
°F AVG MIN	58	58	58	59	58	59	60	60	60	59	59	58
DIURNAL RANGE	17	19	20	20	22	21	20	20	19	20	19	18
RAIN/INCHES	5.8	6.5	8.7	11.1	11.8	11.9	8.9	11.7	11.5	9.9	7.7	5.2
HUMIDITY/%	84	82	82	81	80	80	81	81	82	83	84	84
BLOOM SEASON	*			*	*							
DAYS CLR	N/A											
RAIN/MM	147	165	221	282	300	302	226	297	292	251	196	132
°C AVG MAX	23.8	24.9	25.4	26.0	26.5	26.5	26.5	26.5	26.0	26.0	25.4	24.3
°C AVG MIN	14.3	14.3	14.3	14.9	14.3	14.9	15.4	15.4	15.4	14.9	14.9	14.3
DIURNAL RANGE	9.5	10.6	11.1	11.1	12.2	11.6	11.1	11.1	10.6	11.1	10.5	10.0
S/HEMISPHERE	JUL	AUG	SEP	OCT	NOV	DEC	JAN	FEB	MAR	APR	MAY	JUN

Cultural Recommendations

LIGHT: 2000–3000 fc.

TEMPERATURES: Throughout the year, days average 75–80°F (24–27°C), and nights average 58–60°F (14–15°C), with a diurnal range of 17–22°F (10–12°C).

HUMIDITY: 80–85% year-round.

WATER: Rainfall is heavy all year, but conditions are slightly drier in winter. Cultivated plants should be kept moist but not soggy.

FERTILIZER: ¼–½ recommended strength. A balanced fertilizer should be applied weekly to biweekly throughout the year. The Royal Botanic Garden in Edinburgh uses a seaweed-based fertilizer for high-elevation plants from New Guinea.

REST PERIOD: Growing conditions should be maintained all year. In the habitat, rainfall is slightly lower in winter. Water and fertilizer may be reduced somewhat in winter, especially for plants grown in the dark, short-day conditions common in temperate latitudes. Plants should never be allowed to dry out completely, however. In the habitat, light is slightly higher in winter.

GROWING MEDIA: Plants may be mounted on tree-fern or cork slabs if humidity is high and plants are watered at least once daily in summer. When plants are potted, any open, fast-draining medium may be used. Repotting may be done anytime new roots are growing.

MISCELLANEOUS NOTES: The bloom season shown in the climate table is based on collection records.

Plant and Flower Information

PLANT SIZE AND TYPE: A 1.6–2.4 in. (4–6 cm) sympodial epiphyte.

PSEUDOBULB: 0.3–0.6 in. (0.8–1.5 cm) long. The very small pseudobulbs are ovate-ellipsoid.

LEAVES: 2, rarely 3 per growth. The lanceolate leaves are 0.8–1.6 in. (2–4 cm) long.

INFLORESCENCE: 0.5 in. (1.3 cm) long. Inflorescences emerge from the apex of the stem.

FLOWERS: 2 or more per inflorescence. The flowers are 0.5–0.7 in. (1.3–1.8 cm) long and do not open fully. The pointed sepals and petals are scarlet-red. Blossoms have slender petals and dorsal sepal and somewhat ovate lateral sepals. The sharply pointed lip is golden yellow with scarlet at the tip. All segments are keeled. The unlobed lip curls in along the side margins. It has an inverted, V-shaped ridge.

REFERENCES: 218, 271, 381, 385, 393, 400, 437, 445, 470, 476, 516.

PHOTOS/DRAWINGS: *385*, 437.

Dendrobium puniceum Rolfe not Ridley.
See *D. rutriferum* Rchb. f. REFERENCES: 219, 254, 271, 381, 413, 445.

Dendrobium purissimum Kränzlin.
See *D. inaequale* Rolfe. REFERENCES: 220, 254, 437.

Dendrobium purpurascens Teijsm. and Binn.
See *D. rugosum* (Blume) Lindley. REFERENCES: 216, 254, 469.

Dendrobium purpurascens Thwaites.
Now considered a species of *Coelogyne*. REFERENCES: 216, 254.

Dendrobium purpureiflorum J. J. Smith

ORIGIN/HABITAT: Irian Jaya (western New Guinea). Plants grow on forest trees on the eastern slopes of the Cyclops Range at about 2000 ft. (610 m).

CLIMATE: Station #97690, Sentani/Jayapura, Irian Jaya, Lat. 2.7°S, Long. 140.5°E, at 289 ft. (88 m). Temperatures are calculated for an elevation of 2000 ft. (610 m), resulting in probable extremes of 91°F (33°C) and 62°F (17°C).

N/HEMISPHERE	JAN	FEB	MAR	APR	MAY	JUN	JUL	AUG	SEP	OCT	NOV	DEC
°F AVG MAX	81	83	83	84	84	83	83	82	83	84	84	83
°F AVG MIN	66	66	66	67	67	67	67	67	67	68	67	67
DIURNAL RANGE	15	17	17	17	17	16	16	15	16	16	17	16
RAIN/INCHES	4.1	3.9	5.3	2.9	6.7	7.0	8.3	8.3	8.5	4.6	2.4	5.2
HUMIDITY/%	81	80	80	79	81	81	79	80	80	80	81	80
BLOOM SEASON												*
DAYS CLR @ 9AM	5	3	4	3	2	1	1	0	1	2	2	5
DAYS CLR @ 3PM	4	3	3	3	2	1	3	0	1	2	2	3
RAIN/MM	104	99	135	74	170	178	211	211	216	117	61	132
°C AVG MAX	27.4	28.5	28.5	29.1	29.1	28.5	28.5	28.0	28.5	29.1	29.1	28.5
°C AVG MIN	19.1	19.1	19.1	19.6	19.6	19.6	19.6	19.6	19.6	20.2	19.6	19.6
DIURNAL RANGE	8.3	9.4	9.4	9.5	9.5	8.9	8.9	8.4	8.9	8.9	9.5	8.9
S/HEMISPHERE	JUL	AUG	SEP	OCT	NOV	DEC	JAN	FEB	MAR	APR	MAY	JUN

Cultural Recommendations

LIGHT: 2000–3000 fc.

TEMPERATURES: Throughout the year, days average 81–84°F (27–29°C),

and nights average 66–68°F (19–20°C), with a diurnal range of 15–17°F (8–10°C).

HUMIDITY: Near 80% year-round.

WATER: Rainfall is heavy all year, with brief semidry periods in spring and autumn. Cultivated plants should be kept moist most of the year, but they should be allowed to become somewhat dry for a few weeks in spring and again in autumn.

FERTILIZER: ¼–½ recommended strength. A balanced fertilizer should be applied weekly to biweekly throughout the year.

REST PERIOD: Growing conditions should be maintained year-round. Water and fertilizer might be reduced slightly in winter, especially for plants grown in the dark, short-day conditions common in temperate latitudes. They should never be allowed to dry completely, however. In the habitat, light is slightly higher in winter.

GROWING MEDIA: Plants may be mounted on tree-fern or cork slabs if humidity is high and plants are watered at least once daily in summer. When plants are potted, any open, fast-draining medium may be used. Repotting may be done anytime new roots are growing.

MISCELLANEOUS NOTES: The bloom season shown in the climate table is based on reports from the habitat.

Plant and Flower Information

PLANT SIZE AND TYPE: A 28 in. (70 cm) sympodial epiphyte.

PSEUDOBULB: 28 in. (70 cm) long. The slender, elongated stems branch repeatedly.

LEAVES: Many. The pointed, linear-lanceolate leaves are 0.4–1.7 in. (1.1–4.3 cm) long. The apex is minutely toothed.

INFLORESCENCE: Short.

FLOWERS: 1–5 per inflorescence. The violet-red flowers are 0.8 in. (2.0 cm) long. The dorsal sepal is oval, lateral sepals are obliquely triangular, and the petals are somewhat elliptical. The paler lip equals the length of the column. It is hooded and turned in at the apex. The column is orange-red.

REFERENCES: 221, 470, 476.

Dendrobium purpureostelidium Ames

AKA: *Ephemerantha purpureostelidium* P. F. Hunt and Summerhayes, *Desmotrichum purpureostelidium* (Ames) A. Hawkes, *Flickingeria purpureostelidia* (Ames) A. Hawkes. Seidenfaden (ref. 449) stated that he did not know if it was rightly included as a *Flickingeria*, and Valmayor (ref. 536) considers it a *Dendrobium*.

ORIGIN/HABITAT: The Philippines. Plants grow on forest trees at low elevations. The original collection was made near Dagami on Leyte at 200 ft. (60 m). Plants also occur on Mindanao in Agusan Province, on Basilan Island, and on Luzon in Camarines Sur (Mt. Labo) and Laguna provinces.

CLIMATE: Station #98550, Tacloban, Leyte Island, Philippines, Lat. 11.3°N, Long. 125.0°E, at 52 ft. (16 m). Record extreme temperatures are not available for this location.

N/HEMISPHERE	JAN	FEB	MAR	APR	MAY	JUN	JUL	AUG	SEP	OCT	NOV	DEC
°F AVG MAX	83	85	86	88	89	89	87	88	87	87	86	84
°F AVG MIN	73	73	74	75	77	77	76	76	75	75	75	73
DIURNAL RANGE	10	12	12	13	12	12	11	12	12	12	11	11
RAIN/INCHES	9.4	6.2	4.4	3.3	5.8	7.8	6.9	5.7	8.3	9.1	11.4	8.5
HUMIDITY/%	N/A											
BLOOM SEASON					*	*	*	*	*			
DAYS CLR	N/A											
RAIN/MM	238	157	112	84	147	198	175	145	211	231	290	216
°C AVG MAX	28.3	29.4	30.0	31.1	31.7	31.7	30.6	31.1	30.6	30.6	30.0	28.9
°C AVG MIN	22.8	22.8	23.3	23.9	25.0	25.0	24.4	24.4	23.9	23.9	23.9	22.8
DIURNAL RANGE	5.5	6.6	6.7	7.2	6.7	6.7	6.2	6.7	6.7	6.7	6.1	6.1
S/HEMISPHERE	JUL	AUG	SEP	OCT	NOV	DEC	JAN	FEB	MAR	APR	MAY	JUN

Cultural Recommendations

LIGHT: 2000–3000 fc.

TEMPERATURES: Throughout the year, days average 83–89°F (28–32°C), and nights average 73–77°F (23–25°C), with a diurnal range of 10–13°F (6–7°C).

HUMIDITY: Information is not available for this location. However, reports from other stations in the region indicate that humidity is probably 80–85% most of the year, dropping to 75–80% in late winter and early spring.

WATER: Rainfall is moderate to heavy most of the year with a slightly drier period in late winter and early spring. Cultivated plants should be kept evenly moist with only slight drying allowed between waterings.

FERTILIZER: ¼–½ recommended strength. A balanced fertilizer should be applied weekly to biweekly throughout the year.

REST PERIOD: Growing conditions should be maintained all year. In the habitat, a brief rest may occur during the slightly drier period of late winter and early spring. Water may be reduced for about 2 months, but plants should not be allowed to dry out completely. Fertilizer should be limited anytime water is reduced. In the habitat, seasonal light variation is minor.

GROWING MEDIA: Mounting plants on tree-fern or cork slabs accommodates their pendulous growth habit. However, humidity must be high and plants must be watered at least once a day in summer. If plants cannot be mounted, small pots or hanging baskets may be filled with an open, fast-draining medium. Repotting may be done anytime new roots are actively growing.

MISCELLANEOUS NOTES: The bloom season shown in the climate table is based on collection reports.

Plant and Flower Information

PLANT SIZE AND TYPE: A 12 in. (30 cm) sympodial epiphyte.

PSEUDOBULB: 10 in. (25 cm) long. The yellow stems are elongated, pendulous, and branching.

LEAVES: 1 per branch. Each rigid leathery leaf is 1.2–1.6 in. (3–4 cm) long.

INFLORESCENCE: The inflorescence emerges at the base of the leaf. Blossoms are produced in succession.

FLOWERS: 1 per inflorescence. Flowers are 0.2 in. (0.5 cm) long. The whitish or yellowish flowers are marked with purple. Blossoms have triangular lateral sepals, an oblong-lanceolate dorsal sepal, and linear-lanceolate petals. The white lip is flat, spool-shaped, and tinged with purple.

REFERENCES: 12, 213, 222, 296, 449, 536.

Dendrobium purpureum Roxburgh

AKA: In 1993 Dauncey and Cribb in *Kew Bulletin* 48(3) divided this entity into 2 subspecies and distributed the synonyms as follows. For *D. purpureum* subsp. *purpureum* from the southern Moluccas they include *Angraecum purpureum silvestre* Rumph., *D. viridiroseum* Rchb. f., *D. reinwardtii* Lindley, *D. purpureum* var. *moselyi* Hemsl., *D. praeustum* Kränzlin, *D. scabripes* Kränzlin. For *D. purpureum* subsp. *candidulum* (Rchb. f.) Dauncey and Cribb, they include *D. purpureum* var. *candidulum* Rchb. f. and indicate that *D. purpureum* Roxburgh var. *steffensianum* Schlechter is a possible synonym. Kränzlin (ref. 254) includes *D. chrysocephalum* Kränzlin as a synonym of *D. reinwardtii* Lindley, which is now considered a synonym of *D. purpureum* Roxburgh.

ORIGIN/HABITAT: Vanuatu, Fiji, Bougainville, New Guinea, the Caroline islands, and the islands of the Malay Archipelago. Plants grow in coastal lowlands as well as mountain forests from sea level to 3750 ft. (0–1150 m). *D. purpureum* var. *steffensianum* Schlechter is endemic to Sulawesi (Celebes). It was collected on forest trees at 2600 ft. (800 m) on Mt. Klabat (Minahassa).

CLIMATE: Station #91502, Kieta, Bougainville, Lat. 6.2°S, Long. 155.6°E, at 240 ft. (73 m). Temperatures are calculated for an elevation of 2000 ft. (610 m), resulting in probable extremes of 90°F (32°C) and 58°F (15°C).

N/HEMISPHERE	JAN	FEB	MAR	APR	MAY	JUN	JUL	AUG	SEP	OCT	NOV	DEC
°F AVG MAX	79	79	81	82	82	83	82	82	82	81	81	80
°F AVG MIN	68	68	68	69	69	69	70	69	70	70	69	69
DIURNAL RANGE	11	11	13	13	13	14	12	13	12	11	12	11
RAIN/INCHES	10.9	9.4	8.0	9.8	9.6	9.4	10.5	10.7	11.2	11.7	9.3	9.0
HUMIDITY/%	80	80	79	76	78	76	79	77	78	80	80	82
BLOOM SEASON	*	*	**	**	*	*	*	*	*	*	*	
DAYS CLR	N/A											
RAIN/MM	277	239	203	249	244	239	267	272	284	297	236	229
°C AVG MAX	26.2	26.2	27.3	27.9	27.9	28.4	27.9	27.9	27.9	27.3	27.3	26.8
°C AVG MIN	20.1	20.1	20.1	20.7	20.7	20.7	21.2	20.7	21.2	21.2	20.7	20.7
DIURNAL RANGE	6.1	6.1	7.2	7.2	7.2	7.7	6.7	7.2	6.7	6.1	6.6	6.1
S/HEMISPHERE	JUL	AUG	SEP	OCT	NOV	DEC	JAN	FEB	MAR	APR	MAY	JUN

Cultural Recommendations

LIGHT: 3000–4000 fc. High humidity and strong air movement should be maintained when light is high.

TEMPERATURES: Throughout the year, days average 79–83°F (26–28°C), and nights average 68–70°F (20–21°C), with a diurnal range of 11–14°F (6–8°C).

HUMIDITY: Near 80% year-round.

WATER: Rainfall is very heavy all year. Cultivated plants should be kept moist but not soggy. Warm water might be beneficial.

FERTILIZER: ¼–½ recommended strength. A balanced fertilizer should be applied weekly to biweekly throughout the year.

REST PERIOD: Growing conditions should be maintained all year. Water should be reduced in winter for plants grown in the dark, short-day conditions common in temperate latitudes. They should never be allowed to dry out completely, however. Fertilizer should be reduced or eliminated anytime water is reduced. In the habitat, seasonal light variation is minor.

GROWING MEDIA: Mounting plants on tree-fern or cork slabs accommodates their pendulous growth habit. However, humidity must be high and plants must be watered at least once a day in summer. If plants cannot be mounted, small pots or hanging baskets may be filled with an open, fast-draining medium. Repotting may be done anytime new roots are actively growing.

MISCELLANEOUS NOTES: The primary bloom season shown in the climate table is based on cultivation records, but plants may bloom any time of year. Growers indicate that this species is adaptable and that it grows and blooms reliably.

Plant and Flower Information

PLANT SIZE AND TYPE: A 20–43 in. (50–110 cm) sympodial epiphyte that may grow to a length of 59 in. (150 cm) or be as small as 8 in. (20 cm). The dwarf form may originate at higher elevations.

PSEUDOBULB: 20–43 in. (50–110 cm) long. Initially erect, the clustered stems become curved and pendulous. They may be cylindrical to spindle-shaped. The stems, which are originally fleshy, become grooved with age. The internodes may be somewhat trapezoid. Stems may be slightly swollen at the base. The canes are yellow-green when young and turn purple with age. The silvery sheaths disintegrate in time.

LEAVES: Several at the apex of new growths. The lanceolate, dark green leaves are 2.8–5.5 in. (7–14 cm) long. They alternate along the stem, forming 2 rows. They are deciduous and drop off easily.

INFLORESCENCE: 1 in. (2.5 cm) long. Inflorescences normally arise laterally from nodes along older, leafless stems, but they may also emerge from leafy canes. The blossom clusters are held close to the stems which appear completely covered in flowers.

FLOWERS: 10–25 per densely clustered inflorescence. The flowers are 0.5–0.8 in. (1.3–2.0 cm) long and often remain rather closed. The pointed sepals and rounded petals may be red, purple, rose-purple, or white, but they are always green at the tips and may be paler at the base. The margins of the petals and lip are minutely ciliate. The backs of the sepals are sparsely and minutely warty. The lip is white, very obscurely 3-lobed, constricted below the middle, with infolded sides. The apex of the lip sometimes has a green tip. Dauncey and Cribb indicate that the transverse callus may be low and straight or moderately high and curved. The subspecies they described are differentiated on the basis of lip shape, nectary position, and location. Flower color cannot be used to differentiate the subspecies.

REFERENCES: 17, 25, 79, 95, 179, 212, 216, 252, 254, 262, 270, 271, 310, 317, 353, 359, 433, 436, 445, 466, 468, 479, 516, 552, Dauncey and Cribb 1993 *Kew Bulletin* 48(3).

PHOTOS/DRAWINGS: *270, 271, 540, 552,* Dauncey and Cribb 1993 *Kew Bulletin* 48(3).

Dendrobium pusillum (Blume) Lindley not D. Don or H. B. and K. See *D. pachyphyllum* (Kuntze) Bakhuizen f. REFERENCES: 25, 75, 213, 216, 254, 277, 286, 295, 310, 445, 454, 469.

Dendrobium pusillum D. Don not (Blume) Lindley or H. B. and K. See *D. monticola* Hunt and Summerhayes. REFERENCES: 32, 213, 216, 254, 369, 454.

Dendrobium pusillum H. B. and K. not D. Don or (Blume) Lindley. Now considered a synonym of *Pleurothallis pusilla* Lindley. REFERENCES: 45, 216, 254.

Dendrobium putnamii A. Hawkes and A. H. Heller

AKA: *D. coerulescens* Schlechter.

ORIGIN/HABITAT: Endemic to northern New Guinea. Plants grow in mist-forests at 6900–9850 ft. (2100–3000 m), but they occasionally grow at lower elevations in cool microclimates. Plants are usually found in deep shade, where they form large mats on tree trunks, cliff faces, and rocks.

CLIMATE: Botanical garden records, Laiagam, Papua New Guinea, Lat. 5.5°S, Long. 143.5°E, at 7218 ft. (2200 m). Temperatures are calculated for an elevation of 8500 ft. (2600 m), resulting in probable extremes of 87°F (30°C) and 28°F (–2°C).

N/HEMISPHERE	JAN	FEB	MAR	APR	MAY	JUN	JUL	AUG	SEP	OCT	NOV	DEC
°F AVG MAX	72	73	74	72	74	74	78	73	72	74	74	72
°F AVG MIN	51	50	51	51	52	52	51	52	54	53	52	52
DIURNAL RANGE	21	23	23	21	22	22	27	21	18	21	22	20
RAIN/INCHES	4.0	4.8	6.1	7.8	8.5	9.1	8.4	9.6	9.5	8.9	6.3	4.0
HUMIDITY/%	N/A											
BLOOM SEASON			*	*	*							
DAYS CLR	N/A											
RAIN/MM	102	122	155	198	216	231	213	244	241	226	160	102
°C AVG MAX	22.1	22.6	23.2	22.1	23.2	23.2	25.4	22.6	22.1	23.2	23.2	22.1
°C AVG MIN	10.4	9.9	10.4	10.4	11.0	11.0	10.4	11.0	12.1	11.5	11.0	11.0
DIURNAL RANGE	11.7	12.7	12.8	11.7	12.2	12.2	15.0	11.6	10.0	11.7	12.2	11.1
S/HEMISPHERE	JUL	AUG	SEP	OCT	NOV	DEC	JAN	FEB	MAR	APR	MAY	JUN

Cultural Recommendations

LIGHT: 1200–2300 fc.

TEMPERATURES: Throughout the year, days average 72–78°F (22–25°C), and nights average 50–54°F (10–12°C), with a diurnal range of 18–27°F (10–15°C).

HUMIDITY: Information is not available for this location. However, records from nearby stations indicate that humidity probably averages 70–80% year-round.

WATER: Rainfall is moderate to heavy throughout the year, but conditions are driest for 3–4 months in winter. Cultivated plants should be kept evenly moist.

FERTILIZER: ¼–½ recommended strength. A balanced fertilizer should be applied weekly to biweekly throughout the year.

REST PERIOD: Growing conditions should be maintained year-round. Water and fertilizer should be reduced somewhat in winter, especially for plants grown in the dark, short-day conditions common in temperate latitudes. Plants should never be allowed to dry out completely, however. In the habitat, light is highest in winter.

GROWING MEDIA: The plant probably grows best mounted on tree-fern or cork slabs with a pad of sphagnum. Mounting or repotting may be done anytime new roots are growing.

MISCELLANEOUS NOTES: The bloom season shown in the climate table is based on reports from the habitat. Cultivation records indicate autumn and early winter blooming. *D. putnamii* is considered easy to grow but difficult to bloom. Visitors to the habitat report that even in nature it is a very reluctant bloomer. When the plants do bloom, the flowers open in spring and last until autumn. The climate and habitat suggest that seedlings out of flask should be potted in live sphagnum moss and grown in daytime temperatures near 65°F (18°C), dropping to about 55°F (13°C) at night.

Plant and Flower Information

PLANT SIZE AND TYPE: A prostrate, 0.6–0.8 in. (1.5–2.0 cm) sympodial epiphyte or lithophyte. *D. putnamii* is the smallest of the *Oxyglossum* group.

PSEUDOBULB: 0.1–0.2 in. (0.3–0.5 cm) tall. The minute pseudobulbs are cylindrical and arise from a creeping, elongated rhizome.

LEAVES: 1–2 per pseudobulb. The leaves are lanceolate, erect-spreading, and less than 0.4 (1.0 cm) long.

INFLORESCENCE: 1 per growth. The very short inflorescence rises from nodes near the apex of the pseudobulb.

FLOWERS: 1, rarely 2 per inflorescence. The erect blossoms may be larger than the plant. Plants described as *D. coerulescens* Schlechter had flowers that were about 0.2 in. (0.5 cm) long and did not open fully. Blossoms are pale blue-gray sometimes with a violet tinge. *D. putnamii* produces the brightest blue flowers of any *Oxyglossum*. The lip apex is orange-red, and the sepals are occasionally tinged with orange at the tips. The pointed sepals and petals are keeled. The pointed lip is not lobed.

REFERENCES: 95, 179, 191, 229, 385, 437, 548, 556.

PHOTOS/DRAWINGS: *385, 437, 556.*

Dendrobium pychnostachyum Lindley

AKA: Sometimes spelled *D. pycnostachyum*.

ORIGIN/HABITAT: The mountains of northwestern Thailand and the Tenasserim region of Burma. Plants usually grow at about 3300 ft. (1000 m).

CLIMATE: Station #48325, Mae Sariang, Thailand, Lat. 18.2°N, Long. 97.8°E, at 1030 ft. (314 m). Temperatures are calculated for an elevation of 3000 ft. (910 m), resulting in probable extremes of 104°F (40°C) and 34°F (1°C).

N/HEMISPHERE	JAN	FEB	MAR	APR	MAY	JUN	JUL	AUG	SEP	OCT	NOV	DEC
°F AVG MAX	81	85	89	92	87	82	80	80	82	83	82	79
°F AVG MIN	51	50	57	66	69	68	67	67	67	65	61	53
DIURNAL RANGE	30	35	32	26	18	14	13	13	15	18	21	26
RAIN/INCHES	0.3	0.2	0.3	1.9	5.7	9.0	8.4	10.8	8.7	3.7	1.1	0.6
HUMIDITY/%	72	67	57	55	68	83	83	84	83	81	77	75
BLOOM SEASON			*	*								
DAYS CLR @ 7AM	1	16	0	3	4	0	0	0	0	0	0	1
DAYS CLR @ 1PM	24	18	9	5	2	0	0	1	1	6	13	20
RAIN/MM	8	5	8	48	145	229	213	274	221	94	28	15
°C AVG MAX	27.5	29.7	31.9	33.6	30.8	28.1	26.9	26.9	28.1	28.6	28.1	26.4
°C AVG MIN	10.8	10.3	14.2	19.2	20.8	20.3	19.7	19.7	19.7	18.6	16.4	11.9
DIURNAL RANGE	16.7	19.4	17.7	14.4	10.0	7.8	7.2	7.2	8.4	10.0	11.7	14.5
S/HEMISPHERE	JUL	AUG	SEP	OCT	NOV	DEC	JAN	FEB	MAR	APR	MAY	JUN

Cultural Recommendations

LIGHT: 3000–4000 fc. The heavy summer cloud cover indicates that some shading is needed from spring through autumn, but light should be as high as the plant can tolerate, short of burning the leaves. Strong air movement is very important all year.

TEMPERATURES: Summer days average 80–82°F (27–28°C), and nights average 67–68°F (20°C), with a diurnal range of 13–14°F (7–8°C). The warmest season is spring. Days average 87–92°F (31–34°C), and nights average 57–69°F (14–21°C), with a diurnal range of 18–32°F (10–19°C).

HUMIDITY: 80–85% in summer through early autumn, dropping to near 55% for 2 months in winter.

WATER: Rainfall is heavy for 6 months from spring into early autumn but is very light in winter and early spring. Cultivated plants should be kept moist while actively growing, but water should be gradually reduced in autumn after new growths mature.

FERTILIZER: ¼–½ recommended strength, applied weekly. A high-nitrogen fertilizer is beneficial from spring to midsummer, but a fertilizer high in phosphates should be used in late summer and autumn.

REST PERIOD: Winter days average 79–85°F (26–30°C), and nights average 50–53°F (10–12°C), with a diurnal range of 26–35°F (15–19°C). Rainfall is light for 5–6 months from autumn into spring; but during the early part of the dry period, considerable moisture is available from heavy dew and as mist from low clouds and fog. For 2 months in spring, however, the weather is clear and dry, with humidity so low that even the moisture from dew is uncommon. During most of the winter dry season, cultivated plants should be allowed to dry out between waterings, but they should not remain dry for long periods. For 1–2 months in late winter, however, water should be further decreased and limited only to occasional early morning mistings. Fertilizer should be eliminated until water is increased in spring. In the habitat, light is highest in winter.

GROWING MEDIA: Plants may be mounted on tree-fern or cork slabs if humidity is high and plants are watered at least once daily in summer. When plants are potted, any open, fast-draining medium may be used. Repotting may be done anytime new roots are growing.

MISCELLANEOUS NOTES: The bloom season shown in the climate table is based on cultivation records.

Plant and Flower Information

PLANT SIZE AND TYPE: A 2–12 in. (5–30 cm) sympodial epiphyte.

PSEUDOBULB: 2–12 in. (5–30 cm) long. The swollen stems are covered by leaf-sheaths that are eventually deciduous.

LEAVES: 6 per growth. The leaves are 2 in. (5 cm) long. The leaves are deciduous after a single season.

INFLORESCENCE: 2–4 in. (5–10 cm) long. 1–2 densely flowered racemes emerge from nodes near the apex of leafy pseudobulbs.

FLOWERS: 20 per inflorescence. The flowers are 0.2 in. (0.5 cm) across.

Sepals and petals are white sometimes with faint purple veins. The obscurely 3-lobed lip is green. The ovate midlobe is toothed and ruffled with a point at the tip.

REFERENCES: 157, 179, 202, 216, 254, 278, 454.
PHOTOS/DRAWINGS: *454*.

Dendrobium pygmaeum A. Cunningham. A synonym of *D. caleyi* A. Cunningham, which is now considered a synonym of *Bulbophyllum exiguum*. REFERENCES: 216, 222, 254, 330.

Dendrobium pygmaeum Lindley. See *D. peguanum* Lindley. REFERENCES: 38, 46, 157, 202, 211, 216, 254, 369, 445, 454.

Dendrobium pygmaeum Smith. Now considered a synonym of *Bulbophyllum pygmaeum* (Smith) Lindley. REFERENCES: 211, 216, 316.

Dendrobium pyropum Ridley. See *D. crocatum* Hooker f. REFERENCES: 218, 254, 395, 454.

Dendrobium qnaifei Guillaumin. A misspelling for *D. quaifei* Rolfe ex. Ames, see *D. mooreanum* Lindley. REFERENCES: 17.

Dendrobium quadrangulare Ridley. See *D. pumilum* Parish and Rchb. f. REFERENCES: 402.

Dendrobium quadrangulare Parish and Rchb. f. See *D. hymenanthum* Rchb. f. The name *D. quadrangulare* is sometimes erroneously applied to plants which should be called *D. pachyphyllum* (Kuntze) Bakhuizen f. REFERENCES: 56, 157, 200, 202, 218, 254, 286, 295, 445, 454, 455, 524. PHOTOS/DRAWINGS: 200.

Dendrobium quadriferum Schlechter

ORIGIN/HABITAT: Northeastern Papua New Guinea. Plants grow in the Kani Range at about 3300 ft. (1000 m). They are usually found near the ground on the trunks of mistforest trees.

CLIMATE: Station #200187, Erap, Papua New Guinea, Lat. 6.6°S, Long. 146.7°E, at 850 ft. (260 m). Temperatures are calculated for an elevation of 3300 ft. (1000 m), resulting in probable extremes of 94°F (34°C) and 45°F (7°C).

N/HEMISPHERE	JAN	FEB	MAR	APR	MAY	JUN	JUL	AUG	SEP	OCT	NOV	DEC
°F AVG MAX	80	80	81	82	85	85	85	85	85	84	82	82
°F AVG MIN	61	61	61	62	64	65	64	64	65	63	66	62
DIURNAL RANGE	19	19	20	20	21	20	21	21	20	21	16	20
RAIN/INCHES	3.9	3.9	2.7	3.0	3.0	5.3	5.9	5.9	7.0	3.4	2.4	3.1
HUMIDITY/%	82	81	81	79	75	74	74	74	77	76	80	80
BLOOM SEASON						*						
DAYS CLR	N/A											
RAIN/MM	99	99	69	76	76	135	150	150	178	86	61	79
°C AVG MAX	26.7	26.7	27.2	27.8	29.4	29.4	29.4	29.4	29.4	28.9	27.8	27.8
°C AVG MIN	16.1	16.1	16.1	16.7	17.8	18.3	17.8	17.8	18.3	17.2	18.9	16.7
DIURNAL RANGE	10.6	10.6	11.1	11.1	11.6	11.1	11.6	11.6	11.1	11.7	8.9	11.1
S/HEMISPHERE	JUL	AUG	SEP	OCT	NOV	DEC	JAN	FEB	MAR	APR	MAY	JUN

Cultural Recommendations

LIGHT: 2500–3500 fc.

TEMPERATURES: Throughout the year, days average 80–85°F (27–29°C), and nights average 61–66°F (16–19°C), with a diurnal range of 16–21°F (9–12°C).

HUMIDITY: 75–80% all year. Despite high average humidity, the habitat may be quite dry during hot afternoons.

WATER: Rainfall is moderate most of the year, but conditions are somewhat wetter for 4–5 months in summer and early autumn. Cultivated plants should be thoroughly saturated then allowed to dry slightly between waterings in summer and early autumn. Water should be gradually reduced in autumn.

FERTILIZER: ¼–½ recommended strength. A balanced fertilizer should be applied weekly to biweekly throughout the year.

REST PERIOD: Growing temperatures should be maintained all year. In the habitat, rainfall is lowest in winter, but the high humidity indicates that additional moisture is frequently available from heavy dew. Cultivated plants should be allowed to dry for somewhat longer between waterings than in summer, but they should not remain dry for extended periods. Fertilizer should be reduced until water is increased in spring. In the habitat, seasonal light variation is minor.

GROWING MEDIA: Plants may be mounted on tree-fern or cork slabs or potted in small pots filled with any open, fast-draining medium. Repotting may be done anytime new roots are growing.

MISCELLANEOUS NOTES: The bloom season shown in the climate table is based on reports from the habitat.

Plant and Flower Information

PLANT SIZE AND TYPE: A 25 in. (64 cm) sympodial epiphyte.

PSEUDOBULB: 25 in. (64 cm) long. The stems are laxly leafy near the apex.

LEAVES: Few. The lanceolate to elliptic leaves are 5–7 in. (13–18 cm) long.

INFLORESCENCE: Very short. The inflorescences are clustered.

FLOWERS: 4–7 per inflorescence. The white flowers are 0.7 in. (1.8 cm) long. The blossoms do not open. Whether they are self-pollinated or fertilized by insects is not known, but the plants produce numerous seed capsules. Schlechter (ref. 437) never found an open flower. He suspected that they may open only during wet years, but he was unable to confirm this hypothesis. Blossoms are fragrant even when they do not open.

REFERENCES: 92, 221, 437, 445.

PHOTOS/DRAWINGS: 437.

Dendrobium quadrifidium Llave and Lexarza. Now considered a synonym of *Pleurothallis quadrifida* Lindley. REFERENCES: 216, 254.

Dendrobium quadrialatum J. J. Smith

ORIGIN/HABITAT: Ternate Island in the Moluccas. Plants are common in old forests at 350–2600 ft. (100–800 m).

CLIMATE: Station #97430, Ternate Island, Indonesia, Lat. 0.8°N, Long. 127.4°E, at 75 ft. (23 m). Temperatures are calculated for an elevation of 1800 ft. (550 m). Record extreme temperatures are not available for this location.

N/HEMISPHERE	JAN	FEB	MAR	APR	MAY	JUN	JUL	AUG	SEP	OCT	NOV	DEC
°F AVG MAX	79	79	80	80	81	80	81	80	80	81	81	80
°F AVG MIN	71	70	71	71	71	70	69	69	70	71	71	71
DIURNAL RANGE	8	9	9	9	10	10	12	11	10	10	10	9
RAIN/INCHES	5.3	6.1	6.7	6.6	9.4	8.4	4.6	2.1	3.1	3.2	7.2	8.2
HUMIDITY/%	N/A											
BLOOM SEASON								*	*	*		
DAYS CLR	N/A											
RAIN/MM	135	155	170	168	239	213	117	53	79	81	183	208
°C AVG MAX	26.3	26.3	26.8	26.8	27.4	26.8	27.4	26.8	26.8	27.4	27.4	26.8
°C AVG MIN	21.8	21.3	21.8	21.8	21.8	21.3	20.7	20.7	21.3	21.8	21.8	21.8
DIURNAL RANGE	4.5	5.0	5.0	5.0	5.6	5.5	6.7	6.1	5.5	5.6	5.6	5.0
S/HEMISPHERE	JUL	AUG	SEP	OCT	NOV	DEC	JAN	FEB	MAR	APR	MAY	JUN

Cultural Recommendations

LIGHT: 2500–3500 fc.

TEMPERATURES: Throughout the year, days average 79–81°F (26–27°C), and nights average 69–71°F (21–22°C), with a diurnal range of 8–12°F (5–7°C). The warmest days and coolest nights occur simultaneously in early summer.

HUMIDITY: Information is not available for this location. However, records from nearby stations indicate that humidity probably averages near 85% year-round.

WATER: Rainfall is moderate to heavy most of the year, but conditions are somewhat drier for 2–3 months in late summer and autumn. Cultivated plants should be kept moist, with only slight drying allowed between waterings during most of the year. Plants should become moderately dry between waterings in late summer and early autumn, however; but they should not remain dry for long periods.

FERTILIZER: ¼–½ recommended strength. A balanced fertilizer should be applied weekly to biweekly throughout the year.

REST PERIOD: Growing conditions should be maintained all year. Water should be reduced somewhat in winter for plants grown in the dark, short-day conditions common in temperate latitudes, but they should never be allowed to dry out completely. In the habitat, seasonal light variation is minor.

GROWING MEDIA: Plants may be mounted on tree-fern or cork slabs or potted in small pots filled with any open, fast-draining medium. Repotting may be done anytime new roots are growing.

MISCELLANEOUS NOTES: The bloom season shown in the climate table is based on collection reports. The plant was described in 1922 in *Bull. Jard. Bot. Buit.* 3rd sér. 5:87.

Plant and Flower Information

PLANT SIZE AND TYPE: A 14 in. (36 cm) sympodial epiphyte.

PSEUDOBULB: 14 in. (36 cm) long. The stems are snaky.

LEAVES: Many. The leaves are about 3 in. (8 cm) long or smaller at the apex. They are lanceolate, leathery, and unequally bilobed at the apex. The leaves may be shiny or dull, dark green on the upper surface and lighter green on the underside.

INFLORESCENCE: 0.7 in. (1.8 cm) long. Numerous, densely flowered inflorescences emerge from nodes on leafless stems.

FLOWERS: 8–10 per inflorescence. The flowers are 1 in. (2.5 cm) long. Sepals and petals are rose to violet. Lateral sepals are very narrow, but the dorsal sepal is oblong with a 3-angled, pointed tip. The petals are oblong to subovate and subrectangular at the apex. The red-orange lip is green at the base. It is rounded and recurved along the upper 40%. It has an elevated margin. The column and ovary are light green.

REFERENCES: 223.

Dendrobium quadrilobatum Carr

ORIGIN/HABITAT: Peninsular Malaya. Originally collected along the Tahan River in Pahang State, plants were growing with *D. rhodostele* Ridley on a tree overhanging the river. Plants were recently found near Jengga in Terengganu State.

CLIMATE: Station #49630, Temerloh, Pahang, Malaya, Lat. 3.5°N, Long. 102.4°E, at 163 ft. (50 m). Record extreme temperatures are 97°F (36°C) and 64°F (18°C).

N/HEMISPHERE	JAN	FEB	MAR	APR	MAY	JUN	JUL	AUG	SEP	OCT	NOV	DEC
°F AVG MAX	85	88	90	91	91	90	90	90	90	89	87	86
°F AVG MIN	71	71	72	73	73	73	72	72	72	73	73	72
DIURNAL RANGE	14	17	18	18	18	17	18	18	18	16	14	14
RAIN/INCHES	7.8	3.9	6.0	7.6	6.6	4.3	3.4	5.6	6.5	9.3	9.7	10.1
HUMIDITY/%	87	83	84	85	86	86	87	84	86	87	89	88
BLOOM SEASON	N/A											
DAYS CLR @ 7AM	0	0	2	1	1	0	2	2	2	0	0	0
DAYS CLR @ 1PM	1	1	2	1	1	0	1	1	0	0	0	0
RAIN/MM	198	99	152	193	168	109	86	142	165	236	246	257
°C AVG MAX	29.4	31.1	32.2	32.8	32.8	32.2	32.2	32.2	32.2	31.7	30.6	30.0
°C AVG MIN	21.7	21.7	22.2	22.8	22.8	22.8	22.2	22.2	22.2	22.8	22.8	22.2
DIURNAL RANGE	7.7	9.4	10.0	10.0	10.0	9.4	10.0	10.0	10.0	8.9	7.8	7.8
S/HEMISPHERE	JUL	AUG	SEP	OCT	NOV	DEC	JAN	FEB	MAR	APR	MAY	JUN

Cultural Recommendations

LIGHT: 2500–3500 fc.

TEMPERATURES: Throughout the year, days average 85–91°F (29–33°C), and nights average 71–73°F (22–23°C), with a diurnal range of 14–18°F (8–10°C).

HUMIDITY: 85–90% year-round.

WATER: Rainfall is moderate to heavy for most of the year, but conditions are slightly drier for 1–2 months in winter and again in summer. Cultivated plants should be kept moist with only slight drying allowed between waterings.

FERTILIZER: ¼–½ recommended strength. A balanced fertilizer should be applied weekly to biweekly throughout the year.

REST PERIOD: Growing conditions should be maintained all year. However, water should be reduced for a month or so in summer and again in late winter. Plants should be allowed to become somewhat drier between waterings during these periods but should never dry out completely. Fertilizer should be reduced or eliminated while water is reduced. In the habitat, seasonal light variation is minor.

GROWING MEDIA: Plants may be mounted on tree-fern or cork slabs if humidity is high and plants are watered at least once daily in summer. When plants are potted, any open, fast-draining medium may be used. Repotting may be done anytime new roots are growing.

Plant and Flower Information

PLANT SIZE AND TYPE: A 12 in. (30 cm) sympodial epiphyte.

PSEUDOBULB: 12 in. (30 cm) long. The clustered stems, which are arranged in 2 rows, are borne on a short, creeping rhizome. The pseudobulbs are grooved and flattened.

LEAVES: Many at the apex of each stem. The leaves are 1 in. (2.5 cm) long. They are green with a purple suffusion, oblong-triangular, flattened, and pointed.

INFLORESCENCE: The inflorescences emerge from nodes near the apex of the stem.

FLOWERS: 1 per inflorescence. The pale yellowish flowers, which are 0.4 in. (1.1 cm) long and open fully, are marked with purple stripes and spots. They have oblong-lanceolate sepals and smaller oblanceolate petals. The recurved lip is marked with purple and orange. The midlobe is deeply notched with a hairy callus. The pale yellow sidelobes are erect, covered with hairs, and marked with purple along the margin.

REFERENCES: 56, 200, 224, 445, 455.

PHOTOS/DRAWINGS: 455.

Dendrobium quadrilobum Rolfe.

Now considered a synonym of *Flickingeria quadriloba* (Rolfe) A. Hawkes. REFERENCES: 213, 231, 254.

Dendrobium quadrilobum Rupp.

Clements (ref. 67) lists this as an illegitimate name. REFERENCES: 67.

Dendrobium quadriquetrum J. J. Smith

ORIGIN/HABITAT: Irian Jaya (western New Guinea). Plants grow on moss-covered trees along the Zuidwest River at 1000–2600 ft. (300–800 m).

CLIMATE: Station #97796, Kokenau (Kokonau), Irian Jaya, Lat. 4.7°S, Long. 136.4°E, at 10 ft. (3 m). Temperatures are calculated for an elevation of 2000 ft. (610 m). Record extreme temperatures are not available for this location.

N/HEMISPHERE	JAN	FEB	MAR	APR	MAY	JUN	JUL	AUG	SEP	OCT	NOV	DEC
°F AVG MAX	76	76	79	81	83	82	82	82	83	81	80	77
°F AVG MIN	66	66	67	67	67	68	67	67	67	67	67	66
DIURNAL RANGE	10	10	12	14	16	14	15	15	16	14	13	11
RAIN/INCHES	18.4	15.8	18.9	11.6	9.7	10.6	11.5	15.7	11.6	11.6	16.0	19.9
HUMIDITY/%	N/A											
BLOOM SEASON	N/A											
DAYS CLR	N/A											
RAIN/MM	467	401	480	295	246	269	292	399	295	295	406	505
°C AVG MAX	24.7	24.7	26.4	27.5	28.6	28.0	28.0	28.0	28.6	27.5	26.9	25.2
°C AVG MIN	19.1	19.1	19.7	19.7	19.7	20.2	19.7	19.7	19.7	19.7	19.7	19.1
DIURNAL RANGE	5.6	5.6	6.7	7.8	8.9	7.8	8.3	8.3	8.9	7.8	7.2	6.1
S/HEMISPHERE	JUL	AUG	SEP	OCT	NOV	DEC	JAN	FEB	MAR	APR	MAY	JUN

Dendrobium quadrisulcatum

Cultural Recommendations

LIGHT: 2500–3500 fc.

TEMPERATURES: Throughout the year, days average 76–83°F (25–29°C), with the coolest days in winter. Nights average 66–68°F (19–20°C), with a diurnal range of 10–16°F (6–9°C).

HUMIDITY: Information is not available for this location. However, records from nearby locations indicate that humidity probably averages near 85% year-round.

WATER: Rainfall is very heavy all year. Cultivated plants should be kept evenly moist but not soggy.

FERTILIZER: ¼–½ recommended strength. A balanced fertilizer should be applied weekly to biweekly throughout the year.

REST PERIOD: Growing conditions vary only slightly during the year. Water and fertilizer may be reduced slightly in winter, especially for plants cultivated in the dark, short-day conditions common in the temperate latitudes. Plants should never be allowed to dry out completely, however. In the habitat, seasonal light variation is minor.

GROWING MEDIA: Plants may be potted in small pots filled with any rapidly draining medium. Repotting may be done anytime new roots are growing.

MISCELLANEOUS NOTES: The plant was described from an incomplete specimen.

Plant and Flower Information

PLANT SIZE AND TYPE: A sympodial epiphyte of unreported size.

PSEUDOBULB: The stem is square in cross-section.

LEAVES: 0.5 in. (1.4 cm) wide. The papery leaves are twisted at the base. The leaf-sheaths are prominently nerved and densely warty.

INFLORESCENCE: Short. Inflorescences perforate the leaf sheaths to emerge along the stem.

FLOWERS: 10–12 per inflorescence. The yellow flowers are 0.6 in. (1.5 cm) long. The dorsal sepal is oblong and convex with a long groove. Lateral sepals are oblique, and the petals are linear-lanceolate. The conical lip has no callus. It is hooded and turned in at the apex with long, hairlike structures at the edge.

REFERENCES: 221, 470, 476, 486.

Dendrobium quadrisulcatum J. J. Smith. See *D. uniflorum* Griffith. REFERENCES: 222, 286, 295, 373, 454, 455, 536. PHOTOS/DRAWINGS: 373.

Dendrobium quaifei Rolfe ex Ames. See *D. mooreanum* Lindley. REFERENCES: 17, 83, 225, 270.

Dendrobium quangxiensis S. J. Cheng and C. Z. Tang. See *D. guangxiense*. REFERENCES: 153.

Dendrobium quinarium Rolfe

ORIGIN/HABITAT: New Guinea. Specific habitat location was not reported, but the plants were imported with *D. johnsoniae* F. Mueller. We assume both species grew in approximately the same area, but the following climate data should be used with caution.

CLIMATE: Station #94048, Finschhafen, Papua New Guinea, Lat. 6.6°S, Long. 147.9°E, at 25 ft. (8 m). Temperatures are calculated for an elevation of 2950 ft. (900 m), resulting in probable extremes of 83°F (29°C) and 58°F (15°C).

N/HEMISPHERE	JAN	FEB	MAR	APR	MAY	JUN	JUL	AUG	SEP	OCT	NOV	DEC
°F AVG MAX	74	73	73	74	76	78	79	79	77	76	74	74
°F AVG MIN	63	62	62	61	61	62	64	64	64	64	63	63
DIURNAL RANGE	11	11	11	13	15	16	15	15	13	12	11	11
RAIN/INCHES	25.8	22.4	20.9	15.8	11.7	8.9	5.5	3.7	5.3	11.9	18.3	23.2
HUMIDITY/%	88	87	86	86	84	85	84	85	86	88	88	88
BLOOM SEASON						*	*					
DAYS CLR	N/A											
RAIN/MM	655	568	531	402	297	227	140	95	135	301	464	589
°C AVG MAX	23.5	23.0	23.0	23.5	24.6	25.7	26.3	26.3	25.2	24.6	23.5	23.5
°C AVG MIN	17.4	16.9	16.9	16.3	16.3	16.9	18.0	18.0	18.0	18.0	17.4	17.4
DIURNAL RANGE	6.1	6.1	6.1	7.2	8.3	8.8	8.3	8.3	7.2	6.6	6.1	6.1
S/HEMISPHERE	JUL	AUG	SEP	OCT	NOV	DEC	JAN	FEB	MAR	APR	MAY	JUN

Cultural Recommendations

LIGHT: 2500–3500 fc.

TEMPERATURES: Throughout the year, days average 73–79°F (23–26°C), and nights average 61–64°F (16–18°C), with a diurnal range of 11–16°F (6–9°C).

HUMIDITY: Near 85–90% year-round.

WATER: Rainfall is very heavy most of the year but is somewhat less for 3–4 months in summer. Cultivated plants should be kept evenly moist.

FERTILIZER: ¼–½ recommended strength. A balanced fertilizer should be applied weekly to biweekly throughout the year.

REST PERIOD: Growing conditions should be maintained year-round. In the habitat, rainfall is heaviest in winter, but water and fertilizer should be reduced for cultivated plants grown in the dark, short-day conditions common in temperate latitudes. These plants should never be allowed to dry out completely, however. In the habitat, light is lowest in winter.

GROWING MEDIA: Plants may be mounted on tree-fern or cork slabs or potted in small pots filled with any open, fast-draining medium. Repotting may be done anytime new roots are growing.

MISCELLANEOUS NOTES: The bloom season shown in the climate table is based on bloom records for a plant imported to England.

Plant and Flower Information

PLANT SIZE AND TYPE: A 6–9 in. (15–23 cm) sympodial epiphyte.

PSEUDOBULB: 6–9 in. (15–23 cm) long. The 4-angled stems are slender at the base and swollen near the apex.

LEAVES: 2 at the apex of the stem. The oblong-lanceolate leaves are pointed at the tip.

INFLORESCENCE: Short. Racemes emerge near the apex of the stem.

FLOWERS: 2 per inflorescence. The pale yellow flowers are 1.1 in. (2.8 cm) long. They may not open at the same time. Sepals and petals are oblong-lanceolate, though the petals are somewhat smaller. The nearly round lip is marked with light brown nerves near the apex.

REFERENCES: 219, 254, 413.

Dendrobium quinquecallosum J. J. Smith. Now considered a synonym of *Epigeneium quinquecallosum* (J. J. Smith) Summerhayes. REFERENCES: 222, 229, 499.

Dendrobium quinquecaudatum J. J. Smith

AKA: *D. acuminatissimum* (Blume) Lindley var. *latifolium* J. J. Smith.

ORIGIN/HABITAT: Irian Jaya (western New Guinea). Plants grow on primary forest trees on Nepenthes Hill. Habitat elevation is estimated, so the following climate data should be used with caution.

CLIMATE: Station #97796, Kokenau (Kokonau), Irian Jaya, Lat. 4.7°S, Long. 135.4°E, at 10 ft. (3 m). Temperatures are calculated for an elevation of 1000 ft. (300 m). Record extreme temperatures are not available for this location.

N/HEMISPHERE	JAN	FEB	MAR	APR	MAY	JUN	JUL	AUG	SEP	OCT	NOV	DEC
°F AVG MAX	80	80	83	85	87	86	86	86	87	85	84	81
°F AVG MIN	70	70	71	71	71	72	71	71	71	71	71	70
DIURNAL RANGE	10	10	12	14	16	14	15	15	16	14	13	11
RAIN/INCHES	18.4	15.8	18.9	11.6	9.7	10.6	11.5	15.7	11.6	11.6	16.0	19.9
HUMIDITY/%	N/A											
BLOOM SEASON												
DAYS CLR	N/A											
RAIN/MM	467	401	480	295	246	269	292	399	295	295	406	505
°C AVG MAX	26.5	26.5	28.2	29.3	30.4	29.9	29.9	29.9	30.4	29.3	28.7	27.1
°C AVG MIN	21.0	21.0	21.5	21.5	21.5	22.1	21.5	21.5	21.5	21.5	21.5	21.0
DIURNAL RANGE	5.5	5.5	6.7	7.8	8.9	7.8	8.4	8.4	8.9	7.8	7.2	6.1
S/HEMISPHERE	JUL	AUG	SEP	OCT	NOV	DEC	JAN	FEB	MAR	APR	MAY	JUN

Cultural Recommendations

LIGHT: 2500–3500 fc.

TEMPERATURES: Throughout the year, days average 80–87°F (27–30°C), and nights average 70–72°F (21–22°C), with a diurnal range of 10–16°F (6–9°C).

HUMIDITY: Information is not available for this location. However, averages from nearby stations indicate that humidity is probably near 85% year-round.

WATER: Rainfall is very heavy all year. Cultivated plants should be kept evenly moist but not soggy.

FERTILIZER: ¼–½ recommended strength. A balanced fertilizer should be applied weekly to biweekly throughout the year.

REST PERIOD: Growing conditions vary only slightly during the year. Water and fertilizer may be reduced slightly in winter, especially for plants cultivated in the dark, short-day conditions common in the temperate latitudes. Plants should never be allowed to dry out completely, however. In the habitat, seasonal light variation is minor.

GROWING MEDIA: Plants are best potted in small pots filled with any open, fast-draining medium. Repotting may be done anytime new roots are growing.

MISCELLANEOUS NOTES: The bloom season shown in the climate table is based on reports from the habitat. Plants that produce flowers which last a single day commonly bloom several times during the year. Flowering usually occurs 7–14 days after a sudden 10°F (5°C) drop in daytime temperatures.

Plant and Flower Information

PLANT SIZE AND TYPE: A 39 in. (100 cm) sympodial epiphyte.

PSEUDOBULB: 39 in. (100 cm) long. The stems are shiny.

LEAVES: Many. The stubby leaves are 3–4 in. (8–11 cm) long and broadly linear with 2 unequal rounded teeth at the apex.

INFLORESCENCE: Short. Inflorescences emerge through the leaf sheaths.

FLOWERS: The flowers are 1.6 in. (4 cm) long. The dorsal sepal is covered with wartlike bumps. The sepals and very slender, incurved petals are yellowish white. The fuzzy, 3-lobed lip is pale rose-red below with a very narrow, purple margin. The sidelobes are triangular. The midlobe is lacerated along the margin. The column is marked with orange. Blossoms are short-lived.

REFERENCES: 224, 445, 470.

Dendrobium quinquecostatum Schlechter. See *D. violaceum* Kränzlin. REFERENCES: 151, 154, 179, 187, 221, 304, 385, 430, 437, 445.

Dendrobium quinquecristatum P. van Royen. See *D. brevicaule* Rolfe. REFERENCES: 233, 385, 538. PHOTOS/DRAWINGS: 538.

Dendrobium quinquedentatum J. J. Smith

ORIGIN/HABITAT: Irian Jaya (western New Guinea). Plants were collected near Nepenthes Hill in the Noord River region close to the south coast.

CLIMATE: Station #97796, Kokenau (Kokonau), Irian Jaya, Lat. 4.7°S, Long. 136.4°E, at 10 ft. (3 m). Record extreme temperatures are not available for this location.

N/HEMISPHERE	JAN	FEB	MAR	APR	MAY	JUN	JUL	AUG	SEP	OCT	NOV	DEC
°F AVG MAX	83	83	86	88	90	89	89	89	90	88	87	84
°F AVG MIN	73	73	74	74	74	75	74	74	74	74	74	73
DIURNAL RANGE	10	10	12	14	16	14	15	15	16	14	13	11
RAIN/INCHES	18.4	15.8	18.9	11.6	9.7	10.6	11.5	15.7	11.6	11.6	16.0	19.9
HUMIDITY/%	N/A											
BLOOM SEASON												
DAYS CLR	N/A											
RAIN/MM	467	401	479	295	245	269	293	400	294	296	407	506
°C AVG MAX	28.6	28.4	30.2	31.1	32.1	31.9	31.9	31.7	32.0	31.4	30.7	28.7
°C AVG MIN	22.7	22.6	23.3	23.4	23.5	23.7	23.6	23.5	23.4	23.4	23.5	23.0
DIURNAL RANGE	5.9	5.8	6.9	7.7	8.6	8.2	8.3	8.2	8.6	8.0	7.2	5.7
S/HEMISPHERE	JUL	AUG	SEP	OCT	NOV	DEC	JAN	FEB	MAR	APR	MAY	JUN

Cultural Recommendations

LIGHT: 2500–3500 fc.

TEMPERATURES: Throughout the year, days average 83–90°F (29–32°C), and nights average 73–75°F (23–24°C), with a diurnal range of 10–16°F (6–9°C).

HUMIDITY: Information is not available for this location, but records from nearby stations indicate that humidity probably averages near 85% year-round.

WATER: Rainfall is very heavy all year. Cultivated plants should be kept evenly moist but not soggy.

FERTILIZER: ¼–½ recommended strength. A balanced fertilizer should be applied weekly to biweekly throughout the year.

REST PERIOD: Growing conditions vary only slightly during the year. Water and fertilizer may be reduced slightly in winter, especially for plants cultivated in the dark, short-day conditions common in the temperate latitudes. Plants should never be allowed to dry out completely, however. In the habitat, seasonal light variation is minor.

GROWING MEDIA: Plants may be potted in any open, fast-draining medium. Moisture-retaining additives may be added as needed to keep the plant moist but not soggy. Repotting may be done anytime new roots are growing.

MISCELLANEOUS NOTES: The bloom season shown in the climate table is based on collection reports.

Plant and Flower Information

PLANT SIZE AND TYPE: A 24 in. (60 cm.) sympodial epiphyte.

PSEUDOBULB: 24 in. (60 cm) long. The stems are elongated.

LEAVES: Many. The tiny, lanceolate leaves are 0.8–1.6 in. (2–4 cm) long. They are slightly twisted at the base and bilobed at the apex. The leaf bases are covered with warts.

INFLORESCENCE: Short. The laterally flattened inflorescences emerge through the leaf sheaths.

FLOWERS: The blossoms are less than 0.5 in. (1.3 cm) long. Sepals and petals are very narrow at the tips. The 3-lobed lip is covered with hairs. Flower color was not included in the original plant description.

REFERENCES: 220, 254, 445, 470.

Dendrobium quinquelobatum Schlechter

ORIGIN/HABITAT: Northeastern Papua New Guinea. Plants are found in the Maboro Range of the Waria District at about 3950 ft. (1200 m). They grow on mistforest trees which are thickly covered with moss.

Dendrobium quinquelobum

CLIMATE: Station #200192, Garaina, Papua New Guinea, Lat. 7.9°S, Long. 147.1°E, at 2350 ft. (716 m). Temperatures are calculated for an elevation of 3950 ft. (1200 m), resulting in probable extremes of 89°F (32°C) and 41°F (5°C).

N/HEMISPHERE	JAN	FEB	MAR	APR	MAY	JUN	JUL	AUG	SEP	OCT	NOV	DEC
°F AVG MAX	75	77	78	79	80	80	80	80	79	79	78	76
°F AVG MIN	58	58	58	59	58	59	60	60	60	59	59	58
DIURNAL RANGE	17	19	20	20	22	21	20	20	19	20	19	18
RAIN/INCHES	5.8	6.5	8.7	11.1	11.8	11.9	8.9	11.7	11.5	9.9	7.7	5.2
HUMIDITY/%	84	82	82	81	80	80	81	81	82	83	84	84
BLOOM SEASON												*
DAYS CLR	N/A											
RAIN/MM	147	165	221	282	300	302	226	297	292	251	196	132
°C AVG MAX	23.8	24.9	25.4	26.0	26.5	26.5	26.5	26.5	26.0	26.0	25.4	24.3
°C AVG MIN	14.3	14.3	14.3	14.9	14.3	14.9	15.4	15.4	15.4	14.9	14.9	14.3
DIURNAL RANGE	9.5	10.6	11.1	11.1	12.2	11.6	11.1	11.1	10.6	11.1	10.5	10.0
S/HEMISPHERE	JUL	AUG	SEP	OCT	NOV	DEC	JAN	FEB	MAR	APR	MAY	JUN

Cultural Recommendations

LIGHT: 2000–3000 fc.

TEMPERATURES: Throughout the year, days average 75–80°F (24–27°C), and nights average 58–60°F (14–15°C), with a diurnal range of 17–22°F (10–12°C).

HUMIDITY: 80–85% year-round.

WATER: Rainfall is heavy all year, but conditions are slightly drier in winter. Cultivated plants should be kept moist but not soggy.

FERTILIZER: 1/4–1/2 recommended strength. A balanced fertilizer should be applied weekly to biweekly throughout the year.

REST PERIOD: Growing conditions should be maintained all year. In the habitat, rainfall is slightly lower in winter. Water and fertilizer should be reduced somewhat, especially for plants cultivated in the dark, short-day conditions common in temperate latitudes. Plants should never be allowed to dry out completely, however. In the habitat, light is slightly higher in winter.

GROWING MEDIA: Plants may be mounted on tree-fern or cork slabs if humidity is high and plants are watered at least once daily in summer. When plants are potted, any open, fast-draining medium may be used. Repotting may be done anytime new roots are growing.

MISCELLANEOUS NOTES: The bloom season shown in the climate table is based on collection reports. Plants that produce flowers which last a single day commonly bloom several times during the year. Flowering usually occurs 7–14 days after a sudden 10°F (5°C) drop in daytime temperatures.

Plant and Flower Information

PLANT SIZE AND TYPE: A 31 in. (80 cm) sympodial epiphyte.

PSEUDOBULB: 31 in. (80 cm) long. The flattened, unbranched stems arise from a very short rhizome. They are densely leafy.

LEAVES: Many. The elliptical, suberect leaves are 3.5–5.0 in. (9–13 cm) long.

INFLORESCENCE: Short.

FLOWERS: 2 per inflorescence. The flowers are 1 in. (2.5 cm) long and do not open fully. Blossoms are salmon colored with pale cinnabar-red markings on the midlobe, callus, and at the apex of the column. The 3-lobed lip is nearly round. The front margin has 4, nearly equal notches and a pointed apex. The front margin of the sidelobes is toothed. Blossoms are short-lived.

REFERENCES: 221, 437, 445.

PHOTOS/DRAWINGS: 437.

Dendrobium quinquelobum (Schlechter) J. J. Smith

AKA: *Cadetia quinqueloba* Schlechter. *Cadetia* is now considered a valid genus by some botanists, so this plant may again be considered a *Cadetia*.

ORIGIN/HABITAT: Papua New Guinea. Plants grow in the forests of the Bismarck Range at about 5900 ft. (1800 m).

CLIMATE: Station #94010, Goroka, Papua New Guinea, Lat. 6.1°S, Long. 145.4°E, at 5141 ft. (1567 m). Temperatures are calculated for an elevation of 5900 ft. (1800 m), resulting in probable extremes of 84°F (29°C) and 40°F (5°C).

N/HEMISPHERE	JAN	FEB	MAR	APR	MAY	JUN	JUL	AUG	SEP	OCT	NOV	DEC
°F AVG MAX	73	74	75	76	76	75	76	75	75	75	76	74
°F AVG MIN	53	54	54	54	55	56	56	56	57	56	56	54
DIURNAL RANGE	20	20	21	22	21	19	20	19	18	19	20	20
RAIN/INCHES	2.1	2.8	4.6	5.9	6.6	9.3	9.1	10.1	10.7	8.3	4.6	2.0
HUMIDITY/%	70	67	67	67	67	71	72	73	74	71	70	70
BLOOM SEASON					*							
DAYS CLR	N/A											
RAIN/MM	53	71	117	150	168	236	231	257	272	211	117	51
°C AVG MAX	23.0	23.6	24.1	24.7	24.7	24.1	24.7	24.1	24.1	24.1	24.7	23.6
°C AVG MIN	11.9	12.5	12.5	12.5	13.0	13.6	13.6	13.6	14.1	13.6	13.6	12.5
DIURNAL RANGE	11.1	11.1	11.6	12.2	11.7	10.5	11.1	10.5	10.0	10.5	11.1	11.1
S/HEMISPHERE	JUL	AUG	SEP	OCT	NOV	DEC	JAN	FEB	MAR	APR	MAY	JUN

Cultural Recommendations

LIGHT: 2000–3000 fc.

TEMPERATURES: Throughout the year, days average 73–76°F (23–25°C), and nights average 53–57°F (12–14°C), with a diurnal range of 18–22°F (10–12°C). Plants from this habitat seldom survive continuous high temperatures.

HUMIDITY: 70–75% most of the year, dropping to near 65% in late winter and spring.

WATER: Rainfall is moderate to heavy most of the year, but conditions are slightly drier for 3 months in winter. Cultivated plants should be kept moist but not soggy. Occasional early morning mistings may be beneficial, especially on bright, sunny days.

FERTILIZER: 1/4–1/2 recommended strength. A balanced fertilizer should be applied weekly to biweekly throughout the year.

REST PERIOD: Growing temperatures should be maintained all year. In the habitat, rainfall is lowest in winter, but dew and mist from fog and low clouds are common. Water and fertilizer should be reduced somewhat for cultivated plants, especially those grown in the darker, short-day conditions common during temperate-latitude winters. Plants should be kept on the dry side, but they should never be allowed to dry out completely. In the habitat, light is higher in winter.

GROWING MEDIA: Plants may be mounted on tree-fern or cork slabs, but high humidity must be maintained and plants must be watered at least daily in summer. When plants are potted, medium to coarse fir bark or any open, fast-draining medium may be used. Repotting may be done anytime new roots are growing.

MISCELLANEOUS NOTES: The bloom season shown in the climate table is based on reports from the habitat.

Plant and Flower Information

PLANT SIZE AND TYPE: A 3.2–5.5 in. (8–14 cm) sympodial epiphyte.

PSEUDOBULB: 1.4–3.2 in. (3.5–8.0 cm) long. The erect growths are borne on a very short rhizome.

LEAVES: 1 per growth. The linear leaves are 1.6–3.2 in. (4–8 cm) long. They are rounded but taper to a sharp point at the tip.

INFLORESCENCE: Short.

FLOWERS: 1 blossom opens at a time. Additional flowers may develop after the first one fades. They are 0.2 in. (0.6 cm) long. Blossoms are white on the inside, sometimes green tinged on the back. The 3-lobed lip is totally smooth. The midlobe is broadly kidney-shaped with a notch at the apex.

REFERENCES: 221, 437, 472.

PHOTOS/DRAWINGS: 437.

Dendrobium quisumbingii A. Hawkes and A. H. Heller

AKA: *D. macgregorii* Ames.

ORIGIN/HABITAT: The Philippine Islands including Luzon and Polillo. Plants grow in the highlands of Benquet Province and in mangrove swamps on Polillo Island.

CLIMATE: Station #98328, Baguio, Philippines, Lat. 16.4°N, Long. 120.6°E, at 4962 ft. (1512 m). Record extreme temperatures are 84°F (29°C) and 46°F (8°C).

N/HEMISPHERE	JAN	FEB	MAR	APR	MAY	JUN	JUL	AUG	SEP	OCT	NOV	DEC
°F AVG MAX	72	73	76	77	76	75	71	71	71	73	74	74
°F AVG MIN	55	56	58	60	61	61	60	60	60	60	59	57
DIURNAL RANGE	17	17	18	17	15	14	11	11	11	13	15	17
RAIN/INCHES	0.9	0.9	1.7	4.3	15.8	17.2	42.3	45.7	28.1	15.0	4.9	2.0
HUMIDITY/%	83	83	83	85	89	90	93	93	92	89	86	84
BLOOM SEASON			*							*	*	
DAYS CLR	N/A											
RAIN/MM	23	23	43	109	401	437	1074	1161	714	381	124	51
°C AVG MAX	22.2	22.8	24.4	25.0	24.4	23.9	21.7	21.7	21.7	22.8	23.3	23.3
°C AVG MIN	12.8	13.3	14.4	15.6	16.1	16.1	15.6	15.6	15.6	15.6	15.0	13.9
DIURNAL RANGE	9.4	9.5	10.0	9.4	8.3	7.8	6.1	6.1	6.1	7.2	8.3	9.4
S/HEMISPHERE	JUL	AUG	SEP	OCT	NOV	DEC	JAN	FEB	MAR	APR	MAY	JUN

Cultural Recommendations

LIGHT: 1200–2500 fc. Diffused or dappled light is recommended. Sky-cover records are unavailable, but high elevations are typically cloudy in this region.

TEMPERATURES: Summer days average 71–75°F (22–24°C), and nights average 60–61°F (16°C), with a diurnal range of 11–14°F (6–8°C).

HUMIDITY: 85–95% most of the year, dropping below 85% in winter.

WATER: Rainfall is very heavy from spring to autumn but is greatly reduced in winter. Cultivated plants should be kept moist but not soggy from spring to autumn, but water should be gradually reduced in late autumn.

FERTILIZER: ¼–½ recommended strength, applied weekly. A high-nitrogen fertilizer is beneficial from spring to midsummer, but a fertilizer high in phosphates should be used in late summer and autumn.

REST PERIOD: Winter days average 72–76°F (22–24°C), and nights average 55–58°F (13–14°C), with a diurnal range of 17–18°F (9–10°C). Since plants also grow at low elevations, they should adapt to warmer winter temperatures. Rainfall is low for 2–4 months in winter, but the continuing high humidity indicates that additional moisture is frequently available from dew or fog and mist. Cultivated plants should be allowed to dry somewhat between waterings, but should never remain dry for long periods. Fertilizer should be reduced or eliminated anytime water is reduced or plants are not actively growing. In the habitat, light may be highest in winter.

GROWING MEDIA: Plants may be potted in small pots filled with any open, fast-draining medium. Repotting is best done in early spring when new roots are growing.

MISCELLANEOUS NOTES: The bloom season shown in the climate table is based on collection times.

Plant and Flower Information

PLANT SIZE AND TYPE: A 20 in. (50 cm) sympodial epiphyte.

PSEUDOBULB: 20 in. (50 cm) long. The middle of the stem is leafy.

LEAVES: Many. The slender, grasslike leaves are 1.2–2.0 in. (3–5 cm) long. They are widely spaced and alternate along the stem, forming 2 rows.

INFLORESCENCE: Short. Inflorescences emerge from a cushion of fibrous scales at stem nodes opposite rudimentary leaves. The flowers are held in dense racemes.

FLOWERS: Several per inflorescence. The tiny flowers are 0.2 in. (0.5 cm) long. They may be white or yellowish. The lip is marked with 2 dark carmine lines. The 3-lobed lip is wedge-shaped, oblong, and narrow at the base. The midlobe is rounded with a minutely hairy disk. The sidelobes are round.

REFERENCES: 12, 191, 229, 296, 536.

Dendrobium rabanii Lindley. Sometimes spelled *D. rabani*, it is now considered a synonym of *Flickingeria rabanii* (Lindley) Seidenfaden. REFERENCES: 213, 216, 231, 254, 278, 449, 469.

Dendrobium racemiflorum Swartz. Now considered a synonym of *Pleurothallis oblongifolia* Lindley. REFERENCES: 216, 254.

Dendrobium racemosum (Nicholls) Clemesha and Dockrill

AKA: *D. beckleri* F. Mueller var. *racemosum* Nicholls.

ORIGIN/HABITAT: Australia. Plants are found in only a few areas, including the Atherton and Evelyn Tablelands and the lower Russell and Johnstone Rivers, all in northern Queensland at about 17.5°S Latitude. Plants grow above 2500 ft. (760 m) on rainforest trees in sunny, humid areas with strong air movement, high rainfall and frequent mists.

CLIMATE: Station #94287, Cairns, Australia, Lat. 16.9°S, Long. 145.8°E, at 7 ft. (2 m). Temperatures are calculated for an elevation of 3000 ft. (910 m), resulting in probable extremes of 100°F (38°C) and 33°F (1°C).

N/HEMISPHERE	JAN	FEB	MAR	APR	MAY	JUN	JUL	AUG	SEP	OCT	NOV	DEC
°F AVG MAX	68	70	73	76	78	80	80	79	77	75	71	69
°F AVG MIN	51	52	54	58	60	63	64	64	63	60	56	54
DIURNAL RANGE	17	18	19	18	18	17	16	15	14	15	15	15
RAIN/INCHES	1.6	1.7	1.7	2.1	3.9	8.7	16.6	15.7	18.1	11.3	4.4	2.9
HUMIDITY/%	69	67	65	65	65	68	72	72	74	73	73	72
BLOOM SEASON			*	*	*							
DAYS CLR @ 10AM	9	11	13	11	6	6	4	5	6	7	11	10
DAYS CLR @ 4PM	8	10	12	16	10	7	4	3	4	6	9	10
RAIN/MM	41	43	43	53	99	221	422	399	460	287	112	74
°C AVG MAX	20.1	21.2	22.8	24.5	25.6	26.7	26.7	26.2	25.1	24.0	21.7	20.6
°C AVG MIN	10.6	11.2	12.3	14.5	15.6	17.3	17.8	17.8	17.3	15.6	13.4	12.3
DIURNAL RANGE	9.5	10.0	10.5	10.0	10.0	9.4	8.9	8.4	7.8	8.4	8.3	8.3
S/HEMISPHERE	JUL	AUG	SEP	OCT	NOV	DEC	JAN	FEB	MAR	APR	MAY	JUN

Cultural Recommendations

LIGHT: 3000–4000 fc. Growers report that plants are healthiest with about 50% shading, high humidity, and constant air movement.

TEMPERATURES: Summer days average 79–80°F (26–27°C), and nights average 63–64°F (17–18°C), with a diurnal range of 15–17°F (8–9°C).

HUMIDITY: In the rainforest habitats, relative humidity probably averages 75–85%, or about 10% greater than indicated in the climate table.

WATER: Rainfall is heavy from late spring into autumn, but amounts are much less in winter. Cultivated plants should never be allowed to dry out while actively growing, but water should be reduced gradually in autumn.

FERTILIZER: ¼–½ recommended strength, applied weekly. A high-nitrogen fertilizer is beneficial from spring to midsummer, but a fertilizer high in phosphates should be used in late summer and autumn.

REST PERIOD: Winter days average 68–73°F (20–23°C), and nights average 51–54°F (11–12°C), with a diurnal range of 15–19°F (8–11°C). Although record low temperatures are near freezing, Australian growers report that winter lows should not fall below 41°F (5°C). Rainfall is low in winter, but additional moisture from heavy dew and mist is common. For cultivated plants, water and fertilizer should be reduced somewhat for 4–5 months from late autumn to early spring. Plants should be kept on the dry side, but they should never remain dry for long periods or be allowed to dry out completely. Fertilizer should be reduced to a weak application once every few weeks until water is increased in spring. Light, humidity, and air movement should be high.

GROWING MEDIA: Mounting on cork or hardwood blocks produces the healthiest plants if humidity is high and plants are kept moist. Air circulation around the roots is important. Plants benefit from frequent mistings on hot, dry days. Repotting is best done in early spring when new roots are growing.

MISCELLANEOUS NOTES: The bloom season shown in the climate table is based on reports from the habitat. In the wild, plants may bloom almost any time.

Plant and Flower Information

PLANT SIZE AND TYPE: A 35 in. (90 cm) sympodial epiphyte.

PSEUDOBULB: 35 in. (90 cm) long. The erect, branching stems have a small swelling at the base.

LEAVES: 1 at the apex of each branch. The nearly cylindrical leaves are 4–8 in. (10–20 cm) long. They are seldom much wider than the stem.

INFLORESCENCE: 2–3 in. (5–8 cm) long. The erect racemes emerge near the base of leaves on the upper part of the stem.

FLOWERS: 8–15 per inflorescence. The flowers are 0.8–1.2 in. (2–3 cm) across. They may be creamy white, yellowish, or nearly brown. The 3-lobed lip is uneven along the margin. The midlobe tapers to an extremely long, recurled point. The center of the lip is decorated with 3 raised lines that extend to the apex of midlobe. The sides of the midlobe are uneven and ruffled. The column and anther are purplish. Blossoms are fragrant and last 1–2 weeks.

REFERENCES: 67, 105, 230, 240, 262, 325, 390, 421, 533.

PHOTOS/DRAWINGS: *105, 240, 325, 533.*

Dendrobium rachmatii J. J. Smith

ORIGIN/HABITAT: Endemic to Sulawesi (Celebes). Plants grow in the south on Mt. Pasangmalambe and Mt. Tolmongah. Habitat elevation is estimated, so the following climate data should be used with caution.

CLIMATE: Station #97180, Makassar, Sulawesi, Indonesia, Lat. 5.1°S, Long. 119.6°E, at 46 ft. (14 m). Temperatures are calculated for an estimated elevation of 3300 ft. (1000 m), resulting in probable extremes of 84°F (29°C) and 47°F (9°C).

N/HEMISPHERE	JAN	FEB	MAR	APR	MAY	JUN	JUL	AUG	SEP	OCT	NOV	DEC
°F AVG MAX	75	76	76	76	75	73	73	73	74	75	76	75
°F AVG MIN	59	58	59	61	63	63	63	64	63	63	63	61
DIURNAL RANGE	16	18	17	15	12	10	10	9	11	12	13	14
RAIN/INCHES	1.3	0.4	0.5	1.6	6.7	23.2	28.3	20.9	16.7	6.5	3.6	2.7
HUMIDITY/%	72	67	64	70	77	84	84	85	84	80	79	76
BLOOM SEASON						*						
DAYS CLR @ 8AM	14	17	15	14	8	4	4	1	4	8	8	11
DAYS CLR @ 2PM	7	7	11	13	9	3	1	1	1	2	6	7
RAIN/MM	33	10	13	41	170	589	719	531	424	165	91	69
°C AVG MAX	24.0	24.6	24.6	24.6	24.0	22.9	22.9	22.9	23.5	24.0	24.6	24.0
°C AVG MIN	15.1	14.6	15.1	16.3	17.4	17.4	17.4	17.9	17.4	17.4	17.4	16.3
DIURNAL RANGE	8.9	10.0	9.5	8.3	6.6	5.5	5.5	5.0	6.1	6.6	7.2	7.7
S/HEMISPHERE	JUL	AUG	SEP	OCT	NOV	DEC	JAN	FEB	MAR	APR	MAY	JUN

Cultural Recommendations

LIGHT: 2500–3500 fc. Clear summer days are rare. Cultivated plants need shade.

TEMPERATURES: Summer days average 73°F (23°C), and nights average 63–64°F (17–18°C), with a diurnal range of 9–10°F (5–6°C). Regardless of habitat elevation, seasonal patterns are similar.

HUMIDITY: Near 85% in summer and early autumn, dropping to 65–70% in winter and early spring.

WATER: Rainfall is heavy from late spring to autumn. Conditions are much drier in winter. Cultivated plants should be kept moist from late spring to early autumn, but water should be gradually reduced in late autumn.

FERTILIZER: ¼–½ recommended strength, applied weekly. A high-nitrogen fertilizer is beneficial from spring to midsummer, but a fertilizer high in phosphates should be used in late summer and autumn.

REST PERIOD: Winter days average 75–76°F (24–25°C), and nights average 58–61°F (15–16°C), with a diurnal range of 14–18°F (8–10°C). The increased diurnal range results from both warmer days and cooler nights. Rainfall is much lower for about 4 months in winter. For 2 of these months, conditions are so dry that even dew is uncommon. Water and fertilizer should be reduced for cultivated plants. In early winter, they should be kept barely moist; but for 1–2 months in late winter, plants should be allowed to dry out between waterings. They should not remain completely dry for extended periods, however. In the habitat, light is highest in winter.

- GROWING MEDIA: Plants may be mounted on tree-fern or cork slabs if humidity is high and plants are watered at least once daily in summer. When plants are potted, any open, fast-draining medium may be used. Repotting may be done anytime new roots are growing.
- MISCELLANEOUS NOTES: The bloom season shown in the climate table is based on reports from the habitat. The plant was described in 1917 in *Bull. Jard. Bot. Buit.* 2nd sér. 25:56.

Plant and Flower Information

- PLANT SIZE AND TYPE: A sympodial epiphyte of unreported size.
- PSEUDOBULB: The stems are elongated and rhomboid in cross-section.
- LEAVES: The leaves are 2.8–3.1 in. (7–8 cm) long, recurved, and firmly papery. The leaf sheaths have prominent nerves and a purple suffusion.
- INFLORESCENCE: 0.8–1.6 in. (2–4 cm) long. The laxly flowered inflorescences emerge from nodes on leafy and leafless stems.
- FLOWERS: 4–5 per inflorescence. The dark- to pale-red flowers are 1.7 in. (4.4 cm) long. The blossoms have an ovate-oblong dorsal sepal, triangular lateral sepals, and oblong petals. The narrow, erect lip is 3-lobed with a protruding midlobe.
- REFERENCES: 222, 436.

Dendrobium radians Rchb. f.
Reported to have originated in Borneo, but habitat location and elevation are not available, so climate data cannot be selected. *D. radians* is not known to be in cultivation. The plant and growth habit were originally described as similar to *D. sculptum* Rchb. f. The flowers were 2.4 in. (6 cm) across with milky white sepals and petals. The wavy lip was marked with green and reddish brown stripes and spots on the sidelobes. REFERENCES: 216, 254, 286, 295, 394, 429, 445.

Dendrobium radicosum Ridley.
Now considered a synonym of *Epigeneium radicosum* (Ridley) Summerhayes. REFERENCES: 220, 229, 286, 295, 499.

Dendrobium rajanum J. J. Smith

- ORIGIN/HABITAT: Southwest Borneo. Plants grow in western Kalimantan near Mt. Raja at 4100 ft. (1250 m).
- CLIMATE: Station #96583, Pontianak, Kalimantan, Borneo, Lat. 0.0°N, Long. 109.3°E, at 13 ft. (4 m). Temperatures are calculated for an elevation of 4100 ft. (1250 m), resulting in probable extremes of 83°F (28°C) and 55°F (13°C).

N/HEMISPHERE	JAN	FEB	MAR	APR	MAY	JUN	JUL	AUG	SEP	OCT	NOV	DEC
°F AVG MAX	74	76	76	76	77	77	76	77	77	76	75	74
°F AVG MIN	61	63	62	62	62	62	61	61	62	62	62	61
DIURNAL RANGE	13	13	14	14	15	15	15	16	15	14	13	13
RAIN/INCHES	10.8	8.2	9.5	10.9	11.1	8.7	6.5	8.0	9.0	14.4	15.3	12.7
HUMIDITY/%	85	85	84	84	82	81	79	82	83	87	86	87
BLOOM SEASON				*								
DAYS CLR @ 7AM	1	1	1	3	2	4	5	1	2	1	1	2
DAYS CLR @ 1PM	0	0	1	0	0	0	1	1	1	0	1	0
RAIN/MM	274	208	241	277	282	221	165	203	229	366	389	323
°C AVG MAX	23.1	24.2	24.2	24.2	24.7	24.7	24.2	24.7	24.7	24.2	23.6	23.1
°C AVG MIN	15.8	17.0	16.4	16.4	16.4	16.4	15.8	15.8	16.4	16.4	16.4	15.8
DIURNAL RANGE	7.3	7.2	7.8	7.8	8.3	8.3	8.4	8.9	8.3	7.8	7.2	7.3
S/HEMISPHERE	JUL	AUG	SEP	OCT	NOV	DEC	JAN	FEB	MAR	APR	MAY	JUN

Cultural Recommendations

- LIGHT: 1800–2500 fc.
- TEMPERATURES: Throughout the year, days average 74–77°F (23–25°C), and nights average 61–63°F (16–17°C), with a diurnal range of 13–16°F (7–9°C). Average highs fluctuate only 3°F (1°C), and average lows vary 2°F (1°C), indicating that plants may not tolerate wide temperature fluctuations.
- HUMIDITY: 80–85% year-round.
- WATER: Rainfall is heavy all year. Cultivated plants should be kept moist but not soggy. Constant air movement is highly recommended. Warm water may be beneficial.
- FERTILIZER: ¼–½ recommended strength. A balanced fertilizer should be applied weekly to biweekly throughout the year.
- REST PERIOD: Growing conditions should be maintained all year. Water may be reduced somewhat in winter, especially for plants grown in the dark, short-day conditions common in temperate latitudes. Plants should never be allowed to dry out completely, however. Fertilizer should be reduced if water is reduced. In the habitat, seasonal light variation is minor.
- GROWING MEDIA: Plants may be mounted on tree-fern or cork slabs or potted in small pots filled with any open, fast-draining medium. Repotting may be done anytime new roots are growing.
- MISCELLANEOUS NOTES: The bloom season shown in the climate table is based on collection reports. In 1927, J. J. Smith included a drawing with his description in *Mitt. Inst. Bot. Hamburg* 7:56.

Plant and Flower Information

- PLANT SIZE AND TYPE: An 8 in. (20 cm) sympodial epiphyte.
- PSEUDOBULB: 8 in. (20 cm) long. The clustered stems are flattened at the base, then slender and snaky for most of their length. They become dilated at the apex.
- LEAVES: Many. The somewhat lanceolate leaves are 1–2 in. (2.5–5.0 cm) long. They are erect to spreading, recurved, rigidly leathery, and equally spaced.
- INFLORESCENCE: Inflorescences emerge from nodes on the upper part of leafy stems.
- FLOWERS: Several per inflorescence. Blossoms open in succession. The flowers are 0.3 in. (0.8 cm) long. Blossoms are yellowish and reddish. The dorsal sepal and petals are nearly erect, and the lateral sepals are sharply recurved. The lip has erect sidelobes and a W-shaped notch at the apex.
- REFERENCES: 224, 286, 445.
- PHOTOS/DRAWINGS: See Miscellaneous Notes.

Dendrobium ramificans J. J. Smith

- AKA: Kränzlin (ref. 254) includes *D. ramificans* as a synonym of *D. micranthum* Lindley, but Schlechter (ref. 436) specifically excludes Kränzlin's synonymy.
- ORIGIN/HABITAT: The Soela Islands and Sulawesi (Celebes). Plants were collected near Malino and near Tondano (Tomohon) on the Minahassa Peninsula at 900–2950 ft. (280–900 m). They are found on roadside trees, in secondary forests, and at the edge of the forest.
- CLIMATE: Station #97014, Manado, Sulawesi, Lat. 1.5°N, Long. 124.9°E, at 264 ft. (80 m). Temperatures are calculated for an elevation of 3000 ft. (910 m), resulting in probable extremes of 88°F (31°C) and 56°F (13°C).

Dendrobium ramosii

N/HEMISPHERE	JAN	FEB	MAR	APR	MAY	JUN	JUL	AUG	SEP	OCT	NOV	DEC
°F AVG MAX	76	76	76	77	78	78	78	80	80	80	78	77
°F AVG MIN	64	64	64	64	65	64	64	64	64	63	64	65
DIURNAL RANGE	12	12	12	13	13	14	14	16	16	17	14	12
RAIN/INCHES	18.6	13.8	12.2	8.0	6.4	6.5	4.8	4.0	3.4	4.9	8.9	14.7
HUMIDITY/%	84	83	83	83	81	80	75	72	75	77	82	83
BLOOM SEASON		*			*					*	*	*
DAYS CLR @ 8AM	4	3	6	11	11	12	12	12	14	17	12	8
DAYS CLR @ 2PM	1	1	1	2	1	3	3	4	4	4	1	1
RAIN/MM	472	351	310	203	163	165	122	102	86	124	226	373
°C AVG MAX	24.4	24.4	24.4	25.0	25.5	25.5	25.5	26.7	26.7	26.7	25.5	25.0
°C AVG MIN	17.8	17.8	17.8	17.8	18.3	17.8	17.8	17.8	17.8	17.2	17.8	18.3
DIURNAL RANGE	6.6	6.6	6.6	7.2	7.2	7.7	7.7	8.9	8.9	9.5	7.7	6.7
S/HEMISPHERE	JUL	AUG	SEP	OCT	NOV	DEC	JAN	FEB	MAR	APR	MAY	JUN

Cultural Recommendations

LIGHT: 2500–3500 fc. In the habitat, skies are often clear in the morning and overcast in the afternoon.

TEMPERATURES: Throughout the year, days average 76–80°F (24–27°C), and nights average 63–65°F (17–18°C), with a diurnal range of 12–17°F (7–10°C). The average highs vary only 4°F (2°C), and average lows fluctuate only 2°F (1°C), indicating that plants may not tolerate wide temperature fluctuations. The warmest and coolest temperatures of the year occur in the late summer and early autumn dry season.

HUMIDITY: 80–85% most of the year, dropping to 70–75% in summer.

WATER: Rainfall is moderate to heavy all year. The driest weather occurs in late summer when temperatures are warm. Cultivated plants should be kept moist but not soggy. Warm water might be beneficial.

FERTILIZER: ¼–½ recommended strength. A balanced fertilizer should be applied weekly to biweekly throughout the year.

REST PERIOD: Growing temperatures should be maintained all year. The plants may rest during the 1–2 month drier period which occurs in late summer and coincides with the period of greatest diurnal range. Cultivated plants should dry out slightly during this period, but they should never remain dry for long. The heaviest rainfall in the habitat occurs in winter, but water should not be increased for cultivated plants. In fact, water should be reduced somewhat for plants grown in the dark, short-day conditions common in temperate latitudes, but they should not be allowed to dry out completely.

GROWING MEDIA: Plants may be mounted on tree-fern or cork slabs if humidity is high and plants are watered at least once daily in summer. When plants are potted, any open, fast-draining medium may be used. Repotting may be done anytime new roots are growing.

MISCELLANEOUS NOTES: The bloom season shown in the climate table is based on collection reports.

Plant and Flower Information

PLANT SIZE AND TYPE: A 12 in. (30 cm) sympodial epiphyte.

PSEUDOBULB: 12 in. (30 cm) long. The flattened stems are strongly branching.

LEAVES: Many. The leaves are 0.5 in. (1.3 cm) long, laterally flattened, and arranged in 2 rows.

INFLORESCENCE: Short. Inflorescences are borne near the apex of the stem.

FLOWERS: Few per inflorescence. The flowers are 0.2 in. (0.5 cm) across. The white blossoms have pink stripes on the sepals and petals. They have an ovate, 3-angled dorsal sepal, ovate-triangular lateral sepals, and oblong petals. The 3-lobed lip is wavy.

REFERENCES: 219, 254, 436.

Dendrobium ramosii Ames

ORIGIN/HABITAT: The Philippines, on Luzon Island. The habitat includes Benquet and Quezon Provinces and collections are reported near Bontoc in Mountain Province. The orchids grow on open ground in mountainous areas at 3950–4250 ft. (1200–1300 m).

CLIMATE: Station #98328, Baguio, Luzon, Philippines, Lat. 16.4°N, Long. 120.6°E, at 4962 ft. (1512 m). Temperatures are calculated for an elevation of 4000 ft. (1220 m), resulting in probable extremes of 87°F (31°C) and 49°F (10°C).

N/HEMISPHERE	JAN	FEB	MAR	APR	MAY	JUN	JUL	AUG	SEP	OCT	NOV	DEC
°F AVG MAX	75	76	79	80	79	78	74	74	74	76	77	77
°F AVG MIN	58	59	61	63	64	64	63	63	63	63	62	60
DIURNAL RANGE	17	17	18	17	15	14	11	11	11	13	15	17
RAIN/INCHES	0.9	0.9	1.7	4.3	15.8	17.2	42.3	45.7	28.1	15.0	4.9	2.0
HUMIDITY/%	83	83	83	85	89	90	93	93	92	89	86	84
BLOOM SEASON		*			*				*			*
DAYS CLR	N/A											
RAIN/MM	23	23	43	109	401	437	1074	1161	714	381	124	51
°C AVG MAX	24.0	24.5	26.2	26.8	26.2	25.7	23.4	23.4	23.4	24.5	25.1	25.1
°C AVG MIN	14.5	15.1	16.2	17.3	17.9	17.9	17.3	17.3	17.3	17.3	16.8	15.7
DIURNAL RANGE	9.5	9.4	10.0	9.5	8.3	7.8	6.1	6.1	6.1	7.2	8.3	9.4
S/HEMISPHERE	JUL	AUG	SEP	OCT	NOV	DEC	JAN	FEB	MAR	APR	MAY	JUN

Cultural Recommendations

LIGHT: 3000–4000 fc. Diffused or dappled light is recommended. Sky-cover records are unavailable, but in this region, mountain locations are typically cloudy.

TEMPERATURES: Summer days average 74–78°F (23–26°C), and nights average 63–64°F (17–18°C), with a diurnal range of 11–14°F (6–8°C).

HUMIDITY: 85–95% most of the year, dropping below 85% in winter.

WATER: Rainfall is very heavy from spring to autumn but is greatly reduced in winter. Cultivated plants should be kept moist but not soggy from spring to autumn. Water should be gradually reduced in late autumn.

FERTILIZER: ¼–½ recommended strength, applied weekly. A high-nitrogen fertilizer is beneficial from spring to midsummer, but a fertilizer high in phosphates should be used in late summer and autumn.

REST PERIOD: Winter days average 75–79°F (24–26°C), and nights average 58–61°F (15–16°C), with a diurnal range of 17–18°F (9–10°C). Rainfall is low for 2–4 months in winter, but the continuing high humidity indicates that additional moisture is frequently available from dew or fog and mist. Cultivated plants should be allowed to dry somewhat between waterings, but should never remain dry for long periods. Fertilizer should be reduced or eliminated anytime water is reduced or plants are not actively growing. In the habitat, light may be highest in winter.

GROWING MEDIA: Plants may be mounted on tree-fern or cork slabs or potted in small pots filled with any open, fast-draining medium. Repotting may be done anytime new roots are growing.

MISCELLANEOUS NOTES: The bloom season shown in the climate table is based on collection reports.

Plant and Flower Information

PLANT SIZE AND TYPE: A 12 in. (30 cm) sympodial terrestrial plant.

PSEUDOBULB: 12 in. (30 cm) long. The canelike stems are very slender.

LEAVES: Many. The linear leaves are 2.8 in. (7 cm) long. They are held in 2 rows.

INFLORESCENCE: The racemes emerge from nodes at the tip and along the sides of the stem.

FLOWERS: 5 per inflorescence. The pale purple flowers are 0.4–0.8 in. (1–2 cm) long. Sepals are somewhat hooded at the tip. The ovate-oblong petals and unlobed lip are rounded at the tips and finely toothed along the margin.

HYBRIDIZING NOTES: Chromosome count is $2n = 40$ (ref. 151, 154, 187, 188).

REFERENCES: 12, 151, 154, 187, 188, 221, 296, 373, 536.

Dendrobium ramosissimum Wight. See *D. herbaceum* Lindley. REFERENCES: 216, 244, 254, 278, 317, 369, 424, 445.

Dendrobium ramosum Lindley ex Wallich. See *D. ruckeri* Lindley. Kränzlin (ref. 254) reverses this synonymy. REFERENCES: 38, 46, 179, 202, 216, 254, 277, 369, 445, 504, 580.

Dendrobium ramosum Persoon. Now considered a synonym of *Maxillaria ramosa*. REFERENCES: 216.

Dendrobium randaiense Hayata. See *D. chameleon* Ames. REFERENCES: 61, 192, 208, 221, 274, 279, 536. PHOTOS/DRAWINGS: 274.

Dendrobium rantii J. J. Smith

ORIGIN/HABITAT: Sulawesi (Celebes). Plants were found near Makassar above Malino at about 3450 ft. (1050 m).

CLIMATE: Station #97180, Makassar, Sulawesi, Indonesia, Lat. 5.1°S, Long. 119.6°E, at 46 ft. (14 m). Temperatures are calculated for an elevation of 3450 ft. (1050 m), resulting in probable extremes of 84°F (29°C) and 47°F (8°C).

N/HEMISPHERE	JAN	FEB	MAR	APR	MAY	JUN	JUL	AUG	SEP	OCT	NOV	DEC
°F AVG MAX	75	76	76	76	75	73	73	73	74	75	76	75
°F AVG MIN	59	58	59	61	63	63	63	64	63	63	63	61
DIURNAL RANGE	16	18	17	15	12	10	10	9	11	12	13	14
RAIN/INCHES	1.3	0.4	0.5	1.6	6.7	23.2	28.3	20.9	16.7	6.5	3.6	2.7
HUMIDITY/%	72	67	64	70	77	84	84	85	84	80	79	76
BLOOM SEASON	N/A											
DAYS CLR @ 8AM	14	17	15	14	8	4	4	1	4	8	8	11
DAYS CLR @ 2PM	7	7	11	13	9	3	1	1	1	2	6	7
RAIN/MM	33	10	13	41	170	589	719	531	424	165	91	69
°C AVG MAX	23.8	24.3	24.3	24.3	23.8	22.6	22.6	22.6	23.2	23.8	24.3	23.8
°C AVG MIN	14.9	14.3	14.9	16.0	17.1	17.1	17.1	17.6	17.1	17.1	17.1	16.0
DIURNAL RANGE	8.9	10.0	9.4	8.3	6.7	5.5	5.5	5.0	6.1	6.7	7.2	7.8
S/HEMISPHERE	JUL	AUG	SEP	OCT	NOV	DEC	JAN	FEB	MAR	APR	MAY	JUN

Cultural Recommendations

LIGHT: 2000–3000 fc. Clear, summer days are rare.

TEMPERATURES: Summer days average 73°F (23°C), and nights average 63–64°F (17–18°C), with a diurnal range of 9–10°F (5–6°C).

HUMIDITY: Near 85% in summer and early autumn, dropping to 65–70% in winter and early spring.

WATER: Rainfall is heavy from late spring to autumn. Conditions are much drier in winter. Cultivated plants should be kept moist from late spring to early autumn, but water should be gradually reduced in late autumn.

FERTILIZER: ¼–½ recommended strength, applied weekly. A high-nitrogen fertilizer is beneficial from spring to midsummer, but a fertilizer high in phosphates should be used in late summer and autumn.

REST PERIOD: Winter days average 75–76°F (24–25°C), and nights average 58–61°F (15–16°C), with a diurnal range of 14–18°F (8–10°C). The increased diurnal range results from both warmer days and cooler nights. Rainfall is much lower for about 4 months in winter. For 2 of these months, conditions are so dry that even dew is uncommon. Water and fertilizer should be reduced for cultivated plants. In early winter, they should be kept barely moist; but for 1–2 months in late winter, plants should be allowed to dry out between waterings. They should not remain completely dry for extended periods, however. In the habitat, light is highest in winter.

GROWING MEDIA: Plants may be mounted on tree-fern or cork slabs if humidity is high and plants are watered at least once daily in summer. When plants are potted, any open, fast-draining medium may be used. They may be repotted anytime new roots are growing.

Plant and Flower Information

PLANT SIZE AND TYPE: A 16 in. (40 cm) sympodial epiphyte.

PSEUDOBULB: 16 in. (40 cm) long. The elongated stems are slender, flexuous, and very branching. The branches do not root. When dry, the stems become ridged and dirty yellow.

LEAVES: Many. The linear leaves are 2.0–2.4 in. (5–6 cm) long, and very unequally 2-toothed at the apex. The foliage is deciduous.

INFLORESCENCE: Short. Inflorescences emerge through the leaf sheaths below the nodes of leafy and leafless branches. They occasionally branch.

FLOWERS: 5–8 per inflorescence. The flowers are 0.8 in. (2 cm) long. Sepals and petals are violet with a darker violet lip. The dorsal sepal is broad at the base, tapering to a slender tip. Lateral sepals are linear and concave. The lip has small, triangular sidelobes and a large midlobe that is incurved at the tip.

REFERENCES: 225, 485.

Dendrobium rappardii J. J. Smith

ORIGIN/HABITAT: Sumatra. Plants were originally collected near Bengkulu (Benkule or Bengkoeloe) in primeval forest at about 2150 ft. (650 m).

CLIMATE: Station #96253, Bengkulu, Sumatra, Indonesia, Lat. 3.9°S, Long. 102.3°E, at 49 ft. (15 m). Temperatures are calculated for an elevation of 2150 ft. (660 m). Record extreme temperatures are not available for this location.

N/HEMISPHERE	JAN	FEB	MAR	APR	MAY	JUN	JUL	AUG	SEP	OCT	NOV	DEC
°F AVG MAX	81	80	80	80	80	80	81	81	81	81	82	81
°F AVG MIN	65	65	65	66	66	66	66	65	66	67	66	66
DIURNAL RANGE	16	15	15	14	14	14	15	16	15	14	16	15
RAIN/INCHES	6.9	6.8	9.1	13.9	16.0	12.7	16.0	11.5	12.0	8.3	8.4	8.4
HUMIDITY/%	77	78	77	77	79	80	78	76	77	79	77	78
BLOOM SEASON									*			
DAYS CLR	N/A											
RAIN/MM	175	173	231	353	406	323	406	292	305	211	213	213
°C AVG MAX	27.3	26.7	26.7	26.7	26.7	26.7	27.3	27.3	27.3	27.3	27.8	27.3
°C AVG MIN	18.4	18.4	18.4	18.9	18.9	18.9	18.9	18.4	18.9	19.5	18.9	18.9
DIURNAL RANGE	8.9	8.3	8.3	7.8	7.8	7.8	8.4	8.9	8.4	7.8	8.9	8.4
S/HEMISPHERE	JUL	AUG	SEP	OCT	NOV	DEC	JAN	FEB	MAR	APR	MAY	JUN

Cultural Recommendations

LIGHT: 2000–3000 fc.

TEMPERATURES: Throughout the year, days average 80–82°F (27–28°C), and nights average 65–67°F (18–20°C), with a diurnal range of 14–16°F (8–9°C).

HUMIDITY: 75–80% year-round.

WATER: Rainfall is heavy all year, but conditions are slightly drier in winter. Cultivated plants should be kept moist but not soggy.

FERTILIZER: ¼–½ recommended strength. A balanced fertilizer should be applied weekly to biweekly throughout the year.

REST PERIOD: Growing conditions should be maintained year-round. Water may be reduced somewhat for cultivated plants in winter, especially those grown in the dark, short-day conditions common in temperate latitudes. Plants should never be allowed to dry out completely, however. In the habitat, light is highest in winter.

GROWING MEDIA: Plants may be mounted on tree-fern or cork slabs or potted in small pots filled with any open, fast-draining medium. Repotting may be done anytime new roots are growing.

MISCELLANEOUS NOTES: The bloom season shown in the climate table is based on records from the herbarium at Leiden.

Plant and Flower Information

PLANT SIZE AND TYPE: A 28–35 in. (70–90 cm) sympodial epiphyte. Plants occasionally reach a length of 59 in. (150 cm).

PSEUDOBULB: 28–35 in. (70–90 cm) long, occasionally longer.

LEAVES: The lanceolate leaves are about 6 in. (16 cm) long, but they are smaller near the apex of the stem. They are pointed, rigidly papery, and deciduous.

INFLORESCENCE: Inflorescences emerge from nodes on leafless stems.

FLOWERS: 6–9 per inflorescence. The conspicuous flowers are 2.0–2.4 in. (5–6 cm) across. Blossoms are white, somewhat suffused with violet. J. J. Smith (ref. 488) described the blossoms as a striped form of *D. obrienianum* Kränzlin. The dorsal sepal is lanceolate and rounded at the tip. Lateral sepals are oblong-triangular, curved along the margin, and pointed at the tip. Petals are uneven along the margin. The erect lip is linear with 2, parallel, longitudinal lines.

REFERENCES: 227, 488.

Dendrobium rariflorum J. J. Smith

ORIGIN/HABITAT: Irian Jaya (western New Guinea). Plants grow about 43 mi. (70 km) north of the Jaya (Carstensz) Mountains at 5900–7200 ft. (1800–2200 m).

CLIMATE: Station #97686, Wamena, Irian Jaya, Lat. 4.1°S, Long. 139.0°E, at 5446 ft. (1660 m). Temperatures are calculated for an elevation of 6400 ft. (1950 m). Extreme temperatures are not available for this location.

N/HEMISPHERE	JAN	FEB	MAR	APR	MAY	JUN	JUL	AUG	SEP	OCT	NOV	DEC
°F AVG MAX	72	73	74	73	74	73	74	73	73	76	75	71
°F AVG MIN	57	57	59	59	60	61	60	59	60	62	62	58
DIURNAL RANGE	15	16	15	14	14	12	14	14	13	14	13	13
RAIN/INCHES	3.0	1.9	2.2	4.0	4.6	3.3	2.8	4.2	6.9	3.9	5.4	4.9
HUMIDITY/%	N/A											
BLOOM SEASON			*									
DAYS CLR	N/A											
RAIN/MM	76	48	56	102	117	84	71	107	175	99	137	124
°C AVG MAX	22.1	22.7	23.3	22.7	23.3	22.7	23.3	22.7	22.7	24.4	23.8	21.6
°C AVG MIN	13.8	13.8	14.9	14.9	15.5	16.0	15.5	14.9	15.5	16.6	16.6	14.4
DIURNAL RANGE	8.3	8.9	8.4	7.8	7.8	6.7	7.8	7.8	7.2	7.8	7.2	7.2
S/HEMISPHERE	JUL	AUG	SEP	OCT	NOV	DEC	JAN	FEB	MAR	APR	MAY	JUN

Cultural Recommendations

LIGHT: 2000–2500 fc. In the habitat, light is highest in the morning.

TEMPERATURES: Throughout the year, days average 71–76°F (22–24°C), and nights average 57–62°F (14–17°C), with a diurnal range of 12–16°F (7–9°C). In the habitat, the warmest temperatures of the day occur during late morning when skies are usually clear. Clouds and mist develop near noon, thus preventing additional warming.

HUMIDITY: Information is not available for this location. However, records from nearby stations indicate that humidity probably averages near 80% year-round. High humidity and excellent air circulation are particularly important if temperatures are warm. Placing the plants in front of an evaporative cooler or near a fine mist may be very beneficial on especially warm days.

WATER: Rainfall is light to moderate through most of the year; but in the high elevation habitat, it is probably greater than indicated in the climate table. In addition, large amounts of water are usually available from mist and heavy dew, even during periods of lower rainfall. Cultivated plants should be kept moist. Good air movement is critically important and should be maintained at all times.

FERTILIZER: ¼–½ recommended strength. A balanced fertilizer should be applied weekly to biweekly throughout the year. The Royal Botanic Garden in Edinburgh uses a dilute, seaweed-based fertilizer.

REST PERIOD: Growing conditions should be maintained all year. Conditions are slightly drier for 1–2 months in winter. In cultivation, water may be decreased somewhat, but plants should never be allowed to dry out completely. In the habitat, light is slightly higher in winter.

GROWING MEDIA: Plants may be mounted on tree-fern or cork slabs if humidity is high and plants are watered at least once daily in summer. When plants are potted, any open, fast-draining medium may be used. Repotting may be done anytime new roots are growing.

MISCELLANEOUS NOTES: The bloom season shown in the climate table is based on reports from the habitat.

Plant and Flower Information

PLANT SIZE AND TYPE: A 5 in. (13 cm) sympodial epiphyte. Plants may be larger.

PSEUDOBULB: 3.3 in. (8.5 cm) long. The 3-noded stems are clustered, slightly club-shaped, and about 7-angled. J. J. Smith (ref. 470) indicated that the specimen might have been an immature plant.

LEAVES: 1 per growth. The erect leaves are 1.3 in. (3.4 cm) long. They are linear-lanceolate with 2 short teeth at the apex.

INFLORESCENCE: 1.6 in. (4 cm) long. Inflorescence length varies depending on plant size. Each growth normally produces 2 Inflorescences which exceed the length of the leaves.

FLOWERS: 1–2 per inflorescence. The flowers are 0.7–0.8 in. (1.8–2.0 cm) across. Sepals and petals are ivory white with red-brown dots. The lip may be white or pale green with red-brown dots and streaks. The dorsal sepal is subtriangular-oblong and rounded. Lateral sepals are lanceolate. The parallel petals are rhombic-spathulate and pointed. The 3-lobed lip has erect, slightly wavy sidelobes and a concave, 5-angled midlobe. The callus consists of 3 parallel ridges.

REFERENCES: 83, 224, 445, 470.

Dendrobium rarum Schlechter

ORIGIN/HABITAT: Northern Papua New Guinea and Vanuatu. In New Guinea, plants grow in the Waria district in the Finisterre Range and the Maboro Mountains. In New Guinea, plants grow on moss-covered mist-forest trees at 3950–4250 ft. (1200–1300 m). In Vanuatu, the orchids are found in primary and secondary forests at 150–2600 ft. (40–800 m).

CLIMATE: Station #200192, Garaina, Papua New Guinea, Lat. 7.9°S, Long. 147.1°E, at 2350 ft. (716 m). Temperatures are calculated for an elevation of 3950 ft. (1200 m), resulting in probable extremes of 89°F (32°C) and 41°F (5°C).

N/HEMISPHERE	JAN	FEB	MAR	APR	MAY	JUN	JUL	AUG	SEP	OCT	NOV	DEC
°F AVG MAX	75	77	78	79	80	80	80	80	79	79	78	76
°F AVG MIN	58	58	58	59	58	59	60	60	60	59	59	58
DIURNAL RANGE	17	19	20	20	22	21	20	20	19	20	19	18
RAIN/INCHES	5.8	6.5	8.7	11.1	11.8	11.9	8.9	11.7	11.5	9.9	7.7	5.2
HUMIDITY/%	84	82	82	81	80	80	81	81	82	83	84	84
BLOOM SEASON			*							*		
DAYS CLR	N/A											
RAIN/MM	147	165	221	282	300	302	226	297	292	251	196	132
°C AVG MAX	23.8	24.9	25.4	26.0	26.5	26.5	26.5	26.5	26.0	26.0	25.4	24.3
°C AVG MIN	14.3	14.3	14.3	14.9	14.3	14.9	15.4	15.4	15.4	14.9	14.9	14.3
DIURNAL RANGE	9.5	10.6	11.1	11.1	12.2	11.6	11.1	11.1	10.6	11.1	10.5	10.0
S/HEMISPHERE	JUL	AUG	SEP	OCT	NOV	DEC	JAN	FEB	MAR	APR	MAY	JUN

Cultural Recommendations

LIGHT: 2000–3000 fc.

TEMPERATURES: Throughout the year, days average 75–80°F (24–27°C), and nights average 58–60°F (14–15°C), with a diurnal range of 17–22°F (10–12°C).

HUMIDITY: 80–85% year-round.

WATER: Rainfall is heavy all year, but conditions are slightly drier in winter. Cultivated plants should be kept moist but not soggy.

FERTILIZER: 1/4–1/2 recommended strength. A balanced fertilizer should be applied weekly to biweekly throughout the year.

REST PERIOD: Growing conditions should be maintained all year. In the habitat, rainfall is slightly lower in winter. Water and fertilizer should be reduced somewhat for cultivated plants, especially those grown in the dark, short-day conditions common during temperate-latitude winters. They should never be allowed to dry out completely, however. In the habitat, seasonal light variation is minor.

GROWING MEDIA: Plants may be mounted on tree-fern or cork slabs if humidity is high and plants are watered at least once daily in summer. When plants are potted, fir bark or any open, fast-draining medium may be used. Repotting may be done anytime new roots are growing.

MISCELLANEOUS NOTES: The bloom season shown in the climate table is based on reports from the habitat.

Plant and Flower Information

PLANT SIZE AND TYPE: An 18 in. (45 cm) sympodial epiphyte.

PSEUDOBULB: 14–16 in. (35–40 cm) long. Lewis and Cribb (ref. 270) state that plants may reach a length of 59 in. (150 cm). The clustered, dull purple stems are erect, swollen at the base, and grooved.

LEAVES: Many. The thin-textured leaves are 2–6 in. (5–15 cm) long. They are linear, pointed, more or less erect, and unequally bilobed. They are bright green with a purple flush on the upper surface.

INFLORESCENCE: 1.2 in. (3 cm) long. Inflorescences are olive-green to purple-green and become brick-red. The pendent clusters of flowers emerge from nodes on the upper half of leafless stems.

FLOWERS: 8–15 per cluster. Blossoms are smaller than the closely related *D. roseipes* Schlechter and *D. pseudoglomeratum* J. J. Wood and T. M. Reeve. Flowers are shaped like a flared cone. The segments are deep rose-purple, sometimes with white at the recurved tips. Sepals are hooded at the apex. The ovate dorsal sepal is pointed. Lateral sepals are triangular-ovate and pointed at the tip. The lip is ovate, pointed, and covered with minute bumps.

REFERENCES: 95, 221, 269, 270, 437, 445, 552.

PHOTOS/DRAWINGS: 269, 270, 437.

Dendrobium rechingerorum Schlechter

ORIGIN/HABITAT: Bougainville Island and the Solomon Islands. On Bougainville, plants grow on coastal forest trees near Djup.

CLIMATE: Station #91500, Torokina, Bougainville Island, Lat. 6.2°S, Long. 155.1°E, at 130 ft. (40 m). Record extreme temperatures are 95°F (35°C) and 65°F (18°C).

N/HEMISPHERE	JAN	FEB	MAR	APR	MAY	JUN	JUL	AUG	SEP	OCT	NOV	DEC
°F AVG MAX	86	87	87	86	85	88	89	89	88	87	87	87
°F AVG MIN	71	71	71	71	72	73	72	71	73	72	71	71
DIURNAL RANGE	15	16	16	15	13	15	17	18	15	15	16	16
RAIN/INCHES	19.9	12.7	13.9	22.9	16.4	19.2	22.2	7.5	14.7	11.4	11.2	9.5
HUMIDITY/%	91	90	90	91	86	87	87	86	87	88	88	89
BLOOM SEASON			*									
DAYS CLR	N/A											
RAIN/MM	504	323	353	582	417	488	564	190	373	290	284	241
°C AVG MAX	30.0	30.6	30.6	30.0	29.4	31.1	31.7	31.7	31.1	30.6	30.6	30.6
°C AVG MIN	21.7	21.7	21.7	21.7	22.2	22.8	22.2	21.7	22.8	22.2	21.7	21.7
DIURNAL RANGE	8.3	8.9	8.9	8.3	7.2	8.3	9.5	10.0	8.3	8.4	8.9	8.9
S/HEMISPHERE	JUL	AUG	SEP	OCT	NOV	DEC	JAN	FEB	MAR	APR	MAY	JUN

Cultural Recommendations

LIGHT: 1800–2500 fc.

TEMPERATURES: Throughout the year, days average 85–89°F (29–32°C), and nights average 71–73°F (22–23°C), with a diurnal range of 13–18°F (7–10°C).

HUMIDITY: 85–90% year-round.

WATER: Rainfall is extremely heavy all year. Cultivated plants should be kept moist but not soggy.

FERTILIZER: 1/4–1/2 recommended strength. A balanced fertilizer should be applied weekly to biweekly throughout the year.

REST PERIOD: Growing conditions should be maintained year-round. Water and fertilizer may be reduced somewhat in winter, but plants should never be allowed to dry out completely. In the habitat, seasonal light variation is minor.

GROWING MEDIA: Plants may be mounted on tree-fern or cork slabs if humidity is high and plants are watered at least once daily in summer. When plants are potted, any open, fast-draining medium may be used. Repotting may be done anytime new roots are growing.

MISCELLANEOUS NOTES: The bloom season shown in the climate table is based on reports from the habitat. Plants that produce flowers which last a single day commonly bloom several times during the year. Flowering usually occurs 7–14 days after a sudden 10°F (5°C) drop in daytime temperatures.

Plant and Flower Information

PLANT SIZE AND TYPE: A 20 in. (50 cm) sympodial epiphyte.

PSEUDOBULB: 20 in. (50 cm) long. The upper portion of the stem is leafy.

LEAVES: Many. The ovate leaves are 1.6–3.1 in. (4–8 cm) long, distichous, and unequally bilobed at the apex.

INFLORESCENCE: Short. The lateral inflorescences emerge from flattened bumps along the stem.

FLOWERS: 2 per inflorescence. The paired flowers are 1 in. (2.5 cm) long. They are yellow with mauve stripes. The petals are lighter yellow than the sepals. The sepals and petals arch up then forward. The pointed dorsal sepal is lanceolate. Lateral sepals are sickle-shaped. Petals are slender and pointed. The 3-lobed lip has triangular sidelobes that are about half as long as the triangular midlobe. The callus is densely covered with bumps, especially on the midlobe.

REFERENCES: 221, 271, 437, 440, 445, 516.

PHOTOS/DRAWINGS: 271, 437, 440.

Dendrobium recurvatum (Blume) J. J. Smith.

Originally described as *Cadetia recurvata* Blume. *Cadetia* is again considered a valid genus by some botanists, so this plant may become a *Cadetia*. It originated in Irian Jaya (western New Guinea). Habitat location and elevation are unavailable, so climate data cannot be selected. REFERENCES: 220, 470.

Dendrobium recurvifolium J. J. Smith.

Now considered a synonym of *Diplocaulobium recurvifolium* (J. J. Smith) A. Hawkes.
REFERENCES: 224, 229, 445, 470.

Dendrobium recurvilabre J. J. Smith

ORIGIN/HABITAT: Irian Jaya (western New Guinea). Plants grow on trees in primary forests along the Lorentz River. Habitat elevation is unavailable, so the following climate data should be used with caution.

CLIMATE: Station #97796, Kokenau (Kokonau), Irian Jaya, Lat. 4.7°S, Long. 136.4°E, at 10 ft. (3 m). Record extreme temperatures are not available for this location.

Dendrobium reflexibarbatulum

N/HEMISPHERE	JAN	FEB	MAR	APR	MAY	JUN	JUL	AUG	SEP	OCT	NOV	DEC
°F AVG MAX	83	83	86	88	90	89	89	89	90	88	87	84
°F AVG MIN	73	73	74	74	74	75	74	74	74	74	74	73
DIURNAL RANGE	10	10	12	14	16	14	15	15	16	14	13	11
RAIN/INCHES	18.4	15.8	18.9	11.6	9.7	10.6	11.5	15.7	11.6	11.6	16.0	19.9
HUMIDITY/%	N/A											
BLOOM SEASON	*					*						
DAYS CLR	N/A											
RAIN/MM	467	401	479	295	245	269	293	400	294	296	407	506
°C AVG MAX	28.6	28.4	30.2	31.1	32.1	31.9	31.9	31.7	32.0	31.4	30.7	28.7
°C AVG MIN	22.7	22.6	23.3	23.4	23.5	23.7	23.6	23.5	23.4	23.4	23.5	23.0
DIURNAL RANGE	5.9	5.8	6.9	7.7	8.6	8.2	8.3	8.2	8.6	8.0	7.2	5.7
S/HEMISPHERE	JUL	AUG	SEP	OCT	NOV	DEC	JAN	FEB	MAR	APR	MAY	JUN

Cultural Recommendations

LIGHT: 2500–3500 fc.

TEMPERATURES: Throughout the year, days average 83–90°F (29–32°C), and nights average 73–75°F (23–24°C), with a diurnal range of 10–16°F (6–9°C).

HUMIDITY: Information is not available for this location. However, records from nearby stations indicate that humidity probably averages near 85% year-round.

WATER: Rainfall is very heavy all year. Cultivated plants should be kept evenly moist but not soggy. Warm water might be beneficial.

FERTILIZER: ¼–½ recommended strength. A balanced fertilizer should be applied weekly to biweekly throughout the year.

REST PERIOD: Growing temperatures should be maintained year-round. The smallest diurnal range occurs in winter. Water and fertilizer might be reduced slightly, especially for plants grown in the dark, short-day conditions common in temperate latitudes. Plants should never be allowed to dry out completely, however. In the habitat, seasonal light variation is minor.

GROWING MEDIA: Plants may be mounted on tree-fern or cork slabs or potted in small pots filled with any open, fast-draining medium. Repotting may be done anytime new roots are actively growing.

MISCELLANEOUS NOTES: The bloom season shown in the climate table is based on collection reports.

Plant and Flower Information

PLANT SIZE AND TYPE: A sympodial epiphyte.

PSEUDOBULB: Stems are elongated, flattened, and elliptical in cross-section.

LEAVES: The lanceolate leaves are 5 in. (13 cm) long. They are erect-spreading, somewhat twisted at the base, and unequally 2-toothed at the apex.

INFLORESCENCE: Short. Numerous inflorescences emerge through the leaf bases at nodes along the stem.

FLOWERS: 2 per inflorescence. The flowers are less than 0.7 in. (1.7 cm) long. They are yellow with an orange lip. Sepals and petals are incurved. The concave sepals are warty on the outside. Lateral sepals are oblong-triangular and sickle-shaped. The erect, 3-lobed lip is 5-sided. It is relatively short and broad with small sidelobes and a broadly triangular, recurved midlobe. The spur is white.

REFERENCES: 221, 470, 478.

Dendrobium reflexibarbatulum J. J. Smith

ORIGIN/HABITAT: Southwest Borneo. Plants grow in western Kalimantan near the village of Kruab at about 200 ft. (60 m).

CLIMATE: Station #96583, Pontianak, Borneo, Lat. 0.0°N, Long. 109.3°E, at 13 ft. (4 m). Temperatures are calculated for an elevation of 250 ft. (80 m), resulting in probable extremes of 95°F (35°C) and 67°F (20°C).

N/HEMISPHERE	JAN	FEB	MAR	APR	MAY	JUN	JUL	AUG	SEP	OCT	NOV	DEC
°F AVG MAX	86	88	88	88	89	89	88	89	89	88	87	86
°F AVG MIN	73	75	74	74	74	74	73	73	74	74	74	73
DIURNAL RANGE	13	13	14	14	15	15	15	16	15	14	13	13
RAIN/INCHES	10.8	8.2	9.5	10.9	11.1	8.7	6.5	8.0	9.0	14.4	15.3	12.7
HUMIDITY/%	85	85	84	84	82	81	79	82	83	87	86	87
BLOOM SEASON											*	
DAYS CLR @ 7AM	1	1	1	3	2	4	5	1	2	1	1	2
DAYS CLR @ 1PM	0	0	1	0	0	0	1	1	0	1	0	0
RAIN/MM	274	208	241	277	282	221	165	203	229	366	389	323
°C AVG MAX	30.1	31.2	31.2	31.2	31.8	31.8	31.2	31.8	31.8	31.2	30.7	30.1
°C AVG MIN	22.9	24.0	23.5	23.5	23.5	23.5	22.9	22.9	23.5	23.5	23.5	22.9
DIURNAL RANGE	7.2	7.2	7.7	7.7	8.3	8.3	8.3	8.9	8.3	7.7	7.2	7.2
S/HEMISPHERE	JUL	AUG	SEP	OCT	NOV	DEC	JAN	FEB	MAR	APR	MAY	JUN

Cultural Recommendations

LIGHT: 1800–2500 fc.

TEMPERATURES: Throughout the year, days average 86–89°F (30–32°C), and nights average 73–75°F (23–24°C), with a diurnal range of 13–16°F (7–9°C). Average highs fluctuate only 3°F (1°C), and average lows vary 2°F (1°C), indicating that plants may not tolerate wide temperature fluctuations.

HUMIDITY: 80–85% year-round.

WATER: Rainfall is heavy all year. Cultivated plants should be kept constantly moist but not soggy. Warm water might be beneficial.

FERTILIZER: ¼–½ recommended strength. A balanced fertilizer should be applied weekly to biweekly throughout the year.

REST PERIOD: Growing conditions should be maintained all year. Water and fertilizer may be reduced somewhat in winter, especially for plants grown in the dark, short-day conditions common in temperate latitudes. Plants should never be allowed to dry completely, however. In the habitat, seasonal light variation is minor.

GROWING MEDIA: Plants may be mounted on tree-fern or cork slabs or potted in small pots filled with any open, fast-draining medium. Repotting may be done anytime new roots are actively growing.

MISCELLANEOUS NOTES: The bloom season shown in the climate table is based on collection reports. The plant was described in 1927 in *Mitt. Inst. Bot. Hamburg* 7:54.

Plant and Flower Information

PLANT SIZE AND TYPE: A 7 in. (18 cm) sympodial epiphyte.

PSEUDOBULB: 7 in. (18 cm) long. The branching stems have obliquely triangular internodes. The leafy stems are flattened.

LEAVES: Many. The triangular leaves are 0.2 in. (0.6 cm) long and laterally flattened. They are rigid and appear warty when dry.

INFLORESCENCE: Short. Inflorescences emerge at the apex of the stem.

FLOWERS: Several per inflorescence. The flowers are 0.4 in. (1 cm) long. They have amber-yellow sepals and petals and a rose lip. The dorsal sepal is triangular, concave, and pointed. Lateral sepals are concave and sickle-shaped. The lanceolate petals are pointed at the tip. The erect, recurved lip contracts to a sharp point.

REFERENCES: 224, 286, 445.

Dendrobium reflexitepalum J. J. Smith

ORIGIN/HABITAT: Sumatra and Java. Plants are found throughout Java, but they are especially common in the western and central regions. They usually grow in lightly forested areas at 1000–3300 ft. (300–1000 m).

CLIMATE: Station #96781, Bandung, Java, Indonesia, Lat. 6.9°S, Long. 107.6°E, at 2430 ft. (741 m). Record extreme temperatures are 94°F (34°C) and 52°F (11°C).

N/HEMISPHERE	JAN	FEB	MAR	APR	MAY	JUN	JUL	AUG	SEP	OCT	NOV	DEC
°F AVG MAX	82	83	84	84	82	81	81	80	81	82	82	82
°F AVG MIN	63	63	64	65	66	67	67	67	67	67	66	64
DIURNAL RANGE	19	20	20	19	16	14	14	13	14	15	16	18
RAIN/INCHES	2.7	2.2	2.0	6.0	7.9	8.5	9.5	10.0	9.4	5.6	4.6	4.0
HUMIDITY/%	70	66	62	65	73	77	79	78	78	78	75	72
BLOOM SEASON	*	*	*	*						*	*	*
DAYS CLR @ 7AM	9	10	12	9	4	1	1	1	2	4	5	8
DAYS CLR @ 1PM	8	8	7	2	1	0	0	1	1	1	3	6
RAIN/MM	69	56	51	152	201	216	241	254	239	142	117	102
°C AVG MAX	27.8	28.3	28.9	28.9	27.8	27.2	27.2	26.7	27.2	27.8	27.8	27.8
°C AVG MIN	17.2	17.2	17.8	18.3	18.9	19.4	19.4	19.4	19.4	19.4	18.9	17.8
DIURNAL RANGE	10.6	11.1	11.1	10.6	8.9	7.8	7.8	7.3	7.8	8.4	8.9	10.0
S/HEMISPHERE	JUL	AUG	SEP	OCT	NOV	DEC	JAN	FEB	MAR	APR	MAY	JUN

Cultural Recommendations

LIGHT: 3000–4000 fc. Diffused light is suggested, as clear, summer days are very rare. Plants are normally found on forest trees, but they may also grow fully exposed to available light.

TEMPERATURES: Throughout the year, days average 80–84°F (27–29°C), and nights average 63–67°F (17–19°C), with a diurnal range of 13–20°F (7–11°C). The diurnal range is lowest in summer, when overcast skies prevent warming.

HUMIDITY: Near 80% in summer, dropping to 60–65% in winter and spring.

WATER: Rainfall is moderate to heavy most of the year, but conditions are relatively dry in winter. Cultivated plants should be kept moist but not soggy from spring to early autumn. Water should be gradually reduced in late autumn.

FERTILIZER: ¼–½ recommended strength, applied weekly. A high-nitrogen fertilizer is beneficial from spring to midsummer, but a fertilizer high in phosphates should be used in late summer and autumn.

REST PERIOD: Growing conditions should be maintained all year. The increased diurnal range results from both warmer days and cooler nights. Water and fertilizer should be reduced for 2–3 months in winter. Plants should be allowed to dry slightly between waterings, but they should not remain dry for long periods. In the habitat, winter light is highest.

GROWING MEDIA: Mounting plants on tree-fern or cork slabs accommodates their pendulous growth habit. However, humidity must be high and plants must be watered at least once a day in summer. If plants cannot be mounted, hanging pots or baskets may be filled with an open, fast-draining medium. Repotting may be done anytime new roots are actively growing.

MISCELLANEOUS NOTES: The bloom season shown in the climate table is based on reports from the habitat.

Plant and Flower Information

PLANT SIZE AND TYPE: A 16 in. (40 cm) sympodial epiphyte.

PSEUDOBULB: 16 in. (40 cm) long. Stems are erect when young but become pendulous as they mature.

LEAVES: Many. The leaves are about 1 in. (3 cm) long on the lower part of the stem, but they are smaller near the apex. The ovate leaves are pointed at the apex. They are normally green, but the leaves become dark red when grown in high light.

INFLORESCENCE: Very short. Flowers usually arise from the leaf bracts on the leafless, apical extensions of the stem, but they may also appear from between the leaves.

FLOWERS: 1 per inflorescence. The flowers are 0.2 in. (0.5 cm) across. The blossoms are usually deep pink, but some clones are white with a faint pink flush. The white lip may have a purple margin. When the flower first opens, only the petals and upper sepal are reflexed, but in time, the lateral sepals also curl back. The 3-lobed lip has very small, erect, reddish sidelobes and a deeply notched midlobe.

REFERENCES: 25, 75, 223, 445.

PHOTOS/DRAWINGS: 75.

Dendrobium refractum Teijsm. and Binnend.

AKA: Seidenfaden (ref. 454) discusses the taxonomic difficulties surrounding the names *D. ellipsophyllum* Tang and Wang, *D. refractum* Teijsm. and Binn., *D. revolutum* Lindley, and *D. uniflorum* Griffith. He suggests that the plants might be considered a highly variable alliance rather than individual species.

ORIGIN/HABITAT: Lampong, Sumatra.

CLIMATE: Station #48665, Melaka (Malacca), Malaya, Lat. 2.3°N, Long. 102.3°E, at 40 ft. (12 m). Record extreme temperatures are 99°F (37°C) and 61°F (16°C).

N/HEMISPHERE	JAN	FEB	MAR	APR	MAY	JUN	JUL	AUG	SEP	OCT	NOV	DEC
°F AVG MAX	88	89	89	89	89	88	88	88	88	88	88	88
°F AVG MIN	72	72	72	73	73	73	72	72	72	72	72	72
DIURNAL RANGE	16	17	17	16	16	15	16	16	16	16	16	16
RAIN/INCHES	3.9	3.7	4.9	7.4	6.8	7.9	7.8	10.3	8.8	10.1	8.7	6.5
HUMIDITY/%	79	79	82	85	85	83	84	84	84	84	84	82
BLOOM SEASON	N/A											
DAYS CLR @ 7AM	1	1	1	1	1	1	2	1	1	1	0	1
DAYS CLR @ 1PM	1	1	1	1	1	1	1	1	1	0	0	0
RAIN/MM	99	94	124	188	173	201	198	262	224	257	221	165
°C AVG MAX	31.1	31.7	31.7	31.7	31.7	31.1	31.1	31.1	31.1	31.1	31.1	31.1
°C AVG MIN	22.2	22.2	22.2	22.8	22.8	22.8	22.2	22.2	22.2	22.2	22.2	22.2
DIURNAL RANGE	8.9	9.5	9.5	8.9	8.9	8.3	8.9	8.9	8.9	8.9	8.9	8.9
S/HEMISPHERE	JUL	AUG	SEP	OCT	NOV	DEC	JAN	FEB	MAR	APR	MAY	JUN

Cultural Recommendations

LIGHT: 2000–3000 fc.

TEMPERATURES: Throughout the year, days average 88–89°F (31–32°C), and nights average 72–73°F (22–23°C), with a diurnal range of 15–17°F (8–10°C).

HUMIDITY: 80–85% year-round.

WATER: Rainfall is heavy all year, but conditions are slightly drier for 2 months in winter. Cultivated plants should be kept evenly moist with only slight drying allowed between waterings.

FERTILIZER: ¼–½ recommended strength. A balanced fertilizer should be applied weekly to biweekly throughout the year.

REST PERIOD: Growing conditions should be maintained all year. Water and fertilizer might be reduced somewhat in winter, especially for plants cultivated in the dark, short-day conditions common in temperate latitudes. Plants should never be allowed to dry out completely, however. In the habitat, seasonal light variation is minor.

GROWING MEDIA: Plants may be mounted on tree-fern or cork slabs if humidity is high and plants are watered at least once daily in summer. When plants are potted, any open, fast-draining medium may be used. Repotting may be done anytime new roots are growing.

Plant and Flower Information

PLANT SIZE AND TYPE: A sympodial epiphyte of unreported size.

PSEUDOBULB: The upper portion of the stem is leafy.

LEAVES: Several. The leaves are 1.6 in. (4 cm) long and unequally bilobed at the tip.

FLOWERS: 1 per inflorescence. The flowers are 0.4–0.6 in. (1.0–1.5 cm) across. Sepals and petals are reflexed. The flat, 3-lobed lip is decorated with 7 keels. It projects forward.

REFERENCES: 12, 216, 254, 454.

PHOTOS/DRAWINGS: 454.

Dendrobium regale Schlechter. Now considered a synonym of *Diplocaulobium regale* (Schlechter) A. Hawkes. The red flowered form has blossoms that last 3 days, but the blossoms of the white flowered form lasts a single day. REFERENCES: 92, 221, 229, 437, 445, 470, 486. PHOTOS/DRAWINGS: *383*.

Dendrobium regium Prain

ORIGIN/HABITAT: India. Plants grow in the Orissa region and in Chota Nagpur, an area in southwestern Bihar.

CLIMATE: Station #42701, Ranchi, India, Lat. 23.3°N, Long. 85.3°E, at 2146 ft. (654 m). Record extreme temperatures are not available for this location, but records from nearby stations indicate that extreme highs are probably above 100°F (38°C), and lows are probably near 35°F (2°C).

N/HEMISPHERE	JAN	FEB	MAR	APR	MAY	JUN	JUL	AUG	SEP	OCT	NOV	DEC
°F AVG MAX	72	77	86	95	95	90	84	83	84	83	78	73
°F AVG MIN	51	55	64	71	75	75	73	72	71	65	58	52
DIURNAL RANGE	21	22	22	24	20	15	11	11	13	18	20	21
RAIN/INCHES	0.8	1.0	0.6	1.2	2.4	7.1	11.8	9.9	7.5	1.4	0.4	0.5
HUMIDITY/%	N/A											
BLOOM SEASON				**	**	**						
DAYS CLR	N/A											
RAIN/MM	21	26	15	29	62	181	300	252	192	35	11	12
°C AVG MAX	22.2	24.8	30.1	34.8	35.2	32.3	28.7	28.2	29.0	28.2	25.4	22.7
°C AVG MIN	10.7	12.9	17.5	21.6	24.0	23.7	22.7	22.2	21.9	18.6	14.6	11.3
DIURNAL RANGE	11.5	11.9	12.6	13.2	11.2	8.6	6.0	6.0	7.1	9.6	10.8	11.4
S/HEMISPHERE	JUL	AUG	SEP	OCT	NOV	DEC	JAN	FEB	MAR	APR	MAY	JUN

Cultural Recommendations

LIGHT: 2000–3000 fc. The heavy summer cloud cover indicates that some shading is needed from spring through autumn, but light should be as high as the plant can tolerate, short of burning the leaves. Strong air movement should be provided all year.

TEMPERATURES: Summer days average 83–90°F (28–32°C), and nights average 72–75°F (22–24°C), with a diurnal range of 11–15°F (6–9°C). Spring is the warmest season. Days average 86–95°F (30–35°C), and nights average 64–75°F (18–24°C), with a diurnal range of 20–24°F (11–13°C). Temperatures this warm are not necessary for cultivated plants. The important aspect is the warm, moist growing conditions following the cool, dry winter rest.

HUMIDITY: Information is not available for this location. However, records from nearby locations indicate that humidity probably averages near 80% in summer, dropping to near 60% in autumn and early winter. Humidity in the region drops to 35–50% for about 3 months in late winter and spring, and even moisture from dew is uncommon during this very dry period.

WATER: Rainfall is heavy for 4–5 months during the summer monsoon, but conditions are very dry from late autumn into spring. While actively growing, cultivated plants should be kept moist, with only slight drying allowed between waterings. Water should be gradually reduced after new growths mature in autumn.

FERTILIZER: ¼–½ recommended strength, applied weekly. A high-nitrogen fertilizer is beneficial from spring to midsummer, but a fertilizer high in phosphates should be used in late summer and autumn.

REST PERIOD: Winter days average 72–77°F (22–25°C), and nights average 51–55°F (11–13°C), with a diurnal range of 21–22°F (12°C). Water and fertilizer should be reduced for 3–5 months in winter and early spring. Plants should be allowed to dry out between waterings, but they should not remain completely dry for extended periods. Occasional early morning mistings between waterings may be beneficial if stems start to shrivel. Water and fertilizer should be gradually increased and shading provided as new growth starts in spring. In the habitat, skies are clear and light is high in winter.

GROWING MEDIA: Plants may be mounted on tree-fern or cork slabs if humidity is high and plants are watered at least once daily in summer. When plants are potted, any open, fast-draining medium may be used. Repotting is best done in early spring when new roots are growing.

MISCELLANEOUS NOTES: The bloom season shown in the climate table is based on reports from the habitat. Cultivated plants bloom most heavily in summer.

Plant and Flower Information

PLANT SIZE AND TYPE: A 22 in. (55 cm) sympodial epiphyte, terrestrial, or lithophyte.

PSEUDOBULB: 18 in. (45 cm) long. The fleshy, stem-like pseudobulbs may be erect to arching.

LEAVES: The lanceolate leaves are usually 4 in. (10 cm) long. They are most often deciduous.

INFLORESCENCE: 3 in. (7.5 cm) long. The inflorescences emerge near the apex of the pseudobulb.

FLOWERS: 2–3 per inflorescence. The flowers are 3 in. (7.5 cm) across. Sepals and petals are rosy-red, fading to white at the base. Sepals are oblong and rounded. The petals are elliptic and rounded. The lip is darker magenta red in the throat with a cream or yellow disk. The 3-lobed lip has a small midlobe. The sidelobes curve in to form a tube. The fragrant blossoms are heavy-textured and long-lived. Although closely related to *D. nobile* Lindley, *D. regium* has yellow on the lip and lacks the deep purple in the throat.

HYBRIDIZING NOTES: Chromosome count is $2n = 38$ (ref. 504, 580).

REFERENCES: 38, 46, 179, 190, 210, 219, 254, 389, 445, 504, 580.

PHOTOS/DRAWINGS: 210, *389*.

Dendrobium reineckei Schlechter

AKA: *D. gemellum* as used by Kränzlin not Lindley.

ORIGIN/HABITAT: Upolu Island, Samoa near the Letogo River. A single collection was made near Taveuni, Fiji where the plant grew on moss-covered rocks at about 2750 ft. (840 m).

CLIMATE: Station #91762, Apia, Western Samoa, Lat. 13.8°S, Long. 171.8°W, at 7 ft. (2 m). Temperatures are calculated for an elevation of 2750 ft. (840 m), resulting in probable extremes of 84°F (29°C) and 54°F (12°C).

N/HEMISPHERE	JAN	FEB	MAR	APR	MAY	JUN	JUL	AUG	SEP	OCT	NOV	DEC
°F AVG MAX	76	75	75	76	77	76	77	76	77	77	76	76
°F AVG MIN	65	66	65	66	65	65	66	67	65	66	65	65
DIURNAL RANGE	11	9	10	10	12	11	11	9	12	11	11	11
RAIN/INCHES	3.2	3.5	5.2	6.7	10.5	14.6	17.9	15.2	14.1	10.0	6.3	5.1
HUMIDITY/%	76	75	75	77	77	78	81	80	80	78	77	75
BLOOM SEASON									*			
DAYS CLR @ 1PM	9	10	9	6	3	3	4	2	3	5	9	10
DAYS CLR @ 7PM	12	10	11	7	4	3	2	2	2	5	11	8
RAIN/MM	81	89	132	170	267	371	455	386	358	254	160	130
°C AVG MAX	24.4	23.9	23.9	24.4	25.0	24.4	25.0	24.4	25.0	25.0	24.4	24.4
°C AVG MIN	18.3	18.9	18.3	18.9	18.3	18.3	18.9	19.4	18.3	18.9	18.3	18.3
DIURNAL RANGE	6.1	5.0	5.6	5.5	6.7	6.1	6.1	5.0	6.7	6.1	6.1	6.1
S/HEMISPHERE	JUL	AUG	SEP	OCT	NOV	DEC	JAN	FEB	MAR	APR	MAY	JUN

Cultural Recommendations

LIGHT: 2000–3000 fc

TEMPERATURES: Throughout the year, days average 75–77°F (24–25°C), and nights average 65–67°F (18–19°C), with a diurnal range of 9–12°F (5–7°C).

HUMIDITY: 75–80% year-round.

WATER: Rainfall is moderate to heavy all year, but conditions are slightly drier for 2–3 months in winter. Cultivated plants should be kept moist, with only slight drying allowed between waterings.

FERTILIZER: ¼–½ recommended strength. A balanced fertilizer should be applied weekly to biweekly throughout the year.

REST PERIOD: Growing temperatures should be maintained all year. Water should be reduced somewhat for cultivated plants, especially those grown in the dark, short-day conditions common during temperate-latitude winters. Plants should be allowed to dry slightly between waterings, but they should never dry out completely. In the habitat, light is highest in winter.

GROWING MEDIA: Plants may be mounted on tree-fern or cork slabs if humidity is high and plants are watered at least once daily in summer. When plants are potted, any open, fast-draining medium may be used. Repotting may be done anytime new roots are growing.

MISCELLANEOUS NOTES: The bloom season shown in the climate table is based on collection reports.

Plant and Flower Information

PLANT SIZE AND TYPE: A 39 in. (100 cm) sympodial epiphyte or lithophyte.

PSEUDOBULB: 39 in. (100 cm) long, sometimes smaller. The hard, reedlike stems are smooth and shiny. They are close together and arise from a very short rhizome. The upper part of each stem is leafy.

LEAVES: Many. The linear-lanceolate leaves are 3–6 in. (8–15 cm) long and taper toward the tip. They are papery and nearly erect.

INFLORESCENCE: 0.5 in. (1.3 cm) long. Many inflorescences are borne at nodes opposite the leaves. Developing inflorescences are covered by enlarged, curved sheaths.

FLOWERS: 2 per inflorescence. Blossoms are 1.6 in. (4 cm) long and remain rather closed. Sepals and petals, which taper to a threadlike point, are white with numerous red to pink spots. The 3-lobed lip is fringed on the side of the narrowly triangular midlobe. It has one prominent raised line and 2 minor lines. The short-lived flowers may last from a few hours to a few days.

REFERENCES: 221, 434, 466.

Dendrobium reinwardtii Lindley. See *D. purpureum* Roxburgh. REFERENCES: 216, 254, 278, 310, Dauncey and Cribb 1993 *Kew Bulletin* 48(3).

Dendrobium remiforme J. J. Smith

ORIGIN/HABITAT: Irian Jaya (western New Guinea). Plants grow on forest trees in the Arfak Mountains at about 1950 ft. (600 m).

CLIMATE: Station #97530, Manokwari, Irian Jaya, Lat. 0.9°S, Long. 134.1°E, at 10 ft. (3 m). Temperatures are calculated for an elevation of 1950 ft. (600 m), resulting in probable extremes of 87°F (30°C) and 62°F (16°C).

N/HEMISPHERE	JAN	FEB	MAR	APR	MAY	JUN	JUL	AUG	SEP	OCT	NOV	DEC
°F AVG MAX	80	79	81	81	82	80	80	80	80	80	80	79
°F AVG MIN	68	69	68	68	68	69	67	67	68	68	68	68
DIURNAL RANGE	12	10	13	13	14	11	13	13	12	12	12	11
RAIN/INCHES	5.4	5.6	5.0	4.7	4.5	10.3	12.0	9.4	13.2	11.1	7.8	7.3
HUMIDITY/%	87	87	86	84	85	86	86	85	86	86	86	85
BLOOM SEASON				*								
DAYS CLR @ 9AM	4	3	3	5	3	3	3	1	1	2	3	7
DAYS CLR @ 3PM	2	2	2	3	1	1	1	1	0	1	0	2
RAIN/MM	137	142	127	119	114	262	305	239	335	282	198	185
°C AVG MAX	26.4	25.9	27.0	27.0	27.6	26.4	26.4	26.4	26.4	26.4	26.4	25.9
°C AVG MIN	19.8	20.3	19.8	19.8	19.8	20.3	19.2	19.2	19.8	19.8	19.8	19.8
DIURNAL RANGE	6.6	5.6	7.2	7.2	7.8	6.1	7.2	7.2	6.6	6.6	6.6	6.1
S/HEMISPHERE	JUL	AUG	SEP	OCT	NOV	DEC	JAN	FEB	MAR	APR	MAY	JUN

Cultural Recommendations

LIGHT: 2000–3000 fc.

TEMPERATURES: Throughout the year, days average 79–82°F (26–28°C), and nights average 67–69°F (19–20°C), with a diurnal range of 10–14°F (6–8°C).

HUMIDITY: Near 85% year-round.

WATER: Rainfall is heavy all year, but conditions are slightly drier in winter and spring. Cultivated plants should be kept moist, with only slight drying allowed between waterings.

FERTILIZER: ¼–½ recommended strength. A balanced fertilizer should be applied weekly to biweekly throughout the year.

REST PERIOD: Growing conditions should be maintained all year. Water and fertilizer may be reduced somewhat in winter, especially for plants grown in the dark, short-day conditions common in temperate latitudes. Plants should never be allowed to dry out completely, however. In the habitat, light is slightly higher in winter.

GROWING MEDIA: Plants may be mounted on tree-fern slabs or potted in any open, fast-draining medium. Repotting may be done anytime new roots are growing.

MISCELLANEOUS NOTES: The bloom season shown in the climate table is based on reports from the habitat.

Plant and Flower Information

PLANT SIZE AND TYPE: A 12–16 in. (30–40 cm) sympodial epiphyte.

PSEUDOBULB: 10–12 in. (25–30 cm) long. The clustered stems are slender on the lower part, but they become swollen and flattened on the upper part.

LEAVES: 7 per growth. The oblong, pointed leaves are 2.8–4.0 in. (7–10 cm) long.

INFLORESCENCE: 1 in. (2.5 cm) long. Inflorescences are pendulous and emerge at the leaf axis.

FLOWERS: 3–6 per inflorescence. The flowers are 1.1 in. (2.8 cm) long. They are yellowish white with brown longitudinal stripes on the lip. The oblong sepals and lanceolate petals end abruptly in a short point. The 3-lobed lip is minutely ruffled along the margin with erect, roundly triangular sidelobes.

REFERENCES: 221, 445, 470, 476.

Dendrobium remotisepalum J. J. Smith

ORIGIN/HABITAT: Northern Irian Jaya (western New Guinea). Plants were originally found on the east side of a ridge leading to Mt. Doorman at about 4650 ft. (1420 m). They grow in thin, moss-covered *Vaccinium* forests.

CLIMATE: Station #97686, Wamena, New Guinea, Lat. 4.1°S, Long. 139.0°E, at 5446 ft. (1660 m). Temperatures are calculated for an elevation of 4400 ft. (1340 m). Record extreme temperatures are not available for this location.

N/HEMISPHERE	JAN	FEB	MAR	APR	MAY	JUN	JUL	AUG	SEP	OCT	NOV	DEC
°F AVG MAX	78	79	80	79	80	79	80	79	79	82	81	77
°F AVG MIN	63	63	65	65	66	67	66	65	66	68	68	64
DIURNAL RANGE	15	16	15	14	14	12	14	14	13	14	13	13
RAIN/INCHES	3.0	1.9	2.2	4.0	4.6	3.3	2.8	4.2	6.9	3.9	5.4	4.9
HUMIDITY/%	N/A											
BLOOM SEASON				*								
DAYS CLR	N/A											
RAIN/MM	76	48	56	102	117	84	71	107	175	99	137	124
°C AVG MAX	25.8	26.4	26.9	26.4	26.9	26.4	26.9	26.4	26.4	28.0	27.5	25.3
°C AVG MIN	17.5	17.5	18.6	18.6	19.1	19.7	19.1	18.6	19.1	20.3	20.3	18.0
DIURNAL RANGE	8.3	8.9	8.3	7.8	7.8	6.7	7.8	7.8	7.3	7.7	7.2	7.3
S/HEMISPHERE	JUL	AUG	SEP	OCT	NOV	DEC	JAN	FEB	MAR	APR	MAY	JUN

Cultural Recommendations

LIGHT: 2000–3000 fc. In the habitat, light is highest in the morning.

TEMPERATURES: Throughout the year, days average 78–82°F (26–28°C), and nights average 63–68°F (18–20°C), with a diurnal range of 12–16°F (7–9°C). Autumn is the warmest time of year. In the habitat, the warmest temperatures of the day occur in late morning when skies are clear. Clouds and mist develop near noon, thus preventing additional warming.

Dendrobium rennellii

HUMIDITY: Information is not available for this location. However, records from nearby stations indicate that humidity probably averages near 80% year-round. High humidity and excellent air circulation are particularly important if temperatures are warm. Placing the plants in front of an evaporative cooler or near a fine mist may be very beneficial.

WATER: Rainfall is moderate through most of the year; but in the habitat, it is probably greater than indicated in the climate table. In addition, large amounts of water are available from mist and heavy dew, even during periods of lower rainfall. Cultivated plants should be kept moist. Good air movement is critically important and should be maintained at all times.

FERTILIZER: 1/4–1/2 recommended strength. A balanced fertilizer should be applied weekly to biweekly throughout the year. The Royal Botanic Garden in Edinburgh uses a dilute, seaweed-based fertilizer.

REST PERIOD: Growing conditions should be maintained all year. Conditions are slightly drier for 1–2 months in winter. In cultivation, water may be decreased somewhat, but plants should never be allowed to dry out completely. In the habitat, light is slightly higher in winter.

GROWING MEDIA: Plants may be mounted on tree-fern or cork slabs, but high humidity must be maintained and plants must be watered daily in summer. When plants are potted, any open, fast-draining medium may be used. Repotting may be done anytime new roots are growing.

MISCELLANEOUS NOTES: The bloom season shown in the climate table is based on reports from the habitat.

Plant and Flower Information

PLANT SIZE AND TYPE: A very small sympodial epiphyte. Plants are usually less than 1 in. (2.5 cm) tall.

PSEUDOBULB: Very small. The light green, somewhat ovoid pseudobulbs are borne on a very short, branching rhizome.

LEAVES: 1 per growth. The leaves are 0.5–0.8 in. (1.3–2.0 cm) long. They are dark green with occasional red dots on the upper surface and lighter green on the underside.

INFLORESCENCE: Short. 1–2 inflorescences are borne behind the leaf.

FLOWERS: 1 per inflorescence. The flowers are 0.3 in. (0.7 cm) across. The front sides of the sepals and petals are white with dark red dots on the back of the sepals. The 3-lobed lip is dirty white with a rounded midlobe and narrow sidelobes that are united by a transverse bar.

REFERENCES: 224, 445, 470.

Dendrobium rennellii Cribb

ORIGIN/HABITAT: The Solomon Islands. Plants are found on Rennell and Bellona Islands, which are raised coral islands in the Coral Sea south of Guadalcanal. These endemic plants grow on trees and bare rock on coral islets from sea level to 330 ft. (0–100 m).

CLIMATE: Station #91520, Honiara, Guadalcanal, Solomon Islands, Lat. 9.4°S, Long. 160.6°E, at 10 ft. (3 m). Record extreme temperatures are 95°F (35°C) and 65°F (18°C).

N/HEMISPHERE	JAN	FEB	MAR	APR	MAY	JUN	JUL	AUG	SEP	OCT	NOV	DEC
°F AVG MAX	86	87	88	88	88	88	88	88	87	88	88	87
°F AVG MIN	72	72	72	72	73	73	74	74	73	73	73	72
DIURNAL RANGE	14	15	16	16	15	15	14	14	14	15	15	15
RAIN/INCHES	6.0	4.4	4.6	7.7	7.7	9.5	14.1	13.3	16.7	10.6	8.1	6.7
HUMIDITY/%	84	82	81	80	81	82	83	83	87	85	85	85
BLOOM SEASON	N/A											
DAYS CLR @ 5AM	6	7	7	5	6	4	3	3	4	4	8	7
DAYS CLR @ 11AM	3	2	2	1	1	1	1	0	2	2	4	4
RAIN/MM	152	112	117	196	196	241	358	338	424	269	206	170
°C AVG MAX	30.0	30.6	31.1	31.1	31.1	31.1	31.1	31.1	30.6	31.1	31.1	30.6
°C AVG MIN	22.2	22.2	22.2	22.2	22.8	22.8	23.3	23.3	22.8	22.8	22.8	22.2
DIURNAL RANGE	7.8	8.4	8.9	8.9	8.3	8.3	7.8	7.8	7.8	8.3	8.3	8.4
S/HEMISPHERE	JUL	AUG	SEP	OCT	NOV	DEC	JAN	FEB	MAR	APR	MAY	JUN

Cultural Recommendations

LIGHT: 3000–4000 fc.

TEMPERATURES: Throughout the year, days average 86–88°F (30–31°C), and nights average 72–74°F (22–23°C), with a diurnal range of 14–16°F (8–9°C).

HUMIDITY: 80–85% year-round.

WATER: Rainfall is heavy all year, but for 2–3 months in winter, conditions are slightly drier. Cultivated plants should be kept moist with only slight drying allowed between waterings.

FERTILIZER: 1/4–1/2 recommended strength. A balanced fertilizer should be applied weekly to biweekly throughout the year.

REST PERIOD: Growing conditions should be maintained year-round. Water and fertilizer may be reduced somewhat for cultivated plants in winter, especially those grown in the dark, short-day conditions common in temperate latitudes. Plants should never be allowed to dry out completely, however.

GROWING MEDIA: Plants may be mounted on tree-fern or cork slabs if humidity is high and plants are watered at least once daily in summer. When plants are potted, any open, fast-draining medium may be used. Repotting may be done anytime new roots are growing.

MISCELLANEOUS NOTES: Growers report that plants are often in bloom much of the year. They reproduce vegetatively by forming keikis.

Plant and Flower Information

PLANT SIZE AND TYPE: A 28 in. (70 cm) sympodial epiphyte.

PSEUDOBULB: 28 in. (70 cm) long. The cane-like stems are yellow with dark maroon stripes.

LEAVES: Many. The narrowly elliptical leaves are 4.3 in. (11 cm) long.

INFLORESCENCE: 12 in. (30 cm) long. Inflorescences may be arching or suberect.

FLOWERS: 5–15 per inflorescence. The attractive flowers are 2.0–2.4 in. (5–6 cm) long. Blossoms are white or creamy white with prominent purple veins on the lip. The lanceolate dorsal sepal is somewhat recurved. The petals are nearly erect and may be twisted once. The lip is 3-lobed with a pointed, elliptic-oblong midlobe. The sidelobes are erect, elliptic-oblong, and rounded. The callus consists of 3 longitudinal ridges. Blossoms are fragrant.

HYBRIDIZING NOTES: *D. rennellii* is known to hybridize naturally with *D. sylvanum* Rchb. f. not Kränzlin.

REFERENCES: 82, 84, 86, 234, 271, 516, 526, 551.

PHOTOS/DRAWINGS: *84, 86, 271, 551.*

Dendrobium reptans Franch. and Sav. Now considered a synonym of *Eria reptans* (Franch. and Sav.) Makino. REFERENCES: 139, 216, 254, 275, 279.

Dendrobium reptans Ridley not Swartz. See *D. humifusum* Kränzlin. REFERENCES: 218, 254, 393.

Dendrobium reptans Swartz not Ridley. Now considered a synonym of *Bulbophyllum nutans* Thouars. REFERENCES: 216, 254.

Dendrobium reticulatum J. J. Smith. See *D. spectatissimum* Rchb. f. REFERENCES: 12, 221, 286, 295, 429, 430.

Dendrobium retroflexum J. J. Smith. See *D. vexillarius* Schlechter. REFERENCES: 221, 385, 445, 470, 538. PHOTOS/DRAWINGS: 538.

Dendrobium retusum Llave and Lexarza. Now considered a synonym of *Pleurothallis retusa* Lindley. REFERENCES: 216, 254.

Dendrobium retusum Llanos. Status unknown. Merrill (ref. 296) and Valmayor (ref. 536) indicate that *D. retusum* Llanos may be a synonym of *D. anosmum* Lindley. REFERENCES: 216, 296, 536.

Dendrobium revolutum Hooker f. not Lindley. Merrill (ref. 296) and Valmayor (ref. 536) include this name as a synonym of *D. uniflorum* Griffith, but Tang and Wang (ref. 505) include it as a synonym of *D. ellipsophyllum* T. Tang and F. T. Wang. REFERENCES: 296, 505, 536.

Dendrobium revolutum Lindley not Hooker f.

AKA: Seidenfaden (ref. 454) discusses the taxonomic status of this plant and concludes that *D. revolutum* is an extremely rare plant from Malaya. Although often considered synonymous or confused with *D. uniflorum* Griffith, Schelpe (ref. 429) suggested that *D. revolutum* Lindley not Hooker f. would prove to be a synonym of *D. parthenium* Rchb. f. See note at *D. refractum* Teijsm. and Binnend.

ORIGIN/HABITAT: Singapore and Malaya near Batu Pahat in Johore state. Seidenfaden and Wood (ref. 455) state that this is a rare plant that has been found only in the listed area and that records from other areas refer to *D. uniflorum* Griffith.

CLIMATE: Station #48665, Melaka (Malacca), Malaya, Lat. 2.3°N, Long. 102.3°E, at 40 ft. (12 m). Record extreme temperatures are 99°F (37°C) and 61°F (16°C).

N/HEMISPHERE	JAN	FEB	MAR	APR	MAY	JUN	JUL	AUG	SEP	OCT	NOV	DEC
°F AVG MAX	88	89	89	89	89	88	88	88	88	88	88	88
°F AVG MIN	72	72	72	73	73	73	72	72	72	72	72	72
DIURNAL RANGE	16	17	17	16	16	15	16	16	16	16	16	16
RAIN/INCHES	3.9	3.7	4.9	7.4	6.8	7.9	7.8	10.3	8.8	10.1	8.7	6.5
HUMIDITY/%	79	79	82	85	85	83	84	84	84	84	84	82
BLOOM SEASON			*		*		*		*			
DAYS CLR @ 7AM	1	1	1	1	1	2	1	1	1	1	0	1
DAYS CLR @ 1PM	1	1	1	1	1	1	1	1	1	1	0	0
RAIN/MM	99	94	124	188	173	201	198	262	224	257	221	165
°C AVG MAX	31.1	31.7	31.7	31.7	31.7	31.1	31.1	31.1	31.1	31.1	31.1	31.1
°C AVG MIN	22.2	22.2	22.2	22.8	22.8	22.8	22.2	22.2	22.2	22.2	22.2	22.2
DIURNAL RANGE	8.9	9.5	9.5	8.9	8.9	8.3	8.9	8.9	8.9	8.9	8.9	8.9
S/HEMISPHERE	JUL	AUG	SEP	OCT	NOV	DEC	JAN	FEB	MAR	APR	MAY	JUN

Cultural Recommendations

LIGHT: 2000–3000 fc.

TEMPERATURES: Throughout the year, days average 88–89°F (31–32°C), and nights average 72–73°F (22–23°C), with a diurnal range of 15–17°F (8–10°C).

HUMIDITY: 80–85% year-round.

WATER: Rainfall is moderate to heavy all year, but conditions are slightly drier for 2 months in winter. Cultivated plants should be kept evenly moist, with only slight drying allowed between waterings.

FERTILIZER: ¼–½ recommended strength. A balanced fertilizer should be applied weekly to biweekly throughout the year.

REST PERIOD: Growing conditions should be maintained all year. Water and fertilizer might be reduced somewhat in winter, especially for plants cultivated in the dark, short-day conditions common in temperate latitudes. Plants should never be allowed to dry out completely, however. In the habitat, seasonal light variation is minor.

GROWING MEDIA: Plants may be mounted on tree-fern or cork slabs if humidity is high and plants are watered at least once daily in summer. When plants are potted, any open, fast-draining medium may be used. Repotting may be done anytime new roots are growing.

MISCELLANEOUS NOTES: The bloom season shown in the climate table is based on cultivation records and should be considered questionable. Seidenfaden (ref. 454) indicates that the true *D. revolutum* is very rare, so these reports may apply to other plants.

Plant and Flower Information

PLANT SIZE AND TYPE: An 18–24 in. (45–60 cm) sympodial epiphyte.

PSEUDOBULB: 18–24 in. (45–60 cm) long. The stems have internodes at 0.4–0.8 in. (1–2 cm) intervals.

LEAVES: Many. The stems are densely leafy. The distichous leaves are 1.2–2.0 in. (3–5 cm) long. They are linear-oblong, very close together, slightly narrowed at the base, and somewhat triangular at the tip.

INFLORESCENCE: Short. Inflorescences emerge from the side of the stem near the base of the leaves.

FLOWERS: 1, rarely 2 per inflorescence. The lateral sepals are 0.8 in. (2 cm) long, but other segments are shorter. Sepals and petals are white. The lip may be dull orange to brownish with dark orange keels on the disk. The dorsal sepal and petals are recurved. The large, fleshy lip has small, triangular sidelobes and 4 raised, full-length lines with a partial central line near the tip.

HYBRIDIZING NOTES: Chromosome count is reported as 2n = 40 (ref. 151, 187, 504, 580).

REFERENCES: 151, 187, 190, 200, 202, 210, 216, 254, 296, 317, 395, 402, 429, 445, 448, 454, 455, 504, 580.

PHOTOS/DRAWINGS: 210, 454, 455.

Dendrobium rex M. Clements and D. Jones

AKA: Considered by many to be part of the *D. speciosum* alliance, but Clements (ref. 67) lists it as an independent species and includes the synonyms *D. speciosum* var. *grandiflorum* F. M. Bailey, *D. speciosum* var. *hilli* F. M. Bailey forma *grandiflorum* (F. M. Bailey) F. M. Bailey. In Australia, *D. rex* is commonly called the golden king orchid. Also see discussion at *D. speciosum*.

ORIGIN/HABITAT: Australia in southeastern Queensland. Plants are found from near Brisbane to Gladstone and as far west as Toowoomba. They were originally found growing 75 miles (120 km) north of Brisbane in the same type of habitat as *D. speciosum*. They are frequently found on rocks in open forest, but they also grow on trees in some rainforest areas.

CLIMATE: Station #94551, Toowoomba, Australia, Lat. 27.6°S, Long. 152.0°E, at 1921 ft. (586 m). Record extreme temperatures are 105°F (41°C) and 22°F (–6°C).

N/HEMISPHERE	JAN	FEB	MAR	APR	MAY	JUN	JUL	AUG	SEP	OCT	NOV	DEC
°F AVG MAX	61	65	71	76	80	82	82	81	78	74	67	62
°F AVG MIN	41	42	47	52	56	59	61	61	59	52	46	42
DIURNAL RANGE	20	23	24	24	24	23	21	20	19	22	21	20
RAIN/INCHES	2.1	1.6	2.1	2.6	3.3	4.5	5.0	4.5	3.7	2.6	2.1	2.4
HUMIDITY/%	64	56	55	57	54	54	62	67	66	65	63	67
BLOOM SEASON	*	**	**	*							*	*
DAYS CLR	N/A											
RAIN/MM	53	41	53	66	84	114	127	114	94	66	53	61
°C AVG MAX	16.1	18.3	21.7	24.4	26.7	27.8	27.8	27.2	25.6	23.3	19.4	16.7
°C AVG MIN	5.0	5.6	8.3	11.1	13.3	15.0	16.1	16.1	15.0	11.1	7.8	5.6
DIURNAL RANGE	11.1	12.7	13.4	13.3	13.4	12.8	11.7	11.1	10.6	12.2	11.6	11.1
S/HEMISPHERE	JUL	AUG	SEP	OCT	NOV	DEC	JAN	FEB	MAR	APR	MAY	JUN

Cultural Recommendations

LIGHT: 2000–3000 fc. Australian growers report that *D. rex* requires more shade than other members of what has been known as the *D. speciosum* alliance. Plants that bloom the most often have leaves and pseudobulbs that are bleached and leathery.

TEMPERATURES: Summer days average 81–82°F (27–28°C), and nights

Dendrobium rhabdoglossum

average 59–61°F (15–16°C), with a diurnal range of 20–23°F (11–13°C).

HUMIDITY: Near 65% most of the year, dropping to near 55% in winter and spring.

WATER: Rainfall is moderate to heavy in summer, but conditions are drier from autumn through spring. Cultivated plants should be kept moist in summer, with only slight drying allowed between waterings, but water should be reduced in autumn after new growths mature.

FERTILIZER: 1/4–1/2 recommended strength, applied weekly. A high-nitrogen fertilizer is beneficial from spring to midsummer, but a fertilizer high in phosphates should be used in late summer and autumn.

REST PERIOD: Winter days average 61–65°F (16–18°C), and nights average 41–42°F (5–6°C), with a diurnal range of 20–23°F (11–13°C). Cultivated plants require a decidedly dry winter rest. Water should be reduced and the plants allowed to become somewhat dry between waterings. They should not remain dry for extended periods, however. Water should be increased somewhat if plants appear stressed. Reduce or eliminate fertilizer while water is reduced. Plants produce their masses of flowers only if they have been rested properly.

GROWING MEDIA: Plants may be mounted on tree-fern or cork slabs if humidity is high and plants are watered at least once daily in summer. When plants are potted, the medium must be very open and fast-draining. Frequent repotting is necessary because the plants are extremely robust growers. Repotting is best done after flowering is finished in early spring, as this is when new roots are growing.

MISCELLANEOUS NOTES: The bloom season shown in the climate table is based on reports from the habitat. Plants usually bloom in spring, but blooming is sometimes sporadic. *D. rex* is adaptable and very easy to grow, although growers not providing a proper rest period consider it difficult. Old stems should not be removed when repotting, as they continue to flower for several years.

Plant and Flower Information

PLANT SIZE AND TYPE: A 41 in. (105 cm) sympodial epiphyte or lithophyte. The large plant has a growth habit similar to *D. tarberi* M. Clements and D. Jones.

PSEUDOBULB: 31 in. (80 cm) long. The deep green stems are consistently erect, cylindrical to slightly club-shaped, with a narrow base. The stems produce aerial roots.

LEAVES: Several at the apex of each growth. The dark green leaves are 10 in. (25 cm) long, stiff, and leathery.

INFLORESCENCE: Several. The long, densely flowered inflorescences often appear simultaneously from apical nodes. They may be suberect or pendent.

FLOWERS: Many per inflorescence. The star-shaped blossoms are 1.8 in. (4.5 cm) across. They are bright yellow to cream-colored and become deeper yellow with age. The lip, which is smaller than other forms of *D. speciosum,* is heavily marked with mauve-blue.

HYBRIDIZING NOTES: Although members of the *D. speciosum* alliance are seldom self-fertile, Adams (ref. 4) indicates that this plant produces capsules if the post-pollination conditions are warm, but not if conditions are cool. Pollinations between different clones of the same variety and between different varieties commonly produce seed.

REFERENCES: 4, 67, 235, 240.

PHOTOS/DRAWINGS: 240.

Dendrobium rhabdoglossum Schlechter

ORIGIN/HABITAT: Papua New Guinea. Plants grow in the Sepik River region at 4250–4900 ft. (1300–1500 m).

CLIMATE: Station #200004, Ambunti, Papua New Guinea, Lat. 4.2°S, Long. 142.8°E, at 164 ft. (50 m). Temperatures are calculated for an elevation of 4600 ft. (1400 m), resulting in probable extremes of 84°F (29°C) and 37°F (3°C).

N/HEMISPHERE	JAN	FEB	MAR	APR	MAY	JUN	JUL	AUG	SEP	OCT	NOV	DEC
°F AVG MAX	73	75	75	75	76	75	75	75	75	75	75	74
°F AVG MIN	57	58	59	58	58	58	57	58	58	58	58	59
DIURNAL RANGE	16	17	16	17	18	17	18	17	17	17	17	15
RAIN/INCHES	6.4	7.4	7.7	8.5	9.2	9.4	10.9	10.2	12.2	10.4	8.3	5.2
HUMIDITY/%	N/A											
BLOOM SEASON									*	*	*	*
DAYS CLR	N/A											
RAIN/MM	163	188	196	216	234	239	277	259	310	264	211	132
°C AVG MAX	23.0	24.1	24.1	24.1	24.6	24.1	24.1	24.1	24.1	24.1	24.1	23.5
°C AVG MIN	14.1	14.6	15.2	14.6	14.6	14.6	14.1	14.6	14.6	14.6	14.6	15.2
DIURNAL RANGE	8.9	9.5	8.9	9.5	10.0	9.5	10.0	9.5	9.5	9.5	9.5	8.3
S/HEMISPHERE	JUL	AUG	SEP	OCT	NOV	DEC	JAN	FEB	MAR	APR	MAY	JUN

Cultural Recommendations

LIGHT: 2000–3000 fc.

TEMPERATURES: Throughout the year, days average 73–76°F (23–25°C), and nights average 57–59°F (14–15°C), with a diurnal range of 15–18°F (8–10°C).

HUMIDITY: Information is not available for this location. However, records from nearby stations indicate that humidity probably averages near 80% year-round.

WATER: Rainfall is heavy year-round. The greatest amounts fall in summer and early autumn. Cultivated plants should be moist but not soggy.

FERTILIZER: 1/4–1/2 recommended strength. A balanced fertilizer should be applied weekly to biweekly throughout the year.

REST PERIOD: Growing conditions should be maintained all year. Water and fertilizer should be reduced for plants cultivated in the dark, short-day conditions common in temperate-latitude winters, but they should never be allowed to dry out completely. In the habitat, seasonal light variation is minor.

GROWING MEDIA: Plants may be mounted if humidity is high and plants are watered at least once daily in summer. When plants are potted, any open, fast-draining medium may be used. Repotting may be done anytime new roots are growing.

MISCELLANEOUS NOTES: The bloom season shown in the climate table is based on collection reports from the habitat.

Plant and Flower Information

PLANT SIZE AND TYPE: A 12 in. (30 cm) sympodial epiphyte.

PSEUDOBULB: 12 in. (30 cm) long. The leafy stems are slender and fleshy. They become grooved with age. They arise from a very short, branching rhizome.

LEAVES: Many. The leaves are 1.6–2.4 in. (4–6 cm) long, lanceolate, and sharply pointed.

INFLORESCENCE: Short.

FLOWERS: The flowers are 0.5 in. (1.3 cm) long. The sepals and petals may be orange, orange-red, or dark rose-red. The color is paler at the tips. The lip is yellow to gold with dark bluish-red stripes. The dorsal sepal is oblong. The short, oblong-elliptic petals are minutely fringed along the margin. The hooded lip is concave with a blunt apex. It is serrated or toothed along the margin.

REFERENCES: 223, 443.

Dendrobium rhaphiotes Schlechter. See *D. hellwigianum* Kränzlin. REFERENCES: 222, 385.

Dendrobium rhipidolobum Schlechter. Now considered a synonym of *Flickingeria rhipidoloba* (Schlechter) A. Hawkes. REFERENCES: 92, 213, 219, 230, 231, 254, 436, 437, 444, 445, 449, 470, 537.

Dendrobium rhizophoreti Ridley. See *D. lobatum* (Blume) Miquel. REFERENCES: 254, 395, 455, 469.

Dendrobium rhodobalion Schlechter. Now considered a synonym of *Flickingeria rhodobalion* (Schlechter) F. G. Brieger. REFERENCES: 213, 220, 230, 234, 436, 449.

Dendrobium rhodobotrys Ridley

ORIGIN/HABITAT: Irian Jaya (western New Guinea). Plants were collected on the south side of Mt. Jaya (Mt. Carstensz) at 3900–5500 ft. (1190–1680 m).

CLIMATE: Station #97796, Kokenau (Kokonau), Irian Jaya, Lat. 4.7°S, Long. 135.4°E, at 10 ft. (3 m). Temperatures are calculated for an elevation of 4500 ft. (1370 m). Record extreme temperatures are not available for this location.

N/HEMISPHERE	JAN	FEB	MAR	APR	MAY	JUN	JUL	AUG	SEP	OCT	NOV	DEC
°F AVG MAX	68	68	71	73	75	74	74	74	75	73	72	69
°F AVG MIN	58	58	59	59	59	60	59	59	59	59	59	58
DIURNAL RANGE	10	10	12	14	16	14	15	15	16	14	13	11
RAIN/INCHES	18.4	15.8	18.9	11.6	9.7	10.6	11.5	15.7	11.6	11.6	16.0	19.9
HUMIDITY/%	N/A											
BLOOM SEASON	N/A											
DAYS CLR	N/A											
RAIN/MM	467	401	480	295	246	269	292	399	295	295	406	505
°C AVG MAX	20.1	20.1	21.8	22.9	24.0	23.4	23.4	23.4	24.0	22.9	22.3	20.7
°C AVG MIN	14.5	14.5	15.1	15.1	15.1	15.7	15.1	15.1	15.1	15.1	15.1	14.5
DIURNAL RANGE	5.6	5.6	6.7	7.8	8.9	7.7	8.3	8.3	8.9	7.8	7.2	6.2
S/HEMISPHERE	JUL	AUG	SEP	OCT	NOV	DEC	JAN	FEB	MAR	APR	MAY	JUN

Cultural Recommendations

LIGHT: 2500–3500 fc.

TEMPERATURES: Throughout the year, days average 68–75°F (20–24°C), and nights average 58–60°F (15–16°C), with a diurnal range of 10–16°F (6–9°C).

HUMIDITY: Information is not available for this location. However, records from nearby stations indicate that humidity probably averages near 85% year-round.

WATER: Rainfall is very heavy year-round. Cultivated plants should be kept evenly moist.

FERTILIZER: ¼–½ recommended strength. A balanced fertilizer should be applied weekly to biweekly throughout the year.

REST PERIOD: Growing conditions should be maintained year-round. Water and fertilizer might be reduced slightly in winter for plants cultivated in the dark, short-day conditions common in temperate latitudes. However, plants should never be allowed to dry out completely. In the habitat, seasonal light variation is minor.

GROWING MEDIA: Plants may be mounted on tree-fern or cork slabs or potted in small pots filled with any open, fast-draining medium. Repotting may be done anytime new roots are growing.

Plant and Flower Information

PLANT SIZE AND TYPE: A tall sympodial epiphyte of unreported size.

PSEUDOBULB: Stems are elongated and very slender.

LEAVES: The leaves are 3 in. (8 cm) long, lanceolate to ovate-lanceolate, and leathery. They are pointed at the tip and rounded at the base.

INFLORESCENCE: 0.8 in. (2 cm) long. Inflorescences are densely flowered. They emerge at the apex of the stems.

FLOWERS: 24 per inflorescence. The flowers are 0.4 in. (1 cm) across. Sepals are oblong and rounded. The broad, ovate-oblong petals are rose colored. The lip is 0.5 in. (1.2 cm) long. It is broad at the apex and minutely toothed along the margin. The column and callus have orange markings.

REFERENCES: 222, 400.

Dendrobium rhodocentrum Rchb. f.

ORIGIN/HABITAT: Burma. Plants were originally reported from the Moulmein region. Habitat elevation is unavailable, so the following climate data should be used with caution.

CLIMATE: Station #48103, Moulmein, Burma, Lat. 16.4°N, Long. 97.7°E, at 150 ft. (46 m). Record extreme temperatures are 103°F (39°C) and 52°F (11°C).

N/HEMISPHERE	JAN	FEB	MAR	APR	MAY	JUN	JUL	AUG	SEP	OCT	NOV	DEC
°F AVG MAX	89	92	94	95	89	85	83	83	85	88	89	87
°F AVG MIN	66	68	73	76	76	75	75	75	75	75	73	68
DIURNAL RANGE	23	24	21	19	13	10	8	8	10	13	16	19
RAIN/INCHES	0.3	0.2	0.4	3.0	20.3	35.6	46.3	43.4	28.1	8.5	2.1	0.1
HUMIDITY/%	66	68	68	70	81	91	92	93	91	81	75	64
BLOOM SEASON					*			*		*		
DAYS CLR @ 7AM	12	7	5	6	1	0	0	0	0	3	7	12
DAYS CLR @ 1PM	20	13	10	8	3	0	0	0	0	4	12	17
RAIN/MM	8	5	10	76	516	904	1176	1102	714	216	53	3
°C AVG MAX	31.7	33.3	34.4	35.0	31.7	29.4	28.3	28.3	29.4	31.1	31.7	30.6
°C AVG MIN	18.9	20.0	22.8	24.4	24.4	23.9	23.9	23.9	23.9	23.9	22.8	20.0
DIURNAL RANGE	12.8	13.3	11.6	10.6	7.3	5.5	4.4	4.4	5.5	7.2	8.9	10.6
S/HEMISPHERE	JUL	AUG	SEP	OCT	NOV	DEC	JAN	FEB	MAR	APR	MAY	JUN

Cultural Recommendations

LIGHT: 2000–3000 fc.

TEMPERATURES: Summer days average 83–85°F (28–29°C), and nights average 75°F (24°C), with a narrow diurnal range of 8–10°F (4–6°C). The warmest season is spring. Days average 89–95°F (32–35°C), nights average 73–76°F (23–24°C), with a diurnal range of 13–21°F (7–12°C). The warmest temperatures often coincide with the lowest humidity.

HUMIDITY: 80–90% from late spring to early autumn, dropping to 65–70% in winter and early spring.

WATER: Rainfall is extremely heavy for 5 months in summer, but conditions become quite dry for 4 months in winter. Cultivated plants should be kept moist but not soggy while actively growing, but water should be gradually reduced in autumn. Warm water is highly recommended. Good air circulation and excellent drainage are particularly important.

FERTILIZER: ¼–½ recommended strength, applied weekly. A high-nitrogen fertilizer is beneficial from spring to midsummer, but a fertilizer high in phosphates should be used in late summer and autumn.

REST PERIOD: Winter days average 87–92°F (31–33°C), and nights average 66–68°F (19–20°C), with a diurnal range of 19–24°F (11–13°C). The larger diurnal range results from both warmer days and cooler nights. Rainfall in the habitat is low for 4–5 months, but additional moisture is available from heavy dew and mist for much of the period. Water should be reduced for cultivated plants. They should be allowed to dry between waterings but should not remain dry for extended periods. Although the climate data suggest the need for a 3–4 month dry rest, growers indicate that a 1-month rest is sufficient for other plants from this region. Fertilizer should be reduced until water is increased in spring. In the habitat, light is highest in winter.

GROWING MEDIA: Plants may be mounted on tree-fern or cork slabs if humidity is high and plants are watered at least once a day in summer. When plants are potted, any open, fast-draining medium may be used. Repotting may be done anytime new roots are growing.

MISCELLANEOUS NOTES: The bloom season shown in the climate table is based on cultivation reports.

Plant and Flower Information

PLANT SIZE AND TYPE: A 4–8 in. (10–20 cm) sympodial epiphyte. Plants were described as having the stature and habit of *D. cumulatum* Lindley.

PSEUDOBULB: 4–8 in. (10–20 cm) long.

LEAVES: The papery, lanceolate leaves are about 3 in. (8 cm) long.

INFLORESCENCE: Short.

FLOWERS: 2 per inflorescence. The flowers are 1.6–2.0 in. (4–5 cm) across when the lateral sepals are spread. The blossoms are pale rose with purple at the tips of the petals. The base of the large midlobe is yellowish, and the bearded column is purplish. Seidenfaden (ref. 454) indicates that the flowers are very similar to D. cumulatum Lindley, particularly when dry. However, the spur on D. rhodocentrum is shorter than the dorsal sepal, and it has no free tooth on the claw of the lip.

REFERENCES: 179, 202, 216, 254, 454.

Dendrobium rhododiodes P. van Royen

ORIGIN/HABITAT: Papua New Guinea. Plants grow in subalpine forests at about 10,300 ft. (3150 m) on the south spur of Punpunipon in the Mt. Suckling area.

CLIMATE: Station #200192, Garaina, Papua New Guinea, Lat. 7.9°S, Long. 147.1°E, at 2350 ft. (716 m). Temperatures are calculated for an elevation of 10,150 ft. (3100 m), resulting in probable extremes of 68°F (20°C) and 20°F (−7°C).

N/HEMISPHERE	JAN	FEB	MAR	APR	MAY	JUN	JUL	AUG	SEP	OCT	NOV	DEC
°F AVG MAX	54	56	57	58	59	59	59	59	58	58	57	55
°F AVG MIN	37	37	37	38	37	38	39	39	39	38	38	37
DIURNAL RANGE	17	19	20	20	22	21	20	20	19	20	19	18
RAIN/INCHES	5.8	6.5	8.7	11.1	11.8	11.9	8.9	11.7	11.5	9.9	7.7	5.2
HUMIDITY/%	84	82	82	81	80	80	81	81	82	83	84	84
BLOOM SEASON												*
DAYS CLR	N/A											
RAIN/MM	147	165	221	282	300	302	226	297	292	251	196	132
°C AVG MAX	12.3	13.4	14.0	14.6	15.1	15.1	15.1	15.1	14.6	14.6	14.0	12.9
°C AVG MIN	2.9	2.9	2.9	3.4	2.9	3.4	4.0	4.0	4.0	3.4	3.4	2.9
DIURNAL RANGE	9.4	10.5	11.1	11.2	12.2	11.7	11.1	11.1	10.6	11.2	10.6	10.0
S/HEMISPHERE	JUL	AUG	SEP	OCT	NOV	DEC	JAN	FEB	MAR	APR	MAY	JUN

Cultural Recommendations

LIGHT: 2000–3000 fc.

TEMPERATURES: Throughout the year, days average 54–59°F (12–15°C), and nights average 37–39°F (3–4°C), with a diurnal range of 17–22°F (9–12°C).

HUMIDITY: Near 80–85% year-round.

WATER: Rainfall is heavy all year, but conditions are slightly drier in winter. Cultivated plants should be kept moist but not soggy.

FERTILIZER: ¼–½ recommended strength. A balanced fertilizer should be applied weekly to biweekly throughout the year.

REST PERIOD: Growing conditions should be maintained all year. In the habitat, rainfall is slightly lower in winter. Water and fertilizer should be reduced somewhat for cultivated plants, especially those grown in the dark, short-day conditions common during temperate-latitude winters. They should never be allowed to dry out completely, however. In the habitat, seasonal light variation is minor.

GROWING MEDIA: Mounting plants on tree-fern or cork slabs accommodates their pendulous growth habit. However, humidity must be high and plants must be watered at least once a day in summer. If plants cannot be mounted, hanging pots or baskets may be filled with an open, fast-draining medium. Repotting may be done anytime new roots are actively growing.

MISCELLANEOUS NOTES: The bloom season shown in the climate table is based on reports from the habitat.

Plant and Flower Information

PLANT SIZE AND TYPE: A 5–6 in. (13–15 cm) sympodial epiphyte.

PSEUDOBULB: 5–6 in. (13–15 cm) long. The stems are branching and pendulous. They are medium green above with a purple tinge at the base. The stems are leafy at the apex of each newer branch.

LEAVES: Many. The distichous leaves are 0.8–1.2 in. (2–3 cm) long, and unequally bilobed at the tip.

INFLORESCENCE: Very short. Inflorescences emerge from nodes along the side of newer stems.

FLOWERS: 7–9 per inflorescence. The flowers are 0.6–0.8 in. (1.5–2.0 cm) across. Blossoms are purple-red with an orange-red lip and red at the tip of the spur. The ovate dorsal sepal is smooth with bumps on the margin only at the apex. Lateral sepals are ovate-triangular. The petals are uneven and bumpy along the margin. The lip is covered with fine bumps at the apex and has a half-moon, ruffled crest. It is pointed at the tip.

REFERENCES: 233, 538.

PHOTOS/DRAWINGS: 538.

Dendrobium rhodopterygium Rchb. f.

AKA: Seidenfaden (ref. 454) indicates that Hooker f. considered D. polyphlebium Rchb. f. conspecific with D. rhodopterygium and that he suggested that it might be a natural hybrid of D. pierardii Roxburgh ex Hooker f. [now D. aphyllum (Roxburgh) C. Fischer] and D. parishii Rchb. f. Seidenfaden further states that he can see no difference between D. parishii and D. rhodopterygium. However, he left both as separate species because he was unable to study the type specimens.

ORIGIN/HABITAT: Moulmein, Burma. Plants have been collected in several locations; but habitat elevation was not reported, so the following climate data should be used with caution.

CLIMATE: Station #48103, Moulmein, Burma, Lat. 16.4°N, Long. 97.7°E, at 150 ft. (46 m). Temperatures are calculated for an estimated habitat elevation of 2000 ft. (610 m), resulting in probable extremes of 96°F (36°C) and 45°F (7°C).

N/HEMISPHERE	JAN	FEB	MAR	APR	MAY	JUN	JUL	AUG	SEP	OCT	NOV	DEC
°F AVG MAX	83	86	88	89	83	79	77	77	79	82	83	81
°F AVG MIN	60	62	67	70	70	69	69	69	69	69	67	62
DIURNAL RANGE	23	24	21	19	13	10	8	8	10	13	16	19
RAIN/INCHES	0.3	0.2	0.4	3.0	20.3	35.6	46.3	43.4	28.1	8.5	2.1	0.1
HUMIDITY/%	66	68	68	70	81	91	92	93	91	81	75	64
BLOOM SEASON				*	*							
DAYS CLR @ 7AM	12	7	5	6	1	0	0	0	0	3	7	12
DAYS CLR @ 1PM	20	13	10	8	3	0	0	0	0	4	12	17
RAIN/MM	8	5	10	76	516	904	1176	1102	714	216	53	3
°C AVG MAX	28.3	29.9	31.1	31.6	28.3	26.1	24.9	24.9	26.1	27.7	28.3	27.2
°C AVG MIN	15.5	16.6	19.4	21.1	21.1	20.5	20.5	20.5	20.5	20.5	19.4	16.6
DIURNAL RANGE	12.8	13.3	11.7	10.5	7.2	5.6	4.4	4.4	5.6	7.2	8.9	10.6
S/HEMISPHERE	JUL	AUG	SEP	OCT	NOV	DEC	JAN	FEB	MAR	APR	MAY	JUN

Cultural Recommendations

LIGHT: 2000–3000 fc. The heavy summer cloud cover indicates that shading is needed from spring through autumn, but light should be as high as the plant can tolerate, short of burning the leaves.

TEMPERATURES: Summer days average 77–79°F (25–26°C), and nights average 69°F (21°C), with a diurnal range of 8–10°F (4–6°C). Weather is warmest in spring. Days average 83–89°F (28–32°C), and nights average 67–70°F (19–21°C), with a diurnal range of 13–21°F (7–12°C).

HUMIDITY: 80–90% from late spring to early autumn, dropping to 65–70% in winter and early spring.

WATER: Rainfall is very heavy from late spring into autumn, but conditions are much drier in winter. Cultivated plants should be kept evenly moist while actively growing, but water should be gradually reduced in autumn after new growths mature.

FERTILIZER: ¼–½ recommended strength, applied weekly. A high-nitrogen fertilizer is beneficial from spring to midsummer, but a fertilizer high in phosphates should be used in late summer and autumn.

REST PERIOD: Winter days average 81–86°F (27–30°C), and nights average 60–62°F (16–17°C), with a diurnal range of 19–24°F (11–13°C). The larger diurnal range results from both warmer days and cooler nights. In the habitat, rainfall is low for 4–5 months, but additional moisture is available from frequent heavy deposits of dew. Cultivated plants should be allowed to dry out between waterings, but they should never remain dry for long periods. Occasional early morning mistings between waterings may help prevent plants from becoming too dry. Fertilizer should be reduced or eliminated until water is increased in spring. In the habitat, light is highest in winter.

GROWING MEDIA: Plants may be mounted on slabs of cork or tree-fern fiber with a pad of sphagnum if humidity is high and water is applied daily in summer. If plants are potted, a rapidly draining medium is recommended. Repotting is best done immediately after flowering.

MISCELLANEOUS NOTES: The bloom season shown in the climate table is based on cultivation records. Growers indicate that *D. rhodopterygium* is difficult to grow and flower unless given intermediate temperatures.

Plant and Flower Information

PLANT SIZE AND TYPE: A 12–20 in. (30–50 cm) sympodial epiphyte.

PSEUDOBULB: 12–20 in. (30–50 cm) long. Cylindrical and erect, the stems are longer and more erect than plants known as *D. parishii*.

LEAVES: The deciduous leaves are 2–3 in. (5–8 cm) long. They may be linear, lanceolate or oblong.

INFLORESCENCE: Short. Inflorescences emerge from leafless pseudobulbs.

FLOWERS: 1–3 per inflorescence. The flowers are 2.5–3.0 in. (6.4–7.6 cm) across. Sepals and petals are normally rosy purple or rosy pink with white mottling, but white clones have been found. The purple lip is toothed along the margin and marked with 6 purple streaks. The margin is white or yellow, and the disk is covered with warts. Flowers with white sepals and petals normally have a purple lip. Blossoms are fragrant and moderately long lived.

HYBRIDIZING NOTES: Chromosome count is 2n = 38 (ref. 151, 187).

REFERENCES: 151, 157, 187, 190, 196, 202, 216, 254, 445, 454, 541, 570.

Dendrobium rhodostele Ridley

ORIGIN/HABITAT: Southeastern and peninsular Thailand, Malaya, Sumatra, and Sabah (North Borneo). In Malaya, plants are found in Ulu Kemaman and Pahang State. They are common along rivers in thick jungle.

CLIMATE: Station #49630, Temerloh, Pahang, Malaya, Lat. 3.5°N, Long. 102.4°E, at 163 ft. (50 m). Record extreme temperatures are 97°F (36°C) and 64°F (18°C).

N/HEMISPHERE	JAN	FEB	MAR	APR	MAY	JUN	JUL	AUG	SEP	OCT	NOV	DEC
°F AVG MAX	85	88	90	91	91	90	90	90	90	89	87	86
°F AVG MIN	71	71	72	73	73	73	72	72	72	73	73	72
DIURNAL RANGE	14	17	18	18	18	17	18	18	18	16	14	14
RAIN/INCHES	7.8	3.9	6.0	7.6	6.6	4.3	3.4	5.6	6.5	9.3	9.7	10.1
HUMIDITY/%	87	83	84	85	86	86	87	84	86	87	89	88
BLOOM SEASON	N/A											
DAYS CLR @ 7AM	0	0	2	1	1	0	2	2	2	0	0	0
DAYS CLR @ 1PM	1	1	2	1	1	1	0	1	0	1	0	0
RAIN/MM	198	99	152	193	168	109	86	142	165	236	246	257
°C AVG MAX	29.4	31.1	32.2	32.8	32.8	32.2	32.2	32.2	32.2	31.7	30.6	30.0
°C AVG MIN	21.7	21.7	22.2	22.8	22.8	22.8	22.2	22.2	22.2	22.8	22.8	22.2
DIURNAL RANGE	7.7	9.4	10.0	10.0	10.0	9.4	10.0	10.0	10.0	8.9	7.8	7.8
S/HEMISPHERE	JUL	AUG	SEP	OCT	NOV	DEC	JAN	FEB	MAR	APR	MAY	JUN

Cultural Recommendations

LIGHT: 2500–3500 fc.

TEMPERATURES: Throughout the year, days average 85–91°F (29–33°C), and nights average 71–73°F (22–23°C), with a diurnal range of 14–18°F (8–10°C).

HUMIDITY: 85–90% year-round.

WATER: Rainfall is moderate to heavy for most of the year, but conditions are slightly drier for 1–2 months in winter and again in summer. Cultivated plants should be kept moist, with only slight drying allowed between waterings.

FERTILIZER: ¼–½ recommended strength. A balanced fertilizer should be applied weekly to biweekly throughout the year.

REST PERIOD: Growing conditions should be maintained all year. However, water should be reduced for a month or so in summer and again in late winter. Plants should be allowed to become somewhat drier between waterings during these periods but should never dry out completely. Fertilizer should be reduced or eliminated while water is reduced. In the habitat, seasonal light variation is minor.

GROWING MEDIA: Plants may be mounted on tree-fern or cork slabs if humidity is high and plants are watered at least once daily in summer. When plants are potted, any open, fast-draining medium may be used. Repotting may be done anytime new roots are growing.

MISCELLANEOUS NOTES: Plants are vegetatively similar to *D. aloifolium* (Blume) Rchb. f.

Plant and Flower Information

PLANT SIZE AND TYPE: A 4–10 in. (10–25 cm) sympodial epiphyte.

PSEUDOBULB: 3–8 in. (8–20 cm) long.

LEAVES: Many. The pointed leaves are 1–2 in. (2.5–5.0 cm) long, flattened, and triangular. They are regularly and widely spaced in 2 rows on a single plane.

INFLORESCENCE: Very short. Inflorescences emerge from nodes on the leafless, apical portion of the stem and opposite the leaves along the stem. The clustered flowers are scattered here and there along the stem.

FLOWERS: Several. The tiny flowers are 0.2 in. (0.5 cm) across, which is small for the plant size. The blunt, ovate sepals and linear, pointed petals are not recurved. They may be white or yellow and white, and some segments may be flushed with pink or purple. The 3-lobed lip is linear-oblong with a deeply notched midlobe. The callus nearly covers the lip. The column is red or purple rather than white like *D. aloifolium*.

REFERENCES: 200, 218, 254, 395, 402, 454, 455.

PHOTOS/DRAWINGS: 200, *454, 455.*

Dendrobium rhodostictum F. Mueller and Kränzlin

AKA: *D. madonnae* Rolfe.

ORIGIN/HABITAT: Eastern New Guinea to Bougainville Island, including the islands of New Ireland and New Britain. In New Guinea, plants grow on trees in mountain rainforests or mistforests or on the ground on steep, wet, mossy slopes at 2600–3950 ft. (800–1200 m).

CLIMATE: Station #200192, Garaina, Papua New Guinea, Lat. 7.9°S, Long. 147.1°E, at 2350 ft. (716 m). Temperatures are calculated for an elevation of 3300 ft. (1000 m), resulting in probable extremes of 91°F (33°C) and 43°F (6°C).

N/HEMISPHERE	JAN	FEB	MAR	APR	MAY	JUN	JUL	AUG	SEP	OCT	NOV	DEC
°F AVG MAX	77	79	80	81	82	82	82	82	81	81	80	78
°F AVG MIN	60	60	60	61	60	61	62	62	62	61	61	60
DIURNAL RANGE	17	19	20	20	22	21	20	20	19	20	19	18
RAIN/INCHES	5.8	6.5	8.7	11.1	11.8	11.9	8.9	11.7	11.5	9.9	7.7	5.2
HUMIDITY/%	84	82	82	81	80	80	81	81	82	83	84	84
BLOOM SEASON		*	*	*				*	*			
DAYS CLR	N/A											
RAIN/MM	147	165	221	282	300	302	226	297	292	251	196	132
°C AVG MAX	25.0	26.1	26.6	27.2	27.7	27.7	27.7	27.7	27.2	27.2	26.6	25.5
°C AVG MIN	15.5	15.5	15.5	16.1	15.5	16.1	16.6	16.6	16.6	16.1	16.1	15.5
DIURNAL RANGE	9.5	10.6	11.1	11.1	12.2	11.6	11.1	11.1	10.6	11.1	10.5	10.0
S/HEMISPHERE	JUL	AUG	SEP	OCT	NOV	DEC	JAN	FEB	MAR	APR	MAY	JUN

Dendrobium rhombeum

Cultural Recommendations

LIGHT: 2500–3500 fc.

TEMPERATURES: Throughout the year, days average 77–82°F (25–28°C), and nights average 60–62°F (16–17°C), with a diurnal range of 17–22°F (10–12°C). Highs vary only 5°F (3°C), and lows fluctuate only 2°F (1°C), indicating that plants may not tolerate wide seasonal fluctuations.

HUMIDITY: 80–85% year-round.

WATER: Rainfall is heavy all year, but conditions are slightly drier in winter. Cultivated plants should be kept moist but not soggy.

FERTILIZER: ¼–½ recommended strength. A balanced fertilizer should be applied weekly to biweekly throughout the year.

REST PERIOD: Growing conditions should be maintained all year. Growers indicate that plants tolerate winter lows near 50°F (10°C). In the habitat, rainfall is slightly lower in winter. Water and fertilizer should be reduced somewhat for cultivated plants, especially those grown in the dark, short-day conditions common during temperate-latitude winters. They should never be allowed to dry out completely, however. In the habitat, seasonal light variation is minor.

GROWING MEDIA: Plants may be mounted on tree-fern or cork slabs if humidity is high and plants are watered at least once daily in summer. When plants are potted, any open, fast-draining medium may be used. Repotting may be done anytime new roots are growing.

MISCELLANEOUS NOTES: The bloom season shown in the climate table is based on cultivation records.

Plant and Flower Information

PLANT SIZE AND TYPE: A 5–10 in. (13–25 cm) sympodial epiphyte.

PSEUDOBULB: 3–9 in. (8–23 cm) long. The yellow stems have 3–5 nodes below the leaves. Cruttwell (ref. 95) says, "There are several distinct forms of D. rhodostictum, the Bougainville one having an egg-shaped swelling right at the top of the pseudobulb, whereas the Daga form has long fusiform pseudobulbs."

LEAVES: 2–4 per growth. The dark green leaves are 2–4 in. (5–10 cm) long. They are persistent, leathery, and spreading.

INFLORESCENCE: 3 in. (8 cm) long. Generally erect, the inflorescences emerge near the apex of the pseudobulb.

FLOWERS: 3–8 per inflorescence. The waxy flowers are 2.4–2.8 in. (6–7 cm) across. The white sepals and petals may have green or purple veins. They are keeled and pointed. The lip, which is shaped like a whale's tail, is marked with purple spots on the front margin. The extent of spotting is variable. The apex of the lip has a small point in the center of the notch. Blossoms are fragrant.

HYBRIDIZING NOTES: Chromosome count, 2n = 36 (ref. 152, 243).

REFERENCES: 83, 91, 95, 152, 179, 190, 210, 218, 243, 254, 271, 304, 359, 371, 430, 437, 445, 516, 550.

PHOTOS/DRAWINGS: *83, 91,* 210, *271, 304, 371, 430,* 437.

Dendrobium rhombeum Lindley. See *D. heterocarpum* Lindley. REFERENCES: 75, 190, 216, 254, 296, 430, 436, 445, 454, 469.

Dendrobium rhomboglossum J. J. Smith

ORIGIN/HABITAT: Endemic to Irian Jaya (western New Guinea). In the Goliath mountains and the Angi lakes area of the Arfak Mountains, plants grow on the ground in mountain forests, usually in wet, heath-like terrain on clay soil, and open marshes at 5900–10,500 ft. (1800–3200 m). Plants were abundant on an open, burned-over mountain plateau at 9000 ft. (2740 m).

CLIMATE: Station #97530, Manokwari, Irian Jaya, Lat. 0.9°S, Long. 134.1°E, at 10 ft. (3 m). Temperatures are calculated for an elevation of 8200 ft. (2500 m), resulting in probable extremes of 66°F (19°C) and 41°F (5°C).

N/HEMISPHERE	JAN	FEB	MAR	APR	MAY	JUN	JUL	AUG	SEP	OCT	NOV	DEC
°F AVG MAX	59	58	60	60	61	59	59	59	59	59	59	58
°F AVG MIN	47	48	47	47	47	48	46	46	47	47	47	47
DIURNAL RANGE	12	10	13	13	14	11	13	13	12	12	12	11
RAIN/INCHES	5.4	5.6	5.0	4.7	4.5	10.3	12.0	9.4	13.2	11.1	7.8	7.3
HUMIDITY/%	87	87	86	84	85	86	86	85	86	86	86	85
BLOOM SEASON						*		*		*		
DAYS CLR @ 9AM	4	3	3	5	3	3	3	1	1	2	3	7
DAYS CLR @ 3PM	2	2	2	3	1	1	1	1	0	1	0	2
RAIN/MM	137	142	127	119	114	262	305	239	335	282	198	185
°C AVG MAX	15.0	14.4	15.5	15.5	16.1	15.0	15.0	15.0	15.0	15.0	15.0	14.4
°C AVG MIN	8.3	8.9	8.3	8.3	8.3	8.9	7.8	7.8	8.3	8.3	8.3	8.3
DIURNAL RANGE	6.7	5.5	7.2	7.2	7.8	6.1	7.2	7.2	6.7	6.7	6.7	6.1
S/HEMISPHERE	JUL	AUG	SEP	OCT	NOV	DEC	JAN	FEB	MAR	APR	MAY	JUN

Cultural Recommendations

LIGHT: 2500–3500 fc.

TEMPERATURES: Throughout the year, days average 58–61°F (14–16°C), and nights average 46–48°F (8–9°C), with a diurnal range of 10–14°F (6–8°C). Because of the effects of the microclimate, actual maximum temperatures in the habitat may be as much as 10°F (6°C) warmer than indicated.

HUMIDITY: Near 85% year-round.

WATER: Rainfall is heavy all year, but conditions are somewhat drier in winter and spring. Cultivated plants should be kept moist but not soggy.

FERTILIZER: ¼–½ recommended strength. A balanced fertilizer should be applied weekly to biweekly all year.

REST PERIOD: Growing conditions should be maintained year-round. Water and fertilizer should be reduced somewhat in winter, especially for plants cultivated in the dark, short-day conditions common in temperate latitudes, but plants should never be allowed to dry out completely. In the habitat, light is highest in winter.

GROWING MEDIA: Because of the terrestrial growth habit, plants should be potted using a fast-draining medium that retains some moisture, such as mixtures suitable for *Paphiopedilum* species. Repotting may be done anytime new roots are growing.

MISCELLANEOUS NOTES: The bloom season shown in the climate table is based on collection reports.

Plant and Flower Information

PLANT SIZE AND TYPE: A 12–39 in. (30–100 cm) sympodial terrestrial.

PSEUDOBULB: Commonly 7–8 in. (18–20 cm) long, but plants may reach an overall height of 40 in. (102 cm), including branches. The stems are cylindrical, erect, and ribbed. They consist of 8 nodes.

LEAVES: 2–3 per growth. The linear or narrowly elliptical leaves are 2.4–3.5 in. (6–9 cm) long.

INFLORESCENCE: 4 in. (10 cm) long. The erect inflorescence emerges at the apex.

FLOWERS: 2–6, rarely 14 per inflorescence. The flowers are 1.6–2.0 in. (4–5 cm) across. The pointed, ovate to elliptical sepals and petals are pale purple or violet. In the Arfak Mountains blossoms are magenta on the outside and white on the inside. The 3-lobed lip has a pointed, triangular midlobe and broad, rounded sidelobes. The 3 raised lines in the center terminate behind the apex of the sidelobes.

REFERENCES: 83, 144, 221, 445, 470, 538.

PHOTOS/DRAWINGS: 83, 538.

Dendrobium rhombopetalum Kränzlin. Plants originated in southern Sumatra. However, habitat location and elevation are not

available, and since Sumatra has elevations over 12,500 ft. (3660 m), climate data cannot be selected. The orchid is a sympodial epiphyte with arching, flattened stems about 6 in. (15 cm) long. The many triangular leaves are 1.2 in. (3 cm) long. Short inflorescences emerge along the stem at or near the apex. Each inflorescence carries a single blossom. The flowers are 0.3 in. (0.8 cm) long. They are white with rose on the backside and rose veins on the front. Sepals and petals are somewhat folded lengthwise. The 3-lobed lip is folded and pointed with a fleshy disc. REFERENCES: 220, 254.

Dendrobium rhopalobulbum Schlechter.
Sometimes spelled *D. rhopalobulbon*. Now considered a synonym of *Flickingeria rhopalobulbum* (Schlechter) A. Hawkes. REFERENCES: 92, 213, 220, 231, 254, 433, 437.

Dendrobium rhytidothece Schlechter

ORIGIN/HABITAT: Northern Papua New Guinea. In the Waria District, plants grow on forest trees in the Maboro mountains at about 3950 ft. (1200 m).

CLIMATE: Station #200192, Garaina, Papua New Guinea, Lat. 7.9°S, Long. 147.1°E, at 2350 ft. (716 m). Temperatures are calculated for an elevation of 3950 ft. (1200 m), resulting in probable extremes of 89°F (32°C) and 41°F (5°C).

N/HEMISPHERE	JAN	FEB	MAR	APR	MAY	JUN	JUL	AUG	SEP	OCT	NOV	DEC
°F AVG MAX	75	77	78	79	80	80	80	80	79	79	78	76
°F AVG MIN	58	58	58	59	58	59	60	60	60	59	59	58
DIURNAL RANGE	17	19	20	20	22	21	20	20	19	20	19	18
RAIN/INCHES	5.8	6.5	8.7	11.1	11.8	11.9	8.9	11.7	11.5	9.9	7.7	5.2
HUMIDITY/%	84	82	82	81	80	80	81	81	82	83	84	84
BLOOM SEASON	*	*	*	*	*	*	*	*	*	*	*	*
DAYS CLR	N/A											
RAIN/MM	147	165	221	282	300	302	226	297	292	251	196	132
°C AVG MAX	23.8	24.9	25.4	26.0	26.5	26.5	26.5	26.5	26.0	26.0	25.4	24.3
°C AVG MIN	14.3	14.3	14.3	14.9	14.3	14.9	15.4	15.4	15.4	14.9	14.9	14.3
DIURNAL RANGE	9.5	10.6	11.1	11.1	12.2	11.6	11.1	11.1	10.6	11.1	10.5	10.0
S/HEMISPHERE	JUL	AUG	SEP	OCT	NOV	DEC	JAN	FEB	MAR	APR	MAY	JUN

Cultural Recommendations

LIGHT: 2000–3000 fc.

TEMPERATURES: Throughout the year, days average 75–80°F (24–27°C), and nights average 58–60°F (14–15°C), with a diurnal range of 17–22°F (10–12°C).

HUMIDITY: 80–85% year-round.

WATER: Rainfall is heavy all year, but conditions are slightly drier in winter. Cultivated plants should be kept moist but not soggy.

FERTILIZER: ¼–½ recommended strength. A balanced fertilizer should be applied weekly to biweekly throughout the year. The Royal Botanic Garden in Edinburgh uses a seaweed-based fertilizer for high-elevation plants from New Guinea.

REST PERIOD: Growing conditions vary only slightly during the year. In the habitat, rainfall is slightly lower in winter. Water and fertilizer should be reduced somewhat, especially for plants grown in the dark, short-day conditions common in temperate-latitude winters. Plants should never be allowed to dry out completely, however. In the habitat, light is slightly higher in winter.

GROWING MEDIA: Plants may be mounted on tree-fern or cork slabs if humidity is high and plants are watered at least once daily in summer. When plants are potted, any open, fast-draining medium may be used. Repotting may be done anytime new roots are growing.

MISCELLANEOUS NOTES: In the habitat, blooming occurs throughout the year.

Plant and Flower Information

PLANT SIZE AND TYPE: A 14–18 in. (35–45 cm) sympodial epiphyte.

PSEUDOBULB: 11–13 in. (28–33 cm) long. The flattened, erect stems arise from a very short rhizome. They are densely leafy.

LEAVES: Many. The erect, linear leaves are 3–5 in. (8–13 cm) long.

FLOWERS: 1 per inflorescence. The flowers are 0.4 in. (1 cm) across. They are pale yellow with red spots near the base of the lip and dark purple-brown markings near the front. The column is streaked with red. The anther is dark red. The petals and dorsal sepal are pointed ovals. The large lateral sepals form a large, sack-like spur. The tips of the sepals curve back. The 3-lobed lip has a bumpy, concave midlobe and large, incurved sidelobes.

HYBRIDIZING NOTES: Chromosome count is 2n = 38 (ref. 153, 273).

REFERENCES: 92, 153, 179, 221, 273, 437, 445.

PHOTOS/DRAWINGS: 437.

Dendrobium ridleyanum Kerr.
See *D. hendersonii* A. Hawkes and A. H. Heller. REFERENCES: 224, 249, 454.

Dendrobium ridleyanum Schlechter in obs.
Now considered a synonym of *Diplocaulobium ridleyanum* (Schlechter) W. Kittredge. REFERENCES: 229, 234, 444.

Dendrobium ridleyi Ames.
An invalid name. In Merrill (ref. 295), the name was changed from *Dendrobium intermedium* Ridley to *D. ridleyi* Ames because of the duplication of names. However, the plant was originally described as a *Dendrochilum* not a *Dendrobium*. REFERENCES: 223, 286, 295.

Dendrobium rigens (Blume) Rchb. f.
See *D. concinnum* Miquel. REFERENCES: 25, 75, 216, 254, 266, 317, 448, 454, 469.

Dendrobium rigescens Miquel.
J. J. Smith (ref. 469), Kränzlin (ref. 254), and Hawkes (ref. 190) included *D. rigescens* Miquel as a synonym of *D. mutabile* (Blume) Lindley. This synonymy is not included by Comber (ref. 75), so the current status of this species may be in question. REFERENCES: 75, 190, 216, 254, 310, 469.

Dendrobium rigidifolium Rolfe

AKA: *D. alpinum* P. van Royen, *D. giluwense* P. van Royen, *D. guttatum* J. J. Smith, *D. helenae* Chadim.

ORIGIN/HABITAT: New Guinea. Plants usually grow on the trunks of *Nothofagus* trees in upper mountain forests, but they are occasionally found on the surface of the ground in deep moss. Although this species grows naturally at 7550–12,450 ft. (2300–3800 m), plants from different elevations are successfully cultivated in the botanic garden at Laiagam in Enga Province, which is at 7218 ft. (2200 m).

CLIMATE: Botanical garden records, Laiagam, Papua New Guinea, Lat. 5.5°S, Long. 143.5°E, at 7218 ft. (2200 m). Temperatures are calculated for an elevation of 8500 ft. (2600 m), resulting in probable extremes of 87°F (30°C) and 28°F (-2°C).

N/HEMISPHERE	JAN	FEB	MAR	APR	MAY	JUN	JUL	AUG	SEP	OCT	NOV	DEC
°F AVG MAX	72	73	74	72	74	74	78	73	72	74	74	72
°F AVG MIN	51	50	51	51	52	52	51	52	54	53	52	52
DIURNAL RANGE	21	23	23	21	22	22	27	21	18	21	22	20
RAIN/INCHES	4.0	4.8	6.1	7.8	8.5	9.1	8.4	9.6	9.5	8.9	6.3	4.0
HUMIDITY/%	N/A											
BLOOM SEASON	*	*	*	*	*	*	*	*	*	*	*	*
DAYS CLR	N/A											
RAIN/MM	102	122	155	198	216	231	213	244	241	226	160	102
°C AVG MAX	22.1	22.6	23.2	22.1	23.2	23.2	25.4	22.6	22.1	23.2	23.2	22.1
°C AVG MIN	10.4	9.9	10.4	10.4	11.0	11.0	10.4	11.0	12.1	11.5	11.0	11.0
DIURNAL RANGE	11.7	12.7	12.8	11.7	12.2	12.2	15.0	11.6	10.0	11.7	12.2	11.1
S/HEMISPHERE	JUL	AUG	SEP	OCT	NOV	DEC	JAN	FEB	MAR	APR	MAY	JUN

Dendrobium rigidum

Cultural Recommendations

LIGHT: 2000–3000 fc.

TEMPERATURES: Throughout the year, days average 72–78°F (22–25°C), and nights average 50–54°F (10–12°C), with a diurnal range of 18–27°F (10–15°C). The values in the preceding climate table represent the lower, therefore warmer, portion of the habitat, so plants should easily adapt to conditions that are 6–8°F (3–4°C) cooler than indicated.

HUMIDITY: Information is not available for this location. However, records from nearby stations indicate that averages are probably near 80% year-round.

WATER: Rainfall is moderate to heavy throughout the year, but conditions are driest for 3–4 months in winter. Cultivated plants should be kept evenly moist.

FERTILIZER: ¼–½ recommended strength. A balanced fertilizer should be applied weekly to biweekly throughout the year.

REST PERIOD: Growing conditions should be maintained year-round. Water and fertilizer should be reduced somewhat in winter, especially for plants grown in the dark, short-day conditions common in temperate latitudes. Plants should never be allowed to dry out completely, however. In the habitat, light is highest in winter.

GROWING MEDIA: Plants may be mounted on tree-fern or cork slabs if humidity is high and plants are watered at least once daily in summer. When plants are potted, any open, fast-draining medium may be used. Repotting may be done anytime new roots are growing.

MISCELLANEOUS NOTES: The bloom season shown in the climate table is based on reports from the habitat. *D. rigidifolium* is variable and greatly influenced by environmental conditions. Plants grown in the shade are generally larger leafed, while plants exposed to high light are often stunted.

Plant and Flower Information

PLANT SIZE AND TYPE: A 3–28 in. (8–70 cm) sympodial epiphyte.

PSEUDOBULB: 3–28 in. (8–70 cm) long. The ribbed stems have 12–18 nodes, with 4–8 nodes below the leaves. The stems are orange when dry. Plants are difficult to differentiate from *D. terrestre* J. J. Smith when not in bloom.

LEAVES: 3–9. The erect spreading leaves are 4–5 in. (10–13 cm) long. They are widely spaced on the apical portion of the cane. When young, the leaves are flat, ovate to oblong, and leathery. They are medium green when young, purplish with age, and become golden yellow when dry. The leaf margins are irregular, wavy, and transparent.

INFLORESCENCE: 4–9 in. (10–23 cm) long. Several inflorescences arise laterally from nodes near the tip of the cane. They may be erect or spreading. The blossoms may be horizontal or slightly pendulous.

FLOWERS: 4–15 per inflorescence. The flowers are 1–2 in. (2.5–5.0 cm) across and may not open fully. Sepals and petals are white or yellowish with reddish purple at the base which fades to a delicate rose-pink. The lip is yellowish or greenish white with purple-red streaks along the veins on the margin. The lip is 3-lobed, but the lobes are not clearly divided. It has 2 raised keels. The callus is purple-red.

REFERENCES: 83, 95, 254, 348, 412, 470, 538, 550.

PHOTOS/DRAWINGS: 83, 348, 538.

Dendrobium rigidum (Blume) Miquel. See *D. concinnum* Miquel. REFERENCES: 75, 277, 310, 454, 469.

Dendrobium rigidum R. Brown

ORIGIN/HABITAT: Australia and New Guinea. Plants are widespread and common in New Guinea, where they usually grow on mangroves in swampy coastal lowlands from sea level to 2300 ft. (0–700 m). In Australia, plants are found from the Russell River to the tip of the Cape York Peninsula. They commonly grow in mangrove swamps but are also found on trees along creeks and on rock faces and ironbark trees in low mountains and dry savannas, sometimes considerably inland from the coast.

CLIMATE: Station #94283, Cooktown, Queensland, Australia, Lat. 15.5°S, Long. 145.2°E, at 24 ft. (7 m). Record extreme temperatures are 105°F (41°C) and 46°F (8°C).

N/HEMISPHERE	JAN	FEB	MAR	APR	MAY	JUN	JUL	AUG	SEP	OCT	NOV	DEC
°F AVG MAX	79	80	82	85	88	89	89	88	86	85	82	80
°F AVG MIN	66	67	70	73	75	75	75	75	75	73	70	68
DIURNAL RANGE	13	13	12	12	13	14	14	13	11	12	12	12
RAIN/INCHES	0.9	1.2	0.6	1.0	2.5	6.6	14.4	13.7	15.3	8.8	2.8	2.0
HUMIDITY/%	73	69	68	67	68	71	75	76	77	75	74	75
BLOOM SEASON	*	*		*	*					*	*	*
DAYS CLR	N/A											
RAIN/MM	23	30	15	25	64	168	366	348	389	224	71	51
°C AVG MAX	26.1	26.7	27.8	29.4	31.1	31.7	31.7	31.1	30.0	29.4	27.8	26.7
°C AVG MIN	18.9	19.4	21.1	22.8	23.9	23.9	23.9	23.9	23.9	22.8	21.1	20.0
DIURNAL RANGE	7.2	7.3	6.7	6.6	7.2	7.8	7.8	7.2	6.1	6.6	6.7	6.7
S/HEMISPHERE	JUL	AUG	SEP	OCT	NOV	DEC	JAN	FEB	MAR	APR	MAY	JUN

Cultural Recommendations

LIGHT: 3000–4500 fc. Growers recommend 50% shade in summer. Strong air movement is recommended throughout the year.

TEMPERATURES: Summer days average 88–89°F (31–32°C), and nights average 75°F (24°C), with a diurnal range of 13–14°F (7–8°C). The record highs exceed 100°F (38°C), but growers recommend that highs above 90°F (32°C) be avoided.

HUMIDITY: 70–75% most of the year, falling to 65–70% in late winter and spring.

WATER: Rainfall is moderate to heavy in summer and early autumn. Conditions are dry in winter, but plants grow in wet microclimates. In summer and early autumn, cultivated plants should be kept moist but not soggy. Water should be gradually reduced in late autumn after new growths are mature.

FERTILIZER: ¼–½ recommended strength, applied weekly. A high nitrogen fertilizer is beneficial from spring to midsummer, but a fertilizer high in phosphates should be used in late summer and autumn.

REST PERIOD: Winter days average 79–82°F (26–28°C), and nights average 66–70°F (19–21°C), with a diurnal range of 12–13°F (7°C). Australian growers report that plants survive growing in a brush-house in Sydney, where winter minimum temperatures are about 46°F (8°C), but they grow better in a lightly shaded, warm greenhouse. In the habitat, conditions are dry in winter and early spring. Cultivated plants should be allowed to dry between waterings, but they should not remain dry for long periods. Australian growers indicate that while plants are very tolerant of drought, mounted plants are healthiest if misted enough to keep them just barely moist in winter. Overwatering in winter will kill the plant, especially those grown in pots. In the habitat, light is highest in winter.

GROWING MEDIA: Very slow growing, the plants are healthiest when attached to a cork, tree-fern, hardwood, or other coarse-barked mount. However, humidity must be high, and plants should be misted several times a day during hot weather. Growers recommend that the mount be at least 4 by 6 in. (10 by 15 cm). Air movement is critical. Potted plants are much more difficult to maintain, as *D. rigidum* does not like "wet feet" and must be allowed to dry out between waterings. If pots must be used, a shallow bulb pan or hanging basket may be filled with an open and rapidly draining medium and suspended so the pendulous stems can hang down. The plants must dry briefly between waterings, but the wiry roots should never become desiccated. Remounting is best done in early spring when new roots are growing. Seedlings should be deflasked into a standard seedling mix or directly onto slabs with a small tree-fern pad under each plant. They should not be potted in sphagnum moss, as the moss holds too much water which kills the young plants. Air circulation is essential to keep seedlings alive.

MISCELLANEOUS NOTES: The bloom season shown in the climate table is based on cultivation records. *D. rigidum* blooms sporadically during the year and usually blooms several times a year, but the main flowering is in spring. Blooming is less common in summer.

Plant and Flower Information

PLANT SIZE AND TYPE: A 6–16 in. (15–40 cm) sympodial, colony forming epiphyte that is occasionally lithophytic. Plant size and habit are highly variable.

PSEUDOBULB: 6–16 in. (15–40 cm) long. Cultivated plants are most often about 6 in. (15 cm) long. The thin wiry stems have 1–3 internodes and radiate randomly from the crown of the plant. They branch near the base. Initially erect, the plants start drooping and become pendulous as the slender stems lengthen.

LEAVES: 1 at the apex of each growth. The somewhat flattened leaves, which are 0.8–2.4 in. (2–6 cm) long, may be nearly round to long and slender. They are thick, fleshy, and rough textured. Usually dull gray-green, they may have a purplish tint which is intensified in high light.

INFLORESCENCE: 0.8–2.0 in. (2–5 cm) long. Inflorescences arise from the base of the leaf at the tip of newer, mature branches. The blossoms are held in a cluster, sometimes arranged in a rosette, at the apex of the inflorescence.

FLOWERS: 2–8 per inflorescence. The flowers, which are often upturned, are 0.4–0.8 in. (1–2 cm) across. Sepals and petals are rich cream to yellow, sometimes with pink or russet mottling on the backside. The lip, which may be short and narrow or wide and protruding, is usually somewhat recurved. The lip is cream to pale yellow with varying amounts of orange or rose-red along the margin, which may occasionally extend to the centerline. Some clones have a pure yellow lip. The anther cap is bright green. Growers indicate that all plants have flowers that are slightly different.

HYBRIDIZING NOTES: Chromosome count is 2n = 38 (ref. 154, 188). *D. rigidum* hybridizes naturally with *D. calamiforme* Loddiges to produce *D.* × *foederatum* St. Cloud.

REFERENCES: 23, 36, 67, 105, 154, 179, 186, 188, 216, 240, 254, 262, 291, 304, 325, 330, 390, 421, 445, 533.

PHOTOS/DRAWINGS: *36, 105, 186,* 240, *291, 304,* 325, *533.*

Dendrobium rigidum Lindley. See *D. mutabile* (Blume) Lindley.
REFERENCES: 190, 216, 254, 469.

Dendrobium rimanni Rchb. f. Sometimes spelled *D. rimannii,* see *D. calophyllum* Rchb. f.
REFERENCES: 25, 84, 216, 254.

Dendrobium rindjaniense J. J. Smith

ORIGIN/HABITAT: Lombok in the Sunda Islands. Plants were collected near Segara Anak at 6300–6550 ft. (1925–2000 m).

CLIMATE: Station #97240, Ampenan, Lombok, Lat. 8.6°S, Long. 116.1°E, at 10 ft. (3 m). Temperatures are calculated for an elevation of 6400 ft. (1950 m). Record extremes are not available for this location.

N/HEMISPHERE	JAN	FEB	MAR	APR	MAY	JUN	JUL	AUG	SEP	OCT	NOV	DEC
°F AVG MAX	64	64	66	66	65	64	64	64	65	65	65	65
°F AVG MIN	50	51	53	54	55	55	55	55	54	54	54	52
DIURNAL RANGE	14	13	13	12	10	9	9	9	11	11	11	13
RAIN/INCHES	0.9	1.1	1.1	3.9	8.9	9.0	8.8	8.1	7.4	5.5	4.0	1.8
HUMIDITY/%	N/A											
BLOOM SEASON											*	
DAYS CLR	N/A											
RAIN/MM	24	29	28	99	227	228	225	206	188	139	102	47
°C AVG MAX	17.8	17.8	18.9	18.9	18.3	17.8	17.8	17.8	18.3	18.3	18.3	18.3
°C AVG MIN	10.0	10.6	11.7	12.2	12.8	12.8	12.8	12.8	12.2	12.2	12.2	11.1
DIURNAL RANGE	7.8	7.2	7.2	6.7	5.5	5.0	5.0	5.0	6.1	6.1	6.1	7.2
S/HEMISPHERE	JUL	AUG	SEP	OCT	NOV	DEC	JAN	FEB	MAR	APR	MAY	JUN

Cultural Recommendations

LIGHT: 2000–3000 fc.

TEMPERATURES: Throughout the year, days average 64–66°F (18–19°C), and nights average 50–55°F (10–13°C), with a diurnal range of 9–14°F (5–8°C).

HUMIDITY: Averages are not available for this location, but records from nearby locations indicate humidity is probably 70–75% year-round.

WATER: Rainfall is moderate to heavy most of the year, but conditions are relatively dry for 3–4 months in winter. Cultivated plants should be kept moist from spring to autumn, but water should be gradually reduced in late autumn.

FERTILIZER: ¼–½ recommended strength, applied weekly. A high nitrogen fertilizer is beneficial from spring to midsummer, but a fertilizer high in phosphates should be used in late summer and autumn.

REST PERIOD: Growing temperatures should be maintained all year. Water should be reduced for 3–4 months in winter. Plants should be kept relatively dry but should never remain completely dry for long periods. Fertilizer should be reduced until water is increased in spring.

GROWING MEDIA: Plants may be mounted on tree-fern or cork slabs if humidity is high and plants are watered at least once daily in summer. When plants are potted, any open, fast-draining medium may be used. They may be repotted anytime new roots are growing.

MISCELLANEOUS NOTES: The bloom season shown in the climate table is based on records from the habitat.

Plant and Flower Information

PLANT SIZE AND TYPE: A 3–9 in. (8–23 cm) sympodial epiphyte.

PSEUDOBULB: 2–7 in. (5–17 cm) long. Growths are borne on a creeping, branching rhizome.

LEAVES: The pointed, lanceolate leaves are 1.4–2.2 in. (3.5–5.5 cm) long.

INFLORESCENCE: Short. Inflorescences emerge from the upper nodes of the stem.

FLOWERS: 8 per inflorescence. The flowers are 0.9 in. (2.2 cm) long. Blossoms have an ovate dorsal sepal and oblong-elliptic petals. The ovate-triangular lateral sepals are lacerated. The erect lip is simple and spatula-shaped with a V-shaped callus. Flower color was not included in the description.

REFERENCES: 223, 482.

Dendrobium riparium J. J. Smith. See *D. subclausum* Rolfe.
REFERENCES: 144, 221, 470, 476, 588.

Dendrobium ritaeanum King and Pantling. Now considered a synonym of *Flickingeria ritaeana* (King and Pantling) A. Hawkes.
REFERENCES: 213, 230, 231, 250, 254, 369, 449.

Dendrobium rivesii Gagnepain. See *D. chryseum* Rolfe.
REFERENCES: 136, 224, 266, 447, 448, 454.

Dendrobium robertsianum Hort. ined. See *D. macrophyllum* A. Richard. REFERENCES: 83.

Dendrobium robertsii F. Mueller ex Rupp. See *D. mortii* F. Mueller not Bentham. REFERENCES: 67, 105, 225, 533.

Dendrobium robinsonii Ames. See *D. carinatum* (Linn.) Willdenow. REFERENCES: 12, 13, 221, 296, 536.

Dendrobium robustum Rolfe. See *D. sylvanum* Rchb. f. REFERENCES: 84, 218, 254.

Dendrobium rolfei A. Hawkes and A. H. Heller. See *D. chryseum* Rolfe. REFERENCES: 191, 229, 454.

Dendrobium rorulentum Teijsm. and Binn. See *D. metachilinum* Rchb. f. REFERENCES: 216, 454, 468.

Dendrobium roseatum Ridley

AKA: *D. clarissimum* Ridley.

ORIGIN/HABITAT: Malaya. Plants grow in the Taiping Hills and in the main mountain range, often close to forest streams, at about 4000 ft. (1220 m). They have been collected near Telom, Pahang in mountain forests near a waterfall and along forest streams.

CLIMATE: Station #48625, Ipoh, Malaya, Lat. 4.6°N, Long. 101.1°E, at 123 ft. (37 m). Temperatures are calculated for an estimated elevation of 4000 ft. (1220 m), resulting in probable extremes of 86°F (30°C) and 51°F (11°C).

N/HEMISPHERE	JAN	FEB	MAR	APR	MAY	JUN	JUL	AUG	SEP	OCT	NOV	DEC
°F AVG MAX	77	79	80	79	79	79	78	78	77	76	76	76
°F AVG MIN	59	59	60	60	61	60	59	59	60	59	59	59
DIURNAL RANGE	18	20	20	19	18	19	19	19	17	17	17	17
RAIN/INCHES	7.9	3.1	7.6	8.4	6.2	3.6	7.2	6.9	8.8	11.0	13.0	8.9
HUMIDITY/%	76	74	76	78	78	75	76	77	79	82	82	81
BLOOM SEASON	N/A											
DAYS CLR @ 7AM	3	3	3	1	1	2	1	1	0	0	1	2
DAYS CLR @ 1PM	2	2	2	1	1	1	1	0	0	0	0	2
RAIN/MM	201	79	193	213	157	91	183	175	224	279	330	226
°C AVG MAX	25.1	26.2	26.8	26.2	26.2	26.2	25.7	25.7	25.1	24.6	24.6	24.6
°C AVG MIN	15.1	15.1	15.7	15.7	16.2	15.7	15.1	15.1	15.7	15.1	15.1	15.1
DIURNAL RANGE	10.0	11.1	11.1	10.5	10.0	10.5	10.6	10.6	9.4	9.5	9.5	9.5
S/HEMISPHERE	JUL	AUG	SEP	OCT	NOV	DEC	JAN	FEB	MAR	APR	MAY	JUN

Cultural Recommendations

LIGHT: 1500–2500 fc. Light should be diffused or dappled, and direct sunlight should be avoided. Clear days are quite rare.

TEMPERATURES: Throughout the year, days average 76–80°F (25–27°C), and nights average 59–61°F (15–16°C), with a diurnal range of 17–20°F (9–11°C). The extreme high does not exceed the warmest averages by more than 6°F (3°C), and the average lows fluctuate only 2°F (1°C) indicating that plants may not be able to tolerate wide seasonal fluctuations. Although temperatures are uniform all year, the diurnal range is surprising large.

HUMIDITY: 75–80% year-round.

WATER: Rainfall is heavy most of the year. The heaviest rainfall occurs in autumn with a secondary maximum in spring. Brief semidry periods occur in midwinter and midsummer. Cultivated plants should be kept evenly moist with only slight drying allowed between waterings.

FERTILIZER: ¼–½ recommended strength. A balanced fertilizer should be applied weekly to biweekly throughout the year.

REST PERIOD: Growing conditions should be maintained year-round. Water should be reduced somewhat in winter for plants cultivated in the dark, short-day conditions common in temperate latitudes. They should never be allowed to dry out completely, however. Fertilizer may be reduced when the plant is not actively growing or when water is reduced. In the habitat, light is slightly higher in winter.

GROWING MEDIA: Mounting plants on tree-fern or cork slabs accommodates their pendulous growth habit. However, humidity must be high and plants must be watered at least once a day in summer. If plants cannot be mounted, hanging pots or baskets may be filled with an open, fast-draining medium. Repotting may be done anytime new roots are actively growing.

Plant and Flower Information

PLANT SIZE AND TYPE: A 12–24 in. (30–60 cm) sympodial epiphyte.

PSEUDOBULB: 12–24 in. (30–60 cm) long or longer. The slender stems consist of nodes spaced every 1.2 in. (3 cm). The entire plant is pendulous.

LEAVES: 8–10 per growth. The narrowly lanceolate leaves are 2–6 in. (5–14 cm) long. They have a thin texture and taper to a point at the apex.

INFLORESCENCE: 1–2 in. (2.5–5.0 cm) long. Inflorescences emerge from nodes near the apex of leafless pseudobulbs.

FLOWERS: 3–6 per inflorescence. The flowers are 1.2–1.4 in. (3.0–3.5 cm) long. Blossoms are white tinged with pink, which is darkest at the apex of the petals. The crystalline texture sparkles in the light. The lip is ruffled, slightly toothed on the margins, and decorated with a small golden yellow patch at the back. It has no sidelobes but is thickened at the base. All segments are approximately equal in size and shape. The somewhat recurved sepals and petals overlap at the base. The spur is curved, clubbed, and thickened at the tip.

REFERENCES: 200, 254, 395, 402, 455.

PHOTOS/DRAWINGS: 455.

Dendrobium roseicolor A. Hawkes and A. H. Heller

AKA: *D. roseum* Schlechter.

ORIGIN/HABITAT: Northern Papua New Guinea. Plants grow on mistforest trees in the Torricelli Range at about 2600 ft. (800 m).

CLIMATE: Station #94004, Wewak, Papua New Guinea, Lat. 3.6°S, Long. 143.7°E, at 16 ft. (5 m). Temperatures are calculated for an elevation of 2600 ft. (800 m), resulting in probable extremes of 89°F (32°C) and 53°F (12°C).

N/HEMISPHERE	JAN	FEB	MAR	APR	MAY	JUN	JUL	AUG	SEP	OCT	NOV	DEC
°F AVG MAX	79	79	79	79	79	79	78	77	78	79	79	79
°F AVG MIN	65	65	65	66	66	66	66	66	65	65	66	65
DIURNAL RANGE	14	14	14	13	13	13	12	11	13	14	13	14
RAIN/INCHES	7.6	4.8	5.3	10.0	13.3	14.5	12.1	11.9	14.9	16.9	15.1	10.8
HUMIDITY/%	80	79	79	78	79	81	82	82	81	82	81	80
BLOOM SEASON		*										
DAYS CLR	N/A											
RAIN/MM	193	122	135	254	338	368	307	302	378	429	384	274
°C AVG MAX	26.3	26.3	26.3	26.3	26.3	26.3	25.8	25.2	25.8	26.3	26.3	26.3
°C AVG MIN	18.6	18.6	18.6	19.1	19.1	19.1	19.1	19.1	18.6	18.6	19.1	18.6
DIURNAL RANGE	7.7	7.7	7.7	7.2	7.2	7.2	6.7	6.1	7.2	7.7	7.2	7.7
S/HEMISPHERE	JUL	AUG	SEP	OCT	NOV	DEC	JAN	FEB	MAR	APR	MAY	JUN

Cultural Recommendations

LIGHT: 1800–2500 fc.

TEMPERATURES: Throughout the year, days average 77–79°F (25–26°C), and nights average 65–66°F (19°C), with a diurnal range of 11–14°F (6–8°C).

HUMIDITY: Near 80% year-round.

WATER: Rainfall is heavy all year, but conditions are slightly drier for 1–2 months in winter. Cultivated plants should be kept moist but not soggy.

FERTILIZER: ¼–½ recommended strength. A balanced fertilizer should be applied weekly to biweekly throughout the year.

REST PERIOD: Growing temperatures should be maintained all year. Water and fertilizer should be reduced somewhat for plants grown in the dark, short-day conditions common during temperate-latitude winters, but they should never be allowed to dry out completely. In the habitat, seasonal light variation is minor.

GROWING MEDIA: A very open and fast-draining medium should be used with either baskets or small pots. Repotting may be done anytime new roots are growing.

MISCELLANEOUS NOTES: The bloom season shown in the climate table is based on collection records.

Plant and Flower Information

PLANT SIZE AND TYPE: A 20 in. (50 cm) sympodial epiphyte. Plants are often smaller.

PSEUDOBULB: 16 in. (40 cm) long. The slender, leafy stems may be spreading or erect. They are borne on a very short rhizome.

LEAVES: Many. The erect, linear leaves are 2.8–4.3 in. (7–11 cm) long. They are pointed and unequally bilobed at the apex.

INFLORESCENCE: Short. The densely flowered inflorescences emerge from nodes along the side of the stem.

FLOWERS: Many per inflorescence. The cone-shaped flowers are 0.7 in. (1.7 cm) long. The sepals and petals are rose-red. The dorsal sepal is broadly oval. Lateral sepals are elongated forming a long, cone-shaped spur. Petals are somewhat elliptical. The concave lip, which is not lobed, is blunt at the apex. It has an inverted V-shaped structure at the base.

REFERENCES: 191, 229, 437.

PHOTOS/DRAWINGS: 437.

Dendrobium roseipes Schlechter

ORIGIN/HABITAT: Northeastern Papua New Guinea. Collections are reported from Mt. Gomadjidji near the Waria River, just below the mistforest zone. The orchids usually grow on the lower, moss-covered tree branches at 1500–3300 ft. (450–1000 m).

CLIMATE: Station #200192, Garaina, Papua New Guinea, Lat. 7.9°S, Long. 147.1°E, at 2350 ft. (716 m). Record extreme temperatures are 94°F (34°C) and 46°F (8°C).

N/HEMISPHERE	JAN	FEB	MAR	APR	MAY	JUN	JUL	AUG	SEP	OCT	NOV	DEC
°F AVG MAX	80	82	83	84	85	85	85	85	84	84	83	81
°F AVG MIN	63	63	63	64	63	64	65	65	65	64	64	63
DIURNAL RANGE	17	19	20	20	22	21	20	20	19	20	19	18
RAIN/INCHES	5.8	6.5	8.7	11.1	11.8	11.9	8.9	11.7	11.5	9.9	7.7	5.2
HUMIDITY/%	84	82	82	81	80	80	81	81	82	83	84	84
BLOOM SEASON								*	*	*	*	
DAYS CLR	N/A											
RAIN/MM	148	166	220	282	300	303	227	296	291	251	195	131
°C AVG MAX	26.8	27.5	28.2	28.6	29.3	29.3	29.4	29.4	29.1	28.7	28.2	27.2
°C AVG MIN	16.9	16.9	17.4	17.6	17.4	18.0	18.1	18.2	18.4	17.7	17.7	17.1
DIURNAL RANGE	9.9	10.6	10.8	11.0	11.9	11.3	11.3	11.2	10.7	11.0	10.5	10.1
S/HEMISPHERE	JUL	AUG	SEP	OCT	NOV	DEC	JAN	FEB	MAR	APR	MAY	JUN

Cultural Recommendations

LIGHT: 2500–3500 fc.

TEMPERATURES: Throughout the year, days average 80–85°F (27–29°C), and nights average 63–65°F (17–18°C), with a diurnal range of 17–22°F (10–12°C).

HUMIDITY: 80–85% year-round.

WATER: Rainfall is heavy all year, with a slightly drier period in winter. Cultivated plants should be kept moist but not soggy.

FERTILIZER: ¼–½ recommended strength. A balanced fertilizer should be applied weekly to biweekly throughout the year.

REST PERIOD: Growing conditions vary only slightly during the year. In the habitat, rainfall is lowest in winter. Water should be reduced somewhat for cultivated plants, especially those grown in the dark, short-day conditions common in temperate-latitude winters. Plants should never be allowed to dry out completely, however. Fertilizer should be reduced or eliminated anytime water is reduced. In the habitat, light is slightly higher in winter.

GROWING MEDIA: Mounting plants on tree-fern or cork slabs accommodates their semipendent growth habit. However, humidity must be high and plants must be watered at least once a day in summer. If plants cannot be mounted, hanging pots or baskets may be filled with an open, fast-draining medium. Repotting may be done anytime new roots are actively growing.

MISCELLANEOUS NOTES: The bloom season shown in the climate table is based on collection reports. Plants that produce flowers which last a single day commonly bloom several times during the year. Flowering usually occurs 7–14 days after a sudden 10°F (5°C) drop in daytime temperatures.

Plant and Flower Information

PLANT SIZE AND TYPE: A 14 in. (35 cm) sympodial epiphyte. Plants occasionally reach a length of 28 in. (70 cm). Plants tend to be pendent.

PSEUDOBULB: 12–14 in. (30–35 cm) long. Young stems are yellowish green, but stems become gray-brown as they age.

LEAVES: Many all along new growths. The yellowish green leaves are 2.4–4.3 in. (6–11 cm) long. They are deciduous before flowering.

INFLORESCENCE: 1.6 in. (4 cm) long. Inflorescences emerge laterally from nodes on leafless stems. Only rarely do inflorescences arise at the apex of the stem, but canes can be completely covered with blossoms.

FLOWERS: 8–10 per inflorescence. The fan-shaped flowers are 0.6 in. (1.5 cm) across. Sepals and petals may be nearly solid rose-pink with white tips or white grading to dark pink at the base. The sepals are pointed but the petals are rounded at the tip. The lip, which is not lobed, is incurved along the side with an inverted U-shaped structure near the base. Blossoms have a peculiar odor.

REFERENCES: 95, 221, 304, 437, 445, 552, 554.

PHOTOS/DRAWINGS: *304*, 437, *552*.

Dendrobium rosellum Ridley

ORIGIN/HABITAT: Borneo and Malaya. In Borneo, plants are common at sea level near Marudi in northern Sarawak. In Malaya, they grow in southeastern Johore state, usually on trees near rivers and occasionally on Mt. Pantai (Panti). Plants have been collected from fallen logs.

CLIMATE: Station #48674, Mersing, Malaya, Lat. 2.5°N, Long. 103.8°E, at 151 ft. (46 m). Record extreme temperatures are 99°F (37°C) and 68°F (20°C).

N/HEMISPHERE	JAN	FEB	MAR	APR	MAY	JUN	JUL	AUG	SEP	OCT	NOV	DEC
°F AVG MAX	82	83	86	89	90	89	88	87	87	87	86	82
°F AVG MIN	74	74	74	73	73	72	72	72	72	72	72	73
DIURNAL RANGE	8	9	12	16	17	17	16	15	15	15	14	9
RAIN/INCHES	14.4	6.3	6.1	4.6	7.1	5.1	5.6	6.7	9.3	9.9	13.4	24.3
HUMIDITY/%	82	82	81	82	82	83	84	84	84	84	85	86
BLOOM SEASON	*										*	
DAYS CLR @ 7AM	0	0	1	3	2	2	3	2	1	0	1	1
DAYS CLR @ 1PM	0	0	1	2	1	1	0	1	0	0	0	0
RAIN/MM	366	160	155	117	180	130	142	170	236	251	340	617
°C AVG MAX	27.8	28.3	30.0	31.7	32.2	31.7	31.1	30.6	30.6	30.6	30.0	27.8
°C AVG MIN	23.3	23.3	23.3	22.8	22.8	22.2	22.2	22.2	22.2	22.2	22.2	22.8
DIURNAL RANGE	4.5	5.0	6.7	8.9	9.4	9.5	8.9	8.4	8.4	8.4	7.8	5.0
S/HEMISPHERE	JUL	AUG	SEP	OCT	NOV	DEC	JAN	FEB	MAR	APR	MAY	JUN

Dendrobium rosenbergii

Cultural Recommendations

LIGHT: 2000–3000 fc. Direct sun should be avoided.

TEMPERATURES: Throughout the year, days average 82–90°F (28–32°C), and nights average 72–74°F (22–23°C), with a diurnal range of 8–17°F (5–10°C). The diurnal range is greatest in summer, the result of warmer days and slightly cooler nights.

HUMIDITY: 80–85% year-round.

WATER: Rainfall is heavy to very heavy all year. Cultivated plants should be kept moist, but the medium should not be soggy.

FERTILIZER: ¼–½ recommended strength. A balanced fertilizer should be applied weekly to biweekly throughout the year.

REST PERIOD: Growing conditions should be maintained all year. Lows vary only 2°F (1°C) throughout the year, but winter days are noticeably cooler. Winters are very wet, but excess moisture is harmful in cultivation, particularly for plants grown in the dark, short-day conditions common in temperate latitudes. Water should be reduced in winter for these plants, but they should never be allowed to dry out completely. Fertilizer should be reduced until water is increased in spring. In the habitat, seasonal light variations are minor.

GROWING MEDIA: Plants may be mounted on tree-fern or cork slabs if humidity is high and plants are watered at least once daily in summer. When plants are potted, any open, fast-draining medium may be used. Repotting may be done anytime new roots are growing.

MISCELLANEOUS NOTES: The bloom season shown in the climate table is based on collection reports. The plant was described in 1927 in *Mitt. Inst. Bot. Hamburg* 7:55.

Plant and Flower Information

PLANT SIZE AND TYPE: A 12–18 in. (30–45 cm) sympodial epiphyte. The vegetative characteristics are described as very similar to *D. aloifolium* (Blume) Rchb. f.

PSEUDOBULB: 12–18 in. (30–45 cm) long. The stems are branched.

LEAVES: Many. The leaves, which are about 1 in. (2.5 cm) long, may be widely spaced or very close together.

INFLORESCENCE: Very short. Flowers are borne from between the leaves. They appear to rest on the stem close to the centerline.

FLOWERS: 1 per inflorescence. Among the smallest of the genus, the blossoms are 0.2–0.3 in. (0.5–0.8 cm) across. Sepals and petals, which curve forward, may be magenta or white with bright rose-purple stripes and mottling. The sepals are pointed and the smaller petals are rounded. The 3-lobed lip has small, rounded sidelobes and a much larger, deeply notched midlobe. It has 3 ridges that converge to a yellow callus. Anthers and pollinia are greenish. The flowers are not fragrant.

REFERENCES: 59, 200, 254, 286, 295, 394, 395, 402, 455.

PHOTOS/DRAWINGS: 200, 455.

Dendrobium rosenbergii Teijsm. and Binn. See *D. mirbelianum* Gaudich. REFERENCES: 84, 88, 216, 254, 470, 533.

Dendrobium roseoflavidum Schlechter 1912 not 1923

AKA: Sometimes spelled *D. roseo-flavidum*.

ORIGIN/HABITAT: Northeastern Papua New Guinea. Schlechter found this orchid only once in the Waria District. It grew epiphytically in the forests covering the slopes of Mt. Mimi at about 2300 ft. (700 m).

CLIMATE: Station #200192, Garaina, Papua New Guinea, Lat. 7.9°S, Long. 147.1°E, at 2350 ft. (716 m). Record extreme temperatures are 94°F (34°C) and 46°F (8°C).

N/HEMISPHERE	JAN	FEB	MAR	APR	MAY	JUN	JUL	AUG	SEP	OCT	NOV	DEC
°F AVG MAX	80	82	83	84	85	85	85	85	84	84	83	81
°F AVG MIN	63	63	63	64	63	64	65	65	65	64	64	63
DIURNAL RANGE	17	19	20	20	22	21	20	20	19	20	19	18
RAIN/INCHES	5.8	6.5	8.7	11.1	11.8	11.9	8.9	11.7	11.5	9.9	7.7	5.2
HUMIDITY/%	84	82	82	81	80	80	81	81	82	83	84	84
BLOOM SEASON											*	
DAYS CLR	N/A											
RAIN/MM	148	166	220	282	300	303	227	296	291	251	195	131
°C AVG MAX	26.8	27.5	28.2	28.6	29.3	29.4	29.4	29.4	29.1	28.7	28.2	27.2
°C AVG MIN	16.9	16.9	17.4	17.6	17.4	18.0	18.1	18.2	18.4	17.7	17.7	17.1
DIURNAL RANGE	9.9	10.6	10.8	11.0	11.9	11.3	11.3	11.2	10.7	11.0	10.5	10.1
S/HEMISPHERE	JUL	AUG	SEP	OCT	NOV	DEC	JAN	FEB	MAR	APR	MAY	JUN

Cultural Recommendations

LIGHT: 2500–3500 fc.

TEMPERATURES: Throughout the year, days average 80–85°F (27–29°C), and nights average 63–65°F (17–18°C), with a diurnal range of 17–22°F (10–12°C).

HUMIDITY: Near 80–85% year-round.

WATER: Rainfall is heavy all year, but conditions are slightly drier in winter. Cultivated plants should be kept moist but not soggy.

FERTILIZER: ¼–½ recommended strength. A balanced fertilizer should be applied weekly to biweekly throughout the year.

REST PERIOD: Growing conditions should be maintained all year. In the habitat, rainfall is slightly lower in winter. Water and fertilizer should be reduced somewhat for cultivated plants, especially those grown in the dark, short-day conditions common during temperate-latitude winters. They should never be allowed to dry out completely, however. In the habitat, seasonal light variation is minor.

GROWING MEDIA: Plants may be mounted on tree-fern or cork slabs if humidity is high and plants are watered at least once daily in summer. When plants are potted, any open, fast-draining medium may be used. Repotting may be done anytime new roots are growing.

MISCELLANEOUS NOTES: The bloom season shown in the climate table is based on collection reports. Plants that produce flowers which last a single day commonly bloom several times during the year. Flowering usually occurs 7–14 days after a sudden 10°F (5°C) drop in daytime temperatures.

Plant and Flower Information

PLANT SIZE AND TYPE: A 10–12 in. (25–30 cm) sympodial epiphyte.

PSEUDOBULB: 10–12 in. (25–30 cm) long. The densely leafy stems are flattened and unbranched. They arise from a very short rhizome.

LEAVES: Many. The leaves are rough, pointed, and curved.

INFLORESCENCE: Short.

FLOWERS: 1 per inflorescence. The inverted flowers are 0.3 in. (0.8 cm) across. Sepals and petals are pink with yellowish tips. The lip is pale pink with pale red markings. It is 3-lobed with a small, nearly round midlobe that is pointed at the apex. The midlobe and front of the sidelobes are covered with small warts.

REFERENCES: 221, 437.

PHOTOS/DRAWINGS: 437.

Dendrobium roseoflavidum Schlechter 1923 not 1912. See *D. buffumii* A. Hawkes. REFERENCES: 223, 443, 445.

Dendrobium roseonervatum Schlechter

AKA: Sometimes spelled *D. roseo-nervatum*.

ORIGIN/HABITAT: Sumatra, without location details. *D. roseonervatum* was originally cultivated in the Berlin botanical garden under the name *D. rigens* (Blume) Rchb. f. (now *D. concinnum* Miquel), which suggests that the plant may have been collected and imported with that species. *D. concinnum* was collected in Sumatra near Takengon (Takingeun) at about 3600 ft. (1070 m). The following climate data should be used with extreme caution, since it is based on suppositions, conjecture, and assumptions.

CLIMATE: Station #96009, Lhou, Sumatra, Indonesia, Lat. 5.1°N, Long. 97.2°E, at 7 ft. (2 m). Temperatures are calculated for an elevation of 4000 ft. (1220 m). Record extreme temperatures are not available for this location.

N/HEMISPHERE	JAN	FEB	MAR	APR	MAY	JUN	JUL	AUG	SEP	OCT	NOV	DEC
°F AVG MAX	71	73	74	75	75	76	75	75	73	73	72	71
°F AVG MIN	59	59	60	61	62	61	60	60	60	60	60	60
DIURNAL RANGE	12	14	14	14	13	15	15	15	13	13	12	11
RAIN/INCHES	4.8	1.9	3.3	3.2	6.6	2.2	4.8	2.8	5.0	4.6	9.2	7.6
HUMIDITY/%	N/A											
BLOOM SEASON	N/A											
DAYS CLR	N/A											
RAIN/MM	122	48	84	81	168	56	122	71	127	117	234	193
°C AVG MAX	21.6	22.7	23.2	23.8	23.8	24.3	23.8	23.8	22.7	22.7	22.1	21.6
°C AVG MIN	14.9	14.9	15.5	16.0	16.6	16.0	15.5	15.5	15.5	15.5	15.5	15.5
DIURNAL RANGE	6.7	7.8	7.7	7.8	7.2	8.3	8.3	8.3	7.2	7.2	6.6	6.1
S/HEMISPHERE	JUL	AUG	SEP	OCT	NOV	DEC	JAN	FEB	MAR	APR	MAY	JUN

Cultural Recommendations

LIGHT: 2000–3000 fc.

TEMPERATURES: Throughout the year, days average 71–76°F (22–24°C), and nights average 59–62°F (15–17°C), with a diurnal range of 11–15°F (6–8°C).

HUMIDITY: Information is not available for this location. However, records from nearby stations indicate that humidity probably averages near 80% year-round.

WATER: Rainfall is moderate most of the year with brief semidry periods in midwinter and again in early summer. Cultivated plants should be allowed to dry out somewhat between waterings, but they should never dry out completely or remain dry for long periods.

FERTILIZER: ¼–½ recommended strength. A balanced fertilizer should be applied weekly to biweekly throughout the year.

REST PERIOD: Growing conditions should be maintained year-round. The wettest conditions occur in late autumn and early winter. However, water should not be increased for cultivated plants, especially those grown in the dark, short-day conditions common in temperate-latitude winters. In the habitat, seasonal light variation is minor.

GROWING MEDIA: Plants may be mounted on tree-fern or cork slabs or potted in small pots filled with any open, fast-draining medium. Repotting may be done anytime new roots are growing.

Plant and Flower Information

PLANT SIZE AND TYPE: An 8 in. (20 cm) sympodial epiphyte.

PSEUDOBULB: 8 in. (20 cm) long. The densely leafy stems are erect.

LEAVES: Many. The distichous leaves are 0.8 in. (2 cm) long. They are lanceolate, fleshy, and curved.

INFLORESCENCE: Inflorescences emerge from the leaf axils.

FLOWERS: 1 or a few per inflorescence. The pale rose flowers are 0.4 in. (1 cm) across. The lanceolate dorsal sepal has 5 rose-colored nerves, but each ovate lateral sepal has only one. The petals are rounded, 1-nerved, and somewhat sickle-shaped. The curved, 3-lobed lip is decorated with rose-colored nerves. It has erect sidelobes and an ovate, pointed, curved midlobe.

REFERENCES: 219, 254, 431.

Dendrobium roseopunctatum Ridley.
Sometimes spelled *D. roseo-punctatum*, it was transferred to *Ephemerantha fimbriata* by Hunt and Summerhayes, but Seidenfaden (ref. 449) considers it a possible synonym of *Flickingeria fugax* (Rchb. f.) Seidenfaden. REFERENCES: 213, 395, 449.

Dendrobium roseostriatum Ridley

AKA: Sometimes spelled *D. roseo-striatum*.

ORIGIN/HABITAT: Sumatra. Plants were originally found on the west coast near Lubok Tandai in the Bengkulu (Bencoolen) district. Habitat elevation is estimated, so the following climate data should be used with caution.

CLIMATE: Station #96253, Bengkulu, Sumatra, Indonesia, Lat. 3.9°S, Long. 102.3°E, at 49 ft. (15 m). Temperatures are calculated for an elevation of 2150 ft. (660 m). Record extreme temperatures are not available for this location.

N/HEMISPHERE	JAN	FEB	MAR	APR	MAY	JUN	JUL	AUG	SEP	OCT	NOV	DEC
°F AVG MAX	81	80	80	80	80	80	81	81	81	81	82	81
°F AVG MIN	65	65	65	66	66	66	65	66	67	66	66	66
DIURNAL RANGE	16	15	15	14	14	14	15	16	15	14	16	15
RAIN/INCHES	6.9	6.8	9.1	13.9	16.0	12.7	16.0	11.5	12.0	8.3	8.4	8.4
HUMIDITY/%	77	78	77	77	79	80	78	76	77	79	77	78
BLOOM SEASON	N/A											
DAYS CLR	N/A											
RAIN/MM	175	173	231	353	406	323	406	292	305	211	213	213
°C AVG MAX	27.3	26.7	26.7	26.7	26.7	26.7	27.3	27.3	27.3	27.3	27.8	27.3
°C AVG MIN	18.4	18.4	18.4	18.9	18.9	18.9	18.9	18.4	18.9	19.5	18.9	18.9
DIURNAL RANGE	8.9	8.3	8.4	7.8	7.8	7.8	8.4	8.9	8.4	7.8	8.9	8.4
S/HEMISPHERE	JUL	AUG	SEP	OCT	NOV	DEC	JAN	FEB	MAR	APR	MAY	JUN

Cultural Recommendations

LIGHT: 2000–3000 fc.

TEMPERATURES: Throughout the year, days average 80–82°F (27–28°C), and nights average 65–67°F (18–20°C), with a diurnal range of 14–16°F (8–9°C).

HUMIDITY: 75–80% year-round.

WATER: Rainfall is heavy all year, but conditions are slightly drier in winter. Cultivated plants should be kept moist but not soggy.

FERTILIZER: ¼–½ recommended strength. A balanced fertilizer should be applied weekly to biweekly throughout the year.

REST PERIOD: Growing conditions should be maintained year-round. Water may be reduced somewhat in winter, especially for plants cultivated in the dark, short-day conditions common in temperate latitudes, but plants should never be allowed to dry completely.

GROWING MEDIA: Plants may be mounted on tree-fern or cork slabs or potted in small pots filled with any open, fast-draining medium. Repotting may be done anytime new roots are growing.

Plant and Flower Information

PLANT SIZE AND TYPE: A 14 in. (35 cm) sympodial epiphyte.

PSEUDOBULB: 14 in. (35 cm) long. The stems are bare at the base but the upper portion is flattened and covered with pale leaf sheaths. At the apex, the stem is again leafless.

LEAVES: Many. Leathery and oblong-lanceolate, the leaves are 0.4 in. (1 cm) long.

INFLORESCENCE: The flowers are held in congested clusters at the apex of the stem.

FLOWERS: Many. The flowers are 0.2 in. (0.5 cm) long. The lanolate dorsal sepal and somewhat triangular lateral sepals are streaked with pink. The pale petals are lanceolate-oblong. The erect lip has a semicircular callus and 2 elevated nerves. The anther is white.

REFERENCES: 223, 403.

Dendrobium roseum Dalzell not Schlechter or Swartz. See *D. crepidatum* Lindley. REFERENCES: 190.

Dendrobium roseum Schlechter not Dalzell or Swartz. See *D. roseicolor* A. Hawkes and A. H. Heller. REFERENCES: 221, 437, 445.

Dendrobium roseum Swartz not Dalzell or Schlechter. Now considered a synonym of *Polystachya elastica* Lindley. REFERENCES: 216, 254, 277.

Dendrobium rotundatum Bentham not (Lindley) Hooker f.

AKA: *Bolbophyllum rotundatum* Rchb. f.

ORIGIN/HABITAT: Northeastern India. Plants grow in Sikkim and the Naga and Khasi (Khasia) Hills at 6550–7550 ft. (2000–2300 m). Plants commonly grow at the base of trees, where they receive ample moisture and protection from extreme temperature fluctuations.

CLIMATE: Station #42398, Baghdogra, India, Lat. 26.7°N, Long. 88.3°E, at 412 ft. (126 m). Temperatures are calculated for an elevation of 7000 ft. (2130 m), resulting in probable extremes of 82°F (28°C) and 14°F (−10°C).

N/HEMISPHERE	JAN	FEB	MAR	APR	MAY	JUN	JUL	AUG	SEP	OCT	NOV	DEC
°F AVG MAX	52	55	63	68	68	67	67	67	66	65	60	55
°F AVG MIN	28	32	38	46	51	54	55	55	54	48	38	31
DIURNAL RANGE	24	23	25	22	17	13	12	12	12	17	22	24
RAIN/INCHES	0.3	0.7	1.3	3.7	11.8	25.9	32.2	25.3	21.2	5.6	0.5	0.2
HUMIDITY/%	73	68	57	58	74	84	86	85	85	79	75	76
BLOOM SEASON				*	*							
DAYS CLR @ 6AM	21	18	15	11	5	0	1	1	4	13	23	19
DAYS CLR @ 12PM	23	16	16	11	2	2	0	1	2	10	21	18
RAIN/MM	8	18	33	94	300	658	818	643	538	142	13	5
°C AVG MAX	11.3	12.9	17.4	20.1	20.1	19.6	19.6	19.6	19.0	18.5	15.7	12.9
°C AVG MIN	−2.1	0.1	3.5	7.9	10.7	12.4	12.9	12.9	12.4	9.0	3.5	−0.4
DIURNAL RANGE	13.4	12.8	13.9	12.2	9.4	7.2	6.7	6.7	6.6	9.5	12.2	13.3
S/HEMISPHERE	JUL	AUG	SEP	OCT	NOV	DEC	JAN	FEB	MAR	APR	MAY	JUN

Cultural Recommendations

LIGHT: 2000–3000 fc. Diffused light is suggested.

TEMPERATURES: Summer days average 67–68°F (20°C), and nights average 51–55°F (11–13°C), with a diurnal range of 12–17°F (7–9°C). Because of the effects of microclimate, actual summertime maximum temperatures in the habitat may be 6–10°F (3–6°C) warmer than indicated.

HUMIDITY: 75–85% most of the year, dropping below 60% for 2 months in late winter and early spring.

WATER: Rainfall is extremely heavy in summer, but conditions are very dry in winter. However, more moisture is available at higher elevations than is recorded at the low elevation station. Cultivated plants should be kept wet but not soggy from late spring through summer, but water should be gradually reduced in autumn after new growths mature.

FERTILIZER: ¼–½ recommended strength, applied weekly. A high-nitrogen fertilizer is beneficial from spring to midsummer, but a fertilizer high in phosphates should be used in late summer and autumn.

REST PERIOD: Winter days average 52–55°F (11–13°C), and nights average 28–32°F (−2–0°C), with a diurnal range of 23–24°F (13°C). Growers are cautioned that the calculated temperatures above may not be representative. Observed temperatures at high-elevation stations in nearby regions suggest that average minimum values in winter may be 6–10°F (3–6°C) warmer than indicated. Plants should survive freezing temperatures, providing they are dry, but extreme conditions should be avoided in cultivation. In the habitat, winter rainfall is low but additional moisture is often available from heavy deposits of dew. For about a month in late winter or early spring, however, humidity is so low that even the moisture from dew is uncommon. Cultivated plants should be allowed to dry out between waterings in winter, but they should not remain dry for extended periods. Occasional early morning mistings between waterings, especially on warm, sunny days, may help prevent the plants from becoming too dry. Fertilizer should be eliminated until water is increased in spring. In the habitat, light is highest in winter. The cool, dry rest with increased light may be necessary to initiate blooming.

GROWING MEDIA: Plants may be mounted on tree-fern or cork slabs if humidity is high and plants are watered at least once daily in summer. When plants are potted, any open, fast-draining medium may be used. Repotting is best done in early spring when new roots are growing.

MISCELLANEOUS NOTES: In the habitat, blooming occurs in spring.

Plant and Flower Information

PLANT SIZE AND TYPE: A 7–8 in. (18–20 cm) sympodial plant.

PSEUDOBULB: The stem may have an ovoid or ellipsoid swelling 1–2 in. (2.5–5.0 cm) long.

LEAVES: 2–3 at the apex of each growth. The pointed leaves, which may be elliptic-oblong to lanceolate, are 5–6 in. (13–15 cm) long.

INFLORESCENCE: Short.

FLOWERS: 1 per inflorescence. The fleshy flowers are 1.4 in. (3.5 cm) across. Sepals and petals may be pale yellow or pale chestnut-brown. The dorsal sepal and petals are narrow, oblong, and rounded. The large lip may be pink or yellow with red veins. The lip has large, wavy sidelobes and a nearly round, ruffled midlobe.

HYBRIDIZING NOTES: Chromosome counts are n = 20 (ref. 154, 504, 580) and 2n = 40 (ref. 153, 154).

REFERENCES: 38, 46, 153, 154, 202, 254, 294, 445, 504, 580.

PHOTOS/DRAWINGS: 46, 294.

Dendrobium rotundatum (Lindley) Hooker f. not Bentham. Sometimes listed as a synonym of *Bulbophyllum rotundatum* (Lindley) Rchb. f., but Summerhayes (ref. 499) considers both names to be synonyms of *Epigeneium rotundatum* (Lindley) Summerhayes. REFERENCES: 219, 229, 369, 499.

Dendrobium roxburghii Lindley

AKA: *Aporum roxburghii* Griffith, *Callista calceola* O. K., *Dendrobium calceolum* Roxburgh.

ORIGIN/HABITAT: Ambon Island and Seram. Plants grow in coastal vegetation from sea level to 650 ft. (0–200 m). Lindley (ref. 277) reported the plant as originating in New Guinea. However, J. J. Smith (ref. 470) indicated that he had never seen a specimen from New Guinea.

CLIMATE: Station #97724, Ambon/Pattimura, Indonesia, Lat. 3.7°S, Long. 128.1°E, at 33 ft. (10 m). Record extreme temperatures are 96°F (36°C) and 66°F (19°C).

N/HEMISPHERE	JAN	FEB	MAR	APR	MAY	JUN	JUL	AUG	SEP	OCT	NOV	DEC
°F AVG MAX	81	81	83	85	88	88	88	88	88	86	84	82
°F AVG MIN	74	74	74	74	75	76	76	76	76	76	75	74
DIURNAL RANGE	7	7	9	11	13	12	12	12	12	10	9	8
RAIN/INCHES	23.7	15.8	9.5	6.1	4.5	5.2	5.0	4.7	5.3	11.0	20.3	25.1
HUMIDITY/%	83	82	81	80	79	78	78	77	79	82	83	84
BLOOM SEASON							*		*			
DAYS CLR @ 9AM	1	1	1	6	7	4	3	5	5	3	3	3
DAYS CLR @ 3PM	1	1	2	5	6	1	1	1	2	3	1	3
RAIN/MM	602	401	241	155	114	132	127	119	135	279	516	638
°C AVG MAX	27.2	27.2	28.3	29.4	31.1	31.1	31.1	31.1	31.1	30.0	28.9	27.8
°C AVG MIN	23.3	23.3	23.3	23.3	23.9	24.4	24.4	24.4	24.4	24.4	23.9	23.3
DIURNAL RANGE	3.9	3.9	5.0	6.1	7.2	6.7	6.7	6.7	6.7	5.6	5.0	4.5
S/HEMISPHERE	JUL	AUG	SEP	OCT	NOV	DEC	JAN	FEB	MAR	APR	MAY	JUN

Cultural Recommendations

LIGHT: 2500–3500 fc.

TEMPERATURES: Throughout the year, days average 81–88°F (27–31°C), and nights average 74–76°F (23–24°C), with a diurnal range of 7–13°F (4–7°C).

HUMIDITY: 80–85% year-round.

WATER: Rainfall is moderate to heavy all year, but conditions are slightly drier in late spring and summer. Cultivated plants should be kept evenly moist, with only slight drying allowed between waterings.

FERTILIZER: 1/4–1/2 recommended strength. A balanced fertilizer should be applied weekly to biweekly throughout the year.

REST PERIOD: Growing conditions should be maintained all year. In the habitat, rainfall is heaviest in winter, but water and fertilizer may be reduced somewhat for cultivated plants, especially those grown in the dark, short-day conditions common in temperate latitudes. They should never be allowed to dry completely, however. In the habitat, light is highest in spring.

GROWING MEDIA: Plants may be mounted on tree-fern or cork slabs if humidity is high and plants are watered at least once daily in summer. When plants are potted, any open, fast-draining medium may be used. Repotting may be done anytime new roots are growing.

MISCELLANEOUS NOTES: The bloom season shown in the climate table is based on reports from the habitat.

Plant and Flower Information

PLANT SIZE AND TYPE: A sympodial epiphyte of unreported size.

PSEUDOBULB: The stems are long and straight.

LEAVES: Several. The widely spaced leaves are 1.7 in. (4.3 cm) long. They are deciduous.

INFLORESCENCE: Flowers are borne at the apex and along the side of the leafless, apical portion of the stem.

FLOWERS: The large flowers vary from yellow to dull-orange with red streaks or veins on the lip. The 3-lobed lip is deeply notched at the tip of the midlobe, resulting in the lip appearing nearly 4-lobed.

REFERENCES: 216, 277, 278, 310, 468, 470.

Dendrobium roylei A. Hawkes. See *D. monticola* Hunt and Summerhayes. REFERENCES: 211, 230, 454.

Dendrobium roylei Hiroe. See *D. monticola* Hunt and Summerhayes. REFERENCES: 232, 454.

Dendrobium rubropictum Schlechter

ORIGIN/HABITAT: Northern Papua New Guinea. Plants grow near sea level on forest trees near Peso in the Eitape District.

CLIMATE: Station #94004, Wewak, Papua New Guinea, Lat. 3.6°S, Long. 143.7°E, at 16 ft. (5 m). Record extreme temperatures are 98°F (37°C) and 62°F (17°C).

N/HEMISPHERE	JAN	FEB	MAR	APR	MAY	JUN	JUL	AUG	SEP	OCT	NOV	DEC
°F AVG MAX	88	88	88	88	88	88	87	86	87	88	88	88
°F AVG MIN	74	74	74	75	75	75	75	75	74	74	75	74
DIURNAL RANGE	14	14	14	13	13	13	12	11	13	14	13	14
RAIN/INCHES	7.6	4.8	5.3	10.0	13.3	14.5	12.1	11.9	14.9	16.9	15.1	10.8
HUMIDITY/%	80	79	79	78	79	81	82	82	81	82	81	80
BLOOM SEASON												
DAYS CLR	N/A											
RAIN/MM	193	122	135	254	338	368	307	302	378	429	384	274
°C AVG MAX	31.1	31.1	31.1	31.1	31.1	31.1	30.6	30.0	30.6	31.1	31.1	31.1
°C AVG MIN	23.3	23.3	23.3	23.9	23.9	23.9	23.9	23.9	23.3	23.3	23.9	23.3
DIURNAL RANGE	7.8	7.8	7.8	7.2	7.2	7.2	6.7	6.1	7.2	7.8	7.2	7.8
S/HEMISPHERE	JUL	AUG	SEP	OCT	NOV	DEC	JAN	FEB	MAR	APR	MAY	JUN

Cultural Recommendations

LIGHT: 2000–3000 fc.

TEMPERATURES: Throughout the year, days average 86–88°F (30–31°C), and nights average 74–75°F (23–24°C), with a diurnal range of 11–14°F (6–8°C).

HUMIDITY: Near 80% year-round.

WATER: Rainfall is heavy all year, but conditions are slightly drier for 1–2 months in late winter. Cultivated plants should be kept moist, with only slight drying allowed between waterings.

FERTILIZER: 1/4–1/2 recommended strength. A balanced fertilizer should be applied weekly to biweekly throughout the year.

REST PERIOD: Growing conditions should be maintained year-round. Water should be reduced for plants cultivated in the dark, short-day conditions common during temperate-latitude winters, but they should not be allowed to dry out completely. Fertilizer should also be reduced if water is reduced. In the habitat, light may be slightly higher in winter.

GROWING MEDIA: A very open and fast-draining medium should be used with either baskets or small pots. Repotting may be done anytime new roots are growing.

MISCELLANEOUS NOTES: The bloom season shown in the climate table is based on reports from the habitat. Plants that produce flowers which last a single day commonly bloom several times during the year. Flowering usually occurs 7–14 days after a sudden 10°F (5°C) drop in daytime temperatures.

Plant and Flower Information

PLANT SIZE AND TYPE: A 16–26 in. (40–65 cm) sympodial epiphyte.

PSEUDOBULB: 12–20 in. (30–50 cm) long. The leafy stems are simple, curved, and somewhat flattened.

LEAVES: Many. The narrow leaves are 4–6 in. (10–15 cm) long. They may be erect or spreading.

INFLORESCENCE: Short.

FLOWERS: 2 per inflorescence. The flowers are 0.5 in. (1.3 cm) long and remain rather closed. Sepals and petals are white. The white lip is marked with red on the sidelobes and the midlobe has a golden yellow crest. The apex of the column foot is golden yellow. The lip is 3-lobed with a truncate midlobe which has a small, projecting point in the center. The oblong sidelobes are moderately ruffled along the exterior margin. Blossoms are short-lived.

REFERENCES: 92, 221, 437, 445.

PHOTOS/DRAWINGS: 437.

Dendrobium ruckeri Lindley

AKA: *D. ramosum* Lindley ex Wallich. Kränzlin (ref. 254) reverses this synonymy.

ORIGIN/HABITAT: Northeastern India. Plants grow in Sikkim, Bhutan, and the Khasi (Khasia) Hills at 4250–5600 ft. (1300–1700 m). Plants were once thought to have originated in the Philippines, but Merrill (ref. 296) excludes this species from the Philippines.

CLIMATE: Station #42410, Gauhati, India, Lat. 26.1°N, Long. 91.6°E, at 158 ft. (48 m). Temperatures are calculated for an elevation of 4600 ft. (1400 m), resulting in probable extremes of 89°F (32°C) and 26°F (−3°C).

N/HEMISPHERE	JAN	FEB	MAR	APR	MAY	JUN	JUL	AUG	SEP	OCT	NOV	DEC
°F AVG MAX	61	63	71	73	73	74	75	75	74	72	66	61
°F AVG MIN	36	39	45	53	57	62	63	63	61	56	46	38
DIURNAL RANGE	25	24	26	20	16	12	12	12	13	16	20	23
RAIN/INCHES	0.4	1.2	2.0	5.7	9.3	12.3	12.3	10.3	6.6	2.8	0.6	0.2
HUMIDITY/%	79	72	64	71	82	85	85	86	84	84	83	82
BLOOM SEASON		*	*	**	**							
DAYS CLR @ 6AM	6	12	16	11	3	0	0	1	3	7	6	3
DAYS CLR @ 12PM	17	16	18	15	6	1	0	0	2	11	17	19
RAIN/MM	10	30	51	145	236	312	312	262	168	71	15	5
°C AVG MAX	16.3	17.4	21.9	23.0	23.0	23.5	24.1	24.1	23.5	22.4	19.1	16.3
°C AVG MIN	2.4	4.1	7.4	11.9	14.1	16.9	17.4	17.4	16.3	13.5	8.0	3.5
DIURNAL RANGE	13.9	13.3	14.5	11.1	8.9	6.6	6.7	6.7	7.2	8.9	11.1	12.8
S/HEMISPHERE	JUL	AUG	SEP	OCT	NOV	DEC	JAN	FEB	MAR	APR	MAY	JUN

Dendrobium rudolphii

Cultural Recommendations

LIGHT: 2500–3500 fc. In the habitat, summer light is diffused and relatively low because clouds are heavy during the rainy season. Light increases by midautumn when about half of the afternoons are clear. In autumn and winter, light should be as high as possible, short of burning the leaves.

TEMPERATURES: Summer days average 74–75°F (24°C), and nights average 62–63°F (17°C), with a diurnal range of 12°F (7°C). The effects of the microclimate may cause actual summer maximum and winter minimum temperatures to be 6–8°F (3–4°C) warmer than indicated.

HUMIDITY: Near 85% in summer, dropping to 65–70% for about 2 months in late winter.

WATER: Rainfall is heavy from spring through summer but decreases rapidly in autumn with a 1–2 month transition into the winter dry season. Cultivated plants should be kept moist while actively growing, but water should be gradually reduced after new growths mature in autumn.

FERTILIZER: ¼–½ recommended strength, applied weekly. A high-nitrogen fertilizer is beneficial from spring to midsummer, but a fertilizer high in phosphates should be used in late summer and autumn.

REST PERIOD: Winter days average 61–63°F (16–17°C), and nights average 36–39°F (2–4°C), with a diurnal range of 23–25°F (13–14°C). Growers are cautioned that these calculated night temperatures may be colder than actual habitat values. Observed temperatures at high-elevation stations in nearby regions suggest that actual minimums may be 4–6°F (2–3°C) warmer than indicated. Plants should survive exposure to freezing if they are dry at the time, but extreme conditions should be avoided in cultivation. Although rainfall is low for 4–5 winter months, high humidity and the large temperature range indicate that additional moisture from heavy dew is common. Therefore, although water should be greatly reduced and cultivated plants allowed to dry out between waterings from late autumn into early spring, they should not remain dry for extended periods. Occasional mistings between waterings during bright, sunny weather may help prevent the plants from becoming too dry. Fertilizer should be reduced or eliminated until active growth resumes and water is increased in spring. In the habitat, light is brightest in winter.

GROWING MEDIA: Mounting plants on tree-fern or cork slabs accommodates their pendulous growth habit. However, humidity must be high and plants must be watered at least once a day in summer. If plants cannot be mounted, hanging pots or baskets may be filled with an open, fast-draining medium. Repotting may be done anytime new roots are actively growing.

MISCELLANEOUS NOTES: The bloom season shown in the climate table is based on cultivation records.

Plant and Flower Information

PLANT SIZE AND TYPE: A 12–29 in. (30–74 cm) sympodial epiphyte. Although normally smaller, plants sometimes reach a length of 36 in. (92 cm).

PSEUDOBULB: 12–36 in. (30–92 cm) long. The stems are long, slender, and smooth. They branch and rebranch, becoming pendulous. Nodes are spaced about 2 in. (5 cm) apart. They are not swollen.

LEAVES: The linear-lanceolate leaves are 3–5 in. (8–13 cm) long and pointed at the tip.

INFLORESCENCE: Inflorescences emerge from the uppermost joints of leafless stems.

FLOWERS: 1–2 per inflorescence. The fragrant blossoms are 1.4–1.6 in. (3.5–4.0 cm) across, with primrose yellow sepals and petals. The 3-lobed lip is sub trapezoid-obovate. It may be pink or yellow with brownish purple streaks or red veins. The papillose crest in the center of the lip is a yellow-green. The margins of the large midlobe are reflexed and wavy. The spur is twisted.

HYBRIDIZING NOTES: Chromosome count is 2n = 40 as *D. ramosum* Lindley ex Wallich (ref. 504, 580).

REFERENCES: 38, 46, 179, 202, 216, 254, 296, 317, 369, 445, 504, 541, 580.

PHOTOS/DRAWINGS: 46.

Dendrobium rudolphii A. Hawkes and A. H. Heller. See *D. hendersonii* A. Hawkes and A. H. Heller. REFERENCES: 191, 229, 454.

Dendrobium ruginosum Ames

ORIGIN/HABITAT: South Pacific Islands. On Vanikoro Island in the Santa Cruz group, plants have been collected in rainforest at 2600 ft. (800 m). In the Solomon Islands, they grow on trees and rocks. On Bougainville Island, plants are found in mountain rainforests and scrub habitat at 2300–6250 ft. (700–1900 m).

CLIMATE: Station #91502, Kieta, Bougainville Island, Lat. 6.2°S, Long. 155.6°E, at 240 ft. (73 m). Temperatures are calculated for an elevation of 4250 ft. (1300 m), resulting in probable extremes of 83°F (28°C) and 51°F (10°C).

N/HEMISPHERE	JAN	FEB	MAR	APR	MAY	JUN	JUL	AUG	SEP	OCT	NOV	DEC
°F AVG MAX	72	72	74	75	75	76	75	75	75	74	74	73
°F AVG MIN	61	61	61	62	62	62	63	62	63	63	62	62
DIURNAL RANGE	11	11	13	13	13	14	12	13	12	11	12	11
RAIN/INCHES	10.9	9.4	8.0	9.8	9.6	9.4	10.5	10.7	11.2	11.7	9.3	9.0
HUMIDITY/%	80	80	79	76	78	76	79	77	78	80	80	82
BLOOM SEASON									*			
DAYS CLR	N/A											
RAIN/MM	277	239	203	249	244	239	267	272	284	297	236	229
°C AVG MAX	22.1	22.1	23.2	23.7	23.7	24.3	23.7	23.7	23.7	23.2	23.2	22.6
°C AVG MIN	15.9	15.9	15.9	16.5	16.5	16.5	17.1	16.5	17.1	17.1	16.5	16.5
DIURNAL RANGE	6.2	6.2	7.3	7.2	7.2	7.8	6.6	7.2	6.6	6.1	6.7	6.1
S/HEMISPHERE	JUL	AUG	SEP	OCT	NOV	DEC	JAN	FEB	MAR	APR	MAY	JUN

Cultural Recommendations

LIGHT: 3000–4000 fc. High humidity and strong air movement should be maintained when light levels are high.

TEMPERATURES: Throughout the year, days average 72–76°F (22–24°C), and nights average 61–63°F (16–17°C), with a diurnal range of 11–14°F (6–8°C).

HUMIDITY: Near 75–80% year-round.

WATER: Rainfall is heavy all year. Cultivated plants should be kept moist but not soggy. Warm water might be beneficial.

FERTILIZER: ¼–½ recommended strength. A balanced fertilizer should be applied weekly to biweekly throughout the year.

REST PERIOD: Growing conditions should be maintained all year. Water should be reduced somewhat in winter, especially for plants grown in the dark, short-day conditions common in temperate latitudes. Plants should never be allowed to dry completely, however. Fertilizer should be reduced or eliminated anytime water is reduced. In the habitat, seasonal light variation is minor.

GROWING MEDIA: Because of high water requirements and the lack of drying between waterings, plants are easier to manage if grown in pots with a very open and fast-draining medium. Repotting may be done anytime new roots are growing.

MISCELLANEOUS NOTES: The bloom season shown in the climate table is based on cultivation records. Lewis and Cribb (ref. 270, 271) indicate that *D. mooreanum* Lindley from Vanuatu resembles *D. ruginosum*.

Plant and Flower Information

PLANT SIZE AND TYPE: A 3–10 in. (8–25 cm) sympodial epiphyte.

PSEUDOBULB: 3–10 in. (8–25 cm) long. The clustered, club-shaped stems may be yellow or purple. They are 4-angled with 4 nodes below the leaves.

LEAVES: 2–4 at the apex of each growth. The lanceolate leaves are 1.6–4.7 in. (4–12 cm) long. They are leathery and suberect.

INFLORESCENCE: 8 in. (20 cm) long. The inflorescence emerges at the apex of the pseudobulb.

FLOWERS: 4–8 per inflorescence. The flowers are 1.2–1.6 in. (3–4 cm) across. The pointed sepals and petals are white. The lip may be white, pale yellow, or creamy green with purple-brown stripes. The 3-lobed lip is pointed at the tip. The sidelobes are rounded in front and curve in, forming a cone. The oblong midlobe is longer than the sidelobes. The fleshy callus is obscurely 3-ridged at the base.

HYBRIDIZING NOTES: Chromosome count is 2n = 36 (ref. 152, 243).

REFERENCES: 17, 83, 91, 95, 152, 179, 225, 243, 270, 271, 516, 550.

PHOTOS/DRAWINGS: *83, 271*.

Dendrobium rugosum (Blume) Lindley

AKA: *Grastidium rugosum* Blume, *Dendrobium glaucophyllum* Teijsm. and Binn., *D. purpurascens* Teijsm. and Binn.

ORIGIN/HABITAT: East and West Java. The orchids are common forest epiphytes at 1650–2800 ft. (500–850 m). They usually hang from lower tree branches.

CLIMATE: Station #96755, Bogor, Indonesia, Lat. 6.5°S, Long. 106.8°E, at 558 ft. (170 m). Temperatures are calculated for an elevation of 2600 ft. (790 m), resulting in probable extremes of 89°F (32°C) and 59°F (15°C).

N/HEMISPHERE	JAN	FEB	MAR	APR	MAY	JUN	JUL	AUG	SEP	OCT	NOV	DEC
°F AVG MAX	79	80	81	81	80	78	77	77	78	79	80	79
°F AVG MIN	66	66	66	67	67	67	67	67	67	68	68	67
DIURNAL RANGE	13	14	15	14	13	11	10	10	11	11	12	12
RAIN/INCHES	2.1	1.0	0.5	5.0	8.1	18.8	23.7	20.2	14.4	12.0	11.9	3.4
HUMIDITY/%	72	68	65	66	74	79	84	84	81	79	77	75
BLOOM SEASON								*				
DAYS CLR @ 7AM	14	14	14	11	5	3	1	2	4	6	10	12
DAYS CLR @ 1PM	9	10	8	5	1	1	0	0	1	1	3	7
RAIN/MM	53	25	13	127	206	478	602	513	366	305	302	86
°C AVG MAX	26.3	26.8	27.4	27.4	26.8	25.7	25.2	25.2	25.7	26.3	26.8	26.3
°C AVG MIN	19.1	19.1	19.1	19.6	19.6	19.6	19.6	19.6	19.6	20.2	20.2	19.6
DIURNAL RANGE	7.2	7.7	8.3	7.8	7.2	6.1	5.6	5.6	6.1	6.1	6.6	6.7
S/HEMISPHERE	JUL	AUG	SEP	OCT	NOV	DEC	JAN	FEB	MAR	APR	MAY	JUN

Cultural Recommendations

LIGHT: 1800–2500 fc.

TEMPERATURES: Throughout the year, days average 77–81°F (25–27°C), and nights average 66–68°F (19–20°C), with a diurnal range of 10–15°F (6–8°C). Uniform temperatures may be critical for plant health.

HUMIDITY: 80–85% in summer, dropping to about 65% in winter. Excellent air circulation may be particularly important for plants from this habitat.

WATER: Rainfall is very heavy from spring into autumn, but conditions are very dry for 2–3 months in winter. During the growing season, plants should never be allowed to dry out completely, but water should be gradually reduced in late autumn.

FERTILIZER: ¼–½ recommended strength, applied weekly. A high-nitrogen fertilizer is beneficial from spring to midsummer, but a fertilizer high in phosphates should be used in late summer and autumn.

REST PERIOD: Growing conditions should be maintained all year, but rainfall is very low for 2–3 winter months. In cultivation, water should be reduced and the plants allowed to become somewhat dry between waterings. They should not remain dry for prolonged periods, however. Fertilizer may be reduced or eliminated anytime the plant is not actively growing. In the habitat, light is highest in winter.

GROWING MEDIA: Plants should be mounted on tree-fern or cork slabs to accommodate their stiffly pendulous growth habit. Remounting may be done anytime new roots are growing.

MISCELLANEOUS NOTES: The bloom season shown in the climate table is based on reports from the habitat. Plants that produce flowers which last a single day commonly bloom several times during the year. Flowering usually occurs 7–14 days after a sudden 10°F (5°C) drop in daytime temperatures.

Plant and Flower Information

PLANT SIZE AND TYPE: A 79 in. (200 cm) long sympodial epiphyte.

PSEUDOBULB: 79 in. (200 cm) long. Stems are stiffly pendulous.

LEAVES: Many. The ovate to narrowly lanceolate leaves are 2.8–4.7 in. (7–12 cm) long. They are thick and fleshy. The typical variety has shiny green leaves that are often dark violet when young, but var. *glaucophyllum* (Teijsm. Binn.) J. J. Smith has gray leaves.

INFLORESCENCE: Very short. Inflorescences appear from nodes anywhere along the stem. Both flowers face the same direction, but the upper blossom is erect while the lower one is upside down.

FLOWERS: 2 per inflorescence. The flowers are 1.0–1.2 in. (2.5–3.0 cm) across and somewhat fan-shaped. The dorsal sepal is curved forward at the tip. The edges of the petals curl in so that the margin of each segment touches the opposite edge. Sepals and petals are pale yellow with red speckles. The small, trilobed lip is recurved at the tip. The keel is covered with red tubercles. The yellowish white column is orange at the tip. Blossoms are short-lived.

REFERENCES: 25, 75, 216, 254, 277, 310, 317, 445, 469.

PHOTOS/DRAWINGS: *75, 469*.

Dendrobium rugulosum J. J. Smith

ORIGIN/HABITAT: Irian Jaya (western New Guinea). Plants are rare on the lower slopes of Mt. Goliath, where they were found on the trunks of smooth barked trees at about 500 ft. (150 m).

CLIMATE: Station #97876, Tanahmerah, Irian Jaya, Lat. 6.1°S, Long. 140.3°E, at 75 ft. (23 m). Temperatures are calculated for an elevation of 500 ft. (150 m), resulting in probable extremes of 97°F (36°C) and 63°F (17°C).

N/HEMISPHERE	JAN	FEB	MAR	APR	MAY	JUN	JUL	AUG	SEP	OCT	NOV	DEC
°F AVG MAX	83	84	86	89	90	89	89	88	89	88	86	84
°F AVG MIN	71	70	70	71	72	73	72	72	72	72	73	72
DIURNAL RANGE	12	14	16	18	18	16	17	16	17	16	13	12
RAIN/INCHES	11.5	12.1	14.7	13.2	14.4	15.9	14.5	15.8	17.4	17.3	15.5	11.9
HUMIDITY/%	N/A											
BLOOM SEASON										*		
DAYS CLR	N/A											
RAIN/MM	292	307	373	335	366	404	368	401	442	439	394	302
°C AVG MAX	28.1	28.7	29.8	31.4	32.0	31.4	31.4	30.9	31.4	30.9	29.8	28.7
°C AVG MIN	21.4	20.9	20.9	21.4	22.0	22.6	22.0	22.0	22.0	22.0	22.6	22.0
DIURNAL RANGE	6.7	7.8	8.9	10.0	10.0	8.8	9.4	8.9	9.4	8.9	7.2	6.7
S/HEMISPHERE	JUL	AUG	SEP	OCT	NOV	DEC	JAN	FEB	MAR	APR	MAY	JUN

Cultural Recommendations

LIGHT: 2000–3000 fc.

TEMPERATURES: Throughout the year, days average 83–90°F (28–32°C), and nights average 70–73°F (21–23°C), with a diurnal range of 12–18°F (7–10°C).

HUMIDITY: Information is not available for this location. However, records from nearby stations indicate that humidity probably averages near 85% year-round.

WATER: Rainfall is very heavy all year. Cultivated plants should be kept evenly moist but not soggy.

FERTILIZER: ¼–½ recommended strength. A balanced fertilizer should be applied weekly to biweekly throughout the year.

REST PERIOD: Growing conditions should be maintained year-round. Water and fertilizer might be reduced slightly in winter, especially for plants grown in the dark, short-day conditions common in temperate latitudes; but plants should never be allowed to dry completely.

GROWING MEDIA: Because plants must be kept moist, they are easier to manage when potted. Fir bark or any open, fast-draining medium may be used. Repotting may be done anytime new roots are growing.

MISCELLANEOUS NOTES: The bloom season shown in the climate table is based on reports from the habitat. The plant was described in 1911 in *Bul. Jard. Bot. Buit.* 2nd sér. 2:10.

Plant and Flower Information

PLANT SIZE AND TYPE: An 11 in. (28 cm) sympodial epiphyte.

PSEUDOBULB: 11 in. (28 cm) long. The stems are clustered, leafy, and shiny. They are slightly flattened and elliptical in cross section.

LEAVES: Many. The linear leaves are 3–4 in. (8–10 cm) long, papery, and unequally 2-toothed at the apex.

INFLORESCENCE: Short. Inflorescences emerge from nodes along the stem.

FLOWERS: 2 per inflorescence. The white flowers are 0.5 in. (1.3 cm) long. The dorsal sepal is oblong, pointed, and concave. The lateral sepals are somewhat ovate, sickle-shaped, concave, and pointed at the tip. The wavy, concave petals are subrhomboid. The 3-lobed lip is wavy with a large, broad midlobe. Sidelobes are erect, quadrangular, and ruffled or uneven along the margin.

REFERENCES: 221, 445, 470.

Dendrobium ruidilobum J. J. Smith. See *D. cochliodes* Schlechter. REFERENCES: 25, 84, 225, 485.

Dendrobium rumphiae Rchb. f.

AKA: *Index Kewensis* (ref. 216) indicates that *D. rumphiae* Rchb. f. is a synonym of *Dendrobium angustifolium* (Blume) Lindley, which was originally described as *Desmotrichum angustifolium* Blume. Comber (ref. 75) indicates that *Desmotrichum angustifolium* Blume is now considered a synonym of *Flickingeria angustifolia* (Blume) A. Hawkes. However, J. J. Smith (ref. 470) and Schlechter (ref. 437) indicate that *D. rumphiae* Rchb. f. was originally described as *Cadetia angustifolia* Blume. Due to the confusion, we have included it as a separate species.

D. rumphiae Rchb. f. var. *quinquecostatum* J. J. Smith is now considered a synonym of *D. versteegii* J. J. Smith. *D. rumphiae* Rchb. f. var. *quinquenervium* is now considered a synonym of *Cadetia quinquenervia*.

ORIGIN/HABITAT: Irian Jaya (western New Guinea). Plants grow near sea level along the Noord River south of Nepenthes Hill. They grow on trees in *Metroxylon* swamps or on isolated trees along rocky beaches.

CLIMATE: Station #97796, Kokenau (Kokonau), Irian Jaya, Lat. 4.7°S, Long. 136.4°E, at 10 ft. (3 m). Record extreme temperatures are not available for this location.

N/HEMISPHERE	JAN	FEB	MAR	APR	MAY	JUN	JUL	AUG	SEP	OCT	NOV	DEC
°F AVG MAX	83	83	86	88	90	89	89	89	90	88	87	84
°F AVG MIN	73	73	74	74	74	75	74	74	74	74	74	73
DIURNAL RANGE	10	10	12	14	16	14	15	15	16	14	13	11
RAIN/INCHES	18.4	15.8	18.9	11.6	9.7	10.6	11.5	15.7	11.6	11.6	16.0	19.9
HUMIDITY/%	N/A											
BLOOM SEASON	*			*			*					
DAYS CLR	N/A											
RAIN/MM	467	401	479	295	245	269	293	400	294	296	407	506
°C AVG MAX	28.6	28.4	30.2	31.1	32.1	31.9	31.9	31.7	32.0	31.4	30.7	28.7
°C AVG MIN	22.7	22.6	23.3	23.4	23.5	23.7	23.6	23.5	23.4	23.5	23.4	23.0
DIURNAL RANGE	5.9	5.8	6.9	7.7	8.6	8.2	8.3	8.2	8.6	8.0	7.2	5.7
S/HEMISPHERE	JUL	AUG	SEP	OCT	NOV	DEC	JAN	FEB	MAR	APR	MAY	JUN

Cultural Recommendations

LIGHT: 2500–3500 fc.

TEMPERATURES: Throughout the year, days average 83–90°F (29–32°C), and nights average 73–75°F (23–24°C), with a diurnal range of 10–16°F (6–9°C).

HUMIDITY: Information is not available for this location. However, records from nearby stations indicate that humidity probably averages near 85% year-round.

WATER: Rainfall is very heavy all year. Cultivated plants should be kept evenly moist but not soggy. Warm water might be beneficial.

FERTILIZER: ¼–½ recommended strength. A balanced fertilizer should be applied weekly to biweekly throughout the year.

REST PERIOD: Growing temperatures should be maintained year-round. The smallest diurnal range occurs in winter. Water and fertilizer might be reduced somewhat in winter, especially for plants cultivated in the dark, short-day conditions common in the temperate latitudes. They should never be allowed to dry out completely, however. In the habitat, seasonal light variation is minor.

GROWING MEDIA: Plants are best grown in small containers filled with any open, fast-draining medium which must be kept moist, but not soggy. Moisture-retaining additives may be added as needed to maintain the required moisture levels. Repotting may be done anytime new roots are growing.

MISCELLANEOUS NOTES: The bloom season shown in the climate table is based on collection reports.

Plant and Flower Information

PLANT SIZE AND TYPE: A 2.2–4.1 in. (5.5–10.5 cm) sympodial epiphyte.

PSEUDOBULB: 0.8–2.4 in. (2–6 cm) long. The erect stems are clustered on a very short rhizome.

LEAVES: 1 per growth. The erect, lanceolate leaves are 1.4–1.8 in. (3.5–4.5 cm) long. They are 2-toothed at the apex.

INFLORESCENCE: 0.6 in. (1.5 cm) long. The inflorescence emerges at the apex of the pseudobulb.

FLOWERS: 1 per inflorescence. The flowers are 0.4 in. (1 cm) long. The dorsal sepal is erect, incurved, and pointed at the tip. Lateral sepals are ovate-triangular, pointed, and concave. Petals are pointed, reflexed, somewhat lanceolate, dilated at the base, and uneven along the margin. The lip may be sulfur yellow or orange. Sidelobes are erect. The midlobe is oblong-obovate and incurved. It is papillose in the center.

REFERENCES: 216, 254, 445, 470.

Dendrobium rumphianum Teijsm. and Binn. See *D. bicaudatum* Reinwardt ex Lindley. The International Orchid Commission (ref. 236) registers hybrids under the name *D. rumphianum*. REFERENCES: 25, 216, 236, 254, 343, 436, 445, 468, 483. PHOTOS/DRAWINGS: 343.

Dendrobium rupestre J. J. Smith

ORIGIN/HABITAT: Widespread in New Guinea. In Irian Jaya (western New Guinea), collections are reported in the Jaya (Carstensz), Victor Emanuel, and Traub (Treub) Mountains. They are also found on Mt. Goliath and near Lake Habbema. In Papua, the orchids grow in the Western Highlands, Southern Highlands, Enga, Chimbu, Morobe, and Northern Provinces at 4900–10,150 ft. (1500–3100 m). Plants are usually epiphytic, but they occasionally grow in moss on the surface of the ground or on schist.

CLIMATE: Botanical garden records, Laiagam, Papua New Guinea, Lat.

5.5°S, Long. 143.5°E, at 7218 ft. (2200 m). Record extreme temperatures are 91°F (33°C) and 32°F (0°C).

N/HEMISPHERE	JAN	FEB	MAR	APR	MAY	JUN	JUL	AUG	SEP	OCT	NOV	DEC
°F AVG MAX	76	77	78	76	78	78	82	77	76	78	78	76
°F AVG MIN	55	54	55	55	56	56	55	56	58	57	56	56
DIURNAL RANGE	21	23	23	21	22	22	27	21	18	21	22	20
RAIN/INCHES	4.0	4.8	6.1	7.8	8.5	9.1	8.4	9.6	9.5	8.9	6.3	4.0
HUMIDITY/%	N/A											
BLOOM SEASON	*	*	*				*	*	*			
DAYS CLR	N/A											
RAIN/MM	102	121	154	198	217	230	213	243	241	227	159	102
°C AVG MAX	24.4	25.0	25.6	24.4	25.6	25.6	27.8	25.0	24.4	25.6	25.6	24.4
°C AVG MIN	12.8	12.2	12.8	12.8	13.3	13.3	12.8	13.3	14.4	13.9	13.3	13.3
DIURNAL RANGE	11.7	12.8	12.8	11.7	12.2	12.2	15.0	11.7	10.0	11.7	12.2	11.1
S/HEMISPHERE	JUL	AUG	SEP	OCT	NOV	DEC	JAN	FEB	MAR	APR	MAY	JUN

Cultural Recommendations

LIGHT: 2000–3000 fc.

TEMPERATURES: Throughout the year, days average 76–82°F (24–28°C), and nights average 54–58°F (12–14°C), with a diurnal range of 18–27°F (10–15°C).

HUMIDITY: Information is not available for this location. However, records from nearby stations indicate that averages are probably 70–80% year-round.

WATER: Rainfall is heavy throughout the year, but conditions are slightly drier for 3–4 months in winter. Cultivated plants should be kept evenly moist.

FERTILIZER: ¼–½ recommended strength. A balanced fertilizer should be applied weekly to biweekly throughout the year.

REST PERIOD: Growing conditions should be maintained year-round. Water and fertilizer should be reduced somewhat in winter, especially for plants grown in the dark, short-day conditions common in temperate latitudes. They should never be allowed to dry out completely, however. In the habitat, light is highest in winter.

GROWING MEDIA: Plants may be mounted on tree-fern or cork slabs if humidity is high and plants are watered at least once daily in summer. When plants are potted, any open, fast-draining medium may be used. Repotting may be done anytime new roots are growing.

MISCELLANEOUS NOTES: The bloom season shown in the climate table is based on reports from the habitat.

Plant and Flower Information

PLANT SIZE AND TYPE: A 2 in. (5 cm) sympodial epiphyte.

PSEUDOBULB: 0.8 in. (2 cm) long. The obovoid pseudobulbs have 1–3 nodes. They are borne on a rhizome that is very branching, creeping, and rooting.

LEAVES: 1 per growth. The lanceolate leaves are 0.8–2.4 in. (2–6 cm) long and hooked at the pointed tip. The margins are minutely toothed. They are dark olive green on the upper surface with a lighter shade on the underside.

INFLORESCENCE: 0.8 in. (2 cm) long. One or two inflorescences arise through the leaf sheaths from the nodes near the apex of the newest growths.

FLOWERS: 1–2 per inflorescence. The flowers are 0.8–1.0 in. (2.0–2.5 cm) across, large for the plant size. They open fully. Sepals and petals may be blood-red, pale red, magenta, or silvery gray with violet near the tips. The backsides of the sepals are sparsely covered with dots. The slender lateral sepals are long and spreading. Petals are erect, lanceolate, pointed, and covered with minute hairs. The dorsal sepal is ovate-oblong. The erect lip is dark purple-red with orange, blood-red, or brown at the tip. The concave lip is obscurely 3-lobed and incurved along the margins. The spur is darker brownish-red. Color is variable.

REFERENCES: 221, 379, 395, 445, 470, 538.

PHOTOS/DRAWINGS: *379, 385*, 538.

Dendrobium rupicola Rchb. f. See *D. venustum* Teijsm. and Binn. REFERENCES: 21, 179, 190, 220, 254, 454. PHOTOS/DRAWINGS: *21*.

Dendrobium rupicolum Ridley

AKA: Sometimes spelled *D. rupicola*. Hunt (ref. 211) includes *D. distichophyllum* A. Hawkes and A. H. Heller as a synonym.

ORIGIN/HABITAT: Malaya. Plants grow on rocks and trees on Mt. Tahan, the Cameron Highlands, and the main mountain range. Habitat elevation is estimated, so the following climate data should be used with caution.

CLIMATE: Station #48625, Ipoh, Malaya, Lat. 4.6°N, Long. 101.1°E, at 123 ft. (37 m). Temperatures are calculated for an estimated elevation of 4000 ft. (1220 m), resulting in probable extremes of 86°F (30°C) and 51°F (11°C).

N/HEMISPHERE	JAN	FEB	MAR	APR	MAY	JUN	JUL	AUG	SEP	OCT	NOV	DEC
°F AVG MAX	77	79	80	79	79	79	78	78	77	76	76	76
°F AVG MIN	59	59	60	60	61	60	59	59	60	59	59	59
DIURNAL RANGE	18	20	20	19	18	19	19	19	17	17	17	17
RAIN/INCHES	7.9	3.1	7.6	8.4	6.2	3.6	7.2	6.9	8.8	11.0	13.0	8.9
HUMIDITY/%	76	74	76	78	78	75	76	77	79	82	82	81
BLOOM SEASON							*	*	*	*		
DAYS CLR @ 7AM	3	3	3	1	1	2	1	1	0	0	1	2
DAYS CLR @ 1PM	2	2	2	1	1	1	1	1	0	0	0	2
RAIN/MM	201	79	193	213	157	91	183	175	224	279	330	226
°C AVG MAX	25.1	26.2	26.8	26.2	26.2	26.2	25.7	25.7	25.1	24.6	24.6	24.6
°C AVG MIN	15.1	15.1	15.7	15.7	16.2	15.7	15.1	15.1	15.7	15.1	15.1	15.1
DIURNAL RANGE	10.0	11.1	11.1	10.5	10.0	10.5	10.6	10.6	9.4	9.5	9.5	9.5
S/HEMISPHERE	JUL	AUG	SEP	OCT	NOV	DEC	JAN	FEB	MAR	APR	MAY	JUN

Cultural Recommendations

LIGHT: 1800–2500 fc. Light should be diffused or dappled, and direct sunlight should be avoided. Clear days are quite rare.

TEMPERATURES: Throughout the year, days average 76–80°F (25–27°C), and nights average 59–61°F (15–16°C), with a diurnal range of 17–20°F (9–11°C). The extreme high does not exceed the warmest averages by more than 6°F (3°C), and the average lows fluctuate only 2°F (1°C), indicating that plants may not tolerate wide seasonal temperature fluctuations. Although temperatures are uniform all year, the diurnal range is surprisingly large.

HUMIDITY: 75–80% year-round.

WATER: Rainfall is heavy most of the year. The heaviest rainfall occurs in autumn with a secondary maximum in spring. Brief semidry periods occur in midwinter and midsummer. Cultivated plants should be kept evenly moist, with only slight drying allowed between waterings.

FERTILIZER: ¼–½ recommended strength. A balanced fertilizer should be applied weekly to biweekly throughout the year.

REST PERIOD: Growing conditions should be maintained year-round. Water should be reduced somewhat in winter for plants cultivated in the dark, short-day conditions common in temperate latitudes. They should never be allowed to dry out completely, however. Fertilizer may be reduced when the plant is not actively growing or when water is reduced. In the habitat, light is slightly higher in winter.

GROWING MEDIA: Plants may be mounted on tree-fern or cork slabs if humidity is high and plants are watered at least once daily in summer. When plants are potted, any open, fast-draining medium may be used. Repotting may be done anytime new roots are growing.

MISCELLANEOUS NOTES: The bloom season shown in the climate table is based on cultivation records.

Plant and Flower Information

PLANT SIZE AND TYPE: A 6–14 in. (15–35 cm) sympodial epiphyte or lithophyte.

PSEUDOBULB: 6–14 in. (15–35 cm) long. The stems, which consist of nodes spaced about 0.2 in. (0.6 cm) apart, are covered with leaf sheaths.

LEAVES: Many. The oblong leaves are approximately 0.2–0.7 in. (0.5–1.8 cm) long. They are bilobed at the tip.

INFLORESCENCE: Short. Inflorescences emerge from nodes opposite the leaves.

FLOWERS: 1 per inflorescence. The tiny flowers are 0.3 in. (0.7 cm) across. Sepals and very narrow petals may be dull yellow, greenish yellow, or pale ochre brown. The lip is white or pale yellow with a dull orange, mealy blotch in the center and a slight notch at the apex. It has no side-lobes. The broad lip is upturned along the sides.

REFERENCES: 200, 211, 221, 229, 402, 454, 455.

PHOTOS/DRAWINGS: 455.

Dendrobium ruppianum A. Hawkes. See *D. jonesii* Rendle.
REFERENCES: 36, 67, 105, 151, 152, 154, 179, 187, 230, 240, 243, 262, 390, 495, 533. PHOTOS/DRAWINGS: 262, 390.

Dendrobium × ruppiosum S. C. Clemsha. Upton (ref. 533) indicates that this is a natural hybrid between *D. ruppianum* A. Hawkes (*D. jonesii* Rendle) and *D. speciosum* J. E. Smith [*D. pedunculatum* (Clemsha) M. Clements and D. Jones]. REFERENCES: 67, 234, 240, 533.

Dendrobium ruscifolium Swartz. Now considered a synonym of *Pleurothallis ruscifolia* R. Brown. REFERENCES: 190, 216, 254.

Dendrobium rutriferum Rchb. f.

AKA: *D. moirianum* A. Hawkes, *D. puniceum* Rolfe not Ridley.

ORIGIN/HABITAT: Northern Papua New Guinea. Plants grow on trees at the edge of mistforests in the Torricelli Range at about 1950 ft. (600 m). The orchids are also found on Bougainville, but they are not native to that habitat.

CLIMATE: Station #94004, Wewak, Papua New Guinea, Lat. 3.6°S, Long. 143.7°E, at 16 ft. (5 m). Temperatures are calculated for an elevation of 2000 ft. (610 m), resulting in probable extremes of 91°F (33°C) and 55°F (13°C).

N/HEMISPHERE	JAN	FEB	MAR	APR	MAY	JUN	JUL	AUG	SEP	OCT	NOV	DEC
°F AVG MAX	81	81	81	81	81	81	80	79	80	81	81	81
°F AVG MIN	67	67	67	68	68	68	68	68	67	67	68	67
DIURNAL RANGE	14	14	14	13	13	13	12	11	13	14	13	14
RAIN/INCHES	7.6	4.8	5.3	10.0	13.3	14.5	12.1	11.9	14.9	16.9	15.1	10.8
HUMIDITY/%	80	79	79	78	79	81	82	82	81	82	81	80
BLOOM SEASON		*							*			
DAYS CLR	N/A											
RAIN/MM	193	122	135	254	338	368	307	302	378	429	384	274
°C AVG MAX	27.5	27.5	27.5	27.5	27.5	27.5	26.9	26.4	26.9	27.5	27.5	27.5
°C AVG MIN	19.7	19.7	19.7	20.3	20.3	20.3	20.3	20.3	19.7	19.7	20.3	19.7
DIURNAL RANGE	7.8	7.8	7.8	7.2	7.2	7.2	6.6	6.1	7.2	7.8	7.2	7.8
S/HEMISPHERE	JUL	AUG	SEP	OCT	NOV	DEC	JAN	FEB	MAR	APR	MAY	JUN

Cultural Recommendations

LIGHT: 2000–3000 fc.

TEMPERATURES: Throughout the year, days average 79–81°F (26–28°C), and nights average 67–68°F (20°C), with a diurnal range of 11–14°F (6–8°C).

HUMIDITY: Near 80% year-round.

WATER: Rainfall is heavy all year, but conditions are slightly drier for 1–2 months in late winter. Cultivated plants should be kept moist with only slight drying allowed between waterings.

FERTILIZER: ¼–½ recommended strength. A balanced fertilizer should be applied weekly to biweekly throughout the year.

REST PERIOD: Growing conditions should be maintained year-round. Water should be reduced for plants cultivated in the dark, short-day conditions common during temperate-latitude winters, but they should not be allowed to dry out completely. Fertilizer should also be reduced if water is reduced. In the habitat, light may be slightly higher in winter.

GROWING MEDIA: Mounting plants on tree-fern or cork slabs accommodates their pendulous growth habit. However, humidity must be high and plants must be watered at least once a day in summer. If plants cannot be mounted, hanging pots or baskets may be filled with an open, fast-draining medium. Repotting may be done anytime new roots are actively growing.

MISCELLANEOUS NOTES: The bloom season shown in the climate table is based on reports from the habitat.

Plant and Flower Information

PLANT SIZE AND TYPE: An 18–30 in. (45–75 cm) sympodial epiphyte.

PSEUDOBULB: 18–30 in. (45–75 cm) long. The clustered, pendent stems are longitudinally grooved.

LEAVES: Many. The lanceolate leaves are dark green, distichous, and 3–4 in. (8–10 cm) long.

INFLORESCENCE: 1.4 in. (3.5 cm) long. Racemes emerge from nodes along the side of the stem. The pedicels are light rose-pink. Flowers are borne in axillary fascicles. When describing *D. puniceum*, Rolfe indicated that plants produced racemes, not axillary fascicles.

FLOWERS: Many per inflorescence. The flowers are 0.5 in. (1.2 cm) long. Blossoms may be light rose-pink to dark purplish red, often with light yellow at the tips. The color tends to change as the flowers age. The dorsal sepal is ovate-oblong, and lateral sepals are broadly triangular-ovate. The petals are elliptic-oblong. The lip is narrowly oblong, concave, and minutely toothed.

REFERENCES: 218, 229, 254, 271, 381, 387, 413, 437, 445.

PHOTOS/DRAWINGS: 437.

Dendrobium ruttenii J. J. Smith

ORIGIN/HABITAT: Seram in the Moluccas. A single collection was made near Kali Koea on the northeast coast. The plant was cultivated at the botanical garden at Bogor, Java.

CLIMATE: Station #97748, Ceram-laut, Moluccas, Indonesia, Lat. 3.9°S, Long. 130.9°E, at 10 ft. (3 m). Record extreme temperatures are not available for this location.

N/HEMISPHERE	JAN	FEB	MAR	APR	MAY	JUN	JUL	AUG	SEP	OCT	NOV	DEC
°F AVG MAX	84	83	85	89	90	89	88	88	89	88	86	83
°F AVG MIN	76	77	77	79	80	80	79	77	79	79	79	76
DIURNAL RANGE	8	6	8	10	10	9	9	11	10	9	7	7
RAIN/INCHES	3.9	6.9	5.1	2.2	4.0	7.7	4.5	5.4	3.7	5.4	6.4	8.9
HUMIDITY/%	N/A											
BLOOM SEASON		*										
DAYS CLR	N/A											
RAIN/MM	100	174	130	56	101	195	115	136	94	137	163	227
°C AVG MAX	28.7	28.4	29.6	31.5	32.3	31.9	31.2	31.2	31.8	31.0	30.1	28.5
°C AVG MIN	24.5	24.8	24.8	26.1	26.6	26.5	26.0	25.1	26.1	26.2	26.4	24.7
DIURNAL RANGE	4.2	3.6	4.8	5.4	5.7	5.4	5.2	6.1	5.7	4.8	3.7	3.8
S/HEMISPHERE	JUL	AUG	SEP	OCT	NOV	DEC	JAN	FEB	MAR	APR	MAY	JUN

Cultural Recommendations

LIGHT: 2500–3500 fc.

TEMPERATURES: Throughout the year, days average 84–90°F (29–32°C),

and nights average 76–80°F (25–27°C), with a diurnal range of 6–11°F (4–6°C).

HUMIDITY: Information is not available for this location. However, records from nearby stations indicate that averages are probably 70–80% year-round.

WATER: Rainfall is moderate most of the year with a brief semidry period in spring. Cultivated plants should be kept moist, with only slight drying allowed between waterings.

FERTILIZER: 1/4–1/2 recommended strength, applied weekly. A high-nitrogen fertilizer is beneficial from spring to midsummer, but a fertilizer high in phosphates should be used in late summer and autumn.

REST PERIOD: Growing conditions should be maintained all year. Water and fertilizer should be reduced in winter, especially for plants grown in the dark, short-day conditions common in temperate latitudes. Plants may be allowed to become somewhat dry between waterings, but they should not remain dry for long periods. In the habitat, seasonal light variation is minor.

GROWING MEDIA: Plants may be mounted on tree-fern or cork slabs if humidity is high and plants are watered at least once daily in summer. When plants are potted, any open, fast-draining medium may be used. Repotting may be done anytime new roots are growing.

MISCELLANEOUS NOTES: The bloom season shown in the climate table is based on reports from the habitat.

Plant and Flower Information

PLANT SIZE AND TYPE: A 4–8 in. (10–20 cm) sympodial epiphyte.

PSEUDOBULB: 4–8 in. (10–20 cm) long. The club-shaped stems are pale green with 10–13 longitudinal grooves.

LEAVES: 1 at the apex of each growth. The ovate-lanceolate leaf is fleshy, leathery, pointed, and shiny dark green on the upper surface.

INFLORESCENCE: 0.4 in. (1 cm) long. Inflorescences emerge from nodes at the side of the stem.

FLOWERS: 1–3, commonly 2 per inflorescence. The flowers are 0.7 in. (1.7 cm) across, fleshy, and shiny. Sepals are pale green on the outside, but on the inside, the upper half is yellowish and the lower half is yellowish white. The white petals are oblong and pointed. The erect-incurved side-lobes are white with violet veins, and the midlobe is pale green. The 3-lobed lip is recurved, with a tooth in the apical notch of the midlobe. The callus terminates at the base of the midlobe.

REFERENCES: 83, 222.

Dendrobium sacculiferum J. J. Smith 1922 not 1929

ORIGIN/HABITAT: Ternate Island in the Moluccas. Habitat location and elevation are unavailable, so the following climate data should be used with caution. Plants were cultivated in the botanical garden at Bogor, Java.

CLIMATE: Station #97430, Ternate Island, Indonesia, Lat. 0.8°N, Long. 127.4°E, at 75 ft. (23 m). Temperatures are calculated for an elevation of 500 ft. (150 m). Record extreme temperatures are not available for this location.

N/HEMISPHERE	JAN	FEB	MAR	APR	MAY	JUN	JUL	AUG	SEP	OCT	NOV	DEC
°F AVG MAX	84	84	85	85	86	85	86	85	85	86	86	85
°F AVG MIN	76	75	76	76	76	75	74	74	75	76	76	76
DIURNAL RANGE	8	9	9	9	10	10	12	11	10	10	10	9
RAIN/INCHES	5.3	6.1	6.7	6.6	9.4	8.4	4.6	2.1	3.1	3.2	7.2	8.2
HUMIDITY/%	N/A											
BLOOM SEASON	N/A											
DAYS CLR	N/A											
RAIN/MM	135	155	170	168	239	213	117	53	79	81	183	208
°C AVG MAX	28.7	28.7	29.2	29.2	29.8	29.2	29.8	29.2	29.2	29.8	29.8	29.2
°C AVG MIN	24.2	23.7	24.2	24.2	24.2	23.7	23.1	23.1	23.7	24.2	24.2	24.2
DIURNAL RANGE	4.5	5.0	5.0	5.0	5.6	5.5	6.7	6.1	5.5	5.6	5.6	5.0
S/HEMISPHERE	JUL	AUG	SEP	OCT	NOV	DEC	JAN	FEB	MAR	APR	MAY	JUN

Cultural Recommendations

LIGHT: 2000–3000 fc.

TEMPERATURES: Throughout the year, days average 84–86°F (29–30°C), and nights average 74–76°F (23–24°C), with a diurnal range of 8–12°F (5–7°C).

HUMIDITY: Information is not available for this location. However, records from nearby stations indicate that averages are probably near 80% year-round.

WATER: Rainfall is heavy most of the year, but for 2–3 months in late summer and early autumn, conditions are slightly drier. Cultivated plants should be kept moist and never be allowed to dry out completely.

FERTILIZER: ¼–½ recommended strength. A balanced fertilizer should be applied weekly to biweekly throughout the year.

REST PERIOD: Growing conditions should be maintained all year. In 2–3 months in late summer and autumn, water should be reduced for cultivated plants. They should be allowed to dry slightly between waterings but should never remain dry for extended periods. Although rainfall is moderately high in the habitat during winter, water should not be increased for cultivated plants grown in the dark, short-day conditions common in temperate latitudes. These plants should not be allowed to dry out completely, however.

GROWING MEDIA: Plants may be mounted on tree-fern or cork slabs or potted in small pots filled with any open, fast-draining medium. Repotting may be done anytime new roots are actively growing.

MISCELLANEOUS NOTES: The plant was described in 1922 in *Bull. Jard. Bot. Buit.* 3rd. sér. 5:77.

Plant and Flower Information

PLANT SIZE AND TYPE: A 30 in. (75 cm) sympodial epiphyte.

PSEUDOBULB: 30 in. (75 cm) long. The dark green, clustered stems are borne on a short, creeping, rooting rhizome. They are shiny green, flattened, and unbranched.

LEAVES: Many. The linear leaves are 4 in. (10 cm) long and twisted at the base. They are shiny green, folded, and 2-toothed at the apex.

INFLORESCENCE: Short. The pale green inflorescences emerge through 2 overlapping leaf bases.

FLOWERS: 2 per inflorescence. The flowers are 0.6 in. (1.4 cm) across. Sepals and petals are white with yellow at the apex. The lip is greenish white with yellow brown markings. The spreading sepals and petals are rounded and recurved at the apex. They have a somewhat oblong dorsal sepal, triangular-oblong lateral sepals, and spatula-shaped petals. The 3-lobed lip has a raised center line. The sidelobes are small, linear, sickle-shaped, and minutely ruffled on the outer margin. The oblong midlobe is rounded, with a point in the apical notch. Blossoms are small and short-lived, but they fill the air with a fragrance similar to vanilla.

REFERENCES: 223, 224.

Dendrobium sacculiferum J. J. Smith 1929 not 1922. See *D. dillonionum* A. Hawkes and A. H. Heller. REFERENCES: 224, 229, 445, 470.

Dendrobium sagittatum J. J. Smith

AKA: Sometimes spelled *D. sagitattum*.

ORIGIN/HABITAT: Sumatra and Java. Plants grow throughout Java in open mountain forests at 2300–4900 ft. (700–1500 m). In western Java, plants grow near Garut (Garoet), about 32 mi. (51 km) southeast of Bandung.

CLIMATE: Station #96781, Bandung, Java, Lat. 6.9°S, Long. 107.6°E, at 2450 ft. (741 m). Temperatures are calculated for an elevation of 3600 ft. (1100 m), resulting in probable extremes of 90°F (32°C) and 48°F (9°C).

N/HEMISPHERE	JAN	FEB	MAR	APR	MAY	JUN	JUL	AUG	SEP	OCT	NOV	DEC
°F AVG MAX	78	79	80	80	78	77	77	76	77	78	78	78
°F AVG MIN	59	59	60	61	62	63	63	63	63	63	62	60
DIURNAL RANGE	19	20	20	19	16	14	14	13	14	15	16	18
RAIN/INCHES	2.7	2.2	2.0	6.0	7.9	8.5	9.5	10.0	9.4	5.6	4.6	4.0
HUMIDITY/%	70	66	62	65	73	77	79	78	78	78	75	72
BLOOM SEASON	N/A											
DAYS CLR @ 6AM	9	10	12	9	4	1	1	1	2	4	5	8
DAYS CLR @ 1PM	8	8	7	2	1	0	0	1	1	1	3	6
RAIN/MM	69	56	51	152	201	216	241	254	239	142	117	102
°C AVG MAX	25.6	26.2	26.7	26.7	25.6	25.1	25.1	24.5	25.1	25.6	25.6	25.6
°C AVG MIN	15.1	15.1	15.6	16.2	16.7	17.3	17.3	17.3	17.3	17.3	16.7	15.6
DIURNAL RANGE	10.5	11.1	11.1	10.5	8.9	7.8	7.8	7.2	7.8	8.3	8.9	10.0
S/HEMISPHERE	JUL	AUG	SEP	OCT	NOV	DEC	JAN	FEB	MAR	APR	MAY	JUN

Cultural Recommendations

LIGHT: 1800–3000 fc. Diffused light is preferred, as clear days are very rare in the habitat. Plants most often grow on forest trees, but they also grow fully exposed to available light.

TEMPERATURES: Throughout the year, days average 76–80°F (25–27°C), and nights average 59–63°F (15–17°C), with a diurnal range of 13–20°F (7–11°C). The diurnal range is lowest in summer months when overcast skies reduce both daily warming and nightly cooling. Plants are unlikely to tolerate extremely hot summer weather.

HUMIDITY: 75–80% in summer, dropping to 60–70% in winter and spring.

WATER: Rainfall is moderate to heavy most of the year, but there is a relatively dry season in winter. Cultivated plants should be kept moist but not soggy from spring through autumn, but water should be gradually reduced in late autumn.

FERTILIZER: ¼–½ recommended strength. A balanced fertilizer should be applied weekly to biweekly throughout the year.

REST PERIOD: Growing temperatures should be maintained year-round. Not only is rainfall reduced in the habitat in winter, but humidity is so low that even moisture from dew is uncommon for 2–3 months. For cultivated plants, water, fertilizer, and humidity should be reduced. Plants should be allowed to dry out somewhat between waterings, but should not remain dry for long periods. In the habitat, light is highest in winter.

GROWING MEDIA: Plants may be mounted on tree-fern or cork slabs or potted in small pots filled with any open, fast-draining medium. Repotting may be done anytime new roots are actively growing.

MISCELLANEOUS NOTES: This species seems to tolerate more drying than other members of the section.

Plant and Flower Information

PLANT SIZE AND TYPE: An 11 in. (28 cm) sympodial epiphyte.

PSEUDOBULB: 11 in. (28 cm) long. The unbranched stems are flattened and leafy to the apex with nodes every 0.6 in. (1.4 cm).

LEAVES: Many. The triangular leaves are 0.8 in. (2 cm) long. They are light green and may have violet dots when young.

INFLORESCENCE: Short. The flowers are usually carried at the apex of the stem.

FLOWERS: 1 per inflorescence. The flowers are 0.6 in. (1.4 cm) across and open fully. Sepals and petals are pale pink. The erect lip is pale pink with numerous wide red veins, which are darkest on the incurved side-lobes. The midlobe is recurved at the narrowed tip with a thick band in the center.

REFERENCES: 25, 75, 219, 254, 445, 469.

PHOTOS/DRAWINGS: 75, 469.

Dendrobium salaccense (Blume) Lindley not Hort. ex Rchb. f.

AKA: *Grastidium salaccense* Blume, *Dendrobium bambusifolium* Parish and Rchb. f., *D. intermedium* Teijsm. and Binn. Seidenfaden (ref. 454) indicates that the name *D. salaccense* has been applied to plants which should have been identified as *D. cathcartii* Hooker f. and *D. gemellum* Lindley. He also indicates that Schlechter considered *D. salaccense* conspecific with *D. pensile* Ridley, but Seidenfaden questions this synonymy. Some authors consider *D. haemoglossum* Thwaites to be conspecific with *D. salaccense*.

ORIGIN/HABITAT: Widespread through Southeast Asia. The habitat includes Thailand, Laos, Vietnam near Dalat, the Guangdong and Hainan regions of southern China, Burma near Moulmein, and many parts of Malaya, including Pahang and Johore states, where plants grow at about 3300 ft. (1000 m). The orchid is widespread in Borneo, Sumatra, and Java, where it grows from sea level to 5900 ft. (0–1800 m) on both trees and rocks in forests and open places. The range originally included the Kerala region of southwest India but reports suggest that it may now be extinct in that habitat.

CLIMATE: Station #48564, Phuket, Thailand, Lat. 8.0°N, Long. 98.4°E, at 100 ft. (30 m). Temperatures are calculated for an elevation of 1500 ft. (460 m), resulting in probable extremes of 95°F (35°C) and 57°F (14°C).

N/HEMISPHERE	JAN	FEB	MAR	APR	MAY	JUN	JUL	AUG	SEP	OCT	NOV	DEC
°F AVG MAX	83	85	86	86	84	84	82	82	81	82	82	82
°F AVG MIN	70	70	70	72	71	71	71	71	70	70	70	70
DIURNAL RANGE	13	15	16	14	13	13	11	11	11	12	12	12
RAIN/INCHES	1.4	1.2	2.6	5.9	11.0	11.8	11.1	10.9	12.9	14.3	8.1	2.7
HUMIDITY/%	73	72	73	78	82	81	81	81	83	83	81	77
BLOOM SEASON				*		*				*		
DAYS CLR @ 7AM	13	10	10	3	1	2	4	2	2	3	6	12
DAYS CLR @ 1PM	13	13	14	3	1	3	3	1	2	1	6	10
RAIN/MM	36	30	66	150	279	300	282	277	328	363	206	69
°C AVG MAX	28.5	29.7	30.2	30.2	29.1	29.1	28.0	28.0	27.4	28.0	28.0	28.0
°C AVG MIN	21.3	21.3	21.3	22.4	21.9	21.9	21.9	21.9	21.3	21.3	21.3	21.3
DIURNAL RANGE	7.2	8.4	8.9	7.8	7.2	7.2	6.1	6.1	6.1	6.7	6.7	6.7
S/HEMISPHERE	JUL	AUG	SEP	OCT	NOV	DEC	JAN	FEB	MAR	APR	MAY	JUN

Cultural Recommendations

LIGHT: 2500–3500 fc.

TEMPERATURES: Throughout the year, days average 81–86°F (27–30°C), and nights average 70–72°F (21–22°C), with a diurnal range of 11–16°F (6–9°C). Temperatures are warmest and the diurnal range is greatest in spring, before the start of the summer monsoon. Plants should adapt to temperatures 8–10°F (4–6°C) cooler than indicated, as they also grow at higher elevations.

HUMIDITY: 80–85% most of the year, dropping to 70–75% in winter.

WATER: Rainfall is heavy from spring through early autumn. Conditions are drier in winter. Cultivated plants should be kept evenly moist from spring to autumn, but water should be reduced in late autumn.

FERTILIZER: ¼–½ recommended strength, applied weekly. A high-nitrogen fertilizer is beneficial from spring to midsummer, but a fertilizer high in phosphates should be used in late summer and autumn.

REST PERIOD: Growing temperatures should be maintained all year. In the habitat, rainfall is reduced for 3–4 months in winter, and humidity is so low that even moisture from morning dew is uncommon. Cultivated plants should be allowed to dry out, but they should not remain dry for extended periods. Fertilizer should be reduced or eliminated anytime water is reduced. In the habitat, light is much higher in winter, and light should be as high as possible for cultivated plants, short of burning the foliage.

GROWING MEDIA: Mounting on tree-fern or cork slabs accommodates the semipendulous growth habit. Repotting may be done anytime new roots are growing.

MISCELLANEOUS NOTES: The bloom times shown in the climate table are based on cultivation reports. Plants may bloom several times during the year. Flowering usually occurs 7–14 days after a sudden 10°F (5°C) drop in daytime temperatures.

Plant and Flower Information

PLANT SIZE AND TYPE: A 12–24 in. (30–60 cm) sympodial epiphyte or lithophyte. Plants sometimes reach a length of 39 in. (100 cm).

PSEUDOBULB: 12–24 in. (30–60 cm) long. A bushy plant with slender, often semipendulous stems. They are shiny and woody with nodes spaced 0.8–1.2 in. (2–3 cm) apart. The upper 60% of each growth is leafy. Vegetative growth habit is similar to *D. indragiriense* Schlechter.

LEAVES: Many. The slender, grasslike leaves are 3–5 in. (8–13 cm) long. They are distichous, rigidly papery, and grasslike. They may arch away from the stem or hang down from it.

INFLORESCENCE: 0.8 in. (2 cm) long. Inflorescences emerge from leaf nodes opposite the leaves.

FLOWERS: 1–4 per inflorescence. The flowers are 0.2–0.8 in. (0.5–2.0 cm) across. The larger flowered form originates in Java. The erect sepals and petals may be green, white, or pale yellow. They become narrow at the apex, where they are often marked with dark red. The tongue-shaped lip, which has no sidelobes, is sharply recurved, wavy, and pointed. It is marked with a central yellow band and yellow margins and often tinged with red. The flowers are variable, even on the same stem.

HYBRIDIZING NOTES: Chromosome counts are 2n = 38 as *D. bambusifolium* (ref. 152, 154, 188) and as *D. salaccense* (ref. 152, 243). Johansen (ref. 239) found that seed capsules matured in 43–47 days. Of the seed produced, 82% contained visible embryos but only 14% germinated. When used in hybridizing, *D. salaccense* should be used as the pollen parent. None of Johansens' attempts to use *D. salaccense* as the pod parent were successful, but when used as the pollen parent 6 of 8 attempts were successful.

REFERENCES: 25, 46, 56, 75, 97, 152, 154, 157, 179, 188, 200, 202, 208, 216, 239, 243, 254, 255, 277, 310, 317, 435, 445, 447, 448, 454, 455, 469, 528, 586, 592.

PHOTOS/DRAWINGS: 75, 454, 455, 469.

Dendrobium salaccense Hort. ex Rchb. f. not (Blume) Lindley. See *D. bullenianum* Rchb. f. REFERENCES: 216, 254.

Dendrobium salhutuense J. J. Smith

ORIGIN/HABITAT: Molucca Islands. Plants were originally found on Ambon Island at about 2150 ft. (650 m) on Mt. Salhoetoe (Salhutu?).

CLIMATE: Station #97724, Ambon Island, Indonesia, Lat. 3.7°S, Long. 128.1°E, at 33 ft. (10 m). Temperatures are calculated for an elevation of 2150 ft. (650 m), resulting in probable extremes of 89°F (32°C) and 59°F (15°C).

N/HEMISPHERE	JAN	FEB	MAR	APR	MAY	JUN	JUL	AUG	SEP	OCT	NOV	DEC
°F AVG MAX	74	74	76	78	81	81	81	81	81	79	77	75
°F AVG MIN	67	67	67	67	68	69	69	69	69	69	68	67
DIURNAL RANGE	7	7	9	11	13	12	12	12	12	10	9	8
RAIN/INCHES	23.7	15.8	9.5	6.1	4.5	5.2	5.0	4.7	5.3	11.0	20.3	25.1
HUMIDITY/%	83	82	81	80	79	78	78	77	79	82	83	84
BLOOM SEASON					*							
DAYS CLR @ 9AM	1	1	1	6	7	4	3	3	5	5	3	3
DAYS CLR @ 3PM	1	1	2	5	6	1	1	1	2	3	1	3
RAIN/MM	602	401	241	155	114	132	127	119	135	279	516	638
°C AVG MAX	23.3	23.3	24.5	25.6	27.2	27.2	27.2	27.2	27.2	26.1	25.0	23.9
°C AVG MIN	19.5	19.5	19.5	19.5	20.0	20.6	20.6	20.6	20.6	20.6	20.0	19.5
DIURNAL RANGE	3.8	3.8	5.0	6.1	7.2	6.6	6.6	6.6	6.6	5.5	5.0	4.4
S/HEMISPHERE	JUL	AUG	SEP	OCT	NOV	DEC	JAN	FEB	MAR	APR	MAY	JUN

Cultural Recommendations

LIGHT: 2500–3500 fc.

TEMPERATURES: Throughout the year, days average 74–81°F (23–27°C), and nights average 67–69°F (20–21°C), with a diurnal range of 7–13°F (4–7°C). Record extreme temperatures are only a few degrees above and below the averages, indicating that plants may not tolerate wide seasonal fluctuations.

HUMIDITY: 80–85% year-round.

WATER: Rainfall is moderate to heavy all year, but conditions are slightly drier in late spring and summer. Cultivated plants should be kept evenly moist all year, with only slight drying allowed between waterings.

FERTILIZER: ¼–½ recommended strength. A balanced fertilizer should be applied weekly to biweekly throughout the year.

REST PERIOD: Growing conditions should be maintained all year. In the habitat, a brief, semidry period occurs in late spring. Rainfall is heaviest in winter, but water and fertilizer should be reduced for plants cultivated in the dark, short-day conditions common in temperate-latitude winters. Plants should never be allowed to dry completely, however. In the habitat, light is highest in spring.

GROWING MEDIA: Plants may be mounted on tree-fern or cork slabs or potted in small pots filled with any open, fast-draining medium. Repotting may be done anytime new roots are actively growing.

MISCELLANEOUS NOTES: Bloom season shown in the climate table is based on collector reports. The plant was described in 1927 in *Bull. Jard. Bot. Buit.* 3rd sér. 9:154.

Plant and Flower Information

PLANT SIZE AND TYPE: An 0.8 in. (2 cm) sympodial epiphyte.

PSEUDOBULB: 0.3 in. (0.8 cm) long. The erect stems are clustered, 1-noded, and grooved. They arise from a very short rhizome that is thick, branching, and rooting.

LEAVES: 1 per growth. The erect, oblong leaf is less than 0.5 in. (1.3 cm) long.

INFLORESCENCE: Short. A single Inflorescence arises at the base of the leaf.

FLOWERS: 1 per inflorescence. The white flowers are 0.3 in. (0.8 cm) long. The sepals and petals are somewhat obovate, and the lip is lanceolate. Sepals and petals stretch out and forward. The lip is obscurely 3-lobed, fleshy, and pointed at the tip. It has 2 parallel, raised lines.

REFERENCES: 224.

Dendrobium salicifolium J. J. Smith

ORIGIN/HABITAT: Irian Jaya (western New Guinea). Plants grow in primeval forests near the Rouffaer River at about 800 ft. (250 m).

CLIMATE: Station #200004, Ambunti, Papua New Guinea, Lat. 4.2°S, Long. 142.8°E, at 164 ft. (50 m). Temperatures are calculated for an elevation of 1000 ft. (300 m), resulting in probable extremes of 96°F (36°C) and 49°F (10°C).

N/HEMISPHERE	JAN	FEB	MAR	APR	MAY	JUN	JUL	AUG	SEP	OCT	NOV	DEC
°F AVG MAX	85	87	87	87	88	87	87	87	87	87	87	86
°F AVG MIN	69	70	71	70	70	70	69	70	70	70	70	71
DIURNAL RANGE	16	17	16	17	18	17	18	17	17	17	17	15
RAIN/INCHES	6.4	7.4	7.7	8.5	9.2	9.4	10.9	10.2	12.2	10.4	8.3	5.2
HUMIDITY/%	N/A											
BLOOM SEASON			*									
DAYS CLR	N/A											
RAIN/MM	163	188	196	216	234	239	277	259	310	264	211	132
°C AVG MAX	29.6	30.7	30.7	30.7	31.2	30.7	30.7	30.7	30.7	30.7	30.7	30.1
°C AVG MIN	20.7	21.2	21.8	21.2	21.2	21.2	20.7	21.2	21.2	21.2	21.2	21.8
DIURNAL RANGE	8.9	9.5	8.9	9.5	10.0	9.5	10.0	9.5	9.5	9.5	9.5	8.3
S/HEMISPHERE	JUL	AUG	SEP	OCT	NOV	DEC	JAN	FEB	MAR	APR	MAY	JUN

Cultural Recommendations

LIGHT: 2000–3000 fc.

TEMPERATURES: Throughout the year, days average 85–88°F (30–31°C), and nights average 69–71°F (21–22°C), with a diurnal range of 15–18°F (8–10°C).

HUMIDITY: Information is not available for this location. However, records from nearby stations indicate that humidity probably averages near 80% year-round.

WATER: Rainfall is heavy all year, with the greatest amounts falling in summer and early autumn. Cultivated plants should be kept moist but not soggy.

FERTILIZER: ¼–½ recommended strength. A balanced fertilizer should be applied weekly to biweekly throughout the year.

REST PERIOD: Growing conditions should be maintained all year. Water and fertilizer should be reduced slightly in winter, especially for plants cultivated in the dark, short-day conditions common in temperate latitudes. However, plants should never be allowed to dry between waterings. In the habitat, light is probably highest in winter.

GROWING MEDIA: Plants may be mounted on cork or tree-fern slabs if humidity is high and plants are watered at least once daily in summer. When plants are potted, any open, fast-draining medium may be used, but fir bark is preferred by most growers. Repotting may be done anytime new roots are growing.

MISCELLANEOUS NOTES: The bloom season shown in the climate table is based on reports from the habitat.

Plant and Flower Information

PLANT SIZE AND TYPE: A 28 in. (70 cm) sympodial epiphyte.

PSEUDOBULB: 28 in. (70 cm) long. Stems are connected by a short rhizome.

LEAVES: Many. The lanceolate leaves are 2.0–2.4 in. (5–6 cm) long. They are rigid, leathery, and somewhat irregular along the apical margin.

INFLORESCENCE: Short. Inflorescences emerge through the leaf sheaths.

FLOWERS: 2 per inflorescence. The fleshy flowers are 0.5 in. (1.3 cm) long. Blossoms are white with a dense covering of light violet spots on the inside. The lip is marked with an orange dot. Sepals and petals are concave and incurved at the tips. Blossoms are covered with small wartlike protuberances. The dorsal sepal is elliptical with a point at the tip. Laterals sepals are oblong, sickle-shaped, and incurved along the margin. The petals are oblong-elliptical and concave. The lip is erect, recurved, and fleshy. It has small earlike appendages at the grooved base of the rounded, ruffled midlobe.

REFERENCES: 225, 470.

Dendrobium salicornioides J. J. Smith not Teijsm. and Binn. See *D. shipmani* A. Hawkes. REFERENCES: 436, 470.

Dendrobium salicornioides Teijsm. and Binn. not J. J. Smith. See *D. uncatum* Lindley. REFERENCES: 216, 254, 266, 448, 454, 468.

Dendrobium salmoneum Schlechter 1905

AKA: *D. trichostomum* as used by Kränzlin not Rchb. f. ex Oliver.

ORIGIN/HABITAT: Papua New Guinea. Plants grow on trees, often in creekside forests, in the Kani, Ibo, and Bismarck Mountains at 2600–3350 ft. (800–1100 m).

CLIMATE: Station #94010, Goroka, Papua New Guinea, Lat. 6.1°S, Long. 145.4°E, at 5141 ft. (1567 m). Temperatures are calculated for an elevation of 3300 ft. (1000 m), resulting in probable extremes of 93°F (34°C) and 49°F (10°C).

N/HEMISPHERE	JAN	FEB	MAR	APR	MAY	JUN	JUL	AUG	SEP	OCT	NOV	DEC
°F AVG MAX	82	83	84	85	85	84	85	84	84	84	85	83
°F AVG MIN	62	63	63	63	64	65	65	65	66	65	65	63
DIURNAL RANGE	20	20	21	22	21	19	20	19	18	19	20	20
RAIN/INCHES	2.1	2.8	4.6	5.9	6.6	9.3	9.1	10.1	10.7	8.3	4.6	2.0
HUMIDITY/%	70	67	67	67	67	71	72	75	74	71	70	70
BLOOM SEASON				*		*	*					
DAYS CLR	N/A											
RAIN/MM	53	71	117	150	168	236	231	257	272	211	117	51
°C AVG MAX	27.9	28.4	29.0	29.5	29.5	29.0	29.5	29.0	29.0	29.0	29.5	28.4
°C AVG MIN	16.7	17.3	17.3	17.3	17.9	18.4	18.4	18.4	19.0	18.4	18.4	17.3
DIURNAL RANGE	11.2	11.1	11.7	12.2	11.6	10.6	11.1	10.6	10.0	10.6	11.1	11.1
S/HEMISPHERE	JUL	AUG	SEP	OCT	NOV	DEC	JAN	FEB	MAR	APR	MAY	JUN

Cultural Recommendations

LIGHT: 2000–3000 fc.

TEMPERATURES: Throughout the year, days average 82–85°F (28–30°C), and nights average 62–65°F (17–18°C), with a diurnal range of 18–22°F (10–12°C). Average highs and lows vary only slightly during the year, indicating that plants may not tolerate wide seasonal fluctuations.

HUMIDITY: 70–75% in summer and autumn, dropping to 65–70% in winter and spring.

WATER: Rainfall is moderate to heavy most of the year but is relatively low for 2–3 months in winter. However, additional moisture is available from dew, fog, and mist, even during periods when rainfall is low. Cultivated plants should be kept moist but not soggy. Additional early morning mistings between waterings are often beneficial, especially on warm, bright, sunny days.

FERTILIZER: ¼–½ recommended strength. A balanced fertilizer should be applied weekly to biweekly throughout the year.

REST PERIOD: Growing temperatures should be maintained all year. Water should be reduced in winter. Plants should dry slightly between waterings, but they should never be allowed to dry out completely. Fertilizer should be reduced or eliminated until water is increased in spring. In the habitat, winter light may be slightly higher.

GROWING MEDIA: To accommodate the somewhat pendulous growth habit, plants may be mounted on tree-fern or cork slabs or potted in small hanging pots or baskets filled with any open, fast-draining medium. Repotting may be done anytime new roots are growing.

MISCELLANEOUS NOTES: The bloom season shown in the climate table is based on records from the habitat.

Plant and Flower Information

PLANT SIZE AND TYPE: A 10–16 in. (25–40 cm) sympodial epiphyte.

PSEUDOBULB: 10–16 in. (25–40 cm) long. The green, shiny stems are covered by leaf sheaths. They are slender, cylindrical, and arise from a very short rhizome.

LEAVES: Several per growth. The alternate leaves are elliptical, opposite, pointed at the tip, and 1.2–1.6 in. (3–4 cm) long. The leaf sheaths, which are covered with warty protuberances, are eventually deciduous.

INFLORESCENCE: Short. Inflorescences emerge from leafless stems.

FLOWERS: 4–10 per inflorescence. The flowers are 0.4 in. (0.9 cm) long. The ovate sepals and linear petals are orange-red to orange-yellow, often with yellow at the tips. The oblong lip is concave with erect to incurved margins. The thickened center is teardrop-shaped with a row of fine hairs. The front margin of the lip is uneven with a long, sharp, toothlike fringe.

REFERENCES: 92, 219, 254, 437, 444, 445, 549, 553.

PHOTOS/DRAWINGS: 437, *553*.

Dendrobium salomonense Schlechter

ORIGIN/HABITAT: The Solomon Islands and Bougainville. Plants grow on rainforest trees from sea level to 3750 ft. (0–1150 m). On Bougainville, they have been found near Kieta Bay.

CLIMATE: Station #91502, Kieta, Bougainville, Lat. 6.2°S, Long. 155.6°E, at 240 ft. (73 m). Record extreme temperatures are 96°F (36°C) and 64°F (18°C).

N/HEMISPHERE	JAN	FEB	MAR	APR	MAY	JUN	JUL	AUG	SEP	OCT	NOV	DEC
°F AVG MAX	85	85	87	88	88	89	88	88	88	87	87	86
°F AVG MIN	74	74	74	75	75	75	76	75	76	76	75	75
DIURNAL RANGE	11	11	13	13	13	14	12	13	12	11	12	11
RAIN/INCHES	10.9	9.4	8.0	9.8	9.6	9.4	10.5	10.7	11.2	11.7	9.3	9.0
HUMIDITY/%	80	80	79	76	78	76	79	77	78	80	80	82
BLOOM SEASON			*									
DAYS CLR	N/A											
RAIN/MM	277	239	203	249	244	239	267	272	284	297	236	229
°C AVG MAX	29.4	29.4	30.6	31.1	31.1	31.7	31.1	31.1	31.1	30.6	30.6	30.0
°C AVG MIN	23.3	23.3	23.3	23.9	23.9	23.9	24.4	23.9	24.4	24.4	23.9	23.9
DIURNAL RANGE	6.1	6.1	7.3	7.2	7.2	7.8	6.7	7.2	6.7	6.2	6.7	6.1
S/HEMISPHERE	JUL	AUG	SEP	OCT	NOV	DEC	JAN	FEB	MAR	APR	MAY	JUN

Cultural Recommendations

LIGHT: 3000–4000 fc. High humidity and strong air movement should be maintained when light levels are high.

TEMPERATURES: Throughout the year, days average 85–89°F (29–32°C), and nights average 74–76°F (23–24°C), with a diurnal range of 11–14°F (6–8°C). Because of the wide range of habitat elevation, plants should easily adapt to conditions 12–14°F (7–8°C) cooler than indicated.

HUMIDITY: Near 80% year-round.

WATER: Rainfall is very heavy all year. Cultivated plants should be kept moist but not soggy. Warm water might be beneficial.

FERTILIZER: ¼–½ recommended strength. A balanced fertilizer should be applied weekly to biweekly throughout the year.

REST PERIOD: Growing conditions should be maintained all year. Plants cultivated in the temperate latitudes need less water and fertilizer during the dark, short days of winter, but they should never be allowed to dry completely. In the habitat, seasonal light variation is minor.

GROWING MEDIA: Mounting plants on tree-fern or cork slabs accommodates their pendulous growth habit. However, humidity must be high and plants must be watered at least once a day in summer. If plants cannot be mounted, hanging pots or baskets may be filled with an open, fast-draining medium. Because plants are healthiest when watered frequently, the medium must be very open and fast-draining if pots or baskets are used. Repotting may be done anytime new roots are growing.

MISCELLANEOUS NOTES: The bloom season shown in the climate table is based on reports from the habitat. Plants that produce flowers which last a single day commonly bloom several times during the year. Flowering usually occurs 7–14 days after a sudden 10°F (5°C) drop in daytime temperatures.

Plant and Flower Information

PLANT SIZE AND TYPE: A 39–79 in. (100–200 cm) sympodial epiphyte.

PSEUDOBULB: 39–79 in. (100–200 cm) long. The stems are pendulous.

LEAVES: Many. The lanceolate leaves are 6 in. (15 cm) long. They are distichous.

INFLORESCENCE: Short. The lateral inflorescences emerge from flattened protuberances at the side of the stem.

FLOWERS: 2 per inflorescence. The flowers are 0.4 in. (1 cm) long. Sepals and petals may be white or yellow. The white or yellow lip is marked with purple veins and a central orange callus. It is densely hairy at the tip. The segments are rounded at the tips and tend to bend or hook downward. Blossoms are short-lived.

REFERENCES: 221, 271, 437, 440, 445, 516.

PHOTOS/DRAWINGS: 271, 437, 440.

Dendrobium sambasanum J. J. Smith

AKA: Kränzlin (ref. 254) lists *D. sambasanum* as a synonym of *D. salicornioides* Teijsm. and Binn. (now *D. uncatum* Lindley). However, Seidenfaden (ref. 454) asserts that Kränzlin confused several different plants with *D. salicornioides*. Until this confusion is clarified, we are treating *D. sambasanum* as a valid species.

ORIGIN/HABITAT: Borneo. Plants were originally found along the Sambas River in northwest Kalimantan. Elevation was not included with the original description. Most of the region is low lying, but elevations rise to near 4000 ft. (1220 m) at the headwaters of the river. Habitat elevation is estimated, so the following climate data should be used with caution.

CLIMATE: Station #96583, Pontianak, Borneo, Lat. 0.0°N, Long. 109.3°E, at 13 ft. (4 m) elevation. Temperatures are calculated for an estimated elevation of 500 ft. (150 m), resulting in probable extremes of 94°F (35°C) and 66°F (19°C).

N/HEMISPHERE	JAN	FEB	MAR	APR	MAY	JUN	JUL	AUG	SEP	OCT	NOV	DEC
°F AVG MAX	85	87	87	87	88	88	87	88	88	87	86	85
°F AVG MIN	72	74	73	73	73	73	72	72	73	73	73	72
DIURNAL RANGE	13	13	14	14	15	15	15	16	15	14	13	13
RAIN/INCHES	10.8	8.2	9.5	10.9	11.1	8.7	6.5	8.0	9.0	14.4	15.3	12.7
HUMIDITY/%	85	85	84	84	82	81	79	82	83	87	86	87
BLOOM SEASON	N/A											
DAYS CLR @ 7AM	1	1	1	3	2	4	5	1	2	1	1	2
DAYS CLR @ 1PM	0	0	1	0	0	0	1	1	1	0	1	0
RAIN/MM	274	208	241	277	282	221	165	203	229	366	389	323
°C AVG MAX	29.7	30.8	30.8	30.8	31.3	31.3	30.8	31.3	31.3	30.8	30.2	29.7
°C AVG MIN	22.4	23.6	23.0	23.0	23.0	23.0	22.4	22.4	23.0	23.0	23.0	22.4
DIURNAL RANGE	7.3	7.2	7.8	7.8	8.3	8.3	8.4	8.9	8.3	7.8	7.2	7.3
S/HEMISPHERE	JUL	AUG	SEP	OCT	NOV	DEC	JAN	FEB	MAR	APR	MAY	JUN

Cultural Recommendations

LIGHT: 2000–3000 fc.

TEMPERATURES: Throughout the year, days average 85–88°F (30–31°C), and nights average 72–74°F (22–24°C), with a diurnal range of 13–16°F (7–9°C). The extreme temperatures are very close to the averages, indicating that plants from this habitat may not tolerate wide temperature fluctuations.

HUMIDITY: Near 80–90% year-round.

WATER: Rainfall is heavy all year. Cultivated plants should receive year-round moisture and never be allowed to dry out completely. Constant air movement is highly recommended. Warm water may be beneficial.

FERTILIZER: ¼–½ recommended strength. A balanced fertilizer should be applied weekly to biweekly throughout the year.

REST PERIOD: Growing conditions should be maintained all year. Water may be reduced somewhat in winter, especially for plants grown in the dark, short-day conditions common in temperate latitudes. Fertilizer should be reduced if water is reduced.

GROWING MEDIA: Plants may be mounted on tree-fern or cork slabs or potted in small pots filled with any open, fast-draining medium. Repotting may be done anytime new roots are growing.

Plant and Flower Information

PLANT SIZE AND TYPE: A 14 in. (36 cm) sympodial epiphyte.

PSEUDOBULB: 14 in. (36 cm) long. The leafy stems are elongated, branching, and clustered. The internodes are swollen at the base.

LEAVES: Many. The linear leaves are 1.4–2.0 in. (3.5–5.0 cm) long. They are fleshy, curved, and laterally folded.

INFLORESCENCE: Inflorescences emerge from nodes on the upper part of the stem.

FLOWERS: Several per inflorescence. The flowers are 0.5 in. (1.3 cm) across. The dorsal sepal is oblong-triangular, lateral sepals are sickle-shaped, and petals are lanceolate. The curved, 3-lobed lip is covered with wart-like protuberances. The sidelobes are triangular. The midlobe is notched and uneven along the margin. Flower color was not included in the original description.

REFERENCES: 220, 254, 286, 295.

Dendrobium samoense Cribb

AKA: Originally thought to be *D. tokai* Rchb. f., Cribb (ref. 84) recently described *D. samoense* as a separate species.

ORIGIN/HABITAT: Samoa. These rare plants are found on the islands of Upolu, Savaii, and Tutuila, where they grow in coastal forests at about 650 ft. (200 m). On Suvaii, they have been found above Patamea and were reported near Matautu growing on *Thespesia populnea*.

CLIMATE: Station #91759, Faleolo, Upolu Island, Western Samoa, Lat. 13.8°S, Long. 172.8°W, at 3 ft. (1 m). Record extreme temperatures are 93°F (34°C) and 63°F (17°C).

N/HEMISPHERE	JAN	FEB	MAR	APR	MAY	JUN	JUL	AUG	SEP	OCT	NOV	DEC
°F AVG MAX	85	84	84	85	86	85	86	85	86	86	85	85
°F AVG MIN	74	75	74	75	74	74	75	76	74	75	74	74
DIURNAL RANGE	11	9	10	10	12	11	11	9	12	11	11	11
RAIN/INCHES	3.2	3.5	5.2	6.7	10.5	14.6	17.9	15.2	14.1	10.0	6.3	5.1
HUMIDITY/%	76	75	75	77	77	78	81	80	80	78	77	75
BLOOM SEASON	N/A											
DAYS CLR @ 1PM	9	10	9	6	3	3	4	2	3	5	9	10
RAIN/MM	81	89	132	170	267	371	455	386	358	254	160	130
°C AVG MAX	29.4	28.9	28.9	29.4	30.0	29.4	30.0	29.4	30.0	30.0	29.4	29.4
°C AVG MIN	23.3	23.9	23.3	23.9	23.3	23.3	23.9	24.4	23.3	23.9	23.3	23.3
DIURNAL RANGE	6.1	5.0	5.6	5.5	6.7	6.1	6.1	5.0	6.7	6.1	6.1	6.1
S/HEMISPHERE	JUL	AUG	SEP	OCT	NOV	DEC	JAN	FEB	MAR	APR	MAY	JUN

Cultural Recommendations

LIGHT: 2000–3000 fc. Cultivated plants need some shading from spring through autumn, but light should be as high as the plant can tolerate, short of burning the leaves. Air movement should be excellent.

TEMPERATURES: Throughout the year, days average 84–86°F (29–30°C), and nights average 74–75°F (23–24°C), with a diurnal range of 9–12°F (5–7°C).

HUMIDITY: 75–80% year-round.

WATER: Rainfall is moderate to heavy most of the year, but conditions are

semidry for 2 months in winter. Cultivated plants should be kept moist but not soggy.

FERTILIZER: ¼–½ recommended strength. A balanced fertilizer should be applied weekly to biweekly throughout the year.

REST PERIOD: Growing conditions should be maintained year-round. Water and fertilizer should be reduced in winter, especially for plants grown in the dark, short-day conditions common in temperate latitudes. Plants should never be allowed to dry out completely, however. In the habitat, light is highest in winter.

GROWING MEDIA: Plants may be mounted on tree-fern or cork slabs if humidity is high and plants are watered at least once daily in summer. When plants are potted, any open, fast-draining medium may be used. Repotting may be done anytime new roots are growing.

MISCELLANEOUS NOTES: Plants are often incorrectly identified as *D. tokai*.

Plant and Flower Information

PLANT SIZE AND TYPE: A 20 in. (50 cm) sympodial epiphyte.

PSEUDOBULB: 20 in. (50 cm) long. The clustered stems are canelike.

LEAVES: The elliptic leaves are 2.4–3.5 in. (6–9 cm) long. They are roundly and unequally bilobed at the apex.

INFLORESCENCE: 18 in. (45 cm) long. Inflorescences, which may be erect or suberect, are laxly flowered.

FLOWERS: 10–20 per inflorescence. Normally yellowish, the flowers are 0.8–1.2 in. (2–3 cm) across and do not open fully. Sepals and petals are pointed. The dorsal sepal is narrowly oblong-lanceolate, lateral sepals are lanceolate, and the untwisted petals are oblong. The 3-lobed lip is rounded in front. The midlobe is elliptic, pointed, and wavy along the margin. The erect sidelobes are narrowly oblong. The callus consists of 5 ridges.

REFERENCES: 82, 84, 234, 434.

PHOTOS/DRAWINGS: 84.

Dendrobium sancristobalense Cribb

ORIGIN/HABITAT: The Solomon Islands. Plants are found on Makira and San Cristobal Islands, where they grow on trees in coastal forests and rainforests below 2800 ft. (850 m).

CLIMATE: Station #91520, Honiara, Guadalcanal, Solomon Islands, Lat. 9.4°S, Long. 160.6°E, at 10 ft. (3 m). Record extreme temperatures are 95°F (35°C) and 65°F (18°C).

N/HEMISPHERE	JAN	FEB	MAR	APR	MAY	JUN	JUL	AUG	SEP	OCT	NOV	DEC
°F AVG MAX	86	87	88	88	88	88	88	88	87	88	88	87
°F AVG MIN	72	72	72	72	73	73	74	74	73	73	73	72
DIURNAL RANGE	14	15	16	16	15	15	14	14	14	15	15	15
RAIN/INCHES	6.0	4.4	4.6	7.7	7.7	9.5	14.1	13.3	16.7	10.6	8.1	6.7
HUMIDITY/%	84	82	81	80	81	82	83	83	87	85	85	85
BLOOM SEASON	N/A											
DAYS CLR @ 5AM	6	7	7	5	6	4	3	3	4	4	8	7
DAYS CLR @ 11AM	3	2	2	1	1	1	1	0	2	2	4	4
RAIN/MM	152	112	117	196	196	241	358	338	424	269	206	170
°C AVG MAX	30.0	30.6	31.1	31.1	31.1	31.1	31.1	31.1	30.6	31.1	31.1	30.6
°C AVG MIN	22.2	22.2	22.2	22.2	22.8	22.8	23.3	23.3	22.8	22.8	22.8	22.2
DIURNAL RANGE	7.8	8.4	8.9	8.9	8.3	8.3	7.8	7.8	7.8	8.3	8.3	8.4
S/HEMISPHERE	JUL	AUG	SEP	OCT	NOV	DEC	JAN	FEB	MAR	APR	MAY	JUN

Cultural Recommendations

LIGHT: 3000–4000 fc.

TEMPERATURES: Throughout the year, days average 86–88°F (30–31°C), and nights average 72–74°F (22–23°C), with a diurnal range of 14–16°F (8–9°C). Because of the range of habitat elevation, plants should adapt to temperatures 6–8°F (3–4°C) cooler than indicated in the climate table.

HUMIDITY: Near 80–85% year-round.

WATER: Rainfall is heavy all year, but conditions are slightly drier for 2–3 months in winter. Cultivated plants should be kept moist but not soggy.

FERTILIZER: ¼–½ recommended strength. A balanced fertilizer should be applied weekly to biweekly throughout the year.

REST PERIOD: Growing temperatures should be maintained all year. Water and fertilizer should be reduced somewhat in winter, but plants should never be allowed to dry out completely. In the habitat, light is highest in winter.

GROWING MEDIA: Plants may be mounted on tree-fern or cork slabs if humidity is high and plants are watered at least once daily in summer. When plants are potted, any open, fast-draining medium may be used. Repotting may be done anytime new roots are growing.

MISCELLANEOUS NOTES: Lewis and Cribb (ref. 271) indicate that *D. sancristobalense* is closely related to the variable *D. gouldii* Rchb. f.

Plant and Flower Information

PLANT SIZE AND TYPE: A 39 in. (100 cm) sympodial epiphyte.

PSEUDOBULB: 39 in. (100 cm) long. The stems are canelike.

LEAVES: Many. The elliptic to oblong leaves are 5.5 in. (14 cm) long, distichous, and unequally bilobed at the apex.

INFLORESCENCE: 14 in. (36 cm) long. The laxly flowered inflorescences may be erect or suberect.

FLOWERS: 2 to many per inflorescence. The flowers are 1.6–2.4 in. (4–6 cm) across. They are very similar to the white-flowered forms of *D. gouldii* but differ in the structure of the lamella on the lip. These raised flaps of tissue are rounded at the apex rather than pointed as in *D. gouldii*. Blossoms are cream or white with purple or violet veins on the lip. The petals are suberect, rounded, with a full or half twist. The dorsal sepal projects forward and lateral sepals curve back.

REFERENCES: 82, 84, 234, 270, 271, 516.

PHOTOS/DRAWINGS: 84.

Dendrobium sandaiense Hayata. Probably a misspelling of *D. sanseiense* Hayata, which is now considered a synonym of *Epigeneium sanseiense* (Hayata) Summerhayes. REFERENCES: 208, 499.

Dendrobium sanderae Rolfe

ORIGIN/HABITAT: The Philippine Islands. Plants grow in the mountains of Luzon Island at 3300–5400 ft. (1000–1650 m). They are found in Mountain, Benguet, and Rizal Provinces.

CLIMATE: Station #98328, Baguio, Philippines, Lat. 16.4°N, Long. 120.6°E, at 4962 ft. (1512 m). Record extreme temperatures are 84°F (29°C) and 46°F (8°C).

N/HEMISPHERE	JAN	FEB	MAR	APR	MAY	JUN	JUL	AUG	SEP	OCT	NOV	DEC
°F AVG MAX	72	73	76	77	76	75	71	71	71	73	74	74
°F AVG MIN	55	56	58	60	61	61	60	60	60	60	59	57
DIURNAL RANGE	17	17	18	17	15	14	11	11	11	13	15	17
RAIN/INCHES	0.9	0.9	1.7	4.3	15.8	17.2	42.3	45.7	28.1	15.0	4.9	2.0
HUMIDITY/%	83	83	83	85	89	90	93	93	92	89	86	84
BLOOM SEASON			*		*	**	**	**	*	*	*	
DAYS CLR	N/A											
RAIN/MM	23	23	43	109	401	437	1074	1161	714	381	124	51
°C AVG MAX	22.2	22.8	24.4	25.0	24.4	23.9	21.7	21.7	21.7	22.8	23.3	23.3
°C AVG MIN	12.8	13.3	14.4	15.6	16.1	16.1	15.6	15.6	15.6	15.6	15.0	13.9
DIURNAL RANGE	9.4	9.5	10.0	9.4	8.3	7.8	6.1	6.1	6.1	7.2	8.3	9.4
S/HEMISPHERE	JUL	AUG	SEP	OCT	NOV	DEC	JAN	FEB	MAR	APR	MAY	JUN

Cultural Recommendations

LIGHT: 1500–2500 fc. Diffused or dappled light is recommended. Sky-cover records are unavailable, but high elevations are typically cloudy in this region.

TEMPERATURES: Throughout the year, days average 71–77°F (22–25°C),

and nights average 55–61°F (13–16°C), with a diurnal range of 11–18°F (6–10°C). Since plants also grow at lower elevations, they should adapt to temperatures that are 4–6°F (2–3°C) warmer than indicated.

HUMIDITY: 85–95% most of the year, dropping to 80–85% in winter.

WATER: Rainfall is very heavy from spring to autumn but is greatly reduced in winter. Cultivated plants should be kept moist but not soggy from spring to autumn, but water should be gradually reduced in late autumn.

FERTILIZER: ¼–½ recommended strength, applied weekly. A high-nitrogen fertilizer is beneficial from spring to midsummer, but a fertilizer high in phosphates should be used in late summer and autumn.

REST PERIOD: Growing temperatures should be maintained all year. Some growers indicate that plants tolerate winter temperatures of 43°F (6°C), but it should be noted that this is colder than the record low indicated in the climate data. Rainfall is low for 2–4 months in winter, but the continuing high humidity indicates that additional moisture is frequently available from fog, dew, or mist. Cultivated plants should be allowed to dry somewhat between waterings, but they should never remain dry for long periods. In the habitat, light may be highest in winter.

GROWING MEDIA: Plants may be mounted on tree-fern or cork slabs or potted in small pots filled with any open, fast-draining medium. Repotting may be done anytime new roots are growing.

MISCELLANEOUS NOTES: The bloom season shown in the climate table is based on cultivation records. In nature, var. *major* blooms in spring, but the smaller-flowered var. *parviflorum* blooms in the fall. Growers indicate that plants do not survive cultivation in Manila, but grow well in Honolulu, Hawaii, which is about 5–10°F (3–6°C) cooler. The plants are free flowering when grown in conditions comparable to its native mountain habitat.

Plant and Flower Information

PLANT SIZE AND TYPE: A 16–32 in. (41–81 cm) sympodial epiphyte.

PSEUDOBULB: 16–32 in. (41–81 cm) long. The elongated stems are striped.

LEAVES: Many. The leaves are 2 in. (5 cm) long and arranged in 2 rows. They are spaced about 0.8 in. (2 cm) apart along the stem. The leaves are evergreen, oblong, and leathery. Leaf sheaths are covered with black hairs.

INFLORESCENCE: 0.8–2.4 in. (2–6 cm) long. The racemes emerge from nodes near the apex of the stem.

FLOWERS: 3–4, less often 6–12 per inflorescence. The flowers are 2.8–4.0 in. (7–10 cm) across. They are large, showy, and crystalline white. The petals are broad, flaring, and rounded, but the sepals are narrower and pointed. The lip has a notched, broadly ovate midlobe. The throat is marked with sharply contrasting red or plum-purple parallel stripes. Some pure white clones have been found.

HYBRIDIZING NOTES: Chromosome counts are n = 20 (ref. 580) and 2n = 40 (ref. 154, 188, 580).

REFERENCES: 12, 36, 98, 154, 179, 188, 190, 196, 200, 210, 220, 293, 296, 326, 371, 373, 389, 429, 430, 504, 524, 536, 580.

PHOTOS/DRAWINGS: 98, 210, *371*, 373, *389, 430*.

Dendrobium sanderianum Rolfe. See *D. parthenium* Rchb. f. REFERENCES: 218, 254, 286, 295, 407, 429, 430.

Dendrobium sanguineum Rolfe. See *D. cinnabarinum* Rchb. f. REFERENCES: 211, 218, 254, 286, 445.

Dendrobium sanguineum Swartz. Now considered a synonym of *Broughtonia sanuinea* R. Brown. REFERENCES: 216, 254.

Dendrobium sanguinolentum Lindley

AKA: *D. cerinum* Rchb. f. not Schlechter. Seidenfaden and Wood (ref. 455) indicate that *D. kentrochilum* Hooker f. may be a synonym.

ORIGIN/HABITAT: Widespread in Southeast Asia. The habitat includes Malaya, Sumatra, Borneo, Thailand, Java, the Sulu Archipelago, and the Philippine Islands. Plants grow near Pattani, Thailand at about 2950 ft. (900 m). They are found in the hills of northwest Malaya at 2500–3000 ft. (760–910 m), and were recently collected in Java, southwest of Bogor on Mt. Halimum, at about 2600 ft. (800 m). On Luzon Island in the Philippines, they are found in the mountains east of Manila. Plants normally grow in moderately exposed locations at moderate elevations. In Malaya, plants grow on low trees and stumps.

CLIMATE: Station #96755, Bogor, Java, Indonesia, Lat. 6.5°S, Long. 106.8°E, at 558 ft. (170 m). Temperatures are calculated for an elevation of 2600 ft. (790 m), resulting in probable extremes of 89°F (32°C) and 59°F (15°C).

N/HEMISPHERE	JAN	FEB	MAR	APR	MAY	JUN	JUL	AUG	SEP	OCT	NOV	DEC
°F AVG MAX	79	80	81	81	80	78	77	77	78	79	80	79
°F AVG MIN	66	66	66	67	67	67	67	67	67	68	68	67
DIURNAL RANGE	13	14	15	14	13	11	10	10	11	11	12	12
RAIN/INCHES	2.1	1.0	0.5	5.0	8.1	18.8	23.7	20.2	14.4	12.0	11.9	3.4
HUMIDITY/%	72	68	65	66	74	79	84	84	81	79	77	75
BLOOM SEASON	*							**	**	*	*	*
DAYS CLR @ 7AM	14	14	14	11	5	3	1	2	4	6	10	12
DAYS CLR @ 1PM	9	10	8	5	1	1	0	0	1	1	3	7
RAIN/MM	53	25	13	127	206	478	602	513	366	305	302	86
°C AVG MAX	26.3	26.8	27.4	27.4	26.8	25.7	25.2	25.2	25.7	26.3	26.8	26.3
°C AVG MIN	19.1	19.1	19.1	19.6	19.6	19.6	19.6	19.6	19.6	20.2	20.2	19.6
DIURNAL RANGE	7.2	7.7	8.3	7.8	7.2	6.1	5.6	5.6	6.1	6.1	6.6	6.7
S/HEMISPHERE	JUL	AUG	SEP	OCT	NOV	DEC	JAN	FEB	MAR	APR	MAY	JUN

Cultural Recommendations

LIGHT: 2500–3500 fc. Light should be relatively high.

TEMPERATURES: Throughout the year, days average 77–81°F (25–27°C), and nights average 66–68°F (19–20°C), with a diurnal range of 10–15°F (6–8°C). Uniform temperatures may be critical for plant health; but because of the wide distribution, plants may adapt to temperatures 4–6°F (2–3°C) cooler than indicated.

HUMIDITY: 80–85% in summer, dropping to about 65% in winter. Excellent air circulation may be particularly important for plants from this habitat.

WATER: Rainfall is very heavy from spring into autumn, but conditions are very dry for 1–2 months in winter. During the growing season, plants should never be allowed to dry out completely, but water should be gradually reduced in late autumn.

FERTILIZER: ¼–½ recommended strength, applied weekly. A high-nitrogen fertilizer is beneficial from spring to midsummer, but a fertilizer high in phosphates should be used in late summer and autumn.

REST PERIOD: Growing conditions should be maintained all year, but rainfall is very low for 1–2 months. In cultivation, water should be reduced and the plants allowed to become dry between waterings, but they should not remain dry for prolonged periods. Fertilizer may be reduced or eliminated anytime the plant is not actively growing. In the habitat, light is highest in winter.

GROWING MEDIA: Mounting plants on tree-fern or cork slabs accommodates their pendulous growth habit. However, humidity must be high and plants must be watered at least once a day in summer. If plants cannot be mounted, hanging pots or baskets may be filled with an open, fast-draining medium. Repotting may be done anytime new roots are actively growing. Old canes should not be removed, as they continue to bloom for several years.

MISCELLANEOUS NOTES: The bloom season shown in the climate table is based on cultivation records. Growers indicate that *D. sanguinolentum* grows readily in Singapore but that it rarely blooms, suggesting that either the diurnal range or the dry period may be needed to initiate blooms. Plants reportedly grow well in gardens in Manila. Plants from the Philippines, originally called *D. cerinum* and now known as *D. sanguinolentum* var. *cerinum* (Rchb. f.) Ridley, are small, erect, compact, and deciduous. This variety is more common and lacks the colored tips on the flowers.

Plant and Flower Information

PLANT SIZE AND TYPE: An 18–48 in. (46–122 cm) sympodial epiphyte, terrestrial, or lithophyte.

PSEUDOBULB: 18–48 in. (46–122 cm) long. The purple canes are horizontal when young, but they become thick, cylindrical, and pendulous with age.

LEAVES: Many along the stem. The evergreen leaves, which are reddish or purplish when young, are 3 in. (8 cm) long. Leaves may be deciduous. The leaf sheaths have purple veins.

INFLORESCENCE: 1.0–1.5 in. (2.5–3.8 cm) long. The blossoms are carried in a close bunch. Inflorescences emerge from the upper-most joints.

FLOWERS: 2–6, rarely 1 per inflorescence. The waxy flowers are 1 in. (2.5 cm) across. The broad sepals and petals, which sometimes have deep violet tips, may be pale fawn-beige, deep cream, or amber-yellow. The sepals occasionally have a purplish tint. Shorter than the other segments, the lip is notched at the apex. It has a wavy margin, erect sidelobes, a raised orange patch in the center, and a violet-crimson tip. Blossoms last about 2 weeks.

REFERENCES: 74, 75, 179, 190, 200, 202, 216, 254, 258, 286, 295, 317, 394, 395, 402, 445, 454, 455, 541, 570, 592.

PHOTOS/DRAWINGS: 74, 75, 200, 454, 455.

Dendrobium sanseiense Hayata. Now considered a synonym of *Epigeneium sanseiense* (Hayata) Summerhayes. REFERENCES: 61, 62, 151, 187, 194, 208, 222, 229, 499. PHOTOS/DRAWINGS: 62.

Dendrobium sarasinorum Kränzlin. See *D. furcatum* Reinwardt ex Lindley. REFERENCES: 436.

Dendrobium sarawakense Ames

AKA: *D. multiflorum* Ridley not Parish and Rchb. f. *Index Kewensis* (ref. 223) lists the name as *D. sarawakense* Merrill.

ORIGIN/HABITAT: Borneo near Quop, Sarawak. Habitat elevation is unavailable, so the following climate data should be used with caution.

CLIMATE: Station #96413, Kuching, Sarawak, Lat. 1.5°N, Long. 110.3°E, at 85 ft. (26 m). Record extreme temperatures are 97°F (36°C) and 64°F (18°C).

N/HEMISPHERE	JAN	FEB	MAR	APR	MAY	JUN	JUL	AUG	SEP	OCT	NOV	DEC
°F AVG MAX	88	88	89	90	91	91	91	92	90	90	90	88
°F AVG MIN	72	72	72	72	72	73	72	72	72	72	72	72
DIURNAL RANGE	16	16	17	18	19	18	19	20	18	18	18	16
RAIN/INCHES	27.1	19.7	14.2	9.7	9.0	8.5	6.9	8.8	9.5	12.6	13.1	20.1
HUMIDITY/%	89	88	86	85	85	83	82	83	84	85	87	88
BLOOM SEASON			*									
DAYS CLR @ 7AM	1	0	1	2	3	2	4	1	2	1	1	1
DAYS CLR @ 1PM	0	0	0	0	0	1	1	1	0	0	0	0
RAIN/MM	688	500	361	246	229	216	175	224	241	320	333	511
°C AVG MAX	31.1	31.1	31.7	32.2	32.8	32.8	32.8	33.3	32.2	32.2	32.2	31.1
°C AVG MIN	22.2	22.2	22.2	22.2	22.2	22.8	22.2	22.2	22.2	22.2	22.2	22.2
DIURNAL RANGE	8.9	8.9	9.5	10.0	10.6	10.0	10.6	11.1	10.0	10.0	10.0	8.9
S/HEMISPHERE	JUL	AUG	SEP	OCT	NOV	DEC	JAN	FEB	MAR	APR	MAY	JUN

Cultural Recommendations

LIGHT: 2000–3000 fc.

TEMPERATURES: Throughout the year, days average 88–92°F (31–33°C), and nights average 72–73°F (22–23°C), with a diurnal range of 16–20°F (9–11°C). The diurnal range is unusually large for a habitat with so little seasonal variation.

HUMIDITY: 80–90% year-round. High humidity and excellent air circulation are important.

WATER: Rainfall is very heavy all year. Plants should be kept moist but not soggy. Warm water may be beneficial.

FERTILIZER: ¼–½ recommended strength. A balanced fertilizer should be applied weekly to biweekly throughout the year.

REST PERIOD: Growing conditions should be maintained all year. The record low is only 10°F (6°C) below the average lows. Although rainfall remains heavy, water may be reduced somewhat for cultivated plants, especially those grown in the dark, short-day conditions common in temperate latitudes. Plants should never be allowed to dry out completely, however. In the habitat, light is highest in winter.

GROWING MEDIA: Plants may be mounted on tree-fern or cork slabs if humidity is high and plants are watered at least once daily in summer. When plants are potted, any open, fast-draining medium may be used. They may be repotted anytime new roots are growing.

MISCELLANEOUS NOTES: The bloom season shown in the climate table is based on records from the habitat.

Plant and Flower Information

PLANT SIZE AND TYPE: An 18–24 in. (45–60 cm) sympodial epiphyte.

PSEUDOBULB: 18–24 in. (45–60 cm) long. The slightly flexuous stems are strongly grooved.

LEAVES: Many. The elliptic leaves are about 3 in. (8 cm) long.

INFLORESCENCE: 2–4 in. (5–10 cm) long. The inflorescence is borne at the apex.

FLOWERS: Many. The blossoms are described as large. The petals and lip are yellow. The sepals are red on the outside. The sepals and slightly smaller petals are elliptic-lanceolate. The rounded, ovate lip is 1 in. (2.5 cm) across, thickened in the center, and distinctly nerved. The nerves at the base are raised, forming a wavy keel. The red spur is curved, thick, blunt, and 0.5 in. (1.3 cm) long.

REFERENCES: 223, 286, 295, 398.

Dendrobium sarcanthum Lindley. See *D. cuspidatum* Lindley 1830 not 1858. REFERENCES: 216, 254, 278, 310, 454, 469.

Dendrobium sarcochilus Finet

AKA: *D. megalorhizum* Kränzlin, *D. sarcochilus* Finet var. *megalorhizum*. (Kränzlin) Hallé.

ORIGIN/HABITAT: New Caledonia. Plants grow in the southern district near the Ngoye River along the forest edge at about 500 ft. (150 m).

CLIMATE: Station #91592, Noumea, New Caledonia, Lat. 22.3°S, Long. 166.5°E, at 246 ft. (75 m). Record extreme temperatures are 99°F (37°C) and 52°F (11°C).

N/HEMISPHERE	JAN	FEB	MAR	APR	MAY	JUN	JUL	AUG	SEP	OCT	NOV	DEC
°F AVG MAX	76	76	78	80	83	86	86	85	85	83	79	77
°F AVG MIN	62	61	63	65	68	70	72	73	72	70	66	64
DIURNAL RANGE	14	15	15	15	15	16	14	12	13	13	13	13
RAIN/INCHES	3.6	2.6	2.5	2.0	2.4	2.6	3.7	5.1	5.7	5.2	4.4	3.7
HUMIDITY/%	73	70	69	67	68	69	71	74	75	76	73	73
BLOOM SEASON			*	*	*		*			*	*	
DAYS CLR @ 11AM	7	9	9	15	12	10	7	6	7	7	7	7
DAYS CLR @ 5PM	7	11	6	11	7	6	5	4	4	5	3	7
RAIN/MM	91	66	51	61	66	94	130	145	132	112	94	
°C AVG MAX	24.4	24.4	25.6	26.7	28.3	30.0	30.0	29.4	29.4	28.3	26.1	25.0
°C AVG MIN	16.7	16.1	17.2	18.3	20.0	21.1	22.2	22.8	22.2	21.1	18.9	17.8
DIURNAL RANGE	7.7	8.3	8.4	8.4	8.3	8.9	7.8	6.6	7.2	7.2	7.2	7.2
S/HEMISPHERE	JUL	AUG	SEP	OCT	NOV	DEC	JAN	FEB	MAR	APR	MAY	JUN

Cultural Recommendations

LIGHT: 2500–3500 fc.

TEMPERATURES: Summer days average 85–86°F (29–30°C), and nights

Dendrobium sarcodes

average 70–73°F (21–23°C), with a diurnal range of 12–16°F (7–9°C).

HUMIDITY: 70–75% most of the year, dropping to near 65% in early spring.

WATER: Rainfall is moderate to heavy all year. Cultivated plants should be allowed to dry slightly between waterings.

FERTILIZER: ¼–½ recommended strength, applied weekly. A high-nitrogen fertilizer is beneficial from spring to midsummer, but a fertilizer high in phosphates should be used in late summer and autumn.

REST PERIOD: Winter days average 76–78°F (24–26°C), and nights average 61–64°F (16–18°C), with a diurnal range of 13–15°F (7–8°C). High and low temperatures decline simultaneously, resulting in little change in the diurnal range. Cultivated plants cannot tolerate drying out, but water and fertilizer should be reduced somewhat for plants cultivated in the dark, short-day conditions common during temperate-latitude winters. In the habitat, light is highest in winter.

GROWING MEDIA: Plants may be mounted on tree-fern or cork slabs if humidity is high and plants are watered at least once daily in summer. When plants are potted, any open, fast-draining medium may be used. Repotting is best done in early spring when new roots are growing.

MISCELLANEOUS NOTES: The bloom season shown in the climate table is based on reports from the habitat.

Plant and Flower Information

PLANT SIZE AND TYPE: A 39–118 in. (100–300 cm) sympodial terrestrial.

PSEUDOBULB: 39–118 in. (100–300 cm) long. The tall, woody canes resemble bamboo and grow in a shrublike mass.

LEAVES: Many. The linear-lanceolate leaves are usually about 5 in. (12 cm) long. They are arranged in 2 rows.

INFLORESCENCE: 4 in. (10 cm) long. Several lateral racemes emerge at the base of the leaves. The racemes are leafy.

FLOWERS: 8–15 per inflorescence. The flowers open in succession. They are 0.5 in. (1.3 cm) long. The pointed sepals and petals may be white or greenish. The yellow lip is flushed with rose. It is 3-lobed, with 3 raised keels at the base. The margin of the midlobe is thickened and very wavy.

REFERENCES: 118, 173, 219, 233, 254, 432, 445.

PHOTOS/DRAWINGS: 173.

Dendrobium sarcodes Schlechter

ORIGIN/HABITAT: Northern Papua New Guinea. Plants grow on forest trees in the Kani Mountains at about 3300 ft. (1000 m).

CLIMATE: Station #200187, Erap, Papua New Guinea, Lat. 6.6°S, Long. 146.7°E, at 850 ft. (260 m). Temperatures are calculated for an elevation of 3300 ft. (1000 m), resulting in probable extremes of 94°F (34°C) and 45°F (7°C).

N/HEMISPHERE	JAN	FEB	MAR	APR	MAY	JUN	JUL	AUG	SEP	OCT	NOV	DEC
°F AVG MAX	80	80	81	82	85	85	85	85	85	84	82	82
°F AVG MIN	61	61	61	62	64	65	64	64	65	63	66	62
DIURNAL RANGE	19	19	20	20	21	20	21	21	20	21	16	20
RAIN/INCHES	3.9	3.9	2.7	3.0	3.0	5.3	5.9	5.9	7.0	3.4	2.4	3.1
HUMIDITY/%	82	81	81	79	75	74	74	74	77	76	80	80
BLOOM SEASON						*						
DAYS CLR	N/A											
RAIN/MM	99	99	69	76	76	135	150	150	178	86	61	79
°C AVG MAX	26.7	26.7	27.2	27.8	29.4	29.4	29.4	29.4	29.4	28.9	27.8	27.8
°C AVG MIN	16.1	16.1	16.1	16.7	17.8	18.3	17.8	17.8	18.3	17.2	18.9	16.7
DIURNAL RANGE	10.6	10.6	11.1	11.1	11.6	11.1	11.6	11.6	11.1	11.7	8.9	11.1
S/HEMISPHERE	JUL	AUG	SEP	OCT	NOV	DEC	JAN	FEB	MAR	APR	MAY	JUN

Cultural Recommendations

LIGHT: 2000–3000 fc.

TEMPERATURES: Throughout the year, days average 80–85°F (27–29°C), and nights average 61–65°F (16–18°C), with a diurnal range of 16–21°F (9–12°C).

HUMIDITY: 75–80% year-round.

WATER: Rainfall is moderate most of the year, but for 4–5 months in summer and early autumn, conditions are somewhat wetter. Cultivated plants should be thoroughly saturated then allowed to dry slightly between waterings in summer and early autumn. Water should be gradually reduced in autumn.

FERTILIZER: ¼–½ recommended strength. A balanced fertilizer should be applied weekly to biweekly throughout the year.

REST PERIOD: Growing temperatures should be maintained all year. In the habitat, rainfall is lowest in winter, but the high humidity indicates that additional moisture is frequently available from heavy dew. Cultivated plants should be allowed to dry for somewhat longer between waterings, but should not remain dry for extended periods. Fertilizer should be reduced until water is increased in spring. In the habitat, seasonal light variation is minor.

GROWING MEDIA: Plants may be mounted on tree-fern or cork slabs if humidity is high and plants are watered at least once daily in summer. When plants are potted, any open, fast-draining medium may be used. Repotting may be done anytime new roots are growing.

MISCELLANEOUS NOTES: The bloom season shown in the climate table is based on collection reports. Plants that produce flowers which last a single day commonly bloom several times during the year. Flowering usually occurs 7–14 days after a sudden 10°F (5°C) drop in daytime temperatures.

Plant and Flower Information

PLANT SIZE AND TYPE: A 39–59 in. (100–150 cm) sympodial epiphyte.

PSEUDOBULB: 39–59 in. (100–150 cm) long. The long stems do not branch.

LEAVES: Many per growth. The elliptic leaves are 3.5–6.0 in. (9–15 cm) long.

INFLORESCENCE: Short. Inflorescences emerge from the side of the stem.

FLOWERS: 2 per inflorescence. The flowers are 0.7 in. (1.8 cm) long. Sepals and petals are white with red dots. They are cupped at the thickened tips. The sepals are covered with bumps on the backside. The 3-lobed lip is yellowish with orange-red to orange-brown markings. It is covered with bumps and the center of the midlobe has a cluster of pointed projections. The midlobe is wavy and uneven along the sides and pointed at the tip. The sidelobes extend to the midpoint of the midlobe. They are rounded at the tip and uneven along the margin. Blossoms are short-lived.

REFERENCES: 92, 221 437, 445.

PHOTOS/DRAWINGS: 437.

Dendrobium sarcophyllum Schlechter

ORIGIN/HABITAT: Northern Papua New Guinea. Plants grow on forest trees in the Finisterre Range at about 4250 ft. (1300 m).

CLIMATE: Station #94010, Goroka, Papua New Guinea, Lat. 6.1°S, Long. 145.4°E, at 5141 ft. (1567 m). Temperatures are calculated for an elevation of 4000 ft. (1220 m), resulting in probable extremes of 90°F (32°C) and 46°F (8°C).

N/HEMISPHERE	JAN	FEB	MAR	APR	MAY	JUN	JUL	AUG	SEP	OCT	NOV	DEC
°F AVG MAX	80	81	82	83	83	82	83	82	82	82	83	81
°F AVG MIN	60	61	61	61	62	63	63	63	64	63	63	61
DIURNAL RANGE	20	20	21	22	21	19	20	19	18	19	20	20
RAIN/INCHES	2.1	2.8	4.6	5.9	6.6	9.3	9.1	10.1	10.7	8.3	4.6	2.0
HUMIDITY/%	70	67	67	67	67	71	72	73	74	71	70	70
BLOOM SEASON	*											
DAYS CLR	N/A											
RAIN/MM	53	71	117	150	168	236	231	257	272	211	117	51
°C AVG MAX	26.5	27.1	27.6	28.2	28.2	27.6	28.2	27.6	27.6	27.6	28.2	27.1
°C AVG MIN	15.4	16.0	16.0	16.0	16.5	17.1	17.1	17.1	17.6	17.1	17.1	16.0
DIURNAL RANGE	11.1	11.1	11.6	12.2	11.7	10.5	11.1	10.5	10.0	10.5	11.1	11.1
S/HEMISPHERE	JUL	AUG	SEP	OCT	NOV	DEC	JAN	FEB	MAR	APR	MAY	JUN

Cultural Recommendations

LIGHT: 2000–3000 fc.

TEMPERATURES: Throughout the year, days average 80–83°F (27–28°C), and nights average 60–64°F (15–18°C), with a diurnal range of 18–22°F (10–12°C). The diurnal range is unusually large for a habitat with such constant temperatures.

HUMIDITY: 70–75% in summer and early autumn, dropping to 65–70% in winter and spring. Plants require excellent air movement.

WATER: Rainfall is moderate to heavy most of the year, but conditions are somewhat drier in winter. Cultivated plants should be kept moist while actively growing, but water should be gradually reduced in autumn. Early morning mistings between waterings are often beneficial, especially on warm, sunny days.

FERTILIZER: ¼–½ recommended strength. A balanced fertilizer should be applied weekly to biweekly throughout the year.

REST PERIOD: Growing conditions should be maintained all year. In the habitat, rainfall is lowest in winter, but heavy dew and mist from fog and low clouds are common. Water and fertilizer should be reduced for cultivated plants, especially those grown in the dark, short-day conditions common in temperate-latitude winters. Plants should dry slightly between waterings, but they should never be allowed to dry completely or to remain dry for long periods. In the habitat, light is slightly higher in winter.

GROWING MEDIA: Plants may be mounted on tree-fern or cork slabs if humidity is high and plants are watered at least once daily in summer. When plants are potted, any open, fast-draining medium may be used. Repotting may be done anytime new roots are growing.

MISCELLANEOUS NOTES: The bloom season shown in the climate table is based on collection reports. Plants that produce flowers which last a single day commonly bloom several times during the year. Flowering usually occurs 7–14 days after a sudden 10°F (5°C) drop in daytime temperatures.

Plant and Flower Information

PLANT SIZE AND TYPE: A 12–18 in. (30–45 cm) sympodial epiphyte.

PSEUDOBULB: 12–18 in. (30–45 cm) long. The rigid stems do not branch. They are laxly leafy.

LEAVES: Several. The leaves are 0.7 in. (1.8 cm) long, thick, fleshy, and terete.

INFLORESCENCE: Short.

FLOWERS: 2 per inflorescence. The flowers are 0.4 in. (1 cm) long and may not open fully. They are pale yellow with orange-red in the center of the lip. The dorsal sepal and petals project forward and the lateral sepals curve down. The 3-lobed lip is pointed at the apex, and the side margins are deeply toothed to fringed. The lip is covered with pointed projections except near the margins. The sidelobes are pointed. Blossoms are short-lived.

REFERENCES: 92, 221, 437, 445.

PHOTOS/DRAWINGS: 437.

Dendrobium sarcopodioides J. J. Smith. See *D. simplex* J. J. Smith. REFERENCES: 83, 221, 470, 478, 499.

Dendrobium sarcostemma Teijsm. and Binn. ex Miquel. Sometimes spelled *D. sarcostoma*, see *D. macrophyllum* A. Richard. REFERENCES: 75, 83, 190, 254, 373.

Dendrobium sarcostoma (Blume) Lindley. Now considered a synonym of *Sarcostoma javanica* Blume. REFERENCES: 75, 216, 310, 469.

Dendrobium sarmentosum Rolfe

AKA: *D. fragrans* Hort. ex Hooker f.

ORIGIN/HABITAT: Burma. Plants were originally found 30 miles (48 km) from Inle Lake in Shan state. Habitat elevation is unavailable, so the following climate data should be used with caution.

CLIMATE: Station #48057, Taunggyi, Burma, Lat. 20.8°N, Long. 97.1°E, at 4712 ft. (1436 m). Record extreme temperatures are 93°F (34°C) and 32°F (0°C).

N/HEMISPHERE	JAN	FEB	MAR	APR	MAY	JUN	JUL	AUG	SEP	OCT	NOV	DEC
°F AVG MAX	72	76	81	84	81	77	75	76	76	75	74	71
°F AVG MIN	45	47	52	60	63	64	64	64	63	61	52	47
DIURNAL RANGE	27	29	29	24	18	13	11	12	13	14	22	24
RAIN/INCHES	0.1	0.4	0.1	1.3	9.3	7.8	11.3	13.0	8.5	6.8	1.5	0.6
HUMIDITY/%	66	59	49	55	72	82	83	85	84	82	76	71
BLOOM SEASON		*										
DAYS CLR @ 6AM	17	20	23	17	8	0	0	1	2	6	16	18
DAYS CLR @ 12PM	21	19	22	11	3	0	0	0	0	1	9	16
RAIN/MM	3	10	3	33	236	198	287	330	216	173	38	15
°C AVG MAX	22.2	24.4	27.2	28.9	27.2	25.0	23.9	24.4	24.4	23.9	23.3	21.7
°C AVG MIN	7.2	8.3	11.1	15.6	17.2	17.8	17.8	17.8	17.2	16.1	11.1	8.3
DIURNAL RANGE	15.0	16.1	16.1	13.3	10.0	7.2	6.1	6.6	7.2	7.8	12.2	13.4
S/HEMISPHERE	JUL	AUG	SEP	OCT	NOV	DEC	JAN	FEB	MAR	APR	MAY	JUN

Cultural Recommendations

LIGHT: 2000–3000 fc.

TEMPERATURES: Summer days average 75–77°F (24–25°C), and nights average 64°F (18°C), with a diurnal range of 11–13°F (6–7°C). The warmest season is spring. Days average 81–84°F (27–29°C), and nights average 52–63°F (11–17°C), with a diurnal range of 18–29°F (10–16°C).

HUMIDITY: 80–85% in summer and autumn, dropping to 50–60% in late winter and early spring.

WATER: Rainfall is heavy for 6 months from spring to early autumn. The wet season is followed abruptly by 4–6 very dry months with little if any transition between the 2 seasons. Cultivated plants should be kept moist while actively growing, but water should be greatly reduced in autumn after new growths mature.

FERTILIZER: ¼–½ recommended strength, applied weekly. A high-nitrogen fertilizer is beneficial from spring to midsummer, but a fertilizer high in phosphates should be used in late summer and autumn.

REST PERIOD: Winter days average 71–76°F (22–24°C), and nights average 45–47°F (7–8°C), with a diurnal range of 24–29°F (13–16°C). Plants apparently do not require a certain minimum temperature, but the increased diurnal range in winter seems to be very important. In the habitat, rainfall is lowest in winter, but heavy dew is common during the early part of the dry season. The driest part of the season lasts 2–3 months. Cultivated plants should be allowed to dry out between waterings, but should not remain dry for long periods. Occasional early morning mistings between waterings may help keep plants from becoming too dry. Fertilizer should be reduced or eliminated during the rest period. In the habitat, light is highest in winter.

GROWING MEDIA: Mounting plants on tree-fern or cork slabs accommodates their pendulous growth habit. However, humidity must be high and plants must be watered at least once a day in summer. If plants cannot be mounted, hanging pots or baskets may be filled with an open, fast-draining medium. Repotting may be done anytime new roots are actively growing.

MISCELLANEOUS NOTES: The bloom season shown in the climate table is based on cultivation records.

Plant and Flower Information

PLANT SIZE AND TYPE: A 16 in. (40 cm) sympodial epiphyte.

Dendrobium sarrasinorum

PSEUDOBULB: 16 in. (40 cm) long. The pendulous stems are cylindrical and consist of many nodes. The plants appear twiggy due to the branching growth habit.

LEAVES: The ovate-oblong leaves are 2.4 in. (6 cm) long.

INFLORESCENCE: 2.4 in. (6 cm) long. Inflorescences emerge from leaf nodes along the stem.

FLOWERS: 1, rarely 2 per inflorescence. The flowers are 1.2 in. (3 cm) across. They are white with violet markings. The lip is very light green at the base. The small, rounded sidelobes are yellow with red-brown, radiating stripes. The midlobe is oblong and rounded with a hairy disk. Blossoms have a fragrance like violets.

REFERENCES: 179, 210, 254, 445.

PHOTOS/DRAWINGS: 210.

Dendrobium sarrasinorum Kränzlin. See *D. furcatum* Reinwardt ex Lindley. REFERENCES: 220, 254.

Dendrobium saruwagedicum Schlechter. Reeve and Wood (ref. 385) consider it a possible synonym of *D. brevicaule* Rolfe. REFERENCES: 221, 385, 538.

Dendrobium savannicola Schlechter 1907 not 1923. Now considered a synonym of *Diplocaulobium savannicola* (Schlechter) A. Hawkes. REFERENCES: 221, 229, 437, 445.

Dendrobium sayeri Schlechter (1907) not Schlechter (1912). Now considered a synonym of *Cadetia sayeri* (Schlechter) Schlechter. REFERENCES: 220, 254, 437.

Dendrobium sayeria Schlechter 1912 not 1907. See *D. crutwellii* T. M. Reeve. REFERENCES: 83, 221.

Dendrobium scabrifolium Ridley

ORIGIN/HABITAT: Irian Jaya (western New Guinea). Plants were collected on the south side of Mt. Jaya (Mt. Carstensz) at 8300–11,000 ft. (2530–3350 m).

CLIMATE: Station #97796, Kokenau (Kokonau), Irian Jaya, Lat. 4.7°S, Long. 135.4°E, at 10 ft. (3 m). Temperatures are calculated for an elevation of 9500 ft. (2900 m). Record extreme temperatures are not available for this location.

N/HEMISPHERE	JAN	FEB	MAR	APR	MAY	JUN	JUL	AUG	SEP	OCT	NOV	DEC
°F AVG MAX	52	52	55	57	59	58	58	58	59	57	56	53
°F AVG MIN	42	42	43	43	43	44	43	43	43	43	43	42
DIURNAL RANGE	10	10	12	14	16	14	15	15	16	14	13	11
RAIN/INCHES	18.4	15.8	18.9	11.6	9.7	10.6	11.5	15.7	11.6	11.6	16.0	19.9
HUMIDITY/%	N/A											
BLOOM SEASON	N/A											
DAYS CLR	N/A											
RAIN/MM	467	401	480	295	246	269	292	399	295	295	406	505
°C AVG MAX	10.9	10.9	12.6	13.7	14.8	14.3	14.3	14.3	14.8	13.7	13.2	11.5
°C AVG MIN	5.4	5.4	5.9	5.9	5.9	6.5	5.9	5.9	5.9	5.9	5.9	5.4
DIURNAL RANGE	5.5	5.5	6.7	7.8	8.9	7.8	8.4	8.4	8.9	7.8	7.3	6.1
S/HEMISPHERE	JUL	AUG	SEP	OCT	NOV	DEC	JAN	FEB	MAR	APR	MAY	JUN

Cultural Recommendations

LIGHT: 2500–3500 fc.

TEMPERATURES: Throughout the year, days average 52–59°F (11–15°C), and nights average 42–44°F (5–7°C), with a diurnal range of 10–16°F (6–9°C). Due to the effects of the microclimate, actual high temperatures may average 3–7°F (2–4°C) warmer than indicated.

HUMIDITY: Information is not available for this location. However, records from nearby stations indicate that humidity probably averages near 85% year-round.

WATER: Rainfall is very heavy year-round. Cultivated plants should be kept evenly moist but not soggy.

FERTILIZER: ¼–½ recommended strength. A balanced fertilizer should be applied weekly to biweekly throughout the year.

REST PERIOD: Growing conditions should be maintained year-round. Cultivated plants should never be allowed to dry completely; but water and fertilizer might be reduced somewhat in winter, especially for plants grown in the dark, short-day conditions common during temperate latitudes. In the habitat, seasonal light variation is minor.

GROWING MEDIA: Plants may be mounted on tree-fern or cork slabs or potted in small pots filled with any open, fast-draining medium. Repotting may be done anytime new roots are growing.

Plant and Flower Information

PLANT SIZE AND TYPE: A sympodial epiphyte of unreported size.

PSEUDOBULB: The frequently branching stems are covered with the fibers that remain after the leaf sheaths disintegrate.

LEAVES: 1.2 in. (3 cm) long. The linear-lanceolate leaves are stiff with notches and serrations along the yellow margin.

INFLORESCENCE: 2 in. (5 cm) long. Inflorescences emerge at the apex of the stem. The ovary is red.

FLOWERS: The flowers are 0.8 in. (2 cm) across. The sepals are elliptical. The rosy petals are oblanceolate. The obovate lip is grooved in the center, minutely toothed along the margin, and 0.7 in. (1.8 cm) long.

REFERENCES: 222, 400.

Dendrobium scabrilingue Lindley

AKA: *D. galactanthum* Schlechter, *D. hedyosmum* Bateman. Hawkes (ref. 190) also includes *D. alboviride* Parish.

ORIGIN/HABITAT: Burma, Laos, and Thailand. Plants are usually found in the highlands at 2000–4000 ft. (610–1220 m). In Burma, they grow near Moulmein in the Tenasserim region and along the Salween River.

CLIMATE: Station #48327, Chiang Mai, Thailand, Lat. 18.8°N, Long. 99.0°E, at 1100 ft. (335 m). Temperatures are calculated for an elevation of 2500 ft. (760 m), resulting in probable extremes of 104°F (40°C) and 33°F (1°C).

N/HEMISPHERE	JAN	FEB	MAR	APR	MAY	JUN	JUL	AUG	SEP	OCT	NOV	DEC
°F AVG MAX	80	85	90	91	89	85	84	82	83	84	81	79
°F AVG MIN	51	52	57	65	69	69	69	70	68	66	61	52
DIURNAL RANGE	29	33	33	26	20	16	15	12	15	18	20	27
RAIN/INCHES	0.3	0.4	0.6	2.0	5.5	6.1	7.4	8.7	11.5	4.9	1.5	0.4
HUMIDITY/%	73	65	58	62	73	78	80	83	83	81	79	76
BLOOM SEASON	*		**		*	*	*					
DAYS CLR @ 7AM	5	5	2	2	1	0	0	0	0	1	3	3
DAYS CLR @ 1PM	9	8	4	2	0	0	0	0	0	0	1	3
RAIN/MM	8	10	15	51	140	155	188	221	292	124	38	10
°C AVG MAX	26.9	29.7	32.4	33.0	31.9	29.7	29.1	28.0	28.5	29.1	27.4	26.3
°C AVG MIN	10.8	11.3	14.1	18.5	20.8	20.8	20.8	21.3	20.2	19.1	16.3	11.3
DIURNAL RANGE	16.1	18.4	18.3	14.5	11.1	8.9	8.3	6.7	8.3	10.0	11.1	15.0
S/HEMISPHERE	JUL	AUG	SEP	OCT	NOV	DEC	JAN	FEB	MAR	APR	MAY	JUN

Cultural Recommendations

LIGHT: 2500–3500 fc. The heavy summer cloud cover indicates that some shading is needed from spring through autumn, but light should be as high as the plant can tolerate, short of burning the leaves.

TEMPERATURES: Summer days average 82–85°F (28–30°C), and nights average 69–70°F (21°C), with a diurnal range of 12–16°F (7–9°C).

Spring, before the start of the summer rainy season, is the warmest time of the year. Days average 89–91°F (32–33°C), and nights average 57–69°F (14–21°C), with a diurnal range of 20–33°F (11–18°C).

HUMIDITY: Near 80% most of the year, dropping to near 60% in late winter and early spring.

WATER: Rainfall is moderate to heavy from late spring through early autumn, but conditions are much drier in winter. Cultivated plants should be kept moist while actively growing, but water should be gradually reduced after new growths mature in autumn.

FERTILIZER: ¼–½ recommended strength, applied weekly. A high-nitrogen fertilizer is beneficial from spring to midsummer, but a fertilizer high in phosphates should be used in late summer and autumn.

REST PERIOD: Winter days average 79–85°F (26–30°C), and nights average 51–52°F (11°C), with a diurnal range of 27–33°F (15–18°C). In the habitat, rainfall averages are very low for 4 months in winter, but during the early part of the season the high relative humidity indicates that additional moisture is available from frequent fog, mist, and heavy deposits of dew. Growers sometimes recommend eliminating water in winter, but plants are healthiest if for most of the winter they are allowed to become dry between waterings but do not remain dry for extended periods. However, for 1–2 months in early spring, conditions in the habitat are clear, warm, and dry; and humidity is so low that even the moisture from morning dew is uncommon. During a corresponding time for cultivated plants, water should be limited to an occasional early morning misting if the pseudobulbs start to shrivel, or if an extended period of bright, sunny weather is expected. Fertilizer should be eliminated in winter and resumed only when water is increased in spring. In the habitat, light is highest in winter.

GROWING MEDIA: Plants may be mounted on tree-fern or cork slabs or potted in small pots filled with any open, fast-draining medium. Undersized pots that are barely large enough to hold the roots should be used. Repotting should be done just as seldom as possible, but when necessary, repotting is best done as soon as new root growth starts, or immediately after flowering.

MISCELLANEOUS NOTES: The bloom season shown in the climate table is based on cultivation records. Growers consider *D. scabrilingue* very easy to cultivate if it receives a cool, dry winter rest. Otherwise, it is difficult.

Plant and Flower Information

PLANT SIZE AND TYPE: A 6–12 in. (15–30 cm) sympodial epiphyte.

PSEUDOBULB: 6–12 in. (15–30 cm) long. The erect stems are swollen above the narrow base. They are somewhat lumpy and knobby looking.

LEAVES: 2–6 per growth. The oblong, apical leaves are 2.4–4.0 in. (6–10 cm) long and unequally bilobed at the apex. They are leathery and persistent. The leaf sheaths are covered with blackish hairs.

INFLORESCENCE: Very short. Numerous flowers are produced from apical and upper nodes of leafy stems and on lower nodes of leafless stems.

FLOWERS: 1–3 per inflorescence. The waxy flowers are 1.4 in. (3.5 cm) across. Sepals and petals are green to greenish white when they first open but change to ivory or bluish white within a few days. The 3-lobed lip is yellow-green with green veins when it first opens. The smooth keel starts at the base of the lip and separates into 3 lines at about the midpoint of the midlobe. The tips are warty and uneven. Each side of the keel is flanked by 2 less prominent lines. The sidelobes are green with red markings. The midlobe has a yellow disk with deep orange grooves and crimson stripes. Individual blossoms last about 5 weeks, but the plant is often in bloom for many months as buds continue to form. The flowers have a sweet fragrance reminiscent of wallflowers.

HYBRIDIZING NOTES: Chromosome count is 2n = 38 (ref. 151, 154, 187, 188, 504, 580).

REFERENCES: 36, 151, 154, 157, 179, 187, 188, 190, 202, 210, 216, 245, 254, 266, 278, 295, 310, 371, 429, 430, 445, 447, 448, 454, 504, 521, 541, 570, 580.

PHOTOS/DRAWINGS: 210, *245, 371, 430, 454, 521*.

Dendrobium scabripes Kränzlin. See *D. purpureum* Roxburgh. REFERENCES: 220, 254, 437, Dauncey and Cribb 1993 *Kew Bulletin* 48(3).

Dendrobium scalpelliforme Teijsm. and Binn. See *D. acinaciforme* Roxburgh. REFERENCES: 216, 254, 454, 455, 468.

Dendrobium scariosum Llave and Lexarza. Now considered a synonym of *Pleurothallis scariosa* Lindley. REFERENCES: 216, 254.

Dendrobium scarlatinum Schlechter. See *D. puniceum* Ridley. REFERENCES: 221, 271, 385, 437, 445.

Dendrobium schimperianum A. Richard. Now considered a synonym of *Angraecum schimperianum* Rchb. f. REFERENCES: 216, 254.

Dendrobium schinzianum Kränzlin. See *D. cymatoleguum* Schlechter. REFERENCES: 173, 224.

Dendrobium schinzii Rolfe. Now considered a synonym of *Flickingeria schinzii* (Rolfe) A. Hawkes. REFERENCES: 213, 220, 230, 231, 254.

Dendrobium schistoglossum Schlechter. Now considered a synonym of *Flickingeria schistoglossa* (Schlechter) A. Hawkes. REFERENCES: 213, 221, 230, 231, 435, 449.

Dendrobium schlechterianum J. J. Smith. Synonymous with *D. trilamellatum* Schlechter, which Seidenfaden (ref. 449) includes as a possible synonym of *Flickingeria bancana* (J. J. Smith) A. Hawkes. He does not, however, include *D. schlechterianum* as a synonym. REFERENCES: 221, 449.

Dendrobium schmidtianum Kränzlin. See *D. crumenatum* Swartz. REFERENCES: 67, 221, 254, 266, 448, 454.

Dendrobium schneiderae F. M. Bailey

ORIGIN/HABITAT: Eastern Australia. Plants grow in northeastern New South Wales and southeastern Queensland, especially in the MacPherson Range at about 1500 ft. (450 m). They are found high in rainforest trees where light is high. The orchids usually grow in moss on the lower side of branches, but they are occasionally found on rocks. *D. schneiderae* var. *major* Rupp, a larger, more robust form, grows about 600 mi. (1000 km) away near Mackay in the Eungella Mountains of northern Queensland.

CLIMATE: Station #94576, Brisbane, Australia, Lat. 27.4°S, Long. 153.1°E, at 17 ft. (5 m). Temperatures are calculated for an elevation of 1500 ft. (460 m), resulting in probable extremes of 105°F (41°C) and 30°F (−1°C).

N/HEMISPHERE	JAN	FEB	MAR	APR	MAY	JUN	JUL	AUG	SEP	OCT	NOV	DEC
°F AVG MAX	63	66	71	75	77	80	80	80	77	74	69	64
°F AVG MIN	44	45	50	55	59	62	64	63	61	56	51	46
DIURNAL RANGE	19	21	21	20	18	18	16	17	16	18	18	18
RAIN/INCHES	2.2	1.9	1.9	2.5	3.7	5.0	6.4	6.3	5.7	3.7	2.8	2.6
HUMIDITY/%	62	59	58	57	59	59	63	65	66	64	64	64
BLOOM SEASON							*	*	*			
DAYS CLR @ 10AM	17	20	18	11	12	9	5	4	9	14	18	16
DAYS CLR @ 4PM	15	16	15	12	14	12	8	5	8	10	14	14
RAIN/MM	56	48	48	64	94	127	163	160	145	94	71	66
°C AVG MAX	17.3	18.9	21.7	23.9	25.1	26.7	26.7	26.7	25.1	23.4	20.6	17.8
°C AVG MIN	6.7	7.3	10.1	12.8	15.1	16.7	17.8	17.3	16.2	13.4	10.6	7.8
DIURNAL RANGE	10.6	11.6	11.6	11.1	10.0	10.0	8.9	9.4	8.9	10.0	10.0	10.0
S/HEMISPHERE	JUL	AUG	SEP	OCT	NOV	DEC	JAN	FEB	MAR	APR	MAY	JUN

Cultural Recommendations

LIGHT: 3500–4500 fc. Light should be as high as the plant can tolerate, short of burning the leaves. In the habitat, more than half the days are clear each month except during the summer rainy season when skies are clear approximately 30% of the time. Growers recommend using 40–50% shade cloth, and indicate that high light is required to initiate blooms.

TEMPERATURES: Summer days average 77–80°F (25–27°C), and nights average 61–64°F (16–18°C), with a diurnal range of 16–18°F (9–10°C).

HUMIDITY: 60–65% year-round, although values are probably greater in the rainforest habitat. Growers recommend maximum air circulation.

WATER: Rainfall is moderate in summer and autumn, but conditions are drier in winter. Cultivated plants should be watered frequently during the growing season, but they must dry out slightly between waterings. If temperatures exceed 85°F (30°C), plants should be misted constantly until the temperature falls.

FERTILIZER: ¼–½ recommended strength, applied weekly. A high-nitrogen fertilizer is beneficial from spring to midsummer, but a fertilizer high in phosphates should be used in late summer and autumn.

REST PERIOD: Winter days average 63–71°F (17–22°C), and nights average 44–50°F (7–10°C), with a diurnal range of 18–21°F (10–12°C). In cultivation, water and fertilizer should be greatly reduced in winter. Plants should be allowed to dry out slightly between waterings, but they should not remain dry for extended periods. Water should be increased when growth resumes in spring. Growers indicate that plants from this habitat require a distinct seasonal variation and do not tolerate uniformly warm conditions. In the habitat, light is highest in winter.

GROWING MEDIA: Growers recommend mounting *D. schneiderae* on a cork slab. They indicate that plants are slow to establish and must be attached firmly. Mounted plants need daily watering and high humidity during the summer. Remounting is best done immediately after flowering when new roots are growing.

MISCELLANEOUS NOTES: The bloom season shown in the climate table is based on cultivation records. Although *D. schneiderae* is not vigorous or spectacular, once established it grows and flowers readily. Two varieties are presently recognized: the original species *D. schneiderae* var. *schneiderae* and *D. schneiderae* var. *major* Rupp.

Plant and Flower Information

PLANT SIZE AND TYPE: A 1.4–4.0 in. (3.5–10.0 cm) sympodial epiphyte. Plant size is variable.

PSEUDOBULB: 0.4–1.0 in. (1.0–2.5 cm) long. The squat, round to pear-shaped pseudobulbs are closely packed and form a dense mat on the creeping rhizome. The ribbed pseudobulbs may be dark green or yellowish.

LEAVES: 1–3 per growth. The slender, dark green leaves are 1.0–2.8 in. (2.5–7.0 cm) long. They are often somewhat twisted.

INFLORESCENCE: 2.4–6.7 in. (6–17 cm) long. Inflorescences arise from the apex of each new pseudobulb. They are semipendulous.

FLOWERS: 5–25 per inflorescence. The flowers are less than 0.4 in. (1 cm) across. They are waxy and bell-shaped. The incurved sepals and petals are dull yellowish-green with a pink or maroon margin. The lip, which is shaped something like a whale's tail, is broad at the tip with a prominent callus. Blossoms are fragrant.

HYBRIDIZING NOTES: Chromosome count is 2n = 38 (ref. 151, 153, 154, 188, 273). Pollen from the same plant seldom produces seed, but pods are regularly produced when pollen from another plant is used.

REFERENCES: 23, 67, 105, 151, 153, 154, 179, 188, 218, 240, 254, 262, 273, 291, 325, 390, 421, 533.

PHOTOS/DRAWINGS: 105, 240, *291*, 325, *390, 533*.

Dendrobium schoeninum Lindley

AKA: *D. beckleri* F. Mueller, *D. mortii* Bentham not F. Mueller, *D. striolatum* F. M. Bailey not Rchb. f., *D. striolatum* Rchb. f. var. *beckleri* (F. Mueller) F. M. Bailey. Although known as *D. beckleri* F. Mueller for over 100 years, Clements (ref. 67) indicates that Lindley's description predates F. Mueller's by 23 years. Consequently, under the International Rules of Nomenclature, *D. beckleri* should be considered a synonym.

ORIGIN/HABITAT: Eastern Australia. The habitat extends from near Newcastle in New South Wales to the Burdekin River in northeastern Queensland. Plants grow on trees and rocks in rainforests or open forests with high humidity. The habitat extends from coastal lowlands to about 1950 ft. (0–600 m).

CLIMATE: Station #94576, Brisbane, Australia, Lat. 27.4°S, Long. 153.1°E, at 17 ft. (5 m). Temperatures are calculated for an elevation of 1500 ft. (460 m), resulting in probable extremes of 105°F (41°C) and 30°F (−1°C).

N/HEMISPHERE	JAN	FEB	MAR	APR	MAY	JUN	JUL	AUG	SEP	OCT	NOV	DEC
°F AVG MAX	63	66	71	75	77	80	80	80	77	74	69	64
°F AVG MIN	44	45	50	55	59	62	64	63	61	56	51	46
DIURNAL RANGE	19	21	21	20	18	18	16	17	16	18	18	18
RAIN/INCHES	2.2	1.9	1.9	2.5	3.7	5.0	6.4	6.3	5.7	3.7	2.8	2.6
HUMIDITY/%	62	59	58	57	59	59	63	65	66	64	64	64
BLOOM SEASON		**	**	**	*	*			*		*	*
DAYS CLR @ 10AM	17	20	18	11	12	9	5	4	9	14	18	16
DAYS CLR @ 4PM	15	16	15	12	14	12	8	5	8	10	14	14
RAIN/MM	56	48	48	64	94	127	163	160	145	94	71	66
°C AVG MAX	17.3	18.9	21.7	23.9	25.1	26.7	26.7	26.7	25.1	23.4	20.6	17.8
°C AVG MIN	6.7	7.3	10.1	12.8	15.1	16.7	17.8	17.3	16.2	13.4	10.6	7.8
DIURNAL RANGE	10.6	11.6	11.6	11.1	10.0	10.0	8.9	9.4	8.9	10.0	10.0	10.0
S/HEMISPHERE	JUL	AUG	SEP	OCT	NOV	DEC	JAN	FEB	MAR	APR	MAY	JUN

Cultural Recommendations

LIGHT: 3000–4000 fc. Light should be as high as the plant can tolerate, short of burning the leaves. In the habitat, more than half the days are clear each month except during the summer rainy season, when skies are clear approximately 30% of the time. Growers recommend using 40–50% shade cloth and indicate that high light is required to initiate blooms.

TEMPERATURES: Summer days average 77–80°F (25–27°C), and nights average 62–64°F (17–18°C), with a diurnal range of 16–18°F (9–10°C).

HUMIDITY: 60–65% year-round. However, averages in the habitat are probably greater than indicated in the climate table. Growers recommend high humidity along with strong air circulation.

WATER: Rainfall is moderate to heavy in summer and autumn. Plants should be kept moist during the growing season, but water should be gradually reduced in autumn. Some growers suggest that the smaller plant forms are healthiest if they are allowed to dry slightly between waterings.

FERTILIZER: ¼–½ recommended strength, applied weekly. A high-nitrogen fertilizer is beneficial from spring to midsummer, but a fertilizer high in phosphates should be used in late summer and autumn.

REST PERIOD: Winter days average 63–71°F (17–22°C), and nights average 44–50°F (7–10°C), with a diurnal range of 18–21°F (10–12°C). In cultivation, water and fertilizer should be greatly reduced, but more moisture is available in the habitat than is indicated in the climate data. Plants should be allowed to dry out slightly between waterings, but they should never remain dry for long periods. In the habitat, light is highest in winter.

GROWING MEDIA: Plants should be mounted on slabs of cork, tree-fern, or rough-barked hardwood to accommodate their pendulous growth habit. Although the stems are large, the plant roots only at the base and remains happy on a small mount, even a small stick. However, mounted plants need high humidity and must be watered at least once daily in summer. If plants are potted, a small clay pot should be filled with a rapidly draining medium. Growers report that plastic pots are less satisfactory. Repotting is best done immediately after flowering.

MISCELLANEOUS NOTES: The bloom season shown in the climate table is based on cultivation records. *D. schoeninum* usually blooms during late winter and spring, but the plants may produce flowers in multiple bursts throughout the winter and again in spring.

Plant and Flower Information

PLANT SIZE AND TYPE: A 36 in. (91 cm) sympodial epiphyte.

PSEUDOBULB: 36 in. (91 cm) long. The thin stems are erect when young, but they become pendulous with age, size, and extent of branching. They emerge from a slowly creeping rhizome. The stems become progressively smaller at the tip.

LEAVES: 1 per branch. The terete leaves are 0.8–6.3 in. (2–16 cm) long. They are short, prominently ribbed, and upright. The leaves normally remain erect regardless of the angle of the stem.

INFLORESCENCE: 0.6–1.2 in. (1.5–3.0 cm) long. Inflorescences arise from nodes at the tips of branches.

FLOWERS: 1–4 per inflorescence. The blossoms are 1.0–1.4 in. (2.5–3.5 cm) across and open fully. Sepals and petals may be cream, white, yellow, pale green, or pink with dark purple stripes on the backside. The white lip may be decorated with purple on the margins. The sepals and petals hang down and the lip is uppermost. It is 3-lobed with a sharply pointed, recurved tip. The side margins of the midlobe are ruffled. The lip is decorated with 3 lines that are wavy near the apex. The blossoms are delicately fragrant and last about 2 weeks.

HYBRIDIZING NOTES: Chromosome count is 2n = 38 as *D. beckleri* (ref. 152, 154, 188, 243) and 2n = 19 (ref. 151) and 2n = 38 (ref. 151) as *D. beckleri* var. *superbum*. Rarely self-fertile, pollen from the same plant does not produce seed, but seeds are regularly produced when pollen from another plant is used. Seeds are released 10–14 weeks after pollination.

REFERENCES: 2, 23, 36, 67, 105, 151, 152, 154, 179, 188, 190, 216, 240, 243, 254, 262, 291, 330, 390, 421, 495, 533.

PHOTOS/DRAWINGS: 240, *390, 533*.

Dendrobium schouteniense J. J. Smith. Now considered a synonym of *Diplocaulobium schouteniense* (J. J. Smith) A. Hawkes.
REFERENCES: 224, 229, 445, 470.

Dendrobium schroderi Hort. See *D. densiflorum* Wallich.
REFERENCES: 38, 190, 216, 254.

Dendrobium schroederianum Hort. ex Gentil. Sometimes spelled *D. schroederanum*. Upton (ref. 533) lists the plant name as *D. phalaenopsis* Fitzgerald var. *schroederianum* Hort. ex Masters, which he includes as a synonym of *D. bigibbum* Lindley subsp. *laratensis* Clemesha; however, Clements (ref. 67) indicates that the name is invalid and refers the plant to the new species name *D. striaenopsis* M. Clements and D. Jones. The International Orchid Commission (ref. 236) registers hybrids under the name *D. phalaenopsis*. REFERENCES: 67, 220, 236, 533.

Dendrobium schuetzei Rolfe

AKA: Sometimes spelled *D. schuetzii*, *D. schultzei*, *D. schutezei*, or *D. schutzei*.

ORIGIN/HABITAT: The Philippines. Plants grow on northern Mindanao Island in Surigao and Agusan Provinces. They are frequently found with *D. dearei* Rchb. f. in lush forests at 1000–3000 ft. (300–910 m).

CLIMATE: Station #98653, Surigao, Mindanao, Philippines, Lat. 9.8°S, Long. 125.5°E, at 72 ft. (22 m). Temperatures are calculated for an elevation of 2000 ft. (610 m), resulting in probable extremes of 93°F (34°C) and 59°F (15°C).

N/HEMISPHERE	JAN	FEB	MAR	APR	MAY	JUN	JUL	AUG	SEP	OCT	NOV	DEC
°F AVG MAX	77	78	79	81	83	83	83	83	83	82	80	78
°F AVG MIN	66	66	67	67	68	68	68	69	69	68	68	67
DIURNAL RANGE	11	12	12	14	15	15	15	14	14	14	12	11
RAIN/INCHES	21.4	14.8	19.9	10.0	6.2	4.9	7.0	5.1	6.6	10.7	16.8	24.4
HUMIDITY/%	91	90	87	85	85	82	83	82	83	84	88	89
BLOOM SEASON	*	*			*	*		*		*		
DAYS CLR @ 8AM	1	1	2	4	2	3	2	2	1	2	1	1
DAYS CLR @ 2PM	1	2	2	6	3	1	2	1	2	3	1	1
RAIN/MM	544	376	505	254	157	124	178	130	168	272	427	620
°C AVG MAX	24.8	25.4	25.9	27.0	28.1	28.1	28.1	28.1	28.1	27.6	26.5	25.4
°C AVG MIN	18.7	18.7	19.2	19.2	19.8	19.8	19.8	20.4	20.4	19.8	19.8	19.2
DIURNAL RANGE	6.1	6.7	6.7	7.8	8.3	8.3	8.3	7.7	7.7	7.8	6.7	6.2
S/HEMISPHERE	JUL	AUG	SEP	OCT	NOV	DEC	JAN	FEB	MAR	APR	MAY	JUN

Cultural Recommendations

LIGHT: 2000–3000 fc.

TEMPERATURES: Throughout the year, days average 77–83°F (25–28°C), and nights average 66–69°F (19–20°C), with a diurnal range of 11–15°F (6–8°C). The widest diurnal range, which occurs in summer, results from warmer days.

HUMIDITY: 80–85% most of the year, increasing to near 90% in late autumn and winter.

WATER: Rainfall is moderate to very heavy all year. Cultivated plants should be kept moist but not soggy. Warm water might be beneficial.

FERTILIZER: ¼–½ recommended strength. A balanced fertilizer should be applied weekly to biweekly throughout the year.

REST PERIOD: Growing conditions should be maintained all year. Although rainfall in the habitat is greater in winter, water should not be increased for cultivated plants. Plants should be kept moist with only slight drying allowed between waterings. In the habitat, seasonal light variation is minor.

GROWING MEDIA: Plants may be mounted on tree-fern or cork slabs if humidity is high and plants are watered at least once daily in summer. When plants are potted, any open, fast-draining medium may be used. Repotting may be done anytime new roots are growing.

MISCELLANEOUS NOTES: Cultivation bloom records, as shown in the climate table, indicate that plants may bloom any time of year. In the habitat, blooming usually occurs in late winter or early spring. McVittie (ref. 293) reports that these plants are difficult to grow successfully in Manila unless they are kept cool and moist.

Plant and Flower Information

PLANT SIZE AND TYPE: A 6–16 in. (15–40 cm) sympodial epiphyte.

PSEUDOBULB: 4–12 in. (10–30 cm) long. The erect stems consist of about 12 nodes. They are slender at the base, very thickened in the middle, and deeply furrowed. The upper portions of the stems are leafy.

LEAVES: Many. The elliptic-oblong leaves are 2.4–4.0 in. (6–10 cm) long. They are distichous, leathery, and suberect. Leaf sheaths are covered with black hairs.

INFLORESCENCE: Longer than the leaves. The showy racemes emerge from bracts near the apex of the stem.

FLOWERS: 3–4 per inflorescence. Showy and waxy, flowers are 2.4–3.7 in. (6.0–9.5 cm) across and open flat. All segments are white. The lip may have a purple tinge at the base. The disk is emerald green. The dorsal sepal is oblong-lanceolate, pointed, and incurved. Lateral sepals are triangular, pointed, and keeled. The broad ovate to round petals have a small point at the tip. The 3-lobed lip has incurved sidelobes and a wide, oblong-ovate midlobe that is scalloped along the margin and notched at the apex. The blossoms, which last many weeks, are said to be larger and prettier than *D. sanderae* Rolfe. Some describe the blossoms as fragrant, but others indicate that they have no fragrance.

HYBRIDIZING NOTES: Chromosome counts are n = 20 (ref. 504, 580) and 2n = 40 (ref. 504, 580).

REFERENCES: 12, 25, 36, 98, 179, 190, 196, 200, 210, 221, 293, 296, 326, 373, 429, 430, 445, 504, 524, 536, 580.

PHOTOS/DRAWINGS: *36*, 98, 210, *373, 430*, 536.

Dendrobium schulleri J. J. Smith

AKA: Sometimes spelled *D. schuleri*.

ORIGIN/HABITAT: Northwest New Guinea and adjacent islands. Plants grow on trees at low elevations near swamps, creeks, and lagoons. They are found in areas with high light and high humidity.

CLIMATE: Station #97560, Mokmer, Indonesia, located on Biak Island off the northwest coast of Irian Jaya, Lat. 1.2°S, Long. 136.1°E, at 46 ft. (14 m). Record extreme temperatures are 91°F (33°C) and 70°F (21°C).

N/HEMISPHERE	JAN	FEB	MAR	APR	MAY	JUN	JUL	AUG	SEP	OCT	NOV	DEC
°F AVG MAX	85	86	86	87	87	86	86	85	86	86	87	87
°F AVG MIN	74	75	74	75	75	75	74	74	75	75	75	75
DIURNAL RANGE	11	11	12	12	12	11	12	11	11	11	12	12
RAIN/INCHES	11.3	11.2	7.0	6.1	7.3	12.5	11.0	8.2	11.7	8.3	8.6	10.5
HUMIDITY/%	85	84	83	83	84	85	84	85	86	85	87	86
BLOOM SEASON			*		*							
DAYS CLR @ 9AM	2	2	4	1	2	1	2	1	1	2	2	3
DAYS CLR @ 3PM	3	3	3	3	2	1	2	1	2	2	1	2
RAIN/MM	287	284	178	155	185	318	279	208	297	211	218	267
°C AVG MAX	29.4	30.0	30.0	30.6	30.6	30.0	30.0	29.4	30.0	30.0	30.6	30.6
°C AVG MIN	23.3	23.9	23.3	23.9	23.9	23.9	23.3	23.3	23.9	23.9	23.9	23.9
DIURNAL RANGE	6.1	6.1	6.7	6.7	6.7	6.1	6.7	6.1	6.1	6.1	6.7	6.7
S/HEMISPHERE	JUL	AUG	SEP	OCT	NOV	DEC	JAN	FEB	MAR	APR	MAY	JUN

Cultural Recommendations

LIGHT: 3000–4000 fc. The heavy summer cloud cover indicates that some shading is needed from spring through autumn, but light should be as high as the plant can tolerate, short of burning the leaves. Strong air movement is recommended all year.

TEMPERATURES: Throughout the year, days average 85–87°F (29–31°C), and nights average 74–75°F (23–24°C), with a diurnal range of 11–12°F (6–7°C).

HUMIDITY: Near 85% year-round.

WATER: Rainfall is heavy all year, with no real dry season. Cultivated plants should be kept moist but not soggy. Warm water might be beneficial.

FERTILIZER: ¼–½ recommended strength. A balanced fertilizer should be applied weekly to biweekly throughout the year.

REST PERIOD: Growing temperatures should be maintained year-round. Although rainfall remains heavy, water and fertilizer may be reduced somewhat for cultivated plants, especially those grown in the dark, short-day conditions common in temperate-latitude winters. Plants should never be allowed to dry out completely, however. In the habitat, seasonal light variation is minor.

GROWING MEDIA: Plants may be mounted on tree-fern or cork slabs if humidity is high and plants are watered at least once daily in summer. When plants are potted, any open, fast-draining medium may be used. Repotting may be done anytime new roots are growing.

MISCELLANEOUS NOTES: The bloom season shown in the climate table is based on cultivation records. In the habitat, *D. schulleri* usually blooms in autumn, but it may also bloom in winter and spring. It blooms at a small size and young age.

One specimen plant reached a diameter of 72 in. (183 cm) and consisted of 84 canes. As many as 7 inflorescences were produced on each of 43 canes, and all bloomed simultaneously. The blossoms were said to be too numerous to count.

Plant and Flower Information

PLANT SIZE AND TYPE: A 39 in. (100 cm) sympodial epiphyte. Plants are sometimes larger.

PSEUDOBULB: 39 in. (100 cm) long. The plump, sturdy stems are swollen at the base, but the upper 30% of the stem tapers to a point. Between the swollen base and tapering tip, the stem is uniform.

LEAVES: The oval to oblong leaves are 7 in. (17 cm) long, dark green, glossy, fleshy, and leathery.

INFLORESCENCE: 12–24 in. (30–60 cm) long. Inflorescences are green with dark brown mottling. They emerge from under the leaf bases near the tip of the stem. Each stem usually produces 1–5 inflorescences, but well-grown plants sometimes produce more. The laxly flowered inflorescences may be horizontal or arching.

FLOWERS: 10–35 per inflorescence. The showy flowers are 2.4 in. (6 cm) across. Sepals and petals vary from dull, pale, brownish green to solid green or lemon-yellow. The dorsal sepal is horizontal, oblong, with a small point at the tip. The oblong lateral sepals are laxly wavy along the margin. The broad petals are obovate, shiny, and twisted slightly. The 3-lobed lip, which has 5–6 wavy, waxy keels, is greenish white with violet markings. The erect, rounded sidelobes are green. Flower size and color are variable.

HYBRIDIZING NOTES: Chromosome count is 2n = 38 (ref. 504, 580). Hybridizers indicate that when used as a parent, *D. schulleri* contributes the tendency for numerous spikes with many flowers. It also helps improve flower form and increases flower substance, often transmitting its waxy texture.

REFERENCES: 25, 84, 179, 190, 196, 200, 221, 304, 345, 355, 389, 445, 470, 504, 510, 537, 580.

PHOTOS/DRAWINGS: *84, 304*, 345, *389*.

Dendrobium × *schumannianum* Schlechter.

Schlechter (ref. 437) found this plant growing between *D. antennatum* Lindley and *D. veratrifolium* Lindley *(D. lineale* Rolfe). Cribb (ref. 84) suggests that *D. andersonianum* F. M. Bailey may be a natural hybrid between *D. antennatum* and *D. lineale*. He further indicates that if this parentage is accurate, the name *D.* × *andersonianum* F. M. Bailey will take precedence over the name *D.* × *schumannianum* Schlechter. REFERENCES: 84, 229, 348, 437.

Dendrobium schutzei Rolfe. See *D. schuetzei* Rolfe. REFERENCES: 200.

Dendrobium schwartzkopffianum Kränzlin

AKA: J. J. Smith (ref. 470) suggested that the description of *D. schwartzkopf-*

fianum Kränzlin sounded very like *D. acuminatissimum* (Blume) Lindley. Schlechter (ref. 437) indicated that he was unable to locate the flower for the type specimen.

ORIGIN/HABITAT: Northeast Papua New Guinea. Plants were found near Rabaul (Ralum) on New Britain Island. They were reported growing near the mistforest zone along the Mangrove River.

CLIMATE: Station #94085, Rabaul, New Britain Island, Papua New Guinea, Lat. 4.2°S, Long. 152.2°E, at 28 ft. (9 m). Temperatures are calculated for an elevation of 1150 ft. (350 m), resulting in probable extremes of 96°F (36°C) and 61°F (16°C).

N/HEMISPHERE	JAN	FEB	MAR	APR	MAY	JUN	JUL	AUG	SEP	OCT	NOV	DEC
°F AVG MAX	85	85	87	88	87	86	86	86	86	86	86	86
°F AVG MIN	69	68	69	69	69	69	69	69	69	69	69	69
DIURNAL RANGE	16	17	18	19	18	17	17	17	17	17	17	17
RAIN/INCHES	5.4	3.7	3.5	5.1	7.1	10.1	14.8	10.4	10.2	10.0	5.2	3.3
HUMIDITY/%	74	73	69	70	73	76	77	76	77	77	75	74
BLOOM SEASON	N/A											
DAYS CLR	N/A											
RAIN/MM	137	94	89	130	180	257	376	264	259	254	132	84
°C AVG MAX	29.6	29.6	30.7	31.3	30.7	30.2	30.2	30.2	30.2	30.2	30.2	30.2
°C AVG MIN	20.7	20.2	20.7	20.7	20.7	20.7	20.7	20.7	20.7	20.7	20.7	20.7
DIURNAL RANGE	8.9	9.4	10.0	10.6	10.0	9.5	9.5	9.5	9.5	9.5	9.5	9.5
S/HEMISPHERE	JUL	AUG	SEP	OCT	NOV	DEC	JAN	FEB	MAR	APR	MAY	JUN

Cultural Recommendations

LIGHT: 2500–3500 fc.

TEMPERATURES: Throughout the year, days average 85–87°F (30–31°C), and nights average 68–69°F (20–21°C), with a diurnal range of 16–19°F (9–11°C).

HUMIDITY: Near 75% most of the year, dropping to near 70% in early spring. During each day, however, humidity rises to 90–100% at night and drops as low as 35% in the afternoon during the dry season.

WATER: Rainfall is heavy most of the year, with slightly drier conditions for 2 months in winter. Cultivated plants should be kept moist from spring to early autumn, but water should be gradually reduced in late autumn. Warm water might be beneficial.

FERTILIZER: ¼–½ recommended strength. A balanced fertilizer should be applied weekly to biweekly throughout the year.

REST PERIOD: Growing temperatures should be maintained all year. In the habitat, winter rainfall remains moderately high; but water and fertilizer should be reduced for cultivated plants, especially those grown in the dark, short-day conditions common in temperate latitudes. In the habitat, light may be highest in winter.

GROWING MEDIA: Plants may be mounted on tree-fern or cork slabs if humidity is high and plants are watered at least once daily in summer. When plants are potted, fir bark or any open, fast-draining medium may be used. Repotting may be done anytime new roots are growing.

MISCELLANEOUS NOTES: Plants that produce flowers which last a single day commonly bloom several times during the year. Flowering usually occurs 7–14 days after a sudden 10°F (5°C) drop in daytime temperatures.

Plant and Flower Information

PLANT SIZE AND TYPE: A 40 in. (102 cm) sympodial epiphyte.

PSEUDOBULB: 40 in. (102 cm) long. The tall stems resemble leafy bamboo.

LEAVES: Many. The linear leaves are 8 in. (20 cm) long. They taper to a long, slender point.

INFLORESCENCE: Short. Racemes emerge from leaf scales.

FLOWERS: 2 per inflorescence. The flowers are 4 in. (10 cm) long. The nearly transparent sepals and petals taper to a mere thread at the tips. The triangular midlobe is deeply cut into narrow lacerations. The oblong sidelobes are pointed and minutely toothed along the margin. The elevated callus is located between the sidelobes. Blossoms are short-lived.

REFERENCES: 254, 437, 470.

Dendrobium schweinfurthianum A. Hawkes and A. H. Heller

AKA: *D. leopardinum* Schlechter.

ORIGIN/HABITAT: Northern Papua New Guinea. Plants grow on forest trees in the Finisterre and Kani Ranges at 3300–4600 ft. (1000–1400 m).

CLIMATE: Station #200187, Erap, Papua New Guinea, Lat. 6.6°S, Long. 146.7°E, at 850 ft. (260 m). Temperatures are calculated for an elevation of 3300 ft. (1000 m), resulting in probable extremes of 94°F (34°C) and 45°F (7°C).

N/HEMISPHERE	JAN	FEB	MAR	APR	MAY	JUN	JUL	AUG	SEP	OCT	NOV	DEC
°F AVG MAX	80	80	81	82	85	85	85	85	85	84	82	82
°F AVG MIN	61	61	61	62	64	65	64	64	65	63	66	62
DIURNAL RANGE	19	19	20	20	21	20	21	21	20	21	16	20
RAIN/INCHES	3.9	3.9	2.7	3.0	3.0	5.3	5.9	5.9	7.0	3.4	2.4	3.1
HUMIDITY/%	82	81	81	79	75	74	74	74	77	76	80	80
BLOOM SEASON			*			*						
DAYS CLR	N/A											
RAIN/MM	99	99	69	76	76	135	150	150	178	86	61	79
°C AVG MAX	26.7	26.7	27.2	27.8	29.4	29.4	29.4	29.4	29.4	28.9	27.8	27.8
°C AVG MIN	16.1	16.1	16.1	16.7	17.8	18.3	17.8	17.8	18.3	17.2	18.9	16.7
DIURNAL RANGE	10.6	10.6	11.1	11.1	11.6	11.1	11.6	11.6	11.1	11.7	8.9	11.1
S/HEMISPHERE	JUL	AUG	SEP	OCT	NOV	DEC	JAN	FEB	MAR	APR	MAY	JUN

Cultural Recommendations

LIGHT: 2500–3500 fc.

TEMPERATURES: Throughout the year, days average 80–85°F (27–29°C), and nights average 61–66°F (16–19°C), with a diurnal range of 16–21°F (9–12°C).

HUMIDITY: 75–80% year-round.

WATER: Rainfall is relatively light to moderate most of the year, but morning moisture from heavy dew is commonly available year-round. Cultivated plants should be allowed to dry slightly between waterings, but they should never dry out completely.

FERTILIZER: ¼–½ recommended strength. A balanced fertilizer should be applied weekly to biweekly throughout the year.

REST PERIOD: Growing conditions should be maintained all year. In the habitat, rainfall is lowest in winter. Cultivated plants should be allowed to dry slightly more between waterings than in summer, but they should never remain dry for extended periods. Fertilizer should be reduced in winter.

GROWING MEDIA: Plants may be mounted on tree-fern or cork slabs or potted in small pots filled with any open, fast-draining medium. Repotting may be done anytime new roots are growing.

MISCELLANEOUS NOTES: The bloom season shown in the climate table is based on reports from the habitat. Plants that produce flowers which last a single day commonly bloom several times during the year. Flowering usually occurs 7–14 days after a sudden 10°F (5°C) drop in daytime temperatures.

Plant and Flower Information

PLANT SIZE AND TYPE: A sympodial epiphyte of unreported size.

PSEUDOBULB: The leafy stems are flattened. They are erect to spreading and borne on a very short rhizome.

LEAVES: Many. The linear leaves are 4–5 in. (10–13 cm) long. They are nearly erect. The leaf sheaths are sparsely covered with small warts.

INFLORESCENCE: 0.6 in. (1.5 cm) long. The flattened racemes emerge from nodes along the side of the stem.

Dendrobium schweinfurthianum

FLOWERS: 2 per inflorescence. The flowers are 1.7 in. (4.3 cm) long. Described as bizarre, the exceptionally elongated sepals and petals are yellow with dark brown spots. The white lip is marked with red dots on the margins and sidelobes. It is toothed to fringed along the margin of the midlobe with a large hairy patch inside. The midlobe has a sharp point at the apex. The oblong sidelobes are somewhat sickle-shaped and rounded at the tip. They have an uneven inner margin. Blossoms are short-lived.

REFERENCES: 191, 229, 437, 486.

PHOTOS/DRAWINGS: 437.

Dendrobium schweinfurthianum H. G. Jones not A. Hawkes and A. H. Heller. Cribb (ref. 82, 84) considers this to be a doubtful species. Regardless, it is a later use of this name, so it is illegitimate.
REFERENCES: 82, 84, 466.

Dendrobium sciadanthum F. Mueller. Now considered a synonym of *Epiblastus sciandanthus* (F. Mueller) Schlechter. REFERENCES: 270.

Dendrobium scirpoides Schlechter

ORIGIN/HABITAT: Upolu Island, Samoa. Habitat elevation is unavailable, so the following climate data should be used with caution.

CLIMATE: Station #91762, Apia, Western Samoa, Lat. 13.8°S, Long. 171.8°W, at 7 ft. (2 m). Temperatures are calculated for an estimated elevation of 1300 ft. (400 m), resulting in probable extremes of 89°F (32°C) and 59°F (15°C).

N/HEMISPHERE	JAN	FEB	MAR	APR	MAY	JUN	JUL	AUG	SEP	OCT	NOV	DEC
°F AVG MAX	81	80	80	81	82	81	82	81	82	82	81	81
°F AVG MIN	70	71	70	71	70	70	71	72	70	71	70	70
DIURNAL RANGE	11	9	10	10	12	11	11	9	12	11	11	11
RAIN/INCHES	3.2	3.5	5.2	6.7	10.5	14.6	17.9	15.2	14.1	10.0	6.3	5.1
HUMIDITY/%	76	75	75	77	77	78	81	80	80	78	77	75
BLOOM SEASON	N/A											
DAYS CLR @ 1PM	9	10	9	6	3	3	4	2	3	5	9	10
DAYS CLR @ 7PM	12	10	11	7	4	3	2	2	2	5	11	8
RAIN/MM	81	89	132	170	267	371	455	386	358	254	160	130
°C AVG MAX	27.1	26.5	26.5	27.1	27.6	27.1	27.6	27.1	27.6	27.6	27.1	27.1
°C AVG MIN	21.0	21.5	21.0	21.5	21.0	21.0	21.5	22.1	21.0	21.5	21.0	21.0
DIURNAL RANGE	6.1	5.0	5.5	5.6	6.6	6.1	6.1	5.0	6.6	6.1	6.1	6.1
S/HEMISPHERE	JUL	AUG	SEP	OCT	NOV	DEC	JAN	FEB	MAR	APR	MAY	JUN

Cultural Recommendations

LIGHT: 2000–3000 fc.

TEMPERATURES: Throughout the year, days average 80–82°F (27–28°C), and nights average 70–71°F (21–22°C), with a diurnal range of 9–12°F (5–7°C).

HUMIDITY: 75–80% year-round.

WATER: Rainfall is moderate to heavy all year, but conditions are slightly drier for 2–3 months in winter. Cultivated plants should be kept evenly moist with only slight drying allowed between waterings.

FERTILIZER: ¼–½ recommended strength. A balanced fertilizer should be applied weekly to biweekly throughout the year.

REST PERIOD: Growing conditions should be maintained all year. Although water and fertilizer should be reduced somewhat for plants grown in the dark, short-day conditions common during temperate-latitude winters, plants should not be allowed to dry out completely. In the habitat, light is highest in winter.

GROWING MEDIA: Plants may be mounted on tree-fern or cork slabs or potted in small pots filled with any open, fast-draining medium. Repotting may be done anytime new roots are actively growing.

Plant and Flower Information

PLANT SIZE AND TYPE: A 6–8 in. (15–20 cm) sympodial epiphyte.

PSEUDOBULB: 4–6 in. (10–15 cm) long. Erect new growths arise from a rooting, branching rhizome. They are grooved and spindle-shaped.

LEAVES: 5–8 per growth. The cylindrical leaves are erect-spreading and 1.6–3.1 in. (4–8 cm) long.

INFLORESCENCE: Short. Clusters of flowers are borne at the apex of the stem.

FLOWERS: Few per inflorescence. Blossoms open one at a time. The flowers are 0.2 in. (0.5 cm) long. They have ovate-lanceolate sepals and linear petals that are dilated at the base. The smooth lip is elliptical with a short point at the tip. It is wavy along the margin, with 2 parallel lines.

REFERENCES: 221, 434.

Dendrobium sclerophyllum Lindley. A synonym of *D. firmum* Steudel, which is now considered a synonym of *D. mutabile* (Blume) Lindley. REFERENCES: 216, 254.

Dendrobium scopa Lindley. This plant is sometimes listed as a synonym of *Ephemerantha comata* (Blume) Hunt and Summerhayes. At other times, it is listed as a synonym of *Flickingeria scopa* (Lindley) F. G. Brieger. REFERENCES: 12, 98, 151, 154, 187, 188, 208, 213, 216, 230, 234, 254, 296, 317, 373, 395, 441, 449, 530, 536.

Dendrobium scopula Schlechter

ORIGIN/HABITAT: Northern Papua New Guinea. Plants grow on moss-covered trees in the mistforests of the Finisterre mountains at about 4250 ft. (1300 m).

CLIMATE: Station #94010, Goroka, Papua New Guinea, Lat. 6.1°S, Long. 145.4°E, at 5141 ft. (1567 m). Temperatures are calculated for an elevation of 4000 ft. (1220 m), resulting in probable extremes of 90°F (32°C) and 46°F (8°C).

N/HEMISPHERE	JAN	FEB	MAR	APR	MAY	JUN	JUL	AUG	SEP	OCT	NOV	DEC
°F AVG MAX	80	81	82	83	83	82	83	82	82	82	83	81
°F AVG MIN	60	61	61	61	62	63	63	64	63	63	63	61
DIURNAL RANGE	20	20	21	22	21	19	20	19	18	19	20	20
RAIN/INCHES	2.1	2.8	4.6	5.9	6.6	9.3	9.1	10.1	10.7	8.3	4.6	2.0
HUMIDITY/%	70	67	67	67	67	71	72	73	74	71	70	70
BLOOM SEASON							*					
DAYS CLR	N/A											
RAIN/MM	53	71	117	150	168	236	231	257	272	211	117	51
°C AVG MAX	26.5	27.1	27.6	28.2	28.2	27.6	28.2	27.6	27.6	27.6	28.2	27.1
°C AVG MIN	15.4	16.0	16.0	16.0	16.5	17.1	17.1	17.6	17.6	17.1	17.1	16.0
DIURNAL RANGE	11.1	11.1	11.6	12.2	11.7	10.5	11.1	10.5	10.0	10.5	11.1	11.1
S/HEMISPHERE	JUL	AUG	SEP	OCT	NOV	DEC	JAN	FEB	MAR	APR	MAY	JUN

Cultural Recommendations

LIGHT: 2000–3000 fc.

TEMPERATURES: Throughout the year, days average 80–83°F (27–28°C), and nights average 60–64°F (15–18°C), with a diurnal range of 19–22°F (11–12°C). The diurnal range is unusually large for a habitat with such constant temperatures.

HUMIDITY: 70–75% from summer into autumn, dropping to 65–70% in winter and spring. Plants require excellent air movement.

WATER: Rainfall is moderate to heavy most of the year, but conditions are slightly drier for 3 months in winter. Cultivated plants should be kept moist but not soggy. Daily watering may be necessary during hot, dry, summer weather. In addition, early morning mistings may be beneficial, especially on warm, bright, sunny days.

FERTILIZER: ¼–½ recommended strength. A balanced fertilizer should be applied weekly to biweekly throughout the year.

REST PERIOD: Growing temperatures should be maintained all year. In the habitat, rainfall is lowest in winter, but additional moisture from dew, fog, and low clouds is common. Water and fertilizer should be reduced somewhat for cultivated plants, especially those grown in the dark, short-day conditions common during temperate-latitude winters. Plants should never be allowed to dry completely, however. In the habitat, light is higher in winter.

GROWING MEDIA: Plants may be mounted on tree-fern or cork slabs if humidity is high and plants are watered at least once daily in summer. When plants are potted, any open, fast-draining medium may be used. Repotting may be done anytime new roots are growing.

MISCELLANEOUS NOTES: The bloom season shown in the climate table is based on reports from the habitat.

Plant and Flower Information

PLANT SIZE AND TYPE: A 24 in. (60 cm) sympodial epiphyte. Schlechter (ref. 437) indicated that the plant resembled a broom.

PSEUDOBULB: 24 in. (60 cm) long. The curved, extremely branching stems arise from an elongated, somewhat climbing rhizome. They are very slender and densely leafy.

LEAVES: Many. The linear leaves are 0.4–1.0 in. (1.0–2.5 cm) long. They are erect, or nearly so, and cover the upper part of the stem. The leaves are unequally bilobed at the tip.

INFLORESCENCE: Flowers are borne at nodes along the side of the stem.

FLOWERS: 1 per inflorescence. The tiny flowers are 0.2 in. (0.5 cm) long. The flowers are white with red markings on the lip. The lateral sepals are joined to form a hood over the lip. The 3-lobed lip is uppermost. It is moderately hairy with incurved front margins and a point at the tip. Blossoms last a few days.

REFERENCES: 92, 221, 437, 445.

PHOTOS/DRAWINGS: 437.

Dendrobium scoriarum W. W. Smith

AKA: Tsi (ref. 528) includes *D. scoriarum* as a synonym of *D. aduncum* Wallich ex Lindley, but Seidenfaden (ref. 454) indicates reservations regarding this synonymy so both are included.

ORIGIN/HABITAT: Yunnan Province, southwest China. Plants were found west of Tengyueh at Lat. 25°N, where they grew on rocks and trees near a lava bed at about 5000 ft. (1520 m).

CLIMATE: Station #56739, Teng-Chung, China, Lat. 25.1°N, Long. 98.5°E, at 5340 ft. (1628 m). Record extreme temperatures are 84°F (29°C) and 25°F (−4°C).

N/HEMISPHERE	JAN	FEB	MAR	APR	MAY	JUN	JUL	AUG	SEP	OCT	NOV	DEC
°F AVG MAX	63	64	73	75	75	73	75	76	77	72	68	64
°F AVG MIN	32	35	41	49	55	63	64	63	57	53	40	35
DIURNAL RANGE	31	29	32	26	20	10	11	13	20	19	28	29
RAIN/INCHES	0.5	1.6	1.4	2.7	5.1	9.3	12.3	11.1	6.4	6.2	1.6	0.9
HUMIDITY/%	68	64	61	68	78	88	89	87	84	84	75	73
BLOOM SEASON							*					
DAYS CLR @ 7AM	23	17	22	12	5	1	0	1	3	8	22	22
DAYS CLR @ 1PM	20	9	15	6	3	2	0	1	7	17	21
RAIN/MM	13	41	36	69	130	236	312	282	163	157	41	23
°C AVG MAX	17.2	17.8	22.8	23.9	23.9	22.8	23.9	24.4	25.0	22.2	20.0	17.8
°C AVG MIN	0.0	1.7	5.0	9.4	12.8	17.2	17.8	17.2	13.9	11.7	4.4	1.7
DIURNAL RANGE	17.2	16.1	17.8	14.5	11.1	5.6	6.1	7.2	11.1	10.5	15.6	16.1
S/HEMISPHERE	JUL	AUG	SEP	OCT	NOV	DEC	JAN	FEB	MAR	APR	MAY	JUN

Cultural Recommendations

LIGHT: 2500–3500 fc. Skies are generally overcast during the growing season.

TEMPERATURES: Summer days average 73–76°F (23–24°C), and nights average 63–64°F (17–18°C), with a diurnal range of 10–13°F (6–7°C). The record high is very close to the average highs, indicating that plants from this habitat may not tolerate hot summer weather. Minimum temperatures fall rapidly in autumn, causing a rapid increase in the diurnal range.

HUMIDITY: 85–90% in summer and early autumn, dropping to 60–65% in late winter.

WATER: Rainfall is very heavy from late spring into autumn, but conditions are much drier in winter. Cultivated plants should be kept moist while actively growing, but water should be decreased when new growths mature in autumn.

FERTILIZER: ¼–½ recommended strength, applied weekly. A high-nitrogen fertilizer is beneficial from spring to midsummer, but a fertilizer high in phosphates should be used in late summer and autumn.

REST PERIOD: Winter days average 63–64°F (17–18°C), and nights average 32–35°F (0–2°C), with a diurnal range of 29–32°F (16–18°C). Although rainfall is low in winter, heavy dew is common because of the relatively high humidity and wide temperature range. In cultivation, water and fertilizer should be reduced for 2–3 months in winter. Plants should be allowed to dry slightly between waterings, but they should not remain dry for long periods. In the habitat, light is highest in winter.

GROWING MEDIA: Plants may be mounted on tree-fern or cork slabs if humidity is high and plants are watered at least once daily in summer. When plants are potted, any open, fast-draining medium may be used. Repotting may be done anytime new roots are growing.

MISCELLANEOUS NOTES: The bloom season shown in the climate table is based on collection reports.

Plant and Flower Information

PLANT SIZE AND TYPE: A 24 in. (60 cm) sympodial epiphyte.

PSEUDOBULB: 24 in. (60 cm) long. The slender, sinuous stems, which are not fully erect, are leafy up to near the apex.

LEAVES: Many. The oblong, distichous leaves are 1.6 in. (4 cm) long. The leaf bases remain attached to the pseudobulb.

INFLORESCENCE: 1 in. (2.5 cm) long. Blossoms are borne on long pedicels.

FLOWERS: The dried flowers are 0.6 in. (1.6 cm) long. The ovate-lanceolate dorsal sepal and sickle-shaped lateral sepals are yellowish with a flush of red. The lanceolate petals are pale yellowish white. The tip of the column is brilliant rose-magenta. Sepals and petals are pointed. The lip is crimson with a pale yellow center. The sidelobe margins are minutely toothed, and the tip of the midlobe is hairy. Blossoms are not fragrant.

REFERENCES: 208, 223, 454, 489, 492, 528.

Dendrobium scortechinii Hooker f.

Sometimes spelled *D. scortechini*, see *D. anosmum* Lindley. REFERENCES: 190, 202, 218, 254, 296, 395, 436, 454, 470.

Dendrobium scotiiferum J. J. Smith.

See *D. violaceum* Kränzlin. REFERENCES: 225, 385, 486.

Dendrobium scotiiforme J. J. Smith.

Sometimes spelled *D. scottiforme*, it is now considered a synonym of *Diplocaulobium scotiiforme* (J. J. Smith) Hunt and Summerhayes. REFERENCES: 213, 221, 230, 445, 470, 475.

Dendrobium sculptum Rchb. f.

ORIGIN/HABITAT: Northern Sarawak in western Borneo. Plants grow near Mt. Dulit in mossforests at about 4000 ft. (1220 m).

Dendrobium secundum

CLIMATE: Station #96449, Miri, Sarawak, Lat. 4.4°N, Long. 114.0°E, at 13 ft. (4 m). Temperatures are calculated for an elevation of 4000 ft. (1220 m), resulting in probable extremes of 82°F (28°C) and 54°F (12°C).

N/HEMISPHERE	JAN	FEB	MAR	APR	MAY	JUN	JUL	AUG	SEP	OCT	NOV	DEC
°F AVG MAX	73	73	74	75	75	75	75	75	74	74	74	74
°F AVG MIN	61	61	61	62	62	62	61	61	61	61	61	61
DIURNAL RANGE	12	12	13	13	13	13	14	14	13	13	13	13
RAIN/INCHES	16.8	6.5	5.5	4.4	8.2	12.0	8.5	8.4	11.8	11.7	14.5	11.3
HUMIDITY/%	86	86	85	83	83	82	81	81	82	83	84	85
BLOOM SEASON									*			
DAYS CLR @ 8AM	1	2	4	4	3	2	3	2	2	1	2	2
DAYS CLR @ 2PM	1	1	3	4	2	5	3	2	3	2	1	1
RAIN/MM	427	165	140	112	208	305	216	213	300	297	368	287
°C AVG MAX	22.7	22.7	23.2	23.8	23.8	23.8	23.8	23.8	23.2	23.2	23.2	23.2
°C AVG MIN	16.0	16.0	16.0	16.6	16.6	16.6	16.0	16.0	16.0	16.0	16.0	16.0
DIURNAL RANGE	6.7	6.7	7.2	7.2	7.2	7.2	7.8	7.8	7.2	7.2	7.2	7.2
S/HEMISPHERE	JUL	AUG	SEP	OCT	NOV	DEC	JAN	FEB	MAR	APR	MAY	JUN

Cultural Recommendations

LIGHT: 2000–3000 fc.

TEMPERATURES: Throughout the year, days average 73–75°F (23–24°C), and nights average 61–62°F (16–17°C), with a diurnal range of 12–14°F (7–8°C).

HUMIDITY: 80–85% year-round.

WATER: Rainfall is heavy to very heavy all year, but conditions are slightly drier in winter. Cultivated plants should be kept moist but not soggy.

FERTILIZER: ¼–½ recommended strength. A balanced fertilizer should be applied weekly to biweekly throughout the year.

REST PERIOD: Growing conditions should be maintained all year. In cultivation, water and fertilizer should be reduced somewhat in winter, especially for plants grown in the dark, short-day conditions common in temperate latitudes. These plants should never dry out completely, however. In the habitat, seasonal light variation is minor.

GROWING MEDIA: Plants may be mounted on tree-fern or cork slabs if humidity is high and plants are watered at least once daily in summer. When plants are potted, any open, fast-draining medium may be used. Repotting may be done immediately after flowering or anytime new roots are growing.

MISCELLANEOUS NOTES: The bloom season shown in the climate table is based on collection reports.

Plant and Flower Information

PLANT SIZE AND TYPE: A 2.4–4.0 in. (6–10 cm) sympodial epiphyte.

PSEUDOBULB: 2.4–4.0 in. (6–10 cm) long. The short, greenish stems are terete.

LEAVES: The oblong, sparsely hairy leaves are 1 in. (2.5 cm) long.

INFLORESCENCE: Short.

FLOWERS: Few per inflorescence. The unscented flowers are 2 in. (5 cm) across. Blossoms are ivory white with dark orange spots, especially at the base of the lip. The sepals are lanceolate, and the pointed petals are broadly ovate. The lip is fiddle-shaped with an uneven margin. The disc at the base of the lip is very rough.

REFERENCES: 59, 216, 254, 286, 295, 394, 429, 445, 448, 454, 570.

Dendrobium secundum (Blume) Lindley

AKA: *Pedilonium secundum* Blume, *Dendrobium bursigerum* Lindley, *D. secundum* var. *bursigerum* Ridley, *D. heterostigma* Rchb. f., *D. secundum* f. *album* Valmayor. Merrill (ref. 296) includes *D. bursigerum* as a synonym of *D. secundum* Wallich.

ORIGIN/HABITAT: Widespread. The habitat includes northern and eastern Thailand at 1000–5250 ft. (300–1600 m) and the Tenasserim and Moulmein regions of Burma. Plants are also found in Cambodia, Laos, and Vietnam. In northern Malaya, plants are fairly common in rather exposed places near the sea. The orchid is relatively common in Sumatra, Borneo, Java, Sulawesi (Celebes), and many smaller Indonesian islands. In Borneo, plants are found in hill forests of Sabah, Sarawak, and Kalimantan at about 1950 ft. (600 m). In the Philippines, plants grow on Mindanao and Luzon islands from sea level to 750 ft. (0–230 m). Plants are common in forests with a pronounced dry season.

CLIMATE: Station #48327, Chiang Mai, Thailand, Lat. 18.8°N, Long. 99.0°E, at 1100 ft. (335 m). Temperatures are calculated for an elevation of 2500 ft. (760 m), resulting in probable extremes of 104°F (40°C) and 33°F (1°C).

N/HEMISPHERE	JAN	FEB	MAR	APR	MAY	JUN	JUL	AUG	SEP	OCT	NOV	DEC
°F AVG MAX	80	85	90	91	89	85	84	82	83	84	81	79
°F AVG MIN	51	52	57	65	69	69	69	70	68	66	61	52
DIURNAL RANGE	29	33	33	26	20	16	15	12	15	18	20	27
RAIN/INCHES	0.3	0.4	0.6	2.0	5.5	6.1	7.4	8.7	11.5	4.9	1.5	0.4
HUMIDITY/%	73	65	58	62	73	78	80	83	83	81	79	76
BLOOM SEASON	*	*					*		*	*	*	
DAYS CLR @ 7AM	5	5	2	2	1	0	0	0	0	1	3	3
DAYS CLR @ 1PM	9	8	4	2	0	0	0	0	0	0	1	3
RAIN/MM	8	10	15	51	140	155	188	221	292	124	38	10
°C AVG MAX	26.9	29.7	32.4	33.0	31.9	29.7	29.1	28.0	28.5	29.1	27.4	26.3
°C AVG MIN	10.8	11.3	14.1	18.5	20.8	20.8	20.8	21.3	20.2	19.1	16.3	11.3
DIURNAL RANGE	16.1	18.4	18.3	14.5	11.1	8.9	8.3	6.7	8.3	10.0	11.1	15.0
S/HEMISPHERE	JUL	AUG	SEP	OCT	NOV	DEC	JAN	FEB	MAR	APR	MAY	JUN

Cultural Recommendations

LIGHT: 3000–4000 fc. Bright light and strong air movement are recommended. The heavy summer cloud cover indicates that some shading is needed from spring through autumn, but light should be as high as the plant can tolerate, short of burning the leaves. Plants grown in the temperate latitudes should be placed close to the glass at the brightest end of the greenhouse, especially in winter.

TEMPERATURES: Summer days average 82–85°F (28–30°C), and nights average 69–70°F (21°C), with a diurnal range of 12–16°F (7–9°C). Spring, before the start of the summer rainy season, is the warmest time of the year. Days average 89–91°F (32–33°C), and nights average 57–69°F (14–21°C), with a diurnal range of 20–33°F (11–18°C).

HUMIDITY: Near 80% during the growing season, dropping to about 60% for 2 months in winter.

WATER: Rainfall is moderate to heavy from late spring through early autumn, but conditions are very dry in winter. Cultivated plants should be kept moist while actively growing, but water should be gradually reduced after new growths mature in autumn.

FERTILIZER: ¼–½ recommended strength, applied weekly. A high-nitrogen fertilizer is beneficial from spring to midsummer, but a fertilizer high in phosphates should be used in late summer and autumn.

REST PERIOD: Winter days average 79–85°F (26–30°C), and nights average 51–52°F (11°C), with a diurnal range of 27–33°F (15–18°C). Because of the wide range of distribution and habitat elevation, plants should adapt to winter temperatures 8–10°F (4–6°C) warmer than indicated. However, growers indicate that plants often survive much lower temperatures and will tolerate light frost providing they are dry when temperatures are low. In the habitat, rainfall averages are very low for 4 months in winter, but during the early part of the season the high relative humidity indicates that additional moisture is available from frequent fog, mist, and heavy deposits of dew. Growers sometimes recommend eliminating water in winter, but plants are healthiest if for most of the winter they are allowed to become dry between waterings but do not remain dry for extended periods. However, for 1–2 months in early spring, conditions in the habitat are clear, warm, and dry, and humidity is so low that even the moisture from morning dew is uncommon. Plants should be allowed to dry out completely between waterings and remain dry longer during this time. Occasional early morning mistings between waterings may help keep the plants from becoming too dry. Fertilizer should be eliminated in winter, and resumed only when water is increased in spring. In the habitat, light is highest in winter.

GROWING MEDIA: Growers recommend mounting plants on slabs of cork or tree-fern fiber as the plants are healthiest if they dry between waterings. Mounting also accommodates the frequently pendulous growth habit. If plants must be potted, a very open, fast-draining medium in hanging baskets or clay pots is recommended. Undersized pots that are barely large enough to hold the roots should be used. Repotting should be done as seldom as possible, but when necessary, repotting should be done as soon as new root growth starts, or as soon after flowering as possible.

MISCELLANEOUS NOTES: The bloom season shown in the climate table is based on cultivation records. If well grown, *D. secundum* can be very free-flowering, and may be in bloom most of the year. In the habitat, plants usually bloom during the winter dry season. Because of the large area of distribution and the wide range of habitat elevation, plants should adapt easily to winter minimum temperatures 8–10°F (4–6°C) warmer than indicated above. However, a dry period in winter is common in the areas where this species is found.

Plant and Flower Information

PLANT SIZE AND TYPE: A highly variable, 12–21 in. (30–54 cm) sympodial epiphyte. Growth habit resembles that of *D. erthroxanthum* Rchb. f.

PSEUDOBULB: 12–21 in. (30–54 cm) long in cultivation. However, in the wild, plants may reach a length of 72 in. (183 cm). Individual stems may be erect or pendulous. They are swollen in the middle and taper at each end.

LEAVES: Many. The elliptic-lanceolate leaves are 2.4–4.0 in. (6–10 cm) long. They are rigidly fleshy. Normally deciduous at the beginning of the cool, dry period, the leaves may persist for several seasons if the plants are grown in a more moderate environment.

INFLORESCENCE: 3–6 in. (8–15 cm) long, occasionally shorter. The many flowered racemes emerge from upper nodes of leafless stems. The inflorescences may be erect, but they are often held at a 45° angle to the stem. The one-sided racemes have flowers that all point up in densely packed sprays.

FLOWERS: Many per inflorescence. The small, somewhat tubular to fan-shaped flowers are 0.7 in. (1.8 cm) long. The pointed sepals and petals may be light pink, rose-red, bright purple, or rarely white. The smooth, unlobed lip may be orange or yellow. The brilliant colors are iridescent. The pollen is dark purple. Some sources indicate that blossoms are short-lived, while others indicate that flowers last well.

HYBRIDIZING NOTES: Chromosome counts are n = 20 (ref. 151, 187, 504, 580) and 2n = 40 (ref. 151, 154, 187, 188, 504, 580). Johansen (ref. 239) indicates that the stigma is not receptive for 10–12 days after the flower opens. He also found that plants are self-sterile, with flowers dropping 5–12 days after self-pollination. When cross-pollinated, a high percentage produced capsules which opened 51–97 days after pollination. Seeds ripened in 65 days in 1986 and in 87 days in 1987. Some capsules produced no seed with visible embryos, while 98% of the seed produced in other capsules contained embryos. Germination varied from 0–100%. When *D. secundum* was used as the female parent and crossed with *D. aphyllum* (Roxburgh) C. Fischer and *D. chrysotoxum* Lindley, no viable seed was produced. When used as the pollen parent with *D. farmerii* Paxton, no viable seed was produced.

REFERENCES: 12, 25, 36, 73, 75, 79, 98, 151, 154, 157, 165, 187, 188, 190, 196, 200, 202, 210, 216, 234, 239, 245, 254, 258, 266, 286, 295, 296, 310, 317, 352, 369, 371, 394, 395, 402, 430, 436, 445, 447, 448, 454, 455, 469, 504, 524, 536, 541, 569, 580, 592.

PHOTOS/DRAWINGS: *36, 73, 75, 79,* 200, 210, *245, 369, 371, 430, 454, 455,* 469, *569, 592.*

Dendrobium seemannii L. O. Williams. See *D. vagans* Schlechter 1911 not 1923.
REFERENCES: 152, 179, 226, 243, 252, 270, 353, 466. PHOTOS/DRAWINGS: *270, 540.*

Dendrobium seidelianum Rchb. f. See *D. loddigesii* Rolfe.
REFERENCES: 190, 254.

Dendrobium seidenfadenii K. Senghas and L. Bockemühl. See *D. dickasonii* L. O. Williams.
REFERENCES: 36, 157, 179, 190, 196, 202, 233, 245, 254, 280, 369, 452, 454, 504, 541, 568, 570, 580. PHOTOS/DRAWINGS: *454.*

Dendrobium sematoglossum Schlechter. Transferred to *Ephemerantha sematoglossa* by Hunt and Summerhayes, which is now considered synonymous with *Flickingeria*.
REFERENCES: 213, 221, 230, 435, 449.

Dendrobium semeion P. van Royen. See *D. vexillarius* J. J. Smith.
REFERENCES: 233, 385, 538. PHOTOS/DRAWINGS: *538.*

Dendrobium semifuscum (Rchb. f.) Lavarack and Cribb. See *D. trilamellatum* J. J. Smith.
REFERENCES: 67, 84, 233, 262, 533. PHOTOS/DRAWINGS: *262.*

Dendrobium senile Parish ex Rchb. f.

ORIGIN/HABITAT: Laos, the Tenasserim region of Burma, the Ranong area of peninsular Thailand, and northern and eastern Thailand. Plants grow at 1650–3950 ft. (500–1200 m).

CLIMATE: Station #48353, Loei, Thailand, Lat. 17.5°N, Long. 101.5°E, at 817 ft. (249 m). Temperatures are calculated for an elevation of 3000 ft. (910 m), resulting in probable extremes of 99°F (37°C) and 27°F (−3°C).

N/HEMISPHERE	JAN	FEB	MAR	APR	MAY	JUN	JUL	AUG	SEP	OCT	NOV	DEC
°F AVG MAX	78	82	87	90	86	84	83	82	81	80	80	77
°F AVG MIN	45	51	58	63	66	67	67	67	66	62	57	49
DIURNAL RANGE	33	31	29	27	20	17	16	15	15	18	23	28
RAIN/INCHES	0.2	0.8	1.4	3.6	6.9	6.8	5.0	8.3	8.8	4.3	0.8	0.1
HUMIDITY/%	62	60	59	62	75	77	77	79	82	79	74	69
BLOOM SEASON	*	*	*									
DAYS CLR @ 7AM	1	1	1	2	1	0	1	0	0	1	1	1
DAYS CLR @ 1PM	22	14	8	5	2	0	0	1	1	5	11	15
RAIN/MM	5	20	36	91	175	173	127	211	224	109	20	3
°C AVG MAX	25.4	27.7	30.4	32.1	29.9	28.8	28.2	27.7	27.1	26.6	26.6	24.9
°C AVG MIN	7.1	10.4	14.3	17.1	18.8	19.3	19.3	19.3	18.8	16.6	13.8	9.3
DIURNAL RANGE	18.3	17.3	16.1	15.0	11.1	9.5	8.9	8.4	8.3	10.0	12.8	15.6
S/HEMISPHERE	JUL	AUG	SEP	OCT	NOV	DEC	JAN	FEB	MAR	APR	MAY	JUN

Cultural Recommendations

LIGHT: 2000–3500 fc. Cultivated plants need about 50% shading in summer. Light should be as high as possible without stressing the plant. In the habitat, the heavy cloud cover associated with the summer monsoon causes light to be relatively low. Very strong air movement is required throughout the year.

TEMPERATURES: Summer days average 82–84°F (28–29°C), and nights average 67°F (19°C), with a 15–17°F (8–10°C) diurnal range. In the habitat, the warmest temperatures occur in early spring. Days average 86–90°F (30–32°C), and nights are 58–66°F (14–19°C), with a diurnal range of 20–29°F (11–16°C).

HUMIDITY: 75–80% from late spring through autumn, dropping to about 60% for 4 months in winter and early spring.

WATER: Rainfall is moderate to heavy from late spring through summer, but conditions are quite dry in winter. Cultivated plants should be watered often while actively growing, with only sight drying allowed between waterings. Water should be gradually reduced after new growths mature in autumn.

FERTILIZER: ¼–½ recommended strength, applied weekly. A high-nitrogen fertilizer is beneficial from spring to midsummer, but a fertilizer high in phosphates should be used in late summer and autumn.

REST PERIOD: Winter days average 77–82°F (25–28°C), and nights average 45–51°F (7–10°C), with a diurnal range of 28–33°F (16–18°C). The record low is below freezing in the habitat, but extremes should be avoided in cultivation. Rainfall is low for 3–5 months in winter, but additional moisture is available from heavy dew, fog, and mist during most of the season. Cultivated plants should be allowed to dry out between waterings, but they should not remain completely dry for extended periods. Occasional early morning mistings between waterings may help keep the plants from becoming too dry. Fertilizer should be eliminated until water is increased in spring. In the habitat, light is highest in winter.

GROWING MEDIA: Plants may be mounted on tree-fern or cork slabs if humidity is high and plants are watered at least once daily in summer. When plants are potted, any open, fast-draining medium may be used. Clay pots are recommended so that plants may dry more easily between waterings. They may be repotted anytime new roots are growing.

MISCELLANEOUS NOTES: The bloom season shown in the climate table is based on reports from the habitat. Cultivated plants may bloom anytime from winter to early summer. Although *D. senile* is somewhat adaptable, it is considered difficult by some growers, so careful attention should be paid to its cultural requirements. It must be given a cool, dry rest to be healthy and to bloom.

Plant and Flower Information

PLANT SIZE AND TYPE: A 3.5–8.7 in. (9–22 cm) sympodial epiphyte.

PSEUDOBULB: 2–6 in. (5–15 cm) long. The pseudobulbs, which consist of 4–6 nodes, arise from a short rhizome. They are densely covered with long, soft white hairs which persist for several years.

LEAVES: 2–6 per growth. The ovate-lanceolate leaves are 1.6–2.0 in. (4–5 cm) long. They alternate along the stem. The leaves and persistent leaf sheaths are covered with long, woolly, silver-white hairs. Semideciduous, the stems often retain a few leaves through the dry season.

INFLORESCENCE: 1.2–2.0 in. (3–5 cm) long. Numerous inflorescences emerge from upper nodes along the stems.

FLOWERS: 1–3, rarely up to 7 per stem. The waxy flowers, which are very large relative to the plant size, are 1.6–2.4 in. (4–6 cm) across and open fully. The pointed sepals and petals are bright lemon- or buttercup-yellow. The broad, spade-shaped lip has green blotches on each side of the orange-yellow disk and red speckles deep in the throat. It is more brightly and intensely colored than the sepals and petals. Blossoms are lemon scented and last 3–4 weeks.

HYBRIDIZING NOTES: Chromosome counts are 2n = 38 (ref. 153, 187, 273, 504, 580) and 2n = 40 (ref. 151, 187). Johansen (ref. 239) found that *D. senile* is often self-pollinating. Capsules opened 77 days after pollination, and approximately 70% of the seed contained visible embryos, but none of the seeds germinated.

REFERENCES: 29, 151, 153, 157, 179, 187, 190, 196, 202, 210, 216, 239, 245, 254, 266, 268, 273, 291, 330, 332, 333, 371, 430, 445, 447, 448, 454, 504, 541, 568, 570, 580, 581.

PHOTOS/DRAWINGS: 29, 210, 245, 268, 291, 333, 339, 371, 430, 454, 581.

Dendrobium separatum Ames. See *D. calcaratum* A. Richard. REFERENCES: 16, 225, 270, 271, 516.

Dendrobium sepikanum Schlechter. Now considered a synonym of *Diplocaulobium sepikanum* (Schlechter) P. F. Hunt. REFERENCES: 212, 223, 232, 443, 486.

Dendrobium septemcostulatum J. J. Smith

ORIGIN/HABITAT: The Molucca Islands near Koeda Mati on Ambon. Habitat elevation is unavailable, but plants were cultivated in the botanical gardens at Bogor, Java, indicating at least some tolerance for the warm temperatures at lower elevations. However, the following climate data should be used with caution.

CLIMATE: Station #97724, Ambon/Pattimura, Indonesia, Lat. 3.7°S, Long. 128.1°E, at 33 ft. (10 m). Record extreme temperatures are 96°F (36°C) and 66°F (19°C).

N/HEMISPHERE	JAN	FEB	MAR	APR	MAY	JUN	JUL	AUG	SEP	OCT	NOV	DEC
°F AVG MAX	81	81	83	85	88	88	88	88	88	86	84	82
°F AVG MIN	74	74	74	74	75	76	76	76	76	76	75	74
DIURNAL RANGE	7	7	9	11	13	12	12	12	12	10	9	8
RAIN/INCHES	23.7	15.8	9.5	6.1	4.5	5.2	5.0	4.7	5.3	11.0	20.3	25.1
HUMIDITY/%	83	82	81	80	79	78	78	77	79	82	83	84
BLOOM SEASON	N/A											
DAYS CLR @ 9AM	1	1	1	6	7	4	3	3	5	5	3	3
DAYS CLR @ 3PM	1	1	2	5	6	1	1	1	2	3	1	3
RAIN/MM	602	401	241	155	114	132	127	119	135	279	516	638
°C AVG MAX	27.2	27.2	28.3	29.4	31.1	31.1	31.1	31.1	31.1	30.0	28.9	27.8
°C AVG MIN	23.3	23.3	23.3	23.3	23.9	24.4	24.4	24.4	24.4	24.4	23.9	23.3
DIURNAL RANGE	3.9	3.9	5.0	6.1	7.2	6.7	6.7	6.7	6.7	5.6	5.0	4.5
S/HEMISPHERE	JUL	AUG	SEP	OCT	NOV	DEC	JAN	FEB	MAR	APR	MAY	JUN

Cultural Recommendations

LIGHT: 2500–3500 fc.

TEMPERATURES: Throughout the year, days average 81–88°F (27–31°C), and nights average 74–76°F (23–24°C), with a diurnal range of 7–13°F (4–7°C).

HUMIDITY: 80–85% year-round.

WATER: Rainfall is moderate to heavy all year, with slightly drier conditions in late spring and summer. Cultivated plants should be kept evenly moist all year.

FERTILIZER: ¼–½ recommended strength. A balanced fertilizer should be applied weekly to biweekly throughout the year.

REST PERIOD: Growing conditions should be maintained all year. In the habitat, a brief, semidry period occurs in late spring. Rainfall is heaviest in winter, but water and fertilizer should be reduced for plants cultivated in the dark, short-day conditions common in temperate-latitude winters. These plants should never be allowed to dry completely, however. In the habitat, light is highest in spring.

GROWING MEDIA: Plants may be mounted on tree-fern or cork slabs if humidity is high and plants are watered at least once daily in summer. When plants are potted, any open, fast-draining medium may be used. Repotting may be done anytime new roots are growing.

MISCELLANEOUS NOTES: The plant was described in 1920 in *Bull. Jard. Bot. Buit.* 3rd sér. 2:83.

Plant and Flower Information

PLANT SIZE AND TYPE: A 6–14 in. (15–36 cm) sympodial epiphyte.

PSEUDOBULB: 4–10 in. (10–25 cm) long. The pale, yellow-green stems are very flattened and consist of 9–12 nodes.

LEAVES: 3–7 on the upper part of each stem. The ovate to oblong-lanceolate leaves are 2–4 in. (5–10 cm) long. They are dark green, recurved at the apex, and twisted at the base.

INFLORESCENCE: Short. Inflorescences emerge from nodes on the upper part of the stem.

FLOWERS: 2–4 per inflorescence. The flowers are 1 in. (2.5 cm) long. The shiny sepals are pale yellow-brown, and the incurved petals are pale yellow. The 3-lobed lip is erect, wavy, and sharply recurved at the apex. It is shiny, yellowish white to pale yellow-brown with a purplish suffusion. The sidelobes are white with pale rose nerves. Blossoms fill the air with fragrance.

REFERENCES: 221.

Dendrobium seranicum J. J. Smith

ORIGIN/HABITAT: Molucca Islands. Plants grow in central Seram on Mt. Moerkele (Merkele), at 3300–6250 ft. (1000–1900 m).

CLIMATE: Station #49620, Amahai, Seram, Indonesia, Lat. 3.3°S, Long. 128.9°E, at 10 ft. (3 m). Temperatures are calculated for an elevation of 5000 ft. (1520 m), resulting in probable extremes of 80°F (26°C) and 50°F (10°C).

N/HEMISPHERE	JAN	FEB	MAR	APR	MAY	JUN	JUL	AUG	SEP	OCT	NOV	DEC
°F AVG MAX	65	65	67	69	72	72	72	72	72	70	68	66
°F AVG MIN	58	58	58	58	59	60	60	60	60	60	59	58
DIURNAL RANGE	7	7	9	11	13	12	12	12	12	10	9	8
RAIN/INCHES	23.7	15.8	9.5	6.1	4.5	5.2	5.0	4.7	5.3	11.0	20.3	25.1
HUMIDITY/%	83	82	81	80	79	78	78	77	79	82	83	84
BLOOM SEASON												*
DAYS CLR @ 9AM	1	1	1	6	7	4	3	3	5	5	3	3
DAYS CLR @ 3PM	1	1	2	5	6	1	1	1	2	3	1	3
RAIN/MM	602	401	241	155	114	132	127	119	135	279	516	638
°C AVG MAX	18.1	18.1	19.2	20.3	22.0	22.0	22.0	22.0	22.0	20.9	19.7	18.6
°C AVG MIN	14.2	14.2	14.2	14.2	14.7	15.3	15.3	15.3	15.3	15.3	14.7	14.2
DIURNAL RANGE	3.9	3.9	5.0	6.1	7.3	6.7	6.7	6.7	6.7	5.6	5.0	4.4
S/HEMISPHERE	JUL	AUG	SEP	OCT	NOV	DEC	JAN	FEB	MAR	APR	MAY	JUN

Cultural Recommendations

LIGHT: 2000–3000 fc. In the habitat, clear days are rare.

TEMPERATURES: Throughout the year, days average 65–72°F (18–22°C), and nights average 58–60°F (15°C), with a diurnal range of 7–12°F (4–7°C).

HUMIDITY: 80–85% most of the year, falling briefly to near 75% in late summer.

WATER: Rainfall is moderate to heavy all year, but conditions are driest in spring and summer. Cultivated plants should be allowed to dry slightly between waterings, but they should never be allowed to dry out completely.

FERTILIZER: 1/4–1/2 recommended strength, applied weekly. A high-nitrogen fertilizer is beneficial from spring to midsummer, but a fertilizer high in phosphates should be used in late summer and autumn.

REST PERIOD: Growing conditions should be maintained all year. In the habitat, winter is the wettest season, but water should not be increased for cultivated plants. In fact, water should be reduced, especially for plants grown in the dark, short-day conditions common during temperate-latitude winters. However, cultivated plants should never be allowed to dry completely between waterings. Occasional early morning mistings between waterings may be beneficial, particularly on bright, sunny days. Fertilizer should be reduced or eliminated anytime water is reduced. In the habitat, light is lowest in winter.

GROWING MEDIA: Plants may be mounted on tree-fern or cork slabs or potted in small pots filled with any open, fast-draining medium. Repotting may be done anytime new roots are growing.

Plant and Flower Information

PLANT SIZE AND TYPE: A 1.2–1.6 in. (3–4 cm) sympodial epiphyte.

PSEUDOBULB: 0.4–0.6 in. (1.1–1.5 cm) long. Very small and tightly clustered, the pseudobulbs are somewhat ovoid.

LEAVES: 2–4 per growth. The linear to narrowly lanceolate leaves are 0.5–2.8 in. (1.3–7.1 cm) long.

INFLORESCENCE: Short. Inflorescences emerge near the apex on fully mature, sometimes leafless pseudobulbs.

FLOWERS: 2 per inflorescence. The erect flowers are 0.7–1.1 in. (1.8–2.8 cm) long. J. J. Smith originally described the blossoms as dark violet with a yellow lip. However, Reeve and Woods (ref. 385) indicate that sepals and petals are pale to mid-pink with a pink lip. The lip may have a faint orange mark at the widest point. Flowers have an ovate-oblong dorsal sepal, and lanceolate-triangular lateral sepals, with lanceolate petals. The lip is obscurely 3-lobed with slightly upcurved margins and a pointed, triangular apex.

REFERENCES: 224, 385.

PHOTOS/DRAWINGS: 385.

Dendrobium seriatum Wallich.
An unpublished name for an entity that is now considered a synonym of *Eria acervata* Lindley. REFERENCES: 218, 254.

Dendrobium serpens (Hooker f.) Hooker f.
See *D. panduriferum* Hooker f. REFERENCES: 200, 203, 218, 254, 402, 454, 455. PHOTOS/DRAWINGS: 203.

Dendrobium serra (Lindley) Lindley.
See *D. aloifolium* (Blume) Rchb. f. REFERENCES: 75, 157, 190, 200, 202, 216, 254, 266, 278, 310, 394, 395, 402, 447, 448, 454, 455, 469.

Dendrobium serratilabium L. O. Williams

ORIGIN/HABITAT: The Philippine Islands. Plants are found in Rizal Province on Luzon Island, but little else has been reported about the habitat. Elevation has been estimated, so the following climate data should be used with caution.

CLIMATE: Station #98427, Manila, Philippines, Lat. 14.5°N, Long. 121.0°E, at 85 ft. (26 m). Temperatures are calculated for an estimated elevation of 800 ft. (240 m), resulting in probable extremes of 99°F (37°C) and 56°F (13°C).

N/HEMISPHERE	JAN	FEB	MAR	APR	MAY	JUN	JUL	AUG	SEP	OCT	NOV	DEC
°F AVG MAX	84	86	89	91	91	89	86	85	86	86	85	84
°F AVG MIN	67	67	69	71	73	73	73	73	73	72	70	68
DIURNAL RANGE	17	19	20	20	18	16	13	12	13	14	15	16
RAIN/INCHES	0.9	0.5	0.7	1.3	5.1	10.0	17.0	16.6	14.0	7.6	5.7	2.6
HUMIDITY/%	77	73	70	68	71	81	84	86	87	84	82	89
BLOOM SEASON									*	*	*	
DAYS CLR @ 8AM	6	9	14	14	10	3	2	1	6	7	6
DAYS CLR @ 2PM	3	6	10	10	8	2	1	1	0	2	2	3
RAIN/MM	23	13	18	33	130	254	432	422	356	193	145	66
°C AVG MAX	28.7	29.8	31.4	32.6	32.6	31.4	29.8	29.2	29.8	29.8	29.2	28.7
°C AVG MIN	19.2	19.2	20.3	21.4	22.6	22.6	22.6	22.6	22.6	22.0	20.9	19.8
DIURNAL RANGE	9.5	10.6	11.1	11.2	10.0	8.8	7.2	6.6	7.2	7.8	8.3	8.9
S/HEMISPHERE	JUL	AUG	SEP	OCT	NOV	DEC	JAN	FEB	MAR	APR	MAY	JUN

Cultural Recommendations

LIGHT: 2000–3000 fc.

TEMPERATURES: Throughout the year, days average 84–91°F (29–33°C), and nights average 67–73°F (19–23°C), with a diurnal range of 12–20°F (7–11°C). The warmest temperatures occur in spring.

Dendrobium serratipetalum

HUMIDITY: 80–90% in summer and autumn, dropping to near 70% in late winter and spring.

WATER: Rainfall is heavy in summer, moderate in autumn, and light in winter and spring. Cultivated plants should be kept moist during the growing season, but water should be gradually reduced in autumn.

FERTILIZER: ¼–½ recommended strength, applied weekly. A high-nitrogen fertilizer is beneficial from spring to midsummer, but a fertilizer high in phosphates should be used in late summer and autumn.

REST PERIOD: Growing temperatures should be maintained all year. Rainfall is low for 3–4 months in winter, but additional moisture is available from frequent heavy dew. In cultivation, water should be reduced and the plants allowed to dry out between waterings. They should not remain dry for extended periods, however. Fertilizer should also be reduced or eliminated anytime water is reduced. In the habitat, light is highest in winter.

GROWING MEDIA: Plants may be mounted on tree-fern or cork slabs if humidity is high and plants are watered at least once daily in summer. When plants are potted, any open, fast-draining medium may be used. Repotting is best done in early spring when new roots are growing.

MISCELLANEOUS NOTES: The bloom season shown in the climate table is based on reports from the habitat. Sparse cultivation reports also indicate autumn blooming.

Plant and Flower Information

PLANT SIZE AND TYPE: A 16 in. (40 cm) sympodial epiphyte.

PSEUDOBULB: 16 in. (40 cm) long. The stems are thickened and wrinkled.

LEAVES: Many. The lanceolate leaves, which are 2.4–3.2 in. (6–8 cm) long, are spaced 0.6–0.8 in. (1.5–2.0 cm) apart. The leaf sheaths are yellow and streaked.

INFLORESCENCE: Short. Inflorescences emerge from nodes on the older portion of the stems.

FLOWERS: Few per inflorescence. The flowers are 1.2–1.6 in. (3–4 cm) across. The white, yellow, or greenish yellow blossoms have red-brown stripes and veins. The broadly lanceolate dorsal sepal is joined at the base to the lateral sepals. Petals are elliptic-lanceolate. The somewhat heart-shaped lip is cream-white with irregularly cut or toothed side margins. The spur is long and slender.

REFERENCES: 179, 226, 536.

PHOTOS/DRAWINGS: 536.

Dendrobium serratipetalum Schlechter

ORIGIN/HABITAT: Papua New Guinea. Plants grow in the Sepik River region at 1950–6550 ft. (600–2000 m).

CLIMATE: Station #200004, Ambunti, Papua New Guinea, Lat. 4.2°S, Long. 142.8°E, at 164 ft. (50 m). Temperatures are calculated for an elevation of 4600 ft. (1400 m), resulting in probable extremes of 84°F (29°C) and 37°F (3°C).

N/HEMISPHERE	JAN	FEB	MAR	APR	MAY	JUN	JUL	AUG	SEP	OCT	NOV	DEC
°F AVG MAX	73	75	75	75	76	75	75	75	75	75	75	74
°F AVG MIN	57	58	59	58	58	58	57	58	58	58	58	59
DIURNAL RANGE	16	17	16	17	18	17	18	17	17	17	17	15
RAIN/INCHES	6.4	7.4	7.7	8.5	9.2	9.4	10.9	10.2	12.2	10.4	8.3	5.2
HUMIDITY/%	N/A											
BLOOM SEASON			*	*		*			*			
DAYS CLR	N/A											
RAIN/MM	163	188	196	216	234	239	277	259	310	264	211	132
°C AVG MAX	23.0	24.1	24.1	24.1	24.6	24.1	24.1	24.1	24.1	24.1	24.1	23.5
°C AVG MIN	14.1	14.6	15.2	14.6	14.6	14.6	14.1	14.6	14.6	14.6	14.6	15.2
DIURNAL RANGE	8.9	9.5	8.9	9.5	10.0	9.5	10.0	9.5	9.5	9.5	9.5	8.3
S/HEMISPHERE	JUL	AUG	SEP	OCT	NOV	DEC	JAN	FEB	MAR	APR	MAY	JUN

Cultural Recommendations

LIGHT: 2000–3000 fc.

TEMPERATURES: Throughout the year, days average 73–76°F (23–25°C), and nights average 57–59°F (14–15°C), with a diurnal range of 15–18°F (8–10°C).

HUMIDITY: Information is not available for this location. However, records from other stations in the region indicate that averages are probably near 80% year-round.

WATER: Rainfall is heavy all year, with the greatest amounts falling in summer and early autumn. Cultivated plants should be kept moist but not soggy.

FERTILIZER: ¼–½ recommended strength. A balanced fertilizer should be applied weekly to biweekly throughout the year.

REST PERIOD: Growing temperatures should be maintained all year. Water and fertilizer may be reduced somewhat in winter, especially for plants grown in the dark, short-day conditions common in temperate latitudes, but plants should never be allowed to dry out between waterings.

GROWING MEDIA: Plants may be mounted if humidity is high and plants are watered at least once daily in summer. When plants are potted, any open, fast-draining medium may be used. Repotting may be done anytime new roots are growing.

MISCELLANEOUS NOTES: The bloom season shown in the climate table is based on reports from the habitat.

Plant and Flower Information

PLANT SIZE AND TYPE: A 12–18 in. (30–45 cm) sympodial epiphyte.

PSEUDOBULB: 12–18 in. (30–45 cm) long. The leafy stems are slender and do not branch.

LEAVES: Many. The broadly lanceolate leaves are 2.8–4.3 in. (7–11 cm) long and pointed at the tip.

INFLORESCENCE: Very short.

FLOWERS: Few per inflorescence. The small, white flowers are about 0.4 in. (1 cm) long. The backs of the sepals are darker and covered with a scaly coating. The dorsal sepal is oval, and lateral sepals are somewhat oblong. The petals are obovate-elliptical with a serrated margin. The obscurely 3-lobed lip is obovate. The incurved sidelobes are serrated along the margin. The large, nearly round midlobe is incurved along the unequally serrated margin.

REFERENCES: 223, 443.

Dendrobium sertatum Rolfe.
Sometimes spelled *D. serratum*, see *D. catillare* Rchb. f. REFERENCES: 12, 20, 212, 252, 254, 270, 353, 466.

Dendrobium sertularioides Swartz.
Now considered a synonym of *Pleurothallis sertularioides* Sprengel. REFERENCES: 216, 254.

Dendrobium sessile Gagnepain.
In 1982 Seidenfaden in *Opera Botanica* #62 includes *D. sessile* as a synonym of *Trichotosia velutina* (Loddiges ex Lindley) Kränzlin. REFERENCES: 138, 227, 448.

Dendrobium setifolium Ridley

ORIGIN/HABITAT: Thailand, Malaya, Singapore, the Riau Archipelago, and Borneo. In western Thailand, plants grow south of Tak and south of Omkoi on the mainland. On the peninsula, they are found in the Surat and Satul regions. In Borneo, plants grow near Kuching in Sarawak and in the lower mountain forests of Sabah at 4600–5250 ft. (1400–1600 m).

CLIMATE: Station #49613, Tambunan, Sabah, Borneo, Lat. 5.7°N, Long. 116.4°E, at 1200 ft. (366 m). Temperatures are calculated for an elevation of 4800 ft. (1460 m), resulting in probable extremes of 86°F (30°C) and 42°F (6°C).

N/HEMISPHERE	JAN	FEB	MAR	APR	MAY	JUN	JUL	AUG	SEP	OCT	NOV	DEC
°F AVG MAX	74	75	77	78	78	77	77	77	77	76	75	74
°F AVG MIN	55	53	54	55	56	55	54	54	55	55	55	56
DIURNAL RANGE	19	22	23	23	22	22	23	23	22	21	20	18
RAIN/INCHES	5.8	3.7	5.8	7.5	8.2	7.3	5.1	4.9	6.4	7.0	6.8	6.0
HUMIDITY/%	N/A											
BLOOM SEASON	N/A											
DAYS CLR	N/A											
RAIN/MM	147	94	147	190	208	185	130	124	163	178	173	152
°C AVG MAX	23.4	24.0	25.1	25.6	25.6	25.1	25.1	25.1	25.1	24.5	24.0	23.4
°C AVG MIN	12.8	11.7	12.3	12.8	13.4	12.8	12.3	12.3	12.8	12.8	12.8	13.4
DIURNAL RANGE	10.6	12.3	12.8	12.8	12.2	12.3	12.8	12.8	12.3	11.7	11.2	10.0
S/HEMISPHERE	JUL	AUG	SEP	OCT	NOV	DEC	JAN	FEB	MAR	APR	MAY	JUN

Cultural Recommendations

LIGHT: 3500–4500 fc.

TEMPERATURES: Throughout the year, days average 74–78°F (23–26°C), and nights average 53–56°F (12–13°C), with a diurnal range of 18–23°F (10–13°C).

HUMIDITY: Information is not available for this location. However, records from nearby stations indicate that humidity probably averages 80–85% year-round.

WATER: Rainfall is moderate to heavy all year with a brief, slightly drier period in winter. Cultivated plants should be kept moist, with only slight drying allowed between waterings.

FERTILIZER: ¼–½ recommended strength. A balanced fertilizer should be applied weekly to biweekly throughout the year.

REST PERIOD: Growing temperatures should be maintained all year. Water should be reduced for cultivated plants, especially those grown in the dark, short-day conditions common in temperate-latitude winters, but they should never be allowed to dry out completely. Fertilizer should be reduced or eliminated until water is increased in spring.

GROWING MEDIA: Plants may be mounted on tree-fern or cork slabs if humidity is high and plants are watered at least once daily in summer. When plants are potted, any open, fast-draining medium may be used. New growth begins when rains resume after the dry period, and roots begin actively growing after new growths are partially mature. Plants should be repotted only after roots begin growing.

MISCELLANEOUS NOTES: Plants that produce flowers which last a single day commonly bloom several times during the year. Flowering usually occurs 7–14 days after a sudden 10°F (5°C) drop in daytime temperatures.

Plant and Flower Information

PLANT SIZE AND TYPE: A 10–16 in. (25–40 cm) sympodial epiphyte.

PSEUDOBULB: 10–16 in. (25–40 cm) long. The clustered stems have a short, slender section at the base. It then enlarges, forming a fat, nearly round, pseudobulbous swelling before becoming slender again on the very elongated upper portion. Plants root only at the base. *D. clavator* is vegetatively very similar to *D. setifolium*.

LEAVES: 4–8 per growth. The widely spaced leaves are 1.2–4.0 in. (3–10 cm) long. They are slender, terete, and channeled. The leaves may be held at any angle to the stem.

INFLORESCENCE: Very short. Inflorescences emerge from bracts opposite each leaf. They occur from the middle to the apex of the stem.

FLOWERS: 1 per inflorescence. The flowers, which are 0.7 in. (1.8 cm) long, are upside down and do not open fully. Sepals and petals are white. The lip has a yellow callus. The margin of the small midlobe is notched and ruffled. The large, rounded sidelobes are decorated with red veins. Blossoms are short-lived.

HYBRIDIZING NOTES: Johansen (ref. 239) indicates that plants are self-sterile and that flowers dropped 3–7 days after self-pollination. When crossed with *D. farmerii* Paxton using *D. setifolium* as the female parent, 13% of the seed had visible embryos and 89% germinated.

REFERENCES: 56, 200, 239, 394, 445, 448, 450, 454, 455.

PHOTOS/DRAWINGS: 450, *454*, 455.

Dendrobium setigerum Ames. See *D. macrophyllum* A. Richard. REFERENCES: 83.

Dendrobium setosum Schlechter

ORIGIN/HABITAT: Northern Papua New Guinea. Plants grow on forest trees in the Torricelli Mountains at about 2600 ft. (800 m) and in the Kani and Finisterre Ranges at 3300–3950 ft. (1000–1200 m).

CLIMATE: Station #94004, Wewak, Papua New Guinea, Lat. 3.6°S, Long. 143.7°E, at 16 ft. (5 m). Temperatures are calculated for an elevation of 2600 ft. (800 m), resulting in probable extremes of 89°F (32°C) and 53°F (12°C).

N/HEMISPHERE	JAN	FEB	MAR	APR	MAY	JUN	JUL	AUG	SEP	OCT	NOV	DEC
°F AVG MAX	79	79	79	79	79	79	78	77	78	79	79	79
°F AVG MIN	65	65	65	66	66	66	66	66	65	65	66	65
DIURNAL RANGE	14	14	14	13	13	13	12	11	13	14	13	14
RAIN/INCHES	7.6	4.8	5.3	10.0	13.3	14.5	12.1	11.9	14.9	16.9	15.1	10.8
HUMIDITY/%	80	79	79	78	79	81	82	82	81	82	81	80
BLOOM SEASON			*				*					
DAYS CLR	N/A											
RAIN/MM	193	122	135	254	338	368	307	302	378	429	384	274
°C AVG MAX	26.3	26.3	26.3	26.3	26.3	26.3	25.8	25.2	25.8	26.3	26.3	26.3
°C AVG MIN	18.6	18.6	18.6	19.1	19.1	19.1	19.1	19.1	18.6	18.6	19.1	18.6
DIURNAL RANGE	7.7	7.7	7.7	7.2	7.2	7.2	6.7	6.1	7.2	7.7	7.2	7.7
S/HEMISPHERE	JUL	AUG	SEP	OCT	NOV	DEC	JAN	FEB	MAR	APR	MAY	JUN

Cultural Recommendations

LIGHT: 2000–3000 fc.

TEMPERATURES: Throughout the year, days average 77–79°F (25–26°C), and nights average 65–66°F (19°C), with a diurnal range of 11–14°F (6–8°C).

HUMIDITY: Near 80% year-round.

WATER: Rainfall is heavy all year, but conditions are slightly drier for 1–2 months in winter. Cultivated plants should be kept moist but not soggy.

FERTILIZER: ¼–½ recommended strength. A balanced fertilizer should be applied weekly to biweekly throughout the year.

REST PERIOD: Growing temperatures should be maintained all year. However, water and fertilizer should be reduced somewhat, especially if plants are cultivated in the dark, short-day conditions common during temperate-latitude winters. In the habitat, seasonal light variation is minor.

GROWING MEDIA: A very open and fast-draining medium should be used in baskets or small pots. Repotting may be done anytime new roots are growing.

MISCELLANEOUS NOTES: The bloom season shown in the climate table is based on reports from the habitat. Plants that produce flowers which last a single day commonly bloom several times during the year. Flowering usually occurs 7–14 days after a sudden 10°F (5°C) drop in daytime temperatures.

Plant and Flower Information

PLANT SIZE AND TYPE: A 20 in. (50 cm) sympodial epiphyte.

Dendrobium shepherdii

PSEUDOBULB: The climbing plants are prostrate with their tips turned upwards. The somewhat flattened growths arise from an elongated rhizome that branches repeatedly.

LEAVES: Many. The linear leaves are 1.6–3.0 in. (4.0–7.5 cm) long.

INFLORESCENCE: Short.

FLOWERS: 2 per inflorescence. The flowers are 0.3 in. (0.8 cm) across. The greenish sepals and petals are spreading, but they do not open fully. The lip and column are marked with orange-red. The lip is shaped like a whale's tail with large, pointed sidelobes. The midlobe has a wavy front margin. It is notched with a small point in the center of the notch. The center of the lip is sparsely covered with small, pointed protuberances. Blossoms are short-lived.

REFERENCES: 92, 221, 437, 445.

PHOTOS/DRAWINGS: 437.

Dendrobium shepherdii F. Mueller.
Now considered a synonym of *Bulbophyllum shepherdii*. *Dendrobium shepherdii* F. Mueller var. *platyphyllum* F. Mueller is now known as *Bulbophyllum schillerianum*. REFERENCES: 67, 105, 216, 254.

Dendrobium shipmani A. Hawkes

AKA: *D. confusum* Schlechter not J. J. Smith, *D. salicornioides* J. J. Smith not Teijsm. and Binn. In addition, Schlechter (ref. 436) and J. J. Smith (ref. 470) included *D. parciflorum* Kränzlin as a synonym of *D. confusum* Schlechter.

ORIGIN/HABITAT: Widespread and common in New Guinea and Sulawesi. In Irian Jaya (western New Guinea), plants grow in forests near Manokwari. In the Minahassa district of north Sulawesi (Celebes), this species is abundant on roadside trees between Menado and Tondano (Tomohon) at 50–2600 ft. (20–800 m). Plants often grow in trees overhanging water.

CLIMATE: Station #97530, Manokwari, Irian Jaya, Lat. 0.9°S, Long. 134.1°E, at 10 ft. (3 m). Temperatures are calculated for an elevation of 1950 ft. (600 m), resulting in probable extremes of 87°F (30°C) and 62°F (16°C).

N/HEMISPHERE	JAN	FEB	MAR	APR	MAY	JUN	JUL	AUG	SEP	OCT	NOV	DEC
°F AVG MAX	80	79	81	81	82	80	80	80	80	80	80	79
°F AVG MIN	68	69	68	68	68	69	67	67	68	68	68	68
DIURNAL RANGE	12	10	13	13	14	11	13	13	12	12	12	11
RAIN/INCHES	5.4	5.6	5.0	4.7	4.5	10.3	12.0	9.4	13.2	11.1	7.8	7.3
HUMIDITY/%	87	87	86	84	85	86	86	85	86	86	86	85
BLOOM SEASON		*	*	*	*							
DAYS CLR @ 9AM	4	3	3	5	3	3	3	1	1	2	3	7
DAYS CLR @ 3PM	2	2	2	3	1	1	1	1	0	1	0	2
RAIN/MM	137	142	127	119	114	262	305	239	335	282	198	185
°C AVG MAX	26.4	25.9	27.0	27.0	27.6	26.4	26.4	26.4	26.4	26.4	26.4	25.9
°C AVG MIN	19.8	20.3	19.8	19.8	19.8	20.3	19.2	19.2	19.8	19.8	19.8	19.8
DIURNAL RANGE	6.6	5.6	7.2	7.2	7.8	6.1	7.2	7.2	6.6	6.6	6.6	6.1
S/HEMISPHERE	JUL	AUG	SEP	OCT	NOV	DEC	JAN	FEB	MAR	APR	MAY	JUN

Cultural Recommendations

LIGHT: 2500–3500 fc.

TEMPERATURES: Throughout the year, days average 79–82°F (26–28°C), and nights average 67–69°F (19–20°C), with a diurnal range of 10–14°F (6–8°C).

HUMIDITY: Near 85% year-round.

WATER: Rainfall is very heavy all year, but conditions are driest in winter and spring. Cultivated plants should never be allowed to dry completely.

FERTILIZER: ¼–½ recommended strength. A balanced fertilizer should be applied weekly to biweekly throughout the year.

REST PERIOD: Growing conditions should be maintained all year. Water and fertilizer may be reduced somewhat in winter, especially for plants cultivated in the dark, short-day conditions common in temperate latitudes. In the habitat, light is slightly higher in winter.

GROWING MEDIA: Plants may be mounted on tree-fern or cork slabs if humidity is high and plants are watered at least once daily in summer. When plants are potted, any open, fast-draining medium may be used. Repotting is best done in early spring when new roots are growing.

MISCELLANEOUS NOTES: The bloom season shown in the climate table is based on reports from the habitat.

Plant and Flower Information

PLANT SIZE AND TYPE: A 2.4–12.0 in. (6–31 cm) sympodial epiphyte.

PSEUDOBULB: 2.4–12.0 in. (6–30 cm) long. The pseudobulbs are dark green, clustered, and arise from a very short rhizome. They are not swollen above the base. The stems are densely leafy near the apex.

LEAVES: Many. The linear to linear-lanceolate leaves 0.8–1.2 in. (2–3 cm) long and spaced 1.0–1.2 in. (2.5–3.0 cm) apart. They alternate along the stem in 2 rows. The leaves are thick, terete, somewhat sickle-shaped, and laterally flattened.

INFLORESCENCE: Clusters of flowers emerge from nodes at or near the apex.

FLOWERS: Many. Flowers open in succession. The blossoms are 0.8–1.2 in. (2.0–3.0 cm) long. Sepals and petals are pristine, crystalline white. Sepals are ovate-lanceolate. Petals are somewhat lanceolate. The white lip is 3-lobed with a notch in the center of the midlobe. It has 2 parallel lines and a yellow disc in the throat. The beautiful flowers are thin-textured and very short-lived.

HYBRIDIZING NOTES: Chromosome count is 2n = 38 as *D. confusum* (ref. 153, 273).

REFERENCES: 153, 191, 229, 273, 304, 436, 454, 470, 537.

PHOTOS/DRAWINGS: *304*.

Dendrobium shiraishii T. Yukawa and M. Nishida

ORIGIN/HABITAT: Irian Jaya, in the vicinity of Manokwari. Habitat elevation is estimated so the following data should be used with caution.

CLIMATE: Station #97530, Manokwari, Irian Jaya, Lat. 0.9°S, Long. 134.1°E, at 10 ft. (3 m). Temperatures are calculated for an elevation of 5000 ft. (1520 m), resulting in probable extremes of 77°F (25°C) and 52°F (11°C).

N/HEMISPHERE	JAN	FEB	MAR	APR	MAY	JUN	JUL	AUG	SEP	OCT	NOV	DEC
°F AVG MAX	70	69	71	71	72	70	70	70	70	70	70	69
°F AVG MIN	58	59	59	58	58	59	57	57	58	58	58	58
DIURNAL RANGE	12	10	13	13	14	11	13	13	12	12	12	11
RAIN/INCHES	5.4	5.6	5.0	4.7	4.5	10.3	12.0	9.4	13.2	11.1	7.8	7.3
HUMIDITY/%	87	87	86	84	85	86	86	85	86	86	86	85
BLOOM SEASON	N/A											
DAYS CLR @ 9AM	4	3	3	5	3	3	3	1	1	2	3	7
DAYS CLR @ 3PM	2	2	2	3	1	1	1	1	0	1	0	2
RAIN/MM	137	142	127	119	114	262	305	239	335	282	198	185
°C AVG MAX	20.9	20.3	21.4	21.4	22.0	20.9	20.9	20.9	20.9	20.9	20.9	20.3
°C AVG MIN	14.2	14.7	14.2	14.2	14.2	14.7	13.6	13.6	14.2	14.2	14.2	14.2
DIURNAL RANGE	6.7	5.6	7.2	7.2	7.8	6.2	7.3	7.3	6.7	6.7	6.7	6.1
S/HEMISPHERE	JUL	AUG	SEP	OCT	NOV	DEC	JAN	FEB	MAR	APR	MAY	JUN

Cultural Recommendations

LIGHT: 2000–3000 fc.

TEMPERATURES: Throughout the year, days average 69–72°F (20–22°C), and nights average 57–59°F (14–15°C), with a diurnal range of 10–14°F (6–8°C). Because of microclimate effects, actual maximum temperatures may be as much as 10°F (6°C) warmer than the calculated values in the climate table.

HUMIDITY: Near 85% year-round.

WATER: Rainfall is moderate to very heavy all year. Cultivated plants should be kept moist, with only slight drying allowed between waterings.

FERTILIZER: ¼–½ recommended strength. A balanced fertilizer should be applied weekly to biweekly throughout the year.

REST PERIOD: Growing conditions should be maintained year-round. Water and fertilizer may be reduced somewhat in winter, especially for plants grown in the dark, short-day conditions common in temperate latitudes. Plants should never be allowed to dry out completely, however.

GROWING MEDIA: Plants may be mounted on tree-fern or cork slabs if humidity is high and plants are watered daily in summer. When plants are potted, any open, fast-draining medium may be used. Repotting may be done anytime new roots are growing.

Plant and Flower Information

PLANT SIZE AND TYPE: A 26 in. (65 cm) sympodial epiphyte, terrestrial, or lithophyte.

PSEUDOBULB: 7–17 in. (17–43 cm) long. The greenish brown stems are clustered, grooved, and swollen on the upper part.

LEAVES: 2–4 at the apex of each growth. The elliptic-oblong leaves are 6–10 in. (15–25 cm) long. They are leathery, dark green, and rounded at the tip.

INFLORESCENCE: 11–15 in. (28–37 cm) long. A single inflorescence emerges at the apex of the stem.

FLOWERS: 10 per growth. The long-lasting flowers, which open fully, are about 2 in. (5.5 cm) across. The pointed sepals and petals are greenish yellow with maroon spots on the backside of the sepals. The deflexed petals have a large, irregular, blackish brown stain on the backside. The lip is dull red with greenish yellow at the apex. It is 3-lobed with large triangular sidelobes.

REFERENCES: Yukawa and Nishida 1992 *Lindleyana* 7(2):89–90.

PHOTOS/DRAWINGS: Yukawa and Nishida 1992 *Lindleyana* 7(2):89–90.

Dendrobium siberutense J. J. Smith

ORIGIN/HABITAT: Siberut Island, which is part of the Mentawei Island group just off the west coast of Sumatra. Siberut is a relatively large, low-lying island located west of Padang, Sumatra. Habitat elevation is unavailable; the following climate data should be used with caution.

CLIMATE: Station #96163, Padang, Sumatra, Indonesia, Lat. 0.9°S, Long. 100.4°E, at 19 ft. (6 m). Temperatures are calculated for an elevation of 450 ft. (140 m), resulting in probable extremes of 93°F (34°C) and 67°F (19°C).

N/HEMISPHERE	JAN	FEB	MAR	APR	MAY	JUN	JUL	AUG	SEP	OCT	NOV	DEC
°F AVG MAX	86	86	85	85	85	85	86	86	86	86	87	86
°F AVG MIN	73	73	73	73	73	73	73	73	73	74	74	73
DIURNAL RANGE	13	13	12	12	12	12	13	13	13	12	13	13
RAIN/INCHES	10.9	13.7	6.0	19.5	20.4	18.9	13.8	10.2	12.1	14.3	12.4	12.1
HUMIDITY/%	81	82	83	84	85	84	81	81	82	83	81	81
BLOOM SEASON							*					
DAYS CLR @ 7AM	5	1	1	0	0	2	2	1	2	2	3	5
DAYS CLR @ 1PM	5	2	2	1	1	3	3	4	3	3	6	5
RAIN/MM	277	348	152	495	518	480	351	259	307	363	315	307
°C AVG MAX	29.8	29.8	29.2	29.2	29.2	29.2	29.8	29.8	29.8	29.8	30.3	29.8
°C AVG MIN	22.5	22.5	22.5	22.5	22.5	22.5	22.5	22.5	22.5	23.1	23.1	22.5
DIURNAL RANGE	7.3	7.3	6.7	6.7	6.7	6.7	7.3	7.3	7.3	6.7	7.2	7.3
S/HEMISPHERE	JUL	AUG	SEP	OCT	NOV	DEC	JAN	FEB	MAR	APR	MAY	JUN

Cultural Recommendations

LIGHT: 2000–3000 fc. Diffused light is preferred.

TEMPERATURES: Throughout the year, days average 85–87°F (29–30°C), and nights average 73–74°F (23°C), with a diurnal range of 12–13°F (7°C). Probable extremes vary only a few degrees from the averages, indicating that the plant may not tolerate wide temperature fluctuations.

HUMIDITY: 80–85% year-round.

WATER: Rainfall is heavy all year. Cultivated plants should be kept moist but not soggy. They should never be allowed to dry out completely.

FERTILIZER: ¼–½ recommended strength. A balanced fertilizer should be applied weekly to biweekly throughout the year.

REST PERIOD: Growing conditions should be maintained year-round. For cultivated plants, water and fertilizer may be reduced somewhat in winter, especially for plants grown in the dark, short-day conditions common in temperate latitudes. In the habitat, light is highest in winter.

GROWING MEDIA: Plants may be mounted on tree-fern or cork slabs or potted in small pots filled with any open, fast-draining medium. Repotting may be done anytime new roots are growing.

MISCELLANEOUS NOTES: The bloom season shown in the climate table is based on collection reports. The plant was described in 1922 in *Bull. Jard. Bot. Buit.* 3rd sér. 5:82.

Plant and Flower Information

PLANT SIZE AND TYPE: An 11–13 in. (28–33 cm) sympodial epiphyte.

PSEUDOBULB: 11–13 in. (28–33 cm) long. Growths are about 5 in. (13 cm) apart on an elongated, branching rhizome.

LEAVES: Many. The distichous, lanceolate leaves are 3 in. (8 cm) long, though they may be smaller near the apex. When dry, the leaves are covered with small black dots on the backside. The leaf sheaths are covered with hairs.

INFLORESCENCE: Short. Inflorescences emerge through the leaf bases at nodes along the stem.

FLOWERS: 4–5 per inflorescence. The flowers are 0.8 in. (2 cm) across. The sepals and petals are uneven along the margin. The lip is warty on the inside. The plant was described from an herbarium specimen, and flower color was not available.

REFERENCES: 223.

Dendrobium signatum Rchb. f.

AKA: *D. hildebrandii* Rolfe, *D. tortile* Lindley var. *hildebrandii* (Rolfe) Tang & Wang. The International Orchid Commission (ref. 236) lists *D. signatum* as a synonym of *D. bensoniae* Rchb. f. but registers hybrids as *D. signatum*. However, Seidenfaden (ref. 454) maintains both as separate species.

ORIGIN/HABITAT: Southeast Asia. Plants are found in the Shan States of Burma, northern Thailand, and the Borikhane region of Laos. In Thailand, plants grow at 1000–3950 ft. (300–1200 m).

CLIMATE: Station #48327, Chiang Mai, Thailand, Lat. 18.8°N, Long. 99.0°E, at 1100 ft. (335 m). Temperatures are calculated for an elevation of 2500 ft. (760 m), resulting in probable extremes of 104°F (40°C) and 33°F (1°C).

N/HEMISPHERE	JAN	FEB	MAR	APR	MAY	JUN	JUL	AUG	SEP	OCT	NOV	DEC
°F AVG MAX	80	85	90	91	89	85	84	82	83	84	81	79
°F AVG MIN	51	52	57	65	69	69	69	70	68	66	61	52
DIURNAL RANGE	29	33	33	26	20	16	15	12	15	18	20	27
RAIN/INCHES	0.3	0.4	0.6	2.0	5.5	6.1	7.4	8.7	11.5	4.9	1.5	0.4
HUMIDITY/%	73	65	58	62	73	78	80	83	83	81	79	76
BLOOM SEASON		*	*	*	***	*		*				
DAYS CLR @ 7AM	5	5	2	1	0	0	0	0	1	3	3	
DAYS CLR @ 1PM	9	8	4	2	0	0	0	0	0	1	3	
RAIN/MM	8	10	15	51	140	155	188	221	292	124	38	10
°C AVG MAX	26.9	29.7	32.4	33.0	31.9	29.7	29.1	28.0	28.5	29.1	27.4	26.3
°C AVG MIN	10.8	11.3	14.1	18.5	20.8	20.8	20.8	21.3	20.2	19.1	16.3	11.3
DIURNAL RANGE	16.1	18.4	18.3	14.5	11.1	8.9	8.3	6.7	8.3	10.0	11.1	15.0
S/HEMISPHERE	JUL	AUG	SEP	OCT	NOV	DEC	JAN	FEB	MAR	APR	MAY	JUN

Cultural Recommendations

LIGHT: 2500–3500 fc. The heavy summer cloud cover indicates that some shading is needed from spring through autumn, but light should be as high as the plant can tolerate, short of burning the leaves.

TEMPERATURES: Summer days average 82–85°F (28–30°C), and nights average 69–70°F (21°C), with a diurnal range of 12–16°F (7–9°C). Spring is the warmest season. Days average 89–91°F (32–33°C), and nights average 57–69°F (14–21°C), with a diurnal range of 20–33°F (11–18°C).

HUMIDITY: Near 80% most of the year, dropping to near 60% in late winter and early spring.

WATER: Rainfall is moderate to heavy from late spring through early autumn, but conditions are much drier in winter. Cultivated plants should be kept moist while actively growing, but water should be gradually reduced after new growths mature in autumn.

FERTILIZER: ¼–½ recommended strength, applied weekly. A high-nitrogen fertilizer is beneficial from spring to midsummer, but a fertilizer high in phosphates should be used in late summer and autumn.

REST PERIOD: Winter days average 79–85°F (26–30°C), and nights average 51–52°F (11°C), with a diurnal range of 27–33°F (15–18°C). In the habitat, rainfall is very low for 4 months in winter. During the early part of the season, the high relative humidity indicates that additional moisture is available from frequent fog, mist, and heavy deposits of dew. Growers sometimes recommend eliminating water in winter, but plants are healthiest if for most of the winter they are allowed to become dry between waterings but do not remain dry for extended periods. However, for 1–2 months in early spring, conditions in the habitat are clear, warm, and dry. Humidity is so low that even the moisture from morning dew is uncommon. During a corresponding time for cultivated plants, water should be limited to an occasional early morning misting if the pseudobulbs start to shrivel, or if an extended period of bright, sunny weather is expected. Fertilizer should be eliminated in winter, and resumed only when water is increased in spring. In the habitat, light is highest in winter.

GROWING MEDIA: Plants may be mounted on tree-fern or cork slabs or potted in small pots filled with any open, fast-draining medium. Repotting may be done anytime new roots are actively growing.

MISCELLANEOUS NOTES: The bloom season shown in the climate table is based on cultivation records.

Plant and Flower Information

PLANT SIZE AND TYPE: A 24 in. (61 cm) sympodial epiphyte.

PSEUDOBULB: 24 in. (61 cm) long. The stemlike pseudobulbs are slender and fleshy.

LEAVES: 4 in. (10 cm) long. The leaves are leathery, lanceolate, pointed, and eventually deciduous.

INFLORESCENCE: Short. Inflorescences emerge on leafless canes.

FLOWERS: 2 per inflorescence. The flowers are 3 in. (7.6 cm) across. Sepals and petals, which are sometimes wavy and twisted, are white, greenish-white, or cream. The velvety lip is yellow in the throat, darker yellow on the disk, and white along the recurved front margin. The lip may be marked with 2 purplish blotches near the base. Blossoms are fragrant and long lived.

HYBRIDIZING NOTES: Chromosome counts are 2n = 2x (ref. 504, 580) as *D. signatum*. As *D. hildebrandii*, counts are 2n = 38 (ref. 153, 273) and 2n = 38+1f (ref. 504, 580).

REFERENCES: 179, 190, 216, 236, 273, 359, 389, 408, 430, 447, 454, 504, 505, 568, 580.

PHOTOS/DRAWINGS: *389, 430, 454.*

Dendrobium sikinii Schlechter. Sometimes spelled *D. sikini*, see *D. subquadratum* J. J. Smith. REFERENCES: 83, 92, 221, 437, 445.

Dendrobium sikkimense A. Hawkes and A. H. Heller. See *D. praecinctum* Rchb. f. REFERENCES: 191, 229, 369, 454.

Dendrobium simile Schlechter 1905 not 1906. Now considered a synonym of *Pseuderia similis* (Schlechter) Schlechter. REFERENCES: 219, 221, 271, 437, 444.

Dendrobium simile Schlechter 1906 not 1905. See *D. torricellianum* Kränzlin. REFERENCES: 220, 254, 437, 454, 486.

Dendrobium simile (Blume) J. J. Smith. Originally described as *Cadetia similis* Blume. Since *Cadetia* is now considered a valid genus by some botanists, this plant may again become a *Cadetia*. Plants originated in Irian Jaya (western New Guinea), but habitat location and elevation are unavailable. REFERENCES: 220, 470.

Dendrobium simondii Gagnepain

ORIGIN/HABITAT: Vietnam. Plants were collected near Mt. Tai-ninh in southern Vietnam (Cochinchina), that part of Vietnam lying south of about 10.8°N latitude. Habitat details are unavailable, so the following climate data should be used with caution.

CLIMATE: Station #48900, Ho Chi Minh City (Saigon), Vietnam, Lat. 10.1°N, Long. 106.1°E, at 33 ft. (11 m). Record extreme temperatures are 104°F (40°C) and 57°F (14°C).

N/HEMISPHERE	JAN	FEB	MAR	APR	MAY	JUN	JUL	AUG	SEP	OCT	NOV	DEC
°F AVG MAX	89	91	93	94	92	89	88	89	88	88	87	87
°F AVG MIN	70	71	74	77	76	75	75	75	75	74	73	71
DIURNAL RANGE	19	20	19	17	16	14	13	14	13	14	14	16
RAIN/INCHES	0.6	0.2	0.4	2.0	8.6	12.4	11.7	10.7	13.0	10.2	4.6	2.1
HUMIDITY/%	70	69	69	72	79	82	82	83	85	85	81	76
BLOOM SEASON	N/A											
DAYS CLR @ 7AM	6	5	8	5	2	2	2	1	1	1	3	4
DAYS CLR @ 1PM	3	4	5	1	0	0	9	0	0	0	0	2
RAIN/MM	15	5	10	51	218	315	297	272	330	259	117	53
°C AVG MAX	31.7	32.8	33.9	34.4	33.3	31.7	31.1	31.7	31.1	31.1	30.6	30.6
°C AVG MIN	21.1	21.7	23.3	25.0	24.4	23.9	23.9	23.9	23.9	23.3	22.8	21.7
DIURNAL RANGE	10.6	11.1	10.6	9.4	8.9	7.8	7.2	7.8	7.2	7.8	7.8	8.9
S/HEMISPHERE	JUL	AUG	SEP	OCT	NOV	DEC	JAN	FEB	MAR	APR	MAY	JUN

Cultural Recommendations

LIGHT: 2000–3000 fc.

TEMPERATURES: Throughout the year, days average 87–94°F (31–34°C), and nights average 70–76°F (21–24°C), with a diurnal range of 13–20°F (7–11°C).

HUMIDITY: 80–85% most of the year, dropping to near 70% in winter and early spring.

WATER: Rainfall is heavy from late spring through autumn, but conditions are drier for 3–4 months in winter. Cultivated plants should be kept moist but not soggy while actively growing, but water should be gradually reduced in late autumn.

FERTILIZER: ¼–½ recommended strength, applied weekly. A high nitrogen fertilizer is beneficial from spring to midsummer, but a fertilizer high in phosphates should be used in late summer and autumn.

REST PERIOD: Growing temperatures should be maintained all year. In the habitat, winter rainfall is lower, but heavy dew is common for most of the dry season. Therefore, cultivated plants should be allowed to dry somewhat between waterings, but they should not remain dry for long periods. Occasional early morning mistings between waterings may be beneficial, especially on bright, sunny days. Fertilizer should be reduced until water is increased in spring. In the habitat, light is highest in winter.

GROWING MEDIA: Plants may be mounted on tree-fern or cork slabs or potted in small pots filled with any open, fast-draining medium. Repotting may be done anytime new roots are actively growing.

Plant and Flower Information

PLANT SIZE AND TYPE: A 4–12 in. (10–30 cm) sympodial epiphyte.

PSEUDOBULB: 4–12 in. (10–30 cm) long. The pseudobulbous stems, which are enlarged at the base, consist of nodes 0.4 in. (1 cm) long.

LEAVES: The leaves are 2.4–2.8 in. (6–7 cm) long.

INFLORESCENCE: 3–5 in. (8–12 cm) long. The inflorescence emerges at the apex of the stem. The blossoms are widely spaced on the inflorescence.

FLOWERS: 8–15 per inflorescence. The white and green flowers are 0.8–1.2 in. (2–3 cm) across. The lateral sepals are somewhat sickle-shaped. The lip sidelobes are marked with violet dots. The midlobe is toothed and ruffled. The disk is green.

REFERENCES: 138, 227, 448.

Dendrobium simplex J. J. Smith

AKA: *Dendrobium sarcopodioides* J. J. Smith, *Epigeneium simplex* (J. J. Smith) Summerhayes.

ORIGIN/HABITAT: Irian Jaya (western New Guinea) near Mt. Goliath, north of the Jaya (Carstensz) Mountains, and near Angi Lake in the Arfak Mountains. Plants are also found near Laiagam in Papua New Guinea. They usually grow in scrub or mountain forests at 7850–10,150 ft. (2400–3100 m).

CLIMATE: Botanical garden records, Laiagam, Papua New Guinea, Lat. 5.5°S, Long. 143.5°E, at 7218 ft. (2200 m). Temperatures are calculated for an elevation of 8500 ft. (2600 m), resulting in probable extremes of 87°F (30°C) and 28°F (−2°C).

N/HEMISPHERE	JAN	FEB	MAR	APR	MAY	JUN	JUL	AUG	SEP	OCT	NOV	DEC
°F AVG MAX	72	73	74	72	74	74	78	73	72	74	74	72
°F AVG MIN	51	50	51	51	52	52	51	52	54	53	52	52
DIURNAL RANGE	21	23	23	21	22	22	27	21	18	21	22	20
RAIN/INCHES	4.0	4.8	6.1	7.8	8.5	9.1	8.4	9.6	9.5	8.9	6.3	4.0
HUMIDITY/%	N/A											
BLOOM SEASON							*	*				
DAYS CLR	N/A											
RAIN/MM	102	122	155	198	216	231	213	244	241	226	160	102
°C AVG MAX	22.1	22.6	23.2	22.1	23.2	23.2	25.4	22.6	22.1	23.2	23.2	22.1
°C AVG MIN	10.4	9.9	10.4	10.4	11.0	11.0	10.4	11.0	12.1	11.5	11.0	11.0
DIURNAL RANGE	11.7	12.7	12.8	11.7	12.2	12.2	15.0	11.6	10.0	11.7	12.2	11.1
S/HEMISPHERE	JUL	AUG	SEP	OCT	NOV	DEC	JAN	FEB	MAR	APR	MAY	JUN

Cultural Recommendations

LIGHT: 2000–3000 fc.

TEMPERATURES: Throughout the year, days average 72–78°F (22–25°C), and nights average 50–54°F (10–12°C), with a diurnal range of 18–27°F (10–15°C). The values in the preceding climate table represent the lower, therefore warmer, portion of the habitat, so plants should easily adapt to conditions that are 5–7°F (3–4°C) cooler than indicated.

HUMIDITY: Information is not available for this location. However, records from nearby stations indicate that averages are probably near 80% year-round.

WATER: Rainfall is heavy all year, but conditions are slightly drier for 3–4 months in winter. Rain falls as heavy showers most afternoons. Skies clear by early evening, then low clouds and mist develop again during the evening and continue until midmorning the next day. The mist is so heavy that trees and shrubs drip moisture soon after the mist forms. Cultivated plants should be kept moist with little if any drying allowed between waterings.

FERTILIZER: ¼–½ recommended strength. A balanced fertilizer should be applied weekly to biweekly throughout the year. The Royal Botanic Garden in Edinburgh uses a seaweed-based fertilizer for high-elevation plants from New Guinea.

REST PERIOD: Growing conditions should be maintained year-round. Water and fertilizer may be reduced somewhat in winter, especially for plants grown in the dark, short-day conditions common in temperate latitudes, but they should never be allowed to dry out completely. Occasional early morning mistings between waterings may be beneficial, particularly on bright, sunny days. In the habitat, light may be slightly higher in winter.

GROWING MEDIA: Plants may be mounted on tree-fern or cork slabs or potted in small pots filled with any open, fast-draining medium. Repotting may be done anytime new roots are actively growing.

MISCELLANEOUS NOTES: The bloom season shown in the climate table is based on reports from the habitat.

Plant and Flower Information

PLANT SIZE AND TYPE: A 1.2–2.4 in. (3–6 cm) sympodial epiphyte.

PSEUDOBULB: 0.4–0.8 in. (1–2 cm) long. The clustered pseudobulbs are borne on a creeping, branching rhizome. They are reddish purple and somewhat round.

LEAVES: 2 per growth. The ovate to elliptical leaves are 0.8–1.6 in. (2–4 cm) long.

INFLORESCENCE: 3 in. (8 cm) long. Two inflorescences emerge from between the leaves at the apex of the pseudobulb.

FLOWERS: 1–2, rarely more per inflorescence. The fleshy flowers are up to 1 in. (2.5 cm) across. They may not open fully. Blossoms are greenish white to greenish red with a white callus on the lip. The dorsal sepal is ovate. Lateral sepals are obliquely triangular. Petals are elliptical and wavy at the base. The unlobed lip is concave and incurved at the base.

HYBRIDIZING NOTES: Chromosome counts are 2n = 36 (ref. 152, 153, 243, 273) and 2n = about 36 (ref. 243).

REFERENCES: 83, 95, 152, 153, 221, 229, 243, 273, 445, 470, 499, 538.

PHOTOS/DRAWINGS: 83, 538.

Dendrobium simplicicaule J. J. Smith. Now considered a synonym of *Flickingeria simplicicaulis* (J. J. Smith) A. Hawkes. REFERENCES: 213, 224, 230, 231, 445, 470.

Dendrobium simplicissimum (Loureiro) Kränzlin. See *D. crumenatum* Swartz. REFERENCES: 67, 208, 254, 454.

Dendrobium sinense T. Tang and F. T. Wang

ORIGIN/HABITAT: China. Plants grow on Hainan Island at 1300–3300 ft. (400–1000 m) on Tzu-Shan (Mountain) and in the districts of Ting-An, Pao-T'inf, Le-Tung, and Pai-Sha.

CLIMATE: Station #59849, Yinggen, Hainan Island, China, Lat. 19.1°N, Long. 109.9°E, at 797 ft. (243 m). Average temperatures are calculated for an elevation of 2600 ft. (800 m). Record extreme temperatures are not available for this location.

N/HEMISPHERE	JAN	FEB	MAR	APR	MAY	JUN	JUL	AUG	SEP	OCT	NOV	DEC
°F AVG MAX	64	68	74	78	81	82	83	81	78	75	69	64
°F AVG MIN	50	54	57	62	65	67	67	67	65	62	57	50
DIURNAL RANGE	14	14	17	16	16	15	16	14	13	13	12	14
RAIN/INCHES	1.9	1.4	1.7	5.1	7.6	7.0	6.8	9.7	15.1	19.1	7.1	1.9
HUMIDITY/%	N/A											
BLOOM SEASON							*	*		*		*
DAYS CLR	N/A											
RAIN/MM	48	36	43	130	193	178	173	246	384	485	180	48
°C AVG MAX	17.8	20.0	23.4	25.6	27.3	27.8	28.4	27.3	25.6	23.9	20.6	17.8
°C AVG MIN	10.0	12.3	13.9	16.7	18.4	19.5	19.5	19.5	18.4	16.7	13.9	10.0
DIURNAL RANGE	7.8	7.7	9.5	8.9	8.9	8.3	8.9	7.2	7.2	6.7	7.8	
S/HEMISPHERE	JUL	AUG	SEP	OCT	NOV	DEC	JAN	FEB	MAR	APR	MAY	JUN

Dendrobium singalanense

Cultural Recommendations

LIGHT: 2000–3000 fc.

TEMPERATURES: Summer days average 81–83°F (27–28°C), and nights average 67°F (20°C), with a diurnal range of 14–16°F (8–9°C).

HUMIDITY: Information is not available for this location. However, records from nearby stations indicate that humidity probably averages 80–85% from late spring into autumn, dropping to 70–75% from late autumn into spring.

WATER: Rainfall is heavy from spring through autumn, but conditions are dry for 4 months in winter. Cultivated plants should be kept moist from spring into autumn, but water should be reduced in late autumn.

FERTILIZER: 1/4–1/2 recommended strength, applied weekly. A high nitrogen fertilizer is beneficial from spring to midsummer, but a fertilizer high in phosphates should be used in late summer and autumn.

REST PERIOD: Winter days average 64–68°F (18–20°C), and nights average 50–54°F (10–12°C), with a diurnal range of 14–17°F (8–10°C). While rainfall is lower in winter, additional water is available from heavy dew and overnight mist, which are common during the season. Cultivated plants should be watered less frequently in winter. They should be allowed to dry slightly between waterings but should not dry out completely or remain dry for long periods.

GROWING MEDIA: Plants may be mounted on tree-fern or cork slabs if humidity is high and plants are watered at least once daily in summer. When plants are potted, any open, fast-draining medium may be used. They may be repotted anytime new roots are growing.

MISCELLANEOUS NOTES: The bloom season shown in the climate table is based collection reports.

Plant and Flower Information

PLANT SIZE AND TYPE: A 2.0–4.3 in. (5–11 cm) sympodial epiphyte. *D. sinense* is vegetatively smaller but similar to *D. trigonopus* Rchb. f, which has slightly larger flowers.

PSEUDOBULB: 2.0–4.3 in. (5–11 cm) long. The clustered, erect stems are club shaped and taper toward the tip.

LEAVES: 3–5 per growth. The leaves are 0.7–1.3 in. (1.8–3.3 cm) long, rounded, oblong, and leathery with long black hairs.

INFLORESCENCE: Short. Inflorescences emerge laterally from nodes near the apex of the stem. The bracts on the inflorescence are sparsely covered with long black hairs.

FLOWERS: 1 per inflorescence. The flowers are 1.6–2.4 in. (4–6 cm) across. Blossoms have an elliptic-lanceolate dorsal sepal, asymmetrical ovate-lanceolate lateral sepals, and elliptic-oblong petals. The ovate lip has a heart-shaped, rounded midlobe that is irregularly ruffled at the front margin.

HYBRIDIZING NOTES: Chromosome count, 2n = 38. *D. sinense* is self-fertile. Pollen from a different flower on the same plant produces seed.

REFERENCES: 232, 506, 528.

Dendrobium singalanense Kränzlin. See *D. hymenopterum*
Hooker f. REFERENCES: 220, 254, 454, 455.

Dendrobium singaporense A. Hawkes and A. H. Heller

AKA: *D. teres* Lindley not Roxburgh.

ORIGIN/HABITAT: Malaya, Singapore, Sumatra, Borneo, and the southern part of Peninsular Thailand. In Malaya, plants grow in Pahang State near Kuala Lipis, in Perak State near Taiping, in the states of Penang and Johore, and in Singapore. They are widespread, but uncommon, and usually grow in moist habitats.

CLIMATE: Station #49630, Temerloh, Pahang, Malaya, Lat. 3.5°N, Long. 102.4°E, at 163 ft. (50 m). Temperatures are calculated for an elevation of 1000 ft. (300 m), resulting in probable extremes of 94°F (35°C) and 61°F (16°C).

N/HEMISPHERE	JAN	FEB	MAR	APR	MAY	JUN	JUL	AUG	SEP	OCT	NOV	DEC
°F AVG MAX	82	85	87	88	88	87	87	87	87	86	84	83
°F AVG MIN	68	68	69	70	70	70	69	69	69	70	70	69
DIURNAL RANGE	14	17	18	18	18	17	18	18	18	16	14	14
RAIN/INCHES	7.8	3.9	6.0	7.6	6.6	4.3	3.4	5.6	6.5	9.3	9.7	10.1
HUMIDITY/%	87	83	84	85	86	86	87	84	86	87	89	88
BLOOM SEASON	N/A											
DAYS CLR @ 7AM	0	0	2	1	1	0	2	2	2	0	0	0
DAYS CLR @ 1PM	1	1	2	1	1	1	0	1	1	0	0	0
RAIN/MM	198	99	152	193	168	109	86	142	165	236	246	257
°C AVG MAX	27.9	29.6	30.7	31.2	31.2	30.7	30.7	30.7	30.7	30.1	29.0	28.5
°C AVG MIN	20.1	20.1	20.7	21.2	21.2	21.2	20.7	20.7	20.7	21.2	21.2	20.7
DIURNAL RANGE	7.8	9.5	10.0	10.0	10.0	9.5	10.0	10.0	10.0	8.9	7.8	7.8
S/HEMISPHERE	JUL	AUG	SEP	OCT	NOV	DEC	JAN	FEB	MAR	APR	MAY	JUN

Cultural Recommendations

LIGHT: 2500–3500 fc.

TEMPERATURES: Throughout the year, days average 82–88°F (28–31°C), and nights average 68–70°F (20–21°C), with a diurnal range of 14–18°F (8–10°C).

HUMIDITY: 85–90% year-round.

WATER: Rainfall is moderate to heavy all year, with brief, 1–2 month, slightly drier periods in winter and summer. Cultivated plants should be kept moist, with little if any drying allowed between waterings during most of the year.

FERTILIZER: 1/4–1/2 recommended strength. A balanced fertilizer should be applied weekly to biweekly throughout the year.

REST PERIOD: Growing conditions should be maintained all year. However, water should be reduced for a month or so in summer, and again in late winter. Plants should be allowed to dry slightly between waterings, but should not remain dry for long periods. Fertilizer should be reduced or eliminated anytime the plant is not growing. In the habitat, seasonal light variation is minor.

GROWING MEDIA: Plants may be mounted on tree-fern or cork slabs if humidity is high and plants are watered at least once daily in summer. When plants are potted, any open, fast-draining medium may be used. They may be repotted anytime new roots are growing.

Plant and Flower Information

PLANT SIZE AND TYPE: An 8–16 in. (20–40 cm) sympodial epiphyte.

PSEUDOBULB: 8–16 in. (20–40 cm) long. The rigid stems are somewhat zig-zag and are very slender along their entire length.

LEAVES: 2–10 per growth. The widely spaced leaves are 2–4 in. (5–10 cm) long. They are slightly curved, nearly terete, and held at a wide angle to the stem. The leaves are said to resemble *Vanda teres*.

INFLORESCENCE: Short. Flowers are borne along the leafless, apical 30–50% of the stem. The blossoms open one at a time from tufts of bracts.

FLOWERS: 1 per inflorescence. The flowers are 0.8–1.6 in. (2.0–4.0 cm) across when spread, but they normally do not open fully. The white, fleshy flowers have orange veins and flame-colored keels near the apex of the lip. The lip is upcurved, with erect, broadly triangular sidelobes and a narrow, triangular tip. Blossoms are fragrant.

REFERENCES: 191, 200, 202, 229, 254, 317, 395, 402, 452, 454, 455.

PHOTOS/DRAWINGS: 454, 455.

Dendrobium singkawangense J. J. Smith

AKA: Spelled *D. singkawangeme* in Masamune (ref. 286).

ORIGIN/HABITAT: Borneo. Plants were originally discovered in southwestern Borneo, near the village of Singkawang. They were growing in fields with scattered trees. Habitat elevation was not reported. Plants have since been found growing in lower mountain forests in the Mt. Kinabalu region of Sabah at about 4600 ft. (1400 m).

CLIMATE: Station #49613, Tambunan, Sabah, Borneo, Lat. 5.7°N, Long. 116.4°E, at 1200 ft. (366 m). Temperatures are calculated for an elevation of 4800 ft. (1460 m), resulting in probable extremes of 86°F (30°C) and 42°F (6°C).

N/HEMISPHERE	JAN	FEB	MAR	APR	MAY	JUN	JUL	AUG	SEP	OCT	NOV	DEC
°F AVG MAX	74	75	77	78	78	77	77	77	77	76	75	74
°F AVG MIN	55	53	54	55	56	55	54	54	55	55	55	56
DIURNAL RANGE	19	22	23	23	22	22	23	23	22	21	20	18
RAIN/INCHES	5.8	3.7	5.8	7.5	8.2	7.3	5.1	4.9	6.4	7.0	6.8	6.0
HUMIDITY/%	N/A											
BLOOM SEASON					*							
DAYS CLR	N/A											
RAIN/MM	147	94	147	190	208	185	130	124	163	178	173	152
°C AVG MAX	23.4	24.0	25.1	25.6	25.6	25.1	25.1	25.1	25.1	24.5	24.0	23.4
°C AVG MIN	12.8	11.7	12.3	12.8	13.4	12.8	12.3	12.3	12.8	12.8	12.8	13.4
DIURNAL RANGE	10.6	12.3	12.8	12.8	12.2	12.3	12.8	12.8	12.3	11.7	11.2	10.0
S/HEMISPHERE	JUL	AUG	SEP	OCT	NOV	DEC	JAN	FEB	MAR	APR	MAY	JUN

Cultural Recommendations

LIGHT: 2500–3500 fc.

TEMPERATURES: Throughout the year, days average 74–78°F (23–26°C), and nights average 53–56°F (12–13°C), with a diurnal range of 18–23°F (10–13°C).

HUMIDITY: Information is not available for this location. However, records from nearby locations indicate that humidity probably averages 80–85% year-round.

WATER: Rainfall is moderate to heavy all year, with a brief, slightly drier period in winter. Cultivated plants should be kept moist, with only slight drying allowed between waterings.

FERTILIZER: ¼–½ recommended strength. A balanced fertilizer should be applied weekly to biweekly throughout the year.

REST PERIOD: Growing temperatures should be maintained all year. Water should be reduced for cultivated plants, especially those grown in the dark, short-day conditions common in temperate-latitude winters, but plants should never be allowed to dry out completely. Fertilizer should be reduced or eliminated until water is increased in spring.

GROWING MEDIA: Plants may be mounted on tree-fern or cork slabs if humidity is high and plants are watered at least once daily in summer. When plants are potted, any open, fast-draining medium may be used. They may be repotted anytime new roots are growing.

MISCELLANEOUS NOTES: The bloom season shown in the climate table is based on collection reports.

Plant and Flower Information

PLANT SIZE AND TYPE: An 8 in. (20 cm) sympodial epiphyte.

PSEUDOBULB: 8 in. (20 cm) long. The stems are clustered.

LEAVES: Several per growth. The oblong leaves are about 1.7 in. (4.3 cm) long and recurved at the tip. They have 2 rounded lobes at the apex. They are initially covered with dark hairs.

INFLORESCENCE: 0.4–0.8 in. (1–2 cm) long. Inflorescences emerge through the leaf bases.

FLOWERS: 3–4 per inflorescence. The fleshy flowers are 1.2 in. (3 cm) across. Sepals and petals are creamy white. Blossoms have ovate, acute petals. The lip midlobe, which is bright orange on the inside, is very warty. The sidelobes are large relative to the midlobe.

REFERENCES: 25, 225, 286, 487, 592.

Dendrobium singulare Ames and Schweinfurth

ORIGIN/HABITAT: Sabah, Northern Borneo. Plants grow near Lobong on Mt. Kinabalu. Habitat elevation was not reported, but the elevation at Lobong is about 4800 ft. (1460 m).

CLIMATE: Station #49613, Tambunan, Sabah, Borneo, Lat. 5.7°N, Long. 116.4°E, at 1200 ft. (366 m). Temperatures are calculated for an elevation of 4800 ft. (1460 m), resulting in probable extremes of 86°F (30°C) and 42°F (6°C).

N/HEMISPHERE	JAN	FEB	MAR	APR	MAY	JUN	JUL	AUG	SEP	OCT	NOV	DEC
°F AVG MAX	74	75	77	78	78	77	77	77	77	76	75	74
°F AVG MIN	55	53	54	55	56	55	54	54	55	55	55	56
DIURNAL RANGE	19	22	23	23	22	22	23	23	22	21	20	18
RAIN/INCHES	5.8	3.7	5.8	7.5	8.2	7.3	5.1	4.9	6.4	7.0	6.8	6.0
HUMIDITY/%	N/A											
BLOOM SEASON										*		
DAYS CLR	N/A											
RAIN/MM	147	94	147	190	208	185	130	124	163	178	173	152
°C AVG MAX	23.4	24.0	25.1	25.6	25.6	25.1	25.1	25.1	25.1	24.5	24.0	23.4
°C AVG MIN	12.8	11.7	12.3	12.8	13.4	12.8	12.3	12.3	12.8	12.8	12.8	13.4
DIURNAL RANGE	10.6	12.3	12.8	12.8	12.2	12.3	12.8	12.8	12.3	11.7	11.2	10.0
S/HEMISPHERE	JUL	AUG	SEP	OCT	NOV	DEC	JAN	FEB	MAR	APR	MAY	JUN

Cultural Recommendations

LIGHT: 2000–3000 fc.

TEMPERATURES: Throughout the year, days average 74–78°F (23–26°C), and nights average 53–56°F (12–13°C), with a diurnal range of 18–23°F (10–13°C).

HUMIDITY: Information is not available for this location. However, records from nearby locations indicate that humidity probably averages 80–85% year-round.

WATER: Rainfall is moderate to heavy all year, with a brief, slightly drier period in winter. Cultivated plants should be kept moist, with only slight drying allowed between waterings.

FERTILIZER: ¼–½ recommended strength. A balanced fertilizer should be applied weekly to biweekly throughout the year.

REST PERIOD: Growing temperatures should be maintained all year. Water should be reduced for cultivated plants, especially those grown in the dark, short-day conditions common in temperate-latitude winters, but they should never be allowed to dry out completely. Fertilizer should be reduced or eliminated until water is increased in spring.

GROWING MEDIA: Plants may be potted or mounted on tree-fern slabs. The roots, which do not branch, are fibrous with black spreading hairs. They should never be allowed to dry completely. Repotting may be done anytime new roots are growing.

MISCELLANEOUS NOTES: The bloom season shown in the climate table is based on collection reports.

Plant and Flower Information

PLANT SIZE AND TYPE: A 10 in. (25 cm) sympodial epiphyte.

PSEUDOBULB: 10 in. (25 cm) long. The suberect stems are shiny yellow with dark bands at the nodes. They are somewhat zigzag, flattened, and covered by clasping leaf sheaths. The unbranched roots are more or less covered with spreading black hairs especially on the older parts.

LEAVES: Many. The distichous leaves are 2 in. (5 cm) long. They are rigid, lanceolate, and abruptly taper to a slender tip.

INFLORESCENCE: Short. Inflorescences arise from scales opposite the uppermost leaves.

FLOWERS: 1 per inflorescence. The small flowers, which open in succession, are 0.6 in. (1.5 cm) across. The blossoms are purple and yellow. The dorsal sepal is ovate. Lateral sepals are broadly triangular. The petals are linear and taper to a threadlike tip. The 3-lobed lip has conspicuously spreading sidelobes with uneven, hairy margins. The midlobe, which is shorter than the sidelobes, is notched to the 3-toothed, fleshy callus, thus forming 2 small, linear, diverging lobes.

REFERENCES: 12, 222, 286, 592.

Dendrobium sinuatum (Lindley) Lindley ex Rchb. f. not Schlechter

AKA: *Aporum sinuatum* Lindley. Holttum (ref. 200) lists *D. paniferum* J. J. Smith as a possible synonym.

ORIGIN/HABITAT: Southeast Asia. The habitat includes Sabah, Borneo, Siberut Island in the Mentawi Island group off the west coast of Sumatra, Malaya, and Singapore. In Malaya, plants are found at Batu Pahat in Johore State, and in Pinang (Penang), Melaka (Malacca), and the Cameron Highlands. Ridley (ref. 402) indicated that plants were common on mangroves and orchard trees at about 5500 ft. (1680 m), but plants are reported from both the mountains and lowlands of Malaya.

CLIMATE: Station #48665, Melaka (Malacca), Malaya, Lat. 2.3°N, Long. 102.3°E, at 40 ft. (12 m). Temperatures are calculated for an elevation of 1000 ft. (300 m), resulting in probable extremes of 96°F (36°C) and 58°F (14°C).

N/HEMISPHERE	JAN	FEB	MAR	APR	MAY	JUN	JUL	AUG	SEP	OCT	NOV	DEC
°F AVG MAX	85	86	86	86	86	85	85	85	85	85	85	85
°F AVG MIN	69	69	69	70	70	70	69	69	69	69	69	69
DIURNAL RANGE	16	17	17	16	16	15	16	16	16	16	16	16
RAIN/INCHES	3.9	3.7	4.9	7.4	6.8	7.9	7.8	10.3	8.8	10.1	8.7	6.5
HUMIDITY/%	79	79	82	85	85	83	84	84	84	84	84	82
BLOOM SEASON	N/A											
DAYS CLR @ 7AM	1	1	1	1	1	1	2	1	1	1	0	1
DAYS CLR @ 1PM	1	1	1	1	1	1	1	1	1	1	0	0
RAIN/MM	99	94	124	188	173	201	198	262	224	257	221	165
°C AVG MAX	29.4	29.9	29.9	29.9	29.9	29.4	29.4	29.4	29.4	29.4	29.4	29.4
°C AVG MIN	20.5	20.5	20.5	21.0	21.0	21.0	20.5	20.5	20.5	20.5	20.5	20.5
DIURNAL RANGE	8.9	9.4	9.4	8.9	8.9	8.4	8.9	8.9	8.9	8.9	8.9	8.9
S/HEMISPHERE	JUL	AUG	SEP	OCT	NOV	DEC	JAN	FEB	MAR	APR	MAY	JUN

Cultural Recommendations

LIGHT: 2000–3000 fc.

TEMPERATURES: Throughout the year, days average 85–86°F (29–30°C), and nights average 69–70°F (21°C), with a diurnal range of 15–17°F (8–9°C). These values represent conditions in the lower elevations of the habitat. Because the plants are found over a wide range of elevations, they should adapt to conditions 10–12°F (6–7°C) cooler than indicated above.

HUMIDITY: 80–85% year-round.

WATER: Rainfall is moderate to heavy all year, but conditions are slightly drier for about 2 months in winter. Cultivated plants should be kept moist with only slight drying allowed between waterings.

FERTILIZER: ¼–½ recommended strength. A balanced fertilizer should be applied weekly to biweekly throughout the year.

REST PERIOD: Growing conditions should be maintained all year. Water and fertilizer may be reduced somewhat in winter, especially for plants cultivated in the dark, short-day conditions common in the temperate latitudes. Plants should never be allowed to dry out completely, however. In the habitat, seasonal light variation is minor.

GROWING MEDIA: Mounting plants on tree-fern or cork slabs accommodates their pendulous growth habit. However, humidity must be high and plants must be watered at least once a day in summer. If plants cannot be mounted, small pots or hanging baskets may be filled with an open, fast-draining medium. Repotting may be done anytime new roots are actively growing.

Plant and Flower Information

PLANT SIZE AND TYPE: A 4–8 in. (10–20 cm) sympodial epiphyte.

PSEUDOBULB: 4–8 in. (10–20 cm) long, rarely to 12 in. (30 cm) long. The stems, which may be simple or branching, are leafy and pendulous.

LEAVES: Many. The lanceolate leaves are 0.4–1.0 in. (1.0–2.5 cm) long, flat, and fleshy. They are densely overlapping and alternate along the stem in 2 rows.

INFLORESCENCE: Short. The flowers are clustered at or near the apex of the stem.

FLOWERS: Few per inflorescence. The flowers are 0.4–0.5 in. (1.0–1.2 cm) across. The blossoms may be yellow, orange-yellow, or orange, although some clones may be deep orange-purple. The lateral sepals are triangular while the dorsal sepal and smaller petals are lanceolate. The fleshy lip has toothlike sidelobes and a thickened, fleshy apex. The darker callus is V-shaped. The column is pale red with a darker spot at the base.

REFERENCES: 200, 202, 216, 254, 286, 295, 317, 395, 402, 454, 455.

PHOTOS/DRAWINGS: *454*, 455.

Dendrobium sinuatum Schlechter not Lindley. See *D. cultratum* Schlechter. REFERENCES: 296, 536.

Dendrobium sinuosum Ames

ORIGIN/HABITAT: The Philippine Islands. Plants grow near sea level on Leyte Island near Tacloban.

CLIMATE: Station #98550, Tacloban, Leyte Island, Philippines, Lat. 11.3°N, Long. 125.0°E, at 52 ft. (16 m). Record extreme temperatures are not available for this location.

N/HEMISPHERE	JAN	FEB	MAR	APR	MAY	JUN	JUL	AUG	SEP	OCT	NOV	DEC
°F AVG MAX	83	85	86	88	89	89	87	88	87	87	86	84
°F AVG MIN	73	73	74	75	77	77	76	76	75	75	75	73
DIURNAL RANGE	10	12	12	13	12	12	11	12	12	12	11	11
RAIN/INCHES	9.4	6.2	4.4	3.3	5.8	7.8	6.9	5.7	8.3	9.1	11.4	8.5
HUMIDITY/%	N/A											
BLOOM SEASON						*						
DAYS CLR	N/A											
RAIN/MM	238	157	112	84	147	198	175	145	211	231	290	216
°C AVG MAX	28.3	29.4	30.0	31.1	31.7	31.7	30.6	31.1	30.6	30.6	30.0	28.9
°C AVG MIN	22.8	22.8	23.3	23.9	25.0	25.0	24.4	24.4	23.9	23.9	23.9	22.8
DIURNAL RANGE	5.5	6.6	6.7	7.2	6.7	6.7	6.2	6.7	6.7	6.7	6.1	6.1
S/HEMISPHERE	JUL	AUG	SEP	OCT	NOV	DEC	JAN	FEB	MAR	APR	MAY	JUN

Cultural Recommendations

LIGHT: 2500–3500 fc.

TEMPERATURES: Throughout the year, days average 83–89°F (28–32°C), and nights average 73–77°F (23–25°C), with a diurnal range of 10–13°F (6–7°C).

HUMIDITY: Information is not available for this location. However, reports from other stations in the region indicate that humidity is probably 80–85% most of the year, dropping to 75–80% in late winter and early spring.

WATER: Rainfall is moderate to heavy most of the year. A slightly drier period occurs in late winter and early spring. Cultivated plants should be kept evenly moist, with only slight drying between waterings.

FERTILIZER: ¼–½ recommended strength. A balanced fertilizer should be applied weekly to biweekly throughout the year.

REST PERIOD: Growing conditions should be maintained all year. In the habitat, a brief rest may occur during the slightly drier period in late winter and early spring. Water may be reduced for about 2 months for cultivated plants. They should dry out slightly between waterings, but should not remain dry for long periods. Fertilizer should be limited anytime water is reduced. In the habitat, seasonal light variation is minor.

GROWING MEDIA: Plants may be mounted on tree-fern or cork slabs or potted in small pots filled with any open, fast-draining medium. Repotting may be done anytime new roots are growing.

MISCELLANEOUS NOTES: The bloom season shown in the climate table is based on collection reports.

Plant and Flower Information

PLANT SIZE AND TYPE: A 6–12 in. (15–30 cm) sympodial epiphyte.

PSEUDOBULB: 6–12 in. (15–30 cm) long.

LEAVES: 6–13 per growth. The leaves are less than 2 in. (5 cm) long. They are distichous and alternate along the stem. On the lower 30% of the stem, the leaves are linear-lanceolate, but toward the apex of the stem they are widely spaced and gradually become smaller and more terete.

INFLORESCENCE: Short. The racemes emerge from bracts near the apex of the stem.

FLOWERS: Few per inflorescence. The flowers are 0.4 in. (1 cm) across and open in succession. Sepals and petals are white. Lateral sepals are triangular. The petals and dorsal sepal are narrowly lanceolate. Sepals are pointed. The obscurely 3-lobed lip is white with purple and yellow markings. The margins are irregularly scalloped and toothed. The disk has 3 elevated lines.

REFERENCES: 12, 223, 296, 536.

Dendrobium sitanalae J. J. Smith. Now considered a synonym of *Diplocaulobium sitanalae* (J. J. Smith) Hunt and Summerhayes. REFERENCES: 213, 221, 230, 470, 478.

Dendrobium sladei J. J. Wood and Cribb

AKA: *D. vaupelianum* as used by Yuncker not Kränzlin.

ORIGIN/HABITAT: Numerous Pacific Islands, including Samoa, Vanuatu, and Fiji. On Fiji, plants grow on isolated trees or in open forests from sea level to 2950 ft. (0–900 m). On Vanuatu, plants are found in coastal forests from sea level to 1300 ft. (0–400 m).

CLIMATE: Station #91554, Luganville, Espiritu Santo Island, Vanuatu, Lat. 15.5°S, Long. 167.1°E, at 493 ft. (150 m). Record extreme temperatures are 93°F (34°C) and 61°F (16°C).

N/HEMISPHERE	JAN	FEB	MAR	APR	MAY	JUN	JUL	AUG	SEP	OCT	NOV	DEC
°F AVG MAX	81	81	82	83	83	86	86	87	86	85	83	81
°F AVG MIN	71	71	72	72	73	74	75	74	73	74	73	72
DIURNAL RANGE	10	10	10	11	10	12	11	13	13	11	10	9
RAIN/INCHES	6.4	6.3	4.7	6.3	9.5	9.2	10.6	9.7	10.9	10.1	8.1	6.1
HUMIDITY/%	81	80	83	81	82	81	83	83	88	86	83	80
BLOOM SEASON	*	*		*								
DAYS CLR	N/A											
RAIN/MM	163	160	119	160	241	234	269	246	277	257	206	155
°C AVG MAX	27.2	27.2	27.8	28.3	28.3	30.0	30.0	30.6	30.0	29.4	28.3	27.2
°C AVG MIN	21.7	21.7	22.2	22.2	22.8	23.3	23.9	23.3	22.8	23.3	22.8	22.2
DIURNAL RANGE	5.5	5.5	5.6	6.1	5.5	6.7	6.1	7.3	7.2	6.1	5.5	5.0
S/HEMISPHERE	JUL	AUG	SEP	OCT	NOV	DEC	JAN	FEB	MAR	APR	MAY	JUN

Cultural Recommendations

LIGHT: 2500–3500 fc.

TEMPERATURES: Throughout the year, days average 81–87°F (27–31°C), and nights average 71–75°F (22–24°C), with a diurnal range of 9–13°F (5–7°C).

HUMIDITY: 80–85% year-round.

WATER: Rainfall is moderate to heavy most of the year. Cultivated plants should be kept moist but not soggy, and only slight drying allowed between waterings.

FERTILIZER: ¼–½ recommended strength. A balanced fertilizer should be applied weekly to biweekly throughout the year.

REST PERIOD: Growing conditions should be maintained all year. Water and fertilizer may be reduced somewhat in winter for plants grown in the dark, short-day conditions common in temperate latitudes. They should not be allowed to dry out completely, however.

GROWING MEDIA: Mounting plants on tree-fern or cork slabs accommodates their pendulous growth habit. However, humidity must be high and plants must be watered at least once a day in summer. If plants cannot be mounted, small pots or hanging baskets may be filled with an open, fast-draining medium. Repotting may be done anytime new roots are actively growing.

MISCELLANEOUS NOTES: The bloom season shown in the climate table is based on reports from the habitat. Fruits are present in May (Nov.). Cultivation reports indicate summer blooming.

Plant and Flower Information

PLANT SIZE AND TYPE: A 79 in. (200 cm) sympodial epiphyte.

PSEUDOBULB: 79 in. (200 cm) long. The slender, pendulous stems are covered by sheathlike leaf bases.

LEAVES: Many. The distichous leaves are 2–4 in. (5–10 cm) long. They are lanceolate and rigidly leathery.

INFLORESCENCE: 1.6 in. (4 cm) long. Inflorescences emerge opposite the leaves at nodes along the apical part of the stem.

FLOWERS: 2 per inflorescence. The fleshy flowers are 1.0–1.2 in. (2.5–3.0 cm) long. Blossoms emerge as a pair with their bases together. They are creamy straw-yellow with reddish brown or reddish purple markings on the lip sidelobes and an orange blotch at the base of the column foot. The sepals are more or less pointed, lanceolate, and somewhat incurved. The 3-lobed lip, which is strongly recurved at the tip, has a ruffled, uneven margin. The sidelobes are narrowly triangular, erect, and pointed. The midlobe is triangular-ovate. The disk is roughened and warty, becoming a hairy median nerve behind the sidelobes. Blossoms are fragrant and short-lived.

REFERENCES: 93, 179, 234, 252, 270, 466.

PHOTOS/DRAWINGS: *93, 270,* 540.

Dendrobium smillieae F. Mueller

AKA: Sometimes spelled *D. smilliae*. Clements (ref. 67) includes the Australian names *D. hollrungii* Kränzlin var. *australiense* Rendle, *D. ophioglossum* Rchb. f., and *D. smillieae* var. *ophioglossum* (Rchb. f.) Bailey. J. J. Smith (ref. 470) includes *D. hollrungii* Kränzlin, *D. kaernbachii* Kränzlin, and *D. pachyceras* F. Mueller and Kränzlin as synonyms, but we found no recent use of this synonymy.

ORIGIN/HABITAT: Northeast Australia from the Burdekin River to the tip of the Cape York Peninsula, the islands of the Torres Straits, and across all of New Guinea. In Australia, plants are found from near sea level to 1950 ft. (0–600 m). They usually grow in lowland areas, but they are also plentiful in the lower mountains. The most common habitat is open forest near the edge of rainforests. Plants grow on tree trunks, tree ferns, rocks, and on hollow limbs or tree forks where bark and leaves have accumulated and composted to form a coarse soil. In New Guinea, plants grow on swamp trees, rocky outcrops, and rock faces in lowland forests and old plantations.

CLIMATE: Station #94283, Cooktown, Australia, Lat. 15.5°S, Long. 145.2°E, at 24 ft. (7 m). Temperatures are calculated for an elevation of 1000 ft. (300 m), resulting in probable extremes of 101°F (39°C) and 43°F (6°C).

Dendrobium smithianum

N/HEMISPHERE	JAN	FEB	MAR	APR	MAY	JUN	JUL	AUG	SEP	OCT	NOV	DEC
°F AVG MAX	76	77	79	82	85	86	86	85	83	82	79	77
°F AVG MIN	63	64	67	70	72	72	72	72	72	70	67	65
DIURNAL RANGE	13	13	12	12	13	14	14	13	11	12	12	12
RAIN/INCHES	0.9	1.2	0.6	1.0	2.5	6.6	14.4	13.7	15.3	8.8	2.8	2.0
HUMIDITY/%	73	69	68	67	68	71	75	76	77	75	74	75
BLOOM SEASON	*	*	*	*								*
DAYS CLR	N/A											
RAIN/MM	23	30	15	25	64	168	366	348	389	224	71	51
°C AVG MAX	24.3	24.9	26.0	27.7	29.3	29.9	29.9	29.3	28.2	27.7	26.0	24.9
°C AVG MIN	17.1	17.7	19.3	21.0	22.1	22.1	22.1	22.1	22.1	21.0	19.3	18.2
DIURNAL RANGE	7.2	7.2	6.7	6.7	7.2	7.8	7.8	7.2	6.1	6.7	6.7	6.7
S/HEMISPHERE	JUL	AUG	SEP	OCT	NOV	DEC	JAN	FEB	MAR	APR	MAY	JUN

Cultural Recommendations

LIGHT: 1800–2500 fc. Diffused or barely dappled light is preferred. Direct sunlight should be avoided, as the thin leaves burn easily.

TEMPERATURES: Summer days average 85–86°F (29–30°C), and nights average 72°F (22°C), with a diurnal range of 13–14°F (7–8°C). The diurnal range varies only 3°F (2°C) all year.

HUMIDITY: 70–75% year-round, but humidity is probably greater than indicated in the habitat. Growers recommend a very humid atmosphere.

WATER: Rainfall is moderate to heavy in summer and early autumn, but conditions are drier in winter. Cultivated plants should be kept moist but not soggy while actively growing. Water should be reduced after new growths mature in autumn.

FERTILIZER: ½ recommended strength, applied weekly. A high-nitrogen fertilizer is beneficial from spring to midsummer, but a fertilizer high in phosphates should be used in late summer and autumn. Growers indicate that plants are fast-growing and utilize more fertilizer than many Dendrobium.

REST PERIOD: Winter days average 76–79°F (24–26°C), and nights average 63–67°F (17–19°C), with a diurnal range of 12–13°F (7°C). Some growers recommend winter lows of 59°F (15°C). In the habitat, rainfall is lowest in winter; but heavy dew and mist are common, so additional moisture is usually available. Cultivated plants should be allowed to dry slightly between waterings, but should not dry out completely or remain dry for long periods. Some growers indicate that plants are healthiest when watered frequently, particularly if temperatures are warm. However, other growers recommend a definite rest, with just enough water given so that plants do not dry completely. D. smillieae blooms best if it is allowed to dry enough to lose a few leaves in spring. In the habitat, light is highest in winter. Plants may require higher winter light to bloom.

GROWING MEDIA: Plants may be mounted on tree-fern or cork slabs if humidity is high and plants are watered at least once daily in summer. When plants are potted, any open, fast-draining medium may be used. They may be repotted anytime new roots are growing.

MISCELLANEOUS NOTES: The winter-spring bloom season shown in the climate table is based on reports from the habitat. However, cultivation reports from northern hemisphere growers indicate that D. smillieae may bloom anytime during the year except winter. Cultivated plants often produce their first blooms when only a few inches tall. Growers report that plants are relatively tough, with strong powers of rehabilitation. In nature, new growth is produced in the wet season and these stems retain their leaves for about 1 year. The leaves then fall before the plant blooms.

Plant and Flower Information

PLANT SIZE AND TYPE: Usually about 31 in. (80 cm) tall. Plants are normally robust, sympodial epiphytes that may be as small as 6 in. (15 cm) or as large as 118 in. (300 cm).

PSEUDOBULB: 31 in. (80 cm) long. The stems are canelike. Nodes are more widely spaced at the base than at the apex.

LEAVES: Many. The papery leaves are up to 6–7 in. (15–18 cm) long and quickly deciduous. They are lance-shaped to ovate with a pointed tip.

INFLORESCENCE: 5 in. (13 cm) long. Racemes are densely flowered along their entire length. They arise from leafless stems.

FLOWERS: Many per inflorescence. The nearly tubular flowers are 0.6–0.8 in. (1.5–2.0 cm) long and may remain somewhat closed. The waxy sepals and petals are yellow to greenish yellow with a rose suffusion and green or pink tips. The sepals are obliquely ovate. Petals are obovate-oblong. The fleshy lip, which is not lobed, is decorated with 2 raised lines. It is more intensely colored, with bright green at the tip. The spur is purple.

HYBRIDIZING NOTES: Chromosome counts are 2n = 38 as D. smillieae (ref. 151, 153, 154, 187, 188, 273, 504, 580) and as D. ophioglossum (ref. 151).

REFERENCES: 25, 36, 67, 79, 105, 151, 153, 154, 179, 187, 188, 216, 240, 254, 262, 273, 302, 304, 307, 325, 352, 371, 390, 421, 430, 470, 504, 510, 533, 537, 552, 554, 570, 580, 581.

PHOTOS/DRAWINGS: 24, *36, 79*, 105, 240, *262, 304, 307*, 325, *371, 390, 430, 533, 554, 581*.

Dendrobium smithianum Schlechter

AKA: Schlechter (ref. 436) includes D. concavum J. J. Smith var. celebense J. J. Smith as a possible synonym. He indicated that D. smithianum var. nebularum Schlechter might be a mountain form of D. smithianum.

ORIGIN/HABITAT: Northern Sulawesi (Celebes). Plants were found at about 500 ft. (150 m) near Ayermadidi and at about 250 ft. (80 m) along the Lampasioe River in the Toli-Toli district. Schlechter (ref. 436) collected D. smithianum var. nebularum in mountain forests near Tondano (Tomohon) on the Minahassa Peninsula at about 2600 ft. (800 m).

CLIMATE: Station #97014, Manado, Sulawesi, Indonesia, Lat. 1.5°N, Long. 124.9°E, at 264 ft. (80 m). Temperatures are calculated for an elevation of 1800 ft. (550 m), resulting in probable extremes of 92°F (33°C) and 60°F (16°C).

N/HEMISPHERE	JAN	FEB	MAR	APR	MAY	JUN	JUL	AUG	SEP	OCT	NOV	DEC
°F AVG MAX	80	80	80	81	82	82	82	84	84	84	82	81
°F AVG MIN	68	68	68	68	69	68	68	68	68	67	68	69
DIURNAL RANGE	12	12	12	13	13	14	14	16	16	17	14	12
RAIN/INCHES	18.6	13.8	12.2	8.0	6.4	6.5	4.8	4.0	3.4	4.9	8.9	14.7
HUMIDITY/%	84	83	83	83	81	80	75	72	75	77	82	83
BLOOM SEASON	*										*	*
DAYS CLR @ 8AM	4	3	6	11	11	12	12	12	14	17	12	8
DAYS CLR @ 2PM	1	1	1	2	1	3	3	4	4	4	1	1
RAIN/MM	472	351	310	203	163	165	122	102	86	124	226	373
°C AVG MAX	26.6	26.6	26.6	27.2	27.7	27.7	27.7	28.9	28.9	28.9	27.7	27.2
°C AVG MIN	20.0	20.0	20.0	20.0	20.5	20.0	20.0	20.0	20.0	19.4	20.0	20.5
DIURNAL RANGE	6.6	6.6	6.6	7.2	7.2	7.7	7.7	8.9	8.9	9.5	7.7	6.7
S/HEMISPHERE	JUL	AUG	SEP	OCT	NOV	DEC	JAN	FEB	MAR	APR	MAY	JUN

Cultural Recommendations

LIGHT: 2500–4000 fc. In the habitat, summer skies are frequently clear in the morning but cloudy in the afternoon.

TEMPERATURES: Throughout the year, days average 80–84°F (27–29°C), and nights average 67–69°F (19–21°C), with a diurnal range of 12–17°F (7–10°C). Extreme temperatures are within 10°F (6°C) of the averages, indicating that the plant may not tolerate large seasonal temperature fluctuations. The daily temperature range is greater than the seasonal variation.

HUMIDITY: 70–80% in summer and early autumn, increasing to 80–85% in winter and spring.

WATER: Rainfall is moderate to heavy all year. The driest weather occurs in late summer when temperatures are warm. Cultivated plants should be kept moist but not soggy. Warm water might be beneficial.

FERTILIZER: ¼–½ recommended strength. A balanced fertilizer should be applied weekly to biweekly throughout the year.

REST PERIOD: Growing temperatures should be maintained all year. The plants may rest during the 1–2 month drier period which occurs in late summer and coincides with the period of greatest diurnal range. Cultivated plants should dry out slightly during this period, but they should never remain dry for long. The heaviest rainfall in the habitat occurs in winter, but water should not be increased for cultivated plants. In fact, water should be reduced somewhat for plants grown in the dark, short-day conditions common in temperate latitudes, but they should not be allowed to dry out completely.

GROWING MEDIA: Plants may be mounted on tree-fern or cork slabs or potted in small pots filled with any open, fast-draining medium. Repotting may be done anytime new roots are growing.

MISCELLANEOUS NOTES: The bloom season shown in the climate table is based on reports from the habitat.

Plant and Flower Information

PLANT SIZE AND TYPE: A 6–14 in. (15–35 cm) sympodial epiphyte.

PSEUDOBULB: 6–14 in. (15–35 cm) long. The unbranched stems are erect and clustered. They arise from a very short rhizome.

LEAVES: Many. The lanceolate leaves, which are usually 0.8–2.0 in. (2–5 cm) long, taper to a narrow point at the apex. They are sickle-shaped on the lower portion of the stem, but near the apex, they become bractlike.

INFLORESCENCE: Flowers are carried in small, widely spaced bunches on the apical part of the stem.

FLOWERS: Few per inflorescence. The flowers are 0.4 in. (1 cm) across. The ovate sepals and somewhat lanceolate petals are yellowish. The white lip is marked with purple. The kidney-shaped lip is wavy with erect, oblong sidelobes. The midlobe is notched in the center with a small point in the center. It is wavy along the margin. The callus is 2-grooved.

REFERENCES: 221, 436.

Dendrobium sociale J. J. Smith

AKA: *D. batakense* J. J. Smith, *D. nhatrangense* Gagnepain. In 1992, Seidenfaden (ref. *Opera Botanica* 114) includes *D. alleizettei* Gagnepain as a synonym.

ORIGIN/HABITAT: Near Dalat in Vietnam, near Trat in southeastern Thailand, and near Bataklanden and Siborforong in Sumatra. Plants were collected at about 3600 ft. (1100 m).

CLIMATE: Station #48881, Dalat, Vietnam, Lat. 11.1°N, Long. 108.1°E, at 3156 ft. (962 m). Record extreme temperatures are 93°F (34°C) and 43°F (6°C).

N/HEMISPHERE	JAN	FEB	MAR	APR	MAY	JUN	JUL	AUG	SEP	OCT	NOV	DEC
°F AVG MAX	80	82	84	85	84	81	81	80	80	80	79	79
°F AVG MIN	56	57	59	62	65	65	65	65	65	63	60	58
DIURNAL RANGE	24	25	25	23	19	16	16	15	15	17	19	21
RAIN/INCHES	0.2	0.9	1.6	4.6	9.1	6.1	7.7	8.2	10.1	9.7	2.7	1.3
HUMIDITY/%	68	64	65	71	78	81	82	83	84	82	76	73
BLOOM SEASON	N/A											
DAYS CLR @ 7AM	13	13	13	9	5	3	2	2	2	5	7	10
DAYS CLR @ 1PM	8	8	8	2	0	0	0	0	0	1	3	4
RAIN/MM	5	23	41	117	231	155	196	208	257	246	69	33
°C AVG MAX	26.7	27.8	28.9	29.4	28.9	27.2	27.2	26.7	26.7	26.7	26.1	26.1
°C AVG MIN	13.3	13.9	15.0	16.7	18.3	18.3	18.3	18.3	18.3	17.2	15.6	14.4
DIURNAL RANGE	13.4	13.9	13.9	12.7	10.6	8.9	8.9	8.4	8.4	9.5	10.5	11.7
S/HEMISPHERE	JUL	AUG	SEP	OCT	NOV	DEC	JAN	FEB	MAR	APR	MAY	JUN

Cultural Recommendations

LIGHT: 1800–2500 fc.

TEMPERATURES: Summer days average 80–81°F (27°C), and nights average 65°F (18°C), with a diurnal range of 15–16°F (8–9°C). The warmest temperatures occur in late winter and spring. Days average 84–85°F (29°C), and nights average 59–65°F (15–18°C), with a diurnal range of 19–25°F (11–14°C).

HUMIDITY: 80–85% in summer, dropping to near 65% in late winter.

WATER: Rainfall is moderate to heavy in summer but is very light for 2 months in winter. Cultivated plants should be kept moist while growing, but water should be gradually reduced after new growths mature in autumn.

FERTILIZER: ¼–½ recommended strength, applied weekly. A high-nitrogen fertilizer is beneficial from spring to midsummer, but a fertilizer high in phosphates should be used in late summer and autumn.

REST PERIOD: Winter days average 79–82°F (26–28°C), and nights average 56–58°F (13–14°C), with a diurnal range of 21–25°F (12–14°C). The increased diurnal range results from warmer days and cooler nights. Rainfall is low for 3–4 months. For 1–2 of these months, conditions are so dry that even moisture from dew is uncommon. For cultivated plants, water and fertilizer should be reduced for 2–3 months. Plants should be allowed to dry out between waterings, but they should not remain dry for extended periods. In the habitat, light is highest in winter.

GROWING MEDIA: Plants may be mounted on tree-fern or cork slabs if humidity is high and plants are watered at least once daily in summer. When plants are potted, any open, fast-draining medium may be used. Repotting may be done anytime new roots are growing.

Plant and Flower Information

PLANT SIZE AND TYPE: A 14 in. (35 cm) sympodial terrestrial.

PSEUDOBULB: 14 in. (35 cm) long. The stemlike pseudobulbs, which may branch, are leafy near the apex.

LEAVES: Many. The linear-lanceolate leaves, which are 2 in. (5 cm) long, are minutely toothed at the apex.

INFLORESCENCE: Short. Inflorescences emerge from nodes near the apex of leafless stems.

FLOWERS: 1–3 per inflorescence. The small flowers are 0.4–0.6 in. (1.0–1.5 cm) across. The white blossoms often have a reddish purple tint and light reddish purple veins on the lip. The 3-lobed lip is yellow at the base. It has 5 central nerves, 3 of which extend nearly to the apex of the midlobe. Fine hairs are scattered along the centerline or arranged in a clump in the center. The margins of the sidelobes are uneven to toothed.

REFERENCES: 136, 169, 221, 266, 454.

PHOTOS/DRAWINGS: 454.

Dendrobium somai Hayata

ORIGIN/HABITAT: Taiwan. The plant is found in forests throughout the island at 1650–4900 ft. (500–1500 m) and is cultivated in Taipei.

CLIMATE: Station #46696, Taipei, Taiwan, Lat.25.1°N, Long.121.5°E, at 21 ft. (6 m). Record extreme temperatures are 99°F (37°C) and 33°F (1°C).

N/HEMISPHERE	JAN	FEB	MAR	APR	MAY	JUN	JUL	AUG	SEP	OCT	NOV	DEC
°F AVG MAX	66	67	71	77	84	88	92	91	88	80	75	69
°F AVG MIN	53	55	58	64	69	73	76	76	74	68	63	58
DIURNAL RANGE	13	12	13	13	15	15	16	15	14	12	12	11
RAIN/INCHES	3.8	5.3	4.3	5.3	6.9	8.8	8.8	8.7	8.2	5.5	4.2	2.9
HUMIDITY/%	84	86	86	85	85	85	82	82	83	84	84	84
BLOOM SEASON								*				
DAYS CLR @ 8AM	1	1	1	2	3	2	4	4	4	4	3	2
DAYS CLR @ 2PM	4	4	4	3	2	1	2	4	5	4	5	4
RAIN/MM	97	135	109	135	175	224	224	221	208	140	107	74
°C AVG MAX	18.9	19.4	21.7	25.0	28.9	31.1	33.3	32.8	31.1	26.7	23.9	20.6
°C AVG MIN	11.7	12.8	14.4	17.8	20.6	22.8	24.4	24.4	23.3	20.0	17.2	14.4
DIURNAL RANGE	7.2	6.6	7.3	7.2	8.3	8.3	8.9	8.4	7.8	6.7	6.7	6.2
S/HEMISPHERE	JUL	AUG	SEP	OCT	NOV	DEC	JAN	FEB	MAR	APR	MAY	JUN

Dendrobium sophronites

Cultural Recommendations

LIGHT: 2000–3000 fc. In the habitat, clear days are rare.

TEMPERATURES: Summer days average 88–92°F (31–33°C), and nights average 73–76°F (23–24°C), with a diurnal range of 15–16°F (8–9°C). The widest diurnal range occurs in summer. Because of the large range in habitat elevation, plants should adapt to conditions somewhat cooler than indicated in the climate table.

HUMIDITY: 80–85% year-round.

WATER: Rainfall is moderate to heavy all year, but conditions are slightly drier in winter. Cultivated plants should be kept moist while actively growing, but water should be gradually reduced in autumn.

FERTILIZER: ¼–½ recommended strength, applied weekly. A high-nitrogen fertilizer is beneficial from spring to midsummer, but a fertilizer high in phosphates should be used in late summer and autumn.

REST PERIOD: Winter days average 66–71°F (19–22°C), and nights average 53–58°F (12–14°C), with a diurnal range of 11–13°F (6–7°C). For 1–2 months in winter, conditions are drier, but frequent mist and heavy deposits of dew result in more available moisture than is indicated by the rainfall averages. Cultivated plants should be allowed to dry slightly between waterings, but they should not remain dry for long periods. Fertilizer should be greatly reduced or eliminated until spring.

GROWING MEDIA: Plants may be mounted on tree-fern or cork slabs if humidity is high and plants are watered at least once daily in summer. When plants are potted, any open, fast-draining medium may be used. Repotting is best done in early spring when new roots are growing.

MISCELLANEOUS NOTES: The bloom season shown in the climate table is based on records from the habitat.

Plant and Flower Information

PLANT SIZE AND TYPE: A 24 in. (60 cm) sympodial epiphyte.

PSEUDOBULB: 24 in. (60 cm) long. Pseudobulbs are clustered and erect.

LEAVES: Many on the upper part of the stem. The linear-lanceolate leaves are 0.3 in. (0.8 cm) long.

INFLORESCENCE: 0.4 in. (1 cm) long. Inflorescences emerge at nodes along the stem.

FLOWERS: 1 per inflorescence. The flowers are 0.8 in. (2 cm) across. Blossoms have linear-lanceolate sepals and linear petals. The 3-lobed lip is ovate with a ruffled margin, oblong-triangular sidelobes, and a smooth fleshy disk. Flower color was not included in the original description.

REFERENCES: 61, 194, 208, 222, 274, 279, 528.

PHOTOS/DRAWINGS: *274, 279.*

Dendrobium sophronites Schlechter. See *D. cuthbertsonii* F. Mueller. REFERENCES: 36, 49, 151, 154, 187, 188, 196, 221, 305, 326, 330, 378, 385, 430, 437, 445, 504, 580. PHOTOS/DRAWINGS: *36, 49, 124, 305, 330.*

Dendrobium sordidum King and Pantling. Now considered a synonym of *Flickingeria convexa* (Blume) A. Hawkes. REFERENCES: 213, 250, 254, 449.

Dendrobium sororium Schlechter

ORIGIN/HABITAT: Endemic to Sulawesi (Celebes). Plants grow on large solitary trees near Kakas on the Minahassa Peninsula at about 2150 ft. (650 m). Plants are cultivated in Java.

CLIMATE: Station #97014, Manado, Sulawesi, Indonesia, Lat. 1.5°N, Long. 124.9°E, at 264 ft. (80 m). Temperatures are calculated for an elevation of 2300 ft. (700 m), resulting in probable extremes of 90°F (32°C) and 58°F (15°C).

N/HEMISPHERE	JAN	FEB	MAR	APR	MAY	JUN	JUL	AUG	SEP	OCT	NOV	DEC
°F AVG MAX	78	78	78	79	80	80	80	82	82	82	80	79
°F AVG MIN	66	66	66	66	67	66	66	66	66	65	66	67
DIURNAL RANGE	12	12	12	13	13	14	14	16	16	17	14	12
RAIN/INCHES	18.6	13.8	12.2	8.0	6.4	6.5	4.8	4.0	3.4	4.9	8.9	14.7
HUMIDITY/%	84	83	83	83	81	80	75	72	75	77	82	83
BLOOM SEASON												*
DAYS CLR @ 8AM	4	3	6	11	11	12	12	12	14	17	12	8
DAYS CLR @ 2PM	1	1	1	2	1	3	3	4	4	4	1	1
RAIN/MM	472	351	310	203	163	165	122	102	86	124	226	373
°C AVG MAX	25.7	25.7	25.7	26.3	26.8	26.8	26.8	27.9	27.9	27.9	26.8	26.3
°C AVG MIN	19.0	19.0	19.0	19.0	19.6	19.0	19.0	19.0	19.0	18.5	19.0	19.6
DIURNAL RANGE	6.7	6.7	6.7	7.3	7.2	7.8	7.8	8.9	8.9	9.4	7.8	6.7
S/HEMISPHERE	JUL	AUG	SEP	OCT	NOV	DEC	JAN	FEB	MAR	APR	MAY	JUN

Cultural Recommendations

LIGHT: 1800–3000 fc. Mornings are frequently clear, but afternoons are usually overcast.

TEMPERATURES: Throughout the year, days average 78–82°F (26–28°C), and nights average 65–67°F (19–20°C), with a diurnal range of 12–17°F (7–9°C). The record high is only a few degrees above the average highs.

HUMIDITY: 70–80% in summer and early autumn, increasing to 80–85% in winter and spring.

WATER: Rainfall is moderate to heavy all year. The driest weather occurs in late summer when temperatures are warm. Cultivated plants should be kept moist but not soggy. Warm water might be beneficial.

FERTILIZER: ¼–½ recommended strength. A balanced fertilizer should be applied weekly to biweekly throughout the year.

REST PERIOD: Growing temperatures should be maintained all year. The plants may rest during the 1–2 month drier period which occurs in late summer and coincides with the period of greatest diurnal range. Cultivated plants should dry out slightly during this period, but they should never remain dry for long. The heaviest rainfall in the habitat occurs in winter, but water should not be increased then for cultivated plants. In fact, water should be reduced somewhat for plants grown in the dark, short-day conditions common in temperate latitudes, although they should not be allowed to dry out completely.

GROWING MEDIA: Plants may be mounted on tree-fern or cork slabs if humidity is high and plants are watered at least once daily in summer. When plants are potted, any open, fast-draining medium may be used. Repotting is best done in early spring when new roots are growing.

MISCELLANEOUS NOTES: The bloom season shown in the climate table is based on reports from the habitat.

Plant and Flower Information

PLANT SIZE AND TYPE: A 39 in. (100 cm) sympodial epiphyte.

PSEUDOBULB: 39 in. (100 cm) long. The densely leafy stems are clustered. The entire plant is blue-green to brownish purple-green.

LEAVES: Many. The more or less ovate-oblong leaves are about 2.4 in. (6 cm) long. They are close together, glaucous, and leathery.

INFLORESCENCE: Short. Inflorescences emerge opposite the leaves.

FLOWERS: 2 per inflorescence. Flowers are 0.7 in. (1.8 cm) across. The linear-lanceolate sepals and petals are light yellow. Lateral sepals are slightly sickle-shaped. The light orange lip is covered with long, thick hairs. It is 3-lobed with erect sidelobes and a broadly oval, wavy midlobe. Blossoms have a somewhat fetid odor.

REFERENCES: 25, 220, 436.

Dendrobium spatella Rchb. f. See *D. acinaciforme* Roxburgh. REFERENCES: 38, 46, 179, 202, 216, 254, 454, 369.

Dendrobium spathaceum Lindley

AKA: Kränzlin (ref. 254) includes the synonym *D. candidum* King and Pantling not Wallich and maintains *D. candidum* Wallich as a separate species. Hawkes (ref. 190) includes *D. spathaceum* Lindley as a synonym of *D. candidum* Wallich. Several later references include both plants as separate species.

ORIGIN/HABITAT: India. Plants are found in Sikkim and the Khasi (Khasia) hills of Assam, where they grow on rocks near rivers at 6550–7550 ft. (2000–2300 m).

CLIMATE: Station #42398, Baghdogra, India, Lat. 26.7°N, Long. 88.3°E, at 412 ft. (126 m). Temperatures are calculated for an elevation of 7000 ft. (2130 m), resulting in probable extremes of 82°F (28°C) and 14°F (–10°C).

N/HEMISPHERE	JAN	FEB	MAR	APR	MAY	JUN	JUL	AUG	SEP	OCT	NOV	DEC
°F AVG MAX	52	55	63	68	68	67	67	67	66	65	60	55
°F AVG MIN	28	32	38	46	51	54	55	55	54	48	38	31
DIURNAL RANGE	24	23	25	22	17	13	12	12	12	17	22	24
RAIN/INCHES	0.3	0.7	1.3	3.7	11.8	25.9	32.2	25.3	21.2	5.6	0.5	0.2
HUMIDITY/%	73	68	57	58	74	84	86	85	85	79	75	76
BLOOM SEASON					*							
DAYS CLR @ 6AM	21	18	15	11	5	0	1	1	4	13	23	19
DAYS CLR @ 12PM	23	16	16	11	2	2	0	1	2	10	21	18
RAIN/MM	8	18	33	94	300	658	818	643	538	142	13	5
°C AVG MAX	11.3	12.9	17.4	20.1	20.1	19.6	19.6	19.6	19.0	18.5	15.7	12.9
°C AVG MIN	-2.1	0.1	3.5	7.9	10.7	12.4	12.9	12.9	12.4	9.0	3.5	-0.4
DIURNAL RANGE	13.4	12.8	13.9	12.2	9.4	7.2	6.7	6.7	6.6	9.5	12.2	13.3
S/HEMISPHERE	JUL	AUG	SEP	OCT	NOV	DEC	JAN	FEB	MAR	APR	MAY	JUN

Cultural Recommendations

LIGHT: 2000–3000 fc. Diffused light is suggested.

TEMPERATURES: Summer days average 67–68°F (20°C), and nights average 51–55°F (11–13°C), with a diurnal range of 12–17°F (7–9°C). Because of the effects of microclimate, actual summer maximum and winter minimum temperatures in the habitat may be 8–10°F (4–6°C) warmer than indicated in the climate table.

HUMIDITY: 75–85% most of the year, dropping below 60% for 2 months in late winter or early spring.

WATER: Rainfall is extremely heavy in summer, but conditions are much drier in winter. More moisture is available at higher elevations than is recorded at the weather station. Cultivated plants should be kept wet but not soggy from spring to early autumn. Water should be gradually reduced in late autumn after new growths mature.

FERTILIZER: ¼–½ recommended strength, applied weekly. A high nitrogen fertilizer is beneficial from spring to midsummer, but a fertilizer high in phosphates should be used in late summer and autumn.

REST PERIOD: Winter days average 52–55°F (11–13°C), and nights average 28–32°F (–2–0°C), with a diurnal range of 23–24°F (13°C). Growers are cautioned that the calculated winter minimum temperatures may be too low. Observed temperatures at high-elevation stations in nearby regions suggest that average night temperatures may be 8–10°F (4–6°C) warmer than indicated. Plants should tolerate freezing temperatures, at least for short periods, if they are dry at the time; but extremes should be avoided in cultivation. In the habitat, the dry period is 4–5 months long, but for 3 months, the high humidity indicates that some additional moisture is available from heavy dew. Therefore, conditions are extremely dry for only 1–2 months. Cultivated plants should be allowed to dry out between waterings in winter, but they should not remain dry for extended periods. Occasional early morning mistings between waterings, especially on warm, sunny days, may help prevent the plants from becoming too dry. Fertilizer should be eliminated until water is increased in spring. In the habitat, light is much higher in winter.

GROWING MEDIA: Plants may be mounted on tree-fern or cork slabs if humidity is high and plants are watered at least once daily in summer. When plants are potted, any open, fast-draining medium may be used. They may be repotted anytime new roots are growing.

MISCELLANEOUS NOTES: The bloom season shown in the climate table is based on reports from the habitat. Cultivation records show blooming at the same time.

Plant and Flower Information

PLANT SIZE AND TYPE: A 10–12 in. (25–30 cm) sympodial lithophyte.

PSEUDOBULB: 10–12 in. (25–30 cm) long.

LEAVES: Many. The leaves are 2.0–2.8 in. (5–7 cm) long and spaced 1.6 in. (4 cm) apart.

INFLORESCENCE: Very short.

FLOWERS: 1–3 per inflorescence. The snow-white flowers are 1.7 in. (4.4 cm) across when spread. They are very similar to *D. candidum*. The lip has 2 elevated disks. Blossoms are sweetly fragrant.

REFERENCES: 38, 46, 179, 190, 202, 216, 254, 278, 369, 445.

PHOTOS/DRAWINGS: 46.

Dendrobium spathilabium Ames and Schweinfurth

ORIGIN/HABITAT: Northern Sumatra. Plants were originally collected at 3500–5000 ft. (1070–1520 m) near the top of a mountain along the jungle trail between Kabajakan and Tretet.

CLIMATE: Station #96009, Lhou, Sumatra, Indonesia, Lat. 5.1°N, Long. 97.2°E, at 7 ft. (2 m). Temperatures are calculated for an elevation of 4000 ft. (1220 m). Record extreme temperatures are not available for this location.

N/HEMISPHERE	JAN	FEB	MAR	APR	MAY	JUN	JUL	AUG	SEP	OCT	NOV	DEC
°F AVG MAX	71	73	74	75	75	76	75	75	73	73	72	71
°F AVG MIN	59	59	60	61	62	61	60	60	60	60	60	60
DIURNAL RANGE	12	14	14	14	13	15	15	15	13	13	12	11
RAIN/INCHES	4.8	1.9	3.3	3.2	6.6	2.2	4.8	2.8	5.0	4.6	9.2	7.6
HUMIDITY/%	N/A											
BLOOM SEASON	*											
DAYS CLR	N/A											
RAIN/MM	122	48	84	81	168	56	122	71	127	117	234	193
°C AVG MAX	21.6	22.7	23.2	23.8	23.8	24.3	23.8	23.8	22.7	22.7	22.1	21.6
°C AVG MIN	14.9	14.9	15.5	16.0	16.6	16.0	15.5	15.5	15.5	15.5	15.5	15.5
DIURNAL RANGE	6.7	7.8	7.7	7.8	7.2	8.3	8.3	8.3	7.2	7.2	6.6	6.1
S/HEMISPHERE	JUL	AUG	SEP	OCT	NOV	DEC	JAN	FEB	MAR	APR	MAY	JUN

Cultural Recommendations

LIGHT: 2000–3000 fc.

TEMPERATURES: Throughout the year, days average 71–76°F (22–24°C), and nights average 59–62°F (15–17°C), with a diurnal range of 11–15°F (6–8°C).

HUMIDITY: Information is not available for this location. However, records from nearby stations indicate that humidity probably averages near 80% year-round.

WATER: Rainfall is moderate most of the year, with brief semidry periods in midwinter and again in early summer. Cultivated plants should be allowed to dry out somewhat between waterings, but they should never dry out completely or remain dry for long periods.

FERTILIZER: ¼–½ recommended strength. A balanced fertilizer should be applied weekly to biweekly throughout the year.

REST PERIOD: Growing conditions should be maintained year-round. The wettest conditions occur in late autumn and early winter. However, water should not be increased for cultivated plants, especially those grown in the dark, short-day conditions common in temperate-latitude winters. In the habitat, seasonal light variation is minor.

GROWING MEDIA: Plants may be mounted on tree-fern or cork slabs or potted in small pots filled with any open, fast-draining medium. Repotting may be done anytime new roots are growing.

MISCELLANEOUS NOTES: The bloom season shown in the climate table is based on collection reports.

Plant and Flower Information

PLANT SIZE AND TYPE: A 14 in. (35 cm) sympodial epiphyte. The size estimate was based on an incomplete specimen.

PSEUDOBULB: 14 in. (35 cm) long. The yellow stems are slender near the apex and slightly thickened below. They are completely covered by leaf sheaths when young and become longitudinally ridged with age. Nodes are marked with dark rings. They are spaced 0.8 in. (2 cm) apart.

LEAVES: Many. The narrow, distichous leaves are 4 in. (10 cm) long. They are linear-lanceolate, unequally bilobed, and taper toward the tip. The leaf-sheaths are scaly and covered with dots.

INFLORESCENCE: Very short. The slender inflorescences arise from leafless stems.

FLOWERS: 2 per inflorescence. The tissue-thin flowers have pure white segments 0.4–0.5 in. (1.0–1.3 cm) long. The dorsal sepal is ovate-elliptic. The ovate-oblong lateral sepals are broad and cupped at the tips. Petals are oval with an irregular apical margin. The concave lip is 3-lobed near the front. It has 2 keels on the disk that converge toward the apex.

REFERENCES: 225, 298.

Dendrobium spathilingue J. J. Smith

ORIGIN/HABITAT: Bali and eastern Java. The orchids are common in the lower mountains on the south coast at 1650–2600 ft. (500–800 m). They grow on trees in deep forest, on the ground in open forests, and on rocks. They have been collected on Mt. Jagokereng and on a ridge south of Mt. Semeru.

CLIMATE: Station #97230 Bali, Indonesia, Lat. 8.7°S, Long. 115.2°E, at 16 ft. (5 m). Temperatures are calculated for an elevation of 2600 ft. (800 m), resulting in probable extremes of 88°F (31°C) and 54°F (12°C).

N/HEMISPHERE	JAN	FEB	MAR	APR	MAY	JUN	JUL	AUG	SEP	OCT	NOV	DEC
°F AVG MAX	78	77	79	80	82	81	81	80	81	82	81	79
°F AVG MIN	59	62	62	62	63	62	64	64	64	63	63	61
DIURNAL RANGE	19	15	17	18	19	19	17	16	17	19	18	18
RAIN/INCHES	3.8	1.5	0.4	4.8	7.9	14.7	15.9	8.4	8.1	5.0	1.6	2.0
HUMIDITY/%	74	72	72	72	73	76	76	78	77	75	76	75
BLOOM SEASON									*			
DAYS CLR @ 8AM	8	7	9	8	5	4	6	3	3	10	8	9
DAYS CLR @ 2PM	13	14	16	10	6	2	5	3	5	10	12	12
RAIN/MM	97	38	10	122	201	373	404	213	206	127	41	51
°C AVG MAX	25.8	25.2	26.3	26.9	28.0	27.4	27.4	26.9	27.4	28.0	27.4	26.3
°C AVG MIN	15.2	16.9	16.9	16.9	17.4	16.9	18.0	18.0	18.0	17.4	17.4	16.3
DIURNAL RANGE	10.6	8.3	9.4	10.0	10.6	10.5	9.4	8.9	9.4	10.6	10.0	10.0
S/HEMISPHERE	JUL	AUG	SEP	OCT	NOV	DEC	JAN	FEB	MAR	APR	MAY	JUN

Cultural Recommendations

LIGHT: 1800–2400 fc. Light should be diffused or barely dappled, and direct sunlight avoided.

TEMPERATURES: Throughout the year, days average 77–82°F (25–28°C), and nights average 59–64°F (15–18°C), with a diurnal range of 15–19°F (8–11°C).

HUMIDITY: 70–75% year-round.

WATER: Rainfall is very heavy in summer, but conditions are quite dry for 1–2 months in late winter. Cultivated plants should be kept moist from spring to early autumn, but water should be reduced in late autumn.

FERTILIZER: ¼–½ recommended strength. A balanced fertilizer should be applied weekly to biweekly throughout the year.

REST PERIOD: Growing temperatures should be maintained all year. Water and fertilizer should be reduced in winter. For 1–2 months, plants should be allowed to dry out somewhat between waterings, but they should not remain dry for long periods. In the habitat, light is somewhat higher in winter, but whether this is important in cultivation is unknown.

GROWING MEDIA: Mounting plants on tree-fern or cork slabs accommodates their untidy growth habit. However, humidity must be high and plants must be watered at least once a day in summer. If plants cannot be mounted, hanging pots or baskets may be filled with an open, fast-draining medium. Repotting may be done anytime new roots are actively growing.

MISCELLANEOUS NOTES: The bloom season shown in the climate table is based on reports from the habitat. Plants that produce flowers which last a single day commonly bloom several times during the year. Flowering occurs 8 days after a sudden 10°F (5°C) drop in daytime temperatures.

Plant and Flower Information

PLANT SIZE AND TYPE: A 79 in. (200 cm) sympodial epiphyte, terrestrial, or lithophyte. Plants have a scrambling, untidy growth habit.

PSEUDOBULB: 79 in. (200 cm) long. The stems frequently branch and root. They are dark, elongated, and straggling.

LEAVES: 3–8 per growth. The leaves are 0.8–2.0 in. (2–5 cm) long. They are spaced about 0.6 in. (1.5 cm) apart.

INFLORESCENCE: Several. Inflorescences emerge one at a time from nodes near the apex of mature, normally leafless stems.

FLOWERS: 2–7 per inflorescence. The beautiful flowers are 1.6 in. (4 cm) across. They may be white or bright mauve. The white form often has a pink flush on the sepals and petals, sometimes with a darker spot at the tips. The lip is wavy on the edges and deeply notched at the apex. It is broadest at the tip with a golden yellow patch in the center. Blossoms are short-lived.

REFERENCES: 25, 74, 75, 111, 221, 445.

PHOTOS/DRAWINGS: 74, 75.

Dendrobium spathipetalum J. J. Smith

ORIGIN/HABITAT: Southeastern Borneo near Kota Waringin. Plants were cultivated in the botanical garden at Bogor, Java. Habitat elevation was not reported, so the following climate data should be used with caution.

CLIMATE: Station #96685, Bandjarmasin, Borneo, Lat. 3.4°S, Long. 114.8°E, at 66 ft. (20 m). Record extreme temperatures are not available for this location.

N/HEMISPHERE	JAN	FEB	MAR	APR	MAY	JUN	JUL	AUG	SEP	OCT	NOV	DEC
°F AVG MAX	88	89	91	90	87	86	86	86	87	89	88	88
°F AVG MIN	74	73	74	76	76	76	76	75	75	77	77	76
DIURNAL RANGE	14	16	17	14	11	10	10	11	12	12	11	12
RAIN/INCHES	3.5	3.2	3.9	5.1	8.5	12.2	12.7	11.7	11.9	8.5	6.2	5.6
HUMIDITY/%	78	77	73	75	81	84	84	83	82	81	80	79
BLOOM SEASON	N/A											
DAYS CLR @ 8AM	12	12	13	8	5	3	1	2	3	6	9	11
DAYS CLR @ 2PM	3	2	2	3	1	0	0	0	1	2	2	3
RAIN/MM	89	81	99	130	216	310	323	297	302	216	157	142
°C AVG MAX	31.0	31.9	32.7	32.4	30.7	29.9	29.8	30.0	30.6	31.4	30.9	31.1
°C AVG MIN	23.2	23.0	23.4	24.2	24.3	24.2	24.2	24.1	24.1	24.9	24.9	24.2
DIURNAL RANGE	7.8	8.9	9.3	8.2	6.4	5.7	5.6	5.9	6.5	6.5	6.0	6.9
S/HEMISPHERE	JUL	AUG	SEP	OCT	NOV	DEC	JAN	FEB	MAR	APR	MAY	JUN

Cultural Recommendations

LIGHT: 2000–3000 fc.

TEMPERATURES: Throughout the year, days average 86–91°F (30–33°C), and nights average 73–77°F (23–25°C), with a diurnal range of 10–17°F (6–9°C).

HUMIDITY: 80–85% from late spring through autumn, dropping to about 75% in winter and early spring.

WATER: Rainfall is moderate to heavy all year, but conditions are slightly drier for 3 months in winter. Plants should be kept evenly moist from spring into autumn, but water should be gradually reduced in late autumn. Warm water might be beneficial.

FERTILIZER: 1/4–1/2 recommended strength. A balanced fertilizer should be applied weekly to biweekly throughout the year.

REST PERIOD: Growing conditions should be maintained all year. Water and fertilizer should be reduced somewhat in winter, especially for plants cultivated in the dark, short-day conditions common in temperate latitudes. Plants should be allowed to dry slightly between waterings, but they should not remain dry for long periods. In the habitat, light is highest in winter.

GROWING MEDIA: Plants may be mounted on tree-fern or cork slabs or potted in small pots filled with any open, fast-draining medium. Repotting may be done anytime new roots are growing.

MISCELLANEOUS NOTES: The plant was described in 1914 in *Bull. Jard. Bot. Buit.* 2nd sér. 13:20.

Plant and Flower Information

PLANT SIZE AND TYPE: A 17 in. (43 cm) sympodial epiphyte.

PSEUDOBULB: 17 in. (43 cm) long. The stems are clustered and erect with about 8 grooves. The upper part is leafless.

LEAVES: Many. The broadly lanceolate leaves are up to 2.8 in. (7 cm) long. They are erect-spreading, concave, recurved, not twisted at the base, and unequally 2-toothed at the apex. Young leaf sheaths are covered with a white powder, but with age, they become smooth and turn black.

INFLORESCENCE: Short. Inflorescences emerge through 2 leaf sheaths at nodes on leafy and leafless stems.

FLOWERS: 4–6 per inflorescence. The flowers are 0.7 in. (1.8 cm) across. Sepals and petals are pale yellow with darker nerves. The dorsal sepal is oblong-ovate. Lateral sepals are triangular with a slashed margin. Petals are sickle-shaped. The 3-lobed lip has yellowish white, triangular sidelobes. The truncated midlobe is ovate, ruffled, and rounded. It has a warty-mealy area at the base of the midlobe.

REFERENCES: 221, 286, 295.

Dendrobium spathulatilabratum P. van Royen. See *D. habbemense* P. van Royen. REFERENCES: 233, 385, 538. PHOTOS/DRAWINGS: 538.

Dendrobium spathulatum L. O. Williams

ORIGIN/HABITAT: Endemic to Vitu Levu, Fiji. Plants are found in the southeastern part of the island, apparently below 500 ft. (150 m). They are uncommon.

CLIMATE: Station #91683, Nausori, Vitu Levu, Fiji Islands, Lat. 18.1°S, Long. 178.6°E, at 19 ft. (6 m). Record extreme temperatures are 98°F (37°C) and 55°F (13°C).

N/HEMISPHERE	JAN	FEB	MAR	APR	MAY	JUN	JUL	AUG	SEP	OCT	NOV	DEC
°F AVG MAX	79	79	80	81	83	85	86	86	86	84	82	80
°F AVG MIN	68	68	69	70	71	73	74	74	74	73	71	69
DIURNAL RANGE	11	11	11	11	12	12	12	12	12	11	11	11
RAIN/INCHES	4.9	8.3	7.7	8.3	9.8	12.5	11.4	10.7	14.5	12.2	10.1	6.7
HUMIDITY/%	77	77	76	75	75	76	76	76	79	79	81	78
BLOOM SEASON		*			*				*			
DAYS CLR @ 12PM	3	1	0	0	1	1	2	0	0	0	1	0
RAIN/MM	124	211	196	211	249	318	290	272	368	310	257	170
°C AVG MAX	26.1	26.1	26.7	27.2	28.3	29.4	30.0	30.0	30.0	28.9	27.8	26.7
°C AVG MIN	20.0	20.0	20.6	21.1	21.7	22.8	23.3	23.3	23.3	22.8	21.7	20.6
DIURNAL RANGE	6.1	6.1	6.1	6.1	6.6	6.6	6.7	6.7	6.7	6.1	6.1	6.1
S/HEMISPHERE	JUL	AUG	SEP	OCT	NOV	DEC	JAN	FEB	MAR	APR	MAY	JUN

Cultural Recommendations

LIGHT: 2500–3500 fc. Strong air movement is very important for cultivated plants.

TEMPERATURES: Throughout the year, days average 79–86°F (26–30°C), and nights average 68–74°F (20–23°C), with a diurnal range of 11–12°F (6–7°C).

HUMIDITY: 75–80% year-round.

WATER: Rainfall is very heavy all year. Cultivated plants should be kept moist and never be allowed to dry completely.

FERTILIZER: 1/4–1/2 recommended strength. A balanced fertilizer should be applied weekly to biweekly throughout the year.

REST PERIOD: Growing conditions should be maintained all year. Winter rainfall in the habitat is heavy; but water and fertilizer should be reduced somewhat for cultivated plants, especially those grown in the dark, short-day conditions common in temperate-latitude winters. Cultivated plants should never be allowed to dry out completely, however. In the habitat, seasonal light variation is minor.

GROWING MEDIA: Plants may be mounted on tree-fern or cork slabs or potted in small pots filled with any open, fast-draining medium. Repotting may be done anytime new roots are growing.

MISCELLANEOUS NOTES: The bloom season shown in the climate table is based on reports from the habitat.

Plant and Flower Information

PLANT SIZE AND TYPE: A 24–28 in. (60–70 cm) sympodial epiphyte.

PSEUDOBULB: 20–25 in. (50–64 cm) long. The terete stems, which are somewhat flattened, are leafy at the apex of each growth. They are clustered and arise from a short rhizome.

LEAVES: Many. The elliptic-oblong leaves are 2.8–3.5 in. (7–9 cm) long. They are quickly deciduous.

INFLORESCENCE: 10 in. (25 cm) long. Inflorescences emerge from nodes near the apex of the stem and exceed the length of the leaves. They arise opposite the leaves.

FLOWERS: 10–20 per inflorescence. The showy flowers are 0.8–1.2 in. (2–3 cm) long. Sepals and petals are mustard-yellow with a brownish tinge on the inside. The dorsal sepal and petals are reflexed, but the lateral sepals project forward with recurved tips. The 3-lobed lip has triangular sidelobes and 3 raised lines in the fleshy center. The midlobe is whitish yellow with faint red lines. It is transversely ovate with a broad notch and small point in the center.

REFERENCES: 82, 84, 226, 252, 353, 466, 571.

PHOTOS/DRAWINGS: 84, 466.

Dendrobium speciosissimum Rolfe. Sometimes spelled *D. speciossimum*, see *D. spectatissimum* Rchb. f. REFERENCES: 140, 179, 217, 218, 254, 286, 295, 340, 391, 429, 445.

Dendrobium speciosum J. E. Smith

AKA: Adams (ref. 4) states, "The varieties (of *D. speciosum*) are best regarded as intergrading, forming a species complex in which typical and atypical plants occur." After extensive review, he recommends following the more generally accepted treatment which divides the alliance into the following varieties of *D. speciosum*: *D. speciosum* var. *capricornicum* Clemesha, *D. speciosum* var. *curvicaule* F. M. Bailey, *D. speciosum* var. *hillii* Masters, *D. speciosum* var. *grandiflorum* F. M. Bailey, *D. speciosum* var. *pendunculatum* Clemesha, and *D. speciosum* var. *speciosum*. He notes that the characteristics which separate the varieties overlap considerably.

Clements (ref. 67) split *D. speciosum* into several species and distributes the named varieties as follows. Only time will tell whether his treatment becomes generally accepted or whether a new layer of synonyms have added to the confusion. Most of these newly named species are presently cultivated under the name *D. speciosum*.

Dendrobium speciosum

D. speciosum var. *album* B. S. Williams. See *D.* × *delicatum*. (Bailey) Bailey.

D. speciosum var. *bancroftianum* Rchb. f. See *D. jonesii* Rendle subsp. *bancroftianum* (Rchb. f.) M. Clements and D. Jones.

D. speciosum var. *capricornicum* Clemesha. See *D. curvicaule* (Bailey) M. Clements and D. Jones.

D. speciosum var. *curvicaule* F. M. Bailey. See *D. curvicaule* (Bailey) M. Clements and D. Jones.

D. speciosum var. *delicatum* F. M. Bailey. See *D.* × *delicatum* F. M. Bailey.

D. speciosum var. *fragrans* R. Brown (in part). See *D. curvicaule* (Bailey) M. Clements and D. Jones.

D. speciosum var. *fusiforme* F. M. Bailey. See *D. jonesii* Rendle subsp. *jonesii*.

D. speciosum var. *gracillimum* Rupp. See *D.* × *gracillimum* (Rupp) Leaney.

D. speciosum var. *grandiflorum* F. M. Bailey. See *D. rex* M. Clements and D. Jones.

D. speciosum forma *hillii* Domin. See *D. tarberi*. M. Clements and D. Jones

D. speciosum var. *hillii* author unknown. See *D. tarberi* M. Clements and D. Jones.

D. speciosum var. *hillii* forma *grandiflorum* F. M. Bailey. See *D. rex* M. Clements and D. Jones.

D. speciosum var. *hillii* forma *bancroftianum* (Rchb. f.) F. M. Bailey. See *D. jonesii* Rendle.

D. speciosum var. *nitidum* F. M. Bailey. See *D.* × *nitidum* (Bailey) M. Clements and D. Jones.

D. speciosum var. *pendunculatum* Clemsha. See *D. pendunculatum* (Clemsha) M. Clements and D. Jones.

ORIGIN/HABITAT: Southeast Australia. The habitat extends from just south of Genoa in Victoria (37.7°S) northward to Bulahdelah in central New South Wales (32.4°S). Plants are found from near the coast to about 150 mi. (240 km) inland in the Mudgee area. They usually grow on rocks in open forest and at the base of cliffs, but north of Nowra in the Cambewarra Range, they are found high on rainforest trees in a very moist area with strong air movement. Some of the largest-flowered forms grow in leaf mold on rocks in the foothills of the Blue Mountains west of Sydney. Plants growing in the interior mountains near Mudgee are exposed to frost, snow, and a dry west wind in winter and to searing heat in summer.

CLIMATE: Station #94750, Nowra, New South Wales, Australia, Lat. 34.9°S, Long. 150.6°E, at 350 ft. (107 m). Temperatures are calculated for an elevation of 2500 ft. (760 m), resulting in probable extremes of 100°F (38°C) and 28°F (−2°C).

N/HEMISPHERE	JAN	FEB	MAR	APR	MAY	JUN	JUL	AUG	SEP	OCT	NOV	DEC
°F AVG MAX	52	54	58	62	70	70	70	68	67	65	60	57
°F AVG MIN	36	38	40	44	47	50	52	55	53	48	42	41
DIURNAL RANGE	16	16	18	18	23	20	18	13	14	17	18	16
RAIN/INCHES	3.8	2.2	2.1	2.4	2.2	2.8	4.0	3.2	4.0	3.4	3.5	4.3
HUMIDITY/%	72	70	68	67	59	72	72	82	80	69	74	68
BLOOM SEASON	*	**	**	*								*
DAYS CLR @ 10AM	17	15	14	12	15	11	12	3	5	13	14	14
DAYS CLR @ 4PM	11	9	13	8	12	10	10	2	3	9	11	12
RAIN/MM	97	56	53	61	56	71	102	81	102	86	89	109
°C AVG MAX	11.1	12.2	14.4	16.7	21.1	21.3	21.2	20.0	19.4	18.3	15.6	13.9
°C AVG MIN	2.2	3.3	4.4	6.6	8.3	9.9	11.1	12.7	11.6	8.8	5.5	4.9
DIURNAL RANGE	8.9	8.9	10.0	10.1	12.8	11.4	10.1	7.3	7.8	9.5	10.1	9.0
S/HEMISPHERE	JUL	AUG	SEP	OCT	NOV	DEC	JAN	FEB	MAR	APR	MAY	JUN

Cultural Recommendations

LIGHT: 3000–4500 fc. Australian growers report that the plants which bloom most dramatically often have leaves and pseudobulbs that are bleached and leathery. Very bright light is needed in winter for flower bud development. Air movement should be strong throughout the year.

TEMPERATURES: Summer days average 68–70°F (20–21°C), and nights average 50–55°F (10–13°C), with a diurnal range of 13–20°F (7–11°C).

HUMIDITY: 70–80% most of the year, dropping to 60–65% in late spring

WATER: Rainfall is light to moderate most of the year, but is probably greater in the forest and rainforest habitats. Cultivated plants should be watered frequently while actively growing, with only slight drying allowed between waterings. Water should be reduced after new growths mature in autumn.

FERTILIZER: ¼–½ recommended strength, applied weekly. A high nitrogen fertilizer is beneficial from spring to midsummer, but a fertilizer high in phosphates should be used in late summer and autumn.

REST PERIOD: Winter days average 52–58°F (11–14°C), and nights average 36–41°F (2–5°C), with a diurnal range of 16–18°F (9–10°C). Rainfall in the habitat is lower in winter. Cultivated plants should be allowed to dry out somewhat between waterings, but they should not dry completely or remain dry for extended periods. Fertilizer should be reduced or eliminated until water is increased in spring. Light in the habitat is very bright from late autumn into spring.

GROWING MEDIA: Plants may be mounted on tree-fern or cork slabs if humidity is high and plants are watered at least once daily in summer. Plants may be potted if necessary, but frequent repotting is necessary because they are very robust growers. Plants should never be overpotted in an attempt to delay the need to repot, and a very open, fast-draining medium should be used. Repotting is best done in early spring when new roots are growing. Old stems should not be removed during repotting, as they continue to flower for several years.

MISCELLANEOUS NOTES: The bloom season shown in the climate table is based on cultivation reports. In nature, plants usually bloom in late winter and spring, but blooming is sometimes sporadic. *D. speciosum* is adaptable and very easy to grow, although growers not providing a dry rest consider them difficult to bloom. When plants are not given a rest, they will not bloom; but latent buds may all produce flowers after the required cool dry rest conditions are provided. This tendency to save-up buds results in spectacular floral displays in some years. However, if conditions are excessively cold or wet during the winter, inflorescences may be severely damaged. Some growers hypothesize that it may be hot weather the preceding summer that determines the number of blossoms.

Plant and Flower Information

PLANT SIZE AND TYPE: A 10–20 in. (25–50 cm) sympodial lithophyte which sometimes grows as an epiphyte. Plant size is highly variable, however, and plants may be as small as 2 in. (5 cm) or as large as 40 in. (102 cm).

PSEUDOBULB: 9–12 in. (23–30 cm) long. Plant size is based on cultivated plants. Stems are deep green, sometimes with a brown or purple flush. *D. speciosum* often becomes a large mass of thick, conical pseudobulbs that radiate in all directions from a single point. Each stem is ribbed and consists of several nodes. Clements (ref. 67) indicates that *D. speciosum* does not produce aerial roots like *D. rex* M. Clements and D. Jones and *D. tarberi* M. Clements and D. Jones.

LEAVES: 2–5 near the apex of each growth. The thick, persistent leaves are 2–10 in. (4–25 cm) long. They are flat, oblong, and deep green.

INFLORESCENCE: 4–24 in. (10–60 cm) long. Several inflorescences often appear simultaneously from the apex and upper nodes of mature growths. The densely flowered inflorescences may be semierect or pendent.

FLOWERS: Up to 100 per inflorescence. A healthy plant produces hundreds of waxy, long-lasting flowers. They are 0.8–3.0 in. (2–8 cm) across but often do not expand fully. The greater the number of flowers the smaller the individual blossom size. Sepals and petals may be any shade from white to yellow, and growers indicate that flower color varies from year to year. The lip, which may be nearly enclosed by the sepals and petals, is decorated with red or purple spots. It is shorter than the sepals. Some clones have been reported that have purple spots on all flower segments. The inverted blossoms are fragrant in full sun.

HYBRIDIZING NOTES: Chromosome count is 2n = 38 as *D. speciosum* (ref. 152, 504, 580), as *D. speciosum* var. *fusiforme* (ref. 580), and as *D. speciosum* var. *hillii* (ref. 580). *D. speciosum* and its varieties are not normally self-fertile and pollen from the same plant seldom produces seeds, but pods are regularly produced when pollen from another clone or another variety is used. Self-fertility may increase if post-pollination conditions are warm. As a parent, *D. speciosum* generally increases the number of flowers on the raceme.

REFERENCES: 3, 4, 6, 23, 36, 67, 105, 152, 161, 179, 190, 196, 200, 210, 216, 234, 240, 243, 254, 256, 260, 262, 263, 317, 325, 352, 371, 389, 390, 421, 430, 445, 495, 504, 527, 533, 541, 544, 545, 557, 569, 570, 576, 580.

PHOTOS/DRAWINGS: *4, 6, 27, 36, 105,* 182, *184, 185,* 210, 240, *256,* 325, *371, 389, 390, 430, 492, 520, 527, 532, 533, 544, 545, 569.*

Dendrobium spectabile (Blume) Miquel

AKA: *Latourea spectabilis* Blume, *Dendrobium tigrinum* Rolfe ex Hemsley.

ORIGIN/HABITAT: New Guinea, Bougainville, the Solomon Islands, and Vanuatu. Plants grow on trees in swampy lowland forests, lower mountain forests, or in planted coconut or *Casuarina* trees from sea level to 3600 ft. (0–1100 m). On ridge tops, they grow on the surface of the ground in thick moss and peat. The plants survive exposure to high light and hot temperatures at lower elevations, but they are more abundant in cool, shady locations at higher elevations.

CLIMATE: Station #200187, Erap, Papua New Guinea, Lat. 6.6°S, Long. 146.7°E, at 850 ft. (260 m). Temperatures are calculated for an elevation of 1950 ft. (600 m), resulting in probable extremes of 98°F (37°C) and 49°F (10°C).

N/HEMISPHERE	JAN	FEB	MAR	APR	MAY	JUN	JUL	AUG	SEP	OCT	NOV	DEC
°F AVG MAX	84	84	85	86	89	89	89	89	89	88	86	86
°F AVG MIN	65	65	65	66	68	69	68	68	69	67	70	66
DIURNAL RANGE	19	19	20	20	21	20	21	21	20	21	16	20
RAIN/INCHES	3.9	3.9	2.7	3.0	3.0	5.3	5.9	5.9	7.0	3.4	2.4	3.1
HUMIDITY/%	82	81	81	79	75	74	74	74	77	76	80	80
BLOOM SEASON		*	*								*	*
DAYS CLR	N/A											
RAIN/MM	99	99	69	76	76	135	150	150	178	86	61	79
°C AVG MAX	29.1	29.1	29.6	30.2	31.8	31.8	31.8	31.8	31.8	31.3	30.2	30.2
°C AVG MIN	18.5	18.5	18.5	19.1	20.2	20.7	20.2	20.2	20.7	19.6	21.3	19.1
DIURNAL RANGE	10.6	10.6	11.1	11.1	11.6	11.1	11.6	11.6	11.1	11.7	8.9	11.1
S/HEMISPHERE	JUL	AUG	SEP	OCT	NOV	DEC	JAN	FEB	MAR	APR	MAY	JUN

Cultural Recommendations

LIGHT: 2500–3500 fc. Growers report these plants grow well in half shade to full sun. However, plants should be introduced gradually to high light conditions. Strong air movement should be provided all year.

TEMPERATURES: Throughout the year, days average 84–89°F (29–32°C), and nights average 65–70°F (19–21°C), with a diurnal range of 16–21°F (9–12°C).

HUMIDITY: Near 75–80% year-round. The habitat may be quite dry for a few hours during hot afternoons, however.

WATER: Rainfall is moderate most of the year, but conditions are a little drier from late autumn to spring. However, the high relative humidity and the large diurnal temperature range indicate additional water is available from frequent heavy deposits of dew. Cultivated plants should be allowed to dry slightly between waterings, but they should not remain dry for extended periods.

FERTILIZER: ¼–½ recommended strength. A balanced fertilizer should be applied weekly to biweekly throughout the year.

REST PERIOD: Growing temperatures should be maintained all year. Some growers recommend winter low temperatures of 54°F (12°C), but it should be noted that this is near the record low in the habitat. Water should be reduced somewhat for cultivated plants, especially those grown in the dark, short-day conditions common in temperate-latitude winters, but they should not be allowed to dry out completely. Fertilizer should be reduced in winter.

GROWING MEDIA: Plants may be mounted on tree-fern or cork slabs or potted in any open, fast-draining medium. Repotting may be done anytime new roots are growing. Growers report that plants grow well in roomy tree-fern pots which are well drained.

MISCELLANEOUS NOTES: The bloom season shown in the climate table is based on reports from the habitat. Cultivation records indicate blooming in all seasons with very light blooming in summer and early autumn. Plants grow well but do not flower in Singapore, indicating that *D. spectabile* needs slightly cooler, drier conditions to induce flowering. These conditions rarely occur in lowland tropical areas. Plants grown in temperate latitudes often fail to bloom reliably. Growers indicate that *D. spectabile* must be quite large and very root-bound before it starts to bloom.

Plant and Flower Information

PLANT SIZE AND TYPE: A 12–48 in. (30–122 cm) sympodial epiphyte.

PSEUDOBULB: 12–48 in. (30–122 cm) long. Cultivated plants are commonly 12–16 in. (30–40 cm) long. The stems are enlarged at the base, become slender, then thicken along the upper part. They are yellow-brown and grooved with 5–8 nodes below the leaves.

LEAVES: 3–6 per growth. The leathery leaves are 6–8 in. (15–20 cm) long. They are suberect, sharply pointed, and dark, glossy green.

INFLORESCENCE: 8–16 in. (20–40 cm) long. Inflorescences emerge from below the leaf bases.

FLOWERS: 5–20 per inflorescence. The flowers are 2.8–3.1 in. (7–8 cm) across. They are creamy to pale greenish, with extensive reddish brown to dark purple mottling, blotching, and veining except along the margins. The crested lip is yellowish with a white base. The sharply pointed segments are twisted and curled. Blossoms have been described as grotesquely beautiful.

HYBRIDIZING NOTES: Chromosome count is 2n = 38 (ref. 152, 243, 504, 580).

REFERENCES: 25, 36, 83, 152, 179, 190, 200, 210, 216, 243, 254, 270, 271, 304, 310, 352, 371, 430, 437, 444, 445, 458, 470, 504, 510, 516, 522, 526, 537, 550, 568, 580.

PHOTOS/DRAWINGS: *83,* 200, 210, 254, *271, 304,* 371, *430,* 437, 458, *550.*

Dendrobium spectatissimum Rchb. f.

AKA: *D. reticulatum* J. J. Smith, *D. speciosissimum* Rolfe.

ORIGIN/HABITAT: Borneo. Endemic to the Mt. Kinabalu region of Sabah. This uncommon orchid usually grows in sparse woods at 4900–5600 ft. (1500–1700 m), but plants have been reported as low as 650 ft. (200 m). It is usually found on small *Leptospermum* bushes that are only a few meters tall.

CLIMATE: Station #49613, Tambunan, Sabah (North Borneo), Lat. 5.7°N, Long. 116.4°E, at 1200 ft. (366 m). Temperatures are calculated for an elevation of 5400 ft. (1640 m), resulting in probable extremes of 85°F (30°C) and 42°F (5°C).

Dendrobium speculigerum

N/HEMISPHERE	JAN	FEB	MAR	APR	MAY	JUN	JUL	AUG	SEP	OCT	NOV	DEC
°F AVG MAX	73	74	76	77	77	76	76	76	76	75	74	73
°F AVG MIN	54	52	53	54	55	54	53	53	54	54	54	55
DIURNAL RANGE	19	22	23	23	22	22	23	23	22	21	20	18
RAIN/INCHES	5.8	3.7	5.8	7.5	8.2	7.3	5.1	4.9	6.4	7.0	6.8	6.0
HUMIDITY/%	N/A											
BLOOM SEASON					*							
DAYS CLR	N/A											
RAIN/MM	147	94	147	190	208	185	130	124	163	178	173	152
°C AVG MAX	23.0	23.6	24.7	25.3	25.3	24.7	24.7	24.7	24.7	24.1	23.6	23.0
°C AVG MIN	12.5	11.4	11.9	12.5	13.0	12.5	11.9	11.9	12.5	12.5	12.5	13.0
DIURNAL RANGE	10.5	12.2	12.8	12.8	12.3	12.2	12.8	12.8	12.2	11.6	11.1	10.0
S/HEMISPHERE	JUL	AUG	SEP	OCT	NOV	DEC	JAN	FEB	MAR	APR	MAY	JUN

Cultural Recommendations

LIGHT: 2500–3500 fc.

TEMPERATURES: Throughout the year, days average 73–77°F (23–25°C), and nights average 52–55°F (11–13°C), with a diurnal range of 18–23°F (10–13°C). The plants are unlikely to tolerate hot weather, as the probable extreme high is 85°F (30°C).

HUMIDITY: 75–80% year-round.

WATER: Rainfall is moderate to heavy through the year. Cultivated plants should be kept moist, with only slight drying allowed between waterings.

FERTILIZER: ¼–½ recommended strength. A balanced fertilizer should be applied weekly to biweekly throughout the year.

REST PERIOD: Growing conditions vary only slightly through the year. The diurnal range is slightly lower in winter due to somewhat cooler days. In cultivation, water should be reduced somewhat in winter, especially for plants grown in the dark, short-day conditions common in temperate latitudes. Plants should never be allowed to dry out completely, however. Fertilizer should be decreased when water is reduced and when plants are not actively growing.

GROWING MEDIA: Plants may be potted or mounted on tree-fern or cork slabs. Repotting may be done anytime new roots are growing.

MISCELLANEOUS NOTES: The bloom season shown in the climate table is based on cultivation records.

Plant and Flower Information

PLANT SIZE AND TYPE: A 12–16 in. (30–40 cm) sympodial epiphyte.

PSEUDOBULB: 12–16 in. (30–40 cm) long. The grooved stems are rather slender, erect, and leafy. They are covered with coarse, rigidly erect, black hairs.

LEAVES: Many. The ovate-oblong leaves are 1.7–2.5 in. (4.3–6.5 cm) long. They are covered with black hairs.

INFLORESCENCE: Inflorescences emerge from nodes near the apex of mature leafy or leafless stems.

FLOWERS: 1–2 per inflorescence. The shiny flowers are 3–4 in. (8–10 cm) across. They are described as very similar to *D. formosum* Roxburgh ex Lindley. The keeled, pointed sepals and large, rounded petals are snow-white with a papery texture. Petals may be reflexed when they first open, becoming flat with age. The 3-lobed, fiddle-shaped lip is accented with a golden-yellow blotch on the disk that is red at the base. The fragrant blossoms last up to 6 weeks.

HYBRIDIZING NOTES: Marlow and Butcher (ref. 285) report that dry seeds have been propagated after sterilizing in small filter paper packets with a 5% V/V sodium hypochlorite solution (a drop of Tween 40 was added as a wetting agent) for 10 minutes and then rinsing in sterile deionized water. The seeds were sown on a growth medium (Vacin and Went, 1949) and germinated at 77°F (25°C) with 16 hours of light. Germination occurred in 8–10 weeks.

REFERENCES: 12, 179, 190, 216, 218, 254, 285, 286, 295, 391, 394, 429, 430, 589, 592.

PHOTOS/DRAWINGS: *132, 285, 430, 592*.

Dendrobium speculigerum Schlechter

ORIGIN/HABITAT: Sulawesi (Celebes). Plants grow on trees in mountain forests near Mt. Klabat (Minahassa) at about 2950 ft. (900 m).

CLIMATE: Station #97014, Manado, Sulawesi, Lat. 1.5°N, Long. 124.9°E, at 264 ft. (80 m). Temperatures are calculated for an elevation of 3000 ft. (910 m), resulting in probable extremes of 88°F (31°C) and 56°F (13°C).

N/HEMISPHERE	JAN	FEB	MAR	APR	MAY	JUN	JUL	AUG	SEP	OCT	NOV	DEC
°F AVG MAX	76	76	76	77	78	78	78	80	80	80	78	77
°F AVG MIN	64	64	64	64	65	64	64	64	64	63	64	65
DIURNAL RANGE	12	12	12	13	13	14	14	16	16	17	14	12
RAIN/INCHES	18.6	13.8	12.2	8.0	6.4	6.5	4.8	4.0	3.4	4.9	8.9	14.7
HUMIDITY/%	84	83	83	83	81	80	75	72	75	77	82	83
BLOOM SEASON												*
DAYS CLR @ 8AM	4	3	6	11	11	12	12	14	17	12	8	
DAYS CLR @ 2PM	1	1	1	2	1	3	3	4	4	4	1	1
RAIN/MM	472	351	310	203	163	165	122	102	86	124	226	373
°C AVG MAX	24.4	24.4	24.4	25.0	25.5	25.5	25.5	26.7	26.7	26.7	25.5	25.0
°C AVG MIN	17.8	17.8	17.8	17.8	18.3	17.8	17.8	17.8	17.8	17.2	17.8	18.3
DIURNAL RANGE	6.6	6.6	6.6	7.2	7.2	7.7	7.7	8.9	8.9	9.5	7.7	6.7
S/HEMISPHERE	JUL	AUG	SEP	OCT	NOV	DEC	JAN	FEB	MAR	APR	MAY	JUN

Cultural Recommendations

LIGHT: 2000–3000 fc. In the habitat, skies are clear about half the mornings each month through much of the year, but they are usually overcast by afternoon.

TEMPERATURES: Throughout the year, days average 76–80°F (24–27°C), and nights average 63–65°F (17–18°C), with a diurnal range of 12–17°F (7–10°C). Temperatures vary only slightly through the year, and plants from this habitat may not tolerate wide seasonal fluctuations.

HUMIDITY: 80–85% most of the year, dropping to 70–75% in summer and early autumn.

WATER: Rainfall is moderate to heavy all year. The driest period occurs in late summer and early autumn. Cultivated plants should be kept moist but not soggy.

FERTILIZER: ¼–½ recommended strength. A balanced fertilizer should be applied weekly to biweekly throughout the year.

REST PERIOD: Growing conditions should be maintained all year. In the habitat, rainfall is greatest in winter, but increased water could be detrimental for cultivated plants. In fact, water should be reduced for plants grown in the dreary, short-day conditions common in temperate-latitude winters. They should never be allowed to dry out completely, however. In the habitat, light is lowest in winter.

GROWING MEDIA: Mounting plants on tree-fern or cork slabs accommodates their pendulous growth habit. However, humidity must be high and plants must be watered at least once a day in summer. If plants cannot be mounted, hanging pots or baskets may be filled with an open, fast-draining medium. Repotting may be done anytime new roots are actively growing.

MISCELLANEOUS NOTES: The bloom season shown in the climate table is based on reports from the habitat.

Plant and Flower Information

PLANT SIZE AND TYPE: A 10–28 in. (25–70 cm) sympodial epiphyte.

PSEUDOBULB: 10–28 in. (25–70 cm) long. Stems are lax, pendulous, furrowed, and moderately branched. Nodes are spaced about 1.6 in. (4 cm) apart.

LEAVES: Many. The linear-oblong leaves, which are about 4 in. (10 cm) long, are shiny, greenish brown. They are rather thin and become wrinkled and ridged with age. Leaves are arranged in 2 rows.

INFLORESCENCE: 1 in. (2.5 cm) long. Inflorescences emerge from nodes near the apex of leafless pseudobulbs.

FLOWERS: 4–7 per inflorescence. The flowers are 0.4–0.6 in. (1.0–1.5 cm) across. Blossoms may be pale greenish yellow or brownish. They have ovate sepals, sickle-shaped lateral sepals, and oblong petals. The long, 3-lobed lip has a dark red blotch at the tip, finely toothed margins, and toothlike sidelobes. It is covered with warty projections up to the long, glossy lamina.

REFERENCES: 220, 436.

Dendrobium speculum J. J. Smith. Now considered a synonym of *Epigeneium speculum* (J. J. Smith) Summerhayes. REFERENCES: 220, 229, 286, 295, 445, 499.

Dendrobium sphegidiglossum Rchb. f. See *D. spegidoglossum* Rchb. f. REFERENCES: 202, 216, 254, 369.

Dendrobium spegidoglossum Rchb. f.

AKA: Sometimes spelled *D. sphegidiglossum*, *sphegidglossum*, or *sphegidoglossum*. Generally accepted synonyms include *D. exsculptum* Teijsm. and Binn and *D. flavidulum* Ridley ex Hooker f. Some references consider *D. spegidoglossum* synonymous with *D. stuposum* Lindley, but Seidenfaden (ref. 454) indicates that the plants are separate species.

ORIGIN/HABITAT: Southeast Asia, including southeastern and peninsular Thailand, Burma, Java, Borneo, Malaya, Singapore, and Sumatra. In eastern and western Java, plants grow at about 2300 ft. (700 m). In Borneo, plants are found in Kalimantan, Sarawak, and the Mt. Kinabalu region of Sabah at 3950–4900 ft. (1200–1500 m). On the Malaya Peninsula, plants are found in Singapore and the states of Pinang (Penang) and Kelantan where they are common on old mangrove trees. In some literature, it is listed as occurring in the Khasi (Khasia) Hills of India at 3300–5600 ft. (1000–1700 m).

CLIMATE: Station #48601, Pinang (Penang), Malaya, Lat. 5.3°N, Long. 100.3°E, at 8 ft. (2 m). Temperatures are calculated for an elevation of 1000 ft. (300 m), resulting in probable extremes of 95°F (35°C) and 64°F (18°C).

N/HEMISPHERE	JAN	FEB	MAR	APR	MAY	JUN	JUL	AUG	SEP	OCT	NOV	DEC
°F AVG MAX	87	88	89	88	87	87	87	86	85	86	85	86
°F AVG MIN	70	70	71	72	71	71	71	70	70	70	70	70
DIURNAL RANGE	17	18	18	16	16	16	16	16	15	16	15	16
RAIN/INCHES	3.7	3.1	5.6	7.4	10.7	7.7	7.5	11.6	15.8	16.9	11.9	5.8
HUMIDITY/%	76	77	81	84	84	84	85	85	85	87	86	81
BLOOM SEASON					*							
DAYS CLR @ 7AM	2	1	2	0	0	1	1	0	0	0	1	1
DAYS CLR @ 1PM	3	2	2	1	1	1	1	0	0	0	1	2
RAIN/MM	94	79	142	188	272	196	191	295	401	429	302	147
°C AVG MAX	30.6	31.1	31.7	31.1	30.6	30.7	30.6	30.0	29.4	30.0	29.4	30.0
°C AVG MIN	21.1	21.0	21.5	22.1	21.5	21.5	21.5	21.0	21.0	21.0	21.0	21.0
DIURNAL RANGE	9.5	10.1	10.2	9.0	9.1	9.2	9.1	9.0	8.4	9.0	8.4	9.0
S/HEMISPHERE	JUL	AUG	SEP	OCT	NOV	DEC	JAN	FEB	MAR	APR	MAY	JUN

Cultural Recommendations

LIGHT: 1800–2500 fc.

TEMPERATURES: Throughout the year, days average 85–89°F (29–32°C), and nights average 70–72°F (21–22°C), with a diurnal range of 15–18°F (8–10°C). Because of the range in habitat elevation, plants should adapt to conditions 8–10°F (4–6°C) cooler than indicated.

HUMIDITY: Near 85% most of the year, dropping to 75–80% in winter.

WATER: Rainfall is moderate to heavy most of the year, but conditions are somewhat drier for 2 months in winter. Cultivated plants should be kept moist and never be allowed to dry out completely.

FERTILIZER: ¼–½ recommended strength, applied weekly during periods of active growth.

REST PERIOD: Growing conditions should be maintained all year. Water should be reduced in winter, with slight drying allowed between waterings. Plants should not remain dry for long periods, however. Fertilizer should be reduced until water is increased in spring. In the habitat, seasonal light variation is minor.

GROWING MEDIA: Plants may be mounted on tree-fern or cork slabs if humidity is high and plants are watered at least once daily in summer. When plants are potted, any open, fast-draining medium may be used. Repotting is best done in early spring when new roots begin to grow.

MISCELLANEOUS NOTES: The bloom season shown in the climate table is based on records from the habitat.

Plant and Flower Information

PLANT SIZE AND TYPE: A 10–31 in. (25–80 cm) sympodial epiphyte.

PSEUDOBULB: 10–31 in. (25–80 cm) long. The slender stems are furrowed, clustered and fleshy. The nodes are spaced 1.0–1.6 in. (2.5–4.0 cm) apart.

LEAVES: Many. The linear-oblong to narrowly lanceolate leaves are 3–4 in. (8–10 cm) long. They are shiny, greenish brown, rather thin, and become ridged with age.

INFLORESCENCE: 0.8 in. (2 cm) long. Several very thin inflorescences are borne at nodes near the apex of leafless stems.

FLOWERS: 4–9, occasionally fewer per inflorescence. The flowers are 0.5 in. (1.3 cm) across. The pointed sepals and blunter petals are pale greenish-yellow as they open, but they fade to ivory-white with age. The lip has a row of fine hairs along the entire front margin and a hairy patch at the tip of the midlobe. It is usually pale brownish-yellow with red veins and a yellow band or a red spot at the tip of the midlobe. The triangular sidelobes are nearly as large as the midlobe. Markings are variable.

REFERENCES: 25, 38, 46, 75, 179, 202, 216, 254, 317, 369, 395, 402, 445, 454, 455, 469, 592.

PHOTOS/DRAWINGS: 454, 455.

Dendrobium sphenochilum F. Mueller and Kränzlin. In Papua New Guinea, plants were reportedly found in the mountains, but habitat location and elevation are not available, so climate data cannot be selected. The sympodial epiphyte was 7 in. (19 cm) long. The stems were leafy at the apex, with 12–14 brownish leaves that were 0.8–2.0 in. (2–5 cm) long, linear, and pointed with long leaf sheaths. The raceme emerged at the apex of the pseudobulb. Blossoms were crowded at the apex of the few-flowered inflorescence. The flowers were 0.8 in. (2 cm) long, white, sometimes with a rosy suffusion, and opened in succession. The dorsal sepal and petals were lanceolate and pointed. The pointed lateral sepals were broadly triangular. The lip midlobe was large but the sidelobes were obsolete. The disk had elevated lines. REFERENCES: 218, 253, 254.

Dendrobium spinescens Lindley. Now considered a synonym of *Pseuderia foliosa* (Brogniart) Schlechter. REFERENCES: 216, 254, 278, 310, 437.

Dendrobium spurium (Blume) J. J. Smith

AKA: *Dendrocolla spuria* Blume, *Dendrobium euphlebium* Rchb. f. ex Lindley, *D. unguiculatum* Teijsm and Binn.

ORIGIN/HABITAT: The Philippine Islands, Borneo, Java, New Guinea,

Dendrobium squalens

Sumatra, Singapore, and Malaya. On Luzon Island in the Philippines, plants grow in Bataan, Cagayan, Ilocos Norte, Laguna, and Sorsogon provinces. They are also found in Davao Province on Mindanao Island. Collections are reported at about 2800 ft. (850 m) on Mt. Mariveles in Bataan Province. In most habitats, plants grow on trees at 330–3100 ft. (100–950 m). They are found on mangroves as well as on trees in hillside woods. In Java, they grow in primary forests at 1000–3600 ft. (300–1100 m), where no long dry season occurs, and on low mountain ridges with excellent air movement. In Sarawak, plants grow on limestone rocks.

CLIMATE: Station #98426, Cubi Point NAS, Philippines, Lat. 14.8°N, Long. 120.3°E, at 55 ft. (17 m). Temperatures are calculated for an elevation of 3000 ft. (910 m), resulting in probable extremes of 91°F (33°C) and 52°F (11°C).

N/HEMISPHERE	JAN	FEB	MAR	APR	MAY	JUN	JUL	AUG	SEP	OCT	NOV	DEC
°F AVG MAX	77	78	81	83	82	78	77	76	76	79	78	77
°F AVG MIN	62	62	64	66	67	66	65	65	65	65	65	63
DIURNAL RANGE	15	16	17	17	15	12	12	11	11	14	13	14
RAIN/INCHES	0.1	0.1	0.1	0.8	7.1	25.1	30.5	33.7	29.5	7.8	2.4	0.8
HUMIDITY/%	68	67	68	67	72	82	84	86	86	80	74	71
BLOOM SEASON	*	*	*			*	*					
DAYS CLR @ 8AM	7	7	8	10	6	2	1	0	0	4	3	4
DAYS CLR @ 2PM	4	3	4	4	3	1	0	0	0	2	1	2
RAIN/MM	3	3	3	20	180	638	775	856	749	198	61	20
°C AVG MAX	25.2	25.7	27.4	28.5	27.9	25.7	25.2	24.6	24.6	26.3	25.7	25.2
°C AVG MIN	16.8	16.8	17.9	19.0	19.6	19.0	18.5	18.5	18.5	18.5	18.5	17.4
DIURNAL RANGE	8.4	8.9	9.5	9.3	8.3	6.7	6.7	6.1	6.1	7.8	7.2	7.8
S/HEMISPHERE	JUL	AUG	SEP	OCT	NOV	DEC	JAN	FEB	MAR	APR	MAY	JUN

Cultural Recommendations

LIGHT: 2000–3000 fc. Strong air movement is recommended at all times.

TEMPERATURES: Summer days average 76–78°F (25–26°C), and nights average 65–66°F (19°C), with a diurnal range of 11–12°F (6–7°C). The warmest weather occurs in spring. Days average 81–83°F (27–29°C), and nights 64–67°F (18–20°C), with a diurnal range of 15–17°F (8–10°C).

HUMIDITY: 80–85% in summer and early autumn, dropping to 65–70% in winter and spring.

WATER: Rainfall is very heavy from late spring into autumn, but conditions are very dry in winter. Cultivated plants should be kept evenly moist in summer and autumn, but water should be gradually reduced in late autumn.

FERTILIZER: ¼–½ recommended strength, applied weekly during the growing season. A high-nitrogen fertilizer is beneficial from spring to midsummer, but a fertilizer high in phosphates should be used in late summer and autumn.

REST PERIOD: Winter days average 77–78°F (25–26°C), and nights average 62–63°F (17°C), with a diurnal range of 14–16°F (8–9°C). In the habitat, rainfall is low for 3–5 months in winter; but high humidity and nightly cooling result in heavy deposits of dew during most of the period. In cultivation, water should be reduced and the plants allowed to dry out between waterings. They should not remain completely dry for extended periods, however. Occasional early morning mistings between waterings may be beneficial, especially on bright, sunny days. Fertilizer should reduced or eliminated. In the habitat, light is highest in winter and spring.

GROWING MEDIA: Mounting plants on tree-fern or cork slabs accommodates their pendent growth habit, but humidity must be high and plants must be watered at least once daily in summer. Plants may be potted in hanging pots or baskets filled with any open, fast-draining medium. Repotting is best done in early spring when new roots are growing.

MISCELLANEOUS NOTES: The bloom season shown in the climate table is based on collection records in the Philippines. *D. spurium* blooms every few weeks all year. Plants that produce flowers which last a single day commonly bloom several times during the year. Flowering occurs 10 days after a sudden 10°F (5°C) drop in daytime temperatures.

Plant and Flower Information

PLANT SIZE AND TYPE: A 6–12 in. (15–30 cm) sympodial epiphyte or lithophyte.

PSEUDOBULB: 6–12 in. (15–30 cm) long. Stems are thickened with a ridge on each side above the slender, almost wiry base. Growths emerge from a slender, descending rhizome. Each erect new growth emerges below the preceding growth, causing the entire plant to be horizontal or arching. The stems are spaced about 0.4 in. (1 cm) apart on the rhizome. When young, the stems are covered with thin overlapping sheaths; but with age, the stems are bare.

LEAVES: 2–3 per growth. The terminal leaves are 3–6 in. (8–15 cm) long. They are lanceolate, taper to a fine point, and all tend to point in one direction.

INFLORESCENCE: Inflorescences emerge below the leaves on the lower, leafless portion of the stem.

FLOWERS: 1 per inflorescence. The flowers are 1.2–1.6 in. (3–4 cm) across. Blossoms are not hairy. White sepals and petals open fully. The lip is cream or pinkish purple with prominent purple-brown veins and an orange flush in the center. The cupped midlobe is nearly round near the apex and narrow at the base. Comber (ref. 75) notes that the drawing of a flower from a Philippine plant shows a different lip shape from plants in Java. Blossoms last a single day.

HYBRIDIZING NOTES: Chromosome count is 2n = 40 (ref. 280, 504, 580).

REFERENCES: 12, 25, 75, 111, 190, 200, 219, 254, 278, 280, 286, 295, 296, 310, 317, 394, 395, 402, 445, 455, 469, 504, 536, 580, 592.

PHOTOS/DRAWINGS: 12, *75*, 200, *455*, 469.

Dendrobium squalens Lindley. Now considered a synonym of *Maxillaria (Xylobium?) squalens* Lindley. REFERENCES: 216, 254, 445.

Dendrobium squamiferum J. J. Smith

AKA: Kränzlin (ref. 254) included *D. squamiferum* as a synonym of *D. melanostictum* Schlechter, but J. J. Smith (ref. 470) disagreed.

ORIGIN/HABITAT: Irian Jaya (western New Guinea). Plants grow on Pandamus trees and in *Metroxylon* swamps near sea level along the Noord River. They were also collected at Bivouac Island and near Pandamus Creek.

CLIMATE: Station #97796, Kokenau (Kokonau), Irian Jaya, Lat. 4.7°S, Long. 136.4°E, at 10 ft. (3 m). Record extreme temperatures are not available for this location.

N/HEMISPHERE	JAN	FEB	MAR	APR	MAY	JUN	JUL	AUG	SEP	OCT	NOV	DEC
°F AVG MAX	83	83	86	88	90	89	89	89	90	88	87	84
°F AVG MIN	73	73	74	74	74	75	74	74	74	74	74	73
DIURNAL RANGE	10	10	12	14	16	14	15	15	16	14	13	11
RAIN/INCHES	18.4	15.8	18.9	11.6	9.7	10.6	11.5	15.7	11.6	11.6	16.0	19.9
HUMIDITY/%					N/A							
BLOOM SEASON										*	*	
DAYS CLR					N/A							
RAIN/MM	467	401	479	295	245	269	293	400	294	296	407	506
°C AVG MAX	28.6	28.4	30.2	31.1	32.1	31.9	31.9	31.7	32.0	31.4	30.7	28.7
°C AVG MIN	22.7	22.6	23.3	23.4	23.5	23.7	23.6	23.5	23.4	23.4	23.5	23.0
DIURNAL RANGE	5.9	5.8	6.9	7.7	8.6	8.2	8.3	8.2	8.6	8.0	7.2	5.7
S/HEMISPHERE	JUL	AUG	SEP	OCT	NOV	DEC	JAN	FEB	MAR	APR	MAY	JUN

Cultural Recommendations

LIGHT: 2500–3500 fc.

TEMPERATURES: Throughout the year, days average 83–90°F (28–32°C),

and nights average 73–75°F (23–24°C), with a diurnal range of 10–16°F (6–9°C).

HUMIDITY: Information is not available for this location. However, records from nearby stations indicate that humidity probably averages near 85% year-round.

WATER: Rainfall is very heavy all year. Cultivated plants should be kept evenly moist but not soggy. Warm water might be beneficial.

FERTILIZER: ¼–½ recommended strength. A balanced fertilizer should be applied weekly to biweekly throughout the year.

REST PERIOD: Growing temperatures should be maintained year-round. The smallest diurnal range occurs in winter. Water and fertilizer might be reduced slightly, especially for plants cultivated in the dark, short-day conditions common in the temperate latitudes. However, plants should never be allowed to dry out completely. In the habitat, seasonal light variation is minor.

GROWING MEDIA: Plants may be mounted on tree-fern or cork slabs or potted in small pots filled with any open, fast-draining medium. Probably it is better to pot because of the heavy water requirement. Repotting may be done anytime new roots are growing.

MISCELLANEOUS NOTES: The bloom season shown in the climate table is based on collection reports.

Plant and Flower Information

PLANT SIZE AND TYPE: A 12.0–29.5 in. (30–75 cm) sympodial epiphyte.

PSEUDOBULB: 12.0–29.5 in. (30–75 cm) long. The clustered stems are leafy.

LEAVES: Many. The lanceolate leaves are 3–5 in. (7.5–12.5 cm) long. They have 2 tiny teeth at the apex. Apical and basal leaves are smallest.

INFLORESCENCE: Short. Inflorescences emerge through 2 leaf sheaths on leafy stems. Flowers are held in clusters.

FLOWERS: 6–8 per inflorescence. The ovate dorsal sepal is 0.4 in. (1.1 cm) long. Lateral sepals are somewhat triangular. The petals are oblong. The lip is concave with small sidelobes and a roundly triangular midlobe. Flower color was not included in the original description, but Schlechter (ref. 437) indicates that all related species are yellowish brown on the outside, white on the inside, with a yellow lip and darker yellow to orange markings. Blossoms have peculiar thin brown scales on the backside.

REFERENCES: 220, 254, 437, 445, 470.

Dendrobium squarrosum J. J. Smith

ORIGIN/HABITAT: Borneo, near Samenggaria. Habitat elevation is unavailable, but plants were cultivated at the botanical garden in Bogor, Java. The following climate data should be used with caution.

CLIMATE: Station #96755, Bogor, Indonesia, Lat. 6.5°S, Long. 106.8°E, at 558 ft. (170 m). Record extreme temperatures are 96°F (36°C) and 66°F (19°C).

N/HEMISPHERE	JAN	FEB	MAR	APR	MAY	JUN	JUL	AUG	SEP	OCT	NOV	DEC
°F AVG MAX	86	87	88	88	87	85	84	84	85	86	87	86
°F AVG MIN	73	73	73	74	74	74	74	74	74	75	75	74
DIURNAL RANGE	13	14	15	14	13	11	10	10	11	11	12	12
RAIN/INCHES	2.1	1.0	0.5	5.0	8.1	18.8	23.7	20.2	14.4	12.0	11.9	3.4
HUMIDITY/%	72	68	65	66	74	79	84	84	81	79	77	75
BLOOM SEASON	N/A											
DAYS CLR @ 7AM	14	14	14	11	5	3	1	2	4	6	10	12
DAYS CLR @ 1PM	9	10	8	5	1	1	0	0	1	1	3	7
RAIN/MM	53	25	13	127	206	478	602	513	366	305	302	86
°C AVG MAX	30.0	30.6	31.1	31.1	30.6	29.4	28.9	28.9	29.4	30.0	30.6	30.0
°C AVG MIN	22.8	22.8	22.8	23.3	23.3	23.3	23.3	23.3	23.3	23.9	23.9	23.3
DIURNAL RANGE	7.2	7.8	8.3	7.8	7.3	6.1	5.6	5.6	6.1	6.1	6.7	6.7
S/HEMISPHERE	JUL	AUG	SEP	OCT	NOV	DEC	JAN	FEB	MAR	APR	MAY	JUN

Cultural Recommendations

LIGHT: 1500–2500 fc. Diffused or barely dappled light is preferred. Direct sunlight should be avoided.

TEMPERATURES: Throughout the year, days average 84–88°F (29–31°C), and nights average 73–75°F (23–24°C), with a diurnal range of 10–15°F (6–8°C). Average highs vary only 4°F (2°C) all year, and nights fluctuate even less. Temperatures at higher elevations are a few degrees cooler, but the diurnal range and limited seasonal fluctuation are similar. Cultivated plants may not tolerate wide temperature variations.

HUMIDITY: 75–85% most of the year, dropping to 65–70% in winter and early spring.

WATER: Rainfall is very heavy from spring into autumn, but conditions are very dry for 2 months in winter. During the growing season, plants should never be allowed to dry out completely, but water should be gradually reduced in late autumn.

FERTILIZER: ¼–½ recommended strength, applied weekly. A high-nitrogen fertilizer is beneficial from spring to midsummer, but a fertilizer high in phosphates should be used in late summer and autumn.

REST PERIOD: Growing conditions should be maintained all year; but the diurnal range increases slightly in winter, and rainfall is very low for 2–3 months. In cultivation, water should be reduced and the plants allowed to become dry between waterings. However, they should not remain dry for prolonged periods. Fertilizer may be reduced or eliminated anytime the plant is not actively growing. In the habitat, light is highest in winter.

GROWING MEDIA: Plants may be mounted on tree-fern or cork slabs if humidity is high and the plants are watered daily in summer. When plants are potted, any open, fast-draining medium may be used. Repotting may be done anytime roots are actively growing.

MISCELLANEOUS NOTES: The plant was described in 1914 in *Bull. Jard. Bot. Buit.* 2nd sér. 13:22.

Plant and Flower Information

PLANT SIZE AND TYPE: A 15 in. (38 cm) sympodial epiphyte.

PSEUDOBULB: 15 in. (38 cm) long. Stems are angled, dark green, and 7-grooved.

LEAVES: Many. The leaves are 2–3 in. (4–8 cm) long, somewhat linear, and sickle-shaped. They are dark violet, rigid, and shiny. The leaf sheaths, which may be dirty green or yellow-green, are covered with dark hairs.

INFLORESCENCE: Short. Inflorescences emerge through the leaf sheaths.

FLOWERS: 2 per inflorescence. The flowers are 0.5 in. (1.3 cm) across. They are shiny white with orange stripes. Blossoms have an ovate-oblong dorsal sepal, oblong-triangular lateral sepals, and the recurled petals are somewhat sickle-shaped. The 3-lobed lip is marked with pale yellow and orange. It has 3 raised lines and an uneven margin. The midlobe terminates abruptly.

REFERENCES: 221, 286, 295.

Dendrobium statterianum Hort. ex O'Brien. According to Clements (ref. 67), this as an invalid name. He suggests that the name may have been used for a plant of *D. striaenopsis* M. Clements and D. Jones rather than a plant of *D. bigibbum* Lindley where it is generally placed. REFERENCES: 67.

Dendrobium × *statterianum* (Sander) Rolfe. See *D. statterianum*. Index Kewensis (ref. 220) lists this as a possible hybrid between *D. bigibbum* Lindley and *D. phalaenopsis* Fitzgerald. REFERENCES: 67, 220.

Dendrobium steatoglossum Rchb. f.

ORIGIN/HABITAT: New Caledonia. Plants grow in several locations at 500–2600 ft. (150–800 m), but most collections are made at the south end of the island at about 1000 ft. (300 m).

CLIMATE: Station #91592, Noumea, New Caledonia, Lat. 22.3°S, Long. 166.5°E, at 246 ft. (75 m). Temperatures are calculated for an elevation of 1000 ft. (300 m), resulting in probable extremes of 97°F (36°C) and 50°F (10°C).

N/HEMISPHERE	JAN	FEB	MAR	APR	MAY	JUN	JUL	AUG	SEP	OCT	NOV	DEC
°F AVG MAX	74	74	76	78	81	84	84	83	83	81	77	75
°F AVG MIN	60	59	61	63	66	68	70	71	70	68	64	62
DIURNAL RANGE	14	15	15	15	15	16	14	12	13	13	13	13
RAIN/INCHES	3.6	2.6	2.5	2.0	2.4	2.6	3.7	5.1	5.7	5.2	4.4	3.7
HUMIDITY/%	73	70	69	67	68	69	71	74	75	76	73	73
BLOOM SEASON	*	*	*	*	*	*	*	*	*	*	*	*
DAYS CLR @ 11AM	7	9	9	15	12	10	7	6	7	7	7	7
DAYS CLR @ 5PM	7	11	6	11	7	6	5	4	4	5	3	7
RAIN/MM	91	66	64	51	61	66	94	130	145	132	112	94
°C AVG MAX	23.1	23.1	24.2	25.3	27.0	28.6	28.6	28.1	28.1	27.0	24.7	23.6
°C AVG MIN	15.3	14.7	15.8	17.0	18.6	19.7	20.8	21.4	20.8	19.7	17.5	16.4
DIURNAL RANGE	7.8	8.4	8.4	8.3	8.4	8.9	7.8	6.7	7.3	7.4	7.2	7.2
S/HEMISPHERE	JUL	AUG	SEP	OCT	NOV	DEC	JAN	FEB	MAR	APR	MAY	JUN

Cultural Recommendations

LIGHT: 1800–2500 fc. Despite the relatively high number of clear days in the habitat, the plant grows only in dense forests.

TEMPERATURES: Summer days average 81–84°F (27–29°C), and nights average 68–71°F (20–21°C), with a diurnal range of 12–16°F (7–9°C).

HUMIDITY: 70–75% is recorded at the weather station, but humidity may be greater in the forest habitat.

WATER: Rainfall is light to moderate all year. The wettest period occurs in late summer and early autumn. Cultivated plants should be allowed to dry slightly between waterings but should never remain dry for long periods.

FERTILIZER: ¼–½ recommended strength, applied weekly. A high-nitrogen fertilizer is beneficial from spring to midsummer, but a fertilizer high in phosphates should be used in late summer and autumn.

REST PERIOD: Winter days average 74–76°F (23–24°C), and nights average 59–62°F (15–16°C), with a diurnal range if 13–15°F (7–8°C). Winter rainfall occurs intermittently as showers, and cultivated plants should be allowed to become slightly dry between waterings. In the habitat, light is highest in early spring.

GROWING MEDIA: Plants may be mounted on tree-fern or cork slabs or potted in any open, fast-draining medium. Repotting may be done anytime new roots are growing.

MISCELLANEOUS NOTES: The bloom season shown in the climate table is based on reports from the habitat.

Plant and Flower Information

PLANT SIZE AND TYPE: A 39–118 in. (100–300 cm) sympodial terrestrial.

PSEUDOBULB: 39–118 in. (100–300 cm) long. Tall woody canes resemble a shrublike mass of black bamboo. They are swollen at the base.

LEAVES: Many. The leaves are about 5 in. (12.5 cm) long, oblong, distichous, and covered with black spots.

INFLORESCENCE: Shorter than the leaves. Inflorescences emerge above the leaves from nodes along the side of the stem.

FLOWERS: 1–2 per inflorescence. The long-lasting flowers are described as similar to *D. aduncum* Wallich. The pointed sepals and petals are white. They do not open widely. The green lip has 3 raised lines that terminate below the midpoint and a groove at the tip.

REFERENCES: 173, 216, 254, 432.

PHOTOS/DRAWINGS: 173.

Dendrobium steinii J. J. Smith

ORIGIN/HABITAT: New Guinea. Plants were found at Majalibit Bay on Waigeo Island off the northwest coast. Habitat elevation was not given, but topographical maps of the region indicate that elevations are generally less than 2000 ft. (610 m).

CLIMATE: Station #97502, Jefman, Indonesian New Guinea, Lat. 0.9°S, Long. 131.1°E, at an elevation of 10 ft. (3 m). Record extreme temperatures are 93°F (34°C) and 72°F (22°C).

N/HEMISPHERE	JAN	FEB	MAR	APR	MAY	JUN	JUL	AUG	SEP	OCT	NOV	DEC
°F AVG MAX	85	87	89	89	88	88	88	88	89	90	89	87
°F AVG MIN	77	77	77	78	78	78	79	79	79	79	78	78
DIURNAL RANGE	8	10	12	11	10	10	9	9	10	11	11	9
RAIN/INCHES	13.1	9.7	10.3	8.1	6.9	7.0	7.2	6.6	8.0	9.6	12.4	13.4
HUMIDITY/%	85	86	85	82	82	83	81	81	82	82	85	84
BLOOM SEASON												*
DAYS CLR @ 9AM	2	2	2	5	6	1	6	1	4	5	5	6
DAYS CLR @ 3PM	3	2	3	4	1	1	5	1	2	4	3	5
RAIN/MM	333	246	262	206	175	178	183	168	203	244	315	340
°C AVG MAX	29.4	30.6	31.7	31.7	31.1	31.1	31.1	31.1	31.7	32.2	31.7	30.6
°C AVG MIN	25.0	25.0	25.0	25.6	25.6	25.6	26.1	26.1	26.1	26.1	25.6	25.6
DIURNAL RANGE	4.4	5.6	6.7	6.1	5.6	5.6	5.0	5.0	5.6	6.1	6.1	5.0
S/HEMISPHERE	JUL	AUG	SEP	OCT	NOV	DEC	JAN	FEB	MAR	APR	MAY	JUN

Cultural Recommendations

LIGHT: 3000–4000 fc. or as much light as possible without burning the foliage. Some shading is required from spring into early autumn.

TEMPERATURES: Throughout the year, days average 85–90°F (29–32°C), and nights average 77–79°F (25–26°C), with a diurnal range of 8–12°F (4–7°C). More temperature variation occurs each day than occurs seasonally.

HUMIDITY: 80–85% year-round.

WATER: Rainfall is moderate to heavy all year. Cultivated plants should be kept moist all year.

FERTILIZER: ¼–½ recommended strength. A balanced fertilizer should be applied weekly to biweekly throughout the year.

REST PERIOD: Growing temperatures should be maintained year-round. In the habitat, there is no real dry season. Water should be reduced for plants grown in the dark, short-day conditions common in temperate-latitude winters, but they should never be allowed to dry out completely. Fertilizer should be reduced anytime water is reduced. In the habitat, light is lowest in winter.

GROWING MEDIA: Plants may be mounted on tree-fern or cork slabs if humidity is high and plants are watered daily in summer. If plants are potted, any open, fast-draining medium may be used. Repotting may be done anytime new roots are growing.

MISCELLANEOUS NOTES: The bloom season shown in the climate table is based on reports from the habitat.

Plant and Flower Information

PLANT SIZE AND TYPE: A sympodial epiphyte that exceeds 16 in. (40 cm).

PSEUDOBULB: The pale green stems are elongated, flattened, and shiny. The portion of the stem present at the time the plant was described was 16 in. (41 cm) long.

LEAVES: Many. The oblong to ovate leaves are 3–4 in. (8–10 cm) long. They are dirty green, firmly but thinly textured, and somewhat twisted at the base.

INFLORESCENCE: Short. Inflorescences emerge through the leaf bases.

FLOWERS: 2 per inflorescence. The fleshy flowers are 0.5 in. (1.3 cm) long. The dorsal sepal is oblong, pointed, concave, and incurved near the tip.

Lateral sepals are obliquely triangular overall and somewhat sickle-shaped at the incurved apex. The rounded petals are obovate-oblong. The erect, recurved lip is concave. The erect sidelobes have rounded, uneven margins. The lip ridge is lobed at the base.

REFERENCES: 225, 486.

Dendrobium stelidiiferum J. J. Smith

ORIGIN/HABITAT: Sumatra. Plants were originally found near Padang on Mt. Singgalang at about 5600 ft. (1700 m).

CLIMATE: Station #96163, Padang, Sumatra, Indonesia, Lat. 0.9°S, Long. 100.4°E, at 19 ft. (6 m). Temperatures are calculated for an elevation of 5600 ft. (1700 m), resulting in probable extremes of 76°F (24°C) and 50°F (10°C).

N/HEMISPHERE	JAN	FEB	MAR	APR	MAY	JUN	JUL	AUG	SEP	OCT	NOV	DEC
°F AVG MAX	69	69	68	68	68	68	69	69	69	69	70	69
°F AVG MIN	56	56	56	56	56	56	56	56	56	57	57	56
DIURNAL RANGE	13	13	12	12	12	12	13	13	13	12	13	13
RAIN/INCHES	10.9	13.7	6.0	19.5	20.4	18.9	13.8	10.2	12.1	14.3	12.4	12.1
HUMIDITY/%	81	82	82	84	85	84	81	81	82	83	81	81
BLOOM SEASON	N/A											
DAYS CLR @ 7AM	5	1	1	0	0	2	2	1	2	2	3	5
DAYS CLR @ 1PM	5	2	2	1	1	3	3	4	3	3	6	5
RAIN/MM	277	348	152	495	518	480	351	259	307	363	315	307
°C AVG MAX	20.3	20.3	19.8	19.8	19.8	19.8	20.3	20.3	20.3	20.3	20.9	20.3
°C AVG MIN	13.1	13.1	13.1	13.1	13.1	13.1	13.1	13.1	13.1	13.7	13.7	13.1
DIURNAL RANGE	7.2	7.2	6.7	6.7	6.7	6.7	7.2	7.2	7.2	6.6	7.2	7.2
S/HEMISPHERE	JUL	AUG	SEP	OCT	NOV	DEC	JAN	FEB	MAR	APR	MAY	JUN

Cultural Recommendations

LIGHT: 2000–3000 fc. Diffused light is preferred.

TEMPERATURES: Throughout the year, days average 68–70°F (20–21°C), and nights average 56–57°F (13–14°C), with a diurnal range of 12–13°F (7°C). Probable extremes vary only a few degrees from the averages, indicating that the plant may not tolerate wide temperature fluctuations.

HUMIDITY: 80–85% year-round.

WATER: Rainfall is heavy all year. Cultivated plants should be constantly moist but not soggy.

FERTILIZER: ¼–½ recommended strength. A balanced fertilizer should be applied weekly to biweekly throughout the year.

REST PERIOD: Growing conditions should be maintained year-round. Water may be reduced somewhat for cultivated plants in winter, but they should never be allowed to dry out completely.

GROWING MEDIA: Plants may be mounted on tree-fern or cork slabs or potted in small pots filled with any open, fast-draining medium. Repotting may be done anytime new roots are actively growing.

MISCELLANEOUS NOTES: The plant was described in 1920 in *Bull. Jard. Bot. Buit.* 3rd sér. 2:66.

Plant and Flower Information

PLANT SIZE AND TYPE: A 13 in. (32 cm) sympodial epiphyte.

PSEUDOBULB: 13 in. (32 cm) long. The clustered stems have an oval to subovoid swelling for part of their length.

LEAVES: Many. The leaves are 1.2–2.4 in. (3–6 cm) long, nearly terete, and channeled. Foliage is rudimentary on the upper part of the stem.

INFLORESCENCE: Short. Blossoms are carried at nodes on the leafless, apical portion of the stem.

FLOWERS: 1 per inflorescence. The yellow flowers are 0.6 in. (1.5 cm) long. Sepals have a faint rose-purple flush at the base with 3–4 faint rose-purple veins. The lip sidelobes have rose-purple veins, while the small midlobe is dark yellow with light yellow ridges. The converging sepals and petals are recurved at the tips. Lateral sepals are obliquely triangular with a rectangular apex. The lip is erect, abruptly recurved. The large, somewhat triangular sidelobes are incurved, and the small midlobe in the indentation between the sidelobes.

REFERENCES: 222.

Dendrobium stella-silvae (Loher and Kränzlin) Ames. Now considered a synonym of *Epigeneium stella-silvae* (Loher and Kränzlin) Summerhayes. REFERENCES: 12, 222, 229, 296, 373, 499, 536.

Dendrobium stelliferum J. J. Smith. Now considered a synonym of *Diplocaulobium stelliferum* (J. J. Smith) A. Hawkes. REFERENCES: 224, 229, 445, 470.

Dendrobium stenocentrum Schlechter. Now considered a synonym of *Cadetia stenocentrum* (Schlechter) Schlechter. REFERENCES: 219, 254, 437, 444.

Dendrobium stenoglossum Gagnepain. Now considered a synonym of *Flickingeria stenoglossa* (Gagnepain) Seidenfaden. REFERENCES: 214, 225, 231, 266, 448, 449.

Dendrobium stenophyllum Schlechter

ORIGIN/HABITAT: Papua New Guinea. Plants grow on forest trees in the Maboro Range at about 3950 ft. (1200 m).

CLIMATE: Station #200192, Garaina, Papua New Guinea, Lat. 7.9°S, Long. 147.1°E, at 2350 ft. (716 m). Temperatures are calculated for an elevation of 3950 ft. (1200 m), resulting in probable extremes of 89°F (32°C) and 41°F (5°C).

N/HEMISPHERE	JAN	FEB	MAR	APR	MAY	JUN	JUL	AUG	SEP	OCT	NOV	DEC
°F AVG MAX	75	77	78	79	80	80	80	80	79	79	78	76
°F AVG MIN	58	58	58	59	58	59	60	60	60	59	59	58
DIURNAL RANGE	17	19	20	20	22	21	20	20	19	20	19	18
RAIN/INCHES	5.8	6.5	8.7	11.1	11.8	11.9	8.9	11.7	11.5	9.9	7.7	5.2
HUMIDITY/%	84	82	82	81	80	80	81	81	82	81	84	84
BLOOM SEASON						*						*
DAYS CLR	N/A											
RAIN/MM	147	165	221	282	300	302	226	297	292	251	196	132
°C AVG MAX	23.8	24.9	25.4	26.0	26.5	26.5	26.5	26.5	26.0	26.0	25.4	24.3
°C AVG MIN	14.3	14.3	14.3	14.9	14.3	14.9	15.4	15.4	15.4	14.9	14.9	14.3
DIURNAL RANGE	9.5	10.6	11.1	11.1	12.2	11.6	11.1	11.1	10.6	11.1	10.5	10.0
S/HEMISPHERE	JUL	AUG	SEP	OCT	NOV	DEC	JAN	FEB	MAR	APR	MAY	JUN

Cultural Recommendations

LIGHT: 2000–3000 fc.

TEMPERATURES: Throughout the year, days average 75–80°F (24–27°C), and nights average 58–60°F (14–15°C), with a diurnal range of 17–22°F (10–12°C).

HUMIDITY: 80–85% year-round.

WATER: Rainfall is heavy all year, but conditions are slightly drier in winter. Cultivated plants should be kept moist but not soggy.

FERTILIZER: ¼–½ recommended strength. A balanced fertilizer should be applied weekly to biweekly throughout the year. The Royal Botanic Garden in Edinburgh uses a seaweed-based fertilizer for high-elevation plants from New Guinea.

REST PERIOD: Growing conditions vary only slightly during the year. In the habitat, rainfall is slightly lower in winter. Water and fertilizer should be reduced somewhat, especially for plants cultivated in the darker, short-day conditions common in temperate-latitude winters. However, plants should never be allowed to dry out completely. In the habitat, light is slightly higher in winter.

GROWING MEDIA: Plants may be mounted on tree-fern or cork slabs if humidity is high and plants are watered at least once daily in summer. When plants are potted, any open, fast-draining medium may be used. Repotting may be done anytime new roots are growing.

MISCELLANEOUS NOTES: The bloom season shown in the climate table is based on reports from the habitat. Plants that produce flowers which last a single day commonly bloom several times during the year. Flowering usually occurs 7–14 days after a sudden 10°F (5°C) drop in daytime temperatures.

Plant and Flower Information

PLANT SIZE AND TYPE: A 16–28 in. (40–70 cm) sympodial epiphyte.

PSEUDOBULB: 16–28 in. (40–70 cm) long. The curved stems are erect to arching. They do not branch.

LEAVES: The very narrow leaves are 4.7–5.5 in. (12–14 cm) long and unequally bilobed at the apex.

INFLORESCENCE: Short.

FLOWERS: 2 per inflorescence. The flowers are 0.4 in. (1 cm) long and do not open widely. The keeled sepals and rounded petals are yellowish white. The lip is marked with violet, the column is marked with a red spot, and the callus is orange-yellow. The 3-lobed lip has somewhat sickle-shaped sidelobes that are ruffled on the outer margin. The midlobe is straight across the front with a ruffled front margin and a sprinkling of wartlike areas. Blossoms are short-lived.

REFERENCES: 221, 437, 445.

PHOTOS/DRAWINGS: 437.

Dendrobium stenophyton Schlechter.
Now considered to be a synonym of *Diplocaulobium stenophyton* (Schlechter) Hunt and Summerhayes. However, Kränzlin (ref. 254) described this plant as *Diplocaulobium arachne*, but Schlechter (ref. 436) moved Kränzlin's species to *Dendrobium stenophyton*. REFERENCES: 213, 220, 230, 254, 436, 483.

Dendrobium stictanthum Schlechter

ORIGIN/HABITAT: Northern Papua New Guinea. Plants grow on forest trees in the Torricelli Range at about 2600 ft. (800 m).

CLIMATE: Station #94004, Wewak, Papua New Guinea, Lat. 3.6°S, Long. 143.7°E, at 16 ft. (5 m). Temperatures are calculated for an elevation of 2600 ft. (800 m), resulting in probable extremes of 89°F (32°C) and 53°F (12°C).

N/HEMISPHERE	JAN	FEB	MAR	APR	MAY	JUN	JUL	AUG	SEP	OCT	NOV	DEC
°F AVG MAX	79	79	79	79	79	79	78	77	78	79	79	79
°F AVG MIN	65	65	65	66	66	66	66	66	65	65	66	65
DIURNAL RANGE	14	14	14	13	13	13	12	11	13	14	13	14
RAIN/INCHES	7.6	4.8	5.3	10.0	13.3	14.5	12.1	11.9	14.9	16.9	15.1	10.8
HUMIDITY/%	80	79	79	78	79	81	82	82	81	82	81	80
BLOOM SEASON			*									
DAYS CLR	N/A											
RAIN/MM	193	122	135	254	338	368	307	302	378	429	384	274
°C AVG MAX	26.3	26.3	26.3	26.3	26.3	26.3	25.8	25.2	25.8	26.3	26.3	26.3
°C AVG MIN	18.6	18.6	18.6	19.1	19.1	19.1	19.1	19.1	18.6	18.6	19.1	18.6
DIURNAL RANGE	7.7	7.7	7.7	7.2	7.2	7.2	6.7	6.1	7.2	7.7	7.2	7.7
S/HEMISPHERE	JUL	AUG	SEP	OCT	NOV	DEC	JAN	FEB	MAR	APR	MAY	JUN

Cultural Recommendations

LIGHT: 2000–3000 fc.

TEMPERATURES: Throughout the year, days average 77–79°F (25–26°C), and nights average 65–66°F (19°C), with a diurnal range of 11–14°F (6–8°C).

HUMIDITY: Near 80% year-round.

WATER: Rainfall is moderate to heavy all year, but conditions are slightly drier for 1–2 months in winter. Cultivated plants should be kept moist but not soggy.

FERTILIZER: ¼–½ recommended strength. A balanced fertilizer should be applied weekly to biweekly throughout the year.

REST PERIOD: Growing temperatures should be maintained all year. However, water and fertilizer should be reduced somewhat, especially if plants are cultivated in the darker, short-day conditions common during temperate-latitude winters. Plants should never be allowed to dry out completely, however. In the habitat, seasonal light variation is minor.

GROWING MEDIA: Plants may be mounted on tree-fern or cork slabs if humidity is high and plants are watered at least once daily in summer. When plants are potted, any open, fast-draining medium may be used. They may be repotted anytime new roots are growing.

MISCELLANEOUS NOTES: The bloom season shown in the climate table is based on reports from the habitat. Plants that produce flowers which last a single day commonly bloom several times during the year. Flowering usually occurs 7–14 days after a sudden 10°F (5°C) drop in daytime temperatures.

Plant and Flower Information

PLANT SIZE AND TYPE: A 24–31 in. (60–80 cm) sympodial epiphyte.

PSEUDOBULB: 24–31 in. (60–80 cm) long. The stems are slender, zigzag, and arranged in a loose, spreading growth habit.

LEAVES: Each growth is laxly leafy. The smooth lanceolate leaves, which are erect or nearly so, are 2–4 in. (5–10 cm) long.

INFLORESCENCE: Very short. Inflorescences are borne from nodes along the side of the stem.

FLOWERS: 2 per inflorescence. The flowers are 0.7 in. (1.8 cm) across. Sepals and petals are incurved to nearly a full curl at the tips. The whitish segments are warty and closely dotted with violet-red. The 3-lobed lip has smooth, rounded sidelobes and a ruffled, scalloped midlobe with a point at the apex. The column is marked with violet-red. Blossoms are short-lived.

REFERENCES: 221, 437, 445.

PHOTOS/DRAWINGS: 437.

Dendrobium stolleanum Schlechter

ORIGIN/HABITAT: Papua New Guinea. Plants grow in the Sepik River region at 4600–4900 ft. (1400–1500 m).

CLIMATE: Station #200004, Ambunti, Papua New Guinea, Lat. 4.2°S, Long. 142.8°E, at 164 ft. (50 m). Temperatures are calculated for an elevation of 4600 ft. (1400 m), resulting in probable extremes of 84°F (29°C) and 37°F (3°C).

N/HEMISPHERE	JAN	FEB	MAR	APR	MAY	JUN	JUL	AUG	SEP	OCT	NOV	DEC
°F AVG MAX	73	75	75	75	76	75	75	75	75	75	75	74
°F AVG MIN	57	58	59	58	58	58	57	58	58	58	58	59
DIURNAL RANGE	16	17	16	17	18	17	18	17	17	17	17	15
RAIN/INCHES	6.4	7.4	7.7	8.5	9.2	9.4	10.9	10.2	12.2	10.4	8.3	5.2
HUMIDITY/%	N/A											
BLOOM SEASON		*		*								
DAYS CLR	N/A											
RAIN/MM	163	188	196	216	234	239	277	259	310	264	211	132
°C AVG MAX	23.0	24.1	24.1	24.1	24.6	24.1	24.1	24.1	24.1	24.1	24.1	23.5
°C AVG MIN	14.1	14.6	15.2	14.6	14.6	14.6	14.1	14.6	14.6	14.6	14.6	15.2
DIURNAL RANGE	8.9	9.5	8.9	9.5	10.0	9.5	10.0	9.5	9.5	9.5	9.5	8.3
S/HEMISPHERE	JUL	AUG	SEP	OCT	NOV	DEC	JAN	FEB	MAR	APR	MAY	JUN

Cultural Recommendations

LIGHT: 2000–3000 fc.

TEMPERATURES: Throughout the year, days average 73–76°F (23–25°C),

and nights average 57–59°F (14–15°C), with a diurnal range of 15–18°F (8–10°C).

HUMIDITY: Information is not available for this location. However, records from nearby stations indicate that humidity probably averages near 80% year-round.

WATER: Rainfall is heavy year-round, with the greatest amounts falling in summer and early autumn. Cultivated plants should be kept moist but not soggy.

FERTILIZER: 1/4–1/2 recommended strength. A balanced fertilizer should be applied weekly to biweekly throughout the year.

REST PERIOD: Growing conditions should be maintained all year. Water and fertilizer may be reduced somewhat in winter, especially for plants grown in the dark, short-day conditions common in temperate latitudes. These plants should never be allowed to dry between waterings, however.

GROWING MEDIA: Plants may be mounted on cork or tree-fern slabs if humidity is high and plants are watered at least once daily in summer. When plants are potted, any open, fast-draining medium may be used, but fir bark is preferred by most growers. Repotting may be done anytime new roots are growing.

MISCELLANEOUS NOTES: The bloom season shown in the climate table is based on reports from the habitat.

Plant and Flower Information

PLANT SIZE AND TYPE: A 16–20 in. (40–50 cm) sympodial epiphyte.

PSEUDOBULB: 16–20 in. (40–50 cm) long. The plants consist of numerous branching stems.

LEAVES: Many. The lanceolate leaves, which are 0.8–2.4 in. (2–6 cm) long, are unequally bilobed at the apex.

INFLORESCENCE: Short.

FLOWERS: The flowers are 0.7 in. (1.7 cm) across. Bluish red sepals and petals are rose-red at the apex. Sepals and petals are more or less elliptical. The lip is acutely serrated along the margin.

REFERENCES: 223, 443.

Dendrobium stratiotes Rchb. f.

AKA: *D. strebloceras* Rchb. f. var. *rossianum* Rchb. f.

ORIGIN/HABITAT: Irian Jaya (western New Guinea), Halmahera and Morotai Islands in the Moluccas, and possibly Sulawesi (Celebes). Habitat elevation is unavailable, so the following climate data should be used with caution.

CLIMATE: Station #97406, Galela, Halmahera Island, Indonesia, Lat. 1.8°N, Long. 127.8°E, at 180 ft. (55 m). Record extreme temperatures are not available for this location.

N/HEMISPHERE	JAN	FEB	MAR	APR	MAY	JUN	JUL	AUG	SEP	OCT	NOV	DEC
°F AVG MAX	86	86	86	88	87	86	86	87	87	88	88	87
°F AVG MIN	76	74	76	76	77	75	73	75	75	76	77	76
DIURNAL RANGE	10	12	10	12	10	11	13	12	12	11	11	11
RAIN/INCHES	5.3	6.4	7.4	4.1	10.0	7.1	8.1	9.3	5.2	6.9	7.0	11.4
HUMIDITY/%	N/A											
BLOOM SEASON		*	*	*	*				*	*	*	
DAYS CLR	N/A											
RAIN/MM	134	163	188	104	254	180	205	236	132	175	177	289
°C AVG MAX	30.1	30.0	29.8	30.9	30.6	30.2	30.0	30.5	30.7	31.4	31.2	30.5
°C AVG MIN	24.3	23.6	24.6	24.6	24.9	23.9	22.9	23.7	24.2	24.9	25.2	24.6
DIURNAL RANGE	5.8	6.4	5.2	6.3	5.7	6.3	7.1	6.8	6.5	6.5	6.0	5.9
S/HEMISPHERE	JUL	AUG	SEP	OCT	NOV	DEC	JAN	FEB	MAR	APR	MAY	JUN

Cultural Recommendations

LIGHT: 2500–4000 fc.

TEMPERATURES: Throughout the year, days average 86–88°F (30–31°C), and nights average 73–77°F (23–25°C), with a diurnal range of 10–13°F (5–7°C). It should be noted that these values are based on estimated habitat elevation. Some growers recommend minimum winter temperatures near 59°F (15°C), which suggests a habitat elevation of 4000–5000 ft. (1220–1520 m). It is unknown whether these are the preferred conditions or merely ones to which the plants adapt.

HUMIDITY: Information is not available for this location. However, records from nearby stations indicate that humidity probably averages near 80% year-round.

WATER: Rainfall is moderate to heavy all year. Cultivated plants should be kept moist but not soggy.

FERTILIZER: 1/4–1/2 recommended strength. A balanced fertilizer should be applied weekly to biweekly throughout the year.

REST PERIOD: Growing conditions should be maintained year-round. Water should be reduced slightly in winter, especially for plants grown in the dark, short-day conditions common in temperate latitudes. Fertilizer should be reduced or eliminated if water is reduced. In the habitat, seasonal light variation is minor.

GROWING MEDIA: Plants may be mounted or potted in a basket. Growers indicate that excellent air circulation is particularly critical for this species. The base of the plant should be placed well above the potting medium. The stem should be supported by the stiff, strong roots and should never come in contact with the substrate. Repotting may be done anytime new roots are growing.

MISCELLANEOUS NOTES: The bloom season shown in the climate table is based on cultivation records. Reports from the habitat indicate that plants bloom summer through fall. Growers indicate that plants grown in a bright, moist environment with excellent air movement may bloom more than once a year.

Plant and Flower Information

PLANT SIZE AND TYPE: A 15–79 in. (38–200 cm) sympodial epiphyte.

PSEUDOBULB: 15–79 in. (38–200 cm) long. The canelike stems are commonly about 31 in. (80 cm) long and are swollen at the base.

LEAVES: Few to many per growth. The ovate leaves are 3.1–5.5 in. (8–14 cm) long, stiffly leathery, and persist for several years. The uppermost leaves are the smallest.

INFLORESCENCE: 3–12 in. (8–30 cm) long. Inflorescences are normally erect and emerge laterally from nodes along the middle or upper part of the pseudobulb.

FLOWERS: 3–15 per inflorescence. The flowers, which are 3–4 in. (8–10 cm) long, are considered by many to be the loveliest of the related species. They have fine texture and excellent substance. The shiny sepals are creamy white with wavy edges. The erect petals, which are twice as long as the sepals, are slender, pale greenish, shiny, and twisted several times. The white lip is marked with violet stripes and veins. The dorsal sepal may also be twisted. Blossoms are extremely long-lasting, and plants may be in bloom for 6–9 months.

HYBRIDIZING NOTES: Chromosome count is $2n = 38$ (ref. 504, 580) as *D. stratiotes* and *D. stratiotes* var. *giganteum* (ref. 580). As a parent, it contributes the tendencies toward long blossom life, numerous flowers, and frequent bloom periods so that offspring may be in bloom most of the year. Progeny tend to have short stems, and the erect, twisted petals are dominant for several generations. Seeds are normally ready for green-pod culture in 150–200 days.

REFERENCES: 25, 36, 84, 116, 179, 190, 196, 200, 218, 254, 326, 343, 351, 371, 425, 430, 445, 504, 526, 541, 551, 568, 570, 580.

PHOTOS/DRAWINGS: *36, 48, 84, 116, 343, 351, 371, 430.*

Dendrobium straussianum Schlechter

ORIGIN/HABITAT: New Ireland in the Bismarck Islands. Plants were described without elevation or additional habitat information, so the following climate data should be used with caution.

CLIMATE: Station #94076, Kavieng, New Ireland, Papua New Guinea, Lat. 2.6°S, Long. 150.8°E, at 15 ft. (5 m). Record extreme temperatures are 99°F (37°C) and 66°F (19°C).

N/HEMISPHERE	JAN	FEB	MAR	APR	MAY	JUN	JUL	AUG	SEP	OCT	NOV	DEC
°F AVG MAX	88	88	89	90	90	89	88	88	87	88	88	88
°F AVG MIN	73	73	73	73	74	74	75	75	75	74	74	74
DIURNAL RANGE	15	15	16	17	16	15	13	13	12	14	14	14
RAIN/INCHES	10.7	11.2	7.8	8.0	9.7	10.7	12.2	11.1	11.6	12.5	10.0	9.9
HUMIDITY/%	78	76	76	75	77	78	80	79	79	80	79	79
BLOOM SEASON	N/A											
DAYS CLR	N/A											
RAIN/MM	272	284	198	203	246	272	310	282	295	318	254	251
°C AVG MAX	31.1	31.1	31.7	32.2	32.2	31.7	31.1	31.1	30.6	31.1	31.1	31.1
°C AVG MIN	22.8	22.8	22.8	22.8	23.3	23.3	23.9	23.9	23.9	23.3	23.3	23.3
DIURNAL RANGE	8.3	8.3	8.9	9.4	8.9	8.4	7.2	7.2	6.7	7.8	7.8	7.8
S/HEMISPHERE	JUL	AUG	SEP	OCT	NOV	DEC	JAN	FEB	MAR	APR	MAY	JUN

Cultural Recommendations

LIGHT: 2000–3000 fc.

TEMPERATURES: Throughout the year, days average 87–90°F (31–32°C), and nights average 73–75°F (23–24°C), with a diurnal range of 12–17°F (7–9°C).

HUMIDITY: 75–80% year-round.

WATER: Rainfall is very heavy all year. Cultivated plants should be kept evenly moist but not soggy.

FERTILIZER: ¼–½ recommended strength. A balanced fertilizer should be applied weekly to biweekly throughout the year.

REST PERIOD: Growing conditions should be maintained year-round. In the habitat, rainfall is heavy in winter; but water and fertilizer may be reduced somewhat for cultivated plants, especially those grown in the dark, short-day conditions common in temperate latitudes. Plants should never be allowed dry out completely, however. In the habitat, seasonal light variation is minor.

GROWING MEDIA: Plants may be mounted on tree-fern or cork slabs if humidity is high and plants are watered at least once daily in summer. When plants are potted, any open, fast-draining medium may be used. Repotting may be done anytime new roots are growing.

MISCELLANEOUS NOTES: In 1915, Schlechter included the following information in *Orchis* 9:92.

Plant and Flower Information

PLANT SIZE AND TYPE: A 39 in. (100 cm) sympodial epiphyte.

PSEUDOBULB: 39 in. (100 cm) long. The slender, unbranched stems are borne from a very short rhizome. They are covered with persistent leaf sheaths.

LEAVES: Many. The shiny, oblong leaves are 4 in. (10 cm) long.

INFLORESCENCE: Short.

FLOWERS: The flowers are 0.6 in. (1.5 cm) long. The base of the midlobe is densely covered with warts. The lip margin is rounded and ruffled. Flower color was not included with the original description.

REFERENCES: 221.

Dendrobium strebloceras Rchb. f.

AKA: *D. dammerboerii* J. J. Smith. *D. strebloceras* var. *rossianum* Rchb. f. is now considered a synonym of *D. stratiotes* Rchb. f. *D. strebloceras* and *D. strepsiceros* J. J. Smith are often confused and mislabeled.

ORIGIN/HABITAT: The origin of this species is uncertain. The type specimen is listed only as coming from the Moluccas, and some writers feel it was probably found on Halmahera Island. However, others suggest it may have originated on Seram. Because specific habitat location and elevation are not known, the following climate data should be used with extreme caution.

CLIMATE: Station #97430, Ternate, Indonesia, Lat. 0.8°N, Long. 127.4°E, at 75 ft. (23 m). Record extreme temperatures are not available for this location.

N/HEMISPHERE	JAN	FEB	MAR	APR	MAY	JUN	JUL	AUG	SEP	OCT	NOV	DEC
°F AVG MAX	85	85	86	86	87	86	87	86	86	87	87	86
°F AVG MIN	77	76	77	77	77	76	75	75	76	77	77	77
DIURNAL RANGE	8	9	9	9	10	10	12	11	10	10	10	9
RAIN/INCHES	5.3	6.1	6.7	6.6	9.4	8.4	4.6	2.1	3.1	3.2	7.2	8.2
HUMIDITY/%	N/A											
BLOOM SEASON							*	*	*	*		
DAYS CLR	N/A											
RAIN/MM	135	155	170	168	239	213	117	53	79	81	183	208
°C AVG MAX	29.4	29.4	30.0	30.0	30.6	30.0	30.6	30.0	30.0	30.6	30.6	30.0
°C AVG MIN	25.0	24.4	25.0	25.0	25.0	24.4	23.9	23.9	24.4	25.0	25.0	25.0
DIURNAL RANGE	4.4	5.0	5.0	5.0	5.6	5.6	6.7	6.1	5.6	5.6	5.6	5.0
S/HEMISPHERE	JUL	AUG	SEP	OCT	NOV	DEC	JAN	FEB	MAR	APR	MAY	JUN

Cultural Recommendations

LIGHT: 2500–3500 fc.

TEMPERATURES: Throughout the year, days average 85–87°F (29–31°C), and nights average 75–77°F (24–25°C), with a diurnal range of 8–12°F (4–7°C). The warmest days and coolest nights occur simultaneously in early summer. It should be noted that these values are based on estimated habitat elevation. Some growers recommend minimum winter temperatures near 59°F (15°C) which suggests a habitat elevation of 4000–5000 ft. (1220–1520 m). It is unknown whether these are the preferred conditions or merely ones to which the plants adapt.

HUMIDITY: Information is not available for this location. However, records from nearby stations indicate that humidity probably averages near 80% year-round.

WATER: Rainfall is moderately heavy most of the year, but for 2–3 months in late summer into autumn, conditions are slightly drier. Cultivated plants should be kept evenly moist through most of the year, but water should be reduced and the plants allowed to dry slightly between waterings in late summer and early autumn.

FERTILIZER: ¼–½ recommended strength. A balanced fertilizer should be applied weekly to biweekly throughout the year.

REST PERIOD: Growing conditions should be maintained all year. Water may be reduced somewhat in winter, especially for plants grown in the dark, short-day conditions common in temperate latitudes, but plants should never be allowed to dry completely between waterings. In the habitat, seasonal light variation is minor.

GROWING MEDIA: Plants may be mounted or potted in fir bark or any open, fast-draining medium. Repotting may be done anytime new roots are growing.

MISCELLANEOUS NOTES: The bloom season shown in the climate table is based on cultivation records. Growers report that plants may bloom several times during the year. Although not commonly cultivated, *D. strebloceras* blooms moderately freely in Singapore. Plants often produce keikis which may be detached and potted when the roots are still relatively short.

Plant and Flower Information

PLANT SIZE AND TYPE: A 24–59 in. (60–150 cm) sympodial epiphyte.

PSEUDOBULB: 24–59 in. (60–150 cm) long. The canelike stems emerge from a stout climbing rhizome. The shiny, yellow-green pseudobulbs have a dark ring around each internode. The stems taper abruptly.

LEAVES: Many on the upper 30% of each growth. The variably shaped leaves are 6 in. (15 cm) long, leathery, and dark green. They are curved and held at an angle to the pseudobulb.

INFLORESCENCE: 12–16 in. (30–40 cm) long. Several violet-brown inflorescences, up to 6, are produced from the uppermost nodes.

FLOWERS: 5–12 per inflorescence. The flowers are 2 in. (5 cm) long. Sepals and petals may be pale yellow or tangerine-orange. The recurved sepals are twisted and wavy along the margin. They are marked with 5 brown nerves. The twisted petals are normally stiffly erect, but they may be held at an angle. The white to yellow lip has 5 purple keels and purple margins. The midlobe is wavy along the edge. Individual blossoms, which may last 2 months, have the tendency to become darker and duskier with age. They are delightfully fragrant.

HYBRIDIZING NOTES: Chromosome count is 2n = 38 (ref. 151, 187, 504, 580). As a parent, it contributes the tendencies toward long blossom life, numerous flowers, and frequent bloom periods so that offspring may be in bloom most of the year. Progeny tend to have short stems and the erect, twisted petals are dominant for several generations.

REFERENCES: 25, 84, 151, 187, 190, 196, 200, 218, 254, 304, 343, 371, 445, 504, 541, 568, 570, 580.

PHOTOS/DRAWINGS: *84, 304, 343, 371*.

Dendrobium strepsiceros J. J. Smith

AKA: *D. strebloceras* Rchb. f. and *D. strepsiceros* are often confused and mislabeled.

ORIGIN/HABITAT: Irian Jaya (western New Guinea) and possibly Batjan, an island just off the southwest coast of Halmahera Island in the Moluccas. Plants were cultivated in a private garden at Bogor, Java.

CLIMATE: Station #97430, Ternate, Indonesia, Lat. 0.8°N, Long.127.4°E, at 75 ft. (23 m). Record extreme temperatures are not available for this location.

N/HEMISPHERE	JAN	FEB	MAR	APR	MAY	JUN	JUL	AUG	SEP	OCT	NOV	DEC
°F AVG MAX	85	85	86	86	87	86	87	86	86	87	87	86
°F AVG MIN	77	76	77	77	77	76	75	75	76	77	77	77
DIURNAL RANGE	8	9	9	9	10	10	12	11	10	10	10	9
RAIN/INCHES	5.3	6.1	6.7	6.6	9.4	8.4	4.6	2.1	3.1	3.2	7.2	8.2
HUMIDITY/%	N/A											
BLOOM SEASON	N/A											
DAYS CLR	N/A											
RAIN/MM	135	155	170	168	239	213	117	53	79	81	183	208
°C AVG MAX	29.4	29.4	30.0	30.0	30.6	30.0	30.6	30.0	30.0	30.6	30.6	30.0
°C AVG MIN	25.0	24.4	25.0	25.0	25.0	24.4	23.9	23.9	24.4	25.0	25.0	25.0
DIURNAL RANGE	4.4	5.0	5.0	5.0	5.6	5.6	6.7	6.1	5.6	5.6	5.6	5.0
S/HEMISPHERE	JUL	AUG	SEP	OCT	NOV	DEC	JAN	FEB	MAR	APR	MAY	JUN

Cultural Recommendations

LIGHT: 2500–3500 fc.

TEMPERATURES: Throughout the year, days average 85–87°F (29–31°C), and nights average 75–77°F (24–25°C), with a diurnal range of 8–12°F (4–7°C). The warmest days and coolest nights occur simultaneously in early summer.

HUMIDITY: Information is not available for this location. However, records from nearby stations indicate that humidity probably averages near 80% year-round.

WATER: Rainfall is moderately heavy most of the year, but for 2–3 months in late summer and into autumn, conditions are slightly drier. Cultivated plants should be kept evenly moist through most of the year, but water should be reduced and the plants allowed to dry slightly between waterings in late summer and early autumn.

FERTILIZER: ¼–½ recommended strength. A balanced fertilizer should be applied weekly to biweekly throughout the year.

REST PERIOD: Growing conditions should be maintained all year. Water may be reduced somewhat in winter, especially for plants grown in the dark, short-day conditions common in temperate latitudes, but plants should never be allowed to dry completely between waterings. In the habitat, seasonal light variation is minor.

GROWING MEDIA: Plants may be mounted on tree-fern or cork slabs if humidity is high and plants are watered at least once daily in summer. When plants are potted, any open, fast-draining medium may be used. Repotting may be done anytime new roots are growing.

MISCELLANEOUS NOTES: *D. strepsiceros* is more commonly cultivated than *D. strebloceras*. Growers indicate that the white flowered variety blooms freely in Singapore. Plants often bloom more than once and may bloom several times a year, but bloom seasons are unavailable.

Plant and Flower Information

PLANT SIZE AND TYPE: A 24–40 in. (60–102 cm) sympodial epiphyte.

PSEUDOBULB: 24–40 in. (60–102 cm) long. The thick stems are 4-angled in cross section.

LEAVES: The shiny, pale green leaves are about 5 in. (13 cm) long. They are thick and ovate with 2 teeth at the apex.

INFLORESCENCE: 9–13 in. (23–34 cm) long. Inflorescences emerge from the tips of the canes and may be somewhat drooping.

FLOWERS: 8–12 per inflorescence. The flowers are approximately 2.5 in. (6.4 cm) long. The blossoms are usually light yellow-green, sometimes with faint brownish markings on the sepals, but they are occasionally white. The sepals are twisted, and the petals are narrow, erect, and twisted. The large midlobe of the lip is white to green and is marked with 5 violet keels. Blossoms are fragrant and long-lasting.

HYBRIDIZING NOTES: As a parent, it contributes tendencies toward long blossom life, numerous flowers, and frequent bloom periods so that hybrids are in bloom most of the year. Progeny tend to have short stems. The tendency for erect, twisted petals is a dominant characteristic for several generations.

REFERENCES: 25, 84, 200, 221, 343, 445, 470, 510.

Dendrobium striaenopsis M. Clements and D. Jones

AKA: *D. bigibbum* Lindley subsp. *laratensis* Clemesha, *D. bigibbum* var. *albomarginatum* Linden not F. M. Bailey, *D. bigibbum* var. *albopurpuratum* Hort., *D. phalaenopsis* Fitzgerald var. *schroderianum* Hort. ex Masters.

ORIGIN/HABITAT: The Tanimbar Islands southwest of Irian Jaya. Habitat elevation is unavailable, but the islands are low lying.

CLIMATE: Station #97900, Saumlaki, Pulau Jamdena, Indonesia, Lat. 8.0°S, Long. 131.3°E, at 79 ft. (24 m). Record extreme temperatures are not available for this location.

N/HEMISPHERE	JAN	FEB	MAR	APR	MAY	JUN	JUL	AUG	SEP	OCT	NOV	DEC
°F AVG MAX	83	83	84	87	90	89	87	87	88	87	85	84
°F AVG MIN	73	73	73	74	76	76	76	75	75	76	77	74
DIURNAL RANGE	10	10	11	13	14	13	11	12	13	11	8	10
RAIN/INCHES	2.5	1.1	0.3	0.5	2.4	7.3	9.8	9.1	6.1	5.5	8.5	5.7
HUMIDITY/%	N/A											
BLOOM SEASON	**	*	*	*						**	**	**
DAYS CLR @	N/A											
RAIN/MM	64	27	8	13	61	186	248	230	156	140	215	144
°C AVG MAX	28.1	28.1	29.0	30.6	32.2	31.7	30.8	30.6	31.0	30.6	29.7	28.6
°C AVG MIN	22.6	22.6	22.9	23.6	24.3	24.3	24.7	23.6	23.7	24.5	24.7	23.6
DIURNAL RANGE	5.5	5.5	6.1	7.0	7.9	7.4	6.1	7.0	7.3	6.1	5.0	5.0
S/HEMISPHERE	JUL	AUG	SEP	OCT	NOV	DEC	JAN	FEB	MAR	APR	MAY	JUN

Cultural Recommendations

LIGHT: 3000–4500 fc.

Dendrobium striatellum

TEMPERATURES: Throughout the year, days average 83–90°F (28–32°C), and nights average 73–77°F (23–25°C), with a diurnal range of 8–14°F (5–8°C).

HUMIDITY: Averages are not available for this location. At other stations in the region, however, humidity is about 75% for much of the year; but averages drop to near 60% in winter and spring.

WATER: Rainfall is moderate to heavy in summer and autumn, but conditions are very dry in late winter and early spring. Cultivated plants should be kept moist with only slight drying allowed between waterings from late spring into autumn. Water should be gradually reduced in late autumn after new growths mature.

FERTILIZER: ¼–½ recommended strength, applied weekly. A high-nitrogen fertilizer is beneficial from spring to midsummer, but a fertilizer high in phosphates should be used in late summer and autumn.

REST PERIOD: Growing temperatures should be maintained year-round. A long dry rest is required in winter. Some growers recommend hanging plants high in the greenhouse and forgetting them for 2–3 months in winter. However, a little rain does fall each month, so an occasional early morning misting should help keep plants from becoming too dry. Growers should maintain high light levels, provide strong air movement, and eliminate fertilizer until watering is resumed in spring. Because new growths are susceptible to infection and rot, growers should use care to keep water from them until they are 2–3 in. (5–8 cm) tall.

GROWING MEDIA: Plants may be mounted or potted. If plants are potted, the pots should be as small as possible and the medium should be very open and fast draining. Excellent drainage is essential. Repotting is best done when the new growth is 2–3 in. (5–7 cm) high and new root growth is evident.

MISCELLANEOUS NOTES: The bloom season shown in the climate table is based on reports for *D. bigibbum*.

Plant and Flower Information

PLANT SIZE AND TYPE: A slender, 16–48 in. (40–122 cm) sympodial epiphyte or lithophyte that is very similar to *D. bigibbum*. Plants seldom develop into specimen plants, as they are very prone to die-back.

PSEUDOBULB: 16–48 in. (40–122 cm) long. The cylindrical stems are slightly swollen at the base. The apical 30% of the stem is leafy. Stems that die back at the base may produce new plants near the apex.

LEAVES: 3–5, rarely 12. The oblong-lanceolate leaves are 3–6 in. (8–15 cm) long. They are leathery, rigid, and flushed with red or purple. Leaves last for 2 years.

INFLORESCENCE: 8–16 in. (20–40 cm) long. Over a period of several years, each growth produces 1–4 inflorescences from nodes near the apex of the pseudobulb even after stems are leafless. The inflorescences are usually arching or horizontal, but they may be pendent. Flowers are nicely spaced along the upper half of the raceme.

FLOWERS: 3–20 per inflorescence. The showy flowers are 1.4–2.8 in. (3.5–7.0 cm) across with broad overlapping sepals and petals and a heavy texture. They are similar to but larger than *D. phalaenopsis,* with sepals and petals that are recurved only slightly and a lip midlobe that is usually longer and pointed instead of more or less rounded. Flowers are normally deep-lilac, but they may be white, pale lilac, magenta, or purple. All colors are bright and rich. The lip is usually a darker shade of the same color as the sepals and petals with deeper color in the throat and stripes on the oblong, pointed midlobe. Blossoms are highly variable in size and color. If they do not become water spotted, flowers last for months, so that plants are in nearly continuous bloom. Clements and Jones (ref. 67) indicate that *D. striaenopsis* blossoms are normally marked with distinctly darker stripes. The callus on the very recurved lip is decorated with numerous long dark lines.

REFERENCES: 67, 235, 533.

PHOTOS/DRAWINGS: *533*.

Dendrobium striatellum Carr

ORIGIN/HABITAT: Northern Malaya. Plants were found at about 500 ft. (150 m) near Gua Musang in the southern part of Kelantan state.

CLIMATE: Station #49630, Temerloh, Pahang, Malaya, Lat. 3.5°N, Long. 102.4°E, at 163 ft. (50 m). Temperatures are calculated for a habitat elevation of 1000 ft. (300 m), resulting in probable extremes of 94°F (35°C) and 61°F (16°C).

N/HEMISPHERE	JAN	FEB	MAR	APR	MAY	JUN	JUL	AUG	SEP	OCT	NOV	DEC
°F AVG MAX	82	85	87	88	88	87	87	87	87	86	84	83
°F AVG MIN	68	68	69	70	70	70	69	69	69	70	70	69
DIURNAL RANGE	14	17	18	18	18	17	18	18	18	16	14	14
RAIN/INCHES	7.8	3.9	6.0	7.6	6.6	4.3	3.4	5.6	6.5	9.3	9.7	10.1
HUMIDITY/%	87	83	84	85	86	86	87	84	86	87	89	88
BLOOM SEASON									*			
DAYS CLR @ 7AM	0	0	2	1	1	0	2	2	2	0	0	0
DAYS CLR @ 1PM	1	1	2	1	1	1	0	1	1	0	0	0
RAIN/MM	198	99	152	193	168	109	86	142	165	236	246	257
°C AVG MAX	27.9	29.6	30.7	31.2	31.2	30.7	30.7	30.7	30.7	30.1	29.0	28.5
°C AVG MIN	20.1	20.1	20.7	21.2	21.2	21.2	20.7	20.7	20.7	21.2	21.2	20.7
DIURNAL RANGE	7.8	9.5	10.0	10.0	10.0	9.5	10.0	10.0	10.0	8.9	7.8	7.8
S/HEMISPHERE	JUL	AUG	SEP	OCT	NOV	DEC	JAN	FEB	MAR	APR	MAY	JUN

Cultural Recommendations

LIGHT: 2500–3500 fc.

TEMPERATURES: Throughout the year, days average 82–88°F (28–31°C), and nights average 68–70°F (20–21°C), with a diurnal range of 14–18°F (8–10°C).

HUMIDITY: 85–90% year-round.

WATER: Rainfall is moderate to heavy all year, with brief, 1–2 month slightly drier periods in winter and summer. Cultivated plants should be kept moist and only slight drying allowed between waterings.

FERTILIZER: ¼–½ recommended strength. A balanced fertilizer should be applied weekly to biweekly throughout the year.

REST PERIOD: Growing conditions should be maintained all year. However, water should be reduced for a month or so in summer, and again in late winter. Plants should be allowed to become somewhat drier between waterings during these periods, but they should never dry out completely. Fertilizer should be reduced or eliminated anytime the plant is not growing. In the habitat, seasonal light variation is minor.

GROWING MEDIA: Plants may be mounted on tree-fern or cork slabs or potted in small pots filled with any open, fast-draining medium. Repotting may be done anytime new roots are growing.

MISCELLANEOUS NOTES: The bloom season shown in the climate table is based on records from the habitat. Plants that produce flowers which last a single day commonly bloom several times during the year. Flowering usually occurs 7–14 days after a sudden 10°F (5°C) drop in daytime temperatures. Carr (ref. 57) indicated that this species bloomed one day before *D. pumilum* Roxburgh [now *D. pachyphyllum* (Kuntze) Bakhuizen f.] and a few days after *D. quadrangulare* Parish (now *D. hymenanthum* Rchb. f.).

Plant and Flower Information

PLANT SIZE AND TYPE: A 4 in. (10 cm) sympodial epiphyte.

PSEUDOBULB: 3 in. (8 cm) long. The thickened stems are 8-angled near the apex. They are olive-yellow, often tinged with red. Plants grow as small tufts of erect to suberect stems that are borne on a creeping, branching rhizome.

LEAVES: 2 per growth. The fleshy leaves are 1.3 in. (3.2 cm) long, lanceolate to oblong-lanceolate, and obtuse at the apex with small bristles. They are dark green, often with a red tinge.

INFLORESCENCE: Short. Inflorescences are borne between the leaves from tufts of dry bracts.

FLOWERS: 1 per inflorescence. The flowers are 0.5 in. (1.2 cm) across. Sepals and petals are white with faint reddish purple streaks near the base. The backsides of the sepals have a rough texture. The white lip, which has purplish veins, is edged with purple along the ruffled margin. The orange, moon-shaped keel extends to near the apex of the obovate-oblong lip. The blossoms last a single day.

REFERENCES: 57, 200, 225, 455.

Dendrobium striatiflorum J. J. Smith

ORIGIN/HABITAT: Irian Jaya (western New Guinea). Plants grow on forest trees near Humboldt Bay at about 1000 ft. (300 m).

CLIMATE: Station #97690, Sentani/Jayapura, Irian Jaya, Lat. 2.7°S, Long. 140.5°E, at 289 ft. (88 m). Temperatures are calculated for an elevation of 1000 ft. (300 m), resulting in probable extremes of 95°F (35°C) and 66°F (19°C).

N/HEMISPHERE	JAN	FEB	MAR	APR	MAY	JUN	JUL	AUG	SEP	OCT	NOV	DEC
°F AVG MAX	85	87	87	88	88	87	87	86	87	88	88	87
°F AVG MIN	70	70	70	71	71	71	71	71	71	72	71	71
DIURNAL RANGE	15	17	17	17	17	16	16	15	16	16	17	16
RAIN/INCHES	4.1	3.9	5.3	2.9	6.7	7.0	8.3	8.3	8.5	4.6	2.4	5.2
HUMIDITY/%	81	80	80	79	81	81	79	80	80	80	81	80
BLOOM SEASON			*									
DAYS CLR @ 9AM	5	3	4	3	2	1	1	0	1	2	2	5
DAYS CLR @ 3PM	4	3	3	3	2	1	3	0	1	2	2	3
RAIN/MM	104	99	135	74	170	178	211	211	216	117	61	132
°C AVG MAX	29.3	30.4	30.4	31.0	31.0	30.4	30.4	29.8	30.4	31.0	31.0	30.4
°C AVG MIN	21.0	21.0	21.0	21.5	21.5	21.5	21.5	21.5	21.5	22.1	21.5	21.5
DIURNAL RANGE	8.3	9.4	9.4	9.5	9.5	8.9	8.9	8.3	8.9	8.9	9.5	8.9
S/HEMISPHERE	JUL	AUG	SEP	OCT	NOV	DEC	JAN	FEB	MAR	APR	MAY	JUN

Cultural Recommendations

LIGHT: 2000–3000 fc.

TEMPERATURES: Throughout the year, days average 85–88°F (29–31°C), and nights average 70–72°F (21–22°C), with a diurnal range of 15–17°F (8–9°C). Average highs fluctuate only 3°F (2°C), while the average lows and diurnal ranges vary only 2°F (1°C), indicating that plants may not tolerate wide temperature fluctuations.

HUMIDITY: Near 80% year-round.

WATER: Rainfall is heavy all year with brief semidry periods in spring and autumn. Cultivated plants should be kept evenly moist and only slight drying allowed between waterings.

FERTILIZER: ¼–½ recommended strength. A balanced fertilizer should be applied weekly to biweekly throughout the year.

REST PERIOD: Growing conditions should be maintained year-round. Water may be reduced somewhat for cultivated plants in winter, especially those grown in the dark, short-day conditions common in temperate latitudes. They should never be allowed to dry out completely, however. In the habitat, light is slightly higher in winter.

GROWING MEDIA: Plants may be mounted on tree-fern or cork slabs or potted in any open, fast-draining medium. Repotting is best done in early spring as soon after flowering as new roots start growing.

MISCELLANEOUS NOTES: The bloom season shown in the climate table is based on reports from the habitat.

Plant and Flower Information

PLANT SIZE AND TYPE: A 14 in. (36 cm) sympodial epiphyte.

PSEUDOBULB: 14 in. (36 cm) long. The stems are flexuous.

LEAVES: Many. The lanceolate to linear leaves, which are 0.8–1.4 in. (2.0–3.5 cm) long, have 2, unequal teeth at the apex. The leaf sheaths resemble those of *Malpighia* with long, ascending hairs that are attached at the middle of the upper surface with 2 radiating branches.

INFLORESCENCE: Short.

FLOWERS: 2 per inflorescence. The blossoms are 0.8 in. (2 cm) across the narrow petals. The oblong sepals are 0.3–0.4 in. (0.8–1.0 cm) long and end abruptly in a sharp point. The lateral sepals appear to have been slashed. The 3-lobed lip has triangular sidelobes and a round to oval midlobe with an uneven margin.

REFERENCES: 221, 470, 476.

Dendrobium striatum Griffith. Now considered a synonym of *Bulbophyllum striatum* Rchb. f. REFERENCES: 216, 254, 453.

Dendrobium striatum Hort. See *D. obrienianum* Kränzlin. REFERENCES: 219, 254, 296, 536.

Dendrobium stricklandianum Rchb. f.

AKA: *D. tosaense* Makino, which is the name used by the International Orchid Commission (ref. 236) to register hybrids. Lin (ref. 274) includes *D. pere-fauriei* Hayata and *D. tosaense* var. *pere-fauriei* (Hayata) Masamume as synonyms of *D. tosaense*. Garay and Sweet (ref. 139) list no synonyms.

ORIGIN/HABITAT: Japan on Shikoku and Kyushu, the Yakushima Islands, on Okinawa and other islands in the Ryukyus, Taiwan, and China. On Taiwan, plants grow in the eastern mountains near Hua-Lien (Hualien) at 1000–3950 ft. (300–1200 m). They are found on tree branches or rocks.

CLIMATE: Station #46763, Hua-Lien, Taiwan, Lat. 24.0°N, Long. 121.6°E, at 42 ft. (13 m). Temperatures are calculated for an elevation of 2500 ft. (760 m), resulting in probable extremes of 87°F (31°C) and 36°F (2°C).

N/HEMISPHERE	JAN	FEB	MAR	APR	MAY	JUN	JUL	AUG	SEP	OCT	NOV	DEC
°F AVG MAX	63	62	65	69	75	78	81	80	78	74	69	65
°F AVG MIN	51	50	53	57	62	65	66	66	64	60	55	52
DIURNAL RANGE	12	12	12	12	13	13	15	14	14	14	14	13
RAIN/INCHES	2.3	4.4	4.1	7.7	10.7	7.0	10.6	8.7	12.8	8.7	3.3	2.2
HUMIDITY/%	78	81	80	82	84	84	81	82	80	76	76	76
BLOOM SEASON	*	*	*	*	*							
DAYS CLR	N/A											
RAIN/MM	58	112	104	196	272	178	269	221	325	221	84	56
°C AVG MAX	17.2	16.6	18.3	20.5	23.8	25.5	27.2	26.6	25.5	23.3	20.5	18.3
°C AVG MIN	10.5	9.9	11.6	13.8	16.6	18.3	18.8	18.8	17.7	15.5	12.7	11.0
DIURNAL RANGE	6.7	6.7	6.7	6.7	7.2	7.2	8.4	7.8	7.8	7.8	7.8	7.3
S/HEMISPHERE	JUL	AUG	SEP	OCT	NOV	DEC	JAN	FEB	MAR	APR	MAY	JUN

Cultural Recommendations

LIGHT: 2000–3000 fc.

TEMPERATURES: Summer days average 78–81°F (26–27°C), and nights average 65–66°F (18–19°C), with a diurnal range of 13–15°F (7–8°C).

HUMIDITY: 80–85% from late winter through summer, dropping to about 75% in autumn and early winter.

WATER: Rainfall is moderate to heavy from spring to autumn. The wet season is followed by a 5-month drier season from winter through early spring. Cultivated plants should be kept moist while actively growing, but water should be gradually reduced in autumn.

FERTILIZER: ¼–½ recommended strength, applied weekly. A high nitrogen fertilizer is beneficial from spring to midsummer, but a fertilizer high in phosphates should be used in late summer and autumn.

REST PERIOD: Winter days average 62–65°F (17–18°C), and nights average 50–52°F (10–11°C), with a diurnal range of 12–13°F (7°C). Water and fertilizer should be reduced somewhat, but plants should not be

Dendrobium strictum

allowed to remain dry for any length of time. Fertilizer should be reduced until water is increased in spring.

GROWING MEDIA: Mounting plants on tree-fern or cork slabs accommodates their sometimes pendulous growth habit. However, humidity must be high and plants must be watered at least once a day in summer. If plants cannot be mounted, small pots or hanging baskets may be filled with an open, fast-draining medium. Repotting may be done anytime new roots are actively growing.

MISCELLANEOUS NOTES: The bloom season shown in the climate table is based on cultivation records. Reports from the habitat indicate that blooming occurs primarily in autumn.

Plant and Flower Information

PLANT SIZE AND TYPE: A 10–16 in. (25–40 cm) sympodial epiphyte or lithophyte. Plants are often smaller.

PSEUDOBULB: 10–16 in. (25–40 cm) long. The pale green stems may be erect or pendent and consist of nodes spaced 0.8–2.4 in. (2–6 cm) apart. The stems are tightly clustered.

LEAVES: 12 per growth. The deciduous leaves are 0.8–2.8 in. (2–7 cm) long, elliptic-lanceolate, and distichous.

INFLORESCENCE: 0.8–2.8 in. (2–7 cm) long. The laxly flowered inflorescences emerge from the upper nodes of 2- and 3-year-old, leafless stems.

FLOWERS: 3–8 per inflorescence. The flowers are 1.2 in. (3 cm) across. The lanceolate sepals and petals are pale greenish yellow and slightly recurved at the tips. The lip, which is somewhat recurved at the tip, is marked with a few dark purple lines or streaks below the center. The column is pale green.

HYBRIDIZING NOTES: Chromosome counts are n = 19 (ref. 151, 187), 2n = 38 (ref. 151, 187, 504, 580), and 2n = 40 (ref. 187, 504, 580) as *D. tosaense*. Seeds are ready for green-pod culture in about 120 days.

REFERENCES: 18, 36, 62, 139, 151, 179, 187, 208, 216, 236, 254, 338, 445, 497, 504, 528, 580.

PHOTOS/DRAWINGS: *36.*

Dendrobium strictum Ridley. See *D. subclausum* Rolfe. REFERENCES: 222, 400, 538, 588. PHOTOS/DRAWINGS: 538.

Dendrobium strigosum Schlechter. See *D. tetraedre* (Blume) Lindley. REFERENCES: 75, 221, 435, 454.

Dendrobium striolatum Rchb. f.

AKA: *D. milligani* F. Mueller, *D. teretifolium* Lindley not Blanco or R. Brown.

D. striolatum Rchb. f. var. *beckleri* (F. Mueller) F. M. Bailey is a synonym of *D. schoeninum* Lindley.

Hallé (ref. 173) includes *D. striolatum* Rchb. f. var. *chalandei* Finet as a synonym of *D. chalandei* (A. Finet) Kränzlin. However, Clements (ref. 67) indicates that it should be a synonym of *D. bowmanii* Bentham.

ORIGIN/HABITAT: Tasmania and Australia. The habitat includes the northeast coast of Tasmania near St. Helens, Bicheno, Coles Bay, and the Furneaux Islands in Gass Straits. In Australia, the habitat extends from east of Melbourne northward to the Hunter River near Newcastle, New South Wales. Plants usually grow on rocks in very exposed locations, but they are occasionally found on trees in somewhat shady conditions. The habitat extends from sea level to 2950 ft. (0–900 m). The orchids usually grow in the lower mountains, but they are occasionally found near the coast.

CLIMATE: Station #94767, Sydney, Australia, Lat. 33.9°S, Long. 151.0°E, at 16 ft. (5 m). Temperatures are calculated for an elevation of 2000 ft. (620 m), resulting in probable extremes of 107°F (42°C) and 28°F (−2°C).

N/HEMISPHERE	JAN	FEB	MAR	APR	MAY	JUN	JUL	AUG	SEP	OCT	NOV	DEC
°F AVG MAX	53	56	60	64	67	70	71	71	69	64	59	54
°F AVG MIN	39	41	44	49	53	56	58	58	56	51	45	41
DIURNAL RANGE	14	15	16	15	14	14	13	13	13	13	14	13
RAIN/INCHES	4.6	3.0	2.9	2.8	2.9	2.9	3.5	4.0	5.0	5.3	5.0	4.6
HUMIDITY/%	68	64	61	61	62	64	66	68	69	70	70	69
BLOOM SEASON		*	***	**	**	*						
DAYS CLR @ 10AM	14	15	13	11	11	8	7	4	8	10	11	11
DAYS CLR @ 4PM	13	12	12	11	11	10	10	7	10	10	11	10
RAIN/MM	117	76	74	71	74	74	89	102	127	135	127	117
°C AVG MAX	11.9	13.6	15.8	18.0	19.7	21.4	21.9	21.9	20.8	18.0	15.3	12.5
°C AVG MIN	4.1	5.3	6.9	9.7	11.9	13.6	14.7	14.7	13.6	10.8	7.5	5.3
DIURNAL RANGE	7.8	8.3	8.9	8.3	7.8	7.8	7.2	7.2	7.2	7.2	7.8	7.2
S/HEMISPHERE	JUL	AUG	SEP	OCT	NOV	DEC	JAN	FEB	MAR	APR	MAY	JUN

Cultural Recommendations

LIGHT: 2500–3500 fc. Plants have been found hanging from the roofs of humid caves, so they may tolerate quite low light. Excessive light causes the leaves to become dark purple. Plants also tolerate nearly full sun, but they should be gradually introduced to these conditions. Strong air movement, which helps prevent damage from too much light as well as problems caused by overwatering, should be provided at all times.

TEMPERATURES: Summer days average 70–71°F (21–22°C), and nights average 56–58°F (14–15°C), with a diurnal range of 13–14°F (7–8°C).

HUMIDITY: 65–70% most of the year, dropping to near 60% for 3 months in late winter and early spring.

WATER: Rainfall is moderate most of the year, but conditions are drier for 3 months in late winter and spring. Cultivated plants should be allowed to dry slightly between waterings, but they should never remain dry for long periods. If plants are grown on slabs, they should be watered 2–3 times a day during hot weather. A light misting on hot evenings is usually beneficial. New leaves must be kept dry, however, because rot starts easily if water is allowed to stand on the tender new growth.

FERTILIZER: ¼–½ recommended strength, applied weekly. A high-nitrogen fertilizer is beneficial from spring to midsummer, but a fertilizer high in phosphates should be used in late summer and autumn.

REST PERIOD: Winter days average 53–60°F (12–16°C), and nights average 39–44°F (4–7°C), with a diurnal range of 13–16°F (7–9°C). Australian growers recommend a minimum winter temperature of 34°F (1°C). Water should be reduced so that plants are kept barely damp, but they should never dry out completely. Fertilizer should be reduced or eliminated anytime water is reduced.

GROWING MEDIA: Plants are healthiest when firmly mounted to cork, hardwood, or tree-fern slabs. If plants must be potted, growers recommend filling a hanging basket with an open, fast-draining medium. Repotting is best done in early spring when new roots are growing.

MISCELLANEOUS NOTES: The bloom season shown in the climate table is based on cultivation records. Growers indicate that plants are easy and forgiving, especially if nights are cool. They bloom consistently year after year.

Plant and Flower Information

PLANT SIZE AND TYPE: A 2–24 in. (5–60 cm) sympodial lithophyte that occasionally grows epiphytically on exposed tree roots.

PSEUDOBULB: 2–24 in. (5–60 cm) long. The clustered, branching stems emerge from a creeping, sometimes branching, rhizome. The dark brown stems are slender, almost wiry, and form a dense mass. The plants are most often erect, but they sometimes become pendulous as plant size increases.

LEAVES: 1 per node. Terete and pencil-shaped, the cylindrical, dark green leaves are 1.6–4.3 in. (4–11 cm) long. When exposed to bright light, they turn reddish. The leaves, which are curved, hard, and faintly ridged, may appear to arise almost directly from the rhizome.

INFLORESCENCE: Inflorescences usually equal the length of the leaves. A single inflorescence is produced from the base of each leaf node.

FLOWERS: 1–2 per inflorescence, up to 200 per plant. Blossoms are produced in great profusion. Individual flowers are 0.8–1.0 in. (2.0–2.5 cm) across and open fully. Sepals and petals may be white, cream, or yellow with a few reddish, purplish, or brownish stripes at the base and on the backside. Petals are slender. The pure white lip, which is uppermost, is pointed, recurved at the apex, ruffled, and wavy. It has 3 keels. Blossoms are delicately fragrant.

HYBRIDIZING NOTES: Chromosome count is 2n = 38 (ref. 152, 143). Normally self-fertile, most attempts to self-pollinate are successful.

REFERENCES: 23, 36, 67, 105, 152, 190, 216, 240, 243, 254, 291, 317, 325, 371, 390, 395, 421, 445, 527, 533, 541, 544, 570.

PHOTOS/DRAWINGS: *33, 105, 240, 291*, 325, *371, 390, 404, 533*.

Dendrobium strongylanthum Rchb. f.

AKA: *D. ctenoglossum* Schlechter.

ORIGIN/HABITAT: Northwestern Thailand near Chiang Mai, northern Burma near the southern Chin Hills, and the western and southwestern parts of Yunnan Province in China where habitat elevation is reported as 3300–6650 ft. (1000–2000 m).

CLIMATE: Station #48327, Chiang Mai, Thailand, Lat. 18.8°N, Long. 99.0°E, at 1100 ft. (335 m). Temperatures are calculated for an elevation of 4000 ft. (1220 m), resulting in probable extremes of 99°F (38°C) and 28°F (−2°C).

N/HEMISPHERE	JAN	FEB	MAR	APR	MAY	JUN	JUL	AUG	SEP	OCT	NOV	DEC
°F AVG MAX	75	80	85	86	84	80	79	77	78	79	76	74
°F AVG MIN	46	47	52	60	64	64	64	65	63	61	56	47
DIURNAL RANGE	29	33	33	26	20	16	15	12	15	18	20	27
RAIN/INCHES	0.3	0.4	0.6	2.0	5.5	6.1	7.4	8.7	11.5	4.9	1.5	0.4
HUMIDITY/%	73	65	58	62	73	78	80	83	83	81	79	76
BLOOM SEASON					*	*	*	*				
DAYS CLR @ 7AM	5	5	2	2	1	0	0	0	0	1	3	3
DAYS CLR @ 1PM	9	8	4	2	0	0	0	0	0	0	1	3
RAIN/MM	8	10	15	51	140	155	188	221	292	124	38	10
°C AVG MAX	24.1	26.9	29.7	30.2	29.1	26.9	26.4	25.2	25.8	26.4	24.7	23.6
°C AVG MIN	8.0	8.6	11.3	15.8	18.0	18.0	18.0	18.6	17.5	16.4	13.6	8.6
DIURNAL RANGE	16.1	18.3	18.4	14.4	11.1	8.9	8.4	6.6	8.3	10.0	11.1	15.0
S/HEMISPHERE	JUL	AUG	SEP	OCT	NOV	DEC	JAN	FEB	MAR	APR	MAY	JUN

Cultural Recommendations

LIGHT: 1500–2400 fc. Diffused light is recommended. In the habitat, clear, summer days are exceedingly rare, so direct sunlight should be avoided.

TEMPERATURES: Summer days average 77–80°F (25–27°C), and nights average 64–65°F (18–19°C), with a diurnal range of 12–16°F (7–9°C). The warmest weather occurs in spring. Days average 84–86°F (29–30°C), and nights average 60–64°F (16–18°C), with a diurnal range of 20–26°F (11–14°C). Both highs and lows are more moderate after the start of the summer wet season. Low night temperatures or a wide diurnal range may be necessary to initiate blooming.

HUMIDITY: 80–85% in summer, decreasing to 65–75% for most of the rest of the year. However, averages drop to near 60% for 2 months near the end of the dry season in late winter and early spring.

WATER: Rainfall is heavy while plants are actively growing from spring to early autumn. During this season, cultivated plants should be kept moist with little if any drying allowed between waterings. However, water should be gradually reduced after new growths mature in autumn.

FERTILIZER: ¼–½ recommended strength, applied weekly. A high-nitrogen fertilizer is beneficial from spring to midsummer, but a fertilizer high in phosphates should be used in late summer and autumn. Some growers report good success alternating applications of fish emulsion with their regular fertilizer.

REST PERIOD: Winter days average 74–80°F (24–27°C), and nights average 46–47°F (8–9°C), with a diurnal range of 27–33°F (15–18°C). Overnight lows are below 50°F (10°C) for 3 months. Plants should be able to tolerate temperatures a few degrees below freezing for short periods, but extremes should be avoided in cultivation. During very cold weather, a plant's chance of surviving with minimal damage is better if it is dry when temperatures are low. In the habitat, winter rainfall is low for 4–5 months, and humidity falls to 58–65%, indicating distinctly reduced moisture. During the early part of the dry season, additional moisture is available from dew and as mist from fog and low clouds. Cultivated plants should be allowed to dry out between waterings, but they should not remain dry for extended periods. Fertilizer should be greatly reduced or eliminated anytime water is reduced. In the habitat, light is slightly higher in winter, but increased light may not be critical in cultivation.

GROWING MEDIA: Plants may be mounted on tree-fern or cork slabs if humidity is high and plants are watered at least once daily in summer. When plants are potted, any open, fast-draining medium may be used. Repotting is best done in early spring when new roots are growing.

MISCELLANEOUS NOTES: The bloom season shown in the climate table is based on cultivation records.

Plant and Flower Information

PLANT SIZE AND TYPE: A 6 in. (15 cm) sympodial epiphyte.

PSEUDOBULB: 4 in. (10 cm) long. Plants often consist of a few, very slender stems which are covered with sheaths.

LEAVES: 5 per growth. The leaves are 1.2–2.0 in. (3–5 cm) long.

INFLORESCENCE: Often more than one branching inflorescence emerges laterally from nodes near the apex of leafy pseudobulbs. The upper half of the inflorescences are densely flowered.

FLOWERS: 6–8 per inflorescence. The flowers are 0.4–0.8 in. (1–2 cm) across. Sepals and petals are narrow and erect. The sepals are dark purple on the back, and on the front, they are flushed with dark violet-brown near the base. Petals are greenish yellow with purple speckles. Recurved at the tip, the lip is warty and deeply ruffled along the maroon margins. It is serrate to the middle. The depressed callus is keeled in the middle and papillose in front.

REFERENCES: 179, 202, 208, 216, 254, 454, 528.

PHOTOS/DRAWINGS: 454.

Dendrobium stuartii F. M. Bailey

AKA: Seidenfaden and Wood (ref. 455) include *D. viridicatum* Ridley and plants identified as *D. tetrodon* not Rchb. f. as synonyms. Clements (ref. 67) indicates that *D. stuartii* is often erroneously referred to as *D. tetrodon*. He includes *D. whiteanum* Hunt as a synonym.

ORIGIN/HABITAT: Widespread in Southeast Asia, including Thailand, Vietnam, Malaya, Sumatra, Java, Bali, Borneo (Kalimantan), and Australia. In northeastern Australia, the habitat extends from near Coen on the eastern side of the Cape York Peninsula to Bamaga at the tip of the Peninsula. Plants are found in a variety of habitats, including lowland rainforests, vine scrub in dry gullies, trees on ridge tops and plateaus, and dry scrub bordering mangrove swamps. They occur between sea level and 1150 ft. (0–350 m). In Java, plants grow southwest of Bogor on Salak Volcano. In Sumatra, they occur near Padang and Palembang. In Malaya, they are found on trees in fairly open places in the lowlands.

CLIMATE: Station #94167, Horn Island, Australia, Lat. 10.6°S, Long.

Dendrobium stueberi

142.3°E, at 27 ft. (8 m). Temperatures are calculated for an elevation of 500 ft. (150 m), resulting in probable extremes of 96°F (36°C) and 62°F (17°C).

N/HEMISPHERE	JAN	FEB	MAR	APR	MAY	JUN	JUL	AUG	SEP	OCT	NOV	DEC
°F AVG MAX	80	80	82	84	86	87	85	85	85	84	83	82
°F AVG MIN	71	71	72	74	75	76	75	75	75	75	74	72
DIURNAL RANGE	9	9	10	10	11	11	10	10	10	9	9	10
RAIN/INCHES	0.4	0.2	0.1	0.3	1.5	7.0	13.2	15.8	13.9	8.0	1.6	0.5
HUMIDITY/%	75	72	71	70	69	72	79	80	79	77	75	75
BLOOM SEASON						*	**	**				
DAYS CLR @ 9AM	3	4	3	2	3	1	0	0	1	4	9	5
DAYS CLR @ 3PM	4	5	6	8	7	2	0	1	1	4	8	6
RAIN/MM	10	5	3	8	38	178	335	401	353	203	41	13
°C AVG MAX	26.9	26.9	28.0	29.1	30.2	30.8	29.7	29.7	29.7	29.1	28.6	28.0
°C AVG MIN	21.9	21.9	22.5	23.6	24.1	24.7	24.1	24.1	24.1	24.1	23.6	22.5
DIURNAL RANGE	5.0	5.0	5.5	5.5	6.1	6.1	5.6	5.6	5.6	5.0	5.0	5.5
S/HEMISPHERE	JUL	AUG	SEP	OCT	NOV	DEC	JAN	FEB	MAR	APR	MAY	JUN

Cultural Recommendations

LIGHT: 1500–2500 fc. Heavy shading is recommended, because the soft foliage burns easily. Strong air movement at all times is also recommended.

TEMPERATURES: Summer days average 85–87°F (30–31°C), and nights average 75–76°F (24–25°C), with a diurnal range of 10–11°F (6°C).

HUMIDITY: 75–80% in summer and autumn, dropping to near 70% in late winter and spring.

WATER: Rainfall is heavy in summer and early autumn. Cultivated plants should be watered heavily while actively growing. In some parts of the habitat, the dry season is pronounced, but in other areas, rainfall is heavy most of the year, with brief, slightly drier periods in midwinter and midsummer.

FERTILIZER: ¼–½ recommended strength, applied weekly early in the growing season. Fertilizer should be reduced in late summer and eliminated in winter.

REST PERIOD: Winter days average 80–82°F (27–28°C), and nights average 71–72°F (22–23°C), with a diurnal range of 9–10°F (5–6°C). Australian growers indicate that winter lows should not fall below 60°F (15°C). Water should be gradually reduced in autumn to allow the most recent growths to harden before the dry season. In the Australian habitat, conditions are quite dry for 5–6 months in winter. For cultivated plants, water should be reduced drastically for several months until new growth starts. Climate data from other regions in the area of distribution indicate that the dry season need not be as long or quite as severe as indicated in the above table. Australian growers recommend giving a dry rest when the buds appear and withholding water until new growths are 1.5–2.0 in. (3.7–5.0 cm) long. Fertilizer should be eliminated when conditions are dry.

GROWING MEDIA: Plants should be tightly mounted to cork, hardwood, or tree-fern slabs or blocks, providing humidity is high and plants are watered at least once daily in summer. If plants must be potted, hanging pots or baskets may be filled with any open, fast-draining medium. Repotting may be done anytime new roots are growing.

MISCELLANEOUS NOTES: The bloom season shown in the climate table is based on reports from the habitat. Cultivation records also indicate summer blooming. Ridley (ref. 402) indicated that plants from Malaya were always self-pollinating. Comber (ref. 75) reports that all 3 forms are found in Java. Australian growers report that new growths are produced rapidly during the wet season, but the leaves are shed before the dry season.

Plants may be propagated by cutting old stems into short lengths consisting of several nodes and placing them on damp sphagnum moss. With luck, new growths (keikis) may start at the nodes. These should be removed and potted when the new roots are 1–2 in. (2.5–5.0 cm) long.

Plant and Flower Information

PLANT SIZE AND TYPE: A 6–18 in. (15–45 cm) sympodial epiphyte.

PSEUDOBULB: 6–18 in. (15–45 cm) long. New stems start growing in an upright position, becoming pendulous as they mature. They are slender and zigzag with nodes spaced about 0.8 in. (2 cm) apart.

LEAVES: Many. The thin leaves are 1–3 in. (2.5–7.0 cm) long. They are distichous, lanceolate to ovate, often curved, and deciduous.

INFLORESCENCE: 0.4–5.0 in. (1–13 cm) long. The thin inflorescences emerge from nodes on leafless stems shortly after the leaves drop.

FLOWERS: 1–3 per inflorescence, many per stem. The flowers are 0.8 in. (2 cm) across and may open fully or remain closed and be self-pollinating. The lanceolate sepals and petals may be dull white or light yellowish green with small mauve patches at the recurved tips. The lime green lip ages to yellow with a network of mauve, red, or purple veins. The apical part is hairy on the inside. All margins are ciliate, and the margins of the sidelobes curve inwards at the base, often meeting above the column. Normal flowers open fully. Comber (ref. 75) indicates that some Java plants have self-pollinating flowers that never open, but other plants have greenish white peloric flowers with a lip that is shaped like the sepals and petals. The peloric flowers are not self-pollinating. Blossoms are fragrant.

HYBRIDIZING NOTES: Johansen (ref. 239) indicates (for plants originally identified as *D. tetrodon*) that "the number of days to capsule maturity could not be determined exactly because of spontaneous self-pollination." 93% of the seed produced contained visible embryos and 98% germinated.

REFERENCES: 67, 75, 105, 179, 216, 239, 240, 254, 262, 402, 421, 445, 454, 455, 469, 533.

PHOTOS/DRAWINGS: *75, 105, 240, 454, 455, 533.*

Dendrobium stueberi Stilber ex Zurow. See *D. lasianthera* J. J. Smith. REFERENCES: 84, 190, 225.

Dendrobium stuposum Lindley

AKA: Some writers include *D. sphegidiglossum (spegidoglossum, sphegidglossum)* Rchb. f. as a synonym of *D. stuposum*, but Seidenfaden (ref. 454) considers the plants separate species.

ORIGIN/HABITAT: India, Burma, Thailand, and China. Plants grow at 1300–3300 ft. (400–1000 m) in the Teesta Valley of Sikkim, near Nyoth in Bhutan, and in the Khasi (Khasia) Hills near Shillong in northeastern India. Distribution continues eastward to the Tenasserim region of Burma and the mountains of northwestern Thailand, where plants are found near Chiang Mai at 1650–7500 ft. (500–2285 m). In Yunnan Province, China, plants grow on volcanic rocks at about 5750 ft. (1750 m).

CLIMATE: Station #42410, Gauhati, India, Lat. 26.1°N, Long. 91.6°E, at 158 ft. (48 m). Temperatures are calculated for a habitat elevation of 3000 ft. (910 m), resulting in probable extremes of 95°F (35°C) and 32°F (0°C).

N/HEMISPHERE	JAN	FEB	MAR	APR	MAY	JUN	JUL	AUG	SEP	OCT	NOV	DEC
°F AVG MAX	67	69	77	79	79	80	81	81	80	78	72	67
°F AVG MIN	42	45	51	59	63	68	69	69	67	62	52	44
DIURNAL RANGE	25	24	26	20	16	12	12	12	13	16	20	23
RAIN/INCHES	0.4	1.2	2.0	5.7	9.3	12.3	12.3	10.3	6.6	2.8	0.6	0.2
HUMIDITY/%	79	72	64	71	82	85	85	86	84	84	83	82
BLOOM SEASON						*			*			
DAYS CLR @ 6AM	6	12	16	11	3	0	0	1	3	7	6	3
DAYS CLR @ 12PM	17	16	18	15	6	1	0	0	2	11	17	19
RAIN/MM	10	30	51	145	236	312	312	262	168	71	15	5
°C AVG MAX	19.2	20.3	24.8	25.9	25.9	26.5	27.0	27.0	26.5	25.3	22.0	19.2
°C AVG MIN	5.3	7.0	10.3	14.8	17.0	19.8	20.3	20.3	19.2	16.5	10.9	6.5
DIURNAL RANGE	13.9	13.3	14.5	11.1	8.9	6.7	6.7	6.7	7.3	8.8	11.1	12.7
S/HEMISPHERE	JUL	AUG	SEP	OCT	NOV	DEC	JAN	FEB	MAR	APR	MAY	JUN

Cultural Recommendations

LIGHT: 2500–3500 fc. Cultivated plants need as much light as possible without burning the foliage during autumn and winter.

TEMPERATURES: Summer days average 80–81°F (27°C), and nights average 68–69°F (20°C), with a diurnal range of 12°F (7°C).

HUMIDITY: 80–85% most of the year, dropping to 65–70% for 3 months in late winter and spring.

WATER: Rainfall is heavy from spring through summer but decreases rapidly in autumn with a 1–2 month transition into the winter dry season. Cultivated plants should be kept moist while actively growing, then water should be gradually reduced after new growths mature in autumn.

FERTILIZER: ¼–½ recommended strength, applied weekly. A high nitrogen fertilizer is beneficial from spring to midsummer, but a fertilizer high in phosphates should be used in late summer and autumn.

REST PERIOD: Winter days average 67–69°F (19–20°C), and nights average 42–45°F (5–7°C), with an increased diurnal range of 23–25°F (13–14°C). Although rainfall is low for 4–5 winter months, high humidity and the large temperature range indicate that additional moisture from heavy dew is common. Therefore, while water should be greatly reduced and cultivated plants allowed to dry out between waterings from late autumn into early spring, they should not remain dry for extended periods. Occasional mistings between waterings during bright, sunny weather may help prevent the plants from becoming too dry. Fertilizer should be reduced or eliminated until active growth resumes and water is increased in spring.

GROWING MEDIA: Plants may be mounted on tree-fern or cork slabs if humidity is high and plants are watered at least once daily in summer. When plants are potted, any open, fast-draining medium may be used. Repotting is best done in early spring when new roots are growing.

MISCELLANEOUS NOTES: The bloom season shown in the climate table is based on cultivation records.

Plant and Flower Information

PLANT SIZE AND TYPE: A 6–10 in. (15–25 cm) sympodial epiphyte or lithophyte. Plants from China are reported to be 12–20 in. (30–50 cm) tall.

PSEUDOBULB: 6–10 in. (15–25 cm) long. Stems are slender with a somewhat enlarged area near the apex. They are erect and grooved.

LEAVES: The shiny leaves are yellow-green, linear-oblong, and 2–8 in. (5–20 cm) long.

INFLORESCENCE: Short. Several racemes are produced at nodes of leafless stems just when new growths are leafing out.

FLOWERS: 2 per inflorescence. The flowers are 0.5–0.8 in. (1.2–2.0 cm) across. The erect sepals and petals are pure white. The margins of the broad petals are toothed. The white lip has red veins and a dull yellow or deep orange callus. The lip has a narrow midlobe and triangular sidelobes which are toothed and ruffled. It has hairlike glands scattered on the surface and long hairy projections at the apex. Plants from China have yellow flowers with a rose tinge on the tip of the spur.

HYBRIDIZING NOTES: Chromosome counts are 2n = 38 (ref. 151, 154, 187, 188) and 2n = 40 (ref. 152, 153, 154, 542).

REFERENCES: 38, 46, 151, 152, 153, 154, 157, 187, 188, 203, 208, 216, 254, 278, 317, 369, 376, 445, 454, 489, 542.

PHOTOS/DRAWINGS: 46, 203, *454*.

Dendrobium suaveolens Kränzlin not Schlechter

AKA: We did not find this species or *D. suaveolens* Schlechter renamed or used as synonyms.

ORIGIN/HABITAT: Sorong, Irian Jaya (western New Guinea). Habitat elevation is unavailable, so the following climate data should be used with caution.

CLIMATE: Station #97502, Jefman, Indonesian New Guinea, Lat. 0.9°S, Long. 131.1°E, at an elevation of 10 ft. (3 m). Record extreme temperatures are 93°F (34°C) and 72°F (22°C).

N/HEMISPHERE	JAN	FEB	MAR	APR	MAY	JUN	JUL	AUG	SEP	OCT	NOV	DEC
°F AVG MAX	85	87	89	89	88	88	88	88	89	90	89	87
°F AVG MIN	77	77	77	78	78	78	79	79	79	79	78	78
DIURNAL RANGE	8	10	12	11	10	10	9	9	10	11	11	9
RAIN/INCHES	13.1	9.7	10.3	8.1	6.9	7.0	7.2	6.6	8.0	9.6	12.4	13.4
HUMIDITY/%	85	86	85	82	82	83	81	81	82	82	85	84
BLOOM SEASON										*		
DAYS CLR @ 9AM	2	2	2	5	6	1	6	1	4	5	5	6
DAYS CLR @ 3PM	3	2	3	4	1	1	5	1	2	4	3	5
RAIN/MM	333	246	262	206	175	178	183	168	203	244	315	340
°C AVG MAX	29.4	30.6	31.7	31.7	31.1	31.1	31.1	31.1	31.7	32.2	31.7	30.6
°C AVG MIN	25.0	25.0	25.0	25.6	25.6	25.6	26.1	26.1	26.1	26.1	25.6	25.6
DIURNAL RANGE	4.4	5.6	6.7	6.1	5.5	5.5	5.0	5.0	5.6	6.1	6.1	5.0
S/HEMISPHERE	JUL	AUG	SEP	OCT	NOV	DEC	JAN	FEB	MAR	APR	MAY	JUN

Cultural Recommendations

LIGHT: 3000–4000 fc. The summer cloud cover indicates that some shading is needed from spring through autumn, but light should be as high as the plant can tolerate, short of burning the leaves.

TEMPERATURES: Throughout the year, days average 85–90°F (29–32°C), and nights average 77–79°F (25–26°C), with a diurnal range of 8–12°F (4–7°C). Temperatures vary more each day than they do seasonally.

HUMIDITY: 80–85% year-round.

WATER: Rainfall is moderate to heavy all year with a slightly drier period in summer. Cultivated plants should be kept moist but not soggy.

FERTILIZER: ¼–½ recommended strength. A balanced fertilizer should be applied weekly to biweekly throughout the year.

REST PERIOD: Growing temperatures should be maintained year-round. In the habitat, rainfall is greatest in winter; but water may be reduced somewhat for cultivated plants, especially those grown in the dark, short-day conditions common in temperate-latitude winters. These plants should never be allowed to dry out completely, however. Fertilizer should be reduced anytime water is reduced. In the habitat, light is lowest in winter.

GROWING MEDIA: Plants may be mounted on tree-fern or cork slabs if humidity is high and plants are watered daily in summer. If plants are potted, any open, fast-draining medium may be used. Repotting may be done anytime new roots are growing.

MISCELLANEOUS NOTES: The bloom season shown in the climate table is based on reports from the habitat.

Plant and Flower Information

PLANT SIZE AND TYPE: A 10 in. (25 cm) sympodial epiphyte.

PSEUDOBULB: 10 in. (25 cm) long. The ascending stems are borne on a short creeping rhizome.

LEAVES: Many, especially near the apex of the stem. The triangular leaves are 1.2 in. (3 cm) long.

INFLORESCENCE: 0.4–0.8 in. (1–2 cm) long. Numerous racemes are produced along the side of the stem.

FLOWERS: The flowers are 0.4 in. (1 cm) long. The blossoms have pure white sepals and petals and a pale yellow lip. The dorsal sepal is oblong. The smaller lateral sepals are pointed. Petals are pointed and lanceolate. The 3-lobed lip has minute sidelobes and an ovate-oblong midlobe with 3 ridges on the hairy disk. The collector indicated that the fragrance filled the air and reminded him of vanilla or gardenia blossoms.

REFERENCES: 220, 254.

Dendrobium suaveolens Schlechter not Kränzlin

AKA: We did not find this species or *D. suaveolens* Kränzlin renamed or used as synonyms. Schlechter (ref. 436:1911) included *D. gemmiferum* Kränzlin as a possible synonym of *D. suaveolens* Schlechter, but he later (ref. 436:1925) listed it as a synonym of *D. odoratum* Schlechter.

ORIGIN/HABITAT: North Sulawesi (Celebes). Plants grow near Tolitoli and Tondano (Tomohon) at 350–2950 ft. (100–900 m).

CLIMATE: Station #97014, Manado, Sulawesi, Indonesia, Lat. 1.5°N, Long. 124.9°E, at 264 ft. (80 m). Temperatures are calculated for an elevation of 2300 ft. (700 m), resulting in probable extremes of 90°F (32°C) and 58°F (15°C).

N/HEMISPHERE	JAN	FEB	MAR	APR	MAY	JUN	JUL	AUG	SEP	OCT	NOV	DEC
°F AVG MAX	78	78	78	79	80	80	80	82	82	82	80	79
°F AVG MIN	66	66	66	66	67	66	66	66	66	65	66	67
DIURNAL RANGE	12	12	12	13	13	14	14	16	16	17	14	12
RAIN/INCHES	18.6	13.8	12.2	8.0	6.4	6.5	4.8	4.0	3.4	4.9	8.9	14.7
HUMIDITY/%	84	83	83	83	81	80	75	72	75	77	82	83
BLOOM SEASON	*	*	*								*	
DAYS CLR @ 8AM	4	3	6	11	11	12	12	12	14	17	12	8
DAYS CLR @ 2PM	1	1	1	2	1	3	3	4	4	4	1	1
RAIN/MM	472	351	310	203	163	165	122	102	86	124	226	373
°C AVG MAX	25.7	25.7	25.7	26.3	26.8	26.8	26.8	27.9	27.9	27.9	26.8	26.3
°C AVG MIN	19.0	19.0	19.0	19.0	19.6	19.0	19.0	19.0	19.0	18.5	19.0	19.6
DIURNAL RANGE	6.7	6.7	6.7	7.2	7.2	7.8	7.8	8.9	8.9	9.4	7.8	6.7
S/HEMISPHERE	JUL	AUG	SEP	OCT	NOV	DEC	JAN	FEB	MAR	APR	MAY	JUN

Cultural Recommendations

LIGHT: 2000–3000 fc. Mornings are frequently clear, but afternoons are usually overcast.

TEMPERATURES: Throughout the year, days average 78–82°F (26–28°C), and nights average 65–67°F (19–20°C), with a diurnal range of 12–17°F (8–9°C). The record high is only a few degrees above the average highs.

HUMIDITY: 70–75% in summer, increasing to near 85% in winter.

WATER: Rainfall is moderate to heavy all year. The driest conditions occur in summer and autumn. Cultivated plants should be kept moist year-round, with only slight drying allowed between waterings.

FERTILIZER: 1/4–1/2 recommended strength. A balanced fertilizer should be applied weekly to biweekly throughout the year.

REST PERIOD: Growing conditions should be maintained all year. In the habitat, rainfall is heaviest in winter. In cultivation, however, increasing water could be detrimental, particularly if light is low, days are short, or temperatures are cool. The record low is just a few degrees below the average lows, suggesting that plants may not tolerate wide temperature fluctuations. In the habitat, light is lowest in winter.

GROWING MEDIA: Plants may be mounted on tree-fern or cork slabs or potted in small pots filled with any open, fast-draining medium. Repotting may be done anytime new roots are growing.

MISCELLANEOUS NOTES: The winter bloom seasons shown in the climate table is based on collection reports.

Plant and Flower Information

PLANT SIZE AND TYPE: A 39 in. (100 cm) sympodial epiphyte.

PSEUDOBULB: 39 in. (100 cm) long. The moderately branching stems, which are swollen at the base and slender above, are longitudinally grooved. They are borne from a very short rhizome. The stems are leafless at the apex.

LEAVES: Many. The oblong leaves are usually 2–4 in. (5–10 cm) long, smooth, and leathery.

INFLORESCENCE: Short. Clusters of blossoms emerge from nodes near the apex of the stem.

FLOWERS: Several per inflorescence. The flowers are about 1 in. (2.5 cm) long. Sepals and petals are snow white. The white lip is marked with red veins and yellow keels. The dorsal sepal is ovate-lanceolate. Lateral sepals are triangular. Petals are obliquely oblong to tongue-shaped with a wavy margin. The lip is 3-lobed on the apical quarter with short, rounded sidelobes and a nearly round midlobe with a point at the apex. The margin is slightly wavy. The lip has 2 raised, wavy lines. Blossoms have a lovely fragrance.

REFERENCES: 25, 220, 436, 483.

Dendrobium suavissimum Rchb. f. See *D. chrysotoxum* Lindley.
REFERENCES: 190, 208, 216, 236, 247, 254, 430, 445, 454, 570.

Dendrobium subacaule Reinwardt ex Lindley

AKA: Reeve and Woods (ref. 385) list *D. begoniicarpum* J. J. Smith, *D. junzaingense* J. J. Smith, *D. oreocharis* Schlechter, and *D. tricostatum* Schlechter as synonyms. Lewis and Cribb (ref. 271) include only the later 2 names as synonyms.

ORIGIN/HABITAT: Widespread. Plants grow in the mountains of New Guinea, on Tidore Island in the Moluccas, and on Guadalcanal in the Solomon Islands. In Irian Jaya (western New Guinea), plants are reported from the Vogelkop Peninsula, Mt. Jaya (Mt. Carstensz), and the Cyclop and Orion Mountains. In Papua, plants grow in the provinces of West Sepik, Enga, Southern Highlands, Western Highlands, Eastern Highlands, Madang, Morobe, Central, and Milne Bay. The orchids usually grow at 2450–8200 ft. (750–2500 m) on small moss-covered twigs and branches, but they are occasionally found in the moss on both rocks and the surface of the ground.

CLIMATE: Station #94010, Goroka, Papua New Guinea, Lat. 6.1°S, Long. 145.4°E, at 5141 ft. (1567 m). Record extreme temperatures are 87°F (31°C) and 43°F (6°C).

N/HEMISPHERE	JAN	FEB	MAR	APR	MAY	JUN	JUL	AUG	SEP	OCT	NOV	DEC
°F AVG MAX	76	77	78	79	79	78	79	78	78	78	79	77
°F AVG MIN	56	57	57	57	58	59	59	59	60	59	59	57
DIURNAL RANGE	20	20	21	22	21	19	20	19	18	19	20	20
RAIN/INCHES	2.1	2.8	4.6	5.9	6.6	9.3	9.1	10.1	10.7	8.3	4.6	2.0
HUMIDITY/%	70	67	67	67	67	71	72	73	74	71	70	70
BLOOM SEASON				*	*	*	*	*	*			
DAYS CLR	N/A											
RAIN/MM	54	70	118	151	167	236	230	256	271	211	116	52
°C AVG MAX	24.7	25.1	25.6	26.3	26.2	25.7	25.8	25.6	25.5	25.6	25.9	25.1
°C AVG MIN	13.5	13.8	14.0	14.0	14.2	14.8	15.0	15.2	15.3	15.1	14.7	13.7
DIURNAL RANGE	11.2	11.3	11.6	12.3	12.0	10.9	10.8	10.4	10.2	10.5	11.2	11.4
S/HEMISPHERE	JUL	AUG	SEP	OCT	NOV	DEC	JAN	FEB	MAR	APR	MAY	JUN

Cultural Recommendations

LIGHT: 2000–2500 fc.

TEMPERATURES: Throughout the year, days average 76–79°F (25–26°C), and nights average 56–60°F (14–15°C), with a diurnal range of 18–20°F (10–11°C). Because plants are found over such a wide range of elevations, they should adapt to temperatures 8–10°F (4–6°C) warmer and cooler than indicated above.

HUMIDITY: 70–75% most of the year, dropping to near 65% in late winter and spring.

WATER: Rainfall is moderate to heavy most of the year, but conditions are slightly drier for 3 months in winter. The high relative humidity and wide temperature range causes frequent heavy deposits of dew. Additional moisture is available as mist from fog and low clouds. Cultivated plants should be kept moist and never be allowed to dry completely. In summer, daily watering may be necessary during hot, dry weather. Additional early morning mistings may be beneficial, especially on bright, sunny days.

FERTILIZER: ¼–½ recommended strength. A balanced fertilizer should be applied weekly to biweekly throughout the year.

REST PERIOD: Growing temperatures should be maintained all year. Water should be reduced in winter, especially for plants cultivated in the dark, short-day conditions common in temperate latitudes; but plants should never be allowed to dry completely. Fertilizer should be reduced or eliminated until spring. In the habitat, light is probably highest in winter.

GROWING MEDIA: Plants may be mounted on tree-fern or cork slabs if humidity is high and plants are watered at least once daily in summer. When plants are potted, any open, fast-draining medium may be used. They may be repotted anytime new roots are growing.

MISCELLANEOUS NOTES: The bloom season shown in the climate table is based on cultivation records. Plants are difficult to keep alive in cultivation. Excellent drainage and strong air circulation are evidently critical elements. Northen (ref. 330) indicates that plants need "cool, damp, and good light."

Plant and Flower Information

PLANT SIZE AND TYPE: A 0.8–1.6 in. (2–4 cm) sympodial epiphyte. The tiny plants form mats that often reach 8–12 in. (20–30 cm) across.

PSEUDOBULB: 0.2–0.4 in. (0.5–1.0 cm) long. Pseudobulbs are reddish brown.

LEAVES: 2–3 per growth. The oval, deciduous leaves are 0.2–0.4 in. (0.5–1.0 cm) long. The upper surface is dark green and the underside has a purple suffusion.

INFLORESCENCE: 0.5 in. (1.3 cm) long. Numerous inflorescences are borne on leafless pseudobulbs. The blossoms face each other. Individual pseudobulbs produce flowers for 2 years or longer.

FLOWERS: 2 per inflorescence, but plants are often completely covered with blossoms. The flowers are 0.3–0.4 in. (0.8–1.0 cm) across, large for the plant size. They often last 6 months or more. Sepals and petals with ciliated margins may be brick red or bright scarlet red. The spade-shaped lip, which is uppermost, is commonly yellow or orange, especially at the apex.

REFERENCES: 94, 95, 179, 216, 254, 271, 278, 304, 310, 330, 385, 400, 437, 516, 549, 554.

PHOTOS/DRAWINGS: *94, 304, 330, 385,* 437, *549, 554.*

Dendrobium subarticulatum Teijsm. and Binn. See *D. connatum* (Blume) Lindley. REFERENCES: 75, 216, 254, 469.

Dendrobium subbilobatum Schlechter

ORIGIN/HABITAT: Papua New Guinea. Plants grow in the Sepik River region at about 6800 ft. (2070 m).

CLIMATE: Station #200004, Ambunti, Papua New Guinea, Lat. 4.2°S, Long. 142.8°E, at 164 ft. (50 m). Temperatures are calculated for an elevation of 6800 ft. (2070 m), resulting in probable extremes of 77°F (25°C) and 30°F (−1°C).

N/HEMISPHERE	JAN	FEB	MAR	APR	MAY	JUN	JUL	AUG	SEP	OCT	NOV	DEC
°F AVG MAX	66	68	68	68	69	68	68	68	68	68	68	67
°F AVG MIN	50	51	52	51	51	51	50	51	51	51	51	52
DIURNAL RANGE	16	17	16	17	18	17	18	17	17	17	17	15
RAIN/INCHES	6.4	7.4	7.7	8.5	9.2	9.4	10.9	10.2	12.2	10.4	8.3	5.2
HUMIDITY/%	N/A											
BLOOM SEASON												
DAYS CLR	N/A											
RAIN/MM	163	188	196	216	234	239	277	259	310	264	211	132
°C AVG MAX	18.9	20.1	20.1	20.1	20.6	20.1	20.1	20.1	20.1	20.1	20.1	19.5
°C AVG MIN	10.1	10.6	11.2	10.6	10.6	10.6	10.1	10.6	10.6	10.6	10.6	11.2
DIURNAL RANGE	8.8	9.5	8.9	9.5	10.0	9.5	10.0	9.5	9.5	9.5	9.5	8.3
S/HEMISPHERE	JUL	AUG	SEP	OCT	NOV	DEC	JAN	FEB	MAR	APR	MAY	JUN

Cultural Recommendations

LIGHT: 2000–3000 fc.

TEMPERATURES: Throughout the year, days average 66–69°F (19–21°C), and nights average 50–52°F (10–11°C), with a diurnal range of 15–18°F (8–10°C).

HUMIDITY: Information is not available for this location. However, records from nearby stations indicate that humidity probably averages near 80% year-round.

WATER: Rainfall is heavy all year. The greatest amounts fall in summer and early autumn. Cultivated plants should never be allowed to dry completely.

FERTILIZER: ¼–½ recommended strength. A balanced fertilizer should be applied weekly to biweekly throughout the year.

REST PERIOD: Growing conditions should be maintained all year. Water and fertilizer should be reduced somewhat in winter, especially for plants cultivated in the dark, short-day conditions common in temperate latitudes, but the plants should never be allowed to dry out between waterings. In the habitat, seasonal light variation is minor.

GROWING MEDIA: Plants may be mounted if humidity is high and plants are watered at least once daily in summer. When plants are potted, any open, fast-draining medium may be used. Repotting is best done in early spring when new roots are growing.

MISCELLANEOUS NOTES: The bloom season shown in the climate table is based on reports from the habitat.

Plant and Flower Information

PLANT SIZE AND TYPE: A 20 in. (50 cm) sympodial epiphyte.

PSEUDOBULB: 20 in. (50 cm) long. The flattened stems, which are rigid, slender, and erect, arise from a short rhizome. They resemble a bush or shrub.

LEAVES: Many. The linear leaves are 2.4–3.5 in. (6–9 cm) long, suberect, rigid, and unequally bilobed.

INFLORESCENCE: Short.

FLOWERS: 1 per inflorescence. The inverted flowers are about 0.3 in. (0.8 cm) long. They are uniformly citron-yellow. They are smooth and fleshy. The dorsal sepal is elliptical, and lateral sepals are triangular-ovate. Petals are somewhat oblong. The curved, fleshy lip appears bilobed with a tooth at the apex and lines near the base.

REFERENCES: 223, 443.

Dendrobium subclausum Rolfe

AKA: J. J. Wood (ref. 588) divides *D. subclausum* into 4 varieties, including *D. subclausum* var. *subclausum, D. subclausum* var. *pandanicola* J. J. Wood, *D. subclausum* var. *phlox* (Schlechter) J. J. Wood, and *D. subclausum* var. *speciosum* J. J. Wood. He distributes the synonyms as follows:

For *D. subclausum* var. *phlox,* he includes the generally accepted synonym *D. phlox* Schlechter, which grows at 3950–4250 ft. (1200–1300 m).

For *D. subclausum* var. *subclausum,* he includes *D. angiense* J. J. Smith, which is sometimes spelled *D. argiense.* J. J. Smith apparently intended to name this plant for Angi Lake, the plant's point of origin, but the original publication in 1913 used the spelling *D. argiense.* In later works, Smith spelled the name *D. angiense.* Other synonyms are *D. aurantiflavum* P. van Royen, *D. calyptratum* J. J. Smith, *D. dichroma* Schlechter, *D. flammula* Schlechter, *D. fruticicola* J. J. Smith, *D. infractum* J. J. Smith, *D. mitriferum* J. J. Smith, *D. mitriferum* J. J. Smith f. *alpinum* J. J. Smith, *D. paspalifolium* J. J. Smith, *D. riparium* J. J. Smith, and *D. strictum* Ridley.

Dendrobium subclausum

The original collections for most of the above plant names were found at about 6550 ft. (2000 m). However, *D. infractum* was collected at 9000 ft. (2950 m) and *D. aurantiflavum* and *D. mitriferum* var. *alpinum* were collected at 10,250–10,500 ft. (3120–3200 m). *D. paspalifolium* was found at about 8200 ft. (2500 m). *D. strictum* grew at 3750–10,250 ft. (1140–3150 m).

ORIGIN/HABITAT: The Molucca Islands and northern Papua New Guinea. In New Guinea, plants grow at 1950–10,500 ft. (600–3200 m). Plants found below 3300 ft. (1000 m) usually grow on tall trees in undisturbed, swampy, rainforests. Those found at higher elevations most often grow on rocks and clay cliffs, but they may also grow on the surface of the ground in a layer of peat and humus. Var. *pandanicola* grows epiphytically on *Pandanus* trees. Plants known as *D. angiense* grow near Angi Lake in the Arfak Range above Manokwari at about 6250–8000 ft. (1900–2440 m). They frequently grow on trees in open forests on mountain peaks, but they are also found on moss-covered shrubs that grow in swampy humus covering decomposed granite. At higher elevations, plants grow terrestrially in open spaces on ridges. *D. calyptratum* J. J. Smith, which was found on Mt. Goliath in Irian Jaya, grows at 6400–8500 ft. (1950–2600 m) in mossy, shady areas on both trees and the ground.

CLIMATE: Station #94010, Goroka, Papua New Guinea, Lat. 6.1°S, Long. 145.4°E, at 5141 ft. (1567 m). Temperatures are calculated for an elevation of 6550 ft. (2000 m), resulting in probable extremes of 82°F (28°C) and 38°F (4°C).

N/HEMISPHERE	JAN	FEB	MAR	APR	MAY	JUN	JUL	AUG	SEP	OCT	NOV	DEC
°F AVG MAX	71	72	73	74	74	73	74	73	73	73	74	72
°F AVG MIN	51	52	52	52	53	54	54	54	55	54	54	52
DIURNAL RANGE	20	20	21	22	21	19	20	19	18	19	20	20
RAIN/INCHES	2.1	2.8	4.6	5.9	6.6	9.3	9.1	10.1	10.7	8.3	4.6	2.0
HUMIDITY/%	70	67	67	67	67	71	72	73	74	71	70	70
BLOOM SEASON	*	*	*	*	*				*	*	*	*
DAYS CLR	N/A											
RAIN/MM	53	71	117	150	168	236	231	257	272	211	117	51
°C AVG MAX	21.8	22.4	23.0	23.5	23.5	23.0	23.5	23.0	23.0	23.0	23.5	22.4
°C AVG MIN	10.7	11.3	11.3	11.3	11.8	12.4	12.4	12.4	13.0	12.4	12.4	11.3
DIURNAL RANGE	11.1	11.1	11.7	12.2	11.7	10.6	11.1	10.6	10.0	10.6	11.1	11.1
S/HEMISPHERE	JUL	AUG	SEP	OCT	NOV	DEC	JAN	FEB	MAR	APR	MAY	JUN

Cultural Recommendations

LIGHT: 2500–3500 fc.

TEMPERATURES: Throughout the year, days average 71–74°F (22–24°C), and nights average 51–55°F (11–13°C), with a diurnal range of 18–22°F (10–12°C).

HUMIDITY: Near 70–75% year-round. Growers indicate that other plants from this habitat require a delicate balance among air movement, moisture, and drainage.

WATER: Rainfall is moderate to heavy most of the year, but conditions are slightly drier for 3 months in winter. Cultivated plants should be kept moist. In summer, daily water may be necessary during hot, dry weather. In addition, early morning mistings may be beneficial, especially on bright, sunny days.

FERTILIZER: ¼ recommended strength. A balanced fertilizer should be applied weekly to biweekly throughout the year. Plants require little or no fertilizer if grown in live sphagnum. In any medium, fertilizer should be very weak. The Royal Botanic Garden in Edinburgh uses a weak, seaweed-based fertilizer for plants from this habitat.

REST PERIOD: Growing conditions must be cool year-round. In the habitat, rainfall is lowest in winter, but dew, fog, and low clouds are common. Water should be reduced in winter, especially for plants grown in the dark, short-day conditions common in temperate latitudes, but they should never be allowed to dry out completely. Fertilizer should be reduced or eliminated until water is increased in spring. In the habitat, seasonal light variation is minor.

GROWING MEDIA: Mounting plants on tree-fern or cork slabs accommodates their branching, bushy, sometimes pendulous growth habit. However, humidity must be high and plants must be watered at least once a day in summer. If plants cannot be mounted, small pots or hanging baskets may be filled with an open, fast-draining medium. Repotting may be done anytime new roots are actively growing. When repotting, old canes should not be removed, as they continue to bloom for many years.

MISCELLANEOUS NOTES: The bloom season shown in the climate table is based on cultivation records. Plants may bloom any time of year, but blooming is most frequent in midwinter. Warren (ref. 549, 553) recommends cultivating *D. subclausum* var. *pandanicola*, which is covered with lemon-yellow flowers in midwinter, and the compact *D. subclausum* var. *subclausum*, which has orange sepals and petals with yellow tips. He indicates that these plants form compact, easily managed 12 in. (30 cm) bushes whereas other varieties may reach a length of 48–72 in. (122–183 cm). He also states (ref. 549) that *D. subclausum* seedlings are among the easiest of all seedlings to successfully grow to flowering.

Plant and Flower Information

PLANT SIZE AND TYPE: An 8–28 in. (20–70 cm) sympodial terrestrial, lithophyte, or epiphyte that may reach a length of 72 in. (183 cm).

PSEUDOBULB: 8–28 in. (20–70 cm) long. Plants are extremely variable, and stems may be thick or slender. Each branch may reach a length of 8 in. (20 cm). Plants appear bushy because of their branching growth habit.

LEAVES: 5–8 densely arranged leaves at the apex of the youngest branches. The elliptic-ovate leaves, which are 1–3 in. (2.5–7.5 cm) long, are dark green.

INFLORESCENCE: 0.6 in. (1.5 cm) long. Numerous inflorescences emerge from nodes below the leaves. The flowers are clustered.

FLOWERS: 2–10 per inflorescence, many per plant. The flowers, which are 0.8–1.6 in. (2–4 cm) long, do not open fully. Blossoms are normally bicolored. Sepals and petals are commonly red-orange at the base with golden yellow tips. The spur and lip are orange or orange-red. The plants are frequently described with glowing adjectives because of the color and number of blossoms. J. J. Wood (ref. 588) differentiates the 4 varieties of *D. subclausum* as follows.

D. subclausum var. *subclausum*. Flowers are less than 1.2 in. (3 cm) long, sepals and petals are spreading, and leaf sheaths may be smooth or warty, but they are never hairy. Most often bicolored, the red blossoms have contrasting yellow tips. Plants are probably healthiest with slightly warmer temperatures than are shown in the climate table.

D. subclausum var. *phlox*. Flowers are less than 1.2 in. (3 cm) long, sepals and petals are spreading, and the often deciduous leaf sheaths are papillose-hairy. Mature stems are yellow. Blossoms are flame-colored.

D. subclausum var. *speciosum*. Flowers are 1.2–1.6 in. (3–4 cm) long, and sepals and petals are distinctly reflexed. The persistent leaf sheaths are covered with bumps and warts. The upper portions of the sepals and petals are golden yellow, and the lower portions are orange to orange-red. This variety is uncommon.

D. subclausum var. *pandanicola*. Green buds open to bright yellow or lemon-yellow flowers. The very bushy plants have zigzag, very branching stems that become yellow and ribbed when dry. Plants are normally epiphytic on *Pandanaceae*. This variety requires intermediate rather than cool temperatures.

HYBRIDIZING NOTES: Chromosome count is $2n = 38$ as *D. subclausum* (ref. 153, 273), as *D. phlox* (ref. 152, 153, 154, 188, 273), as *D. phlox* var. *flava* (ref. 151, 187), and as *D. flammula* (ref. 504, 580). Plants originally known as *D. flammula* are known to hybridize naturally with *D. lawesii* F. Mueller, creating *D.* × *von-paulsenianum* A. Hawkes.

REFERENCES: 95, 96, 144, 146, 151, 152, 153, 154, 179, 187, 188, 218, 235,

254, 273, 304, 305, 318, 371, 400, 409, 430, 437, 445, 470, 476, 486, 504, 549, 553, 554, 580, 588.

PHOTOS/DRAWINGS: *95, 304, 318, 319, 371, 430,* 437.

Dendrobium subelobatum J. J. Smith not *D. sublobatum* J. J. Smith

ORIGIN/HABITAT: Irian Jaya (western New Guinea). Plants grow in an interior valley near the Idenberg River at 1300 ft. (400 m).

CLIMATE: Station #200004, Ambunti, Papua New Guinea, Lat. 4.2°S, Long. 142.8°E, at 164 ft. (50 m). Temperatures are calculated for an elevation of 1000 ft. (300 m), resulting in probable extremes of 96°F (36°C) and 49°F (10°C).

N/HEMISPHERE	JAN	FEB	MAR	APR	MAY	JUN	JUL	AUG	SEP	OCT	NOV	DEC
°F AVG MAX	85	87	87	87	88	87	87	87	87	87	87	86
°F AVG MIN	69	70	71	70	70	70	69	70	70	70	70	71
DIURNAL RANGE	16	17	16	17	18	17	18	17	17	17	17	15
RAIN/INCHES	6.4	7.4	7.7	8.5	9.2	9.4	10.9	10.2	12.2	10.4	8.3	5.2
HUMIDITY/%	N/A											
BLOOM SEASON				*								
DAYS CLR	N/A											
RAIN/MM	163	188	196	216	234	239	277	259	310	264	211	132
°C AVG MAX	29.6	30.7	30.7	30.7	31.2	30.7	30.7	30.7	30.7	30.7	30.7	30.1
°C AVG MIN	20.7	21.2	21.8	21.2	21.2	21.2	20.7	21.2	21.2	21.2	21.2	21.8
DIURNAL RANGE	8.9	9.5	8.9	9.5	10.0	9.5	10.0	9.5	9.5	9.5	9.5	8.3
S/HEMISPHERE	JUL	AUG	SEP	OCT	NOV	DEC	JAN	FEB	MAR	APR	MAY	JUN

Cultural Recommendations

LIGHT: 2000–3000 fc.

TEMPERATURES: Throughout the year, days average 85–88°F (30–31°C), and nights average 69–71°F (21–22°C), with a diurnal range of 15–18°F (8–10°C).

HUMIDITY: Information is not available for this location. However, records from nearby locations indicate that humidity probably averages near 80% year-round.

WATER: Rainfall is heavy all year, with the greatest amounts falling in summer and early autumn. Cultivated plants should never be allowed to dry completely.

FERTILIZER: 1/4–1/2 recommended strength. A balanced fertilizer should be applied weekly to biweekly throughout the year.

REST PERIOD: Growing conditions should be maintained all year. Water and fertilizer should be reduced somewhat in winter, especially for plants grown in the dark, short-day conditions common in temperate latitudes, but plants should never be allowed to dry out completely between waterings. In the habitat, seasonal light variation is minor.

GROWING MEDIA: Plants may be mounted on cork or tree-fern slabs if humidity is high and plants are watered at least once daily in summer. When plants are potted, any open, fast-draining medium may be used, but fir bark is preferred by most growers. Repotting may be done anytime new roots are growing.

MISCELLANEOUS NOTES: The bloom season shown in the climate table is based on reports from the habitat.

Plant and Flower Information

PLANT SIZE AND TYPE: A 25 in. (64 cm) sympodial epiphyte.

PSEUDOBULB: 25 in. (64 cm) long. The elongated, clustered stems are carried on a short, branching rhizome.

LEAVES: Many. The lanceolate, red-brown leaves are 1.6–2.4 in. (4–6 cm) long.

INFLORESCENCE: Short. Inflorescences emerge through the leaf sheaths at nodes along the stem.

FLOWERS: Few per inflorescence. The white flowers are 0.6 in. (1.5 cm) across. Sepals are oblong and incurved at the tip. The petals are concave and incurved at the tip. The small, 3-lobed lip is erect and very recurved.

REFERENCES: 224, 445, 470.

Dendrobium suberectum (Ridley) Masamune. Now considered a synonym of *Epigeneium suberectum* (Ridley) Summerhayes.

REFERENCES: 229, 286, 499.

Dendrobium subfalcatum J. J. Smith. Schlechter (ref. 443) considered this a synonym of *Cadetia subfalcata* (J. J. Smith) Schlechter.

REFERENCES: 221, 223, 443, 445, 470, 475.

Dendrobium subflavidum Ridley

AKA: *D. chloroleucum* Ridley.

ORIGIN/HABITAT: Malaya. Plants grow in exposed locations on Mt. Tahan, Mt. Tapis, and Mt. Korbu (Kerbau) at 3000–6000 ft. (910–1820 m).

CLIMATE: Station #48625, Ipoh, Malaya, Lat. 4.6°N, Long. 101.1°E, at 123 ft. (37 m). Temperatures are calculated for an elevation of 4900 ft. (1500 m), resulting in probable extremes of 83°F (28°C) and 48°F (9°C).

N/HEMISPHERE	JAN	FEB	MAR	APR	MAY	JUN	JUL	AUG	SEP	OCT	NOV	DEC
°F AVG MAX	74	76	77	76	76	76	75	75	74	73	73	73
°F AVG MIN	56	56	57	57	58	57	56	56	57	56	56	56
DIURNAL RANGE	18	20	20	19	18	19	19	19	17	17	17	17
RAIN/INCHES	7.9	3.1	7.6	8.4	6.2	3.6	7.2	6.9	8.8	11.0	13.0	8.9
HUMIDITY/%	76	74	76	78	78	75	76	77	79	82	82	81
BLOOM SEASON	*	*										*
DAYS CLR @ 7AM	3	3	3	1	1	2	1	1	0	0	1	2
DAYS CLR @ 1PM	2	2	2	1	1	1	1	1	0	0	0	2
RAIN/MM	201	79	193	213	157	91	183	175	224	279	330	226
°C AVG MAX	23.4	24.5	25.1	24.5	24.5	24.5	24.0	24.0	23.4	22.9	22.9	22.9
°C AVG MIN	13.4	13.4	14.0	14.0	14.5	14.0	13.4	13.4	14.0	13.4	13.4	13.4
DIURNAL RANGE	10.0	11.1	11.1	10.5	10.0	10.5	10.6	10.6	9.4	9.5	9.5	9.5
S/HEMISPHERE	JUL	AUG	SEP	OCT	NOV	DEC	JAN	FEB	MAR	APR	MAY	JUN

Cultural Recommendations

LIGHT: 1500–2500 fc. Light should be diffused or dappled, and direct sunlight should be avoided. Clear days are quite rare.

TEMPERATURES: Throughout the year, days average 73–77°F (23–25°C), and nights average 56–58°F (13–15°C), with a diurnal range of 17–20°F (9–11°C).

HUMIDITY: 75–80% year-round.

WATER: Rainfall is heavy most of the year. The heaviest rainfall occurs in autumn with a secondary maximum in spring. Brief semidry periods occur in midwinter and midsummer. Cultivated plants should be kept evenly moist, with only slight drying allowed between waterings.

FERTILIZER: 1/4–1/2 recommended strength. A balanced fertilizer should be applied weekly to biweekly throughout the year.

REST PERIOD: Growing conditions should be maintained year-round. Water should be reduced somewhat in winter for plants cultivated in the dark, short-day conditions common in temperate latitudes. They should never be allowed to dry out completely, however. Fertilizer may be reduced when the plant is not actively growing or when water is reduced. In the habitat, light is slightly higher in winter.

GROWING MEDIA: Plants may be mounted on tree-fern or cork slabs if humidity is high and plants are watered at least once daily in summer. When plants are potted, any open, fast-draining medium may be used. Repotting may be done anytime new roots are growing.

MISCELLANEOUS NOTES: The bloom season shown in the climate table is based on cultivation records.

Plant and Flower Information

PLANT SIZE AND TYPE: An 18–28 in. (45–70 cm) sympodial epiphyte.

PSEUDOBULB: 18–28 in. (45–70 cm) long. The purplish stems appear dirty.

Dendrobium subhastatum

LEAVES: Many. The leaves, which are about 5.5 in. (14 cm) long, are spaced 1.2–2.0 in. (3–5 cm) apart. They are thin, lanceolate, and pointed at the tip. They may be dark green or suffused with dark violet.

INFLORESCENCE: 0.9 in. (2.2 cm) long. Inflorescences are pendulous. Racemes emerge from nodes on old stems.

FLOWERS: 1–2 per inflorescence. The flowers are 1.6–1.8 in. (4.0–4.5 cm) long. The large sepals and much smaller petals are cream to pale greenish yellow. The canary yellow lip is often marked with crimson or red-brown spots at the base. It is unlobed with a wavy, uneven margin. The column may be green at the base.

REFERENCES: 179, 200, 220, 402, 455.

PHOTOS/DRAWINGS: 455.

Dendrobium subhastatum J. J. Smith.
Although not correctly transferred, Schlechter (ref. 443) considered this plant to be a synonym of *Cadetia subhastata* (J. J. Smith) Schlechter. REFERENCES: 221, 223, 443, 445, 470.

Dendrobium sublobatum J. J. Smith.
Now considered a synonym of *Diplocaulobium sublobatum* (J. J. Smith) Hunt and Summerhayes. REFERENCES: 213, 221, 230, 445, 470, 475.

Dendrobium subpandifolium J. J. Smith

ORIGIN/HABITAT: Bangka Island, off the southeast coast of Sumatra. Habitat elevation was not reported. Bangka is a low-lying island with the highest point about 2300 ft. (700 m). Since plants were cultivated in the botanical garden at Bogor, Java, low-elevation climate data are provided, but they should be used with caution.

CLIMATE: Station #96237, Pangkalpinang, Bangka Island, Indonesia, Lat. 2.2°S, Long. 106.1°E, at 109 ft. (33 m). Record extreme temperatures are 94°F (34°C) and 68°F (20°C).

N/HEMISPHERE	JAN	FEB	MAR	APR	MAY	JUN	JUL	AUG	SEP	OCT	NOV	DEC
°F AVG MAX	86	86	86	87	86	85	84	85	86	87	87	86
°F AVG MIN	78	78	77	76	74	74	74	74	74	75	76	77
DIURNAL RANGE	8	8	9	11	12	11	10	11	12	12	11	9
RAIN/INCHES	8.6	6.0	5.9	6.3	11.6	16.3	15.1	12.4	9.9	11.8	9.7	7.5
HUMIDITY/%	76	72	71	75	80	86	84	85	84	82	81	79
BLOOM SEASON	N/A											
DAYS CLR @ 7AM	6	6	6	3	1	0	2	2	2	3	4	3
DAYS CLR @ 1PM	1	2	5	2	0	0	0	0	0	0	0	0
RAIN/MM	218	152	150	160	295	414	384	315	251	300	246	190
°C AVG MAX	30.0	30.0	30.0	30.6	30.0	29.4	28.9	29.4	30.0	30.6	30.6	30.0
°C AVG MIN	25.6	25.6	25.0	24.4	23.3	23.3	23.3	23.3	23.3	23.9	24.4	25.0
DIURNAL RANGE	4.4	4.4	5.0	6.2	6.7	6.1	5.6	6.1	6.7	6.7	6.2	5.0
S/HEMISPHERE	JUL	AUG	SEP	OCT	NOV	DEC	JAN	FEB	MAR	APR	MAY	JUN

Cultural Recommendations

LIGHT: 2000–3000 fc.

TEMPERATURES: Throughout the year, days average 84–87°F (29–31°C), and nights average 74–78°F (23–26°C), with a diurnal range of 8–12°F (4–7°C).

HUMIDITY: 80–85% from late spring through autumn, dropping to 70–75% in winter and early spring.

WATER: Rainfall is heavy year-round, but conditions are driest in winter. Cultivated plants should never be allowed to dry out completely. Warm water might be beneficial.

FERTILIZER: ¼–½ recommended strength. A balanced fertilizer should be applied weekly to biweekly throughout the year.

REST PERIOD: Growing conditions should be maintained year-round. Water may be reduced somewhat in winter, especially for plants grown in the dark, short-day conditions common in temperate latitudes. However, plants should never be allowed to dry out completely. In the habitat, light is slightly higher in winter.

GROWING MEDIA: Plants may be mounted on tree-fern or cork slabs or potted in small pots filled with any open, fast-draining medium. Repotting may be done anytime new roots are actively growing.

MISCELLANEOUS NOTES: The plant was described in 1927 in *Bull. Jard. Bot. Buit.* 3rd sér. 9:157.

Plant and Flower Information

PLANT SIZE AND TYPE: A 9.5 in. (24 cm) sympodial epiphyte.

PSEUDOBULB: 9.5 in. (24 cm) long. The elongated stems are dark, shiny yellow when dry. The lower part is leafy, but the upper part has only rudimentary leaves.

LEAVES: Many. The linear leaves are 0.8–1.6 in. (2–4 cm) long, curved, pointed, somewhat fleshy, laterally folded, and sickle-shaped.

INFLORESCENCE: Inflorescences emerge along the upper part of the stem.

FLOWERS: 1–2 per inflorescence. The small flowers are 0.3 in. (0.8 cm) long. Segments are light yellow with pale purple stripes. Blossoms have a triangular dorsal sepal, oblong-falcate, concave lateral sepals, and lanceolate petals. The erect lip is recurved along the margin with 3 raised, parallel ridges in the center. It is essentially unlobed.

REFERENCES: 224.

Dendrobium subpetiolatum Schlechter

ORIGIN/HABITAT: Northern Papua New Guinea. Plants grow on thickly moss-covered mistforest trees in the Torricelli Range at about 2600 ft. (800 m).

CLIMATE: Station #94004, Wewak, Papua New Guinea, Lat. 3.6°S, Long. 143.7°E, at 16 ft. (5 m). Temperatures are calculated for an elevation of 2600 ft. (800 m), resulting in probable extremes of 89°F (32°C) and 53°F (12°C).

N/HEMISPHERE	JAN	FEB	MAR	APR	MAY	JUN	JUL	AUG	SEP	OCT	NOV	DEC
°F AVG MAX	79	79	79	79	79	79	78	77	78	79	79	79
°F AVG MIN	65	65	65	66	66	66	66	66	65	65	66	65
DIURNAL RANGE	14	14	14	13	13	13	12	11	13	14	13	14
RAIN/INCHES	7.6	4.8	5.3	10.0	13.3	14.5	12.1	11.9	14.9	16.9	15.1	10.8
HUMIDITY/%	80	79	79	78	79	81	82	82	81	82	81	80
BLOOM SEASON			*									
DAYS CLR	N/A											
RAIN/MM	193	122	135	254	338	368	307	302	378	429	384	274
°C AVG MAX	26.3	26.3	26.3	26.3	26.3	26.3	25.8	25.2	25.8	26.3	26.3	26.3
°C AVG MIN	18.6	18.6	18.6	19.1	19.1	19.1	19.1	19.1	18.6	18.6	19.1	18.6
DIURNAL RANGE	7.7	7.7	7.7	7.2	7.2	7.2	6.7	6.1	7.2	7.7	7.2	7.7
S/HEMISPHERE	JUL	AUG	SEP	OCT	NOV	DEC	JAN	FEB	MAR	APR	MAY	JUN

Cultural Recommendations

LIGHT: 1500–2500 fc.

TEMPERATURES: Throughout the year, days average 77–79°F (25–26°C), and nights average 65–66°F (19°C), with a diurnal range of 11–14°F (6–8°C).

HUMIDITY: Near 80% year-round.

WATER: Rainfall is heavy all year, but conditions are slightly drier in winter. Cultivated plants should never be allowed to dry out completely. Warm water might be beneficial.

FERTILIZER: ¼–½ recommended strength. A balanced fertilizer should be applied weekly to biweekly throughout the year.

REST PERIOD: Growing conditions should be maintained year-round. Water and fertilizer may be reduced somewhat in winter, especially for plants grown in the dark, short-day conditions common in temperate latitudes. However, plants should never be allowed to dry out completely. In the habitat, light is highest in winter.

GROWING MEDIA: A very open and fast-draining medium should be used with either baskets or small pots. Repotting may be done anytime new roots are growing.

MISCELLANEOUS NOTES: The bloom season shown in the climate table is based on collection reports. Plants that produce flowers which last a single day commonly bloom several times during the year. Flowering usually occurs 7–14 days after a sudden 10°F (5°C) drop in daytime temperatures.

Plant and Flower Information

PLANT SIZE AND TYPE: A 31 in. (80 cm) sympodial epiphyte.

PSEUDOBULB: 31 in. (80 cm) long. The flattened, nearly erect stems arise from a short rhizome. They are densely leafy.

LEAVES: Many. The elliptical, suberect leaves are 2.8–4.0 in. (7–10 cm) long.

INFLORESCENCE: Short.

FLOWERS: 2 per inflorescence. The flowers are 0.9 in. (2.3 cm) long and do not open fully. Sepals and petals are white with a pink flush on the backside. The lip is white with brown on the side fringe on the front lobe. It has short, scattered warts on the pointed midlobe and a tuft of hairs near the base. It has a 3-part midlobe with small, ear-like projections on each side of the larger midlobe. The margins of the sidelobes are uneven. The column is orange-yellow. Blossoms are short-lived.

REFERENCES: 92, 221, 437, 445.

PHOTOS/DRAWINGS: 437.

Dendrobium subquadratum J. J. Smith

AKA: *D. sikinii* Schlechter, *D. kingianum* Bidwell var. *subquadratum* Kränzlin.

ORIGIN/HABITAT: New Guinea. In Papua, *D. sikinii* was collected in the Minjem Valley above Kelel. In Irian Jaya, plants grow on trees in primary forests along the Noord River. The orchids usually grow in cool, moist locations along mountain creeks at 1000–1650 ft. (300–500 m).

CLIMATE: Station #94014, Madang, Papua New Guinea, Lat. 5.2°S, Long. 145.8°E, at 13 ft. (4 m). Temperatures are calculated for an elevation of 1150 ft. (350 m), resulting in probable extremes of 94°F (35°C) and 58°F (15°C).

N/HEMISPHERE	JAN	FEB	MAR	APR	MAY	JUN	JUL	AUG	SEP	OCT	NOV	DEC
°F AVG MAX	79	79	81	81	81	81	81	81	81	83	83	80
°F AVG MIN	73	74	74	74	73	73	73	73	73	72	73	74
DIURNAL RANGE	6	5	7	7	8	8	8	8	8	11	10	6
RAIN/INCHES	4.0	3.4	3.2	8.5	11.2	11.1	10.1	11.3	9.4	11.3	10.5	6.7
HUMIDITY/%	88	87	86	86	86	86	86	85	85	87	88	89
BLOOM SEASON	*											
DAYS CLR	N/A											
RAIN/MM	102	86	81	216	284	282	257	287	239	287	267	170
°C AVG MAX	26.2	26.2	27.4	27.4	27.4	27.4	27.4	27.4	27.4	28.5	28.5	26.8
°C AVG MIN	22.9	23.5	23.5	23.5	22.9	22.9	22.9	22.9	22.9	22.4	22.9	23.5
DIURNAL RANGE	3.3	2.7	3.9	3.9	4.5	4.5	4.5	4.5	4.5	6.1	5.6	3.3
S/HEMISPHERE	JUL	AUG	SEP	OCT	NOV	DEC	JAN	FEB	MAR	APR	MAY	JUN

Cultural Recommendations

LIGHT: 2000–3000 fc.

TEMPERATURES: Throughout the year, days average 79–83°F (26–29°C), and nights average 72–74°F (22–24°C), with a diurnal range of 5–11°F (3–6°C). The warmest highs, the coolest lows, and the greatest diurnal range occur in autumn.

HUMIDITY: 85–90% year-round.

WATER: Rainfall is heavy from spring through autumn, but conditions are somewhat drier in winter. Cultivated plants should be kept moist but not soggy while actively growing.

FERTILIZER: ¼–½ recommended strength. A balanced fertilizer should be applied weekly to biweekly throughout the year.

REST PERIOD: Growing temperatures should be maintained all year. In the habitat, rainfall decreases somewhat for 3–4 months in winter. In cultivation, water should be reduced and the plants allowed to dry slightly between waterings. Fertilizer should be reduced until water is increased in spring. In the habitat, light is highest in winter.

GROWING MEDIA: Mounting plants on tree-fern or cork slabs accommodates their pendulous growth habit. However, humidity must be high and plants must be watered at least once a day in summer. If plants cannot be mounted, small pots or hanging baskets may be filled with an open, fast-draining medium. Repotting may be done anytime new roots are actively growing.

MISCELLANEOUS NOTES: The bloom season shown in the climate table is based on collection reports. Plants have not been collected recently.

Plant and Flower Information

PLANT SIZE AND TYPE: An 8–12 in. (20–30 cm) sympodial epiphyte.

PSEUDOBULB: 2.4–12.0 in. (6–30 cm) long. The stems are many edged with 7–9 concave sides. They have about 5 nodes and become yellow when dry.

LEAVES: 2 per growth. Erect and somewhat elliptical, the leaves are 5–6 in. (12–15 cm) long. They are twisted at the base so that both leaves face front.

INFLORESCENCE: 1.2–4.7 in. (3–12 cm) long. Inflorescences emerge near the apex of the stem. They are very slender, almost wiry, and may be erect or arching.

FLOWERS: 6–10 per inflorescence. The fleshy flowers are 0.5–0.8 in. (1.3–2.0 cm) long and do not open fully. The white or pale green sepals and petals are long and pointed. The pale green lip becomes pale, dull yellow with age. The midlobe is very thick, rough, and folded. It cannot be flattened. The 3-ridged callus terminates near the base of the midlobe.

REFERENCES: 83, 92, 220, 254, 437, 445, 470.

PHOTOS/DRAWINGS: 437.

Dendrobium subradiatum J. J. Smith. Schlechter (ref. 443) considered this plant to be a synonym of *Cadetia subradiata* (J. J. Smith) Schlechter. REFERENCES: 144, 221, 223, 443, 445, 470, 475.

Dendrobium subretusum J. J. Smith

AKA: *Cadetia imitans* Schlechter. *Cadetia* is now considered a valid genus by some botanists, so this plant may again be a *Cadetia*.

ORIGIN/HABITAT: Papua New Guinea. In the Waria District, plants grow on trees in the forests of the Dischore Mountains at about 4250 ft. (1300 m).

CLIMATE: Station #200192, Garaina, Papua New Guinea, Lat. 7.9°S, Long. 147.1°E, at 2350 ft. (716 m). Temperatures are calculated for an elevation of 4250 ft. (1300 m), resulting in probable extremes of 88°F (31°C) and 40°F (4°C).

N/HEMISPHERE	JAN	FEB	MAR	APR	MAY	JUN	JUL	AUG	SEP	OCT	NOV	DEC
°F AVG MAX	74	76	77	78	79	79	79	79	78	78	77	75
°F AVG MIN	57	57	57	58	57	58	59	59	59	58	58	57
DIURNAL RANGE	17	19	20	20	22	21	20	20	19	20	19	18
RAIN/INCHES	5.8	6.5	8.7	11.1	11.8	11.9	8.9	11.7	11.5	9.9	7.7	5.2
HUMIDITY/%	84	82	82	81	80	80	81	81	82	83	84	84
BLOOM SEASON												*
DAYS CLR	N/A											
RAIN/MM	147	165	221	282	300	302	226	297	292	251	196	132
°C AVG MAX	23.1	24.3	24.8	25.4	25.9	25.9	25.9	25.9	25.4	25.4	24.8	23.7
°C AVG MIN	13.7	13.7	13.7	14.3	13.7	14.3	14.8	14.8	14.8	14.3	14.3	13.7
DIURNAL RANGE	9.4	10.6	11.1	11.1	12.2	11.6	11.1	11.1	10.6	11.1	10.5	10.0
S/HEMISPHERE	JUL	AUG	SEP	OCT	NOV	DEC	JAN	FEB	MAR	APR	MAY	JUN

Dendrobium subserratum

Cultural Recommendations

LIGHT: 2000–3000 fc.

TEMPERATURES: Throughout the year, days average 74–79°F (23–26°C), and nights average 57–59°F (14–15°C), with a diurnal range of 17–22°F (9–12°C).

HUMIDITY: 80–85% year-round.

WATER: Rainfall is heavy all year, but conditions are slightly drier in winter. Cultivated plants should be kept moist but not soggy.

FERTILIZER: ¼–½ recommended strength. A balanced fertilizer should be applied weekly to biweekly throughout the year. The Royal Botanic Garden in Edinburgh uses a seaweed-based fertilizer for plants from high-elevation New Guinea habitats.

REST PERIOD: Growing conditions should be maintained all year. In the habitat, rainfall is slightly lower in winter. Water and fertilizer may be reduced somewhat in winter, especially for plants grown in the dark, short-day conditions common in temperate latitudes. Plants should never be allowed to dry out completely, however. In the habitat, light is probably higher in winter.

GROWING MEDIA: Plants may be mounted on tree-fern or cork slabs if humidity is high and plants are watered at least once daily in summer. When plants are potted, any open, fast-draining medium may be used. Repotting may be done anytime new roots are growing.

MISCELLANEOUS NOTES: The bloom season shown in the climate table is based on collection reports. Schlechter (ref. 437) reported that *D. subretusum* occasionally grows with *D. dischorense* Schlechter.

Plant and Flower Information

PLANT SIZE AND TYPE: A 1.0–1.6 in. (2.5–4.0 cm) sympodial epiphyte.

PSEUDOBULB: 0.3–1.2 in. (0.8–3.0 cm) long. The cylindrical stems are clustered on a very short rhizome.

LEAVES: 1 per growth. The somewhat oblong-lanceolate leaves are 0.3–0.8 in. (0.8–2.0 cm) long. They are pointed at the tip.

INFLORESCENCE: Very short. Inflorescences emerge at the apex of the stem.

FLOWERS: 2–3 per inflorescence. Blossoms open in succession. The snow white flowers are 0.2 in. (0.5 cm) long. The narrow, pointed sepals are sharply recurved, nearly hiding the spur. The lip and pointed, narrow petals project forward. The 3-lobed lip has a slight depression at the apex of the rounded midlobe and small pointed sidelobes.

REFERENCES: 221, 437, 472.

PHOTOS/DRAWINGS: 437.

Dendrobium subserratum Schlechter

ORIGIN/HABITAT: Northern Papua New Guinea. Plants grow on forest trees in the Finisterre Range at about 4250 ft. (1300 m).

CLIMATE: Station #94010, Goroka, Papua New Guinea, Lat. 6.1°S, Long. 145.4°E, at 5141 ft. (1567 m). Temperatures are calculated for an elevation of 4000 ft. (1220 m), resulting in probable extremes of 90°F (32°C) and 46°F (8°C).

N/HEMISPHERE	JAN	FEB	MAR	APR	MAY	JUN	JUL	AUG	SEP	OCT	NOV	DEC
°F AVG MAX	80	81	82	83	83	82	83	82	82	82	83	81
°F AVG MIN	60	61	61	61	62	63	63	63	64	63	63	61
DIURNAL RANGE	20	20	21	22	21	19	20	19	18	19	20	20
RAIN/INCHES	2.1	2.8	4.6	5.9	6.6	9.3	9.1	10.1	10.7	8.3	4.6	2.0
HUMIDITY/%	70	67	67	67	67	71	72	73	74	71	70	70
BLOOM SEASON		*	*	*	*	*			*	*	*	
DAYS CLR	N/A											
RAIN/MM	53	71	117	150	168	236	231	257	272	211	117	51
°C AVG MAX	26.5	27.1	27.6	28.2	28.2	27.6	28.2	27.6	27.6	27.6	28.2	27.1
°C AVG MIN	15.4	16.0	16.0	16.0	16.5	17.1	17.1	17.1	17.6	17.1	17.1	16.0
DIURNAL RANGE	11.1	11.1	11.6	12.2	11.7	10.5	11.1	10.5	10.0	10.5	11.1	11.1
S/HEMISPHERE	JUL	AUG	SEP	OCT	NOV	DEC	JAN	FEB	MAR	APR	MAY	JUN

Cultural Recommendations

LIGHT: 2000–3000 fc.

TEMPERATURES: Throughout the year, days average 80–83°F (27–28°C), and nights average 60–64°F (15–18°C), with a diurnal range of 18–22°F (10–12°C). The diurnal range is unusually large for a habitat with such constant temperatures.

HUMIDITY: 70–75% from summer into autumn, dropping to near 65% in winter and spring. Plants require excellent air movement.

WATER: Rainfall is moderate to heavy most of the year, with slightly drier conditions for 3 months in winter. Cultivated plants should be kept moist but not soggy. Daily watering may be necessary during hot weather. In addition, early morning mistings may be beneficial, especially on bright, sunny days.

FERTILIZER: ¼–½ recommended strength. A balanced fertilizer should be applied weekly to biweekly throughout the year.

REST PERIOD: Growing temperatures should be maintained all year. In the habitat, rainfall is lowest in winter, but heavy dew and mist from fog and low clouds are common. Water and fertilizer should be reduced for cultivated plants, especially those grown in the dark, short-day conditions common in temperate latitudes. However, they should never be allowed to dry out completely. In the habitat, light is higher in winter.

GROWING MEDIA: Plants may be mounted on tree-fern or cork slabs if humidity is high and plants are watered at least once daily in summer. When plants are potted, any open, fast-draining medium may be used. Repotting may be done anytime new roots are growing.

MISCELLANEOUS NOTES: The bloom season shown in the climate table is based on cultivation records. *D. subserratum* may bloom at any time of year.

Plant and Flower Information

PLANT SIZE AND TYPE: A 12–16 in. (30–40 cm) sympodial epiphyte.

PSEUDOBULB: 12–16 in. (30–40 cm) long. The erect stems are flattened, densely leafy, and unbranched. They are clustered and arise from a very short rhizome.

LEAVES: Many. The erect, linear leaves are 1.6–2.8 in. (4–7 cm) long. They are unequally bilobed at the apex.

FLOWERS: 1 per inflorescence. The inverted flowers are 0.4 in. (1.1 cm) long and do not open widely. Sepals and narrow petals are yellowish pink. The roundly oblong lip is yellow with reddish brown along the minutely toothed margins. The lip has 4 longitudinal folds in the center of the midlobe.

REFERENCES: 92, 179, 221, 437, 445.

PHOTOS/DRAWINGS: 437.

Dendrobium subsessile Gagnepain.

Often listed as a synonym of *D. indochinese* A. Hawkes and A. H. Heller, but In 1982 Seidenfaden in *Opera Botanica* #62 indicates that this name is a synonym of *Eria corneri*. REFERENCES: 138, 227, 448.

Dendrobium subsessile Schlechter

ORIGIN/HABITAT: Northern Papua New Guinea. Plants grow on trunks and branches of mistforest trees in the Kani Range at about 3600 ft. (1100 m).

CLIMATE: Station #200187, Erap, Papua New Guinea, Lat. 6.6°S, Long. 146.7°E, at 850 ft. (260 m). Temperatures are calculated for an elevation of 3300 ft. (1000 m), resulting in probable extremes of 94°F (34°C) and 45°F (7°C).

N/HEMISPHERE	JAN	FEB	MAR	APR	MAY	JUN	JUL	AUG	SEP	OCT	NOV	DEC
°F AVG MAX	80	80	81	82	85	85	85	85	85	84	82	82
°F AVG MIN	61	61	61	62	64	65	64	64	65	63	66	62
DIURNAL RANGE	19	19	20	20	21	20	21	21	20	21	16	20
RAIN/INCHES	3.9	3.9	2.7	3.0	3.0	5.3	5.9	5.9	7.0	3.4	2.4	3.1
HUMIDITY/%	82	81	81	79	75	74	74	74	77	76	80	80
BLOOM SEASON				*								
DAYS CLR	N/A											
RAIN/MM	99	99	69	76	76	135	150	150	178	86	61	79
°C AVG MAX	26.7	26.7	27.2	27.8	29.4	29.4	29.4	29.4	29.4	28.9	27.8	27.8
°C AVG MIN	16.1	16.1	16.1	16.7	17.8	18.3	17.8	17.8	18.3	17.2	18.9	16.7
DIURNAL RANGE	10.6	10.6	11.1	11.1	11.6	11.1	11.6	11.6	11.1	11.7	8.9	11.1
S/HEMISPHERE	JUL	AUG	SEP	OCT	NOV	DEC	JAN	FEB	MAR	APR	MAY	JUN

Cultural Recommendations

LIGHT: 2500–3500 fc.

TEMPERATURES: Throughout the year, days average 80–85°F (27–29°C), and nights average 61–65°F (16–18°C), with a diurnal range of 16–21°F (9–12°C).

HUMIDITY: 75–80% year-round.

WATER: Rainfall is relatively light most of the year, but for 4–5 months in summer and early autumn, conditions are much wetter. Cultivated plants should be thoroughly saturated then allowed to dry slightly between waterings.

FERTILIZER: ¼–½ recommended strength. A balanced fertilizer should be applied weekly to biweekly throughout the year.

REST PERIOD: Growing temperatures should be maintained all year. In the habitat, rainfall is lowest in winter, but additional moisture is frequently available from fog and mist. Cultivated plants should be allowed to dry out between waterings, but they should not remain dry for long periods. Fertilizer should be reduced until water is increased in spring. In the habitat, seasonal light variation is minor.

GROWING MEDIA: Mounting plants on tree-fern or cork slabs accommodates their pendent growth habit. Plants are best remounted when roots are actively growing.

MISCELLANEOUS NOTES: The bloom season shown in the climate table is based on collection reports.

Plant and Flower Information

PLANT SIZE AND TYPE: A 24 in. (60 cm) sympodial epiphyte.

PSEUDOBULB: 24 in. (60 cm) long. The leafy stems occasionally branch.

LEAVES: Many. The equitant, lanceolate leaves are 0.8–1.4 in. (2.0–3.6 cm) long.

INFLORESCENCE: Short. Inflorescences emerge from nodes along the side and at the apex of the stems.

FLOWERS: 1 per inflorescence. The dark carmine flowers are 0.3 in. (0.7 cm) long. They are thick and fleshy and do not open fully. The lip is approximately the same size as sepals and petals. Sepals are keeled with a sharp point where the keel extends beyond the margin of the blade. The apex of the unlobed lip is folded along the rounded sides making it appear pointed.

REFERENCES: 92, 221, 437, 445.

PHOTOS/DRAWINGS: 437.

Dendrobium subteres Lindley. See *D. acerosum* (Griffith) Lindley. REFERENCES: 216, 278, 310, 454.

Dendrobium subterrestre Gagnepain. In 1982 Seidenfaden in *Opera Botanica* #62 indicates that *D. subterrestre* is a synonym of *Eria bractescens* Lindley. REFERENCES: 136, 224, 266, 448.

Dendrobium subtricostatum J. J. Smith

ORIGIN/HABITAT: Irian Jaya (western New Guinea). Plants were collected on a mountain ridge about 43 miles (70 km) north of Mt. Jaya (Mt. Carstensz). Habitat elevation is not included with the original description, so the following climate data should be used with caution.

CLIMATE: Station #97686, Wamena, New Guinea, Lat. 4.1°S, Long. 139.0°E, at 5446 ft. (1660 m). Record extreme temperatures are not available for this location.

N/HEMISPHERE	JAN	FEB	MAR	APR	MAY	JUN	JUL	AUG	SEP	OCT	NOV	DEC
°F AVG MAX	75	76	77	76	77	76	77	76	76	79	78	74
°F AVG MIN	60	60	62	62	63	64	63	62	63	65	65	61
DIURNAL RANGE	15	16	15	14	14	12	14	14	13	14	13	13
RAIN/INCHES	3.0	1.9	2.2	4.0	4.6	3.3	2.8	4.2	6.9	3.9	5.4	4.9
HUMIDITY/%	N/A											
BLOOM SEASON	N/A											
DAYS CLR	N/A											
RAIN/MM	76	48	56	102	117	84	71	107	175	99	137	124
°C AVG MAX	23.9	24.4	25.0	24.4	25.0	24.4	25.0	24.4	24.4	26.1	25.6	23.3
°C AVG MIN	15.6	15.6	16.7	16.7	17.2	17.8	17.2	16.7	17.2	18.3	18.3	16.1
DIURNAL RANGE	8.3	8.8	8.3	7.7	7.8	6.6	7.8	7.7	7.2	7.8	7.3	7.2
S/HEMISPHERE	JUL	AUG	SEP	OCT	NOV	DEC	JAN	FEB	MAR	APR	MAY	JUN

Cultural Recommendations

LIGHT: 1800–2500 fc. In the habitat, light is highest in the morning.

TEMPERATURES: Throughout the year, days average 74–77°F (23–25°C), and nights average 60–65°F (16–18°C), with a diurnal range of 12–16°F (7–9°C). In the habitat, the warmest temperatures of the day occur during late morning when skies are usually clear. Clouds and mist develop near noon, thus preventing additional warming.

HUMIDITY: Information is not available for this location. However, records from nearby stations indicate that humidity probably averages near 80% year-round. High humidity and excellent air circulation are particularly important if temperatures are warm. Placing the plants in front of an evaporative cooler or near a fine mist may be very beneficial on especially warm days.

WATER: Rainfall is light to moderate through most of the year; but in the high elevation habitat, it is probably greater than indicated in the climate table. In addition, large amounts of water are usually available from mist and heavy dew, even during periods of lower rainfall. Cultivated plants should be kept moist with only slight drying allowed between waterings. Good air movement is critically important and should be maintained at all times.

FERTILIZER: ¼–½ recommended strength. A balanced fertilizer should be applied weekly to biweekly throughout the year. The Royal Botanic Garden in Edinburgh uses a dilute, seaweed-based fertilizer.

REST PERIOD: Growing conditions should be maintained all year. Seasonal high and low temperatures vary about 5°F (3°C). Conditions are slightly drier for 1–2 months in winter. In cultivation, water may be decreased somewhat, but plants should never be allowed to dry out completely. In the habitat, light is slightly higher in winter.

GROWING MEDIA: Plants may be mounted on tree-fern or cork slabs if humidity is high and plants are watered daily in summer. Repotting may be done anytime new roots are growing.

Plant and Flower Information

PLANT SIZE AND TYPE: A sympodial epiphyte of unreported size.

PSEUDOBULB: The elongated stems are elliptical in cross-section with nodes about 1 in. (2.7 cm) apart.

LEAVES: Many. The linear leaves are about 3 in. (8 cm) long and obtusely 2-toothed at the apex. The leaf-sheaths are warty.

INFLORESCENCE: Short. Inflorescences emerge through the leaf bases of leafy stems. Blossoms alternate on the inflorescence.

FLOWERS: 2 per inflorescence. The fleshy flowers are 0.7 in. (1.8 cm) long. Blossoms have cream colored sepals and petals and a pale yellow or brown lip. The dorsal sepal is oblong-triangular, lateral sepals are somewhat triangular-sickle-shaped with 3 ridges. Petals are linear-lanceolate. Segments are concave. The 3-lobed lip is erect and recurved. The erect sidelobes are triangular, sickle-shaped, and incurved. The broadly triangular midlobe is toothed to slashed along the margin.

REFERENCES: 224, 445, 470.

Dendrobium subulatoides Schlechter

ORIGIN/HABITAT: Sarawak, Borneo near Kuching and Mt. Matang. Habitat elevation was not reported, but plants were described at the same time as *D. xiphophyllum* Schlechter, which was collected on Mt. Matang at about 2500 ft. (760 m). Because habitat elevation is estimated, the following climate data should be used with caution.

CLIMATE: Station #96413, Kuching, Sarawak, Borneo, Lat. 1.5°N, Long. 110.3°E, at 85 ft. (26 m). Temperatures are calculated for an elevation of 2500 ft. (760 m), resulting in probable extremes of 89°F (32°C) and 56°F (13°C).

N/HEMISPHERE	JAN	FEB	MAR	APR	MAY	JUN	JUL	AUG	SEP	OCT	NOV	DEC
°F AVG MAX	80	80	81	82	83	83	83	84	82	82	82	80
°F AVG MIN	64	64	64	64	64	65	64	64	64	64	64	64
DIURNAL RANGE	16	16	17	18	19	18	19	20	18	18	18	16
RAIN/INCHES	27.1	19.7	14.2	9.7	9.0	8.5	6.9	8.8	9.5	12.6	13.1	20.1
HUMIDITY/%	89	88	86	85	85	83	82	83	84	85	87	88
BLOOM SEASON						*	*					
DAYS CLR @ 7AM	1	0	1	2	3	2	4	1	2	1	1	1
DAYS CLR @ 1PM	0	0	0	0	0	1	1	1	0	0	0	0
RAIN/MM	688	500	361	246	229	216	175	224	241	320	333	511
°C AVG MAX	26.7	26.7	27.2	27.8	28.4	28.4	28.4	28.9	27.8	27.8	27.8	26.7
°C AVG MIN	17.8	17.8	17.8	17.8	17.8	18.4	17.8	17.8	17.8	17.8	17.8	17.8
DIURNAL RANGE	8.9	8.9	9.4	10.0	10.6	10.0	10.6	11.1	10.0	10.0	10.0	8.9
S/HEMISPHERE	JUL	AUG	SEP	OCT	NOV	DEC	JAN	FEB	MAR	APR	MAY	JUN

Cultural Recommendations

LIGHT: 2000–3000 fc.

TEMPERATURES: Throughout the year, days average 80–84°F (27–29°C), and nights average 64–65°F (18°C), with a diurnal range of 16–20°F (9–11°C). This habitat has essentially no seasonal temperature fluctuations.

HUMIDITY: 85–90% most of the year, dropping to near 80% for a brief period in summer. High humidity and excellent air circulation are important for cultivated plants.

WATER: Rainfall is heavy all year. Cultivated plants should be kept very moist but not soggy. Warm water is suggested.

FERTILIZER: ¼–½ recommended strength. A balanced fertilizer should be applied weekly to biweekly throughout the year.

REST PERIOD: Growing conditions should be maintained all year. The smaller diurnal range in winter results from cooler days, not cooler nights. The record low temperature is only 10°F (6°C) below the average lows, indicating that plants may not tolerate wide temperature fluctuations. Moisture and humidity levels should be maintained. Water may be reduced somewhat for plants cultivated in the dark, short-day conditions common in temperate-latitude winters; but they should never be allowed to dry out completely. In the habitat, light is slightly lower in winter.

GROWING MEDIA: Plants may be mounted on tree-fern or cork slabs or potted in small pots filled with any open, fast-draining medium. Repotting may be done anytime new roots are growing.

MISCELLANEOUS NOTES: The bloom season shown in the climate table is based on reports from the habitat. In 1911, Schlechter described this plant in Fedde's *Repert. Sp. Nov.* 9:290.

Plant and Flower Information

PLANT SIZE AND TYPE: A 4 in. (10 cm) sympodial epiphyte.

PSEUDOBULB: 4 in. (10 cm) long. The stems are cylindrical, sometimes curved, and densely leafy. They are carried on a very short, ascending rhizome.

LEAVES: Many. The oblong, somewhat sickle-shaped leaves are smooth, leathery, folded, and 0.3 in. (0.8 cm) long.

INFLORESCENCE: Short. Inflorescences are widely spaced on the leafless, apical portion of the stem.

FLOWERS: 1 per inflorescence. The flowers are 0.8 in. (2 cm) across. They are white with brownish markings. Sepals are ovate. Petals are tongue-shaped to lanceolate. The smooth, 3-lobed lip has short, rounded sidelobes and a nearly round midlobe that is deeply notched at the apex and unevenly ruffled along the margin.

REFERENCES: 221, 286, 295.

Dendrobium subulatum Hooker f. See *D. subulatum* (Blume) Lindley. REFERENCES: 202, 218, 394, 395, 469.

Dendrobium subulatum (Blume) Lindley

AKA: *Onychium subulatum* Blume, *Dendrobium subulatum* Hooker f. Ridley (ref. 402) includes *Podochilus bicolor* Miquel as a synonym.

ORIGIN/HABITAT: Widespread in Southeast Asia. Collections have been made in southern Peninsular Thailand, Malaya, Sumatra, Java, and Borneo. On the Malay Peninsula, plants grow in the lowlands of Perak, Selanor, and Singapore. In all the wetter parts of Java, plants are found high on old trees in sheltered locations from sea level to 2150 ft. (0–650 m).

CLIMATE: Station #48625, Ipoh, Malaya, Lat. 4.6°N, Long. 101.1°E, at 123 ft. (37 m). Record extreme temperatures are 99°F (37°C) and 64°F (18°C).

N/HEMISPHERE	JAN	FEB	MAR	APR	MAY	JUN	JUL	AUG	SEP	OCT	NOV	DEC
°F AVG MAX	90	92	93	92	92	92	91	91	90	89	89	89
°F AVG MIN	72	72	73	73	74	73	72	72	73	72	72	72
DIURNAL RANGE	18	20	20	19	18	19	19	19	17	17	17	17
RAIN/INCHES	7.9	3.1	7.6	8.4	6.2	3.6	7.2	6.9	8.8	11.0	13.0	8.9
HUMIDITY/%	76	74	76	78	78	75	76	77	79	82	82	81
BLOOM SEASON		*			*							
DAYS CLR @ 7AM	3	3	3	1	1	2	1	1	1	0	1	2
DAYS CLR @ 1PM	2	2	2	1	1	1	1	1	0	0	0	2
RAIN/MM	201	79	193	213	157	91	183	175	224	279	330	226
°C AVG MAX	32.2	33.3	33.9	33.3	33.3	33.3	32.8	32.8	32.2	31.7	31.7	31.7
°C AVG MIN	22.2	22.2	22.8	22.8	23.3	22.8	22.2	22.2	22.8	22.2	22.2	22.2
DIURNAL RANGE	10.0	11.1	11.1	10.5	10.0	10.5	10.6	10.6	9.4	9.5	9.5	9.5
S/HEMISPHERE	JUL	AUG	SEP	OCT	NOV	DEC	JAN	FEB	MAR	APR	MAY	JUN

Cultural Recommendations

LIGHT: 2000–3000 fc.

TEMPERATURES: Throughout the year, days average 89–93°F (32–34°C), and nights average 72–74°F (22–23°C), with a diurnal range of 17–20°F (9–11°C). These values represent the warmer, lower portion of the habitat. Because plants are also found at higher elevations, they should adapt to temperatures 6–8°F (3–4°C) cooler than indicated.

HUMIDITY: 75–80% year-round.

WATER: Rainfall is heavy most of the year. The heaviest rainfall occurs in autumn with a secondary maximum in spring. Brief semidry periods occur in midwinter and midsummer. Cultivated plants should be kept evenly moist, with only slight drying allowed between waterings.

FERTILIZER: ¼–½ recommended strength. A balanced fertilizer should be applied weekly to biweekly throughout the year.

REST PERIOD: Growing conditions should be maintained year-round. Water should be reduced somewhat in winter for plants cultivated in the dark, short-day conditions common in temperate latitudes. They should never be allowed to dry out completely, however. Fertilizer may be reduced when the plant is not actively growing or when water is reduced. In the habitat, light is slightly higher in winter.

GROWING MEDIA: Plants may be mounted on tree-fern or cork slabs if humidity is high and plants are watered at least once daily in summer. When plants are potted, any open, fast-draining medium may be used. Repotting may be done anytime new roots are growing.

MISCELLANEOUS NOTES: The bloom season shown in the climate table is based on reports from the habitat. Plants that produce flowers which last a single day commonly bloom several times during the year. Flowering usually occurs 7–10 days after a sudden 10°F (5°C) drop in daytime temperatures.

Plant and Flower Information

PLANT SIZE AND TYPE: A 2–6 in. (5–15 cm) sympodial epiphyte. Plants are very similar to *D. acerosum* Lindley but parts are smaller.

PSEUDOBULB: 2–6 in. (5–15 cm) long. The slender, erect stems are somewhat zigzag. They do not branch. The lower part of the stem is sparsely leafy while the upper part has only scalelike leaves and flowers.

LEAVES: Several. The somewhat flattened, terete leaves are 0.6 in. (1.5 cm) long, widely spaced, and recurved. They are held at right angles to the stem.

INFLORESCENCE: Short. The pedicels are reddish.

FLOWERS: 1 per inflorescence. The small, nearly transparent flowers are 0.3–0.6 in. (0.8–1.5 cm) long. Fan-shaped blossoms may be white, pale greenish yellow, light brown, or pale orange with a crystalline texture. The white lip is yellow in the center. The sepals and smaller, linear petals have pink or purple veins. The 3-lobed lip has a notched midlobe and large sidelobes that extend nearly to the apex of the midlobe. It is lightly wavy along the margins.

HYBRIDIZING NOTES: Chromosome count is 2n = 38 (ref. 154, 188). Johansen (ref. 239) indicates that plants are self-sterile and that flowers dropped 4–6 days after self-pollination.

REFERENCES: 25, 75, 154, 188, 200, 216, 239, 254, 277, 286, 295, 310, 395, 402, 435, 445, 454, 455, 469.

PHOTOS/DRAWINGS: *75, 454*, 455, 469.

Dendrobium subuliferum J. J. Smith

ORIGIN/HABITAT: New Guinea. In Irian Jaya (western New Guinea), plants grow on the Vogelkop Peninsula, in the Gautier and Star Mountains, and on Mt. Goliath. In Papua, they grow in West Sepik, Southern Highlands, and Morobe provinces. The orchids are usually epiphytic in primary and secondary forests at 1000–6550 ft. (300–2000 m), but they occasionally grow on the surface of the ground in shady, moss-covered locations.

CLIMATE: Station #200590, Bulolo, Papua New Guinea, Lat. 7.2°S, Long. 146.6°E, at 2440 ft. (745 m). Temperatures are calculated for an elevation of 4000 ft. (1220 m), resulting in probable extremes of 91°F (33°C) and 47°F (8°C).

N/HEMISPHERE	JAN	FEB	MAR	APR	MAY	JUN	JUL	AUG	SEP	OCT	NOV	DEC
°F AVG MAX	78	79	81	81	83	82	82	82	82	82	81	79
°F AVG MIN	60	59	60	61	60	62	61	61	61	60	61	60
DIURNAL RANGE	18	20	21	20	23	20	21	21	21	22	20	19
RAIN/INCHES	4.1	4.4	5.1	5.7	6.1	7.2	5.2	4.9	6.2	5.4	5.0	3.5
HUMIDITY/%	76	74	72	74	71	73	71	72	73	73	75	75
BLOOM SEASON	*	*	*	*	*						*	*
DAYS CLR	N/A											
RAIN/MM	104	112	130	145	155	183	132	124	157	137	127	89
°C AVG MAX	25.5	26.0	27.1	27.1	28.3	27.7	27.7	27.7	27.7	27.7	27.1	26.0
°C AVG MIN	15.5	14.9	15.5	16.0	15.5	16.6	16.0	16.0	16.0	16.0	15.5	16.0	15.5
DIURNAL RANGE	10.0	11.1	11.6	11.1	12.8	11.1	11.7	11.7	11.7	12.2	11.1	10.5
S/HEMISPHERE	JUL	AUG	SEP	OCT	NOV	DEC	JAN	FEB	MAR	APR	MAY	JUN

Cultural Recommendations

LIGHT: 2000–3000 fc.

TEMPERATURES: Throughout the year, days average 78–83°F (26–28°C), and nights average 59–62°F (15–17°C), with a diurnal range of 18–23°F (10–13°C).

HUMIDITY: 70–75% year-round.

WATER: Rainfall is moderate throughout the year. Conditions are slightly drier for 1–2 months in winter. Cultivated plants should be allowed to dry only slightly between waterings.

FERTILIZER: ¼–½ recommended strength. A balanced fertilizer should be applied weekly to biweekly throughout the year.

REST PERIOD: Growing conditions should be maintained year-round. Water and fertilizer should be reduced somewhat in winter, especially for plants cultivated in the dark, short-day conditions common in temperate latitudes. However, they should never be allowed to dry completely. In the habitat, seasonal light variation is minor.

GROWING MEDIA: Plants may be potted in live sphagnum moss over bark or mounted on tree-fern slabs if humidity is high. Repotting may be done anytime new roots are growing.

MISCELLANEOUS NOTES: The bloom season shown in the climate table is based on reports from the habitat. Cultivated plants bloom from winter to early summer.

Plant and Flower Information

PLANT SIZE AND TYPE: A 1.2 in. (3 cm) sympodial epiphyte.

PSEUDOBULB: 0.1–0.3 in. (0.3–0.9 cm) long. The ovoid pseudobulbs are contracted at the base. They are tightly clustered.

LEAVES: 1–3 at the apex of each growth. The leaves are 0.7–1.1 in. (1.8–2.8 cm) long. They are linear, pointed at the tip, rigid, and curved. The margin has minute warts.

INFLORESCENCE: Very short. The erect inflorescences emerge near the apex of the stem.

FLOWERS: 1 per inflorescence. The erect flowers are 0.3–0.5 in. (0.8–1.2 cm) across and open fully. The pointed segments are arranged like an open, 5-pointed star. Blossoms are white with purple along the margin of the lip. The dorsal sepal has a few tiny dots along the backside of the margin. The nearly ovate petals have tiny warts along the margin. The pointed lip is linear-lanceolate, erect, and recurved. It is somewhat 3-lobed with a 2-lobed, transverse callus.

REFERENCES: 179, 221, 385, 445, 470, 538.

PHOTOS/DRAWINGS: *385*, 538.

Dendrobium × *suffusum* Cady. A natural hybrid between *D. kingianum* Bidwell ex Lindley and *D. macropus* (Endl.) Rchb. f. ex Lindley subsp. *gracilicaule* (F. Mueller) P. S. Green *(D. gracilicaule* F. Mueller). HYBRIDIZING NOTES: Chromosome count is 2n = 57. Plants are not self-fertile, and seed is produced only when pollen from a different plant is used. REFERENCES: 67, 105, 152, 179, 230, 240, 243, 430, 533. PHOTOS/DRAWINGS: 105.

Dendrobium sulcatum Lindley

ORIGIN/HABITAT: India and Southeast Asia including Burma, China, northern Thailand, Laos, and Vietnam. In India, the habitat extends from tropical valleys near Kalimpong and Darjeeling in Sikkim to the Khasi (Khasia) Hills, Assam, Manipur, and Megahalaya. In northeastern India, plants grow at 1650–3300 ft. (500–1000 m).

CLIMATE: Station #42410, Gauhati, India, Lat. 26.1°N, Long. 91.6°E, at 158 ft. (48 m). Temperatures are calculated for a habitat elevation of

Dendrobium sulphuratum

2000 ft. (610 m), resulting in probable extremes of 98°F (37°C) and 35°F (2°C).

N/HEMISPHERE	JAN	FEB	MAR	APR	MAY	JUN	JUL	AUG	SEP	OCT	NOV	DEC
°F AVG MAX	70	72	80	82	82	83	84	84	83	81	75	70
°F AVG MIN	45	48	54	62	66	71	72	72	70	65	55	47
DIURNAL RANGE	25	24	26	20	16	12	12	12	13	16	20	23
RAIN/INCHES	0.4	1.2	2.0	5.7	9.3	12.3	12.3	10.3	6.6	2.8	0.6	0.2
HUMIDITY/%	79	72	64	71	82	85	85	86	84	84	83	82
BLOOM SEASON				**	**							
DAYS CLR @ 6AM	6	12	16	11	3	0	0	1	3	7	6	3
DAYS CLR @ 12PM	17	16	18	15	6	1	0	0	2	11	17	19
RAIN/MM	10	30	51	145	236	312	312	262	168	71	15	5
°C AVG MAX	21.1	22.2	26.6	27.7	27.7	28.3	28.8	28.8	28.3	27.2	23.8	21.1
°C AVG MIN	7.2	8.8	12.2	16.6	18.8	21.6	22.2	22.2	21.1	18.3	12.7	8.3
DIURNAL RANGE	13.9	13.4	14.4	11.1	8.9	6.7	6.6	6.6	7.2	8.9	11.1	12.8
S/HEMISPHERE	JUL	AUG	SEP	OCT	NOV	DEC	JAN	FEB	MAR	APR	MAY	JUN

Cultural Recommendations

LIGHT: 2500–3500 fc.

TEMPERATURES: Summer days average 83–84°F (28–29°C), and nights average 71–72°F (22°C), with a diurnal range of 12–13°F (7°C).

HUMIDITY: 80–85% most of the year, dropping to 65–70% for 3 months in late winter and early spring.

WATER: Rainfall is heavy during the growing season from spring to early autumn, but conditions are dry for 2–3 months in winter. Cultivated plants should be kept moist but not soggy in spring and summer, but water should be gradually reduced after new growths mature in autumn.

FERTILIZER: ¼–½ recommended strength, applied weekly. A high-nitrogen fertilizer is beneficial from spring to midsummer, but a fertilizer high in phosphates should be used in late summer and autumn.

REST PERIOD: Winter days average 70–80°F (21–27°C), and nights average 45–54°F (7–12°C), with a diurnal range of 23–26°F (13–14°C). Although rainfall is low in winter, additional moisture is available from fog, mist, or heavy dew. For cultivated plants, water should be reduced for 2–3 months in winter. They should be allowed to dry out between waterings, but should not remain dry for extended periods. Fertilizer should be reduced or eliminated until water is increased in spring. In the habitat, winter days are frequently clear. The cool, dry rest is usually necessary to induce flowering. Other species from this habitat may grow in the warm, uniform Singapore climate, but they seldom bloom.

GROWING MEDIA: Plants may be mounted on tree-fern or cork slabs if humidity is high and plants are watered at least once daily in summer. When plants are potted, any open, fast-draining medium may be used. They may be repotted anytime new roots are growing.

MISCELLANEOUS NOTES: The bloom season shown in the climate table is based on cultivation records. Reports from the habitat indicate spring blooming.

Plant and Flower Information

PLANT SIZE AND TYPE: An 8–18 in. (20–45 cm) sympodial epiphyte.

PSEUDOBULB: 8–18 in. (20–45 cm) long. The somewhat flattened stems are grooved and spindle-shaped with a slender base.

LEAVES: 2 at the apex of each stem. The large, ovate leaves are 4–8 in. (10–20 cm) long. They are wavy along the margins.

INFLORESCENCE: 4–8 in. (10–20 cm) long. Pendulous inflorescences emerge from upper leaf axils of both leafy and leafless stems. Blossoms are tightly clustered on the apical part of the inflorescence.

FLOWERS: 3–15 per inflorescence. The flowers are 1.0–1.4 in. (2.5–3.5 cm) across, but they remain cupped or bell-like. Sepals and petals may be bright or dingy yellow or orange-yellow with darker lines. The orange lip has red veins and brown or red-brown patches of nerves on either side at the base. The boat-shaped lip, which appears to have been folded, is pubescent along the edge. It has a small, toothlike projection at the apex.

HYBRIDIZING NOTES: Chromosome count is 2n = 40 (ref. 154, 187, 188).

REFERENCES: 38, 46, 154, 157, 179, 187, 188, 190, 202, 210, 216, 254, 317, 369, 376, 445, 447, 448, 454, 507, 541.

PHOTOS/DRAWINGS: 46, 210, *369*, *454*.

Dendrobium sulphuratum Ridley.
Now considered a synonym of *Epigeneium zebrinum* (J. J. Smith) Summerhayes. REFERENCES: 220, 286, 295, 449, 499.

Dendrobium sulphureum Schlechter

AKA: *D. cellulosum* J. J. Smith. Reeve and Woods (ref. 385) recognize 3 varieties: *D. sulphureum* var. *sulphureum*, *D. sulphureum* var. *rigidifolium* T. M. Reeve and P. Woods, and *D. sulphureum* var. *cellulosum* (J. J. Smith) T. M. Reeve and P. Woods.

ORIGIN/HABITAT: New Guinea. In Irian Jaya (western New Guinea), a few collections are reported near Mt. Doorman and in the Cyclop Mountains. In Papua, plants are found in numerous high-elevation provinces. The orchids grow on mossy tree trunks and twigs at 5900–12,000 ft. (1800–3660 m). The original collection was made at 2600 ft. (800 m). Plants grow in mountain cloudforests, at forest edges in subalpine grasslands, and on trees in open grassland.

CLIMATE: Botanical garden records, Laiagam, Papua New Guinea, Lat. 5.5°S, Long. 143.5°E, at 7218 ft. (2200 m). Temperatures are calculated for an elevation of 8000 ft. (2440 m), resulting in probable extremes of 88°F (31°C) and 29°F (−1°C).

N/HEMISPHERE	JAN	FEB	MAR	APR	MAY	JUN	JUL	AUG	SEP	OCT	NOV	DEC
°F AVG MAX	73	74	75	73	75	75	79	74	73	75	75	73
°F AVG MIN	52	51	52	52	53	53	52	53	55	54	53	53
DIURNAL RANGE	21	23	23	21	22	22	27	21	18	21	22	20
RAIN/INCHES	4.0	4.8	6.1	7.8	8.5	9.1	8.4	9.6	9.5	8.9	6.3	4.0
HUMIDITY/%	N/A											
BLOOM SEASON	*	*	*	*	*	*	*	*	*	*	*	*
DAYS CLR	N/A											
RAIN/MM	102	122	155	198	216	231	213	244	241	226	160	102
°C AVG MAX	23.0	23.6	24.1	23.0	24.1	24.1	26.3	23.6	23.0	24.1	24.1	23.0
°C AVG MIN	11.3	10.8	11.3	11.3	11.9	11.9	11.3	11.9	13.0	12.5	11.9	11.9
DIURNAL RANGE	11.7	12.8	12.8	11.7	12.2	12.2	15.0	11.7	10.0	11.6	12.2	11.1
S/HEMISPHERE	JUL	AUG	SEP	OCT	NOV	DEC	JAN	FEB	MAR	APR	MAY	JUN

Cultural Recommendations

LIGHT: 2000–3000 fc.

TEMPERATURES: Throughout the year, days average 73–79°F (23–26°C), and nights average 51–55°F (11–13°C), with a diurnal range of 18–27°F (10–15°C). The values in the preceding climate table represent the lower, therefore warmer, portion of the habitat, so plants should easily adapt to conditions that are 8–10°F (4–6°C) cooler than indicated.

HUMIDITY: Information is not available for this location. However, records from nearby stations indicate that averages are probably near 80% year-round.

WATER: Rainfall is moderate to heavy all year, but conditions are slightly drier for 3–4 months in winter. Rain falls as heavy showers most afternoons. Skies clear by early evening. Low clouds and mist develop again during the evening and continue until midmorning the next day. The mist is so heavy that trees and shrubs drip moisture soon after the mist forms. Cultivated plants should be kept moist.

FERTILIZER: ¼–½ recommended strength. A balanced fertilizer should be applied weekly to biweekly throughout the year. The Royal Botanic Garden in Edinburgh uses a seaweed-based fertilizer for high-elevation plants from New Guinea.

REST PERIOD: Growing conditions should be maintained year-round. However, water and fertilizer should be reduced in winter, especially for plants grown in the dark, short-day conditions common in temperate latitudes. Plants should never be allowed to dry out completely, however. In the habitat, light may be slightly higher in winter.

GROWING MEDIA: Plants may be mounted on tree-fern or cork slabs or potted in small pots filled with any open, fast-draining medium. Repotting may be done anytime new roots are growing.

MISCELLANEOUS NOTES: The bloom season shown in the climate table is based on cultivation records.

Plant and Flower Information

PLANT SIZE AND TYPE: A 1.0–1.2 in. (2.5–3.0 cm) sympodial epiphyte.

PSEUDOBULB: 0.2–0.4 in. (0.5–1.0 cm) long. Pseudobulbs may be ellipsoid or oval.

LEAVES: 2 to several per growth. The elliptic leaves are 0.3–0.5 in. (0.7–1.3 cm) long. They may be erect or held at an angle. The leaves are eventually deciduous, but the leaf-sheaths are persistent.

INFLORESCENCE: 0.7 in. (1.8 cm) long. Inflorescences emerge at the apex of leafy and leafless stems.

FLOWERS: 1–2, rarely 4 per inflorescence. The flowers are about 0.4 in. (1.0 cm) long, large for the plant size. The fan-shaped sepals and petals are light sulfur-yellow. The dorsal sepal and petals are smaller than the lateral sepals. The slender, erect lip is orange-yellow with green at the pointed tip.

HYBRIDIZING NOTES: Chromosome count 2n = 76 (ref. 152, 243).

REFERENCES: 152, 179, 221, 235, 243, 385, 437, 445, 556.

PHOTOS/DRAWINGS: 385, 437, 556.

Dendrobium sumatranum A. Hawkes and A. H. Heller

AKA: *D. cultriforme* J. J. Smith not Thouars.

ORIGIN/HABITAT: Sumatra. Plants were originally found on the small island of Telo, northwest of Padang. Habitat elevation is not reported, but topographical maps indicate that the island is low-lying with elevations below 350 ft. (100 m). Plants were cultivated at the botanical garden at Bogor, Java.

CLIMATE: Station #96163, Padang, Sumatra, Indonesia, Lat. 0.9°S, Long. 100.4°E, at 19 ft. (6 m). Record extreme temperatures are 94°F (34°C) and 68°F (20°C).

N/HEMISPHERE	JAN	FEB	MAR	APR	MAY	JUN	JUL	AUG	SEP	OCT	NOV	DEC
°F AVG MAX	87	87	86	86	86	86	87	87	87	87	88	87
°F AVG MIN	74	74	74	74	74	74	74	74	74	75	75	74
DIURNAL RANGE	13	13	12	12	12	12	13	13	13	12	13	13
RAIN/INCHES	10.9	13.7	6.0	19.5	20.4	18.9	13.8	10.2	12.1	14.3	12.4	12.1
HUMIDITY/%	81	82	82	84	85	84	81	81	82	83	81	81
BLOOM SEASON	N/A											
DAYS CLR @ 7AM	5	1	1	0	2	2	2	1	2	2	3	5
DAYS CLR @ 1PM	5	2	2	1	1	3	3	4	3	3	6	5
RAIN/MM	277	348	152	495	518	480	351	259	307	363	315	307
°C AVG MAX	30.6	30.6	30.0	30.0	30.0	30.0	30.6	30.6	30.6	30.6	31.1	30.6
°C AVG MIN	23.3	23.3	23.3	23.3	23.3	23.3	23.3	23.3	23.3	23.9	23.9	23.3
DIURNAL RANGE	7.3	7.3	6.7	6.7	6.7	6.7	7.3	7.3	7.3	6.7	7.2	7.3

Cultural Recommendations

LIGHT: 2000–3000 fc. Diffused light is preferred.

TEMPERATURES: Throughout the year, days average 86–88°F (30–31°C), and nights average 74–75°F (23–24°C), with a diurnal range of 12–13°F (7°C). Probable extremes vary only a few degrees from the extremely uniform averages, indicating that the plant may not tolerate wide temperature fluctuations.

HUMIDITY: 80–85% year-round.

WATER: The rainfall is heavy all year. Cultivated plants should be kept moist but not soggy. Warm water may be beneficial.

FERTILIZER: ¼–½ recommended strength. A balanced fertilizer should be applied weekly to biweekly throughout the year.

REST PERIOD: Growing conditions should be maintained year-round. Water should be reduced somewhat for plants grown in the dark, short-day conditions common in temperate-latitude winters, but they should never be allowed to dry out completely.

GROWING MEDIA: Plants may be mounted on tree-fern or cork slabs if humidity is high and plants are watered at least once daily in summer. When plants are potted, any open, fast-draining medium may be used. They may be repotted anytime new roots are growing.

Plant and Flower Information

PLANT SIZE AND TYPE: A 59 in. (150 cm) sympodial epiphyte.

PSEUDOBULB: 59 in. (150 cm) long. The elongated stems are clustered, flattened, and flexuous. They are shiny yellowish green. The lower 24 in. (60 cm) is leafy, but the upper portion is branching with only rudimentary leaves.

LEAVES: Many. The oblong, 3-angled leaves are 2 in. (5 cm) long. They are pale green, fleshy, pointed, and very flattened.

INFLORESCENCE: Short. Inflorescences emerge from nodes on the upper part of the stem.

FLOWERS: The flowers are 0.4 in. (1 cm) across. They are yellowish-white with 3 purplish stripes on the ovate dorsal sepal and 2 purplish stripes on the lateral sepals. The oblong petals are marked with 3 purple stripes. The erect, 3-lobed lip is fleshy and wavy. It is yellowish-white with purple markings on the large, rounded sidelobes. The midlobe is abruptly truncated with an uneven margin.

REFERENCES: 191, 229, 254, 471.

PHOTOS/DRAWINGS: 471.

Dendrobium summerhayesianum A. Hawkes and A. H. Heller

AKA: *D. pictum* Schlechter.

ORIGIN/HABITAT: New Guinea. In northern Papua, plants grow on forest trees in the Torricelli Range at 1950–2300 ft. (600–700 m). In Irian Jaya (western New Guinea), plants grow along the Lorentz River. They were cultivated in the botanical garden at Bogor, Java.

CLIMATE: Station #94004, Wewak, Papua New Guinea, Lat. 3.6°S, Long. 143.7°E, at 16 ft. (5 m). Temperatures are calculated for an elevation of 2000 ft. (610 m), resulting in probable extremes of 91°F (33°C) and 55°F (13°C).

N/HEMISPHERE	JAN	FEB	MAR	APR	MAY	JUN	JUL	AUG	SEP	OCT	NOV	DEC
°F AVG MAX	81	81	81	81	81	81	80	79	80	81	81	81
°F AVG MIN	67	67	67	68	68	68	68	68	67	67	68	67
DIURNAL RANGE	14	14	14	13	13	13	12	11	13	14	13	14
RAIN/INCHES	7.6	4.8	5.3	10.0	13.3	14.5	12.1	11.9	14.9	16.9	15.1	10.8
HUMIDITY/%	80	79	79	78	79	81	82	82	81	82	81	80
BLOOM SEASON			*									
DAYS CLR	N/A											
RAIN/MM	193	122	135	254	338	368	307	302	378	429	384	274
°C AVG MAX	27.5	27.5	27.5	27.5	27.5	27.5	26.9	26.4	26.9	27.5	27.5	27.5
°C AVG MIN	19.7	19.7	19.7	20.3	20.3	20.3	20.3	20.3	19.7	19.7	20.3	19.7
DIURNAL RANGE	7.8	7.8	7.8	7.2	7.2	7.2	6.6	6.1	7.2	7.8	7.2	7.8
S/HEMISPHERE	JUL	AUG	SEP	OCT	NOV	DEC	JAN	FEB	MAR	APR	MAY	JUN

Cultural Recommendations

LIGHT: 1800–2500 fc.

TEMPERATURES: Throughout the year, days average 79–81°F (26–28°C), and nights average 67–68°F (20°C), with a diurnal range of 11–14°F (6–8°C).

HUMIDITY: Near 80% year-round.

WATER: Rainfall is moderate to heavy all year, but conditions are slightly drier for 1–2 months in winter. Cultivated plants should be kept moist.

FERTILIZER: ¼–½ recommended strength. A balanced fertilizer should be applied weekly to biweekly throughout the year.

REST PERIOD: Growing temperatures should be maintained year-round. Rainfall is lowest in winter, and water should be reduced somewhat for cultivated plants, especially those grown in the dark, short-day conditions common in temperate-latitude winters. Plants should never be allowed to dry out completely, however. Fertilizer should be reduced until water is increased in spring. In the habitat, light is highest in winter.

GROWING MEDIA: A very open and fast-draining medium should be used with either baskets or small pots. Repotting may be done anytime new roots are growing.

MISCELLANEOUS NOTES: The bloom season shown in the climate table is based on collection reports.

Plant and Flower Information

PLANT SIZE AND TYPE: A 12–20 in. (30–50 cm) sympodial epiphyte.

PSEUDOBULB: 10–17 in. (25–43 cm) long. The stems, which are rigid and unbranched, may be erect or suberect.

LEAVES: The elliptical leaves are 2.0–3.5 in. (5–9 cm) long. They are often erect.

INFLORESCENCE: Very short. Flattened inflorescences arise from nodes along the stem. Flowers are held opposite each other.

FLOWERS: 2 per inflorescence. The flowers are 0.8 in. (2 cm) across. The variegated sepals and petals are brownish yellow. They are rounded and incurved at the tips, causing the blossom to resemble a lumpy, uneven ball. The oblong to somewhat fiddle shaped lip has dark violet markings around the centerline. The midlobe is pointed at the apex with small, ruffled scallops along the margin. The column is white.

REFERENCES: 191, 229, 437, 470.

PHOTOS/DRAWINGS: 437.

Dendrobium sumneri F. Mueller. See *D. bigibbum* Lindley.

REFERENCES: 67, 105, 216, 254, 421, 533.

Dendrobium superans J. J. Smith

ORIGIN/HABITAT: Sulawesi (Celebes) near Bolaäng Mongondou. Habitat elevation is unavailable, so the following climate data should be used with extreme caution.

CLIMATE: Station #97014, Manado, Sulawesi, Indonesia, Lat. 1.5°N, Long. 124.9°E, at 264 ft. (80 m). Temperatures are calculated for an estimated elevation of 1800 ft. (550 m), resulting in probable extremes of 92°F (33°C) and 60°F (16°C).

N/HEMISPHERE	JAN	FEB	MAR	APR	MAY	JUN	JUL	AUG	SEP	OCT	NOV	DEC
°F AVG MAX	80	80	80	81	82	82	82	84	84	84	82	81
°F AVG MIN	68	68	68	68	69	68	68	68	68	67	68	69
DIURNAL RANGE	12	12	12	13	13	14	14	16	16	17	14	12
RAIN/INCHES	18.6	13.8	12.2	8.0	6.4	6.5	4.8	4.0	3.4	4.9	8.9	14.7
HUMIDITY/%	84	83	83	83	81	80	75	72	75	77	82	83
BLOOM SEASON						•						
DAYS CLR @ 8AM	4	3	6	11	11	12	12	14	17	12	8	
DAYS CLR @ 2PM	1	1	1	2	1	3	4	4	4	1	1	
RAIN/MM	472	351	310	203	163	165	122	102	86	124	226	373
°C AVG MAX	26.6	26.6	26.6	27.2	27.7	27.7	27.7	28.9	28.9	28.9	27.7	27.2
°C AVG MIN	20.0	20.0	20.0	20.0	20.5	20.0	20.0	20.0	20.0	19.4	20.0	20.5
DIURNAL RANGE	6.6	6.6	6.6	7.2	7.2	7.7	7.7	8.9	8.9	9.5	7.7	6.7
S/HEMISPHERE	JUL	AUG	SEP	OCT	NOV	DEC	JAN	FEB	MAR	APR	MAY	JUN

Cultural Recommendations

LIGHT: 2000–3000 fc. In the habitat, summer skies are frequently clear in the morning and cloudy in the afternoon.

TEMPERATURES: Throughout the year, days average 80–84°F (27–29°C), and nights average 67–69°F (19–21°C), with a diurnal range of 12–17°F (7–10°C). The daily temperature range is greater than the seasonal variation, and extreme temperatures are within 10°F (6°C) of the averages. Therefore, plants may not tolerate large seasonal temperature fluctuations.

HUMIDITY: Near 80% most of the year, dropping to 70–75% in summer and early autumn.

WATER: Rainfall is moderate to heavy all year. The driest period occurs in late summer and early autumn. Cultivated plants should be kept moist most of the year, but slight drying between waterings should be allowed in late summer and early autumn.

FERTILIZER: ¼–½ recommended strength. A balanced fertilizer should be applied weekly to biweekly throughout the year.

REST PERIOD: Growing conditions should be maintained all year. In the habitat, rainfall is greatest in winter; but in cultivation, increasing water could be detrimental, particularly if light is low, days are short, or temperatures are cool. In the habitat, light is lowest in winter.

GROWING MEDIA: Plants may be mounted on tree-fern or cork slabs if humidity is high and plants are watered at least once daily in summer. When plants are potted, any open, fast-draining medium may be used. They may be repotted anytime new roots are growing.

MISCELLANEOUS NOTES: The bloom season shown in the climate table is based on collection reports.

Plant and Flower Information

PLANT SIZE AND TYPE: A 16 in. (40 cm) sympodial epiphyte.

PSEUDOBULB: 16 in. (40 cm) long. The leafy stems are erect, flexuous, and occasionally branching.

LEAVES: Many. The ovate-lanceolate leaves are 1.6 in. (4 cm) long. They are partially twisted at the base and unequally 2-toothed at the apex.

INFLORESCENCE: Short. Inflorescences are borne on the upper part of the stem.

FLOWERS: 1–3 per inflorescence. The flowers are 1.3–1.5 in. (3.2–3.8 cm) long. The attractive blossoms have white sepals and petals and a purple lip. The pointed dorsal sepal is oblong-elliptical. Lateral sepals are very slender. Petals are broadly oval and slightly contracted at the base. The unlobed lip is small, tongue-shaped, partially incurved along the margin, and recurved at the tip.

REFERENCES: 224, 483.

Dendrobium × *superbiens* Rchb. f. A natural hybrid

between *D. bigibbum* Lindley and *D. discolor* Lindley. Over the years plants have been called *D. bigibbum* var. *albomarginatum* F. M. Bailey Mar. 1891 not Linden Aug. 1891, *D. bigibbum* var. *superbiens* (Rchb. f.) F. M. Bailey, *D. brandtiae* Kränzlin, *D. fitzgeraldii* F. Mueller ex F. M. Bailey, *D. goldiei* Rchb. f., *D. superbiens* Fitzgerald, and *D.* × *vinicolor* St. Cloud. HYBRIDIZING NOTES: Chromosome counts are n = 19 (ref. 187, 504) and 2n = 38 (ref. 150, 151, 154, 187, 188, 504, 542, 580). Seeds are normally ready for green-pod culture in 160–250 (186) days. Plants are considered easy in flask. REFERENCES: 6, 23, 25, 24, 67, 105, 150, 151, 154, 179, 187, 188, 200, 216, 230, 236, 240, 254, 262, 325, 326, 348, 390, 421, 425, 430, 445, 458, 461, 504, 533, 541, 542, 557, 570. PHOTOS/DRAWINGS: 105, 200, *262, 390*, 458, 510, 570, 580.

Dendrobium superbiens Fitzgerald. See *D.* × *superbiens* Rchb. f. REFERENCES: 67.

Dendrobium superbum Rchb. f. See *D. anosmum* Lindley.
REFERENCES: 6, 12, 25, 151, 196, 216, 236, 254, 266, 286, 296, 317, 402, 425, 430, 436, 448, 454, 455, 468, 470, 541, 557, 569, 570, 580.
PHOTOS/DRAWINGS: 569.

Dendrobium sutepense Rolfe ex Downie

ORIGIN/HABITAT: Northwestern Thailand. Plants grow near Chiang Mai at 4900–6250 ft. (1500–1900 m). A single collection was made in Burma near the Mogok ruby mine.

CLIMATE: Station #48327, Chiang Mai, Thailand, Lat. 18.8°N, Long. 99.0°E, at 1100 ft. (335 m). Temperatures are calculated for an elevation of 5000 ft. (1520 m), resulting in probable extremes of 96°F (36°C) and 25°F (–4°C).

N/HEMISPHERE	JAN	FEB	MAR	APR	MAY	JUN	JUL	AUG	SEP	OCT	NOV	DEC
°F AVG MAX	72	77	82	83	81	77	76	74	75	76	73	71
°F AVG MIN	43	44	49	57	61	61	61	62	60	58	53	44
DIURNAL RANGE	29	33	33	26	20	16	15	12	15	18	20	27
RAIN/INCHES	0.3	0.4	0.6	2.0	5.5	6.1	7.4	8.7	11.5	4.9	1.5	0.4
HUMIDITY/%	73	65	58	62	73	78	80	83	83	81	79	76
BLOOM SEASON		*	*									
DAYS CLR @ 7AM	5	5	2	2	1	0	0	0	0	1	3	3
DAYS CLR @ 1PM	9	8	4	2	0	0	0	0	0	0	1	3
RAIN/MM	8	10	15	51	140	155	188	221	292	124	38	10
°C AVG MAX	22.3	25.1	27.9	28.4	27.3	25.1	24.5	23.4	24.0	24.5	22.9	21.7
°C AVG MIN	6.2	6.7	9.5	14.0	16.2	16.2	16.2	16.7	15.6	14.5	11.7	6.7
DIURNAL RANGE	16.1	18.4	18.4	14.4	11.1	8.9	8.3	6.7	8.4	10.0	11.2	15.0
S/HEMISPHERE	JUL	AUG	SEP	OCT	NOV	DEC	JAN	FEB	MAR	APR	MAY	JUN

Cultural Recommendations

LIGHT: 1800–2400 fc. Cultivated plants need bright light and strong air movement. The heavy summer cloud cover indicates that some shading is needed from spring through autumn; but light should be as high as the plants can tolerate, short of burning the foliage.

TEMPERATURES: Summer days average 74–77°F (23–25°C), and nights average 61–62°F (16–17°C), with a diurnal range of 12–16°F (7–9°C). The warmest temperatures occur in spring. Days average 81–83°F (27–28°C), and nights average 49–61°F (10–16°C), with a diurnal range of 20–33°F (11–18°C).

HUMIDITY: 75–80% most of the year, dropping to about 60% in late winter and early spring.

WATER: Rainfall is moderate to heavy from spring through autumn, but conditions are quite dry for 4–5 months over winter. Cultivated plants should be kept moist while actively growing, but water should be gradually reduced after new growths mature in autumn.

FERTILIZER: 1/4–1/2 recommended strength, applied weekly. A high-nitrogen fertilizer is beneficial from spring to midsummer, but a fertilizer high in phosphates should be used in late summer and autumn.

REST PERIOD: Winter days average 71–77°F (22–25°C), and nights average 43–44°F (6–7°C), with a diurnal range of 27–33°F (15–18°C). The average low temperatures are below 50°F (10°C) for 3 months and then warm rapidly in spring. Plants should be able to tolerate temperatures a few degrees below freezing, but extremes should be avoided in cultivation. During very cold weather, a plant's chance of surviving with minimal damage is better if it is dry. In the habitat, rainfall averages are very low for 4–5 months in winter, but during the early part of the season the high relative humidity indicates that additional moisture is available from frequent fog, mist, and heavy deposits of dew. Growers sometimes recommend eliminating water in winter, but plants are healthiest if for most of the winter they are allowed to become somewhat dry between waterings but do not remain dry for extended periods. For 1–2 months in late winter, however, conditions are clear, warm, and dry, with humidity so low that even the moisture from morning dew is uncommon. Plants should be allowed to dry out completely between waterings and remain dry longer during this time. Occasional early morning mistings between waterings may help keep the plants from becoming too dry. Fertilizer should be greatly reduced or eliminated until water is increased in spring. A cool, dry rest is essential for cultivated plants and should be continued until new growth starts in spring. In the habitat, light is highest in winter, but increased light may not be critical in cultivation.

GROWING MEDIA: Plants may be mounted on tree-fern or cork slabs or potted in small pots filled with any open, fast-draining medium. Repotting may be done anytime new roots are growing.

MISCELLANEOUS NOTES: The bloom season shown in the climate table is based on reports from the habitat.

Plant and Flower Information

PLANT SIZE AND TYPE: A 5–8 in. (13–20 cm) sympodial epiphyte.

PSEUDOBULB: 5–8 in. (13–20 cm) long. The unbranched stems are smallest at the base.

LEAVES: 4–5 per growth. The narrowly elliptic leaves are 1.3–2.7 in. (3.2–6.8 cm) long, persistent, and unequally bilobed at the apex.

INFLORESCENCE: Short. An inflorescence emerges from each node opposite the leaves on leafy canes.

FLOWERS: 1–2 per inflorescence. The flowers are 0.6–1.0 in. (1.5–2.5 cm) long. The glossy white sepals and petals are pointed at the tip. The 3-lobed lip is recurved, ruffled at the edge, and decorated with a raised yellow disk and yellow lines on the sidelobes.

HYBRIDIZING NOTES: Chromosome counts are 2n = 2x (ref. 187, 504, 580) and 2n = 38 (ref. 151, 154, 187, 188, 504, 580).

REFERENCES: 151, 154, 187, 188, 223, 245, 266, 418, 429, 448, 454, 504, 580.

PHOTOS/DRAWINGS: *245, 454.*

Dendrobium swartzii A. Hawkes and A. H. Heller. Originally described as *D. lilacinum* Rchb. f. not Teijsm. and Binn. The plant originated in Borneo, but habitat location and elevation are not available, so climate data cannot be selected. The tidy plants produced lilac flowers without any contrasting color on the lip. Reichenbach f. compared the blossoms to *D. picto* Lindley and *D. lucenti* Rchb. f. REFERENCES: 191, 229, 254, 286, 295, 394.

Dendrobium sylvanum Kränzlin not Rchb. f. See *D. tokai* Rchb. f. REFERENCES: 434.

Dendrobium sylvanum Rchb. f. not Kränzlin

AKA: *D. cogniauxianum* Kränzlin (in part), *D. robustum* Rolfe, *D. validum* Schlechter [for which Schlechter (ref. 437) included the synonym *D. veratrifolium* Kränzlin], *D. warianum* Schlechter. Hallé (ref. 173) includes *D. casuarinae* Schlechter and *D. daenikerianum* Kränzlin as synonyms. Cribb (ref. 84) includes *D. prionochilum* F. Mueller and Kränzlin, but Clements (ref. 67) indicates that *D. prionochilum* is a synonym of *D. mirbelianum* Gaudich not J. J. Smith. Cribb (ref. 84) also lists *D. kennedyi* Schlechter as a possible synonym.

ORIGIN/HABITAT: New Guinea, New Ireland, the Solomon Islands, and possibly New Caledonia and Samoa. Plants usually grow in forests below 250 ft. (70 m).

CLIMATE: Station #94085, Rabul, New Britain Is., Papua New Guinea, Lat. 4.2°S, Long. 152.2°E, at 28 ft. (9 m). Record extreme temperatures are 100°F (38°C) and 65°F (18°C).

Dendrobium sylvanum

N/HEMISPHERE	JAN	FEB	MAR	APR	MAY	JUN	JUL	AUG	SEP	OCT	NOV	DEC
°F AVG MAX	89	89	91	92	91	90	90	90	90	90	90	90
°F AVG MIN	73	72	73	73	73	73	73	73	73	73	73	73
DIURNAL RANGE	16	17	18	19	18	17	17	17	17	17	17	17
RAIN/INCHES	5.4	3.7	3.5	5.1	7.1	10.1	14.8	10.4	10.2	10.0	5.2	3.3
HUMIDITY/%	74	73	69	70	73	76	77	76	77	77	75	74
BLOOM SEASON	**	*	*								*	**
DAYS CLR	N/A											
RAIN/MM	137	94	89	130	180	257	376	264	259	254	132	84
°C AVG MAX	31.7	31.7	32.8	33.3	32.8	32.2	32.2	32.2	32.2	32.2	32.2	32.2
°C AVG MIN	22.8	22.2	22.8	22.8	22.8	22.8	22.8	22.8	22.8	22.8	22.8	22.8
DIURNAL RANGE	8.9	9.5	10.0	10.5	10.0	9.4	9.4	9.4	9.4	9.4	9.4	9.4
S/HEMISPHERE	JUL	AUG	SEP	OCT	NOV	DEC	JAN	FEB	MAR	APR	MAY	JUN

Cultural Recommendations

LIGHT: 2500–3000 fc.

TEMPERATURES: Throughout the year, days average 89–92°F (32–33°C), and nights average 72–73°F (22–23°C), with a diurnal range of 16–19°F (9–11°C). Average highs and lows vary less than 3°F (2°C) all year.

HUMIDITY: 70–80% most of the year. Humidity increases to 90–100% at night but drops as low as 35% during the day.

WATER: Rainfall is moderate to heavy most of the year, but conditions are somewhat drier for 2 months in late winter.

FERTILIZER: ¼–½ recommended strength. A balanced fertilizer should be applied weekly to biweekly throughout the year.

REST PERIOD: Growing conditions should be maintained all year. Water should be reduced somewhat in winter and the plants allowed to dry slightly between waterings. Fertilizer should be reduced anytime water is reduced. In the habitat, light may be slightly higher in winter.

GROWING MEDIA: Plants may be most easily managed when mounted. Potted plants are likely to be tipsy. Repotting may be done anytime new roots are growing.

MISCELLANEOUS NOTES: The bloom season shown in the climate table is based on reports from the habitat. Cultivation records indicate blooming in summer and autumn. Singapore growers indicate that plants are strong and healthy in their climate, that plants regularly bloom during the dry weather following the rainy season, and that they occasionally flower at other times.

Plant and Flower Information

PLANT SIZE AND TYPE: A 20–48 in. (50–122 cm) sympodial epiphyte.

PSEUDOBULB: 20–48 in. (50–122 cm) long. The leafy stems may be cylindrical or tapered at each end. Growers indicate that cultivated plants are often small.

LEAVES: Many. The dark, glossy green leaves, which are elongated ovals, are 3–6 in. (8–15 cm) long. They are smooth, tough, and somewhat erect. The tips have 2 small points that turn inward.

INFLORESCENCE: 10–20 in. (25–50 cm) long. Inflorescences emerge near the top of the canes. Flowers are attractively but densely arranged on the erect racemes.

FLOWERS: 15–40 per inflorescence. The flowers are 2.4 in. (6 cm) long and do not open fully. Sepals and petals may be any shade of green, yellow, gold- or chocolate-brown. They are often marked with violet on the inside at the base of the segments. The sepals are recurved at the tips. The petals are slightly twisted. The 3-lobed lip is narrow, recurved, and pointed. It is white, ruffled, and marked with violet or purple veins. The white callus is 3-ridged, wavy, and tipped with violet.

REFERENCES: 82, 84, 92, 173, 179, 216, 254, 271, 304, 344, 346, 351, 437, 444, 516, 526

PHOTOS/DRAWINGS: *84, 173, 271, 304, 344, 346, 351,* 437.

Dendrobium takadui (Schlechter) J. J. Smith. Now considered a synonym of *Cadetia takadui* Schlechter. REFERENCES: 92, 221, 437, 472.

Dendrobium takahashii Carr. See *D. ovipostoriferum* J. J. Smith. REFERENCES: 25, 58, 200, 225, 429.

Dendrobium talasea. Although never described as *D. talasea*, plants have been popularly known by this name for some time. In 1980, however, the plant was formally described as *D. helix* Cribb. REFERENCES: 80.

Dendrobium talaudense J. J. Smith

ORIGIN/HABITAT: The Talaud Islands, which are between the Moluccas and the Philippines. The plants were found on Salibabu Island at about 850 ft. (260 m) in old forests on the south slope of Mt. Ajambana.

CLIMATE: Station #97008, Naha, Pulau Sangine, Indonesia, Lat. 3.6°N, Long. 125.5°E, at 125 ft. (38 m). Temperatures are calculated for an elevation of 850 ft. (260 m). Record extreme temperatures are not available for this location.

N/HEMISPHERE	JAN	FEB	MAR	APR	MAY	JUN	JUL	AUG	SEP	OCT	NOV	DEC
°F AVG MAX	82	82	82	79	84	83	83	84	84	84	84	83
°F AVG MIN	75	75	76	73	77	75	74	75	75	75	76	75
DIURNAL RANGE	7	7	6	6	7	8	9	9	9	9	8	8
RAIN/INCHES	8.0	9.2	6.9	7.7	8.9	7.7	5.0	4.0	3.4	8.2	9.2	8.0
HUMIDITY/%	N/A											
BLOOM SEASON					*							
DAYS CLR	N/A											
RAIN/MM	203	234	175	196	226	196	127	102	86	208	234	203
°C AVG MAX	27.6	27.6	27.6	25.9	28.7	28.1	28.1	28.7	28.7	28.7	28.7	28.1
°C AVG MIN	23.7	23.7	24.2	22.6	24.8	23.7	23.1	23.7	23.7	23.7	24.2	23.7
DIURNAL RANGE	3.9	3.9	3.4	3.3	3.9	4.4	5.0	5.0	5.0	5.0	4.5	4.4
S/HEMISPHERE	JUL	AUG	SEP	OCT	NOV	DEC	JAN	FEB	MAR	APR	MAY	JUN

Cultural Recommendations

LIGHT: 1800–2500 fc.

TEMPERATURES: Throughout the year, days average 79–84°F (26–29°C), and nights average 73–77°F (23–25°C), with a diurnal range of 6–9°F (3–5°C).

HUMIDITY: Information is not available for this location. However, records from nearby stations indicate that humidity probably averages near 80–85% most of the year, dropping to about 75% in late summer and early autumn.

WATER: Rainfall is moderate to heavy most of the year with a short drier period in late summer and early autumn. Cultivated plants should be kept evenly moist.

FERTILIZER: ¼–½ recommended strength. A balanced fertilizer should be applied weekly to biweekly throughout the year.

REST PERIOD: Growing conditions should be maintained year-round. Water and fertilizer should be reduced somewhat in winter, especially for plants cultivated in the dark, short-day conditions common in temperate latitudes. However, plants should never be allowed to dry completely. In the habitat, seasonal light variation is minor.

GROWING MEDIA: Plants may be mounted on tree-fern or cork slabs if humidity is high and plants are watered at least once daily in summer. When plants are potted, any open, fast-draining medium may be used. They may be repotted anytime new roots are growing.

MISCELLANEOUS NOTES: The bloom season shown in the climate table is based on collection reports. The plant was described in 1930 in *Bull. Jard. Bot. Buit.* 3rd sér. 11:78.

Plant and Flower Information

PLANT SIZE AND TYPE: A 48 in. (122 cm) sympodial epiphyte.

PSEUDOBULB: 48 in. (122 cm) long. The stems are fleshy.

LEAVES: Many. The leaves are 5 in. (13 cm) long, lanceolate, deciduous, and dark green. They are thin-textured.

INFLORESCENCE: Short. The densely flowered inflorescences are borne at nodes on leafless stems.

FLOWERS: Many. The flowers are 0.5 in. (1.3 cm) long. The fleshy sepals and petals are white with blue tips. Blossoms have a triangular dorsal sepal and very narrow lateral sepals. They are hairy on the backside. The upper margins of the petals are hairy. The unlobed lip is oblong-6-angled, concave, and wavy. The upper surface is hairy with a transverse bar. The ovary is white.

REFERENCES: 224.

Dendrobium tangerinum Cribb

AKA: *D. tangerinum* is often grown and sold as *D. strepsiceros* J. J. Smith.

ORIGIN/HABITAT: Papua New Guinea. Plants are found in the provinces of Madang, Morobe, and Milne Bay from sea level to 4100 ft. (0–1250 m). They usually grow in the crowns of trees at about 800 ft. (250 m), but collections have been made above 3950 ft. (1200 m) where plants grew on rocks in landslide areas.

CLIMATE: Station #200187, Erap, Papua New Guinea, Lat. 6.6°S, Long. 146.7°E, at 850 ft. (260 m). Record extreme temperatures are 102°F (39°C) and 53°F (12°C).

N/HEMISPHERE	JAN	FEB	MAR	APR	MAY	JUN	JUL	AUG	SEP	OCT	NOV	DEC
°F AVG MAX	88	88	89	90	93	93	93	93	93	93	92	90	90
°F AVG MIN	69	69	69	70	72	73	72	72	73	71	74	70
DIURNAL RANGE	19	19	20	20	21	20	21	21	20	21	16	20
RAIN/INCHES	3.9	3.9	2.7	3.0	3.0	5.3	5.9	5.9	7.0	3.4	2.4	3.1
HUMIDITY/%	82	81	81	79	75	74	74	74	77	76	80	80
BLOOM SEASON	*	*	*	*	*	*	*	*	*	*	*	*
DAYS CLR	N/A											
RAIN/MM	98	99	68	77	76	135	149	149	179	87	60	78
°C AVG MAX	30.9	30.9	31.7	32.3	34.0	33.9	33.8	33.9	34.0	33.6	32.3	32.0
°C AVG MIN	20.4	20.5	20.7	21.1	22.0	22.5	22.1	22.4	22.5	21.7	23.3	20.9
DIURNAL RANGE	10.5	10.4	11.0	11.2	12.0	11.4	11.7	11.5	11.5	11.0	9.0	11.1
S/HEMISPHERE	JUL	AUG	SEP	OCT	NOV	DEC	JAN	FEB	MAR	APR	MAY	JUN

Cultural Recommendations

LIGHT: 2500–3500 fc. Growers report that plants from this habitat often tolerate full sun, providing it is introduced gradually.

TEMPERATURES: Throughout the year, days average 88–93°F (31–34°C), and nights average 69–74°F (20–23°C), with a diurnal range of 16–21°F (9–12°C).

HUMIDITY: 75–80% year-round. Despite high average humidity, the habitat may be quite dry during hot afternoons.

WATER: Rainfall is moderate most of the year, but conditions are somewhat wetter for 4–5 months in summer and early autumn. Cultivated plants should be thoroughly saturated then allowed to dry slightly between waterings in summer and early autumn. Water should be gradually reduced in autumn.

FERTILIZER: ¼–½ recommended strength. A balanced fertilizer should be applied weekly to biweekly throughout the year.

REST PERIOD: Growing temperatures should be maintained all year. In the habitat, rainfall is lowest in winter, but the high humidity indicates that additional moisture is frequently available from heavy dew. Cultivated plants should be allowed to dry for somewhat longer between waterings than in summer, but they should not remain dry for extended periods. Fertilizer should be reduced until water is increased in spring. In the habitat, seasonal light variation is minor. Growers indicate that *D. tangerinum* is healthiest if kept slightly dry.

GROWING MEDIA: Plants may be mounted on tree-fern or cork slabs or potted in small pots filled with any open, fast-draining medium. Plants should be repotted only when absolutely necessary, as they resent being divided or disturbed. When disturbed, hormones activate dormant buds along the cane, initiating numerous keikis or aerial vegetative growths. This characteristic might be used advantageously to propagate numerous identical plants.

MISCELLANEOUS NOTES: The bloom season shown in the climate table is based on cultivation records. Growers indicate that plants bloom any time of year except autumn.

Plant and Flower Information

PLANT SIZE AND TYPE: A 20–24 in. (50–60 cm) sympodial epiphyte.

PSEUDOBULB: 20–24 in. (50–60 cm) long. The erect, canelike stems are slightly swollen at the base. The upper half of the stem is leafy.

LEAVES: Many. The leaves are 2.8–3.5 in. (7–9 cm) long, leathery, and oblong to elliptic.

INFLORESCENCE: 14 in. (35 cm) long. One to several inflorescences are produced from nodes near the apex of leafy canes. They emerge through the leaf sheaths.

FLOWERS: Up to 15 per inflorescence. The flowers are 2.0–2.4 in. (5–6 cm) long and 1.2 in. (3 cm) across. Blossoms may be orange, orange-yellow, or reddish with maroon veins on the sepals. Sepals are often marked with red-brown or maroon speckles. The oblong dorsal sepal is recurved and inrolled with a wavy margin. The sickle-shaped lateral sepals are recurved-inrolled on the apical half. Petals are stiffly erect and twisted 2–3 times. The lip is recurved at the tip, white at the base, and decorated with 3–5 lilac keels. The erect sidelobes have an uneven margin. Flowers may last 6 months.

HYBRIDIZING NOTES: Chromosome count is 2n = 38 (ref. 152, 243). Until recently, hybrids have been registered as progeny of *D. strepsiceros*. When used as a parent, *D. tangerinum* contributes long-lasting flowers, frequent bloom periods, a short plant stature, and stiffly erect petals. The slender, erect petals persist for several generations of hybridizing.

REFERENCES: 80, 84, 152, 179, 233, 243, 343, 430, 526, 551.

PHOTOS/DRAWINGS: 80, *84, 343, 430, 551.*

Dendrobium tapingense W. W. Smith

ORIGIN/HABITAT: Bhamo, Burma. Plants grow on trees in shady jungles along the banks of the Taping River at about 2000 ft. (610 m).

CLIMATE: Station #48019, Bhamo, Burma, Lat. 24.3°N, Long. 97.3°E, at 360 ft. (110 m). Temperatures are calculated for an elevation of 2000 ft. (610 m), resulting in probable extremes of 100°F (38°C) and 32°F (0°C).

N/HEMISPHERE	JAN	FEB	MAR	APR	MAY	JUN	JUL	AUG	SEP	OCT	NOV	DEC
°F AVG MAX	71	77	83	88	88	84	83	83	84	82	76	71
°F AVG MIN	42	48	55	62	68	70	71	70	70	65	56	47
DIURNAL RANGE	29	29	28	26	20	14	12	13	14	17	20	24
RAIN/INCHES	0.4	0.6	0.7	1.8	6.1	14.1	16.7	16.1	9.8	4.6	1.7	0.5
HUMIDITY/%	79	75	66	59	69	84	88	88	86	86	83	82
BLOOM SEASON			**									
DAYS CLR @ 6AM	6	12	13	8	5	1	0	0	2	3	7	4
DAYS CLR @ 12PM	18	16	16	11	5	1	0	0	2	6	17	20
RAIN/MM	10	15	18	46	155	358	424	409	249	117	43	13
°C AVG MAX	21.4	24.8	28.1	30.9	30.9	28.7	28.1	28.1	28.7	27.5	24.2	21.4
°C AVG MIN	5.3	8.7	12.5	16.4	19.8	20.9	21.4	20.9	20.9	18.1	13.1	8.1
DIURNAL RANGE	16.1	16.1	15.6	14.5	11.1	7.8	6.7	7.2	7.8	9.4	11.1	13.3
S/HEMISPHERE	JUL	AUG	SEP	OCT	NOV	DEC	JAN	FEB	MAR	APR	MAY	JUN

Cultural Recommendations

LIGHT: 1800–2500 fc. The heavy summer cloud cover indicates that shading is needed from spring through autumn, but light should be as high as the plant can tolerate, short of burning the leaves.

TEMPERATURES: Summer days average 83–84°F (28–29°C), and nights average 70–71°F (21°C), with a diurnal range of 12–14°F (7–8°C). The warmest weather occurs in spring. Days average 83–88°F (28–31°C), and nights average 55–68°F (13–20°C), with a diurnal range of 20–28°F (11–16°C).

HUMIDITY: 85–90% in summer and autumn, dropping to 60–65% for 2 months in late winter and early spring.

WATER: Rainfall is heavy for 6 months from late spring through early autumn, but conditions are much drier for 4 months in winter. The wet and dry seasons are separated by 1-month transitional periods in spring and autumn. Cultivated plants should be kept moist while actively growing, but water should be gradually reduced after new growths mature in autumn.

FERTILIZER: ¼–½ recommended strength, applied weekly. A high-nitrogen fertilizer is beneficial from spring to midsummer, but a fertilizer high in phosphates should be used in late summer and autumn.

REST PERIOD: Winter days average 71–77°F (21–25°C), and nights average 42–48°F (5–9°C), with a diurnal range of 24–29°F (13–16°C). In the habitat, the record low temperatures are near freezing, but extremes should be avoided for cultivated plants. Water should be greatly reduced for several months in winter, but it should not be eliminated. Winter rainfall is very low, but additional moisture is available from mist and dew. Cultivated plants should be allowed to dry out between waterings, but they should not remain dry for extended periods. Occasional early morning mistings between waterings may help keep plants from becoming too dry. Fertilizer should be reduced or eliminated until spring. In the habitat, light is highest in winter.

GROWING MEDIA: Plants may be mounted on tree-fern or cork slabs if humidity is high and plants are watered at least once daily in summer. When plants are potted, any open, fast-draining medium may be used. They may be repotted anytime new roots are growing.

MISCELLANEOUS NOTES: The bloom season shown in the climate table is based on collection reports.

Plant and Flower Information

PLANT SIZE AND TYPE: An 8–18 in. (20–45 cm) sympodial epiphyte.

PSEUDOBULB: 8–18 in. (20–45 cm) long. The slender, tightly clustered stems consist of numerous nodes 0.8–1.2 in. (2–3 cm) long. They occasionally branch. The leaf sheaths are initially white, but they turn black after the leaves drop.

LEAVES: The leaves are deciduous before flowering.

INFLORESCENCE: 0.6 in. (1.6 cm) long. Inflorescences emerge at the apex of each branch.

FLOWERS: 1 per inflorescence. The tiny blossoms are 0.2 in. (0.5 cm) long. Flowers are dull, creamy-yellow flushed with rose. They have an oblong dorsal sepal, ovate lateral sepals, and oblanceolate petals which are somewhat truncated at the apex. The lip, which is 0.4 in. (1 cm) long, is twice as long as the other segments. It is incurved and somewhat truncated at the apex with a ruffled margin. Blossoms are fragrant.

REFERENCES: 223, 489.

Dendrobium tapiniense T. M. Reeve

ORIGIN/HABITAT: Papua New Guinea. Plants grow on trees in mountain forests in the region north of Port Moresby near Tapini. They are usually found at 4900–6400 ft. (1500–1950 m).

CLIMATE: Station #94035, Port Moresby, Papua New Guinea, Lat. 9.5°S, Long. 147.2°E, at 126 ft. (38 m). Temperatures are calculated for an elevation of 5600 ft. (1700 m), resulting in probable extremes of 80°F (27°C) and 46°F (8°C).

N/HEMISPHERE	JAN	FEB	MAR	APR	MAY	JUN	JUL	AUG	SEP	OCT	NOV	DEC
°F AVG MAX	65	64	66	68	70	72	71	69	70	69	68	66
°F AVG MIN	55	55	56	57	58	58	58	58	58	58	57	56
DIURNAL RANGE	10	9	10	11	12	14	13	11	12	12	11	10
RAIN/INCHES	1.1	0.7	1.0	1.4	1.9	4.4	7.0	7.6	6.7	4.2	2.5	1.3
HUMIDITY/%	78	77	78	76	73	71	71	73	74	75	77	78
BLOOM SEASON					*	**	**	**	*	*		
DAYS CLR	N/A											
RAIN/MM	28	18	25	36	48	112	178	193	170	107	64	33
°C AVG MAX	18.3	17.8	18.9	20.0	21.1	22.2	21.7	20.6	21.1	20.6	20.0	18.9
°C AVG MIN	12.8	12.8	13.3	13.9	14.4	14.4	14.4	14.4	14.4	13.9	13.9	13.3
DIURNAL RANGE	5.5	5.0	5.6	6.1	6.7	7.8	7.3	6.2	6.7	6.7	6.1	5.6
S/HEMISPHERE	JUL	AUG	SEP	OCT	NOV	DEC	JAN	FEB	MAR	APR	MAY	JUN

Cultural Recommendations

LIGHT: 2500–3000 fc. Plants require moderately high light with strong air movement year-round. About 50% shading should be provided in summer. Light should be as high as the plants can tolerate, short of burning the foliage.

TEMPERATURES: Throughout the year, days average 64–72°F (18–22°C), and nights average 55–58°F (13–14°C), with a diurnal range of 9–14°F (5–8°C).

HUMIDITY: 70–75% most of the year, increasing to near 80% in winter. Humidity is probably somewhat greater in the higher elevation forest habitat, however.

WATER: Rainfall is moderate for 5 months in summer, but conditions are dry in winter. Cultivated plants should dry slightly between waterings from spring to early autumn, but water should be gradually reduced in late autumn.

FERTILIZER: ¼–½ recommended strength, applied weekly. A high-nitrogen fertilizer is beneficial from spring to midsummer, but a fertilizer high in phosphates should be used in late summer and autumn.

REST PERIOD: Growing conditions should be maintained all year. In the habitat, rainfall is low for 6–7 months in winter, but additional water is available from dew and mist in the high elevation habitat. Water should be reduced somewhat for cultivated plants, especially those grown in the dark, short-day conditions common in temperate latitudes. Plants should be kept somewhat moist, however, and never be allowed to dry out completely. In addition to regular waterings, occasional light mistings on clear, sunny mornings may be beneficial. Fertilizer should be reduced anytime water is reduced. In the habitat, winter light is highest.

GROWING MEDIA: Plants are best mounted on tree-fern or cork slabs providing humidity is high and plants are watered at least once daily in summer. If plants are potted, a very open, fast-draining medium should be used in an undersized pot that is barely large enough to hold the roots. Repotting is best done in early spring when new roots are growing.

MISCELLANEOUS NOTES: The bloom season shown in the climate table is based on records from the habitat. *D. tapiniense* is grown at the botanical garden at Laiagam, New Guinea where roots are vigorous and even small plants flower freely. However, it has proved difficult for some growers, so careful attention should be given the cultural requirements. In the northern latitudes, some cultivated plants grown from seed have required 15 years to bloom.

Plant and Flower Information

PLANT SIZE AND TYPE: A 15–24 in. (38–60 cm) sympodial epiphyte.

PSEUDOBULB: 15–24 in. (38–60 cm) long. Pseudobulbs are stocky, furrowed, and taper to a very slender base. Each stem consists of about 9 nodes. Plants are vigorous and produce many leads.

LEAVES: 2 per growth. The elliptic leaves are 6 in. (15 cm) long.

INFLORESCENCE: 4–6 in. (10–15 cm) long. Inflorescences emerge at the apex of the pseudobulb.

FLOWERS: 10–15 per inflorescence. Plants often produce hundreds of blossoms. The attractive flowers are 1.6 in. (4 cm) long. They are smooth, stiff, fleshy, and completely hairless. The greenish to creamy white segments are heavily spotted with purple. The sepals are broad. The petals are oblong with wavy margins and a half twist. The broad, strongly recurved lip is marked with purple veins on the sidelobes. The midlobe is distinctly wavy and finely serrated along the margin. It has a glossy callus and a sharply divided midlobe. Blossoms last 3–4 months.

HYBRIDIZING NOTES: Northen (ref. 331) reports that *D. tapiniense* can be self-pollinated.

REFERENCES: 83, 91, 95, 234, 331, 526, 550.

PHOTOS/DRAWINGS: *83, 91, 95, 331, 550.*

Dendrobium tarberi M. Clements and D. Jones

AKA: Plants are still considered by most to be part of the *D. speciosum* alliance. Also see discussion at *D. speciosum*. Clements (ref. 67) states that further research on the *D. speciosum* alliance is in progress, but in the meantime, he includes the synonyms *D. hillii* Hooker not F. Mueller, *D. speciosum* Smith forma *hillii* Domin, and *D. speciosum* Smith var. *hillii* author unknown. Only time will tell whether the name *D. tarberi* will be generally accepted.

ORIGIN/HABITAT: Australia. The habitat extends from the Brisbane Valley to Dungog. Plants commonly grow on trees, but they are occasionally found on rocks in rainforests and other moist forests.

CLIMATE: Station #94791, Coffs Harbour, Australia, Lat. 30.3°S, Long. 153.1°E, at 14 ft. (4 m). Temperatures are calculated for an elevation of 2000 ft. (610 m), resulting in probable extremes of 99°F (38°C) and 23°F (−5°C).

N/HEMISPHERE	JAN	FEB	MAR	APR	MAY	JUN	JUL	AUG	SEP	OCT	NOV	DEC
°F AVG MAX	58	60	64	67	72	73	73	73	72	70	64	61
°F AVG MIN	37	38	43	48	52	56	58	59	57	52	43	38
DIURNAL RANGE	21	22	21	19	20	17	15	14	15	18	21	23
RAIN/INCHES	3.8	2.1	2.9	3.8	4.0	5.8	6.9	7.7	8.7	7.7	5.7	4.5
HUMIDITY/%	74	72	70	74	72	76	79	83	79	78	75	74
BLOOM SEASON			*	*								
DAYS CLR @ 4AM	8	9	10	10	12	11	9	8	10	7	11	8
DAYS CLR @ 10AM	16	18	18	12	15	11	8	5	10	10	14	15
RAIN/MM	97	53	74	97	102	147	175	196	221	196	145	114
°C AVG MAX	14.7	15.8	18.0	19.7	22.5	23.0	23.0	23.0	22.5	21.4	18.0	16.4
°C AVG MIN	3.0	3.6	6.4	9.1	11.4	13.6	14.7	15.2	14.1	11.4	6.4	3.6
DIURNAL RANGE	11.7	12.2	11.6	10.6	11.1	9.4	8.3	7.8	8.4	10.0	11.6	12.8
S/HEMISPHERE	JUL	AUG	SEP	OCT	NOV	DEC	JAN	FEB	MAR	APR	MAY	JUN

Cultural Recommendations

LIGHT: 2000–3000 fc. Growers report that *D. tarberi* requires more shade than most plants in the *D. speciosum* alliance.

TEMPERATURES: Summer days average 73°F (23°C), and nights average 56–59°F (14–15°C), with a diurnal range of 14–17°F (8–9°C).

HUMIDITY: 75–80% in summer and autumn, dropping to near 70% in winter. Humidity may well be somewhat greater in the moist forest habitat.

WATER: Rainfall is moderate to heavy through most of the year, but for 2–3 months in winter, conditions are slightly drier. Cultivated plants should kept moist.

FERTILIZER: ¼–½ recommended strength, applied weekly. A high nitrogen fertilizer is beneficial from spring to midsummer, but a fertilizer high in phosphates should be used in late summer and autumn.

REST PERIOD: Winter days average 58–64°F (15–18°C), and nights average 37–43°F (3–6°C), with a diurnal range of 21–23°F (12–13°C). For 2–3 months in winter, cultivated plants should be allowed to dry briefly between waterings. Fertilizer should be reduced until water is increased in spring. In the habitat, the probable extreme low is 23°F (−5°C), indicating that plants probably survive freezing temperatures, at least for short periods. However, extremes should be avoided for cultivated plants. If plants are exposed to cold temperatures, they are more likely to survive if they are dry at the time. In the habitat, light is highest in winter.

GROWING MEDIA: Mounting plants on tree-fern or cork slabs accommodates their long, pendent flower spikes, but humidity must be high and the plants watered at least once daily in summer. Plants may be potted in hanging pots or baskets filled with any open, fast-draining medium. Repotting may be done anytime new roots are growing.

MISCELLANEOUS NOTES: The bloom season shown in the climate table is based on reports from the habitat.

Plant and Flower Information

PLANT SIZE AND TYPE: A 24 in. (60 cm) sympodial epiphyte. Plants may form clumps 79–118 in. (200–300 cm) across.

PSEUDOBULB: 16 in. (40 cm) long. Pseudobulbs are consistently erect, cylindrical to slightly club-shaped, and narrow at the base. The stems produce aerial roots. The roots that emerge from the base of the stem often grow upwards.

LEAVES: 3–5 per growth. The leaves are about 8 in. (20 cm) long. They are clustered at the apex of the stem.

INFLORESCENCE: Long. Numerous inflorescences appear simultaneously from nodes near the apex. They are densely flowered and may be suberect or pendent.

FLOWERS: Many per inflorescence. The numerous white or cream flowers are 0.8–1.0 in. (2.0–2.5 cm) across. The lip is smaller than that of a typical *D. speciosum*. Also see *D. speciosum*.

HYBRIDIZING NOTES: *D. tarberi* is known to hybridize naturally with *D. kingianum* Bidwill ex Lindley to produce *D.* × *delicatum* (F. M. Bailey) F. M. Bailey and with *D. gracilicaule* to form *D.* × *gracillimum* F. Mueller. Although members of the *D. speciosum* alliance are seldom self-fertile, Adams (ref. 4) indicates that cross-pollination between different clones of the same variety and between different varieties commonly produce seed.

REFERENCES: 4, 67, 235, 240, 254, 580.

PHOTOS/DRAWINGS: 240.

Dendrobium tattonianum Bateman

AKA: *D. canaliculatum* R. Brown var. *tattonianum* (Bateman ex Rchb. f.) Rchb. f.

ORIGIN/HABITAT: Australia. Plants grow in eastern Queensland from Cairns southward to about Rockhampton. They are usually found in coastal swamps growing on paper-bark trees.

CLIMATE: Station #94294, Townsville, Australia, Lat. 19.3°S, Long. 146.8°E, at 18 ft. (5 m). Record extreme temperatures are 110°F (43°C) and 39°F (4°C).

N/HEMISPHERE	JAN	FEB	MAR	APR	MAY	JUN	JUL	AUG	SEP	OCT	NOV	DEC
°F AVG MAX	75	77	80	83	85	87	87	87	86	84	81	77
°F AVG MIN	59	61	66	71	74	76	76	75	73	70	65	61
DIURNAL RANGE	16	16	14	12	11	11	11	12	13	14	16	16
RAIN/INCHES	0.6	0.5	0.7	1.3	1.9	5.4	10.9	11.2	7.2	3.3	1.3	1.4
HUMIDITY/%	61	61	62	64	66	70	72	71	70	64	63	63
BLOOM SEASON		*	*	*								
DAYS CLR @ 10AM	16	18	15	10	7	7	5	5	9	13	14	15
DAYS CLR @ 4PM	16	18	20	20	17	15	8	5	7	11	14	15
RAIN/MM	15	13	18	33	48	137	277	284	183	84	33	36
°C AVG MAX	23.9	25.0	26.7	28.3	29.4	30.8	30.6	30.6	30.0	28.9	27.2	25.0
°C AVG MIN	15.0	16.1	18.9	21.7	23.3	24.4	24.4	23.9	22.8	21.1	18.3	16.1
DIURNAL RANGE	8.9	8.9	7.8	6.6	6.1	6.4	6.2	6.7	7.2	7.8	8.9	8.9
S/HEMISPHERE	JUL	AUG	SEP	OCT	NOV	DEC	JAN	FEB	MAR	APR	MAY	JUN

Cultural Recommendations

LIGHT: 3000–4000 fc. In the habitat, plants tolerate nearly full sun. Growers indicate that plants are the most floriferous when light is very bright.

TEMPERATURES: Summer days average 87°F (31°C), and nights average 75–76°F (24°C), with a diurnal range of 11–12°F (6–7°C).

HUMIDITY: Near 70% in summer, dropping to 60–65% during the rest of the year. In the swampy habitat, however, values are probably 10–15% greater than indicated by the climate data. Humidity for cultivated plants should be 75–85% year-round.

WATER: At lower elevations, rainfall is moderate to heavy during a 5-month summer wet season, followed by a 6–7 month dry season. Cultivated plants should be kept moist with only slight drying allowed between waterings in summer and early autumn. Water should be gradually reduced in autumn after new growths mature.

FERTILIZER: ¼–½ recommended strength, applied weekly. A high-nitrogen fertilizer is beneficial from spring to midsummer, but a fertilizer high in phosphates should be used in late summer and autumn.

REST PERIOD: Winter days average 75–77°F (24–25°C), and nights average 59–61°F (15–16°C), with a diurnal range of 16°F (9°C). Plants are widely distributed, so they should adapt to winter minimum temperatures 6–8°F (3–4°C) cooler than indicated. Water and humidity should be reduced in autumn to allow the plants to dry out between waterings. For 3–4 months in winter, plants should be very dry, with only enough water given to keep the pseudobulbs from shriveling too much. As inflorescences start to grow, water should be gradually increased so that plants are slightly moist. However, the plants should be kept quite dry until new growths are about 2 in. (5 cm) tall because young growths are very susceptible to disease. Fertilizer should be eliminated during the winter dry season. In the habitat, light is highest during the rest period.

GROWING MEDIA: Plants are best mounted on a cork slab, as they are healthiest when the roots are exposed to air. Plants are less vigorous when potted. Remounting is best done in early spring when new roots are actively growing. Some Australian growers report good results when plants are potted with wine corks as a medium.

MISCELLANEOUS NOTES: The bloom season shown in the climate table is based on reports from the habitat.

Plant and Flower Information

PLANT SIZE AND TYPE: A 3–10 in. (8–25 cm) sympodial epiphyte.

PSEUDOBULB: 1–2 in. (2.5–5.0 cm) long, rarely to 6 in. (15 cm). The pear-shaped pseudobulbs resemble clumps of 4–7 onions. Growths are densely clustered and form small to medium mats or clumps.

LEAVES: 3–6 per growth. The fleshy, nearly terete leaves are variable. They are usually 2–4 in. (5–10 cm) long, but may reach a length of 8 in. (20 cm). Environmental conditions, particularly the amount of light, strongly influence leaf size, thickness, and shape, which varies from terete to straplike to linear.

INFLORESCENCE: 4–16 in. (10–41 cm) long. Inflorescence length varies with plant size. The slender, rigidly erect inflorescences emerge from nodes near the apex of each growth. Each growth produces 1 to several flower spikes every year and continues to bloom for several years, resulting in well-grown plants being covered with blossoms.

FLOWERS: 12–25, sometimes 60 per inflorescence. The flowers are 1 in. (2.5 cm) across with a sweet honey-like fragrance. They are attractive and curious rather than showy. The slender sepals and petals are normally white to pale yellow-green at the base with varying shades of yellow on the apical half. The petals are longer than the sepals and all are twisted less than once. The lip is white with 3 raised keels and purple-lavender markings on the sidelobes and disk. The long-lived blossoms last about 5 weeks.

REFERENCES: 67, 84, 105, 216, 254, 430, 445, 533.

Dendrobium taurinum Lindley

AKA: Merrill (ref. 296) and Valmayor (ref. 536) include *D. veratrifolium* Naves not Lindley as a possible synonym.

ORIGIN/HABITAT: The Philippine Islands. The orchids are found near Manila on Luzon Island, near Davao on Mindanao Island, on the small Dinagat Islands, and on Guimaras, just off the south coast of Panay Island. Plants usually grow in coastal mangrove swamps below 1000 ft. (300 m), but they are also found on open, woody plateaus exposed to the hot dry winds from nearby plains.

CLIMATE: Station #98653, Surigao, Philippines, Lat. 9.8°N, Long. 125.5°E, at 72 ft. (22 m). Temperatures are calculated for an elevation of 800 ft. (240 m), resulting in probable extremes of 96°F (36°C) and 63°F (17°C).

N/HEMISPHERE	JAN	FEB	MAR	APR	MAY	JUN	JUL	AUG	SEP	OCT	NOV	DEC
°F AVG MAX	81	82	83	85	87	87	87	87	87	86	84	82
°F AVG MIN	70	70	71	71	72	72	72	73	73	72	72	71
DIURNAL RANGE	11	12	12	14	15	15	15	14	14	14	12	11
RAIN/INCHES	21.4	14.8	19.9	10.0	6.2	4.9	7.0	5.1	6.6	10.7	16.8	24.4
HUMIDITY/%	91	90	88	85	85	82	83	82	83	84	88	89
BLOOM SEASON				*	*	*				*	*	
DAYS CLR @ 8AM	1	1	1	4	2	3	2	2	1	2	1	1
DAYS CLR @ 2PM	1	2	2	6	3	1	2	1	2	3	1	1
RAIN/MM	544	376	505	254	157	124	178	130	168	272	427	620
°C AVG MAX	27.0	27.6	28.1	29.2	30.3	30.3	30.3	30.3	30.3	29.8	28.7	27.6
°C AVG MIN	20.9	20.9	21.4	21.4	22.0	22.0	22.0	22.6	22.6	22.0	22.0	21.4
DIURNAL RANGE	6.1	6.7	6.7	7.8	8.3	8.3	8.3	7.7	7.7	7.8	6.7	6.2
S/HEMISPHERE	JUL	AUG	SEP	OCT	NOV	DEC	JAN	FEB	MAR	APR	MAY	JUN

Cultural Recommendations

LIGHT: 2500–3500 fc.

TEMPERATURES: Throughout the year, days average 81–87°F (27–30°C), and nights average 70–73°F (21–23°C), with a diurnal range of 11–15°F (6–8°C). The widest diurnal range occurs in summer and results from warmer days.

HUMIDITY: 80–90% year-round.

WATER: Rainfall is moderate to very heavy all year. Cultivated plants should be kept moist but not soggy. Warm water, about 70°F (21°C), might be beneficial.

FERTILIZER: ¼–½ recommended strength. A balanced fertilizer should be applied weekly to biweekly throughout the year.

REST PERIOD: Growing conditions should be maintained all year. Wide seasonal temperature fluctuations should be avoided. In the habitat, the heaviest rainfall occurs in winter; but in cultivation, increasing water could be detrimental. This is especially true for plants grown in the dark, short-day conditions common in temperate latitudes. Cultivated plants should be kept moist, with only slight drying allowed between waterings. In the habitat, light is lowest in winter. Some growers report that plants grow well with intermediate winter temperatures and recommend a minimum winter temperature of 59°F (15°C). However, it should be noted that this is colder than the extreme low in the habitat.

GROWING MEDIA: Plants may be mounted on tree-fern or cork slabs if humidity is high and plants are watered at least once daily in summer. When plants are potted, any open, fast-draining medium may be used. Repotting may be done anytime new roots are growing.

MISCELLANEOUS NOTES: The bloom season shown in the climate table is based on cultivation records. In the wild, plants bloom twice a year in midwinter and early autumn. Growers indicate that plants do not survive cultivation outdoors in Manila.

Plant and Flower Information

PLANT SIZE AND TYPE: A 35–49 in. (90–125 cm) sympodial epiphyte. In the wild, plants may reach a length of 157 in. (400 cm).

PSEUDOBULB: 35–157 in. (90–400 cm) long. The canelike stems, which are stiffly erect, may be cylindrical or strongly spindle shaped. They are leafy in the middle and along the upper part of each growth.

LEAVES: Many. The elliptical leaves are 3–8 in. (8–20 cm) long and unequally bilobed at the apex. They are dark, shiny green, broad, thick, leathery, and somewhat persistent.

INFLORESCENCE: Normally 4–20 in. (10–50 cm) long, the inflorescences may reach a length of 48 in. (122 cm). The racemes are erect, somewhat zigzag, and emerge from nodes near the apex of the stem. Blossoms are widely-spaced.

FLOWERS: 6–30 per inflorescence. The flowers are 2.0–2.6 in. (5.0–6.5 cm) long. Sepals are white with a yellowish green suffusion that may have a pinkish tinge. They are waxy, wavy, and curve backward. The petals may be reddish brown, purple, or rose, often with white at the base. They are long, erect, and twisted once or twice. The very large, 3-lobed lip is white with a heavy rose or purple flush near the margin and purple veins. It is transversely oblong and frilled with an uneven margin. The raised, 3-ridged callus is white. Some clones may be nearly all white with brown or purple spots at the tips of the sepals and petals. Blossoms last several weeks.

HYBRIDIZING NOTES: Chromosome count is 2n = 38 (ref. 151, 187, 504, 580). When used as a parent, *D. taurinum* contributes good flower substance, a large full lip, and bright colors.

REFERENCES: 12, 25, 36, 84, 98, 151, 179, 187, 190, 196, 200, 216, 234, 254, 293, 296, 317, 326, 347, 371, 373, 430, 445, 458, 468, 504, 524, 526, 536, 541, 570, 580.

PHOTOS/DRAWINGS: *84*, *98*, *347, 371*, *430*, *458*, *536*.

Dendrobium taurulinum J. J. Smith

ORIGIN/HABITAT: Seram Island in the Moluccas. Plants grow in the northern and central parts of the island at 2600–2950 ft. (800–900 m). One collection originated on a sandy beach. Plants were cultivated in the botanic garden at Bogor, Java.

CLIMATE: Station #49620, Amahai, Seram, Indonesia, Lat. 3.3°S, Long. 128.9°E, at 10 ft. (3 m). Record extreme temperatures are 96°F (36°C) and 66°F (19°C).

N/HEMISPHERE	JAN	FEB	MAR	APR	MAY	JUN	JUL	AUG	SEP	OCT	NOV	DEC
°F AVG MAX	81	81	83	85	88	88	88	88	88	86	84	82
°F AVG MIN	74	74	74	74	75	76	76	76	76	76	75	74
DIURNAL RANGE	7	7	9	11	13	12	12	12	12	10	9	8
RAIN/INCHES	23.7	15.8	9.5	6.1	4.5	5.2	5.0	4.7	5.3	11.0	20.3	25.1
HUMIDITY/%	83	82	81	80	79	78	78	77	79	82	83	84
BLOOM SEASON	*	*										*
DAYS CLR @ 9AM	1	1	1	6	7	4	3	5	5	3	3	3
DAYS CLR @ 3PM	1	1	2	5	6	1	1	2	3	1	3	3
RAIN/MM	602	401	241	155	114	132	127	119	135	279	516	638
°C AVG MAX	27.2	27.2	28.3	29.4	31.1	31.1	31.1	31.1	31.1	30.0	28.9	27.8
°C AVG MIN	23.3	23.3	23.3	23.3	23.9	24.4	24.4	24.4	24.4	24.4	23.9	23.3
DIURNAL RANGE	3.9	3.9	5.0	6.1	7.2	6.7	6.7	6.7	6.7	5.6	5.0	4.5
S/HEMISPHERE	JUL	AUG	SEP	OCT	NOV	DEC	JAN	FEB	MAR	APR	MAY	JUN

Cultural Recommendations

LIGHT: 2000–3000 fc. In the habitat, clear days are rare.

TEMPERATURES: Throughout the year, days average 81–88°F (27–31°C), and nights average 74–76°F (23–24°C), with a diurnal range of 7–13°F (4–7°C). Because of the range in habitat elevation, plants should adapt to temperatures 6–8°F (3–4°C) cooler than indicated.

HUMIDITY: 75–80% most of the year, increasing to near 85% in winter.

WATER: Rainfall is moderate to heavy all year with a slightly drier season in spring and summer. Plants should be kept moist, with only slight drying allowed between waterings.

FERTILIZER: ¼–½ recommended strength. A balanced fertilizer should be applied weekly to biweekly throughout the year.

REST PERIOD: Growing conditions should be maintained all year. In the habitat, winter is the wettest season, but water should not be increased for cultivated plants. In fact, it should be reduced for plants grown in the dark, short-day conditions common in temperate-latitude winters. Plants should never be allowed to dry out completely, however. Fertilizer should be reduced or eliminated anytime water is reduced. In the habitat, light is highest in early spring.

- GROWING MEDIA: Plants may be mounted on tree-fern or cork slabs if humidity is high and plants are watered at least once daily in summer. When plants are potted, any open, fast-draining medium may be used. They may be repotted anytime new roots are growing.
- MISCELLANEOUS NOTES: The bloom season shown in the climate table is based on reports from the habitat.

Plant and Flower Information

- PLANT SIZE AND TYPE: A 3–18 in. (7–45 cm) sympodial epiphyte.
- PSEUDOBULB: 3–18 in. (7–45 cm) long. The canelike stems are swollen in the middle.
- LEAVES: Several. The leathery leaves are 1.6–3.1 in. (4–8 cm) long with 2 points at the tip. They are ovate to elliptical.
- INFLORESCENCE: 3.5–5.1 in. (9–13 cm) long. The suberect inflorescences emerge from the upper nodes.
- FLOWERS: 4–6 per inflorescence. The flowers are 1.2–1.4 in. (3.0–3.5 cm) across, smaller than the closely related *D. bicaudatum* Reinwardt ex Lindley. The dorsal sepal is oblong-triangular, pointed, and recurved on the apical half. Lateral sepals are oblong-lanceolate and pointed. Sepals are white with a pale green suffusion. Petals are linear and sharply pointed with a half twist. They are yellow-green to light green with a white margin. The 3-lobed lip is pale green with 3 violet keels. The longer center keel is continuous with interrupted side keels.
- REFERENCES: 84, 222, 344.
- PHOTOS/DRAWINGS: 344.

Dendrobium taveuniense Dauncey and Cribb

- AKA: Plants were once thought to be *D. catillare*.
- ORIGIN/HABITAT: Fiji. This species occurs on the islands of Tavenui, Vanua Levu, and Viti Levu. The epiphytic plants grow in dense forest, often on ridges, at 2150–4900 ft. (650–1500 m).
- CLIMATE: Station #91661, Savusavu, Fiji Island, Lat. 16.8°S, Long. 179.3°E, at 10 ft. (3 m). Temperatures are calculated for an elevation of 3600 ft. (1100 m), resulting in probable extremes of 86°F (30°C) and 43°F (6°C).

N/HEMISPHERE	JAN	FEB	MAR	APR	MAY	JUN	JUL	AUG	SEP	OCT	NOV	DEC
°F AVG MAX	67	67	68	69	71	73	74	74	74	72	70	68
°F AVG MIN	56	56	57	58	59	61	62	62	62	61	59	57
DIURNAL RANGE	11	11	11	11	12	12	12	12	12	11	11	11
RAIN/INCHES	4.9	8.3	7.7	8.3	9.8	12.5	11.4	10.7	14.5	12.2	10.1	6.7
HUMIDITY/%	77	77	76	75	75	76	76	78	79	79	81	78
BLOOM SEASON	N/A											
DAYS CLR @ 12PM	1	4	1	1	2	1	1	0	0	1	1	2
RAIN/MM	124	211	196	211	249	318	290	272	368	310	257	170
°C AVG MAX	19.4	19.4	20.0	20.6	21.7	22.9	23.4	23.3	23.3	22.2	21.1	20.0
°C AVG MIN	13.3	13.4	14.0	14.5	15.1	16.2	16.8	16.8	16.8	16.2	15.1	14.0
DIURNAL RANGE	6.1	6.0	6.0	6.1	6.6	6.7	6.6	6.5	6.5	6.0	6.0	6.0
S/HEMISPHERE	JUL	AUG	SEP	OCT	NOV	DEC	JAN	FEB	MAR	APR	MAY	JUN

Cultural Recommendations

- LIGHT: 2500–3500 fc.
- TEMPERATURES: Throughout the year, days average 67–74°F (19–23°C), and nights average 56–62°F (13–17°C), with a diurnal range of 11–12°F (6–7°C).
- HUMIDITY: 75–80% year-round.
- WATER: Rainfall is moderate to heavy all year with a brief, slightly drier period in winter. Cultivated plants should be kept moist with only slight drying allowed between waterings.
- FERTILIZER: ¼–½ recommended strength. A balanced fertilizer should be applied weekly to biweekly throughout the year.
- REST PERIOD: Growing conditions should be maintained all year. Cultivated plants should never be allowed to dry out completely, but water should be reduced slightly in winter, especially for plants grown in the dark, short-day conditions common in temperate latitudes.
- GROWING MEDIA: Plants may be mounted on tree-fern or cork slabs if humidity is high and plants are watered at least once daily in summer. When plants are potted, any open, fast-draining medium may be used. Repotting may be done anytime new roots are growing.

Plant and Flower Information

- PLANT SIZE AND TYPE: An 8–16 in. (20–41 cm) sympodial epiphyte.
- PSEUDOBULB: 8–16 in. (20–41 cm) long. The yellow stems are very slender and become grooved with age. They may be straight or curved.
- LEAVES: 1.6–2.8 in. (4–7 cm) long. The thin papery leaves are bilobed and pointed. They often have an uneven margin.
- INFLORESCENCE: 0.4 in. (1 cm) long. Inflorescences emerge along the side of leafless stems.
- FLOWERS: 3–10. The flowers are about 0.7 in. (1.8 cm) long and open widely. They are smooth and may be white or pink. The mentum equals the free parts of the lateral sepals. The pointed lip is slightly uneven along the margin. It has prominent sidelobes. The ovary, which is winged and shortly curved, lies against the column foot.
- REFERENCES: Dauncey and Cribb 1993 *Kew Bulletin* 48(3).
- PHOTOS/DRAWINGS: Dauncey and Cribb 1993 *Kew Bulletin* 48(3).

Dendrobium taylori (F. Mueller) Fitzgerald. Now considered a synonym of *Cadetia taylori*. REFERENCES: 67, 105, 190, 219, 254, 445.

Dendrobium teijsmannii Miquel. Sometimes spelled *D. teysmannii*, see *D. lobbii* Teijsm. and Binn. REFERENCES: 67, 216, 254, 310, 454.

Dendrobium teligerum P. van Royen. See *D. brevicaule* Rolfe. REFERENCES: 233, 385, 538. PHOTOS/DRAWINGS: 538.

Dendrobium teloense J. J. Smith

- AKA: Kränzlin (ref. 254) listed *D. teloense* as a synonym of *D. concavum* J. J. Smith, but Schlechter (ref. 436) strongly disagreed.
- ORIGIN/HABITAT: Telo Island, off the west coast of central Sumatra. Habitat elevation is unavailable, but Telo is a low-lying island.
- CLIMATE: Station #96163, Padang, Sumatra, Indonesia, Lat. 0.9°S, Long. 100.4°E, at 19 ft. (6 m). Record extreme temperatures are 94°F (34°C) and 68°F (20°C).

N/HEMISPHERE	JAN	FEB	MAR	APR	MAY	JUN	JUL	AUG	SEP	OCT	NOV	DEC
°F AVG MAX	87	87	86	86	86	86	87	87	87	87	88	87
°F AVG MIN	74	74	74	74	74	74	74	74	74	75	75	74
DIURNAL RANGE	13	13	12	12	12	12	13	13	13	12	13	13
RAIN/INCHES	10.9	13.7	6.0	19.5	20.4	18.9	13.8	10.2	12.1	14.3	12.4	12.1
HUMIDITY/%	81	82	82	84	85	84	81	81	82	83	81	81
BLOOM SEASON	N/A											
DAYS CLR @ 7AM	5	1	1	0	0	2	2	1	2	2	3	5
DAYS CLR @ 1PM	5	2	2	1	1	3	3	4	3	3	6	5
RAIN/MM	277	348	152	495	518	480	351	259	307	363	315	307
°C AVG MAX	30.6	30.6	30.0	30.0	30.0	30.0	30.6	30.6	30.6	30.6	31.1	30.6
°C AVG MIN	23.3	23.3	23.3	23.3	23.3	23.3	23.3	23.3	23.3	23.9	23.9	23.3
DIURNAL RANGE	7.3	7.3	6.7	6.7	6.7	6.7	7.3	7.3	7.3	6.7	7.2	7.3
S/HEMISPHERE	JUL	AUG	SEP	OCT	NOV	DEC	JAN	FEB	MAR	APR	MAY	JUN

Cultural Recommendations

LIGHT: 2000–3000 fc. Diffused light is preferred.

TEMPERATURES: Throughout the year, days average 86–88°F (30–31°C), and nights average 74–75°F (23–24°C), with a diurnal range of 12–13°F (7°C). Probable extremes vary only a few degrees from the averages, indicating that the plant may not tolerate wide temperature fluctuations.

HUMIDITY: 80–85% year-round.

WATER: Rainfall is heavy all year. Cultivated plants should be kept moist but not soggy.

FERTILIZER: 1/4–1/2 recommended strength. A balanced fertilizer should be applied weekly to biweekly throughout the year.

REST PERIOD: Growing conditions should be maintained year-round. Water may be reduced somewhat for cultivated plants in winter, especially those grown in the dark, short-day conditions common in temperate latitudes. They should never be allowed to dry out completely, however.

GROWING MEDIA: Plants may be mounted on tree-fern or cork slabs if humidity is high and plants are watered at least once daily in summer. When plants are potted, any open, fast-draining medium may be used. Repotting may be done anytime new roots are growing.

Plant and Flower Information

PLANT SIZE AND TYPE: A 15 in. (38 cm) sympodial epiphyte.

PSEUDOBULB: 15 in. (38 cm) long. The shiny green stems are flattened, erect, and flexuous. The lower part of the stem is leafless, the midportion is leafy, and the upper portion has only rudimentary leaves. The nodes have dark rings. Each segment is narrow at the base and wide at the top, producing a somewhat zigzag appearance when leafless.

LEAVES: Many. The distichous leaves are 1.4 in. (3.6 cm) long and become smaller near the apex of the stem. They are held in 2 rows at an acute angle to the stem. The foliage is fleshy, laterally compressed, and pointed.

INFLORESCENCE: Short. Clustered inflorescences emerge laterally from nodes along the upper part of the stem.

FLOWERS: Few per inflorescence. The pale yellow flowers are 0.5 in. (1.2 cm) long. Sepals are oblong-lanceolate with parallel longitudinal nerves. The linear petals are marked with fine red nerves. The erect lip is curved and channeled along the centerline with a wavy, rounded, notched apex. It is marked with a faint yellow spot. Blossoms are extremely fragrant.

REFERENCES: 220, 254, 445, 471.

PHOTOS/DRAWINGS: 471.

Dendrobium tenellum (Blume) Lindley

AKA: *D. latilabre* J. J. Smith. *D. tenellum* is sometimes listed as a synonym of *D. gracile* (Blume) Lindley, but Seidenfaden (ref. 450) specifically excludes this synonymy. *D. tenellum* var. *setifolium* Guillamin is a synonym of *D. pseudotenellum* Guillamin.

ORIGIN/HABITAT: Java and Lombok Island. Plants are found in the western and central parts of Java, but they are most common in east Java, where they grow in both humid and dry mountain forests at 4900–7200 ft. (1500–2200 m).

CLIMATE: Station #96881, Madiun, Java, Indonesia, Lat. 7.6°S, Long. 111.4°E, at 361 ft. (110 m). Temperatures are calculated for an elevation of 5900 ft. (1800 m), resulting in probable extremes of 77°F (25°C) and 44°F (7°C).

N/HEMISPHERE	JAN	FEB	MAR	APR	MAY	JUN	JUL	AUG	SEP	OCT	NOV	DEC
°F AVG MAX	67	68	69	70	68	67	66	66	67	69	68	68
°F AVG MIN	51	51	53	54	54	54	54	54	54	54	54	52
DIURNAL RANGE	16	17	16	16	14	13	12	12	13	15	14	16
RAIN/INCHES	1.3	0.8	1.2	2.9	7.6	10.2	11.9	10.9	10.4	8.8	5.1	3.2
HUMIDITY/%	60	54	52	52	64	72	77	78	78	74	70	64
BLOOM SEASON					*	*	*					
DAYS CLR @ 7AM	18	22	21	16	8	4	2	2	3	6	9	16
DAYS CLR @ 1PM	15	17	14	9	4	2	1	1	1	3	6	11
RAIN/MM	33	20	30	74	193	259	302	277	264	224	130	81
°C AVG MAX	19.3	19.8	20.4	21.0	19.8	19.3	18.7	18.7	19.3	20.4	19.8	19.8
°C AVG MIN	10.4	10.4	11.5	12.1	12.1	12.1	12.1	12.1	12.1	12.1	12.1	11.0
DIURNAL RANGE	8.9	9.4	8.9	8.9	7.7	7.2	6.6	6.6	7.2	8.3	7.7	8.8
S/HEMISPHERE	JUL	AUG	SEP	OCT	NOV	DEC	JAN	FEB	MAR	APR	MAY	JUN

Cultural Recommendations

LIGHT: 1800–3000 fc. The heavy summer cloud cover indicates that some shading is needed from spring through autumn, but light should be as high as the plant can tolerate, short of burning the leaves.

TEMPERATURES: Throughout the year, days average 66–70°F (19–21°C), and nights average 51–54°F (10–12°C), with a diurnal range of 12–17°F (7–9°C). Due to the effects of the microclimate, maximum temperatures may be 6–10°F (3–6°C) warmer than indicated.

HUMIDITY: 75–80% in summer, dropping to 50–55% for 3 months in winter and spring. However, values may be greater in the high-elevation habitat.

WATER: At the weather station, rainfall is heavy from spring through autumn, followed by a 2–3 month winter dry season when humidity is so low that even moisture from dew is uncommon. Rainfall is much heavier in the high-elevation cloudforest, however, and moisture from mist, fog, and dew is usually available, even during periods of low rainfall. Cultivated plants should be kept moist but not soggy while growing, but water should be gradually reduced in autumn.

FERTILIZER: 1/4–1/2 recommended strength. A balanced fertilizer should be applied weekly to biweekly throughout the year.

REST PERIOD: Growing temperatures should be maintained year-round. In the habitat, conditions are very dry in winter. For cultivated plants, water and fertilizer should be reduced for 2–3 months. Plants should be allowed to dry slightly between waterings, but they should not remain dry for long periods. In the habitat, light is much higher in winter.

GROWING MEDIA: Plants may be mounted on tree-fern or cork slabs if humidity is high and plants are watered at least once daily in summer. When plants are potted, any open, fast-draining medium may be used. Repotting may be done anytime new roots are growing.

MISCELLANEOUS NOTES: The bloom season shown in the climate table is based on reports from the habitat. Related plants that produce flowers which last a single day commonly bloom several times during the year, and flowering usually occurs 7–14 days after the sudden 10°F (5°C) drop in daytime temperatures. However, the correlation between blooming and the temperature drop is less specific for this species and the bloom initiators have not been identified.

Plant and Flower Information

PLANT SIZE AND TYPE: A 24 in. (60 cm) sympodial epiphyte. Plants occasionally grow terrestrially.

PSEUDOBULB: 24 in. (60 cm) long. About 0.8 in. (2 cm) above the base, the erect stems have a red, shiny pseudobulbous swelling 0.8–1.2 in. (2–3 cm) long. The higher the light, the redder the swollen section.

LEAVES: 10–12. The leaves are 1.6–2.0 in. (4–5 cm) long, pale green, and nearly terete. They become small and rudimentary near the apex of the stem.

INFLORESCENCE: A single inflorescence emerges near the apex of the stem.

FLOWERS: 1. The flowers are 0.4–0.5 in. (1.0–1.2 cm) long and do not open fully. The lateral sepals spread widely, but the dorsal sepal and petals arch over the column. Blossoms are normally yellowish with violet veins, but coloring is highly variable. Plants known as *D. tenellum* var. *latilarabe* J. J. Smith have white flowers with reddish veins and dirty purple on the backside, but those known as *D. tenellum* var. *flavescens* J. J. Smith have pale yellow blossoms with dark purple papillae and a violet anther. The fan-shaped, ruffled lip is truncate and incurved at the apex. It may be white or yellow with a red flush and orange papillae. Blossoms last a few hours.

REFERENCES: 25, 75, 216, 254, 277, 310, 445, 450, 469, 482.

PHOTOS/DRAWINGS: 75, 450, 469.

Dendrobium tenens J. J. Smith. See *D. vexillarius* J. J. Smith.
REFERENCES: 224, 385, 445.

Dendrobium tennuissimum Rupp. Sometimes spelled *D. tenuissimum*, see *D. mortii* F. Mueller. REFERENCES: 23, 67, 105, 153, 179, 224, 240, 273, 325, 390, 421. PHOTOS/DRAWINGS: 105, 325, *390*.

Dendrobium tentaculatum Schlechter. Now considered a synonym of *Diplocaulobium tentaculatum* (Schlechter) Kränzlin. REFERENCES: 219, 220, 254, 437, 444, 445.

Dendrobium tenue J. J. Smith

ORIGIN/HABITAT: Southeastern Borneo. Plants were originally collected near Martapoera, a small town east of Bandjarmasin. Specific habitat information is unavailable, so the following climate data should be used with caution.

CLIMATE: Station #96685, Bandjarmasin, Borneo, Lat. 3.4°S, Long. 114.8°E, at 66 ft. (20 m). Record extreme temperatures are not available for this location.

N/HEMISPHERE	JAN	FEB	MAR	APR	MAY	JUN	JUL	AUG	SEP	OCT	NOV	DEC
°F AVG MAX	88	89	91	90	87	86	86	86	87	89	88	88
°F AVG MIN	74	73	74	76	76	76	76	75	75	77	77	76
DIURNAL RANGE	14	16	17	14	11	10	10	11	12	12	11	12
RAIN/INCHES	3.5	3.2	3.9	5.1	8.5	12.2	12.7	11.7	11.9	8.5	6.2	5.6
HUMIDITY/%	78	77	73	75	81	84	84	83	82	81	80	79
BLOOM SEASON	N/A											
DAYS CLR @ 8AM	12	12	13	8	5	3	1	2	3	6	9	11
DAYS CLR @ 2PM	3	2	2	3	1	0	0	0	1	2	2	3
RAIN/MM	89	81	99	130	216	310	323	297	302	216	157	142
°C AVG MAX	31.0	31.9	32.7	32.4	30.7	29.9	29.8	30.0	30.6	31.4	30.9	31.1
°C AVG MIN	23.2	23.0	23.4	24.2	24.3	24.2	24.2	24.1	24.1	24.9	24.9	24.2
DIURNAL RANGE	7.8	8.9	9.3	8.2	6.4	5.7	5.6	5.9	6.5	6.5	6.0	6.9
S/HEMISPHERE	JUL	AUG	SEP	OCT	NOV	DEC	JAN	FEB	MAR	APR	MAY	JUN

Cultural Recommendations

LIGHT: 2000–3000 fc.

TEMPERATURES: Throughout the year, days average 86–91°F (30–33°C), and nights average 73–77°F (23–25°C), with a diurnal range of 10–17°F (6–9°C).

HUMIDITY: 80–85% from late spring through autumn, dropping to about 75% in winter and early spring.

WATER: Rainfall is moderate to heavy all year, but conditions are slightly drier for 3 months in winter. Plants should be kept evenly moist from spring into autumn, but water should be gradually reduced in late autumn. Warm water might be beneficial.

FERTILIZER: ¼–½ recommended strength. A balanced fertilizer should be applied weekly to biweekly throughout the year.

REST PERIOD: Growing conditions should be maintained all year. Water and fertilizer should be reduced somewhat in winter, especially for plants cultivated in the dark, short-day conditions common in temperate latitudes. Plants should be allowed to dry slightly between waterings, but they should not remain dry for long periods. In the habitat, light is highest in winter.

GROWING MEDIA: Plants may be mounted on tree-fern or cork slabs or potted in small pots filled with any open, fast-draining medium. Repotting may be done anytime new roots are growing.

MISCELLANEOUS NOTES: The plant was described in 1917 in *Bull. Jard. Bot. Buit.* 2nd sér. 25:31.

Plant and Flower Information

PLANT SIZE AND TYPE: A 7 in. (18 cm) sympodial epiphyte.

PSEUDOBULB: 7 in. (18 cm) long. The clustered stems are very slender, laxly leafy, and club-shaped at the base. They are dark olive-green.

LEAVES: Several. The dirty green leaves are 2.8 in. (7 cm) long, terete, and fleshy.

INFLORESCENCE: Blossoms are borne near the apex of the stem.

FLOWERS: 1 to a few per inflorescence. The yellowish flowers are 0.4 in. (1 cm) long. The dorsal sepal is ovate-oblong. Lateral sepals are pointed, somewhat triangular, and sickle-shaped at the tip. The petals have an uneven margin at the apex. The yellowish white lip is marked with purple lines. It is erect, concave, and recurved with erect sidelobes.

REFERENCES: 222, 286, 295.

Dendrobium tenuicalcar J. J. Smith. See *D. violaceum* Kränzlin. REFERENCES: 221, 385, 445.

Dendrobium tenuicaule Hayata not Hooker f. or Ridley. See *D. leptocladum* Hayata. REFERENCES: 61, 192, 193, 221, 279.

Dendrobium tenuicaule Hooker f. not Hayata or Ridley

ORIGIN/HABITAT: Andaman Islands. Specific habitat location and elevation are unavailable, but the islands are low lying with only a few points above 1000 ft. (300 m).

CLIMATE: Station #43333, Port Blair, Andaman Islands, Lat. 11.7°N, Long. 92.7°E, at 259 ft. (79 m). Record extreme temperatures are 99°F (37°C) and 62°F (17°C).

N/HEMISPHERE	JAN	FEB	MAR	APR	MAY	JUN	JUL	AUG	SEP	OCT	NOV	DEC
°F AVG MAX	84	86	88	89	87	84	84	83	83	84	84	84
°F AVG MIN	72	71	72	75	75	75	75	75	74	74	74	73
DIURNAL RANGE	12	15	16	14	12	9	9	8	9	10	10	11
RAIN/INCHES	1.8	1.1	1.1	2.4	15.1	21.8	15.4	16.3	17.4	12.5	10.5	7.9
HUMIDITY/%	79	76	79	79	86	87	87	89	89	86	84	81
BLOOM SEASON			*									
DAYS CLR @ 6AM	1	5	6	2	0	1	0	0	0	1	5	3
DAYS CLR @ 12PM	1	6	11	2	0	0	0	0	0	0	4	2
RAIN/MM	46	28	28	61	384	554	391	414	442	318	267	201
°C AVG MAX	28.9	30.0	31.1	31.7	30.6	28.9	28.9	28.3	28.3	28.9	28.9	28.9
°C AVG MIN	22.2	21.7	22.2	23.9	23.9	23.9	23.9	23.9	23.3	23.3	23.3	22.8
DIURNAL RANGE	6.7	8.3	8.9	7.8	6.7	5.0	5.0	4.4	5.0	5.6	5.6	6.1
S/HEMISPHERE	JUL	AUG	SEP	OCT	NOV	DEC	JAN	FEB	MAR	APR	MAY	JUN

Cultural Recommendations

LIGHT: 2000–3000 fc.

TEMPERATURES: Throughout the year, days average 83–89°F (28–32°C), and nights average 71–75°F (22–24°C), with a diurnal range of 8–16°F (4–9°C).

HUMIDITY: 85–90% from late spring into autumn, dropping to 75–80% in winter and early spring.

WATER: Rainfall is heavy from late spring through autumn. The winter dry season lasts 3–4 months. Cultivated plants should be kept moist while actively growing, but water should be reduced in late autumn.

FERTILIZER: ¼–½ recommended strength. A balanced fertilizer should be applied weekly to biweekly throughout the year.

REST PERIOD: Growing temperatures should be maintained all year. Water and fertilizer should be reduced in winter. Plants should be allowed to dry out somewhat between waterings, but they should not remain dry for extended periods. In the habitat, light is highest in winter.

GROWING MEDIA: Plants may be mounted on tree-fern or cork slabs or potted in small pots filled with any open, fast-draining medium. Repotting may be done anytime new roots are growing.

MISCELLANEOUS NOTES: The bloom season shown in the climate table is based on reports from the habitat.

Plant and Flower Information

PLANT SIZE AND TYPE: A 10–12 in. (25–30 cm) sympodial epiphyte.

PSEUDOBULB: 10–12 in. (25–30 cm) long. The clustered stems have a bulbous swelling at the basal node. Above the base they are slender for several nodes then swell for several nodes before becoming slender again. The upper nodes are covered with sheaths.

LEAVES: 3–4 on each young stem. Very narrowly linear, the recurved leaves are 3–5 in. (8–13 cm) long and pointed at the tip. They are deciduous.

INFLORESCENCE: Flowers are borne near the apex of leafless stems.

FLOWERS: 1–3 per inflorescence. The flowers are 0.6 in. (1.5 cm) long. Sepals and small petals may be pure white, yellow, or white with a yellow suffusion. Blossoms are membranelike and may age to yellowish brown. The yellow lip is 3-lobed and trumpet-shaped. It is marked with 5 distinct nerves and a pubescent disk on the small, round midlobe.

REFERENCES: 157, 202, 203, 218, 254, 369, 445.

PHOTOS/DRAWINGS: 203, 369.

Dendrobium tenuicaule Ridley not Hayata or Hooker f. See *D. exilicaule* Ridley. REFERENCES: 200, 219, 455.

Dendrobium tenuissimum Rupp. See *D. mortii* F. Mueller. REFERENCES: 67, 224, 533.

Dendrobium teres Blanco not Lindley or Roxburgh. Now considered a synonym of *Luisia teretifolia* Gaudich. REFERENCES: 296, 536.

Dendrobium teres Lindley not Blanco or Roxburgh. See *D. singaporense* A. Hawkes and A. H. Heller. REFERENCES: 202, 203, 216, 254, 317, 395, 402, 445, 452, 454, 455.

Dendrobium teres Roxburgh not Blanco or Lindley. Now considered a synonym of *Vanda teres* Lindley. REFERENCES: 190, 216, 254, 369.

Dendrobium teretifolium Blanco not R. Brown or Lindley. Now considered a synonym of *Luisia teretifolia* Gaudich. REFERENCES: 296.

Dendrobium teretifolium R. Brown not Blanco or Lindley

AKA: The following names are commonly considered synonyms of *D. teretifolium*, but Clements (ref. 67) distributes them to his new species as follows: *D. teretifolium* var. *fairfaxii* (F. Mueller and Fitzgerald) F. M. Bailey is referred to *D. fairfaxii* F. Mueller, and *D. teretifolium* var. *fasciculatum* Rupp is considered a synonym of *D. calamiforme* Loddiges. *D. teretifolium* var. *album* C. White, *D. teretifolium* var. *aureum* F. M. Bailey, and *D. teretifolium* var. *fairfaxii* forma *aureum* (F. M. Bailey) Clemsha are considered synonyms of *D. dolichophyllum* D. Jones and M. Clements.

ORIGIN/HABITAT: Eastern Australia. The habitat extends from Bega in southeastern New South Wales to Rockhampton in southeastern Queensland. Plants generally grow on trees at low elevations, but they are occasionally found on rocks. They prefer high light in coastal gullies and river estuaries. The orchids are frequently found on trees overhanging water in creeks, lakes, or swamps.

CLIMATE: Station #94576, Brisbane, Australia, Lat. 27.4°S, Long. 153.1°E, at 17 ft. (5 m). Record extreme temperatures are 110°F (43°C) and 35°F (2°C).

N/HEMISPHERE	JAN	FEB	MAR	APR	MAY	JUN	JUL	AUG	SEP	OCT	NOV	DEC
°F AVG MAX	68	71	76	80	82	85	85	85	82	79	74	69
°F AVG MIN	49	50	55	60	64	67	69	68	66	61	56	51
DIURNAL RANGE	19	21	21	20	18	18	16	17	16	18	18	18
RAIN/INCHES	2.2	1.9	1.9	2.5	3.7	5.0	6.4	6.3	5.7	3.7	2.8	2.6
HUMIDITY/%	62	59	58	57	59	59	63	65	66	64	64	64
BLOOM SEASON	*	*	*	*	***							
DAYS CLR @ 10AM	17	20	18	11	12	9	5	4	9	14	18	16
DAYS CLR @ 4PM	15	16	15	12	14	12	8	5	8	10	14	14
RAIN/MM	56	48	48	64	94	127	163	160	145	94	71	66
°C AVG MAX	20.0	21.7	24.4	26.7	27.8	29.4	29.4	29.4	27.8	26.1	23.3	20.6
°C AVG MIN	9.4	10.0	12.8	15.6	17.8	19.4	20.6	20.0	18.9	16.1	13.3	10.6
DIURNAL RANGE	10.6	11.7	11.7	11.1	10.0	10.0	8.9	9.4	8.9	10.0	10.0	10.0
S/HEMISPHERE	JUL	AUG	SEP	OCT	NOV	DEC	JAN	FEB	MAR	APR	MAY	JUN

Cultural Recommendations

LIGHT: 2000–3000 fc. A shady, sheltered location with strong air movement is required. Summer shading is required most of the day. Plants are healthiest with bright, early morning light and filtered shade the rest of the day. In the habitat, more than half the days are clear each month except during the summer rainy season, when skies are clear approximately 30% of the time. Growers recommend using 40–50% shade cloth. High light is required to initiate blooms. Strong air movement should be provided at all times.

TEMPERATURES: Summer days average 85°F (29°C), and nights average 67–69°F (19–21°C), with a diurnal range of 16–18°F (9–10°C).

HUMIDITY: 60–65% year-round. However, humidity may be greater in the habitat, since plants are usually found overhanging water.

WATER: Rainfall is moderate in summer and autumn with drier winters. Cultivated plants should be kept moist during the growing season, but water should be gradually reduced in autumn.

FERTILIZER: ¼–½ recommended strength, applied weekly. A high-nitrogen fertilizer is beneficial from spring to midsummer, but a fertilizer high in phosphates should be used in late summer and autumn.

REST PERIOD: Winter days average 68–76°F (20–24°C), and nights average 49–55°F (9–13°C), with a diurnal range of 18–21°F (10–12°C). Growers recommend that winter lows be kept above 35°F (2°C). Rainfall is relatively low in winter. Cultivated plants should be allowed to become somewhat dry between waterings but should never dry out completely. Growers indicate that plants should be kept just barely moist in winter. Fertilizer should be reduced or eliminated until water is increased in spring. Plants from this habitat require distinct seasonal variation to be healthy. In the habitat, light is highest in winter.

GROWING MEDIA: Plants should be firmly mounted to cork or hardwood mounts to accommodate their pendulous growth habit. If plants cannot be mounted, hanging baskets or the smallest possible hanging pot should be used. Growers report that clay pots are preferable to plastic ones. Plants should be disturbed as little as possible. If plants must be remounted, it is best done immediately after flowering when roots are actively growing.

MISCELLANEOUS NOTES: The bloom season shown in the climate table is based on reports from the habitat. Cultivation reports show blooming every month with peak blooming in early spring. Growers indicate that plants grow quickly into specimen plants. Young actively growing plants are adaptable and easy to establish, but large, old plants may be difficult, as new roots grow very slowly.

Plant and Flower Information

PLANT SIZE AND TYPE: A 106 in. (270 cm) sympodial epiphyte.

PSEUDOBULB: 106 in. (270 cm) long. The stems, which are long, branching, and wiry, emerge from a creeping rhizome. The plants hang like a chandelier.

LEAVES: 1 at the tip of each branch, many per plant. The leaves are 4–24 in. (10–60 cm) long, terete, and pendulous.

INFLORESCENCE: 2 near the apex of each branch. Numerous inflorescences emerge from nodes at the leaf bases producing a cloud of flowers. Inflorescences are slender and branching.

FLOWERS: 4–16 per inflorescence. The spidery flowers are 1.6 in. (4 cm) across. The very slender sepals and petals may be creamy white or yellowish with a purple stain at the base. The backs of the sepals may have red or purple streaks. The purple to purple-brown lip is recurved and ruffled along the margin. Flower number, size, and shape are highly variable. The fragrant blossoms last about 3 weeks.

HYBRIDIZING NOTES: Chromosome count as *D. teretifolium* is 2n = 76 (ref. 152), as *D. teretifolium* R. Brown var. *fasciculatum* Rupp, 2n = 76 (ref. 243), 2n = 2x (ref. 504, 580), and 2n = 40 (ref. 151, 187). *D. teretifolium* hybridizes naturally with *D. rigidum* R. Brown forming *D. × foederatum* St. Cloud.

REFERENCES: 23, 24, 25, 67, 105, 151, 152, 179, 187, 190, 196, 210, 216, 240, 243, 254, 260, 262, 277, 304, 317, 325, 352, 371, 390, 421, 430, 445, 504, 527, 533, 541, 544, 570, 580.

PHOTOS/DRAWINGS: 182, 210, *240*, 254, 325, *304, 371, 390, 430, 533*.

Dendrobium teretifolium Lindley not Blanco or R. Brown.
See *D. striolatum* Rchb. f. not F. M. Bailey. REFERENCES: 67, 105, 216.

Dendrobium terminale Parish and Rchb. f.

AKA: *D. verlaquii* Constantin. Seidenfaden and Wood (ref. 455) indicate that *D. mannii* Ridley is sometimes incorrectly identified as *D. terminale*. In 1992 *Opera Botanica* #114, Seidenfaden includes *D. leonis* (Lindley) Rchb. f. var. *strictum* Finet as a synonym.

ORIGIN/HABITAT: Widespread. The habitat includes India, Burma, Malaya, peninsular Thailand, Vietnam near Dalat and Hue, and Yunnan Province of southwestern China. In India, plants are found from Darjeeling to near Jowai in Meghalaya at 1650–5250 ft. (500–1600 m).

CLIMATE: Station #42398, Baghdogra, India, Lat. 26.7°N, Long. 88.3°E, at 412 ft. (126 m). Temperatures are calculated for an elevation of 2000 ft. (610 m), resulting in probable extremes of 99°F (37°C) and 31°F (−1°C).

N/HEMISPHERE	JAN	FEB	MAR	APR	MAY	JUN	JUL	AUG	SEP	OCT	NOV	DEC
°F AVG MAX	69	72	80	85	85	84	84	84	83	82	77	72
°F AVG MIN	45	49	55	63	68	71	72	72	71	65	55	48
DIURNAL RANGE	24	23	25	22	17	13	12	12	12	17	22	24
RAIN/INCHES	0.3	0.7	1.3	3.7	11.8	25.9	32.2	25.3	21.2	5.6	0.5	0.2
HUMIDITY/%	73	68	57	58	74	84	86	85	85	79	75	76
BLOOM SEASON	*	*	*						*			
DAYS CLR @ 6AM	21	18	15	11	5	0	1	1	4	13	23	19
DAYS CLR @ 12PM	23	16	16	11	2	2	0	1	2	10	21	18
RAIN/MM	8	18	33	94	300	658	818	643	538	142	13	5
°C AVG MAX	20.4	22.1	26.5	29.3	29.3	28.8	28.8	28.8	28.2	27.6	24.9	22.1
°C AVG MIN	7.1	9.3	12.6	17.1	19.9	21.5	22.1	22.1	21.5	18.2	12.6	8.8
DIURNAL RANGE	13.3	12.8	13.9	12.2	9.4	7.3	6.7	6.7	6.7	9.4	12.3	13.3
S/HEMISPHERE	JUL	AUG	SEP	OCT	NOV	DEC	JAN	FEB	MAR	APR	MAY	JUN

Cultural Recommendations

LIGHT: 1800–2500 fc. Light is lowest in summer when clear days are rare.

TEMPERATURES: Summer days average 84°F (29°C), and nights average 71–72°F (22°C), with a diurnal range of 12–13°F (7°C).

HUMIDITY: Near 85% in summer. Humidity decreases to 75–80% in autumn, and to near 60% in late winter and early spring.

WATER: Conditions are very wet for 5 months in summer, very dry for 5 months in winter, with short transition periods in autumn and spring. Cultivated plants should be kept evenly moist from spring to early autumn, but water should be gradually reduced after new growths mature in late autumn.

FERTILIZER: ¼–½ recommended strength, applied weekly. A high-nitrogen fertilizer is beneficial from spring to midsummer, while a fertilizer high in phosphates should be used in late summer and autumn. Summer growth should be rapid to improve flowering the following year.

REST PERIOD: Winter days average 69–72°F (20–22°C), and nights average 45–49°F (7–9°C), with a diurnal range of 23–24°F (13°C). In the habitat, winter rainfall is low but additional moisture is often available from heavy deposits of dew. For about a month in late winter or early spring, however, humidity is so low that even the moisture from dew is uncommon. Cultivated plants should be allowed to dry out between waterings in winter, but they should not remain dry for extended periods. Occasional early morning mistings between waterings, especially on warm, sunny days, may help prevent the plants from becoming too dry. Fertilizer should be eliminated until water is increased in spring. In the habitat, light is highest in winter. The cool, dry rest with increased light may be necessary to initiate blooming.

GROWING MEDIA: Plants may be mounted on tree-fern or cork slabs if humidity is high and plants are watered at least once daily in summer. When plants are potted, any open, fast-draining medium may be used. They may be repotted anytime new roots are growing.

MISCELLANEOUS NOTES: The bloom season shown in the climate table is based on cultivation records. Reports from the habitat show autumn blooming.

Plant and Flower Information

PLANT SIZE AND TYPE: A 5–7 in. (13–18 cm) sympodial plant.

PSEUDOBULB: 4–6 in. (10–15 cm) long. The stems are covered by leaf sheaths.

LEAVES: Many. The triangular leaves are usually 0.8 in. (2 cm) long, succulent, and deciduous. They are arranged in 2 rows and form a narrow angle with the stem.

INFLORESCENCE: Short. Inflorescences arise near the apex of the stem before the leaves drop.

FLOWERS: 1–5 per inflorescence. The tubular blossoms are 0.4–0.8 in. (1.0–2.0 cm) long. They may be white or pale pink. The white or yellowish lip has purple markings and a yellow line along the center. It is triangular without sidelobes. The midlobe is deflexed with a notch at the center of the broader apex.

HYBRIDIZING NOTES: Chromosome counts are 2n = 38 (ref. 151, 187) and 2n = 40 (ref. 153, 273).

REFERENCES: 38, 46, 151, 153, 157, 179, 187, 202, 216, 254, 266, 273, 369, 376, 395, 402, 445, 448, 454, 455, 528.

PHOTOS/DRAWINGS: 46, *454*, 455.

Dendrobium ternatense J. J. Smith. See *D. macrophyllum* A. Richard. REFERENCES: 12, 83, 220, 254, 270, 271, 296, 373, 445, 483, 536. PHOTOS/DRAWINGS: *373*.

Dendrobium terrestre J. J. Smith

AKA: *D. magnificum* Schlechter, *D. terrestre* var. *sublobatum* J. J. Smith.

ORIGIN/HABITAT: New Guinea and New Britain Island. In Irian Jaya (western New Guinea) plants grow on Mt. Goliath and the Arfak Range at about 3950 ft. (1200 m). In Papua New Guinea, they are found in numerous high altitude locations in mountain forests at 4900–8550 ft. (1500–2600 m).

CLIMATE: Botanical garden records, Laiagam, Papua New Guinea, Lat. 5.5°S, Long. 143.5°E, at 7218 ft. (2200 m). Record extreme temperatures are 91°F (33°C) and 32°F (0°C).

N/HEMISPHERE	JAN	FEB	MAR	APR	MAY	JUN	JUL	AUG	SEP	OCT	NOV	DEC
°F AVG MAX	76	77	78	76	78	78	82	77	76	78	78	76
°F AVG MIN	55	54	55	55	56	56	55	56	58	57	56	56
DIURNAL RANGE	21	23	23	21	22	22	27	21	18	21	22	20
RAIN/INCHES	4.0	4.8	6.1	7.8	8.5	9.1	8.4	9.6	9.5	8.9	6.3	4.0
HUMIDITY/%	N/A											
BLOOM SEASON					*				*			
DAYS CLR	N/A											
RAIN/MM	102	121	154	198	217	230	213	243	241	227	159	102
°C AVG MAX	24.4	25.0	25.6	24.4	25.6	25.6	27.8	25.0	24.4	25.6	25.6	24.4
°C AVG MIN	12.8	12.2	12.8	12.8	13.3	13.3	12.8	13.3	14.4	13.9	13.3	13.3
DIURNAL RANGE	11.6	12.8	12.8	11.6	12.3	12.3	15.0	11.7	10.0	11.7	12.3	11.1
S/HEMISPHERE	JUL	AUG	SEP	OCT	NOV	DEC	JAN	FEB	MAR	APR	MAY	JUN

Cultural Recommendations

LIGHT: 2000–3000 fc.

TEMPERATURES: Throughout the year, days average 76–82°F (24–28°C), and nights average 54–58°F (12–14°C), with a diurnal range of 18–27°F (10–15°C). The table represents only the mid portions of the habitat, and plants should easily adapt to conditions that are 5–7°F (3–4°C) warmer or cooler than indicated.

HUMIDITY: Information is not available for this location. However, records from nearby locations indicate that humidity probably averages 70–80% year-round.

WATER: Rainfall is moderate to heavy throughout the year, but conditions are driest for 3–4 months in winter. Cultivated plants should be kept evenly moist.

FERTILIZER: ¼–½ recommended strength. A balanced fertilizer should be applied weekly to biweekly throughout the year.

REST PERIOD: Growing conditions should be maintained year-round. Water and fertilizer should be reduced somewhat in winter, especially for plants grown in the dark, short-day conditions common in temperate latitudes. They should never be allowed to dry out completely, however. In the habitat, light is highest in winter.

GROWING MEDIA: Plants may be mounted on tree-fern or cork slabs or potted in any open, fast-draining medium. Repotting may be done anytime new roots are growing.

MISCELLANEOUS NOTES: The bloom season shown in the climate table is based on reports from the habitat. Cultivation records show blooming in summer and winter.

Plant and Flower Information

PLANT SIZE AND TYPE: A 24–39 in. (60–100 cm) sympodial terrestrial that is occasionally epiphytic. Plants are difficult to differentiate from *D. rigidifolium* Rolfe unless they are in bloom.

PSEUDOBULB: 20–35 in. (50–90 cm) long. The stems have 9–11 nodes below the leaves.

LEAVES: 3–7 per growth. The oval leaves are 3.1–4.3 in. (8–11 cm) long with 2 teeth at the apex.

INFLORESCENCE: 4–8 in. (10–20 cm) long. Inflorescences arise at or near the apex of the pseudobulb. They are erect and laxly flowered.

FLOWERS: 5–20 per inflorescence. The flowers are 1.0–2.4 in. (2.5–6.0 cm) across. The keeled, pointed sepals and petals are creamy white with red-purple spots on the outer surface, but they turn ochre-yellow to orange-yellow with age. Longitudinal brown stripes and red veins decorate the orange to yellow-green lip. The erect, 3-lobed lip is pointed at the tip. The sidelobes are uneven along the front margin. The column is flushed with violet at the base. In a rare use of superlatives, Schlechter described the blossoms as having the loveliest coloring of any *Dendrobium* in New Guinea. Flower size and color are highly variable.

HYBRIDIZING NOTES: Chromosome count is 2n = 36 (ref. 152, 243).

REFERENCES: 83, 95, 96, 152, 179, 221, 236, 243, 437, 445, 470, 486.

PHOTOS/DRAWINGS: 83, 437.

Dendrobium testiculatum Swartz.

Now considered a synonym of *Ionopsis testiculata* Lindley. REFERENCES: 190, 216, 254.

Dendrobium tetrachromum Rchb. f.

ORIGIN/HABITAT: Borneo. Plants are found in Sabah and Kalimantan. They have been collected along the Kinateki River at about 1650 ft. (500 m).

CLIMATE: Station #49613, Tambunan, Sabah, Borneo, Lat. 5.7°N, Long. 116.4°E, at 1200 ft. (366 m). Temperatures are calculated for an elevation of 1650 ft. (500 m), resulting in probable extremes of 97°F (36°C) and 53°F (11°C).

N/HEMISPHERE	JAN	FEB	MAR	APR	MAY	JUN	JUL	AUG	SEP	OCT	NOV	DEC
°F AVG MAX	85	86	88	89	89	88	88	88	88	87	86	85
°F AVG MIN	66	64	65	66	67	66	65	65	66	66	66	67
DIURNAL RANGE	19	22	23	23	22	22	23	23	22	21	20	18
RAIN/INCHES	5.8	3.7	5.8	7.5	8.2	7.3	5.1	4.9	6.4	7.0	6.8	6.0
HUMIDITY/%	N/A											
BLOOM SEASON	N/A											
DAYS CLR	N/A											
RAIN/MM	147	94	147	191	208	185	130	124	163	178	173	152
°C AVG MAX	29.4	30.0	31.1	31.7	31.7	31.3	31.2	31.1	31.1	30.6	30.0	29.4
°C AVG MIN	18.9	17.5	18.1	18.6	19.2	18.6	18.1	18.1	18.6	18.6	18.6	19.2
DIURNAL RANGE	10.5	12.5	13.0	13.1	12.5	12.7	13.1	13.0	12.5	12.0	11.4	10.2
S/HEMISPHERE	JUL	AUG	SEP	OCT	NOV	DEC	JAN	FEB	MAR	APR	MAY	JUN

Cultural Recommendations

LIGHT: 2000–3000 fc.

TEMPERATURES: Throughout the year, days average 85–89°F (29–32°C), and nights average 64–67°F (18–19°C), with a diurnal range of 18–23°F (10–13°C).

HUMIDITY: Information is not available for this location. However, records from nearby locations indicate that humidity is probably 80–85% year-round.

WATER: Rainfall is moderate to heavy all year with a brief, slightly drier period in winter. Cultivated plants should be allowed to dry slightly between waterings.

FERTILIZER: ¼–½ recommended strength. A balanced fertilizer should be applied weekly to biweekly throughout the year.

REST PERIOD: Growing conditions should be maintained all year. Water should be reduced slightly in winter, but plants should never be allowed to dry out completely. Fertilizer should be reduced anytime plants are not actively growing. In the habitat, seasonal light variation is minor.

GROWING MEDIA: Plants may be mounted on tree-fern or cork slabs if humidity is high and plants are watered at least once daily in summer. When plants are potted, any open, fast-draining medium may be used. Repotting is best done in early spring when new roots begin to grow.

Plant and Flower Information

PLANT SIZE AND TYPE: A 12 in. (30 cm) sympodial epiphyte.

PSEUDOBULB: 8 in. (20 cm) long. The stems are long and thin with numerous joints. The apex of the stem is leafy.

LEAVES: 3 in. (8 cm) long. The relatively long, pointed leaves are deciduous and somewhat twisted at the base.

INFLORESCENCE: 0.7 in. (1.7 cm) long. The short inflorescences emerge from the upper nodes of leafy or leafless stems.

FLOWERS: 1–2 per inflorescence. The flowers are about 1.6 in. (4 cm) across. The white sepals and petals are pointed. The white, 3-lobed lip is marked with yellow to deep orange. The lip is uneven and wavy along the margin with incurved sidelobes and upcurved sides on the midlobe. The spur is greenish on the back.

REFERENCES: 216, 254, 286, 295, 592.

PHOTOS/DRAWINGS: 592.

Dendrobium tetraedre (Blume) Lindley

AKA: *Onychium tetraedre* Blume, *Dendrobium strigosum* Schlechter.

ORIGIN/HABITAT: Borneo, Java, and Sumatra. In Sumatra, plants grow on forest trees on Mt. Djarat near Pandangpandjang, a small town north of Padang, at about 3950 ft. (1200 m). Plants are common throughout Java in moist, rather dark forests at 1650–5900 ft. (500–1800 m).

CLIMATE: Station #96163, Padang, Sumatra, Indonesia, Lat. 0.9°S, Long. 100.4°E, at 19 ft. (6 m). Temperatures are calculated for an elevation of 3950 ft. (1200 m), resulting in probable extremes of 81°F (27°C) and 55°F (13°C).

N/HEMISPHERE	JAN	FEB	MAR	APR	MAY	JUN	JUL	AUG	SEP	OCT	NOV	DEC
°F AVG MAX	74	74	73	73	73	73	74	74	74	74	75	74
°F AVG MIN	61	61	61	61	61	61	61	61	61	62	62	61
DIURNAL RANGE	13	13	12	12	12	12	13	13	13	12	13	13
RAIN/INCHES	10.9	13.7	6.0	19.5	20.4	18.9	13.8	10.2	12.1	14.3	12.4	12.1
HUMIDITY/%	81	82	82	84	85	84	81	81	82	83	81	81
BLOOM SEASON		*										
DAYS CLR @ 7AM	5	1	1	0	0	2	2	1	2	2	3	5
DAYS CLR @ 1PM	5	2	2	1	1	3	3	4	3	3	6	5
RAIN/MM	277	348	152	495	518	480	351	259	307	363	315	307
°C AVG MAX	23.3	23.3	22.8	22.8	22.8	22.8	23.3	23.3	23.3	23.3	23.9	23.3
°C AVG MIN	16.1	16.1	16.1	16.1	16.1	16.1	16.1	16.1	16.1	16.7	16.7	16.1
DIURNAL RANGE	7.2	7.2	6.7	6.7	6.7	6.7	7.2	7.2	7.2	6.6	7.2	7.2
S/HEMISPHERE	JUL	AUG	SEP	OCT	NOV	DEC	JAN	FEB	MAR	APR	MAY	JUN

Cultural Recommendations

LIGHT: 1500–2000 fc. Diffused light is recommended.

TEMPERATURES: Throughout the year, days average 73–75°F (23–24°C), and nights average 61–62°F (16–17°C), with a diurnal range of 12–13°F (7°C). Because plants are found over such a wide range of elevations, they are not extremely temperature sensitive and should adapt to conditions that are 6–8°F (3–4°C) warmer or cooler than indicated.

HUMIDITY: 80–85% year-round.

WATER: Rainfall is heavy all year. Cultivated plants should be kept moist but not soggy.

FERTILIZER: ¼–½ recommended strength. A balanced fertilizer should be applied weekly to biweekly throughout the year.

REST PERIOD: Growing conditions should be maintained year-round. Water may be reduced somewhat for cultivated plants in winter, especially those grown in the dark, short-day conditions common in temperate latitudes. They should never be allowed to dry out completely, however.

GROWING MEDIA: Plants may be mounted on tree-fern or cork slabs if humidity is high and plants are watered at least once daily in summer. When plants are potted, any open, fast-draining medium may be used. Repotting may be done anytime new roots are growing.

MISCELLANEOUS NOTES: The bloom season shown in the climate table is based on reports from the habitat. The nearly round fruit is shiny green.

Plant and Flower Information

PLANT SIZE AND TYPE: An 8–12 in. (20–30 cm) sympodial epiphyte.

PSEUDOBULB: 8–12 in. (20–30 cm) long. The stems, which arise from a short rhizome, are erect, slender, and clustered. Part of the stem is leafy. A ribbed thickening at the base is about 1.2 in. (3 cm) long.

LEAVES: Many. The linear leaves are 0.6–1.4 in. (1.5–3.6 cm) long with unequal teeth at the apex. They may be erect or spreading.

INFLORESCENCE: Short. Inflorescences are borne at or near the apex of leafy stems. The pedicels are bright red.

FLOWERS: Few per inflorescence. Blossoms develop in succession. The tiny flowers are 0.3 in. (0.8 cm) long and do not open fully. They have pink sepals and white petals. The toothed lip has a pale yellow band in the center. It is hairy on the front, the characteristic that separates *D. tetraedre* from other closely related species.

REFERENCES: 25, 75, 216, 254, 310, 435, 445, 448, 469.

PHOTOS/DRAWINGS: 75, 469

Dendrobium tetragonum A. Cunningham

AKA: *D. tetragonum* var. *hayesianum* P. A. Gilbert, *D. tetragonum* var. *variabilis* P. A. Gilbert. *D. tetragonum* is considered by many to be a variable species for which all of the following names are synonyms. See also *D. cacatua* M. Clements and D. Jones and *D. capitisyork* M. Clements and D. Jones.

Clements (ref. 67), however, divides the *D. tetragonum* alliance into several species, based partially on different habitats. He distributes the synonyms as follows:

D. tetragonum var. *giganteum* Leaney. Clements considers it a synonym of *D. cacatua* M. Clements and D. Jones.

D. tetragonum var. *giganteum* P. A. Gilbert. Clements maintains that part of the original description belonged to *D. cacatua* M. Clements and D. Jones and part should be applied to *D. capitisyork* M. Clements and D. Jones.

D. tetragonum var. *hayesianum* as used by Dockrill not P. A. Gilbert. Clements considers it a synonym of *D. cacatua* M. Clements and D. Jones. It was previously considered a color form of the type variety which appeared as individual plants in normal colonies.

D. tetragonum var. *tomentosum* Nicholls. Clements considers it a synonym of *D. capitisyork* M. Clements and D. Jones.

ORIGIN/HABITAT: Southeastern Australia. The habitat extends from south of Sydney northward to near Brisbane. Usually found near the coast, the orchids sometimes grow on the lower eastern slopes of the Dividing Range, as much as 60 mi. (100 km) inland. Plants are occasionally found as high as 3300 ft. (1000 m), but they most often grow at much lower elevations. In the northern (warmer) part of the habitat, however, plants seldom grow above 1650 ft. (500 m). They are most often found in moist, very shady areas with continuous air movement, such as ravines and gullies. They also grow on rainforest trees near swamps and along mountain creeks.

CLIMATE: Station #94791, Coffs Harbour, Australia, Lat. 30.3°S, Long. 153.1°E, at 14 ft. (4 m). Temperatures are calculated for an elevation of 1000 ft. (300 m), resulting in probable extremes of 102°F (39°C) and 27°F (−3°C).

N/HEMISPHERE	JAN	FEB	MAR	APR	MAY	JUN	JUL	AUG	SEP	OCT	NOV	DEC
°F AVG MAX	62	64	68	71	76	77	77	77	76	74	68	65
°F AVG MIN	41	42	47	52	56	60	62	63	61	56	47	42
DIURNAL RANGE	21	22	21	19	20	17	15	14	15	18	21	23
RAIN/INCHES	3.8	2.1	2.9	3.8	4.0	5.8	6.9	7.7	8.7	7.7	5.7	4.5
HUMIDITY/%	74	72	70	74	72	76	79	83	79	78	75	74
BLOOM SEASON	**	**	**	**	*	*	*	*				*
DAYS CLR @ 4AM	8	9	10	10	12	11	9	8	10	7	11	8
DAYS CLR @ 10AM	16	18	18	12	15	11	8	5	10	10	14	15
RAIN/MM	97	53	74	97	102	147	175	196	221	196	145	114
°C AVG MAX	16.5	17.6	19.9	21.5	24.3	24.9	24.9	24.9	24.3	23.2	19.9	18.2
°C AVG MIN	4.9	5.4	8.2	11.0	13.2	15.4	16.5	17.1	16.0	13.2	8.2	5.4
DIURNAL RANGE	11.6	12.2	11.7	10.5	11.1	9.5	8.4	7.8	8.3	10.0	11.7	12.8
S/HEMISPHERE	JUL	AUG	SEP	OCT	NOV	DEC	JAN	FEB	MAR	APR	MAY	JUN

Cultural Recommendations

LIGHT: 1500–3000 fc. Australian growers suggest about 60% shade and strong air movement. Some growers recommend low light and indicate that plants burn easily, but others feel that the plants grow and bloom better with bright light.

TEMPERATURES: Summer days average 77°F (25°C), and nights average 60–63°F (15–17°C), with a diurnal range of 14–17°F (8–10°C).

HUMIDITY: 75–80% most of the year, dropping to near 70% in winter. Values in the rainforest, swamp, or stream-side habitat may be greater than the averages at the weather station, however.

WATER: Rainfall is moderate to heavy most of the year, but conditions are somewhat drier for 2–3 months in winter. Cultivated plants should be kept moist and never allowed to dry out completely.

FERTILIZER: ¼–½ recommended strength, applied weekly. A high-nitrogen fertilizer is beneficial from spring to midsummer, but a fertilizer high in phosphates should be used in late summer and autumn.

REST PERIOD: Winter days average 62–68°F (17–20°C), and nights average 41–47°F (5–8°C), with a diurnal range of 21–23°F (12–13°C). Growers recommend that winter lows should be kept above 35°F (2°C). Cultivated plants should be allowed to dry slightly between waterings, but they should remain dry only briefly. Some growers indicate that intermediate temperatures are adequate year-round but recommend eliminating water in winter. Others suggest that cool temperatures are required and that water should be reduced, allowing plants to dry between mistings. Still others recommend summer growing temperatures with heavy watering all year. The warmer climatic conditions preferred by plants known as *D. tetragonum* var. *giganteum* are provided under the name *D. cacatua*. Fertilizer should be reduced or eliminated anytime water is reduced. In the habitat, light is highest in winter.

GROWING MEDIA: Mounting plants on hardwood or cork accommodates their pendent growth habit. Growers indicate that it is easy to rot the roots when plants are mounted on tree fern because the material holds so much water. Plants should be allowed to dry slightly between waterings. Remounting is best done when new roots are actively growing, but growers report that plants suffer tremendous setback when disturbed.

MISCELLANEOUS NOTES: The bloom season shown in the climate table is based on cultivation reports. Considered difficult to cultivate by some, growers indicate that it is easy, providing the plant is given a drier rest. Growers also indicate that the small forms of *D. tetragonum* are adaptable, but the larger forms are not.

Plant and Flower Information

PLANT SIZE AND TYPE: A 2–20 in. (5–50 cm) sympodial epiphyte.

PSEUDOBULB: 2–4 in. (5–10 cm) long. Stems are normally quite small, but they may reach a length of 20 in. (50 cm). They are slender and wiry from the base to the middle with a swollen 4-angled section at the top. The stems are usually pendulous, but some forms from Queensland are surprisingly erect.

LEAVES: 2–5 per growth. The oblong to ovate leaves are thin, leathery, and 1.2–4.0 in. (3–10 cm) long. They are glossy and dark green, wavy along the margin, curved, curled, and often twisted. The leaves persist for more than a single season.

INFLORESCENCE: Short. Inflorescences are borne between the leaves near the apex of the pseudobulb.

FLOWERS: 1–9 per inflorescence. The spidery flowers may be as small as 1.6 in. (4 cm) long, but they are normally larger and may exceed a length of 4.8 in. (12 cm). Sepals are yellow-green with a red, brown, or purplish edge of variable width. The smaller petals are pale yellow-green and very slender. All segments taper to a long, pointed tip. The lip may be white or pale yellow with reddish markings, and the apex is pointed and sharply recurved. Individual flowers last 10–20 days, but new blossoms may continue to develop for several months. Blossoms have a pronounced vanilla fragrance.

HYBRIDIZING NOTES: Chromosome count is 2n = 38 as *D. tetragonum* var. *giganteum* (ref. 151, 153, 187, 273). Plants are commonly self-sterile. Pollen from the same plant rarely produces seed, but fruits are regularly produced when pollen from another plant is used. When used as a parent, *D. tetragonum* is dominant in shape, size, and flower color. It is widely used in Australian hybrids.

REFERENCES: 23, 24, 25, 36, 67, 105, 151, 153, 179, 187, 190, 210, 216, 240, 254, 260, 262, 273, 309, 313, 317, 325, 330, 352, 371, 390, 421, 430, 445, 495, 527, 533, 534, 541, 544, 564.

PHOTOS/DRAWINGS: 24, *36*, 105, 210, *240*, 313, 325, *371*, *390*, *430*, *533*, *534*, *535*, *544*, *564*.

Dendrobium tetralobum Schlechter

ORIGIN/HABITAT: Borneo. Plants were originally found near Samarinda, just north of Balikpapan in eastern Kalimantan (Koetei). Habitat elevation is unreported, so the following climate data should be used with caution.

CLIMATE: Station #96633, Balikpapan, Borneo, Lat. 1.3°S, Long. 116.9°E, at 10 ft. (3 m). Record extreme temperatures are 92°F (33°C) and 60°F (16°C).

N/HEMISPHERE	JAN	FEB	MAR	APR	MAY	JUN	JUL	AUG	SEP	OCT	NOV	DEC
°F AVG MAX	83	84	84	85	85	85	85	86	86	85	85	84
°F AVG MIN	73	74	74	74	73	73	73	73	73	73	74	74
DIURNAL RANGE	10	10	10	11	12	12	12	13	13	12	11	10
RAIN/INCHES	7.1	6.4	5.5	5.2	6.6	8.1	7.9	8.9	9.1	8.2	9.1	7.6
HUMIDITY/%	82	80	77	78	80	79	82	81	81	82	83	82
BLOOM SEASON	*											
DAYS CLR @ 8AM	4	2	3	3	3	2	3	2	4	4	2	5
DAYS CLR @ 2PM	6	4	5	5	3	1	2	1	2	3	4	5
RAIN/MM	180	163	140	132	168	206	201	226	231	208	231	193
°C AVG MAX	28.3	28.9	28.9	29.4	29.4	29.4	29.4	30.0	30.0	29.4	29.4	28.9
°C AVG MIN	22.8	23.3	23.3	23.3	22.8	22.8	22.8	22.8	22.8	22.8	23.3	23.3
DIURNAL RANGE	5.5	5.6	5.6	6.1	6.6	6.6	6.6	7.2	7.2	6.6	6.1	5.6
S/HEMISPHERE	JUL	AUG	SEP	OCT	NOV	DEC	JAN	FEB	MAR	APR	MAY	JUN

Cultural Recommendations

LIGHT: 2000–3000 fc.

TEMPERATURES: Throughout the year, days average 83–86°F (28–30°C), and nights average 73–74°F (23°C), with a diurnal range of 10–13°F (6–7°C).

HUMIDITY: Near 80% year-round.

WATER: Rainfall is heavy all year. Cultivated plants should be kept moist.

FERTILIZER: ¼–½ recommended strength. A balanced fertilizer should be applied weekly to biweekly throughout the year.

REST PERIOD: Growing conditions should be maintained year-round. Water and fertilizer should be reduced somewhat in winter, especially for plants cultivated in the dark, short-day conditions common in temperate latitudes. Plants should never be allowed to dry out completely, however. In the habitat, seasonal light variation is minor.

GROWING MEDIA: Mounting plants on tree-fern or cork slabs accommodates their often pendulous growth habit. However, humidity must be high and plants must be watered at least once a day in summer. If plants cannot be mounted, hanging pots or baskets may be filled with an open, fast-draining medium. Repotting may be done anytime new roots are actively growing.

MISCELLANEOUS NOTES: The bloom season shown in the climate table is based on reports from the habitat.

Plant and Flower Information

PLANT SIZE AND TYPE: A 40 in. (102 cm) sympodial epiphyte.

PSEUDOBULB: 40 in. (102 cm) long. The flattened, densely leafy stems are arching to pendent and arise from a short rhizome. They are leafless at the apex and rarely branch.

LEAVES: Many. The ovate-lanceolate leaves are 1 in. (2.5 cm) long.

INFLORESCENCE: Inflorescences emerge at leaf axils. The blossoms are arranged in 2 rows.

FLOWERS: Many per inflorescence. The tiny flowers are 0.1 in. (0.3 cm) long, which may be the smallest in the genera. Sepals are ovate-oblong. The smooth petals are linear-tongue-shaped. The lip was described as 4-lobed with an oblong-quadrate callus.

REFERENCES: 220, 254, 286, 295, 433.

Dendrobium tetrodon Rchb. f. ex Lindley

AKA: Clements (ref. 67) and Seidenfaden and Wood (ref. 455) indicate that plants from Malaya and Indonesia that are commonly known as *D. tetrodon* are actually *D. stuartii* F. M. Bailey. Clements states that the plants called *D. tetrodon* from Java represent yet another species closely allied to *D. aphyllum* (Roxburgh) C. Fischer. However, in a 1994 personal communication, Seidenfaden expressed reservations regarding these conclusions. He recommended that *D. tetrodon* be included.

ORIGIN/HABITAT: Southern Thailand to Java. In Malaya, plants grow on orchard trees in fairly open lowlands near Taiping and Ipoh. In Thailand, they are found on islands off the southwest coast. In Sumatra, plants occur near Padang and Palembang. In Java, they are found on Salak Volcano southwest of Bogor. *D. tetrodon* var. *vanvuurenii* J. J. Smith was collected on Sulawesi (Celebes).

CLIMATE: Station #48625, Ipoh, Malaya, Lat. 4.6°N, Long. 101.1°E, at 123 ft. (37 m). Record extreme temperatures are 99°F (37°C) and 64°F (18°C).

N/HEMISPHERE	JAN	FEB	MAR	APR	MAY	JUN	JUL	AUG	SEP	OCT	NOV	DEC
°F AVG MAX	90	92	93	92	92	92	91	91	90	89	89	89
°F AVG MIN	72	72	73	73	74	73	72	72	73	72	72	72
DIURNAL RANGE	18	20	20	19	18	19	19	19	17	17	17	17
RAIN/INCHES	7.9	3.1	7.6	8.4	6.2	3.6	7.2	6.9	8.8	11.0	13.0	8.9
HUMIDITY/%	76	74	76	78	78	75	76	77	79	82	82	81
BLOOM SEASON					*							
DAYS CLR @ 7AM	3	3	3	1	1	2	1	1	0	0	1	2
DAYS CLR @ 1PM	2	2	2	1	1	1	1	1	0	0	0	2
RAIN/MM	201	79	193	213	157	91	183	175	224	279	330	226
°C AVG MAX	32.2	33.3	33.9	33.3	33.3	33.3	32.8	32.8	32.2	31.7	31.7	31.7
°C AVG MIN	22.2	22.2	22.8	22.8	23.3	22.8	22.2	22.2	22.8	22.2	22.2	22.2
DIURNAL RANGE	10.0	11.1	11.1	10.5	10.0	10.5	10.6	10.6	9.4	9.5	9.5	9.5
S/HEMISPHERE	JUL	AUG	SEP	OCT	NOV	DEC	JAN	FEB	MAR	APR	MAY	JUN

Cultural Recommendations

LIGHT: 2000–3000 fc.

TEMPERATURES: Throughout the year, days average 89–93°F (32–34°C), and nights average 72–74°F (22–23°C), with a diurnal range of 17–20°F (9–11°C). Average highs fluctuate only 4°F (2°C) all year, and average lows vary only 2°F (1°C).

HUMIDITY: 75–80% year-round.

WATER: Rainfall is heavy most of the year. The heaviest rainfall occurs in autumn, with a secondary maximum in spring. Brief semidry periods occur in midwinter and midsummer. Cultivated plants should be kept evenly moist with only slight drying allowed between waterings.

FERTILIZER: ¼–½ recommended strength. A balanced fertilizer should be applied weekly to biweekly throughout the year.

REST PERIOD: Growing conditions should be maintained year-round. Water should be reduced somewhat in winter for plants cultivated in the dark, short-day conditions common in temperate latitudes. They should never be allowed to dry out completely, however. Fertilizer may be reduced when the plant is not actively growing or when water is reduced. In the habitat, light is slightly higher in winter.

GROWING MEDIA: Plants may be mounted on tree-fern or cork slabs if humidity is high and plants are watered at least once daily in summer. When plants are potted, any open, fast-draining medium may be used. Repotting may be done anytime new roots are growing.

MISCELLANEOUS NOTES: The bloom season shown in the climate table is based on reports from the habitat. Ridley (ref. 402) indicated that his specimens were always self-pollinating.

Plant and Flower Information

PLANT SIZE AND TYPE: A 12 in. (31 cm) sympodial epiphyte.

PSEUDOBULB: 12 in. (31 cm) long. The stems are thin and pendulous.

LEAVES: Many. The thin, lanceolate leaves are 2–3 in. (5–7 cm) long. They are deciduous.

INFLORESCENCE: 4–5 in. (10–13 cm) long. The thin inflorescences emerge from nodes on leafless stems shortly after the leaves drop.

FLOWERS: 2–3 per inflorescence, many per stem. Flowers are numerous on leafless stems. The light yellowish green sepals and petals are lanceolate and measure 0.8 in. (2 cm) across. The yellow lip has red to purple veins, and the apical part is hairy on the inside. All margins are ciliate, and the margins of the sidelobes curve inwards at the base, often meeting above the column. Normal flowers open fully. Comber (ref. 75) indicates that some Java plants are cleistogamous, with self-pollinating flowers that never open, while other plants have greenish white peloric flowers with a lip that is shaped like the sepals and petals. The peloric flowers are not self-pollinating.

HYBRIDIZING NOTES: Johansen (ref. 229) indicates that "the number of days to capsule maturity could not be determined exactly because of spontaneous self-pollination." 93% of the seed produced contained visible embryos and 98% germinated.

REFERENCES: 25, 67, 75, 200, 216, 239, 254, 278, 310, 402, 436, 445, 454, 455, 467, 469.

PHOTOS/DRAWINGS: 75, 454, 469.

Dendrobium textile J. J. Smith. Now considered a synonym of *Diplocaulobium textile* (J. J. Smith) Hunt and Summerhayes. REFERENCES: 213, 225, 230.

Dendrobium teysmanni Miquel. A misspelling for *D. teijsmannii*, which is considered a synonym of *D. lobbii* Teijsm and Binn. REFERENCES: 216.

Dendrobium theionanthum Schlechter. See *D. masarangense* Schlechter. REFERENCES: 94, 179, 221, 235, 305, 330, 385, 437, 445, 538. PHOTOS/DRAWINGS: 94, 538.

Dendrobium theionochilum Schlechter. Upper Burma. No additional habitat information is available, so climate data cannot be selected. The plant was imported to Germany, where it bloomed in late

winter or early spring. It was a 12 in. (30 cm) sympodial epiphyte. The short inflorescences carried 2 blossoms and emerged laterally from leafless stems. The flowers, which were 2.8 in. (7 cm) across, were described as similar to *D. pierardii* Roxburgh [now *D. aphyllum* (Roxburgh) C. Fischer]. REFERENCES: 223.

Dendrobium thyrsiflorum Rchb. f.

AKA: Sometimes spelled *D. thrysiflorum*. Synonyms include *D. densiflorum* var. *albolutea* Hooker f. and *D. galliceanum* Linden. The name *D. densiflorum* is sometimes erroneously applied to plants that should be labeled *D. thyrsiflorum*. *D. thyrsiflorum* is often included as a synonym of *D. densiflorum* Lindley, but Seidenfaden (ref. 454) lists it as a separate species. The International Orchid Commission (ref. 236) lists *D. thyrsiflorum* Rchb. f. as a synonym of *D. densiflorum* Lindley but registers hybrids under *D. thyrsiflorum*.

ORIGIN/HABITAT: Widespread in southeast Asia from India to Vietnam. In India, plants grow in Nagaland, Manipur, and Sikkim, where they are found near Darjeeling at about 6550 ft. (2000 m). In Burma, plants have been collected in the northern Tenasserim Range, near Lake Inle, and near Bhamo. In northern and eastern Thailand, plants grow in semi-shaded areas at about 4000 ft. (1220 m). *D. thyrsiflorum* var. *parviflora* Rchb. f. was collected at 5000 ft. (1520 m) in Yunnan Province, southwestern China.

CLIMATE: Station #48327, Chiang Mai, Thailand, Lat. 18.8°N, Long. 99.0°E, at 1100 ft. (335 m). Temperatures are calculated for an elevation of 4000 ft. (1220 m), resulting in probable extremes of 99°F (38°C) and 28°F (−2°C).

N/HEMISPHERE	JAN	FEB	MAR	APR	MAY	JUN	JUL	AUG	SEP	OCT	NOV	DEC
°F AVG MAX	75	80	85	86	84	80	79	77	78	79	76	74
°F AVG MIN	46	47	52	60	64	64	64	65	63	61	56	47
DIURNAL RANGE	29	33	33	26	20	16	15	12	15	18	20	27
RAIN/INCHES	0.3	0.4	0.6	2.0	5.5	6.1	7.4	8.7	11.5	4.9	1.5	0.4
HUMIDITY/%	73	65	58	62	73	78	80	83	83	81	79	76
BLOOM SEASON	*	*	**	**	***	**	*	*	*	*		
DAYS CLR @ 7AM	5	5	2	2	1	0	0	0	0	1	3	3
DAYS CLR @ 1PM	9	8	4	2	0	0	0	0	0	0	1	3
RAIN/MM	8	10	15	51	140	155	188	221	292	124	38	10
°C AVG MAX	24.1	26.9	29.7	30.2	29.1	26.9	26.4	25.2	25.8	26.4	24.7	23.6
°C AVG MIN	8.0	8.6	11.3	15.8	18.0	18.0	18.0	18.6	17.5	16.4	13.0	8.0
DIURNAL RANGE	16.1	18.3	18.4	14.4	11.1	8.9	8.4	6.6	8.3	10.0	11.1	15.0
S/HEMISPHERE	JUL	AUG	SEP	OCT	NOV	DEC	JAN	FEB	MAR	APR	MAY	JUN

Cultural Recommendations

LIGHT: 2000–3500 fc. Diffused light is appropriate as clear summer days are exceedingly rare. Light should be bright, but direct sunlight should be avoided. Air movement should be excellent.

TEMPERATURES: Summer days average 77–80°F (25–27°C), and nights average 64–65°F (18–19°C), with a diurnal range of 12–16°F (7–9°C). The warmest weather occurs in spring. Days average 84–86°F (29–30°C), and nights average 52–64°F (11–18°C), with a diurnal range of 20–33°F (11–18°C). Both highs and lows are more moderate after the start of the summer wet season. Low night temperatures or wide diurnal range may be necessary to initiate blooming.

HUMIDITY: 75–85% during most of the year, dropping to near 60% for 2 months in late winter and early spring.

WATER: Rainfall is moderate to heavy from late spring through early autumn, but conditions are much drier in winter. Cultivated plants should be kept moist while actively growing, but water should be gradually reduced after new growths mature in autumn.

FERTILIZER: ¼–½ recommended strength, applied weekly. A high-nitrogen fertilizer is beneficial from spring to midsummer, but a fertilizer high in phosphates should be used in late summer and autumn. Some growers report good success alternating applications of fish emulsion with their regular fertilizer.

REST PERIOD: Winter days average 74–80°F (24–27°C), and nights average 46–47°F (8–9°C), with a diurnal range of 27–33°F (15–18°C). Overnight lows are below 50°F (10°C) for 3 months. Some growers recommend winter minimum temperatures of 41°F (5°C). Plants should be able to tolerate temperatures a few degrees below freezing for short periods, but extremes should be avoided in cultivation. During very cold weather, a plant's chance of surviving with minimal damage is better if it is dry when temperatures are low. In the habitat, rainfall averages are very low for 4–5 months in winter, but during the early part of the season the high relative humidity indicates that additional moisture is available from frequent fog, mist, and heavy deposits of dew. Growers sometimes recommend eliminating water in winter, but plants are healthiest if for most of the winter they are allowed to become somewhat dry between waterings but do not remain dry for extended periods. For 1–2 months in late winter, however, conditions are clear, warm, and dry, with humidity so low that even the moisture from morning dew is uncommon. Plants should be allowed to dry out completely between waterings and remain dry longer during this time. Occasional early morning mistings between waterings may help keep the plants from becoming too dry. Fertilizer should be greatly reduced or eliminated until water is increased in spring. A cool, dry rest is essential for cultivated plants and should be continued until new growth starts in spring. In the habitat, light is highest in winter.

GROWING MEDIA: Plants may be mounted on tree-fern or cork slabs if humidity is high and plants are watered at least once daily in summer. When plants are potted, any open, fast-draining medium may be used. They may be repotted anytime new roots are growing.

MISCELLANEOUS NOTES: The bloom season shown in the climate table is based on cultivation records. Plants are considered difficult to grow by many growers; but those who provide the needed cool, dry rest find them easy to grow.

Plant and Flower Information

PLANT SIZE AND TYPE: A 9–24 in. (23–60 cm) sympodial epiphyte.

PSEUDOBULB: 9–24 in. (23–60 cm) long. The slender stems are ridged, rounded not angled, and club-shaped. They are often yellowish near the apex and turn brownish when mature. The characteristics of the pseudobulbs are the most obvious differences between *D. thyrsiflorum* and *D. densiflorum*.

LEAVES: 5–7. The leaves are 4–6 in. (10–15 cm) long and last for several years. They are smooth, flexible, and dark green.

INFLORESCENCE: 8–12 in. (20–30 cm) long. Inflorescences emerge as a round swelling from a joint near the top of the stem. Inflorescences may be arching or pendulous. The closely spaced blossoms spiral around the inflorescence.

FLOWERS: 30–50 per inflorescence. The flowers are 1.2–2.0 in. (3–5 cm) across. The ovate sepals and round, finely toothed petals are white to cream and nearly transparent. The blossoms may be yellowish near the center or tinged with violet or rose. The funnel-shaped lip, which is bright orange to yellow-orange, is sharply contrasting. Blossoms are beautiful and very showy but only last about a week.

HYBRIDIZING NOTES: Chromosome counts are n = 20 (ref. 154, 187, 504, 580) and 2n = 40 (ref. 151, 152, 153, 187, 243, 504, 580). Johansen (ref. 239) indicates that plants are self-sterile and that flowers dropped 6–10 days after self-pollination.

REFERENCES: 25, 38, 46, 78, 151, 152, 153, 154, 161, 179, 187, 190, 196, 200, 208, 210, 216, 236, 239, 243, 245, 247, 254, 326, 369, 371, 389, 428, 430, 445, 447, 448, 454, 489, 495, 504, 507, 523, 524, 541, 557, 570, 580, 581.

PHOTOS/DRAWINGS: 78, 210, *245, 247, 327, 371, 389, 428, 430, 454,* 522, 524, 541, 557, 570, *581, 596.*

Dendrobium thyrsodes Rchb. f. See *D. kuhlii* (Blume) Lindley. REFERENCES: 75, 216, 254, 317, 469.

Dendrobium thysanochilum Schlechter. Often considered a synonym of *Flickingeria comata* (Lindley) A. Hawkes, but Valmayor (ref. 536) includes it as a synonym of *D. scopa* Lindley, which is now a synonym of *Flickingeria scopa* (Lindley) F. G. Brieger. However, Hunt and Summerhayes (ref. 214) specifically retain *D. comata* (Blume) Lindley and *D. thysanochilum* Schlechter as separate species. REFERENCES: 67, 105, 211, 213, 214, 219, 230, 254, 271, 296, 437, 444, 445, 536.

Dendrobium thysanophorum Schlechter

ORIGIN/HABITAT: Endemic to northern Sulawesi (Celebes). Plants were originally collected near Tomohon on the Minahassa Peninsula at about 3300 ft. (1000 m).

CLIMATE: Station #97014, Manado, Sulawesi, Lat. 1.5°N, Long. 124.9°E, at 264 ft. (80 m). Temperatures are calculated for an elevation of 3000 ft. (910 m), resulting in probable extremes of 88°F (31°C) and 56°F (13°C).

N/HEMISPHERE	JAN	FEB	MAR	APR	MAY	JUN	JUL	AUG	SEP	OCT	NOV	DEC
°F AVG MAX	76	76	76	77	78	78	78	80	80	80	78	77
°F AVG MIN	64	64	64	64	65	64	64	64	64	63	64	65
DIURNAL RANGE	12	12	12	13	13	14	14	16	16	17	14	12
RAIN/INCHES	18.6	13.8	12.2	8.0	6.4	6.5	4.8	4.0	3.4	4.9	8.9	14.7
HUMIDITY/%	84	83	83	83	81	80	75	72	75	77	82	83
BLOOM SEASON										•		
DAYS CLR @ 8AM	4	3	6	11	11	12	12	12	14	17	12	8
DAYS CLR @ 2PM	1	1	1	2	1	3	3	4	4	4	1	1
RAIN/MM	472	351	310	203	163	165	122	102	86	124	226	373
°C AVG MAX	24.4	24.4	24.4	25.0	25.5	25.5	25.5	26.7	26.7	26.7	25.5	25.0
°C AVG MIN	17.8	17.8	17.8	17.8	18.3	17.8	17.8	17.8	17.8	17.2	17.8	18.3
DIURNAL RANGE	6.6	6.6	6.6	7.2	7.2	7.7	7.7	8.9	8.9	9.5	7.2	6.7
S/HEMISPHERE	JUL	AUG	SEP	OCT	NOV	DEC	JAN	FEB	MAR	APR	MAY	JUN

Cultural Recommendations

LIGHT: 2000–3000 fc. In the habitat, morning light is highest. Skies are usually overcast by afternoon.

TEMPERATURES: Throughout the year, days average 76–80°F (24–27°C), and nights average 63–65°F (17–18°C), with a diurnal range of 12–17°F (7–10°C). The average highs vary only 4°F (2°C), and average lows fluctuate only 2°F (1°C), indicating that plants may not tolerate wide temperature fluctuations.

HUMIDITY: 80–85% most of the year, dropping to 70–75% in summer.

WATER: Rainfall is moderate to heavy all year. The driest weather occurs in late summer when temperatures are warm. Cultivated plants should be kept moist but not soggy. Warm water might be beneficial.

FERTILIZER: ¼–½ recommended strength. A balanced fertilizer should be applied weekly to biweekly throughout the year.

REST PERIOD: Growing temperatures should be maintained all year. The plants may rest during the 1–2 month drier period which occurs in late summer and coincides with the period of greatest diurnal range. Cultivated plants should dry out slightly during this period, but they should never remain dry for long. The heaviest rainfall in the habitat occurs in winter, but water should not be increased for cultivated plants. In fact, water should be reduced somewhat for plants grown in the dark, short-day conditions common in temperate latitudes, but they should not be allowed to dry out completely.

GROWING MEDIA: Plants may be mounted on tree-fern or cork slabs or potted in small pots filled with any open, fast-draining medium. Repotting may be done anytime new roots are growing.

MISCELLANEOUS NOTES: The bloom season shown in the climate table is based on reports from the habitat.

Plant and Flower Information

PLANT SIZE AND TYPE: An 8–14 in. (20–35 cm) sympodial epiphyte, terrestrial, or lithophyte.

PSEUDOBULB: 8–14 in. (20–35 cm) long. The flattened stems arise from a very short rhizome. They may be erect or spreading.

LEAVES: Many. The leaves are ovate-lanceolate to ovate-triangular and 0.4–1.0 in. (1.0–2.5 cm) long. They are somewhat sickle-shaped.

INFLORESCENCE: Short. Clusters of blossoms emerge at the apex and laterally along the stem.

FLOWERS: Many per inflorescence, but blossoms open in succession. The flowers are less than 0.2 in. (0.5 cm) long. They may be wide-opening or rather closed. Sepals are broadly ovate. The petals are minutely serrated along the margin. The lip is undivided. Schlechter (ref. 436) indicated that without careful examination of the flower, the plant and flowers cannot be differentiated from *D. distichum* (Presl) Rchb. f. from the Philippines, which has a distinctly 3-lobed lip.

REFERENCES: 221, 436.

Dendrobium tibeticum Schlechter. See *D. chryseum* Rolfe. REFERENCES: 208, 223, 454.

Dendrobium tigrinum Rolfe ex Hemsley. See *D. spectabile* (Blume) Miquel. REFERENCES: 83, 190, 218, 254, 270, 271, 430, 437, 470.

Dendrobium tipula J. J. Smith. Now considered a synonym of *Diplocaulobium tipula* (J. J. Smith) Kränzlin. REFERENCES: 220, 254, 445, 470.

Dendrobium tipuliferum Rchb. f. Now considered a synonym of *Diplocaulobium tipuliferum* (Rchb. f.) Kränzlin. REFERENCES: 179, 216, 220, 254, 353, 466.

Dendrobium tixieri Guillaumin. See *D. oligophyllum* Gagnepain. REFERENCES: 169, 179, 230, 448, 454.

Dendrobium tmesipteris Lindley

ORIGIN/HABITAT: Sarawak, Borneo. Habitat elevation is unavailable, so the following climate data should be used with caution. Although sometimes listed as originating in the Philippines, Merrill (ref. 296) includes *D. tmesipteris* in his list of excluded or synonymous species for the Philippines.

CLIMATE: Station #96413, Kuching, Sarawak, Lat. 1.5°N, Long. 110.3°E, at 85 ft. (26 m). Record extreme temperatures are 97°F (36°C) and 64°F (18°C).

N/HEMISPHERE	JAN	FEB	MAR	APR	MAY	JUN	JUL	AUG	SEP	OCT	NOV	DEC
°F AVG MAX	88	88	89	90	91	91	91	92	90	90	90	88
°F AVG MIN	72	72	72	72	72	73	72	72	72	72	72	72
DIURNAL RANGE	16	16	17	18	19	18	19	20	18	18	18	16
RAIN/INCHES	27.1	19.7	14.2	9.7	9.0	8.5	6.9	8.8	9.5	12.6	13.1	20.1
HUMIDITY/%	89	88	86	85	85	83	82	83	84	85	87	88
BLOOM SEASON	N/A											
DAYS CLR @ 7AM	1	0	1	2	3	2	4	1	2	1	1	1
DAYS CLR @ 1PM	0	0	0	0	0	1	1	0	0	0	0	0
RAIN/MM	688	500	361	246	229	216	175	224	241	320	333	511
°C AVG MAX	31.1	31.1	31.7	32.2	32.8	32.8	32.8	33.3	32.2	32.2	32.2	31.1
°C AVG MIN	22.2	22.2	22.2	22.2	22.2	22.8	22.2	22.2	22.2	22.2	22.2	22.2
DIURNAL RANGE	8.9	8.9	9.5	10.0	10.6	10.0	10.6	11.1	10.0	10.0	10.0	8.9
S/HEMISPHERE	JUL	AUG	SEP	OCT	NOV	DEC	JAN	FEB	MAR	APR	MAY	JUN

Cultural Recommendations

LIGHT: 1500–2500 fc.

TEMPERATURES: Throughout the year, days average 88–92°F (31–33°C), and nights average 72–73°F (22–23°C), with a diurnal range of 16–20°F (9–11°C). The diurnal range is unusually large for a habitat with so little seasonal variation.

HUMIDITY: 80–90% year-round. High humidity and excellent air circulation are important.

WATER: Rainfall is very heavy all year. Plants should be kept moist but not soggy. Warm water may be beneficial.

FERTILIZER: ¼–½ recommended strength. A balanced fertilizer should be applied weekly to biweekly throughout the year.

REST PERIOD: Growing conditions should be maintained all year. The record low is only 10°F (6°C) below the average lows. Although rainfall remains heavy in winter, water may be reduced somewhat for cultivated plants, especially those grown in the dark, short-day conditions common in temperate latitudes. They should never be allowed to dry out completely, however. In the habitat, light is highest in winter.

GROWING MEDIA: Plants may be mounted on tree-fern or cork slabs if humidity is high and plants are watered at least once daily in summer. When plants are potted, any open, fast-draining medium may be used. They may be repotted anytime new roots are growing.

Plant and Flower Information

PLANT SIZE AND TYPE: A 5 in. (13 cm) sympodial epiphyte.

PSEUDOBULB: 4 in. (10 cm) long. The leafy stems are densely clustered.

LEAVES: Many. The distichous leaves are 1 in. (2.5 cm) long. They are fleshy, linear-lanceolate, sharply pointed, and widely spaced.

FLOWERS: Few per inflorescence. Blossoms open in succession 1–2 at a time. Flowers are less than 0.2 in. (0.5 cm) long. The apex of the dorsal sepal is recurved. Lateral sepals are bow-shaped at the tip. The petals are curved. The obovate lip is concave and ruffled along the margin. It has a sharp point at the apex of the midlobe and 2 lines in the center.

REFERENCES: 216, 254, 278, 286, 295, 296, 310, 394.

Dendrobium toadjanum J. J. Smith.
Schlechter (ref. 443) considered this plant to be a synonym of *Cadetia toadjana* (J. J. Smith) Schlechter. REFERENCES: 221, 223, 443, 445, 470, 475.

Dendrobium tobaense J. J. Wood and J. B. Comber

ORIGIN/HABITAT: Northern Sumatra. The type specimen was collected northeast of Lake Toba at about 4900 ft. (1500 m). Plants also grow in pine or fir woods on Mt. Dolok south of Lake Toba at 3300–4250 ft. (1000–1300 m).

CLIMATE: Station #96035, Medan, Sumatra, Indonesia, Lat. 3.6°N, Long. 98.7°E, at 87 ft. (27 m). Temperatures are calculated for an elevation of 4750 ft. (1450 m), resulting in probable extremes of 84°F (29°C) and 45°F (7°C).

N/HEMISPHERE	JAN	FEB	MAR	APR	MAY	JUN	JUL	AUG	SEP	OCT	NOV	DEC
°F AVG MAX	70	72	73	74	74	74	74	74	73	71	71	70
°F AVG MIN	56	56	57	58	58	57	57	57	57	57	57	57
DIURNAL RANGE	14	16	16	16	16	17	17	17	16	14	14	13
RAIN/INCHES	5.4	3.6	4.1	5.2	6.9	5.2	5.3	7.0	8.3	10.2	9.7	9.0
HUMIDITY/%	80	79	78	78	79	78	79	79	81	83	83	82
BLOOM SEASON					*							
DAYS CLR @ 7AM	4	2	2	2	2	2	2	0	0	0	1	1
DAYS CLR @ 1PM	0	1	0	0	1	0	2	1	0	0	0	0
RAIN/MM	137	91	104	132	175	132	135	178	211	259	246	229
°C AVG MAX	20.9	22.0	22.6	23.1	23.1	23.1	23.1	23.1	22.6	21.5	21.5	20.9
°C AVG MIN	13.1	13.1	13.7	14.2	14.2	13.7	13.7	13.7	13.7	13.7	13.7	13.7
DIURNAL RANGE	7.8	8.9	8.9	8.9	8.9	9.4	9.4	9.4	8.9	7.8	7.8	7.2
S/HEMISPHERE	JUL	AUG	SEP	OCT	NOV	DEC	JAN	FEB	MAR	APR	MAY	JUN

Cultural Recommendations

LIGHT: 2000–3000 fc.

TEMPERATURES: Throughout the year, days average 70–74°F (21–23°C), and nights average 56–58°F (13–14°C), with a diurnal range of 13–17°F (7–9°C). Average lows vary only 2°F (1°C) during the year.

HUMIDITY: 75–80% year-round.

WATER: Rainfall is moderate to heavy all year with a brief slightly drier period in winter. Cultivated plants should be kept moist with only slight drying allowed between waterings.

FERTILIZER: ¼–½ recommended strength. A balanced fertilizer should be applied weekly to biweekly throughout the year.

REST PERIOD: Growing conditions should be maintained all year. Water may be reduced somewhat in winter for plants grown in the dark, short-day conditions common in temperate latitudes, but they should never be allowed to dry out completely. In the habitat, light is slightly higher for about 3 months in winter.

GROWING MEDIA: Plants may be mounted on tree-fern or cork slabs or potted in small pots filled with any open, fast-draining medium. Repotting may be done anytime new roots are growing.

MISCELLANEOUS NOTES: The bloom season shown in the climate table is based on collection records.

Plant and Flower Information

PLANT SIZE AND TYPE: A 9.5–12.0 in. (24–30 cm) sympodial epiphyte.

PSEUDOBULB: 9.5–12.0 in. (24–30 cm) long.

LEAVES: 8–9. The oblong-elliptic leaves are 1.2–3.2 in. (3–8 cm) long and unequally bilobed at the apex. They are smooth on the upper surface and densely covered with black hairs on the underside. Sheaths are densely covered with short, blackish hairs.

INFLORESCENCE: Very short. Inflorescences emerge from the base of the leaf sheath opposite the leaf.

FLOWERS: 1 at a time. Blossoms open in succession. The flowers are 3 in. (8 cm) across. The ovate sepals and petals taper to a slender, elongated tip. Segments are stiffly fleshy and reflexed at the tips. The pale yellow sepals and petals have green veins that are raised and netlike. The lip has erect, somewhat sickle-shaped sidelobes. The thick, fleshy midlobe is densely covered with slender warty protuberances. The orange-red lip has slender, longitudinal red lines on the orange sidelobes.

REFERENCES: 593.

PHOTOS/DRAWINGS: 593.

Dendrobium tofftii F. M. Bailey.
Sometimes spelled *D. toftii*, see *D. nindii* W. Hill. REFERENCES: 25, 67, 84, 105, 217, 219, 236, 254, 262, 325, 421, 445, 504, 533, 580.

Dendrobium tokai Rchb. f.

AKA: Schlechter (ref. 434) includes *D. sylvanum* Kränzlin not Rchb. f. as a synonym. *D. tokai* var. *crassinerve* Finet is now considered a synonym of *D. macranthum* A. Richard.

ORIGIN/HABITAT: Fiji and Tonga. In Fiji, plants grow in both dense and open forests from sea level to 2600 ft. (0–800 m). Plants are most often found in low lying areas.

CLIMATE: Station #91683, Nausori, Viti Levu, Fiji, Lat. 18.1°S, Long. 178.6°E, at 19 ft. (6 m). Temperatures are calculated for an elevation of 1500 ft. (460 m), resulting in probable extremes of 93°F (34°C) and 50°F (10°C).

Dendrobium tomohonense

N/HEMISPHERE	JAN	FEB	MAR	APR	MAY	JUN	JUL	AUG	SEP	OCT	NOV	DEC
°F AVG MAX	74	74	75	76	78	80	81	81	81	79	77	75
°F AVG MIN	63	63	64	65	66	68	69	69	69	68	66	64
DIURNAL RANGE	11	11	11	11	12	12	12	12	12	11	11	11
RAIN/INCHES	4.9	8.3	7.7	8.3	9.8	12.5	11.4	10.7	14.5	12.2	10.1	6.7
HUMIDITY/%	77	77	76	75	75	76	76	78	79	79	81	78
BLOOM SEASON								*	*			
DAYS CLR @ 12PM	3	1	0	0	1	1	2	0	0	0	1	0
RAIN/MM	124	211	196	211	249	318	290	272	368	310	257	170
°C AVG MAX	23.4	23.4	24.0	24.5	25.6	26.7	27.3	27.3	27.3	26.2	25.1	24.0
°C AVG MIN	17.3	17.3	17.8	18.4	19.0	20.1	20.6	20.6	20.6	20.1	19.0	17.8
DIURNAL RANGE	6.1	6.1	6.2	6.1	6.6	6.6	6.7	6.7	6.7	6.1	6.1	6.2
S/HEMISPHERE	JUL	AUG	SEP	OCT	NOV	DEC	JAN	FEB	MAR	APR	MAY	JUN

Cultural Recommendations

LIGHT: 2500–3500 fc.

TEMPERATURES: Summer days average 80–81°F (27°C), and nights average 68–69°F (20–21°C), with a diurnal range of 12°F (7°C).

HUMIDITY: 75–80% year-round.

WATER: Rainfall is moderate to heavy all year. Cultivated plants should be kept moist and never allowed to dry completely.

FERTILIZER: ¼–½ recommended strength, applied weekly. A high-nitrogen fertilizer is beneficial from spring to midsummer, but a fertilizer high in phosphates should be used in late summer and autumn.

REST PERIOD: Winter days average 74–75°F (23–24°C), and nights average 63–64°F (17–18°C), with a diurnal range of 11°F (6°C). Seasonal temperature variation is minor. Winter rainfall is high, but water should be reduced somewhat for cultivated plants, especially those grown in the dark, short-day conditions common in temperate-latitude winters. Plants should never be allowed to dry completely, however. Fertilizer should be reduced or eliminated anytime water is reduced.

GROWING MEDIA: Plants are best potted in small pots filled with any open, fast-draining medium. Repotting may be done anytime new roots are growing.

MISCELLANEOUS NOTES: The bloom season shown in the climate table is based on reports from the habitat. In the habitat, fruits are most common in autumn and winter.

Plant and Flower Information

PLANT SIZE AND TYPE: A 31 in. (80 cm) sympodial epiphyte. Plants occasionally grow lithophytically.

PSEUDOBULB: 16–28 in. (40–70 cm) long. The stems arise from a very short rhizome. They are fleshy and cylindrical with many ridges.

LEAVES: 2 at the apex of each growth. The narrowly oblong leaves are 3–6 in. (8–15 cm) long, leathery, and bilobed at the tip.

INFLORESCENCE: 12 in. (30 cm) long. Inflorescences arise from nodes near the apex of the stem. The upper half of the inflorescence is densely flowered.

FLOWERS: 8–20 per inflorescence. The flowers are 1.2–2.0 in. (3–5 cm) long and do not open fully. They are yellow to greenish yellow with reddish purple markings on the lip. The sepals and erect petals are slender and pointed. The 3-lobed lip, which is broader than the other segments, is sharply and abruptly pointed at the apex of the broadly elliptic midlobe. The callus terminates in 3 raised lines on the lower half of the midlobe.

HYBRIDIZING NOTES: Chromosome counts are n = 19 (ref. 504, 580) and 2n = 38 (ref. 504, 580). When used as a parent, *D. tokai* enhances the shape, floriferousness, and flower longevity of the offspring.

REFERENCES: 82, 84, 173, 216, 252, 254, 270, 271, 344, 353, 434, 445, 466, 504, 580.

PHOTOS/DRAWINGS: *344, 466.*

Dendrobium tomohonense Kränzlin. See *D. macrophyllum* A. Richard. REFERENCES: 83, 220, 254, 270, 271, 436.

Dendrobium tonkinense Wildeman. See *D. uniflorum* Griffith. REFERENCES: 93, 103, 190, 220, 254, 454.

Dendrobium topaziacum Ames. See *D. bullenianum* Rchb. f. REFERENCES: 12, 151, 179, 190, 222, 280, 296, 430, 504, 536, 580.

Dendrobium toressae (F. M. Bailey) Dockrill

AKA: *Bulbophyllum toressae* F. M. Bailey.

ORIGIN/HABITAT: Northeastern Australia. The habitat is located along the eastern side of the Cape York Peninsula between the Tully and Broomfield Rivers. Plants grow on trees and shady rocks in open forests and rainforests. Plants are often found in exposed locations at 3000–4000 ft. (910–1220 m), but they also grow near sea level.

CLIMATE: Station #94287, Cairns, Australia, Lat. 16.9°S, Long. 145.8°E, at 7 ft. (2 m). Temperatures are calculated for an elevation of 3000 ft. (910 m), resulting in probable extremes of 100°F (38°C) and 33°F (1°C).

N/HEMISPHERE	JAN	FEB	MAR	APR	MAY	JUN	JUL	AUG	SEP	OCT	NOV	DEC
°F AVG MAX	68	70	73	76	78	80	80	79	77	75	71	69
°F AVG MIN	51	52	54	58	60	63	64	64	63	60	56	54
DIURNAL RANGE	17	18	19	18	18	17	16	15	14	15	15	15
RAIN/INCHES	1.6	1.7	1.7	2.1	3.9	8.7	16.6	15.7	18.1	11.3	4.4	2.9
HUMIDITY/%	69	65	65	65	65	68	72	72	74	73	73	72
BLOOM SEASON			**	**	**							
DAYS CLR @ 10AM	9	11	13	11	6	6	4	5	6	7	11	10
DAYS CLR @ 4PM	8	10	12	16	10	7	4	3	4	6	9	10
RAIN/MM	41	43	43	53	99	221	422	399	460	287	112	74
°C AVG MAX	20.1	21.2	22.8	24.5	25.6	26.7	26.7	26.2	25.1	24.0	21.7	20.6
°C AVG MIN	10.6	11.2	12.3	14.5	15.6	17.3	17.8	17.8	17.3	15.6	13.4	12.3
DIURNAL RANGE	9.5	10.0	10.5	10.0	10.0	9.4	8.9	8.4	7.8	8.4	8.3	8.3
S/HEMISPHERE	JUL	AUG	SEP	OCT	NOV	DEC	JAN	FEB	MAR	APR	MAY	JUN

Cultural Recommendations

LIGHT: 1800–3000 fc. About 50% shade in summer. Strong air movement should be provided year-round. Some growers recommend bright shade, but plants tolerate both shade and bright light.

TEMPERATURES: Summer days average 79–80°F (26–27°C), and nights average 63–64°F (17–18°C), with a diurnal range of 15–17°F (8–9°C).

HUMIDITY: 70–75% most of the year, dropping to 65% in late winter and spring. In the rainforest habitat, relative humidity may average 10% more than indicated in the climate table. Cultivated plants are healthiest if humidity is high.

WATER: Rainfall is heavy from late spring into autumn, with much drier conditions in winter. Growers indicate that mounted plants should be misted frequently and never be allowed to dry out completely for any length of time.

FERTILIZER: ¼–½ recommended strength, applied weekly. A high-nitrogen fertilizer is beneficial from spring to midsummer, but a fertilizer high in phosphates should be used in late summer and autumn.

REST PERIOD: Winter days average 68–73°F (20–23°C), and nights average 51–54°F (11–12°C), with a diurnal range of 15–19°F (8–11°C). Australian growers recommend that winter lows not fall below 43°F (6°C). Water and fertilizer should be reduced for 4–5 months from late autumn to early spring. Plants should be allowed to dry slightly between waterings, but they should not remain dry for long periods. Fertilizer may be reduced when temperatures are cool or light is low. In the habitat, winter skies are frequently clear.

GROWING MEDIA: Plants should be mounted firmly to hardwood, tree-fern, or cork slabs if humidity is high and plants are watered at least once daily in summer. They may need to be watered several times a day during very hot weather. Plants are not vigorous and are rather slow to establish. The older portions of the plant tend to die back when disturbed, so they should be divided or remounted only when absolutely necessary.

MISCELLANEOUS NOTES: The bloom season shown in the climate table is based on reports from the habitat, but growers report that plants may bloom at any time of year. *D. toressae* is very slow growing, and many growers consider it difficult to cultivate. Plants are seldom found in patches larger than 4 in. (10 cm).

Plant and Flower Information

PLANT SIZE AND TYPE: A 2 in. (5 cm) sympodial epiphyte or lithophyte that resembles a tiny succulent.

PSEUDOBULB: The prostrate plants produce leaves all along the branching rhizome and root at each node. At the base of each leaf is a vestigial pseudobulb.

LEAVES: 0.2–0.3 in. (0.4–0.8 cm) long. The numerous leaves alternate on either side of the creeping rhizome. Rounded on the bottom and channeled on top, they resemble sparkling grains of wheat. The surface is rough with many indentations or large pores.

INFLORESCENCE: Extremely short. Inflorescences emerge along the centerline of the rhizome. The flowers are borne at the apex of the vestigial pseudobulb and rest on the hollow of the leaf.

FLOWERS: 1 per inflorescence. The match head sized flowers may reach a diameter of 0.2 in. (0.5 cm) when spread. The cupped sepals and much smaller petals are translucent yellowish white to pinkish tan. The relatively large, 3-lobed lip is yellow with red markings at the base. It is uppermost. Blossoms last 2–6 weeks.

HYBRIDIZING NOTES: Chromosome counts are 2n = about 36 (ref. 153, 273) and 2n = 38 (ref. 152, 243).

REFERENCES: 23, 67, 105, 152, 153, 179, 230, 240, 243, 262, 263, 273, 291, 325, 330, 352, 390, 527, 533.

PHOTOS/DRAWINGS: 105, *240, 291, 325, 390, 533*.

Dendrobium torquisepalum Kränzlin. See *D. pensile* Ridley.
REFERENCES: 220, 254, 286, 295.

Dendrobium torricellense Schlechter

ORIGIN/HABITAT: New Guinea. In northern Papua, plants grow in the peaty layers of roots on the ground in ridge-top forests of the Torricelli Range. They are usually found in mistforests at 2600–5100 ft. (800–1550 m). Collections are also reported from the Vogelkop Peninsula in Irian Jaya (western New Guinea).

CLIMATE: Station #94004, Wewak, Papua New Guinea, Lat. 3.6°S, Long. 143.7°E, at 16 ft. (5 m). Temperatures are calculated for an elevation of 3800 ft. (1160 m), resulting in probable extremes of 86°F (30°C) and 50°F (10°C).

N/HEMISPHERE	JAN	FEB	MAR	APR	MAY	JUN	JUL	AUG	SEP	OCT	NOV	DEC
°F AVG MAX	76	76	76	76	76	76	75	74	75	76	76	76
°F AVG MIN	62	62	62	63	63	63	63	63	62	62	63	62
DIURNAL RANGE	14	14	14	13	13	13	12	11	13	14	13	14
RAIN/INCHES	7.6	4.8	5.3	10.0	13.3	14.5	12.1	11.9	14.9	16.9	15.1	10.8
HUMIDITY/%	80	79	79	78	79	81	82	82	81	82	81	80
BLOOM SEASON			*						*			
DAYS CLR	N/A											
RAIN/MM	193	122	135	254	338	368	307	302	378	429	384	274
°C AVG MAX	24.2	24.2	24.2	24.2	24.2	24.2	23.6	23.1	23.6	24.2	24.2	24.2
°C AVG MIN	16.4	16.4	16.4	17.0	17.0	17.0	17.0	17.0	16.4	16.4	17.0	16.4
DIURNAL RANGE	7.8	7.8	7.8	7.2	7.2	7.2	6.6	6.1	7.2	7.8	7.2	7.8
S/HEMISPHERE	JUL	AUG	SEP	OCT	NOV	DEC	JAN	FEB	MAR	APR	MAY	JUN

Cultural Recommendations

LIGHT: 2000–3000 fc.

TEMPERATURES: Throughout the year, days average 74–76°F (23–24°C), and nights average 62–63°F (16–17°C), with a diurnal range of 11–14°F (6–8°C). The probable record high is 86°F (30°C), and growers indicate that many plants from this habitat do poorly in continuous high temperatures.

HUMIDITY: Near 80% year-round.

WATER: Rainfall is heavy all year, but conditions are slightly drier for 1–2 months in late winter. Cultivated plants should be kept moist with only slight drying allowed between waterings.

FERTILIZER: ¼–½ recommended strength. A balanced fertilizer should be applied weekly to biweekly throughout the year.

REST PERIOD: Growing conditions should be maintained year-round. Water should be reduced for plants cultivated in the dark, short-day conditions common during temperate-latitude winters, but they should not be allowed to dry out completely. Fertilizer should also be reduced if water is reduced. In the habitat, light may be slightly higher in winter.

GROWING MEDIA: A very open and fast-draining medium should be used with either baskets or small pots. Repotting may be done anytime new roots are growing.

MISCELLANEOUS NOTES: The bloom season shown in the climate table is based on reports from the habitat.

Plant and Flower Information

PLANT SIZE AND TYPE: A 12 in. (30 cm) sympodial terrestrial.

PSEUDOBULB: 12 in. (30 cm) long. The slender, yellow stems are clustered and swollen at the base. Each round stem consists of about 7 nodes.

LEAVES: 2 at the apex of each growth. The leaves are 6 in. (15 cm) long. They are thin, linear-lanceolate, and suberect.

INFLORESCENCE: 5 in. (12 cm) long. Erect inflorescences emerge from between the leaves at the apex of the pseudobulb.

FLOWERS: 2, rarely more per inflorescence. The flowers are 0.8 in. (2 cm) across. They are white with red or violet on the lip. The narrower petals are uneven along the margin. The 3-lobed lip has large sidelobes and a notched, ruffled midlobe. The 3 keels terminate below the midlobe.

REFERENCES: 83, 92, 219, 254, 437, 444, 445, 550.

PHOTOS/DRAWINGS: *83, 437*.

Dendrobium torricellianum Kränzlin

AKA: *D. atrorubens* Schlechter not Ridley, *D. simile* Schlechter 1906 not 1905.

ORIGIN/HABITAT: Northern Papua New Guinea. Plants grow on forest trees in the Torricelli Range and near Sattelberg at 3600–4600 ft. (1100–1400 m).

CLIMATE: Station #94004, Wewak, Papua New Guinea, Lat. 3.6°S, Long. 143.7°E, at 16 ft. (5 m). Temperatures are calculated for an elevation of 3800 ft. (1160 m), resulting in probable extremes of 86°F (30°C) and 50°F (10°C).

N/HEMISPHERE	JAN	FEB	MAR	APR	MAY	JUN	JUL	AUG	SEP	OCT	NOV	DEC
°F AVG MAX	76	76	76	76	76	76	75	74	75	76	76	76
°F AVG MIN	62	62	62	63	63	63	63	63	62	62	63	62
DIURNAL RANGE	14	14	14	13	13	13	12	11	13	14	13	14
RAIN/INCHES	7.6	4.8	5.3	10.0	13.3	14.5	12.1	11.9	14.9	16.9	15.1	10.8
HUMIDITY/%	80	79	79	78	79	81	82	82	81	82	81	80
BLOOM SEASON							*		*			
DAYS CLR	N/A											
RAIN/MM	193	122	135	254	338	368	307	302	378	429	384	274
°C AVG MAX	24.2	24.2	24.2	24.2	24.2	24.2	23.6	23.1	23.6	24.2	24.2	24.2
°C AVG MIN	16.4	16.4	16.4	17.0	17.0	17.0	17.0	17.0	16.4	16.4	17.0	16.4
DIURNAL RANGE	7.8	7.8	7.8	7.2	7.2	7.2	6.6	6.1	7.2	7.8	7.2	7.8
S/HEMISPHERE	JUL	AUG	SEP	OCT	NOV	DEC	JAN	FEB	MAR	APR	MAY	JUN

Dendrobium tortile

Cultural Recommendations

LIGHT: 2000–3000 fc.

TEMPERATURES: Throughout the year, days average 74–76°F (23–24°C), and nights average 62–63°F (16–17°C), with a diurnal range of 11–14°F (6–8°C). The probable record high is 86°F (30°C), and growers indicate that many plants from this habitat do poorly in continuous high temperatures.

HUMIDITY: Near 80% year-round.

WATER: Rainfall is heavy all year, but conditions are slightly drier for 1–2 months in late winter. Cultivated plants should be kept moist and never be allowed to dry out.

FERTILIZER: ¼–½ recommended strength. A balanced fertilizer should be applied weekly to biweekly throughout the year.

REST PERIOD: Growing conditions should be maintained year-round. Water should be reduced for plants cultivated in the dark, short-day conditions common during temperate-latitude winters, but they should still not be allowed to dry out completely. Fertilizer should also be reduced if water is reduced. In the habitat, light may be slightly higher in winter.

GROWING MEDIA: A very open and fast-draining medium should be used with either baskets or small pots. Repotting may be done anytime new roots are growing.

MISCELLANEOUS NOTES: The bloom season shown in the climate table is based on collection reports.

Plant and Flower Information

PLANT SIZE AND TYPE: A 4–6 in. (10–15 cm) sympodial epiphyte.

PSEUDOBULB: 4–6 in. (10–15 cm) long. The densely leafy stems rarely branch.

LEAVES: Many. The leaves are 1.6–2.0 in. (4–5 cm) long and appear linear. They are leathery, flattened, and distichous.

INFLORESCENCE: Clusters of flowers emerge near the apex of the stem.

FLOWERS: Several per inflorescence. The flowers are 0.2 in. (0.6 cm) long. Blossoms are dark red-purple, thick, and fleshy. The keeled sepals are pointed. The petals are small. The segments are arranged like an open fan. The erect lip is oval with a recurved point at the apex. It is not lobed.

REFERENCES: 220, 254, 304, 437, 444, 445, 454, 486.

PHOTOS/DRAWINGS: *304*, 437.

Dendrobium tortile A. Cunningham not Lindley. See *D. monophyllum* F. Mueller. REFERENCES: 67, 105, 216, 254, 533.

Dendrobium tortile Lindley not A. Cunningham

AKA: Hunt (ref. 211) includes *D. dartoisianum* Wildeman and *D. haniffii* var. *dartoisianum* (Wildeman) Hawkes. Seidenfaden and Wood (ref. 455) list only *D. haniffii* Ridley. In 1992 *Opera Botanica* 114, Seidenfaden also includes *D. tortile* var. *dartoisianum* (Wildeman) O'Brien and *D. tortile* var. *simondii* Gagnepaign.

ORIGIN/HABITAT: Northeastern India, the Andaman Islands, Malaya, the Tenasserim district in Burma, Thailand, and the mountains between Laos and Vietnam. In Thailand, plants grow at about 4000 ft. (1220 m). In Malaya, they have been collected along the banks of the Kelantan River and in the states of Pinang (Penang), Kedah, Kelantan, and Pahang.

CLIMATE: Station #48300, Mae Hong Son, Thailand, Lat. 19.3°N, Long. 97.9°E, at 711 ft. (217 m). Temperatures are calculated for an elevation of 3000 ft. (910 m), resulting in probable extremes of 100°F (38°C) and 35°F (2°C).

N/HEMISPHERE	JAN	FEB	MAR	APR	MAY	JUN	JUL	AUG	SEP	OCT	NOV	DEC
°F AVG MAX	78	82	89	90	87	81	79	79	80	82	80	77
°F AVG MIN	49	49	54	64	68	67	66	66	66	64	60	51
DIURNAL RANGE	29	33	35	26	19	14	13	13	14	18	20	26
RAIN/INCHES	0.4	0.2	0.3	1.7	6.1	7.1	9.6	9.9	8.1	3.9	1.2	0.4
HUMIDITY/%	67	60	50	50	68	81	82	83	83	82	75	71
BLOOM SEASON		*	**	**	**	*	*					
DAYS CLR @ 7AM	2	8	10	9	3	0	0	0	0	1	1	2
DAYS CLR @ 1PM	20	20	20	13	3	0	0	0	0	3	13	17
RAIN/MM	10	5	8	43	155	180	244	251	206	99	30	10
°C AVG MAX	25.8	28.0	31.9	32.5	30.8	27.5	26.4	26.4	26.9	28.0	26.9	25.2
°C AVG MIN	9.7	9.7	12.5	18.0	20.2	19.7	19.1	19.1	19.1	18.0	15.8	10.8
DIURNAL RANGE	16.1	18.3	19.4	14.5	10.6	7.8	7.3	7.3	7.8	10.0	11.1	14.4
S/HEMISPHERE	JUL	AUG	SEP	OCT	NOV	DEC	JAN	FEB	MAR	APR	MAY	JUN

Cultural Recommendations

LIGHT: 2000–3000 fc. The heavy summer cloud cover indicates that some shading is needed from spring through autumn, but light should be as high as the plant can tolerate, short of burning the leaves. Strong air movement is important at all times.

TEMPERATURES: Summer days average 79–81°F (26–28°C), and nights average 66–67°F (19–20°C), with a diurnal range of 13–14°F (7–8°C). The warmest temperatures occur in late winter and spring. Days average 87–90°F (31–33°C), and nights average 54–68°F (13–20°C), with a diurnal range of 19–35°F (11–19°C).

HUMIDITY: 80–85% from summer into autumn, dropping to near 50% for 2 months in late winter and spring.

WATER: Rainfall is very heavy during the growing season, but winters are very dry. Cultivated plants should be kept moist while actively growing, but water should be gradually reduced after new growths mature in autumn.

FERTILIZER: ¼–½ recommended strength, applied weekly. A high-nitrogen fertilizer is beneficial from spring to midsummer, but a fertilizer high in phosphates should be used in late summer and autumn.

REST PERIOD: Winter days average 77–82°F (25–28°C), and nights average 49–51°F (10–11°C), with a diurnal range of 26–33°F (14–18°C). In the habitat, rainfall is low for 4–5 months in winter. For 2–3 of these months, high humidity and nightly cooling result in frequent, heavy deposits of dew with even more moisture available from fog and mist. Therefore, the driest season is only 1–2 months long. For cultivated plants, water should be reduced from late autumn to early spring. During most of the winter, plants should be allowed to dry out between waterings, but they should not remain completely dry for extended periods. Occasional early morning mistings between waterings may help prevent the plants from becoming too dry. For 1–2 months in late winter, however, water should be limited to occasional early morning mistings. Fertilizer should be reduced or eliminated, until new growth starts in spring. In the habitat, the large number of clear, winter afternoons indicates very bright conditions.

GROWING MEDIA: Plants may be mounted on tree-fern or cork slabs if humidity is high and plants are watered at least once daily in summer. When plants are potted, any open, fast-draining medium may be used. Repotting is best done in early spring when new roots are growing.

MISCELLANEOUS NOTES: The bloom season shown in the climate table is based on cultivation records. In the habitat, plants bloom winter and spring. One cultivated plant reached 36 in. (90 cm) in diameter, and observers estimated 1000 flowers. Plants grow well but do not flower freely in the warm conditions in Singapore.

Plant and Flower Information

PLANT SIZE AND TYPE: A 6–18 in. (15–45 cm) sympodial epiphyte, terrestrial, or lithophyte.

PSEUDOBULB: 6–18 in. (15–45 cm) long. The stems, which become yellow with age, are covered with tubular leaf sheaths. They are club- to spindle-shaped, grooved and flattened in the middle. They are not swollen at the nodes.

LEAVES: 3–4 per growth. The thin, deciduous leaves are about 4 in. (10 cm) long, but the lower ones are usually shorter and broader. They are curved, leathery, and sharply pointed.

INFLORESCENCE: 1.6–3.1 in. (4–8 cm) long. Inflorescences emerge from the upper leaf axils of leafless stems.

FLOWERS: Normally 2–3, rarely 6 or more per inflorescence. The flowers are 2.8–3.1 in. (7–8 cm) across. Selected clones may be as large as 5 in. (12.5 cm). The lanceolate sepals and petals twist and curl. They are normally white with a faint rose or lilac tinge, but they may be rosy purple or have a pale yellow tint. The woolly, funnel-shaped lip is nearly round when spread. It may be white, cream, or lemon-yellow with purple at the tip and a patch of pale mauve to deep purple veins on both sides near the base. Flower color is variable. Blossoms are long-lasting and extremely fragrant.

HYBRIDIZING NOTES: Chromosome counts are n = 19 (ref. 542) and 2n = 38 (ref. 151, 152, 154, 187, 188, 243, 504, 580). Johansen (ref. 239) found that all self-pollinations were successful. The seed capsules opened 358 days after pollination. Only 12% of the seed had visible embryos, but 61% of those germinated.

REFERENCES: 38, 46, 151, 152, 154, 157, 179, 187, 188, 190, 200, 202, 210, 211, 216, 239, 243, 245, 254, 266, 402, 430, 445, 448, 454, 455, 504, 541, 542, 557, 568, 570, 580.

PHOTOS/DRAWINGS: 200, 210, *245, 359, 430, 454, 455*.

Dendrobium tortitepalum J. J. Smith. Now considered a synonym of *Diplocaulobium tortitepalum* (J. J. Smith) A. Hawkes. REFERENCES: 224, 229, 445, 470.

Dendrobium tosaense Makino. See *D. stricklandianum* Rchb. f. The International Orchid Commission (ref. 236) registers hybrids under *D. tosaense*. REFERENCES: 61, 62, 139, 151, 187, 208, 218, 235, 236, 254, 274, 279, 338, 445, 497, 504, 528, 580. PHOTOS/DRAWINGS: *62, 274, 497*.

Dendrobium toxopei J. J. Smith

ORIGIN/HABITAT: Buru Island in the Moluccas. Plants were collected near Wa'Katin at about 2000 ft. (610 m).

CLIMATE: Station #97700, Namlea, Pulau Buru, Indonesia, Lat. 3.3°S, Long. 127.0°E, at 66 ft. (20 m). Temperatures are calculated for an elevation of 2000 ft. (610 m). Record extreme temperatures are not available for this location.

N/HEMISPHERE	JAN	FEB	MAR	APR	MAY	JUN	JUL	AUG	SEP	OCT	NOV	DEC
°F AVG MAX	78	78	80	81	81	80	79	78	79	80	80	78
°F AVG MIN	69	71	71	72	74	72	71	71	71	71	71	70
DIURNAL RANGE	9	7	9	9	7	8	8	7	8	9	9	8
RAIN/INCHES	3.1	4.4	1.3	1.6	4.0	5.8	6.1	5.3	6.9	2.8	2.0	5.5
HUMIDITY/%	N/A											
BLOOM SEASON												
DAYS CLR	N/A											
RAIN/MM	79	112	33	41	102	147	155	135	175	71	51	140
°C AVG MAX	25.3	25.3	26.5	27.0	27.0	26.5	25.9	25.3	25.9	26.5	26.5	25.3
°C AVG MIN	20.3	21.5	21.5	22.0	23.1	22.0	21.5	21.5	21.5	21.5	21.5	20.9
DIURNAL RANGE	5.0	3.8	5.0	5.0	3.9	4.5	4.4	3.8	4.4	5.0	5.0	4.4
S/HEMISPHERE	JUL	AUG	SEP	OCT	NOV	DEC	JAN	FEB	MAR	APR	MAY	JUN

Cultural Recommendations

LIGHT: 2000–3000 fc.

TEMPERATURES: Throughout the year, days average 78–81°F (25–27°C), and nights average 69–74°F (20–23°C), with a diurnal range of 7–9°F (4–5°C).

HUMIDITY: Information is not available for this location. However, records from nearby stations indicate that humidity probably averages near 85% year-round.

WATER: Rainfall is moderate most of the year. Semidry periods, which last 1–2 months, occur in early spring and again in autumn. Cultivated plants should be allowed to dry slightly between waterings.

FERTILIZER: ¼–½ recommended strength. A balanced fertilizer should be applied weekly to biweekly throughout the year.

REST PERIOD: Growing temperatures should be maintained year-round. For cultivated plants, water should be reduced somewhat in autumn and spring and the plants allowed to become somewhat drier between waterings. However, they should not remain dry for long periods. Fertilizer should be reduced anytime water is reduced. In the habitat, seasonal light variation is minor.

GROWING MEDIA: Plants may be mounted on tree-fern or cork slabs or potted in small pots filled with any open, fast-draining medium. Repotting may be done anytime new roots are growing.

MISCELLANEOUS NOTES: The bloom season shown in the climate table is based on reports from the habitat. The plant was described in 1928 in *Bul. Jard. Bot. Buit.* 3rd sér. 9:467.

Plant and Flower Information

PLANT SIZE AND TYPE: A 33 in. (84 cm) sympodial epiphyte.

PSEUDOBULB: 33 in. (84 cm) long. The clustered stems arise from a short, branching rhizome. They are shiny and do not branch. The stems are leafy on the upper part.

LEAVES: Many. The nearly linear leaves are 5.5–6.3 in. (14–16 cm) long, spreading, and somewhat twisted at the base.

INFLORESCENCE: Short. The flattened inflorescences emerge through the leaf bases at nodes along the stem.

FLOWERS: 2 per inflorescence. The flowers are 0.4 in. (1 cm) long. Sepals are oblong-triangular, concave, and pointed. Petals are broadly linear and pointed. The erect, 3-lobed lip has small, erect sidelobes. The very large, notched midlobe is rounded, broadly oval and notched at the apex with a triangular tooth in the indentation. The plant was described from a dried specimen, and flower color was not reported.

REFERENCES: 224.

Dendrobium tozerensis Lavarack

ORIGIN/HABITAT: Australia. Plants are found on Cape York Peninsula in a relatively small area between Coen and the Tozer and Janet Ranges at about 12.7°S latitude. They usually grow on rainforest trees in open, rocky areas where light is bright such as near waterfalls. The orchids occasionally grow on cliffs and large rocks.

CLIMATE: Station #94185, Coen, Australia, Lat. 14.0°S, Long. 143.2°E, at 633 ft. (193 m). Record extreme temperatures are not available for this location, but nearby stations report winter extremes at 50–55°F (10–13°C) and summer extremes near 105°F (41°C).

N/HEMISPHERE	JAN	FEB	MAR	APR	MAY	JUN	JUL	AUG	SEP	OCT	NOV	DEC
°F AVG MAX	74	75	76	80	82	83	81	81	81	82	80	74
°F AVG MIN	66	67	69	72	75	76	75	75	75	74	72	65
DIURNAL RANGE	8	8	7	8	7	7	6	6	6	8	8	9
RAIN/INCHES	0.2	0.1	0.1	0.4	1.0	2.7	7.4	7.4	4.7	2.2	1.4	0.6
HUMIDITY/%	N/A											
BLOOM SEASON					*	*	*	*				
DAYS CLR	N/A											
RAIN/MM	4	2	2	9	25	67	189	188	120	56	37	15
°C AVG MAX	23.3	23.9	24.7	26.6	27.7	28.2	27.3	27.0	27.0	27.7	26.4	23.3
°C AVG MIN	19.0	19.6	20.5	22.2	23.7	24.3	24.1	24.1	24.0	23.4	22.3	18.4
DIURNAL RANGE	4.3	4.3	4.2	4.4	4.0	3.9	3.2	2.9	3.0	4.3	4.1	4.9
S/HEMISPHERE	JUL	AUG	SEP	OCT	NOV	DEC	JAN	FEB	MAR	APR	MAY	JUN

Cultural Recommendations

LIGHT: 2500–3500 fc. Strong air movement is recommended all year.

TEMPERATURES: Summer days average 81–83°F (27–28°C), and nights average 75–76°F (24°C), with a diurnal range of 6–7°F (3–4°C).

HUMIDITY: Information is not available for this location. However, records from nearby stations indicate that humidity is probably near 70–75% year-round. Humidity may be even higher in the rainforest habitat.

WATER: Rainfall is very light to moderate all year. Rainfall is heavier in the rainforest habitat, however, and additional water is available from mist and heavy dew. Cultivated plants should be watered frequently while actively growing. Although they should dry quickly after watering, plants should never be allowed to dry out completely.

FERTILIZER: 1/4–1/2 recommended strength, applied weekly. A high-nitrogen fertilizer is beneficial from spring to midsummer, but a fertilizer high in phosphates should be used in late summer and autumn.

REST PERIOD: Winter days average 74–75°F (23–24°C), and nights average 65–67°F (18–20°C), with a diurnal range of 8–9°F (4–5°C). Growers indicate that plants do not survive temperatures below 54°F (12°C). The dry season in the region is long and severe; but in the habitat, moisture is available from mist and heavy dew. Although water should be reduced in winter, plants should never be allowed to dry completely. Water and fertilizer should be reduced or eliminated until new growth begins in spring. Rot starts easily in young tissue, so water should be kept off new growths until they are 2–3 in. (5–8 cm) tall. In the habitat, light is highest in winter.

GROWING MEDIA: Plants may be mounted on tree-fern or cork slabs or potted in small pots filled with any open, fast-draining medium. Repotting is best done in early spring when new roots are growing.

MISCELLANEOUS NOTES: The bloom season shown in the climate table is based on reports from the habitat; but growers indicate that plants usually bloom several times during the bloom season and may bloom anytime during the year. Plants that produce flowers which last a single day commonly bloom several times during the year. Flowering usually occurs 7–14 days after a sudden 10°F (5°C) drop in daytime temperatures. Plants begin blooming while very young.

Plant and Flower Information

PLANT SIZE AND TYPE: An 8–24 in. (20–60 cm) sympodial epiphyte or lithophyte.

PSEUDOBULB: 8–24 in. (20–60 cm) long. The stems are slender, woody, and generally erect. They frequently form large clumps consisting of hundreds of stems.

LEAVES: Many. The leaves are 1.2–3.1 in. (3–8 cm) long, stiff, persistent, and dark green. Young growths are leafy along their entire length; but as the stems mature, the lower leaves drop, leaving a few near the apex. The leaves are distinctly and unequally bilobed.

INFLORESCENCE: Short. Inflorescences emerge opposite and below the leaf bases from any node on the upper 65% of mature stems. Stems begin blooming when about half mature. The paired blossoms are back to back.

FLOWERS: 2 per inflorescence, up to 30–40 per stem. Nearly pure white, the flowers are 1.2 in. (3 cm) across. The tapering segments are sharply pointed. The lip has an uneven, ruffled margin and a hairy patch in the center of the midlobe. The short-lived flowers last a few hours, but plants produce quantities of flowers 10–14 times a year.

REFERENCES: 67, 145, 233, 240, 259, 262, 533.

PHOTOS/DRAWINGS: *145,* 240, *259, 262, 533.*

Dendrobium trachychilum Kränzlin. Now considered a synonym of *Pseuderia trachychila* (Kränzlin) Schlechter. REFERENCES: 219, 221, 437, 444.

Dendrobium trachyphyllum Schlechter. See *D. cuthbertsonii* F. Mueller. REFERENCES: 221, 385, 437, 445.

Dendrobium trachyrhizum Schlechter

ORIGIN/HABITAT: Northern Papua New Guinea. Plants grow in lowland forests in the Torricelli, Kani, and Finisterre Ranges. They are most often found in partial shade on moss-free trees in gallery forests along wet-weather water courses below 1950 ft. (600 m).

CLIMATE: Station #94004, Wewak, Papua New Guinea, Lat. 3.6°S, Long. 143.7°E, at 16 ft. (5 m). Record extreme temperatures are 98°F (37°C) and 62°F (17°C).

N/HEMISPHERE	JAN	FEB	MAR	APR	MAY	JUN	JUL	AUG	SEP	OCT	NOV	DEC
°F AVG MAX	88	88	88	88	88	88	87	86	87	88	88	88
°F AVG MIN	74	74	74	75	75	75	75	75	74	74	75	74
DIURNAL RANGE	14	14	14	13	13	13	12	11	13	14	13	14
RAIN/INCHES	7.6	4.8	5.3	10.0	13.3	14.5	12.1	11.9	14.9	16.9	15.1	10.8
HUMIDITY/%	80	79	79	78	79	81	82	82	81	82	81	80
BLOOM SEASON			*									*
DAYS CLR	N/A											
RAIN/MM	193	122	135	254	338	368	307	302	378	429	384	274
°C AVG MAX	31.1	31.1	31.1	31.1	31.1	31.1	30.6	30.0	30.6	31.1	31.1	31.1
°C AVG MIN	23.3	23.3	23.3	23.9	23.9	23.9	23.9	23.9	23.3	23.3	23.9	23.3
DIURNAL RANGE	7.8	7.8	7.8	7.2	7.2	7.2	6.7	6.1	7.3	7.8	7.2	7.8
S/HEMISPHERE	JUL	AUG	SEP	OCT	NOV	DEC	JAN	FEB	MAR	APR	MAY	JUN

Cultural Recommendations

LIGHT: 2000–3000 fc.

TEMPERATURES: Throughout the year, days average 86–88°F (30–31°C), and nights average 74–75°F (23–24°C), with a diurnal range of 11–14°F (6–8°C). Average highs vary only 2°F (1°C), and average lows fluctuate even less, indicating that plants may not tolerate wide temperature fluctuations.

HUMIDITY: Near 80% year-round.

WATER: Rainfall is heavy all year, but conditions are slightly drier for 1–2 months in winter. However, rain often comes as heavy showers, so plants dry between the showers. Cultivated plants should be kept moist, with only slight drying allowed between waterings.

FERTILIZER: 1/4–1/2 recommended strength. A balanced fertilizer should be applied weekly to biweekly throughout the year.

REST PERIOD: Growing temperatures should be maintained year-round. Water and fertilizer should be reduced somewhat in winter, especially for plants cultivated in the dark, short-day conditions common in temperate latitudes. Plants should not be allowed to dry out completely, however. In the habitat, light is somewhat higher in winter.

GROWING MEDIA: Baskets or small pots should be filled with a very open and fast-draining medium. When repotting, old canes should not be removed, as they continue to produce blossoms for several years. Repotting may be done anytime new roots are growing.

MISCELLANEOUS NOTES: The bloom season shown in the climate table is based on reports from the habitat. Cultivated plants bloom in winter. The roots are covered with wartlike bumps.

Plant and Flower Information

PLANT SIZE AND TYPE: A 12–24 in. (30–60 cm) sympodial epiphyte.

PSEUDOBULB: 12–24 in. (30–60 cm) long. The ridged stems have beige and brown bands.

LEAVES: Several. The pointed, oblong leaves are 2–4 in. (5–10 cm) long. They are thin textured, dark green, and deciduous.

INFLORESCENCE: 1.6–3.1 in. (4–8 cm) long. Several inflorescences arise from nodes along the stem.

FLOWERS: 3–8 per inflorescence. Sepals and petals are creamy-white to yellowish. The dorsal sepal and petals are erect. The pointed lateral sepals are somewhat triangular. The lip has dark purple and green markings. It is very broad with a deep notch at the apex of the slightly ruffled margin.

REFERENCES: 92, 179, 221, 304, 437, 445.

PHOTOS/DRAWINGS: *304*, 437.

Dendrobium trachythece Schlechter

ORIGIN/HABITAT: Papua New Guinea. Plants grow in the Sepik River region. Habitat elevation is unavailable, so the following climate data should be used with caution.

CLIMATE: Station #200004, Ambunti, Papua New Guinea, Lat. 4.2°S, Long. 142.8°E, at 164 ft. (50 m). Record extreme temperatures are 99°F (37°C) and 52°F (11°C).

N/HEMISPHERE	JAN	FEB	MAR	APR	MAY	JUN	JUL	AUG	SEP	OCT	NOV	DEC
°F AVG MAX	88	90	90	90	91	90	90	90	90	90	90	89
°F AVG MIN	72	73	74	73	73	73	72	73	73	73	73	74
DIURNAL RANGE	16	17	16	17	18	17	18	17	17	17	17	15
RAIN/INCHES	6.4	7.4	7.7	8.5	9.2	9.4	10.9	10.2	12.2	10.4	8.3	5.2
HUMIDITY/%	N/A											
BLOOM SEASON												
DAYS CLR	N/A											
RAIN/MM	163	187	196	217	233	240	277	260	311	265	211	132
°C AVG MAX	31.2	32.2	32.4	32.1	32.6	32.2	32.3	31.9	32.1	31.9	31.9	31.7
°C AVG MIN	22.4	22.8	23.2	22.8	23.0	22.8	22.4	22.5	22.7	22.8	22.9	23.1
DIURNAL RANGE	8.8	9.4	9.2	9.3	9.6	9.4	9.9	9.4	9.4	9.1	9.0	8.6
S/HEMISPHERE	JUL	AUG	SEP	OCT	NOV	DEC	JAN	FEB	MAR	APR	MAY	JUN

Cultural Recommendations

LIGHT: 2000–3000 fc.

TEMPERATURES: Throughout the year, days average 88–91°F (31–33°C), and nights average 72–74°F (22–23°C), with a diurnal range of 15–18°F (9–10°C).

HUMIDITY: Information is not available for this location. Reports from other stations in the region suggest that humidity probably averages 75–85% year-round.

WATER: Rainfall is heavy year-round. The greatest amounts fall in summer and early autumn. Cultivated plants should be moist but not soggy.

FERTILIZER: ¼–½ recommended strength. A balanced fertilizer should be applied weekly to biweekly throughout the year.

REST PERIOD: Growing conditions should be maintained all year. Water and fertilizer should be reduced for plants cultivated in the dark, short-day conditions common in temperate-latitude winters, but they should never be allowed to dry out completely. In the habitat, seasonal light variation is minor.

GROWING MEDIA: Plants may be mounted on tree-fern or cork slabs if humidity is high and plants are watered daily in summer. When plants are potted, any open, fast-draining medium may be used. Repotting may be done anytime new roots are growing.

MISCELLANEOUS NOTES: The bloom season shown in the climate table is based on reports from the habitat.

Plant and Flower Information

PLANT SIZE AND TYPE: A 12–20 in. (30–50 cm) sympodial epiphyte.

PSEUDOBULB: 12–20 in. (30–50 cm) long. The cylindrical stems emerge from a short rhizome. They occasionally branch.

LEAVES: Many. The lanceolate leaves are 1.2–2.0 in. (3–5 cm) long with a short point at the tip. The leaf sheaths are covered with a dense granular coating.

INFLORESCENCE: Short.

FLOWERS: The flowers are 0.5 in. (1.2 cm) long. Blossoms have an elliptical dorsal sepal, with large, somewhat triangular lateral sepals, and obovate-elliptical petals. The conical to hooded lip is toothed to deeply cut along the margin.

REFERENCES: 223, 443.

Dendrobium transparens Wallich ex Lindley

AKA: *D. henshalli* Rchb. f.

ORIGIN/HABITAT: India, Nepal, and Burma. In Nepal, the habitat ranges from 2300–5900 ft. (700–1800 m). Plants also grow Sikkim, the Khasi (Khasia) Hills, and the Chin Hills of Burma. They grow in the Garhwal region of northern India. Plants are common in Arunachal Pradesh in northeast India, where they grow on trees at 650–6550 ft. (200–2000 m). Plants grow high in trees in open forests or at the base of trees in denser forests.

CLIMATE: Station #42147, Mukteswar, India, Lat. 29.5°N, Long. 79.7°E, at 7592 ft. (2314 m). Temperatures are calculated for an elevation of 4000 ft. (1220 m), resulting in probable extremes of 102°F (39°C) and 33°F (1°C).

N/HEMISPHERE	JAN	FEB	MAR	APR	MAY	JUN	JUL	AUG	SEP	OCT	NOV	DEC
°F AVG MAX	63	66	73	81	87	87	81	81	80	77	73	67
°F AVG MIN	48	50	56	64	69	71	71	70	68	62	56	51
DIURNAL RANGE	15	16	17	17	18	16	10	11	12	15	17	16
RAIN/INCHES	1.0	2.1	1.7	1.0	0.3	4.6	11.4	12.8	4.6	3.5	0.3	0.2
HUMIDITY/%	61	55	50	39	44	67	91	93	83	66	55	56
BLOOM SEASON			**	**								
DAYS CLR @ 5PM	17	17	15	18	18	12	1	1	6	25	26	21
RAIN/MM	25	53	43	25	8	117	290	325	117	89	8	5
°C AVG MAX	17.1	18.8	22.7	27.1	30.5	30.5	27.1	27.1	26.6	24.9	22.7	19.4
°C AVG MIN	8.8	9.9	13.3	17.7	20.5	21.6	21.6	21.0	19.9	16.6	13.3	10.5
DIURNAL RANGE	8.3	8.9	9.4	9.4	10.0	8.9	5.5	6.1	6.7	8.3	9.4	8.9
S/HEMISPHERE	JUL	AUG	SEP	OCT	NOV	DEC	JAN	FEB	MAR	APR	MAY	JUN

Cultural Recommendations

LIGHT: 2500–3500 fc. Some shading is needed from spring through autumn, but light should be as high as the plant can tolerate, short of burning the leaves.

TEMPERATURES: Summer days average 81–87°F (27–31°C), and nights average 70–71°F (21–22°C), with a diurnal range of 10–16°F (6–9°C). Plants grow over a wide range of elevations, so they should adapt to temperatures 6–8°F (3–4°C) warmer or cooler than indicated.

HUMIDITY: Near 90% in summer, dropping to 55–60% in winter. The driest season occurs in spring when humidity drops to near 40% for 2 months.

WATER: Rainfall is moderate to heavy for 5 months in summer. The wet season is followed immediately by 7 very dry months from autumn through spring. Several months are so dry that even morning dew is uncommon. Cultivated plants should be kept moist while actively growing, but water should be gradually reduced after new growths mature in autumn.

FERTILIZER: ¼–½ recommended strength, applied weekly. A high-nitrogen fertilizer is beneficial from spring to midsummer, but a fertilizer high in phosphates should be used in late summer and autumn.

REST PERIOD: Winter days average 63–67°F (17–19°C), and nights average 48–51°F (9–11°C), with a diurnal range of 15–16°F (8–9°C). Water should be reduced for cultivated plants in winter. They should be allowed to dry out between waterings but should not remain dry for extended periods. Occasional early morning mistings between waterings may be beneficial in keeping plants from becoming too dry. In the habitat, winter is the brightest season.

GROWING MEDIA: Mounting plants on tree-fern or cork slabs accommodates their often pendulous growth habit. However, humidity must be high and plants must be watered at least once a day in summer. If plants cannot be mounted, hanging pots or baskets may be filled with an open, fast-draining medium. Repotting may be done anytime new roots are actively growing.

MISCELLANEOUS NOTES: The bloom season shown in the climate table is based on reports from the habitat. Cultivation records show blooming from winter into summer with peak blooming in spring. Growers indicate that although *D. transparens* is not widely cultivated, it is free-flowering and attractive when well grown.

Plant and Flower Information

PLANT SIZE AND TYPE: A 12–24 in. (30–60 cm) sympodial epiphyte.

PSEUDOBULB: 12–24 in. (30–60 cm) long. The slender stems, which are swollen at the base, may be erect or pendulous. They are mottled with dark gray and faintly yellow at the thickened nodes.

LEAVES: 5–7. The leaves are 3.1–4.3 in. (8–11 cm) long, thin textured, and linear-lanceolate. The margin is uneven at the tip. The leaves are found only on younger stems, as they are quickly deciduous.

INFLORESCENCE: The purplish inflorescences arise from numerous nodes along the prior year's leafless stems.

FLOWERS: 2, rarely 3 per inflorescence. The flowers are 1.2–2.0 in. (3–5 cm) across. Sepals and petals are normally transparent white with varying amounts of pink or purple at the tips, but pure white clones do occur. The fringed lip is white with pink or purple at the apex. It is inrolled at the base, without distinct sidelobes, and finely fringed along the margin. The midlobe is wavy and undulate along the edge. The throat is decorated with 1–2 dark purple or blood red blotches. Blossoms are short-lived and delicately fragrant.

HYBRIDIZING NOTES: Chromosome counts are n = 20 (ref. 150, 154, 504, 542, 580), n = 19 (ref. 151, 152), 2n = 38 (ref. 152, 542, 580), 2n = 20 (ref. 154), and 2n = 40 (30) (ref. 504, 542).

REFERENCES: 36, 38, 46, 102, 150, 151, 152, 154, 157, 179, 190, 202, 210, 216, 254, 277, 278, 294, 317, 358, 369, 376, 430, 445, 458, 504, 523, 541, 542, 557, 569, 570, 580.

PHOTOS/DRAWINGS: *36,* 46, 102, 210, 294, 369, *430,* 458, *569.*

Dendrobium transtilliferum J. J. Smith

ORIGIN/HABITAT: The west coast of Sumatra. Plants grow near Pariaman, Solok, and several other locations near Padang. Habitat elevation is unreported, so the following climate data should be used with caution.

CLIMATE: Station #96163, Padang, Sumatra, Indonesia, Lat. 0.9°S, Long. 100.4°E, at 19 ft. (6 m). Temperatures are calculated for an elevation of 450 ft. (140 m), resulting in probable extremes of 93°F (34°C) and 67°F (19°C).

N/HEMISPHERE	JAN	FEB	MAR	APR	MAY	JUN	JUL	AUG	SEP	OCT	NOV	DEC
°F AVG MAX	86	86	85	85	85	85	86	86	86	86	87	86
°F AVG MIN	73	73	73	73	73	73	73	73	73	74	74	73
DIURNAL RANGE	13	13	12	12	12	12	13	13	13	12	13	13
RAIN/INCHES	10.9	13.7	6.0	19.5	20.4	18.9	13.8	10.2	12.1	14.3	12.4	12.1
HUMIDITY/%	81	82	82	84	85	84	81	81	82	83	81	81
BLOOM SEASON	N/A											
DAYS CLR @ 7AM	5	1	1	0	0	2	2	1	2	2	3	5
DAYS CLR @ 1PM	5	2	2	1	1	3	3	4	3	3	6	5
RAIN/MM	277	348	152	495	518	480	351	259	307	363	315	307
°C AVG MAX	29.8	29.8	29.2	29.2	29.2	29.2	29.8	29.8	29.8	29.8	30.3	29.8
°C AVG MIN	22.5	22.5	22.5	22.5	22.5	22.5	22.5	22.5	22.5	23.1	23.1	22.5
DIURNAL RANGE	7.3	7.3	6.7	6.7	6.7	6.7	7.3	7.3	7.3	6.7	7.2	7.3
S/HEMISPHERE	JUL	AUG	SEP	OCT	NOV	DEC	JAN	FEB	MAR	APR	MAY	JUN

Cultural Recommendations

LIGHT: 2000–2500 fc. Diffused light is preferred.

TEMPERATURES: Throughout the year, days average 85–87°F (29–30°C), and nights average 73–74°F (23°C), with a diurnal range of 12–13°F (7°C). Probable extremes vary only a few degrees from the averages, indicating that the plant may not tolerate wide temperature fluctuations.

HUMIDITY: 80–85% year-round.

WATER: Rainfall is heavy all year. Cultivated plants should be constantly moist but not soggy.

FERTILIZER: ¼–½ recommended strength. A balanced fertilizer should be applied weekly to biweekly throughout the year.

REST PERIOD: Growing conditions should be maintained year-round. Water may be reduced somewhat for cultivated plants in winter, especially those grown in the dark, short-day conditions common in temperate latitudes. They should never be allowed to dry out completely, however. In the habitat, light is slightly brighter in winter.

GROWING MEDIA: Plants may be mounted on tree-fern or cork slabs or potted in small pots filled with any open, fast-draining medium. Repotting may be done anytime new roots are growing.

MISCELLANEOUS NOTES: The plant was described in 1922 in *Bull. Jard. Bot. Buit.* 3rd sér. 5:85.

Plant and Flower Information

PLANT SIZE AND TYPE: A 24 in. (60 cm) sympodial epiphyte.

PSEUDOBULB: 24 in. (60 cm) long. Stems are slender, elongated, and grooved. They may be greenish yellow or yellowish brown.

LEAVES: The leaves are about 3.5 in. (9 cm) long, but they are smaller near the apex. They are lanceolate to linear-lanceolate, deciduous, and papery.

INFLORESCENCE: Short. Inflorescences emerge from nodes along the upper, leafless part of the stem.

FLOWERS: 2–6 per inflorescence. The flowers are 0.8 in. (2 cm) long. Sepals and petals are pale yellow and nearly transparent. The backsides of the sepals are tinged or dotted with light purple. The light yellow lip is marked with a yellow-brown or orange longitudinal band. The somewhat ovate dorsal sepal is erect and recurved at the apex. Lateral sepals are obliquely triangular. Petals are elliptical with an uneven margin. The erect lip is recurved. The nearly round midlobe is toothed or uneven along the margin. Blossoms are honey-scented.

REFERENCES: 223.

Dendrobium transversilobium J. J. Smith. Now considered a synonym of *Cadetia transversiloba* (J. J. Smith) Schlechter. REFERENCES: 220, 254, 437, 445, 470.

Dendrobium treacherianum Rchb. f. Now considered a synonym of *Epigeneium treacherianum* (Rchb. f.) Summerhayes. REFERENCES: 25, 179, 200, 216, 229, 254, 286, 394, 445, 499, 541, 570.

Dendrobium treubii J. J. Smith

ORIGIN/HABITAT: The Molucca Islands. Plants grow on Ambon and near Wahaai on Seram. Habitat elevation is not available, so the following climate data should be used with caution. Plants were cultivated in the botanical garden at Bogor, Java.

CLIMATE: Station #97724, Ambon/Pattimura, Indonesia, Lat. 3.7°S, Long. 128.1°E, at 33 ft. (10 m). Record extreme temperatures are 96°F (36°C) and 66°F (19°C).

N/HEMISPHERE	JAN	FEB	MAR	APR	MAY	JUN	JUL	AUG	SEP	OCT	NOV	DEC
°F AVG MAX	81	81	83	85	88	88	88	88	88	86	84	82
°F AVG MIN	74	74	74	74	75	76	76	76	76	76	75	74
DIURNAL RANGE	7	7	9	11	13	12	12	12	12	10	9	8
RAIN/INCHES	23.7	15.8	9.5	6.1	4.5	5.2	5.0	4.7	5.3	11.0	20.3	25.1
HUMIDITY/%	83	82	81	80	79	78	78	77	79	82	83	84
BLOOM SEASON					*							
DAYS CLR @ 9AM	1	1	1	6	7	4	3	3	5	5	3	3
DAYS CLR @ 3PM	1	1	2	5	6	1	1	1	2	3	1	3
RAIN/MM	602	401	241	155	114	132	127	119	135	279	516	638
°C AVG MAX	27.2	27.2	28.3	29.4	31.1	31.1	31.1	31.1	31.1	30.0	28.9	27.8
°C AVG MIN	23.3	23.3	23.3	23.3	23.9	24.4	24.4	24.4	24.4	24.4	23.9	23.3
DIURNAL RANGE	3.9	3.9	5.0	6.1	7.2	6.7	6.7	6.7	6.7	5.6	5.0	4.5
S/HEMISPHERE	JUL	AUG	SEP	OCT	NOV	DEC	JAN	FEB	MAR	APR	MAY	JUN

Cultural Recommendations

LIGHT: 2500–3500 fc.

TEMPERATURES: Throughout the year, days average 81–88°F (27–31°C), and nights average 74–76°F (23–24°C), with a diurnal range of 7–13°F (4–7°C).

HUMIDITY: 80–85% year-round.

WATER: Rainfall is moderate to heavy all year, but conditions are slightly drier in late spring and summer. Cultivated plants should be kept evenly moist with only slight drying allowed between waterings.

FERTILIZER: ¼–½ recommended strength. A balanced fertilizer should be applied weekly to biweekly throughout the year.

REST PERIOD: Growing conditions should be maintained all year. In the habitat, rainfall is heaviest in winter, but water and fertilizer may be reduced somewhat for cultivated plants, especially those grown in the dark, short-day conditions common in temperate latitudes. They should never be allowed to dry completely, however. In the habitat, light is highest in spring.

GROWING MEDIA: Plants may be mounted on tree-fern or cork slabs if humidity is high and plants are watered daily in summer. When plants are potted, medium or coarse fir bark or any open, fast-draining medium may be used. Repotting may be done anytime new roots are growing.

MISCELLANEOUS NOTES: The bloom season shown in the climate table is based on cultivation records.

Plant and Flower Information

PLANT SIZE AND TYPE: An 18 in. (45 cm) sympodial epiphyte.

PSEUDOBULB: 10–14 in. (25–35 cm) long. The flattened stems are slender at the base and swollen above. They are elliptical in cross-section.

LEAVES: 10–12 per growth. The oblong leaves are 4–6 in. (10–15 cm) long, deciduous, pale green, somewhat wavy along the margin, and slightly twisted at the base. They are arranged in 2 rows along the stem.

INFLORESCENCE: 2.4 in. (6 cm) long. The pendulous, laxly flowered inflorescences emerge from upper nodes.

FLOWERS: 5–6 per inflorescence. The shiny, yellowish white flowers are 2.4 in. (6 cm) across. Blossoms have an ovate-lanceolate dorsal sepal, 3-angled lateral sepals, and lanceolate petals. The 3-lobed lip is erect, curved at the tip, and wavy along the margin. Sidelobes are broadly 3-angled. The oblong midlobe is pale yellow at the base. The disk is purple.

REFERENCES: 65, 25, 179, 219, 220, 254, 445, 468, 471.

PHOTOS/DRAWINGS: 471.

Dendrobium triadenium Lindley. See *D. mutabile* (Blume) Lindley. REFERENCES: 21, 190, 254, 445, 469.

Dendrobium trialamellatum Schlechter. Transferred to *Ephemerantha trilamellata* (Schlechter) Hunt and Summerhayes, which is now considered synonymous with *Flickingeria*. REFERENCES: 213, 230.

Dendrobium trialatum Schlechter. See *D. vexillarius* J. J. Smith. REFERENCES: 221, 385, 437, 445.

Dendrobium triangulum J. J. Smith

ORIGIN/HABITAT: Irian Jaya (western New Guinea). Plants grow on forest trees near the Giriwo River along the east coast of Teluk Cenderawasih (Geelvink Bay).

CLIMATE: Station #97682, Nabire, Irian Jaya, Lat. 3.3°S, Long. 135.5°E, at 10 ft. (3 m). Record extreme temperatures are not available for this location.

N/HEMISPHERE	JAN	FEB	MAR	APR	MAY	JUN	JUL	AUG	SEP	OCT	NOV	DEC
°F AVG MAX	86	86	86	86	87	87	86	86	87	87	87	87
°F AVG MIN	75	75	76	77	77	76	77	75	75	76	76	76
DIURNAL RANGE	11	11	10	9	10	11	9	11	12	11	11	11
RAIN/INCHES	7.4	11.1	8.5	8.5	7.5	9.0	9.2	10.6	12.1	11.3	10.2	9.8
HUMIDITY/%	N/A											
BLOOM SEASON			*									
DAYS CLR	N/A											
RAIN/MM	190	283	217	217	192	228	233	270	308	286	259	248
°C AVG MAX	30.1	29.9	30.1	30.3	30.5	30.6	30.0	30.0	30.5	30.5	30.3	30.3
°C AVG MIN	24.0	24.0	24.3	24.7	24.9	24.5	24.8	24.0	23.8	24.6	24.3	24.2
DIURNAL RANGE	6.1	5.9	5.8	5.6	5.6	6.1	5.2	6.0	6.7	5.9	6.0	6.1
S/HEMISPHERE	JUL	AUG	SEP	OCT	NOV	DEC	JAN	FEB	MAR	APR	MAY	JUN

Cultural Recommendations

LIGHT: 2000–3000 fc.

TEMPERATURES: Throughout the year, days average 86–87°F (30–31°C), and nights average 75–77°F (24–25°C), with a diurnal range of 9–12°F (5–7°C).

HUMIDITY: Information is not available for this location. However, records from nearby stations indicate that humidity probably averages near 85% year-round.

WATER: Rainfall is heavy year-round. Cultivated plants should be kept evenly moist with only slight drying between waterings. Warm water might be beneficial.

FERTILIZER: ¼–½ recommended strength. A balanced fertilizer should be applied weekly to biweekly throughout the year.

REST PERIOD: Growing conditions should be maintained year-round. Water and fertilizer may be reduced slightly in winter, especially for plants grown in the dark, short-day conditions common in temperate latitudes. Plants should never be allowed to dry completely, however.

GROWING MEDIA: Plants may be mounted if humidity is high and plants are watered daily in summer. When plants are potted, any open, fast-draining medium may be used. Repotting may be done anytime new roots are growing.

MISCELLANEOUS NOTES: The bloom season shown in the climate table is based on reports from the habitat. The plant was described in 1914 in *Bull. Jard. Bot. Buit.* 2nd sér. 13:65

Plant and Flower Information

PLANT SIZE AND TYPE: A 10 in. (25 cm) sympodial epiphyte.

PSEUDOBULB: 10 in. (25 cm) long. The flattened stems are branching and rooting.

LEAVES: Many. The leaves are 0.6–0.9 in. (1.5–2.3 cm) long. The leaves are unequally bilobed at the apex and somewhat twisted at the base.

INFLORESCENCE: Short. Inflorescences emerge through the leaf bases.

Dendrobium tribuloides

FLOWERS: 2 per inflorescence. The small, yellow flowers are 0.3 in. (0.8 cm) long. Blossoms have an oblong dorsal sepal, obliquely triangular lateral sepals, and lanceolate petals. Sepals and petals are concave and except for the dorsal sepal the segments are somewhat sickle-shaped. The tiny, 3-lobed lip is erect and recurved. The triangular midlobe is short and wavy. The large sidelobes are triangular.

REFERENCES: 221, 470.

Dendrobium tribuloides Swartz. Now considered a synonym of *Pleurothallis tribuloides* Lindley. REFERENCES: 190, 216, 254, 445.

Dendrobium tricallosum Ames and Schweinfurth. Now considered a synonym of *Epigeneium tricallosum* (Ames and Schweinfurth) J. J. Wood. REFERENCES: 12, 222, 235, 286, 590.

Dendrobium trichosepalum A. Gilli

ORIGIN/HABITAT: Papua New Guinea. Plants grow in the forests west of Laiagam at about 9500 ft. (3000 m).

CLIMATE: Botanical garden records, Laiagam, Papua New Guinea, Lat. 5.5°S, Long. 143.5°E, at 7218 ft. (2200 m). Temperatures are calculated for an elevation of 9500 ft. (2900 m), resulting in probable extremes of 83°F (29°C) and 24°F (−4°C).

N/HEMISPHERE	JAN	FEB	MAR	APR	MAY	JUN	JUL	AUG	SEP	OCT	NOV	DEC
°F AVG MAX	68	69	70	68	70	70	74	69	68	70	70	68
°F AVG MIN	47	46	47	47	48	48	47	48	50	49	48	48
DIURNAL RANGE	21	23	23	21	22	22	27	21	18	21	22	20
RAIN/INCHES	4.0	4.8	6.1	7.8	8.5	9.1	8.4	9.6	9.5	8.9	6.3	4.0
HUMIDITY/%	N/A											
BLOOM SEASON	N/A											
DAYS CLR	N/A											
RAIN/MM	102	122	155	198	216	231	213	244	241	226	160	102
°C AVG MAX	20.2	20.8	21.4	20.2	21.4	21.4	23.6	20.8	20.2	21.4	21.4	20.2
°C AVG MIN	8.6	8.0	8.6	8.6	9.1	9.1	8.6	9.1	10.2	9.7	9.1	9.1
DIURNAL RANGE	11.6	12.8	12.8	11.6	12.3	12.3	15.0	11.7	10.0	11.7	12.3	11.1
S/HEMISPHERE	JUL	AUG	SEP	OCT	NOV	DEC	JAN	FEB	MAR	APR	MAY	JUN

Cultural Recommendations

LIGHT: 2000–3000 fc.

TEMPERATURES: Throughout the year, days average 68–74°F (20–24°C), and nights average 46–50°F (8–10°C), with a diurnal range of 18–27°F (10–15°C).

HUMIDITY: Information is not available for this location. However, records from other stations in the region indicate that values are probably 70–80% year-round.

WATER: Rainfall is heavy throughout the year, but conditions are slightly drier for 3–4 months in winter. Cultivated plants should be kept moist.

FERTILIZER: ¼–½ recommended strength. A balanced fertilizer should be applied weekly to biweekly throughout the year.

REST PERIOD: Growing conditions should be maintained all year. Water and fertilizer should be reduced somewhat in winter, especially when plants are grown in the dark, short-day conditions common in temperate latitudes. Plants should dry slightly between waterings, but they should never be allowed to dry out completely. Water and fertilizer should be gradually increased when plants begin growing in spring.

GROWING MEDIA: Mounting plants on tree-fern or cork slabs accommodates their pendulous growth habit. However, humidity must be high and plants must be watered at least once a day in summer. If plants cannot be mounted, small pots or hanging baskets may be filled with an open, fast-draining medium. Repotting may be done anytime new roots are actively growing.

Plant and Flower Information

PLANT SIZE AND TYPE: A sympodial epiphyte of unreported size.

PSEUDOBULB: The long, branching stems are pendent.

LEAVES: Many. The linear-lanceolate leaves are 2–4 in. (5–10 cm) long, with a rough, warty surface.

INFLORESCENCE: Short. The blossoms are held opposite each other.

FLOWERS: 2 per inflorescence. Flowers are 1.6–2.0 in. (4–5 cm) long. Sepals and petals are white with lilac dots at the base and yellow veins. They taper from the somewhat triangular base to a long slender tip. Blossoms turn lilac with age. The lanceolate to tongue-shaped lip, which is not lobed, is densely fringed along the margin and sparsely hairy along the upper surface.

REFERENCES: 146, 234.

PHOTOS/DRAWINGS: 146.

Dendrobium trichostomum Rchb. f. ex Oliver

ORIGIN/HABITAT: Northern Papua New Guinea. Plants grow on mistforest trees in the Kani and Ibo Mountains at about 3300 ft. (1000 m). They are found on creek-side trees near the Bismarck Range at about 2600 ft. (800 m). Collections are reported in Irian Jaya (western New Guinea), but habitat information is not available.

CLIMATE: Station #200187, Erap, Papua New Guinea, Lat. 6.6°S, Long. 146.7°E, at 850 ft. (260 m). Temperatures are calculated for an elevation of 3300 ft. (1000 m), resulting in probable extremes of 94°F (34°C) and 45°F (7°C).

N/HEMISPHERE	JAN	FEB	MAR	APR	MAY	JUN	JUL	AUG	SEP	OCT	NOV	DEC
°F AVG MAX	80	80	81	82	85	85	85	85	85	84	82	82
°F AVG MIN	61	61	61	62	64	65	64	64	65	63	66	62
DIURNAL RANGE	19	19	20	20	21	20	21	21	20	21	16	20
RAIN/INCHES	3.9	3.9	2.7	3.0	3.0	5.3	5.9	5.9	7.0	3.4	2.4	3.1
HUMIDITY/%	82	81	81	79	75	74	74	74	77	76	80	80
BLOOM SEASON			*			*	*	*				
DAYS CLR	N/A											
RAIN/MM	99	99	69	76	76	135	150	150	178	86	61	79
°C AVG MAX	26.7	26.7	27.2	27.8	29.4	29.4	29.4	29.4	29.4	28.9	27.8	27.8
°C AVG MIN	16.1	16.1	16.1	16.7	17.8	18.3	17.8	17.8	18.3	17.2	18.9	16.7
DIURNAL RANGE	10.6	10.6	11.1	11.1	11.6	11.1	11.6	11.6	11.1	11.7	8.9	11.1
S/HEMISPHERE	JUL	AUG	SEP	OCT	NOV	DEC	JAN	FEB	MAR	APR	MAY	JUN

Cultural Recommendations

LIGHT: 3000–4000 fc.

TEMPERATURES: Throughout the year, days average 80–85°F (27–29°C), and nights average 61–66°F (16–19°C), with a diurnal range of 16–21°F (9–12°C).

HUMIDITY: 75–80% year-round. Despite high average humidity, the habitat may be quite dry during hot afternoons.

WATER: Rainfall is moderate most of the year, but conditions are somewhat wetter for 4–5 months in summer and early autumn. Cultivated plants should be thoroughly saturated then allowed to dry slightly between waterings in summer and early autumn. Water should be gradually reduced in autumn.

FERTILIZER: ¼–½ recommended strength. A balanced fertilizer should be applied weekly to biweekly throughout the year.

REST PERIOD: Growing temperatures should be maintained all year. In the habitat, rainfall is lowest in winter, but the high humidity indicates that additional moisture is frequently available from heavy dew. Cultivated plants should be allowed to dry for somewhat longer between waterings than in summer, but they should not remain dry for extended periods. Fertilizer should be reduced until water is increased in spring. In the habitat, seasonal light variation is minor.

GROWING MEDIA: To accommodate the pendulous growth habit, plants may be mounted on tree-fern or cork slabs or potted in small hanging pots or baskets filled with any open, fast-draining medium. Repotting may be done anytime new roots are growing.

MISCELLANEOUS NOTES: The bloom season shown in the climate table is based on collection reports.

Plant and Flower Information

PLANT SIZE AND TYPE: A 10 in. (25 cm) sympodial epiphyte.

PSEUDOBULB: 10 in. (25 cm) long. The pendulous, cylindrical stems emerge from a short rhizome.

LEAVES: Many. The elliptical, spreading leaves are 1.2–1.6 in. (3–4 cm) long. The undersides of the leaves are a uniform olive-purple. The leaves and leaf sheaths are often tinged with purple.

INFLORESCENCE: Short. Inflorescences most often emerge from nodes along the upper portion of the stem.

FLOWERS: Few per inflorescence, many per plant. The flowers are 0.4 in. (1 cm) across. They may be purple-carmine, orange-yellow, or orange-red. The dorsal sepal is ovate, and the lateral sepals are very dilated at the apex. The petals are linear. The margin of the lip is minutely fringed and turned in.

REFERENCES: 216, 254, 393, 470, 486, 553.

Dendrobium tricolor Kränzlin. See *D. correllianum* A. Hawkes and A. H. Heller. REFERENCES: 220, 229, 254.

Dendrobium tricolor Persoon. Now considered a synonym of *Maxillaria tricolor* Ruiz and Pavon. REFERENCES: 216, 254.

Dendrobium tricostatum Schlechter. See *D. subacaule* Reinwardt ex Lindley. REFERENCES: 94, 221, 271, 385, 437, 445. PHOTOS/DRAWINGS: 94.

Dendrobium tricuspe (Blume) Lindley.

AKA: *Onychium tricuspe* Blume, *Dendrobium kohlmeyerianum* Teijsm. and Binn.

ORIGIN/HABITAT: West Java and Sumatra. Comber (ref. 75) indicates that the orchid is rare in lowland forests. It has not been found recently.

CLIMATE: Station #96755, Bogor, Java, Indonesia, Lat. 6.5°S, Long. 106.8°E, at 558 ft. (170 m). Record extreme temperatures are 96°F (36°C) and 66°F (19°C).

N/HEMISPHERE	JAN	FEB	MAR	APR	MAY	JUN	JUL	AUG	SEP	OCT	NOV	DEC
°F AVG MAX	86	87	88	88	87	85	84	84	85	86	87	86
°F AVG MIN	73	73	73	74	74	74	74	74	74	75	75	74
DIURNAL RANGE	13	14	15	14	13	11	10	10	11	11	12	12
RAIN/INCHES	2.1	1.0	0.5	5.0	8.1	18.8	23.7	20.2	14.4	12.0	11.9	3.4
HUMIDITY/%	72	68	65	66	74	79	84	84	81	79	77	75
BLOOM SEASON	N/A											
DAYS CLR @ 7AM	14	14	14	11	5	3	1	2	4	6	10	12
DAYS CLR @ 1PM	9	10	8	5	1	1	0	0	1	1	3	7
RAIN/MM	53	25	13	127	206	478	602	513	366	305	302	86
°C AVG MAX	30.0	30.6	31.1	31.1	30.6	29.4	28.9	28.9	29.4	30.0	30.6	30.0
°C AVG MIN	22.8	22.8	22.8	23.3	23.3	23.3	23.3	23.3	23.3	23.9	23.9	23.3
DIURNAL RANGE	7.2	7.8	8.3	7.8	7.3	6.1	5.6	5.6	6.1	6.1	6.7	6.7
S/HEMISPHERE	JUL	AUG	SEP	OCT	NOV	DEC	JAN	FEB	MAR	APR	MAY	JUN

Cultural Recommendations

LIGHT: 1200–2400 fc. Diffused or barely dappled light is preferred. Direct sunlight should be avoided.

TEMPERATURES: Throughout the year, days average 84–88°F (29–31°C), and nights average 73–75°F (23–24°C), with a diurnal range of 10–15°F (6–8°C). Cultivated plants may not tolerate wide seasonal temperature fluctuations.

HUMIDITY: Near 75–85% most of the year, dropping to about 65% for 3 months in winter.

WATER: Rainfall is very heavy from spring to autumn, but conditions are very dry for 2–3 months in winter. During the growing season, plants should never be allowed to dry out completely, but water should be gradually reduced in late autumn.

FERTILIZER: ¼–½ recommended strength, applied weekly. A high-nitrogen fertilizer is beneficial from spring to midsummer, but a fertilizer high in phosphates should be used in late summer and autumn.

REST PERIOD: Growing conditions should be maintained all year, but rainfall is very low for 2–3 winter months. Cultivated plants should become somewhat dry between waterings, but they should not remain dry for prolonged periods. Fertilizer may be reduced or eliminated anytime the plant is not actively growing. In the habitat, light is highest in winter.

GROWING MEDIA: Plants may be mounted on tree-fern or cork slabs if humidity is high and plants are watered at least once daily in summer. When plants are potted, any open, fast-draining medium may be used. Repotting is best done in spring when new growth starts.

Plant and Flower Information

PLANT SIZE AND TYPE: A 39 in. (100 cm) sympodial epiphyte.

PSEUDOBULB: 39 in. (100 cm) long. The swollen portion of the stem, which is about 5 in. (13 cm) long, is lanceolate and flattened. The slender, elongated portion is flattened. The older stems may branch.

LEAVES: The leaves are thin, lanceolate, and about 2.4 in. (6 cm) long.

FLOWERS: The fan-shaped flowers are 0.6 in. (1.5 cm) long. The wide sepals are white on the inner surface and yellowish with red at the base on the outside. The white, narrow petals, which are rounded at the tip, have an uneven margin. The lip has a triangular outline with narrow sidelobes. The midlobe is divided into 2 parts with a short fringe at the apex. The disk has 3 ridges of yellow papillae with red tips.

REFERENCES: 25, 75, 216, 254, 310, 445, 469.

PHOTOS/DRAWINGS: 469.

Dendrobium tridentatum Ames and Schweinfurth

ORIGIN/HABITAT: Northern Borneo. In Sabah, plants grow on the Marei Parei Spur of Mt. Kinabalu. Plants grow in both lower and upper mountain forests at 4900–7200 ft. (1500–2200 m).

CLIMATE: Station #49613, Tambunan, Sabah, Borneo, Lat. 5.7°N, Long. 116.4°E, at 1200 ft. (366 m). Temperatures are calculated for an elevation of 6000 ft. (1830 m), resulting in probable extremes of 82°F (28°C) and 38°F (3°C).

N/HEMISPHERE	JAN	FEB	MAR	APR	MAY	JUN	JUL	AUG	SEP	OCT	NOV	DEC
°F AVG MAX	70	71	73	74	74	73	73	73	73	72	71	70
°F AVG MIN	51	49	50	51	52	51	50	50	51	51	51	52
DIURNAL RANGE	19	22	23	23	22	22	23	23	22	21	20	18
RAIN/INCHES	5.8	3.7	5.8	7.5	8.2	7.3	5.1	4.9	6.4	7.0	6.8	6.0
HUMIDITY/%	N/A											
BLOOM SEASON											*	
DAYS CLR	N/A											
RAIN/MM	147	94	147	190	208	185	130	124	163	178	173	152
°C AVG MAX	21.2	21.8	22.9	23.4	23.4	22.9	22.9	22.9	22.9	22.3	21.8	21.2
°C AVG MIN	10.6	9.5	10.1	10.6	11.2	10.6	10.1	10.1	10.6	10.6	10.6	11.2
DIURNAL RANGE	10.6	12.3	12.8	12.8	12.2	12.3	12.8	12.8	12.3	11.7	11.2	10.0
S/HEMISPHERE	JUL	AUG	SEP	OCT	NOV	DEC	JAN	FEB	MAR	APR	MAY	JUN

Cultural Recommendations

LIGHT: 2000–3000 fc.

TEMPERATURES: Throughout the year, days average 70–74°F (21–23°C), and nights average 49–52°F (10–11°C), with a diurnal range of 18–23°F (10–13°C).

HUMIDITY: Information is not available for this location. However, reports from nearby stations indicate that humidity is probably 80–85% year-round. Excellent air circulation should be provided.

WATER: Rainfall is moderate to heavy through the year. Cultivated plants should be kept moist with only slight drying allowed between waterings.

FERTILIZER: ¼–½ recommended strength. A balanced fertilizer should be applied weekly to biweekly throughout the year.

REST PERIOD: Growing conditions vary only slightly through the year. The diurnal range is slightly lower in winter due to somewhat cooler days. In cultivation, water should be reduced somewhat in winter, especially for plants grown in the dark, short-day conditions common in temperate latitudes. Plants should never be allowed to dry out completely, however. Fertilizer should be decreased when water is reduced and when plants are not actively growing.

GROWING MEDIA: Plants may be mounted on tree-fern or cork slabs or potted in small pots filled with any open, fast-draining medium. Repotting may be done anytime new roots are growing.

MISCELLANEOUS NOTES: The bloom season shown in the climate table is based on collection reports. The very long roots, which rarely branch, occasionally develop at upper nodes.

Plant and Flower Information

PLANT SIZE AND TYPE: A 16 in. (40 cm) sympodial epiphyte.

PSEUDOBULB: 16 in. (40 cm) long. The many jointed, gently arched stems have a 1.2 in. (3 cm) swelling at the base. They may be yellow to greenish brown with dark rings around the numerous joints.

LEAVES: Many. The linear leaves are 2 in. (5 cm) long. They are thick and rigid with a sharp, pointed projection at the rounded tip.

INFLORESCENCE: Short. Inflorescences emerge from upper nodes opposite the leaves.

FLOWERS: 1 per inflorescence. The white flowers are 1.4–1.6 in. (3.5–4.0 cm) across. Lateral sepals are narrowly triangular-lanceolate and taper to a long point. The dorsal sepal and petals are very narrow. The lip is 3-lobed. The flower strongly resembles *D. crumenatum* Swartz, but the growth habit is similar to *D. singaporense* A. Hawkes and A. H. Heller.

REFERENCES: 12, 222, 286, 592.

PHOTOS/DRAWINGS: 592.

Dendrobium tridentiferum Lindley.

Plants reportedly originated in Papua New Guinea, but habitat location and elevation were not reported, so climate data cannot be selected. An elongated sympodial epiphyte of unreported size. The long, branching stems consist of many nodes. The many leaves are 4.3–6.0 in. (11–15 cm) long. They are fleshy and broadly oblong-lanceolate. The short inflorescences emerge at the tips of the branches. Each inflorescence bears 2 blossoms. The fleshy, spreading flowers are 0.8 in. (2 cm) across. Flowers were described as possibly being purple and some pale color. The blossoms have an oblong dorsal sepal, ovate lateral sepals, and pointed, oblong-lanceolate petals. The lip has a pointed midlobe with coarse protuberances and somewhat ovate sidelobes. REFERENCES: 216, 254, 310, 317.

Dendrobium triflorum (Blume) Lindley.

Now considered a synonym of *Epigeneium triflorum* (Blume) Summerhayes. REFERENCES: 25, 75, 179, 213, 216, 229, 254, 277, 310, 445, 469, 499.

Dendrobium trifolium J. J. Smith.

See *D. vexillarius* J. J. Smith. REFERENCES: 144, 222, 385.

Dendrobium trigonellodorum Kränzlin.

Plants originated in Papua New Guinea, but neither habitat location nor elevation were included with the original description, so climate data cannot be selected. Plants are 12–16 in. (30–40 cm) sympodial epiphytes with numerous, oblong leaves which are 3.1–4.0 in. (8–10 cm) long. The short inflorescences carry 2 or more blossoms per inflorescence. The flowers, which open in succession, are 1.2 in. (3 cm) across the spread sepals. The dorsal sepal is broadly oblong, lateral sepals are ovate with a broad base, and petals are slender ovals. The 3-lobed lip is incurved, and slightly wavy along the margin, with a minutely warty disk. The midlobe is triangular. The oval sidelobes are incurved. The entire plant has an unpleasant odor. REFERENCES: 220, 254.

Dendrobium trigonocarpum Schlechter.

Now considered a synonym of *Cadetia trigonocarpa* (Schlechter) Schlechter. REFERENCES: 219, 254, 437, 444.

Dendrobium trigonopus Rchb. f.

AKA: *D. velutinum* Rolfe.

ORIGIN/HABITAT: The Shan States of Burma, Laos, Yunnan Province of southwestern China, and the mountains of northern Thailand. Plants grow at 1000–4900 ft. (300–1500 m).

CLIMATE: Station #48327, Chiang Mai, Thailand, Lat. 18.8°N, Long. 99.0°E, at 1100 ft. (335 m). Temperatures are calculated for an elevation of 4000 ft. (1220 m), resulting in probable extremes of 99°F (38°C) and 28°F (–2°C).

N/HEMISPHERE	JAN	FEB	MAR	APR	MAY	JUN	JUL	AUG	SEP	OCT	NOV	DEC
°F AVG MAX	75	80	85	86	84	80	79	77	78	79	76	74
°F AVG MIN	46	47	52	60	64	64	64	65	63	61	56	47
DIURNAL RANGE	29	33	33	26	20	16	15	12	15	18	20	27
RAIN/INCHES	0.3	0.4	0.6	2.0	5.5	6.1	7.4	8.7	11.5	4.9	1.5	0.4
HUMIDITY/%	73	65	58	62	73	78	80	83	83	81	79	76
BLOOM SEASON		*	*									
DAYS CLR @ 7AM	5	5	2	2	1	0	0	0	0	1	3	3
DAYS CLR @ 1PM	9	8	4	2	0	0	0	0	0	0	1	3
RAIN/MM	8	10	15	51	140	155	188	221	292	124	38	10
°C AVG MAX	24.1	26.9	29.7	30.2	29.1	26.9	26.4	25.2	25.8	26.4	24.7	23.6
°C AVG MIN	8.0	8.6	11.3	15.8	18.0	18.0	18.0	18.6	17.5	16.4	13.6	8.6
DIURNAL RANGE	16.1	18.3	18.4	14.4	11.1	8.9	8.4	6.6	8.3	10.0	11.1	15.0
S/HEMISPHERE	JUL	AUG	SEP	OCT	NOV	DEC	JAN	FEB	MAR	APR	MAY	JUN

Cultural Recommendations

LIGHT: 2500–3500 fc. In the habitat, clear, summer days are exceedingly rare, but growers indicate that plants prefer bright light.

TEMPERATURES: Summer days average 77–80°F (25–27°C), and nights average 64–65°F (18–19°C), with a diurnal range of 12–16°F (7–9°C). The warmest weather occurs in spring. Days average 84–86°F (29–30°C), and nights average 60–64°F (16–18°C), with a diurnal range of 20–26°F (11–14°C). Both highs and lows are more moderate after the start of the summer wet season. Low night temperatures or a wide diurnal range may be necessary to initiate blooming.

HUMIDITY: 80–85% in summer, decreasing to 65–75% for most of the rest of the year. However, averages drop to near 60% for 2 months near the end of the dry season in late winter and early spring.

WATER: Rainfall is moderate to heavy from late spring through early autumn, but conditions are much drier in winter. Cultivated plants should be kept moist while actively growing, but water should be gradually reduced after new growths mature in autumn.

FERTILIZER: ¼–½ recommended strength, applied weekly. A high-nitrogen fertilizer is beneficial from spring to midsummer, but a fertilizer high in phosphates should be used in late summer and autumn.

REST PERIOD: Winter days average 74–80°F (24–27°C), and nights average 46–47°F (8–9°C), with a diurnal range of 27–33°F (15–18°C). Overnight lows are below 50°F (10°C) for 3 months, and some growers recommend minimum winter temperatures near this value. Plants should be able to tolerate temperatures a few degrees below freezing for short periods, but extremes should be avoided in cultivation. During very cold weather, a plant's chance of surviving with minimal damage is better if it is dry when temperatures are low. In the habitat, rainfall averages are very low for 4–5 months in winter, but during the early part of the season the high relative humidity indicates that additional moisture is available from frequent fog, mist, and heavy deposits of dew. Growers sometimes recommend eliminating water in winter, but plants are healthiest if for most of the winter they are allowed to become somewhat dry between waterings but do not remain dry for extended periods. For 1–2 months in late winter, however, conditions are clear, warm, and dry, with humidity so low that even the moisture from morning dew is uncommon. Plants should be allowed to dry out completely between waterings and remain dry longer during this time. Occasional early morning mistings between waterings may help keep the plants from becoming too dry. Fertilizer should be greatly reduced or eliminated until water is increased in spring. A cool, dry rest is essential for cultivated plants and should be continued until new growth starts in spring. In the habitat, light is highest in winter.

GROWING MEDIA: Plants are best mounted on tree-fern or cork slabs if humidity is high and plants are watered daily in summer. If plants must be potted, any open, coarse, fast-draining medium may be used. Repotting is best done immediately after flowering when roots are actively growing. When repotting, the old canes should not be removed as they continue to bloom for several years.

MISCELLANEOUS NOTES: The bloom season shown in the climate table is based on reports from the habitat. Cultivation records show blooming from winter to early summer with the peak season in spring. Blooming occurs while conditions are quite dry and temperatures are cool, suggesting that increased day length may initiate flowers. Plants cultivated in the temperate-latitudes tend to bloom later in spring.

Plant and Flower Information

PLANT SIZE AND TYPE: A 9–12 in. (23–30 cm) sympodial epiphyte.

PSEUDOBULB: 6–8 in. (15–20 cm) long. The spindle-shaped stems are fleshy, furrowed, and consist of 4 internodes. With age, the stems turn yellow or purplish brown.

LEAVES: 1–5 near the apex of the stem. The narrowly oblong leaves are 3–4 in. (7.5–10.0 cm) long. They are dull green and leathery. The backside of the leaves and the leaf sheaths are covered with short, black or dark brown hairs.

INFLORESCENCE: Very short. Inflorescences are borne on the upper portion of both old and new growths.

FLOWERS: Normally 1–2, rarely 4 per inflorescence. The very waxy flowers are 2 in. (5 cm) across, which is large for the plant size. Sepals and petals, which may be bright golden yellow or pale straw yellow, taper to a sharp point. The darker yellow lip is green in the center with red lines on each side. The broadly triangular midlobe is covered with small glands. The sidelobes are finely toothed along the front edge. Blossoms are fragrant and last 2–3 months.

HYBRIDIZING NOTES: Chromosome count is 2n = 38 (ref. 153, 273, 504, 580). Commonly self-fertile when pollen from another flower on the same plant is used. Seedlings are considered easy to maintain in flask.

REFERENCES: 36, 153, 157, 179, 190, 196, 202, 208, 218, 245, 254, 266, 273, 291, 371, 429, 430, 447, 448, 454, 504, 528, 580.

PHOTOS/DRAWINGS: *36, 245, 291, 371, 430, 454.*

Dendrobium trilamellatum Schlechter. Transferred to *Ephemerantha trilamellatum* by Hunt and Summerhayes, but Seidenfaden (ref. 449) considers it a possible synonym of *Flickingeria bancana* (J. J. Smith) A. Hawkes. REFERENCES: 213, 221, 230, 435, 449.

Dendrobium trilamellatum J. J. Smith

AKA: *D. johannis* Rchb. f. var. *semifuscum* Rchb. f., *D. semifuscum* (Rchb. f.) Lavarack and Cribb.

ORIGIN/HABITAT: Australia, the islands of the Torres Straits, and southern New Guinea. In Australia, plants are found on Melville Island in the Northern Territory and in Queensland from Cooktown to Cape York. They are often found in *Melaleuca* (paperbark) woodlands where conditions are very dry in winter and spring and very wet the remainder of the year. In New Guinea, plants usually grow in low-lying, swampy flats near the coast.

CLIMATE: Station #94167, Horn Island, Australia, Lat. 10.6°S, Long. 142.3°E, at 27 ft. (8 m). Temperatures are calculated for an elevation of 500 ft. (150 m), resulting in probable extremes of 96°F (36°C) and 62°F (17°C).

N/HEMISPHERE	JAN	FEB	MAR	APR	MAY	JUN	JUL	AUG	SEP	OCT	NOV	DEC
°F AVG MAX	80	80	82	84	86	87	85	85	85	84	83	82
°F AVG MIN	71	71	72	74	75	76	75	75	75	75	74	72
DIURNAL RANGE	9	9	10	10	11	11	10	10	10	9	9	10
RAIN/INCHES	0.4	0.2	0.1	0.3	1.5	7.0	13.2	15.8	13.9	8.0	1.6	0.5
HUMIDITY/%	75	72	71	70	69	72	79	80	79	77	75	75
BLOOM SEASON		**	**	**	**							
DAYS CLR @ 9AM	3	4	3	2	3	1	0	0	1	4	9	5
DAYS CLR @ 3PM	4	5	6	8	7	2	0	1	1	4	8	6
RAIN/MM	10	5	3	8	38	178	335	401	353	203	41	13
°C AVG MAX	26.9	26.9	28.0	29.1	30.2	30.8	29.7	29.7	29.7	29.1	28.6	28.0
°C AVG MIN	21.9	21.9	22.5	23.6	24.1	24.7	24.1	24.1	24.1	24.1	23.6	22.5
DIURNAL RANGE	5.0	5.0	5.5	5.5	6.1	6.1	5.6	5.6	5.6	5.0	5.0	5.5
S/HEMISPHERE	JUL	AUG	SEP	OCT	NOV	DEC	JAN	FEB	MAR	APR	MAY	JUN

Cultural Recommendations

LIGHT: 3000–4000 fc. Some growers recommend very high light with continuous strong air movement. Other growers suggest growing in a location that receives morning sun. However, the heavy summer cloud cover indicates that some shading is needed from spring through autumn, but light should be as high as the plant can tolerate, short of burning the leaves.

TEMPERATURES: Summer days average 85–87°F (30–31°C), and nights average 75–76°F (24–25°C), with a diurnal range of 10–11°F (6°C).

HUMIDITY: 75–80% in summer and autumn, dropping to near 70% in late winter and spring.

WATER: Rainfall is moderate to heavy from late spring through early autumn. Potted plants should be kept evenly moist in summer and early autumn. Water should be gradually reduced in late autumn. If plants are mounted, they should be watered at least once daily during hot, sunny weather.

FERTILIZER: ¼–½ recommended strength, applied weekly. A high-nitrogen fertilizer is beneficial from spring to midsummer, but a fertilizer high in phosphates should be used in late summer and autumn.

REST PERIOD: Winter days average 80–82°F (27–28°C), and nights average 71–72°F (22–23°C), with a diurnal range of 9–10°F (5–6°C). The most recent growths need to harden before winter, so water should be gradually reduced in autumn. Winters are very dry for 5–6 months. Not only is rainfall low, but conditions are so dry that even moisture from dew is uncommon. Plants should be allowed to dry out with only occasional water given to keep pseudobulbs from shriveling excessively. When new growth starts in spring, water should be withheld until the growth is 1.5–2.0 in. (3.7–5.0 cm) long. Fertilizer should be eliminated anytime water is reduced.

GROWING MEDIA: Plants grow best when tightly mounted to cork, hardwood, or tree-fern slabs or blocks. Growers report that plants are very sensitive to an excess of moisture. Because excellent drainage is essential, a very open medium should be used if plants are grown in pots. Repotting is best done in early spring when new roots are growing.

MISCELLANEOUS NOTES: The bloom season shown in the climate table is based on reports from the habitat. Cultivated plants may bloom any time of year, but growers indicate that it is not free-flowering in the lowland tropics.

The blossoms are very similar to those of *D. johannis* Rchb. f. The most easily identifiable difference is that *D. trilamellatum* blooms heaviest in spring and usually has a yellow to dark brown spur. *D. johannis*, on the other hand, blooms most heavily in autumn and usually has a deep purple spur.

Plant and Flower Information

PLANT SIZE AND TYPE: A 12–24 in. (30–60 cm) sympodial epiphyte.

PSEUDOBULB: 12–24 in. (30–60 cm) long. The clustered stems consist of nodes 1.2–2.0 in. (3–5 cm) apart. They are canelike with a swelling at the base.

LEAVES: Several. The dark green leaves are about 5.5 in. (14 cm) long. They are fleshy, linear-lanceolate, and clustered near the apex of each growth.

INFLORESCENCE: 16 in. (40 cm) long. The erect inflorescences emerge at the apex of the stem.

FLOWERS: 13 or less per inflorescence. The glossy flowers are 2 in. (5 cm) across. Sepals and crisped petals are waxy, narrow, and twisted. They may be light yellow, greenish yellow, brownish yellow, or russet with 3–6 dark brown lines. The light yellow lip is marked with purple or dark yellow lines. Blossoms are fragrant and long-lived.

HYBRIDIZING NOTES: Early hybrid registrations may apply to *D. johannis* or *D. trilamellatum*.

REFERENCES: 25, 67, 84, 190, 200, 220, 240, 254, 262, 304, 344, 445, 470, 526, 533, 537.

PHOTOS/DRAWINGS: *84*, 240, *262*, 265, *304*, 344, *533*.

Dendrobium trilobulatum Kores

ORIGIN/HABITAT: Endemic to Fiji. Plants grow near Lautoka on Viti Levu and at the southern base of Mathuata Mountain north of Natua on Vanua Levu. They usually grow in drainage areas or near waterfalls in dense forests at 350–800 ft. (100–250 m). Normally pendulous in tall trees, they occasionally grow on fallen logs or among rocks.

CLIMATE: Station #91680, Nadi, Vitu Levu, Fiji Islands, Lat. 17.8°S, Long. 177.4°E, at 63 ft. (19 m). Temperatures are calculated for an elevation of 500 ft. (150 m), resulting in probable extremes of 94°F (34°C) and 54°F (12°C).

N/HEMISPHERE	JAN	FEB	MAR	APR	MAY	JUN	JUL	AUG	SEP	OCT	NOV	DEC
°F AVG MAX	82	84	84	85	85	86	88	87	87	87	85	82
°F AVG MIN	63	65	66	67	68	70	71	71	72	70	67	64
DIURNAL RANGE	19	19	18	18	17	16	17	16	15	17	18	18
RAIN/INCHES	0.5	1.4	3.7	3.5	2.8	4.7	12.7	10.0	15.1	6.8	5.3	4.3
HUMIDITY/%	74	73	73	75	73	78	80	80	83	82	78	78
BLOOM SEASON			*	*	*	*						
DAYS CLR @ 12PM	10	15	7	9	8	5	5	3	3	6	9	11
DAYS CLR @ 6PM	12	10	4	6	3	2	1	1	3	6	8	
RAIN/MM	13	36	94	89	71	119	323	254	384	173	135	109
°C AVG MAX	27.5	28.6	28.6	29.2	29.2	29.8	30.9	30.3	30.3	30.3	29.2	27.5
°C AVG MIN	17.0	18.1	18.6	19.2	19.8	20.9	21.4	21.4	22.0	20.9	19.2	17.5
DIURNAL RANGE	10.5	10.5	10.0	10.0	9.4	8.9	9.5	8.9	8.3	9.4	10.0	10.0
S/HEMISPHERE	JUL	AUG	SEP	OCT	NOV	DEC	JAN	FEB	MAR	APR	MAY	JUN

Cultural Recommendations

LIGHT: 1500–2500 fc.

TEMPERATURES: Summer days average 86–88°F (30–31°C), and nights average 70–71°F (21°C), with a diurnal range of 16–17°F (9–10°C).

HUMIDITY: Near 80% in summer and early autumn, dropping to near 75% in winter and spring. Averages may be somewhat greater in the microclimate of the habitat, however.

WATER: Rainfall is moderate to heavy from spring through autumn, but conditions are slightly drier for 2–3 months in winter. Cultivated plants should be kept evenly moist while in actively growing, but water should be gradually reduced in late autumn.

FERTILIZER: ¼–½ recommended strength, applied weekly. A high-nitrogen fertilizer is beneficial from spring to midsummer, but a fertilizer high in phosphates should be used in late summer and autumn.

REST PERIOD: Winter days average 82–84°F (28–29°C), and nights average 63–65°F (17–18°C), with a diurnal range of 18–19°F (10–11°C). Cultivated plants should be allowed to dry out between waterings, but should not remain completely dry for any length of time. Fertilizer should be reduced until water is increased in spring.

GROWING MEDIA: Mounting plants on tree-fern or cork slabs accommodates their pendulous growth habit. However, humidity must be high and plants must be watered at least once a day in summer. If plants cannot be mounted, hanging pots or baskets may be filled with an open, fast-draining medium. Repotting may be done anytime new roots are actively growing.

MISCELLANEOUS NOTES: The bloom season shown in the climate table is based on reports from the habitat. Fruits are seen in summer and autumn.

Plant and Flower Information

PLANT SIZE AND TYPE: A 39–79 in. (100–200 cm) sympodial epiphyte.

PSEUDOBULB: 39–79 in. (100–200 cm) long. The pendulous stems emerge from a very short rhizome. Stems are leafy near the apex.

LEAVES: Many. The oblong-elliptic leaves are 3.1–5.5 in. (8–14 cm) long, distichous, and twisted at the base.

INFLORESCENCE: Short. Inflorescences emerge directly above the leaves along the upper part of the stem.

FLOWERS: 1, rarely 2 per inflorescence. The small white and yellow flowers are 0.6 in. (1.5 cm) long and do not open fully. The dorsal sepal is erect and ovate-elliptical. The pointed lateral sepals are broadly sickle-shaped. Petals are oblong to oblong-lanceolate. The lip is uppermost and lightly fringed or toothed along the front margin. It expands abruptly to 3-lobes at the apex.

REFERENCES: 235, 252, 466.

PHOTOS/DRAWINGS: 466.

Dendrobium trinervium Ridley

ORIGIN/HABITAT: Northern Malaya and southern Thailand. Although uncommon, plants have been collected on Kedah Peak in northwestern Malaya and near Phang-nga, Thung Nui, Satul, Khao Bo Ngu Luam, and Takuantung in southern Thailand. Plants were cultivated in the Penang Botanical Garden.

CLIMATE: Station #48603, Alor Setar, Malaya, Lat. 6.2°N, Long. 100.4°E, at 13 ft. (4 m). Temperatures are calculated for an elevation of 1500 ft. (460 m), resulting in probable extremes of 95°F (35°C) and 56°F (13°C).

N/HEMISPHERE	JAN	FEB	MAR	APR	MAY	JUN	JUL	AUG	SEP	OCT	NOV	DEC
°F AVG MAX	85	87	88	88	85	84	83	83	82	82	83	83
°F AVG MIN	66	66	68	69	70	69	69	69	69	69	68	67
DIURNAL RANGE	19	21	20	19	15	15	14	14	13	13	15	16
RAIN/INCHES	2.5	2.2	5.8	9.0	10.7	7.8	7.7	10.4	12.8	11.9	8.1	5.2
HUMIDITY/%	71	66	70	75	79	79	79	79	82	84	83	77
BLOOM SEASON	*				*	*	*	*	*	*	*	*
DAYS CLR @ 7AM	5	4	5	2	0	1	1	1	1	1	2	5
DAYS CLR @ 1PM	2	2	2	1	0	1	1	1	0	0	1	2
RAIN/MM	64	56	147	229	272	198	196	264	325	302	206	132
°C AVG MAX	29.5	30.6	31.2	31.2	29.5	28.9	28.4	28.4	27.8	27.8	28.4	28.4
°C AVG MIN	18.9	18.9	20.1	20.6	21.2	20.6	20.6	20.6	20.6	20.6	20.1	19.5
DIURNAL RANGE	10.6	11.7	11.1	10.6	8.3	8.3	7.8	7.8	7.2	7.2	8.3	8.9
S/HEMISPHERE	JUL	AUG	SEP	OCT	NOV	DEC	JAN	FEB	MAR	APR	MAY	JUN

Cultural Recommendations

LIGHT: 2000–3000 fc.

TEMPERATURES: Throughout the year, days average 82–88°F (28–31°C), and nights average 66–70°F (19–21°C), with a diurnal range of 13–21°F (7–12°C). The warmest weather occurs at the end of the dry season in late winter and spring.

HUMIDITY: 75–85% most of the year, dropping to 65–75% in late winter and spring.

WATER: Rainfall is moderate to heavy most of the year, with a semidry period in winter. Cultivated plants should be kept moist but not soggy from spring into autumn.

FERTILIZER: ¼–½ recommended strength, applied weekly. A high-nitrogen fertilizer is beneficial from spring to midsummer, but a fertilizer high in phosphates should be used in late summer and autumn.

REST PERIOD: Growing temperatures should be maintained all year. However, slightly warmer days and cooler nights increase the diurnal range to about 20°F (11°C) in winter. Water should be gradually reduced as the new growths mature in autumn. In the habitat, rainfall is low, but heavy dew is common, making more water available than is indicated by the rainfall averages. For 1–2 months, water should be reduced and the plants allowed to dry slightly between waterings. They should not remain dry for long periods, however. Fertilizer should be reduced or eliminated until water is increased in spring. In the habitat, light is highest in winter.

GROWING MEDIA: Plants may be mounted on tree-fern or cork slabs if humidity is high and plants are watered daily in summer. When plants are potted, any open, fast-draining medium may be used. Repotting may be done anytime new roots are growing.

MISCELLANEOUS NOTES: The bloom season shown in the climate table is based on cultivation records.

Plant and Flower Information

PLANT SIZE AND TYPE: A 2.4–3.1 in. (6–8 cm) sympodial epiphyte.

PSEUDOBULB: 1.6–2.4 in. (4–6 cm) long. The crowded, thick, knobby looking stems are somewhat zigzag. They are covered by leaf sheaths.

LEAVES: 4–9 on the upper portion of each new growth. The lanceolate to ovate leaves are 2.5 in. (6.4 cm) long. They are deciduous.

INFLORESCENCE: 0.3 in. (0.8 cm) long. The short inflorescences hold the flowers near the tips of the leaves. Inflorescences emerge opposite the leaves.

FLOWERS: 1–3 per inflorescence. The pendent flowers are 0.4–0.6 in. (1.0–1.5 cm) long and do not open fully, but they appear large on the small plants. The dorsal sepal is much smaller than the lateral sepals. The white petals are lanceolate. The fiddle-shaped lip, which is white with yellow at the thickened tip, has red or purple spots at the base and 3 bright green keels. The sidelobes are streaked with purple lines.

REFERENCES: 179, 254, 395, 402, 448, 454, 455.

PHOTOS/DRAWINGS: 454, *455*.

Dendrobium tripetaloides Roxburgh. Now considered a synonym of *Bulbophyllum auricomum* Lindley. REFERENCES: 75, 190, 216, 254.

Dendrobium triphyllum Persoon. Now considered a synonym of *Maxillaria triphylla* Ruiz and Pavon. REFERENCES: 216, 254.

Dendrobium tripterum Wallich. Now considered a synonym of *Trias oblonga* Lindley. REFERENCES: 190, 218, 254.

Dendrobium triquetrum Ridley. Now considered a synonym of *Cadetia triquetra* (Ridley) Schlechter. REFERENCES: 218, 254, 393.

Dendrobium trisaccatum Kränzlin. See *D. bracteosum* Rchb. f. REFERENCES: 190, 220, 254, 437, 470.

Dendrobium triste Schlechter

ORIGIN/HABITAT: Northern Papua New Guinea. Plants grow on forest trees in the Torricelli Range at about 2950 ft. (900 m).

CLIMATE: Station #94004, Wewak, Papua New Guinea, Lat. 3.6°S, Long. 143.7°E, at 16 ft. (5 m). Temperatures are calculated for an elevation of 2600 ft. (800 m), resulting in probable extremes of 89°F (32°C) and 53°F (12°C).

N/HEMISPHERE	JAN	FEB	MAR	APR	MAY	JUN	JUL	AUG	SEP	OCT	NOV	DEC
°F AVG MAX	79	79	79	79	79	79	78	77	78	79	79	79
°F AVG MIN	65	65	65	66	66	66	66	66	65	66	66	65
DIURNAL RANGE	14	14	14	13	13	13	12	11	13	13	13	14
RAIN/INCHES	7.6	4.8	5.3	10.0	13.3	14.5	12.1	11.9	14.9	16.9	15.1	10.8
HUMIDITY/%	80	79	79	78	79	81	82	82	81	82	81	80
BLOOM SEASON												
DAYS CLR	N/A											
RAIN/MM	193	122	135	254	338	368	307	302	378	429	384	274
°C AVG MAX	26.3	26.3	26.3	26.3	26.3	26.3	25.8	25.2	25.8	26.3	26.3	26.3
°C AVG MIN	18.6	18.6	18.6	19.1	19.1	19.1	19.1	19.1	18.6	19.1	19.1	18.6
DIURNAL RANGE	7.7	7.7	7.7	7.2	7.2	7.2	6.7	6.1	7.2	7.7	7.2	7.7
S/HEMISPHERE	JUL	AUG	SEP	OCT	NOV	DEC	JAN	FEB	MAR	APR	MAY	JUN

Cultural Recommendations

LIGHT: 2000–3000 fc.

TEMPERATURES: Throughout the year, days average 77–79°F (25–26°C), and nights average 65–66°F (19°C), with a diurnal range of 11–14°F (6–8°C).

HUMIDITY: Near 80% year-round.

WATER: Rainfall is heavy all year, but conditions are slightly drier for 1–2 months in winter. Cultivated plants should be kept moist but not soggy.

FERTILIZER: ¼–½ recommended strength. A balanced fertilizer should be applied weekly to biweekly throughout the year.

REST PERIOD: Growing temperatures should be maintained all year. Water and fertilizer should be reduced somewhat in winter, especially if plants are cultivated in the dark, short-day conditions common in temperate latitudes. In the habitat, seasonal light variation is minor.

GROWING MEDIA: A very open and fast-draining medium should be used with either baskets or small pots. Repotting may be done anytime new roots are growing.

MISCELLANEOUS NOTES: The bloom season shown in the climate table is based on reports from the habitat. Plants that produce flowers which last a single day commonly bloom several times during the year. Flowering usually occurs 7–14 days after a sudden 10°F (5°C) drop in daytime temperatures.

Plant and Flower Information

PLANT SIZE AND TYPE: A 59–79 in. (150–200 cm) sympodial epiphyte.

PSEUDOBULB: 59–79 in. (150–200 cm) long. The elongated stems are densely leafy.

LEAVES: Many. The leaves are 3.5–5.5 in. (9–14 cm) long, smooth, and lanceolate-elliptic.

INFLORESCENCE: Short. Inflorescences emerge from the side of the stem.

FLOWERS: 2 per inflorescence. The flowers are 0.6 in. (1.5 cm) across. Sepals and petals are dark purple. Sepals and petals are cupped and thickened at the tips. The sepals are bumpy on the exterior. The small, 3-lobed lip has an orange-red crest, triangular sidelobes, and a sharply pointed midlobe. The midlobe has an extremely jagged margin. The reddish column is marked with orange-yellow. Blossoms are very short-lived.

REFERENCES: 92, 221, 437, 445.

PHOTOS/DRAWINGS: 437.

Dendrobium triviale Kränzlin. See *D. calcaratum* A. Richard.
REFERENCES: 179, 254, 270, 271, 434, 445.

Dendrobium tropaeoliflorum Hooker f. Kränzlin (ref. 254) included *D. perula* Rchb. f. as a synonym, but more recent writers do not include this synonymy. The plant was reportedly collected in Perak, Malaya, but it is known only from the original description which was based on a plant cultivated in Calcutta, India. Habitat location and elevation are unavailable, so climate data cannot be selected. The orchid was a 12 in. (30 cm) sympodial epiphyte with leaves 2.4 in. (6 cm) long. Up to 6 blossoms were borne on a 2 in. (5 cm) long inflorescences. Flowers were 1 in. (2.5 cm) across. The small sepals and petals were deep red-purple. The lip was said to be similar to *D. panduriferum* Hooker f. with a smooth margin on the midlobe. REFERENCES: 200, 202, 203, 218, 254, 402, 455. PHOTOS/DRAWINGS: 203, 455.

Dendrobium tropidoneuron Schlechter

ORIGIN/HABITAT: Sumatra. Plants grow on trees at about 2950 ft. (900 m) near Pandangpandjang, a village close to Padang.

CLIMATE: Station #96163, Padang, Sumatra, Indonesia, Lat. 0.9°S, Long. 100.4°E, at 19 ft. (6 m). Temperatures are calculated for an elevation of 2950 ft. (900 m), resulting in probable extremes of 84°F (29°C) and 58°F (15°C).

N/HEMISPHERE	JAN	FEB	MAR	APR	MAY	JUN	JUL	AUG	SEP	OCT	NOV	DEC
°F AVG MAX	77	77	76	76	76	76	77	77	77	77	78	77
°F AVG MIN	64	64	64	64	64	64	64	64	64	65	65	64
DIURNAL RANGE	13	13	12	12	12	12	13	13	13	12	13	13
RAIN/INCHES	10.9	13.7	6.0	19.5	20.4	18.9	13.8	10.2	12.1	14.3	12.4	12.1
HUMIDITY/%	81	82	82	84	85	84	81	81	82	83	81	81
BLOOM SEASON						*						
DAYS CLR @ 7AM	5	1	1	0	2	2	1	2	2	2	3	5
DAYS CLR @ 1PM	5	2	2	1	1	3	3	4	3	3	6	5
RAIN/MM	277	348	152	495	518	480	351	259	307	363	315	307
°C AVG MAX	25.2	25.2	24.6	24.6	24.6	24.6	25.2	25.2	25.2	25.2	25.7	25.2
°C AVG MIN	18.0	18.0	18.0	18.0	18.0	18.0	18.0	18.0	18.0	18.5	18.5	18.0
DIURNAL RANGE	7.2	7.2	6.6	6.6	6.6	6.6	7.2	7.2	7.2	6.7	7.2	7.2
S/HEMISPHERE	JUL	AUG	SEP	OCT	NOV	DEC	JAN	FEB	MAR	APR	MAY	JUN

Cultural Recommendations

LIGHT: 2000–3000 fc. Diffused light is preferred.

TEMPERATURES: Throughout the year, days average 76–78°F (25–26°C), and nights average 64–65°F (18–19°C), with a diurnal range of 12–13°F (7°C). Probable extremes vary only a few degrees from the averages, indicating that the plant may not tolerate wide temperature fluctuations.

HUMIDITY: 80–85% year-round.

WATER: Rainfall is extremely heavy all year. Cultivated plants should be constantly moist but not soggy.

FERTILIZER: ¼–½ recommended strength. A balanced fertilizer should be applied weekly to biweekly throughout the year.

REST PERIOD: Growing conditions should be maintained year-round. Water should be reduced somewhat in winter for cultivated plants, especially those grown in the dark, short-day conditions common in temperate latitudes. Plants should never be allowed to dry out completely, however.

GROWING MEDIA: Plants may be mounted on tree-fern or cork slabs if humidity is high and plants are watered at least once daily in summer. When plants are potted, any open, fast-draining medium may be used. Repotting may be done anytime new roots are growing.

MISCELLANEOUS NOTES: The bloom season shown in the climate table is based on reports from the habitat.

Plant and Flower Information

PLANT SIZE AND TYPE: A 4–5 in. (10–13 cm) sympodial epiphyte.

PSEUDOBULB: 4–5 in. (10–13 cm) long. The clustered stems are covered by persistent leaf sheaths. The stems are unbranched.

LEAVES: Many. The leaves are 1 in. (2.5 cm) long, fleshy, smooth, and lanceolate-triangular. They are equally spaced along the stem.

INFLORESCENCE: Short. Blossoms are held in clusters near the top of the stem.

FLOWERS: Several. The dark purple flowers are less than 0.4 in. (1 cm) across. The pointed dorsal sepal is ovate oblong. Lateral sepals are somewhat triangular and pointed. Petals are oblong and pointed. The tongue-shaped lip has a minutely wavy, uneven margin. When dried, the lip and sepals each have 3 prominent, keel-shaped veins. Schlechter (ref. 435) indicated that except for the color, the blossoms are easily confused with *D. carnosum* Lindley.

REFERENCES: 221, 435.

Dendrobium tropidophorum Schlechter. Now considered a synonym of *Diplocaulobium tropidophorum* (Schlechter) A. Hawkes.
REFERENCES: 221, 229, 437, 445.

Dendrobium trullatum J. J. Wood and A. Lamb

ORIGIN/HABITAT: Borneo. Plants were collected near Nabawan in the Keningau District of Sabah. The habitat is located southeast of Keningau at 1500–1750 ft. (450–540 m). The plants grow in forests which occur on infertile, acid, sandstone soils. Other plants in the vicinity include Rhododendron, ferns, and other orchids.

CLIMATE: Station #49613, Tambunan, Sabah, Borneo, Lat. 5.7°N, Long. 116.4°E, at 1200 ft. (366 m). Temperatures are calculated for an elevation of 1650 ft. (500 m), resulting in probable extremes of 97°F (36°C) and 53°F (11°C).

N/HEMISPHERE	JAN	FEB	MAR	APR	MAY	JUN	JUL	AUG	SEP	OCT	NOV	DEC
°F AVG MAX	85	86	88	89	89	88	88	88	88	87	86	85
°F AVG MIN	66	64	65	66	67	66	65	65	66	66	66	67
DIURNAL RANGE	19	22	23	23	22	22	23	23	22	21	20	18
RAIN/INCHES	5.8	3.7	5.8	7.5	8.2	7.3	5.1	4.9	6.4	7.0	6.8	6.0
HUMIDITY/%	N/A											
BLOOM SEASON		*							*	*		
DAYS CLR	N/A											
RAIN/MM	147	94	147	191	208	185	130	124	163	178	173	152
°C AVG MAX	29.4	30.0	31.1	31.7	31.7	31.3	31.2	31.1	31.1	30.6	20.0	29.4
°C AVG MIN	18.9	17.5	18.1	18.6	19.2	18.6	18.1	18.1	18.6	18.6	18.6	19.2
DIURNAL RANGE	10.5	12.5	13.0	13.1	12.5	12.7	13.1	13.0	12.5	12.0	11.4	10.2
S/HEMISPHERE	JUL	AUG	SEP	OCT	NOV	DEC	JAN	FEB	MAR	APR	MAY	JUN

Cultural Recommendations

LIGHT: 2000–3000 fc.

TEMPERATURES: Throughout the year, days average 85–89°F (29–32°C), and nights average 64–67°F (18–19°C), with a diurnal range of 18–23°F (10–13°C).

HUMIDITY: Information is not available for this location. However, records from nearby locations indicate that humidity is probably 80–85% year-round.

WATER: Rainfall is moderate to heavy all year with a brief, slightly drier period in winter. Cultivated plants should be allowed to dry slightly between waterings.

FERTILIZER: ¼–½ recommended strength. A balanced fertilizer should be applied weekly to biweekly throughout the year.

REST PERIOD: Growing conditions should be maintained year-round. Water should be reduced slightly in winter, but the plants should never be allowed to dry out completely. Fertilizer should be reduced anytime plants are not actively growing. In the habitat, seasonal light variation is minor.

GROWING MEDIA: Plants may be mounted on tree-fern or cork slabs if humidity is high and plants are watered at least once daily in summer. When plants are potted, any open, fast-draining medium may be used. Repotting is best done in early spring when new roots begin to grow.

MISCELLANEOUS NOTES: The bloom season shown in the climate table is based on collection times.

Plant and Flower Information

PLANT SIZE AND TYPE: A 4.8–5.5 in. (12–14 cm) sympodial epiphyte.

PSEUDOBULB: 4.8–5.5 in. (12–14 cm) long. The slender, somewhat sinuous stems are clustered at the base.

LEAVES: Many, along most of the stem. The smooth, stiff leaves are linear to tongue-shaped, unequally bilobed, slightly pointed at the tips, and about 0.5–0.8 in. (1.2–2.0 cm) long.

INFLORESCENCE: Very short. Flowers appear to rest on the stem. Inflorescences emerge from the base of the smooth sheaths opposite the leaves.

FLOWERS: 1–2. The fragrant flowers are 0.5 in. (1.3 cm) across. The dorsal sepal is triangular-ovate, pointed, and shorter than the lateral sepals. Lateral sepals are pale green or bright yellow, stiff, spreading, triangular-ovate, pointed at the tip, and joined at the base, forming a conical spur less than 0.1 in. (0.2 cm) long. The 3-lobed lip, which is stiff and fleshy, is uppermost. It is cream with a fuzzy midlobe and a grainy disk. Sidelobes are erect, rounded, and broadly triangular.

REFERENCES: Wood, J. J. and P. Cribb. 1994. *A checklist of the orchids of Borneo*. Royal Botanic Gardens, Kew.

PHOTOS/DRAWINGS: Wood, J. J. and P. Cribb. 1994. *A checklist of the orchids of Borneo*. Royal Botanic Gardens, Kew.

Dendrobium truncatum Lindley

AKA: *D. clavipes* Hooker f.

ORIGIN/HABITAT: Southeast Asia. In Malaya, plants grow in dense forests in the lowlands of Kedah, Perak, Selangor, and Pahang states. They are found in first growth jungles of Sumatra and the Sabah region of Borneo at about 3600 ft. (1100 m). In East and West Java, plants grow in high light on the trunks of roadside trees from sea level to 3300 ft. (0–1000 m). Plants are also found in peninsular Thailand.

CLIMATE: Station #96881, Madiun, Java, Indonesia, Lat. 7.6°S, Long. 111.4°E, at 361 ft. (110 m). Temperatures are calculated for an elevation of 2600 ft. (800 m), resulting in probable extremes of 88°F (31°C) and 55°F (13°C).

N/HEMISPHERE	JAN	FEB	MAR	APR	MAY	JUN	JUL	AUG	SEP	OCT	NOV	DEC
°F AVG MAX	78	79	80	81	79	78	77	77	78	80	79	79
°F AVG MIN	62	62	64	65	65	65	65	65	65	65	65	63
DIURNAL RANGE	16	17	16	16	14	13	12	12	13	15	14	16
RAIN/INCHES	1.3	0.8	1.2	2.9	7.6	10.2	11.9	10.9	10.4	8.8	5.1	3.2
HUMIDITY/%	60	54	52	52	64	72	77	78	78	74	70	64
BLOOM SEASON							*					
DAYS CLR @ 7AM	18	22	21	16	8	4	2	2	3	6	9	16
DAYS CLR @ 1PM	15	17	14	9	4	2	1	1	1	3	6	11
RAIN/MM	33	20	30	74	193	259	302	277	264	224	130	81
°C AVG MAX	25.3	25.9	26.5	27.0	25.9	25.3	24.8	24.8	25.3	26.5	25.9	25.9
°C AVG MIN	16.5	16.5	17.6	18.1	18.1	18.1	18.1	18.1	18.1	18.1	18.1	17.0
DIURNAL RANGE	8.8	9.4	8.9	8.9	7.8	7.2	6.7	6.7	7.2	8.4	7.8	8.9
S/HEMISPHERE	JUL	AUG	SEP	OCT	NOV	DEC	JAN	FEB	MAR	APR	MAY	JUN

Cultural Recommendations

LIGHT: 3000–4000 fc.

TEMPERATURES: Throughout the year, days average 77–81°F (25–27°C), and nights average 62–65°F (17–18°C), with a diurnal range of 12–17°F (7–9°C).

HUMIDITY: 70–80% most of the year, dropping to 50–55% in late winter and early spring.

WATER: At the weather station, rainfall is heavy from spring through autumn. The wet season is followed by a 2–3 month winter dry season when humidity is so low that even moisture from dew is uncommon. Cultivated plants should be watered frequently during the growing season from late spring to early autumn, but water should be gradually reduced in late autumn.

FERTILIZER: ¼–½ recommended strength. A balanced fertilizer should be applied weekly to biweekly throughout the year.

REST PERIOD: Growing conditions should be maintained year-round. Water and fertilizer should be reduced in winter and the plants allowed to dry out somewhat between waterings. They should not remain dry for long periods, however. In the habitat, light may be higher in winter.

GROWING MEDIA: Plants may be mounted on tree-fern or cork slabs if humidity is high and plants are watered at least once daily in summer. When plants are potted, any open, fast-draining medium may be used. Repotting may be done anytime new roots are growing.

MISCELLANEOUS NOTES: The bloom season shown in the climate table is based on reports from the habitat. Blooming occurs sporadically during the year. Plants that produce flowers which last a few days commonly bloom several times during the year. Flowering frequently occurs 7–14 days after a sudden 10°F (5°C) drop in daytime temperatures.

Plant and Flower Information

PLANT SIZE AND TYPE: A 6–12 in. (15–30 cm) sympodial epiphyte.

PSEUDOBULB: 6–12 in. (15–30 cm) long. The slender stems have 1–2 swollen internodes near the base. The swollen area may be round or ovoid and becomes warty with age. The leafy stems are somewhat flattened and sometimes branch.

LEAVES: Many. The hooked, narrowly linear leaves are 1.0–1.3 in. (2.5–3.3 cm) long. They are held so that they appear to avoid direct sun.

INFLORESCENCE: Short. Inflorescences emerge on the apical, leafless portion of the stem. Plants may develop successive inflorescences from the same nodes.

FLOWERS: 1 per inflorescence. The flowers are 0.4 in. (1.0 cm) long. The normally white blossoms often have pink sepals and darker, orchid-colored petals. The lip has large rounded sidelobes with red or purple veins and a green ridge on the smaller, tonguelike midlobe. The fragrant blossoms only last a few days.

REFERENCES: 25, 75, 200, 202, 216, 254, 278, 286, 295, 298, 310, 395, 402, 445, 454, 455, 469.

PHOTOS/DRAWINGS: *75, 254, 454, 455.*

Dendrobium truncicola Schlechter

ORIGIN/HABITAT: Sulawesi (Celebes). Plants were discovered near Lansot on the Minahassa Peninsula. They grow 10–13 ft. (3–4 m) above the ground on the trunks of large trees in moderately open, hilly areas at about 2300 ft. (700 m) often with *D. imitans* Schlechter.

CLIMATE: Station #97014, Manado, Sulawesi, Indonesia, Lat. 1.5°N, Long. 124.9°E, at 262 ft. (80 m). Temperatures are calculated for an elevation of 2300 ft. (700 m), resulting in probable extremes of 90°F (32°C) and 58°F (15°C).

Dendrobium tuadenum

N/HEMISPHERE	JAN	FEB	MAR	APR	MAY	JUN	JUL	AUG	SEP	OCT	NOV	DEC
°F AVG MAX	78	78	78	79	80	80	80	82	82	82	80	79
°F AVG MIN	66	66	66	66	67	66	66	66	66	65	66	67
DIURNAL RANGE	12	12	12	13	13	14	14	16	16	17	14	12
RAIN/INCHES	18.6	13.8	12.2	8.0	6.4	6.5	4.8	4.0	3.4	4.9	8.9	14.7
HUMIDITY/%	84	83	83	83	81	80	75	72	75	77	82	83
BLOOM SEASON												*
DAYS CLR @ 8AM	4	3	6	11	11	12	12	12	14	17	12	8
DAYS CLR @ 2PM	1	1	1	2	1	3	3	4	4	4	1	1
RAIN/MM	472	351	310	203	163	165	122	102	86	124	226	373
°C AVG MAX	25.7	25.7	25.7	26.3	26.8	26.8	26.8	27.9	27.9	27.9	26.8	26.3
°C AVG MIN	19.0	19.0	19.0	19.0	19.6	19.0	19.0	19.0	19.0	18.5	19.0	19.6
DIURNAL RANGE	6.7	6.7	6.7	7.3	7.2	7.8	7.8	8.9	8.9	9.4	7.8	6.7
S/HEMISPHERE	JUL	AUG	SEP	OCT	NOV	DEC	JAN	FEB	MAR	APR	MAY	JUN

Cultural Recommendations

LIGHT: 1800–2500 fc. Mornings are frequently clear, but afternoons are usually overcast.

TEMPERATURES: Throughout the year, days average 78–82°F (26–28°C), and nights average 65–67°F (19–20°C), with a diurnal range of 12–17°F (7–9°C). The probable extremes vary only a few degrees above and below the averages.

HUMIDITY: 70–75% in summer and early autumn, increasing to 80–85% the remainder of the year.

WATER: Rainfall is moderate to heavy all year. The driest conditions occur in summer and autumn. Cultivated plants should be allowed to dry slightly between waterings, but they should never be allowed to dry out completely.

FERTILIZER: ¼–½ recommended strength. A balanced fertilizer should be applied weekly to biweekly throughout the year.

REST PERIOD: Growing conditions should be maintained all year. In the habitat, rainfall is heaviest in winter. However, increasing water for cultivated plants could be detrimental, particularly if plants are grown in the dark, short-day conditions common in temperate latitudes. In the habitat, light is lowest in winter.

GROWING MEDIA: Plants may be mounted on tree-fern or cork slabs if humidity is high and plants are watered at least once daily in summer. When plants are potted, any open, fast-draining medium may be used. Repotting may be done anytime new roots are growing.

MISCELLANEOUS NOTES: The bloom season shown in the climate table is based on reports from the habitat.

Plant and Flower Information

PLANT SIZE AND TYPE: A 39 in. (100 cm) sympodial epiphyte.

PSEUDOBULB: 39 in. (100 cm) long. The clustered stems are erect to spreading, and emerge from a very short rhizome.

LEAVES: Many. The long, pointed leaves are 3–4 in. (8–10 cm) long.

INFLORESCENCE: Short. Inflorescences emerge from the side of the stem.

FLOWERS: 2 per inflorescence. The flowers are 1.8 in. (4.5 cm) long. Blossoms are whitish, sometimes lightly suffused with rose-red. Sepals and petals taper to mere threads at the tips. The smooth lip is slashed along the margin.

REFERENCES: 221, 436.

Dendrobium tuadenum Boxall ex Naves. Considered an invalid name by Kränzlin (ref. 254) and Merrill (ref. 296). REFERENCES: 216, 254, 296.

Dendrobium tuberculatum J. J. Smith. Now considered a synonym of *Diplocaulobium tuberculatum* (J. J. Smith) Hunt and Summerhayes. REFERENCES: 213, 221, 230, 445, 470, 475.

Dendrobium tuberiferum Hooker f.

AKA: Seidenfaden (ref. 454) includes *D. tuberiferum* as a synonym of *D. blumei*, but stated that the confusion cannot be resolved until botanists who are familiar with both Philippine plants and plants from other regions review the related plants. *D. tuberiferum* is often included as a synonym of both *D. planibulbe* Lindley and *D. blumei* Lindley, but some botanists consider *D. planibulbe* and *D. tuberiferum* as separate species. Valmayor (ref. 536) includes *D. blumei* Lindley as a synonym of *D. planibulbe*. Because their status is so confused, all are being included as separate species.

ORIGIN/HABITAT: Singapore and Borneo. In the central part of eastern Borneo, plants were found in primeval forests in West Koetai at about 2300 ft. (700 m). Ridley (ref. 395) indicates that plants are isolated and never common. They grow in low country.

CLIMATE: Station #96633, Balikpapan, Borneo, Indonesia, Lat. 1.3°S, Long. 116.9°E, at 10 ft. (3 m). Temperatures are calculated for an elevation of 2300 ft. (700 m), resulting in probable extremes of 84°F (29°C) and 52°F (11°C).

N/HEMISPHERE	JAN	FEB	MAR	APR	MAY	JUN	JUL	AUG	SEP	OCT	NOV	DEC
°F AVG MAX	75	76	76	77	77	77	77	78	78	77	77	76
°F AVG MIN	65	66	66	66	65	65	65	65	65	65	66	66
DIURNAL RANGE	10	10	10	11	12	12	12	13	13	12	11	10
RAIN/INCHES	7.1	6.4	5.5	5.2	6.6	8.1	7.9	8.9	9.1	8.2	9.1	7.6
HUMIDITY/%	82	80	77	78	80	79	82	81	81	82	83	82
BLOOM SEASON		*										
DAYS CLR @ 8AM	4	2	3	3	3	2	3	4	4	2	5	
DAYS CLR @ 2PM	6	4	5	5	3	1	2	1	2	3	4	5
RAIN/MM	180	163	140	132	168	206	201	226	231	208	231	193
°C AVG MAX	24.1	24.7	24.7	25.2	25.2	25.2	25.2	25.8	25.8	25.2	25.2	24.7
°C AVG MIN	18.6	19.1	19.1	19.1	18.6	18.6	18.6	18.6	18.6	18.6	19.1	19.1
DIURNAL RANGE	5.5	5.6	5.6	6.1	6.6	6.6	6.6	7.2	7.2	6.6	6.1	5.6
S/HEMISPHERE	JUL	AUG	SEP	OCT	NOV	DEC	JAN	FEB	MAR	APR	MAY	JUN

Cultural Recommendations

LIGHT: 2000–3000 fc.

TEMPERATURES: Throughout the year, days average 75–78°F (24–26°C), and nights average 65–66°F (19°C), with a diurnal range of 10–13°F (6–7°C).

HUMIDITY: Near 80% year-round.

WATER: Rainfall is heavy all year. Cultivated plants should be kept moist.

FERTILIZER: ¼–½ recommended strength. A balanced fertilizer should be applied weekly to biweekly throughout the year.

REST PERIOD: Growing conditions should be maintained year-round. Water and fertilizer should be reduced somewhat in winter, especially for plants cultivated in the dark, short-day conditions common in temperate latitudes. Plants should never be allowed to dry out completely, however. In the habitat, seasonal light variation is minor.

GROWING MEDIA: Plants may be mounted on tree-fern or cork slabs or potted in small pots filled with any open, fast-draining medium. Repotting may be done anytime new roots are growing.

MISCELLANEOUS NOTES: The bloom season shown in the climate table is based on collection reports.

Plant and Flower Information

PLANT SIZE AND TYPE: A 12–18 in. (30–45 cm long) sympodial epiphyte.

PSEUDOBULB: 12–18 in. (30–45 cm) long. The stems are leafy.

LEAVES: Many. The oblong leaves are 1.5–2.0 in. (3.8–5.0 cm) long, leathery, and recurved along the margin.

INFLORESCENCE: Short. Inflorescences appear from nodes at the leafless ends of the stem.

FLOWERS: 1–2 per inflorescence. The small flowers are 0.3–0.5 in. (0.8–1.3 cm) long. The blossoms have a thin texture. Sepals and petals vary in size and shape. Petals are hairy along the margin. The lip has large rounded sidelobes and a small hairy midlobe.

REFERENCES: 190, 200, 202, 218, 254, 286, 295, 395, 445, 454.

Dendrobium tubiflorum J. J. Smith

ORIGIN/HABITAT: Irian Jaya (western New Guinea). Plants grow in secondary forests of the Nassau Range in the eastern part of the Oroh Valley at about 4250 ft. (1300 m).

CLIMATE: Station #97686, Wamena, Irian Jaya, Lat. 4.1°S, Long. 139.0°E, at 5446 ft. (1660 m). Temperatures are calculated for an elevation of 4400 ft. (1340 m). Record extreme temperatures are not available for this location.

N/HEMISPHERE	JAN	FEB	MAR	APR	MAY	JUN	JUL	AUG	SEP	OCT	NOV	DEC
°F AVG MAX	78	79	80	79	80	79	80	79	79	82	81	77
°F AVG MIN	63	63	65	65	66	67	66	65	66	68	68	64
DIURNAL RANGE	15	16	15	14	14	12	14	14	13	14	13	13
RAIN/INCHES	3.0	1.9	2.2	4.0	4.6	3.3	2.8	4.2	6.9	3.9	5.4	4.9
HUMIDITY/%	N/A											
BLOOM SEASON						*						
DAYS CLR	N/A											
RAIN/MM	76	48	56	102	117	84	71	107	175	99	137	124
°C AVG MAX	25.8	26.4	26.9	26.4	26.9	26.4	26.9	26.4	26.4	28.0	27.5	25.3
°C AVG MIN	17.5	17.5	18.6	18.6	19.1	19.7	19.1	18.6	19.1	20.3	20.3	18.0
DIURNAL RANGE	8.3	8.9	8.3	7.8	7.8	6.7	7.8	7.8	7.3	7.7	7.2	7.3
S/HEMISPHERE	JUL	AUG	SEP	OCT	NOV	DEC	JAN	FEB	MAR	APR	MAY	JUN

Cultural Recommendations

LIGHT: 2000–2500 fc. In the habitat, light is highest in the morning.

TEMPERATURES: Throughout the year, days average 78–82°F (26–28°C), and nights average 63–68°F (18–20°C), with a diurnal range of 12–16°F (7–9°C). In the habitat, the warmest temperatures of the day occur during late morning when skies are usually clear. Clouds and mist develop near noon, thus preventing additional warming.

HUMIDITY: Information is not available for this location. However, records from nearby stations indicate that humidity probably averages near 80% year-round. High humidity and excellent air circulation are particularly important if temperatures are warm. Placing the plants in front of an evaporative cooler or near a fine mist may be very beneficial on especially warm days.

WATER: Rainfall is light to moderate through most of the year, but large amounts of water are usually available from mist and heavy dew, even during periods of lower rainfall. Cultivated plants should be kept moist with only slight drying allowed between waterings. Good air movement is critically important and should be maintained at all times.

FERTILIZER: ¼–½ recommended strength. A balanced fertilizer should be applied weekly to biweekly throughout the year.

REST PERIOD: Growing conditions should be maintained all year. Conditions are slightly drier for 1–2 months in winter. In cultivation, water may be decreased somewhat, but plants should never be allowed to dry out completely or remain dry for long periods. In the habitat, light is slightly higher in winter.

GROWING MEDIA: Plants may be mounted on tree-fern or cork slabs if humidity is high and plants are watered at least once daily in summer. When plants are potted, any open, fast-draining medium may be used. Repotting may be done anytime new roots are growing.

MISCELLANEOUS NOTES: The bloom season shown in the climate table is based on reports from the habitat. The plant was described in 1914 in *Bull. Jard. Bot. Buit.* 2nd sér. 13:66.

Plant and Flower Information

PLANT SIZE AND TYPE: A 16 in. (40 cm) sympodial epiphyte.

PSEUDOBULB: 16 in. (40 cm) long. The stems do not branch.

LEAVES: The somewhat ovate to lanceolate leaves are 2.5–4.0 in. (6.4–10.0 cm) long. They have a long, sharp point at the tip.

INFLORESCENCE: Short. Inflorescences arise from lower nodes of leafless stems.

FLOWERS: 6–10 per inflorescence. The flowers are about 1 in. (2.5 cm) long. The blossoms are long and narrow. The ovate dorsal sepal, somewhat triangular lateral sepals, and the oval to oblong petals may be white or a pale shade of pink-violet. The nearly white lip is fringed at the apex.

REFERENCES: 221, 470.

Dendrobium tumidulum Schlechter. See *D. nebularum* Schlechter. REFERENCES: 223, 385, 443.

Dendrobium tumoriferum J. J. Smith

ORIGIN/HABITAT: Irian Jaya (western New Guinea) and the islands of Bougainville, Guadalcanal, and New Georgia. In Irian Jaya, plants grow on trees in swamps along the Noord River from sea level to 1950 ft. (0–600 m).

CLIMATE: Station #97796, Kokenau (Kokonau), Irian Jaya, Lat. 4.7°S, Long. 136.4°E, at 10 ft. (3 m). Record extreme temperatures are not available for this location.

N/HEMISPHERE	JAN	FEB	MAR	APR	MAY	JUN	JUL	AUG	SEP	OCT	NOV	DEC
°F AVG MAX	83	83	86	88	90	89	89	90	88	87	84	
°F AVG MIN	73	73	74	74	74	75	74	74	74	74	74	73
DIURNAL RANGE	10	10	12	14	16	14	15	15	16	14	13	11
RAIN/INCHES	18.4	15.8	18.9	11.6	9.7	10.6	11.5	15.7	11.6	11.6	16.0	19.9
HUMIDITY/%	N/A											
BLOOM SEASON			*									
DAYS CLR	N/A											
RAIN/MM	467	401	479	295	245	269	293	400	294	296	407	506
°C AVG MAX	28.6	28.4	30.2	31.1	32.1	31.9	31.9	31.7	32.0	31.4	30.7	28.7
°C AVG MIN	22.7	22.6	23.3	23.4	23.5	23.7	23.6	23.5	23.4	23.4	23.5	23.0
DIURNAL RANGE	5.9	5.8	6.9	7.7	8.6	8.2	8.3	8.2	8.6	8.0	7.2	5.7
S/HEMISPHERE	JUL	AUG	SEP	OCT	NOV	DEC	JAN	FEB	MAR	APR	MAY	JUN

Cultural Recommendations

LIGHT: 2500–3500 fc.

TEMPERATURES: Throughout the year, days average 83–90°F (28–32°C), and nights average 73–75°F (23–24°C), with a diurnal range of 10–16°F (6–9°C).

HUMIDITY: Information is not available for this location. However, records from nearby stations indicate that humidity is probably near 85% year-round.

WATER: Rainfall is very heavy all year. Cultivated plants should be kept evenly moist but not soggy. Warm water might be beneficial.

FERTILIZER: ¼–½ recommended strength. A balanced fertilizer should be applied weekly to biweekly throughout the year.

REST PERIOD: Growing temperatures should be maintained year-round. The smallest diurnal range occurs in winter. Water and fertilizer might be reduced somewhat in winter, especially for plants cultivated in the dark, short-day conditions common in the temperate latitudes. They should never be allowed to dry out completely, however. In the habitat, seasonal light variation is minor.

GROWING MEDIA: Mounting plants on tree-fern or cork slabs accommodates their pendulous growth habit. However, humidity must be high and plants must be watered at least once a day in summer. If plants can-

not be mounted, hanging pots or baskets may be filled with an open, fast-draining medium. Repotting may be done anytime new roots are actively growing.

MISCELLANEOUS NOTES: The bloom season shown in the climate table is based on reports from the habitat.

Plant and Flower Information

PLANT SIZE AND TYPE: A 26 in. (66 cm) sympodial epiphyte.

PSEUDOBULB: 26 in. (66 cm) long. The clumps of flattened stems are pendulous.

LEAVES: Many. The linear leaves are 1.3 in. (3.4 cm) long, alternating in 2 rows, and flattened lengthwise.

INFLORESCENCE: Very short. Inflorescences emerge from the leaf axils along the stem.

FLOWERS: 1 per inflorescence. The fleshy flowers are 0.2–0.3 in. (0.4–0.8 cm) long and do not open fully. They may be self-pollinating. The dorsal sepal is ovate, and concave lateral sepals are obliquely triangular. The petals are triangular-lanceolate, pointed, and recurved at the tip. The lateral sepals are pale yellow and other parts are tinged with maroon. The erect lip is curved, concave, and fringed.

REFERENCES: 220, 254, 445, 470, 516.

Dendrobium tunense J. J. Smith

AKA: Kränzlin (ref. 254) included *D. tunense* as a variety of *D. dendrocolla* (J. J. Smith) Kränzlin, which is now considered a synonym of *Diplocaulobium dendrocolla* (J. J. Smith) Kränzlin. Since Kränzlins' synonyms are so often disputed, it is included here.

ORIGIN/HABITAT: Molucca Islands. Plants were originally found near Toena on Ambon Island at about 450 ft. (130 m).

CLIMATE: Station #97724, Ambon Island, Moluccas, Indonesia, Lat. 3.7°S, Long. 128.1°E, at 33 ft. (10 m). Temperatures are calculated for an elevation of 500 ft. (150 m), resulting in probable extremes of 94°F (35°C) and 64°F (18°C).

N/HEMISPHERE	JAN	FEB	MAR	APR	MAY	JUN	JUL	AUG	SEP	OCT	NOV	DEC
°F AVG MAX	79	79	81	83	86	86	86	86	86	84	82	80
°F AVG MIN	72	72	72	72	73	74	74	74	74	74	73	72
DIURNAL RANGE	7	7	9	11	13	12	12	12	12	10	9	8
RAIN/INCHES	23.7	15.8	9.5	6.1	4.5	5.2	5.0	4.7	5.3	11.0	20.3	25.1
HUMIDITY/%	83	82	81	80	79	78	78	77	79	82	83	84
BLOOM SEASON	N/A											
DAYS CLR @ 9AM	1	1	1	6	7	4	3	3	5	5	3	3
DAYS CLR @ 3PM	1	1	2	5	6	1	1	1	2	3	1	3
RAIN/MM	602	401	241	155	114	132	127	119	135	279	516	638
°C AVG MAX	26.4	26.4	27.5	28.6	30.3	30.3	30.3	30.3	30.3	29.1	28.0	26.9
°C AVG MIN	22.5	22.5	22.5	22.5	23.0	23.6	23.6	23.6	23.6	23.6	23.0	22.5
DIURNAL RANGE	3.9	3.9	5.0	6.1	7.3	6.7	6.7	6.7	6.7	5.5	5.0	4.4
S/HEMISPHERE	JUL	AUG	SEP	OCT	NOV	DEC	JAN	FEB	MAR	APR	MAY	JUN

Cultural Recommendations

LIGHT: 2500–3500 fc.

TEMPERATURES: Throughout the year, days average 79–86°F (26–30°C), and nights average 72–74°F (23–24°C), with a diurnal range of 7–13°F (4–7°C).

HUMIDITY: 80–85% year-round.

WATER: Rainfall is moderate to heavy all year, but conditions are slightly drier in late spring and summer. Cultivated plants should be kept evenly moist.

FERTILIZER: ¼–½ recommended strength. A balanced fertilizer should be applied weekly to biweekly throughout the year.

REST PERIOD: Growing temperatures should be maintained all year. Rainfall is highest in winter, but water should be reduced for plants cultivated in the dark, short-day conditions common in temperate latitudes. Plants should never be allowed to dry out completely, however.

GROWING MEDIA: Plants may be mounted on tree-fern or cork slabs if humidity is high and plants are watered at least once daily in summer. When plants are potted, any open, fast-draining medium may be used. Repotting is best done in early spring when new roots are growing.

MISCELLANEOUS NOTES: Plants that produce flowers which last a single day commonly bloom several times during the year. Flowering usually occurs 7–14 days after a sudden 10°F (5°C) drop in daytime temperatures. The plant was described in 1909 in *Bull. Dép. Agric. Indes Néerl.* 22:22.

Plant and Flower Information

PLANT SIZE AND TYPE: A 5 in. (13 cm) sympodial epiphyte.

PSEUDOBULB: 0.8 in. (2 cm) long. The pseudobulbs are oblong-ovoid, swollen, and clustered.

LEAVES: 1 per growth. The linear-lanceolate leaf is 4 in. (10 cm) long. It is leathery, dark green on the upper surface and pale green on the underside. The apex of the leaf is 2-toothed.

INFLORESCENCE: 0.8 in. (2 cm) long. The inflorescence emerges near the apex of the pseudobulb. Blossoms are clustered at the apex of the inflorescence.

FLOWERS: Several. The flowers are 2.8 in. (7 cm) across. The lanceolate sepals and petals are yellowish white in the center and pale yellow near the tips. The backside is darker with a reddish tinge. The lip is yellowish white with red to dark purple markings near the base. It is erect, recurved, and 3-lobed. The erect sidelobes are ruffled on the margin. The midlobe is wavy. Blossoms are very short lived.

REFERENCES: 220, 254.

Dendrobium tysanochilum Schlechter. Now considered a synonym of *Flickingeria comata*. REFERENCES: 67, 434.

Dendrobium uliginosum J. J. Smith

ORIGIN/HABITAT: Irian Jaya (western New Guinea). Plants were found on trees in the swamps on the coastal plain along the Noord River.

CLIMATE: Station #97796, Kokenau (Kokonau), Irian Jaya, Lat. 4.7°S, Long. 136.4°E, at 10 ft. (3 m). Record extreme temperatures are not available for this location.

N/HEMISPHERE	JAN	FEB	MAR	APR	MAY	JUN	JUL	AUG	SEP	OCT	NOV	DEC
°F AVG MAX	83	83	86	88	90	89	89	89	90	88	87	84
°F AVG MIN	73	73	74	74	74	75	74	74	74	74	74	73
DIURNAL RANGE	10	10	12	14	16	14	15	15	16	14	13	11
RAIN/INCHES	18.4	15.8	18.9	11.6	9.7	10.6	11.5	15.7	11.6	11.6	16.0	19.9
HUMIDITY/%	N/A											
BLOOM SEASON			*									
DAYS CLR	N/A											
RAIN/MM	467	401	479	295	245	269	293	400	294	296	407	506
°C AVG MAX	28.6	28.4	30.2	31.1	32.1	31.9	31.9	31.7	32.0	31.4	30.7	28.7
°C AVG MIN	22.7	22.6	23.3	23.4	23.5	23.7	23.6	23.5	23.4	23.4	23.5	23.0
DIURNAL RANGE	5.9	5.8	6.9	7.7	8.6	8.2	8.3	8.2	8.6	8.0	7.2	5.7
S/HEMISPHERE	JUL	AUG	SEP	OCT	NOV	DEC	JAN	FEB	MAR	APR	MAY	JUN

Cultural Recommendations

LIGHT: 2500–3500 fc.

TEMPERATURES: Throughout the year, days average 83–90°F (28–32°C), and nights average 73–75°F (23–24°C), with a diurnal range of 10–16°F (6–9°C).

HUMIDITY: Information is not available for this location. However, records from nearby stations indicate that humidity probably averages near 85% year-round.

WATER: Rainfall is very heavy all year. Cultivated plants should be kept evenly moist but not soggy. Warm water might be beneficial.

FERTILIZER: ¼–½ recommended strength. A balanced fertilizer should be applied weekly to biweekly throughout the year.

REST PERIOD: Growing temperatures should be maintained year-round. The smallest diurnal range occurs in winter. Water and fertilizer might be reduced slightly, especially for plants cultivated in the dark, short-day conditions common in the temperate latitudes. However, plants should never be allowed to dry out completely. In the habitat, seasonal light variation is minor.

GROWING MEDIA: Plants may be potted in any open, fast-draining medium; but the water requirement is high, so a moisture retaining medium should be used if plants are not watered regularly. Repotting may be done anytime new roots are growing.

MISCELLANEOUS NOTES: The bloom season shown in the climate table is based on reports from the habitat. The plant was described in 1910 in *Bull. Dép. Agric. Indes. Néerl.* 39:11.

Plant and Flower Information

PLANT SIZE AND TYPE: A sympodial epiphyte of unreported size.

PSEUDOBULB: Stems are terete.

INFLORESCENCE: 0.6–1.0 in. (1.5–2.5 cm) long. The densely flowered inflorescences emerge along the side of the stem.

FLOWERS: 20 per inflorescence. The violet-red flowers are 1.1 in. (2.8 cm) long. Blossoms have an obovate-oblong dorsal sepal, with somewhat ovate-oblong lateral sepals, and spatula-shaped petals. The concave petals have an uneven upper margin. The erect lip has a broadly rounded, incurved front margin and a V-shaped callus.

REFERENCES: 220, 254, 445, 470.

Dendrobium umbellatum (Gaudich.) Rchb. f. not J. J. Smith

AKA: *Cadetia umbellata* Gaudich. *Cadetia* is considered a valid genus by some botanists, so this plant may again be a *Cadetia*.

ORIGIN/HABITAT: Eastern Indonesia. Plants are found on the Molucca Islands, Ambon Island, and Yapen (Jobie or Yobi) Island, which is located off the north coast of Irian Jaya (western New Guinea). Habitat elevation is unreported, so the following climate data should be used with caution.

CLIMATE: Station #97724, Ambon/Pattimura, Indonesia, Lat. 3.7°S, Long. 128.1°E, at 33 ft. (10 m). Record extreme temperatures are 96°F (36°C) and 66°F (19°C).

N/HEMISPHERE	JAN	FEB	MAR	APR	MAY	JUN	JUL	AUG	SEP	OCT	NOV	DEC
°F AVG MAX	81	81	83	85	88	88	88	88	88	86	84	82
°F AVG MIN	74	74	74	74	75	76	76	76	76	76	75	74
DIURNAL RANGE	7	7	9	11	13	12	12	12	12	10	9	8
RAIN/INCHES	23.7	15.8	9.5	6.1	4.5	5.2	5.0	4.7	5.3	11.0	20.3	25.1
HUMIDITY/%	83	82	81	80	79	78	78	77	79	82	83	84
BLOOM SEASON	N/A											
DAYS CLR @ 9AM	1	1	1	6	7	4	3	3	5	5	3	3
DAYS CLR @ 3PM	1	1	2	5	6	1	1	1	2	3	1	3
RAIN/MM	602	401	241	155	114	132	127	119	135	279	516	638
°C AVG MAX	27.2	27.2	28.3	29.4	31.1	31.1	31.1	31.1	31.1	30.0	28.9	27.8
°C AVG MIN	23.3	23.3	23.3	23.3	23.9	24.4	24.4	24.4	24.4	24.4	23.9	23.3
DIURNAL RANGE	3.9	3.9	5.0	6.1	7.2	6.7	6.7	6.7	6.7	5.6	5.0	4.5
S/HEMISPHERE	JUL	AUG	SEP	OCT	NOV	DEC	JAN	FEB	MAR	APR	MAY	JUN

Cultural Recommendations

LIGHT: 2000–3000 fc.

TEMPERATURES: Throughout the year, days average 81–88°F (27–31°C), and nights average 74–76°F (23–24°C), with a diurnal range of 7–13°F (4–7°C).

HUMIDITY: 80–85% year-round.

WATER: Rainfall is moderate to heavy all year, but conditions are slightly drier in late spring and summer. Cultivated plants should be kept evenly moist all year with only slight drying allowed between waterings.

FERTILIZER: ¼–½ recommended strength. A balanced fertilizer should be applied weekly to biweekly throughout the year.

REST PERIOD: Growing conditions should be maintained all year. In the habitat, a brief, semidry period occurs in late spring. Rainfall is heaviest in winter, but water and fertilizer should be reduced for plants cultivated in the dark, short-day conditions common in temperate-latitude winters. Plants should never be allowed to dry completely, however. In the habitat, light is highest in spring.

GROWING MEDIA: Plants may be mounted on tree-fern or cork slabs if humidity is high and plants are watered at least once daily in summer. When plants are potted, any open, fast-draining medium may be used. They may be repotted anytime new roots are growing.

Plant and Flower Information

PLANT SIZE AND TYPE: A 3–4 in. (8–10 cm) sympodial epiphyte.

PSEUDOBULB: 1.4–2.0 in. (3–5 cm) long.

LEAVES: 1 per growth. The leaves are 1.6–2.4 in. (4–6 cm) long. They are oblong-lanceolate and rigid.

INFLORESCENCE: Short.

FLOWERS: 6–10 per inflorescence. The blossoms open in succession. The white flowers are 0.2 in. (0.5 cm) across. The ovary is hairy.

REFERENCES: 216, 254, 317, 468.

Dendrobium umbellatum J. J. Smith not Rchb. f. A synonym of *D. pseudo-umbellatum* J. J. Smith, which Schlechter (ref. 437) considered a synonym of *Cadetia pseudo-umbellata* (J. J. Smith) Schlechter. REFERENCES: 437.

Dendrobium umbonatum Seidenfaden

ORIGIN/HABITAT: Southeastern Thailand. Plants are found near Khao Kuap, Trat.

Dendrobium uncatum

CLIMATE: Station #48480, Chanthaburi, Thailand, Lat. 12.6°N, Long. 102.1°E, at 16 ft. (5 m). Record extreme temperatures are 103°F (39°C) and 48°F (9°C).

N/HEMISPHERE	JAN	FEB	MAR	APR	MAY	JUN	JUL	AUG	SEP	OCT	NOV	DEC
°F AVG MAX	91	92	92	93	91	88	87	87	87	89	89	88
°F AVG MIN	67	70	72	74	75	76	75	75	74	73	71	67
DIURNAL RANGE	24	22	20	19	16	12	12	12	13	16	18	21
RAIN/INCHES	0.8	1.4	2.7	4.8	12.4	19.3	19.3	17.9	19.6	9.9	2.8	0.5
HUMIDITY/%	71	75	78	80	85	86	86	87	88	84	77	71
BLOOM SEASON					*							
DAYS CLR @ 7AM	5	1	1	1	0	0	0	0	0	1	5	7
DAYS CLR @ 1PM	7	3	1	1	0	0	0	0	0	0	4	8
RAIN/MM	20	36	69	122	315	490	490	455	498	251	71	13
°C AVG MAX	32.8	33.3	33.3	33.9	32.8	31.1	30.6	30.6	30.6	31.7	31.7	31.1
°C AVG MIN	19.4	21.1	22.2	23.3	23.9	24.4	23.9	23.9	23.3	22.8	21.7	19.4
DIURNAL RANGE	13.4	12.2	11.1	10.6	8.9	6.7	6.7	6.7	7.3	8.9	10.0	11.7
S/HEMISPHERE	JUL	AUG	SEP	OCT	NOV	DEC	JAN	FEB	MAR	APR	MAY	JUN

Cultural Recommendations

LIGHT: 1800–2500 fc.

TEMPERATURES: Summer days average 87–88°F (31°C), and nights average 75–76°F (24°C), with a diurnal range of 12°F (7°C). The warmest temperatures occur in spring. Days average 91–93°F (33–34°C), nights average 72–75°F (22–24°C), and the diurnal range is 16–20°F (9–11°C).

HUMIDITY: Near 85% in summer and autumn, dropping to 70–75% for 3–4 months in winter.

WATER: Rainfall is very heavy for 6 months from late spring through autumn, but amounts are much lower for 2–3 months in winter. Cultivated plants should be kept moist from late spring to early autumn. Daily watering may be necessary during bright, hot weather. Water should be gradually reduced after new growths mature in autumn.

FERTILIZER: ¼–½ recommended strength, applied weekly. A high-nitrogen fertilizer is beneficial from spring to midsummer, but a fertilizer high in phosphates should be used in late summer and autumn.

REST PERIOD: Winter days average 88–92°F (31–33°C), and nights average 67–70°F (19–21°C), with a diurnal range of 21–24°F (12–13°C). In the habitat, rainfall is low for 2–3 months in winter, but considerable additional moisture is available from nightly deposits of dew. Water should be reduced for cultivated plants in winter. They should be allowed to become almost dry between waterings, but should never remain dry for long periods. Fertilizer should be reduced or eliminated until water is increased in spring. In the habitat, light is much higher in winter.

GROWING MEDIA: Plants may be mounted on tree-fern or cork slabs if humidity is high and plants are watered at least once daily in summer. When plants are potted, any open, fast-draining medium may be used. Repotting is best done in early spring when new roots are growing.

MISCELLANEOUS NOTES: The bloom season shown in the climate table is based on reports from the habitat.

Plant and Flower Information

PLANT SIZE AND TYPE: A sympodial epiphyte that exceeds a length of 14 in. (35 cm).

PSEUDOBULB: Longer than 14 in. (35 cm) long. The slender, leafy stems consist of internodes 0.8 in. (2 cm) long.

LEAVES: Many. The lanceolate leaves are deciduous and 2.8–3.1 in. (7–8 cm) long. They are arranged in 2 rows.

INFLORESCENCE: 0.4 in. (1 cm) long. Inflorescences emerge from nodes opposite the leaves on both leafy and leafless stems.

FLOWERS: 4 per inflorescence. The small flowers are about 0.6 in. (1.5 cm) long. Sepals and petals are white. The fan-shaped, 3-lobed lip is greenish white with a raised yellow patch near the front of the midlobe and dark purplish red veins on the sidelobes. The midlobe and sidelobes have a long, dense, hairlike fringe along the front margins.

REFERENCES: 234, 454.

PHOTOS/DRAWINGS: 454.

Dendrobium uncatum Lindley

AKA: *D. salicornioides* Teijsm. and Binnend.

ORIGIN/HABITAT: Common in West Java. Plants grow at 650–1000 ft. (200–300 m) south of Bogor. Plants are also found in Borneo, where they grow in lower mountain forests in Sabah at about 4600 ft. (1400 m). They are also reported from Krakatau and, as *D. salicornioides*, from southern Vietnam. Unlike most orchids, *D. uncatum* grows on rubber trees.

CLIMATE: Station #96755, Bogor, Java, Indonesia, Lat. 6.5°S, Long. 106.8°E, at 558 ft. (170 m). Temperatures are calculated for an elevation of 1000 ft. (300 m), resulting in probable extremes of 95°F (35°C) and 65°F (18°C).

N/HEMISPHERE	JAN	FEB	MAR	APR	MAY	JUN	JUL	AUG	SEP	OCT	NOV	DEC
°F AVG MAX	85	86	87	87	86	84	83	83	84	85	86	85
°F AVG MIN	72	72	72	73	73	73	73	73	73	74	74	73
DIURNAL RANGE	13	14	15	14	13	11	10	10	11	11	12	12
RAIN/INCHES	2.1	1.0	0.5	5.0	8.1	18.8	23.7	20.2	14.4	12.0	11.9	3.4
HUMIDITY/%	72	68	65	66	74	79	84	84	81	79	77	75
BLOOM SEASON	*	*	*									*
DAYS CLR @ 7AM	14	14	14	11	5	3	1	2	4	6	10	12
DAYS CLR @ 1PM	9	10	8	5	1	1	0	0	1	1	3	7
RAIN/MM	53	25	13	127	206	478	602	513	366	305	302	86
°C AVG MAX	29.2	29.7	30.3	30.3	29.7	28.6	28.1	28.1	28.6	29.2	29.7	29.2
°C AVG MIN	22.0	22.0	22.0	22.5	22.5	22.5	22.5	22.5	22.5	23.1	23.1	22.5
DIURNAL RANGE	7.2	7.7	8.3	7.8	7.2	6.1	5.6	5.6	6.1	6.1	6.6	6.7
S/HEMISPHERE	JUL	AUG	SEP	OCT	NOV	DEC	JAN	FEB	MAR	APR	MAY	JUN

Cultural Recommendations

LIGHT: 2000–3000 fc. Diffused or barely dappled light is preferred. Direct sunlight should be avoided.

TEMPERATURES: Throughout the year, days average 83–87°F (28–30°C), and nights average 72–74°F (22–23°C), with a diurnal range of 10–15°F (6–8°C). The warmest temperatures occur in spring. The small seasonal variation indicates that plants may not tolerate wide temperature fluctuations. Because of the difference in habitat elevation, temperatures for plants originating in Borneo should be 8–10°F (4–6°C) cooler than indicated. We do not know whether plants from Java will adapt to cooler conditions.

HUMIDITY: 80–85% in summer, dropping to near 65% for 2–3 months in late winter and early spring.

WATER: Rainfall is very heavy from spring into autumn, but conditions are very dry for 2 months in winter. During the growing season, plants should never be allowed to dry out completely, but water should be gradually reduced in late autumn.

FERTILIZER: ¼–½ recommended strength, applied weekly. A high-nitrogen fertilizer is beneficial from spring to midsummer, but a fertilizer high in phosphates should be used in late summer and autumn.

REST PERIOD: Growing conditions should be maintained all year, but the diurnal range increases slightly in winter, and rainfall is very low for 2–3 months. In cultivation, water should be reduced and the plants allowed to become dry between waterings. However, they should not remain dry for prolonged periods. Fertilizer may be reduced or eliminated anytime the plant is not actively growing. In the habitat, light is highest in winter.

GROWING MEDIA: Mounting plants on tree-fern or cork slabs accommodates their pendulous growth habit. However, humidity must be high and plants must be watered at least once a day in summer. If plants cannot be mounted, hanging pots or baskets may be filled with an open, fast-draining medium. Repotting may be done anytime new roots are actively growing.

MISCELLANEOUS NOTES: The bloom season shown in the climate table is based on cultivation records.

Plant and Flower Information

PLANT SIZE AND TYPE: A 10 in. (25 cm) sympodial epiphyte.

PSEUDOBULB: 10 in. (25 cm) long. The zigzag stems emerge upright and become pendulous as they lengthen. The stems are leafy.

LEAVES: Many. The bright green leaves are 0.3 in. (0.7 cm) long, terete, flattened, and slightly recurved. They are held at nearly right angles to the stem. The stem and leaves appear to be part of a single structure.

INFLORESCENCE: Short. Inflorescences emerge at the apex of the stem.

FLOWERS: 1–2 per inflorescence. The erect, fan-shaped flowers are 0.8 in. (2 cm) across. Sepals and petals may be white or rosy orange with pure orange tips. The dorsal sepal and petals are small. The relatively large lateral sepals are somewhat triangular. The base of the lip is flushed with a crimson or yellow blotch even when the blossoms are primarily white. The slender lip is recurved at the apex with a scalloped, wavy, incurved margin. It is faintly 3-lobed with subtriangular sidelobes and a short midlobe.

REFERENCES: 25, 75, 179, 216, 254, 266, 278, 310, 330, 445, 454, 469, 592.

PHOTOS/DRAWINGS: 75, 469.

Dendrobium uncinatum Schlechter. See *D. vexillarius* J. J. Smith. REFERENCES: 179, 221, 304, 307, 385, 437, 445, 538. PHOTOS/DRAWINGS: *307*, 538.

Dendrobium uncipes J. J. Smith

AKA: J. J. Smith (ref. 470) originally placed *D. uncipes* in the section *Sarcopodium*. It was later transferred to *Katherina uncipes* (J. J. Smith) A. Hawkes, then to *Epigeneium uncipes* (J. J. Smith) Summerhayes, and then included in the *Dendrobium* section *Latouria* by Cribb (ref. 83).

ORIGIN/HABITAT: Irian Jaya (western New Guinea). Near Jayapura, plants grow in forests of the Goliath Mountains at about 2950 ft. (900 m).

CLIMATE: Station #97690, Sentani/Jayapura, Irian Jaya, Lat. 2.7°S, Long. 140.5°E, at 289 ft. (88 m). Temperatures are calculated for an elevation of 3000 ft. (910 m), resulting in probable extremes of 88°F (31°C) and 59°F (15°C).

N/HEMISPHERE	JAN	FEB	MAR	APR	MAY	JUN	JUL	AUG	SEP	OCT	NOV	DEC
°F AVG MAX	78	80	80	81	81	80	80	79	80	81	81	80
°F AVG MIN	63	63	63	64	64	64	64	64	64	65	64	64
DIURNAL RANGE	15	17	17	17	17	16	16	15	16	16	17	16
RAIN/INCHES	4.1	3.9	5.3	2.9	6.7	7.0	8.3	8.3	8.5	4.6	2.4	5.2
HUMIDITY/%	81	80	80	79	81	81	79	80	80	80	81	80
BLOOM SEASON												*
DAYS CLR @ 9AM	5	3	4	3	2	1	1	0	1	2	2	5
DAYS CLR @ 3PM	4	3	3	3	2	1	3	0	1	2	2	3
RAIN/MM	104	99	135	74	170	178	211	211	216	117	61	132
°C AVG MAX	25.6	26.7	26.7	27.3	27.3	26.7	26.7	26.1	26.7	27.3	27.3	26.7
°C AVG MIN	17.3	17.3	17.3	17.8	17.8	17.8	17.8	17.8	17.8	18.4	17.8	17.8
DIURNAL RANGE	8.3	9.4	9.4	9.5	9.5	8.9	8.9	8.3	8.9	8.9	9.5	8.9
S/HEMISPHERE	JUL	AUG	SEP	OCT	NOV	DEC	JAN	FEB	MAR	APR	MAY	JUN

Cultural Recommendations

LIGHT: 2000–3000 fc.

TEMPERATURES: Throughout the year, days average 78–81°F (26–27°C), and nights average 63–65°F (17–18°C), with a diurnal range of 15–17°F (8–10°C).

HUMIDITY: Near 80% year-round.

WATER: Rainfall is heavy all year, with brief semidry periods in spring and autumn. Cultivated plants should be kept moist most of the year, but they should be allowed to become somewhat dry for a few weeks in spring and again in autumn.

FERTILIZER: ¼–½ recommended strength. A balanced fertilizer should be applied weekly to biweekly throughout the year.

REST PERIOD: Growing conditions should be maintained year-round. Water and fertilizer might be reduced slightly in winter, especially for plants grown in the dark, short-day conditions common in temperate latitudes. They should never be allowed to dry completely, however. In the habitat, light is slightly higher in winter.

GROWING MEDIA: Plants may be mounted on tree-fern or cork slabs if humidity is high and plants are watered at least once daily in summer. When plants are potted, fir bark or any open, fast-draining medium may be used. Repotting may be done anytime new roots are growing.

MISCELLANEOUS NOTES: The bloom season shown in the climate table is based on collection records. *D. uncipes* is related to plants which bloom while quite young.

Plant and Flower Information

PLANT SIZE AND TYPE: A 2 in. (5 cm) sympodial epiphyte.

PSEUDOBULB: 0.7 in. (1.7 cm) long. The ovoid pseudobulbs are brownish yellow with 8 angles.

LEAVES: 2 at the apex. The ovoid leaves are 1.2 in. (3 cm) long, dark green, and fleshy but flexible. The narrow apex is 2-toothed.

INFLORESCENCE: 1.4 in. (3.6 cm) long. The inflorescence is erect.

FLOWERS: 3 per inflorescence. Flowers are 0.4 in. (1 cm) long, fleshy, and yellow-brown. The oblong-elliptic sepals are mealy on the backside. The dorsal sepal is 2-toothed at the apex. Petals are somewhat sickle-shaped with an uneven margin. The conspicuously 3-lobed lip has narrowly elliptical sidelobes and a notched midlobe with a blunt point in the center. The lip has a fleshy, 3-ridged callus that extends half the length of the midlobe.

REFERENCES: 83, 221, 445, 470, 499.

Dendrobium undatialatum Schlechter

AKA: *D. maboroense* Schlechter.

ORIGIN/HABITAT: Widespread in Papua New Guinea. Plants grow in the Torricelli, Finisterre, and Maboro Mountains. They are usually found on horizontal branches of mistforest trees at 2950–4250 ft. (900–1300 m). The orchids have also been found at about 2500 ft. (760 m) on Kolombangara Island in the Solomon Islands.

CLIMATE: Station #200192, Garaina, Papua New Guinea, Lat. 7.9°S, Long. 147.1°E, at 2350 ft. (716 m). Temperatures are calculated for an elevation of 3300 ft. (1000 m), resulting in probable extremes of 91°F (33°C) and 43°F (6°C).

N/HEMISPHERE	JAN	FEB	MAR	APR	MAY	JUN	JUL	AUG	SEP	OCT	NOV	DEC
°F AVG MAX	77	79	80	81	82	82	82	82	81	81	80	78
°F AVG MIN	60	60	60	61	60	61	62	62	62	61	61	60
DIURNAL RANGE	17	19	20	20	22	21	20	20	19	20	19	18
RAIN/INCHES	5.8	6.5	8.7	11.1	11.8	11.9	8.9	11.7	11.5	9.9	7.7	5.2
HUMIDITY/%	84	82	82	81	80	80	81	81	82	83	84	84
BLOOM SEASON	*	*										*
DAYS CLR	N/A											
RAIN/MM	147	165	221	282	300	302	226	297	292	251	196	132
°C AVG MAX	25.0	26.1	26.6	27.2	27.7	27.7	27.7	27.7	27.2	27.2	26.6	25.5
°C AVG MIN	15.5	15.5	15.5	16.1	15.5	16.1	16.6	16.6	16.6	16.1	16.1	15.5
DIURNAL RANGE	9.5	10.6	11.1	11.1	12.2	11.6	11.1	11.1	10.6	11.1	10.5	10.0
S/HEMISPHERE	JUL	AUG	SEP	OCT	NOV	DEC	JAN	FEB	MAR	APR	MAY	JUN

Dendrobium undatiflorum

Cultural Recommendations

LIGHT: 2000–3000 fc.

TEMPERATURES: Throughout the year, days average 77–82°F (25–28°C), and nights average 60–62°F (16–17°C), with a diurnal range of 17–22°F (10–12°C). Highs vary only 5°F (3°C), and lows fluctuate only 2°F (1°C), indicating that plants may not tolerate wide temperature variations.

HUMIDITY: 80–85% year-round.

WATER: Rainfall is heavy all year, but conditions are slightly drier in winter. Cultivated plants should be kept moist but not soggy.

FERTILIZER: ¼–½ recommended strength. A balanced fertilizer should be applied weekly to biweekly throughout the year.

REST PERIOD: Growing conditions should be maintained all year. In the habitat, rainfall is slightly lower in winter. Water and fertilizer should be reduced somewhat for cultivated plants, especially those grown in the dark, short-day conditions common during temperate-latitude winters. They should never be allowed to dry out completely, however. In the habitat, seasonal light variation is minor.

GROWING MEDIA: Plants may be mounted on tree-fern or cork slabs if humidity is high and plants are watered at least once daily in summer. When plants are potted, any open, fast-draining medium may be used. Repotting may be done anytime new roots are growing.

MISCELLANEOUS NOTES: The bloom season shown in the climate table is based on collection records and reports from the habitat. This orchid has not yet been introduced to greenhouse cultivation.

Plant and Flower Information

PLANT SIZE AND TYPE: A 2–4 in. (5–10 cm) sympodial epiphyte.

PSEUDOBULB: 0.6 in. (1.5 cm) long. The clustered pseudobulbs are ovoid and consist of 2–4 nodes. The sheath around the basal node deteriorates leaving hairlike strands.

LEAVES: 1, rarely 2 per growth. The oblong to elliptic-lanceolate leaves are 1.6–3.4 in. (4.0–8.6 cm) long. Leaves are deciduous.

INFLORESCENCE: 0.5 in. (1.3 cm) long. The inflorescences, which are covered with bracts, emerge at the apex of the pseudobulb.

FLOWERS: 3–8 per inflorescence. The flowers are 0.7 in. (1.8 cm) long. The pointed oblong sepals and elliptic petals are white and remain nearly closed. The obscurely 3-lobed lip is orange-yellow in the middle and white at the pointed tip with 5 red veins that fade near the base. It is sharply pointed at the apex, and the margin behind the point is minutely toothed. The ovary has 5–7 wavy wings that are readily apparent on the backside of each blossom.

REFERENCES: 221, 385, 437, 445.

PHOTOS/DRAWINGS: 385, 437.

Dendrobium undatiflorum Persoon. Sometimes spelled *D. undulatiflorum* Persoon, it is now considered a synonym of *Maxillaria undatiflora* Ruiz and Pavon. REFERENCES: 216, 254.

Dendrobium undatiflorum Steudel. Now considered a synonym of *Maxillaria undulata* Ruiz and Pavon. REFERENCES: 216, 254.

Dendrobium undulans Bakhuizen f. See *D. discolor* Lindley. REFERENCES: 25, 84, 211, 230.

Dendrobium undulatiflorum Steudel. Now considered a synonym of *Maxillaria undulata* Ruiz and Pavon. REFERENCES: 216, 254.

Dendrobium undulatum R. Brown not Persoon. See *D. discolor* Lindley. *D. undulatum* R. Brown var. *johannis* (Rchb. f.) F. M. Bailey is considered a synonym of *D. johannis* Rchb. f. and *D. undulatum* R. Brown var. *woodfordianum* Maiden is considered a synonym of *D. gouldii* Rchb. f. The International Orchid Commission (ref. 236) registers hybrids under the name *D. undulatum*. REFERENCES: 67, 84, 105, 190, 200, 211, 216, 236, 240, 254, 262, 270, 271, 277, 317, 326, 421, 430, 445, 470, 504, 533, 537, 568, 580. PHOTOS/DRAWINGS: 568.

Dendrobium undulatum Persoon not R. Brown. Now considered a synonym of *Maxillaria undulata* Ruiz and Pavon. REFERENCES: 216, 254.

Dendrobium undulatum Rich. Kränzlin (ref. 254) included this name in a discussion of *D. tofftii* Bailey. No other references were found. REFERENCES: 254.

Dendrobium unguiculatum Teijsm. and Binn. See *D. spurium* (Blume) J. J. Smith. REFERENCES: 216, 254, 296, 310, 317, 469, 536.

Dendrobium unicarinatum Kores

AKA: Kores (ref. 466) indicates that the plant discussed by Lewis and Cribb (ref. 270) under the name *D. bilobum* is actually a new species endemic to Fiji.

ORIGIN/HABITAT: Fiji. These rare plants, which are endemic to Mba province, have been found only in the forests of north-central Viti Levu and near Nandarivatu at 2450–2950 ft. (750–900 m).

CLIMATE: Station #91680, Nadi, Vitu Levu, Fiji, Lat. 17.8°S, 177.4°E, at 63 ft. (19 m). Temperatures are calculated for an elevation of 2600 ft. (790 m), resulting in probable extremes of 87°F (30°C) and 47°F (8°C).

N/HEMISPHERE	JAN	FEB	MAR	APR	MAY	JUN	JUL	AUG	SEP	OCT	NOV	DEC
°F AVG MAX	75	77	77	78	78	79	81	80	80	80	78	75
°F AVG MIN	56	58	59	60	61	63	64	64	65	63	60	57
DIURNAL RANGE	19	19	18	18	17	16	17	16	15	17	18	18
RAIN/INCHES	0.5	1.4	3.7	3.5	2.8	4.7	12.7	10.0	15.1	6.8	5.3	4.3
HUMIDITY/%	74	73	73	75	73	78	80	80	83	82	78	78
BLOOM SEASON					*							
DAYS CLR @ 12PM	10	15	7	9	8	5	5	3	3	6	9	11
DAYS CLR @ 6PM	12	10	4	6	3	2	1	1	1	3	6	8
RAIN/MM	13	36	94	89	71	119	323	254	384	173	135	109
°C AVG MAX	23.7	24.8	24.8	25.3	25.3	25.9	27.0	26.5	26.5	26.5	25.3	23.7
°C AVG MIN	13.1	14.2	14.8	15.3	15.9	17.0	17.6	17.6	18.1	17.0	15.3	13.7
DIURNAL RANGE	10.6	10.6	10.0	10.0	9.4	8.9	9.4	8.9	8.4	9.5	10.0	10.0
S/HEMISPHERE	JUL	AUG	SEP	OCT	NOV	DEC	JAN	FEB	MAR	APR	MAY	JUN

Cultural Recommendations

LIGHT: 2000–3000 fc.

TEMPERATURES: Summer days average 79–81°F (26–27°C), and nights average 63–64°F (17–18°C), with a diurnal range of 16–17°F (9°C).

HUMIDITY: Near 80% in summer and autumn, dropping to 70–75% in winter and spring.

WATER: Rainfall is moderate to heavy from spring through autumn, but conditions are drier for 1–2 months in winter. Cultivated plants should be kept evenly moist while in actively growing, but water should be gradually reduced in autumn.

FERTILIZER: ¼–½ recommended strength, applied weekly. A high-nitrogen fertilizer is beneficial from spring to midsummer, but a fertilizer high in phosphates should be used in late summer and autumn.

REST PERIOD: Winter days average 75–77°F (24–25°C), and nights average 56–59°F (13–15°C), with a diurnal range of 18–19°F (10–11°C).

In cultivation, water and fertilizer should be reduced for 1–2 months in winter and plants allowed to dry out between waterings. They should never remain dry for long periods, however. In the habitat, winter skies are frequently clear.

GROWING MEDIA: Plants may be mounted on tree-fern or cork slabs or potted, in any open, fast-draining medium. Repotting is best done in early spring when new roots are growing.

MISCELLANEOUS NOTES: The bloom season shown in the climate table is based on reports from the habitat. Plants are in fruit in late summer and autumn.

Plant and Flower Information

PLANT SIZE AND TYPE: A 24 in. (60 cm) sympodial epiphyte.

PSEUDOBULB: 22 in. (55 cm) long. The erect, reedlike stems arise from a very short rhizome. The stems are leafy at the apex.

LEAVES: Many. The leaves are 1.8–2.4 in. (4.5–6.0 cm) long, distichous, oblong-lanceolate, and unequally bilobed at the apex. They are erect or nearly so. The leaf sheaths are bilobed at the apex opposite the leaves.

INFLORESCENCE: Very short. Inflorescences emerge from flattened protuberances along the stem.

FLOWERS: 1 per inflorescence. The yellow and white flowers are 0.4 in. (1 cm) long and remain rather closed. They have an ovate dorsal sepal, a pointed somewhat triangular lateral sepals, and small, ovate petals. The unlobed lip is uppermost with a central, linear callus. The apical part is oval and the edges of the apex are incurved, making it appear pointed.

REFERENCES: 235, 252, 255, 466.

PHOTOS/DRAWINGS: 466.

Dendrobium unicorne Ames. Now considered a synonym of *Flickingeria unicornis* (Ames) A. Hawkes. REFERENCES: 12, 213, 222, 230, 231, 296, 536.

Dendrobium unicum Seidenfaden

ORIGIN/HABITAT: Northern Thailand, Laos, and Vietnam. In Thailand, plants have been found near Omkoi at 2600–3300 ft. (800–1000 m) and near Loei at 4600–5100 ft. (1400–1550 m). In Laos, they have been reported in Vientiane and Sedone. They grow on rocks or bushes in areas with low, scrublike vegetation.

CLIMATE: Station #48325, Mae Sariang, Thailand, Lat. 18.2°N, Long. 97.8°E, at 1030 ft. (314 m). Temperatures are calculated for an elevation of 3000 ft. (910 m), resulting in probable extremes of 104°F (40°C) and 34°F (1°C).

N/HEMISPHERE	JAN	FEB	MAR	APR	MAY	JUN	JUL	AUG	SEP	OCT	NOV	DEC
°F AVG MAX	81	85	89	92	87	82	80	80	82	83	82	79
°F AVG MIN	51	50	57	66	69	68	67	67	67	65	61	53
DIURNAL RANGE	30	35	32	26	18	14	13	13	15	18	21	26
RAIN/INCHES	0.3	0.2	0.3	1.9	5.7	9.0	8.4	10.8	8.7	3.7	1.1	0.6
HUMIDITY/%	72	67	57	55	68	83	83	84	83	81	77	75
BLOOM SEASON	*	*	*	**	**	*						
DAYS CLR @ 7AM	1	16	0	3	4	0	0	0	0	0	0	1
DAYS CLR @ 1PM	24	18	9	5	2	0	0	1	1	6	13	20
RAIN/MM	8	5	8	48	145	229	213	274	221	94	28	15
°C AVG MAX	27.5	29.7	31.9	33.6	30.8	28.1	26.9	26.9	28.1	28.6	28.1	26.4
°C AVG MIN	10.8	10.1	14.2	19.2	20.8	20.3	19.7	19.7	19.7	18.6	16.4	11.9
DIURNAL RANGE	16.7	19.4	17.7	14.4	10.0	7.8	7.2	7.2	8.4	10.0	11.7	14.5
S/HEMISPHERE	JUL	AUG	SEP	OCT	NOV	DEC	JAN	FEB	MAR	APR	MAY	JUN

Cultural Recommendations

LIGHT: 2500–4000 fc. The heavy summer cloud cover indicates that some shading is needed from spring through autumn, but light should be as high as the plant can tolerate, short of burning the leaves. Strong air movement is very important all year.

TEMPERATURES: Summer days average 80–82°F (27–28°C), and nights average 67–68°F (20°C), with a diurnal range of 13–14°F (7–8°C). The warmest season is spring. Days average 87–92°F (31–34°C), and nights average 57–69°F (14–21°C), with a diurnal range of 18–32°F (10–19°C).

HUMIDITY: 80–85% in summer through early autumn, dropping to near 55% for 2 months in winter.

WATER: Rainfall is heavy for 6 months from spring into early autumn but is very light for 4–5 months in winter and early spring. Cultivated plants should be kept moist while actively growing, but water should be gradually reduced in autumn after new growths mature.

FERTILIZER: $1/4$–$1/2$ recommended strength, applied weekly. A high-nitrogen fertilizer is beneficial from spring to midsummer, but a fertilizer high in phosphates should be used in late summer and autumn.

REST PERIOD: Winter days average 79–85°F (26–30°C), and nights average 50–53°F (10–12°C), with a diurnal range of 26–35°F (15–19°C). Rainfall is light for 5–6 months from autumn into spring; but during the early part of the dry period, considerable moisture is available from heavy dew and as mist from low clouds and fog. However, for 2 months in spring the weather is clear and dry, with humidity so low that even the moisture from dew is uncommon. During most of the winter dry season, cultivated plants should be allowed to dry slightly between waterings, but they should not remain dry for long periods. For 1–2 months in late winter, however, water should be further decreased and the plants allowed to dry completely. Fertilizer should be eliminated. In the habitat, light is highest in winter.

GROWING MEDIA: Plants may be mounted on tree-fern or cork slabs if humidity is high and plants are watered at least once daily in summer. When plants are potted, any open, fast-draining medium may be used. Repotting is best done in early spring when new roots are growing.

MISCELLANEOUS NOTES: The bloom season shown in the climate table is based on cultivation records. Growers indicate that plants may bloom anytime from winter to summer.

Plant and Flower Information

PLANT SIZE AND TYPE: A 2.8–3.5 in. (7–9 cm) sympodial epiphyte or lithophyte.

PSEUDOBULB: 2.8–3.5 in. (7–9 cm) long. The blackish stems are short and less than fully erect. When cultivated in a humid environment, the stems elongate and may become pendulous. Most of the year, the plants resemble a cluster of dead twigs.

LEAVES: 2–3 at the apex of each growth. The narrow leaves, which are 2.0–2.8 in. (5–7 cm) long, are borne near the apex of the pseudobulb. They are sometimes suffused with red. Leaves may persist for 2 years. Plants called *D. unicum* var. *variegata* have alternating green and white strips on the leaves.

INFLORESCENCE: 1.2–2.0 in. (3–5 cm) long. Inflorescences emerge at the apex and laterally from nodes on mature, leafy and leafless stems. Each pseudobulb usually produces several inflorescences.

FLOWERS: 1–3 per inflorescence, many per plant. The flowers are 1.4–2.0 in. (3.5–5.0 cm) across when spread. The strangely-shaped blossoms have long slender sepals and petals that are deep orange or bright red-orange. They may open fully or be so strongly curled that they appear tangled. The large lip, which is uppermost, is tubular and strongly veined. It juts forward and may be white, cream, or beige. It is finely toothed along the margin. The fragrance resembles tangerines.

HYBRIDIZING NOTES: Chromosome count is $2n = 38$ (ref. 152, 153, 273). Johansen (ref. 239) found that most attempts to pollinate *D. unicum* failed.

Dendrobium uniflorum

REFERENCES: 152, 153, 179, 196, 230, 239, 273, 291, 330, 359, 369, 430, 447, 448, 454, 514, 524.

PHOTOS/DRAWINGS: *291, 330, 359, 430, 454*, 514, 524.

Dendrobium uniflorum Finet ex Gagnepain not Griffith or Teijsm. and Binn. See *D. intricatum* Gagnepain. REFERENCES: 454.

Dendrobium uniflorum Griffith not Finet ex Gagnepain or Teijsm. and Binn.

AKA: *D. quadrisulcatum* J. J. Smith. In 1992 *Opera Botanica* 114, Seidenfaden included *D. tonkinense* Wildeman as a synonym. Many authors consider *D. revolutum* Lindley and *D. uniflorum* Griffith as synonyms, so information about them has been mixed and matched in various references. Seidenfaden and Wood (ref. 455) state that *D. revolutum* is a rare plant that has been found only in the lowlands of Singapore and Jahore state in Malaya and that records from other areas refer to *D. uniflorum*.

ORIGIN/HABITAT: Widespread in Southeast Asia. In Malaya, plants grow at 3000–5000 ft. (910–1520 m) in Melaka (Malacca) state. They are also found on Mt. Jerai in Kedah State, on Mt. Tapis near Kuantan, the Laurt Hills in Perak, on Mt. Blumset in Johore, on Kedah Peak, and near Pahang. The orchids also grow near Pattani in the southern part of peninsular Thailand, at several locations in Laos, and near Dalat and Quangtri in Vietnam. In Borneo, they are found in Sarawak and on Mt. Kinabalu in Sabah, where they grow on shrubs at 2000–3600 ft. (610–1100 m). In the Philippines, they grow at 200–2300 ft. (60–700 m) on Dinagat, Luzon, Leyte, Mindanao, Negros, Polillo, and Samar Islands.

CLIMATE: Station #48657, Kuantan, Malaya, Lat. 3.8°N, Long. 103.2°E, at 58 ft. (18 m). Temperatures are calculated for an elevation of 4900 ft. (1500 m), resulting in probable extremes of 83°F (28°C) and 46°F (8°C).

N/HEMISPHERE	JAN	FEB	MAR	APR	MAY	JUN	JUL	AUG	SEP	OCT	NOV	DEC
°F AVG MAX	68	70	73	74	75	75	74	74	74	73	71	69
°F AVG MIN	56	56	56	57	58	57	57	57	57	57	57	56
DIURNAL RANGE	12	14	17	17	17	18	17	17	17	16	14	13
RAIN/INCHES	16.4	7.5	10.6	8.3	7.8	7.3	7.4	7.8	8.4	10.6	11.1	20.9
HUMIDITY/%	88	88	87	86	87	86	86	86	86	87	90	90
BLOOM SEASON							*	*	*	*		
DAYS CLR @ 7AM	1	1	2	1	1	1	0	0	0	0	0	1
DAYS CLR @ 1PM	0	0	0	0	0	0	0	0	0	0	0	0
RAIN/MM	417	190	269	211	198	185	188	198	213	269	282	531
°C AVG MAX	20.1	21.2	22.8	23.4	23.9	23.9	23.4	23.4	23.4	22.8	21.7	20.6
°C AVG MIN	13.4	13.4	13.4	13.9	14.5	13.9	13.9	13.9	13.9	13.9	13.9	13.4
DIURNAL RANGE	6.7	7.8	9.4	9.5	9.4	10.0	9.5	9.5	9.5	8.9	7.8	7.2
S/HEMISPHERE	JUL	AUG	SEP	OCT	NOV	DEC	JAN	FEB	MAR	APR	MAY	JUN

Cultural Recommendations

LIGHT: 1500–2500 fc. Low diffused light is suggested as clear days are rare.

TEMPERATURES: Throughout the year, days average 68–75°F (20–24°C), and nights average 56–58°F (13–15°C), with a diurnal range of 12–18°F (7–10°C).

HUMIDITY: 85–90% year-round.

WATER: Rainfall is heavy all year. Plants should be kept moist but not soggy.

FERTILIZER: ¼–½ recommended strength. A balanced fertilizer should be applied weekly to biweekly throughout the year.

REST PERIOD: Growing conditions should be maintained all year. In the habitat, rainfall is greatest in winter, but water should not be increased for cultivated plants. Plants should be kept somewhat moist and never be allowed to dry out completely. In the habitat, seasonal light variation is minor.

GROWING MEDIA: Plants may be mounted on tree-fern or cork slabs if humidity is high and plants are watered at least once daily in summer. When plants are potted, any open, fast-draining medium may be used. Repotting is best done in early spring when new roots are growing.

MISCELLANEOUS NOTES: The bloom season shown in the climate table is based on plants cultivated as *D. uniflorum*.

Plant and Flower Information

PLANT SIZE AND TYPE: A 12–16 in. (30–40 cm) sympodial lithophyte or epiphyte.

PSEUDOBULB: 12–16 in. (30–40 cm) long. The erect stems are grooved, swollen, or 4-angled above the middle and often marked with red stripes.

LEAVES: Many. The variable leaves are 1.0–1.2 in. (2.5–3.0 cm) long. They may be elliptic to oblong-lanceolate with a broad, slightly bilobed apex. Leaves are distichous and twisted at the base so all leaves lie on a single plane. Plants described as *D. quadrisulcatum* had linear-lanceolate leaves.

INFLORESCENCE: Short. Inflorescences emerge opposite leaves at the nodes of mature pseudobulbs. Flowers are held at the tips of the leaves.

FLOWERS: 1 per inflorescence. The heavily textured flowers are 0.5–1.1 in. (1.3–2.7 cm) across. They are initially creamy white, becoming dull yellow with age. The pointed sepals and rounded petals are generally flat but may be somewhat recurved. The 3-lobed lip is white to pale green and may be marked with yellow and brown. It has large, deeply notched sidelobes that tend to curl under the midlobe. The lip has 2 full-length and one partial keel that may be violet, orange, or crimson. The long-lived blossoms are not fragrant.

HYBRIDIZING NOTES: Chromosome count is 2n = 40 (ref. 154, 188).

REFERENCES: 12, 154, 179, 188, 190, 200, 216, 254, 286, 295, 296, 373, 394, 395, 402, 445, 447, 454, 455, 536, 592.

PHOTOS/DRAWINGS: 373, 454, *455*, 536, *592*.

Dendrobium uniflorum Teijsm. and Binn. See note at *D. prostratum* Ridley. REFERENCES: 216, 254, 454.

Dendrobium uniflos F. M. Bailey. Now considered a synonym of *Cadetia taylori* (F. Mueller) Schlechter. REFERENCES: 67, 105, 216, 254.

Dendrobium unifoliatum Schlechter. See *D. petiolatum* Schlechter. REFERENCES: 223, 271, 385.

Dendrobium urvillei Finet. See *D. affine* (Decaisne) Steudel. REFERENCES: 67, 118, 219, 254, 445, 470, 533.

Dendrobium usterii Schlechter. Sometimes spelled *D. usteri*, it is now considered a synonym of *Flickingeria usterii* (Schlechter) F. G. Brieger. REFERENCES: 12, 213, 220, 230, 234, 254, 296, 433, 536.

Dendrobium usterioides Ames

ORIGIN/HABITAT: The Philippine Islands. Plants grow at the tops of trees along the Bongabong River in southeastern Mindoro Island. They are also reported in Agusan, Davao, and Surigao provinces on Mindanao Island.

CLIMATE: Station #98431, Calapan, Mindoro Island, Philippines, Lat. 13.4°N, Long. 121.2°E, at 128 ft. (39 m). Temperatures are calculated for an elevation of 2000 ft. (610 m). Record extreme temperatures are not available for this location.

N/HEMISPHERE	JAN	FEB	MAR	APR	MAY	JUN	JUL	AUG	SEP	OCT	NOV	DEC
°F AVG MAX	77	79	81	83	85	84	83	83	82	81	80	78
°F AVG MIN	67	67	69	70	71	70	70	70	69	69	69	67
DIURNAL RANGE	10	12	12	13	14	14	13	13	13	12	11	11
RAIN/INCHES	2.2	1.7	1.9	3.6	3.8	6.1	7.8	5.3	4.8	10.3	5.6	3.4
HUMIDITY/%	N/A											
BLOOM SEASON			*									
DAYS CLR	N/A											
RAIN/MM	56	43	48	91	97	155	198	135	122	262	142	86
°C AVG MAX	24.9	26.0	27.1	28.2	29.3	28.8	28.2	28.2	27.7	27.1	26.6	25.5
°C AVG MIN	19.3	19.3	20.5	21.0	21.6	21.0	21.0	21.0	20.5	20.5	20.5	19.3
DIURNAL RANGE	5.6	6.7	6.6	7.2	7.7	7.8	7.2	7.2	7.2	6.6	6.1	6.2
S/HEMISPHERE	JUL	AUG	SEP	OCT	NOV	DEC	JAN	FEB	MAR	APR	MAY	JUN

Cultural Recommendations

LIGHT: 2500–3500 fc. The plants grow at the tops of trees, so they may tolerate higher light than indicated if it is introduced gradually. Light should be reduced if plants show signs of stress. Strong air movement is recommended.

TEMPERATURES: Throughout the year, days average 77–85°F (25–29°C), and nights average 67–71°F (19–22°C), with a diurnal range of 10–14°F (6–8°C).

HUMIDITY: Information is not available for this location. However, records from nearby locations indicate that humidity probably averages near 80% year-round.

WATER: Rainfall is moderate to heavy most of the year, with a 2–3 month dry period in late winter or early spring. Cultivated plants should be kept moist while actively growing, but water should be gradually reduced in autumn.

FERTILIZER: ¼–½ recommended strength. A balanced fertilizer should be applied weekly to biweekly throughout the year.

REST PERIOD: Growing conditions should be maintained all year. Water and fertilizer should be reduced for 2–3 months in winter. Plants should be allowed to dry somewhat between waterings, but they should never remain dry for long periods. Light should be as high as possible, short of burning the foliage.

GROWING MEDIA: Plants may be mounted on tree-fern or cork slabs if humidity is high and plants are watered daily in summer. When plants are potted, any open, fast-draining medium may be used. Repotting may be done anytime new roots are growing.

MISCELLANEOUS NOTES: The bloom season shown in the climate table is based on collection records. Plants that produce flowers which last 1–2 days commonly bloom several times during the year. Flowering usually occurs 7–14 days after a sudden 10°F (5°C) drop in daytime temperatures.

Plant and Flower Information

PLANT SIZE AND TYPE: A 4 in. (10 cm) sympodial epiphyte.

PSEUDOBULB: 4 in. (10 cm) long. The erect stems emerge from a short rhizome. They are spindle-shaped, longitudinally grooved, swollen at the lower nodes, and loosely covered with white or gray sheaths. Stems become yellow with age.

LEAVES: 1 per growth. The very thick, fleshy leaves are 1–2 in. (2.5–5.0 cm) long.

INFLORESCENCE: Short. The rigid, slightly zigzag inflorescences are borne on the apical, leafless portion of the stem. The inflorescences are covered with grayish sheaths.

FLOWERS: The flowers are 0.6 in. (1.5 cm) long. They are pale, clear, greenish yellow with pale rosy lines on the backsides of the sepals and petals. Lateral sepals are obliquely triangular, and the dorsal sepal and petals are oblong-lanceolate. The 3-lobed lip is wedge-shaped. Sidelobes are toothed along the margin. The midlobe has a small point at the apex.

REFERENCES: 12. 222, 296, 536.

Dendrobium ustulatum Carr

ORIGIN/HABITAT: Malaya and western Borneo. In Malaya, plants grow in the Jeriau Valley near Ulu Jeriau below Fraser's Hill at about 3500 ft. (1070 m). In Borneo, plants were found in Sarawak near Mt. Dulit at less than 1000 ft. (300 m) and in Sabah near Mt. Kinabalu at 2950 ft. (900 m).

CLIMATE: Station #49630, Temerloh, Pahang, Malaya, Lat. 3.5°N, Long. 102.4°E, at 163 ft. (50 m). Temperatures are calculated for an elevation of 3500 ft. (1070 m), resulting in probable extremes of 86°F (30°C) and 53°F (12°C).

N/HEMISPHERE	JAN	FEB	MAR	APR	MAY	JUN	JUL	AUG	SEP	OCT	NOV	DEC
°F AVG MAX	74	77	79	80	80	79	79	79	79	78	76	75
°F AVG MIN	60	60	61	62	62	62	61	61	61	62	62	61
DIURNAL RANGE	14	17	18	18	18	17	18	18	18	16	14	14
RAIN/INCHES	7.8	3.9	6.0	7.6	6.6	4.3	3.4	5.6	6.5	9.3	9.7	10.1
HUMIDITY/%	87	83	84	85	86	86	87	84	86	87	89	88
BLOOM SEASON							*					
DAYS CLR @ 7AM	0	0	2	1	1	0	2	2	2	0	0	0
DAYS CLR @ 1PM	1	1	2	1	1	1	0	1	1	0	0	0
RAIN/MM	198	99	152	193	168	109	86	142	165	236	246	257
°C AVG MAX	23.3	25.0	26.1	26.7	26.7	26.1	26.1	26.1	26.1	25.5	24.4	23.9
°C AVG MIN	15.5	15.5	16.1	16.7	16.7	16.7	16.1	16.1	16.1	16.7	16.7	16.1
DIURNAL RANGE	7.8	9.5	10.0	10.0	10.0	9.4	10.0	10.0	10.0	8.8	7.7	7.8
S/HEMISPHERE	JUL	AUG	SEP	OCT	NOV	DEC	JAN	FEB	MAR	APR	MAY	JUN

Cultural Recommendations

LIGHT: 2500–3500 fc.

TEMPERATURES: Throughout the year, days average 74–80°F (23–27°C), and nights average 60–62°F (16–17°C), with a diurnal range of 14–18°F (8–10°C).

HUMIDITY: 85–90% year-round.

WATER: Rainfall is moderate to heavy for most of the year, but conditions are slightly drier for 1–2 months in winter and again in summer. Cultivated plants should be kept moist with only slight drying allowed between waterings.

FERTILIZER: ¼–½ recommended strength. A balanced fertilizer should be applied weekly to biweekly throughout the year.

REST PERIOD: Growing conditions should be maintained all year. In cultivation, water should be reduced slightly for a month or so in summer and again in late winter to simulate the drier periods in the habitat. Plants should not be allowed to dry out completely, however. Fertilizer should be reduced or eliminated anytime water is reduced. In the habitat, seasonal light variation is minor.

GROWING MEDIA: Plants may be mounted on tree-fern or cork slabs if humidity is high and plants are watered daily in summer. When plants are potted, any open, fast-draining medium may be used. Repotting may be done anytime new roots are growing.

MISCELLANEOUS NOTES: The bloom season shown in the climate table is based on a single collection time. Plants that produce flowers which last a single day commonly bloom several times during the year. Flowering usually occurs 7–14 days after a sudden 10°F (5°C) drop in daytime temperatures.

Plant and Flower Information

PLANT SIZE AND TYPE: A 1.5–2.5 in. (3.8–6.4 cm) sympodial epiphyte.

Dendrobium utile

PSEUDOBULB: 1–2 in. (2.5–5.0 cm) long. The prostrate, swollen stems alternate along a creeping, branching rhizome. They are olive-yellow.

LEAVES: 2 at the apex of each stem. The leaves are 0.6 in. (1.5 cm) long, ovate-oblong, and very fleshy. They are dark green, often with a red suffusion.

INFLORESCENCE: 0.8 in. (2 cm) long. Inflorescences emerge singly from tufts of dry bracts near the apex of the stem.

FLOWERS: 1 per inflorescence. The flowers are 0.4 in. (1 cm) across. Blossoms are cream to pale yellow with faint red to purplish veins. The backside of the sepals is covered with scalelike dots. The white lip has a small, yellow-green, warty patch in the center and about 5 longitudinal purple veins on the outside. Flowers are not fragrant.

REFERENCES: 57, 59, 200, 225, 286, 455, 592.

Dendrobium utile J. J. Smith. Now considered a synonym of *Diplocaulobium utile* (J. J. Smith) Kränzlin. REFERENCES: 219, 220, 254, 445, 468.

Dendrobium utricularioides Swartz. Now considered a synonym of *Ionopsis utricularioides* Lindley. REFERENCES: 190, 216, 254.

Dendrobium utriculariopsis Kränzlin. See *D. cuneilabrum* J. J. Smith. REFERENCES: 220, 254, 436.

Dendrobium vacciniifolium J. J. Smith

ORIGIN/HABITAT: Irian Jaya (western New Guinea). Plants grow in moss-covered forests in the western Nassau Mountains at 8200–8550 ft. (2500–2600 m).

CLIMATE: Station #97686, Wamena, New Guinea, Lat. 4.1°S, Long. 139.0°E, at 5446 ft. (1660 m). Temperatures are calculated for an elevation of 8500 ft. (2600 m). Record extreme temperatures are not available for this location.

N/HEMISPHERE	JAN	FEB	MAR	APR	MAY	JUN	JUL	AUG	SEP	OCT	NOV	DEC
°F AVG MAX	65	66	67	66	67	66	67	66	66	69	68	64
°F AVG MIN	50	50	52	52	53	54	53	52	53	55	55	51
DIURNAL RANGE	15	16	15	14	14	12	14	14	13	14	13	13
RAIN/INCHES	3.0	1.9	2.2	4.0	4.6	3.3	2.8	4.2	6.9	3.9	5.4	4.9
HUMIDITY/%	N/A											
BLOOM SEASON							*					
DAYS CLR	N/A											
RAIN/MM	76	48	56	102	117	84	71	107	175	99	137	124
°C AVG MAX	18.2	18.8	19.3	18.8	19.3	18.8	19.3	18.8	18.8	20.5	19.9	17.7
°C AVG MIN	9.9	9.9	11.0	11.0	11.6	12.1	11.6	11.0	11.6	12.7	12.7	10.5
DIURNAL RANGE	8.3	8.9	8.3	7.8	7.7	6.7	7.7	7.8	7.2	7.8	7.2	7.2
S/HEMISPHERE	JUL	AUG	SEP	OCT	NOV	DEC	JAN	FEB	MAR	APR	MAY	JUN

Cultural Recommendations

LIGHT: 2000–3000 fc.

TEMPERATURES: Throughout the year, days average 64–69°F (18–21°C), and nights average 50–55°F (10–13°C), with a diurnal range of 12–16°F (7–9°C). In the habitat, the warmest temperatures of the day occur in late morning when skies are clear. Because of microclimate effects, actual maximum temperatures may be somewhat warmer than indicated. Reports from the habitat indicate a sharp contrast between day and night temperatures.

HUMIDITY: Information is not available for this location. However, records from nearby stations indicate that humidity probably averages near 80% year-round. High humidity and excellent air circulation are particularly important if temperatures are warm. Placing the plants in front of an evaporative cooler or near a fine mist is very beneficial.

WATER: Rainfall is moderate through most of the year. In the higher-elevation habitat, rainfall amounts may be greater than indicated in the climate table. In addition, large amounts of water are available from mist and heavy dew, even during periods of reduced rainfall. Cultivated plants should be kept moist, with only slight drying allowed between waterings. They should be misted several times daily on the hottest days, but the foliage should always be dry before evening. Good air movement is critically important and should be maintained at all times.

FERTILIZER: ¼–½ recommended strength. A balanced fertilizer should be applied weekly to biweekly throughout the year. The Royal Botanic Garden in Edinburgh uses a dilute, seaweed-based fertilizer.

REST PERIOD: Growing conditions should be maintained all year. Rainfall averages are somewhat lower for a month or so in winter and again in midsummer. In cultivation, water may be decreased, but plants should never be allowed to dry out completely. In the habitat, light is slightly higher in winter.

GROWING MEDIA: Plants may be mounted on tree-fern or cork slabs or potted in small pots filled with any open, fast-draining medium. Repotting may be done anytime new roots are actively growing.

MISCELLANEOUS NOTES: The bloom season shown in the climate table is based on reports from the habitat.

Plant and Flower Information

PLANT SIZE AND TYPE: A 31 in. (80 cm) sympodial epiphyte.

PSEUDOBULB: 31 in. (80 cm) long. The slender, branching stems have roots on the lower 25%.

LEAVES: Many. The small, ovate leaves are 0.4–1.1 in. (0.9–2.8 cm) long.

INFLORESCENCE: Short. Inflorescences are borne at nodes along the stem.

FLOWERS: 3–5 per inflorescence. The brick red flowers are 1 in. (2.5 cm) across. The oval dorsal sepal is erect and minutely toothed at the apex. The margin of the lateral sepals is fringed. The lip is serrated only at the top margin.

REFERENCES: 225, 470.

Dendrobium vagabundum A. Hawkes and A. H. Heller

AKA: *D. vagans* Schlechter 1923 (ref. 443) not 1911 (ref. 434) and not Gagnepain.

ORIGIN/HABITAT: Papua New Guinea. Plants grow in the Sepik River region at about 3750 ft. (1140 m).

CLIMATE: Station #200004, Ambunti, Papua New Guinea, Lat. 4.2°S, Long. 142.8°E, at 164 ft. (50 m). Temperatures are calculated for an elevation of 3750 ft. (1140 m), resulting in probable extremes of 87°F (31°C) and 40°F (5°C).

N/HEMISPHERE	JAN	FEB	MAR	APR	MAY	JUN	JUL	AUG	SEP	OCT	NOV	DEC
°F AVG MAX	76	78	78	78	79	78	78	78	78	78	78	77
°F AVG MIN	60	61	62	61	61	61	60	61	61	61	61	62
DIURNAL RANGE	16	17	16	17	18	17	18	17	17	17	17	15
RAIN/INCHES	6.4	7.4	7.7	8.5	9.2	9.4	10.9	10.2	12.2	10.4	8.3	5.2
HUMIDITY/%	N/A											
BLOOM SEASON							*					
DAYS CLR	N/A											
RAIN/MM	163	188	196	216	234	239	277	259	310	264	211	132
°C AVG MAX	24.5	25.6	25.6	25.6	26.2	25.6	25.6	25.6	25.6	25.6	25.6	25.1
°C AVG MIN	15.6	16.2	16.8	16.2	16.2	16.2	15.6	16.2	16.2	16.2	16.2	16.8
DIURNAL RANGE	8.9	9.4	8.8	9.4	10.0	9.4	10.0	9.4	9.4	9.4	9.4	8.3
S/HEMISPHERE	JUL	AUG	SEP	OCT	NOV	DEC	JAN	FEB	MAR	APR	MAY	JUN

Cultural Recommendations

LIGHT: 2000–3000 fc.

TEMPERATURES: Throughout the year, days average 76–79°F (25–26°C), and nights average 60–62°F (16–17°C), with a diurnal range of 15–18°F (8–10°C).

HUMIDITY: Information is not available for this location. However, records from nearby stations indicate that humidity is probably near 80% year-round.

WATER: Rainfall is heavy all year. The greatest amounts fall in summer and early autumn. Cultivated plants should be kept moist.

FERTILIZER: ¼–½ recommended strength. A balanced fertilizer should be applied weekly to biweekly throughout the year.

REST PERIOD: Growing temperatures should be maintained all year. Water and fertilizer should be reduced for plants cultivated in the dark, short-day conditions common during temperate-latitude winters. However, plants should never be allowed to dry out completely. In the habitat, light is highest in winter.

GROWING MEDIA: Plants may be mounted on cork or tree-fern slabs if humidity is high and plants are watered at least once daily in summer. When plants are potted, any open, fast-draining medium may be used, but fir bark is preferred by most growers. Repotting may be done anytime new roots are growing.

MISCELLANEOUS NOTES: The bloom season shown in the climate table is based on collection reports.

Plant and Flower Information

PLANT SIZE AND TYPE: A 20 in. (50 cm) sympodial epiphyte.

PSEUDOBULB: 20 in. (50 cm) long. The stems are pendent to spreading, densely leafy, and branching. They are nearly black when dried.

LEAVES: Many. The broadly linear leaves are 1.4–2.4 in. (3.5–6.0 cm) long and unequally bilobed at the apex.

INFLORESCENCE: Short.

Dendrobium vagans

FLOWERS: 1 per inflorescence. The white flowers are inverted. The very small, oval sepals and elliptical petals are about 0.1 in. (0.3 cm) long, thus making the flowers among the smallest in the genus. The lip is 3-lobed on the apical quarter. It is sparsely hairy with nearly round side-lobes and a half-moon callus.

REFERENCES: 191, 223, 229, 443.

Dendrobium vagans Gagnepain not Schlechter 1911 or 1923.
See *D. fimbriatum* Hooker. REFERENCES: 138, 227, 448.

Dendrobium vagans Schlechter 1911 not 1923 and not Gagnepain.

AKA: Kores (ref. 466) includes *D. calamiforme* Rolfe, *D. crispatum* Seemann not (Forster) Swartz, and *D. seemannii* L. O. Williams as synonyms, but Lewis and Cribb (ref. 270) list the plant name as *D. seemannii*.

ORIGIN/HABITAT: Samoa, Fiji, Vanuatu (New Hebrides), and perhaps other nearby islands. Plants usually grow on branches and tree trunks, but they occasionally grow directly on limestone outcroppings. On Fiji, they are found below 2800 ft. (850 m), but in other locations, they grow as high as 5400 ft. (1650 m). The orchids most frequently occur along water courses or near seashores, often overhanging the ocean or salt marshes.

CLIMATE: Station #91683, Nausori, Vitu Levu, Fiji, Lat. 18.1°S, Long. 1787.6°E, at 19 ft. (6 m). Temperatures are calculated for an elevation of 2000 ft. (610 m), resulting in probable extremes of 91°F (33°C) and 48°F (9°C).

N/HEMISPHERE	JAN	FEB	MAR	APR	MAY	JUN	JUL	AUG	SEP	OCT	NOV	DEC
°F AVG MAX	72	72	73	74	76	78	79	79	79	77	75	73
°F AVG MIN	61	61	62	63	64	66	67	67	67	66	64	62
DIURNAL RANGE	11	11	11	11	12	12	12	12	12	11	11	11
RAIN/INCHES	4.9	8.3	7.7	8.3	9.8	12.5	11.4	10.7	14.5	12.2	10.1	6.7
HUMIDITY/%	77	77	76	75	75	76	76	78	79	79	81	78
BLOOM SEASON	*	*				*						*
DAYS CLR @ 12PM	3	1	0	0	1	1	2	0	0	0	1	0
RAIN/MM	124	211	196	211	249	318	290	272	368	310	257	170
°C AVG MAX	22.5	22.5	23.0	23.6	24.7	25.8	26.4	26.4	26.4	25.3	24.1	23.0
°C AVG MIN	16.4	16.4	16.9	17.5	18.0	19.1	19.7	19.7	19.7	19.1	18.0	16.9
DIURNAL RANGE	6.1	6.1	6.1	6.1	6.7	6.7	6.7	6.7	6.7	6.2	6.1	6.1
S/HEMISPHERE	JUL	AUG	SEP	OCT	NOV	DEC	JAN	FEB	MAR	APR	MAY	JUN

Cultural Recommendations

LIGHT: 2500–3500 fc. Strong air movement is very important for cultivated plants.

TEMPERATURES: Summer days average 78–79°F (26°C), and nights average 66–67°F (19–20°C), with a diurnal range of 12°F (7°C).

HUMIDITY: 75–80% year-round.

WATER: Rainfall is very heavy all year. Cultivated plants should be kept moist but not soggy.

FERTILIZER: ¼–½ recommended strength. A balanced fertilizer should be applied weekly to biweekly throughout the year.

REST PERIOD: Growing conditions should be maintained all year. Although rainfall in winter remains heavy, water and fertilizer should be reduced somewhat for cultivated plants, especially those grown in the dark, short-day conditions common in temperate latitudes. Plants should never be allowed to dry out completely, however. In the habitat, seasonal light variation is minor.

GROWING MEDIA: To accommodate the pendent growth habit, plants may be grown on slabs or rafts if humidity is high. Mounted plants should be watered at least daily all year, and several times each day during hot, dry summer weather. If plants are potted, the smallest hanging pot or basket possible should be used with medium to large-sized bark or cork nuggets. Plants are healthiest if they are watered frequently, so the medium must be very open and fast draining. Repotting may be done anytime new roots are growing.

MISCELLANEOUS NOTES: The bloom season shown in the climate table is based on cultivation records for plants grown as *D. seemannii*.

Plant and Flower Information

PLANT SIZE AND TYPE: A 79 in. (200 cm) sympodial epiphyte.

PSEUDOBULB: 79 in. (200 cm) long. The slender stems are branching and pendent.

LEAVES: 1 at the apex of each branch. The leaves are 3–8 in. (8–20 cm) long, terete, pendent, and dark green.

INFLORESCENCE: 3–6 in. (8–15 cm) long. Slender and laxly flowered, the inflorescence emerges at the base of a leaf near the apex of the stem.

FLOWERS: 5–15 per inflorescence. Flowers are 0.8–1.2 in. (2–3 cm) long. The creamy yellow sepals and petals are slender and pointed. The white lip is marked with purple spots on the side. It is linear-lanceolate with a wavy, ruffled margin. The column is purple-green. Blossoms are fragrant.

HYBRIDIZING NOTES: Chromosome count 2n = 38 as *D. seemannii* (ref. 152, 243).

REFERENCES: 152, 179, 221, 243, 252, 270, 353, 417, 434, 466.

PHOTOS/DRAWINGS: 466, *540*.

Dendrobium vagans Schlechter 1923 (ref. 443) not 1911 (ref. 434) and not Gagnepain.
See *D. vagabundum* A. Hawkes and A. H. Heller. REFERENCES: 223, 229, 443.

Dendrobium vaginatum Wallich.
Now considered a synonym of *Appendicula anceps* Blume. REFERENCES: 536.

Dendrobium validicolle J. J. Smith.
Now considered a synonym of *Diplocaulobium validicolle* (J. J. Smith) Kränzlin. REFERENCES: 111, 220, 254, 445, 470.

Dendrobium validipecten J. J. Smith

ORIGIN/HABITAT: The west coast of Sumatra. Plants grow in the forests of Mt. Kerintji at about 5600 ft. (1700 m).

CLIMATE: Station #96163, Padang, Sumatra, Indonesia, Lat. 0.9°S, Long. 100.4°E, at 19 ft. (6 m). Temperatures are calculated for an elevation of 5600 ft. (1700 m), resulting in probable extremes of 76°F (24°C) and 50°F (10°C).

N/HEMISPHERE	JAN	FEB	MAR	APR	MAY	JUN	JUL	AUG	SEP	OCT	NOV	DEC
°F AVG MAX	69	69	68	68	68	68	69	69	69	69	70	69
°F AVG MIN	56	56	56	56	56	56	56	56	56	57	57	56
DIURNAL RANGE	13	13	12	12	12	12	13	13	13	12	13	13
RAIN/INCHES	10.9	13.7	6.0	19.5	20.4	18.9	13.8	10.2	12.1	14.3	12.4	12.1
HUMIDITY/%	81	82	82	84	85	84	81	81	82	83	81	81
BLOOM SEASON							*					
DAYS CLR @ 7AM	5	1	1	0	2	2	2	1	2	2	3	5
DAYS CLR @ 1PM	5	2	2	1	3	3	4	3	3	3	6	5
RAIN/MM	277	348	152	495	518	480	351	259	307	363	315	307
°C AVG MAX	20.3	20.3	19.8	19.8	19.8	19.8	20.3	20.3	20.3	20.3	20.9	20.3
°C AVG MIN	13.1	13.1	13.1	13.1	13.1	13.1	13.1	13.1	13.1	13.7	13.7	13.1
DIURNAL RANGE	7.2	7.2	6.7	6.7	6.7	6.7	7.2	7.2	7.2	6.6	7.2	7.2
S/HEMISPHERE	JUL	AUG	SEP	OCT	NOV	DEC	JAN	FEB	MAR	APR	MAY	JUN

Cultural Recommendations

LIGHT: 2000–3000 fc. Diffused light is preferred.

TEMPERATURES: Throughout the year, days average 68–70°F (20–21°C), and nights average 56–57°F (13–14°C), with a diurnal range of 12–13°F (7°C). Probable extremes vary only a few degrees from the averages, indicating that plants may not tolerate wide temperature fluctuations.

HUMIDITY: 80–85% year-round.

WATER: Rainfall is heavy all year. Cultivated plants should be constantly moist but not soggy.

FERTILIZER: ¼–½ recommended strength. A balanced fertilizer should be applied weekly to biweekly throughout the year.

REST PERIOD: Growing conditions should be maintained year-round. Water may be reduced somewhat in winter for cultivated plants, especially those grown in the dark, short-day conditions common in temperate latitudes. They should never be allowed to dry out completely, however. In the habitat, light is slightly higher in winter.

GROWING MEDIA: Plants may be mounted on tree-fern or cork slabs or potted in small pots filled with any open, fast-draining medium. Repotting may be done anytime new roots are actively growing.

MISCELLANEOUS NOTES: The bloom season shown in the climate table is based on collection reports. The plant was described in 1928 in *Bull. Jard. Bot. Buit.* 3rd sér. 10:59.

Plant and Flower Information

PLANT SIZE AND TYPE: An 8–16 in. (20–40 cm) sympodial epiphyte.

PSEUDOBULB: 8–16 in. (20–40 cm) long. The stems are elongated, flattened, and leafy. They are borne on a short, very branching rhizome.

LEAVES: Many. The somewhat linear-lanceolate leaves are 1.5–2.2 in. (3.8–5.6 cm) long, distichous, fleshy, and laterally flattened.

INFLORESCENCE: Short. Branching inflorescences emerge at or near the apex of the stem.

FLOWERS: The fleshy, shiny brown flowers are 0.5 in. (1.3 cm) across. The ovate dorsal sepal is erect, recurved, convex, and pointed. Lateral sepals are rounded triangles with a short point at the apex. The oblong petals, which are minutely uneven along the margin, are contracted on the upper part with a short point at the tip. The lip is recurved, fleshy, uneven along the margin. The apical part is transversely oval. The roughened, thickened part covers less than half the lip.

REFERENCES: 224.

Dendrobium validum Schlechter. See *D. sylvanum* Rchb. f.
REFERENCES: 84, 92, 219, 254, 437, 444, 445.

Dendrobium vandaefolium Finet

AKA: Sometimes spelled *D. vandifolium*.

ORIGIN/HABITAT: Northwestern New Caledonia. The habitat extends from sea level to 2300 ft. (0–700 m).

CLIMATE: Station #91577, Koumac, New Caledonia, Lat. 20.6°S, Long. 164.3°E, at 75 ft. (23 m). Record extreme temperatures are not available for this location, but information from other stations on the island indicate that extremes are probably near 100°F (38°C) and 50°F (10°C).

N/HEMISPHERE	JAN	FEB	MAR	APR	MAY	JUN	JUL	AUG	SEP	OCT	NOV	DEC
°F AVG MAX	75	76	77	80	82	84	85	86	84	83	81	77
°F AVG MIN	61	61	63	66	69	71	74	74	72	70	68	64
DIURNAL RANGE	14	15	14	14	13	13	11	12	12	13	13	13
RAIN/INCHES	1.5	0.8	1.6	1.2	2.8	3.3	6.1	5.1	3.3	1.8	2.7	2.1
HUMIDITY/%	N/A											
BLOOM SEASON				**								**
DAYS CLR	N/A											
RAIN/MM	37	20	42	30	71	84	155	129	84	46	68	53
°C AVG MAX	23.9	24.4	25.0	26.7	27.8	28.9	29.4	30.0	28.9	28.3	27.2	25.0
°C AVG MIN	16.1	16.1	17.2	18.9	20.6	21.7	23.3	23.3	22.2	21.1	20.0	17.8
DIURNAL RANGE	7.8	8.3	7.8	7.8	7.2	7.2	6.1	6.7	6.7	7.2	7.2	7.2
S/HEMISPHERE	JUL	AUG	SEP	OCT	NOV	DEC	JAN	FEB	MAR	APR	MAY	JUN

Cultural Recommendations

LIGHT: 2000–3000 fc.

TEMPERATURES: Summer days average 84–86°F (29–30°C), and nights average 71–74°F (22–23°C), with a diurnal range of 11–13°F (6–7°C).

HUMIDITY: Information is not available for this location. However, records from nearby stations indicate that humidity is probably 70–80% year-round.

WATER: Rainfall is moderate in summer but is relatively light through the rest of the year. Cultivated plants should be allowed to dry slightly between waterings in summer, and water should be gradually reduced in autumn.

FERTILIZER: ¼–½ recommended strength, applied weekly. A high-nitrogen fertilizer is beneficial from spring to midsummer, but a fertilizer high in phosphates should be used in late summer and autumn.

REST PERIOD: Winter days average 75–77°F (24–25°C), and nights average 61–64°F (16–18°C), with a diurnal range of 13–15°F (7–8°C). Water and fertilizer should be reduced in winter. Cultivated plants should dry out between waterings, but they should not remain dry for extended periods. In the habitat, seasonal light variation is minor.

GROWING MEDIA: Plants may be mounted on tree-fern or cork slabs or potted in small pots filled with any open, fast-draining medium. Repotting may be done anytime new roots are actively growing.

MISCELLANEOUS NOTES: The bloom season shown in the climate table is based on reports from the habitat.

Plant and Flower Information

PLANT SIZE AND TYPE: A 39–157 in. (100–400 cm) sympodial terrestrial.

PSEUDOBULB: 39–157 in. (100–400 cm) long. The vigorous, bamboolike stems are swollen at the base and do not branch. The apex of the stem is leafy.

LEAVES: Several. The lanceolate leaves are 5–8 in. (13–20 cm) long.

INFLORESCENCE: 4–6 in. (10–15 cm) long. Inflorescences emerge from nodes below the leafy portion of the stem.

FLOWERS: 10–30 per inflorescence. The flowers are 0.4 in. (1 cm) long and do not open fully. The pointed sepals and petals may be pale yellow or green with a white lip, but one collection was white with rose markings on the lip. The unlobed lip has a toothed to scalloped margin along the sides of the apical oval. It has 3 raised ridges and upturned sides near the back. Blossoms have a fragrance resembling hyacinths.

REFERENCES: 118, 173, 219, 254, 445.

PHOTOS/DRAWINGS: 173.

Dendrobium vanderwateri Ridley

ORIGIN/HABITAT: Irian Jaya (western New Guinea). Plants were collected south of Mt. Jaya (Mt. Carstensz) at about 3100 ft. (940 m).

CLIMATE: Station #97796, Kokenau (Kokonau), Irian Jaya, Lat. 4.7°S, Long. 135.4°E, at 10 ft. (3 m). Temperatures are calculated for an elevation of 3000 ft. (910 m). Record extreme temperatures are not available for this location.

N/HEMISPHERE	JAN	FEB	MAR	APR	MAY	JUN	JUL	AUG	SEP	OCT	NOV	DEC
°F AVG MAX	73	73	76	78	80	79	79	79	80	78	77	74
°F AVG MIN	63	63	64	64	64	65	64	64	64	64	64	63
DIURNAL RANGE	10	10	12	14	16	14	15	15	16	14	13	11
RAIN/INCHES	18.4	15.8	18.9	11.6	9.7	10.6	11.5	15.7	11.6	11.6	16.0	19.9
HUMIDITY/%	N/A											
BLOOM SEASON	N/A											
DAYS CLR	N/A											
RAIN/MM	467	401	480	295	246	269	292	399	295	295	406	505
°C AVG MAX	22.9	22.9	24.5	25.6	26.7	26.2	26.2	26.2	26.7	25.6	25.1	23.4
°C AVG MIN	17.3	17.3	17.9	17.9	17.9	18.4	17.9	17.9	17.9	17.9	17.9	17.3
DIURNAL RANGE	5.6	5.6	6.6	7.7	8.8	7.8	8.3	8.3	8.8	7.7	7.2	6.1
S/HEMISPHERE	JUL	AUG	SEP	OCT	NOV	DEC	JAN	FEB	MAR	APR	MAY	JUN

Cultural Recommendations

LIGHT: 2500–3500 fc.

TEMPERATURES: Throughout the year, days average 73–80°F (23–27°C), and nights average 63–65°F (17–18°C), with a diurnal range of 10–16°F (6–9°C).

HUMIDITY: Information is not available for this location. However, records from nearby stations indicate that humidity is probably near 85% year-round.

WATER: Rainfall is very heavy all year. Cultivated plants should be kept evenly moist but not soggy.

FERTILIZER: ¼–½ recommended strength. A balanced fertilizer should be applied weekly to biweekly throughout the year.

REST PERIOD: Growing conditions should be maintained year-round. Water and fertilizer may be reduced somewhat for cultivated plants in winter, especially those grown in the dark, short-day conditions common in temperate latitudes. Plants should never be allowed to dry completely, however. In the habitat, seasonal light variation is minor.

GROWING MEDIA: Plants may be mounted on tree-fern or cork slabs or potted in small pots filled with any open, fast-draining medium. Repotting may be done anytime new roots are growing.

Plant and Flower Information

PLANT SIZE AND TYPE: A sympodial epiphyte of unreported size.

PSEUDOBULB: The stems resemble bamboo.

LEAVES: Many. The lanceolate leaves, which are 4–5 in. (11–12 cm) long, taper to a long narrow point.

INFLORESCENCE: 0.6 in. (1.5 cm) long.

FLOWERS: 2 per inflorescence. The flowers are 1.6–2.0 in. (4–5 cm) across. The linear-lanceolate sepals and petals are threadlike near the tip. The citrus colored lip is has short sidelobes and a yellow callus near the base.

REFERENCES: 222, 400.

Dendrobium vandiflorum Rchb. f.

A poorly described plant thought to have originated in New Guinea. Insufficient habitat information is available to select climate data. Kränzlin (ref. 254) indicated that, based on the original description, the raceme was laxly flowered. The pointed sepals and petals were tongue-shaped, wavy and twisting, and probably white. The fiddle-shaped lip had small, obtusely angled sidelobes and a deeply notched midlobe with 2 grooved keels to the base of the disk. The lip may have been green. REFERENCES: 216, 254, 348.

Dendrobium vandoides Schlechter

ORIGIN/HABITAT: Northern Papua New Guinea. Plants grow on forest trees in the Kani and Gati Ranges and in the Minjem Valley at about 1300 ft. (400 m). On Bougainville, *D. vandoides* is probably not native, but it is cultivated at sea level.

CLIMATE: Station #200187, Erap, Papua New Guinea, Lat. 6.6°S, Long. 146.7°E, at 850 ft. (260 m). Record extreme temperatures are 102°F (39°C) and 53°F (12°C).

N/HEMISPHERE	JAN	FEB	MAR	APR	MAY	JUN	JUL	AUG	SEP	OCT	NOV	DEC
°F AVG MAX	88	88	89	90	93	93	93	93	93	92	90	90
°F AVG MIN	69	69	69	70	72	73	72	72	73	71	74	70
DIURNAL RANGE	19	19	20	20	21	20	21	21	20	21	16	20
RAIN/INCHES	3.9	3.9	2.7	3.0	3.0	5.3	5.9	5.9	7.0	3.4	2.4	3.1
HUMIDITY/%	82	81	81	79	75	74	74	74	77	76	80	80
BLOOM SEASON				*			*					
DAYS CLR	N/A											
RAIN/MM	98	99	68	77	76	135	149	149	179	87	60	78
°C AVG MAX	30.9	30.9	31.7	32.3	34.0	33.9	33.8	33.9	34.0	33.6	32.3	32.0
°C AVG MIN	20.4	20.5	20.7	21.1	22.0	22.5	22.1	22.4	22.5	21.7	23.3	20.9
DIURNAL RANGE	10.5	10.4	11.0	11.2	12.0	11.4	11.7	11.5	11.5	11.9	9.0	11.1
S/HEMISPHERE	JUL	AUG	SEP	OCT	NOV	DEC	JAN	FEB	MAR	APR	MAY	JUN

Cultural Recommendations

LIGHT: 2000–3000 fc.

TEMPERATURES: Throughout the year, days average 88–93°F (31–34°C), and nights average 69–74°F (20–23°C), with a diurnal range of 16–21°F (9–12°C).

HUMIDITY: 75–80% year-round. However, the habitat may be quite dry during hot afternoons.

WATER: Rainfall is moderate most of the year, but for 4–5 months in summer and early autumn, conditions are somewhat wetter. Cultivated plants should be thoroughly saturated then allowed to dry slightly between waterings in summer and early autumn. Water should be gradually reduced in autumn.

FERTILIZER: ¼–½ recommended strength. A balanced fertilizer should be applied weekly to biweekly throughout the year.

REST PERIOD: Growing temperatures should be maintained all year. In the habitat, rainfall is lowest in winter, but the high humidity indicates that additional moisture is frequently available from heavy dew. Cultivated plants should be allowed to dry for somewhat longer between waterings, but should not remain dry for extended periods. Fertilizer should be reduced until water is increased in spring. In the habitat, seasonal light variation is minor.

GROWING MEDIA: Plants may be mounted on tree-fern or cork slabs if humidity is high and plants are watered at least once daily in summer. When plants are potted, any open, fast-draining medium may be used. Repotting may be done anytime new roots are growing.

MISCELLANEOUS NOTES: The bloom season shown in the climate table is based on reports from the habitat. Plants that produce flowers which last a single day commonly bloom several times during the year. Flowering usually occurs 7–14 days after a sudden 10°F (5°C) drop in daytime temperatures.

Plant and Flower Information

PLANT SIZE AND TYPE: A 24–28 in. (60–70 cm) epiphyte that resembles a *Vanda*.

PSEUDOBULB: 24–28 in. (60–70 cm) long. The stems arise from a very short rhizome. They are flattened and densely leafy.

LEAVES: Many. The leaves are 8–10 in. (20–25 cm) long, curved, and spreading.

INFLORESCENCE: 0.8 in. (2 cm) long.

FLOWERS: 2 per inflorescence. The flowers are 0.8 in. (2 cm) long. They are pale yellow with red dots and spots. The elliptical sepals and petals taper to a rounded point. The 3-lobed lip is roundly oblong and pointed at the tip with a fringe of hairs along the margin of the midlobe. It has a rough surface texture with short hairs and central callus near the base. The narrow sidelobes are sharply pointed. Blossoms are short-lived.

REFERENCES: 25, 221, 271, 437, 445, 516.

PHOTOS/DRAWINGS: 437.

Dendrobium vanhulstijnii J. J. Smith

ORIGIN/HABITAT: The Sula Islands on Mt. Bapenghaja. Habitat details are unavailable, so the following climate data should be used with caution. Plants were cultivated in the botanical garden at Bogor, Java.

CLIMATE: Station #97600, Sanana, Pulau Sulabesi, Indonesia, Lat. 2.1°S, Long. 126.0°E, at 7 ft. (2 m). Record extreme temperatures are not available for this location.

N/HEMISPHERE	JAN	FEB	MAR	APR	MAY	JUN	JUL	AUG	SEP	OCT	NOV	DEC
°F AVG MAX	86	85	87	88	88	88	88	88	87	88	87	86
°F AVG MIN	76	76	75	77	77	78	78	76	76	76	78	76
DIURNAL RANGE	10	9	12	11	11	10	10	11	12	11	9	10
RAIN/INCHES	2.8	2.7	1.2	1.8	4.8	5.4	4.1	4.1	5.7	6.6	6.5	7.3
HUMIDITY/%	N/A											
BLOOM SEASON	N/A											
DAYS CLR	N/A											
RAIN/MM	72	69	31	47	122	137	105	104	146	168	165	185
°C AVG MAX	29.9	29.6	30.3	31.0	31.3	31.0	31.0	30.8	30.9	30.3	30.4	29.8
°C AVG MIN	24.4	24.3	24.0	25.2	25.1	25.4	25.3	24.5	24.4	24.6	25.3	24.2
DIURNAL RANGE	5.5	5.3	6.3	5.8	6.2	5.6	5.7	6.3	6.5	5.7	5.1	5.6
S/HEMISPHERE	JUL	AUG	SEP	OCT	NOV	DEC	JAN	FEB	MAR	APR	MAY	JUN

Cultural Recommendations

LIGHT: 2000–3000 fc.

TEMPERATURES: Throughout the year, days average 85–88°F (30–31°C), and nights average 75–78°F (24–25°C), with a diurnal range of 9–12°F (5–6°C).

HUMIDITY: Information is not available for this location. However, records from other stations in the region indicate that humidity probably exceeds 80% year-round.

WATER: Rainfall is moderate most of the year with a semidry period in winter and early spring. Cultivated plants should be allowed to dry slightly between waterings from late spring through autumn.

FERTILIZER: ¼–½ recommended strength. A balanced fertilizer should be applied weekly to biweekly throughout the year.

REST PERIOD: Growing conditions should be maintained year-round. Water and fertilizer should be reduced in winter. Cultivated plants should be allowed to dry between waterings, but they should not remain dry for long periods. In the habitat, seasonal light variation is minor.

GROWING MEDIA: Plants may be mounted on tree-fern or cork slabs or potted in small pots filled with any open, fast-draining medium. Repotting may be done anytime new roots are actively growing.

MISCELLANEOUS NOTES: The plant was described in 1917 in *Bull. Jard. Bot. Buit.* 2nd sér. 25:39.

Plant and Flower Information

PLANT SIZE AND TYPE: A 15 in. (38 cm) sympodial epiphyte.

PSEUDOBULB: 15 in. (38 cm) long. The clustered stems are slender, shiny, dark green, zigzag, and leafy below the apex. They are not swollen at the base. Otherwise, they are very similar to *D. juncifolium* Schlechter.

LEAVES: The terete leaves are fleshy and pointed.

INFLORESCENCE: Blossoms are borne near the apex of the stem.

FLOWERS: 1–2 per inflorescence. The flowers are 0.5 in. (1.3 cm) across. Sepals and petals are white with purple on the backside. The dorsal sepal is erect and somewhat elliptical. It is convex except at the tip where it is concave. Lateral sepals are broadly triangular at the base and slender at the tip. They are recurved at the margin. The ovate petals are pointed at the tip. The erect, 3-lobed lip is yellow-green with orange markings. It has a warty surface and 3 keels. The midlobe is erect and notched at the apex. The triangular sidelobes are erect, recurved, and ruffled.

REFERENCES: 222.

Dendrobium vanikorense Ames

AKA: Lewis and Cribb (ref. 270) included *D. vanikorense* Ames as a synonym of *D. biflorum* Swartz. However, in later work (ref. 271), they found sufficient differences to consider them separate species.

ORIGIN/HABITAT: The Santa Cruz Islands, Bougainville, and most of the Solomon Islands. Plants usually grow in rainforests at 50–1550 ft. (15–480 m).

CLIMATE: Station #91520, Honiara, Guadalcanal, Solomon Islands, Lat. 9.4°S, Long. 160.0°E, at 10 ft. (3 m). Temperatures are calculated for an elevation of 1200 ft. (370 m), resulting in probable extremes of 91°F (33°C) and 61°F (16°C).

N/HEMISPHERE	JAN	FEB	MAR	APR	MAY	JUN	JUL	AUG	SEP	OCT	NOV	DEC
°F AVG MAX	82	83	84	84	84	84	84	84	83	84	84	83
°F AVG MIN	68	68	68	68	69	69	70	70	69	69	69	68
DIURNAL RANGE	14	15	16	16	15	15	14	14	14	15	15	15
RAIN/INCHES	6.0	4.4	4.6	7.7	7.7	9.5	14.1	13.3	16.7	10.6	8.1	6.7
HUMIDITY/%	84	82	81	80	81	82	83	83	87	85	85	85
BLOOM SEASON	N/A											
DAYS CLR @ 5AM	6	7	7	5	6	4	3	3	4	4	8	7
DAYS CLR @ 11AM	3	2	2	1	1	1	0	2	2	4	4	
RAIN/MM	152	112	117	196	196	241	358	338	424	269	206	170
°C AVG MAX	27.8	28.4	28.9	28.9	28.9	28.9	28.9	28.9	28.4	28.9	28.9	28.4
°C AVG MIN	20.0	20.0	20.0	20.0	20.6	20.6	21.2	21.2	20.6	20.6	20.6	20.0
DIURNAL RANGE	7.8	8.4	8.9	8.9	8.3	8.3	7.7	7.7	7.8	8.3	8.3	8.4
S/HEMISPHERE	JUL	AUG	SEP	OCT	NOV	DEC	JAN	FEB	MAR	APR	MAY	JUN

Cultural Recommendations

LIGHT: 1800–2500 fc.

TEMPERATURES: Throughout the year, days average 82–84°F (28–29°C), and nights average 68–70°F (20–21°C), with a diurnal range of 14–16°F (8–9°C).

HUMIDITY: 80–85% year-round.

WATER: Rainfall is heavy all year, but for 2–3 months in winter, conditions are slightly drier. Cultivated plants should be kept moist with only slight drying allowed between waterings.

FERTILIZER: ¼–½ recommended strength. A balanced fertilizer should be applied weekly to biweekly throughout the year.

REST PERIOD: Growing conditions should be maintained year-round. Water and fertilizer may be reduced somewhat for cultivated plants in winter, especially those grown in the dark, short-day conditions common in temperate latitudes. They should never be allowed to dry out completely, however.

GROWING MEDIA: Mounting plants on tree-fern or cork slabs accommodates their pendulous growth habit. However, humidity must be high and plants must be watered at least once a day in summer. If plants cannot be mounted, hanging pots or baskets may be filled with an open, fast-draining medium. Repotting may be done anytime new roots are actively growing.

Plant and Flower Information

PLANT SIZE AND TYPE: A 39 in. (100 cm) sympodial epiphyte.

PSEUDOBULB: 39 in. (100 cm) long. The slender stems are clustered and pendulous.

LEAVES: Many. The linear-lanceolate, distichous leaves are 3.0–4.3 in. (7.5–11.0 cm) long.

INFLORESCENCE: Short. Inflorescences emerge from flattened protuberances along the side of the stem.

FLOWERS: 2 per inflorescence. The flowers are about 0.4 in. (0.8 cm) long and do not open widely. Blossoms may be white or creamy yellow with a purple tinge. Sepals and petals are pointed. The 3-lobed lip has small, erect, crescent-shaped sidelobes that are uneven along the margin. The hairy, oblong midlobe is recurved with a deeply uneven margin.

REFERENCES: 16, 225, 270, 271, 516.

PHOTOS/DRAWINGS: 271.

Dendrobium vanilliodorum J. J. Smith. Now considered a synonym of *Diplocaulobium vanilliodorum* (J. J. Smith) A. Hawkes.

REFERENCES: 221, 229, 230, 470, 477.

Dendrobium vanleeuwenii J. J. Smith. Now considered a synonym of *Diplocaulobium vanleeuwenii* (J. J. Smith) Hunt and Summerhayes. REFERENCES: 213, 225, 230, 470.

Dendrobium vannouhuysii J. J. Smith

ORIGIN/HABITAT: Common in Irian Jaya (western New Guinea) at 6900–10,650 ft. (2100–3250 m). Plants grow in alpine shrubbery, in open mountain forests, in open places between boulders, along mountain ridges, on bare or mossy rocks, and in alpine grasslands on Mt. Goliath and Mt. Doorman. On Mt. Gahavisuka, they creep along the ground in mossy bogs. In Papua, plants have been found only in Enga Province.

CLIMATE: Station #97686, Wamena, Irian Jaya, Lat. 4.1°S, Long. 139.0°E, at 5446 ft. (1660 m). Temperatures are calculated for an elevation of 8500 ft. (2600 m). Record extreme temperatures are not available for this location.

N/HEMISPHERE	JAN	FEB	MAR	APR	MAY	JUN	JUL	AUG	SEP	OCT	NOV	DEC
°F AVG MAX	65	66	67	66	67	66	67	66	66	69	68	64
°F AVG MIN	50	50	52	52	53	54	53	52	53	55	55	51
DIURNAL RANGE	15	16	15	14	14	12	14	14	13	14	13	13
RAIN/INCHES	3.0	1.9	2.2	4.0	4.6	3.3	2.8	4.2	6.9	3.9	5.4	4.9
HUMIDITY/%	N/A											
BLOOM SEASON				*		*	*		*			
DAYS CLR	N/A											
RAIN/MM	76	48	56	102	117	84	71	107	175	99	137	124
°C AVG MAX	18.2	18.8	19.3	18.8	19.3	18.8	19.3	18.8	18.8	20.5	19.9	17.7
°C AVG MIN	9.9	9.9	11.0	11.0	11.6	12.1	11.6	11.0	11.6	12.7	12.7	10.5
DIURNAL RANGE	8.3	8.9	8.3	7.8	7.7	6.7	7.7	7.8	7.2	7.8	7.2	7.2
S/HEMISPHERE	JUL	AUG	SEP	OCT	NOV	DEC	JAN	FEB	MAR	APR	MAY	JUN

Cultural Recommendations

LIGHT: 2000–2500 fc. In the habitat, conditions are brightest in late morning.

TEMPERATURES: Throughout the year, days average 64–69°F (18–21°C), and nights average 50–55°F (10–13°C), with a diurnal range of 12–16°F (7–9°C). In the habitat, the warmest temperatures of the day occur during late morning when skies are usually clear. Clouds and mist develop near noon, thus preventing additional warming. Because of microclimate effects, actual maximum temperatures may be somewhat warmer than indicated. Reports from the habitat indicate a sharp contrast between day and night temperatures.

HUMIDITY: Information is not available for this location. However, records from nearby stations indicate that humidity probably averages near 80% year-round. High humidity and excellent air circulation are particularly important when temperatures are warm. Placing the plants in front of an evaporative cooler or near a fine mist is very beneficial.

WATER: Rainfall is moderate through most of the year. In the higher-elevation habitat, rainfall amounts may be greater than indicated in the climate table. In addition, large amounts of water are available from mist and heavy dew, even during periods of reduced rainfall. Cultivated plants should be kept moist with only slight drying allowed between waterings. They should be misted several times daily on the hottest days, but the foliage should always be dry before evening. Good air movement is critically important and should be maintained at all times.

FERTILIZER: ¼–½ recommended strength. A balanced fertilizer should be applied weekly to biweekly throughout the year. The Royal Botanic Garden in Edinburgh uses a dilute, seaweed-based fertilizer.

REST PERIOD: Growing conditions should be maintained all year. Rainfall averages are somewhat lower for a month or so in winter and again in midsummer. In cultivation, water may be decreased, but plants should never be allowed to dry out completely. In the habitat, light is slightly higher in winter.

GROWING MEDIA: Plants may be mounted on tree-fern or cork slabs if humidity is high and plants are watered at least once daily in summer. When plants are potted, any open, fast-draining medium may be used. Repotting may be done anytime new roots are growing.

MISCELLANEOUS NOTES: The bloom season shown in the climate table is based on reports from the habitat.

Plant and Flower Information

PLANT SIZE AND TYPE: A 1.8 in. (4.5 cm) sympodial terrestrial.

PSEUDOBULB: 1.8 in. (4.5 cm) long. The slender, 10-noded stems, which occasionally branch, arise from a creeping, rooting rhizome. The stems are evenly spaced on the rhizome.

LEAVES: Several near the apex of the stem. The oblong-ovate leaves are 0.3–0.4 in. (0.8–1.1 cm) long and somewhat distichous. They are wavy along the margin and warty at the tip. The leaf sheaths are distinctly warty.

INFLORESCENCE: Inflorescences emerge near the apex of the stem.

FLOWERS: 1–2 per inflorescence. The flowers are about 1 in. (2.5 cm) long. Sepals and petals may be cinnabar to brick-red. Blossoms have an obovate dorsal sepal, triangular lateral sepals, and spatula-shaped petals. The obovate lip is yellow to orange with an uneven to fringed apical margin. It is deeply notched at the apex and folded along the centerline.

HYBRIDIZING NOTES: Chromosome count, 2n = 38 (ref. 152, 243).

REFERENCES: 95, 96, 152, 221, 243, 379, 445, 470, 538.

PHOTOS/DRAWINGS: 538.

Dendrobium vanoverberghii Ames. Sometimes spelled *D. vanoberghii*, see *D. papilio* Loher. REFERENCES: 13, 98, 221, 296, 445, 536.

Dendrobium vanroemeri J. J. Smith

ORIGIN/HABITAT: Dutch New Guinea. Plants grow in the Cyclops mountains near Ostabhang and Agathodamonsberg at 5250–8450 ft. (1600–2580 m).

CLIMATE: Station #97690, Sentani/Jayapura, Irian Jaya, Lat. 2.7°S, Long. 140.5°E, at 289 ft. (88 m). Temperatures are calculated for an elevation of 6550 ft. (2000 m), resulting in probable extremes of 76°F (25°C) and 47°F (9°C).

N/HEMISPHERE	JAN	FEB	MAR	APR	MAY	JUN	JUL	AUG	SEP	OCT	NOV	DEC
°F AVG MAX	66	68	68	69	69	68	68	67	68	69	69	68
°F AVG MIN	51	51	51	52	52	52	52	52	52	53	52	52
DIURNAL RANGE	15	17	17	17	17	16	16	15	16	16	17	16
RAIN/INCHES	4.1	3.9	5.3	2.9	6.7	7.0	8.3	8.3	8.5	4.6	2.4	5.2
HUMIDITY/%	81	80	80	79	81	81	79	80	80	80	81	80
BLOOM SEASON					*							*
DAYS CLR @ 9AM	5	3	4	3	2	1	1	0	1	2	2	5
DAYS CLR @ 3PM	4	3	3	3	2	1	3	0	1	2	2	3
RAIN/MM	104	99	135	74	170	178	211	211	216	117	61	132
°C AVG MAX	19.1	20.2	20.2	20.7	20.7	20.2	20.2	19.6	20.2	20.7	20.7	20.2
°C AVG MIN	10.7	10.7	10.7	11.3	11.3	11.3	11.3	11.3	11.3	11.9	11.3	11.3
DIURNAL RANGE	8.4	9.5	9.5	9.4	9.4	8.9	8.9	8.3	8.9	8.8	9.4	8.9
S/HEMISPHERE	JUL	AUG	SEP	OCT	NOV	DEC	JAN	FEB	MAR	APR	MAY	JUN

Cultural Recommendations

LIGHT: 1500–2500 fc.

TEMPERATURES: Throughout the year, days average 66–69°F (19–21°C), and nights average 51–53°F (11–12°C), with a diurnal range of 15–17°F (8–10°C). Because of microclimate effects, actual maximum temperatures may be somewhat warmer than indicated.

HUMIDITY: Near 80% year-round.

WATER: Rainfall is heavy all year with brief semidry periods in spring and autumn. Cultivated plants should be kept evenly moist with only slight drying allowed between waterings.

FERTILIZER: ¼–½ recommended strength. A balanced fertilizer should be applied weekly to biweekly throughout the year.

REST PERIOD: Growing conditions should be maintained year-round. Water may be reduced somewhat for cultivated plants in winter, especially those grown in the dark, short-day conditions common in temperate latitudes. They should never be allowed to dry out completely, however. In the habitat, light is slightly higher in winter.

GROWING MEDIA: Plants may be mounted on tree-fern or cork slabs if humidity is high and plants are watered at least once daily in summer. When plants are potted, any open, fast-draining medium may be used. Repotting may be done anytime new roots are growing.

MISCELLANEOUS NOTES: The bloom season shown in the climate table is based on collection reports.

Plant and Flower Information

PLANT SIZE AND TYPE: A 1.3 in. (3.3 cm) sympodial epiphyte.

PSEUDOBULB: 0.4 in. (1 cm) long. The slender pseudobulbs are flattened.

LEAVES: 0.9 in. (2.3 cm) long. The very tiny lanceolate leaves are erect-spreading, twisted at the base, and bilobed at the tip. They are grooved, fleshy, and shiny. The leaf sheaths are marked with dots and warts.

INFLORESCENCE: Short. Inflorescences perforate 2 leaf sheaths to emerge at the leaf axils along the side of the stem.

FLOWERS: 1 per inflorescence. The flowers are 0.3 in. (0.8 cm) across. Blossoms are white with violet flecks on the lip. The oblong dorsal sepal is concave. The petals and slender lateral sepals are oval-oblong, recurved, and somewhat sickle-shaped. The erect, 3-lobed lip has erect, broadly triangular sidelobes with an uneven margin and a short, rounded midlobe. Blossoms last several days.

REFERENCES: 437, 470.

Dendrobium variabile Nicholls. See *D. prenticei* (F. Mueller) Nicholls. REFERENCES: 67, 105, 227, 228, 421, 533.

Dendrobium variegatum Persoon. Now considered a synonym of *Maxillaria variegata* Ruiz and Pavon. REFERENCES: 216, 254.

Dendrobium vaupelianum Kränzlin. See *D. dactylodes* Rchb. f. REFERENCES: 220, 252, 254, 434, 466.

Dendrobium veitchianum Lindley. See *D. macrophyllum* A. Richard. REFERENCES: 75, 83, 190, 216, 254, 310, 430, 436, 445, 469.

Dendrobium velutinum Rolfe. See *D. trigonopus* Rchb. f. REFERENCES: 179, 190, 218, 254, 430, 454.

Dendrobium ventricosum Kränzlin

AKA: Su (ref. 497) lists *D. equitans* Kränzlin as a synonym, but later works do not include this synonymy.

ORIGIN/HABITAT: The Philippine Islands. Plants are reported from Sorsogon and Zambales Provinces on Luzon and from Agusan, Davao, and Surigao Provinces on Mindanao. The orchids grow in low elevation rainforests. They have also been found on the small island of Botel Tobago, just off the Taiwan coast, growing on tree trunks and branches at 350–1000 ft. (100–300 m).

CLIMATE: Station #98444, Legaspi, Luzon Island, Philippines, Lat. 13.1°N, Long. 123.8°E, at 62 ft. (19 m). Record extreme temperatures are 100°F (38°C) and 62°F (17°C).

N/HEMISPHERE	JAN	FEB	MAR	APR	MAY	JUN	JUL	AUG	SEP	OCT	NOV	DEC
°F AVG MAX	83	84	85	87	89	90	89	89	89	88	86	84
°F AVG MIN	72	73	73	75	76	75	75	75	74	74	74	73
DIURNAL RANGE	11	11	12	12	13	15	14	14	15	14	12	11
RAIN/INCHES	15.4	11.5	7.7	5.9	6.4	7.9	10.2	7.9	10.2	13.7	18.3	20.3
HUMIDITY/%	82	81	81	80	80	80	82	83	83	83	84	84
BLOOM SEASON						*	*	*		*		
DAYS CLR @ 8AM	4	4	6	5	5	4	3	2	2	4	3	3
DAYS CLR @ 2PM	1	1	4	5	4	1	0	0	0	1	1	1
RAIN/MM	391	292	196	150	163	201	259	201	259	348	465	516
°C AVG MAX	28.3	28.9	29.4	30.6	31.7	32.2	31.7	31.7	31.7	31.1	30.0	28.9
°C AVG MIN	22.2	22.8	22.8	23.9	24.4	23.9	23.9	23.9	23.3	23.3	23.3	22.8
DIURNAL RANGE	6.1	6.1	6.6	6.7	7.3	8.3	7.8	7.8	8.4	7.8	6.7	6.1
S/HEMISPHERE	JUL	AUG	SEP	OCT	NOV	DEC	JAN	FEB	MAR	APR	MAY	JUN

Cultural Recommendations

LIGHT: 2500–3500 fc.

TEMPERATURES: Throughout the year, days average 83–90°F (28–32°C), and nights average 72–76°F (22–24°C), with a diurnal range of 11–15°F (6–8°C).

HUMIDITY: 80–85% year-round.

WATER: Rainfall is very heavy all year. Cultivated plants should be kept moist. They should never be allowed to dry out completely.

FERTILIZER: ¼–½ recommended strength. A balanced fertilizer should be applied weekly to biweekly throughout the year.

REST PERIOD: Growing conditions should be maintained all year. In the habitat, rainfall is high, but water and fertilizer should be reduced for cultivated plants in winter, especially those grown in the dark, short-day conditions common in temperate latitudes. However, plants should never be allowed to dry out completely.

GROWING MEDIA: Plants may be grown on slabs or rafts if humidity is high. Plants should be watered at least daily all year, and several times each day during hot, dry summer weather. Because plants are healthiest if watered frequently, a potting medium must be very open and fast-draining. If plants are potted, the smallest pot possible should be used, and medium to large-sized bark or cork nuggets used as a medium. Repotting may be done anytime new roots are growing.

MISCELLANEOUS NOTES: The bloom season shown in the climate table is based on collection reports. Flowers are normally produced every 4 months.

Plant and Flower Information

PLANT SIZE AND TYPE: A 12–24 in. (30–60 cm) sympodial epiphyte.

PSEUDOBULB: 12–24 in. (30–60 cm) long. The erect, many noded stems are slender, yellow, and shiny. The lower nodes are swollen.

LEAVES: Many. The 2-ranked leaves are 2 in. (5 cm) long and 0.8 in (2 cm) apart. They are knife-shaped, thick, and fleshy.

INFLORESCENCE: 4–8 in. (10–20 cm) long. Inflorescences emerge from the cushion of fibrous scales opposite the rudimentary leaves at the apex of the stem.

FLOWERS: 1 per inflorescence. The small, highly variable flowers are 0.8 in. (2 cm) long. The petals and united sepals may be white or yellowish green. The 3-lobed lip is decorated with bluish pink veins in the throat and yellow along the center with large, triangular sidelobes. The midlobe is transversely oblong and notched at the apex with 3, toothed, raised lines. The apical margin may be minutely toothed or almost fringed. Blossoms are fragrant.

HYBRIDIZING NOTES: Chromosome counts are 2n = 20 (ref. 504) and 2n = 38 (ref. 280, 504, 580).

REFERENCES: 12, 61, 151, 208, 220, 280, 254, 279, 280, 296, 497, 504, 528, 536, 580.

Dendrobium ventrilabium J. J. Smith

PHOTOS/DRAWINGS: 279.

ORIGIN/HABITAT: Western Sumatra, near Padang. Habitat elevation is unavailable, so the following climate data should be used with caution.

CLIMATE: Station #96163, Padang, Sumatra, Indonesia, Lat. 0.9°S, Long. 100.4°E, at 19 ft. (6 m). Temperatures are calculated for an elevation of 450 ft. (140 m), resulting in probable extremes of 93°F (34°C) and 67°F (19°C).

N/HEMISPHERE	JAN	FEB	MAR	APR	MAY	JUN	JUL	AUG	SEP	OCT	NOV	DEC
°F AVG MAX	86	86	86	85	85	85	86	86	86	86	87	86
°F AVG MIN	73	73	73	73	73	73	73	73	73	74	74	73
DIURNAL RANGE	13	13	12	12	12	12	13	13	13	12	13	13
RAIN/INCHES	10.9	13.7	6.0	19.5	20.4	18.9	13.8	10.2	12.1	14.3	12.4	12.1
HUMIDITY/%	81	82	82	84	85	84	81	81	82	83	81	81
BLOOM SEASON	N/A											
DAYS CLR @ 7AM	5	1	1	0	0	2	1	2	2	2	3	5
DAYS CLR @ 1PM	5	2	2	1	1	3	3	4	3	3	6	5
RAIN/MM	277	348	152	495	518	480	351	259	307	363	315	307
°C AVG MAX	29.8	29.8	29.2	29.2	29.2	29.2	29.8	29.8	29.8	29.8	30.3	29.8
°C AVG MIN	22.5	22.5	22.5	22.5	22.5	22.5	22.5	22.5	22.5	23.1	23.1	22.5
DIURNAL RANGE	7.3	7.3	6.7	6.7	6.7	6.7	7.3	7.3	7.3	6.7	7.2	7.3
S/HEMISPHERE	JUL	AUG	SEP	OCT	NOV	DEC	JAN	FEB	MAR	APR	MAY	JUN

Cultural Recommendations

LIGHT: 2000–3000 fc. Diffused light is preferred.

TEMPERATURES: Throughout the year, days average 85–87°F (29–30°C), and nights average 73–74°F (23°C), with a diurnal range of 12–13°F (7°C). Probable extremes vary only a few degrees from the averages, indicating that the plant may not tolerate wide temperature fluctuations.

HUMIDITY: 80–85% year-round.

WATER: Rainfall is heavy all year. Cultivated plants should be constantly moist but not soggy.

FERTILIZER: ¼–½ recommended strength. A balanced fertilizer should be applied weekly to biweekly throughout the year.

REST PERIOD: Growing conditions should be maintained year-round. Rainfall is only slightly lower for a month in late winter. Although water should be reduced somewhat for cultivated plants, especially those grown in the dark, short-day conditions common in temperate latitudes, they should never be allowed to dry out completely. In the habitat, light is highest in winter.

GROWING MEDIA: Plants may be mounted on tree-fern or cork slabs or potted in small pots filled with any open, fast-draining medium. Repotting may be done anytime new roots are actively growing.

MISCELLANEOUS NOTES: The plant description in 1922 in *Bull. Jard. Bot. Buit.* 3rd sér. 5:84 was based on preserved flowers. The other plant parts were unavailable.

Plant and Flower Information

INFLORESCENCE: Short. The bracts and inflorescences are violet-brown.

FLOWERS: 2–3 per inflorescence. The flowers are 1.4 in. (3.6 cm) long. They are light yellowish green with purple veins. The column and anther are white. The dorsal sepal is ovate, pointed, and nearly flat. Lateral sepals are concave, pointed, and somewhat triangular. Petals are elliptical with a short point at the apex. The erect lip is obscurely 3-lobed with 5 raised lines. The erect sidelobes are triangular. The lip is rounded at the back with a truncated, folded-ruffled margin on the front. The midlobe is slightly elongated. It has a notch in the center with a point between the 2 short, round lobes.

REFERENCES: 223.

Dendrobium ventripes Carr

ORIGIN/HABITAT: Borneo. In northern Sarawak, plants grow on mossforest trees on a ridge leading to Mt. Dulit at about 4000 ft. (1220 m). In Sabah, plants are found in the Mt. Kinabalu region in both upper and lower mountain forests at 3950–8550 ft. (1200–2600 m).

CLIMATE: Station #96449, Miri, Sarawak, Lat. 4.4°N, Long. 114.0°E, at 13 ft. (4 m). Temperatures are calculated for an elevation of 4000 ft. (1220 m), resulting in probable extremes of 82°F (28°C) and 54°F (12°C).

N/HEMISPHERE	JAN	FEB	MAR	APR	MAY	JUN	JUL	AUG	SEP	OCT	NOV	DEC
°F AVG MAX	73	73	74	75	75	75	75	75	74	74	74	74
°F AVG MIN	61	61	61	62	62	62	61	61	61	61	61	61
DIURNAL RANGE	12	12	13	13	13	13	14	14	13	13	13	13
RAIN/INCHES	16.8	6.5	5.5	4.4	8.2	12.0	8.5	8.4	11.8	11.7	14.5	11.3
HUMIDITY/%	86	86	85	83	83	82	81	81	82	83	84	85
BLOOM SEASON								*				
DAYS CLR @ 8AM	1	2	4	4	3	2	3	2	2	1	2	2
DAYS CLR @ 2PM	1	1	3	4	2	5	3	2	3	2	1	1
RAIN/MM	427	165	140	112	208	305	216	213	300	297	368	287
°C AVG MAX	22.7	22.7	23.2	23.8	23.8	23.8	23.8	23.8	23.2	23.2	23.2	23.2
°C AVG MIN	16.0	16.0	16.0	16.6	16.6	16.6	16.0	16.0	16.0	16.0	16.0	16.0
DIURNAL RANGE	6.7	6.7	7.2	7.2	7.2	7.2	7.8	7.8	7.2	7.2	7.2	7.2
S/HEMISPHERE	JUL	AUG	SEP	OCT	NOV	DEC	JAN	FEB	MAR	APR	MAY	JUN

Cultural Recommendations

LIGHT: 1800–2500 fc.

TEMPERATURES: Throughout the year, days average 73–75°F (23–24°C), and nights average 61–62°F (16–17°C), with a diurnal range of 12–14°F (7–8°C). Because of the wide range of habitat elevation, plants should adapt to conditions that are 10–12°F (6–7°C) cooler than indicated.

HUMIDITY: 80–85% year-round.

WATER: Rainfall is heavy to very heavy all year, but conditions are slightly drier in winter. Cultivated plants should be kept moist but not soggy.

FERTILIZER: ¼–½ recommended strength. A balanced fertilizer should be applied weekly to biweekly throughout the year.

REST PERIOD: Growing conditions should be maintained all year. In cultivation, water and fertilizer should be reduced in winter, especially for plants grown in the dark, short-day conditions common in temperate latitudes. They should never be allowed to dry out completely, however. In the habitat, seasonal light variation is minor.

GROWING MEDIA: Plants may be mounted on tree-fern or cork slabs if humidity is high and plants are watered at least once daily in summer. When plants are potted, any open, fast-draining medium may be used. They may be repotted anytime new roots are growing.

MISCELLANEOUS NOTES: The bloom season shown in the climate table is based on records from the habitat.

Plant and Flower Information

PLANT SIZE AND TYPE: A 24 in. (61 cm) sympodial epiphyte.

PSEUDOBULB: 24 in. (61 cm) long. The clustered stems are slightly flattened and leafy to the apex. Above the basal 2–3 nodes, stems are swollen for about 4 in. (10 cm).

LEAVES: Many. The leaves are 0.4–1.5 in. (1.1–3.7 cm) long, lanceolate to oblong-lanceolate, abruptly narrowed below the bilobed apex, and twisted at the base. They are leathery with a thin texture. The leaves are grooved above and keeled below.

INFLORESCENCE: Very short. Inflorescences emerge from tufts of dry scales on the apical portion of the stem. Flowers are borne from between the leaves on the underside of the stem so they are hidden by the leaves when viewed from above.

FLOWERS: 1 per inflorescence. The fleshy flowers are 0.4 in. (1 cm) across with sickle-shaped lateral sepals, an ovate dorsal sepal and lanceolate petals. The 3-lobed lip has erect, twisted sidelobes which are much larger than the toothed, incurved midlobe. The margin of the midlobe is hairy toward the apex and fringed along the margin. Blossoms are green with crimson markings on the petals and lip.

REFERENCES: 59, 225, 286, 592.

PHOTOS/DRAWINGS: 592.

Dendrobium venustum Teijsm. and Binn.

AKA: *D. ciliatum* Parish ex Hooker f. not Ruiz and Pavon, *D. ciliferum* Bakhuizen, *D. rupicola* Rchb. f. not *D. rupicolum* Ridley, *D. ciliatum* var. *rupicola* Rchb. f. The name *D. delacourii* has sometimes been applied to plants which should have been identified as *D. venustum*. *D. ciliatum* var. *breve* Rchb. f. is considered a synonym of *D. delacourii*.

ORIGIN/HABITAT: Northern and western Thailand, the Moulmein and Maymyo regions of Burma, near Vientaiane in Laos, Cambodia, and near Dalat in Vietnam. In Thailand, plants grow near Chiang Mai at 1000–1500 ft. (300–460 m).

CLIMATE: Station #48327, Chiang Mai, Thailand, Lat. 18.8°N, Long. 99.0°E at 1100 ft. (335 m). Record extreme temperatures are 109°F (43°C) and 38°F (3°C).

N/HEMISPHERE	JAN	FEB	MAR	APR	MAY	JUN	JUL	AUG	SEP	OCT	NOV	DEC
°F AVG MAX	85	90	95	96	94	90	89	87	88	89	86	84
°F AVG MIN	56	57	62	70	74	74	74	75	73	71	66	57
DIURNAL RANGE	29	33	33	26	20	16	15	12	15	18	20	27
RAIN/INCHES	0.3	0.4	0.6	2.0	5.5	6.1	7.4	8.7	11.5	4.9	1.5	0.4
HUMIDITY/%	73	65	58	62	73	78	80	83	83	81	79	76
BLOOM SEASON							**	**	*	*		
DAYS CLR @ 7AM	5	5	2	2	1	0	0	0	0	1	3	3
DAYS CLR @ 1PM	9	8	4	2	0	0	0	0	0	0	1	3
RAIN/MM	8	10	15	51	140	155	188	221	292	124	38	10
°C AVG MAX	29.4	32.2	35.0	35.6	34.4	32.2	31.7	30.6	31.1	31.7	30.0	28.9
°C AVG MIN	13.3	13.9	16.7	21.1	23.3	23.3	23.3	23.9	22.8	21.7	18.9	13.9
DIURNAL RANGE	16.1	18.3	18.3	14.5	11.1	8.9	8.4	6.7	8.3	10.0	11.1	15.0
S/HEMISPHERE	JUL	AUG	SEP	OCT	NOV	DEC	JAN	FEB	MAR	APR	MAY	JUN

Cultural Recommendations

LIGHT: 3500–4500 fc. Bright light and strong, constant air movement should be provided. The heavy summer cloud cover indicates that some shading is needed from spring through autumn, but light should be as high as the plant can tolerate, short of burning the leaves.

TEMPERATURES: Summer days average 87–90°F (31–32°C), and nights average 74–75°F (23–24°C), with a diurnal range of 12–16°F (7–9°C). Spring is the warmest time of the year. Days average 94–96°F (35–36°C), and nights average 62–74°F (17–23°C), with a diurnal range of 20–33°F (11–18°C).

HUMIDITY: 80–85% in summer and early autumn, dropping to about 60–65% in late winter and early spring.

WATER: Rainfall is moderate to heavy from late spring through early autumn, but conditions are much drier in winter. Cultivated plants should be kept moist while actively growing, but water should be gradually reduced after new growths mature in autumn.

FERTILIZER: ¼–½ recommended strength, applied weekly. A high-nitrogen fertilizer is beneficial from spring to midsummer, but a fertilizer high in phosphates should be used in late summer and autumn.

REST PERIOD: Winter days average 84–90°F (29–32°C), and nights average 56–57°F (13–14°C), with a diurnal range of 27–33°F (15–18°C). In the habitat, rainfall averages are very low for 4–5 months in winter, but during the early part of the season the high relative humidity indicates that additional moisture is available from frequent fog, mist, and heavy deposits of dew. Growers sometimes recommend eliminating water in winter, but plants are healthiest if for most of the winter they are allowed to become somewhat dry between waterings but do not remain dry for extended periods. For 1–2 months in late winter, however, conditions are clear, warm, and dry, with humidity so low that even the moisture from morning dew is uncommon. Plants should be allowed to dry out completely between waterings and remain dry longer during this time. Occasional early morning mistings between waterings may help keep the plants from becoming too dry. Fertilizer should be greatly reduced or eliminated until water is increased in spring. A cool, dry rest is essential for cultivated plants and should be continued until new growth starts in spring. In the habitat, light is highest in winter.

GROWING MEDIA: Mounting plants on tree-fern or cork slabs accommodates their often pendulous growth habit. However, humidity must be high and plants must be watered at least once a day in summer. If plants cannot be mounted, hanging pots or baskets may be filled with an open, fast-draining medium. Repotting should be done as seldom as possible. When repotting is necessary, it is best done as soon as new root growth starts or as soon after flowering as possible.

MISCELLANEOUS NOTES: The bloom season shown in the climate table is based on cultivation records for plants grown as *D. rupicola*.

Growers indicate that this species is very difficult to flower in warm, uniform climates. Plants cultivated as *D. ciliatum* are small with multiple spikes. Blossoms have yellow sepals and petals and a pale yellow and brown fringed lip with prominent cilia.

Plant and Flower Information

PLANT SIZE AND TYPE: A 12–18 in. (30–45 cm) sympodial epiphyte. Plants occasionally reach a length of 24 in. (60 cm).

PSEUDOBULB: 4–24 in. (10–60 cm) long. The stems may be arching or pendulous.

LEAVES: Up to 7 per growth. The oblong or straplike leaves are 4.0–5.5 in. (10–14 cm) long, leathery, glossy, and bright green. They are persistent, especially near the apex.

INFLORESCENCE: 6–12 in. (15–30 cm) long. Inflorescences may be arching or horizontal. They arise from upper nodes along the stem and at the apex. Flowers are carried on the apical 60% of the inflorescence.

FLOWERS: 5–25 per inflorescence. The flowers are 1 in. (2.5 cm) across. The lanceolate sepals and petals may be creamy white or greenish yellow with or without dull red veins. The lip is often rust colored with yellow-green markings. Seidenfaden (ref. 454) indicates that plants known as *D. venustum* have longer cilia on the midlobe than *D. delacourii*.

HYBRIDIZING NOTES: Chromosome count is $2n = 38$ (ref. 580) and $2n = 40$ (ref. 154, 188, 580) as *D. ciliatum*.

REFERENCES: 21, 25, 154, 167, 179, 188, 202, 216, 254, 266, 348, 454, 580.

PHOTOS/DRAWINGS: *21, 454*.

Dendrobium veratrifolium as used by Kränzlin not Lindley, Naves, A. Richard, or Roxburgh.

Schlechter (ref. 437) included *D. veratrifolium* as used by Kränzlin as a synonym of *D. validum* Schlechter, which is now considered a synonym of *D. sylvanum* Rchb. f. REFERENCES: 84, 437.

Dendrobium veratrifolium Lindley not Kränzlin, Naves, A. Richard, or Roxburgh.

See *D. lineale* Rolfe. REFERENCES: 25, 84, 190, 211, 216, 236, 254, 310, 317, 437, 444, 445, 470, 537.

Dendrobium veratrifolium as used by Naves not Kränzlin, Lindley, A. Richard, or Roxburgh.

Merrill (ref. 296) and Valmayor (ref. 536) include this name as a possible synonym of *D. taurinum* Lindley. REFERENCES: 296, 536.

Dendrobium veratrifolium A. Richard not Kränzlin, Lindley, Naves, or Roxburgh.

This name was used by Kränzlin (ref. 254) in a discussion of *D. scopa* (Lindley) Kränzlin. No additional information was found. REFERENCES: 254.

Dendrobium veratrifolium Roxburgh not Kränzlin, Lindley, Naves, or A. Richard.

Now considered a synonym of *Phaius veratrifolius* Lindley. REFERENCES: 216, 254.

Dendrobium veratroides Bakhuizen f. See *D. lineale* Rolfe.
REFERENCES: 25, 84, 211, 230, 516.

Dendrobium verlaquii Costantine. See *D. terminale* Parish and Rchb. f.
REFERENCES: 222, 454.

Dendrobium vernicosum Schlechter

ORIGIN/HABITAT: Northern Papua New Guinea and several islands in the Solomons. In New Guinea, plants grow on trees in the mossy rainforests of the Kani Range at about 3500 ft. (1070 m). In the Solomon Islands, they grow at 2600–4900 ft. (800–1500 m)

CLIMATE: Station #200187, Erap, Papua New Guinea, Lat. 6.6°S, Long. 146.7°E, at 850 ft. (260 m). Temperatures are calculated for an elevation of 3300 ft. (1000 m), resulting in probable extremes of 94°F (34°C) and 45°F (7°C).

N/HEMISPHERE	JAN	FEB	MAR	APR	MAY	JUN	JUL	AUG	SEP	OCT	NOV	DEC
°F AVG MAX	80	80	81	82	85	85	85	85	85	84	82	82
°F AVG MIN	61	61	61	62	64	65	64	64	65	63	66	62
DIURNAL RANGE	19	19	20	20	21	20	21	21	20	21	16	20
RAIN/INCHES	3.9	3.9	2.7	3.0	3.0	5.3	5.9	5.9	7.0	3.4	2.4	3.1
HUMIDITY/%	82	81	81	79	75	74	74	74	77	76	80	80
BLOOM SEASON							*					
DAYS CLR	N/A											
RAIN/MM	99	99	69	76	76	135	150	150	178	86	61	79
°C AVG MAX	26.7	26.7	27.2	27.8	29.4	29.4	29.4	29.4	29.4	28.9	27.8	27.8
°C AVG MIN	16.1	16.1	16.1	16.7	17.8	18.3	17.8	17.8	18.3	17.2	18.9	16.7
DIURNAL RANGE	10.6	10.6	11.1	11.1	11.6	11.1	11.6	11.6	11.1	11.7	8.9	11.1
S/HEMISPHERE	JUL	AUG	SEP	OCT	NOV	DEC	JAN	FEB	MAR	APR	MAY	JUN

Cultural Recommendations

LIGHT: 2500–3500 fc.

TEMPERATURES: Throughout the year, days average 80–85°F (27–29°C), and nights average 61–66°F (16–19°C), with a diurnal range of 16–21°F (9–12°C).

HUMIDITY: 75–80% year-round. Despite high average humidity, the habitat may be quite dry during hot afternoons.

WATER: Rainfall is moderate most of the year, but for 4–5 months in summer and early autumn, conditions are somewhat wetter. Cultivated plants should be thoroughly saturated then allowed to dry slightly between waterings in summer and early autumn. Water should be gradually reduced in autumn.

FERTILIZER: ¼–½ recommended strength. A balanced fertilizer should be applied weekly to biweekly throughout the year.

REST PERIOD: Growing temperatures should be maintained all year. In the habitat, rainfall is lowest in winter, but the high humidity indicates that additional moisture is frequently available from heavy dew. Cultivated plants should be allowed to dry for somewhat longer between waterings, but should not remain dry for extended periods. Fertilizer should be reduced until water is increased in spring. In the habitat, seasonal light variation is minor.

GROWING MEDIA: Plants may be mounted on tree-fern or cork slabs or potted in small pots filled with any open, fast-draining medium. Repotting may be done anytime new roots are growing.

MISCELLANEOUS NOTES: The bloom season shown in the climate table is based on collection reports. Plants that produce flowers which last a single day commonly bloom several times during the year. Flowering usually occurs 7–14 days after a sudden 10°F (5°C) drop in daytime temperatures.

Plant and Flower Information

PLANT SIZE AND TYPE: A 39–59 in. (100–150 cm) sympodial epiphyte.

PSEUDOBULB: 39–59 in. (100–150 cm) long. The erect stems are borne on a very short rhizome.

LEAVES: Many. The linear-lanceolate leaves are 5–6 in. (13–16 cm) long. They are pointed, shiny, closely set, and somewhat spreading. The slightly roughened leaf sheaths have small raised warts.

INFLORESCENCE: Short. The inflorescences emerge from the side of the stem. Blossoms are held opposite each other.

FLOWERS: 2 per inflorescence. The flowers are 1.6 in. (4 cm) long. The snow white sepals and petals are dilated at the base and very long, slender, and pointed near the apex. The lip and column are marked with brownish yellow at the base. The 3-lobed lip is hairy and deeply fringed. Side-lobes are ovate triangular. Blossoms are short-lived.

REFERENCES: 221, 271, 437, 445, 470.

PHOTOS/DRAWINGS: 437.

Dendrobium verruciferum Rchb. f. not J. J. Smith

ORIGIN/HABITAT: Endemic to New Caledonia. Plants are commonly found at 150–1000 ft. (50–300 m), but they occasionally grow as high as 2550–3100 ft. (780–950 m). The orchids, which grow on the forest floor, are often found near water.

CLIMATE: Station #91592, Noumea, New Caledonia, Lat. 22.3°S, Long. 166.5°E, at 246 ft. (75 m). Record extreme temperatures are 99°F (37°C) and 52°F (11°C).

N/HEMISPHERE	JAN	FEB	MAR	APR	MAY	JUN	JUL	AUG	SEP	OCT	NOV	DEC
°F AVG MAX	76	76	78	80	83	86	86	85	85	83	79	77
°F AVG MIN	62	61	63	65	68	70	72	73	72	70	66	64
DIURNAL RANGE	14	15	15	15	15	16	14	12	13	13	13	13
RAIN/INCHES	3.6	2.6	2.5	2.0	2.4	2.6	3.7	5.1	5.7	5.2	4.4	3.7
HUMIDITY/%	73	70	69	67	68	69	71	74	75	76	73	73
BLOOM SEASON	*	*	*	*				*	**	*	*	**
DAYS CLR @ 11AM	7	9	9	15	12	10	7	6	7	7	7	7
DAYS CLR @ 5PM	7	11	6	11	7	6	5	4	4	5	3	7
RAIN/MM	91	66	64	51	61	66	94	130	145	132	112	94
°C AVG MAX	24.4	24.4	25.6	26.7	28.3	30.0	30.0	29.4	29.4	28.3	26.1	25.0
°C AVG MIN	16.7	16.1	17.2	18.3	20.0	21.1	22.2	22.8	22.2	21.1	18.9	17.8
DIURNAL RANGE	7.7	8.3	8.4	8.4	8.3	8.9	7.8	6.6	7.2	7.2	7.2	7.2
S/HEMISPHERE	JUL	AUG	SEP	OCT	NOV	DEC	JAN	FEB	MAR	APR	MAY	JUN

Cultural Recommendations

LIGHT: 2500–3500 fc.

TEMPERATURES: Summer days average 85–86°F (29–30°C), and nights average 70–73°F (21–23°C), with a diurnal range of 12–16°F (7–9°C).

HUMIDITY: 70–75% most of the year, dropping to near 65% for 1–2 months in spring.

WATER: Rainfall is relatively low and consistent most of the year. The driest season is in late winter and spring, and the heaviest rain falls in late summer and early autumn. Cultivated plants should be allowed to become somewhat dry between waterings but should never dry out completely.

FERTILIZER: ¼–½ recommended strength, applied weekly. A high-nitrogen fertilizer is beneficial from spring to midsummer, but a fertilizer high in phosphates should be used in late summer and autumn.

REST PERIOD: Winter days average 76–78°F (24–26°C), and nights average 61–64°F (16–18°C), with a diurnal range of 13–15°F (7–8°C). High and low temperatures decline simultaneously, resulting in little change in the diurnal range. In the habitat, rainfall is somewhat lower in late winter and spring. In cultivation, water and fertilizer should be reduced and the plants allowed to dry even more between waterings than in summer. They should not dry out completely or remain dry for long periods, however. In the habitat, light is highest in winter.

GROWING MEDIA: Plants may be mounted on tree-fern or cork slabs if humidity is high and plants are watered at least once daily in summer.

When plants are potted, any open, fast-draining medium may be used. Repotting is best done in early spring when new roots are growing.

MISCELLANEOUS NOTES: The bloom season shown in the climate table is based on reports from the habitat.

Plant and Flower Information

PLANT SIZE AND TYPE: A 12 in. (30 cm) sympodial terrestrial.

PSEUDOBULB: 12 in. (30 cm) long. The stems are swollen at the base, slender above, and slightly zigzag near the tip.

LEAVES: 10–12 per growth. The variable leaves, which are 1–2 in. (2.5–5.0 cm) long, are bilobed at the tip and twisted at the base to lie on a single plane. They are arranged in 2, alternate rows on the upper portion of the stem.

INFLORESCENCE: Short. Inflorescences emerge from between the leaves.

FLOWERS: 1 per inflorescence. The flowers are 0.6–1.0 in. (1.5–2.5 cm) long. The slender sepals and petals may not open fully. Flower color is variable and may be shades of mauve, red, greenish yellow, and white. The unlobed lip may be green, yellow, or red. It has 3 raised lines in the center. The upturned margin is deeply ruffled near the apex.

REFERENCES: 173, 216, 254, 445.

PHOTOS/DRAWINGS: 173.

Dendrobium verruciferum J. J. Smith not Rchb. f. Now considered a synonym of *Epigeneium verruciferum* (Rolfe) Summerhayes. Summerhayes (ref. 499) discusses the nomenclature for this species name. REFERENCES: 220, 254, 445, 499.

Dendrobium verruciflorum Schlechter

ORIGIN/HABITAT: Papua New Guinea. Plants were collected only once from forest trees near the Djamu River at about 1000 ft. (300 m). Climate information is included for the reported collection site, but the lack of additional collections suggest that this may not be its preferred habitat.

CLIMATE: Station #94014, Madang, Papua New Guinea, Lat. 5.2°S, Long. 145.8°E, at 13 ft. (4 m). Temperatures are calculated for an elevation of 1000 ft. (300 m), resulting in probable extremes of 95°F (35°C) and 59°F (15°C).

N/HEMISPHERE	JAN	FEB	MAR	APR	MAY	JUN	JUL	AUG	SEP	OCT	NOV	DEC
°F AVG MAX	80	80	82	82	82	82	82	82	82	84	84	81
°F AVG MIN	74	75	75	75	74	74	74	74	74	73	74	75
DIURNAL RANGE	6	5	7	7	8	8	8	8	8	11	10	6
RAIN/INCHES	4.0	3.4	3.2	8.5	11.2	11.1	10.1	11.3	9.4	11.3	10.5	6.7
HUMIDITY/%	88	87	86	86	86	86	86	85	85	87	88	89
BLOOM SEASON				•								
DAYS CLR	N/A											
RAIN/MM	102	86	81	216	284	282	257	287	239	287	267	170
°C AVG MAX	26.6	26.6	27.7	27.7	27.7	27.7	27.7	27.7	27.7	28.8	28.8	27.1
°C AVG MIN	23.2	23.8	23.8	23.8	23.2	23.2	23.2	23.2	23.2	22.7	23.2	23.8
DIURNAL RANGE	3.4	2.8	3.9	3.9	4.5	4.5	4.5	4.5	4.5	6.1	5.6	3.3
S/HEMISPHERE	JUL	AUG	SEP	OCT	NOV	DEC	JAN	FEB	MAR	APR	MAY	JUN

Cultural Recommendations

LIGHT: 2500–3000 fc.

TEMPERATURES: Throughout the year, days average 80–84°F (27–29°C), and nights average 73–75°F (23–24°C), with a diurnal range of 5–11°F (3–6°C). The warmest highs, the coolest lows, and the greatest diurnal range occur in autumn.

HUMIDITY: 85–90% year-round.

WATER: Rainfall is moderate to heavy all year. The driest conditions occur in late winter. Cultivated plants should be kept moist but not soggy.

FERTILIZER: ¼–½ recommended strength. A balanced fertilizer should be applied weekly to biweekly throughout the year.

REST PERIOD: Growing temperatures should be maintained all year. In the habitat, rainfall decreases for 4 months in winter. Water should be reduced for cultivated plants, but they should not be allowed to dry out completely. Fertilizer should be reduced or eliminated while water is reduced. In the habitat, light is slightly higher in late winter.

GROWING MEDIA: Plants may be mounted on tree-fern or cork slabs if humidity is high and plants are watered at least once daily in summer. If plants are potted, any open, fast-draining medium may be used. Repotting may be done anytime new roots are growing.

MISCELLANEOUS NOTES: The bloom season shown in the climate table is based on reports from the habitat. Plants that produce flowers which last a single day commonly bloom several times during the year. Flowering usually occurs 7–14 days after a sudden 10°F (5°C) drop in daytime temperatures.

Plant and Flower Information

PLANT SIZE AND TYPE: A 16 in. (40 cm) sympodial epiphyte.

PSEUDOBULB: 16 in. (40 cm) long. The unbranched stems are flattened. They are borne on a very short rhizome.

LEAVES: Many. The oblong, somewhat erect leaves are 3.1–3.5 in. (8–9 cm) long. The are flattened.

INFLORESCENCE: Very short.

FLOWERS: 2 per inflorescence. The flowers are 1 in. (2.5 cm) long. The sepals are brown and densely bumpy on the exterior with white on the inside. Lateral sepals point down, but the dorsal sepal and petals project forward. The oblong, recurved lip is covered with hairs that extend beyond the front margin. It is not lobed. Blossoms are short lived.

REFERENCES: 221, 437.

PHOTOS/DRAWINGS: 437.

Dendrobium verruculosum Ames. See *D. blanche-amesii* A. Hawkes and A. H. Heller. REFERENCES: 12, 13, 191, 221, 229, 296, 536.

Dendrobium verruculosum Schlechter

ORIGIN/HABITAT: Northern Papua New Guinea. Plants grow on mistforest trees in the Waria District and in the Dischore Range at 4250–5600 ft. (1300–1700 m). Plants have also been collected in the Arfak Range of Irian Jaya (western New Guinea) at about 5600 ft. (1700 m).

CLIMATE: Station #200192, Garaina, Papua New Guinea, Lat. 7.9°S, Long. 147.1°E, at 2350 ft. (716 m). Temperatures are calculated for an elevation of 4250 ft. (1300 m), resulting in probable extremes of 88°F (31°C) and 40°F (4°C).

N/HEMISPHERE	JAN	FEB	MAR	APR	MAY	JUN	JUL	AUG	SEP	OCT	NOV	DEC
°F AVG MAX	74	76	77	78	79	79	79	79	78	78	77	75
°F AVG MIN	57	57	57	58	57	58	59	59	59	58	58	57
DIURNAL RANGE	17	19	20	20	22	21	20	20	19	20	19	18
RAIN/INCHES	5.8	6.5	8.7	11.1	11.8	11.9	8.9	11.7	11.5	9.9	7.7	5.2
HUMIDITY/%	84	82	82	81	80	80	81	81	82	83	84	84
BLOOM SEASON											•	•
DAYS CLR	N/A											
RAIN/MM	147	165	221	282	300	302	226	297	292	251	196	132
°C AVG MAX	23.1	24.3	24.8	25.4	25.9	25.9	25.9	25.9	25.4	25.4	24.8	23.7
°C AVG MIN	13.7	13.7	13.7	14.3	13.7	14.3	14.8	14.8	14.8	14.3	14.3	13.7
DIURNAL RANGE	9.4	10.6	11.1	11.1	12.2	11.6	11.1	11.1	10.6	11.1	10.5	10.0
S/HEMISPHERE	JUL	AUG	SEP	OCT	NOV	DEC	JAN	FEB	MAR	APR	MAY	JUN

Cultural Recommendations

LIGHT: 2000–3000 fc.

TEMPERATURES: Throughout the year, days average 74–79°F (23–26°C), and nights average 57–59°F (14–15°C), with a diurnal range of 17–22°F (9–12°C).

Dendrobium versicolor

HUMIDITY: 80–85% year-round.

WATER: Rainfall is heavy all year, but conditions are slightly drier in winter. Cultivated plants should be kept moist but not soggy.

FERTILIZER: ¼–½ recommended strength. A balanced fertilizer should be applied weekly to biweekly throughout the year. The Royal Botanic Garden in Edinburgh uses a seaweed-based fertilizer for plants from high-elevation New Guinea habitats.

REST PERIOD: Growing conditions should be maintained all year. In the habitat, rainfall is slightly lower in winter. Water and fertilizer should be reduced for cultivated plants, especially those grown in the dark, short-day conditions common during temperate-latitude winters. They should never be allowed to dry out completely, however. In the habitat, light is probably higher in winter.

GROWING MEDIA: Plants may be mounted on tree-fern or cork slabs if humidity is high and plants are watered at least once daily in summer. When plants are potted, any open, fast-draining medium may be used. Repotting may be done anytime new roots are growing.

MISCELLANEOUS NOTES: The bloom season shown in the climate table is based on collection reports.

Plant and Flower Information

PLANT SIZE AND TYPE: An 18 in. (45 cm) sympodial epiphyte.

PSEUDOBULB: 18 in. (45 cm) long. The stems are somewhat erect.

LEAVES: Many. The lanceolate, spreading leaves are 1.8–2.2 in. (4.5–5.5 cm) long.

INFLORESCENCE: Very short. The blossoms are held in clusters.

FLOWERS: 5–7 per inflorescence. The flowers are 0.5 in. (1.3 cm) long. The orange-yellow blossoms resemble a flared cone. Sepals and petals are paler at the tips. The column is pale yellow, and the anther is violet. The nearly erect dorsal sepal and petals are very small compared to the relatively large, triangular lateral sepals. The hooded lip is squared off at the serrated apex like an elongated triangle with incurved margins.

REFERENCES: 221, 437, 445, 486.

PHOTOS/DRAWINGS: 437.

Dendrobium versicolor Cogniaux.
Plants originated in the Assam region of India, but habitat location and elevation are unavailable, so climate data cannot be selected. They bloomed in July. (Jan.). *D. versicolor* was described as a 16–20 in. (40–50 cm) sympodial epiphyte with slender, elongated stems that were swollen at the nodes. Inflorescences were 2.8–3.5 in. (7–9 cm) long. The greenish red raceme was produced on leafless stems. Blossoms appeared 3–5 per inflorescence. They were 1 in. (2.5 cm) long. Sepals were yellowish green but turned yellowish purple with age. The petals were pale yellow but turned sulfur yellow. The lip may have been greenish or pale yellow. The spur was primarily green with yellow and rose areas. REFERENCES: 70, 218, 254.

Dendrobium versteegii J. J. Smith

AKA: *Cadetia quinquecostata* Schlechter, *D. rumphiae* Rchb. f. var. *quinquecostatum* J. J. Smith and *D. rumphiae* Rchb. f. var. *quinquenervium* Kränzlin. Since *Cadetia* is again considered a valid genus, this plant may belong in that genus.

ORIGIN/HABITAT: Irian Jaya (western New Guinea). Plants grow on trees in primary forests along the Giriwo and Lorentz Rivers.

CLIMATE: Station #97682, Nabire, Irian Jaya (western New Guinea), Lat. 3.3°S, Long. 135.5°E, at 10 ft. (3 m). Record extreme temperatures are not available for this location.

N/HEMISPHERE	JAN	FEB	MAR	APR	MAY	JUN	JUL	AUG	SEP	OCT	NOV	DEC
°F AVG MAX	86	86	86	86	87	87	86	86	87	87	87	87
°F AVG MIN	75	75	76	77	77	76	77	76	75	75	76	76
DIURNAL RANGE	11	11	10	9	10	11	9	11	12	11	11	11
RAIN/INCHES	7.4	11.1	8.5	8.5	7.5	9.0	9.2	10.6	12.1	11.3	10.2	9.8
HUMIDITY/%	N/A											
BLOOM SEASON	*							*				
DAYS CLR	N/A											
RAIN/MM	190	283	217	217	192	228	233	270	308	286	259	248
°C AVG MAX	30.1	29.9	30.1	30.3	30.5	30.6	30.0	30.0	30.5	30.5	30.3	30.3
°C AVG MIN	24.0	24.0	24.3	24.7	24.9	24.5	24.8	24.0	23.8	24.6	24.3	24.2
DIURNAL RANGE	6.1	5.9	5.8	5.6	5.6	6.1	5.2	6.0	6.7	5.9	6.0	6.1
S/HEMISPHERE	JUL	AUG	SEP	OCT	NOV	DEC	JAN	FEB	MAR	APR	MAY	JUN

Cultural Recommendations

LIGHT: 2000–3000 fc.

TEMPERATURES: Throughout the year, days average 86–87°F (30–31°C), and nights average 75–77°F (24–25°C), with a diurnal range of 9–12°F (5–7°C).

HUMIDITY: Information is not available for this location. However, records from nearby stations indicate that humidity is probably about 85% year-round.

WATER: Rainfall is heavy all year. Cultivated plants should be kept evenly moist. Warm water might be beneficial.

FERTILIZER: ¼–½ recommended strength. A balanced fertilizer should be applied weekly to biweekly throughout the year.

REST PERIOD: Growing conditions should be maintained year-round. Water and fertilizer might be reduced slightly in winter, especially for plants grown in the dark, short-day conditions common in temperate latitudes. However, plants should never be allowed to dry out completely. In the habitat, seasonal light variation is minor.

GROWING MEDIA: Plants may be mounted on tree-fern or cork slabs or potted in small pots filled with any open, fast-draining medium. Repotting may be done anytime new roots are growing.

MISCELLANEOUS NOTES: The bloom season shown in the climate table is based on reports from the habitat.

Plant and Flower Information

PLANT SIZE AND TYPE: A 3–7 in. (8–18 cm) sympodial epiphyte.

PSEUDOBULB: 1.4–4.0 in. (3.5–10.0 cm) long. The stems are densely clustered on a very short rhizome.

LEAVES: 1 per growth. The fleshy, lanceolate leaves are 1.8–3.2 in. (4.5–8.0 cm) long, erect, and 2-toothed at the apex.

INFLORESCENCE: 0.3–0.5 in. (0.8–1.3 cm) long. Inflorescences emerge at the apex and from nodes on the side of the stem.

FLOWERS: 1 per inflorescence. The flowers are 0.4 in. (1 cm) long. Blossoms are white, sometimes with pale rose markings at the base of the lip. The erect dorsal sepal is concave and incurved on the upper part and the lower margin is very recurved. Lateral sepals are nearly ovate. The reflexed petals are linear-lanceolate. The 3-lobed lip has erect sidelobes.

REFERENCES: 221, 470, 472.

Dendrobium vestigiiferum J. J. Smith

ORIGIN/HABITAT: Northern Papua New Guinea. Plants grow in the Saruwaged Range near Ogeramnang at about 5900 ft. (1800 m) and near Sattelberg at 2600–5900 ft. (800–1800 m).

CLIMATE: Station #94048, Finschhafen, Papua New Guinea, Lat. 6.6°S, Long. 147.9°E, at 25 ft. (8 m). Temperatures are calculated for an elevation of 4000 ft. (1220 m), resulting in probable extremes of 80°F (27°C) and 55°F (13°C).

N/HEMISPHERE	JAN	FEB	MAR	APR	MAY	JUN	JUL	AUG	SEP	OCT	NOV	DEC
°F AVG MAX	71	70	70	71	73	75	76	76	74	73	71	71
°F AVG MIN	60	59	59	58	58	59	61	61	61	61	60	60
DIURNAL RANGE	11	11	11	13	15	16	15	15	13	12	11	11
RAIN/INCHES	25.8	22.4	20.9	15.8	11.7	8.9	5.5	3.7	5.3	11.9	18.3	23.2
HUMIDITY/%	88	87	86	86	84	85	84	85	86	88	88	88
BLOOM SEASON					*			*				
DAYS CLR	N/A											
RAIN/MM	655	569	531	401	297	226	140	94	135	302	465	589
°C AVG MAX	21.6	21.0	21.0	21.6	22.7	23.8	24.4	24.4	23.3	22.7	21.6	21.6
°C AVG MIN	15.5	14.9	14.9	14.4	14.4	14.9	16.0	16.0	16.0	16.0	15.5	15.5
DIURNAL RANGE	6.1	6.1	6.1	7.2	8.3	8.9	8.4	8.4	7.3	6.7	6.1	6.1
S/HEMISPHERE	JUL	AUG	SEP	OCT	NOV	DEC	JAN	FEB	MAR	APR	MAY	JUN

Cultural Recommendations

LIGHT: 2000–3000 fc.

TEMPERATURES: Throughout the year, days average 70–76°F (21–24°C), and nights average 58–61°F (14–16°C), with a diurnal range of 11–16°F (6–9°C).

HUMIDITY: 85–90% year-round.

WATER: Rainfall is very heavy most of the year, but conditions are slightly drier for 3–4 months in summer. Cultivated plants should be kept evenly moist.

FERTILIZER: ¼–½ recommended strength. A balanced fertilizer should be applied weekly to biweekly throughout the year.

REST PERIOD: Growing conditions should be maintained year-round. In the habitat, rainfall is heaviest in winter. In cultivation, water and fertilizer may be reduced somewhat, especially for plants grown in the dark, short-day conditions common in temperate latitudes. These plants should never be allowed to dry completely, however. In the habitat, seasonal light variation is minor.

GROWING MEDIA: Plants may be mounted on tree-fern or cork slabs or potted in small pots filled with any open, fast-draining medium. Repotting may be done anytime new roots are actively growing.

MISCELLANEOUS NOTES: The bloom season shown in the climate table is based on collection reports.

Plant and Flower Information

PLANT SIZE AND TYPE: A sympodial epiphyte of unreported size.

PSEUDOBULB: The slender stems have erect to spreading branches.

LEAVES: Many. The small leaves are 0.6–1.1 in. (1.4–2.9 cm) long, folded at the base, truncated and unequally bilobed at the tip, and slightly ruffled along the margin. The shiny leaves have dark grooves. They are arranged in 2 rows.

INFLORESCENCE: Short. Inflorescences emerge through 2 leaf sheaths.

FLOWERS: 1 per inflorescence. The white flowers are 0.2 in. (0.5 cm) long. The converging, somewhat sickle-shaped sepals and petals are slender at the tips. The erect, 3-lobed lip has a triangular, incurved midlobe, with erect, angular sidelobes. It has 2 raised, V-shaped lines in the center and a warty, uneven margin.

REFERENCES: 225, 486.

Dendrobium vestitum Wallich.
Now considered a synonym of *Eria vestita* Lindley. REFERENCES: 190, 216, 254, 277.

Dendrobium × *vexabile* Rchb. f.
An apparent natural hybrid described in the 1884 *Gardeners' Chronicle* I, p. 271. Reichenbach indicated that this plant appeared in a group of *D. luteolum* Bateman. The flowers reminded him of *D. ruckeri* Lindley. The stem was said to resemble *D. luteolum*, but it is also compared to *D. falconeri* Hooker. REFERENCES: 216.

Dendrobium vexans Dammer.
See *D. hercoglossum* Rchb. f. REFERENCES: 220, 254, 445, 454.

Dendrobium vexillarius J. J. Smith

AKA: *D. albiviride* P. van Royen, *D. albiviride* var. *minor* P. van Royen, *D. bilamellatum* R. S. Rogers, *D. caenosicallainum* P. van Royen, *D. microblepharum* Schlechter, *D. retroflexum* J. J. Smith, *D. tenens* J. J. Smith, *D. trialatum* Schlechter, *D. trifolium* J. J. Smith, *D. uncinatum* Schlechter, *D. xiphiphorum* P. van Royen. Reeve and Woods (ref. 385) indicate that after additional study *D. brachyphyta* Schlechter and *D. semeion* P. van Royen may be recognized as synonyms.

ORIGIN/HABITAT: New Guinea, New Ireland, and the Molucca Islands. Plants grow at the tips of horizontal tree branches in mistforests, alpine forests, shrubbery, and grasslands. At higher elevations, the normally epiphytic plants grow on the surface of the ground in a deep layer of peat, humus, and moss. They are usually found at 6550–11,500 ft. (2000–3500 m), but some varieties occur as low as 3600 ft. (1100 m).

D. vexillarius var. *albiviride* (P. van Royen) T. M. Reeve and P. Wood grows in the Central and Milne Bay provinces of eastern New Guinea on alpine shrubs at 9200–11,150 ft. (2800–3400 m). The climate table represents the lower, therefore warmer, portion of the habitat. This variety should easily adapt to conditions that are 5–7°F (3–4°C) cooler than indicated. Sepals and petals are pale greenish white to primrose yellow. The lip is green with an orange tip.

D. vexillarius var. *elworthyi* T. M. Reeve and P. Wood occurs in eastern New Guinea on Mt. Michael in Eastern Highlands Province at about 9500 ft. (2900 m) and in the Musa Mountains along the border between the Central and Northern provinces at 3600–4250 ft. (1100–1300 m). Plants grow on elfin trees with many other epiphytic plants on exposed ridge tops at high elevations. Sepals and petals are orange to reddish orange. The dark lip may be purple to nearly black with orange at the tip.

D. vexillarius var. *microblepharum* (Schlechter) T. M. Reeve and P. Wood grows in Irian Jaya (western New Guinea) near Lake Habbema. In Papua, it is found in West Sepik, Enga, East Sepik, and Southern Highlands provinces. Plants are usually found low on mountain trees or shrubs at 5900–9500 ft. (1800–2900 m). The climate table represents the higher, therefore cooler, portion of the habitat. This variety should easily adapt to conditions 3–5°F (2–3°C) warmer than indicated. Sepals and petals are orange, orange-red, or orange-yellow.

D. vexillarius var. *retroflexum* (J. J. Smith) T. M. Reeve and P. Wood. In Irian Jaya (western New Guinea), plants grow on Mt. Jaya (Mt. Carstensz), Mt. Wilhelmina, and near Lake Habbema. In Papua, plants occur west of Laiagam in West Sepik, Enga, and Southern Highlands provinces. Plants grow low on trees or embedded in clumps of moss on alpine shrubbery at 8850–11,300 ft. (2700–3450 m). They are often semipendulous. Sepals and petals are greenish blue, blue, bluish gray, or gray, often suffused with violet. The lip is very dark violet, almost black, with dark orange-red at the tip.

D. vexillarius var. *uncinatum* (Schlechter) T. M. Reeve and P. Wood is found in Irian Jaya (western New Guinea) on the Vogelkop Peninsula, on Mt. Doorman, and along the Idenburg River. In eastern New Guinea, plants grow in many provinces. This variety may also grow on Seram Island in the Moluccas. Plants usually grow on trees at the edges of primary forests, in secondary forest, or in subalpine grasslands at 5250–9200 ft. (1600–2800 m). Sepals and petals are usually pinkish purple, but some clones are pale yellow, orange, carmine, crimson, purplish red, or blue. Blossoms are rarely white and only occasionally yellow or greenish yellow. The lip is dark with dark, pinkish red at the tip. Plants growing in direct sun are more brightly colored. This variety prefers higher light and constant air movement.

D. vexillarius var. *vexillarius* is widespread in eastern and western New Guinea. In the west, plants grow on Mt. Jaya (Mt. Carstensz), Mt. Doorman, Mt. Wilhelmina, and near Lake Habbema. In the east, they occur in numerous provinces. Plants normally grow on small branches and twigs in mountain and alpine forests at 6550–11,500 ft. (2000–3500 m). Flowers are yellow to greenish yellow.

CLIMATE: Botanical garden records, Laiagam, Papua New Guinea, Lat. 5.5°S, Long. 143.5°E, at 7218 ft. (2200 m). Temperatures are calculated for an elevation of 9500 ft. (2900 m), resulting in probable extremes of 83°F (29°C) and 24°F (–4°C).

N/HEMISPHERE	JAN	FEB	MAR	APR	MAY	JUN	JUL	AUG	SEP	OCT	NOV	DEC
°F AVG MAX	68	69	70	68	70	70	74	69	68	70	70	68
°F AVG MIN	47	46	47	47	48	48	47	48	50	49	48	48
DIURNAL RANGE	21	23	23	21	22	22	27	21	18	21	22	20
RAIN/INCHES	4.0	4.8	6.1	7.8	8.5	9.1	8.4	9.6	9.5	8.9	6.3	4.0
HUMIDITY/%	N/A											
BLOOM SEASON	*	*	*	*	*	*				*	*	*
DAYS CLR	N/A											
RAIN/MM	102	122	155	198	216	231	213	244	241	226	160	102
°C AVG MAX	20.2	20.8	21.4	20.2	21.4	21.4	23.6	20.8	20.2	21.4	21.4	20.2
°C AVG MIN	8.6	8.0	8.6	8.6	9.1	9.1	8.6	9.1	10.2	9.7	9.1	9.1
DIURNAL RANGE	11.6	12.8	12.8	11.6	12.3	12.3	15.0	11.7	10.0	11.7	12.3	11.1
S/HEMISPHERE	JUL	AUG	SEP	OCT	NOV	DEC	JAN	FEB	MAR	APR	MAY	JUN

Cultural Recommendations

LIGHT: 2000–3000 fc.

TEMPERATURES: Throughout the year, days average 68–74°F (20–24°C), and nights average 46–50°F (8–10°C), with a diurnal range of 18–27°F (10–15°C).

HUMIDITY: Information is not available for this location. However, records from other stations in the region indicate that humidity probably averages near 80% year-round.

WATER: Rainfall is heavy throughout the year, but conditions are slightly drier for 3–4 months in winter. Cultivated plants should be kept moist.

FERTILIZER: ¼–½ recommended strength. A balanced fertilizer should be applied weekly to biweekly throughout the year.

REST PERIOD: Growing conditions should be maintained all year. Water and fertilizer should be reduced somewhat in winter, especially when plants are grown in the dark, short-day conditions common in temperate latitudes. Plants should dry slightly between waterings, but they should never be allowed to dry out completely. Water and fertilizer should be gradually increased when plants begin growing in spring.

GROWING MEDIA: Plants may be mounted on tree-fern or cork slabs if humidity is high and plants are watered at least once daily in summer. When plants are potted, any open, fast-draining medium may be used. Repotting may be done anytime new roots are growing.

MISCELLANEOUS NOTES: The bloom season is variable. Growers indicate that *D. vexillarius* is difficult to grow, even when they successfully grow other high-altitude New Guinea dendrobiums. They recommend that seedlings be deflasked in early spring.

Plant and Flower Information

PLANT SIZE AND TYPE: A bushy, 5–10 in. (13–25 cm) sympodial epiphyte.

PSEUDOBULB: 5–10 in. (13–25 cm) long. The cylindrical stems consist of 7–10 nodes. Sometimes swollen near the base, they may emerge from a tightly packed root system or, in some habitats, a creeping rhizome. They are often light green.

LEAVES: 2–5 at the apex of each growth. The pointed leaves are 2–6 in. (5–15 cm) long and V-shaped in cross section. They may be linear, elliptic, or ovate. The leaves are dark green on the upper surface and gray-green on the underside. The leaf sheaths are often reddish or dark purple.

INFLORESCENCE: Short. Several inflorescences emerge at or near the apex of leafy and leafless stems, including immature new growths.

FLOWERS: 1–5, rarely as many as 7 per inflorescence. The shiny, fan-shaped flowers are 0.9–2.0 in. (2.2–5.0 cm) long and last up to 6 months. They have an ovate to oblong-elliptic dorsal sepal, with ovate-triangular lateral sepals and somewhat oblong petals. The lip is nearly linear with incurved upper margins and small, rounded sidelobes. The ovary is 3-winged. Flower color is highly variable depending on the variety, as described in the preceding list of varieties.

HYBRIDIZING NOTES: Chromosome count is 2n = 38 (ref. 152, 243).

REFERENCES: 91, 95, 96, 144, 152, 179, 220, 224, 235, 243, 254, 304, 307, 318, 371, 379, 385, 406, 430, 437, 443, 445, 470, 525, 526, 538, 556.

PHOTOS/DRAWINGS: *91, 115, 304, 307, 318, 371, 379, 385, 430, 437, 526, 538, 556.*

Dendrobium victoria-reginae Loher

AKA: Sometimes spelled *D. victoriae-reginae. D. coeleste* Loher is a synonym. *D. victoria-reginae* Loher var. *miyakei* (Schlechter) Liu and Su is considered a synonym of *D. miyakei* Schlechter.

ORIGIN/HABITAT: The Philippine islands. Plants are found on Camiguin, Luzon, Mindanao, Mindoro, and Negros Islands. They grow in dense, mossy forests with oak, rhododendron, azalea, and myrtle at 4250–8700 ft. (1300–2650 m). On Luzon, plants are found near Baguio in Benguet Province, near Bontoc in Mountain Province, as well as in the provinces of Ifugao, Pampanga, and Nueva Vizcaya.

CLIMATE: Station #98328, Baguio, Luzon, Philippines, Lat. 16.4°N, Long. 120.6°E, at 4926 ft. (1512 m). Temperatures are calculated for an elevation of 6500 ft. (1980 m), resulting in probable extremes of 79°F (26°C) and 41°F (5°C).

N/HEMISPHERE	JAN	FEB	MAR	APR	MAY	JUN	JUL	AUG	SEP	OCT	NOV	DEC
°F AVG MAX	67	68	71	72	71	70	66	66	66	68	69	69
°F AVG MIN	50	51	53	55	56	56	55	55	55	55	54	52
DIURNAL RANGE	17	17	18	17	15	14	11	11	11	13	15	17
RAIN/INCHES	0.9	0.9	1.7	4.3	15.8	17.2	42.3	45.7	28.1	15.0	4.9	2.0
HUMIDITY/%	83	83	83	85	89	90	93	93	92	89	86	84
BLOOM SEASON	*	*	*	*	***	***	**	*	*	*	*	*
DAYS CLR	N/A											
RAIN/MM	23	23	43	109	401	437	1074	1161	714	381	124	51
°C AVG MAX	19.4	20.0	21.6	22.2	21.6	21.1	18.8	18.8	18.8	20.0	20.5	20.5
°C AVG MIN	10.0	10.5	11.6	12.7	13.3	13.3	12.7	12.7	12.7	12.7	12.2	11.1
DIURNAL RANGE	9.4	9.5	10.0	9.5	8.3	7.8	6.1	6.1	6.1	7.3	8.3	9.4
S/HEMISPHERE	JUL	AUG	SEP	OCT	NOV	DEC	JAN	FEB	MAR	APR	MAY	JUN

Cultural Recommendations

LIGHT: 1500–2500 fc. Diffused or dappled light is recommended. Sky-cover records are unavailable, but high elevations are typically cloudy in this region. Growers indicate that excessive light causes premature leaf-drop.

TEMPERATURES: Throughout the year, days average 66–72°F (19–22°C), and nights average 50–56°F (10–13°C), with a diurnal range of 11–18°F (6–10°C). Plants do not tolerate hot temperatures, but they may grow well in conditions slightly warmer than indicated.

HUMIDITY: 85–90% year-round.

WATER: Rainfall is very heavy from late spring into autumn, but conditions are much drier in winter. Cultivated plants should be kept moist but not soggy during the growing season. Water should be gradually reduced after new growths mature in autumn.

FERTILIZER: ¼–½ recommended strength, applied weekly. A high nitrogen fertilizer is beneficial from spring to midsummer, but a fertilizer high in phosphates should be used in late summer and autumn.

REST PERIOD: Growing temperatures should be maintained all year. Growers recommend keeping winter lows above 41°F (5°C). Rainfall is low for 2–4 months in winter, but the continuing high humidity indicates that additional moisture is frequently available from fog, dew, or mist. Cultivated plants should be allowed to dry somewhat between waterings, but should never remain dry for long periods. In the habitat, light may be highest in winter.

GROWING MEDIA: Plants are most easily managed when placed in a basket or mounted on a cork slab or raft with a moisture-retaining pad. This accommodates the pendulous growth habit. If plants must be potted, small pots may be filled with an open, fast-draining medium. Repotting is best done in early spring when new roots are growing.

MISCELLANEOUS NOTES: The bloom season shown in the climate table is based on cultivation records. Plants bloom intermittently, often twice a year. Growers indicate that plants do not survive cultivation in Manila, but grow well in Honolulu, which is about 10°F (6°C) cooler. Constant air movement is particularly important if light is high or temperatures are warm.

Plant and Flower Information

PLANT SIZE AND TYPE: A 10–24 in. (25–60 cm) sympodial epiphyte. Plants occasionally reach a length of 48 in. (122 cm).

PSEUDOBULB: 10–48 in. (25–122 cm) long. The stemlike pseudobulbs are orange-yellow and profusely branching. The internodes taper then become swollen at the nodes. They are covered with gradually deteriorating sheaths. The branches often form a tangled mass of roots and branches. They are pendulous because the stems are too slender to support their own weight.

LEAVES: 10–14 per growth. The leaves are 2.4 in. (6 cm) long, pointed, shiny, and linear- to oblong-lanceolate. They are deciduous with a papery texture.

INFLORESCENCE: Very short. The small clusters of flowers are usually borne at nodes on older leafless stems.

FLOWERS: 1–6, rarely 12 per cluster. The waxy flowers are 1.2–1.6 in. (3–4 cm) across, but do not open widely. The slender sepals and petals are white with blue-violet on the apical part of the segments. The unlobed lip is marked with 5 violet, deep blue-violet, or purplish red lines. It is ovate, pointed, and flattened or concave. The disk is yellow or orange. Clones with white and pink blossoms have been found. Blossoms are not fragrant.

HYBRIDIZING NOTES: Chromosome count is 2n = 38 (ref. 152, 504, 580). Plants are self-fertile.

REFERENCES: 6, 12, 20, 36, 79, 98, 152, 154, 179, 190, 196, 210, 234, 236, 254, 293, 296, 371, 389, 430, 445, 497, 504, 524, 536, 580.

PHOTOS/DRAWINGS: 6, *36, 79, 98,* 210, *287, 371, 389, 430, 497, 539.*

Dendrobium villosipes J. J. Smith

ORIGIN/HABITAT: Irian Jaya (western New Guinea). Plants grow on rocks on steep, south-facing schist slopes in the Treub Range at 6550–7850 ft. (2000–2400 m).

CLIMATE: Station #97686, Wamena, New Guinea, Lat. 4.1°S, Long. 139.0°E, at 5446 ft. (1660 m). Temperatures are calculated for an elevation of 7850 ft. (2400 m). Extreme temperatures, relative humidity, and cloud cover records are not available for this location.

N/HEMISPHERE	JAN	FEB	MAR	APR	MAY	JUN	JUL	AUG	SEP	OCT	NOV	DEC
°F AVG MAX	67	68	69	68	69	68	69	68	68	71	70	66
°F AVG MIN	52	52	54	54	55	56	55	54	55	57	57	53
DIURNAL RANGE	15	16	15	14	14	12	14	14	13	14	13	13
RAIN/INCHES	3.0	1.9	2.2	4.0	4.6	3.3	2.8	4.2	6.9	3.9	5.4	4.9
HUMIDITY/%	N/A											
BLOOM SEASON												
DAYS CLR	N/A											
RAIN/MM	76	48	56	102	117	84	71	107	175	99	137	124
°C AVG MAX	19.4	20.0	20.5	20.0	20.5	20.0	20.5	20.0	20.0	21.7	21.1	18.9
°C AVG MIN	11.1	11.1	12.2	12.2	12.8	13.3	12.8	12.2	12.8	13.9	13.9	11.7
DIURNAL RANGE	8.3	8.9	8.3	7.8	7.7	6.7	7.7	7.8	7.2	7.8	7.2	7.2
S/HEMISPHERE	JUL	AUG	SEP	OCT	NOV	DEC	JAN	FEB	MAR	APR	MAY	JUN

Cultural Recommendations

LIGHT: 1500–2500 fc. Plants may tolerate higher light levels, especially in the morning.

TEMPERATURES: Throughout the year, days average 67–71°F (19–22°C), and nights average 52–57°F (11–14°C), with a diurnal range of 12–16°F (7–9°C). In the habitat, the warmest temperatures of the day occur during late morning. Clouds and mist develop near noon, thus preventing additional warming. Because of microclimate effects, actual maximum temperatures may be somewhat warmer than indicated. Reports from the habitat indicate a sharp contrast between day and night temperatures.

HUMIDITY: Information is not available for this location. However, average humidity in mistforest habitats normally exceeds 80% year-round.

WATER: Rainfall is moderate through most of the year. In the higher-elevation habitat, rainfall amounts may be greater than indicated in the climate table. In addition, large amounts of water are available from mist and heavy dew, even during periods of reduced rainfall. Cultivated plants should be kept moist, with only slight drying allowed between waterings. They may need to be misted several times daily on the hottest days, but the foliage should always be dry before evening. Good air movement is critically important and should be maintained at all times.

FERTILIZER: ¼–½ recommended strength. A balanced fertilizer should be applied weekly to biweekly throughout the year. The Royal Botanic Garden in Edinburgh uses a dilute, seaweed-based fertilizer.

REST PERIOD: Growing conditions should be maintained all year. Rainfall averages are somewhat lower for a month or so in winter and again in midsummer. In cultivation, water may be decreased, but plants should never be allowed to dry out completely. In the habitat, light is slightly higher in winter.

GROWING MEDIA: Plants may be mounted on tree-fern or cork slabs if humidity is high and plants are watered at least once daily in summer. When plants are potted, any open, fast-draining medium may be used. Repotting may be done anytime new roots are growing.

MISCELLANEOUS NOTES: The bloom season shown in the climate table is based on reports from the habitat. The plant was described in 1914 in *Bull. Jard. Bot. Buit.* 2nd sér. 13:64.

Plant and Flower Information

PLANT SIZE AND TYPE: A 39 in. (100 cm) sympodial epiphyte.

PSEUDOBULB: 39 in. (100 cm) long. The clustered stems are elliptical in cross-section. They are borne on a short rhizome.

LEAVES: Many. The lanceolate to ovate-oblong leaves are 1.4–3.1 in. (3.5–8.0 cm) long. They are bilobed with 2 teeth at the apex and recurved along the margin.

INFLORESCENCE: 1.0–1.8 in. (2.5–4.5 cm) long. The inflorescences emerge through the sheaths at nodes on leafy stems.

FLOWERS: 3–9 per inflorescence. The fleshy flowers are 0.4 in. (1 cm) long. The concave sepals and petals are pale green and red. The ovate dorsal sepal is rounded with a short point at the apex and an uneven margin. Lateral sepals are broadly triangular. The oblong petals have 2 tiny teeth at the apex. The erect lip is yellow with violet at the base. It is 3-lobed, warty, recurved at the tip, with a somewhat T-shaped callus and a slightly wavy, uneven margin.

REFERENCES: 221, 470.

Dendrobium villosulum Lindley (1852)

AKA: Seidenfaden and Wood (ref. 455) include *D. melanochlamys* Holttum as a synonym for which Holttum (ref. 200) included *D. villosulum* Wallich as a synonym. Hunt (ref. 211) includes *D. villosulum* Lindley 1852 not Lindley 1829 as a synonym of *D. nutans* Lindley.

Dendrobium villosulum

ORIGIN/HABITAT: Malaya, including Kedah Peak, Mt. Ophir (Mt. Ledang), and the lowlands of Singapore. Plants grow on the surface of the ground in decaying leaves and other forest litter in dry, lightly shaded places. In Borneo, they grow near Matang at 2000–3000 ft. (600–900 m). On Gurulau Spur of Mt. Kinabalu, the orchids are found on rotting logs at 3500–5500 ft. (1070–1680 m).

CLIMATE: Station #48625, Ipoh, Malaya, Lat. 4.6°N, Long. 101.1°E, at 123 ft. (37 m). Temperatures are calculated for an estimated plant elevation of 3500 ft. (1070 m), resulting in probable extremes of 88°F (31°C) and 53°F (12°C).

N/HEMISPHERE	JAN	FEB	MAR	APR	MAY	JUN	JUL	AUG	SEP	OCT	NOV	DEC
°F AVG MAX	79	81	82	81	81	81	80	80	79	78	78	78
°F AVG MIN	61	61	62	62	63	62	61	61	62	61	61	61
DIURNAL RANGE	18	20	20	19	18	19	19	19	17	17	17	17
RAIN/INCHES	7.9	3.1	7.6	8.4	6.2	3.6	7.2	6.9	8.8	11.0	13.0	8.9
HUMIDITY/%	76	74	76	78	78	75	76	77	79	82	82	81
BLOOM SEASON		*										
DAYS CLR @ 7AM	3	3	3	1	1	2	1	1	0	0	1	2
DAYS CLR @ 1PM	2	2	2	1	1	1	1	1	0	0	0	2
RAIN/MM	201	79	193	213	157	91	183	175	224	279	330	226
°C AVG MAX	26.0	27.1	27.7	27.1	27.1	27.1	26.6	26.6	26.0	25.5	25.5	25.5
°C AVG MIN	16.0	16.0	16.6	16.6	17.1	16.6	16.0	16.0	16.6	16.0	16.0	16.0
DIURNAL RANGE	10.0	11.1	11.1	10.5	10.0	10.5	10.6	10.6	9.4	9.5	9.5	9.5
S/HEMISPHERE	JUL	AUG	SEP	OCT	NOV	DEC	JAN	FEB	MAR	APR	MAY	JUN

Cultural Recommendations

LIGHT: 2500–3500 fc.

TEMPERATURES: Throughout the year, days average 78–82°F (26–28°C), and nights average 61–63°F (16–17°C), with a diurnal range of 17–20°F (9–11°C).

HUMIDITY: 75–80% year-round.

WATER: Rainfall is heavy most of the year. The heaviest rainfall occurs in autumn with a secondary maximum in spring. Brief semidry periods occur in midwinter and midsummer. Cultivated plants should be kept evenly moist, with only slight drying allowed between waterings.

FERTILIZER: ¼–½ recommended strength. A balanced fertilizer should be applied weekly to biweekly throughout the year.

REST PERIOD: Growing conditions should be maintained year-round. Water should be reduced somewhat in winter for plants cultivated in the dark, short-day conditions common in temperate latitudes. They should never be allowed to dry out completely, however. Fertilizer may be reduced when the plant is not actively growing or when water is reduced. In the habitat, light is slightly higher in winter.

GROWING MEDIA: Plants may be mounted on tree-fern or cork slabs if humidity is high and plants are watered at least once daily in summer. When plants are potted, any open, fast-draining medium may be used. Repotting may be done anytime new roots are growing.

MISCELLANEOUS NOTES: The bloom season shown in the climate table is based on reports from the habitat.

Plant and Flower Information

PLANT SIZE AND TYPE: A 24–39 in. (60–100 cm) sympodial terrestrial.

PSEUDOBULB: 24–39 in. (60–100 cm) long. The stems, which sometimes branch, are slender, wiry, and graceful with 0.4–0.8 in. (1–2 cm) internodes.

LEAVES: Many. The linear-lanceolate leaves are usually 2 in. (5 cm) long, rigid, channeled, recurved along the margin, unequally bilobed at the tip, and arranged in 2 rows. Leaves are held at right angles to the stem. The leaf sheaths are spotted and covered with long black hairs.

INFLORESCENCE: Short. The inflorescence emerges from sheaths.

FLOWERS: 1 per inflorescence. The pendulous flowers are 0.6 in. (1.5 cm) across. The slender sepals and petals may be white or yellowish with pale red veins. The linear petals are recurved. The lip is 3-lobed. The rounded midlobe is primrose yellow with a thickened area on each side at the apex. The blunt sidelobes are erect.

REFERENCES: 12, 59, 200, 202, 211, 225, 254, 277, 286, 295, 310, 394, 395, 402, 454, 455, 586.

PHOTOS/DRAWINGS: 455.

Dendrobium villosulum Wallich.

Holttum (ref. 200) and Schlechter (ref. 437) include this name as a member of the section *Conostalix*. Holttum considered *D. villosulum* Wallich the basis for *D. melanochlamys* Holttum. However, Seidenfaden and Wood (ref. 455) include *D. melanochlamys* as a synonym of *D. villosulum* Lindley. REFERENCES: 200, 216, 437, 445, 586.

Dendrobium × *vinicolor* St. Cloud.

See *D.* × *superbiens* Rchb. f. REFERENCES: 67, 105, 229, 240, 262, 533.

Dendrobium vinosum Schlechter

ORIGIN/HABITAT: Papua New Guinea. Plants grow in the Sepik River region at about 3450 ft. (1050 m).

CLIMATE: Station #200004, Ambunti, Papua New Guinea, Lat. 4.2°S, Long. 142.8°E, at 164 ft. (50 m). Temperatures are calculated for an elevation of 3750 ft. (1140 m), resulting in probable extremes of 87°F (31°C) and 40°F (5°C).

N/HEMISPHERE	JAN	FEB	MAR	APR	MAY	JUN	JUL	AUG	SEP	OCT	NOV	DEC
°F AVG MAX	76	78	78	78	79	78	78	78	78	78	78	77
°F AVG MIN	60	61	62	61	61	61	60	61	61	61	61	62
DIURNAL RANGE	16	17	16	17	18	17	18	17	17	17	17	15
RAIN/INCHES	6.4	7.4	7.7	8.5	9.2	9.4	10.9	10.2	12.2	10.4	8.3	5.2
HUMIDITY/%	N/A											
BLOOM SEASON		*										
DAYS CLR	N/A											
RAIN/MM	163	188	196	216	234	239	277	259	310	264	211	132
°C AVG MAX	24.5	25.6	25.6	25.6	26.2	25.6	25.6	25.6	25.6	25.6	25.6	25.1
°C AVG MIN	15.6	16.2	16.8	16.2	16.2	16.2	15.6	16.2	16.2	16.2	16.2	16.8
DIURNAL RANGE	8.9	9.4	8.8	9.4	10.0	9.4	10.0	9.4	9.4	9.4	9.4	8.3
S/HEMISPHERE	JUL	AUG	SEP	OCT	NOV	DEC	JAN	FEB	MAR	APR	MAY	JUN

Cultural Recommendations

LIGHT: 2000–3000 fc.

TEMPERATURES: Throughout the year, days average 76–79°F (25–26°C), and nights average 60–62°F (16–17°C), with a diurnal range of 15–18°F (8–10°C).

HUMIDITY: Information is not available for this location. However, records from nearby locations indicate that humidity probably averages near 80% year-round.

WATER: Rainfall is heavy year-round, with the greatest amounts falling in summer and early autumn. Cultivated plants should never be allowed to dry completely.

FERTILIZER: ¼–½ recommended strength. A balanced fertilizer should be applied weekly to biweekly throughout the year.

REST PERIOD: Growing temperatures should be maintained all year. Water and fertilizer should be reduced for plants cultivated in the dark, short-day conditions common during temperate-latitude winters. However, plants should never be allowed to dry out completely. In the habitat, light is highest in winter.

GROWING MEDIA: Plants may be mounted on cork or tree-fern slabs if humidity is high and plants are watered at least once daily in summer. When plants are potted, any open, fast-draining medium may be used, but fir bark is preferred by most growers. Repotting may be done anytime new roots are growing.

MISCELLANEOUS NOTES: The bloom season shown in the climate table is based on reports from the habitat.

Plant and Flower Information

PLANT SIZE AND TYPE: A shrublike, 28 in. (70 cm) sympodial epiphyte.

PSEUDOBULB: 28 in. (70 cm) long. The leafy stems, which emerge from a very short rhizome, are flattened and do not branch.

LEAVES: Many. The somewhat linear leaves are 1.2–2.6 in. (3.0–6.5 cm) long and unequally bilobed at the apex.

INFLORESCENCE: Short.

FLOWERS: 1 per inflorescence. The flowers are wine-red, inverted, and less than 0.5 in. (1.3 cm) across. Blossoms have an ovate-oblong dorsal sepal, triangular-ovate lateral sepals, and somewhat tongue-shaped petals. The 3-lobed lip is roundly oval with short, nearly oblong side-lobes. The midlobe is nearly circular with a ruffled margin.

REFERENCES: 223, 443.

Dendrobium violaceoflavens J. J. Smith

AKA: Sometimes spelled *D. violaceo-flavens*.

ORIGIN/HABITAT: Irian Jaya (western New Guinea). Plants grow near sea level. They have been found in the region around Jayapura, along the Mamberamo River, and in southern New Guinea along the Kepulauan (Becking) River. Occasionally found on rocks, the orchid also grows on tall trees as high as 100 ft. (30 m) above the ground.

CLIMATE: Station #97690, Sentani/Jayapura, Irian Jaya, Lat. 2.7°S, Long. 140.5°E, at 289 ft. (88 m). Record extreme temperatures are 97°F (36°C) and 68°F (20°C).

N/HEMISPHERE	JAN	FEB	MAR	APR	MAY	JUN	JUL	AUG	SEP	OCT	NOV	DEC
°F AVG MAX	87	89	89	90	89	89	89	88	89	90	90	89
°F AVG MIN	72	72	72	73	73	73	73	73	73	74	73	73
DIURNAL RANGE	15	17	17	17	17	16	16	15	16	16	17	16
RAIN/INCHES	4.1	3.9	5.3	2.9	6.7	7.0	8.3	8.3	8.5	4.6	2.4	5.2
HUMIDITY/%	81	80	80	79	81	81	79	80	80	80	81	80
BLOOM SEASON	*									*		
DAYS CLR @ 9AM	5	3	4	3	2	1	1	0	1	2	2	5
DAYS CLR @ 3PM	4	3	3	3	2	1	3	0	1	2	2	3
RAIN/MM	104	99	135	74	170	178	211	211	216	117	61	132
°C AVG MAX	30.6	31.7	31.7	32.2	32.2	31.7	31.7	31.1	31.7	32.2	32.2	31.7
°C AVG MIN	22.2	22.2	22.2	22.8	22.8	22.8	22.8	22.8	22.8	23.3	22.8	22.8
DIURNAL RANGE	8.3	9.4	9.4	9.4	9.4	8.9	8.9	8.3	8.9	8.9	9.4	8.9
S/HEMISPHERE	JUL	AUG	SEP	OCT	NOV	DEC	JAN	FEB	MAR	APR	MAY	JUN

Cultural Recommendations

LIGHT: 1500–3000 fc. Growers report that plants grow well in shade to half-shade.

TEMPERATURES: Throughout the year, days average 87–90°F (31–32°C), and nights average 72–74°F (22–23°C), with a diurnal range of 15–17°F (8–9°C).

HUMIDITY: Near 80% year-round.

WATER: Rainfall is moderate to heavy most of the year, with brief, semidry periods in spring and autumn. Cultivated plants should be kept moist with only slight drying allowed between waterings.

FERTILIZER: ¼–½ recommended strength. A balanced fertilizer should be applied weekly to biweekly throughout the year.

REST PERIOD: Growing conditions should be maintained year-round. Cultivated plants should never be allowed to dry out completely. However, water and fertilizer should be reduced somewhat for plants grown in the dark, short-day conditions common in temperate-latitude winters. In the habitat, light is highest in winter.

GROWING MEDIA: Plants may be mounted on tree-fern or cork slabs if humidity is high and plants are watered at least once daily in summer. When plants are potted, any open, fast-draining medium may be used. Repotting may be done anytime new roots are growing.

MISCELLANEOUS NOTES: The bloom season shown in the climate table is based on cultivation and collection records. Growers indicate that plants grow well in Java but do poorly in Singapore.

Plant and Flower Information

PLANT SIZE AND TYPE: A 59–79 in. (150–200 cm) sympodial epiphyte or lithophyte. Plants sometimes reach a length of 217 in. (550 cm).

PSEUDOBULB: 59–79 in. (150–200 cm) long. This giant plant is one of the tallest pseudobulbous orchids known. The leafy stems are erect, cane-like, and taper toward the apex.

LEAVES: Many. The elliptic to lanceolate leaves are 5.5–9.0 in. (14–23 cm) long. They are leathery, persistent, recurved along the margin, and grooved on the upper surface.

INFLORESCENCE: 12–24 in. (30–60 cm) long. The laxly flowered inflorescences emerge from upper nodes on leafy stems. They may be erect or horizontal.

FLOWERS: 10–20, sometimes more per inflorescence. The flowers are 1.8–2.4 in. (4.5–6.0 cm) across. Sepals and petals are usually yellow, but they may be pea green or creamy white. The dorsal sepal is oblong, truncate, and rounded. The slender lateral sepals are somewhat triangular. The twisted petals are linear. The lip is erect, linear, and 3-lobed. It has 5 keels which are decorated with blue, violet, or dark purple spotting. A single awarded plant carried 810 blossoms on 54 inflorescences.

HYBRIDIZING NOTES: When used as a parent, *D. violaceoflavens'* colors tend to be dominant. It also contributes a heavy, waxy flower texture, spikes with numerous flowers, long flower life, and a rounded flower form.

REFERENCES: 25, 84, 179, 190, 196, 200, 224, 345, 351, 445, 470, 537.

PHOTOS/DRAWINGS: *84, 342, 345, 351*.

Dendrobium violaceominiatum Schlechter

AKA: Sometimes spelled *D. violaceo-miniatum*.

ORIGIN/HABITAT: The Caroline and Solomon Islands. In the Caroline Islands, plants are found on Ponape near Patapat. The orchids usually grow in low-elevation mossforests at 650–1000 ft. (200–300 m), but they are also found on Mt. Tolotom and Mt. Kubersoh at 2000–2100 ft. (610–640 m). Plants often grow in open sunny areas on *Hibicus tiliaceus*. In the Solomons, plants are found on New Georgia and Kolombangara in mountain forests at 800–1950 ft. (240–600 m).

CLIMATE: Station #91348, Ponape, Caroline Islands, Lat. 7.0°N, Long. 158.2°E, at 121 ft. (37 m). Temperatures are calculated for an elevation of 800 ft. (240 m). Record extreme temperatures are not available for this location.

N/HEMISPHERE	JAN	FEB	MAR	APR	MAY	JUN	JUL	AUG	SEP	OCT	NOV	DEC
°F AVG MAX	84	84	85	86	86	85	85	86	86	86	86	85
°F AVG MIN	75	75	75	75	74	74	73	72	73	73	73	74
DIURNAL RANGE	9	9	10	11	12	11	12	14	13	13	13	11
RAIN/INCHES	13.7	9.4	11.2	12.6	15.2	23.8	22.9	17.1	17.4	15.7	17.0	16.7
HUMIDITY/%	N/A											
BLOOM SEASON										*		
DAYS CLR	N/A											
RAIN/MM	348	239	284	320	386	605	582	434	442	399	432	424
°C AVG MAX	28.8	28.8	29.3	29.9	29.9	29.3	29.3	29.9	29.9	29.9	29.9	29.3
°C AVG MIN	23.8	23.8	23.8	23.8	23.2	23.2	22.6	22.1	22.6	22.6	22.6	23.2
DIURNAL RANGE	5.0	5.0	5.6	6.1	6.7	6.1	6.7	7.8	7.2	7.2	7.2	6.1
S/HEMISPHERE	JUL	AUG	SEP	OCT	NOV	DEC	JAN	FEB	MAR	APR	MAY	JUN

Cultural Recommendations

LIGHT: 2500–3500 fc.

TEMPERATURES: Throughout the year, days average 84–86°F (29–30°C), and nights average 72–75°F (22–24°C), with a diurnal range of 9–14°F (5–8°C).

HUMIDITY: Information is not available for this location. However, records from nearby stations indicate that humidity is probably near 80% year-round.

WATER: Rainfall is heavy to very heavy all year. Cultivated plants should be kept wet but not soggy.

FERTILIZER: ¼–½ recommended strength. A balanced fertilizer should be applied weekly to biweekly throughout the year.

REST PERIOD: Growing temperatures should be maintained all year. Water and fertilizer should be reduced in winter, especially for plants grown in the dark, short-day conditions common in temperate latitudes. Plants should never be allowed to dry out completely, however. In the habitat, seasonal light variation is minor.

GROWING MEDIA: Plants may be mounted on tree-fern or cork slabs if humidity is high and plants are watered at least once daily in summer. When plants are potted, any open, fast-draining medium may be used. Repotting may be done anytime new roots are growing.

MISCELLANEOUS NOTES: The bloom season shown in the climate table is based on collection reports.

Plant and Flower Information

PLANT SIZE AND TYPE: A 1.2–2.0 in. (3–5 cm) sympodial epiphyte.

PSEUDOBULB: 0.4 in. (1 cm) long. The tufted growths arise from a very short rhizome. They develop longitudinal grooves when dry.

LEAVES: 2 at the apex of each growth. The smooth, linear leaves are 0.8–1.4 in. (2.0–3.5 cm) long.

INFLORESCENCE: Short. The erect inflorescences arise from the apex of mature leafy and leafless pseudobulbs.

FLOWERS: 2 per inflorescence. The tiny flowers are 0.5–0.6 in. (1.2–1.6 cm) long. The sepals and petals may be white, bluish, or violet. Blossoms have lanceolate sepals and linear petals. The apex of the white lip is often marked with orange-red or brick-red. It is linear with a sharp, triangular point at the apex.

REFERENCES: 189, 223, 271, 385, 441.

PHOTOS/DRAWINGS: 385.

Dendrobium violaceopictum Schlechter

AKA: Sometimes spelled *D. violaceo-pictum.*

ORIGIN/HABITAT: Papua New Guinea. Plants grow on forest trees in the Ibo and the Finisterre Ranges at 3300–3950 ft. (1000–1200 m).

CLIMATE: Station #200187, Erap, Papua New Guinea, Lat. 6.6°S, Long. 146.7°E, at 850 ft. (260 m). Temperatures are calculated for an elevation of 3300 ft. (1000 m), resulting in probable extremes of 94°F (34°C) and 45°F (7°C).

N/HEMISPHERE	JAN	FEB	MAR	APR	MAY	JUN	JUL	AUG	SEP	OCT	NOV	DEC
°F AVG MAX	80	80	81	82	85	85	85	85	85	84	82	82
°F AVG MIN	61	61	61	62	64	65	64	64	65	63	66	62
DIURNAL RANGE	19	19	20	20	21	20	21	21	20	21	16	20
RAIN/INCHES	3.9	3.9	2.7	3.0	3.0	5.3	5.9	5.9	7.0	3.4	2.4	3.1
HUMIDITY/%	82	81	81	79	75	74	74	74	77	76	80	80
BLOOM SEASON					*	*						
DAYS CLR	N/A											
RAIN/MM	99	99	69	76	76	135	150	150	178	86	61	79
°C AVG MAX	26.7	26.7	27.2	27.8	29.4	29.4	29.4	29.4	29.4	28.9	27.8	27.8
°C AVG MIN	16.1	16.1	16.1	16.7	17.8	18.3	17.8	17.8	18.3	17.2	18.9	16.7
DIURNAL RANGE	10.6	10.6	11.1	11.1	11.6	11.1	11.6	11.6	11.1	11.7	8.9	11.1
S/HEMISPHERE	JUL	AUG	SEP	OCT	NOV	DEC	JAN	FEB	MAR	APR	MAY	JUN

Cultural Recommendations

LIGHT: 2500–3500 fc.

TEMPERATURES: Throughout the year, days average 80–85°F (27–29°C), and nights average 61–66°F (16–19°C), with a diurnal range of 16–21°F (9–12°C).

HUMIDITY: 75–80% year-round. Despite high average humidity, the habitat may be quite dry during hot afternoons.

WATER: Rainfall is moderate most of the year, but for 4–5 months in summer and early autumn, conditions are wetter. Cultivated plants should be thoroughly saturated then allowed to dry slightly between waterings.

FERTILIZER: ¼–½ recommended strength. A balanced fertilizer should be applied weekly to biweekly throughout the year.

REST PERIOD: Growing temperatures should be maintained all year. In the habitat, rainfall is lowest in winter, but the high humidity indicates that additional moisture is frequently available from heavy dew. Cultivated plants should be allowed to dry for somewhat longer between waterings, but should not remain dry for extended periods. Fertilizer should be reduced until water is increased in spring. In the habitat, seasonal light variation is minor.

GROWING MEDIA: Plants may be mounted on tree-fern or cork slabs or potted in small pots filled with any open, fast-draining medium. Repotting may be done anytime new roots are growing.

MISCELLANEOUS NOTES: The bloom season shown in the climate table is based on collection reports. Plants that produce flowers which last a single day commonly bloom several times during the year. Flowering usually occurs 7–14 days after a sudden 10°F (5°C) drop in daytime temperatures.

Plant and Flower Information

PLANT SIZE AND TYPE: A 12–18 in. (30–45 cm) sympodial epiphyte.

PSEUDOBULB: 12–18 in. (30–45 cm) long.

LEAVES: Many. The smooth, lanceolate leaves are 2.4–3.5 in. (6–9 cm) long and somewhat erect.

INFLORESCENCE: Short. The blossoms are held almost opposite each other.

FLOWERS: 2 per inflorescence. The short-lived white flowers are 0.9 in. (2.2 cm) long. Sepals and petals have a full, inward curl at the tip. The deeply 3-lobed lip is closely spotted with violet-red. It is recurved with a raised ridge in the center. The column is white.

REFERENCES: 92, 221, 437, 445.

PHOTOS/DRAWINGS: 437.

Dendrobium violaceum Kränzlin

AKA: Reeve and Woods (ref. 385) recognize the following synonyms:

For *D. violaceum* subsp. *violaceum*, they include *D. allioides* J. J. Smith, *D. brachyacron* Schlechter, *D. dryadum* Schlechter, *D. geminiflorum* Schlechter, *D. pityphyllum* Schlechter, *D. quinquecostatum* Schlechter, and *D. tenuicalcar* J. J. Smith.

For *D. violaceum* subsp. *cyperifolium* (Schlechter) T. M. Reeve and P. J. B. Woods, they include the synonyms *D. cyperifolium* Schlechter, *D. igneoviolaceum* J. J. Smith, and *D. scotiiferum* J. J. Smith.

ORIGIN/HABITAT: New Guinea. *D. violaceum* subsp. *violaceum* is found from the West Nassau Mountains in Irian Jaya (western New Guinea) to Milne Bay Province at the southeastern tip of the island. Plants usually grow at 2450–6550 ft. (750–2000 m) in the higher-light conditions of juvenile secondary forest or at the margins of primary mountain forests. Plants are epiphytic, but they occasionally grow on rocks or the surface of the ground. *D. violaceum* subsp. *cyperifolium* occurs primarily in Irian Jaya (western New Guinea), where it grows on Mt. Jaya (Mt. Carstensz), in the Cyclop Mountains, and near Wissel Lakes. However, the orchids also grow in the western part of Papua New Guinea in East Sepik, West Sepik, and Enga provinces. They are frequently found on the horizontal branches of mistforest trees on the open slopes of the Finisterre Range at 3950–6550 ft. (1200–2000 m).

CLIMATE: Station #200243, Mt. Hagen, Papua New Guinea, Lat. 5.8°S, Long. 144.3°E, at 5350 ft. (1630 m). Extreme temperatures are 88°F (31°C) and 35°F (2°C).

N/HEMISPHERE	JAN	FEB	MAR	APR	MAY	JUN	JUL	AUG	SEP	OCT	NOV	DEC
°F AVG MAX	72	73	74	75	76	76	76	76	75	75	76	74
°F AVG MIN	55	55	55	55	55	56	56	56	56	57	56	54
DIURNAL RANGE	17	18	19	20	21	20	20	20	19	18	20	20
RAIN/INCHES	5.2	6.7	8.7	8.7	8.2	10.2	10.4	10.7	11.2	10.0	7.2	4.7
HUMIDITY/%	84	83	82	78	79	81	81	80	82	81	82	82
BLOOM SEASON			*	*	*	*	*	*	*	*	*	
DAYS CLR	N/A											
RAIN/MM	131	171	221	221	208	258	264	271	285	253	184	119
°C AVG MAX	22.4	22.7	23.2	23.9	24.3	24.2	24.2	24.4	23.8	23.9	24.3	23.1
°C AVG MIN	12.5	12.7	12.6	12.5	12.7	13.3	13.4	13.3	13.4	13.7	13.4	12.4
DIURNAL RANGE	9.9	10.0	10.6	11.4	11.6	10.9	10.8	11.1	10.4	10.2	10.9	10.7
S/HEMISPHERE	JUL	AUG	SEP	OCT	NOV	DEC	JAN	FEB	MAR	APR	MAY	JUN

Cultural Recommendations

LIGHT: 2500–3500 fc. Strong air movement should be provided year-round.

TEMPERATURES: Throughout the year, days average 72–76°F (22–24°C), and nights average 54–57°F (12–14°C), with a diurnal range of 17–21°F (10–12°C).

HUMIDITY: Near 80% year-round.

WATER: Rainfall is moderate to heavy all year. Cultivated plants should be kept moist, with only slight drying allowed between waterings.

FERTILIZER: ¼–½ recommended strength. A balanced fertilizer should be applied weekly to biweekly throughout the year.

REST PERIOD: Growing temperatures should be maintained all year. Water should be reduced somewhat in winter for plants grown in the dark, short-day conditions common in temperate latitudes. They should never be allowed to dry out completely, however. Fertilizer should be reduced or eliminated when water is reduced.

GROWING MEDIA: Plants may be mounted on tree-fern if humidity is high and plants are watered at least once daily in summer. When plants are potted, sphagnum moss or chopped tree-fern may be used. Repotting may be done anytime new roots are growing.

MISCELLANEOUS NOTES: The bloom season shown in the climate table is based on cultivation records. Growers indicate that *D. violaceum* is the warmest growing of the *Oxyglossum* group. Plants from the wild are sometimes difficult to establish, but those grown from seed adapt easily to cultivation.

Plant and Flower Information

PLANT SIZE AND TYPE: A 2.4–10.0 in. (6–25 cm) sympodial epiphyte. Plants form a large, brownish green clump.

PSEUDOBULB: 1.2–2.0 in. (3–5 cm) long. The stems, which are thick and fleshy, are swollen at the base and narrower at the apex.

LEAVES: 2–4 at the apex of each growth. The linear leaves are usually 5–7 in. (13–18 cm) long. They may be light to dark green or light yellow when light levels are high. The leaves are channeled along the midline. *D. violaceum* subsp. *violaceum* has broader leaves than *D. violaceum* subsp. *cyperifolium*.

INFLORESCENCE: 1.2 in. (3 cm) long. The Inflorescence arises from the base of the pseudobulb. If the plant is exposed to sun, inflorescences are short, with tight clusters of flowers held at the base of the leaves. The flowers emerge laterally from nodes on the upper portion of the inflorescence.

FLOWERS: 2–10 per inflorescence. Several blossoms are open at the same time. The flowers are 0.9–1.6 in. (2.2–4.0 cm) across and resemble a flared fan. Blossoms may be light or dark with color ranging from bright purple to bright pink-violet with white markings on the lip and linear petals. The dorsal sepal is oblong-ovate, and lateral sepals are somewhat triangular. The unlobed lip is linear with a triangular point at the tip and an upturned margin near the apex. It may be greenish brown tipped with dark orange or dark muddy-violet with bright scarlet at the apex. *D. violaceum* has the largest flowers of closely related plants. Blossoms last 6 months or more, so the plants are nearly always in bloom.

HYBRIDIZING NOTES: Chromosome counts are 2n = 38 as *D. violaceum* (ref. 152, 154, 243) and as *D. quinquecostatum* (ref. 151, 188).

REFERENCES: 91, 92, 95, 151, 152, 154, 179, 188, 220, 235, 243, 254, 304, 326, 385, 430, 437, 443, 486, 525, 549.

PHOTOS/DRAWINGS: *91, 304, 385, 430, 437, 549.*

Dendrobium violascens J. J. Smith

ORIGIN/HABITAT: The Molucca Islands. On Ternate Island, plants grow in forests at about 3300 ft. (1000 m).

CLIMATE: Station #97430, Ternate Island, Indonesia, Lat. 0.8°N, Long. 127.4°E, at 75 ft. (23 m). Temperatures are calculated for an elevation of 3300 ft. (1000 m). Record extreme temperatures are not available for this location.

N/HEMISPHERE	JAN	FEB	MAR	APR	MAY	JUN	JUL	AUG	SEP	OCT	NOV	DEC
°F AVG MAX	74	74	75	75	76	75	76	75	75	76	76	75
°F AVG MIN	66	65	66	66	66	65	64	64	65	66	66	66
DIURNAL RANGE	8	9	9	9	10	10	12	11	10	10	10	9
RAIN/INCHES	5.3	6.1	6.7	6.6	9.4	8.4	4.6	2.1	3.1	3.2	7.2	8.2
HUMIDITY/%	N/A											
BLOOM SEASON									*			
DAYS CLR	N/A											
RAIN/MM	135	155	170	168	239	213	117	53	79	81	183	208
°C AVG MAX	23.6	23.6	24.1	24.1	24.7	24.1	24.7	24.1	24.1	24.7	24.7	24.1
°C AVG MIN	19.1	18.6	19.1	19.1	19.1	18.6	18.0	18.0	18.6	19.1	19.1	19.1
DIURNAL RANGE	4.5	5.0	5.0	5.0	5.6	5.5	6.7	6.1	5.5	5.6	5.6	5.0
S/HEMISPHERE	JUL	AUG	SEP	OCT	NOV	DEC	JAN	FEB	MAR	APR	MAY	JUN

Cultural Recommendations

LIGHT: 2000–3000 fc.

TEMPERATURES: Throughout the year, days average 74–76°F (24–25°C), and nights average 64–66°F (18–19°C), with a diurnal range of 8–12°F (5–7°C). The warmest days and coolest nights occur simultaneously in early summer.

HUMIDITY: Information is not available for this location. However, records from nearby stations indicate that humidity is probably near 85% year-round.

WATER: Rainfall is moderate to heavy most of the year, but conditions are somewhat drier for 2–3 months in late summer and autumn. Cultivated plants should be kept moist, with only slight drying allowed between waterings during most of the year. Plants should become moderately dry between waterings in late summer and early autumn, however, but they should not remain dry for long periods.

FERTILIZER: ¼–½ recommended strength. A balanced fertilizer should be applied weekly to biweekly throughout the year.

REST PERIOD: Growing temperatures should be maintained all year. Water may be reduced somewhat in winter, especially for plants grown in the dark, short-day conditions in temperate latitudes. They should not be allowed to dry out completely, however. In the habitat, seasonal light variation is minor.

GROWING MEDIA: Plants may be mounted on tree-fern or cork slabs if humidity is high and plants are watered at least once daily in summer.

When plants are potted, any open, fast-draining medium may be used. Repotting may be done anytime new roots are growing.

MISCELLANEOUS NOTES: The bloom season shown in the climate table is based on cultivation records.

Plant and Flower Information

PLANT SIZE AND TYPE: A 7–11 in. (18–28 cm) sympodial epiphyte.

PSEUDOBULB: 7–11 in. (18–28 cm) long. The greenish-brown stems are clustered.

LEAVES: 2–3 per growth. The leathery, ovate-lanceolate leaves are 4.0–4.3 in. (10–11 cm) long. They are 2-toothed at the apex.

INFLORESCENCE: 2.8–4.0 in. (7–10 cm) long. Inflorescences emerge near the apex of the stem.

FLOWERS: Many per inflorescence. The pale violet-white flowers are 1 in. (2.5 cm) across. The dorsal sepal is pointed, lanceolate-triangular, and strongly recurved at the tip. Lateral sepals are slender and obliquely triangular. Petals are somewhat spoon-shaped. The 3-lobed lip has a large ovate midlobe and rounded sidelobes, with a fleshy, 3-ridged callus.

REFERENCES: 83, 179, 224.

Dendrobium virescens Ridley. See *D. panduriferum* Hooker f. REFERENCES: 254, 395, 402, 455.

Dendrobium virgineum Rchb. f.

AKA: *D. kontumense* Gagnepain.

ORIGIN/HABITAT: Burma, Laos, Vietnam, and eastern Thailand. In Thailand, plants grow near Seta, Nongkhai, Ubon Ratchathani, Nakon Phanom, and in the Phu Won National Park. Habitat elevation is not available, so the following climate data should be used with caution.

CLIMATE: Station #48357, Nakhon Phanom, Thailand, Lat. 17.4°N, Long. 104.7°E, at 562 ft. (171 m). Record extreme temperatures are 106°F (41°C) and 36°F (2°C).

N/HEMISPHERE	JAN	FEB	MAR	APR	MAY	JUN	JUL	AUG	SEP	OCT	NOV	DEC
°F AVG MAX	82	85	91	95	93	89	88	88	88	88	87	84
°F AVG MIN	56	62	70	74	76	76	75	74	74	69	64	59
DIURNAL RANGE	26	23	21	21	17	13	13	14	14	19	23	25
RAIN/INCHES	0.2	0.7	1.1	3.5	9.1	15.8	18.7	20.5	12.2	2.5	0.2	0.2
HUMIDITY/%	61	63	62	63	74	82	81	83	82	73	66	63
BLOOM SEASON							*	*	*			
DAYS CLR @ 7AM	12	11	11	8	4	2	1	2	2	11	13	14
DAYS CLR @ 1PM	22	16	13	8	1	0	1	0	1	5	10	15
RAIN/MM	5	18	28	89	231	401	475	521	310	64	5	5
°C AVG MAX	27.8	29.4	32.8	35.0	33.9	31.7	31.1	31.1	31.1	31.1	30.6	28.9
°C AVG MIN	13.3	16.7	21.1	23.3	24.4	24.4	23.9	23.3	23.3	20.6	17.8	15.0
DIURNAL RANGE	14.5	12.7	11.7	11.7	9.5	7.3	7.2	7.8	7.8	10.5	12.8	13.9
S/HEMISPHERE	JUL	AUG	SEP	OCT	NOV	DEC	JAN	FEB	MAR	APR	MAY	JUN

Cultural Recommendations

LIGHT: 2500–3500 fc. The heavy summer cloud cover indicates that some shading is needed from spring through autumn, but light should be as high as the plant can tolerate, short of burning the leaves.

TEMPERATURES: Summer days average 88–89°F (31–32°C), and nights average 74–76°F (23–24°C), with a diurnal range of 13–14°F (7–8°C). The warmest temperatures occur in spring when days average 91–95°F (33–35°C), and nights average 70–76°F (21–24°C), with a diurnal range of 17–21°F (10–12°C).

HUMIDITY: Near 80% from late spring through summer, decreasing to near 60% in winter and early spring.

WATER: Rainfall is heavy from late spring to early autumn, but conditions are very dry from late autumn through winter. Cultivated plants should be kept moist from late spring through summer, but water should be gradually reduced after new growths mature in autumn.

FERTILIZER: A fertilizer mixed at about ½ recommended strength should be applied weekly during periods of active growth in spring and summer. A fertilizer higher in nitrogen should be used until about mid-summer, especially if fir bark is used as a potting medium. One high in phosphates should be used from mid-summer into autumn in order to promote blooming and to allow the new growth to harden off before winter.

REST PERIOD: Winter days average 82–85°F (28–29°C), nights average 56–62°F (13–17°C), and the diurnal range is 23–26°F (13–15°C). Rainfall is low for 4–5 months from late autumn through winter. During part of the dry season, additional moisture is available from mist and heavy dew; but in late winter, conditions are so dry for about 2 months that even dew is uncommon. Cultivated plants should be allowed to dry out between waterings, but they should not remain dry for extended periods. Occasional early morning mistings between waterings may help prevent plants from becoming too dry. Fertilizer should be reduced or eliminated until water is increased in spring. In the habitat, light is highest in winter.

GROWING MEDIA: Plants may be mounted on tree-fern or cork slabs if humidity is high and plants are watered at least once daily in summer. When plants are potted, any open, fast-draining medium may be used. Repotting is best done in early spring when new roots are growing.

MISCELLANEOUS NOTES: The bloom season shown in the climate table is based on reports from the habitat. Cultivation records indicate blooming in late autumn and winter.

Plant and Flower Information

PLANT SIZE AND TYPE: A 12–16 in. (30–40 cm) sympodial epiphyte.

PSEUDOBULB: 12–16 in. (30–40 cm) long. The slender stems are round in cross-section, somewhat swollen in the middle, and taper at each end. The leaves and sheaths are covered with black hairs.

LEAVES: Many per growth. The somewhat oblong to elliptic-ovate leaves are 2.6 in. (6.5 cm) long. They are deep green, flat, somewhat downcurved, and bilobed at the apex.

INFLORESCENCE: Short. 1–3 racemes emerge from nodes near or at the apex of the stem.

FLOWERS: 4–6 per inflorescence. The flowers are about 1.6 in. (4 cm) across. Sepals and petals are primarily white. The dorsal sepal has a low keel on the back. The somewhat lanceolate sepals are pointed, but the broadly ovate petals are more rounded. The 3-lobed lip is marked with an orange spot in the middle. The red veining on the lip is variable, as is the presence of a red flush that may extend down the spur. The midlobe is nearly round, notched at the apex, and wavy along the margin.

HYBRIDIZING NOTES: Johansen (ref. 239) found *D. virgineum* to be self-sterile, and blossoms drop 21–28 days after self-pollination. When crossed with *D. aphyllum* using *D. virgineum* as the female parent, 48% of the seed had visible embryos and 79% germinated. When crossed with *D. cariniferum*, 61% had visible embryos and 87% germinated. When crossed with *D. formosum* var. *giga*, 98% had visible embryos and 32% germinated.

REFERENCES: 157, 179, 202, 216, 239, 254, 266, 429, 454, 570.

PHOTOS/DRAWINGS: 454.

Dendrobium viridicatum Ridley. See *D. stuartii* F. M. Bailey. REFERENCES: 75, 219, 254, 454, 455, 469.

Dendrobium viridiflorum F. M. Bailey. Habitat location and elevation are not available, so climate data cannot be selected. Plants bloomed in May (Nov.). Plants were sympodial epiphytes 4–6 in. (10–15 cm) long. The stems consisted of internodes 0.5 in. (1.3 cm) long with a 1 in. (2.5 cm) swelling at the base. The linear leaves are 2 in. (5 cm) long. A single flower is carried on each short inflorescence. Blos-

soms open in succession. The flowers are 0.4 in. (1 cm) long with ovate-lanceolate sepals and linear petals. The fleshy 3-lobed lip has a broadly heart-shaped midlobe decorated with 2 elevated ridges on the disk and semiobovate-oblong sidelobes. Sepals and petals are green with a white margin. The lip is white. REFERENCES: 254.

Dendrobium viridiroseum Rchb. f.
Sometimes spelled *D. viridi-roseum* Rchb. f., see *D. purpureum* Roxburgh. REFERENCES: 212, 216, 254, 317.

Dendrobium viriditepalum J. J. Smith

ORIGIN/HABITAT: Southwestern Sumatra. Plants are found at several locations near Bengkulu at about 3300 ft. (1000 m).

CLIMATE: Station #96253, Bengkulu, Sumatra, Indonesia, Lat. 3.9°S, Long. 102.3°E, at 49 ft. (15 m). Temperatures are calculated for an elevation of 3300 ft. (1000 m). Record extreme temperatures are not available for this location.

N/HEMISPHERE	JAN	FEB	MAR	APR	MAY	JUN	JUL	AUG	SEP	OCT	NOV	DEC
°F AVG MAX	77	76	76	76	76	76	77	77	77	77	78	77
°F AVG MIN	61	61	61	62	62	62	62	61	62	63	62	62
DIURNAL RANGE	16	15	15	14	14	14	15	16	15	14	16	15
RAIN/INCHES	6.9	6.8	9.1	13.9	16.0	12.7	16.0	11.5	12.0	8.3	8.4	8.4
HUMIDITY/%	77	78	77	77	79	80	78	76	77	79	77	78
BLOOM SEASON	N/A											
DAYS CLR @ 7AM	5	1	1	1	0	0	2	1	1	1	2	3
DAYS CLR @ 1PM	5	4	3	1	2	3	2	2	2	3	7	5
RAIN/MM	175	173	231	353	406	323	406	292	305	211	213	213
°C AVG MAX	25.2	24.6	24.6	24.6	24.6	24.6	25.2	25.2	25.2	25.2	25.7	25.2
°C AVG MIN	16.3	16.3	16.3	16.8	16.8	16.8	16.8	16.3	16.8	17.4	16.8	16.8
DIURNAL RANGE	8.9	8.3	8.3	7.8	7.8	7.8	8.4	8.9	8.4	7.8	8.9	8.4
S/HEMISPHERE	JUL	AUG	SEP	OCT	NOV	DEC	JAN	FEB	MAR	APR	MAY	JUN

Cultural Recommendations

LIGHT: 2000–3000 fc.

TEMPERATURES: Throughout the year, days average 76–78°F (25–26°C), and nights average 61–63°F (16–17°C), with a diurnal range of 14–16°F (8–9°C).

HUMIDITY: 75–80% year-round.

WATER: Rainfall is heavy all year, but winter is slightly drier than summer. Cultivated plants should be kept moist but not soggy.

FERTILIZER: ¼–½ recommended strength. A balanced fertilizer should be applied weekly to biweekly throughout the year.

REST PERIOD: Growing conditions should be maintained year-round. Water and fertilizer may be reduced somewhat in winter, especially for plants grown in the dark, short-day conditions common in temperate latitudes. They should never be allowed to dry out completely between waterings, however. In the habitat, light is highest in winter.

GROWING MEDIA: Plants may be mounted on tree-fern or cork slabs or potted in small pots filled with any open, fast-draining medium. Repotting may be done anytime new roots are actively growing.

MISCELLANEOUS NOTES: The plant was described in 1917 in *Bull. Jard. Bot. Buit.* 2nd sér. 25:54.

Plant and Flower Information

PLANT SIZE AND TYPE: A 9.4 in. (24 cm) sympodial epiphyte.

PSEUDOBULB: 9.4 in. (24 cm) long. The dark green stems are marked with dark spots. They are close together, club-shaped, and elliptical in cross-section.

LEAVES: The pale green leaves are 2.4–2.8 in. (6–7 cm) long. They may be papery or fleshy. They are oblong, slightly twisted at the base, and recurved at the apex.

INFLORESCENCE: Short. Inflorescences emerge from nodes on leafless stems.

FLOWERS: 1–2 per inflorescence. The pale green flowers are 0.1 in. (0.3 cm) across. The dorsal sepal is ovate-oblong. Lateral sepals are subtriangular-oblong, longitudinally grooved, with prominent nerves. The oblong petals are rounded and dilated at the apex. Sepals and petals are reflexed. The unlobed lip is heart-shaped with a notch at the apex. It is shiny with 2 converging, raised lines and a triangular disk.

REFERENCES: 222.

Dendrobium viridulum Ridley

ORIGIN/HABITAT: The southern part of peninsular Thailand and northern Malaya. In Malaya, plants are reported on Langkawi island, in Kedah, and in the Cameron Highlands.

CLIMATE: Station #48625, Ipoh, Malaya, Lat. 4.6°N, Long. 101.1°E, at 123 ft. (37 m). Temperatures are calculated for an elevation of 2000 ft. (610 m), resulting in probable extremes of 93°F (34°C) and 58°F (14°C).

N/HEMISPHERE	JAN	FEB	MAR	APR	MAY	JUN	JUL	AUG	SEP	OCT	NOV	DEC
°F AVG MAX	84	86	87	86	86	86	85	85	84	83	83	83
°F AVG MIN	66	66	67	67	68	67	66	66	67	66	66	66
DIURNAL RANGE	18	20	20	19	18	19	19	19	17	17	17	17
RAIN/INCHES	7.9	3.1	7.6	8.4	6.2	3.6	7.2	6.9	8.8	11.0	13.0	8.9
HUMIDITY/%	76	74	76	78	78	75	76	77	79	82	79	81
BLOOM SEASON	N/A											
DAYS CLR @ 7AM	3	3	3	1	1	2	1	1	0	0	1	2
DAYS CLR @ 1PM	2	2	2	1	1	1	1	1	0	0	0	2
RAIN/MM	201	79	193	213	157	91	183	175	224	279	330	226
°C AVG MAX	28.8	29.9	30.4	29.9	29.9	29.9	29.3	29.3	28.8	28.2	28.2	28.2
°C AVG MIN	18.8	18.8	19.3	19.3	19.9	19.3	18.8	18.8	19.3	18.8	18.8	18.8
DIURNAL RANGE	10.0	11.1	11.1	10.6	10.0	10.6	10.5	10.5	9.5	9.4	9.4	9.4
S/HEMISPHERE	JUL	AUG	SEP	OCT	NOV	DEC	JAN	FEB	MAR	APR	MAY	JUN

Cultural Recommendations

LIGHT: 2500–3500 fc.

TEMPERATURES: Throughout the year, days average 83–87°F (28–30°C), and nights average 66–68°F (19–20°C), with a diurnal range of 17–20°F (9–11°C).

HUMIDITY: 75–80% year-round.

WATER: Rainfall is heavy most of the year. The heaviest rainfall occurs in autumn, with a secondary maximum in spring. Brief semidry periods occur in midwinter and midsummer. Cultivated plants should be kept evenly moist, with only slight drying allowed between waterings.

FERTILIZER: ¼–½ recommended strength. A balanced fertilizer should be applied weekly to biweekly throughout the year.

REST PERIOD: Growing conditions should be maintained year-round. Water should be reduced somewhat in winter for plants cultivated in the dark, short-day conditions common in temperate latitudes. They should never be allowed to dry out completely, however. Fertilizer may be reduced when the plant is not actively growing or when water is reduced. In the habitat, light is slightly higher in winter.

GROWING MEDIA: Plants may be mounted on tree-fern or cork slabs if humidity is high and plants are watered at least once daily in summer. When plants are potted, any open, fast-draining medium may be used. Repotting may be done anytime new roots are growing.

Plant and Flower Information

PLANT SIZE AND TYPE: A sympodial epiphyte of unreported size.

PSEUDOBULB: The leafy stems are slender.

LEAVES: Many. The linear-lanceolate leaves, which have 3 veins, are very unequally bilobed at the apex. They are about 3 in. (7.5 cm) long.

INFLORESCENCE: Short. Inflorescences are borne at numerous nodes on leafless stems.

FLOWERS: 1–2 per inflorescence. The flowers are 0.6–0.8 in. (1.5–2.0 cm) long, and do not open fully. They are light green to yellow. The linear to lanceolate sepals and slightly broader petals are nearly equal in size and shape. The unlobed lip is oblong-elliptic with a small point at the apex and a minutely serrated margin. It has no callus or keels.

REFERENCES: 254, 395, 454, 455.

PHOTOS/DRAWINGS: 454, 455.

Dendrobium virotii Guillaumin

ORIGIN/HABITAT: Endemic to New Caledonia. Plants normally grow on tree trunks in humid forests, but some occasionally fall from the trees and root in forest litter. They are found on mountain slopes at 650–3300 ft. (200–1000 m).

CLIMATE: Station #91590, La Tontouta, New Caledonia, Lat. 22.0°S, Long. 166.2°E, at 52 ft. (16 m). Temperatures are calculated for an elevation of 1650 ft. (500 m), resulting in probable extremes of 90°F (32°C) and 42°F (5°C).

N/HEMISPHERE	JAN	FEB	MAR	APR	MAY	JUN	JUL	AUG	SEP	OCT	NOV	DEC
°F AVG MAX	69	70	72	75	79	81	82	82	79	75	73	71
°F AVG MIN	53	53	54	56	59	62	65	65	65	61	56	54
DIURNAL RANGE	16	17	18	19	20	19	17	17	14	14	17	17
RAIN/INCHES	3.6	2.6	2.5	2.0	2.4	2.6	3.7	5.1	5.7	5.2	4.4	3.7
HUMIDITY/%	78	76	74	71	67	72	72	75	81	79	78	76
BLOOM SEASON						*				*	*	*
DAYS CLR @ 11AM	8	7	7	11	10	6	4	3	5	7	6	7
DAYS CLR @ 5PM	8	9	5	9	8	3	3	1	2	3	4	6
RAIN/MM	91	66	64	51	61	66	94	130	145	132	112	94
°C AVG MAX	20.4	21.0	22.1	23.8	26.0	27.1	27.6	27.6	26.0	23.8	22.6	21.5
°C AVG MIN	11.5	11.5	12.1	13.2	14.9	16.5	18.2	18.2	18.2	16.0	13.2	12.1
DIURNAL RANGE	8.9	9.5	10.0	10.6	11.1	10.6	9.4	9.4	7.8	7.8	9.4	9.4
S/HEMISPHERE	JUL	AUG	SEP	OCT	NOV	DEC	JAN	FEB	MAR	APR	MAY	JUN

Cultural Recommendations

LIGHT: 1800–2500 fc.

TEMPERATURES: Summer days average 81–82°F (27–28°C), and nights average 62–65°F (17–18°C), with a diurnal range of 17–19°F (9–11°C).

HUMIDITY: 70–80% year-round.

WATER: Rainfall is light to moderate all year, but amounts may be greater in the mountain habitat than those measured at the weather station. Cultivated plants should be allowed to dry slightly between waterings, but they should never dry out completely.

FERTILIZER: ¼–½ recommended strength, applied weekly. A high-nitrogen fertilizer is beneficial from spring to midsummer, but a fertilizer high in phosphates should be used in late summer and autumn.

REST PERIOD: Winter days average 69–72°F (20–22°C), and nights average 53–54°F (12°C), with a diurnal range of 16–18°F (9–10°C). High and low temperatures decline simultaneously, resulting in little change in the diurnal range. Water should be reduced somewhat for cultivated plants. Plants should be allowed to become somewhat drier between waterings but should not remain dry for extended periods. In the habitat, light is highest in winter.

GROWING MEDIA: Plants may be mounted on tree-fern or cork slabs if humidity is high and plants are watered at least once daily in summer. When plants are potted, any open, fast-draining medium may be used. Repotting is best done in early spring when new roots are growing.

MISCELLANEOUS NOTES: The bloom season shown in the climate table is based on reports from the habitat.

Plant and Flower Information

PLANT SIZE AND TYPE: A sympodial epiphyte or terrestrial of unreported size.

PSEUDOBULB: The leafy stems are grooved and somewhat zigzag. They branch and rebranch. Each branch develops roots.

LEAVES: Many. The largest leaves are about 3 in. (7.5 cm) long, but they are smallest at the tip of the stem.

INFLORESCENCE: 2–5 in. (5–13 cm) long. Inflorescences emerge from nodes on the upper portion of the stem. They rarely branch. The blossoms open from the base to the apex.

FLOWERS: 6–22 per inflorescence. The flowers are 0.3 in. (0.7 cm) long. The pointed sepals and petals are widest near the apex and nearly equal in size and shape. They may be brown, red-brown, or greenish brown, and each have 3 veins. The lip is white with red or orange markings and a white edge. The side margins are upturned, uneven, and slightly wavy. The lip has a somewhat U-shaped callus at the base of the midlobe.

REFERENCES: 173, 227.

PHOTOS/DRAWINGS: 173.

Dendrobium vitellinum Kränzlin. See *D. mohlianum* Rchb. f.

REFERENCES: 220, 254, 270, 271, 445.

Dendrobium vitiense Kränzlin not Rolfe. See *D. kraenzlinii* L. O. Williams. REFERENCES: 224, 226.

Dendrobium vitiense Rolfe not Kränzlin

ORIGIN/HABITAT: Endemic to Fiji. On Viti Levu, plants are found along the upper Singatoka River in Nandronga and Navosa Provinces near Nandrau. Rolfe (ref. 417) reported the habitat elevation as 4900 ft. (1500 m), but Kores (ref. 466) indicates that the primary habitat is closer to 1500 ft. (460 m). Other collections have been made at 500–1500 ft. (150–460 m).

CLIMATE: Station #91683, Nausori, Viti Levu, Fiji, Lat. 18.1°S, Long. 178.6°E, at 19 ft. (6 m). Temperatures are calculated for an elevation of 1500 ft. (460 m), resulting in probable extremes of 93°F (34°C) and 50°F (10°C).

N/HEMISPHERE	JAN	FEB	MAR	APR	MAY	JUN	JUL	AUG	SEP	OCT	NOV	DEC
°F AVG MAX	74	74	75	76	78	80	81	81	81	79	77	75
°F AVG MIN	63	63	64	65	66	68	69	69	69	68	66	64
DIURNAL RANGE	11	11	11	11	12	12	12	12	12	11	11	11
RAIN/INCHES	4.9	8.3	7.7	8.3	9.8	12.5	11.4	10.7	14.5	12.2	10.1	6.7
HUMIDITY/%	77	77	76	75	75	76	76	78	79	79	81	78
BLOOM SEASON					*							
DAYS CLR @ 12PM	3	1	0	0	1	2	0	0	0	1	0	
RAIN/MM	124	211	196	211	249	318	290	272	368	310	257	170
°C AVG MAX	23.4	23.4	24.0	24.5	25.6	26.7	27.3	27.3	27.3	26.2	25.1	24.0
°C AVG MIN	17.3	17.3	17.8	18.4	19.0	20.1	20.6	20.6	20.6	20.1	19.0	17.8
DIURNAL RANGE	6.1	6.1	6.2	6.1	6.6	6.6	6.7	6.7	6.7	6.1	6.1	6.2
S/HEMISPHERE	JUL	AUG	SEP	OCT	NOV	DEC	JAN	FEB	MAR	APR	MAY	JUN

Cultural Recommendations

LIGHT: 2500–3500 fc. With high light, high relative humidity and strong air movement are very important at all times for cultivated plants.

TEMPERATURES: Summer days average 80–81°F (27°C), and nights average 68–69°F (20–21°C), with a diurnal range of 12°F (7°C).

HUMIDITY: 75–80% year-round.

WATER: Rainfall is moderate to heavy all year. Cultivated plants should be kept moist but not soggy.

FERTILIZER: ¼–½ recommended strength. A balanced fertilizer should be applied weekly to biweekly throughout the year.

REST PERIOD: Winter days average 74–75°F (23–24°C), and nights average 63–64°F (17–18°C), with a diurnal range of 11°F (6°C). Seasonal temperature variation is minor, but lows occasionally drop to 55–60°F

(13–16°C). Winter rainfall is high in the habitat; but water should be reduced for cultivated plants, especially those grown in the dark, short-day conditions common in temperate latitudes. Plants should never be allowed to dry completely, however. Fertilizer should be reduced or eliminated anytime water is reduced.

GROWING MEDIA: Plants may be mounted on tree-fern or cork slabs if humidity is high and plants are watered at least once daily in summer. When plants are potted, the medium must be very open and fast draining. Repotting may be done anytime new roots are growing.

MISCELLANEOUS NOTES: The bloom season shown in the climate table is based on reports from the habitat.

Plant and Flower Information

PLANT SIZE AND TYPE: A 6–10 in. (15–25 cm) sympodial epiphyte.

PSEUDOBULB: 3.5–8.0 in. (9–20 cm) long. The stems arise from a creeping, slightly elongated rhizome. They are cylindrical, fleshy, and grooved.

LEAVES: 3–5 at the apex of each growth. The oblong-lanceolate leaves are 1.4–2.8 in. (3.5–7.0 cm) long and unequally bilobed at the apex.

INFLORESCENCE: 0.6–2.0 in. (1.5–5.0 cm) long. The erect, laxly flowered inflorescences arise from nodes along the upper part of the stem.

FLOWERS: 3–6 per inflorescence. The very small flowers are 0.2 in. (0.5 cm) long. They are greenish yellow with an erect dorsal sepal, spreading lateral sepals, and weakly spreading petals. The 3-lobed lip has 2 slightly raised lines. The heart-shaped midlobe is slightly reflexed, broadly rounded, and notched at the apex. The sidelobes are small, ovate, and upturned.

REFERENCES: 223, 252, 353, 417, 466.

PHOTOS/DRAWINGS: 466.

Dendrobium × *von-paulsenianum* A. Hawkes.

Originally described as *D.* × *intermedium* Schlechter, it is now considered to be a natural hybrid between *D. lawesii* F. Mueller not Schlechter and *D. flammula* Schlechter. REFERENCES: 191, 229.

Dendrobium vonroemeri J. J. Smith

AKA: Originally spelled *D. vonrömeri*.

ORIGIN/HABITAT: Irian Jaya (western New Guinea). Plants grow on trees on the eastern slopes of the Cyclops Range at about 5250 ft. (1600 m). They are found along ridges of the Hellwig Range and on Mt. Agathodämons, where the orchids grow on the surface of the ground at about 8450 ft. (2580 m).

CLIMATE: Station #97686, Wamena, Irian Jaya, Lat. 4.1°S, Long. 139.0°E, at 5446 ft. (1660 m). Temperatures are calculated for an elevation of 8500 ft. (2600 m). Record extreme temperatures are not available for this location.

N/HEMISPHERE	JAN	FEB	MAR	APR	MAY	JUN	JUL	AUG	SEP	OCT	NOV	DEC
°F AVG MAX	65	66	67	66	67	66	67	66	66	69	68	64
°F AVG MIN	50	50	52	52	53	54	53	52	53	55	55	51
DIURNAL RANGE	15	16	15	14	14	12	14	14	13	14	13	13
RAIN/INCHES	3.0	1.9	2.2	4.0	4.6	3.3	2.8	4.2	6.9	3.9	5.4	4.9
HUMIDITY/%	N/A											
BLOOM SEASON				*		*						*
DAYS CLR	N/A											
RAIN/MM	76	48	56	102	117	84	71	107	175	99	137	124
°C AVG MAX	18.2	18.8	19.3	18.8	19.3	18.8	19.3	18.8	18.8	20.5	19.9	17.7
°C AVG MIN	9.9	9.9	11.0	11.0	11.6	12.1	11.6	11.0	11.6	12.7	12.7	10.5
DIURNAL RANGE	8.3	8.9	8.3	7.8	7.7	6.7	7.7	7.8	7.2	7.8	7.2	7.2
S/HEMISPHERE	JUL	AUG	SEP	OCT	NOV	DEC	JAN	FEB	MAR	APR	MAY	JUN

Cultural Recommendations

LIGHT: 2000–2500 fc.

TEMPERATURES: Throughout the year, days average 64–69°F (18–21°C), and nights average 50–55°F (10–13°C), with a diurnal range of 12–16°F (7–9°C). In the habitat, the warmest temperatures of the day occur during late morning when skies are usually clear. Clouds and mist develop near noon, thus preventing additional warming. Because of microclimate effects, actual maximum temperatures may be somewhat warmer than indicated. Reports from the habitat indicate a sharp contrast between day and night temperatures.

HUMIDITY: Information is not available for this location. However, records from nearby stations indicate that humidity probably averages near 80% year-round. High humidity and excellent air circulation are particularly important if temperatures are warm. Placing the plants in front of an evaporative cooler or near a fine mist is very beneficial.

WATER: Rainfall is moderate through most of the year. In the higher-elevation habitat, rainfall amounts may be greater than indicated in the climate table. In addition, large amounts of water are available from mist and heavy dew, even during periods of reduced rainfall. Cultivated plants should be kept moist with only slight drying allowed between waterings. They may need to be misted several times daily on the hottest days, but the foliage should always be dry before evening. Good air movement is critically important and should be maintained at all times.

FERTILIZER: ¼–½ recommended strength. A balanced fertilizer should be applied weekly to biweekly throughout the year. The Royal Botanic Garden in Edinburgh uses a dilute, seaweed-based fertilizer.

REST PERIOD: Growing conditions should be maintained all year. Rainfall averages are somewhat lower for a month or so in winter and again in midsummer. In cultivation, water may be decreased, but plants should never be allowed to dry out completely. In the habitat, light is slightly higher in winter.

GROWING MEDIA: Plants may be mounted on tree-fern or cork slabs if humidity is high and plants are watered at least once daily in summer. When plants are potted, any open, fast-draining medium may be used. Repotting may be done anytime new roots are growing.

MISCELLANEOUS NOTES: The bloom season shown in the climate table is based on reports from the habitat. The plant was described in 1910 in *Bull. Dép. Agric. Indes Néerl.* 39:12.

Plant and Flower Information

PLANT SIZE AND TYPE: A sympodial epiphyte of unreported size.

PSEUDOBULB: Short. The slender stems are flattened.

LEAVES: Many. The very small leaves are lanceolate, somewhat erect, bilobed at the apex, and twisted at the base. They are shiny, fleshy, rough, and grooved.

INFLORESCENCE: Short. Inflorescences emerge through the overlapping leaf sheaths along the side of the stem.

FLOWERS: 1 per inflorescence. The small flowers are 0.3 in. (0.8 cm) long. They are white with violet flecks on the lip. The dorsal sepal is oblong. Lateral sepals and petals are somewhat sickle shaped. The 3-lobed lip has a nearly round midlobe with an uneven, serrated margin. The sidelobes are triangular.

REFERENCES: 220, 254, 445, 470.

Dendrobium vulcanicum Schlechter. See *D. lancifolium* A. Richards. REFERENCES: 220, 254, 433, 436, 470.

Dendrobium wallichii A. Hawkes and A. H. Heller. See *D. peguanum* Lindley. REFERENCES: 191, 211, 229, 454.

Dendrobium wangii Tso. See *D. hercoglossum* Rchb. f. REFERENCES: 153, 208, 225, 454.

Dendrobium warburgianum Kränzlin. See *D. lawesii* F. Mueller. REFERENCES: 217, 218, 254, 437.

Dendrobium wardianum Warner

AKA: Hawkes (ref. 190) includes *D. falconeri* Hooker var. *wardianum* Hooker and *D. album* Williams as synonyms.

ORIGIN/HABITAT: Widespread in southeast Asia. In India, plants grow near Gangtok in Sikkim, in Bhutan, the Khasi (Khasia) Hills of Assam, and the Manipur region. The habitat extends eastward across Burma, through the mountains of northwestern Thailand, and into Yunnan Province of southwestern China. Plants commonly grow on trees in mixed or deciduous forests at 3300–6550 ft. (1000–2000 m), but in China, they are found on rocks and cliffs.

CLIMATE: Station #48327, Chiang Mai, Thailand, Lat. 18.8°N, Long. 99.0°E, at 1100 ft. (335 m). Temperatures are calculated for an elevation of 5000 ft. (1520 m), resulting in probable extremes of 96°F (36°C) and 25°F (−4°C).

N/HEMISPHERE	JAN	FEB	MAR	APR	MAY	JUN	JUL	AUG	SEP	OCT	NOV	DEC
°F AVG MAX	72	77	82	83	81	77	76	74	75	76	73	71
°F AVG MIN	43	44	49	57	61	61	61	62	60	58	53	44
DIURNAL RANGE	29	33	33	26	20	16	15	12	15	18	20	27
RAIN/INCHES	0.3	0.4	0.6	2.0	5.5	6.1	7.4	8.7	11.5	4.9	1.5	0.4
HUMIDITY/%	73	65	58	62	73	78	80	83	83	81	79	76
BLOOM SEASON	**	**	***	**	**					*		*
DAYS CLR @ 7AM	5	5	2	2	1	0	0	0	0	1	3	3
DAYS CLR @ 1PM	9	8	4	2	0	0	0	0	0	0	1	3
RAIN/MM	8	10	15	51	140	155	188	221	292	124	38	10
°C AVG MAX	22.3	25.1	27.9	28.4	27.3	25.1	24.5	23.4	24.0	24.5	22.9	21.7
°C AVG MIN	6.2	6.7	9.5	14.0	16.2	16.2	16.2	16.7	15.6	14.5	11.7	6.7
DIURNAL RANGE	16.1	18.3	18.3	14.4	11.1	8.9	8.3	6.7	8.3	10.0	11.1	15.0
S/HEMISPHERE	JUL	AUG	SEP	OCT	NOV	DEC	JAN	FEB	MAR	APR	MAY	JUN

Cultural Recommendations

LIGHT: 2500–3500 fc. The heavy summer cloud cover indicates that some shading is needed spring through autumn, but light should be as high as the plants can tolerate, short of burning the foliage.

TEMPERATURES: Summer days average 74–77°F (23–25°C), and nights average 61–62°F (16–17°C), with a diurnal range of 12–16°F (7–9°C). The warmest temperatures occur in spring. Days average 81–83°F (27–28°C), and nights average 49–61°F (10–16°C), with a diurnal range of 20–33°F (11–18°C).

HUMIDITY: 75–85% from late spring through autumn, dropping to near 60% in late winter and early spring.

WATER: Rainfall is moderate to heavy from late spring through early autumn, but conditions are very dry in winter. Cultivated plants should be kept moist while actively growing, but water should be gradually reduced after new growths mature in autumn.

FERTILIZER: ¼–½ recommended strength, applied weekly. A high-nitrogen fertilizer is beneficial from spring to midsummer, but a fertilizer high in phosphates should be used in late summer and autumn.

REST PERIOD: Winter days average 71–77°F (22–25°C), and nights average 43–44°F (6–7°C), with a diurnal range of 27–33°F (15–18°C). The average low temperatures are below 50°F (10°C) for 3 months and then warm rapidly in spring. Plants should be able to tolerate temperatures a few degrees below freezing, but extremes should be avoided in cultivation. During very cold weather, a plant's chance of surviving with minimal damage is better if it is dry. In the habitat, rainfall averages are very low for 4–5 months in winter, but during the early part of the season the high relative humidity indicates that additional moisture is available from frequent fog, mist, and heavy deposits of dew. Growers sometimes recommend eliminating water in winter, but plants are healthiest if for most of the winter they are allowed to become somewhat dry between waterings but do not remain dry for extended periods. For 1–2 months in late winter, however, conditions are clear, warm, and dry, with humidity so low that even the moisture from morning dew is uncommon. Plants should be allowed to dry out completely between waterings and remain dry longer during this time. Occasional early morning mistings between waterings may help keep the plants from becoming too dry. Fertilizer should be greatly reduced or eliminated until water is increased in spring. A cool, dry rest is essential for cultivated plants and should be continued until new growth starts in spring. In the habitat, light is highest in winter.

GROWING MEDIA: Plants may be mounted on tree-fern or cork slabs but the canes must be tied to grow vertically. Many growers place plants in hanging baskets and allow them to cascade naturally. Baskets should be filled with an open, fast-draining medium. Repotting is best done in early spring when new roots are growing.

MISCELLANEOUS NOTES: The bloom season shown in the climate table is based on cultivation reports. Growers indicate that dry rest is needed to mature growths and induce flowering. Plants cultivated in Singapore do not bloom.

Plant and Flower Information

PLANT SIZE AND TYPE: A 12–47 in. (30–120 cm) sympodial epiphyte or lithophyte.

PSEUDOBULB: 12–47 in. (30–120 cm) long. Stems may be erect or pendulous. They are normally thickened at the nodes, but the stems may be slender and elongated when cultivated plants are given regular water.

LEAVES: Many on young growths. The deciduous leaves are 3–6 in. (8–15 cm) long. They are glossy, leathery, bright green, and pointed. Leaves may be oblong- to linear-lanceolate.

INFLORESCENCE: Short. Inflorescences emerge from opposite sides of the nodes all along the prior year's leafless stem.

FLOWERS: 2–3 per inflorescence. Described as magnificent, the waxy flowers are 3–4 in. (8–10 cm) across. The broad sepals and petals are thick and blunt at the tips. They are white with a variable amount of bright magenta-rose near the tips. The white lip has a rich orange to lemon yellow blotch, purple veins, 2 purple blotches near the base, and magenta-rose at the apex. It is in-rolled at the base. The fragrant blossoms are moderately long-lasting if kept cool and dry.

HYBRIDIZING NOTES: Chromosome counts are n = 19 (ref. 150, 187, 542), n = 20 (ref. 152, 542), 2n = 2x (ref. 580), 2n = 38 (ref. 151, 154, 187, 188, 542), and 2n = 40 (ref. 152, 542). When varieties were tested, the count for *D. wardianum* var. *wardianum* was 2n = 2x (ref. 187, 504); however, *D. wardianum* var. *album* was 2n = about 57 (ref. 504, 580), and *D. wardianum* var. *giganteum* was 2n = 40 (ref. 504, 580).

REFERENCES: 6, 25, 36, 38, 46, 150, 151, 152, 154, 157, 179, 187, 188, 190, 196, 200, 202, 208, 210, 216, 245, 254, 326, 369, 376, 389, 430, 445, 454, 461, 489, 504, 528, 541, 542, 557, 569, 570, 580.

PHOTOS/DRAWINGS: 6, *36*, 46, 210, *245, 369, 389, 430, 454,* 541, 557, *569,* 570.

Dendrobium warianum Schlechter. See *D. sylvanum* Rchb. f. REFERENCES: 84, 179, 221, 271, 304, 346, 351, 437, 445. PHOTOS/DRAWINGS: *346, 351.*

Dendrobium warianum (Schlechter) J. J. Smith. Originally described as *Cadetia wariana* Schlechter, the plant was transferred to *Dendrobium* by J. J. Smith. He stated later, however, that "*D. warianum*

(Schlechter) J. J. Smith can hardly be separated from *D. funiforme* Blume," which Schlechter considered a synonym of *Cadetia funiformis* (Blume) Schlechter. REFERENCES: 221, 437, 470, 472, 500.

Dendrobium wassellii S. T. Blake

ORIGIN/HABITAT: Northeastern Australia. Plants are found only in the McIlwraith Range on the Cape York Peninsula. They grow at the edge of *Araucaria* vine forests in areas with good light and strong air movement at about 1000 ft. (300 m). Commonly epiphytic on tree trunks, they sometimes grow on rocks. For unknown reasons, plants that grow on rocks are generally much larger than those found on trees.

CLIMATE: Station #94185, Coen, Australia, Lat. 14.0°S, Long. 143.2°E, at 633 ft. (193 m). Temperatures are calculated for an elevation of 1000 ft. (300 m). Record extreme temperatures are not available for this location, but reports from nearby stations indicate that winter minimums are probably 50–55°F (10–13°C), and summer maximums are probably near 105°F (41°C).

N/HEMISPHERE	JAN	FEB	MAR	APR	MAY	JUN	JUL	AUG	SEP	OCT	NOV	DEC
°F AVG MAX	73	74	75	79	81	82	80	80	80	81	79	73
°F AVG MIN	65	66	68	71	74	75	74	74	74	73	71	64
DIURNAL RANGE	8	8	7	8	7	7	6	6	6	8	8	9
RAIN/INCHES	0.2	0.1	0.1	0.4	1.0	2.7	7.4	7.4	4.7	2.2	1.4	0.6
HUMIDITY/%	N/A											
BLOOM SEASON											*	*
DAYS CLR	N/A											
RAIN/MM	5	3	3	10	25	69	188	188	119	56	36	15
°C AVG MAX	22.7	23.3	23.8	26.0	27.1	27.7	26.6	26.6	26.6	27.1	26.0	22.7
°C AVG MIN	18.3	18.8	19.9	21.6	23.3	23.8	23.3	23.3	23.3	22.7	21.6	17.7
DIURNAL RANGE	4.4	4.5	3.9	4.4	3.8	3.9	3.3	3.3	3.3	4.4	4.4	5.0
S/HEMISPHERE	JUL	AUG	SEP	OCT	NOV	DEC	JAN	FEB	MAR	APR	MAY	JUN

Cultural Recommendations

LIGHT: 2500–3500 fc. Strong air movement is recommended all year.

TEMPERATURES: Summer days average 80–82°F (27–28°C), and nights average 74–75°F (23–24°C), with a diurnal range of 6–7°F (3–4°C).

HUMIDITY: Information is not available for this location. However, average humidity normally exceeds 70–75% at other stations in the region, and may be higher near rainforests.

WATER: Rainfall is moderate during the 5-month summer wet season. However, in the rainforest habitat, water is available all year from mist and heavy dew. Plants should be watered frequently, with only slight drying allowed between waterings in summer and early autumn. Water should be gradually reduced in late autumn.

FERTILIZER: ¼–½ recommended strength, applied weekly. A high-nitrogen fertilizer is beneficial from spring to midsummer, but a fertilizer high in phosphates should be used in late summer and autumn.

REST PERIOD: Winter days average 73–75°F (23–24°C), and nights average 64–68°F (18–20°C), with a diurnal range of 7–9°F (4–5°C). Growers indicate that winter temperatures should not fall below 50°F (10°C). While the dry season in the region is long and severe, moisture from mist and heavy dew is available in the rainforest habitat. Water should be reduced in winter, keeping plants on the dry side, but they should not remain dry for long periods. Fertilizer should be reduced or eliminated until new growth begins in spring. In the habitat, light is highest in winter.

GROWING MEDIA: Mounting plants on tree-fern or cork slabs accommodates the creeping, branching growth habit, but humidity must be high and plants must be watered at least once daily in summer. If plants cannot be mounted, pots or baskets may be filled with an open, fast-draining medium. Repotting may be done anytime new roots are actively growing.

MISCELLANEOUS NOTES: The bloom season shown in the climate table is based on reports from the habitat. Cultivated plants also bloom at other times. Australian growers report that a temperature drop is sometimes necessary to induce flowering. In nature, the primary flowering period is early winter. Although *D. wassellii* has a very limited range in nature, growers report that plants are adaptable, easy to cultivate, and quickly form large clumps.

Plant and Flower Information

PLANT SIZE AND TYPE: A 2.4–3.5 in. (6–9 cm) sympodial epiphyte.

PSEUDOBULB: The leaves appear to emerge directly from the prostrate, rooting rhizome.

LEAVES: 1 per growth. The erect leaves are 2.4–3.5 in. (6–9 cm) long. They have 5 longitudinal furrows.

INFLORESCENCE: 4–8 in. (10–20 cm) long. Racemes emerge from the base of the leaf on the most recently matured growths. They are erect and densely flowered.

FLOWERS: Many per inflorescence. There may be as many as 40–50 per inflorescence, but cultivated plants usually seem to have about 30. The white to creamy-white flowers, which open fully and are large for the plant size, may reach a diameter of 1 in. (2.5 cm). Sepals are narrowly linear and somewhat recurved, and the equally slender petals are sufficiently incurved to cross each other. Flowers are often arranged with the lip uppermost. The long, slender lip is white and yellow with purple stripes and spots near the base. It is ruffled along the sides and recurved at the pointed tip.

HYBRIDIZING NOTES: Chromosome count is 2n = 38 (ref. 151, 152, 154, 187, 188, 243).

REFERENCES: 24, 67, 105, 151, 152, 154, 179, 187, 188, 230, 240, 243, 262, 263, 264, 533.

PHOTOS/DRAWINGS: 105, *240, 262, 533.*

Dendrobium waterhousei Carriere. See *D. punamense* Schlechter. REFERENCES: 83, 225, 271.

Dendrobium wattii (Hooker f.) Rchb. f.

AKA: *D. cariniferum* Rchb. f. var. *wattii* Hooker f., *D. evrardii* Gagnepain. Seidenfaden (ref. 454) discusses the confusion surrounding the names *D. wattii*, *D. cariniferum* Rchb. f., and *D. williamsonu* Day and Rchb. f. In 1992 *Opera Botanica* #114, Seidenfaden tentatively differentiates the plants with characteristics included in the following Plant and Flower Information.

ORIGIN/HABITAT: Northern Thailand, northeastern India, northern Burma near Bhamo, the Phong Saly region of northern Laos, and in the Langbian region of Vietnam. In Thailand, plants grow at 4900–6250 ft. (1500–1900 m), but they are reported at about 6900 ft. (2100 m) in Vietnam.

CLIMATE: Station #48327, Chiang Mai, Thailand, Lat. 18.8°N, Long. 99.0°E, at 1100 ft. (335 m). Temperatures are calculated for an elevation of 5000 ft. (1520 m), resulting in probable extremes of 96°F (36°C) and 25°F (–4°C).

N/HEMISPHERE	JAN	FEB	MAR	APR	MAY	JUN	JUL	AUG	SEP	OCT	NOV	DEC
°F AVG MAX	72	77	82	83	81	77	76	74	75	76	73	71
°F AVG MIN	43	44	49	57	61	61	61	62	60	58	53	44
DIURNAL RANGE	29	33	33	26	20	16	15	12	15	18	20	27
RAIN/INCHES	0.3	0.4	0.6	2.0	5.5	6.1	7.4	8.7	11.5	4.9	1.5	0.4
HUMIDITY/%	73	65	58	62	73	78	80	83	83	81	79	76
BLOOM SEASON		*	*	*								
DAYS CLR @ 7AM	5	5	2	2	1	0	0	0	0	1	3	3
DAYS CLR @ 1PM	9	8	4	2	0	0	0	0	0	0	1	3
RAIN/MM	8	10	15	51	140	155	188	221	292	124	38	10
°C AVG MAX	22.3	25.1	27.9	28.4	27.3	25.1	24.5	23.4	24.0	24.5	22.9	21.7
°C AVG MIN	6.2	6.7	9.5	14.0	16.2	16.2	16.2	16.7	15.6	14.5	11.7	6.7
DIURNAL RANGE	16.1	18.3	18.3	14.4	11.1	8.9	8.3	6.7	8.3	10.0	11.1	15.0
S/HEMISPHERE	JUL	AUG	SEP	OCT	NOV	DEC	JAN	FEB	MAR	APR	MAY	JUN

Cultural Recommendations

LIGHT: 2500–3500 fc. The heavy summer cloud cover indicates that some shading is needed spring through autumn, but light should be as high as the plants can tolerate, short of burning the foliage.

TEMPERATURES: Summer days average 74–77°F (23–25°C), and nights average 61–62°F (16–17°C), with a diurnal range of 12–16°F (7–9°C). The warmest temperatures occur in spring. Days average 81–83°F (27–28°C), and nights average 49–61°F (10–16°C), with a diurnal range of 20–33°F (11–18°C).

HUMIDITY: 75–85% from late spring through autumn, dropping to near 60% in late winter and early spring.

WATER: Rainfall is moderate to heavy from late spring through early autumn, but conditions are very dry in winter. Cultivated plants should be kept moist while actively growing, but water should be gradually reduced after new growths mature in autumn.

FERTILIZER: ¼–½ recommended strength, applied weekly. A high-nitrogen fertilizer is beneficial from spring to midsummer, but a fertilizer high in phosphates should be used in late summer and autumn.

REST PERIOD: Winter days average 71–77°F (22–25°C), and nights average 43–44°F (6–7°C), with a diurnal range of 27–33°F (15–18°C). The average low temperatures are below 50°F (10°C) for 3 months and then warm rapidly in spring. Plants should be able to tolerate temperatures a few degrees below freezing, but extremes should be avoided in cultivation. During very cold weather, a plant's chance of surviving with minimal damage is better if it is dry. In the habitat, rainfall averages are very low for 4–5 months in winter, but during the early part of the season the high relative humidity indicates that additional moisture is available from frequent fog, mist and heavy deposits of dew. Growers sometimes recommend eliminating water in winter, but plants are healthiest if for most of the winter they are allowed to become somewhat dry between waterings but do not remain dry for extended periods. For 1–2 months in late winter, however, conditions are clear, warm, and dry, with humidity so low that even the moisture from morning dew is uncommon. Plants should be allowed to dry out completely between waterings and remain dry longer during this time. Occasional early morning mistings between waterings may help keep the plants from becoming too dry. Fertilizer should be greatly reduced or eliminated until water is increased in spring. A cool, dry rest is essential for cultivated plants and should be continued until new growth starts in spring. In the habitat, light is highest in winter.

GROWING MEDIA: Plants may be mounted on tree-fern or cork slabs if humidity is high and plants are watered at least once daily in summer. When plants are potted, any open, fast-draining medium may be used. Repotting is best done in early spring when new roots are growing.

MISCELLANEOUS NOTES: The bloom season shown in the climate table is based on reports from the habitat. Cultivation records indicate blooming from autumn to spring with the peak season in winter.

Plant and Flower Information

PLANT SIZE AND TYPE: A 10–12 in. (25–30 cm) sympodial epiphyte.

PSEUDOBULB: 10–12 in. (25–30 cm) long. The slender stems are cylindrical.

LEAVES: 4–8 per growth. The leaves are 3–4 in. (8–10 cm) long, leathery, and narrowly linear. The leaf sheaths are covered with black hairs.

INFLORESCENCE: Short. Inflorescences are borne at the apex of normally leafless pseudobulbs.

FLOWERS: 2–3 per inflorescence. The flowers are 2 in. (5 cm) across. The ovate-lanceolate sepals and much broader, lanceolate petals are white. The sepals and petals have no keels. The lip has a thick golden yellow disk and yellow veins on the sidelobes. The midlobe, which is smaller than the sidelobes, is ruffled and deeply toothed. The lip surface is not papilose or fimbriate. The callus is divided into 3 close low keels through the blade.

REFERENCES: 38, 46, 136, 179, 190, 202, 218, 254, 266, 447, 448, 454.

PHOTOS/DRAWINGS: 454.

Dendrobium wentianum J. J. Smith

ORIGIN/HABITAT: Irian Jaya (western New Guinea). Plants grow on trees in primary forests between the Wichmann and Hubrect Mountains at 9200–9850 ft. (2800–3000 m).

CLIMATE: Station #97686, Wamena, Irian Jaya, Lat. 4.1°S, Long. 139.0°E, at 5446 ft. (1660 m). Temperatures are calculated for an elevation of 9500 ft. (2900 m). Record extreme temperatures are not available for this location.

N/HEMISPHERE	JAN	FEB	MAR	APR	MAY	JUN	JUL	AUG	SEP	OCT	NOV	DEC
°F AVG MAX	62	63	64	63	64	63	64	63	63	66	65	61
°F AVG MIN	47	47	49	49	50	51	50	49	50	52	52	48
DIURNAL RANGE	15	16	15	14	14	12	14	14	13	14	13	13
RAIN/INCHES	3.0	1.9	2.2	4.0	4.6	3.3	2.8	4.2	6.9	3.9	5.4	4.9
HUMIDITY/%	N/A											
BLOOM SEASON	*								*			
DAYS CLR	N/A											
RAIN/MM	76	48	56	102	117	84	71	107	175	99	137	124
°C AVG MAX	16.5	17.0	17.6	17.0	17.6	17.0	17.6	17.0	17.0	18.7	18.1	15.9
°C AVG MIN	8.1	8.1	9.2	9.2	9.8	10.3	9.8	9.2	9.8	10.9	10.9	8.7
DIURNAL RANGE	8.4	8.9	8.4	7.8	7.8	6.7	7.8	7.8	7.2	7.8	7.2	7.2
S/HEMISPHERE	JUL	AUG	SEP	OCT	NOV	DEC	JAN	FEB	MAR	APR	MAY	JUN

Cultural Recommendations

LIGHT: 1500–2500 fc. In the habitat, light is highest in the morning.

TEMPERATURES: Throughout the year, days average 62–66°F (17–19°C), and nights average 47–52°F (8–11°C), with a diurnal range of 12–16°F (7–9°C). In the habitat, the warmest temperatures of the day occur during late morning, when skies are usually clear. Clouds and mist develop near noon, thus preventing additional warming. Because of microclimate effects, actual maximum temperatures may be somewhat warmer than indicated. Reports from the habitat indicate a sharp contrast between day and night temperatures.

HUMIDITY: Information is not available for this location. However, records from nearby stations indicate that humidity probably averages near 80% year-round. High humidity and excellent air circulation are particularly important when temperatures are warm. Placing the plants in front of an evaporative cooler or near a fine mist is very beneficial.

WATER: Rainfall is moderate through most of the year. In the higher-elevation habitat, rainfall amounts may be greater than indicated in the climate table. In addition, large amounts of water are available from mist and heavy dew, even during periods of reduced rainfall. Cultivated plants should be kept evenly moist, with only slight drying allowed between waterings. They may need to be misted several times daily on the hottest days, but the foliage should always be dry before evening.

FERTILIZER: ¼–½ recommended strength. A balanced fertilizer should be applied weekly to biweekly throughout the year. The Royal Botanic Garden in Edinburgh uses a dilute, seaweed-based fertilizer.

REST PERIOD: Growing conditions should be maintained all year. Rainfall averages are somewhat lower for a month or so in winter and again in midsummer. In cultivation, water may be decreased, but plants should never be allowed to dry out completely. In the habitat, light is slightly higher in winter.

GROWING MEDIA: Mounting plants on tree-fern or cork slabs accommodates their pendulous growth habit. However, humidity must be high and plants must be watered at least once a day in summer. If plants cannot be mounted, small pots or hanging baskets may be filled with an open, fast-draining medium. Repotting may be done anytime new roots are actively growing.

MISCELLANEOUS NOTES: The bloom season shown in the climate table is based on reports from the habitat.

Plant and Flower Information

PLANT SIZE AND TYPE: A 6–11 in. (16–28 cm) sympodial epiphyte. Plants sometimes reach a length of 26 in. (67 cm).

PSEUDOBULB: 6–26 in. (16–67 cm) long. The stems are strongly branched and pendulous. They root only at the base.

LEAVES: Few on younger branches. The small oval leaves, which are bent-back, are 1.0–1.3 in. (2.5–3.4 cm) long.

INFLORESCENCE: Inflorescences are borne near the apex of older branches.

FLOWERS: 2–3 per inflorescence. The waxy, orange flowers are 0.7–0.9 in. (1.7–2.2 cm) long. They have a long spur. The dorsal sepal is oblong-ovate, and the part of the lateral sepals that do not form the spur are ovate. The spoon-shaped lip is thickened along the strongly cupped margin. It is notched at the apex of the center line.

REFERENCES: 95, 221, 445, 470, 538, 549, 553.

PHOTOS/DRAWINGS: 95, 538, 549, 553.

Dendrobium wenzelii Ames

ORIGIN/HABITAT: The Philippine Islands. Plants are found on Mindanao in Lanao and Surigao Provinces, on Luzon in Quezon Province, and on Leyte. They usually grow below 350 ft. (100 m).

CLIMATE: Station #98653, Surigao, Philippines, Lat. 9.8°N, Long. 125.5°E, at 72 ft. (22 m). Record extreme temperatures are 99°F (37°C) and 65°F (18°C).

N/HEMISPHERE	JAN	FEB	MAR	APR	MAY	JUN	JUL	AUG	SEP	OCT	NOV	DEC
°F AVG MAX	83	84	85	87	89	89	89	89	89	88	86	84
°F AVG MIN	72	72	73	73	74	74	74	75	75	74	74	73
DIURNAL RANGE	11	12	12	14	15	15	15	14	14	14	12	11
RAIN/INCHES	21.4	14.8	19.9	10.0	6.2	4.9	7.0	5.1	6.6	10.7	16.8	24.4
HUMIDITY/%	91	90	88	85	85	82	83	82	83	84	88	89
BLOOM SEASON			*	*	*	*		*		*		
DAYS CLR @ 8AM	1	1	2	4	2	3	2	2	1	2	1	1
DAYS CLR @ 2PM	1	2	2	6	3	1	2	1	2	3	1	1
RAIN/MM	544	376	505	254	157	124	178	130	168	272	427	620
°C AVG MAX	28.3	28.9	29.4	30.6	31.7	31.7	31.7	31.7	31.7	31.1	30.0	28.9
°C AVG MIN	22.2	22.2	22.8	22.8	23.3	23.3	23.3	23.9	23.9	23.3	23.3	22.8
DIURNAL RANGE	6.1	6.7	6.6	7.8	8.4	8.4	8.4	7.8	7.8	7.8	6.7	6.1
S/HEMISPHERE	JUL	AUG	SEP	OCT	NOV	DEC	JAN	FEB	MAR	APR	MAY	JUN

Cultural Recommendations

LIGHT: 1800–2500 fc.

TEMPERATURES: Throughout the year, days average 83–89°F (28–32°C), and nights average 72–75°F (22–24°C), with a diurnal range of 11–15°F (6–8°C). The widest diurnal range occurs in summer and results from warmer days.

HUMIDITY: 80–90% year-round.

WATER: Rainfall is moderate to very heavy all year. Cultivated plants should be kept moist but not soggy. Warm water might be beneficial.

FERTILIZER: ¼–½ recommended strength. A balanced fertilizer should be applied weekly to biweekly throughout the year.

REST PERIOD: Growing conditions should be maintained all year. Wide temperature fluctuations should be avoided. In the habitat, the heaviest rainfall occurs in winter; but water should not be increased for cultivated plants. In fact, water should be reduced for plants grown in the dark, short-day conditions common in temperate-latitude winters. Plants should never be allowed to dry out completely, however. In the habitat, light is lowest in winter.

GROWING MEDIA: Plants may be mounted on tree-fern or cork slabs if humidity is high and plants are watered at least once daily in summer. When plants are potted, any open, fast-draining medium may be used. Repotting may be done anytime new roots are growing.

MISCELLANEOUS NOTES: The bloom season shown in the climate table is based on collection reports.

Plant and Flower Information

PLANT SIZE AND TYPE: A 1.6–4.0 in. (4–10 cm) sympodial epiphyte.

PSEUDOBULB: 1.6–4.0 in. (4–10 cm) long. The stems are slender.

LEAVES: Many. The rigid leaves are 0.5 in. (1.2 cm) long on the longest edge. They are triangular, somewhat sickle-shaped, and 2-ranked along the stem. The apical pair of leaves are glossy orange.

INFLORESCENCE: The inflorescence emerges from a cushion of fibrous scales at stem nodes opposite rudimentary leaves.

FLOWERS: 1 at a time per inflorescence. The flowers are 0.4 in. (1 cm) long. Sepals and petals are white. Blossoms have an oblong-elliptical dorsal sepal and triangular, sickle-shaped lateral sepals. The unlobed lip is purple with yellow at the notched tip.

REFERENCES: 12, 222, 296, 536.

Dendrobium whiteanum Hunt. See *D. stuartii* F. M. Bailey.

REFERENCES: 67, 105, 228, 533.

Dendrobium whitmeei Kränzlin

ORIGIN/HABITAT: Samoa. Plants grow at low elevations near Apia on Upolu Island.

CLIMATE: Station #91762, Apia, Western Samoa, Lat. 13.8°S, Long. 171.8°W, at 7 ft. (2 m). Record extreme temperatures are 93°F (34°C) and 63°F (17°C).

N/HEMISPHERE	JAN	FEB	MAR	APR	MAY	JUN	JUL	AUG	SEP	OCT	NOV	DEC
°F AVG MAX	85	84	84	85	86	85	86	85	86	86	85	85
°F AVG MIN	74	75	74	75	74	74	75	76	74	75	74	74
DIURNAL RANGE	11	9	10	10	12	11	11	9	12	11	11	11
RAIN/INCHES	3.2	3.5	5.2	6.7	10.5	14.6	17.9	15.2	14.1	10.0	6.3	5.1
HUMIDITY/%	76	75	75	77	77	78	81	80	80	78	77	75
BLOOM SEASON		*										
DAYS CLR @ 1PM	9	10	9	6	3	3	4	2	3	5	9	10
DAYS CLR @ 7PM	12	10	11	7	4	3	2	2	2	5	11	8
RAIN/MM	81	89	132	170	267	371	455	386	358	254	160	130
°C AVG MAX	29.4	28.9	28.9	29.4	30.0	29.4	30.0	29.4	30.0	30.0	29.4	29.4
°C AVG MIN	23.3	23.9	23.3	23.9	23.3	23.3	23.9	24.4	23.3	23.9	23.3	23.3
DIURNAL RANGE	6.1	5.0	5.6	5.5	6.7	6.1	6.1	5.0	6.7	6.1	6.1	6.1
S/HEMISPHERE	JUL	AUG	SEP	OCT	NOV	DEC	JAN	FEB	MAR	APR	MAY	JUN

Cultural Recommendations

LIGHT: 2000–3000 fc.

TEMPERATURES: Throughout the year, days average 84–86°F (29–30°C), and nights average 74–76°F (23–24°C), with a diurnal range of 9–12°F (5–7°C).

HUMIDITY: 75–80% year-round.

WATER: Rainfall is moderate to heavy all year, but conditions are slightly drier for 2–3 months in winter. Cultivated plants should be kept moist with only slight drying allowed between waterings.

FERTILIZER: ¼–½ recommended strength. A balanced fertilizer should be applied weekly to biweekly throughout the year.

REST PERIOD: Growing temperatures should be maintained all year. Water should be reduced somewhat for cultivated plants, especially those grown in the dark, short-day conditions common during temperate-latitude winters; but they should never be allowed to dry out completely.

Dendrobium wichersii

Fertilizer should be reduced or eliminated anytime water is reduced. In the habitat, light is highest in winter.

GROWING MEDIA: Plants may be mounted on tree-fern or cork slabs or potted in small pots filled with any open, fast-draining medium. Repotting may be done anytime new roots are growing.

MISCELLANEOUS NOTES: The bloom season shown in the climate table is based on cultivation records.

Plant and Flower Information

PLANT SIZE AND TYPE: A sympodial epiphyte of unreported size.

PSEUDOBULB: The plant was described from an incomplete specimen 12–16 in. (30–40 cm) long. The elongated stems were probably pendulous.

LEAVES: Many. The leaves are 3.1 in. (8 cm) long, ovate-oblong, and papery.

INFLORESCENCE: Very short. Inflorescences are borne along the stem.

FLOWERS: The flowers are 1.6 in. (4 cm) across. They are pale sulfur yellow. The ovate sepals and petals are similar. The small, 3-lobed lip has elevated lines. The midlobe is triangular and hairy along the margin and disk. The small, ovate sidelobes are serrated along the margin.

REFERENCES: 220, 254.

Dendrobium wichersii Schlechter. Now considered a synonym of *Epigeneium wichersii* (Schlechter) Summerhayes. REFERENCES: 220, 229, 435, 499.

Dendrobium wightii Balakr. See *D. wightii* A. Hawkes and A. H. Heller. REFERENCES: 31, 231.

Dendrobium wightii A. Hawkes and A. H. Heller

AKA: *D. graminifolium* Wight not Ames or Willdenow, *D. wightii* Balakr.

ORIGIN/HABITAT: Southern India. Plants are found in the Kerala and Tamil Nadu regions from sea level to 2300 ft. (0–700 m), and Joseph (ref. 244) reported plants in the Nilgiris region at 3350–6250 ft. (1030–1900 m).

CLIMATE: Station #43314, Calicut, India, Lat. 11.3°N, Long. 75.8°E, at 17 ft. (5 m). Temperatures are calculated for an elevation of 1500 ft. (460 m), resulting in probable extremes of 94°F (35°C) and 52°F (11°C).

N/HEMISPHERE	JAN	FEB	MAR	APR	MAY	JUN	JUL	AUG	SEP	OCT	NOV	DEC
°F AVG MAX	83	84	85	86	85	80	77	78	79	81	82	83
°F AVG MIN	66	68	71	73	73	70	69	69	70	70	69	66
DIURNAL RANGE	17	16	14	13	12	10	8	9	9	11	13	17
RAIN/INCHES	0.4	0.2	0.7	3.6	9.3	33.1	32.5	17.2	7.9	10.3	5.5	1.0
HUMIDITY/%	71	73	73	74	82	87	91	91	87	85	77	74
BLOOM SEASON				*	*							
DAYS CLR @ 5AM	19	18	21	12	5	4	2	2	4	4	19	20
DAYS CLR @ 11AM	16	18	23	15	5	3	0	1	6	5	12	14
RAIN/MM	10	5	18	91	236	841	826	437	201	262	140	25
°C AVG MAX	28.4	28.9	29.5	30.1	29.5	26.7	25.1	25.6	26.2	27.3	27.8	28.4
°C AVG MIN	18.9	20.1	21.7	22.8	22.8	21.2	20.6	20.6	21.2	21.2	20.6	18.9
DIURNAL RANGE	9.5	8.8	7.8	7.3	6.7	5.5	4.5	5.0	5.0	6.1	7.2	9.5
S/HEMISPHERE	JUL	AUG	SEP	OCT	NOV	DEC	JAN	FEB	MAR	APR	MAY	JUN

Cultural Recommendations

LIGHT: 3000–4000 fc. The heavy summer cloud cover indicates that some shading is needed from spring through autumn, but light should be as high as the plant can tolerate, short of burning the leaves.

TEMPERATURES: Throughout the year, days average 77–86°F (25–30°C), and nights average 66–73°F (19–23°C), with a diurnal range of 8–17°F (4–10°C). The coolest days and the smallest diurnal range occur in summer.

HUMIDITY: 85–90% in summer, dropping to 70–75% in winter.

WATER: Rainfall is heavy to extremely heavy most of the year, but conditions are very dry for 3–4 months in winter. Cultivated plants should be watered liberally in summer, as often as several times a week during bright, hot weather. Water should be gradually reduced through autumn, greatly reduced in winter, then gradually increased in spring when new growth starts.

FERTILIZER: ¼–½ recommended strength, applied weekly. A high-nitrogen fertilizer is beneficial from spring to midsummer, but a fertilizer high in phosphates should be used in late summer and autumn.

REST PERIOD: Growing temperatures should be maintained year-round. For cultivated plants, water should be greatly reduced for 3–4 months. Plants should be allowed to dry out between waterings, but they should not remain completely dry for extended periods. Occasional early morning mistings between waterings may be beneficial, especially on warm, sunny days. Fertilizer should be greatly reduced or eliminated until water is increased in spring. In the habitat, light is highest in winter.

GROWING MEDIA: Growers recommend mounting on tree-fern slabs if humidity is high. Plants may need daily watering in midsummer. If plants are potted, any open, fast-draining medium may be used. Repotting should be done in late spring when new roots begin to grow.

MISCELLANEOUS NOTES: The bloom season shown in the climate table is based on reports from the habitat. Because of the wide range of habitat elevation, plants should adapt to conditions 8–10°F (4–6°C) cooler than indicated.

Plant and Flower Information

PLANT SIZE AND TYPE: A 6–11 in. (15–28 cm) sympodial epiphyte.

PSEUDOBULB: 4–8 in. (10–20 cm) long. The ascending stems arise from a long, slender, creeping rhizome.

LEAVES: 6 per growth. The leaves are 2–3 in. (5.0–7.5 cm) long. They are pointed at the tip, narrowly linear, and grasslike.

INFLORESCENCE: Shorter than the leaves. The slender raceme emerges at the apex of the stem. It is somewhat zigzag.

FLOWERS: 1–6 per inflorescence. The tiny white flowers are 0.6 in. (1.5 cm) across. The lanceolate lateral sepals are somewhat sickle-shaped. The petals are linear-lanceolate. The oblong lip is flat with wavy margins and small spreading sidelobes. The spur is short and straight.

HYBRIDIZING NOTES: Chromosome count is 2n = 38 as *D. graminifolium* (ref. 504).

REFERENCES: 31, 38, 119, 202, 230, 231, 244, 254, 255, 317, 504.

PHOTOS/DRAWINGS: 244.

Dendrobium wildianum (Rolfe ex Downie) T. Tang and F. T. Wang. Now considered a synonym of *Eria wildiana* Rolfe ex Downie. REFERENCES: 228, 418, 505.

Dendrobium wilkianum Rupp. See *D. mirbelianum* Gaudich. REFERENCES: 67, 84, 88, 105, 227, 228, 236, 240, 262, 345, 421, 533. PHOTOS/DRAWINGS: 105, 345, 421.

Dendrobium williamsianum Rchb. f.

ORIGIN/HABITAT: Papua New Guinea. Plants usually grow on small *Antidesma* trees in hot, dry savannas, often with little or no rain for 6 months. They are often found with *Acriopsis javanica*, *Coelogyne asperata*, *Dendrobium bifalce*, and *Vanda hindsii*. Plants may also be found, although in smaller numbers, growing in tree tops along the borders of lowland forests and savannas.

CLIMATE: Station #94003, Daru, Papua New Guinea, Lat. 9.1°S, Long. 143.2°E, at 20 ft. (6 m). Record extreme temperatures are 98°F (37°C) and 63°F (17°C).

N/HEMISPHERE	JAN	FEB	MAR	APR	MAY	JUN	JUL	AUG	SEP	OCT	NOV	DEC
°F AVG MAX	81	82	83	85	88	88	88	87	87	86	84	82
°F AVG MIN	74	74	74	76	76	76	76	76	76	76	77	75
DIURNAL RANGE	7	8	9	9	12	12	12	11	11	10	7	7
RAIN/INCHES	3.0	2.2	1.8	2.3	4.6	8.1	11.9	10.4	12.5	12.6	9.4	3.8
HUMIDITY/%	94	93	91	88	85	88	85	87	84	88	91	94
BLOOM SEASON				*	**	**	**	*				*
DAYS CLR	N/A											
RAIN/MM	76	56	46	58	117	206	302	264	318	320	239	97
°C AVG MAX	27.2	27.8	28.3	29.4	31.1	31.1	31.1	30.6	30.6	30.0	28.9	27.8
°C AVG MIN	23.3	23.3	23.3	24.4	24.4	24.4	24.4	24.4	24.4	24.4	25.0	23.9
DIURNAL RANGE	3.9	4.5	5.0	5.0	6.7	6.7	6.7	6.2	6.2	5.6	3.9	3.9
S/HEMISPHERE	JUL	AUG	SEP	OCT	NOV	DEC	JAN	FEB	MAR	APR	MAY	JUN

Cultural Recommendations

LIGHT: 3000–4000 fc. Provide 50% shade in summer, with no shade in midwinter.

TEMPERATURES: Throughout the year, days average 81–88°F (27–31°C), and nights average 74–77°F (23–25°C), with a diurnal range of 7–12°F (4–7°C).

HUMIDITY: 85–90% from spring to autumn, increasing to 90–95% in winter.

WATER: Rainfall is heavy from late spring through autumn, with a 2–3 month drier season in late winter and early spring. Cultivated plants should be kept wet but not soggy from late spring through early autumn, but water should be gradually reduced in late autumn.

FERTILIZER: ¼–½ recommended strength. A balanced fertilizer should be applied weekly to biweekly throughout the year.

REST PERIOD: Growing temperatures should be maintained all year. Rainfall is low for about 5 months, but the driest part of the season lasts only 2–3 months. However, large quantities of water are available from nightly dew. Cultivated plants should be allowed to dry out between waterings, but they should not remain dry for long periods. Growers indicate that these plants require the same conditions as *D. bigibbum* Lindley, with a prolonged dry rest after flowering. Fertilizer should be reduced or eliminated until water is increased in spring. In the habitat, light is probably greater in winter.

GROWING MEDIA: Plants may be mounted on tree-fern or cork slabs if humidity is high and plants are watered at least once daily in summer. When plants are potted, any open, fast-draining medium may be used. Repotting may be done anytime new roots are growing.

MISCELLANEOUS NOTES: The bloom season shown in the climate table is based on cultivation records. Plants tend to be shorter in higher light habitats.

Plant and Flower Information

PLANT SIZE AND TYPE: A variable, 18–138 in. (45–350 cm) sympodial epiphyte.

PSEUDOBULB: 18–138 in. (46–350 cm) long. Some plants have canes more than 197 in. (500 cm) long. The stems are slender but very strong.

LEAVES: Many. The oblong, persistent leaves are 2 in. (5 cm) long with a blunt tip. They may be pale green to medium yellow. The leaves are arranged in 2 rows.

INFLORESCENCE: 8–10 in. (20–25 cm) long. The arching inflorescences rise from the upper part of the stems.

FLOWERS: 3–10 per inflorescence. The flowers are 0.8–2.0 in. (2–5 cm) across and may last for 2–3 months. The broad sepals and petals are white to pale yellow with a mauve flush on the outside. They are oblong to broadly ovate with a point at each apex. The lip is rich dark purple with a pale margin and raised blackish-purple keels. The margins are upturned to incurled at the back of the large round lip. The nodding, downward facing flowers are most attractive when viewed from below.

HYBRIDIZING NOTES: Chromosome count is 2n = 38 (ref. 153, 154, 188, 273).

REFERENCES: 153, 154, 179, 188, 190, 216, 233, 254, 273, 301, 304, 351, 430, 445, 461, 570.

PHOTOS/DRAWINGS: 301, *304*, *430*, 570.

Dendrobium williamsonii Day and Rchb. f.

AKA: Sometimes spelled *D. williamsoni*. Seidenfaden (ref. 454) discusses the confusion regarding the species *D. cariniferum* Rchb. f., *D. wattii* (Hooker f.) Rchb. f., and *D. williamsonii*. Pradhan (ref. 369) lists *D. cariniferum* and *D. wattii* as synonyms. Schelpe (ref. 429) includes *D. cariniferum* and *D. luebbersianum* Rchb. f. as synonyms. In 1992 *Opera Botanica*, Seidenfaden tentatively differentiates the plants with characteristics included in the following Plant and Flower Information.

ORIGIN/HABITAT: India and Southeast Asia. In India, plants grow near Gangtok in Sikkim, in the Khasi (Khasia) Hills in Assam, and in the Manipur district. They are also found near Nam Hat in upper Burma and in western Yunnan Province of China. Plants usually grow at 3600–5900 ft. (1100–1800 m). Plants called *D. wattii* originated in Manipur and West Bengal, India, *D. williamsonii* originated in Assam and the Khasi (Khasia) Hills, and *D. luebbersianum* originated in Borneo. Seidenfaden (ref. 454) indicates that plants have been reported in Thailand and Vietnam, but he questions their actual occurrence in these areas.

CLIMATE: Station #42410, Gauhati, India, Lat. 26.1°N, Long. 91.6°E, at 158 ft. (48 m). Temperatures are calculated for an elevation of 4600 ft. (1400 m), resulting in probable extremes of 89°F (32°C) and 26°F (−3°C).

N/HEMISPHERE	JAN	FEB	MAR	APR	MAY	JUN	JUL	AUG	SEP	OCT	NOV	DEC
°F AVG MAX	61	63	71	73	73	74	75	75	74	72	66	61
°F AVG MIN	36	39	45	53	57	62	63	63	61	56	46	38
DIURNAL RANGE	25	24	26	20	16	12	12	12	13	16	20	23
RAIN/INCHES	0.4	1.2	2.0	5.7	9.3	12.3	12.3	10.3	6.6	2.8	0.6	0.2
HUMIDITY/%	79	72	64	71	82	85	85	86	84	84	83	82
BLOOM SEASON	*	*	*	*								
DAYS CLR @ 6AM	6	12	16	11	3	0	0	3	3	6	6	3
DAYS CLR @ 12PM	17	16	18	15	6	1	0	0	2	11	17	19
RAIN/MM	10	30	51	145	236	312	312	262	168	71	15	5
°C AVG MAX	16.3	17.4	21.9	23.0	23.0	23.5	24.1	24.1	23.5	22.4	19.1	16.3
°C AVG MIN	2.4	4.1	7.4	11.9	14.1	16.9	17.4	17.4	16.3	13.5	8.0	3.5
DIURNAL RANGE	13.9	13.3	14.5	11.1	8.9	6.6	6.7	6.7	7.2	8.9	11.1	12.8
S/HEMISPHERE	JUL	AUG	SEP	OCT	NOV	DEC	JAN	FEB	MAR	APR	MAY	JUN

Cultural Recommendations

LIGHT: 2500–3500 fc. The heavy summer cloud cover indicates that some shading is needed from spring through autumn, but light should be as high as the plant can tolerate, short of burning the leaves.

TEMPERATURES: Summer days average 74–75°F (24°C), and nights average 62–63°F (17°C), with a diurnal range of 12°F (7°C).

HUMIDITY: 80–85% most of the year, dropping to 65–70% for 3 months in late winter and spring.

WATER: Rainfall is heavy from spring through summer but decreases rapidly in autumn with a 1–2 month transition into the winter dry season. Cultivated plants should be kept moist while actively growing. Water should be gradually reduced after new growths mature in autumn.

FERTILIZER: ½ recommended strength, applied weekly. A high-nitrogen fertilizer is beneficial from spring to midsummer, but a fertilizer high in phosphates should be used in late summer and autumn.

REST PERIOD: Winter days average 61–63°F (17–22°C), and nights average 36–39°F (2–4°C), with a diurnal range of 23–25°F (13–14°C). Growers are cautioned that these calculated lows may be too cold. Observed temperatures at high-elevation stations in nearby regions suggest that averages may be 4–6°F (2–3°C) warmer than indicated in the table. Plants should survive exposure to freezing if they are dry at the time, but extreme conditions should be avoided in cultivation. Although rainfall is low for 4–5 winter months, high humidity and the large temperature range indicate that additional moisture from heavy dew is common. Therefore, while water should be greatly reduced and cultivated plants allowed to dry out between waterings from late autumn into early spring, they should not remain dry for extended periods. Occasional mistings between waterings during bright, sunny weather may help prevent the plants from becoming too dry. Fertilizer should be reduced or eliminated until active growth resumes and water is increased in spring. In the habitat, light is brightest in winter.

GROWING MEDIA: Plants may be mounted on tree-fern or cork slabs or potted in small pots filled with any open, fast-draining medium. Repotting may be done anytime new roots are growing.

MISCELLANEOUS NOTES: The bloom season shown in the climate table is based on cultivation records. Growers indicate that *D. williamsonii* survives but does not thrive in lowland Thailand. It is considered difficult to establish. *D. williamsonii* is sometimes found growing with *D. draconis* Rchb. f.

Plant and Flower Information

PLANT SIZE AND TYPE: A 6–12 in. (15–30 cm) sympodial epiphyte.

PSEUDOBULB: 6–12 in. (15–30 cm) long. The erect stems are spindle-shaped and densely covered with black hairs.

LEAVES: 2–5 near the apex of young stems. The narrowly oblong leaves are usually 2–5 in. (5–13 cm) long. The leaf sheaths are covered with black hairs. Some reports indicate that leaves are evergreen, while others indicate that the leaves are deciduous. While this discrepancy may indicate that leaves are persistent in milder habitats, the confusion surrounding the use of names for this plant alliance may indicate that reports for different species are applied to the wrong species name.

INFLORESCENCE: Very short. Inflorescences are borne at nodes of the most recently matured pseudobulbs.

FLOWERS: 1–3 per inflorescence. The flowers are 2–3 in. (5–8 cm) across. The pointed sepals and petals are white with a pale, fawn yellow flush that may be darkest on the tips of the sepals. The keels on the backs of the sepals do not extend into the ovary as in *D. cariniferum*. The ovary is circular in cross-section. The 3-lobed lip has a yellow, bright red, or red-brown disk, a toothed and wavy margin, and woolly hairs along the veins. The long curved spur is brownish purple. Some flowers are dusted with red on the inside. Flowers known as *D. luebbersianum* were described as having "3 carnation blotches" on the lip. Blossoms are fragrant and long-lived. Unlike *D. cariniferum*, the ovary is not keeled.

HYBRIDIZING NOTES: Chromosome counts are 2n = 38 (ref. 152, 243) and 2n = 57 (ref. 150, 154, 542) as *D. williamsonii* and 2n = 38 (ref. 504) as *D. cariniferum*.

REFERENCES: 36, 38, 39, 46, 150, 152, 154, 179, 190, 196, 202, 203, 210, 216, 243, 245, 254, 266, 364, 369, 429, 430, 445, 448, 454, 504, 528, 541, 542, 569, 570.

PHOTOS/DRAWINGS: *36, 39, 125,* 203, 210, *364, 369, 430, 454, 569.*

Dendrobium wilmsianum Schlechter

ORIGIN/HABITAT: Burma and Thailand. In Burma, plants grow at about 4500 ft. (1370 m) in the southern Shan States. The orchids are also found in the mountains of northern and western Thailand. Although they are reported as high as 7550 ft. (2300 m), the plants generally grow at 3300–4900 ft. (1000–1500 m).

CLIMATE: Station #48325, Mae Sariang, Thailand, Lat. 18.2°N, Long. 97.8°E, at 1030 ft. (314 m). Temperatures are calculated for an elevation of 3900 ft. (1190 m), resulting in probable extremes of 101°F (39°C) and 32°F (0°C).

N/HEMISPHERE	JAN	FEB	MAR	APR	MAY	JUN	JUL	AUG	SEP	OCT	NOV	DEC
°F AVG MAX	79	83	87	90	85	80	78	78	80	81	80	77
°F AVG MIN	49	48	55	64	67	66	65	65	65	63	59	51
DIURNAL RANGE	30	35	32	26	18	14	13	13	15	18	21	26
RAIN/INCHES	0.3	0.2	0.3	1.9	5.7	9.0	8.4	10.8	8.7	3.7	1.1	0.6
HUMIDITY/%	72	67	57	55	68	83	83	84	83	81	77	75
BLOOM SEASON												*
DAYS CLR @ 7AM	1	16	0	3	4	0	0	0	0	0	0	1
DAYS CLR @ 1PM	24	18	9	5	2	0	0	1	1	6	13	20
RAIN/MM	8	5	8	48	145	229	213	274	221	94	28	15
°C AVG MAX	25.8	28.1	30.3	32.0	29.2	26.4	25.3	25.3	26.4	27.0	26.4	24.7
°C AVG MIN	9.2	8.6	12.5	17.5	19.2	18.6	18.1	18.1	18.1	17.0	14.7	10.3
DIURNAL RANGE	16.6	19.5	17.8	14.5	10.0	7.8	7.2	7.2	8.3	10.0	11.7	14.4
S/HEMISPHERE	JUL	AUG	SEP	OCT	NOV	DEC	JAN	FEB	MAR	APR	MAY	JUN

Cultural Recommendations

LIGHT: 3000–4000 fc. Heavy cloud cover reduces light levels considerably during what should be the brightest part of the year. Winter is actually the brightest season in the habitat, as indicated by the large number of clear afternoons and the deciduous nature of the forests. Consequently, cultivated plants should be shaded from late spring into autumn, but shading should be reduced or removed in winter and as much light as possible provided, short of burning the leaves. Strong air movement is very important throughout the year.

TEMPERATURES: Summer days average 78–80°F (25–26°C), and nights average 65–66°F (18–19°C), with a diurnal range of 13–14°F (7–8°C). The warmest weather occurs in spring. Days average 85–90°F (29–32°C), and nights average 55–67°F (13–19°C), with a diurnal range of 18–32°F (10–18°C).

HUMIDITY: 80–85% in summer and early autumn, dropping to near 55% in late winter and early spring.

WATER: Rainfall is moderate to heavy from late spring through early autumn. Conditions are very dry in winter and early spring, however. Cultivated plants should be kept moist while they are actively growing, but water should be gradually reduced in autumn after new growths mature.

FERTILIZER: ¼–½ recommended strength, applied weekly. A high-nitrogen fertilizer is beneficial from spring to midsummer, but a fertilizer high in phosphates should be used in late summer and autumn.

REST PERIOD: Winter days average 77–83°F (25–28°C), and nights average 48–51°F (9–10°C), with a diurnal range of 26–35°F (14–20°C). In the habitat, winter rainfall is low for 4–5 months. During the early part of the dry season, overnight fog, mist, and very heavy dew results in more available moisture than is indicated by the rainfall averages. For most of the winter dry season, cultivated plants should be allowed to dry out between waterings, but they should not remain dry for extended periods. However, for 1–2 months in late winter, conditions are clear, warm, and dry, with humidity so low that even the moisture from morning dew is uncommon. Cultivated plants should be allowed to become dry during this time with only an occasional watering or early morning misting provided if excessive shriveling is noted. Fertilizer should be eliminated when plants are dry.

GROWING MEDIA: Plants may be mounted on tree-fern or cork slabs if humidity is high and plants are watered at least once daily in summer. When plants are potted, any open, fast-draining medium may be used. Repotting is best done in early spring when new roots are growing.

MISCELLANEOUS NOTES: The bloom season shown in the climate table is based on collection reports. *D. wilmsianum* differs from *D. compactum* Rolfe ex W. Hackett only in the shape of the callus on the lip.

Plant and Flower Information

PLANT SIZE AND TYPE: A 2–5 in. (5–13 cm) sympodial epiphyte.

PSEUDOBULB: 2–5 in. (5–13 cm) long. The leafy stems taper toward the apex.

LEAVES: 8–10. The pale, yellow-green leaves are 1.2–2.0 in. (3–5 cm) long.

INFLORESCENCE: 1.2 in. (3 cm) long. Several inflorescences emerge from nodes on the upper part of the stem.

FLOWERS: 1–3, rarely as many as 15 per inflorescence. The flowers are 0.3 in. (0.8 cm) long. The lanceolate sepals and narrower petals are pointed at the tip. They are white, shading to green. The 3-lobed lip is uppermost. It is uneven and deeply ruffled along the margin with a broad notch at the apex. The raised callus is lyre-shaped.

REFERENCES: 220, 254, 266, 448, 454.

PHOTOS/DRAWINGS: 454.

Dendrobium wilsonii Rolfe

AKA: *D. kosepangii* Tso, *D. kwangtungense* Tso.

ORIGIN/HABITAT: China. In western Szechuan Province, plants grow at about 4100 ft. (1250 m). They are also found in Hunan, Kwangsi, Kwangtung, and Kweichow provinces of southwestern China and have been reported at 3300–4250 ft. (1000–1300 m).

CLIMATE: Station #56671, Hui-li, China, Lat. 26.8°N, Long. 102.3°E, at 6299 ft. (1920 m). Temperatures are calculated for an elevation of 4100 ft. (1250 m), resulting in probable extremes of 100°F (38°C) and 28°F (–2°C).

N/HEMISPHERE	JAN	FEB	MAR	APR	MAY	JUN	JUL	AUG	SEP	OCT	NOV	DEC
°F AVG MAX	68	70	79	85	88	86	87	86	84	77	73	69
°F AVG MIN	39	42	49	56	64	69	71	69	66	61	48	41
DIURNAL RANGE	29	28	30	29	24	17	16	17	18	16	25	28
RAIN/INCHES	N/A											
HUMIDITY/%	59	58	49	47	53	72	73	77	74	77	70	68
BLOOM SEASON			*									
DAYS CLR @ 7AM	20	16	20	17	13	3	2	3	6	4	18	20
DAYS CLR @ 1PM	17	10	15	12	4	2	1	2	4	3	11	15
RAIN/MM	N/A											
°C AVG MAX	20.1	21.3	26.3	29.6	31.3	30.1	30.7	30.1	29.0	25.1	22.9	20.7
°C AVG MIN	4.0	5.7	9.6	13.5	17.9	20.7	21.8	20.7	19.0	16.3	9.0	5.1
DIURNAL RANGE	16.1	15.6	16.7	16.1	13.4	9.4	8.9	9.4	10.0	8.8	13.9	15.6
S/HEMISPHERE	JUL	AUG	SEP	OCT	NOV	DEC	JAN	FEB	MAR	APR	MAY	JUN

Cultural Recommendations

LIGHT: 2000–3000 fc. The heavy summer cloud cover indicates that some shading is needed from spring through autumn, but light should be as high as the plant can tolerate, short of burning the leaves.

TEMPERATURES: Summer days average 86–87°F (30–31°C), and nights average 69–71°F (21–22°C), with a diurnal range of 16–17°F (9°C). Spring is the warmest season. Days are 79–88°F (26–31°C), and nights are 49–64°F (10–18°C), with a diurnal range of 24–30°F (13–17°C).

HUMIDITY: 70–75% in summer and autumn, dropping to near 60% in early winter, then dropping further to 45–50% for 2–3 months in late winter and early spring.

WATER: Rainfall records are not available for this location. However, reports from other stations in the region show a pronounced wet/dry pattern. Rainfall is probably moderate to heavy from spring into autumn, followed by a 4–5 month winter dry period when monthly rainfall is likely to average less than 1 in. (25 mm). Cultivated plants should be kept moist while actively growing, but water should be gradually reduced after new growths mature in autumn.

FERTILIZER: ¼–½ recommended strength, applied weekly. A high-nitrogen fertilizer is beneficial from spring to midsummer, but a fertilizer high in phosphates should be used in late summer and autumn.

REST PERIOD: Winter days average 68–70°F (20–21°C), and nights average 39–42°F (4–6°C), with a diurnal range of 28–29°F (16°C). Rainfall is low for 4–5 months, but during the early part of the dry season, additional moisture is available from heavy dew. During this time, plants should be allowed to dry out between waterings, but they should not remain dry for long periods. When humidity drops below 50% for 2–3 months, conditions are too dry even for dew to form. During a corresponding time, cultivated plants should be allowed to become quite dry between waterings. Occasional early morning mistings may be given between waterings if excessive shriveling is noted. Fertilizer should be reduced or eliminated. Winter light should be as high as the plant can tolerate, short of burning the foliage.

GROWING MEDIA: Plants may be mounted on tree-fern or cork slabs or potted in small pots filled with any open, fast-draining medium. Repotting may be done anytime new roots are actively growing.

MISCELLANEOUS NOTES: The bloom season shown in the climate table is based on cultivation records. Plants are dried and used in Chinese medicine.

Plant and Flower Information

PLANT SIZE AND TYPE: An 18–24 in. (45–60 cm) sympodial epiphyte or terrestrial.

PSEUDOBULB: 18–24 in. (45–60 cm) long. The stems are cylindrical and slender.

LEAVES: Many. The somewhat oblong leaves are 2–3 in. (5–8 cm) long. They have 2 unequal teeth at the apex.

INFLORESCENCE: Short.

FLOWERS: Few per inflorescence. The flowers are 1.0–1.6 in. (2.5–4.0 cm) long. The oblong petals and narrower sepals are rounded at the tip. The unlobed lip is shorter than the sepals. All segments are pale rose, but the lip is decorated with a yellow disk and purple dots. The column is yellow with purple spots. Blossoms are fragrant.

REFERENCES: 179, 208, 220, 254, 528.

Dendrobium wisselense Cribb

ORIGIN/HABITAT: Western New Guinea. Plants grow in the Wissel Lakes region near Digitaria Pass at about 5750 ft. (1750 m).

CLIMATE: Station #97686, Wamena, Irian Jaya, Lat. 4.1°S, Long. 139.0°E, at 5446 ft. (1660 m). Record extreme temperatures are not available for this location.

N/HEMISPHERE	JAN	FEB	MAR	APR	MAY	JUN	JUL	AUG	SEP	OCT	NOV	DEC
°F AVG MAX	75	76	77	76	77	76	77	76	76	79	78	74
°F AVG MIN	60	60	62	62	63	64	63	62	63	65	65	61
DIURNAL RANGE	15	16	15	14	14	12	14	14	13	14	13	13
RAIN/INCHES	3.0	1.9	2.2	4.0	4.6	3.3	2.8	4.2	6.9	3.9	5.4	4.9
HUMIDITY/%	N/A											
BLOOM SEASON	N/A											
DAYS CLR	N/A											
RAIN/MM	76	48	56	102	117	84	71	107	175	99	137	124
°C AVG MAX	23.9	24.4	25.0	24.4	25.0	24.4	25.0	24.4	24.4	26.1	25.6	23.3
°C AVG MIN	15.6	15.6	16.7	16.7	17.2	17.8	17.2	16.7	17.2	18.3	18.3	16.1
DIURNAL RANGE	8.3	8.8	8.3	7.7	7.8	6.6	7.8	7.7	7.2	7.8	7.3	7.2
S/HEMISPHERE	JUL	AUG	SEP	OCT	NOV	DEC	JAN	FEB	MAR	APR	MAY	JUN

Cultural Recommendations

LIGHT: 1500–2500 fc. In the habitat, morning light is highest.

TEMPERATURES: Throughout the year, days average 74–79°F (23–26°C), and nights average 60–65°F (16–18°C), with a diurnal range of 12–16°F (7–9°C). In the habitat, the warmest temperatures of the day occur in late morning, when skies are clear. Clouds and mist develop near noon and continue through the afternoon, thus preventing additional warming.

HUMIDITY: Information is not available for this location. However, records from nearby stations indicate that humidity probably averages near 80% year-round. High humidity and excellent air circulation are particularly important if temperatures are warm. Placing the plants in front of an

Dendrobium wollastonii

evaporative cooler or near a fine mist may be very beneficial on especially warm days.

WATER: Rainfall is light to moderate through most of the year, but in the habitat, it is probably greater than indicated in the climate table. In addition, large amounts of water are usually available from mist and heavy dew, even during periods of lower rainfall. Cultivated plants should be kept moist, with only slight drying allowed between waterings. Good air movement is critically important and should be maintained at all times.

FERTILIZER: ¼–½ recommended strength. A balanced fertilizer should be applied weekly to biweekly throughout the year.

REST PERIOD: Growing conditions should be maintained all year. Rainfall averages are somewhat lower for a month or so in winter and again in midsummer. In cultivation, water may be decreased, but plants should never be allowed to dry out completely. In the habitat, light is slightly higher in winter.

GROWING MEDIA: Plants may be mounted on tree-fern or cork slabs if humidity is high and plants are watered at least once daily in summer. When plants are potted, any open, fast-draining medium may be used. Repotting may be done anytime new roots are growing.

MISCELLANEOUS NOTES: *D. wisselense* is unlikely to be available for cultivation.

Plant and Flower Information

PLANT SIZE AND TYPE: A 15 in. (38 cm) sympodial epiphyte or terrestrial.

PSEUDOBULB: 15 in. (38 cm) long. The slender stems are club-shaped and consist of 2–5 nodes.

LEAVES: 2 at the apex of each growth. The leaves are about 3 in. (8 cm) long, linear to narrowly oblong, and nearly erect.

INFLORESCENCE: 3–6 in. (8–16 cm) long. Inflorescences may be erect or suberect.

FLOWERS: 8–20 per inflorescence. The flowers are 0.8–1.2 in. (2–3 cm) across. The pointed sepals and narrower petals are lanceolate. The pointed lip is spatula-shaped with a linear callus consisting of 3 ridges. It is obscurely 3-lobed. Flower color is not known.

REFERENCES: 83, 234.

Dendrobium wollastonii Ridley. Sometimes spelled *D. woolastonii*, see *D. eximium* Schlechter. REFERENCES: 83, 222, 445.

Dendrobium wolterianum Schlechter. Plants originated in New Guinea. Habitat location and elevation are unavailable, so climate data cannot be selected. In the habitat, plants bloomed in Aug. (Feb.). This sympodial epiphyte has stems 6–8 in. (15–20 cm) long. The cylindrical stems, which arise from a very short rhizome, may be erect or suberect. They do not branch. Each stem carries 4–6 leaves that were not present at the time the plant was described. The short inflorescences produce a densely flowered cluster of 4–6 blossoms. The rose-red flowers are 0.4 in. (1 cm) across. The sepals, which are smaller than the petals, are ovate and pointed, while the elliptical petals are minutely toothed along the margin. The pointed lip is hairy to toothed at the apex. REFERENCES: 221, 438, 445.

Dendrobium woluense J. J. Smith

AKA: The name should perhaps be spelled *D. woloense* for Mt. Woloe, but the spelling in the original description was *D. woluense*.

ORIGIN/HABITAT: Molucca Islands. In southern Seram, the orchids grow in the forests on limestone mountains at 5600–6550 ft. (1700–2000 m). They were originally found near the summit of Mt. Woloe.

CLIMATE: Station #49620, Amahai, Seram, Indonesia, Lat. 3.3°S, Long. 128.9°E, at 10 ft. (3 m). Temperatures are calculated for an elevation of 6000 ft. (1830 m), resulting in probable extremes of 76°F (25°C) and 46°F (8°C).

N/HEMISPHERE	JAN	FEB	MAR	APR	MAY	JUN	JUL	AUG	SEP	OCT	NOV	DEC
°F AVG MAX	61	61	63	65	68	68	68	68	68	66	64	62
°F AVG MIN	54	54	54	54	55	56	56	56	56	56	55	54
DIURNAL RANGE	7	7	9	11	13	12	12	12	12	10	9	8
RAIN/INCHES	23.7	15.8	9.5	6.1	4.5	5.2	5.0	4.7	5.3	11.0	20.3	25.1
HUMIDITY/%	83	82	81	80	79	78	78	77	79	82	83	84
BLOOM SEASON					*							
DAYS CLR @ 9AM	1	1	1	6	7	4	3	3	5	5	3	3
DAYS CLR @ 3PM	1	1	2	5	6	1	1	1	2	3	1	3
RAIN/MM	602	401	241	155	114	132	127	119	135	279	516	638
°C AVG MAX	16.2	16.2	17.4	18.5	20.1	20.1	20.1	20.1	20.1	19.0	17.9	16.8
°C AVG MIN	12.4	12.4	12.4	12.4	12.9	13.5	13.5	13.5	13.5	13.5	12.9	12.4
DIURNAL RANGE	3.8	3.8	5.0	6.1	7.2	6.6	6.6	6.6	6.6	5.5	5.0	4.4
S/HEMISPHERE	JUL	AUG	SEP	OCT	NOV	DEC	JAN	FEB	MAR	APR	MAY	JUN

Cultural Recommendations

LIGHT: 2000–3000 fc. In the habitat, clear days are rare.

TEMPERATURES: Throughout the year, days average 61–68°F (16–20°C), and nights average 54–56°F (12–14°C), with a diurnal range of 7–13°F (4–7°C). Because of the effects of microclimate, actual maximum temperatures in the habitat may be somewhat warmer than indicated.

HUMIDITY: 75–80% year-round.

WATER: Rainfall is moderate to heavy all year, but conditions are driest in spring and summer. Cultivated plants should be allowed to dry slightly between waterings, but they should never be allowed to dry out completely.

FERTILIZER: ¼–½ recommended strength. A balanced fertilizer should be applied weekly to biweekly throughout the year.

REST PERIOD: Growing conditions should be maintained all year. In the habitat, winter is the wettest season, but water should not be increased for cultivated plants. In fact, water should be reduced, especially for plants cultivated in the dark, short-day conditions common during temperate-latitude winters. However, cultivated plants should never be allowed to dry completely between waterings. Fertilizer should be reduced or eliminated anytime water is reduced. In the habitat, light is lowest in winter.

GROWING MEDIA: Plants may be mounted on tree-fern or cork slabs or potted in small pots filled with any open, fast-draining medium. Repotting may be done anytime new roots are actively growing.

MISCELLANEOUS NOTES: The bloom season shown in the climate table is based on collection reports. The plant was described in 1928 in *Bull. Jard. Bot. Buit.* 3rd sér. 10:153.

Plant and Flower Information

PLANT SIZE AND TYPE: A 24 in. (60 cm) sympodial epiphyte.

PSEUDOBULB: 24 in. (60 cm) long. The branching stems are clustered.

LEAVES: Many. The ovate-lanceolate leaves are about 2.3 in. (5.8 cm) long but become smaller near the apex. They are rigidly papery and deciduous.

INFLORESCENCE: Short. Inflorescences emerge from nodes on leafless stems.

FLOWERS: 3 per inflorescence. The flowers are 1.2 in. (3 cm) long. The rounded sepals and petals are red. Blossoms have an erect, ovate-elliptical dorsal sepal, somewhat triangular lateral sepals, and oblong-elliptical petals with an uneven margin. The white lip is recurved and fringed along the front margin.

REFERENCES: 224.

Dendrobium womersleyi T. M. Reeve

ORIGIN/HABITAT: Papua New Guinea. Although uncommon, plants have been found in the provinces of Enga, Western Highlands, and Southern Highlands. They grow in filtered shade at 4900–5900 ft. (1500–1800 m). The plants appear terrestrial, but their roots remain above the ground in the loose litter and moss that collects at the base of trees and *Miscanthus* clumps.

CLIMATE: Station #200243, Mt. Hagen, Papua New Guinea, Lat. 5.8°S, Long. 144.3°E, at 5350 ft. (1630 m). Extreme temperatures are 88°F (31°C) and 35°F (2°C).

N/HEMISPHERE	JAN	FEB	MAR	APR	MAY	JUN	JUL	AUG	SEP	OCT	NOV	DEC
°F AVG MAX	72	73	74	75	76	76	76	76	75	75	76	74
°F AVG MIN	55	55	55	55	55	56	56	56	56	57	56	54
DIURNAL RANGE	17	18	19	20	21	20	20	20	19	18	20	20
RAIN/INCHES	5.2	6.7	8.7	8.7	8.2	10.2	10.4	10.7	11.2	10.0	7.2	4.7
HUMIDITY/%	84	83	82	78	79	81	81	80	82	81	82	82
BLOOM SEASON	**			*						*		
DAYS CLR	N/A											
RAIN/MM	131	171	221	221	208	258	264	271	285	253	184	119
°C AVG MAX	22.4	22.7	23.2	23.9	24.3	24.2	24.2	24.4	23.8	23.9	24.3	23.1
°C AVG MIN	12.5	12.7	12.6	12.5	12.7	13.3	13.4	13.3	13.4	13.7	13.4	12.4
DIURNAL RANGE	9.9	10.0	10.6	11.4	11.6	10.9	10.8	11.1	10.4	10.2	10.9	10.7
S/HEMISPHERE	JUL	AUG	SEP	OCT	NOV	DEC	JAN	FEB	MAR	APR	MAY	JUN

Cultural Recommendations

LIGHT: 2000–3000 fc.

TEMPERATURES: Throughout the year, days average 72–76°F (22–24°C), and nights average 54–57°F (12–14°C), with a diurnal range of 17–21°F (10–12°C).

HUMIDITY: Near 80% year-round.

WATER: Rainfall is moderate to heavy all year with a 1–2 month slightly drier period in winter. Cultivated plants should be kept moist and never be allowed to dry completely.

FERTILIZER: ¼–½ recommended strength. A balanced fertilizer should be applied weekly to biweekly throughout the year.

REST PERIOD: Growing temperatures should be maintained year-round. Water and fertilizer should be reduced somewhat in winter, especially for plants grown in the dark, short-day conditions common in temperate latitudes. In the habitat, light is higher in winter.

GROWING MEDIA: In the botanical gardens at Laiagam, Papua New Guinea, plants grow terrestrially in soil with a loose tree-fern fiber mulch on top, but they do not grow on tree-fern slabs. Plants are best transplanted when new roots are growing.

MISCELLANEOUS NOTES: The bloom season shown in the climate table is based on records from the habitat.

Plant and Flower Information

PLANT SIZE AND TYPE: A 4–48 in. (10–122 cm) sympodial epiphyte or terrestrial.

PSEUDOBULB: 4–48 in. (10–122 cm) long. The brown, leafy stems are cylindrical, more or less erect, and slightly zigzag near the tip. They are borne on a very short rhizome. After the leaves drop, the original stem develops new branches. New growths are dark purple.

LEAVES: Many. The sharply pointed, lanceolate leaves are 0.4–1.6 in. (1–4 cm) long.

INFLORESCENCE: Short. Inflorescences arise at the upper nodes of both leafy and leafless stems.

FLOWERS: 1–3 per inflorescence. The spreading flowers, which are 0.8–1.0 in. (2.0–2.5 cm) long, may be orange to golden yellow. The dorsal sepal and petals are elliptic to lanceolate and taper to a point. The lateral sepals are larger and somewhat triangular. The erect lip is unlobed. The pollinia are yellow.

REFERENCES: 234, 381, 552.

PHOTOS/DRAWINGS: 381.

Dendrobium woodfordianum (Maiden) Schlechter. See *D. gouldii* Rchb. f. REFERENCES: 84, 221, 270, 271.

Dendrobium woodsii Cribb

AKA: *D. fantasticum* as used by P. Taylor and J. J. Wood.

ORIGIN/HABITAT: Southern Papua New Guinea. Plants grow on shady tree trunks in mountain forests east of Port Moresby and in Milne Bay Province near the southeastern tip of the island. The orchids are usually found at 1650–6550 ft. (500–2000 m).

CLIMATE: Station #94035, Port Moresby, Papua New Guinea, Lat. 9.5°S, Long. 147.2°E, at 126 ft. (38 m). Temperatures are calculated for an elevation of 4500 ft. (1370 m), resulting in probable extremes of 84°F (29°C) and 50°F (10°C).

N/HEMISPHERE	JAN	FEB	MAR	APR	MAY	JUN	JUL	AUG	SEP	OCT	NOV	DEC
°F AVG MAX	69	68	70	72	74	76	75	73	74	73	72	70
°F AVG MIN	59	59	60	61	62	62	62	62	62	61	61	60
DIURNAL RANGE	10	9	10	11	12	14	13	11	12	12	11	10
RAIN/INCHES	1.1	0.7	1.0	1.4	1.9	4.4	7.0	7.6	6.7	4.2	2.5	1.3
HUMIDITY/%	78	77	78	76	73	71	71	73	74	75	77	78
BLOOM SEASON										*		
DAYS CLR	N/A											
RAIN/MM	28	18	25	36	48	112	178	193	170	107	64	33
°C AVG MAX	20.3	19.8	20.9	22.0	23.1	24.2	23.6	22.5	23.1	22.5	22.0	20.9
°C AVG MIN	14.8	14.8	15.3	15.9	16.4	16.4	16.4	16.4	16.4	15.9	15.9	15.3
DIURNAL RANGE	5.5	5.0	5.6	6.1	6.7	7.8	7.2	6.1	6.7	6.6	6.1	5.6
S/HEMISPHERE	JUL	AUG	SEP	OCT	NOV	DEC	JAN	FEB	MAR	APR	MAY	JUN

Cultural Recommendations

LIGHT: 3000–4000 fc. Plants require high light with strong air movement year-round. About 50% shading should be provided in summer, but as much light as possible, short of burning the foliage, should be given all year.

TEMPERATURES: Throughout the year, days average 68–76°F (20–24°C), and nights average 59–62°F (15–16°C), with a diurnal range of 9–14°F (5–8°C). Because plants are found at a wide range of elevations, cultivated plants should easily adapt to conditions 8–10°F (4–6°C) warmer or cooler than indicated.

HUMIDITY: 70–75% most of the year, increasing to about 80% in winter.

WATER: Rainfall is moderate for 5 months in summer, but conditions are dry in winter. Cultivated plants should dry slightly between waterings from spring to early autumn, but water should be gradually reduced in late autumn.

FERTILIZER: ¼–½ recommended strength. A balanced fertilizer should be applied weekly to biweekly throughout the year.

REST PERIOD: Growing conditions should be maintained all year. In the habitat, rainfall is low for 6–7 months in winter. Water and fertilizer should be reduced considerably in winter. Plants should be allowed to dry between waterings but should not remain dry for extended periods. Occasional mistings on clear, sunny mornings are usually beneficial. In the habitat, winter light is high.

GROWING MEDIA: Slab culture generally proves superior, providing that high humidity is maintained and plants are watered at least once daily during summer. If plants are potted, an undersized pot barely large enough to hold the roots should be filled with a very open, fast-draining medium. Repotting may be done anytime new roots are growing.

MISCELLANEOUS NOTES: The bloom season shown in the climate table is based on cultivation records.

Plant and Flower Information

PLANT SIZE AND TYPE: A 16 in. (40 cm) sympodial epiphyte.

PSEUDOBULB: 16 in. (40 cm) long. The yellowish green stems are club-shaped and clustered with about 5 nodes.

LEAVES: 2 at the apex of each growth. The glossy, dark green leaves are 7 in. (18 cm) long.

INFLORESCENCE: 6–7 in. (15–18 cm) long. Inflorescences may arise laterally through the base of the leaf sheaths or at the apex of the stem. Blossoms are pendent on a wiry inflorescence.

FLOWERS: 4–7 per inflorescence. The pleasantly fragrant flowers are 0.8 in. (2 cm) across. Sepals and petals are white tinged with green. The ovate-oblong dorsal sepal has an uneven margin. Lateral sepals are somewhat ovate-oblong and very large relative to the dorsal sepal and petals. Petals are somewhat linear, sickle-shaped, chopped off or rounded at the apex with uneven margins near the tip. The lip is pink to purple with darker tones at the base. The apex of the midlobe is very deeply notched, resulting in 4 nearly equal lobes. The obscurely 3-ridged callus is raised and fleshy.

HYBRIDIZING NOTES: Chromosome count 2n = 36 (ref. 152, 243).

REFERENCES: 83, 95, 152, 179, 234, 243, 526, 550.

PHOTOS/DRAWINGS: *83*.

Dendrobium wulaiense N. H. S. Howcroft

AKA: Until recently, this plant was considered a variety of *D. lineale* Rolfe. It was discussed by Millar (ref. 304) as Wulai Island white.

ORIGIN/HABITAT: Papua New Guinea. Plants grow on Wulai Island in Kinbe Bay on the north-central coast of New Britain. They often grow on trees overhanging the sea but are sometimes found on coral cliffs. Plants also grow on Long Island, which is part of Madang Province.

CLIMATE: Station #94085, Rabul, New Britain Is., Papua New Guinea, Lat. 4.2°S, Long. 152.2°E, at 28 ft. (9 m). Record extreme temperatures are 100°F (38°C) and 65°F (18°C).

N/HEMISPHERE	JAN	FEB	MAR	APR	MAY	JUN	JUL	AUG	SEP	OCT	NOV	DEC
°F AVG MAX	89	89	91	92	91	90	90	90	90	90	90	90
°F AVG MIN	73	72	73	73	73	73	73	73	73	73	73	73
DIURNAL RANGE	16	17	18	19	18	17	17	17	17	17	17	17
RAIN/INCHES	5.4	3.7	3.5	5.1	7.1	10.1	14.8	10.4	10.2	10.0	5.2	3.3
HUMIDITY/%	74	73	69	70	73	76	77	76	77	77	75	74
BLOOM SEASON					*					*	*	
DAYS CLR	N/A											
RAIN/MM	137	94	89	130	180	257	376	264	259	254	132	84
°C AVG MAX	31.7	31.7	32.8	33.3	32.8	32.2	32.2	32.2	32.2	32.2	32.2	32.2
°C AVG MIN	22.8	22.2	22.8	22.8	22.8	22.8	22.8	22.8	22.8	22.8	22.8	22.8
DIURNAL RANGE	8.9	9.5	10.0	10.5	10.0	9.4	9.4	9.4	9.4	9.4	9.4	9.4
S/HEMISPHERE	JUL	AUG	SEP	OCT	NOV	DEC	JAN	FEB	MAR	APR	MAY	JUN

Cultural Recommendations

LIGHT: Near 5000 fc. Growers indicate that although the plant will tolerate light shade, it is healthiest in very high light.

TEMPERATURES: Throughout the year, days average 89–92°F (32–33°C), and nights average 72–73°F (22–23°C), with a diurnal range of 16–19°F (9–11°C). Average highs and lows vary less than 3°F (2°C) all year, indicating that plants may not tolerate wide temperature fluctuations.

HUMIDITY: 70–80% most of the year. Humidity increases to 90–100% at night but may drop as low as 35% during hot afternoons.

WATER: Rainfall is moderate to heavy most of the year, but conditions are slightly drier for 2 months in late winter. Cultivated plants should be kept moist in spring and summer, but water should be gradually reduced in autumn.

FERTILIZER: ¼–½ recommended strength. A balanced fertilizer should be applied weekly to biweekly throughout the year.

REST PERIOD: Growing conditions should be maintained all year. Water and fertilizer should be reduced somewhat in winter. Plants should dry slightly between waterings, but they should never be allowed to dry completely. In the habitat, light may be slightly higher in winter.

GROWING MEDIA: Plants may be mounted on tree-fern or cork slabs if humidity is high and plants are watered at least once daily in summer. When plants are potted, any open, fast-draining medium may be used. Repotting may be done anytime new roots are growing.

MISCELLANEOUS NOTES: The bloom season shown in the climate table is based on cultivation records. The plants are self-pollinating.

Plant and Flower Information

PLANT SIZE AND TYPE: A 67 in. (170 cm) sympodial epiphyte. Plants are occasionally lithophytic.

PSEUDOBULB: 67 in. (170 cm) long. The erect stems are canelike with a pseudobulbous swelling at the base. They are more or less striped with maroon.

LEAVES: 5–7 per growth. The ovate to elliptic leaves are 3–7 in. (7–17 cm) long. They are leathery.

INFLORESCENCE: 5–19 in. (13–48 cm) long. 1–3 inflorescences emerge near the apex of the pseudobulb.

FLOWERS: 4–30 per inflorescence. The flowers are 2.0–2.4 in. (5–6 cm) across. The sepals and petals are more or less pointed, wavy, curled, and twisted. The oblong petals have a single twist, and the narrowly oblong dorsal sepal is incurved and rolled. Lateral sepals are obliquely oblong-triangular. All segments are ivory white, with violet lines decorating the large sidelobes on the lip. The small, broadly ovate midlobe appears ruffled with an uneven margin. The callus consists of 5 ridges.

REFERENCES: 84, 206, 234, 304.

PHOTOS/DRAWINGS: *84, 206, 304*.

Dendrobium xanthellum Ridley

ORIGIN/HABITAT: Irian Jaya (western New Guinea). Plants were collected on the south side of Mt. Jaya (Mt. Carstensz) at about 3100 ft. (940 m).

CLIMATE: Station #97796, Kokenau (Kokonau), Irian Jaya, Lat. 4.7°S, Long. 135.4°E, at 10 ft. (3 m). Temperatures are calculated for an elevation of 3000 ft. (910 m). Record extreme temperatures are not available for this location.

N/HEMISPHERE	JAN	FEB	MAR	APR	MAY	JUN	JUL	AUG	SEP	OCT	NOV	DEC
°F AVG MAX	73	73	76	78	80	79	79	79	80	78	77	74
°F AVG MIN	63	63	64	64	64	65	64	64	64	64	64	63
DIURNAL RANGE	10	10	12	14	16	14	15	15	16	14	13	11
RAIN/INCHES	18.4	15.8	18.9	11.6	9.7	10.6	11.5	15.7	11.6	11.6	16.0	19.9
HUMIDITY/%	N/A											
BLOOM SEASON	N/A											
DAYS CLR	N/A											
RAIN/MM	467	401	480	295	246	269	292	399	295	295	406	505
°C AVG MAX	22.9	22.9	24.5	25.6	26.7	26.2	26.2	26.2	26.7	25.6	25.1	23.4
°C AVG MIN	17.3	17.3	17.9	17.9	17.9	18.4	17.9	17.9	17.9	17.9	17.9	17.3
DIURNAL RANGE	5.6	5.6	6.6	7.7	8.8	7.8	8.3	8.3	8.8	7.7	7.2	6.1
S/HEMISPHERE	JUL	AUG	SEP	OCT	NOV	DEC	JAN	FEB	MAR	APR	MAY	JUN

Cultural Recommendations

LIGHT: 2500–3500 fc.

TEMPERATURES: Throughout the year, days average 73–80°F (23–27°C), and nights average 63–65°F (17–18°C), with a diurnal range of 10–16°F (6–9°C).

HUMIDITY: Information is not available for this location. However, records from nearby stations indicate that humidity is probably near 85% year-round.

WATER: Rainfall is very heavy year-round. Cultivated plants should be kept evenly moist but not soggy.

FERTILIZER: ¼–½ recommended strength. A balanced fertilizer should be applied weekly to biweekly throughout the year.

REST PERIOD: Growing conditions should be maintained year-round. Water and fertilizer might be reduced slightly in winter, especially for plants cultivated in the dark, short-day conditions common in temperate latitudes; but plants should never be allowed to dry out completely. In the habitat, seasonal light variation is minor.

GROWING MEDIA: Plants may be mounted on tree-fern or cork slabs if humidity is high and plants are watered at least once daily in summer. When plants are potted, any open, fast-draining medium may be used. Repotting may be done anytime new roots are growing.

Plant and Flower Information

PLANT SIZE AND TYPE: A 16 in. (40 cm) sympodial epiphyte.

PSEUDOBULB: 16 in. (40 cm) long. Nodes are spaced about 0.4 in. (1 cm) apart on the flexuous stems.

LEAVES: The deciduous leaves were missing when the plant was described.

INFLORESCENCE: 1.3 in. (3.3 cm) long. Racemes emerge near the apex of leafless stems.

FLOWERS: 15 per inflorescence. The tiny orange flowers are 0.5 in. (1.3 cm) long. The lanceolate sepals and petals are pointed. Lateral sepals are wider than the dorsal sepal. The lip is linear and pointed. It is smaller than the other segments.

REFERENCES: 222, 400.

Dendrobium xanthoacron Schlechter. See note at *D. prostratum* Ridley. REFERENCES: 220, 254, 286, 295, 433, 455.

Dendrobium xanthocaulon Schlechter. Now considered a synonym of *Diplocaulobium xanthocaulon* (Schlechter) A. Hawkes.
REFERENCES: 92, 221, 229, 437, 445.

Dendrobium xanthogenium Schlechter

ORIGIN/HABITAT: Papua New Guinea. Plants grow in the Sepik River region at 4600–4900 ft. (1400–1500 m).

CLIMATE: Station #200004, Ambunti, Papua New Guinea, Lat. 4.2°S, Long. 142.8°E, at 164 ft. (50 m). Temperatures are calculated for an elevation of 4600 ft. (1400 m), resulting in probable extremes of 84°F (29°C) and 37°F (3°C).

N/HEMISPHERE	JAN	FEB	MAR	APR	MAY	JUN	JUL	AUG	SEP	OCT	NOV	DEC
°F AVG MAX	73	75	75	75	76	75	75	75	75	75	75	74
°F AVG MIN	57	58	59	58	58	58	57	58	58	58	58	59
DIURNAL RANGE	16	17	16	17	18	17	18	17	17	17	17	15
RAIN/INCHES	6.4	7.4	7.7	8.5	9.2	9.4	10.9	10.2	12.2	10.4	8.3	5.2
HUMIDITY/%	N/A											
BLOOM SEASON	*	*										*
DAYS CLR	N/A											
RAIN/MM	163	188	196	216	234	239	277	259	310	264	211	132
°C AVG MAX	23.0	24.1	24.1	24.1	24.6	24.1	24.1	24.1	24.1	24.1	24.1	23.5
°C AVG MIN	14.1	14.6	15.2	14.6	14.6	14.1	14.1	14.6	14.6	14.6	14.6	15.2
DIURNAL RANGE	8.9	9.5	8.9	9.5	10.0	9.5	10.0	9.5	9.5	9.5	9.5	8.3
S/HEMISPHERE	JUL	AUG	SEP	OCT	NOV	DEC	JAN	FEB	MAR	APR	MAY	JUN

Cultural Recommendations

LIGHT: 2000–3000 fc.

TEMPERATURES: Throughout the year, days average 73–76°F (23–25°C), and nights average 57–59°F (14–15°C), with a diurnal range of 15–18°F (8–10°C).

HUMIDITY: Information is not available for this location. However, records from nearby stations indicate that humidity is probably near 80% year-round.

WATER: Rainfall is heavy year-round, with the greatest amounts falling in summer and early autumn. Cultivated plants should be kept moist but not soggy.

FERTILIZER: ¼–½ recommended strength. A balanced fertilizer should be applied weekly to biweekly throughout the year.

REST PERIOD: Growing temperatures should be maintained all year. Water and fertilizer should be reduced somewhat in winter, especially for plants cultivated in the dark, short-day conditions common in temperate latitudes; but plants should never be allowed to dry out completely. In the habitat, seasonal light variation is minor.

GROWING MEDIA: Plants may be mounted on cork or tree-fern slabs if humidity is high and plants are watered at least once daily in summer. When plants are potted, any open, fast-draining medium may be used. Repotting may be done anytime new roots are growing.

MISCELLANEOUS NOTES: The bloom season shown in the climate table is based on reports from the habitat.

Plant and Flower Information

PLANT SIZE AND TYPE: A 16–24 in. (40–60 cm) sympodial epiphyte.

PSEUDOBULB: 16–24 in. (40–60 cm) long. The slender, fleshy stems are deeply grooved. They emerge from a very short rhizome.

LEAVES: Many. The oblong-lanceolate leaves are 1.1–1.8 in. (2.8–4.5 cm) long.

INFLORESCENCE: Short.

FLOWERS: Described as pretty, the flowers are about 1 in. (2.5 cm) long. The elliptical sepals and petals are rosy lilac. The small lip is roundly oblong, concave, and deeply toothed at the apex. The spur is orange.

Dendrobium xantholeucum

REFERENCES: 223, 443.

Dendrobium xantholeucum Rchb. f. Sometimes spelled *D. xantholeuchum*, it is now considered a synonym of *Flickingeria xantholeuca* (Rchb. f.) A. Hawkes. REFERENCES: 25, 75, 111, 200, 213, 216, 230, 231, 254, 286, 445, 449, 455, 469. PHOTOS/DRAWINGS: 469.

Dendrobium xanthomeson Schlechter

ORIGIN/HABITAT: Northern Papua New Guinea. In the Torricelli Range, plants grow low on mistforest trees at about 2600 ft. (800 m).

CLIMATE: Station #94004, Wewak, Papua New Guinea, Lat. 3.6°S, Long. 143.7°E, at 16 ft. (5 m). Temperatures are calculated for an elevation of 2600 ft. (800 m), resulting in probable extremes of 89°F (32°C) and 53°F (12°C).

N/HEMISPHERE	JAN	FEB	MAR	APR	MAY	JUN	JUL	AUG	SEP	OCT	NOV	DEC
°F AVG MAX	79	79	79	79	79	79	78	77	78	79	79	79
°F AVG MIN	65	65	65	66	66	66	66	66	65	65	66	65
DIURNAL RANGE	14	14	14	13	13	13	12	11	13	14	13	14
RAIN/INCHES	7.6	4.8	5.3	10.0	13.3	14.5	12.1	11.9	14.9	16.9	15.1	10.8
HUMIDITY/%	80	79	79	78	79	81	82	82	81	82	81	80
BLOOM SEASON									*			
DAYS CLR	N/A											
RAIN/MM	193	122	135	254	338	368	307	302	378	429	384	274
°C AVG MAX	26.3	26.3	26.3	26.3	26.3	26.3	25.8	25.2	25.8	26.3	26.3	26.3
°C AVG MIN	18.6	18.6	18.6	19.1	19.1	19.1	19.1	19.1	18.6	18.6	19.1	18.6
DIURNAL RANGE	7.7	7.7	7.7	7.2	7.2	7.2	6.7	6.1	7.2	7.7	7.2	7.7
S/HEMISPHERE	JUL	AUG	SEP	OCT	NOV	DEC	JAN	FEB	MAR	APR	MAY	JUN

Cultural Recommendations

LIGHT: 1800–2500 fc.

TEMPERATURES: Throughout the year, days average 77–79°F (25–26°C), and nights average 65–66°F (19°C), with a diurnal range of 11–14°F (6–8°C).

HUMIDITY: Near 80% year-round.

WATER: Rainfall is heavy all year, but conditions are slightly drier for 1–2 months in winter. Cultivated plants should be kept moist but not soggy.

FERTILIZER: ¼–½ recommended strength. A balanced fertilizer should be applied weekly to biweekly throughout the year.

REST PERIOD: Growing temperatures should be maintained all year. Water and fertilizer should be reduced somewhat in winter, especially for plants cultivated in the dark, short-day conditions common in temperate latitudes. Plants should never be allowed to dry out completely, however. In the habitat, seasonal light variation is minor.

GROWING MEDIA: A very open and fast-draining medium should be used with either baskets or small pots. Repotting may be done anytime new roots are growing.

MISCELLANEOUS NOTES: The bloom season shown in the climate table is based on collection reports.

Plant and Flower Information

PLANT SIZE AND TYPE: A 12 in. (30 cm) sympodial epiphyte. Plants sometimes reach a length of 39 in. (100 cm).

PSEUDOBULB: 12 in. (30 cm) long. The slender stems are swollen in the middle and taper at each end.

LEAVES: Many. The stems are sparsely leafed near the apex. The herblike leaves are oblong-lanceolate and 4.0–9.5 in. (10–24 cm) long.

INFLORESCENCE: Short. The flower clusters are 1.6 in. (4 cm) across.

FLOWERS: 6–10 per inflorescence. The fleshy flowers are 0.8 in. (2 cm) long and do not open fully. The oblong sepals and ovate petals are yellowish on the outside and white inside. The round lip is pale yellow in the center with regular teeth on the margin. The front of the lip resembles a scallop shell.

REFERENCES: 219, 254, 437, 444, 445.

PHOTOS/DRAWINGS: 437.

Dendrobium xanthophaeum Schlechter

ORIGIN/HABITAT: Northeastern Papua New Guinea. Plants grow in the Dischore Range and near the Waria River at 1500–3300 ft. (450–1000 m). They are found in lower hill country and the mistforests.

CLIMATE: Station #200192, Garaina, Papua New Guinea, Lat. 7.9°S, Long. 147.1°E, at 2350 ft. (716 m). Record extreme temperatures are 94°F (34°C) and 46°F (8°C).

N/HEMISPHERE	JAN	FEB	MAR	APR	MAY	JUN	JUL	AUG	SEP	OCT	NOV	DEC
°F AVG MAX	80	82	83	84	85	85	85	85	84	84	83	81
°F AVG MIN	63	63	63	64	63	64	65	65	65	64	64	63
DIURNAL RANGE	17	19	20	20	22	21	20	20	19	20	19	18
RAIN/INCHES	5.8	6.5	8.7	11.1	11.8	11.9	8.9	11.7	11.5	9.9	7.7	5.2
HUMIDITY/%	84	82	82	81	80	80	81	81	82	83	84	84
BLOOM SEASON									*	*	*	*
DAYS CLR	N/A											
RAIN/MM	148	166	220	282	300	303	227	296	291	251	195	131
°C AVG MAX	26.8	27.5	28.2	28.6	29.3	29.3	29.4	29.4	29.1	28.7	28.2	27.2
°C AVG MIN	16.9	16.9	17.4	17.6	17.4	18.0	18.1	18.2	18.4	17.7	17.7	17.1
DIURNAL RANGE	9.9	10.6	10.8	11.0	11.9	11.3	11.3	11.2	10.7	11.0	10.5	10.1
S/HEMISPHERE	JUL	AUG	SEP	OCT	NOV	DEC	JAN	FEB	MAR	APR	MAY	JUN

Cultural Recommendations

LIGHT: 2500–3500 fc.

TEMPERATURES: Throughout the year, days average 80–85°F (27–29°C), and nights average 63–65°F (17–18°C), with a diurnal range of 17–22°F (10–12°C).

HUMIDITY: 80–85% year-round.

WATER: Rainfall is heavy all year with a slightly drier period in winter. Cultivated plants should be kept moist but not soggy.

FERTILIZER: ¼–½ recommended strength. A balanced fertilizer should be applied weekly to biweekly throughout the year.

REST PERIOD: Growing temperatures should be maintained all year. Water and fertilizer should be reduced somewhat in winter, especially for plants grown in the dark, short-day conditions common in temperate latitudes. In the habitat, light is slightly higher in winter.

GROWING MEDIA: Plants may be mounted on tree-fern or cork slabs if humidity is high and plants are watered at least once daily in summer. When plants are potted, any open, fast-draining medium may be used. Repotting may be done anytime new roots are growing.

MISCELLANEOUS NOTES: The bloom season shown in the climate table is based on collection reports. Plants that produce flowers which last a single day commonly bloom several times during the year. Flowering usually occurs 7–14 days after a sudden 10°F (5°C) drop in daytime temperatures.

Plant and Flower Information

PLANT SIZE AND TYPE: A 16 in. (40 cm) sympodial epiphyte.

PSEUDOBULB: 16 in. (40 cm) long. The densely leafy stems become ridged with age.

LEAVES: Many. The oblong leaves are 0.8–1.6 in. (2–4 cm) long.

INFLORESCENCE: Inflorescences emerge laterally from nodes along the stem.

FLOWERS: 1 per inflorescence. The pale yellow-brown flowers are about 0.4 in. (1 cm) long. The pointed, keeled sepals and petals are erect-recurved. The 3-lobed lip juts forward. It is incurved along the side margins. The midlobe is indented at the apex, with small evenly spaced scallops along the margin. It has 3 raised lines that terminate near the apex of the midlobe. The sidelobes are slender, elongated, and pointed.

REFERENCES: 221, 437, 445.

PHOTOS/DRAWINGS: 437.

Dendrobium xanthophlebium Lindley

AKA: *D. marginatum* Bateman.

ORIGIN/HABITAT: Burma. Plants were originally collected near Moulmein in the Tenasserim region at about 4500 ft. (1370 m).

CLIMATE: Station #48103, Moulmein, Burma, Lat. 16.4°N, Long. 97.7°E, at 150 ft. (46 m). Temperatures are calculated for an elevation of 4500 ft. (1370 m), resulting in probable extremes of 89°F (32°C) and 38°F (3°C).

N/HEMISPHERE	JAN	FEB	MAR	APR	MAY	JUN	JUL	AUG	SEP	OCT	NOV	DEC
°F AVG MAX	75	78	80	81	75	71	69	69	71	74	75	73
°F AVG MIN	52	54	59	62	62	61	61	61	61	61	59	54
DIURNAL RANGE	23	24	21	19	13	10	8	8	10	13	16	19
RAIN/INCHES	0.3	0.2	0.4	3.0	20.3	35.6	46.3	43.4	28.1	8.5	2.1	0.1
HUMIDITY/%	66	68	68	70	81	91	92	93	91	81	75	64
BLOOM SEASON									*			
DAYS CLR @ 7AM	12	7	5	6	1	0	0	0	0	3	7	12
DAYS CLR @ 1PM	20	13	10	8	3	0	0	0	0	4	12	17
RAIN/MM	8	5	10	76	516	904	1176	1102	714	216	53	3
°C AVG MAX	23.7	25.4	26.5	27.0	23.7	21.5	20.4	20.4	21.5	23.1	23.7	22.6
°C AVG MIN	10.9	12.0	14.8	16.5	16.5	15.9	15.9	15.9	15.9	15.9	14.8	12.0
DIURNAL RANGE	12.8	13.4	11.7	10.5	7.2	5.6	4.5	4.5	5.6	7.2	8.9	10.6
S/HEMISPHERE	JUL	AUG	SEP	OCT	NOV	DEC	JAN	FEB	MAR	APR	MAY	JUN

Cultural Recommendations

LIGHT: 2000–3000 fc. The heavy summer cloud cover indicates that shading is needed from spring through autumn, but light should be as high as the plant can tolerate, short of burning the leaves.

TEMPERATURES: Summer days average 69–71°F (20–22°C), and nights average 61°F (16°C), with a diurnal range of 8–10°F (5–6°C). Weather is warmest in spring. Days average 75–81°F (24–27°C), and nights average 59–62°F (15–17°C), with a diurnal range of 13–21°F (7–12°C).

HUMIDITY: 80–90% from late spring to midautumn, dropping to about 65–70% in winter.

WATER: Rainfall is very heavy from late spring into autumn, but conditions are much drier in winter. Cultivated plants should be kept evenly moist while actively growing, but water should be gradually reduced in autumn after new growths mature.

FERTILIZER: ¼–½ recommended strength, applied weekly. A high-nitrogen fertilizer is beneficial from spring to midsummer, but a fertilizer high in phosphates should be used in late summer and autumn.

REST PERIOD: Winter weather is moderately cool and dry. Days average 73–78°F (23–25°C), and nights average 52–54°F (11–12°C), with a diurnal range of 19–24°F (11–13°C). In the habitat, rainfall is low for 4 months, but additional moisture is available from frequent heavy deposits of dew. Cultivated plants should be allowed to dry out between waterings, but they should never remain dry for long periods. Occasional early morning mistings between waterings may help prevent plants from becoming too dry. Fertilizer should be reduced or eliminated. In the habitat, light is highest in winter.

GROWING MEDIA: Plants may be mounted on slabs of cork or tree-fern fiber with a pad of sphagnum, but humidity must be high and water should be applied daily in summer. If plants are potted, a rapidly draining medium is recommended. Repotting is best done immediately after flowering.

MISCELLANEOUS NOTES: The bloom season shown in the climate table is based on cultivation records. *D. xanthophlebium* is unlikely to be available for cultivation.

Plant and Flower Information

PLANT SIZE AND TYPE: A 6–18 in. (15–45 cm) sympodial epiphyte.

PSEUDOBULB: 6–18 in. (15–45 cm) long. Smooth and quill-like, the angular stems are green and white striped.

LEAVES: 2, rarely more at the apex of the stem. The linear-lanceolate leaves are 2–4 in. (5–10 cm) long. They are soft-textured and deciduous.

INFLORESCENCE: Short. Inflorescences may emerge at the apex, but they are usually lateral from nodes below the leaves.

FLOWERS: 2 per inflorescence. The flowers are 1.2–2.0 in. (3–5 cm) across. The pointed sepals and more rounded petals are white with a waxy texture. The 3-lobed lip has large, somewhat triangular sidelobes that are spotted and veined with orange or orange-yellow. The nearly round midlobe is deeply ruffled with an orange disk and a white border. It has a short point at the apex. The fragrant blossoms are relatively short-lived.

REFERENCES: 157, 179, 190, 202, 210, 216, 254, 278, 445, 454, 541, 570.

PHOTOS/DRAWINGS: 454.

Dendrobium xanthothece Schlechter

ORIGIN/HABITAT: Northern Papua New Guinea. Plants grow on forest trees in the Finisterre Range at about 4000 ft. (1220 m).

CLIMATE: Station #94010, Goroka, Papua New Guinea, Lat. 6.1°S, Long. 145.4°E, at 5141 ft. (1567 m). Temperatures are calculated for an elevation of 4000 ft. (1220 m), resulting in probable extremes of 90°F (32°C) and 46°F (8°C).

N/HEMISPHERE	JAN	FEB	MAR	APR	MAY	JUN	JUL	AUG	SEP	OCT	NOV	DEC
°F AVG MAX	80	81	82	83	83	82	83	82	82	82	83	81
°F AVG MIN	60	61	61	61	62	63	63	63	64	63	63	61
DIURNAL RANGE	20	20	21	22	21	19	20	19	18	19	20	20
RAIN/INCHES	2.1	2.8	4.6	5.9	6.6	9.3	9.1	10.1	10.7	8.3	4.6	2.0
HUMIDITY/%	70	67	67	67	67	72	73	74	71	70	70	70
BLOOM SEASON							*					
DAYS CLR	N/A											
RAIN/MM	53	71	117	150	168	236	231	257	272	211	117	51
°C AVG MAX	26.5	27.1	27.6	28.2	28.2	27.6	28.2	27.6	27.6	27.6	28.2	27.1
°C AVG MIN	15.4	16.0	16.0	16.0	16.5	17.1	17.1	17.1	17.6	17.1	17.1	16.0
DIURNAL RANGE	11.1	11.1	11.6	12.2	11.7	10.5	11.1	10.5	10.0	10.5	11.1	11.1
S/HEMISPHERE	JUL	AUG	SEP	OCT	NOV	DEC	JAN	FEB	MAR	APR	MAY	JUN

Cultural Recommendations

LIGHT: 2000–3000 fc.

TEMPERATURES: Throughout the year, days average 80–83°F (27–28°C), and nights average 60–64°F (15–18°C), with a diurnal range of 18–22°F (10–12°C). The diurnal range is unusually large for a habitat with such constant temperatures.

HUMIDITY: 70–75% from summer into autumn, dropping to 65–70% in winter and spring. Plants require excellent air movement.

WATER: Rainfall is moderate to heavy most of the year, but conditions are slightly drier for 3 months in winter. Cultivated plants should be kept moist but not soggy. Occasional early morning mistings may be beneficial, especially on bright, sunny days.

FERTILIZER: ¼–½ recommended strength. A balanced fertilizer should be applied weekly to biweekly throughout the year.

REST PERIOD: Growing temperatures should be maintained all year. In the habitat, rainfall is lowest in winter, but dew and mist from fog and low clouds are common. Water and fertilizer should be reduced somewhat for cultivated plants, especially those grown in the darker, short-day conditions common during temperate-latitude winters. Plants should be kept on the dry side, but they should never be allowed to dry out completely. In the habitat, light is higher in winter.

GROWING MEDIA: Plants may be mounted on tree-fern or cork slabs if humidity is high and plants are watered at least once daily in summer. When plants are potted, any open, fast-draining medium may be used. Repotting is best done in early spring when new roots are growing.

Dendrobium xichouensis

MISCELLANEOUS NOTES: The bloom season shown in the climate table is based on cultivation records.

Plant and Flower Information

PLANT SIZE AND TYPE: A 12–16 in. (30–40 cm) sympodial epiphyte.

PSEUDOBULB: 12–16 in. (30–40 cm) long. The upright stems are curved, flattened, and do not branch. They are densely leafy and arise from a very short rhizome.

LEAVES: Many. The erect, linear leaves are 1.4–2.4 in. (3.5–6.0 cm) long and unequally bilobed at the tip.

FLOWERS: 1 per inflorescence. The white and yellow flowers are 0.2 in. (0.6 cm) across. Sepals are ovate, and the petals are oblong. The 3-lobed lip is uppermost. It is marked with brown spots except along the smooth white margin. The midlobe is broadly oblong. The small sidelobes are incurved along the margin. The column is marked with brown spots. The anther is red-brown and white.

REFERENCES: 221, 437, 445.

PHOTOS/DRAWINGS: 437.

Dendrobium xichouensis S. J. Cheng and Z. Z. Tang

ORIGIN/HABITAT: China. Plants grow in southeast Yunnan province at about 6250 ft. (1900 m). They are also found near Xichou, Fadou Commune, and Donzuncao. The orchids are usually found in forest trees on limestone mountains.

CLIMATE: Station #56985, Mengtze, Yunnan, China, Lat. 23.3°N, Long. 103.4°E, at 4262 ft. (1299 m). Temperatures are calculated for an elevation of 6250 ft. (1900 m), resulting in probable extremes of 90°F (33°C) and 21°F (–6°C).

N/HEMISPHERE	JAN	FEB	MAR	APR	MAY	JUN	JUL	AUG	SEP	OCT	NOV	DEC
°F AVG MAX	58	60	70	76	78	75	75	74	74	68	66	60
°F AVG MIN	38	42	48	54	59	60	61	59	56	52	47	40
DIURNAL RANGE	20	18	22	22	19	15	14	15	18	16	19	20
RAIN/INCHES	0.2	1.0	1.2	1.5	5.4	6.9	10.2	9.3	2.9	2.7	2.2	0.5
HUMIDITY/%	68	69	62	61	64	74	78	79	74	74	71	70
BLOOM SEASON							*					
DAYS CLR @ 7AM	13	11	13	11	7	2	2	3	5	4	12	14
DAYS CLR @ 1PM	12	10	10	11	3	1	1	2	2	7	13	
RAIN/MM	5	25	30	38	137	175	259	236	74	69	56	13
°C AVG MAX	14.7	15.8	21.4	24.7	25.8	24.1	24.1	23.6	23.6	20.2	19.1	15.8
°C AVG MIN	3.6	5.8	9.1	12.5	15.2	15.8	16.4	15.2	13.6	11.4	8.6	4.7
DIURNAL RANGE	11.1	10.0	12.3	12.2	10.6	8.3	7.7	8.4	10.0	8.8	10.5	11.1
S/HEMISPHERE	JUL	AUG	SEP	OCT	NOV	DEC	JAN	FEB	MAR	APR	MAY	JUN

Cultural Recommendations

LIGHT: 3000–4000 fc. Dappled light is recommended.

TEMPERATURES: Summer days average 74–75°F (24°C), and nights average 59–61°F (15–16°C), with a diurnal range of 14–15°F (8°C). The warmest days and the greatest diurnal range occur in spring. Days average 70–78°F (21–26°C), and nights average 48–59°F (9–15°C), with a diurnal range of 19–22°F (11–12°C).

HUMIDITY: 75–80% in summer and early autumn, dropping gradually to near 60% for 2–3 months in late winter and early spring.

WATER: Rainfall is heavy from late spring through summer with much drier conditions in winter and early spring. Cultivated plants should be constantly moist while actively growing, but water should be gradually reduced after new growths mature in autumn.

FERTILIZER: ¼–½ recommended strength, applied weekly. A high nitrogen fertilizer is beneficial from spring to midsummer, but a fertilizer high in phosphates should be used in late summer and autumn.

REST PERIOD: Winter days average 58–60°F (15–16°C), and nights average 38–42°F (4–6°C), with a diurnal range of 18–20°F (10–11°C). Although rainfall is low in winter, considerable additional moisture is available from heavy dew. In cultivation, water should be reduced for 4–5 months. Plants should be allowed to dry out between waterings, but they should not remain dry for extended periods. Occasional early morning mistings on sunny days may help prevent plants from becoming too dry. Fertilizer should be reduced or eliminated until water is increased in spring. In the habitat, light is highest in winter.

GROWING MEDIA: Plants may be mounted on tree-fern or cork slabs if humidity is high and plants are watered at least once daily in summer. When plants are potted, any open, fast-draining medium may be used. They may be repotted anytime new roots are growing.

MISCELLANEOUS NOTES: The bloom season shown in the climate table is based on records from the habitat.

Plant and Flower Information

PLANT SIZE AND TYPE: A 4–12 in. (10–30 cm) sympodial epiphyte.

PSEUDOBULB: 4–12 in. (10–30 cm) long. The yellow-green stems are somewhat zigzag, especially toward the apex.

LEAVES: 7–10 per growth. The oblong to oblong-lanceolate leaves are 0.7–1.6 in. (1.8–4.0 cm) long and unequally bilobed at the apex.

INFLORESCENCE: Short. Inflorescences emerge from upper nodes on leafless stems.

FLOWERS: 1–2 per inflorescence. The flowers are 0.6 in. (1.5 cm) across and do not open fully. The oblong to ovate sepals and petals are pointed. They are pale rosy white. The brownish lip has a yellow disk and is covered with pale yellow hairs. The rounded midlobe is incurved on each side so that it appears pointed. The obscure sidelobes have uneven margins. Blossoms are fragrant.

REFERENCES: 234, 507.

PHOTOS/DRAWINGS: 507.

Dendrobium xiphiphorum P. van Royen. See *D. vexillarius* J. J. Smith. REFERENCES: 233, 385, 538. PHOTOS/DRAWINGS: 538.

Dendrobium xiphophyllum Schlechter

ORIGIN/HABITAT: Sarawak, Borneo. Plants grow on Mt. Matang at about 2500 ft. (760 m).

CLIMATE: Station #96413, Kuching, Sarawak, Borneo, Lat. 1.5°N, Long. 110.3°E, at 85 ft. (26 m). Temperatures are calculated for an elevation of 2500 ft. (760 m), resulting in probable extremes of 89°F (32°C) and 56°F (13°C).

N/HEMISPHERE	JAN	FEB	MAR	APR	MAY	JUN	JUL	AUG	SEP	OCT	NOV	DEC
°F AVG MAX	80	80	81	82	83	83	83	84	82	82	82	80
°F AVG MIN	64	64	64	64	64	65	64	64	64	64	64	64
DIURNAL RANGE	16	16	17	18	19	18	19	20	18	18	18	16
RAIN/INCHES	27.1	19.7	14.2	9.7	9.0	8.5	6.9	8.8	9.5	12.6	13.1	20.1
HUMIDITY/%	89	88	86	85	85	83	82	83	84	85	87	88
BLOOM SEASON					*		*					
DAYS CLR @ 7AM	1	0	1	2	3	2	4	1	2	1	1	1
DAYS CLR @ 1PM	0	0	0	0	0	1	1	1	0	0	0	0
RAIN/MM	688	500	361	246	229	216	175	224	241	320	333	511
°C AVG MAX	26.7	26.7	27.2	27.8	28.4	28.4	28.4	28.9	27.8	27.8	27.8	26.7
°C AVG MIN	17.8	17.8	17.8	17.8	17.8	18.4	17.8	17.8	17.8	17.8	17.8	17.8
DIURNAL RANGE	8.9	8.9	9.4	10.0	10.6	10.0	10.6	11.1	10.0	10.0	10.0	8.9
S/HEMISPHERE	JUL	AUG	SEP	OCT	NOV	DEC	JAN	FEB	MAR	APR	MAY	JUN

Cultural Recommendations

LIGHT: 2000–3000 fc.

TEMPERATURES: Throughout the year, days average 80–84°F (27–29°C), and nights average 64–65°F (18°C), with a diurnal range of 16–20°F (9–11°C). This habitat has essentially no seasonal temperature fluctuations.

HUMIDITY: 80–90% year-round. High humidity and excellent air circulation are important.

WATER: Rainfall is heavy all year. Cultivated plants should be kept very moist but not soggy. Warm water is suggested.

FERTILIZER: 1/4–1/2 recommended strength. A balanced fertilizer should be applied weekly to biweekly throughout the year.

REST PERIOD: Growing conditions should be maintained all year. The smaller diurnal range results from cooler days, not cooler nights. The record low is only 10°F (6°C) below the average lows. In the habitat, light is slightly lower in winter. Although rainfall remains heavy all year, water should be reduced somewhat in winter for cultivated plants, especially those grown in the dark, short-day conditions common in temperate latitudes. They should never be allowed to dry out completely, however.

GROWING MEDIA: Plants may be mounted on tree-fern or cork slabs or potted in small pots filled with any open, fast-draining medium. Repotting may be done anytime new roots are growing.

MISCELLANEOUS NOTES: The bloom season shown in the climate table is based on reports from the habitat.

Plant and Flower Information

PLANT SIZE AND TYPE: A 12–16 in. (30–40 cm) sympodial epiphyte. The growth habit was described as similar to that of *D. grande* Hooker f.

PSEUDOBULB: 10–13 in. (25–33 cm) long. The erect, densely leafy stems are flattened lengthwise. They are borne on a very short rhizome.

LEAVES: Many. The leaves are 3 in. (8 cm) long, distichous, and persistent.

INFLORESCENCE: Clusters of flowers are borne along the side of the stem.

FLOWERS: Several per inflorescence. The flowers are 0.3 in. (0.8 cm) across. The sepals are ovate, but the lateral sepals are dilated at the base. Petals are obliquely spatula-shaped. The 3-lobed lip has oblong, rounded sidelobes and a very large midlobe that is notched in the center. The transverse callus is 4-lobed. Flower color was not included in the original description. The blossoms were described as similar to *D. grande*.

REFERENCES: 221, 286, 295.

Dendrobium xylophyllum Kränzlin

ORIGIN/HABITAT: Papua New Guinea. Plants were originally found at Cape Frere, near the eastern tip of the island. Habitat elevation is unavailable, so the following climate data should be used with caution.

CLIMATE: Station #94075, Samarai, Sideia Island, Papua New Guinea, Lat. 10.6°S, Long. 150.7°E, at 20 ft. (6 m). Record extreme temperatures are 104°F (40°C) and 64°F (18°C).

N/HEMISPHERE	JAN	FEB	MAR	APR	MAY	JUN	JUL	AUG	SEP	OCT	NOV	DEC
°F AVG MAX	81	81	82	83	85	87	87	88	87	86	84	82
°F AVG MIN	74	73	74	74	75	76	77	77	76	75	75	74
DIURNAL RANGE	7	8	8	9	10	11	10	11	11	11	9	8
RAIN/INCHES	8.1	8.6	10.1	8.7	8.4	6.1	7.0	7.8	10.0	9.8	12.0	11.3
HUMIDITY/%	N/A											
BLOOM SEASON	N/A											
DAYS CLR	N/A											
RAIN/MM	206	218	257	221	213	155	178	198	254	249	305	287
°C AVG MAX	27.2	27.2	27.8	28.3	29.4	30.6	30.6	31.1	30.6	30.0	28.9	27.8
°C AVG MIN	23.3	22.8	23.3	23.3	23.9	24.4	25.0	25.0	24.4	23.9	23.9	23.3
DIURNAL RANGE	3.9	4.4	4.5	5.0	5.5	6.2	5.6	6.1	6.2	6.1	5.0	4.5
S/HEMISPHERE	JUL	AUG	SEP	OCT	NOV	DEC	JAN	FEB	MAR	APR	MAY	JUN

Cultural Recommendations

LIGHT: 2500–3000 fc.

TEMPERATURES: Throughout the year, days average 81–88°F (27–31°C), and nights average 73–77°F (23–25°C), with a diurnal range of 7–11°F (4–6°C).

HUMIDITY: Information is not available for this location. However, records from nearby stations indicate that humidity is probably 70–80% year-round.

WATER: Rainfall is very heavy year-round. Cultivated plants should be kept moist but not soggy.

FERTILIZER: 1/4–1/2 recommended strength. A balanced fertilizer should be applied weekly to biweekly throughout the year.

REST PERIOD: Growing conditions should be maintained year-round. In the habitat, winter rainfall is high; but water and fertilizer should be reduced for cultivated plants, especially those grown in the dark, short-day conditions in temperate-latitude winters. Plants should never be allowed to dry out completely, however. In the habitat, seasonal light variation is minor.

GROWING MEDIA: Plants may be mounted on tree-fern or cork slabs if humidity is high and plants are watered daily at least once daily in summer. When plants are potted, any open, fast-draining medium may be used. Repotting is best done in early spring when new roots are growing.

Plant and Flower Information

PLANT SIZE AND TYPE: An 8 in. (20 cm) sympodial epiphyte.

PSEUDOBULB: 8 in. (20 cm) long. The stems are curved, rigid, and densely leafy.

LEAVES: Many. The leaves are 1.6 in. (4 cm) long, ovate, and bilobed at the apex.

INFLORESCENCE: Short.

FLOWERS: 1 at a time. The yellow flowers are 1.6–2.0 in. (4–5 cm) across. They open in succession. Sepals and petals are linear, pointed, and incurved. The 3-lobed lip has triangular sidelobes. The triangular midlobe is toothed and deflexed along the margin. The disk has long hairs.

REFERENCES: 220, 254.

Dendrobium yeageri Ames and Quisumbing

ORIGIN/HABITAT: The Philippine Islands. Plants were collected in hardwood forests on Mt. Pauai in Benguet Province on Luzon Island. Habitat elevation is unavailable, so the following climate data should be used with caution.

CLIMATE: Station #98328, Baguio, Luzon, Philippines, Lat. 16.4°N, Long. 120.6°E, at 4962 ft. (1512 m). Temperatures are calculated for an elevation of 4000 ft. (1220 m), resulting in probable extremes of 87°F (31°C) and 49°F (10°C).

N/HEMISPHERE	JAN	FEB	MAR	APR	MAY	JUN	JUL	AUG	SEP	OCT	NOV	DEC
°F AVG MAX	75	76	79	80	79	78	74	74	74	76	77	77
°F AVG MIN	58	59	61	63	64	64	63	63	63	63	62	60
DIURNAL RANGE	17	17	18	17	15	14	11	11	11	13	15	17
RAIN/INCHES	0.9	0.9	1.7	4.3	15.8	17.2	42.3	45.7	28.1	15.0	4.9	2.0
HUMIDITY/%	83	83	83	85	89	90	93	93	92	89	86	84
BLOOM SEASON					*							
DAYS CLR	N/A											
RAIN/MM	23	23	43	109	401	437	1074	1161	714	381	124	51
°C AVG MAX	24.0	24.5	26.2	26.8	26.2	25.7	23.4	23.4	23.4	24.5	25.1	25.1
°C AVG MIN	14.5	15.1	16.2	17.3	17.9	17.9	17.3	17.3	17.3	17.3	16.8	15.7
DIURNAL RANGE	9.5	9.4	10.0	9.5	8.3	7.8	6.1	6.1	6.1	7.2	8.3	9.4
S/HEMISPHERE	JUL	AUG	SEP	OCT	NOV	DEC	JAN	FEB	MAR	APR	MAY	JUN

Cultural Recommendations

LIGHT: 2000–2500 fc. Diffused or dappled light is recommended. Sky-cover records are unavailable, but in this region, high elevations are typically cloudy.

TEMPERATURES: Throughout the year, days average 74–80°F (23–27°C), and nights average 58–64°F (15–18°C), with a diurnal range of 11–17°F (6–10°C). The coolest nights and greatest diurnal range occur in winter.

HUMIDITY: 85–90% year-round.

WATER: Rainfall is very heavy from late spring into autumn, but conditions are much drier in winter. Cultivated plants should be kept moist while actively growing, but water should be gradually reduced in autumn.

FERTILIZER: ¼–½ recommended strength. A balanced fertilizer should be applied weekly to biweekly throughout the year.

REST PERIOD: Growing temperatures should be maintained all year. Winter lows occasionally drop below 55°F (13°C). Rainfall is low for 2–4 months in winter, but the continuing high humidity indicates that additional moisture is frequently available from fog, dew, or mist. Cultivated plants should be allowed to dry somewhat between waterings, but should never remain dry for long periods. In the habitat, light may be highest in winter.

GROWING MEDIA: Mounting plants on tree-fern or cork slabs accommodates their pendulous growth habit. However, humidity must be high and plants must be watered at least once a day in summer. If plants cannot be mounted, hanging pots or baskets may be filled with an open, fast-draining medium. Repotting may be done anytime new roots are actively growing.

MISCELLANEOUS NOTES: The bloom season shown in the climate table is based on collection reports.

Plant and Flower Information

PLANT SIZE AND TYPE: An 8–20 in. (20–50 cm) sympodial epiphyte.

PSEUDOBULB: 8–20 in. (20–50 cm) long. The pendulous stems are slender, clustered, and rarely branch. The nodes are very swollen.

LEAVES: Many. The leaves are 2–4 in. (5–10 cm) long, pointed, and lanceolate.

INFLORESCENCE: Short. Inflorescences emerge along the side of the stem.

FLOWERS: 2–6 per inflorescence. The showy flowers are 1.2–1.6 in. (3–4 cm) across when spread. Sepals and petals are narrowly oblong. The floral segments are lavender-violet at the apex and deep violet-purple at the base with dark purple veins. The lip is oblong, unlobed, and smooth with a broad, blunt point at the apex. Flowers are closely related to *D. victoriae-reginae,* but the color pattern is reversed, and the lip has no callus. Blossoms are not fragrant.

REFERENCES: 225, 373, 536.

PHOTOS/DRAWINGS: *373.*

Dendrobium × *yengiliense* T. M. Reeve.
Now considered a natural hybrid between *D. alaticaulinum* P. van Royen and *D. leucocyanum* T. M. Reeve. REFERENCES: 234, 381.

Dendrobium ypsilon Seidenfaden

ORIGIN/HABITAT: Southwestern Thailand. Plants are reported in the Tomoh National Park near Pathalung. Habitat elevation is estimated, so the following climate data should be used with caution.

CLIMATE: Station #48569, Hat Yai, Thailand, Lat. 6.9°N, Long. 100.4°E, at 89 ft. (27 m). Temperatures are calculated for an elevation of 1000 ft. (300 m). Record extreme temperatures are not available for this location.

N/HEMISPHERE	JAN	FEB	MAR	APR	MAY	JUN	JUL	AUG	SEP	OCT	NOV	DEC
°F AVG MAX	85	88	91	91	87	89	89	88	87	86	83	82
°F AVG MIN	68	68	70	71	69	71	71	71	71	71	71	69
DIURNAL RANGE	17	20	21	20	18	18	18	17	16	15	12	13
RAIN/INCHES	1.2	0.4	1.6	4.5	7.7	3.5	4.0	4.6	6.5	7.5	11.4	11.2
HUMIDITY/%	N/A											
BLOOM SEASON		*										
DAYS CLR	N/A											
RAIN/MM	30	10	41	114	196	89	102	117	165	190	290	284
°C AVG MAX	29.4	31.1	32.8	32.8	30.6	31.7	31.7	31.1	30.6	30.0	28.3	27.8
°C AVG MIN	20.0	20.0	21.1	21.7	20.6	21.7	21.7	21.7	21.7	21.7	21.7	20.6
DIURNAL RANGE	9.4	11.1	11.7	11.1	10.0	10.0	10.0	9.4	8.9	8.3	6.6	7.2
S/HEMISPHERE	JUL	AUG	SEP	OCT	NOV	DEC	JAN	FEB	MAR	APR	MAY	JUN

Cultural Recommendations

LIGHT: 2000–3000 fc.

TEMPERATURES: Throughout the year, days average 82–91°F (28–33°C), and nights average 68–71°F (20–22°C), with a diurnal range of 12–20°F (7–11°C). Spring is the warmest season.

HUMIDITY: Information is not available for this location. However, records from nearby stations indicate that humidity is probably 75–80% year-round.

WATER: Rainfall is moderate to heavy most of the year. Autumn is the wettest season, followed immediately by a relatively short dry season in winter. Cultivated plants should be thoroughly saturated then allowed to dry slightly between waterings from spring through autumn.

FERTILIZER: ¼–½ recommended strength, applied weekly. A high-nitrogen fertilizer is beneficial from spring to midsummer, but a fertilizer high in phosphates should be used in late summer and autumn.

REST PERIOD: Growing temperatures should be maintained all year. Rainfall is low for 2–3 months, but additional moisture is frequently available from heavy dew. Water and fertilizer should be reduced for cultivated plants, but they should never be allowed to remain dry for long periods. In the habitat, light is highest in winter.

GROWING MEDIA: Plants may be mounted on tree-fern or cork slabs if humidity is high and plants are watered at least once daily in summer. When plants are potted, any open, fast-draining medium may be used. Repotting is best done in early spring when new roots are growing.

MISCELLANEOUS NOTES: The bloom season shown in the climate table is based on reports from the habitat.

Plant and Flower Information

PLANT SIZE AND TYPE: A 2–8 in. (5–20 cm) sympodial epiphyte. Seidenfaden (ref. 454) indicated that vegetatively *D. ypsilon* could not be distinguished from *D. lamellatum* (Blume) Lindley, and the vegetative information given below is based on the latter species.

PSEUDOBULB: 2–5 in. (5–13 cm) long. The green stems resemble smooth cactus leaves. They are wide, very thin and flat, and somewhat curved or cupped. The stems may be nearly as wide as they are tall. The plant is very branched and each branch consists of 3–4 nodes.

LEAVES: 1–3 per growth. The oval leaves are carried at upper nodes of young stems. They are 1.5–3.0 in. (3.8–7.5 cm) long.

INFLORESCENCE: Short. The arching to pendulous racemes arise near the apex of the pseudobulb.

FLOWERS: 2–5 per inflorescence. The flowers are up to 0.8 in. (2 cm) across. They are yellow with an orange tint. The small petals, which are broadest near the tips, are uneven and minutely toothed along the margin. Lateral sepals are broadly triangular. The Y-shaped lip has a recurved, uneven margin at the broad apex.

REFERENCES: 234, 454.

PHOTOS/DRAWINGS: 454.

Dendrobium yunnanense Finet. See *D. moniliforme* (Linn.) Swartz.

REFERENCES: 117, 208, 254, 414, 445.

Dendrobium zamboangense Ames

ORIGIN/HABITAT: The Philippine Islands. On Mindanao Island, plants grow in Agusan, Davao, and Zamboango provinces. In Zamboanga, the orchids grow in the Sax River Mountains at about 3600 ft. (1100 m).

CLIMATE: Station #98836, Zamboanga, Mindanao, Philippines, Lat. 6.9°, Long. 122.1°E, at 17 ft. (5 m). Temperatures are calculated for an elevation of 3600 ft. (1100 m), resulting in probable extremes of 84°F (29°C) and 48°F (9°C).

N/HEMISPHERE	JAN	FEB	MAR	APR	MAY	JUN	JUL	AUG	SEP	OCT	NOV	DEC
°F AVG MAX	77	77	78	78	77	76	76	76	76	76	77	76
°F AVG MIN	59	59	60	61	62	62	61	61	61	61	60	59
DIURNAL RANGE	18	18	18	17	15	14	15	15	15	15	17	17
RAIN/INCHES	2.1	2.2	1.5	2.0	3.5	4.2	4.9	4.0	4.7	5.6	4.2	3.4
HUMIDITY/%	78	76	76	77	79	80	80	80	80	81	80	79
BLOOM SEASON										*	*	
DAYS CLR @ 8AM	6	6	8	7	3	1	3	2	4	7	6	5
DAYS CLR @ 2PM	4	3	5	3	1	1	1	2	2	2	2	3
RAIN/MM	53	56	38	51	89	107	124	102	119	142	107	86
°C AVG MAX	25.1	25.1	25.7	25.7	25.1	24.5	24.5	24.5	24.5	24.5	25.1	24.5
°C AVG MIN	15.1	15.1	15.7	16.2	16.8	16.8	16.2	16.2	16.2	16.2	15.7	15.1
DIURNAL RANGE	10.0	10.0	10.0	9.5	8.3	7.7	8.3	8.3	8.3	8.3	9.4	9.4
S/HEMISPHERE	JUL	AUG	SEP	OCT	NOV	DEC	JAN	FEB	MAR	APR	MAY	JUN

Cultural Recommendations

LIGHT: 2500–3500 fc.

TEMPERATURES: Throughout the year, days average 76–78°F (25–26°C), and nights average 59–62°F (15–17°C), with a diurnal range of 14–18°F (8–10°C).

HUMIDITY: 75–80% year-round.

WATER: Rainfall is moderate most of the year. Cultivated plants should be allowed to dry slightly between waterings from late spring into autumn. Water should be gradually reduced in late autumn and early winter.

FERTILIZER: ¼–½ recommended strength. A balanced fertilizer should be applied weekly to biweekly throughout the year.

REST PERIOD: Warm growing temperatures should be maintained year-round. Water and fertilizer should be reduced slightly in winter. Plants should be allowed to dry out between waterings, but they should not remain dry for long periods. In the habitat, light is brightest from late autumn into spring.

GROWING MEDIA: Plants may be mounted on tree-fern or cork slabs if humidity is high and plants are watered at least once daily in summer. When plants are potted, any open, fast-draining medium may be used. Repotting may be done anytime new roots are growing.

MISCELLANEOUS NOTES: The bloom season shown in the climate table is based on collection reports.

Plant and Flower Information

PLANT SIZE AND TYPE: An 8–12 in. (20–30 cm) sympodial epiphyte.

PSEUDOBULB: 8–12 in. (20–30 cm) long. The slender, leafy stems are narrowest at the base. They consist of nodes spaced 0.4 in. (1 cm) apart.

LEAVES: Many. The leathery leaves are 1.2–1.4 in. (3.0–3.5 cm) long and unequally bilobed at the apex. The leaves are similar to those of *D. clavipes* Hooker f.

INFLORESCENCE: Very short. The purple racemes emerge from nodes opposite the leaves. They are laxly flowered.

FLOWERS: 6 per inflorescence. The purple flowers are 0.4 in. (1 cm) across. Segments are nearly transparent. Blossoms have oblong lateral sepals, an elliptic-lanceolate dorsal sepal, and oblong-lanceolate petals. Floral segments are pointed. The spoon-shaped lip has a smooth margin.

REFERENCES: 12, 222, 296, 536.

Dendrobium zaranense P. van Royen. See *D. brevicaule* Rolfe. REFERENCES: 233, 385, 538. PHOTOS/DRAWINGS: 538.

Dendrobium zebrinum J. J. Smith. Now considered a synonym of *Epigeneium zebrinum* (J. J. Smith) Summerhayes. REFERENCES: 25, 200, 219, 229, 254, 286, 445, 449, 455, 499.

Dendrobium zenkeri Schindl. This name is included in Index Kewensis (ref. 223), but no information was found at the reference given. Since the plant originated in the Cameroons, it is unlikely to be a *Dendrobium*. REFERENCES: 223.

Dendrobium zhaojuense S. C. Sun and L. G. Xu

ORIGIN/HABITAT: China. Plants grow in southwest Sichuan (Szechwan) province. They are found on rocks near Zhaojue (Chao-chiao) at 5600–5900 ft. (1700–1800 m).

CLIMATE: Station #56571, Hsi-Chang (Hsicha), Sichuan, China, Lat. 27.9°N, Long. 102.3°E, at 5246 ft. (1599 m). Temperatures are calculated for an elevation of 5750 ft. (1750 m), resulting in probable extremes of 95°F (35°C) and 23°F (−5°C).

N/HEMISPHERE	JAN	FEB	MAR	APR	MAY	JUN	JUL	AUG	SEP	OCT	NOV	DEC
°F AVG MAX	59	61	73	79	80	77	81	80	77	69	65	60
°F AVG MIN	37	40	48	55	59	62	65	63	60	53	45	39
DIURNAL RANGE	22	21	25	24	21	15	16	17	17	16	20	21
RAIN/INCHES	0.3	0.4	1.1	1.2	3.4	10.7	7.1	8.2	9.1	4.4	1.3	0.1
HUMIDITY/%	49	51	40	42	52	72	74	73	70	72	61	58
BLOOM SEASON					*							
DAYS CLR @ 7AM	18	16	20	16	9	3	3	4	6	5	17	19
DAYS CLR @ 1PM	20	15	17	17	9	4	5	5	8	9	19	22
RAIN/MM	8	10	28	30	86	272	180	208	231	112	33	3
°C AVG MAX	15.2	16.3	23.0	26.3	26.9	25.2	27.4	26.9	25.2	20.7	18.5	15.7
°C AVG MIN	3.0	4.6	9.1	13.0	15.2	16.9	18.5	17.4	15.7	11.9	7.4	4.1
DIURNAL RANGE	12.2	11.7	13.9	13.3	11.7	8.3	8.9	9.5	9.5	8.8	11.1	11.6
S/HEMISPHERE	JUL	AUG	SEP	OCT	NOV	DEC	JAN	FEB	MAR	APR	MAY	JUN

Cultural Recommendations

LIGHT: 2500–3500 fc.

TEMPERATURES: Summer days average 77–81°F (25–27°C), and nights average 62–65°F (17–19°C), with a diurnal range of 15–17°F (8–10°C).

HUMIDITY: 70–75% in summer and autumn, dropping to 40–50% in winter and spring.

WATER: Rainfall is moderate to heavy from late spring into autumn, but conditions are drier for 5–6 months. While actively growing, cultivated plants should be watered frequently with only slight drying allowed between waterings, but water should be gradually reduced after new growths mature in autumn.

FERTILIZER: ¼–½ recommended strength, applied weekly. A high nitrogen fertilizer is beneficial from spring to midsummer, but a fertilizer high in phosphates should be used in late summer and autumn.

REST PERIOD: Winter days average 59–61°F (15–16°C), and nights average 37–40°F (3–5°C), with a diurnal range of 21–22°F (12°C). Rainfall is low for 5–6 months from late autumn into early spring. For 3 of these months, conditions are so dry that even moisture from dew is uncommon. Water should be reduced for cultivated plants. They should be allowed to dry out between waterings but should not remain completely dry for extended periods. Occasional early morning mistings between waterings may help prevent plants from becoming too dry. Water should be gradually increased as new growth starts in spring.

GROWING MEDIA: Plants should be potted in a very open, fast-draining medium that retains moisture. They may be repotted anytime new roots are growing.

MISCELLANEOUS NOTES: The bloom season shown in the climate table is based on collection reports.

Plant and Flower Information

PLANT SIZE AND TYPE: A 9–14 in. (23–35 cm) sympodial lithophyte.

PSEUDOBULB: 8–12 in. (20–30 cm) long. The stems are erect, slender, and clustered. They are dark yellow when dry.

LEAVES: 2–5 per growth. The lanceolate leaves, which are 1.2–4.0 in. (3–10 cm) long, taper to a point.

INFLORESCENCE: 10–14 in. (25–35 cm) long. The inflorescence arises from the base of the stems and holds the blossoms at the tips of the leaves.

FLOWERS: 1–2 per inflorescence. The flowers are 2.4 in. (6 cm) across and open fully. Blossoms have oblong-lanceolate sepals and ovate-lanceolate petals. Sepals and petals are pointed. The broadly ovate lip has an irregularly serrated margin. Sepals are yellowish with purplish-green on the backside. Petals are yellowish. The yellow lip has a purple margin and 2 velvety, purple patches at the base of the lip.

REFERENCES: 235, 502.

PHOTOS/DRAWINGS: 502.

Dendrobium zippelii J. J. Smith

AKA: *D. ansusanum* Schlechter.

ORIGIN/HABITAT: New Guinea and the Admiralty Islands. Plants are found in open areas of mangrove swamps near sea level. They often grow with *Diplocaulobium nitidissimum*. In Irian Jaya (western New Guinea), plants grow on mangroves near Etna Bay, on rocks along river banks at about 150 ft. (40 m) near Humboldt Bay, and at about 800 ft. (250 m) on Waigeo Island.

CLIMATE: Station #97690, Sentani/Jayapura, Irian Jaya, Lat. 2.7°S, Long. 140.5°E, at 289 ft. (88 m). Record extreme temperatures are 97°F (36°C) and 68°F (20°C).

N/HEMISPHERE	JAN	FEB	MAR	APR	MAY	JUN	JUL	AUG	SEP	OCT	NOV	DEC
°F AVG MAX	87	89	89	90	90	89	89	88	89	90	90	89
°F AVG MIN	72	72	72	73	73	73	73	73	73	74	73	73
DIURNAL RANGE	15	17	17	17	17	16	16	15	16	16	17	16
RAIN/INCHES	4.1	3.9	5.3	2.9	6.7	7.0	8.3	8.3	8.5	4.6	2.4	5.2
HUMIDITY/%	81	80	80	79	81	81	79	80	80	80	81	80
BLOOM SEASON										*	*	*
DAYS CLR @ 9AM	5	3	4	3	2	1	1	0	1	2	2	5
DAYS CLR @ 3PM	4	3	3	3	2	1	3	0	1	2	2	3
RAIN/MM	104	99	135	74	170	178	211	211	216	117	61	132
°C AVG MAX	30.6	31.7	31.7	32.2	32.2	31.7	31.7	31.1	31.7	32.2	32.2	31.7
°C AVG MIN	22.2	22.2	22.2	22.8	22.8	22.8	22.8	22.8	22.8	23.3	22.8	22.8
DIURNAL RANGE	8.4	9.5	9.5	9.4	9.4	8.9	8.9	8.3	8.9	8.9	9.4	8.9
S/HEMISPHERE	JUL	AUG	SEP	OCT	NOV	DEC	JAN	FEB	MAR	APR	MAY	JUN

Cultural Recommendations

LIGHT: 2000–3000 fc.

TEMPERATURES: Throughout the year, days average 87–90°F (31–32°C), and nights average 72–74°F (22–23°C), with a diurnal range of 15–17°F (8–10°C).

HUMIDITY: Near 80% year-round.

WATER: Rainfall is moderate to heavy most of the year with brief, semidry periods in spring and autumn. Cultivated plants should be kept moist with only slight drying allowed between waterings.

FERTILIZER: ¼–½ recommended strength. A balanced fertilizer should be applied weekly to biweekly throughout the year.

REST PERIOD: Growing conditions should be maintained year-round. Cultivated plants should never be allowed to dry out completely. However, water and fertilizer should be reduced somewhat, especially for plants cultivated in dark, short-day conditions common during temperate-latitude winters. In the habitat, light is highest in winter.

GROWING MEDIA: Plants may be mounted on tree-fern or cork slabs if humidity is high and plants are watered at least once daily in summer. When plants are potted, any open, fast-draining medium may be used. Repotting may be done anytime new roots are growing.

MISCELLANEOUS NOTES: The bloom season shown in the climate table is based on reports from the habitat. The slender roots are very rough.

Plant and Flower Information

PLANT SIZE AND TYPE: A 10 in. (25 cm) sympodial epiphyte or lithophyte.

PSEUDOBULB: 10 in. (25 cm) long. The erect, wiry stems are spaced 0.6 in. (1.5 cm) apart on the creeping, rooting rhizome that curves up at the growing tip. The stems are yellow when dry.

LEAVES: Many. The spreading, lanceolate leaves are 1.6–2.4 in. (4–6 cm) long. They are unequally bilobed at the apex.

INFLORESCENCE: Short. The inflorescences have branches that each carry a single blossom. The racemes emerge from the side of the stem at the base of each leaf.

FLOWERS: 2–4 per inflorescence. The flowers are 0.5 in. (1.2 cm) long. Blossoms have an oblong, pointed dorsal sepal; 3-angled, recurved lateral sepals; and lanceolate petals. The fleshy, erect lip is recurved. Sepals and petals are apple-green. The lip is cream colored. All segments turn yellowish apricot with age.

REFERENCES: 219, 254, 445, 470, 486, 583.

PHOTOS/DRAWINGS: 583.

Dendrobium zollingerianum Teijsm. and Binn. Now considered a synonym of *Flickingeria comata* (Blume) A. Hawkes. REFERENCES: 211, 213, 216, 254, 395, 449, 469.

Dendrobium zonatum Rolfe. See *D. moniliforme* (Linn.) Swartz. REFERENCES: 139, 208, 219, 254, 414, 528.

Appendix A
Orchid Growing Problems

Appendix Contents

I. Preventing Disease
    Disease Development 785
    Techniques for Avoiding Orchid Diseases 785

II. Identifying and Treating Plant Problems
    Glossary of Terms 787
    Guide to Symptoms
        Flowers (Including Buds, Fruit, and Sheaths) 788
        Leaves 789
        New Leads, Pseudobulbs, Rhizomes, Roots, and Stems 794
    Pathogens
        General Information 796
        List of Pathogens 796
        Disease Treatment Summary 812
    Pests
        General Information 820
    List of Pests 821
        Orchid Pests Summary 824
    Nutrients
        General Information 826
        List of Nutrients 826
        Nutrients Summary 830

III. Using Chemicals Safely
    Chemical Toxicity 833
    General Rules for Chemical Use 833
    Chemical Classifications and Methods of Application 834

I. Preventing Disease

Disease Development

Plant scientists take a broad view of disease, defining it as any plant abnormality due to a causative agent. Thus, in the broad sense, disease includes problems resulting from unfavorable environmental conditions, pests, and nutrient imbalances as well as infection by pathogens, whether bacteria, fungi, or viruses.

The environmental and cultural requirements of individual orchid species have been the primary focus of this book, because vigorous, healthy plants grow and bloom better. Despite growers' best efforts, however, problems occasionally arise. This is when the most important benefit of paying careful attention to cultural requirements becomes apparent. When insects or disease attack, healthy plants usually survive, while stressed or sickly plants often die.

Disease caused by a pathogen requires 4 elements in order to become established:

1. The disease-producing organism must be present in the environment. All pathogens are not necessarily present in all areas.
2. The pathogen must be in the infectious stage of development and must come in contact with the host plant.
3. Environmental conditions must be suitable for the growth and reproduction of the disease-producing organism. Cool, wet weather increases the likelihood of infection by some pathogens, while warm weather increases the likelihood of infection by others.
4. The host plant must be susceptible to the infecting pathogen. Some plants are naturally resistant.

Plants cannot become infected if any one of these preconditions is missing. A strong, healthy plant exposed to a disease pathogen may ward off infection. Growers are usually unaware of this process, just as we are not always aware when our immune system protects us from disease.

Infectious diseases develop in 5 distinct phases. Understanding this progression may help growers more effectively prevent and control infections. When the risk of inoculation is high, preventive action is a far better approach than allowing the disease to develop and then attempting to treat it after the plant is damaged. On the other hand, when the risk is low, preventive sprays are unnecessary and potentially harmful to the plant. Treating plants after the problem has progressed to the point that signs or symptoms are evident is the least effective way of dealing with disease.

Inoculation occurs when the pathogen is introduced to the plant tissue. The infecting agents may be carried by environmental elements such as wind, rain, or dripping water. They may also be carried from one plant to another by insects or people.

Incubation is the period during which the pathogen changes to a form that can infect or penetrate the plant. Fungi, for instance, develop a structure called a penetration peg which grows through cell walls.

Penetration may be active or passive. It is the process whereby the pathogen enters the plant, which may be accomplished by penetrating the surface or by entering through openings in the leaves.

Infection occurs when a parasitic relationship is established between the pathogen and the host plant.

Disease is the final stage of infection and may be described as the host plant's response to the pathogen. It is at this stage in disease development when symptoms such as chlorosis (yellow discoloration of tissue), necrosis (death of tissue), or spotting begin to show. This is also the time when treatment often begins.

Plants respond to disease in a limited number of ways, and different problems frequently cause similar symptoms. Moreover, a given problem does not necessarily affect all plants the same way, nor do the same diseases attack all orchid species or genera around the world. Unfortunately, there is no simple means of diagnosis. But a careful analysis of plant signs and symptoms is a necessary step in dealing with plant abnormalities. Symptoms of plant diseases are discussed in Section II of this Appendix.

Treatment involves such actions as removing an infected portion of a plant or applying curative chemicals. Both techniques help control disease within the plant as well as reducing the risk that infection will spread to other plants. Eradication is usually impossible once a pathogen has been introduced, but control may be achieved through the use of general disinfectants. Control is possible only if plants with serious infections are removed or destroyed and the growing area is carefully disinfected. Treatments for controlling individual pathogens are discussed in Section III of this Appendix.

Techniques for Avoiding Orchid Diseases

Avoidance measures include selecting plants that are not susceptible to prevailing pathogens, keeping infected plants out of the growing area, isolating new or diseased plants, applying preventive treatments to plants being introduced into the environment, or preventing inoculation by controlling insects or sterilizing contaminated tools.

Protection is best achieved through careful environmental control, which results in a strong, healthy plant able to protect itself. The environment may be manipulated within the range of plant tolerance so that temperature and moisture conditions are outside the range necessary for the pathogens' survival. Preventive applications of fungicides, bactericides, or disinfectants together with insect control measures are effective techniques for plant protection.

Greenhouse cleanliness and good cultural practices cannot be emphasized too strongly. Experts have found that good culture together with good sanitation measures, both in the growing area and with respect to the plants themselves, prevents the vast majority of infections.

The following practices help to reduce the risk of infection.

- Always use new or sterile potting medium.
- Avoid cutting roots unnecessarily.
- Avoid physical injury to the plants since this provides a point of entry for disease.
- Avoid working with plants when they are wet.

Preventing Disease

- Control insects that may transmit diseases from plant to plant.
- Do not crowd plants.
- Identify and remove or isolate any diseased plants.
- Intermix plants so that susceptible plants are not close together.
- Keep greenhouses clean and free from plant debris.
- Keep new plants in isolation until a healthy new growth emerges. An isolation period of 3–4 months is recommended.
- Keep plants clean. Old sheaths, leaves, or other plant tissue should be removed. These serve as hiding places for various pests and allow infections or infestations to develop unnoticed.
- Maintain excellent air movement.
- Never allow water to drip from one plant to another.
- Observe plants carefully for signs of stress, particularly during seasonal shifts in temperature, light, and moisture. Whenever environmental conditions change, a preventive application of a disinfectant to the plants and growing area might be beneficial.
- Sterilize pots and tools after each use.

Sterilizing tools and equipment after each use is critically important to prevent the transmission of disease pathogens. As a safeguard, trays and benches (especially wooden ones) should be disinfected any time a diseased plant is discovered. Sterilizing every surface the plants might touch prevents the spread of bacterial diseases which are transmitted through splashing or dripping water.

Greenhouse disinfectants are available commercially. They must be mixed according to the instructions on the label, as different concentrations are recommended for sterilizing tools, pots, and trays, washing benches, and spraying plants.

Flaming has been the standard method for sterilizing tools. Heat destroys pathogens and is considered by many to be the surest means of deactivating viruses. Single-edged razor blades may be dipped in denatured or isopropyl alcohol then passed over a flame to ignite the alcohol. The blade should be cooled before reuse.

The University of California at Riverside recommends the following method as an alternative to flaming.

- Dip tool for 2 seconds in a fresh solution of
  1 part sodium hypochlorite (household bleach)
  5 parts water
- Immediately dip the tool into a neutralizing mixture consisting of
  1 part vinegar, 5 parts water, 1 tsp. salad oil
- Dry the tool before reusing or storing it.

The vinegar in the second dip neutralizes the corrosive action of the bleach, and the oil lubricates the tool. The same technique, with the oil omitted from the neutralizing mixture, should be used to sterilize pots and trays.

II. Identifying and Treating Plant Problems

Using the plant pathologist's definition of disease as any plant abnormality due to a causal agent means that disease must be considered the rule rather than the exception, for all plants are subject to disease. It also means that in determining the cause of a plant problem, symptoms of inappropriate light, temperature, and moisture levels must be considered together with other causal agents such as physical or chemical injury, disease pathogens, pests, or nutrient imbalances. This Appendix is designed as a tool to help growers identify the cause of plant problems and find possible solutions quickly, in order to reduce damage to their plants.

Signs and symptoms of many plant problems are described briefly in the following lists. Each symptom is classified under the plant part affected; thus the symptoms appear under 3 headings:

    Flowers (Including Buds, Fruit, and Sheaths)
    Leaves
    New Leads, Pseudobulbs, Rhizomes, Roots, and Stems

In the symptom lists, which are arrannged alphabetically, the color of the affected area is a primary clue to identifying the probable source of the problem. Symptoms are further described in terms of size, shape, or location of the abnormality. Growers noticing a problem should carefully examine the particular plant, note the plant parts showing symptoms, then scan the lists for the description which most closely matches the observed abnormality. Cross-references are provided to the general information in Chapter 1; to individual species listings; and to the headings Pathogens, Pests, and Nutrients in this Appendix. For further information on prevention and recommended treatments or controls, we urge you to contact your local universities, agricultural agents, or other local growers.

The process of describing symptoms and matching them with causal agents is at best an uncertain science. Descriptive lists are subjective and require interpretation, as different observers would no doubt describe the same symptoms in different words. It is also important to remember that symptoms may differ from species to species and genus to genus. Still, the effort of careful analysis and interpretation is well worth making, since symptoms provide the grower's best clues to plant problems.

Glossary of Terms

The following terms are used repeatedly in symptom descriptions.

Chlorosis or chlorotic. Yellow or faded tissue that is normally green. The change in color results from the loss of chlorophyll.

Color break. A streaking or separating of flower color, usually caused by viral infections. It normally occurs on the sepals and petals as intensified streaks of color. White streaking on lavender *Cattleya* petals is usually caused by a genetic disorder rather than a virus.

Lesions. Abnormal tissue caused by disease or injury.

Mosaic mottling. A pattern of yellow or pale green tissue separated by areas of green tissue which appears normal. The overall effect resembles mosaic tile.

Mycelia. Hairlike filaments that are the vegetative growths of fungi and some bacteria.

Necrosis or necrotic. Dead or dying tissue which may be white, brown, or black. Necrotic spots may occur in larger chlorotic patches.

Pathogen. A specific cause of disease (such as a bacterium, fungus, or virus).

Pustules. Blisters or pimples, usually raised, which develop on diseased tissue.

Ringspot. Yellowish or dead tissue, usually circular, which surrounds green tissue.

Rosetting. Abnormal whorls formed by the leaves.

Sclerotia. Hardened masses of fungal threads which often remain dormant for an extended period.

Spores. Reproductive bodies which are capable of developing into new individual fungi. They are the fungal equivalent of seeds.

Sporing or fruiting bodies. Small, raised fungal structures where spores are produced. They are the fungal equivalent of seed pods and the fungi's means of propagation.

Guide to Symptoms

Flowers (Including Buds, Fruit, and Sheaths)

Black necrotic flecks. See Pathogens—*Alternaria alternata*.

Black or brown watery pustules. The raised areas usually occur on the underside of the sepals and petals of older flowers. See Pathogens—*Colletotrichum gloeosporioides*.

Black or light brown water-soaked spots. The spots start very small but may enlarge and cover the entire flower. See Pathogens—*Botrytis cinerea*; *Vanda* transit rot.

Black spots on the lip. The petals may also be discolored. See Pathogens—*Colletotrichum* species; *Glomerella* species.

Black spots or streaks on flower sheaths. Several fungi may also cause rotting of flower buds. See Pathogens—*Botrytis cinerea*, *Colletotrichum* species; *Curvularia geniculata*; *Glomerella* species.

Black to dark brown lesions. Usually sunken, the lesions are often covered with white, powdery mycelia and small pink sporing bodies. See Pathogens—*Fusarium moniliforme*.

Bleached spots on flowers. See Pathogens—*Cymbidium* mosaic.

Brown lesions. The areas may be light or dark, circular or oval. They appear on the sepals, petals, or flower spikes. See Pathogens—*Curvularia geniculata*.

Brown spots on the blossoms. They may be caused by water droplets. See Chapter 1—Flowers.

Brown spots on *Vanilla* flowers and beans. See Pathogens—*Nectria vanillae*.

Brown streaks or spots which develop on flowers approximately 1 week after the buds open. See Pathogens—Blossom necrotic streak.

Buds that develop improperly. See Nutrients—Calcium (deficiency); Cobalt (deficiency); Copper (deficiency); Iron (deficiency); Magnesium (excess); Manganese (excess); Potassium (excess); Zinc (deficiency or excess).

Buds that drop. The flower buds drop before opening. This is usually caused by incorrect temperatures or air pollution. See Chapter 1—Flowers; Species listings—Rest period; Temperatures.

Buds that fail to open properly. See Pests—Thrips.

Buds that rot. The flower buds rot before opening. See Pathogens—*Botrytis cinerea*; *Colletotrichum* species; *Curvularia geniculata*; *Glomerella* species; *Pseudomonas aeruginosa*.

Buds that yellow and drop. Symptoms are usually caused by incorrect light or temperature. See Chapter 1—Flowers; Pathogens—*Fusarium moniliforme*; Species listings—Light; Temperatures.

Color break. Particularly in *Vanda* flowers, color break may be caused by insect damage. See Pests—Thrips.

Color break (mild) in flowers. See Pathogens—Cucumber mosaic; *Odontoglossum* mosaic.

Color break with mottling and distortion of flowers. See Pathogens—*Odontoglossum* ringspot.

Color break with symmetrical variegations. The colored areas of the petals and the margins of the sepals are most likely to be affected. The center of the petals is not normally affected. See Pathogens—Flower break, symmetrical.

Color variegation and distortion of flowers. See Pathogens—*Cymbidium* bar mottle.

Damaged flowers. The damage may result from mechanical injury or inappropriate growing conditions. See Pests—Thrips; Species listings—Light; Rest period; Temperatures.

Few flowers. Poor flowering is usually caused by low light levels, incorrect photoperiods, or a lack of phosphorus. See Nutrients—Phosphorus (deficiency); Species listings—Light; Rest period.

Gray fungus on diseased or decaying flowers. See Pathogens—*Botrytis cinerea*.

Holes and notches in flowers. See Pests—Slugs and snails.

Malformed flowers. See Chapter 1—Flowers; Pathogens—Tobacco rattle.

Misshapen buds, flowers, or new growths. Affected areas may become stunted or distorted. See Pests—Aphids.

Necrotic flecks on sepals and petals. See Pathogens—*Alternaria alternata*; *Botrytis cinerea*; *Vanda* transit rot.

Necrotic specks with water-soaked margins on sepals and petals. See Pathogens—*Pseudomonas aeruginosa*.

Necrotic streaks and spots on flowers. Symptoms do not show on the leaves. See Pathogens—Flower necrosis.

Necrotic veins. See Pathogens—*Dendrobium* vein necrosis.

No flowers. Failure to flower usually indicates a cultural problem such as inappropriate growing temperatures or a lack of diurnal or seasonal temperature fluctuations. See Chapter 1—Flowers; Species listings—Rest period; Temperatures.

Orange spots on flower spikes. The oval spots are raised and often have a yellow halo. See Pathogens—*Coleosporium bletiae*.

Pink sporing bodies. These are usually associated with powdery, white mycelia and black to dark brown, sunken lesions. See Pathogens—*Fusarium moniliforme*.

Raised, watery pustules. Usually black or brown, they normally occur on the underside of aging sepals and petals. See Pathogens—*Colletotrichum gloeosporioides*.

Sepal wilt or premature aging. See Chapter 1—Flowers.

Sheaths that brown or discolor. The damaged sheath may prevent normal flowering. See Pathogens—Fungi species; *Paphiopedilum* flower sheath browning.

Sunken, black to dark brown lesions. White, powdery mycelia and small pink sporing bodies often cover the lesions. See Pathogens—*Fusarium moniliforme*.

Tan or light brown watery spots. They may have somewhat darker centers. See Pathogens—*Phytophthora cactorum*.

Tan to dark brown lesions. The circular or oval areas are usually slightly sunken and approximately 0.02 in. (0.5 mm) across. Sepals, petals, and flower spikes may be affected. See Pathogens—*Botrytis cinerea*; *Curvularia geniculata*.

Vanilla beans with brown spots. See Pathogens—*Nectria vanillae*.

Vanilla beans with brown tips. They are eventually covered with a white powder. See Pathogens—*Phytophthora jatrophae*.

Vein necrosis. See Pathogens—*Dendrobium* vein necrosis.

Water-soaked spots. The very small, black to light brown spots may enlarge and cover the entire flower. See Pathogens—*Botrytis cinerea*.

Watery pustules. The raised black or brown spots appear on the underside of sepals and petals, normally on older flowers. See Pathogens—*Colletotrichum gloeosporioides*.

White cell necrosis. The cause may be ethylene gas or other air pollutants. See Chapter 1—Flowers.

White cell necrosis on *Cattleya*. See Pathogens—*Cymbidium* mosaic.

White, powdery mycelia. Small pink sporing bodies may also be present on the black to dark brown, sunken lesions. See Pathogens—*Fusarium moniliforme*.

White streaks on flowers. (White streaks on lavender *Cattleya* petals are usually caused by a genetic disorder, not a virus.) See Pathogens—*Dendrobium* white streak.

Wilting flowers. Sepal wilt is usually caused by ethylene gas, but premature aging may occur if pollinia are dislodged or the flower is injured. See Chapter 1—Flowers.

Yellow buds in winter. These may indicate incorrect light or temperature. See Chapter 1—Flowers; Pathogens—*Fusarium moniliforme*; Species listings—Light; Temperatures.

Leaves

Black flecks and streaks on older leaves. As spots enlarge, they become necrotic and merge, forming hieroglyphic patterns. Leaves may show reddish purple ring lesions or elongated, mottled, diamond-shaped chlorotic areas. Plants may be stunted or develop abnormally. See Pathogens—*Odontoglossum* ringspot.

Black leaf tips on new leaves. Affected area may have an advancing yellow band. See Nutrients—Calcium (deficiency).

Black lesions. These are dry and appear old. See Pathogens—*Phytophthora cactorum*.

Black newer and older leaves. See Nutrients—Nitrogen (excess).

Black or orange pustules. The spots are arranged in concentric rings on the leaf undersurface. See Pathogens—*Sphenospora kevorkianii*.

Black spots, streaks, or lines. See Pathogens—Black streak.

Black spots that are usually sunken. See Pathogens—*Cymbidium* mosaic: *Erwinia chrysanthemi*.

Black streaks, lines, or spots that are usually sunken. See Pathogens—Black streak.

Black streaks or flecks which develop on older leaves. As the spots enlarge, they become necrotic and merge to form hieroglyphic patterns. Leaves may show reddish purple ring lesions or elongated, mottled, diamond-shaped chlorotic areas. Plants may be stunted and develop abnormally. See Pathogens—*Odontoglossum* ringspot.

Black tissue between veins. See Nutrients—Boron (excess).

Black to brown lesions which are small and usually sunken. See Pathogens—*Fusarium moniliforme*.

Black to brown rings, streaks, or blotches. They usually occur first on older leaves. See Pathogens—*Cymbidium* mosaic.

Black to brown spots or lesions which appear greasy. See Pathogens—*Diplodia laeliocattleyae*.

Black to brown spots or lesions which are circular or irregularly shaped. See Pathogens—*Septoria selenophomoides*.

Black to brown spots that ooze liquid. They are most common near the leaf tip. See Pathogens—*Pseudomonas cattleyae*.

Black to brown spots which are ring-shaped. See Pathogens—*Dendrobium* viral disease.

Black to brown spots which are usually sunken and oval. Often arranged in concentric rings, they usually occur on the underside of leaves. Plants may be stunted. See Pathogens—*Cymbidium* mosaic.

Black to brown spots which occur first on the leaf tips. The areas enlarge and merge until the entire leaf tip dies. They may be covered with powdery spore masses. See Pathogens—*Botrytis* species.

Black to dark brown lesions. The tiny spots may be circular or irregular and are usually sunken. They are yellow initially but darken with age. See Pathogens—*Septoria selenophomoides*.

Black to dark brown spots surrounded by a water-soaked brown area. They may ooze water if pressed. The affected area is usually small and irregular with a yellowish advancing margin. See Pathogens—*Phytophthora cactorum*.

Black to dark grey patchy deposits on the leaves. Discolored areas may be wiped off with a damp cloth. See Pathogens—*Gloeodes pomigena*.

Black to reddish brown areas. They may be spots, streaks, necrotic rings, or diamond-shaped lesions that begin as chlorotic tissue. Leaves may drop prematurely. See Pathogens—*Spathoglottis* diamond spot.

Blistered leaf cells, particularly on the underside of leaves. See Pests—Thrips.

Bronze leaves. See Nutrients—Chlorine (deficiency).

Brown areas which are dried and shriveled. See Pathogens—*Erwinia cypripedii*.

Brown blotches. Normally found on older leaves, the areas are watery. They are round or elongated and about 1.4–2.0 in. (3.5–5.0 cm) across. The blotches usually have a pale brown margin. See Pathogens—*Penicillin thomii*.

Brown circular areas on the underside of leaves. The spots have an advancing orange margin. See Pathogens—*Uredo oncidii*.

Brown circular areas which appear suddenly on a curved leaf surface. These are usually caused by sunburn. See Chapter 1—Leaves; Species listings—Light.

Brown leaf tips or leaf margins. These are usually caused by accumulated fertilizer salts, or the symptoms may result from applying chemicals inappropriately. See Chapter 1—Fertilizer.

Brown leaf tips which proceed from the tip toward the base. See Nutrients—Chlorine (excess); Pathogens—*Glomerella cincta*.

Brown leaves. They start by yellowing and end by dying back. This may be a normal process for plants with deciduous leaves. See Nutrients—Calcium (deficiency); Cobalt (deficiency); Copper (deficiency); Iron (deficiency); Potassium (excess); Magnesium (excess); Manganese (deficiency); Zinc (deficiency or excess).

Brown lesions. The areas are watery and usually located at the base of the stem. The roots and leaf bases often collapse rapidly. See Pathogens—*Sclerotium rolfsii*.

Brown pustules. The areas are usually raised, often have reddish borders, and occur on the underside of leaves. With age, the pustules become purple-black. See Pathogens—*Uredo epidendri*.

Brown spots on either leaf surface. They start small and develop into round, oval, or irregular lesions. They become discolored in the center, and sporing bodies appear on older spots. See Pathogens—*Selenophoma dendrobii*.

Brown spots on the leaves. See Nutrients—Iron (deficiency); Manganese (excess); Zinc (excess).

Brown spots on the leaves which increase in size. The leaves turn yellow, and the tissue between the veins may collapse. See Pathogens—Short orchid rhabdovirus.

Brown spots on the underside of leaves. They are tiny and slightly raised. See Pathogens—*Cercospora angraeci*; *Cercospora* species I–IV.

Brown to grey areas in concentric zones or rings. The discolorations usually occur near the leaf apex. See Pathogens—*Colletotrichum gloeosporiodes*.

Brown to light grey areas without concentric zones or rings. See Pathogens—*Botryodiplodia theobromae*.

Brown to tan areas with well-defined margins. They often have a yellow outer band and with time develop black or dark brown sporing bodies. See Pathogens—*Phyllostictina citricarpa*.

Brown to tan spore pustules. See Pathogens—*Uredo nigropuncta*.

Brown to tan spots. The tiny spots have a slightly raised, red to purple-black margin, a tan or brown center, and raised black spore structures. See Pathogens—*Phyllostictina pyriformis*.

Brown, water-soaked spots on the leaves. See Pathogens—*Erwinia chrysanthemi*.

Brown, water-soaked spots that may ooze water if pressed. The spots are small and irregular and often have a yellowish advancing margin. The center becomes dark brown or black as the lesions age. See Pathogens—*Phytophthora cactorum*.

Burned leaves. A sudden increase in light levels or severe overexposure to excessive light may result in burning. See Chapter I—Light; Species listings—Light.

Chestnut-brown areas on the leaves. See Pathogens—*Erwinia cypripedii*.

Chlorosis. Some forms of chlorosis may result from inappropriate use of chemicals. Also see listings beginning with the words "Yellow" or "Light green."

Chlorosis and ringspots on the leaves. The discolorations are sometimes quite faint. See Pathogens—*Cymbidium* ringspot.

Chlorosis between the veins on newer leaves. Affected leaf tissue is usually light yellow to white. See Nutrients—Zinc (deficiency).

Chlorosis between the veins on older leaves, usually light yellow. See Nutrients—Molybdenum (deficiency).

Chlorosis, light yellow. See Nutrients—Molybdenum (deficiency).

Chlorosis on middle or older leaves. Light yellow discoloration between veins or along the leaf margins is usually caused by a magnesium deficiency. See Nutrients—Calcium (excess); Cobalt (deficiency); Copper (deficiency); Iron (deficiency); Magnesium (deficiency); Manganese (deficiency); Potassium (excess); Zinc (deficiency or excess).

Chlorosis on new leaves. See Nutrients—Zinc (deficiency).

Chlorosis on new leaves which often produces mild discolorations. See Pathogens—*Cymbidium* mosaic.

Chlorosis on older leaves. The discoloration is usually light yellow and is usually caused by a nitrogen deficiency. See Nutrients—Cobalt (deficiency); Copper (deficiency); Iron (deficiency); Manganese (deficiency); Nitrogen (deficiency); Phosphorus (excess); Potassium (excess); Zinc (deficiency or excess).

Chlorosis with deep furrowing and ridging. The necrotic, water-soaked areas are most pronounced on the underside of leaves. Leaves may drop. See Pathogens—*Cymbidium* mosaic.

Chlorotic areas which are elongated or diamond-shaped. The areas may be mottled with pale, reddish purple ring lesions. As the spots enlarge, they become necrotic and merge to form hieroglyphic patterns. Older leaves may develop black flecks and streaks. Plants may be stunted and develop abnormally. See Pathogens—*Odontoglossum* ringspot.

Chlorotic areas which become large, dark brown or black, ring shaped spots. See Pathogens—*Dendrobium* viral disease.

Chlorotic or dark areas on the leaves. Plants appear unhealthy. See Pests—Mealybugs; Scale.

Chlorotic patches and rings which are usually faint. They have a subtly different appearance from chlorosis caused by *Cymbidium* mosaic. See Pathogens—Cucumber mosaic.

Chlorotic patches on the upper leaf surface. Orange-yellow patches in a roughly circular pattern may cover the lower surface. See Pathogens—*Uredo behickiana*.

Chlorotic patches which are diamond-shaped and become necrotic. See Pathogens *Cymbidium* mosaic.

Chlorotic spots and streaks. The necrotic rings or diamond-shaped lesions become reddish brown or black with age. Leaves may drop prematurely. See Pathogens—*Spathoglottis* diamond spot.

Chlorotic spots, streaks, or stippling. The area eventually becomes sunken and turns brown. See Pests—Mites.

Chlorotic streaks. Usually faint, the basal necrotic streaking may cause premature leaf drop. See Pathogens—Tomato ringspot.

Collapsed leaf bases and roots. Watery brown lesions appear at the base of the stem. See Pathogens—*Sclerotium rolfsii*.

Creamy-yellow discoloration which soon turns brown. See Pathogens—*Sclerotium rolfsii*.

Curled, desiccated leaves. Fungal growth and brown rot may be evident on the roots. See Pathogens—*Rhizoctonia solani*.

Curled or cupped mature leaves. These may result from inappropriate use of chemicals. Also see Nutrients—Calcium (deficiency or excess); Cobalt (deficiency); Copper (deficiency); Iron (deficiency); Magnesium (deficiency); Manganese (deficiency); Potassium (excess); Zinc (deficiency or excess).

Dark green leaves which are often succulent and brittle. See Nutrients—Nitrogen (excess); Potassium (deficiency).

Dark green leaves with purplish coloring along the veins. Affected plants are usually also stunted. See Nutrients—Phosphorus (deficiency).

Dark green or limp leaves. Soft leaves often indicate that the plant is receiving insufficient light or that temperatures are too low. See Chapter I—Leaves; Species listings—Light; Temperatures.

Dark or chlorotic areas on the leaves. Plants appear unhealthy. See Pests—Mealybugs; Scale.

Dark streaks. They may rapidly cover the entire leaf. See Pathogens—*Erwinia carotovora*.

Dead tissue. The underside of leaves shows irregular, elongated streaks. See Pathogens—*Cymbidium* mosaic.

Dead tissue between veins. See Nutrients—Boron (excess).

Die-back of mature leaves. Even evergreen plants have a few leaves that die back each year. If all leaves die back, the plant may be deciduous. See Species listings—Leaves.

Die-back of new leaves. Apical buds, growing tips, or terminal leaves may be affected. Symptoms may result from inappropriate use of chemicals. See Nutrients—Boron (deficiency).

Distorted or deformed leaves. Symptoms usually result from inappropriate use of chemicals.

Dry, black lesions that look old. See Pathogens—*Phytophthora cactorum*.

Faded leaves or wilted terminal shoots. See Nutrients—Copper (deficiency).

Flyspeck-like spots. They appear in large groups on leaf surfaces and may be wiped off with a damp cloth. See Pathogens—*Microthyriella rubi*.

Furrowing and ridging. Chlorosis and necrotic, water-soaked areas also appear. See Pathogens—*Cymbidium* mosaic.

Gray to black patchy deposits on the leaves. They may be removed with a damp cloth. See Pathogens—*Gloeodes pomigena*.

Gray to brown areas. They have no concentric zones or rings. See Pathogens—*Botryodiplodia theobromae*.

Gray to brown concentric zones or rings. They occur primarily near the leaf apex. See Pathogens—*Colletotrichum gloeosporiodes*.

Greasy-looking black to brown spots or lesions. See Pathogens—*Diplodia laeliocattleyae*.

Green mosaic on older leaves. The mosaic forms concentric ring patterns. See Pathogens—*Dendrobium* mosaic.

Green veins on yellow mature leaves. See Nutrients—Magnesium (deficiency).

Holes and notches in new leaves. See Pests—Cockroaches; Grasshoppers; Slugs and snails.

Holes in the center of dark spots. See Pathogens—*Cercospora angraeci*; *Cercospora* species I–IV.

Irregular streaks and spots on the leaves. See Pathogens—*Oncidium* severe mosaic streaking.

Leaf drop. Premature leaf drop, sometimes resulting in plant death, may result from high night temperatures. See Species listings—Rest period; Temperatures.

Leaf drop of middle and older leaves. Leaves fall prematurely. See Nutrients—Calcium (deficiency or excess); Cobalt (deficiency); Copper (deficiency); Iron (deficiency); Manganese (deficiency); Nitrogen (deficiency); Phosphorus (deficiency); Potassium (excess); Zinc (deficiency or excess).

Leaf drop which may be accompanied by chlorosis. Other symptoms include deep furrowing and ridging and necrotic, water-soaked areas which are most pronounced on the underside of leaves. See Pathogens—*Cymbidium* mosaic.

Leaf drop with faint chlorotic streaks or basal necrotic streaking. The streaking is usually the first symptom. See Pathogens—Tomato ringspot.

Leaf drop with rotting leaves. See Pathogens—*Pseudomonas andropogonis*.

Leaf-tip die-back is frequently caused by a lack of moisture. Other causes of similar symptoms include excess water resulting in root loss, chemical damage from salt buildup or chemical applications, or overfertilization. See Chapter 1—Fertilizer; Leaves; Nutrients—Calcium (deficiency); Species listings—Water.

Light green. Also see listings beginning with the words "Chlorosis" and "Yellow."

Light green mosaic mottling. See Pathogens—*Oncidium* light green mosaic mottle.

Light green mosaic patches. Other symptoms include chlorosis on the leaves, tissue collapse, necrosis, broad chlorotic furrows, or water-soaked areas on the underside of leaves. See Pathogens—*Phalaenopsis* mosaic.

Light green to yellow rings. The rings may be small and irregular and may turn reddish black with age. See Pathogens—*Odontoglossum* streak.

Limp leaves. They are usually dark green, indicating that the plant is receiving insufficient light. See Chapter 1—Leaves; Species listings—Light.

Malformed leaves which may be mottled. Plants become stunted and weak and produce few flowers. See Pathogens—*Cymbidium* bar mottle.

Mold. Usually found on dead plant material, mold may spread to living tissue. See Pathogens—*Saprophytic* fungi.

Mosaic mottling on leaf tips. Usually inconspicuous, the mottling is often first noticed as a problem with the blossoms. See Pathogens—*Vanda* mosaic.

Mosaic mottling on older leaves. Usually green, it appears in concentric rings. See Pathogens—*Dendrobium* mosaic.

Mosaic mottling on the leaves which is usually light green. See Pathogens—*Oncidium* light green mosaic mottle.

Mosaic mottling on the leaves which may be very faint. See Pathogens—Flower break, symmetrical.

Mosaic mottling on the underside of leaves. It may be accompanied by diffuse, light green or yellow patches, tissue collapse, broad chlorotic furrows, or water-soaked areas. Necrosis and light green chlorosis may show on the upper surface. See Pathogens—*Phalaenopsis* mosaic.

Mosaic mottling on young leaves. It is usually quite pale. See Pathogens—*Cymbidium* bar mottle; *Dendrobium* mosaic.

Mosaic mottling, rings, or streaks. See Pathogens—*Paphiopedilum* viral infection.

Mosaic mottling, usually sunken. See Pathogens—Bean yellow mosaic.

Necrosis. Symptoms frequently result from inappropriate use of chemicals.

Necrotic concentric rings. They surround apparently healthy tissue and may merge to form faint mosaic patterns, chlorotic streaks, or diamond mottling. See Pathogens—*Odontoglossum* mosaic.

Necrotic lines or semicircular rings on the leaves. See Pathogens—*Laelia* etch.

Necrotic or chlorotic flecks on the leaves. See Pathogens—Orchid fleck.

Necrotic streaking and premature leaf drop. See Pathogens—Tomato ringspot.

Necrotic veins on the leaves and flowers. See Pathogens—*Dendrobium* vein necrosis.

Orange pustules in concentric rings on the underside of leaves. The pustules become black with age. See Pathogens—*Sphenospora kevorkianii*.

Orange pustules on both leaf surfaces. Affected areas often have a yellow halo. See Pathogens—*Coleosporium bletiae*.

Orange pustules on the underside of leaves. The pustules are small, and the affected area is usually circular. See Pathogens—*Uredo oncidii*.

Orange pustules which become black with age. See Pathogens—*Uredo nigropuncta*.

Orange to rust-brown pustules. The tiny, raised spots appear on the underside of leaves and turn dark brown with age. See Pathogens—*Sphenospora saphena*.

Orange-yellow patches on the underside of leaves. Patches appear in roughly circular patterns. The top surface develops chlorotic patches. See Pathogens—*Uredo behickiana*.

Pale leaves. They are also desiccated and curl inward. The roots may have fungal growth and brown rot. See Pathogens—*Rhizoctonia solani*.

Purple-black old-looking pustules. The spots, which appear on the underside of leaves, may have started as raised, brown pustules with reddish borders. See Pathogens—*Uredo epidendri*.

Purple-brown sunken spots on the underside of leaves. See Pathogens—*Cercospora angraeci*; *Cercospora* species I–IV.

Purple-brown to purplish black patches. Often irregularly shaped, they sometimes have either an advancing yellow margin or a darker raised margin. See Pathogens—*Cercospora angraeci*; *Cercospora* species I–IV.

Purple lesions. Usually elongated and parallel to the veins, the lesions become streaks, irregular blotches, or diamond-shaped areas. With age, the center turns tan and becomes raised, and black fungal structures develop. See Pathogens—*Guignardia* species.

Purplish to dark green leaves. Red coloring is strongest along the veins. Affected plants are usually stunted. See Nutrients—Phosphorus (deficiency).

Raised black spore structures on tiny brown to tan spots. The pustules may have a slightly raised, red to purple-black margin. See Pathogens—*Phyllostictina pyriformis*.

Raised black spore structures which develop in the brown center of purple lesions. They are usually elongated and parallel to the veins. They may become streaks, irregular blotches, or diamond-shaped areas. See Pathogens—*Guignardia* species.

Guide to Symptoms—Leaves

Raised brown pustules, often with reddish borders. They occur on the underside of leaves, and with age, the pustules become purple-black. See Pathogens—*Uredo epidendri*.

Raised brown spots. Usually tiny, they appear on the underside of seedling leaves. See Pathogens—*Cercospora angraeci*; *Cercospora* species I–IV.

Raised orange to rust-brown pustules on the underside of leaves. Usually tiny, they turn dark brown with age. See Pathogens—*Sphenospora saphena*.

Reddish black deposits. See Pests—Thrips.

Reddish black rings. These may be small or irregular and often start as light green or yellow discolorations. See Pathogens—*Odontoglossum* streak.

Reddish brown or black areas. These may show as spots, streaks, necrotic rings, or diamond-shaped lesions that begin as chlorotic areas. Leaves may drop prematurely. See Pathogens—*Spathoglottis* diamond spot.

Reddish brown spots. They are sunken and well defined. Usually small initially, they may grow and merge, killing the leaf. The first spots usually appear near the leaf tip. See Pathogens—*Gloeosporium* species.

Reddish purple lesions. They may be ring-shaped or elongated, diamond-shaped chlorotic areas which may be mottled. As the areas enlarge, they become necrotic and merge to form hieroglyphic patterns. Older leaves may develop black flecks and streaks, and plants may be stunted and develop abnormally. See Pathogens—*Odontoglossum* ringspot.

Reddish purple spots. Usually sunken, they occur on the underside of leaves and may have a slightly raised, tan center. See Pathogens—*Cercospora angraeci*; *Cercospora* species I–IV.

Red or purple coloring along the veins. See Nutrients—Phosphorus (deficiency).

Red or purple coloring on the leaves. The chief causes are excessive light and macronutrient imbalances. See Chapter I—Leaves; Nutrients—Cobalt (deficiency); Copper (deficiency); Iron (deficiency); Manganese (deficiency); Nitrogen (deficiency); Phosphorus (excess); Potassium (excess); Zinc (deficiency or excess); Species listings—Light.

Red spots on mature leaves. The spots eventually disappear, leaving sunken areas. See Pathogens—*Laelia* red leaf spots.

Ringspot, usually very distinct. See Pathogens—Ringspot.

Ringspot with faint chlorotic areas. Plants may be stunted, and old growths may die. See Pathogens—*Cymbidium* ringspot.

Rings which may be black to brown. See *Dendrobium* viral disease.

Rings which may be small or irregular and reddish black, light green, or yellow. See Pathogens—*Odontoglossum* streak.

Rosetting of the leaves. See Nutrients—Zinc (deficiency).

Rotting, dropping leaves. See Pathogens—*Pseudomonas andropogonis*.

Silvery sheen on the topside of leaves. It eventually becomes sunken and turns brown. See Pests—Mites; Thrips.

Small leaves. See Nutrients—Zinc (deficiency).

Small leaves on normally large-leaved species. See Chapter 1—Leaves.

Soft leaves. They may result from high moisture, low light, or high night temperatures. See Species listings—Light; Rest period; Temperatures; Water.

Soft rot of the leaves. See Pathogens—*Erwinia chrysanthemi*.

Spots on *Vanilla* leaves. See Pathogens—*Seuratia coeffeicola*.

Stippled streaks on the leaves. See Pathogens—*Oncidium* stippled streak.

Streaking, stippling, or spotting. Due to the loss of chlorophyll, the affected areas eventually become sunken and brown. See Pests—Mites.

Streaks of dead tissue on the underside of leaves. The areas are usually elongated and irregular. See Pathogens—*Cymbidium* mosaic.

Streaks, usually dark, that rapidly cover the entire leaf. See Pathogens—*Erwinia carotovora*.

Stunted plants. See Nutrients—Boron (deficiency); Calcium (deficiency).

Sunken mosaic mottling. See Pathogens—Bean yellow mosaic.

Sunken, purple-brown spots on the underside of leaves. See Pathogens—*Cercospora angraeci*; *Cercospora* species I–IV.

Sunken streaks or pebbling on new leaves in early spring. Initially yellow, the streaks become tan, and black pits develop with age. Although the damage resembles a virus, it is caused by low temperatures and occurs only on new leaves. Subsequent leaves are normal. See Species listings—Rest period; Temperatures.

Tan areas on the underside of leaves. Pitting and irregular depressions may also be present. See Pathogens—*Cymbidium* mosaic.

Tan growths resembling mustard seeds. See Pathogens—*Sclerotium rolfsii*.

Tan patches with dark brown borders. See Pathogens—*Macrophomina phaseolina*.

Tan spots with a purple margin. See Pathogens—*Cercospora angraeci*; *Cercospora* species I–IV.

Tan spots with darker brown margins. They are usually elongated. See Pathogens—*Sphaeropsis* species.

Tan, sunken streaks or pebbling on new leaves in early spring. Initially yellow, the streaks become sunken, and black pits develop with age. Although the damage resembles a virus, it is caused by low temperatures and occurs only on new leaves. Subsequent leaves are normal. See Species listings—Rest period; Temperatures.

Tan to dark brown areas with yellow margins. The margins are well defined, and black or dark brown sporing bodies may be present. See Pathogens—*Phyllostictina citricarpa*.

Tan to dark brown spore pustules. See Pathogens—*Uredo nigropuncta*.

Tan to dark brown spots. The tiny spots have a slightly raised, red to purple-black margin and a tan or brown center. Black, raised spore structures may be present. See Pathogens—*Phyllostictina pyriformis*.

Tan, water-soaked spots. They are often located near the middle of the leaf. See Pathogens—*Erwinia cypripedii*.

Translucent blisters. They may have a yellowish or pale green halo. See Pathogens—*Pseudomonas cattleyae*.

Translucent, water-soaked areas. Usually small and soft, they eventually turn brown or black and become sunken. The affected areas ooze liquid, especially near the leaf tip. See Pathogens—*Pseudomonas cattleyae*.

Translucent, water-soaked areas on the underside of leaves. See Pathogens—*Cymbidium* mosaic.

Translucent, water-soaked patches on the leaves. See *Erwinia chrysanthemi*.

Translucent, water-soaked spots on seedlings. The areas turn yellow then black. See Pathogens—*Phytophthora cactorum*.

Translucent, water-soaked spots on the upper leaf surface. See Pathogens—*Pseudomonas cypripedii*.

Translucent, water-soaked spots which are usually small. See Pathogens—*Erwinia carotovora*.

Twisted leaves. See Nutrients—Molybdenum (deficiency).

Unopened leaves. See Nutrients—Molybdenum (deficiency).

Water-soaked areas. Affected plants may also show light green chlorosis, mosaic patches, tissue collapse, or broad, chlorotic furrows on the underside of leaves. Necrosis and light green chlorosis may show on the upper surface. See Pathogens—*Phalaenopsis* mosaic.

Water-soaked areas on the underside of leaves. The leaves are usually chlorotic or necrotic with deep furrowing or ridging. They may drop prematurely. See Pathogens—*Cymbidium* mosaic.

Water-soaked brown spots. Usually small and irregular, they may have a yellowish advancing margin. The center becomes dark brown or black as the lesions age, and the spots may ooze water if pressed. See Pathogens—*Phytophthora cactorum*.

Water-soaked brown spots on the leaves. See Pathogens—*Erwinia chrysanthemi*.

Water-soaked tan spots. Affected areas are often located near the middle of the leaf. See Pathogens—*Erwinia cypripedii*.

Water-soaked, translucent areas on the underside of leaves. See Pathogens—*Cymbidium* mosaic.

Water-soaked, translucent lesions. Usually small and soft, they eventually become sunken, turn brown to black, and ooze liquid, especially from the leaf tip. See Pathogens—*Pseudomonas cattleyae*.

Water-soaked, translucent patches on the leaves. See Pathogens—*Erwinia chrysanthemi*.

Water-soaked, translucent spots. They turn yellow then black. See Pathogens—*Phytophthora cactorum*.

Water-soaked, translucent spots on the upper leaf surface. See Pathogens—*Pseudomonas cypripedii*.

Water-soaked, translucent spots which are usually small. See Pathogens—*Erwinia carotovora*.

Water-soaked, yellow leaves. See Pathogens—*Erwinia chrysanthemi*.

Water-soaked, yellow spots. Usually small and round, they eventually become reddish brown and sunken. See Pathogens—*Erwinia cypripedii*.

Watery brown blotches on older leaves. The round or elongated spots are 1.4–2.0 in. (3.5–5.0 cm) across with a pale brown margin. See Pathogens—*Penicillin thomii*.

Watery brown lesions at the base of the stem. The roots and leaf bases collapse rapidly. See Pathogens—*Sclerotium rolfsii*.

Wavy leaf margins. See Nutrients—Zinc (deficiency).

Webs. They are usually small and inconspicuous. See Pests—Mites.

Wet rot with a foul odor. See Pathogens—*Erwinia carotovora*.

White fungal mycelia. The filaments cover *Vanilla* plants and turn brown with age. See Pathogens—*Sporoschisma* species.

White leaves or streaks. New leaves may be pale or white, and older leaves may develop white streaks. Growth is often stunted. See Nutrients—Zinc (deficiency).

White to yellow mottling on new leaves. Veins usually remain green. Most frequent cause is lack of iron. See Nutrients—Copper (excess); Iron (deficiency); Zinc (excess).

Wilted, dying leaves. See Pests—Thrips.

Wilted leaf tips. Leaves do not become erect when the plants are watered. See Nutrients—Chlorine (deficiency).

Wilted terminal shoots or faded leaves. See Nutrients—Copper (deficiency).

Wrinkled or hard leaves. Inadequate moisture or high light may cause this problem. See Chapter I—Leaves; Species listings—Light; Rest period; Water.

Wrinkling between the leaf veins. See Nutrients—Potassium (deficiency).

Yellow. Also see listings beginning with the words "Chlorosis," "Light green," and "Necrotic."

Yellow area with well-defined margins. The areas often have a yellow outer band and turn to brown. Black or dark brown sporing bodies may be present. As the lesion gets larger, the adjacent tissue becomes sunken and may become yellow or pale green. See Pathogens—*Phyllostictina citricarpa*.

Yellow areas on the underside of leaves. The affected areas are usually round or irregular and sunken. A chlorotic spot may show on the upper surface. See Pathogens—*Cercospora angraeci*; *Cercospora* species I–IV.

Yellow between green veins. Stems are often yellowish green. See Nutrients—Manganese (deficiency).

Yellow blotches and streaks. The blotches may be pronounced rectangular chlorotic areas or broken lines of bar-shaped discolorations. The discolored area is usually yellow or light to dark green at first and later becomes necrotic. It may be ridged and bumpy. See Pathogens—*Cymbidium* bar mottle.

Yellow chlorosis. See Nutrients—Molybdenum (deficiency).

Yellow chlorotic areas. They may become large, dark brown or black, ring-shaped spots. See Pathogens—*Dendrobium* viral disease.

Yellow chlorotic streaks. The leaves may be ridged, thickened, or curled. See Pathogens—Chlorotic leaf streak of *Oncidium*.

Yellow-green leaves. If the leaves are normally dark green, the change may indicate inappropriate light levels. See Chapter 1—Leaves; Species listings—Light.

Yellow, irregular patches. See Pathogens—*Cymbidium* mosaic.

Yellow leaves. The cause is usually inappropriate light or nitrogen deficiency. A sudden increase in light, prolonged high light levels, severe light deprivation, or incorrect photoperiods all cause leaves to yellow. See Chapter 1—Light; Nutrients—Molybdenum (deficiency); Nitrogen (deficiency); Pathogens—Mycoplasmal diseases; Species listings—Light.

Yellow leaves that turn brown and die with age. See Nutrients—Calcium (deficiency); Cobalt (deficiency); Copper (deficiency); Iron (deficiency); Magnesium (excess); Manganese (deficiency); Nitrogen (deficiency); Potassium (excess); Zinc (deficiency or excess).

Yellow leaves which are thin, shriveled, and twisted. See Pathogens—*Rhizoctonia solani*.

Yellow leaves which may be thin, shriveled, or wilted and eventually turn grey. See Pathogens—*Fusarium oxysporum*.

Yellow leaves with collapsed tissue between the veins. The problem first shows as brown spots on the leaves. See Pathogens—Short orchid rhabdovirus.

Yellow lesions. The circular or irregular lesions are normally tiny and sunken. They become dark brown or black with age. See Pathogens—*Septoria selenophomoides*.

Yellow margins on the leaves. See Nutrients—Potassium (deficiency).

Yellow mature leaves with green veins. See Nutrients—Magnesium (deficiency).

Yellow rings and spots. The affected area increases in size as the leaf grows. See Pathogens—*Stanhopea* yellow spot.

Yellow spots on both leaf surfaces. The spots are usually tiny. See Pathogens—*Coleosporium bletiae*.

Yellow spots on either leaf surface. As they enlarge, they become greasy, brown or black lesions. See Pathogens—*Diplodia laeliocattleyae*.

Yellow streaks or pebbling on new leaves in early spring. The affected area is usually slightly sunken. With age, the streaks become tan, and black pits develop. Although it resembles a virus, it is caused by low temperatures and occurs only on new leaves. Subsequent leaves are normal. See Species listings—Rest period; Temperatures.

Yellow streaks which are long and irregular. See Pathogens—Blossom necrotic streak.

Yellow to light green leaves. The stem is often slender. See Nutrients—Sulfur (deficiency).

Yellow to light green rings. They are small and irregular and become reddish black with age. See Pathogens—*Odontoglossum* streak.

Yellow to light green spots. Circular, sunken spots appear on the leaves and pseudobulbs. The spots may merge to cover the leaf tip. With age, they turn light brown, and darker spots of fungal sporing bodies may appear. See Pathogens—*Gloeosporium affine*.

Yellow to white mottling on new leaves. Veins usually remain green. The primary cause is lack of iron. See Nutrients—Copper (excess); Iron (deficiency); Zinc (excess).

Yellow, water-soaked leaves. See Pathogens—*Erwinia chrysanthemi*.

Yellow, water-soaked spots which are usually small and round and eventually become reddish brown and sunken. See Pathogens—*Erwinia cypripedii*.

Yellow, wilted leaves which may be dying. See Pathogens—P*hytophthora cactorum*; *Sclerotium rolfsii*.

New Leads, Pseudobulbs, Rhizomes, Roots, and Stems

Black or brown roots or pseudobulbs. They soften and rot. See Pathogens—*Pythium ultimum*.

Black stems. See Nutrients—Boron (deficiency).

Black to dark brown pseudobulbs. The bulbs are usually soft and shriveled. The rot expands, and the advancing margin is water-soaked. See Pathogens—*Erwinia carotovora*.

Brown areas on pseudobulbs. Affected tissue may be light to dark brown with well-defined margins and often has a yellow or pale green outer band. As the lesion gets larger, the adjacent tissue becomes sunken. Black or dark brown sporing bodies may be present. See Pathogens—*Phyllostictina citricarpa*.

Brown rot on the leaves. The cause is a root disease which is often first noticed on aerial parts of the plant. See Pathogens—*Rhizoctonia solani*.

Chewed or missing growing tips or roots. See Pests—Cock roaches; Grasshoppers; Millipedes; Sowbugs.

Chlorotic blotches. Mild discolorations develop on new shoots. See Pathogens—*Cymbidium* mosaic.

Collapsed roots. See Pathogens—*Phytophthora cactorum*.

Creamy yellow discolorations. They occur on one or both sides of *Cattleya* family pseudobulbs. See Pathogens—*Pythium ultimum*.

Damaged or unhealthy-looking new growths. See Pests—Whiteflies.

Dead growing tip or bud. Symptoms usually result from inappropriate use of chemicals. See Section III of this Appendix.

Dead root-tips. These are probably caused by salt buildup resulting from hard water or excess fertilizer. See Chapter 1—Leaves; Nutrients—Calcium (deficiency); Cobalt (deficiency); Copper (deficiency); Iron (deficiency); Magnesium (excess); Manganese (deficiency); Potassium (excess); Zinc (deficiency or excess).

Deformed roots. See Nutrients—Chlorine (deficiency).

Distorted or stunted new growths. See Pests—Aphids.

Fungal mycelia on *Vanilla* stems. See Pathogens—*Fusicladium vanillae*.

Hard, mummified pseudobulbs. See Pathogens—*Pythium ultimum*.

Holes in canes or pseudobulbs. A yellow margin or chlorotic area surrounds the small, shot-sized holes. See Pests—Orchid beetle.

Malformed, twisted, or shriveled pseudobulbs. See Pathogens—*Fusarium oxysporum*.

Pale green or yellowish plants. See Nutrients—Sulfur (deficiency).

Poor growth or vigor. Often caused by nutrient problems, poor growth may also result from high night temperatures. See Nutrients—Calcium (deficiency); Cobalt (deficiency); Copper (deficiency); Iron (deficiency); Magnesium (excess); Manganese (deficiency); Nitrogen (deficiency); Phosphorus (deficiency or excess); Potassium (excess); Zinc (deficiency or excess); Species listings—Rest period; Temperatures.

Purple band or circle on the rhizome or roots. The symptom usually occurs on recently divided plants. A pinkish purple discoloration may show on the connective tissue. See Pathogens—*Fusarium oxysporum*.

Purple or purplish-brown areas on new growths. The areas are sharply defined and have a yellowish, advancing margin. See Pathogens—*Phytophthora cactorum*.

Root die-back. The problem is often first noticed when the disease affects the stem. See Pathogens—*Pseudomonas aeruginosa*.

Rotting *Cattleya* pseudobulbs. See Pests—Orchid beetle.

Soft rot of pseudobulbs. See Pathogens—*Erwinia chrysanthemi*.

Soft, shriveled pseudobulbs. A dark brown or black progressive rot with a water-soaked advancing margin. See Pathogens—*Erwinia carotovora*.

Stunted growths. Leaves are dark green. See Nutrients—Phosphorus (deficiency).

Stunted plants or new growths. Growths may be distorted and lack vigor. Symptoms usually result from inappropriate use of chemicals. Also see Nutrients—Boron (deficiency); Calcium (deficiency); Cobalt (deficiency); Copper (deficiency); Iron (deficiency); Magnesium (excess); Manganese (deficiency); Nitrogen (deficiency); Phosphorus (excess); Potassium (deficiency or excess); Zinc (deficiency or excess).

Stunted roots. They are often poorly developed. See Nutrients—Boron (deficiency); Calcium (deficiency); Cobalt (deficiency); Copper (deficiency); Iron (deficiency); Magnesium (excess); Manganese (deficiency); Potassium (deficiency or excess); Sulfur (deficiency); Zinc (deficiency or excess).

Swollen pseudobulbs with an exit hole. See Pests—Wasps.

Tan to dark brown areas on pseudobulbs. The margins are red to purple-black and slightly raised, while the center is tan or brown. Tiny, black, raised spore structures may be present. See Pathogens—*Phyllostictina pyriformis*.

Tan to dark brown areas on pseudobulbs, usually with well-defined margins. The areas often have a yellow outer band. Black or dark brown sporing bodies may be present. See Pathogens—*Phyllostictina citricarpa*.

Tan, watery lesions at the base of the stem. The roots, stems, and leaf bases may collapse rapidly. See Pathogens—*Sclerotium rolfsii*.

Thin stems. See Nutrients—Phosphorus (deficiency); Sulfur (deficiency).

Watery, tan lesions at the base of the stem. The roots, stems, and leaf bases may collapse rapidly. See Pathogens—*Sclerotium rolfsii*.

Weak, spindly growth. See Nutrients—Nitrogen (excess); Potassium (deficiency).

Wet rot with a foul odor on any plant part. See Pathogens—*Erwinia carotovora*.

White, powdery growth on organic potting media. See Pathogens—*Ptychogaster* species.

Withered new pseudobulbs. The cause is insufficient water. See Species listings—Rest period; Water.

Yellowish green stems. See Nutrients—Manganese (deficiency).

Yellowish or pale green plants. See Nutrients—Sulfur (deficiency).

Yellow or pale green areas on the pseudobulb. The well-defined margins often have a yellow outer band. They become light to dark brown with age. Black or dark brown sporing bodies may be present. As the lesion enlarges, the adjacent tissue becomes sunken. See Pathogens—*Phyllostictina citricarpa*.

Yellow, shriveled new growths. Usually thin and twisted, the growths are progressively smaller. See Pathogens—*Rhizoctonia solani*.

Yellow, sunken lesions on any plant part. The round to oval spots are usually tiny and turn tan to dark brown with age. They have slightly raised, red to purple-black margins and a tan or brown center. Tiny, black, raised spore structures may be present. See Pathogens—*Phyllostictina pyriformis*.

Pathogens

General Information

Diseases known to affect one species or genus often occur in closely related species and genera. If one plant in the growing area is infected by a particular pathogen, species not normally considered susceptible may also become infected. It is important to note that symptoms may be distinctly different depending on the plant part affected. Symptoms may also differ from one plant to another and from one genus to another.

Infectious organisms may be divided into the following categories.

Bacteria are single-celled, microscopic organisms without chlorophyll that reproduce by division. They are usually the infecting agent in oozing or soft, wet-rot orchid diseases. Bacteria frequently spread rapidly and are often quickly fatal.

Fungi are filamentlike plant organisms without chlorophyll that reproduce and spread by means of sporing bodies. In orchids, they cause diseases ranging from deadly root and rhizome rots to annoying leaf and flower spotting. During the sexual stage of the fungal life cycle (when the fungus is known by a different Latin name), each sporing body produces enough spores to infect the entire growing area. Common fungi include molds, yeasts, and mushrooms.

The vast majority of infectious plant diseases are caused by fungi. Visible sporing bodies or mycelia (masses of fungal threads) confirm the presence of a fungal infection. The rate at which the infection spreads depends on the stage of fungal growth.

Mycoplasa are microscopic organisms similar to bacteria which lack cell walls, causing them to appear filamentlike. They are uncommon in orchids, but when present, they interfere with plant metabolism. Mycoplasa may be controlled and destroyed in the growing area, but they cannot be eliminated once they have invaded a plant.

Viruses are submicroscopic, subcellular organisms that require a host cell in which to multiply. They cause a number of diseases in cultivated orchids but are rare or nonexistent in the wild. While viral infections may be prevented, they cannot be cured once a plant is infected.

Only 2 orchid viruses are known to occur world-wide: *Cymbidium* mosaic virus (CyMV) and *Odontoglossum* ringspot virus, which is the orchid strain of tobacco mosaic (TMV-O).

Viral diseases are transmitted by insects, mites, nematodes, fungi, parasitic plants, and human handling. They may also be spread by contact between plants and contaminated pots, benches, and tools, or through exchange of pollen, dripping sap, or the sale or exchange of infected plant divisions. Several practices help prevent the spread of viruses: sterilizing tools and pots after each use, eliminating insect carriers, removing or destroying infected plants, eliminating weeds which might be infected, and isolating new plants so that viruses are not brought into the growing area. Unfortunately, infected plants may appear free from symptoms, so that other plants become infected before symptoms of the disease show in the host plant.

Propagating virus-infected *Cymbidium* plants through shoot-tip culture is considered a means of salvaging a valuable plant; but the procedure is difficult to do correctly, and when done incorrectly, it results in spreading infected plants. Meristeming genera such as *Cattleya* does not result in virus-free plants. Using dry pollen from infected plants was once considered a safe means of propagation. Since infected pollen has been found, this is no longer considered a safe technique.

Indicator plants are sometimes used to detect viruses. When an indicator plant is inoculated with sap from a diseased orchid, it develops symptoms which confirm the presence of a virus. In the following list, known indicator plants are included under "Miscellaneous Notes" for each pathogen. Among orchids, *Spathoglottis* species are often used as indicators since they are highly susceptible to infection by viruses which attack other orchid genera. The *Handbook on Orchid Pests and Diseases* published by the American Orchid Society in 1986 discusses indicator plants, methods of inoculation, and the symptoms produced.

Symptoms of viral infection often resemble symptoms of other problems. Before assuming that a problem is a virus, it is wise to consider other possible causes. For example, chemicals may be toxic to some plants, so consider whether the symptoms are showing on the first new growth following treatment with a chemical. Because symptoms vary from plant to plant, it is nearly impossible to confirm viral infection without using indicator plants or obtaining a laboratory analysis. To prevent possible contamination of other plants, isolate any plant suspected of infection until a determination is made.

Viroids are particles which resemble viruses but lack the protein coat of a virus. They frequently cause abnormalities in coloration, often in the form of chlorotic streaking or mosaic patterns, and they may also cause stunting and growth distortion. Like mycoplasa and viruses, viroids may be controlled and destroyed in the growing area before plants are infected, but they cannot be eliminated once they have invaded a plant.

List of Pathogens

The following list corresponds to pathogens named in the preceding Guide to Symptoms. For information about suggested chemical treatments, refer to the "Disease Treatment Summary" at the end of the list of pathogens. Note that numbers denoting classes of bactericides, fungicides, and so on correspond to this table. Thus "Fungicide-7" refers to several different chemicals and brand-name products which are grouped together in the table for ease of reference. "N/A" following any heading indicates that information is not available. See Section III for information about using chemicals.

Alternaria alternata (fungus). The following pathogens cause similar symptoms and respond to similar treatment: *Bipolaris setariae, Bipolaris sorokiniana, Bipolaris urochloae, Botrytis cinerea, Exserohilum rostratum,* and *Stemphylium* species of fungi.

COMMON NAMES: Necrotic flecks.

PLANTS AFFECTED: *Dendrobium.*

SYMPTOMS: Dark necrotic flecks on the flowers.

TREATMENT: Apply Fungicide-7.

CONTROL/PREVENTION: Methods of control are not established, but the information given for *Botrytis cinerea* may be helpful.

MISCELLANEOUS NOTES: The symptoms are thought to be aborted infections caused by one of the fungi listed. The disease is a common problem in Hawaii. Also see *Vanda* transit rot.

American anthracnose. See *Colletotrichum gloeosporiodes.*

Anthracnose orchid spot. See *Colletotrichum gloeosporiodes.*

Bacterial brown rot. See *Erwinia cypripedii.*

Bacterial brown spot. See *Pseudomonas cattleya.*

Bacterial leaf rot. See *Erwinia chrysanthemi.*

Bacterial rot. See *Pseudomonas aeruginosa.*

Bacterial soft rot. See *Erwinia cartovora.*

Bacterial tip burn. See *Miltonia* scorch.

Bacterium cattleyae. See *Pseudomonas cattleyae.*

Bar mottle. See *Cymbidium* bar mottle.

Bean yellow mosaic (virus)

COMMON NAMES: Abbreviated BYMV.

PLANTS AFFECTED: *Calanthe, Masdevallia*.

SYMPTOMS: The leaves show a sunken mosaic or mottled pattern. The flowers are apparently unaffected.

TREATMENT: Destroy the plant when infection is confirmed.

CONTROL/PREVENTION: Isolate any plant suspected of infection. Sterilize cutting tools, control insects, and disinfect the growing area.

MISCELLANEOUS NOTES: The virus is reported in Japan and the United States. *Chenopodium quinoa* and *Vicia faba* are known indicator plants.

Bipolaris setariae. See *Alternaria alternata*.

Bipolaris sorokiniana. See *Alternaria alternata*.

Bipolaris urochloae. See *Alternaria alternata*.

Black rot. See *Phytophthora cactorum*.

Black sheath. See Fungi species.

Black spot on *Vanda*. See *Colletotrichum* and *Glomerella* species.

Black streak. See *Cymbidium* mosaic.

Blossom brown necrotic streak. See *Cymbidium* ringspot.

Blossom necrosis. See *Cymbidium* ringspot.

Blossom necrotic streak (virus)

COMMON NAMES: Information not available.

PLANTS AFFECTED: *Cattleya*.

SYMPTOMS: Flowers develop brown streaks or spots approximately a week after opening. Leaves may develop long, irregular, yellowish streaks.

TREATMENT: Destroy the plant when infection is confirmed.

CONTROL/PREVENTION: Isolate any plant suspected of infection. The pathogen is known to be spread by contaminated cutting tools, so it is possible that insects also transmit the disease. Disinfect the growing area.

MISCELLANEOUS NOTES: *Chenopodium amaranticolor* is an indicator plant. Also see *Odontoglossum* ringspot.

Botryodiplodia theobromae (fungus)

COMMON NAMES: Brown spot.

PLANTS AFFECTED: Information not available.

SYMPTOMS: Similar to anthracnose (*Colletotrichum gloeosporiodes*) without the concentric zones.

TREATMENT: Apply Fungicide, germicide-2. Also see treatments for *Colletotrichum gloeosporiodes*.

CONTROL/PREVENTION: Normal sanitation with good air movement in the growing area.

MISCELLANEOUS NOTES: A weak fungus that seldom attacks healthy plants, *B. theobromae* usually invades a cut or broken surface.

Botrytis cinerea (fungus). Pathogens known to cause similar symptoms include *Sclerotinia fuckeliana* (the sexual stage of *Botrytis*) and *Cladosporium oxysporum*. Other fungi may cause similar problems. Also see *Alternaria alternata* and *Vanda* transit rot.

COMMON NAMES: *Botrytis* blossom blight, *Botrytis* rot, *Dendrobium* blossom blight, flower blight, flower brown rot, flower brown speck, flower speck, flower spotting, petal blight, petal speck, *Vanilla* fruit deformation.

PLANTS AFFECTED: *Cattleya, Cymbidium, Dendrobium, Oncidium, Phalaenopsis, Spathoglottis, Vanda*, and older, fading flowers of many other genera.

SYMPTOMS: Very small, black or light brown, water-soaked spots on the flowers. The spots may enlarge and cover the entire flower. If conditions are moist, a gray fungal growth may appear on severely infected or decaying flowers. Also see *Curvularia geniculata*. *Vanilla* beans may be deformed.

TREATMENT: Remove infected flowers, then treat the plant with bactericide, fungicide, nematocide-1, Fungicide-7, or Systemic fungicide-1 or -3.

CONTROL/PREVENTION: Remove and destroy affected flowers and old or infected plant material, since these are reservoirs of infection. In general, infection by these common gray molds may be reduced through careful sanitation, increased air circulation, reduced humidity, and warmer night temperatures. The fungus is most active during damp, cool weather but may occur anytime. It is common and cannot be eradicated. Since it is often transmitted by scale and insects, the growing area should be treated to control them as well as to control the fungus itself.

Botrytis species (fungus)

COMMON NAMES: *Cymbidium* tip burn.

PLANTS AFFECTED: *Cymbidium*.

SYMPTOMS: Dark spots that enlarge and merge until the entire leaf tip dies. Tips may be covered by powdery spore masses.

TREATMENT: Remove infected tissue and treat the plant with a fungicide. Bactericide, fungicide, nematocide-1, Fungicide-3 or -7, and Systemic fungicide-1 or -3 are recommended.

CONTROL/PREVENTION: Some growers believe the symptoms occur when salts are concentrated in the leaf tips, suggesting that *Botrytis* infection may be a particular problem in areas with hard water or when excess chemical fertilizers are used, damaging leaf tissues and making the plants more susceptible. If *Botrytis* is a recurring problem, flush the pots frequently and reduce the strength and frequency of fertilizer applications.

MISCELLANEOUS NOTES: *Botrytis* disease is reported world-wide.

Brown rot. See *Erwinia cypripedii*.

Brown spot. See *Botryodiplodia theobromae*.

Capnodium species. See *Gloeodes pomigena*.

Cattleya flower disease. See *Cymbidium* ringspot.

Cattleya leaf necrosis. See *Cymbidium* mosaic.

Cattleya severe flower break. See *Cymbidium* bar mottle.

Cercospora angraeci (fungus). Other *Cercospora* pathogens listed below cause similar symptoms and require similar treatment.

COMMON NAMES: *Cercospora* leaf spot.

PLANTS AFFECTED: *Angraecum, Dendrobium, Odontoglossum*.

SYMPTOMS: Infection shows first as a yellow spot on the underside of the leaf. As the spots enlarge in irregular patterns, they become sunken and turn purplish brown to purplish black. The top surface of the leaf first becomes chlorotic and finally necrotic.

TREATMENT: Remove and burn affected tissue. Spray or soak plants with Fungicide-2, -7, or -15 or Systemic fungicide-1 with a wetting agent. If fungicides are applied as a spray, the underside of the leaves must be treated in order for the fungicide to be effective. Three fungicide applications at intervals of 7–15 days should control the fungus.

CONTROL/PREVENTION: Normal sanitation with good air movement in the growing area. Apply a preventive spray at monthly intervals if needed, or when new plants are brought into the growing area.

MISCELLANEOUS NOTES: The disease is reported in England, France, Malaysia, and Florida in the United States. It is known to affect *Dendrobium* only in Malaysia. In Florida, only *Angraecum* infections are reported. Spider-mite damage is easily confused with *Cercospora* leaf spots.

Cercospora dendrobii (fungus)

PLANTS AFFECTED: *Dendrobium, Odontoglossum.*

SYMPTOMS: The first symptom is light yellow spots on the underside of leaves. Soon after infection occurs, the yellow-green area may be noted on the top surface of the leaf. The spots continue to enlarge in a circular or irregular pattern and may eventually cover the entire leaf. With age, the spots become slightly sunken and necrotic and change to purple-brown or purple-black. The advancing margin remains yellow. Heavily infected leaves usually fall from the plant prematurely, especially if the infection started near the base of the leaf.

TREATMENT: Remove and burn infected tissue. Plants may be sprayed or soaked with Fungicide-2, -7, or -15. Systemic fungicide-1 with a wetting agent is effective against most *Cercospora* species. It should be applied weekly until the infection is controlled. If fungicides are applied as a spray, the underside of the leaves must be treated in order for the fungicide to be effective.

Other susceptible plants should receive at least 3 fungicide applications at intervals of 7–15 days to control the fungus. Repeat the spray at monthly intervals if needed, or when new plants are brought into the growing area.

CONTROL/PREVENTION: Normal sanitation with good air movement in the growing area.

MISCELLANEOUS NOTES: This pathogen affects only *Dendrobium*—both deciduous and evergreen—and *Odontoglossum*. Spider-mite damage is easily confused with *Cercospora* leaf spots. The disease is reported in Florida and Japan.

Cercospora epipactidis (fungus)

PLANTS AFFECTED: *Anguloa, Ansellia, Bletia, Brassia, Calanthe, Catasetum, Coelogyne, Cycnoches, Cyrtopodium, Dendrochilum, Epipactis, Eulophia, Gongora, Lycaste, Maxillaria, Monomeria, Neomoorea, Phaius, Spathoglottis, Stanhopea, Xylobium, Zygopetalum.*

SYMPTOMS: On *Phaius tankervilleae*, the initial symptoms are tiny, sunken yellow spots on the underside of leaves. As the disease progresses, the spots continue to enlarge to approximately ¼ in. (6 mm) across. They then turn purplish black with a somewhat darker, slightly raised margin. The spots may merge to form large, irregular lesions. The center of the spots may fall out with age.

TREATMENT: Spraying or soaking the plants with Fungicide-2, -7, -15, or Systemic fungicide-1 with a wetting agent is effective against some *Cercospora* species. Other susceptible plants should receive 3 fungicide applications at intervals of 7–15 days to control the fungus. If fungicides are applied as a spray, the underside of the leaves must be treated in order for the fungicide to be effective.

CONTROL/PREVENTION: Normal sanitation with good air movement in the growing area. If the fungus is a continuing problem, monthly fungicide sprays may offer effective prevention. New plants should be treated before they are brought into the growing area.

MISCELLANEOUS NOTES: Spider-mite damage is easily confused with *Cercospora* leaf spots. This pathogen is reported in Italy, Germany, Mexico, Russia, and numerous areas in the United States.

Cercospora leaf spot. See *Cercospora angraeci.*

Cercospora odontoglossi (fungus)

PLANTS AFFECTED: *Brassavola, Broughtonia, Cattleya, Caularthron, Epidendrum, Laelia, Schomburgkia, Sophronitis.*

SYMPTOMS: This is the most serious leaf-spotting fungus that attacks the *Cattleya* family. Seedlings and small plants first show signs of infection as tiny, slightly raised, dark brown spots on the underside of leaves. The spots are first chlorotic and finally necrotic. The disease spreads rapidly, eventually affecting and killing the entire leaf. Seedlings and small plants may be killed by this fungus. If all the leaves on small seedlings become infected, the plant dies. If the infected seedling is strong enough, it may produce a new growth; but if the disease is untreated, the new growth is also infected.

Older seedlings and mature plants first show symptoms as slightly sunken, yellow, round or irregular areas on the underside of leaves. With age these spots turn purplish black. The top surface is chlorotic initially but becomes necrotic. The disease is seldom fatal to mature plants.

TREATMENT: Remove and destroy affected tissue. Spray or soak plants with Fungicide-2, -7, or -15, or Systemic fungicide-1 with a wetting agent. Three fungicide applications at intervals of 7–15 days should control the fungus. If fungicides are applied as a spray, the underside of the leaves must be treated in order for the fungicide to be effective.

CONTROL/PREVENTION: Normal sanitation with good air movement in the growing area. Preventive fungicide sprays may be applied at monthly intervals if reinfection is a problem. New plants should be treated before they are brought into the growing area.

MISCELLANEOUS NOTES: Both species and hybrids may be affected. Infections are reported in Brazil, France, Venezuela, and several areas in the United States. Spider-mite damage is easily confused with *Cercospora* leaf spots.

Cercospora peristeriae (fungus)

PLANTS AFFECTED: *Peristeria elata* is the only known host.

SYMPTOMS: Infections show first on the lower leaf surface as yellowish to pale brown oval or elongated spots. Within a few days, spots may appear on both surfaces of the leaf. As the disease progresses, the spots become tan with a purple border and enlarge to 0.2–2.0 in. (5–50 mm) across. Sporing bodies develop on the underside of the leaf.

TREATMENT: Remove and destroy affected tissue. Spray or soak affected plants with Fungicide-2, -7, or -15 or Systemic fungicide-1 with a wetting agent. Three applications at intervals of 7–15 days should control the fungus in a growing area. If fungicides are applied as a spray, the underside of the leaves must be treated in order for the fungicide to be effective.

CONTROL/PREVENTION: Normal sanitation with good air movement in the growing area. Fungicide sprays may be used at monthly intervals if needed. New plants should be treated before they are brought into the growing area.

MISCELLANEOUS NOTES: Spider-mite damage is easily confused with *Cercospora* leaf spots.

Cercospora species I (fungus)

PLANTS AFFECTED: *Aerides, Arachnis, Ascocentrum, Doritis, Phalaenopsis, Renanthera, Rhynchostylis, Vanda.*

SYMPTOMS: Purple-brown spots appear on the underside of leaves. The tiny, sunken spots are usually less than 0.05 in. (1 mm) across but may merge to form a larger spot. The upper leaf surface is initially yellow-green but may become purple-brown with age.

TREATMENT: Soak or spray plants with Fungicide-2, -7, or -15 or Systemic fungicide-1 with a wetting agent. Three applications at 15-day intervals should control the fungus. If fungicides are applied as a spray, the underside of the leaves must be treated in order for the fungicide to be effective.

CONTROL/PREVENTION: Normal sanitation with good air movement in the growing area. If infection is a continuing problem, monthly preventive sprays may be applied. New plants should be treated before they are brought into the growing area.

MISCELLANEOUS NOTES: The symptoms may be slightly different, depending on the genus infected. Spider-mite damage is easily confused with *Cercospora* leaf spots.

Cercospora species II (fungus)

PLANTS AFFECTED: *Cattleya* and related genera.

SYMPTOMS: Tiny, purple-brown spots occur on the underside of leaves. They are usually slightly sunken and 0.05 in. (1 mm) or less in diameter. The upper leaf surface is light yellow-green. When entire leaves are infected, they may fall prematurely. The oldest leaves are usually the most severely infected, but leaves which are not fully mature may also be attacked.

TREATMENT: Spraying or soaking the plants with Fungicide-2, -7, or -15 or Systemic fungicide-1 with a wetting agent is effective against some *Cercospora* species. Three applications at 15-day intervals should eradicate the fungus from a growing area. Repeat the spray at monthly intervals if needed, or when new plants are brought into the growing area. If fungicides are applied as a spray, the underside of the leaves must be treated in order for the fungicide to be effective.

CONTROL/PREVENTION: Normal sanitation with good air movement in the growing area.

MISCELLANEOUS NOTES: Reported primarily from the southern United States, the disease has also been found in the northeastern states. Spider-mite damage is easily confused with *Cercospora* leaf spots.

Cercospora species III (fungus)

PLANTS AFFECTED: *Comparettia, Miltonia, Oncidium, Rodriguezia*.

SYMPTOMS: Tiny, sunken spots appear on the underside of leaves. Usually less than 0.05 in. (1 mm) across, they are reddish purple with a slightly raised tan center. With age, the spots merge and become longer, but they retain the reddish purple color.

TREATMENT: Remove and burn infected tissue. Plants may be soaked or sprayed with Fungicide-2, -7, or -15 or Systemic fungicide-1 with a wetting agent. Three applications at intervals of 7–15 days should control the fungus. If fungicides are applied as a spray, the underside of the leaves must be treated in order for the fungicide to be effective.

CONTROL/PREVENTION: Normal sanitation with good air movement in the growing area. Repeat the spray at monthly intervals if needed, or when new plants are brought into the growing area.

MISCELLANEOUS NOTES: The symptoms may differ slightly depending on the genus infected. The disease affects both species and hybrids and is reported in the southern United States. Spider-mite damage is easily confused with *Cercospora* leaf spots.

Cercospora species IV (fungus)

PLANTS AFFECTED: *Cymbidiella, Cymbidium, Grammatophyllum*.

SYMPTOMS: Tiny, round spots appear on the underside of leaves. The slightly sunken spots are dark brown and usually less than 0.05 in. (1 mm) across, but several spots may merge to form a larger spot. A yellow-green spot shows on the upper leaf surface; with age, it becomes brown with a slight yellow halo. The symptoms are usually more severe on older leaves.

TREATMENT: Spraying or soaking the plants with Fungicide-2, -7, or -15 or Systemic fungicide-1 with a wetting agent is effective against many *Cercospora* species. Three applications at intervals of 7–15 days should control the fungus. If fungicides are applied as a spray, the underside of the leaves must be treated in order for the fungicide to be effective.

CONTROL/PREVENTION: Normal sanitation and good air movement in the growing area may help reduce the spread of this disease. Preventive sprays may be applied at monthly intervals if needed, and new plants should be treated before they are placed in the growing area.

MISCELLANEOUS NOTES: Symptoms may be slightly different depending on the genus infected. The symptoms are easily confused with spider-mite damage. The disease is reported in the southern United States.

Chlorotic leaf streak of *Oncidium* (virus)

PLANTS AFFECTED: The hybrid *Oncidium* Golden Shower is the primary host, but *Cattleya, Phalaenopsis,* and *Renanthera* have also been infected.

SYMPTOMS: Chlorotic streaks of varying length, often with ridging, thickening, or curling of the leaves.

TREATMENT: Destroy the plant when infection is confirmed.

CONTROL/PREVENTION: Isolate any plant suspected of infection. Sterilize cutting tools, control insects, and disinfect the growing area with Algicide, bactericide, fungicide-1, or with a disinfectant.

MISCELLANEOUS NOTES: These symptoms are caused by *Cymbidium* mosaic (CyMV) and tobacco mosaic-orchid strain (TMV-O) in combination. The disease is currently reported only in the Philippines.

Cladosporium oxysporum. See *Botrytis cinerea.*

Coleosporium bletiae (fungus)

COMMON NAMES: Rust.

PLANTS AFFECTED: *Phaius*.

SYMPTOMS: Orange rust pustules on either leaf surface or on the flower spike. The earliest symptom is the appearance of tiny yellow spots, which become orange spore masses in just a few days. The spots enlarge in a circular pattern. The outside margin is orange, due to the spore masses, while the center turns brown and often falls out. A yellow halo surrounds the spots. Individual lesions on the leaves are usually less than ½ in. (13 mm) across. The oval lesions on the flower stalks are often larger.

TREATMENT: Isolate infected plants and remove all affected tissue. Spray plants with either Fungicide-7 or -15, or Systemic Fungicide-12 to which a suitable wetting agent has been added. New chemicals that are effective against rust are being introduced and may soon be approved for orchids. Consult local agricultural agents or orchid growers.

CONTROL/PREVENTION: Isolate the plant and disinfect the growing area.

Colletotrichum and *Glomerella* species (fungus)

COMMON NAMES: Black spot of *Vanda* flowers.

PLANTS AFFECTED: *Vanda tricolor*.

SYMPTOMS: Discoloration of the petals with black spots on the lip. Also see *Vanda* transit rot.

TREATMENT: Spray blossoms with Disinfectant-4.

CONTROL/PREVENTION: Normal sanitation with good air movement in the growing area.

MISCELLANEOUS NOTES: The disease is reported in the United States. The same fungi may also cause other orchid diseases.

Colletotrichum cinctum: See *Colletotrichum gloeosporiodes.*

Colletotrichum gloeosporiodes (fungus).
Other pathogens which cause similar symptoms include *Calospora vanillae, Colletotrichum cinctum, Colletotrichum orchidearum, Gloeosporium orchidearum, Glomerella cincta, Glomerella cingulata,* and *Glomerella vanillae*. The *Colletotrichum* stage is the most destructive and is nearly always the stage causing disease in orchids.

COMMON NAMES: American anthracnose, Anthracnose orchid spot.

PLANTS AFFECTED: *Aerides, Angraecum, Brassia, Cattleya, Coelia, Coelogyne, Cymbidium, Cypripedium, Dendrobium, Dichaea, Epidendrum, Eria, Gongora, Isochilus, Laelia, Lycaste, Malaxis, Maxillaria, Milto-*

Pathogens—Colletotrichum orchidearum

nia, *Odontoglossum, Oncidium, Ornithidium, Paphiopedilum, Phaius, Phalaenopsis, Pholidota, Pleurothallis, Polystachya, Sobralia, Spiranthes, Stanhopea, Tetramicra, Trichopilia, Vanda, Vandopsis, Vanilla, Xylobium, Zygopetalum,* and other genera.

SYMPTOMS: This disease infects the aerial portion of the plant. Flowers develop watery, black or brown pustules which are usually raised and occur on the underside of older sepals and petals. The spots may merge and cover the entire flower. The leaves are most often attacked. Leaf tips turn brown beginning at the apex and proceeding toward the base. Dark brown or light gray patches develop, sometimes as concentric rings or as numerous dark bands across the leaf. The affected area is usually sharply defined and somewhat sunken, while the remainder of the leaf appears normal. Sporing bodies develop in the infected area.

TREATMENT: Remove dead tissue by cutting through healthy tissue 1–2 in. (2.5–5.0 cm) below the diseased area. Paint the cut surface with Systemic fungicide-1 mixed with a wetting agent, or paint it with Fungicide, germicide-2. In addition to treating the cut surface, plants should be sprayed or drenched with Systemic fungicide-3 or Fungicide-1, -2, -7, or -15. Spraying with Systemic fungicide-1 is also effective for *Fusarium,* which often attacks the flowers of plants weakened by *Colletotrichum.*

CONTROL/PREVENTION: Normal sanitation, good air movement, lower temperatures, and increased light may help reduce the spread of this disease.

MISCELLANEOUS NOTES: The pathogen is most active in warm weather when light is low and moisture is high. Conditions which increase plants' susceptibility to attack include excessive nitrogen, exposure to some chemicals, and generally poor cultivation. *C. gloeosporioides* always infects the aerial portion of the plant and tends to invade weak or injured plants. It often spreads rapidly toward the base of the plant, which may die if left untreated. The disease symptoms occur worldwide but may be caused by different pathogens in different regions.

Colletotrichum orchidearum. See *Colletotrichum gloeosporioides.*

Color break. See *Cymbidium* ringspot.

Crown rot. See *Phytophthora cactorum.*

Cucumber mosaic (virus)

COMMON NAMES: Abbreviated CMV.

PLANTS AFFECTED: *Dendrobium, Miltonia.*

SYMPTOMS: Flowers may be affected with mild color break. The leaves show faint chlorotic patches and rings. The appearance is different from that of chlorosis caused by *Cymbidium* mosaic (CyMV).

TREATMENT: Destroy the plant when infection is confirmed.

CONTROL/PREVENTION: Isolate any plant suspected of infection. This highly infectious pathogen is present in sap and is easily transmitted by aphids or contaminated tools. Sterilize cutting tools, control insects, and disinfect the growing area.

MISCELLANEOUS NOTES: The disease is reported in Korea and Japan. Fortunately this virus does not cause infection in *Cattleya, Cymbidium, Oncidium,* or *Zygopetalum.* Known indicator plants include *Chenopodium amaranticolor, Citrullus vulgaris, Datura stramonium,* and *Sesamum.*

Curvularia flower blight. See *Curvularia geniculata.*

Curvularia geniculata (fungus)

COMMON NAMES: *Curvularia* leaf spot, flower blight.

PLANTS AFFECTED: Information not available.

SYMPTOMS: Many tiny, slightly sunken, light to dark brown, circular or oval lesions on either or both surfaces of sepals, petals, or flower spikes. Similar symptoms are caused by *Botrytis cinerea.* Infections are usually first noticed on the flowers.

TREATMENT: Remove damaged tissue and paint the cut with Systemic fungicide-1. Spray leaves and flowers with Systemic fungicide-1, Fungicide-7, or use the treatments listed for *Colletotrichum gloeosporioides.*

CONTROL/PREVENTION: Increasing air movement and decreasing humidity may help prevent the disease from spreading.

MISCELLANEOUS NOTES: The disease invades the plant through damaged leaf tissue. It is reported world-wide.

Curvularia leaf spot. See *Curvularia geniculata.*

Cymbidium bar mottle (virus)

COMMON NAMES: Bar mottle, *Cattleya* severe flower break.

PLANTS AFFECTED: *Cattleya, Cymbidium,* and possibly other orchid genera.

SYMPTOMS: *Cattleya* plants are most likely to show signs of infection in the flowers. Symptoms include strong color variegation, mottling, distortion, and malformation. Weakened plants become stunted and produce few flowers. In *Cymbidium* plants, the infection usually shows first in the leaves.

Affected leaves show yellow blotches or streaks or bar-shaped discolorations which may be yellow or light to dark green. The discolorations often appear in broken lines. The affected area later becomes necrotic and develops ridges and bumps.

TREATMENT: Destroy the plant when infection is confirmed.

CONTROL/PREVENTION: Remove infected plants from the growing area, control aphids, screen greenhouse vents, and disinfect the growing area. The disease is spread from area to area through propagation of infected plants. The green peach aphid is the only insect known to carry the disease from plant to plant.

MISCELLANEOUS NOTES: Symptoms may result from *Cymbidium* mosaic (CyMV) either alone or in combination with other viruses.

Cymbidium chlorotic leaf streak. See Tomato ringspot.

Cymbidium diamond mottle. See *Cymbidium* ringspot.

Cymbidium mosaic. See *Cymbidium* mosaic.

Cymbidium mild mosaic (virus). Abbreviated CyMMV. This virus is known to affect *Cymbidium,* but information on symptoms is not available. The primary means of transmission is infected sap, carried by insects or contaminated tools. *Chenopodium amaranticolor* is a known indicator plant. The virus is reported in Korea.

Cymbidium mosaic (virus)

COMMON NAMES: Often abbreviated CyMV. This virus may be called black streak, *Cattleya* leaf necrosis, mosaic, necrotic mosaic, necrotic spot, necrotic streak, orchid mosaic, or white cell necrosis.

PLANTS AFFECTED: *Ada, Aerides, Angraecum, Arundina, Brassavola, Calanthe, Catasetum, Cattleya, Cymbidium, Dendrobium, Epidendrum, Gongora, Grammatophyllum, Laelia, Lycaste, Miltonia, Odontoglossum, Oncidium, Peristeria, Phaius, Phalaenopsis, Phragmipedium, Pleurothallis, Rhynchostylis, Schomburgkia, Selenipedium, Spathoglottis, Trichopilia, Vanda, Vanilla, Zygopetalum,* and probably other genera.

SYMPTOMS: The disease has variable symptoms depending on the species, the plant part affected, and the environmental conditions. This variability has resulted in numerous common names for a single disease organism.

Flowers on infected plants may be symptom-free. White *Cattleya* flowers show necrotic spots and streaks. Infected flowers may appear healthy until several days after they open when the symptoms begin to show.

Lavender *Cattleya* flowers show white cell necrosis, usually along the center rib of the petals, 1–2 weeks after the flowers open. However, bleached spots on lavender *Cattleya* flowers may result from air pollution rather than a virus, while color breaking in lavender *Cattleya* is consistently associated with tobacco mosaic-orchid strain (TMV-O). *Dendrobium superbum* may have color break in the flowers. *Phalaenopsis* flowers show symptoms similar to those of *Cattleya. Cymbidium, Dendrobium, Epidendrum, Laelia,* and *Vanda* flowers are also affected.

In the early stage of infection, the leaves usually develop irregular yellow patches known as chlorotic mosaic. Later, irregular, elongated streaks of dead tissue are often found on the underside of leaves, and some leaves may die. Black necrotic spots may develop, and the area is sometimes sunken. Other patterns may appear; or, in the right environment, infected plants may be symptom-free.

The leaves of *Cattleya* and related orchids show light brown pitting and irregular sunken areas on the underside of leaves, particularly near the tip. Black or brown rings, streaks, or blotches are usually the first symptoms on older leaves, but the leaves are eventually covered with spots and blotches. Infected plants may die within a few months. When the disease is indicated by these symptoms, it is often called *Cattleya* leaf necrosis.

Cymbidium develop mild chlorotic mosaic or blotches in new shoots about 3 weeks after infection. The affected areas enlarge, and symptoms become more pronounced as the leaves mature. *Dendrobium* leaves and flowers may show symptoms similar to those described for *Cattleya*. Sometimes, however, *Dendrobium* plants show no symptoms yet test positive for the virus.

Infected *Epidendrum* plants are very stunted, with sunken, brown or black, oval spots which usually occur on the underside of leaves.

Oncidium Golden Shower plants show the infection as sunken brown or black spots on the underside of leaves. The spots sometimes appear in concentric rings, with a few spots breaking through to the upper leaf surface.

Phalaenopsis symptoms are highly variable; they include light green and chlorotic patches, deep furrowing and ridging, and necrotic, water-soaked areas. Necrosis is more pronounced on the underside of leaves. Leaves may drop if the infection is severe. Sometimes, however, *Phalaenopsis* plants show no symptoms yet test positive for the virus.

Spathoglottis plants usually show diamond-shaped chlorotic patches which become necrotic.

TREATMENT: Destroy the plant if infection is confirmed.

CONTROL/PREVENTION: Isolate any plant suspected of infection. Infected cutting tools are the most common means of transmission, but the virus is present in the sap and may be transmitted by contaminated pots, dripping water, and insects. Disinfect the growing area. Because plants may carry CyMV without showing symptoms, other plants may be contaminated before the grower is aware of a problem. Careful sanitation is important.

MISCELLANEOUS NOTES: Unlike many viruses, CyMV occurs naturally only in orchids. *Cassia occidentalis* (and possibly other *Cassia* species), *Chenopodium amaranticolor, C. quinoa, Datura stramonium,* and *Tetragonia expansa* can be artificially infected and therefore serve as indicator plants.

Cymbidium ringspot (virus)

COMMON NAMES: Abbreviated CyRV, this virus is sometimes called necrotic ringspot or severe leaf necrosis. Apparently it is a form of white clover virus.

PLANTS AFFECTED: *Cymbidium* is the primary host, but *Cattleya, Spathoglottis,* and *Trichosma* may also be susceptible.

SYMPTOMS: Leaves may have faint chlorotic ringspot patterns. Plants may be stunted, and old shoots may die. No symptoms were indicated for flowers.

TREATMENT: Destroy the plant.

CONTROL/PREVENTION: Isolate plant suspected of infection. The virus is carried in sap and soil. Sterilize cutting tools, control insects, and disinfect the growing area.

MISCELLANEOUS NOTES: Reported in southern England, this disease is severe, highly contagious, and often lethal to plants. Fortunately, it is uncommon. *Chenopodium amaranticolor, Emilia sangitota, Nicotiana clevelandii,* and *Phaseolus vulgaris* 'The Prince' are known indicator plants.

Cymbidium soft rot. See *Erwinia carotovora*.

Cypripedium filamentous (virus).
Abbreviated CF, this virus was reported in Germany in *Cypripedium calceolus*. Information on symptoms or means of transmission is not available.

Damping off. See *Fusarium; Phytophthora cactorum; Pythium ultimum; Rhizoctonia*.

Dendrobium blossom blight. See *Botrytis cinerea*.

Dendrobium leaf spot. See *Septoria selenophomoides;* Short orchid rhabdovirus.

Dendrobium mosaic (virus)

COMMON NAMES: Abbreviated DeMV.

PLANTS AFFECTED: *Dendrobium*.

SYMPTOMS: Sharply defined mosaic and green concentric ring patterns on older leaves. Young leaves may show light mottling, but flowers are not affected.

TREATMENT: Destroy the plant when infection is confirmed.

CONTROL/PREVENTION: Isolate any plant suspected of infection. The virus is transmitted by aphids and contaminated cutting tools. Sterilize cutting tools, control insects, and disinfect the growing area.

MISCELLANEOUS NOTES: *Chenopodium amaranticolor* and *C. quinoa* serve as indicator plants. This virus, currently reported only in Japan, does not cause infection in *Cattleya, Cymbidium, Miltonia, Oncidium,* or *Zygopetalum* even when deliberately inoculated.

Dendrobium vein necrosis (virus).
Abbreviated DVN, this virus was reported in Germany in *Dendrobium* plants. Flowers and leaves develop vein necrosis. The disease is uncommon.

Dendrobium viral disease (virus)

COMMON NAMES: Abbreviated DV.

PLANTS AFFECTED: *Dendrobium ionoglossum* and *D. antennatum* are the primary hosts, but other *Dendrobium* species and hybrids may also be susceptible.

SYMPTOMS: Yellow chlorotic areas and large, dark brown or black, ring-shaped spots appear on the leaves.

TREATMENT: Destroy the plant when infection is confirmed.

CONTROL/PREVENTION: Isolate any plant suspected of infection. Sterilize cutting tools, control insects, and disinfect the growing area.

MISCELLANEOUS NOTES: DV is reported in New Guinea and Germany.

Dendrobium white streak (virus).
This disease is reported in Hawaii. *Dendrobium* is the primary host, but *Phalaenopsis* may also be susceptible. The virus causes white streaks on the flowers. Information on means of transmission or indicator plants is not available.

Diplodia laeliocattleyae (fungus)

COMMON NAMES: *Diplodia* leaf spot, leaf spot.

PLANTS AFFECTED: *Cattleya* and related genera.

SYMPTOMS: Small yellow spots on either leaf surface. They enlarge with age and become greasy, brown to black lesions. Black sporing bodies may be visible on older lesions.

TREATMENT: Apply Fungicide-1.

CONTROL/PREVENTION: Normal sanitation measures should prevent the spread of this disease.

MISCELLANEOUS NOTES: This fungus is rare and affects only old or damaged tissues.

Diplodia leaf spot. See *Diplodia laeliocattleyae*.

Erwinia carotovora (bacterium)

COMMON NAMES: Bacterial soft rot, *Cymbidium* soft rot, soft rot.

PLANTS AFFECTED: *Brassavola, Cattleya* and closely related genera, *Cymbidium, Cycnoches, Lockhartia, Odontoglossum, Oncidium, Paphiopedilum, Phalaenopsis,* and probably other orchid genera.

SYMPTOMS: Small, water-soaked spots appear on the leaves and eventually become dark streaks. If unchecked, the infection may rapidly cover the entire leaf. The rot spreads rapidly in the leaves and roots and more slowly in the rhizomes or pseudobulbs. This wet rot may have a foul odor.

Pseudobulbs or crown develop a progressive rot which has a water-soaked advancing margin, while the tissues behind it are brown. The oldest portion of the infection may be black. Infected bulbs are often soft, shriveled, and dark.

In *Phalaenopsis,* the disease spreads so rapidly that plants may be completely rotted in 2–3 days. Bacteria enter the plant through wounds.

TREATMENT: If the plant is valuable and the disease is localized, remove the plant from the growing area, then cut off and destroy all tissue showing infection. Spray or paint cuts with Algicide, bactericide, fungicide-1 or a paste of Fungicide, germicide-1. Localized infection may be swabbed with mercuric chloride (1 : 1,000 dilution).

CONTROL/PREVENTION: *Erwinia carotovora* is a highly contagious disease. Destroy affected plants and immediately disinfect the entire growing area with a 10% sodium hypochlorite (bleach) solution or a 1 : 1000 (¾ tsp. per gal.—0.98 ml/liter) mercuric chloride solution. Wear protective clothing when using mercuric chloride and handle the compound very cautiously.

Avoid overhead watering if the disease is present, as the infection is spread through fluids from infected plants. Treat nearby plants as well as those that are diseased, and take measures to control insects. Periodic sprays of Algicide, bactericide, fungicide-1 help to prevent infection.

When dividing plants, use careful sanitation measures to prevent the slower rot of pseudobulbs and rhizomes. Disinfect tools after each cut. Paint cut surfaces with a paste of Fungicide-9 or asphaltum paint.

MISCELLANEOUS NOTES: The disease is rare in orchids, affecting *Cattleya* most seriously. But it affects many vegetables and ornamentals and is so devastating that infected plants are best destroyed. Infection enters the plant through wounds or breaks in the plant's outer skin, which may result from insects, mechanical injury, or fungal infection.

Erwinia chrysanthemi (bacterium)

COMMON NAMES: Bacterial leaf rot, *Erwinia chrysanthemi* soft rot.

PLANTS AFFECTED: *Cymbidium, Dendrobium, Grammatophyllum, Oncidium, Phalaenopsis, Vanda.*

SYMPTOMS: Soft rot of the leaves and pseudobulbs. *Dendrobium* leaves appear yellow and water-soaked and become black and sunken. *Vanda* leaves develop translucent patches which become black and sunken. *Grammatophyllum* leaves have water-soaked, brownish spots which become black and sunken.

TREATMENT: Remove diseased tissue and spray with Fungicide, germicide-2 or Algicide, bactericide, fungicide-1. Disinfectant-2 is specifically recommended for *Cymbidium, Oncidium,* and *Phalaenopsis,* as are Bactericide-1 and -2. Bactericides are toxic to many orchids and should be used cautiously.

CONTROL/PREVENTION: Normal sanitation and increased air movement may reduce the risk of infecting other plants. Preventive sprays of Fungicide, germicide-2 may be applied before and during wet weather.

MISCELLANEOUS NOTES: This disease occurs primarily in Hawaii.

Erwinia chrysanthemi soft rot. See *Erwinia chrysanthemi*.

Erwinia cypripedii (bacterium)

COMMON NAMES: *Erwinia* f. *cypripedii,* commonly called bacterial brown rot, brown rot, *Paphiopedilum* brown rot, *Paphiopedilum* brown spot.

PLANTS AFFECTED: *Cypripedium, Paphiopedilum.* The disease also occurs occasionally in *Brassia* and *Miltonia* hybrids, *Phalaenopsis, Phragmipedium,* and many other orchid genera.

SYMPTOMS: Water-soaked spots appear, often near the center of the leaf. They are usually small and may be either round or oval. As the disease progresses, the color of the spot changes from light brown to very dark chestnut-brown. The spot enlarges in all directions and may reach the growing crown before the leaf tip is affected. If untreated, the disease quickly spreads throughout the plant, leaving it a dark, shriveled mass. *Paphiopedilum* leaves develop small, round spots that are initially yellow and water-soaked but eventually become reddish brown and sunken.

TREATMENT: Remove infected tissue down to the rhizome, and disinfect tools after each cut. Soak the plant for several hours in Fungicide, germicide-2 or Disinfectant-4. Repeat this treatment 2–3 times every few days. An alternative treatment is spraying with Algicide, bactericide, fungicide-1.

CONTROL/PREVENTION: The pathogen favors warm, moist conditions, so if infection occurs, keep leaves dry, reduce temperature and humidity if possible, and increase air circulation. Give adjacent plants a preventive spray with Fungicide-3 or Algicide, bactericide, fungicide-1, since the disease can be devastating if not controlled. Periodic sprays with Algicide, bactericide, fungicide-1 may be used throughout the year to help prevent infection.

MISCELLANEOUS NOTES: The symptoms are easily confused with the disease caused by *Pseudomonas cypripedii*.

European anthracnose. See *Gloeosporium affine*.

Exserohilum rostratum. See *Alternaria alternata*.

Flower blight. See *Botrytis cinerea; Fusarium moniliforme*.

Flower break. See *Cymbidium* ringspot; *Vanda* mosaic.

Flower break, symmetrical (virus)

PLANTS AFFECTED: *Cattleya* and possibly other orchids.

SYMPTOMS: Symmetrical variegations appear in colored areas of the petals and at the sepal margins. The center of the petals is not usually affected. Leaves may develop a light mosaic mottling.

TREATMENT: Destroy the plant when infection is confirmed.

CONTROL/PREVENTION: Isolate any plant suspected of infection. Infections are transmitted by insects and contaminated cutting tools. Sterilize cutting tools, control insects, and disinfect the growing area.

MISCELLANEOUS NOTES: The unnamed virus that causes this condition occurs world-wide.

Flower brown rot. See *Botrytis cinerea*.

Flower brown speck. See *Botrytis cinerea*.

Flower necrosis (virus). White-flowered *Cattleya* develop necrotic streaks and spots on the flowers without foliage symptoms. Symptoms are apparently caused by a strain of *Cymbidium* mosaic (CyMV), perhaps in combination with *Odontoglossum* ringspot. Also see *Cymbidium* ringspot. The disease occurs in Europe, Italy, and the United States.

Flower speck. See *Botrytis cinerea*.

Flower spotting. See *Botrytis cinerea*.

Fly speck. See *Microthyriella rubi*.

Fungi species

COMMON NAMES: Black sheath.

PLANTS AFFECTED: All orchids that produce flowers in sheaths.

SYMPTOMS: The sheath is discolored and may rot, spreading the infection to flower buds.

TREATMENT: Remove the sheath, and allow the area to dry. Apply Fungicide-2 or -3, or Fungicide, germicide-2.

CONTROL/PREVENTION: This disease usually occurs when water, from either excessively high humidity or careless watering, is allowed to soak the sheath or stand in the area between the leaf and the sheath.

MISCELLANEOUS NOTES: If the sheath is treated quickly and kept dry, the infection may not spread to the buds. The problem is reported in the United States, though it probably occurs world-wide.

Fusarium batatis* var. *vanillae (fungus)

COMMON NAMES: *Vanilla* root rot, *Vanilla* wilt.

PLANTS AFFECTED: *Vanilla planifolia*. *V. barbellata* and *V. pompona* are also susceptible, while *V. phaeantha* is somewhat resistant.

SYMPTOMS: The roots turn brown and rot. Depending on available moisture, the rot may be dry or soft and watery. Underground roots are usually destroyed before the aerial roots begin to show signs of infection. When the infection is firmly established, growth slows, and the plant eventually dies.

TREATMENT: Systemic fungicide-1 is being used experimentally.

CONTROL/PREVENTION: Use only disease-free plants for propagating or stem cuttings.

MISCELLANEOUS NOTES: The disease was originally thought to be caused by *Fusarium oxysporum*. It occurs in commercial *Vanilla*-growing areas of the world.

Fusarium flower blight. See *Fusarium moniliforme*.

Fusarium moniliforme* f. *cattleyae (fungus)

COMMON NAMES: Flower blight, *Fusarium* flower blight.

PLANTS AFFECTED: *Arachnis, Dendrobium,* and perhaps others.

SYMPTOMS: Flowers, buds, and inflorescence develop sunken, dark brown to black lesions which are often covered with powdery white mycelia and small pink sporing bodies. Severe infections cause the flowers to yellow and drop, usually in the bud stage. This pathogen is related to the fungi known to cause wilt.

Dendrobium leaves develop small spots, as do the leaves of several other orchids. The disease organism usually invades through wounded tissue. The symptoms are similar to those found on the flowers, except that sporing bodies are not usually present.

TREATMENT: Remove infected areas, and spray plants every 4–7 days with Fungicide-1, -2, or -15. For additional control measures, see *Colletotrichum gloeosporioides*.

CONTROL/PREVENTION: Normal sanitation with good air movement in the growing area.

MISCELLANEOUS NOTES: The disease is prevalent throughout the United States and is reported world-wide. It is apparently one of the causes of bud drop in Singapore.

Fusarium oxysporum (fungus). *F. oxysporum* f. *cattleyae*, f. *vanillae*, and f. *vasinfectus* cause similar problems. *Fusarium, Phytophthora, Pythium,* and *Rhizoctonia* all cause damping off and much the same symptoms.

COMMON NAMES: *Fusarium* rot, *Fusarium* wilt, *Paphiopedilum* wilt.

PLANTS AFFECTED: *Ascocenda, Brassavola, Catasetum, Cattleya* and most related genera, *Cirrhopetalum, Coelogyne, Cymbidium, Dendrobium, Doritis, Encyclia, Oncidium, Paphiopedilum, Phalaenopsis,* and *Vanilla* are specifically listed. The disease is widespread and may affect all orchid genera.

SYMPTOMS: Infected leaves are yellow, thin, shriveled, or wilted and eventually die. Leaf margins may become gray or grayish green.

Symptoms on aerial portions of the plant are similar to those of *Rhizoctonia solani*, but *Fusarium* wilt produces a circle or band of purple or pinkish-purple discoloration on the outer layers of the rhizome. If the disease is extensive, the entire rhizome may turn purple, and the discoloration may extend to the pseudobulbs. The pathogen attacks the plant through roots or through the cut ends of rhizomes on recently divided plants. Severely infected plants may die in 3–9 weeks, while mildly infected plants gradually decline over a year or so.

Pseudobulbs may be malformed, twisted, or shriveled, symptoms very similar to those caused by root rot. Rot eventually sets in and extends an inch (2.5 cm) or so up the pseudobulb after the disease reaches an advanced stage. The rot may be the result of invasion by other organisms.

Vanilla plants become yellow then wither and die. Wilting is often an early symptom which occurs when the pathogen affects the roots. The roots blacken on the outside and are stained brown in the center.

TREATMENT: Remove all parts of the plant that show purple discoloration, sterilizing the cutting tool after each cut. Then treat the plant, repot it, and destroy the old medium. Systemic fungicide-1 may be used as a drench or soak for the entire plant. Alternatively, Fungicide-8 may be used as a spray on the diseased plant, bench, and nearby plants; use it cautiously, as the chemical is toxic. Repeat sprays every 3 days, for 3 applications. Repot only in new potting material with good drainage. If osmunda is used as the medium, pre-drench with 4% formalin solution, since osmunda can carry *Fusarium* spores.

CONTROL/PREVENTION: Burn diseased plant tissue. Disinfect benches in areas of possible contamination with a 4% formalin solution. Decrease moisture levels in the growing area. Excellent drainage and good air movement help prevent the spread of the disease.

MISCELLANEOUS NOTES: The disease is reported in Australasia and the United States and probably occurs world-wide.

Fusarium rot. See *Fusarium oxysporum*.

Fusarium wilt. See *Fusarium oxysporum*.

Fusicladium vanillae (fungus). *Vanilla* stems are covered with fungal mycelia. The disease is reported in Java, but no information about controls or treatment is available.

Gloeodes pomigena (fungus). *Capnodium* species and *Meliola* species cause similar problems and require the same treatment.

COMMON NAMES: Sooty blotch, sooty mold.

PLANTS AFFECTED: This pathogen is thought to affect *Vanilla* and numerous other orchid genera.

SYMPTOMS: Patchy, dark gray or black residue on the leaves that may be removed by wiping with a damp cloth.

TREATMENT: Wipe leaves or spray with Systemic fungicide-1. Other fungicides are also effective. The fungus usually dies out when plants are moved to a new location.

CONTROL/PREVENTION: Good air movement in the growing area may be beneficial.

MISCELLANEOUS NOTES: *Gloeodes pomigena* often occurs with *Microthyriella rubi*. Both pathogens live on aphid honeydew on the leaf surface and seldom invade healthy plant tissue. They generally appear during warm, humid weather or when the plants are grown outdoors, particularly under trees infested with aphids and affected with sooty mold. The pathogen usually affects the aerial portions of plants. It apparently affects *Vanilla* in Madagascar and probably in other *Vanilla*-growing areas.

Gloeosporium affine (fungus)

COMMON NAMES: European anthracnose.

PLANTS AFFECTED: *Aerides, Angraecum, Brassia, Cattleya, Coelia, Coelogyne, Cymbidium, Cypripedium, Dendrobium, Dichaea, Epidendrum, Eria, Gongora, Isochilus, Laelia, Lycaste, Malaxis, Maxillaria, Miltonia, Odontoglossum, Oncidium, Ornithidium, Paphiopedilum, Phaius, Phalaenopsis, Pholidota, Pleurothallis, Polystachya, Sobralia, Spiranthes, Stanhopea, Tetramicra, Trichopilia, Vanda, Vandopsis, Vanilla, Xylobium, Zygopetalum,* and other orchid genera.

SYMPTOMS: Slightly sunken, yellow to light green circular areas develop on leaves and pseudobulbs. As the lesions dry, black spots (fungal sporing bodies) develop. The spots develop in concentric rings, circular patches, or diamond-shaped areas, which at first glance resemble a virus infection. As the infected area spreads and the spots merge, the area becomes thin, dry, and light brown, while the outer portion dies. Infections spread rapidly in *Dendrobium, Odontoglossum,* and *Oncidium*.

TREATMENT: Remove infected areas and spray with Fungicide-2 or -3 or Systemic fungicide-1 mixed with a wetting agent. Repeat sprays at the recommended interval until the disease is under control. See *Colletotrichum gloeosporioides* for additional treatment options.

CONTROL/PREVENTION: This fungus is most active when temperatures are warm, moisture is high, and light is low. If plants develop symptoms, lower temperatures and reduce the humidity in the growing area. Careful sanitation and increased air movement are also important. When infection occurs, apply a preventive spray of a long-acting systemic fungicide to other orchids in the area.

MISCELLANEOUS NOTES: *G. affine* usually infects the aerial portions of weak plants. It seldom invades healthy plants except through injured tissue. Also see *Colletotrichum gloeosporioides* (American anthracnose) and *Vanda* transit rot.

Gloeosporium species (fungus)

COMMON NAMES: *Gloeosporium* leaf spot.

PLANTS AFFECTED: *Cattleya, Pholidota,* and other orchid genera.

SYMPTOMS: Prominent, reddish-brown spots on leaves are well defined and sunken. The spots usually start small, frequently near the tip of the leaf, but they may merge to cover the entire leaf.

TREATMENT: See recommended treatments for *Colletotrichum gloeosporiodes*.

CONTROL/PREVENTION: Avoid damp conditions, and do not allow water to stand on the leaves.

MISCELLANEOUS NOTES: The disease is reported in Hawaii and Singapore.

Glomerella cincta. See *Colletotrichum gloeosporioides*.

Glomerella cingulata. See *Colletotrichum gloeosporiodes*.

Glomerella orchidearum. See *Colletotrichum gloeosporiodes*.

Grammatophyllum bacilliform (virus).
Abbreviated GBV, this virus was reported in *Grammatophyllum* in the United States. Information on symptoms and means of transmission is not available.

Guignardia species (fungus)

PLANTS AFFECTED: *Ascocentrum* and *Vanda*, and their hybrids.

SYMPTOMS: The first signs of infection are tiny, dark purple, elongated lesions on either leaf surface. These lesions run parallel to the veins and elongate into purple streaks or diamond-shaped areas. Spots often merge to form large irregular lesions that may affect a large part of the leaf. With age, the center of the lesions turns tan. Raised, black sporing bodies develop in the affected area.

TREATMENT: Definite control measures have not been established for this disease.

CONTROL/PREVENTION: Protect other plants from contamination by practicing good sanitation and increasing air movement in the growing area. Preliminary tests indicate that Systemic fungicide-1 helps control the spread of the disease.

MISCELLANEOUS NOTES: See *Phyllostictina citricarpa*.

Heart rot. See *Phytophthora cactorum*.

Laelia etch (virus).
Laelia anceps foliage is marked with necrotic lines and semicircular rings. This unnamed virus occurs primarily in California and may prove to be *Cymbidium* mosaic (CyMV).

Laelia red leaf spots (virus)

COMMON NAMES: Abbreviated LRLS.

PLANTS AFFECTED: *Laelia purpurata*, other *Laelia* species, *Laelia* and *Cattleya* hybrids. The virus may also affect *Cymbidium*.

SYMPTOMS: Leaves are marked with dark red, 0.05–0.20 in. (1–5 mm) spots which eventually disappear leaving sunken areas on the mature leaves.

TREATMENT: Destroy the plant when infection is confirmed.

CONTROL/PREVENTION: Isolate any plant suspected of infection. Sterilize cutting tools, control insects, and disinfect the growing area.

MISCELLANEOUS NOTES: This virus, reported in Germany, may also occur elsewhere.

Leaf blight. See *Sphaeropsis* species.

Leaf necrotic fleck. See Orchid fleck.

Leaf spot. See *Diplodia laeliocattleyae; Macrophomina phaseolina; Phyllostictina pyriformis*.

Leptothyrium pomi. See *Microthyriella rubi*.

Long orchid rhabdovirus (virus).
Abbreviated LORV, it was found in *Cattleya, Epidendrum, Laelia, Paphiopedilum,* and *Phragmipedium* plants in Germany. Information on symptoms or means of transmission is not available.

Macrophomina leaf spot. See *Macrophomina phaseolina*.

Macrophomina phaseolina (fungus)

COMMON NAMES: Leaf spot, *Macrophomina* leaf spot.

PLANTS AFFECTED: *Calanthe* and probably other orchid genera.

SYMPTOMS: Light brown patches with dark brown borders on the leaves.

TREATMENT: Information not available.

CONTROL/PREVENTION: Normal sanitation and good air movement in the growing area.

MISCELLANEOUS NOTES: This common root fungus, normally found in tropical areas, is reported in Southeast Asia.

Masdevallia isometric (virus). Known as MI-virus unnamed, it was reported in *Masdevallia* in Colombia. Information on symptoms and treatment is not available.

Meliola fungus species. See *Gloeodes pomigena*.

Microthyriella rubi (fungus)

COMMON NAMES: Flyspeck. *Leptothyrium pomi* is the sexual stage of the fungus.

PLANTS AFFECTED: *Cattleya, Dendrobium, Epidendrum, Vanda,* and other orchid genera.

SYMPTOMS: Large groups of flyspeck-sized spots appear on leaf surfaces.

TREATMENT: Any common fungicide or Systemic fungicide-1 is recommended.

CONTROL/PREVENTION: Move the plants to a different location. Good air movement in the growing area may be beneficial.

MISCELLANEOUS NOTES: Reported primarily in Florida in the United States. *Microthyriella rubi* often occurs with *Gloeodes pomigena*. Both pathogens live on aphid honeydew on the leaf surface and seldom invade healthy plant tissue. They generally appear during warm, humid weather when the plants are grown outdoors, particularly under trees infested with aphids and affected with sooty mold. The pathogen usually affects the aerial portions of plants.

Mild flower break. See *Cymbidium* ringspot.

Miltonia leaf scorch. See *Miltonia* scorch.

Miltonia scorch (bacterium)

COMMON NAMES: Bacterial tip burn, *Miltonia* leaf scorch, and streak are some of the common names given to this unidentified pathogen.

PLANTS AFFECTED: *Miltonia*.

SYMPTOMS: Water-soaked spots develop on the tips or margins of the leaves. When the disease spreads to the pseudobulbs, they become yellow to orange with necrotic areas that appear burned or injured.

TREATMENT: Remove and destroy infected leaves or growths. Soak plants in a solution of Disinfectant-4 or Fungicide, germicide-2 for several hours.

CONTROL/PREVENTION: This is a cool-temperature disease that is extremely infectious, dictating extremely careful sanitation. Increase temperatures and air circulation, and decrease moisture in the growing area.

Mosaic. See *Cymbidium* mosaic.

Mycoplasmal disease. Called yellowing, this uncommon disease causes yellowing of the leaves. It was isolated from a *Dactylorhiza majalis* plant in Germany. Further information is not available.

Necrotic fleck. See *Alternaria alternata;* Orchid fleck.

Necrotic mosaic. See *Cymbidium* mosaic.

Necrotic ringspot. See *Cymbidium* ringspot.

Necrotic spot. See *Cymbidium* mosaic.

Necrotic streak. See *Cymbidium* mosaic.

Nectria vanillae (fungus). *Nectria vanillicola* and *Negria tjibodensis* cause similar symptoms. These pathogens cause malformed *Vanilla* buds and brown spots on the flowers and *Vanilla* beans. It is thought to be a saprophytic fungus that may respond to similar treatment. Reported only from Réunion in the Mascarene Islands, no treatment information is available.

Nectria vanillicola. See *Nectria vanillae*.

Negria tjibodensis. See *Nectria vanillae*.

Odontoglossum mosaic (virus)

PLANTS AFFECTED: *Cattleya, Cymbidium, Odontoglossum.*

SYMPTOMS: Concentric rings of necrotic tissue which may develop around apparently healthy green tissue. The rings often merge to form a variety of patterns. Symptoms are frequently more pronounced in the early stages of infection and may cause the leaves to drop. Although the plant appears to improve with time, it is still infected with the virus. *Cymbidium* leaves may show faint mosaic patterns, chlorotic streak, or diamond mottle. This virus may cause a form of mild color break in *Cattleya* flowers.

TREATMENT: Destroy the plant when infection is confirmed.

CONTROL/PREVENTION: Isolate any plant suspected of infection. Sterilize cutting tools, control insects, and disinfect the growing area.

MISCELLANEOUS NOTES: This unidentified virus is known to occur in Europe and the United States and may occur world-wide. It affects a wide variety of orchids and may have different strains.

Odontoglossum ringspot (virus). A form of tobacco mosaic-orchid strain (TMV-O).

COMMON NAMES: This virus often occurs in combination with *Cymbidium* mosaic (CyMV), the virus that causes *Cymbidium* diamond mottle and mild flower break. In some cases, a combination of these 2 viruses causes other conditions known as blossom brown necrotic streak, blossom necrosis, *Cattleya* flower disease, color break, flower break, flower necrosis, and mild flower break.

PLANTS AFFECTED: *Cattleya, Cymbidium, Epidendrum, Odontoglossum, Oncidium.* The disease is common in *Cattleya*. Similar problems are recorded for *Angraecum, Arundina, Brassavola, Calanthe, Catasetum, Cochleanthes, Dendrobium, Grammatophyllum, Laelia, Miltonia, Phaius, Phalaenopsis, Vanda, Vanilla, Zygopetalum,* and probably other orchid genera.

SYMPTOMS: The leaves are marked with elongated, diamond-shaped chlorotic areas and may be mottled with light red-purple, ring-shaped lesions. As the disease progresses, the spots enlarge, become necrotic, and merge to form hieroglyphic patterns. Older leaves may develop black flecks and streaks. Other common symptoms include mottling, color breaking, and flower distortion. The plants may be stunted and develop abnormally.

Plants which test positive for infection may not show symptoms in the flowers. *Cattleya, Cymbidium, Odontoglossum, Phalaenopsis,* and plants of other genera show the infection as broken or variegated flower color, usually described as mild color break. Sepals and petals are generally not deformed, and any symptoms on the leaves are mild and scarcely noticeable.

TREATMENT: Destroy the plant when infection is confirmed.

CONTROL/PREVENTION: The virus is transmitted by insects and contaminated cutting tools. Isolate any plant suspected of infection. Sterilize cutting tools, control insects, and disinfect the growing area.

MISCELLANEOUS NOTES: *Odontoglossum* ringspot is considered the same as tobacco mosaic-orchid strain (TMV-O) for cultivation purposes. It is reported in Europe, Japan, and the United States and may be found world-wide.

Indicator plants may be used to confirm infection by this virus. *Chenopodium amaranticolor* and *Gomphrena globosa* are indicators for mild flower break caused by *Odontoglossum* ringspot. *Chenopodium quinoa* is an indicator for the form of the virus that causes *Cattleya* blossom brown necrotic streak. *Tetragonia expansa* is an indicator for all forms of the disease.

Odontoglossum streak (virus). In *Odontoglossum* it causes yellow to light green rings on the leaves. The rings may be small or irregular and turn reddish black with age. The virus is currently reported in the United States but may also occur elsewhere. Information on means of transmission is not available.

Oncidium light green mosaic mottle (virus). This pathogen was reported in *Oncidium altissimum* in the United States. The virus causes light green mosaic mottling on the leaves. Information on means of transmission is not available.

Oncidium severe mosaic streaking (virus). Reported in *Oncidium concolor* and *Oncidium varicosum* in the United States, the virus causes irregular streaks and spots on the leaves. This may be the same virus which causes *Cymbidium* mosaic and *Cattleya* mild flower break. Information on means of transmission is not available.

Oncidium stippled streak (virus). Reported in *Oncidium flexuosum* in the United States, this virus causes stippled streaks on the leaves. No additional information is available.

Orchid fleck (virus). In Japan, orchid fleck is the common name given to Short orchid rhabdovirus.
COMMON NAMES: Leaf necrotic fleck, necrotic fleck.
PLANTS AFFECTED: *Anguloa, Cymbidium, Dendrobium, Odontoglossum, Oncidium, Pescatorea,* and probably other orchid genera. Leaf spots on *Dendrobium* and *Phalaenopsis* may result from this virus.
SYMPTOMS: Necrotic or chlorotic flecks on the leaves.
TREATMENT: Destroy the plant when infection is confirmed.
CONTROL/PREVENTION: The disease may be spread by infected sap. Isolate any plant suspected of infection. Sterilize cutting tools, control insects, and disinfect the growing area.
MISCELLANEOUS NOTES: Reported in Brazil, Europe, and Japan. Indicator plants include *Chenopodium amaranticolor, C. quinoa, Nicotiana glutinosa,* and *N. tabacum.*

Orchid mosaic. See *Cymbidium* mosaic.

Orchid wilt. See *Sclerotium rolfsii.*

Paphiopedilum brown rot. See *Erwinia cypripedii.*

Paphiopedilum brown spot. See *Erwinia cypripedii.*

Paphiopedilum flower sheath browning (fungus?).
PLANTS AFFECTED: *Paphiopedilum* and possibly other orchids that produce flower sheaths.
SYMPTOMS: Flower sheaths turn brown and die, preventing normal blooming.
TREATMENT: Information not available.
CONTROL/PREVENTION: These symptoms may also be caused by wide temperature fluctuations, excessive humidity, waterlogging, and air pollution. Correcting these conditions in the growing area may help prevent the disease.
MISCELLANEOUS NOTES: Fungal infection is the suspected cause, but specific microorganisms have not been identified.

Paphiopedilum leaf blotch. See *Penicillin thomii.*

Paphiopedilum viral infection (virus). Mosaic rings and streaks have been reported on *Paphiopedilum* leaves in the United States and elsewhere. Viral diseases in *Paphiopedilum* have not been confirmed, and viruses that attack other orchids—such as *Cymbidium* mosaic (CyMV) and tobacco mosaic-orchid strain (TMV-O)—are the suspected cause of these symptoms.

Paphiopedilum wilt. See *Fusarium oxysporum.*

Pellicularia filamentosa. See *Rhizoctonia solani.*

Penicillin thomii (fungus)
COMMON NAMES: *Paphiopedilum* leaf blotch.
PLANTS AFFECTED: *Paphiopedilum.*
SYMPTOMS: Watery, deep brown blotches 1.4–2.0 in. (3.5–5.0 cm) across occur on older leaves. The blotches are usually round or elongated with a pale brown margin.
TREATMENT: Spray with a standard fungicide.
CONTROL/PREVENTION: Normal sanitation and good air movement in the growing area.
MISCELLANEOUS NOTES: This pathogen normally infects plants only through unhealthy or injured tissue.

Pestalotiopsis leaf spot. See *Pestalotiopsis disseminata; P. versi.*

Pestalotiopsis disseminata (fungus). *P. versi* causes similar symptoms and requires similar controls.
COMMON NAMES: *Pestalotiopsis* leaf spot.
PLANTS AFFECTED: *Cymbidium aloifolium* and possibly other orchid species. A wide variety of other plants are affected by this pathogen.
SYMPTOMS: Information not available.
TREATMENT: Information not available.
CONTROL/PREVENTION: Normal sanitation and good air movement in the growing area.
MISCELLANEOUS NOTES: The disease occurs in India.

Pestalotiopsis versi. See *P. disseminata.*

Petal blight. See *Botrytis cinerea.*

Phalaenopsis mosaic (virus)
PLANTS AFFECTED: *Cymbidium, Phalaenopsis, Spathoglottis.*
SYMPTOMS: Leaves are marked with a diffuse mosaic consisting of light green or chlorotic patches. Leaf tissue collapses, and broad chlorotic furrows or water-soaked areas appear on the underside of leaves, while the upper surface shows necrosis or light green chlorosis.
TREATMENT: Destroy the plant when infection is confirmed.
CONTROL/PREVENTION: Isolate any plant suspected of infection. Sterilize cutting tools, control insects, and disinfect the growing area.
MISCELLANEOUS NOTES: The symptoms are apparently caused by a combination of *Cymbidium* mosaic (CyMV) and tobacco mosaic-orchid strain (TMV-O). The disease is reported in the United States and elsewhere.

Phyllosticta citricarpa. See *Phyllostictina citricarpa.*

Phyllosticta leaf spot. See *Phyllostictina citricarpa.*

Phyllostictina citricarpa (fungus). *Guignardia citricarpa* is the sexual stage. In Hawaii, *Phyllostictina capitalensis* and *P. pyriformis* are said to cause similar symptoms.
COMMON NAMES: *Phyllosticta, Phyllostictina* leaf spot.
PLANTS AFFECTED: *Dendrobium, Vanilla,* and numerous other orchid genera.
SYMPTOMS: Areas on the leaves and pseudobulbs turn yellow; with age the spots become light to dark brown. The discolorations have a well-defined margin, often with a yellow outer band. As the infection progresses, black or dark brown sporing bodies may appear. The lesions increase in size, and the adjacent tissue becomes yellow or pale green and sunken.
TREATMENT: Spray with Systemic fungicide-1.

CONTROL/PREVENTION: Normal sanitation and good air movement help prevent the infection.

MISCELLANEOUS NOTES: Not normally a devastating disease, *P. citricarpa*. may become serious in *Dendrobium*. It is reported in Asia and the United States and probably occurs world-wide. It is known to affect *Vanilla* in Madagascar.

Phyllostictina leaf spot. See *Phyllostictina citricarpa*.

Phyllostictina pyriformis (fungus)

COMMON NAMES: Leaf spot.

PLANTS AFFECTED: *Aerides, Angraecum, Arachnis, Ascocenda, Ascocentrum, Aspasia, Bifrenaria, Brassavola, Brassia, Broughtonia, Catasetum, Cattleya, Caularthron, Chondrorhyncha, Cochleanthes, Cymbidiella, Cymbidium, Cyrtopodium, Cyrtorchis, Dendrobium, Encyclia, Epidendrum, Eulophiella, Gongora, Grammatophyllum, Isochilus, Laelia, Laeliopsis, Lockhartia, Masdevallia, Maxillaria, Miltonia, Odontoglossum, Oncidium, Paphiopedilum, Pescatorea, Phalaenopsis, Pleurothallis, Renanthera, Rhynchostylis, Schomburgkia, Spathoglottis, Stanhopea, Stelis, Trichopilia, Vanda, Vanilla, Xylobium, Zygopetalum.*

SYMPTOMS: Spotting may start anywhere on the leaf or pseudobulb. The lesions are tiny, yellow, and slightly sunken. As they enlarge, they become round to oval and more sunken, especially if the infection is on the leaves. With age, they turn tan to dark brown and develop a slightly raised, red to purple-black margin. Eventually, tiny, black, raised spore structures develop in the center of the spots. Individual spots are about ¼ in. (6 mm) across. Severely infected leaves may drop prematurely.

TREATMENT: Spray with Systemic fungicide-1 mixed with a wetting agent.

CONTROL/PREVENTION: Normal sanitation with good air movement in the growing area.

MISCELLANEOUS NOTES: The disease is reported in Australasia, the Caribbean islands, Central America, India, the Pacific islands, the Netherlands, South America, and the United States. It probably occurs world-wide.

Phytomonas cattleyae. See *Pseudomonas cattleyae*.

Phytophthora cactorum (fungus)

COMMON NAMES: Black rot, crown rot, damping off, and heart rot are some common names for infections caused by *Phytophthora* pathogens. *Phytophthora omnivora* and *P. palmivora* cause similar symptoms and require the same treatment. Other pathogens such as *Fusarium, Pythium,* or *Rhizoctonia* may also cause damping off.

PLANTS AFFECTED: *Brassavola, Cattleya, Coelogyne, Cymbidium, Dendrobium, Epidendrum, Gongora, Grammatophyllum, Laelia, Oncidium, Paphiopedilum, Phaius, Phalaenopsis, Rhynchostylis, Rodriguezia, Trichocentrum, Vanda, Vanilla,* and other, less commonly cultivated genera. *Phalaenopsis* and *Vanda* are particularly susceptible.

SYMPTOMS: Symptoms vary with plant age. The infection usually starts on the leaves, new leads, or roots, though all plant parts are susceptible.

On flowers, the infection shows as light brown, watery spots with a somewhat darker center.

Leaves usually show the first signs of infection. Symptoms first appear on the underside as small, irregular, watery, brown spots which rapidly become purplish brown or purplish black. The spots may have a yellowish advancing margin. The lesions enlarge with age and may ooze water if pressed. Old lesions sometimes become dry and black, often allowing other diseases to attack the plant. The disease may spread rapidly to the rhizome and roots, particularly when the humidity is high.

New leads show a purple or purple-brown area with a yellowish advancing margin and may be pulled off easily. Only under extremely wet conditions does the infection start in the shoot tip.

Pseudobulbs, roots, or rhizomes show infection as a purplish-black, often sharply delineated, discolored area in the center of the plant. The infection often starts in the roots and may spread to the base of the pseudobulb or leaf, causing the plant to wilt. Sometimes the leaves do not appear infected but become brittle and fall from the plant.

The seedlings of many species are susceptible, but the disease is a particular problem with *Cattleya* and semiterete *Vanda* seedlings. It first appears as small, water-soaked spots which turn yellow and then black. Infected roots collapse, killing the seedlings.

TREATMENT: Remove infected tissue, then treat the plant with a commercial fungicide. Spray with a disinfectant or with Fungicide-2 or -9. An alternative treatment is to dip entire plant in Fungicide-3 or Disinfectant-2. Recommended drenches include Fungicide, germicide-1 or Fungicide-9, or -12. Plants may be dusted with Fungicide-3. Spraying regularly with Fungicide-1, -3, or -7 is reported to be an effective protective measure.

Seedlings in community pots are particularly susceptible and may be lost in 1–2 days. The disease is devastating when soft-tissued young plants are crowded and conditions are moist. Infected seedlings rarely recover. Very dilute solutions of Fungicide, germicide-2 or drenches of Fungicide-9 or -12 may be applied weekly to control the spread of the disease.

CONTROL/PREVENTION: Unless the plant is valuable, the best approach is to remove and burn it, as the disease is highly contagious. If left untreated, the disease spreads from plant to plant when contaminated water splashes from the plant or drips through the growing medium. Warm temperatures, high humidity, and water-soaked medium all contribute to the spread of this disease.

MISCELLANEOUS NOTES: If the growing tip of *Vanda* is infected, cut well below the infected site to promote growth of a healthy side shoot. If the newest growth of a sympodial orchid becomes infected, remove the growth. The disease is specifically reported in Asia, the Caribbean, Europe, New Zealand, and the United States, but it probably occurs world-wide.

Phytophthora jatrophae (fungus). Commonly called *Vanilla* mildew, the tips of *Vanilla* beans turn brown and are eventually covered with a white powder. No treatment information is available, but the treatments recommended for *Phytophthora cactorum* might be effective. The disease is reported in the Cormoro Islands, Java, Madagascar, Puerto Rico, and on Réunion in the Mascarene Islands.

Phytophthora omnivora. See *Phytophthora cactorum*.

Phytophthora palmivora. See *Phytophthora cactorum*.

Pseudomonas aeruginosa (bacterium). *Pseudomonas fluorescens* causes similar symptoms and requires similar treatment.

COMMON NAMES: Bacterial rot.

PLANTS AFFECTED: *Cattleya, Cymbidium, Paphiopedilum.*

SYMPTOMS: Buds may rot, and the sepals and petals may develop small necrotic specks with water-soaked margins.

Infected roots die back, but the infection often goes unnoticed until it spreads upward to the base of the stem.

TREATMENT: See *Pseudomonas cattleyae*.

CONTROL/PREVENTION: Normal sanitation with good air movement in the growing area.

MISCELLANEOUS NOTES: *Pseudomonas* is normally a secondary infection that does not invade healthy plants.

Pseudomonas andropogonis (bacterium). Also called *Vanda* firm rot, it affects *Dendrobium, Phalaenopsis, Vanda,* and possibly other orchids. The leaf rots and drops. The disease occurs primarily in Hawaii. No additional information is available.

Pseudomonas cattleyae (bacterium). *Bacterium cattleyae* and *Phytomonas cattleyae* cause similar symptoms and require the same treatment.

COMMON NAMES: Bacterial brown spot.

PLANTS AFFECTED: *Aerides, Ascocenda, Ascocentrum, Brassia, Catasetum, Cattleya* and related genera, *Cymbidium, Cyrtopodium, Dendrobium, Doritaenopsis, Epidendrum, Oncidium, Ornithocephalus, Paphiopedilum, Phalaenopsis, Phragmipedium, Renanthopsis, Rhynchostylis, Rodriguezia, Sophronitis, Vanda,* and other, less commonly cultivated orchid genera.

SYMPTOMS: The infection may appear anywhere on the leaf as a small, soft, water-soaked blister. Initially dirty green in color, the infected spot enlarges and eventually becomes brown or black and sunken. It oozes a bacteria-laden liquid, particularly when the disease reaches the tip of the leaf.

In *Cattleya,* the infection enters through wounds on older plants and usually affects only older leaves. It advances slowly and is rarely fatal.

In *Phalaenopsis,* the blister-like spots may be surrounded with a yellowish or pale green halo. Spots coalesce, and the infection spreads rapidly. If the diseased area invades the crown, the plant will die.

In seedlings, the infection enters through the stomata rather than just damaged tissue and is particularly severe. It rapidly kills young *Phalaenopsis* plants.

TREATMENT: Remove infected plants from the growing area. Cut away infected tissue, leaves, and growths, and soak the entire plant for several hours in Algicide, bactericide, fungicide-1 or Fungicide, germicide-2. Fungicide, germicide-2 is suggested for seedlings, since Algicide, bactericide, fungicide-1 is sometimes harmful. Diseased plants should also be drenched or thoroughly sprayed with broad-spectrum, systemic fungicide because secondary infections are likely to develop in weakened plants. Several repeat treatments a few days apart are usually necessary.

CONTROL/PREVENTION: Reduce humidity and overhead watering. *Pseudomonas cattleyae* is a water-borne pathogen which prefers warm, moist conditions. Increase air circulation and reduce temperatures if possible. Sterilize wooden benches by painting them with a copper naphthenate compound. The exudate from diseased tissue is laden with infectious bacteria, which are easily spread to other plants through dripping or splashing water, insect carriers, or contaminated tools.

MISCELLANEOUS NOTES: This is the most common and severe disease affecting *Phalaenopsis.* It is reported in Asia, the Philippines, and the United States.

Pseudomonas cypripedii (bacterium)

COMMON NAMES: *Paphiopedilum* brown spot.

PLANTS AFFECTED: *Paphiopedilum.*

SYMPTOMS: Soft, water-soaked spots appear on the upper leaf surface. These enlarge and eventually destroy the plant.

TREATMENT: Cut out infected tissue down to the rhizome, and soak plants for several hours in Fungicide, germicide-2 or Disinfectant-4. Repeat this treatment several times. Another recommended treatment is spraying with Algicide, bactericide, fungicide-1.

CONTROL/PREVENTION: Normal sanitation procedures and good air movement are important protective measures. Plants and the entire growing area should be sprayed with Algicide, bactericide, fungicide-1.

MISCELLANEOUS NOTES: Symptoms are easily confused with those of *Erwinia cypripedii,* and treatment is similar. The disease is reported in the United States and probably occurs elsewhere.

Pseudomonas fluorescens. See *Pseudomonas aeruginosa.* Although these are different bacteria, they cannot be differentiated without laboratory diagnosis. Plant symptoms and recommended treatments are the same for both pathogens.

***Ptychogaster* species** (fungus)

COMMON NAMES: Snow mold.

PLANTS AFFECTED: Plants grown in organic potting media are subject to infection. In some regions, snow mold is a problem for *Vanda* growers.

SYMPTOMS: White, powdery growth on the medium or near the base of the stem. The mold, which repels water, covers the roots and rhizome, suffocating and dehydrating the plant.

TREATMENT: Unpot the plant, then treat it with Fungicide-13 mixed with a suitable wetting agent, or soak it in Algicide, bactericide, fungicide-1. Inspect and treat nearby plants also. Several treatments may be necessary, as the fungus is quite water repellent. After treatment, repot the plant in new medium.

CONTROL/PREVENTION: Repot plants according to the recommended schedule, as this problem seldom occurs when plants receive regular care.

MISCELLANEOUS NOTES: Plant symptoms may be similar to those caused by *Fusarium oxysporum* f. *cattleyae* and *Rhizoctonia solani.* Other molds in the potting medium respond to similar treatment. Also see Saprophytic fungi.

***Pythium* rot.** See *Pythium ultimum.*

Pythium ultimum (fungus). *Pythium* is one of the fungi which cause damping off. Other pathogens such as *Fusarium, Phytophthora,* and *Rhizoctonia* also cause damping off and similar symptoms.

COMMON NAMES: Black rot, *Cattleya* soft rot, damping off, *Pythium* rot.

PLANTS AFFECTED: *Cattleya, Cymbidium, Epidendrum, Oncidium,* and other orchid genera.

SYMPTOMS: The infection usually starts in the roots then spreads to the rhizome, pseudobulbs, and leaves. Information on the symptoms of *Phytophthora* rot also applies to *Pythium* rot: see *Phytophthora cactorum.* When infected, the tissue of the pseudobulb often remains firm and gradually dries, becoming hard and mummified.

Cattleya may show a creamy yellow discoloration on one or both sides of the pseudobulbs. The discoloration eventually turns black or brown and softens, and the bulb rots.

Seedlings are particularly susceptible to infection and die rapidly unless treated immediately. The affected plants turn translucent brown, sometimes with black spots near the base.

TREATMENT: Destroy seriously infected seedlings and isolate other infected plants. Older plants may recover if infected tissue is cut well beyond the affected area. Soak plants, particularly *Phalaenopsis* and seedlings, for several hours in Fungicide, germicide-2. In the case of seedlings or plants in community pots, even unaffected plants should be soaked.

CONTROL/PREVENTION: Destroy or carefully isolate the plant. A water-borne mold, *Pythium* is often carried from plant to plant through dripping or splashing water. As a preventive measure, growers suggest watering seedlings and plants in community pots each month using Disinfectant-4 or Fungicide, germicide-2. *Pythium* is most active when humidity is high and temperatures are cool, so reducing humidity and raising temperatures should help stop the infection from spreading.

MISCELLANEOUS NOTES: Reported in Asia and the United States, this disease probably occurs world-wide.

Rhizoctonia solani (fungus). The names *Pellicularia filamentosa* and *Thanatephorus cucumeris* apply to the sexual stage of the fungus. *Rhizoctonia* is one of the fungi thought to cause damping off and other symptoms similar to those caused by *Fusarium, Phytophthora,* and *Pythium.*

COMMON NAMES: Root rot, *Paphiopedilum* root rot.

PLANTS AFFECTED: Seedlings of *Cattleya* and related genera, *Oncidium*, *Paphiopedilum*, and *Phalaenopsis*. Adult plants of *Brassavola*, *Cattleya*, *Cypripedium*, *Dendrobium*, *Epidendrum*, *Oncidium*, *Paphiopedilum*, *Phalaenopsis*, *Trichocentrum*, and *Vanda*.

SYMPTOMS: *Rhizoctonia* is primarily a root disease, but the symptoms are usually first noticed on aerial parts of the plant and are similar to those caused by *Fusarium oxysporum*. If the disease is not controlled, infected plants develop brown rot and die. The process is quite gradual in mature plants.

Leaves and pseudobulbs become yellow, shriveled, thin, and twisted, and new growths become progressively smaller. *Paphiopedilum* leaves become pale and desiccated and curl inward.

The roots usually show a brown rot with white or brown fungal growth. In severe infections, the fungus girdles and kills the plant. The infection quickly invades the lower leaves and rhizomes of small seedlings.

TREATMENT: Remove infected portions of the roots and leaves, and repot the plant in sterile medium. Drench several times with Systemic fungicide-1 or -3 or Fungicide, germicide-2, or spray with Fungicide-2 or -3. To treat seedlings, submerge them in Fungicide, germicide-2 or Fungicide-2, or -3.

CONTROL/PREVENTION: *Rhizoctonia solani* is very contagious. If not controlled immediately, it spreads rapidly, causing severe damage. When disease is suspected in other plants or when repotting is overdue, unpot the plants and check their roots. If the roots are not firm and healthy, they should be trimmed, and the plants should be treated with a fungicide, then repotted in new, sterile medium.

Root rot usually occurs when the medium breaks down, drainage is poor, or plants are overwatered. Rot sets in quickly when roots are damaged by injury or salt buildup from hard water or overfertilizing. In hard-water areas, pots should be flushed at least monthly to prevent root damage.

Ringspot (virus). This disease is known to affect *Aspasia*, *Bifrenaria*, *Brassia*, *Dendrobium*, *Hormidium*, *Miltonia*, *Oncidium*, *Phalaenopsis*, and *Trigonidium*. Distinct ringspots develop on the leaves. The virus is currently reported in Europe and Brazil. No additional information is available.

Rust. See *Sphenospora kevorkianii*, *S. saphena*, *Uredo behickiana*, *U. epidendri*, *U. nigropuncta*, *U. oncidii*.

Saprophytic fungi (fungus). These are species that live on dead matter.

COMMON NAMES: Molds.

PLANTS AFFECTED: All dead or dying vegetable matter.

SYMPTOMS: These fungi are usually found on dead plant material, but they may spread to living tissue. The mycelia and fruiting bodies may appear on potting medium or other organic material.

TREATMENT: Treat the plant with Fungicide-13, then repot it in new, sterile medium.

CONTROL/PREVENTION: Remove dead plant material, increase spacing between plants, and spray with a fungicide. Excessively wet or humid conditions are conducive to the spread of the infection, so moisture levels should be reduced. General cleanup of the growing area is indicated, including removal of dead plant parts. Avoid mold in seedling flasks by maintaining sterile conditions.

MISCELLANEOUS NOTES: Saprophytic fungi are seldom serious except for young plants in seedling flasks or community pots.

Sclerotinia fuckeliana. See *Botrytis cinerea*.

Sclerotium rolfsii (fungus). This is the asexual stage of the fungus *Pellicularia rolfsii* (*Corticium rolfsii*), which occurs only rarely. *Sclerotium vanillae* and other closely related *Sclerotium* fungi cause symptoms similar to those caused by *Botrytis cinerea*, and respond to the same treatments.

COMMON NAMES: Basal rot, collar rot, crown rot, *Cymbidium* collar rot, *Cymbidium Sclerotium* rot, orchid wilt, southern blight, *Vanilla* bean deformation.

PLANTS AFFECTED: *Cattleya*, *Cycnoches*, *Cymbidium*, *Oncidium*, *Phaius*, *Phalaenopsis*, *Spathoglottis*, *Vanda*, *Vanilla*, and probably other orchid genera.

SYMPTOMS: Roots, pseudobulbs, leaf bases, and the lower part of stems turn cream-yellow. The affected tissue becomes brown (resulting from invasion by secondary pathogens), collapses, and rots very rapidly. The disease eventually girdles and destroys the entire basal portion of the plant and attacks young leaves. Affected leaves become yellow, wilt, and die. If left untreated, the infection leads to the death of the entire plant. In *Vanilla*, the beans may be deformed. Seedlings are particularly susceptible to infection.

Small yellow or tan sclerotia about the size and color of mustard seed form on the affected tissue. This is the resting form of the fungus and often persists for years in soil, medium, and on benches or other surfaces in the growing area.

TREATMENT: If this disease becomes established in the growing area, it can be devastating and difficult to eradicate. Remove and burn diseased plants. If the infected plant is very valuable, and if the infection is just starting, remove the affected plant parts, and dip the entire plant in a solution of Fungicide, germicide-2 or Disinfectant-2 for at least an hour. This treatment sometimes controls the disease.

CONTROL/PREVENTION: Isolate the plant until it is disease-free. Sterilize the pot with a solution of 4% formalin or 10% bleach before reusing it. Also sterilize benches and the surrounding area with a 2% formalin solution or with Fungicide-13. Temperatures below 85°F (29°C), good sanitation, and increased air movement help limit the spread of this disease.

MISCELLANEOUS NOTES: Reported world-wide, *Sclerotium* is most prevalent in warmer climates, where it also affects beans, peppers, marigolds, and phlox.

Sclerotium vanillae. See *Sclerotium rolfsii*.

Selenophoma dendrobii (fungus)

COMMON NAMES: *Selenophoma* leaf spot.

PLANTS AFFECTED: *Dendrobium*.

SYMPTOMS: Small brown spots on the leaves which rapidly develop into round, oval, or irregular lesions. The spots may occur on either side of the leaves and eventually become discolored in the center. Sporing is evident on older spots. Severely infected leaves drop off.

CONTROL/PREVENTION: Normal sanitation with good air movement in the growing area.

MISCELLANEOUS NOTES: This disease is reported only in Japan.

Selenophoma leaf spot. See *Selenophoma dendrobii*.

Septoria leaf spot. See *Septoria selenophomoides*.

Septoria selenophomoides (fungus)

COMMON NAMES: *Dendrobium* leaf spot, *Septoria* leaf spot.

PLANTS AFFECTED: *Brassia*, *Bulbophyllum*, *Coelogyne*, *Cymbidium*, *Dendrobium*, *Encyclia*, *Laelia*, *Masdevallia*, *Miltonia*, *Odontoglossum*, *Oncidium*, *Paphiopedilum*, *Pleurothallis*, *Stanhopea*, *Stenocoryne*. *Dendrobium nobile* and its hybrids are extremely susceptible.

SYMPTOMS: The tiny spots may start on either leaf surface as sunken, yellow lesions. They continue to enlarge, becoming dark brown to black, circular or irregular lesions. Spots may merge to form large, irregular patches on the leaf. Heavily infected leaves fall prematurely.

TREATMENT: Spray the plant with Fungicide-2 or Systemic fungicide-1.

CONTROL/PREVENTION: Water on the leaves may lead to infection by this pathogen.

MISCELLANEOUS NOTES: The disease is most frequently reported in Hawaii and Japan, but it also occurs in Brazil, Colombia, Costa Rica, the Dominican Republic, England, Guatemala, India, Mexico, the Philippines, Thailand, and Florida in the United States. In the United States it most often appears on recently imported orchids, which should be given a preventive fungicide treatment.

Seuratia coeffeicola (fungus). *S. pinicola* and *S. vanillae* cause similar problems and require to the same treatment.

COMMON NAMES: *Vanilla seuratia*.

PLANTS AFFECTED: *Vanilla*.

SYMPTOMS: Sporing bodies on the leaves and stem.

TREATMENT: Treating the plant with Fungicide-13 may be helpful.

CONTROL/PREVENTION: Excessively wet or humid conditions are conducive to the spread saprophytic fungi, so planting in areas with improved air circulation might be beneficial.

MISCELLANEOUS NOTES: This is a rare disease from Madagascar that is not normally parasitic.

Seuratia pinicola. See *Seuratia coeffeicola*.

Seuratia vanillae. See *Seuratia coeffeicola*.

Severe leaf necrosis. See *Cymbidium* ringspot.

Short orchid rhabdovirus (virus)

PLANTS AFFECTED: *Coelogyne, Dendrobium, Dendrobium phalaenopsis, Miltonia, Odontoglossum, Oncidium, Paphiopedilum, Phalaenopsis, Renanthera, Stanhopea, Vanda, Zygopetalum*. This virus has been found in more than 26 orchid genera throughout the world. It may be a single strain or multiple strains of the virus.

SYMPTOMS: Brown spots on the leaves. As the spots increase in size, the leaves turn yellow, and the tissues between the veins may collapse.

TREATMENT: Destroy the plant when infection is confirmed.

CONTROL/PREVENTION: Isolate any plant suspected of infection, since the infection is transmitted through contaminated sap.

MISCELLANEOUS NOTES: This virus was first reported during a study of *Fusarium moniliforme* a fungus that causes flower blight. Symptoms of the fungal infection may hide the symptoms of the viral infection. Possible indicator plants include *Chenopodium amaranticolor, C. quinoa*, and *Nicotiana clevelandii*. The disease occurs in Denmark, Germany, and Japan. In Japan it is called orchid fleck.

Snow mold. See *Ptychogaster* species.

Soft rot. See *Erwinia carotovora; Pythium ultimum*.

Sooty blotch. See *Gloeodes pomigena*.

Sooty mold. See *Gloeodes pomigena*.

Spathoglottis diamond spot (virus)

PLANTS AFFECTED: *Cattleya, Cymbidium, Dendrobium, Miltonia, Spathoglottis, Vanda*.

SYMPTOMS: The leaves develop chlorotic streaks or spots, necrotic rings, or diamond-shaped lesions. With age, the affected areas become reddish brown or black, and the leaves drop prematurely.

TREATMENT: Destroy the plant when infection is confirmed.

CONTROL/PREVENTION: Isolate any plant suspected of infection. Sterilize cutting tools, control insects, and disinfect the growing area.

MISCELLANEOUS NOTES: *Spathoglottis* may be used as an indicator plant since it is highly susceptible to infection by viruses which attack other orchid genera. Symptoms are fairly consistent regardless of the host plant being tested, although several different viruses cause similar symptoms. The disease is reported in the United States.

Sphaeropsis species (fungus)

COMMON NAMES: Leaf blight.

PLANTS AFFECTED: *Spathoglottis*.

SYMPTOMS: Light brown, linear markings with darker brown margins. With age, the spots increase in size to cover most of the leaf.

TREATMENT: Fungicides used for other blights or leaf spots may be effective. See *Cercospora angraeci*.

CONTROL/PREVENTION: Normal sanitation with good air movement in the growing area.

MISCELLANEOUS NOTES: The disease is reported in Assam.

Sphenospora kevorkianii (fungus)

COMMON NAMES: Rust.

PLANTS AFFECTED: *Batemania, Bletia, Brassia, Bulbophyllum, Capanemia, Catasetum, Caularthron, Cycnoches, Cyrtopodium, Epidendrum, Gongora, Hexisea, Huntleya, Ionopsis, Laelia, Leochilus, Lockhartia, Lycaste, Masdevallia, Maxillaria, Miltonia, Mormodes, Notylia, Odontoglossum, Oeceoclades, Oncidium, Ornithocephalus, Pelexia, Peristeria, Pescatorea, Pleurothallis, Plocoglottis, Polystachya, Rodriguezia, Schomburgkia, Sigmatostalix, Stanhopea, Trichoceros, Trichopilia, Trigonidium, Xylobium, Zygopetalum, Zygostates*, and probably other orchid genera.

SYMPTOMS: Small, orange spore pustules appear on the underside of leaves. The disease rarely infects the stem. As the lesion enlarges, the pustules eventually break through to the top leaf surface. The orange pustules, which turn black with age, often develop in a concentric pattern, giving the infected area the appearance of a target.

TREATMENT: Remove and burn all leaves that show infection. If all plant parts are infected, destroy the entire plant. Spray plants with either Fungicide-7 or -15, or Systemic Fungicide-12 mixed with a suitable wetting agent. Because rust is capable of infecting numerous genera, it is usually best to destroy infected plants. New chemicals that are effective against rust are being introduced and may soon be approved for orchids. Consult local agricultural agents or orchid growers.

CONTROL/PREVENTION: Isolate or destroy the plant and disinfect the growing area. Periodically inspect plants for symptoms of this disease.

MISCELLANEOUS NOTES: Rust seldom kills a plant but weakens it, reducing or eliminating flowering. The disease is known to occur in the Caribbean islands, Central America, Florida in the United States, and northern South America.

Sphenospora mera (fungus)

COMMON NAMES: Rust.

PLANTS AFFECTED: *Bletia, Bletilla, Cycnoches, Epidendrum, Ionopsis, Mormodes, Oncidium, Pleurothallis, Rodriguezia*.

SYMPTOMS: Only leaves are affected. The tiny, raised spots are cinnamon-brown and appear on the underside of leaves. The sporing bodies rupture when mature, dispersing the spores via wind or splashing water.

TREATMENT: Remove and burn all leaves showing infection. Spray plants with Fungicide-7 or -15, or Systemic Fungicide-12 mixed with a suitable wetting agent. New chemicals that are effective against rust are being introduced and may soon be approved for orchids. Consult local agricultural agents or orchid growers.

CONTROL/PREVENTION: Isolate infected plants until they are free of disease. Give plants in susceptible genera a preventive spray, and periodically inspect them for symptoms of this disease.

MISCELLANEOUS NOTES: This pathogen is reported in Brazil, Central America, and Mexico.

Sphenospora saphena (fungus)

COMMON NAMES: Rust.

PLANTS AFFECTED: *Cochlioda, Epidendrum, Ionopsis, Laelia, Masdevallia, Oncidium, Pescatorea, Rodriguezia, Sobralia.*

SYMPTOMS: Tiny, raised, orange or rust-brown pustules appear on the underside of leaves, which eventually become covered with these spore-bearing pustules. The spots turn dark brown with age.

TREATMENT: Because rust is capable of infecting numerous genera, it is usually advisable to destroy infected plants. To treat the plant, isolate it and remove and burn all leaves showing infection. Spray plants with either Fungicide-7 or -15, or Systemic Fungicide-12 mixed with a suitable wetting agent. New chemicals that are effective against rust are being introduced and may soon be approved for orchids. Consult local agricultural agents or orchid growers.

CONTROL/PREVENTION: Disinfect the growing area and apply a preventive spray to other plants in the growing area. Periodically inspect plants for symptoms of this disease.

MISCELLANEOUS NOTES: The disease occurs from Brazil to Mexico.

Sporoschisma species (fungus)

COMMON NAMES: *Vanilla* sporoschisma.

PLANTS AFFECTED: *Vanilla.*

SYMPTOMS: White fungal mycelia cover the plant and turn brown with age.

TREATMENT: Information not available.

CONTROL/PREVENTION: Plant debris in the growing area may encourage disease development, since this fungus is apparently saprophytic.

MISCELLANEOUS NOTES: Reported only in *Vanilla planifolia* in Indochina, the disease does not weaken the plant severely.

Stanhopea yellow spot (virus). *Stanhopea* leaves develop yellow rings and spots that increase in size as the leaf grows. The disease is uncommon. It was reported in California in the United States on plants imported from an unnamed location. No information on the virus is available.

Stemphylium **species.** See *Alternaria alternata.*

Streak. See *Miltonia* scorch.

Thanatephorus cucumeris (fungus). This is the sexual stage of *Rhizoctonia solani.*

Tobacco mosaic (virus). Abbreviated TMV. Unlike *Cymbidium* mosaic virus, TMV has many strains and variants and infects numerous plant families. Tobacco mosaic-orchid strain (TMV-O) has many of the same properties as TMV, but it has a unique chemical makeup and infects only a few plants other than orchids. Similarly, most vegetable strains of TMV do not invade orchids. TMV-O often occurs with other viruses and causes somewhat different symptoms in different orchid genera. For further information, see Chlorotic leaf streak of *Oncidium, Odontoglossum* ringspot, *Paphiopedilum* viral infection, and *Phalaenopsis* mosaic.

Tobacco rattle (virus). Abbreviated TRV, it was reported to affect *Orchis* in Germany. The virus causes misshapen flowers and is transmitted by contaminated tools. Indicator plants include *Nicotiana tabacum* 'Xanthi' and 'Samsun'. A strain of this virus is common in crop plants, but no other instances of orchid infection have been recorded.

Tomato ringspot (virus)

COMMON NAMES: Abbreviated TRSV, it is also known as *Cymbidium* chlorotic leaf streak.

PLANTS AFFECTED: *Cymbidium.*

SYMPTOMS: Faint chlorotic streaks on leaves, basal necrotic streaking, and premature leaf drop. No flower symptoms were reported. Plants with no visible symptoms sometimes test positive for the virus.

TREATMENT: Destroy the plant when infection is confirmed.

CONTROL/PREVENTION: Isolate any plant suspected of infection. Sterilize cutting tools, control insects, and disinfect the growing area.

MISCELLANEOUS NOTES: *Cassia quinoa, Nicotiana tabacum* 'Kentucky 35', *Vigna sinensis,* and *V. unguiculata* are indicator plants. The infected sap can be transmitted to indicator plants but not back to orchids. The disease is reported in the United States.

Trichopilia isometric (virus). Known as TI—virus unnamed, this virus was isolated in Germany from a *Trichopilia* plant. It is probably uncommon. No further information is available.

Turnip mosaic (virus). Abbreviated TuMV, this virus was isolated in Germany from an *Orchis* plant. It is apparently transmitted by contaminated tools. Information on symptoms is not available. *Nicotiana clevelandii* is an indicator plant.

Unnamed bacilliform (virus). Abbreviated PhBV, this virus reportedly affects *Phalaenopsis* in Germany. Information on symptoms and means of transmission is not available.

Unnamed rhabdovirus (virus) Known as RV—unnamed, this virus reportedly affects *Bifrenaria harrisoniae, Brassia, Hormidium fragrans, Miltonia,* and *Oncidium* plants in Brazil. Information on symptoms and means of transmission is not available.

Uredo behickiana (fungus)

COMMON NAMES: Rust.

PLANTS AFFECTED: *Cattleya, Bletia, Dendrobium, Encyclia, Hexisea, Laelia, Masdevallia, Maxillaria, Oncidium, Phaius, Pleurothallis, Schomburgkia, Spathoglottis, Stanhopea.*

SYMPTOMS: Orange-yellow patches enlarge in a roughly circular pattern, eventually covering the entire underside of the leaf. The top surface of the leaf becomes chlorotic. Even severely infected plants may bloom, but the inflorescences are smaller than normal, with fewer and smaller flowers.

TREATMENT: Cut off and destroy all leaves showing infection. A chemical control for this disease has not been established.

CONTROL/PREVENTION: Isolate or destroy infected plants, and disinfect the growing area. Inspect plants frequently for signs of reinfection.

MISCELLANEOUS NOTES: Rust is seldom fatal, but it weakens the plant, thus reducing or eliminating flowering. This fungus is reported from Brazil to Mexico, and in the Caribbean islands. It is sometimes found in the United States in imported plants.

Uredo epidendri (fungus)

COMMON NAMES: Rust.

PLANTS AFFECTED: *Caularthron, Encyclia, Epidendrum, Ionopsis, Laelia, Oncidium, Rodriguezia, Trigonidium.*

SYMPTOMS: The first symptoms, which appear on the underside of leaves, are raised brown pustules, often with a reddish border. As the disease progresses, the developing spore pustules break through to the upper leaf surfaces. With age, the pustules change from brown to purple-black. Only the leaves are affected.

TREATMENT: Cut off and burn all leaves showing infection, and spray plants with Fungicide-7 or -15, or Systemic Fungicide-12 mixed with a suitable wetting agent.

CONTROL/PREVENTION: Because rust is capable of infecting many plant genera, it is usually best to destroy infected plants. Disinfect the growing area, and periodically inspect plants for signs of reinfection. Isolate infected plants, remove all infected tissue, and spray with Fungicide-7 or -15, or Systemic Fungicide-12. New chemicals that are effective against rust are being introduced and may soon be approved for orchids. Consult local agricultural agents or orchid growers.

MISCELLANEOUS NOTES: Rust is seldom fatal, but it weakens the plant and thus reduces or eliminates flowering.

Uredo nigropuncta (fungus)

COMMON NAMES: Rust.

PLANTS AFFECTED: *Bletia, Cyrtopodium, Encyclia, Stanhopea.*

SYMPTOMS: On *Stanhopea,* the symptoms are light to dark brown spore pustules on the underside of the leaf. As the infection progresses, the pustules break through to the upper leaf surface. In other orchid genera, the symptoms are similar, but the pustules may be orange and turn black with age.

TREATMENT: Cut off and burn all leaves showing infection, and spray plants with either Fungicide-7 or -15, or Systemic Fungicide-12 mixed with a suitable wetting agent. New chemicals that are effective against rust are being introduced and may soon be approved for orchids. Consult local agricultural agents or orchid growers.

CONTROL/PREVENTION: Because rust is difficult to control once it becomes established, it is usually best to destroy infected plants. Disinfect the growing area, and inspect plants periodically for signs of this disease.

MISCELLANEOUS NOTES: Rust is seldom fatal, but it weakens the plant, thus reducing or eliminating flowering.

Uredo oncidii (fungus)

COMMON NAMES: Rust.

PLANTS AFFECTED: *Epidendrum, Lycaste, Odontoglossum, Oncidium.*

SYMPTOMS: Small orange pustules appear on the underside of leaves. The infected area is usually circular with an advancing orange margin. With age, the center turns brown.

TREATMENT: Cut off and burn all leaves showing infection, and spray plants with Fungicide-7 or -15, or Systemic Fungicide-12 mixed with a suitable wetting agent. New chemicals that are effective against rust are being introduced and may soon be approved for orchids. Consult local agricultural agents or orchid growers.

CONTROL/PREVENTION: Because rust is capable of infecting numerous genera, it is usually best to destroy infected plants. Disinfect the growing area, and inspect plants periodically for signs of this disease.

MISCELLANEOUS NOTES: Rust is seldom fatal, but it weakens the plant, thus reducing or eliminating flowering. This pathogen is reported from Brazil to Mexico and in the Caribbean islands.

Uredo scabies (fungus)

COMMON NAMES: Rust, *Vanilla* rust.

PLANTS AFFECTED: *Vanilla.*

SYMPTOMS: Small pustules appear on the underside of leaves. The infected area is usually circular with an advancing margin of infected tissue. With age, the spots may change color.

TREATMENT: It is usually best to burn infected plants. If infection is just beginning, cut off and burn all leaves showing infection, sterilizing the tool after each cut. Spray plants with either Fungicide-7 or -15, or Systemic Fungicide-12 mixed with a suitable wetting agent. New chemicals that are effective against rust are being introduced and may soon be approved for use on orchids. Consult local agricultural agents or orchid growers.

CONTROL/PREVENTION: Periodically inspect plants for signs of this disease.

MISCELLANEOUS NOTES: Rust is the most serious disease affecting *Vanilla* plantations. It seldom kills plants but weakens them, thus reducing or eliminating flowering. The disease is reported in all commercial *Vanilla*-growing areas.

Uromyces joffrini. See *Uredo scabies.*

***Vanda* firm rot.** See *Pseudomonas andropogonis.*

Vanda mosaic (virus)

COMMON NAMES: Flower break.

PLANTS AFFECTED: *Vanda.*

SYMPTOMS: Symptoms include distorted sepals and petals, variegated flower color, and faint or inconspicuous mosaic on the leaf tips.

TREATMENT: Destroy the plant when infection is confirmed.

CONTROL/PREVENTION: Isolate any plant suspected of infection. Sterilize cutting tools, control insects, and disinfect the growing area.

MISCELLANEOUS NOTES: This virus is different from other flower break viruses. It occurs wherever *Vanda* is grown.

***Vanda* transit rot** (fungus). This is a complex of fungi including *Alternaria, Botrytis,* and *Gloeosporium.*

PLANTS AFFECTED: *Vanda.*

SYMPTOMS: Small, chocolate-brown spots appear 3–5 days after cut flowers have been packed for shipping. The spots continue to enlarge until they cover the blossom.

TREATMENT: Before *Vanda* flowers are packed for shipping, they should be sprayed with Fungicide, germicide-2, diluted to 1:2000.

CONTROL/PREVENTION: Pretreat blossoms before shipping.

MISCELLANEOUS NOTES: The disease probably occurs world-wide.

***Vanilla* anthracnose.** See *Colletotrichum gloeosporiodes.*

***Vanilla* astérinées.** See *Gloeodes pomigena.*

***Vanilla* bud malformation.** See *Nectria vanillae.*

***Vanilla* fruit deformation.** See *Botrytis cinerea.*

***Vanilla* mildew.** See *Phytophthora jatrophae.*

***Vanilla* root rot.** See *Fusarium batatis* var. *vanillae.*

***Vanilla* rouille or rust.** See *Uredo scabies.*

***Vanilla* seuratia.** See *Seuratia coeffeicola.*

***Vanilla* sporoschisma.** See *Sporoschisma* species.

***Vanilla* wilt.** See *Fusarium oxysporum.*

White cell necrosis. See *Cymbidium* mosaic.

Yellowing. See Mycoplasmal disease.

Disease Treatment Summary

Despite all efforts at prevention, orchid growing problems that require more drastic measures occur from time to time. A wide variety of chemicals are specifically formulated to deal with these problems. Given the ever-changing nature of the chemical arsenal and the complexity of regulations regarding their sale and use, we do not recommend specific chemical compounds but urge readers instead to consult their local agricultural agents for information on accepted chemical preventatives and their use. For information on interpreting product labels and using chemicals safely, see Section III of this Appendix.

To facilitate cross-referencing, we have divided widely used chemicals into the following broad classifications: bactericides, disinfectants, fungicides, and systemic fungicides.

Bactericides, as used in horticulture, are broad-spectrum antibiotics that effectively destroy a wide variety of bacteria that cause plant diseases.

Disinfectants, which kill pathogens on contact, are used for general control of a variety of organisms. They have a short residual effect but may be highly toxic to plants. Sterilizing with a disinfectant kills viruses on pots, tools, benches, and equipment in the growing area, but no chemical is selective enough to kill only a virus once it has infected plant cells.

Fungicides kill fungi on contact.

Systemic fungicides provide longer-term protection but are sometimes not effective until they are absorbed by the plant.

The products listed in the following tables may be available and approved for use only in certain parts of the world. The inclusion of a chemical on this list does not indicate that it has been registered for use on orchids. Other, equally effective products may be available. Consult with local agricultural agents for the names of products currently approved for use on orchids.

The use of product names implies no endorsement by the authors or publisher, nor do the authors or publisher assume liability for any accidents resulting from use of the chemicals named. *The information on applications given below is not a substitute for the information on the product label.*

It is the responsibility of the user to comply with the directions on the container of the product used and with the laws of the area in which the chemical is applied.

Readers should be aware that because of rapid changes in both state and national laws and regulations governing horticultural chemicals, products in the following tables may or may not be available in any particular state or country. The products listed are known to be effective against the indicated diseases but are not necessarily available or certified for use with orchids. After a disease has been identified, growers are cautioned to check with local agricultural agents, nurseries, commercial growers, or garden supply stores to determine currently approved treatments in their area.

The list of chemicals in the Treatment Tables, following, known to be effective against particular pathogens was compiled from information in the following works:

American Orchid Society, Inc. 1986. *Handbook on orchid pests and diseases.* American Orchid Society, Inc., 6000 South Olive Ave., West Palm Beach, Fla., U.S.A. 33405.

Extension Services of Oregon State University, Washington State University, and the University of Idaho. 1993. *Pacific Northwest disease control handbook.* Pacific Northwest Extension Services, c/o Agricultural Communications, Oregon State University, Corvallis, Ore., U.S.A. 97331–2119.

Hadley, G., M. Arditti, and J. Arditti. 1987. Orchid diseases—a compendium. In: *Orchid biology: reviews and perspectives.* Vol. IV. Edited by J. Arditti. Comstock Publishing, Cornell University Press, Ithaca, N.Y.

Disease Treatment Summary

Treatment Tables

Readers should be aware that because of rapid changes in both state and national laws and regulations governing horticultural chemicals, products in the following tables may or may not be available in any particular state or country. The products listed are known to be effective against the indicated diseases but are not necessarily available or certified for use with orchids. After a disease has been identified, growers are cautioned to check with local agriculture agents, nurseries, commercial growers, or garden supply stores to determine currently approved treatments in their area.

Chemical Type	Chemical Name—Active Ingredient	Product Names	Product Applications
Treatment categories used in Section III—Identifying and Treating Plant Problems	The primary active ingredient. Information on chemical composition is followed by more general chemical names.	Generic and brand-name products containing the primary active ingredient.	General information on usage.
Algicide, bactericide, fungicide-1	dimethyl benzyl ammonium chlorides *or* dimethylethyl-benzyl ammonium chlorides	Consan Consan 20 Physan 20 RD-20 Triconsan	A broad-spectrum bactericide and fungicide used to treat *Erwinia*, *Phytophthora*, *Pseudomonas*, and *Pythium* infections. Used as a disinfectant, it helps prevent the spread of all pathogens, including viral pathogens.
Bactericide-1	4-(dimethylamino)-1,4,4a,5,5a-6,11,12-octahydro-3, 5,6,10,12,12a-hexahydroxy-6-methyl-1,11-dioxo-2-naphthacenecarboxamide	Oxytetracycline Terramycin	Available as a dust or a wettable powder, it is an antibiotic used specifically to treat bacterial infections caused by *Erwinia* and *Pseudomonas*.
Bactericide-2	o-2-deoxy-2-(methylamino)-a-L-glucopyranosyl-(1d)-o-5-deoxy-3-C-formyl-a-L-lyxofuranosyl-(1d4)-N, N²-bis (ammoniomethyl)-a-streptamine *or* cycloheximide *or* streptomycin sulfate, sometimes combined with oxytetracycline (terramycin)	Agrimycin Agristrep Phytomycin Streptomycin	Available as a dust or a wettable powder, it is an antibiotic used specifically to treat bacterial infections caused by *Erwinia* and *Pseudomonas*.
Bactericide, fungicide, nematocide-1	tetrachloroisophthalonitrile	Bravo Chlorothalonil Ole Daconil Exotherm-Termil Funginil	A broad-spectrum fungicide, available as a liquid or a wettable powder, that is effective against *Botrytis* infections.
Disinfectant-1	8-quinolinol	8-hydroxyquinoline	Used to sterilize pots, tools, benches, and the growing area.

Disease Treatment Summary

Chemical Type	Chemical Name—Active Ingredient	Product Names	Product Applications
Disinfectant-2	8-quinolinol sulfate *or* oxyquinoline sulfate	8-Hydroxyquinoline sulfate 8-Quinol sulfate Chinosol Quinosol	Used to treat petal blights and *Erwinia, Phytophthora, Pseudomonas, Pythium,* and *Sclerotium* infections.
Disinfectant-3	37% formaldehyde solution	Formaldehyde Formalin Karsan Steriform	Used to sterilize pots, tools, benches, and the growing area.
Disinfectant-4	oxyquinolinol benzoate *or* quinolinol benzoate	8-Hydroxyquinoline benzoate Wilson's Anti-Damp	Used to treat *Colletotrichum, Erwinia,* and *Glomerella* species and to counteract *Miltonia* scorch.
Disinfectant-5	sodium hypochlorite	Clorox Purex	Common household bleach, used to sterilize pots, tools, benches, and the growing area.
Fungicide-1	1,2-ethanediylbis[carbamo-dithioato](2-)manganese *or* manebmanganese ethylene bisdithio carbamate with manganese or zinc ions	Dithane M-22 Dithane M-45 Fore Mancozeb Maneb Tersan LSR Dithane S-31 Manzate	Available as a dust, liquid, or wettable powder, these compounds are used to treat blight, *Diplodia* leaf spot, *Fusarium, Phythphthora,* rust, and *Septoria* leaf spot. Brand names at the left include varying amounts of Maneb plus various other substances such as zinc, nickel sulfate, or manganese.
Fungicide-2	zinc ethylene bisdithiocarbamate	Zineb	Available as a dust or a wettable powder, these compounds have a long residual action. They are used to treat *Cercospora, Colletotrichum,* fungi species, *Fusarium, Gloeosporium, Phytophthora, Rhizoctonia, Sclerotium,* and *Septoria.*

Disease Treatment Summary

Chemical Type	Chemical Name—Active Ingredient	Product Names	Product Applications
Fungicide-3	1,4,-dichloro-2,5-dimethoxybenzene or tetramethylthiuram disulfide or thiram or thiram plus cadmium chloride or thiram plus phenyl mercuric acetate	Cad-Treto Chloroneb Panoram 75 Scutl Spotreto Terraneb SP Tersan SP Thimer Thiram Thiramed	Available as a dust or a wettable powder, these compounds are used to treat *Phytophthora*.
Fungicide-4	3-(3,5-dichlorophenyl)-5-ethenyl-5-methyl-2,4-oxazolidinedione	Ornalin Ronilan Vinclozolin 50% WP	Available as a wettable powder, it is used to control *Botrytis*.
Fungicide-5	3-(3,5-dichlorophenyl)-N-(1-methyl-ethyl)-2,4-dioxo-1-imidzolidine-carboxamide	Chipco 26019 Eouc 30 Iprodione Roval 50W	Effective as a preventative for *Diplodia*, other dark-spored fungi, and *Rhizoctonia*. The compound reportedly offers particularly dependable protection when rotated with Systemic fungicide-1.
Fungicide-6	3a,4,7,7a-tetrahydro-2-[(1,1,2,2-tetra-chloroethyl)thiol]-1H-isoin-dole-1,3(2H)-dione	Capatafol Difolatan	Available as a liquid. No information on specific applications.
Fungicide-7	3a,4,7,7a-tetrahydro-2-[(trichloromethyl)thiol]-1H-isoin-dole-1,3(2H)-dione or N-[(trichloromethyl)thiol]-4-cyclohexene-1,2,dicarboxamide	Captan Orthocide	A broad-spectrum fungicide, available as a liquid, dust, or wettable powder, used to treat *Alternaria*, black spot, *Botrytis*, *Cercospora*, *Colletotrichum*, *Curvularia*, *Gloeosporium*, leaf spot, *Phytophthora*, rust, *Sphenospora*, *Uredo*, and perhaps other infections.
Fungicide-8	3-[2-(3,5-dimethyl-2-oxocyclohexyl)-2-hydroxyethyl]glutarimide	Actidione Cycloheximide	Used to treat *Fusarium*.
Fungicide-9	5-ethoxy-3-trichloromethyl-1,2,4-thiadiazole or etridiazole	Terrazole Truban ETAT Truban 30WP Etridiazole	A wettable powder that should be applied as a drench. This fungicide is best used for preventing rather than treating infections. It is reported to be effective against black rot diseases such as damping off, or infections caused by *Phytophthora* and *Pythium*. One application is effective for 12 weeks.

Disease Treatment Summary

Chemical Type	Chemical Name—Active Ingredient	Product Names	Product Applications
Fungicide-10	methylmercury dicyandiamide	Morosodren	Used to treat *Phytophthora*.
Fungicide-11	N-alkyl dimethyl benzyl and ethyl ammonium chlorides *or* N-alkyl methyl isoquinolinium chlorides	Shield 10WP	Used as a drench to treat *Ptychogaster* and other molds that occur in the medium.
Fungicide-12	sodium [4-(dimethylamino) phenyl] diazene sulfonate	Fenaminosulf Lesan	Used to treat *Phytophthora* and *Pythium*, this compound is more effective against the latter. It deteriorates rapidly in sunlight and should be used immediately after mixing. After the roots are drenched, it should be watered in.
Fungicide-13	pentachloronitrobenzene	PCNB Terraclor Turfcide	Available as a liquid, dust, or wettable powder, this compound should be used as a drench. It is reported to be an effective treatment for *Rhizoctonia* and *Sclerotium*. Only one application is required.
Fungicide-14	tetrachloroisophthalonitrile	Bravo Chlorothalonil	Available as a liquid or a wettable powder. No information on specific applications.
Fungicide-15	tris (dimethylcarbamodithoato-S,S,') iron *or* ferric dimethyl dithiocarbamate	Carbamate WDG Ferbam	Available in several forms, this compound is used to treat *Cercospora*, *Coleosporium*, *Colletotrichum*, *Fusarium*, *Gloeosporium*, *Rhizoctonia*, rust, *Sphenospora*, *Uredo*, and probably other infections.
Fungicide, germicide-1	cupric hydroxide *or* cupric sulfate + lime *or* micronized tribasic copper sulfate *or* cuprous oxide	Bordeaux Mix Champ Kocide 101 Microcop Nordox OrthoCop-53	Copper compounds are available as water suspensions or dusts, since fixed copper is insoluble. Copper is used to treat *Erwinia*, *Phytophthora*, and *Pseudomonas* infections, but it is toxic to some orchids and should be used cautiously. Copper-based compounds should never be mixed with other chemicals. Most copper compounds require repeat applications at 7–10 day intervals.

Disease Treatment Summary

Chemical Type	Chemical Name—Active Ingredient	Product Names	Product Applications
Fungicide, germicide-2	o-phenylphenol, sodium salt tetrahydrate *or* sodium 2-hydroxy diphenyl *or* sodium orthophenylphenate *ot* sodium o-phenylphenate	Dowicide A Natriphene Stopmold B	Available as a liquid, it is used as a drench or soak. This is a stable chemical with short residual effects. Compatible with most water-soluble chemicals, it is effective in treating bacterial infections such as *Miltonia* scorch, or those caused by *Erwinia* and *Pseudomonas*. It is used to treat *Phytophthora*, *Pythium*, and other fungal diseases such as *Colletotrichum*, *Rhizoctonia*, and *Sclerotium*.
Systemic fungicide-1	methyl-1-(butylcarbamoyl)-2-benzimi-dazolecarbamate.	Benlate Benomyl Tersan 1991	A broad-spectrum fungicide effective against most orchid diseases except those caused by *Pythium ultimum*, *Phytophthora cactorum*, and bacteria. It both cures and prevents infections of black spot, *Botrytis*, *Cercospora*, *Colletotrichum*, *Curvularia*, *Fusarium*, *Gloeodes*, *Gloeosporium*, *Guignardia*, *Microthyriella*, *Phyllostictina*, *Rhizoctonia*, *Septoria*, and others. Treatments must be repeated at 10–14 day intervals until the disease is controlled.
Systemic fungicide-2	1-(4-chlorophenyxy)-3,3 dimethyl-1-(1H-1,2,4-triazol-1-yl)-2 butanone	Bayleton 50WP Tridimefon	Recommended as a control for powdery mildew. Applied as a spray, the chemical enters plants through the foliage.
Systemic fungicide-3	15% 5-ethoxy-3-(trichloromethyl)-1,2,4-thiadiazole plus 25% dimethyl 4,4'-0-phenylene bis (3-thicallophanate)	Banrot (40WP)	Available as a wettable powder, this compound contains the active ingredient in Fungicide-9 together with a systemic fungicide. It is used to treat *Botrytis*, *Colletotrichum*, *Fusarium*, *Gloeosporium*, *Pythium*, *Phytophthora*, *Rhizoctonia*, *Sclerotinia*, and other infections.
Systemic fungicide-4	aluminum tris-o-ethyl phosphate *or* fosetyl aluminum	Aliette Fosetyl-A1	A plant-activated compound considered very safe for the environment, this fungicide reportedly improves or enhances plant resistance and is effective as both a preventative and curative for *Phytophthora* and *Pythium*. It is absorbed by both roots and leaves and moves both up and down through the plant.
Systemic fungicide-5	N-(2,6-dimethylphenyl)-N-(methoxyacetyl) alanine methyl ester	Metalaxyl Ridomil Subdue 2E Apron FL Apron 25W	Supplied as a liquid, this compound should be applied as a drench. Although it is absorbed by both roots and leaves, it only moves up the plant. It is effective as both preventative and curative for *Phytophthora* and *Pythium*.

Disease Treatment Summary

Chemical Type	Chemical Name—Active Ingredient	Product Names	Product Applications
Systemic fungicide-6	N,N-[1,4-piperazinediyl bis (2,2,2-trichloroethylidene)]-bis(formamide)	Cela W-524 Funginex Saprol Triforine	An effective treatment and systemic protectant against rust and other diseases, this compound should be applied as a spray, since plants take it up through the foliage.
Systemic fungicide-7	propamocarb hydrochloride	Banol	Effective as both a curative and preventative for *Phytophthora* and *Pythium*.
Systemic fungicide-8	thiophanate-methyl, (dimethyl [(1,2-phenylene) bis (iminocarbonothioyl)] bis [carbamate]), with zinc++ ions and manganese++ ethylenebis dithiocarbamate	Zyban	A contact and systemic fungicide that should be applied as a foliar spray. It is reportedly effective against *Alternaria*, *Botrytis*, *Cercospora*, *Colletotrichum*, *Curvularia*, *Fusarium*, *Gloeosporium*, *Rhizoctonia*, and *Septoria*.
Systemic fungicide-9	2-(4-thiazolyl) benzimidazole, hypophosphite salt	Arbotect 20-S Mertect 340-F thiabendazole	A systemic fungicide in the same family of chemicals as Benlate. Used as a protectant against many storage rot fungi and leaf spotting diseases.
Systemic fungicide-10	Dimethyl 4,4-0-phenylene bis (3-thioallophanate)	Fungo Duosan Topsin M thiophanate methyl	A systemic fungicide in the same family of chemicals as Benlate.
Systemic fungicide-11	N/A.	Bromosan Clearys 3336 Spot Klean thiophanate	A systemic fungicide in the same family of chemicals as Benlate.
Systemic fungicide-12	2,3-dihydro-5-carboxanilid-6-methyl-1,4-oxathiin-4,4-dioxide	Oxycarboxin Plantvax	Used as a foliar application for control of rusts.

WARNING: READ AND FOLLOW THE INSTRUCTIONS ON THE LABEL

Growers are warned that chemicals may damage plants if applied in a manner or to a plant not specifically recommended on the label. Chemicals may alter a plant's sensitivity to light or cause damage that results in deformed new growths. See the discussion under "General Rules for Chemical Use" in the preceding pages.

Pests

General Information

Greenhouse pests usually fall into one of 2 groups: the phylum *Arthropoda*, which includes insects, mites, and millipedes, and the phylum *Mollusca*, which includes slugs and snails. Insects may be the oldest, most numerous creatures on earth, and the vast majority are either beneficial or harmless to plants.

The few insects that pose problems in horticulture often cause considerable damage by chewing and sucking. In addition to direct injury, insects play a role in transferring disease pathogens. There is evidence that insects contribute to the spread of approximately 150 viral diseases, 25 fungal diseases, and 15 or more bacterial diseases.

Overall health is a plant's first line of defense against pests. Most gardeners have seen weak plants devastated by attack while nearby healthy plants were completely unaffected. Our understanding of the means by which healthy plants protect themselves from insects and diseases is currently quite limited. Scientists have learned that plant varieties which are resistant to certain insects or diseases naturally produce more chemicals than those which are affected. Recent research further indicates that forest trees rapidly increase their production of chemical defenses when a nearby tree is under attack. While a similar phenomenon has not been confirmed for orchids, it is a fascinating possibility.

Protective, preventive measures are the grower's second line of defense against pests. When plants are growing in an enclosed area, all vents and openings should be screened. In addition, new plants should be inspected and sprayed before they are introduced into the growing area. Plants that are summered outside should be carefully sprayed before they are reintroduced into the enclosed growing area.

An option available to greenhouse owners is using positive pressure (fans that blow air in) rather than negative pressure (fans that pull air out). Growers with positive-pressure greenhouses experience dramatically fewer problems with insects and hypothesize that the pests are destroyed as they are blown through the fan. Even in a positive-pressure greenhouse, however, the safest approach is to screen the air vents.

Applying chemicals should be the last pest-control option considered by a grower. Pesticide applications should be carefully timed to coincide with the appropriate phase of the insect's life-cycle. The only effective time to spray for armored scale, for example, is when eggs are hatching in spring. One way to monitor insect populations is to install and periodically inspect sticky strips or yellow boards coated with a sticky substance such as Stick-em or Tangle-foot. The panels may be cleaned with turpentine and recoated as needed. The time to apply control sprays is just as insect populations begin to increase.

Beneficial insects are sometimes used to help keep pest populations under control in the garden. Ladybugs and praying mantises are familiar predatory insects, and parasitic insects may be available locally. Beneficial insects should not be released until after the pest population begins to increase, or they will simply move on to other gardens where food is available. Using beneficial insects is less practical in a greenhouse, since most orchid growers prefer to control pests before their numbers increase to this level.

Small frogs are very effective at controlling insects. Growers can encourage green frogs to take up residence by providing places where the frogs are safe during the day. Hiding places must be shaded, moist, and protected. A pot turned upside down and buried with the drainage holes above the surface of the ground is an ideal frog-house.

Local agricultural agents are an excellent source of information regarding local pest populations, recommended pesticides, and effective timing of pest-control measures.

Adding a spreader-sticker or wetting agent often increases the effectiveness of a spray. Follow the label directions. An alternative to a commercial spreader-sticker is liquid dishwashing soap (not detergent) mixed at ½ tsp. per gal. (2.5 ml per 3.8 liters) of water.

Pesticides are classified as either botanical or synthetic, indicating whether they are derived from plants or manmade. Regardless of their source, pesticides should be used cautiously and conservatively. Even natural pesticides are potent chemical substances that are as devastating to beneficial insects as they are to pests.

Botanical Pesticides

Botanical pesticides are natural pesticidal products which often act rapidly but tend to have a short life. Because of their short life, they are generally considered safer to use than synthetic pesticides. Unlike many of the latter, botanical pesticides are not stored in the tissue of plants, so they are potentially less harmful to the environment.

Insecticidal soap is considered the least toxic form of insect control. A special formulation of fatty acids, it is effective against aphids, mealybugs, mites, scale, thrips, and whiteflies. Some formulations include pyrethrum. Orchid growers commonly use insecticidal soaps successfully.

The following botanical insecticides are powerful natural chemicals that should be used carefully. The general rules for using chemicals included in Section III of this Appendix, "Using Chemicals Safely," also apply to the use of botanical insecticides.

Pyrethrum, derived from *Chrysanthemum cinerariaefolium*, is a contact insecticide that kills rapidly by paralyzing insects. It is available as a dust. Pyrethrum is considered a safe insecticide for people and other warm-blooded animals, but the dust should not be inhaled. Cats are sometimes sensitive to pyrethrum, and it is toxic to fish. Synthetic or concentrated pyrethrum, shown on the label as "pyrethrin," is usually formulated as a liquid and is available under a variety of brand names. It is effective against aphids, beetles, mealybugs, exposed thrips, mites, and whiteflies. Orchid growers commonly use it successfully.

Rotenone is another strong pesticide derived from plants, including the roots of *Tephrosia virginiana* (a weed commonly called devil's shoe string), which contain 5% rotenone. This chemical works as a slow-acting poison, and a 1% solution should kill any insect. Rotenone is often adulterated with other chemicals, however, so read the label. It also has a short period of effectiveness with little residual effect. Pyrethrum and rotenone, the most frequently used botanicals, are often combined to form a strong, effective, short-lived insecticide which is considered safe for warm-blooded animals. Rotenone should not be inhaled, and it is extremely toxic to fish. Orchid growers commonly use it successfully.

Ryania and *Sabadilla* are less commonly available botanicals. Ryania is usually sold as a dust, which is sometimes mixed with water for spraying. It is a mildly alkaline insecticide known to be effective against many moths, borers, larvae, and other insects. Information regarding its effect on orchids is not available. Sabadilla, also sold as a dust, is derived from a lily originating in Mexico and South America. It is also effective against many pest larvae as well as aphids and some beetles.

Nicotine is derived from *Nicotiana tabacum* (commonly known as tobacco). It kills by fumes and on contact. Unlike most botanicals, however, it is extremely toxic to warm-blooded animals, including people and pets. It should be used with great caution. Nicotine is available commercially as a dust or in a liquid formulation called nicotine sulfate. In contrast to many synthetic compounds, it does not cause discoloration when sprayed directly on blossoms, and it is used by many orchid growers. No insect has ever developed a tolerance or immunity to nicotine.

Nicotine pesticide solutions were originally made by soaking tobacco leaves in water. Orchid growers thinking of preparing their own nicotine solution should remember that one of the viral diseases which affects orchids is tobacco mosaic-orchid strain (TMV-O). While orchids are not a host for the form of tobacco mosaic virus that affects tobacco, viruses do mutate, and there is no point in risking contamination.

Veratrum or *false hellebore*, also called skunk cabbage or Indian poke, is derived from several species of *Veratrum*. The roots of all plants in this genus are extremely poisonous. All parts of the plant known as Indian poke (*V. viride*) are also poisonous. *Veratrum* is applied to garden plants as a spray—0.5 oz. (15 ml) of hellebore dissolved in 1 gal. (3.8 liters) of water. Information regarding its effect on orchids is not available. It is a stomach poison that is effective against many chewing insects such as beetles, caterpillars, grasshoppers, and sawflies.

Wormwood tea, made from the leaves of *Artemesia* species, is sometimes used as a pesticide and also serves as a repellent for pests such as flea beetles and butterflies. Information regarding its effect on orchids is not available. (Note that *A. absinthium* should not be used as a companion plant since it also produces a growth retardant which inhibits the growth of nearby plants.)

Synthetic Pesticides

Synthetic pesticides are chemical compounds made by man. They are sometimes designed to resemble a botanical. Synthetic chemicals are readily available, easy to use, and specifically labeled for approved uses. They are sometimes very selective, often particularly effective, and frequently long-lasting, but many are considered potentially more dangerous than botanicals. Systemic insecticides should not be used with orchids. They can cause severe damage, particularly to soft-leaved orchids.

Except for synthetic baits, such as those used for slugs and snails, we have found that botanical insecticides are as effective as synthetics, and we prefer to use pesticides with the shorter life of these natural chemicals.

Laws concerning the use and registration of synthetic insecticides vary enormously from region to region. Consequently, we do not recommend specific chemicals. Consult a local nursery or agricultural agent for information on specific synthetic insecticides.

List of Pests

The most common pests affecting orchids—pests which occur worldwide—are listed below. A summary of pests and treatment information follows this list.

Ants

DESCRIPTION: Ants, which belong to the family Formicidae, are usually 1/6–1/4 in. (4–6 mm) long and may be black, brown, or red. They have an enlarged abdomen and are true insects. During certain periods, female ants may have wings.

SYMPTOMS: Ants may cause spotting on flowers but do little direct damage. Apparent damage is usually caused by the insects exuding the honeydew to which the ants are attracted.

TREATMENT: Controlling aphids, mealybugs, or scale usually solves any problem with ants. Pyrethrum is reportedly effective. Honey placed strategically around the greenhouse lures ants from orchids.

MISCELLANEOUS NOTES: When ants are present, plants should be inspected for aphids, mealybugs, or scale.

Aphids

DESCRIPTION: Aphids that attack orchids belong to several genera in the suborder Homoptera. Also called plant lice, these small, soft-bodied, slow-moving pests are 0.05–0.35 in. (1–6 mm) long. They cause damage by sucking plant juices and, more importantly, by transmitting disease from plant to plant. Aphids are somewhat pear-shaped and may be pale green, yellow, brown, or black. They mature rapidly, so that numerous generations are produced each season.

SYMPTOMS: Aphids attack buds, flowers, or new growths, which may become stunted or distorted. Buds or flowers may fail to open. Leaves may have a sticky deposit.

TREATMENT: The simplest approach is to wash aphids from the plant with a jet of water. Botanical insecticides such as pyrethrum, rotenone, and nicotine are particularly effective against aphids. Applying a systemic fungicide may help prevent a fungal infection from developing in plant tissue damaged by aphids.

MISCELLANEOUS NOTES: Various aphid species occur in most parts of the world. The honeydew excreted by aphids and other sucking insects is very attractive to ants and is also an ideal medium for sooty mold. When sooty mold or ants are present, plants should be inspected for aphids, mealybugs, or scale.

Cockroaches

DESCRIPTION: Members of the order Orthoptera, cockroach species are usually flattened and broadly oval. They are active at night and hide in dark, moist places during the day.

SYMPTOMS: Cockroaches occasionally cause damage to orchid flowers, roots, and new growths.

TREATMENT: Treatment is usually unnecessary unless populations are very high. Reported botanical controls include pyrethrum and nicotine. One method of reducing populations is to trap the insects in the dark nooks where they customarily hide.

MISCELLANEOUS NOTES: The damage caused by cockroaches may be similar to that caused by grasshoppers.

Grasshoppers

DESCRIPTION: Grasshoppers or locusts are classified as *Acrididae* and belong to the order Orthoptera. Varied in size and color, they have narrow wings and strong, oversized back legs. While many species are capable of flying, these pests usually move by jumping. Grasshoppers are active during the day.

SYMPTOMS: These chewing insects can quickly destroy orchid leaves and roots. They are unlikely to be a problem unless conditions are dry and other vegetation is not available.

TREATMENT: Partially bury jars which contain a mixture of molasses and water. These will attract grasshoppers, which fall into the water and drown. Other controls are probably unnecessary unless the population increases rapidly and conditions are dry. *Veratrum* is the only botanical pesticide reported to be effective.

MISCELLANEOUS NOTES: The damage caused by grasshoppers may be similar to that caused by cockroaches.

Mealybugs

DESCRIPTION: Mealybugs belong to several genera in the suborder Homoptera and are closely related to scale. Mealybugs are 0.1–0.2 in. (2–5 mm) long and tend to live in colonies. They are most mobile when young but become sluggish as their bodies develop a characteristic waxy coating. These soft-bodied, sucking insects may be recognized by the soft, mealy covering, which makes them appear white and waxy.

SYMPTOMS: Severe infestations cause darkened or chlorotic areas on the leaves. Plants appear unhealthy, and symptoms may be more obvious than the insects themselves. Plant damage is similar to that caused by scale.

TREATMENT: Mealybugs need constant attention, as many generations are produced each year. Mealybugs may attack any part of the plant, but they tend to stay tucked away at the junction of the leaf and stem. Old leaf and pseudobulb sheaths should be removed regularly.

Treatments with insecticidal soap, nicotine, or a cotton swab dipped in soapy water, rubbing alcohol, kerosene, or methylated spirits (turpentine, paint thinner, or mineral spirits) dissolve the waxy covering that normally protects the insect. It is difficult to control mealybugs effectively by spraying, since their waxy covering tends to repel liquids. Mixing a spreader sticker or wetting agent with the insecticide solution helps it to penetrate the waxy covering and remain in place long enough to be effective. The underside of leaves should be thoroughly coated with the spray. Repeat applications may be necessary to control overlapping generations.

MISCELLANEOUS NOTES: Various mealybug species occur in most parts of the world. Ants may signal a mealybug infestation since mealybugs deposit a sweet honeydew which attracts the ants. The honeydew is also an ideal medium for sooty mold. When sooty mold or ants are present, plants should be inspected for aphids, mealybugs, or scale.

Millipedes

DESCRIPTION: Commonly called thousand-legged worms, millipedes may have up to 400 legs. Classified as Diplopoda, they are hard-bodied and coil like a spring when disturbed. These pests may be brown, pinkish brown, or grey.

SYMPTOMS: Millipedes may occasionally damage orchid roots, though they feed primarily on dead plant material.

TREATMENT: Reduce watering. The presence of millipedes indicates that plants may need repotting. A nicotine drench is reportedly an effective control.

MISCELLANEOUS NOTES: Millipedes contribute to the breakdown of natural media. They prefer moist places and are unlikely to be a problem unless plants are overwatered. The greatest threat they pose to orchids is the possibility of transmitting fungal infection.

Mites

DESCRIPTION: Often called spider mites, these sucking insects are closely related to spiders, ticks, and scorpions and belong to the class Arachnida. They usually appear in spring during warm, dry weather. They multiply rapidly if left unchecked; at 60°F (16°C) new generations mature in approximately 3 weeks, while at 90°F (32°C) they mature in 6 days. Mites are red to brown, very small, and difficult to see without a hand lens.

SYMPTOMS: Damage to the upper surface of the leaves is often the first symptom of mite infestation. The affected area may be darkened or develop a silvery sheen that eventually becomes sunken and turns brown. The leaves may be streaked, stippled, or spotted due to loss of chlorophyll. Small webs may be present, and damaged leaves may drop prematurely.

TREATMENT: Insecticidal soap, pyrethrum, rotenone, nicotine, and commercial miticides are effective. To control mites, it is often necessary to make 6–8 applications repeated at intervals of 2–4 days. Treating once or twice is not enough to control the pest. Hosing off the plants washes away mites and breaks down their webs. Increasing humidity and lowering temperatures help prevent infestations. Applying a systemic fungicide may help prevent a fungal infection from developing in the damaged tissue.

MISCELLANEOUS NOTES: Various mite species occur in most parts of the world. Spider-mite damage is easily confused with *Cercospora* leaf spots. To check a plant for mites, rub a piece of white paper or cloth on the underside of the leaves. If it is streaked with red or brown, mites are present.

Orchid beetles

DESCRIPTION: These members of the genus *Xylosandrus* are classified as *Coleoptera*. They are also called black twig borers and dendrobium beetles. Mature beetles measure about 0.2–0.4 in. (4–10 mm) long. These chewing pests bore into plant tissue to lay their eggs, causing unusual swelling in *Dendrobium* canes and *Cattleya* pseudobulbs.

SYMPTOMS: Old pseudobulbs may be abnormally swollen with small, shot-sized holes. A yellow or chlorotic margin surrounds the infested area. *Dendrobium* are not normally killed by the insect, but rot often follows infestation of *Cattleya* pseudobulbs.

TREATMENT: Adult beetles are easily seen and may be picked off the plants; but they tend to fall off the leaf when they feel threatened, so it is best to hold a container under the leaf during inspection. Pyrethrum, rotenone, and nicotine are effective against mature beetles. If new growths become abnormally swollen, they should be removed and burned to prevent the maturation of hidden beetle larvae.

MISCELLANEOUS NOTES: If these pests become established in the growing area, they can be extremely difficult to control. Various species occur in most tropical areas. The beetles seldom appear in temperate areas unless they are imported along with a new plant. The canes and pseudobulbs of plants imported from infested areas should be carefully examined. Remove old leaf and pseudobulb sheaths to inspect for abnormal swelling, chlorotic areas, or small holes that may otherwise be hidden.

Orchid fly. See Wasps.

Scale

DESCRIPTION: Scale refers to several species of sucking insects belonging to various genera of the suborder Homoptera. Usually smaller than 0.1 in. (1–2 mm) in length, these insects attach to and feed on the underside of leaves and are often hidden under old leaf and pseudobulb sheaths.

Female armored scale secrete a waxy protective coating that is raised, nearly round, often with concentric ridges, and feels hard to the touch. Different species vary in color and may be brown, grey, reddish, white, or yellow. The males are usually smaller, with a protective shell that is often oval with ridges rather than concentric rings. Once the insects attach to a plant, they remain in the same location throughout their life.

Soft scale (such as mealybugs, which are listed separately) also damage by sucking. These insects are smaller than 0.2 in. (1–5 mm) in length. Some species are fully exposed, while others are protected by a soft, waxy covering.

SYMPTOMS: Severe infestations cause darkened or chlorotic areas to appear on the leaves. The leaves may yellow and drop prematurely. Plants appear unhealthy, and leaf symptoms, which are similar to those caused by mealybugs, may be more obvious than the insects themselves.

TREATMENT: Scale is best removed immediately. It may be scraped off or wiped away with a cotton swab soaked in methylated spirits (turpentine, paint thinner, or mineral spirits). The mature scale may be scrubbed off with a toothbrush dipped in any pesticide which will kill young scale in the crawler stage. When plants are inspected regularly, scale is unlikely to become a serious problem. Old leaf and flower sheaths should be removed and the exposed surfaces checked for scale and mealybugs. New plants should be carefully inspected before they are introduced into the growing area. If it is necessary to treat scale with chemicals, they should be applied just as the young hatch and begin to move from plant to plant (i.e., at the crawler stage). The underside of leaves must be carefully sprayed in order for the treatment to be effective. Repeat applications are usually necessary to control overlapping generations.

MISCELLANEOUS NOTES: Various scale species occur in most parts of the world. Ants may signal a scale infestation since these pests deposit a sweet honeydew of plant sap which attracts ants. The honeydew is also an ideal medium for sooty mold. When sooty mold or ants are present, plants should be inspected for aphids, mealybugs, or scale.

Slugs and snails

DESCRIPTION: These familiar chewing pests belonging to the phylum *Mollusca* may be grey, black, or brown, often with spots or stripes. Their soft bodies are usually 0.5–3 in. (13–76 mm) long. Snails are protected by a hard shell, but slugs do not have a protective covering. These pests can cause considerable damage, particularly to young seedlings and tender new growths.

SYMPTOMS: Slugs and snails leave holes and notches in the leaves and may chew off growing tips. Chewed areas may also appear on buds. These nocturnal pests travel on a layer of slime which they excrete to protect their undersides, and this trail is evidence of a potential problem.

TREATMENT: Chemical baits are commercially available. Growers who prefer not to use chemicals may bait slugs and snails with a saucer of beer. The pests are attracted to the beer, in which they drown. Nicotine dust or wormwood (*Artemesia* species) tea may offer effective control. The tea should be applied as a drench, though we have no knowledge of the effect wormwood may have on orchids. Slugs and snails can be difficult to eradicate from the growing area because they enter pots through the drainage holes and stay safely hidden in the damp medium. These pests are often found in damp debris and under rocks or boards. They can be attracted to pieces of cut potato where they can be crushed or killed with salt or ammonia (substances which should not be applied directly to plants).

MISCELLANEOUS NOTES: Various slug and snail species occur in most parts of the world. Slugs and snails frequently return each night to the same plant to feed—a characteristic growers can use to good advantage in setting out bait or hand-picking.

Sowbugs

DESCRIPTION: Sowbugs or pillbugs have hard, segmented, greyish brown bodies and roll into a ball when disturbed. They are classified as Crustacea.

SYMPTOMS: Sowbugs may occasionally damage orchid roots and leaves, though they feed primarily on dead plant material.

TREATMENT: Reduce watering. Many botanical pesticides, including pyrethrum, rotenone, and nicotine, control sowbugs if applied as a drench. The presence of sowbugs may indicate that plants need repotting.

MISCELLANEOUS NOTES: Sowbugs contribute to the breakdown of natural media. They prefer moist places and are unlikely to be a problem unless plants are overwatered.

Thrips

DESCRIPTION: A number of different insects of the order Thysanoptera are known as thrips, a term used for tiny, slender, winged insects measuring 0.02–0.20 in. (0.5–5.0 mm) long. They are usually dark brown or black, but at least one species is yellowish white. Most species produce 3–5 generations per year. These sucking insects are barely visible. They move rapidly when disturbed.

SYMPTOMS: Infested buds may not open properly, and flowers may be deformed. Flowers are damaged when the insects break through cell walls and suck the plant juices. Flowers may appear to have a virus-caused color break that is actually the result of thrip damage. Damaged flowers, buds, and new leaves appear pitted, stippled, silvery, or bleached. Some species feed on the underside of leaves, moving to the upper surface as populations increase. When damage is extensive, the leaves may wilt and die. The leaves may also be spotted with reddish black deposits of excrement. Some species lay eggs in the leaf cells, causing small blisters.

TREATMENT: Insecticidal soaps, pyrethrum, rotenone, and nicotine are very effective against exposed thrips, but because these pests often remain hidden, sprays frequently fail to reach them. Repeat applications are often necessary to control overlapping generations. Applying a systemic fungicide may help prevent a fungal infection from developing in damaged tissue.

MISCELLANEOUS NOTES: Various species of thrips occur in most parts of the world, particularly in warmer climates and in greenhouses. Flowers, beans, and fruit, particularly citrus, are common hosts. Thrips are especially bothersome in that they carry disease from plant to plant.

Wasps

DESCRIPTION: A chalcid wasp, of the order Hymenoptera, has transparent wings and lays its eggs in plant tissue. It is 0.1 in. (1.5–3.0 mm) long. Sometimes called the orchid fly, this insect is not a true fly.

SYMPTOMS: Pseudobulbs are enlarged or swollen, and old canes and pseudobulbs have an exit hole, usually near the base. The wasp pierces the plant tissue to lay its eggs. As the eggs mature, the larvae feed inside the canes and pseudobulbs, causing abnormal swelling. If the insect becomes established in the growing area, it can be extremely difficult to control.

TREATMENT: Pyrethrum, rotenone, and nicotine are effective controls for adult wasps, but killing larvae in the pseudobulb is more difficult. Swollen new growths should be removed and destroyed to prevent the larvae from maturing.

MISCELLANEOUS NOTES: Plant damage results when the larvae feed on the pseudobulb and cut their way out as they mature.

Whiteflies

DESCRIPTION: *Trialeurodes vaporariorum* is commonly known as the greenhouse whitefly. This mothlike sucking insect is tiny, usually less than $1/16$ in. (1.6 mm) long, with wings covered by a white, powdery substance.

SYMPTOMS: New growth may appear damaged or unhealthy. Whitefly attacks weaken the plant, making it more susceptible to disease. Fungal infections often invade plants where whiteflies have punctured the tissue.

TREATMENT: Insecticidal soap, pyrethrum, rotenone, and particularly nicotine are effective. Sprays repeated at 4-day intervals are necessary for control of overlapping generations. Applying a systemic fungicide may help prevent a secondary infection.

MISCELLANEOUS NOTES: The insect lays eggs on the underside of leaves. Initially yellow, the eggs become white or grey, which results in a chalky-looking spot. Many broods are produced each year. Various whitefly species occur in most parts of the world.

Orchid Pests Summary

Pests	Plant Symptoms	Miscellaneous Notes	Botanical Pesticides in order of increasing toxicity to humans
Ants	Damaged flowers	Honey placed strategically around the greenhouse lures ants from orchids.	Pyrethrum
Aphids	Buds or flowers that fail to open Distorted or stunted flowers, buds, or new leaves Sticky deposits on leaves	Aphids may be washed off flowers and foliage.	Insecticidal soap Pyrethrum Rotenone Nicotine
Cockroaches	Damaged flowers, roots, and new growths	These nocturnal pests may be controlled by trapping.	Pyrethrum Nicotine
Grasshoppers	Damaged roots and new growths	Grasshoppers may be baited with jars of molasses water.	Veratrum
Mealybugs	Chlorotic or darkened areas on leaves Sticky deposits on leaves	Mealybugs appear as a white, cottony-looking mass. Treat with compounds that dissolve the waxy protective covering. Repeat applications to control overlapping generations.	Insecticidal soap Nicotine
Millipedes	Damaged roots	Millipedes prefer moist places and may indicate that plants are overwatered or in need of repotting.	Nicotine
Mites	Darkened areas on leaves Leaves that are pitted, stippled, bleached, white, or silvery Sunken areas on leaves	Mites may be washed off foliage. Reducing temperatures and increasing humidity help prevent infestations. Mites are seldom visible, but minute webs may be evident. Sprays should be repeated at 2–4 day intervals 6–8 times.	Insecticidal soap Pyrethrum Rotenone
Orchid beetles	Swollen pseudobulbs with small, visible holes	Pesticides are effective only against adults. Abnormally swollen new growths indicate the presence of larvae. The growths should be removed and burned.	Pyrethrum Rotenone Nicotine
Scale	Chlorotic or darkened areas on leaves Leaves that appear yellow and drop prematurely Sticky deposits on leaves	These sucking insects attach to leaves and pseudobulbs. A cotton swab dipped in methylated spirits (paint thinner) may be used to remove scale. Sprays should be repeated to control overlapping generations.	Insecticidal soap Nicotine
Slugs and snails	Chewed areas on buds, leaves, young roots, and new growths	Slugs and snails are nocturnal, but shiny slime trails confirm their presence. They may be baited with beer or pieces of cut potato. Damp debris, rocks, and boards serve as hiding places. Commercial baits are available.	Nicotine dust Wormwood tea

Orchid Pests Summary

Pests	Plant Symptoms	Miscellaneous Notes	Botanical Pesticides in order of increasing toxicity to humans
Sowbugs	Damaged roots and leaves	Sowbugs prefer moist places and may indicate that plants are overwatered or in need of repotting.	Pyrethrum Rotenone Nicotine
Thrips	Blossoms with color break Buds that fail to open Deformed buds or flowers Flowers, buds, and new leaves that are stunted, pitted, stippled, or blistered Leaves that wilt and die prematurely Reddish black deposits of excrement on leaves	Thrips, which are barely visible, often hide deep in buds and may be difficult to eradicate. Sprays should be repeated to control overlapping generations.	Rotenone Nicotine
Wasps	Swollen pseudobulbs with small, visible holes	Pesticides are effective only against adults. Abnormally swollen new growths indicate the presence of larvae. The growths should be removed and burned.	Pyrethrum Rotenone Nicotine
Whiteflies	Chalky spots on the underside of leaves New growths that are damaged or unhealthy looking	The tiny, sucking insects are white and mothlike. Sprays should be repeated at 4-day intervals to control overlapping generations.	Insecticidal soap Pyrethrum Rotenone Nicotine

WARNING: READ AND FOLLOW THE INSTRUCTIONS ON THE LABEL.

Growers are warned that chemicals may damage plants if applied in a manner or to a plant not specifically recommended on the label. Chemicals may alter a plant's sensitivity to light or cause damage that results in deformed new growths. See the discussion under "General Rules for Chemical Use" in Section III.

Nutrients

General Information

Adequate nutrition is normally provided by the fertilizer applications recommended in the species listings throughout this volume. Nutrition is not a simple matter, however, since plants differ widely in their nutritional needs and the availability of different nutrients varies with pH. Though individual orchid species may have different nutrient requirements, these differences are often subtle and are seldom identified.

Essential plant nutrients are classified as either macronutrients or micronutrients. Macronutrients, required in relatively large amounts, include carbon (C), hydrogen (H), and oxygen (O), which are available directly from the atmosphere.

Other macronutrients needed in large quantities are

Nitrogen (N)
Phosphorus (P)
Potassium (K)

Also classified as macronutrients but needed in much smaller quantities are

Calcium (Ca)
Magnesium (Mg)
Sulfur (S)

Micronutrients, needed in minute quantities, include

Boron (B)
Chlorine (Cl)
Cobalt (Co)
Copper (Cu)
Iron (Fe)
Manganese (Mn)
Molybdenum (Mo)
Zinc (Zn)

Cultivated orchids are much more likely to suffer from an excess of nutrients than from a deficiency. Fertilizers and micronutrient supplements are readily available and easy to apply. The tendency to apply too much fertilizer must be avoided as diligently as the tendency to overwater. Recommended fertilizer type, strength, and frequency of application are discussed in Chapter 1 under the heading "Fertilizer."

Accidental overfertilization may be remedied by immediately flushing the pot several times to leach the fertilizer from the medium. This prevents the plants from absorbing the nutrients. Growers often include charcoal in the medium to help remedy slight to moderate overfertilization. Once a plant has absorbed the nutrients, nothing will draw the nutrients out of the plant. Repotting will prevent the plant from absorbing still more, but only time will tell whether the plant is able to survive.

Macronutrients are usually mobile in the plant, while most micronutrients are not. When nutrients are mobile in the plant, they are pulled from older growths and used for new growth anytime they are in short supply. Consequently, deficiencies of mobile nutrients show first in older leaves or mature growths. On the other hand, nutrients that are not mobile in the plant are locked up in older growths and cannot be further utilized by the plant. Deficiencies of these elements usually show first in the new leaves or growths.

Micronutrients are generally available from organic media in amounts adequate for orchids. The stored nutrients are released by the microbial action that breaks down the medium. Little work has been done on which micronutrients are available from different media. In addition to these naturally occurring micronutrients, many fertilizers contain micronutrients in varying amounts which may not be shown on the label. Many micronutrients are mutually antagonistic in such a way that an excess of one crowds out another and shows as a deficiency of the nutrient no longer available.

Brief descriptions of the various nutritional elements and symptoms of both excesses and deficiencies are given below to assist growers in determining and correcting possible nutritional problems. Although various plant species react differently to imbalances, most indicate an excess or deficiency of a particular nutrient with a variation of the symptoms given.

Research has shown that symptoms of micronutrient deficiencies, which might show in days or weeks in garden plants, usually do not occur for several months in orchids. Symptoms of excess are more common. High levels of micronutrients are toxic to all plants, but orchids are particularly sensitive. If a commercial micronutrient supplement is used, care must be taken to ensure that recommended levels are not exceeded. In fact, since orchids are very efficient at absorbing nutrients, it is a good practice to make 1 or 2 applications at ¼–½ the recommended strength. Toxicity is more likely if micronutrients are applied to any dry medium, but this is particularly true of dry rock wool. An excess of micronutrients is much worse for a plant than a deficiency.

List of Nutrients

For ease of reference, all nutrients are listed alphabetically below. When imbalances of several macro- or micronutrients could cause a plant symptom, macronutrients are most likely to be the problem. A summary of nutrients and problems related to nutrient balance follows this list.

Boron (B). Not mobile in the plant.

Boron, a micronutrient, is required as a catalyst in plant nutrition and metabolism, and it is essential for flowering and fruiting.

SYMPTOMS OF EXCESS: Excess boron causes blackening or death of tissue between veins. Boron in excessive amounts is very toxic to all plants, but it is especially harmful to orchids.

SYMPTOMS OF DEFICIENCY: Boron deficiency can lead to failure to set seed and to death of apical buds, terminal leaves, or growing tips. Plants are usually stunted, roots may be short, and stems may be black and dying. Boron is less available when the pH is above 7. Excess calcium can reduce a plant's ability to use boron.

MISCELLANEOUS NOTES: Boron balance is unlikely to be a problem in orchid cultivation, since adequate amounts of boron are normally available to plants from natural media, regularly applied natural fertilizers, or 1–2 applications each year of a micronutrient supplement. Boron is potentially so toxic that a laboratory tissue analysis should be performed and deficiency determined before boron is added.

Calcium (Ca). Somewhat mobile in the plant.

Calcium, a lesser macronutrient, is used to build cell walls, helps plants neutralize certain toxic acids produced as by-products of plant metabolism, and raises the pH of the medium.

SYMPTOMS OF EXCESS: Excess calcium interferes with magnesium absorption. Consequently, symptoms of magnesium deficiency such as chlorosis on middle or older leaves, light yellow discoloration between the veins or along the leaf margins, curled or cupped mature leaves, or leaf drop of middle and older leaves may indicate a calcium excess. High calcium levels may raise the pH to such a level that some micronutrients are unavailable to the plant.

SYMPTOMS OF DEFICIENCY: Deficiencies usually occur in spring and summer during periods of active growth. Possible symptoms range widely.

Poor growth or vigor are early symptoms; however, these symptoms can result from other cultural problems including root rot due to overwatering or deteriorated medium, high night temperatures, and inappropriate rest-period conditions. Plants should be unpotted and the roots examined for damage before fertilizer is increased.

New leaves may turn black at the tips. The affected area has an advancing yellow band. How far the discoloration extends down the leaf depends on the severity of the deficiency. Similar symptoms are caused by lack of water or excess fertilizing, so it is important to review watering and fertilizing practices before increasing nutrients.

Yellow leaves may turn brown and die prematurely.

Mature leaves may become cupped. A similar symptom may be caused by chemical damage.

Bud growth may be inhibited, or buds may develop improperly. Buds that yellow and drop prematurely usually indicate light or temperature problems rather than a nutrient imbalance, while deformed buds usually result from insect or chemical damage.

A calcium deficiency may cause death of root tips.

Excess potassium or magnesium may cause symptoms of calcium deficiency. Likewise, too much or too little water can cause symptoms of calcium deficiency in the growth which occurred during the period of water stress. At low pH, calcium binds with other elements and is unavailable to the plant.

MISCELLANEOUS NOTES: Calcium is seldom included in commercial fertilizers or micronutrient preparations because the calcium content in water varies so greatly that calcium levels may already be excessive in some hard-water areas. If calcium is needed, 1 Tbs. of dolomitic limestone may be added to each gal. (3.8 liters) of medium to provide both calcium and magnesium in the correct ratio. Dolomite lime has a natural balance of calcium and magnesium. Using garden lime, which contains no magnesium, can result in an excess of calcium which interferes with the plant's ability to absorb magnesium. Other sources of calcium include steamed bone meal and crushed shells. Growers in soft-water areas often add dolomitic limestone as a rapidly available form of calcium and crushed shells for a longer term calcium supply.

Chlorine (Cl). Not mobile in the plant.

Chlorine, a micronutrient, is required in extremely small amounts.

SYMPTOMS OF EXCESS: Excess chlorine shows as salt injury and may cause leaves to turn brown from the tip toward the base. Soft-leaved orchids are sometimes extremely sensitive to chlorinated water. If chlorinated water is the suspected cause of brown leaf tips, try storing water overnight in an open container, which allows the chlorine to dissipate before the water is applied to sensitive plants.

SYMPTOMS OF DEFICIENCY: Leaves become bronze then chlorotic and finally die. Wilted leaf tips that do not become erect when watered usually indicate insufficient chlorine. A deficiency may also cause deformed roots. Chlorine deficiency is very unlikely, since chlorine is normally available in adequate quantities from natural media or from the water supply. A laboratory tissue analysis should be performed before chlorine is added.

MISCELLANEOUS NOTES: Chlorine balance is unlikely to be a problem in orchid cultivation.

Cobalt (Co). Degree of mobility is not known.

Only recently established as a necessary micronutrient, cobalt is required for nitrogen fixation.

SYMPTOMS OF EXCESS: N/A.

SYMPTOMS OF DEFICIENCY: Cobalt deficiency may cause chlorosis in older leaves or red or purple coloring on the leaves. Excess phosphorus or potassium may interfere with cobalt availability.

MISCELLANEOUS NOTES: Cobalt balance is unlikely to be a problem in orchid cultivation. Cobalt should be added only as part of a micronutrient supplement.

Copper (Cu). Not mobile in the plant.

Copper, a micronutrient, is essential for plant growth and serves as a catalyst in plant respiration and the utilization of iron.

SYMPTOMS OF EXCESS: Excess copper may be toxic to orchids. It often shows as symptoms of iron deficiency, such as yellow to white mottling on new leaves with green veins. The condition may occur at low pH levels.

SYMPTOMS OF DEFICIENCY: New growths may be small and mis-shapen. Terminal shoots may wilt, and leaf color may be faded. Excess potassium interferes with copper utilization, causing symptoms of copper deficiency.

MISCELLANEOUS NOTES: Copper balance is unlikely to be a problem in orchid cultivation. Copper should be applied only as part of a micronutrient supplement, as it can be highly toxic to orchids. When the pH is above 7, copper is less available to the plant.

Iron (Fe). Not mobile in the plant.

Iron, a micronutrient, is used in chlorophyll and carbohydrate production.

SYMPTOMS OF EXCESS: Excess iron is rarely a problem in cultivated plants. Research indicates that excess iron is particularly harmful to orchids, but no information on symptoms is available.

SYMPTOMS OF DEFICIENCY: Interveinal chlorosis (yellowing) usually occurs in new leaves. If the deficiency continues, the yellow tissue may become white. Brown spots on the leaves, which may indicate iron deficiency, are more likely to be caused by fungal infection or insect damage. Iron deficiencies may occur, even in a natural medium, if oxygen is deficient or if the pH is 7 or greater.

MISCELLANEOUS NOTES: Iron balance is unlikely to be a problem in orchid cultivation. Iron is pH sensitive and is more likely to be deficient at extremely high or low pH levels. It is normally available to the plant in sufficient amounts from natural media. Orchids are known to be extremely sensitive to excess iron. Since iron is available in many fertilizers and commercial micronutrient supplements, additional iron should be applied only if a tissue analysis has determined a deficiency.

Magnesium (Mg). Mobile in the plant.

Magnesium, a lesser macronutrient, is necessary for the production of chlorophyll. In addition, it aids in protein formation, corrects plant pH, and is necessary to the plant's utilization of other nutrients.

SYMPTOMS OF EXCESS: Excess magnesium interferes with calcium uptake, so plants may show signs of calcium deficiency.

SYMPTOMS OF DEFICIENCY: Cupped leaves, reduction in growth, and marginal or interveinal chlorosis (yellow along leaf edges or between veins) are symptoms of deficiency in some species. Deficiencies usually show in the middle or older leaves. If the local water supply is high in calcium but low in magnesium, plants may benefit from increased magnesium.

MISCELLANEOUS NOTES: Like calcium, magnesium is seldom included in commercial fertilizers. In addition, it is easily leached from the medium. Magnesium may be applied alone in the form of Epsom salts, mixed at the rate of 1 tsp. per gal. of water (1 tsp. per 3.8 liters), every few weeks during periods of active growth. Adding 1 Tbs. of dolomitic limestone to each gal. (3.8 liters) of medium provides both calcium and magnesium in the correct ratio. Dolomite lime has a calcium to magnesium ratio of 62 to 38. At very low pH levels, plants are unable to use magnesium.

Manganese (Mn). Not mobile in the plant.

Manganese, a micronutrient, is necessary as a catalyst in plant nutrition and influences growth and maturation.

SYMPTOMS OF EXCESS: An excess of manganese causes reduced growth and brown spotting on the leaves. An excess usually occurs under acid conditions (low pH). It may show as symptoms of iron deficiency, since too much manganese can interfere with iron uptake.

SYMPTOMS OF DEFICIENCY: Manganese deficiency causes interveinal chlorosis of new leaves. The yellowing occurs between green veins. Later, the discolored areas become brown, producing a checked or mottled effect. Stems may be yellowish green. Symptoms of manganese deficiency can be caused by excess potassium. Plants are less able to use manganese when the pH is above 7.

MISCELLANEOUS NOTES: Manganese balance is unlikely to be a problem in orchid cultivation. Manganese is seldom deficient in orchids grown in organic media, and growers using inorganic media can provide adequate supplies with a micronutrient supplement. Extremely high or low pH levels may cause poor manganese utilization.

Molybdenum (Mo). Somewhat mobile in the plant.

Molybdenum, a micronutrient, is normally considered a pollutant, but plants need it in very small amounts in order to utilize nitrogen.

SYMPTOMS OF EXCESS: N/A.

SYMPTOMS OF DEFICIENCY: Molybdenum deficiency may cause pale yellow interveinal chlorosis on older leaves. Leaves may be twisted or fail to expand. Plants are seldom deficient in molybdenum unless the pH is below 5.2.

MISCELLANEOUS NOTES: Molybdenum balance is unlikely to be a problem in orchid cultivation. A laboratory tissue analysis should be performed and deficiency determined before molybdenum is added.

Nitrogen (N). Mobile in the plant.

Nitrogen, a macronutrient, is directly used in the growth of green, leafy portions of the plant. Plants with an appropriate supply are sturdy and mature rapidly.

SYMPTOMS OF EXCESS: When nitrogen levels are too high, new growth is weak, spindly, and dark green. It may also be brittle, especially when temperatures are high. An imbalance of nitrogen and potassium is a possible cause of dark green leaves, but nutrient imbalances are unlikely if a balanced fertilizer is used at the recommended frequency. Excess nitrogen combined with low light can cause leaf curl in some plants, as can any chemical injury. Leaves may turn black when nitrogen is grossly excessive. Exceedingly low temperatures may produce a similar plant response.

Excess nitrogen results in soft, rapid growth that is more susceptible to disease. In agriculture, high nitrogen with moderate levels of phosphate is known to increase many plants' susceptibility to fungal, bacterial, and mosaic diseases. High nitrogen may be one of the reasons viral diseases are found in cultivated orchids, while they are seldom found in plants growing in the wild.

SYMPTOMS OF DEFICIENCY: Inadequate nitrogen results in reduced growth, poor vigor, and yellowing (chlorosis) of the older growth. Low light or excess moisture are other possible causes. Red or purple coloring may intensify in the leaves of some plants. A different fertilizer mix should be considered since nitrogen is seldom deficient when a balanced fertilizer is applied regularly. An excess of phosphorus or potassium may cause symptoms of nitrogen deficiency.

MISCELLANEOUS NOTES: The best nitrogen to potassium (N/K) ratio is 1/1 unless a medium requiring high nitrogen is used. Orchids need much less nitrogen than most plants, and fertilizers should normally be diluted to $1/4$–$1/2$ the strength recommended for garden plants. Growers report good success with most orchids when an even weaker solution is applied every watering.

Phosphorus (P). Mobile in the plant.

Phosphorus, a macronutrient, is needed for cell division, is essential to root growth, and is particularly important in producing flowers, fruit, and seed.

SYMPTOMS OF EXCESS: Excess phosphorus prevents plants from taking up micronutrients, resulting in deficiencies of zinc, iron, or cobalt. It may also cause symptoms of nitrogen deficiency. Phosphorus is unlikely to be excessive if a balanced fertilizer is used regularly.

SYMPTOMS OF DEFICIENCY: Common plant responses to phosphorus deficiency are reduced growth, stunted plants with dark green leaves, and red to purple coloring along leaf veins. The leaves of some plants develop intensified color, while the leaves of other plants become brown or purple. Reddish or purplish leaves also may be caused by high light.

Thin stems and spindly growth may be caused by phosphorus deficiency but usually result from low light levels.

Older leaves may drop prematurely. Unless a high-nitrogen fertilizer is used exclusively, light levels are probably the problem.

Phosphorus deficiency may result in reduced flowering, but this symptom is more likely to result from low light levels, incorrect photoperiods, insufficient rest, or inappropriate temperatures.

A deficiency seldom occurs if a balanced fertilizer is used at the recommended frequency.

MISCELLANEOUS NOTES: Phosphorus is especially critical for seedlings and young or actively growing plants. A periodic application of high-phosphorus fertilizer is sometimes suggested for young plants, and many growers use a high phosphate fertilizer near the end of the growing season to promote blooming the following year. Phosphorus leaches easily from a medium which is high in bark or peat. In acid (low pH) conditions, it combines with other elements and is unavailable to the plant. In alkaline conditions (pH above 7), phosphorus binds with other elements, forming compounds which the plant cannot use. High levels of phosphorus interfere with micronutrient and nitrogen absorption.

Potassium (K). Mobile in the plant.

Potassium, a macronutrient, is necessary for the production of plant sugars. It also increases resistance to disease, reduces dehydration during dry weather, increases resistance to cold, and helps to counteract the effects of excess nitrogen.

SYMPTOMS OF EXCESS: Excess potassium shows as a deficiency of other nutrients (including nitrogen, magnesium, calcium, iron, zinc, copper, manganese, and cobalt) because it interferes with a plant's ability to use those nutrients.

SYMPTOMS OF DEFICIENCY: Common symptoms of potassium deficiency are reduced growth, dwarfed plants, and shortened internodes. Other symptoms include chlorosis, burned leaf margins, and necrotic or dead spots on the leaf. Leaves may be wrinkled between the veins.

MISCELLANEOUS NOTES: The nitrogen/potassium balance is important. High nitrogen/low potassium favors vegetative growth; low nitrogen/high potassium promotes reproductive (flowering and fruiting) growth.

Potassium is seldom deficient if a balanced fertilizer is applied at the recommended strength and frequency. If other symptoms of macronutrient deficiency are present, fertilizer should be applied more frequently. Increasing the frequency of application is preferable to increasing strength. If a high nitrogen fertilizer has been used exclusively, a more balanced formula should be considered.

Sulfur (S). Not mobile in the plant.

Sulfur, a micronutrient, helps plants to produce chlorophyll.

SYMPTOMS OF EXCESS: Excess sulfur is rarely a problem. Since sulfur is acidifying, an excess would probably show as micronutrient deficiencies resulting from low pH.

SYMPTOMS OF DEFICIENCY: Stunted or reduced roots, slender stems, light green leaves, or a general yellowing of the leaves or the entire plant may indicate a sulfur deficiency. Sulfur is rarely deficient, however, since it may be absorbed from the air, and it is often used as a carrier or an impurity in fertilizers.

MISCELLANEOUS NOTES: Sulfur balance is unlikely to be a problem in orchid cultivation. In agriculture, sulfur is used as a fungicide and to lower the soil pH.

Zinc (Zn). Not mobile in the plant.

Zinc, a micronutrient, is critical in the production of amino acids.

SYMPTOMS OF EXCESS: Zinc excess usually shows as iron or magnesium deficiency, since too much zinc interferes with the utilization of these nutrients.

SYMPTOMS OF DEFICIENCY: Symptoms of zinc deficiency include wavy, distorted, or puckered leaf margins; rosetting of the leaves; small or white-streaked leaves; and leaves that are necrotic or chlorotic, with yellowing between the veins on newer leaves. Shortened internodes may result in stunted plants. Excess phosphorus or potassium may cause symptoms of zinc deficiency.

MISCELLANEOUS NOTES: Zinc balance is unlikely to be a problem in orchid cultivation. Zinc is seldom deficient when a natural medium is used or a micronutrient supplement is applied to inorganic media. A laboratory tissue analysis should be performed and deficiency determined before zinc is added. A pH above 7 may interfere with a plant's ability to use zinc, but this is unlikely in orchid cultivation.

Nutrients Summary

Nutrients Summary

Nutrient	Symptoms of Excess	Symptoms of Deficiency	Miscellaneous Notes
Boron	Black or dead tissue between veins	Black stems Die-back of apical buds or terminal leaves Failure to set seed Short roots Stunted plants	Boron balance is unlikely to be a problem in orchid cultivation. Excess boron is highly toxic. Deficiency of boron seldom occurs, since boron is usually available from natural media and is included in most micronutrient preparations. A laboratory tissue analysis should be performed and deficiency determined before boron is added.
Calcium	Chlorosis on middle or older leaves, between veins, or along leaf margins Curled or cupped mature leaves Leaf drop of middle and older leaves Leaves that fall prematurely	Black leaf tips on new leaves Buds that develop improperly Cupped leaves Dying roots tips Poor growth or vigor Yellow leaves that turn brown and die prematurely	Excess calcium blocks magnesium absorption and causes symptoms of magnesium deficiency. It may also raise the pH to such a level that some micronutrients are unavailable to the plant. Deficiency of calcium usually occurs during periods of active growth and is more likely to be a problem than most other nutrient imbalances. Before adding calcium, growers should review other possible causes of symptoms. Dark leaf tips may be caused by too little water or too much fertilizer. Bud problems are usually caused by improper light or temperature, while deformed buds usually result from insect or chemical damage. Poor growth or yellow leaves may be caused by various nutrient deficiencies or root damage. Imbalances of magnesium and phosphorus are other possible problems.
Chlorine	Browning of leaves from the tip toward the base	Bronze leaves Chlorotic, dying leaves Deformed roots Wilted leaf tips that do not become erect when plants are watered	Chlorine balance is unlikely to be a problem in orchid cultivation. Excess chlorine may be a problem with soft-leaved orchids. Store water overnight in an open container to allow the chlorine to dissipate before watering sensitive plants. Deficiency of chlorine occurs rarely. A laboratory tissue analysis should be performed and deficiency determined before chlorine is added.
Cobalt	N/A	Chlorosis in older leaves Red or purple coloring on leaves	Cobalt balance is unlikely to be a problem in orchid cultivation. Excess cobalt seldom occurs. Deficiency of cobalt is very rare. Cobalt should be added only as a part of a micronutrient supplement.
Copper	Signs of iron deficiency Yellow to white mottling on new leaves with green veins	Faded leaves New growths that are small or misshapen Wilted terminal shoots	Copper balance is unlikely to be a problem in orchid cultivation. Excess copper can be highly toxic to orchids. Deficiency of copper may be caused by excess potassium. Copper should be added only as a part of a micronutrient supplement.

Nutrients Summary

Iron	N/A	Brown spots on leaves Yellow or white leaf tissue	Iron balance is unlikely to be a problem in orchid cultivation. Excess iron can be highly toxic to orchids. Deficiency of iron seldom occurs. A laboratory tissue analysis should be performed and deficiency determined before iron is added.
Magnesium	Signs of calcium deficiency	Cupped leaves Reduced growth Yellow mature leaves with green veins	Excess magnesium can be highly toxic to orchids. Deficiency of magnesium is more likely to be a problem than most other nutrient imbalances. If the water supply is low in magnesium but high in calcium, plants may benefit from increased magnesium.
Manganese	Brown spotting on leaves Reduced growth Signs of iron deficiency	Brown discoloration on leaves Yellow between green veins on new leaves Yellowish green stems	Manganese balance is unlikely to be a problem in orchid cultivation. Excess manganese may occur under very acid conditions (low pH). Too much manganese can interfere with iron uptake. Deficiency of manganese seldom occurs. Manganese should be added only as part of a micronutrient supplement.
Molybdenum	N/A	Pale yellow chlorosis between veins on older leaves Twisted leaves that fail to open	Molybdenum balance is unlikely to be a problem in orchid cultivation. Excess molybdenum can be highly toxic to orchids. Deficiency of molybdenum seldom occurs. A laboratory tissue analysis should be performed and deficiency determined before molybdenum is added.
Nitrogen	Blackened leaves Brittle new growth Dark green leaves New growth that is weak and spindly	Chlorosis of older growth Red or purple coloring on leaves Reduced growth	Excess nitrogen is a fairly common problem resulting from poorly balanced fertilizer. Moderately high levels may increase the plant's susceptibility to disease. Grossly excessive nitrogen causes blackened leaves, which may also result from very cold temperatures. Deficiency of nitrogen is unlikely to occur when a balanced fertilizer is used at the recommended frequency. An excess of phosphorus or potassium may cause symptoms of nitrogen deficiency.
Phosphorus	Signs of deficiencies in other nutrients	Dark green leaves with reddish or purplish coloring along veins Premature leaf drop Purplish leaves Reduced flowering Spindly new growth Stunted plants Thin stems	Excess phosphorus is unlikely to be a problem. Deficiency of phosphorus seldom occurs if a balanced fertilizer is applied at the recommended frequency. Unless a high-nitrogen fertilizer is used exclusively, spindly growth and discolored leaves probably result from problems with light levels. Poor flowering is usually due to low light levels, incorrect photoperiods, insufficient rest, or inappropriate temperatures.

Nutrients Summary

Nutrient	Symptoms of Excess	Symptoms of Deficiency	Miscellaneous Notes
Potassium	Signs of deficiencies in other nutrients	Burned leaf margins Chlorosis of leaves Dead spots on leaves Dwarfed plants Shortened internodes Wrinkling between leaf veins Yellow leaf margins	Excess potassium is unlikely to be a problem. Deficiency of potassium seldom occurs if a balanced fertilizer is applied at the recommended strength and frequency. If a high-nitrogen fertilizer has been used exclusively, a more balanced formula should be considered. The nitrogen/potassium balance is important.
Sulfur	Signs of deficiencies in other nutrients	Slender stems Stunted or reduced roots Yellowish to pale green plants or leaves	Sulfur balance is unlikely to be a problem in orchid cultivation. Excess sulfur seldom occurs. Deficiency of sulfur is rare. Discoloration of leaves is more likely to result from inappropriate light or macronutrient imbalances; short roots, from insufficient watering; and slender stems, from phosphorus deficiency.
Zinc	Signs of iron or magnesium deficiency	Chlorosis between the veins on newer leaves Chlorotic leaves Pale or white new leaves Rosetting of the leaves Small leaves Stunted growth Wavy leaf margins White streaks on older leaves	Zinc balance is unlikely to be a problem in orchid cultivation. Excess zinc seldom occurs. Deficiency of zinc rarely occurs if a natural medium is used or a micronutrient supplement is applied to inorganic media. A laboratory tissue analysis should be performed and deficiency determined before zinc is added.

WARNING: READ AND FOLLOW THE INSTRUCTIONS ON THE LABEL.

Growers are warned that chemicals may damage plants if applied in a manner or to a plant not specifically recommended on the label. Chemicals may alter a plant's sensitivity to light or cause damage that results in deformed new growths. See the discussion under "General Rules for Chemical Use" in Section III.

III. Using Chemicals Safely

Chemical Toxicity

Chemicals are designed to kill—treat them with the respect they deserve.
Chemicals are best avoided if possible. When their use is appropriate, remember that most pathogen-related plant diseases are caused by fungi which are a form of plant life. Any chemical applied to save the host plant is a chemical designed to kill another plant form. This is why some chemicals may be fatal to young seedlings and sometimes damage adult plants.

An important rule of thumb is to select *the least toxic chemical that will do the job*. All chemicals are rated with an LD_{50} number. This number sounds innocuous until one realizes that it means the amount given was a **L**ethal **D**ose to **50%** of the animals tested. Thus, if the LD_{50} number is 1–5 mg, the chemical is extremely toxic. In human terms, this means that for someone weighing 154 lbs. (70 kg), about 6 drops could be fatal 50% of the time. For a 50 lb. (23 kg) child, 2 drops could be fatal 50% of the time. For a toddler or small family pet, less than a drop could be fatal. An LD_{50} of 5000 mg indicates that an amount equal to a pint of chemical for a 154 lb. (70 kg) person killed 50% of the test animals. LD_{50} ratings are not printed on labels, but this information is available from local agricultural agents. The lower the LD_{50} number, the more dangerous the chemical, and the stronger the precautionary statement on the label.

Danger—Poison with a skull and crossbones symbol means that the substance is highly toxic, and the lethal dosage ranges from a taste to a teaspoon. Children might be killed by merely putting the bottle to their mouth.

Warning indicates that the chemical is moderately toxic. A dose lethal to humans ranges from a single teaspoon to a single tablespoon.

Caution indicates that the toxicity level is relatively low. A dose lethal to humans ranges from an ounce to more than a pint.

The importance of the information on the label cannot be over emphasized: *Read the label, and follow the instructions*. Labels indicate the dangers of the particular chemical and whether swallowing it, inhaling it, or bringing it into contact with skin or eyes can result in serious injury or accidental poisoning. Emergency first-aid measures are printed on the label. If accidental poisoning should occur, the pesticide label is the most important information you can take to the physician.

In addition to indicating toxicity, the label should also provide information about environmental hazards such as the risk of fire or explosion or physical dangers, including the risk of harming the eyes or inhaling fumes. Local agricultural agents are the best source of information regarding toxicity ratings.

Another aspect of toxicity is the long-term carcinogenic effect of certain chemicals. Dr. Bruce Ames, Chairman of the Biochemistry Department, University of California at Berkeley, is one of the leading researchers exploring the possible mutagenic effects of chemical substances. His research has shown that we are continuously exposed to mutagens from such common substances as citrus oil, peanut butter, and broiled steak. Until the interactions between our immune systems and these potentially carcinogenic substances is more fully understood, however, it is unlikely that definitive standards or a danger-rating system will be established. In the meantime, growers should be aware of the serious possible side effects from exposure to chemicals and take every possible precaution when mixing or applying any chemical.

General Rules for Chemical Use

Protect yourself and others. Read and follow the precautionary statements on the label. Always remember that these chemicals are designed to be toxic to living things. Recent evidence indicates that agricultural workers may develop severe health problems as a result of regular or prolonged exposure to many of the chemicals used in greenhouses.

When using chemicals, the most dangerous phase is during mixing, when the chemical is still in concentrated form. An accidental spill or splash of the concentrate on exposed skin can easily result in a dangerous amount of the chemical being rapidly absorbed through the skin. It is therefore important to wear protective clothing. The grower who mixes and applies a spray wearing only shorts or lightweight summer clothing is running a great risk.

Gloves which are impervious to chemicals should be worn during all phases of pesticide use, but most particularly when the chemical concentrate is being measured.

A respirator, designed to prevent the inhalation of fumes and vapor, should be considered a necessity, not a luxury.

Goggles or face shields to protect the eyes and face are also critical, since the optic nerves may be permanently damaged if even dilute mixtures of certain chemicals are absorbed through the eyes.

Many chemicals are specifically designed to be absorbed through the living "skin" of the plant or insect. Long-sleeved shirts and long-legged pants or coveralls help prevent absorption through the skin. Clothing should be changed and washed separately immediately after chemicals are used. After the clothes are removed from the machine, it should be run through another complete cycle with soap before it is again used for the family wash.

Do not ignore illness which occurs during or shortly after exposure to or use of pesticides. Read the label, follow the instructions for emergency first-aid, and contact a doctor, hospital, or poison control center immediately.

Protect your plants. The risk of chemical damage to orchid plants is high. These general guidelines will help reduce that risk.

- Avoid spraying stressed plants. They are more likely to be damaged than healthy, actively growing plants.

- Do not apply aerosols at less than the recommended distance. If the can indicates spraying at 12 in. (30 cm), and it is held at 8 in. (20 cm), it is very likely to cause damage.

- Do not spray during cool, humid weather. The risk of injury increases when plants do not dry quickly after they are sprayed.

- Do not spray during hot, sunny weather. The risk of plant injury increases when temperatures are warm or light levels are high. When air or plant temperatures are as high as 90°F (32°C), damage is likely since some chemical actions are intensified.

- Do not apply chemicals more frequently than recommended.
- Mix at the correct strength, and avoid overdosing plants.
- Water plants thoroughly before spraying. Dry plants absorb more chemical than is needed, which often causes injury.
- Spray only to the point of runoff. Excess chemicals do not benefit the plant but may increase the risk of chemical damage.
- Spray early in the day, preferably between 6 and 10 a.m.
- Use only chemicals that are known to be safe for the particular plant.

Avoid noxious fumes, which harm plants. Some chemicals produce fumes that are quickly fatal to many plants. Weed control compounds containing 2-4-D should not be sprayed in the vicinity of orchids. Other chemical compounds also produce fumes, often for an extended period, that are extremely harmful to orchids. Fumes from tar oil (sometimes found in rust preventatives used on greenhouse pipes) can injure orchids in a closed greenhouse. Likewise, fumes from wood preserved with Penta compounds or creosote may be toxic, particularly in winter when air circulation is reduced. Fumes from some preservative paints may also affect plants adversely. Use paints designated for greenhouse use.

Use caution in combining chemicals. Mixing chemicals in an attempt to control several diseases or pests in a single application may change a plant's response to chemicals that are safe when used separately. Information regarding chemical compatibility is sometimes found on the product label, but generally, wettable powders may be mixed with other wettable powders and emulsifiable concentrates with other emulsifiable concentrates. Chemical compatibility charts are published annually by the Meister Publishing Co., Willoughby, OH, U.S.A. 44094.

Pesticides are often mixed as a convenience, allowing a grower to apply treatments for several pests at one time, and in many instances mixing may be done safely. When there is any room for doubt, however, it is safer to make separate applications of the different chemicals, spaced a few days apart. Chemical brands from a single manufacturer are more likely to be compatible than those from different manufacturers. Only chemicals of similar toxicity—such as the group marked "Danger," the group marked "Warning," and the group marked "Caution"—should be mixed. Growers sometimes make the mistake of diluting each chemical separately then combining the 2 solutions in a sprayer. This dilutes each chemical to less than the recommended strength. If each chemical should be mixed in a gallon of water, only one gallon of water should be used.

Symptoms of phytotoxicity (plant toxicity) normally show within 18–72 hours and nearly always within a week. Chemical toxicity may cause problems such as burn, necrosis, or chlorosis. Injury is most likely to be evident at leaf tips and margins, but the damage may also show as spotting or discoloration of the entire leaf, and growing tips or buds may die. Distortion such as crinkling, cupping, or curling of the leaves may occur quickly, while stunting or abnormal growth appears more gradually.

Sprays are more likely to damage new leaves, while drenches are more likely to damage older leaves and roots.

If many plants of a single species are to be sprayed, it is wise to test spray a few plants before making a general application.

Follow the package instructions, and mix chemicals at the recommended strength. This is important because the recommended application strength is necessary to kill the pathogen without harming the orchid. Using a single chemical exclusively for a prolonged period may result in the survival of only strains of pathogens that are unaffected by that chemical. It is always wise to complete a treatment with one chemical, then to use a different chemical if the problem continues.

Apply at the recommended frequency. Instructions for the application of chemicals include the frequency. This is based on the life of the chemical or the reproductive life of the pest. Repeated applications are often necessary to control pests that hatch after the chemical is applied. In the case of systemics, several applications are necessary for the plant to build-up the necessary chemical levels to be toxic to the pest or disease.

Mix only what you need. Most chemicals rapidly lose their effectiveness after being mixed, so mix only the amount that can be used that day. Never put mixed chemicals in a food-storage container. These are not child-proof, and if accidentally left out, they could easily lead a curious child to sample the contents.

Store chemicals safey. Safe storage means always keeping the chemical in the original container, which was designed with safety in mind. Also, when chemicals are kept in the original container, the label is available to be read before each use. A locked cabinet is highly recommended. This protects both people and the chemicals, since the effective life of a chemical can be prolonged by storage in a cool, dark place.

Dispose of containers and extra solution as instructed. Rinse empty containers several times by filling them with water and emptying the rinse into the solution being mixed. Dispose of the empty, well-rinsed container and any leftover solution as the label advises.

Clean sprayers and mixing containers. After using chemicals, it is very important to thoroughly clean mixing containers and spraying equipment. When wettable powders or other suspended solids are used, the containers are easily cleaned by carefully rinsing and flushing the spray mechanism with fresh, clean water. For some chemicals, however, especially liquids using an oil base or those mixed with sticker/spreaders, rinsing may not be sufficient to remove all the chemical from the equipment. Any chemical solution left clinging to the equipment may be neutralized by first rinsing with a solution of 2 parts household ammonia and 1 part water. The ammonia reacts with most agricultural and horticultural chemicals, changing them into substances that are safe for plants and animals. This solution should be pumped through the spray mechanism, and the equipment allowed to stand for 24 hours then given a final rinsing with clean water. The equipment is then safe to use with another chemical.

Chemical Classifications and Methods of Application

Pesticides are categorized by their intended use. All chemicals used to control pests (such as disease and insects) are considered pesticides.

Acaricides control mites, ticks, and spiders.

Attractants lure pests.

Bactericides control bacteria.

Fungicides control fungi.

Herbicides kill plants (not just weeds).

Insecticides control insects.

Miticides control mites.

Repellents keep pests away.

Pesticides are further classified by how they work.

Broad-spectrum formulations kill a wide variety of pests.

Contact poisons kill by touching.

Disinfectants are used to sterilize and normally kill on contact.

Fumigants are gasses which kill when inhaled or absorbed.

Selective chemicals are designed to treat only specific problems.

Stomach poisons kill when swallowed by the pest.

Systemic poisons circulate through the plant, killing pests when they attack.

Treatments are applied in several ways, and the application method is often critical. Chemicals absorbed by the leaves should be applied as a spray, while chemicals absorbed by plant roots should be used as a drench. Spraying a chemical that should be applied as a drench provides little benefit to the plant.

The following terms are used in labeling to describe application methods.

Band: Apply in a strip.

Broadcast: Scatter over the surface.

Dip: Submerge the entire plant.

Direct: Aim at a specific location.

Drench: Saturate the medium.

Side dress: Place beside the plant.

Spot treat: Apply to the affected area.

Spray or foliar spray: Apply to both sides of the leaves until the chemical drips off the tips of the leaves.

Chemicals are available in various forms depending on how they should be applied. Following is a list of formulation types. Common abbreviations that may appear on labels are included in parentheses.

Aerosol (A): A low concentrate applied as a fine mist.

Bait (B): A solid or liquid, often with an attractant, used to combat slugs and snails.

Dust (D): A powder which is dusted on the leaves or surface of the medium.

Emulsified concentrate (EC or E): An oil-based solution designed to be diluted with water.

Flowable (F or L): A liquid which forms a suspension when mixed with water.

Granules (G): Coarse particles which are usually broadcast. The pesticide is often mixed with clay for easy handling.

Soluble powder (SP): A powder which dissolves when mixed with water.

Wettable powder (WP or P): A dust designed to be mixed with water and sprayed. Wettable powders are held in suspension rather than dissolved, so the solution must be continuously agitated during spraying. These powders should first be mixed with a small quantity of water to form a slurry, then diluted to the required strength.

Certain products, called surfactants or simply additives, are mixed with some chemicals to improve dispersal of the spray, alter droplet size, increase coverage, keep the chemical in suspension, or allow oil and water to mix. Different brand-name products have different formulations; the brand recommended on the label is the one designed to be compatible with that pesticide formulation. Follow the instructions on the label.

Spreaders increase the deposit and coverage on plant surfaces. Often used with wettable powder insecticides, they improve contact between the pesticide and the plant surface.

Stickers are compounds which help the spray adhere to the leaf surface. They are particularly beneficial when used with wettable powders and are frequently recommended for use with fungicides.

Wetting agents are usually oily additives which prevent the droplets from beading up and rolling off the leaf surface, thereby allowing the pesticide to dry on the plant.

Chemicals are valuable tools that should be used only when necessary. This approach makes the chemicals more effective and is safer for people, pets, plants, and the environment. We hope the information in this Appendix will help growers understand and identify plant problems that may occur. We also hope that it will assist the grower in selecting the safest and most effective possible remedial action when intervention is required.

Appendix B
Unit Conversions and Formulas for Greenhouse Management

English and Metric-System Equivalents

1 inch	=	25.4 millimeters
1 foot	=	30.48 centimeters
1 yard	=	91.44 centimeters
1 mile	=	1.609 kilometers
1 gallon	=	3.785 liters
1 ounce	=	28.35 grams
1 pound	=	453.6 grams
1 millimeter	=	0.03937 inches
1 centimeter	=	0.3937 inches
1 meter	=	39.37 inches
1 kilometer	=	0.62137 miles
1 liter	=	1.057 quarts
1 gram	=	15.43 grains
1 kilogram	=	2.205 pounds

Metric Prefixes

Names of multiples of metric and other units are formed by adding a prefix (representing a power of 10) to "meter," "gram," "liter," and so on.

tera	=	one trillion	or 10^{12}	or	1,000,000,000,000
giga	=	one billion	or 10^{9}	or	1,000,000,000
mega	=	one million	or 10^{6}	or	1,000,000
kilo	=	one thousand	or 10^{3}	or	1,000
hecto	=	one hundred	or 10^{2}	or	100
deka	=	ten	or 10^{1}	or	10
deci	=	one tenth	or 10^{-1}	or	0.1
centi	=	one hundredth	or 10^{-2}	or	0.01
milli	=	one thousandth	or 10^{-3}	or	0.001
micro	=	one millionth	or 10^{-6}	or	0.000001
nano	=	one billionth	or 10^{-9}	or	0.000000001
pico	=	one trillionth	or 10^{-12}	or	0.000000000001

NOTE: The special case of one millionth of a meter is called a micron.

Abbreviations

BTU	=	British thermal unit	Tbs.	=	tablespoon
CFM	=	cubic feet per minute	tsp.	=	teaspoon
cu.	=	cubic	yd.	=	yard
ft.	=	foot	cm	=	centimeter
gal.	=	gallon	g	=	gram
in.	=	inch	kg	=	kilogram
lb.	=	pound	km	=	kilometer
oz.	=	ounce	l	=	liter
pt.	=	pint	l/sec	=	liters per second
qt.	=	quart	m	=	meter
sec.	=	second	ml	=	milliliter
sq.	=	square	mm	=	millimeter

Approximate Conversion Factors and Relationships Among Units of Measure

Liquid Measure

1 ounce (fluid) = 2 Tbs. = 6 tsp. = 1.805 cu. in. = 29.54 ml

1 teaspoon = 50–60 drops = 0.33 Tbs. = 0.167 oz. = 0.301 cu. in. = 4.93 ml

1 tablespoon = 3 tsp. = 0.5 oz. = 0.0625 cup = 0.9025 cu. in. = 14.79 ml

1 cup = 16 Tbs. = 8 oz. = 0.5 pt. = 0.25 qt. = 14.44 cu. in. = 236.32 ml

1 pint = 32 Tbs. = 16 oz. = 2 cups = 0.5 qt. = 28.88 cu. in. = 472.65 ml

1 quart = 64 Tbs. = 32 oz. = 4 cups = 0.25 gal. = 57.76 cu. in. = 946 ml

1 gallon = 4 qt. = 8 pt. = 16 cups = 128 oz. = 231 cu. in. = 3.785 liter

1 milliliter = 1 cu. cm = 0.001 liter = 0.203 tsp.

1 liter = 1000 cu. cm = 1.057 qt. = 0.2642 gal. = 61.02 cu. in.

Dry Measure

1 teaspoon = 0.33 Tbs.	1 quart = 2 pt.
1 tablespoon = 3 tsp.	1 gallon = 4 qt.
1 cup = 16 Tbs. = 48 tsp.	1 peck = 2 gal.
1 pint = 2 cups	

Weight

1 ounce = 0.0625 lb. = 28.35 g = 3 Tbs. (dry) = 2 Tbs. (liquid)

1 pound = 16 oz. = 453.6 g = 2 cups

1 gram = 15.43 grains = 0.0353 oz. = 0.1058 Tbs. = 0.3175 tsp.

1 kilogram = 1000 g = 2.205 lb. = 35.28 oz.

Length

1 inch = 25.4 mm = 2.54 cm = 0.0833 ft.
1 foot = 12 in. = 30.48 cm = 0.333 yd. = 0.3048 m
1 yard = 36 in. = 3 ft. = 91.44 cm = 0.914 m
1 mile = 5280 ft. = 1609.344 m = 1.609 km

1 millimeter = 0.001 m = 0.03937 in.
1 centimeter = 0.01 m = 0.3937 in.
1 meter = 1000 mm = 100 cm = 0.001 km = 39.37 in. = 3.281 ft.
1 kilometer = 1000 m = 3281 ft. = 0.62137 mile

Square Measurements

1 square inch (in.^{2}) = 6.452 sq. cm = 0.0069 sq. ft.
1 square foot (ft.^{2}) = 144 sq. in. = 929.03 sq. cm = 0.0929 sq. m = 0.1109 sq. yd.
1 square meter (m^2) = 1550 sq. in. = 10.765 sq. ft.
1 square mile = 27,878,400 sq. ft. = 2.59 sq. km = 640 acres
1 acre = 43,560 sq. ft. = 4,045.13 sq. m = 0.4 hectare
1 hectare = 10,000 sq. m = 2.47 acres

Cubic Measurements

1 cubic inch (in.^{3}) = 0.03463 pt. = 0.01732 qt. = 16.39 cu. cm = 0.01639 liter
1 cubic foot (ft.^{3}) = 1728 cu. in. = 0.028 cu. m = 0.03704 cu. yd. = 7.4805 gal. = 29.92 qt. = 28.32 liter = 1.25 bushels
1 cubic yard (yd.^{3}) = 27 cu. ft. = 808 qt. = 202 gal. = 764.6 liter = 0.7646 cu. m = 22 bushels
1 cubic centimeter (cm^3) = 1 ml = 0.001 liter = 0.06102 cu. in. = 0.002113 pt.
1 cubic meter (m^3) = 1,000,000 cu. cm = 1000 liter = 35.31 cu. ft. = 1.308 cu. yd. = 2113 pt. = 1057 qt. = 264.2 gal.

Miscellaneous Measurements

1 palm = 3 in.
1 hand = 4 in.
1 span = 6 in.
1 cubit = 18 in.
1 biblical cubit = 21.8 in.
1 furlong = 660 ft. = 0.125 mile
1 league = 3 miles

Per-Gallon Equivalents for Diluting Concentrated Fertilizers and Chemicals

Some commercial products give dilution rates per 100 gal. (380 liters). Listed below are the approximate equivalents for 1 gal. (3.8 liters).

Liquids

2 gal./100 gal.	=	5 Tbs./gal.
1 gal./100 gal.	=	7.5 tsp./gal.
2 qt./100 gal.	=	3.75 tsp./gal.
1 qt./100 gal.	=	2 tsp./gal.
1 pt./100 gal.	=	1 tsp./gal.
8 oz./100 gal.	=	0.5 tsp./gal.
4 oz./100 gal.	=	0.25 tsp./gal.

Solids

5 lb./100 gal.	=	4.75 tsp./gal.
4 lb./100 gal.	=	3.75 tsp./gal.
2 lb./100 gal.	=	2 tsp./gal.
1 lb./100 gal.	=	1 tsp./gal.
8 oz./100 gal.	=	0.5 tsp./gal.

Dilutions

For some chemicals, dilution rates are given as a ratio. The following are approximate equivalent rates for a single gallon.

1:100	= 2 Tbs. + 2 tsp./gal.	= 10.0 ml/l
1:200	= 4 tsp./gal.	= 5.2 ml/l
1:400	= 2 tsp./gal.	= 2.6 ml/l
1:800	= 1 tsp./gal.	= 1.3 ml/l
1:1000	= ¾ tsp./gal.	= 1.0 ml/l
1:2000	= ⅜ tsp./gal.	= 0.5 ml/l

For some chemicals, dilution rates are given as parts per million (ppm). The following are approximate equivalents.

% sol.*	dilution	ppm†	tsp./gal.			ml/l
0.001	1:100,000	10	0.00768	or	¾ tsp./100 gal.	0.01
0.005	1:50,000	20	0.0154	or	¾ tsp./50 gal.	0.02
0.01	1:10,000	100	0.0768	or	¾ tsp./10 gal.	0.1
0.02	1:5000	200	0.1536	or	¾ tsp./5 gal.	0.2
0.05	1:2000	500	0.384	or	⅜ tsp./gal.	0.5
0.10	1:1000	1000	0.768	or	¾ tsp./gal.	1.0
1.00	1:100	10,000	7.68	or	7⅔ tsp./gal.	10.0

*This assumes an initial concentration of 100%. To use with different concentrations, divide 100 by the % of concentration and multiply the tsp./gal. or ml/l by the answer. For example, when using a fertilizer containing 20% nitrogen, divide 100 by 20, which yields 5. Then multiply 5 by the amount shown under **tsp./gal.** or **ml/l**.

†If a solution of 100 ppm is desired when using a 20% concentration, multiply 0.0768 tsp./gal. or 0.1 ml/l by 5. In other words, it requires 0.0768 tsp./gal. or 0.1 ml/l of 100% concentrate to give a solution with 100 ppm, but it takes 5 times these amounts of 20% concentrate to produce a mixture with the same strength.

Approximate Pot Volumes

The following volumes are approximate. Pot volumes vary dramatically depending on pot shape. These volumes may be used to approximate the amount of medium needed or to estimate the quantity of a supplement that is appropriate for small to medium-sized pots.

Round Azalea Pots (height = ¾ diameter of top)

4 in. (10 cm) = 1½ cups (354 ml)
5 in. (13 cm) = 3⅝ cups (857 ml)
6 in. (15 cm) = 5½ cups (1300 ml)
7 in. (18 cm) = 8 cups (1890 ml)

Round Bulb Pans (height = ½ diameter of top)

5 in. (13 cm) = 2¾ cups (473 ml)
6.5 in. (17 cm) = 5¾ cups (1359 ml)
8 in. (20 cm) = 8 cups (1890 ml)

Unit Conversions and Formulas

Round Standard Pots (height = diameter of top)
1.5 in. (4 cm) = ⅛ cup (29.5 ml)
2 in. (5 cm) = ¼ cup (59 ml)
2.5 in. (6 cm) = ⅜ cup (89 ml)
3 in. (8 cm) = ¾ cup (178 ml)
3.5 in. (9 cm) = 1¼ cup (295 ml)
4 in. (10 cm) = 1⅞ cup (443 ml)
5 in. (13 cm) = 3¾ cup (886 ml)
6 in. (15 cm) = 6½ cup (1536 ml)

Square Pots (height = width of top)
2¼ in. (5.7 cm) = ⅜ cup (89 ml)
2½ in. (6 cm) = ½ cup (118 ml)
3 in. (8 cm) = ⅞ cup (206 ml)
3½ in. (9 cm) = 1¼ cup (295 ml)
4 in. (10 cm) = 1¾ cup (413 ml)
4½ in. (11 cm) = 2¾ (532 ml)

Temperature Conversions

Conversion Formulas

$$°C = (5/9)(°F - 32) \qquad °F = (9/5)(°C) + 32$$

Conversion Table

Fahrenheit to Celsius and Celsius to Fahrenheit

°F	0	1	2	3	4	5	6	7	8	9
	°C	°C	°C	°C	°C	°C	°C	°C	°C	°C
-10	-23	-24	-24	-25	-26	-26	-27	-27	-28	-28
-0	-18	-18	-19	-19	-20	-21	-21	-22	-22	-23
0	-18	-17	-17	-16	-16	-15	-14	-14	-13	-13
10	-12	-12	-11	-11	-10	-9	-9	-8	-8	-7
20	-7	-6	-6	-5	-4	-4	-3	-3	-2	-2
30	-1	-1	0	1	1	2	2	3	3	4
40	4	5	6	6	7	7	8	8	9	9
50	10	11	11	12	12	13	13	14	14	15
60	16	16	17	17	18	18	19	19	20	21
70	21	22	22	23	23	24	24	25	26	26
80	27	27	28	28	29	29	30	31	31	32
90	32	33	33	34	34	35	36	36	37	37
100	38	38	39	39	40	41	41	42	42	43
110	43	44	44	45	46	46	47	47	48	48

To convert from °F to °C, find the appropriate tens line on the left and move to the right to the column under the appropriate units digit (the line of numbers at the top of the table). The number at the intersection of the column and the line is the °C value. For example, to convert 64°F, locate the 60 line and move to the right to the column under 4. The number at this intersection is 18. Thus 64°F = 18°C.

To convert from °C to °F, simply work backwards. Find the desired °C value in the table and determine the corresponding °F value by combining the numbers at the left and the top of the table. For example, 13°C falls at the intersection of the 50 line and the 5 and 6 columns. Consequently, 13°C = 55-56°F. (If it is desirable to find °F in tenths of degrees, the best procedure is to use the formula given above. Thus, for the present example, °F = (9/5)(13°C) + 32 = 55.4.)

Some Equations Useful in Greenhouse Management

$$Watts = Amps \times Volts$$

$$Volts = \frac{Watts}{Amps}$$

$$Amps = \frac{Watts}{Volts}$$

1 BTU = 0.252 kilocalorie   1 CFM = 0.472 liters per second

Greenhouse Ventilation

Due to the engineering constants in the following equations, they are appropriate only for use with English units of measure.

Fans used for greenhouse ventilation should be of sufficient size to provide a complete exchange of air every 1.5 minutes. The following equation gives the fan size necessary to meet this requirement:

$$V \times 0.7 = CFM$$

where V is the volume of the greenhouse, obtained by multiplying the length times the width times the average height of the structure, and where CFM is the required fan size given in cubic feet per minute.

Air removed by a fan must be replaced if the fan is to operate properly, so inlet vents that allow passage of the required volume of air should be provided. To determine the size of the necessary vent area, divide the CFM (as determined above) by 250. This will give the total shutter area in square feet. Divide this number by the number of shutters that will be used to determine the size of each shutter.

Greenhouse Heating

The following formula determines the approximate heating requirements of a greenhouse:

$$A \times D \times 1.1 = BTU$$

where A is the total wall and roof area of the greenhouse in square feet, D is the °F difference between the coldest outdoor winter temperature and the night temperature desired in the greenhouse, and BTU is the required output of the heater expressed in British thermal units. Subtract 30% from this value if the greenhouse is double-glazed or has a polyethylene liner.

Bibliography

References

Citations of journal articles include name(s) of author(s), year of publication, article title, and journal name, followed by volume number, issue number (in parentheses), and page numbers. The issue number corresponds to the month of publication, or in the case of quarterlies, the 3-month period for which the issue was released.

1 Adams, P. 1988. Multiple bee pollinators of *Dendrobium kingianum* Bidw. in the natural habitat. *The Orchadian* 9(5):103.

2 ———, ed. 1988. *Reproductive biology of species orchids: principles and practice*. Orchid Species Society of Victoria Inc. and The School of Botany, University of Melbourne, Australia.

3 ———. 1989. The capacity of *Dendrobium speciosum* Sm. to carry seed capsules to maturity. *The Orchadian* 9(9):201.

4 ———. 1991. Variation, multiple pollinators and breeding system in *Dendrobium speciosum* Smith: A biological review. *The Orchadian* 10(5):124.

5 ———. 1992. Chromosome analysis of some *Dendrobium kingianum* used in breeding. *The Orchadian* 10(9):300.

6 Adnams, T. 1981. Selected dendrobiums. *The Orchid Review* 89(7): 205–207, 237–239.

7 *Aeronautical navigation charts*. Prepared and published by the U. S. Defense Mapping Agency, Washington, D. C. The charts are updated periodically as additional mapping is accomplished.

8 American Orchid Society. 1974, *An orchidist's glossary*. American Orchid Society, Inc., 6000 S. Olive Ave., West Palm Beach, Fla., U. S. A., 33405.

9 ———. 1980. *Handbook on orchid photography*. American Orchid Society, Inc., 6000 S. Olive Ave., West Palm Beach, Fla., U.S.A. 33405.

10 ———. 1986. *Handbook on orchid culture*. American Orchid Society, Inc., 6000 S. Olive Ave., West Palm Beach, Fla., U.S.A. 33405.

11 ———. 1986. *Handbook on orchid pests and diseases*. American Orchid Society, Inc., 6000 S. Olive Ave., West Palm Beach, Fla., U.S.A. 33405.

12 Ames, O. [1905–1922] 1982. *Orchidaceae*. Fasc. I, II, III, IV, V, VI, and VII. Merrymount Press, Boston. Reprint, Twin Oaks Books, Greenfield, Wis.

13 ———. 1913. Notes on Philippine orchids. *The Philippine Journal of Science* 8:423–426.

14 ———. 1914. *The Philippine Journal of Science* 9:14.

15 ———. [1923] 1983. *Schedulae orchidianae*. Vols. V and VI. Merrymount Press, Boston. Reprint, Twin Oaks Books, Greenfield, Wis.

16 ———. 1932. Contribution to the flora of the New Hebrides and Santa Cruz Islands. *Journal of the Arnold Arboretum* 13(2):127–144. Harvard University, Boston.

17 ———. 1933. Additional notes on the orchids of the New Hebrides and Santa Cruz Islands. *Journal of the Arnold Arboretum* 14(2):106–111. Harvard University, Boston, Mass.

18 Arditti, J. 1982. Orchid seed germination and seedling culture—a manual. Appendix in *Orchid biology: reviews and perspectives*, Vol. II. Edited by J. Arditti. Comstock Publishing, Cornell University Press, Ithaca, N.Y.

19 Arditti, J., and G. Boutillier. 1972. Kalimpong—an orchid heaven. *American Orchid Society Bulletin* 41(5):400.

20 Arnold, R. [1940] 1990. *Dendrobium victoriae reginae*. fifty years ago. *The Orchid Review* 98(5):149–150.

21 Atwood, J. 1983. Notes from the O. I. C.—*Dendrobium rupicola*. *American Orchid Society Bulletin* 52(1):22.

22 ———. 1984. The Identity of *Dendrobium alexandrae*. *American Orchid Society Bulletin* 53(11):1178.

23 Australasian Native Orchid Society (Victoria Group). 1984. *Cultivation of Australian native orchids*. Australasian Native Orchid Society, Inc., Melbourne, Australia.

24 Australasian Native Orchid Society. 1990. *'Proceedings' first Australasian native orchid conference and show*. Australasian Native Orchid Society, Inc., Wollongong, N. S. W., Australia.

25 Backer, C., and R. Bakhuizen Van Den Brink. 1968. *Flora of Java*, Vol. III. Wolters-Noordhoff N. V., Groningen, The Netherlands.

26 Bailey, F. [1906] 1910. Species novae ex: F. M. Bailey, contributions of the flora of Queensland and New Guinea. *Repertorium specierum novarum regni vegetabilis* Fasc. VIII:9–10, 80–81. Originally published in the *Queensland Agricultural Journal*.

27 Bailey, J. 1988. Mona Vale spring show. *The Orchadian* 9(6):125, 132.

28 Baker, G. 1975. A color by any other name. *American Orchid Society Bulletin* 44(1):44.

29 ———. 1992. Scaling down. *American Orchid Society Bulletin* 61(7):664.

30 Baker, J. 1884. The flora of Fiji. *Journal of the Linnean Society*, Botany 20:372–373.

31 Balakrishnan, N. 1970. Nomenclatural notes on some flowering plants—II. *Journal of the Bombay Natural History Society* 67(1): 327.

32 Banerji, M., and P. Pradhan. 1984. *The orchids of Nepal Himalaya*. J. Cramer, Vaduz, India.

33 Banks, D. 1993. Show photos. *The Orchadian* 10(10):369.

34 Batchelor, S. 1980. The Butterworth Prize for most outstanding specimen plant. *American Orchid Society Bulletin* 49(8):871.

35 ———. 1981. Beginner's series—Orchid culture—10—Repotting. *American Orchid Society Bulletin* 50(12):1437.

36 Bechtel, H., P. Cribb, and E. Launert. 1980. *Manual of cultivated orchid species*. MIT Press, Cambridge, Mass.

37. Begaud, J. 1987. A 'hairy' *Dendrobium* from New Caledonia. *American Orchid Society Bulletin* 56(11):1133.
38. Bhattacharjee, S. 1976. India: Major *Dendrobium* habitat of the world. *American Orchid Society Bulletin* 45(8):713.
39. ———. 1977. Distribution of orchid genera in India. *Orchid Digest* 41(1):7.
40. Bigham, R. 1987. Orchids on stamps—an update. *American Orchid Society Bulletin* 56(6):591.
41. ———. 1988. The orchid stamps of 1987. *American Orchid Society Bulletin* 57(7):753.
42. ———. 1989. The orchid stamps of 1988. *American Orchid Society Bulletin* 58(12):1230.
43. Bishop, D. 1974. *Dendrobium phalaenopsis* culture. *American Orchid Society Bulletin* 43(8):709.
44. Blake, S. 1962. *Dendrobium bigibbum*, *Dendrobium phalaenopsis* and the Cooktown orchid. *Proceedings of the Royal Society of Queensland*, issued 1964. LXXIV:29–44.
45. Bonpland, A., A. de Humboldt, and C. Kunth. [1815] 1963. *Nova genera et species plantarum*. Lutetiae Parisiorum, Sumtibus Librariae Graeco-Latino-Germanicae. Reprint by Hafner Publishing Co., New York, N. Y.
46. Bose, T., and S. Bhattacharjee. 1980. *Orchids of India*. Naya Prokash, Calcutta, India.
47. Bostwick, M. 1986. Papua New Guinea, 1985. *American Orchid Society Bulletin* 55(10):1016.
48. Boyett, E. 1990. Cover photograph. *American Orchid Society Bulletin* 59(3):BC.
49. Braem, G. 1990. *Dendrobium sophronitis—Dendrobium cuthbersonii*. An endless confusion. *Schlechteriana* 1(3):98.
50. ———. 1991. Miniature Orchids. *Schlechteriana* 2(4):150.
51. Brieger, F. 1981. Subtribus *Dendrobiinea*. *Die Orchideen*, Band 1, 11. u. 12. Lieferung Bogen 40b–47: 636–752.
52. Brown, F. 1930. New Polynesian plants. *Bernice P. Bishop Museum, Occasional Papers* 9(3):15.
53. Burkhill, I. 1918. A new *Dendrobium*, *D. gracilipes*, from the Rhio Archipelago. *Journal of the straits Branch of the Royal Asiatic Society* 79:45–46.
54. Burns-Balogh, P. 1989. *A reference guide to orchidology*. Koeltz Scientific Books, P. O. Box 1360, D-6240 Koenigstein/West Germany.
55. Cameron, R. 1973. Ink-brush painting. *American Orchid Society Bulletin* 42(2):104.
56. Carr, C. 1929. Some Malayan orchids. *The Gardens' Bulletin Straits Settlements,* Vol. V. Singapore.
57. ———. 1932. Some Malayan orchids III. *The Gardens' Bulletin Straits Settlements* Vol. VII. Singapore.
58. ———. 1934. *Dendrobium takahashii*, sp. nov. *The Orchid Review* 42:44–46.
59. ———. 1935. Some Malayan orchids V. *The Gardens' Bulletin Straits Settlements* Vol. VIII. Singapore.
60. Chandrabose, M., V. Chandrasekaran, and N. Nair. 1981. A new species of *Dendrobium* Sw. *(Orchidaceae)* from South India. *Journal of the Bombay Natural History Society* 78(3):575.
61. Chen, Sing-Chi, and T. Tang. 1982. A general review of the orchid flora of China. *Orchid biology: reviews and perspectives* Vol. II. Ed. by J. Arditti. Comstock Publishing, Cornell University Press, Ithaca, N. Y.
62. Cheng, C. [Not dated] *Chow Cheng orchids*. Missouri Botanical Garden, St. Louis, Mo.
63. Cheng, S., and Z. Tang. 1984. Dendrobiums new to China. *Acta Botanica Yunnanica* 6(3):280–284.
64. Chowdhury, S. 1988. A new species of *Dendrobium (Orchidaceae)* from Assam, India. *Kew Bulletin* 43(4):667–669.
65. Clark, W. 1977. A spectrum of miniature species. *American Orchid Society Bulletin* 46(4):305.
66. Clements, M. 1986. *Orchidaceae* of Green, Norfolk and Lord Howe Islands, II. *Journal of the Arnold Arboretum* 67(1):115–116.
67. ———. 1989. Catalogue of Australian *Orchidaceae*. *Australian Orchid Research* Vol. 1. D. Jones, ed. Australian Orchid Foundation, 107 Roberts St., Essendon 3040, Victoria, Australia.
68. Clements, M., and D. Jones. 1990. Recently named Australian Orchid taxa—1: *Dendrobium*. *Lindleyana* 5(4):235–243.
69. Clemesha, S. 1980. *Dendrobium bigibbum* Lindl. and *Dendrobium phalaenopsis* R. D. Fitzg. *American Orchid Society Bulletin* 49(9):991.
70. Cogniaux, A. 1895. *Dendrobium versicolor* Cogn. *Journal des Orchidées* 130:153.
71. Coleman, R. 1986. Growing orchids as epiphytes. *American Orchid Society Bulletin* 55(4):376.
72. Collins, R., and R. Peterson. 1975. Choosing your first orchids—2—vegetative habits—Basic orchid culture—3. *American Orchid Society Bulletin* 44(3):217.
73. Comber, J. 1981. *Dendrobium pedilonum* in Java. *Orchid Digest* 45(2):73.
74. ———. 1983. The section *Calcarifera* of the genus *Dendrobium* in Java. *Orchid Digest* 47(5):191.
75. ———. 1990. *Orchids of Java*. The Bentham-Moxon Trust, Royal Botanic Gardens, Kew, Richmond, Surrey, England.
76. Coombes, A. 1985. *Dictionary of plant names*. Timber Press, Portland, Ore.
77. Craig, D. 1989. The *Dendrobium* that only its mother loved. *American Orchid Society Bulletin* 58(1):6.
78. Crawford, D. 1972. The beginner—some hints on the housing headache. *American Orchid Society Bulletin* 41(4):301.
79. Crawford, D., and M. Crawford. 1986. Growing some *Pedilonum* dendrobiums. *American Orchid Society Bulletin* 55(8):788.
80. Cribb, P. 1980. Three new species of *Dendrobium* sect. *Ceratobium* from Papua New Guinea. *The Orchid Review* 88 (1043):143–147.
81. ———. 1981. Two new orchids from the highlands of Papua New Guinea. *The Orchadian* 6(12):274.
82. ———. 1983. *Dendrobium* sect. *Ceratobium (Orchidaceae)* in the Pacific Islands. *Kew Bulletin* 37(4):577–588.
83. ———. 1983. A revision of *Dendrobium* sect. *Latouria (Orchidaceae)*. Reprint *Kew Bulletin* 38(2):229–306.
84. ———. 1986. The 'antelope' dendrobiums. A revision of *Dendrobium* sect. *Spatulata (Orchidaceae)*. *Kew Bulletin* 41(3):615–692.
85. ———. 1990. *Dendrobium alexandrae*. *The Kew Magazine* 7(3):117–121.
86. ———. 1990. Desert island discoveries—Orchid hunting on a coral island. *The Orchadian* 10(1):5.
87. ———. 1991. The genus *Diplocaulobium* (Reichb. f.) Kränzlin *(Orchidaceae)* in the Solomon Islands and Bougainville. *Lindleyana* 6(1):27–35.

88 Cribb, P., and D. Blaxell. 1983. A reassessment of *Dendrobium mirbelianum* Gaud. and the true identity of *D. wilkianum* Rupp. *The Orchadian* 7(8):175–176.

89 Cribb, P., and B. Lewis. 1989. Orchids of Vanuatu. *The Orchid Review* 97(9): 279–285.

90 ———. 1989. New orchids from Vanuatu in the southwest Pacific, part 3. *The Orchid Review* 97(11): 360–362.

91 Cribb, P., T. Reeve, and P. Woods. 1985. The genus *Dendrobium* in New Guinea. *The Kew Magazine* 2, 3:291–308.

92 Cribb, P., and S. Robbins. 1990. New Guinea orchid collections of Rudolf Schlechter in Herbarium Bogoriense. *Lindleyana* 5(4): 244–248.

93 Cribb, P., and J. J. Wood. 1982. A new species of *Dendrobium* from Vanuatu. *The Orchid Review* 90(1):14–15.

94 Cruttwell, C. 1977. Twigs aflame—dendrobiums in New Guinea. *Orchid Digest* 41(1):12.

95 Cruttwell, N. 1989. Orchids of Mount Gahavisuka—part 2: *Dendrobium*. *The Orchadian* 9(7):144–164.

96 ———. 1990. Orchids of Mount Gahavisuka—part 4: The terrestrials. *The Orchadian* 9(11):246.

97 Dassanayake, M., and E. Fosberg. 1981. *Flora of Ceylon: a revised handbook*. Oxford and IBH Publishing Co., New Delhi, India.

98 Davis, R., and M. Steiner. 1982. *Philippine orchids*. M & L Licudine Enterprises, 941 Quirino Avenue, Dongalo, Paranaque, Metro Manila, Philippines.

99 Davydov, N. 1962. *Botanical dictionary, Russian—English—German—French—Latin*. Central Editorial Board, Foreign-Language Scientific and Technical Dictionaries, Moscow.

100 De la Bathie, H. Perrier. [1939, 1941] 1981. *Flora of Madagascar* vols. I–II. The Government of Madagascar and the National Museum of Natural History, Paris. Translated and published in one vol. by Steven D. Beckman, 621 Palm Ave., Lodi, Calif., U.S.A. 95240.

101 De Martini, B. 1976. Orchids of Botanical Merit. *American Orchid Society Bulletin* 45(9):788.

102 Deva, S., and H. Naithani. 1986. *Orchid flora of North West Himalaya*. Print & Media Assoc., New Delhi, India.

103 De Wildeman, E. 1906. Plantes nouvelles ou intéressantes. *Dendrobium tonkinense* De Wild. and *D. ochraceum* De Wild. *La Tribune Horticole* Vol.1.

104 Dietrich, H. 1980, 1981, 1985, 1988. *Bibliographia orchidacearum* vols. 2.1, 2.2, 3, 4. Bibliographische Mitteilungen der Universiatsbibliothek, Friedrich-Schiller-Universitat, Jena, East Germany.

105 Dockrill, A. 1969. *Australian indigenous orchids*. Society for Growing Australian Plants, Halstead Press, Sydney, Australia.

106 Dodson, C., and R. Gillespie. 1967. *The biology of the orchids*. The Mid-America Orchid Congress, Inc.

107 Dokkum, J. A. van. 1988. *Dendrobium luteolum* Batem. *Die Orchidee* 39(4):152–153.

108 Dourado, F. 1978. *Dendrobium anosmum*. *Orchid Digest* 42(2):77.

109 ———. 1981. Photograph. *Orchid Digest* 45(6):FC.

110 ———. 1982. *Dendrobium anosmum*—Variations in a spectacular species. *American Orchid Society Bulletin* 51(6):576–578.

111 Dressler, R. 1981. *The orchids, natural history and classification*. Harvard University Press, Cambridge, Mass.

112 Ducharme, B. 1974. A novice's experience with *Dendrobium phalaenopsis*. *American Orchid Society Bulletin* 43(8):679.

113 Durheim, L. 1987. Growing orchids in the home: pests and diseases, more specifics. *Orchid Digest* 51(3):153–154.

114 Ellsworth, L. 1974. Cover photograph. *American Orchid Society Bulletin* 43(8):FC.

115 Featherstone, F. 1990. Photographs. *The Orchadian* 9(11):244.

116 Fennell, T., III. 1986. Evergreen *Dendrobium* culture—a practical guide for the beginner. *American Orchid Society Bulletin* 55(11): 1109.

117 Finet, M. 1897. VII. Orchidées nouvelles de la Chine. *Bulletin de la Société Botanique de France* Tome XLIV:419–424.

118 ———. 1903. *Dendrobium* nouveaux de L'Herbier du Muséum. *Bulletin de la Société Botanique de France* 50(III)5–6:372–376.

119 Fischer, C. [Not dated] 1984. *Flora of the Presidency of Madras* Vol. 3:1399–1478. *Orchidaceae* by J. S. Gamble. Adlard & Son, London. Reprint, Bishen Singh Mahendra Pal Singh, Dehra Dun, India.

120 Fitch, C. 1979. Orchids at Bogor botanic gardens of Indonesia. *American Orchid Society Bulletin* 48(5):459.

121 ———. 1979. Singapore botanic gardens orchid center. *American Orchid Society Bulletin* 48(7):675.

122 ———. 1980. Indonesian orchid species specialist, 2. *American Orchid Society Bulletin* 49(3):261.

123 ———. 1983. Malaysian orchid conservationist. *American Orchid Society Bulletin* 52(7):705.

124 ———. 1984. Photograph. *American Orchid Society Bulletin* 53(8): FC, BC.

125 ———. 1985. Photograph. *American Orchid Society Bulletin* 54(10):BC.

126 ———. 1986. Photograph. *American Orchid Society Bulletin* 55(12):FC.

127 ———. 1989. Techniques for photographing orchid flowers in the field. *American Orchid Society Bulletin* 58(4):373.

128 ———. 1990. Photograph. *American Orchid Society Bulletin* 59(2): FC.

129 Flanagan, A. 1992. *Dendrobium kingianum*—origins of the 'red' breeding programme and search for the ultimate red. *The Orchadian* 10(9):304.

130 Folsom, J. 1991. Book review: *Dendrobiums* by Sybella Schelpe and Joyce Stewart. *Orchid Digest* 55(3):123.

131 Fowlie, J. 1981. Speciation amongst the *Orchidaceae* as a function of climate change and topophysiography. *Orchid Digest* 45(2):44–49.

132 ———. 1985. Malaya revisited part XXIX: Rediscovering the habitat of *Paphiopedilum dayanum* on serpentine cliffs on Mount Kinabalu in eastern Malaysia (formerly North Borneo). *Orchid Digest* 49(4):125.

133 ———. 1988. China: Awash in the bitter sea—part I. The past. *Orchid Digest* 52(4):155.

134 ———. 1990. Photograph *D. crepidatum* Lindl. & Paxt *Orchid Digest* 54(2):559.

135 Fukuyama, N. 1937. Studia orchidacearum Japonicarum. IX. *Orchidaceae* Novae Micronesianae a T. Hosokawa Collectae. *The Botanical Magazine* LI(612):900–903.

136 Gagnepain, F. 1930. Quelques *Dendrobium* nouveaux D'Indochine. *Bulletin du Muséum National D'histoire Naturelle*, 2 Série.-Tome 2: 232–240, No. 2. Paris.

137 ———. 1949. Orchidacées nouvelles D'Indochine. *Bulletin du*

Muséum National D'histoire Naturelle, 2 Série.-Tome 21:737–743, No. 6. Paris.

138 ———. 1950. Orchidacées nouvelles D'Indochine (suite). *Bulletin du Muséum National D'histoire Naturelle,* 2 Série.-Tome 22: 396–403, No. 3, May 1950. Paris.

139 Garay, L., and H. Sweet. 1974. *Orchids of the southern Ryukyu Islands.* Botanical Museum, Harvard University, Cambridge, Mass.

140 *Gazetteers.* 1955–. U.S. Board of Geographic Names. Prepared and published by the U.S. Defense Mapping Agency, Washington, D.C. The *Gazetteers*, in numerous volumes, are updated periodically.

141 Geernick, D. 1984. *Flore d'Afrique central: Orchidaceae.* Jardin botanique national de Belgique, Meise, Belgium.

142 Gibbs, L. S. 1909–1911. The montane flora of Fiji. *Orchidaceae* by R. A. Rolfe. *Journal of the Linnean Society,* Botany 39:174–175.

143 ———. 1914. A contribution to the flora and plant formations of Mount Kinabalu and the highlands of British North Borneo. *Orchidaceae* by R. A. Rolfe. *Journal of the Linnean Society,* Botany 42:146–161.

144 ———. 1917. *Dutch N. W. New Guinea; a contribution to the phytogeography and flora of the Arfak Mountains, &c. Orchidaceae* by J. J. Smith. Taylor and Francis, London.

145 Gifford, R. 1992. The Australian dendrobiums of section *Grastidium. The Orchadian* 10(9): 306–312.

146 Gilli, A. 1983. Beiträge zur flora von Papua–New Guinea. *Annalen des Naturhistorischen Museums in Wein,* #84 Band 1980 Serie B für Botanik und Zoologie. (pub. May 1983). Wein, Germany.

147 Glicenstein, L. 1988. Reminiscences of orchids. *American Orchid Society Bulletin* 57(5):500.

148 Glikbarg, W. 1978. An orchid collecting experience (fantasy?) in Sumatra. *Orchid Digest* 42(5):165.

149 Goh, Chong Jin, M. Strauss, and J. Arditti. 1982. Flower induction and physiology in orchids. In: *Orchid biology: reviews and perspectives* Vol. II. Edited by J. Arditti. Comstock Publishing, Cornell University Press, Ithaca, N. Y.

150 Goldblatt, P., ed. 1981. Index to plant chromosome numbers. 1975–1978. *Monographs in Systematic Botany from the Missouri Botanical Garden* 5.

151 ———. 1984. Index to plant chromosome numbers. 1979–1981. *Monographs in Systematic Botany from the Missouri Botanical Garden* 8.

152 ———. 1985. Index to plant chromosome numbers. 1982–1983. *Monographs in Systematic Botany from the Missouri Botanical Garden* 13.

153 ———. 1988. Index to plant chromosome numbers. 1984–1985. *Monographs in Systematic Botany from the Missouri Botanical Garden* 23.

154 Goldblatt, P. and D. Johnson, eds. 1990. *Index to plant chromosome numbers. 1986–1987. Monographs in Systematic Botany from the Missouri Botanical Garden* 30.

155 ———. 1991. *Index to plant chromosome numbers. 1988–1989. Monographs in Systematic Botany from the Missouri Botanical Garden* 40.

156 Gopalan, P., and A. Henry. 1990. A new subspecies of *Dendrobium panduratum* Lindl. *(Orchidaceae)* from southern India. *Journal of the Bombay Natural History Society* 87(1):128.

157 Grant, B. [1895] 1966. *Orchids of Burma (including the Andaman Islands).* Hanthawaddy Press, Rangoon, Burma. Reprint, Twin Oaks Books, Greenfield, Wis.

158 Gregory, T. 1991. Line breeding Australian dendrobiums. *The Orchadian* 10(5):160–163.

159 Griesbach, J. 1983. Orchid flower color: genetic and cultural interactions. *American Orchid Society Bulletin* 52(10):1056.

160 Griesbach, R. 1981. Genetics and taxonomy. *Orchid Digest* 45(6): 219–221.

161 Gripp, P. 1978. Low-energy orchids. *American Orchid Society Bulletin* 47(1):39.

162 Guillaumin, A. 1929. La flore des Nouvelles-Hebrides-3. *Bulletin de la Société Botanique de France* March 1929(3–4):299–300.

163 ———. 1953. Plantes nouvelles, rares ou critiques des serres du muséum. (Notules sur quelques Orchidées d'Indochine, V.) *Bulletin du Muséum National D'histoire Naturelle,* 2 Série.-Tome 25:329–331.

164 ———. 1955. Plantes nouvelles, rares ou critiques des serres du muséum. (Notules sur quelques Orchidées d'Indochine, X.) *Bulletin du Muséum National D'histoire Naturelle,* 2 Série.-Tome 27:143–144.

165 ———. 1956. Plantes nouvelles, rares ou critiques des serres du muséum. (Notules sur quelques Orchidées d'Indochine, XIV.) *Bulletin du Muséum National D'histoire Naturelle,* 2 Série.-Tome 28:483–488.

166 ———. 1956. Plantes nouvelles, rares ou critiques des serres du muséum. (Notules sur quelques Orchidées d'Indochine, XV.) *Bulletin du Muséum National D'histoire Naturelle,* 2 Série.-Tome 28:547–549.

167 ———. 1958. Plantes nouvelles, rares ou critiques des serres du muséum. (Notules sur quelques Orchidées d'Indochine, XIX.) *Bulletin du Muséum National D'histoire Naturelle,* 2 Série.-Tome 30:458–459.

168 ———. 1962. Plantes nouvelles, rares ou critiques des serres du muséum. (Notules sur quelques Orchidées d'Indochine, XXVIII.) *Bulletin du Muséum National D'histoire Naturelle,* 2 Série.-Tome 34(3):262–263.

169 ———. 1962. Plantes nouvelles, rares ou critiques des serres du muséum. (Notules sur quelques Orchidées d'Indochine, XXIX.) *Bulletin du Muséum National D'histoire Naturelle,* 2 Série.-Tome 34(5):408–411.

170 ———. 1965. Plantes nouvelles, rares ou critiques des serres du muséum. (Notules sur quelques Orchidées d'Indochine, XXXVIII.) *Bulletin du Muséum National D'histoire Naturelle,* 2 Série., Tome 37(1):199–201.

171 Hadley, G., M. Arditti, and J. Arditti. 1987. Orchid diseases—a compendium. in *Orchid biology: reviews and perspectives* Vol. IV. Edited by J. Arditti. Comstock Publishing, Cornell University Press, Ithaca, N. Y.

172 Hagar, G. 1979. *Dendrobium phalaenopsis*—the "Cooktown orchid." *American Orchid Society Bulletin* 48(10):1034.

173 Hallé, N. 1977. *Flore de la Nouvelle Caledonie et dépendencies.* Vol. 8, *Orchidacées.* Musée national d'histoire naturelle, Paris.

174 Hamilton, R. 1972. *Index to plant illustrations. 1932–1971*, vols. 1–40 of the *American Orchid Society Bulletin.* R. M. Hamilton, 9211 Beckwith Road, Richmond, B.C., Canada V6X 1V7.

175 ———. [1980] 1988. *Orchid doctor.* Robert M. Hamilton, 9211 Beckwith Road, Richmond, B.C., Canada V6X 1V7.

176 ———. 1986. *Supplementary index to plant illustrations.* 1972–

1985, vols. 41–54 of the *American Orchid Society Bulletin*. R. M. Hamilton, 9211 Beckwith Road, Richmond, B.C., Canada V6X 1V7.

177 ———. 1988. *New orchid doctor*. Robert M. Hamilton, 9211 Beckwith Road, Richmond, B.C., Canada V6X 1V7.

178 ———. 1988. *When does it flower?* 2nd ed. Robert M. Hamilton, 9211 Beckwith Road, Richmond, B.C., Canada V6X 1V7.

179 ———. 1990. Flowering months of orchid species under cultivation. *Orchid Biology Reviews and Perspectives* Vol. 5. J. Arditti, ed. Timber Press, Portland, Ore.

180 Hamzah, A., M. Toha, and C. G. G. J. Van Steenis. 1972. *The mountain flora of Java*. E. J. Brill, Leiden.

181 Hanko, R. 1989. Cool masdevallias in hot Houston. *American Orchid Society Bulletin* 58(2):139.

182 Harrison, M. 1988. ANOS Sydney group spring show. *The Orchadian* 9(6):122.

183 ———. 1989. Show reports. *The Orchadian* 9(10):222.

184 ———. 1992. ANOS Sydney Group Inc. spring show. *The Orchadian* 10(6):174.

185 ———. 1992. Thoughts on *Dendrobium speciosum* Smith. *The Orchadian* 10(8):268.

186 ———. 1993. *Dendrobium rigidum* R. Br. *The Orchadian* 10(10): 355.

187 Hashimoto, K. 1981. Chromosome count in *Dendrobium* 1. 87 species. *Bulletin of the Hiroshima Botanical Garden* 4:63–80.

188 ———. 1987. Karyomorphological studies of some 80 taxa of *Dendrobium, Orchidaceae. Bulletin of the Hiroshima Botanical Garden* 9:1–5.

189 Hawkes, A. 1952. Notes on a collection of orchids from Ponape, Caroline Islands. *Pacific Science* VI:(1)6–9.

190 ———. [1965] 1987. *Encyclopaedia of cultivated orchids*. Faber and Faber, London.

191 Hawkes, A., and A. H. Heller. 1957. Nomenclatorial notes on the *Dendrobium* alliance. *Lloydia* 20(2).

192 Hayata, B. 1911–1912. Materials for a flora of Formosa. *The Journal of the College of Science* Vol. 30. Imperial University of Tokyo.

193 ———. 1914. *Icones plantarum Formosanarum* Vol. IV. Bureau of Productive Industries, Government of Formosa, Taihoku.

194 ———. 1916. *Icones plantarum Formosanarum* Vol. VI. Bureau of Productive Industries, Government of Formosa, Taihoku.

195 Head, P. 1988. *The* Dendrobium *family*. Peter R. Head, P.O. Box 551, Alderley, Queensland 4051, Australia.

196 Heeseler, R. 1987. *Orchid species culture guide*. Richard C. Heeseler, P.O. Box 1525, Seaford, N. Y., U.S.A. 11783.

197 Hegde, S., and A. Rao. 1982. *Dendrobium kentrophyllum* Hook. f.—A new record from Arunachal Pradesh, India. *The Orchid Review* 90(12):386.

198 Helleiner, M. 1984. Growing more orchids in a windowsill greenhouse. *American Orchid Society Bulletin* 53(3):266.

199 Holmgren, P., W. Keuken, and E. Schofield. 1981. *Index herbariorum*, part 1, ed. 7. *Regnum vegetabile* Vol. 106. F. A. Stafleu, ed. International Bureau for Plant Taxonomy and Nomenclature. Utrecht, Netherlands.

200 Holttum, R. 1964. *A revised flora of Malaya*. Vol. 1, *orchids*. Government Printing Office, Singapore

201 Holttum, R., F. Brieger, and P. Cribb. 1979. A proposal for the retypification of *Dendrobium* Sw., nom. cons. *Taxon* 28(4):409.

202 Hooker, J. 1890–1894. *Flora of British India* Vols. V and VI. L. Reeve & Co., London.

203 ———. [1895] 1967. *A century of Indian orchids*. Annals of the Royal Botanic Garden, Calcutta. Reprint, J. Cramer, Lehre, West Germany.

204 Horridge, W. 1920. *Dendrobium* × *primulardi*. *The Gardeners' Chronicle* sér. III, XLVII:308.

205 Hosokawa, T. 1942. Materials of the botanical research towards the flora of Micronesia XXIII. *Transactions of the Natural History Society of Taiwan (Formosa)* XXXII:12.

206 Howcroft, N. 1981. *Dendrobium wulaiense*—a new species of section *Ceratobium* from West New Britain Province, Papua New Guinea. *The Orchadian* 6(12): 284.

207 ———. 1990. Contributions to the orchid flora of the Araucaria forests in New Guinea—7—*Dendrobium anosmum* Lindl. *The Orchadian* 9(11):263.

208 Hu, Shiu-Ying. 1973. The *Orchidaceae* of China 5. *Quarterly Journal-Taiwan Museum*, 26, 1–2:150–165.

209 ———. 1977. *The genera of* Orchidaceae *in Hong Kong*. The Chinese University Press, Hong Kong.

210 Hunt, D. 1981. *Orchids from Curtis's botanical magazine*. Bentham-Moxon Trust, Curwen Books, Plaistow, London.

211 Hunt, P. 1970. Notes on Asiatic Orchids: V. *Kew Bulletin* 24(1):86–92.

212 ———. 1971. Notes on Asiatic Orchids: VI. *Kew Bulletin* 26(1): 171–179.

213 Hunt, P., and V. Summerhayes. 1961. Notes on Asiatic Orchids: III. *Taxon* X:101–110.

214 ———. 1966. Notes on Asiatic Orchids:IV. *Kew Bulletin* 2:259–268.

215 *Index herbariorum*. [1952] 1981. 7th edition. S. Stafleu, ed. Part 1. The herbaria of the world. *Regnum Vegetabile* Vol. 106. International Association of Plant Taxonomists, The Hague/Boston.

216 *Index Kewensis*. [1895] 1977. Vol. I–II (–1885). An enumeration of the genera and species of flowering plants. Oxford University Press, Amen House, London E. C. 4. Reprint by Otto Koeltz Science Publishers, D-6240 Koenigstein/West Germany.

217 *Index Kewensis*. [1901] 1981. Supplement I (1886–1895). Plantarum Phanerogameram. An enumeration of the genera and species of flowering plants. Oxford University Press, Amen House, London E. C. 4. Reprint by Otto Koeltz Science Publishers, D-6240 Koenigstein/West Germany.

218 *Index Kewensis*. [Not dated] 1979. Supplement II (1896–1900). Plantarum Phanerogameram. An enumeration of the genera and species of flowering plants. Oxford University Press, Amen House, London E. C. 4. Reprint by Otto Koeltz Science Publishers, D-6240 Koenigstein/West Germany.

219 *Index Kewensis*. [1908] 1978. Supplement III (1901–1905). Plantarum Phanerogameram. An enumeration of the genera and species of flowering plants. Oxford University Press, Amen House, London E. C. 4. Reprint by Otto Koeltz Science Publishers, D-6240 Koenigstein/West Germany.

220 *Index Kewensis*. [1913] 1982. Supplement IV (1906–1910). Plantarum Phanerogameram. An enumeration of the genera and species of flowering plants. Oxford University Press, Amen House, London E. C. 4. Reprint by Otto Koeltz Science Publishers, D-6240 Koenigstein/West Germany.

221 *Index Kewensis*. [1921] 1978. Supplement V (1911–1915). Plan-

Bibliography

222 *Index Kewensis*. [1926] 1989. Supplement VI (1916–1920). Plantarum Phanerogameram. An enumeration of the genera and species of flowering plants. Oxford University Press, Amen House, London E. C. 4. Reprint by Otto Koeltz Science Publishers, D-6240 Koenigstein/West Germany.

223 *Index Kewensis*. [1929] 1984. Supplement VII (1921–1925). Plantarum Phanerogameram. An enumeration of the genera and species of flowering plants. Oxford University Press, Amen House, London E. C. 4. Reprint by Otto Koeltz Science Publishers, D-6240 Koenigstein/West Germany.

224 *Index Kewensis*. [1933] 1960. Supplement VIII (1926–1930). Plantarum Phanerogameram. An enumeration of the genera and species of flowering plants. Oxford University Press, Amen House, London E. C. 4.

225 *Index Kewensis*. [1938] 1978. Supplement IX (1931–1935). Plantarum Phanerogameram. An enumeration of the genera and species of flowering plants. Oxford University Press, Amen House, London E. C. 4. Reprint by Otto Koeltz Science Publishers, D-6240 Koenigstein/West Germany.

226 *Index Kewensis*. [1947] 1981. Supplement X (1936–1940). Plantarum Phanerogameram. An enumeration of the genera and species of flowering plants. Oxford University Press, Amen House, London E. C. 4. Reprint by Otto Koeltz Science Publishers, D-6240 Koenigstein/West Germany.

227 *Index Kewensis*. [1953] 1978. Supplement XI (1941–1950). Plantarum Phanerogameram. An enumeration of the genera and species of flowering plants. Oxford University Press, Amen House, London E. C. 4. Reprint by Otto Koeltz Science Publishers, D-6240 Koenigstein/West Germany.

228 *Index Kewensis*. [1959] 1980. Supplement XII. 1964. (1951–1955). Plantarum Phanerogameram. An enumeration of the genera and species of flowering plants. Oxford University Press, Amen House, London E. C. 4. Reprint by Otto Koeltz Science Publishers, D-6240 Koenigstein/West Germany.

229 *Index Kewensis*. 1966. Supplement XIII (1956–1960). Plantarum Phanerogameram. An enumeration of the genera and species of flowering plants. Oxford University Press, Amen House, London E. C. 4.

230 *Index Kewensis*. [1970] 1985. Supplement XIV (1961–1965). Plantarum Phanerogameram. An enumeration of the genera and species of flowering plants. Oxford University Press, Amen House, London E. C. 4. Reprint by Otto Koeltz Science Publishers, D-6240 Koenigstein/West Germany.

231 *Index Kewensis*. [1974] 1983. Supplement XV (1966–1970). Plantarum Phanerogameram. An enumeration of the genera and species of flowering plants. Oxford University Press, Amen House, London E. C. 4. Reprint by Otto Koeltz Science Publishers, D-6240 Koenigstein/West Germany.

232 *Index Kewensis*. [1981] 1987. Supplement XVI (1971–1975). Plantarum Phanerogameram. An enumeration of the genera and species of flowering plants. Oxford University Press, New York.

233 *Index Kewensis*. 1987. Supplement XVII (1976–1980). Names of seed-bearing plants at the rank of family and below. Clarendon Press, Oxford.

234 *Index Kewensis*. 1987. Supplement XVIII (1981–1985). Names of seed-bearing plants at the rank of family and below. Clarendon Press, Oxford.

235 *Index Kewensis*. 1991. Supplement XVIV (1986–1990). Names of seed-bearing plants at the rank of family and below. Clarendon Press, Oxford.

236 International Orchid Commission. 1993. *Handbook on orchid nomenclature and registration*. 4th ed., rev. International Orchid Commission, London.

237 Irwin, J. 1991. Peloric dendrobiums of Norfolk Island. *The Orchadian* 10(4):100.

238 Jain, S., and P. Hajra. 1976. Orchids in some protected habitats in Assam in Eastern India. *American Orchid Society Bulletin* 45(12):1103.

239 Johansen, B. 1990. Incompatibility in *Dendrobium* (Orchidaceae). *Botanical Journal of the Linnean Society* 103:165–196 with 10 figures.

240 Jones, D. 1988. *Native orchids of Australia*. Reed books Pty. Ltd., 2 Aquatic Drive, Frenchs Forest, NSW 2086, Australia.

241 Jones, D. 1993. A new species of *Dendrobium* Sw. Section *Dendrocoryne (Orchidaceae)* from Australia. *The Orchadian* 10(12):457.

242 Jones, D., and B. Gray. 1976. The pollination of *Dendrobium lichenastrum* (F. Muell.) Krzl. *American Orchid Society Bulletin* 45(11):981.

243 Jones, K., K. Lim, and P. Cribb. 1982. The chromosomes of orchids VII. *Dendrobium*. *Kew Bulletin* 37(2):221.

244 Joseph, J. 1982. Orchids of Nilgiris. *Records of the botanical survey of India* Vol. 22. Botanical Survey of India, P.O. Botanic Garden, Howrah, India.

245 Kamemoto, H., and R. Sagarik. 1975. *Beautiful Thai orchid species*. Orchid Society of Thailand, Aksornsampan Press, Bangkok, Thailand.

246 Kamemoto, K. 1978. Photograph. *American Orchid Society Bulletin* 47(8):FC.

247 Kennedy, G. 1975. Dendrobiums of the Sikkim Himalaya and the Burmese-India border. *American Orchid Society Bulletin* 44(9):797.

248 ———. 1977. Peloric orchids. *Orchid Digest* 41(5):169.

249 Kerr, A. F. G. 1927. XXVIII.—Contributions to the Flora of Siam. Additamentum XXII (continued from p. 174). *Bulletin of Miscellaneous Information* No. 5. Royal Botanic Gardens, Kew, London.

250 King, G., and R. Pantling. 1897. Materials for a flora of the Malayan Peninsula—new Indo-Malayan orchids. *Journal of the Asiatic Society of Bengal* part II.—Natural Science, Vol. LXVI(3):583–585.

251 King, J. 1984. A miscellany of orchids—*Dendrobium infundibulum*. *The Orchid Review* 92(1): 28–29.

252 Kores, P. 1989. Fijian orchids. *Allertonia* 5(1):73–98.

253 Kränzlin, F. 1894. *Orchidaceae* Papuanae. *Österreichische Botanische Zeitschrift* XLIV:161–164, 253–257, 333–338.

254 ———. [1910] 1957. Orchidaceae-Monandrae-Dendrobiinae. In *Das Pflanzenreich. Regni vegetabilis conspectus*, ed. by A. Engler. Reprinted Im Verlag von H. R. Engelmann (J. Cramer). Weinheim/Bergstr.

255 Kumar, M., and N. Sasidharan. 1986. Orchids of Kerala and their conservation. In *Biology, conservation, and culture of orchids*, ed. by S. P. Vij. The Orchid Society of India. Affiliated East-West Press Private Ltd. New Delhi, India.

256 Kunze, H. 1982. The 7th Australian orchid conference. *American Orchid Society Bulletin* 51(5):501.

257 Lager, J. 1978. Reminiscences of an orchid collector. *Orchid Digest* 42(6):231–232.

258 Lamb, A. 1982. The wild orchid species of Sabah. *Orchid Digest* 46(1):25.

259 Lavarack, P. 1977. Notes on Queensland *Orchidaceae*, I. *Austrobaileya* 1(1):63–74.

260 ———. 1991. An appraisal of the species concept in the taxonomy of Australian orchids. *The Orchadian* 10(5):141–143.

261 Lavarack, P., and P. Cribb. 1983. *Dendrobium carronii*—a new species from Cape York Peninsula and New Guinea. *The Orchadian* 7(8):177–179.

262 Lavarack, P., and B. Gray. 1985. *Tropical orchids of Australia*. Thomas Nelson, Melbourne, Australia.

263 Lawler, L. 1989. Native orchids of tropical Queensland. *The Orchadian* 9(8):168.

264 ———. 1991. Orchids in far north Queensland. *The Orchadian* 10(3):63.

265 Lea, R. 1988. Wollongong and district Native Orchid Society spring show. *The Orchadian* 9(6):134.

266 Lecomte, H., and H. Humbert, ed. 1932. *Orchidacées* by F. Gagnepain. *Flore Génerale de L'Indo-Chine* Vol. 6 (sixieme).

267 Lemieux, C. 1978. Photograph. *American Orchid Society Bulletin* 47(11):FC.

268 Levy, R., Mrs. 1987. *Dendrobium senile*—the fuzzy facts. *American Orchid Society Bulletin* 56(11):1129.

269 Lewis, B. 1990. Orchids of Vanuatu. *The Orchadian* 10(2):36.

270 Lewis, B., and P. Cribb. 1989. *Orchids of Vanuatu*. Royal Botanic Gardens, Kew, England.

271 ——— 1991. *Orchids of the Solomon Islands and Bougainville*. Royal Botanic Gardens, Kew, England.

272 Light, M. 1990. Doing your part for conservation—1. Getting seeds. *American Orchid Society Bulletin* 59(8):787.

273 Lim, K. 1985. The chromosomes of orchids at Kew—2—*Dendrobium*. *American Orchid Society Bulletin* 54(9):1122.

274 Lin, Tsian-Piao. 1975. *Native orchids of Taiwan* Vol. 1. Southern Materials Center, P.O. Box 13-342, Taipei, Taiwan, Republic of China.

275 ———. 1977. *Native orchids of Taiwan* Vol. 2. Southern Materials Center, P.O. Box 13-342, Taipei, Taiwan, Republic of China.

276 Linden, L. 1895. *Le Journal des Orchidées* p. 153. Paris.

277 Lindley, J. 1830–1840. *The genera and species of orchidaceous plants*. Ridgways, Piccadilly, London.

278 ———. 1859. Contributions to the Orchidology of India—II. *Journal of the Proceedings of the Linnean Society. Supplement to Botany* 1:1–17, 3:1–21. London.

279 Liu, Tang-Shui. 1978. *Flora of Taiwan* Vol. 5—*Angiospermae*. Orchidaceae by Su, Horng-Jye. Epoch Publishing Co., Ltd. Taipei, Taiwan, Republic of China. Sponsored by the National Science Foundations of the Republic of China and of the United States under a cooperative Science Program.

280 Löve, A., and O. Solbrig. 1965–1966. IOPB chromosome number reports. *Taxon* 14–15:52–57, 86–87.

281 Lower, P., and B. Lower. 1992. A gallery of fragrant orchids. *American Orchid Society Bulletin* 61(3):238.

282 Lu, Jiong-Lin and Gao Li-Xian. 1990. A new species of *Dendrobium* from Henan, China. *Bulletin of Botanical Research* 10(4):29–31.

283 Manilal, K., and C. Sathish Kumar. 1985. *Dendrobium panduratum* Lindl. *(Orchidaceae)*—a new record for India. *Journal of the Indian Botanical Society* 64:299.

284 Mark, F. 1980. The *Pleione* of Taiwan—*Pleione formosana* Hayata with temperature and rainfall data of Taiwan. *Orchid Digest* 44(6):236–237.

285 Marlow, S., and D. Butcher. 1987. Propagation of two rare orchid species from seed. *The Orchid Review* 95(10):331–334.

286 Masamune, G. 1942. *Enumeratio Phanerogamarum Bornearum*.

287 Mattes, P. 1982. A discovery trip to the Philippines with notes on the habitat of *Paphiopedilum fowliei* on Palawan Island. *Orchid Digest* 46(1):5.

288 McAlpine, J., and G. Keig, with R. Falls. 1983. *Climate of Papua New Guinea*. Commonwealth Scientific and Industrial Research Organization with the Australian National University Press, Canberra, Australia.

289 McDonald, M. 1990. The native orchids of New Zealand. *The Orchid Review* 98(7):216:220.

290 McIntosh, S. 1992. Grand prix. *American Orchid Society Bulletin* 61(7):654.

291 McQueen, J,. and B. McQueen. 1992. *Miniature orchids*. Timber Press, Portland, Ore.

292 McQuerry, M. 1987. A.O.S. acquires original Reichenbachia paintings. *American Orchid Society Bulletin* 56(6):588.

293 McVittie, M. 1971. Philippine dendrobiums and how they grow. *Orchid Digest* 35(5):143.

294 Mehra, P., and S. Vij. 1974. Some observations on the ecological adaptations and distribution pattern of the East Himalayan orchids. *American Orchid Society Bulletin* 43(4):301–315.

295 Merrill, E. 1921. A bibliographic enumeration of Bornean plants, Orchidaceae by O. Ames. *Journal of the Straits Branch of the Royal Asiatic Society* Special Number 164: 134–204.

296 ———. 1924. An enumeration of Philippine flowering plants. *Bureau of Science* No. 18(1) Fasc. 3, Manila, Philippines.

297 ———. 1929. *Plantae elmerianae Borneenses*. University of California Press, Berkeley, Calif..

298 ———. 1934. An enumeration of plants collected in Sumatra by W. Bangham and C. Bangham. *Contributions from the Arnold Arboretum of Harvard University* VIII. The Arnold Arboretum of Harvard University, Jamaica Plain, Mass.

299 Milan, L. 1982. Preservation through pictures ... a guide to simple or complex flower and plant photography. *Orchid Digest* 46(4):156.

300 Millar, A. 1972. The gardens and orchid collection of the University of Papua New Guinea. *American Orchid Society Bulletin* 41(4):292.

301 ———. 1972. Orchid work in Papua New Guinea. *American Orchid Society Bulletin* 41(8):676.

302 ———. 1975. Collecting in the Western District of Papua New Guinea. *American Orchid Society Bulletin* 44(6):485.

303 ———. 1976. New Guinea orchids—Sepik blue or May River red? *American Orchid Society Bulletin* 45(5):411.

304 ———. 1978. *Orchids of Papua, New Guinea: an introduction*. University of Washington Press, Seattle, Wash.

305 ———. 1978. Orchids of the misty highlands of Papua New Guinea. *American Orchid Society Bulletin* 47(11):1031.

306 ———. 1987. The Sepik blue and the May River red. *American Orchid Society Bulletin* 56(9):913.

307 ———. 1987. The pastor's orchid. *American Orchid Society Bulletin* 56(10):1019.

308 ———. 1990. Conservation and preservation of our native species. *American Orchid Society Bulletin* 59(1):5.

309 ———. 1990. Hybrids of Australian Native Orchids. *American Orchid Society Bulletin* 59(2):123.

310 Miquel, F. 1855. *Flora van Nederlandsch Indié.* C. G. Van Der Post, Amsterdam, C. Van Der Post, Jr. Utrecht, and Fried Fleischer, Leipzig.

311 Miyamoto, C. 1988. Hawaiian achievements with *Dendrobium phalaenopsis. Orchid Digest* 52(3):101.

312 Mohr, H. 1990. Australian dendrobiums. *Schlechteriana* 1(4):159.

313 ———. 1991. Australian dendrobiums-2. *Schlechteriana* 2(1):31.

314 Montefusco, M. 1981. Sander's Reichenbachia—a Victorian masterpiece. *American Orchid Society Bulletin* 50(5):541.

315 Moore, J. 1933. Raiatean plants. *Bulletin of the Bernice P. Bishop Museum* 102:24.

316 Moore, L., and E. Edgar. 1970. *Flora of New Zealand* Vol. 2. A. R. Shearer, Government Printer, Wellington, New Zealand.

317 Mueller, G. 1861. *Orchides.* 1369. *Dendrobium* Sw. *G. G. Walpers. Annales Botanices Systematicae* 6:279–308.

318 Mulder, D., and T. Mulder-Roelfsema. 1992. Papua New Guinea. *American Orchid Society Bulletin* 61(11):1090.

319 Mulder-Roelfsema, T. 1992. Photograph *D. subclausum. American Orchid Society Bulletin* 61(10):1087.

320 Naithani, H. 1986. A new species of *Dendrobium* Sw. *(Orchidaceae)* from Arunachal Pradesh (India). *Indian Forester* 112(1):66–68.

321 Nax and Butterworth Winners. 1989. *American Orchid Society Bulletin* 58(3):255.

322 Neptune, W. 1984. The culture of nobile dendrobiums. *American Orchid Society Bulletin* 53(5):462.

323 ———. 1989. The growing of specimen plants. *American Orchid Society Bulletin* 58(12):1202.

324 New and recently named orchids. 1988. *Orchid Digest* 52(4):165.

325 Nicholls, W. 1969. *Orchids of Australia.* Edited by D. Jones and T. Muir. Nelson Publishing, Melbourne, Australia.

326 Northen, R. 1970. *Home orchid growing.* Van Nostrand Reinhold, New York.

327 ———. 1972. Cover photograph. *American Orchid Society Bulletin* 41(10):BC.

328 ———. 1973. Orchids for the beginner—5—flowering. *American Orchid Society Bulletin* 42(5):423.

329 ———. 1973. Orchids for the beginner—9—orchid ailments: part 2, diseases. *American Orchid Society Bulletin* 42(9):810.

330 ———. 1980. *Miniature orchids.* Van Nostrand Reinhold, New York.

331 ———. 1988. Fifteen years to flower: *Dendrobium tapiniense. American Orchid Society Bulletin* 57(1):41.

332 ———. 1988. The kingdom of Lilliput: miniature orchids. *American Orchid Society Bulletin* 57(2):116–124.

333 ———. 1988. The lure of miniatures. *Orchid Digest* 52(1):4.

334 North Shore Orchid Society of Australia. 1983. *World of orchids.* North Shore Orchid Society of Australia, Sydney, Australia.

335 Obata, J. 1987. Native and naturalized orchids of Hawaii. *American Orchid Society Bulletin* 56(7):695.

336 O'Byrne, P. 1992. Two members of *Dendrobium* section *Rhopalanthe* and *Aporum. The Orchadian* 10(8):274.

337 Oertle, C. ed. 1987. *Index periodicarum orchidacearum.* Tipografia Poncioni, Losone, Switzerland.

338 Ohwi, J., F. Meyer, and E. Walker. 1965. *Flora of Japan.* Smithsonian Institution, Washington, D. C.

339 Olmo, J. 1987. Photograph. *American Orchid Society Bulletin* 56(11):FC.

340 Orchid Review. 1935. Notes. A new Bornean *Dendrobium—D. paathii. The Orchid Review* XLIII: 289–290.

341 Oregon Orchid Society. 1977. *Your first orchids and how to grow them.* Oregon Orchid Society, P. O. Box 14182, Portland, OR 97214, U.S.A.

342 Ossian, C. 1981. A review of the "Antelope" dendrobiums (section *Ceratobium*)—part 1—introduction. *American Orchid Society Bulletin* 50(10):1213–1219.

343 ———. 1981. A review of the "Antelope" dendrobiums (section *Ceratobium*)—part 2—subsection *Minacea. American Orchid Society Bulletin* 50(11):1333–1343.

344 ———. 1981. A review of the "Antelope" dendrobiums (section *Ceratobium*)—part 3—Tricostate *Platypetala* species. *American Orchid Society Bulletin* 50(12):1446.

345 ———. 1982. Review of the "Antelope" dendrobiums (section *Ceratobium*)—part 4—Pentacostate *Platypetala* species. *American Orchid Society Bulletin* 51(1):23.

346 ———. 1982. A review of the "Antelope" dendrobiums (Section *Ceratobium*)—part 5—Subsection *Mirbeliana. American Orchid Society Bulletin* 51(2):139.

347 ———. 1982. A review of the "Antelope" dendrobiums (section *Ceratobium*)—part 6—subsection *Taurina* and subsection *Undulata. American Orchid Society Bulletin* 51(3):249.

348 ———. 1982. A review of the "Antelope" dendrobiums (section *Ceratobium*)—part 7—"incertae sedis" and conclusions. *American Orchid Society Bulletin* 51(4):353.

349 ———. 1983. *Dendrobium bellatulum* Rolfe—a special species. *American Orchid Society Bulletin* 52(7):699.

350 ———. 1990. *Dendrobium* culture: Introduction and general suggestions. *Orchid Digest* 54(2): 52–59.

351 ———. 1992. *Dendrobium* culture: part 2 care and feeding of the sections *Phalaenanthe* and *Spatulata. Orchid Digest* 56(3):117.

352 ———. 1993. Growing Australasian dendrobiums in the United States. *The Orchadian* 10(10):348–350.

353 Parham, J. 1972. *Plants of the Fiji Islands: Orchidaceae.* Rev. ed. The Government Printer, Suva, Fiji.

354 Peterson, R. 1974. Ten small orchids for the beginner. *American Orchid Society Bulletin* 43(8):672.

355 ———. 1976. *Dendrobium* hybrids—Hawaii's endemic orchids. *American Orchid Society Bulletin* 45(3):235.

356 ———. 1977. A Preview of the 9th World Orchid Conference—and Beyond. *American Orchid Society Bulletin* 46(6):535.

357 Photos Great Britain. 1992. *Dendrobium miyakei. Orchid Review* 100(1181):107. March 1992.

358 Polunin, O., and A. Stainton. 1984. *Flowers of the Himalaya*. Oxford University Press, New York.

359 Pottinger, M., C. Bailes, and D. Menzies. 1984. Orchids flowering at Kew. *The Orchid Review* 92(7):204–207.

360 Pradhan, G. 1972. *Dendrobium primulinum. American Orchid Society Bulletin* 41(3):196.

361 ———. 1972. Purple beauties—*Dendrobium parishii* and *D. lituiflorum. American Orchid Society Bulletin* 41(5):414.

362 ———. 1972. *Dendrobium aduncum. American Orchid Society Bulletin* 41(12):1098.

363 ———. 1973. *Dendrobium candidum. American Orchid Society Bulletin* 42(1):39.

364 ———. 1974. Indian species of the *Nigrohirsutae* section of *Dendrobium* part 1. *Orchid Digest* 38(4):124.

365 ———. 1976. *Dendrobium densiflorum* and its allies. *American Orchid Society Bulletin* 45(11):984.

366 ———. 1977. Indian species of the *Nigrohirsutae* section of *Dendrobium* part 2. *Orchid Digest* 41(1):4.

367 Pradhan, J. 1972. Orchids in Nepal. *American Orchid Society Bulletin* 41(8):699.

368 Pradhan, U. 1972. Beautiful orchid species—*Dendrobium crepidatum* Lindl. *American Orchid Society Bulletin* 41(6):525.

369 ———. 1979. *Indian orchids: guide to identification and culture* Vol. 2. Udai C. Pradhan, Kalimpong, India.

370 Pridgeon, A. 1986. Cover photograph. *American Orchid Society Bulletin* 55(10):FC.

371 Pridgeon, A., ed. 1992. *The illustrated encyclopedia of orchids*. Timber Press, Portland, Ore.

372 Quisumbing, E. 1964. Orchid hunting in Borneo. *Araneta Journal of Agriculture* 11(2):76–78.

373 Quisumbing, E. 1981. *The complete writings of Dr. Eduardo A. Quisumbing*. Eugenio Lòpez Foundation, Inc. Chronicle Building, Meralco Avenue, Pasig, Metro Manila, Philippines.

374 Raizada, M., H. Naithani, and H. Saxena. 1981. *Orchids of Mussoorie*. Bishen Singh Mahendra Pal Singh, 23-A, Connaught Place, Dehra Dun, India 248001.

375 Rakpaibulsombat, T. 1977. A judging trip to the orchid jungles in northern Thailand. *American Orchid Society Bulletin* 46(6):532.

376 Rao, A. 1986. Orchid flora of Arunachal Pradesh—a conspectus, in *Biology, conservation, and culture of orchids,* ed. by S. P. Vij. The Orchid Society of India. Affiliated East-West Press Private Ltd. New Delhi, India.

377 Rao, P. 1991. A new species of *Dendrobium (Orchidaceae)* from Andaman Islands, India. *Nordic Journal of Botany* 12(2):227–229.

378 Reeve, T. 1978. "The most beautiful orchid in Papua New Guinea." *Dendrobium sophronites* Schltr. *The Orchadian* 6(2):36–39.

379 ———. 1981. Orchids of the Enga Province, Papua New Guinea. *Australian Orchid Review* 46:104–110.

380 ———. 1983. *Dendrobium geotropum* T. M. Reeve a new species in section *Latouria* from Papua New Guinea. *The Orchadian* 7(6):183–185.

381 ———. 1983. Some new species of *Dendrobium* section *Pedilonum* from the highlands of Papua New Guinea. *The Orchadian* 7(6):130–137.

382 ———. 1983. A revision of *Dendrobium* section *Microphytanthe (Orchidaceae). The Orchadian* 7(9):203–206.

383 ———. 1989. Photographs. *The Orchadian* 9(9):192.

384 Reeve, T., and P. Woods. 1981. *Dendrobium delicatulum* Kränzlin. *The Orchadian* 7(1):18–21.

385 ———. 1989. A revision of *Dendrobium* section *Oxyglossum* (Orchidaceae). *Notes from the Royal Botanic Garden Edinburgh*. 46(2):161–304.

386 Reichenbach, H. G., Jr. 1881. *Dendrobium cobbianum* Rchb. f. *The Gardeners' Chronicle*, p. 780.

387 ———. 1887. *Dendrobium rutriferum* Rchb. f. *Lindenia* III:49.

388 Reis, J. 1972. Orchid portraits. *American Orchid Society Bulletin* 41(3):212.

389 Rentoul, J. 1982. *Growing orchids, book 3. Vandas, dendrobiums and others*. Timber Press, Portland, Ore.

390 ———. 1985. *Growing orchids, book 4. The Australasian families*. Timber Press, Portland, Ore.

391 Revue Horticole. 1895. *Société Nationale d'Horticulture de France*, Paris.

392 Richards, P. 1964. *The tropical rain forest*. Cambridge University Press, New York.

393 Ridley, H. 1886. On the monocotyledonous plants of New Guinea collected by Mr. H. O. Forbes. *The Journal of Botany British and Foreign* 24:321–327, 353–356.

394 ———. 1895–1897. An enumeration of all *Orchidaceae* hitherto recorded from Borneo. *The Journal of the Linnean Society, Botany* 31:267–272.

395 ———. 1896. *Orchidaceae* and *Apostasiceae* of the Malay Peninsula. *The Journal of the Linnean Society* 32:231–265.

396 ———. 1900. *Journal of Botany British and Foreign* 38:70.

397 ———. 1907. New or rare Malayan plants. *Journal of the Straits Branch of the Royal Asiatic Society* 48:132–134.

398 ———. 1908. New or rare Malayan plants. *Journal of the Straits Branch of the Royal Asiatic Society* 50:126–143.

399 ———. 1910. New or rare Malayan plants—V. *Journal of the Straits Branch of the Royal Asiatic Society* 54:47–55.

400 ———. 1916–1922. Report on the botany of the Wollaston Expedition to Dutch New Guinea, 1912–13. *Transactions of The Linnean Society of London*. Second Series, Botany 9:1–9, 165–178. London.

401 ———. 1917. Results of an expedition to Korinchi Peak, Sumatra. *Journal of the Federated Malay States Museums* 8(4):90–93.

402 ———. 1924. *The flora of the Malay Peninsula*. L. Reeve and Co. Ltd., 6 Henrietta St., Covent Garden, W. C., England.

403 ———. 1925. XII.—Plants from Bencoolen, Sumatra. Collected by Mr. C. J. Brooks. *Bulletin of Miscellaneous Information*, Royal Botanic Gardens, Kew, England.

404 Riley, J. 1992. Painting. *The Orchadian* 10(6):BC.

405 Rittershausen, W. 1991. *Dendrobium phalaenopsis* and its hybrids. *The Orchid Review* 99(10):310–316.

406 Rogers, R. 1925. Contributions to the orchidology of Papua and New Guinea. *Transactions and proceedings of the Royal Society of South Australia* XLIX:254–265.

407 Rolfe, R. 1894. CCCLXXXII.—New orchids—decade 8. *Bulletin of Miscellaneous Information*, p. 154–159. Royal Botanic Gardens, Kew, London.

408 ———. 1894. CCCLXXXIII.—New orchids—decade 9. *Bulletin of Miscellaneous Information*, p. 182–187. Royal Botanic Gardens, Kew, London.

409 ———. 1894. CCCCXV.—New orchids—decade 10. *Bulletin of Miscellaneous Information*, p. 361–362. Royal Botanic Gardens, Kew, London.

410 ———. 1896. DXXXIV.—New orchids—decades 17–20. *Bulletin of Miscellaneous Information*, p. 193. Royal Botanic Gardens, Kew, London.

411 ———. 1898. DCXX.—New orchids—decades 21 and 22. *Bulletin of Miscellaneous Information*, p. 192–199. Royal Botanic Gardens, Kew, London.

412 ———. 1899. DCLIII.—Flora of British New Guinea. *Bulletin of Miscellaneous Information*, p. 95–112. Royal Botanic Gardens, Kew, London.

413 ———. 1901. III.—New Orchids—decade 25. *Bulletin of Miscellaneous Information*, p. 146–150. Royal Botanic Gardens, Kew, London.

414 ———. 1903. *Orchidaceae. Epidendreae.* Enumeration of all the plants known from China proper by F. Forbes and W. Hemsley. *Journal of the Linnean Society, Botany* 36:9–13.

415 ———. 1906. XXI.—New orchids—decade 28. *Kew Bulletin:* 112. Royal Botanic Gardens, Kew, London.

416 ———. 1906. LI.—New orchids—decade 29. *Kew Bulletin:* 375. Royal Botanic Gardens, Kew, London.

417 ———. 1921. IV.—New orchids—decades XLVIII–XLIX. *Kew Bulletin:* 55:52–56. Royal Botanic Gardens, Kew, London.

418 ———. 1925. *Bulletin of Miscellaneous Information*, p. 373–374, 377. Royal Botanic Gardens, Kew, London.

419 Royal Botanic Gardens, Kew. 1986–1991. *The Kew record of taxonomic literature-vascular plants.* Royal Botanic Gardens, Kew.

420 Royal Horticultural Awards. 1992. *Dendrobium miyakei. The Orchid Review* 100(3):107.

421 Rupp, H., and T. Hunt. 1947. A review of the genus *Dendrobium* (Orchidaceae) in Australia. *The Proceedings of the Linnean Society of New South Wales* Vol. LXXII: 233–251.

422 Sagarik, R. 1977. Trend of vandaceous orchid hybridization in Thailand. *American Orchid Society Bulletin* 46(6):511.

423 ———. 1977. Photograph—*Dendrobium parishii. American Orchid Society Bulletin* 46(6):502.

424 Santapau, H., and Z. Kapadia. 1966. *The orchids of Bombay.* Government of India Press, Calcutta, India.

425 Sauleda, R. 1976. Harvesting times of orchid seed capsules for the green pod culture process. *American Orchid Society Bulletin* 45(4):305–309.

426 ———. 1984. *Dendrobium fimbriatum* Hooker and its varieties. *American Orchid Society Bulletin* 53(9):947.

427 Saunders, W., H. G. Reichenbach, and W. Fitch. [1869, 1873, 1882] 1980. *Refugium botanicum* or figures and descriptions from living specimens or little known or new plants of botanical interest, Vol. II. Earl M. Coleman, Pub. Stanfordville, New York.

428 Schelpe, E. 1981. A review of the genus *Dendrobium* section *Callista. Orchid Digest* 45(6):204.

429 ———. 1985. The section *Formosae* of the genus *Dendrobium.* In K. W. Tan (Ed.), *Proceedings of the 11th World Orchid Conference March 1984, Miami*, p. 308–310.

430 Schelpe, S., and J. Stewart. 1990. *Dendrobiums—an introduction to the species in cultivation.* Orchid Sundries, Ltd., New Gate Farm, Stour Provost, Gillingham, Dorset SB8 5LT, Great Britain.

431 Schlechter, R. 1904. VI. *Dendrobium (Aporum) roseo-nervatum. Notizblatt des Königllichen Botanischen Gartens und Museums zu Berlin* 33:131.

432 ———. [1906] 1986. Contributions to the knowledge of the Flora of New Caledonia. Engler's *Botanische Jahrbucher* 39:33–91. Reprint translated by H. Katz, and J. Simmons and edited by D. Blaxell. *Australian Orchid Foundation,* 107 Roberts St., Essendon 3040, Victoria, Australia.

433 ———. 1906. Neue Orchidaceen der flora des Monsum-Gebietes. *Bulletin de L'Herbier Boissier*, 2nd. series, 6:453–460.

434 ———. [1910–1911] 1986. Revision of the orchids of German Samoa. *Fedde's Repertorium specierum novarum regni vegetabilis* 9:82–96, 98–112. Reprint edited and translated by H. Katz, and J. Simmons. *Australian Orchid Foundation,* 107 Roberts St., Essendon 3040, Victoria, Australia.

435 ———. [1911] 1986. Contributions to knowledge of the orchid flora of Sumatra. A. Engler, ed. *Beiblatt zu Den Botanischen Jahrbüchern* No. 104, XLV(3):1–61. Reprint edited and translated by H. Katz and J. Simmons. *Australian Orchid Foundation,* 107 Roberts St., Essendon 3040, Victoria, Australia.

436 ———. [1911, 1925] 1986. The *Orchidaceae* of the Celebes (1911) and the *Orchidaceae* of the island of Celebes (1925). *Fedde's Repertorium specierum novarum regni vegetabilis* Vol. 10:1–40, 66–96, 177–213 and Vol. 21:113–212. Berlin, Germany. Reprint edited and translated by H. Katz and J. Simmons. *Australian Orchid Foundation,* 107 Roberts St., Essendon 3040, Victoria, Australia.

437 ———. [1911–1914] 1982. *The Orchidaceae of German New Guinea. Fedde's Repertorium specierum novarum regni vegetabilis* Beiheft 1 fascicle No. 1–68, and I–V. Translated by H. Katz and J. Simmons and edited by D. Blaxell. *Australian Orchid Foundation,* 107 Roberts St., Essendon 3040, Victoria, Australia.

438 ———. 1912. Neue und seltene garten-orchideen. *Orchis* 6(4):65.

439 ———. 1912. XXXIX. *Orchidaceae* novae et criticae. Decade 25. *Fedde's Repertorium specierum novarum regni vegetabilis* 10(11):251. Berlin, Germany.

440 ———. 1914. Orchidaceae in Botanische und Zoologische Ergebnisse einer Wissenschaftlichen Forschungsreise nach den Samoainseln, Dem Newguinea-archipel und den Salomonsinseln. K. Rechinger, ed. *Denkschriften der Kaiserlichen Akademie Der Wissenschaften, Mathematisch-Naturwissenschaftliche Klasse,* 89:59, 523–526.

441 ———. [1914, 1921] 1986. The orchids of Micronesia. Engler's *Botanische Jahrbucher* 52:9–13 and 56:434–501. Edited and translated by H. Katz and J. Simmons. *Australian Orchid Foundation,* 107 Roberts St., Essendon 3040, Victoria, Australia.

442 ———. 1915. *Die Orchideen ihre beschreibung, kulture and züchter and botaniker.* Verlagsbachhandlung Paul Parey, Berlin.

443 ———. [1923]. Not dated. Neue orchidaceen Papuasiens. C. Lauterbach, Beiträge zur Flora von Papuasien. IX. Engler's *Botanische Jahrbücher* 58:50–154. Reprinted by the Johnson Reprint Corporation, New York.

444 Schumann, K., and K. Lauterbach, ed. 1905. *Nachträge zur flora der Deutschen Schutzgebiete in der südsee. Orchidaceae, Dendrobium* by R. Schlechter. Verlag Von Gebrüder Borntraeger, Leipzig.

445 Schuster, C. [1931–1943] 1981. Orchidacearum iconum index. *Fedde's Repertorium specierum novarum regni vegetabilis* Beiheft 60. Reprinted by Otto Koeltz Science Publishers, D-634 Koenigstein, Germany.

446 Scully, R. 1992. Checklist February. *American Orchid Society Bulletin* 61(2):154.

447 Seidenfaden, G. 1972. An enumeration of Laotian orchids. *Bulletin du Musée national d'histoire naturelle botanique* 71(5):141–142.

448 ———. 1975. *Contributions to a revision of the orchid flora of Cambodia, Laos, and Vietnam*. Kai Olsen, 10 Helstedsvej, DK-3480, Fredensborg, Denmark.

449 ———. 1980. Orchid genera in Thailand IX. *Flickingeria* Hawkes & *Epigeneium* Gagnep. *Dansk Botanisk Arkiv* Bind 34—Nr. 1.

450 ———. 1981. Contributions to the orchid flora of Thailand IX. *Nordic Journal of Botany* 1(2) April 1981.

451 ———. 1982. Orchid Genera in Thailand X. *Trichotosia* Bl. and *Eria* Lindl. *Opera Botanica* 62.

452 ———. 1982. Contributions to the orchid flora of Thailand X. *Nordic Journal of Botany* 2(3).

453 ———. 1985. Contributions to the orchid flora of Thailand XI. *Nordic Journal of Botany* 5(2).

454 ———. 1985. Orchid genera in Thailand, XII. *Dendrobium* Sw. *Opera Botanica* 83, Copenhagen, Denmark.

455 Seidenfaden, G., and J. J. Wood. 1992. *The orchids of peninsular Malaysia and Singapore*. Published in association with The Royal Botanic Gardens, Kew and Botanic Gardens, Singapore. Olsen & Olsen, Helstedsvej 10, DK-3480 Fredensborg, Denmark.

456 Sheehan, T., and M. Sheehan. 1972. Orchid genera, Illustrated—XXVII. *American Orchid Society Bulletin* 41(5):440.

457 Shooter, R. 1990. *Dendrobium fleckeri* and some progeny. *The Orchadian* 10(1):27–28

458 Shuttleworth, H., H. Zim, and G. Dillon. 1970. *Orchids, a golden guide*. Golden Press, New York.

459 Singh, F. 1975. Exquisite Orchids from Western Ghats (India)—1. *Dendrobium barbatulum*. *American Orchid Society Bulletin* 44(12):1086.

460 ———. 1983. *Dendrobium crassinode*—the jointed *Dendrobium*. *The Orchid Review* 91(11): 346

461 Skelsey, A. 1979. Orchids. In *Time-Life encyclopedia of gardening*. Time-Life Books, Alexandria, Va.

462 Slade, G. 1980. *Dendrobium mohlianum*—A case of pollination by birds. *American Orchid Society Bulletin* 49(8):869.

463 ———. 1990. My voyage through orchids—part 1. *The Orchadian* 10(1):24–25.

464 Smedley, D. 1989. Notes on the pollination of *D. kingianum*. *The Orchadian* 9(8):177–178.

465 ———. 1991. The search for the perfect mount. *The Orchadian* 10(4):114–118, BC.

466 Smith, A., ed. 1991. *Flora Vitiensis nova*, Vol. V. *Orchidaceae* by P. Kores. National Tropical Botanical Garden, Lawai, Kauai, Hawaii, U.S.A.

467 Smith, J. J. [1905] 1984. *Die Orchideen von Java*. E. J. Brill, Leiden, The Netherlands. Reprint, Bishen Singh Mahendra Pal Singh, Dehra Dun, India.

468 ———. 1905–1908. *Die Orchideen von Ambon*. Landsdrukkerjj, Batavia.

469 ———. [1908] 1984. *Die Orchideen von Java—figuren-atlas*. E. J. Brill, Leiden. Reprinted by Bishen Singh Mahendra Pal Singh, Dehra Dun-248001, India.

470 ———. 1911–1936. Orchidaceae *in Nova Guinea. Resultats de l'expédition Scientifique Néerlandaise à la Nouvelle-Guinée en 1907–1936*, Vol. VIII part 1, pp. 1–142 (1909), part III, pp. 522–608 (1911); 1912–1913 Vol. XII part 1, pp 1–104 (1912), part III, pp. 173–272 (1915), part IV, pp. 272–469; Vol. XIV pp. 337–515 (1929); Vol. XVIII pp. 9–85 (1936). *Die Orchideen von Niederländisch Neu-Guinea*. E. J. Brill, Leiden, The Netherlands. The German text is translated without plant descriptions in 1990 as *The Orchids of Dutch New Guinea*, by J. J. Smith. The Australian Orchid Foundation, 107 Roberts Rd., Essendon, Victoria 3040, Australia.

471 ———. 1903–1909. Icones Bogorienses Vol. II, tab CXIV–CXXI and Vol. III, tab CCV, CCVII, CCVIII. *Jardin Botanique de Buitenzorg*. E. J. Brill, Leide.

472 ———. 1912. *Dendrobium* Sw. sect. *Cadetia*. *Bulletin du Jardin Botanique* Série II, Vol. 8:15–18.

473 ———. 1912. Neue Malaiische Orchideen. *Bulletin du Jardin Botanique* Série II, Vol. 8:38–42.

474 ———. [1913] Not dated. *Orchidaceae*. In H. Winkler's, *Beiträge zur Kenntnis der Flora und Pflanzengeographie von Borneo* II: 98–101. A. Engler, ed. *Botanische Jahrbücher für Systematik, Pflanzengeschichte und Pflanzengeographie* XLVIII. Leipzig. Reprinted by the Johnson Reprint Corporation, New York.

475 ———. 1913. V. Vorläufige Beschreibungen neuer papuanishcher Orchideen IX. *Fedde's Repertorium specierum novarum regni vegetabilis* 12:24–34. Berlin, Germany.

476 ———. 1913. XXI. Vorläufige Beschreibungen neuer papuanischer Orchideen. X. *Fedde's Repertorium specierum novarum regni vegetabilis* 12:110–121. Berlin, Germany.

477 ———. 1913. LXXVI. Vorläufige Beschreibungen neuer papuanischer Orchideen. XI. *Fedde's Repertorium specierum novarum regni vegetabilis* 12:394–398. Berlin, Germany.

478 ———. 1914–1915. XXIII. Vorläufige Beschreibungen neuer papuanischer Orchideen, XIII. *Mededeelingen Van's Rijks Herbarium* 21–27(25):1–21.

479 ———. 1917. The Amboina *Orchidaceae* collected by C. B. Robinson. *The Philippine Journal of Science*, C. Botany 12(5):256–258.

480 ———. 1917. *Orchidaceae* Novae Malayanses VIII. *Bulletin du Jardin Botanic Buitenzorg* Série II, 25:1–103.

481 ———. 1920. *Orchidaceae* novae Malayenses IX. *Bulletin du Jardin Botanique* Série III, 2:58–85.

482 ———. 1925. Die Orchideen der zweiten Frankfurter Sunda-Expedition 1909–1910. *Mededeelingen Van's Rijks Herbarium*, Leiden. 48–53(53):8–11.

483 ———. 1926. *Orchidaceae* from the Selebes. *Svensk Botanisk Tidskrift* 20:475–478.

484 ———. 1931. On a collection of *Orchidaceae* from central Borneo. *Bulletin du Jardin Botanique* Série III, II(2):83–160.

485 ———. 1934. VII *Orchidaceae* Novae Malayenses. XV. *Fedde's Repertorium specierum novarum regni vegetabilis* Vol. XXXVI: 110–119. Berlin.

486 ———. [1934] 1984. *New Papuasian orchids*. A translation of Neue Orchideen Papuasiens, from "Beitrage zur flora von Papuasien XX." Engler's, *Botanische Jahrbücher* LXVI:161–215. Edited by D. Blaxell, and translated by H. Katz and J. Simmons. Australian Orchid Foundation, 107 Roberts St. Essendon, Victoria, Australia 3040.

487 ———. 1938. A few orchids from the Malayan Archipelago. *The Gardens' Bulletin Straits Settlements* Vol. IX:89–92. Singapore.

Bibliography

488 ———. 1943. *Orchidaceae novae Malayenses* XVII. *Blumea* 5(2): 308–309.

489 Smith, W. W. 1921. New orchids from Yunnan and northern Burma. *Notes from the Royal Botanic Garden*, Edinburgh 13:189.

490 Soule, L. 1984. Grower's Corner—*Dendrobium capillipes*. *American Orchid Society Bulletin* 53(3):255.

491 South Florida Orchid Society. 1984. *Introduction to orchids*. South Florida Orchid Society, Miami, Florida.

492 Spence, P. 1988. Hybridizing with Australian native orchids. *American Orchid Society Bulletin* 57(3):257.

493 Sprunger, S., ed. 1992. *Orchids from the Botanical Register* 1815–1847. Birkhäuser Verlag, Basel, Boston, and Berlin.

494 Stearn, W. 1986. *Botanical Latin*. 3rd ed. David and Charles, North Pomfret, Vt.

495 Stephens, J. 1979. Orchids in a cold glasshouse "down under." *American Orchid Society Bulletin* 48(5):473.

496 Stern, R. 1974. Orchids off the beaten path—New Guinea. *American Orchid Society Bulletin* 43(5):415.

497 Su, Horng-Jye. 1975. *Taiwan orchids*. 2nd ed. Horng-Jye Su, Department of Forestry, National Taiwan University, Taipei, Republic of China.

498 Sullivan, J. 1986. Growing *Dendrobium cuthbertsonii* under lights. *American Orchid Society Bulletin* 55(12):1224.

499 Summerhayes, V. 1957. Notes on Asiatic orchids: II. *Kew Bulletin* 2:259–268.

500 ———. 1964. African orchids: XXIX. *Kew Bulletin* 17(3).

501 Sun, Shao-Chi, and Li-Guo Xu. 1986. A new species of *Dendrobium* from China. *Bulletin of Botanical Research* 6(2):113–116.

502 ———. 1988. A new species of *Dendrobium* from Sichuan, China. *Bulletin of Botanical Research* 8(2):59–61.

503 Tabor, L. 1977. Photograph. *American Orchid Society Bulletin* 46(2):FC.

504 Tanaka, R., and H. Kamemoto. 1984. Chromosomes in orchids: counting and numbers. Appendix. In *Orchid biology: reviews and perspectives*. Vol. III. Edited by J. Arditti. Comstock Publishing, Cornell University Press, Ithaca, N.Y.

505 Tang, T., and F. Wang. 1951. Contributions to the knowledge of Eastern Asiatic Orchidaceae II. *Acta Phytotaxonomica Sinica* 1:82.

506 ———. 1974. Plantae novae Orchidacearum Hainanensium. *Acta Phytotaxonomica Sinica* 12(1):35–49.

507 Tang, Zhen-Zi, and Shi-Jun Cheng. 1984. A study on the raw plants for the Chinese traditional medicine "Houshand shi-hu." *Bulletin of Botanical Research* 4(3):141–145.

508 Tempera, L., and A. Pridgeon. 1987. The wizard of Copiague, or . . . what does Lu do? *American Orchid Society Bulletin* 56(8):792.

509 Teo, C. K. 1985. *Native orchids of peninsula Malaysia*. Times Books International, Singapore.

510 Teoh, E. S. 1980. *Asian orchids*. Times Books International, Singapore.

511 Teuscher, H. 1972. Collector's item—*Dendrobium heterocarpum*. *American Orchid Society Bulletin* 41(1):37.

512 ———. 1972. Collector's item—*Dendrobium devonianum*. *American Orchid Society Bulletin* 41(9):793.

513 ———. 1974. Collector's item—*Dendrobium brymerianum*. *American Orchid Society Bulletin* 43(12):1051.

514 ———. 1977. Collector's item—*Dendrobium unicum*. *American Orchid Society Bulletin* 46(5):423.

515 Thompson, P. [1977] 1980. *Orchids from seed*. Royal Botanic Gardens, Kew, London.

516 Thorne, A., and P. Cribb. 1984. *Orchids of the Solomon Islands and Bougainville—a preliminary checklist*. Royal Botanic Gardens, Kew, London.

517 Thwaites, G. H. K. 1864. *Enumeratio plantarum Zelaniae*. Dulau and Co., London.

518 *The Times atlas of the world*. 1988. 7th ed. Times Books, Random House, New York.

519 Titmuss, D. 1992. Photograph. *The Orchadian* 10(9):BC.

520 ———. 1992/1993. Show photo. *The Orchadian* 10(10):368.

521 Tokunaga, R. 1990. The *Nigrohirsutae* dendrobiums of Thailand and their hybrids. *American Orchid Society Bulletin* 59(6):567.

522 Trussell, R. and A. Trussell. 1991. Dendrobiums—a personal view. Part I. An introduction to the geography. *The Orchid Review* 99(8):254–258.

523 ———. 1991. Dendrobiums—a personal view. Part II: Dendrobiums of the Raj, of the Himalayas and Upper Burma. *The Orchid Review* 99(9):281–286.

524 ———. 1991. Dendrobiums—a personal view. Part III: west of the Wallace line. *The Orchid Review* 99(10):316–321.

525 ———. 1991. Dendrobiums—a personal view. Part IV: of Antelopes and Kangaroos. *The Orchid Review* 99(11):385–390.

526 ———. 1991. Dendrobiums—a personal view. Part IV: of Antelopes and Kangaroos (Continued). *The Orchid Review* 99(12):421–424.

527 ———. 1992. Dendrobiums—a personal view. Part V: The genus in Australia. *The Orchid Review* 100(1):23–28.

528 Tsi, Z. H. 1980. A preliminary study of the orchid genus *Dendrobium* Sw. in China. *Acta Phytotaxonomica Sinica* 18:427–449.

529 ———. 1989. New taxa of *Orchidaceae* from China. *Bulletin of Botanical Research* 9(2):21–31.

530 Tuyama, T. 1941. *Orchidaceae* novae Micronesiacae (V). *The Journal of Japanese Botany*. 17(1–12):507–515.

531 Upton, W. 1987. *Dendrobium macropus* subsp. *gracilicaule* (F. Muell.) P. S. Green. *The Orchadian* 9(1):11.

532 ———. 1988. Central coast group 8th annual show. *The Orchadian* 9(6):124.

533 ———. 1989. *Dendrobium* orchids of Australia. Timber Press, Inc., Portland, Ore., 97225, U.S.A.

534 ———. 1991. The genus *Dendrobium* in Australia, its species and hybrids. *The Orchadian* 10(4):92.

535 ———. 1992. Photograph. *The Orchadian* 10(9):320.

536 Valmayor, H. 1984. *Orchidiana Philippiniana* vols. 1–2. Eugenio Lopez Foundation, Manila, Philippines.

537 Van Bodegom, J. [1954–1962] 1985. *Enige Orchideeén van west Nieuw Guinea. Some Orchids of West New Guinea*. Translated by G. Nieuwenhoven, edited by J. Simmons. Australian Orchid Foundation, 107 Roberts St., Essendon 3040, Victoria, Australia.

538 Van Royen, P. 1980. *The orchids of the high mountains of New Guinea*. J. Cramer, Vaduz. A reprint edition of the orchid part of *The alpine flora of New Guinea*.

539 Vasiljev, A. 1989. The main botanical garden of the USSR. *American Orchid Society Bulletin* 58(11):1103.

540 Vaughan, M. 1982. A new orchid stamp issue from Vanuatu. *American Orchid Society Bulletin* 51(12):1260.

541 Veitch, J., and Sons. [1887–1894] 1963, 1981. *Manual of orchidaceous plants*, Vol. I. James Veitch and Sons, Royal Exotic Nursery, Chelsea, London. Reprint, A. Asher and Co., Amsterdam, The Netherlands.

542 Vij, S., ed. 1986. *Biology, conservation, and culture of orchids*. The Orchid Society of India. Affiliated East-West Press Private Ltd. New Delhi, India.

543 Walker, H. 1977. *Dendrobium loddigesii* 'Malvern'. *American Orchid Society Bulletin* 46(2):104.

544 Walsh, G. 1990. The epiphytic orchids of the Illawarra. *The Orchadian* 10(1):16.

545 ———. 1992. Speciosum speculations. *The Orchadian* 10(8):271.

546 ———. 1993. Extension of the distribution of *Bulbophyllum weinthalii* and *Dendrobium linguiforme* var. *nugentii*. *The Orchadian* 10(10):384–386.

547 Wang, L., and J. Xu. 1989. The chromosome number in *Dendrobium*. 10 species. *Journal of Wuhan Botanical Research* 7(1): 113.

548 Warren, R. 1982. Lesser known dendrobiums: *D. atroviolaceum* and *D. lawesii*. *The Orchid Review* 90(5):144–145.

549 ———. 1990. *Equatorial plants newsletter*. Equatorial Plant Co., 73 Dundas St., Edinburgh, Scotland EH3 6RS.

550 ———. 1990. New Guinea orchids—I: *Dendrobium* section *Latouria*. *American Orchid Society Bulletin* 59(2):128.

551 ———. 1990. New Guinea orchids—II: The antelope dendrobiums. *American Orchid Society Bulletin* 59(3):252–259.

552 ———. 1990. New Guinea dendrobiums—III: section *Pedilonum*. *American Orchid Society Bulletin* 59(5):473–479.

553 ———. 1990. New Guinea orchids—IV: *Dendrobium* section *Calyptrochilum*. *American Orchid Society Bulletin* 59(6):590–597.

554 ———. 1991. New Guinea dendrobiums—a growing fascination. *Schlechteriana* 2(3):97.

555 ———. 1992. Photograph. *Schlechteriana* 3(1):8.

556 Warren, R., and P. Woods. 1990. New Guinea dendrobiums—V: section *Oxyglossum*—"The jewels in the canopy." *American Orchid Society Bulletin* 59(7):704.

557 Watson, W., and W. Bean. [1890] 1979. *Orchids: their culture and management*. L. Upcott Gill, London.

558 Webb, A., and M. Webb. 1991. The orchids of Australia—1: introduction. *American Orchid Society Bulletin* 60(10):964.

559 ———. 1991. The orchids of Australia—2: *Dendrobium kingianum*. *American Orchid Society Bulletin* 60(11):1084.

560 Webb, M. 1988. Photograph. *The Orchadian* 9(6):120.

561 ———. 1989. Photographs. *The Orchadian* 9(10):220–221, 236–237.

562 Webb, M., and A. Webb. 1992. Australian Orchids. *American Orchid Society Bulletin* 61(1):12.

563 ———. 1992. Australian Orchids. *American Orchid Society Bulletin* 61(4):348.

564 ———. 1992. Australian Orchids. *American Orchid Society Bulletin* 61(6):560.

565 *Webster's new geographical dictionary*. 1977. G. and C. Merriam Co., Springfield, Mass.

566 Wells, G. 1988. Photograph. *The Orchadian* 9(6):133.

567 Whitmore, T. 1984. *Tropical rain forests of the Far East* 2nd ed. Oxford University Press, New York.

568 Wilfret, G., and H. Kamemoto. 1969. Genome and karyotype relationships in the genus *Dendrobium (Orchidaceae)*. I. crossability. *American Journal of Botany* 56(5):521–526.

569 Williams, B., with J. Kramer. 1987. *Orchids for everyone*. W. H. Smith Publishers, New York.

570 Williams, B. S. [1894] 1973. *Orchid growers' manual*. 7th ed. Victoria and Paradise Nurseries, London. Reprint, Weldon & Wesley, Codicote, Herts, United Kingdom and Verlag J. Cramer, Lehre, West Germany.

571 Williams, L. 1938. Orchid studies IV. The orchids of the Fiji Islands. *Botanical Museum Leaflets,* Harvard University 5(7):119–129.

572 ———. 1940. Orchid studies, XI. New species of *Epidendrum* and *Dendrobium*. *Botanical Museum Leaflets,* Harvard University 8(5):107–108.

573 ———. 1941. A new *Dendrobium* from Burma. *American Orchid Society Bulletin* (3):272.

574 ———. 1946. *Orchidaceae* Novae Guineae 1. *Botanical Museum Leaflets,* Harvard University 12(5):156–161.

575 Wilson, K. 1980. The difference between alba, alba form, and white. *American Orchid Society Bulletin* 49(8):863.

576 Wirth, G. 1992. "Red" speciosums. *The Orchadian* 10(7):229.

577 Wishinski, P. 1978. Some orchids of the Nepal Himalayas. *American Orchid Society Bulletin* 47(7):623.

578 Wisler, G. 1991. *How to control orchid viruses: the complete handbook*. Maupin House Publishers, P. O. Box 90148, Gainesville, Fla. 32607, U.S.A.

579 Wisniewski, J. 1980. Fluorescent light culture for orchids. *American Orchid Society Bulletin* 49(7):691.

580 Withner, C. 1974. *The orchids, scientific studies*. John Wiley and Sons, New York.

581 Wood, H. 1979. A trip to the ninth world orchid conference, with the accent on *Dendrobium* species. *American Orchid Society Bulletin* 48(3):229.

582 ———. 1992. Personal communication, growers notes.

583 Wood, J. J. 1980. Some orchids of the Admiralty Islands. *The Orchid Review* 88:38.

584 ———. 1981. A new species of *Dendrobium* from Indonesia—*D. courtauldii* Summerh. ex J. J. Wood. *The Orchid Review* 89(10): 322.

585 ———. 1983. A new species of *Dendrobium (Orchidaceae)* from Borneo. *Kew Bulletin:* 38:79–81.

586 ———. 1984. A preliminary annotated checklist of the orchids of Gunung Mulu National Park with a key to genera. In Jermy (ed.), *Studies on the flora of Gunung Mulu National Park*, Sarawak. Kuching.

587 ———. 1984. New orchids from Sarawak. *Kew Bulletin:* 39(1):82–84.

588 ———. 1986. Notes on Asiatic and New Guinea *Orchidaceae*. *Kew Bulletin* 41(4):811.

589 ———. 1988. The diversity of Bornean *Dendrobium*. *Die Orchidee* 39(6):213.

590 ———. 1990. New orchids from Borneo. *Lindleyana* 5(2):89–101.

591 ———. 1993. *Thesaurus woolwardiae*. Orchids of the Marquis of

Lothian. Dendrobium. Part Two. Missouri Botanical Garden, St Louis, Missouri.

592 Wood, J. J., R. S. Beaman, and J. H. Beaman. 1993. *The plants of Mt. Kinabalu*, Vol. 2, *Orchids*. Royal Botanic Gardens, Kew, Richmond, Surrey TW9 3AE, England.

593 Wood, J. J., and J. B. Comber. 1993. A new species of *Dendrobium* Sw. (Section *Formosae*) from Sumatra *(Orchidaceae)*. *Lindleyana* 8(3):115.

594 *World weather records, 1961–1970*. 1979–1985. Vols. 1–5. U.S. Department of Commerce, National Oceanic and Atmospheric Administration, National Climatic Center, Asheville, N. C.

595 *World-wide airfield summaries*. 1967, 1968, 1974. Vols. I–VII, IX, XII. U.S. Naval Weather Service, National Technical Information Service, Washington, D. C.

596 Yamamoto, J. 1972. A history of nobile type *Dendrobium* breeding with a contribution towards recent improvements. *Orchid Digest* 36(2):41.

597 Zettler, F., G. Wisler, M. Elliott, and N. Ko. 1987. Some new, potentially significant viruses of orchids and their probable means of transmission. *American Orchid Society Bulletin* 56(10):1045.

598 Zoufaly, H. 1986. Light up your orchids. *American Orchid Society Bulletin* 55(12):1204.

List of Sources

The following indexes, books, and articles are helpful.

Dietrich, Helga. 1980, 1981, 1985, 1988. *Bibliographia orchidacearum*. Vols. 2.1, 2.2, 3, 4. Bibliographische Mitteilungen der Universiatsbibliothek, Friedrich-Schiller-Universitat, Jena, East Germany.

Oertle, Charles F. (ed.). 1987. *Index periodicarum orchidacearum*. Tipografia Poncioni, Losone, Switzerland.

On Geographic Names

The following maps and gazetteers were used to correlate obsolete or uncommon place names with names in current usage:

Gazetteers. 1955–present. U.S. Board of Geographic Names. Prepared and published by the U.S. Defense Mapping Agency, Washington, D.C. The *Gazetteers*, in numerous volumes, are updated periodically.

O.N.C. aeronautical navigation charts. Prepared and published by the U.S. Defense Mapping Agency, Washington, D.C. The charts are updated periodically as additional mapping is accomplished.

The Times atlas of the world. 7th ed. 1988. Times Books, Random House, New York.

Webster's new geographical dictionary. 1977. G. and C. Merriam Co., Springfield, Mass.

On Specific Climates

Published weather records appear in the following publications.

World weather records, 1961–1970. 1979–1985. Vols. 1–5. U.S. Department of Commerce, National Oceanic and Atmospheric Administration, National Climatic Center, Asheville, N.C.

World wide airfield summaries. 1967, 1968, 1974. Vols. I–VII, IX, XII. U.S. Naval Weather Service, National Technical Information Service, Washington, D.C.

Readers seeking weather data for special projects are invited to contact Margaret and Charles Baker, 3526 S. E. Johnson Creek Blvd., Portland, OR, U.S.A. 97222.

On Botanical Names

The following volume offers general information on botanical names:

Coombes, A. J. 1985. *Dictionary of plant names*. Timber Press, Portland, Ore.

On Foreign-Language Publications

The following references are useful in translating botanical terms from various languages:

Davydov, N. N. 1962. *Botanical dictionary, Russian—English—German—French—Latin*. Central Editorial Board, Foreign-Language Scientific and Technical Dictionaries, Moscow.

Stearn, W. T. 1986. *Botanical Latin*. 3rd ed. David and Charles, North Pomfret, Vt.

Suppliers of Books on Botany and Horticulture

American Orchid Society, 6000 S. Olive Ave., West Palm Beach, Fla., U.S.A. 33405. Catalog available.

Koeltz Scientific Books, Herrnwaldstr. 6, 6240 Koenigstein/TS, Germany. Catalog available.

Koeltz Scientific Books, RR7, Box 39 Champaign, IL 61821. U.S.A. Catalog available.

McQuerry Orchid Books, 5700 W. Salerno Road, Jacksonville, Fla., U.S.A. 32244. Catalog available.

Timber Press, 9999 S.W. Wilshire, Portland, OR, U.S.A. 97225. Catalog available.

Touchwood Books, P. O. Box 610, Hastings, New Zealand. Catalog available.